Pseudonyms and Nicknames Dictionary

Related Gale Titles

Biography Almanac. Covers over 23,000 famous and infamous newsmakers from Biblical times to the present. Volume 1 is arranged alphabetically and provides brief biographical data together with citations to biographical sketches appearing in over 300 widely held sources. Volume 2 is an index volume that arranges the entries chronologically by year and day of month and geographically, using dates and places of birth and death.

Biography and Genealogy Master Index. Contains 3.25 million citations to biographical articles appearing in more than 350 contemporary who's whos and other works of collective biography, including historical as well as present-day men and women of note. Updated and expanded by annual supplements through 1986, the 1981 through 1985 supplements have been cumulated into a five-volume single alphabetically sequenced set.

Contemporary Newsmakers. Furnishes up-to-date biographical profiles on people in the news. Covering all fields, from business and international affairs to literature and the arts, the articles feature photographs of individuals along with biographical and career data. This publication is issued in quarterly installments and is annually cumulated into a hardbound volume.

Eponyms Dictionaries Index. Identifies biographical sources and dictionaries for 33,000 eponymous terms and the people upon which they are based. Also available: interedition supplement.

ISSN 0277-0350

THIRD EDITION

Pseudonyms and Nicknames Dictionary

A Guide to 80,000 Aliases, Appellations, Assumed Names, Code Names, Cognomens, Cover Names, Epithets, Initialisms, Nicknames, Noms de Guerre, Noms de Plume, Pen Names, Pseudonyms, Sobriquets, and Stage Names of 55,000 Contemporary and Historical Persons, Including the Subjects' Real Names, Basic Biographical Information, and Citations for the Sources from Which the Entries Were Compiled

Covers: Actors, Aristocrats, Artists, Athletes, Authors, Clergymen, Criminals, Entertainers, Film Stars, Journalists, Military Leaders, Monarchs, Musicians, Playwrights, Poets, Politicians, Popes, Rogues, Saints, Theatrical Figures, and Other Prominent Personalities of All Nations Throughout the Ages

Jennifer Mossman,
Editor

Volume 2
L-Z

Gale Research Company ● Book Tower ● Detroit, Michigan 48226

Editor: Jennifer Mossman
Assistant Editor: Chris Jones Wehrli

Production Supervisor: Mary Beth Trimper
Senior Production Associate: Dorothy Kalleberg
Art Director: Arthur Chartow

Editorial Data Systems Director: Dennis LaBeau
Supervisor of Programming and Systems: Diane H. Belickas
Program Design: Barry M. Trute

Editorial Data Entry Supervisor: Doris D. Goulart
Editorial Data Entry Associate: Jean Hinman Portfolio
Senior Data Entry Assistant : Anna Marie Woolard

Publisher: Frederick G. Ruffner
Editorial Director: Dedria Bryfonski
Associate Editorial Director: Ellen T. Crowley
Senior Editor, Dictionaries: Donna Wood

Library of Congress Cataloging-in-Publication Data

Pseudonyms and nicknames dictionary.

Includes bibliographies.
1. Bibliographies--20th century. 2. Nicknames.
3. Anonyms and pseudonyms. I. Mossman, Jennifer.
CT120.P8   1987   920.02   86-19522
ISBN 0-8103-0541-0

Computerized photocomposition by
Amtec Information Services, Inc.
Lakewood, California

Printed in the United States of America

Contents

Volume 1
A-K

Volume 2
L-Z

Editorial Policies and Arrangement of Names

Pseudonyms and Nicknames Dictionary (PND) and its supplements, *New Pseudonyms and Nicknames (NPN)*, index original and assumed names in one alphabetic sequence. Both contemporary and historical figures throughout the world are included.

Entries are coded to indicate the sources from which information was gathered. The List of Sources Cited decodes these symbols, and provides complete bibliographic data, where applicable, for users who wish to find additional information about a particular individual. Entries were frequently based on a compilation of information from several sources and do not necessarily represent an exact duplication of material found in any one source. Those entries without source-identification codes were collected through independent research by the editors.

Form of Entries

Within *PND*'s single alphabet, there are two types of entry:

1. The main entry, which consists of six elements:

> Original name
> Dates of birth and (where applicable) death
> Up to eight source-identification codes
> Nationality
> Occupation
> Assumed name (or names) by which the individual has become known, highlighted by an asterisk

> **Blair, Eric Arthur** 1903-1950
> [EWL, SF, TCL]
> *British author*
> *Orwell, George

Supplements *(New Pseudonyms and Nicknames)* contain the notation "See also base volume" at the end of each entry for which additional pseudonyms or nicknames can be found in the main edition.

2. The cross reference, which refers the user from the assumed name (pen name, nickname, stage name, etc.) to the original name:

> **Orwell, George**
> *See* Blair, Eric Arthur

Source Conflicts

A variety of sources may have been used to compile an entry, and the editors sometimes found conflicting information. If additional research failed to resolve these discrepancies, various methods were employed to indicate that some uncertainty still exists:

When correct birth dates could not be determined, the earliest date was arbitrarily selected, and a question mark was added to show that some doubt remains. It was particularly necessary to use this procedure with some stage and screen personalities, whose age is traditionally a closely guarded secret.

If differences were found in the form or spelling of a name, both possibilities were incorporated into an entry: Badawi, Mohamed [or Muhammad] Mustafa.

Sources occasionally gave conflicting information in their description of nationalities. For example, one source might determine the nationality based upon place of birth, while a second source might consider length of residence to be of greater importance, and the actual legal status might be difficult to determine in any case. In these instances, *PND* would use a designation such as "British-born" to indicate that, while the place of birth may be known, the actual citizenship is unclear.

Alphabetical Arrangement

All words and letters are considered in alphabetizing except those that are enclosed in brackets. Spacing generally affects alphabetical position, except in the case of surnames compounded of two or more names. These are arranged after the single surname. Particles (De, La, Von, etc.) are considered to be the first element of a surname and will, unless common usage dictates otherwise, be alphabetized as such:

> De Angelis, Alberto
> De Mille, Agnes
> Dean, Mary
> Dean, Robert George
> Dean-Andrews, Simon Paul
> Dean Norwood, Victor
> Deane, Joseph
> Deane, P. Virginia

Articles that begin a nickname, whether in English or other languages, are not considered for alphabetizing purposes. El Gato, for example, will be found in the G's.

Some common abbreviations (Mr., Dr., St., Ste.) are alphabetized as if they were spelled out (Mister, Doctor, Saint, Sainte).

Name Reversals

Most names found in *PND* are alphabetized by surname, followed by the given name(s). There are some entries, however, that do not have the form of first and last names and must, therefore, be handled differently:

> Given names followed by a single initial can be found under the given name:
> *M*alcolm X, *J*ackie O.

> Initials that replace the entire name are alphabetized under the first of the initials:
> *J*.F.K., *L*.B.J.

> When titles are combined with a given name, the entry will be found under the title:
> *U*ncle Miltie, *M*iss Lillian.

Treatment of Nicknames

Some nicknames are quite clearly meant to replace a given name, and thus fit the usual method of handling assumed names: Lefty Aber and Dusty Baker can be found under the surnames (in the A's and B's respectively).

Others cannot logically be made to fit this pattern since they are not commonly used in conjunction with a surname. These nicknames will stand alone: Calamity Jane, [The] Sultan of Swat.

It is not always immediately obvious whether a given nickname is generally used in combination with a surname or whether it should stand alone. In order to ensure that the user is able to locate the nickname, even though the surname may not be known, a double cross reference (by surname and by nickname) is given:

Mehlhorn, Wild Bill
See Mehlhorn, William

Wild Bill Mehlhorn
See Mehlhorn, William

In some cases, the editors had difficulty in deciding when a nickname should be combined with a surname and when it can correctly stand alone. In approaching this and other editorial problems, attempts were made to be as logical as circumstances permitted. Unfortunately, complete consistency was impossible, and the user who is unable to locate a particular name is encouraged to check other possible forms.

List of Sources Cited

AES   Hollander, Zander. *The American Encyclopedia of Soccer.* New York: Everest House, 1980.

ALR   *American League Red Book.* 48th ed. Los Angeles: Baseball Fact Books, 1977.

ALY   Traub, Hamilton. *The American Literary Yearbook.* Reprint of the 1919 ed. Detroit: Gale Research Co., 1968.

AM   Vallance, Tom. *The American Musical.* New York: Castle Books, 1970.

AN   Nykoruk, Barbara. *Authors in the News.* Vol. 1. Detroit: Gale Research Co., 1976.

ANT   Warfel, Harry R. *American Novelists of Today.* Westport, Conn.: Greenwood Press, 1972.

ART   *Who's Who in Art.* 19th ed. Havant, Hants., England: Art Trade Press, 1980.

AS   Hickok, Ralph. *Who Was Who in American Sports.* New York: Hawthorn Books, Inc., 1971.

ASC   The Lynn Farnol Group Inc. *The ASCAP Biographical Dictionary of Composers, Authors and Publishers.* 3rd ed. New York: The American Society of Composers, Authors and Publishers, 1966.

AW   *The Author's and Writer's Who's Who.* 6th ed. Darien, Conn.: Hafner Publishing Co. Inc., 1971.

BA   *Who's Who Among Black Americans.* 2nd ed. Northbrook, Ill.: Who's Who Among Black Americans Inc., 1978.

BAB   Appel, Martin, and Goldblatt, Burt. *Baseball's Best.* New York: McGraw-Hill, 1977.

BB   Mendell, Ronald L. *Who's Who in Basketball.* New Rochelle, N.Y.: Arlington House, 1973.

BBD   Slonimsky, Nicolas. *Baker's Biographical Dictionary of Musicians.* 5th ed. New York: G. Schirmer, 1971.

BBH   Soderberg, Paul, and Washington, Helen. *The Big Book of Halls of Fame in the United States and Canada.* New York: R. R. Bowker Co., 1977.

BDF   Thomson, David. *A Biographical Dictionary of Film.* New York: William Morrow and Co. Inc., 1976.

BDSA   Knight, Lucian Lamar. *Biographical Dictionary of Southern Authors.* Reprint of the 1929 ed. Detroit: Gale Research Co., 1978.

BDW   Tunney, Christopher. *A Biographical Dictionary of World War II.* New York: St. Martin's Press, 1972.

BE   *The Baseball Encyclopedia.* 3rd ed. New York: Macmillan Publishing Co. Inc., 1976.

BEW   Rigdon, Walter. *The Biographical Encyclopedia and Who's Who of the American Theatre.* New York: James H. Heineman, 1966.

BF   Gifford, Denis. *The Illustrated Who's Who in British Films.* London: B. T. Batsford Ltd., 1978.

BI   *Biography Index.* Vols. 1-11. New York: The H. W. Wilson Co., 1949-1980.

BL   Wallechinsky, David; Wallace, Irving; and Wallace, Amy. *The People's Almanac Presents the Book of Lists.* New York: William Morrow and Co. Inc., 1977.

BLB   Nash, Jay Robert. *Bloodletters and Badmen.* New York: M. Evans and Co., 1973.

BMH   Busby, Roy. *British Music Hall.* Salem, N.H.: Paul Elek Inc., 1976.

BN   *Baseball Nicknames, 1870-1946.* Hingham, Mass.: Gates-Vincent Publications, 1946.

BP   Andersen, Christopher P. *The Book of People.* New York: Perigee Books, 1981.

BR   Marcin, Joe, and Byers, Dick, eds. *Official Baseball Register.* St. Louis: The Sporting News Publishing Co., 1977.

BS   Severn, Bill. *Bill Severn's Guide to Magic as a Hobby.* New York: David McKay Co. Inc., 1979.

BTB   Olan, Ben, ed. *Big-Time Baseball.* New York: Hart Publishing Co., 1958.

BWG   Bartlett, Michael, ed. *Bartlett's World Golf Encyclopedia.* New York: Bantam Books, 1973.

BWW   Harris, Sheldon. *Blues Who's Who.* New Rochelle, N.Y.: Arlington House, 1979.

BX   Burrill, Bob. *Who's Who in Boxing.* New Rochelle, N.Y.: Arlington House, 1974.

CA   *Contemporary Authors.* Vols. 1-109. New Revision Series, Vols. 1-10. Detroit: Gale Research Co., 1962-1983.

CAA   Millett, Fred B. *Contemporary American Authors.* Reprint of the 1940 ed. New York: AMS Press, 1970.

CAL   Foy, Felician A. *Catholic Almanac.* Huntington, Ind.: Our Sunday Visitor Inc., 1979.

CAN   Thomas, Clara. *Canadian Novelists, 1920-1945.* New York: Longmans, Green & Co., 1946.

CAP   *Contemporary Authors Permanent Series.* Vols 1-2. Detroit: Gale Research Co., 1975, 1978.

CAR   Naylor, Colin, and P-Orridge, Genesis. *Contemporary Artists.* New York: St. Martin's Press, 1977.

CAT   Hoehn, Matthew. *Catholic Authors.* Newark: St. Mary's Abbey, 1948 and 1952.

CBS   Bacheller, Martin A., ed. *The CBS News Almanac, 1977.* Maplewood, N.J.: Hammond Almanac Inc., 1976.

CC   Barzun, Jacques, and Taylor, Wendell Hertig. *A Catalogue of Crime.* New York: Harper & Row Publishers, 1971.

CCL   Watters, Reginald Eyre. *A Checklist of Canadian Literature and Background Materials, 1628-1960.* 2nd ed. Toronto: University of Toronto Press, 1972.

CD   Smith, Horatio. *Columbia Dictionary of Modern European Literature.* New York: Columbia University Press, 1971.

CEC   Scott, Sir Harold. *The Concise Encyclopedia of Crime and Criminals.* New York: Hawthorn Books Inc., 1961.

CED   Rust, Brian. *The Complete Entertainment Discography.* New Rochelle, N.Y.: Arlington House, 1973.

CEI   Hollander, Zander, and Bock, Hal, eds. *The Complete Encyclopedia of Ice Hockey.* Rev. ed. Englewood Cliffs, N.J.: Prentice-Hall, 1974.

CFH   Smith, Larry, ed. *Canadian Football Hall of Fame.* Hamilton, Ontario: Canadian Football Hall of Fame.

CLC   *Contemporary Literary Criticism.* Vols. 1-25. Detroit: Gale Research Co., 1973-1983.

CM   *Country Music Who's Who.* Record World Publications, 1972.

CMA   Zalkind, Ronald. *Contemporary Music Almanac, 1980/81.* New York: Schirmer Books, 1980.

CME   Shestack, Melvin. *The Country Music Encyclopedia.* New York: Thomas Y. Crowell Co., 1974.

CN   Vinson, James. *Contemporary Novelists.* 2nd ed. New York: St. Martin's Press, 1976.

CND   Ruffner, Frederick G., Jr., and Thomas, Robert C., eds. *Code Names Dictionary.* Detroit: Gale Research Co., 1974.

CR   Blackwell, Earl. *Celebrity Register.* New York: Simon and Schuster, 1973.

CRI   Burke, Joan Martin. *Civil Rights.* 2nd ed. New York: R. R. Bowker Co., 1974.

CSH   Wise, S. F., and Fisher, Douglas. *Canada's Sporting Heroes.* Don Mills, Ontario: General Publishing Co. Ltd., 1974.

CU   Finch, John R. *Close-Ups.* New York: A. S. Barnes and Co., 1978.

CW   Herdeck, Donald E. *Caribbean Writers.* Washington, D.C.: Three Continents Press, 1979.

CWG   Gentry, Linnell. *A History and Encyclopedia of Country, Western, and Gospel Music.* 2nd ed. Nashville, Tenn.: Clairmont Corp., 1969.

DAM   Claghorn, Charles Eugene. *Biographical Dictionary of American Music.* West Nyack, N.Y.: Parker Publishing Co. Inc., 1973.

DBA   Waters, Grant M. *Dictionary of British Artists Working 1900-1950.* 2 vols. Eastbourne, England: Eastbourne Fine Art, 1975.

DBQ   Kenin, Richard, and Wintle, Justin. *The Dictionary of Biographical Quotation.* New York: Alfred A. Knopf, 1978.

DC   Sproat, Iain. *Debrett's Cricketers' Who's Who.* London: Debrett's Peerage Ltd., 1980.

DEA   Sharp, R. Farquharson. *A Dictionary of English Authors.* Reprint of the 1904 ed. Detroit: Gale Research Co., 1978.

DEL   Adams, W. Davenport. *Dictionary of English Literature.* Reprint of the 2nd ed. Detroit: Gale Research Co., 1966.

DEP   Hyamson, Albert M. *A Dictionary of English Phrases.* Reprint of the 1922 ed. Detroit: Gale Research Co., 1970.

DF   *Detroit Free Press.* 1982-1986.

DFM   Sadoul, Georges. *Dictionary of Film Makers.* Los Angeles: University of California Press, 1972.

DGS   Mac Farlane, Paul, ed. *Daguerreotypes of Great Stars of Baseball.* St. Louis: The Sporting News Publishing Co., 1971.

DHA   Harbottle, Thomas Benfield. *Dictionary of Historical Allusions.* Reprint of the 1904 ed. Detroit: Gale Research Co., 1968.

DI   Green, Jonathon. *The Directory of Infamy.* Toronto: Mills & Boon, 1980.

DIL   Hogan, Robert. *Dictionary of Irish Literature.* Westport, Conn.: Greenwood Press, 1979.

DLE   Myers, Robin. *A Dictionary of Literature in the English Language from 1940 to 1970.* New York: Pergamon Press, 1978.

DLE1   Myers, Robin. *A Dictionary of Literature in the English Language from Chaucer to 1940.* New York: Pergamon Press, 1970.

DN   *Detroit News.* 1985.

DNA   Wallace, W. Stewart. *A Dictionary of North American Authors Deceased before 1950.* Reprint of the 1951 ed. Detroit: Gale Research Co., 1968.

DNNF   Wheeler, William A. *An Explanatory and Pronouncing Dictionary of the Noted Names of Fiction.* Reprint of the 1889 ed. Detroit: Gale Research Co., 1966.

DNNS   Latham, Edward. *A Dictionary of Names, Nicknames and Surnames of Persons, Places and Things.* Reprint of the 1904 ed. Detroit: Gale Research Co., 1966.

DSB   Gillespie, Charles Coulston. *Dictionary of Scientific Biography.* 14 vols. New York: Charles Scribner's Sons, 1970-1976.

EAR   Cutter, Robert, and Fendell, Bob. *Encyclopedia of Auto Racing Greats.* Englewood Cliffs, N.J.: Prentice-Hall Inc., 1973.

EC   Golesworthy, Maurice. *Encyclopaedia of Cricket.* 1st and 6th eds. London: Robert Hale, 1962 and 1977.

ECM   Dellar, Fred; Thompson, Roy; and Green, Douglas B. *The Illustrated Encyclopedia of Country Music.* New York: Harmony Books, 1977.

EE   Seth, Ronald. *Encyclopedia of Espionage.* London: New English Library, 1972.

EF   Treat, Roger. *The Encyclopedia of Football.* 13th ed. New York: A. S. Barnes and Co., 1975.

EG   Evans, Webster. *Encyclopedia of Golf.* 2nd ed. New York: St. Martin's Press Inc., 1974.

EJ   Feather, Leonard. *The Encyclopedia of Jazz.* Rev. ed. New York: Horizon Press, 1960.

EJ7   Feather, Leonard, and Gitler, Ira. *The Encyclopedia of Jazz in the Seventies.* New York: Horizon Press, 1976.

EJS   Postal, Bernard; Silver, Jesse; and Silver, Roy. *Encyclopedia of Jews in Sports.* New York: Bloch, 1965.

EMD   Steinbrunner, Chris, and Penzler, Otto, eds. *Encyclopedia of Mystery and Detection.* New York: McGraw-Hill Book Co., 1976.

EMT   Green, Stanley. *Encyclopaedia of the Musical Theatre.* New York: Dodd, Mead & Co., 1976.

EOP   Shepard, Leslie. *Encyclopedia of Occultism & Parapsychology.* 2 vols. and supplement. Detroit: Gale Research Co., 1978-1982.

EPM   Stambler, Irwin. *Encyclopedia of Popular Music.* New York: St. Martin's Press, 1965.

ESF   Nicholls, Peter. *The Encyclopedia of Science Fiction.* New York: Granada Publishing Ltd., 1979.

ET   Brown, Les. *The New York Times Encyclopedia of Television.* New York: Times Books, 1977.

EWG   O'Neal, Bill. *Encyclopedia of Western Gunfighters.* Norman, Okla.: University of Oklahoma Press, 1979.

EWL   Fleishmann, Wolfgang Bernard, ed. *Encyclopedia of World Literature in the 20th Century.* Vols. 1-3. New York: Frederick Ungar Publishing Co., 1967.

F1   Stewart, John. *Filmarama.* Vol. 1: The Formidable Years, 1893-1919. Metuchen, N.J.: The Scarecrow Press Inc., 1975.

F2   Stewart, John. *Filmarama.* Vol. 2: The Flaming Years, 1920-1929. Metuchen, N.J.: The Scarecrow Press Inc., 1977.

FAA   Young, William C. *Famous Actors and Actresses on the American Stage.* New York: R. R. Bowker Co., 1975.

FAP   Kane, Joseph Nathan. *Facts about the Presidents.* 4th ed. New York: The H. W. Wilson Co., 1981.

FB   Mendell, Ronald L., and Phares, Timothy B. *Who's Who in Football.* New Rochelle, N.Y.: Arlington House, 1974.

FBJ   De Montreville, Doris, and Crawford, Elizabeth D. *Fourth Book of Junior Authors and Illustrators.* New York: The H. W. Wilson Co., 1978.

FC   Halliwell, Leslie. *The Filmgoer's Companion.* 3rd ed. New York: Avon Books, 1970.

FCW   Stambler, Irwin, and Landon, Grelun. *Encyclopedia of Folk, Country and Western Music.* New York: St. Martin's Press, 1969.

FD   Parish, James Robert, and Pitts, Michael R. *Film Directors: A Guide to Their American Films.* Metuchen, N.J.: The Scarecrow Press Inc., 1974.

FDG   Parish, James Robert. *Film Directors Guide-Western Europe.* Metuchen, N.J.: The Scarecrow Press Inc., 1976.

FF   Phyfe, William Henry P. *5,000 Facts and Fancies.* Reprint of the 1901 ed. Detroit: Gale Research Co., 1966.

FFA   Lawless, Ray M. *Folksingers and Folksongs in America.* 2nd ed. New York: Duell, Sloan & Pearce, 1965.

FFF   Reddall, Henry Frederic. *Fact, Fancy, and Fable.* Reprint of the 1889 ed. Detroit: Gale Research Co., 1968.

FHE   Fischler, Stan, and Fischler, Shirley. *Fischler's Hockey Encyclopedia.* New York: Thomas Y. Crowell Co., 1975.

FIR   *Films in Review.* New York: National Board of Review of Motion Pictures Inc., Feb., 1972- June/July, 1984.

FR   Marcin, Joe, and Byers, Dick. *Football Register.* St. Louis: The Sporting News Publishing Co., 1977.

GA   Amstutz, Walter. *Who's Who in Graphic Art.* Zurich: Amstutz & Herdeg Graphis Press, 1962.

GF   Elliott, Len, and Kelly, Barbara. *Who's Who in Golf.* New Rochelle, New York: Arlington House, 1976.

GLET   Lee, Frederick George. *A Glossary of Liturgical and Ecclesiastical Terms.* Reprint of the 1877 ed. Detroit: Gale Research Co., 1971.

GME   Scharff, Robert, ed. *Golf Magazine's Encyclopedia of Golf.* New York: Harper & Row Publishers, 1970.

GS   Smith, George B. Taurine Bibliophiles of America. Private communication.

GSH   Davis, Mac. *100 Greatest Sport Heroes.* Rev. ed. New York: Grosset & Dunlap, 1958.

GW   Williams, George. National Cowboy Hall of Fame, Rodeo Division. Private communication.

GWP   Nares, Robert. *A Glossary of Words, Phrases, Names and Allusions in the Works of English Authors.* Reprint of the 1905 ed. Detroit: Gale Research Co., 1966.

HCA   Parish, James Robert. *Hollywood Character Actors.* New Rochelle, N.Y.: Arlington House, 1978.

HDM   Bullock, Alan, and Stallybrass, Oliver, eds. *The Harper Dictionary of Modern Thought.* New York: Harper & Row Publishers, 1977.

HFF   Ashley, Mike. *Who's Who in Horror and Fantasy Fiction.* New York: Taplinger Publishing Co., 1977.

HFN   Hamst, Olphar, Esq. *Handbook of Fictitious Names.* Reprint of the 1868 ed. Detroit: Gale Research Co., 1969.

HHF   Walsh, William S. *Heroes and Heroines of Fiction*. Reprint of the 1914 ed. Detroit: Gale Research Co., 1966.

HK   Kariher, Harry C. *Who's Who in Hockey*. New Rochelle, N.Y.: Arlington House, 1973.

HN   Brewer, E. Cobham. *The Historic Note-Book*. Reprint of the 1891 ed. Detroit: Gale Research Co., 1966.

HPPN   Sharp, Harold S. *Handbook of Pseudonyms and Personal Nicknames*. 5 vols. Metuchen, N.J.: The Scarecrow Press Inc., 1972-1982.

HR   Elk, Herb. *The Hockey Register, 1976-77*. St. Louis: The Sporting News Publishing Co., 1976.

HT   Billings, Pat, and Eyles, Allen. *Hollywood Today*. New York: A. S. Barnes & Co., 1971.

IA   Thompson, Donald E. *Indiana Authors and Their Books, 1917-1966*. Crawfordsville, Ind.: Wabash College, 1974.

IAW   Gaster, Adrian. *The International Authors and Writers Who's Who*. 8th ed. Cambridge, England: Melrose Press Ltd., 1977.

IBW   Spradling, Mary Mace. *In Black and White*. 3rd ed. Detroit: Gale Research Co., 1980.

IBY   Ward, Martha E., and Marquardt, Dorothy A. *Illustrators of Books for Young People*. 2nd ed. Metuchen, N.J.: Scarecrow Press, 1975.

ICB   *Illustrators of Children's Books, 1946-56, 1957-66, 1967-76*. Boston: The Horn Book Inc., 1958, 1968, and 1978.

IEJ   Case, Brian. *The Illustrated Encyclopedia of Jazz*. New York: Harmony Books, 1978.

IP   Cushing, William. *Initials and Pseudonyms: A Dictionary of Literary Disguises*. Reprint of the 1885 ed. Detroit: Gale Research Co., 1982.

IPA   Golenpaul, Ann, ed. *Information Please Almanac, Atlas and Yearbook, 1977*. New York: Information Please Almanac, 1976.

ITA   Gertner, Richard, ed. *International Television Almanac, 1977*. New York: Quigley Publishing Co. Inc., 1977.

IWM   Gaster, Adrian. *International Who's Who in Music and Musician's Directory*. 8th ed. Cambridge, England: Melrose Press Ltd., 1977.

JF   Franklin, Joe. *Joe Franklin's Encyclopedia of Comedians*. Secaucus, N.J.: The Citadel Press, 1979.

JL   Greenberg, Martin H. *The Jewish Lists*. New York: Schocken Books, 1979.

LAO   Lawrence, A., ed. *Who's Who Among Living Authors of Older Nations*. Reprint of the 1931 ed. Detroit: Gale Research Co., 1966.

LBA   Shockley, Ann Allen, and Chandler, Sue P. *Living Black American Authors*. New York: R. R. Bowker Co., 1973.

LC   Ward, A. C. *Longman Companion to Twentieth Century Literature*. London: Longman Group Ltd., 1970.

LFW   Nash, Jay Robert. *Look for the Woman*. New York: M. Evans and Co., 1981.

LRR   *Lillian Roxon's Rock Encyclopedia*. New York: Grosset & Dunlap Inc., 1971.

MA   *Michigan Authors*. 2nd ed. Ann Arbor, Mich.: Michigan Association for Media in Education, 1980.

MBF   Lofts, W. O. G., and Adley, D. J. *The Men Behind Boy's Fiction*. London: Howard Baker, 1970.

MBL	Temple, Ruth Z., and Tucker, Martin. *Modern British Literature. A Library of Literary Criticism.* Vols. 1-3. New York: Frederick Ungar Publishing Co., 1966.
MEB	Hollander, Zander, ed. *The Modern Encyclopedia of Basketball.* New York: Four Winds Press, 1969.
MGL	Domandi, Agnes Koerner. *Modern German Literature. A Library of Literary Criticism.* 2 vols. New York: Frederick Ungar Publishing Co., 1972.
MJA	Fuller, Muriel. *More Junior Authors.* New York: The H. W. Wilson Co., 1963.
MK	Kleinknecht, Merl F. Society for American Baseball Research, Negro Leagues Research Committee. Private communication.
MM	Messick, Hank, and Goldblatt, Burt. *The Mobs and the Mafia.* New York: Thomas Y. Crowell Co., 1972.
MS	Ewen, David. *Musicians Since 1900.* New York: The H. W. Wilson Co., 1978.
MWD	Matlaw, Myron. *Modern World Drama.* New York: E. P. Dutton & Co. Inc., 1972.
MY	Miller, Paul Eduard. *Miller's Yearbook of Popular Music.* Chicago: Pem Publications, 1943.
NAA	Lawrence, Alberta, ed. *Who Was Who Among North American Authors 1921-1939.* Reprint of the 1921-1939 series. Detroit: Gale Research Co., 1976.
NAD	Jack, Alex, ed. *The New Age Dictionary.* Brookline, Mass.: Kanthaka Press, 1976.
NBA	Winick, Matt, ed. *National Basketball Association Official Guide for 1976-77.* St. Louis: The Sporting News Publishing Co., 1976.
NBB	Leadbitter, Mike. *Nothing but the Blues.* London: Hanover Books, 1971.
NLC	*Nineteenth-Century Literature Criticism.* Vols. 1-3. Detroit: Gale Research Co., 1981-1983.
NLG	*National League Green Book-1977.* Los Angeles: Baseball Fact Books, 1977.
NN	Noble, Vernon. *Nicknames Past and Present.* London: Hamish Hamilton Ltd., 1976.
NND	Attwater, Donald. *Names and Name-Days.* Reprint of the 1939 ed. Detroit: Gale Research Co., 1968.
NOJ	Rose, Al, and Souchon, Edmond. *New Orleans Jazz.* Baton Rouge. La.: Louisiana State University Press, 1978.
NP	Wells, Dicky. *The Night People.* London: Robert Hale & Co., 1971.
NPS	Dawson, Lawrence H. *Nicknames and Pseudonyms.* Reprint of the 1908 ed. Detroit: Gale Research Co., 1974.
NW	*Newsweek.* 1982-1986.
NY	*New York Times.* 1983-1986.
OBW	Peterson, Robert. *Only the Ball Was White.* Englewood Cliffs, N.J.: Prentice-Hall Inc., 1970.
OCF	Bawden, Liz-Anne, ed. *The Oxford Companion to Film.* New York: Oxford University Press, 1976.
OCS	Arlott, John, ed. *The Oxford Companion to Sports and Games.* New York: Oxford University Press, 1975.
OET	*United States Lawn Tennis Association Official Encyclopedia of Tennis.* New York: Harper & Row Publishers, 1972.
OP	Rich, Maria F., ed. *Who's Who in Opera.* New York: Arno Press Inc., 1976.

PA   Haynes, John Edward. *Pseudonyms of Authors.* Reprint of the 1882 ed. Detroit: Gale
           Research Co., 1969.

PAC   Ewen, David. *Popular American Composers.* 1st suppl. New York: The H. W. Wilson Co.,
           1972.

PB   Karst, Gene, and Jones, Martin J. Jr. *Who's Who in Professional Baseball.* New Rochelle,
           N.Y.: Arlington House, 1973.

PHM   Maclean, Don. *Pictorial History of the Mafia.* New York: Pyramid Books, 1974.

PI   O'Donoghue, D. J. *The Poets of Ireland.* Reprint of the 1912 ed. Detroit: Gale Research
           Co., 1968.

PMJ   Kinkle, Roger D. *The Complete Encyclopedia of Popular Music and Jazz, 1900-1950.* New
           Rochelle, N.Y.: Arlington House, 1974.

PPN   Payton, Geoffrey. *Payton's Proper Names.* New York: Frederick Warne, 1969.

PRS   Stambler, Irwin. *Encyclopedia of Pop, Rock and Soul.* New York: St. Martin's Press, 1974.

PW   *Publishers Weekly.* 1982-1986.

RBE   Loubet, Nat, and Ort, John. *The Ring Boxing Encyclopedia and Record Book.* 1977 ed. New
           York: The Ring Book Shop, 1976.

RH   Brewer, E. Cobham. *The Reader's Handbook of Famous Names in Fiction, Allusions,
           References, Proverbs, Plots, Stories, and Poems.* Reprint of the 1899 ed. Detroit: Gale
           Research Co., 1966.

RM   York, William. *Who's Who in Rock Music.* Seattle: Atomic Press, 1978.

RO1   Nite, Norm N. *Rock On.* Vol. 1: The Solid Gold Years. New York: Thomas Y. Crowell Co.,
           1974.

RO2   Nite, Norm N. *Rock On.* Vol. 2: The Modern Years. New York: Thomas Y. Crowell Co.,
           1978.

SA   *The Official Associated Press Sports Almanac 1975.* New York: Dell Publishing Co. Inc.,
           1975.

SAT   Commire, Anne. *Something about the Author.* Vols. 1-33. Gale Research Co., 1971-1983.

SC   Truitt, Evelyn Mack. *Who Was Who on Screen.* 2nd ed. New York: R. R. Bowker Co.,
           1977.

SF   Ash, Brian. *Who's Who in Science Fiction.* New York: Taplinger Publishing Co., 1976.

SFL   Reginald, R. *Fiction and Fantasy Literature.* 2 vols. Detroit: Gale Research Co., 1979.

SFP   McGhan, Barry. *Science Fiction and Fantasy Pseudonyms.* Dearborn, Mich., Howard
           DeVore, 1978.

SG   Gallelo, Al 'Scoop.' International Veteran Boxers Association. Private communication.

SI   *Sports Illustrated.* 1980-1984.

SMG   Sports Media Guides. Official press guides for professional baseball, basketball, football,
           and hockey teams.

SN   Frey, Albert R. *Sobriquets and Nicknames.* Reprint of the 1888 ed. Detroit: Gale Research
           Co., 1966.

SR   Frommer, Harvey. *Sports Roots.* New York: Atheneum, 1979.

SSS   Wieder, Judy, and Mattern, Lynn. *Right On's 100 Super-Soul Stars.* Hollywood, Calif.:
           Laufer Co., 1972.

SW   Willis, John, ed. *Screen World.* Vol. 27. New York: Crown Publishers Inc., 1976.

SWI	Besford, Pat. *Encyclopaedia of Swimming.* New York: St. Martin's Press, 1971.
TBJ	De Montreville, Doris, and Hill, Donna. *Third Book of Junior Authors.* New York: The H. W. Wilson Co., 1972.
TC	Kunitz, Stanley J., and Haycraft, Howard, eds. *Twentieth Century Authors.* New York: The H. W. Wilson Co., 1942.
TC1	Kunitz, Stanley J., and Colby, Vineta, eds. *Twentieth Century Authors.* First Supplement. New York: The H. W. Wilson Co., 1955.
TCC	Kirkpatrick, D. L. *Twentieth-Century Children's Writers.* New York: St. Martin's Press, 1978.
TCCM	Reilly, John M. *Twentieth-Century Crime and Mystery Writers.* New York: St. Martin's Press, 1980.
TCL	Seymour-Smith, Martin. *Who's Who in Twentieth Century Literature.* New York: Holt, Rinehart and Winston, 1976.
TF	Hanley, Reid M. *Who's Who in Track and Field.* New Rochelle, N.Y.: Arlington House, 1973.
THR	*Who Was Who in the Theatre: 1912-1976.* 4 vols. Reprint of the 1912-1972 eds. Detroit: Gale Research Co., 1978.
TI	*Time.* 1982-1986.
TLC	*Twentieth-Century Literary Criticism.* Vols. 1-11. Detroit: Gale Research Co., 1978-1983.
TR	Herbert, Ian. *Who's Who in the Theatre.* 16th ed. Detroit: Gale Research Co., 1977.
UH	Gerwig, Henrietta. *University Handbook for Readers and Writers.* New York: Thomas Y. Crowell Co., 1965.
WA	Delury, George E., ed. *The World Almanac and Book of Facts 1977.* New York: Newspaper Enterprise Association Inc., 1976.
WBC	McCallum, John D. *The Encyclopedia of World Boxing Champions Since 1882.* Radnor, Pa.: Chilton Book Co., 1975.
WBD	*Webster's Biographical Dictionary.* Springfield, Mass.: G. & C. Merriam Co., 1974.
WD	*The Writers Directory, 1974-76.* New York: St. Martin's Press, 1974.
WEC	Horn, Maurice. *The World Encyclopedia of Cartoons.* 2 vols. New York: Chelsea House Publishers, 1980.
WECO	Horn, Maurice. *The World Encyclopedia of Comics.* 2 vols. New York: Chelsea House Publishers, 1976.
WEF	Cawkwell, Tim, and Smith, John M. *The World Encyclopedia of Film.* New York: World Publishing, 1972.
WF	Cowie, Peter. *World Filmography, 1967 and 1968.* 2 vols. New York: A. S. Barnes and Co., 1977.
WFA	Lambert, Eleanor. *World of Fashion.* New York: R. R. Bowker Co., 1976.
WGT	Rock, James A. *Who Goes There.* Bloomington, Ind.: James A. Rock and Co., 1979.
WOA	Wakeman, John. *World Authors, 1950-1970 and 1970-1975.* 2 vols. New York: The H. W. Wilson Co., 1975 and 1980.
WP	*Washington Post.* 1981-1985.
WW	Gribbin, Lenore S. *Who's Whodunit.* University of North Carolina Library Studies, No. 5. Reprint of the 1969 ed. Ann Arbor, Mich.: University Microfilms International, 1978.

WWB   Siwoff, Seymour, ed. *Who's Who in Baseball.* 62nd ed. New York: Who's Who in Baseball Magazine Co. Inc., 1977.

WWJ   Chilton, John. *Who's Who of Jazz.* New York: Chilton Book Co., 1970.

WWL   *Who Was Who in Literature, 1906-1934.* 2 vols. Reprint of 'Literary Yearbook' (1906-1922) and 'Who's Who in Literature' (1924-1934). Detroit: Gale Research Co., 1979.

WWS   McCormick, Donald. *Who's Who in Spy Fiction.* New York: Taplinger Publishing Co. Inc., 1977.

WWW   Keegan, John. *Who Was Who in World War II.* London: Arms and Armour Press, 1978.

WYA   Sarkissian, Adele. *Writers for Young Adults: Biographies Master Index.* 1st ed. Detroit: Gale Research Co., 1979.

YAB   Commire, Anne, ed. *Yesterday's Authors of Books for Children.* Vols. 1-2. Detroit: Gale Research Co., 1977-1978.

Pseudonyms and Nicknames Dictionary

Volume 2
L-Z

L

Asterisk (*) indicates assumed name.

L.
See Beltz, George Frederick

L.
See Chapman, Edward John

L.
See Lachlan, Robert

L.
See Lamson, Alvan

L.
See Landon, Letitia Elizabeth

L.
See Laycock, Thomas

L.
See Lennox, James

L.
See Littledale, Richard

L.
See Lothrop, Samuel Kirkland

L.
See Lunt, William Parsons

L.
See Lyons, Lady, of Strathmore

L.
See O'Neill, John

L.
See Petty, [Sir] William

L.
See Swanwick, Catherine

L. A.
See Anthony, Louisa

L. A.
See Atthill, Lombe

L. A. C.
See Mudge, Henry

L. B. J.
See Johnson, Lyndon Baines

L. B. T.
See Thomas, Lawrence Buckley

L. C.
See Coleman, Lyman

L. C.
See Coward, William

L. C. H.
See Hill, L. C.

L. C. M.
See Moulton, Ellen Louise Chandler

L. D.
See Digges, Leonard

L. D. Y.
See Buckley, Michael Bernard

L. E.
See Eden, Eleanor

L. E.
See Edwards, Mrs.

L. E.
See Engel, Louis

L. E.
See Eusden, Laurence

L. E.
See Pegge, Samuel

L. E. B.
See Bather, Lucy Elizabeth Bloomfield

L. E. L.
See Landon, Letitia Elizabeth

L. F.
See Hawker, Mary Elizabeth

L. F. F. M.
See Miller, Lydia Falconer

L. G.
See Gill, Lilly K. E.

L. G. C.
See Condon, Lizzie G.

L. H.
See Hooper, Lucy

L. H. C.
See Lueders, Charles Henry

L. H. S.
See Sigourney, Lydia Howard Huntley

L. I.
See Pratt, Jacob Loring

L. K.
See Kinsella, Linda Iris

L. K. Y.
See Hickey, Michael Patrick

L. L. A. V.
See Very, Lydia Louisa Ann

L. L. L.
See Foe, Daniel

L. L. L.
See Lauren, L. L.

L. L. T.
See Toynbee, Lawrence

L. M.
See Lim, Boon Keng

L. M.
See Tucker, Eleonora C.

L. M. C.
See Childs, Lydia Maria Francis

L. M. C.
See Cole, L. M.

L. M. H.
See Hubbard, L. M.

L. M. J.
See Ellemjay, Louise

L. M. W. M., Rt. Hon.
See Montagu, Mary Wortley

L. N.
See Cushman, George Francis

L. N. F.
See Fitzsimon, Ellen

L. N. R.
See Ranyard, Ellen Henrietta White

L. P.
See Munday, Anthony

L. P.
See Potocki, Leon

L. P. W.
See Wright, Lucy Pauline

L. R. G.
See Griffith, Lawrence Rector

L. S.
See Sharpe, Lancelot

L. S.
See Stephen, [Sir] Leslie

L. S. A.
See Auger, Louis Simon

L. S. C.
See Cushing, Luther Stearns

[The] L. S. D. King
See Stanley, Augustus Owsley, III

L. S. D., Mr.
See Stanley, Augustus Owsley, III

[The] L. S. D. Tycoon
See Stanley, Augustus Owsley, III

L. S. E.
See Gathercole, Michael Augustus

L. S. G.
See Glanzman, Louis S.

L. S. T.
See Temple, Laura Sophia

L. T.
See Twining, Louisa

L. W.
See Waldo, Leonard

L. W.
See Whistler, Laurence

L. W.
See Whitney, Louisa [Goddard]

L. W. J. S.
See Thisted, V[aldemar] Adolph

La
See Second element of name for further listings

La Barbera, Pascel 1944-   [EJ7]
American jazz musician
* La Barbera, Pat

La Barbera, Pat
See La Barbera, Pascel

La Barr, Creighton
See Von Block, Bela

La Beaumelle, Laurent Angliviele De 1727-1773   [HPPN]
French author
* Le Voyageur, Krinebol

La Belle, Chemet
See Lanham, Ceora B.

La Bolina, Jack
See Vacchi, Augustus Victor

La Bruyere, Jean de 1645-1696   [DNNS, RH]
French author
* [The] Theophrastus of France

La Cock, Joanne Letitia 1923-   [BDF, FC, WEF]
American actress
* Dru, Joanne
* Marshall, Joanne

La Cock, Pierre 1917?-   [HPPN, WP 10-5-85]
American entertainer and television personality
* Marshall, Peter

La Colere [or Lacolere], Francois
See Aragon, Louis

La Coste, Guy Robert 20th c.   [WW]
Author
* Berton, Guy [joint pseudonym with Eadfrid A. Bingham]

La Due, Hubert 1891-   [NAA]
American author, critic, journalist
* Moore, Kenneth

La Farge, John 1835-1910   [HPPN]
American attorney, painter, inventor
* [The] Father of Opalescent Glass

La Faye, Julian 1907?-   [F2, FC]
American actor and singer
* Carroll, John

La Fayette, Comtesse de
See Pioche de la Vergne, Marie Madeleine

La Flesche, Joseph 1822-1889   [BI]
American Indian chief
* Iron Eyes

La Flesche, Susette
See Bright Eyes

La Follette, Battling Bob
See La Follette, Robert Marion, Sr.

La Follette, Robert Marion, Sr. 1855-1925   [HPPN]
American politician
* La Follette, Battling Bob

La Fontaine, Blanche
See Schwalberg, Carol[yn Ernestine Stein]

La Fontaine, Jean de 1621-1695   [DNNF, SN]
French poet and author
* [The] Aesop of France
* [The] French Homer
* Polyphile

[The] La Fontaine of the Vaudeville
See Panard, Charles-Francois

La Fontaine, Pierre Dewey, Jr. 1930-   [HPPN]
American jazz musician
* Fountain, Pete

La Forrounnays, Mlle.   [PA]
Author
* Craven, Mrs.

La Fruelen, Mademoiselle ?-1801   [FFF]
Daughter of Emperor Francis Joseph I of Austria
* [The] Lady of the Haystack?

La Gierse, Edyth 1881-1954   [BBD]
American opera singer
* De Treville, Yvonne

La Guardia, Fiorello Henry 1882-1947   [HPPN, PW 2-25-83]
American politician
* Butch
* [The] Little Flower

La Harpe, Jean Francois de 1739-1803   [DNNS, SN]
French poet and critic
* [The] Fontenelle of His Generation
* [The] French Quintilian

La Hiff, Anne Veronica 1905?-1965   [BEW, CED, F2]
American actress
* Carroll, Nancy

La La, Prince
See Mackenzie, Foster, III

La Lupe
See Raymond, Lupe Victoria Jolie

La Marck, Guillaume [or William] de 1446?-1485   [DNNF, FFF, WBD]
Belgian soldier
* Sanglier des Ardennes
* [The] Wild Boar of the Ardennes

La Marck, Robert III de 1491?-1537?   [WBD]
Marshal of France
* Bouillon, Comte de
* Fleuranges, Seigneur de
* [Le] Jeune Aventureux

La Marr, Barbara
See Watson, Reatha

La Menthe, Ferdinand Joseph 1885-1941   [BBD, IBW, WWJ]
American jazz musician
* Morton, Jelly Roll
* Morton, William Ferdinand Joseph

La Moille, [Dr.] Tom G.
See Olmsted, George La Moille

La Mont, Harry
See Gilbert, Alfred

La Mothe Le Vayer, Francois de 1583?-1672   [DEP, DNNS, RH]
French philosopher and author
* [The] Modern Plutarch
* [The] Plutarch of France

La Mothe, N. Pere 1680-1740   [PA]
Author
* [La] Hode

La Plante, Laura 1904-   [HPPN]
American actress
* [The] Blue Eyed Blonde

La Plante, Sandra
See Lyons, Luella B.

La Remnee, Francine 1898-   [BEW]
French-born actress
* Larrimore, Francine

La Reyniere
See Courtine, Robert

La Roca, Pete
See Sims, Peter

[The] La Rochefoucauld of England
See Stanhope, Philip Dormer

La Rocque De La Rour, Roderick
1896?-1969 [F1, F2, FC]
American actor
* La Rocque, Rod

La Rocque, Rod
See La Rocque De La Rour, Roderick

La Roe, James 1928?- [HPPN]
American entertainer
* Dixon, Richard M.

La Roque
See Boyer, Louis

La Rose, Anthony
See La Rose, John A.

La Rose, Harry
See O'Neill, Lally

La Rose, John A. 1917- [CW]
Trinidadian poet, critic, publisher
* La Rose, Anthony

La Rouchefoucauld-Chamfort
See Chamfort, Nicolas Sebastian Roch

La Roy, Rita
See Stuart, Ina

La Roze, Claude 1640?-1686 [HPPN]
French actor
* Rosimond

La Rue, Danny
See Carroll, Daniel Patrick

La Rue, Jack
See Biondolillo, Gaspare

La Rue, Jean
See Bailey, Eugene Marcus

La Rue, Leonard P. 1915?- [BI]
American sea captain and monk
* Marinus, [Brother]

La Salle, Victor [house pseudonym, John Spencer]
See Fanthorpe, R[obert] Lionel

La Salle, Victor [house pseudonym]
See Glasby, John [Stephen]

La Santera [The Sanctuary Keeper]
See Martin, Jose

La Spina, Greye Bragg 1880-1969
[HFF, NAA, SFP]
American writer
* Di Savuto, Baroness
* Kofoed, J. C.
* Putnam, Isra

La Thorne, Jean
See Dilks, John M.

La Torre, Charles A.
See Dottore, Charles A.

La Torre, Giuseppe 20th c. [WF]
Italian cinematographer
* Tower, Joseph L.

La Touche, Geoffry
See Snow, Theodore William

La Tour d'Auvergne, Henri de [Duc de Bouillon] 1555-1623 [DEP]
Marshal of France
* [The] Demon of Rebellions

La Tour [or Latour] d'Auvergne, Theophile Malo Corret de 1743-1800
[DEP, DNNS, SN]
French soldier
* [The] First Grenadier of France
* [Le] Premier Grenadier de France
* [Le] Premier Grenadier de la Republique

La Tour, Tomline
See Gilbert, [Sir] William Schwenck

La Valliere, Duchesse de
See Baume Le Blanc, Francoise Louise de la

La Varre, John Merton 1901-1959 [SC]
American actor
* Merton, John

La Vernie, Laura
See Anderson, Laura

La Vinder, Gracille
See Mattox, Hazel

Laage, Barbara
See Colombat, Claire

Laar [or Laer], Pieter van 1613?-1674?
[DNNS, NPS, RH, SN]
Dutch painter
* [Il] Bamboccio
* [The] Deformed
* Michael Angelo de Kermesses
* [Le] Michel Ange des Bamboches

Laaveg, Bronco
See Laaveg, Paul

Laaveg, Paul 20th c.
American football player
* Laaveg, Bronco

Labadie, Joseph Gilles Michel 1932-
[CEI]
Canadian-born hockey player
* Labadie, Mike

Labadie, Mike
See Labadie, Joseph Gilles Michel

Labadie, Mrs. Francis [FFF]
Entertainer
* Russell, Hattie

Labaigt, Laurent 1859-1942 [WBD]
French poet and author
* Rameau, Jean

Labarnas
See Suppiluliumas

Labarre, Louis 1810-? [IP]
Belgian journalist
* Bienaise, Jacques

LaBastille, Anne 1938- [CA]
American author and illustrator
* Bowes, Anne LaBastille

Labat, Jean-Yves 20th c. [CMA]
Musician
* Frog, M.

L'Abbe, Joseph Barnabe Saint-Sevin
See Saint Sevin, Joseph Barnabe

L'Abbe, Maurice Joseph 1947- [CEI]
Canadian-born hockey player
* L'Abbe, Moe

L'Abbe, Moe
See L'Abbe, Maurice Joseph

Labby
See Labouchere, Henry

Labe, Louise 1526-1566 [DNNS, FFF, SN]
French poet
* [The] Aspasia of Lyons
* [The] Beautiful Ropemaker
* [La] Belle Cordiere
* Captain Louisa
* Loys, Captain

LaBelle, Patti
See Holt, Patricia

Labenette
See Corsee, Jean Baptiste

Labeo [The Thick-Lipped]
See Notker

Laberius Crispinus, Rufus
See Shakespeare, William

LaBlanche, George
See Blais, George

[The] Labor Baron
See Lewis, John Llewellyn

[The] Labor Mayor
See Dore, John Francis

Labor, Mr.
See Turner, James Castle, Jr.

LaBorde, Rene
See Neuffer, Irene LaBorde

Labor's Gray Mystery
See Wilson, [James] Harold

Labor's Rugged Individualist
See Reuther, Walter Philip

Labor's Troubadour
See Glazer, Joe

Labouchere, Henry 1831-1912 [FFF, IP]
British author, journalist, politician
* Besieged Resident
* Labby
* Our Member for Paris
* Scrutator

Laboulaye, Edouard 1811-1883 [HPPN, IP, NPS]
French jurist, statesman, author
* Alceste
* Lefebvre, [Dr.] Rene
* Nadie, X.

Laboy, Coco
See Laboy, Jose Alberto

Laboy, Jose Alberto 1939-   [BE]
Puerto Rican-born baseball player
* Laboy, Coco

Labraaten, Dan 1951-   [SMG]
Swedish-born hockey player
* Labraaten, Rusty

Labraaten, Rusty
See Labraaten, Dan

Labronio, G.
See Marradi, Giovanni

Labrousse, M.   [PA]
Author
* Carbon

Labrunie, Gerard 1808-1855   [WBD]
French author
* Nerval, Gerard de

Labuchin, Rassoul 1939-   [CW]
Haitian poet, author, playwright
* Medard, Yves

LaBuna, Virginia 1905?-1980
American actress
* Faire, Virginia Brown

Labus, Marta Haake 1943-   [CA]
American author
* McCormick, Claire

Lacanal, Joseph 1762-1845   [WBD]
French educator and politician
* Lakanal, Joseph

Lacanza, Manuel   [PA]
Author
* Ben-Ezra, Juan J.

Lace [Secret Service code name]
See Onassis, Jacqueline Lee [Bouvier] [Kennedy]

Lacenaire, Pierre-Francois 1800-1836 [CEC]
French assassin, thief, forger
* Gaillard

Lacepede, Comte de
See De la Ville, Bernard Germain Etienne

Lacey, Ginger
See Lacey, J. H.

Lacey, J. H. 1917-   [BDW]
British fighter pilot
* Lacey, Ginger

Lacey, John
See Alexander, Boyd

Lacey, Mrs. Henry   [FFF]
Entertainer
* Hawthorne, Kate

Lacey, Paul 1851-1900   [BMH]
British entertainer
* Godfrey, Charles

Lach-Szyrma, Wladislaw Somerville 1841-1915   [SFL, WGT]
British author
* W. S. L. S.

LaChance, Candy
See LaChance, George Joseph

LaChance, George Joseph 1870-1932 [AS, BE]
American baseball player
* LaChance, Candy

Lachlan, Robert 19th c.   [IP]
British army officer and author
* L.

Lachoff, Sol 1911-   [ASC]
American composer
* Lake, Sol

Lack, B. D.
See Lack, Barbara Dacia

Lack, Barbara Dacia 20th c.   [ART]
British artist
* Lack, B. D.

Lack, Pearl 20th c.   [BEW]
American choreographer and dancer
* Lang, Pearl

Lack, Simon
See Macalpine, Simon

[The] Lackey
See Leclerc du Tremblay, Francois

Lackland
See John

Lackland, Thomas
See Hill, George Canning

Lackritz, Steven 1934-   [EJ]
American jazz musician
* Lacy, Steve

Lacks, Cecilia 1945-   [CA]
American author and educator
* Lacks, Cissy

Lacks, Cissy
See Lacks, Cecilia

Lacks, Henrietta
Author
* Lane, Helen

Laclede, Pierre
See Liguest, Pierre Laclede

Laco
See Higginson, Stephen

LaCock, Pete
See LaCock, Ralph Pierre, II

LaCock, Ralph Pierre, II 1952-   [SMG, WWB]
American baseball player
* LaCock, Pete

Lacon
See Watson, Edmund Henry Lacon

[The] Lacordaire of America
See Esquin, Mamertus

LaCosta
See Tucker, LaCosta

Lacoste, Jean Amand 1797-1885   [FFF]
French playwright
* Saint Amand

Lacoste, Jean-Rene 1905-   [BBH]
French tennis player
* [The] Crocodile

Lacoste, Mathilde de   [FFF]
French author
* Gerald, Louise

Lacoume, Emile 1885-1946   [NOJ]
American jazz musician
* Lacoume, Stalebread

Lacoume, Stalebread
See Lacoume, Emile

LaCount, Sherwood Keith 1912-1972 [SC]
American actor
* Keith, Sherwood

Lacretie, Arnold
See Claretie, Arsene Arnaud

Lacroix, Paul 1806-1884   [FFF, HPPN, PA, WBD]
French author
* Bibliophile Jacob
* Dubourg, Antony
* Dufour, Pierre
* Jacob, P. L., Bibliophile

Lacroix, Ramon
See McKeag, Ernest L[ionel]

Lactantius, Lucius Coelius ?-330 [DNNF, HN, SN]
Author and religious leader
* [The] Christian Cicero

Lactilla
See Yearsley, Ann

Lacy, Charles
See Hippisley Coxe, Antony D[acres]

Lacy, Ed
See Zinberg, Leonard

Lacy, Francis Maurice 1725-1801 [WBD]
Irish-born army officer
* Lascy, Franz Moritz

Lacy, Frank
See Stocken, Frank

Lacy, George Carleton 1888-1951 [BI]
American clergyman
* Trask, Jeremy

Lacy, Joe
See Elorrieta, Jose Maria

Lacy, John
See Darley, George

Lacy, Lee
See Lacy, Leondaus

Lacy, Leondaus 1948-   [BE, SMG]
American baseball player
* Lacy, Lee

Lacy, Peter 1678-1751   [WBD]
Irish-born army officer
* Lascy, Pierre

Lacy, Rube
See Lacy, Rubin

Lacy, Rubin 1901-1972? [BWW]
American singer
* Lacy, Rube

Lacy, Sam 20th c. [IBW]
American columnist
* [The] Dean of Black Sports Writers

Lacy, Steve
See Lackritz, Steven

Lacy, Willoughby 18th c. [PI]
Irish poet
* One Formerly Possessed of the Place

[The] Lad
See Almagro, Diego de

[The] Lad from Maine
See Oakes, [Sir] Harry

[The] Lad from Wigan
See Booth, James

Ladd, Alan, Jr. 1938?-
American film studio executive
* Ladd, Laddie

Ladd, Big Cat
See Ladd, Ernest [Ernie]

Ladd, Big Ernie
See Ladd, Ernest [Ernie]

Ladd, Catherine Stratton 1809-? [FFF]
Writer
* Alida
* Arcturus
* Mayflower, Minnie
* Morna

Ladd, Cheryl
See Stoppelmoor, Cheryl

Ladd, Diane
See Ladnier, Diane

Ladd, Ernest 1875-1940 [SC]
American actor
* Howard, Ernest

Ladd, Ernest [Ernie] 20th c. [HPPN]
American wrestler and football player
* [The] King of Wrestling
* Ladd, Big Cat
* Ladd, Big Ernie

Ladd, Fred
See Laderman, Fred

Ladd, H. Dexter, Sr. 1873-1926
[HPPN]
American musician and director
* Harrington, Jim

Ladd, Joseph Brown 1764-1786 [FFF]
American poet
* Arouet

Ladd, Laddie
See Ladd, Alan, Jr.

Ladd, Marion Frances 1916-1971 [SC]
American actress
* Robinson, Frances

Ladd, Pete 20th c. [DF 4-19-83]
American baseball player
* Bigfoot

Ladd, Veronica
See Miner, Jane Claypool

Ladd, William 1778-1841 [HPPN, PA]
American author
* [The] Apostle of Peace
* Philanthropos

Lade, Doyle Marion 1921- [BE]
American baseball player
* Lade, Porky

Lade, Porky
See Lade, Doyle Marion

Ladenis, Carlos
See Sykowski, Abram

Laderman, Fred 1927- [WEC]
American animator and producer
* Ladd, Fred

Ladewig, Marion 1914- [HPPN]
American bowler
* [The] Lady of the Lanes

Ladislas Posthumus
See Ladislas V [or VI]

Ladislas I 1040?-1095 [WBD]
King of Hungary
* [The] Saint

Ladislas IV 1262-1290 [WBD]
King of Hungary
* [The] Cuman

Ladislas V [or VI] 1440-1457 [WBD]
King of Hungary
* Ladislas Posthumus

Ladislaus [or Lancelot] 1379?-1414 [SN]
King of Naples
* [The] Victorious

Ladnek, Odlaw
See Kendall, Carlton

Ladner, Kurt
See DeMille, Nelson

Ladnier, Diane 1932- [SW]
French-born actress
* Ladd, Diane

Lados, Carlos
See Sycowski, Abraham Albert

LaDoux, Scott 20th c. [RBE]
American boxer
* Ledoux, Scott

[A] Lady
See Amory, Thomas

[A] Lady
See Anne

[A] Lady
See Astell, Mary

[A] Lady
See Austen, Jane

[A] Lady
See Battier, Henrietta

Lady
See Black, Lillian

[A] Lady
See Blennerhasset, Margaret [Agnew]

[A] Lady
See Blount, Martha

[A] Lady
See Bonhote, Elizabeth

[A] Lady
See Botsford, Margaret

[A] Lady
See Bouligny, Mrs. M. E. Parker

[A] Lady
See Budge, Jane

[A] Lady
See Celesia, Dorothea Mallet

[A] Lady
See Cooper, Susan Fenimore

[A] Lady
See Cursham, Mary Ann

[A] Lady
See Douglas, Catharine [Duchess of Queensberry]

[A] Lady
See Elliott, Charlotte

[A] Lady
See Fielding, Sarah

[A] Lady
See Finch, Anne [Countess of Winchilsea]

[A] Lady
See French, Sarah

[A] Lady
See Gamble, Elizabeth Washington

[A] Lady
See Gunn, Harriet

[A] Lady
See Gwynn, Albinia

[A] Lady
See Halkett, [Lady] Anne

[A] Lady
See Hicks, Emilie Earle [Steele]

[A] Lady
See Hill, [Sir] John

[A] Lady
See Howe, Julia Ward

[A] Lady
See Jackson, M. E.

[A] Lady
See Jameson, Anna Murphy

[A] Lady
See Jourdan, Mary J.

[A] Lady
See Kitching, Mrs. H. St. A.

[A] Lady
See Mackenzie, Mary Jane

[A] Lady
See Martin, Mrs. E. Throop

[The] Lady
See Milton, John

[A] Lady
See Nicol, Martha

[A] Lady
See O'Brien, Mary

[A] Lady
See Palmer, Mrs. James F. [Reynolds]

[A] Lady
See Perkins, Eliza

[A] Lady
See Pickard, Hannah Maynard [Thompson]

[A] Lady
See Plumptre, Annabella

[A] Lady
See Porter, Jane

[A] Lady
See Rawson, Mrs. Harry

[A] Lady
See Ritchie, Anna Cora [Ogden Mowatt]

[A] Lady
See Rundell, Mrs.

[A] Lady
See St. Clair, Rosalind

[A] Lady
See Sewell, Elizabeth Missing

[A] Lady
See Smith, Sarah Pogson

[A] Lady
See Spence, Elizabeth Isabella

[A] Lady
See Wallis, Mary Davis [Cook]

[A] Lady
See White, Hannah

[A] Lady
See Wirt, Elizabeth Washington [Gamble]

[A] Lady
See Wray, Mary

Lady Bird Johnson
See Johnson, Claudia Alta [Taylor]

Lady Calantha
See Lamb, [Lady] Caroline

Lady Deloraine ?-1744 [SN]
* Delia

Lady Di
See Diana [Frances]

[The] Lady Drag Racer
See Goins, Nellie Louise

[The] Lady Explorer
See Barreto, [Dona] Isabel

[The] Lady Freemason
See St. Leger, Elizabeth

[The] Lady from Philadelphia
See Anderson, Marian

[The] Lady Governor
See Barreto, [Dona] Isabel

Lady Gustine
See Weaver, Gustine Courson

[The] Lady in Black
See Jiang Qing

[The] Lady in Black
See Mefford, Ditra Helena

[A] Lady in England
See Tickell, Thomas

[The] Lady in Pants
See Bloomer, Amelia Jenks

[The] Lady in Red
See Franklin, Polly

[A] Lady Lately Deceased
See Bowdler, Henrietta

[The] Lady Lazarus
See Gumm, Frances

Lady Lindy
See Earhart, Amelia

[The] Lady Magistrate
See Berkley, Lady

[The] Lady Margaret Professor of Divinity
See Blunt, John James

Lady Monteagle
See Lamb, [Lady] Caroline

[The] Lady Mountaineer
See Peck, Annie S.

[A] Lady of Boston
See Nickerson, Susan D.

[A] Lady of Charleston, S. C.
See Murden, Eliza

[The] Lady of Christ College
See Milton, John

[The] Lady of Christ's
See Milton, John

[The] Lady of England
See Matilda [or Maud]

[A] Lady of Fashion
See Blackwell, Miss

[A] Lady of Fashion
See Thackeray, William Makepeace

[The] Lady of Godey's
See Hale, Sarah Josepha Buell

[The] Lady of Literature
See Evans, Marian

[A] Lady of Maine
See Barrell, Sarah Sayward

[A] Lady of Massachusetts
See Barrell, Sarah Sayward

[A] Lady of Massachusetts
See Child, Lydia Maria [Francis]

[A] Lady of Massachusetts
See Foster, Hannah [Webster]

[The] Lady of Mercia
See Ethelflaeda

[A] Lady of New Hampshire
See Hale, Sarah Josepha Buell

[A] Lady of New Orleans
See Southwood, Marion

[A] Lady of New York
See Haight, Sarah [Rogers]

[A] Lady of Philadelphia
See Botsford, Margaret

[A] Lady of Philadelphia
See Hall, Sarah [Ewing]

[A] Lady of Philadelphia
See Leslie, Eliza

[A] Lady of Quality
See Bagnold, Enid

[A] Lady of Quality
See Chudleigh, [Lady] Mary Lee

[A] Lady of Quality
See Vane, Ann

[A] Lady of Quality
See Wynn, Frances Williams

[A] Lady of Rank
See Bury, Charlotte Susan Maria [Campbell]

[A] Lady of Rank
See Egerton, Mary Margaret

Lady of Seneca Falls
See Mott, Lucretia Coffin

[The] Lady of the Camelias
See Du Plessis, Marie [Rose Alphonsine Plessis]

[The] Lady of the Haystack?
See La Fruelen, Mademoiselle

[The] Lady of the Iron Watchdog
See Ingalls, Marilla Baker

[The] Lady of the Lanes
See Ladewig, Marion

[A] Lady of the Last Century
See Montagu, Elizabeth Robinson

[The] Lady of the Mercians
See Aethelflaed [Aethelfled or Elflida]

[The] Lady of the Stars
See Proctor, Mary

[The] Lady of the Sun
See Perrers [or Pierce?], Alice

Lady of the Vale
See Butler, Eleanor

Lady of the Vale
See Ponsonby, Sarah

[A] Lady of Virginia?
See Elwes, A. W.

Lady of Virginia
See McGuire, Mrs. J. P.

Lady Olga
See Barnell, Jane

Lady Pearl
See Mitchell, Lottie Pearl

[The] Lady Who Loves Libraries
See Durham, Marilyn

Lady Who Prefers to be Anonymous
See Jolly, Emily

Lady with a Sceptre
See Elizabeth I

[The] Lady With Muscle
See Prudden, Bonnie

[The] Lady With the Hatchet
See Nation, Carry Amelia Moore
Gloyd

[The] Lady with the Lamp
See Nightingale, Florence

[The] Ladykiller
See Landru, Henri Desire

[The] Ladykiller
See Smith, George Joseph

Ladylift
See Hutchinson, John

Laelius
See Boswell, James

Laelius
See Disraeli, Benjamin

Laelius, Gaius 2nd c. BC [DEP, NPS,
WBD]
Roman general and statesman
* [The] Roman Socrates
* Sapiens
* [The] Wise

Laengsdorff, Julia Virginia 1878-?
[LAO]
German author
* Julia Virginia

Laennec, Rene T. H. 1781-1826 [HPPN]
French physician and inventor
* [The] Father of the Stethoscope

Laertes
See Townsend, George Alfred

Laertes, Joseph
See Saltzman, Joseph [Joe]

Laevastu, Taivo
See Granfeldt, Taivo

Lafarge, Marie
See Capella, Marie-Fortunee

Lafargue, Philip
See Philpot, Joseph Henry

Lafayette, Carlos
See Boiles, Charles Lafayette, Jr.

Lafayette, Marquis de
See Du Motier, Marie Joseph Paul
Yves Roch Gilbert

[The] Lafayette of the Greek Revolution
See Howe, Samuel Gridley

Lafayette, Rene
See Hubbard, Lafayette Ronald

Laffan, Kevin [Barry] 1922- [CA]
British playwright, actor, director
* Barry, Kevin

Laffeaty, Christina 1932- [AW]
South African-born author
* Carstens, Netta
* Fortina, Martha

Laffemas, Isaac de 1587-1657 [SN]
Public executioner
* [The] Cardinal's Hangman

Laffer, Arthur 20th c.
American economist
* Laffer, Curve

Laffer, Curve
See Laffer, Arthur

Lafferty, Flip
See Lafferty, Frank Bernard

Lafferty, Frank Bernard 1854-1910 [BE]
American baseball player
* Lafferty, Flip

Lafferty, Kid
See Lafferty, Louis

Lafferty, Louis 20th c. [BBH]
Boxer
* Lafferty, Kid

Lafferty, Martha Janet 1921- [BEW,
FC, HPPN, PMJ]
American actress, singer, dancer
* Blair, Janet
* Blake, Janet

Lafferty, R. A.
See Lafferty, Raphael Aloysius

Lafferty, Raphael Aloysius 1914- [SF]
American author
* Lafferty, R. A.

Lafferty, Wilson
See Wilson, Gene

Laffin, John [Alfred Charles] 1922-
[AW, CA, WD]
Australian-born author
* Dekker, Carl
* Napier, Mark
* Sabre, Dirk

Lafitte, Doc
See Lafitte, Edward Francis

Lafitte, Edward Francis 1886- [BE]
American baseball player
* Lafitte, Doc

Lafitte, Jean 1780?-1826? [DNNS,
HPPN]
French privateer and smuggler
* [The] Boss
* [The] Gentleman Smuggler
* [The] Last of the Buccaneers
* [The] Pirate of the Gulf
* [The] Terror of the Gulf

Lafitte, [Colonel] Leon
See Ingraham, Prentiss

Lafitte, Louis 1917- [ESF]
French writer
* Curtis, Jean-Louis

LaFleur, Guy Damien 1951-
Canadian-born hockey player
* [The] Flower

Lafontaine, August Heinrich Julius
1758-1831 [WBD]
German clergyman and author
* Freier, Gustav
* Miltenberg
* Selchow

LaFontaine, Franny [The Franchise]
See LaFontaine, Pat

LaFontaine, Pat 1966?- [TI 1-30-84]
American hockey player
* LaFontaine, Franny [The Franchise]

Lafontant-Medard, Michaelle 1949-
[CW]
Haitian poet and author
* Deschamps, Marguerite

LaForest, Byron Joseph 1919-1947 [BE]
Canadian-born baseball player
* LaForest, Ty

Laforest, Mark 20th c.
Canadian-born hockey player
* Laforest, Trees

Laforest, Trees
See Laforest, Mark

LaForest, Ty
See LaForest, Byron Joseph

Laforest-Divonne, Philomene De 1887-
[WGT]
Author
* Silve, Claude

Laforet, Georg
See Seitz, Franz

Lafrensen, Nils 1737-1807 [WBD]
Swedish painter
* Lavreince, Nicolas

Lafrentz, Ferdinand William 1859-?
[NAA]
German-born poet
* Von Fehmarn

Lafuente [or La Fuente], Modesto
1806-1866 [WBD]
Spanish historian and author
* Fray Gerundio
* Tirabeque

Lagaboeter [Reformer of the Laws]
See Magnus VI

Lagartija [The Rogue]
See Ruiz y Vargas, Juan

Lagartijillo [Little Lizard]
See Moreno y Fernandez, Antonio

Lagartijillo-Chico [Tiny Lizard]
See Moreno del Moral, Jose

Lagartijo [Lizard]
See Molina y Martinez, Rafael

Lagartijo [Lizard]
See Molina y Sanchez, Rafael

Lagartijo Chico [Little Lizard]
See Molina y Martinez, Rafael

Lagenevais, F. de
See Blaze, Ange Henri

Lageniensis
See Mangan, James Clarence

Lageniensis
See O'Hanlon, John

Lagerwall, Edna 20th c. [CA]
American editor and author
* Traynor, Alex

Lagevi, Bo
See Blom, Karl Arne

Lagevi, Bo
See Bolinder, Jean Adolf

Lagger, Alexander 1942- [OP]
Swiss opera singer
* Malta, Alexander

Lagneau-Kesteloot, Lilyan
See Kesteloot, Lilyan

Lago Severino, Francisco 1875-1964 [SC]
Actor
* Salas, Paco

Lagrange
See Cardeilhac, Augustin

Lagrange-Chancel, Joseph de
See Chancel, Joseph

LaGrone, John Kerr 1891-1953 [BI]
American aviator
* LaGrone, Tex

LaGrone, Oliver 20th c. [LBA]
American sculptor and poet
* Oliver, Clarence

LaGrone, Tex
See LaGrone, John Kerr

Lahainaluna
See Dibble, [Rev.] Sheldon

Lahany, Kristin Elaine Eggleston 1931-
[IAW]
American author
* Horter, Kristin

Laharpe, Jean Francois de
See Delharpe [or Delaharpe], Jean
Francois

Lahm, Frank 1887-1963 [HPPN]
American army officer
* [The] Army's First Pilot

[Der] Lahme
See Hermann von Reichenau

Lahor, Jean
See Cazalis, Henry

Lahoud, Duck
See Lahoud, Joseph Michael

Lahoud, Joseph Michael 1947- [BE]
American baseball player
* Lahoud, Duck

Lahr, Bert
See Lahrheim, Irving

Lahrheim, Irving 1895-1967 [BEW,
EMT, FC]
American actor
* Lahr, Bert

Lahtinen, Duke
See Lahtinen, Warner H.

Lahtinen, Warner H. 1910-1968 [SC]
American actor
* Lahtinen, Duke

Laicus
See Abbott, Lyman

Laicus, Phillipe
See Wasserburg, Philipp

Laidlaw, A. K.
See Grieve, Christopher Murray

Laidler, Gavin Graham 1908-1940
[WEC]
British cartoonist
* Pont

L'Aigle de la France
See Ailly, Pierre d'

Laimbeer, Clara Stephens 1870-1907
[HPPN]
American actress
* Bloodgood, Clara

Laine
See Gomez Leon, Diego

Laine, Alfred 1895-1957 [NOJ, WWJ]
American jazz musician
* Laine, Baby
* Laine, Pantsy

Laine, Baby
See Laine, Alfred

Laine, Cleo
See Campbell, Clementina Dinah

Laine, Denny
See Haynes, Brian Arthur

Laine, Digger
See Laine, Julian

Laine, Frankie
See LoVecchio, Frank Paul

Laine, George Vitelle 1873-1966 [DAM,
EJ, HPPN, NOJ, WWJ]
American jazz musician
* Laine, Jack
* Papa Jack

Laine, Gloria
See Hanna, David

Laine, Jack
See Laine, George Vitelle

Laine, Julian 1907-1957 [NOJ]
American jazz musician
* Laine, Digger

Laine, Pantsy
See Laine, Alfred

Laing, A. S. 19th c. [SN]
British jurist
* Fang, Mr.

Laing, Alexander 1787-1857 [DEL]
British poet
* [The] Brechin Poet

Laing, Anne C.
See Schachterle, Nancy [Lange]

Laing, David 1793-1878 [HPPN]
Scottish antiquarian, librarian, editor
* D. L.

Laing, Hugh
See Skinner, Hugh

Laing, Martha
See Celestino, Martha Laing

Laing, Patrick
See Long, Amelia Reynolds

Laing, Ronald David 1927?- [HPPN]
Scottish psychiatrist
* [The] Philosopher of Madness

Laini, Safisha
See Easton, Carol D.

Lair, Clara
See Negron Munoz, Mercedes

Lair, Grace
See Gaylor, Grace

Laird
See Lowther, Armstrong John

Laird, Dorothy
See Carr, Dorothy Stevenson Laird

Laird, Francis C. 1794-? [FFF, PA]
British author
* Howard, George, Esq.

Laird, G. F. 20th c. [BBH]
American baseball coach
* Laird, Red

Laird, Jean E[louise] 1930- [CA]
American writer
* Drial, J. E.
* McKeever, Marcia
* Wakefield, Jean L.

Laird of Auchinleck
See Boswell, James

[The] Laird of Cockpen
See Caross, Mark

[The] Laird of Lag
See Grierson, [Sir] Robert

[The] Laird of Littlegrange
See FitzGerald, Edward

[The] Laird of Skibo
See Carnegie, Andrew

[The] Laird of Skibo Castle
See Carnegie, Andrew

[The] Laird of the Halls
See MacLennan, Harry

[The] Laird of Woodchuck Lodge
See Burroughs, John

Laird, Red
See Laird, G. F.

Laire, Criad
See Rooney, William

Laisne, Jeanne 1454-? [WBD]
French heroine
* Fourquet, Jeanne
* Hachette, Jeanne

Laissing, W. K. 20th c. [SFP]
Author
* Edwards, Dolton

Lait, Jack
See Lait, Jacquin

Lait, Jacquin 1882-1954 [ALY, SC]
American author
* Lait, Jack

Lajeunesse, Marie Louise Cecilia Emma
1847-1930 [BBD, BEW, HPPN]
Canadian opera singer
* Albani, Emma
* Albani, Madame

Lajoie, Larry
See Lajoie, Napoleon

Lajoie, Nap
See Lajoie, Napoleon

Lajoie, Napoleon 1875-1959 [AS, BE, PB]
American baseball player and manager
* King Larry
* Lajoie, Larry
* Lajoie, Nap

Lakaitel [Little Lackey]
See Keitel, Wilhelm

Lakanal, Joseph
See Lacanal, Joseph

Lake, Arthur
See Silverlake, Arthur

Lake, Claude
See Blind, Mathilde

Lake, Edward Erving [Eddie] 1916-
[BN]
American baseball player
* Lake, Inky

Lake Elbe
See Bleloch, Archibald

Lake, Florence
See Silverlake, Florence

Lake, Harriette 1909- [EMT, F2, FC]
American actress and singer
* Sothern, Ann

Lake, Inky
See Lake, Edward Erving [Eddie]

Lake, Joe Barry 20th c. [WW]
Author
* Barry, Joe

Lake, John
See Laycock, John W.

Lake, Kenneth R[obert] 1931- [CA, WD]
British writer
* Boyer, Robert
* King, Arthur
* Market Man
* Mentor
* Roberts, K.
* Roberts, Ken
* Soutter, Fred
* Xeno

Lake, Mrs. W. P. [FFF]
Entertainer
* Byron, Clara

[The] Lake Poet
See Campbell, [William] Wilfred

Lake, Sarah
See Weiner, Margery Sarah

Lake, Simon 1866-1945 [HPPN]
American naval architect, inventor, mechanical engineer
* [The] Father of the Modern Submarine

Lake, Sol
See Lachoff, Sol

Lake, Veronica
See Ockleman, Constance Frances Marie

Lakeman, Albert Wesley 1918- [BE]
American baseball player
* Lakeman, Moose

Lakeman, Moose
See Lakeman, Albert Wesley

Lakeman, Stephen 1812-1897 [JL]
British army officer
* Mazar Pasha

Laker, Cecil
See Bainbridge, Harriette Smith

Laker, Rosalind
See Ovstedal, Barbara

Laklan, Carli
See Laughlin, Virginia Carli

Lakomska, Sylvia Jadviga 1931- [BEW]
Polish-born actress
* Daneel, Sylvia

Lakritz, Esther 1928- [WD]
American author
* Collingswood [M.D.], Frederick

Laks, S.
See Izbitsky [or Ishbitsky], Samuel

Lalawethika 1768?-1834? [WBD]
American Indian religious leader
* Elskwatawa

Lalawethika (cont.)
* [The] Prophet
* [The] Shawnee Prophet
* Tenskwatawa

Lalita
See Johnson, Maud Lalita

Lalitananda, Swami
See Rego, Leonora

Lalla, Mohan Bulchand 1930- [IAW]
Indian author
* Kalpana, Mohan

L'Allemand, Pauline
See Elsasser, Pauline

Lalli, Cele G[oldsmith] 1933- [WGT]
American author
* Goldsmith, Cele

Lallo, Moose
See Lallo, Morris

Lallo, Morris 20th c. [SMG]
Hockey executive
* Lallo, Moose

Lally, Bud
See Lally, Daniel J.

Lally, Daniel J. 1867-1936 [BE]
American baseball player
* Lally, Bud

Lally, Patrick Joseph 1868-1956 [CSH]
Canadian lacrosse player
* [The] Knight of the Whistle

Lally, William 1908-1956 [SC]
American actor and film editor
* Wallace, Bill

Lalonde, Edouard 1887-1970 [CEI, FHE, HK]
Canadian-born hockey player
* Lalonde, Newsy

Lalonde, Newsy
See Lalonde, Edouard

Lalonde, Newsy
See Lalonde, Ron

Lalonde, Ron 1952- [SMG]
Canadian-born hockey player
* Lalonde, Newsy

Lamabe, John Alexander [Jack] 1936-
American baseball player
* Lamabe, Tomato Face

Lamabe, Tomato Face
See Lamabe, John Alexander [Jack]

LaMancusa, Katherine C.
See Koop, Katherine C.

LaManna, Frank 1919- [BE]
American baseball player
* LaManna, Hank

LaManna, Hank
See LaManna, Frank

Lamanske, Frank James 1906-1971 [BE]
American baseball player
* Lamanske, Lefty

Lamanske, Lefty
See Lamanske, Frank James

Lamar, Ashton
See Sayler, Harry Lincoln

Lamar, Bo
See Lamar, Dwight

Lamar, Dwight 1951- [BB, BI, SMG]
American basketball player
* Lamar, Bo
* Little Bo Pete

Lamar, Kenneth
See Kernan, Will Hubbard

Lamar, Pete
See Lamar, Pierre

Lamar, Pierre 1874-1970 [BE]
American baseball player
* Lamar, Pete

Lamar, William Harmong 1897-1970 [BE]
American baseball player
* Good Time Bill

Lamare, Hilton Napoleon 1907?- [ASC, DAM, PMJ]
American jazz musician
* Lamare, Nappy

Lamare, Nappy
See Lamare, Hilton Napoleon

Lamarr, Hedy
See Kiesler, Hedwig Eva Marie

LaMarsh, Judy
See LaMarsh, Julia Verlyn

LaMarsh, Julia Verlyn 1924-1980 [CA]
Canadian writer
* LaMarsh, Judy

Lamartine, Alphonse Marie Louis de Prat de 1790-1869 [SN]
French poet
* [The] Narcissus of France

[The] Lamb
See Eric III

[The] Lamb
See Pringle, Thomas

[The] Lamb
See Sampson, Edgar Melvin

Lamb, Allan Joseph 1954- [DC]
South African cricketer
* Lamb, Lambie

Lamb, Antonia 1943- [IAW]
American author
* Foerster-Nietschze, Elisabeth

Lamb, [Lady] Caroline 1785-1828 [SN]
British author
* Lady Calantha
* Lady Monteagle
* Lorraine, Mrs. Felix

Lamb, Charles 1775-1834 [DEL, HPPN, SN]
British author and poet
* Burton Junior
* Crito

Lamb, Charles (cont.)
* Edax
* Elia
* [An] Eye Witness
* [The] Mitre Courtier
* Old Honesty
* Suspensurus
* Upright Telltruth, Esq.
* [A] Water Drinker

Lamb, Charles Bentall 1914-1981 [CA]
British author and naval officer
* Achilles

Lamb, Charlotte
See Holland, Sheila

Lamb, Clifford 1888- [THR]
British actor
* Heatherley, Clifford

Lamb, Elizabeth Searle 1917- [CA]
American author
* Mitchell, K. L.

Lamb, Geoffrey Frederick [CA, SAT, WD]
British author
* Balaam

Lamb, Helen B.
See Lamont, Helen Lamb

Lamb, Herbert 1855-1917 [BEW]
British-born actor
* Kelcey, Herbert

Lamb, J. [PA]
Author
* [A] Manchester Man

Lamb, Lambie
See Lamb, Allan Joseph

Lamb, Martha Joanna Reade 1829-? [HPPN]
American journalist
* Crisp

Lamb, Mary Ann 1765-1847 [HPPN, NPS, PA]
British author
* Cousin Bridget
* Elia, Bridget
* M. B.

Lamb, Natalie
See Elston, Natalie

[The] Lamb of God
See Jesus Christ

Lamb, Ruth 19th c. [FFF]
American author
* Buck, Ruth

Lamb, William 1835-1909 [HPPN]
American army officer
* [The] Hero of Fort Fisher

Lamb, William
See Jameson, [Margaret] Storm

Lambart, Richard
See Leighton, Eric

Lambe, F. 20th c. [MBF]
British author
* Reid, Desmond [house pseudonym]

Lambeau, Curly
See Lambeau, Earl L.

Lambeau, Earl L. 1898-1965 [AS, FB, SMG]
American football player and coach
* Lambeau, Curly

Lambec, Zoltan
See Kimbro, John M.

Lambecius
See Lambeck, Peter

Lambeck, Peter 1628-1680 [PA]
Author
* Lambecius

Lamber, Juliette
See Adam, Juliette

Lambert, Arthur
See Widner, Arthur L.

Lambert, Basil Garwood 1891?-1950 [BI, HPPN]
American musician
* Lambert, Professor
* Lamberti, Professor

Lambert, Charles Frederick 1887-? [HPPN]
American law officer
* Lambert, Kid

Lambert, Christine
See Freybe, Heidi Huberta

Lambert, David 1770-1809 [RH]
Weighed 739 lbs. at death
* [The] Fat

Lambert, Derek 1929- [CA, WD]
British author
* Falkirk, Richard

Lambert, Edward 1809-1894 [HPPN]
British actor and playwright
* Stirling, Edward

Lambert, Elisabeth
See Ortiz, Elisabeth Lambert

Lambert, Elizabeth [Minnie] 1933- [CA]
Canadian author and playwright
* Lee, Betty

Lambert, Eric 1918-1966 [CAP]
British author
* Brennand, Frank
* Kay, George

Lambert, F. A. Heygate 20th c. [WWL]
Welsh author and poet
* Arthur, Frederick

Lambert, Francois 1487-1530 [PA]
Author
* Serranus

Lambert, Franz 1486?-1530 [WBD]
Theologian
* Lambert of Avignon

Lambert, Harold 1901- [PMJ]
American singer
* Lambert, Scrappy

Lambert, John ?-1538 [BI]
British martyr
* Nicholson, John

Lambert, Jonathan 17th c. [HPPN]
American pirate
* Brother Jonathan

Lambert, Kid
See Lambert, Charles Frederick

Lambert, Leslie Harrison 1883-1940
[LC, WW]
British author and broadcaster
* Alan, A. J.

Lambert, Louis
See Gilmore, Patrick Sarsfield

Lambert, Marion
See Perry, Montanye

Lambert, May 1876-1929 [LFW]
*Irish-born American bank robber and
swindler*
* Chicago May
* Churchill, May Vivienne
* Latimer, May
* [The] Queen of the Badgers

Lambert of Avignon
See Lambert, Franz

Lambert, Piggy
See Lambert, Ward L.

Lambert, Professor
See Lambert, Basil Garwood

Lambert, S. H.
See Southwold, Stephen

Lambert, Scrappy
See Lambert, Harold

Lambert, T. H. 20th c. [MBF]
British author
* Lumberjack

Lambert, Ward L. 1888-1958 [AS, BB]
American basketball coach
* Lambert, Piggy

Lamberti, Michael ?-1950 [SC]
American actor
* Lamberti, Professor

Lamberti, Professor
See Lambert, Basil Garwood

Lamberti, Professor
See Lamberti, Michael

Lambertini, Prospero 1675-1758 [WBD]
Pope
* Benedict XIV

Lambot, Isobel Mary 1926- [AW, CA,
WD]
British author
* Ingham, Daniel
* Rees, Meriel
* Turner, Mary

Lambourne, John
See Lamburn, John Battersby
Crompton

Lambton, Hedworth 1856-1929 [WBD]
British naval officer
* Meux, [Sir] Hedworth

**Lambton, John George [First Earl of
Durham]** 1792-1840 [NPS]
British politician
* [The] Coal Master

Lamburn, John Battersby Crompton
1893- [CAP]
British author
* Crompton, John
* Lambourne, John

Lamburn, Richmal Crompton 1890-1969
[CAP, LC, SAT]
British author
* Crompton, Richmal

[The] Lame
See Albert II

[The] Lame
See Charles I

[The] Lame
See Charles II

[The] Lame
See Eric XI

[The] Lame
See Henry II [or Heinrich]

[The] Lame
See Jean [or Jehan] de Meung

[The] Lame
See Prusias I

[The] Lame
See Reichenau, Hermann Von

[The] Lame
See Tyrtaeus

Lame Deer 1902?- [HPPN]
American Indian medicine man
* Fire Lame Deer, John
* [The] Seeker of Visions

[The] Lame Vicegerent
See Cromwell, Richard

Lamech
See Lynch, Michael

Lamey, Bob 1939- [SMG]
American sportscaster
* Lamey, Hockey Bob

Lamey, Hockey Bob
See Lamey, Bob

Lamhdearg
See Holland, Denis

Lamia
See Austin, Alfred

Lamline, Dutch
See Lamline, Fred[erick Arthur]

Lamline, Fred[erick Arthur] 1891-1970
[BE]
American baseball player
* Lamline, Dutch

Lamm, Baron
See Lamm, Herman K.

Lamm, Herman K. ?-1930 [BLB]
German-born American bank robber
* Lamm, Baron

Lamm, Richard D. 1936?- [NW 5-27-85,
PW 8-30-85]
American politician
* Gloom, Governor
* Gloom, Professor

Lamme, Buck
See Lamme, Emerald

Lamme, Emerald 20th c. [EF]
American football player
* Lamme, Buck

Lamoignon, Chretien 1644-1709 [NPS]
French politician
* Aristus

Lamont, Duncan
See Tubb, Edwin Charles

Lamont, Gil
See Lamont, Gilvan Derwent

Lamont, Gilvan Derwent 1947- [SFL]
British-born author
* Lamont, Gil

Lamont, Helen Lamb 1906?-1975 [CA]
American economist, educator, author
* Lamb, Helen B.

Lamont, Jack
See Capitola, Jack

Lamont, Jack
See Mastin, James

Lamont, Marianne
See Rundle, Anne

Lamont, N. B.
See Barnitt, Nedda Lemmon

Lamont, Nedda
See Barnitt, Nedda Lemmon

Lamont, Rosette C[lementine] 20th c.
[CA]
*French-born American educator and
author*
* Farmer, R. L.

Lamont, Victor
See Maiorana, Victor E.

LaMoore, Louis [Dearborn] 1908- [CA,
CLC, WD]
American author and screenwriter
* Burns, Tex
* L'Amour, Louis [Dearborn]
* Mayo, Jim

LaMotta, Jacob [Jake] 1921- [BX, RBE]
American boxer
* [The] Bronx Bull

Lamotte-Houdar
See De La Motte, Antoine Houdar

Lamotte-Houdar
See Houdar de La Motte, Antoine

Lamour, Dorothy
See Kaumeyer, Dorothy

L'Amour, Louis [Dearborn]
See LaMoore, Louis [Dearborn]

Lamp
See Watson, George B.

[The] Lamp of India
See Pandit, Vijaya Lakshmi

[The] Lamp of the Law
See Irnerius

[A] Lamp to Light the Way
See Madison, James

Lampley, James 1949- [HPPN]
American television sports announcer
* [The] Cronkite of Oddball Sports

Lamplugh, Lois
See Davis, Lois Carlile

Lampman, Archibald 1861-1899 [DLE1]
Canadian poet
* [The] Canadian Keats

Lampman, Evelyn Sibley 1907-1980
[CA, MJA, SAT]
American author
* Bronson, Lynn

Lamprecht 12th c. [DNNS]
Frankish poet
* [The] Priest

Lamprecht, Kurt
See Heymann, Ernest F.

Lamprey, A. C.
See Fish, Robert L.

Lamptey, Jonathan Kwesi 1909- [IAW]
Ghanaian writer
* J. K.
* Uncle Kwesi

Lampton, Austen
See Dent, Anthony Austen

Lampton, W. J. [FFF]
American writer
* Mary Jane
* Waxem of Wayback, Jedge

Lamson, Alvan 1792-1864 [HPPN]
American clergyman
* A. L.
* L.

Lamson, Frank 1851-1938 [WBD]
American botanist
* Lamson-Scribner, Frank

Lamson, Gertrude 1874-? [BEW]
American actress
* O'Neil, Nance

Lamson-Scribner, Frank
See Lamson, Frank

Lamy, Douglas N. 1919-1951 [SC]
American actor
* Drake, Douglas
* Mitchell, John

Lan [or Lang?] Ping 20th c. [NW 7-30-84, TI 7-30-84]
Chinese volleyball player
* [The] Iron Hammer

Lan Ping
See Mao Chiang Ching

Lan, Viggo
See Tolderlund, Hother

Lana
See Kemp, Alan

[A] Lancashire Artisan
See Macleod, Malcolm

[The] Lancashire Burns
See Waugh, Edwin

[The] Lancashire Hogarth
See Collier, John

[A] Lancashire Incumbent
See Hume, Abraham

[The] Lancashire Lad
See Cash, Morny

[A] Lancashire Lad
See Sowden, Thomas

[The] Lancashire Poet
See Waugh, Edwin

Lancashire's Own Principal Boy
See Wood, Daisy

Lancaster, Burt[on Stephen] 1913-
[HPPN]
American actor and producer
* Lang

Lancaster, Captain
See Hook, Samuel Clarke

Lancaster, Evelyn
See Sizemore, Chris[tine] Costner

Lancaster, G. B.
See Lyttelton, Edith Joan Balfour

Lancaster, Jack
See Burrage, Alfred McLelland

Lancaster, Lydia
See Meaker, Eloise

Lancaster, Robert A.
See Cohen, Paul Arthur

Lancaster, Sheila
See Holland, Sheila

Lancaster, Thunderbird
See Lancaster, William Byard

Lancaster, Time Honored
See John of Gaunt

Lancaster, William
See Warren, John Byrne Leicester
[Baron de Tabley]

Lancaster, William Byard 1942- [EJ7]
American jazz musician
* Lancaster, Thunderbird

Lancaster, William Joseph Cosens
1851-1922 [MBF, SFL, WGT]
British author
* Collingwood, Harry

Lancaster, William P.
See Leicester-Warren, John Byrne
[Baron de Tabley]

Lance, Albert
See Ingram, Lancelot Albert

Lance, John
See Bungay, E. Newton

Lance, Leslie
See Swatridge, Charles [John]

Lancelotz, Corneille 1547-1622 [PA]
Author
* Lancilottus

Lancer [Secret Service code name]
See Kennedy, John Fitzgerald [Jack]

Lancer [code name]
See Salinger, Pierre Emil George

Lancer
See Stouder, O. C.

Lancet
See McSwiney, Stephen Myles

Lancewood, Lawrence
See Wise, Daniel

Lanchester, Elsa
See Sullivan, Elizabeth

Lancia, Joseph 20th c. [BLB]
American underworld figure
* Lancia, Jumbo

Lancia, Jumbo
See Lancia, Joseph

Lancilottus
See Lancelotz, Corneille

Lancing, George
See Hunter, Bluebell Matilda

Lancour, Gene
See Fisher, Gene L[ouis]

Land
See Landry, Robert John

[The] Land Admiral
See Reeside, James

Land, Doc
See Land, William Gilbert

Land, Edwin Herbert 1909- [HPPN]
American inventor and manufacturer
* [The] Father of Polaroid
* [The] Father of Retinex
* [The] Father of the One Step Camera

Land, George Thomas Lock 1933-
[IAW]
American author
* Lock, Thomas

[The] Land Hero of 1812
See Jackson, Andrew

Land, Jane and Ross [joint pseudonym
with Helen Ross (Smith) Speicher]
See Borland, Kathryn Kilby

Land, Jane and Ross [joint pseudonym
with Kathryn Kilby Borland]
See Speicher, Helen Ross [Smith]

Land, Rosina
See Hastings, Phyllis Dora Hodge

Land, William Gilbert 1903-   [BE]
American baseball player
* Land, Doc

Landau, Abe 20th c.   [BLB]
American underworld figure
* Landau, Misfit

Landau, Dorothea
See Da Fano, Dorothea Natalie Sophia

Landau, Edwin Maria 1904-   [IAW]
German-born author
* Devin, Marius

Landau, Mark Aleksandrovich
1886?-1957 [CD, EWL, TC]
Russian author
* Aldanov, Mark Aleksandrovich

Landau, Misfit
See Landau, Abe

Lande, Jules
Musician
* [The] Troubador of the Violin

Lande, Lawrence Montague 1906-   [WD]
Canadian author and poet
* Verval, Alain [joint pseudonym with
   Thomas Greenwood]

Landeau, Max
See Sykowski, Abram

Landels, D. H.
See Henderson, Donald Landels

Landenberger, Ken[neth Henry]
1928-1960 [BE]
American baseball player
* Landenberger, Red

Landenberger, Red
See Landenberger, Ken[neth Henry]

Lander, Dane
See Clarke, Percy A.

Lander, Jean
See Hello, Mme. Ernst

Lander, Jean Margaret Davenport
See Donald, Jean Margaret Davenport

Lander, Meta
See Lawrence, Margaret Woods

Lander, Toni
See Petersen, Toni Phil

Landers, Ann
See Crowley, Ruth

Landers, Ann
See Lederer, Esther Pauline [Friedman]

Landers, Lew
See Friedlander, Lewis

Landesberg, Phyllis G. 1927-   [HPPN]
American composer
* Fairbanks, Phyllis

Landesman, Irving Ned 1919-   [BEW]
American producer and playwright
* Landesman, Jay

Landesman, Jay
See Landesman, Irving Ned

Landesmann, Heinrich 1821-1902
[WBD]
German author and poet
* Lorm, Hieronymus

[The] Landgrave
See Montague, Eleonora Louisa

[The] Landgrave of Hesse
See Rosen, Michael

[A] Landholder
See Bell, Benjamin

[A] Landholder
See Updike, Wilkins

Landi, Elissa
See Zanardi-Landi, Elizabeth Marie

Landino, Francesco 1325?-1397 [WBD]
Florentine muscian and composer
* Francesco Cieco
* Francesco degli Organi

Landis, Carole
See Ridste, Frances Lillian Mary

Landis, Doc
See Landis, Samuel H.

Landis, Houston 20th c.   [HPPN]
American football player
* Landis, Judge

Landis, Jerry
See Simon, Paul Frederick

Landis, Jessie Royce
See Medbury, Jessie Royse

Landis, Judge
See Landis, Houston

Landis, Judge
See Landis, Kenesaw Mountain

Landis, Kenesaw Mountain 1866-1944
[HPPN]
*American attorney and baseball
commissioner*
* [The] Czar of American Baseball
* [The] Czar of Baseball
* [The] Czar of the National Pastime
* Landis, Judge

Landis, Samuel H. 1854-?   [BE]
American baseball player
* Landis, Doc

[The] Landlord
See Howe, Lyman

[The] Landlord of Holmes' Castle
See Mudgett, Herman Webster

[The] Landlord of New York
See Astor, William Backhouse

Landon, Alf[red Mossman] 1887-
[HPPN]
American politician
* [The] Coolidge of the West
* [The] Kansas Coolidge

Landon, Batesy
See Landon, Bruce

Landon, Bruce 1949-   [SMG]
American hockey player
* Landon, Batesy

Landon, Letitia Elizabeth 1802-1838
[HPPN]
British author and poet
* [The] English Sappho
* L.
* L. E. L.

Landon, Louise
See Hauck, Louise [Platt]

Landon, Melville De Lancey 1839-1910
[FFF, SFL, WGT]
American author
* Perkins, Eli

Landon, Michael
See Orowitz, Eugene Maurice

Landor, Charles
See Stickney, Caroline

Landor, Walter Savage 1775-1864 [NPS,
SN]
British author and poet
* Boythorne, Lawrence
* [The] Gebir
* That Deep-Mouthed Boeotian

Landreaux, Elizabeth Mary 1895-1963
[BWW, PMJ, WWJ]
American singer
* [The] Creole Songbird
* Miles, Lizzie
* Queen Elleezee
* [La] Rose Noire de Paris [The Black
   Rose of Paris]
* Smith, Mandy

Landrith, Hobert Neal 1930-   [BE]
American baseball player
* Landrith, Hobie

Landrith, Hobie
See Landrith, Hobert Neal

Landru
See Colombres, Juan Carlos

Landru, Henri Desire 1869-1922
[HPPN, PPN]
French murderer
* Bluebeard
* [The] Busy Bluebeard
* Diard, Raymond
* DuPont, Francois
* France's Gift to Infamy
* Fremyet
* [The] Ladykiller
* Petit, Francois

Landrum, Terry Lee 1954- [SMG]
American baseball player
* Landrum, Tito

Landrum, Tito
See Landrum, Terry Lee

Landry, Robert John 1903- [CA]
American editor and critic
* Land

Landsborough, G. H. 20th c. [MBF]
British author
* Cody, Stone
* M'Cracken, Mike

Landseer
See Murray, Bromley

[The] Landseer of Sculpture
See Gatley, Alfred

[The] Landseer of the Present
See Ansdell, Richard

Landsfeldt, Countess
See Salomen, Edith

Landslide Lyndon Johnson
See Johnson, Lyndon Baines

Landsteiner, Karl 1868-1943 [HPPN]
Austrian-American physician and pathologist
* [The] Father of Blood Grouping

Landwirth, Heinz 1927- [BI]
Austrian author
* Lind, Jakov

Landy, Dad
See Landy, G. W.

Landy, G. W. ?-1930 [BLB]
American bank robber
* Landy, Dad

Landy, Tonny
See Nuppenau, Tonny Landy

Lane, Allan
See Albershart, Harry

Lane, Arthur
See Tremaine, F[rederick] Orlin

Lane, Bay Bay
See Lane, Calvin

Lane, Burton
See Levy, Burton

Lane, Calvin 1954- [SMG]
American football player
* Lane, Bay Bay

Lane, Chancery, Esq.
See Wilson, James Edwin

Lane, Chappy
See Lane, George M.

Lane, Charles
See Gatti, Arthur Gerard

Lane, Charles
See Lucania, Salvatore

Lane, D. P.
See Lane, David Pulaski

Lane, David Pulaski 1912- [BA]
American dentist
* Lane, D. P.

Lane, Denny 1818-1895 [PI]
Irish poet
* D. L.?
* Doinnall-na-glanna
* Donall-na-Glanna

Lane, Dick 20th c.
American billiard player
* Lane, Night Train

Lane, Dodo
See Lane, [James] Hunter

Lane, Elizabeth
See Farmers, Eileen Elizabeth [Honeyman]

Lane, Fighting Jim
See Lane, James Henry

Lane, Frank C. 1896- [PB]
American baseball executive
* Lane, Frantic Frankie

Lane, Franklin Knight 1864-1921 [HPPN]
American secretary of the Interior
* [The] Despoiler of Public Lands
* [The] Mystic Materialist

Lane, Frantic Frankie
See Lane, Frank C.

Lane, George M. ?-1896 [BE]
American baseball player
* Lane, Chappy

Lane, Gerald
See Fanning, David Christopher Patrick St. John

Lane, Gloria
See Siet, Gloria

Lane, Grant
See Fisher, Stephen Gould

Lane, Helen
See Lacks, Henrietta

Lane, Horace
See Greaves, Horace

Lane, [James] Hunter 1900- [BE]
American baseball player
* Lane, Dodo

Lane, James A. 1924- [BWW, NBB]
American singer
* Rogers, James [Jimmy]

Lane, James Henry 1814-1866 [HPPN]
American abolitionist and army officer
* [The] Grim Chieftain
* Lane, Fighting Jim

Lane, James Woods 19th c. [FFF]
American writer
* Cameroy

Lane, Jane
See Dakers, Elaine Kidner

Lane, Jerry
See Martin, Patricia Miles

Lane, David Pulaski 1912- [BA]

Lane, John 19th c. [HPPN]
American blacksmith and inventor
* [The] Father of the Steel Plow

Lane, John [house pseudonym, Curtis Warren]
See Hughes, Den[n]is [Talbot]

Lane, John [house pseudonym]
See MacDonald, John D[ann]

Lane, Joseph 1801-1881 [HPPN]
American army officer
* [The] Marion of the Mexican Army

Lane, Katharine A. 20th c. [NAA]
American author
* Ike

Lane, Kenneth Westmacott 1893- [BI, WW]
British author
* West, Keith

Lane, Laurie
See Clapsaddle, Hilda R.

Lane, Leota
See Day, Leota Lane

Lane, Lola
See Mullican, Dorothy

Lane, Lupino
See Lupino, Henry George

Lane, Marion
See Judd, Ruth Marian McKinnell

Lane, Mary D.
See Delaney, Mary Murray

Lane, Mary E. Bradley 19th c. [SFL, WGT]
Author
* Zarovitch, [Princess] Vera

Lane, Mary Louisa 1894- [WWL]
Australian writer
* Emel
* Lee, Mariel

Lane, Master Juba
See Lane, William Henry

Lane, Michael
See Orowitz, Eugene Maurice

Lane, Neva ?-1956 [HPPN]
American missionary
* [The] Beloved of Guatemala

Lane, Night Train
See Lane, Dick

Lane, Night Train
See Lane, Richard

Lane, Nipper
See Lupino, Henry George

Lane, Plonk
See Lane, Ronnie

Lane, Priscilla
See Mullican, Priscilla

Lane, R.
See Vanderbilt, Cornelius, Jr.

Lane, Ralph Norman Angell 1872-1967
[LC, TC]
British economist and author
* Angell, [Sir] Norman

Lane, Richard 1899?-1982
American entertainer
* [The] Singing and Dancing Juvenile

Lane, Richard 1928- [FB]
American football player
* Lane, Night Train

Lane, Rocky
See Albershart, Harry

Lane, Ronnie 1948- [CMA]
Musician
* Lane, Plonk

Lane, Rose Wilder 1887-1968 [WYA]
American author
* Wilder, Rose

Lane, Rosemary
See Mullican, Rosemary

Lane, Sarah 19th c. [DNA, FFF, HPPN]
American author
* Kingston, Mary
* Kingston, May

Lane, Sheena Porter 1935- [TBJ]
British author
* Porter, Sheena

Lane, Sherry
See Smith, Richard Rein

Lane, Temple
See Leslie, Mary Isabel

Lane, Wallace
See Lupino, Wallace

Lane, Wickliffe
See Jenings, Elizabeth Janet

Lane, William Henry 1825-1853 [IBW]
American dancer
* Lane, Master Juba

Lane, Yoti 20th c. [CA]
Irish-born author, director, critic
* Mayo, Mark

Lane Fox, Augustus Henry 1827-1900
[WBD]
British army officer
* Pitt-Rivers, Augustus Henry

Lane-Jackson, Nicholas 1849-? [LAO]
British journalist
* Creston

Lanes, Selma Gordon 1929- [CA, SAT]
American author
* Gordon, Selma

Lanford, Lewis Grover 1886- [BE]
American baseball player
* Lanford, Sam

Lanford, Sam
See Lanford, Lewis Grover

Lang
See Lancaster, Burt[on Stephen]

Lang, Andrew 1844-1912 [HPPN, SFL,
TCC, WGT]
Scottish author and poet
* Langway, Hugo
* Longway, A. Huge
* [A] Well Known Author

Lang, Anthony
See Vahey, John George Haslette

Lang, Bunny
See Lang, Violet Ranney

Lang, Chip
See Lang, Robert David

Lang, Don
See Whitney, Walter Langdon

Lang, Eddie
See Massaro, Salvatore

Lang, Frances
See Mantle, Winifred Langford

Lang, Gerry
See Langella, Gennaro

Lang, Grace
See Floren, Lee

Lang, Gregor
See Birren, Faber

Lang, Howard
See Lange, Frederick

Lang, Isaac 1891-1950 [BI, TCL, WOA]
French-born poet, author, playwright
* Goll, Iwan [or Yvan]
* Lassang, Iwan
* Thor, Johannes
* Thor, Tristan
* Torsi, Tristan

Lang, Jim
See Sellers, Connie Leslie, Jr.

Lang, Jimmy
See Robinson, James

Lang, June
See Vlasek, June

Lang, King [house pseudonym, Curtis
Warren]
See Griffiths, David Arthur

Lang, King [house pseudonym, Curtis
Warren]
See Hay, George

Lang, King [house pseudonym, Curtis
Warren]
See Holloway, Brian

Lang, King [house pseudonym, Curtis
Warren]
See Jennison, John W[illiam]

Lang, King [house pseudonym, Curtis
Warren]
See Tubb, Edwin Charles

Lang, Lefty
See Lang, Martin John [Marty]

Lang, Maria
See Lange, Maria Dagmar

Lang, Martin
See Birren, Faber

Lang, Martin John [Marty] 1906-1968
[BE]
American baseball player
* Lang, Lefty

Lang, Maud
See Williams, Claerwen

Lang, Pearl
See Lack, Pearl

Lang, Peter
See Fearn, C. Eaton

Lang, Rex
See Lyttle, Richard B[ard]

Lang, Robert David 1952- [SMG]
American baseball player
* Lang, Chip

Lang, Ronny
See Langinger, Ronald

Lang, S.
See Stoddard, Richard Henry

Lang, Simon
See Hartman, Darlene

Lang, Stewart
See Muir, Wardrop Openshaw

Lang Syne
See McKoy, William

Lang, T. T.
See Taylor, Theodore

Lang, Theo
See Langbehn, Theo

Lang, Thomas [PA]
Author
* Mofussillite

Lang, Violet Ranney 1924-1956 [BI]
American poet
* Lang, Bunny

Langa-Langa
See Hermon-Hodge, Harry Baldwin

Langan, Jack 1799?-1846 [RBE]
Irish boxer
* [The] Irish Champion

Langan, Mary Magdalene 1872?-1950
[BI]
American educator
* Cecilia Rose, [Sister]

Langart, Darrel T.
See Garrett, [Gordon] Randall [Philip
David]

Langbehn, Theo 20th c. [WW]
Author
* Lang, Theo
* Piper, Peter

Langdale, Eve
See Craig, Evelyn Quita

Langdale, Launcelot
See Graham, George I.

Langdon, John [Franklin Coasten] 1913-
[IAW]
American author
* Gannold, John
* Russell, Rex

Langdon, Mary
See Pike, Mary Hayden Green

Lange, Carl Gustav Albert 1885- [LAO]
German author
* Penklub

Lange, Ernst Philipp Karl 1813-1899
[WBD]
German author
* Galen, Philipp

Lange, Frederick 1876?-1941 [BEW]
Actor
* Lang, Howard

Lange, John
See Crichton, [John] Michael

Lange, John Frederick, Jr. 1931- [ESF,
SFL, WGT]
American author
* Norman, John

Lange, Little Eva
See Lange, William Alexander

Lange, Maria Dagmar 1914- [AW]
Swedish-born author
* Lang, Maria

Lange, Ned
See Sheckley, Robert

Lange, William Alexander 1871-1950
[BE, PB]
American baseball player
* Lange, Little Eva

Langel
See Orleans, Louis Philippe Albert d'

Langell, Sears
See Glasser, Allen

Langella, Gennaro 1939?- [WP 10-25-84]
American underworld figure
* Lang, Gerry

Langenstein, Heinrich 1320-1397 [PA]
Author
* Von Hassia, Henricus

Langer, Alfons 1859-? [LAO]
German author and chemist
* Komed
* Schultze, Paul

Langer, Dollar John
See Langer, John

Langer, John 20th c. [HPPN]
American gambler
* Langer, Dollar John

Langeveldt, George
See Macropedius, Georgius

Langey, Guillaume du Bellay 1491-1553
[NPS]
French army officer, diplomat, author
* Ogdoades

Langford, Elton 1900- [BE]
American baseball player
* Langford, Sam

Langford, Frances
See Newbern, Frances

Langford, James R[ouleau] 1937- [CA]
American editor and author
* Langford, Jerome J.

Langford, Jane
See Mantle, Winifred Langford

Langford, Jerome J.
See Langford, James R[ouleau]

Langford, Sam 1880?-1956 [AS, BX,
RBE]
Canadian-born boxer
* [The] Boston Tar Baby

Langford, Sam
See Langford, Elton

Langgaesser, Elisabeth
See Hoffmann, E. L.

Langguth, A. J.
See Langguth, Arthur John

Langguth, Arthur John 1933- [SFL]
American author
* Langguth, A. J.

Langhanke, Lucille Vasconcellos 1906-
[BDF, BEW, CA, HPPN]
American actress
* Astor, Mary
* [The] Cameo Beauty

Langheimer, Charles 1806?-1883 [FFF]
American prison inmate
* Dicken's Dutchman

Langholm, Neil
See Bulmer, [Henry] Kenneth

Langier, Joseph Tidele 1802-? [PA]
Author
* Le Genie, Toulounais

Langiewicz, Marjan 1827-1887 [WBD]
Polish patriot
* Langle

Langinger, Ronald 1927- [EJ, PMJ]
American jazz musician
* Lang, Ronny

Langland, William
See Muntz, [Isabelle] Hope

Langle
See Langiewicz, Marjan

Langley, Ansel ?-1911 [HPPN]
American dancer and singer
* Doyle, Biddy

Langley, Batty
See Langley, Daniel

Langley, Daniel 1696-1751 [BI]
British architect
* Langley, Batty

Langley, [Rev.] Daniel Baxter 19th c.
[HPPN]
British clergyman
* [An] Anxious Enquirer After Truth

Langley, Dorothy
See Kissling, Dorothy Hight
[Richardson]

Langley, F. E. [FFF]
Author
* Douglas, Frank

Langley, Frank
See Torrio, John [Johnny]

Langley, Helen
See Rowland, Donald Sydney

Langley, John Prentice
See Rathborne, St. George Henry

Langley, Lee
See Langley, Sarah

Langley, Roger 1930- [CA]
American author and journalist
* Power, Rex

Langley, Samuel Pierpont 1834-1906
[HPPN]
American inventor, astronomer, aviator
* [The] Father of the Bolometer

Langley, Sarah 20th c. [CC]
Author
* Langley, Lee

Langley, Tania
See Armstrong, Tilly

Langlin, Henry [FFF]
Entertainer
* Vokes, Harry

Langlois, Albert 1934- [CEI, FHE]
Canadian-born hockey player
* Langlois, Junior

Langlois, Junior
See Langlois, Albert

Langmann, Claude 1934- [FC, FDG]
French director
* Berri, Claude

Langner, Armina [Marshall] [BI]
American playwright and producer
* Loudon, Isabelle

Langrenus, Manfred
See Hecht, Friedrich

Langsford, Robert William [Bob]
See Lankswert, Robert William

Langshank, Laurence, Gent.
See Mudie, Robert

Langstaff, Josephine
See Herschberger, Ruth [Margaret]

Langstaff, Launcelot [joint pseudonym
with William Irving and James Kirke
Paulding]
See Irving, Washington

Langstaff, Launcelot [joint pseudonym with Washington Irving and James Kirke Paulding]
See Irving, William

Langstaff, Launcelot [joint pseudonym with Washington Irving and William Irving]
See Paulding, James Kirke

Langstaff, Tristram
See Lord, William Wilberforce

Langston, Murray 20th c.
American comedian
* [The] Unknown Comic

Langstroth, Lorenzo Lorraine 1810-1895 [HPPN]
American apiarist, educator, clergyman
* [The] Father of American Apiculture

Langton, Basil C.
See Calvert-Langton, Basil

Langtry, Baby
See Edwards, Lillie

Langtry, Lillie
See Edwards, Lillie

Langtry, Lily [or Lillie]
See Le Breton, Emilie Charlotte

Languereau, Maurice 20th c. [WECO]
French writer and publisher
* Caumery

Languichatte
See Beaubrun, Theodore

Languid Bob Meusel
See Meusel, Robert William [Bob]

Langway, Hugo
See Lang, Andrew

Langworthy, Yolande
See Reade, Frances Lawson

Lanham, Ceora B. 20th c. [NAA]
American entertainer and author
* Bee, Betty
* La Belle, Chemet

Lania, Leo
See Herrmann, Lazar

Lanier, Alison Raymond 1917- [CA]
American author
* Raymond, G. Alison

Lanier, Bob 1948-
American basketball player
* Lanier, Bob-A-Dob

Lanier, Bob-A-Dob
See Lanier, Bob

Lanier, [Dr.] Clement 1879-1967 [CW]
Haitian author
* Robion, Jean

Lanier, Contact
See Lanier, Willie E.

Lanier, Honey Bear
See Lanier, Willie E.

Lanier, Lorenzo 1948- [BE]
American baseball player
* Lanier, Rimp

Lanier, Rimp
See Lanier, Lorenzo

Lanier, Sidney 1842-1881 [HPPN]
American poet
* [The] Sunrise Poet

Lanier, Warren, Sr. 1927- [BA]
American journalist
* [The] Black Prince

Lanier, Willie E. 1945- [FB, IBW]
American football player
* Lanier, Contact
* Lanier, Honey Bear

Lanigan, Catherine 20th c.
Author
* Wilder, Joan

Lanigan, George Thomas 1845-1886 [DLE1, PA, PI]
Canadian journalist and poet
* Aesop, George Washington
* Allid
* G. T. L.
* Toxopholite

Lanigan, Richard 19th c. [CCL]
Canadian author
* [An] Ex Journalist

Lanigan, William 1820?-? [PI]
Irish clergyman and poet
* Alpha

Lanihan, Peter 19th c.
American frontiersman
* Lanihan, Rattlesnake Pete

Lanihan, Rattlesnake Pete
See Lanihan, Peter

Lanin, E. B.
See Dillon, Emile Joseph

Lankswert, Robert William ?-1907 [BE]
American baseball player
* Langsford, Robert William [Bob]

Lanktree, J. W. 19th c. [PI]
Irish author and poet
* J. W. L.?

[The] Lanky Cornishman
See Fitzsimmons, Robert Prometheus [Bob]

Lanman, Charles 1819-1895 [HPPN]
American author and painter
* [The] Picturesque Explorer of the United States

Lanna, A. August 1914?-1976 [BI]
American labor mediator and tennis umpire
* Lanna, Gus

Lanna, Gus
See Lanna, A. August

Lanne, William F.
See Leopold, Nathan F.

Lannen, [Mother] Clement
See Lannen, Ellen

Lannen, Ellen 1841-1910 [BI]
American educator
* Lannen, [Mother] Clement

Lanning, John Young 1910- [BE]
American baseball player
* Tobacco Chewin' Johnny

Lanning, Les[ter Alfred] 1895-1962 [BE]
American baseball player
* Lanning, Red

Lanning, Red
See Lanning, Les[ter Alfred]

Lanoe, Jacques
See Lanoe, Jiquel

Lanoe, Jiquel [F2]
Actor
* Lanoe, Jacques

Lanoue, Conrad 1908- [ASC]
American musician
* Lanoue, Tee

Lanoue, Francois de 1531-1591 [DNNF, RH, SN]
French army officer
* Bras de Fer
* Iron Arm

Lanoue, Tee
See Lanoue, Conrad

Lanphere, Gladys ?-1948 [SC]
Actress
* Banjamin, Gladys

Lansberry, Paula Vivien 1922- [IAW]
British author
* Batchelor, Paula

[The] Lansdowne Laureate
See Moore, Thomas

Lansdowne, Marquis of
See Petty, [Sir] William

Lansford, Alex 20th c. [EF]
American football player
* Lansford, Buck

Lansford, Buck
See Lansford, Alex

Lansing, [Eu]gene [Hewitt] 1898-1945 [BE]
American baseball player
* Lansing, Jigger

Lansing, Henry
See Rowland, Donald Sydney

Lansing, Jessie
See St. Martin, Anna

Lansing, Jigger
See Lansing, [Eu]gene [Hewitt]

Lansing, Joi
See Wasmansdoff, Joyce

Lansing, Robert
See Brown, Robert Howell

Lansky, Meyer
See Suchowljansky, Maier

Lanson, Roy 1919- [PMJ]
American singer
* Lanson, Snooky

Lanson, Snooky
See Lanson, Roy

Lant, Harvey
See Rowland, Donald Sydney

Lantern
See Marquis, Donald Robert Perry

Lanternbug, Mr.
See Loutherbourg, Philip James de

Lantree, Ann 1943- [RO2]
British musician
* Lantree, Honey

Lantree, Honey
See Lantree, Ann

Lantry, Mike
See Tubb, Edwin Charles

Lanty the Flint
See Donnelly, James

Lantz, Constantine P. 1934?-
American jurist
* Lantz, Dick

Lantz, Dick
See Lantz, Constantine P.

Lantz, Kid
See Lantz, Russell

Lantz, Russell 20th c. [BBH]
Boxer
* Lantz, Kid

Lanum, Jake
See Lanum, R.

Lanum, R. 20th c. [SMG]
American football player
* Lanum, Jake

Lanza, Black Jack
See Lanza, John

Lanza, Cowboy Jack
See Lanza, John

Lanza, Isabel 1952?- [HPPN]
Cuban-born fashion model
* Ardigo, Isabella
* [The] Pet of the Year

Lanza, John 20th c. [HPPN]
American wrestler
* Lanza, Black Jack
* Lanza, Cowboy Jack

Lanza, Joseph 20th c. [CEC, PHM]
American underworld figure
* Lanza, Socks

Lanza, Mario
See Cocozza, Alfredo Arnold

Lanza, Silverio
See Amoros, Juan Bautista

Lanza, Socks
See Lanza, Joseph

[El] Lanzallama
See Lopez, Aurelio Alejandro

Lao She
See Shu Ch'ing-ch'un

Lao-tzu [or Lao-tse]
See Li Erh

Laoide, Seosamh
See Lloyd, Joseph H.

Laon
See Le Sieur, W. D.

[The] Lap King
See Olaf

Lapage
See Boccage, Marie Anne

LaPalme, Lefty
See LaPalme, Paul Edmore

LaPalme, Paul Edmore 1923- [BE]
American baseball player
* LaPalme, Lefty

Lapaquellerie, Yvon
See Bizardel, Yvon

Lapauze, Jeanne Loiseau 1860-1921
[WBD]
French author
* Lesueur, Daniel

Lapham, William Berry 1828-? [HPPN]
American physician and author
* W. B. L.

Lapide, Phinn E.
See Lapide, Pinchas E.

Lapide, Pinchas E. 1922- [CA]
Israeli diplomat, army officer, author
* Lapide, Phinn E.

Lapidus, Elaine 1939- [CA]
*American author and television
scriptwriter*
* Coleman, Lee
* Peters, Lane

LaPierre, Cherilyn
See Sarkisian, Cheryl

LaPietra, Mary 1929- [CA]
American writer
* Patanne, Maria

Lapihuska, Andrew [Andy] 1922- [BE]
American baseball player
* Lapihuska, Apples

Lapihuska, Apples
See Lapihuska, Andrew [Andy]

Lapin, Adam 1914?-1961 [BI]
American author
* Adams, Ben

Lapize, Alice 1888- [EMT]
French-born actress and singer
* Delysia, Alice

Laplace, Pierre Simon de 1749-1827
[SN]
French astronomer
* [The] Modern Newton

Lapland Willie Weaver
See Weaver, William [Bill]

LaPlante, Violet Virginia 20th c. [FIR]
American actress
* Avon, Violet

Lapointe, Jumbo
See Lapointe, Rick

Lapointe, Rick 1955- [SMG]
Canadian-born hockey player
* Lapointe, Jumbo

LaPore, James
See Marino, James

Laporte
See Le Febvre, Mathieu

LaPorte, Frank Breyfogle 1880-1939
[BE]
American baseball player
* LaPorte, Pot

LaPorte, Pot
See LaPorte, Frank Breyfogle

Lara
See Griffith-Jones, George Chetwynd

Lara, Jose 1837-1902 [GS]
Spanish bullfighter
* Chicorro [Husky Young Man]

Lara y Merino, Matias 1887-1957 [GS]
Spanish bullfighter
* Larita [Little Lara]

Lara y Reyes, Manuel 1867-1912 [GS]
Spanish bullfighter
* Jerezano [Man from Jerez]

Laracy, Larry
See Doherty, John

Laraia, Carol Maria 1932- [EMT, IPA,
SW]
American actress, singer, dancer
* Lawrence, Carol

Laramie, Jacques
See Lorimer, Jacques

Laramy, Grant
See Longo, Germano

Laraque, Paul 1920- [CW]
Haitian poet and author
* Lenoir, Jacques

Larbalestier, Philip George 20th c.
[WW]
Author
* Scott, Archer G.

Larbaud, Valery 1881-1957 [TLC]
French poet, author, translator
* Hagiosy, L.

Larche, Doug 20th c.
Author
* Gander, Father

Larco, Isabel Granda 1911?-1983 [CA]
Peruvian-born singer and songwriter
* Granda, Chabuca

Lardner, Dionysius 1793-1859 [HPPN, SN]
Irish author and editor
* Gander, Diabolus
* [A] Resident of Paris

Lardner, Ring
See Lardner, Ringgold Wilmer

Lardner, Ringgold Wilmer 1885-1933
[AS, IPA, LC]
American author
* Lardner, Ring

Laredo, Betty
See Codrescu, Andrei

Laredo, Johnny
See Caesar, [Eu]gene [Lee]

Lariar, Lawrence
See Rosenblum, Lawrence

Larin, Yuri
See Lurye, Mikhail

Larios Alvarez, Jose 1912- [GS]
Mexican bullfighter
* [El] Indio [The Indian]

Larista, Pepe
See Schweizer, Marc

Larita [Little Lara]
See Lara y Merino, Matias

Larius, R. Q.
See Arcularius, Henry W.

Larivey, Pierre de
See Giunta, Pierre

Lariviere, Bimbo
See Lariviere, Garry Joseph

LaRiviere, Edmond 1895-1964 [BE]
Canadian-born baseball player
* Wingo, Ed[mund Armand]

Lariviere, Garry Joseph 1954- [SMG]
Canadian-born hockey player
* Lariviere, Bimbo

Lark, J. C.
See Ackerman, Forrest J[ames]

Lark, Jody
See Sellers, Connie Leslie, Jr.

Larkelle, Nellie
See Colligan, Mrs. George W.

Larkfin
See Satterthwaite, Franklin

Larkin
See Cassidy, Charles

Larkin
See Cassidy, John L.

Larkin, Frank [BE]
American baseball player
* Larkin, Terry

Larkin, James Patrick
See Vizzini, Sal[vatore]

Larkin, Joseph A. 1951- [SMG]
American football player
* Larkin, Meadow

Larkin, Maia
See Wojciechowska, Maia [Teresa]

Larkin, Meadow
See Larkin, Joseph A.

Larkin, Milton 1910- [WWJ]
American jazz musician
* Larkin, Tippy

Larkin, Peter O'Neill 19th c. [PI]
Irish poet
* P. L.

Larkin, Philip 1922?-1985 [WP 12-3-85]
British poet and librarian
* [The] Hermit of Hull

Larkin, R. T.
See Larkin, Rochelle

Larkin, Rochelle 1935- [CA]
American author and editor
* Larkin, R. T.

Larkin, Sarah
See Loening, Sarah Larkin

Larkin, Terry
See Larkin, Frank

Larkin, Thomas 1795?-1850? [PI]
Irish poet
* [The] Bard of Ballydine

Larkin, Tippy
See Larkin, Milton

Larkin, Tippy
See Pilleteri, Tony

Larkin, William
See Stiles, William Larkin [Billy]

Larking, G. B.
See Shaw, George Bernard

Larkins, Mary 1889- [HPPN]
American industrial employee
* Miss Mary

Larkins, Ned
See Larkins, Wayne

Larkins, Wayne 1953- [DC]
British cricketer
* Larkins, Ned

Larkins, William Frederick 1931- [AW]
Australian author
* Long, Gerry

Larminie, Margaret Rivers
See Tragett, Margaret Rivers

Larmore, Red
See Larmore, Robert McCahan [Bob]

Larmore, Robert McCahan [Bob]
1896-1964 [BE]
American baseball player
* Larmore, Red

Larner, Jeremy 1937- [CA]
American author
* Gouge, Orson

Larneuil, Michel
See Batbedat, Jean

LaRocca, Dominick James 1889-1961
[ASC]
American jazz musician
* LaRocca, Nick

LaRocca, Nick
See LaRocca, Dominick James

LaRocca, Pasquale
See Lilly, Patrick J.

LaRocca, Patty
See Lilly, Patrick J.

Laroche, Rene
See McKeag, Ernest L[ionel]

Larocque, Bunny
See Larocque, Michel Raymond

Larocque, Michel Raymond 1952- [HR, SMG]
Canadian-born hockey player
* Larocque, Bunny

Larose, Claude 1955- [SMG]
Canadian-born hockey player
* [The] Rocket

LaRoss, Harry Raymond 1891-1954
[BE]
American baseball player
* LaRoss, Spike

LaRoss, Spike
See LaRoss, Harry Raymond

Larr, Sven
See Lyngstad, Sverre

Larra, Mariano Jose de 1809-1837
[FFF, WBD]
Spanish poet, playwright, author
* Figaro

Larralde, Romulo, Jr. 1902- [BEW SW]
Mexican actor, director, playw⟩
* Brent, Romney

Larrette, C. H. 1846-? [NPS]
Journalist and author
* Old Athlete

Larrimore, Francine
See La Remnee, Francine

Larrimore, Lida
See Turner, Lida Larrimore

Larrowe, Marcus Dwight 183⟩
Author
* Loisette, Alphonso

Larrupin' Lou Gehrig
See Gehrig, [Henry] Lou[is]

Larry
See Parkes, Terence

Larry of Macedonia
See Eagleburger, Lawrence

Larry the Aviator
See Banghart, Basil

Larsen, Arthur 1925-
American tennis player
* Larsen, Tappy
* Larsen, Tuppy

Larsen, Carl 1934- [CA]
American poet, author, playwright
* Poots-Booby, Edna

Larsen, Egon
See Lehrburger, Egon

Larsen, Erik 1911- [IAW]
Austrian-born author
* Petronius

Larsen, Erling 1909- [CA]
American author
* Brand, Peter

Larsen, Erling Arthur 1913- [BE]
American baseball player
* Larsen, Swede

Larsen, Geraldine 20th c. [BS]
American magician
* [The] Magic Lady

Larsen, Henry Hertzberg 1867-1922
[WBD]
Australian author
* Lawson, Henry Hertzberg

Larsen, Lola
See Franco, Fulvia

Larsen, Peter
See Lehrburger, Peter

Larsen, Suzan 1924- [FC]
American opera singer and actress
* Foster, Susanna

Larsen, Swede
See Larsen, Erling Arthur

Larsen, Tappy
See Larsen, Arthur

Larsen, Tuppy
See Larsen, Arthur

Larsocchi, Eduard
See Neagu, Paul

Larson, Butch
See Larson, Frank

Larson, Eve
See St. John, Wylly Folk

Larson, Frank 20th c. [HPPN]
American football player
* Larson, Butch

Larson, Frederic 20th c. [EF]
American football player
Larson, Ojay

Larson, Harry 20th c. [EF]
American football player
Larson, Pete

Larson, Ojay
Larson, Frederic

Larson, Pete
Larson, Harry

Shirley Elizabeth Crosman
[HPPN]
actress
Shirl

Larssen, Pedar
See Mallette, Gertrude Ethel

Larsson, Carl Filip 1877-? [CD]
Swedish poet and author
* Larsson I By, Carl

Larsson, Signe 20th c.
Swedish-born actress
* Hasso, Signe

Larsson I By, Carl
See Larsson, Carl Filip

Larteguy, Jean
See Osty, Lucien Pierre Jean

LaRue, Alfred 1921- [BI]
American actor
* LaRue, Lash

LaRue, Dione 1945- [RO1]
American singer
* Sharp, Dee Dee

LaRue, Lash
See LaRue, Alfred

Larusdottir, Elinborg 1891- [IAW]
Icelandic author
* Sunna

Laruska, Dianne 1928- [FC]
Canadian actress
* Foster, Dianne

LaRusso, Dominic A[nthony] 1924-
[CA]
American educator and author
* Domini, Jon

Larwood, Harold 1904- [EC]
British cricketer
* Larwood, Lol

Larwood, Jacob
See Sadler, L. R.

Larwood, Joshua 19th c. [HFN]
British author and clergyman
* [A] Sailor

Larwood, Lol
See Larwood, Harold

Lary, Broadway
See Lary, Lynford Hobart

Lary, Bulldog
See Lary, Frank Strong

Lary, Frank Strong 1931- [BE, PB,
SMG]
American baseball player
* Lary, Bulldog
* Lary, Mule
* Lary, Taters
* [The] Yankee Killer

Lary, Lyn
See Lary, Lynford Hobart

Lary, Lynford Hobart 1906-1973 [BE,
PB]
American baseball player
* Lary, Broadway
* Lary, Lyn

Lary, Mule
See Lary, Frank Strong

Lary, Taters
See Lary, Frank Strong

Las Casas, Bartolome de 1474-1566
[DNNF, HN, SN]
Spanish missionary
* [The] Apostle of the Indians
* [The] Indian Apostle
* Protector of the Indians

**Las Cases, Emmanuel Augustin
Dieudonne de** 1766-1842 [FFF, RH, SN]
French historian
* [Le] Sage
* [The] Wise

Lasalle, George E.
See Ellis, Edward S[ylvester]

Lasalle, Jean Baptiste de 1651-1719
[HPPN]
Saint
* [The] Patron of All Teachers

[Il] Lasca [The Roach]
See Grazzini, Antonio Francesco [or
Antonfrancesco]

Lascaris
See John IV

Lascaris
See Theodore I

Lascaris
See Theodore II

Lascaris, Andreas Johannes [or Janus]
1445?-1535 [WBD]
Greek scholar and educator
* Rhyndacenus

Lascelles, Alison
See Parris, John

Lascelles, [Lady] Caroline
See Maxwell, Mary Elizabeth [Braddon]

Lascelles, Emma
See Queen, Mrs. Frederick E.

Lascelles, Robert [NPS]
Author
* Piscator

Lascelles, Tony
See Green, Hubert Unsworth

Lascelles, Walter 1898- [HPPN]
Irish author
* Downe, Patrick

Laschever, Barnett D. 1924- [CA]
American journalist and author
* Barnett, L. David

Lasco, John
See Laski, Jan

Lascy, Franz Moritz
See Lacy, Francis Maurice

Lascy, Pierre
See Lacy, Peter

Lasell, Fen H.
See Calvert, Elinor H.

Lasha, Prince
See Lasha, William B.

Lasha, William B. 1929-   [DAM]
American musician
* Lasha, Prince

Lashwood, George 1863-1942   [BMH]
British comedian and singer
* [The] Beau Brummell of the Halls

Lasker, Albert Davis 1880-1952   [HPPN]
American baseball official
* [The] Advertising Wizard
* [The] Father of the Lasker Plan

Lasker, Edward 1885-1981
German-born chess player, author,
engineer, inventor
* Lasker Minor

Lasker, Emmanuel 20th c.
Chess player
* Lasker Major

Lasker Major
See Lasker, Emmanuel

Lasker Minor
See Lasker, Edward

Laski, Jan 1499-1560   [HPPN]
Polish-British scholar and reformer
* Lasco, John

Laski, Marghanita 1915-   [LC]
British author
* Russell, Sarah

Laskowski, Janina Domanska 20th c.
[TBJ]
Polish-born author and illustrator
* Domanska, Janina

Lasky, Jesse Louis, Jr. 1910-   [AW]
American author, poet, playwright
* Smeed, Frances

Laslett, Peter 1915-   [CA]
British author
* Russell, Thomas

Lasley, Bill
See Lasley, Willard Almond

Lasley, Willard Almond 1902-   [BE]
American baseball player
* Lasley, Bill

[The] Lass with the Golden Locks
See Smart, Anna Maria

Lassal, Ferdinand 1825-1864   [JL, UH]
German political organizer and theorist
* Alvan, [Dr] Sigismund
* Lassalle, Ferdinand

Lassalle, C. E.
See Ellis, Edward S[ylvester]

Lassalle, Ferdinand
See Lassal, Ferdinand

Lassang, Iwan
See Lang, Isaac

Lasselle, Hyacinth 1777-1810?   [HPPN]
American army officer, pioneer, Indian
fighter
* [The] Frontier Baby

Lasser, David 1902-   [WGT]
American author
* Penny, Richard

Lasseran-Massencome [Seigneur de Montluc] 1501-1577   [HPPN, NPS]
French marshal
* [Le] Boucher Royaliste [The Royalist Butcher]
* [Le] Royaliste Boucher

[Das] Lasseter
See Lasseter, L. Harold Bell

Lasseter, L. Harold Bell ?-1931?
[HPPN]
Australian gold prospector
* [Das] Lasseter

Lassez, M.
See Bedford-Jones, Henry [James O'Brien]

Lassie's Master
See Rettig, Thomas Noel [Tommy]

Lassiter, Luther 20th c.   [IBW]
American billiard player
* Lassiter, Wimpy

Lassiter, Wimpy
See Lassiter, Luther

Lasso, Orlando di
See Delattre [or de Lattre], Roland

Lassus, Orlandus [or Roland] de
See Delattre [or de Lattre], Roland

[The] Last Astrologer
See Lilly, William

[The] Last Caesar
See Trujillo Molina, Rafael Leonidas

[The] Last Cold Warrior
See Ulbricht, Walter

[The] Last Draftee in American History
See Stone, [Private] Dwight Elliot

Last Elizabethan
See Raleigh, [Sir] Walter

[The] Last English Maecenas
See Rogers, Samuel

[The] Last English Witch
See Wenham, Jane

[The] Last Genro
See Saionji, [Prince] Kimmochi

[The] Last Gleeman
See Moran, Michael

[The] Last Great American Hero
See Ellsberg, Daniel

[The] Last Great Englishman
See Mountbatten, Louis

Last, Jef
See Last, Josephus Carel Franciscus

Last, Josephus Carel Franciscus
1898-1972   [CAP]
Dutch poet, author, translator
* Last, Jef

[The] Last King of America
See George III

[The] Last King of Paradise
See Kalakaua, David

[The] Last King of the Matabele
See Lobengula

[The] Last King of the Ohio
See Tecumseh

[The] Last Knight of the King's Gambit
See Spielmann, Rudolf

[The] Last Laocoon
See Fitzgerald, F[rancis] Scott [Key]

[The] Last Literary Cavalier
See Hayne, Paul Hamilton

[The] Last Log Cabin Statesman
See Fairbanks, Charles Warren

[The] Last Man
See Charles I

[The] Last Marine
See Somoza Debayle, Anastasio

[The] Last Minstrel of the English Stage
See Shirley, James

[The] Last of Dillinger's Boys
See Shaw, William A.

[The] Last of Monsters
See Braschi, Giovanni Angelo

[The] Last of Philadelphia's Free Quakers
See Ross, Betsy Griscom

[The] Last of the Barons
See Neville, Richard

[The] Last of the Big Bats
See Aaron, Henry Louis [Hank]

[The] Last of the Big City Bosses
See Daley, Richard Joseph

[The] Last of the Big Spenders
See Gulbenkian, Nubar Sarkis

[The] Last of the Big Time Amateurs
See Wade, Virginia

[The] Last of the Big Time Grafters
See Sullivan, Timothy Daniel

[The] Last of the Boatmen
See Fink, Mike

[The] Last of the Buccaneers
See Lafitte, Jean

[The] Last of the Buffalo Hunters
See Wades in the Water

[The] Last of the Bushrangers
See Kelly, Edward [Ned]

[The] Last of the Cocked Hats
See Mease, John

[The] Last of the Cocked Hats
See Monroe, James

[The] Last of the Cold War L
See Jackson, Henry Martin

[The] **Last of the Dandies**
See D'Orsay, Alfred Guillaume Gabriel

[The] **Last of the Elizabethans**
See Ford, John

[The] **Last of the English**
See Hereward

[The] **Last of the Fathers**
See Bernard of Clairvaux

[The] **Last of the Fullblooded Hurons**
See Vincent, Zacherie

[The] **Last of the Giants**
See Wilkins, Roy

[The] **Last of the Golden Age Producers**
See Zanuck, Darryl Francis

[The] **Last of the Goths**
See Roderick

[The] **Last of the Great Adventurers**
See Halliburton, Richard

Last of the Great American Clowns
See Skelton, [Richard] Red

[The] **Last of the Great Asian Conquerors**
See Nadir Shah

[The] **Last of the Great Bohemians**
See Rexroth, Kenneth

[The] **Last of the Great New York Bosses**
See De Sapio, Carmine

[The] **Last of the Great Scouts**
See Cody, William Frederick

[The] **Last of the Great Southern Belles**
See Mitchell, Martha Elizabeth Beall Jennings

[The] **Last of the Greeks**
See Philopoemen

[The] **Last of the Incas**
See Atahualpa [or Atahuallpa]

[The] **Last of the Incas**
See Condorcanqui, Jose Gabriel

[The] **Last of the Irish Bards**
See Carolan, Turlough

[The] **Last of the Kennedy Brothers**
See Kennedy, Edward Moore [Ted]

[The] **Last of the Knights**
See Maximilian I

[The] **Last of the Lion Comiques**
See Lloyd, Arthur

[The] **Last of the Magi**
See Constant, Alphonse Louis

[The] **Last of the Makars**
Lindsay [or Lyndsay], [Sir] David

Last of the Medici
dici, Anna Maria Ludovica de

[The] **Last of the Medici**
See Medici, Cosimo de

[The] **Last of the Oklahoma Bad Men**
See Hamon, Jacob L. [Jake]

[The] **Last of the Oldtime Gangsters**
See Orgen, Jacob

[The] **Last of the Parnassians**
See Flecker, Herman Elroy

[The] **Last of the Platonists**
See Scotus, Johannes [or John]

[The] **Last of the Puritans**
See Adams, Samuel

[The] **Last of the Red Hot Mamas**
See Abuza, Sophie

[The] **Last of the Romans**
See Aetius, Flavius

[The] **Last of the Romans**
See Boethius, Anicius Manlius Severinus

[The] **Last of the Romans**
See Bonifacius

[The] **Last of the Romans**
See Brutus, Marcus Junius

[The] **Last of the Romans**
See Cassius Longinus, Caius

[The] **Last of the Romans**
See Congreve, William

[The] **Last of the Romans**
See Desbillons, Francois Joseph Terasse

[The] **Last of the Romans**
See Fox, Charles James

[The] **Last of the Romans**
See Gabrini, Niccolo

[The] **Last of the Romans**
See Stilicho, Flavius

[The] **Last of the Romans**
See Walpole, Horatio [Fourth Earl of Orford]

[The] **Last of the Saxons**
See Harold II

[The] **Last of the Schoolmen**
See Biel [or Byll], Gabriel

[The] **Last of the Schoolmen**
See Major [or Mair], John

[The] **Last of the Schoolmen**
See Suarez, Francisco [or Francois]

[The] **Last of the Scottish Chaucerians**
See Lindsay [or Lyndsay], [Sir] David

[The] **Last of the Silly Asses**
See Buchanan, Jack

[The] **Last of the Spitball Pitchers**
See Grimes, Burleigh Arland

[The] **Last of the Stuarts**
See Stuart, Henry Benedict Maria Clemens

[The] **Last of the Tories**
See Johnson, Samuel

[The] **Last of the Tribunes**
See Gabrini, Niccolo

[The] **Last of the Troubadours**
See Baline, Israel

[The] **Last of the Troubadours**
See Boe, Jacques

[The] **Last of the Troubadours**
See Rene I

[The] **Last of the Tycoons**
See Eaton, Cyrus

[The] **Last of the Tycoons**
See Hitotsubashi

[The] **Last of the Unholy Trio**
See Sheil, Lily

[The] **Last of the Western Train Robbers**
See Carlile, William L. [Bill]

[The] **Last of the Wild Indians**
See Ishi

[The] **Last Poet of Rome**
See Juvenal [Decimus Junius Juvenalis]

[The] **Last Protestant**
See Dewey, John

[The] **Last Rower**
See Pound, Ezra [Loomis]

[The] **Last Stone Age Man in the United States**
See Ishi

[The] **Last Tragedian**
See Booth, Edwin Thomas

[The] **Last True Bard of Ireland**
See O'Carolan, Turloch

[The] **Last Universal Man**
See Goethe, Johann Wolfgang von

[The] **Last Virgin on Broadway**
See Golden, Matilda

[The] **Last who Spoke Cornish**
See Pentreath, Doll

Lata, Bibhuti 1915- [DFM]
Indian cinematographer
* Agradoot [joint pseudonym with Nishith Bannerjee Agragami]

Latas, Michael 1806-1871 [HPPN]
Turkish army officer
* Omar Pasha

Latchinian, Gerard 1938?- [TI 11-12-84]
Honduran arms dealer and alleged assassination plot conspirator
* [The] Ambassador of Death

[A] **Late Author**
See Brevint, Daniel

[A] **Late Author**
See Coward, William

[A] **Late Author**
See Galloway, Joseph

[The] Late Ben Smith
See Mathews, Cornelius

[A] Late Commentator
See Romaine, [Rev.] William

[A] Late Deceased Satirist
See Potter, John

[A] Late Eminent Advocate
See Melmoth, William

[A] Late Eminent Citizen of Dublin
See Latouche, James Digges

[A] Late Eminent Divine
See Law, William

[A] Late Eminent Hand
See Cooke, [Sir] George

[A] Late Fellow of King's College,
Cambridge
See Ashton, Thomas

[The] Late Gilbert Earle, Esq.
See St. Leger, Francis Barry Boyle

[A] Late Graduate of Oxford
See Naghten, Frederick

[A] Late Inhabitant
See Hasted, Edward

[The] Late J. J. S., Esq.
See Anstey, John

[A] Late Learned Judge
See Gilbert, [Sir] Geoffry

[A] Late Lord Mayor of London
See Barnard, [Sir] John

[A] Late Member of the General Court
See Swan, [Colonel] James

[A] Late Noble Commander
See Sackville, [Lord] George [First
Viscount Sackville]

[A] Late Noble Writer
See Burke, Edmund

[A] Late Officer in the U. S. Army
See Cutler, Jervase

[A] Late Prime Minister
See Bentinck, William Henry Cavendish
[Duke of Portland]

[A] Late Professor in the University of
Oxford
See Lowth, Robert

[A] Late Railway Chaplain
See Nowers, [Rev.] James Henry

[A] Late Resident at Bhagulpore
See Hopkins, David

[A] Late Staff Sergeant of the 13th
Light Infantry
See MacMullen, John

[A] Late Stipendiary Magistrate in
Jamaica
See Bourne, Stephen

[A] Late Teacher
See Singleton, William

[A] Late Under Secretary of State
See Knox, William

[A] Late Very Learned and Reverend
Divine
See Pegge, Samuel

[A] Late Vicar
See Masters, Robert

Lateef, Yusef
See Evans, William

Latell, Lyle
See Zeiem, Lyle

Lateral Pass
See Stern, Bill

Latessa, James 1934-1964 [SC]
American actor
* Eaton, James

Lateur, Frank 1871-1969 [BI, CD]
Flemish author
* Streuvels, Stijn

Latham, Arlie
See Latham, Walter Arlington

Latham, Dwight 20th c.
American singer
* Latham, Red

Latham, Edward Bryan 1895- [IAW]
British author
* Bryan, E.

Latham, Fat
See Latham, George

Latham, George 20th c. [HPPN]
American football player
* Latham, Fat

Latham, George Warren 1852-1914 [BE]
American baseball player
* Latham, Juice

Latham, Henry Jepson [PA]
Author
* Jepson, Ring

Latham, Hope
See Kemper, Louise Brega

Latham, Jean Lee 1902- [CLC, TCC]
American author, poet, playwright
* Campion, Rose [joint pseudonym with
Arthur LeRoy Kaser and Ruth Perry]
* Gard, Janice
* Lee, Julian

Latham, Juice
See Latham, George Warren

Latham, Mavis
See Clark, Mavis Thorpe

Latham, O'Neill
See O'Neill, Rose Cecil

Latham, Philip
See Richardson, Robert S[hirley]

Latham, Red
See Latham, Dwight

Latham, Sade 1889-1940 [SC]
British-born actress
* Carr, Sade

Latham, Walter Arlington 1859-1952
[BE]
American baseball player
* [The] Freshest Man on Earth
* Latham, Arlie

Lathbury, Mary Artemisia 1841-1913
[FFF, PA]
American author
* Aunt Mary

Lathe, Herbert William 1851-? [ALY]
American clergyman and author
* Nichols, Nicholas

[A] Lathe Painted to Look Like Iron
See Cecil, Robert Arthur Talbot [Third
Marquis of Salisbury]

Lathen, Emma [joint pseudonym with
Mary J. Latis]
See Henissart, Martha

Lathen, Emma [joint pseudonym with
Martha Hennissart]
See Latsis, Mary Jane

Lathers, Charles Ten Eyck 1888- [BE]
American baseball player
* Lathers, Chick

Lathers, Chick
See Lathers, Charles Ten Eyck

Lathrop, Annie Wakeman 20th c. [NPS]
Author
* Wakeman, Annie

Lathrop, Cornelia Sterrett [Penfield]
1892-1938 [WW]
Author
* Penfield, Cornelia

Lathrop, Francis
See Leiber, Fritz

Lathrop, G. P. [PA]
Author
* [The] Masque of Poets

Lathrop, Lorin Andrews 1858-? [NPS,
WW]
Author
* Gambier, Kenyon
* Kaye, Lorin [joint pseudonym with F.
Konstam]
* Loring, Andrew

Lathrop, Mary Torrans [FFF]
Author
* Lena

Lathrop, Rose [Hawthorne] 1851-1926
[BI]
American missionary
* Mary Alphonsa, [Mother]

Lathy, Thomas P. 19th c. [PA]
British author
* Piscator

Lathyros
See Ptolemy IX [or VIII]

Latimer, Clifford Wesley 1875-1936
[BE]
American baseball player
* Latimer, Tacks

Latimer, Faith
See Miller, Mrs. John A.

Latimer, Hugh 1472?-1555 [HN]
British religious reformer
* [The] Apostle of England

Latimer, Jonathan [Wyatt] 1906-
[EMD]
American author
* Coffin, Peter

Latimer, May
See Lambert, May

Latimer, Rupert
See Mills, Algernon Victor

Latimer, Tacks
See Latimer, Clifford Wesley

Latimore, Frank
See Kline, Frank

Latimore, Jewel C. 1935- [LBA]
American poet
* Amini, Johari
* Kunjufu, Johari M. Amini

[The] Latin Ulysses
See Bohemond I

[The] Latin Walt Whitman
See Reyes Basualto, [Ricardo Eliezer]
Neftali

[The] Latine
See Galindo, Beatriz

Latissioner, John
See Jefferys, William Hamilton

Latman, Arnold Barry 1936- [EJS]
American baseball player
* Latman, Shoulders

Latman, Shoulders
See Latman, Arnold Barry

Latner, Helen [Stambler] 1918- [CA]
American author
* Stambler, Helen

Latner, Pat Wallace
See Wallace, Pat

Latona
See Battey, Sallie J. [Hancock]

Latonius
See Masson, Barthelemy

Latorre, Mariano 1886-? [HPPN]
Chilean author
* [The] Chilean Pereda

Latouche, James Digges 18th c.
[HPPN]
Irish politician
* [A] Late Eminent Citizen of Dublin

Latouche, John
See Crawfurd, Oswald John Frederick

Latour, M. Chabaud
See Louis Philippe

Latourelle, James 1835-1908 [HPPN]
American composer and director
* Little Jimmy

Latreaumont
See May, Karl Friedrich

Latroon, M.
See Head, Richard

Latsios, Nickolas C. 1920?-1983 [WP
10-2-83]
American boxer
* [The] Golden Greek

Latsis, Mary Jane 1928?- [CC, EMD,
WD]
American attorney and author
* Dominic, R. B. [joint pseudonym with
Martha Hennissart]
* Lathen, Emma [joint pseudonym with
Martha Hennissart]

Latta, G-Man
See Latta, Gregory Edwin

Latta, Gregory Edwin 1952- [BA]
American football player
* Latta, G-Man

Latta, Marguerite
See Greenbie, Marjorie Barstow

Lattas, Michael 1806-1871 [WBD]
Turkish army officer
* Omer [or Omar] Pasha

Lattiff, Ann Veronica 1905-1965
[HPPN]
American actress
* Carroll, Nancy

Lattimore, Lattie
See Lattimore, Oliver Louis

Lattimore, Oliver Louis 1893- [BA]
American dentist and businessman
* Lattimore, Lattie

Lattimore, Owen 1900- [HPPN]
American author and historian
* [The] China Lobby Man

Lattimore, Sloathful Bill
See Lattimore, William Hershel [Bill]

Lattimore, William Hershel [Bill]
1884-1920 [BE]
American baseball player
* Lattimore, Sloathful Bill

Lattin, Ann
See Cole, Lois Dwight

Lattin, Big Daddy
See Lattin, David

Lattin, David 1943- [BB]
American basketball player
* Lattin, Big Daddy

Latto, Thomas C. 1818-? [FFF, PA]
American writer
* Dunn, Aiken

Latude, Jean Henry 1725-1805 [WBD]
French army officer
* Danger
* Danry, Jean
* Jedor
* Masers d'Aubrespy
* Masers de Latude

Latzo, Pete 1902-1968 [WBC]
American boxer
* Clancy, Young

Lau, Charley 20th c.
American baseball player and coach
* [The] Svengali of Swat

Lau, Chino
See Lau, [Col.] Ricardo

Lau, [Col.] Ricardo 20th c. [DN 1-28-85]
Nicaraguan military officer
* Lau, Chino

Lau Shaw
See Shu Ch'ing-ch'un

Laub, Phoebe 1951-
American singer
* Snow, Phoebe

Laubach, Frank Charles 1884-1970
[HPPN]
American missionary and educator
* [The] Teacher of Millions

L'Aubanelenco
See Drutel, Marcelle Louise Marie

Laubenthal Horst R.
See Neumaier, Horst R.

Lauchheimer, Alan 1906-1979 [CA]
American journalist and author
* Barth, Alan
* [The] Liberal Conscience of
Washington

Lauchlan, Isabel [FFF]
Scottish eccentric
* Mad Bell

Lauchmonen
See Kempadoo, Peter

Lauck, Chester 20th c. [HPPN, JF]
American comedian
* Lum

Laud, William 1573-1645 [SN]
British prelate
* [The] Hocuspocus
* [The] Little Vermin
* Parva Laus [Little Laud]
* [The] Urchin

Laudenbach, Pierre Jules Louis
1897-1975 [BEW, FC, OCF]
French actor
* Fresnay, Pierre

Lauder, Agnes 1880-? [DBA]
Scottish painter
* Lauder, Nancy

Lauder, Estee
See Mentzer, Josephine Esther

Lauder, George [Dick]
See Dick-Lauder, [Sir] George Andrew

Lauder, Harry
See MacLennan, Harry

Lauder, Maria Elise Turner 19th c.
[CCL]
Canadian author
* Lauder, Toofie

Lauder, Nancy
See Lauder, Agnes

Lauder, [Sir] Thomas Dick 1784-1848
[HPPN]
Scottish author
* Montgomery, Charles Montague

Lauder, Toofie
See Lauder, Maria Elise Turner

Lauder, William ?-1771 [HPPN]
Scottish scholar and literary impostor
* W. L.

Laudet, Fernand Charles 1860-? [LAO]
French author
* Film

Laufenberg, Babe
See Laufenberg, Brandon Hugh

Laufenberg, Brandon Hugh 1959- [WP
12-8-85]
American football player
* Laufenberg, Babe

Lauffer, Pierre
See Martes, Jose Antonio

[The] Laughing Blacksmith
See Nash, John

Laughing Charley
See Hicks, Charlie

[The] Laughing Gas Man
See Short, Dewey

**[The] Laughing Killer of the Woodside
Glens**
See Selz, Ralph Jerome Von Braun

[The] Laughing Lady
See O'Neil, Kitty

Laughing Larry Doyle
See Doyle, Lawrence Joseph

[The] Laughing Philosopher
See Democritus

Laughing Sam Carey
See Carey, Sam

Laughlin, John William 19th c. [PI]
Irish clergyman and author
* J. W. L.

Laughlin, Tom 1938- [BI]
American actor and director
* Frank, T. C.

Laughlin, Virginia Carli 1907- [BI, CA,
SAT]
American author
* Clarke, John
* Laklan, Carli

Laughton, Thomas R. [PA]
Author
* Wallis, Ik

Laugier, R.
See Cumberland, Marten

Laujon, Pierre 1727-1811 [DEP, RH]
French poet
* [The] Anacreon of the French
* [The] French Anacreon

Lauler, Michael
See Osenburg, Richard

Laumer, [John] Keith 1925- [SFL,
WGT]
American author
* LeBaron, Anthony

Laumer, March 20th c. [SFL, WGT]
Author
* Severance, Felix
* Xanthus, Xavier

Launay, Andrew [Joseph] 1930- [CA,
WW]
British author
* Adony, Raoul
* Launay, Droo

Launay, [Vicomte] Charles de
See Girardin, Delphine Gay De

Launay, Droo
See Launay, Andrew [Joseph]

Launcelot, Dom Claude
See Schimmelpenninck, Mary Anne
Galton

Launis, Armas Emanuel
See Lindberg, Armas Emanuel

Laura
See De Noves, Laure

Laura
See Perdomo y Heredia, Josefa Antonia

Laura Maria
See Robinson, Mary Darby

Laurac, Serge
See Schweizer, Marc

Laurati da Siena
See Lorenzetti, Pietro

Laurati, Pietro
See Lorenzetti, Pietro

[A] Laureat
See Southey, Robert

Laureate Gabriel
See Harvey, Gabriel

[The] Laureate of Song
See Longfellow, Henry Wadsworth

Laureate of the Bluestockings
See More, Hannah

[The] Laureate of the Dago
See Daly, T. A.

[The] Laureate of the Gentle Craft
See Sachs, Hans

Laureate of the Nursery
See Miller, William

[The] Laureate of the Nursery
See Rands, William Brighty

[The] Laureate of the South
See Hayne, Paul Hamilton

Laurel, Countess
See Battier, Henrietta

Laurel, Doy
See Laurel, Salvador

Laurel, Salvador 1929-
Philippine politician
* Laurel, Doy

Laurel, Stan
See Jefferson, Arthur Stanley

[A] Laurelled Bard
See Eusden, Laurence

Lauremberg, Johann 1590-1658 [HPPN]
German author
* Rost, Hans Wilmsen L.

Lauren, L. L. 19th c. [HPPN]
Swedish author
* L. L. L.

Lauren, Linda
See Bunce, Linda Susan [Staines]

Laurence, Clarice
See Sadler, Clarice Laurence

Laurence, Frances Elsie [Fry] 1893-
[CCL]
Canadian author
* Field, Christine

Laurence, John
See Pritchard, John Laurence

Laurence, Johnnie
See Biers, Clarence

Laurence, Paula
See De Lugo, Paula

Laurence, Richard 1760-1839 [HPPN]
British clergyman
* R. C.

Laurence, Will
See Smith, Willard L[aurence]

Laurence, William Leonard
See Siew, William Leonard

Laurens, John 1756?-1782 [FFF]
American army officer
* [The] Bayard of the Revolution

Laurent
See Meslin, Michael Neure

Laurent de la Resurrection
See Herman, Nicolas

Laurent, Emmanuel 1899- [IAW]
Belgian author
* Renault

Laurent, Henry
See Gesling, Henry L.

Laurent, Jaques
See Laurent-Cely, Jacques

Laurent, Marie-Jeanne 1744-1812?
[WFA]
French fashion designer
* Bertin, Rose
* [The] Minister of Fashion

Laurent-Cely, Jacques 1919- [CD, WGT]
French author
* Laurent, Jaques
* Saint Laurent, Cecil
* Varenne, Alberic

Laurentis, Dino de 1919- [HPPN]
Italian film producer
* [The] Dynamo of the Italian Motion
  Picture Industry
* [The] Garibaldi of the Italian Motion
  Picture Industry
* [The] Kingfish of the Italian Motion
  Picture Industry

Lauri
See Salola, Eeero

Lauri, Pikku
See Salola, Eeero

Laurice, Carmine 1905?-1948 [BI]
American welder and baseball fan
* Laurice, Jack

Laurice, Jack
See Laurice, Carmine

Laurie, Andre
See Grousset, Paschal

Laurie, Harry C.
See Cahn, Zvi

Laurie, Piper
See Jacobs, Rosetta

Laurier, Jay
See Chapman, Jay

Laurier, Silver Tongued
See Laurier, [Sir] Wilfrid

Laurier, [Sir] Wilfrid 1841-1919
Canadian statesman
* Laurier, Silver Tongued

Laurin, Anne
See McLaurin, Anne

Lauritsen, John [Phillip] 1939- [CA]
American author
* Red Butterfly

Lauscher, Hermann
See Hesse, Hermann

Lausen, John R. 1911- [EJ, PMJ, WWJ]
American jazz musician
* Lawson, John R.
* Lawson, Yank

Lausin y Lopez, Braulio 1898-1967
[GS]
Spanish bullfighter
* Gitanillo [Little Gypsy]

Lauter
See Chamson, Andre J[ules] L[ouis]

Lauthe, Alfredo Di Stephano 1926-
[HPPN]
Argentine soccer player
* Di Stephano, Alfredo

Lautreamont, le Comte de
See Ducasse, Isidore Lucien

Laux, E. F. 1919- [HPPN]
*American automobile manufacturing
executive*
* Laux, Gar

Laux, Gar
See Laux, E. F.

Lauzun, Duc de
See Nompar de Caumont, Antonin

Lavaden, Leon [PA]
Author
* Grandlien, Doctor

Lavado, Joaquin 1932- [WECO]
Argentinian cartoonist
* Quino

Lavagetto, Cookie
See Lavagetto, Harry Arthur

Lavagetto, Harry Arthur 1914- [BE, BI,
PB]
American baseball player and manager
* Lavagetto, Cookie

Laval, Pierre 1883-1945 [CND]
French attorney and politician
* Mossbank [code name used during
  World War II]

Lavan, Doc
See Lavan, John Leonard

Lavan, Henry 1921- [EMT]
American composer and lyricist
* Merrill, Bob

Lavan, John Leonard 1890-1952 [BE]
American baseball player
* Lavan, Doc

Lavant, Christine
See Habernig, Christine

Lavater, Johann Caspar 1741-1801
[DNNS, HN, HPPN, SN]
Swiss poet and theologian
* Asahel, Jonathan
* [The] Crane
* [The] Father of Physiognomy
* [The] Fenelon of Germany
* [The] Founder of Physiognomy

Lavedan, Henri L. E. 1859-? [NPS]
French author
* Manchecourt

Lavelle, Gary Robert 1949- [SMG]
American baseball player
* Lavelle, Pudge

Lavelle, Mike 1933?- [HPPN]
American columnist
* [The] Blue Collar Pundit

Lavelle, Pudge
See Lavelle, Gary Robert

Lavelli, Dante 1923- [BBH]
American football player
* Lavelli, Glue Fingers

Lavelli, Glue Fingers
See Lavelli, Dante

Lavender, Glenn 1930- [HPPN]
American singer
* Williams, Andy

Lavender, Grover C. 1932- [CM]
American booking agent and musician
* Lavender, Shorty

Lavender, Shorty
See Lavender, Grover C.

Lavengro
See Borrow, George Henry

Laver, James 1899-1975 [CA]
British fashion historian, poet, author
* Reval, Jacques

Laver, Rocket
See Laver, Rod[ney George]

Laver, Rod[ney George] 1938- [CR,
HPPN]
Australian tennis player
* Laver, Rocket
* [The] Millionaire of Tennis
* [The] Rocket
* [The] Rockhampton Rocket

Laverack, Julian
See Brown, Alfred J.

LaVere, Charles
See Johnson, Charles LaVere

Laverne, Maud
See Barlow, Maud

Laverty, Donald [joint pseudonym with
Damon F(rancis) Knight]
See Blish, James [Benjamin]

Laverty, Donald [joint pseudonym with
James (Benjamin) Blish]
See Knight, Damon F[rancis]

LaVey, Anton Szandor 1930- [EOP]
Leader of American religious cult
* [The] Black Pope

Lavi
See Diaz Cantoral, Manuel

Lavigne, George 1869-1928? [AS, BX,
RBE]
American boxer
* Lavigne, Kid
* [The] Saginaw Kid

Lavigne, Kid
See Lavigne, George

Lavigne, Mark
See Leopold, Emmanuel-Flavia

Lavin, Mary
See Walsh, Mary

Lavine, Lewis H[erbert] 1934- [CA]
American historian and author
* Carlson, Lewis H[erbert]

Lavington, Hubert?
See Carrington, Hereward Hubert Lavington

Lavinia
See Ponti, Diana da

Lavinson, Joseph
See Kaye, Marvin [Nathan]

Laviolette, Jack
See Laviolette, Jean Baptiste

Laviolette, Jean Baptiste 1879-1960 [CSH, HK]
Canadian-born hockey player
* Laviolette, Jack
* [The] Speed Merchant

Lavoie, Kent 1943- [RO2]
American singer
* Lobo

Lavoix, Jean
See Sauvageau, Juan

Lavond, Paul Dennis [joint pseudonym with F. Pohl, R. Lowndes, C. Kornbluth] [house pseudonym]
See Dockweiler, Joseph Harold

Lavond, Paul Dennis [joint pseudonym with J. H. Dockweiler, R. A. Lowndes, F. Pohl]
See Kornbluth, Cyril M.

Lavond, Paul Dennis [joint pseudonym with J. H. Dockweiler, C. Kornbluth, F. Pohl]
See Lowndes, Robert Augustine Ward

Lavond, Paul Dennis [joint pseudonym with J. Dockweiler, C. Kornbluth, R. Lowndes]
See Pohl, Frederik

Lavreince, Nicolas
See Lafrensen, Nils

Lavritch, Sophie Bentkowski 1905- [EOP]
Russian-born editor and writer
* Bentkowski, Sophie
* Bentkowski-Lavritch, Sonia
* De Trabeck, Sophie

[The] Law
See Jordan, [Dr.] Paul

[A] Law Abiding Revolutionist
See Wellman, Bert J.

Law, Beau
See Law, John

[A] Law Clerk
See Russell, William

Law, Deacon
See Law, Vernon Sanders

Law, Elizabeth Susan [Lady Colchester] 1799-? [IP, PA]
British poet
* E. S. L.

Law, Ep
See Law, M. Eprevel

Law, George 1806-1881 [FFF]
American shipbuilder
* Live Oak George

[The] Law Giver
See Frederick II

[The] Law Giver
See Suleiman II [or Soliman]

Law, Janice
See Trecker, Janice Law

Law, Jessamy John
See Law, John

Law, John 1671-1729 [DNNF, HN, HPPN, SN]
Scottish financier
* Law, Beau
* Law, Jessamy John
* [The] Paper King
* [The] Projector

Law, M. Eprevel 1943- [BA]
American educator and businessman
* Law, Ep

Law, Michael Haldane 1925- [AW]
British author
* Kreuzenau, Michael

Law, Ruth Helen 1909- [ART]
British painter
* Woodbridge, Ruth

Law, Sallie Chapman Gordon 1805-1894 [HPPN]
American Confederate sympathizer
* [The] Mother of the Confederacy

Law, Vernon Sanders 1930- [PB]
American baseball player
* Law, Deacon

Law, Virginia W.
See Shell, Virginia Law

[The] Law West of the Pecos
See Bean, Roy

Law, William 1686-1761 [HPPN]
British author
* [A] Late Eminent Divine

Lawes, Henry 1596-1662 [SN]
British composer
* Tuneful Harry

[The] Lawgiver of Parnassus
See Boileau-Despreaux, Nicolas

Lawing, Garland Fred 1919- [BE]
American baseball player
* Lawing, Knobby

Lawing, Knobby
See Lawing, Garland Fred

Lawlars, Ernest 1900-1961 [BWW]
American singer
* Little Son Joe
* Son Joe

Lawler, C. F. 19th c. [PA]
British author
* Pindar, Peter?

Lawler, Debbie 1951?- [HPPN]
American motorcyclist
* [The] Female Evel Knievel
* [The] Flying Angel

Lawless, Anthony
See MacDonald, Philip

Lawless, Bettyclare Hamilton 1915- [CA]
American author
* Hamilton, Clare

Lawless, Eve?
See Finn, Frank Stanislaus

Lawless, John 1772-1837 [SN]
Irish agitator
* Honest Jack

Lawlor, Denis Shine 1808-1887 [PI]
Irish poet
* Oscotian
* Oscotiensis

Lawlor, Glenn 20th c. [BBH]
American coach and collegiate athletic director
* Lawlor, Jake

Lawlor, Jake
See Lawlor, Glenn

Lawlor, Pat[rick Anthony] 1893- [AW, CAP, WD]
New Zealand author
* Bagarag, Shibli
* Penn, Christopher

[The] Lawman Turned Gunfighter
See Stoudenmire, Dallas

Lawonda, Signor
Circus performer
* [The] Iron Jawed Man

Lawrence
See Stephens, Lawrence Sterne

Lawrence, A. R.
See Foff, Arthur R[aymond]

Lawrence, Andrea Mead 20th c. [BBH]
American skier
* Lawrence, Andy

Lawrence, Andy
See Lawrence, Andrea Mead

Lawrence, Arnie
See Finkelstein, Arnold Lawrence

Lawrence, [Lieut.] Ashbury
See Calhoun, Alfred R.

Lawrence, Babe
See Lawrence, William

Lawrence, Bessie [PA]
Author
* Agatha

Lawrence, Birdie
See Lawrence, Edith Bird

Lawrence, Bud
See Lawrence, George H.

Lawrence, Carol
See Laraia, Carol Maria

Lawrence, Charlie
See Lorenzon, Livio

Lawrence, Chester
See Campbell, Sydney G.

Lawrence, Christopher George Holman
1866-1950 [MBF]
British author
* Abbott, Lawrence
* Jackspur
* Lynn, Escott
* Metcalfe, [Captain] W. C.

Lawrence, Cornelius C. 1902- [HPPN]
American composer, publisher, actor
* Lawrence, Neil

Lawrence, D. H.
See Lawrence, David Herbert

Lawrence, David Herbert 1885-1930
[HPPN, LC]
British author
* Davidson, Lawrence H.
* Dawson, Lawrence H.
* Lawrence, D. H.
* Prophet of the Midlands

Lawrence, Dorset William 1853-1931
[BEW]
British actor
* D'Orsay, Lawrence

Lawrence, E. S.
See Bradburne, E[lizabeth] Sutton

Lawrence, Edith Bird 1914- [MY]
American musician
* Lawrence, Birdie

Lawrence, Elliot
See Broza, Elliot Lawrence

Lawrence, Ernest Orlando 1901-1958
[HPPN]
American physicist
* [The] Father of the Cyclotron

Lawrence, Florence 1886-1939 [CU, SC]
Canadian-born actress
* Baby Flo
* [The] Biograph Girl
* [The] Imp Girl

Lawrence, Frederick 1821?-1867 [HFN]
British author and barrister
* [A] Barrister

Lawrence, George H. 20th c.
American business executive
* Lawrence, Bud

Lawrence, Gertrude
See Klasen, Gertrud Alexandra Dagmar
Lawrence

Lawrence, H. L
See Lawrence, Henry Lionel

Lawrence, Harold G. 1928- [IBW]
American author, poet, editor
* Wangara, Harun Kofi

Lawrence, Henry Lionel 1908- [SFL]
British author
* Lawrence, H. L

Lawrence, Irene
See Marsh, John

Lawrence, J. T.
See Rowland-Entwistle, [Arthur]
Theodore [Henry]

Lawrence, Jack
See Fitzgerald, Lawrence P[ennybaker]

Lawrence, Jack
See Schwartz, Jacob Lawrence

Lawrence, James [or Jimmie]
See Dillinger, John Herbert

Lawrence, James
See Tames, Richard Lawrence

Lawrence, James Henry 1774-1841
[HPPN]
British poet and playwright
* [A] Detenu

Lawrence, Jerome
See Schwartz, Jerome Lawrence

Lawrence, Jodi 1938- [CA]
American author, playwright, screenwriter
* Kebin, Jody
* Kevin, Jodi
* Lawrence, John

Lawrence, Jody
See Goddard, Josephine Lawrence

Lawrence, Joe 20th c. [BMH]
British comedian
* [The] Upside Down Comedian

Lawrence, John 1753-1839 [BI]
British author and sportsman
* Moubray, Bonington
* Scott, William Henry

Lawrence, John
See Lawrence, Jodi

**Lawrence, John Laird Mair [First
Baron Lawrence]** 1811-1879 [HPPN]
British statesman and administrator
* [The] Saviour of the Punjab

Lawrence, Joyce 1898- [FC, OCF]
British actress
* Carey, Joyce

Lawrence, Joyce Whitsett 1938- [IBW]
American poet
* Wangara, Malaika Ayo

Lawrence, Karl
See Foff, Arthur R[aymond]

Lawrence, Kennedy 20th c.
American police officer
* [The] Green Hornet

Lawrence, Kenneth G.
See Ringgold, Gene

Lawrence, Larry
See Dow, Lawrence T.

Lawrence, Larry
See Lawrence, Robert Andrew [Bob]

Lawrence, Lesley
See Lewis, Lesley

Lawrence, Lou
See Lazarin, Louis

Lawrence, Louise
See Wintle, Elizabeth Rhoda

Lawrence, Louise De Kiriline 1894-
[CA, SAT]
Canadian writer
* De Kiriline, Louise

Lawrence, Margaret Woods 1813-1901
[DNA, FFF]
American author
* Lander, Meta

Lawrence, Martin [joint pseudonym with
Lawrence Grow]
See Greif, Martin

Lawrence, Martin [joint pseudonym with
Martin Greig]
See Grow, Lawrence

Lawrence, Michael
See Rosenblum, Lawrence

Lawrence, Neil
See Lawrence, Cornelius C.

Lawrence of Arabia
See Lawrence, Thomas Edward

[The] Lawrence of Manchuria
See Doihara, Kenji

Lawrence, P.
See Tubb, Edwin Charles

Lawrence, Peter Lee
See Hirenbach, Karl

Lawrence, Richard
See Bartle, L. E.

Lawrence, Richard A.
See Leopold, Nathan F.

Lawrence, Robert
See Beum, Robert [Lawrence]

Lawrence, Robert Andrew [Bob] 1899-
[BE]
American baseball player
* Lawrence, Larry

Lawrence, Slingsby
See Lewes, George Henry

Lawrence, Stacy 1928?-1982
American entertainer
* Stormy

Lawrence, Stephen
See Stephens, Lawrence Sterne

Lawrence, Steve
See Liebowitz, Sidney

Lawrence, Steven C.
See Murphy, Lawrence A[ugustus]

Lawrence, Stringer 1697-1775 [WBD]
British army officer
* [The] Father of the Indian Army

Lawrence, T. E.
See Lawrence, Thomas Edward

Lawrence, [Sir] Thomas 1769-1830
[HN]
British painter
* [The] Wonderful Boy of Devizes

Lawrence, Thomas
See Roberts, Thom[as Sacra]

Lawrence, Thomas Edward 1888-1935
[CBS, DLE1, HPPN, IPA, LC, PPN]
British author, soldier, adventurer
* [El] Aurens
* Lawrence of Arabia
* Lawrence, T. E.
* Ross, Aircraftsman
* Ross, J. H.
* Shaw, [Private] T. E.
* Shaw, Thomas Edward

Lawrence, Trudy
See Halpern, Gertrude

Lawrence, Ulysses Brooks 1925- [BE, BTB]
American baseball player
* [The] Bull

Lawrence, Vera Brodsky 1909- [CA]
American musician, music historian, author
* Brodsky, Vera

Lawrence, Vesta 1873-1951 [BEW, BMH, THR]
British comedienne and singer
* Baby Victoria
* Little Victoria
* Victoria, Vesta

[The] Lawrence Welk of American Painting
See Rockwell, Norman Percival

Lawrence, William 1896-1947 [SC]
American actor
* Lawrence, Babe

Lawrence, William Beach 1800-1880
[PA]
American author
* [An] American Citizen

Lawrence, William John 1862-? [HPPN]
Irish theatrical historian and author
* Scaramuccio

Lawrenson, Helen 1907-1982 [CA]
American author, critic, journalist
* Norden, Helen Brown

Lawrie, Marie McDonald McLaughlin 1948- [FC, LRR, RO2]
Scottish singer
* Lulu

Lawry, Otis Carroll 1893-1965 [BE]
American baseball player
* Lawry, Rabbit

Lawry, Rabbit
See Lawry, Otis Carroll

[The] Law's Expounder
See Romilly, [Sir] Samuel

Laws, Joe 20th c. [BBH]
American football player
* Laws, Tiger

Laws, Samuel Spahr 1824-1921 [HPPN]
American educator, clergyman, inventor
* [The] Father of the Ticker Tape

Laws, Tiger
See Laws, Joe

Laws, Tony 1935- [ART]
British silversmith designer
* T. L.

Lawson, Big Jim
See Lawson, Harry

Lawson, Chet
See Tubb, Edwin Charles

Lawson, Edward
See Reulbach, Edward Marvin

Lawson, Eleanor
See Smith, Eleanor

Lawson, Harry 1904- [WWJ]
American jazz musician
* Lawson, Big Jim

Lawson, Henry Hertzberg
See Larsen, Henry Hertzberg

Lawson, Horace Lowe 1900- [CA]
American author, journalist, educator
* Lawson, M. C.
* Summers, John A.

Lawson, Humanity
See Lawson, John

Lawson, Jacob
See Burgess, Michael Roy

Lawson, Jahun 1779-? [PA]
Author
* Cosmopolite

Lawson, Jessie [Kerr] 1838-1917 [CCL]
Canadian author
* Airlie, O'Hugh

Lawson, John 1867-1920 [BMH]
British entertainer
* Lawson, Humanity

Lawson, [Rev.] John 19th c. [HPPN]
British poet and clergyman
* [A] Village Pastor

Lawson, John Daniel 1816-1896 [HPPN]
American politician
* Sitting Bull

Lawson, John R.
See Lausen, John R.

Lawson, Kate
See Drain, Kathryn

Lawson, M. C.
See Lawson, Horace Lowe

Lawson, Michael
See Ryder, Michael Lawson

Lawson, O. C.
See Lawson, Oscar Clifton

Lawson, Oscar Clifton 1921- [BA]
American local government official
* Lawson, O. C.

Lawson, Patrick
See Eby, Lois Christine

Lawson, [Dr.] Philip
See Trimmer, Eric James

Lawson, Ruth Penelope 1890- [IAW]
British author
* [A] Member of CSMV
* [A] Religious of CSMV

Lawson, Smirle 20th c. [CFH]
Canadian football player
* [The] Big Train

Lawson, Steve
See Turner, Robert [Harry]

Lawson, Ted
See Lehrman, Theodore H.

Lawson, W. B.
See Cook, William Wallace

Lawson, W. B.
See Ingraham, Prentiss

Lawson, W. B.
See Jenks, George Charles

Lawson, W. B.
See Rathborne, St. George Henry

Lawson, W. B.?
See Stratemeyer, Edward L.

Lawson, Warren J.
See Bobin, Donald E. M.

Lawson, Wilfrid
See Worsnop, Wilfrid

Lawson, Yank
See Lausen, John R.

Lawton, Bud
See Lawton, Charles C.

Lawton, Charles
See Heckelmann, Charles N[ewman]

Lawton, Charles C. 1904-1965 [HPPN]
American cinematographer
* Lawton, Bud

Lawton, Dennis
See Faust, Frederick [Schiller]

Lawton, Effie
See Bell, Mrs. S. May

Lawton, Ethel Chapin 1903- [MA]
American author and poet
* [The] Poetry Lady

Lawton, Henry W. 1843-1900 [HPPN]
American army officer
* Lawton, Long Hank

Lawton, Long Hank
See Lawton, Henry W.

Lawton, Mrs. W. H. [FFF]
Singer
* Beebe, Henrietta

Lawton, Sherman P[axton] 1908- [CAP]
American author and educator
* Paxton, Jack
* Paxton, [Dr.] John

Lawton, Thomas 1911-1979 [HPPN]
American actor, producer, author
* Bennett, Raymond

Lawton, [Capt.] Wilbur
See Goldfrap, John Henry

[The] Lawyer
See Blackstone, [Sir] William

[A] Lawyer
See Cowley, Charles

[A] Lawyer
See Fine, John

[A] Lawyer
See Hext, Francis

[A] Lawyer
See Reeves, John

[A] Lawyer
See Stewart, [Sir] James

[The] Lawyer
See Thomas, Wade Hamilton, Sr.

Lawyer, Mr.
See Davis, John William

Laxness, Halldor Kiljan
See Gudjonsson, Halldor Kiljan

[A] Lay Baronet
See Martin, [Sir] Henry

[The] Lay Bishop
See Savile, [Sir] Henry

Lay, Dilys 1934- [TR]
British actress
* Laye, Dilys

Lay, Elzy
See Lay, William Ellsworth

[A] Lay Gentleman
See Lee, Francis

[A] Lay Hand
See Cox, [Sir] Richard

[A] Lay Hand
See Curll, Edmund

Lay Member of the British and Foreign Bible Society
See Stokes, George

[A] Lay Member of the Church of England
See Stow, John

[A] Lay Member of the Committee
See Rivington, William

[The] Lay Preacher
See Dennie, Joseph

[A] Lay Preacher to the Largest Congregation in the United States
See Bok, Edward William

Lay, William Ellsworth 1862-1934 [EWG, HPPN]
American gunfighter
* [The] Educated Outlaw
* Johnson, William
* Lay, Elzy
* McGinnis, William

Layamon 13th c. [DEP, FFF, SN]
British poet
* [The] English Ennius

Laycock, John W. 1904-1960 [SC]
American actor
* Lake, John

Laycock, Lucky
See Laycock, Robert E.

Laycock, Robert E. 1907-1968 [WWW]
British military leader
* Laycock, Lucky

Laycock, Thomas 1812-1876 [HPPN]
British physician
* L.

Layden, Elmer 1902?-1973 [HPPN]
American football player
* [The] Thin Man

Laye, Dilys
See Lay, Dilys

[A] Layman
See Abbott, Lyman

[A] Layman
See Adams, Samuel

[A] Layman
See Alderson, [Sir] Edward Hall

[A] Layman
See Alexander, Richard Dykes

[A] Layman
See Allen, John

[A] Layman
See Allibone, Samuel Austin

[A] Layman
See Anderdon, John Lavicount

[A] Layman
See Barrington, John Shute [First Viscount Barrington]

[A] Layman
See Bartlett, Bailey

[A] Layman
See Bayley, [Sir] John

[A] Layman
See Bevans, J.

[A] Layman
See Bowles, John

[A] Layman
See Burgh, William

[A] Layman
See Bush, Harold Richard

[A] Layman
See Chambers, J. D.

[A] Layman
See Chandler, Peleg Whitman

[A] Layman
See Cogan, Thomas

[A] Layman
See Colebrooke, [Sir] George

[A] Layman
See Colman, George

[A] Layman
See Comegys, Benjamin Bartis

[A] Layman
See Curtis, Charles Bewick

[A] Layman
See De Peyster, John Watts

[A] Layman
See Domville, [Sir] William

[A] Layman
See Dryden, John

[A] Layman
See Duigenan, Patrick

[A] Layman
See Eames, Jane Anthony

[A] Layman
See Ellis, Arthur

[A] Layman
See Ellis, William

[A] Layman
See Falconer, William

[A] Layman
See Falconer, William

[A] Layman
See Foe, Daniel

[A] Layman
See Gordon, Thomas

[A] Layman
See Gough, Richard

[A] Layman
See Grafton, Augustus Henry Fitzroy [Third Duke of Grafton]

[A] Layman
See Hardinge, Thomas

[A] Layman
See Heywood, Samuel

[A] Layman
See Hitherley, W.

[A] Layman
See Hoare, P.

[A] Layman
See Hook, Walter Farquhar

[A] Layman
See Innes, Duncan

[A] Layman
See Irving, Theodore

[A] **Layman**
See Kynaston, Thomas

[A] **Layman**
See Lofft, Capel

[A] **Layman**
See Lowe, Solomon

[A] **Layman**
See Lowell, John

[A] **Layman**
See Mathias, Thomas James

[A] **Layman**
See Milnes, Richard Monckton [First Baron Houghton]

[A] **Layman**
See Muir, John

[A] **Layman**
See Norton, James

[A] **Layman**
See Paine, Thomas

[A] **Layman**
See Park, James Allan

[A] **Layman**
See Penney, William, [Lord Kinloch]

[A] **Layman**
See Peter, William

[A] **Layman**
See Plumer, William

[A] **Layman**
See Poynder, John

[A] **Layman**
See Ribbans, Frederick Bolingbroke

[A] **Layman**
See Rivington, William

[A] **Layman**
See Robinson, Solon

[A] **Layman**
See Rowland, D.

[A] **Layman**
See St. John, James Augustus

[A] **Layman**
See Sanden, Thomas

[A] **Layman**
See Scott, [Sir] Walter

[A] **Layman**
See Seeley, Robert Benton

[A] **Layman**
See Simpson, [Rev.] Samuel

[A] **Layman**
See Skinner, John

[A] **Layman**
See Smith, Goldwin

[A] **Layman**
See Stock, John Edmonds

[A] **Layman**
See Talbot, George Foster

[A] **Layman**
See Taylor, Jeremy

[A] **Layman**
See Taylor, John

[A] **Layman**
See Tempest, Stephen

[A] **Layman**
See Turner, Sharon

[A] **Layman**
See Waldo, Peter

[A] **Layman**
See Witherby, William

[A] **Layman**
See Wornum, Ralph Nicholson

[A] **Layman**
See Wright, James A.

[A] **Layman of Boston**
See Appleton, Nathan

[A] **Layman of the Church**
See Aytoun, William Edmonstoune

[A] **Layman of the Church of England**
See Knox, William

[A] **Layman of the Church of England**
See Watson, John

[A] **Layman of the Church of Scotland**
See Blackwood, Thomas

[A] **Layman of the County of Suffolk**
See Deck, P.

Layne, Ivoria Hillis 1918-   [BE]
American baseball player
* Layne, Tony

Layne, Laura
See Knott, William Cecil, Jr. [Bill]

Layne, Pyngle
See Turner, J. Fox

Layne, Robert Lawrence [Bobby] 1926-
[HPPN]
American football player
* [The] Built In Timepiece

Layne, Tony
See Layne, Ivoria Hillis

Layton, Andrea
See Bancroft, Iris [Nelson]

Layton, Dennis 1948-   [BB]
American basketball player
* Layton, Mo

Layton, F. G.
See Layton, Frank George

Layton, Frank George 1872-1941
[WGT, WWL]
British author
* Andrew, Stephen
* Layton, F. G.

Layton, Henry 18th c.   [HPPN]
British clergyman
* [A] Lover of Truth

Layton, Irving
See Lazarovitch, Irving

Layton, Joe
See Lichtman, Joseph

Layton, Mo
See Layton, Dennis

Layton, Phil 1917-   [MY]
American jazz musician
* Layton, Skippy

Layton, Skippy
See Layton, Phil

Lazar, Irving Paul 1907-
American literary representative
* Lazar, Swifty

Lazar, Swifty
See Lazar, Irving Paul

Lazarin, Louis 1905?-1954   [BI]
American cantor
* Lawrence, Lou

Lazarovitch, Irving 1912-   [JL]
Canadian poet
* Layton, Irving

Lazarro, Sofia
See Scicolone, Sofia Villani

Lazarus
See Boswell, James

Lazarus, Arnold Leslie 1914-   [IAW]
American author and poet
* Leslie, A. L.

Lazarus, Ebenezer
See Mason, Robert

Lazarus, Felix
See Cable, George Washington

Lazarus, Israel 1812-1867   [HPPN]
British boxer
* Lazarus, Izzy

Lazarus, Izzy
See Lazarus, Israel

Lazarus, Jack David 1930-   [CA]
American author
* Holmes, Jack D[avid] L[azarus]

Lazarus, Marguerite 1916-   [CA]
British author
* Gascoigne, Marguerite
* Gilbert, Anna

Lazarus, Mel 1927-   [WECO]
American cartoonist
* Fulton
* Mell

Lazeroff, Bernard 1921-   [PMJ]
American musician
* Leighton, Bernie

Lazerowitz, Alice Ambrose 1906-   [WD]
American writer
* Ambrose, Alice

Lazetich, Mike
See Lazetich, Milan

Lazetich, Milan 20th c. [EF]
American football player
* Lazetich, Mike

Lazlo, Kate
See Angus, Sylvia

Lazo, Alonzo Carillo 18th c. [HPPN]
British clergyman
* [The] Chaplain

Lazy Bill Lucas
See Lucas, William [Bill]

Lazy Dan Kaufman
See Kaufman, Irving

Lazy Jim Day
See Day, Jim

Lazy Lester
See Johnson, Leslie

Lazy Slim Jim
See Harris, Ed[ward P.]

Lazzara, Bernadette 1948- [TR]
American actress and singer
* Peters, Bernadette

Lazzari
See D'Agnolo [or D'Angelo], Donato

Lazzaro, Samuel 1902- [BX, RBE]
Italian-born American boxer
* Dundee, Joe

Lazzaro, Vincent 1904-1949 [AS, BX, RBE]
Italian-born American boxer
* Dundee, Vince

Lazzeri, Anthony Michael [Tony]
1903-1946 [AS, BE, PB]
American baseball player
* Push 'em Up Tony

Le
See   Second element of name for further listings

Le Bargy, Simone
See Benda, Simone

Le Baron, Grace
See Upham, Grace Le Baron [Locke]

Le Baron, Marie
See Bielby, Mrs.

Le Baron, Marie
See Urie, Mary Le Baron [Andrews]

Le Barron, Betty
See Hudnall, Floris M.

Le Bas, R. A.
See Le Bas, Rachel Ann

Le Bas, Rachel Ann 1923- [ART]
British painter and engraver
* Le Bas, R. A.

Le Blanc, Jean Bernard 1707-1781
[HPPN]
French author
* [Un] Francois

Le Blanc, M.
See Germain, Sophie

Le Blond, Louis Vincent Joseph [Comte de St. Hilaire] 1766-1809 [DNNF, FFF, SN]
French army officer
* [The] Roland of the Army

Le Bonnieres, Robert 1850-1895 [NPS]
French journalist and author
* Estienne, Robert
* Janus

Le Bossu, Jacques 1546-1626 [PA]
Author
* Bossolus

Le Bouvier, Gillies 1386-1460 [PA]
Author
* Berry

Le Bozec, Marcel 1894-1947 [BEW]
French-born director
* Varnel, Marcel

Le Breton, Anna Letitia [Aikin] 19th c.
[IP]
British author
* One of a Literary Family

Le Breton, Auguste
See Montfort, Auguste

Le Breton, Emilie Charlotte 1852-1929
[BEW, IPA, NN]
British actress and courtesan
* [The] Jersey Lily
* Langtry, Lily [or Lillie]

Le Breton, Mrs. John
See Murray-Ford, Alice May [Harte-Potts]

Le Breton, Thomas
See Murray-Ford, Thomas

Le Brock, Kelly 1961?- [NW 1-10-83]
American model
* [The] Mouth

Le Brun, Jean Baptiste ?-1731 [PA]
Author
* Desmarettes

Le Caron 1536-1617 [PA]
Author
* Charondas

Le Caron, Henry
See Beach, Thomas Miller

Le Caron, Michault 15th c. [BI]
French poet
* Taillevent, Michault

Le Carre, John
See Cornwell, David [John Moore]

Le Chanois, Jean-Paul
See Dreyfus, Jean-Paul

Le Clerc
See Cowen, Samuella Mardis

Le Clerc, Clara 19th c. [IP]
American author
* Holt, Harry
* Holt, Polly

Le Clerc, Jean 1587-1633 [FFF, RH]
* [The] Cavalier
* [Le] Chevalier

Le Clercq, Jacques George Clemenceau
1898-1972 [CA]
Austrian-born American educator and poet
* Tanaquil, Paul

Le Clerq, Augustus Howard 1884-1969
[FC]
British actor
* McNaughton, Gus

Le Conner, Hans Patrick
See Bowman, J. L.

Le Coq, Monsieur
See Simenon, Georges [Joseph Christian]

Le Corbusier
See Jeanneret-Gris, Charles Edouard

Le Couteur, Brember 1883?-1948 [THR]
British actor
* Wills, Brember

Le Duan 1908-
Vietnamese Communist leader
* Ba [Second Son]

Le Fanu, J[oseph] Sheridan 1814-1873
[WGT]
Irish author
* Figwood, John, Barrister-at-Law

Le Feber, David 1903- [IAW]
Dutch author
* Cronieckschrijver
* Eerfeld, B.

Le Febvre, Mathieu 1584?-1621?
[HPPN]
French actor-manager
* Laporte

Le Feuvre, Amy ?-1929 [TCC]
British author
* Dodge, Mary Thurston

Le Fevre, Felicite
See Smith-Masters, Margaret

Le Fevre, Paul 1885- [CD]
French poet and playwright
* Geraldy, Paul

Le Fontaine, Joseph [Raymond] 1927-
[CA]
American author and publisher
* Raymond, Joseph H.

Le Fre, Albert
See De Voy, Albert

Le Gallienne, Irma Hinton 1876?-1955
[BEW]
French actress
* Perry, Irma

Le Gallienne, Richard 1866-? [WWL]
Author and poet
* Logroller

Le Genie, Toulounais
See Langier, Joseph Tidele

Le Grand, Franc 20th c.   [BEW]
French author
* Nohain, Franc

Le Grand, Margaret 1896-1976   [BEW]
Canadian actress
* Bannerman, Margaret

Le Grand, Pierre
See Francois, Pierre

Le Grice, Charles Valentine 1773-1858
[IP]
British clergyman and author
* C. V. Le G.
* Civis
* Gronovius
* Vigilans

Le Gurdeur, Stephen 1904-1950   [HPPN]
American actor
* Reed, Steve

Le Hay, John
See Healy, John

Le Jemlys
See Jelley, Symmes M.

Le Louarn, Yvan 1915-1968   [WEC]
French cartoonist and illustrator
* Chaval

Le Marchant, Jacques 1537-1609   [PA]
Author
* Merchantius

Le Meingre, Jean ?-1368   [WBD]
French soldier
* Bouciquaut

Le Mesurier, Thomas 19th c.   [IP]
British clergyman and author
* [A] Clergyman of the Diocese of
  Durham

Le Moyne, Charles
See Lemon, Charles J.

Le Moyne, Roy
See Hersey, Harold

Le Moyne, Seymour
See Hersey, Harold

Le Moyne, W. J.
See Le Moyne, William

Le Moyne, William 1831-1905   [BEW]
Actor
* Le Moyne, W. J.

Le Ngo Nhi
See Gregory, Gene

Le Noire, Felicia
See Bliss, Lena Edith

Le Nord
See Killen, James Bryce

Le Normand, Marie 1772-1843   [EOP]
French occultist
* [The] Sybil of the Faubourg Saint
  Germain

Le Normand, Michelle
See Desrosiers, Marie Antoinette Tardif

Le Page, Rand [house pseudonym,
Curtis Warren]
See Bird, William Henry Fleming

Le Page, Rand [joint pseudonym with
Arthur O. Roberts] [house pseudonym,
Curtis Warren]
See Glasby, John [Stephen]

Le Page, Rand [house pseudonym,
Curtis Warren]
See Holloway, Brian

Le Page, Rand [house pseudonym,
Curtis Warren]
See O'Brien, David

Le Page, Rand [house pseudonym,
Curtis Warren]
See Protheroe, Cyril

Le Page, Rand [joint pseudonym with
John (Stephen) Glasby] [house
pseudonym, Curtis Warren]
See Roberts, Arthur O.

Le Paul, Paul
See Braden, Paul

Le Pelley, Guernsey 1910-   [CA]
American playwright and cartoonist
* Norman, Kerry
* Richard, Lee

Le Pinski, Gwendolyn 1906-
American actress
* Lee, Gwen

Le Poitevin Saint-Alme, Auguste
1791-1854   [HPPN]
French author
* De Villergle

Le Querrec, A. Charles 20th c.   [THR]
French playwright
* Mirande, Yves

Le Reboullet, Adolphe Louis Auguste
1845-?   [IP, PA]
French author
* Chazel, Prosper

Le Reveur
See Holland, Denis

Le Roi, David [De Roche] 1905-   [CA]
American author and journalist
* Roche, John

Le Roux, Henri 1860-1925   [HPPN,
WBD]
French journalist
* Le Roux, Hughes

Le Roux, Hughes
See Le Roux, Henri

Le Roux, S. P. Daniel 1922-   [TCL]
Afrikaans author
* Leroux, Etienne

Le Roy, William Edgar 1818-1888
[HPPN]
American naval officer
* [The] Chesterfield of the Navy

Le Sage, Aimard
See Backer, Desaix

Le Sage, Rene-Andre 1695-1743   [HPPN]
French actor
* Montmenil

Le Sieg, Theo
See Geisel, Theodor Seuss

Le Sieur, W. D.   [IP]
Canadian author
* Laon

Le Sueur [or **Lesueur**], **Eustache**
1617-1655   [DEP, DNNF, FFF]
French painter
* [The] French Raphael
* [The] Raphael of France

Le Sueur, Lucille 1904?-1977   [BDF, FC,
WEF]
American actress
* Cassin, Billie
* Crawford, Joan

Le Tonnelier de Breteuil, Gabrielle
Emilie 1706-1749   [HN]
French author
* Chatelet, Marquise du
* [The] Divine Emilie

Le Toulon, Guillaume 1493-1568   [PA]
Author
* Fullonius

Le Vayer, Franoise De La Mothe
1583-1672   [HPPN]
French philosopher and author
* [The] Plutarch of France

Le Vert, Octavia Walton 1810-1877
[HPPN]
American actress
* [The] Belle of the Union

Le Voe, Spivy 1907-1971   [SC]
American entertainer
* Madame Spivy

Le Voyageur, Krinebol
See La Beaumelle, Laurent Angliviele
De

Lea
See Vettergrund, Josephina Vilhelmina
Lundberg

Lea, Alec 1907-   [SAT]
Canadian-born author
* Lea, Richard

Lea, Biffy
See Lea, Langdon

Lea, Constance Nicholson 1881-?   [NAA]
British-born writer
* Shorthouse, Rebecca

Lea, Fannie Heaslip
See Agee, Mrs. H. P.

Lea, Henry Charles 1825-?   [IP]
American author and publisher
* Mizpah

Lea, Joan
See Lowry, Joan [Catlow]

Lea, Langdon 1874-1937   [AS, FB]
American football player
* Lea, Biffy

Lea, Luke 1879-? [HPPN]
American politician
* Young Thunderbolt

Lea, Richard
See Lea, Alec

Lea, Terrea 20th c. [SFL]
Author
* Stacy, Terry

Lea, Timothy
See Wood, Christopher [Hovelle]

Lea, William H. 1867-1932 [HPPN]
American actor
* Cho Cho the Clown

Leabo, Betty 1918- [FC]
American actress
* Joyce, Brenda

Leach, Ann 1859?-1952 [BI]
American author
* Duane, A. S.
* McDonald, Robert

Leach, Archibald Alexander 1904-
[BDF, BS, SW]
British-born American actor
* Grant, Cary
* [The] Great Carini

Leach, Bone
See Leach, Richard Max [Rick]

Leach, Buddy
See Leach, Claude

Leach, Claude 1935?-
American politician
* Leach, Buddy

Leach, Clifford
See Clark, Kenneth Sherman

Leach, Felix 20th c. [HPPN]
American football player
* Leach, Lefty

Leach, Harry Harwood [PA]
Author
* [A] Sentimental Idler

Leach, Harvey 1804-1847 [DI]
American entertainer
* Nano, Hervio

Leach, Lefty
See Leach, Felix

Leach, Michael 1940- [CA]
American author
* Jeffrey, Christopher

Leach, Reginald Joseph 1950- [FHE]
Canadian-born hockey player
* [The] Chief

Leach, Richard Max [Rick] 1957-
American baseball player
* Leach, Bone

Leach, Thomas W. 1877-1969 [AS]
American baseball player
* Leach, Wee Tommy

Leach, Wee Tommy
See Leach, Thomas W.

Leachman, Cloris W. 1901-1967 [HPPN]
American theatrical manager
* Wallace, Cloris

Leacroft, Eric
See Young, Eric Brett

Leadbeater, Barrie 1943- [DC]
British cricketer
* Leadbeater, Bungalow
* Leadbeater, Leady

Leadbeater, Bungalow
See Leadbeater, Barrie

Leadbeater, Leady
See Leadbeater, Barrie

Leadbelly
See Ledbetter, Huddie [William]

Leadbetter, J. 19th c. [IP]
British author
* J. L.

[The] Leader
See Sinatra, Francis Albert [Frank]

Leader, [Evelyn] Barbara [Blackburn]
1898- [CA]
British author
* Blackburn, Barbara
* Castle, Frances
* Grant, Jane

Leader, Benjamin Williams
See Williams, Benjamin

Leader, Charles
See Smith, Robert Charles

Leader, James
See Tanner, James T.

[The] Leader of American Labor
See Meany, [William] George

[The] Leader of Men
See Pelley, William Dudley

[The] Leader of the Amsterdam School
See Looy, Jacobus Van

[The] Leader of the Gunpowder Plot
See Catesby, Robert

[The] Leader of the Modern Pharisees
See Gaetano [or Caetani], Benedetto

[The] Leader of the Oil Gang
See Rockefeller, William

[The] Leader of the Pop Art Movement
See Warhola, Andrew

[The] Leader of the Publishing Revolution
See Curtis, Cyrus Hermann Kotzschmar

[The] Leader of the Reformation
See Luther, Martin

Leaderman, George
See Robinson, Richard Blundell

[The] Leading Authority in His Field
See Goren, Charles Henry

[The] Leading Figure of the Yiddish Theater
See Schwartz, Maurice

[The] Leading Lady
See Hood, Darla

[The] Leading Lady of Silent Pictures
See Percy, Eileen

[The] Leading Muckraker of His Time
See Pearson, Andrew Russel

[The] Leading Spokesman for Jews
See Seixas, Gershom

Leadlay, Frank R. 20th c. [CFH]
Canadian football player
* Leadlay, Pep

Leadlay, Pep
See Leadlay, Frank R.

[The] Leadville Storekeeper Millionaire
See Tabor, Horace Austin Warner

Leaf, [Wilbur] Munro 1905-1976 [CA, TC1, TCC]
American author and illustrator
* Calvert, John
* Mun

Leahy, Francis William [Frank]
1908-1973 [HPPN]
American football coach
* [The] Prussian Leprechaun

Leak, C. J.
See Leak, Curtis James

Leak, Curtis James 1953- [SMG]
American football player
* Leak, C. J.

Leake, John 18th c. [HPPN]
British scholar
* [A] Gentleman of Oxford

Leake, [Colonel] William Martin 19th c.
[HPPN]
British army officer
* [An] Old Brother Officer

Leaks, Roosevelt 1953- [BA]
American football player
* Leaks, Rosey

Leaks, Rosey
See Leaks, Roosevelt

Leal
See Disosway, E.

Leal, Orlando
See Ramirez, Orlando

Leal Kuri, Alfredo 1930- [GS]
Mexican bullfighter
* Principe del Toreo [Prince of Bullfighting]

Leal y Casado, Cayetano 1865-1950
[GS]
Spanish bullfighter
* Pepe Hillo [Little Joe]

Leal y Casado, Eduardo 1875-1931 [GS]
Spanish bullfighter
* Llavarito

Leamy, Edmund 1848-1904 [PI]
Irish poet
* Eos

Lean, Blanche Harris 1750-1815
[HPPN]
British poet
* Harris, [Miss] Blanche

Lean, Garth Dickinson 1912- [CA]
Welsh-born journalist and editor
* Tenax

Lean Jimmy Jones
See Jones, James Chamberlain

Lean, Joseph F. 1834-1854 [HPPN]
British miner
* [The] Young Mining Captain

[The] Lean Man
See Neill, Patrick

Lean Mean Cuisine
See Icahn, Carl

Lean, Sidney
See Fago, Giovanni

Leander
See Hughes, John

Leander, Ed
See Richelson, Geraldine

Leander, Richard
See Volkmann, Richard von

[The] Leaning Tower of Pizza
See Barkley, Charles

Leanord, Old Bill
See Leanord, William

Leanord, William 19th c. [HPPN]
American gambler
* Leanord, Old Bill

Leaphart, Vincent 20th c. [NW 5-27-85]
American social cult leader
* Africa, John

Leaping Mike Menosky
See Menosky, Michael William

Leapor, Mary 1722-1746 [DEL, SN]
British poet
* [The] Untaught Poetess

Lear, Charles Bernard 1891- [BE]
American baseball player
* Lear, King

Lear, Edward 1812-1888 [HPPN, SAT]
British author and illustrator
* Derry Down Derry
* Lear, Limerick

Lear, Fred[rick Francis] 1894-1955 [BE]
American baseball player
* Lear, King

Lear, Hal 1935- [BB]
American basketball player
* Lear, King

Lear, Henrietta Louisa Farrer 19th c.
[HPPN]
British author
* H. L. F.

Lear, King
See Lear, Charles Bernard

Lear, King
See Lear, Fred[rick Francis]

Lear, King
See Lear, Hal

Lear, King
See Lear, Norman

Lear, King
See Lear, William Powell

Lear, Limerick
See Lear, Edward

Lear, Norman 1922-
American television producer
* Lear, King

Lear, Peter
See Lovesey, Peter

Lear, William Powell 1902-1978
American business executive
* Lear, King
* Navcom, Mr.

Leard, Wild Bill
See Leard, William Wallace [Bill]

Leard, William Wallace [Bill] 1885-1970
[BE]
American baseball player
* Leard, Wild Bill

Learmont, Thomas 13th c. [DNNF,
HPPN, RH, SN]
Scottish magician, prophet, poet
* [The] Merlin of Scotland
* Thomas of Erceldoune
* Thomas Rhymour of Ercildoune
* Thomas the Rhymer
* True Thomas

[The] Learned
See Coloman

[The] Learned
See Ferdinand VI

[The] Learned
See George II

[A] Learned Attila
See Johnson, Samuel

[The] Learned Blacksmith
See Burritt, Elihu

[The] Learned Cabbage-Eater
See Ritson, Joseph

[The] Learned Dr. Gill
See Gill, John

[A] Learned Gorilla
See White, Richard Grant

[A] Learned Hand
See Hale, [Sir] Matthew

[A] Learned Judge
See Buller, [Sir] Francis

[The] Learned Knight
See Elyot, [Sir] Thomas

[The] Learned Painter
See Lebrun, Charles

[The] Learned Printer
See Bowyer, William

[The] Learned Selden
See Selden, John

[The] Learned Shoemaker
See Sherman, Roger

[The] Learned Tailor
See Hill, Robert

[The] Learned Tailor
See Wild, Henry

[The] Learned Weaver
See Young, Joseph

Learsi, Rufus
See Goldberg, Israel

Leary, John 19th c. [LFW]
American gang member
* Leary, Red

Leary, Red
See Leary, John

Leary, Timothy 1920-
American psychologist and author
* [The] High Priest of LSD

Leask, William [IP]
British clergyman and author
* [A] Dissenting Minister

Leasley, F. W. [PA]
Author
* Almon, Caspar

Least Heat Moon, William
See Trogdon, William

Leatham, Louis Salisbury 1902- [IAW]
American author
* Lou

Leather Apron
See Pizer [or Kosminski?]

Leather, George
See Swallow, Norman

Leather, Joe
See Lehder, Carlos

Leather-Lungs, Lady
See Zimmerman, Ethel Agnes

Leatherhead, Lanthorn
See Jones, Inigo

Leathers, Thomas Paul 1816-1896
[HPPN]
American riverboat captain
* [The] Hero of the Lower Mississippi
* Old Push
* Old Pushmataha

Leatherstocking
See Dolby, Doctor

Leathes, Mrs. Stanley 19th c. [IP]
British author
* M. G.

Leaver, Philip 1904- [THR]
British actor and playwright
* Brandon, Philip

Leaver, Ruth
See Tomalin, Ruth

Leavis, F. R.
See Leavis, Frank Raymond

Leavis, Frank Raymond 1895- [LC, TC1]
British critic and educator
* Leavis, F. R.

Leavitt, Abe
See Leavitt, Douglas

Leavitt, Douglas 1883-1960 [SC]
American actor
* Leavitt, Abe

Leavitt, Dudley 1772-1851 [HPPN]
American educator and almanac maker
* Leavitt, Old Master

Leavitt, Frank S. 1890-1953 [SC]
American actor and wrestler
* Dean, Man Mountain

Leavitt, Joshua 1794-1873 [HPPN]
American clergyman
* [A] Trinitarian

Leavitt, Old Master
See Leavitt, Dudley

Leavitt, Ruby R.
See Rohrlich, Ruby

Lebar, John
See Wright, Gilbert Munger

LeBaron, Anthony
See Laumer, [John] Keith

LeBaron, Eddie 20th c.
American football player
* [The] Little General

Lebeau, Eugene [IP]
French poet
* Ruy-Blas, Eugene

Lebeck, Fats
See Lebeck, George

Lebeck, George [F1]
Actor
* Lebeck, Fats

Lebengood, Fungy
See Lebengood, Howard

Lebengood, Howard 20th c. [EF]
American football player
* Lebengood, Fungy

Lebensohn, Abraham Dob 1794?-1878 [BI, HPPN]
Lithuanian author
* Adam

Lebenson
See Kahn, Yitzhak

Leberecht, Peter
See Tieck, Johann Ludwig

Lebert, Randy
See Brannon, William T.

Lebert, Siegmund
See Levy, Siegmund

Lebies, Rene
See Seibel, Werner

Lebitsky, Leonard 1911-1973 [HPPN]
American entertainer
* Insult, Mr.
* Leonard, Fat Jack
* Leonard, Jack E.
* Libitsky, Fat
* [The] Master of the Oneliner
* [The] Mean Mr. Clean

Leblanc, Dudley J. 1894- [HPPN]
American politician and manufacturing executive
* Couzin Dud
* Hadacol, Mr.
* Uncle Dud

LeBlanc, Georgette
See Maeterlinck, Georgette

LeBlanc, J. P.
See LeBlanc, Jean-Paul

LeBlanc, Jean-Paul 1946- [SMG]
Canadian-born hockey player
* LeBlanc, J. P.

Lebo, Deli
See Lebo, Dell

Lebo, Dell 1922- [IAW]
American author and poet
* Bell, [Prof.] Leo D.
* Lebo, Deli

Leborgne
See Boigne, Beuvit

LeBourveau, Bevo
See LeBourveau, DeWitt Wiley

LeBourveau, DeWitt Wiley 1896-1947 [BE]
American baseball player
* LeBourveau, Bevo

Lebreo, Steward
See Weiner, Stewart

Lebreo, Stewart
See Weiner, Stewart

Lebrowitz, Barney 1891-1949 [AS, BX, HPPN, RBE]
American boxer
* Levinsky, Battling
* Levinsky, King
* Williams, Barney

Lebrun, Camille
See Lebrun, Pauline Guyot

Lebrun, Charles 1619-1690 [DNNS, FFF, SN]
French painter
* [The] Learned Painter

LeBrun, Gautier
See Gibson, Walter B[rown]

Lebrun, M.
See Louis Philippe

Lebrun, Pauline Guyot 1805-? [IP, PA]
French author
* Dartigue, Laure
* De Camille
* Lebrun, Camille
* Saint Leger, Fabien de

Lebrun Pindare
See Lebrun, Ponce Denis Ecouchard

Lebrun, Ponce Denis Ecouchard 1729-1807 [DEP, FFF, WBD]
French poet
* [The] French Pindar
* Lebrun Pindare
* [The] Pindar of France

Lebrunie, Gerard
See De Marval, Gerard

Lebzelter, Jack Warden 1920-
American actor
* Warden, Jack

Lecale, Errol
See McNeilly, Wilfred Glassford

Lecapenus
See Romanus I

Lecavele, L.
See Lecavele, Roland

Lecavele, Roland 1886-1973 [CD, EWL, HPPN, WBD]
French author
* Dorgeles, Roland
* Lecavele, L.

Lechanteur, M. E. [IP]
French author
* De Pontaumont

Lechmere, Edmund 17th c. [IP]
British author
* Stratford, Edmund

Lechmere, Edmund 18th c. [HPPN]
British poet
* [A] Young Gentleman of Oxford

Lechon, Jan
See Serafinowicz, Leszek

Leckenby, Derek 1945- [RO2]
British musician
* Leckenby, Lek

Leckenby, Lek
See Leckenby, Derek

Leckie, Peter Martin 1890- [ESF, SFL, WGT]
British author
* Martin, Peter

Leckie, Robert [Hugh] 1920- [CA]
American author
* Barlow, Roger
* Porter, Mark

Lecky, Walter
See McDermott, William

Lecky, William Edward Hartpole
1838-1903 [DLE1]
Irish historian and author
* Hibernicus

L'Eclair
See Odum, Mary Hunt McCaleb

Leclerc
See De Hautecloque, Vicomte

Leclerc du Tremblay, Francois
1577-1638 [DHA, NPS, SN, WBD]
French monk and diplomat
* Alter Ego of Richelieu
* Bras Droit du Cardinal
* [The] Cardinal's Right Arm
* [L']Eminence Grise
* Joseph, [Father]
* [The] Lackey
* [A] Nero
* Patelin

Leclerc, Georges Louis [Comte de Buffon] 1707-1788 [NPS]
French scientist, naturalist, author
* [The] King of Phrases

Leclerc, Jacques Philippe
See Hautecloque, Philippe de

Leclerc, Louis 1799-1854 [IP]
French economist and author
* Celler, Ludovic

Leclerc, Renald 1947- [CEI, HR]
Canadian-born hockey player
* Leclerc, Rene

Leclerc, Rene
See Leclerc, Renald

Leclerc, Thomas
See Francoeur, Robert Thomas

Leclerc, Victor
See Parry, Albert

Leclere, Leon 1874-1966 [WBD]
French poet, painter, musician
* Klingsor, Tristan

Lecluse, Charles De 1525-1609 [HPPN]
French botanist
* Clusius

LeCompte, Jane
Author
* Ashford, Jane

Lecomte, Jules 1814-1864 [IP]
French journalist
* Du Camp, Jules
* Van Engelyom

Leconte, Antoine 1526-1586 [PA]
Author
* Contius

Leconte, Charles Marie 1818-1894 [WBD]
French poet
* Leconte de Lisle, Charles Marie

Leconte de Lisle, Charles Marie
See Leconte, Charles Marie

Lecoq de Boisbaudran, Francois
See Lecoq de Boisbaudran, Paul Emile

Lecoq de Boisbaudran, Paul Emile
1838?-1912? [WBD]
French chemist
* Lecoq de Boisbaudran, Francois

Lecoustellier, Simon [or Simonet]
15th c. [HPPN]
French insurgent
* Caboche, Simon

Lectron, E.
See Fine, Louis

[The] Lecturer
See Mansel, Henry Longueville

Lecuyer, Andree [Husson] 1885-1952 [BI]
French author
* Corthis, Andre

Ledain, Olivier ?-1484 [HN, RH, SN]
Flemish barber
* [The] Devil
* [Le] Diable

Ledan, Marie 1875-1932 [BBD, HPPN]
French opera singer
* Delna, Marie

Ledbetter, Huddie [William] 1885?-1949 [BBD, BWW, FCW]
American singer and composer
* King of the 12 String Guitar Players
* Leadbelly

Ledbetter, Ralph Overton 1894- [BN]
American baseball player
* Ledbetter, Razor
* Ledbetter, Slats

Ledbetter, Razor
See Ledbetter, Ralph Overton

Ledbetter, Slats
See Ledbetter, Ralph Overton

Leder, Rudolf 1915- [MGL]
German poet
* Hermlin, Stephan

Lederer, Edith Madelon
See Weiner, Edith

Lederer, Eppie
See Lederer, Esther Pauline [Friedman]

Lederer, Esther Pauline [Friedman]
1918- [BI]
American columnist
* Landers, Ann
* Lederer, Eppie

Lederer, Evelyn 1907?- [F2, FC]
American actress
* Carol, Sue

Lederer, Francis
See Lederer, Frantisek [or Franz]

Lederer, Frantisek [or Franz] 1906- [BEW, F2]
Czech-born actor and director
* Lederer, Francis

Lederer, Rhoda Catharine [Kitto] 1910- [CA]
British author
* Barrow, Rhoda

Ledesma, Gonzales 20th c. [WECO]
Spanish cartoonist
* Silver Kane

Ledford, Minnie Lena 1922- [CWG]
American country-western performer
* Black Eyed Susan

[The] Ledge
See Odam, Norman

Led'huy, Jean Baptiste Alphonse [FFF, IP]
French author
* Dagobert, Chrysostome

Ledoux, John Walter 1860-1932 [SFL]
Author
* Calson, Isaac

Ledoux, Mary Hall 1876-1960 [HPPN]
American actress
* Hall, Mary

Ledoux, Scott
See LaDoux, Scott

Ledoux, Urbain 20th c. [HPPN]
American political theorist
* [The] Flophouse Humanitarian
* Zero, Mr.

Ledsam
See Savory, [Sir] Reginald Arthur

Leduc, Albert 1901- [CEI, FHE, HK]
Canadian-born hockey player
* Leduc, Battleship

Leduc, Battleship
See Leduc, Albert

Leduc, Claudine
See Lindsay, Sadi

Ledyard, Hope
See Harris, C. L.

Ledyard, Hope
See Harris, Frances McCready

Lee, A. E. [IP]
British author
* A. E. L.

Lee, A. R.
See Ash, Rene Lee

Lee, Abby [IP]
American author
* A. L.

Lee, Agnes
See Freer, Martha Agnes Rand

Lee, [Rev.] Albert 1858-? [LAO]
British author
* Mason, Adrian
* Romaine, Linton

Lee, Alexander ?-1831 [SN]
* Lord Barrymore's Tiger

Lee, Alfred
See Ferguson, John Clark

Lee, Alfred E. 1896-1954 [SC]
American actor
* Powell, Lee

Lee, Alice G.
See Bradley, Emily

Lee, Alice Louise 1868-1952 [ALY, BI]
American author
* Garland, John

Lee, Amber
See Baldwin, Faith

Lee, Andrew
See Auchincloss, Louis Stanton

Lee, Ann 1736-1784 [DEP, HPPN, NAD, RH, WBD]
British-born religious leader
* Ann of the Word
* Ann the Word
* Lee, Mother
* Mother Ann
* Wisdom, Mother

Lee, Anna
See Winnifrith, Joanna

Lee, Anne S.
See Murphy, Mabel Ansley

Lee, Anthony
See Ayers, William [Bill]

Lee, Archibald Edward John 1881-? [WWL]
British author
* Esterre, Neville D'

Lee, Arlene
See Schrader, Alma

Lee, Arthur 1740-1792 [HPPN, IP, NPS, PA]
American diplomat and author
* [An] American
* [An] American Wanderer
* Junius Americanus
* Monitor
* [An] Old Member of Parliament
* Raleigh

Lee, Arthur Stanley Gould 1894-1975 [SFL, WGT]
Author
* Gould, Arthur Lee

Lee, Aura
See Urziceanu, Aura

Lee, Austin 1904-1965 [CAP, WW]
British author
* Austwick, John
* Callender, Julian

Lee, Babs
See Lee, Marion [Van Der Veer]

Lee, Barbara [Moore] 1934- [CA]
American author
* Moore, Barbara

Lee, [Brother] Basil Leo 1909-1974 [CA]
American educator and author
* Lee, George Leslie

Lee, Bessie
See Smith, Trixie

Lee, Betty
See Lambert, Elizabeth [Minnie]

Lee, Big Bill
See Lee, William Crutcher

Lee, Bill
See Williams, James Edwards Lee

Lee, Billy
See Levise, William S., Jr. [Billy]

Lee, Blah
See Lee, Blair, III

Lee, Blair, III 20th c.
American politician
* Lee, Blah

Lee, Bob 20th c.
American football player
* Lee, Brook Trout

Lee, Bob
See McGrath, Robert L[ee]

Lee, Bonafide
See Lee, Ron

Lee, Brenda
See Tarpley, Brenda Mae

Lee, Brook Trout
See Lee, Bob

Lee, Bruce
See Lee Yuen Kam

Lee, Buck
See Lee, Ford Washington

Lee, C. Y.
See Li Chin-yang

Lee, Canada
See Canegata, Leonard Lionel Cornelius

Lee, Carol
See Fletcher, Helen Jill

Lee, Caroline
See Brown, Bessie

Lee, Caroline
See Dern, Peggy Gaddis

Lee, Cecile
See Lee, Mary Emily Frances

Lee, Charles 1731-1782 [HPPN, IP]
British-born army officer and author
* Boiling Water
* [The] Hero of Charleston
* Junius Americanus

Lee, Charles
See Graham, Roger Phillips

Lee, Charles
See Levy, Charles

Lee, Charles C.
See Rose, Martha Emily [Parmelee]

Lee, Charles H.
See Story, Rosamond Mary

Lee, Chauncey 1763-1842 [HPPN]
American clergyman
* Aristarchus

Lee chee-men 597?-626 [RH]
Chinese emperor
* [The] Solomon of China
* Tae-tsong I

Lee, Chief
See Lee, Edward E.

Lee, Ching
See Lee, Willis A., Jr.

Lee, Chuku Emeka
See Lee, Howard Frederick

Lee, Courthouse
See Lee, John C. H.

Lee, Devon
See Pohle, Robert W[arren], Jr.

Lee, Dickey
See Lipscomb, Dickey

Lee, Dixie
See Crosby, Wilma Wyatt

Lee, Dixie
See Williamson, LaVerne

Lee, Dixie
See Wyatt, Wilma Winifred

Lee, Don[ald] L[uther] 1942- [CA, IBW]
American poet
* Madhubuti, Haki R.

Lee, Doris
See Emrich, Doris

Lee, Dorothy
See Millsap, Marjorie

Lee, Dud
See Lee, Ernest Dudley

Lee, Edith
See Burckett, Florence

Lee, Edward
See Fouts, Edward Lee

Lee, Edward
See Seabrooke, Edward

Lee, Edward D. 1844-1927 [HPPN]
American sponsor of children's picnics
* [The] Ain't Gonna Rain No Mo' Man

Lee, Edward E. 20th c. [IBW]
American politician
* Lee, Chief

Lee, Elsie 1912- [CA]
American author
* Cromwell, Elsie
* Gordon, Jane
* Sheridan, Lee [joint pseudonym with Michael Sheridan]

Lee, Eric
See Blitch, Fleming Lee

Lee, Eric
See Page, Gerald W[ilburn]

Lee, Ernest Dudley 1899-1971 [BE]
American baseball player
* Dudley, Dud
* Lee, Dud

Lee, Ernie
See Cornelison, Ernest Eli

Lee, Fitzhugh 1835-1905 [HPPN]
American army officer
* Flea

Lee, Fleming
See Blitch, Fleming Lee

Lee, Ford Washington ?-1955 [IBW]
American entertainer
* Lee, Buck

Lee, Francis 17th c. [IP]
British author
* [A] Lay Gentleman

Lee, Francis Nigel 1934- [CA]
British-born author
* Nik

Lee, Franz John Tennyson 1938- [IAW]
South African-born author
* Lesizwe, Ilizwi
* Letromache, Maeng

Lee, Frederick George 19th c. [IP]
British clergyman and poet
* F. G. L.

Lee, Gabby
See Woolridge, Anna Marie

Lee, George B.
See Harbaugh, Thomas Chalmers

Lee, George Leslie
See Lee, [Brother] Basil Leo

Lee, Griffin
See Randolph, Paschal Beverley

Lee, Guy Carlton
See Ayer, John

Lee, Gwen
See Le Pinski, Gwendolyn

Lee, Gypsy Rose
See Hovick, Rose Louise

Lee, Hannah Farnham Sawyer
1780-1865 [HPPN]
American author
* [A] Friend

Lee, Harold Burnham 1905- [BE]
American baseball player
* Lee, Sheriff

Lee, Harper
See Gillete, Harper Lee

Lee, Harry
See Fellinge, Harry Lee

Lee, Henry 1756-1818 [DNNS, FFF, HPPN, SN]
American army officer
* Legion Harry
* Light Horse Harry
* [The] Sage of Ashland

Lee, Henry Boyle 19th c. [SFL, WGT]
Author
* M'Crib, Theophilus

Lee, Herbert d'H.
See Kastle, Herbert D[avid]

Lee, Holme
See Parr, Harriet

Lee, Holsey S. 1899-1974 [MK]
American baseball player
* Lee, Scrip

Lee, Honest Jack
See Lee, John

Lee, Horse
See Lee, Jerry

Lee, Horse
See Lee, Robert Dean

Lee, Howard [house pseudonym]
See Goulart, Ron[ald Joseph]

Lee, Howard Frederick 1948- [BA]
American editor and businessman
* Lee, Chuku Emeka

Lee, Irving B.
See Blumenstock, Irving

Lee, Ivy Ledbetter 1877-1934 [HPPN]
American public relations consultant
* [The] Corporate Dog Robber
* [The] Image Maker for P. R.
* Lee, Poison Ivy
* [The] Little Brother of the Rich
* Minnesinger to Millionaires
* [The] Physician to Corporate Bodies
* [The] Public Relations Genius

Lee, J. S.
See Li Ssu-Kuang

Lee, J. Waye 1902?-1955 [BI]
American restaurateur
* Lee, Shavey

Lee, Jacques L.
See Weinstein, Harry

Lee, James Richard [Jimmy] 1880-1930 [HPPN]
American actor
* Lee, Vaudeville

Lee, Jane
See D'Arcy, Ruth

Lee, Jennie 1846?-1930 [BEW]
British-born actress
* Lee, Jo

Lee, Jerry 1953- [SMG]
American football player
* Lee, Horse

Lee, Jesse 1758-1816 [BDSA]
American author and clergyman
* [The] Apostle of Methodism

Lee, Jimmy
See Robinson, Jimmy Lee

Lee, Jo
See Lee, Jennie

Lee, John 1733-1793 [HPPN]
British barrister
* Lee, Honest Jack

Lee, John 1780-1859 [IP]
Scottish clergyman and author
* Alumni of the University of Edinburgh

Lee, John 1953- [SMG]
American football player
* Lee, Shaft

Lee, John
See Henley, John Lee

Lee, John
See Li, Shu-T'ien

Lee, John C. H. 1887-1958
American military leader
* Jesus Christ Himself
* Lee, Courthouse

Lee, Johnny
See Hooker, John Lee

Lee, Joshua Bryan 1892- [HPPN]
American politician
* [The] Boy Orator
* [The] Boy Wonder
* Bryan, Silver Tongued Josh
* Lee, One Speech
* [The] Second William Jennings Bryan

Lee, Judy
See Carlson, Judith Lee

Lee, Julian
See Latham, Jean Lee

Lee, Kamikaze
See Lee, Ron

Lee, Katherine
See Jenner, Katherine Lee

Lee, Kay
See Kelly, Karen

Lee, Keng-Yen
See Li, Shu-T'ien

Lee, Kenneth
See Carmichael, Kenneth

Lee, Larry
See Levine, Lawrence

Lee, Laura
See Smith, Laura Newton Rundless

Lee, Leapy
See Lee, Peter Granville

Lee, Lefty
See Lee, Thornton Starr

Lee, Leonidas Pyrrhus
See Funkhouser, Leonidas Pyrrhus

Lee, Lila
See Appel, Augusta

Lee, Lincoln 1922- [CA]
British airline pilot and writer
* Collen, Neil

Lee, Lonesome
See Robinson, Jimmy Lee

Lee, Louisa Carter
See Jenkins, Will[iam] F[itzgerald]

Lee, Lucy
See Talbot, Charlene Joy

Lee, M. F.
See Lee, Man-Fong

Lee, Man-Fong 1913- [ART]
Chinese painter
* Lee, M. F.

Lee, Manfred B[ennington]
See Lepofsky, Manfred

Lee, Maria Berl 1924- [CA]
Austrian-born American author
* Berl-Lee, Maria

Lee, Mariel
See Lane, Mary Louisa

Lee, Marion [Van Der Veer] 1914-
[WW]
Author
* Lee, Babs

Lee, Marion
See Hanshaw, Annette

Lee, Mary Ann 1826-1899
American dancer
* Our Mary Ann

Lee, Mary Elizabeth 1813-1849 [IP, IP,
PA]
American author and poet
* [A] Friend
* M. E. L.

Lee, Mary Emily Frances 20th c.
[HPPN]
British author
* Lee, Cecile

Lee, Matt
See Merwin, [W.] Sam[uel], Jr.

Lee, Michele
See Dusiak [or Dusick?], Michele Lee

Lee, Mildred
See Scudder, Mildred Lee

Lee, Minnie Mary
See Wood, Julia Amanda [Sargent]

Lee, Moose
See Lee, Robert Dean

Lee, Mother
See Lee, Ann

Lee, Nata
See Frackman, Nathaline

Lee, Nathaniel 1657?-1690? [DNNF,
DNNS, HN]
British playwright
* [The] Crazy Poet
* [The] Mad Poet

Lee, Norah
See Barstow, Norah Lee Haymond
Bradley

Lee, Norman 1905-1962 [CC, TCCM,
WW]
British author
* Armstrong, Raymond
* Corrigan, Mark
* Hobart, Robertson

Lee, O. H.
See Oswald, Lee Harvey

Lee, Old Spades
See Lee, Robert Edward

Lee, Olga
See Hammaersbough, Olga

Lee, One Speech
See Lee, Joshua Bryan

Lee, Palmer 1927- [FC, ITA, SW]
American actor
* Palmer, Gregg

Lee, Parker
See Turner, Robert [Harry]

Lee, Patty
See Carey, Alice

Lee, Peggy
See Egstrom, Norma Dolores

Lee, Peter Granville 1945- [DC]
British cricketer
* Lee, Leapy

Lee, Pinky
See Leff, Pincus

Lee, Poison Ivy
See Lee, Ivy Ledbetter

Lee, Rachel Frances Antonina Dashwood
1770?-1829 [IP]
British author
* Philopatria
* R. F. A.

Lee, Ranger
See Snow, Charles Horace

Lee, Raymond
See Martin, E. Le Breton

Lee, Rebecca Smith 1894- [CA]
American author
* Smith, Rebecca

Lee, Richard Henry 1732-1794 [HPPN,
IP]
American statesman and author
* [The] American Cicero
* [The] Cicero of the Revolution
* [The] Federal Farmer

Lee, Robert
See Fairman, Paul W.

Lee, Robert Dean 1937- [BE]
American baseball player
* Lee, Horse
* Lee, Moose

Lee, Robert E. 1861-? [HPPN]
American gambler and outlaw
* Curry, Bob

Lee, Robert Edward 1807-1870 [DEP,
HPPN, SN]
American army officer
* [The] Bayard of the Confederate
Army
* [The] Gentle General
* Lee, Old Spades
* Massa Bob
* Old Ace of Spades
* Uncle Robert

Lee, Roberta
See McGrath, Robert L[ee]

Lee, Ron 1952-
American basketball player
* Lee, Kamikaze
* [The] Tasmanian Devil

Lee, Ron 1952- [SMG]
American football player
* Lee, Bonafide

Lee, Ronny
See Leventhal, Ronald

Lee, Rooney
See Lee, William Henry Fitzhugh

Lee, Rose
See McQuoid, Rose Lee

Lee, Rosie
See Aiken, Joan Delano

Lee, Rowena
See Bartlett, Marie [Swan]

Lee, Roy
See Hopkins, Clark

Lee, Ruth
See Rhodes, Ruth

Lee, Sammy
See Levy, Samuel

Lee, Sarah [Willis Bowdich] 1791-1856
[IP]
British author
* [A] Traveller

Lee, Scrip
See Lee, Holsey S.

Lee, Shaft
See Lee, John

Lee, Shavey
See Lee, J. Waye

Lee, Sheriff
See Lee, Harold Burnham

Lee, [Sir] Sidney
See Levy, Solomon Lazarus

Lee Siu Loong
See Lee Yuen Kam

Lee, Sondra
See Gash, Sondra Lee

Lee, Sonny
See Lee, Thomas Ball

Lee, Spaceman
See Lee, William Francis [Bill]

Lee, Stan
See Lieber, Stanley Martin

Lee, Stannie
See Webb, Laura S.

Lee, Steve
See Parry, Michel Patrick

Lee, Stuart 1938- [CA]
American author
* Woods, Stuart

Lee, Susan Richmond 20th c. [NPS]
Author
* Yorke, Curtis

Lee, Theodis 1946-1979 [IBW]
American basketball player
* Lee, Wolfman

Lee, Thomas Ball 1904- [PMJ, WWJ]
American jazz musician
* Lee, Sonny

Lee, Thornton Starr 1906- [BE]
American baseball player
* Lee, Lefty

Lee, Ting
See Tingley, Richard Hoadley

Lee, Vanessa
See Moule, Winifred Ruby

Lee, Vaudeville
See Lee, James Richard [Jimmy]

Lee, Vernon
See Paget, Violet

Lee, Veronica
See Woodford, [Irene] Cecile

Lee, Warren
See Jackson, Lee

Lee, Watty
See Lee, Wyatt Arnold

Lee, Wayne Cyril 1917- [ESF, IAW, SFL]
American author
* Havens, Stewart
* Sheldon, Lee

Lee, William ?-1610 [HPPN]
British clergyman and inventor
* [The] Father of the Stocking Frame

Lee, William ?-1840 [IP]
American author
* [Un] Americain Citoyen
* [The] High Constable

Lee, William [or Willy]
See Burroughs, William [Seward]

Lee, William C. 1895-1948
American military officer
* [The] Father of American Airborne Forces

Lee, William Crutcher 1909- [BE]
American baseball player
* Lee, Big Bill

Lee, William Francis [Bill] 1946- [SMG]
American baseball player
* Lee, Spaceman
* [The] Spaceman

Lee, William Henry Fitzhugh 1837-1891 [WBD]
American army officer
* Lee, Rooney

Lee, Willis A., Jr. 1888-1945
American naval officer
* Lee, Ching

Lee, Winifred
See Gombell, Minna

Lee, Wolfman
See Lee, Theodis

Lee, Wyatt Arnold 1879-1936 [BE]
American baseball player
* Lee, Watty

Lee Yuen Kam 1940-1973 [HPPN, SC]
American-born actor and martial arts expert
* Kung Fu
* Lee, Bruce
* Lee Siu Loong
* [The] Little Dragon

Lee-Doolan, Tom 1903- [THR]
American actor
* Douglas, Tom

Lee-Hankey, Edith Mary 1881-? [DBA]
British painter
* Garner, E. M.

Lee Howard, Leon Alexander 1914-1979? [CA]
British author, editor, journalist
* Howard, Leigh
* Krislov, Alexander

Lee-Richardson, James 1913- [AW]
Irish-born author
* Dunne, Desmond

Leech, H. E. S. [IP]
British author
* H. E. S. L.

Leech, Harper 1885-1951 [BI]
American journalist
* Scrutator

Leech, John 1817-1864 [NPS]
Caricaturist
* Pen, A., Esq.

Leech, Margaret 1893-1974 [CA]
American historian and author
* Pulitzer, Margaret Leech

Leech, Richard
See McClelland, Richard Leeper

Leeds, Andrea
See Lees, Antoinette

Leeds, Duchess of [NPS]
Author
* Carmarthen, K.

Leeds, Herbert I.
See Levy, Herbert I.

Leeds, Homer Stansbury
See Bernard, Pierre A.

[A] Leeds Layman
See Rawson, George

Leeds, William Henry [IP]
British architect and author
* W. H. L.

Leef, David
See Lefkowitz, David

Leek, Sybil
See Falk, Sybil

Leemans, Alphonse E. 1912-1979 [BI, FB]
American football player
* Leemans, Tuffy

Leemans, Tuffy
See Leemans, Alphonse E.

Leeming, Jo Ann
See Leeming, Joseph

Leeming, Joseph 1897-1968 [CA]
American author
* Leeming, Jo Ann
* Swift, Merlin
* Zingara, Professor

Lees, Antoinette 1914- [FC, HPPN]
American actress
* Leeds, Andrea

Lees, Hannah
See Fetter, Elizabeth Head

Lees, James Cameron [IP, PA]
Scottish clergyman and author
* A. R. A.
* M'Rory, [Rev] Rory
* Rag, Tag, and Bobtail

Lees, John Morton
See Middleton, Ellis

Lee's Old War Horse
See Longstreet, James

Lees-Craston, Eily Sophie 1879-1961 [SC]
British-born actress
* Malyon, Eily

Leese, George 19th c. [BLB]
American gangleader
* Leese, Snatchem

Leese, Snatchem
See Leese, George

Leeson, R. A.
See Leeson, Robert [Arthur]

Leeson, Robert [Arthur] 1928- [CA]
British author and journalist
* Leeson, R. A.

Leete, Frederick De Land 1866-? [NAA]
American clergyman and author
* DeLand, Tracy

Leeteg, Edgar 1904-1953 [HPPN]
American artist
* [The] American Gauguin
* [The] Master

Leever, Deacon
See Leever, Samuel

Leever, Samuel 1871-1953 [BE, BI]
American baseball player
* [The] Goshen Schoolmaster
* Leever, Deacon

Leevitt, Don T. B.
See Spence, James Mudie

LeFaivre, Georgiana 1873?-1951 [BI]
Canadian editor
* Ginevra

Lefaur, Andre
See Lefaurichon, Andre

Lefaurichon, Andre 1879-1952 [SC]
French actor
* Lefaur, Andre

Lefebure-Wely, Louis James Alfred
See Lefebvre, Louis James Alfred

Lefebvre, Catherine Hubscher [Duchess of Dantzig] 18th c. [DEP, DHA, DNNS]
Wife of Napoleon's marshal, Francois Lefebvre
* Sans Gene, Madame

Lefebvre, Frenchy
See Lefebvre, James Kenneth [Jim]

Lefebvre, Germaine 1933?- [FC, ITA, SW]
French-born actress
* Capucine

Lefebvre, James Kenneth [Jim] 1943- [PB, SMG]
American baseball player
* Lefebvre, Frenchy

LeFebvre, Lefty
See LeFebvre, Wilfrid Henry [Bill]

Lefebvre, Louis James Alfred 1817-1870 [WBD]
French musician and composer
* Lefebure-Wely, Louis James Alfred

Lefebvre, [Dr.] Rene
See Laboulaye, Edouard

LeFebvre, Wilfrid Henry [Bill] 1915- [BE, SMG]
American baseball player and scout
* LeFebvre, Lefty

LeFevre, Al
See LeFevre, Alfredo Modesto

LeFevre, Alfredo Modesto 1898- [BE]
American baseball player
* LeFevre, Al

Lefevre, Francois Antoine 1670-1737 [PA]
Author
* Faber

Lefevre, [Sir] George William 1797-1846 [IP]
British physician and author
* [A] Travelling Physician

Lefevre, Gui
See Bickers, Richard Leslie Townshend

Lefevre, Laura Zenobia 20th c. [HPPN]
American author
* Bird, Zenobia

Lefevre, Lily Alice 19th c. [PI]
Irish poet
* Fleurange

Lefevre, [Lieut.] Paul
See Cooper, Charles Henry St. John

Lefevre d'Etaples, Jacques 1450?-1537? [WBD]
French scholar, theologian, religious reformer
* Stapulensis

Leff, Pincus 1916- [ITA]
American entertainer
* Lee, Pinky

Lefferd, Vera ?-1919 [HPPN]
American actress
* Anderson, Vera

Leffingwell, Albert 1895-1946 [WW]
Author
* Chambers, Dana
* Jackson, Giles

Lefkowicz, Mel 1893-1935 [HPPN, JF]
American comedian
* Klee, Mel

Lefkowitz, David 20th c. [BI]
American singer
* Leef, David

Lefleur, Victoria 1914-1957 [HPPN]
American actress
* Ward, Victoria

Lefley, Charles Thomas 1950- [SMG]
Canadian-born hockey player
* [The] Break Away Kid

LeFlore, Flo
See LeFlore, Ron[ald]

LeFlore, Ron[ald] 1952- [IBW]
American baseball player
* LeFlore, Flo
* Twinkle Toes

Lefroy, E. N. [NPS]
Author
* Fry, E. N. Leigh

[The] Left Bank Mother Confessor
See Powell, Altivia Edwards

[The] Left's Lawyer's Lawyer
See Boudin, Leonard

Lefty Louis Rosenberg
See Rosenberg, Louis

Lefy, Nora
See Russell, Hanora Mary

[The] Legal Interpreter of the Constitution
See Marshall, John

[The] Legal Killer
See Elliott, Robert G.

[The] Legal Succesor of Houdini
See Weiss, Theo

Legalist
See Philpott, J. P.

Legate, Charles 19th c. [HPPN]
Canadian gambler, forger, swindler
* Charley Black Eyes
* Jacobs, Colonel
* Montford, Charles L.

Legatee, Residuary
See Sargent, Henry Jackson

[A] Legend of Impropriety
See Boswell, James

[The] Legendary Figure of the Screen
See Asther, Nils

[The] Legendary Stardust Cowboy
See Odam, Norman

Legendre, Frenchy
See Legendre, Henri A.

Legendre, Henri A. 1924- [BA]
American business executive
* Legendre, Frenchy

Legendre, Louis 1756?-1797 [DNNF, DNNS, SN]
French politician
* [Le] Paysan du Danube
* [The] Peasant of the Danube

Leger, [Marie-Rene] Alexis Saint-Leger 1887-1975 [CA, EWL, TC]
French diplomat and poet
* Leger, Saintleger
* Saint John, Perse

Leger, Jack-Alain 1949- [IAW]
French author
* Hedayat, Dashiell

Leger, Raymond Alfred 1883- [SFL, WGT]
Author
* McDonald, Raymond [joint pseudonym with Edward Richard McDonald]

Leger, Saintleger
See Leger, [Marie-Rene] Alexis Saint-Leger

Legett, Doc
See Legett, Lou[is Alfred]

Legett, Lou[is Alfred] 1901- [BE]
American baseball player
* Legett, Doc

Legg, W. Dorr 20th c. [SFL]
Author
* Auctor Ignotus?

Leggatt, Albert G. 1880-1959 [BEW]
American actor
* Sterling, Richard

Legge, Alfred Owen [IP, PA]
British author
* One of her Sons
* Stawell, Augustus

Leggett, Eric
See Rimel, Duane [Weldon]

Leggett, William 1802-1839 [IP]
American journalist
* [A] Country Schoolmaster
* [A] Midshipman of the U.S. Navy

Leggio, Carmelo John 1927- [EJ]
American jazz musician
* Leggio, Carmen

Leggio, Carmen
See Leggio, Carmelo John

Legh, Gerard 17th c. [IP]
Scottish author
* [A] Christian
* Dalrymple, Gilbert, D. D.

Leginska, Ethel
See Liggins, Ethel

Legion
See Sullivan, Robert Baldwin

Legion Harry
See Lee, Henry

[The] Legislator of Parnassus
See Boileau-Despreaux, Nicolas

Legman, G[ershon]
See Legman, George Alexander

Legman, George Alexander 1917- [CA, CC]
American author
* De La Glannege, Roger-Maxe
* Legman, G[ershon]

Legnon, Albert 1898?- [NOJ]
American jazz musician
* Legnon, Red

Legnon, Red
See Legnon, Albert

Legrady, Thomas Theodore
See Tassy, Tamas

Legrand
See Belleville, Henri

Legrand
See Davy, Poupart

LeGrand
See Henderson, LeGrand

LeGrand, Claude Maria Eugent 1903?-
[BEW, TR]
French-born actor and director
* Dauphin, Claude

Legrand, Francois
See Antel, Franz

Legrand, Henri 1587?-1637 [HPPN]
French comic actor
* Turlupin

Legrand, Louis, M.D.? [joint pseudonym
with Orville J. Victor]
See Victor, Metta Victoria Fuller

Legrand, Louis, M.D.? [joint pseudonym
with Metta Victoria Fuller Victor]
See Victor, Orville J.

Legrand, Martin
See Rice, James

Legs Larry Smith
See Smith, Larry

Legurregui, Jose 17th c. [GS]
Spanish bullfighter
* [El] Pamplones [Man from Pamplona]

LeHand, Marguerite Alice ?-1944
[HPPN]
*Secretary to American president, Franklin
Roosevelt*
* LeHand, Missy

LeHand, Missy
See LeHand, Marguerite Alice

Lehder, Carlos 20th c. [NW 2-25-85]
Reputed Colombian drug smuggler
* Leather, Joe
* Lemon, Joe

Lehigh, [Colonel] Rutherford B.
See Weil, Joseph R.

Lehman, George 19th c. [HPPN]
American resort proprietor
* George the Baker
* Lehman, Round House George

Lehman, Helen Miller 1893- [NAA]
American writer
* Mann, H. Leigh

Lehman, Round House George
See Lehman, George

Lehmann
See Hoedel, Emil Heinrich Max

**Lehmann, Elizabeth Nina Mary
Frederika** 1862-1918 [HPPN]
British singer and composer
* Lehmann, Liza

Lehmann, Liza
See Lehmann, Elizabeth Nina Mary
Frederika

Lehmann, Lotte 1888- [HPPN]
German opera singer
* [The] Great Soprano from the Golden
  Age of Opera
* Lehmann, Madame

Lehmann, Madame
See Lehmann, Lotte

Lehmann, R. C.
See Lehmann, Rudolf Chambers

Lehmann, Rudolf Chambers 1856-1929
[LC, NPS]
British author
* Lehmann, R. C.
* Vagrant

Lehmann, Theodore H. 1929- [HPPN]
American composer and educator
* Lawson, Ted

Lehndorff, Vera 1942?- [NW 4-1-85]
Fashion model and actress
* Veruschka

Lehner, Gulliver
See Lehner, Paul Eugene

Lehner, Paul Eugene 1920-1967 [BE]
American baseball player
* Lehner, Gulliver

Lehnert, Josephine 1894- [BI]
German nun
* Pasqualina, [Sister]

Lehnhoff, Laura [FFF]
Entertainer
* Clairon, Laura

Lehnus, Opal [Hull] 1920- [CA, WD]
American author
* Hull, Opal

Lehovich, Eugenie Ouroussow
See Ouroussow, Eugenie

Lehr, Anna
See McKim, Ann

Lehr, Clarence Emanuel 1886-1948 [BE]
American baseball player
* Lehr, King

Lehr, King
See Lehr, Clarence Emanuel

Lehr, King
See Lehr, Norm[an Carl Michael]

Lehr, Lew 1895-1950 [HPPN]
American comedian
* Dribblepuss

Lehr, Norm[an Carl Michael] 1901-1968
[BE]
American baseball player
* Lehr, King

Lehrburger, Egon 20th c. [CA]
Author
* Larsen, Egon

Lehrburger, Peter 1933- [CA]
British-born writer and photographer
* Larsen, Peter

Lehrman, Henry 1886-1946 [DFM,
HPPN]
American actor, director, producer
* Lehrman, Pathe
* Lehrman, Suicide

Lehrman, Liza
See Williams, Liza

Lehrman, Pathe
See Lehrman, Henry

Lehrman, Suicide
See Lehrman, Henry

Lehrman, Theodore H. 1929- [ASC]
American composer
* Lawson, Ted

Lehrmann, Chanan
See Lehrmann, Charles C[uno]

Lehrmann, Charles C[uno] 1905- [CA]
Austrian-born rabbi and author
* Lehrmann, Chanan
* Lehrmann, Cuno Chanan

Lehrmann, Cuno Chanan
See Lehrmann, Charles C[uno]

Lei Chen Yuan
See De Jaegher, Raymond-Joseph

Leibenguth, Charla Ann
See Banner, Charla Ann Leibenguth

Leiber, Fritz 1910- [CA, WW]
American author
* Lathrop, Francis

Leibich, Augusta [FFF]
American writer
* March, Marjorie

Leibnitz [or Leibniz], Gottfried Wilhelm von 1646-1716 [DEP, DNNS, SN]
German philosopher and mathematician
* [The] First of Philosophers
* [A] Living Dictionary

Leibold, Harry Loran 1892-1977 [BE]
American baseball player
* Leibold, Nemo

Leibold, Nemo
See Leibold, Harry Loran

Leibowicz, Jankiew 1726?-1791 [WBD]
Polish founder of religious sect
* Frank, Jacob

Leibowitz, Michael 1941- [RO2]
South African-born musician
* Mann, Manfred

Leibowitz, Samuel Simon 1894?-1978
Rumanian-born American jurist
* Leibowitz, Sentencing Sam

Leibowitz, Sentencing Sam
See Leibowitz, Samuel Simon

Leibrook, Min
See Leibrook, Wilford F.

Leibrook, Wilford F. 1903-1943 [WWJ]
American jazz musician
* Leibrook, Min

Leicester-Warren, John Byrne [Baron de Tabley] 1835-1895 [DEA]
British author and poet
* Lancaster, William P.

Leicestershire
See Foe, Daniel

Leidesdorf, Franz 19th c. [IP, PA]
German author
* Wallner, Franz

Leidhof, Charles [PA]
Author
* Mohr, Frederick

Leifchild, John R. 1815-? [HPPN]
British author
* J. R. L.

Leifield, Albert Peter 1883-1970 [BE]
American baseball player
* Leifield, Lefty

Leifield, Lefty
See Leifield, Albert Peter

Leigh, [Capt.] Arthur
See Steffens, Arthur

Leigh, Aurora
See Browning, Elizabeth Barrett

Leigh, Benjamin Watkins 1781-1849 [IP]
American attorney, statesman, author
* [An] Eminent Citizen of Viriginia
* Sydney, Algernon

Leigh, Carolyn
See Rosenthal, Carolyn

Leigh, Chandos 1791-1850 [IP]
British poet
* [A] Gloucestershire County Gentleman

Leigh, Dorma
See Woodleigh, Dorma

Leigh, Eugene
See Seltzer, Leon E[ugene]

Leigh, Florence
See Wilbur, Anna T.

Leigh, George 1743-1816 [HPPN]
British auctioneer
* [The] Rafaelle of Auctioneers

Leigh, Gracie
See Ellis, Gracie

Leigh, Hart
See Denny, John Thomas

Leigh, Ione
See Massada, Ione

Leigh, Janet
See Morrison, Jeanette Helen

Leigh, Johanna
See Sayers, Dorothy L[eigh]

Leigh, Kathy
See Killough, [Karen] Lee

Leigh, Larry
See Warner, L. T.

Leigh, Magda
See Shirley, Florence Henderson

Leigh, Mary
See Eveleigh, Mary

Leigh, Mary
See Everleigh, Mary

Leigh, Mitch
See Michnick, Irwin S.

Leigh, Olivia
See Clamp, Helen Mary Elizabeth

Leigh, P. Brady 19th c. [IP]
British barrister and author
* [A] Member of Gray's Inn

Leigh, Palmer
See Palmer, Pamela Lynn

Leigh, Percival 1813-1889 [HPPN, IP, PA]
British author and journalist
* Pipps, Mr.
* Prendergast, Paul
* Professor

Leigh, Ruth
See Sclater, Ruth Leigh

Leigh, Stuart
See Clarke, Mary Bayard Devereux

Leigh, Ursula
See Gwynn, Ursula Grace

Leigh, Vivien
See Hartley, Vivian Mary

Leigh, W. Rye
See Riley, Willie

Leigh-Pemberton, Nigel Douglas 1934- [OP]
British opera singer
* Douglas, Nigel

Leighninger, Lanny
See Leighninger, R. E.

Leighninger, R. E. 20th c.
Horseracing official
* Leighninger, Lanny

Leighton
See Appleton, Jesse

Leighton, Ann
See Smith, Isadore Leighton Luce

Leighton, Bernie
See Lazeroff, Bernard

Leighton, Bert
See Leighton, James Albert

Leighton, Eric ?-1924 [BEW]
British actor
* Lambart, Richard

Leighton, F. S. [PA]
Author
* Lernier, Luke

Leighton, Florence
See Pfalzgraf, Florence Leighton

Leighton, Frederick 1830-1896 [FFF]
British painter
* Limmer, Luke, Esq.

Leighton, George N.
See Leitao, George Neves

Leighton, James Albert 1877?-1964 [BEW]
American theatrical performer and songwriter
* Leighton, Bert

Leighton, John 1822-1912 [IP, PA, WWL]
British author and illustrator
* Limner, Luke

Leighton, Lee
See Overholser, Wayne D.

Leighton, Lillie
See Gerard, Lillie

Leighton, Mauri Lynn
See Kilroy, Marilyn

Leighton, Queenie
See Gerard, Lillie

Leighton, Robert 1611-1684 [SN]
Scottish prelate
* [The] Fenelon of Scotland

Leijel, Carl F. 1875-1925 [BEW]
British-born producer
* Leyel, Carl F.

Leila
See Barlow, Emma

Leila
See Caldwell, Ella

Leina, Wil. D', Esq., of the Outer Temple
See Wilson, Daniel

Leinad
See Crilly, Daniel

Leiner, Benjamin 1896-1947 [AS, BX, EJS]
American boxer
* [The] Ghetto Wizard
* Leonard, Benny
* [The] Mama's Boy

Leino, Eino
See Loennbohm, Armas Eino Leopold

Leinster, Murray
See Jenkins, Will[iam] F[itzgerald]

Leipiar, Louise 20th c. [WGT]
Author
* Reynolds, L. Major

Leipziger, Nathan [Nate] 1873-1939 [HPPN]
American magician
* [The] International King of Cards

Leird, Henry J. 20th c.
Author
* Palmer, Tom

Leisenring, Margaret 1904-1926 [SC]
American actress
* Stuart, Jean

Leishman, J. B.
See Leishman, James Blair

Leishman, James Blair 1902-1963 [LC]
British educator and author
* Leishman, J. B.

Leisk, David Johnson 1906-1975 [CA, SAT, TBJ]
American cartoonist, author, illustrator
* Johnson, Crockett

Leisure, Piddleton
See Vawter, L. P.

Leisurely Saunterer
See Eggleston, Edward

Leisy, James Franklin 1927- [CA, WD]
American song editor and writer
* Lynn, Frank

Leitao, George Neves 20th c. [IBW]
American politician
* Leighton, George N.

Leitch, Cecil
See Leitch, [Charlotte] Cecilia

Leitch, [Charlotte] Cecilia 1891- [BBH, EG]
British golfer
* Leitch, Cecil

Leitch, Donovan P. 1946- [LRR, NAD]
Scottish-born singer
* Donovan

Leitch, Lavinia
See Hynd, Lavinia Leitch

Leitch, Robert 1891-1956 [HPPN]
American dancer
* Allan, Roy

Leite, George Thurston 1920- [WW]
Author
* Scott, Thurston [joint pseudonym with Jody Scott]

Leitersdorf, Fini 1906- [WFA]
Israeli fashion designer
* [The] Godmother of the Israeli Fashion Image

Leith, Elizabeth
See Julyan, Louise Elizabeth

Leith, Shady Bill
See Leith, William [Bill]

Leith, William [Bill] 1874-1940 [BE]
American baseball player
* Leith, Shady Bill

Leitner, Doc
See Leitner, George Aloysius

Leitner, Dummy
See Leitner, George Michael

Leitner, George Aloysius 1865-1937 [BE]
American baseball player
* Leitner, Doc

Leitner, George Michael 1871-1960 [BE]
American baseball player
* Leitner, Dummy

Leito, Arturo 1910- [CW]
Curacaon author
* Chobil
* Tuyuchi

Leitzel, Lillian
See Pelikan, Leopeldina Alize Elianore

Leivick, H.
See Halpern, Leivick

Lejeune, Anthony
See Thompson, Edward Anthony

Lejeune, Francois 1908- [WEC]
French cartoonist and illustrator
* Effel, Jean

LeJeune, Larry
See LeJeune, Sheldon Aldenbury

LeJeune, Sheldon Aldenbury 1885-1952 [BE]
American baseball player
* LeJeune, Larry

Lejeunesse, Marie Louise Cecilia Emma 1847-1930 [HPPN]
Canadian opera singer
* Dame Emma

Lekain, Henri Louis
See Cain, Henri Louis

Leland, Aaron Whitney 1787-1871 [IP]
American clergyman and author
* Expositor

Leland, Charles Godfrey 1824-1903 [DEL, PA]
American author and poet
* Breitmann, Hans
* Meister Karl
* Sloper, Mace

Leland, George 1945- [IBW]
American politician
* Leland, Mickey

Leland, John 1506-1552 [NPS]
British scholar and antiquary
* [The] Antiquarian Poet

Leland, Mickey
See Leland, George

Lelia
See Dudevant, Amandine Aurore Lucile Dupin

Lelio
See Riccoboni, Luigi

Lell, Jennie
See Smith, Jane Luella Dowd

Lelland, Frank
See Burrage, Alfred McLelland

Lelong, Lucien 1889- [HPPN]
French fashion designer
* [The] First Gentleman of Fashion

LeLorrain, Charles
See Mellin, Charles

Lely, [Sir] Peter
See Van der Faes, Pieter

Lema, Anthony David 1934-1966 [AS, EG, GF]
American golfer
* Lema, Champagne Tony

Lema, Champagne Tony
See Lema, Anthony David

LeMair, H[enriette] Willebeek 1889-1966 [BI, HPPN, SAT]
Dutch artist and illustrator
* Saida

Lemaire, M. 19th c. [HN]
French diplomat
* Jaunot

Lemaitre, Antoine Louis Prosper 1800-1876 [SN, WBD]
French actor
* [Le] Grand Frederic
* Lemaitre, Frederic [or Frederick]
* [The] Talma of the Boulevards

Lemaitre, Frederic [or Frederick]
See Lemaitre, Antoine Louis Prosper

Lemaster, Bones
See Lemaster, Johnnie Lee

Lemaster, Denny
See Lemaster, Denver Clayton

Lemaster, Denver Clayton 1939- [BE]
American baseball player
* Lemaster, Denny

Lemaster, Johnnie Lee 1954- [SMG]
American baseball player
* Lemaster, Bones

LeMay, Curtis 1906-
American military leader
* Iron Ass

Lembo, Diana L.
See Spirt, Diana L[ouise]

Lemesurier, Peter
See Britton, Peter Ewart

Lemieux, Kenneth 20th c. [CCL]
Canadian author
* Orvis, Kenneth

Lemieux, Marc 1948- [CA]
American author
* Best, Marc

Lemir, Andre
See Rimel, Duane [Weldon]

Lemire, Aubert 1573-1640 [PA]
Author
* Miroeus

Lemke, Henry E.
See Tooker, Richard

Lemke, Moratorium Bill
See Lemke, William

Lemke, William 1878-? [HPPN]
American politician
* Lemke, Moratorium Bill

Lemm-Margadant, Simon 1511?-1550
[WBD]
German author and poet
* Lemnius, Simon

Lemmitz, Hans
See Brauer-Tuchorze, Johann Ernst

Lemmon, Laura Elizabeth 1917- [WW]
Author
* Wilson, Lee

Lemnius, Simon
See Lemm-Margadant, Simon

Lemoine
See Didier, Eugene Lemoine

Lemoine, Adolphe 1812?-1880 [IP, PA]
French playwright
* Montigny, Lemoine

Lemoine, Ernest
See Roy, Ewell Paul

LeMoine, James MacPherson 1825-1912
[CCL]
Canadian author
* Cosmopolite

Lemoine, Sauvelle 1671-1701 [FFF]
Governor of Louisiana
* [The] American Prodigy

Lemon, [Sir] Charles 1784-1868 [HPPN]
British author
* C. L.

Lemon, Charles J. 1880-1956 [SC]
American actor
* Le Moyne, Charles

Lemon, Joe
See Lehder, Carlos

Lemon, Lem
See Lemon, Robert Granville [Bob]

LeMon, Lynn
See Wert, Lynette L[emon]

Lemon, Mark 1809-1870 [HPPN, IP]
British author, playwright, journalist
* Lemon, Thickhead
* Uncle Mark

Lemon, Meadow George, III 1934- [BB,
HPPN, IBW]
American basketball player
* [The] Clown Prince of Basketball
* [The] Comedy King of the Sports
  World
* Lemon, Meadowlark
* [The] Undisputed King of Basketball
  Comedy

Lemon, Meadowlark
See Lemon, Meadow George, III

Lemon, Mrs. Henry W.   [FFF]
Entertainer
* Melrose, Julia

Lemon, Robert Granville [Bob] 1920-
[PB]
American baseball player and manager
* Lemon, Lem

Lemon, Thickhead
See Lemon, Mark

Lemon, [Sir] William 1748-1824
[HPPN]
British author
* His Representative

Lemonade Lucy Hayes
See Hayes, Lucy Ware Webb

LeMond, Alan 1938- [CA]
American author
* Tahlaquah, David

Lemons, Overton Amos 1920-1966
[BWW]
American singer
* Lewis, Smiley
* Lewis, Smiling

Lena
See Lathrop, Mary Torrans

Lena
See Stiles, Rolland Mays

Lena, Lily
See Archer, Lily

Lenanton, C.
See Oman, Carola [Mary Anima]

Lenanton, Carola Mary Anima Oman
See Oman, Carola [Mary Anima]

Lenard, Darryl 20th c.
American basketball player
* Lenard, Pee Wee

Lenard, Pee Wee
See Lenard, Darryl

Lenarduzzi, Sam
See Lenarduzzi, Silvano

Lenarduzzi, Silvano 1948- [AES]
Italian-born Canadian soccer player
* Lenarduzzi, Sam

Lenau, Nikolaus
See Von Strehlenau, Nikolaus
Niembsch

L'Enclos, Anne 1615?-1705 [HN, SN,
WBD]
French coutesan
* [The] Aspasia of France
* [The] Aspasia of the Seventeenth
  Century
* Ninon de Lenclos

Lency, C.
See Train, Arthur

Lender, Marcelle
See Bastien, Marie

Lendon, Alfred Austin 1856-? [HPPN]
British physician and author
* Harding, Austin

Lendon, Kenneth Harry 1928- [CA,
WD]
Canadian-born author
* Vaughan, Leo

Lenel
See O'Leary, Ellen

Leneru, Marie 1875-1918 [HPPN]
French playwright
* Morsain, Antoine

LeNeve, Ethel 1885?-? [HPPN]
*British secretary and mistress of
American murderer, Hawley Crippen*
* Robinson, John Philo, Jr.

L'Enfant, Pierre C. 1754-1825 [HPPN]
*French-American army officer and
architect*
* [The] Architect of the Capital

Lengel, Frances
See Trocchi, Alexander

Lengel, William Charles 1888- [NAA]
American author
* Grant, Charles
* Spencer, Warren

L'Engle, Madeleine
See Camp, Madeleine L'Engle

Lengsfelder, Hans Jan 1903- [ASC]
*Austrian-born American composer, author,
recording executive*
* Lenk, Harry

Lengyel, Cornel Adam 1915- [CA]
American author
* Adam, Cornel

Lengyel, Geza 1904- [ASC]
Hungarian-born American composer
* Adams, George

Lenhardt, Donald Eugene 1922- [BE]
American baseball player
* Lenhardt, Footsie

Lenhardt, Footsie
See Lenhardt, Donald Eugene

Lenhart, Jason Gregory 1920?- [BEW, FC]
American actor, producer, talent representative
* Gregory, Paul

Lenhart, William 1864-1942 [SC]
American actor
* Hart, Billy

Lenihan, Albert John 1888-1974 [HPPN]
American actor and singer
* Lenihan, Burton

Lenihan, Bish
See Lenihan, Edward T.

Lenihan, Burton
See Lenihan, Albert John

Lenihan, D. M.   [PI]
Irish poet
* D. M. L.

Lenihan, Edward T. 1883-1972 [HPPN]
American stage manager
* Lenihan, Bish

Lenihan, F. J.   [PA]
Author
* Romanus

Lenin, Nicolai
See Ulyanov, Vladimir Ilich

Lenin, Vladimir Ilyich
See Ulyanov, Vladimir Ilich

Lenk, Harry
See Lengsfelder, Hans Jan

Lenkaitis, William Edward 1946- [SMG]
American football player
* [The] Doctor

Lennehan, Helen Theresa Eucharia Flaherty   [BI]
American columnist
* Muir, Helen

Lennon, Arch
See Lennon, Robert Albert [Bob]

Lennon, Florence 1891?-1972 [HPPN]
American entertainer
* Roxanne

Lennon, Florence Becker [Tanenbaum] 1895- [CA]
American author and poet
* Becker, Florence

Lennon, Helen M.
See Goulart, Frances Sheridan

Lennon, John 1940-1980
British musician, singer, songwriter
* Dream, Dr.
* Ghurkin, [Rev.] Fred
* Ghurkin, [Rev.] Thumbs
* Johnson, [Hon.] John St. John

Lennon, John (cont.)
* Kundalini, Kaptain
* McDougal, Dwarf
* Nohnn, Joel
* O'Boogie, [Dr.] Winston
* O'Cean, John
* O'Ghurkin, [Dr.] Winston
* O'Reggae, [Dr.] Winston
* Torment, Mel

Lennon, Mrs. Nestor   [FFF]
Entertainer
* McCall, Lizzie

Lennon, Robert Albert [Bob] 1928- [BE]
American baseball player
* Lennon, Arch

Lennox, Charles Henry Gordon [Sixth Duke of Richmond] 1818-1903 [HPPN]
British politician
* Lennox, Miss

Lennox, Charlotte Ramsay 1720-1804 [HPPN]
British-American author and poet
* [The] Author of the Female Quixote
* Stuart, Harriet

Lennox, Edward
See Nixson, Maisie Mayer

Lennox, Eggie
See Lennox, James Edgar

Lennox, George St. Leger Gordon 1845-1919 [BI, HPPN]
South African outlaw
* Smith, Scotty

Lennox, James ?-1878 [PA]
American author
* L.

Lennox, James Edgar 1885-1939 [BE]
American baseball player
* Lennox, Eggie

Lennox, Miss
See Lennox, Charles Henry Gordon [Sixth Duke of Richmond]

Lenny, Christian 19th c. [IP]
British clergyman and author
* [A] Clergyman of the Church of England

Lenny, Jack
See Hannoch, Leonard John

[The] Lenny of the Seventies
See Thomas, Michael Tilson

Leno, Dan
See Galvin, George

Leno, Dan, Jr.
See Galvin, Sydney Paul

Lenoir, Carlos 1878-1906 [WEC]
Brazilian cartoonist
* Gil
* Vaz, Gil

Lenoir, J. B. 1929-1967 [BWW]
American singer
* Lenore, J. B.

Lenoir, Jacques
See Laraque, Paul

Lenoir, Jean Joseph Etienne 1822-1900 [HPPN]
French inventor
* [The] Father of the Internal Combustion Engine

Lenoir, Lucie 1873-? [IBW]
American singer
* [The] Creole Nightingale
* Walker, Rachel

Lenon, Edmund Fitz-Maurice 1863?-1928 [BEW]
British actor
* Maurice, Edmund

Lenore, J. B.
See Lenoir, J. B.

Lenormand, Henri-Rene 1882-1951 [MWD]
French playwright
* [The] Eugene O'Neill of the French Stage

Lenormand, Marie Anne Adelaide 1772-1843 [HPPN, WBD]
French fortune teller
* [The] Great Lenormand
* [La] Sibylle du Faubourg Saint-Germain

Lenotre, Andre 1613-1700 [DEP, DNNS, FFF, HPPN]
French landscape architect
* [The] Creator of French Landscape Gardening
* [The] Father of Landscape Gardening

Lenox, James 1800-1880 [HPPN]
American bibliophile and philanthropist
* L.

Lens
See Saleeby, Caleb Williams

Lenska, Rula 1948?-
British actress
* [The] Fair One

Lent, Blair 1930- [CA, SAT, TBJ]
American author and illustrator
* Small, Ernest

Lent, D[ora] Geneva 1904- [CA]
Canadian artist and author
* Dorant, Gene

Lentfoehr, Florence Mae 1902- [BI]
American poet
* Mary Therese, [Sister]

Lentulus, Lucius Cornelius 1st c. BC [WBD]
Roman politician
* Crus [or Cruscello]

Lentulus, Publius Cornelius 1st c. BC [WBD]
Roman politician
* Sura

Lentulus, Publius Cornelius 1st c. BC
[WBD]
Roman politician
* Spinther

Lentz, Harry 20th c. [EF]
American football player
* Lentz, Jack

Lentz, Jack
See Lentz, Harry

Lenya, Lotte
See Blamauer, Karoline

Lenz, Carolyn Ruth Swift
See Swift, Carolyn Ruth

Lenz, George Montgomery 1916-
[HPPN]
American actor
* Montgomery, George

Lenz, Peter 1832-1928 [WBD]
German painter, architect, sculptor
* Desiderius, [Father]

Leo [HN]
Army commander
* [The] Ajax of the East

Leo
See Casey, John Keegan

Leo
See Martin, Egbert

Leo
See Pemberton, Col.

Leo Africanus 16th c. [HPPN, WBD]
Arabian geographer
* Eliberitanus
* Johannes Leo
* Leone, Giovanni

Leo, Alan
See Allan, Frederick William

Leo, Andre
See Champseix, Mme.

Leo, Bessie
See Murray, Leslie

Leo, Bob 1881-1929 [HPPN]
American actor
* Topping, Leo

Leo, Frank
See Peers, Frank

Leo Hebraeus
See Abrabanel, Judah Leon

Leo, Jessie
See Chapman, Jessie Leo

Leo, Jim 20th c.
American football player
* Leo, Nomad

Leo, Juan 1483-1522 [PA]
Moorish geographer
* [The] African

Leo, Ma
See Fullard-Leo, Ellen

Leo, Nomad
See Leo, Jim

Leo I 390?-461 [DNNS]
Pope
* [The] Great

Leo I 400?-474 [DNNS, WBD]
Byzantine emperor
* [The] Great
* Makeles [The Butcher]
* [The] Thracian

Leo III 680?-741 [DNNS, WBD]
Byzantine emperor
* [The] Isaurian

Leo IV 750?-780 [WBD]
Byzantine emperor
* [The] Khazar

Leo IX
See Bruno

Leo V ?-820 [DNNS, WBD]
Byzantine emperor
* [The] Armenian

Leo VI 866-912 [DNNS, HN]
Byzantine emperor
* [The] Philosopher
* [The] Wise

Leo X
See Medici, Giovanni de

Leo XI
See Medici, Alessandro Ottaviano de

Leo XII
See Della Genga, Annibale Francesco

Leo XIII
See Pecci, Gioacchino Vincenzo

Leola
See Rogers, Loula K.

Leolin
See Renan, Joseph Ernest

Leoline
See Dunham, Emma B. Sargent

Leon
See Boitel, Leonard

Leon, [Brother]
See Sauget, Joseph Sylvestre

Leon
See Van Roey, Leon

Leon, Casper
See Leoni, Gaspare

Leon, Eddie
See Leon, Eduardo Antonio

Leon, Eduardo Antonio 1946- [BE]
American baseball player
* Leon, Eddie

Leon, Elizabeth Lucie 1899?-1972 [BI]
American journalist
* Noel, Lucie

Leon Felipe
See Camino, Leon Felipe

Leon Hebreo
See Abrabanel, Judah Leon

Leon, Henry Cecil 1902-1976 [CC,
EMD, TR]
British author and playwright
* Cecil, Henry

Leon, John 1934- [TR]
British actor
* Standing, John

Leon, Max
See Leon, Maximino Molina

Leon, Maximino Molina 1950- [SMG]
Mexican-born baseball player
* Leon, Max

Leon, W. D.
See Glasscock, W. D.

Leon y Lopez, Juan 1788-1854 [GS,
HPPN]
Spanish bullfighter
* Leoncillo [Little Lion]

Leona
See Button, Margaret Helen

Leonard
See Lewis, Leonard

Leonard
See Perrugia, Vincenzo

Leonard, A. B.
See Aldrich, Earl Augustus

Leonard, Agnes 19th c. [IP]
American author and poet
* Mollie Myrtle

Leonard, Baird
See Zogbaum, Baird Leonard

Leonard, Benny
See Leiner, Benjamin

Leonard, Billie 20th c. [THR]
British actress and singer
* Hill, Billie

Leonard, Bob 1932- [BB]
American basketball player
* Leonard, Slick

Leonard, Buck
See Leonard, Walter Fenner

Leonard, Charles C. 19th c. [IP]
American author
* Crocus

Leonard, Charles Hall 19th c. [IP]
American clergyman and author
* C. H. L.

Leonard, Charles L.
See Heberden, Mary Violet

Leonard, Cotton
See Leonard, Jeffrey

Leonard, Daniel 1740-1829 [FFF, IP, PA]
American author
* Massachusettenis
* [A] Native of New England
* [A] Person of Honor

Leonard, Dutch
See Leonard, Elmore

Leonard, Dutch
See Leonard, Emil John

Leonard, Dutch
See Leonard, Hubert Benjamin

Leonard, Eddie
See Toney, Lemuel Gordon

Leonard, Edith Jewell 1923- [BEW]
American talent representative and casting consultant
* Leonard, Julie

Leonard, Elmer Ellsworth 1888- [BE]
American baseball player
* Leonard, Tiny

Leonard, Elmore 1925- [CA, PW 2-25-83, WP 2-17-85]
American author
* [The] Dickens of Detroit
* Leonard, Dutch
* Long, Emmett

Leonard, Emil John 1910- [BE, DGS]
American baseball player
* Leonard, Dutch

Leonard, Fat Jack
See Lebitsky, Leonard

Leonard, Florence Peltier [NAA]
American writer
* Peltier, Florence

Leonard, Frederick 1881-1954 [LC]
British playwright
* Lonsdale, Frederick

Leonard, George H. 20th c. [SFL]
Author
* Cooper, Hughes

Leonard, Gus
See Lerond, Gustav

Leonard, H. C. [PA]
Author
* H. C. L.

Leonard, Harlan Quentin 1905- [WWJ]
American jazz musician
* Leonard, Mike

Leonard, Helen Louise 1861-1922 [BEW, EMT, F1]
American actress and singer
* American Beauty Rose
* Clinton, Mr.
* Russell, Lillian

Leonard, Henry Charles 19th c. [IP]
American clergyman and author
* [The] Minister of the Church

Leonard, Hubert Benjamin 1892-1952 [AS, BE, PB]
American baseball player
* Leonard, Dutch

Leonard, Hugh
See Byrne, John Keyes

Leonard, Jack E.
See Lebitsky, Leonard

Leonard, Jeffrey 1955- [SMG]
American baseball player
* Leonard, Cotton

Leonard, Joe 20th c.
Auto racer
* [The] Pelican
* [The] Penguin

Leonard, John 1901-1956 [SC]
British-born actor, bandleader, singer
* Little, Little Jack

Leonard, John 20th c.
American author
* Cyclops

Leonard, Julie
See Leonard, Edith Jewell

Leonard, Mary
See Barclay, May [Hartley]

Leonard, Mike
See Leonard, Harlan Quentin

Leonard, Nellie Mabel 1875-? [NAA]
American author
* Stuart, Fay

Leonard, Ray Charles 1956- [HPPN]
American boxer
* America's Darling
* Boxing's Darling
* Leonard, Sugar Ray
* [The] Sugar Man

Leonard, Sheldon
See Bershad, Sheldon Leonard

Leonard, Slick
See Leonard, Bob

Leonard, Sugar Ray
See Leonard, Ray Charles

Leonard, Susan 1865-1944 [BEW]
American entertainer
* Westford, Susanne

Leonard, Tiny
See Leonard, Elmer Ellsworth

Leonard, Walter Fenner 1907- [MK, PB]
American baseball player
* [The] Black Lou Gehrig
* Leonard, Buck

Leonard-Boyne, Eva
See Boyne, Eva

Leonardi, Biki
See Leonardi, Elvira

Leonardi, Elvira 20th c. [WFA]
Italian fashion designer
* Leonardi, Biki

Leonardi, Leon
See Leonardi, Leonid

Leonardi, Leonid 1901- [ASC]
Russian-born American composer, conductor, pianist
* Leonardi, Leon

Leonardo
See Marquez, Horatio

Leonardo da Cutri
See Leonardo, Giovanni

Leonardo da Pisa
See Fibonacci, Leonardo

[The] Leonardo da Vinci of the Drums
See Balassoni, Louis

Leonardo, Giovanni 1542-1587 [HPPN]
Italian chess player
* Leonardo da Cutri
* [Il] Puttino [The Boy]

Leonardo, Harry
See Gottsacker, H. L.

Leonardo, Leo
See De Leo, Lionardo Oronzo Salvatore

[The] Leonardo of Forgers
See Bojarsky, Czeslaw

Leoncillo [Little Lion]
See Leon y Lopez, Juan

Leone, Giovanni
See Leo Africanus

Leone, Sarah
See Brown, Polly

Leone, Scott
See Bonnell, Kenneth

Leone, Sergio 1921- [FDG]
Italian director
* Robertson, Bob

Leong, Gor Yun
See Ellison, Virginia Howell

Leonhardt, Anna 20th c. [SC]
Actress
* Belle, Nancy

Leonhart, [Dr.] Raphael W.
See Wybraniec, Peter F[rank]

Leoni, Francesca Bussa di 1384-1440 [HPPN]
Saint
* Frances of Rome

Leoni, Gaspare 1872-1926 [BX, RBE]
Italian-born American boxer
* Leon, Casper

Leoni, Leone 1509-1590 [BI, WBD]
Italian medalist, goldsmith, sculptor
* Aretino, Leone
* [Il] Cavaliere Aretino

Leoni, Leone
See Osborne, John D.

Leoni, Meyer
See Levin, Meyer

Leonid
See Bosworth, Willan George

Leonidas 5th c. BC [FFF]
King of Sparta
* [The] Defender of Thermopylae

Leonidas
See Da Silva, Leonidas

[The] Leonidas of America
See Stark, John

[The] Leonidas of Hungary
See Nicholas

[The] Leonidas of Modern Greece
See Bozzaris, Marco

[The] Leonidas of the Day
See Peel, [Sir] Robert

Leonide [or Leonid]
See Berman, Leonide [or Leonid]

Leonie
See Sachs, Nelly

Leonora, Lili
See Winkler, Lillian

Leonore
See Sikes, William Wirt

Leonowens, Anna Harriette [Crawford]
1834-? [IP]
British author
* [The] English Governess

Leontes
See Bindley, James

Leont'ev, A.
See Leont'ev, Lev Abramovich

Leont'ev, Lev Abramovich 1901-1974
[BI]
Russian economist
* Leont'ev, A.

Leontius of Byzantium 485?-543?
[WBD]
Byzantine monk
* Byzantinus
* [The] First of the Scholastics
* Scholasticus

Leonty
See Turkevich, Leonid

Leonzo, Vic
See Lessinger, Louis

Leopardi, Alessandro 16th c. [HPPN]
Venetian sculptor and architect
* Del Cavallo

Leopold   [RH]
Prince
* Peu-a-Peu

Leopold, Aldo 20th c. [BBH]
Hunter and educator
* [The] Father of Ecology

Leopold, Alexander 19th c. [IP]
German author
* [A] Rational Christian

Leopold, Babe
See Leopold, Nathan F.

Leopold, Carolyn Clugston 1923- [CA]
American author
* Michaels, Carolyn Leopold

Leopold, Emmanuel-Flavia 1896-1962
[CW]
West Indian poet and author
* Lavigne, Mark

Leopold, Isaiah Edwin 1886-1966 [F2,
FAA, FC, HPPN, IPA]
American entertainer
* [The] Clown Prince of Comedy
* [The] Fire Chief
* [The] Perfect Fool
* Wynn, Ed

Leopold, John ?-1958 [BI]
Canadian police official
* Esselwein, Jack

Leopold, Nathan F. 1904-1971 [BLB,
CA, CAP]
American murderer and author
* Ballard, Morton D.
* Johnson, George
* Lanne, William F.
* Lawrence, Richard A.
* Leopold, Babe

Leopold, Winnie 1896- [THR]
British actress and singer
* Collins, Winnie

Leopold I 1640-1705 [HN, SN]
Emperor of Germany
* [The] Great
* [The] Little Man in Red Stockings

Leopold I 1676-1747 [DEP, DNNF, SN]
Prince of Anhalt-Dessau
* [Der] Alte Dessauer
* [The] Old Dessauer

Leopold I 1790-1865 [DEP, DNNS, FFF,
HPPN]
King of Belgium
* [The] Nestor of Europe
* Uncle Leopold

Leopold II 15th c. [SN]
Duke of Austria
* [The] Big
* [The] Courtly

Leopold II
See Louis Philippe Marie Victor

Leopold III 1096-1136 [WBD]
Margrave of Austria
* [The] Pious

Leopold VI 1176-1230 [WBD]
Duke of Austria
* [Der] Glorreiche [The Glorious]

**Leopoldine, Marie Charlotte Amelie
Augustine Victoire Clementine** 1840-1927
[HPPN]
*Empress consort of Maximilian, Emperor
of Mexico*
* [The] American Empress
* [The] Empress Carlotta

Leotard Lady
See Strong, Shirley

Lepcio, Ted
See Lepcio, Thaddeus Stanley

Lepcio, Thaddeus Stanley 1930- [BE]
American baseball player
* Lepcio, Ted

Lepel, H.
See Gurster, Eugen

Lepenski
See Jones, Rudolph Lepenski

[The] Leper
See Amalrich

[The] Leper
See Baldwin IV

[The] Leper Priest
See Veuster, Joseph Damien de

Lepidus
See Gosset, Isaac

Lepin, Ella-Marta
See Egorova, Evgeniia Nikolaevna

Lepine, Alfred 1901-1955 [CEI, FHE]
Canadian-born hockey player
* Lepine, Pit

L'Epine, Ernest Louis Victor Jules
1826-1893 [IP, PA]
French author and playwright
* Manuel, Ernest
* Quatrelles

LePine, Louis Joseph 1876-1949 [BE]
Canadian-born baseball player
* LePine, Pete

LePine, Pete
See LePine, Louis Joseph

Lepine, Pit
See Lepine, Alfred

Lepito, Michael [or Mike]
See Malone, Michael F.

Lepley, Jean Elizabeth 1934- [CA]
British-born author and educator
* Darcy, Jean

Lepofsky, Manfred 1905-1971 [AW, CA,
EMD]
American author and editor
* Lee, Manfred B[ennington]
* Queen, Ellery [joint pseudonym with
  Daniel Nathan]
* Queen, Ellery, Jr. [joint pseudonym
  with Daniel Nathan]
* Ross, Barnaby [joint pseudonym with
  Daniel Nathan]

Leppert, Alice Jean 1915- [CED, FC,
OCF]
American actress and singer
* Faye, Alice

Leppert, Don Eugene 1930- [BE]
American baseball player
* Leppert, Tiger

Leppert, Tiger
See Leppert, Don Eugene

Leppoc, Derfla
See De Marini y Coppel, Alfredo Jose

Leprohon, Pierre 1903- [CA]
French film critic and historian
* Valbonne, Jean

Lerch, Ethelyn [Countess d'Esternaux]
1878?-1971 [BI]
American painter and poet
* Emelde

Lerchbaum, Dora 20th c. [NAA]
Polish-born writer
* Love, D.

Lerchen, Bertram Roe 1889-1962 [BE]
American baseball player
* Lerchen, Dutch

Lerchen, Dutch
See Lerchen, Bertram Roe

Lerian, Peck
See Lerian, Walt[er Irvin]

Lerian, Walt[er Irvin] 1903-1929 [BE]
American baseball player
* Lerian, Peck

Leriche, Jeanne 1869-1934 [SC]
French actress
* Cheirel, Jeanne

Leris, Claire Josephe 1723-1803 [SN, WBD]
French actress
* Clairon, Claire Josephe Hippolyte de la Tude
* [The] Queen of Carthage

L'Ermite, Daniel 1584-1613 [PA]
Author
* Eremita

L'Ermite, Tristan 1405-1493 [NPS]
Servant of King Louis XI of France
* [The] Gossip

Lermoliev, Ivan
See Morelli, Giovanni

Lermont, L. 19th c. [IP]
American author
* Cousin Cicely

Lermontoff, Mikhail Yurievitch
1814-1841 [NPS]
Russian poet and author
* [The] Poet of the Caucasus

Lernier, Luke
See Leighton, F. S.

Lerond, Gustav 1856-1939 [SC]
French-born actor
* Leonard, Gus

LeRos, Christian
See Sorel, W. J.

Leroux, Etienne
See Le Roux, S. P. Daniel

Leroy
See Barnwell, Annie M.

Leroy
See Chatman, John Len

Leroy
See Roy, Hippolyte

Leroy from Eloy
See Malone, Art Lee

LeRoy, Hal
See Schotte, John LeRoy

LeRoy, Jack
See Levy, Jacob

LeRoy, Ken
See Klopfenstein, Kenneth Vladimir

Leroy, Louis [PA]
Author
* Regius

Leroy's Buddy
See Gaither, Bill

Lerrovitch
See Hersey, Harold

Lerski, George Jan 1917- [CA]
Polish-born American historian and author
* Jur, Jerzy

Lerteth, Oban
See Fanthorpe, R[obert] Lionel

Lesage, Alain Rene 1668-1747 [HPPN]
French author and playwright
* [The] Father of the Picaresque Novel

Lesbia
See Clodia

Lesbia
See Lewis, Lydia T.

[The] Lesbian Citizen
See Alcaeus

Lescaille, Catherine 1649-1711 [DNNF]
Dutch poet
* [The] Dutch Sappho

Leschziner, Oscar 1873-1948 [HPPN]
German murder suspect
* Slater, Oscar

Lesdiguieres, Duc de
See De Bonne, Francois

Leser, Tina
See Shillard-Smith, Christine Wetherill

LeShan, Lawrence L[ee] 1920- [CA]
American author
* Grendon, Edward

Lesher, Phyllis 1912- [IAW]
American author
* Livingston-Matthews, Asenath

Lesizwe, Ilizwi
See Lee, Franz John Tennyson

Leskov, Nikolai Semenovich 1831-1895
Russian author
* Stebnitski

Lesky, John 1888-1955 [BX, RBE]
American boxer
* Buff, Johnny

Lesley, Carole
See Rippingale, Maureen

Lesley, J. P.
See Lesley, Peter

Lesley, Peter 1819-1903 [HPPN]
American geologist
* Allen, John W., Jr.
* J. P. L.

Lesley, W. W.
See Mason, William Lasley

Leslie, A. L.
See Lazarus, Arnold Leslie

Leslie, Alfred 1874-1925 [THR]
British actor
* Lester, Alfred

Leslie, Amy
See West, Lillie

Leslie Ann
See Cameron, Leslie Georgiana

Leslie, Arthur
See Grieve, Christopher Murray

Leslie, Blake
See Duckworth, Leslie Blakey

Leslie, Buckskin Frank
See Leslie, Nashville Franklin

Leslie, Captain
See Bradley, J. J. G.

Leslie, Cecilie 1914- [CA]
British author and critic
* MacAdam, Eve

Leslie, Charles 1650-1722 [HPPN, IP]
Irish author
* [A] Churchman
* [A] Free Churchman
* [A] Gentleman in Scotland
* [A] Gentleman in the City
* [A] Lover of Truth
* [A] Member of the Church of England
* Miso Dolos
* One Called an High Churchman
* One Misco Dolos
* Philalethes
* [A] Student of the Temple

Leslie, Doris
See Fergusson Hannay, Doris

Leslie, Eliza 1787-1858 [HPPN]
American author
* [A] Lady of Philadelphia

Leslie, Emma
See Dixon, Mrs.

Leslie, Frances
See Schmitz, Frances

Leslie, Frank
See Carter, Henry

Leslie, Frank
See Collier, Frank

Leslie, Frank
See Leslie, Miriam Florence Folline

Leslie, Gene
See Halverson, Leslie Eugene

Leslie, George K.
See Leslie, George Leonidas

Leslie, George Leonidas 1842-1884
[BLB, HPPN]
American bankrobber
* Allison, J. G.
* America's Ace Burglar
* Green, G. C.
* Herbert, George
* Howard, George
* [The] King of the Bankrobbers
* Leslie, George K.
* Lester, George L.
* [The] Original Raffles
* Western George

Leslie, Henrietta
See Schuetze, Gladys Henrietta
[Raphael]

Leslie, Hugh 19th c. [HPPN]
Scottish author
* Loy, Hugo de la

Leslie, James
See Powell, John

Leslie, Joan
See Brodell, Joan

Leslie, John 1571-1671 [HPPN]
British clergyman
* [The] Fighting Bishop

Leslie, John
See Howitt, John Leslie Despard

Leslie, John Randolph 1885- [WWL]
British author
* Leslie, Shane

Leslie, Josephine Aimee Campbell
1898-1979 [AW, CA]
British author
* Dick, R. A.

Leslie, Lawrence
See Rathborne, St. George Henry

Leslie, Lew
See Lessinsky, Lewis

Leslie, Lilian [joint pseudonym with
Violet Lilian Perkins]
See Hood, Archer Leslie

Leslie, Lilian [joint pseudonym with
Arthur Leslie Hood]
See Perkins, Violet Lilian

Leslie, [Mrs.] Madeline
See Baker, Harriette Newell

Leslie, Madeline
See Baker, Mrs. H. N. Woods

Leslie, Marion
See Tooley, Sarah Anne

Leslie, Mary 1842-1920 [DNA]
Canadian author and poet
* Jones, James Thomas

Leslie, Mary Isabel 1899-? [DIL, SFL,
WGT]
Irish author and poet
* Lane, Temple

Leslie, Miriam Florence Folline
1836?-1914 [HPPN]
American editor and author
* Leslie, Frank
* Squire, Miriam F.

Leslie, Nashville Franklin ?-1925?
[EWG]
American gunfighter
* Leslie, Buckskin Frank

Leslie, O. H.
See Slesar, Henry

Leslie, Peter 1922- [ESF, WGT]
British author, journalist, actor
* MacNee, Patrick

Leslie, Robert
See Roberts, Sonia Leslie

Leslie, Robert B.
See Wooley, John [Steven]

Leslie, Rochelle
See Diamond, Graham

Leslie, Sambo
See Leslie, Samuel Andrew

Leslie, Samuel Andrew 1905- [BE]
American baseball player
* Leslie, Sambo

Leslie, San
See Crook, Bette [Jean]

Leslie, Sarah
See McGuire, Leslie Sarah

Leslie, Shane
See Leslie, John Randolph

Leslie, Sharon
See Luster, Shirley

Leslie, Sylvia
See Ward, Sylvia

Leslie, Tom
See Veale, Thomas

Leslie, Val
See Knights, Leslie Douglas

Leslie, Walter
See Levinsky, Walter

Leslie, Ward S.
See Ward, Elizabeth Honor [Shedden]

Leslie-Satie, Alfred Erikit 1866-1925
[HPPN]
French composer
* Satie, Erik

Leslie-Stuart, May
See Stuart, May

Lesman, Boleslaw 1878-1937 [CD, TCL]
Polish poet
* Lesmian, Boleslaw

Lesmian, Boleslaw
See Lesman, Boleslaw

Lesnevich, Gus 1915-1964 [WBC]
American boxer
* [The] Russian Lion

LeSourd, Catherine
See Marshall, [Sarah] Catherine [Wood]

Lesperance, David 20th c. [WGT]
Author
* Davidson, Gene A.

Lespes, Leo
See Girardin, Delphine Gay De

Lespes, Napoleon 1811-? [PA]
Author
* Trimm, Timothy

Lesseps, Ferdinand Marie de 1805-1894
[HPPN]
French diplomat
* [The] Father of the Suez Canal

[The] Lesser
See James

Lesser, Columbus
See Cowen, Laurence

Lesser, Derwin
See Hornig, Charles D.

Lesser, Milton 1928- [CA, WD, WGT]
American author
* Chase, Adam [joint pseudonym with
Paul W. Fairman]
* Frazer, Andrew
* Granger, Darius John
* Marlowe, Stephen
* Ridgway, Jason
* Tenneshaw, S. M. [house pseudonym,
Ziff-Davis]
* Thames, C[hristopher] H.
* Wilder, Stephen

Lesser, Roger Harold 1928- [CA]
British-born author and clergyman
* Damor, Hakji

Lessey, May Abbey 1872-1952 [HPPN]
American actress
* Abbey, May

Lessing, Bruno
See Bloch, Rudolph Edgar

Lessing, Doris 1920?- [NW 10-1-84, NY
9-23-84, TI 10-1-84, TI 10-7-85, WP 9-24-84]
British author
* Somers, Jane

Lessing, Gotthold Ephraim 1729-1781
[DEP, DNNF, FFF, HPPN]
German playwright and critic
* [The] Aesop of Germany
* [The] Father of German Criticism
* [The] Father of German Literature
* [The] Frederick the Great of Thought

Lessinger, Louis 1857-1914 [HPPN]
American actor
* Leonzo, Vic

Lessinsky, Lewis 1886-1963 [BEW, EMT]
American producer and director
* Leslie, Lew

Lester, Ada 1875-? [HPPN]
American brothel proprietress
* Everleigh, Ada

Lester, Alfred
See Leslie, Alfred

Lester, Andrew
See Greenhough, Terence [Terry]

Lester, Anthony
See Boyce, Christopher John

Lester, Bruce
See Lister, Bruce

Lester, Charles Edward 1815-? [PA]
Author
* Berkeley

Lester, Frank
See Usher, Frank Hugh

Lester, Gene
See Mercer, Jean

Lester, George L.
See Leslie, George Leonidas

Lester, Irvin
See Pratt, [Murray] Fletcher

Lester, James
See Blake, Leslie James

Lester, Jane
See Walker, Emily Kathleen

Lester, John
See Werner, Vivian

Lester, Katherine 1911- [FC]
American actress
* De Mille, Katherine

Lester, Ketty
See Frierson, Revoyda

Lester, Louise
See Nathal, Mrs.

Lester, Mark
See Russell, Martin

Lester, Minna 1877-? [HPPN]
American brothel proprietress
* Everleigh, Minna

Lester the Molester
See Conner, Lester

Lester-Rands, A.
See Judd, Frederick Charles

Lestocq, William
See Wooldridge, Lestocq Boileau

L'Estoilo, Pierre
See Housset, Arsene

L'Estrange, Anna
See Ellerbeck, Rosemary [Anne L'Estrange]

L'Estrange, Charles James 1880?-1947 [BI, LC, SFL]
British author
* Strang, Herbert [joint pseudonym with George Herbert Ely]

L'Estrange, Corinne
See Hartshorne, Henry

L'Estrange, Dick
See Von Strensch, Gunther

Lestrange, Joseph 1775?-? [PI]
Irish poet
* Brass Pen
* J. L'E

L'Estrange, Joseph
See Merimee, Prosper

L'Estrange, [Sir] Roger 1616-1704 [HN, RH, SN]
British journalist
* Old Noll's Fiddler
* Oliver's Fiddler
* Sheva

Lesueur, Daniel
See Lapauze, Jeanne Loiseau

Lesueur, Nicolas 1545-1594 [PA]
Author
* Sudorius

Lesuk, Bill 1946- [SMG]
Canadian-born hockey player
* Lesuk, Tractor

Lesuk, Tractor
See Lesuk, Bill

Lesure, Thomas B[arbour] 1923- [CA]
American author
* Barbour, Thomas L.

Leszlei, Marta
See Dosa, Marta Leszlei

Leszynski, Werner Jacques 1898-1962 [BI]
German-American metallurgist and author
* Schelle, Werner

Let-'em-Go Joe
See Durant, Joseph

Letellier, Francois Michel [Marquis de Louvois] 1641-1691 [SN]
French minister of war
* Protesilaus

Lethaby, John W. 20th c. [WGT]
Author
* J. W. L.

Lethbridge, Rex
See Meyers, Roy [Lethbridge]

Lethington, Secretary
See Maitland, William

Letine
See Gorin, George

Leto, Pomponio
See Vitelleschi, Marchese

Letob, O. H.
See Botelho, Francis Martin

Letoriere, Georges
See Peyronney, Vicomtesse de

Letory, John Bruno 1918- [IBW]
American clergyman and musician
* Sayles, Bartholomew

Letromache, Maeng
See Lee, Franz John Tennyson

Letrusco
See Martini, Virgilio

Lett, William Pittman 1810?-? [PI]
Irish-born journalist and poet
* Ryan, Sweeney

[The] Letter Carrier's Friend
See Cox, Samuel Sullivan

[The] Letter H.
See Halpine, Charles Graham

Lettieri, Al
See Lettieri, Alfredo

Lettieri, Alfredo 1928-1975 [SC]
American actor and screenwriter
* Lettieri, Al

Letts, W. M.
See Verschoyle, Winifred Mabel Letts

Letz, George Montgomery 1916- [FC, ITA, SW]
American actor
* Montgomery, George

Leucadio Doblado, Don
See White, Joseph Blanco

Leucophaeus
See Brown, John

Leumas, William S.
See Scantlan, Samuel William

LeVake, Dorothy Jean 1925- [BEW]
American singer and actress
* Darling, Jean

Levance, Cal
See Waite, Charles

Levane, Andrew 1920- [BB, MEB]
American basketball player
* Levane, Fuzzy

Levane, Fuzzy
See Levane, Andrew

Levary, Tibor
See Tiberiu, Farkas

Levasseur, Marie Claude Josephe 1749-1826 [BBD]
French singer
* Levasseur, Rosalie
* Mlle. Rosalie

Levasseur, Rosalie
See Levasseur, Marie Claude Josephe

Levater, Louis
See Spach, Louis Adolphe

Levee Joe
See Weldon, Will

[The] Leveller in Poetry
See Quarles, Francis

Leven, Benny
See Levin, Benjamin

Levene, Ben 1938- [ART]
British painter
* B. L.

Levene, Israel George 1885-1930
[HPPN]
American football player
* Levene, Izzy

Levene, Izzy
See Levene, Israel George

Levene, Phoebus A. T.
See Levin, Fishel

Levene, Sam
See Levine, Samuel

Levenson, Louis 1896?-1969 [BI]
American author
* Dexter, Charles

Leventhal, Albert Rice 1907-1976 [CA]
American publisher, editor, author
* Rice, Albert

Leventhal, Ronald 1927- [ASC]
American musician and author
* Lee, Ronny

Leventon, Vladimir Ivan 1904-1951
[BDF, OCF, WEF]
Russian-born American producer
* Lewton, Val

Lever, Charles James 1806-1872 [DEA,
DEP, HPPN, NPS, PA, SN]
Irish author
* Gosebett, Paul
* Gosslet, Paul
* [The] Irish Smollett
* Lorrequer, Harry
* O'Dowd, Cornelius
* O'Malley, C.
* [The] Prince of Neck-or-Nothing
  Novelists
* Shirley
* Templeton, Horace
* Tramp, Tilbury

Lever, J. K.
See Lever, John Kenneth

Lever, Jake
See Lever, John Kenneth

Lever, John Kenneth 1949- [DC]
British cricketer
* Lever, J. K.
* Lever, Jake

Leverenz, Tiny
See Leverenz, Walt[er Fred]

Leverenz, Walt[er Fred] 1888-1973 [BE]
American baseball player
* Leverenz, Tiny

Leverett, Dixie
See Leverett, Gorham Vance

Leverett, Gorham Vance 1894-1957
[BE]
American baseball player
* Leverett, Dixie

Leverette, Hod
See Leverette, Horace William

Leverette, Horace William 1889-1958
[BE]
American baseball player
* Leverette, Hod

Leverone, Nathaniel 1884-? [HPPN]
American business pioneer
* [The] Father of Automatic
  Merchandising

Leverson, Ada 1865-1936 [LC]
British author
* Elaine
* [The] Sphinx

Leveson, Henry Astbury 1828-1875
[DEL]
British author
* H. A. L., The Old Shekarry
* [The] Old Shekarry

Leveson-Gower, Granville George
1815-1891 [SN]
British statesman
* Glaucus

**Leveson-Gower, [Sir] Henry Dudley
Gresham** 1873-1954 [EC]
British cricketer
* Leveson-Gower, Shrimp

Leveson-Gower, Shrimp
See Leveson-Gower, [Sir] Henry Dudley
Gresham

Levesque, Leo A. 1905- [NAA]
American poet
* Dion-Levesque, Rosaire

Levesque, Paul 1913- [CCL]
Canadian author
* Lovitt, Will U.

Levesque, Rene 1922-
Canadian politician
* Rene the Red

Levey, Ethel
See Fowler, Ethelia

Levey, Lorne 1870-1933 [HPPN]
American actor
* Haskell, Loney

Levi
See Dowling, Levi H.

Levi, Aristotle
See Schoeb, Erika

Levi ben Gershon [or Gerson]
1288?-1344? [WBD]
French mathematician and philosopher
* Gersonides

Levi, Eliphas
See Constant, Alphonse Louis

Levi, Isaac [FFF]
Musician
* Levy, Jules

Levi, Johanan ben 1st c. [BI]
Hebrew patriot
* John of Giscala

Levi, Peter 1931- [DLE]
British poet
* Tigar, Chad

Levi, Renato 1926- [BI]
Italian boat-builder
* Levi, Sonny

Levi, Sonny
See Levi, Renato

[The] Leviathan
See Walpole, [Sir] Robert [First Earl of
Orford]

[The] Leviathan of Book-Collectors
See Rawlinson, Thomas

[The] Leviathan of Literature
See Johnson, Samuel

Levick, Mrs. Gustavus [FFF]
Entertainer
* Bartling, Ada

Levie, Isaac 1867?-1945 [BEW]
*American theatrical performer and
producer*
* Watson, Billy

Levielle [or Leuvielle?], Gabriel
1883-1925 [CU, F1, FC]
French actor and director
* Linder, Max
* Lonesome Luke

Levien, Ilse 1852-1908 [WBD]
German author
* Frapan-Akunian, Ilse

Levien, Sonya
See Hovey, Sonya Levien

Levin, Benjamin 1903- [BMH]
British comedian and singer
* Bonn, Issy
* Leven, Benny

Levin, David Iulevich 1889- [HPPN]
Russian author
* Dallin, David J.

Levin, Edwina
See Macdonald, Edwina Le Vin

Levin, Fishel 1869-1940 [JL]
Russian-born chemist
* Levene, Phoebus A. T.

Levin, Jane Whitbread 1914- [CA]
American author
* Whitbread, Jane

Levin, Kim 20th c. [CA]
American artist and writer
* Pateman, Kim

Levin, Marcia Obrasky 1918- [CA,
SAT]
American author
* Martin, Jeremy [joint pseudonym with
  Martin P. Levin]
* Martin, Marcia

Levin, Martin P. 20th c. [CA, SAT]
American author
* Martin, Jeremy [joint pseudonym with
  Marcia Obrasky Levin]

Levin, Meyer 18th c.
British opera singer
* Leoni, Meyer
* Lyon, Meyer

Levin, Richard 20th c. [WGT]
Author
* Mand, Cyril [joint pseudonym with George R. Hahn]

Levine, Ben 20th c. [EJS]
American boxer
* [The] Grand Old Man

Levine, Betty K[rasne] 1933- [CA]
American author
* Krasne, Betty

Levine, Diana 20th c. [PW 7-5-85]
Author
* Henstell, Diana

Levine, Dutch
See Levine, John Nathan

Levine, Harry 1899-1965 [HPPN]
American actor
* Dunn, Henry

Levine, Henry 1907- [PMJ, WWJ]
American jazz musician
* Levine, Hot Lips

Levine, Hot Lips
See Levine, Henry

Levine, Hymie 20th c. [HPPN]
American criminal
* Levine, Loud Mouth

Levine, Isaac Don 1892- [NAA]
Russian-born author
* Monitor

Levine, Jack 1905- [HPPN]
American painter
* America's Colorful Expressionist
* City Boy
* Precocious Pencil

Levine, James 1943-
American conductor
* [The] Met's Young Master
* Orpheus in the Gray Shades
* Wunderkind

Levine, John Nathan 1881-? [HPPN]
Polish American football player
* Levine, Dutch

Levine, Joseph 1906?- [HPPN]
American producer
* Levins, Jolly Joe

Levine, Lainie 1940- [CR]
American singer
* Kazan, Lainie

Levine, Lawrence 20th c. [MS]
American musician
* Lee, Larry

Levine, Lillian [Epstein] 1900-1960 [BI]
American poet
* Everts, Lillian

Levine, Lou 1939?- [HPPN]
American marksman and television news director
* Nice Gun, Mr.

Levine, Loud Mouth
See Levine, Hymie

Levine, Mara 1914-1965 [SC]
American actress
* Alexander, Mara

Levine, Philip 1928- [CA]
American poet
* Poe, Edgar

Levine, Pretty
See Levine, Sam

Levine, Red
See Levine, Sam

Levine, Sam 20th c. [BLB, PHM]
American underworld figure
* Levine, Pretty
* Levine, Red

Levine, Samuel 1905- [BEW, EMT]
American actor
* Levene, Sam

Levine, William 1881-? [WW]
Author
* Levinrew, Will

Levinger, Lowell 1946- [RO2]
American musician
* Banana

Levinrew, Will
See Levine, William

Levins, Jolly Joe
See Levine, Joseph

Levinsky, Alexander H. 1910?- [CEI, EJS, FHE]
American hockey player
* Levinsky, Kingfish
* Levinsky, Mein Boy

Levinsky, Battling
See Lebrowitz, Barney

Levinsky, King
See Lebrowitz, Barney

Levinsky, Kingfish
See Levinsky, Alexander H.

Levinsky, Mein Boy
See Levinsky, Alexander H.

Levinsky, Walter 1929- [ASC]
American musician
* Leslie, Walter

Levinson, Bob
See Wells, Robert

Levinson, Charles 1921?- [HPPN]
Canadian author
* Levinson, Chip

Levinson, Chip
See Levinson, Charles

Levinson, Irene
See Zahava, Irene

Levinson, Jerry 1909- [PMJ]
American composer
* Livingston, Jerry

Levinson, Norman 1900-1972 [IPA, WFA]
American fashion designer
* [The] Dean of American Fashion Designers
* Norell, Norman

Levis, Oscal
See Levis, Oscar

Levis, Oscar 20th c. [OBW]
American baseball player
* Levis, Oscal

Levise, William S., Jr. [Billy] 1947- [RO2]
American singer
* Lee, Billy
* Ryder, Mitch

Levison, William H. 1822-1857 [DNA, PA]
American author
* Hannibal, Julius Caesar

Levister, Wendell W. 1926- [IBW]
American-born transport pilot and flight instructor
* [The] Ebon Eagle

Levita, Elijah 1469-1549 [HPPN]
Bavarian scholar
* Ashkenazi, Elijah
* Bachur [or Bahur]
* Tishbi, Elijah

Levitch, Gary 1946- [RO2]
American musician
* Lewis, Gary

Levitch, Joseph 1926- [BDF, FC, HT]
American actor, producer, director
* Lewis, Jerry

Levitin, George 1916- [CA]
Russian-born American author
* Levitine, George

Levitine, George
See Levitin, George

Levitor, Morton
See Sobell, Morton

Levitt, Bunny
See Levitt, Harold

Levitt, Harold 1911?- [BB]
American basketball free-throw expert
* Levitt, Bunny

Levitt, I. M.
See Levitt, Israel Monroe

Levitt, Israel Monroe 1908- [WYA]
American author
* Levitt, I. M.

Levitzka, Sarah 1858?-1953 [BEW]
Russian-born actress
* Adler, Sarah

Levkowitz, Isidore 1881-? [BEW, PMJ]
German-born actor and vaudevillian
* Howard, Eugene

Levkowitz, Wilhelm 1886-1949 [BEW, EMT, PMJ]
German-born vaudevillian
* Howard, Willie

Levon, Fred
See Ayvazian, L. Fred

Levsen, Dutch
See Levsen, Emil Henry

Levsen, Emil Henry 1898-1972 [BE, PB]
American baseball player
* Levsen, Dutch

Levshin, Peter 1737-1812 [WBD]
Russian prelate
* Platon

Levy, Abraham [Abe] 1861?-1920 [HPPN]
American attorney
* [The] Mighty Abe Levy

Levy, Adele [FFF]
Entertainer
* Belgarde, Adele

Levy, Angelina 19th c. [HFN]
Songwriter
* Angelina

Levy, Arthur 1878-1946 [JL]
German philosopher
* Liebert, Arthur

Levy, Benjamin
See Lumley, Benjamin

Levy, Brigid Antonia Brophy 1929- [WGT]
British author
* Brophy, Brigid

Levy, Burton 1912- [BEW, EMT, TR]
American composer
* Lane, Burton

Levy, Butch
See Levy, Leonard

Levy, Charles 1913- [CA]
American author
* Lee, Charles

Levy, Ed[ward Clarence]
See Whitner, Edward Clarence

Levy, Estelle
Actress
* Davies, Gwen

Levy, Frederick 1878?-1938 [F1, F2, FC]
American actor
* Tearle, Conway

Levy, George Morton 20th c. [BBH]
American harness racing pioneer
* [The] Father of Modern Harness Racing

Levy, Henry 1813-1900 [JL]
British composer
* Russell, Henry

Levy, Herbert I. 1900?- [FC, FD]
American director
* Leeds, Herbert I.

Levy, Herta Hess
See Kahn, Herta Hess

Levy, Irish
See Levy, Milton Lambert

Levy, Jacob 1888-1932 [HPPN]
American singer
* LeRoy, Jack

Levy, Jacques Fromental Elie 1799-1862 [WBD]
French composer
* Halevy

Levy, Joseph [Joe] 1897- [HPPN]
American confidence man
* Adler, Jerome
* Cohen, Alex
* Goldsmith, Morris
* Meredith, Crad
* Wolfe, Sam

Levy, Jules
See Levi, Isaac

Levy, Julien 1906?-1981
American art dealer
* [The] Modernist Maestro

Levy, Julius 1831-1914 [WBD]
German poet and author
* Rodenberg, Julius

Levy, Leonard 20th c. [EJS]
American football player and wrestler
* Levy, Butch

Levy, Lorelei
See Schwalberg, Carol[yn Ernestine Stein]

Levy, Louis 1855-1932 [HPPN]
German financier
* Hagen, Louis

Levy, Louis Henry 1883-1960 [BI, EJS]
American football historian
* Baker, Louis Henry

Levy [or Levee?], Marian 1911- [HPPN]
American actress
* [The] Girl on the Moon
* Goddard, Paulette
* Peaches

Levy, Milton 1894-1948 [SC]
American actor and bandleader
* Britton, Milt

Levy, Milton Lambert ?-1958 [EJS]
American football player
* Levy, Irish

Levy, Moe
See Cohen, Harry

Levy, Newman 1888- [WWL]
American author
* Flaccus

Levy, Norma
See Russell, Hanora Mary

Levy, Paul 1889-1932 [FC]
American director
* Bern, Paul

Levy, Phil
See Fox, Phil

Levy, Roland Alexis Manuel 1891-1966 [BBD, JL]
French composer and author
* Roland-Manuel, Alexis

Levy, Samuel 1890-1968 [EMT]
American choreographer and dancer
* Lee, Sammy

Levy, Siegmund 1822-1884 [BBD]
German musician
* Lebert, Siegmund

Levy, Solomon Lazarus 1859-1926 [LL]
British editor and author
* Lee, [Sir] Sidney

Levy, Stephen 1939- [FC]
Canadian actor
* Young, Stephen

Levy, Uriah Phillips 1792-1862 [HPPN]
American naval officer
* [The] Commodore

Levy, Victor Miles, Jr. 1931- [BA]
American television newscaster
* Miles, Vic

Levy, Walter James 1911- [HPPN]
German-American economist
* [The] Dean of Petroleum Analysts
* [The] Dean of Petroleum Consultants

Levya, Fred F. ?-1921 [HPPN]
American actor
* Lyons, Fred

Lew
See Clayton, Cyril James

Lewald, Fanny
See Stahr, Mme. Adolf W. T.

Lewandowski, Herbert 1896- [WGT]
Author
* Van Dovski, Lee

Lewars, Mrs. Harold
Author
* Singmaster, Elsie

Leweck, Gustave Wilhelm 1846-1914 [HPPN]
American actor
* Williams, Gus

Lewes, George Henry 1817-1878 [DEL, HPPN, PA]
British author, critic, historian
* Churchill, Frank
* G. H. L.
* Lawrence, Slingsby
* Vivian

Lewes, Lettie
See Cleveland, Philip Jerome

Lewes, Marian
See Evans, Marian

Lewes, William James
See Fine, David

Lewesdon, John
See Daniell, Albert Scott

Lewin, Arthur [FFF]
Entertainer
* Terriss, William

Lewin, Breezy Bill
See Lewin, William Charles

Lewin, C. L.
See Brister, Richard

Lewin, Dore 1879-1932 [THR]
Polish-born actor
* Mannering, Dore Lewin

Lewin, Ellaline 1871-1971 [EMT]
British actress and singer
* Terriss, Ellaline

Lewin, Kurt Z. 1890-1947 [JL]
German-born psychologist
* [The] Father of Field Theory

Lewin, Leonard C[ase] 1916- [CA]
American writer and editor
* Case, L. L.

Lewin, William Charles 1847-1897
[HPPN]
British actor
* Lewin, Breezy Bill
* Terriss, Number 1 Adelphi
* Terriss, William

Lewine, Ethel [BI]
American author
* Lewis, Ethel G.

Lewing, Anthony Charles 1933- [AW]
British author
* Bannerman, Mark

Lewins, C. A. 20th c. [MBF]
British author
* Rivers, Tex

Lewis, Abby
See Lewis, Camelia Albon

Lewis, Abigail Victoria Harding
1876-1935 [HPPN]
*Sister of American president, Warren
Harding*
* Lewis, Daisy

Lewis, Albert Ehrlich 1908- [BEW]
American educator, critic, director
* Lewis, Allan

Lewis, Alethea [Brereton] 1749-1827
[WGT]
British author
* De Acton, Eugenia
* [A] Person Without A Name

Lewis, Alfred Henry 1858-1914 [EMD]
American editor and author
* Quin, Dan

Lewis, Allan
See Lewis, Albert Ehrlich

Lewis, Alma [FFF]
Entertainer
* Ormsby, Clara

Lewis, Alonzo 1794-1861 [PA]
Author
* [The] Lynn Bard

Lewis, Alvin 1943- [IBW]
American boxer
* Lewis, Blue

Lewis, Angelo John 1839-? [BS, MBF]
British author
* Hoffmann, [Professor] Louis

Lewis, Art 1911-1962 [FB]
American football coach
* Lewis, Pappy

Lewis, Augustin
See Austin, Lewis

Lewis, Ben
See Smolar, Boris

Lewis, Big Ed
See Lewis, Edward

Lewis, Big Jim
See Lewis, James Wilson

Lewis, Big Lewie
See Lewis, David R.

Lewis, Blue
See Lewis, Alvin

Lewis, Bob
See Lubbers, Robert

Lewis, Bubbles
See Lewis, R. S.

Lewis, Buddy
See Lewis, John Kelly

Lewis, Buddy
See Lewis, [William] Morgan

Lewis, Buddy
See Lewis, William Henry [Bill]

Lewis, C. S.
See Lewis, Clive Staples

Lewis, Caleb
See Lewis, Edwin Herbert

Lewis, Camelia Albon 1910- [BEW]
American actress
* Lewis, Abby

Lewis, Caroline [joint pseudonym with
(James) Stafford Ransome and M. H.
Temple]
See Begbie, [Edward] Harold

Lewis, Caroline [joint pseudonym with
(Edward) Harold Begbie and M. H.
Temple]
See Ramsome, [James] Stafford

Lewis, Caroline [joint pseudonym with
James S. Ransome and (Edward) Harold
Begbie]
See Temple, M. H.

Lewis, Carson
See Milton, John R.

Lewis, Catherine
See Robertson, Mrs. Donald

Lewis, Charles 20th c. [EF]
American football player
* Lewis, Mac

Lewis, Charles
See Dixon, Roger

Lewis, Charles
See Rowe, John Gabriel

Lewis, Charles Bertrand 1842-1924
American journalist
* [The] Free Press Man
* Quad, M.

Lewis, Clarence 20th c. [OBW]
American baseball player
* Lewis, Foots

Lewis, Clifford 1912- [AW]
British author
* Berrisford, Judith M. [joint
pseudonym with Judith Mary
(Berrisford) Lewis]

Lewis, Clive Staples 1898-1963 [LC,
SAT, WGT]
British author
* Clerk, N. W.
* Hamilton, Clive
* Lewis, C. S.
* Whilk, Nat

Lewis, Connie
See Wilson, Constance

Lewis, Count Lorenzo
See Lewis, Lorenzo

Lewis, Country
See Lewis, Gaston F.

Lewis, Curigwen
See Jones-Lewis, Curigwen

Lewis, Cyclone Louis
See Lewis, Vach

Lewis, D. B.
See Bixby, Jerome Lewis

Lewis, D. B. Wyndham
See Lewis, Dominic Bevan Wyndham

Lewis, D. D.
See Lewis, Dwight Douglas

Lewis, Daddy
See Lewis, James H.

Lewis, Daisy
See Lewis, Abigail Victoria Harding

Lewis, David 1942- [CA]
British-born author and journalist
* Hodgson, David

Lewis, David John 1869-? [HPPN]
American coal miner and politician
* Little Davey
* [The] Little Giant

Lewis, David R. 1953- [SMG]
Canadian-born hockey player
* Lewis, Big Lewie

Lewis, Dominic Bevan Wyndham
1894-1969 [DLE, LC, TC]
British author and columnist
* Beachcomber [newspaper column
pseudonym, 1919-1924]

Lewis, Dominic Bevan Wyndham (cont.)
* Lewis, D. B. Wyndham
* Shy, Timothy [joint pseudonym with Ronald William Fordham Searle]

Lewis, Don 1934- [IBW]
American jazz musician and political activist
* Lewis, Sports

Lewis, [An]Drew, [Jr.] 1932- [HPPN]
American politician
* [The] Management Troubleshooter

Lewis, Duffy
See Lewis, George Edward

Lewis, Dwight Douglas 1945- [SMG]
American football player
* Lewis, D. D.

Lewis, E. M. 20th c. [CA]
British educator, playwright, author
* Melwood, Mary

Lewis, Ed
See Friedrich, Robert

Lewis, Edward 1909- [EJ, NP]
American jazz musician
* Big D
* Lewis, Big Ed
* Lewis, Rags

Lewis, Edward Morgan 1872-1936 [BE]
Welsh-born American baseball player
* Lewis, Parson

Lewis, Edwin Herbert 1866-1938 [DNA]
American author and educator
* Lewis, Caleb

Lewis, Eleanor Parke Custis 1779?-1852 [HPPN]
Granddaughter of American president, George Washington
* Custis, Nellie

Lewis, Elliott
See Remley, Frank

Lewis, Elmer 1877?-1896 [HPPN]
American outlaw
* [The] Mysterious Kid
* [The] Slaughter Kid

Lewis, Eric
See Tuffley, Fred Eric Lewis

Lewis, Ernest 20th c. [NBB]
American musician
* Country Slim

Lewis, Essington 1881-1961 [HPPN]
Australian industrialist
* [The] Steel Master

Lewis, Estelle Anna Blanche Robinson 1824-1880 [HPPN, PA]
American author, poet, playwright
* [The] Female Petrarch
* Lewis, S. Anna
* Lewis, Sarah Anna
* [The] Rival of Sappho
* Stella

Lewis, Ethel G.
See Lewine, Ethel

Lewis, Ethelreda ?-1946 [DLE1]
South African author
* Baptist, R. Hernekin

Lewis, Fielding
See Byars, William Vincent

Lewis, Foots
See Lewis, Clarence

Lewis, Francine
See Weinstock, Helen

Lewis, Frank 20th c. [LFW]
American gangleader
* Lewis, Jumbo

Lewis, Fred 1944- [BB, BI]
American basketball player
* Lewis, Fritz

Lewis, Fred 20th c. [SA]
American handball player
* Lewis, Steady Freddie

Lewis, Fred
See Till, Fred

Lewis, Fritz
See Lewis, Fred

Lewis, Furry
See Lewis, Walter

Lewis, Gary
See Levitch, Gary

Lewis, Gaston F. 1904- [IBW]
American track and field coach
* Lewis, Country

Lewis, Gentleman
See Lewis, William Thomas

Lewis, George
See Zenon [or Zeno], George Louis Francis

Lewis, [Sir] George Cornewall 1806-1863 [HPPN]
British statesman and man of letters
* Brownius, Johannes, A. M.

Lewis, George Edward 1888-1979 [BE]
American baseball player
* Lewis, Duffy

Lewis, Gilbert Newton 1875-1946 [HPPN]
American educator and chemist
* [The] Founder of the Valence Theory

Lewis, Harriet Newell 1841-1878
American author
* Constellano, Mrs. Illion
* Harrington, Grace D.
* Old Contributor [joint pseudonym with Julius Warren Lewis]

Lewis, Harry
See Besterman, Henry

Lewis, Henry
See Gehrig, [Henry] Lou[is]

Lewis, Henry Clay 1825-1850 [BI, HPPN]
American physician and humorist
* Louisiana Swamp Doctor
* Tensas, Madison

Lewis, Ian
See Bensman, Joseph

Lewis, Ida 1841-1911 [DEP, FFF]
American lighthouse keeper
* [The] Grace Darling of America

Lewis, Ida 1869-1950 [BEW]
Canadian-born actress
* Arthur, Julia

Lewis, J. R.
See Lewis, Roy

Lewis, Jack 20th c. [MBF]
British author and editor
* Hood, Stephen
* Jackson, Lewis
* Lewis, Phylis

Lewis, James H. 1850-1928 [SC]
American actor
* Lewis, Daddy

Lewis, James Hamilton 1866-1939 [HPPN]
American politician
* [The] Beau Brummel of the Senate
* [The] Fashion Plate
* Pink Whiskers

Lewis, James W. 1946?- [TI 10-25-82, TI 11-1-82, TI 12-27-82]
American extortion suspect
* Richardson, Robert

Lewis, James Wilson 1915- [HPPN]
American army officer
* Lewis, Big Jim
* Lewis, Jungle Jim

Lewis, James Window 1934-1981 [HPPN]
American narcotics dealer, racketeer, pimp
* [The] King of the Dope Trade
* Six, Jimmy

Lewis, Janet
See Winters, Janet Lewis

Lewis, Jeffreys
See Mainhall, Mrs. Henry

Lewis, Jennie
See Egnor, Virginia Ruth

Lewis, Jerry
See Levitch, Joseph

Lewis, Jerry Lee 1935- [CME]
American singer and musician
* [The] Killer

Lewis, [Rev.] John 1675-1746 [HPPN]
British clergyman and antiquary
* [A] Minister in the Country

Lewis, John Delaware [PA]
Author
* Smith, John

Lewis, John Frederick 1805-1876 [NPS]
British painter and etcher
* Lewis, Spanish

Lewis, John Kelly 1916- [BE]
American baseball player
* Lewis, Buddy

Lewis, John Llewellyn 1880-1969
[HPPN]
American labor leader
* [The] Grand Old Man of Labor
* [The] Labor Baron

Lewis, John Noel Claude 1912- [IAW]
Welsh-born author
* Venner, J. G.

Lewis, John Woodruff 1835-1919
American author and poet
* Constellano, Juan
* Lewis, Juan

Lewis, Johnny
See Hill, Lester

Lewis, Joseph [OBW]
American baseball player
* Lewis, Sleepy

Lewis, Juan
See Lewis, John Woodruff

Lewis, Judith Mary [Berrisford] 1912-
[AW, IAW, WD]
British author
* Berrisford, Judith M. [joint
  pseudonym with Clifford Lewis]
* Farr, Fiona
* Hope, Amanda

Lewis, Julius Warren 1833-1920 [HBA,
PA, WW]
American author
* Constellano, Illion
* Lewis, Leon
* Old Contributor [joint pseudonym
  with Harriet Newell Lewis]
* Piper, A. G.

Lewis, Jumbo
See Lewis, Frank

Lewis, Jungle Jim
See Lewis, James Wilson

Lewis, Kate
See Cox, Ida

Lewis, Kid
See Mendeloff, Gershon

Lewis, Lange
See Brandt, Jane Lewis

Lewis, LeAnn 1947?- [TI 11-1-82]
American extortion suspect
* Richardson, Nancy

Lewis, Lefty
See Lewis, Wilmarth

Lewis, Leo [CFH]
American-born football player
* [The] Lincoln Locomotive

Lewis, Leo Rich 1865-? [NAA]
American educator and author
* Rich, C. B.

Lewis, Leon
See Lewis, Julius Warren

Lewis, Leonard 20th c. [WFA]
British hairstylist
* Leonard

Lewis, Lesley 1909- [WD]
British author
* Lawrence, Lesley

Lewis, Lorenzo 19th c. [HPPN]
American gambler
* Lewis, Count Lorenzo

Lewis, Lucia Z.
See Anderson, Lucia [Lewis]

Lewis, Lux
See Lewis, Meade Anderson

Lewis, Lydia T. 20th c. [CCL]
Canadian poet
* Lesbia

Lewis, M. G.
See Lewis, Matthew Gregory

Lewis, Mabel 1872-1957 [THR]
British actress
* Terry-Lewis, Mabel

Lewis, Mac
See Lewis, Charles

Lewis, Mack 20th c. [TI 11-29-82]
American boxing trainer
* Mr. Mack

Lewis, Margaret Cameron 1867-? [ALY]
American author
* Cameron, Margaret

Lewis, Mary
See Kidd, Mary

Lewis, Mary Christianna [Milne] 1907-
[CA, CC, EMD]
British author
* Ashe, Mary Ann
* Brand, Christianna
* Jones, Annabel
* Roland, Mary
* Thompson, China

Lewis, Mary Edmonia 1845-1890 [IBW]
American sculptor
* Lewis, Wildfire

Lewis, Mary F. W.
See Bond, Mary Fanning Wickham

Lewis, Matthew Gregory 1775-1818
[DEP, HN, NPS, RH, WGT]
British poet, playwright, author
* Dark Musgrave
* Lewis, M. G.
* Lewis, Monk
* [The] Monk
* [The] Prince of Dandies

Lewis, May
See Goldstone, Aline Lewis

Lewis, Meade Anderson 1905-1964
[HDM, WWJ]
American jazz musician
* [The] Duke of Luxembourg
* Lewis, Lux

Lewis, Mel
See Sokoloff, Melvin

Lewis, Meriwether 1774-1809 [HPPN]
American explorer
* Long Knife
* [The] Sublime Dandy

Lewis, Mervyn
See Frewer, Glyn [M.]

Lewis, Mildred D. 1912- [CA]
American author
* DeWitt, James

Lewis, Monk
See Lewis, Matthew Gregory

Lewis, [William] Morgan 1906-1968
[EMT]
American composer
* Lewis, Buddy

Lewis, Mrs. Sinclair 1894- [HPPN]
American newspaper columnist
* [The] Cassandra of the Columnists
* [The] Contemporary Cassandra
* Thompson, Dorothy

Lewis, Myrtle Ehrlich
See Lewis, Tillie Ehrlich

Lewis, Nina?
See Buck, Marilyn Jean

Lewis, Pappy
See Lewis, Art

Lewis, Parson
See Lewis, Edward Morgan

Lewis, Paul
See Gerson, Noel Bertram

Lewis, Pete
See Crown, Peter J.

Lewis, Phylis
See Lewis, Jack

Lewis, R. Edward
See Wolfe, LeRoy E.

Lewis, R. S. 20th c. [OBW]
American baseball player
* Lewis, Bubbles

Lewis, Rags
See Lewis, Edward

Lewis, Ras
See Christianson, Willard Erastus

Lewis, Robert 1900-1965 [NOJ]
American jazz musician
* Son Fewclothes

Lewis, Roger
See Zarchy, Harry

Lewis, Roy 1933- [AW]
British barrister and author
* Lewis, J. R.
* Springfield, David

Lewis, S. Anna
See Lewis, Estelle Anna Blanche
Robinson

Lewis, Sabby
See Lewis, William Sebastian

Lewis, Sarah Anna
See Lewis, Estelle Anna Blanche
Robinson

Lewis, Shari
See Hurwitz, Shari

Lewis, Sherman 1942- [FB]
American football player
* Lewis, Tank

Lewis, [Harry] Sinclair 1885-1951
[ANT, HPPN]
American author and playwright
* [The] Chronicler of Main Street
* Graham, Tom
* Red

Lewis, Sleepy
See Lewis, Joseph

Lewis, Smiley
See Lemons, Overton Amos

Lewis, Smiling
See Lemons, Overton Amos

Lewis, Spanish
See Lewis, John Frederick

Lewis, Sports
See Lewis, Don

Lewis, Steady Freddie
See Lewis, Fred

Lewis, Stephen 1946?-1981 [BI]
American author
* Sills, Jennifer

Lewis, Strangler
See Friedrich, Robert

Lewis, Stuart 1756?-1818 [NPS]
Scottish poet
* [The] Mendicant Bard

Lewis, Sylvan R.
See Aronson, Virginia

Lewis, Tad
See Friedman, Theodore Leopold

Lewis, Tank
See Lewis, Sherman

Lewis, Ted
See Mendeloff, Gershon

Lewis, Thomas H. 20th c. [WWL]
British editor and poet
* Riot, Pat

Lewis, Tillie Ehrlich 1904- [HPPN]
American business executive
* Lewis, Myrtle Ehrlich

Lewis, Tom 1940- [CA]
American author, poet, editor
* Babcock, Nicolas

Lewis, Tommy
See Watts, Lou[is Thomas]

Lewis, Vach ?-1908 [BLB]
American underworld figure
* Lewis, Cyclone Louis

Lewis, Vance
See Vanzi, Luigi

Lewis, Voltaire
See Ritchie, Edwin

Lewis, W. W. [PA]
Author
* Binnacle

Lewis, Waller 1711-1781 [FFF]
British author and physician
* Cam

Lewis, Walter 1893-1981 [BWW]
American singer
* Lewis, Furry

Lewis, Whitey
See Seidenschmer, Jacob

Lewis, Wildfire
See Lewis, Mary Edmonia

Lewis, William Henry [Bill] 1904- [BE]
American baseball player
* Lewis, Buddy

Lewis, William Sebastian 1914- [WWJ]
American jazz musician
* Lewis, Sabby

Lewis, William Thomas 1748-1811
[DEP, RH, WBD]
British comedian
* Lewis, Gentleman
* [The] Mercutio of Actors

Lewis, William Waller 1860-1915
[BEW]
Spanish-born actor and producer
* Waller, Lewis

Lewis, Wilmarth 1896-
American editor of Walpole letters
* Lewis, Lefty

Lewis, [Percy] Wyndham 1884-1957
[HPPN]
British artist, essayist, author
* [The] Father of Vorticism

Lewiton, Mina
See Simon, Mina Lewiton

Lewittes, Mordecai Henry
See Lewittes, Morton H[enry]

Lewittes, Morton H[enry] 1911- [CA]
American educator and author
* Lewittes, Mordecai Henry

Lewton, Val
See Leventon, Vladimir Ivan

Lewyn, Joey Marion·
Actor
* Mack, Marion

Lexau, Joan M. 20th c. [CA, SAT]
American author
* Nodset, Joan L.

Lexiphanes
See Colman, George

Lexy, Edward
See Little, Edward Gerald

Ley, Arthur Gordon 1921-1968 [ESF,
SFL, WGT]
British author
* Luther, Ray
* Sellings, Arthur

Ley, Brea R.
See McCalment, Maebelle [Brearley]

Ley, Willy 1906-1969 [CA, SAT]
German-born American author
* Willey, Robert

Leybourne, George
See Saunders, Joe

Leyel, Carl F.
See Leijel, Carl F.

Leyhart, Edward
See Edwards, Elwyn Hartley

Leylio
See Andreini, Giovanni Battista

Leynard, Martin
See Berger, Ivan [Bennett]

Leyne, Maurice Richard 1820-1854 [PI]
Irish journalist and poet
* Carrick-on-Suir, L.?
* M. R. L.
* Zozimus

Leypoldt, Frederick 1837?-1884 [FFF,
HPPN]
*German-born American publisher and
bibliographer*
* [The] Father of the Library Journal
* Pylodet, L.

Leys, Simon
See Ryckmans, Pierre

Leyva, Fred F. ?-1921 [SC]
Actor
* Lyons, Fred

Leyva, Ricardo
See Valdes, Nelson P.

Leywood, A. E. 1884-1970 [HPPN]
American animator
* Leywood, Bert

Leywood, Bert
See Leywood, A. E.

Lezama, Jose
See Lima, Jose Lezama

L'Hermite, Francois 1601-1655 [WBD]
French poet, playwright, author
* L'Hermite, Tristan

L'Hermite, Tristan
See L'Hermite, Francois

Li Chin-yang 1917- [WOA]
Chinese-American author and journalist
* Lee, C. Y.

Li Erh 5th c. BC [HPPN, WBD]
Chinese philosopher
* [The] Father of Taoism
* Lao-tzu [or Lao-tse]

Li Fei-kan 1904- [CA, CLC]
Chinese author
* Pa Chin

Li Hung-chang 1823-1901 [DEP, DHA, DNNS]
Chinese statesman
* [The] Bismarck of Asia

Li Lorenzo, Maurizio 1933?-1979
Italian actor and faith healer
* Arena, Maurizio

Li, Shu-T'ien 1900- [IAW]
Chinese-born engineer and writer
* Lee, John
* Lee, Keng-Yen

Li Ssu-Kuang 1889?- [HPPN]
Chinese geologist and educator
* Lee, J. S.

Li Yuan 565-635 [WBD]
Chinese emperor
* Kao Tsu

Lia
See Felix, Adelaide

Liancourt, Raoul de
See Wingenbach, Charles Edward

Liang, [Father]
See Angelini-Larghetti, Ambrose

Liao Cheng-Chih 1908- [HPPN]
Chinese Communist politician and publicist
* Ho Liu-hua

Liao Chung-K'Al, [Madame] 1880?-?
[HPPN]
Chinese painter, poet, revoultionary leader
* Ho Hsiang-ning

[The] Liar
See Aswad, al-

[The] Liar
See Moseilma

Libb, Richard 1890-1935 [SC]
Canadian-born actor
* Travers, Richard C.

Libbey, Pauline 1885-1938 [BEW]
American actress
* Frederick, Pauline

Libby, Wild Bill
See Libby, Willard Frank

Libby, Willard Frank 1908-1980
[HPPN]
American nuclear chemist
* [The] Father of Radiocarbon Dating
* Libby, Wild Bill

Liberace
See Liberace, Wladziu Valentino

Liberace, George J. 1911- [HPPN]
American jazz musician
* Brother George

[The] Liberace of London
See Atwell, Winifred

[The] Liberace of the Accordion
See Welk, Lawrence LeRoy

Liberace, Wladziu Valentino 1919-
[BMH, BP, FC, ITA]
American pianist
* Busterkeys, Walter
* Liberace
* [The] Rhinestone Rubinstein

[The] Liberal Conscience of Washington
See Lauchheimer, Alan

[The] Liberal Philosopher of the Middle West
See White, William Allen

[The] Liberal Politician
See Perkins, Frances

[The] Liberator
See Bolivar, Simon

[The] Liberator
See MacGahan, Januarius Aloysius

[The] Liberator
See O'Connell, Daniel

[The] Liberator of Africa
See Philip, John

[The] Liberator of Chile
See O'Higgins, Bernardo

[The] Liberator of Genoa
See Doria, Andrea

[The] Liberator of Haiti
See Toussaint L'Ouverture, Pierre Dominique

[The] Liberator of His People
See Arango, Doroteo

[The] Liberator of Italy
See Garibaldi, Giuseppe

[The] Liberator of Missouri
See Pillow, Gideon Johnson

Liberator of Rome
See Gabrini, Niccolo

[The] Liberator of the New World
See Franklin, Ben[jamin]

Liberator of the Territory
See Thiers, Louis Adolphe

Liberi, Pietro 1605-1687 [WBD]
Venetian painter
* [Il] Libertino

Liberito, Joe 20th c. [PHM]
American underworld figure
* [The] Baker

Liberius
See Priestley, Joseph

[El] Libertador
See Bolivar, Simon

Libertas
See Ellis, Charles Mayo

Libertas
See Foe, Daniel

Libertas
See Norton, Caroline Elizabeth Sarah

Libertas
See O'Callaghan, Thomas O'Donnell

[Il] Libertino
See Liberi, Pietro

Liberty
See Foe, Daniel

Libitsky, Fat
See Lebitsky, Leonard

Libke, Al[bert Walter] 1918- [BE]
American baseball player
* Libke, Big Al

Libke, Big Al
See Libke, Al[bert Walter]

Libni
See Oates, Titus

Libose, Jean
See Ambroise, Lys

Libra
See Brotherton, Edward

Libra
See Cobden, Richard

[The] Librarian
See Anastasius

[The] Librarian
See Betts, [Rev.] Beverley Robinson

[The] Librarian
See Jones, William Alfred

[The] Librarian
See Pearson, Edmund Lester

[The] Librarian of the Republic of Letters
See Fabricius, John Albert

[The] Library Profession's
See Cheney, Frances Neel

[The] Libyan Sibyl
See Van Wagener, Isabelle

Licavoli, Horseface
See Licavoli, Peter, Sr.

Licavoli, Jack
See Licavoli, James

Licavoli, James 20th c.
American underworld figure
* Licavoli, Jack

Licavoli, Peter, Sr. 20th c.
American underworld figure
* Licavoli, Horseface

Licavoli, Thomas 20th c. [MM]
American underworld figure
* Licavoli, Yonnie

Licavoli, Yonnie
See Licavoli, Thomas

[El] Licenciado Tome de Burguillos
See Vega Carpio, Lope Felix de

Lichenstein, Irving Herbert 1923-
[BEW]
American actor and fencing master
* Colbin, Rod

Lichfield, Richard 16th c. [HPPN]
British poet
* Medico Campo, Don Richardo de

Lichine, David
See Lichtenstein, David

Licht, Hans
See Brandt, Paul

Lichtenberg, Byron 20th c. [TI 12-12-83]
American biomedical engineer and astronaut
* [The] Vampire

Lichtenberg, Elisabeth Jacoba 1913-
[CA]
Dutch-born British author
* Van Someren, Liesje

Lichtenstein, David 1909?-1972 [JL, THR]
Russian-born dancer and choreographer
* Lichine, David

Lichtenstein, George Maurice 1905-
[WEC]
American cartoonist
* Lichty

Lichtenstein, Mortimer Haig 1918-
[BEW]
American actor
* Marshall, Mort

Lichtheim, George 1912-1973 [CA]
German-born historian and author
* Arnold, G. L.

Lichtman, Joseph 1931- [BEW, EMT, TR]
American director and choreographer
* Layton, Joe

Lichtveld, Lodewijk Alphonsus Maria 1906-? [BBD, CW]
Surinamese author, poet, playwright, composer
* Helman, Albert
* Lichtveld, Lou

Lichtveld, Lou
See Lichtveld, Lodewijk Alphonsus Maria

Lichty
See Lichtenstein, George Maurice

[The] Lickety Split Technician
See Haldeman, Harry Robbins

Lickfold, Charles 1846-1909 [BEW]
British-born actor
* Warner, Charles

Lickfold, Henry Bryon 1876-1958
[BEW]
British-born actor
* Warner, Henry Bryon

Licks, H. E.
See Merriman, Mansfield

Lickshingle, Grandfather
See Criswell, Robert W.

Liddell, C. H. [joint pseudonym with Catherine Lucile Moore]
See Kuttner, Henry

Liddell, C. H. [joint pseudonym with Henry Kuttner]
See Moore, Catherine Lucile

Liddell, Dick
See Liddell, James Andrew

Liddell, James Andrew 1847?-1893?
[HPPN]
American outlaw
* Liddell, Dick
* Little, Dick
* Smith, Joe

Liddell, Thomas 1801-? [HPPN]
British printer
* [A] Contributor to the Way Rate
* [A] Parish Waywarden
* [A] Traveller
* [A] Triggite

Liddell Hart, B. H.
See Liddell Hart, [Sir] Basil Henry

Liddell Hart, [Sir] Basil Henry
1895-1970 [LC]
British journalist, lecturer, military advisor
* Liddell Hart, B. H.

Liddington, Liddie
See Liddington, Robert Allen

Liddington, Robert Allen 1948- [SMG]
Canadian-born hockey player
* Liddington, Liddie

Liddle, Christina Catherine Fraser Tytler 19th c. [NPS]
Author
* Tytler, C. C. Fraser

Liddy, Eleanor Jane 1870-1948 [BEW, BMH, THR]
Scottish-born actress, singer, dancer
* [The] Essence of Eccentricity
* [La] Petite Nellie
* Wallace, Nellie

Liddy, James [Daniel Reeves] 1934-
[CA, DLE]
Irish author and poet
* Lynch, Brian
* O'Connor, Liam
* Reeves, Daniel

Lidin, Vladimir
See Gomberg, Vladimir Germanovich

Lieb, Dick
See Lieb, Ziskind

Lieb, John William 1860-1929 [HPPN]
American electrician and inventor
* Apostle of Light and Power
* [The] Father of the Electric Light in Europe

Lieb, Michael 1844-1900 [FFF, WBD]
Hungarian painter
* Munkacszy, Mihaly von

Lieb, Yehudah
See Ben Asher, Judah Loeb

Lieb, Ziskind 1930- [ASC]
American musician
* Lieb, Dick

Liebeler, Jean [Mayer] 20th c. [WW]
Author
* Mather, Virginia

Lieber, Charles Edwin 1909-1961 [BE]
American baseball player
* Lieber, Dutch

Lieber, Dutch
See Lieber, Charles Edwin

Lieber, Francis 1800-1872 [FFF, HPPN, PA]
German-born historian and author
* Americus
* [The] Father of Political Science

Lieber, Stanley Martin 1922- [CA]
American author, editor, publisher
* Lee, Stan

Lieber [or Liebler], Thomas 1524-1583
[DHA, WBD]
German-Swiss theologian, physician, philosopher
* Erastus, Thomas

Lieberman, M. I. 20th c. [CSH]
Canadian football player
* Lieberman, Moe

Lieberman, Moe
See Lieberman, M. I.

Lieberman, Morris 1912?- [HPPN]
American salesman and gate crasher
* Morris the Crasher

Lieberman, Mortimer 1905?-1963 [BEW]
American columnist
* Mortimer, Lee

Liebermann, David 1887-1971 [FC]
American actor
* Mann, Hank

Liebert, Arthur
See Levy, Arthur

Liebhard, Joachim 1500-1574 [HPPN]
German scholar
* Camerarius, Joachim

Liebhardt, Glenn Ignatius 1910- [BE]
American baseball player
* Liebhardt, Sandy

Liebhardt, Sandy
See Liebhardt, Glenn Ignatius

Liebling, A. J.
See Liebling, Abbott Joseph

Liebling, Abbott Joseph 1904-1963 [LC, TC1]
American journalist
* Liebling, A. J.

Liebmann, Yisrol Paul Mann 1915- [BEW]
Canadian-born actor, director, educator
* Mann, Paul

Liebowicz, Jankiew 1726-1791 [HPPN]
Polish theologian and mystic
* Frank, Jacob

Liebowitz, Sidney 1935- [BEW, EMT]
American singer
* Lawrence, Steve

Liebstadter, Anschel B. 1879-1955 [HPPN]
American producer
* Seymoure, Schnitz

Liebstein, Jacov 1898- [JL]
Lithuanian-born American political activist
* Lovestone, Jay

Lief, N. H.
See Bayes, Ronald H[omer]

Lieknis, Edvarts 1883-1940 [EWL]
Latvian poet
* Virza, Edvarts

Lieksman, Anders
See Haavikko, Paavo Juhani

Lien, Chi
See Wong, Elizabeth

Lien, Edirb Cam
See McBride, Neil

Lieven, Albert
See Lieven-Lieven, Albert Fritz

Lieven, Dariya Khristoforovna 1784-1857 [WBD]
Latvian-born society leader
* [The] Sibyl of Europe

Lieven, Prince
See Domela, Harry

Lieven-Lieven, Albert Fritz 1906- [THR]
German-born actor
* Lieven, Albert

Lievin, Dorothea 1784-1857 [HPPN]
Russian politician
* [The] Egeria of Guizot

Life, John
See Chadwick, Charles

Liggett, Charles 1865-1920 [HPPN]
American entertainer
* Wayne, Charles

Liggett, Genevieve Gauntier 1885-1966 [CU, NAA]
American author and actress
* Gauntier, Gene
* [The] Kalem Girl

Liggett, Hunter
See Paine, Lauran [Bosworth]

Liggins, Ethel 1886- [BBD]
British pianist
* Leginska, Ethel

Liggins, Joe 1915- [PMJ]
American singer and bandleader
* [The] Honeydripper

Light, Ben 1894-1965 [HPPN]
American jazz musician
* Lightning Fingers

Light Bulb Johnson
See Johnson, Lyndon Baines

Light Cast
See Roberts, [Sir] Randal H.

Light, Daisy Mae 1883-1965 [SC]
American actress
* Harte, Betty

Light, Golden
See Hicks, William Watkin

Light Horse Harry
See Lee, Henry

Light Horse Harry Cooper
See Cooper, Harry E.

Light Horse Harry Wilson
See Wilson, Harry E.

Light, Maude Ellen 1881-1934 [BEW]
American actress
* Illington, Margaret

[The] Light of the Age
See Maimonides [or Moses ben Maimon]

[The] Light of the Exile
See Gershom

[The] Light of the Town
See Oates, Titus

[The] Light of the West
See Maimonides [or Moses ben Maimon]

[The] Light of the Western Churches
See Hooker, Thomas

[The] Light of the World
See Jesus Christ

[The] Light of the World
See Sigismund

Light, Paul
See Kahn, Howard

Light Speed Stone
See Stone, Jeffery

Light, Walter Herrod 1888- [MBF, WWL]
British author and editor
* Herrod, Walter
* Willson, Wingrove

Lightfoot
See Adams, John Isaac Ira

Lightfoot, Alexander 1924-1971 [BWW]
American singer
* Lightfoot, George
* Lightfoot, Papa

Lightfoot, Alexander (cont.)
* Little Papa Walter
* Papa George

Lightfoot, Captain
See Martin, Michael

Lightfoot, George
See Lightfoot, Alexander

Lightfoot, Hannah 18th c. [DEP, DHA, DNNS]
Wife of King George III of England
* [The] Fair Quakeress

Lightfoot, Papa
See Lightfoot, Alexander

Lighthall, William Douw 1857-1954 [BI, CCL]
Canadian author
* Chateauclair, Wilfrid

Lightner, A. M.
See Hopf, Alice L[ightner]

Lightner, Winnie
See Hanson, Winifred

Lightnin'
See Gosden, Freeman Fisher

Lightnin'
See Mitchell, Doris

Lightnin' Joe Collins
See Collins, Joseph Lawton

Lightnin' Jr.
See Dupree, William Thomas

Lightnin' Jr.
See Williams, L. C.

Lightnin' Slim
See Hicks, Otis V.

Lightning
See Ellsworth, George A.

Lightning
See Hamilcar

Lightning [Secret Service code name]
See Humphrey, Hubert Horatio

[The] Lightning
See Stephen II

Lightning Destroyer
See Foreman, George

Lightning Fingers
See Light, Ben

Lightning Hutch Hutchinson
See Hutchinson, Charles

[The] Lightning Pilot
See Bixby, Horace Ezra

Lightning Rod Junior
See Bache, Benjamin Franklin

[The] Lightning Story-Writer
See Crawford, Francis Marion

Lightstone, Pauline 1882- [BBD]
Canadian opera singer
* Donalda, Pauline

Lignac, Xavier de 1912?- [BI]
French journalist
* Chauveau, Jean

Ligne, Charles Joseph 1735-1814
[DNNF, FFF, SN]
Austrian army officer
* [The] Prince of Coxcombs

Lignon, Etienne Frederic 1779-1833
[SN]
French engraver
* [The] Prince of Portrait Engravers

Ligon, Jim 20th c. [IBW]
American basketball player
* [The] Great Goose

Ligonier
See Burleigh, William Henry

Ligonier, Jean Louis
See Ligonier, John

Ligonier, John 1680-1770 [HPPN]
British military officer
* Ligonier, Jean Louis

Ligouri, Alphonsus 1696-1787 [HPPN]
Saint
* Alphonsus

Liguest, Pierre Laclede 1724?-1778
[WBD]
*French-born fur trader and pioneer in
America*
* Laclede, Pierre

Liguquka, Iphiva Elilala
See Mazibuko, Mandla Thomas

[The] Ligurian Sage
See Persius Flaccus, Aulus

Liholiho, A. 19th c. [HFN]
Author
* [A] Haole

Liholiho, Alexander 1834-1863
King of the Hawaiian Islands
* Kamehameha IV

Liholiho, Kalaninui 1797-1824
King of the Hawaiian Islands
* Kamehameha II

Lijn, Liliane
See Segall, Liliane

Like, Jim   [GW]
American rodeo performer
* Like, Powder Horn

Like, Powder Horn
See Like, Jim

Lil
See Ormsby, Waterman L., Jr.

Li'l Abner
See Erickson, Paul Walford

Lil Abner
See Hagan, Cliff

Li'l Jackie Paterson
See Paterson, Jackie

Li'l Lou Kaplan
See Kaplan, Louis

Li'l Papa Moliere
See Moliere, Frank

Lil Son Jackson
See Jackson, Melvin

Lil Ty Barkley
See Barkley, Tyrone

Lilburne
See Ralph, James

Lilburne, John 1613-1657 [DNNS, FFF,
HPPN, NPS, RH, SN]
British political agitator
* [The] Champion of Individual
  Freedom
* Freeborn John
* [The] Haberdasher
* [The] Hero of the Age
* Sturdy John

Liles, Elvin 20th c. [EF]
American football player
* Liles, Sonny

Liles, Sonny
See Liles, Elvin

Liletts [or Liletta], Marta Maria 1897-
[F1, F2, FC]
German actress
* Daghofer, Lillitts
* Dagover, Lil

Liliencron, Friedrich [Axel Adolf]
1844-1909 [EWL]
German poet and author
* Von L., Detlev

Lilienthal, David E. 20th c.
American author
* Ely, David

Lilina, Maria Petrovna
See Perevozchikova, Maria Petrovna

Liljenfors, Bennie Mads Carl 1938-
[IAW]
Swedish author
* Matiason, K. G.
* Wilding, Sten

Lillebakken, J. P. 1879-1967 [EWL]
Norwegian author
* Falkberget, Johan [Petter]

Lilley, Alan William 1959- [DC]
British cricketer
* Lilley, Peanut

Lilley, Arthur Frederick Augustus
1867-1929 [EC]
British cricketer
* Lilley, Dick

Lilley, Dick
See Lilley, Arthur Frederick Augustus

Lilley, John 1876-1910 [HPPN]
American vaudeville performer
* Artois, Jack

Lilley, Peanut
See Lilley, Alan William

Lilley, Peter 20th c. [CC, WW]
Author
* Buckingham, Bruce [joint pseudonym
  with Anthony Stansfeld]
* Chandos, Dane [joint pseudonym with
  N. Stansbury-Millett, later with A.
  Stansfeld]

Lillie, Beatrice [or Bea]
See Munston, Constance Sylvia

Lillie, [Major] Gordon W. 1860-1942
[HPPN]
American frontier scout and showman
* Pawnee Bill
* [The] White Chief of the Pawnees

Lillie, Grasshopper
See Lillie, James J. [Jim]

Lillie, James J. [Jim] 1862-1890 [BE]
American baseball player
* Lillie, Grasshopper

Lillies, Arthur 1858-1932 [THR]
British theatrical manager
* Chudleigh, Arthur

Lillo
See Galante, Carmine

[A] Lillo Among Painters
See Hogarth, William

Lilly, Isabella Purvis 1907- [IAW]
New Zealand author
* Allan, Ann
* Cousin Ann

Lilly, Leon 1884-1960 [THR]
British actor and playwright
* Gordon, Leon

Lilly, Patrick J. 1949-
American police officer
* LaRocca, Pasquale
* LaRocca, Patty

Lilly, Ray
See Curtis, Richard [Alan]

Lilly, Robert Lewis 1939-
American football player
* Lilly, Tiger

Lilly, Tiger
See Lilly, Robert Lewis

Lilly, William 1602-1681 [DEP, DNNS,
FFF, HPPN, SN]
British astrologer
* [The] English Merlin
* Erra Pater ?
* [The] Last Astrologer
* [The] Merlin of England
* Merlinus Anglicus
* Sidrophel
* Zadkiel

Liltin' Martha Tilton
See Tilton, Martha

Lily [code name used during World
War II]
See Carre, Mathilde [Belard]

[The] Lily of the Mohawks
See Tekakwitha, Kateri

Lim, Boon Keng 1869-? [HPPN]
Chinese physician and author
* L. M.
* Wen Ching

Lima, Jose Lezama 1911?-1976 [CA]
Cuban poet, author, editor
* Lezama, Jose

Limac, Nassour el-
See Camille, Roussan

[A] Limb of Shakespeare
See Fletcher, John

Limbach, Cornelius 1889-1965 [SC]
American actor
* Edwards, Neely

[The] Lime and Mortar Knight
See Chambers, [Sir] William

Limeno [From Lima]
See Garate Echenique, Enrique

Limeno [From Lima]
See Garate y Hernandez, Jose

Limentani, Giacoma
See Limentani Cantatore, Giacometta

Limentani Cantatore, Giacometta 1927-
[IAW]
Italian translator
* Limentani, Giacoma

Limet, Stephanie 1933-1966 [HPPN]
American dancer
* Ariel, Stephanie

Limey Stomper
See Washington, George

Liminana, Eva 1899-1953 [SC]
Mexican actress, producer, screenwriter
* Duchess Olga

Limmer, Luke, Esq.
See Leighton, Frederick

Limnelius, George
See Robinson, Lewis George

Limner, Luke
See Leighton, John

Limon, Bazooka
See Limon, Rafael

Limon, Rafael 20th c. [WP 12-12-82]
Boxer
* Limon, Bazooka

[The] Limosin Scholar
See Helisane de Crenne

Lin, Adet J[usu] 1923- [CA]
Chinese-born author
* Tan Yun

Lin, Anor 1926- [CA]
Chinese editor, author, translator
* Lin, Tai-yi
* Lin, Wu-shuang

Lin Cho-Liang
Musician
* Lin, Jimmy

Lin, Frank
See Atherton, Gertrude [Franklin Horn]

Lin, Jimmy
See Lin Cho-Liang

Lin, Po-ch'u
See Lin, Tsu-han

Lin, Richard
See Lin Show Yu

Lin Shao-Yang
See Johnston, [Sir] Reginald Fleming

Lin Show Yu 1933- [CAR]
British artist
* Lin, Richard

Lin, Tai-yi
See Lin, Anor

Lin, Tsu-han 1882-? [BI]
Chinese communist leader
* Lin, Po-ch'u

Lin, Wu-shuang
See Lin, Anor

Lincoln, Abbey
See Woolridge, Anna Marie

Lincoln, Abe
See Pearson, Charles M.

Lincoln, Abraham 1809-1865 [DEP, DF 4-20-83, FAP, HPPN, SN]
American president
* [The] Ancient
* [The] Buffoon
* Caesar
* [The] DeWitt Clinton of Illinois
* [The] Emancipation President
* Father Abraham
* [The] Flatboat Man
* [The] Gorilla from Illinois
* [The] Grand Wrestler
* [The] Great Emancipator
* [The] Great Wrestler
* Honest Abe
* [The] Illinois Baboon
* [The] Jester
* Linkum, Massa
* [The] Little Giant
* [The] Long 'Un
* [The] Man of the People
* [The] Martyr President
* Old Abe
* [The] Rail Splitter
* [The] Sage of Springfield
* [The] Sectional President
* [The] Tycoon
* [The] Tyrant
* Uncle Abe

Lincoln, Arthur
See Haydon, Arthur Lincoln

Lincoln, Charlie
See Hicks, Charlie

Lincoln, E. K.
See Lincoln, Edward Kline

Lincoln, E. R.
See Van Horn, Dale R.

Lincoln, Edward Kline ?-1958 [SC]
American actor
* Lincoln, E. K.

Lincoln, Elmo
See Linkenhelter, Otto Elmo

Lincoln, Geoffrey
See Mortimer, John [Clifford]

Lincoln, George
See Freda, Riccardo

Lincoln, George
See Sample, Omer W.

Lincoln, Howard
See Harbaugh, Thomas Chalmers

Lincoln, Isaac
See Trebitsch, Isaac

Lincoln, Jane Elizabeth [Larcombe]
1829-? [FFF]
American author
* Campbell, Kate

[The] Lincoln Locomotive
See Lewis, Leo

Lincoln, Lucy
See Warren, Ina Russelle

Lincoln, Mary Todd 1818-1882 [DF 3-26-86, HPPN]
Wife of American president, Abraham Lincoln
* [The] She Wolf

Lincoln, Myrtle 1888-1938 [HPPN]
American actress
* Stedman, Myrtle

Lincoln, Nancy 1807-1828
Sister of American president, Abraham Lincoln
* Lincoln, Sarah

Lincoln, Nancy Hanks 1783-1818
[HPPN]
Mother of American president, Abraham Lincoln
* Hanks, Nancy

[The] Lincoln of Labor
See Haywood, William Dudley

Lincoln, Robert O.
See Mason, George Champlin

Lincoln, Robert Todd 1843-1926
American government official and corporate executive
* [The] Prince of the Rails

Lincoln, Sarah
See Lincoln, Nancy

Lincoln, Scott Free
See Lincoln, Warren

Lincoln, Tad
See Lincoln, Thomas

Lincoln, Thomas 1853-1871 [HPPN]
Son of American president, Abraham Lincoln
* Lincoln, Tad

Lincoln, Victoria 1904-1981 [CA]
American author
* Lowe, Victoria Lincoln

Lincoln, Warren ?-1941 [HPPN]
*American attorney, horticulturist,
murderer*
* Lincoln, Scott Free

Lincoln's Commando
See Cushing, [Commander] William
Barker

[A] Lincolnshire Grazier
See Horne, Thomas Hartwell

[The] Lincolnshire Thrasher
See Richardson, Charles

L'Inconnue
See Benson, Janie [Ollivar]

Lind, Abraham 1933- [OP]
American opera singer
* Lind-Oquendo, Abraham

Lind, Gertrude
See Donnelly, Gertrude

Lind, Harry 20th c. [EF]
American football player
* Lind, Mike

Lind, Jack
See Lind, Jackson Hugh

Lind, Jackson Hugh 1946- [BE]
American baseball player
* Lind, Jack

Lind, Jakov
See Landwirth, Heinz

Lind, [Dr.] James 1716-1794 [HPPN]
Scottish physician
* [The] Father of Nautical Medicine

Lind, Jenny
See Lind, Johanna Maria

Lind, Johanna Maria 1820-1887
[DNNF, FFF, HPPN, WBD]
Swedish singer
* Goldschmidt, Madame Otto
* Lind, Jenny
* [The] Swedish Nightingale
* Sweet Warbler

Lind, Joseph Conrad 1915- [BEW]
American actor
* Hayes, Peter Lind

Lind, Letty
See Rudge, Letty

Lind, Mike
See Lind, Harry

Lind, Ragnar Godfrey 1909- [BEW, FC]
American actor
* Lynn, Jeffrey

Lind, Ruby
See Lindsay, Ruby

Lind-Oquendo, Abraham
See Lind, Abraham

Lindamour
See Gildon, Charles

Lindars, Barnabas
See Lindars, Frederick Chevallier

Lindars, Frederick Chevallier 1923-
[WD]
British clergyman and author
* Lindars, Barnabas

Lindbeck, Em
See Lindbeck, Emerit Desmond

Lindbeck, Emerit Desmond 1935- [BE]
American baseball player
* Lindbeck, Em

Lindberg, Armas Emanuel 1884- [BBD]
Finnish musicologist and composer
* Launis, Armas Emanuel

Lindberg, Arthur A. 1887-1938 [HPPN]
American dancer and singer
* Wilson, Whitney

Lindberg, Karl Sivert 1933- [IAW]
Swedish author and poet
* Veits, Ulf

Lindbergh, Charles Augustus 1902-1974
[HPPN]
American aviator
* [The] Ambassador of the Air
* Lindbergh, Slim
* Lindy
* [The] Lone Eagle
* Lucky Lindy

Lindbergh, Charles Augustus, Jr.
1930-1932 [HPPN]
*Son of American aviator, Charles
Lindbergh*
* [The] Little Eaglet

[The] Lindbergh of Russia
See Herman, Victor

[The] Lindbergh of the Sea
See D'Aboville, Gerard

Lindbergh, Richard Franklin
See Speck, Richard Franklin

Lindbergh, Slim
See Lindbergh, Charles Augustus

Lindegger, Albert 1904- [GA]
Swiss graphic artist
* Lindi

Lindell, Jack 20th c.
Circus performer and horse trainer
* Lindell, Swede

Lindell, Mary
See Milleville, Mary Ghita Lindell

Lindell, Swede
See Lindell, Jack

Lindeman, Edith
See Calisch, Edith

Lindeman, Gladys 1895-1929 [HPPN]
American actress
* Brockwell, Gladys

Lindemann, Frederick Alexander 1886-
1957
British physicist
* [The] Prof

Lindemann, Kelvin
Danish author
* Hareng, Alexis

Linden, Erik Hugo Emanuel 1918-
[IAW]
Swedish author and poet
* Lowo, Hans
* Ristare, Bo

Linden, Hal
See Lipshitz, Harold

Linden, Oliver
See Abrahams, Doris Caroline

Linden, Robert
See Jacobson, Robert Navra

Linden, Sara
See Bartlett, Marie [Swan]

Lindenbaum, Edward 20th c. [HPPN]
American restaurateur
* Lindenbaum, Lindy

Lindenbaum, Lindy
See Lindenbaum, Edward

Lindenberg, Hedda 1916- [HPPN]
Romanian artist
* Sterne, Hedda

Lindenthal, Gustav 1850-1935 [HPPN]
Austrian-American engineer
* America's Greatest Bridge Builder

Linder, Max
See Levielle [or Leuvielle?], Gabriel

Linderman, Bill 1920-1965 [GW]
American rodeo performer
* [The] King

Linderman, Bud
See Linderman, Elmer

Linderman, Elmer 20th c. [GW]
American rodeo performer
* Linderman, Bud

Linders, Carl
See Geibel, Adam

Lindfors, Viveca
See Torstensdotter, Elsa Viveca

Lindholm, Anna Chandler 1870-? [WW]
Author
* Fay, Dorothy

Lindi
See Lindegger, Albert

Lindley, Erica
See Quigley, Aileen

Lindley, Louis Bert, Jr. 1919-1983 [FC,
ITA, SW]
American actor and rodeo performer
* Pickens, Slim

Lindner, D. Berry
See DuBreuil, Elizabeth Lorinda

Lindo, Mark Prager 1819-1879 [WBD]
Dutch author
* [De] Oude Heer Smits [Old Mr.
Smits]

Lindon-Travers, Florence 1913- [FC]
British actress
* Travers, Linden

Lindquist, Carl Emil 1919- [BE]
American baseball player
* Lindquist, Lindy

Lindquist, Lindy
See Lindquist, Carl Emil

Linds, Mark Prager [PA]
Author
* Smitts, Mr.

Lindsay
See Johnson, F. R.

Lindsay, Alexander ?-1454 [NPS]
Fourth Earl of Crawford
* Beardie, Earl
* [The] Tiger Earl

Lindsay, Barbara 20th c. [CA]
Author
* James, Josephine [joint pseudonym with Emma Gelders Sterne]

Lindsay, Charles
See Murphy, Charles

Lindsay, Christian H. 1878-1941 [BE]
American baseball player
* Lindsay, Pinky

Lindsay, D'Auvergne Sharon 1904-1963
American actress and songwriter
* Lynn, Sharon E.

Lindsay [or Lyndsay], [Sir] David
1490-1555 [HPPN, WBD]
Scottish poet
* [The] Last of the Makars
* [The] Last of the Scottish Chaucerians
* Lindsay of the Mount

Lindsay, David
See Walls, Ian Gascoigne

Lindsay, Donald 1946?- [HPPN]
American bagpipe player and educator
* [The] Dean of the Bagpipers

Lindsay, Ersatz John
See Lindsay, John Vliet

Lindsay, Frog
See Lindsay, Robert

Lindsay, Harold Arthur 1900- [CA]
Australian author
* Bogaduck
* Carrick, A. B.
* Ex-R.S.M.

Lindsay, Harry
See Hudson, H. Lindsay

Lindsay, Honest John
See Lindsay, John Vliet

Lindsay, Jack 1900- [CA, WD]
Australian historian, author, editor
* Meadows, Peter
* Preston, Richard

Lindsay, John
See Muriel, John Saint Clair

Lindsay, John Vliet 1921- [HPPN]
American politician
* Fairest Dark Horse of Them All
* Golden Boy
* Lindsay, Ersatz John
* Lindsay, Honest John
* Mayor For the Times
* Mayor On the Move
* Odd-Man In
* Ringmaster of Fun City

Lindsay, Josephine
See Story, Rosamond Mary

Lindsay, Kathleen 1903- [AW, WW]
British author
* Cameron, Margaret
* Richmond, Mary

Lindsay, Lord 1812-? [PA]
Author
* Crawford, A. W.

Lindsay, Margaret
See Kies, Margaret

Lindsay, Mark
See Chapman, Mark

Lindsay, [John] Maurice 1918- [CA]
Scottish poet, editor, author
* Brock, Gavin

Lindsay, Mayne
See Clarke, Mrs.

Lindsay of the Mount
See Lindsay [or Lyndsay], [Sir] David

Lindsay, Perry
See Dern, Peggy Gaddis

Lindsay, Pinky
See Lindsay, Christian H.

Lindsay, Robert 20th c. [OBW]
American baseball player
* Lindsay, Frog

Lindsay, Robert Blake Theodore [Ted]
1925- [CEI, FHE, HK]
Canadian-born hockey player and executive
* Lindsay, Scarface
* Lindsay, Terrible Ted

Lindsay, Robert James 1832-1901
[WBD]
British army officer
* Loyd-Lindsay, Robert James
* Wantage, Baron

Lindsay, Ruby 1887-1919 [DBA]
British painter and illustrator
* Lind, Ruby

Lindsay, Sadi ?-1969 [SC]
French-born actress and writer
* Leduc, Claudine

Lindsay, Scarface
See Lindsay, Robert Blake Theodore
[Ted]

Lindsay, Terrible Ted
See Lindsay, Robert Blake Theodore
[Ted]

Lindsay, Vera
See Poliakoff, Vera

Lindsay, William Schaw 1816-1877
[HPPN]
Scottish merchant and shipowner
* [A] Sailor

Lindsay-Thomson, Beatrix 1900- [THR]
British actress
* Thomson, Beatrix

Lindsey, Ben[jamin Barr] 1869-1943
[HPPN]
American jurist
* [The] Father of the Juvenile Court

Lindsey, Joseph 1899-? [NOJ]
American jazz musician
* Lindsey, Little Joe
* Lindsey, Seefus

Lindsey, Little Joe
See Lindsey, Joseph

Lindsey, Seefus
See Lindsey, Joseph

Lindsley, Mary F[lora] 20th c. [CA]
American educator and author
* Jaffee, Mary L.

Lindstroem, Kirsten
See Fischer, Marie Louise

Lindstrom, Alf
See Lundholm, Anja

Lindstrom, Frederick Charles 1905-1981
[BE, DGS]
American baseball player
* Lindstrom, Lindy

Lindstrom, Lindy
See Lindstrom, Frederick Charles

Lindstrom, Willy 1951- [SMG]
Swedish-born hockey player
* Willy the Wisp

Lindt, Gillian 1932- [CA]
British-born American sociologist and author
* Gollin, Gillian Lindt

Lindy
See Lindbergh, Charles Augustus

Line, Francis 1595-1675 [BI]
British clergyman and scientist
* Hall, Francis

Linebarger, Paul M[yron] A[nthony]
1913-1966 [CA, ESF, SF]
American author
* Bearden, Anthony
* Forest, Felix C.
* Smith, Carmichael
* Smith, Cordwainer

Linebarger, Paul Myron Wentworth
1871-? [NAA]
American author
* Myron, Paul

Linecar, Arthur 20th c. [WWL]
British author
* Grim, Anthony

Linedecker, Clifford L. 1931- [CA]
American author
* Clifton, Lewis

Lineham, Richard 20th c. [BBH]
Boxer
* [The] Lion

Linesman
See Grant, Maurice Harold

Linfield, Mary Barrow 1891- [NAA]
American author
* Highland, Lawrence

Linfield, Sam
See Clifton, Sam

Ling, James Joseph 1922- [HPPN]
American manufacturer
* [The] Texas Titan

Lingard, Dickey
See Dunning, Harriet Sarah

Lingard, Mrs. William [FFF]
Entertainer
* Dunning, Alice

Lingard, Nellie
See Burbeck, Mrs. F. M.

Lingeman, Richard R[oberts] 1931-
[CA]
American author
* Chignon, Niles
* Hirsch, William Randolph [joint
  pseudonym with Marvin Kitman and
  Victor S. Navasky]

Lingenfelter, Charles David 1887-1934
[SC]
American actor
* Percival, Walter C.

[The] Lingerer
See Fabius Maximus Verrucosus,
Quintus

Lingerlong, Reuben
See Carpenter, James M.

Lingle, Alfred 1892?-1930 [HPPN]
*American police reporter and murder
victim*
* Lingle, Jake

Lingle, Jake
See Lingle, Alfred

Lingley, Big Bill
See Lingley, William

Lingley, William ?-1915 [BLB]
American murderer and gangster
* Lingley, Big Bill

Linhart, Anton Hansjorg 1942- [SMG]
Austrian-born football player
* Linhart, Toni

Linhart, Toni
See Linhart, Anton Hansjorg

Linington, Elizabeth 1921- [AW, CA,
CC]
American author
* Blaisdell, Anne
* Egan, Lesley

Linington, Elizabeth (cont.)
* O'Neill, Egan
* Shannon, Dell

Linke, Babe
See Linke, Ed[ward Karl]

Linke, Ed[ward Karl] 1911- [BN]
American baseball player
* Linke, Babe

Linke, Fred[erick L.] 20th c. [BE]
American baseball player
* Linke, Laddie

Linke, Laddie
See Linke, Fred[erick L.]

Linke Poot
See Doeblin, Alfred

Linkenhelter, Otto Elmo 1889-1952
[BEW, F1, FC]
American actor
* Lincoln, Elmo

Linkensale
See Ingersoll, L. D.

Linkinwater, Tim
See Waldo, James Curtis

Linklater, J. Lane
See Watkins, Alex

Linkletter, Art
See Kelley, Arthur Gordon

Linkum, Massa
See Lincoln, Abraham

Linley, Elizabeth Ann 1754-1792
[DNNF, RH, SN]
British singer
* [The] Maid of Bath

Linley, Julian
See Pearson, Alec George

Linley, Mark
See Samways, George Richmond

Linn, Alexander P. 1885?-1960 [BI]
American clergyman and philosopher
* Alphonsus Fidelis, [Brother]

Linn, Bambi
See Linnemier, Bambina Aennchen

Linn, Buck
See Linn, Charlie

Linn, Bud
See Linn, Grafton E.

Linn, Charlie 19th c. [BLB]
American gunfighter
* Linn, Buck

Linn, Grafton E. 1909-1968 [SC]
American actor and singer
* Linn, Bud

Linnaeus
See Davis, Emerson

Linnaeus, Carl
See Linne, Carl von

Linnaeus, Carolus
See Linne, Carl von

[The] Linnaeus of Hogarth
See Ireland, John

Linnankoski, Johannes
See Peltonen, Vihtori

Linne, Carl von 1707-1778 [HPPN]
Swedish botanist
* [The] Beloved Botanist
* [The] Father of Modern Systematic
  Botany
* Linnaeus, Carl
* Linnaeus, Carolus

Linnemier, Bambina Aennchen 1926-
[BEW]
American actress and dancer
* Linn, Bambi

Linnit, Bill
See Linnit, Sidney

Linnit, Sidney 1898-1956 [HPPN]
American executive
* Linnit, Bill

Lino
See Martinez, Lino

Linois, Georges
See Batz-Trenqueleon, Charles de

Linseman, Ken 1958-
Canadian-born hockey player
* [The] Rat

Linskill, Doris Joy 1908- [IAW]
British author and playwright
* Trevor, Joy

Linskill, Mary 1840-1891 [NPS]
Author
* Yorke, Stephen

Linsley, Ladd. E.
See Sellers, Connie Leslie, Jr.

Lintner, Grace
See Ingraham, Ellen M.

Linton, A. H.
See Hopkins, Alphonso A.

Linton, Barbara Leslie 1945- [CA]
American author
* Austin, Barbara Leslie

Linton, Bob
See Linton, Claud C.

Linton, Claud C. 1902- [BE]
American baseball player
* Linton, Bob

Linton, John James Edmonstoune
1804-1869 [CCL]
Canadian author
* [A] Settler, at Stratford

Linton, Mabel 1905- [F2, ITA]
American actress
* Morley, Karen

Linton, Phyllis Margaret 1929- [SWI]
British swimmer
* Linton, Pip

Linton, Pip
See Linton, Phyllis Margaret

Linton, William James 1812-? [PA]
Author
* Spartacus

Linus ?-76 [HN]
Pope
* [The] Great Light [Llever Mawr]

Linval, Paule Cassius de 1890-1970
[CW]
West Indian author
* Marx, Jean

Linwood, Lottie
See Cooke, Helen M.

Linwood, Lucy-Anne
See Ellwood, Gracia-Fay

Linz, Amelie Speyer 1824-? [HPPN]
German author
* Godin, Amelie

Linz, Philip Francis 1939- [BE]
American baseball player
* Linz, Supersub

Linz, Supersub
See Linz, Philip Francis

[The] Lion
See Damelowicz

[The] Lion
See Doenitz, Karl

[The] Lion
See Henry

[The] Lion
See James II

[The] Lion
See Lineham, Richard

[The] Lion
See Louis VIII

[The] Lion
See Nomelleni, Leo

[The] Lion
See Otto I [or Otho]

[The] Lion
See Smith, William Henry Joseph
Berthol Bonaparte Bertholoff

[The] Lion
See Thompson, William

[The] Lion
See William

[The] Lion Hearted
See Richard I

Lion Hearted Thomas
See Thomas, George Henry

[The] Lion Hunter
See Cumming, Roualeyn George
Gordon

[The] Lion Hunter
See Tinkham, George Holden

[The] Lion Killer
See Gerard, Jules

[The] Lion King of Assyria
See Arioch al Asser

[The] Lion Man
See Debranski, Stephen

[The] Lion of Defence
See Model, Walther

[The] Lion of God
See Ali

[The] Lion of God and His Prophet
See Hamza

[The] Lion of Janina
See Ali

[The] Lion of Judah
See Makonnen, Ras Tafari

[The] Lion of Justice
See Henry I

[The] Lion of Kashmir
See Abdullah, Mohammad

[The] Lion of Kent
See Mynn, Alfred

[The] Lion of Munster
See Galen, Graf Clemens von

[The] Lion of Paris
See Paderewski, Ignace Jan

[The] Lion of Pisa
See Titta, Ruffo Cafiero

[The] Lion of Swaziland
See Sobhuza II

[The] Lion of Sweden
See Baner [Banier or Banner], Johan

[The] Lion of the Caribbean
See Bustamante, [Sir] William
Alexander

[The] Lion of the Fold of Judah
See MacHale, John

[The] Lion of the Lyceum
See Price, Joseph Charles

[The] Lion of the North
See Gustavus II

[The] Lion of the North
See Parr, George

[The] Lion of the Punjab
See Ranjit [or Runjeet], Singh

[The] Lion of the Senate
See Borah, William Edgar

[The] Lion of the South
See Hindman, Thomas Carmichael

[The] Lion of the Vigilantes
See Coleman, William Tell

[The] Lion of Panjshir
See Massoud, Ahmad Shah

[Le] Lion Rouge
See Ney, Michel [Duc d'Elchingen]

[The] Lion Tamer
See Goulding, Edmund

Lion, Yehudah
See Ben Asher, Judah Loeb

[The] Lion-Killer
See Gerard, Cecile Jules Basile

Lionel
See Debranski, Stephen

Lionel, Robert
See Fanthorpe, R[obert] Lionel

[The] Lioness
See Elizabeth I

[La] Lionne
See Paulet, Mlle.

Liotta, Leonardo 1932- [BX, RBE, WBC]
American boxer
* [The] Boston Bomber
* Demarco, Tony

[The] Lip
See Durocher, Leo Ernest

[The] Lip
See Schmidt, Helmut

Lipchitz, Chaim Jacob 1891-1973 [CAR]
French sculptor
* Lipchitz, Jacques

Lipchitz, Jacques
See Lipchitz, Chaim Jacob

Lipkind, William 1904-1974 [SAT, TCC]
American author
* Will

Lipon, John Joseph 1922- [BE, PB]
American baseball player and manager
* Lipon, Skids

Lipon, Skids
See Lipon, John Joseph

Lipp, Helen Louise 1917- [BEW, TR]
American singer and actress
* Bliss, Helena

Lipp, Joseph Julius
See Lipski, Joseph Julius

Lippard, George 1822-1854 [HPPN, PA]
American author
* Darppil
* Our Talisman

Lipper, Bette 1922?-1954 [BEW]
Actress
* Grayson, Bette

Lippert, Clarissa Start 1917- [CA]
American author
* Davidson, Clarissa Start
* Start, Clarissa

Lippert, Thomas Ray 1950?- [HPPN]
American kidnaper
* [The] Love Kidnaper

Lippi, [Fra] Filippo 1406?-1469 [HPPN, WBD]
Florentine painter
* Filippo del Carmine
* Lippi, Lippo

Lippi, Lippo
See Lippi, [Fra] Filippo

Lippi, Lorenzo 1606-1664 [WBD]
Florentine poet and painter
* Zipoli, Perlone

Lippincott, Martha Shepard ?-1949
[HPPN]
American poet
* [The] Quaker Poetess

Lippincott, Sara
See Richards, Sara Lippincott

Lippincott, Sara Jane [Clarke]
1825?-1904 [DEL, DNNF, FFF]
American journalist
* Greenwood, Grace

Lippmann, Walter 1889- [HPPN]
American author, journalist, columnist
* [The] Dean of American
 Newspapermen

[Il] Lippo [The Blear Eyed]
See Brandolini, Aurelius

Lipschitz, [Rabbi] Chaim U. 1912-
[AW]
Israeli-born author and clergyman
* Yerushalmi, Chaim

Lipschitz, Israel 1903- [BI]
South African sculptor
* Lipschitz, Lippy

Lipschitz, Lippy
See Lipschitz, Israel

Lipscomb, Andrew Adgate 1816-1890
[HPPN]
American clergyman
* [The] Boy Preacher

Lipscomb, Big Daddy
See Lipscomb, [Eu]gene

Lipscomb, Dickey 1941- [ECM]
American singer and songwriter
* Lee, Dickey

Lipscomb, [Commander] F. W.
See Lipscomb, Frank Woodgate

Lipscomb, Frank Woodgate 1903- [CA]
British naval officer and author
* Lipscomb, [Commander] F. W.

Lipscomb, [Eu]gene 1931-1963 [AS, FB]
American football player
* Lipscomb, Big Daddy

Lipscomb, Gerard 1911- [BE]
American baseball player
* Lipscomb, Nig

Lipscomb, Nig
See Lipscomb, Gerard

Lipsett, Marianne 20th c. [THR]
British actress
* Caldwell, Marianne

Lipshitz, Harold 1931- [BEW, EMT, TR]
American actor and singer
* Linden, Hal

Lipsian Dicke
See Harvey, Richard

Lipsitz, Dean 1919- [CA]
American author
* Lipton, Dean

Lipsius, Marie 1837-1927 [BBD, WBD]
German author
* [La] Mara

Lipski, Joseph Julius 1889-1958 [EJS]
American football official
* Lipp, Joseph Julius

Lipson, Fredda 1926- [JL, RO1]
American singer
* Gibbons, Fredda
* Gibbs, Georgia
* Gibson, Fredda [or Freddie]
* Her Nibs

Lipson, Gertrude 20th c. [DLE]
British author
* Charles, Gerda

Lipton, Dean
See Lipsitz, Dean

Lipton, Robert 20th c. [SFL]
Author
* Sterling, Barry

Lipton, Thomas
British merchant and yachtsman
* Tea, Sir

[The] Liquor Czar
See Morgan, William Forbes

Liquori, Marty 20th c. [CR]
American track and field athlete
* [The] Hustler

Liranzo, Pedro Rafael 1953- [SMG]
Dominican-born baseball player
* Liranzo, Raf

Liranzo, Raf
See Liranzo, Pedro Rafael

Lisboa, Antonio Francisco 1730-1814
[IBW]
Brazilian architect and sculptor
* [The] Little Cripple

Lisbona, Edward 1915- [ASC]
*British-born American composer and
pianist*
* Miller, Eddie
* Miller, Piano

Lisciotti, Larry 20th c.
American billiard player
* Lisciotti, Oil Can

Lisciotti, Oil Can
See Lisciotti, Larry

Liscombe, Carl
See Liscombe, Harry Carlyle

Liscombe, Harry Carlyle 1915- [CEI,
FHE, HK]
Canadian-born hockey player
* Liscombe, Carl

Lisenbee, Hod
See Lisenbee, Horace Milton

Lisenbee, Horace Milton 1898- [BE]
American baseball player
* Lisenbee, Hod

Lisi, Virna
See Pieralisi, Virna

Lisideius
See Sedley, [Sir] Charles

Lisle
See Ellis, George Edward

L'Isle, Jean de
See Daudet, Alphonse

Lisle, Lester
See Walker, Emmeline Lisle

Lisle, Mary
See Cornish, [Doris] Mary

Lisle, Seward D.
See Ellis, Edward S[ylvester]

Lismore
See Walsh, John

[The] Lisping
See Eric XI

Liss, Peggy K[orn] 1927- [CA]
American historian and author
* Korn, Peggy

Lissandrino
See Magnasco, Alessandro

Lissenden, George B. 1879-? [WWL]
British author
* Whitstable, George

Lissitzky, El.
See Lissitzky, Lazar Markovich

Lissitzky, Lazar Markovich 1890-1941
[CAR]
Russian artist
* Lissitzky, El.

List, Eugene 1918?-1985
American pianist
* [The] Potsdam Pianist

List, Ilka Katherine 1935- [CA, SAT]
American artist and author
* Maidoff, Ilka List

[The] Listener
See Chamberlain, Nathan Henry

[The] Listener
See Wilson, Caroline [Fry]

Listener, Richard
See Menetrier, Charles

Lister, Bruce 1912- [FC]
South African actor
* Lester, Bruce

Lister, Eve
See Watson, Eve

Lister, Joseph 1827-1912 [HPPN]
British nobleman and surgeon
* [The] Father of Antiseptic Surgery

Lister, Lance
See Watson, Solomon Lancelot Inglis

Lister, Morris Elmer 1881-1948 [BE]
American baseball player
* Lister, Pete

Lister, Pete
See Lister, Morris Elmer

Liston, B. E.
See Livingston, Berkeley

Liston, Big Lis
See Liston, Emil S.

Liston, Charles 1932?-1970? [AS, BI, BX]
American boxer
* [The] Bear
* Liston, Sonny

Liston, Emil S. 1890-1949 [BBH]
American basketball coach
* Liston, Big Lis
* Liston, Liz

Liston, Harry 1843-1929 [BMH]
British comedian
* [The] Stage-Struck Hero

Liston, Jack
See Maloney, Ralph Liston

Liston, Liz
See Liston, Emil S.

[The] Liston of His Age
See Nokes, James

Liston, Sonny
See Liston, Charles

Liston, Victor ?-1913 [BMH]
British comic singer
* [The] Robson of the Halls

Liszt, Abbe
See Liszt, Franz

Liszt, Franz 1811-1886 [HPPN]
Hungarian pianist and composer
* Liszt, Abbe

Lite, Jams
See Schneck, Stephen

[A] Literary Antiquary
See Fairholt, Frederick William

[The] Literary Anvil
See Johnson, Samuel

[The] Literary Baker
See Jeacock, Caleb

[The] Literary Bull-Dog
See Warburton, William

[The] Literary Castor
See Johnson, Samuel

[The] Literary Colossus
See Johnson, Samuel

[The] Literary Drayman
See Young, Samuel

[The] Literary Leather-Dresser
See Dowse, Thomas

[A] Literary Lounger
See Willis, John Howard

[A] Literary Machiavel
See Addison, Joseph

[The] Literary Pollux
See Goldsmith, Oliver

[The] Literary Pride of His Home Town
See Saroyan, William

[A] Literary Proteus
See Hill, [Sir] John

[The] Literary Radical
See Bourne, Randolph Silliman

[A] Literary Revolutionist
See Warburton, William

[A] Literary Sinbad
See Hall, Basil

[The] Literary Sir Plume
See Dutens, Louis

[A] Literary Sycophant
See Hurd, Richard

[The] Literary Tailor
See Brown, Theophilis

[A] Literary Vassal
See Byron, George Gordon Noel

Lithotomus
See Ammonius

[The] Lithuanian
See Cukoschay [or Zukauskas], Joseph Paul

Litri
See Baez, Manuel

Litri
See Baez, Miguel

Litri
See Baez Espuny, Miguel

Litri
See Baez y Quintero, Miguel

Litster, John ?-1381 [NPS]
Leader of British peasants' revolt
* [The] King of the Commons

Littauer, Emanuel Victor 1895- [HPPN]
American football player
* Littauer, Manny

Littauer, Manny
See Littauer, Emanuel Victor

Littell, Country
See Littell, Mark Alan

Littell, Mark Alan 1953- [SMG]
American baseball player
* Littell, Country

[The] Little
See Dionysius Exiguus

[The] Little
See James

[The] Little
See John of Salisbury

[The] Little
See Procop

Little, A. Edward
See Klein, Aaron E.

Little Abbie Brunies
See Brunies, Albert

Little Al Gunter
See Gunter, Al

Little Albie Booth
See Booth, Albert James, Jr.

Little Alby Barkley
See Barkley, Alben William

Little Alec Bannerman
See Bannerman, Alexander Chambers

Little Aleck Stephens
See Stephens, Alexander Hamilton

Little All Right
See Ritchey, Claude Cassius

Little Andrew Odom
See Odom, Andrew

[The] Little Angel of Radio
See Dragonette, Jessica

Little Angie Tuminaro
See Tuminaro, Angelo

Little Ann Bunn
See Bunn, Ann

Little Anthony
See Gourdine, Anthony

Little Apples
See Reggione, Michael

Little Arkansas
See Hardin, John Wesley

Little Artha Johnson
See Johnson, John Arthur [Jack]

Little Augie Carfano
See Carfano, Anthony

Little Augie Orgen
See Orgen, Jacob

Little Augie Pisano
See Carfano, Anthony

Little Bat
See Garnier, Baptiste

Little, Bathless Bob
See Little, Robert

[The] Little Beagle
See Cecil, William [First Baron Burleigh]

Little Bear Zardis
See Zardis, Chester

Little Beaver Rowe
See Rowe, Frank

Little Ben
See Harrison, Benjamin

Little Ben Crenshaw
See Crenshaw, Ben

Little Benny Harris
See Harris, Benjamin

Little, Big Devil
See Little, John

[The] Little Big Man
See Archibald, Nathaniel [Nate]

[The] Little Big Man
See Hoffman, Dustin

Little Big Man
See Minacore, Calogero

Little, Big Tiny
See Little, Dudley

Little Bill
See Stephenson, [Sir] William Samuel

Little Bill Johnston
See Johnston, William M.

Little Bill Raidler
See Raidler, Bill

Little, Billy
See Rhodes, Billy

Little Billy Cody the Messenger
See Cody, William Frederick

Little Billy Smith
See Smith, Billy

Little Billy Smith
See Smith, William Russell

Little Billy Whiting
See Whiting, William Henry Chase

Little Bird
See Heath, James Edward [Jimmy]

Little Black Dan
See Webster, Daniel

Little Black John
See Slaughter, John Horton

[The] Little Blue-Cloak
See Champion, Edme

Little Bo
See Robinson, Fannie Clay

Little Bo Pete
See Lamar, Dwight

[The] Little Boatman
See Wordsworth, William

Little Bobby Hunter
See Hunter, Bobby Lee

Little Bobby Scumbag
See Crumb, Robert

[The] Little Boswell of His Day
See Aubrey, John

Little Box o' Tricks
See Palmer, Thomas

Little Boy Blue
See Booth, Albert James, Jr.

Little Boy Blue
See Ford, Aleck

Little Boy Fuller
See Trice, Rich[ard]

Little Bozo
See Pizzo, John F.

Little Breeches
See Hay, John Milton

Little Britches
See Stevens, Jennie

[The] Little Bronze Statue from Florida
See Desjardins, Pete[r]

Little Brother Griffin
See Griffin, Roosevelt

Little Brother Montgomery
See Montgomery, Eurreal Wilford

[The] Little Brother of the Rich
See Lee, Ivy Ledbetter

[The] Little Bugler
See Roger, George Munroe

Little, Byrd
See Lomax, E. Victoria

Little Caesar
See Burnett, Carl

Little Caesar
See DiVarco, Joseph Vincent

Little Caesar
See Petrillo, James Caesar

Little Caesar
See Saperstein, Abraham M. [Abe]

Little Caesar
See Varco, Joseph Vincent di

[The] Little Captain
See George II

Little Carl Carlton
See Carlton, Carl

Little, Carleton B. 1872-1933   [HPPN]
American actor
* Carleton, Lloyd B.

Little Casino
See Taral, Fred

Little, Chicken
See Little, Larry

Little Chief
See Thatcher, Moses

Little Chink Martin
See Abraham, Martin, Jr.

Little Chis Chism
See Chism, Elijah

Little Chocolate
See Dixon, George

Little Chrissie Evert
See Evert, Chris[tine Marie]

[The] Little Colonel
See Reese, Harold Henry

Little Comedy
See Bunbury, Catharine Horneck

Little, Constance 20th c.   [CC]
Author
* Little, Conyth [joint pseudonym with Gwenyth Little]

Little, Conyth [joint pseudonym with Gwenyth Little]
See Little, Constance

Little, Conyth [joint pseudonym with Constance Little]
See Little, Gwenyth

[The] Little Corporal
See Bonaparte, Napoleon

[The] Little Corporal
See Nelson, Knute

Little Corporal of Unsought Fields
See McClellan, George Brinton

[The] Little Cowboy
See Gobel, George Leslie

Little Coz
See Henderson, Eloise Cozens

[The] Little Cripple
See Lisboa, Antonio Francisco

Little Daddy
See Braddix, Ben

Little Dan Brown
See Brown, Daniel

[The] Little Dasher
See Graham, H.

[The] Little Dauphin
See Louis de France

Little Dave Klodny
See Klodny, David

Little Davey
See Lewis, David John

Little David
See Felton, John

Little David
See Randolph, John

Little David Alexander
See Alexander, David

Little David O'Brien
See O'Brien, David

Little Davy
See Garrick, David

[The] Little Deacon
See John of Salisbury

Little, Dick
See Liddell, James Andrew

Little Dick
See West, Richard

Little Dicky
See Steele, [Sir] Richard

Little Dingus
See James, Jesse Woodson

Little Do Doherty
See Doherty, Hugh Lawrence

Little Doc Severinsen
See Severinsen, Carl

[The] Little Doctor
See Aubrey, William

[The] Little Doctor
See Houghton, Douglass

[The] Little Doctor
See Meanwell, Walter E.

[The] Little Doctor
See Teichelmann, Ebenezer

Little Dove
See Dyveke, [or Duiveke]

[The] Little Dragon
See Lee Yuen Kam

[A] Little Druid-Wight
See Pope, Alexander

Little Dud Vincent
See Vincent, Clarence

Little, Dudley 1930-   [ASC, DAM]
American musician
* Little, Big Tiny
* Little, Tiny

[The] Little Duke
See Scott, James

[The] Little Dutchman
See Zuppke, Robert C.

[The] Little Dynamo
See Faulkner, Walt

Little Eagle 1785?-1851   [BI]
American Indian chief
* War Eagle

Little Eagle 1913-
American-Indian actor
* Cody, Iron Eyes

[The] Little Eaglet
See Lindbergh, Charles Augustus, Jr.

Little Ed Masterson
See Masterson, Edward J.

Little Eddie Boyd
See Boyd, Edward Riley

Little Eddie Burns
See Burns, Eddie

Little Eddie Kirkland
See Kirkland, Eddie

Little Eddie Spann
See Spann, Charles Edward, III

Little, Edward Gerald 1897-   [FC]
British actor
* Lexy, Edward

Little Egypt
See Spyropolous, Frieda

[The] Little Electra
See Byron, Augusta Ada

Little Elsie
See Bierbower [or Bierbauer], Elsie

Little Elsie
See Morgan, Helen

Little Esther
See Jones, Esther Mae

Little Eva
See Boyd, Eva Narcissus

Little Eva Lange
See Lange, William Alexander

Little Eva Wilhelm
See Wilhelm, Irvin Key

Little Evalyn McLean
See McLean, Evalyn Walsh

Little Farvel Kovolick
See Kovolick, Philip

[The] Little Father
See Nicholas II

[The] Little Feller
See Little, Robert

[The] Little Feller
See Sullivan, Timothy P.

[The] Little Flower
See La Guardia, Fiorello Henry

Little Flower of Jesus
See Martin, Therese

[The] Little Flying Devil
See Kestner, Paul

Little, Frances
See Macaulay, Fannie Caldwell

[The] Little General
See LeBaron, Eddie

[The] Little General
See Theobald, Ron[ald M.]

Little, George A. 1883-   [NAA]
Canadian clergyman and editor
* Graham, Homer

Little George Buford
See Buford, George

Little George Smith
See Smith, George

[The] Little Georgian David
See Carter, James Earl, Jr. [Jimmy]

Little Georgie Gobel
See Gobel, George Leslie

[The] Little Giant
See Albert, Carl

[The] Little Giant
See Douglas, Stephen Arnold

[The] Little Giant
See Green, David

[The] Little Giant
See Howard, Frank J.

[The] Little Giant
See Hurt, Edward Paisley [Eddie]

[The] Little Giant
See Joliat, Aurel Emile

[The] Little Giant
See Lewis, David John

[The] Little Giant
See Lincoln, Abraham

Little Giant
See Margo, Peter

Little Giant
See Morgan, Joseph Leonard [Joe]

[The] Little Giant of Alexandria
See Nelson, Knute

[The] Little Giant of the Blues
See Blackmore, Amos

[The] Little Giant of Twentieth Century Music
See Stravinsky, Igor Feadorovich

[The] Little Giant of Wall Street
See Harriman, E[dward] H[enry]

[The] Little Girl from Little Rock
See Channing, Carol

[The] Little Globetrotter
See Earle, William Moffat

Little Gloria Vanderbilt
See Vanderbilt, Gloria

Little Goldilocks
See Black, Shirley Temple

Little, Gordon W. 1860-1942   [SC]
American actor and circus performer
* Pawnee Bill

Little, Gwenyth 20th c.   [CC]
Author
* Little, Conyth [joint pseudonym with Constance Little]

Little Hartley
See Coleridge, David Hartley

[The] Little Hatchet
See Nation, Carry Amelia Moore Gloyd

[The] Little Hebrew
See Attell, Abraham Washington [Abe]

Little Henry
See Gray, Henry

Little Hercules
See Wilding, Anthony F.

[The] Little Hero
See Wheeler, Joseph

Little Hillock
See Confucius [or K'ung Fu-tzu]

Little Hudson
See Shower, Hudson

Little Hymie Weiss
See Wajcieckowski, Earl

[The] Little Ice Maiden
See Evert, Chris[tine Marie]

[The] Little Indian
See Moore, Wilbur

[The] Little Indian Fighter
See Standish, Miles

Little, Jack
See Little, William Arthur

Little Jack Little
See Leonard, John

Little Jack Little
See Little, John

Little Jack McGill
See McGill, John Edward

Little Jackie Heller
See Heller, Jackie

Little Jackie Sharkey
See Cervati, Giovanni

Little Jake of Saginaw
See Seligman, Jake

Little Jake Seligman
See Seligman, Jake

Little Jazz Eldridge
See Eldridge, [David] Roy

Little, Jim
See Brown, Sidney

Little Jim Folsom
See Folsom, Jim

Little Jim Rushing
See Rushing, James Andrew [Jimmy]

Little Jimmie Henderson
See Henderson, Jimmie

Little Jimmie Turrell
See Turrell, James Archie [Jim]

Little Jimmy
See Latourelle, James

Little Jimmy Dempsey
See Dempsey, James Clifford

Little Jimmy Dickens
See Dickens, Jimmy

Little Jimmy Sizemore
See Sizemore, Jimmy

Little, Joan 1954- [IBW]
American prison rape victim
* Nadir, Hadiyah Joan

Little Joe
See Cook, Joe

Little Joe
See Hill, Lester

Little Joe Blue
See Valery, Joseph, Jr.

Little Joe Bonanno
See Bonanno, Joseph, Jr.

Little Joe Calabriese
See Calabriese, Joseph

Little Joe Gehrig
See Gehrig, [Henry] Lou[is]

Little Joe Lindsey
See Lindsey, Joseph

Little Joe Montoya
See Montoya, Joseph M.

Little Joe Presko
See Presko, Joseph Edward

Little Joe Wheeler
See Wheeler, Joseph

Little Joe Yeager
See Yeager, Joseph F.

Little Joey
See Hall, Joseph

Little, John 1900-1956 [HPPN]
British-American entertainer, singer, pianist, composer
* Little, Little Jack
* Radio's Cheerful Little Earful

Little, John 1947- [SMG]
American football player
* Little, Big Devil

Little John
See Nailor, John

Little John Badanjek
See Badanjek, John

Little John Hartman
See Hartman, John

Little Johnny Jones
See Jones, John

Little Johnny Taylor
See Young, Johnny

Little Jr.
See Johnson, Luther, Jr.

Little Junior Parker
See Parker, Herman

Little Junior Wells
See Blackmore, Amos

Little Junior Williams
See Williams, Emery H.

Little Katie Crippen
See Crippen, Catherine [Katie]

Little, Kenneth
See Scotland, James

Little King Pepin
See Channing, William Ellery

[The] Little Lady of the Stars
See Proctor, Mary

Little, Larry 1945- [SMG]
American football player
* Little, Chicken

Little Laura Dukes
See Dukes, Laura

Little Lauro Salas
See Salas, Lauro

Little, Lawrence 1893- [FB]
American football coach
* Little, Lou

Little Lepke
See Bookhouse, Louis

[A] Little Liar
See Pope, Alexander

Little Linda Ludgrove
See Ludgrove, Linda

[The] Little Lion
See Hamilton, Alexander

Little, Little Jack
See Leonard, John

Little, Little Jack
See Little, John

Little Looie Aparicio
See Aparicio, Luis Ernesto

Little, Lou[is Lawrence] 1893- [HPPN]
American football coach
* [The] Caesar of Football

Little, Lou
See Little, Lawrence

Little Lou Goldstein
See Goldstein, Lou

Little Loving Henry
See Byrd, Henry Roeland

Little Luther
See Johnson, Lucius Brinson

Little Lynn
See Carlin, Karin

Little M
See Mahovlich, Pete[r]

Little Mac Macullar
See Macullar, James F.

Little Mac McSwiggin
See McSwiggin, William H. [Bill]

Little Mac the Young Napoleon
See McClellan, George Brinton

Little Maceo
See Merriweather, Rozier

Little Machiavel
See Cooper, Anthony Ashley [First Earl of Shaftesbury]

[A] Little Machiavelli
See Galiani, Ferdinand

Little Mack McCarthy
See McCarthy, Thomas Francis Michael [Tommy]

Little Mack Simmons
See Simmons, Mack

Little Mackey Sanders
See Sanders, Charlie

[The] Little Magician
See Van Buren, Martin

[The] Little Magnet
See Deagon, Lyda

[The] Little Major
See Corum, Martene Windsor

Little, Malcolm 1925-1965 [CBS, HPPN, IBW, NAD]
American Black Muslim leader
* Big Red
* Detroit Red
* Malcolm X
* Shabazz, El-Hajj Malik el-

Little Man
See Johnson, James

[The] Little Man
See Minacore, Calogero

[The] Little Man in Pro Football
See Walker, [Ewell] Doak, Jr.

[The] Little Man in Red Stockings
See Leopold I

[The] Little Man of Nuremberg
See Birchinger, Matthew

[The] Little Man of Twickenham
See Pope, Alexander

Little Man Wagner
See Wagner, Danny, Jr.

[The] Little Man With the Goatee
See Ulbricht, Walter

[The] Little Marlborough
See Schwerin, Kurt Christoph von

[The] Little Master
See Beham, Hans Sebald

Little, Master
See Moore, Thomas

Little Matty
See Van Buren, Martin

Little Michael Lord
See Lord, Michael

Little Mike Genna
See Genna, Michael

Little Mike McKendrick
See McKendrick, Gilbert Michael

Little Milton
See Campbell, Milton James

Little Milton Anderson
See Anderson, Milton

[The] Little Minister
See Nietzsche, Friedrich Wilhelm

Little Minnie Maddern
See Davey, Mary Augusta

Little Miss Bab-O
See Small, Mary

Little Miss Dynamite
See Tarpley, Brenda Mae

Little Miss Hollywood
See Black, Shirley Temple

Little Miss Moffitt
See King, Billie Jean Moffitt

Little Miss Poker Face
See Wills, Helen Newington

Little Miss Roosevelt
See Longworth, Alice Lee Roosevelt

Little Miss Sharecropper
See Baker, LaVern

Little Mr. Everywhere
See Huggins, Miller James

Little Mo Connolly
See Connolly, Maureen

Little Mo Modzelewski
See Modzelewski, Richard [Dick]

Little Moses
See Olajuwon, Akeem Abdul

[The] Little Mother of all the Russians
See Catherine II

[The] Little Mother of Colored Drama
See Bush, Anita

Little Mouse Metidieri
See Metidieri, Carlos

Little, Mrs. J. Z.   [FFF]
Entertainer
* Campbell, Lizzie

[The] Little Musketeer
See Cochet, Henri

[The] Little Napoleon
See Beauregard, Pierre Gustave Toutant

Little Napoleon
See Brumbaugh, Carl L.

Little Napoleon
See Chadd, Archie

Little Napoleon
See Kaplan, Louis

[The] Little Napoleon
See McClellan, George Brinton

[The] Little Napoleon
See McGraw, John Joseph

[The] Little Napoleon of the West Coast Bar
See Delmas, Delphin Michael

Little Nemo
See Hill, Bennett

Little Nemo Stephens
See Stephens, James Walter

Little New York
See Campagna, Louis

Little Nick Montos
See Montos, Nick George

[The] Little Nightingale
See Pope, Alexander

[The] Little Norwegian
See Nelson, Knute

Little Orphan Annie in Hollywood
See Mortensen, Norma Jean

Little Otis
See Rush, Otis

Little Owen the Epigrammaker
See Owen, John

[The] Little Ox
See Knox, Henry

[The] Little Pale Star from Georgia
See Stephens, Alexander Hamilton

Little Papa Joe
See Williams, Joseph Leon [Joe]

Little Papa Walter
See Lightfoot, Alexander

Little Patsy Doyle
See Doyle, Patrick

Little, Paul H.
See Litwinsky, Paul

Little, Paula
See Litwinsky, Paul

Little Peetie Wheatstraw
See Hogg, Andrew

Little Peggy March
See March, Peggy

Little Pepper
See Arden, [Sir] Richard Pepper [Lord Alvanley]

Little Pete
See Fong, Ching

Little Pete
See Fung Jing Toy

Little Pharaoh
See Tutankhamen

Little Phil
See Sheridan, Philip Henry

Little Phil Geier
See Geier, Louis Phillip

Little Phil Thompson
See Thompson, Philip Burton, Jr.

Little Pickle
See Jordan, Mrs.

Little Pod Ellingsen
See Ellingsen, H. Bruce

[The] Little Poet
See Oldys, Alexander

Little Poison
See Runyan, Paul Scott

Little Poison
See Waner, Lloyd James

Little, Poor
See Moore, Thomas

[The] Little Potato
See Pascual, Camilo Alberto

[The] Little Preacher
See De Marets, Samuel

[The] Little Prince of Soul
See Jackson, Michael Joseph

[The] Little Princess
See Gampel, Lillit

[The] Little Professor
See DiMaggio, Dominic Paul

[The] Little Professor of the Piney Woods
See Jones, Laurence Clifton

[The] Little Queen
See Isabella of Valois

[The] Little Queen
See Victoria

Little Ray
See Agee, Ray[mond Clinton]

Little Red
See Barton, David

Little Red
See Rudd, W. L.

Little Red Cagney
See Cagney, James Francis [Jimmy]

[The] Little Red Fox
See Alexander II

Little Red Lopez
See Lopez, Danny

Little Red Starkweather
See Starkweather, Charles

Little Reddie from Texas
See McKimie, Robert

Little Richard
See Penniman, Richard Wayne

Little, Richard Henry 1870?-1946 [BI, HPPN]
American columnist
* R. H. L.

Little, Robert 1928- [HPPN]
American bookshelver
* [The] Bellwether
* God's Gift to the Stacks
* Little, Bathless Bob
* [The] Little Feller

[The] Little Round Man
See Butts, James Wallace, Jr.

Little, Ruby A. Black 1896- [NAA]
American journalist
* Black, Ruby Aurora

[The] Little Russian in Pigtails
See Korbut, Olga

Little Sam
See Broonzy, William Lee Conley

Little Sax Crowder
See Crowder, Robert Henry [Bob]

[The] Little Sculptor
See Roubillac, Louis Francois

Little Sister
See Scruggs, Irene

Little Slug of the Boston Red Sox
See Stephens, Vernon Decatur

Little Smokey Smothers
See Smothers, Abraham

Little Son
See Broonzy, William Lee Conley

Little Son Joe
See Lawlars, Ernest

Little Son Willis
See Willis, Aaron

Little Son Willis
See Willis, Malcolm

[The] Little Songbird from Italy
See Van Dine, Harvey

Little Sonny Brown
See Brown, Samuel

Little, Sophia Louise Robbins 1799-? [HPPN]
American author
* Rowena

[The] Little Spaniard
See Ribera, Jose

[The] Little Sparrow
See Gassion, Edith Giovanna

[The] Little Sparrow
See Korbut, Olga

[The] Little Sparrow of Paris
See Gassion, Edith Giovanna

[The] Little Steam Engine
See Galvin, James Francis

[The] Little Steinitz
See Atkins, Henry Ernest

Little Steven
See Van Zandt, Steve

Little Stevie Wonder
See Cauthen, Steve

Little Stevie Wonder
See Morris, Steveland

Little Stevie Wright
See Wright, Steve

Little Sure Shot
See Moses, Phoebe Anne Oakley

Little Susy
See Prentiss, Mrs.

Little Sylvia
See Vanderpool, Sylvia

Little T Bone
See Gaines, Roy

Little T Bone
See Rankin, R. S.

Little T Teagarden
See Teagarden, Charlie

Little Temple
See Jenkins, Gus

Little, Thomas
See Moore, Thomas

Little Tich
See Hanif Mohammad

Little Tich
See Relph, Harry

Little Tiger Thompson
See Thompson, Esau

Little Tim Sullivan
See Sullivan, Timothy P.

Little, Tiny
See Little, Dudley

Little, Tobe
See Slaughter, Marion T.

Little Tom Jefferson
See Jefferson, Thomas

Little Tom Maguire
See Maguire, Tom

[The] Little Tramp
See Chaplin, Charles Spencer

Little Tubby Raskin
See Raskin, Julius

Little Turtle
See Me Che Kan Nah Quah

Little Van
See Van Buren, Martin

[The] Little Van Dyck
See Dyck [or Dijk], Philip van

[The] Little Van Dyck
See Van Dyck, Philip

[The] Little Vermin
See Laud, William

Little Victoria
See Lawrence, Vesta

Little Victoria
See Monks, Victoria

[The] Little Villain
See Raymond, Henry Jarvis

Little Walter
See Jacobs, Marion Walter

Little Walter Ellworthy
See Ellworthy, Walter

Little Walter J
See Jacobs, Marion Walter

Little Walter J.
See Westbrook, Walter J.

Little Walter Jr.
See Smith, George

[The] Little Whig
See Anne

Little, William Arthur 1891-1961 [BE]
American baseball player
* Little, Jack

Little Willie
See Friedrich Wilhelm

Little Willie Foster
See Foster, Willie [or Willy]

Little Willie John
See Woods, William J.

Little Willie Johnson
See Johnson, William Edward John

Little Willie Littlefield
See Littlefield, Willie

Little Wolf
See Shines, John Ned [Johnny]

[The] Little Wolf With The Little Hammer
See Jakubek, Wolfgang

[The] Little Wonder
See Gravelet, Jean Francois

[The] Little Wonder
See Sayers, Tom

[The] Little Wonder
See Wisden, John

Littleboy, Sheila M.
See Ary, Sheila M[ary Littleboy]

Littledale, Richard 1833-1890 [PI]
Irish clergyman and author
* A. L. P. [A London Priest]
* B.
* B. T.
* D. L.
* F.
* F. R.
* L.
* P. C. E.
* P. P. B. K.

Littlefield, Little Willie
See Littlefield, Willie

Littlefield, Willie 1931- [BWW]
American singer
* Littlefield, Little Willie

Littlejohn
See Mackenzie, Robert Shelton

Littlejohn
See Tomlins, Frederick Guest

Littlejohn, Hugh
See Lockhart, John Hugh

Littlejohn, John
See Funchess, John

Littlepage, Cornelius
See Cooper, James Fenimore

Littler, [Eu]gene [Alex] 1930- [GF]
American golfer
* Gene the Machine

[The] Littlest Defector
See Polovchak, Walter

Littleton, Classy Cleo
See Littleton, Cleophus

Littleton, Cleophus 1932- [BB]
American basketball player
* Littleton, Classy Cleo

Littleton, Mark
See Kennedy, John Pendleton

Littlewit, Humphrey
See Lovecraft, Howard Phillips

Littlewood, Alan 1936- [IAW]
British writer
* Ceres

Littlewood, S. R.
See Littlewood, Samuel Robinson

Littlewood, Samuel Robinson 1875-1963 [LC]
British author and drama critic
* Littlewood, S. R.

Litton, Marie
See Lowe, Mary

Littricebey, Clara Alma Allen 20th c. [BWW]
American entertainer
* Littricebey, Granny

Littricebey, Granny
See Littricebey, Clara Alma Allen

Litvak, Anatole
See Lutwak, Michael Anatol

Litvinne, Felia
See Schuetz, Francoise-Jeanne

Litvinov, Ivy 1890?-1977 [CA]
British-born author
* Low, Ivy

Litvinov, Maksim Maksimovich
See Finkelstein, Meyer

Litvinov, Maxim M.
See Wallach, Meir

Litwack, Harry 1907- [BB]
Austrian-born American basketball player
* [The] Chief

Litwinsky, Paul 1915- [CA, HPPN, SFL]
American author
* Little, Paul H.
* Little, Paula
* Minton, Paula
* Paul, Hugo

Litwos
See Sienkiewicz, Henryk [Adam Aleksander Pius]

Liu An 2nd c. BC [WBD]
Chinese ruler and scholar
* Huai-nan Tzu

Liu, Henry 1932?-1984 [TI 1-28-85]
Chinese-American author, journalist, businessman
* Chiang Nam [River South]

Liu, James T[zu] C[hien]
See Liu, Tzu-chien

Liu Po-Ch'eng 1893?- [HPPN]
Chinese Communist army officer
* [The] One Eyed General

Liu, Sydney [Chieh] 1920- [CA]
Chinese author
* Feng, Chin
* Hsiang, Yeh

Liu, Tzu-chien 1919- [CA]
Chinese-born educator and author
* Liu, James T[zu] C[hien]

Liu, Wu-chi 1907- [CA, WD]
Chinese-born American historian, critic, author
* Hsia Hsiao

Liutprand [or Liudprand] 922?-972? [WBD]
Italian prelate and historian
* Liutprand of Cremona

Liutprand of Cremona
See Liutprand [or Liudprand]

Livandais, Augustus M. D. [PA]
Author
* Knutt, A. P.

Live Again, Dr.
See Rusk, Howard

Live Oak George
See Law, George

Lively, Bud
See Lively, Everett Adrian

Lively, Everett Adrian 1925- [BE]
American baseball player
* Lively, Bud
* Lively, Red

Lively, Henry Everett 1885-1967 [BE]
American baseball player
* Lively, Jack

Lively, Jack
See Lively, Henry Everett

Lively, Red
See Lively, Everett Adrian

Lively, Walter
See Elliott, Bruce [Walter Gardner Lively Stacy]

Liver Eating Johnson
See Johnson, John

Livermore, Abiel Abbott 1811-? [HPPN]
American clergyman
* A. A. L.

Livermore, George 1809-1865 [HPPN]
American antiquarian
* [The] Antiquary
* G. L.

Livermore, James
See Livermore, Joseph Mason

Livermore, Jean
See Sanville, Jean

Livermore, Jesse Lauriston 1877-1940 [HPPN, TI 6-13-83]
American financier
* [The] Boy Plunger of Wall Street
* [The] King of Speculators
* [The] Speculator King
* [The] Wolf of Wall Street

Livermore, Joseph Mason 1892?-1977 [BI]
American engineer
* Livermore, James

[The] Livermore Larruper
See Baer, Max[imilian Adelbert]

[The] Liverpool Landseer
See Huggins, William

Livers, Virgil Chester, Jr. 1952- [SMG]
American football player
* Mighty Mouse

Liverton, Joan 1913- [AW, CAP]
British author
* Medhurst, Joan

Livery Man
See Foe, Daniel

[The] Livery Muse
See Dodsley, Robert

Livi, Ivo [or Yvo] 1921- [BDF, ITA, WEF]
French actor and singer
* Montand, Yves

[The] Living Archive
See Traglia, Luigi

[The] Living Computer
See Sheng Ke Gon

[The] Living Cyclopaedia
See Longinus, Dionysius Cassius

[A] Living Dictionary
See Leibnitz [or Leibniz], Gottfried Wilhelm von

[The] Living Legend
See Morganfield, McKinley

[The] Living Library
See Longinus, Dionysius Cassius

[A] Living Library
See Toussain, Jacques

[The] Living Pentecost
See Mezzofanti, Giuseppe

[The] Living Skeleton
See Robinson, Peter

[The] Living Sophism
See Robespierre, Maximilien

[A] Living Statesman
See Stanley, Edward Henry Smith [15th Earl of Derby]

Livingston, Berkeley 1908- [ESF, SFP, WGT]
American writer
* Barclay, Lester
* Blade, Alexander [house pseudonym, Ziff-Davis]
* Hickey, H. B.
* Liston, B. E.
* Steele, Morris J. [house pseudonym, Ziff-Davis]

Livingston, Camille
See Livingston, Livingston

Livingston, Carole 1941- [CA]
American author
* Aphrodite, J.

Livingston, Don Leslie 1892- [NAA]
American author
* Gable, Rufe

Livingston, Fud
See Livingston, Joseph Anthony

Livingston, Goo Goo
See Livingston, L. D.

Livingston, Harrison Edward 1937- [HPPN]
American poet, educator, author
* Fairfield, John

Livingston, Herb 1916- [WGT]
American author
* Blade, Alexander [house pseudonym, Ziff-Davis]
* Hickey, H. B.

Livingston, Jerry
See Levinson, Jerry

Livingston, John Henry 1746-1825 [FFF]
American clergyman
* [The] Father of the Dutch Reformed Church in America

Livingston, Joseph Anthony 1906-1957 [ASC, EJ, PMJ]
American jazz musician
* Livingston, Fud

Livingston, Kenneth
See Stewart, Kenneth Livingston

Livingston, L. D. 20th c. [OBW]
American baseball player
* Livingston, Goo Goo

Livingston, Libby
See Livingston, Warren

Livingston, Livingston ?-1908 [HPPN]
American vaudeville performer
* Livingston, Camille

Livingston, M. Jay
See Livingston, Myran Jabez, Jr.

Livingston, Mickey
See Livingston, Thompson Orville

Livingston, Mollie Parnis 1905- [IPA]
American fashion designer
* Parnis, Mollie

Livingston, Myran Jabez, Jr. 1934- [CA]
American author, director, producer
* Livingston, M. Jay

Livingston, Neville 1948?- [NW 2-21-83]
Jamaican musician
* Wailer, Bunny

Livingston, Paddy
See Livingston, Patrick Joseph

Livingston, Patrick 1945?-
American FBI undercover agent
* Salamone, Pat

Livingston, Patrick Joseph 1880-? [BE]
American baseball player
* Livingston, Paddy

Livingston, Peter Van Rensselaer
See Townsend, James B[arclay] J[ermain]

Livingston, Robert R. 1746-1813 [HPPN]
American attorney, politician, orator
* Cato
* [The] Cicero of America

Livingston, Thompson Orville 1914- [ALR, BE]
American baseball player
* Livingston, Mickey

Livingston, Warren
American football player
* Livingston, Libby

Livingston, William 1723-1790 [FFF, HPPN]
American politician
* [The] Author of the Watch Tower
* Despot In Chief in and Over the Rising State of New Jersey
* [The] Don Quixote of New Jersey
* [The] Don Quixote of the Jerseys
* [The] Extraordinary Chancellor of the Rising State of New Jersey
* [The] Itinerant Dey of New Jersey
* [The] Knight of the Most Honorable Order of Starvation
* [The] Spurious Governor
* [The] Whipping Post

Livingston-Matthews, Asenath
See Lesher, Phyllis

Livingstone, David 1813-1873 [HPPN]
Scottish physician, missionary, explorer
* [The] Greatest of Africa's Explorers

Livingstone, Harrison Edward 1937- [CA, WD]
American author and poet
* Fairfield, John

Livingstone, Ken[neth] 1945-
British politician
* Livingstone, Red Ken

Livingstone, Margaret
See Flynn, Mary Margaret

Livingstone, Mary
See Marks, Sadye

Livingstone, Red Ken
See Livingstone, Ken[neth]

Livinsky, Walter 1929- [HPPN]
American composer, musician, arranger
* Leslie, Walter

Livinus 7th c. [NPS]
Saint
* [The] Apostle of Brabant

Livius, Titus 1st c. BC [BI]
Roman historian
* Livy

Livy
See Livius, Titus

[The] Livy of France
See Mariana, Juan de [or John]

[The] Livy of Portugal
See Barros, Joao de

[The] Livy of Spain
See Ginez de Sepulveda, Juan

[The] Livy of Spain
See Mariana, Juan de [or John]

Liz the Lion Killer
See Holtzman, Elizabeth

Lizana, Curly
See Lizana, Florin J.

Lizana, Florin J. 1895-1967 [NOJ]
American jazz musician
* Lizana, Curly

[The] Lizard King
See Morrison, Jim

Lizaso, Felix
See Lizaso y Gonzalez, Felix

Lizaso y Gonzalez, Felix 1891- [HPPN]
Cuban author
* Lizaso, Felix

Lizzani, Carlo 1922- [FDG]
Italian director
* Beaver, Lee

Lizzie
See Condon, Lizzie G.

Ll. G.
See Lloyd George, David

[A] Llanbrynmair Farmer
See Roberts, S.

Llavarito
See Leal y Casado, Eduardo

Llaverito
See Guerra y Bejarano, Rafael

Llenas, Chilote
See Llenas, Winston Enriquillo

Llenas, Winston Enriquillo 1943- [BE]
Dominican-born baseball player
* Llenas, Chilote

Llenodo
See O'Donnell, Francis Hugh

Llerena, Mario 1913- [CA]
Cuban-born American author
* Niemoller, Ara

Llergo, Josefina Pellicer Lopez
1940-1964 [HPPN]
Spanish actress
* Dellicer, Pina

Llero, Auguste
See Rolle, Christian

Llewellyn
See Saunders, Robert

Llewellyn, Clement Manly 1895- [BE]
American baseball player
* Llewellyn, Lew

Llewellyn, D[avid] W[illiam] Alun 1903-
[CA]
British author
* Taffy

Llewellyn, E. L.
See Sheppard, Lydia H.

Llewellyn, Edward
See Llewellyn-Thomas, Edward

Llewellyn, Fewlass
See Jones, Fewlass

Llewellyn, Frederick 1924- [FC]
British actor
* Bartholemew, Freddie

Llewellyn, Lew
See Llewellyn, Clement Manly

Llewellyn, Louise
See Snoddy, Abbie [Llewellyn]

Llewellyn, M. J.
See Llewellyn, Michael John

Llewellyn, Michael John 1953- [DC]
Welsh cricketer
* Llewellyn, M. J.

Llewellyn, Richard
See Llewellyn Lloyd, Richard Dafydd
Vyvyan

**Llewellyn Lloyd, Richard Dafydd
Vyvyan** 1906?-1983 [CA, LC, SAT]
Welsh-born author, playwright, journalist
* Llewellyn, Richard

Llewellyn-Thomas, Edward 1917- [CA]
British-born author
* Llewellyn, Edward

Llewelyn ab Iorwerth ?-1240 [WBD]
Prince of Wales
* [The] Great

Llewelyn, T. Harcourt
See Hamilton, Charles Harold St. John

Lleyon, Gutto
See Jones, Griffith Robert

Lloyd, Alice
See Wood, Alice

Lloyd, Alison 1905-1935 [F2, HPPN]
American actress
* Hot Toddy
* [The] Ice Cream Blonde
* Todd, Thelma

Lloyd, Arthur 1840-1904 [BMH]
Scottish-born entertainer
* [The] Last of the Lion Comiques

Lloyd, Barry John 1953- [DC]
Welsh cricketer
* Lloyd, Lloydy

Lloyd, Bumble
See Lloyd, David

Lloyd, Charles
See Birkin, Charles [Lloyd]

Lloyd, Clive Hubert 1944- [DC]
Guyanese-born cricketer
* Big C

Lloyd, David 1635-1692 [NPS]
Author
* Foulis, Oliver

Lloyd, David 1947- [DC]
British cricketer
* Lloyd, Bumble

Lloyd, Dennis 1915- [CA]
British barrister and author
* Lloyd of Hampstead, Baron

Lloyd, Duke
See Lloyd, Harold Clayton, Jr.

Lloyd, Edward ?-1713 [HPPN]
*British coffee house proprietor and
publisher*
* [The] Father of Lloyd's News

Lloyd, Emma F. 19th c. [HFN]
Author
* [A] Clergyman's Daughter
* E. F. L.

Lloyd, Evans
See Pregarty, John M.

Lloyd, Flossie
See Lloyd, John

Lloyd, Francis Bartow 19th c. [BDSA]
American author, attorney, journalist
* Saunders, Rufus, The Sage of Rocky
Creek

Lloyd, Grace
See Hyman, Grace Lloyd

Lloyd, Harold Clayton 1893-1971
[HPPN]
American comedian
* Lonesome Luke

Lloyd, Harold Clayton, Jr. 1931-1971
[SC]
American actor and singer
* Lloyd, Duke

Lloyd, Henry Demarest 1847-1903
[HPPN]
American journalist and author
* [The] First of the Muckrakers
* [The] Middle Class Conscience

Lloyd, Herbert
See Fearn, John Russell

Lloyd, Hugh
See Fitzhugh, Percy Keese

Lloyd, Ian
See Buonconciglio, Ian

Lloyd, Jane
See Roberts, John S[torm]

Lloyd, Jasper
See Lloyd, Timothy Andrew

Lloyd, Jerome [Jerry]
See Hurwitz, Jerome

Lloyd, Joe 20th c. [EG]
British golfer
* [The] General

Lloyd, John 20th c. [BP]
British tennis player
* Lloyd, Flossie

Lloyd, John Henry 1884-1965 [AS,
BAB, MK]
American baseball player
* [The] Black Wagner
* [El] Cuchara [The Shovel]
* Lloyd, Pops

Lloyd, John Ivester 1905- [HPPN]
British author
* Babbler

Lloyd, John Ivester (cont.)
* Farmer, Peter
* [The] Lodger

Lloyd, Joseph H. 20th c. [WWL]
Irish author, editor, poet
* Laoide, Seosamh

Lloyd, Kathleen [Kathy]
See Gackle, Kathleen

Lloyd, Lloydy
See Lloyd, Barry John

Lloyd, Margaret
See Sloper, Margaret [Thayer]

Lloyd, Marie
See Wood, Matilda Alice Victoria

Lloyd, Marie, Jr.
See Courtney, Marie

Lloyd, Mary 1890-1973 [F2, FC, THR]
British actress
* Merrall, Mary
* Merrall, Queenie

Lloyd of Hampstead, Baron
See Lloyd, Dennis

Lloyd, Pops
See Lloyd, John Henry

Lloyd, Richard
See Brotherton, Alice Williams

Lloyd, Ronald
See Friedland, Ronald Lloyd

Lloyd, Rosie
See Wood, Rosie

Lloyd, Samuel Jones 1796-1883 [FFF]
British economist
* Mercator

Lloyd, Sarah 18th c. [SN]
British educator
* [The] School Mistress

Lloyd, Stephanie
See Golding, Morton J[ay]

Lloyd, Stephen
See Bond, Stephen

Lloyd, Teflon
See Lloyd, Timothy Andrew

Lloyd, Timothy Andrew 1956- [DC]
British cricketer
* Lloyd, Jasper
* Lloyd, Teflon

Lloyd, Wallace
See Algie, James

Lloyd George, David 1863-1945 [NN, PPN]
British prime minister
* Ll. G.
* [The] Welsh Wizard

Lloyd-Thomas, Catherine 1917- [CA]
British playwright and director
* Muschamp, Thomas

Llucen
See Cullen, John

Lo
See Piccolo, Fillippo

Lo
See   Second element of name for further listings

Loader, William Reginald 1916- [AW, CA]
British author
* Nash, Daniel

Loan, Mike
See Loan, William Joseph

Loan, William Joseph 1895-1966 [BE]
American baseball player
* Loan, Mike

Lobaugh, Elma K. 1907- [WW]
Author
* Lowe, Kenneth

Lobb, Stephen 17th c. [SN]
Jesuit leader
* [The] Hypocrite

Lobengula 1833?-1893 [HPPN]
African king
* [The] Last King of the Matabele

Lobert, Hans
See Lobert, John Bernard

Lobert, Honus
See Lobert, John Bernard

Lobert, John Bernard 1881-1968 [AS, BE, PB]
American baseball player
* Lobert, Hans
* Lobert, Honus

Lobingier, Elizabeth Miller 1889- [NAA]
American educator and author
* Miller, Elizabeth Erwin

Lobo
See Lavoie, Kent

Lobo, George Edmund 1894- [WWL]
British author and editor
* Sherry, Oliver

Lobrano, Josie
See Deubler, Mary

[La] Loca
See Juana [Joanna or Jane]

[A] Local Artist
See Fernihough, John C.

[A] Local Preacher
See Rodd, William Henry

Locas, Jacques 1954- [SMG]
Canadian-born hockey player
* [The] Jet Man

Loch, Joice NanKivell 1893-1981 [CA]
Australian-born relief worker and author
* NanKivell, Joice M.

Lochard, Doc
See Lochard, Metz Tullus Paul

Lochard, Metz Tullus Paul 20th c.
[IBW]
Haitian-born journalist
* Lochard, Doc

Lochee, John ?-1815 [HPPN]
British book auctioneer
* [The] Parmegiano of Auctioneers

Locher, Charles Hall 1913-1979 [FC, HPPN]
American actor
* Crane, Lloyd
* Hall, Jon

Locher, Donald 1902- [FC]
American actor
* Terry, Don

Locher, Jacob 1470-1528 [PA]
Author
* Philomessus

Lochiel
See Cameron, [Sir] Evan

Lochlons, Colin
See Jackson, C[aary] Paul

Lochnagar
See Mowat, Magnus

Lock, Arnold Charles Cooper 20th c. [WW]
Author
* Cooper, Charles

[A] Lock Keeper
See Sadler, J.

Lock, Thomas
See Land, George Thomas Lock

Lockard, Francis Marion [Frank] 1855-? [NAA]
American author
* F. M.

Lockard, Leonard
See Thomas, Theodore L. [Ted]

Lockart, Lucia A[licia] Fox 1930- [CA]
Peruvian-born author and educator
* Ugaro De Fox, Lucia

Locke, Alain L. 1886-1954 [HPPN]
American educator and author
* [The] First Black Rhodes Scholar

Locke, Arthur D'Arcy 1917- [BWG, EG, GF]
South African golfer
* Locke, Bobby

Locke, Bobby
See Locke, Arthur D'Arcy

Locke, Bobby
See Locke, Lawrence Donald

Locke, Charles F. 20th c. [WGT]
Author
* McLociard, George

Locke, Clinton W. [house pseudonym]
[Stratemeyer Syndicate]
See Stratemeyer, Edward L.

Locke, David Ross 1833-1888 [DEL, DNNF, FFF]
American author
* Nasby, [Rev.] Petroleum Vesuvius

Locke, George [Walter] 1936- [ESF, SFP]
British author
* Walters, Gordon

Locke, Gipper
See Locke, Roland A.

Locke, John 1632-1704 [DEA, HPPN]
British author and philosopher
* [The] Father of the Enlightenment in England
* P. A. P. O. I. L. A.
* Philanthropus

Locke, John 1847-1889 [FFF, PI]
Irish poet and journalist
* Southern Gael

Locke, Lawrence Donald 1934- [BE]
American baseball player
* Locke, Bobby

Locke, Lucie
See Price, Lucie Locke

Locke, Martin
See Duncan, W[illiam] Murdoch

Locke, Peter
See McCutchan, J[ohn] Wilson

Locke, Prescott
See Wakefield, Homer

Locke, R. E.
See Raffelock, David

Locke, Richard Adams 1800-1871 [HPPN, WGT]
British-born American author
* [The] Contriver of the Moon Hoax
* Herschel, [Sir] John

Locke, Robert Donald 20th c. [WGT]
Author
* Arcot, Roger

Locke, Roland A. 1903?-1952 [AS]
American track and field athlete
* Locke, Gipper

Locke, Una
See Bailey, Urania Locke Stoughton

Locke, W. J.
See Locke, William John

Locke, William John 1863-1930 [LC]
British author
* Locke, W. J.

Locke-Elliott, Sumner
See Elliott, Sumner Locke

Locker, Arthur
See Forbes, J. H.

Locker, Frederick 1821-1895 [WBD]
British poet
* Locker-Lampson, Frederick

Locker-Lampson, Frederick
See Locker, Frederick

Lockett, Animal
See Lockett, Frank

Lockett, Buck
See Lockett, Lester

Lockett, Frank 1958?- [SI 4-16-84]
American football player
* Lockett, Animal

Lockett, Lester 1912- [MK]
American baseball player
* Lockett, Buck

Lockfast
See Simmons, William Hammatt

Lockhart, Arthur John 1850-1926 [DNA]
Canadian-born author and clergyman
* Felix, Pastor

Lockhart, Carl Ford 1943- [FB, SMG]
American football player
* Lockhart, Spider

Lockhart, Frank ?-1928
Auto racer
* [The] Boy Wonder

Lockhart, Holes
See Lockhart, Howard

Lockhart, Howard 20th c. [CEI]
Hockey player
* Lockhart, Holes

Lockhart, John Gibson 1794-1854 [DEA, DEL, DLE1, FFF, RH]
Scottish author and critic
* [The] Aristarch of British Criticism
* J. G. L.
* Morris, Peter
* Peter
* [The] Scorpion
* Wastle, William

Lockhart, John Hugh 19th c. [FFF, PA]
Grandson of Scottish author, Sir Walter Scott
* Littlejohn, Hugh

Lockhart, Spider
See Lockhart, Carl Ford

Lockhart, T. C.
See Stammel, Heinz-Josef

Locklear, Chief
See Locklear, Gene

Locklear, Gene 1949- [SMG]
American baseball player
* Locklear, Chief

Locklear, Omer ?-1920 [HPPN]
American stunt aviator and barnstormer
* [The] Man Who Walked on Wings

Lockman, Carroll Walter 1926- [BE, PB]
American baseball player
* Lockman, Whitey

Lockman, Whitey
See Lockman, Carroll Walter

Lockridge, Frances Louise [Davis] 20th c. [CC, WW]
Author
* Richards, Francis [joint pseudonym with Richard (Orson) Lockridge]

Lockridge, Hildegarde [Dolson] 1908-1981 [CA]
American author
* Dolson, Hildegarde

Lockridge, Norman
See Roth, Samuel

Lockridge, Richard [Orson] 1898- [CC, WW]
Author
* Richards, Francis [joint pseudonym with Frances Louise (Davis) Lockridge]

Lockroy, Edourard Etienne Antoine
See Simon, Edouard Etienne Antoine

Lockroy, Joseph Philippe
See Simon, Joseph Philippe

[The] Locksmith King
See Louis XVI

Lockwood, Claude Edward 1946- [BE, SMG, WWB]
American baseball player
* Lockwood, Skip

Lockwood, Clyde 20th c. [HPPN]
American jazz musician
* Lockwood, Red

Lockwood, Gary
See Yusolfsky, John Gary

Lockwood, Ingersoll 1841-1918 [DNA]
American author, attorney, editor
* Longman, Irwin

Lockwood, Margaret
See Day, Margaret

Lockwood, Mary
See Spelman, Mary

Lockwood, Ralph Ingersoll 1798-1858 [HPPN]
American author and attorney
* Smith, Mr.

Lockwood, Red
See Lockwood, Clyde

Lockwood, Skip
See Lockwood, Claude Edward

Lockyer, Roger Walter 1927- [CA, WD]
British author and historian
* Francis, Philip

Loco, Joe
See Esteves, Jose, Jr.

Locomotive
See Harvey, Moses

Lode, Rex
See Goldstein, William Isaac

Loden, James [Jimmie] 1929-   [CME, CWG]
American country-western performer
* James, Sonny
* [The] Southern Gentleman

Loder, John
See Lowe, John

Loder, Vernon
See Vahey, John George Haslette

Lodge, Henry Cabot 1850-1924   [HPPN]
American legislator and author
* [The] Destroyer of the League of Nations

Lodge, John 1801-1873   [BBD]
British poet and composer
* Ellerton, John Lodge

Lodge, Maureen Roffey
See Roffey, Maureen

Lodge, Mrs. Benjamin   [FFF]
Entertainer
* Maddigan, Gertie

Lodge, Thomas 1555-1625   [DEP, DNNS, RH]
British author, playwright, poet
* [The] Young Juvenal

[The] Lodger
See Lloyd, John Ivester

Lodigiani, Dario Joseph 1916-   [BE]
American baseball player
* Lodigiani, Lodi

Lodigiani, Lodi
See Lodigiani, Dario Joseph

Loeb, Albert Lorch 1890-   [EJS]
American football player
* [Der] Yiddisher Vild-Kat

Loeb, Milton E. 1888-1972   [HPPN]
American manufacturing executive and inventor
* [The] Father of the Brillo Pad

Loeb, Richard A. 1907-1936   [BLB]
American murderer and kidnapper
* Johnson, George
* Mason, Louis

Loehr, Dolores 1926-1971   [BEW, FC]
American actress
* Lynn, Diana

Loening, Sarah Larkin 1896-   [CA]
American author and poet
* Larkin, Sarah

Loennbohm, Armas Eino Leopold 1878-1925   [HPPN]
Finnish poet, author, playwright
* Leino, Eino

Loennquist, Carl Adolph 20th c.   [ALY]
Swedish-born clergyman and author
* Teofilus

Loeper, John J[oseph] 1929-   [CA, SAT]
American educator and author
* Lowe, Jay, Jr.

Loesser, Frank Henry 1910-   [HPPN]
American songwriter
* [The] Army's One Man Hit Parade
* [The] G. I.'s Own Songwriter

Loew, Grace [Klein] 1910?-1965   [BI, HPPN]
American author
* Farewell, Mina

Loewe, Frederick 1904-   [PAC]
American composer
* Loewe, Fritz

Loewe, Fritz
See Loewe, Frederick

Loewe Kalbe
See Loewe, Wilhelm

Loewe, Wilhelm 1814-1886   [WBD]
German politician
* Loewe Kalbe

Loewenbrugger, Nikolaus 1417-1487 [WBD]
Swiss hermit
* Bruder Klaus
* Nicholas of Flue

Loewenstein, Laszlo 1904-1964   [BDF, FC]
Hungarian-born actor
* Lorre, Peter

Loewenthal, Leonard Joseph Alfonso 1903-   [CA]
British physician and author
* Lowe, Alfonso

Loewy, Raymond 1893-   [HPPN]
French-American industrial designer
* [The] Father of Industrial Design

Loff, Jeanette
See Lov, Janette

Lofft, Capel 1751-1824   [HPPN, SN]
British author
* [A] Layman
* [The] Maecenas of Shoemakers
* That Modern Midas

Lofland, John   [PA]
Author
* [The] Milford Bard

Loftin, J. C.   [FFF, PA]
Author
* Ace Clubs

Loftin, John 20th c.   [SI 11-28-83]
American basketball coach
* [The] Road Runner

Loftin, Louis Santop 1890-1945   [MK]
American baseball player
* Loftin, Top
* Santop, Louis

Loftin, Top
See Loftin, Louis Santop

Lofting, Hugh 1886-1947   [HPPN]
British-American author and illustrator
* Dolittle, Dr.

Lofton, Clarence 1896-1956?   [BWW, EJ, WWJ]
American jazz musician
* Clemens, Albert?
* Lofton, Cripple Clarence

Lofton, Cripple Clarence
See Lofton, Clarence

Lofton, Lawrence 1930-   [DAM]
American musician
* Lofton, Tricky

Lofton, Tricky
See Lofton, Lawrence

Lofts, Norah [Robinson] 1904-   [CA, CC, WGT]
British author
* Astley, Juliet
* Curtis, Peter

Loftus, Cissie
See Loftus, Marie Cecilia

Loftus, Marie 1857-1940   [THR]
Scottish-born comedienne
* [The] Hibernian Hebe

Loftus, Marie Cecilia 1876-1943   [BEW]
Scottish-born actress
* Loftus, Cissie

Loftus, Mrs. W. F.   [FFF]
Entertainer
* Adair, Marie

Lofty
See Isaacs, Marcel Godfrey

Log Cabin Harrison
See Harrison, William Henry

[The] Log Cabin President
See Harrison, William Henry

Log Hall Philips
See Philips, Mardin Wilson

Logan
See Dillon, Thomas

Logan
See Thorpe, Thomas Bangs

Logan
See Ward, Townsend

Logan, Agnes
See Adams, Agnes

Logan, [Rev.] Allan 18th c.   [HPPN]
Scottish clergyman
* [A] Gentleman in the Country

Logan, Black Jack
See Logan, John Alexander

Logan, Celia   [PA]
Author
* C. L.

Logan, Don
See Crawford, William [Elbert]

Logan, Ella
See Armour-Allan, Ella

Logan, Ford
See Newton, Dwight Bennett

Logan, George 1753-1821 [HPPN]
American physician and politician
* [An] American Farmer
* [A] Farmer

Logan, Harvey 1868?-1900? [BLB, HPPN]
American criminal
* Curry, Harvey
* Curry, Kid
* Howard, Ed
* Johnson, Charles

Logan, Jacqueline 1904- [HPPN]
American actress
* [The] Smoky Eyed Beauty of the Silent Screen

Logan, Jake [house pseudonym, Playboy Press]
See Krepps, Robert W[ilson]

Logan, Jake [house pseudonym, Playboy Press]
See Riefe, Alan

Logan, Jake [house pseudonym, Playboy Press]
See Rifkin, Shepard

Logan, Jake
See Smith, Martin William

Logan, James [or John]
See Tah Gah Jute

Logan, John Alexander 1826-1886 [DNNS, HPPN, NPS, SN, UH]
American officer and statesman
* [The] Black Eagle of Illinois
* Jack of Spades
* Logan, Black Jack
* [The] Murat of the Union Army

Logan, John Daniel 1869-1929 [DLE1]
Canadian poet, author, scholar
* Novicius, Aloysius

Logan, John, Jr. [Johnny] 1927- [PB]
American baseball player
* Logan, Yachta

Logan, Joseph Leroy 1922- [BA]
American physician
* [The] Country Doctor

Logan, Lefty
See Logan, Robert Dean

Logan, Lillian Mee 1909- [IAW]
American-born educator and author
* Nagol [joint pseudonym with Virgil Glen Logan]

Logan, M. C. [PA]
Author
* Vincent, Ellerton

Logan, Mark
See Nicole, Christopher Robin

Logan, Martha
See Olmstead, Agnes [Reasor]

Logan, Mary
See Smith, Mary Pearsall

Logan, Olive 1839-1909 [DNA, FFF, PA]
American writer, actress, journalist
* Belle, Clara
* Chroniqueuse

Logan, Olive
See Sikes, Olive [Logan]

Logan, Robert Dean 1910- [BE]
American baseball player
* Logan, Lefty

Logan, Sara [joint pseudonym with Judy Simpson]
See Haydon, June

Logan, Sara [joint pseudonym with June Haydon]
See Simpson, Judy

Logan, Thomas A. [PA]
Author
* Gloan

Logan, Virgil Glen 1904- [IAW]
American-born educator and author
* Nagol [joint pseudonym with Lillian Mee Logan]

Logan, William 18th c. [HPPN]
Scottish author
* [A] Gentleman in Scotland

Logan, William
See Harris, Larry M[ark]

Logan, Yachta
See Logan, John, Jr. [Johnny]

Logau, Friedrich von 1604-1655 [WBD]
German poet and author
* Golaw, Salomon von

Loges, Francois des
See Montcorbier, Francois de

[The] Loggerhead of London
See Pitt, William [Earl of Chatham]

Loghem, Martinus Gesinus Lambert van 1849-1934 [WBD]
Dutch poet and author
* Fiore della Neve

[The] Logic Chopping Machine
See Mill, John Stuart

Logie, [Rev] William 1786-1856 [HPPN]
Scottish clergyman
* [A] Minister

Logistes
See Glasgow, George

Logroller
See Le Gallienne, Richard

Logroscino [or Lo Groscino], **Nicola** 1700?-1763? [WBD]
Italian composer
* [Il] Dio dell'Opera Buffa

Logue, Christopher 1926- [CA, WD]
British author, poet, playwright
* Vicarion, [Count] Palmiro

Lohier, Michel 1891-1973 [CW]
West Indian author
* Oubo, Irac

Lohman, George F. 1864-1928 [BE]
American baseball player
* Lohman, Pete

Lohman, Pete
See Lohman, George F.

Lohrke, Jack Wayne 1924- [BE]
American baseball player
* Lohrke, Lucky

Lohrke, Lucky
See Lohrke, Jack Wayne

Lohrman, Paul [house pseudonym, Ziff-Davis]
See Fairman, Paul W.

Lohrman, Paul [house pseudonym, Ziff-Davis]
See Shaver, Richard S[harpe]

Loinger, Silvia Mary 1917- [IAW]
Austrian author
* Simalo

Loisette, Alphonso
See Larrowe, Marcus Dwight

Loison, Louis Henri 1770?-1816 [SN]
French army officer
* [The] Bloody One-Handed
* Maneta

Lokayat, Suri
See Chaudhari, Raghuveer

Lokelani, [Princess] Lei
See Shaw, Elizabeth Jonia Leilokelani

Lokhvitskaya, Nadezhda Alexandrovna 1872-1952
Russian author
* Teffi, Nadezhda

Lokman 5th c. [NPS]
Arabic philosopher
* [The] Aesop of Arabia

Loknayak [The Peoples Hero]
See Narayan, Jayaprakash

Lola
See Israel, Leon

Lola
See Wynne, Emma [Moffett]

Lolewski-Cassini, Oleg 1913- [HPPN, IPA]
French fashion designer
* Cassini, Oleg
* [The] Fashion World's Most Irrepressible Master of Ceremonies
* [The] Rebel of Seventh Avenue

Lolita
See Ditta, Lolita

Lollard, Walter ?-1322 [SN]
Leader of religious cult
* [The] Morning Star of the Reformation in Germany

Lolli, Countess 1850-1922 [FFF]
Italian opera singer
* Scalchi, Sofia

[The] Lollipop Governor
See Milliken, William Grawn

Lollobrigida, Guido 20th c. [WF]
Italian actor
* Burton, Lee

Lolly
See Parsons, Louella

L'Olonnois, Francois
See Nau, Jacques Jean David

Lolordo, Pasquale ?-1929 [PHM]
American underworld figure
* Lolordo, Patsy

Lolordo, Patsy
See Lolordo, Pasquale

Lom, Herbert
See Kuchacevich Ze Schluderpacheru, Herbert Charles Angelo

Lom, Josephine
See Lomnicka, [Azdis] Josephine

Lomas, Doris 1900-1975 [SC]
British actress
* Pender, Doris

Lomas, Steve
See Brennan, Joseph L[omas]

Lomax, Bliss
See Drago, Harry Sinclair

Lomax, E. Victoria [PA]
Author
* Little, Byrd

Lomax, W. J. 20th c. [MBF]
British author
* Fulke, Commissioner
* Maxwell, Herbert

Lombard, Carole
See Peters, Jane Alice

Lombard, Nap [joint pseudonym with Neil Stewart]
See Johnson, Pamela Hansford

Lombard, Nap [joint pseudonym with Pamela Hansford Johnson]
See Stewart, Neil

Lombard, Peter [or Pietro] 1100-1164 [DNNF, DNNS, HN]
Italian theologian
* Magister Sententiarum
* [The] Master of Sentences

Lombard, Peter
See Benham, William

Lombardi, Alfonso
See Cittadella, Alfonso

Lombardi, Beezer
See Lombardi, Ernesto Natali

Lombardi, Bocci
See Lombardi, Ernesto Natali

Lombardi, Claudio 1922- [EJ]
American jazz musician
* Lombardi, Clyde

Lombardi, Clyde
See Lombardi, Claudio

Lombardi, Cynthia
See Lombardi, Georgina M. [Richmond]

Lombardi, Ernesto Natali 1908-1977 [BE, BI, BN, PB]
American baseball player
* Lombardi, Beezer
* Lombardi, Bocci
* Lombardi, Ernie
* Lombardi, Lom
* Lombardi, Schnozz

Lombardi, Ernie
See Lombardi, Ernesto Natali

Lombardi, Georgina M. [Richmond] 20th c. [NAA, WW]
American author
* Lombardi, Cynthia

Lombardi, Lella 1943- [SA]
Italian auto racer
* [The] Tigress of Turin

Lombardi, Lom
See Lombardi, Ernesto Natali

Lombardi, Pasquale
See Vizzini, Sal[vatore]

Lombardi, Schnozz
See Lombardi, Ernesto Natali

Lombardo, Antonio ?-1928 [PHM]
Italian-born American underworld figure
* Lombardo, Tony

Lombardo, Antonio
See Solaro, Antonio

Lombardo, Gaetano Alberto 1902-1977 [BEW, HPPN]
Canadian bandleader
* [The] King of Corn
* Lombardo, Guy
* New Year's Eve, Mr.

Lombardo, Guy
See Lombardo, Gaetano Alberto

Lombardo, Joey 20th c. [WP 3-6-83]
Underworld figure
* Joey the Clown

Lombardo, Lombo
See Lombardo, Thomas A.

Lombardo, Pietro
See Solaro, Pietro

Lombardo, Thomas A. 1922-1950 [AS, FB]
American football player
* Lombardo, Lombo

Lombardo, Tony
See Lombardo, Antonio

Lombardo, Tullio
See Solaro, Tullio

Lombino, Dominic 1943?- [TI 2-28-83]
Italian attorney
* Dimanso, Andrew

Lombino, Salvatore A. 1926- [CA, EMD, WGT]
American author
* Cannon, Curt
* Collins, Hunt
* Hunter, Evan
* Marsten, Richard
* McBain, Ed
* Rice, Craig [joint pseudonym with Georgiana Ann Randolph]

Lome, Mike
See Pinkwater, Daniel Manus

Lomenie de Brienne, Etienne Charles 1727-1794 [HN]
French prelate and statesman
* [Le] Cardinal de l'Ignominie

Lomi, Artemisia 1590-1642? [HPPN]
Italian painter
* Gentileschi, Artemisia

Lomi, Orazio 1563-1647 [HPPN]
Italian painter
* Gentileschi, Orazio

Lomnicka, [Azdis] Josephine 20th c. [WD]
Polish-born artist and writer
* Lom, Josephine

Lomov, A.
See Lomov-Oppokov, Georgii Ippolitovich

Lomov-Oppokov, Georgii Ippolitovich 1888-1938 [BI]
Russian Communist leader
* Lomov, A.

Lomski, Leo 1903?-1975 [BI]
American boxer
* [The] Aberdeen Assassin

Lon, Alice ?-1981
American singer
* [The] Champagne Lady

Lon Nol 1913- [HPPN]
Cambodian army officer
* [The] Marshal's Backstreet Astrologer

Lonardo, Angelo 1911?- [WP 11-23-85]
American underworld figure
* Lonardo, Big Ange

Lonardo, Big Ange
See Lonardo, Angelo

Lonardo, Big Joe
See Lonardo, Joseph

Lonardo, Joseph 20th c. [MM]
American underworld figure
* Lonardo, Big Joe
* Lonardo, Peppino

Lonardo, Peppino
See Lonardo, Joseph

Lonati 17th c. [HN]
Italian musician
* [Il] Gobbo [The Hunchback]

Lonborg, Arthur 1899- [BB]
American basketball coach
* Lonborg, Dutch

Lonborg, Dutch
See Lonborg, Arthur

Lonborg, Gentleman Jim
See Lonborg, James Reynold

Lonborg, James Reynold 1943- [SMG]
American baseball player
* Lonborg, Gentleman Jim
* Lonborg, Lonnie

Lonborg, Lonnie
See Lonborg, James Reynold

Lonchar, John Anthony 1952- [SMG]
American baseball player
* Lonchar, Lonch

Lonchar, Lonch
See Lonchar, John Anthony

Lonchit [or Loncit], Vilma?
See Baulsy, Banky Vilma

[Il] Londinese
See Sammartini [or San Martini],
Giuseppe

London Antiquary
See Fairholt, Frederick William

[A] London Antiquary
See Hotten, John Camden

London, Art
See Lund, Arthur

London, Babe
See London, Jean

[The] London Bach
See Bach, Johann Christian

[The] London Citizen
See Cruden, Alexander

[A] London Clergyman
See Portal, [Rev.] George Raymond

[A] London Clerk
See Hughes, Thomas

London, George
See Burnstein, George

[The] London Hermit
See Parke, F.

[The] London Idol
See Powles, Matilda Alice

London, Jane
See Geis, Darlene [Stern]

London, Jean 1901?-1980 [FIR]
Entertainer
* London, Babe

London, John
See Kuehne, John

London, John Griffith [Jack] 1876-1916
[HPPN, TLC]
American author
* [The] American Kipling
* [The] Boy Socialist
* [The] King of the Adventure Story
* Prince of the Oyster Pirates
* [The] Sailor Kid

London, Julie
See Peck, Julie

London, Lisa
See Martin, Gloria Ann

London Little-Grace
See Bonner, Edmund

[A] London Merchant
See Ellis, William

[A] London Merchant
See Stokes, C. W.

[A] London Physician
See Dickson, Samuel Henry

[A] London Physician
See Guy, William Augustus

[A] London Physician
See Howard, James

[The] London Star
See De Melvin, Henri

London, Stewart
See Wilson, Roger C.

[A] London Tailor
See Place, Francis

London, Tom
See Clapham, Leonard

London W.
See Dean, Joseph H.

[The] Londoner
See Barron, Oswald

[A] Londoner
See White, Walter

London's Lancashire Comedian
See Stansfield, Thomas

Londos, Jim 20th c. [CSH]
Boxer and wrestler
* [The] Golden Greek
* [The] Greek Adonis

Lone Cat Fuller
See Fuller, Jesse

[The] Lone Cowboy
See Aliff, Hamilton C.

[The] Lone Cowboy
See Kissinger, Henry Alfred

[The] Lone Eagle
See Lindbergh, Charles Augustus

[The] Lone Heretic
See Unamuno Y Jugo, Miguel de

[The] Lone Highwayman
See Holzhay, Reimund

[the] Lone Lion
See Borah, William Edgar

[The] Lone Pillar
See Wash A Kie

Lone Pine, Hal
See Breau, Harold

Lone Ranger
See Beemer, Brace Bell

[The] Lone Ranger
See Moore, Clayton

[The] Lone Star
See Starr, Frederick

Lone Star Dietz
See Dietz, William

[The] Lone Star Ranger
See Slaughter, Marion T.

[The] Lone Star Ranger
See White, John I[rwin]

[The] Lone Twister
See Kaufman, Murray

Lone Wolf
See Schultz, Hart Merriam

[The] Lone Wolf
See Woods, Oscar

[The] Lone Wolf of the Senate
See Morse, Wayne Lyman

[The] Lone Wolf of the Underworld
See Millman, Harry

[The] Lone Wolf of Uruguayan Letters
See Onetti, Juan Carlos

[The] Lone Wolf Politician
See Mitchell, Clarence M., III

[The] Lonely Cowboy
See Fletcher, Tex

[The] Lonely Hearts Killer
See Fernandez, Raymond

[The] Lonely Hero of Hockey
See Worsley, Lorne John

[The] Lonely Queen
See Elizabeth I

[The] Lonely Troubadour
See Friedman, Theodore Leopold

[The] Loner
See Hinckley, John W., Jr.

Lonergan, Michael ?-1953 [BI]
Irish-American journalist
* Shandon

Lonergan, Peg Leg
See Lonergan, Richard

Lonergan, Richard 20th c. [BLB]
American gangster
* Lonergan, Peg Leg

Lonergan, Thomas S. 1861-? [PI]
Irish-born poet and journalist
* Hibernicus

Lonesome Charley Reynolds
See Reynolds, Charles Alexander

[The] Lonesome Cowboy
See White, John I[rwin]

Lonesome Dave
See Peverett, David

Lonesome George
See Gobel, George Leslie

Lonesome George Romney
See   Romney, George

Lonesome George Wallace
See   Wallace, George Corley

Lonesome George Weiss
See   Weiss, George Martin

Lonesome Luke
See   Levielle [or Leuvielle?], Gabriel

Lonesome Luke
See   Lloyd, Harold Clayton

[The] Lonesome Road Racer
See   Wiltshire, George

[The] Lonesome Singer of the Air
See   Marvin, Johnny

Lonesome Sundown
See   Green, Cornelius

Loney, Carolyn Patricia 1944-   [BA]
American business executive
* Loney, Cookie

Loney, Cookie
See   Loney, Carolyn Patricia

Loney, Glenn [Meredith] 1928-   [CA]
American educator and author
* Meredith, Jeff

[Le] Long
See   Philip V [or Philippe]

Long, Amelia Reynolds 1904-   [WGT, WW]
Author
* Coxe, Kathleen Buddington [joint pseudonym with Edna McHugh]
* Laing, Patrick
* Reynolds, Adrian
* Reynolds, Peter
* Weir, Mordred

Long, Andy Iona 1902-   [ASC]
Hawaiian composer
* Iona, Andy

Long, Ann Marie
See   Jensen, Pauline Marie [Long]

Long, Arnold 1940-   [DC]
British cricketer
* Long, Buzby
* Long, Oblong

Long Ben
See   Avery, [Captain] John

Long Ben Every
See   Every, Henry

Long, Big Steve
See   Long, Steve

Long Bob Ewing
See   Ewing, George Lemuel

Long Bob Meusel
See   Meusel, Robert William [Bob]

Long, Buzby
See   Long, Arnold

Long, Clair 20th c.   [HPPN]
American football player
* Long, Shorty

Long, Clarence D. 1909?-   [WP 11-8-84]
American politician
* Long, Doc

Long, Crawford W. 1815-1878   [HPPN]
American surgeon
* [The] First Discoverer of Anesthesia

Long, Doc
See   Long, Clarence D.

Long, Don 1910?-   [WWJ]
American jazz musician
* Long, Slats

Long, Earl Kemp 1895-1960
American politician
* Bitin Man
* Earl of Louisiana
* Ole Earl
* Wild Steed
* Winnfield Frog
* Younger Brother

Long, Edward 1734-1813   [IP]
British author
* Babble, Nicholas, Esq.
* [A] Planter

Long, Edward Noel ?-1809   [IP]
British author
* Cleon

Long, Emmett
See   Leonard, Elmore

Long, Frank Belknap 1903-   [SFL, WGT]
American author
* Long, Lyda Belknap
* Northern, Leslie [house pseudonym]

Long, Fred T. 20th c.   [IBW]
American football coach
* Long, Pop

Long, Frederick 1940-1969   [RO2]
American singer
* Long, Shorty

Long, Gabrielle Margaret Vere [Campbell] 1886-1952   [LAO, TC, WGT]
British author and playwright
* Bowen, Marjorie
* Campbell, Margaret
* Costanza, Senora
* Paye, Robert
* Preedy, George
* Shearing, Joseph
* Vere, Margaret
* Winch, John

Long, George 1800-?   [IP]
British scholar
* [A] Member of the University of Cambridge

Long, Germany
See   Long, Herman C.

Long, Gerry
See   Larkins, William Frederick

Long, Glynn Lea 1895-1945   [NOJ]
American jazz musician
* Long, Red

Long Gone Miles
See   Miles, Luke

Long Hair
See   Custer, George Armstrong

Long Haired Sam
See   Brown, Sam

[The] Long Haired Samian
See   Pythagoras

[The] Long Haired Wonder
See   Clark, Steve

Long Hank Lawton
See   Lawton, Henry W.

Long, Harold B.   [BI]
American clergyman and painter
* Zenos, G. M.

Long Harry
See   Wilkinson, Henry, Jr.

Long, Helen Beecher [house pseudonym]
[Stratemeyer Syndicate]
See   Stratemeyer, Edward L.

Long Henry Pell
See   Pell, Henry

Long Herm Besse
See   Besse, Herman

Long, Herman C. 1866-1909   [AS, BE]
American baseball player
* Long, Germany

Long, Hooey
See   Long, Huey Pierce

Long, Huey
See   Long, Sumner

Long, Huey Pierce 1893-1935   [HPPN]
American politician
* American Demagogue
* American Dictator
* [The] Boss
* [The] Dictator of Louisiana
* [The] Kingfish
* Long, Hooey
* Louisiana's Loud Speaker

Long, Huey Pierce, Jr. 1918-
American politician
* Billiu, Russell

Long, Isaac 1899?-
American banker
* Long, Zack

[The] Long Island Farmer Poet
See   Cutter, Bloodgood H.

Long, James Sebastian 1954-   [IBW]
American jockey
* [The] Black Shoemaker

Long Jim Barnes
See   Barnes, James M.

Long Jim Holdsworth
See   Holdsworth, James [Jim]

Long Jim Whitney
See Whitney, James E.

Long, John [Jack] 19th c. [EWG]
American law officer
* Long John

Long, John 1956-
American basketball player
* B. B.
* Long, Lightning

Long John
See Long, John [Jack]

Long John
See Wentworth, John

Long John Andre
See Andre, John Edward

Long John Baldry
See Baldry, John

Long, John Frederick Lawrence 1917-
[CA, IAW]
British air force officer and author
* Longo, Juan
* Longsword, John

Long John Henderson
See Henderson, John Duncan

Long John Nebel
See Nebel, John

Long John Reilly
See Reilly, John Good

Long John Woodruff
See Woodruff, John

Long, Juanita 1901-1968 [EMT]
American actress and singer
* Hall, Juanita

Long, Kien, Emperor of China
See Mathias, Thomas James

Long Knife
See Boone, Daniel

Long Knife
See Lewis, Meriwether

Long, Lep
See Long, Lester

Long, Lester 1888-1958 [BE]
American baseball player
* Long, Lep

Long Levi Meyerle
See Meyerle, Levi Samuel

Long, Lightning
See Long, John

Long, Lily Augusta ?-1927 [WW]
Author
* Doubleday, Roman

Long, Linda 20th c. [HPPN]
American entertainer
* Phaedra

Long Liz Stride
See Stride, Elizabeth

Long, Lucile
See Brandt, Lucile [Long Strayer]

Long, Lyda Belknap
See Long, Frank Belknap

Long, Margaret 1938?- [HPPN]
American marksman
* Marksman, Little Miss

Long, Mason 1842-? [HPPN]
American gambler
* [The] Converted Gambler

Long, Naomi Cornelia
See Madgett, Naomi Long

Long Neck Woman
See Cheatham, K[aryn] Follis

Long, Nelson 1876-1929 [BE]
Canadian-born baseball player
* Long, Red

Long, Oblong
See Long, Arnold

Long Peter
See Aartsen, Peter

Long, Peter
See Hecht, Ben

Long, Pop
See Long, Fred T.

Long, Red
See Long, Glynn Lea

Long, Red
See Long, Nelson

Long, Richard A[lexander] 1927- [CA]
American educator and author
* Alexander, Ric

Long, Roger 1680-1770 [IP]
British clergyman, astronomer, author
* Dicaiophilus Cantabrigiensis

Long, Russell 20th c.
American politician
* Long, Sugar Ray

Long, Russell Billiu 1918-
American politician
* Kingfish's Son
* Lord of the Manor
* Master of the Maze
* People's Capitalist
* Princefish
* Senate's Rising Star
* Whip's Lash

Long Sam Thompson
See Thompson, Samuel Tommy

Long, Samuel 20th c. [HPPN]
American hobo
* Long, Scissor Sam

Long, Scissor Sam
See Long, Samuel

[The] Long Scribe
See Dowling, Vincent

Long, Shorty
See Long, Clair

Long, Shorty
See Long, Frederick

Long, Silent
See Lynch, Thomas Took

Long Sir Thomas
See Robinson, [Sir] Thomas

Long, Slats
See Long, Don

Long, Steve ?-1868 [EWG]
American gunfighter
* Long, Big Steve

Long, Sugar Ray
See Long, Russell

Long, Sumner 20th c.
American shipping broker and sailboat racer
* Long, Huey

Long Tom
See Jefferson, Thomas

Long Tom Hughes
See Hughes, Thomas J.

Long Tom Parsons
See Parsons, Thomas Anthony [Tom]

Long Tom Perkins
See Perkins, Thomas Handasyd

Long Tom Winsett
See Winsett, John Thomas

[The] Long 'Un
See Lincoln, Abraham

Long, Wesley
See Smith, George O[liver]

Long, William Joseph 1866-1952
[HPPN]
American author, naturalist, clergyman
* Rabbit, Peter

Long, William Stuart
See Stuart, Vivian [Finlay]

Long, Zack
See Long, Isaac

Long-Holloway, A.
See Holloway, Arthur Thomas

Longalius
See De Longueil, Christophe

Longbaugh, Harry 1870?-1909? [BI,
BLB, HPPN]
American outlaw
* Brown, Henry
* [The] Sundance Kid

Longbaugh, Harry
See Goldman, William W.

Longbaugh, Robert 1901-1972 [HPPN]
American outlaw
* [The] Cimarron Kid

Longbeard
See FitzOsbert, William

Longbeard, Frederick
See Longyear, Barry Brookes**

Longden, Johnny 1910- [CSH, HPPN]
Canadian jockey
* [The] Master Reinsman
* [The] Pumper

Longdon, George
See Rayer, Francis G.

[The] Longest Running Newscaster in History
See Thomas, Lowell Jackson

Longfellow, Henry Wadsworth 1807-1882
[FFF, HPPN, IP, PA, SN]
American poet
* [An] American
* [The] Children's Poet
* Coffin, Joshua
* Drift-Wood
* H. W. L.
* Hammergafferstein, Hans
* [The] Laureate of Song
* [The] Poet of the Commonplace
* Strongfellow, Professor

[The] Longfellow of the South
See Hayne, Paul Hamilton

Longfellow, [Rev.] Samuel 1819-1892
[HPPN]
American clergyman and hymn writer
* S. L.

Longford, Francis Aungier Pakenham
1905- [HPPN]
British diplomat
* Porn, Lord

Longford, Frank Pakenham
See Pakenham, Francis Aungier

Longhair, Dr.
See Byrd, Henry Roeland

Longhair, Professor
See Byrd, Henry Roeland

Longhaired Jim Courtright
See Courtright, Timothy Isaiah

Longhi, Pietro
See Falca, Pietro

Longhurst, Percy William 1874-? [MBF]
British author
* Agent 55
* Hockley, Lewis
* Kingston, Brian
* Spence, Hubert

Longimanus [The Long-Handed]
See Artaxerxes I

Longinus
See Dlugosz, Jean

Longinus, Dionysius Cassius 213-273
[FFF, RH, SN]
Roman philosopher
* [The] Living Cyclopaedia
* [The] Living Library
* [The] Prince of Critics
* [The] Walking Library
* [The] Walking Museum

Longinus the Pope
See Pearce, Zachary

Longleigh, Peter J., Jr.
See Korges, James

Longley, Clint 1952- [SMG]
American football player
* [The] Mad Bomber

Longley, John [IP]
British barrister and author
* [An] Eminent English Counsel

Longley, Lydia 1674-1758 [BI]
American nun
* Sainte Madeleine, [Sister]

Longley, Rattling Bill
See Longley, William Preston

Longley, Red
See Longley, Wyman

Longley, Wild Bill
See Longley, William Preston

Longley, William Preston 1850?-1878
[DI, EWG, HPPN]
American murderer and bandit
* Black, Bill
* Black, William
* Henry, Bill
* Jackson, Bill
* Jones, Tom
* Longley, Rattling Bill
* Longley, Wild Bill
* Patterson, Jim
* Webb, Jim

Longley, Wyman 20th c. [OBW]
American baseball player
* Longley, Red

Longlooker Mick Denfeld
See Denfield, Mick

Longman, Irwin
See Lockwood, Ingersoll

Longmuir, John 19th c. [HPPN]
Scottish poet
* J. L.

Longo, Bruce 1939?-1978 [HPPN]
American religious fanatic
* David, Immanuel
* God the Father
* [The] Holy Ghost
* Jesus Christ
* [The] True Prophet

Longo, Germano 20th c. [WF]
Italian actor
* Laramy, Grant

Longo, Juan
See Long, John Frederick Lawrence

Longo, Luigi 1900- [HPPN]
Italian Communist leader
* Italy's Middle of the Road Tactician

Longomontanus
See Severin, Christian

Longrigg, Jane Chichester 1929- [CA]
British author
* Chichester, Jane

Longrigg, Roger [Erskine] 1929- [AW, CA, WD]
Scottish-born author
* Drummond, Ivor
* Erskine, Rosalind

Longshanks
See Edward I

Longstreet, Augustus Baldwin 1790-1870
[HPPN, IP, PA]
American author
* Crabshaw, Timothy
* [A] Native Georgian
* Short, Bob

Longstreet, James 1821-1904 [BDSA, FFF, HPPN]
American army officer and author
* [The] Bulldog
* Lee's Old War Horse
* Old Pete
* Pete
* [The] War Horse of the Confederacy

Longstreet, [Henry] Stephen [Weiner]
1907- [CA, HPPN, TC1, WW]
American author and playwright
* Burton, Thomas
* Buxton, Thomas
* Haggard, Paul
* Ormsbee, David
* Weiner, Henri

Longsword
See Henry II

Longsword
See William

Longsword
See William I

Longsword, John
See Long, John Frederick Lawrence

Longton, Scruffie
See Longton, Walter H.

Longton, Walter H. 20th c.
British military aviator
* Longton, Scruffie

Longueville, Anne 1619-1679 [HPPN]
French noblewoman and politician
* [The] Soul of the Fronde

Longueville, Peter 18th c. [WGT]
Author
* Dorrington, Edward?

Longueville, T. [NPS]
Author
* [The] Prig

Longway, A. Huge
See Lang, Andrew

Longworth, Alice Lee Roosevelt
1884?-1980 [CR, DF 10-17-82, HPPN]
Daughter of American president, Theodore Roosevelt
* Mrs. L.
* Princess Alice
* Queen Alice
* Roosevelt, Little Miss
* Washington's Other Monument

Longworth, Bert 1898-1964 [HPPN]
American photographer
* Longworth, Buddy

Longworth, Buddy
See Longworth, Bert

Longworth, Nicholas 1782-1863 [WBD]
American horticulturist
* [The] Father of American Grape
  Culture

Longyear, Barry Brookes 1942- [CA]
American author
* Ango, Fan D.
* Longbeard, Frederick
* Rant, Tol E.
* Ringdalh, Mark
* Vinest, Shaw

Lonnen, Beatrice Helen 1886- [THR]
British actress
* Lonnen, Jessie

Lonnen, Ellen Farren 1887- [THR]
British actress
* Lonnen, Nellie

Lonnen, Jessie
See Lonnen, Beatrice Helen

Lonnen, Nellie
See Lonnen, Ellen Farren

Lonnon, Alice
See Perkins, Alice

Lonsberry, Roscoe 1947- [SMG]
Canadian-born hockey player
* Lonsberry, Ross

Lonsberry, Ross
See Lonsberry, Roscoe

Lonsdale, Frederick
See Leonard, Frederick

Lonsdale, Gordon Arnold
See Molody, Konon Trofimovich

Lonsdale, Mrs. [FFF]
Entertainer
* Eyre, Sophie

Lonzo
See George, Lloyd

Lonzo
See Hooten, David

Lonzo
See Sullivan, John Y.

Look [code name used during World
War II]
See Eisenhower, David Dwight

Looker, Antonina [Hansell] 1898- [CA]
American author and poet
* Hansell, Antonina
* Jones, Orlando
* Macdonald, Nina Hansell

Looker, O. N.
See Urner, Nathan Dane

[A] Looker On
See Dix, John Ross

[A] Looker Out
See Harris, H.

Looker-On
See Meldrum, David S.

Looker-On
See Stainton, J.

[A] Looker-on from America
See Boynton, Charles Brandon

[A] Looker-On-Here in Vienna
See Andersen, Mary E.

Lookout
See Noble, John [Appelbe]

[The] Looks
See Perske, Betty Joan

Loomis, Alfred Fullerton 1890-1968 [BI]
American author
* Spun Yarn

Loomis, Amy
See Brooks, Amy

Loomis, George Washington, Jr.
1813-1865 [BLB]
American murderer and robber
* Loomis, Wash

Loomis, Noel M[iller] 1905-1969 [CA]
American author
* Allison, Sam
* Miller, Benj.
* Miller, Frank
* Water, Silas

Loomis, Rae
See Steger, Shelby

Loomis, Wash
See Loomis, George Washington, Jr.

Loonie, Janice Hays
See Hays, Janice Nicholson

[The] Loose Girt Boy
See Caesar, [Gaius] Julius

Loose, H.
See Lourie, Dick

Loose, Katharine Riegel 1877-? [NAA]
American author
* Schock, George

Looy, Jacobus Van 1855-1930 [HPPN]
Dutch painter and author
* Horen, Theo van
* [The] Leader of the Amsterdam
  School

Lopana
See De La Llana, Pedro

Lopat, Ed
See Lopatnyski, Edmund Walter

Lopat, Steady Eddie
See Lopatnyski, Edmund Walter

Lopate, Carol
See Ascher, Carol

Lopatnyski, Edmund Walter 1918- [BE,
SR]
American baseball player
* [The] Junk Man
* Lopat, Ed
* Lopat, Steady Eddie

**[The] Lope de Vega of the American
Drama**
See Davis, Owen

Lopes, Baltasar 1907- [CD]
Portuguese author and poet
* Alcanbara, Osvaldo

Lopes, Jose Laurentino 1922-1947
[HPPN]
Spanish bullfighter
* Joselillo

Lopes, Tony
See Lopez, Tony

Lopes Pontes, Maria Rita 1913- [BI]
Brazilian social worker and nun
* Dulce, [Sister]

Lopez, Aaron 1731-1782 [HPPN]
*Portuguese-American shipowner and
merchant*
* [The] Father of America's Whaling
  Industry

Lopez, Al
See Lopez, Alfonso Raymond

Lopez, Alfonso Raymond 1908- [BAB,
BE]
American baseball player and manager
* Lopez, Al
* [The] Senor

Lopez, Angel 1825-1898 [GS]
Spanish bullfighter
* [El] Regatero [The Haggler]

Lopez, Antonio 20th c. [GS]
Spanish bullfighter
* [El] Ronquillo [The Raucous One]

Lopez, Art
See Lopez, Arturo

Lopez, Arturo 1937- [BE]
Puerto Rican-born baseball player
* Lopez, Art

Lopez, Aurelio Alejandro 1948- [BE,
SMG]
Mexican-born baseball player
* [El] Lanzallama
* Lopez, Lopey
* Rios, Aurelio
* Smoke, Senor

Lopez, Carlos
See Lopez y Valles, Carlos Chaflan

Lopez, Danny 1952?- [BI]
American boxer
* Lopez, Little Red

Lopez, Emerito, Jr. 1945- [SMG]
American baseball player
* Lopez, Junior

Lopez, Encarnacion 1905-1945 [BEW]
Argentinian-born dancer
* Argentinita

Lopez, Enrique 20th c. [SFL]
Author
* Lopez, Hank

Lopez, Felix 20th c. [GS]
Spanish bullfighter
* [El] Regio [The Gorgeous One]

Lopez, Francisca Marquez 1888?-1962
[HPPN]
Spanish actress and singer
* Meller, Raquel

Lopez, Hank
See Lopez, Enrique

Lopez, Joseph 1890-1959 [BEW, EMT,
PMJ]
American entertainer
* Cook, Joe

Lopez, Junior
See Lopez, Emerito, Jr.

Lopez, Little Red
See Lopez, Danny

Lopez, Lopey
See Lopez, Aurelio Alejandro

Lopez, Magda
See Lopez de Victoria y Fernandez,
Magdalena

Lopez, Pedro Alonso 1949-
Colombian murderer
* [The] Colombian Monster

Lopez, Perfecto Macabata 1924- [EJ]
American jazz musician
* Lopez, Perry

Lopez, Perry
See Lopez, Perfecto Macabata

Lopez, Richard 20th c. [RO2]
American musician
* Lopez, Scar

Lopez, Scar
See Lopez, Richard

Lopez, Tony 20th c. [RBE]
American boxer
* Lopes, Tony

Lopez, Trini
See Lopez, Trinidad, III

Lopez, Trinidad, III 1937- [IPA]
American singer
* Lopez, Trini

Lopez, Vincent 1895- [HPPN]
American jazz musician
* [The] Pianner Kid

Lopez de Ayala, Pedro 1332-1407
[HPPN]
Spanish chronicler, poet, translator
* [The] Chancellor Ayala

**Lopez de Victoria y Fernandez,
Magdalena** 1900- [CW]
Puerto Rican poet
* Lopez, Magda

Lopez Llergo, Josefina Pellicer
1940-1964 [SC]
Mexican actress
* Pellicer, Pina

Lopez Ostoloza, Beatriz 20th c. [WFA]
Mexican writer
* Trixie

Lopez Parejo, Francisco 1899-1932 [GS]
Spanish bullfighter
* Parejito [Little Smooth One]

Lopez Pinillos, Jose 1875-1922 [HDM]
Spanish author and playwright
* Parmeno

Lopez-Portillo y Rojas, Jose 1850-?
[ALY]
Mexican author
* Ben Issa, Isuf

Lopez Rega, Jose 1922?- [HPPN]
*Argentine politician and presidential
adviser*
* [The] Rasputin of the Presidential
Villa

Lopez Sibrian, Rodolfo Isidro 1956?-
[TI 10-18-82]
Salvadoran police officer
* Posorito [Little Match]

Lopez y Portal, Gabriel 1855-1902 [GS]
Spanish bullfighter
* Mateito [Little Matthew]

Lopez y Portana, Vicente 1772-1850
[HPPN]
Spanish painter
* Retratos, Pintor de

Lopez y Valles, Carlos Chaflan
1887-1942 [SC]
Mexican actor
* Lopez, Carlos

Lopokoff, Lydia 1892- [THR]
Russian-born dancer and actress
* Lopokova, Lydia

Lopokova, Lydia
See Lopokoff, Lydia

Lopresti, Lucia Longhi 1895- [BI]
Italian author and critic
* Banti, Anna

**[The] Loquatious Linguist Whom Labor
Loves**
See Perkins, Frances

Lora, Happy
See Lora, Miquel

Lora, Josephine
See Alexander, Josephine

Lora, Miquel 20th c. [WP 9-14-84]
Boxer
* Lora, Happy

Lora Trejo, Francisco 1907- [GS]
Mexican bullfighter
* Pericas

Lorac, E. C. R.
See Rivett, Edith Caroline

Lorac, H. R. C.?
See Crossen, Ken[dell Foster]

Loraine, Philip
See Estridge, Robin

Loran, Martin [joint pseudonym with
Ron Smith]
See Baxter, John

Loran, Martin [joint pseudonym with
John Baxter]
See Smith, Ron[ald] L[oran]

Lorand, Colette
See Grauaug, Colette

Lorber, Max J. 20th c. [EJS]
American football player
* Lorber, Mugs

Lorber, Mugs
See Lorber, Max J.

[The] Lord
See Crisler, Herbert Orin

Lord B.
See Brougham, Henry Peter

Lord, Barbara
See Gratz, Barbara Jeannette

Lord Barrymore's Tiger
See Lee, Alexander

[The] Lord Bishop of Norwich
See Butts, Robert

[The] Lord Bishop of Oxford
See Lowth, Robert

Lord, Bris
See Lord, Bristol Robotham

Lord, Bristol Robotham 1883-1964 [BE]
American baseball player
* Lord, Bris

Lord Byron
See Nelson, Byron

Lord, Carl
See Lord, Carleton

Lord, Carleton 1900-1947 [BE]
American baseball player
* Lord, Carl

[The] Lord Chamberlain
See Cecil, James [First Marquis of
Salisbury]

[The] Lord Chesterfield of Italy
See Della Casa, Giovanni

Lord Chief Commissioner
See Adam, William

Lord, Claire Cynthia Sweeney 1928-
[HPPN]
American literary representative
* Degener, Claire S.

Lord, Doreen Mildred Douglas 1904-
[WD]
British author, poet, translator
* Ireland, Doreen

Lord Dudley
See Heath, Neville George Clevely

Lord, Elaezar 1788-1871 [IP, PA]
British author
* E. L.

Lord Fanny
See Hervey, John [Baron Hervey of Ickworth]

Lord, Garland [joint pseudonym with Mindret Lord]
See Garland, [Mary] Isabel

Lord, Garland [joint pseudonym with (Mary) Isabel Garland]
See Lord, Mindret

Lord George
See Sanger, George

Lord God the Pope
See Borghese, Camillo

Lord, Grace Virginia ?-1885 [DNA, DNNF, IP]
American author
* Champlin, Virginia

Lord, Grantley
See Norton, Richard Henry Brinsley

Lord, Halkett [FFF]
Author
* Klett, Harold

Lord Henry
See Somerset, Henry Richard Charles

[The] Lord High Executioner
See Anastasia, Albert

Lord, Jack
See Ryan, John Joseph

Lord, Jeffrey [house pseudonym]
See Engel, Lyle Kenyon

Lord, Jeffrey [house pseudonym]
See Green, Roland [James]

Lord, Jeremy
See Redman, Ben Ray

Lord John
See Sanger, John

Lord, John Keast 1817-1872 [HPPN, IP]
British author
* [The] Naturalist
* [The] Wanderer

Lord, Justin
See Cook, Justin Lord

Lord, Little Michael
See Lord, Michael

Lord, Lonnie
See Haydock, Ron

Lord M.
See Morres, Hervey Redmond

Lord, M. L.
See Christian, Sydney

Lord Mayor of the Theatric Sky
See Hunt, [James Henry] Leigh

Lord, Michael 1973?- [HPPN]
American child evangelist and faith healer
* Lord, Little Michael
* [The] Normal Little Boy

Lord, Mindret [WW]
Author
* Lord, Garland [joint pseudonym with (Mary) Isabel Garland]

Lord, Nancy
See Titus, Eve

Lord, Nathan 1793-1870 [IP]
American clergyman and author
* [A] Northern Presbyter

[The] Lord of Alaska
See Baranov, Aleksandr Andreevich

[The] Lord of Beasts
See Jones, Charles Jesse

[The] Lord of Crazy Castle
See Hall, John

[The] Lord of his Age
See Suleiman II [or Soliman]

[The] Lord of Irony
See Arouet, Francois Marie

[The] Lord of Leasowes
See Shenstone, William

Lord of Roanoke
See Randolph, John

[The] Lord of San Simeon
See Hearst, William Randolph

[The] Lord of the British Pandemonium
See Shakespeare, William

[The] Lord of the Imperial Surname
See Cheng Sen

Lord of the Isles
See Donald

Lord of the Manor
See Long, Russell Billiu

[The] Lord of the Ring
See Gebel, Guenther

[The] Lord of the Seas
See Cheng Sen

[The] Lord of the Straits of Formosa
See Iquan, Nicholas

Lord of Tyre
See Conrad [Marquis of Montferrat]

Lord Oxford's Miss
See Davenport, Elizabeth

Lord Peter
See Pope, Alexander

Lord, Phillips H.
See Yolen, Will [Hyatt]

Lord, Phillips Haynes 1902-1975 [SC]
American actor, producer, writer
* Parker, Seth

[The] Lord Protector
See Cromwell, Oliver

Lord Rector of the University of Glasgow
See Cockburn, Henry Thomas

Lord S.
See Addington, Henry [First Viscount Sidmouth]

Lord, Shirley
See Anderson, Shirley Lord

Lord Ted
See Dexter, Roy Evatt

Lord Timothy
See Dexter, Timothy

Lord, Vivian
See Wallace, Pat

Lord, W. B. 19th c. [IP]
British artist
* W. B. L.

Lord, William Wilberforce 1819-1907 [HPPN]
American poet and clergyman
* [The] American Milton
* Langstaff, Tristram
* [The] Rector

Lorde, Athena
See Boles, Athena Lorde

Lorde, Audre 1934- [CA]
American educator and author
* Domini, Rey

Lore, James
See Demara, Ferdinand Waldo, Jr.

Lorel, Phil
See De Pietro, Albert

Loren, Sophia
See Scicolone, Sofia Villani

Lorenz, Ellen Jane 1907- [ASC]
American composer
* James, Allen

Lorenz, Sarah E.
See Winston, Sarah

Lorenzen, Adolph Andreas 1893-1963 [BE]
American baseball player
* Lorenzen, Lefty

Lorenzen, Al 20th c.
American basketball player
* [The] Vanilla Gorilla

Lorenzen, Lefty
See Lorenzen, Adolph Andreas

Lorenzetti, Ambrogio 1300?-1348? [WBD]
Italian painter
* Di Lorenzo, Ambrogio

Lorenzetti, Pietro 1280?-1348? [HPPN, WBD]
Italian painter
* Laurati da Siena
* Laurati, Pietro

Lorenzini, Carlo 1826-1890 [WBD]
Italian author
* Collodi, Carlo

Lorenzo 1370?-1425? [HPPN]
Italian painter
* [Il] Monaco

Lorenzo
See Sykes, [Sir] Mark Masterman

[The] Lorenzo de Medici of Hungary
See Matthias Corvinus

Lorenzo, Don
See Piero di Giovanni

Lorenzo, El Magnifico [Lorenzo the Magnificent]
See Garza Arrambide, Lorenzo

Lorenzo, Francisco 1940?-
American business executive
* Lorenzo, Pancho

Lorenzo Monaco [Lorenzo the Monk]
See Piero di Giovanni

Lorenzo, Pancho
See Lorenzo, Francisco

[The] Lorenzo the Magnificent of the Stage
See Ziegeld, Florenz

Lorenzon, Livio 1926-1971 [SC]
Italian actor
* Lawrence, Charlie

Loreto, Giorgio 1941- [OP]
Italian opera singer
* Lormi, Giorgio

Lorillard, Pierre 1833-1901 [HPPN]
American sportsman and tobacco processor
* [The] Tobacco Prince

Lorimer, Adam
See Watson, William Lorimer

Lorimer, Jacques ?-1821 [HPPN]
American fur trapper and pioneer
* Laramie, Jacques

Lorimer, John Gordon [IP]
Scottish clergyman and author
* [A] Churchman

Lorimer, Mary
See Dunning, M. O. B.

Lorimer, Maxwell George 1908- [TR]
British actor and dancer
* Wall, Max

Lorimer, Scat
See Fuentes, Martha Ayers

Lorin, Kenneth 1909- [AM]
American vocal arranger and composer
* Darby, Ken

Loring, Andrew
See Lathrop, Lorin Andrews

Loring, Ellis Gray 1802-1858 [HPPN]
American attorney and abolitionist
* [The] Board of Managers

Loring, Emilie [Baker] ?-1951 [ANT, WW]
American author
* Story, Josephine

Loring, Eugene
See Kerpestein, Leroy

Loring, J. M.
See Crozetti, Ruth G. Warner [Lora]

Loring, Jules [joint pseudonym with Julia Josephine (Gunther) MacKaye]
See MacKaye, David Loring

Loring, Jules [joint pseudonym with David Loring MacKaye]
See MacKaye, Julia Josephine [Gunther]

Loring, Laurie
See Pratt, L. Maria

Loring Pasha
See Loring, William Wing

Loring, Peter
See Shellabarger, Samuel

Loring, William Wing 1818-1886 [FFF]
American army officer
* Loring Pasha
* Old Blizzard

Loriot
See Buelow, Bernhard-Viktor von

Loris
See Hofmannsthal, Hugo [Laurenz August Hofmann Edler] Von

Loris, Heinrich 1488-1563 [WBD]
Swiss scholar
* Glareanus, Henricus

Lorm, Hieronymus
See Landesmann, Heinrich

Lormi, Giorgio
See Loreto, Giorgio

Lorne, Charles
See Brand, [Charles] Neville

Lorne, Constance
See MacLaurin, Constance

Lorne, Marion
See MacDougall, Marion Lorne

Lorne, Tommy
See Corcoran, Hugh Gallagher

Lorner
See Stoddart, Jane T.

Lorning, Ray
See Braly, Malcolm

Lornquest, Olaf
See Rips, Ervine M[ilton]

Lorrain, Camille
See Babou, Hippolyte

Lorrain [or Lorraine], Claude
See Gellee [or Gelee], Claude

Lorrain, Jean
See Duval, Martin Paul Alexandre

Lorraine, Alden
See Ackerman, Forrest J[ames]

Lorraine, Anne
See Chisholm, Lilian Mary

Lorraine, Francois de 1519-1563 [HN, WBD]
French soldier and politician
* [Le] Balafre [The Scarred]
* [The] Butcher of Vassy
* Guise, 2nd Duc de
* [The] Preserver of His Country

Lorraine, Harry
See Herd, Henry

Lorraine, Henry I [or Henri] de 1550-1589? [FFF, HN, SN]
French soldier
* [Le] Balafre [The Scarred]
* [The] Gashed
* Guise, 3rd Duc de
* [The] King of Paris
* [The] People's King

Lorraine, Henry II [or Henri] de 1614-1664 [DEP, FFF, RH]
French soldier
* Guise, Duc de
* [The] Hero of Fable

Lorraine, Irma
See Berenyi, Maria

Lorraine, Lilith
See Wright, Mary M.

Lorraine, Lillian
See De Jacques, Ealallean [or Eulallean?]

Lorraine, Lillian
See Jacques, Eulallean De

Lorraine, Mrs. Felix
See Lamb, [Lady] Caroline

Lorraine, Paul [house pseudonym, Curtis Warren]
See Bird, William Henry Fleming

Lorraine, Paul [house pseudonym, Curtis Warren]
See Fearn, John Russell

Lorraine, Paul [joint pseudonym with Arthur O. Roberts] [house pseudonym, Curtis Warren]
See Glasby, John [Stephen]

Lorraine, Paul [joint pseudonym with John (Stephen) Glasby] [house pseudonym, Curtis Warren]
See Roberts, Arthur O.

Lorraine, Sid
See Johnson, Sidney Richard

Lorre, Peter
See Loewenstein, Laszlo

Lorrequer, Harry
See Lever, Charles James

Lorrett, Lulu
See Darrow, Harriet Louise

Lorrimer, Laura
See Shelton, Julia Finley

Lorring, Joan
See Ellis, Dellie Madeline [or Magdalen?]

Lorring, Joan
See Ellis, Magdalen

Lorrnel, Marlise ?-1978 [FIR]
Actress
* Rey, Anita

Lortel, Lucille
See Wadler, Lucille

Los, George
See Amabile, George

Losada, Manuel 1825-1873 [FFF]
Mexican bandit
* [The] Tiger of Alica

Loscalzo, Joseph Robert 1910-1955 [AS, BX, RBE]
American boxer
* Wolgast, Midget

Losch, Ottilie Ethel 1902-1975 [BEW, EMT, TR]
Austrian-born dancer, actress, choreographer
* Losch, Tilly

Losch, Tilly
See Losch, Ottilie Ethel

Loscutoff, James 1930- [BB]
American basketball player
* Loscutoff, Jungle Jim

Loscutoff, Jungle Jim
See Loscutoff, James

Loser, J. Carlton 1893?-1984 [WP 8-1-84]
American attorney and politician
* [The] Man Who Cleaned Up Nashville

[The] Losing Pitcher
See Mulcahy, Hugh Noyes

[The] Lost Dauphin
See Williams, Eleazar

[The] Lost Leader
See Cannon, [Bishop] James, Jr.

[The] Lost Leader
See Wordsworth, William

[The] Lost Mistress
See Talbot, Elizabeth

[The] Lost Star of the House of Judah
See Aguilar, Grace

Lot, Arthur
See Bunner, Henry Cuyler

Lot, Parson
See Kingsley, Charles

Lotarev, Igor Vasilyevich 1887-1942 [CD]
Russian poet
* Severyanin, Igor

Lothair I 795?-855 [HPPN]
Holy Roman Emperor
* [The] Pious

Lothair II 1070?-1137 [DNNS, WBD]
King of Germany and Holy Roman emperor
* [The] Saxon

Lothar, Ernest
See Mueller, Ernst

Lothar, Hanns
See Neutze, Hanns Lothar

Lothar, Louis
See Dupin, Paul

Lothario
See Jenner, [Rev.] Charles

Lothian, Jane 1863?-1938 [BEW]
American actress
* Kennard, Jane

Lothian, Maurice [IP]
Scottish barrister and author
* [A] Sincere Friend of the People

Lothrop, Amy
See Warner, Anna Bartlett

Lothrop, Harriet Mulford Stone 1844-1924 [SAT]
American author
* Sidney, Margaret

Lothrop, Samuel Kirkland 1804-1886 [HPPN]
American clergyman
* L.
* S. K. L.

Loti, Pierre
See Viaud, Louis Marie Julien

Lotich, Peter 1528-1560 [PA]
Author
* Secundus

Lotinga, Ernest 1876-1951 [F2]
British actor, screenwriter, producer
* Roy, Dan

Lotinga, W. [NPS]
Author
* Lynx, Larry
* Magpie

Lott, Monroe
See Howard, Edwin

Lott, Noah
See Hobart, George Vere

Lotta, Charlotte
See Crabtree, Carlotta

Lotte [code name used during World War II]
See Bonnesen, Edith

Lottich, Kenneth V[erne] 1904- [AW, CA]
American educator and author
* Conrad, Kenneth

Lottie
See Walker, C.

Lottimer, Ebb
See Lottimer, Edmund

Lottimer, Edmund 1951?- [BI]
American songwriter
* Lottimer, Ebb

Lottman, Eileen 1927- [CA]
American author and screenwriter
* Willis, Maud

Lotz, Joseph Peter [Joe] 1891-1971 [BE]
American baseball player
* Lotz, Smokey

Lotz, Smokey
See Lotz, Joseph Peter [Joe]

Lou
See Leatham, Louis Salisbury

Lou
See Van Voorthuizen [or Voorthuyzen], Louwrens

Loubat
See Bohan, Francois-Phillippe

Loud Larry McPhail
See McPhail, Leland Stanford

Loud Mouth Levine
See Levine, Hymie

Louden, Baldy
See Louden, William

Louden, William 1885-1935 [BE]
American baseball player
* Louden, Baldy

Loudermilk, Charlie 1927- [ECM]
American country-western performer
* Louvin, Charlie

Loudermilk, Ira 1924-1965 [ECM]
American country-western performer
* Louvin, Ira

Loudermilk, John D. 1934- [PAC]
American composer
* Dee, Johnny

Loudon, Isabelle
See Langner, Armina [Marshall]

Loudon, John Claudius 1783-1843 [IP]
Scottish author
* [A] Scottish Farmer and Land Agent

Loughery, Kevin 1940-
American basketball player
* Loughery, Murph

Loughery, Murph
See Loughery, Kevin

Louie Bluie
See Armstrong, Howard

Louie the Lump
See Pioggi, Louis

Louis 880-928? [HPPN]
King of Provence
* [The] Blind

Louis [or Ludwig] 1042-? [DNNF, DNNS, SN]
Margrave of Thuringia
* Ludwig der Springer
* [The] Springer

Louis 14th c. [WBD]
King of Hungary and Poland
* [The] Great

Louis 1661-1711 [DNNS, HN, RH, SN]
Son of King Louis XIV of France
* [Le] Grand Dauphin
* [The] Great Dauphin
* Monseigneur
* Sephi-Mirza

Louis 1729-1765 [HN]
Son of King Louis XV of France
* [The] French Germanicus

Louis Charles de France
See Louis XVII

Louis de France 1682-1712 [DNNS, UH]
Grandson of King Louis XIV of France
* Bourgogne, Duc de
* [The] Little Dauphin
* [The] Second Dauphin

Louis de Male
See Louis II

Louis, Jean
See Berthault, Jean Louis

Louis, Joe
See Barrow, Joseph Louis

Louis, Joe Hill
See Hill, Lester

Louis, [Father] M.
See Merton, Thomas [James]

Louis, M.
See Napolitan, Louis

Louis, Marilyn 1922?- [BDF, FC, IPA]
American actress
* Fleming, Rhonda

Louis, Morris
See Bernstein, Morris Louis

Louis, Murray
See Fuchs, Murray Louis

Louis Napoleon
See Bonaparte, Charles Louis Napoleon

Louis of Nassau 1538-1574 [DNNS, HN, RH]
Founder of the Dutch Republic
* [The] Bayard of the Netherlands

Louis Philippe 1773-1850 [DEP, HN, HPPN, SN]
King of France
* [The] Citizen King
* Corby, M.
* Egalite
* [The] King of the Barricades
* Latour, M. Chabaud
* Lebrun, M.
* Mueller, Herr
* [The] Napoleon of Peace
* [La] Poire
* [Le] Roi Bourgeois

Louis Philippe (cont.)
* [Le] Roi Citoyen
* [Le] Roi des Barricades
* Smith, King
* Smith, Mr.
* Smith, William

Louis Philippe Marie Victor 1835-1909 [WBD]
King of Belgium
* Leopold II

Louis, Pierre-Felix 1870-1925 [CD, EWL, LC]
French poet and author
* Louys, Pierre

Louis, Ray Baldwin 1949- [CA]
American author, filmmaker, playwright
* Saltboy, Razor

Louis, Seraphine 1864-1934 [BI]
French painter
* Seraphine de Senlis

Louis, Tommy
See Watts, Lou[is Thomas]

Louis William I 1655-1707 [SN]
German soldier and military engineer
* [Der] Tuerken Louis

Louis X
See Walcott, Louis Eugene

Louis I 778-840 [DNNS, FFF, SN]
King of France and Holy Roman emperor
* [Le] Debonnaire
* [The] Meek
* [Le] Pieux
* [The] Pious

Louis I 1326-1382 [DNNS, SN, WBD]
King of Hungary
* [The] Great

Louis II [or Ludwig] 804?-876 [DNNS, HN, WBD]
King of Germany
* [The] German

Louis II [or Ludwig] 822?-874? [HN]
King of Lorraine and Holy Roman emperor
* [The] Young

Louis II 846-879 [FFF, RH, SN]
King of France
* [Le] Begue
* [The] Stammerer

Louis II 1228-1294 [WBD]
Duke of Bavaria
* [The] Strict

Louis II 1330-1384? [HN]
Count of Flanders
* Louis de Male

Louis II [or Ludwig] 1845-1886
King of Bavaria
* [The] Dream King

Louis III [or Ludwig] 880-923? [HN, HPPN, SN]
Holy Roman Emperor
* [The] Blind
* [The] Blind Emperor

Louis III [or Ludwig] 893-911 [DNNS, HN, WBD]
King of Germany
* [The] Child
* [The] Infant

Louis IV 921-954 [HN, NPS, SN, WBD]
King of France
* D'Outre Mer
* [The] Foreigner
* From Beyond the Seas
* Transmarine

Louis IV 1287?-1347 [DNNS]
King of Germany and Holy Roman emperor
* [The] Bavarian

Louis IX 1215?-1270 [DHA, HN, SN]
King of France
* St. Louis
* [The] Solomon of France

Louis IX 1417-1479 [SN]
Duke of Bavaria
* [The] Rich

Louis V 966-987 [HN, SN, WBD]
King of France
* [Le] Faineant
* [The] Indolent
* [The] Sluggard

Louis VI 1081-1137 [DNNS, FFF, SN]
King of France
* [The] Fat
* [Le] Gros
* [The] Wide Awake

Louis VII 1121?-1180 [DNNS, SN, WBD]
King of France
* [The] Foolish
* [Le] Jeune
* [Le] Pieux [The Pious]
* [The] Young

Louis VIII 1187-1226 [DNNS, FFF, SN]
King of France
* Coeur de Lion [Lion-Hearted]
* [The] Lion

Louis X 1289-1316 [RH, SN, WBD]
King of France
* [Le] Hutin
* [The] Quarreler

Louis XI 1423-1483 [DNNS, FFF, HN, SN]
King of France
* Christianissimus Rex
* [The] French Tiberius
* Most Christian King
* [A] Perjur'd Prince
* [Le] Renard [The Fox]
* [The] Spider King
* [The] Universal Spider

Louis XII 1462-1515 [DNNS, FFF, HN, SN]
King of France
* [The] Father of Letters
* [The] Father of the People
* Grangousier ?
* [The] Just
* [Le] Pere du Peuple

Louis XIII 1601-1643 [DNNS, HN, SN]
King of France
* Cyaxares
* [The] Just

Louis XIV 1638-1715 [DNNS, FFF, NPS, SN]
King of France
* Ahasuerus
* Augustus
* Baboon, Lewis
* Cha-abas
* [The] Destroyer of Heresy
* Dieu-Donne [God-Given]
* [The] Father of His Country
* [The] Gallic Pharaoh
* [Le] Grand
* [Le] Grand Monarque
* [The] Great
* Idomeneo
* Idomeneus
* [The] New Constantine
* Old Bonafide
* Pharaoh
* Pygmalion
* [Le] Roi Soleil
* [The] Ruler of Kings
* Sesostris
* [The] Sun God
* [The] Sun King
* [The] Wolf of France

Louis XV 1710-1774 [DEP, FF, IP, SN]
King of France
* [Le] Bien Aime
* [The] Well Beloved
* Zeokinizul

Louis XVI 1754-1793 [DEP, HN, SN]
King of France
* [The] Baker
* [Le] Charpentier [The Joiner]
* [The] Crowned Sancho
* [Le] Desire
* [The] Locksmith King
* [The] Martyr King
* [The] Restorer of French Liberty
* Veto, Monsieur

Louis XVII 1785-1795 [HPPN]
Titular King of France
* [The] Child of the Temple
* Louis Charles de France

Louis XVII
See Williams, Eleazar

Louis XVIII 1755-1824 [HN, RH, SN]
King of France
* [Le] Desire
* [The] Father of His Country
* [The] Father of the People
* Jehu
* [The] King of England's Viceroy
* [The] King of Slops
* [Le] Roi Panade

Louisa 1776-1810 [SN]
Queen of Prussia
* Armida

Louisa
See Wallace, Lewis

Louise, Anita
See Fremault, Anita Louise

Louise, Edouard 1941- [EJ7]
French jazz musician
* Louiss, Eddy

Louise Ellen
See Moulton, Ellen Louise Chandler

Louise, Tina
See Blacker, Tina

Louiseboulanger
See Boulanger, Louise

Louisiana Earl Nelson
See Nelson, Earl

[The] Louisiana Lady
See Nickerson, Camille Lucie

[The] Louisiana Lark
See Jones, Ernest Mahlon

Louisiana Lightning
See Guidry, Ron[ald Ames]

[The] Louisiana Ram
See Mouton, Robert L.

Louisiana Red
See Minter, Iverson

Louisiana Swamp Doctor
See Lewis, Henry Clay

Louisiana's Hard-Luck Gambler
See Grymes, John Randolph

Louisiana's Loud Speaker
See Long, Huey Pierce

Louiss, Eddy
See Louise, Edouard

[The] Louisville Legend
See Griffith, Darrell

[The] Louisville Lip
See Clay, Cassius Marcellus, Jr.

Louisville Lou Hines
See Hines, Louella

Lounds, Stanley Samuel 1906- [ART]
British artist
* S. L.

[A] Lounger
See Bromet, William

[The] Lounger
See Curtis, George William

[A] Lounger
See Fowler, Frank

[The] Lounger
See Gilder, Joseph B.

Lounger at the Clubs
See Yates, Edmund Hodgson

Lounger in the Lobby
See Merrill, Royal W.

Lourant, Arthur 20th c. [IBW]
American actor
* Lourant, Chico

Lourant, Chico
See Lourant, Arthur

Lourdoneix, Paul de [IP]
French author
* Pierre et Paul

Lourens-Koop, Adriana Luberta Klazina 1920- [IAW]
Dutch author
* Toussaint, Jackie

Lourie, Dick 1937- [CA]
American poet and educator
* Loose, H.
* Wonder, Alvin

Lourie, Helen
See Storr, Catherine [Cole]

[The] Louse
See Cohen, Mickey

Loutherbourg, Philip James de 1740-1812 [SN]
French painter
* Lanternbug, Mr.

Louvier, Pierre
See Lucas, Gerald

Louvigny, Andre
See Ruellan, Andre

Louvin, Charlie
See Loudermilk, Charlie

Louvin, Ira
See Loudermilk, Ira

Louvish, Misha 1909- [CA]
Rumanian-born editor and translator
* Bar-Natan, Moshe

L'Ouvrier Albert
See Martin, Alexandre

Louwen, Jan 1924- [IAW]
Dutch author
* Viking, Ted

Louys, Pierre
See Louis, Pierre-Felix

Lov, Janette 1906-1942
American actress
* Loff, Jeanette

[The] Lovable Egghead
See Ustinov, Peter Alexander

Love, Bessie
See Horton, Juanita

Love, Billy 20th c. [BWW, NBB, RO1]
American musician
* Love, Red

[The] Love Boat
See Barkley, Charles

Love, Bob 1942-   [BB]
American basketball player
* Love, Butterbean

Love, Butterbean
See Love, Bob

Love, Christopher 1618-1651   [SN]
British theologian
* Venn's Principal Fireman at Windsor

Love, D.
See Lerchbaum, Dora

Love, Elmer Haughton 1893-1942   [BE]
American baseball player
* Love, Slim

Love, George Oliver
See Smith, George Joseph

[The] Love Goddess
See Cansino, Margarita Carmen

Love, James
See Dance, James

Love, Janet
See Ferrier, Janet Mackay

Love, John Arthur 1916-   [HPPN]
American politician
* [The] Deputy Energy Czar

Love, John, Jr. 18th c.   [IP]
British author
* J. L.

[The] Love Kidnaper
See Lippert, Thomas Ray

Love, Larry
See Khaury, Herbert Buckingham

Love, Mabel
See Watson, Mabel

Love, Nat 19th c.
American cowboy and gunfighter
* Deadwood Dick

Love, Red
See Love, Billy

Love, Roosevelt 1933-   [BA]
American business executive
* Love, Sam

Love, Sam
See Love, Roosevelt

Love, Slim
See Love, Elmer Haughton

Love Wit, Leonard
See Foe, Daniel

LoVecchio, Frank Paul 1913-   [FC, IPA, PMJ]
American singer
* Laine, Frankie

Lovechild, Laurence
See Fenn, Eleanor

Lovechild, Mrs.
See Fenn, Eleanor

Lovechild, Solomon
See Fenn, Eleanor

Lovecraft, H. P.
See Lovecraft, Howard Phillips

Lovecraft, Howard Phillips 1890-1937
[CA, SF, TLC, WGT]
American author
* Appleton, Laurence
* Bickerstaffe, Isaac, Jr.
* Dunne, John T.
* Gent
* Houdini?
* Jones, John J.
* Littlewit, Humphrey
* Lovecraft, H. P.
* Maynwaring, Archibald
* Paget-Lowe, H[enry]
* Phillips, Ward
* Raleigh, Richard
* Rowley, Ames Dor[r]ance
* Senectissimus, Theobaldus, Esq.
* Softly, Edgar
* Softly, Edward
* Swift, Augustus T.
* Theobald
* Theobald, Lewis, Jr.
* Theobaldus
* Willie, Albert Frederic
* Willie, Frederick
* Zoilus

Lovecraft, Linda
See Parry, Michel Patrick

Loveday, John 1742-1809   [FFF, IP]
British author
* Academicus
* Antiquarius
* Scrutator
* Vindex

Lovegood, John
See Grant Watson, Elliot Lovegood

Lovehill, C. B.
See Nutt, Charles

Lovejoy, Cornelia   [PA]
Author
* Everett, Paul

Lovejoy, Elijah Parish 1802-1837
[WBD]
American abolitionist
* [The] Martyr Abolitionist

Lovejoy, Mary Evelyn [Wood]
1847-1928   [DNA]
American author and historian
* Traine, Gypsey

Lovel, Baron 18th c.   [HPPN]
British barrister and jurist
* Baron L., Mr.

Lovel, Robert   [IP]
British poet
* Moschus

Lovelace, Linda
See Traynor, Linda Borman

[The] Lovelace of His Time
See De Vignerot du Plessis, Louis
Francois Armand

[The] Lovelace of His Time
See Du Plessis, Armand Jean

Loveland, Joy
See Wasmansdoff, Joyce

Loveless, [Dr.] Miguelito
See Miller, Gary Neil

Lovell, Arthur
See Lovell-Williams, David Arthur

Lovell, Francis 1454-1487   [NN]
*Lord Chamberlain to King Richard III
of England*
* [The] Dog

Lovell, Ingraham
See Bacon, Josephine Dodge [Daskam]

Lovell, John 1710-1778   [HPPN]
American educator
* [The] Busby of New England

Lovell, John 1835-?   [IP]
British journalist
* Zeta

Lovell, Marc
See McShane, Mark

Lovell, Mark 1934-   [CA]
British author
* Rowlands, Peter

Lovell, Mark
See Tollemache, David

Lovell, Mrs. 19th c.   [PA]
Author
* Halm

Lovell, Raymond
See Lovell-Robinson, Raymond

Lovell-Robinson, Raymond 1900-1953
[THR]
Canadian-born actor
* Lovell, Raymond

Lovell-Williams, David Arthur 1864-?
[WWL]
British author
* Lovell, Arthur

[The] Lovelorn Killer
See Ray, James Earl

[The] Lovely Bessie
See Raleigh, Elizabeth

[The] Lovely Georgius
See Washington, George

Lovely, Louise
See Welch, Louise

Lovely, Maureen Patey 1906-   [ART]
British painter, engraver, designer
* Proudman, M. Eyre

Lovemore, [Sir] Charles
See Manley, Mary de la Riviere

Loven, [Rev.] Nils ?-1858   [HPPN]
Swedish clergyman, author, translator
* Nicolovius

Lovenberg, Maurice ?-1908 [HPPN]
American singer
* Harris, Charles M.

Lovequist, Gwendlelynn
See Stafford, Linda

Lover Boy Gray
See Gray, [Henry] Judd

[A] **Lover of Candour**
See Hopkinson, Francis

[A] **Lover of Christ**
See Ryland, John Collett

[A] **Lover of Fine Arts**
See Thomas, Vaughan

[A] **Lover of Good English and Common Sense**
See Wesley, John

[A] **Lover of her Sex**
See Astell, Mary

[A] **Lover of his Country**
See Fielding, Henry

[A] **Lover of his Country**
See Macintosh, William

[A] **Lover of His Country**
See Mather, Cotton

[A] **Lover of His Country**
See Rawle, Francis

[A] **Lover of Literature**
See Greene, Thomas

[A] **Lover of Mankind**
See Benezet, Anthony

[The] **Lover of Mankind**
See Debs, Eugene Victor

[A] **Lover of Order**
See Montagu, Basil

[A] **Lover of Peace and Truth in this Church**
See Adams, James

[A] **Lover of Quiteness and Liberty of Conscience**
See De La Flechere, John William

[A] **Lover of Social Order**
See Thornton, Robert John

Lover of Stability
See Webster, Noah

[A] **Lover of the Church of England**
See Drewe, Patrick

Lover of the Fine Arts
See Brooks, Maria Gowen

[A] **Lover of the Protestant Religion**
See Wright, William

[A] **Lover of the Truth**
See Prentiss, Charles

[A] **Lover of the World**
See Ingham, Harvey A.

[A] **Lover of Truth**
See Layton, Henry

[A] **Lover of Truth**
See Leslie, Charles

[A] **Lover of Truth**
See Sharpe, Gregory

[A] **Lover of Truth**
See Wilson, David

[A] **Lover of Truth and Liberty**
See Bourn, Samuel

[A] **Lover of Truth and Liberty**
See Ralph, James

[A] **Lover of Truth and Liberty**
See Williams, Elisha

[A] **Lover of Truth and Mankind universally**
See Hatt, Francis

[A] **Lover of Truth and Peace**
See Nation, William

[A] **Lover of Truth and Peace**
See Rand, [Rev.] William

Lover, Samuel 1797-1868 [DEA, NPS, PI]
Irish musician, painter, songwriter, author
* Jove's Poet
* Trovato, Ben

Loveridge, Marguerite
See Marsh, Margaret

Lovering, John 1788-? [IP]
American author
* Notional, Nehemiah

Lovesey, Peter 1936- [CA]
British author
* Lear, Peter

Lovestone, Jay
See Liebstein, Jacov

Lovett, Blue
See Lovett, Winifred

Lovett, Eddie 1916- [IBW]
American farmer
* [The] Piney Woods Thoreau

Lovett, John 1765-1818 [IP]
American poet
* [A] Washingtonian

Lovett, Mem
See Lovett, Merritt Marwood

Lovett, Merritt Marwood 1912- [BE]
American baseball player
* Lovett, Mem

Lovett, Wild Bill
See Lovett, William L.

Lovett, William L. ?-1923 [BLB]
American gangster
* Lovett, Wild Bill

Lovett, Winifred 1943- [RO2]
American singer
* Lovett, Blue

Lovewit, Theophilus
See Foe, Daniel

Lovey Joe Powell
See Powell, Joe

Lovin' Putty Annixter
See Annixter, Julius

Lovin, Roger Robert 1941- [CA, IAW]
American writer
* Clemens, Rogers
* Clemens, Rogers
* Driver, Cynthia C.
* Zweit, Adam

Loving, Cockeyed Frank
See Loving, Frank

Loving, Frank 1854?-1882 [EWG]
American gunfighter
* Loving, Cockeyed Frank

Lovingood, Alvin 1892- [NAA]
American writer
* Kole, A. K.

Lovingood, Sut
See Harris, George Washington

Lovitt, Will U.
See Levesque, Paul

Lovley, Jim
See Lovley, Leonard

Lovley, Leonard 1900- [BB]
American basketball player
* Lovley, Jim

Low
See Low, [Sir] David

Low, [Sir] David 1891-1963 [HPPN]
British cartoonist
* Blimp, Colonel
* Low

Low, Dorothy Mackie
See Low, Lois Dorothea

Low, Gardner
See Rodda, Charles

Low, Hanns
See Tralow, Johannes

Low, Ivy
See Litvinov, Ivy

Low, Juliette Gordon 1860-1927 [HPPN]
American philanthropist and civic leader
* [The] Mother of the Girl Scouts

Low, Lois Dorothea 1916- [AW, CA, WD]
Scottish-born author
* Low, Dorothy Mackie
* Paxton, Lois

Low, Mary [IP]
British author
* Aunt Mary

Low, Rachael
See Whear, [Dr.] Rachael

Low, Samuel 1765-? [IP]
American poet and playwright
* [An] American

Lowden, Frank Orren 1861-1943
[HPPN]
American attorney and politician
* [The] Farmer's Friend
* [The] Sage of Sinnissippi

Lowdermilk, Grover Cleveland 1885-1968
[BE]
American baseball player
* Lowdermilk, Slim

Lowdermilk, Slim
See Lowdermilk, Grover Cleveland

Lowe, Alfonso
See Loewenthal, Leonard Joseph
Alfonso

Lowe, Anne 1899-1966 [IBW]
American fashion designer
* [The] Dean of Black American
Designers

Lowe, Bennett [IP, PA]
British photographer and author
* Justitia

Lowe, Bull
See Lowe, George

Lowe, Charles K.
See Swicegood, Thomas L. P.

Lowe, Claud D. 20th c. [MBF]
British scriptwriter
* Clifford, Martin [house pseudonym]
* Griffiths, Maurice
* Hardy, Phillip

Lowe, Corke
See Pepper, Choral

Lowe, Florence 1902-1975 [SC]
American stunt performer
* Barnes, Florence
* Barnes, Pancho

Lowe, George 20th c. [EF]
American football player
* Lowe, Bull

Lowe, Helen Porter 1876-? [WWL]
British author
* Lowe-Porter, H. T.

Lowe, [Sir] Hudson 1769-1844 [NPS]
Governor of St. Helena
* Turnkey

Lowe, Jay, Jr.
See Loeper, John J[oseph]

Lowe, Jim
See Parker, Robert LeRoy

Lowe, John 1898- [F2, FC]
British actor
* Loder, John

Lowe, Joseph 1845?-1899? [BLB, EWG,
HPPN]
American gunfighter
* Lowe, Monte Joe
* Lowe, Red Joe
* Lowe, Rowdy Joe

Lowe, Kate 1851-? [HPPN]
*American prostitute and brothel
proprietress*
* Lowe, Rowdy Kate

Lowe, Kenneth
See Lobaugh, Elma K.

Lowe, Kevin 1959- [SMG]
Canadian-born hockey player
* Lowe, Viscious

Lowe, Link
See Lowe, Robert Lincoln

Lowe, Martha A. [Perry] [IP]
American poet
* His Wife

Lowe, Mary 1847-1884 [HPPN]
British actress
* Litton, Marie

Lowe, Monte Joe
See Lowe, Joseph

Lowe, Norman E. 1928- [CEI]
Canadian-born hockey player
* Lowe, Odie

Lowe, Odie
See Lowe, Norman E.

Lowe, Red Joe
See Lowe, Joseph

Lowe, Robert [Viscount Sherbrooke]
1811-1892 [HPPN]
British statesman
* [The] Member for Kidderminster

Lowe, Robert Lincoln 1868-1951 [BE]
American baseball player
* Lowe, Link

Lowe, Rowdy Joe
See Lowe, Joseph

Lowe, Rowdy Kate
See Lowe, Kate

Lowe, Sherman
See Lowenstein, Sherman

Lowe, Solomon 18th c. [IP]
British author
* [A] Layman

Lowe, Victoria Lincoln
See Lincoln, Victoria

Lowe, Viscious
See Lowe, Kevin

Lowe, William Herman 1897- [NAA]
American writer
* Suds

Lowe-Porter, H. T.
See Lowe, Helen Porter

Lowell, Alan
See Thomas, William B. [Bill]

Lowell, Amy 1874-1925 [CAA]
American poet
* [A] Dreamer
* [A] Poker of Fun

Lowell, Cal
See Lowell, Robert Taill Spence

Lowell, Charles 1782-1861 [HPPN]
American clergyman
* [The] Senior Minister of the West
Church in Boston

Lowell, Francis Cabot 1855-1911 [DNA]
American author and jurist
* Orne, Philip

Lowell, Helen
See Robb, Helen

Lowell, J. R. [joint pseudonym with
Robert Lowell]
See Lowell, Jan

Lowell, J. R. [joint pseudonym with Jan
Lowell]
See Lowell, Robert

Lowell, James Russell 1819-1891 [DEL,
DNNF, HFN, HPPN, IP, PA]
American author, poet, diplomat
* [The] Best Read Man of the Century
* Biglow, Hosea
* Elmwood
* J. R. L.
* Nye, Columbus
* Wilbur, Homer
* [A] Wonderful Quiz

Lowell, Jan 20th c. [SFL]
Author
* Lowell, J. R. [joint pseudonym with
Robert Lowell]

Lowell, Joan 1900-1967 [SC]
Actress and author
* Trask, Helen

Lowell, John 1769-1840 [FFF, HPPN,
IP, PA]
American attorney and author
* [An] Alumnus of that College
* [The] Boston Rebel
* [A] Bostonian
* [A] Citizen of Massachusetts
* [A] Citizen of New England
* [The] Columella of New England
* [A] Friend of That College
* [A] Friend to Peace
* His Intimate Friend
* [A] Layman
* [A] Massachusetts Lawyer
* [A] New England Farmer
* No bel-esprit
* [An] Old Farmer
* [A] Roxbury Farmer
* [A] Yankee Farmer

Lowell, John
See Russell, John L.

Lowell, Robert 20th c. [SFL]
Author
* Lowell, J. R. [joint pseudonym with
Jan Lowell]

Lowell, Robert Taill Spence 1917-1977
[TI 11-8-82]
American poet
* Lowell, Cal

Lowell, Tex
See Turner, George E[ugene]

Lowell, Theodore [Teddy] 1905- [HPPN]
American seller of Christmas trees
* [The] Christmas Tree Boy

Lowenkopf, Shelly A[lan] 1931- [CA]
American editor and author
* Chambers, Howard V.

Lowenstein, Allard Kenneth 1929-
[HPPN]
American attorney and politician
* [The] Two Time Loser

Lowenstein, Kenneth 1919- [ITA]
American television executive
* Lowenstein, Larry

Lowenstein, Larry
See Lowenstein, Kenneth

Lowenstein, Sherman 1894-1968 [HPPN]
American playwright
* Lowe, Sherman

Lowenthal, Marjorie Fiske 20th c. [CA]
American author
* Fiske, Marjorie

Lower, Richard 1782-1865 [IP, PA]
British author
* Cladpole, Tim
* [An] Octogenarian
* Uncle Tim

Lowery, Nick 1956-
German-born football player
* Nick the Kick

Lowery, Robert
See Hanke, Robert Lowery

Lowery, Robert
See Hanks, Robert Lowery

Lowing, Anne
See Geach, Christine

Lowmyer, Harvey
See Ray, James Earl

Lown, Omar Joseph 1924- [BE, BTB, SMG]
American baseball player
* Lown, Turk

Lown, Turk
See Lown, Omar Joseph

Lowndes, Doc
See Lowndes, Robert Augustine Ward

Lowndes, Marie [Adelaide] Belloc
1868-1947 [CA, TCCM]
British author
* Belloc, M. A.
* Belloc-Lowndes, Mrs.
* Curtin, Philip

Lowndes, R. W.
See Lowndes, Robert Augustine Ward

Lowndes, Robert Augustine Ward 1916-
[ESF, SF, WGT]
American author and editor
* Cooke, Arthur [joint pseudonym with
  E. Balter, C. Kornbluth, J. Michel,
  D. Wollheim]
* Gottesman, S. D. [joint pseudonym
  with Cyril M. Kornbluth and Frederik
  Pohl]
* Grey, Carol
* Kent, Mallory
* Lavond, Paul Dennis [joint
  pseudonym with J. H. Dockweiler, C.
  Kornbluth, F. Pohl]
* Lowndes, Doc
* Lowndes, R. W.
* MacDougal, John [joint pseudonym
  with James (Benjamin) Blish]
* Morley, Wilfred Owen
* Morrison, Richard
* Morrison, Robert
* Sherman, Michael
* Sherman, Peter Michael
* Woods, Lawrence [joint pseudonym
  with Donald A(llen) Wollheim]
* Wright, Robert [joint pseudonym with
  Forrest J. Ackerman]

Lowndes, Susan
See Lowndes Marques, Susan

Lowndes Marques, Susan 20th c. [AW]
British-born author
* Lowndes, Susan

Lowo, Hans
See Linden, Erik Hugo Emanuel

Lowrey, Harry Lee 1918-1986 [BE, PB,
SMG]
American baseball player and coach
* Lowrey, Peanuts

Lowrey, Peanuts
See Lowrey, Harry Lee

Lowrie, Randolph W. 19th c. [IP]
American clergyman and author
* R. W. L.

Lowrie, Walter 1784-1868 [IP]
American statesman and author
* His Father

Lowry, Henry Dawson 1869-? [WWL]
Author
* [The] Impertinent

Lowry, Joan [Catlow] 1911- [CA, WD]
British author
* Catlow, Joanna
* Lea, Joan

Lowry, Mose
See Lowry, Sam[uel Joseph]

Lowry, Nan
See MacLeod, Ruth

Lowry, Robert [James Collas] 1919-
[CA]
American author
* Caldwell, James

Lowry, Sam[uel Joseph] 1920- [BE]
American baseball player
* Lowry, Mose

Lowth, Robert 1710-1787 [HPPN, IP]
British author
* [A] Late Professor in the University
  of Oxford
* [The] Lord Bishop of Oxford
* [A] Young Gentleman of Winchester
  School

Lowth, Thomas Henry 18th c. [IP]
British author
* T. H. L.

Lowther, Armstrong John 1880-1948
[CCL]
Canadian poet
* Laird

Lowther, [Sir] James 1736-1802 [HPPN,
NPS, SN]
British politician
* [The] Bad Earl
* [The] Brazen Bully
* Farthing Jamie
* Seventy Four, Lord

**Lowther, William [Third Earl of
Lonsdale]** 1787-1872 [SN]
British politician
* Eskdale, Lord

Loxley, Raymond
See Murray, C. Geoffrey

Loxley, Violet
See Humphreys, Violet

Loxmith, John
See Brunner, John [Kilian Houston]

Loy, Barbara
See Gentilini, Maria Teresa

Loy, Hugo de la
See Leslie, Hugh

Loy, Mino 20th c. [WF]
Italian director
* Donan, J. Lee

Loy, Myrna
See Williams, Myrna

Loyacano, Arnold 1889-1962 [NOJ]
American jazz musician
* Loyacano, Deacon

Loyacano, Bud
See Loyacano, John

Loyacano, Deacon
See Loyacano, Arnold

Loyacano, Hook
See Loyacano, Joe

Loyacano, Joe 1893-1967 [NOJ]
American jazz musician
* Loyacano, Hook

Loyacano, John 1879-1960 [NOJ]
American jazz musician
* Loyacano, Bud

[The] Loyal Hard Hat
See Brennan, Peter J.

[The] Loyal Poet
See Fitzgerald, William Thomas

[La] Loyale Epee [The Loyal Sword]
See MacMahon, Marie Edme Patrice
Maurice de

Loyd, Ed
See Kirkeby, Wallace Theodore

Loyd, John
See Smith, George Joseph

Loyd, Samuel Jones [First Baron
Overstone] 1796-? [IP]
British author
* Mercator

Loyd-Lindsay, Robert James
See Lindsay, Robert James

Loyes, Charles Auguste 1841-? [NPS]
French artist, journalist, author
* Montbard, Georges

Loyola y Balda, Ingio de 1491-1556
Saint
* Ignatius of Loyola

Loys, Captain
See Labe, Louise

Loyseau, Jacques
See Collin, Jacques Albin Simon

Loyson, Charles Jean Marie 1827-1912
[DNNS, WBD]
French clergyman
* Hyacinthe, Pere

Lozano, [Don] Pedro 19th c. [HPPN]
Spanish historian
* Philolethus

Lozovskii, Aleksandr
See Dridzo, Solomon Abramovich

Lozzi, Edmondo 20th c. [WF]
Italian film editor
* Zimmerwal, Edmond

Lu, Cheng-hsiang 1870-1949 [BI]
Chinese monk
* Celestin, [Dom] Pierre

Lu ch'iao
See Wu, Nelson I[kon]

Lu Hsun
See Chou Shu-jen

Lu, K'uan-yu
See Luk, Charles

Lu Liang Huan 1936- [EG]
Golfer
* Lu, Mr.

Lu, Mr.
See Lu Liang Huan

Luaces, Joaquin Lorenzo 1826-1867
[CW]
Cuban poet, playwright, author
* Fornaris y Joaquin, lorenzo Luaces

Luahne, Iolani 1915?-1978 [FIR]
Hawaiian actress and dancer
* Auntie Io

Luandrew, Albert 1907- [BWW]
American singer
* Delta Joe

Luandrew, Albert (cont.)
* Doctor Clayton's Buddy
* Sunnyland Slim

Luard, Nicholas Lambert 1937- [CA,
WWS]
British author
* [The] King of Satire
* McVean, James

Luba
See Marks, Rudenko

Lubanski, Jules Clement Ladislas ?-1907
[NPS]
Author
* Heldau
* Star, Jean

Lubbers, Robert 1922- [WECO]
American cartoonist
* Lewis, Bob

Luber, Jet
See Meulenbelt-Luber, Henrietta C. A.

Lubin
See Perrault, Claude

Lubin, Howard 20th c. [RO2]
British musician
* Lubin, Lem

Lubin, Lem
See Lubin, Howard

Lubin, Maurice Alcibiade 1917- [CW]
Haitian author and critic
* Malu

Lubliner, Hugo 1846-1911 [HPPN, IP]
German businessman, playwright, author
* Buerger, Hugo

Luboshits, Lea 1887- [BBD]
Russian musician
* Luboshutz, Lea

Luboshutz, Lea
See Luboshits, Lea

Lubotsky, Charlotte Rae 1926- [BEW,
TR]
American actress and singer
* Rae, Charlotte

Luby, Hal
See Luby, Hugh Max

Luby, Hugh Max 1913- [BE]
American baseball player
* Luby, Hal

Luby, John Perkins 1868-1899 [BE]
American baseball player
* Luby, Pat

Luby, Kate [PA]
Author
* O'Dowd, Darby

Luby, Pat
See Luby, John Perkins

Luc [Luke]
See Frederick II

Luc Gabrielle, [Sister]
See Deckers, Jeannine

Luca, Cleve
See Luca, Cleveland O.

Luca, Cleveland O. 1827-1872 [IBW]
American musician
* Luca, Cleve

Luca da Cortona
See Signorelli, Luca d'Egidio di
Ventura de

Lucan, Arthur
See Towle, Arthur

Lucanese, Dominic 1898?- [HPPN]
American singer
* [The] Crooning Troubador
* Lucas, Nick
* [The] Singing Troubador

Lucania, Salvatore 1897-1962 [BI,
HPPN]
American underworld figure
* Cusak, John T.
* [The] King of the New York Rackets
* [The] King of the Pimps
* Lane, Charles
* Luciano, Charles
* Luciano, Charlie Lucky
* Luciano, Lucky
* [The] Man
* Ross, Charles
* Three Twelve

Lucas, Barbara
See Wall, Barbara

Lucas, Buster
See Lucas, John Charles [Johnny]

Lucas, Charles ?-1774 [HPPN]
Irish author
* Britannicus
* Hellebore, Dr.

Lucas, Charles 1713-1771 [HN]
Irish politician
* [The] Incorruptible Lucas

Lucas, Charles Fred 1902- [BE, PB]
American baseball player
* Lucas, Red
* [The] Nashville Narcissus

Lucas, Christopher Norman 1912- [ASC]
*British-born songwriter and recording
executive*
* Davis, Norman

Lucas, Daniel Bedinger 1836-1909
[HPPN]
American poet
* [The] Poet of the Shenandoah Valley

Lucas, E. V.
See Lucas, Edward Verrall

Lucas, Edward Verrall 1868-1938
[DLE1, LC, WWL]
British author
* E. V. L.
* Lucas, E. V.
* Ward, E. D.

Lucas, Emily Beatrix Coursolles
See Jones, Emily Beatrix Coursolles

Lucas, Eugene 1901-1972 [SC]
American actor, singer, songwriter
* Austin, Gene
* [The] Voice of the Southland
* [The] Whispering Tenor

Lucas, F. L.
See Lucas, Frank Laurence

Lucas, Francois 1812-? [PA]
Author
* Brugensis

Lucas, Frank Laurence 1894-1967 [LC]
British author, scholar, critic
* Lucas, F. L.

Lucas, Gerald 1935- [IAW]
Swiss author
* Louvier, Pierre
* Melvier, Laurent

Lucas, Hans
See Godard, Jean-Luc

Lucas, Henry 1843-? [HPPN]
British barrister
* [A] Student of the Middle Temple

Lucas, J. K.
See Paine, Lauran [Bosworth]

Lucas, Jane
See Spivey, Victoria Regina [Vicky]

Lucas, John Charles [Johnny] 1903-1970
[BE]
American baseball player
* Lucas, Buster

Lucas, Jonathan
See Giarraputo, Lucas Thomas Aco

Lucas, Laddie
See Lucas, Percy Belgrave

Lucas, Lazy Bill
See Lucas, William [Bill]

Lucas, Luke
See Lucas, Ray Wesley

Lucas, Nick
See Lucanese, Dominic

Lucas, Percy Belgrave 1915- [EG, OCS]
British politician and golfer
* Lucas, Laddie

Lucas, Ray Wesley 1908-1969 [BE]
American baseball player
* Lucas, Luke

Lucas, Red
See Lucas, Charles Fred

Lucas, Richard 1648-1715 [HN]
British clergyman
* [The] Blind Prebendary of
  Westminster

Lucas, Robert
See Ehrenzweig, Robert

Lucas van Leyden
See Hugensz, Lucas

Lucas, Victoria
See Plath, Sylvia

Lucas, William 18th c. [IP]
British barrister and author
* A. Z.

Lucas, William [Bill] 1918- [BWW]
American singer
* Lucas, Lazy Bill

Lucas Garcia, Benedicto 20th c.
Guatemalan army officer
* Lucas Garcia, Benny

Lucas Garcia, Benny
See Lucas Garcia, Benedicto

Lucasta
See Sacheverell, Lucy

Lucasta
See Waite, Ada Lakeman

Lucca, Pauline
See Von Walhofen, Baroness

Lucchese, Thomas Gaetano 1903-1967
[BLB, HPPN, PHM]
American underworld figure
* Brown, Three Finger
* Brown, Tommy

Lucchesi, Aldo
See Von Block, Bela

Lucchetto da Genova
See Cambiaso, Luca

Lucci, Mike 20th c.
American football player
* Lucci, Owl

Lucci, Owl
See Lucci, Mike

Lucciola, John 1926- [ASC]
American musician
* Luce, Johnnie

Luce, Alfred 19th c. [HPPN]
American author
* Darf, Esel

Luce, Clare Boothe 1903- [HPPN]
American playwright and diplomat
* Boothe, Clare

Luce, Henry Robinson 1898-1967
[HPPN]
American publisher of news magazines
* [The] Father of Photojournalism

Luce, Johnnie
See Lucciola, John

Luce, Polly
See Marion, Pauline

Luce, Robert 1862-1946 [HPPN]
American politician
* [The] Parliamentarian

Luce, Stephen Bleekard 1827-1917
[HPPN]
American naval officer
* [The] Man Who Taught the Navy to
  Think

Lucebert
See Swanswijk, L. G.

[The] Lucerna Juris
See Irnerius

Lucero, Roberto
See Meredith, Robert C[hidester]

Lucey, James D[ennis] 1923- [CA, WD]
American author
* James, Matthew

Lucey, Joseph Earl [Joe] 1897- [BE]
American baseball player
* Lucey, Scootch

Lucey, Scootch
See Lucey, Joseph Earl [Joe]

Lucey, Thomas Elmore 1874-? [BDSA]
American poet
* [The] Poet Entertainer of the Ozarks

Luchino
See Cambiaso, Luca

Lucia
See Hunting, M. E.

Lucian ?-290 [HN]
Saint
* [The] Apostle of Beauvais

Lucian 120-180 [DEP, FFF, HPPN, NPS]
Greek author
* [The] Blasphemer
* [The] Cerberus of the Muses
* [The] Philosopher of Samosata
* [The] Samosatian Philosopher
* [The] Voltaire of Grecian Literature

Lucian 240?-312 [WBD]
Syrian-born theologian
* Lucian of Antioch
* [The] Martyr

Lucian of Antioch
See Lucian

[The] Lucian of France
See Rabelais, Francois

Luciani, Albino 1912-1978
Pope
* Gianpaolo
* John Paul I

Luciani, Sebastiano 1485?-1547 [WBD]
Italian painter
* Sebastiano del Piombo

Luciano, Charles
See Lucania, Salvatore

Luciano, Charlie Lucky
See Lucania, Salvatore

Luciano, Lucky
See Lucania, Salvatore

Lucid, Pate 1912-1981 [FC, ITA]
American actor
* Hayden, Lucky
* Hayden, Russell
* [The] Rootin', Tootin', Ridin' Romeo
  of the Screen

Lucie-Smith, [John] Edward [McKenzie]
1933- [WD]
British poet, translator, writer
* Kershaw, Peter

Lucien, Jon
See Harrigan, Jon Lucien

Lucier, Mrs. Frederick   [FFF]
Entertainer
* Archmere, Halie

Lucifer
See Ball, John

Lucile
See Sutherland, Lucy Christina

Lucilius, Caius 2nd c. BC [DEP, DNNS, FFF, NPS]
Roman poet
* [The] Father of Roman Satire
* [The] Great Auruncian

Lucinda B.
See Bowser, Lucinda

Lucio
See Phillips, Gordon

Luciolli, Mario 1910- [IAW]
Italian-born author
* Donosti, Mario

Lucioni, Luigi 1900- [HPPN]
Italian-American painter
* [The] Painter Laureate of Vermont

Lucis Amator
See Burton, Doris

Lucius [code name used during World War II]
See Nguyen That Thanh

Lucius II
See Caccianemici, Gerardo

Lucius III
See Allucingoli, Ubaldo

Luck, Georgia
See Jessup, Georgia Mills

Luck, Lucky
See Luck, Robert

Luck, Robert ?-1977 [FIR]
Actor
* Luck, Lucky

Luckett, Edith 20th c. [TI 1-14-85]
Mother of American First Lady, Nancy Reagan
* Luckett, Lucky

Luckett, Lucky
See Luckett, Edith

Luckey, John 19th c. [IP]
American clergyman and author
* [A] Chaplain

[The] Luckiest Fool Alive
See Kelly, Alvin Anthony

Luckless, John [joint pseudonym with Clifford Irving]
See Burkholz, Herbert

Luckless, John [joint pseudonym with Herbert Burkholz]
See Irving, Clifford Michael

[The] Lucky
See Ericsson, Leif

Lucky Bing
See Crosby, Harry Lillis

Lucky Dan Tobin
See Tobin, Daniel

Lucky Eddie Rosenbaum
See Rosenbaum, Edward

Lucky Lindy
See Lindbergh, Charles Augustus

Lucrece
See Daniels, Coralin

Lucretius
See Tytler, William

Lucretius Carus, Titus 1st c. BC [SN]
Roman poet
* [The] Sculptor Poet

Lucullus
See Bennis, Wessel Johannes

Lucullus
See Bernard, Samuel

Lucy
See Ball, Lucille

Lucy [code name used during World War II]
See Roesseler, Rudolf

Lucy, [Sir] Henry William 1845-1924 [FFF, NPS, WWL]
British author
* De Bookworms, Baron
* H. W. L.
* Member of the Chiltern Hundreds
* My Baritone
* Toby, M. P.

Lucy, Thomas Elmore 1874-? [NAA]
American author
* Elmore, Carol

Luddeckens, Werner Louis Georg 1889?-1945 [SC]
German actor
* Alexander, Georg

Ludden, Allen [Ellsworth] 1918?-1981 [CA, SAT]
American television and radio producer, game show host, author
* [The] Happy Highbrow

Ludendorff, Erich Friedrich Wilhelm 1865-1937 [HPPN]
German army officer and politician
* [The] Tormented Warrior

Luder, Doctor
See Luther, Martin

Luders, Catherine 1828?-? [FFF, PA]
American poet
* Hermann, Emily

Ludgrove, Linda 1947- [SWI]
British swimmer
* Ludgrove, Little Linda

Ludgrove, Little Linda
See Ludgrove, Linda

Ludlam, George 19th c. [IP]
British playwright
* G. L.

Ludlow, Dwight 1889- [CU]
American actor
* Washburn, Bryant

Ludlow, Fitz-Hugh 1837-1870 [IP]
American author
* [A] Pythagorean

Ludlow, Geoffrey
See Meynell, Laurence [Walter]

Ludlow, George
See Kay, Ernest

Ludlow, Johnny
See Wood, Ellen Price

Ludlow, Louis Leon 1873-? [HPPN]
American journalist and politician
* Ludlow, Peace

Ludlow, Park
See Brown, Theron

Ludlow, Peace
See Ludlow, Louis Leon

Ludlow, Roger 1590- [HPPN]
British-American attorney
* [The] Father of Connecticut Jurisprudence

Ludlum, Mabel Cleland
See Widdemer, Mabel Cleland

Ludlum, Robert 1927- [CA, CLC, TCCM, WD]
American author
* Ryder, Jonathan
* Shephard, Michael

Ludolph, Wee Willie
See Ludolph, William Francis [Willie]

Ludolph, William Francis [Willie] 1900-1952 [BE]
American baseball player
* Ludolph, Wee Willie

Ludovici, Anthony M[ario] 1882-? [CAP]
British author and illustrator
* Cobbett
* Paterson, Huntley
* Valentine, David

Ludovici, L. J.
See Ludovici, Lorenz [or Laurence] James

Ludovici, Lorenz [or Laurence] James 1910- [CA]
Ceylonese-born author
* Ludovici, L. J.

Ludovicus, M.
See Campbell, John

Ludovisi, Alessandro 1554-1623 [WBD]
Pope
* Gregory XV

Ludvigsen, Karl [Eric] 1934- [CA]
American writer
* Miles, Elliot
* Nielssen, Eric

Ludvigson, Susan 1942- [CA]
American poet
* Bartels, Susan Ludvigson

Ludwell, Bernice
See Stokes, Manning Lee

Ludwig
See Griswold, Rufus Wilmot

Ludwig der Springer
See Louis [or Ludwig]

Ludwig, Emil
See Cohn, Emil

Ludwig, Eric
See Grunwald, Stefan

Ludwig, Frederic
See Grunwald, Stefan

Ludwig, Myles Eric 1942- [CA]
American author
* Williams, J. X.

Lueders, Charles Henry 1858-? [FFF, IP]
American writer
* C. H. L.
* Karlsten, Henry
* L. H. C.

Luetgert, Adolph Louis 1848-1911
[HPPN]
American butcher and murderer
* [The] Sausage Maker Murder

Lueth, Julia 1864?-1950 [BEW]
Danish-born actress and playwright
* Anderson, Julia

Luff, Stanley George Anthony 1921-
[CA]
British author
* Farnash, Hugh

Lufft, Hans 1495-1584 [WBD]
German printer
* [The] Bible Printer

Luganski, Kosak
See Dahl, Vladimir Ivanovitch

Lugard, Flora Louisa Shaw 1852-1929
[SAT]
Irish-born journalist and author
* Shaw, Flora Louisa

[El] Lugareno
See Betancourt Cisneros, Gaspar

Lugman, Adbullah
See Swafford, Johnny C.

Lugosi, Bela
See Blasko, Bela Lugosi

Lugow
See Gow, Lucienne

Luhan, Mabel Dodge
See Luhan, Mabel Ganson

Luhan, Mabel Ganson 1879-1962
[HPPN]
American author
* Luhan, Mabel Dodge

Luhar, Tribhuvandas Purushottandas
20th c. [IAW]
Indian author and poet
* Sundaram

Luhrsen, Wild Bill
See Luhrsen, William Ferdinand [Bill]

Luhrsen, William Ferdinand [Bill]
1884-1973 [BE]
American baseball player
* Luhrsen, Wild Bill

Luigi
See Facciuto, Eugene Louis

Luigi
See Pelletier, Alexis

Luimardel
See Martinez-Delgado, Luis

Luisetti, Angelo Enrico 1916- [BB, BI, OCS]
American basketball player
* Luisetti, Hank

Luisetti, Hank
See Luisetti, Angelo Enrico

Luisi, Marie 1936?-
American advertising executive
* [The] Godmother

Luisillo
See Perez Davila, Luis

Luisinus
See Luvigini, Francesco

Luiskovo, Andrey
See Pedachenko, Alexander

Luiz, Washington
See Pereira de Souza, Washington Luiz

Luk, Charles 1898- [AW, CA]
Chinese editor and translator
* Lu, K'uan-yu

Lukacs, Pal 1891?-1971 [FC, WEF]
Hungarian-born actor
* Lukas, Paul

Lukas, Charlotte Koplinka 1954- [CA]
American author and poet
* Koplinka, Charlotte

Lukas, Paul
See Lukacs, Pal

Luke 1st c. [DEP, DNNF, FF]
Saint
* [The] Beloved Physician

Luke
See Clarke, Gordon Luke

Luke, Frank, Jr. 1897-1918 [HPPN]
American military aviator
* [The] Balloon Buster

Luke, [Sir] Samuel 17th c. [SN]
British justice of the peace and army officer
* Hudibras

Luke, Steve Norman 1953- [BA]
American football player
* Doom, Dr.

Luke the Drifter
See Williams, Hiram King

Luke, Thomas
See Masterton, Graham

Lukeman, Alex 20th c. [SFL]
Author
* Dain, Alex

Lukens, Adam
See De Reyna, Diane Detzer

Lukens, Alan R., III 20th c. [BBH]
American sailboat racer
* Lukens, Doc

Lukens, Doc
See Lukens, Alan R., III

Lukens, Henry Clay 1838-1900? [DNA, FFF, HPPN, PA]
American author and journalist
* Erratic Enrique
* Kingsbury, Vernon L.
* Snekul, Heinrich Yale

Lukens, Mary C. [Painter] 1842-? [IP]
American author
* Dawdle, Dolly

Lukin, James 19th c. [IP]
British clergyman and author
* J. L.

Lukon, Edward Paul [Eddie] 1920-
[BE]
American baseball player
* Lukon, Mongoose

Lukon, Mongoose
See Lukon, Edward Paul [Eddie]

Luks, George Benjamin 1867-1933
American painter
* Chicago Whitey

Lulli, Giovanni Battista 1632-1687
[HPPN, SN]
Italian-born French composer
* [Le] Bouffon Odieux
* [Le] Coeur Bas [The Base Heart]
* [Un] Coquin Tenebreux [A Dark Knave]
* [The] Hateful Clown
* Lully, Jean Baptiste

Lully, Jean Baptiste
See Lulli, Giovanni Battista

Lully, Raymond 1234?-1315 [FFF, HN]
Spanish philosopher
* [The] Enlightened Doctor
* [The] Illuminated Doctor
* Illuminatus, Doctor
* [The] Most Enlightened Doctor

Lulu
See Bonaparte, Napoleon Eugene Louis
Jean Joseph

Lulu
See Hall, Louise G.

Lulu
See Lawrie, Marie McDonald McLaughlin

Lulu Belle
See Wiseman, Myrtle Eleanor Cooper

Lulubelle
See Cooper, Myrtle

Lum
Lauck, Chester

Lum, Dyer Daniel 19th c. [IP]
British author
* [A] Gentile

Lum, Peter
See Crowe, [Lady] Bettina [Lum]

Lumb, E. 19th c. [IP]
British poet
* E. L.

Lumb, Emmeline 20th c. [WWL]
British author
* Brittain, Noel

Lumb, Lummy
See Lumb, Richard Graham

Lumb, Richard Graham 1950- [DC]
British cricketer
* Lumb, Lummy

[The] Lumber King
See Weyerhaeuser, Frederick

Lumberjack
See Lambert, T. H.

Lumenti, Commuter
See Lumenti, Ralph Anthony

Lumenti, Ralph Anthony 1936- [BE]
American baseball player
* Lumenti, Commuter

Luminus
See Melling, Leonard

Lumley, Apple Cheeks
See Lumley, Harry

Lumley, Benjamin 1812-1875 [IP]
British barrister, opera manager, author
* Hermes
* Levy, Benjamin

Lumley, Dave 1954- [SMG]
Canadian-born hockey player
* Lumley, Lummer

Lumley, H. R. 19th c. [IP]
British journalist, author, playwright
* Lyulph

Lumley, Harry 1926- [CEI, FHE, HK]
Canadian-born hockey player
* Lumley, Apple Cheeks

Lumley, Harry G. 1880-1938 [BN]
American baseball player
* Lumley, Yock

Lumley, Lummer
See Lumley, Dave

Lumley, Yock
See Lumley, Harry G.

Lummis, Charles Fletcher 1859-1928
[HPPN]
American author and editor
* [The] Crusader in Corduroy

Lumpkin, Chief
See Lumpkin, Claude C., II

Lumpkin, Claude C., II 1918- [HPPN]
American army officer
* Lumpkin, Chief

Lumpkin, Father
See Lumpkin, Roy

Lumpkin, Roy 20th c. [EF]
American football player
* Lumpkin, Father

Lumpwitz, Prof.
See Bunbury, Henry William

Lumpy Willie
See Chapelski, Alex Samuel

Lumsden, James 19th c. [IP]
Scottish author
* [A] Mercantile Man

Lun
See Rich, John

Luna, Donyale
See Freeman, Peggy Anne Donyale Aragonea Pegeon

Luna, Guillermo Romero 1930- [BE]
Mexican-born baseball player
* Luna, Memo

Luna, Kris [house pseudonym, Curtis Warren]
See Bird, William Henry Fleming

Luna, Kris [house pseudonym, Curtis Warren]
See O'Brien, David

Luna, Memo
See Luna, Guillermo Romero

Lunaeus, Peter 1586-1638 [PA]
Author
* Van der Kun

Lunalilo
See Canaina, William

Lunar, Dennis
See Mungo, Raymond

[A] Lunar Wray
See Savage, M. J.

Lunatic, [Sir] Humphrey, Bart.
See Gentleman, Francis

Lunchbasket, Roger
See Reeve-Jones, Alan Edmond

Lund, A. Morten 1926- [CA]
American author
* Borch, Ted

Lund, Arthur 1915- [MY]
American singer
* London, Art

Lund, Francis L. 1913- [FB]
American football player
* Lund, Pug

Lund, Penny
See Lund, Pentti Alexander

Lund, Pentti Alexander 1925- [CEI]
Finnish-born hockey player
* Lund, Penny

Lund, Philip R[eginald] 1938- [CA]
New Zealand-born author
* Confucius

Lund, Pug
See Lund, Francis L.

Lund, Troels Frederik 1840-1921 [WBD]
Danish historian
* Troels-Lund

Lundberg, Eleanor Jewett 1892- [NAA]
American journalist
* Jewett, Eleanor

Lundberg, Kai
See Potthoff, Margot Maria

Lunden, Joan
See Blunden, Joan

Lundgren, Paul Arthur 1925-1981
[IAW]
American writer
* McCutcheon, James

Lundholm, Anja 20th c. [IAW]
German-born author
* Lindstrom, Alf

Lundigan, William 1914- [HPPN]
American actor
* Chrysler, Mr.
* Parks, Larry

Lundquist, Lunk
See Lundquist, Steve

Lundquist, Steve 20th c. [TI 8-13-84]
American swimmer
* Lundquist, Lunk

Lundy, Benjamin 1789-1839 [HPPN, IP]
American author and abolitionist leader
* [A] Citizen of the United States
* Peter the Hermit of the Abolitionist Movement

Lundy, John Patterson 1823-? [IP]
American clergyman and author
* [A] Presbyter of the Church in Phila

Lundy, Richard 1898-1965 [MK]
American baseball player
* King Richard

Lunettes, Henry
See Conkling, Margaret Cockburn

Lungstrum, Frank Alan 1919- [HPPN]
American singer and disc jockey
* Allan, Frank

Luni, Enrique
See Luning, Heinrich August

Luning, Heinrich August ?-1942 [BI]
German spy
* Luni, Enrique

Lunn, Arnold [Henry Moore] 1888-1974
[CA, CAT, HPPN]
British author
* Croft, Sutton
* [The] Father of the Slalom
* Rubicon

Lunn, Hugh Kingsmill 1889-1949 [LC,
TC, TC1]
British author and critic
* Kingsmill, Hugh

Lunn, Robert 1912-1966 [ECM]
American country-western performer
* [The] Talking Blues Boy
* [The] Talking Blues Man

Lunt, Arthur Milton 1881-1971 [F1, FC,
SC]
British actor
* Rosmer, Milton

Lunt, George 1807?-1885 [DNA, FFF]
American attorney, author, poet
* Brooke, Wesley

Lunt, Irene
See Bradbury, Irene

Lunt, Lois
See Metz, Lois Lunt

Lunt, Lynn Fontanne 1887- [HPPN]
British-American actress
* Fontanne, Lynn

Lunt, William Parsons 1805-1857
[HPPN]
American clergyman
* L.
* W. P.
* W. P. L.

Luola
See Miller, Mary [Ayer]

Luola
See Niller, Mary Ager

Lupescu, Elena 1896?-1977
Wife of King Carol of Rumania
* [The] Jewish Pompadour
* Lupescu, Magda

Lupescu, Magda
See Lupescu, Elena

Lupien, Tony
See Lupien, Ulysses John

Lupien, Ulysses John 1917- [BE]
American baseball player
* Lupien, Tony

Lupino, Henry George 1892-1959 [F2,
FC, SC]
British actor
* Lane, Lupino
* Lane, Nipper

Lupino, Wallace 1898-1961 [SC]
Scottish-born actor
* Lane, Wallace

Lupo, Joseph
See Saietta, Ignazio

Lupo the Wolf
See Saietta, Ignazio

Lupoff, Richard Allen [Dick] 1935-
[CA, CA, ESF, SFP]
American author
* Hamlet, Ova
* O'Donnell, Dick [joint pseudonym
  with Don(ald) (Arthur) Thompson]
* Pascudniak, Pascal
* Steele, Addison, II

Lupton, Marie 1875-1930 [THR]
British actress
* Studholme, Marie

Lupton, Netta 1893?-1953 [BEW]
British-born actress
* Westcott, Netta

Lupu-Pick
See Pick, Lupu

Lupulus
See Woelflein, Heinrich

Lupus, Michael
See De Wolf, Michael

Luque, Adolfo 1890-1957 [BE, DGS]
Cuban-born baseball player
* Luque, Dolf
* [The] Pride of Havana

Luque, Antonio 1838-1887 [GS]
Spanish bullfighter
* Cuchares de Cordoba

Luque, Dolf
See Luque, Adolfo

Luque y Gonzalez, Antonio 1814-1859
[GS]
Spanish bullfighter
* Camara

Luqueer, Helen
See Bushnell, Mrs. William H.

Lurch
See Brabender, Eugene Mathew

Lurgan, Lester
See Knowles, Mabel Winifred

Lurie, Ranan R. 1932- [HPPN]
American cartoonist
* [The] World's Most Widely Syndicated
  Cartoonist

[A] Lurking, Way-Laying Coward
See Pope, Alexander

Lurye, Mikhail 1882-1932 [JL]
Russian economist and politician
* Larin, Yuri

Luscious John Valiant
See Valiant, John

Lush, Lieutenant
See O'Dowd, George Alan

[The] Lusian Scipio
See Nunio

Lusian's Luckless Queen
See Maria I

Lusitano, Candido
See Freire, Francisco Jose

Luska, Sidney
See Harland, Henry

Lussier, Yvonne 1904?-1983 [DF 12-4-83]
Canadian-born actress
* D'Orsay, Fifi
* [The] French Bombshell

Lussu, Joyce [Salvadori] 1912- [CA]
Italian writer and translator
* Salvadori, Joyce

Lustarria, Eduardo De La Barra 19th c.
[HPPN]
Chilean author
* Gesuit, V. Erasmo

Luster, Shirley 1925- [HPPN, PMJ]
American singer
* Christy, June
* Leslie, Sharon

Lustig, [Count] Victor
See Miller, Robert

Lustiger, Aaron 1927?-
French clergyman
* Lustiger, Jean-Marie

Lustiger, Jean-Marie
See Lustiger, Aaron

[The] Lusty Blonde Bandleader
See Cowan, Odessa

Lusus, Larry, Esq.
See O'Brien, William

Lutchman, Martinus Haridat 1926-
[CW]
Surinamese poet
* Shrinivasi, Asjantenu

Lutenberg, Charles William 1864-1938
[BE]
American baseball player
* Lutenberg, Luke

Lutenberg, Luke
See Lutenberg, Charles William

Lutetius
See Stearns, Harold Edmund

Luther, Frank
See Crow, Francis Luther [Frank]

Luther, G. C.
See Williams, Theodore Samuel [Ted]

Luther, Irene 1891?- [F1, F2, FC,
HPPN]
American actress
* [The] Number 1 Slim Woman of the
  Air
* Rich, Irene

Luther, Martin 1483-1546 [DEP, HN,
HPPN, NPS, SN]
German religious reformer
* [The] Father of Protestantism
* [The] Father of the Reformation
* [The] German Paul
* [The] Great Iconoclast
* [The] Great Reformer
* [The] Hot Headed Monk
* [The] Leader of the Reformation
* Luder, Doctor
* Martin, [Brother]

Luther, Martin (cont.)
* * [The] Michael Angelo of the Reformation
* * [The] Monk of Eisleben
* * [The] Monk of Wittenberg
* * [The] Nightingale of Wittenberg
* * [The] Solitary Monk
* * [The] Third Elias
* * [The] Wittenberg Monk

[The] Luther of England
See Cranmer, Thomas

[The] Luther of Sweden
See Petri, Olaus [or Olaf]

[The] Luther of the Early Temperance Reformation
See Hewit, Nathaniel

Luther, Ray
See Ley, Arthur Gordon

Lutoslawski, Wincenty 1863-?   [WWL]
British philosopher and author
* * Ezami, Henri

Lutschitsch-Dalmatoff, B. 1862-?   [THR]
Russian actor
* * Dalmatoff, B.

Lutterby, Francis
See Scudder, Samuel Hubbard

Luttringer, Al
See Luttringer, Alfonse

Luttringer, Alfonse 1879-1953   [SC]
American actor
* * Luttringer, Al

Luttwak, Edward Nicolae 1942-   [IAW]
Rumanian-born author
* * Ignotus, Miles

Lutwak, Michael Anatol 1902-   [FD, WEF]
Russian-born director
* * Litvak, Anatole

Lutyens, Mary 1908-   [CA, WD]
British author and editor
* * Wyndham, Esther

Lutz, Calvin Jack Von Reinhold 1927- [HPPN]
Canadian dancer and choreographer
* * Von Reinhold, Calvin

Lutz, E. O.
See Lutz, Edward Oscar

Lutz, Edward Oscar 1919-   [BEW]
American accountant, educator, executive
* * Lutz, E. O.

Lutz, Louis William 1898-   [BE]
American baseball player
* * Lutz, Red

Lutz, Michael 1949-   [RO2]
American musician
* * Lutz, Sam

Lutz, Red
See Lutz, Louis William

Lutz, Sam
See Lutz, Michael

Lutzke, Rube
See Lutzke, Walter John

Lutzke, Walter John 1897-1938   [BE]
American baseball player
* * Lutzke, Rube

Luvigini, Francesco 1523-1568   [PA]
Author
* * Luisinus

Lux
See Jones, Lucy M.

Lux, Adam
See Pic, Ulysse

Lux Dux
See Howard, Anna Holyoke [Cutts]

Lux Mundi
See Wessel, Johann [or John]

[The] Luxembourg Hercules
See Grunn, John

Luxemburg, Rosa 1870-1919   [WBD]
German Socialist leader
* * Red Rosa

Luxton, Leonora Kathrine 1895-   [CA]
American astrologer and author
* * Howard, Nona

Luz y Caballero, Jose Cipriano de la 1800-1862   [CW]
Cuban author
* * Filolezes

Luzinski, Gregory Michael 1950-   [SMG]
American baseball player
* * [The] Bull
* * Luzinski, Hoss

Luzinski, Hoss
See Luzinski, Gregory Michael

Lyall, David
See Reeves, Helen Buckingham [Mathers]

Lyall, David
See Swan, Annie S[hepherd]

Lyall, Edna
See Bayly, Ada Ellen

Lyall, Katharine Elizabeth 1928-   [CA]
British journalist and author
* * Whitehorn, Katharine

Lyautey, Louis Hubert Gonzalve 1854-1934   [NW 2-7-83]
French army officer
* * [The] Prince of Proconsuls

[The] Lycanthrope
See Borel, Pierre Bord d'Hautoine

Lyceus
See Fitzgibbon, John [Earl of Clare]

Lycidas
See King, Edward

[The] Lycurgus of the Lower House
See Russell, [Lord] John Earl

Lycurgus, Solon
See Clemens, Samuel Langhorne

Lycus
See Fitzgibbon, John

Lyddal
See Garrick, David

Lyde, Edward 1620?-1695?   [BI, HPPN]
British author
* * Joyner

Lydgate, John 1375-1460   [HN, RH, SN]
British poet
* * [The] Monk of Bury

[The] Lydgate of His Day
See Jean [or Jehan] de Meung

[The] Lydian Poet
See Alcman

Lydon, James [Jimmy] 1923-   [HPPN]
American actor
* * [The] Henry Aldrich of the Movies

Lydon, John 20th c.
British musician
* * Rotten, Johnny

Lye Alone, Lionel
See Foe, Daniel

Lyel, Viola
See Watson, Violet

Lyell, [Sir] Charles 1797-1875
British geologist
* * [The] Father of Modern Geology

Lyfick, Warren
See Reeves, Lawrence F.

Lygo, Mary
See Goodall, Irene

Lying Dick Talbot
See Talbot, Richard

[The] Lying Nun
See Monk, Maria

Lying Old Fox
See Walpole, Horatio [Fourth Earl of Orford]

[The] Lying Scot
See Burnet, Gilbert

[The] Lying Traveller
See Mandeville, [Sir] John

Lykiard, Alexis [Constantine] 1940- [CA]
Greek-born poet and author
* * Piano, Celeste

Lyle, Albert Walter 1944-   [BE, PB, WWB]
American baseball player
* * Lyle, Sparky

Lyle, Cecil 1892?-1955   [BEW]
Magician
* * [The] Great Lyle

Lyle, Gwladys M. [Morgan] 1888- [NAA]
American author and poet
* * Morgan, Gwladys M.

Lyle, Lyston
See Gibson, Edward

Lyle, Sparky
See Lyle, Albert Walter

Lyle-Smythe, Alan 1914- [CA, TCCM]
British-born American author,
screenwriter, playwright
* Caillou, Alan

Lyly, John 1554?-1606 [NPS, SN]
British author
* [The] Ape of Envie
* Euphues
* [The] Euphuist
* Pap-Hatchet
* Tullius Anglorum
* [The] Vayn Pap-Hatchet

Lyman, Abe
See Simon, Abraham

Lyman, Albert Robison 1880-1973
[CAP]
American author
* [The] Old Settler

Lyman, Elwood 1905- [HPPN]
American athletic coach
* Lyman, Mose

Lyman, G. H. [PA]
Author
* De Leon, Stuart

Lyman, Helen Hoyt 20th c. [NAA]
American author and poet
* Hoyt, Helen

Lyman, Link
See Lyman, William Roy

Lyman, Mose
See Lyman, Elwood

Lyman, William Roy 1898-1972 [BBH,
FB, SMG]
American football player
* Lyman, Link

Lymington, John
See Chance, John Newton

Lynam, Joan 20th c. [IAW]
Irish author
* Lynam, Shevawn

Lynam, Shevawn
See Lynam, Joan

Lynch, Ann Marie 1937- [HPPN]
American wrestler
* Antonelli, Ann Marie

Lynch, Benny 1913-1946 [HPPN]
Scottish boxer
* Scotland's First World Champion

Lynch, Brian
See Liddy, James [Daniel Reeves]

Lynch, Brid
See Ni Loinsigh, Brid

Lynch, Dummy
See Lynch, Matthew Daniel

Lynch, Edward
See Sutton, William Francis [Willie]

Lynch, Eric
See Bingley, David Ernest

Lynch, Frances
See Compton, David Guy

Lynch, Gentleman Jack
See Lynch, John

Lynch, Grey
See Dorworth, Alice Grey

Lynch, Harriet Louise 20th c. [NAA]
American author
* St. Felix, Marie

Lynch, James
See Andreyev, Leonid [Nikolaevich]

Lynch, John 1918?-
Irish politician
* Lynch, Gentleman Jack

Lynch, John A. 19th c. [HPPN]
American author
* Than, John A.

Lynch, John Gilbert Bohun 20th c.
[MBF]
British author
* Bloomer, Jack

Lynch, Lawrence L.
See Van Deventer, Emma Murdock

Lynch, Marilyn 1938- [CA]
American author
* Ward, Melanie

Lynch, Matthew Daniel 1927- [BE]
American baseball player
* Lynch, Dummy

Lynch, Michael 1852-? [PI]
American poet
* Lamech

Lynch, Mrs. Henry 19th c. [PI]
Irish poet
* Personne

Lynch, Mrs. Samuel [FFF]
Entertainer
* Meserole, Fannie

Lynch, Robert Clyde 1880-1931 [HPPN]
American physician
* [The] Father of the Lynch Operation

Lynch, Ruth Sproule 1910-1968 [HPPN]
American dancer
* Sproule, Ruth

Lynch, Thomas Took 1818-1871 [PI]
British author and hymn writer
* Long, Silent

Lynch, William 1782-1820 [HPPN]
American army officer
* [The] Father of Lynch Law

Lynd, Robert 1879-1949 [BI, HPPN, LC]
Irish-born author
* O'London, John
* Y. Y.

Lynd, Rosa
See Secor, Rosa

Lyndhurst, [Rev.] John Singleton Copley
1772-1863 [HPPN]
British jurist
* [The] Chancellor

Lyndon
See Bright, Matilda A.

Lyndon, Amy
See Radford, Richard F[rancis], Jr.

Lyndon, Barre?
See Edgar, Alfred

Lyndon, Barry
See Austin, George Lowell

Lynds, Dennis 1924- [AW, CA, SFL,
WGT]
American author
* Arden, William
* Carter, Nick
* Collins, Michael
* Crowe, John
* Dekker, Carl
* Grant, Maxwell [house pseudonym]
* Sadler, Mark

Lyne, [Rev.] Augustus Adolphus 19th c.
[HPPN]
British clergyman and naval officer
* [The] Midshipman

Lyne, Joseph Leycester 1837-1908 [BI,
RH]
British monk
* Ignatius, [Father]

Lyngstad, Sverre 1922- [IAW]
Norwegian-born author
* Larr, Sven

Lynk, Warder
See Bowman, Gerald

Lynkeus
See Popper, Josef

Lynley, Carol
See Jones, Carol

Lynn
See Brown, Velma Darbo

Lynn, Barbara
See Ozone, Barbara Lynn

[The] Lynn Bard
See Lewis, Alonzo

Lynn, Benjamin 18th c. [FFF]
American pioneer
* [The] Daniel Boone of Southern
  Kentucky
* [The] Hunter Preacher

Lynn, Cheryl
See Smith, Cherry George

Lynn, Cora
See Cunati, Caroline

Lynn, Diana
See Loehr, Dolores

Lynn, Eddie
See Meminger, Edward Lynn

Lynn, Elwyn Augustus 1917- [AW]
Australian author and editor
* Augustus

Lynn, Escott
See Lawrence, Christopher George
Holman

Lynn, Ethel
See Beers, Ethelinda Elliot

Lynn, Fragile Freddie
See Lynn, Frederick Michael

Lynn, Frank
See Leisy, James Franklin

Lynn, Frederick A. 1947?- [HPPN]
American investment counsellor
* Lynn, Junkman

Lynn, Frederick Michael 1952- [WP 5-14-85]
American baseball player
* Lynn, Fragile Freddie

Lynn, Gerrie
See Robeck, Geraldine Cecilia

Lynn, Irene
See Rowland, Donald Sydney

Lynn, Jane Thursten 1915- [ASC]
American composer
* Willadsen, Gene

Lynn, Janet
See Nowicki, Janet Lynn

Lynn, Janet
See Salomon, Janet Lynn [Nowicki]

Lynn, Japhet Monroe 1913- [BE]
American baseball player
* Lynn, Red

Lynn, Jeffrey
See Lind, Ragnar Godfrey

Lynn, Junkman
See Lynn, Frederick A.

Lynn, Loretta 1935?- [HPPN]
*American country-western performer and
songwriter*
* [The] Coal Miner's Daughter
* [The] Country Queen
* [The] First Lady of Country Music
* [The] Foremost Lady of Country
 Music
* [The] Queen of Country Music

Lynn, Mara
See Mosier, Marilyn

Lynn, Margaret
See Battye, Gladys

Lynn, Mary
See Brokamp, Marilyn

Lynn, Max
See Anderson, G. J. B.

Lynn, Patricia
See Watts, Mabel Pizzey

Lynn, Red
See Lynn, Japhet Monroe

Lynn, Sharon E.
See Lindsay, D'Auvergne Sharon

Lynn, Tracy
See Rose, Mary Kay

Lynn, Vera 1916- [NN]
British singer
* [The] Forces' Sweetheart

Lynne, Becky
See Zawadsky, Patience

Lynne, Carole
See Haymen, Helen Violet Carolyn

Lynne, Glenys 20th c. [RO2]
South African singer
* Jill

Lynne, James Broom 1920- [WD]
British author and playwright
* Quartermain, James

Lynott, Jessica 1930- [NAD]
Yoga instructor
* Savitri Priya, [Swami]

Lynton, Ann
See Rayner, Claire

Lynton, Harriet Ronken 1920- [CA]
American author
* Ronken, Harriet

LYNX
See Angermayer, Fred Antoine

Lynx
See Fairfield, Cecily Isabel

Lynx, Larry
See Lotinga, W.

Lyon, Babe
See Lyon, George

Lyon, Bebe Daniels 1901-1971 [HPPN]
American actress
* Daniels, Bebe

Lyon, Bess 18th c. [HPPN]
*Associate of British criminal John
Sheppard*
* Edgeworth Bess

Lyon, Buck
See Paine, Lauran [Bosworth]

Lyon, David Gordon [Dave] 1911-
[HPPN]
*American advertising executive and
author*
* [The] Campus Radical
* Lyon, Soggy

Lyon, Elinor
See Wright, Elinor Bruce

Lyon, Francis D. 20th c. [ITA]
American director
* Lyon, Pete

Lyon, General [code name used during
World War II]
See George VI

Lyon, George 20th c. [EF]
American football player
* Lyon, Babe

Lyon, Isaac S. 19th c. [FFF]
American writer
* Old Cartman

Lyon, Jessica
See De Leeuw, Cateau Wilhelmina

Lyon, John 1951- [DC]
British cricketer
* Lyon, Lenny

Lyon, Johnny 20th c. [WP 12-29-84]
American singer
* Southside Johnny

Lyon, Katherine
See Mix, Katherine Lyon

Lyon, Lenny
See Lyon, John

Lyon, Louis 1843-1901 [HPPN]
American actor
* Aldrich, Louis
* [The] Ohio Roscius

Lyon, Lyman R.
See De Camp, L[yon] Sprague

Lyon, Marjorie
See Meredyth-Starmer, Marjorie

Lyon, Mary 1797-1849 [HPPN]
American educator
* Fiske, Fidelia

Lyon, Meyer
See Levin, Meyer

Lyon, Pete
See Lyon, Francis D.

Lyon, Soggy
See Lyon, David Gordon [Dave]

Lyons, A. Neil 1880-? [HPPN]
South African author and playwright
* Michael, Albert

Lyons, Ace
See Lyons, James A.

Lyons, Alexander M. 1863-1945 [SC]
British-born actor
* Crimmins, Dan[iel]

Lyons, Clifford Williams 1902-1974
[SC]
American actor, director, stunt performer
* Lyons, Tex

Lyons, Delphine C.
See Smith, Evelyn E.

Lyons, Ed[ward Hoyte] 1923- [BE]
American baseball player
* Lyons, Mouse

Lyons, Elena
See Fairburn, Eleanor

Lyons, Francis Lunakiaki 1909-1960
[SC]
American actor, musician, singer
* Lyons, Freckles

Lyons, Freckles
See Lyons, Francis Lunakiaki

Lyons, Fred
See Levya, Fred F.

Lyons, Fred
See Leyva, Fred F.

Lyons, George
See Martoccio, Dominic

Lyons, George Tony 1891- [BE]
American baseball player
* Lyons, Smooth

Lyons, Gino
See Lyons, Lewis Melville

Lyons, J. B. 1922- [CA]
Irish physician and author
* Fitzwilliam, Michael

Lyons, James A. 20th c. [WP 6-23-84]
American naval officer
* Lyons, Ace

Lyons, John Maguire 1926- [IAW]
Scottish-born author and cartoonist
* O'Liathain, Sesu

Lyons, Lady, of Strathmore [PA]
Author
* L.

Lyons, Leonard
See Sucher, Leonard

Lyons, Lewis Melville 1962-
British artist
* Lyons, Gino

Lyons, Luella B. 1897- [NAA]
American writer
* La Plante, Sandra
* Rider, Jane

Lyons, Marc
American football player
* Lyons, Mountain

Lyons, Marcus
See Blish, James [Benjamin]

Lyons, Mountain
See Lyons, Marc

Lyons, Mouse
See Lyons, Ed[ward Hoyte]

Lyons, Smooth
See Lyons, George Tony

Lyons, Sophie 1848-1924 [LFW]
American swindler
* Owens, Fannie
* [The] Queen of Crime
* Wilson, Kate
* Wilson, Mary

Lyons, Tex
See Lyons, Clifford Williams

Lyons, Thomas A. 1869-1920 [BE]
American baseball player
* Lyons, Toby

Lyons, Toby
See Lyons, Thomas A.

Lyra, Carmen
See Carvalal, Maria Isabel

Lyra, Nicholas de 1270-1340 [HN]
French monk and author
* Utilis, Doctor

Lyre, Pinchbeck
See Sassoon, Siegfried [Lorraine]

[The] Lyric Muse
See Corinna

[The] Lyrical Special Librarian
See Guenther, Charles

[The] Lyrist
See Randles, E.

Lys, Christian
See Brebner, Percy James

Lysander
See Dibdin, Thomas Frognall

Lysberg, Charles-Samuel
See Bovy-Lysberg, Charles-Samuel

Lyscidias
See Boursault, Edme

Lysogorskii, Ondra
See Goy, Erwin

Lyss
See Grant, Hiram Ulysses

Lyte, Charles 1935- [CA]
British author
* Ewart, Charles

Lyte, Richard
See Whelpton, [George] Eric

Lytell, Bert 1888-1954 [HPPN]
American actor
* Valentine, Jimmy

Lytell, Jimmy
See Sarrapede, James

Lytle, Dad
See Lytle, Edward Benson

Lytle, Donald 1941- [CME]
American country-western performer
* [The] Ohio Kid
* Paycheck, Johnny
* Young, Donnie

Lytle, Edward Benson 1862-1950 [BE]
American baseball player
* Lytle, Dad
* Lytle, Pop

Lytle, George Brett
See Fellows, Dick

Lytle, Joy Oleny Mann
See Buor, Joy Olney

Lytle, Mrs. W. J. A. 20th c. [CCL]
Canadian poet
* Berney, Beryl

Lytle, Pop
See Lytle, Edward Benson

Lyttelton, Edith Joan Balfour
1865?-1948 [HPPN]
British author and public official
* Lancaster, G. B.

**Lyttelton, George [First Baron
Lyttelton]** 1709-1773 [HPPN, SN]
British public official and author
* [The] Good Lord Lyttelton
* Scrag, Gosling
* Selim the Persian

**Lyttelton, Thomas [Second Baron
Lyttelton]** 1744-1779 [HPPN, WBD]
British politician
* [The] Bad
* [The] Wicked Lord Lyttelton

Lyttelton, William Henry 19th c.
[HPPN]
British clergyman
* [A] Clergyman

Lyttle, Jean
See Garrett, Eileen J[eanette]

Lyttle, Richard B[ard] 1927- [CA]
American author
* Lang, Rex

Lyttle, Wesley Guard 1844-1896 [PI]
Irish writer and poet
* Robin

Lyttleton, Edith J. 1873-1945 [WBD]
New Zealand author
* Lancaster, G. B.

Lytton, Doris
See Partington, Doris

Lytton, Edward
See Morris, Charles Smith

Lytton, Edward
See Wheeler, Edward Lytton

Lytton, Jane
See Clarke, Percy A.

Lyulph
See Lumley, H. R.

Lyzwinski, Michal 1888?- [HPPN]
Polish soldier and politician
* Zymirski, Michal

M

Asterisk (*) indicates assumed name.

M.
See Gillison, Margaret

M.
See Maclean, [Sir] John

M.
See MacPherson, George Gordon

M.
See Madden, [Sir] Frederick

M.
See Malone, Michael

M.
See May, Samuel, Jr.

M.
See McCarthy, Denis Florence

M.
See McGee, Thomas D'Arcy

M.
See Merrick, John Mudge

M.
See Miles, James Warley

M.
See Monckton, Rose C.

M.
See Moody, Michael David

M.
See Moore, George Henry

M.
See Moultrie, Gerard

M.
See Mulchinock, William Pembroke

M.
See Murphy, James

M.
See Pender, Margaret T.

M.
See Pope, Alexander

M
See Stone, Susan Berch

M
See Warner, Cornell

M. A.
See Abdy, Maria Smith

M. A.
See Andrews, Marcia

M. A.
See Arnold, Matthew

M. A.
See Blagdon, Francis William

M. A.
See Calder, [Rev.] Robert

M. A. C.
See Cursham, Mary Ann

M. A. C.
See MacFayden, Dugald

M. A. D.
See Denison, Mary Andrews

M. A. F.
See Fisher, M. A.

M. A. K.
See Kelty, Mary Ann

M. A. of the Same University
See Bentley, Richard

M. A. T.
See Tincker, Mary Agnes

M. B.
See Balfour, Maria

M. B.
See Brook, Mary

M. B.
See Drew, Mona

M. B.
See Faust, Frederick [Schiller]

M. B.
See Lamb, Mary Ann

M. B. G.
See Grosvenor, Melville Bell

M. B. M. T.
See Toland, Mary B. M.

M. C.
See Chudleigh, [Lady] Mary Lee

M. C.
See Constable, Michael

M. C.
See Cook, Mabel Collins

M. C.
See Cooke, Matthew

M. C.
See Cooper, Mary

M. C.
See Cousin, Charles Yves

M. C.
See Mullen [or Mullins?], Michael

M. C. S.
See Sparks, Mary [Crowninshield]

M. D.
See Black, F. R.

M. D.
See Davis, Marcus

M. D.
See Dawes, Matthew

M. D.
See Doheny, Michael

M. D.
See McAleese, Daniel

M. D. and F. R. S.
See Trusler, John

M. D. C.
See Brooks, Erastus

M. D., Heslingden
See Davitt, Michael

M. de P.
See Pauw, Cornelis van

M. de V.
See De Vere, Mary

M. della R. W.
See Whitehead, Margaret della Rovere

M. E. A.
See Arnold, M. E.

M. E. B.
See Bennett, Mary E.

M. E. B.
See Maxwell, Mary Elizabeth [Braddon]

M. E. C. W.
See Walcott, Mackenzie Edward Clarke

M. E. E.
See Edwards, Mary Ellen

M. E. L.
See Lee, Mary Elizabeth

M. E. M.
See Martin, M. E.

M. E. M.
See Powell, H. W.

M. E. M. J.
See Jones, Margaret Elizabeth Mary

M. E. M. S.
See Sangster, Margaret Elizabeth Munson

M. E. W. S.
See Sherwood, Mary Elizabeth Wilson

M. F.
See Fisher, Myrta

M. F.
See Foy, Mathilda

M. F. A.
See Atkinson, Marshall Foster

M. F. D.
See Douglas, Marguerite France

M. F. D.
See Downing, Mary

M. G.
See Foe, Daniel

M. G.
See Giergielewicz, Mieczyslaw

M. G.
See Gillison, Margaret

M. G.
See Leathes, Mrs. Stanley

M. G. B.
See Buchanan, George

M. H.
See Hack, Maria

M. H.
See Hadfield, Miles

M. H.
See Heffernan, Michael J.

M. H.
See Horsburgh, Matilda

M. H.
See Hullah, Mrs.

M. H. B.
See Burnham, Mary Hewins

M. H. H.
See Haseltine, Mayo H.

M. H. S.
See Seymour, Mary H.

M. H. S.
See Spielmann, Marion Harry Alexander

M. H. T.
See Fiske, Mrs. Stephen

M. H., Thomond
See Hogan, Michael

M. I. B.
See Bromley, M. I.

M. I. D.
See Horne, Richard Henry

M. I. M.
See Motte, Mellish Irving

M. J. B.
See Barry, Michael Joseph

M. J. C.
See Carrington, Margaret Jirvin

M. J. C.
See Clark, James

M. J. I.
See O'Donovan Rossa, Mary Jane

M. J. M.
See King, Katharine

M. J. M. D.
See Dunbar, Margaret Juliana Maria

M. J. R.
See Ryan, Michael

M. J. S.
See O'Sullivan, Michael John

M J. W.
See Whitty, Michael James

M. K.
See Kreeger, Marianne

M. K.?
See McKenna, Andrew James

M. L. D.
See Dodds, M. L.

M. L. R.
See Smith, May Riley

M. M.
See Meredith, Mark

M. M.
See Mitchell, Maria

M. M.
See Montagu, Matthew

M. M.
See Mortensen, Norma Jean

M. M. C.
See Coatman, Maureen Margaret

M. M. D.
See Dodge, Mary Elizabeth Mapes

M. M. D.
See Pearle, Mary

M. M. M.
See Tooke, William

M. M. P.
See Manning, Patrick M.

M. McD.
See McDermott, Martin

M. McD.
See McDermott, Mary

M. My. R.
See Ryan, Margaret Mary

M. N.
See Camden, William

M. N.
See Kennedy, James

M. N.
See Wotton, William

M. N. M.
See Bleecker, Mary Noel

M. N-g-t
See Nugent, Michael

M. O'C.
See O'Connell, Maurice

M. O'D.
See Maginn, William

[AN] M. P.
See Dickie, Charles Herbert

M. P.
See O'Connell, John

M. P.
See Patrick, Marion

M. P.
See Potter, Mary

[An] M. P.
See Urquhart, William Pollard

M. P. H.
See Heaslip, Mark Patrick

M. P. H.
See Hickey, Michael Patrick

M. R.
See Ranking, B. Montgomerie

M. R.
See Russell, Matthew

M. R.
See Ryan, Margaret Mary

M. R. B.
See Bethel, Marion Ross

M. R. C.
See Calder, [Rev.] Robert

M. R. H.
See Higham, Mary R.

M. R. L.
See Leyne, Maurice Richard

M. S.
See Nevins, William

M. S.
See Safford, Mary J.

M. S.
See Smedley, Menella Bute

M. S.
See Smedley, Menella Bute

M. S.
See Stokes, Margaret MacNair

M. S.
See Stringer, Moses

M. T. F.
See Porter, Callie Russell

M. T. P.
See Pender, Margaret T.

M. U.
See Uniacke, Mary

M. W.
See Wilson, Miles

M. W.
See Woodthorpe, Patricia Mariella

M. W. H.
See Hazeltine, Mayo H.

M. W. R.
See Rooney, M. W.

M. W. S.
See Savage, Marmion Wilmo

M. W. T.
See Tileston, Mary Wilder [Foote]

Ma, Nancy Chih
See Chih, Po-Chang

Ma-ka-tae-mish-kia-kiak 1767-1838
[WBD]
American Indian chieftain
* Black Hawk

Maartens, Maarten
See Schwartz, Jozua Marius Willem
Van Der Poorten

Maas, Duane Frederick 1931-1976 [BE,
BI]
American baseball player
* Maas, Duke

Maas, Duke
See Maas, Duane Frederick

Maas, Melvin Joseph 1898- [HPPN]
American aviator and politician
* [The] Marine Aviator

Mab-y-Drycin
See James, David Emrys

Mabel
See Hazen, M. P.

Mabley, Edward [Howe] 1906- [CA]
American playwright
* Ware, John

Mabley, Jackie
See Aiken, Loretta Mary

Mabley, Moms
See Aiken, Loretta Mary

Mabon
See Abraham, William

Mabon, Willie 1925- [BWW]
American singer
* Big Willie

Mabrie, Herman James, III 1948- [BA]
American physician
* Mabrie, Skip

Mabrie, Skip
See Mabrie, Herman James, III

Mabrouk, Djelloul 1934- [CA]
Algerian-born American author
* Marbrook, Del
* Marbrook, Djelloul

Mabry, Thomas
See Dalton, Christopher

Mabuse [or Malbodius]
See Gossaert [Gossart], Jan

Mac
See MacManus, Seumas

Mac
See McConnell, Wallace Robert

Mac
See McGeachy, C. E. A.

Mac
See McGinley, Peter Toner

Mac
See McMahon, George Yielding

Mac A'Ghobhainn, Iain
See Smith, Iain Crichton

Mac A'Ghobhainn, Seamus
See Smith, Iain Crichton

Mac A'Ghreidhir, Gillechriosd
See Grieve, Christopher Murray

Mac An Bhaird, Seaghan
See Ward, John C.

Mac Aoidh
See Mackie, Albert D[avid]

Mac, Chairman
See McGregor, Douglas Murray

Mac Erin
See McHenry, James

Mac Gilla Cuddy
See Archdekin, Richard

Mac Giolla Eain, Eoin
See MacErlean, John C.

Mac, Johnny
See McMillan, John Lanneau

Mac, Mr.
See McDonnell, James Smith

Mac, Mr.
See McLaughlin, Walter T.

Mac, Mr.
See McMillan, John Lanneau

Mac the Knife
See Macmillan, Harold

Mac the Knife
See McNamara, Robert Strange

Mac the Maestro
See McEnroe, John

Mac the Mouth
See McEnroe, John

Mac the Unready
See McClellan, George Brinton

MacAdam, [Reginald] Al[an] 1952?-
Canadian-born hockey player
* MacAdam, Spud

MacAdam, Eve
See Leslie, Cecilie

Macadam, Ian
See Adamson, Iaian Beaton

Macadam, John Loudon 1756-1836
[DEP, DNNS, SN]
Scottish engineer
* [The] King of Roads

MacAdam, Sawney
See Townshend, George [Fourth
Viscount and First Marquis Townshend]

MacAdam, Spud
See MacAdam, [Reginald] Al[an]

Macadams, Tobi
See Crews, Judson [Campbell]

Macaedhagain
See Keegan, James

MacAedhagan, Eamon
See Egan, Edward Welstead

Macall, William ?-1781 [BI]
*British steward and founder of gaming
club*
* Almack, William

Macallan, Daniel [PA]
Author
* Scrutator

MacAlpin, Rory
See MacKinnon, Charles Roy

MacAlpine
See Kenneth I

MacAlpine, Margaret H[esketh Murray]
1907- [CAP]
Scottish-born author
* Carmichael, Ann

Macalpine, Simon 1917- [TR]
Scottish actor
* Lack, Simon

Macaluso, Iron Legs
See Macaluso, Len

Macaluso, Len 20th c. [HPPN]
American football player
* Macaluso, Iron Legs

Macandro
See Rubio, Antonio

Macao, Marshall
See Tuleja, Thaddeus F[rancis]

MacApp, C. C.
See Capps, Carroll M.

Macarone
See Arnold, George

MacArone, Mat
See Cook, Theodore P.

[The] Macaroni Painter
See Cosway, Richard

[The] Macaroni Parson
See Dodd, William

[The] Macaroni Parson
See Horne, John

MacArthur, Arthur 1845-1912 [HPPN]
American army officer
* [The] Boy Colonel of the West

MacArthur, Burke
See Burks, Arthur J.

MacArthur, D[avid] Wilson 1903- [CA, WD, WWL]
Scottish-born author and journalist
* Sinclair, Gavin
* Wilson, David

MacArthur, Douglas 1880-1964 [HPPN]
American military leader
* [The] American Caesar
* America's Superhero
* [The] Beau Brummel of the Army
* [The] Buck Private's Gary Cooper
* [The] D'Artagnan of the A. E. F.
* [The] Defiant General
* [The] Disraeli of the Chiefs of Staff
* Dugout Doug
* [The] Magnificent
* [The] Military Legend
* [The] Napoleon of Luzon

Macarthur, John 1767-1834 [HPPN]
British pioneer and entrepreneur
* Bodice, Jack

Macartney, Charles George 1886-1958 [EC]
Australian cricketer
* [The] Governor General

Macartney, Edith Hyde Robbins 20th c. [HPPN]
American beauty contest winner and fortune teller
* America of 1919, Miss
* [The] First Miss America
* Pandora

MacAskill, Angus 1825-1863
Canadian strongman
* [The] Cape Breton Giant

Macaulay
See Frothingham, Washington

Macaulay, Aula [FFF]
Writer
* Academicus

Macaulay, Clarendon
See Adams, Walter Marsham

Macaulay, Fannie Caldwell 1863-1941 [ALY, WBD]
American author
* Little, Frances

[The] Macaulay of the South
See Jones, Charles Colcock

Macaulay, Thomas Babington [First Baron Macaulay] 1800-1859 [DEL, DEP, NPS, RH]
British statesman and author
* Benengeli, Cid Hamet
* [A] Book in Breeches
* [The] Burke of Our Age
* Merton, Tristram
* Quongti, Richard
* [The] Son of the Saint

Macauley, Easy Ed
See Macauley, Edward C.

Macauley, Edward C. 1928- [BB]
American basketball player
* Macauley, Easy Ed

Macauley, Robie [Mayhew] 1919- [CN]
American author
* Dumbarton, A.

Macaw
See Hannays, Kitty

Macbeath, Innis [Stewart] 1928- [IAW]
Irish-born author
* Maloney, Tighe
* Stewart, Rattray
* Tissant-Bernac, Mathieu

Macbeth, Lydia 1888- [THR]
British actress
* Bilbrooke, Lydia

Macbeth, Madge Hamilton [Lyons] 1878-1965 [CCL]
Canadian author
* Dill, W. S.
* Knox, Gilbert

MacBeth the Great
See MacDonald, Patrick

MacBrady, Thady
See O'Flanagan, Theophilus

MacBride, Melchoir
See Quinton, John P[urcell]

Maccabaeus
See Judas Asmonaeus

Maccabee, Dan
See Segal, Samuel

Maccall, Isobel
See Boyd, Elizabeth Orr

MacCall, Libby
See Machol, Libby

Maccall, William 1812-? [FFF]
British author
* Atticus

MacCarthy, [Sir] Desmond 1878-1952 [LC, TC1]
British author, editor, critic
* Affable Hawk

MacCathmhaoil, Seaghan
See Campbell, John Patrick

MacCathmhaoil, Seosamh
See Campbell, Joseph

Maccheta, Blanche Roosevelt [Tucker] 1853-1898 [DNA, HPPN]
American-born author and opera singer
* Pandora
* Roosevelt, Blanche

Macchirole, Pasquale 20th c. [WP 2-28-85]
American underworld figure
* Mack, Patty

MacClure, Victor 1887- [CC, HPPN, WW]
Scottish author
* Craig, Peter

MacColl, Malcolm 1838-? [PA, WWL]
British author
* Expertus
* Scrutator

MacCormack, Sabine G[abriele] 1941- [CA]
German-born American author
* Oswalt, Sabine

MacCraig, Hugh
See Ward, Craig

MacCrie, Thomas 1772-1835 [SN]
Scottish clergyman and author
* [The] Griffin

MacDaniel, Charles
See Garrison, Charles M.

MacDermot, Robert
See Barbour, Robert MacDermot

MacDermot, Thomas H. 1870-1933 [CW]
Jamaican-born poet, journalist, author
* Redcam, Tom

Macdermott, G. H.
See Farrell, Gilbert Hastings

Macdermott the Great
See Farrell, Gilbert Hastings

MacDiarmid, Hugh
See Grieve, Christopher Murray

MacDonald, Aeneas
See Thomson, George Malcolm

MacDonald, Andrew 1755?-1788? [FFF, PA]
Scottish poet
* Bramble, Matthew

Macdonald, Andrew
See Pierce, William

MacDonald, Angus
See MacDonald Douglas, Ronald Angus

MacDonald, Anson
See Heinlein, Robert A[nson]

MacDonald, B. J.
See MacDonald, Blair

MacDonald, Bettie
See Young, Mary Elizabeth

MacDonald, Betty
See Heskett, Anne Elizabeth Campbell Bard

Macdonald, Blackie
See Emrich, Duncan [Black Macdonald]

MacDonald, Blair 1953- [SMG]
Canadian-born hockey player
* MacDonald, B. J.

MacDonald, Edith 20th c.
American actress
* Blake, Marie
* Rock, Blossom

Macdonald, Edwina Le Vin 1886-
[WWL]
American author
* Levin, Edwina

MacDonald, Eric
See Allan, F. Carney

MacDonald, Flora 20th c.
Canadian politician
* [The] Red Tory

MacDonald, George [PA]
Author
* Dalmocand

MacDonald, Golden
See Brown, Margaret Wise

MacDonald, J. Hay [PA]
Author
* Jambon, Jean

MacDonald, [Sir] James 1741-1766 [SN]
Seventh Baronet of Sleat
* [The] Scottish Marcellus

MacDonald, James Aloysius 1874-1964
[BI]
American columnist
* Stingo, John R.

MacDonald, Jeanette
American actress and singer
* [The] Iron Butterfly

MacDonald, John 1779-1849 [WBD]
Scottish clergyman
* [The] Apostle of the North

Macdonald, John
See Millar, Kenneth

Macdonald, [Sir] John Alexander
1815-1891 [BBH, DNNS]
Canadian prime minister
* [The] Father of Modern Canada
* Old To-morrow

MacDonald, John D[ann] 1916- [EMD]
American author
* Farrell, John Wade [house pseudonym]
* Henry, Robert [house pseudonym]
* Lane, John [house pseudonym]
* O'Hara, Scott [house pseudonym]
* Reed, Peter [house pseudonym]
* Rieser, Henry [house pseudonym]

Macdonald, John James 1849-? [CCL]
Canadian poet
* MacRae, James

Macdonald, John Ross
See Millar, Kenneth

MacDonald, Katherine 1894-1956 [CU]
American actress
* [The] American Beauty

Macdonald, Lucy Maude Montgomery
1874-1942 [HPPN]
Canadian author
* Montgomery, L. M.

Macdonald, Malcolm John Ross 1932-
[CA, WD]
British author, playwright, editor
* Ross-Macdonald, Malcolm J[ohn]

MacDonald, Marcia
See Hill, Grace [Livingston]

Macdonald, Mary
See Gifford, Griselda

Macdonald, Mrs. Edmond [FFF]
Entertainer
* Howard, Cordelia

Macdonald, Mrs. W. H. [FFF]
Entertainer
* Stone, Marie

MacDonald, Murray
See Honeyman, Walter MacDonald

MacDonald, Neil 1719-1788 [BI]
Scottish patriot
* MacEachin, Neil

MacDonald, Nina Hansell
See Looker, Antonina [Hansell]

Macdonald of Glengarry 17th c.
[DNNF]
Scottish chieftain
* Glengarry

MacDonald, Patrick 20th c. [IBW]
American bandleader
* MacBeth the Great

MacDonald, Philip 1896?- [CA, EMD, LC]
British author
* Fleming, Oliver [joint pseudonym with Ronald MacDonald]
* Lawless, Anthony
* Porlock, Martin
* Stuart, W. J.
* Stuart, Warren

MacDonald, Ronald 20th c.
Scottish playwright and author
* Fleming, Oliver [joint pseudonym with Philip MacDonald]

Macdonald, Ross
See Millar, Kenneth

MacDonald, S. W.
See MacDonald, Stuart Wyllie

MacDonald, Stuart Wyllie 1948- [ART]
Scottish painter
* MacDonald, S. W.

Macdonald, Wilson 1880-? [FFF]
Canadian poet
* Spiral Groove

Macdonald, Zillah K[atherine] 1885-
[CAP, SAT]
Canadian-born author
* Zillah

MacDonald Douglas, Ronald Angus
1906- [IAW]
Scottish author and playwright
* MacDonald, Angus

[The] MacDonalds of Process Serving
See Glassner, Frank

Macdonell, Alastair Ruadh 1725?-1761
[WBD]
Scottish soldier
* Pickle the Spy

Macdonell, Archibald Gordon 1895-1941
[CC, TC, WW]
Scottish author
* Cameron, John
* Gordon, Neil

Macdonnaill, Brian
See McDonald, Bernard

Macdonnell, Alexander Ranaldson ?-1828
[SN]
Scottish chieftain
* MacIvor, Fergus

Macdonnell, James Edmond 1917- [CA]
Australian author
* MacNell, James

MacDonnell, James Francis Carlin
1881-1945 [CAT]
American poet
* Carlin, Francis

Macdonough, Augustus Rodney 1820-?
[HPPN]
American author
* Armac

MacDougal, John [joint pseudonym with Robert Augustine Ward Lowndes]
See Blish, James [Benjamin]

MacDougal, John [joint pseudonym with James (Benjamin) Blish]
See Lowndes, Robert Augustine Ward

MacDougall, Fiona
See MacLeod, Robert F.

Macdougall, Harrison Miller, Jr.
1921-1965 [HPPN]
American actor, producer, director
* Thorpe, Clarke Harrison

MacDougall, Leslie Grahame
See Grahame-Thomson, Leslie

Macdougall, Margaret ?-1943 [SFL]
Author
* Armour, Margaret

MacDougall, Marion Lorne 1886?-1968
[BEW, FC]
American actress
* Lorne, Marion

MacDougall, Robertson
See Mair, George Brown

MacDowell, Edward Alexander
1861-1908 [BBD]
American composer
* Thorn, Edgar

Macdowell, Katherine Sherwood Bonner
1849-1883 [HPPN]
American author
* Bonner, Sherwood

MacDuff, Andrew
See Fyfe, Horace Brown

Mace, Aurelia Gay 1835-1910 [DNA]
Author
* Aurelia

Mace, Harry L. 19th c. [BE]
American baseball player
* Mace, Jimmy

Mace, Jem 1831-1910 [RBE]
British boxer
* [The] Gypsy

Mace, Jimmy
See Mace, Harry L.

MacEachin, Neil
See MacDonald, Neil

[The] Macedonian
See Basil I [or Basilius]

[The] Macedonian
See Polyaenus, Julius

Macedonia's Madman
See Alexander III

Macedonicus
See Aemilius Paulus, Lucius

Macedonicus
See Metellus, Quintus Caecilius

Macedonicus
See Paulus, Lucius Aemilius

MacElroy, Andrew Jackson 20th c.
[NAA]
American publisher and writer
* MacGregor, Jack

MacEnri, Seaghan
See Henry, John Patrick

Maceo, Antonio 1848-1896 [IBW]
*American-born leader of the Cuban
revolution, 1849*
* [The] Bronze Titan

Macer
See Philips, Ambrose

MacErlean, John C. 20th c. [WWL]
Irish editor
* Mac Giolla Eain, Eoin

Macero, Attilio Joseph 1925- [EJ]
American jazz musician and composer
* Macero, Teo

Macero, Teo
See Macero, Attilio Joseph

Macfadden, Bernarr 1868?-?
American publisher
* Body Beautiful

MacFadden, Gertrude 1900-1967 [SC]
American actress
* MacFadden, Mickey

MacFadden, Mickey
See MacFadden, Gertrude

Macfadyen, Dugald 19th c. [PI]
Scottish poet and composer
* Cruck-a-leaghan

MacFall, Chambers Haldane Cooke
1860-1928 [WWL]
British author
* Hal, Dane

Macfarlane, Ian 1888-1969 [THR]
Australian-born actor
* Fleming, Ian

Macfarlane, John 20th c. [WWL]
Canadian author and poet
* Arbory, John

MacFarlane, Kenneth
See Walker, Kenneth MacFarlane

Macfarlane, Robert ?-1883 [FFF]
Scottish-born journalist and author
* Rutherglen

MacFarlane, Stephen
See Cross, John Keir

MacFayden, Daniel Knowles 1905-1972
[BE, PB]
American baseball player
* MacFayden, Deacon Danny

MacFayden, Deacon Danny
See MacFayden, Daniel Knowles

MacFayden, Dugald 1867-? [LAO]
British clergyman, author, poet
* M. A. C.

MacFee, Maxwell
See Rennie, James Alan

MacFhionnlaoich, Peadar
See MacGinley, Peter T.

MacFlecknoe
See Shadwell, Thomas

MacGahan, Januarius Aloysius
1844-1878 [HPPN]
American war correspondent
* [The] Liberator

MacGeachy, Charles E. A.   [PA]
Author
* [The] Danburian

MacGibbon, Jean 1913- [TCC]
British author
* Howard, Jean

MacGill, Moyna
See McIldowie, Chattie

MacGillivray, James Pittendrigh 1856-?
[LAO]
Scottish sculptor and writer
* Maitland, Peter
* P. M.

MacGinley, Peter T. 20th c. [WWL]
Irish author and playwright
* MacFhionnlaoich, Peadar

MacGlashan, Helen ?-1969 [SC]
American actress and screenwriter
* Meredyth, Bess

Macgowan
See Smyth, John

MacGrawler, Peter
See Maginn, William

MacGregor, Alasdair Alpin [Douglas]
1899-1970 [CA, CAP]
Scottish journalist and poet
* Featherstonehaugh, Francis

MacGregor, Carol
See Holter, Carol

MacGregor, Chummy
See MacGregor, John Chalmers

MacGregor, D. R.
See MacGregor, David Roy

MacGregor, David Roy 1925- [ART]
British artist
* MacGregor, D. R.

MacGregor, Irvine T. 1915- [ASC]
Scottish-born musician
* MacGregor, Scotty

Macgregor, J. 1797-1857 [PA]
Author
* South, Simeon

MacGregor, Jack
See MacElroy, Andrew Jackson

MacGregor, James [Murdoch] 1925-
[AW, CA, WGT]
Scottish author
* Francis, Gregory [joint pseudonym
  with Frank Parnell]
* McIntosh, J. T.

Macgregor, John 1825-1892 [WBD]
British author and canoe designer
* Rob Roy

MacGregor, John 1848-? [LAO]
Scottish author
* Ralph

MacGregor, John Chalmers 1903- [ASC,
EJ]
American musician
* MacGregor, Chummy

Macgregor, Malcolm
See Mason, William

MacGregor, Mary
See Jameson, Malcolm

MacGregor, Mary Esther [Miller]
1876-1961 [BI, CCL]
Canadian author
* Keith, Marian

Macgregor, Robert 1671-1734 [HN, SN,
UH, WBD]
Scottish chieftain
* Campbell, Robert
* Rob Roy
* Robert the Red
* [The] Robin Hood of the Lowlands

MacGregor, Sandy
See White, John

MacGregor, Scotty
See MacGregor, Irvine T.

MacGregory
See Gregory, Malcolm

MacGrian, Michael
See West, Anthony C.

MacGrom, John
See McMaster, Guy Humphries

MacGuire, Philip
See Burton, Harry McGuire

Machado, Paulo Sergio Mastrotti 1947-
[IAW]
Brazilian author
* Rocket, Captain

Machado y Ruiz, Antonio 1875-1939
[TLC]
Spanish poet and playwright
* Cabellera

MacHale, John 1791-1881 [SN]
Archbishop of Tuam
* [The] Lion of the Fold of Judah

Machan, Tibor R[ichard] 1939- [CA]
Hungarian-born author and educator
* Polony, Raymond

Machaquito [Little Strong One]
See Gonzalez y Madrid, Rafael

Machar, Agnes Maule 1837-1917
[DLE1]
Canadian poet and author
* Fidelis

MacHaye, Eric
See Roche, Arthur Somers

Machemer, David Ritchie 1951- [SMG]
American baseball player
* Machemer, Mac

Machemer, Mac
See Machemer, David Ritchie

Machen, Arthur
See Jones, Arthur Llewellyn

[Der] Macher [The Doer]
See Schmidt, Helmut

Macher, Daniel J.   [FFF]
Entertainer
* Shelby, Daniel

Macheside, Candia
See Mario, Giuseppe

Machiavelli
See McCready, Warren T[homas]

[A] Machiavelli
See Necker, Jacques [or James]

Machiavelli, Niccolo [or Nicholas]
1469-1527 [HN, HPPN, SN]
*Italian statesman and political
philosopher*
* Old Nick
* [The] Prince of Politicians
* [Il] Segretario

[The] Machiavellian Belshazzar
See Van Buren, Martin

Machine Gun Butera
See Butera, Lou

Machine Gun Jack
See De Mora, James Vincenzo

Machine Gun Kelly
See Kelly, George R.

Machine, Mr.
See Burton, Mike

Machito
See Grillo, Frank

Machlin, Milton Robert 1924- [AW]
American author
* Jason, Wm.
* Roberts, McLean

Machlis, Joseph 1906- [AW]
Latvian-born author
* Selcamm, George

Machol, Libby 1916- [CA]
American writer
* MacCall, Libby

MacHugh, Edward 20th c.
Singer
* Your Gospel Singer

Machuisdean, Hamish 1883- [WWL]
Scottish author
* Gates, Michael

Maciarz, Joseph John 1915- [BE]
American baseball player
* Mack, Joseph John [Joe]

Macias, Raton
See Macias, Raul

Macias, Raul 1934- [BX]
Mexican boxer
* Macias, Raton

Macie, James Lewis [or Louis]
1765-1829 [WBD]
British chemist and mineralogist
* Smithson, James

Maciel, Judi[th Anne] 1942- [CA]
American educator and author
* Stewart, Judith Anne

MacInnes, Helen 1907-1985 [SAT]
Scottish-born American author
* Highet, Helen

Macinnes, Tom 1867-? [WWL]
Canadian author
* Roy, Julien

Macintire, Farrington 19th c. [HPPN]
American clergyman
* F. M.

Macintosh, Edith Joan [Burbridge] 1919-
[WW]
Author
* Cockin, Joan

MacIntosh, Joan 1924- [CA]
New Zealand author
* Blaike, Avona

MacIntosh, Peter 1944- [IBW]
Jamaican-born singer and musician
* Tosh, Peter

Macintosh, William 18th c. [IP]
Scottish author
* [A] Lover of his Country

Macintyre, Duncan 1724-1812 [SN]
Gaelic poet
* [The] Fair Haired

MacIntyre, John Horton 1863-? [CCL]
Canadian poet
* Mack

Macioci, Nicholas 1935- [RO1]
American musician
* Massi, Nick

Macip, Vicente Juan 1500?-1579 [WBD]
Spanish painter
* De Juanes [or Joanes], Juan
* [The] Spanish Raphael

MacIre, Esor B.
See Ambrose, Eric [Samuel]

Maciste
See Pagano, Bartolomeo

Maciulevicius-Maciulis, Jonas 1862-1932
[EWL]
Lithuanian author
* Maironis

MacIver, Muriel 1888-1950 [BEW]
Canadian-born actress
* Starr, Muriel

MacIvor, Fergus
See Macdonnell, Alexander Ranaldson

Mack
See MacIntyre, John Horton

Mack
See McCullough, Joseph B.

Mack
See Menchan, W. McKinley

Mack, Andrew
See McAloon, William Andrew

Mack, Bill
See Maclaughlin, Charles W.

Mack, Billy
See McBride, William

Mack, Brearley
See McCalment, Maebelle [Brearley]

Mack, Buck
See Mack, James

Mack, Cecil
See McPherson, Richard C.

Mack, Charles
See McGaughey, Charles

Mack, Charles
See Sellers, Charles E.

Mack, Claire 1921?-1978 [FIR]
Comedienne
* Mack, Cookie

Mack, Connie
See McGillicuddy, Cornelius Alexander

Mack, Cookie
See Mack, Claire

Mack, Dennis Joseph [Denny]
See McCrohan, Dennis Joseph

Mack, Dr.
See McLaughlin, John Belton, M. D.

Mack, Dorothy
See McKittrick, Dorothy

Mack, Earle Thaddeus
See McGillicuddy, Earle Thaddeus

Mack, Edwin 1946- [RBE]
Dutch boxer
* Mack, Fighting

Mack, Elsie Frances [Wilson] 1909-1967
[CCL]
Canadian author
* Moore, Frances Sarah

Mack, Ernest
See Stone, Ernest

Mack, Evalina
See McNamara, Lena Randolph
[Brooke]

Mack, Fighting
See Mack, Edwin

Mack, Frank George 1900- [BE]
American baseball player
* Mack, Stubby

Mack, Gene
See McGillicuddy, Eugene

Mack, Hughie
See McGowan, Hugh

Mack, J. G. O. 1872-? [NPS]
Author
* Callum Beg

Mack, James ?-1959 [SC]
American actor
* Mack, Buck

Mack, Jerry
See Johnson, Jerry Mack

Mack, Joseph
See McNamara, Joseph

Mack, Joseph John [Joe]
See Maciarz, Joseph John

Mack, Kirby
See McEvoy, Harry K[irby]

Mack, Lonnie
See McIntosh, Lonnie

Mack, Louise
See Creed, Mrs. J. P.

Mack, Maebelle
See McCalment, Maebelle [Brearley]

Mack, Marion
See Lewyn, Joey Marion

Mack, Marjorie
See Dixon, Marjorie [Mack]

Mack, Mrs. Will H. [FFF]
Entertainer
* Woodson, Kittie

Mack, Nila
See MacLoughlin, Nila

Mack, Noreen
See O'Flynn, Honoria

Mack, Patty
See Macchirole, Pasquale

Mack, Pearl 1941- [BA]
American educator
* Mack, Willie

Mack, Ray
See Mlckovsky, Raymond James

Mack, Red
See Mack, William

Mack, Reddy
See McNamara, Joseph

Mack, Stubby
See Mack, Frank George

Mack, Ted
See Maguiness, William Edward

Mack the Knife
See Jones, Mack

Mack the Knife
See Mouskos, Mikhail

Mack von Leiberich, Karl 1752-1828
[SN]
Austrian army officer
* That Nonpareil of Generals

Mack, Warner
See McPherson, Warner

Mack, Willard
See McLaughlin, Charles W.

Mack, William 20th c. [EF]
American football player
* Mack, Red

Mack, Willie
See Mack, Pearl

Mackail, J. W.
See Mackail, John William

Mackail, John William 1859-1945 [LC]
Scottish educator and author
* Mackail, J. W.

Mackamotzki, Kunigunde ?-1910 [DI,
HPPN]
American entertainer and murder victim
* Elmore, Belle
* Marsangar, Cora
* Turner, Cora

Mackarness, John Fielder 19th c. [IP]
British clergyman and author
* One of Themselves

Mackarness, Matilda Anne [IP]
British author
* Planche, Matilda Anne
* Sunbeam, Susie

Mackay, Aberigh 1849-1881 [IP]
Indian author
* Ali Baba

Mackay, Andrew 1759-1809 [IP]
Scottish mathematician and author
* Andrew, James

Mackay, Angus 1865-1923 [CCL]
Canadian poet
* Dhu, Oscar

MacKay, Baldy
See MacKay, Calum

MacKay, Calum 1927- [CEI]
Canadian-born hockey player
* MacKay, Baldy

Mackay, Charles 1814-? [IP, PA]
Scottish poet and journalist
* Grimbosh, Herman
* Wagstaffe, Launcelot, Jr.
* Wagstffe, John, Esq., of Wilbye
  Grange

MacKay, Duncan McMillan 1894?-1943?
[CEI, FHE, HK]
Canadian-born hockey player
* MacKay, Mickey
* [The] Wee Scot

Mackay, Elsie ?-1928 [BF]
Scottish-born actress
* Wyndham, Poppy

Mackay, Eric 1851-1899 [HPPN]
Scottish poet
* [A] Violinist

Mackay, Francis Alexander 19th c. [IP]
Scottish poet
* Fitzhugh, Francis

Mackay, George ?-1913 [HPPN]
British murderer
* [The] Real Life Raffles
* Williams, John

Mackay, James [IP]
British clergyman and author
* [A] Chaplain in H. M. Indian Service

Mackay, James [Alexander] 1936- [CA,
WD]
Scottish writer and translator
* Angus, Ian
* Finlay, William
* Garden, Bruce
* Whittington, Peter

Mackay, John Henry 20th c. [PW 1-25-
85]
German author
* Sagitta

Mackay, K. 20th c. [EC]
Australian cricketer
* Mackay, Slasher

Mackay, Lewis Hugh 1897- [SFL,
WGT]
American author
* Matheson, Hugh

MacKay, Louis Alexander 1901- [CCL]
Canadian poet
* Smalacombe, John

Mackay, Mary 1855-1924 [BI, HPPN, LC, TC]
British author and musician
* Corelli, Marie
* Mackay, Minnie

MacKay, Mickey
See MacKay, Duncan McMillan

Mackay, Minnie
See Mackay, Mary

Mackay, Miss [PA]
Author
* Dods, Jeanie

Mackay, Mrs. John A. [FFF]
Entertainer
* Bennett, Lavinia

Mackay, Rita Eleanore 1928- [BEW]
American actress
* Gam, Rita

Mackay, Robert 1714-1771 [HPPN, NPS]
Irish poet
* [The] Brown
* Rob Donn

Mackay, Robert 19th c. [HFN]
American author
* [A] Citizen of the West

Mackay, Slasher
See Mackay, K.

Mackaye, Alberigh 1849-1881 [FFF]
British author
* Ali Baba

MacKaye, David Loring 1890- [BI]
American author and educator
* Julian, David [joint pseudonym with Julia Josephine (Gunther) MacKaye]
* Loring, Jules [joint pseudonym with Julia Josephine (Gunther) MacKaye]
* MacKaye, Loring [joint pseudonym with Julia Josephine (Gunther) MacKaye]

MacKaye, Julia Josephine [Gunther] 1892- [BI]
American author and librarian
* Julian, David [joint pseudonym with David Loring MacKaye]
* Loring, Jules [joint pseudonym with David Loring MacKaye]
* MacKaye, Loring [joint pseudonym with David Loring MacKaye]

MacKaye, Loring [joint pseudonym with Julia Josephine (Gunther) MacKaye]
See MacKaye, David Loring

MacKaye, Loring [joint pseudonym with David Loring MacKaye]
See MacKaye, Julia Josephine [Gunther]

Mackee, [Rev.] Thomas John 19th c. [HPPN]
Irish clergyman
* [An] Old Pastor

MacKeever, Maggie
See Clark, Gail

MacKellar, Billie
See MacKellar, Lillian

MacKellar, Lillian 20th c. [BBH]
New Zealand-born swimmer and coach
* MacKellar, Billie

MacKellar, Thomas 1812-? [IP, PA]
American poet
* Tam

Mackelworth, R. W.
See Mackelworth, Ronald Walter

Mackelworth, Ronald Walter 1930- [SF]
British author
* Mackelworth, R. W.

Macken, John 1784-1823 [PI]
Irish poet
* Fitzadam, Ismael

Mackendrick, Alexander 1912- [FC]
American-born director
* Mackendrick, Sandy

Mackendrick, Sandy
See Mackendrick, Alexander

MacKendrick, William Gordon 1864-? [NAA]
Canadian author
* [The] Roadbuilder

MacKenna, Kenneth
See Mielziner, Leo, Jr.

MacKenna, Theobald ?-1809 [IP]
Irish barrister and author
* [A] Catholic and a Burkist

Mackenzie, Alexander Slidell
See Slidell, Alexander

Mackenzie, Alice 1842?-1889 [BL]
Prostitute and murder victim
* Clay Pipe Alice

Mackenzie, Andrew 1780-1839 [PI]
Irish poet
* Gallius [or Gaelus]

Mackenzie, Anne Maria [IP]
British author
* Ellen of Exeter

Mackenzie, Bloody
See Mackenzie, [Sir] George

Mackenzie, C. F. 19th c. [IP]
British author
* [Il] Musannif

Mackenzie, Charles 1805-1877 [HPPN]
British actor
* Compton, Henry

Mackenzie, Compton
See Compton, [Sir] Edward Montagu

Mackenzie, Edward 1854-1918 [BEW]
British-born actor and producer
* Compton, Edward

Mackenzie, Emperor
See Mackenzie, Kenneth

Mackenzie, Foster, III 1945?-
American singer
* La La, Prince

Mackenzie, Foster, III (cont.)
* Mackenzie, Ken
* Root Boy Slim

Mackenzie, Francis Sidney 1885-1964 [BEW]
British actor
* Compton, Francis

Mackenzie, G. A. [FFF]
Canadian writer
* Dale, Ellis

Mackenzie, George [First Earl of Cromarty] 1630-1714 [HPPN]
British politician and author
* G. E. of C.

Mackenzie, [Sir] George 1636-1691 [HPPN, SN, WBD]
Scottish attorney and author
* [The] Bloodthirsty Advocate
* Mackenzie, Bloody
* Mackenzie of Rosehaugh
* [The] Noble Wit of Scotland

Mackenzie, H. H. ?-1916 [BEW]
Producer and actor
* Morrell, H. H.

Mackenzie, H. Millicent 1863-? [WWL]
British educator and author
* H. M. K.

Mackenzie, Henry 1745-1831 [DEL, DNNS, IP, NPS, PA, SN]
Scottish author
* [The] Addison of the North
* [The] Aged Man
* Brutus
* H. M. K.
* [The] Man of Feeling
* [The] Northern Addison

Mackenzie, James ?-1761 [IP]
Scottish physician and author
* [A] Physician

MacKenzie, Joan 1925- [AW, CA]
Canadian author and poet
* Bedard, Michelle
* Finnigan, Joan

Mackenzie, Ken
See Mackenzie, Foster, III

Mackenzie, Kenneth 1779-1861 [HPPN]
Scottish-American fur trader
* [The] Emperor of the West
* [The] King of the Missouri
* Mackenzie, Emperor

Mackenzie, Kenneth 1913-1955 [TCL]
Australian author and poet
* Mackenzie, Seaforth

Mackenzie, Kenneth Robert H. 19th c. [IP, PA]
Author
* Cryptonymus

Mackenzie, Mary Jane [IP]
British author
* [A] Lady

Mackenzie, Nan 1913- [HPPN]
British author
* Fairbrother, Nan

Mackenzie of Rosehaugh
See Mackenzie, [Sir] George

Mackenzie, Peter [IP]
Scottish author
* [The] Odd Fellow
* [A] Ten Pounder

MacKenzie, Rhoda Elizabeth 1939?-
[CW]
Jamaican poet
* Auntie Lizzie

MacKenzie, Robert [SMG]
American football coach
* MacKenzie, Sarge

Mackenzie, Robert Shelton 1809-1881
[IP, PA, PI]
Irish author and journalist
* Littlejohn
* R. S. M.
* Sholto

MacKenzie, Sarge
See MacKenzie, Robert

Mackenzie, Sawney
See Townshend, George [Fourth
Viscount and First Marquis Townshend]

Mackenzie, Seaforth
See Mackenzie, Kenneth

Mackenzie, [Dr.] Willard
See Stratemeyer, Edward L.

Mackenzie, William 19th c. [IP]
Scottish clergyman and author
* W. M.

Mackenzie, William Henry 1862-1883
[PI]
Irish author and poet
* Skez

Mackenzie, William Lyon 1795-1861
[IP]
Canadian journalist
* Swift, Patrick

Mackercher, Daniel 18th c. [SN]
* [The] Melting Scot

Mackey, Biz
See Mackey, Raleigh

Mackey, Charles 1812-? [PA]
Author
* Grimbosh, Herman

Mackey, Ernan
See McInerny, Ralph

Mackey, Guy ?-1971 [BBH]
American collegiate athletic director
* Mackey, Red

Mackey, Mrs. F. A. [FFF]
Entertainer
* Sylvester, Louise

Mackey, Raleigh 1897- [MK]
American baseball player
* Mackey, Biz

Mackey, Red
See Mackey, Guy

Mackie, Albert D[avid] 1904- [AW,
CAP, HPPN, WD]
Scottish poet and playwright
* Mac Aoidh
* MacNib
* [The] Walrus

Mackie, Bert
See Mackie, Robert James

Mackie, Frank 1904-1969 [NOJ]
American jazz musician
* Mackie, Red

Mackie, George 1920- [ART]
Scottish graphic artist
* G. M.

Mackie, Maron
See McNeely, Jeannette

Mackie, Pauline Bradford
See Hopkins, Pauline Mackie

Mackie, Red
See Mackie, Frank

Mackie, Robert James 1893-1967 [SC]
American actor
* Mackie, Bert

Mackie, S. G.
See Mackie, Sheila Gertrude

Mackie, Sheila Gertrude 1928- [ART]
British artist
* Mackie, S. G.

MacKillop, J. 1871-? [BI]
British army officer
* Wetherby

Mackin, Anita
See Donson, Cyril

Mackin, Cassie
See Mackin, Catherine

Mackin, Catherine 1940?-1982
American reporter
* Mackin, Cassie

Mackinlay, Leila Antoinette Sterling
1910- [CAP, WD]
British author
* Grey, Brenda

Mackinlock, Duncan
See Watts, Peter Christopher

Mackinnon, Campbell 19th c. [IP]
British poet
* C. M.

MacKinnon, Charles Roy 1924- [AW,
CA, HPPN, IAW]
Scottish-born author
* Brown, F.
* Conte, Charles
* Donald, Vivian
* MacAlpin, Rory
* Montrose, Graham
* Rose, Hilary
* Stuart, Charles
* Torr, Iain

Mackintosh, Craig M. 20th c. [ESF]
Author
* Craig, Brian [joint pseudonym with
Brian M(ichael) Stableford]

Mackintosh, Elizabeth 1896-1952 [BEW,
CC, EMD]
Scottish-born playwright and author
* Daviot, Gordon
* Tey, Josephine

Mackintosh, [Sir] James 1765-1832 [IP,
SN]
Scottish philosopher and historian
* [The] Apostate
* [A] Barrister
* [The] Ghost of Vandegrab
* Subscription Jamie

Mackintosh, Kevin Scott 1957- [DC]
British cricketer
* Mackintosh, Mac
* Mackintosh, Toffo

Mackintosh, Mac
See Mackintosh, Kevin Scott

Mackintosh, Toffo
See Mackintosh, Kevin Scott

Mackittrick, Richard Kendall [IP]
Author
* R. K. M.

Mackle, Jeff
See McLeod, John F[reeland]

Macklem, Friday
See Macklem, Roy

Macklem, Roy 20th c. [SMG]
American football team staff member
* Macklem, Friday

Macklin, Charles
See MacLaughlin, Charles

MacKnight, Ninon 1908- [IBY, ICB]
Australian-born illustrator
* Ninon

Macknight, Sarah 1836-1899 [HPPN]
British actress and producer
* Thorne, Sarah

MacKrell, Claude
See Prothero, Ron

Macksey, [Major] K. J.
See Macksey, Kenneth J.

Macksey, Kenneth J. 1923- [CA]
British author and editor
* Macksey, [Major] K. J.

Mackworth
See Rhondda, [Viscountess] Margaret
Haig

Mackworth, Cecily 1911- [CAT]
Welsh-born author and columnist
* Rhiannon

Mackworth, [Sir] Digby 1789-1852 [IP]
British army officer and author
* [A] Field Officer of Cavalry

Mackworth, [Sir] Humphrey 18th c.
[IP]
British author
* H. M., Sir
* [A] Member of Parliament

Macky, John 18th c. [IP]
British author
* [A] Gentleman Here

MacL.
See McLaughlin, Patrick O'Conor

MacLachlan, Kenneth D. 1902-1972
[SC]
Canadian-born actor and stunt performer
* Duncan, Keene

Maclagan, Bridget
See Borden, Mary

Maclagan, Dorothea F. 1895- [ART]
British painter
* D. F. M.

Maclaine, James 18th c. [DI]
Irish-born British highwayman
* [The] Gentleman Highwayman

MacLaine, Shirley
See Beaty, Shirley Maclean

MacLane, Armand Ralph
See McLane, Armand Ralph

Maclane, Mary 1881-1929 [HPPN]
Canadian author
* [The] Butte Bashkirtseff

MacLaren, Gordon
See Patten, William George

Maclaren, Ian
See Watson, John

MacLaren, James
See Grieve, Christopher Murray

Maclaren, John 19th c. [IP]
Scottish author
* [A] Fellow Labourer

MacLaughlin, Charles 1690-1797 [DEA,
RH]
British actor and author
* C. M.
* Macklin, Charles

Maclaughlin, Charles W. 1878-1934
[HPPN]
Canadian-born actor, playwright, director
* Mack, Bill

MacLaurin, Constance 1914-1969 [SC]
Scottish-born actress
* Lorne, Constance

Maclaurin, John 1693-1754 [HPPN]
Scottish clergyman
* Chandler, Tallow
* X. Y.

MacLean, Alistair [Stuart] 1922- [CA,
WD, WWS]
Scottish author
* Stuart, Ian

MacLean, Art
See Shirreffs, Gordon D[onald]

Maclean, Arthur
See Tubb, Edwin Charles

MacLean, Arthur George 20th c. [MBF]
British author
* Kirby, Arthur

Maclean, Charles 1946- [CA]
British author
* Konrad, James

Maclean, Christina
See Casement, Christina

Maclean, Donald Duart 1913-1983 [CA]
*British diplomat, author, and intelligence
agent for Russia*
* Frazer, Mark Petrovich

Maclean, [Sir] John 1811-? [HPPN]
British author
* [A] Churchman
* M.

Maclean, John 1851-1928 [DNA]
Scottish-born author
* Rustler, Robin

Maclean, Katherine 1925- [CA, ESF]
American author
* Dye, Charles
* Morris, G. A.

Maclean, Lachlan 19th c. [IP]
Scottish author
* Seneachie

MacLean, R. D.
See MacLean, Rezin Donald

MacLean, Rezin Donald 1859-1948 [SC]
American actor and director
* MacLean, R. D.

MacLean, Sallie 20th c. [CR]
Dancer
* [La] Trianita

Maclean, Walter A. 1853-1921 [HPPN]
*British-American playwright and
journalist*
* Potter, Paul Meredith

Maclehose, Agnes Craig 1759-1841
[DEL, RH, SN]
*Corresponded with Scottish poet, Robert
Burns*
* Clarinda

MacLennan, Harry 1870-1950 [BMH,
IPA]
Scottish singer
* [The] Laird of the Halls
* Lauder, Harry

Macleod, [Dr.] Archibald
See Bowles, William Lisle

MacLeod, Charlotte [Matilda Hughes]
1922- [CA, SAT]
Canadian-born author
* Craig, Alisa
* Hughes, Matilda

MacLeod, Ellen Jane 1916- [AW, SAT,
WD]
Scottish-born author and playwright
* Anderson, Ella

Macleod, Fiona
See Sharp, William

Macleod, George ?-1921 [HPPN]
American actor
* Grand, George

Macleod, Jean Sutherland 1908- [AW,
CA]
Scottish author
* Airlie, Catherine

Macleod, Joseph [Todd Gordon] 1903-
[CA, WD]
British author, poet, playwright
* Drinan, Adam

Macleod, Malcolm 19th c. [IP]
British author
* [A] Lancashire Artisan

Macleod, Mevrouw Sophia 19th c.
[HPPN]
Scottish author
* Sophia, Mevrouw

MacLeod, Robert
See Knox, William [Bill]

MacLeod, Robert F. 1917- [CA]
American publisher and illustrator
* MacDougall, Fiona

MacLeod, Ruth 1903- [CA]
American author
* Lowry, Nan

Macleod, Xavier Donald 1821-1865 [IP]
American clergyman and author
* Pynnshurst

MacLiammoir, Micheal
See Willmore, Alfred

Maclise, Daniel 1811?-1870 [FFF, PA,
WBD]
Irish painter
* Croquis, Alfred

Macliver, Colin 1792-1863 [HPPN,
WBD]
British army officer
* Campbell, [Sir] Colin
* [The] Red Fox

MacLoughlin, Nila 1891?-1953 [BEW]
American actress, writer, producer
* Mack, Nila

Maclure, William 1763-1840 [FFF]
American geologist
* [The] Father of American Geology

Macmahon, Joseph Parkyns 18th c.
[HPPN]
British artist
* [The] English Limner

**MacMahon, Marie Edme Patrice
Maurice de** 1808-1893 [DEP, DHA]
French president
* [La] Loyale Epee [The Loyal Sword]

MacMahon, Paul 1924- [FC]
American dancer
* Gilbert, Paul

MacMahon, Robert Carrier 1924-
American-born restaurateur
* Carrier, Robert

Macmann, Elaine
See Willoughby, Elaine Macmann

MacManus, Anna 1866-1902 [PI]
Irish poet
* Carbery, Ethna
* Ethna

MacManus, James
See MacManus, Seumas

MacManus, Seumas 1869-1960 [CA]
Irish author, playwright, poet
* Mac
* MacManus, James

MacMillan, Annabelle
See Quick, Annabelle

Macmillan, Daft Pate
See Macmillan, Kirkpatrick

Macmillan, Douglas 1884- [WWL]
British author
* Cary, D. M.

Macmillan, Georgina Fitzgerald 20th c.
[WWL]
British author
* Fitzgerald, Ena

Macmillan, Harold 1894- [NN]
British prime minister
* Mac the Knife
* Supermac

Macmillan, Kirkpatrick 19th c. [BBH]
Scottish inventor
* Macmillan, Daft Pate

MacMillan, Mac
See MacMillan, William Stewart

MacMillan, William Stewart 1943-
[SMG]
Canadian-born hockey player
* MacMillan, Mac
* MacMillan, Yaky

MacMillan, Yaky
See MacMillan, William Stewart

MacMullan, Charles Walden Kirkpatrick
1889-1973 [LAO, LC]
Irish-born playwright
* Munro, C[harles] K[irkpatrick]

Macmullen, Edward Allen 1903-1942
[HPPN]
American actor
* Allen, Edward

MacMullen, John 19th c. [IP]
British soldier and author
* [A] Late Staff Sergeant of the 13th
  Light Infantry

Macmurchada, Diarmaid
See MacMurrough, Dermot

MacMurray, John 1745-1793 [WBD]
British publisher
* Murray, John

MacMurrough, Dermot 1110?-1171
[HN, WBD]
King of Leinster
* [The] Foreigners' Friend
* Macmurchada, Diarmaid

MacNab, Barney
See MacNab, L. B.

MacNab, Frances
See Fraser, Agnes Maude

MacNab, L. B. 1902-1968 [BBH]
American ski patrol founder
* MacNab, Barney

MacNamara, Brinsley
See Weldon, John

MacNamara, Gerald
See Morrow, Harry C.

MacNeal, F. A.
See MacNeal, Frank Ashby

MacNeal, Frank Ashby 1867-1918 [SC]
American actor
* MacNeal, F. A.

MacNee, Patrick
See Leslie, Peter

MacNeice, [Frederick] Louis 1907-1963
[CA, LC, TC]
Irish poet
* Malone, Louis

MacNeil, Al
See MacNeil, Allister Wences

MacNeil, Allister Wences 1935- [FHE,
HK]
Canadian-born hockey player and coach
* MacNeil, Al

MacNeil, Duncan
See McCutchan, Philip [Donald]

Macneil, Hermon Atkins 1866-1947
[HPPN]
American sculptor and designer
* Macneil, Liberty

Macneil, Liberty
See Macneil, Hermon Atkins

MacNeil, Neil
See Ballard, [Willis] Todhunter

MacNeill, Dand
See Fraser, George MacDonald

Macneill, Hector 1746-1818 [IP]
Scottish poet
* [An] Eminent Editor

Macneill, Janet
See McNeely, Jeannette

MacNell, James
See Macdonnell, James Edmond

MacNeven, William James 1763-1841
[IP]
Irish physician and author
* [An] Irish Catholic

MacNib
See Mackie, Albert D[avid]

Macnie, John 1836-1909 [ESF, SFL,
WGT]
American author
* Thiusen, Ismar

Macnish, Robert 1802-1837 [FFF, PA]
Scottish author and physician
* Modern Pythagorean

Macomb, Robert 19th c. [IP]
American author
* [A] Whig of '76

Macomber, A. K. 1875-1955
American horse owner
* Macomber, King

Macomber, Daria
See Robinson, Patricia Colbert

Macomber, George 1927- [BBH]
American skier
* [The] Cat

Macomber, King
See Macomber, A. K.

Macon, David Harrison 1870-1952
[CME, DAM, ECM]
American country-western performer
* [The] Dixie Dew Drop
* [The] Grand Old Man
* King of the Banjo Players
* King of the Hillbillies
* Macon, Uncle Dave

Macon, John Wesley 1923-1973 [BWW]
American singer
* Shortstuff, Mr.

Macon, Nathaniel 1758-1837 [HPPN]
American politician
* [The] Father of the House

Macon, Uncle Dave
See Macon, David Harrison

Maconaquah
See Slocum, Frances

MacOrlan, Pierre
See Dumarchais, Pierre MacOrlan

Macouba, Auguste
See Armeth, Auguste

MacOwen, Arthur H. [DNA]
Author
* Wheeler, Chris

MacOwen, Robert 1744?-1812 [PI]
Irish poet and actor
* Owenson, Robert
* R. N. O.

MacPatterson, F.
See Ernsting, Walter

MacPeek, Walter G. 1902-1973 [CAP,
NAA, SAT]
American author and editor
* Jumpp, Hugo

MacPhail, James A. 20th c. [WW]
Author
* Crockett, James [joint pseudonym
  with Cornelia Warriner]

MacPhail, Larry
See MacPhail, Leland Stanford

MacPhail, Leland Stanford 1890- [PB]
American baseball executive
* MacPhail, Larry

MacPhee, Waddy
See MacPhee, Walter Scott

MacPhee, Walter Scott 1899- [BE]
American baseball player
* MacPhee, Waddy

MacPherson, Bruce Ian 1954- [SMG]
American baseball player
* MacPherson, Mac

MacPherson, Bud
See MacPherson, James Albert

MacPherson, George Gordon 1910-
[ART]
British sculptor and painter
* M.

Macpherson, Ian
See Macpherson, John Cook

Macpherson, James 1738-1796 [PA, SN]
Scottish translator
* Ossian
* [The] Sire of Ossian

MacPherson, James Albert 1927- [CEI]
Canadian-born hockey player
* MacPherson, Bud

MacPherson, Jessie Ingram 1893- [AW]
Scottish-born author
* Kennie, Jessie

Macpherson, John 18th c. [IP]
American author
* [A] Pennsylvania Sailor

Macpherson, John Cook 20th c. [SFL]
Author
* Macpherson, Ian

MacPherson, Mac
See MacPherson, Bruce Ian

Macpherson, Mrs. Brewster 19th c.
[IP]
Scottish author
* X. H.

Macpherson, Quinton 1871?-1940 [BEW]
Actor
* Hymack, Mr.

MacPherson, Thomas George 1915-
[CA]
British-born author
* Parsons, Tom

MacPiarais, Padraic
See Pearse, Patrick Henry

MacQueen, James William 1900-1954
[WW]
American author
* Edwards, James G.
* McHugh, Jay

Macrabin, Mark
See Cunningham, Allan

MacRae, Archibald Oswald 1869-?
[CCL]
Canadian author
* Politicus

Macrae, Arthur
See Schroepfer, Arthur

MacRae, Donald G. 1921- [CA]
Scottish-born sociologist and author
* Campbell, Clive

Macrae, Hawk
See Barker, Albert W.

Macrae, Herbert
See Fearn, C. Eaton

MacRae, James
See Macdonald, John James

MacRae, Travis
See Feagles, Anita MacRae

Macready, William Charles 1793-1873
[HPPN, SN]
British actor
* [The] English Bulldog
* [The] King Arthur of the Stage

Macrembolites
See Eustathius [or Eumathius]

Macri, Teresa [or Theresa] 1797?-1876
[DNNS, SN]
*Friend of British poet, George Gordon
Byron*
* [The] Maid of Athens

Macrillo, Gonzaluo 1866-1918 [HPPN]
American actress and playwright
* McCree, Junie

Macrinus [or Salmon?], Jean 1490-1557
[DEP, FFF, SN]
French poet
* [The] French Horace
* [The] Horace of France

Macropedius, Georgius 1475-1558
[HPPN]
Dutch author
* Langeveldt, George

Macropodio, Gino 1930- [HPPN]
Italian gondolier
* Gino the Gondolier
* Rooster

Macroton [A Slow Speaker]
See Guenault, Francois

Macsarconica, Archy, F. R. S.
See Hastings, Thomas

MacSarin, Kenneth
See Sarin, Max Kenneth

Macsaroni, A.
See Anstey, Christopher

Macshimi, Gillespie
See Simson, Archibald

MacShinie, Gillespie
See Simpson, Archibald

Macsparran, James ?-1757 [IP]
*Irish-born American clergyman and
author*
* [A] Divine of the Church of England

Macsweeny, Joseph 19th c. [IP]
Irish author
* J. M'S.

Macswell
See Russ, W. L.

MacThomais, Ruaraidh
See Thomson, Derick Smith

MacTyre, Paul
See Adam, Robert James

Macullar, James F. 1855-1924 [BE]
American baseball player
* Macullar, Little Mac

Macullar, Little Mac
See Macullar, James F.

Macumber, Mari
See Sandoz, Mari [Susette]

Macurdy, John
See McCurdy, John Edward

MacVean, Phyllis 1892- [WWL]
British author
* Hambledon, Phyllis

MacVeigh, Sue
See Nearing, Elizabeth [Custer]

MacVicar, Martha 1925-1971 [FC]
American actress
* Vickers, Martha

MacWherter, Rod
See McWherter, Rodney

Macy, Dora
See Oursler, Grace Perkins

Macy, Rowland Hussey 1822-1877
[HPPN]
American retail merchant
* [The] Father of the Department Store

Mad Anne Bailey
See Bailey, Anne Hennis Trotter

Mad Anthony Wayne
See Wayne, Anthony

[The] Mad Austrian
See Bluhdorn, Charles G.

Mad Bell
See Lauchlan, Isabel

[The] Mad Bomber
See Fuqua, Richard

[The] Mad Bomber
See Longley, Clint

[The] Mad Bomber
See Metesky, George Peter

[The] Mad Caliph
See Hakim, al-

[The] Mad Canadian
See Carter, Ken[neth]

[The] **Mad Cavalier**
See Rupert

[The] **Mad Colonel**
See Boyd, John

[The] **Mad Cornarus**
See Cornarus, John

[The] **Mad Czar**
See Paul I

Mad Dan the Murrimbidgee Terror
See Morgan, Daniel

[The] **Mad Diarist**
See Mew, Thomas Joseph, III
[Tommy]

[The] **Mad Dog**
See Tracy, Harry

Mad Dog Carter
See Carter, Fred

Mad Dog Coll
See Coll, Vincent

Mad Dog Garner
See Garner, Gary

Mad Dog Hatcher
See Hatcher, Gene

Mad Dog Manders
See Manders, Dave

Mad Dog Mandich
See Mandich, Jim

Mad Dog McGawley
See McGawley, John

Mad Dog McGlinchey
See McGlinchey, Dominic

Mad Dog O'Billovich
See O'Billovich, Jack

Mad Dog Ross
See Ross, Edgar

Mad Dog Sanders
See Sanders, Clarence

Mad Dog White
See White, Dwight

[The] **Mad Duck**
See Karras, Alex[ander George]

Mad Fred Deeming
See Deeming, Frederick Bailey

[The] **Mad Hatter**
See Anastasia, Albert

[The] **Mad Hatter**
See Crab, Roger

[The] **Mad Hungarian**
See Hrabosky, Alan Thomas

Mad Jack
See Percival, John

Mad Jack Byron
See Byron, [Captain] John

[The] **Mad King of Lacedaemon**
See Cleomenes

Mad Mab Barnet
See Barnet, Charles Daly [Charlie]

Mad Mad Joe Califano
See Califano, Joseph Anthony, Jr.

[The] **Mad Major**
See Draper, Christopher

Mad Man
See Rabelais, Francois

Mad Marcus Arnheiter
See Arnheiter, Marcus Aurelius

Mad Marshall Goldberg
See Goldberg, Marshall

Mad Matt Zunic
See Zunic, Matt

Mad Mike Calvert
See Calvert, Michael

Mad Mike Hoare
See Hoare, Michael

[The] **Mad Monk**
See Meyer, Russell Charles

[The] **Mad Monk**
See Rasputin, Grigori Efimovich

[The] **Mad Monk in the Monastery**
See Reed, B. Mitchel

[The] **Mad Monk of Deregulation**
See Fowler, Mark

[The] **Mad Monk of Massachusetts**
See Drinan, [Rev.] Robert

[The] **Mad Mullah**
See Bordino, Pietro

[The] **Mad Mullah**
See Mohammed ibn-Abdullah

[The] **Mad Parson**
See Allen, John Edward

[The] **Mad Parson**
See Swift, Jonathan

[The] **Mad Pittsburgh Playboy**
See Thaw, Harry Kendall

[The] **Mad Poet**
See Clarke [or Clark?], McDonald

[The] **Mad Poet**
See Collins, William

[The] **Mad Poet**
See Lee, Nathaniel

[The] **Mad Poet of Broadway**
See Clarke [or Clark?], McDonald

[The] **Mad Poet of California**
See Kendall, W. S.

[The] **Mad Poet of New York**
See Clarke [or Clark?], McDonald

[The] **Mad Pole of the Civil War**
See Gurowski, [Count] Adam

[The] **Mad Priest of Kent**
See Ball, John

[The] **Mad Programmer**
See Antonowsky, Marvin

[The] **Mad Queen**
See Juana [Joanna or Jane]

Mad Rudi Hess
See Hess, Rudolf

[The] **Mad Russian**
See Gorodetsky, Barney

[The] **Mad Russian**
See Novikoff, Lou[is Alexander]

[The] **Mad Russian**
See Vucerovich, William

[The] **Mad Sculptor**
See Irwin, Fenelon Arroyo Seco

[The] **Mad Socrates**
See Diogenes

[The] **Mad Stork**
See Hendricks, Ted

Mad Tom
See Sherman, William Tecumseh

Mad Tom Davey
See Davey, Thomas

Mada
See Clark, Mary L.

Madam Ambassador From and to Broadway
See Zimmerman, Ethel Agnes

Madame Clarice
See Waters, Clarice C.

[The] **Madame Defarge of the Washington Press Corps**
See McGrory, Mary

Madame Helena
See Jackson, Editha Salomon

Madame Jenny
See Sacerdote, Jenny

Madame Jenny D.
See Bastide, Jenny Dufourquet

Madame Queen
See Randolph, Lillian

Madame Simone
See Benda, Simone

Madame Spivy
See Le Voe, Spivy

Madame Wanda
See O'Rourke, Sarah

Madan, Martin 1726-1790 [HPPN]
British clergyman
* Anti Profanus
* [A] Sincere Well Wisher to the Public

Madau, Antonio 1931- [OP]
Italian opera producer, set designer, author
* Madau Diaz, Antonello

Madau Diaz, Antonello
See Madau, Antonio

[The] Madcap
See Dumond, Normand

Madcap Betsy
See Von Furstenberg-Hedringen, Elizabeth Caroline Maria Agatha Felicitas

Madcap Maggie Whiting
See Whiting, Margaret Eleanore

Madcap Maxie Baer
See Baer, Max[imilian Adelbert]

[The] Madcap Princess of Monaco
See Charlotte

Madden, Bernard Joseph 19th c.   [PI]
Irish poet
* [An] Irish Helot

Madden, Bunny
See Madden, Thomas J.

Madden, Daniel Owen 19th c.   [PA]
Author
* North, Darby

Madden, [Jerry] David 1933-   [CN]
American author
* Travis, Jack

Madden, Dick
See Sellers, Connie Leslie, Jr.

Madden, [Sir] Frederick 1801-1873
[HPPN, PA]
British author
* F. M.
* M.

Madden, J. P. A. 19th c.   [HPPN]
British bibliographer
* [Un] Bibliographe

Madden, John 20th c.
American football coach
* Madden, Pinky

Madden, Kid
See Madden, Michael Joseph

Madden, Lefty
See Madden, Leonard Joseph [Len]

Madden, Leonard Joseph [Len]
1890-1949   [BE]
American baseball player
* Madden, Lefty

Madden, M. A.
See Sadleir, Mary Anne

Madden, Michael Joseph 1866-1896
[BE]
American baseball player
* Madden, Kid

Madden, Owen 1892-1964   [BLB, HPPN, MM]
British-born American murderer and bootlegger
* [The] Killer
* Madden, Owney
* Owney the Killer

Madden, Owney
See Madden, Owen

Madden, Pinky
See Madden, John

Madden, Richard Robert 1798-1886
[HPPN, PI]
Irish poet
* Her Physician
* Ierne
* R. R. M.

Madden, T. E. 20th c.   [WWL]
British author and journalist
* Field Officer

Madden, Thomas J. 1884-   [BE]
American baseball player
* Madden, Bunny

Madden, Warren
See Cameron, Kenneth Neill

Maddern, Al
See Ellison, Harlan [Jay]

Maddern, Little Minnie
See Davey, Mary Augusta

Maddern, Minnie
See White, Mrs. Legrand

Maddigan, Gertie
See Lodge, Mrs. Benjamin

Maddison, Angela Mary 1923-   [AW, CA, SAT]
British author and illustrator
* Banner, Angela

Maddock, Larry
See Jardine, Jack Owen

Maddock, Mrs. E. A. 19th c.   [PA]
Author
* E. A. M.

Maddock, Stephen
See Walsh, James Morgan

Maddocks
See Greenall, Jack

Maddolo
See Byron, George Gordon Noel

Maddow, Ben
See Wolff, David

Maddox, Buggy Whip
See Maddox, Garry Lee

Maddox, Carl
See Tubb, Edwin Charles

Maddox, Claude
See Moore, J. E.

Maddox, Claude
See Moore, John Edward

Maddox, Garry Lee 1949-   [PB]
American baseball player
* Maddox, Buggy Whip

Maddox, Lester
See Hauss, Len

Maddox, Lester Garfield 1915-   [HPPN]
American restaurateur and politician
* White Backlash, Mr.

Maddox, Max
See Jeans, Herbert

Maddox, May 1877-1938   [SC]
American actress
* Wallace, May

Maddox, No Name 1934-   [BP, HPPN]
American murderer
* [The] Demon of Death Valley
* [The] Hippie Murderer
* [The] Hypnotic Hippie
* Manson, Charles

Maddox, Rose
See Brogdon, Roseea Arbana

Maddux, Rachel
See Baker, Rachel Maddux

Madeira, Antonio 1905-   [EWL]
Portuguese poet, author, playwright
* Branquinho Da Fonseca, Antonio Jose

Madeleine [code name used during World War II]
See Khan, Noor Inayat

Madeleva, [Sister] M.
See Wolff, Mary Evaline

Mademoiselle
See Orleans, Anne Marie Louise d'

Mademoiselle Hortense
See Manning, Maria de Roux

Mademoiselle Judith
See Bernat, Julie

Mader, Fred 20th c.   [HPPN]
American labor union racketeer
* Mader, Frenchy

Mader, Frenchy
See Mader, Fred

Maderis, Elma 1909-   [HPPN]
American librarian
* Maderis, Peach

Maderis, Peach
See Maderis, Elma

Madetoja, Onerva 1882-?   [WBD]
Finnish author and poet
* O'nerva, L.

Madge
See Humphry, Mrs. C. E.

Madgett, Naomi Long 1923-   [CA]
American author
* Long, Naomi Cornelia
* Witherspoon, Naomi Long

Madhavikutty
See Das, Kamala

Madhubuti, Haki R.
See Lee, Don[ald] L[uther]

Madiana
See Ricord, J. B.

Madigan, Anthony J. 1868-1954   [BE]
American baseball player
* Madigan, Pony

Madigan, Connie
See Madigan, Cornelius Dennis

Madigan, Cornelius Dennis 1934-   [CEI]
Canadian-born hockey player
* Madigan, Connie

Madigan, Edward P. 1896?-1966   [AS, FB]
American football coach
* Madigan, Slip

Madigan, Mrs. H. P.   [FFF]
Entertainer
* Yates, Mary E.

Madigan, Pony
See Madigan, Anthony J.

Madigan, Slip
See Madigan, Edward P.

Madison, Dolly
See Madison, Dorothy Payne Todd

Madison, Dorothy Payne Todd
1768-1849   [BI, HPPN, WP 1-20-85]
Wife of American president, James Madison
* [The] Dowager
* First Lady in Fashion
* First Lady of the Land
* [The] Incomparable Dolly
* Madison, Dolly
* Madison, Quaker Dolly
* Madison, Queen Dolly
* Mistress of the White House
* [The] Nation's Hostess
* [The] Queen Dowager
* Queen of Hearts
* [The] Velvet Glove

Madison, Eleanor Rose Conway 1731-1829
Mother of American president, James Madison
* Madison, Nellie

Madison, Frank
See Hutchins, Francis Gilman

Madison, Guy
See Moseley, Robert

Madison, Hank
See Rowland, Donald Sydney

Madison, James 1751-1836   [FAP, NPS]
American president
* [The] American Plutarch
* [The] Father of the Constitution
* Framer of the Constitution
* Helvidius
* [A] Lamp to Light the Way
* Master Builder of the Constitution
* Philosopher of the Constitution
* Publius
* [The] Sage of Montpelier
* [The] Unimperial President
* Virginia Revolutionist

Madison, James 20th c.   [NBB]
American musician
* Madison, Pee Wee

Madison, Jane
See Horne, Hugh Robert

Madison, John Rodrigo 1896-1970
[HPPN]
American author, playwright, man of letters
* Dos
* Dos Passos, John
* Jack

Madison, Joyce
See Mintz, Joyce Lois

Madison, Louis 1899-1948   [EJ, WWJ]
American jazz musician
* Shots, Kid

Madison, Marilyn
See Picken, Mary Brooks

Madison, Matilda
See Denison, Mrs.

Madison, Nat
See Moscovitch, Nathaniel

Madison, Nellie
See Madison, Eleanor Rose Conway

Madison, Noel
See Moscovitch, Nathaniel

Madison, Pee Wee
See Madison, James

Madison, Quaker Dolly
See Madison, Dorothy Payne Todd

Madison, Queen Dolly
See Madison, Dorothy Payne Todd

Madison, Thomas A[lvin] [Tom] 1926-
[CA]
American author
* Campbell, Luke

Madison, Virginia
See Putnam, Sarah A.

Madjeski, Ed[ward William]
See Majewski, Edward William

Madlee, Dorothy [Haynes] 1917-   [CA]
American author and journalist
* Haynes, Anne
* Rogers, Wade

Madlock, Bill, Jr. 1951-   [SMG]
American baseball player
* Madlock, Mad

Madlock, Mad
See Madlock, Bill, Jr.

[The] Madman
See Apollodorus

[The] Madman
See Sebastian

Madman Mark Fowler
See Fowler, Mark

[The] Madman of Donner Summitt
See Buek, Richard

[The] Madman of Halberstadt
See Christian of Brunswick

[The] Madman of Macedonia
See Alexander III

[The] Madman of St. Malo
See Von Aulock, Andreas

[The] Madman of the North
See Charles XII

Madonilla [or Madonella]
See Astell, Mary

Madonna
See Ciccone, Madonna Louise

[The] Madonna
See Mary

[The] Madonna of Contemporary Gospel
See Grant, Amy

[The] Madonna of Hall Moody
See Hall, Musa L.

Madrid, Sal
See Madrid, Salvador

Madrid, Salvador 1920-   [BE]
American baseball player
* Madrid, Sal

Madrilenito [Little Fellow from Madrid]
See Diaz Cordero, Luis

Madsen, Axel 1930-   [CA]
Danish-born author and journalist
* Brion, Guy

Madsen, Carl 20th c.   [BBH, CSH]
Canadian lacrosse player
* Madsen, Gus

Madsen, Gus
See Madsen, Carl

Madsen, Merdin Prince Gunnar 1943-
[RO2]
Danish-born musician
* Madsen, Mert

Madsen, Mert
See Madsen, Merdin Prince Gunnar

Mae, Eleanor
See Penner, Eleanor May

Mae, Eydie
See Hunsberger, Edith Mae

Mae, Jimsey
See Rawley, Charlotte

[A] Maecenas
See Blount, William [Fourth Baron Mountjoy]

[A] Maecenas
See Montagu, Charles [First Earl of Halifax]

[The] Maecenas and Lucullus of His Island
See Cavendish, William Spencer

[The] Maecenas and Petronius of His Age
See Stanhope, Philip Dormer

[The] Maecenas of Book-Lovers
See Grolier, Jean

[The] Maecenas of Danish Letters
See Rahbeck, Knud Lyne

[The] Maecenas of Embryo Players
See Hardham, John

[The] Maecenas of England
See Rogers, Samuel

[The] Maecenas of France
See Francis I or [Francois]

[The] Maecenas of His Day
See Mazarin, Jules

[The] Maecenas of His Time
See Visconti, Galeazzo II

[The] Maecenas of Shoemakers
See Lofft, Capel

Mael, Peter [joint pseudonym with Charles Vincent]
See Causse, Charles

Mael, Peter [joint pseudonym with Charles Causse]
See Vincent, Charles

Maelmuire
See Condon, Thomas

[The] Maeonian Poet
See Homer

[The] Maeonian Swan
See Homer

Maeonides
See Homer

Maepen, Hugh
See Kuttner, Henry

Maepen, K. H.
See Kuttner, Henry

Maer, Stephen 1933- [ART]
British artist
* S. M.

Maera
See Garcia y Lopez, Manuel

Maerlant, Jakob 1235-1300 [DEP, DNNF, SN]
Belgian poet
* [The] Father of Dutch Poetry
* [The] Father of Flemish Poets

Maery, Helen
See Mug, [Sister] Mary Theodosia

Maestro
See Blau, Jeno

[El] Maestro [The Master]
See Dihogo, Martin

[Il] Maestro
See Fellini, Federico

Maestro
See Kostelanetz, Andre

[Il] Maestro
See Nuvolari, Tazio

[El] Maestro [The Teacher]
See Shoemaker, William [Willie]

[El] Maestro [The Master]
See Valdes, Angel

Maestro, Johnny
See Mastrangelo, Johnny

[The] Maestro Kid
See Simmons, Calvin

[The] Maestro of Massed Strings
See Mantovani, Annunzio Paulo

[The] Maestro of Money
See Martin, William McChesney, Jr.

[The] Maestro of the Omelet
See Stanish, Rudolph

Maeterlinck, Georgette 1876-1941 [BEW]
French-born actress
* LeBlanc, Georgette

Maeterlinck, Maurice [Polydore Marie Bernard] 1862-1949 [LC]
Belgian poet and playwright
* [The] Belgian Shakespeare

Maevius
See Russell, Richard

Maffei, Andrea 1800-1885 [SN]
Italian author
* [The] Nestor of Modern Italian Authors

Maffie, Jazz
See Maffie, John

Maffie, John 20th c. [DI]
American robber
* Maffie, Jazz

Maffit, John Newland 1794-1850 [HPPN]
Irish-American clergyman
* J. N. M.

Maffy
See Falay, Almes Muvaffax

Maga
See Blackwood, William

Magaddino, Stefano 1891- [BLB]
Italian-born American underworld figure
* Magaddino, Steve

Magaddino, Steve
See Magaddino, Stefano

Magalhaes, Fernao De 1480?-1521 [HPPN, NPS]
Portuguese navigator and explorer
* Magallanes, Fernando de
* Magellan, Ferdinand
* Mighty Eagle
* [The] Most Eminent and Renowned Navigator

Magallanes, Fernando de
See Magalhaes, Fernao De

Magallon, Paul de 1784-1859 [BI]
French clergyman
* John of God, [Brother]

[A] Magazine Editor
See Watts, Alaric Alexander

Magda F.
See Ferrer-Peralta, Magda

Magdalena
See Bay, Magdalena

Magdeleine
See Carbet, Marie-Magdalene

Magee, James 1929- [AW]
Irish author
* Taylor, John

Magee, Lee
See Hoernschemeyer, Leopold Christopher

Magee, Leo Christopher
See Hoernschemeyer, Leopold Christopher

Magee, Sherry
See Magee, Sherwood Robert

Magee, Sherwood Robert 1884-1929 [AS, BE]
American baseball player
* Magee, Sherry

Magee, William Kirkpatrick 1868-1961 [LC]
Irish author
* Eglinton, John

Magellan, Ferdinand
See Magalhaes, Fernao De

Magennis, Bernard 1833-1911 [PI]
Irish poet
* B. McG.
* Hofer
* Iveagh

Mager, Doris 1926?- [HPPN]
American Audubon Society spokeswoman
* [The] Eagle Lady

Maggie
See Browne, Maurice

Maggio, Dante 20th c. [WF]
Italian actor
* May, Dan

Maggiolo, Achille 20th c. [EF]
American football player
* Maggiolo, Chick

Maggiolo, Chick
See Maggiolo, Achille

Maghett, Sam[uel] 1937-1969 [BWW, DAM]
American singer
* Good Rocking Sam
* Magic Sam
* Magic Singing Sam

Magic Charlie Spencer
See Spencer, Charles [Charlie]

[The] Magic Fingers of Radio
See Duchin, Edwin Frank [Eddie]

[The] Magic Lady
See Larsen, Geraldine

[The] Magic Maker
See Cummings, Edward Estlin

[The] Magic Man
See Bennett, Lonnie

[The] **Magic Man**
See Robert-Houdin, Jean Eugene

[The] **Magic Man**
See Starling, Marlon

Magic, Mr.
See Monroe, Earl

Magic Sam
See Maghett, Sam[uel]

Magic Singing Sam
See Maghett, Sam[uel]

Magic Slim
See Holt, Morris

[The] **Magical Maker of Mobiles**
See Calder, Alexander

[The] **Magical Maker of Stabiles**
See Calder, Alexander

[The] **Magician**
See Abreu, Joseph Lawrence [Joe]

[The] **Magician**
See Briscoe, Marlin

[The] **Magician**
See Cawston, Mervyn

[The] **Magician**
See Davies, Robert E. [Bob]

[The] **Magician**
See Kissinger, Henry Alfred

[The] **Magician**
See Peter Lee, Sidney

[The] **Magician**
See Scott, [Sir] Walter

[The] **Magician**
See Van Buren, Martin

[The] **Magician of the North**
See Hamann, Johann Georg

[The] **Magician of the North**
See Scott, [Sir] Walter

Magician of the Screen
See Melies, Georges

Magill, Marcus [joint pseudonym with Brian (Merrikin) Hill?]
See Giles, Joanna Elder

Magill, Marcus [joint pseudonym with Joanna Elder Giles?]
See Hill, Brian [Merrikin]

Magill, Rory
See Faulkner, Dorothea M.

Magin, Joseph 19th c. [PI]
Irish poet
* J. M.?

Maginn, William 1793-1842 [DEL, FFF, HPPN, NPS, PI, SN]
Irish author and journalist
* [The] Adjutant
* Augustinus
* Barrett, [Rev.] J.
* Bombardinio
* Buller, Bob
* Crossman, C. O.

Maginn, William (cont.)
* Crossman, P. J.
* Crossman, P. P.
* Dowden, Richard
* [The] Dromedary
* Duggan, Dionysius
* [The] Ensign
* Eubulus
* Fitztravesty, Blaize, Esq.
* Forager, Philip
* Hincks, [Rev.] E.
* Holt, William
* Howley, John, Esq.
* [An] Irish Gentleman Lately Deceased
* J. T--n
* Jennings, Thomas
* M. O'D.
* MacGrawler, Peter
* Middlestitch, Giles
* [The] Modern Rabelais
* Mulligan, Morty Macnamara
* Mullion, Mordecai
* Mummius
* North, Christopher
* Odoherty, [Sir] Morgan
* O'Toole, Bryan, Esq., of Gray's Inn
* P. P. P.
* P. T. T.
* Paloemon
* Petre, Olinthus
* Polyglott, Pandemus, L. L. D.
* Potts, Philips, Esq.
* [The] Prince of Pedagogues
* R. D. R.
* R. F. P.
* R. T. S.
* Scott, Ralph Tuckett
* Seward, W.
* [The] Standard Bearer
* Sussex, Jasper
* T. C.
* Titus
* Trollope, Susanna

Magister Abstractionum
See De Mairone, Francois

Magister Contradictionis
See Grossetete, Robert

Magister Contradictionum
See Wessel, Johann [or John]

Magister Islebius
See Sneider, Johannes

Magister, Joseph
See Goldberg, Louis T[heodore]

Magister, Juras
See Zagorski, Jerzy

Magister Scolarum
See Grossetete, Robert

Magister Sententiarum
See Lombard, Peter [or Pietro]

[A] **Magistrate**
See Fellowes, Robert

[A] **Magistrate in the Country**
See Grant, [Sir] Francis [Lord Cullen]

Magito, Suria
See Saint Denis, Valia Maria [Suria]

Maglanowich, Hyacinthe
See Merimee, Prosper

Magliabecchi, Antonio [or Anthony] 1633-1714 [NPS, RH, SN]
Florentine bibliophile
* [Il] Biblioteca Animata [The Living Library]
* [The] Book Prodigy of His Age
* [Il] Divoratore de Libri [The Devourer of Books]
* [The] Glutton of Literature
* Helluo
* [The] Universal Index and Living Cyclopaedia

Maglie, Salvatore Anthony 1917- [BE, PB]
American baseball player
* [The] Barber
* Maglie, Sinister Sal
* [The] Renaissance Assassin

Maglie, Sinister Sal
See Maglie, Salvatore Anthony

Maglio, Paul
See DeLucia, Felice

Magliocco, Giuseppe ?-1963 [PHM]
Italian-born American underworld figure
* Magliocco, Joseph

Magliocco, Joseph
See Magliocco, Giuseppe

Magloire, Auguste 1872-1948 [CW]
Haitian historian, journalist, sociologist
* Fureteur, Jean Le

Magloire, Clement, fils 1912-1971 [CW]
Haitian poet and author
* Saint Aude, Magloire

Magloire, Francis L.
See Sejour-Magloire, Francis L.

Maglone, Barney
See Donnelly, James

Maglone, Barney
See Wilson, Robert A.

Magnani, Anna 1908- [HPPN]
Italian actress
* Nannerella

[El] **Magnanimo**
See Alfonso V [or Alphonso]

[The] **Magnanimous**
See Albert V [or Albrecht]

[The] **Magnanimous**
See Alfonso V [or Alphonso]

[The] **Magnanimous**
See John Frederick

[The] **Magnanimous**
See Khosru I [or Chosroes]

[The] **Magnanimous**
See Philip

[The] **Magnanimous**
See Philip II [or Philippe]

Magnano
See Wait, Simeon

Magnasco, Alessandro 1667?-1749 [WBD]
Italian painter
* Lissandrino

Magner, Edmund Burke 1888-1956 [BE]
American baseball player
* Magner, Stubby

Magner, Stubby
See Magner, Edmund Burke

Magnes, Judah Leon 1877-1948 [HPPN]
American educator, clergyman, community leader
* [The] Founder of the Kehillah

[The] Magnet
See Addy, Robert Edward [Bob]

Magnetic Man
See Blaine, James Gillespie

[The] Magnetic Statesman
See Blaine, James Gillespie

Magnetica, Electra
Fox, Hugh [Bernard, Jr.]

[The] Magnificent
See Alfonso III [or Alphonso]

[The] Magnificent
See Arundell, [Sir] John

[The] Magnificent
See Edmund I [or Eadmund]

[The] Magnificent
See George IV

[The] Magnificent
See Khosru I [or Chosroes]

[The] Magnificent
See MacArthur, Douglas

[The] Magnificent
See Medici, Lorenzo de

[The] Magnificent
See Robert I

[The] Magnificent
See Suleiman II [or Soliman]

[The] Magnificent Giant
See Melchior, Lauritz

[The] Magnificent Heber
See Heber, Richard

[The] Magnificent Mongoose
See Wright, Archibald Lee

[The] Magnificent Rube
See Rickard, George Lewis

[The] Magnificent Screwball
See Baer, Max[imilian Adelbert]

[The] Magnificent Skeptic
See Dobie, Gilmour

[The] Magnificent Vestvali
See Vestvali, Felicita

[The] Magnificent Wildcat
See Chalupec, Apolonia

[Le] Magnifique
See Roux, Paul Pierre

Magnin, Cyril 20th c.
American business executive
* San Francisco, Mr.

[EL] Magno
See Ferdinand I

Magnoeus
See Magnusson, Arne

Magnus ?-1449 [SN]
Earl of Northumberland
* Red Mane

Magnus
See Mansel, William

Magnus
See Raviola, Antonio

Magnus Eriksson
See Magnus II

Magnus, Gerald
See Bowman, Gerald

Magnus, Gerardus
See Groote [or Groete], Gerhard

Magnus, John
See Ellison, Harlan [Jay]

Magnus, Jonas 1583-1651 [PA]
Author
* Wexisnensis

Magnus Ladulas [Barn Lock]
See Magnus I

Magnus, Philip
See Magnus-Allcroft, [Sir] Philip [Montefiore]

Magnus-Allcroft, [Sir] Philip [Montefiore] 1906- [CAP]
British author and editor
* Magnus, Philip

Magnus I ?-1047 [DNNS, WBD]
King of Norway and Denmark
* [The] Good

Magnus I 1240-1290 [WBD]
King of Sweden
* Magnus Ladulas [Barn Lock]

Magnus II 1035-1069 [HPPN]
King of Norway
* Haradlsson

Magnus II 1316-1374 [DNNS, WBD]
King of Sweden
* Magnus Eriksson
* Smek

Magnus III 1073-1103 [DNNS, WBD]
King of Norway
* Barefoot
* Barfod

Magnus IV 1115?-1139 [WBD]
King of Norway
* [The] Blind

Magnus V 1156-1184 [HPPN]
King of Norway
* Erlingsson

Magnus VI 1238-1280 [DNNS, WBD]
King of Norway
* Lagaboeter [Reformer of the Laws]

Magnusdottir, Magnea 1930- [IAW]
Icelandic author
* Kleifum, [Fra] Magnea

Magnuson, Maggie
See Magnuson, Warren G.

Magnuson, Warren G. 1905-
American politician
* Magnuson, Maggie

Magnusson, Arne 1663-1730 [PA]
Author
* Magnoeus

Magnusson, Guomundur 1873-1918 [CD, EWL]
Icelandic author and poet
* Trausti, Jon

[El] Mago [The Magician]
See Gardes, Charles Romuald

Magoogin
See Jennings, John J.

Magoon, Bob
See Magoon, Eaton, Jr.

Magoon, Carey [joint pseudonym with Marian Austin (Waite) Magoon]
See Carey, Elisabeth

Magoon, Carey [joint pseudonym with Elisabeth Carey]
See Magoon, Marian Austin [Waite]

Magoon, Eaton, Jr. 1922- [ASC]
American composer
* Magoon, Bob

Magoon, George Henry 1875-1943 [BE]
American baseball player
* Magoon, Topsy

Magoon, Marian Austin [Waite] 1885- [WW]
Author
* Magoon, Carey [joint pseudonym with Elisabeth Carey]

Magoon, Topsy
See Magoon, George Henry

Magor, W. L.
See Magor, William Laurence

Magor, William Laurence 1913- [ART]
Welsh-born painter
* Magor, W. L.

Magoun, Frederick Alexander 1896- [HPPN]
American educator and author
* Wright, Amos

Magpie
See Lotinga, W.

Magpie
See Webb, William H.

Magrath, E. [PA]
Author
* E. M.

Magrath, Peter
See Beresford, William

Magraw, Beatrice Irene [May] 1888-
[AW]
British author
* Padeson, Mary

Magraw, Lucy Cotton 1891-1948 [SC]
American actress
* Cotton, Lucy

Magriel, Paul 1947?-
Mathematician and backgammon player
* [The] Human Computer
* X 22

Magriska, Helene
See Brockies, Enid Florence

Magruder, Jeb Stuart 1934- [HPPN]
American presidential aide
* [The] Brown Nose of the Year

Magruder, Julia 1854-1907 [FFF]
American author
* Kerr, Sherrill

Magrum, Bud
See Magrum, Francis

Magrum, Francis 1949- [SMG]
American football player
* Magrum, Bud

Maguen, David
See Markish, David

Maguilevsky, Leonide 1899- [FC]
Russian producer and director
* Moguy, Leonide

Maguiness, William Edward 1904-
[HPPN]
American radio and television personality
* Mack, Ted

Maguire, Anne
See Munn, Meryl Lucile

Maguire, Aunt
See Berry, Frances Miriam

Maguire, Francis 1839-? [FFF, PA]
Entertainer
* Mayo, Frank

Maguire, H. N.
Author
* Hegmun, Ira

Maguire, Little Tom
See Maguire, Tom

Maguire, Robert Augustine Joseph 1898-
[AW, CA]
Irish-born author
* Taaffe, Michael

Maguire, Shandy
See Fennell, Patrick

Maguire, Tom 1869-1934 [SC]
American actor
* Maguire, Little Tom

Magus aus dem Norden
See Hamann, Johann Georg

Magus of the North
See Hamann, Johann Georg

[The] Magus of the Times
See Sterling, Edward

Mahaffey, Lee Roy 1903-1969 [BE]
American baseball player
* Mahaffey, Popeye

Mahaffey, Popeye
See Mahaffey, Lee Roy

Mahaffy-Wilson, Mary Ruth 1902-
[IAW]
American columnist
* Moms Musings

Mahal, Taj
See Fredricks, Henry Sainte Claire

Mahan, Bull
See Mahan, Larry

Mahan, Edward W. 1882- [FB]
American football player
* Mahan, Natick Eddie

Mahan, Larry 1943?- [BI, GW]
American rodeo performer
* Mahan, Bull

Mahan, Natick Eddie
See Mahan, Edward W.

Mahan, Pat
See Wheat, Patte

Mahan, Patrick Herbert 1891?-1924
[HPPN]
British murderer
* [The] Crumbles Murderer

Mahan, Patte Wheat
See Wheat, Patte

Mahan, Red
See Mahan, Walter

Mahan, Walter 20th c. [EF]
American football player
* Mahan, Red

Maharba
See Abraham, John

Maharg, S. A.
See Graham, Angus A.

Maharil
See Moellin, Jacob ben Moses

Mahaskah 1810-? [HPPN]
American Indian chief
* [The] Younger

[The] Mahatma
See Rickey, [Wesley] Branch

Mahavishnu
See McLaughlin, John

[The] Mahdi
See Mohammed Ahmed

Mahdi, Imam
See Ali Mohammed of Shiraz

Mahdi, Tarik Shakir
See Audeh, Muhammad Daoud

Maher, Beaver
See Maher, Bruce D.

Maher, Bruce D. 1937- [FB]
American football player
* Maher, Beaver

Maher, Ramona 1934- [CA]
American author
* Mayer, Agatha

Mahidol, Anata 1925-1946 [HPPN]
King of Thailand
* Rama VIII

Mahler, Gustav 1860-1911 [HPPN]
Austrian composer
* [The] Song Symphonist

Mahler-Kalkstein, Menaham 1908-
[BBD]
Israeli composer
* Avidom, Menaham

Mahmud 971?-1030 [DNNS, WBD]
Sultan of Ghazni
* [The] Great
* [The] Idol Smasher

Mahn, Mack
See McMahon, Patrick James

Mahner-Mons, Hans 20th c. [SFL]
Author
* Possendorf, Hans

Mahnken, Elaine 20th c. [FIR]
Fashion model
* Davis, Elaine

[The] Mahogany Maimer
See Barrow, Joseph Louis

Mahon, Al[fred Gwin] 1910- [BE]
American baseball player
* Mahon, Lefty

Mahon, Charles James Patrick
1800-1891 [DNNS, WBD]
Irish politician and adventurer
* [The] O'Gorman Mahon

Mahon, Lefty
See Mahon, Al[fred Gwin]

Mahon, Natasha 1917- [THR]
Brazilian-born dancer and actress
* Sokolova, Natasha

Mahon, Patrick Herbert 20th c.
[HPPN]
British murderer
* Waller, P. H.

Mahon, Tommy 1880-1955 [BX, RBE]
British boxer
* Bowker, Joe

Mahone, William 1826-1895 [FFF, SN]
American army officer
* Hero of the Crater
* Skin and Bone

Mahoney, Elizabeth 1911- [AW]
American author
* Mara, Thalia

Mahoney, Elmer J. ?-1976 [BI]
American educator
* Mahoney, Pat

Mahoney, Francis 20th c. [SMG]
American basketball player
* Mahoney, Mo

Mahoney, Frank 20th c. [EF]
American football player
* Mahoney, Ike

Mahoney, George W. 1873-1940 [BE]
American baseball player
* Mahoney, Mike

Mahoney, Ike
See Mahoney, Frank

Mahoney, James 20th c. [HPPN]
American businessman
* [The] Poolroom King

Mahoney, James Thomas 1935- [SMG]
American baseball coach
* Mahoney, Moe

Mahoney, Jock
See O'Mahoney, Jacques

Mahoney, Klondike Mike
See Mahoney, Michael Ambrose

Mahoney, M. F. [PA]
Author
* Stradling, Matthew

Mahoney, Michael Ambrose 1878-1951
[BI, HPPN]
Canadian prospector
* Mahoney, Klondike Mike

Mahoney, Mike
See Mahoney, George W.

Mahoney, Mo
See Mahoney, Francis

Mahoney, Moe
See Mahoney, James Thomas

Mahoney, Pat
See Mahoney, Elmer J.

Mahoney, Suzanne 1946-
American actress and singer
* Somers, Suzanne

Mahony, Elizabeth Ann Katherine
1857-1896 [BMH]
Irish-born comedienne
* Bellwood, Bessie

Mahony, Elizabeth Winthrop 1948-
[CA, SAT]
American editor and author
* Winthrop, Elizabeth

Mahony, Francis Sylvester 1804-1866
[DEL, HPPN, PA, PI]
Irish-born journalist
* O'Dryskull, Teddy
* Prout, Father
* Pungent, Pierce
* Savonarola, Jeremy
* Yorke, Oliver, Esq.

Mahony, Patrick 1911- [CA]
American author
* O'Mahony, Patrick

Mahovlich, Francis William [Frank]
1938- [HK, SMG]
Canadian-born hockey player
* [The] Big M

Mahovlich, Pete[r] 1946- [HPPN]
Canadian-born hockey player
* Little M
* Mahovlich, Young Pete

Mahovlich, Young Pete
See Mahovlich, Pete[r]

Mahr, Curley
See Mahr, Herman Carl

Mahr, Herman Carl 1901-1964 [ASC, BEW]
American composer and arranger
* Mahr, Curley

[The] Maid
See Joan of Arc [or Jeanne d'Arc]

[The] Maid of Athens
See Black, Teresa Macri

[The] Maid of Athens
See Macri, Teresa [or Theresa]

[The] Maid of Bath
See Linley, Elizabeth Ann

[The] Maid of Brittany
See Eleanor

[The] Maid of Kent
See Barton, Elizabeth

[The] Maid of Kent
See Bocher, Joan

[The] Maid of Kent
See Heathorne, Caroline

Maid of Llangollen
See Butler, Eleanor

Maid of Llangollen
See Ponsonby, Sarah

[The] Maid of Magic
See Thurston, Jane

[The] Maid of Norway
See Margaret

[The] Maid of Orleans
See Joan of Arc [or Jeanne d'Arc]

[The] Maid of Saragossa [or Saragoza]
See Augustina

[The] Maid of Stockholm
See Bergman, Ingrid

[The] Maid of the Mountains
See Collins, Jose

[The] Maid of the Oaks
See Farren, Elizabeth

Maida
See Crowe, Maida

[The] Maiden
See Malcolm IV

[The] Maiden King
See Malcolm IV

[The] Maiden Queen
See Elizabeth I

Maidoff, Ilka List
See List, Ilka Katherine

Maier, Booby
See Maier, E.

Maier, E. 20th c. [OET]
Spanish tennis player
* Maier, Booby

Maier, Walter A. 1893-1950 [HPPN]
American clergyman
* [The] Father of the International
  Lutheran Hour

Maigrot, Emile 1889-1961 [WBD]
French poet and author
* Henriot, Emile

Maik, Henri
See Hecht, Henri Joseph

[The] Mail Clad Desperado
See Burrow, Reuben Houston

[The] Mail Order Magician
See Sears, Richard Warren

Mailho, Emil Pierre 1909- [BE]
American baseball player
* Mailho, Lefty

Mailho, Lefty
See Mailho, Emil Pierre

Mailings, Malachi
See Galt, John

Maillart, Aime
See Maillart, Louis

Maillart, Louis 1817-1871 [WBD]
French composer
* Maillart, Aime

Maillaud, Pierre 1909-1948 [BI, HPPN]
*French politician, journalist, radio
announcer*
* Bourdan, Pierre

Maillet-Duclairon, Antoine 1721-1809
[HPPN]
French author
* [Un] Americain

Maillot, Antoine Francois 1747-1814
[PA]
Author
* Eve

Mails, Duster
See Mails, John Walter

Mails, John Walter 1895?-1974 [BE, BI, HPPN, PB]
American baseball player
* [The] Big Lip
* [The] Cock o' the Walk of Baseball
* [The] Great
* [The] Great Left Handed Press Agent
* [The] Great Mails
* Mails, Duster
* Mails, King of Kings

Mails, King of Kings
See Mails, John Walter

Maiman, Theodore A. 1927- [HPPN]
American physicist
* [The] Father of the Laser
* [The] Father of the Maser

Maimonides [or Moses ben Maimon]
1135-1204 [DNNS, HN, RH, TI 12-23-85]
Spanish scholar, philosopher, author
* [The] Great Eagle
* [The] Light of the Age
* [The] Light of the West
* Rambam
* [The] Second Moses

Main, Alex
See Main, Miles Grant

Main, Forrest Harry 1922- [BE]
American baseball player
* Main, Woody

Main, John
See Parsons, Elsie Worthington [Clews]

Main, Marjorie
See Krebs, Mary Tomlinson

Main, Miles Grant 1884-1965 [BE]
American baseball player
* Main, Alex

Main, Woody
See Main, Forrest Harry

Mainbocher
See Bocher, Main Rousseau

Maine, Bruno
See Manninen, Bruno Jalmar

Maine, C. E.
See McIlwain, David

Maine, Charles Eric
See McIlwain, David

Maine, David
See Avice, Claude

Maine de Biran
See Gonthier de Biran, Marie Francois Pierre

Maine, Harold
See Winslow, Walker

Maine, Harry Carlton 1899- [NAA]
American writer
* Osofer, Phil

Maine, Henry James Stuart 1822-1888 [DEA]
British author
* H. S. M.

Maine, Trevor
See Catherall, Arthur

Mainhall, Mrs. Henry [FFF]
Entertainer
* Lewis, Jeffreys
* Virgil, Laura

Mainprize, Don[ald Charles] 1930- [CA]
American author
* Rock, Richard

Mainquene, Louise 1885- [THR]
French actress
* Sylvie, Louise

Mains, Grasshopper
See Mains, Willard Eben

Mains, Wee Willie
See Mains, Willard Eben

Mains, Willard Eben 1868-1923 [BN]
American baseball player
* Mains, Grasshopper
* Mains, Wee Willie

Maintenon, Marquise de
See D'Aubigne, Francoise

Maintop
See Forbes, W. B.

Mainwaring, Daniel 1901?-1977 [CC, EMD, WW]
American author and screenwriter
* Homes, Geoffrey

Maiorana, Victor E. 1897-1964 [ASC]
Italian-born musician
* Lamont, Victor

Mair, E. H. 19th c. [HPPN]
Scottish author
* E. H. M.

Mair, G. H.
See Mair, George Henry

Mair, George Brown 1914- [AW, CA, WD]
Scottish physician and author
* Bok, Kooshti
* MacDougall, Robertson

Mair, George Henry 1887-1926 [LC]
British author
* Mair, G. H.

Mair, Margaret
See Crompton, Margaret [Norah Mair]

Maire
See Murray, John Fisher

Mairet, Jean 1604-1686 [NPS]
Playwright
* [The] French Marston

Maironis
See Maciulevicius-Maciulis, Jonas

Mais, S. P. B.
See Mais, Stuart Petre Brodie

Mais, Stuart Petre Brodie 1885- [LC, TC]
British author and radio broadcaster
* Mais, S. P. B.

Maisel, Flash
See Maisel, Frederick Charles

Maisel, Frederick Charles 1889-1967 [BE]
American baseball player
* Maisel, Flash
* Maisel, Fritz

Maisel, Fritz
See Maisel, Frederick Charles

Maisels, Maxine S. 1939- [CA]
American author
* Amishai-Maisels, Ziva

Maisels, Misha 20th c. [CA]
American author
* Amishai, M. H.

Maisky, Michael
See Maisky, Mischa

Maisky, Mischa 1948- [IWM]
Russian-born musician
* Maisky, Michael

Maison, Margaret M[ary Bowles] 1920- [CA]
British author
* Clare, Margaret

[La] Maisonneuve
See Heroet, Antoine

Maitland
See Bartlett, J.

Maitland, E. [PA]
Author
* Ainslie, Herbert

Maitland, James A.
See Smith, Frances Shubael

Maitland, John Wilson
See Watson, William

Maitland, Margaret
See DuBreuil, Elizabeth Lorinda

Maitland, Peter
See MacGillivray, James Pittendrigh

Maitland, Reginald T. 20th c. [EMD, SFP]
Author
* Scott, R. T. M.
* Stockbridge, Grant [house pseudonym]

Maitland, Ruth
See Erskine, Ruth

Maitland, T. G. Dowling 20th c. [MBF]
British author
* Chandos, Herbert
* Gale, H. Winter
* Monck, Tristam K.

Maitland, [Sir] Thomas [HN]
Governor of the Ionian Islands
* King Tom

Maitland, Thomas
See Buchanan, Robert Williams

Maitland, Thomas
See Swinburne, Algernon Charles

Maitland, William 1528?-1573 [WBD]
Scottish politician
* Lethington, Secretary

Maitre
See Des Essaut, M. Davrelle

Maitre Adam
See Billaut, Adam

Maitre Jean
See Gallus, Johannes

Maizel, C. L.
See Maizel, Clarice Matthews

Maizel, Clarice Matthews 1919- [CA]
British author
* Maizel, C. L.
* Maizel, Leah

Maizel, Leah
See Maizel, Clarice Matthews

Maj
See Valles, Charles

Maj, M. A.
See Jacobson, Marcus A. I.

Majeski, Heeney
See Majeski, Henry

Majeski, Henry 1916- [BE]
American baseball player
* Majeski, Heeney

Majeski, William [Bill] 1927- [CA]
American author and playwright
* Fredericks, Vic [house pseudonym]

Majewski, Edward William 1909- [BE]
American baseball player
* Madjeski, Ed[ward William]

Majharajah of Swirl
See Valles, Charles

Majo, Giovanni 1732-1770 [BBD]
Italian composer
* Ciccio di Majo

Major
See Balbus, Lucius Cornelius

[The] Major
See Houk, Ralph George

[The] Major
See Jackson, Robert R.

[The] Major
See Poore, Benjamin Perley

Major A.
See Coles, Charles Barwell

Major, Alan P[ercival] 1929- [CA]
British author
* John, Dane

Major Bob
See Astles, Robert

Major Bob
See D'Aubuisson, Roberto

Major, Charles 1856-1913 [WBD]
American author
* Caskoden, [Sir] Edwin

Major, Dagney
See Major, J. D.

Major, Geraldyn Hodges 1894- [CA]
American author
* Major, Gerri

Major, Gerri
See Major, Geraldyn Hodges

Major, J. D. 20th c. [MBF]
British author
* Hayward, Dagney
* Major, Dagney

Major, Jakab Gyula
See Mayer, Jakab Gyula

Major [or Mair], John 1470?-1550
[HPPN]
British educator and historian
* [The] Last of the Schoolmen

Major Mite
See Howerton, Clarence

[The] Major of St. Lo
See Howie, Thomas D.

Majorano, Gaetano 1703-1783 [SN,
WBD]
Italian singer
* Caffarelli
* [The] Insolent

Majors, Lee
See Yeary, Lee Harvey

Majors, Simon
See Fox, Gardner Francis

Mak, Marii
See Ferrari, Raquel

Makanowitzky, Barbara
See Norman, Barbara

Makarios III
See Mouskos, Mikhail

Makary
See Iranek-Osmecki, Kazimierz

Makathini, Elijah [RBE]
South African boxer
* Makathini, Tap Tap

Makathini, Tap Tap
See Makathini, Elijah

Makeles [The Butcher]
See Leo I

Makemie, Francis 1658-1708 [HPPN]
Irish-American clergyman
* [The] Apostle of Accomac
* [The] Saint Francis of Presbyterianism

Makemson, Donald Emmet 1915- [CA]
American historian and author
* Worcester, Donald E[mmet]

Makepeace, Joan
See Joan

Makepeace, Joanna
See York, Margaret Elizabeth

[The] Maker of Champions
See Cromwell, Dean

[The] Maker of Modern Egypt
See Baring, Evelyn [First Earl of
Cromer]

[The] Maker of Stars
See Bonesteele, Laura Justine

Makgill, [Sir] George 1868-? [WWL]
British author
* Grant, Francis
* Waite, Victor

Maki, Chico
See Maki, Ronald Patrick

Maki, Ronald Patrick 1939- [CEI, FHE,
HK]
Canadian-born hockey player
* Maki, Chico

Makley, Charles 20th c. [BLB]
American criminal
* Makley, Fat Charley

Makley, Fat Charley
See Makley, Charles

Makonnen, Ras Tafari 1891-1975 [NN]
Emperor of Ethiopia
* Haile Selassie
* [The] Lion of Judah

Makowicz, Adam
See Matyszkowicz, Adam

Makowsky, Harry Duquesne 1923-
[EJS]
French-born American baseball player
* Markell, Duke
* Markell, Harry Duquesne

Makumbi, Eseza 20th c. [IBW]
Ugandan-born actress and educator
* Makumbi, Esther

Makumbi, Esther
See Makumbi, Eseza

Mal
See Hancock, Malcolm

Mala
See Wise, Ray

Mala, Yenomdrah
See Byers, Charles Alma

Malachi
See Scott, [Sir] Walter

Malack, Muly
See Noah, Mordecai Manuel

Malacrida, Marchese 1890- [LAO]
Italian-born author
* Piermarini

Malagrida
See Petty, [Sir] William

Malagrowther, Malachi
See Scott, [Sir] Walter

Malakoff
See Johnson, Samuel

Malakoff
See Johnson, W. F.

Malakoff
See Johnston, W. F.

Malan, Adolph 1910- [BDW]
South African fighter pilot
* Malan, Sailor

Malan, Cesar Jean Salomon 1812-1894
[WBD]
British scholar
* Malan, Solomon Caesar

Malan, Renato Marco 1911-　[CA]
Italian-born author
* Mark Alan, Roy

Malan, Sailor
See Malan, Adolph

Malan, Solomon Caesar
See Malan, Cesar Jean Salomon

Malaparte, Curzio
See Suckert, Curzio

Malaparte, Curzio
See Suckert, Kurt Erich

Malara 16th c.　[SN]
Spanish poet
* [The] Betisian Menander

Malarcher, Cap
See Malarcher, David Julius

Malarcher, David Julius 1894-　[MK]
American baseball player
* Malarcher, Cap
* Malarcher, Gentleman Dave

Malarcher, Gentleman Dave
See Malarcher, David Julius

Malatesta, Guido 20th c.　[FDG]
Italian director
* Read [or Reed?], James

Malchus 223-304　[FFF, HN, WBD]
Greek scholar
* [The] Philosopher
* Porphyry

Malcolm
See Sinclair, Coll McLean

Malcolm, Charles
See Hincks, Cyril Malcolm

Malcolm, Dan
See Silverberg, Robert

Malcolm, [Sir] John 1769-1833　[HPPN]
Scottish colonial administrator and army officer
* [A] Traveller in the East

Malcolm, John
See Uren, Malcolm John Leggoe

Malcolm, Margaret
See Kuether, Edith Lyman

Malcolm the Maiden
See Malcolm IV

Malcolm X
See Little, Malcolm

Malcolm III 1024-1093　[FFF, RH, SN]
King of Scotland
* Canmore
* Great Head

Malcolm IV 1141-1165　[DHA, FFF, HPPN, SN]
King of Scotland
* [The] Maiden

Malcolm IV (cont.)
* [The] Maiden King
* Malcolm the Maiden

Malcolmson, Anne
See Von Storch, Anne B.

Maldclewith, Ronsby
See Smith, Byron Caldwell

Malden, Henry 19th c.　[PA]
Author
* Murray, Hamilton

Malden, Henry, Chapel Clerk
See James, Thomas

Malden, Karl
See Sekulovich, Mladen

Malden, R. H.
See Malden, Richard Henry

Malden, Richard Henry 1879-1951
[HFF]
British clergyman and author
* Malden, R. H.

Maldonado, Bob 20th c.　[BI]
American painter
* Ah-swan

Maldonado y Rodriguez, Edmundo
1910-1964　[GS]
Mexican bullfighter
* Tato de Mexico [Lisper from Mexico]

Male, Christopher Parr 19th c.　[HFN]
Author
* C. P. M.

Malebranche, Nicolas 1638-1715　[SN]
French philosopher
* [The] Plato of His Age

Malefammi, Baron
See Donati, Corso

Malek, Leona [Alford] 1878-1951　[BI]
American home economist
* Prudence Penny

Malerich, Edward P. 1940-　[CA, WD]
American actor and author
* Easton, Edward

Malesevich, Bronislaw 20th c.　[EF]
American football player
* Malesevich, Bronko

Malesevich, Bronko
See Malesevich, Bronislaw

Malet, Lucas
See Harrison, Mary St. Leger
[Kingsley]

Malet, Oriel
See Vaughan, Auriel Rosemary Malet

Malevole
See Shakespeare, William

Malherbe, Francois de 1555-1628　[NPS, SN]
French poet
* [The] Father of Modern French Poetry
* [The] Oracle of Good-Sense

Malherbe, Francois de (cont.)
* [The] Purist of Language
* [The] Tyrant of Words and Syllables

Mali
See Nair, V. Madhavan

Maliades
See Henry

Malick, Terrence 1943-　[CA]
American screenwriter, producer, director
* Whitney, David

Malicky, Lillian Joyce 1944-　[OP]
American opera singer
* Castle, Joyce

[A] Malignant Plant
See Philip IV [or Philippe]

Malik, Abdul
See De Coteau, Delano

Malik, Michael Abdul
See De Freitas, Michael

Malik Shah 11th c.　[WBD]
Sultan of the Seljuk Turks
* Jalal-al-Din [Majesty of Religion]

Malin, Peter
See Conner, [Patrick] Reardon

Malin, Peter
See Connor, Patrick Reardon

Malinche
See Malintzin

Malinche
See Marina, Dona Xaramillo

Malinovsky, Alexander 20th c.　[SFP]
Author
* Bogdanov, Alexander

Malins, M. H.
See Malins, Margery Helen

Malins, Margery Helen 20th c.　[ART]
British painter and illustrator
* Malins, M. H.

Malintzin 1501?-1550　[HPPN]
Mistress of Spanish explorer, Hernando Cortez
* Malinche
* Marina
* Marina, Dona

Maliszewski, Miguel 1948-　[AES]
Argentinian-born soccer player
* Maliszewski, Mike

Maliszewski, Mike
See Maliszewski, Miguel

Malkoff, Buzz
See Malkoff, Jay

Malkoff, Jay 20th c.　[SMG]
American football team physician
* Malkoff, Buzz

[The] Mall of Italy
See Hannibal

Malla
See Garcia y Diaz, Agustin

Mallard, Bo
See Mallard, Louis

Mallard, Louis 20th c.   [BBH]
American basketball player and coach
* Mallard, Bo

Mallarme, Stephane 1842-1898   [CD]
French poet
* De Ponty, Marguerite
* Satin, Miss

Mallecho, Miching, Esq.
See Shelley, Percy Bysshe

Malleolus
See Hammerlein, Felix

Malleson, [Lieut. Colonel] George Bruce
19th c.   [HPPN]
British army officer
* One Who Has Served Under Sir
  Charles Napier

Malleson, Lucy Beatrice 1899-1973
[CA, CC, WW]
British author
* Egerton, Lucy
* Gilbert, Anthony
* Keith, J. Kilmeny
* Meredith, Anne

Mallet, David
See Malloch, David

Mallette, Gertrude Ethel 1887-   [BI,
CCL]
Canadian-American author
* Gregg, Alan
* Larssen, Pedar

Malleus Arianorum
See Hilary

Malleus Asiaticorum
See Hammer-Purgstall, Joseph Freiherr
von

Malleus Hereticorum
See Ailly, Pierre d'

Malleus Hereticorum
See Caster, Francois

Malleus Hereticorum
See Heigerlin, Johannes

Malleus Monachorum
See Cromwell, Thomas [Earl of Essex]

Malleus Scotorum
See Edward I

Malley, Ern [joint pseudonym with
Harold Stewart]
See McAuley, James Phillip

Malley, Ern [joint pseudonym with
James Phillip McAuley]
See Stewart, Harold

Malliard, Mlle. 18th c.   [RH]
French actress
* [The] Goddess of Liberty

Mallinckrodt, Edward 1845-1928
[HPPN]
American chemical manufacturer
* [The] Ammonia King

Mallinson, Russell
See Stannard, Russell

Mallison, William M.   [FFF, PA]
American writer
* O'Pake

Malloch, David 1705-1765   [WBD]
Scottish poet
* Mallet, David

Malloch, George Reston 1875-?   [WWL]
British author, playwright, poet
* Paulus, Jan

Malloch, Peter
See Duncan, W[illiam] Murdoch

Mallock, W. H.
See Mallock, William Hurrell

Mallock, William Hurrell 1849-1923
[LC, NPS]
British author
* Mallock, W. H.
* Moore, Wentworth

Mallon, Henry J. 1868?-1950   [BI]
American educator
* Vallesian, [Brother]

Mallon, Isabel Allderdice [Sloan]
1857-1898   [DNA]
American author and journalist
* Ashmore, Ruth

Mallon, Mary ?-1938   [BL]
American disease carrier
* Typhoid Mary

Mallonee, Ben
See Mallonee, Howard Bennett

Mallonee, Howard Bennett 1894-   [BE]
American baseball player
* Mallonee, Ben
* Mallonee, Lefty

Mallonee, Lefty
See Mallonee, Howard Bennett

Mallory, Boots
See Mallory, Patricia

Mallory, Bull
See Mallory, William Neely

Mallory, Drew
See Garfield, Brian [Francis] Wynne

Mallory, James Baugh [Jim] 1918-
[BE]
American baseball player
* Mallory, Sunny Jim

Mallory, Mark
See Reynolds, Dallas McCord

Mallory, Memphis Bill
See Mallory, William Neely

Mallory, Patricia 1913?-1958   [BEW]
American actress
* Mallory, Boots

Mallory, Sheldon 1953-   [SMG]
American baseball player
* Mallory, Shell

Mallory, Shell
See Mallory, Sheldon

Mallory, Sunny Jim
See Mallory, James Baugh [Jim]

Mallory, William Neely 1901-1945   [FB,
HPPN]
American football player
* Mallory, Bull
* Mallory, Memphis Bill

Mallowan, A[gatha] C[hristie]
See Christie, Agatha [Mary Clarissa]

Malloy, [Archibald] Alex[ander]
1886-1961   [BE]
American baseball player
* Malloy, Lick

Malloy, Durable Mike
See Malloy, Michael [Mike]

Malloy, Indestructible Mike
See Malloy, Michael [Mike]

Malloy, John 1888?-1940   [FC, SC]
American actor
* Wray, John

Malloy, Lick
See Malloy, [Archibald] Alex[ander]

Malloy, Marie Louise ?-1947   [HPPN]
American journalist
* Wink, Josh

Malloy, Michael [Mike] ?-1933   [CEC,
HPPN]
American murder victim
* [The] Durable Alcoholic
* Malloy, Durable Mike
* Malloy, Indestructible Mike
* [The] Somniferous Malloy

Malm, Margaretha
See Pettersson, H. Bertil N.

Malmberg, Carl 1904-   [CA, SAT]
American author
* Trent, Timothy

Malmberg, Harry William 1926-   [BE]
American baseball player
* Malmberg, Swede

Malmberg, Swede
See Malmberg, Harry William

Malmquist, Eve Theodor 1915-   [IAW]
Swedish educator and author
* E. M.

Malo, Gina
See Flynn, Janet

Malone, Andrew E.
See Byrne, Laurence Patrick

Malone, Art Lee 20th c.
American football player
* Leroy from Eloy

Malone, Carroll
See McBurney, M.

Malone, Carroll
See McBurney, William B.

Malone, Cement Head
See Malone, John F.

Malone, Dorothy
See Maloney, Dorothy

Malone, Edmund 1741-1812 [NPS]
Critic and author
* Marcellus

Malone, Elmer Taylor, Jr. 1943- [CA]
American poet
* Malone, Ted

Malone, Ferguson G. 1842-1905 [BE]
American baseball player and manager
* Malone, Fergy

Malone, Fergy
See Malone, Ferguson G.

Malone, James H. 1887?-1955 [BI, HPPN]
American detective
* Malone, Shooey

Malone, John F. 20th c.
American FBI agent
* Malone, Cement Head

Malone, Karl 20th c. [WP 4-11-85]
American basketball player
* Malone, Mailman

Malone, Katie 1863-1949 [BI]
American nun
* Stanislaus, [Sister]

Malone, Lew[is Aloysius] 1897-1973 [BE]
American baseball player
* Ryan, Lew

Malone, Louis
See MacNeice, [Frederick] Louis

Malone, M.
See Cream, [Dr.] Thomas Neil

Malone, Mailman
See Malone, Karl

Malone, Mervin Haskell 1927- [CWG]
American country-western performer
* Malone, Red

Malone, Michael ?-1891? [PI]
Irish writer and poet
* M.

Malone, Michael F. 20th c. [HPPN]
American federal agent
* [The] Great Masquerader
* Lepito, Michael [or Mike]
* Malone, Mysterious Mike

Malone, Michael Francis 1950- [DC]
Australian-born cricketer
* Malone, Mick

Malone, Mick
See Malone, Michael Francis

Malone, Mr.
See Guion, Raymond

Malone, Mysterious Mike
See Malone, Michael F.

Malone, Pat
See Malone, Perce Leigh

Malone, Patricia
See Marsden-Clark, Patricia

Malone, Perce Leigh 1902-1943 [AS, BE, HPPN, PB]
American baseball player
* [The] Black Knight of the Border
* Malone, Pat

Malone, Percy Sylvester
See Caswell, Wilbur Larremore

Malone, Pick
See Maloney, Andrew Pickens

Malone, Red
See Malone, Mervin Haskell

Malone, Shooey
See Malone, James H.

Malone, Ted
See Malone, Elmer Taylor, Jr.

Malone, Ted
See Russell, Frank Alden

Maloney, Andrew Pickens 1893?-1962 [BEW]
American theatrical performer
* Malone, Pick

Maloney, David Wilfred 1956- [SMG]
Canadian-born hockey player
* [The] Kid

Maloney, Dorothy 1925- [BDF, FC, WEF]
American actress
* Malone, Dorothy

Maloney, Francis [Joseph] T[erence] 20th c. [WGT]
British author
* Terry

Maloney, Happy
See Maloney, Patrick

Maloney, James Monte 20th c. [PMJ]
American bandleader
* Joy, Jimmy

Maloney, Janette 1905- [THR]
American-born actress and singer
* Gilmore, Janette

Maloney, Pat
See Markun, Patricia Maloney

Maloney, Patrick 20th c. [BLB]
American underworld figure
* Maloney, Happy

Maloney, Ralph Liston 1927-1973 [CA]
American author
* Liston, Jack

Maloney, Terry 20th c. [SFP]
Author
* Rubios, Jose

Maloney, Tighe
See Macbeath, Innis [Stewart]

Malossis, Auguste Paul Poulet [PA]
Author
* Rouillon, Paul

Maloy, Biff
See Maloy, Paul Augustus

Maloy, Paul Augustus 1892-1976 [BE]
American baseball player
* Maloy, Biff

Malpass, Barbara Ann 20th c. [BL]
American runaway who masqueraded as a male
* Williams, Charles Richard

Malpede, Karen
See Taylor, Karen Malpede

Malpott, Virgule
See Ghnassia, Maurice [Jean-Henri]

Malraux, [Georges-] Andre 1901-1976 [CAP, EWL]
French author
* Berger, [Colonel] A.

Malser, Hans
See Rosegger, Petri Kettenfeier

Malsin, Lane Bryant 20th c. [HPPN]
Lithuanian-American fashion designer and business executive
* Bryant, Lane

Malta, Alexander
See Lagger, Alexander

Maltby, Edward 1770-1859 [HPPN]
British clergyman
* Hellenophilus

Maltby, H. F.
See Maltby, Henry Francis

Maltby, Henry Francis 1880-1963 [LC]
South African-born actor and playwright
* Maltby, H. F.

Malte-Brun [or Maltebrun], Conrad
See Bruun, Malte Conrad

Malten, Therese
See Mueller, Therese

Malthus, Thomas Robert 1766-1834 [HPPN]
British economist
* [The] Economic Pessimist

Maltitz, Hermann von
See Klencke, Hermann

Maltzan, Adolf Georg Otto von 1877-1927 [WBD]
German diplomat
* Maltzan, Ago von

Maltzan, Ago von
See Maltzan, Adolf Georg Otto von

Maltzberger, Gordon Ralph 1912-1974 [BE]
American baseball player
* Maltzberger, Maltzy

Maltzberger, Maltzy
See Maltzberger, Gordon Ralph

Malu
See Lubin, Maurice Alcibiade

Malumba, Voodoo
See Reese, Jerry

Malvern, Gladys ?-1962 [CA]
American author and actress
* Corbin, Sabra Lee
* Von Klopp, Vahrah

Malyon, Eily
See Lees-Craston, Eily Sophie

Malzberg, Barry N[orman] 1939- [CA, SFL, SFP]
American author
* O'Donnell, K. M.
* Schaefer, Robin

Mama Can Can
See Rainey, Gertrude Malissa Nix [Pridgett]

Mama Cass
See Cohen, Ellen Naomi

Mama G.
See Davis, Grania

Mama Lu
See Parks, Louise

Mama, Officer
See Schnabel, Martha

Mamalick, Gordon 1931- [IWM]
Canadian musician
* Mann, Gordie

[The] Mama's Boy
See Leiner, Benjamin

[The] Mambo Kid
See Puente, Ernest, Jr.

[The] Mambo King
See Prado, [Domase] Perez

Mambrino
See McKinney, H. D.

Mamin, Dmitrii Narkisovich 1852-1912 [BI, ICB]
Russian author
* Mamin-Siberiak
* Sibiriak

Mamin-Siberiak
See Mamin, Dmitrii Narkisovich

Mammarella, Anthony [Tony] 20th c.
American songwriter
* September, Anthony

[El] Mamon [The Nursling]
See De La Cruz, Pedro

Mamoun, al- 786-833 [SN]
Seventh Caliph of Baghdad
* [The] Augustus of Arabian Literature
* [The] Father of Arabic Literature

[A] Man
See Barker, Joseph

[The] Man
See Friedhofer, Hugo Wilhelm

[The] Man
See Lucania, Salvatore

[The] Man
See Morris, Steveland

[The] Man
See Musial, Stanislaus

[The] Man
See Sinatra, Francis Albert [Frank]

[A] Man
See Walpole, Horatio [Fourth Earl of Orford]

[The] Man about Town
See Muldoon, William H.

[The] Man Behind the Frown
See McClellan, John

[The] Man Behind the Music
See Jones, Quincy Delight, Jr.

[The] Man Behind the Sixty-Four Thousand Dollar Question
See Mendelson, Harold

[The] Man Behind the Smile
See Hoffman, Dustin

[The] Man Eater
See Keseberg, Lewis

[A] Man for all Seasons
See More, [Sir] Thomas

Man from Maine
See Blaine, James Gillespie

[The] Man from Margaree
See Coady, Moses Michael

[The] Man from Missouri
See Truman, Harry S.

[The] Man From Nowhere
See Kipling, [Joseph] Rudyard

[The] Man from Steamtown
See Blount, Francis Nelson

[The] Man from the North
See Hobman, Joseph Burton

Man from the Wine Country
See Adenauer, Konrad

Man From TRASH
See Kissinger, Henry Alfred

[The] Man in Black
See Cash, John R. [Johnny]

[A] Man in Business
See Hope, John

[The] Man in the Brown Suit
See Rupp, Adolph

[The] Man in the Claret Colored Coat
See Gould, Edward S.

[The] Man in the Cloak
See Mangan, James Clarence

[The] Man in the Front-Row
See Henderson, Henrietta

[The] Man in the Green Suit
See O'Doul, Francis Joseph [Frank]

[The] Man in the Iron Mask
See Hartnett, Charles Leo

[The] Man in the Iron Mask?
See Mattioli, Ercole Antonio

[The] Man in the Iron Mask
See Moody, William Vaughan

[The] Man in the Iron Mask
See Sullivan, Edward Vincent

[The] Man in the Mask
See Moore, Clayton

[The] Man in the Moon
See Anstruther, Capt.

[The] Man in the Moon
See Foe, Daniel

[The] Man in the Moon
See Thomson, William

Man in the Polka-Dot Tie
See Moynihan, [Daniel] Patrick

[The] Man in the Straw Hat
See Chevalier, Maurice Auguste

[The] Man in the Velvet Suit
See Williams, William Holt [Billy]

[The] Man Milliner
See Henry III [or Henri]

Man Mountain Dean
See Leavitt, Frank S.

[The] Man Mountain of Professional Ball
See Earp [or Earpe?], Francis

[The] Man Mouse
See More, Henry

Man o' War
See Rice, Edgar Charles

[A] Man of a Million
See De Quincey, Thomas

[The] Man of a Thousand Curves
See Sain, John Franklin [Johnny]

[The] Man of a Thousand Faces
See Chaney, Alonso

[The] Man of a Thousand Faces
See Guinness, [Sir] Alec

[The] Man of a Thousand Moves
See Baylor, Elgin

[The] Man of Bath
See Allen, Ralph

[The] Man of Black Renown
See Wilberforce, William

[The] Man of Blood
See Charles I

[The] Man of Blood
See Simmons, Thomas

[The] Man of Blood and Iron
See Bismarck, Otto Eduard Leopold von

[A] Man of Business
See Ashton, John

[A] **Man of Business**
See Davys, John

[The] **Man of Business**
See Decker, T.

[A] **Man of Business**
See Dicker, Thomas

[The] **Man of Business**
See Rathbone, William

[The] **Man of Chios**
See Homer

[The] **Man of December**
See Bonaparte, Charles Louis Napoleon

[The] **Man of Destiny**
See Bonaparte, Napoleon

[The] **Man of Destiny**
See Cleveland, [Stephen] Grover

Man of Destiny
See Nasser, Gamal Abdel

[The] **Man of Dimension**
See Connors, Kevin Joseph

[A] **Man of Fashion**
See Mills, John

[The] **Man of Feeling**
See Mackenzie, Henry

Man of Fire
See Simon

[The] **Man of Ghent**
See Guizot, M.

[The] **Man of God**
See Alexis [or Alexius]

[The] **Man of Great Heart**
See Hoover, Herbert Clark

[The] **Man of Happy Unhappy Answers**
See Tarlton, Richard

[The] **Man of Independence**
See Truman, Harry S.

[The] **Man of Iron**
See Bismarck, Otto Eduard Leopold von

[A] **Man of Kent**
See Cowtan, Robert

Man of Kent
See Nicoll, [Sir] William Robertson

[The] **Man of Many Faces**
See Weisenfreund, Muni

[The] **Man of Many Medals**
See Goethe, Johann Wolfgang von

[The] **Man of Mass Confusion**
See Kim, Chin Ho

[The] **Man of Mercy**
See Schweitzer, [Dr.] Albert

[The] **Man of Mutinies**
See Bligh, William

[The] **Man of One Thousand Voices**
See Chatton, Sydney

[The] **Man of Reason**
See Paine, Thomas

[The] **Man of Ross**
See Higginson, Stephen

[The] **Man of Ross**
See Kyrle, John

[The] **Man of Sedan**
See Bonaparte, Charles Louis Napoleon

[The] **Man of Sedition**
See Claude, Jean

[The] **Man of Silence**
See Bonaparte, Charles Louis Napoleon

[The] **Man of Sin**
See Cromwell, Oliver

[The] **Man of Steel**
See Origen

[The] **Man of Steel**
See Zaleski, Anthony Florian

[The] **Man of Stove**
See Thompson, Benjamin [Count Rumford]

[The] **Man of the Black Manifesto**
See Forman, James

Man of the Century
See Shaw, George Bernard

[The] **Man of the Migrants**
See Chavez, Cesar

[The] **Man of the People**
See Fox, Charles James

[The] **Man of the People**
See Henry, Patrick

[The] **Man of the People**
See Jefferson, Thomas

[The] **Man of the People**
See Lincoln, Abraham

[The] **Man of the People**
See Thomson, William

[The] **Man of the Revolution**
See Adams, Samuel

[The] **Man of the Second November**
See Bonaparte, Napoleon

[The] **Man of the Third Republic**
See Bonaparte, Charles Louis Napoleon

Man of the Town Meeting
See Adams, Samuel

Man of the Wooden Walls
See Drake, [Sir] Francis

[The] **Man of Truth**
See Thomson, Charles

[A] **Man of 25**
See Keegan, John

Man of Two Worlds
See Raleigh, [Sir] Walter

[The] **Man of Wax**
See Moore, George

Man on a Winged Horse
See Goethe, Johann Wolfgang von

[The] **Man on Horseback**
See Boulanger, Georges Ernest Jean Marie

[The] **Man on Horseback**
See Roosevelt, Theodore [Teddy]

[The] **Man on the Ledge**
See Warde, John

[The] **Man on the Street**
See Edelson, Dave

[The] **Man Salamander**
See Potter, Richard

[The] **Man Sent from God**
See Franson, Fredrik

[The] **Man to See**
See Rothstein, Arnold

[The] **Man to See in New Jersey**
See Zwillman, Abner

[The] **Man to Whom Hall-Moody Owes Most**
See Penick, [Issac] Newt[on]

[The] **Man Uptown**
See Rothstein, Arnold

[The] **Man Who Banned the Corset**
See Poiret, Paul

[The] **Man Who Broke a Thousand Chains**
See Burns, Robert Elliott

[The] **Man Who Broke Purple**
See Friedman, William Frederic

[The] **Man Who Broke the Bank at Monte Carlo**
See Wells, Charles

[The] **Man Who Broke the Mold**
See Tanaka, Kakuei

[The] **Man Who Built San Francisco**
See Ralston, William Chapman

[The] **Man Who Bumped Fulbright**
See Bumpers, Dale

[The] **Man Who Can Say Anything and Make Everybody Like It**
See Rogers, Will[iam Penn Adair]

[The] **Man Who Cannot Be Lifted**
See Coulon, Johnny

[The] **Man Who Cleaned Up Nashville**
See Loser, J. Carlton

[The] **Man Who Freed Music**
See Beethoven, Ludwig Van

[The] **Man Who Gets Things Done**
See Moses, Robert

[The] **Man Who had it Won**
See Dewey, Thomas Edmund

[The] **Man Who Hated Sherlock Holmes**
See Doyle, [Sir] Arthur Conan

[The] Man Who Invented Panama
See Bunau-Varilla, Phillipe Jean

[The] Man Who Invented the 20th
Century
See Tesla, Nikola

[The] Man Who Invented Tomorrow
See Wells, Herbert George

[The] Man Who Is Always Somebody
Else
See Weisenfreund, Muni

[The] Man Who Keeps his Eyes and
Ears Open
See Beecher, Henry Ward

[The] Man Who Killed Kennedy
See Oswald, Lee Harvey

[The] Man Who Lit Up Broadway
See Gaess, William C., Jr.

Man Who Lost His Halo
See Kissinger, Henry Alfred

Man Who Made A Mountain Out of
Sex
See Kinsey, Alfred Charles

[The] Man Who Made the Trombone
Laugh
See Raderman, Harry

[The] Man Who Menaced America
See Yamamoto, Isoroku

[The] Man Who Never Died
See Hagglund [or Hillstrom?], Joel

[The] Man Who Never Forgets
See Chernenko, Konstantin

[The] Man Who Owned Broadway
See Cohan, George Michael

[The] Man Who Resurrected Troy
See Schliemann, Heinrich

[The] Man Who Sold the Eiffel Tower
See Miller, Robert

[The] Man Who Started It All
See Ellsberg, Daniel

[The] Man Who Sued Baseball
See Flood, Curtis Charles

[The] Man Who Swindled Goering
See Meegeren, Hans van

[The] Man Who Talked With the Dead
See Ford, Arthur A.

[The] Man who taught America to sing
See Waring, Fred

[The] Man Who Taught the Navy to
Think
See Luce, Stephen Bleekard

[The] Man Who Took a Chance
See Brodie, Steve

[The] Man Who Walked on Wings
See Locklear, Omer

[The] Man Who was a Private
See Quincy, Samuel Miller

[The] Man Who Was Never Asked
Back
See Harris, James Thomas

[The] Man Who was Warned
See Begbie, [Edward] Harold

[The] Man Who Westernized Japan
See Saionji, [Prince] Kimmochi

[The] Man Who Would Be King
See Roosevelt, Theodore [Teddy]

[The] Man Who Would Not Die
See Young, James Arthur

[The] Man with a Golden Needle
See Goldhirsch, Harry Lewis

[The] Man With A Hoe
See Wallace, Henry A[gard]

Man With a Memory
See Pound, Roscoe

[The] Man With a Message
See Carnegey, Dale

[The] Man with a Million Friends
See Myrick, David Luke

[The] Man with a Thousand Fingers
See Hayes, Edgar Junius

[The] Man with a Thousand Songs
See Donovan, Tony

[The] Man with a Thousand Voices
See Graham, Frank

[The] Man with a Thousand Voices
See Masilongan, Christobal

[The] Man With a Wig
See Parr, Samuel

[The] Man With 586 Blood Brothers
See Young, Ernest

[The] Man with no Master but God
See Delamarre, Victor

[The] Man With Qualities
See Wittgenstein, Ludwig

[The] Man with Six Senses
See Kraus, Josef

[The] Man With the Finest Sneer in the
Movies
See Rathbone, Basil

[The] Man with the Funny Horn
See Mosley, Lawrence Leo

[The] Man with the Golden Arm
See Davis, A. W.

[The] Man With the Golden Arm
See Koufax, Sanford [Sandy]

[The] Man with the Golden Gut
See Silverman, Fred

[The] Man With the Hard Head
See Carroll, Billy

[The] Man With the Hoe
See Millet, Jean Francois

[The] Man With the Hunting Horn
See Moorman, Watt

[The] Man With the Iron Grip
See Vansittart, Charles

[The] Man with the Leather Breeches
See Fox, George

[The] Man with the Midas Touch
See Rickard, George Lewis

[The] Man with the Million Dollar
Hands
See Garcia, Frank

[The] Man With the Miracle Mind
See Dunninger, Joseph

[The] Man With the Mustache
See Rose, Mauri

[The] Man with the Perfect Profile
See Brough, Spangler Arlington

Man With The Pink Hair
See Veeck, William Louis, Jr. [Bill]

[The] Man with the Sling
See Randolph, John

Man With the Wry Eye
See Kissinger, Henry Alfred

[The] Man With Whiskers
See Barboncito, Chief

[The] Man without a Skin
See Cumberland, Richard

[A] Man without a Spleen
See Chekhov, Anton [Pavlovich]

[The] Man Without a Theory
See Tudor, Antony

[The] Man You Love To Hate
See Von Nordenwald, Erich Oswald
Hans Carl Stroheim

Mana-Zucca
See Zuckermann, Augusta

Manach [or Maynard], Abbe 18th c.
French clergyman and author
* [A] French Missionary

[The] Management Troubleshooter
See Lewis, [An]Drew, [Jr.]

Managing Clerk
See Spero, Leopold

Manaois, Joseph 1903- [HPPN]
Philippine composer and conductor
* Don Jose

Manassa Jack Dempsey
See Dempsey, William Harrison

[The] Manassa Mauler
See Dempsey, William Harrison

Manastersky, Timothy 1929- [CEI]
Canadian-born hockey player
* Manastersky, Tom

Manastersky, Tom
See Manastersky, Timothy

Mance, Elizabeth Hope 1883- [WWL]
British author
* Hope, Elizabeth

Mance, Julian Clifford, Jr. 1928-
[DAM, EJ, PMJ]
American jazz musician
* Mance, Junior

Mance, Junior
See Mance, Julian Clifford, Jr.

[El] Manchao [The Spotted One]
See Parrondo, Tomas

Manchecourt
See Lavedan, Henri L. E.

Manchee, Carol M. [Cassidy] 20th c.
[CCL]
Canadian author
* Cole, Carol Cassidy

[El] Manchequito [The Little Fellow from La Mancha]
See Martinez y Pingarron, Candido

[A] Manchester Man
See Lamb, J.

[A] Manchester Manufacturer
See Bleckley, Henry

[A] Manchester Manufacturer
See Cobden, Richard

[The] Manchester Poet
See Swain, Charles

[The] Manchester Prison Philanthropist
See Wright, Thomas

[The] Manchester Prophet
See Hall, Ellis

Manchester, William 1922- [HPPN]
American historian, author, educator
* Billa
* Sashweight
* Slim
* Tripod

Manchet, Eliane
See Schaaf, Eliane

Mancini, Boom Boom
See Mancini, Lenny

Mancini, Boom Boom
See Mancini, Ray

Mancini, Lenny 20th c.
American boxer
* Mancini, Boom Boom

Mancini, Pat McNees
See McNees, Pat

Mancini, Ray 1961?-
American boxer
* Mancini, Boom Boom

Mancini, Tony
See England, Cecil Louis

Manco Capac 1500?-1544 [HPPN, WBD]
Ruler of Peru
* Inca Manco
* Yupanqui, Manco Inca

[El] Manco de Lapanto
See Cervantes Saavedra, Miguel de

Mancuso, August Rodney 1905- [BE, PB]
American baseball player
* Mancuso, Blackie
* Mancuso, Gus

Mancuso, Blackie
See Mancuso, August Rodney

Mancuso, Felix 1913- [CEI]
Canadian-born hockey player
* Mancuso, Gus

Mancuso, Gus
See Mancuso, August Rodney

Mancuso, Gus
See Mancuso, Felix

Mancuso, Gus
See Mancuso, Ronald Bernard

Mancuso, Ronald Bernard 1933- [DAM, EJ]
American jazz musician
* Mancuso, Gus

Mand, Cyril [joint pseudonym with Richard Levin]
See Hahn, George R.

Mand, Cyril [joint pseudonym with George R. Hahn]
See Levin, Richard

Mand [or Maend], Ewald [or Evald] 1906- [CA]
Estonian-born clergyman and author
* Kalmus, Ain

Mandar, Michael Phillips 1759-1823 [PA]
Author
* Theophile

[The] Mandarin
See Navin, Frank

Mandel, Georges
See Rothchild, Jeroboam

Mandel, Joseph 1880-1954 [BDF, FC, FD]
Austrian-born director
* May, Joe

Mandel, Leon 1928- [CA]
American author
* Dalmas, John

Mandela, Winnie 1935?- [TI 1-6-86]
South African anti-apartheid leader
* [The] Mother of the Nation

Mandelbaum, Fredericka 1818?-1889? [BLB, CEC]
American criminal
* Mandelbaum, Marm
* Mandelbaum, Mother

Mandelbaum, Marm
See Mandelbaum, Fredericka

Mandelbaum, Mother
See Mandelbaum, Fredericka

Mandelkorn, Eugenia Miller 1916- [CA]
American author
* Miller, Eugenia

Mandell, Sammy
See Mandella, Samuel R.

Mandella, Samuel R. 1904-1961? [BX, RBE, WBC]
American boxer
* Mandell, Sammy
* [The] Rockford Sheik

Mander, Lionel 1888-1946 [F1, FC, SC]
British actor
* Mander, Luther
* Mander, Miles
* Miles, Luther

Mander, Luther
See Mander, Lionel

Mander, Miles
See Mander, Lionel

Manders, Automatic Jack
See Manders, John

Manders, Clarence 20th c. [EF]
American football player
* Manders, Pug

Manders, Dave 20th c.
American football player
* Manders, Mad Dog

Manders, Harry
See Farmer, Philip Jose

Manders, John 1910-1977 [BI, FB]
American football player
* Manders, Automatic Jack

Manders, Mad Dog
See Manders, Dave

Manders, Pug
See Manders, Clarence

Mandeville, Bernard de 1670?-1733 [DEA]
British author
* Phil-Porney

Mandeville, [Sir] John 1300-1372 [NPS, UH]
British author and explorer
* [The] Bruce of the Fourteenth Century
* [The] Lying Traveller

Mandeville, John
See Haines, E[dwin] Irvine

Mandich, Jim 1948- [SMG]
American football player
* Mandich, Mad Dog

Mandich, Mad Dog
See Mandich, Jim

Mandot, Baker Boy
See Mandot, Joe

Mandot, Joe 1891-1956 [BX]
American boxer
* Mandot, Baker Boy

Mandrake, Ethel Belle
See Thurman, Wallace

Mandrake the Magician
See Mueller, Donald Frederick

Mandrepelias, Loizos
See Hartocollis, Peter

[The] Maneater
See Packer, Alfred

Manera, Jesus Franco 20th c. [WF]
Director
* Franco, Jess

Manery, Randy 1949- [SMG]
Canadian-born hockey player
* Manery, Straw

Manery, Straw
See Manery, Randy

Manet, Edouard 1832-1883 [HPPN]
French painter
* [The] Fundamentalist
* [The] Proper Iconoclast

Maneta
See Loison, Louis Henri

Manetta, Fess
See Manetta, Manuel

Manetta, Manuel 1889-1969 [WWJ]
American jazz musician
* Manetta, Fess

Manetti, Lido 1899-1928 [SC]
Italian-born actor
* Kent, Arnold

Manfred
See Preston, Elliott W.

Manfred, Frederick Feikema
See Feikema, Frederick

Manfred, Robert
See Marx, Erica Elizabeth

Mangan, James Clarence 1803-1849
[PI]
Irish poet
* Clarence
* J. C. M.
* Lageniensis
* [The] Man in the Cloak
* Monos
* [The] Mourner
* Terrae Filius
* Vacuus
* [A] Yankee

Mangano, Dago Lawrence
See Mangano, Lawrence

Mangano, Lawrence 20th c. [BLB,
PHM]
American underworld figure
* Mangano, Dago Lawrence

Mangano, Silvana 1930-
Italian actress
* [The] Most Beautiful Woman in the
World

Mangasarian, Flora 1880?-1968 [THR]
Turkish-born actress and singer
* Zabelle, Flora

Mangeur [or Comeston]
See Pierre

Mangin, Edward ?-1852 [PI]
Irish poet
* E. M.

Mangione, Gap
See Mangione, Gaspare Charles

Mangione, Gaspare Charles 1938- [EJ7]
American jazz musician
* [The] Happy Honker
* Mangione, Gap

Mangrum, Dandy
See Mangrum, Jim

Mangrum, Jim 1948- [RM, RO2]
American singer
* Mangrum, Dandy

Mangual, Jose Manuel 1952- [SMG,
WWB]
Puerto Rican-born baseball player
* Mangual, Pepe

Mangual, Pepe
See Mangual, Jose Manuel

Mangum, Blackie
See Mangum, Leon Allen

Mangum, Ernest G. 20th c. [SMG]
American football player
* Mangum, Pete

Mangum, Leon Allen 1898-1974 [BE]
American baseball player
* Mangum, Blackie

Mangum, Pete
See Mangum, Ernest G.

Manhattan
See Scoville, Joseph A.

Manhattan's Mad Bomber
See Metesky, George Peter

Manhoff, Bill
See Manhoff, Wilton

Manhoff, Wilton 1919-1974 [CA]
American playwright
* Manhoff, Bill

[The] Maniac
See Shore, Edward William [Eddie]

Maniere, J. E.
See Giraudoux, Jean [Hippolyte]

Manigault, G. 19th c. [PA]
Author
* Saint Cecilia

Manik
See Memon, Munir Ahmed

[The] Manikin
See Ellis, Welbore

Manila Boy
See Santiago, Tomas

Manili
See Ruiz, Manuel

Manilow, Barry
See Pincus, Barry Allen

Manion, Clyde Jennings 1896-1967 [BE]
American baseball player
* Manion, Pete

Manion, Pete
See Manion, Clyde Jennings

Manion, Red
See Friedman, Max Motel

Manivannan
See Naa Parthasarathy, Naarayana-
Parthasarathy

Mankad, Mulvantrai 1917- [EC]
Indian cricketer
* Mankad, Vinoo

Mankad, Vinoo
See Mankad, Mulvantrai

Manke, Douglas Everine 1911-1955
[HPPN]
American authority on cable codes
* Manke, Lanky

Manke, Lanky
See Manke, Douglas Everine

Mankiewicz, Herman 1897-1953
American screenwriter and journalist
* Mankiewicz, Mank

Mankiewicz, Mank
See Mankiewicz, Herman

Mankittrick, Richard Kendall [PA]
Author
* R. K. M.

Mankowska, Joyce Kells Batten 1919-
[CAP]
Scottish-born author
* Batten, Joyce Mortimer

Manley, Charles 1830-1916 [SC]
Irish-born actor
* Manley, Daddy

Manley, Daddy
See Manley, Charles

Manley, Dexter 20th c. [NW 9-5-83]
American football player
* Mr. D.

Manley, Jack
See Webb, Charles Hull

Manley, Mary de la Riviere 1663?-1724
[HPPN, SFL, WGT]
British playwright
* Eginardus
* J. B.
* Lovemore, [Sir] Charles
* Rivella

Manley, Ruth Rodney King 1907?-1973
[CA]
American poet and author
* King, Ruth Rodney

Manlio
See Helfrich-Guberti, Manlio

Manlius
See Douglas, John

Manlius
See Gore, Christopher

Manly, Charles Matthews 1876-1927 [HPPN]
American engineer
* [The] Father of the Radial Engine

Manly, Marline
See Rathborne, St. George Henry

Mann, A. Chester
See Roberts, Philip Ilott

Mann, A. Sufferan
See Bangs, John Kendrick

Mann, Abby
See Goodman, Abraham

Mann, Abel
See Creasey, John

Mann, Anthony [or Anton]
See Bundsmann, Anton [or Emil]

Mann, Avery
See Breetveld, Jim Patrick

Mann, Ben Garth 1915- [BE]
American baseball player
* Mann, Red

Mann, Bert
See Mann, Robert E.

Mann, Charles
See Graham, Roger Phillips

Mann, D. J.
See Freedman, James Dillet

Mann, Deborah
See Bloom, Ursula [Harvey]

Mann, Delos H. 1824-1906 [DNA]
American author and physician
* Gray, Rosalie

Mann, Edward
See Fried, Emanuel

Mann, Frank Hollister 20th c. [BBH]
American athletic trainer
* Mann, Skipper

Mann, Golo
See Mann, Gottfried

Mann, Gordie
See Mamalick, Gordon

Mann, Gottfried 1909- [CA]
German historian and author
* Mann, Golo

Mann, H. Leigh
See Lehman, Helen Miller

Mann, Hank
See Liebermann, David

Mann, Henry J. 1843-1878 [FFF, HPPN]
British actor
* Montague, Harry
* Montague, Henry James

Mann, Herbie
See Solomon, Herbert Jay

Mann, Horace 1796-1859 [HPPN]
American educator, legislator, attorney
* [The] Father of the American Public School
* Our Nation's First Educator

Mann, Jack
See Vivian, Evelyn Charles H.

Mann, James R. 1856-1922 [HPPN]
American politician
* [The] Father of the Mann Act
* [The] Father of the Mann-Elkins Act

Mann, Larnard 20th c. [BBH]
American athletic trainer
* Mann, Lon

Mann, Lon
See Mann, Larnard

Mann, Manfred
See Leibowitz, Michael

Mann, Milton
See Graham, Roger Phillips

Mann, Patricia
See Earnshaw, Patricia

Mann, Patrick
See Waller, Leslie

Mann, Paul
See Liebmann, Yisrol Paul Mann

Mann, Peggy
See Germano, Margaret

Mann, Red
See Mann, Ben Garth

Mann, Rheta
See Zell, Mrs.

Mann, Richard [Dick] 1934- [HPPN]
American motorcycle racer
* [The] Motorcycle Ace

Mann, Robert E. 1902- [ASC]
American composer and comedian
* Mann, Bert

Mann, Skipper
See Mann, Frank Hollister

Mann, Theodore
See Goldman, Theodore

Mann, Thomas 1875-1955 [TC]
German author
* Thomas, Paul

[Der] Mann Vom Rinn
See Speckbacher, Joseph

Mann, W. Berg
See Bergmann, Werner

Manna, Charles J. [Charlie] 1925- [HPPN]
American comedian
* DeForest, Barry

Mannan, Laila
See Sanchez, Sonia Knight

Manne, Macho
See Omari, Cuthbert Kashingo

Manne, Sheldon 1920- [PMJ]
American musician
* Manne, Shelly

Manne, Shelly
See Manne, Sheldon

Mannering, Dore Lewin
See Lewin, Dore

Mannering, Julia
See Bingham, Madeleine [Mary Ebel]

Mannering, Mary
See Friend, Florence

Mannering, Max
See Holland, Josiah Gilbert

Mannering, May
See Nowell, Harriett P. [Hardy]

Mannering, Moya
See Doyle, Moya

Manners, Alexandra
See Rundle, Anne

Manners, Charles
See Mansergh, Southcote

Manners, David
See Acklom, Rauff De Ryther Duan

Manners, Dudley
See Krupp, D. Dudley

Manners, Julia
See Greenaway, Gladys

Manners, Julia
See Judson, Edward Zane Carroll

Manners, Lorain
See Price, Lorain Manners

Manners, Lucille
See McClinchy, Marie Emily

Manners, Miss
See Martin, Judith Sylvia

Manners, Motley
See Duganne, Augustine Joseph Hickey

Manners, Mrs.
See Richards, Cornelia Holroyd [Bradley]

Manners, Mrs. Horace
See Swinburne, Algernon Charles

Manners, Zeke
See Mannes, Leo

Mannes, Leo 1911- [ASC]
American composer and singer
* Manners, Zeke

Mannes, Marya
See Blow, Marya Mannes

Manney, Henrietta 1875-1942 [HCA]
American actress
* Westley, Helen

Manngian, Peter
See Monger, [Ifor] David

Mannheim, L. Andrew 1925- [IAW]
Czech-born author
* Matheson, Andrew

Manninen, Bruno Jalmar 1896-1962
[BEW]
Finnish-born designer
* Maine, Bruno

Manning, Adelaide Frances Oke
1891-1959 [CC, EMD, WW]
British author
* Coles, Manning [joint pseudonym with
  Cyril Henry Coles]
* Gaite, Francis [joint pseudonym with
  Cyril Henry Coles]

Manning, Anne 1807-1879 [HPPN, IP,
NPS, PA]
British author
* Beatrice
* [An] English Girl
* Moldwarp, Nicholas, B. A.
* More, Margareta
* Osborne, Edward
* Powell, Mary

Manning, Catharine
See Frazier, Corinne Reid

Manning, David
See Faust, Frederick [Schiller]

Manning, Doc
See Manning, George Felix

Manning, Ed
See Manning, Ernest Devon [Ernie]

Manning, Ernest Devon [Ernie] 1890-
[BE]
American baseball player
* Manning, Ed

Manning, Frances Duncan 20th c.
[NAA]
American author and horticulturist
* Duncan, Frances

Manning, Frederic 1887-1935 [LC, TC]
Australian-born author and poet
* Private 19022

Manning, George Felix 19th c. [BLB]
American cattle rancher
* Manning, Doc

Manning, Henry Edward 1808-1892
[HPPN, PA]
British author and clergyman
* Catholicus
* H. E. M.

Manning, Hilda
See Reach, James

Manning, Howard, Jr. 1943- [BA]
American attorney
* Manning, Nick

Manning, Irene
See Harvuot, Inez

Manning, Jack
See Marks, Jack Wilson Manning

Manning, Lee
See Stokes, Manning Lee

Manning, Leo
See Hallbing, Kjell Kare

Manning, Maria de Roux 1825-1849
[SN]
Swiss-born murderer
* Mademoiselle Hortense

Manning, Marie 1875?-1945 [BI]
American columnist
* Fairfax, Beatrice

Manning, Mary Louise
See Cameron, Lou

Manning, Nick
See Manning, Howard, Jr.

Manning, Patrick M. 19th c. [PI]
Irish poet
* M. M. P.

Manning, Roosevelt 20th c. [EF]
American football player
* Manning, Rosie

Manning, Rosemary
See Cole, Margaret Alice

Manning, Rosemary Joy 1911- [AW,
CA, IAW]
British author
* Davys, Sarah
* Voyle, Mary

Manning, Rosie
See Manning, Roosevelt

Manning, Rube
See Manning, Walter S.

Manning, Thomas 1772-1840 [SN]
British linguist and mathematician
* [The] Darling of the Nine

Manning, Val
See Miller, Val

Manning, Walter S. 1883-1930 [BE]
American baseball player
* Manning, Rube

Manning, William Henry 1852-1929
[HPPN, WW]
American author
* DeForest, Barry
* Edwards, Warren
* Halliday, Ben
* Hoyt, W. M.
* Inman, Robert Randolph?
* Kent, Warren F.
* Pierce, Jo
* St. Vrain, [Major] E. L.
* Walters, Warren
* Waring, Marcus H.
* Warren, Hugh
* Warren, J. T.
* Warren, Ned
* Warren, V. S.
* Wilton, [Capt.] Mark

Manningham, Basil
See Homersham, Basil Henry

Manningham, T. Raymond
See Weil, Joseph R.

Mannix, Mary Walsh 1846-1938 [CAT]
American poet
* Ashburton, Sarah Frances
* Hunting, Sylvia
* Willis, Hope

Manno, Jeff
See Manno, Nick

Manno, Mousey
See Manno, Tom

Manno, Nick 20th c. [PHM]
American underworld figure
* Manno, Jeff

Manno, Tom 20th c. [PHM]
American underworld figure
* Manno, Mousey

Mannon, M. M. [joint pseudonym with
Mary Ellen Mannon]
See Mannon, Martha

Mannon, M. M. [joint pseudonym with
Martha Mannon]
See Mannon, Mary Ellen

Mannon, Martha 1909- [WW]
Author
* Mannon, M. M. [joint pseudonym
  with Mary Ellen Mannon]

Mannon, Mary Ellen 1913- [WW]
Author
* Mannon, M. M. [joint pseudonym
  with Martha Mannon]

Mannon, W. 1891-1967 [BF]
British actor and producer
* Ward, Warwick

Mannon, Warwick
See Hopkins, Kenneth

Mannone, Joseph 1900?- [ASC, DAM,
PMJ]
American jazz musician
* Juke Box King of Jive
* Manone, Joseph
* Manone, Wingy

Mannstein, Fritz Erich von
See Von Lewinski, Fritz Erich

Mannyng, Robert 1288-1338 [WBD]
British author and poet
* De Brunne, Robert

Manola, Marion
See Mould, Mrs. Henry S.

Manolesco, George 1871-1911 [HPPN]
Rumanian thief and cardsharp
* [The] Duke of Otranto
* His Highness Prince Lahovary
* [The] Prince of Thieves

Manolete [Big Manuel]
See Rodriguez Sanchez, Manuel

Manolete [Big Manuel]
See Rodriguez Sanchez, Manuel

Manolo
See Martinez Hugue, Manuel

Manon, Marcia
See Ankewich, Camille

Manone, Joseph 1904?-1982 [FIR]
American musician
* Manone, Wingy

Manone, Joseph
See Mannone, Joseph

Manone, Wingy
See Mannone, Joseph

Manone, Wingy
See Manone, Joseph

Manor, Jason
See Hall, Oakley [Maxwell]

Manos, Charley
See Moustakas, Alkiviadis

Manos de Piedra [Hands of Stone]
See Duran, Roberto

Manotoc, Tomas 1950?-
Son-in-law of Philippine president,
Ferdinand Marcos
* Manotoc, Tommy

Manotoc, Tommy
See Manotoc, Tomas

Manouche
See Germain, Germaine

[A] Man's Man and the Idol of Women
See O'Brien, George

Mansbridge, Pamela
See Course, Pamela Mary

Mansel, Henry Longueville 1820-1871
[HPPN]
British clergyman
* [The] Lecturer

Mansel, William ?-1820 [SN]
* Magnus

Mansell, Mrs. C. B. 20th c. [CCL]
Canadian author
* St. Clair, Everett

Mansergh, Southcote 1857-1935 [BBD]
British opera singer and impresario
* Manners, Charles

Mansfield, Arthur 20th c. [BBH]
American baseball coach
* Mansfield, Dynie

Mansfield, Dynie
See Mansfield, Arthur

Mansfield, Eddy 1957?-
American wrestler
* [The] Continental Lover

Mansfield, Edward Deering 1801-1880?
[FFF, HPPN, PA]
American journalist
* E. D. M.
* Veteran Observer

Mansfield, Elizabeth
See Schwartz, Paula

Mansfield, Estrith
See Harris, Edna Edith

Mansfield, Jayne
See Palmer, Vera Jane

Mansfield, Joseph 1889?-1971 [EMT,
FD, PMJ]
American actor and singer
* Santley, Joseph

Mansfield, Joyce 1920- [ICB]
British illustrator
* Bee, Joyce

Mansfield, Katherine
See Beauchamp, Kathleen Mansfield

Mansfield, L. W. [PA]
Author
* Z. P.

Mansfield, Lawrence
See Forrest, William Mentzel

Mansfield, Libby
See Schwartz, Paula

Mansfield, Martha
See Ehrlich, Martha

Mansfield, Mary Lou
See Daly, Pauline

Mansfield, Maynard 1910- [PMJ]
American jazz musician
* Mansfield, Saxie

Mansfield, Michael Joseph [Mike] 1903-
[HPPN]
American politician
* Mansfield, Montana Mike

Mansfield, Milburg Francisco 1871-?
[HPPN]
American author
* Miltoun, Francis

Mansfield, Montana Mike
See Mansfield, Michael Joseph [Mike]

Mansfield, Mrs. M. F.
Author
* McManus, Blanche

Mansfield, Norman
See Gladden, E[dgar] Norman

[The] Mansfield of the Screen
See Walthall, Henry B.

Mansfield, Portia
See Swett, Portia

Mansfield, Richard
See Rudersdorff, Richard

Mansfield, Saxie
See Mansfield, Maynard

Mansfield, Walworth
See Walton, W. H.

Mansfield, Willette 1890-1960 [BEW]
American actress and producer
* Kershaw, Willette

Mansion, Gracie
See Young, Joanne Mayhew

Manske, Edgar 20th c. [EF]
American football player
* Manske, Eggs

Manske, Eggs
See Manske, Edgar

Manson, Charles
See Maddox, No Name

Manson, George 1844-1922 [HPPN]
Scottish physician
* Manson, Mosquito

Manson, James B. [PA]
Author
* Warmley, Ernst

Manson, Janet 1922-1961 [SC]
American actress
* Kalionzes, Janet

Manson, Margaret
See Aldiss, Margaret [Christie]

Manson, Mosquito
See Manson, George

Manson, [Sir] Patrick 1844-1922 [WBD]
British physician and parasitologist
* [The] Father of Tropical Medicine

Mansouri, Lotfi
See Mansouri, Lotfollah

Mansouri, Lotfollah 1929- [OP]
Iranian-born opera producer and stage
designer
* Mansouri, Lotfi

Mansur ?-775 [HPPN]
Abbasid caliph
* [The] Founder of Baghdad

Mansur [or Hasan?], Abul Qasim
940-1020 [DEP, HN, WBD]
Persian poet
* Firdusi [or Firdausi]
* [The] Homer of Khorasan
* [The] Homer of Persia
* [The] Oriental Homer

Mant, Richard 1776-1848 [HPPN]
British clergyman
* [A] Curate
* One Who Is Also an Elder

Mant, Richard
See Hearne, George Richard Mant

Mantell, Frank
See Mintell, Frank Otto

Mantell, Robert Bruce 1854-1928
[THR]
Scottish-born actor and theatrical
manager
* Hudson, Robert

Mantequilla
See Soto, Fernando

Mantilla, Felix Lamela 1934-
Puerto Rican-born baseball player
* [The] Cat

Mantinband, James H. 20th c. [WW]
Author
* Keystone, Oliver

Mantle, [Robert] Burns 1873-1948
[HPPN]
American dramatic critic
* [The] Dean of the Dramatic Critics

Mantle, Mickey Charles 1931- [ALR, BE, HPPN]
American baseball player
* [The] Commerce Comet
* [The] Great Mick
* [The] Infant Prodigy
* [The] Million Dollar Invalid
* [The] Wounded Hero

Mantle, Winifred Langford 1911- [AW, CA, WD]
British author
* Fellowes, Anne
* Lang, Frances
* Langford, Jane

Manton, Jo
See Gittings, Jo [Grenville] Manton

Manton, Kate
See Knight, Mrs. S. G.

Manton, Martin 20th c. [HPPN]
American attorney
* Manton, Preying

Manton, Mr.
See Montrose, Duchess of

Manton, Paul
See Walker, Peter Norman

Manton, Peter
See Creasey, John

Manton, Preying
See Manton, Martin

Mantooth, Lawrence 20th c. [BBH]
American wrestler
* [The] Scissor King

Mantovani
See Mantovani, Annunzio Paulo

Mantovani, Annunzio Paulo 1908-1980 [PMJ]
British conductor
* [The] Maestro of Massed Strings
* Mantovani

Mantovano, Alberto
See Ripa, Alberto da

[The] Mantuan
See Spagnolus, Baptista

Mantuan
See Townson, Thomas

[The] Mantuan Bard
See Vergilius Maro, Publius

[The] Mantuan Muse
See Vergilius Maro, Publius

[The] Mantuan Swan
See Vergilius Maro, Publius

Mantuano, Marco
See Benevides, Marco

Mantz, [Albert] Paul 1903-1965 [HPPN]
American stunt aviator
* [The] Hollywood Pilot
* [The] Honeymoon Pilot
* [The] King of the Hollywood Air Devils

Manuel, Ernest
See L'Epine, Ernest Louis Victor Jules

Manuel, George 1915- [IAW]
South African author
* Gemel

Manuel, Jose 20th c. [GS]
Spanish bullfighter
* Tinin

Manuel, Nikolaus 1484-1530 [WBD]
Swiss painter and engraver
* Deutsch, Nikolaus

Manuel I Comnenus 1120-1180 [FFF, HN, RH]
Byzantine emperor
* Captain
* [The] Great Captain

Manuel II 1350-1425 [HPPN]
Byzantine emperor
* Palaeologus

Manuel II 1889-1932 [HPPN]
King of Portugal
* Dom Manoel

Manuela
See De Rochechouart-Mortemart, Marie Clementine

[A] Manufacturer
See Hustler, John

Manugupta
See Shastri, Prithvinath

Manush, Heinie
See Manush, Henry Emmett

Manush, Henry Emmett 1901-1971 [BE, CBS, DGS]
American baseball player
* Manush, Heinie

Manville, George
See Fenn, George Manville

Manville, W. H.
See Manville, William Henry

Manville, William Henry 1930- [CA]
American author
* Manville, W. H.
* Williams, Henry

Manwood, Thomas ?-1612? [SN]
* Philarete

[The] Manx Poet
See Brown, Thomas Edward

Many, Seth E[dward] 1939- [CA]
American author
* NO, Dr.

[The] Many Sided Franklin
See Franklin, Ben[jamin]

Many Treaties, Chief
See Hazlett, William

Manyase, Lenchman Thozamile 1915- [IAW]
South African author and poet
* Joli-Ox

Manypenny, George W. 19th c. [HPPN]
American author
* [The] Commissioner of Indian Affairs

Manywife, Tom
See Foe, Daniel

Manzano y Pelayo, Jose 1828-1869 [GS]
Spanish bullfighter
* [El] Nili

Manzoni, Giacomo 1908- [CAR]
Italian sculptor
* Manzu, Giacomo

Manzu, Giacomo
See Manzoni, Giacomo

Mao?
See Addis, Hazel Iris Wilson

Mao Chiang Ching 1913?- [HPPN]
Actress and wife of Chinese Communist leader, Mao Tse-tung
* Lan Ping

Mao Tse-tung 1893-1976 [HPPN]
Chinese Communist leader
* [The] Founder of Communist China
* [The] Great Helmsman
* [The] Romantic Revolutionary

Mao Tun [Contradiction]
See Shen Yen-ping

Maori
See Inglis, James

Mapel, Lefty
See Mapel, Rolla Hamilton

Mapel, Rolla Hamilton 1890-1966 [BE]
American baseball player
* Mapel, Lefty

Mapes, Cliff Franklin 1922- [BE]
American baseball player
* Mapes, Tiger

Mapes, Mary A.
See Ellison, Virginia Howell

Mapes, Tiger
See Mapes, Cliff Franklin

Mapes, Victor 1870-? [NAA]
American playwright and author
* Post, Maveric
* Sharp, Sidney

Mapes, Walter 1150-1196 [DEL, FFF, SN]
Welsh poet
* [The] Anacreon of the Twelfth Century
* [The] Jovial Toper

Maphis, Joe
See Maphis, Otis W.

Maphis, Otis W. 1921- [CWG, DAM]
American country-western performer
* [The] King of the Strings
* Maphis, Joe

Maphis, Rose Lee 1922- [FCW]
American country-western performer
* Rose of the Mountains

Maple, Eddie 20th c.
American jockey
* [The] Anchor

Maple Knot
See Clemo, Ebenezer

Maples, Evelyn Lucille [Palmer] 1919-
[IAW]
American author
* Dalby, B. J.

Maplesden, Ray
See Pearce, Raymond Maplesden

Mapleton, Mark
See Wilson, Robert

Mapleton, S. E. [PA]
Author
* [A] Clergyman's Wife

Mapother, Edith Rubel 20th c. [NAA]
American educator, musician, poet
* Rubel, Edith

Mappelbeck, John
See Collins, James H.

Maps
See Nicholson, John

Mar, Helen
See Walker, Mrs. D. M. F.

[La] Mara
See Lipsius, Marie

Mara, Adele
See Delgado, Adelaida

Mara, Barney
See Roth, Arthur J[oseph]

Mara, Jeanette
See Cebulash, Mel

Mara, Sally
See Queneau, Raymond

Mara, Thalia
See Mahoney, Elizabeth

Maraini, Yoi 20th c. [WWL]
Author
* Pawlowska, Yoi

Marais
See Brown, Mary Rachel

Marais, Jaap
See Marais, Jacob

Marais, Jacob 20th c.
South African politician
* Marais, Jaap

Marais, Jean
See Villain-Marais, Jean

Marais, Miranda
See Baruch de la Pardo, Rosa Lily
Odette

Marama
See Cilento, Phyllis Dorothy

Marano, Doretta 1928-1968 [BEW,
EMT]
American actress and singer
* Morrow, Doretta

Maranville, Rabbit
See Maranville, Walter James Vincent

Maranville, Walter James Vincent
1891-1954 [AS, DGS, PB]
American baseball player
* Maranville, Rabbit

Maranzano, Salvatore 1868-1931
[HPPN]
Sicilian-American underworld figure
* [The] Boss of All Bosses
* [The] Father of the Cosa Nostra

Maras, Karl [house pseudonym,
Comyns]
See Bulmer, [Henry] Kenneth

Maras, Karl [house pseudonym]
See Hawkins, Peter

Marasco, Georges
See Mrazek, Bertha

Marasmus, Seymour
See Rivoli, Mario

Marat, Jean Paul 1744-1793 [DNNF,
FF, HN]
French revolutionary leader
* Ami du Peuple
* [The] Apostle of Massacre
* [The] Friend of the People
* [The] People's Friend
* [The] Republican Martyr

Marath, Laurie
See Roberts, Suzanne

Marath, Sparrow
See Roberts, Suzanne

Marathon
See McNish, James Thomas

Marauder, Father
See De Vignerot du Plessis, Louis
Francois Armand

Maravan, Lila
See Muschamp, Lila

Maravich, Peter 1948- [BB]
American basketball player
* Maravich, Pistol Pete

Maravich, Pistol Pete
See Maravich, Peter

Maraviglia, Guiseppe Maria ?-1684
[PA]
Author
* Mirabilia

Marberry, Firpo
See Marberry, Fred

Marberry, Fred 1898- [BE, PB]
American baseball player
* Marberry, Firpo

Marble, Alice 1913- [HPPN]
American tennis player
* [The] Golden Girl of Tennis

Marble, Anna 1881?-1946 [BEW]
American author and press representative
* Pollock, Anna

Marble, Dan
See Marble, Danforth

Marble, Danforth 1810-1849 [FAA,
HPPN]
American actor
* [The] Gamecock of the Wilderness
* Marble, Dan

Marble, Harriet Clement 1903-1975
[CA]
American author
* Jones, Harriet

Marble, Major
See Cheever, Henry T.

Marblestone, Eddie 1907?- [PMJ]
American singer
* Stone, Eddie

Marbo, Camille
See Borel, Marguerite [Appell]

Marbode, M. [PA]
Author
* Pellicarius

Marbourg, Dolores
See Bacon, Mary Schell [Hoke]

Marbrook, Del
See Mabrouk, Djelloul

Marbrook, Djelloul
See Mabrouk, Djelloul

Marc, Alessandra
See Borden, Judith

Marc, Elizabeth
See Mirza, Nusrat Ali

Marca, Francois de [HN]
Medieval scholar
* Illustratus, Doctor

Marcano, Jesus Manuel
See Trillo, Jesus Manuel

Marcantonio
See Raimondi, Marcantonio

Marcantonio, Vito 1902-1954 [HPPN]
American politician
* [The] Firebrand

Marceau, Felicien
See Carette, Louis Albert

Marceau, Francois Severin
See Marceau-Desgraviers, Francois
Severin

Marceau, Marcel 1923- [HPPN]
French pantomimist
* Bip

Marceau-Desgraviers, Francois Severin
1769-1796 [WBD]
French army officer
* Marceau, Francois Severin

Marcel
See Allen, William Francis

Marcel, Eugene 1862-1941 [EWL]
French author
* Prevost, Marcel

Marcel, Lucille
See Wasself, Lucille

[The] Marcel Marceau of Television
See Skelton, [Richard] Red

Marceline
See Orbes, Marceline

Marcelino
See Agnew, Edith J[osephine]

Marcella, Fatso Marco
See Marcella, Marco

Marcella, Marco 1909?-1962 [BEW]
American theatrical performer
* Marcella, Fatso Marco

Marcelle, Ghost
See Marcelle, Oliver H.

Marcelle, Oliver H. 20th c. [OBW]
American baseball player
* Marcelle, Ghost

Marcelle-Maurette
See Maurette, Marcelle Marie Josephine

Marcellini, Siro 1921- [FDG]
Italian director
* Markson, Sean

Marcellino, Jocko
See Marcellino, John

Marcellino, John 1950- [RO2]
American singer
* Marcellino, Jocko

Marcellinus, Animianus
See Nadel, Aaron

Marcello
See D'Affry, Adele

Marcello, Alessandro 1684-1750
Italian composer
* Stinfalico, Eterio

Marcello, Carlos
See Minacore, Calogero

Marcellus
See Adams, John Quincy

Marcellus
See Malone, Edmund

Marcellus
See Marteau, Amedee

Marcellus
See Ramsay, Allan, Jr.

Marcellus
See Webster, Noah

Marcellus, Marcus Claudius 3rd c. BC
[DEP, DNNF, DNNS]
Roman general and statesman
* [The] Sword of Rome

[The] Marcellus of Our Tongue
See Oldham, John

[The] Marcellus of Spain
See John

[The] Marcellus of the English Nation
See Sidney, [Sir] Philip

Marcellus, P. H.
See Cronmiller, George, Jr.

Marcellus, W. B.
See Bergstrand, Vilhelm Alexander

Marcellus II
See Cervini, Marcello

Marcet, Mary 1769-1858 [PA]
Author
* Haldimand

Marcetta, Mike
See Marcetta, Milan

Marcetta, Milan 1936- [CEI]
Canadian-born hockey player
* Marcetta, Mike

March, Anne
See Woolson, Constance Fenimore

March, Ausias 1397?-1460 [SN]
Valencian poet
* [The] Petrarch of Catalonia

March, Charles W. 1815-1864 [FFF,
PA]
American author
* Pequot

March, Fredric
See Bickel, Frederick McIntyre

March, Hal
See Mendelson, Harold

March Hare
See Walmsley, Leo

March, Harold C. 1908- [CEI, FHE,
HK]
Canadian-born hockey player
* March, Mush

March, Hilary
See Adcock, Almey St. John

March, Hilary
See Pulvertaft, Lalage Isobel

March, Jermyn
See Webb, Dorothy Anna Maria

[The] March King
See Sousa, John Philip

March, Little Peggy
See March, Peggy

March, Major
See Willcox, Orlando Bolivar

March, Marjorie
See Leibich, Augusta

March, Miles Standish 1860-1932 [SC]
American actor
* Walsh, Frank

March, Mush
See March, Harold C.

March Pane
See Perugini, Mark

March, Peggy 1948- [RO1]
American singer
* March, Little Peggy

March, Stella
See Marshall, Marjorie Bell

March, Walter
See Willcox, Orlando Bolivar

March, Wenzeslaus
See Messenhauser, Casar Wenzel

March, William
See Campbell, William Edward March

Marchand, Marie Francoise 1711-1803
[WBD]
French actress
* Dumesnil, Marie Francoise

Marchant, Bessie
See Comfort, Mrs. J. A.

Marchant, Catherine
See Cookson, Catherine Ann
[McMullen]

Marchant, Charles
See White, John Duncan

Marchant, Ella 20th c. [SFL, WGT]
Author
* Two Women of the West [joint
pseudonym with Alice Ilgenfritz
Jones]

Marchant, R[omano Isabel]
See Colbron, Grace Isabel

Marchant, R. A.
See Marchant, Rex Alan

Marchant, Rex Alan 1933- [WYA]
Author
* Marchant, R. A.

Marchaud, Alfred
See Kaufman, M.

Marchbanks, Samuel
See Davies, Robertson

Marchegiano, Rocco Francis 1923-1969
[AS, BX, HPPN, RBE]
American boxer
* [The] Brockton Blockbuster
* [The] Brockton Bomber
* [The] Brockton Bull
* [The] Brockton Buster
* Marciano, Rocky

Marchelle, Ponce Kiah 20th c.
American columnist
* Heloise

Marchena de Leyba, Amelia Francisco
1850-1941 [CW]
Dominican author
* Francasi [or Francasci], Amelia

[The] Marcher
See Chavez, Cesar

Marchese, Malacrida 1890- [HPPN]
Italian author
* Piermarini

Marchese, Paul 20th c. [BLB]
American underworld figure
* Di Cristina, Paul

Marchesi, Luigi 1754-1829 [BBD]
Italian singer
* Marchesini

Marchesini
See Marchesi, Luigi

Marchetti, Gino 1927- [HPPN]
American football player
* History's Greatest Defensive End

Marchi, Giacomo
See Bassani, Giorgio

Marchioni, Mark 20th c. [SFP]
Author
* Marconette

Marchmont, Frederick
See Torriano, Hugh Arthur

Marcia
See Warren, Mercy Otis

Marcial
See Carpio, Salvador Cayetano

Marciano, Rocky
See Marchegiano, Rocco Francis

Marcinkus, Paul 1922?- [NW 9-13-82]
American-born prelate and banker
* Chink
* [The] Gnome of Rome
* [Il] Gorilla

Marcliffe, Theophilus
See Godwin, William

Marco di Tiziano
See Vecelli, Marco

Marco, Lou
See Gottfried, Theodore Mark

Marco the Magi
See Pelaez, Cesareo

Marco Gomez, Jaime 1920- [GS]
Spanish bullfighter
* [EL] Choni

Marcol, Chester
See Marcol, Czelslaw C.

Marcol, Czelslaw C. 1949- [FB]
Polish-born American football player
* Marcol, Chester
* [The] Polish Messiah

Marcombe, Edith Marion
See Shiffert, Edith [Marcombe]

Marconette
See Marchioni, Mark

Marconi, [Marchese] Guglielmo
1874-1937 [HPPN]
Italian engineer and inventor
* [The] Father of Wireless Telegraphy

Marcos, [Fray]
See Niza, Marcos de

Marcos, Imee
See Marcos, Maria Imelda

Marcos, Imelda 1930- [NW 9-13-82]
Wife of Philippine president, Ferdinand Marcos
* [The] Iron Butterfly
* [The] Orchid
* [The] Rose of Tacloban

Marcos, Jesus 20th c. [GS]
Spanish bullfighter
* Monedero [The Minter]

Marcos, Maria Imelda 1956?-
Daughter of Philippine president, Ferdinand Marcos
* Marcos, Imee

Marcou-Ferrand, Juan Victor Sejour
1817-1874 [IBW]
American playwright and poet
* Sejour, Victor

Marcoureau, Guillaume 1638-1685
[HPPN]
French actor and playwright
* Brecourt

Marcous, Louis 1883-1941 [JL]
French painter
* Marcoussis, Louis

Marcousis, Louis Casimir Ladislas
See Markus, Louis Casimir Ladislas

Marcoussis, Louis
See Marcous, Louis

Marcoux, Jean Emile Diogene
1877-1962 [BBD]
Italian-born opera singer
* Marcoux, Vanni

Marcoux, Vanni
See Marcoux, Jean Emile Diogene

Marcovitch, M. A. 19th c. [HPPN]
Russian author
* Vovchok, Marc

Marcoy, Paul
See De Saint Cricq, Lorenzo

Marcoy, Paul
See Saint Cricq, Lorenzo de

Marcum, Footsie
See Marcum, John Alfred

Marcum, John Alfred 1908- [BE]
American baseball player
* Marcum, Footsie

Marcus
See Blunt, Joseph

Marcus
See Davis, Matthew Livingston

Marcus
See Swift, Deane

Marcus, Anne M[ulkeen] 1927- [CA]
American author and educator
* Mulkeen, Anne

Marcus Aurelius
See Annius Verus, Marcus

[The] Marcus Aurelius of the Base Empire
See John II Comnenus

Marcus, Betty ?-1982 [FIR]
American actress
* Curtis, Pepper

Marcus, Carol 20th c. [BEW]
American actress
* Grace, Carol

Marcus, David 1902-1948 [EJS, HPPN]
American boxer
* Marcus, Mickey
* Mars, Danny
* Mars, Mickey

Marcus, Mickey
See Marcus, David

Marcy, Oliver 1820-1899 [HPPN]
American scientist
* [The] Methodist Agassiz

Marczali, Henrik
See Morgenstern, Henrik

Marczlewicz, Charles Anthony 1919-
[BE]
American baseball player
* Marshall, Charles Anthony [Charlie]

Marden, Lucky
See Marden, Orison Swett

Marden, Orison Swett 1850-1924
[HPPN]
American editor and essayist
* Marden, Lucky

[The] Mare
See Ryan, Hermine Braunsteiner

Marek
See Zulawski, Marek

Marek, Kurt W[illi] 1915-1972 [AW,
BI, CAP]
German-born journalist, archaeologist, author
* Ceram, C. W.

Mareno, Francisco Ildefonse 1748-1829
[BI]
Spanish clergyman
* Antoine, [Father]

Mareth, Glenville [joint pseudonym with Jack Weinstock]
See Gomberg, William Gilbert

Mareth, Glenville [joint pseudonym with William Gilbert Gomberg]
See Weinstock, Jack

Maretzek, Max 1821-1897 [HPPN]
Moravian conductor and composer
* [An] Opera Manager

Marevna
See Vorobeva, Maria

Margaret 1283-1290 [DNNF, FFF, SN]
Granddaughter of King Alexander III of Scotland
* [The] Fair Maid of Norway
* [The] Maid of Norway

Margaret 1353-1412 [DEP, HN, SN]
Queen of Denmark, Norway, and Sweden
* [The] Northern Semiramis

Margaret (cont.)
* [The] Scandinavian Semiramis
* [The] Semiramis of the North

Margaret [or Marguerite] 1430-1482
[HN]
Wife of King Henry VI of England
* Anjou, Marguerite d'
* [The] She Wolf of France

Margaret 1489-1541 [SN]
Wife of King James IV of Scotland
* [The] Rose

Margaret 15th c. [HPPN]
Wife of William Douglas, Earl of Douglas
* [The] Fair Maid of Galloway

Margaret, Karla
See Billings, Karla Margaret Crosier

Margaret Mary
See Alacoque, Margaret Mary

Margaret of Angouleme
See Margaret [or Marquerite] of Navarre

Margaret of Austria
See Margaret of Parma

Margaret of Carinthia 1318-1369
[WBD]
Daughter of Henry, Duke of Carinthia
* Maultasch

Margaret of Constantinople
See Margaret of Flanders

Margaret of Flanders 1200?-1280
[WBD]
Daughter of Emperor Baldwin I, Count of Flanders and Hainault
* Margaret of Constantinople

Margaret [or Marguerite] of France
1523?-1574 [HN, RH, WBD]
Daughter of King Francis I of France
* Margaret of Savoy
* [La] Mere des Peuples
* [The] Mother of the People

Margaret of France
See Margaret of Valois

Margaret [or Marquerite] of Navarre
1492-1549 [HN, WBD]
Queen of Navarre
* Margaret of Angouleme
* Margaret of Orleans
* Marguerite des Marguerites [Pearl of Pearls]
* [The] Tenth Muse

Margaret of Orleans
See Margaret [or Marquerite] of Navarre

Margaret of Parma 1522-1586 [WBD]
Daughter of Emperor Charles V
* Margaret of Austria

Margaret of Savoy
See Margaret [or Marguerite] of France

Margaret of Valois 1553-1615 [HPPN]
Queen consort of Navarre
* Margaret of France
* Margot

Margaret Rose 1930-
British princess
* P. M.

[The] Margaret Thatcher of Yugoslavia
See Planinc, Milka

Marge
See Buell, Marjorie Henderson

Margerie, Pet
See Fleming, Margaret

Margerison, John S. 20th c. [MBF]
British author
* Grey, Gilbert
* Mellalieu, James S.

Margerson, David
See Davies, David Margerison

Margery
See Crandon, Mina [Stinson]

Margery the Boston Medium
See Crandon, Mina [Stinson]

Margetic, Magnetic
See Margetic, Pato

Margetic, Pato 1961?-
Argentinian soccer player
* Margetic, Magnetic

Margheriti, Antonio 1916- [FDG]
Italian director
* Daisies, Anthony
* Dawson, Anthony

Marginalia
See Poe, Edgar Allan

Margites [The Booby]
See Theobald, Lewis

Margo
See Bolado y Castilla, Maria Marguerita Guadalupe

Margo, Peter 20th c.
American billiard player
* Little Giant

Margoliouth, George Edward 1901-
[THR]
British theatrical press representative
* Fearon, George Edward

Margoliouth, Moses 19th c. [HFN]
Author
* [A] Clergyman of the Church of England

Margolis, Charles 1874-1926 [SC]
American actor
* Margolis, Doc

Margolis, Doc
See Margolis, Charles

Margolis, Susanna 1944- [CA]
American author
* Gowar, Antonia [joint pseudonym with Judith Dunford]

Margot
See Margaret of Valois

Margot of Hainault 15th c. [BBH]
French tennis player
* [The] Joan of Arc of Tennis

Margrethe II 1940-
Queen of Denmark
* Daisy
* Grathmer, Ingahild

Marguerita
See Bornstein, Marguerita

Marguerite
See Godwin, Mary

Marguerite
See Pender, Margaret T.

Marguerite, Babe
See Sterling, Babe

Marguerite des Marguerites [Pearl of Pearls]
See Margaret [or Marguerite] of Navarre

Margulois, David 1911- [EMT, HPPN, IPA]
American producer
* [The] Barnum of Broadway Producers
* Merrick, David

Marholm, Laura
See Hansson, Laura

Maria
See English, Anastasia Mary

Maria
See Frazer, John de Jean

Maria
See Wilkin, Maria

Maria Christina 1806-1878 [HPPN]
Queen of Spain
* Christina of Spain

Maria Christina 1947-
Dutch princess
* Van Oranje, Christina

Maria da Gloria
See Maria II

Maria de Jesus
See Fernandez Coronel, Maria

Maria de la Virgen Dolorosa, [Mother]
See Murator, Antonita

Maria Del Rey, [Sister]
See Danforth, Ethel M.

Maria Di Gesu, [Sister]
See Felicita, Maria

Maria, Giuseppe
See Racagni, Giovanni

Maria, Jennie
See Renard, Celine

Maria Louisa 1791-1847 [SN]
Wife of Napoleon Bonaparte
* [The] Deadly Austrian

Maria Mour, Jean Hubert
See Papailler, Hubert

Maria Teresa, [Mother]
See Dudzik, Jozefa

Maria Theresa 1717-1780 [HN, SN]
Queen of Austria
* [The] Modern Hippolyta
* [The] Mother of Her Country

Maria I 1734-1816 [NPS]
Queen of Portugal
* Lusian's Luckless Queen

Maria II 1819-1853 [HPPN]
Queen of Brazil
* Maria da Gloria

Mariaker, Elie
See Boulay-Paty, Evariste Cyprien

Marian Anderson of the Blues
See Hunter, Alberta

Marian Dolores, [Sister]
See Robinson, [Sister] Marian Dolores

Marian, Sahle Sellassie Berhane 1936-
Ethiopian author
* Sellassie, Sahle

Mariana
See Foster, Marian Curtis

Mariana, Juan de [or John] 1537-1624
[DNNS, RH, SN]
Spanish historian
* [The] Father of Spanish History
* [The] Livy of France
* [The] Livy of Spain

Marianne
See Katona, Edita

Marianne of Jesus, [Mother]
See Gurney, Marion Frances

Mariano, Luis
See Gonzalez, Luis

Mariano de Aguiar, Sinesio 20th c.
[FIR]
Brazilian actor
* De Conde, Syn

Marianus, Doctor
See Duns Scotus, Johannes

Maric, Boze
See Maric, Bozidar

Maric, Bozidar 1942- [AES]
Yugoslav soccer player
* Maric, Boze

Marichal, Juan Antonio Sanchez 1937-
[BE]
Dominican-born baseball player
* [The] Dominican Dandy
* Marichal, Manito
* Strike, Mister

Marichal, Manito
See Marichal, Juan Antonio Sanchez

Marichaud, Alphonse
See Wilson, Florence Roma Muir

Marie
See Blake, Mary Elizabeth

Marie
See Kindberg, Agnes Marie

Marie
See Skidmore, Harriet M.

[Josephe Jeanne] Marie Antoinette
1755-1793 [DEP, DHA, HPPN, SN]
Wife of King Louis XVI of France
* [The] Austrian
* [The] Austrian Wench
* [The] Austrian Woman
* Autrichienne
* [The] Baker's Wife
* Deficit, Madame
* [The] Guardian Angel of France
* Veto, Madame
* [The] Widow Capet

Marie Celine, [Sister]
See Castang, Jeanne Germaine

Marie Charlotte 1724-1800 [DNNS]
Countess of Boufflers-Rouveret
* Idole du Temple [Idol of the Temple]

Marie de la Passion, [Mother]
See Chappotin de Neuville, Helene de

Marie de la Providence, [Mother]
See Smet, Eugenie Marie Joseph

Marie, Jeanne
See Gayette-Georgens, Jeanne Marie

Marie, Jeanne
See Wilson, Marie B[eatrice]

Marie, [Father] Raymond
See Bruckberger, Raymond Leopold

Marie St. Ignatius, [Mother]
See Thevenet, Claudine

Marie St. Justin, [Mother]
See Rene-Bazin, Marie

Marie Suzanne, [Sister]
See Novial, Alice

Mariel
See Moorien, M.

Mariella, [Sister]
See Gable, Mary

Mariem, Sahala 1844-1913 [HPPN, IBW]
Abyssinian emperor
* Menelik II
* Negus Negusti [King of Kings]

Marietta
See Bradley, Harriet M.

Marietta, [Sister]
See Murray, Mary

Marijac
See Dumas, Jacques

Marilue
See Johnson, Marilue Carolyn

Marilyn
See Robinson, Peter

[The] Marilyn Monroe of Burlesque
See Evans, Dixie

Marin, A. C.
See De Marini y Coppel, Alfredo Jose

Marin, Alfred
See De Marini y Coppel, Alfredo Jose

Marin, Jean
See Morvan, Yves

Marin, Richard 1947- [RO2]
American entertainer
* Cheech

Marina
See Malintzin

Marina, Dona
See Malintzin

Marina, Dona Xaramillo 1505-1529
[PA]
Author
* Malinche

Marinacci, Gloria
See Cutsforth, Gloria

[The] Marine
See Blais, George

[The] Marine Aviator
See Maas, Melvin Joseph

Marine Bob Mouton
See Mouton, Robert L.

Marine, Nick
See Oursler, Will[iam Charles]

Mariner, David
See Smith, David MacLeod

Mariner, Scott [joint pseudonym with
Frederik Pohl]
See Kornbluth, Cyril M.

Mariner, Scott [joint pseudonym with
Cyril M. Kornbluth]
See Pohl, Frederik

Mariner, Will 1791-1853 [HPPN]
British adventurer
* [The] Boy Chief of Tonga

[El] Marinero [The Sailor]
See Ortega y Ramirez, Antonio

Maring, Helen
See Samsel, Helen Maring

Marini, Giovanni Battista 1569-1625
[FFF, HPPN]
Italian poet
* [The] Cavalier
* [Il] Cavalier Marino
* Marini, Jean Baptiste

Marini, Jean Baptiste
See Marini, Giovanni Battista

[El] Marino [The Mariner]
See Palomares Del Pino, Francisco

Marino, Big Bobby
See Marino, Francis

Marino, Dado
See Marino, Salvador

Marino, Danny 1962?- [SI 9-1-82]
American football player
* Marino, Ice

Marino, Enrico 1889- [BBH]
Italian-born American bowler
* Marino, Hank

Marino, Francis ?-1976
American labor union organizer
* Marino, Big Bobby

Marino, Hank
See Marino, Enrico

Marino, Ice
See Marino, Danny

Marino, James ?-1931 [BLB]
American underworld figure
* LaPore, James

Marino, Rinaldo R. 1916-1963 [ASC]
American composer
* Martin, Lennie

Marino, Salvador 1916- [BX, RBE]
American boxer
* Marino, Dado

Marinoni, Rosa Zagnoni 1890- [NAA]
Italian-born poet and author
* Morrison, Ross Zane
* Rosca, the Jester

Marinotti, Franco
See Torri, Francesco

Marinus, [Brother]
See La Rue, Leonard P.

Marinus
See Martin, Jacques

Marinus, R.
See Jonah

Mario
See Baletti, Giuseppe

Mario, Giuseppe 1810-? [PA]
Author
* Macheside, Candia

Mario, Giuseppe
See Candia, Don Giovanni De

Mario, Jessie Meriton White 1832-1906
[HPPN]
British journalist, lecturer, reformer
* [The] Risorgimento Revolutionary

Mario, Queena
See Tillotson, Queena

Mario S.
See Scopoli-Biasi, Isabella

Mariolino Il Faisario
See Feraboli, Mario

Marion, Dave
See Graves, David Marion

Marion, Edna
See Hannam, Edna

Marion, Elias ?-1730 [PA]
Author
* Allut, Jean

Marion, Francis 1732?-1795 [HPPN, SN, WBD]
American army officer
* [The] Bayard of the South
* [The] Old Swamp Fox
* [The] Swamp Fox

Marion, Frederick
See Kraus, Josef

Marion, Frieda 1912- [CA]
American author
* Kent, Arden
* Von Castelhun, Friedl

Marion, Henry
See Alvarez Del Rey, Ramon Felipe
San Juan Mario Silvio Enrico

Marion, Joan
See Nicholls, Joan

Marion, John Wyeth 1914- [BE]
American baseball player
* Marion, Red

Marion, Martin Whiteford 1917- [BE, BN, PB]
American baseball player and manager
* Ely, Bones
* Marion, Slats
* [The] Octopus
* Shortstop, Mr.

[The] Marion of the Mexican Army
See Lane, Joseph

Marion, Pauline ?-1973 [TR]
Actress
* Luce, Polly

Marion, Red
See Marion, John Wyeth

Marion, Slats
See Marion, Martin Whiteford

Marion, Stella
See Boyle, Mrs. Charles H.

Marion, Zelia 1840-1920 [HPPN]
American actress
* Rose, Nera

[The] Marionette Emperor
See Maximillian, Ferdinand Joseph

Mariotti, Luigi
See Gallenga, Antonio Carlo Napoleone

Maris, Mona
See Cap de Vielle, Maria

Maris, Paul
See Zelmanowitz, Gerald Martin

Maris, Roger 1934- [HPPN]
American baseball player
* [The] New Home Run Champion

Maris Stella, [Sister]
See Smith, Alice Gustava

Marisa
See Nucera, Marisa Lonette

Marisol
See Escobar, Marisol

Marissa
See Chudleigh, [Lady] Mary Lee

[The] Maritime Maverick
See Morrissey, James [Jim]

Maritote, Frank 20th c. [BLB, PHM]
American underworld figure
* Diamond, Frank

Maritz, Empie
See Maritz, Magdalena Petronella

Maritz, Magdalena Petronella 1922-
[IAW]
South African author
* Maritz, Empie

Maritza, Sari
See Detering-Nathan, Patricia

Maritzburg, Pieter
See Jackson, Thomas

Mariucci, John 1916- [FHE]
American hockey player
* Mariucci, Maroosh

Mariucci, Maroosh
See Mariucci, John

Marius
See Benedict, Steve

Marius
See Day, Thomas

Marius
See Wells, William Charles

Marius, Caius 2nd c. BC [FFF, HN, RH, UH]
Roman general
* [The] Saviour of Rome
* [The] Third Founder of Rome
* [The] Third Romulus

Marius, Madame [FFF]
Entertainer
* St. John, Florence

Marius, Simon 1564-1624 [PA]
Author
* Mayer

Marixa
See Fernandez, Maria Luisa

Marjane
See Gendebian, Marie Jane Therese

Marjoe
See Gortner, Hugh Marjoe Ross

Marjoram, J.
See Mottram, Ralph Hale

Marjory, Lady
See Foe, Daniel

Mark ?-74? [SN]
Saint
* [The] Stump Fingered

Mark
See Smith, Andrew

Mark Alan, Roy
See Malan, Renato Marco

Mark, David
See Buitenkant, Nathan

Mark, Edwina
See Fadiman, Edwin, Jr.

Mark, John
See Tindall, Frederick Cryer

Mark, Jon
See DuBreuil, Elizabeth Lorinda

Mark, Matthew
See Babcock, Frederic

Mark, Pauline [Dahlin] 1913- [CA]
American author
* Mark, Polly

Mark, Polly
See Mark, Pauline [Dahlin]

[The] Mark Tapley of Kings
See Charles VII

Mark, Ted
See Gottfried, Theodore Mark

[The] Mark Twain of Cartoonists
See Webster, Harold Tucker

[The] Mark Twain of Country Music
See Hall, Tom T.

[The] Mark Twain of France
See Moinaux, Georges-Victor Marcel

Markandaya, Kamala
See Taylor, Kamala [Purnaiya]

Markell, Charles Frederick 1855-?
[ALY]
American author
* Chaskell

Markell, Duke
See Makowsky, Harry Duquesne

Markell, Harry Duquesne
See Makowsky, Harry Duquesne

Marker, Chris
See Bouche-Villeneuve, Christian
Francois

Marker, Clare
See Witcombe, Rick Trader

Marker, Connie 20th c. [HPPN]
Greek-American wrestling referee
* [The] Dean of Referees
* [The] Golden Greek

Markes, Albert Ernest 1865-1901
[DBA]
British painter
* Albert

[The] Market Gardener
See Blackmore, Richard Doddridge

Market Man
See Lake, Kenneth R[obert]

Markevitch, Igor 1913?-1983 [TI 3-21-83]
Russian-born Swiss conductor
* Igor III

Markewich, Maurice 1936- [EJ]
American jazz musician
* Markewich, Reese

Markewich, Reese
See Markewich, Maurice

Markham, David
See Harrison, Peter Basil

Markham, Dewey Alamo 1904-1981
[IBW]
American comedian
* Markham, Pigmeat

Markham, [Charles] Edwin 1852-1940
[HPPN]
American poet
* [The] Dean of American Poets

Markham, Gervasse 1570-1655 [PA]
Author
* G. M.

Markham, Howard
See Hay, Mary Cecil

Markham, Lucia Clark
See Markham, Lula Clark

Markham, Lula Clark 1870-? [NAA]
American poet
* Markham, Lucia Clark

Markham, Mary
See Frith, Mary

Markham, Mrs.
See Penrose, Elizabeth [Cartwright]

Markham, Pauline
See Hall, Margaret

Markham, Pauline
See McMahon, Margaret [Hale]

Markham, Pigmeat
See Markham, Dewey Alamo

Markham, Robert
See Amis, Kingsley [William]

Markham, Russ
See Hall, Steve

Markina, Mademoiselle
See Taylor, Mary A.

Markins, W. S.
See Jenkins, Marie M[agdalen]

Markish, David 1938- [CA]
Russian-born author
* Maguen, David

Markkula, A. C. 20th c. [TI 1-3-83]
American business executive
* Markkula, Mike

Markkula, Mike
See Markkula, A. C.

Markland, [Cleneth Eu]gene 1919- [BE]
American baseball player
* Markland, Mousey

Markland, Mousey
See Markland, [Cleneth Eu]gene

Markland, Russell 1892- [WWL]
British author and poet
* Ingersley, R. M.

Markle, George Buscher 1827-1888
[HPPN]
American inventor
* [The] Father of the Breaker

Marko Kraljevic 1335-1394 [HPPN]
Serbian hero
* [The] Son of the King

Marko [or Markoski?], Vincent
1903-1954 [SC]
American actor
* Tyler, Tom

Markoosie
See Patsauq, Markoosie

Markov, Georgi 1929?-1978 [CA]
Bulgarian author and playwright
* St. George, David [joint pseudonym
  with David Atlee Phillips]

Markova, Alicia
See Marks, Lilian Alicia

**Markovich, Mariia Aleksandrovna
[Velinskaia]** 1834-1907 [BI]
Russian author
* Vovchok, Marko

Markowitz, Ernest H. 1919- [BEW,
EMT]
American producer and playwright
* Martin, Ernest H.

Markowitz, Irvin 1923- [EJ]
American jazz musician
* Markowitz, Marky

Markowitz, Leila 1936- [BEW]
American actress and singer
* Martin, Leila

Markowitz, Marky
See Markowitz, Irvin

Markowitz, Richard 1926- [ASC]
American composer
* Allen, Richard

Markowitz, Sandra 1937- [SW, TR]
American actress
* Harris, Barbara

Marks, Albert A. 1911?- [WP 9-12-84]
*American stockbroker and pageant
official*
* Miss America, Mr.

Marks, Charles 1881-1971 [F2]
American actor and comedian
* Dale

Marks, Edith Bobroff 1924- [CA]
American educator and author
* Bobroff, Edith

Marks, Elias J. 1880-1960 [ASC]
American composer and singer
* Dawson, Eli

Marks, Harry H. [FFF]
American writer
* Grinder

Marks, J.
See Highwater, Jamake

Marks, Jack Wilson Manning 1916-
[BEW]
American actor, director, educator
* Manning, Jack

Marks, Lilian Alicia 1910- [CAP]
British ballet dancer
* Markova, Alicia

Marks, Mrs. L. S.
Author
* Peabody, Josephine Preston

Marks, Nora
See Atkinson, Eleanor [Stackhouse]

Marks, Pat R.
See Feinman, Jeffrey

Marks, Peter
See Smith, Robert Kimmel

Marks, Richard 19th c. [HFN, PA]
British author and clergyman
* Aliquis
* One Who Loves the Souls of the
Lambs

Marks, Robert Walter 20th c.
Author
* Colleton, John

Marks, Rudenko 20th c. [WFA]
French-born fashion designer
* Luba

Marks, Sadye 1906?-1983
American entertainer
* Livingstone, Mary

Marks, Sallie
See Showles, Mrs. William

Marks, Stan[ley] 1929- [CA]
Australian author
* King, Martin

Marks, Winston K[itchener] 20th c.
[WGT]
Author
* Winney, Ken

Marks-Highwater, J.
See Highwater, Jamake

Marksman, Little Miss
See Long, Margaret

Markson, Sean
See Marcellini, Siro

Markun, Patricia Maloney 1924- [CA,
SAT]
American author
* Forrest, Sybil
* Maloney, Pat
* Marroquin, Patricio
* O'Carroll, Ryan

Markus, Louis Casimir Ladislas
1882?-1941 [HPPN]
Polish painter
* Marcousis, Louis Casimir Ladislas

Markwell, Mary
See Hayes, Catherine E. [Simpson]

Marland, Ernest Whitworth 1874-?
[HPPN]
American politician
* Marland, Hot Oil

Marland, Hot Oil
See Marland, Ernest Whitworth

Marlay
See Chapman, D. W.

Marlborough
See Oaksey, [Lord] John Geoffrey
Tristram

Marlee, Paul
See Nijbroek, Paul Armand

Marler, Walt A.
See Dawley, Thomas Robinson, Jr.

Marley
See Marlowe, Christopher

Marley, B. B.
See Marley, Robert Nesta [Bob]

Marley, Frank Elsworth 1862-? [NAA]
American author and editor
* Historian

Marley, King
See Marley, Robert Nesta [Bob]

Marley, Robert Nesta [Bob] 1945-1981
[HPPN]
Jamaican guitarist and singer
* [The] King of Reggae
* Marley, B. B.
* Marley, King
* [The] Reggae Master
* [The] Reggae Musician

Marlin, Henry
See Giggal, Kenneth

Marlin, Hilda
See Van Stockum, Hilda

Marlin, Morris Wayne 1915- [CWG,
DAM]
American country-western performer
* Marlin, Sleepy

Marlin, Roy
See Ashmore, Basil Norton

Marlin, Sleepy
See Marlin, Morris Wayne

Marling, Ilse   [THR]
German-born actress and singer
* Marvenga, Ilse

Marling, Matt
See Webb, Charles Hull

Marlinski, Cossack
See Bestuzhev [or Bestuschew],
Aleksandr Aleksandrovich

Marlitt, E.
See John, Eugenie

Marlitt, E. P.
See John, Eugenie

Marlo, Karl
See Winkelbleich, Karl Georg

Marlot, Raymond
See Angremy, Jean-Pierre

Marlow, Edwina
See Huff, Tom Elmer

Marlow, [Lady] Harriet
See Beckford, William

Marlow, Joyce
See Connor, Joyce Mary

Marlow, Louis
See Wilkinson, Louis Umfreville

Marlow, Lucy
See McAleer, Lucy Ann

Marlow, Mary
See Orlando, Ada

Marlow, Sidney
See Coggins, Paschal Heston

Marlowe, Alan Stephen 1937- [HPPN]
American actor and author
* Alexander, Kyle

Marlowe, Amy Bell [house pseudonym]
[Stratemeyer Syndicate]
See Stratemeyer, Edward L.

Marlowe, Charles
See Jay, Harriet

Marlowe, Christopher 1564-1593
[HPPN, NPS, SN]
British playwright
* [The] Father of English Dramatic
Poetry
* Marley
* Marlowe, Kit
* [A] Second Shakespeare
* That Atheist Tamburian

Marlowe, Dan J[ames] 1914- [EMD]
American writer
* Sandaval, Jaime

Marlowe, Hugh
See Hipple, Hugh Herbert

Marlowe, Hugh
See Patterson, Harry

Marlowe, Jerry
See Mautner, Jerome

Marlowe, Joan
See Mintz, Joan

Marlowe, Julia
See Frost, Sarah Frances

Marlowe, Kenneth 1926- [CA]
American author and hair stylist
* Mr. Kenneth
* Stuart, Leslie

Marlowe, Kit
See Marlowe, Christopher

Marlowe, Louis J.
See Goetten, L. J.

Marlowe, Marion
See Townsend, Marion

Marlowe, Stephen
See Lesser, Milton

Marlowe, Sylvia
See Sapira, Sylvia

Marlowe, Webb
See McComas, J[esse] Francis

Marly, Florence
See Smekalova, Hana

Marmaduke, Sir
See Tilton, Theodore

Marmarosa, Dodo
See Marmarosa, Michael

Marmarosa, Michael 1925-   [EJ, PMJ]
American jazz musician
* Marmarosa, Dodo

Marmora, Dagoberto
See Bobadilla y Lunar, Emilio

Marm's Poodle Dog
See Steid, Herman

Marneck, F. H.
See Bolza, Oskar

Marnell, Joseph 20th c.   [SFL, WGT]
Author
* Koomoter, Zeno

Marner, Robert
See Budrys, Algirdas Jonas

Marni, Nicole
See Pelide, Nicole

Marnie, Hal
See Marnie, Harry Sylvester

Marnie, Harry Sylvester 1918-   [BE]
American baseball player
* Marnie, Hal

Marnix, Philip Van [Baron Sainte Aldegonde] 1538-1598   [NPS]
Dutch statesman
* Rabbotenus, Isaac

Marno, Anne
See Italiano, Anna Maria Luisa

Marny, Suzanne
See Johnston, Mabel Annesley

Marolewski, Fred Daniel 1928-   [BE]
American baseball player
* Marolewski, Fritz

Marolewski, Fritz
See Marolewski, Fred Daniel

Maronic, Duke
See Maronic, Dusan

Maronic, Dusan 20th c.   [EF]
American football player
* Maronic, Duke

Marontz, Louis Aston
See Simpson, Louis

Marossi, Ruth
See Krefetz, Ruth

Marot, Clement 1484?-1544   [HN, SN]
French poet
* [The] Chaucer of France
* [The] French Chaucer

Marot, Clement (cont.)
* [The] Poet of Princes
* [The] Valet Poet

Marot, Jean
See Desmaretz, Jean

Marot, Marc
See Koch, Kurt E[mil]

Maroto
See Cheng Sen

Marotte, Jean Gilles 1945-   [FHE, SMG]
Canadian-born hockey player
* Crunch, Captain

Marprelate, Martin
See Barrow, Henry

Marprelate, Martin
See Harvey, Gabriel

Marprelate, Martin
See Penry, John

Marprelate, Martin
See Throckmorton, Job

Marprelate, Martin
See Udall, John

Marpriest, Martin
See Overton, Richard

Marquand, J. P.
See Marquand, John Phillips

Marquand, John Phillips 1893-1960
[HPPN, LC, WW]
American author
* Marquand, J. P.
* Phillips, John
* [The] Portrayer of Brahmins

Marquand, Josephine
See Gladstone, Josephine

Marquard, Brick
See Marquard, Carl

Marquard, Carl ?-1978   [FIR]
Cinematographer
* Marquard, Brick

Marquard, Leo[pold] 1897-   [CA]
South African author
* Burger, John

Marquard, Richard William 1889-1980
[BAB, PB, SR]
American baseball player
* [The] Eleven Thousand Dollar Beauty
* [The] Eleven Thousand Dollar Lemon
* [The] Eleven Thousand Dollar Wonder
* Marquard, Rube

Marquard, Rube
See Marquard, Richard William

Marquardt, Albert Ludwig 1902-1968
[BE]
American baseball player
* Marquardt, Ollie

Marquardt, Ollie
See Marquardt, Albert Ludwig

Marquart, Gaston Jean 1887?-1955   [BI]
American mathematician and clergyman
* Defendant, [Brother] Felix

Marques, Zaccaria
See Marques, Zacharias Cyrilo

Marques, Zacharias Cyrilo 1937-   [OP]
Brazilian opera singer
* Marques, Zaccaria

Marquess, Clarence Emmett 1925-
[CEI]
Canadian-born hockey player
* Marquess, Mark

Marquess, Mark
See Marquess, Clarence Emmett

[The] Marquess of Carabas
See Copley, John Singleton [Baron Lyndhurst]

Marquette, Bud
See Marquette, Clayton

Marquette, Clayton 20th c.   [BBH]
American gymnastics coach
* Marquette, Bud

Marquette, Jacques 1637-1675   [HPPN]
French missionary and explorer
* Marquette, Pere

Marquette, Pere
See Marquette, Jacques

Marquez, Canena
See Marquez, Luis Angel

Marquez, Francisco 20th c.   [RBE]
Mexican boxer
* Marquez, Trompo

Marquez, Gonzalo 1946-   [PB]
Venezuelan-born baseball player
* Marquez, Hurricane

Marquez, Horatio 1913?-   [HPPN]
American ventrilquist
* Leonardo

Marquez, Hurricane
See Marquez, Gonzalo

Marquez, Leonardo 1818-?   [DNNS, FFF]
Mexican army officer
* [The] Tiger of Tacayuba [or Tacubaya?]

Marquez, Luis Angel 1925-   [BE]
Puerto Rican-born baseball player
* Marquez, Canena

Marquez, Raymond 20th c.   [PHM]
American underworld figure
* Marquez, Spanish Raymond

Marquez, Spanish Raymond
See Marquez, Raymond

Marquez, Trompo
See Marquez, Francisco

Marquez Lopez, Francisca 1888-1962
[BEW, CED]
Spanish actress and singer
* Meller, Raquel

Marquez y Gispert, Matias Felipe
1851-1887 [CW]
Cuban author
* Aclea, Damaso Gil

[The] Marquis
See Aubusson, Francois d'

Marquis au Courtnez
See Guillaume d'Orange

[Le] Marquis de Brandenbourg
See Frederick II

Marquis, Donald Robert Perry
1878-1937 [DLE1]
American author, poet, journalist
* Lantern

[The] Marquis Duke of Cadiz
See Ponce de Leon, Rodrigo

Marquis, Jean-Robert 20th c. [WF]
Film art director
* Altan, Francesco Tullio

Marquis, M. 20th c. [MBF]
British author
* Williams, Richard [house pseudonym]

Marquis, Noonie
See Marquis, Roger Julian

[The] Marquis of Douro
See Bronte, Charlotte

[The] Marquis of Lorne
See Campbell, George John Douglas
[Eighth Duke of Argyle]

Marquis, Roger Julian 1937- [BE]
American baseball player
* Marquis, Noonie

Marr, Charles W. 1862-1912 [BE]
American baseball player
* Marr, Lefty

Marr, Lefty
See Marr, Charles W.

Marr, N. J.
See Marr-Johnson, Nancy

Marr, William
See Dobie, William

Marr-Johnson, Diana [Maugham] 1908-
[CA]
British author
* Maugham, Diana

Marr-Johnson, Nancy 1921?- [CW]
British-born author and journalist
* Marr, N. J.

Marrack, J. F. 20th c. [CA]
Author
* Potiphar [joint pseudonym with
  (George) Anthony Hern]

Marradi, Giovanni 1852-1922 [WBD]
Italian poet
* Labronio, G.

Marre, Albert
See Moshinski, Albert

Marreco, Anne
See Wignall, Anne

Marrero, Adriano 20th c. [RBE]
Dominican boxer
* Marrero, Nani

Marrero, Connie
See Marrero, Conrado Eugenio Ramos

Marrero, Conrado Eugenio Ramos 1917-
[BE]
Cuban-born baseball player
* Marrero, Connie

Marrero, Jose 1870-1909 [HPPN]
Cuban bullfighter
* Cheche

Marrero, Nani
See Marrero, Adriano

Marric, J. J.
See Creasey, John

[A] Married Critic
See Janin, Jules Gabriel

Marriner, Edythe 1918-1975 [BDF, FC,
WEF]
American actress
* Hayward, Susan

Marriott, Alice
See Edgar, Mrs. R.

Marriott, Buck
See Meagher, M.

Marriott, [Sir] James 1731-1803
[HPPN]
British author
* [A] Candid Man

Marriott, James William 1884-1953
[SFL]
Author
* Wray, Roger

Marriott, Moore
See Moore-Marriott, George Thomas

Marrison, Leslie William 1901- [AW,
CA, WD]
Irish-born author
* Dowley, D. M.

Marron Eufrasio, Alejandro 1916- [GS]
Mexican bullfighter
* Farolito [Little Lighthouse]

Marroquin, Patricio
See Markun, Patricia Maloney

Marrou, Henri Irenee 1904- [IAW]
French music critic
* Davenson, Henri

Marrow, Bernard
See Moore, Brian

Marrow, Buck
See Marrow, Charles Kennon

Marrow, Charles Kennon 1909- [BE]
American baseball player
* Marrow, Buck

Marrs, Stella 1932- [EJ7]
American singer
* Soft Soul, Ms.

Marryatt, Florence
See Ross-Church, Florence M.

Marryatt, Frederick 1792-1848 [NPS,
PA]
Author
* [A] Sea Fielding
* Violet, M.

**[The] Marrying Justice of Worcester
County**
See Davis, Walter Alonzo

Marryshow, Theophilus Albert 1887-1958
[CW]
Grenadan poet and legislator
* Golden, Max T.

Mars, Andre 1515-1576 [PA]
Author
* Massius

Mars, Danny
See Marcus, David

Mars, E. C.
See Mazani, Eric C. F. Nhando

Mars, Forrest, Sr. 1905?- [DF 10-17-82]
American business executive
* [The] Howard Hughes of Candy

Mars, Jean Price
See Price-Mars, Jean

Mars, Marjorie
See Brown, Marjorie

Mars, Mickey
See Marcus, David

Mars, Mlle.
See Boutet, Anne Francoise Hippolyte

[The] Mars of China
See Quang-yoo

[The] Mars of Portugal
See Alfonso [or Affonso] de
Albuquerque

Mars, W. T.
See Mars, Witold Tadeusz J.

Mars, Witold Tadeusz J. 1912- [CA,
SAT]
Polish-born artist and illustrator
* Mars, W. T.

Marsala, Mario Salvatore 1909-1975
[PMJ, WWJ]
American jazz musician
* Marsala, Marty

Marsala, Marty
See Marsala, Mario Salvatore

Marsales, Pierre Paul 1863-1927
[HPPN]
American singer
* Polin

Marsangar, Cora
See Mackamotzki, Kunigunde

Marsano, Ramon
See Dinges, John [Charles]

Marschalk, Andrew 18th c. [HPPN]
American journalist
* [The] Father of Journalism in
Mississippi

Marsden, Anthony
See Sutton, Eric Graham Sutton

Marsden, Frederick
See Silver, W. A.

Marsden, Gerrard 1942- [RO2]
British musician
* Gerry

Marsden, James
See Creasey, John

Marsden, John Howard [PA]
Author
* Philomon

Marsden, Samuel 1764-1838 [DNNF, HPPN]
Australian clergyman and missionary
* [The] Apostle of New Zealand
* Apostle to the Maoris

Marsden-Clark, Patricia 1899- [THR]
British actress and singer
* Malone, Patricia

Marse Henry
See Watterson, Henry

Marse Joe McCarthy
See McCarthy, Joseph Vincent

Marsee, Susanne
See Dowell, Susan Irene

Marseille, Hans Joachim 1919-1942
German fighter pilot
* [The] Star of Africa

Marseilles' Good Bishop
See De Belsunce, Henri Francois
Xavier

Marsh, A-Mo
See Marsh, Amos

Marsh [or de Marisco], Adam 13th c.
[NPS]
British monk
* [The] Illustrious Doctor

Marsh, Amos 20th c.
American football player
* Marsh, A-Mo

Marsh, Analyticus
See Morrison, Marsh

Marsh, Andrew
See O'Donovan, John

Marsh, Carol
See Simpson, Norma

Marsh, Constance Crane 19th c. [FFF]
American poet
* Gabriel, Virginia

Marsh, Crazy
See Marsh, Sylvester

Marsh, E. 19th c. [HPPN, PA]
British author
* Apostle to the Maoris
* Nellie

Marsh, Edwin
See Schorb, Edwin Marsh

Marsh, Garry
See Geraghty, Leslie March

Marsh, George Perkins 1801-1882
[HPPN]
American attorney, diplomat, philologist
* P.

Marsh, Henry
See Saklatvala, Beram

Marsh, [Rev.] Herbert 1757-1839
[HPPN]
British clergyman
* [The] Translator of Michaelis

Marsh, J. E.
See Marshall, Evelyn

Marsh, James 1794-1842 [IP]
*American philosopher, theologian,
educator*
* Philopis

Marsh, Jean
See Marshall, Evelyn

Marsh, Joan
See Marsh, John

Marsh, John 1907- [CAP, WD, WGT]
British author and historian
* Davis, Julia
* Elton, John
* Harley, John
* Hastings, Harrington
* Lawrence, Irene
* Marsh, Joan
* Richmond, Grace
* Sawley, Petra
* Ware, Monica
* Woodward, Lilian

Marsh, Leonard 1800-1871 [HPPN]
American physician
* One of Them

Marsh, Mae
See Marsh, Mary Warne

Marsh, Margaret 1892-1925 [SC]
American actress
* Loveridge, Marguerite

Marsh, Margaret Munnerlyn Mitchell
1900-1949 [HPPN, NAA]
American author
* Mitchell, Margaret
* [The] One Book Author

Marsh, Marion
See Krauth, Violet

Marsh, Mary Warne 1895-1968 [BDF,
F1, FC]
American actress
* Marsh, Mae

Marsh, Muriel 1898- [THR]
Irish-born actress
* Alexander, Muriel

Marsh, Patrick
See Hiscock, Leslie

Marsh, Paul
See Hopkins, Kenneth

Marsh, Rebecca
See Neubauer, William Arthur

Marsh, Richard 20th c. [RO2]
American singer
* Saxon, Sky

Marsh, Sylvester 1803-1884 [HPPN]
American railroad builder
* Marsh, Crazy

Marsh, [Rev.] William 19th c. [HPPN]
British clergyman
* [A] Clergyman

Marshak, Il'ia Iakovlevich 1895- [ICB]
Russian author
* Ilin, M.

Marshal de Saxe
See Saxe, [Hermann] Maurice de

Marshal, James
See Bounds, Sydney J[ames]

**[The] Marshal of the Army of God and
Holy Church**
See FitzWalter, Robert

Marshal, Omer
See Mersan, Omer

Marshal, William ?-1219 [SN]
First Earl of Pembroke and Strigul
* [The] Protector

Marshall, A. J. P. 19th c. [IP]
British author
* [A] Bachelor of Arts

Marshall, Alan John 1911-1967 [BI]
Australian author and zoologist
* Marshall, Jock

Marshall, Albert Leroy 1943- [SMG]
Canadian-born hockey player
* Marshall, Cat
* Marshall, Moose

Marshall, Archibald
See Marshall, Arthur Hammond

Marshall, Arthur C. 20th c. [MBF]
British author and editor
* Brooke, Arthur
* Crane, Berkeley
* Steele, Howard [house pseudonym]
* Yorke, Carras

Marshall, Arthur Hammond 1866-1934
[SFL]
Author
* Marshall, Archibald

Marshall, B. R.
See Marshall, Brian Roberts

Marshall, Bart
See Marshall, Herbert

Marshall, Boisy
See Marshall, William

Marshall, Brenda
See Ankerson, Ardis

Marshall, Brian Roberts 1935- [ART]
British artist
* Marshall, B. R.

Marshall, Buck
See Marshall, David

Marshall, Buster
See Marshall, Vivian Burey

Marshall, Cat
See Marshall, Albert Leroy

Marshall, [Sarah] Catherine [Wood]
1914-1983 [CA]
American author and editor
* LeSourd, Catherine

Marshall, Catherine
See DuBreuil, Elizabeth Lorinda

Marshall, Cecelia A. Suyat 1928- [IBW]
*Wife of American Supreme Court Justice,
Thurgood Marshall*
* Marshall, Cissy

Marshall, Charles [IP]
British clergyman and author
* C. M., Vicar of Brixworth

Marshall, Charles 1899?-1975 [SW]
American actor
* Marshall, Red

Marshall, Charles 19th c. [IP, PA]
British author
* Grey, Heraclitus
* Harkaway

Marshall, Charles Anthony [Charlie]
See Marczlewicz, Charles Anthony

Marshall, Charles C., III 1945?-
American student activist
* Marshall, Chip

Marshall, Charles Hunt 20th c. [WW]
Author
* Hunt, Peter [joint pseudonym with
George Worthing Yates]

Marshall, Chester Alan
See Chess, Stanley

Marshall, Chip
See Marshall, Charles C., III

Marshall, Christabel ?-1960 [LC]
British author
* St. John, Christopher Marie

Marshall, Cissy
See Marshall, Cecelia A. Suyat

Marshall, Clarence Westly 1925- [BE]
American baseball player
* Marshall, Cuddles

Marshall, Cuddles
See Marshall, Clarence Westly

Marshall, Cy
See Marshall, Roy DeVerne

Marshall, David 20th c. [BBH, CSH]
Canadian lacrosse player
* Marshall, Buck

Marshall, Denz
See Marshall, Malcolm Denzil

Marshall, Doc
See Marshall, Edward Herbert

Marshall, Doc
See Marshall, William Riddle

Marshall, Douglas
See McClintock, Marshall

Marshall, E. G.
See Marshall, Everett G.

Marshall, E. P.
See Montgomery, Rutherford George

Marshall, Edison 1894- [HPPN]
American author
* Hunter, Hall

Marshall, Edmund 1724-1797 [FFF]
British clergyman and author
* Cantianus

Marshall, Edmund
See Hopkins, Kenneth

Marshall, Edward Herbert 1906- [BE]
American baseball player
* Marshall, Doc

Marshall, Elizabeth Margaret 1926-
[IAW]
Scottish author
* Sutherland, Elizabeth

Marshall, Emily
See Hall, Bennie Caroline [Humble]

Marshall, Eric 20th c. [CA]
American author
* Brown, Turner, Jr. [joint pseudonym
with Stuart Hample]

Marshall, Evelyn 1897- [AW, CA, SAT]
British author
* Bourne, Lesley
* Marsh, J. E.
* Marsh, Jean

Marshall, Everett G. 1910- [FC]
American actor
* Marshall, E. G.

Marshall, Frances 20th c. [NPS]
Author
* St. Aubyn, Alan

Marshall, Francis 20th c. [ART]
British illustrator, painter, author
* F. M.

Marshall, Frank James 1877-1944
[HPPN]
American chess player
* America's Ambassador of Chess
* [The] Father of the Marshall Swindle

Marshall, Gary
See Snow, Charles Horace

Marshall, George Catlett 1880-1959
[CND]
American military leader
* Braid [code name used during World
War II]

Marshall, George Catlett (cont.)
* Fourfold [code name used during
World War II]
* Mell, Mr. [code name used during
World War II]

Marshall, George W. 19th c. [IP]
British author
* G. W. M.

Marshall, H. H.
See Jahn, Joseph Michael

Marshall, H. P. 20th c. [MBF]
British author
* Stark, Jonathan

Marshall, Henry
See Battcock, Marshall King

Marshall, Herbert 1890-
British actor
* Marshall, Bart

Marshall, Iron Eyes
See Marshall, Samuel Lyman Atwood

Marshall, Iron Mike
See Marshall, Michael Grant

Marshall, Jack
See Marshall, William

Marshall, Jack
See Martin, Hugh

Marshall, James Vance 1887-1964
[CAP]
Australian author
* Doone, Jice

Marshall, James Vance
See Payne, Donald Gordon

Marshall, Jim 20th c. [IBW]
American football player
* Marshall, Wrong Way

Marshall, Joanne
See La Cock, Joanne Letitia

Marshall, Joanne
See Rundle, Anne

Marshall, Jock
See Marshall, Alan John

Marshall, John 1755-1835 [HPPN, SN]
American Supreme Court justice
* [The] Ablest Constitutionalist
* [The] Expounder of the Constitution
* [The] Great American Jurist
* [The] Legal Interpreter of the
Constitution
* Marshall, Silver Heels

Marshall, John
See Pepper, Frank S.

Marshall, Joseph 1902-1948 [PMJ,
WWJ]
American jazz musician
* Marshall, Kaiser

Marshall, Joseph
See Krechniak, Joseph Marshall

Marshall, Kaiser
See Marshall, Joseph

Marshall, Katherine Helen Maud ?-1945
[LC]
British author
* Diver, Maud

Marshall, Kim
See   Marshall, Michael [Kimbrough]

Marshall, Lloyd?
See   Wilding, Philip

Marshall, Lovat
See   Duncan, W[illiam] Murdoch

Marshall, Maco
See   Marshall, Malcolm Denzil

Marshall, Malcolm Denzil 1958- [DC]
West Indian cricketer
* Marshall, Denz
* Marshall, Maco

Marshall, Margaret Lenore Wiley 1908-
[CAP, WD]
American author
* Wiley, Margaret L.

Marshall, Marguerite Mooers
See   Dean, Marguerite Mooers Marshall

Marshall, Marjorie Bell 1916- [AW]
British author
* March, Stella

Marshall, Mel[vin] 1911- [CA]
American author
* Cory, Ray

Marshall, Michael [Kimbrough] 1948-
[CA]
American author and educator
* Marshall, Kim

Marshall, Michael Grant 1943- [SMG]
American baseball player
* Marshall, Iron Mike

Marshall, Mr.
See   Mitchell, John Kearsley

Marshall, Moose
See   Marshall, Albert Leroy

Marshall, Mort
See   Lichtenstein, Mortimer Haig

Marshall, Mrs. Frank   [FFF]
Entertainer
* Cavendish, Ada

Marshall, Nathaniel ?-1729 [HPPN]
British clergyman
* [A] Presbyter of the Church of
  England

Marshall, Oliver P.   [PA]
Author
* Revilo

Marshall, Percy
See   Young, Percy M[arshall]

Marshall, Peter
See   La Cock, Pierre

Marshall, Preston 20th c. [HPPN]
*American laundry tycoon and baseball
club owner*
* Marshall, Wet Wash

Marshall, Raymond
See   Raymond, Rene

Marshall, Red
See   Marshall, Charles

Marshall, Robert 20th c.   [EF]
American football player
* Marshall, Rube

Marshall, Roy DeVerne 1890- [BE]
American baseball player
* Marshall, Cy
* Marshall, Rube

Marshall, Rube
See   Marshall, Robert

Marshall, Rube
See   Marshall, Roy DeVerne

Marshall, S. L. A.
See   Marshall, Samuel Lyman Atwood

Marshall, Sallie
See   Chase, Sallie Marshall

Marshall, Samuel Lyman Atwood
1900-1977 [HPPN]
American general, historian, journalist
* Marshall, Iron Eyes
* Marshall, S. L. A.
* Marshall, Slam

Marshall, Silver Heels
See   Marshall, John

Marshall, Slam
See   Marshall, Samuel Lyman Atwood

Marshall, Stephen 1594?-1655 [DEP,
DNNS, FFF]
British clergyman
* [The] Geneva Bull

Marshall, Thomas Riley 1854-1925
[HPPN]
American vice president
* [The] Advocate of the Five Cent
  Cigar
* [The] Hoosier Statesman

Marshall, Thomas William 1815-1877
[IP]
British clergyman and author
* Chasuble, Archdeacon

Marshall, Thoroughgood 1908- [IBW]
American Supreme Court Justice
* Civil Rights, Mr.
* Marshall, Thurgood

Marshall, Thurgood
See   Marshall, Thoroughgood

Marshall, Tully
See   Phillips, Tully

Marshall, Tully
See   Phillips, William

Marshall, Vivian Burey ?-1955 [IBW]
*Wife of American Supreme Court Justice,
Thurgood Marshall*
* Marshall, Buster

Marshall, Wet Wash
See   Marshall, Preston

Marshall, William 1907- [IBW, OBW]
American baseball player and bowler
* Marshall, Boisy
* Marshall, Jack

Marshall, William
See   Walpole, Horatio [Fourth Earl of
Orford]

Marshall, William Riddle 1875-1959
[BE]
American baseball player
* Marshall, Doc

Marshall, Willie
See   Marshall, Willmott Charles

Marshall, Willmott Charles 1931- [CEI]
Canadian-born hockey player
* Marshall, Willie

Marshall, Wrong Way
See   Marshall, Jim

[The] Marshalltown Infant
See   Anson, Adrian Constantine

[The] Marshal's Backstreet Astrologer
See   Lon Nol

Marshner, Connaught Coyne 1951- [CA]
American writer
* Sarsfield, C. P.

Marsland, Bishop of
See   Duncan, Ronald [Frederick Henry]

Marsland, Maj. Gen.
See   Duncan, Ronald [Frederick Henry]

Marson, Aileen
See   Pitt-Marson, Aileen

Marsten, Richard
See   Lombino, Salvatore A.

Marston, Adelaide [joint pseudonym
with Lynn Stone]
See   Richton, Addy

Marston, Adelaide [joint pseudonym
with Addy Richton]
See   Stone, Lynn

Marston, Edward 1825-1914 [IP, WWL]
British author and publisher
* Amateur Angler
* [A] Publisher

Marston, Hyde
See   Carlton, Captain

Marston, [Major] Jeffery Eardley 1887-
[LAO]
Welsh-born author
* Jeffery, Jeffery E.

Marston, John 1575-1634 [DEA, DEL,
NPS, SN, WBD]
British playwright
* Brabant Junior
* Clove
* Crispinus
* J. M.
* Kinsayder, W.
* Millidus
* Publius Ovid

Marston, John (cont.)
* [The] Rugged Timon of the Elizabethan Drama
* W. K.

Marston, [Col.] Marvin R. 20th c. [BBH]
American sled dog racer
* Marston, Muktuk

Marston, Max
See Marston, Maxwell R.

Marston, Maxwell R. 1892- [EG]
American golfer
* Marston, Max

Marston, Mildred
See Scott, Anna [Kay]

Marston, Muktuk
See Marston, [Col.] Marvin R.

Marston, Philip Bourke 1850-1887 [HPPN]
British poet
* Philip the King

Marston, William Moulton 1893-1947 [WECO]
American author and cartoonist
* Moulton, Charles

Mart, Donovan
See Martin, E. Le Breton

Marteau, Amedee [IP]
Author
* Marcellus

[Le] Marteau des Heretiques
See Ailly, Pierre d'

Martel
See Frothingham, Washington

Martel, Charles
See Charles [or Karl]

Martel, Charles
See Delf, Thomas

Martel, Doc
See Martel, Leon Alphonse

Martel, Don Robert 1939- [CWG]
American country-western performer
* Martel, Marty

Martel, Felicien 1879?-1948 [BI]
French actor
* Tramel

Martel, Leon Alphonse 1883-1947 [BE]
American baseball player
* Martel, Doc
* Martel, Marty

Martel, Marty
See Martel, Don Robert

Martel, Marty
See Martel, Leon Alphonse

Martel, Marty
See Martel, Wilbert

Martel, Wilbert 1887-1958 [BBH, CSH]
Canadian bowler
* King of the Candlepins
* Martel, Marty

Martel de Janville, Comtesse de
See Riqueti de Mirabeau, Sibylle Gabrielle Marie Antoinette

Martell, Claudia
See Wolff, Victoria

Martell, James
See Bingley, David Ernest

Martens, Adolphe-Adhemar-Louis-Michel 1898-1962 [CA, TCL]
Belgian playwright and author
* De Ghelderode, Michel

Martens, Fernand 1904-1970 [FC]
French actor
* Gravet, Fernand

Martens, Paul
See Southwold, Stephen

Martequilla, Angel 1940- [BX]
Cuban-born boxer
* Napoles, Jose

Martes, Jose Antonio 1920- [CW]
Curacaon poet and author
* Lauffer, Pierre

Martha, Henry
See Finkelstein, Mark

Martha Jean, the Queen
See Steinberg, Martha Jean Jones

Marti, Isidro 1884-1921 [HPPN]
Spanish bullfighter
* Flores

Marti, Pepe
See Marti Perez, Jose Julian

Marti Perez, Jose Julian 1853-1895 [CW, HPPN]
Cuban poet, playwright, author
* Marti, Pepe
* [The] Martyr of Cuban Independence

Martial
See Martialis, Marcus Valerius

Martialis, Marcus Valerius 40?-104? [BI, HPPN]
Roman epigrammatist
* Martial

Martin 316?-397? [SN, WBD]
Saint
* [The] Apostle of Gaul
* [The] Apostle of the Gauls
* Martin of Tours

Martin, [Frater]
See Gillet, Stanislaus

Martin, [Brother]
See Luther, Martin

Martin, A. L. 20th c. [MBF]
British author
* Reid, Desmond [house pseudonym]

Martin, Abe
See Hubbard, Frank McKinney

Martin, Abe
See Martin, Glen

Martin, Albert
See Martin, Alexandre

Martin, Albert
See Mehan, Joseph Albert

Martin, Albert
See Nussbaum, Al[bert F.]

Martin, Alexandre 1815-1895 [HPPN, WBD]
French mechanic and politician
* Albert the Workingman
* L'Ouvrier Albert
* Martin, Albert

Martin, Alfred Manuel
See Pesano, Alfred Manuel

Martin, Alfred Tobias John 1802-1850 [IP]
British poet
* [A] Cosmopolite

Martin, Alphonse Case 1845-1933 [BE]
American baseball player
* Martin, Phoney

Martin, Amos
See Martin, Anthony

Martin, Andre
See Jacoby, Henry

Martin, Anne 1920- [HPPN]
American statistician
* [The] Pride of Pittsburgh
* [The] Savior of Terre Haute

Martin, Anne E.
See Patterson, Anna Eliza

Martin, Anthony 1949- [SMG]
American football player
* Martin, Amos

Martin, Anthony
See Glynn, Anthony Arthur

Martin, April
See Sherrill, Dorothy

Martin, Babe
See Martinovich, Boris Michael

Martin, Barnes Robertson 1923- [BE]
American baseball player
* Martin, Barney

Martin, Barney
See Martin, Barnes Robertson

Martin, Biddie
See Martin, Frank L.

Martin, Big Jim
See Martin, James

Martin, Bill
See Joel, William Martin [Billy]

Martin, Billy
See Pesano, Alfred Manuel

Martin, Blind George
See Phelps, Arthur

Martin, Bob 1898- [BX, RBE]
American boxer
* Martin, Fighting Bob

Martin, Bon Louis Henri 1810-1883
[IP, PA]
French historian and author
* Felix
* Irner

Martin, Boris Michael
See Martinovich, Boris Michael

Martin, Bradlee
See Martin, George E.

Martin, Bruce
See Paine, Lauran [Bosworth]

Martin, Butch
See Martin, Oliver, Jr.

Martin, Cannonball
See Martino, Edward Vittorio

Martin, Carol
See Martin, Frances

Martin, Cecilia 1903- [HPPN]
American photographer and journalist
* Martin, Jackie

Martin, Charles 1917-1974 [BI]
French fashion designer and composer
* Esterel

Martin, Charles
See Fernandez, Raymond

Martin, Chink
See Abraham, Martin

Martin, Chris-Pin
See Martin Piaz, Ysabel Ponciana
Chris-Pin

Martin, Christopher
See Hoyt, Edwin P[almer], Jr.

Martin, Clara [Barnes] 19th c. [IP]
American author
* C. B. M.

Martin, Clarence 1895?- [HPPN]
American aviator
* Martin, Mercury

Martin, Cort
See Sherman, Jory [Tecumseh]

Martin, Cye
See Martin, Seymore

Martin, Daisy
See James, Daisy

Martin, David 1915- [TCC]
Hungarian-born author and poet
* Spinifex

Martin, [Brother] David
See Martin, Edward Sylvester

Martin, Dean
See Crocetti, Dino

Martin, Dickie
See Martin, Harry B.

Martin, Doc
See Martin, Harold Winthrop

Martin, Dorothea
See Hewitt, Kathleen Douglas

Martin, Dugie
See Martin, Slater

Martin, E. Le Breton 1874-1944 [MBF]
British author
* Lee, Raymond
* Mart, Donovan
* Shaw, Martin

Martin, Eddie
See Martino, Edward Vittorio

Martin, Edward
See McCord, James W., Jr.

Martin, Edward Sanford 1856-? [IP]
American poet
* E. S. M.

Martin, Edward Sylvester 1901- [BI]
American librarian
* Martin, [Brother] David

Martin, Edward Winslow
See McCabe, James Dabney

Martin, Egbert 1859-1887 [CW]
Guyanese poet
* Leo

Martin, Elizabeth 1869-1941 [SC]
American actress
* Weldon, Lillian

Martin, Ellis
See Ryan, Marah Ellis

Martin, Elwood Goode 1893- [BE]
American baseball player
* Martin, Speed

Martin, Ernest H.
See Markowitz, Ernest H.

Martin, Errol 20th c. [WP 9-17-82]
Jamaican-born musician
* Martin, Honey Boy

Martin, Eugene
See De Vaux, Baron

Martin, Eugene [house pseudonym]
[Stratemeyer Syndicate]
See Stratemeyer, Edward L.

Martin, Eugenie 1879?-1959 [BEW]
Russian-born actress
* Geniat, Marcelle

Martin, Eusebe
See Morel, Henri

Martin, Fiddlin'
See Martin, Frank

Martin, Fiddlin' Joe
See Martin, Joe

Martin, Fighting Bob
See Martin, Robert

Martin, Frances 1948- [BA]
American journalist
* Martin, Carol

Martin, Francis
See Reid, Charles [Stuart]

Martin, Francois Xavier 1764?-1846
[FFF]
American jurist
* [The] Father of the Jurisprudence of
Louisiana

Martin, Frank 20th c. [BWW]
American musician
* Martin, Fiddlin'

Martin, Frank
See Golodnotzky, Harry

Martin, Frank L. 1881-1935 [HPPN]
American minstrel
* Martin, Biddie

Martin, Freddy 1907?- [HPPN]
American jazz musician
* Silvertone, Mr.

Martin, Frederick ?-1864 [IP]
British clergyman and author
* F. M.

Martin, Fredric
See Christopher, Matt[hew F.]

Martin, G. A.
See Martin, Gloria Ann

Martin, Ged
See Martin, Gerald Warren

Martin, George 1889- [NAA]
American editor and writer
* Pepper, George

Martin, George 20th c. [GW]
American rodeo performer
* Martin, Tex

Martin, George
See Martin, Jorge

Martin, George Alfred 1911- [BBH]
American wrestling coach
* [The] Father of High School
Wrestling

Martin, George E. 1875-1955 [HPPN]
American actor
* Martin, Bradlee

Martin, George Madden
See Martin, Mrs. Atwood R.

Martin, George Robert
See Cohen, Paul Arthur

Martin, Gerald Warren 1945- [CA]
British-born historian and author
* Martin, Ged

Martin, Glen 20th c. [BBH]
American baseball coach
* Martin, Abe

Martin, Glenn L. 1886-1955 [HPPN]
American designer, inventor, pilot
* [The] Father of the B-10

Martin, Gloria Ann 1937- [IAW]
American author and poet
* London, Lisa
* Martin, G. A.
* Tramin, A. G.

Martin, Gloria Ann (cont.)
* Tramin, Ed
* Tramin, Lisa

Martin, Greg
See Miller, George Louquet

Martin, Harold Winthrop 1887-1925
[BE]
American baseball player
* Martin, Doc

Martin, Harry B. 1874-1959 [GF]
American golf writer
* Martin, Dickie

Martin, Harvey 1950- [SMG]
American football player
* Martin, Too Mean

Martin, Helena Faucit 1817-1898
[HPPN]
British actress
* Faucit, Helen
* One Who Has Impersonated Them

Martin, [Sir] Henry 1801-1863 [FFF,
IP, PA]
British author
* [A] Lay Baronet
* Phoenix

Martin, Herschel Ray 1909- [BE]
American baseball player
* Martin, Hersh

Martin, Hersh
See Martin, Herschel Ray

Martin, Honest Abe
See Martin, Othol H.

Martin, Honey Boy
See Martin, Errol

Martin, Hubert Jacques 1943- [BI, CEI,
FHE]
Canadian-born hockey player and aviator
* Martin, Pit

Martin, Hugh 20th c. [HPPN]
American singer
* Marshall, Jack

Martin, Hugh Whitfield 1874-1952
[BBD]
American opera singer
* Martin, Riccardo

Martin, Humanity
See Martin, Richard

Martin, J. C.
See Martin, Joseph Clifton

Martin, J. F. [FFF]
American writer
* Hydrant Chuck

Martin, J. L. ?-1848 [IP]
American poet
* J. L. M.

Martin, Jack [NN]
Boxer
* [The] Baker
* Master of the Rolls

Martin, Jackie
See Martin, Cecilia

Martin, Jacques ?-1562 [PA]
Author
* Marinus

Martin, James 1783-1860 [PI]
Irish poet
* Clarke, Owen
* McBlab, Thady
* O'Connell, Philip

Martin, James 1886- [IBW]
American businessman
* Martin, Big Jim

Martin, James 1902-1961 [HPPN]
American producer
* Morelle, Jay

Martin, James Green 1819-1878
[HPPN]
American army soldier
* Old One Wing

Martin, James R. 1919- [FB]
American football player
* Martin, Jungle Jim

Martin, James Sullivan [IP]
American author
* [A] Revolutionary Soldier

Martin, Janet
See Garfinkel, Bernard

Martin, Jay
See Golding, Morton J[ay]

Martin, Jean Baptiste 1659-1735 [RH]
French painter
* [Des] Batailles [Of Battles]

Martin, Jeremy [joint pseudonym with
Martin P. Levin]
See Levin, Marcia Obrasky

Martin, Jeremy [joint pseudonym with
Marcia Obrasky Levin]
See Levin, Martin P.

Martin, Joe 1900-1975 [BWW]
American singer
* Martin, Fiddlin' Joe

Martin, John
Jazz musician
* Martin, Spider

Martin, John 1791-1855 [IP, PA]
British bookseller and author
* J. M.

Martin, John
See Shepard, Morgan Van Roorbach

Martin, John
See Tatham, Laura

Martin, John Leonard 1904-1965 [AS,
BE, PB]
American baseball player
* Martin, Pepper
* [The] Wild Horse of the Osage

Martin, John [[code name used during
World War II]]
See Churchill, Winston Spencer

Martin, Jorge 20th c. [WF]
Actor
* Martin, George

Martin, Jose 1843-1910 [GS]
Spanish bullfighter
* La Santera [The Sanctuary Keeper]

Martin, Jose L[uis] 1921- [CA]
Puerto Rican-born author and educator
* Yunkel, Ramar

Martin, Joseph Clifton 1936- [BE]
American baseball player
* Martin, J. C.

Martin, Joseph Samuel [Joe] 1876-1964
[BE]
American baseball player
* Martin, Silent Joe

Martin, Josiah 18th c. [IP]
British author
* J. M.

Martin, Joy 1922- [CA]
American author and educator
* Crandall, Joy

Martin, Judith Sylvia 1938- [CA]
American author and columnist
* Manners, Miss

Martin, Judy
See Overstake, Eva Alaine

Martin, June Hall
See McCash, June Hall

Martin, Jungle Jim
See Martin, James R.

Martin, Kevin
See Pelton, Robert W[ayne]

Martin, Kimberly Ann 1960?-1977
[HPPN]
American prostitute and murder victim
* Wright, Donna

Martin, [Basil] Kingsley 1897-1969
[CA]
British editor and writer
* Critic

Martin, Lady Theodore 19th c. [FFF]
British actress
* Fawcitt, Helen

Martin, Lance 1918- [IAW]
American author
* Ancel, Martin

Martin, Lawrence 1895- [NAA]
American educator and writer
* Aylesworth, Allison
* Rutherford, Chas.

Martin le Pondeur
See Cautel, Martin Gilles

Martin, Lee
See Wingate, Anne

Martin, Leila
See Markowitz, Leila

Martin, Lennie
See Marino, Rinaldo R.

Martin, Lillie J. 1852-1943   [HPPN]
American psychologist
* [The] Unretired Psychologist

Martin, Linda Lou
See Martin, Wanda Frances Arnold

Martin, Little Chink
See Abraham, Martin, Jr.

Martin, Lloyd 1916-   [EJ, PMJ]
American jazz musician
* Martin, Skip

Martin, Lucien
See Gabel, Joseph

Martin, Luther 1748-1826   [HPPN]
American attorney
* [The] Federal Bull Dog

[The] Martin Luther of Switzerland
See Zwingli, Ulrich [or Huldreich]

Martin, Lynn 20th c.
American politician
* [The] Ax

Martin, M. E. 19th c.   [PI]
Irish poet
* M. E. M.

Martin, Malachi 20th c.   [CA]
Irish-born American author
* Serafian, Michael

Martin, Marcia
See Levin, Marcia Obrasky

Martin, Mariano 1937-   [HPPN]
Spanish bullfighter
* Carriles

Martin, Marie Guyard 1599-1672
[HPPN]
French nun and educator
* Mary of the Incarnation

Martin, Mario, Jr.
See Monteleone, Thomas F.

Martin, Mary Letitia 1815-1850
[HPPN, IP, NPS]
Irish author
* Bell, Mrs. Martin
* [The] Irish Heiress
* Martin, Mrs. Bell
* [The] Princess of Connemara

Martin, Mary Steichen
See Calderone, Mary S[teichen]

Martin, Maude
See Bruno, Guido

Martin, Mercury
See Martin, Clarence

Martin, Michael 1775-1822   [BLB, DI,
IP]
Irish-born highwayman
* Lightfoot, Captain

Martin, Mr.
See Burroughs, William [Seward]

Martin, Morris 20th c.
American soil-conservation expert
* Martin, Red

Martin, Mrs. Atwood R.
Author
* Martin, George Madden

Martin, Mrs. Bell
See Martin, Mary Letitia

Martin, Mrs. E. Throop   [IP]
American author
* [A] Lady

Martin, Mrs. Leon Gaines
See Patterson, Anna Eliza

Martin, Mrs. T. J.   [FFF]
Entertainer
* Fiske, Marion

Martin, Nancy 20th c.
American entertainer
* [The] Pride of the West Virginia Hills

Martin, Nancy
See Salmon, Annie Elizabeth [Martin]

Martin, Nell Columbia Boyer 1890-
[WW]
Author
* Boyer, Columbia

Martin, Netta 20th c.   [AW]
Scottish journalist and broadcaster
* Ashton, Lucy

Martin, Ninnie
See Martin, Peggy Annette

Martin, Octave
See Maurras, Charles-Marie-Photius

Martin of the Fed
See Martin, William McChesney, Jr.

Martin of Tours
See Martin

Martin of Troppau ?-1278   [WBD]
Prelate and author
* Martinus Polonus
* [The] Pole

Martin, Oliver
See Davies, Ernest

Martin, Oliver, Jr. 1936-   [IBW]
American bicycle racer
* Martin, Butch

Martin, Othol H. 1908-   [FB]
American football coach
* Martin, Honest Abe

Martin, Patricia Miles 1899-   [CA, SAT,
WD]
American author and poet
* Lane, Jerry
* Miles, Miska

Martin, Paul
See Deale, Kenneth Edwin Lee

Martin, Paul
See Rade, Paul Martin

Martin, Paul R.
See Martin-Dillon, Paul

Martin, Peggy Annette 1931-   [BA]
American government official
* Martin, Ninnie

Martin, Pepper
See Martin, John Leonard

Martin, Pete
See Halfpenny, Peter

Martin, Pete
See Martin, William Thornton

Martin, Peter
See Chaundler, Christine

Martin, Peter
See Leckie, Peter Martin

Martin, Peter
See Waterman, Nixon

Martin, Phoney
See Martin, Alphonse Case

Martin, Pit
See Martin, Hubert Jacques

Martin, Plugger Bill
See Martin, William

Martin, R. J.
See Mehta, Rustam Jehangir

Martin, R. Johnson
See Mehta, Rustam Jehangir

Martin, Ray 20th c.
American billiard player
* Midnight Cowboy

Martin, Red
See Martin, Morris

Martin, Reginald Alec 1900-   [SFL,
WGT]
Author
* Cameron, Brett
* Dixon, Rex
* Eliott, E. C.
* Martin, Rex
* Martin, Robert
* Martin, Scott

Martin, Rex
See Martin, Reginald Alec

Martin, Riccardo
See Martin, Hugh Whitfield

Martin, Richard 1754-?   [HN]
British politician
* Martin, Humanity

Martin, Richard
See Creasey, John

Martin, Richard A.
See Rosenblatt, Richard Andrew

Martin, Rick
See Martin, Robert L.

Martin, Robert 1898-   [HPPN]
American boxer
* Martin, Fighting Bob

Martin, Robert [Lee] 1908-1976   [CA,
HPPN]
American author
* Roberts, Lee

Martin, Robert
See Martin, Reginald Alec

Martin, Robert Bernard 1918- [CA, CC, WD]
American author, critic, educator
* Bernard, Robert

Martin, Robert Jasper ?-1905 [PI]
Irish poet
* Ballyhooley
* R. J. M.

Martin, Robert L. 1919?- [BI]
American gambler
* Martin, Rick

Martin, Robert W.
See Pelton, Robert W[ayne]

Martin, Ross
See Rosenblatt, Martin

Martin, Ruth [house pseudonym]
See Rayner, Claire

Martin, Sallie M. D. 19th c. [FFF, IP]
American author
* Sibyl

Martin, Sam 18th c. [RBE]
British boxer
* [The] Bath Butcher

Martin, Sam
See Moskowitz, Sam

Martin, Samuel 18th c. [SN]
British politician
* [The] Duellist

Martin, Sara
See Dunn, Sara

Martin, Scott
See Martin, Reginald Alec

Martin, Selina [IP]
British author
* S. M.

Martin, Seymore 1914-1972 [SC]
American actor
* Martin, Cye

Martin, Shane
See Johnston, George Henry

Martin, Shel
See Rooney, William

Martin, Silent Joe
See Martin, Joseph Samuel [Joe]

Martin, Skip
See Martin, Lloyd

Martin, Slater 1925- [BB]
American basketball player
* Martin, Dugie

Martin, Smokey Joe
See Martin, William Joseph [Joe]

Martin, Speed
See Martin, Elwood Goode

Martin, Spider
See Martin, John

Martin, Stella
See Heyer, Georgette

Martin, Strother, Jr. 1919-1980 [FIR]
American actor
* [The] Andy Devine for the Age of Anxiety
* [A] Gabby Hayes Without Honor
* Martin, T-Bone

Martin, T-Bone
See Martin, Strother, Jr.

Martin, Tex
See Martin, George

Martin, [Sir] Theodore 1816-1909 [DEA, WWL]
Scottish-born British author
* Gaultier, Bon [joint pseudonym with William Edmonstoune Aytoun]
* T. M.

Martin, Therese 1873-1897 [WBD]
Saint
* Little Flower of Jesus
* Therese de Lisieux

Martin, Thomas [IP]
Irish barrister and author
* [An] Irish Land Owner

Martin, Thomas Hector 1913- [ESF, SFL, WGT]
British author
* Saxon, Peter [house pseudonym]
* Thomas, Martin

Martin, Tom
See Paine, Lauran [Bosworth]

Martin, Tony
See Morris, Alvin

Martin, Too Mean
See Martin, Harvey

Martin, Vicky
See Storey, Victoria Carolyn

Martin, Violet Florence 1865-1915 [LC, TC]
Irish author
* Ross, Martin
* Somerville and Ross [joint pseudonym with Edith Anna Oenone Somerville]

Martin, W. 20th c. [MBF]
British author
* Kingsley, Hamilton

Martin, Wanda Frances Arnold 1926- [CWG]
American country-western performer
* Martin, Linda Lou

Martin, Webber
See Silverberg, Robert

Martin, Wendy
See Martini, Teri

Martin, William 1801-1867 [DEL, IP, RH]
British author and publisher
* Old Chatty Cheerful
* Parley, Peter

Martin, William 19th c. [BBH]
American bicycle racer
* Martin, Plugger Bill

Martin, William Joseph [Joe] 1911-1960 [BE]
American baseball player
* Martin, Smokey Joe

Martin, William McChesney, Jr. 1906-
American government official
* Head of the Fed
* [The] Maestro of Money
* Martin of the Fed

Martin, William Thornton 1901?-1980
American author and editor
* Martin, Pete

Martin-Beaulieu, Marie Desire 1791-1863 [BBD]
French composer and author
* Beaulieu, Marie-Desire

Martin Caro Cases, Francisco 1915- [GS]
Spanish bullfighter
* Curro Caro [Dear Little Curro]

Martin Caro Cases, Juan 1910- [GS]
Spanish bullfighter
* Chiquito de la Audiencia

Martin-Dillon, Paul 1886- [CAT]
American author and journalist
* Martin, Paul R.

Martin IV
See De Brie, Simon

Martin Piaz, Ysabel Ponciana Chris-Pin 1893-1953 [F1, HCA]
American actor
* [El] Comico
* Martin, Chris-Pin

Martin Ramos, Baldomero 1940- [GS]
Spanish bullfighter
* Terremoto de Malaga [Earthquake from Malaga]

Martin Sanchez, Santiago 1938- [GS, OCS]
Spanish bullfighter
* [El] Viti

Martin Sevilla, Francisco 1857-1888 [GS]
Spanish bullfighter
* [El] Corneta [The Bugle]

Martin V
See Colonna, Ottone [or Oddone]

Martin y Solar, Vicente 1754-1810 [WBD]
Spanish composer
* Martini, Vicente

Martina, Joseph John [Joe] 1889-1962 [BE]
American baseball player
* Martina, Oyster Joe

Martina, Oyster Joe
See Martina, Joseph John [Joe]

Martincho
See Ebassun, Antonio

Martindale, [Rev.] C. C.
See Martindale, Cyril Charlie

Martindale, Cyril Charlie 1879-1963
[LC]
British clergyman and author
* Martindale, [Rev.] C. C.

Martindale, Spencer
See Wolff, William Deakin

Martindale, Wink
See Martindale, Winston Conrad

Martindale, Winston Conrad 1933-
American television performer
* Martindale, Wink

Martine, [Maj.] Max
See Avery, Henry M.

Martineau, Harriet 1802-1876 [DEL,
PA]
British author
* Angelina
* H. M.
* [An] Invalid

Martinelli, Giovanni 1885-1969 [HPPN]
Italian opera singer
* [The] Great Tenor from the Golden
Age of Opera

Martinelli, Ricardo
See Brandon, Johnny

Martinelli, Viola ?-1967 [SC]
American actress
* Holden, Viola

Martines, Julia
See O'Faolain, Julia

Martinetti, Adele
See Pullini, Adele Martinetti

Martinetti, Mme. Ignacio [FFF]
Entertainer
* Murillo, Edith

Martinetz, Vivian L. 1927- [CA]
American author
* Broussard, Vivian L.

Martinez, Buck
See Martinez, John Albert

Martinez, Chuchu
See Martinez, Jose de Jesus

Martinez, Eugenio R. 1924?- [HPPN]
*Cuban-American defendant in Watergate
trial*
* Valdes, Jene

Martinez, Felix Anthony 1950- [SMG,
WWB]
American baseball player
* Martinez, Tippy

Martinez, Gabriel Antonio 1941- [BE]
Cuban-born baseball player
* Martinez, Tony

Martinez, Horacio 20th c. [OBW]
American baseball player
* Martinez, Rabbit

Martinez, Isabel
See Peron, Maria Estela Martinez de

Martinez, Isabelita
See Peron, Maria Estela Martinez de

Martinez, Isidora
See King, Mrs. John J.

Martinez, John Albert 1948- [BE, SMG,
WWB]
American baseball player
* Martinez, Buck

Martinez, Jose 20th c. [HPPN]
Mexican wrestler
* [El] Brasero
* [The] Fastest Man on Land or Sea

Martinez, Jose de Jesus 20th c. [NW
9-27-82, TI 10-22-84]
*Panamanian educator, linguist, army
officer*
* Martinez, Chuchu

Martinez, Julio 1876-1930 [GS]
Spanish bullfighter
* Templaito [The Valiant One]

Martinez, Limonar
See Martinez, Rogelio Ulloa

Martinez, Lino 20th c. [WFA]
Spanish fashion designer
* Lino

Martinez, Lorencillo
See Martinez, Lorenzo Manuel

Martinez, Lorenzo Manuel 17th c. [GS]
Spanish bullfighter
* Martinez, Lorencillo

Martinez, Luis 1930- [EJ7]
American jazz musician
* Martinez, Sabu

Martinez, Marty
See Martinez, Orlando Olivo

Martinez, Octavio 1934- [HPPN]
Spanish bullfighter
* Nacional

Martinez, Orlando Olivo 1941- [BE]
Cuban-born baseball player
* Martinez, Marty

Martinez, Rabbit
See Martinez, Horacio

Martinez, Rogelio Ulloa 1918- [BE]
Cuban-born baseball player
* Martinez, Limonar

Martinez, Rudy 1945- [RO2]
American singer
* Question Mark

Martinez, Sabu
See Martinez, Luis

Martinez, Silvino Garcia 1944-
Cuban chess player
* Garcia, Silvino

Martinez, Teddy
See Martinez, Teodoro Noel

Martinez, Teodoro Noel 1947- [BE]
Dominican-born baseball player
* Martinez, Teddy

Martinez, Tippy
See Martinez, Felix Anthony

Martinez, Tony
See Martinez, Gabriel Antonio

Martinez Alvarez, Rafael 1882-1959
[CW, NAA]
Puerto Rican author and playwright
* Alva, Martin

Martinez Davila, Manuel 1883-1934
[CW]
Puerto Rican poet and author
* Arce, Jose de

Martinez de Hoz, Jose Alfredo *MB
*Argentinian landowner, industrialist,
government official*
* Dr. Joe

Martinez de Jarava, Elio Antonio
1444-1532 [WBD]
Spanish author
* Nebrija [or Lebrija], Elio Antonio de

Martinez-Delgado, Luis 1896- [AW]
Colombian author
* Luimardel

Martinez Gonzalez, Pedro 1932- [GS]
Spanish bullfighter
* Pedres [Big Pedro]

Martinez Hugue, Manuel 1872-1945
[BI]
Spanish sculptor
* Manolo

Martinez Ruiz, Jose 1873?-1967 [CD,
CLC, EWL]
Spanish author and playwright
* Ahriman
* Azorin
* Candido

Martinez y Pingarron, Candido
1867-1925 [GS]
Spanish bullfighter
* [El] Manchequito [The Little Fellow
from La Mancha]

Martinez y Riesco, Manuel 1855-1937
[HPPN]
Spanish bullfighter
* Agujetas

Martinez Zuviria, Gustavo Adolfo
1883-1962 [EWL, TC, WBD]
Argentinian author
* Wast, Hugo

Marting, Ruth Lenore 1907- [WW]
Author
* Bailey, Hilea

Martingale
See White, Charles

Martingale, Hawser
See Sleeper, John Sherburne

Martini, George
See Matrisciano, George

Martini, Giambattista 1706-1784 [BBD]
Italian composer
* Martini, Padre

Martini, Guido Joe 1913- [BE]
American baseball player
* Martini, Southern
* Martini, Wedo

Martini il Tedesco
See Schwarzendorf, Johann Paul
Agidius

Martini, Jean Paul Egide
See Schwarzendorf, Johann Paul
Agidius

Martini, Padre
See Martini, Giambattista

Martini, Simone 1283?-1344 [HPPN]
Sienese painter
* Di Martino

Martini, Southern
See Martini, Guido Joe

Martini, Teri 1930- [CA]
American author
* King, Alison
* Martin, Wendy
* Martini, Therese

Martini, Therese
See Martini, Teri

Martini, Vicente
See Martin y Solar, Vicente

Martini, Virgilio 1903- [CA]
Italian author
* Letrusco

Martini, Wedo
See Martini, Guido Joe

Martino, Al
See Cini, Alfred

Martino, Edward Vittorio 1903- [BX,
RBE, SA]
American boxer
* Martin, Cannonball
* Martin, Eddie

Martino, Pat
See Azzara, Pat

Martinot, Sadie
See Stinson, Mrs. Frederick

Martinovich, Boris Michael 1920- [BE]
American baseball player
* Martin, Babe
* Martin, Boris Michael

Martins, Jay
See Tener, Martin J.

Martins, Maria Isabel Barreno de Faria
1939- [CA]
Portuguese author
* Barreno, Maria Isabel

Martins de Miranda, David
Brazilian faith healer
* [The] Envoy of the Messiah

Martinson, Marty
See Martinson, Michael Anthony

Martinson, Michael Anthony 1956-
[BR]
American baseball player
* Martinson, Marty

Martinson, Moa
See Svarts, Helga

Martinus, [Efraim] Frank 1936- [CW,
IAW]
West Indian author
* Arion, F. M.

Martinus Polonus
See Martin of Troppau

Martinuzzi, George 1482-1551 [HN,
WBD]
Hungarian statesman
* Frater Georgius
* Utjesenovic, Juraj
* [The] Wolsey of Hungary

Martius
See Rose, Frederick W.

Martlet
See Davis, Richard Bingham

Martlew, Mary
See Greenhalgh, Mary

Martley, John 1844-1882 [PI]
Irish poet
* Coelebs in Search of a Wife

Martley, John 19th c. [CCL]
Canadian poet
* Viking, Erl

Martoccio, Dominic 1890-1958 [HPPN]
American musician
* Lyons, George

Martoff, Nickoli 1922- [BEW]
American producer and director
* Mayo, Nick

Marton, Francesca
See Bellasis, Margaret Rosa

Martorano, Joseph 1927-1972 [SC]
American actor
* Corey, Joseph

Martorell, John ?-1460 [SN]
Spanish author
* [The] Boccaccio of the Provencal
Language

Martov, Julius
See Tsederbaum, Iulii O.

Marttin, Paul 1937- [AW]
German-born physician and writer
* Plaut, Martin

Martyn, Barry 1941- [EJ7]
British-born jazz musician
* Martyn, Kid

Martyn, Edward 1859-1923 [SFL, WGT]
Irish author
* Sirius

Martyn, [Rev.] Henry 1781-1812?
[HPPN]
British missionary
* Gwynne, Francis

Martyn, Henry
See Perry, Martin Henry

Martyn, Ivor
See Smith, Bernard

Martyn, John 1699-1768 [HPPN, IP]
British author and botanist
* B.
* Bavius

Martyn, Kid
See Martyn, Barry

Martyn, Myles
See Elliott-Cannon, Arthur Elliott

Martyn, Oliver
See White, Herbert [Martyn] Oliver

Martyn, Phillip
See Tubb, Edwin Charles

Martyn, William 1562-1617 [PA]
Author
* Old Chatty Cheerful

Martyn, Wyndham 1875-? [NAA, WW]
British author
* Grenvil, William

Martyn-Green, William 1899-1975
[BEW, TR]
British actor and singer
* Green, Martyn

[The] Martyr
See Edmund [or Eadmund]

[The] Martyr
See Edward [or Eadward]

[The] Martyr
See Justin

[The] Martyr
See Lucian

[The] Martyr Abolitionist
See Lovejoy, Elijah Parish

[The] Martyr Earl
See Stanley, James

[The] Martyr Hero
See Brown, John

[A] Martyr in the Search for Peace
See Fernandez, Daniel

[The] Martyr King
See Charles I

[The] Martyr King
See Henry VI

[The] Martyr King
See Louis XVI

[The] Martyr of Cuban Independence
See Marti Perez, Jose Julian

[The] Martyr of Erromango
See Williams, John

[The] Martyr of the Renaissance
See Dolet, Etienne

[The] Martyr of the Solway
See Wilson, Margaret

Martyr, Peter
See Anghiera, Pietro Martire

Martyr, Peter
See Vermigli, Pietro Martire

[The] Martyr President
See Garfield, James Abram

[The] Martyr President
See Lincoln, Abraham

[The] Martyr to Science
See Berthollet, Claude Louis

Marugg, Silvio A. 1923- [CW]
Curacaon poet and author
* Tip

Maruna, Annikki
See Aaltonen, [Ilta] Annikki [Tyyne]

Marut, Ret 1890-1969 [BI]
German actor and author
* Croves, Hal?
* Torsvan, Traven?
* Traven, B.?

Maruyama Okyo
See Okyo

Marvel, Andrew
See Middleton, Arthur

Marvel, Carl Shipp 1894- [IAW]
American chemist and writer
* Speed

Marvel, Ik [of Ike]
See Mitchell, Donald Grant

Marvel, J. K.
See Mitchell, Donald Grant

Marvel, Louise 20th c. [HPPN]
American cattle rancher
* [The] Cattle Lady

[The] Marvel of Hockey
See Morenz, Howarth William

Marvel, Scott
See Findlay, J. Dawson

Marvell, Andrew 1621-1678 [DEA, DEL, HN, RH]
British poet and satirist
* A. M.
* [The] British Aristides
* [The] Incorruptible
* Rivetus, Andreas, Junior
* [The] Uncorruptible Commoner

Marvell, Andrew
See Davies, Howell

Marvell, Holt
See Maschwitz, Eric

[The] Marvellous Boy
See Chatterton, Thomas

Marvelous Mal Whitfield
See Whitfield, Malvin Greston

Marvelous Marlene
See Dietrich, Marie Magdalene

Marvelous Marv Galliher
See Galliher, Marvin Gene

Marvelous Marv Throneberry
See Throneberry, Marvin Eugene

Marvelous Marvin Hagler
See Hagler, Marvin Nathaniel

Marvelous Mel Parnell
See Parnell, Melvin Lloyd

Marvelous Mel Weldon
See Weldon, Melvin

Marvenga, Ilse
See Marling, Ilse

Marvil, Dal
See Marvil, Dallas

Marvil, Dallas 20th c. [HPPN]
American football player
* Marvil, Dal

Marville, Pierre Nicolas 1754-1815 [PA]
Author
* Andre

Marvin, F. S.
See Marvin, Francis Sydney

Marvin, Francis Sydney 1863-1943 [LC]
British author
* Marvin, F. S.

Marvin, Joe
See Jurmanowitz, Joseph

Marvin, John T. 1906- [CA]
American author and columnist
* Richards, Charles

Marvin, Johnny 1898-1945 [ECM, HPPN]
American country-western performer
* [The] Lonesome Singer of the Air
* [The] Ukulele Ace

Marvin, Ken
See George, Lloyd

Marvin, Monkey
See Jordan, Marvin A.

Marvin, Muscles
See Jordan, Marvin A.

Marvin the Magnificent
See Barnes, Marvin

Marvin, W. R.
See Cameron, Lou

Marvin's Boy
See Eccles, Charles

Marwedi, Friedrich Carl 20th c. [EE]
German intelligence agent
* Pfalzgraf, Dr.

Marwick, Ernest Walker 1915- [IAW]
Scottish author
* E. W. M.

Marx, Adolph Arthur 1888-1964 [ASC, BDF, BEW]
American comic actor
* Marx, Harpo

Marx, Albert A. 1892-1960 [SC]
American actor and clown
* Almar the Clown

Marx, Chico
See Marx, Leonard

Marx, Erica Elizabeth 1909-1967 [CAP]
British author
* Manfred, Robert

Marx, Groucho
See Marx, Julius Henry

Marx, Gummo
See Marx, Milton

Marx, Harpo
See Marx, Adolph Arthur

Marx, Herbert 1901-1979 [BDF, BEW, EMT]
American comic actor
* Marx, Zeppo

Marx, Jean
See Linval, Paule Cassius de

Marx, Jerry
See Bernstein, Jerry Marx

Marx, John
See Grunn, John

Marx, Julius Henry 1890-1977 [BDF, BEW, EMT]
American comic actor
* Marx, Groucho

Marx, Karl 1818-1883 [HPPN, JL]
German political theorist
* [The] Father of Communism
* [The] Founder of Modern Socialism

Marx, Leonard 1887-1961 [BDF, EMT, F2]
American comic actor
* Marx, Chico

Marx, Milton 1897-1977 [BEW]
American comic actor
* Marx, Gummo

Marx, Minnie Palmer 1864-1929 [HPPN]
American actress
* Palmer, Minnie

Marx, Zeppo
See Marx, Herbert

Mary [HN, PPN, RH]
Mother of Jesus
* [The] Blessed Virgin
* [The] Madonna
* Mater Dolorosa
* [The] Mother of God
* Our Lady of O
* [The] Queen of Heaven
* [The] Virgin Mary

Mary [code name used during World War II]
See Donovan, William Joseph

Mary
See Downing, Ellen Mary Patrick

Mary [code name]
See Gardiner, Muriel

Mary
See Jackson, Mary Hilliard

Mary
See St. John, Mary

Mary Alfreda, [Sister]
See Elsensohn, Edith M.

Mary Aloysia, [Mother]
See Kelly, Catherine Ann

Mary Aloysius, [Sister]
See Becraft, Ann Marie

Mary Aloysius, [Sister]
See Schaldenbrand, Mary

Mary Alphonsa, [Mother]
See Lathrop, Rose [Hawthorne]

Mary Angelita, [Sister]
See Stackhouse, Mary Agnes

Mary Annette, [Sister]
See Buttimer, Anne

Mary Anthony, [Mother]
See Weinig, Jean Maria

Mary Aquina, [Sister]
See Weinrich, Anna Katharina
Hildegard

Mary Beatrice 1658-1718 [DHA, FFF, WBD]
Wife of King James II of England
* Mary of Modena
* [The] Queen of Tears

Mary Benita, [Mother]
See Kane, Mary

Mary Beth
See Miller, Mary Beth

Mary Catherine, [Sister]
See Anderson, Kathleen Agness Cicely

Mary Catherine, [Sister]
See Denning, Genevieve

Mary Cecilia, [Sister]
See Dierolf, Frieda

Mary Consolata, [Sister]
See Carroll, Alice Viola

Mary Consolata, [Sister]
See Carroll, Consolata

Mary de Paul, [Sister]
See Cogan, Claire I.

Mary Demetrias, [Mother]
See Cunningham, Mary

Mary Dominic, [Sister]
See Gallagher, Mary Dominic

Mary Dominic, [Sister]
See Parker, Marion Dominica Hope

Mary Edward, [Sister]
See Feehan, Agnes M.

Mary Edwardine, [Sister]
See O'Connor, Regina Mary

Mary Eleanor, [Sister]
See Brosnahan, Katherine Mary

Mary Eleanor, [Sister]
See Slater, Eleanor

Mary Estelle, [Sister]
See Casalandra, Estelle

Mary Florisenda, [Mother]
See Egan, Mary

Mary Francis, [Mother]
See Aschmann, Alberta

Mary Francis of Jesus, [Sister] 1878-?
[CCL]
Canadian poet
* Miriam

Mary Francis Terese, [Sister]
See Gay, Lucille

[The] Mary Garden of Ragtime
See Abuza, Sophie

Mary Gilbert, [Sister]
See DeFrees, Madeline

Mary Jane
See Lampton, W. J.

Mary Jean, [Sister]
See Dorcy, Mary Jean

Mary Jeanne Madeleine, [Sister]
See Gay, Isabelle

Mary Jeremy, [Sister]
See Finnegan, Alice Winifred

Mary John, [Mother]
See Considine, Honora

Mary Joseph, [Mother]
See Dunn, Mary

Mary Joseph, [Mother]
See Rogers, Mary Josephine

Mary Just, [Sister]
See David, Florence D.

Mary Justine, [Sister]
See Sabourin, Anne Winifred

Mary Liguori, [Sister]
See O'Hara, Abigail

Mary Loyola, [Mother]
See Gannon, Sabina

Mary Lucille, [Sister]
See Clark, Sylvia

Mary Madeleva, [Sister]
See Wolff, Mary Evaline

Mary Magdalen, [Mother]
See Kinsella, Mary M.

Mary Mercedes, [Sister]
See Hitchman, Mary Elizabeth

Mary of Buttermere
See Robinson, Mary

Mary of Guise 1515-1560 [WBD]
Queen of Scotland
* Mary of Lorraine

Mary of Lorraine
See Mary of Guise

Mary of Modena
See Mary Beatrice

Mary of the Cross, [Mother]
See McKillop, Mary

[The] Mary of the Gael
See Bridget [or Brigette]

Mary of the Incarnation
See Guyard, Marie

Mary of the Incarnation
See Martin, Marie Guyard

[The] Mary Pickford of Egypt
See Hamama, Faten

[The] Mary Pickford of France
See Grandais, Susanne

[The] Mary Pickford of This War
See Kaumeyer, Dorothy

Mary, Queen of Scots 1542-1587 [DEP, HPPN, SN, WBD]
Daughter of King James V of Scotland
* Jezebel
* [The] Mermaid
* [The] Queen of Paradox
* [La] Reine Blanche
* [The] Soft Medusa
* Stuart, Mary
* [The] White Queen

Mary Raymond, [Sister]
See Sandiford, Marie

Mary Rose, [Sister] 1903- [CCL]
Canadian author
* Ray, Rena

Mary Salesia, [Sister]
See Poggel, Mary

Mary Scholastica, [Sister]
See Jenkins, Marie M[agdalen]

Mary Simon, [Father]
See Smith, Vincent

[The] Mary Stuart of Italy
See Jane I

Mary Teresa, [Mother]
See Moran, Mary

Mary Teresa of St. Joseph, [Mother]
See Van Den Bosch, Anna Maria
Tauscher

Mary Theodore, [Sister]
See Hegeman, Mary

Mary Therese, [Sister]
See Lentfoehr, Florence Mae

Mary Vincentia, [Mother]
See Fannon, Eleanor E.

Mary Xavier, [Sister]
See Holworthy, Mercedes Claire

Mary I 1516-1558 [DNNF, SN, WBD]
Queen of England
* Bloody Mary
* Tudor, Mary

Mary II 1662-1694   [SN]
Queen of England
* Chelonis

Maryan
See Burstein, Pinchas

Maryanna, [Sister]
See Childs, Maryanna

[The] Maryland Strongboy
See Foxx, James Emory [Jimmy]

Marynen, Joannes
See Matthyssen, Joannes Michael

Maryon, Edward
See Maryon-D'Aulby, John Edward

Maryon-D'Aulby, John Edward
1867-1954   [BBD]
British composer
* Maryon, Edward

Masaccio
See Bartolommeo, Maso Di

Masaccio
See Guidi, Tommaso

Masaniello
See Aniello, Tommaso

Mascall, Margery D.
See Netherclift, Beryl Constance

Mascall, Norman 1931?-   [HPPN]
British swindler
* [The] Enthusiastic Pig Man

Mascara, Red
See Mascari, Joseph Rocco

Mascari, Joseph Rocco 1922-   [ASC]
American composer
* Mascara, Red

Maschler, Tom 20th c.   [CA]
Author
* Caine, Mark [joint pseudonym with
  Frederic (Michael) Raphael]

Maschwitz, Eric 1901-   [EMD, LAO,
WW]
British author
* Marvell, Holt

Masci, Girolamo ?-1292   [CAL]
Pope
* Nicholas IV

Masdama
See Buck, Benjamin

Maseres, Francis 1731-1824   [IP]
British barrister and author
* [A] Friend to the Church of England

Masers d'Aubrespy
See Latude, Jean Henry

Masers de Latude
See Latude, Jean Henry

Masfar ben Bedreddin, Al- 6th c.   [SN]
Spanish orator
* [The] Torch of Eloquence

Masha
See Stern, Marie

Masilongan, Christobal 1925-1974   [SC]
Actor
* De Vera, Cris
* [The] Man with a Thousand Voices

Mask
See Grant, James

[The] Mask of Liberalism
See Moynihan, [Daniel] Patrick

[The] Masked Marvel
See Patton, Charley

**[The] Masked Marvel of Modern
Letters**
See Vidal, Eugene Luther, Jr.

[The] Masked Singer of Country Songs
See Walker, William Marvin [Billy]

Maskell, Dan 20th c.   [WP 7-8-84]
British broadcaster
* Maskell, Faultless Dan
* Uncle Dan

Maskell, Faultless Dan
See Maskell, Dan

Maskell, William 1814-?   [IP]
British clergyman and author
* W. M., A Beneficed Priest

Maskipitoon ?-1869?   [HPPN]
American Indian chief
* Broken Arm

Masler, Jacob
See Maza, Yacov Moshe

Maslin, Alice 1914?-1981   [CA]
American broadcaster and editor
* Craig, Nancy

Mason, A. E. W.
See Mason, Alfred Edward Woodley

Mason, Adelbert William 1883-1962
[BE]
American baseball player
* Mason, Del

Mason, Adrian
See Lee, [Rev.] Albert

Mason, Alfred Edward Woodley
1865-1948   [LC, WWS]
British author
* Mason, A. E. W.

Mason, Arthur Telford 20th c.   [LC]
Author
* Artemas

Mason, Bonnie Joe [or Bonny Jo]
See Sarkisian, Cheryl

Mason, C. P. 20th c.   [WGT]
Author
* Snooks, Epaminondas T.

Mason, Carola
See Zentner, Carola

Mason, Caroline Atherton [Briggs]
1823-?   [IP, PA]
American poet
* Caro
* Thekla

Mason, Charles 19th c.   [HPPN]
American attorney
* C. M.

Mason, Charles 20th c.   [WW]
Author
* Mason, S. C.

Mason, Chuck
See Rowland, Donald Sydney

Mason, Cryin
See Mason, Norman

Mason, Dan
See Grassman, Dan

Mason, Del
See Mason, Adelbert William

Mason, Douglas R[ankine] 1918-   [AW,
CA, SF]
British author
* Douglas, R. M.
* Rankine, John

Mason, Edna Warren
See Pfizenmayer, Edna Warren Mason

Mason, Ernst
See Pohl, Frederik

Mason, Eudo C[olecestra] 1901-1969
[CAP]
British educator and author
* Maurer, Otto

Mason, F. V. W.
See Mason, F[rancis] Van Wyck

Mason, F[rancis] Van Wyck 1897?-1978
[ANT, CA, WGT]
American author
* Coffin, Geoffrey
* Mason, F. V. W.
* Mason, Frank W.
* Weaver, Ward

Mason, Frank
See De Masi, Francesco

Mason, Frank W.
See Mason, F[rancis] Van Wyck

Mason, Frankie
See McCan, Frank

Mason, Fred 1865-1895   [BMH]
American-born entertainer
* [The] Whistling Coster

Mason, George 1735-1806   [IP]
British author
* [A] British Freeholder

Mason, George Champlin 1820-1894
[DNA, IP, PA]
American author
* Champlin
* Lincoln, Robert O.

Mason, Gregory [joint pseudonym with
Doris Meek]
See Jones, Adrienne

Mason, Gregory [joint pseudonym with
Adrienne Jones]
See Meek, Doris

Mason, Howard
See Ramage, Jennifer

Mason, Ida
See Fisher, Eliza M. A.

Mason, Jackie
See Maza, Yacov Moshe

Mason, John 19th c. [IP]
American soldier and author
* [An] Ex Orderly Sergeant?

Mason, John 1900- [THR]
American author and critic
* Brown, John Mason

Mason, John 20th c. [IBW]
American comedian
* Spider Bruce

Mason, John Monck 1727-1809 [HPPN]
Irish author
* [A] Gentleman of Ireland

Mason, Louis
See Loeb, Richard A.

Mason, Lowell 1792-1872 [HPPN]
American hymn writer
* [The] Father of American Church
  Music

Mason, Madeline 1913- [CA]
American author and lecturer
* Bartlett, David
* Mason, Tyler

Mason, Michael Henry 1900- [AW]
British author
* Blake, Cameron

Mason, Miriam Evangeline 1900-1973
[IA]
American author
* Swain, Miriam

Mason, Mrs. C. A. B. [FFF]
American poet
* Caro

Mason, Mrs. W. J. [FFF]
Entertainer
* Temple, Victoria

Mason, Norman 20th c. [GW]
American rodeo performer
* Mason, Cryin

Mason, Pamela
See Kellino, Pamela

Mason, Philip 1906- [AW, CA, WD]
British author
* Woodruff, Philip

Mason, R. A. K.
See Mason, Ronald Alison Kells

Mason, Richard 1601-1678 [NPS]
British clergyman
* Angelus a Sancto Francisco

Mason, Richard Sharp 1795-1874 [IP]
American clergyman and author
* [The] Chairman of the Committee on
  the State of the Church

Mason, Robert 18th c. [IP]
Scottish author
* Lazarus, Ebenezer

Mason, Ronald Alison Kells 1905- [LC]
New Zealand author
* Mason, R. A. K.

Mason, S. C.
See Mason, Charles

Mason, Shirley
See Flugrath, Leona

Mason, Smiling Billy
See Mason, William C.

Mason, Stevens Thomson 1811-1843
[HPPN]
American politician
* [The] Boy Governor

Mason, Stuart
See Millard, Christopher Sclater

Mason, Tally
See Derleth, August [William]

Mason, Tex
See Mix, Tom

Mason, Theodore Charles [Ted]
See Bowman, Theodore C[harles]

Mason, Thomas [IP]
Author
* Peck, I. X.

Mason, Thomas 19th c. [IP]
Scottish bibliographer
* [An] Assistant Librarian

Mason, Thomson 1730-1785 [IP]
American jurist, statesman, author
* [A] British American

Mason, Tyler
See Mason, Madeline

Mason, Val
See Hackleman, Wauneta

Mason, Walt 1862-1939 [HPPN]
Canadian humorist and poet
* [The] Homer of the Middle West

Mason, William 1725?-1797 [DEL, IP,
SN]
British poet, painter, musician
* [A] Gentleman of Cambridge
* Macgregor, Malcolm
* Scroddles

Mason, William C. 1888-1941 [SC]
American actor
* Mason, Smiling Billy

Mason, William Lasley 1861-? [ALY]
American author
* Lesley, W. W.

Mason, William Shaw 19th c. [IP]
Irish author
* W. S. M.

Masque
See Dowling, Bartholomew

[The] Masque of Poets
See Lathrop, G. P.

Mass, William
See Gibson, William

Massa Bob
See Lee, Robert Edward

Massa, Duke
See Massa, Gordon Richard

Massa, Gordon Richard 1935- [BE]
American baseball player
* Massa, Duke
* Massa, Moose

Massa, Moose
See Massa, Gordon Richard

Massachusettenis
See Leonard, Daniel

Massachusetts
See Derby, Elias Haskett

[The] Massachusetts Giant
See Webster, Daniel

[A] Massachusetts Lawyer
See Lowell, John

[The] Massachusetts Madman
See Adams, John Quincy

[The] Massachusetts Thunderer
See Webster, Daniel

Massachusetts Yankee
See Bagg, Lyman Hotchkiss

Massada, Ione 1899- [HPPN]
British author
* Leigh, Ione

Massalsky, Helen Koltzoff [PA]
Author
* D'Istria, Dora

Massarik, Friederike 1882-1969 [JL,
THR]
Austrian-born actress and singer
* Massary, Fritzi

Massaro, Salvatore 1902?-1933 [ASC,
EJ, HPPN, PMJ]
American jazz musician
* Dunn, Blind Willie
* Lang, Eddie

Massary, Fritzi
See Massarik, Friederike

Massary, Isabel 19th c. [IP]
British author
* [A] Resident

Massasoit
See Ousamequin [or Wousamequin]

Masse, Felix Marie 1822-1884 [WBD]
French composer
* Masse, Victor

Masse, James
See Tyssot de Patot, Simon

Masse, Victor
See Masse, Felix Marie

Masselink, Ben 1919- [CA]
American author and television scriptwriter
* Toliver, George

Masselli, William 1927?- [TI 9-6-82, TI 9-13-82]
American underworld figure
* Billy the Butcher

Massen, Mrs. L. F. [FFF]
Entertainer
* Burroughs, Marie

Massena, Andre 1758-1817 [DNNS, HN, HPPN, SN]
French army officer
* [The] Child of Fortune
* [L']Enfant Cheri de la Victorie
* [L']Enfant de la Fortune
* [The] Favored Child of Victory
* [The] Spoilt Child of Fortune
* Victory's Darling Child

Massena, Mrs. A. M. C. 1845-? [IP]
American author
* Creole

Massens, Jakob
See Tyssot de Patot, Simon

Masseria, Giuseppe ?-1931 [BLB, HPPN, MM, PHM]
Italian-born American underworld figure
* [The] Boss
* Joe the Boss
* Masseria, Joseph

Masseria, Joseph
See Masseria, Giuseppe

Massett, Stephen C. 19th c. [IP, PA]
American author and composer
* Pipes, Jeemes, of Pipesville

Massey, Big Bill
See Massey, William Harry [Bill]

Massey, E. C. [FFF, IP]
British author
* Whatshisname

Massey, Erika 1900- [CA]
American author
* Zastrow, Erika

Massey, Guy
See Slaughter, Marion T.

Massey, Harry [IBW]
American football coach
* King Leo

Massey, Ilona
See Hajmassy, Ilona

Massey, James
See Tyssot de Patot, Simon

Massey, Lucy Fletcher 19th c. [HPPN]
British hymn writer
* [The] Same Compiler

Massey, Mike
See Massey, William Herbert

Massey, Red
See Massey, Roy Hardee

Massey, Roy Hardee 1890-1954 [BE]
American baseball player
* Massey, Red

Massey, Ruth
See Tovell, Ruth Massey

Massey, William Harry [Bill] 1871-1940 [BE]
American baseball player
* Massey, Big Bill

Massey, William Herbert 1893-1971 [BE]
American baseball player
* Massey, Mike

Massi, Gentile 1370?-1427? [WBD]
Italian painter
* Gentile da Fabriano

Massi, Nick
See Macioci, Nicholas

Massicot, Butz
See Massicot, Percy

Massicot, Percy 1910- [NOJ]
American jazz musician
* Massicot, Butz

Massie, Joseph 18th c. [IP]
British author
* J. M.

Massillon, Jean Baptiste 1663-1742 [DEP, DNNS, SN]
French prelate and orator
* [The] Cicero of France
* [The] Peaceful Prelate

Massine, Leonide
See Myassin, Leonid Fedorovich

Massinger, Philip 1583-1640 [DEA, NPS, SN]
British playwright
* Apollo's Messenger
* Our Mercurie
* P. M.
* [A] Sot

Massingham, H. W.
See Massingham, Henry William

Massingham, Harold John 1888- [HPPN]
British author
* H. J. M.

Massingham, Henry William 1860-1924 [LC]
British journalist
* Massingham, H. W.

Massis, Henri 1886-1970 [CD]
French author
* Agathon [joint pseudonym with Alfred de Tarde]

Massis, John
See Morbee, Wilfried Oscar

Massius
See Mars, Andre

Masskoff, Maurice 1871-1940 [BEW]
Russian-born actor
* Moscovitch, Maurice

Masso, Justo 1886-1971 [SC]
Spanish actor
* Oh Gran, Gilbert

Masson, Barthelemy 1485-1566 [PA]
Author
* Latonius

Masson, Clemence Harding [FFF, IP]
French author
* Dixon

Masson, Georgina
See Johnson, Marion Georgina [Wikeley]

Massopust, A. H. 1895- [BBH]
American volleyball player and coach
* Massopust, Dick

Massopust, Dick
See Massopust, A. H.

Massoud, Ahmad Shah 1954?- [TI 5-7-84]
Afghan guerrilla leader
* [The] Lion pf Panjshir

Mast, Jane
See West, Mae

Mastai-Ferretti, Giovanni Maria 1792-1878 [DEP, DNNS, FFF]
Pope
* Pius IX
* [The] Prisoner of the Vatican

Mastenbroek, Hendrika 20th c. [BBH, SWI]
Dutch swimmer
* Mastenbroek, Rie

Mastenbroek, Rie
See Mastenbroek, Hendrika

[The] Master
See Arcaro, George Edward [Eddie]

[The] Master
See Corlett, John

[The] Master
See Goethe, Johann Wolfgang von

[The] Master
See Hobbs, [Sir] John Berry

[The] Master
See Leeteg, Edgar

Master Adam
See Billaut, Adam

[The] Master Among Masters
See Read, Herbert

Master and Model of Ten Thousand Generations
See Confucius [or K'ung Fu-tzu]

[The] Master Builder
See Moses, Robert

Master Builder of the Constitution
See Madison, James

[The] Master Criminal
See Peace, Charles Frederick

[The] Master Gambler
See Skaggs, Elijah

Master Joe Peterson
See O'Rourke, Mary

Master Juba Lane
See Lane, William Henry

[The] Master Maker of the Queer
See Becker, Charles

Master Melvin
See Ott, Mel[vin Thomas]

[The] Master Miler of the Thirties
See Cunningham, Glenn

[The] Master Mind
See McGraw, John Joseph

[The] Master Mind of Mental Mystery
See Dunninger, Joseph

[The] Master Mind of the Federal Rum Ferrets
See Einstein, Isidor

[The] Master of a Grammar School
See Goodluck, W. R.

[The] Master of Agent 007
See Fleming, Ian [Lancaster]

[The] Master of Air Defense
See Kelly, James J.

[A] Master of Arts
See King, William

[A] Master of Arts of the University of Oxford
See Asplin, William

[A] Master of Arts of Trinity College, Cambridge
See Allen, Robert

[The] Master of Ballyhoo
See Rickard, George Lewis

[The] Master of Color
See Bellegambe, Jean

[The] Master of Contradiction
See Wessel, Johann [or John]

[The] Master of Counterpoint
See Clement, Jacques

[The] Master of Crime
See Rothstein, Arnold

Master of Flemalle
See Campin, Robert

[The] Master of His Master's Voice
See Victor, Alexander F.

[The] Master of History
See Comestor, Peter [or Petrus]

[The] Master of Illusion
See Bergman, [Ernst] Ingmar

[The] Master of Insult Comedy
See Rickles, Don

[The] Master of Jazz
See Ellington, Edward Kennedy

[The] Master of Limited Color
See Whistler, James Abbott McNeill

[The] Master of Love
See Ovidius Naso, Publius

[The] Master of Magic
See Raymond, Maurice

[The] Master of Middle Earth
See Tolkien, John Ronald Reuel

Master of Moulins
See Clouet, Jean

Master of Music
See Ravel, Maurice Joseph

Master of Paradox
See Chesterton, Gilbert Keith

[The] Master of Scapegoating
See Carter, James Earl, Jr. [Jimmy]

[The] Master of Sentences
See Lombard, Peter [or Pietro]

[The] Master of Stone-Cutting
See Dolcebono, Giacomo

[The] Master of Stories
See Comestor, Peter [or Petrus]

[The] Master of Surrealism
See Dali, Salvador

[The] Master of Suspense
See Hitchcock, Alfred Joseph

[The] Master of the Aerial Circus
See Morrison, [Jesse] Ray

[The] Master of the Bush
See Matta, Raphael

[The] Master of the Company for the Year 1873-1874
See Clode, Charles Mathew

[The] Master of the Epithet
See Pegler, [James] Westbrook

[The] Master of the Feast
See Waller, Edmund

[The] Master of the Fosbury Flop
See Fosbury, Richard D. [Dick]

Master of the Human Form
See Renoir, Pierre Auguste

Master of the Macabre
See Albright, Ivan LeLorraine

Master of the Maze
See Long, Russell Billiu

[The] Master of the Monumentalists
See Smith, Tony

[The] Master of the Multinational Enterprise
See Grace, William Russell

[The] Master of the Oneliner
See Lebitsky, Leonard

Master of the Orchestra
See Strauss, Richard

Master of the Rolls
See Martin, Jack

Master of the Sacred Palace
See Dominic

[The] Master of the School of Design
See Dyce, William

Master of the Swamps
See Hatfield, Bazil Muse

[The] Master of the Tenderloin
See Becker, Charles

Master of the Usk Grammar School
See Wrenford, W. H.

[The] Master of Those Who Knew
See Aristotle

[The] Master of Trinity
See Wordsworth, Christopher

Master of Undergraduate Humor
See Shulman, Max

[The] Master of Violence
See Peckinpah, Sam[uel]

[The] Master of White House Dirty Tricks
See Colson, Charles W. [Chuck]

[The] Master of Words and Guardian of Magazines
See Pollak, Felix

[The] Master Photographer
See Steichen, Edward

[The] Master Pianist
See Friedberg, Carl

[The] Master Pilot of the Mississippi
See Clemens, Samuel Langhorne

[The] Master Political Craftsman
See Bliss, Ray C.

[The] Master Reinsman
See Longden, Johnny

[The] Master Showman
See Grauman, Sid

[The] Master Spy
See Yariv, Aharon

[The] Master Storyteller
See Hunt, E[verette] Howard, Jr.

Master Surveyor
See Jones, Inigo

Master Timothy
See Reynolds, George William Macarthur

[The] Master Wrecker
See McGovern, George Stanley

Master X
See Boland, Jesse Lee

Master-The-Fifth of the Great White Lodge of the Himalayas
See Cannon, Alexander

Masterman, C. F. G.
See Masterman, Charles Frederick Gurney

Masterman, Charles Frederick Gurney
1874-1927 [LC]
British statesman and author
* Masterman, C. F. G.

Masterman, Frank Evans 1910- [HPPN]
American jazz musician
* Masters, Frankie

Masterman, J. C.
See Masterman, John Cecil

Masterman, John Cecil 1891- [WWS]
British author
* Masterman, J. C.

Masters, Anthony 20th c. [CA]
British author
* Tate, Richard

Masters, Bat
See Buley, Bernard

Masters, Edgar Lee 1868?-1950 [CAA, TLC]
American poet, author, playwright
* Atherton, Lucius
* Chubb, Elmer
* Ford, Webster
* Prowler, Harley
* Puckett, Lute
* Wallace, Dexter

Masters, Eliza Bailey 1845-1921
[HPPN]
American educator
* [The] American Schoolmistress

Masters, Frankie
See Masterman, Frank Evans

Masters, Juan
See Eames, Juanita

Masters, Kelly R. 1897- [AW, CA, HPPN, SAT]
American author
* Ball, Zachary [joint pseudonym with Frankie-Lee Janas]

Masters, Paul
See Samways, George Richmond

Masters, Pewee
See Masters, Rene

Masters, Rene 1902-1930 [HPPN]
American actor and dancer
* Masters, Pewee

Masters, Robert 1713-1798 [IP]
British clergyman and author
* [A] Late Vicar

Masters, W. W.
See Masters, William Walter

Masters, William
See Cousins, Margaret

Masters, William Walter 1894- [AW]
British author
* Masters, W. W.

Masters, Zeke
See Bensen, Donald R.

Masters, Zeke [house pseudonym]
See Goulart, Ron[ald Joseph]

Masterson, Bat
See Masterson, Bernard E.

Masterson, Bat
See Masterson, William Bartholomiew

Masterson, Bernard E. 1911-1963 [FB]
American football player
* Masterson, Bat

Masterson, Edward J. 1852-1878
[HPPN]
American law officer
* Masterson, Little Ed

Masterson, Lefty
See Masterson, Paul Nickalis

Masterson, Little Ed
See Masterson, Edward J.

Masterson, Louis
See Hallbing, Kjell Kare

Masterson, Paul Nickalis 1915- [BE]
American baseball player
* Masterson, Lefty

Masterson, Robert 19th c. [HPPN]
American law officer
* Masterson, Smiling Bob

Masterson, Smiling Bob
See Masterson, Robert

Masterson, Val
See Wright, W. George

Masterson, Whit [joint pseudonym]
See McIlwain, David

Masterson, Whit [joint pseudonym with Robert (Bob) Wade]
See Miller, Bill

Masterson, Whit [joint pseudonym with Bill Miller]
See Wade, Robert [Bob]

Masterson, William Barclay
See Masterson, William Bartholomiew

Masterson, William Bartholomiew
1853-1921 [BI, EWG]
American sheriff and sportswriter
* Masterson, Bat
* Masterson, William Barclay

Masterton, Bat
See Masterton, William

Masterton, Graham 1946- [CA]
British author
* Luke, Thomas

Masterton, William 1938-1968 [CEI, FHE, HK]
Canadian-born hockey player
* Masterton, Bat

Mastiff Cur
See Wolsey, Thomas

Mastin, James 1897-1948 [HPPN]
American vauderville performer
* Lamont, Jack

Maston, T. B.
See Maston, Thomas Bufford

Maston, Thomas Bufford 1897- [WYA]
American author
* Maston, T. B.

Mastrangelo, Johnny 1939- [RO1]
American singer
* Maestro, Johnny
* Mastro, Johnny

Mastriana, Louis P. 1922?- [HPPN]
American swindler
* [The] Flim Flam Man

Mastro, Johnny
See Mastrangelo, Johnny

Mastrogany, August 20th c. [EF]
American football player
* Mastrogany, Gus

Mastrogany, Gus
See Mastrogany, August

Masuccio di Salerno
See Dei Guardati, Tommaso

Masudi, al ?-957 [NPS]
Arabic historian
* [The] Herodotus of Arabian History

Masur, Harold Q. 1909- [CA]
American author
* Fleming, Guy
* James, Edward

Masurius
See Desmasures, Louis

Mata
See Thompson, William R.

Mata, Daya
See Wright, Faye

Mata Hari
See Zelle, Margarete Gertrude

[The] Mata Hari of the Civil War
See Fryer, Pauline Cushman

Mataincourt, Pierre de
See Fourier, Pierre

Matal, Red
See Matal, Tony

Matal, Tony 20th c. [HPPN]
American football player
* Matal, Red

Matalon, Isaac Moses 1928- [BEW]
British actor, singer, dancer
* Matalon, Zack

Matalon, Zack
See Matalon, Isaac Moses

[The] Match King
See Kreuger, Ivar

Match, Pincus 1904-1944 [EJS]
American basketball player
* Match, Pinky

Match, Pinky
See Match, Pincus

Matcha, Jack 1919-   [CA]
American author
* Mitchel, Jackson
* Tanner, John

[The] Matchless
See Shakespeare, William

[The] Matchless Orinda
See Philips, Katherine

Matchmaker
See Kissinger, Henry Alfred

[The] Mate
See Dugdale, [Sir] John [Third Baronet Astley]

Mate, Rudolph
See Matheh, Rudolf

Mateito [Little Matthew]
See Lopez y Portal, Gabriel

Matelot
See Uren, Malcolm John Leggoe

Mateo Salcedo, Miguel 1939-   [GS]
Spanish bullfighter
* Miguelin [Little Mike]

Mater Dolorosa
See Mary

Materfamilias
See Bell, Mrs. C. M.

Matey
See Van Buren, Martin

Mateyko, Gladys Mary 1921-1968 [BI, SFP]
American author
* Mayfield, M. I. [joint pseudonym with Henry I. Hirshfield]

Mathalin
See Taillasson, Gaillard

Mathe, Albert
See Camus, Albert

Matheh, Rudolf 1898-1964 [BDF, FD]
Polish-born director
* Mate, Rudolph

Mather, Berkely
See Davies, Jasper

Mather, Berkely
See Davies, John Evan Weston

Mather, Cotton 1663-1728 [HPPN, IP]
American clergyman, author, scholar
* [An] American
* C. M.
* [A] Christian
* [A] Christian in a Cold Season Sitting Before It
* [An] English Minister
* [A] Fellow of the Royal Society
* [A] Gentleman Lately Restored from Threatening Sickness
* Her Father
* [A] Lover of His Country
* [A] Minister in Boston
* [A] Native of Boston
* One Intimately Acquainted With Him
* One of the Hearers

Mather, Cotton (cont.)
* One of the Ministers in Boston
* One of the Ministers in the North Part of Boston
* One That Has Had Experience of Them
* One That Once Was a Scholar to Him
* One Who, As a Son With a Father, Served With Him in the Gospel
* Philalethes

Mather [or Mathers], David 1844?-?
[BLB, EWG, HPPN]
American murderer and robber
* [The] Killer of Killers
* Mather, Mysterious Dave

Mather, Increase 1639-1723 [HPPN, IP]
American clergyman, author, educator
* [A] Friend to the Churches
* Philadelphus

Mather, Margaret
See Haberkom, Mrs. Emil

Mather, Melissa
See Ambros, Melissa Brown

Mather, Mysterious Dave
See Mather [or Mathers], David

Mather, Samuel 1706-1785 [HPPN, IP]
American clergyman and author
* [An] American Englishman
* Aurelius Prudentius, Americanus
* One of the Readers

Mather, Virginia
See Liebeler, Jean [Mayer]

Mathers, Diana
See Cooper, [Lady] Diana

Mathers, Edward Powys 1892-   [WWL]
British author
* Torquemada

Mathers, Helen
See Reeves, Helen Buckingham [Mathers]

Mathers, Patrick
See Sanders, William

Mathers, Patrick, Arch-Bedel to the University of St. Andrews
See Gregory, James

Matheson, Andrew
See Mannheim, L. Andrew

Matheson, Hugh
See Mackay, Lewis Hugh

Matheson, Joan 1924-   [SFL, WGT]
American author
* Transue, Jacob

Matheson, Richard [Burton] 1926-
[WGT]
American author
* Swanson, Logan

Matheson, Rodney
See Creasey, John

Matheson, Sylvia A.
See Schofield, Sylvia Anne

Mathetes
See Jones, John

Mathetes
See Wilson, John

Mathew, Theobald 1790-1856 [DEP, FF, FFF]
Irish clergyman
* [The] Apostle of Temperance
* [The] Sinner's Friend

Mathews, Albert 1820-1903 [DNA, FFF, PA]
American author and attorney
* Siegvolk, Paul

Mathews, Benjamin Kenny Ollard 1889-
[ART]
British painter
* B. M.

Mathews, Charles 1776-1835 [HN]
British comedian
* Prism, Brother

Mathews, Charles Elkin 19th c.   [IP]
British author
* Ch. El. Ma.

Mathews, Cornelius 1817-1889 [HPPN, IP]
American editor, playwright, author
* Hopkins, Puffer
* [The] Late Ben Smith

Mathews, Denise [joint pseudonym with Patricia J. Mathews]
See Hrivnak, Denise

Mathews, Denise [joint pseudonym with Denise Hrivnak]
See Mathews, Patricia J.

Mathews, Evelyn Craw 1906-   [CAP]
Canadian author
* Cleaver, Nancy

Mathews, G. H. 19th c.   [IP]
American author
* Porte

Mathews, Larry
See Mazzeo, Larry

Mathews, Louise
See Tooke, Louise Mathews

Mathews, Lucia Elizabeth 1797-1856
[HPPN]
British actress and stage manager
* Vestris, Madame

Mathews, Mrs. Brander   [FFF]
Entertainer
* Harland, Ada

Mathews, Patricia J. 1929?-1983 [CA]
American author
* Mathews, Denise [joint pseudonym with Denise Hrivnak]

Mathewson, Christopher 1880-1925 [AS, DGS, HPPN, PB]
American baseball player
* Big Six
* Husk
* Mathewson, Christy

Mathewson, Christy
See Mathewson, Christopher

Mathewson, Dorothy Cohen ?-1918
[HPPN]
American actress
* Randolph, Dorothy

Mathias, Carl Lynwood 1936- [BE]
American baseball player
* Mathias, Stubby

Mathias, Charles, Jr. 1922?- [TI 10-7-85]
American politician
* Mathias, Mac

Mathias, Mac
See Mathias, Charles, Jr.

Mathias, Robert Bruce [Bob] 1930-
[HPPN]
American athlete
* [The] Champion of Champions

Mathias, Stubby
See Mathias, Carl Lynwood

Mathias, Thomas James 1750-1835
[HPPN, IP, SN]
British author and poet
* [A] Layman
* Long, Kien, Emperor of China
* [The] Nameless Bard
* That Miserable Imp
* [The] Translator

Mathieson, Una Cooper
See Gibson, Amanda Melvina Thorley

Mathieu, J. P. 1932?-1980
Interior designer and painter
* Mathieu, Pepe

Mathieu, Noel 1916- [EWL]
French poet
* Emmanuel, Pierre

Mathieu, Pepe
See Mathieu, J. P.

Mathis, Big Bus
See Mathis, Buster

Mathis, Buster 1944- [IBW]
American boxer
* Mathis, Big Bus

Mathis, Dean
See Mathis, Lewis

Mathis, Elmertha Burton 1948- [BA]
American physician
* Mathis, Mert

Mathis, Lewis 1939- [RO2]
American singer
* Mathis, Dean

Mathis, Mert
See Mathis, Elmertha Burton

Mathur, Yaduvansh Bahadur 1929-
[IAW]
Indian author
* Baby

Mathura, Mustapha 1939- [TR]
West Indian author
* Matura, Mustapha

Matias
See Henrioud, Charles

Matiason, K. G.
See Liljenfors, Bennie Mads Carl

Matilda [or Maud] 1080-1118 [HN,
HPPN]
Wife of King Henry I of England
* [The] Empress Maud
* Godithe [or Godiva]
* [The] Good
* Good Queen Maud

Matilda [or Maud] 1102-1167 [DNNF,
DNNS, HN]
Daughter of King Henry I of England
* Domina Anglorum
* [The] Lady of England

Matilda
See Piozzi, Hester Lynch Salusbury

Matilda, Julia
See Byrne, Julia C.

Matilda of Tuscany 1046-1115 [WBD]
Countess of Tuscany
* [The] Great Countess

Matilda, Rosa
See Byrne, Charlotte Dacre

[The] Matinee Burglar
See Williams, Albert [Albie]

Matison, Steven Martin 20th c. [WFA]
Mexican fashion designer
* Esteban

Matlock, Alec
See Cooper, Robert Andrew

Matlock, Julian Clifton 1907?-1978
[DA, ASC, MEJ]
American jazz musician
* Matlock, Matty

Matlock, Matty
See Matlock, Julian Clifton

Matoaka 1595?-1617 [HPPN, SN, WBD]
American Indian princess
* [The] Chief's Daughter
* [The] First Lady of America
* Pocahontas
* Rebecca
* Virginia's Tutelary Saint

Matos, Jose Verissimo Dias De
1857-1916 [HPPN]
Brazilian critic, journalist, author
* Verissimo, Jose

Matos, Maria
See Ferreira du Silva, Maria De
Conceicaode Matos

Matranga, Charles 20th c. [BLB]
American underworld figure
* Matranga, Millionaire Charlie

Matranga, Millionaire Charlie
See Matranga, Charles

Matray, Erno 20th c.
Hungarian-born director, writer, actor
* Matray, Ernst

Matray, Ernst
See Matray, Erno

Matrice, H. Ogram
See Keary, C. F.

[A] Matrimonial Monomaniac
See Abbot, L. A.

Matrisciano, George 20th c. [BLB,
HPPN]
Italian-American underworld figure
* Martini, George

Matson, Oliver Genoa 1930- [EF]
American football player
* Matson, Ollie

Matson, Ollie
See Matson, Oliver Genoa

Matson, [James] Randel 1945- [HPPN,
TF]
American track and field athlete
* [The] Gentle Giant
* Matson, Randy

Matson, Randy
See Matson, [James] Randel

Matsuba, Moshe
See Ben Yosef, Avraham Chaim

Matsumoto, Hidehiko 1926- [EJ]
Japanese jazz musician and actor
* Matsumoto, Sleepy

Matsumoto, Sleepy
See Matsumoto, Hidehiko

Matsuno, Masako
See Kobayashi, Masako Matsuno

Matsuo Basho
See Matsuo Munefusa

Matsuo Munefusa 1644-1694 [WBD]
Japanese poet
* Basho
* Matsuo Basho

Matsuobasho
See Munefusa, Matsuo

Matsys, Quentin 1460-1529 [DNNF,
NPS]
Flemish painter
* [The] Blacksmith of Antwerp
* [The] Flemish Blacksmith

Matsys, Quintin
See Sikes, William Wirt

Matt, Anton Josef 20th c. [BBH]
Austrian-born skier
* Matt, Toni

Matt, Toni
See Matt, Anton Josef

Matta, Raphael ?-1960 [HPPN]
French game warden
* [The] Master of the Bush

Mattaniah 6th c. BC [WBD]
King of Judah
* Zedekiah

Mattathias
See Antigonus II

Matte, Kid
See Matte, Thomas R.

Matte, Thomas R. 1939-   [FB]
American football player
* Matte, Kid

Mattei, Bruno 20th c.   [WF]
Film editor
* Matthews, Jordan B.

Mattei, Enrico 1906-1962   [HPPN]
Italian oil executive
* Oil's Gadfly

Matteo
See Vittucci, Matteo

Matteo, P. B., Jr.
See Ringgold, Gene

Mattern, Al
See Mattern, Alonzo Albert

Mattern, Alonzo Albert 1883-1958   [BE]
American baseball player
* Mattern, Al

Matthau, Walter
See Matuschanskayasky, Walter

Matthes, Oscar
American athlete
* [The] Miniature Sandow

Matthew, [Brother]
See Brown, Boyce

Matthew, [Father] Theobald 1790-1856
[HPPN]
Irish clergyman and temperance advocate
* [The] Apostle of Temperance
* [The] Sinner's Friend

Matthew, Thomas
See Rogers, John

Matthew, Tobias [or Tobie] 1546-1628
[SN]
British prelate
* [The] Preaching Bishop

Matthew, [Sir] Tobias [or Tobie]
1577-1655   [NPS]
British courtier, diplomat, author
* Bacon's Alter Ego

Matthew, Wentworth Arthur
See Benyehuda, Yoseh Ben Moshea

Matthews, A. E.
See Matthews, Alfred Edward

Matthews, Alfred Edward 1869-1960
[BEW, SC]
British actor
* Matthews, A. E.
* Matthews, Matty

Matthews and Co.
See Buckingham, Leicester Silk

Matthews, Anthony
See Barker, Dudley

Matthews, Arthur Bache 19th c.   [HFN]
Author
* A. B. M.

Matthews, Banjo
See Matthews, Edwin K.

Matthews, Bebe
See Matthews, Nathaniel

Matthews, Billy
See Matthews, Jacob B.

Matthews, Bo
See Matthews, William

Matthews, Brad
See DeMille, Nelson

Matthews, Channing
See Channing-Renton, Ernest Matthews

Matthews, Chif
See Matthews, Lewis

Matthews, Clayton 1918-   [CA]
American author
* Brisco, Patty [joint pseudonym with
   Patricia (Brisco) Matthews]

Matthews, Constance Mary 1908-   [CA]
New Zealand-born author
* Carrington, Molly

Matthews, Coots
See Matthews, Edward

Matthews, Denise 1961?-   [DF 11-2-84]
Canadian actress and musician
* Vanity

Matthews, Dora ?-1975   [SC]
American actress
* Merande, Doro

Matthews, Edward 1923-
American oilwell troubleshooter
* Matthews, Coots

Matthews, Edwin K. 1932-   [EAR]
American auto racer
* Matthews, Banjo

Matthews, Gary Nathaniel 1950-
American baseball player
* [The] Sarge

Matthews, George 1818?-1847   [PI]
Irish poet
* G. M., Esq.

Matthews, George 20th c.   [NP]
American jazz musician
* Matthews, Truce

Matthews, Hewitt William 1944-   [BA]
American educator
* Matthews, Teddy

Matthews, Honor 19th c.   [HPPN]
American whaling voyager
* Earle, Honor

Matthews, Ian
See McDonald, Ian

Matthews, [Rev.] Isaac Constantine
19th c.   [HPPN]
British clergyman
* [A] Pastor

Matthews, Jacklyn Meek
See Meek, Jacklyn O'Hanlon

Matthews, Jacob B. 1847-1903   [HPPN]
American law officer
* Matthews, Billy

Matthews, James Brander 1852-1929
[DNA]
American author and educator
* Penn, Arthur

Matthews, Jessie 1907-   [HPPN]
British actress and dancer
* [The] Dancing Divinity
* England's Dancing Divinity
* Personality, Princess

Matthews, JoAnn 1931?-   [HPPN]
American acrobat
* [The] Flip Flap Champ
* [The] Tumbling Queen

Matthews, John 1859-1927   [SC]
Welsh-born actor
* Ray, Johnny

Matthews, Jordan B.
See Mattei, Bruno

Matthews, Joseph W. ?-1864?   [HPPN]
American politician
* [The] Well Digger

Matthews, Kevin
See Fox, Gardner Francis

Matthews, Laura
See Rotter, Elizabeth

Matthews, Lewis 1885?-?   [NOJ]
American jazz musician
* Matthews, Chif

Matthews, Mary Jo 1909-   [HPPN]
American composer
* Rush, Mary Jo

Matthews, Matty
See Matthews, Alfred Edward

Matthews, Matty
See Matthews, William R.

Matthews, Nathaniel 1890?-1961   [NOJ]
American jazz musician
* Matthews, Bebe

Matthews, Pamela 1930-   [BF]
British actress
* Morris, Lana

Matthews, Patricia [Brisco] 1927-   [CA,
SAT]
American author
* Brisco, Pat A.
* Brisco, Patty [joint pseudonym with
   Clayton Matthews]
* Wylie, Laura [or Laurie]

Matthews, Pauline 1947-   [RO2]
British singer
* Dee, Kiki

Matthews, Rags
See Matthews, Raymond

Matthews, Raymond 1905-   [FB]
American football player
* Matthews, Rags

Matthews, Stanley 1915?- [HPPN, NN, SR]
British soccer player
* [The] Prince of Dribblers
* [The] Soccer Wizard
* [The] Wizard Dribbler

Matthews, Stanley G[oodwin] 1924-
[CA]
Canadian-born author
* Goodwin, Mark

Matthews, Teddy
See Matthews, Hewitt William

Matthews, Thomas Soady 1864-? [LAO]
British author
* T. S. M.

Matthews, Tom
See Klewin, W[illiam] Thomas

Matthews, Truce
See Matthews, George

Matthews, William 1951- [SMG]
American football player
* Matthews, Bo

Matthews, William R. 1873-1948 [AS, BX, RBE]
American boxer
* Matthews, Matty

Matthewson, Buffalo Bill
See Matthewson, William

Matthewson, William 19th c. [HPPN]
American pioneer scout and buffalo hunter
* [The] Buffalo Killer
* Matthewson, Buffalo Bill

Matthias, [Brother]
See Comeford, Walter

Matthias Corvinus 1442?-1490 [DNNS, NPS, SN, WBD]
King of Hungary
* [The] Conqueror
* [The] Cosmo de Medici of Hungary
* [The] Great
* [The] Lorenzo de Medici of Hungary
* Matyas Hollos

Matthiessen, F. O.
See Matthiessen, Francis Otto

Matthiessen, Francis Otto 1902-1950
[LC]
American author and educator
* Matthiessen, F. O.

Matthyssen, Joannes Michael 1902-
[IAW]
Belgian author
* Marynen, Joannes

Mattice, Butch
See Mattice, Lionel

Mattice, Lionel 1941- [RO1]
American musician
* Mattice, Butch

Mattick, Chick
See Mattick, Walter Joseph [Wally]

Mattick, Walter Joseph [Wally] 1887-1968 [BE]
American baseball player
* Mattick, Chick

Mattioli, Ercole Antonio 1640-1703
[WBD]
Italian statesman and diplomat
* [The] Man in the Iron Mask?

Mattox, Cloy Mitchell 1902- [BE]
American baseball player
* Mattox, Monk

Mattox, Harold Henry 1921- [BEW]
American dancer, singer, actor
* Mattox, Matt

Mattox, Hazel ?-1973 [FIR]
American actress and writer
* Hancock, Hazel
* La Vinder, Gracille

Mattox, Matt
See Mattox, Harold Henry

Mattox, Monk
See Mattox, Cloy Mitchell

Mattson, Eric
See Mattson, Rudolph

Mattson, Rudolph 1908- [BEW]
American producer and director
* Mattson, Eric

Matty the Horse
See Ianniello, Matthew

Matura, Mustapha
See Mathura, Mustapha

Mature, Victor John 1916- [HPPN]
American actor
* Hollywood's Number 1 Glamour Boy
* [The] Hunk
* Young, Ricardo

Maturin, Charles Robert 1782-1824
[DEL, PA]
Irish author and playwright
* Murphy, Dennis Jasper

Matus, Juan 1891- [BI]
Yaqui Indian
* Don Juan

Matuschanskayasky, Walter 1920-
[BDF, IPA, SW]
American actor
* Matthau, Walter

Matusow, Harvey Marshall 1926- [AW]
American author, journalist, broadcaster
* Muldoon, Omar

Matuszak, John 20th c. [WP 5-11-83]
American football player
* [The] Tooz

Matuzak, Harry George 1910- [BE]
American baseball player
* Matuzak, Matty

Matuzak, Matty
See Matuzak, Harry George

Matyas Hollos
See Matthias Corvinus

Matyszkowicz, Adam 1940- [EJ7]
Czech-born jazz musician
* Makowicz, Adam

Matz, Bertram Waldrom 1865-? [WWL]
British author
* Sack, O.

Matza, Ike
See Matza, Isaac

Matza, Isaac 20th c. [HPPN]
American track athlete
* Matza, Ike

Matzo, Emma 1922- [FC, WEF]
American actress
* Scott, Lizabeth

Mau-Mau Bett
See Baumfree, Betsy

Mauch, Gene William 1925- [BE]
American baseball player and manager
* Mauch, Skip

Mauch, Skip
See Mauch, Gene William

Mauck, Alfred Maris 1869-1921 [BE]
American baseball player
* Mauck, Hal

Mauck, Hal
See Mauck, Alfred Maris

Mauclair, Camille
See Faust, Camille

Maud, Victoria 20th c. [SC]
Actress
* Ray, Thelma

Maude
See Jennings, Clotilda

Maude, Lillian Nancy 1880?-1970 [BF, SC]
British actress and author
* Price, Nancy

Mauder, Dutch
See Mauder, Louis

Mauder, Louis 20th c. [EF]
American football player
* Mauder, Dutch

Maudet, Christian 1904- [BDF, FC, OCF]
French director
* Christian Jaque

Maugham, Diana
See Marr-Johnson, Diana [Maugham]

Maugham, Robert Cecil Romer 1916-1981 [CA, LC, WD]
British author
* Griffin, David
* Maugham, Robin

Maugham, Robin
See Maugham, Robert Cecil Romer

Maugham, W[illiam] Somerset 1874-1965
[WWS]
British author and playwright
* Somerville

Maughn, Donald 20th c. [RO2]
Singer
* Fardon, Don

Maul, Albert Joseph 1865-1958 [AS,
BE]
American baseball player
* Maul, Smiling Al

[The] Maul of Monks
See Cromwell, Thomas [Earl of Essex]

Maul, Smiling Al
See Maul, Albert Joseph

M'Aulay, Allan
See Stewart, Charlotte

Maulbetsch, John 20th c.
American football player
* Maulbetsch, Maulie

Maulbetsch, Maulie
See Maulbetsch, John

Mauldin, Mark
See Mauldin, Marshall Reese

Mauldin, Marshall Reese 1914- [BE]
American baseball player
* Mauldin, Mark

Maule, Fox 1801-1874 [HPPN]
British politician
* Ramsay, Fox Maule

Maule, Hamilton Bee 1915- [BI, CA]
American sportswriter
* Maule, Tex

Maule, Tex
See Maule, Hamilton Bee

Maule, Thomas 1645-1724 [HPPN, PA]
American author
* Philalethes [or Lover of Truth]
* T. M.
* Theodorus Philalethes

Maulnier, Thierry 1909- [IAW]
French author and playwright
* Talagrand, Jacques Louis

Maultasch
See Margaret of Carinthia

Maultsby, Emmaline 1928- [EJ]
American singer
* Moore, Debby

Maunoir, Madame
See Adam, Madame Edmond

Maupin, Helen Christine Bennett 1881-?
[NAA]
American writer
* Bennett, Helen Christine

Maura, [Sister]
See Eichner, Maura

Maura, [Sister]
See Power, Mary

Maurault, Olivier 1886- [NAA]
Canadian clergyman and author
* Deligny, Louis

Maurer, Maurice 1914- [ITA]
American theatre executive
* Maurer, Ziggy

Maurer, Mrs. George W. [FFF]
Entertainer
* Quick, Ida

Maurer, Otto
See Mason, Eudo C[olecestra]

Maurer, Rose
See Somerville, Rose M[aurer]

Maurer, Ziggy
See Maurer, Maurice

Maurette, Marcelle Marie Josephine
1903- [BEW]
French writer and playwright
* Marcelle-Maurette

Mauriac, Francois [Charles] 1885-1970
[CAP]
French author and journalist
* Forez

Maurice
See Mouvet, Maurice

Maurice, David [John Kerr] 1899-
[CAP]
Australian author
* Wunnakyawhtin U Ohn Ghine

Maurice, Edmund
See Lenon, Edmund Fitz-Maurice

Maurice, Furnley
See Wilmot, Frank Leslie Thomson

Maurice, John Frederick Denison
1805-1872 [HPPN]
British theologian
* [A] Clergyman
* Nobody [The Writer]
* Rusticus

Maurice, Mary 1844-1918 [F1, SC]
American actress
* Maurice, Mother

Maurice, Michael
See Skinner, Conrad Arthur

Maurice, Mother
See Maurice, Mary

Maurice, Roger
See Asselineau, Roger [Maurice]

Maurice, Walter
See Besant, [Sir] Walter

**Mauricius [or Mauritius], Flavius
Tiberius** 539?-602 [HN, WBD]
Byzantine emperor
* Avaricious Tyrant

Mauriello, Ralph 1934- [BE]
American baseball player
* Mauriello, Tami

Mauriello, Tami
See Mauriello, Ralph

Maurin, Patrick 1947-1982
French actor
* Dewaere, Patrick

Maurina, Zenta
See Raudive-Maurina, Zenta

Mauris, Maurice
See Caglengano, Marchese d'

Mauritius, Pfaffe
See Hartmann, Moritz

[Il] Mauro
See Arcano, Giovanni

Maurois, Andre
See Herzog, Emile [Salomon Wilhelm]

Maurras, Charles-Marie-Photius
1868-1952 [EWL]
French author
* Garnier, Pierre
* Martin, Octave
* Rameau, Leon
* Xenophon XIII

Maurus
See Blackmore, [Sir] Richard

Maury, Chip
See Maury, Donald P.

Maury, Donald P. 1939?- [BI]
American photographer
* Maury, Chip

Maury, J. C. F.
See Tillet, Auguste

Maury, Lou
See Maury, Lowndes

Maury, Lowndes 1911-1975 [HPPN]
American composer and musician
* Maury, Lou

Maury, Matthew Fontaine 1806-1873
[FFF, HPPN]
American oceanographer and author
* Bluff, Harry
* [The] Father of Modern Oceanography
* [The] Pathfinder of the Seas

Mauthe, J. L. 1890-1967 [AS, FB]
American football player
* Mauthe, Pete

Mauthe, Pete
See Mauthe, J. L.

Mautner, Jerome 1913- [ASC]
American musician
* Marlowe, Jerry

Mauzolli, Pietro Angelo [PA]
Author
* Palingenesius

Maverick, Augustus [FFF, PA]
Journalist
* Peebles, Paul

Mavin, John [joint pseudonym with
(John) Edgell Rickword]
See Garman, Douglas Mavin

Mavin, John [joint pseudonym with
Douglas Mavin Garman]
See Rickword, [John] Edgell

Mavity, Hubert
See Bond, Nelson S[lade]

Mavor, Osborne Henry 1888-1951 [LC, TCL, TLC]
Scottish playwright
* Bridie, James
* Henderson, Mary
* Kellock, Archibald P.

Mavor, [Rev.] William 1758-1837 [HPPN]
British clergyman
* [A] Father

Mavromichalis, Petros 1775-1848 [PA, WBD]
Greek patriot
* Petro Bey

Mawdsley, Norman
See Hargreaves-Mawdsley, W[illiam] Norman

Mawe, Thomas
See Abercrombie, John

Mawr, Eta
See Colling, Elizabeth

[Der] Max
See Klein-Luckow, Max

Max
See Maxwell, W. H.

Max [code name used during World War II]
See Moulin, Jean

Max, Edwin 1909?-1980 [FIR]
Actor
* Miller, Edwin

Max, Lucy
See Bogue, Lucile Maxfield

Max, Nicholas
See Asbell, Bernard

Max, Peter
See Finkelstein, Peter Max

Max, Raymond
See Hart, Cyril Charles

Maxfield, Elizabeth
See Miller, Elizabeth Maxfield

Maxfield, Prudence M. 1921- [AW]
British author
* Hill, Prudence

Maxhim, Tristan
See Jones, [Max Him] Henri

Maxick
See Sick, Max

Maxim, Hiram Percy 1869-1936 [HPPN]
American inventor
* [The] Father of the Maxim Silencer

Maxim, Hiram S. 1840-1918 [HPPN]
American inventor
* [The] Father of the Machine Gun

Maxim, Hudson
See Maxim, Isaac

Maxim, Isaac 1853-1927 [WBD]
American engineer and inventor
* Maxim, Hudson

Maxim, Joey
See Berardinelli, Guiseppe Antonio

Maximian [Marcus Aurelius Valerius Maximianus] ?-310 [NPS, WBD]
Roman emperor
* Augustus
* Herculius

Maximilian Joseph 1808-1888 [WBD]
Bavarian duke, author, playwright
* Phantasus

Maximilian I 1459-1519 [DNNF, FFF, HN]
Emperor of Germany
* [The] Last of the Knights
* [The] Penniless
* Pochi Danari
* [The] Taciturn
* Theuerdank [Dear Thanks]

Maximilian I 1573-1651 [DNNS, FFF, NPS, SN]
Duke of Bavaria
* [The] Conqueror
* [The] Great

Maximilian II 1527-1576 [DNNS, FF, SN]
Archduke of Austria and Holy Roman emperor
* [The] Delight of Mankind
* [A] German Mithridates
* [The] Prince of Peace

Maximillian, Ferdinand Joseph 1832-1861 [HPPN]
Emperor of Mexico
* [The] Marionette Emperor

Maximin, [Father]
See Piette, Charles Joseph Ghislain

Maximinus, Gaius Julius Verus 173-238 [WBD]
Roman emperor
* Thrax [The Thracian]

Maximinus, Galerius Valerius
See Daza

Maximov, Leon Samsonov 1930- [CA]
Russian-born author and playwright
* Maximov, Vladimir [Yemelyanovich]

Maximov, Vladimir [Yemelyanovich]
See Maximov, Leon Samsonov

Maximum John Sirica
See Sirica, John Joseph

Maximum John Wood
See Wood, John H., Jr.

Maximus 580?-662 [WBD]
Saint
* [The] Confessor

Maxine
See Allenbraugh, Maxine

Maxine
See Fortier, Cora B.

Maxino the Great
See Thiel, Max

Maxon, Anne
See Best, [Evangel] Allena Champlin

Maxton, Hugh
See McCormack, William John

Maxtone Graham, James Anstruther 1924- [AW, CA]
British writer
* Anstruther, James

Maxtone Graham, Joyce [Anstruther] 1901- [TC]
British author
* Struther, Jan

Maxtone-Grahame, Margaret Ethel
See Oliphant, Kington Blair

Maxvill, Charles Dallan 1939- [BE]
American baseball player
* Maxvill, Dal

Maxvill, Dal
See Maxvill, Charles Dallan

Maxwell
See Parker, Robert LeRoy

Maxwell, A. E. [joint pseudonym with Evan Maxwell]
See Maxwell, Ann [Elizabeth]

Maxwell, A. E. [joint pseudonym with Ann (Elizabeth) Maxwell]
See Maxwell, Evan

Maxwell, Allan
See Bayfield, William John

Maxwell, Ann [Elizabeth] 1944- [CA]
American author
* Maxwell, A. E. [joint pseudonym with Evan Maxwell]

Maxwell, Anna Caroline 1851-1929 [WBD]
American nurse
* [The] American Florence Nightingale

Maxwell, Bert 20th c. [BMH]
American entertainer
* Bernard, Bert

Maxwell, Billy
See Maxwell, W. J.

Maxwell, C. L. 19th c. [EWG]
American gunfighter
* Maxwell, Gunplay

Maxwell, Cattle Kate
See Watson, Ella

Maxwell, Cedric 20th c.
American basketball player
* Maxwell, Cornbread

Maxwell, Charles Richard 1927- [BE, SMG]
American baseball player
* Maxwell, Paw Paw
* Maxwell, Smokey

Maxwell, Cornbread
See Maxwell, Cedric

Maxwell, Eddie
See Cherkose, Eddie

Maxwell, Edward
See Herman, Alan

Maxwell, Edward
See Pollock, Courtnay

Maxwell, Ellen Blackmar
See Barker, Ellen Blackmar

Maxwell, Elsa 1883-1963 [HPPN]
American party-giver
* America's Number 1 Hostess

Maxwell, Evan 20th c. [CA]
American author
* Maxwell, A. E. [joint pseudonym with Ann (Elizabeth) Maxwell]

Maxwell, Fred G. 1890- [HK]
Canadian-born hockey player and coach
* Maxwell, Steamer

Maxwell, Gerald
See Braddon, Gerald

Maxwell, Gordon
See Shute, Walter

Maxwell, Gunplay
See Maxwell, C. L.

Maxwell, Herbert
See Lomax, W. J.

Maxwell, Herbert M.
See Wyman, Walter Forestus

Maxwell, Jack
See McKeag, Ernest L[ionel]

Maxwell, James Clerk 1831-1879 [HPPN]
Scottish physicist
* [The] Greatest Theoretical Physicist of the Nineteenth Century

Maxwell, Jiggs
See Maxwell, Zearlee

Maxwell, John
See Freemantle, Brian [Harry]

Maxwell, Joslyn
See Ireland, M. J.

Maxwell, Kate
See Watson, Ella

Maxwell, Lois
See Hooker, Lois

Maxwell, Marilyn
See Maxwell, Marvel

Maxwell, Marina 1934- [CW]
Trinidadian singer, producer, poet
* Omowale, Marina

Maxwell, Marvel 1921?-1972 [FC, PMJ]
American singer and actress
* Maxwell, Marilyn

Maxwell, Mary Elizabeth [Braddon] 1837-1915 [DEL, HPPN, WGT]
British author
* Braddon, [Miss] Mary E.
* Lascelles, [Lady] Caroline

Maxwell, Mary Elizabeth [Braddon] (cont.)
* M. E. B.
* White, Babington

Maxwell, Mary Mortimer
See Banks, Elizabeth

Maxwell, Mrs.
See Payne, Winona [Wilcox]

Maxwell, Patricia Anne 1942- [CA, WD]
American author
* Blake, Jennifer
* Trehearne, Elizabeth [joint pseudonym with Carol Albritton]

Maxwell, Paul
See Gian, Paolo

Maxwell, Paw Paw
See Maxwell, Charles Richard

Maxwell, Richard [FFF]
Entertainer
* Ogden, Richard D'Orsay

Maxwell, Robert 1923?- [NY 11-11-84]
Czech-born British publisher
* Wilberforce, Charles

Maxwell, Robert W. 1884-1922 [FB]
American football player and sportswriter
* Maxwell, Tiny

Maxwell, Ronald
See Smith, Ronald Gregor

Maxwell, Smokey
See Maxwell, Charles Richard

Maxwell, Steamer
See Maxwell, Fred G.

Maxwell Street Jimmy
See Thomas, Charles

Maxwell, Tiny
See Maxwell, Robert W.

Maxwell, Vicky
See Worboys, Annette Isobel

Maxwell, W. B.
See Maxwell, William Babington

Maxwell, W. H. 1852-? [PA]
Author
* Max

Maxwell, W. J. 1929- [EG]
American golfer
* Maxwell, Billy

Maxwell, William Babington 1866-1938 [LC]
British author
* Maxwell, W. B.

Maxwell, William Holden 1884-1949 [BI]
American magician
* Holden, Max

Maxwell, [Sir] William Stirling
See Stirling, William

Maxwell, Zearlee 20th c. [OBW]
American baseball player
* Maxwell, Jiggs

May, Ada
See Weeks, Ada Mae

May, Alice
See Raymond, Mrs. Lewis

May, Bernice
See Cross, Zora Bernice May

May, Boone
See May, D. B.

May, Bubba
See May, Robert Earl, Jr.

May, Buckshot
See May, William Herbert

May, Butler 20th c. [BWW]
American entertainer
* May, Stringbeans

May, Chopper
See May, David LaFrance

May, D. B. 1849?-? [HPPN]
American stagecoach guard
* May, Boone
* [The] Terror to Road Agents

May, Dan
See Maggio, Dante

May, Dave
See May, Davis Edwards

May, David LaFrance 1943- [SMG]
American baseball player
* May, Chopper

May, Davis Edwards 1951- [SMG]
American baseball player
* May, Dave

May, Edith
See Drinker, Anna

May, Edna
See Pettie [or Petty], Edna May

May, Elaine
See Berlin, Elaine

May Fly
See Somerset, Wellington

May, Frank Spuriell 1895-1970 [AS, BE, PB]
American baseball player
* May, Jakie

May, Geoffrey 1900-1964 [BI]
American attorney and author
* Hawthorn, E. M. D.

May, George W. 1889-1969 [HPPN]
American horseshoe player
* [The] Father of Horseshoe Pitching

May, Hannah
See Spivey, Addie

May, Harley 20th c. [GW]
American rodeo performer
* May, Ladder

May, Henry John 1903-   [CA]
Rhodesian-born barrister and author
* Schlosberg, H[ershel] J[oshua]

May, Herbert Richard Duffield 1878-?
[WWL]
British author
* Hardy, Mark

May, Ida
See Pike, Mary Hayden Green

May, J. C.
See Dikty, Julian May

May, Jakie
See May, Frank Spuriell

May, Janine
See Andonian, Jeanne [Beghian]

May, Joe
See Mandel, Joseph

May, Joseph 1916-1972   [IBW]
American singer
* Brother Joe
* Thunderbolt of the Middle West

May, Julian 1931-   [SAT]
American author
* Feilen, John
* Grant, Matthew G.
* Thorne, Ian

May, Julian [C.]
See Dikty, Julian May

May, Karl Friedrich 1842-1912   [HPPN]
German author
* Hohenthal, Karl
* Latreaumont
* Von Linden, E.

May, Kenneth
See Aveling, Edward Bibbins

May, Ladder
See May, Harley

May, Leola
See McLean, Leola

May, Margery Land
See Foster, Margery Land May

May, Mattie
See Brown, Mrs. C. R.

May, Merrill Glend 1911-   [BE]
American baseball player
* May, Pinky

May, Paul
See Ostermayr, Paul

May, Pinky
See May, Merrill Glend

May, Red
See May, Walter O.

May, Reginald
See Stokes, J. Lemacks

May, Robert Earl, Jr. 1956-   [IBW]
American prison inmate
* May, Bubba

May, Robert Stephen 1929-   [CA, WD]
British author and journalist
* May, Robin

May, Robin
See May, Robert Stephen

May, Rudolph, Jr. 1944-   [SMG]
American baseball player
* [The] Dude

May, Samuel, Jr. 19th c.   [HPPN]
American clergyman
* M.

May, Sophie
See Clarke, Rebecca

May, Sophie
See Meyer, Sophie Frederika Elizabeth

May, Stewart
See De Mejo, Carlo

May, Stringbeans
See May, Butler

May, Thomas 1595-1650   [DEA, FFF,
SN]
British poet and historian
* [The] Historian of the Long
  Parliament
* T. M.

May, Val
See May, Valentine

May, Valentine 1927-   [TR]
British director
* May, Val

May, Walter O. 20th c.   [SMG]
American football player
* May, Red

May, William Herbert 1899-   [BE]
American baseball player
* May, Buckshot

May, Winifred Arnold 20th c.   [NAA]
American author
* Arnold, Winifred

May, Winifred Jean 1921-   [IAW]
South African author
* Wynne, May

Maya [or Moya?], Victoria 1935?-   [FC,
SW]
Mexican actress
* Cristal, Linda

Mayakovsky, Vladimir Vladimirovich
1893-1930   [MWD]
Russian poet
* [The] Iron Poet
* [The] Poet of the Revolution

Mayall, John 1933?-   [BWW, PRS]
British musician
* [The] Father of British Blues
* [The] Grandfather of British Rock

Mayberry, Big John
See Mayberry, John Claiborn

Mayberry, John Claiborn 1950-   [SMG]
American baseball player
* Mayberry, Big John

Maybray-King, Horace
See King, Horace Maybray

Maybrick, Michael 1844-1913   [BBD,
BEW, FFF]
British singer and composer
* Adams, Stephen

Maye, Bernyce
See Moore, Bernyce Atz

Maye, Carrie
See Beecher, Carrie M.

Mayer
See Marius, Simon

Mayer, Agatha
See Maher, Ramona

Mayer, Arthur Loeb 1887?-1981
*American film distributor, exhibitor,
historian*
* [The] Merchant of Menace

Mayer, Bernadette 1945-   [CA]
American poet
* Memory

Mayer, Carl 1894-1944   [FIR]
Austrian-born screenwriter
* [The] First Poet of the Screen

Mayer, Charles E. E. 1901-1971   [CSH]
*Canadian sportswriter, commentator,
official*
* Trois Etoiles [Three Stars]
* Uncle Charles

Mayer, Charles Leopold 1881-?   [CA]
French scientist and author
* Reyam

Mayer, Christa Charlotte
See Thurman, Christa C[harlotte]
Mayer

Mayer, Deborah Anne [Debby] 1946-
[CA]
American author and editor
* Christensen, Anna

Mayer, Eduard Heinrich 1821-1907
[NPS]
German poet
* Fest, Ernst

Mayer, Ellen Moers
See Moers, Ellen

Mayer, Erskine
See Erskine, James

Mayer, Franz Xaver   [FFF]
Author
* Ackermann, Gottlieb

Mayer, Hannelore 1929-   [IAW]
Austrian author
* Valencak, Hannelore

Mayer, Henry 1868-1954   [WEC]
American cartoonist
* Mayer, Hy

Mayer, Hy
See Mayer, Henry

Mayer, Jakab Gyula 1858-1925 [BBD]
Hungarian pianist, conductor, composer
* Major, Jakab Gyula

Mayer, Jane Rothschild 1903- [ANT, AW, CA]
American author
* Jaynes, Clare [joint pseudonym with Clara Gatzert Spiegel]

Mayer, Johann 1486-1543 [SN, WBD]
German theologian
* Dreck [Dirt]
* Eck, Johann

Mayer, Julius 19th c.
American trader
* Box ka re sha has ta ka [Curly-headed white chief with one tongue]

Mayer, Sam[uel Frankel]
See Erskine, Samuel Frankel

Mayer, Scissors
See Erskine, James

Mayer, Selma 1884?-1984 [WP 2-6-84]
German-born nurse
* [The] Jewish Florence Nightingale

Mayer, Sydney Louis 1937- [CA]
American-born author and editor
* Jennings, Patrick

Mayer, Werner 1901-1983 [NY 7-12-83]
German composer
* Egk, Werner

Mayer, Wilhelm 1831-1898 [BBD]
Czech musician
* Remy, W. A.

Mayer-Boerckel, Ferdy 1920- [TR]
British actor
* Mayne, Ferdy

Mayer-Thurman, Christa C.
See Thurman, Christa C[harlotte] Mayer

Mayerl, Billy
See Mayerl, Joseph W.

Mayerl, Joseph W. 1902-1959 [BEW]
British-born composer and conductor
* Mayerl, Billy

Mayes, Adair Bushyhead 1885-1962 [BE]
American baseball player
* Mayes, Paddy

Mayes, Ethel
See Moore, Monette

Mayes, Paddy
See Mayes, Adair Bushyhead

Mayfair, Bertha
See Raborg, Frederick A[shton], Jr.

Mayfair, Franklin
See Mendelsohn, Felix, Jr.

Mayfield, Ann Todd 1932- [FC]
American actress
* Todd, Ann

Mayfield, Catfish
See Mayfield, Rufus

Mayfield, Cleo
See Empy, Cleo

Mayfield, Frank
See Starnes, Daniel

Mayfield, Jack
See Cooper, Parley J[oseph]

Mayfield, John
See Cook, William [Bill]

Mayfield, Julia
See Hastings, Phyllis Dora Hodge

Mayfield, M. I. [joint pseudonym with G. M. Mateyko]
See Hirshfield, Henry I.

Mayfield, M. I. [joint pseudonym with Henry I. Hirshfield]
See Mateyko, Gladys Mary

Mayfield, Marlys
See Frey, Marlys

Mayfield, Millie
See Homes, Mary Sophie Shaw

Mayfield, Rufus 20th c. [IBW]
American community organizer
* Mayfield, Catfish

[The] Mayflower Madam
See Barrows, Sydney Biddle

Mayflower, Minnie
See Ladd, Catherine Stratton

Mayhar, Ardath F[rances] 1930- [CA, WD]
American poet and author
* Cannon, Ravenna
* Hurst, Ardath Frances

Mayhew, Charles
See Smith, Charles

Mayhew, Elizabeth
See Bear, Joan

Mayhew, Katie
See Widmer, Mrs. Harry

Mayhew, Stella
See Sadler, Izetta Estelle

Mayhew, Thomas 1592-1682 [HPPN]
British-American politician
* [The] Patriarch of the Indians

Maylem, John 1739-1762? [HPPN]
American poet
* Phoenix, John

Mayme, Lennie
See Bramwell, P.

Maynard, Belvin W. 20th c.
American clergyman and aviator
* [The] Flying Parson

Maynard, Bill
See Maynard, Christopher

Maynard, Bob 20th c. [GW]
American rodeo performer
* Maynard, Flash

Maynard, Buster
See Maynard, James Walter

Maynard, Chick
See Maynard, Leroy Evans

Maynard, Christopher 1958- [DC]
British cricketer
* Maynard, Bill
* Maynard, Fish

Maynard, Claire
See McCarthy, Marie

Maynard, Colonel [FFF]
American writer
* Kentucky Colonel

Maynard, Country
See Maynard, Don[ald]

Maynard, Don[ald] 1937- [FB, HPPN]
American football player
* Maynard, Country
* Maynard, Monkey Shine
* Maynard, Sunshine

Maynard, Fish
See Maynard, Christopher

Maynard, Flash
See Maynard, Bob

Maynard, George W. 19th c. [HPPN]
American artist
* [The] Eagle

Maynard, Horace 1814-1882 [HPPN]
American politician
* [The] Narragansett

Maynard, James Walter 1913- [BE]
American baseball player
* Maynard, Buster

Maynard, Leroy Evans 1896-1957 [BE]
American baseball player
* Maynard, Chick

Maynard, Monkey Shine
See Maynard, Don[ald]

Maynard, Richard Wheeler 20th c. [BE]
American baseball player
* Wheeler, Richard [Dick]

Maynard, Ruth
See Coffin, Ruth Maynard

Maynard, Sunshine
See Maynard, Don[ald]

Maynard, Walter
See Beale, Thomas Willert

Mayne, Arthur
See Batchelor, Richard A. C.

Mayne, Clarice
See Dulley, Clarice

Mayne, Ernie
See Barratt, Percy Ernest

Mayne, Ethel Colburn ?-1941 [LC]
Irish author
* Huntly, Frances E.

Mayne, Ferdy
See Mayer-Boerckel, Ferdy

Mayne, H. H.
See Wilson, Helen Helga

Mayne, Leger D.
See Dick, William Brisbane

Mayne, Rutherford
See Waddell, Samuel J.

Mayne, William [James Carter] 1928-
[CA, CLC, SAT]
British author
* Cobalt, Martin
* James, Dynely [joint pseudonym with R. D. Caesar]
* Molin, Charles

Maynwaring, Archibald
See Lovecraft, Howard Phillips

Mayo, Cass
See Stevens, Casandra Mayo

Mayo, Charles Horace 1865-1939
[HPPN]
American surgeon
* Doctor Charlie

Mayo, Edward Joseph
See Mayoski, Edward Joseph

Mayo, Frank
See Maguire, Francis

Mayo, Goat
See Mayo, Paul

Mayo, Harry A.
See Sampson, Ray

Mayo, Herbert 1796-1852 [NPS]
British physiologist and surgeon
* [The] Middlesex Owl

Mayo, Isabella Fyvie ?-1914 [DEL, PA, WWL]
Author
* Garrett, Edward
* Garrett, Ruth

Mayo, James
See Coulter, Stephen

Mayo, Jim
See LaMoore, Louis [Dearborn]

Mayo, Johann [FFF]
German painter
* [The] Bearded

Mayo, Margaret
See Clatten, Lilian

Mayo, Mark
See Lane, Yoti

Mayo, Mary
See Woodson, Mary Blake

Mayo, Moose
See Mayo, Paula

Mayo, Mrs. William H. [FFF]
Entertainer
* Sutherland, Josie

Mayo, Nick
See Martoff, Nickoli

Mayo, Paul 20th c. [GW]
American rodeo performer
* Mayo, Goat

Mayo, Paula 20th c.
American basketball player
* Mayo, Moose

Mayo, Sam
See Cowan, Samuel

Mayo, Virginia
See Jones, Virginia

Mayo, William James 1861-1939
[HPPN]
American surgeon
* Doctor Will

Mayoe, Franklin and Marian
See Rosewater, Frank

[The] Mayor
See Quincy, Josiah

Mayor Bill
See McNichols, William, Jr.

Mayor De Luxe
See White, Kevin Hagan

Mayor For the Times
See Lindsay, John Vliet

[The] Mayor of Bayou Pom Pom
See Coquille, Walter J.

[The] Mayor of Beirut
See Gemayel, Amin

[The] Mayor of Broadway
See Connors, Kevin Joseph

[The] Mayor of Castro Street
See Milk, Harvey

[The] Mayor of Gower Gulch
See Dalroy, Harry

[The] Mayor of Kneesville
See Schleier, Gregory

[The] Mayor of Playhouse Square
See Gallagher, Martin J.

[The] Mayor of Rush Street
See King, Henry

[The] Mayor of the Midway
See Rogers, Joseph [Joe]

[The] Mayor of the Palace
See Du Plessis, Armand Jean

[The] Mayor of the Poor
See Curley, James Michael

Mayor On the Move
See Lindsay, John Vliet

Mayoski, Edward Joseph 1910- [BE]
American baseball player
* Mayo, Edward Joseph

[The] Maypole
See Schulemberg, Erangard Melrose de [Duchess of Kendal]

Mayrant, Drayton
See Simons, Katherine Drayton Mayrant

Mayrseidl, Caroline 1902- [THR]
Austrian-born actress and singer
* Seidl, Lea

Mays, Amazing
See Mays, William Howard, Jr. [Willie]

Mays, Billy Wayne 1936?- [HPPN]
American shuffleboard player
* Mays, Texas Billy

Mays, Buckduck
See Mays, William Howard, Jr. [Willie]

Mays, Carl William 1893-1971 [BE, DGS]
American baseball player
* Mays, Sub

Mays, Cedric Wesley 1907- [AW, CA]
British author
* Mays, Spike

Mays, Junie
See Mays, Junior Allen

Mays, Junior Allen 1914- [MY]
American musician
* Mays, Junie

Mays, Spike
See Mays, Cedric Wesley

Mays, Sub
See Mays, Carl William

Mays, Texas Billy
See Mays, Billy Wayne

Mays, William Howard, Jr. [Willie]
1931- [BE, HPPN, PB]
American baseball player
* Mays, Amazing
* Mays, Buckduck
* [The] Say Hey Kid
* Willie the Wallop

Maysi, Kadra
See Simons, Katherine Drayton Mayrant

Mayson, Marina
See Rogers, Rosemary

Maytag, Bud
See Maytag, Lewis B.

Maytag, Lewis B. 1926-
American airline executive
* Maytag, Bud

Mayuto
See Correa, Mailto

Maza, Yacov Moshe 1930- [JF]
American comedian
* Masler, Jacob
* Mason, Jackie

Mazal Tov
See Czaczkes, Shmuel Yosef

Mazani, Eric C. F. Nhando 1948-
[DLE]
Rhodesian poet
* Mars, E. C.

Mazar Pasha
See Lakeman, Stephen

Mazare
See Gassion, Jean de

Mazarin, Jules 1602-1661 [SN]
French prelate and statesman
* [The] Maecenas of His Day

[The] Mazarin of Letters
See Alembert, Jean Le Rond d'

Mazarini, Giulio 1797-1868 [HPPN]
French ballet dancer and choreographer
* Mazilier, Joseph

Maze, Henry 1956- [SMG]
Canadian-born hockey player
* Maze, Rocky

Maze, Rocky
See Maze, Henry

Mazeppa, Rose Marie 1926?- [HPPN]
American singer and actress
* Baby Rose Marie
* Barney
* [The] Darling of the Air
* [The] Five Year Old Child Wonder
* [The] Queen of the Game Shows
* Rose Marie

Mazeroski, Maz
See Mazeroski, William Stanley

Mazeroski, William Stanley 1936- [BE]
American baseball player
* Mazeroski, Maz

Mazibuko, Mandla Thomas 1946-
[IAW]
South African poet
* Liguquka, Iphiva Elilala

Mazilier, Joseph
See Mazarini, Giulio

Mazimoff, Alla 1879-1945 [CU]
Russian-born actress
* Nazimova, Alla

Mazquiaran y Torrontegui, Diego
1895-1940 [GS, OCS]
Spanish bullfighter
* Fortuna [Fortune]

Mazumbo
See Gordon, Edgar Fitzgerald

Mazur, Edward Joseph 1929- [CEI,
FHE]
Canadian-born hockey player
* Mazur, Spider

Mazur, Richard F. 1932?- [HPPN]
*American insurance agent, real estate
operator, pension consultant*
* [The] Polish Prince

Mazur, Spider
See Mazur, Edward Joseph

Mazurki, Mike
See Mazurwski, Mikhail

Mazursky, Irwin 1930-
American screenwriter and director
* Mazursky, Paul

Mazursky, Paul
See Mazursky, Irwin

Mazurwski, Mikhail 1909- [FC]
American actor
* Mazurki, Mike

Mazza, Adriana 1928- [SAT]
Italian illustrator
* Saviozzi, Adriana

Mazzantinito [Little Mazzantino]
See Alarcon, Tomas

Mazzei, Filippo [or Philip] 1730-1816
[HPPN]
*Italian physician, wine merchant,
viticulturist*
* [Un] Citoyen de Virginie

Mazzeo, Larry 1956?-
American actor
* Mathews, Larry

Mazzera, Melvin Leonard 1914- [BE]
American baseball player
* Mazzera, Mike

Mazzera, Mike
See Mazzera, Melvin Leonard

Mazzini, Giuseppe 1808?-1872 [HN]
Italian patriot
* [The] Stormy Petrel of European
Politics

Mazziotta, Choppy
See Mazziotta, John

Mazziotta, John 1916?- [HPPN]
American bookmaker and racketeer
* Mazziotta, Choppy

Mazzochi, Alessio Simmacho 1684-1771
[PA]
Author
* Mazzochole

Mazzochole
See Mazzochi, Alessio Simmacho

Mazzolari, Guiseppe Marione 1712-1786
[PA]
Author
* Parthenia

Mazzoletti, Collette Helene 1907-1968
[SC]
American actress
* Merton, Collette

Mazzoli [or Mazzuoli], Lodovico
1478?-1528 [WBD]
Italian painter
* [Il] Ferrarese
* Mazzolino

Mazzolino
See Mazzoli [or Mazzuoli], Lodovico

Mazzoni, Guido 1450-1518 [WBD]
Italian sculptor
* [Il] Modanino

**Mazzuoli [or Mazzola], Girolamo
Francesco Maria** 1503-1540 [WBD]
Italian painter
* [Il] Parmigianino [or Parmigiano]

Mbali, Ona
See Omari, Cuthbert Kashingo

Mberi, Antar Sudan Katara
See Henderson, Thomas Louis

M'Blashmole, Pat
See Campbell, Thomas

Mboya, Thomas Joseph [Tom] 1930-
[HPPN]
African leader
* Africa's Angry Young Man

McAdams, George D. 1886-1937 [BE]
American baseball player
* McAdams, Jack

McAdams, Jack
See McAdams, George D.

McAdoo, Bob 1951- [SMG]
American basketball player
* McAdoo, Mac

McAdoo, Mac
See McAdoo, Bob

McAdoo, William Gibbs 1863-1941
[HPPN]
American politician
* Bill the Builder
* [The] Crown Prince
* Daddy Longlegs
* [The] Dancing Fool
* [The] World War Croesus

McAfee, B.
See Slaughter, Marion T.

McAfee, Carlos
See Slaughter, Marion T.

McAfee, George A. 1918- [BBH, FB]
American football player
* McAfee, Lefty
* McAfee, One Play

McAfee, Lefty
See McAfee, George A.

McAfee, Nella Marshall [PA]
Author
* San Souce

McAfee, One Play
See McAfee, George A.

McAleer, Lucy Ann 1932- [ITA]
American actress
* Marlow, Lucy

McAleese, Daniel 1833?-1900 [PI]
Irish journalist and poet
* M. D.
* Ossian
* Ruadh

McAlexander, Ulysses Grant 1864-1936
[HPPN]
American army officer
* [The] Rock of the Marne

McAllister, Alister 1877-1943 [CC,
EMD, WW]
Irish playwright and author
* Brock, Lynn
* Wharton, Anthony

McAllister, Amanda
See Dowdell, Dorothy [Florence] Karns

McAllister, Amanda
See Hager, Jean

McAllister, Amanda
See Meaker, Eloise

McAllister, Cassie
See McAllister, Lewis William

McAllister, Chip
See McAllister, Frank

McAllister, Frank 20th c.   [OBW]
American baseball player
* McAllister, Chip

McAllister, Jack
See Coakley, Andrew James

McAllister, Lewis William 1874-1962
[BE, BN]
American baseball player
* McAllister, Cassie
* McAllister, Sport

McAllister, Mary H. 1947-   [GF]
American golfer
* McAllister, Susie

McAllister, Sport
See McAllister, Lewis William

McAllister, Susie
See McAllister, Mary H.

McAlmon, Robert 1896-1956
Author, poet, publisher
* Urquhart, Guy

McAloon, William Andrew 1864?-1931
[BEW]
American actor and singer
* Mack, Andrew

McAlpin, Grant
See McCulley, Johnston

McAlpine, Robert W.   [FFF, PA]
American writer
* Ancient, Oliver
* Brittle, Gath
* Sonica
* Uncle Jake

McArdle, Brian 20th c.   [MBF]
British author
* Reid, Desmond [house pseudonym]

McArdle, Joe 20th c.   [HPPN]
American football player and coach
* Bligh, Captain

McArthur, Dixie
See McArthur, Oland Alexander

McArthur, John
See Wise, Arthur

McArthur, Mac
See McArthur, Malcolm

McArthur, Malcolm 1862-?   [BE]
American baseball player
* McArthur, Mac

McArthur, Oland Alexander 1892-   [BE]
American baseball player
* McArthur, Dixie

McAstocker, David Plante 1884-?   [BI]
American clergyman and author
* Dorley, David

McAtee, Bub
See McAtee, Michael James

McAtee, Jerome 1920-   [CEI]
Canadian-born hockey player
* McAtee, Jud

McAtee, Jud
See McAtee, Jerome

McAtee, Linus 20th c.   [BBH]
American jockey
* McAtee, Pony

McAtee, Michael James 1845-1876   [BE]
American baseball player
* McAtee, Bub

McAtee, Pony
See McAtee, Linus

McAuley, Ike
See McAuley, James Earl

McAuley, James Earl 1893-1928   [BE]
American baseball player
* McAuley, Ike

McAuley, James Phillip 1917-1976
[CA]
Australian poet
* Malley, Ern [joint pseudonym with
  Harold Stewart]

McAuley, Kenneth Leslie 1921-   [FHE]
Canadian-born hockey player
* McAuley, Tubby

McAuley, Tubby
See McAuley, Kenneth Leslie

McAuliffe, John J. 1899?-1953   [BI]
American educator
* Alfred Patrick, [Brother]

McAuliffe, Muggs
See McAuliffe, Richard John [Dick]

McAuliffe, Richard John [Dick] 1939-
[PB]
American baseball player
* McAuliffe, Muggs

McAvoy, James Eugene 1894-1973   [BE]
American baseball player
* McAvoy, Wickey

McAvoy, Jock
See Bamford, Joseph

McAvoy, Wickey
See McAvoy, James Eugene

McBain, Ed
See Lombino, Salvatore A.

McBean, Alvin O'Neal 1938-   [SMG]
American baseball player
* Double O
* [The] Gay Blade
* McBean, Jumping

McBean, Jumping
See McBean, Alvin O'Neal

McBee, Lefty
See McBee, Pryor Edward

McBee, Pryor Edward 1901-1965   [BE]
American baseball player
* McBee, Lefty

McBlab, Thady
See Martin, James

McBride, Algernon Briggs 1869-1956
[BE]
American baseball player
* McBride, Algie

McBride, Algie
See McBride, Algernon Briggs

McBride, Arnold Ray 1949-   [SMG,
WWB]
American baseball player
* [The] Callaway Kid
* McBride, Bake

McBride, Arthur 1887-1972   [FB, MM,
PHM]
American football team owner
* McBride, Mickey

McBride, Bake
See McBride, Arnold Ray

McBride, Floyd 1902-   [BB]
American basketball coach
* McBride, Mickey

McBride, Mary Margaret 1899-1976
[BI, HPPN]
American radio commentator
* Deane, Martha

McBride, Mickey
See McBride, Arthur

McBride, Mickey
See McBride, Floyd

McBride, Neil 20th c.   [PI]
Irish-born poet
* Lien, Edirb Cam

McBride, Patricia
See Bartz, Patricia McBride

McBride, Peter 1854-?   [LAO]
German-born physician and author
* E. C. M.

McBride, Robert Medill 1879-?   [HPPN]
American author
* Medill, Robert

McBride, William 1889-   [IBW]
American comedian
* Mack, Billy

McBroom, Marden 1914-   [FC]
American actor
* Bruce, David

McBroom, R. Curtis 1910-   [CAP]
American author
* Dring, Nathaniel

McBurney, Alvin 1911-   [HPPN, PMJ]
American jazz musician
* [The] King of the Electric Guitar
* Rey, Alvino

McBurney, M. [PA]
Author
* Malone, Carroll

McBurney, William B. ?-1892 [PI]
Irish poet
* Malone, Carroll

McC.
See McCausland, Dominick

McCabe, Cameron
See Borneman, Ernest Wilhelm Julius

McCabe, Charles Cardwell 1836-1906
[HPPN]
American clergyman
* [The] Singing Bishop
* [The] Singing Chaplain
* [The] Singing Secretary

McCabe, James Arthur 1881-1944 [BE]
American baseball player
* McCabe, Swat

McCabe, James Dabney 1842-1883
[DNA]
American author and historian
* Martin, Edward Winslow

McCabe, Joseph 1867-1955 [LC]
British author and clergyman
* Anthony, [Father]

McCabe, Ralph 1909?-1966 [BI]
American author
* Pyrrho

McCabe, Swat
See McCabe, James Arthur

McCabe, William Bernard 1801-1891
[PI]
Irish poet
* W. B. M.

McCaffree, Charles 20th c. [BBH]
*American swimmer, coach, organization
officer*
* McCaffree, Mac

McCaffree, Mac
See McCaffree, Charles

McCaffrey, Bull
See McCaffrey, Frank

McCaffrey, Charles P. ?-1894 [BE]
American baseball player
* McCaffrey, Sparrow

McCaffrey, Frank 20th c. [HPPN]
American football player
* McCaffrey, Bull

McCaffrey, John 1938- [BB]
American basketball player
* McCaffrey, Pete

McCaffrey, Pete
See McCaffrey, John

McCaffrey, Sparrow
See McCaffrey, Charles P.

McCahan, Robert C. 1899-1958 [SC]
American actor
* Dease, Bobby

McCaig, Donald 20th c. [CA, PW 4-6-
84]
American author and poet
* Ashley, Steven
* McCaig, Snee

McCaig, Edith 20th c. [CA]
American author
* Engren, Edith [joint pseudonym with
Robert Jesse McCaig]

McCaig, Robert Jesse 1907- [CA]
American author
* Engren, Edith [joint pseudonym with
Edith McCaig]

McCaig, Snee
See McCaig, Donald

McCain, Boogie
See McCain, Jerry

McCain, Constance 20th c. [ITA]
American actress
* Cain, Sugar

McCain, Jerry 1930- [BWW]
American singer
* McCain, Boogie

McCall, Anthony
See Kane, Henry

McCall, Bam
See McCall, Brian Allen

McCall, Brian Allen 1943- [BE]
American baseball player
* McCall, Bam

McCall, Buffalo Curly
See McCall, John

McCall, C. W.
See Fries, William [Bill]

McCall, Charles
See Fish, Charles D.

McCall, Creighton
See Melcher, Gilbert W[ayne]

McCall, Curly
See McCall, John

McCall, Dutch
See McCall, Robert Leonard

McCall, John 1820-1902 [PI]
Irish author and poet
* Scrutator

McCall, John 1850?-1877 [EWG, HPPN]
American gunfighter
* Broken Nose Jack
* McCall, Buffalo Curly
* McCall, Curly
* Sutherland, Bill

McCall, John Corey
See Morland, Nigel

McCall, John William 1925- [BE]
American baseball player
* McCall, Windy

McCall, Lizzie
See Lennon, Mrs. Nestor

McCall, Patrick Joseph 1861-? [PI]
Irish poet and translator
* Cavellus

McCall, Robert Leonard 1920- [BE]
American baseball player
* McCall, Dutch

McCall, Sidney
See Fenellosa, Mary McNeil

McCall, Vincent
See Morland, Nigel

McCall, Virginia Nielsen 1909- [CA,
SAT]
American author
* Nielsen, Virginia

McCall, William 1821-1881 [PI]
Irish poet
* Dhearg, Lamh

McCall, Windy
See McCall, John William

McCalla, Daniel 1748-1809 [HPPN]
American clergyman
* Artemas

McCallister, Bud [or Buddy]
See McCallister, Herbert Alonzo

McCallister, Herbert Alonzo 1923-
[HPPN]
American actor
* McCallister, Bud [or Buddy]
* McCallister, Lon
* [The] Young Richard Barthelmess

McCallister, Lon
See McCallister, Herbert Alonzo

McCallum, Colin Whitton 1852-1945
[BEW, BMH, FC]
British entertainer and songwriter
* Coborn, Charlie [or Charles]
* [The] Comic of the Day
* [The] Father of the Profession

McCallum, Francis McNeill 1824-1857
[DI]
Scottish-born Australian bushranger
* Melville, Captain

McCallum, Leo 1929- [BA]
American dentist
* Salaam, Abdul

McCalment, Maebelle [Brearley] 20th c.
[NAA]
American writer
* Ley, Brea R.
* Mack, Brearley
* Mack, Maebelle

McCan, Frank 1896- [BX, RBE]
American boxer
* Mason, Frankie

McCann, Arthur
See Campbell, John W[ood], Jr.

McCann, Coolidge
See Fawcett, F[rank] Dubrez

McCann, Edson [joint pseudonym with Frederik Pohl]
See Alvarez Del Rey, Ramon Felipe San Juan Mario Silvio Enrico

McCann, Edson [joint pseudonym with Ramon Felipe San Juan Mario Alvarez Del Rey]
See Pohl, Frederik

McCann, Lawrence
See Beatty, Jerome

McCann, Philip
See Felstein, Ivor

McCarl, John Raymond 1879-1940 [HPPN]
Comptroller General of the United States
* [The] Watchdog of the Treasury

McCarren, Laurence Anthony 1951- [SMG]
American football player
* McCarren, Rock

McCarren, Rock
See McCarren, Laurence Anthony

McCarroll, James 1815-1896 [CCL, FFF]
American author and editor
* Dubh, Scian
* Finnegan, Terry

McCarroll, Marion C[lyde] 1893?-1977 [CA]
American author and columnist
* Fairfax, Beatrice

McCarter, Jody [joint pseudonym with Vermille McCarter]
See Demelikoff, Jodi

McCarter, Jody [joint pseudonym with Jodi Demelikoff]
See McCarter, Vermille

McCarter, Vermille 20th c. [SFP]
Author
* McCarter, Jody [joint pseudonym with Jodi Demelikoff]

McCarter, Willie 20th c.
American basketball player
* [The] Worm

McCarthy, Babe
See McCarthy, James

McCarthy, Cal
See McCarthy, Charles, Jr.

McCarthy, Charles J. 1903-1960 [ASC]
American musician
* McCarthy, Pat

McCarthy, Charles, Jr. 1869-1895 [AS, RBE]
American boxer
* McCarthy, Cal

McCarthy, Charles L. 1882-1962 [AS]
American sportscaster
* McCarthy, Clem

McCarthy, Clean Gene
See McCarthy, Eugene Joseph

McCarthy, Clem
See McCarthy, Charles L.

McCarthy, Denis Florence 1817-1882 [PA, PI]
Irish poet and playwright
* Antonio
* D.
* D. F. McC.
* Desmond
* J. H.
* M.
* S. E. Y.
* Trifolium
* Vig

McCarthy, Eugene Joseph 1916-
American politician
* McCarthy, Clean Gene

McCarthy, Fitzjames 19th c. [PI]
American journalist and poet
* Fitz Mac

McCarthy, Foster J. 1900-1948 [HPPN]
American actor and announcer
* Williams, Foster

McCarthy, Herbert 20th c. [THR]
British actor and playwright
* Darnley, Herbert

McCarthy, J. P.
See McCarthy, Joseph Priestley

McCarthy, J. T.
See Torrio, John [Johnny]

McCarthy, James 1923-1975 [BB, BI]
American basketball coach
* McCarthy, Babe

McCarthy, Joseph Priestley
American radio broadcaster
* McCarthy, J. P.

McCarthy, Joseph Raymond 1908-1957
American politician
* Tail Gunner Joe

McCarthy, Joseph Vincent 1887-1978 [BE, DGS, PB]
American baseball manager
* McCarthy, Marse Joe

McCarthy, Julia 1897?-1974 [BI]
American columnist
* Randolph, Nancy

McCarthy, Justine 1926?-1959 [BDF, BEW, FC]
British actress
* Kendall, Kay

McCarthy, Little Mack
See McCarthy, Thomas Francis Michael [Tommy]

McCarthy, Mac
See Southerland, McCarthy

McCarthy, Marie 1912-1941 [SC]
American actress
* Maynard, Claire

McCarthy, Marse Joe
See McCarthy, Joseph Vincent

McCarthy, Mary Stanislaus 1850?-1897 [PI]
Irish poet
* S. M. S.

McCarthy, Mrs. Daniel [FFF]
Entertainer
* Coleman, Kitty

McCarthy, Pat
See Cook, Patricia

McCarthy, Pat
See McCarthy, Charles J.

McCarthy, Roger L. 1949- [HPPN]
American mechanical engineer
* [The] Disaster Detective

McCarthy, Shaun [Lloyd] 1928- [CA]
British author and journalist
* Callas, Theo
* Cory, Desmond

McCarthy, Teresa
See Anderson, Teresa

McCarthy, Thomas Francis Michael [Tommy] 1864-1922 [BAB]
American baseball player
* [The] Kid
* McCarthy, Little Mack

McCartney, Paul 1942-
British singer, composer, producer
* Ramon, Paul
* Vermouth, Apollo C.
* Webb, Bernard

McCartney, Peter Michael [Mike] 1944- [CA]
British songwriter and author
* McGear, Mike

McCartney, William H. [FFF, PA]
American author
* Muldoon, Major

McCarton, Benjamin F. 1879-1917 [HPPN]
American actor and author
* Carter, Frank

McCarty, Bones
See McCarty, James

McCarty, George S. 1868-1945 [HPPN]
American trapshooter
* [The] Father of Amateur Trapshooting

McCarty, Henry 1859-1881
American gunfighter
* Antrim, Henry
* Antrim, Kid
* Antrim, William
* Billy the Kid
* Bonney, William

McCarty, James 19th c.
American gunfighter
* McCarty, Bones

McCarty, Luther 1892-1913 [HPPN]
American boxer
* [The] White Hope Champion

McCarty, Norma
See Crandall, Norma

McCarty, Wilson 20th c. [CA]
Author
* Chamberlain, Wilson [joint pseudonym
  with Norma Crandall]

McCash, June Hall 1938- [CA]
American author
* Martin, June Hall

McCauley, Elfrieda B[abnick] 1915-
[CA]
American editor
* House, Anne W.

McCauley, Mary Ludwig Hays
1754?-1832 [HPPN, WBD]
American Revolutionary War heroine
* Captain Molly
* Pitcher, Molly

McCaull, M. E.
See Bohlman, [Mary] Edna McCaull

McCausland, Dominick 1806-1873 [PI]
Irish author and attorney
* McC.

McCay, Winsor 1869-1934 [WECO]
American cartoonist
* Silas

McChesney, Harry Vincent 1880-1960
[BE]
American baseball player
* McChesney, Pud

McChesney, Mary F. 20th c. [WW]
Author
* Rayter, Joe

McChesney, Pud
See McChesney, Harry Vincent

McChester, George 19th c. [RBE]
Boxer
* McCloskey, Country

McClain, Boots
See McClain, Edward

McClain, Edward 20th c. [OBW]
American baseball player
* McClain, Boots

McClain, Houndog
See McClain, Ted

McClain, Ted 1947?- [BB, SMG]
American basketball player
* [The] Hound
* McClain, Houndog

McClannin, Mrs. R. F. [FFF]
Entertainer
* Skerrett, Emma

McClary, Jane Stevenson 1919- [CA]
American journalist and author
* McIlvaine, Jane

McClary, Thomas Calvert [ESF, WGT]
American author
* Peregoy, Calvin

McClaskey, Harry 20th c. [PMJ]
Canadian singer
* Burr, Henry

McClatchy, C. K.
See McClatchy, Charles Kenny

McClatchy, Charles Kenny 1858-?
[NAA]
American journalist
* McClatchy, C. K.

McClean, Don 1939?-1984
*American female impersonator, producer,
director*
* Shannon, Lori

McClean, Kathleen
See Hale, Kathleen

McCleary, Eleanor
See Picken, Mary Brooks

McCleese, James 1942- [RO1]
American singer
* Soul, Jimmy

McClellan, George Brinton 1826-1885
[DEP, DNNS, HPPN, NPS, NW 7-18-83,
SN]
American army officer
* [The] General of the Mackerel
  Brigade
* Little Corporal of Unsought Fields
* Little Mac the Young Napoleon
* [The] Little Napoleon
* Mac the Unready
* McClellan, Tardy George
* [The] Modern Belisarius
* [The] Young Napoleon

McClellan, Harriet [Hare] 1873-1913
[DNA]
American author
* Flemming, Harford

McClellan, John 1896- [CR]
American politician
* [The] Craggy-Faced Inquisitor
* [The] Gangster's Nightmare
* [The] Man Behind the Frown

McClellan, Tardy George
See McClellan, George Brinton

McClellan, William
See Strong, Charles Stanley

McClelland, Diane Margaret 1931-
[CA]
British author
* Pearson, Diane

McClelland, M. G.
See McClelland, Mary Greenway

McClelland, Mary Greenway 1853-1895
[WGT]
American author
* McClelland, M. G.

McClelland, Richard Leeper 1922- [TR]
Irish actor
* Leech, Richard

McClendon, Charles Y. 1923- [FB]
American football coach
* McClendon, Cholly Mac

McClendon, Cholly Mac
See McClendon, Charles Y.

McClendon, Ernestine
See Epps, Ernestine

McClendon, Marie Millicent Dancy
1900- [NAA]
American author
* Dancy, M. M.

**McClendon, Rosalie Virginia Scott
[Rose]** 1884-1936 [IBW]
American actress and poet
* [The] Black Duse

McClendon, Sarah 1913- [HPPN]
American journalist
* [The] Holy Terror from Texas
* [The] White House Reporter

McClenny, Patsy 20th c.
American model and actress
* Fairchild, Morgan

McClinchy, Marie Emily 1912-
American singer
* Manners, Lucille

McClintic, James V. 1878-? [HPPN]
American politician
* McClintic, Rivet

McClintic, Rivet
See McClintic, James V.

McClintock, Harry Kirby 1882-1957
[CME]
American country-western performer
* Haywire Mac

McClintock, Marshall 1906-1967 [CAP,
SAT]
American author
* Duncan, Gregory
* Marshall, Douglas
* McClintock, Mike
* Starret, William

McClintock, Mike
See McClintock, Marshall

McClintock, Minda Agnes 1856-?
[NAA]
American physician and author
* Agnes

McClinton, O. B.
See McClinton, Obie Burnett

McClinton, Obie Burnett 1942- [ECM]
American country-western performer
* McClinton, O. B.

McCloskey, Country
See McChester, George

McCloskey, Henry 1829?-1869 [PI]
Irish-born journalist and poet
* Paddy

McCloskey, Honest John
See McCloskey, John

McCloskey, John 1810-1885 [HPPN]
American religious leader
* America's First Cardinal

McCloskey, John 1862-1940 [BE]
American baseball manager
* McCloskey, Honest John

McCloskey, John 1898?-1947? [NOJ]
American jazz musician
* Rogers, Emmett

McCloskey, Paul N. 1927-
American politician
* McCloskey, Pete

McCloskey, Pete
See McCloskey, Paul N.

McCloskey, [John] Robert 1914- [CA, SAT]
American author and illustrator
* Dangerfield, Balfour

McCloud, David
See Coonradt, Paul Talbot

McCloy, Helen [Clarkson] 1866?-1950 [BI]
American columnist
* Benedict, Joan

McCloy, Helen [Worrell Clarkson] 1904- [CA]
American author
* Clarkson, Helen

McClung, Alexander 1855-? [HPPN]
American editor and orator
* [The] Black Knight of the South

McClung, Bum
See McClung, Thomas Lee

McClung, Thomas Lee 1870-1914? [AS, FB]
American football player and U.S. treasurer
* McClung, Bum

McClure, Adrienne Ruth 1908?-1947 [BEW]
American theatrical performer
* Ames, Adrienne

McClure, Greg
See Easton, Dale

McClure, Harold Murray [Hal] 1859-1919 [BE]
American baseball player
* McClure, Mac

McClure, Mac
See McClure, Harold Murray [Hal]

McClure, Mac
See McClure, Robert Craig

McClure, Peggy
See Pierce, Lillian Elizabeth

McClure, Robert Craig 1953- [SMG]
American baseball player
* McClure, Mac

McClure, Samuel Sidney 1857-1949 [HPPN]
British-American editor and publisher
* [The] Father of the Fiction Syndicate

McCluskey, Harold 1913?- [NW 6-20-83]
American nuclear plant technician
* [The] Atomic Man

McCluskey, Harry Roberts 1892-1962 [BE]
American baseball player
* McCluskey, Lefty

McCluskey, Henry 1827-1870 [PA]
Author
* Paddy

McCluskey, Lefty
See McCluskey, Harry Roberts

McCluskey, Roger 1930?- [HPPN]
American auto racer
* [The] Champ

McCluskie, Mike ?-1871 [BLB, EWG]
American gunfighter
* Delaney, Art[hur]

McCobb, Mary Selden [FFF, PA]
Writer
* Densel, Mary

McColl, Alex[ander Boyd] 1894- [BE]
American baseball player
* McColl, Red

McColl, Ewan
See Miller, Jimmy

McColl, Red
See McColl, Alex[ander Boyd]

McCollum, Elmer V. ?-1967 [HPPN]
American biochemist
* [The] Vitamin Researcher

McCollum, J. C. [PA]
Author
* Trumps

McCollum, Robert Lee 1909-1967 [BWW, NBB]
American singer
* McCoy, Robert Lee
* Nighthawk, Robert
* Pettie's Boy
* Ramblin' Bob

McComas, I. V. 20th c. [WWL]
British author
* Somerville, H. B.

McComas, J[esse] Francis 1911-1978 [ESF, WGT]
American author and editor
* Marlowe, Webb

McComb, Big Mac
See McComb, Jeff

McComb, Florence
See Melim, Mary M.

McComb, Frederick Wilson Henry 1927- [IAW]
Irish-born author
* Habershon, Keith

McComb, Jeff 20th c. [HPPN]
American basketball player
* McComb, Big Mac

McComb, Katherine Woods 1895- [CA]
American author
* Woods, Constance

McComb, Robert [Bob] 20th c. [HPPN]
American acrobatic aviator
* Uncle Fudd

McCombe, W. J. 1871-? [PI]
Irish poet
* Ivanhoe

McConn, Charles Maxwell 1881-? [WWL]
American educator and author
* McConn, Max

McConn, Max
See McConn, Charles Maxwell

McConnell, Ambrose Moses 1883-1942 [BE]
American baseball player
* McConnell, Amby

McConnell, Amby
See McConnell, Ambrose Moses

McConnell, Edward 20th c. [HPPN]
American singer
* McConnell, Smilin' Ed

McConnell, Forrest W. 1911?-1962 [BEW]
American theatrical performer
* McConnell, Peewee

McConnell, James Douglas Rutherford 1915- [CA, CC, EMD]
Irish-born author
* Rutherford, Douglas
* Temple, Paul [joint pseudonym with Francis Durbridge]

McConnell, John Lithgow Chandos 1918- [CA]
Scottish-born author
* Chandos, John

McConnell, John Preston ?-1941 [HPPN]
American educator and philosopher
* Eci
* [The] Serving Knight

McConnell, Peewee
See McConnell, Forrest W.

McConnell, Smilin' Ed
See McConnell, Edward

McConnell, Wallace Robert 1881-? [WWL]
American geographer and author
* Mac

McConnell, Will
See Snodgrass, William DeWitt

McCook, Alexander McDowell 1831-1903 [SN]
American army officer
* McCook, Fighting

McCook, Fighting
See McCook, Alexander McDowell

McCoole, Mike 1837-1886 [RBE]
Irish-born American boxer
* [The] Deck Hand Champion of America

McCord, Guy
See Reynolds, Dallas McCord

McCord, James W., Jr. 20th c. [HPPN]
American government official involved in Watergate scandal
* Martin, Edward

McCord, Lewis
See Wanbaugh, Landis

McCord, May Kennedy 1880-1943 [FFA]
American singer
* [The] Queen of the Hillbillies

McCord, Whip
See Norwood, Victor G[eorge] C[harles]

McCord, William, Jr. 1944- [RO2]
American singer
* Vera, Billy

McCormac, Brian
See Swan, Cormac

McCormack, Billie
See Burke, Blanche E.

McCormack, Goose
See McCormack, John Ronald

McCormack, James 20th c. [MBF]
British author
* Patrick, Max

McCormack, John 1884-1945 [HPPN]
Irish-born American opera singer
* Foli, Giovanni
* Ireland's Favorite Tenor

McCormack, John Ronald 1925- [CEI]
Canadian-born hockey player
* McCormack, Goose

McCormack, John W. 1892?-1980 [HPPN]
American politician
* [The] Fighting Irishman of South Boston
* Uncle John

McCormack, Mark H. 1931?- [TI 8-27-84]
American business manager and author
* [The] Abominable Snowjob Man

McCormack, Patty
See Russo, Patricia Ellen

McCormack, William John 1947- [DIL]
Irish poet
* Maxton, Hugh

McCormick, Alice 1875-1958 [HPPN]
American actress
* McCormick, Ma

McCormick, Alyce 1904-1932 [SC]
American actress
* Auburn, Joy

McCormick, Barry
See McCormick, William J.

McCormick, Brooks
See Adams, William Taylor

McCormick, Buck
See McCormick, Frank Andrew

McCormick, Claire
See Labus, Marta Haake

McCormick, Cyrus Hall 1809-1884 [HPPN]
American inventor and industrialist
* [The] Father of the Reaper

McCormick, [George] Donald [King] 1911- [AW, CA, WD]
Welsh-born author and historian
* Deacon, Richard

McCormick, F. J.
See Judge, Peter

McCormick, Frank Andrew 1913- [BE, PB]
American baseball player
* McCormick, Buck

McCormick, Harry Elwood 1881-1962 [BE]
American baseball player
* McCormick, Moose

McCormick, Hyannis Port
See McCormick, John

McCormick, Jerry
See McCormick, John

McCormick, John ?-1905 [BE]
American baseball player
* McCormick, Jerry

McCormick, John 20th c.
American football player
* McCormick, Hyannis Port

McCormick, Ma
See McCormick, Alice

McCormick, Mary 1914- [CA]
American author
* McCormick, [Sister] Rose M[atthew]

McCormick, Merla Jean 1938- [CA]
American author
* Sparks, Merla Jean

McCormick, Mike
See McCormick, Myron Winthrop

McCormick, Moose
See McCormick, Harry Elwood

McCormick, Mrs. Loudon [FFF]
Entertainer
* Miller, Maud

McCormick, Myron Winthrop 1917- [BE]
American baseball player
* McCormick, Mike

McCormick, Philip
See Wilson, Edwin P.

McCormick, Robert Rutherford 1880-1955 [HPPN]
American newspaper publisher, attorny, army officer
* [The] Colonel of Chicago

McCormick, [Sister] Rose M[atthew]
See McCormick, Mary

McCormick, Wilfred 1903- [CA]
American author
* Allison, Rand
* Dunlap, Lon

McCormick, William J. 1874-1956 [BE]
American baseball player
* McCormick, Barry

McCorquodale, Barbara
See Cartland, Barbara [Hamilton]

McCorry, Peter 19th c. [PI]
Irish-born journalist and poet
* McSherry, Shandy

McCovey, Stretch
See McCovey, Willie Lee

McCovey, Wallopin Willie
See McCovey, Willie Lee

McCovey, Willie Lee 1938- [BE, IBW, PB]
American baseball player
* McCovey, Stretch
* McCovey, Wallopin Willie

McCoy, Al
See Rudolph, Al[bert]

McCoy, Arch
See Miller, Victor [Brooke]

McCoy, Big Frank
See McCoy, Francis

McCoy, Charles [Charlie] 1909-1950 [BWW]
American singer
* McCoy, Papa
* Mississippi Mudder
* Papa Charlie

McCoy, Charles
See Selby, Norman

McCoy, Chink
See McCoy, Frank

McCoy, Cyclone
See McCoy, Robert Jesse

McCoy, Elijah J. 1843-1929 [HPPN, IBW]
American inventor
* [The] Father of the Oil Cup
* [The] Father of the Steam Dome
* [The] Real McCoy

McCoy, Flintstone
See McCoy, Leon

McCoy, Francis 19th c. [HPPN]
American bank robber and safe cracker
* McCoy, Big Frank

McCoy, Frank 1906- [MK]
American baseball player
* McCoy, Chink

McCoy, Gertrude
See McRae, Gertrude Lyon

McCoy, Grandpa
See McCoy, Jim

McCoy, Iola Fuller 1906- [CA, SAT]
American author
* Fuller, Iola

McCoy, Jim 1885?-1984   [TI 2-27-84]
American coal miner
* McCoy, Grandpa

McCoy, Joe 1905-1950   [BWW]
American singer
* Big Joe
* Georgia Pine Boy
* Hallelujah Joe
* Hamfoot Ham
* Kansas Joe
* Mississippi Mudder
* Mud Dauber Joe
* Wilber, Bill

McCoy, John 20th c.   [WGT]
Author
* Commissioner, Lord

McCoy, Kathleen [Kathy] 1945-   [CA]
American author and actress
* McCoy, Kaylin

McCoy, Kaylin
See   McCoy, Kathleen [Kathy]

McCoy, Kid
See   McGee, Bill

McCoy, Kid
See   Selby, Norman

McCoy, Leon 20th c.   [GW]
American rodeo performer
* McCoy, Flintstone

McCoy, M. C.
See   McCoy, Michael Charles

McCoy, Malachy
See   Caulfield, Malachy Francis

McCoy, Michael Charles 1953-   [FR]
American football player
* McCoy, M. C.

McCoy, Minnie
See   Douglas, Lizzie

McCoy, Mother
See   McCoy, Peter

McCoy, Mrs. U. E.   [FFF]
Entertainer
* Hodgson, Ethelyn

McCoy, Papa
See   McCoy, Charles [Charlie]

McCoy, Peter 20th c.   [WP 12-21-82]
American government official
* McCoy, Mother

McCoy, Robert Edward
See   McCoy, Robert Jesse

McCoy, Robert Jesse 1910-   [BWW]
American singer
* McCoy, Cyclone
* McCoy, Robert Edward

McCoy, Robert Lee
See   McCollum, Robert Lee

McCoy, Tim 1893-   [CU]
American actor
* [The] White Eagle

McCoy, Van Allen 1941-1979   [IBW]
American dance creator, conductor, singer
* [The] Disco Kid

McCoy, Viola 1900?-1956?   [BWW]
American singer
* Brown, Amanda
* Cliff, Daisy
* Johnson, Fannie
* Johnson, Gladys
* McCoy, Violet
* White, Clara
* Williams, Bessie
* Williams, Susan

McCoy, Violet
See   McCoy, Viola

McCoy, [Captain] William ?-1948
[HPPN]
American bootlegger and rum runner
* [The] Founder of Rum Row
* [The] King of Rum Runners
* [The] Real McCoy

McCrabb, Buster
See   McCrabb, Lester William

McCrabb, Lester William 1914-   [BE]
American baseball player
* McCrabb, Buster

McCracken, Elizabeth A. M. 20th c.
[WWL]
Irish journalist and author
* Priestley, L. A. M.

McCracken, James 1920?-
American opera singer
* McCracken, Moose

McCracken, John D. 1911-1958   [AS,
BB]
American basketball player
* McCracken, Jumping Jack

McCracken, Jumping Jack
See   McCracken, John D.

McCracken, Moose
See   McCracken, James

McCracken, Robert 1899-1961   [HPPN]
American actor
* McTurk, Joe

McCrary, Benny Loyd 1946-
American wrestler
* McGuire, Benny

McCrary, Billy Leon 1946-1979
American wrestler
* McGuire, Billy

McCrary, John Reagan 1910-
American entertainer and journalist
* McCrary, Tex

McCrary, Tex
See   McCrary, John Reagan

McCravey, Leonard 20th c.   [GW]
American rodeo performer
* McCravey, Sinner

McCravey, Sinner
See   McCravey, Leonard

McCready, Jack
See   Powell, Talmage

McCready, Warren T[homas] 1915-
[CA]
American author
* Machiavelli

McCreary, Conn 1921-   [BBH]
American jockey
* McCreary, Convertible Conn

McCreary, Convertible Conn
See   McCreary, Conn

McCreary, Doug 1948-   [HPPN]
American wrestler
* McGuire, Doug

McCreary, Jay
See   McCreary, Lawrence J.

McCreary, Lawrence J. 20th c.   [BBH]
American basketball player and coach
* McCreary, Jay

McCree, Junie
See   Macrillo, Gonzaluo

McCree, Wade H. 1920?-
American solicitor general
* [The] Poet Laureate of the Sixth
Circuit

McCreedie, Judge
See   McCreedie, Walter Henry

McCreedie, Walter Henry 1876-1934
[BE]
American baseball player
* McCreedie, Judge

McCreery, Bud
See   McCreery, Walker William

McCreery, Thomas C. 1817-?   [SN]
American politician
* [The] Silver Tongued Sluggard of the
Senate

McCreery, Walker William 1921?-
[ASC, BEW]
American composer
* McCreery, Bud

McCreigh [or MacCreigh], James
See   Pohl, Frederik

McCrohan, Dennis Joseph 1851-1888
[BE]
American baseball player
* Mack, Dennis Joseph [Denny]

McCrorey, Sanders
See   Counselman, Mary Elizabeth

McCrory, Florence 1917-   [PMJ]
American singer
* Keene, Linda

McCrum, Myra Daisy   [FFF, PA]
Author
* Howard, Daisy

McCue, Duke
See   McCue, W. L.

McCue, Lillian Bueno 1902- [CA, WD]
American author and playwright
* De La Torre, Lillian
* De La Torre-Bueno, Lillian

McCue, W. L. 20th c.
Horse trainer
* McCue, Duke

McCue, William 1874-1913 [HPPN]
American civic leader
* Captain Billy

McCullers, Carson
See McCullers, Lula Carson

McCullers, Lula Carson 1917-1967
[HPPN]
American author
* McCullers, Carson

McCulley, Johnston 1883-1958 [EMD,
MBF, NAA]
American author
* Brien, Raley
* Carter, Nicholas?
* Drayne, George
* McAlpin, Grant
* Morton, Monica
* Phelps, Frederic
* Pierson, Walter
* Raley, Rowena
* Stone, John Mack
* Strong, Harrington

McCulloch, Derek 1897-1967 [MBF]
British author
* Uncle Mac

McCulloch, Earl 1936- [FB]
American football player
* McCulloch, Pearl

McCulloch, Ernie 1926- [BBH]
Canadian skier
* [The] Grand Slam Champion

McCulloch, Hugh [PA]
Author
* J. R. M.

McCulloch, J. H. 20th c. [MBF]
British author
* Rawlings, J. R.

McCulloch, John Tyler
See Burroughs, Edgar Rice

McCulloch, Pearl
See McCulloch, Earl

McCulloch, Sarah [or Sara?] 20th c.
British author
* Ure, Jean

McCulloch, Thomas 1776-1843 [CCL]
Canadian author
* Stepsure, Mephibosheth

McCullough, Big Bob
See McCullough, Robert

McCullough, Harold Taylor 20th c.
[BBH]
American basketball coach
* McCullough, Mack

McCullough, James H.
See Clark, Neil McCullough

McCullough, Joseph B. [FFF, PA]
American editor
* Mack

McCullough, Mack
See McCullough, Harold Taylor

McCullough, Phil
See McCullough, Pinson Lamar

McCullough, Pinson Lamar 1917- [BE]
American baseball player
* McCullough, Phil

McCullough, Robert 20th c. [PHM]
American underworld figure
* McCullough, Big Bob

McCully, Alice Woodruff [Anderson]
[BI]
American author and horticulturist
* McCully, Anderson

McCully, Anderson
See McCully, Alice Woodruff
[Anderson]

McCully, Emily Arnold
See Arnold, Emily

McCurdy, John Edward 1929- [OP]
American opera singer
* Macurdy, John

McCurdy, Nancy
See Parrish, [Emma] Kenyon

McCurry, Betsy
See Moore, Bertha B.

McCurry, Clarence Earl 20th c.
American singer and songwriter
* Ashley, Thomas Clarence

McCutchan, J[ohn] Wilson 1909- [CA]
American author and educator
* Locke, Peter

McCutchan, Philip [Donald] 1920- [CA,
TCCM, WD, WWS]
British author
* Galway, Robert Conington
* MacNeil, Duncan
* Wigg, T. I. G.

McCutcheon, Ben Frederick 1875-1934
[DNA]
American author and journalist
* Brace, Benjamin

McCutcheon, George Barr 1866-1928
[WGT]
American author
* Greaves, Richard

McCutcheon, Hugh Davie-Martin 1909-
[IAW]
Scottish author
* Davie-Martin, Hugh

McCutcheon, James
See Lundgren, Paul Arthur

McDaniel, A. T.
See McDaniel, Adam Theodore

McDaniel, Adam Theodore 1925-
American dentist
* McDaniel, A. T.

McDaniel, David [Edward] 1939- [CA]
American author
* Johnstone, Ted

McDaniel, Deacon
See McDaniel, Sam[uel Rufus]

McDaniel, Ed 1938- [FB, SMG]
American football player and wrestler
* Chief Wahoo
* McDaniel, Wahoo

McDaniel, Ellas
See Bates, Otha Ellas

McDaniel, Evelyn
See Bryan, Evelyn McDaniel Frazier

McDaniel, Hattie 1895-1952 [BWW,
HPPN]
American singer and actress
* Beulah
* [The] Colored Sophie Tucker
* [The] Female Bert Williams
* Hi Hat Hattie

McDaniel, Henry 1867-1948
American horse owner
* McDaniel, Uncle Henry

McDaniel, Ira C. 1877-1954 [HPPN]
American farmer and stock breeder
* Red Rat

McDaniel, James 1915-1963 [CWG]
American country-western performer
* McDaniel, Sleepy

McDaniel, Lindy
See McDaniel, Lyndall Dale

McDaniel, Lyndall Dale 1935- [BE]
American baseball player
* McDaniel, Lindy

McDaniel, Sam[uel Rufus] 1886-1962
[BWW, SC]
American actor
* McDaniel, Deacon

McDaniel, Samuel Walton [FFF]
American writer
* Parsonus Rusticus

McDaniel, Sleepy
See McDaniel, James

McDaniel, Uncle Henry
See McDaniel, Henry

McDaniel, Wahoo
See McDaniel, Ed

McDaniel, Wilma Elizabeth 20th c.
American poet
* Gravy Poet

McDaniel, X-Man
See McDaniel, Xavier

McDaniel, Xavier 20th c. [SI 12-5-83]
American basketball player
* McDaniel, X-Man

McDaniels, Booker T. ?-1974? [MK]
American baseball player
* McDaniels, Cannonball

McDaniels, Cannonball
See McDaniels, Booker T.

McDaniels, Jim 1948- [SMG]
American basketball player
* McDaniels, Mac

McDaniels, Mac
See McDaniels, Jim

McDavid, Raven I[oor], Jr. 1911- [CA]
American author
* Darwin, M. B.
* Hatteras, Owen, III
* Pyles, Aitken

McDermit, Patrick Michael 1956?-
[HPPN]
American practical joker
* Alrea, Andrea

McDermott, Aubrey [or Paul?] 20th c.
[ESF, WGT]
Author
* McDermott, Dennis [joint pseudonym
with Walter Dennis and P. Schuyler
Miller]

McDermott, Dennis [joint pseudonym
with P. Schuyler Miller and Aubrey
McDermott]
See Dennis, Walter L.

McDermott, Dennis [joint pseudonym
with Walter Dennis and P. Schuyler
Miller]
See McDermott, Aubrey [or Paul?]

McDermott, Dennis [joint pseudonym
with Aubrey McDermott and Walter
Dennis]
See Miller, P[eter] Schuyler

McDermott, Frank A. 1889- [BE]
American baseball player
* McDermott, Red

McDermott, George 19th c. [PI]
Irish poet and barrister
* D. G. M.
* G. M. D.

McDermott, Hugh Farrar 1833-1890
[PA, PI]
Irish-born journalist and poet
* Pax

McDermott, Martin 1823-1905 [PI]
Irish poet
* M. McD.

McDermott, Mary 19th c. [PI]
Irish poet
* M. McD.

McDermott, Maurice Joseph 1928- [BE]
American baseball player
* McDermott, Mickey

McDermott, Michael 20th c. [BBH]
American swimmer
* McDermott, Turk

McDermott, Mickey
See McDermott, Maurice Joseph

McDermott, Red
See McDermott, Frank A.

McDermott, Richard Terrance 1940-
[HPPN]
American speed skater
* McDermott, Terry

McDermott, Terry
See McDermott, Richard Terrance

McDermott, Turk
See McDermott, Michael

McDermott, William 1863-1913 [DNA,
PI]
Irish poet, author, clergyman
* Lecky, Walter

McDevitt, Neil 19th c. [PI]
Irish poet
* N. M.?
* Naas, N.

McDevitt, Ruth
See Shoecraft, Ruth Thane

McDole, Carol
See Farley, Carol

McDole, Roland Owen 1939-
American football player
* [The] Dancing Bear
* McDole, Ron
* McDole, Rubber Man

McDole, Ron
See McDole, Roland Owen

McDole, Rubber Man
See McDole, Roland Owen

McDonald, Ab
See McDonald, Alvin Brian

McDonald, Alvin Brian 1936- [CEI,
FHE, HK]
Canadian-born hockey player
* McDonald, Ab

McDonald, Babe
See McDonald, Patrick J.

McDonald, Bernard 1923- [SFL]
Author
* Macdonnaill, Brian

McDonald, Bucko
See McDonald, Wilfred Kennedy

McDonald, Captain Bill
See McDonald, William Jesse [Bill]

McDonald, Cathy
See Wallis, Geraldine McDonald

McDonald, Charles E.
See Crabtree, Charles C.

McDonald, D. A. 20th c. [CCL]
Canadian poet
* Ex Convict No. 1999, Kingston
Penitentiary

McDonald, Daniel ?-1830 [HPPN]
American clergyman and educator
* P.

McDonald, Daniel 1847-1880 [BE]
American baseball player
* McDonald, Jack

McDonald, Dianna
See Shomaker, Dianna

McDonald, Edward 1865-1929 [BI]
American youth leader
* Barnabas Edward, [Brother]

McDonald, Edward Richard 1873-?
[SFL, WGT]
Author
* McDonald, Raymond [joint
pseudonym with Raymond Alfred
Leger]

McDonald, Enos William 1915-1968
[CWG, DAM]
American country-western performer
* McDonald, Skeets

McDonald, Erwin L[awrence] 1907-
[CA]
American clergyman and author
* Hankins, Clabe

McDonald, Garry 1948?- [BI]
Australian actor and television performer
* Gunston, Norman

McDonald, Gooseneck Bill
See McDonald, William

McDonald, Hot Rod
See McDonald, James LeRoy

McDonald, Ian 20th c. [RO2]
British singer
* Matthews, Ian

McDonald, Jack
See McDonald, Daniel

McDonald, James 19th c. [PI]
Irish poet
* J. McD.

McDonald, James LeRoy 1927- [BE]
American baseball player
* McDonald, Hot Rod

McDonald, James Preston 1904- [WWJ]
American jazz musician
* Jackson, Preston

McDonald, Jamie
See Heide, Florence Parry

McDonald, Joe 20th c. [BI]
American singer
* Country Joe

McDonald, John 1846-? [PI]
Irish poet
* J. McD.

McDonald, Joseph Ewing 1819-1891
[FFF]
American politician
* Old Saddlebags

McDonald, Julie 1929- [CA]
American author and playwright
* Jensen, Julie

McDonald, Luther 20th c. [OBW]
American baseball player
* McDonald, Vet

McDonald, Mac
See McDonald, Webster

McDonald, Marie
See Frye, Marie

McDonald, Martha
See Blair, Linda

McDonald, Maurice James 1902-1971
[HPPN]
American business executive
* [The] Hamburger King

McDonald, Michael Cassius [Mike]
1839-1907 [HPPN]
American gambler, politician, newspaper owner
* Chicago's Boss Sharper
* [The] Well Known Gambler

McDonald, Patrick J. 1878?-1954 [AS]
Irish-born track and field athlete
* McDonald, Babe

McDonald, Paula 1939?- [BI]
American author
* Herrigan, Jackie

McDonald, Peter 1836?-1890 [PI]
Irish poet
* P. McD.?
* Roc Noir

McDonald, Raymond [joint pseudonym
with Edward Richard McDonald]
See Leger, Raymond Alfred

McDonald, Raymond [joint pseudonym
with Raymond Alfred Leger]
See McDonald, Edward Richard

McDonald, Richard C. 1935?- [BI]
American author
* Herrigan, Jeff

McDonald, Robert
See Leach, Ann

McDonald, Rocco
See Kroc, Ray

McDonald, Ronald
See Kroc, Ray

McDonald, Skeets
See McDonald, Enos William

McDonald, Stump
See McDonald, Tommy

McDonald, Tex
See Crabtree, Charles C.

McDonald, Tommy 20th c.
American football player
* [The] Elf
* McDonald, Stump

McDonald, Vet
See McDonald, Luther

McDonald, Webster 1900- [IBW, MK]
American baseball player
* [The] Giant Killer
* McDonald, Mac

McDonald, Wilfred Kennedy 1911-
[CEI, FHE, HK]
Canadian-born hockey player
* McDonald, Bucko

McDonald, William 1867-1950 [IBW]
American banker
* McDonald, Gooseneck Bill

McDonald, William Jesse [Bill]
1852-1918 [HPPN]
American rancher and deputy sheriff
* McDonald, Captain Bill

McDonald, Willie Ruth 1931- [BA]
American educator
* Miss M

[The] McDonald's of Con Men
See Weinberg, Melvin

McDonnell, Arthur 1883-1951 [BEW]
Irish actor
* Sinclair, Arthur

McDonnell, James Smith 1899?-1980
[HPPN]
American business executive
* Mac, Mr.
* McDonnell, Old Mac
* Old Man Mac

McDonnell, James William [Jim] 1922-
[BE]
American baseball player
* McDonnell, Mack

McDonnell, Jinny
See McDonnell, Virginia B[leecker]

McDonnell, John 20th c. [EF]
American football player
* McDonnell, Mickey

McDonnell, John W. 1856-? [FFF]
American writer
* Fitzgibbons, Patrick

McDonnell, Mack
See McDonnell, James William [Jim]

McDonnell, Mickey
See McDonnell, John

McDonnell, Old Mac
See McDonnell, James Smith

McDonnell, Sandy
See McDonnell, Sanford

McDonnell, Sanford 20th c. [NW 1-24-
83]
American business executive
* McDonnell, Sandy

McDonnell, Virginia B[leecker] 1917-
[CA, HPPN]
American author
* Barclay, Virginia
* Kirby, Jean [house pseudonym,
Whitman Publishing]
* McDonnell, Jinny

McDonough, Al
See McDonough, James Allison

McDonough, C. J. [PA]
Author
* Warwick, Charles

McDonough, James Allison 1950- [CEI,
HK, HR]
Canadian-born hockey player
* McDonough, Al

McDonough, Paul A. ?-1928 [HPPN]
American actor
* Arthur, Paul

McDougal, David Stockton 1809-1882
[HPPN]
American naval officer
* [The] American Devil

McDougal, Dwarf
See Lennon, John

McDougal, James A. 1878-1910 [BE]
American baseball player
* McDougal, Sandy

McDougal, Lem
See McDougal, Lemuel

McDougal, Lemuel 20th c. [OBW]
American baseball player
* McDougal, Lem

McDougal, McGregor 1831?-1858
[HPPN]
Canadian-American outlaw
* [The] Horse Thief of Northport

McDougal, Sandy
See McDougal, James A.

McDougal, Stan
See Diamant, Lincoln

McDougald, Gilbert James 1928-
[HPPN]
American basketball player
* Casey's Kid

McDougall, E. Jean [Taylor] 20th c.
[CCL]
Canadian author
* Rolyat, Jane

McDougall, Margaret [Dixon] 1826-1898
[CCL]
Canadian author
* Norah
* Peppergrass, Paul

McDoulet [or McDougal], Annie 1877?-
[HPPN]
American outlaw
* McDoulet, Cattle Annie

McDoulet, Cattle Annie
See McDoulet [or McDougal], Annie

McDow, Gerald
See Scortia, Thomas N[icholas]

McDowall, Roddy
See McDowall, Roderick Andrew

McDowall, Roderick Andrew 1928-
[BEW, TR]
British actor
* McDowall, Roddy

McDowell, Crosby
See Freeman, John Crosby

McDowell, Frederick 1904-1972 [DAM]
American singer and composer
* McDowell, Mississippi Fred

McDowell, J. [BI]
British undercover agent
* McDowell, Paddy

McDowell, Jack ?-1864 [HPPN]
American outlaw
* McDowell, Three Fingered Jack

McDowell, Joseph 1756-1799 [FFF, HPPN]
American revolutionary soldier and politician
* Pleasant Gardens Joe
* Quaker Meadows Joe

McDowell, Katherine Sherwood 1849-1883 [FFF, WBD]
American author
* Bonner, Sherwood

McDowell, Malcolm
See Taylor, Malcolm

McDowell, Michael 1950- [CA]
American author
* Aldyne, Nathan [joint pseudonym with Dennis Schuetz]

McDowell, Mississippi Fred
See McDowell, Frederick

McDowell, Mrs. E. A. [FFF]
Entertainer
* Reeves, Fannie

McDowell, Paddy
See McDowell, J.

McDowell, Samuel Edward Thomas 1942- [BE, PB]
American baseball player
* McDowell, Sudden Sam

McDowell, Sudden Sam
See McDowell, Samuel Edward Thomas

McDowell, Three Fingered Jack
See McDowell, Jack

McDuff, Brother Jack
See McDuffy, Eugene

McDuffie, Terris 1911- [MK]
American baseball player
* Elmer the Great

McDuffy, Eugene 1926- [EJ7]
American jazz musician
* McDuff, Brother Jack

McEachern, Malcolm 1884?-1945 [BMH]
Australian-born entertainer
* Jetsam

McEdwards, William Blake 1922- [FC]
American writer, producer, director
* Edwards, Blake

McElfresh, [Elizabeth] Adeline 1918- [CA, WW]
American author
* Cleveland, John
* Scott, Jane
* Wesley, Elizabeth

McElhanon, Kenneth Andrew 1939- [CA]
American author
* Saqorewec, E.

McElhenny, Hugh Edward 1928- [BI, FB, HPPN]
American football player
* [The] King
* McElhenny, King

McElhenny, King
See McElhenny, Hugh Edward

McElhinney, Jane 1836-1874 [FFF, PA]
American actress and author
* Clare, Ada
* Noyes, Mrs. J. F.
* [The] Queen of Bohemia
* Stanfield, Agnes

McElmury, Jim 1949- [SMG]
American hockey player
* McElmury, Mac

McElmury, Mac
See McElmury, Jim

McElroy, Bucky
See McElroy, William

McElroy, Hercules
See McElroy, James Dennis

McElroy, James Dennis 1945- [IBW]
American strongman
* McElroy, Hercules

McElroy, Jim 1953- [SMG]
American basketball player
* McElroy, Mac

McElroy, John 19th c. [HPPN]
American soldier and author
* [A] Private Soldier

McElroy, Kenneth Rex 1934-1981 [HPPN]
American murder victim
* McElroy, Kenrex

McElroy, Kenrex
See McElroy, Kenneth Rex

McElroy, Lee
See Kelton, Elmer

McElroy, Mac
See McElroy, Jim

McElroy, William 20th c. [EF]
American football player
* McElroy, Bucky

McElroy, William E. [PA]
Author
* Hubbell, Myron

McElveen, Humpy
See McElveen, Pryor Mynatt

McElveen, Pryor Mynatt 1880-1951 [BE]
American baseball player
* McElveen, Humpy

McElwee, Lee
See McElwee, Leland Stanford

McElwee, Leland Stanford 1894-1957 [BE]
American baseball player
* McElwee, Lee

McEnery, David 1914- [ASC, CWG, DAM]
American country-western performer
* Red River Dave

McEnroe, John 1959- [HPPN]
American tennis player
* [The] Fiery American Rebel
* Mac the Maestro
* Mac the Mouth
* McTantrum
* Superbrat

McEntee, Maurice Wurts ?-1883 [FFF]
American author and journalist
* Blue Jacket, Uncle

McEntee, P. 19th c. [PI]
Irish poet
* P. McG.

McEnvoy, C. N. 20th c. [MBF]
British author
* Strange, Kemble

McErin, Hugh
See Heinrick, Hugh

McErlane, Frank 20th c. [HPPN]
American underworld figure
* [The] Most Brutal Gunman in Chicago

McEver, Eugene T. 1908- [FB]
American football player
* McEver, Mack
* McEver, Wild Bull

McEver, Mack
See McEver, Eugene T.

McEver, Wild Bull
See McEver, Eugene T.

McEvoy, Arthur 1901-1957 [FC]
British entertainer
* Randle, Frank

McEvoy, Bernard 1842-1932 [NAA]
British-born journalist and author
* Diogenes
* Redbarn, Thomas

McEvoy, Harry K[irby] 1910- [CA]
American author
* Mack, Kirby

McEvoy, J. P.
See McEvoy, Joseph Patrick

McEvoy, Joseph Patrick 1894-1958 [BEW]
American librettist and playwright
* McEvoy, J. P.

McEvoy, Mac
See McEvoy, Michael Stephen Anthony

McEvoy, Marjorie Harte 20th c. [AW, CA, WD]
British author and journalist
* Harte, Marjorie

McEvoy, Michael Stephen Anthony 1956- [DC]
British cricketer
* McEvoy, Mac

McEwan, Cap
See McEwan, John J.

McEwan, Geraldine
See McKeown, Geraldine

McEwan, John J. 1893-1970 [FB]
American football player and coach
* [The] Giant from Minnesota
* McEwan, Cap
* [The] Rover Center

McEwan, Josephine 1892- [BF]
American-born actress
* Earle, Josephine

McEwen, Jessie Evelyn 1911- [CCL]
Canadian author
* Fisher, Agnes

McEwen, Tom 20th c.
American auto racer
* [The] Mongoose

McEwen, William Dalzell 1787-1828
[PI]
Irish poet and clergyman
* Walsingham

McFadden, Bernarr 1868-1955 [HPPN]
American publisher and physical culturist
* [The] Body
* [The] Fighter

McFadden, Elbows
See McFadden, George

McFadden, Flash
See McFadden, Samuel

McFadden, George 20th c. [RBE]
Boxer
* McFadden, Elbows

McFadden, Gertrude V. 20th c. [WWL]
British author
* Milbrook, John

McFadden, Ken 20th c.
American basketball player
* McFadden, Mouse
* [The] Mouse

McFadden, Mouse
See McFadden, Ken

McFadden, Samuel 1952- [RO2]
American musician
* McFadden, Flash

McFadin, Bud
See McFadin, Lewis B.

McFadin, Lewis B. 1928- [FB, SMG]
American football player
* McFadin, Bud

McFall, Bim
See McFall, Donald Jefferson

McFall, Donald Jefferson 1951- [HR]
Canadian-born hockey player
* McFall, Bim

McFall, Frances Elizabeth [Clark]
1862-1943 [LC, TC, TC1]
Irish-born author
* Grand, Sarah

McFarlan, James 1832-1862 [PI]
Scottish poet
* [The] Pedlar Poet

McFarland, Black Dan
See McFarland, Daniel

McFarland, Chappie
See McFarland, Charles Edward

McFarland, Charles Edward 1924- [BE]
American baseball player
* McFarland, Chappie

McFarland, Daniel 1825-1900 [HPPN]
American politician
* McFarland, Black Dan

McFarland, Dorothy Tuck 1938- [CA]
American author
* Tuck, Dorothy

McFarland, George Emmett 1928- [FC,
WA]
American actor
* McFarland, Spanky

McFarland, Herm
See McFarland, Hermus W.

McFarland, Hermus W. 1870-1935 [BE]
American baseball player
* McFarland, Herm

McFarland, LaMont A. 1871-1913 [BE]
American baseball player
* McFarland, Monte

McFarland, Lester 1902- [CWG, DAM]
American country-western performer
* McFarland, Mac

McFarland, Mac
See McFarland, Lester

McFarland, Monte
See McFarland, LaMont A.

McFarland, Packey
See McFarland, Patrick

McFarland, Patrick 1888-1938 [BX,
RBE]
American boxer
* McFarland, Packey

McFarland, Spanky
See McFarland, George Emmett

McFarlane, Alexis 1906- [THR]
Rhodesian-born actress
* France, Alexis

McFarlane, Anti
See McFarlane, William Doddridge

McFarlane, Bud
See McFarlane, Robert

McFarlane, David 1949- [AW]
British writer
* Tyson, Teilo

McFarlane, Elaine 1942- [RO2]
American singer
* McFarlane, Spanky

McFarlane, Leslie 1902-1977 [SAT]
Canadian author
* Dixon, Franklin W. [house
  pseudonym] [Stratemeyer Syndicate]
* Ferris, James Cody [house pseudonym]
  [Stratemeyer Syndicate]
* Keene, Carolyn [house pseudonym]
  [Stratemeyer Syndicate]
* Rockwood, Roy [house pseudonym]
  [Stratemeyer Syndicate]

McFarlane, Robert 1937- [TI 10-21-85]
American presidential adviser
* McFarlane, Bud

McFarlane, Spanky
See McFarlane, Elaine

McFarlane, William Doddridge 1894-
[HPPN]
American politician
* McFarlane, Anti

McFerran, Ann
See Townsend, Doris McFerran

McFerran, Doris
See Townsend, Doris McFerran

McFerran, Douglass David 1934- [CA]
American author
* Farren, David

McFinn, Denis
See O'Connell, Maurice

McFlimsey, Flora
See Johnson, Evelyn Kimball

McGady, Bossy
See McGady, Francis J.

McGady, Francis J. 1895?-1952 [BI]
American columnist
* McGady, Bossy

McGaffigan, Martin A. 1888-1940 [BE]
American baseball player
* McGaffigan, Patsy

McGaffigan, Patsy
See McGaffigan, Martin A.

McGann, Dan
See McGann, Dennis L.

McGann, Dennis L. 1872-1910 [AS, BE]
American baseball player
* McGann, Dan

McGargle
See Dukinfield, William Claude

McGarr, Chippy
See McGarr, James B.

McGarr, James B. 1863-1904 [BE]
American baseball player
* McGarr, Chippy

McGarr, James Vincent [Jim] 1888-
[BE]
American baseball player
* McGarr, Reds

McGarr, Reds
See McGarr, James Vincent [Jim]

McGarragh, Gates White 1863-1940
American banker
* McGarragh, Silent Gates

McGarragh, Silent Gates
See McGarragh, Gates White

McGarrigle, John 1900?-1953 [BI]
American boxing referee
* Daggert, Charley

McGarrity, Mark 1943- [CA]
American author
* Gill, Bartholomew

McGarry, William Rutledge 1868?-?
[WWS]
American author
* Smythe, James P.

McGaughey, Charles 1878-1956 [SC]
American actor and producer
* Mack, Charles

McGaughy, Dudley Dean 20th c. [ESF, SFL, WGT]
American author
* Dean, Dudley
* Owen, Dean

McGaura, Conner
See Ryan, James

McGavin, Moyra
See Crichton, Eleanor Moyra
[McGavin]

McGaw, Naomi Blanche Thoburn 1920-
[CA]
British author
* Hervey, Jane

McGawley, John 1951?- [HPPN]
American criminal
* McGawley, Mad Dog

McGawley, Mad Dog
See McGawley, John

McGeachy, C. E. A. [PA]
Author
* Mac

McGeachy, Irving Harding 1889-
[NAA]
American columnist
* Chatfield, Caroline

McGear, Mike
See McCartney, Peter Michael [Mike]

McGee
See Means, David Macgregor

McGee, Bill 20th c. [BBH]
Boxer
* McCoy, Kid

McGee, Darky
See McGee, Thomas D'Arcy

McGee, Ernest Timothy 1921-
American Hanafi Muslim leader
* Abdul Khaalis, Hamaas

McGee, Fibber
See Jordan, James Edward

McGee, Fiddler Bill
See McGee, William Henry

McGee, Francis D. 1899-1934 [BE]
American baseball player
* McGee, Tubby

McGee, John 19th c. [HPPN]
American gambler
* McGee, Rattlesnake Jack

McGee, Molly
See Jordan, Marian Driscoll

McGee, Molly
See McGee, Sylvester

McGee, Rattlesnake Jack
See McGee, John

McGee, Speed
See Johnson, Harold

McGee, Sylvester 20th c. [EF]
American football player
* McGee, Molly

McGee, Thomas D'Arcy 1825-1868
[FFF, PI]
Irish-born Canadian author, poet, statesman
* Amergin
* Amhergin
* Backwoodsman
* Feargail
* Gilla-Erin
* Gilla-Patrick
* [An] Irish Exile
* M.
* McGee, Darky
* Montanus
* Sarsfield
* T. D. M.

McGee, Tubby
See McGee, Francis D.

McGee, William Henry 1909- [BE]
American baseball player
* McGee, Fiddler Bill

McGeehan, Conny
See McGeehan, Cornelius Bernard

McGeehan, Cornelius Bernard 1883-1907
[BE]
American baseball player
* McGeehan, Conny

McGeehan, Sheriff
See McGeehan, William [Bill]

McGeehan, William [Bill] 20th c.
[HPPN]
American columnist
* McGeehan, Sheriff

McGeoch, Andrew Jackson 1900- [AW]
Scottish poet and playwright
* Paul, Adrian

McGeoghegan, Bucky
See McGeoghegan, John T.

McGeoghegan, John T. 1910?- [HPPN]
American airline pilot and jazz musician
* McGeoghegan, Bucky

McGeoghegan, Thomas J. 1836-? [PI]
Irish-born poet
* Mel

McGhee, Brownie
See McGhee, Walter Brown

McGhee, Donnie 20th c.
American football player
* McGhee, Floater

McGhee, Edward
See Harper, Edward M.

McGhee, Fibber
See McGhee, William Mac [Bill]

McGhee, Floater
See McGhee, Donnie

McGhee, Globetrotter
See McGhee, Granville H.

McGhee, Granville H. 1918-1961
[BWW, NBB]
American singer
* McGhee, Globetrotter
* McGhee, Stick[s]

McGhee, Howard 1918- [IBW]
American jazz musician
* McGhee, Maggie

McGhee, Maggie
See McGhee, Howard

McGhee, Norman L., Jr. 1928- [IBW]
American astrologer
* Ke-Kumbha, Kanya

McGhee, Stick[s]
See McGhee, Granville H.

McGhee, Walter Brown 1915- [BWW, DAM, FCW]
American musician
* Brother George
* Collins, Big Tom
* Fuller, Blind Boy, 2
* Johnson, Henry
* McGhee, Brownie
* Spider Sam
* Tennessee Gabriel
* Williams, Blind Boy

McGhee, William Mac [Bill] 1908-
[BE]
American baseball player
* McGhee, Fibber

McGill, Big Jack
See McGill, John George

McGill, Bill 1939- [BB]
American basketball player
* [The] Hill

McGill, Donald Fraser Gould 1875-1962
[WEC]
British cartoonist
* [The] King of the Seaside Postcard

McGill, Ian
See Allegro, John Marco

McGill, John Edward 1923- [FHE]
Canadian-born hockey player
* McGill, Little Jack

McGill, John George 1921- [CEI, FHE]
Canadian-born hockey player
* McGill, Big Jack

McGill, Kid
See McGill, William Vaness

McGill, Little Jack
See McGill, John Edward

McGill, Marci
See Balterman, Marcia Ridlon

McGill, Parson
See McGill, William John [Bill]

McGill, Patrick 1891-? [PI]
Irish poet
* [The] Navvy Poet

McGill, William John [Bill] 1880-1959
[BE]
American baseball player
* McGill, Parson

McGill, William Vaness 1873-1944 [BE]
American baseball player
* McGill, Kid

McGillicuddy, Cornelius Alexander
1862-1956 [BAB, BE, PB]
American baseball manager
* Mack, Connie
* McGillicuddy, Slats
* [The] Tall Tactician

McGillicuddy, Earle Thaddeus 1889-1967
[BE]
American baseball player
* Mack, Earle Thaddeus

McGillicuddy, Eugene 1890?-1953 [BI]
American cartoonist
* Mack, Gene

McGillicuddy, Mr.
See Abisch, Roslyn Kroop [Roz]

McGillicuddy, Slats
See McGillicuddy, Cornelius Alexander

McGillycuddy, Father
See McGillycuddy, Valentine Trant
O'Connell

McGillycuddy, Strong Man
See McGillycuddy, Valentine Trant
O'Connell

McGillycuddy, Valentine Trant
O'Connell 1849-1939 [HPPN]
American Indian agent
* [The] Autocrat of the Pine Ridge
  Sioux Reservation
* McGillycuddy, Father
* McGillycuddy, Strong Man

McGilvery, Laurence 1932- [CA]
American editor and publisher
* Van Geil, Mercury E. C. L.

McGilvray, Big Bill
See McGilvray, William Alexander
[Bill]

McGilvray, William Alexander [Bill]
1883-1952 [BE]
American baseball player
* McGilvray, Big Bill

McGinley, Bridget
See Gallagher, Bridget

McGinley, Peter Toner 1857-? [PI]
Irish poet
* Mac

McGinn, Maureen Ann
See Sautel, Maureen Ann

McGinness, Martha 1946?- [BI]
American poet
* Alice

McGinnis, Big Mac
See McGinnis, George

McGinnis, Duane 1938- [CA]
American poet
* Niatum, Duane

McGinnis, George [SMG]
American basketball player
* McGinnis, Big Mac

McGinnis, George W. 1864-1934 [BE]
American baseball player
* McGinnis, Jumbo

McGinnis, James Anthony 1847-1906
[HPPN]
American circus impresario
* Bailey, James A.

McGinnis, Jumbo
See McGinnis, George W.

McGinnis, K. K.
See Page, Grover, Jr.

McGinnis, William
See Lay, William Ellsworth

McGinnity, Joseph Jerome 1871-1929
[BE, DGS, PB]
American baseball player
* [The] Iron Man

McGinty, Bonaventure Thomas
1895?-1971 [BI]
American educator
* Thomas, [Brother]

McGirr, Edmund
See Giles, Kenneth

McGirt, William Archibald 1923- [CA]
American poet
* Inman, Will

McGiver, John
See Morris, George

McGivern, Ed[ward] ?-1957 [HPPN]
American pistol marksman
* [The] Grand Old Man of
  Sixshooterology

McGivern, Maureen Daly 20th c. [CA]
Irish-born author
* Daly, Maureen

McGivern, William P[eter] 1924-
[EMD, ESF, WGT]
American author and screenwriter
* Blade, Alexander [house pseudonym,
  Ziff-Davis]
* Peters, Bill

McGlane, Jere ?-1929 [HPPN]
*American procurer, brothel proprietor,
criminal*
* Bassity, Jerome

McGleno, Phillip 1952?- [SI 4-16-84]
American golfer
* O'Grady, Mac

McGlinchey, Dominic 1954?- [TI 3-26-84,
TI 12-5-83]
Irish terrorist
* McGlinchey, Mad Dog

McGlinchey, Mad Dog
See McGlinchey, Dominic

McGlinchy, Fabia Drake 1904- [FC]
British actress
* Drake, Fabia

McGlinn, Dwight
See Brannon, William T.

McGloin, Joseph Thaddeus 1917- [CA,
WW]
American author and clergyman
* O'Finn, Thaddeus

McGlothen, Lynn Everratt 1950- [SMG]
American baseball player
* McGlothen, Mac

McGlothen, Mac
See McGlothen, Lynn Everratt

McGlothin, Ezra Mac 1920- [BE]
American baseball player
* McGlothin, Pat

McGlothin, Pat
See McGlothin, Ezra Mac

McGlothlin, James Milton [Jim] 1943-
[BE, PB]
American baseball player
* McGlothlin, Red

McGlothlin, Red
See McGlothlin, James Milton [Jim]

McGluphy
See Harrison, Hank

McGlynn, Christopher
See Ginder, Richard

McGlynn, Stoney
See McGlynn, Ulysses Simpson Grant

McGlynn, Ulysses Simpson Grant
1872-1941 [BE]
American baseball player
* McGlynn, Stoney

McGonegal, Alfred 1900-1974 [FC,
HCA]
American actor
* Jenkins, Allen

McGoo, Mr.
See Brown, John Y.

McGoon, Earthquake
See McGovern, James B.

McGoorty, Eddie
See Van Dusart, Eddie

McGoughy, Hugh Dilman 20th c.   [FIR]
American actor
* Dilman, Hugh

McGovern, George Stanley 1922-
[HPPN]
American politician
* [The] Master Wrecker
* McGovern, Honest George
* St. George

McGovern, Honest George
See   McGovern, George Stanley

McGovern, Hugh 20th c.   [BLB, PHM]
American underworld figure
* McGovern, Stubby

McGovern, James B. ?-1954
American pilot
* McGoon, Earthquake

McGovern, John Terrence 1880-1918
[BX, RBE]
American boxer
* McGovern, Terrible Terry

McGovern, Stubby
See   McGovern, Hugh

McGovern, Terrible Terry
See   McGovern, John Terrence

McGovern's Man from Missouri
See   Eagleton, Thomas Francis [Tom]

McGowan, Beauty
See   McGowan, Frank Bernard

McGowan, Bridget   [FFF]
Entertainer
* Vernon, Ida

McGowan, Francis Oliver 1907-
[HPPN]
American actor and director
* Oliver, Sherling

McGowan, Frank Bernard 1901-   [BE]
American baseball player
* McGowan, Beauty

McGowan, Hugh 1884-1927   [SC]
American actor
* Mack, Hughie

McGowan, Inez
See   Graham, Roger Phillips

McGowan, Lieutenant Colonel [code
name used during World War II]
See   Murphy, Robert D.

McGowan, Mickey
See   McGowan, Tullis Earl

McGowan, Tullis Earl 1921-   [BE]
American baseball player
* McGowan, Mickey

McGrady, James ?-1855   [PI]
Irish poet
* Shemus of Ullinagh
* [The] Talking Man

McGranary, Al
See   McGranary, Aloysius Cornelius

McGranary, Aloysius Cornelius
1902-1971   [SC]
American actor
* McGranary, Al

McGraner, Howard 1889-1952   [BE]
American baseball player
* McGraner, Muck

McGraner, Muck
See   McGraner, Howard

McGrant, Terence
See   Peck, George Wilbur

McGrath, Doyle
See   Schorb, Edwin Marsh

McGrath, Fidgy
See   McGrath, Fulton

McGrath, Fulton 1908-1958   [WWJ]
American jazz musician
* McGrath, Fidgy

McGrath, John 1864-?   [PI]
Irish poet and journalist
* Cuan

McGrath, John James 1919-   [EAR]
American auto racer
* McGrath, Smiling Jack

McGrath, Mary
See   Murranka, Mary

McGrath, Morgan
See   Rae, Hugh C[rauford]

McGrath, Robert L[ee] 1920-   [CA]
American author
* Lee, Bob
* Lee, Roberta

McGrath, Smiling Jack
See   McGrath, John James

McGrath, Terence
See   Blake, Henry A.

McGraw, B. T.
See   McGraw, Booker Tanner

McGraw, Booker Tanner 1898-   [BA]
American government official
* McGraw, B. T.
* McGraw, Doc
* McGraw, Mac

McGraw, Doc
See   McGraw, Booker Tanner

McGraw, Donnie 1953-   [SMG]
American football player
* McGraw, Quick Draw

McGraw, Frank Edwin 1944-   [BI, PB,
SMG]
American baseball player
* McGraw, Tug

McGraw, J. H. 20th c.   [MBF]
British author
* Jackson, Howard

McGraw, James 19th c.   [HPPN]
American swindler
* McGraw, Phonograph Jimmy
* Tilbury, John

McGraw, John Joseph 1873-1934   [BE,
DGS, HPPN, PB]
American baseball manager
* [The] Father of Inside Baseball
* [The] Little Napoleon
* [The] Master Mind
* McGraw, Muggsy
* McGraw of the Giants

McGraw, Mac
See   McGraw, Booker Tanner

McGraw, Muggsy
See   McGraw, John Joseph

McGraw of the Giants
See   McGraw, John Joseph

McGraw, Phonograph Jimmy
See   McGraw, James

McGraw, Quick Draw
See   McGraw, Donnie

McGraw, Tug
See   McGraw, Frank Edwin

McGraw, William Corbin 1916-   [CA,
MJA, SAT]
American author
* Corbin, William

McGready, James 1758-1817   [HPPN]
American clergyman
* Boanerges

McGreal, E. B. 1905-   [ITA]
American film executive
* McGreal, Mike

McGreal, Elizabeth
See   Yates, Elizabeth

McGreal, Mike
See   McGreal, E. B.

McGregor
See   Hurley, Doran

McGregor, Charles 1931-   [IBW]
American actor
* Fat Freddie

McGregor, Donald Alexander 1939-
[CEI]
Canadian-born hockey player
* McGregor, Sandy

McGregor, Douglas Murray 1906-1964
[HPPN]
American college president
* Mac, Chairman

McGregor, Edward 1873-1917   [BEW,
CED]
American entertainer
* [The] Happy Tramp
* Wills, Nat M.

McGregor, Gregor 1786-1845   [DI]
British swindler
* [The] Prince of Poyais

McGregor, Parke
See   Cushnie, Parke

McGregor, Sandy
See   McGregor, Donald Alexander

McGrew, Alex 1826-? [PA]
Author
* Brandywine

McGrew, Fenn [joint pseudonym with Julia McGrew]
See Fenn, Caroline K.

McGrew, Fenn [joint pseudonym with Caroline K. Fenn]
See McGrew, Julia

McGrew, Julia 20th c. [WW]
Author
* McGrew, Fenn [joint pseudonym with Caroline K. Fenn]

McGrew, Slim
See McGrew, Walter Howard

McGrew, Walter Howard 1899-1967 [BE]
American baseball player
* McGrew, Slim

McGroarty, John Steven 1862-1944 [HPPN]
American poet
* [The] Poet Laureate of California
* [The] Sage of the Verduga Hills

McGrory, Mary 20th c. [WP 2-1-83]
American newspaper columnist
* [The] Madame Defarge of the Washington Press Corps

McGuffey, William Holmes 1800-1873 [HPPN]
American educator and author
* [The] Creator of the Eclectic Readers

McGuffy, Moaner
See Reeve, Edward H. [Ted]

McGuinn, James Joseph, III 1942- [RO2]
American singer
* McGuinn, Roger

McGuinn, Roger
See McGuinn, James Joseph, III

McGuire, Benny
See McCrary, Benny Loyd

McGuire, Biff
See McGuire, William Joseph, Jr.

McGuire, Billy
See McCrary, Billy Leon

McGuire, Deacon
See McGuire, James Thomas

McGuire, Doug
See McCreary, Doug

McGuire, Edna
See Boyd, Edna McGuire

McGuire, Elmer
See McGuire, Thomas Patrick [Tom]

McGuire, Harp
See McGuire, Henry Herbert

McGuire, Henry Herbert 1921-1966 [SC]
American actor
* McGuire, Harp

McGuire, James Thomas 1863-1936 [AS, BE]
American baseball player and manager
* McGuire, Deacon

McGuire, Leslie Sarah 1945- [CA]
American author and illustrator
* Britton, Louisa
* Burton, Leslie
* Eyre, Dorothy
* Keyser, Sarah
* Leslie, Sarah
* Robinson, Shari
* Strong, David

McGuire, M.
See McPherson, Malcolm

McGuire, Marcy
See McGuire, Marilyn

McGuire, Marilyn 20th c. [AM]
American actress and singer
* McGuire, Marcy

McGuire, Mickey
See Yule, Joe, Jr.

McGuire, Mrs. J. P. [PA]
Author
* Lady of Virginia

McGuire, P.
See Penick, Clifton Hewitt

McGuire, Peter James 1852-1906 [HPPN]
American labor leader and social reformer
* [The] Father of Labor Day

McGuire, Richard 1926- [BB]
American basketball player
* McGuire, Tricky Dick

McGuire, Thomas Patrick [Tom] 1892-1959 [BE]
American baseball player
* McGuire, Elmer

McGuire, Tricky Dick
See McGuire, Richard

McGuire, William Joseph, Jr. 1926?- [BEW, TR]
American actor and playwright
* McGuire, Biff

McGuirk, Harriet
See Nawrot, Harriet

McGunnigle, Gunner
See McGunnigle, William Henry [Bill]

McGunnigle, William Henry [Bill] 1855-1899 [BE]
American baseball manager
* McGunnigle, Gunner

McGurk, Slater
See Roth, Arthur J[oseph]

McGurn, Jack
See De Mora, James Vincenzo

McGurn, Joseph 1872?-1952 [BEW]
American actor
* Allen, Joseph

McHale, Frank [PA]
Author
* Geraint

McHale, John 1791-? [IP]
Irish prelate and author
* Hierophilus

McHale, M. J. 1845?-1887 [PI]
Irish clergyman and poet
* [A] Country Curate

McHale, Richard 1862-? [PI]
Irish poet
* Ricardo

McHargue, Georgess 20th c. [CA, SAT]
American author
* Chase, Alice
* Usher, Margo Scegge

McHargue, James Eugene 1907- [EJ, PMJ, WWJ]
American jazz musician
* McHargue, Rosy

McHargue, Rosy
See McHargue, James Eugene

McHenry, James 1785?-1845 [DNA, PI, WGT]
Irish author and poet
* Mac Erin
* Secondsight, Solomon

McHenry, Nellie
See Webster, Mrs. John

McHenry, [Col.] Oram R.
See Rolfe, Maro Orlando

McHouston, Ed
See Baker, McHouston

McHugh, Edna 20th c. [WW]
Author
* Coxe, Kathleen Buddington [joint pseudonym with Amelia Reynolds Long]

McHugh, Edward 20th c. [HPPN]
American singer
* [The] Gospel Singer

McHugh, Hugh
See Hobart, George Vere

McHugh, Jay
See MacQueen, James William

McHugh, Maxine Davis 1899?-1978 [CA, IA]
American journalist and author
* Davis, Maxine

McHugh, Pat
See McHugh, William

McHugh, Ruth Nelson
See Nelson, Ruth

McHugh, Stuart
See Rowland, Donald Sydney

McHugh, William 20th c. [EF]
American football player
* McHugh, Pat

McIldowie, Chattie 1895-1975 [SC, THR]
Irish-born actress
* MacGill, Moyna

McIlraith, Dorothy Ann 1937- [OP]
Canadian opera singer
* Protero, Dodi

McIlvaine, Charles 1840-1909 [WGT]
American author
* Hodge, Toby

McIlvaine, Clara ?-1890? [PI]
Irish poet
* C. L. M.

McIlvaine, Jane
See McClary, Jane Stevenson

McIlveen, Henry Cooke 1880-1960 [BE]
Irish-born baseball player
* McIlveen, Irish

McIlveen, Irish
See McIlveen, Henry Cooke

McIlwain, David 1921- [CA, ESF, SF, SFL]
British author
* Maine, C. E.
* Maine, Charles Eric
* Masterson, Whit [joint pseudonym]
* Rayner, Richard
* Wade, Robert [Bob]

McIlwain, Smokey
See McIlwain, [William] Stover

McIlwain, [William] Stover 1939-1966 [BE]
American baseball player
* McIlwain, Smokey

McIlwraith, Jean Newton 1859-1938 [DLE1]
Canadian author
* Forsyth, Jean

McIlwraith, Maureen Mollie Hunter 1922- [AW, CA, SAT]
Scottish author and playwright
* Hunter, Mollie

McInerny, Ralph 1929- [CA]
American philosopher and author
* Austin, Harry
* Mackey, Ernan
* Quill, Monica

McInnis, John Phalen 1890-1960 [AS, DGS, PB]
American baseball player
* McInnis, Stuffy

McInnis, Stuffy
See McInnis, John Phalen

McIntire, Carl 1906- [HPPN]
American clergyman
* [The] Pirate Preacher

McIntire, Harry
See McIntire, John Reed

McIntire, John Reed 1879-1949 [AS, BE]
American baseball player
* McIntire, Harry
* McIntire, Rocks

McIntire, Rocks
See McIntire, John Reed

McIntosh, Alec 1907-1959 [BI]
American artist
* Blue Eagle, Acee

McIntosh, Alexander 1947- [CA]
American poet and editor
* McIntosh, Sandy

McIntosh, Dutch
See McIntosh, Russell

McIntosh, J. T.
See MacGregor, James [Murdoch]

McIntosh, John Everett ?-1948 [BI]
American farmer
* Fraser, Sandy

McIntosh, Kenneth 20th c. [WGT]
Author
* Casey, Kent

McIntosh, Kinn Hamilton 1930- [AW, CA, EMD]
British author
* Aird, Catherine

McIntosh, Lonnie 1941- [RO1]
American musician
* Mack, Lonnie

McIntosh, Louis
See Johnson, Christopher

McIntosh, Maria Jane 1803-1878 [FFF, PA]
American author
* Aunt Kitty
* Cousin Kate

McIntosh, Professor
See McIntosh, William Carmichael

McIntosh, Randy
See McIntosh, Simeon Charles

McIntosh, Russell 20th c. [HPPN]
American football player
* McIntosh, Dutch

McIntosh, Sandy
See McIntosh, Alexander

McIntosh, Simeon Charles 1944- [BA]
American educator
* McIntosh, Randy

McIntosh, William Carmichael 20th c. [LAO]
Scottish psychiatrist, zoologist, author
* McIntosh, Professor

McIntyre
See Ruttan, Kate [McIntyre]

McIntyre, Hugh D. [FFF, PA]
Author
* Aberdeen

McIntyre, James Francis 1886?-1979
American religious leader
* [The] Brick and Mortar Priest

McIntyre, John 1869-? [LAO]
Scottish author and playwright
* Brandane, John

McIntyre, John T[homas] 1871-1951 [CC, WW]
American author
* O'Neil, Kerry

McIntyre, Marion
See Gray, Marion

McIntyre, O. O.
See McIntyre, [Oscar] Odd

McIntyre, [Oscar] Odd 1884-1938 [HPPN]
American newspaper columnist and author
* [The] First Citizen of New York
* McIntyre, O. O.

McIver, Jock
See Parrot, William

McIver, Muriel 1888-1950 [HPPN]
Canadian actress
* Starr, Muriel

McIver, Tennie Stewart 1873-? [NAA]
American writer
* G. M., Mrs.

McIvor, Ivor Ben
See Welsh, Charles

McJames, Doc
See James, James McCutchen

McJames, James McCutchen
See James, James McCutchen

McKahan, Rufus Alan 1892-1950 [F1, FC]
American actor
* Hale, Alan

McKain, Archie Richard 1911- [BE]
American baseball player
* McKain, Happy

McKain, Happy
See McKain, Archie Richard

McKale, James Fritz 20th c. [BBH]
American baseball coach and collegiate athletic director
* McKale, Pop

McKale, Pop
See McKale, James Fritz

McKane, James Niall 1849-1878 [PI]
Irish-born poet
* J. N. McK.

McKay, Claude 1890-1948 [CA]
Jamaican-born author and poet
* Edwards, Eli

McKay, Donald 1810-1880 [HPPN]
Canadian-American ship designer and builder
* [The] Father of the Clipper Ship

McKay, Eleanor Gough 1915-1959
[BEW, EJ, WWJ]
American singer
* Day, Lady
* Holiday, Billie

McKay, George W.
See Reuben, George

McKay, Grif
See Kirkpatrick, M. Glen

McKay, Harold 1916?- [HPPN]
American criminal and procurer
* McKay, Meathead
* McKay, Moron
* McKay, Stinker

McKay, J. K.
See McKay, John Kenneth

McKay, Jim
See McManus, James Kenneth

McKay, John Kenneth 1953- [FR]
American football player
* McKay, J. K.

McKay, Kevin
See Strong, Charles Stanley

McKay, Meathead
See McKay, Harold

McKay, Moron
See McKay, Harold

McKay, Scott
See Gose, Carl Chester

McKay, Stinker
See McKay, Harold

McKeag, Ernest L[ionel] 1896- [CAP]
British author
* Braza, Jacque
* Griff [house pseudonym?]
* Grimshaw, Mark
* Haynes, Pat
* King, John
* Lacroix, Ramon
* Laroche, Rene
* Maxwell, Jack
* McKeay, Eileen
* Vane, Roland

McKean, Henry Swasey 1810-1857
[HPPN]
American author
* Smith, John

McKean, Joseph 1776-1818 [HPPN]
American clergyman and educator
* [A] Member of the Massachusetts
  Historical Society

McKeay, Eileen
See McKeag, Ernest L[ionel]

McKechnie, Deacon Bill
See McKechnie, William Boyd

McKechnie, Florence 1901- [BEW, FC, IPA]
American actress
* Eldridge, Florence

McKechnie, McKech
See McKechnie, Walter Thomas John

McKechnie, Walter Thomas John 1947-
[SMG]
Canadian-born hockey player
* McKechnie, McKech

McKechnie, William Boyd 1887-1965
[BE, DGS, PB]
American baseball player, coach, manager
* McKechnie, Deacon Bill

McKee, Eva Sue 1926- [ECM, FCW, RO1]
American country-western performer
* Thompson, Sue

McKee, Isabelle Coe ?-1919 [HPPN]
American actress
* Coe, Isabelle

McKee, Lafayette Stocking 1872-1959
[SC]
American actor
* McKee, Lafe

McKee, Lafe
See McKee, Lafayette Stocking

McKee, Raymond Ellis 1890- [BE]
American baseball player
* McKee, Red

McKee, Red
See McKee, Raymond Ellis

McKeen, Captain
See St. John, Percy Bollingbroke

McKeen, Lawrence D., Jr. 1925-1933
[SC]
American actor
* McKeen, Snookums

McKeen, Snookums
See McKeen, Lawrence D., Jr.

McKeever, Marcia
See Laird, Jean E[louise]

McKeever, Mrs. John T., Jr. [FFF]
Entertainer
* Bishop, Frances

McKeithan, Emmett James 1906-1969
[BE]
American baseball player
* McKeithan, Tim

McKeithan, Tim
See McKeithan, Emmett James

McKeithen, Big John
See McKeithen, John Julian

McKeithen, John Julian 1918- [HPPN]
American politician
* McKeithen, Big John

McKelway, St. Clair 1905-1980 [CA]
American author and editor
* Hall, J. De P.

McKendrick, Big Mike
See McKendrick, Reuben Michael

McKendrick, Gilbert Michael 1903?-1961
[WWJ]
American jazz musician
* McKendrick, Little Mike

McKendrick, Little Mike
See McKendrick, Gilbert Michael

McKendrick, Reuben Michael 1901-1965
[WWJ]
American jazz musician
* McKendrick, Big Mike

McKenna, A. Daniel
See Finnerty, Adam Daniel

McKenna, Andrew James 1833-1872
[PI]
Irish poet and journalist
* A. J. M.
* A. J. McK.
* M. K.?

McKenna, Edward Lawrence 1893?-1953
[BI]
American author
* Wingshot, Leo

McKenna, Evelyn
See Joscelyn, Archie Lynn

McKenna, James
See McParlan, James

McKenna, James William 1873-? [BE]
American baseball player
* McKenna, Kit

McKenna, Kit
See McKenna, James William

McKenna, Margaret Mary 1930- [CA]
American author
* McKenna, [Sister] Mary Lawrence

McKenna, [Sister] Mary Lawrence
See McKenna, Margaret Mary

McKenna, Patricia
See Goedicke, Patricia [McKenna]

McKenna, R. M.
See McKenna, Richard Milton

McKenna, Richard Milton 20th c.
[WGT]
Author
* McKenna, R. M.

McKenna, Theobald ?-1808 [PI]
Irish poet and physician
* Dr. McK.

McKenney, R. Armstrong
See Claiborne, Robert [Watson, Jr.]

McKenney, Thomas Loraine 1785-1859
[DNA]
American author
* Aristides

McKenny, Howie
See McKenny, Jim

McKenny, Jim 1946- [SMG]
Canadian-born hockey player
* McKenny, Howie

McKenry, Frank Gordon 1888-1956
[BE]
American baseball player
* McKenry, Limb

McKenry, Limb
See McKenry, Frank Gordon

McKenzie, Altamont 1951-   [AES]
Jamaican soccer player
* McKenzie, Altie

McKenzie, Altie
See McKenzie, Altamont

McKenzie, Christian
See Duffell, Anne

McKenzie, Everett 1888-1923 [HPPN]
American actor and dancer
* Savoy, Bert

McKenzie, Fred
See McKenzie, Wilford Clifton

McKenzie, Grace E. 1913- [NAA]
British-born poet
* Hastings, Elizabeth

McKenzie, James 1892?-1953 [BI]
American educator
* Adelphus Patrick, [Brother]

McKenzie, John 1763-1828 [HPPN]
American pioneer and fur trader
* Kinzie, John

McKenzie, John Albert 1937-   [FHE]
Canadian-born hockey player
* McKenzie, Pie

McKenzie, Paige
See Blood, Marje

McKenzie, Pie
See McKenzie, John Albert

McKenzie, Ray?
See Silverberg, Robert

McKenzie, Red
See McKenzie, William

McKenzie, Wilford Clifton 1918-   [BA]
Jamaican-born business executive
* McKenzie, Fred

McKenzie, William 1899?-1948   [DAM,
EJ, PMJ]
American singer
* McKenzie, Red

McKeon, Jack 20th c.
American baseball executive
* McKeon, Trader Jack
* [The] Sultan of Swap

McKeon, Trader Jack
See McKeon, Jack

McKeown, Geraldine 1932- [BEW, TR]
British actress
* McEwan, Geraldine

McKern, Leo
See McKern, Reginald

McKern, Reginald 1920- [TR]
Australian actor and director
* McKern, Leo

McKernan, John Leo 1882-1963 [AS,
BX]
American boxing manager
* Kearns, Doc
* Kearns, Jack
* McKernan, Perfume Jack

McKernan, Perfume Jack
See McKernan, John Leo

McKernan, Pigpen
See McKernan, Ron

McKernan, Ron 1946-1973 [RO2]
American musician
* McKernan, Pigpen

McKerrow, R. B.
See McKerrow, Ronald Brunlees

McKerrow, Ronald Brunlees 1872-1940
[LC]
British author and editor
* McKerrow, R. B.

McKey, Tom
See Holliday, John Henry

McKibbin, Archibald 1863-1925 [CCL]
Canadian author
* Cloie, Mack

McKibbon, J. E. 20th c. [MBF]
British author
* Ellis, John
* Probyn, Elise
* Probyn, John E.

McKillop, Mary 1832-1909 [BI]
Australian nun
* Mary of the Cross, [Mother]

McKillop, Norman 1892-1974 [CA]
Scottish locomotive engineer and author
* Beg, Toran

McKim, Ann 1912-1979 [F2, FC, HPPN,
SW]
American actress
* Dvorak, Ann
* Lehr, Anna

McKim, William W. 19th c. [HPPN]
American army officer and author
* [An] Ex Army Officer

McKimie, Robert 19th c. [HPPN]
American outlaw and stagecoach robber
* [The] Daredevil of the Black Hills
* Little Reddie from Texas

McKimmey, James 1923- [CA]
American author
* Swift, Benjamin

McKinley, Bill
See Gillum, William McKinley [Bill]

McKinley, Carl
See McKinley, Carlyle

McKinley, Carlyle 1847-1904 [HPPN]
American poet, editor, essayist
* McKinley, Carl

McKinley, William 1843-1901 [FAP]
American president
* [The] Advance Agent of Prosperity
* [The] High Priest of Protective Tariffs
* [The] Idol of Ohio
* [The] Napoleon of Princeton
* [The] Napoleon of Protection
* Prosperity's Advance Agent
* [The] Stocking-Foot Orator
* Wobbly Willie

McKinley's Voice
See Fairbanks, Charles Warren

McKinney, Alice Jane Chandler Webster
1876-1916 [HPPN]
American author
* Webster, Jean

McKinney, Bones
See McKinney, Horace

McKinney, Charles 20th c. [SMG]
American baseball player
* McKinney, Rich

McKinney, D. J.
See Cooper, Parley J[oseph]

McKinney, Ernest Lee, Sr. 1923-   [BA]
American educator
* McKinney, Mac

McKinney, H. D.   [FFF]
American writer
* Mambrino

McKinney, Horace 1919- [BB, SMG]
American basketball player and coach
* McKinney, Bones

McKinney, Kate Slaughter 1859-?
[NAA]
American author and poet
* Katydid

McKinney, Mac
See McKinney, Ernest Lee, Sr.

McKinney, Mac
See McKinney, William

McKinney, Rich
See McKinney, Charles

McKinney, T. L. ?-1859 [PA]
Author
* Aristides

McKinney, Thomas L. 19th c. [EWG]
American law officer
* McKinney, Tip

McKinney, Tip
See McKinney, Thomas L.

McKinney, William 1895?- [MY]
American musician and manager
* McKinney, Mac

McKinnies, Henry H. 1925?-1969 [BDF,
FC, WEF]
American actor
* Hunter, Jeffrey

McKinnis, Gread 1913- [MK]
American baseball player
* McKinnis, Lefty

McKinnis, Lefty
See McKinnis, Gread

McKinnon, Archie 1878-1915 [HPPN]
American vaudeville performer
* McKinnon, Red

McKinnon, Neil 1873?-1946 [BEW]
Scottish-born comedian
* Kenyon, Neil

McKinnon, Red
See McKinnon, Archie

McKisson, Curly Bob
See McKisson, Robert S.

McKisson, Robert S. 19th c. [HPPN]
American politician
* McKisson, Curly Bob

McKittrick, Anna Margaret 1860-1939
[LC]
Irish author
* Ros, Amanda McKittrick

McKittrick, Dorothy
Author
* Mack, Dorothy

McKnight, Harmen Packard 1855-?
[WWL]
American author
* Browne, George N.

McKowen, James 1814-1889 [PI]
Irish poet
* Connor, Kitty
* Curlew

McKoy, Clem
See McKoy, Clemencio Augustino

McKoy, Clemencio Augustino 1928-
[BA]
Cuban-born editor
* McKoy, Clem

McKoy, William 19th c. [IP]
American author
* Lang Syne

McKready, Kelvin
See Murphy, Edgar Gardner

McLachlan, Murray 20th c. [SWI]
South African swimmer
* McLachlan, Tich

McLachlan, Tich
See McLachlan, Murray

McLaglen, Victor 1886-1959 [HPPN]
British-American actor
* [The] Beloved Brute

McLamore, Claire 1927- [OP]
American opera singer
* Watson, Claire

McLandress, Herschel
See Galbraith, John Kenneth

McLane, Armand Ralph 1936- [OP]
American opera singer
* MacLane, Armand Ralph

McLane, Mary Jane 18th c. [IP]
American author
* Windle, Mary Jane

McLaren, Daniel 1823-1900 [HPPN]
*American circus performer and
entrepreneur*
* Rice, Dan

McLaren, George W. ?-1967 [AS, FB]
American football player
* McLaren, Tank

McLaren, J. A. 20th c. [MBF]
British author
* Adams, John

McLaren, Moray [David Shaw]
1901-1971 [CA]
Scottish author and playwright
* Murray, Michael

McLaren, Tank
See McLaren, George W.

McLarnin, Baby Face
See McLarnin, Jimmy

McLarnin, Jimmy 1905- [BX, RBE]
Irish-born boxer
* McLarnin, Baby Face

McLarry, Howard Bell 1891-1971 [BE]
American baseball player
* McLarry, Polly

McLarry, Polly
See McLarry, Howard Bell

McLarty, Margaret Elizabeth 20th c.
[BEW]
American actress and singer
* Fulton, Eileen

McLaughlin, Bill
See Phillips, James W.

McLaughlin, Bo
See McLaughlin, Michael Duane

McLaughlin, Boss
See McLaughlin, John J.

McLaughlin, Charles W. 1878-1934
[BEW]
Canadian-born actor, playwright, director
* Mack, Willard

McLaughlin, Charley
See Dalton, Emmett

McLaughlin, Emma Maude 1901- [CA]
American author
* Weir, Alice M.

McLaughlin, James Anson 1888-1934
[BE]
American baseball player
* McLaughlin, Kid

McLaughlin, James Fairfax 1839-1903
[HPPN, IP]
American attorney and author
* Pasquino

McLaughlin, John 1942- [NAD]
British musician
* Mahavishnu

McLaughlin, John Belton, M. D. 1903-
[BA]
American physician
* Mack, Dr.

McLaughlin, John J. 20th c. [HPPN]
American politician and criminal
* McLaughlin, Boss

McLaughlin, Jud
See McLaughlin, Justin Theodore

McLaughlin, Justin Theodore 1912-1964
[BE]
American baseball player
* McLaughlin, Jud

McLaughlin, Katherine Elizabeth
1921-1975 [ITA, SC]
American actress
* Ryan, Sheila

McLaughlin, Kid
See McLaughlin, James Anson

McLaughlin, Melvin 1960-
American basketball player
* McLaughlin, Sugar

McLaughlin, Mercia 1901- [THR]
South African-born actress
* Gregori, Mercia

McLaughlin, Michael Duane 1953-
[SMG]
American baseball player
* McLaughlin, Bo

McLaughlin, Patrick O'Conor 1851-?
[PI]
Irish author and poet
* MacL.

McLaughlin, Sugar
See McLaughlin, Melvin

McLaughlin, Walter T. 20th c. [BBH]
American collegiate athletic director
* Mac, Mr.

McLaughry, DeOrmond 1893-1974 [BI,
FB]
American football coach
* McLaughry, Tuss

McLaughry, Tuss
See McLaughry, DeOrmond

McLaurin, Anne 1953- [SAT]
American author
* Laurin, Anne

McLaverty, Edmund 1882-1951 [FC]
British actor
* Breon, Edmund

McLean, Alexander 1827-1864 [CCL]
Canadian author
* [A] Protestant

McLean, Barney
See McLean, Robert L.

McLean, Caroline Crawford 20th c.
[NAA]
American author and educator
* Crawford, Caroline

McLean, Eric W. 1900- [MBF, WWL]
British author
* Rayle, Geoffrey
* Townsend, Eric W.

McLean, Evalyn Walsh 1886-1947
[HPPN]
American socialite
* McLean, Little Evalyn
* Washington's Cinderella Woman

McLean, J. Sloan [joint pseudonym
with Josephine M. Wunsch]
See Gillette, Virginia M[ary]

McLean, J. Sloan [joint pseudonym
with Virginia M(ary) Gillette]
See Wunsch, Josephine M.

McLean, John Bannerman 1881-1921
[BE, BN]
American baseball player
* McLean, Larry
* McLean, Slashaway
* McLean, Slasher

McLean, John David Ruari 1917-
[IAW]
Scottish author
* Hardie, David

McLean, Kathryn [Anderson] 1909-1966
[BI, CAP, SAT]
American author
* Forbes, Karine
* Forbes, Kathryn

McLean, Larry
See McLean, John Bannerman

McLean, Leola 1891-1928 [HPPN]
American actress
* May, Leola

McLean, Little Evalyn
See McLean, Evalyn Walsh

McLean, Raymond 1915-1964 [AS,
SMG]
American football player and coach
* McLean, Scooter

McLean, Robert L. 1917- [BBH]
American skier
* McLean, Barney

McLean, Sally Pratt
See Greene, Sarah Pratt McLean

McLean, Scooter
See McLean, Raymond

McLean, Slashaway
See McLean, John Bannerman

McLean, Slasher
See McLean, John Bannerman

McLean, Vinson Walsh 1909-1919
[HPPN]
*Son of American publisher, Edward
McLean*
* [The] Hundred Million Dollar Baby

McLean, Virginia Katherine 1916- [MY]
American singer
* Verrill, Virginia

McLeish, Garen
See Stine, Whitney Ward

McLeland, Nubbin
See McLeland, Wayne Gaffney

McLeland, Wayne Gaffney 1924- [BE]
American baseball player
* McLeland, Nubbin

McLellan, Charles Morton Stewart
See Morton, Hugh

McLellan, Diana 20th c.
American columnist and editor
* [The] Ear

McLellan, Isaac 1806-1899 [HPPN]
American poet
* I. M.
* [The] Poet Sportsman

McLendon, Benson Rayfield, Jr. 1945-
[BWG, GF]
American golfer
* McLendon, Mac

McLendon, Gordon 20th c. [HPPN]
American sports announcer
* [The] Old Scotsman

McLendon, John B., Jr. 1915- [BA]
American basketball player and coach
* Johnny Mc

McLendon, Mac
See McLendon, Benson Rayfield, Jr.

McLennan, J. [FFF]
Author
* Pungent, Pierce

McLeod, Alexander D'Avila 1896-1973
[SC]
*American actor, circus and rodeo
performer*
* McLeod, Tex

McLeod, Allan S. 1949- [SMG]
Canadian-born hockey player
* McLeod, Moose

McLeod, Barbara
See Fielding, Barbara

McLeod, Daniel [IP]
American author
* [A] Native of Virginia

McLeod, Georgie A. 19th c. [FFF, IP]
American author
* Neale, Flora

McLeod, John F[reeland] 1917- [CA]
American journalist
* Freeland, Jay
* Mackle, Jeff

McLeod, Kirsty
See Hudson, [Margaret] Kirsty

McLeod, Margaret Vail
See Holloway, Teresa [Bragunier]

McLeod, Moose
See McLeod, Allan S.

McLeod, Mrs. J. F. [FFF]
Entertainer
* Wilkes, Ada

McLeod, N. R. 20th c.
Horse trainer
* McLeod, Yorkie

McLeod, Ross
See Feldman, Herbert [H. S.]

McLeod, Tex
See McLeod, Alexander D'Avila

McLeod, Yorkie
See McLeod, N. R.

McLiam, John
See Williams, John Joseph

McLin, Samuel Blair 1867-1940 [HPPN]
American executive
* Blair, Sam

McLinn, George 1884?-1953 [BI]
American sportswriter and broadcaster
* McLinn, Stoney

McLinn, Stoney
See McLinn, George

McLish, Bus [or Buster]
See McLish, Calvin Coolidge Julius
Caesar Tuskahoma

**McLish, Calvin Coolidge Julius Caesar
Tuskahoma** 1925- [BE, PB]
American baseball player
* McLish, Bus [or Buster]

McLlelan, George H. H. 1907?- [CW]
Guyanese folklorist and journalist
* Puncuss, Pugagee

McLlhargey, Jack 1952- [SMG]
Canadian-born hockey player
* McLlhargey, Wolfman

McLlhargey, Wolfman
See McLlhargey, Jack

McLociard, George
See Locke, Charles F.

McLoughlin, Diamond Jim
See McLoughlin, James

McLoughlin, James 1877?-1955 [BI]
American fisherman
* McLoughlin, Diamond Jim

McLoughlin, Maurice E. 1890-1957
[AS, HPPN, OET]
American tennis player
* [The] California Comet
* McLoughlin, Red

McLoughlin, R. B.
See Mencken, Henry Louis [Harry]

McLoughlin, Red
See McLoughlin, Maurice E.

McLowery, Frank
See Keevill, Henry J[ohn]

McLure, R. 20th c. [MBF]
British author
* Knowles, Thomas E.

McMacken, Bill 20th c. [GW]
American rodeo performer
* [The] Count

McMahon, Andrew 1926- [BWW]
American singer
* McMahon, Blueblood

McMahon, Big Ed
See McMahon, Ed[ward]

McMahon, Bingo
See McMahon, William [Bill]

McMahon, Blueblood
See McMahon, Andrew

McMahon, Doc
See McMahon, Henry John

McMahon, Ed[ward] 1923-
American television performer
* Carson's Second Banana
* Carson's Straight Man
* McMahon, Big Ed

McMahon, George Yielding ?-1886 [PI]
Irish poet and barrister
* Mac

McMahon, Heber 1851-1880 [PI]
Irish poet
* Celticus
* Noham, Cam
* Skian

McMahon, Henry John 1886-1929 [BE]
American baseball player
* McMahon, Doc

McMahon, J. A. 20th c. [CSH]
Canadian lacrosse player
* McMahon, Wandy

McMahon, James, Jr. 1912-1974 [BBH]
American bowler
* McMahon, Junie

McMahon, Jess
See McMahon, Roderick

McMahon, John Joseph 1867-1954 [AS, BE, DGS]
American baseball player
* McMahon, Sadie

McMahon, Junie
See McMahon, James, Jr.

McMahon, Margaret [Hale] [IP]
Author
* Markham, Pauline

McMahon, Pat
See Hoch, Edward D[entinger]

McMahon, Patrick James 1860-? [PI]
Scottish poet
* Mahn, Mack

McMahon, Robert
See Weverka, Robert

McMahon, Roderick 1882?-1954 [BI]
American boxing promoter
* McMahon, Jess

McMahon, Sadie
See McMahon, John Joseph

McMahon, Wandy
See McMahon, J. A.

McMahon, William [Bill] 20th c. [HPPN]
American football player
* McMahon, Bingo

McMakin, John Weaver 1878-1956 [BE]
American baseball player
* McMakin, Spartanburg John

McMakin, Spartanburg John
See McMakin, John Weaver

McManus, Blanche
See Mansfield, Mrs. M. F.

McManus, Declan Patrick 1955?-
British musician
* Costello, Elvis

McManus, George 1884-1954 [HPPN]
American cartoonist
* McManus, Jiggs

McManus, George 20th c. [BLB, HPPN]
American gambler
* McManus, Hump
* McManus, Humpty
* Richards, George

McManus, Hump
See McManus, George

McManus, Humpty
See McManus, George

McManus, James Kenneth 1921- [CA]
American sports commentator and author
* McKay, Jim

McManus, Jiggs
See McManus, George

McManus, Joab Logan 1887-1955 [BE]
American baseball player
* McManus, Joe

McManus, Joe
See McManus, Joab Logan

McManus, Patrick 1863-1886 [PI]
Irish poet
* Donard, Slieve
* Sunbeam

McMartin, L. E. 20th c. [CCL]
Canadian poet
* Pendragon

McMaster, Bryce 20th c. [CCL]
Canadian poet
* Clansman

McMaster, Guy Humphries 1829-1887 [HPPN]
American jurist, poet, historian
* MacGrom, John

McMath, Virginia Katherine 1911- [BDF, BEW, EMT]
American actress, singer, dancer
* Rogers, Ginger

McMeekan, Wayne James 1914- [BEW, EMT, TR]
American actor
* Wayne, David

McMeekin, Clark [joint pseudonym with Isabel (McLennan) McMeekin]
See Clark, Dorothy [Park]

McMeekin, Clark [joint pseudonym with Dorothy (Park) Clark]
See McMeekin, Isabel [McLennan]

McMeekin, Isabel [McLennan] 1895- [ANT, CA, SAT]
American author
* McMeekin, Clark [joint pseudonym with Dorothy (Park) Clark]

McMichen, Clayton 1900- [BI]
American musician
* McMichen, Pappy

McMichen, Pappy
See McMichen, Clayton

McMickle, Mick
See McMickle, R. D.

McMickle, R. D. 1907- [MY]
American jazz musician
* McMickle, Mick

McMillan, Bub
See McMillan, Norman Alexis

McMillan, Edwin 1907- [HPPN]
American scientiest
* [The] Father of the Synchrocyclotron

McMillan, George A. 20th c. [BE]
American baseball player
* McMillan, Reddy

McMillan, James 1925- [AW, WD]
Scottish-born author
* Coriolanus

McMillan, James C. 1925- [BA]
American artist and educator
* McMillan, Mac

McMillan, John Lanneau 1898- [HPPN]
American politician
* Mac, Johnny
* Mac, Mr.

McMillan, Lida
See Snow, Lida

McMillan, Mac
See McMillan, James C.

McMillan, Norman Alexis 1895-1969 [BE]
American baseball player
* McMillan, Bub

McMillan, Rebel
See McMillan, Thomas Law [Tommy]

McMillan, Reddy
See McMillan, George A.

McMillan, Thomas Law [Tommy] 1888-1966 [BE]
American baseball player
* McMillan, Rebel

McMillen, Thomas 20th c. [WP 1-19-85]
American basketball player
* [The] Senator

McMillian, Butterball
See McMillian, Jim

McMillian, Jim 20th c.
American basketball player
* McMillian, Butterball

McMillin
See Dunaeva, Maria Biconish

McMillin, Alvin N. 1895-1952 [AS, FB, SMG]
American football player and coach
* McMillin, Bo

McMillin, Benton 1845-1933 [HPPN]
American politician
* [The] Democratic War Horse
* [The] Democratic War Horse of
  Tennessee
* [The] Grandest Roman of Them All
* [The] Noblest Roman of Them All

McMillin, Bo
See McMillin, Alvin N.

McMinn, Ursula 1906-1973 [F2, FC]
British actress
* Jeans, Ursula

McMinoway, Michael W. 1947?-
[HPPN]
American detective
* Sedan Chair

McMorrow, Fred 1925- [CA]
American writer
* Redfield, Clark

McMullan, Big Mac
See McMullan, John

McMullan, John 1921- [TI 7-25-83]
American journalist
* McMullan, Big Mac

McMullan, William John 1813-1863
[PI]
Irish poet
* Oge, Hector
* Paddy, Scot, the Piper

McMullen, Catherine
See Cookson, Catherine Ann
[McMullen]

McMullen, John F. 1849-1881 [BE]
American baseball player
* McMullen, Lefty

McMullen, Joseph Carl 1882- [NAA]
American playwright
* Carlton, Joseph

McMullen, Kenneth Lee 1942- [SMG]
American baseball player
* McMullen, Pound Cake

McMullen, Lefty
See McMullen, John F.

McMullen, Mary
See Reilly, Mary

McMullen, Mary A. 19th c. [IP]
American poet
* Una

McMullen, Pound Cake
See McMullen, Kenneth Lee

McMullin, Ruth R[oney] 1942- [CA]
American author and editor
* Roney, Ruth Anne

McMurray, Lillita Louise 1908-
[HPPN]
American actress
* Chaplin, Lita Grey

McMurray, Nancy A[rmistead] 1936-
[CA]
American author and illustrator
* Yowa

McMurrogh-Kavanagh, Douglas Gerrard
1888-1950 [SC]
Irish-born actor and director
* Gerrard, Douglas

McMurry, Lolita 1908- [F2]
Actress
* Grey, Lita

McNabb, Carl Mac 1917- [BE]
American baseball player
* McNabb, Skinny

McNabb, Skinny
See McNabb, Carl Mac

McNair, Boob
See McNair, Donald Eric

McNair, Donald Eric 1909-1949 [BE,
HPPN]
American baseball player
* McNair, Boob
* McNair, Rabbit

McNair, Rabbit
See McNair, Donald Eric

McNally, Andrew 1836-1904 [HPPN]
Irish-American printer and cartographer
* [The] Father of the Highway Map

McNally, Blood
See McNally, John Victor

McNally, Curtis
See Birchall, Ian H[arry]

McNally, Horace 1913- [FC, ITA, SW]
American actor
* McNally, Stephen

McNally, John Victor 1904- [FB,
HPPN, SMG]
American football player
* Blood, Johnny
* [The] Joe Namath of the Thirties
* McNally, Blood
* [The] Vagabond Halfback

McNally, Leonard 1752-1820 [IP, PI]
Irish playwright, author, poet
* [A] Barrister of the Inner Temple
* Plunder

McNally, Stephen
See McNally, Horace

McNally, Walter [FFF]
Entertainer
* Wilson, George

McNamara, Barbara Willard 1913-
[AW]
Australian author
* O'Conner, Elizabeth

McNamara, Big Mac
See McNamara, Gerry

McNamara, Computer Bob
See McNamara, Robert Strange

McNamara, Dinny
See McNamara, John Raymond

McNamara, Gerry 20th c. [SMG]
Hockey scout
* McNamara, Big Mac

McNamara, Iron Man
See McNamara, Reginald James
[Reggie]

McNamara, James B. 20th c. [HPPN]
American labor agitator
* Bryson, J. B.
* Sullivan

McNamara, John Raymond 1905-1963
[BE]
American baseball player
* McNamara, Dinny

McNamara, Joseph 1866-1916 [BE]
Irish-born baseball player
* Mack, Joseph
* Mack, Reddy

McNamara, Lena Randolph [Brooke]
1891- [CAP, WW]
American author and illustrator
* Mack, Evalina

McNamara, [Sister] Marie Aquinas
See Schaub, Marilyn McNamara

McNamara, Reginald James [Reggie]
1887-1971 [HPPN]
Australian bicycle racer
* McNamara, Iron Man

McNamara, Robert Strange 1916- [CR,
HPPN]
*American business executive and
government official*
* [The] Creator of the Department of
  Defense
* Mac the Knife
* McNamara, Computer Bob

McNamara, William Franklin 1855-?
[PI]
American poet
* Hazelton, Harry

McNary, Charles Linza 1874-1944
[HPPN]
American attorney and politician
* McNary, Wise Charley

McNary, Wise Charley
See McNary, Charles Linza

McNaught, Rosamond Livingstone
20th c. [NAA]
American writer and poet
* Hancock, Frances

McNaughton, Gus
See Le Clerq, Augustus Howard

McNaughton, James 19th c. [IP]
American physician and author
* [An] Observer

McNaughton, John H. [FFF]
American poet
* Babble Brook

McNaughton, Violet 1873?-1953 [BEW]
Canadian-born actress
* Adair, Jean

McNeal, Harry
See McNeal, John Harley

McNeal, John Harley 1878-1945 [BE]
American baseball player
* McNeal, Harry

McNeely, Big Jay
See McNeely, Cecil

McNeely, Cecil 1928- [EJ]
American musician
* McNeely, Big Jay

McNeely, Jeannette 1918- [CA]
American author
* Mackie, Maron
* Macneill, Janet

McNees, Pat 1940- [CA]
American author and editor
* Mancini, Pat McNees

McNeil, Brownie
See McNeil, Norman L.

McNeil, Clifton A. 1940- [FB]
American football player
* McNeil, Spider
* McNeil, Sticks

McNeil, Minnie
See Dayton, Mrs. Peter

McNeil, Norman L. 1915- [FFA]
American singer
* McNeil, Brownie

McNeil, Spider
See McNeil, Clifton A.

McNeil, Sticks
See McNeil, Clifton A.

McNeile, Herman Cyril 1888-1937
[EMD, LC, TC]
British author
* Sapper

McNeill, Don 1908?- [NW 1-17-83]
American radio performer
* [The] King of Corn

McNeill, Janet
See Alexander, Janet

McNeill, Robert 20th c.
American news reporter
* McNeill, Robin

McNeill, Robin
See McNeill, Robert

McNeillie, John 20th c. [BI]
British author
* Niall, Ian

McNeilly, Mildred Masterson 1910-
[ANT]
American author
* Dewey, James
* Kelly, Glenn

McNeilly, Wilfred Glassford 1921- [CA,
ESF, SFL]
Scottish-born author
* Baker, W[illiam] Howard
* Ballinger, W. A.
* Glassford, Wilfred
* Gregg, Martin
* Hunter, Joe
* Lecale, Errol

McNeilly, Wilfred Glassford (cont.)
* Reid, Desmond
* Saxon, Peter [house pseudonym]

McNellis, Maggi
See Roche, Margaret Eleanor

McNelly, Willis E[verett] 1920- [CA]
American author, editor, educator
* Tabard, Geoffrey

McNelly's Bulldog
See Armstrong, John Barclay

McNemar, Richard 1770-1839 [HPPN]
American religious leader and author
* Philos Harmoniae
* Wright, Eleazar

McNichols, William, Jr. 1910?- [TI 7-4-
83]
American politician
* Mayor Bill

McNish, George 1660-1722 [FFF]
American clergyman
* [The] Father of Presbyterianism in
New York

McNish, James Thomas 1898- [IAW]
South African author
* Marathon

McNulty, Dorothy 1908- [FC, ITA]
American actress
* Singleton, Penny

McNulty, Eugene Dennis 1917- [PMJ,
SW]
American singer
* Day, Dennis

McNutt, Boob
See McNutt, Paul Vories

McNutt, Charles
See Nutt, Charles

McNutt, George Washington Morrison
1843-? [HPPN]
Circus midget
* Nutt, Commodore

McNutt, Paul Vories 1891-1955 [HPPN]
American attorney and politician
* McNutt, Boob

McPadden, Gunner
See McPadden, William

McPadden, William 20th c. [BLB]
American underworld figure
* McPadden, Gunner

McParlan, James 1844?-1919 [HPPN]
Irish-American detective and labor spy
* McKenna, James

McPartland, Kid
See McPartland, William Lawrence

McPartland, William Lawrence
1875-1953 [BI, HPPN, RBE]
American boxer
* McPartland, Kid

McPeake, Big Red
See McPeake, William Curtis

McPeake, William Curtis 1927- [CWG,
DAM]
American country-western performer
* McPeake, Big Red

McPhail, Buck
See McPhail, Howard

McPhail, Howard 20th c. [EF]
American football player
* McPhail, Buck

McPhail, Larry
See McPhail, Leland Stanford

McPhail, Leland Stanford 1890-1975
[BI, HPPN]
American baseball official
* McPhail, Larry
* McPhail, Loud Larry
* [The] Wizard of Baseball

McPhail, Loud Larry
See McPhail, Leland Stanford

McPhee, Bid [or Biddy]
See McPhee, John Alexander

McPhee, John Alexander 1859-1943
[AS, BE, DGS]
American baseball player
* McPhee, Bid [or Biddy]

McPherrin, Jones
See Day, Thomas Franklin

McPherson, Aimee Semple 1890-1944
Canadian-born evangelist
* Aimee, [Sister]
* [The] World's Most Pulchritudinous
Evangelist

McPherson, Amy
See McPherson, Forrest

McPherson, [Captain] Angus
See Colinski, A. J.

McPherson, Forrest 20th c. [EF]
American football player
* McPherson, Amy

McPherson, Hugh 1921- [CA]
Canadian author
* McPherson, Hugo [Archibald]

McPherson, Hugo [Archibald]
See McPherson, Hugh

McPherson, Malcolm 1850-? [PA]
Author
* McGuire, M.

McPherson, Mrs. H. M.
Author
* West, Jessamyn

McPherson, Newt[on] 1943- [WP 1-3-85]
American politician
* Gingrich, Newt[on Leroy]

McPherson, Richard C. 1883-1944
[ASC, PMJ]
American composer
* Mack, Cecil

McPherson, Warner 1936- [CWG]
American country-western performer
* Mack, Warner

McQuade, Ann Aikman 1928- [CA]
American author
* Aikman, Ann

McQueen, Butterfly
See McQueen, Thelma

McQueen, Justus E. 1936-
American actor
* Jones, L. Q.

McQueen, Mildred Hark 1908- [CAP, SAT]
American author and playwright
* Hark, Mildred

McQueen, Thelma 1911- [FC]
American actress
* McQueen, Butterfly

McQuery, Mox
See McQuery, William Thomas

McQuery, William Thomas 1861-1900
[BE]
American baseball player
* McQuery, Mox

McQuill, Thursty
See Bruce, Wallace

McQuillan, Handsome Hugh
See McQuillan, Hugh A.

McQuillan, Hugh A. 1897-1947 [BE, BN]
American baseball player
* [The] Astoria Eagle
* McQuillan, Handsome Hugh

McQuillen, Glen Richard 1915- [BE]
American baseball player
* McQuillen, Red

McQuillen, Red
See McQuillen, Glen Richard

McQuin, [Abbe] Ange Denis 1756-1823
[PI]
French-born poet and author
* [The] Gleaner

McQuoid, Rose Lee 20th c. [SC]
American actress
* Lee, Rose

M'Cracken, Mike
See Landsborough, G. H.

McRae, Carmen 1922- [BA]
American singer
* Clarke, Carmen

McRae, Cassius
See McRae, Graham

McRae, Ellen
See Gillooly, Edna Rae

McRae, Evander 20th c. [HPPN]
American football player
* McRae, Pete

McRae, Gertrude Lyon ?-1967 [HPPN]
American actress
* McCoy, Gertrude

McRae, Graham 1940- [EAR]
New Zealand auto racer
* McRae, Cassius

McRae, James Wendell 1952- [BA]
American business executive
* McRae, Jimbo

McRae, Jimbo
See McRae, James Wendell

McRae, Lindsay
See Sowerby, Arthur Lindsay McRae

McRae, Pete
See McRae, Evander

McRae, Roy
See Buley, Bernard

M'cready, Max
See M'cready, Samuel Maxwell

M'cready, Samuel Maxwell 1918- [EG]
British golfer
* M'cready, Max

McRealsham, E. D.
See Mead, Charles Marsh

M'Crib, Theophilus
See Lee, Henry Boyle

McRoberts, Agnesann
See Meek, Pauline Palmer

McRuer, Helen ?-1945 [SC]
American actress and playwright
* Mitchell, Helen

McShane, Mark 1929?- [CA, WD]
Australian-born author
* Lovell, Marc

McShann, Hootie
See McShann, Jay

McShann, Jay 1909- [DAM, EJ, PMJ]
American jazz musician
* McShann, Hootie

McSherry, Shandy
See McCorry, Peter

McSorley, John Bernard 1858-1936
[BE]
American baseball player
* McSorley, Trick

McSorley, Trick
See McSorley, John Bernard

McSpadden, Joseph Walker 1874-1960
[BI, HPPN]
American author and editor
* Walker, Joseph

McSpaden, Harold 1908- [BWG, GF]
American golfer
* McSpaden, Jug

McSpaden, Jug
See McSpaden, Harold

McSparran, James ?-1757 [HPPN]
Irish clergyman
* [A] Reverend Divine of the Church of England

McSweeney, Virginia 1898-1968 [F1, F2, FC, HPPN]
American actress
* [The] Outdoor Girl of the Films
* Valli, Virginia

McSwiggin, Little Mac
See McSwiggin, William H. [Bill]

McSwiggin, William H. [Bill] ?-1926
[HPPN]
American attorney
* [The] Hanging Prosecutor
* McSwiggin, Little Mac

McSwiney, Stephen Myles ?-1890 [PI]
Irish physician and poet
* Lancet

McTammany, John 1845-1915 [HPPN]
Scottish-American musician and inventor
* [The] Father of the Player Piano

McTantrum
See McEnroe, John

McTell, Blind Willie
See McTell, Willie Samuel

McTell, Willie Samuel 1901-1959
[BWW]
American singer
* Barrelhouse Sammy
* Blind Doogie
* Blind Sammy
* Georgia Bill
* Glaze, Red Hot Willie
* Hot Shot Willie
* McTell, Blind Willie
* Pig 'n' Whistle Red
* Red Hot Willie

McTurk, Joe
See McCracken, Robert

McTurk, Michael 1858?-? [CW]
Guyanese folklorist
* Quow

McVea, Samuel 1885-1921 [BX, IBW]
American boxer
* [The] Black Globetrotter
* McVey, Sam

McVean, James
See Luard, Nicholas Lambert

McVeigh, Charles 1898- [CEI, HK]
Canadian-born hockey player
* McVeigh, Rabbit

McVeigh, Rabbit
See McVeigh, Charles

McVey, Lucille 1868-1925 [FC]
American actress
* Drew, Mrs. Sidney

McVey, Sam
See McVea, Samuel

McVey, Thomas Glenory ?-1933
[HPPN]
American vaudeville performer
* Glenory, Thomas

McVicker, Brock [PA]
Author
* Edgerton, Wild

McVicker, Mrs. Horace [FFF]
Entertainer
* Weaver, Effie

McVicor, John 20th c. [CEI]
Hockey player
* McVicor, Slim

McVicor, Slim
See McVicor, John

McVitie, Jack ?-1967 [DI]
British underworld figure
* [The] Hat

McWeeny, Buzz
See McWeeny, Douglas Lawrence

McWeeny, Douglas Lawrence 1896-1953
[BE]
American baseball player
* McWeeny, Buzz

McWherter, Rodney 1936- [OP]
American opera singer
* MacWherter, Rod

McWhirter, Glenna S. 1929- [CA]
American columnist
* McWhirter, Nickie

McWhirter, Nickie
See McWhirter, Glenna S.

McWilliam, Andrew 1883-1958 [HPPN]
American actor and singer
* Williams, Danny

McWilliams, Calm Daddy
See McWilliams, Stanley W.

McWilliams, Stanley W. 1939- [IBW]
American Air Patrol pilot
* McWilliams, Calm Daddy

McWorter, Gerald 20th c.
American educator
* Alkalamit, Abdul

Me
See Bunner, Henry Cuyler

Me Che Kan Nah Quah 1747?-1812
[HPPN]
American Indian chief
* Little Turtle

Me Too
See Platt, Thomas Collier

Mea
See Angerer, Mea

Meabey, Leonard
See Gander, Leonard Marsland

Meachum, Dad
See Meachum, James H.

Meachum, James H. 1893?-1963 [BEW]
American theatrical performer
* Meachum, Dad

Mead, Charles Marsh 1836-1911 [BI]
American clergyman
* McRealsham, E. D.

Mead, Edwin Doak 1849-1937 [HPPN]
American author
* [An] Independent

Mead, Jude 1919- [CA]
American clergyman, educator, author
* Jude, [Father]

Mead, Matt
See Richards, Ross

Mead, Russell
See Koehler, Margaret [Hudson]

Mead, Sidney Moko 1927- [AW]
New Zealand author
* Moko

Meade, Claire
See Fields, Marguerite

Meade, Ellen
See Roddick, Ellen

Meade, George Gordon 1815-1872
[DNNS, FFF, SN]
American army officer
* Four Eyed George

Meade, Julia
See Kunze, Julia

Meade, L[illie] T[homas]
See Smith, Elizabeth Thomasina
[Meade]

Meade, Mary
See Church, Ruth Ellen [Lovrien]

Meade, Richard
See Haas, Ben[jamin] L[eopold]

Meade, William 1789-1862 [HPPN]
American clergyman
* [The] Assistant Bishop of Virginia
* [The] Bishop of Virginia

Meader, Vaughn 1936?-
American entertainer
* Sunday, Johnny

Meadley, George Wilson   [PA]
Author
* G. W. M.

Meador, James H. 1912- [FC, SW]
American actor
* Craig, James

Meadowcroft, Enid LaMonte
See Wright, Enid Meadowcroft
[LaMonte]

Meadowcroft, Ernest [William] 1914-
[WD]
British author and poet
* William, Arnold

Meadowcroft, John 1767-1805 [FAA]
British-born actor
* Hodgkinson, John

Meadowes, Pauline
See Megroz, Phyllis

Meadows, Country
See Meadows, Edward

Meadows, Edward 1932- [FB]
American football player
* Meadows, Country

Meadows, Henry Lee 1894-1963 [BE,
⟩GS, PB]
American baseball player
* Meadows, Specs

Meadows, Jayne
See Allen, Jane Cotter

Meadows, Lindon
See Greatrex, Charles

Meadows, Peter
See Lindsay, Jack

Meadows, Specs
See Meadows, Henry Lee

Meagher, John Francis 1848-? [PI]
Irish poet and author
* Slievenamon

Meagher, M. 20th c. [MBF]
British author
* Marriott, Buck

Meagher of the Sword
See Meagher, Thomas Francis

Meagher, Patrick J. 1810-1880 [PI]
Irish-born journalist
* O'Meagher, Patrick J.

Meagher, Thomas Francis 1823-1867
[HN, PI]
*Irish-born American politician and army
officer*
* Meagher of the Sword
* O'Keeffe, Cornelius

Meaker, Eloise 1915- [CA]
American author and columnist
* Clark, Lydia Benson
* Hunter, Valancy
* Lancaster, Lydia
* McAllister, Amanda

Meaker, M. J.
See Meaker, Marijane

Meaker, Marijane 1927- [CLC, FBJ,
SAT]
American author
* Aldrich, Ann
* Kerr, M. E.
* Meaker, M. J.
* Packer, Vin

[The] Meal Ticket
See Hubbell, Carl Owen

Mean Joe Greene
See Greene, Charles Edward

Mean, Mr.
See Micheaux, Larry

[The] Mean Mr. Clean
See Lebitsky, Leonard

[The] Meanest Gambler in New York
See Adams, Al[bert J.]

Means, David Macgregor 1847-?
[HPPN]
American attorney
* McGee

Means, Gaston Bullock 1879-1938
[HPPN]
American investigator and confidence man
* German Agent E-13
* [The] Muenchausen in Modern Dress
* [The] Spectacular Rogue
* [The] Swindler of the Century

Means, Mary 20th c.   [WW]
Author
* Scott, Denis [joint pseudonym with Theodore Saunders]

Meanwell, M.
See Cowper, William

Meanwell, Miranda
See Foe, Daniel

Meanwell, Walter E. 1884-1953   [AS, BB]
British-born American basketball coach
* [The] Little Doctor

Meany, Big George
See Meany, [William] George

Meany, [William] George 1894-1980
[HPPN]
American labor leader
* [The] Leader of American Labor
* Meany, Big George
* [The] Old Curmudgeon of Labor
* [The] Silver Haired Elderly Statesman of American Labor

Meany, Stephen Joseph 1825-1888   [PI]
Irish poet and journalist
* Abelard
* Werner

Meara, Charles Edward [Charlie] 1891-
[BE]
American baseball player
* Meara, Goggy

Meara, Goggy
See Meara, Charles Edward [Charlie]

Mearns, David Chambers 1899-1981
[CA]
American author
* Fraddle, Farragut

Mears, Otto 19th c.
Russian-born road builder and politician
* [The] Pathfinder of San Juan

Measday, George
See Soderberg, Percy Measday

Mease, John 1746-1826   [FFF]
American soldier
* [The] Last of the Cocked Hats

Meason, Gilbert Laing 19th c.   [PA]
Author
* G. L. M.

Measor, Adele
See Buckstone, Mrs. J. C.

Measor, C. P.   [PA]
Author
* Scrutator

[The] Measuring Man
See DeSalvo, Albert

Meat Cleaver Weaver
See Weaver, Eddie

Meat Loaf
See Aday, Marvin Lee

Meaux, Huey 20th c.   [CMA]
American disc jockey
* [The] Crazy Cajun

Mebane, John [Harrison] 1909-   [CA]
American author
* DeVilbiss, Philip
* Heartman, Harold

Mec, Dinah 1920-   [BF]
British actress
* Sheridan, Dinah

[Il] Meccherino
See Di Pace, Domenico

Mecham, William 1853-1902   [WEC]
British cartoonist
* Merry, Tom

[The] Mechanical Man
See Gehringer, Charles Leonard

[The] Mechanical Man
See Nelson, Byron

[The] Mechanical Man
See Williams, Billy Leo

[The] Mechanical Specialist
See Weitzel, Lawrence M.

Meco
See Monardo, Meco

Mecom, Big John
See Mecom, John W., Sr.

Mecom, Jane Franklin 1712-1794
[HPPN]
Sister of American statesman, Benjamin Franklin
* [The] Favorite Sister

Mecom, John W., Sr. 1911?-1981
American industrialist
* Mecom, Big John

Medard, Yves
See Labuchin, Rassoul

Medaris, John B. 1902-
American army officer and priest
* Bruce, [Father]

Medaro
See Nibbi, Gino

Medary, Samuel 1801-1864   [FFF]
American editor
* [The] Old Wheel Horse of Democracy

Medbury, Jessie Royse 1904-1972
[BEW, FC]
American actress
* Landis, Jessie Royce

[The] Meddler
See Roosevelt, Theodore [Teddy]

[The] Meddler
See Trumbull, John

[The] Meddlesome Friar
See Savonarola, Girolamo Maria Francesco Matteo

Mede, Joseph
See Garland, David John

Medeiros, Pep
See Medeiros, Ray Antone

Medeiros, Ray Antone 1926-   [BE]
American baseball player
* Medeiros, Pep

Medes Macial, Antonio Vicente
1835-1897   [EOP]
Brazilian cult leader
* Conselheiro, Antonio

Medford, Kay
See Regan, Kathleen Patricia

Medhurst, Joan
See Liverton, Joan

Medhurst, Mr. 19th c.   [EOP]
Astrologer and author
* Raphael III

Medhurst, Walter Henry 1796-1857
[HPPN]
British clergyman
* Philosinensis

Mediana, Patricia 1923-   [BEW]
British actress
* Medina, Patricia

[A] Medical Man
See Watson, Forbes

Medical Mother
See Cilento, Phyllis Dorothy

Medich, Doc
See Medich, George Francis

Medich, George Francis 1948-   [SMG]
American baseball player
* Medich, Doc

Medici, Alessandro Ottaviano de
1535-1605   [WBD]
Pope
* Leo XI

Medici, Anna Maria Ludovica de
1667-1743   [WBD]
Daughter of Cosimo III, Grand Duke of Tuscany
* [The] Last of the Medici

Medici, Catherine de 1519-1589   [HPPN]
Italian-born Queen of France
* [The] Italian Woman

Medici, Cosimo de 1642-1723   [HPPN]
Grand Duke of Florence
* [The] Last of the Medici

Medici, Cosmo [or Cosimo] de
1389-1464   [DHA, HN, WBD]
Florentine ruler
* Cosimo the Elder
* [The] Father of His Country
* [The] Invincible

Medici, Cosmo [or Cosimo] de
1519-1574 [DNNS, FFF, SN]
Grand Duke of Tuscany
* [The] Great

Medici, Francesco de 1541-1587 [SN]
Son of Cosmo, Grand Duke of Tuscany
* [The] Second Brutus

Medici, Giovanni Angelo 1499-1565
[WBD]
Pope
* Pius IV

Medici, Giovanni de 1475-1521 [RH,
WBD]
Pope
* Divine Majesty
* Husband of the Church
* [The] Key of all the Universe
* Leo X
* Prince of the Apostles

Medici, Giovanni de 1498-1526 [HN,
SN, WBD]
Italian general
* [The] Devil
* Giovanni delle Bande Nere [John of
  the Black Bands]
* [Il] Gran Diavolo

Medici, Giulio de 1478-1534 [WBD]
Pope
* Clement VII

Medici, Lorenzino de
See Medici, Lorenzo de

Medici, Lorenzo de 1395-1440 [WBD]
Florentine banker
* [The] Elder

Medici, Lorenzo de 1448-1492 [DNNF,
HN, RH]
Florentine ruler
* [The] Father of Letters
* [The] Magnificent
* [The] Patron of the Fine Arts
* [The] Restorer of Learning

Medici, Lorenzo de 1463-1507 [WBD]
Florentine politician
* [The] Younger

Medici, Lorenzo de 1514-1548 [WBD]
*Murdered Alessandro de Medici, First
Duke of Florence*
* Medici, Lorenzino de

[The] Medici of the Middle West
See Miller, J. Irwin

Medici, Piero de 1414-1469 [WBD]
Ruler of Florence
* [The] Gouty

Medicine Bill Mountjoy
See Mountjoy, William R. [Billy]

[The] Medicine Man
See Bevan, Aneurin

[The] Medicine Man for Your Blues
See Friedman, Theodore Leopold

Medicine Man Graydon
See Graydon, [Dr.] Thomas

Medico Campo, Don Richardo de
See Harvey, Gabriel

Medico Campo, Don Richardo de
See Lichfield, Richard

Medicus
See Slade, Daniel Denison

Medicus
See Watson, George Bott Churchill

Medicus
See Winslow, Forbes Benignus

Medicus II
See Philipp, Elliot Elias

[The] Medieval Pliny
See Qazwini, al-

Medill, Joseph 1823-1899 [HPPN]
American attorney, politician, journalist
* [The] Founder of the Republican
  Party

Medill, Robert
See McBride, Robert Medill

Medina, Hector 20th c. [RBE]
Mexican boxer
* Casanova, Young

Medina, Patricia
See Mediana, Patricia

Medina, Roberto
See Garcia, John

Meding, Oskar 1829-1903 [PA]
Author
* Samarow, Gregor

Medley?
See Etherege, [Sir] George

Medley, Anne
See Borchard, Ruth [Berendsohn]

Medley, Matthew
See Aston, Anthony

Medlicott, Margaret P[aget] 1913- [CA]
British author
* Paget, Margaret

Mednick, Stanley Robert 1930- [BEW]
American playwright
* Roberts, Meade

Medolla [or Meldolla], Andrea
1522?-1582 [WBD]
Italian painter
* Schiavone, Andrea

Medtner, Nikolai 1879-1951 [HPPN]
Russian pianist and composer
* [The] Russian Brahms

Medveczky
See Hatar, Gyozo Victor John

Medved, Alexander 1937- [HPPN]
Russian wrestler
* [The] Great Champion

Medvedev, Mikhail
See Bernstein, Meyer Y.

Medwall, Henry 15th c. [HPPN]
British clergyman and playwright
* [The] Father of the English Secular
  Play

Medway, Lewis
See Paterson, William

Medwick, Ducky
See Medwick, Joseph Michael

Medwick, Joseph Michael 1911-1975
[BE, HPPN, PB, SR]
American baseball player
* Duckie Wuckie
* [The] Hungarian Rhapsody
* Medwick, Ducky
* Medwick, Mickey
* Medwick, Muscles

Medwick, Mickey
See Medwick, Joseph Michael

Medwick, Muscles
See Medwick, Joseph Michael

Mee, Arthur 1875-? [WWL]
British author
* Idris

Mee, Judge
See Mee, Thomas William [Tommy]

Mee, Mary
See Dean, Mary

Mee, Thomas William [Tommy] 1890-
[BE]
American baseball player
* Mee, Judge

Meech, Edward Raymond ?-1952 [SC]
American actor and circus performer
* Meech, Montana

Meech, Montana
See Meech, Edward Raymond

Meegan, Pete[r J.] 1863-1905 [BE]
American baseball player
* Meegan, Steady Pete

Meegan, Steady Pete
See Meegan, Pete[r J.]

Meegeren, Hans van 1890?-1947
Dutch painter
* Art's Fabulous Forger
* [The] Man Who Swindled Goering
* [The] Old Dutch Faker

Meehan, Alexander S. ?-1852 [PI]
Irish poet
* Astroea
* [The] Spirit of the Nation

Meehan, Charles Patrick 1812-1890 [PI]
Irish author and poet
* C. P. M.
* Clericus
* D. M'L.
* Father Charles
* Sister Mary

Meehan, Chick
See Meehan, John Francis

Meehan, Francis 1898-1968　[BB]
American basketball player
* Meehan, Stretch

Meehan, Francis Joseph 1881-?　[CAT]
American author and critic
* Scarlet, Will
* Zachary Leo, [Brother]

Meehan, John Francis 1893-1972　[BI, FB]
American football coach
* Meehan, Chick

Meehan, Stretch
See Meehan, Francis

Meehan, Thomas 18th c.　[PI]
Irish poet
* T. M.

Meehan, Willie
See Walcott, Eugene

[The] Meek
See Frederick II

[The] Meek
See Louis I

Meek, Alexander Beaufort 1814-1865
[HPPN]
American politician and educator
* [The] Father of the Public Schools of Alabama

Meek, Dad
See Meek, Frank J.

Meek, Doris 20th c.　[WW]
Author
* Gregory, Mason [joint pseudonym with Adrienne Jones]
* Mason, Gregory [joint pseudonym with Adrienne Jones]

Meek, Frank J. ?-1922　[BE]
American baseball player
* Meek, Dad

Meek, Freddie
See Meek, Fredericka

Meek, Fredericka 1971-　[IBW]
American child prodigy
* Meek, Freddie

Meek, Jacklyn O'Hanlon 1933-　[CA, WYA]
American author
* Matthews, Jacklyn Meek
* O'Hanlon, Jacklyn

Meek, Joseph L. 1810-1875　[HPPN]
American politician
* Colonel

Meek, Lois Hayden
See Stolz, Lois Meek

Meek, Margaret
See Spencer Meek, Margaret [Diston]

Meek, Matthew
See Ramsay, Richard

Meek, Pauline Palmer 1917-　[CA]
American author
* McRoberts, Agnesann

Meek, [Major] S. P.
See Meek, Sterner St. Paul

Meek, [Captain] S. P.
See Meek, Sterner St. Paul

Meek, Sterner St. Paul 1894-　[NAA, SF]
American author
* Meek, [Major] S. P.
* Meek, [Captain] S. P.
* St. Paul, Sterner

Meeke, Mary ?-1816?　[HPPN]
British author
* Gabrielli

Meeker, Mildred
See Bruno, Guido

Meeker, N. C.
See Meeker, Nathan Cook

Meeker, Nathan Cook 1817-1879
[WGT]
American author
* Armstrong, [Captain] Jacob D.
* Meeker, N. C.

Meeker, Nellie J. 19th c.　[DNA]
American author
* Valentine, Jane

Meeker, Ralph
See Rathgeber, Ralph

Meeker, W. Johns 20th c.　[WGT]
Author
* Johns, Willy

Meeks, Bud
See Meeks, Charles

Meeks, Charles 1917?-　[HPPN]
American law enforcement officer
* Meeks, Bud

Meeks, Linda A.
See Brower, Linda A.

Meeropol, Abel 20th c.　[ASC]
American composer and educator
* Allan, Lewis

Meeropol, Michael
See Rosenberg, Michael

Meeropol, Robert [or Robbie]
See Rosenberg, Robert

Meers, Babe
See Meers, Russ[ell Harlan]

Meers, Russ[ell Harlan] 1918-　[BE]
American baseball player
* Meers, Babe

Mees, Steve
See Flexner, Stuart Berg

Meese, Edwin, III 1931-　[NW 2-6-84]
American presidential counselor
* Billy Club Ed
* No Problems Ed

Meeting House
See Foe, Daniel

Meeus, Marcel 1934-　[IAW]
Belgian writer
* Cremer, Samuel

Mefford, Ditra Helena 1906?-1984
[HPPN, TI 3-12-84]
American musician and missionary
* Flame, Ditra
* [The] Lady in Black
* Sorellina

Megaletor
See Cromwell, Oliver

[The] Megalomaniac
See Clarke, Norham Pfardt

[The] Megalomaniac
See Jordan, Marvin A.

[The] Megalomaniac Master of Tripoli
See Khadafi [or Qaddafi], [Colonel] Muammar el

[The] Megamidget
See Moore, Dudley

Megard, Andree
See Chamonal, Marie

Megas
See Antiochus III

Megerdichian, Vahan Leon 1923-　[EJ]
American jazz musician
* Merian, Leon

Megerle, Hans Ulrich 1644-1709　[WBD]
Austrian clergyman and satirist
* Abraham a Sancta [or Santa] Clara

Megged [or Meged], Aharon [or Aron]
1920-　[CA]
Israeli journalist
* A. M.

Meggott, John 1714-1789　[HPPN]
British miser
* Elwes, John

Meggs, George 18th c.　[HPPN]
British boxer
* [The] Collier

Meggs, Mary ?-1691　[HPPN]
British orange seller
* Orange Moll

Meghor, Camillo
See Van Peteghem, Camille

Mego, Al
See Roberts, Arthur O.

Megroz, Phyllis 20th c.　[WWL]
British author
* Meadowes, Pauline

Megson, Neil Andrew 1950-　[CAR]
British artist
* P-Orridge, Genesis

Mehaffey, Leroy 1904-　[HPPN]
American baseball player
* Mehaffey, Pop Eye

Mehaffey, Pop Eye
See Mehaffey, Leroy

Mehan, Joseph Albert 1929- [CA]
American author
* Martin, Albert

Mehboob
See Mehboobkhan, Ramjankhan

Mehboobkhan, Ramjankhan 1907- [FC]
Indian director
* Mehboob

Mehegan, Catherine Josephine 1847-1937
[BI, HPPN]
American educator
* Xavier, [Mother]

Mehemet [or Mohammed] Ali
1769?-1848? [DNNS, HN, RH]
Viceroy of Egypt
* [The] Napoleon of the East
* [The] Peter the Great of Egypt

Mehemet Ali Pasha
See Detroit, Karl

Meher, [Baba]
See Irani, Merwan S.

Mehle, Aileen 1952- [BI]
American columnist
* Knickerbocker, Suzy
* Suzy

Mehlhorn, Wild Bill
See Mehlhorn, William

Mehlhorn, William 1894?- [EG, GF]
American golfer
* Mehlhorn, Wild Bill

Mehmed Namik 1840-1888 [WBD]
Turkish poet, author, patriot
* Kemal Bey

Mehmet Suleiman ?-1572? [WBD]
Turkish poet
* Fuzuli

Mehre, Harry J. 20th c. [HPPN]
American football coach
* Mehre, Horse
* [The] True Athenian

Mehre, Horse
See Mehre, Harry J.

Mehta, Rustam Jehangir 1912- [AW,
CA, HPPN]
Indian author
* Hartman, Roger
* Martin, R. J.
* Martin, R. Johnson
* Plutonius

Mei Sheng 2nd c. BC [WBD]
Chinese poet
* [The] Father of Modern Chinese
Poetry

Meibes, Joseph 1927- [BEW, FC]
German-born actor
* Ericson, John

Meidinger-Geise, Inge
See Meidinger-Geise, Ingeborg Lucie

Meidinger-Geise, Ingeborg Lucie 1923-
[IAW]
German author
* Meidinger-Geise, Inge

Meier, Arthur Ernst 1879-? [BE]
American baseball player
* Meier, Dutch

Meier, Dutch
See Meier, Arthur Ernst

Meier, Sally 1928- [HPPN]
American animal lover
* [The] Cat Lady of San Francisco

Meiggs, Henry 1811-1877 [HPPN]
American entrepreneur, and politician
* Don Enrique

Meighan, Donald Charles 1929- [CA,
SAT]
American author and illustrator
* Charles, Donald

Meighan, Thaddeus W. [PA]
Author
* Asmodeus

Meigs, Cornelia Lynde 1884-1973 [CA,
SAT]
American author
* Aldon, Adair

Meigs, Montgomery 1847-1931 [HPPN]
American engineer and inventor
* [The] Father of the Canvas Cofferdam

Meikle, Arthur Francis 1871-1945 [BE]
American baseball player
* Nichols, Arthur Francis

Meikle, Buster
See Meikle, David

Meikle, Clive
See Brooks, Jeremy

Meikle, David 20th c. [RO2]
British musician
* Meikle, Buster

Meiklejohn, J. M. D.
See Meiklejohn, John Miller Dow

Meiklejohn, John Miller Dow 1836-1902
[LC]
Scottish educator and author
* Meiklejohn, J. M. D.

Meilach, Dona Z[weigoron] 1926- [CA]
American author
* Stanli, Sue

Meilhac, Henri 1832-1897 [NPS]
French playwright and author
* Baskoff, Ivan

Mein Boy Levinsky
See Levinsky, Alexander H.

Mein, Jenny
See Geddes, Jenny

Meine, Heinie
See Meine, Henry William

Meine, Heinrich
See Meine, Henry William

Meine, Henry William 1896-1968 [AS,
BE]
American baseball player
* [The] Count of Luxemburg
* Meine, Heinie
* Meine, Heinrich

Meineke, Don 1930- [BB]
American basketball player
* Meineke, Monk

Meineke, Monk
See Meineke, Don

Meingre, Jean le ?-1368 [HPPN]
French army officer
* Bouciquaut

Meingre, Jean le 1366?-1421 [HPPN]
French army officer
* Bouciquaut II

Meinhold, Carl 1925-
American basketball player
* Meinhold, Red

Meinhold, Johann Wilhelm 1797-1851
[WGT]
German author
* Schweidler, Abraham

Meinhold, Red
See Meinhold, Carl

Meir, Golda
See Meyerson, Golda [Mabovitz]

Meiring, Desmond
See Rice, Desmond Charles

Meirion
See Owen, William

Meissner, Hans-Otto 1909- [CA]
German author
* Roos, Hans

Meissonier, Jean Louis Ernst 1815-1891
* [The] Great Painter of Little Pictures

[Der] Meister
See Goethe, Johann Wolfgang von

[Der] Meister
See Wieland, Christoph Martin

Meister, Dutch
See Meister, Karl Daniel

Meister Karl
See Leland, Charles Godfrey

Meister, Karl Daniel 1891-1967 [BE]
American baseball player
* Meister, Dutch

Meister Leu
See Jud, Leo

Meistermann, Georg 1911- [ART]
*German painter and stained-glass window
designer*
* G. M.

Meistier, Gilbert 1900- [NOJ]
American jazz musician
* Blind Gilbert

Meistrell, Harland W. 1900-1962 [BBH]
American lacrosse coach
* Meistrell, Tots

Meistrell, Tots
See Meistrell, Harland W.

Meixel, Merten Merrill 1887- [BE]
American baseball player
* Meixel, Moxie

Meixel, Moxie
See Meixel, Merten Merrill

Mejia Victores, Oscar Humberto 1931?-
[TI 8-22-83]
Guatemalan president
* [The] Scholar

Mejias, Jose 1914- [HPPN]
Spanish bullfighter
* Bienvenida
* Pepe

Mejias, Juan 1936- [HPPN]
Spanish bullfighter
* Bienvenida

Mejias y Jimenez, Antonio 1922-1975
[GS, OCS]
Venezuelan-born bullfighter
* Bienvenida [Welcome]

Mejias y Jimenez, Manuel 1912-1938
[GS]
Spanish bullfighter
* Bienvenida [Welcome]

Mejias y Rapela, Manuel 1884-1964
[GS]
Spanish bullfighter
* Bienvenida [Welcome]

[El] Mejicano [The Mexican]
See Rodriguez, Gonzalo

Mejorcito [Best Little One]
See Ortega, Santiago

Mekum, Friedrich 1491-1546 [WBD]
German theologian
* Myconius [or Mykonius], Friedrich

Mel
See McGeoghegan, Thomas J.

Mel, Mary
See Bennett, Mary E.

Mel-Bonis
See Bonis, Melanie

Melamed, Samuel Max 1885- [NAA]
Russian-born editor and author
* Krieger, Maxime
* Krieger, William

[The] Melancholy
See Cowley, Abraham

[The] Melancholy Jacques
See Rousseau, Jean-Jacques

Melanchthon, Philip
See Schwarzert, Philipp

Melanie
See Safka, Melanie

Melanie
See Schekeryk, Melanie Safka

Melanie, [Sister]
See Willingham, Saundra

Melanter
See Blackmore, Richard Doddridge

Melanthon
See Schwarzert, Philipp

Melaro, Constance L[oraine] 1929- [CA]
American educator and author
* Bruce, Monica

Melaro, H. J. M. 1928- [ASC]
American composer and producer
* Melaro, Speed

Melaro, Speed
See Melaro, H. J. M.

Melata, Don Macario Padua
See Amat, Felix

Melati Van Java
See Sloot, Marie

Melba, Nellie
See Mitchell, Helen Porter

Melbourne, Ivor
See Ransome, L. E.

Melcher, Bertha Corbett 1872-? [NAA]
American writer and poet
* Mother of the Sun-Bonnet Babies

Melcher, Gilbert W[ayne] 1910- [NAA]
American writer
* Aachen, C. V.
* Burt, Gill
* G. W. M.
* McCall, Creighton

Melcher, John 1924?- [TI 9-27-82]
American politician
* PAC Man

Melchior, Lauritz 1890-1973 [HPPN]
Danish singer and actor
* [The] Great Dane
* [The] Magnificent Giant

Melchiorre, Eugene 1927- [BB]
American basketball player
* Melchiorre, Squeaky

Melchiorre, Squeaky
See Melchiorre, Eugene

Meldon, H. Percy
See O'Hara, H. Percy

Meldrum, David S. 1865-? [NPS]
Author and journalist
* Foulis, Hugh
* Looker-On

Meldrum, Helen Myers
See Scott, Helen Myers

Meldrum, James
See Broxholme, John Franklin

Mele, Albert Ernest 1915- [BE]
American baseball player
* Mele, Dutch

Mele, Dutch
See Mele, Albert Ernest

Mele, Sabath Anthony 1922- [BE, PB, SMG]
American baseball manager
* Mele, Sam

Mele, Sam
See Mele, Sabath Anthony

Melekh, Igor Yakovlevich 20th c. [EE]
Russian intelligence agent
* Stephens, Peter

[El] Melenas [The Long-Haired One]
See Rojas, Jose

Melendez Melendez, Gabriel 1930- [GS]
Mexican bullfighter
* Coca Cola

Melendez Valdes, Juan 1754-1817
[DNNF, DNNS, FFF, HPPN]
Spanish poet
* Restaurador del Parnaso
* [The] Restorer of Parnassus

Melesh, Alex
See Melesher, Alexander

Melesher, Alexander 1890-1949 [SC]
Russian-born actor
* Melesh, Alex

Melesigenes
See Homer

Melesville
See Duveyrier, Anne Honore Joseph

Melford
See Reeve, John

Melhorn, Nathan R. 1871-? [NAA]
American clergyman, editor, author
* Etan, Raymond

Meli, Giovanni 1740-1815 [DNNS, FFF, SN]
Sicilian poet
* [The] Anacreon of Sicily
* [The] Sicilian Anacreon
* [The] Sicilian Theocritus

Melies, Georges 1861-1938
French motion picture pioneer
* [The] Alchemist of Light
* [The] Jules Verne of the Cinema
* King of the Phantasmagoria
* Magician of the Screen

Melikian, Saro
See Teilerian, Salomon

Melikow, Loris
See Hofmannsthal, Hugo [Laurenz
August Hofmann Edler] Von

Melillo, Oscar Donald 1899-1963 [AS, BE]
American baseball player
* Melillo, Ski
* Melillo, Spinach

Melillo, Ski
See Melillo, Oscar Donald

Melillo, Spinach
See Melillo, Oscar Donald

Melim, Mary M. 19th c. [PA]
Author
* McComb, Florence

Melin, A. K. 20th c.
American frisbee manufacturer
* Melin, Spud

Melin, Spud
See Melin, A. K.

Melina the Greek
See Mercouri, Maria Amalia

Melis, Jose
See Melis Guiu, Jose

Melis Guiu, Jose 1920- [ASC]
Cuban-born American musician
* Melis, Jose

Melissa
See Brereton, Jane Hughes

Mell
See Lazarus, Mel

Mell, Mr. [code name used during
World War II]
See Marshall, George Catlett

Mell, Patrick Hues 1814-1888 [HPPN]
American clergyman
* [The] Prince of Parliamentarians

Mellalieu, James S.
See Margerison, John S.

Melland, Frank Hulme [WWL]
British author
* Africanus

Melland, Sylvia 20th c. [ART]
British painter and etcher
* S. M.

Melle
See Oldeboerrigter, Melle Johannes

Mellen, Grenville 1799-1841 [DNA]
American author and poet
* Reverie, Reginald

Mellen, Ida M[ay] 1877-? [CA]
American author
* De Mar, Esmeralda
* Otis, George

Mellenbruch, Giles Edward 1911- [ASC]
American musician
* Giles, Johnny

Meller, Raquel
See Lopez, Francisca Marquez

Meller, Raquel
See Marquez Lopez, Francisca

Mellett, John Calvin 1888- [IA]
American author and journalist
* Brooks, Jonathan

Mellick, Henry George 1857-1937
[CCL]
Canadian author
* Timothy, a Country Boy

[The] Mellifluous Doctor
See Bernard of Clairvaux

Mellilo, James 1880?-1946 [AS]
American bowler
* Smith, James

Mellin, Charles 1597?-1649 [BI]
French painter
* LeLorrain, Charles

Mellin, Jeanne 1929- [CA]
American horsewoman, artist, illustrator
* Herrick, Jean Mellin

Melling, Leonard 1913- [AW]
British author
* Luminus

Mellinger, Frederick N. 1914?- [HPPN]
American fashion designer and retailer
* Mr. Frederick

Mellinger, Max
See Mellinger, Maxon

Mellinger, Maxon 1906-1968 [SC]
American actor
* Mellinger, Max

Mello, Francisco de 17th c. [SN]
*Spanish army officer and Governor of the
Netherlands*
* Thomiris

Mellody, Honey
See Mellody, William [Billy]

Mellody, William [Billy] 1884-1919
[AS, BX, RBE]
American boxer
* Mellody, Honey

Mellon, Andrew William 1855-1937
[HPPN]
*American financier, business executive,
statesman*
* [The] Mentor of Aluminum
* [The] Ubiquitous Financier of the
Universe
* [The] World's Second Richest Man

Mellon, Bunny
See Mellon, Rachel

Mellon, Rachel 20th c.
Wife of American financier Paul Mellon
* Mellon, Bunny

Mellos, Ilias 1904- [EWL]
Greek author
* Venezis, Ilias

Mellot, Claude
See Taylor, Tom

Mellowed Militant
See Shahn, Ben[jamin]

Melman, Bud
See DeForest, Calvert

Melman, Larry
See DeForest, Calvert

Melmoth, Courtney
See Pratt, Samuel Jackson

Melmoth, Sebastian
See Wilde, Oscar [Fingal O'Flahertie
Wills]

Melmoth, William 1666-1743 [NPS]
Author and attorney
* Cicero, Marcus Tullius

Melmoth, William 1710-1799 [DEL,
FFF, HPPN, PA]
British author
* Fitzosborne, [Sir] Thomas
* [A] Late Eminent Advocate

Meloan, Molly
See Meloan, Paul

Meloan, Paul 1888-1950 [BE]
American baseball player
* Meloan, Molly

Meloney, Franken [joint pseudonym
with William Brown Meloney]
See Franken, Rose

Meloney, Franken [joint pseudonym
with Rose Franken]
See Meloney, William Brown

Meloney, William Brown 1903- [AW]
American author, producer, director
* Grant, Margaret [joint pseudonym
with Rose Franken]
* Meloney, Franken [joint pseudonym
with Rose Franken]

Melrose, Julia
See Lemon, Mrs. Henry W.

Melrose, Julia
See Semon, Julia Melrose

Mels, August
See Cohn, Martin

Mel'shin, L.
See Iakubovich, Petr Filippovich

[The] Melting Scot
See Mackercher, Daniel

Melton, Barry 1949- [RO2]
American musician
* [The] Fish

Melton, Clifford George 1912- [BE]
American baseball player
* Melton, Mountain Music

Melton, Mel
See Melton, Orrin

Melton, Mountain Music
See Melton, Clifford George

Melton, Mrs. William [FFF]
Entertainer
* Mitchell, Dolly

Melton, Orrin 1916?-1982 [FIR]
American entertainment executive
* Melton, Mel

Melton, Reuben Franklin 1917-1971
[BE]
American baseball player
* Melton, Rube

Melton, Rube
See Melton, Reuben Franklin

Melton, William Edwin 1945- [SMG]
American baseball player
* Belt'n Melt'n

Meltzer, Bernard 1917?-
American radio broadcaster
* Uncle Bernie

Meltzer, Gregor 1501-1531 [WBD]
German jurist
* Haloander, Gregor

Meltzer, R. 1945- [HPPN]
American author
* Borneo Jimmy
* Murphy, Audie, Jr.

Melvier, Laurent
See Lucas, Gerald

Melville, Ada
See Hazleton, Mrs. J. H.

Melville, Alan
See Caverhill, William Melville

Melville, Andrew 1545-1622 [HPPN]
Scottish theologian
* [The] Father of Scottish Presbytery

Melville, Andrew
See Emm, Andrew

Melville, Anne
See Potter, Margaret [Newman]

Melville, Captain
See McCallum, Francis McNeill

Melville, Herman 1819-1891 [UH]
American author
* [The] American Rabelais

Melville, Ida
See Young, Ida Melville

Melville, Jean
See Cummins, Mary Warmington

Melville, Jean-Pierre
See Grumbach, Jean-Pierre

Melville, Jennie
See Butler, Gwendoline [Williams]

Melville, Kathleen 1904- [F2]
Actress
* O'Regan, Katherine

Melville, Lewis
See Beckford, William

Melville, Lewis [joint pseudonym with Reginald Hargreaves]
See Benjamin, Lewis Saul

Melville, Lewis [joint pseudonym with Lewis Saul Benjamin]
See Hargreaves, Reginald [Charles]

Melville, Lewis
See Thackeray, William Makepeace

Melville, Maud
See Anderson, Mrs. Oscar

Melville, Pearl
See Baldwin, Mrs. Walter S.

Melville, Scotty
See Melville, Tom

Melville, Tom 20th c. [CCL]
Canadian poet
* Melville, Scotty

Melville, Virginia
See Murray, Mrs. J. J.

Melville, Winifred
See Wright, Winifred

Melvin, G. S. 1886-1946 [BMH]
Scottish-born comedian
* Donovan, Hugh

Melwood, Mary
See Lewis, E. M.

[A] Member
See Arthington, Maria

[A] Member
See Foe, Daniel

[A] Member
See Milnor, William

[A] Member
See Sparkes, Joseph

[A] Member
See Wakefield, Edward Gibbon

[The] Member for Kidderminster
See Lowe, Robert [Viscount Sherbrooke]

Member for Paris
See Murray, Eustace Clare Grenville

Member for Treorky
See Bowen-Rowlands, Ernest Bowen Brown

[A] Member of Both Syndicates
See Whewell, William

[A] Member of Brazen-Nose College, Oxford
See Ellis, John

[A] Member of CSMV
See Lawson, Ruth Penelope

[A] Member of Gray's Inn
See Leigh, P. Brady

[A] Member of His Flock
See Edmonds, Richard, Jr.

[A] Member of Lincoln's Inn
See Raithby, John

[A] Member of Neither Syndicate
See Addington, Henry [First Viscount Sidmouth]

[A] Member of One of the Societies
See Dale, W.

[A] Member of Parliament
See Abbott, Charles [Second Baron Colchester]

[A] Member of Parliament
See Carte, [Rev.] Thomas

[A] Member of Parliament
See Ellis, George

[A] Member of Parliament
See Grant, [Sir] Francis [Lord Cullen]

[A] Member of Parliament
See Hay, William

[A] Member of Parliament
See Mackworth, [Sir] Humphrey

[A] Member of Parliament
See Seton, William, Jr.

[A] Member of Parliament
See Wilkes, John

[The] Member of Sussex
See Curteis, Edward Jeremiah

[A] Member of the American Bar
See Greenleaf, Simon

[A] Member of the Arcadian Academy of Rome
See Walker, Joseph Cooper

[A] Member of the Athenian Society
See Dunton, John

[A] Member of the Bar
See Hart, C. W.

[A] Member of the Bar
See Kip, Leonard

[A] Member of the Board of Directors of Girard College
See Packard, Frederick Adolphus

[A] Member of the Board of Education
See Whitney, James S.

[A] Member of the Boston Bar
See Austin, Ivers James

[A] Member of the Boston Bar
See Chandler, Peleg Whitman

[A] Member of the Boston Society of the New Jerusalem
See Parsons, Theophilus

Member of the Burton Hunt
See Braddon, [Sir] Henry Yule

Member of the Chiltern Hundreds
See Lucy, [Sir] Henry William

[A] Member of the Church at Oxford
See Palmer, [Sir] William

[A] Member of the Church of England
See Appleyard, Ernest Silvanus

[A] Member of the Church of England
See Hopkins, William

[A] Member of the Church of England
See Leslie, Charles

[A] Member of the Church of England
See Palmer, [Sir] William

[A] Member of the Church of England
See Thornthwaite, J. A.

[A] Member of the Church of God at Oxford
See Palmer, [Sir] William

[A] Member of the Church of Scotland
See Findlay, Robert

[A] **Member of the Church of Scotland**
See Pollock, John

Member of the Class of '67
See Benjamin, Park

[A] **Member of the College of Justice**
See Spink, William

[A] **Member of the College of Justice**
See Watson, James

[A] **Member of the College of Physicians**
See Moyle, John

[A] **Member of the College of Physicians**
See Pearson, Richard

[A] **Member of the College of Physicians**
See Wainewright, Jeremiah

[A] **Member of the College of Surgeons of London**
See Crisp, Edwards

[A] **Member of the Committee**
See Fyffe, Charles Alan

[A] **Member of the Committee of Peace in Paris**
See Gibbs, George M.

[A] **Member of the Congregation**
See Moule, Joseph

[A] **Member of the Consociation and Association**
See Todd, [Rev.] Jonathan

[A] **Member of the Convention of Royal Burghs of Scotland**
See Scott, David Dundas

[A] **Member of the Corporation**
See Eliot, Samuel Atkins

[A] **Member of the Council**
See Goffe, Joseph

[A] **Member of the Council of the National Union**
See Charley, [Sir] William Thomas

[A] **Member of the Duddingston Curling Society**
See Ramsay, James

[A] **Member of the Episcopal Church**
See Seabury, Samuel

[A] **Member of the Established Church**
See Bayley, [Sir] John

[A] **Member of the Executive Committee**
See Mott, Jordan L.

[A] **Member of the Faculty of Advocates**
See Alison, [Sir] Archibald

Member of the Faculty of Advocates
See Ferguson, Charles

[A] **Member of the First Syndicate**
See Peacock, George

[A] **Member of the Gild**
See Stothert, James Augustine

[A] **Member of the H. of A. of Newfoundland**
See Morris, Patrick

[A] **Member of the Honourable House of Commons**
See Foe, Daniel

[A] **Member of the House of Commons**
See Arnall, William

[A] **Member of the House of Commons**
See Benson, William

[A] **Member of the House of Commons**
See Gordon, Thomas

[A] **Member of the House of Commons**
See Hervey, John [Baron Hervey of Ickworth]

[A] **Member of the House of Commons**
See Pulteney, William [Earl of Bath]

[A] **Member of the House of Commons**
See Steele, [Sir] Richard

[A] **Member of the House of Commons**
See Webb, Philip Carteret

[A] **Member of the Howard Association of New Orleans**
See Robinson, William L.

[A] **Member of the Humane Society**
See Davis, Wendell

[A] **Member of the Incorporated Society**
See Stephens, David

[A] **Member of the Inner Temple**
See Wilson, James Holbert

[A] **Member of the Irish Bar**
See Kelly, Peter Burrowes

[A] **Member of the Lower House of Convocation**
See Atterbury, Francis

[A] **Member of the Massachusetts Bible Society**
See Holmes, Abiel

[A] **Member of the Massachusetts Historical Society**
See McKean, Joseph

[A] **Member of the New Athenian Society**
See Dunton, John

[A] **Member of the New York Bar**
See Hall, Abraham Oakey

[A] **Member of the N.Y. Geneal. and Biog. Society**
See Kip, William Ingraham

[A] **Member of the Political Economy Club**
See Torrens, Robert

[A] **Member of the Press**
See Ure, George P.

[A] **Member of the Protestant Episcopal Association, in South Carolina**
See Purcell, [Rev.] Henry

[A] **Member of the Rock County Bar**
See Bundy, J. M.

[A] **Member of the Roxburghe Club**
See Dibdin, Thomas Frognall

[A] **Member of the Said Synod**
See Thomson, [Rev.] John

[A] **Member of the Same**
See Simmons, [Rev.] George Frederick

[A] **Member of the Scottish Bar**
See Grahame, James

[A] **Member of the Society**
See Arnee, Frank

[A] **Member of the Society**
See Ash, Edward

[A] **Member of the Society**
See Spence, David

[A] **Member of the Society for Constitutional Information**
See Jones, [Sir] William

[A] **Member of the Society of Antiquaries of Scotland**
See M'Neill, Archibald

[A] **Member of the Society of Friends**
See Bowden, James

[A] **Member of the Society of Friends**
See Collier, William Bengo

[A] **Member of the Suffolk Committee**
See Gassett, Henry

[A] **Member of the Synod of United Original Seceders**
See Graham, John

[A] **Member of the Univ. of Camb.**
See Nixon, Edward John

[A] **Member of the University**
See Ayscough, Francis

[A] **Member of the University**
See Blayney, Benjamin

[A] **Member of the University**
See Jones, [Sir] William

[A] **Member of the University of Cambridge**
See Burdon, William

[A] **Member of the University of Cambridge**
See Dodd, Philip Stanhope

[A] **Member of the University of Cambridge**
See Jones, [Sir] William

[A] **Member of the University of Cambridge**
See Long, George

[A] **Member of the University of Cambridge**
See Rowe, Samuel

[A] **Member of the University of Oxford**
See Bowles, William Lisle

[A] Member of the University of Oxford
See Churton, Ralph

[A] Member of the University of Oxford
See Golightly, Charles Portales

[A] Member of the University of Oxford
See Keble, John

[A] Member of the University of Oxford
See Wintle, Thomas

[A] Member of the Vermont Bar
See Thompson, Daniel P.

[A] Member of the Worcester Angler's Society
See George, William

[A] Member of Trinity College, Cambridge
See Bentley, Richard

Members of the Mercurie, etc.
See Smith, R. C.

[Un] Membre du Parlement
See Merivale, John Herman

[Un] Membre du Parlement d'Angleterre
See Parnell, [Sir] Henry Brooke

Meminger, Dean 1948- [BB]
American basketball player
* [The] Dream

Meminger, Edward Lynn 1905-1975 [SC]
American actor and producer
* Lynn, Eddie

Memnon
See Ramses V [or Rameses]

Memon, Fahmida 1948- [IAW]
Pakistani writer and poet
* Yakub, Tasnim

Memon, Munir Ahmed 1943- [IAW]
Pakistani author
* Manik

Memor, Andreas
See Gramont, Antoine Agenor Alfred, Duc de

[The] Memorable
See Eric II

Memoriter
See Pae, David

Memory
See Mayer, Bernadette

[The] Memory Man
See Bottle, J. M.

Memphis Bill Mallory
See Mallory, William Neely

Memphis Bill Terry
See Terry, William Harold

Memphis Blues Boy
See Nix, Willie

[The] Memphis Heat
See Parrish, Larry

Memphis Jim
See Dorsey, Thomas A[ndrew] [Tommy]

[The] Memphis Mesmerizer
See Presley, Elvis Aron

Memphis Minnie
See Douglas, Lizzie

Memphis Mose
See Dorsey, Thomas A[ndrew] [Tommy]

Memphis Pal Moore
See Moore, Thomas Wilson

Memphis Slim
See Chatman, John Len

Memphis Slim
See Davenport, Charles [Edward]

Memphis Willie B
See Borum, William [Willie]

Mena, Juan de 1411-1456 [DEP, DNNS, SN]
Spanish poet
* [The] Spanish Ennius

Mena, Maria Cristina
See Chambers, Maria Cristina

[The] Menace
See Conner, Dennis

[The] Menace
See Tueart, Dennis

Menalcas
See Clark, Bracy

Menalcas
See Drury, Henry Joseph Thomas

Menander 4th c. BC [DNNS, RH]
Athenian poet
* Creator of the New Comedy
* [The] Prince of New Comedy

Menander 2nd c. BC [WBD]
Greek king of India
* Milinda

Menander
See Morgan, Charles [Langbridge]

Menander
See Paine, Robert Treat, Jr.

Menander
See Warton, Thomas

Menantes
See Hunold, Christian Friedrich

Menaptus, Wilhelm [PA]
Author
* Insulaneus

Menasco, John
See Sellers, Connie Leslie, Jr.

Menasco, Norman
See Guin, Wyman [Woods]

Menchan, W. McKinley 1898- [IAW]
American educator and writer
* Judge
* Mack

Mencher, Murray 1898- [ASC, PMJ]
American composer
* Murry, Ted

Mencke [or Mencken], Johann Burkhard 1674-1732 [WBD]
German author and historian
* Von der Linde, Philander

Mencken, H. L.
See Mencken, Henry Louis [Harry]

Mencken, Henry Louis [Harry] 1880-1956 [CAA, HPPN, LC]
American author and editor
* Allison, George W.
* Anderson, C. Farley
* Archer, Herbert Winslow
* Bell, W. L. D.
* Bellamy, Atwood C.
* Brownell, Charles F.
* Brownell, John F.
* D'Aubigy, Pierre
* De Verdi, Marie
* Della Torre, Raoul
* [The] Disturber of the Peace
* Drayham, William
* Dryham, James
* Fink, William
* Gilray, J. D.
* Hatteras, Amelia
* Hatteras, Owen [joint pseudonym with George Jean Nathan]
* Henderson, F. C.
* [The] Irreverent Mr. Mencken
* Jefferson, Janet
* McLoughlin, R. B.
* Mencken, H. L.
* Morgan, Harriet
* Peregoy, George Weems
* Ratcliffe, James P.
* [The] Ringmaster
* [The] Sage of Baltimore
* Thompson, Francis Clegg
* Trimball, W. H.
* W. G. L.
* Watson, Irving S.
* Wharton, James
* Woodruff, Robert W.

Menczer, Augustus 1856-1882 [HPPN]
American saloon keeper
* [The] Kid
* Menczer, Gus

Menczer, Gus
See Menczer, Augustus

Mendel
See Smith, James Samuel

Mendel, David 1789-1850 [WBD]
German historian and theologian
* Neander, Johann August Wilhelm

Mendel, Jo [house pseudonym, Albert Whitman & Co.]
See Bond, Gladys Baker

Mendel, Jo [house pseudonym, Albert Whitman & Co.]
See Gilbertson, Mildred [Geiger]

Mendele Mocher Sforim [Mendele the Bookseller]
See Abromowitz, Sholem Yakob

Mendeloff, Gershon 1894-1970 [BX, EJS, RBE]
British boxer
* [The] Aldgate Sphinx
* Lewis, Kid
* Lewis, Ted

Mendelsohn, Felix, Jr. 1906- [CA]
American author
* Mayfair, Franklin

Mendelsohn, Oscar [Adolf] 1896- [CA]
Australian author and composer
* Milsen, Oscar

Mendelson, Harold 1920-1970 [BEW, HPPN]
American actor
* [The] Man Behind the Sixty-Four Thousand Dollar Question
* March, Hal

Mendelssohn, [Jakob Ludwig] Felix 1809-1847 [SN, WBD]
German composer
* Mendelssohn-Bartholdy, Felix
* Meritis, Felix
* [The] Mozart of the Nineteenth Century

Mendelssohn, Moses 1729-1785 [HN, SN, WBD]
German philosopher
* [The] German Socrates
* [The] Jewish Socrates
* Nathan
* [The] Plato of Germany
* [The] Socrates of the Jews

Mendelssohn-Bartholdy, Felix
See Mendelssohn, [Jakob Ludwig] Felix

Mendenhall, John Rufus 1948- [SMG]
American football player
* Mendenhall, Mendy

Mendenhall, Mendy
See Mendenhall, John Rufus

Mendes, Black Cat
See Mendes, Joe

Mendes, Catulle 1841-1909 [CD]
French poet, author, playwright
* Valerius, C.

Mendes, Joe [GW]
American rodeo performer
* Mendes, Black Cat

Mendesia, Gracia 16th c. [BI]
Portuguese philanthropist
* De Luna, Beatrice

Mendez, Alice
See Stovall, Alice

Mendez, Cachin
See Mendez, Oscar

Mendez, Joe
See Mendez, Jose

Mendez, Jose 20th c. [OBW]
American baseball player
* Mendez, Joe

Mendez, Oscar 1945- [RBE]
Argentinian boxer
* Mendez, Cachin

Mendez Pinto, Ferdinand 1509?-1583 [DNNF, FFF, SN]
Portuguese traveller
* [The] Prince of Liars

Mendicant, Arch?
See Aldiss, Brian W[ilson]

[The] Mendicant Bard
See Lewis, Stuart

Mendis, Gehan Dixon 1955- [DC]
Sri Lankan cricketer
* Mendis, Jack
* Mendis, Mendo
* Mendis, Sergio

Mendis, Jack
See Mendis, Gehan Dixon

Mendis, Judith [PA]
Author
* Chailness

Mendis, Mendo
See Mendis, Gehan Dixon

Mendis, Sergio
See Mendis, Gehan Dixon

Mendl, Gladys
See Schuetze, Gladys Henrietta [Raphael]

Mendl, Gladys
See Schutze, Gladys Henrietta

Mendl, Lady
See De Wolfe, Elsie

Mendonca, Susan 1950- [CA]
British-born author
* Sinclair, Rose

Mendoza, Daniel 1764-1836 [HPPN]
British boxer
* [The] Father of Scientific Boxing
* [The] Fighter from Whitechapel
* Mendoza the Jew

Mendoza, Mario 1950- [BE]
Mexican-born baseball player
* Aizpuru, Mario

Mendoza, Pedro Gonzalez de 1428-1495 [UH]
Spanish prelate, statesman, soldier
* [The] Great

Mendoza the Jew
See Mendoza, Daniel

Mendoza Romero, Maria Luisa 1934- [IAW]
Mexican author
* Catay
* China

Mendrock, William
See Nicote, Piere

Mendsoale, My Heele
See Taylor, John

Menedemos 4th c. BC [RH, SN]
Greek philosopher
* [The] Eretrian Bull

Menefee, Jocko
See Menefee, John

Menefee, John 1868-1953 [BE]
American baseball player
* Menefee, Jocko

Meneghel, Antonietta 1893- [BBD]
Italian opera singer
* Monte, Toti Dal

Menelik II
See Mariem, Sahala

Menen, Aubrey
See Menon, Salvator Aubrey Clarence

Menenius
See Starkey, Digbey Pilot

Menes, [or Mena] [HPPN]
King of Egyptian Thinite dynasty
* [The] First Pharaoh
* [The] King of Upper Egypt and Lower Egypt
* Narmer

Meneses, Enrique 1929- [CA]
Spanish journalist
* Carvajal, Ricardo
* Crain, Jeff

Menetrier, Charles 1804-? [HPPN]
French author and critic
* Listener, Richard

Menezes, Tobias Barreto De 1839-1889 [HPPN]
Brazilian poet, critic, jurist
* Barreto, Tobias

Mengel, Paul Fritz 1810-? [HPPN]
Swedish author and journalist
* Bla, Ivar
* Goeran

Mengele, [Dr.] Josef 1911-? [WP 3-8-85]
German physician during Nazi regime
* [The] Angel of Auschwitz
* [The] Angel of Death
* Fischer, [Dr.] Fritz
* Gregor, [Dr.] Helmut
* Gregori, Gregorio?
* Wollman, [Dr.] Enrique?

[Il] Menghino del Violoncello
See Gabrielli, Domenico

Mengs, Anton Rafael 1728-1779 [SN]
German painter
* [The] Prince of Bohemian Artists

Menippus
See Easton, Thomas

Menippus
See Sealy, Robert

Menken, Adah Bertha
See Fuertes, Dolores Adios

Menken, Adah Isaacs
See Fuertes, Dolores Adios

Menken, Adah Isaacs
See Theodore, Adah Bertha

Mennin, Peter
See Mennini, Peter

Mennini, Peter 1923- [BBD, IPA]
American composer
* Mennin, Peter

Menon, Salvator Aubrey Clarence 1912-
[EWL]
British author
* Menen, Aubrey

Menor, Gypsy Marpessa Dawn 1935-
[IBW]
American singer and actress
* Dawn, Marpessa

Menosky, Leaping Mike
See Menosky, Michael William

Menosky, Michael William 1894- [BE]
American baseball player
* Menosky, Leaping Mike

Menot, Michael 15th c. [SN]
French clergyman
* [The] Golden Tongued

Menotti, Gian Carlo 1911-
Italian-born American composer
* Wizard of the Opera

[The] Men's Dior
See Savini-Brioni, Gaetano

Menter, Sophie
See Popper, Frau

Mentor
See Fenelon, Francois de Salignac de la
Mothe

Mentor
See Jones, Frank H.

Mentor
See Lake, Kenneth R[obert]

Mentor
See Quincy, Josiah

Mentor
See Urner, Nathan Dane

[The] Mentor of Aluminum
See Mellon, Andrew William

[The] Mentor of Serpentine Dance
See Fuller, Loie

[The] Mentor of the Algonquin
See Case, Frank

[The] Mentor of the Atomic Bomb
See Groves, Leslie R.

[The] Mentor of the Drake Swindle
See Hartzell, Oscar Merril

[The] Mentor of the Mustache
See Burdette, Robert Jones

**[The] Mentor of the New York Safety
Fund Plan**
See Forman, Joshua

[The] Mentor of the Pop Art Movement
See Oldenburg, Claes

[The] Mentor of the Rule of Reason
See White, Edward Douglass

Mentzer
See Fischart, Johann

Mentzer, Josephine Esther 20th c. [NY
10-13-85]
American business executive
* Lauder, Estee

Menzel, Johanna
See Meskill, Johanna Menzel

Menzel, Roderich 1907- [CA, IAW]
Czech-born author
* Morawa, Michael
* Parma, Clemens

Menzies, Archibald 1943- [HPPN]
Scottish undersea researcher
* Menzies, Jock

Menzies, Jock
See Menzies, Archibald

Menzies, Sutherland
See Stone, Elizabeth

Meoli, Randolph Bart, Jr. 1951- [SMG]
American baseball player
* Meoli, Rudy

Meoli, Rudy
See Meoli, Randolph Bart, Jr.

Mephibosheth
See Pordage, Samuel

Mephistopheles
See Speer, Albert

[The] Mephistopheles of the Ocean
See Schley, Winfield Scott

Merak, A. J.
See Glasby, John [Stephen]

Merande, Doro
See Matthews, Dora

Merante, Mrs. Louis [FFF]
Entertainer
* Richard, Zina

Merauges
See Chanorrier, Antoine

Mercado, Jose Ramon 1863-1911 [CW]
Puerto Rican poet and journalist
* Momo

Mercantelli, Eugene Rudolph 1906-
[BE]
American baseball player
* Rye, Eugene Rudolph
* Rye, Half-Pint

[A] Mercantile Man
See Lumsden, James

Mercator
See Anderson, James

Mercator
See Brewer, William A.

Mercator
See Ellice, Edward

Mercator
See Loyd, Samuel Jones [First Baron
Overstone]

Mercator, Gerhardus
See Kremer, Gerhard

Mercator, J. A.
See Chapman, John A.

Mercator, John
See Kaufmann, Walter

Mercator, Nicolaus
See Kaufmann, Nicolaus

Merce, Antonia 1891?-1936 [BEW]
Argentinian-born dancer
* Argentina

Mercedes, [Sister] 1846-? [DNA]
American poet
* Alexander, [Rev.] Richard W.

Mercein, Eleanor
See Kelly, Eleanor Mercein

Mercer, Cecil William 1885-1960 [CC,
EMD, LC]
British author
* Yates, Dornford

Mercer, Frances
See Hills, Frances Elizabeth

Mercer, George Barclay 1874-1903 [AS,
BE]
American baseball player
* Mercer, Win

Mercer, Guy Carleton 1877-1958
[HPPN]
American actor, producer, playwright
* Guy, Carleton

Mercer, [Major] James 1734-1804
[HPPN]
Scottish poet, scholar, soldier
* Peter the Plowman

Mercer, Jean 1941- [CA]
American author
* Lester, Gene

Mercer, Jessie 20th c. [CA]
American author
* Shannon, Terry

Mercer, Joan Bodger 1923- [CA]
American-born author
* Bodger, Joan

Mercer, John Louis 1869-1941 [BE]
American baseball player
* Johnson, John Louis
* Johnson, Youngy

Mercer, Margaret 1791-1846 [HPPN]
American author
* [The] Hannah More of America

Mercer, Mike
American football player
* Mercer, Moco

Mercer, Moco
See Mercer, Mike

Mercer, Win
See Mercer, George Barclay

[A] Merchant
See Carr, Frank

[A] Merchant
See Hanway, Jonas

[A] Merchant
See Kauffman, C. H.

[A] Merchant
See Koster, John Theodore

Merchant, Andy
See Merchant, James Anderson

[The] Merchant Evangelist
See Crittenton, Charles Nelson

Merchant, James Anderson 1950-
[SMG]
American baseball player
* Merchant, Andy

[The] Merchant King
See Solomon, Saul

Merchant, Matthew
See Wood, W. S.

[A] Merchant of Boston
See Hooper, Samuel

[The] Merchant of Menace
See Biondolillo, Gaspare

[The] Merchant of Menace
See Mayer, Arthur Loeb

[The] Merchant of the Ruby
See Warbeck, Perkin

[The] Merchant of Venom
See Rickles, Don

Merchant, Paul
See Ellison, Harlan [Jay]

[The] Merchant Prince
See Morris, Robert

[The] Merchant Prince of the Middle Ages
See Coeur, Jacques

Merchant, T.
See Dibdin, Thomas John

Merchant, Vivien
See Thomson, Ada

Merchantius
See Le Marchant, Jacques

Mercier, Bartholomew 1734-1799 [SN]
French bibliographer
* [The] Ulysses of Bibliographers

Merck, Johann Heinrich 1741-1791
[SN]
German author
* Merck, Mephistopheles

Merck, Mephistopheles
See Merck, Johann Heinrich

Mercouri, Maria Amalia 1925- [BP]
Greek actress
* Greece's Gifted Gypsy
* [The] Greek Goddess
* Melina the Greek
* Mercouri, Melina
* Mercouri, Mercurial

Mercouri, Melina
See Mercouri, Maria Amalia

Mercouri, Mercurial
See Mercouri, Maria Amalia

Mercurial Miles Davis
See Davis, Miles Dewey, Jr.

Mercurio, Skang
See Mercurio, Walter

Mercurio, Walter 1896-1972 [BBH]
Italian-born American bowler
* Mercurio, Skang

Mercurius ?-535 [DNNS]
Pope
* John II

Mercurius
See Roos, Philipp Peter

Mercurius Rusticus
See Dibdin, Thomas Frognall

Mercury
See Allen, Cecil J[ohn]

Mercury
See Baird, George D.

Mercury
See Bruce, Leslie C.

Mercury, Currier
See Brooks, Charles Timothy

Mercury, Fred
See Bulsara, Frederick

Mercutio
See Winter, William

[The] Mercutio of Actors
See Lewis, William Thomas

Mercy, Lee
See Mercy, Leland, Jr.

Mercy, Leland, Jr. 1942- [BA]
American educator
* Mercy, Lee

[The] Mercy-Killer
See More, [Sir] Thomas

[La] Mere
See Alfassa, Mirra

[The] Mere Dandini
See George IV

Mere des Pauvres [Mother of the Poor]
See Epremesnil, Francoise Augustine d'

[La] Mere des Peuples
See Margaret [or Marguerite] of France

[A] Mere Irishman
See Killen, James Bryce

Meredith, Anne
See Malleson, Lucy Beatrice

Meredith, Arnold
See Hopkins, Kenneth

Meredith, Billy 20th c. [NN]
British soccer player
* [The] Welsh Wizard

Meredith, Buford 20th c. [OBW]
American baseball player
* Meredith, Geetchie

Meredith, Burgess
See Burgess, George

Meredith, C. Leon
See Aiken, George L.

Meredith, Crad
See Levy, Joseph [Joe]

Meredith, Dandy Don
See Meredith, Joe Don

Meredith, David William
See Miers, Earl Schenck

Meredith, Geetchie
See Meredith, Buford

Meredith, Hal
See Blyth, Harry

Meredith, James 1933- [HPPN]
American social reformer
* [The] Most Segregated Negro in America

Meredith, James E. 1892-1957 [AS, TF]
American track and field athlete
* Meredith, Ted

Meredith, Jeff
See Loney, Glenn [Meredith]

Meredith, Joe Don 1938- [FB]
American football player and sportscaster
* Meredith, Dandy Don

Meredith, Lee
See Sauls, Judi Lee

Meredith, Louisa 1812-? [PA]
Author
* Twomby, Louisa

Meredith, Lucille
See Couch, Lizzie

Meredith, Mark 20th c. [WWL]
British writer
* M. M.

Meredith, Mary G.
See Webb, Mary

Meredith, Nicolete
See Stack, Nicolete Meredith

Meredith, Owen
See Bulwer-Lytton, Edward Robert

Meredith, Peter
See Worthington-Stuart, Brian Arthur

Meredith, Robert C[hidester] 1921-
[CA]
American educator and author
* Lucero, Roberto

Meredith, Scott
See Feldman, Scott

Meredith, Ted
See Meredith, James E.

Meredyth, Bess
See MacGlashan, Helen

Meredyth-Starmer, Marjorie 1914-
[IAW]
British author
* Lyon, Marjorie

Merena, John Joseph 1909- [BE]
American baseball player
* Merena, Spike

Merena, Spike
See Merena, John Joseph

Meres, Francis 1565-1647 [NPS]
Clergyman and author
* Gallant Young Juvenal

Meretricious
See Watkinson, Frank

Mereweather, [Rev.] John Davies
19th c. [HPPN]
British clergyman
* [A] Working Clergyman

Merewether, Art[hur Francis] 1902-
[BE]
American baseball player
* Merewether, Merry

Merewether, Merry
See Merewether, Art[hur Francis]

Merezhkovskaya, Zinaida Nikolaevna
1869-1945 [WBD]
Russian poet, author, critic
* Hippius

Mergenthaler, Ottmar 1854-1899
[HPPN]
German-American inventor
* [The] Father of the Linotype

[La] Meri
See Hughes, Russell Meriwether

Merian, Leon
See Megerdichian, Vahan Leon

Merillat, Louis A., Jr. ?-1948 [FB]
American football player
* [The] Forward Pass King

Merimee, Prosper 1803-1870 [HPPN]
French author and historian
* [Un] Des Quarante
* Gazul, Clara
* L'Estrange, Joseph
* Maglanowich, Hyacinthe

Merin, Peter
See Bihalji-Merin, Oto

Merino, Ricardo Montalban 1920-
[HPPN]
Mexican actor
* Montalban, Ricardo

Merisi [or Merisio], Michelangelo
1565?-1609 [WBD]
Italian painter
* Caravaggio, Michelangelo da

Merit, Modest
See Thackeray, William Makepeace

Meritis, Felix
See Mendelssohn, [Jakob Ludwig] Felix

Meriton, Peter
See Hunter, [Alfred] John

Meritt, Lucy Shoe 1906- [CA]
American archaeologist and author
* Shoe, Lucy T.

Merivale, John Herman 1779-1844
[HPPN]
British barrister, translator, poet
* [Un] Membre du Parlement

Meriwether, Del
See Meriwether, Wilhelm Delano

Meriwether, Elizabeth [Avery] 1832-1917
[DNA]
American author and playwright
* Edmonds, George

Meriwether, Wilhelm Delano 1943-
[IBW]
American physician
* Meriwether, Del

Merkle, Fred[erick Charles] 1888-1956
[HPPN, SR]
American baseball player
* Merkle, George
* One of the Gamest Players in the
  Game

Merkle, George
See Merkle, Fred[erick Charles]

Merland, Oliver 20th c. [MBF]
British author
* Collins, Colin
* Grant, Douglas
* Pound, Singleton

Merlin
See Murray, David Christie

Merlin, [Brother]
See Reuss, Theodor

Merlin
See Tennyson, Alfred [First Baron
Tennyson]

Merlin
See Wilder, Alexander

Merlin, Antoine Christophe 1762-1833
[WBD]
French politician
* Merlin de Thionville

Merlin, David
See Moreau, David Merlin

Merlin de Douai
See Merlin, Philippe Antoine

Merlin de Thionville
See Merlin, Antoine Christophe

Merlin, Jan
See Wasylewski, Jan

Merlin, Jean Raymond 1510-1578 [PA]
Author
* Mouray

Merlin, Joanna
See Ratner, Joann

[The] Merlin of England
See Lilly, William

[The] Merlin of Scotland
See Learmont, Thomas

Merlin, Philippe Antoine 1754-1838
[WBD]
French jurist and politician
* Merlin de Douai

Merlin the Second
See Henry, David

Merlini, [The] Great
See Rawson, Clayton

Merlino, Merlin Mesmer
See Carpenter, Donald G.

Merlinus Anglicus
See Lilly, William

Merlotti, Claudio 1533-1604 [WBD]
Italian musician and composer
* Da Correggio, Claudio
* Merulo, Claudio

Merlyn, Arthur
See Blish, James [Benjamin]

[The] Merm
See Zimmerman, Ethel Agnes

[The] Mermaid
See Mary, Queen of Scots

Merman, Ethel
See Zimmerman, Ethel Agnes

Merman, Sureshot
See Zimmerman, Ethel Agnes

Mero, Caldius Biberius
See Domitius Ahenobarbus, Lucius

Meronek, Smiley
See Meronek, William

Meronek, William 1917- [CEI]
Canadian-born hockey player
* Meronek, Smiley

Merrall, Mary
See Lloyd, Mary

Merrall, Queenie
See Lloyd, Mary

Merrett, John Donald 1908-1954 [BI,
HPPN]
British adventurer
* Chesney, Ronald

Merriam, Florence A.
See Bailey, Florence M.

Merriam, Henry Clay 1837-1912
[HPPN]
American soldier
* [The] Father of the Merriam Pack

Merrick, David
See Margulois, David

Merrick, Hugh
See Meyer, Harold Albert

Merrick, Jim
See Fearn, C. Eaton

Merrick, John ?-1890
British victim of neurological disorder
* [The] Elephant Man

Merrick, John Mudge 19th c.   [HPPN]
American clergyman
* J. M. M.
* M.

Merrick, Leonard
See Miller, Leonard

Merrick, M. M.
See Cecily, [Mother]

Merrick, Mark
See Rathborne, St. George Henry

Merrick, May
See Bell, May Merrick

Merrick, Williston
See Ford, Williston Merrick

Merridew, Arthur
See Gaskoin, Charles Jacinth Bellairs

Merrifield, Mrs. Reuben
Author
* Forrester, Izola

Merril, Judith
See Grossman, Josephine Judith

Merrill, Al
See Merrill, C. Allison

Merrill, Antoinette June 1912-   [CA]
American author
* Merrill, Toni

Merrill, Bob
See Lavan, Henry

Merrill, C. Allison 1924-   [BBH]
American skiing coach
* Merrill, Al

Merrill, Carl 20th c.   [WP 11-5-85]
American baseball coach
* Merrill, Stump

Merrill, Dick
See Merrill, Henry Tindall

Merrill, Dina
See Hutton, Nedinia

Merrill, H. R.   [PA]
Author
* Old Scout

Merrill, Helen
See Milcetic, Helen

Merrill, Henry Tindall 1894?-1982   [CA, DF 11-3-82, TI 11-15-82]
American aviator and author
* Merrill, Dick

Merrill, James Milford 1847-1936
American author
* Old Timer
* Parrish, Wendal
* Redwing, Morris

Merrill, Jan 1956-
American track and field athlete
* [The] Mummy

Merrill, Linda 1951?-
American ballerina
* Ashley, Merrill

Merrill, Linda
See Rosenthal, Linda

Merrill, P. J.
See Roth, Holly

Merrill, Robert
See Miller, Morris

Merrill, Royal W.   [FFF]
American writer
* Lounger in the Lobby

Merrill, Stump
See Merrill, Carl

Merrill, Toni
See Merrill, Antoinette June

Merrill, Tony
See Merrill, Walter

Merrill, Walter 20th c.
Actor
* Merrill, Tony

Merriman, Alex
See Silverberg, Robert

Merriman, Beth
See Taylor, Demetria

Merriman, Citation
See Merriman, Lloyd Archer

Merriman, Henry Seton
See Scott, Hugh Stowell

Merriman, Lloyd Archer 1924-   [BE]
American baseball player
* Merriman, Citation

Merriman, Mansfield 1848-1925   [DNA]
American author and engineer
* Licks, H. E.

Merriman, Maurice
See Hook, Samuel Clarke

Merriman, Pat
See Atkey, Philip

Merrit, Katarin Markov
See Ackerman, Forrest J[ames]

Merriton, Mervyn
See Coade, H. C.

Merritt, Aime
See Ackerman, Forrest J[ames]

Merritt, E. B.
See Waddington, Miriam

Merritt, Henry 19th c.   [HPPN]
British author
* [A] Connoisseur

Merritt, [John] Howard 1894-1955   [BE]
American baseball player
* Merritt, Lefty

Merritt, James 1926-   [HPPN]
American jazz musician
* Merritt, Jymie

Merritt, Jymie
See Merritt, James

Merritt, Lefty
See Merritt, [John] Howard

Merritt, Onera Amelia 1887-   [BI]
American-British author
* Weston, Mary

Merritt, Si
See Hoyer, Mildred N.

Merriweather, Bob
See Merriweather, Rozier

Merriweather, Maceo
See Merriweather, Major

Merriweather, Magnus
See Talbot, Charles Remington

Merriweather, Major 1905-1953   [BWW, EJ]
American singer
* Big Maceo
* Merriweather, Maceo

Merriweather, Rozier 20th c.   [BWW]
American musician
* Little Maceo
* Merriweather, Bob

Merriwell, Frank
See Whitson, John Harvey

Merry Andrew
See Borde, Andrew

Merry Andrew
See Freeman, John Henry Gordon

Merry, Captain, U. S. N.
See Rymer, James Malcolm

[The] Merry Devil of Edmonton
See Fabell, Peter

Merry, Doctor
See Wyndham, J.

Merry Droll
See Killigrew, Thomas

Merry, Felix
See Duyckinck, Evert Augustus

Merry Fellow, Dick
See Gardiner, Richard

Merry, Harley
See Britton, Ebenezer

[The] Merry Magician
See Christman, Paul C.

Merry, Malcolm J.
See Rymer, James Malcolm

[The] Merry Mexican
See Trevino, Lee

[The] Merry Mime
See Mills, Hayley

[The] Merry Monarch
See Bodie, Sam

[The] Merry Monarch
See Charles II

[The] Merry Monarch
See Kalakaua, David

[The] Merry Mortician
See Hoyt, Waite Charles

Merry, Robert 1755-1798 [DEP, FFF, NPS, RH]
British poet and playwright
* Della Crusca
* O. P. Q.
* Oziosi [The Lazybones]

Merry, Robert
See Stearns, J. N.

Merry Saint
See More, [Sir] Thomas

Merry, Tom
See Mecham, William

Merryfellow, Malthus
See Clark, Charles

Merrypebble, Mr.
See Gladstone, William Ewart

Mersan, Omer 20th c. [WP 10-14-84]
Bulgarian implicated in plot to assassinate Pope John Paul II
* Marshal, Omer

Merson, Billy
See Thompson, William Henry

Merson, H. A.
See Watson, Harold

Mertes, Bernard James 1923- [SMG]
American football player and coach
* Mertes, Bus

Mertes, Bus
See Mertes, Bernard James

Mertes, Samuel Blair 1872-1945 [BE]
American baseball player
* Mertes, Sandow

Mertes, Sandow
See Mertes, Samuel Blair

Merton, Ambrose, Gent.
See Thoms, William John

Merton, Collette
See Mazzoletti, Collette Helene

Merton, Giles
See Curran, Mona [Elisa]

Merton, John
See La Varre, John Merton

Merton, Richard
See Moses, Richard

Merton, Thomas [James] 1915-1968 [BI, CA, LC]
French-born clergyman, author, poet
* Louis, [Father] M.

Merton, Tristram
See Macaulay, Thomas Babington [First Baron Macaulay]

Mertz, Barbara [Gross] 1927- [AW, CA, WD]
American author and historian
* Michaels, Barbara
* Peters, Elizabeth

Mertz, George
See Mushrush, Obadiah

Merulan
See Joyce, Robert Dwyer

Merulo, Claudio
See Merlotti, Claudio

Merva
See Kilgallen, Mary

Merville, Pierre Francois 1783-1853 [PA]
Author
* Camus

Mervyn, William
See Pickwoad, William

Merwe, A. v.d.
See Geyl, Pieter [Catharinus Arie]

Merwin, [W.] Sam[uel], Jr. 1910- [ESF, SFP, WGT]
American author
* Curson, Stanley
* Lee, Matt
* Saturn, Sergeant [house pseudonym]
* Sprague, Carter

Merwin, W. S.
See Merwin, William Stanley

Merwin, William Stanley 1927- [WYA]
American author
* Merwin, W. S.

Mesa
See Selimovic, Mehmed

Mesa, Johnny
See Meza, Johnny

Mesaros, Stjepan 1903?-
Croatian-born political activist
* Nelson, Steve

[La] Meschinerie
See Enoch, Pierre

Mesec, Iggy
See Mesec, Ignatius

Mesec, Ignatius 20th c. [EF]
American football player
* Mesec, Iggy

Meserole, Fannie
See Lynch, Mrs. Samuel

Meserve, Arthur Livermore 1838-1896
American author
* Cuyler, Duke
* Saco

Meservey, Robert Preston 1918- [BEW, EMT, HPPN, IPA]
American actor and singer
* Preston, Robert

[El] Mesias [The Messiah]
See Benete, Antonio

Mesirow, Milton 1899-1972 [DAM, HPPN, PMJ, WWJ]
American jazz musician
* [The] Ananias of Jazz
* Mezzrow, Mezz
* Mezzrow, Milton

Meske, Eunice Boardman 1926- [CA]
American author and educator
* Boardman, Eunice

Meskill, Johanna Menzel 1930- [CA]
German-born historian and author
* Menzel, Johanna

Meskin, Morton 1916- [WECO]
American cartoonist
* Morton, Mort, Jr.

Meslin, Michael Neure ?-1677 [PA]
Author
* Laurent

Mesmer, Friedrich Anton 1734-1815 [HN, HPPN, SN]
Austrian physician
* [The] Father of Animal Magnetism
* [The] Father of Mesmerism

Mesritz, Andre 1909- [FC]
British actor
* Morell, Andre

Messager, Charles 1882-1971 [CA, CD]
French poet, author, playwright
* Vildrac, Charles

[The] Messalina of Germany
See Barbara of Cilley

[The] Messalina of the North
See Catherine II

Messell, Hank
See Everts, Henry

[The] Messenger
See Baker, George

Messenger, Andrew Warren 1898- [BE]
American baseball player
* Messenger, Bud

Messenger, Bob
See Messina, Roberto

Messenger, Bobby
See Messenger, Charles Walter

Messenger, Bud
See Messenger, Andrew Warren

Messenger, Charles Walter 1884-1951 [BE]
American baseball player
* Messenger, Bobby

Messenger, Lilian T. R. 1844-? [FFF, IP]
American poet
* Clifton, Zena

Messenger of Allah
See Poole, Elijah

Messenger of the King
See Dix, Dorothea Lynde

[The] Messenger of Wandsbeck
See Claudius, Matthias

Messenhauser, Casar Wenzel 1813-? [HPPN]
German author
* March, Wenzeslaus

Messent, Charles 1857-? [WWL]
British author
* Baring, Max

Messer, [Dr.] Asa 1769-1836 [HPPN]
American educator
* [The] Cunning President

Messer, August 1867-1937 [WBD]
German philosopher and author
* Friedwalt, A.

Messer, Mona Naomi Anne [Hocking] 20th c. [WW]
Author
* Hocking, Anne

Messer, Samuel G. 1911- [FC, HT, ITA]
American actor
* Middleton, Robert

Messersmith, Andy
See Messersmith, John Alexander

Messersmith, Bluto
See Messersmith, John Alexander

Messersmith, Channel
See Messersmith, John Alexander

Messersmith, John Alexander 1945- [BE, PB, SMG]
American baseball player
* Messersmith, Andy
* Messersmith, Bluto
* Messersmith, Channel

[The] Messiah
See Crowley, Edward Alexander

Messick, Dale
See Messick, Dalia

Messick, Dalia 1906-
American cartoonist
* Messick, Dale

Messidi, Kathy[anne] Groehn el- 1946- [CA]
American writer
* Cosseboom, Kathy Groehn

Messier, Mark 1961- [SMG]
Canadian-born hockey player
* Messier, Mess

Messier, Mess
See Messier, Mark

Messier, Pierre le 1600?-1670? [HPPN]
French actor and theatrical producer
* Bellerose

Messina, Roberto 20th c. [WF]
Italian actor
* Messenger, Bob

Messina, Santo 1927- [ITA]
American entertainment executive
* Sina, Sandy

[La] Messine
See Adam, Juliette

Messinger, Buddy
See Messinger, Melvin Joe

Messinger, Melvin Joe 1909-1965 [SC]
American actor
* Messinger, Buddy

Messino, Wee Willie
See Messino, William

Messino, William 1917- [BLB]
American underworld figure
* Messino, Wee Willie

Messmann, John 20th c. [SFL]
Author
* Nicole, Claudette

Mesta, Perle 1889-1975 [HPPN]
American diplomat
* [The] Hostess With the Mostes'

Mestayer, Mrs. W. A. [FFF]
Entertainer
* Vaughn, Theresa

Mestayer, William
See Hoppe, William

Mester, Jorge 1935- [HPPN]
Mexican conductor
* [The] Portrait in Sound

Meston, William 1688?-1745 [HPPN]
Scottish poet
* Grimmus, Jodocus
* Quidam

Mestre Jhan
See Gallus, Johannes

Mestre, Noza
See Nick, Inocencio da Costa

Mestrovic, Ivan 1883-1962 [HPPN]
Yugoslav sculptor
* [The] Patriot Sculptor

Meta
See Tomkiewicz, Mina

Metacomet ?-1676 [HPPN, WBD]
American Indian chieftain
* King Philip
* Philip
* Pometacom

Metador
See Alden, William L.

[The] Metal Market Man
See Stahl, Charles

[The] Metaphysical Jester
See Shaw, George Bernard

Metaphysics
See Alden, Henry Mills

Metastasio
See Trapassi, Pietro Antonio Domenico Bonaventura

Metcalf, George
See Johnson, George Metcalf

Metcalf, Jack 1717-1810 [HPPN]
British soldier, smuggler, engineer
* Blind Jack of Knaresborough

Metcalf, Suzanne
See Baum, L[yman] Frank

Metcalfe, Francis
See Egerton, J. K.

Metcalfe, Frederick 1817?-? [IP]
British clergyman and author
* [The] Oxonian

Metcalfe, Ralph 1910- [HPPN]
American politician and track athlete
* One of the World's Fastest Humans

Metcalfe, Thomas 1780-1855 [FFF]
American politician
* Old Stone Hammer

Metcalfe, [Captain] W. C.
See Lawrence, Christopher George Holman

Metellus, Quintus Caecilius 2nd c. BC [WBD]
Roman general and politician
* Macedonicus
* Numidicus

Metellus, Quintus Caecilius 1st c. BC [SN, WBD]
Roman general
* Creticus
* Pius

Meteor
See Foe, Daniel

Metesky, George
See Hoffman, Abbott [Abbie]

Metesky, George Peter 1900- [HPPN, TI 10-18-82]
Lithuanian-American criminal
* F. P.
* [The] Mad Bomber
* Manhattan's Mad Bomber

Meteyard, Eliza 1824?-1879 [DEL, DNNF, FFF]
British author
* Silverpen

Metha, Frank Joseph 1913- [BE]
American baseball player
* Metha, Scat

Metha, Scat
See Metha, Frank Joseph

Metheny, Arthur Beauregard 1915- [BE]
American baseball player
* Metheny, Bud

Metheny, Bud
See Metheny, Arthur Beauregard

Methodicus, Doctor
See Bassol, John

[The] Methodist Agassiz
See Marcy, Oliver

[A] Methodist Preacher in Cambridgeshire
See Berridge, John

[A] Methodist Saint
See Asbury, Francis

Methodius 826-885 [DNNS]
Saint
* [The] Apostle of the Slavs

Methold, Kenneth Walter 1931- [AW, CA, HPPN]
British author
* Cade, Alexander
* Kent, Alexander

Methuen, [Sir] Algernon Methuen Marshall
See Stedman, Algernon Methuen Marshall

Methuen, John
See Bell, John Keble

Methuselah
See Shaw, George Bernard

Methven, Ralph
See Thomson, Ralph Methven

Metidieri, Carlos 1942- [AES]
Brazilian soccer player
* Metidieri, Little Mouse
* Metidieri, Topolino

Metidieri, Little Mouse
See Metidieri, Carlos

Metidieri, Topolino
See Metidieri, Carlos

Metin
See Agca, Mehmet Ali

Metius, Adriaan 1571-1635 [WBD]
Dutch mathematician
* Adriaanszoon, Adriaan

Metkovich, Catfish
See Metkovich, George Michael

Metkovich, Catso
See Metkovich, George Michael

Metkovich, George Michael 1921- [BE, BN]
American baseball player
* Metkovich, Catfish
* Metkovich, Catso

Metlova, Maria 20th c. [SFL, WGT]
Author
* Hathaway, Louise

Metress, James F[rancis]
See Metress, Seamus P.

Metress, Seamus P. 1933- [CA]
American author and anthropologist
* Metress, James F[rancis]

Metro, Charles [Charlie]
See Moreskonich, Charles

Metropolitan Opera, Mr.
See Robinson, Francis [Arthur]

[The] Met's Big Man
See Ticker, Reuben

[The] Met's Second Caruso
See Ticker, Reuben

[The] Met's Young Master
See Levine, James

Metsanurk, Mait
See Hubel, Eduard

Metternich, Clemens Wenzel Lothar 1773-1859 [SN]
Austrian statesman
* [The] Autocrat of Austria

Metz, Alice [FFF]
Entertainer
* Harrison, Alice

Metz, Lois Lunt 1906- [CAP]
American author and educator
* Lunt, Lois

Metz, Louis [FFF]
Entertainer
* Harrison, Louis

Metzetti, Sylvester Ricardo 1896- [F1, F2, FC]
American actor
* Talmadge, Richard

Metzger, Butch
See Metzger, Clarence Edward

Metzger, Clarence Edward 1952- [SMG, WWB]
American baseball player
* Metzger, Butch

Metzger, Ros
See Metzger, Roswell William

Metzger, Roswell William 1906- [ASC]
American musician
* Metzger, Ros

Meulenbelt-Luber, Henrietta C. A. 1889- [LAO]
Dutch author
* Luber, Jet

Meunier, Francois
See Miller, Francis Trevelyn

Meurice, Blanca
See Von Block, Bela

Meurisse, Lucien 1890-1972 [SC]
Actor
* Mussiere, Luciene

Meusel, Emil Frederick 1893-1963 [AS, DGS, PB]
American baseball player
* Meusel, Irish

Meusel, Irish
See Meusel, Emil Frederick

Meusel, Languid Bob
See Meusel, Robert William [Bob]

Meusel, Long Bob
See Meusel, Robert William [Bob]

Meusel, Robert William [Bob] 1896- [BE]
American baseball player
* Meusel, Languid Bob
* Meusel, Long Bob

Meusnier, Georges [IP]
Author
* Robert, Karl

Meux, [Sir] Hedworth
See Lambton, Hedworth

Mew, Thomas Joseph, III [Tommy] 1942- [CAR]
American artist
* [The] Mad Diarist

Mewburn, Martin
See Hitchin, Martin Mewburn

[The] Mexican Nightingale
See Peralta, Angela

[The] Mexican Spitfire
See Velez De Villalobos, Guadelupe

[The] Mexican Washington
See Juarez, Benito Pablo

[The] Mexican Wildcat
See Ybarra, Jose

Mexico's Charlie Chaplin
See Moreno, Mario

Meyer, Adolph
See Goldschmidt, Meyer Aaron

Meyer, [Dr.] Alexander 20th c. [HPPN]
Russian entertainer
* [The] Prewar Rocking Chair Sensation of Russia

Meyer, Annie Nathan 1867-1951 [HPPN]
American playwright
* Nathan, Annie

Meyer, August Friedrich 1811-? [IP]
German poet
* Brunold, Friedrich

Meyer, Benny
See Meyer, Bernhard

Meyer, Bernhard 1888-1974 [BE]
American baseball player
* Meyer, Benny
* Meyer, Earache

Meyer, Berta 1878-1952 [BBD]
German opera singer
* Morena, Berta

Meyer, Bonnie
See Thorne, Mrs. J. H.

Meyer, Charles R[obert] 1926- [CA]
American writer, photographer, public relations consultant
* Jay, Donald

Meyer, Conrad Ferdinand 1825-1898 [WBD]
Swiss poet and author
* Meyer-Ziegler, Conrad Ferdinand

Meyer, David Harold 1930-1980 [HT, SW]
American actor
* Janssen, David

Meyer, Dorothy Quick 1900- [WGT]
American author
* Quick, Dorothy

Meyer, Dutch
See Meyer, Lambert Daniel

Meyer, Dutch
See Meyer, Leo Robert

Meyer, Earache
See Meyer, Bernhard

Meyer, Edward 20th c.
American army officer
* Meyer, Shy

Meyer, George
See Mundviller, Joseph-Louis

Meyer, Gustav 1868-1932 [HFF, SFP]
Austrian-born author
* Meyrink, Gustave

Meyer, H. K. Houston
See Meyer, Heinrich

Meyer, Hans
See Meyer, John F.

Meyer, Harold Albert 1898- [CA, WD]
British author, photographer, translator
* Merrick, Hugh

Meyer, Heinrich 1904- [CA]
German-born author
* Barlow, Robert O.
* Meyer, H. K. Houston

Meyer, Hy
See Meyer, Hyman

Meyer, Hyman 1875-1945 [SC]
American actor
* Meyer, Hy

Meyer, Jacob 1735-1795 [BI, HPPN]
American scientist
* Philadelphia, Jacob

Meyer, Jean Shepherd 1929- [SAT]
American author and illustrator
* Berwick, Jean

Meyer, Jerome Sydney 1895-1975 [CA, SAT]
American editor and writer
* Jennings, S. M.

Meyer, Johann Georg 1813-1886 [WBD]
German painter
* Meyer von Bremen

Meyer, John F. 20th c. [BBH]
American sailboat racer
* Meyer, Hans

Meyer, John M. 1897- [NAA]
German-born naturalist, author, editor
* Morley, Mathew

Meyer, June
See Jordan, June

Meyer, Lambert Daniel 1915- [BE]
American baseball player
* Meyer, Dutch

Meyer, Leo Robert 1898- [BI, FB]
American football coach
* Meyer, Dutch
* Old Iron Pants
* [The] Saturday Fox

Meyer, Lou[is] 1905?- [HPPN]
American auto racer
* [The] Office Builder

Meyer, Mathilde 1851-1933 [BEW]
German-born theatrical performer
* Cottrelly, Mathilde

Meyer, Russ 1922?- [HPPN]
American film producer and director
* [The] King of the Nudie Movie
* Mr. X

Meyer, Russell Charles 1923- [BE]
American baseball player
* [The] Mad Monk

Meyer, Shy
See Meyer, Edward

Meyer, Siegbert 1841-? [IP]
German author
* Siegmey

Meyer, Sophie Frederika Elizabeth
[FFF]
Author
* May, Sophie

Meyer the Bug
See Suchowljansky, Maier

Meyer von Bremen
See Meyer, Johann Georg

Meyer-Ziegler, Conrad Ferdinand
See Meyer, Conrad Ferdinand

Meyerbeer, Giacomo
See Beer, Jakob Liebmann

Meyerle, Levi Samuel 1849-1921 [BE]
American baseball player
* Meyerle, Long Levi

Meyerle, Long Levi
See Meyerle, Levi Samuel

Meyerowitz, Bruce 1937?- [NY 9-12-85]
American radio personality
* Cousin Brucie
* Morrow, Bruce

Meyers, Chief
See Meyers, John Tortes

Meyers, John Tortes 1880-1971 [BE, PB]
American baseball player
* Meyers, Chief

Meyers, Louie
See Myers, Louis

Meyers, Roy [Lethbridge] 1910-1974
[CAP]
British physician and author
* Lethbridge, Rex

Meyers, Sidney 1906-1969 [BI]
American director
* Stebbins, Robert

Meyerson, Bess 1924?- [HPPN]
American actress and politician
* Meyerson, Queen Bess

Meyerson, Golda [Mabovitz] 1898-1978
[BI, CA, IPA]
Israeli prime minister
* Meir, Golda

Meyerson, Queen Bess
See Meyerson, Bess

Meyerson, Tuvia
See Shulvass, Moses A.

Meyerstein, E. H. W.
See Meyerstein, Edward Harry William

Meyerstein, Edward Harry William
1889-1952 [MBL, WWL]
British author
* E. H. W. M.
* Meyerstein, E. H. W.

Meyler, Walter Thomas 19th c. [PI]
Irish poet
* W. T. M.

Meynell, Alice [Christiana Gertrude Thompson] 1847-1922 [TLC]
British author, editor, poet
* Oldcastle, Alice
* Phillimore, Francis
* Thompson, A. C.

Meynell, Clyde
See Van Straubenzee, Clyde

Meynell, Laurence [Walter] 1899- [CC, HPPN, WW]
British author and editor
* Baxter, Valerie
* Bedford, Sidney
* Eton, Robert
* Ludlow, Geoffrey
* Tring, A. Stephen

Meynell, Wilfrid 1852-1948 [FFF]
British author and journalist
* Oldcastle, John [or Jonathan]

Meyrick, [Canon]
See Meyrick, Frederick James

Meyrick, Frederick James 1871-?
[LAO]
British clergyman and author
* Meyrick, [Canon]

Meyrink, Gustave
See Meyer, Gustav

Meysenburg, Janet B. 1884-1955 [FC, HCA]
American actress
* Beecher, Janet

Meza, Johnny 20th c. [RBE]
American boxer
* Mesa, Johnny

Mezaros, Mihaly 1940?- [WP 3-31-83]
Hungarian circus performer
* Michu

Mezzofanti, Giuseppe 1774-1849 [DHA, FFF, HPPN, SN]
Italian linguist and prelate
* [The] Briareus of Languages
* [The] Living Pentecost
* [A] Monster of Languages
* [La] Pentecote Vivante
* [The] Walking Polyglot

Mezzrow, Mezz
See Mesirow, Milton

Mezzrow, Milton
See Mesirow, Milton

M'Fall, Haldane 1860-? [NPS]
Soldier, author, art critic
* Dane, Hal

M'Govan, James
See Honeyman, William C.

Mia
See Parsons-Irwin, Maureen

Miali, Roberto 20th c. [WF]
Italian actor
* Wilson, Jerry

Miall, Edward 1809-1881 [HPPN]
British clergyman and journalist
* [An] Editor Off the Line

Miall, Robert
See Burke, John [Frederick]

Miami's Unmiraculous Miracle Worker
See Shula, Don[ald]

Micantoni, Adriano 20th c. [WF]
Italian actor
* Anthony, Mike

Micelotta, Mickey
See Micelotta, Robert Peter [Bob]

Micelotta, Robert Peter [Bob] 1928- [BE]
American baseball player
* Micelotta, Mickey

Michael
See Wheeler, Joseph Trank

Michael, Albert
See Lyons, A. Neil

Michael Angelo de Kermesses
See Laar [or Laer], Pieter van

[The] Michael Angelo of America
See Cabrera, Miguel

[The] Michael Angelo of Battle Scenes
See Cerquozzi, Michael Angelo

[The] Michael Angelo of France
See Cousin, Jean

[The] Michael Angelo of France
See Puget, Pierre

[The] Michael Angelo of Modern Literature
See Hugo, Victor Marie

[The] Michael Angelo of Music
See Gluck, Christoph Willibald

[The] Michael Angelo of Opera
See Wagner, [Wilhelm] Richard

[The] Michael Angelo of Sculptors
See Puget, Pierre

[The] Michael Angelo of Sculptors
See Slodtz, Rene Michael

[The] Michael Angelo of Spain
See Cano, Alonso [or Alonzo]

[The] Michael Angelo of the Lyre
See Palestrina, Giovanni Pierluigida

[The] Michael Angelo of the Middle Ages
See Arnolfo di Cambio

[The] Michael Angelo of the Reformation
See Luther, Martin

Michael, Big Mike
See Michael, J. E.

Michael, Blaunpayn 13th c. [NPS]
British poet
* [The] Cornish Poet

Michael, Gene Richard 1938- [BE]
American baseball player
* Michael, Stick

Michael, J. E. 20th c.
American football player
* Michael, Big Mike

[The] Michael Jackson of Christian Music
See Grant, Amy

Michael, James
See Scagnetti, Jack

Michael, Jerry Dean 1938?- [BI]
American automobile executive and transvestite
* Carmichael, Geraldine Elizabeth

Michael, John
See Sempill, Ernest

Michael, John D.
See Krown, Kevin

Michael, Judith [joint pseudonym with Michael Fain]
See Barnard, Judith

Michael, Judith [joint pseudonym with Judith Barnard]
See Fain, Michael

Michael, Manfred
See Winterfeld, Henry

Michael, Miona 1870-1944 [HPPN]
American founder of the Memorial Poppy movement
* [The] Poppy Lady

Michael of Kent
See Von Reibnitz, Marie Christine

Michael of Walachia ?-1601 [WBD]
Prince of Walachia
* [The] Bold

Michael, Paul
See Sempill, Ernest

Michael, Ralph
See Shotter, Ralph Champion

Michael, Stick
See Michael, Gene Richard

Michael X
See De Freitas, Michael

Michael I ?-845 [HPPN]
Byzantine emperor
* Rhangabe

Michael II ?-829 [DNNS, FFF, WBD]
Byzantine emperor
* [The] Amorian
* [Le] Begue
* [The] Stammerer

Michael III 9th c. [WBD]
Byzantine emperor
* [The] Drunkard

Michael IV 11th c. [DNNS, WBD]
Byzantine emperor
* [The] Paphlagonian

Michael IX ?-1320 [HPPN]
Byzantine emperor
* Palaeologus

Michael V Calaphrates 11th c. [DNNS]
Byzantine emperor
* [The] Calker

Michael VI Stratioticus 11th c. [DNNS]
Byzantine emperor
* [The] Warrior

Michael VII 11th c. [HPPN]
Byzantine emperor
* Ducas

Michael VIII 1234-1282 [HPPN]
Byzantine emperor
* Palaeologus

Michaeles, M. M.
See Golding, Morton J[ay]

Michaelis, Karin
See Stangeland, Katharina Marie [Bech-Brondum] Michaelis

Michaels, Barbara
See Mertz, Barbara [Gross]

Michaels, Carolyn Leopold
See Leopold, Carolyn Clugston

Michaels, Casimir Eugene
See Kwietniewski, Casimir Eugene

Michaels, Cass
See Kwietniewski, Casimir Eugene

Michaels, Dale
See Rifkin, Shepard

Michaels, Fern [joint pseudonym with Mary Kuczkir]
See Anderson, Roberta

Michaels, Fern [joint pseudonym with Roberta Anderson]
See Kuczkir, Mary

Michaels, Joe
See Saltzman, Joseph [Joe]

Michaels, Kasey
See Seidick, Kathryn A[melia]

Michaels, Kristin
See Williams, Jeanne

Michaels, Lynn
See Strongin, Lynn

Michaels, Peter
See Jackson, Carol

Michaels, Ralph
See Filicchia, Ralph

Michaels, Ruth Gruber
See Gruber, Ruth

Michaels, Steve
See Avallone, Michael [Angelo], Jr.

Michaelson, John August 1893-1968
[BE]
Finnish-born baseball player
* Michaelson, Mike

Michaelson, Mike
See Michaelson, John August

Michalska, Marianna 1899?-1959 [F1,
F2, FC, HPPN]
Polish-born American entertainer
* [The] Box Office Girl
* Gray, Gilda

Michalske, August 1903-1983 [FB,
SMG]
American football player
* Michalske, Iron Mike
* Michalske, Mike

Michalske, Iron Mike
See Michalske, August

Michalske, Mike
See Michalske, August

Michaud, Georges 1888-1970 [SC]
French actor
* Milton, Georges

Michaux, Elder
See Michaux, Solomon Lightfoot

Michaux, Solomon Lightfoot
Evangelist
* Michaux, Elder

Miche, Giuseppe
See Bochenski, Joseph M.

Micheaux, Larry 20th c. [SI 11-28-83]
American basketball player
* Mean, Mr.

Michel
See Churchill, Peter

[Le] Michel Ange des Bamboches
See Laar [or Laer], Pieter van

[Le] Michel Ange Francais
See Cousin, Jean

[Le] Michel Ange Francais
See Puget, Pierre

Michel, Claude 1738-1814 [WBD]
French sculptor
* Clodion

Michel de Notredame 1503-1566
French astrologer
* Nostradamus

Michel, F. Fernand 19th c. [IP]
French author
* Real, Anthony

Michel, John B. 1917- [ESF, WGT]
American author
* Conway, Bowen
* Cooke, Arthur [joint pseudonym with
  C. Kornbluth, R. Lowndes, E. Balter,
  D. Wollheim]
* Raymond, Hugh
* Tara, John
* Woods, Lawrence [joint pseudonym
  with Donald A(llen) Wollheim]

Michel, Maria Johanna 1932- [OP]
Dutch-born opera singer
* Bazuky, Maya

Michel, Tom
See Michel, William

Michel, William 20th c. [EF]
American football player
* Michel, Tom

Michelangeli
See Michelangeli, Arturo Benedetti

Michelangeli, Arturo Benedetti 1920-
[MS]
Italian musician
* Michelangeli

Michelangelo [or Michael Angelo]
See Buonarroti, Michelangelo [or
Michael Angelo]

[The] Michelangelo of Capitol Hill
See Cox, Allyn

Michelborne, John 18th c. [IP]
Irish historian and author
* [A] Gentleman Who Was In the
  Town

Micheli, Ornella 20th c. [WF]
Italian film editor
* Christie, Donna

Micheli, Ugo 1883-? [HPPN]
Italian boxer
* Kelly, Hugo

Michelin, Edouard 1859-1940 [HPPN]
*French industrialist, inventor,
philanthropist*
* [The] Father of the Balloon Tire
* [The] Father of the Pneumatic Rubber
  Tire

Michell, [Sir] Francis 17th c. [SN]
* Greedy, Justice

Michell, Grace [Angove] 1839-? [IP]
British author
* Angove, Grace

Michell, Nicholas 1807-1880 [IP]
British author and poet
* [An] Essayist on the Passions

Michelle, Niccolaiih el-
See Flemming, Herb

Michelman, Stanley 20th c. [TI 3-12-84]
American attorney
* Stork, Mr.

Michels, Nicholas Aloysius 20th c.
[SFL, WGT]
Author
* Mikalowitch, Nicolai

Michi, Orazio 1595?-1641 [BBD]
Italian composer
* Della Arpa

Michie, Archibald [IP]
British critic
* Robinson, Jack

Michieli [or Micheli], Dominico ?-1130
[HN]
Doge of Venice
* [The] Terror of the Greeks

Michiels, Alfred John Xavier 1813-
[HPPN]
French author
* Perrier, Jules

[The] Michigan Assassin
See Kiecal, Stanislaus

[The] Michigan Terror
See Heston, William M. [Willie]

[The] Michigan Wildcat
See Wolgust, Adolphus

Michigan's First Black Congressman
See Diggs, Charles C., Jr.

Michnick, Irwin S. 1928- [EJ]
American jazz musician
* Leigh, Mitch

Michon, Pierre 1610-1685 [PA]
Author
* Bocadelot, Abbe

Michu
See Mezaros, Mihaly

Mick
See Wilson, Michael

[The] Mick
See Yule, Joe, Jr.

Mick the Quick
See Rivers, John Milton

Mickel, Owen Harlan [BI]
American horseman
* Montana, Montie

Mickens, Robert 20th c. [RO2]
American musician
* Mickens, Spike

Mickens, Spike
See Mickens, Robert

Mickey Mouse Haefner
See Haefner, Milton Arnold

Mickiewicz, Adam 1798-1855 [DEP,
DNNF, SN]
Polish poet
* [The] Polish Byron

Mickle, Charles Julius   [IP]
British author
* C. J. M., Mr.

Mickle, Elmon 1919-1977 [BWW, NBB]
American singer
* Driftin' Slim
* Harmonica Harry
* Model T Slim
* Smith, Drifting

Mickle, William Julius 1735-1788
[HPPN]
Scottish poet and translator
* More, William

Micklewhite, Maurice Joseph 1933-
[BDF, FC, IPA]
British actor
* Caine, Michael

Mickley, [Dr.] Jack 20th c. [HPPN]
American pathologist
* [The] Detective of the Microscope

Micky the Magician
See Hades, Micky

[The] Microphone of God
See Sheen, Peter

Micyllus
See Moltzer, Jacob

[The] Mid Victorian Modern
See Butler, Samuel

[The] Midas of Mutual Funds
See Cornfeld, Bernard

[The] Midas of the Rockies
See Stratton, Winfield Scott

[The] Midday Murderer
See Gosman, Klaus

[A] Middle Aged Citizen
See Russell, R.

[A] Middle Aged Man
See Dix, John Ross

Middle America, Mr.
See King, Leslie Lynch, Jr.

[The] Middle Class Conscience
See Lloyd, Henry Demarest

Middle Templar
See Bedwell, Cyril Edward Alfred

Middle Wallop
See Sprake, Leslie

Middlebrook, David
See Rosenus, Alan [Harvey]

Middlecoff, Cary 1921- [GF]
American golfer
* Middlecoff, Doc

Middlecoff, Doc
See Middlecoff, Cary

Middlemass, Hume 19th c. [IP]
British author
* Mignionette
* Thistle

Middlesex
See Robinson, William Stevens

[The] Middlesex Owl
See Mayo, Herbert

Middlestitch, Giles
See Maginn, William

Middleton, Anne ?-1952   [BI]
American educator
* Sea Lord

Middleton, Arthur 1742-1787 [BDSA]
American politician and author
* Marvel, Andrew

Middleton, Arthur
See O'Brien, Edward Joseph Harrington

Middleton, Conyers 1683-1750 [NPS]
Theologian and scholar
* Fiddling Conyers

Middleton, Doc
See Middleton, Thomas

Middleton, Doc
See Riley, James

Middleton, Edgar Charles 1894- [WWL]
British author and journalist
* [An] Air Pilot

Middleton, Ellis 20th c. [WWL]
British author
* Lees, John Morton

Middleton, George 1880-? [BEW]
American playwright
* Saisson, Pierre [joint pseudonym with
   St. George Guy Reginald Bolton]

Middleton, Guy
See Middleton-Powell, Guy

Middleton, Harry 20th c. [WD]
Author
* Kiefer, Middleton [joint pseudonym
   with Warren David Kiefer]

Middleton, Henry 1771-1846 [IP]
American statesman and author
* [A] South Carolinian

Middleton, James Blaine [Jim]
1889-1974 [BE]
American baseball player
* Middleton, Rifle Jim

Middleton, John 1578-? [DNNF, FFF,
HN]
British giant
* [The] Child of Hale

Middleton, Josephine
See Alcock, Josephine

Middleton, Julia 20th c. [IBW]
American culture center organizer
* Aunt Bee

Middleton, Patrick 18th c. [IP]
British clergyman and author
* P. M.

Middleton, Peggy Yvonne 1922- [BDF,
FC, WEF]
Canadian actress
* De Carlo, Yvonne

Middleton, Richard ?-1304 [DNNF,
DNNS, HN]
British theologian
* Fundatus et Copiosus, Doctor
* [The] Profound Doctor
* Profundus, Doctor
* [The] Solid Doctor
* Solidus, Doctor

Middleton, Rifle Jim
See Middleton, James Blaine [Jim]

Middleton, Robert
See Messer, Samuel G.

Middleton, Thomas 1570?-1627 [DEA]
British author and playwright
* Hubburd, Oliver
* T. M.

Middleton, Thomas 1851-1913 [HPPN]
American outlaw
* Middleton, Doc

Middleton-Murry, Colin 1926- [CA, SF,
WD]
British author
* Cowper, Richard
* Murry, Colin

Middleton-Powell, Guy 1907- [THR]
British actor
* Middleton, Guy

Middling, Theophilus
See Snider, Denton Jacques

Midge
See Gillars, Mildred Elizabeth

Midge at the Mike
See Gillars, Mildred Elizabeth

Midgely, R. L.
See Pulsifer, D.

[The] Midget King of Swing
See Short, Robert Waltrip [Bobby]

Midgett, Elwin W. 1911- [CAP]
American author
* Midgett, Wink

Midgett, Wink
See Midgett, Elwin W.

Midgley, Thomas 1889-1944 [HPPN]
*American mechanical engineer and
chemist*
* [The] Father of Ethyl Gasoline
* [The] Father of Freon

Midkiff, Ezra Millington 1882-1957
[BE]
American baseball player
* Midkiff, Salt Rock

Midkiff, Salt Rock
See Midkiff, Ezra Millington

Midler, Bette 1945-
American singer and actress
* [The] Divine Miss M

Midnight, Captain
See Tibbs, Casey

[The] Midnight Cowboy
See Hoffman, Dustin

Midnight Cowboy
See Martin, Ray

[The] Midnight Express
See Tolan, Eddie

Midnight Idol
See Carson, John William [Johnny]

[The] Midnight Idol
See Newton, Wayne

Midnight, [Mrs.] Mary
See Smart, Christpher

Midnight, Mr.
See Gaye, Marvin [Pentz]

[The] Midshipman
See Lyne, [Rev.] Augustus Adolphus

[A] Midshipman of the U.S. Navy
See Leggett, William

[The] Midsummer Night's Dreamer
See Segal, Marc

[A] Midwestern Larry McPhail
See Veeck, William Louis, Jr. [Bill]

[The] Midwife of Men's Thoughts
See Socrates

Midwinter, Ozias
See Hearn, [Patricios] Lafcadio
[Tessima Carlos]

Mieczislaw, Jan 1850-1925 [WBD]
Polish opera singer
* Reszke, Jean de

Mieczyslawa
See Radzyminska, Jozefa

Miedcke, Karl August 1804-1880 [BBD]
German composer
* Krebs, Karl August

Mieg, Peter 1906- [ART]
Swiss painter
* P. M.

Miel [or Meel], Jan 1599-1663 [WBD]
Flemish painter and engraver
* Della Vite, Giovanni

Mielants, Florent Constant Albert 1917-
[MWD]
Belgian poet and playwright
* Hensen, Herwig

Mielziner, Leo, Jr. 1899-1962 [BEW]
American actor, director, editor
* MacKenna, Kenneth

Mier Jimenez, Ramon 1925- [GS]
Mexican bullfighter
* Nino de la Rose [Boy of the Rose]

Mierkowicz, Butch
See Mierkowicz, Edward Frank

Mierkowicz, Edward Frank 1924- [BE]
American baseball player
* Mierkowicz, Butch

Miers, Earl Schenck 1910-1972 [CA,
SAT, WW]
American author and editor
* Meredith, David William

Mies, Ludwig 1886-1969 [HPPN, NW 2-
17-86]
German-born American architect
* [The] Builder in Glass and Steel
* Friend of Steel
* Mies Van Der Rohe, Ludwig
* [The] Modern Classicist
* [The] Puritan

Mies Van Der Rohe, Ludwig
See Mies, Ludwig

Miesel, Sandra [CA]
American author
* Black, Roberta [joint pseudonym with
Robert (Stratton) Coulson]

Mifune, Kyuzo 1883-1965
Martial artist
* [The] Genius of Judo

Mifune, Toshiro 1920?- [NW 3-19-84, TI
10-4-82]
Japanese actor
* [The] John Wayne of Japan

[The] MiG-mad Marine
See Glenn, John Herschel

Miggins, Irish
See Miggins, Lawrence Edward [Larry]

Miggins, Lawrence Edward [Larry]
1925- [BE]
American baseball player
* Miggins, Irish

Miggy, Mrs.
See Krentel, Mildred White

Mighels, Ella Sterling Cummins 1853-?
[NAA]
American author
* Esmeralda, Aurora

[The] Mighty Abe Levy
See Levy, Abraham [Abe]

[The] Mighty Atom
See Booth, Albert James, Jr.

[The] Mighty Atom
See Bradford, David

[The] Mighty Atom
See Grant, Bryan M., Jr.

[The] Mighty Atom
See Greenstein, Joseph L.

[The] Mighty Atom
See Joliat, Aurel Emile

[The] Mighty Atom
See Wilde, James [Jimmy]

[The] Mighty Bambino
See Ruth, George Herman

Mighty Eagle
See Magalhaes, Fernao De

Mighty Flea Conners
See Conners, Gene

Mighty Jack Dempsey
See Dempsey, William Harrison

Mighty Joe Young
See Young, Joseph

[The] Mighty Leviathan
See Hobbes, Thomas

Mighty Little Mo
See Connolly, Maureen

Mighty Loose
See Carr, Michael Leon

Mighty Maggie Thatcher
See Thatcher, Margaret Hilda [Roberts]

[The] Mighty Manager
See Huggins, Miller James

[The] Mighty Medicine Man
See Powell, [David] Frank

[The] Mighty Midget of Corsicana
See Wilson, Robert E. [Bobby]

[The] Mighty Minstrel
See Scott, [Sir] Walter

[The] Mighty Minstrel of Old Mole
See Spenser, Edmund

[The] Mighty Mite
See Booth, Albert James, Jr.

[The] Mighty Mite
See Huggins, Miller James

Mighty Mite
See Stafford, Tammy

Mighty Mouse
See Livers, Virgil Chester, Jr.

Mighty Mouse
See Tanner, Elaine

Mighty Mouth
See Moschitta, John

[The] Mighty Sparrow
See Slinger, Francisco

Migliaccio, Edward 1881-1946 [SC]
Italian-born actor
* Farfariello

Mignard, Pierre 1610-1695 [SN]
French painter
* [The] Roman

Mignionette
See Middlemass, Hume

[Le] Mignon
See Henry III [or Henri]

Mignon, August
See Darling, John A.

Mignonette
See Moore, Emily H.

Miguel, Louis 20th c.
Spanish bullfighter
* Dominguin

Miguelin [Little Mike]
See Mateo Salcedo, Miguel

Miguez, Joao 1520?-1579 [BI]
Portuguese statesman and financier
* Nasi, Joseph [Duke of Naxos]

Mihalek, Jim 20th c. [GW]
American rodeo performer
* Mihalek, Weasel

Mihalek, Weasel
See Mihalek, Jim

Mihilakis, Ulysses George 20th c.
[WGT]
Author
* Hassen, Silaki Ali

Mik
See Mikkelsen, Henning Dahl

Mik, Al
See Plastino, Al

Mikado Milt Scott
See Scott, Milt[on Parker]

Mikalowitch, Nicolai
See Michels, Nicholas Aloysius

Mikan, Baron
See Barba, Harry

Mikan, George 1924- [HPPN]
American basketball player
* Basketball, Mr.

Mike
See Donnet, [Baron] Michael Gabriel
Libert Marie

Mike
See Hughes, Patrick Cairns

Mike
See Muir, Mary

Mike de Pike
See Heitler, Michael

Mike the Devil
See Genna, Michael

Mike the Greek
See Potzin, Mike

Mike the Pike
See Heitler, Michael

Mike-Mayer, Istvan 1947- [SMG]
Hungarian-born football player
* Mike-Mayer, Steve

Mike-Mayer, Steve
See Mike-Mayer, Istvan

Mikes, George
See Mikes, Gyorgy

Mikes, Gyorgy 1912- [SFL]
Author
* Mikes, George

Mikesell, William Henry 1887- [HPPN]
American author
* Dr. Mike

Miketta, Bob
See Morris, Robert

Mikhailov, A.
See Scheller, Aleksandr Konstantinovich

Mikhailov, Peter
See Peter I [Petr Alekseevich]

Mikhailovskii, Nikolai Georgievich
1852-1906 [BI]
Russian author
* Garin, N.

Mikhoels, Salomon
See Vovsky, Salomon Mikhailovich

Mikita, Stan
See Gvoth, Stanislov

Mikkelsen, Hans
See Holberg, Louis [or Ludvig]

Mikkelsen, Henning Dahl 20th c.
[WECO]
Danish cartoonist
* Mik

Mikkelson, Mick
See Mikkelson, Peter J.

Mikkelson, Peter J. 1939- [SMG]
American baseball player
* Mikkelson, Mick

Miklos, Hank
See Miklos, John Joseph

Miklos, John Joseph 1910- [BE]
American baseball player
* Miklos, Hank

Mikol, Jim
See Mikol, John Stanley

Mikol, John Stanley 1938- [CEI]
Canadian-born hockey player
* Mikol, Jim

Mikulich, V.
See Veselitskaia, Lydiia Ivanovna

Milam, Pauline
See Abrahams, Pauline

[The] Milan Bach
See Bach, Johann Christian

Milan, Deerfoot
See Milan, Jesse Clyde

Milan, Jesse Clyde 1887-1953 [AS,
DGS, PB]
American baseball player
* Milan, Deerfoot
* Milan, Zeb

Milan, Zeb
See Milan, Jesse Clyde

[The] Milanese
See Bach, Johann Christian

[Il] Milanese
See Sammartini [or San Martini],
Giovanni Battista

Milani, Chef
See Milani, Joseph L.

Milani, Joseph L. 1892-1965 [SC]
American actor and cooking-show host
* Milani, Chef

Milbourne, Luke ?-1720 [IP]
British author
* Tom of Bedlam

Milbrook, John
See McFadden, Gertrude V.

Milburn, William Henry 1823-? [DNNF,
FF, SN]
American clergyman
* [The] Blind Preacher

Milcetic, Helen 1929- [EJ]
American singer
* Merrill, Helen

[The] Mild
See Frederick II

Mildred, [Sister] M.
See Hill, Margaret Shirley

Mile A Minute Harry
See Selfridge, Harry Godron

Mile a Minute Murphy
See Murphy, Charles W.

Milecete, Helen
See Jones, Susan [Morrow]

Miles
See Sitwell, [Sir] Osbert

Miles
See Southwold, Stephen

Miles, Alfred 1796-1851 [IP]
British author
* A. M.

Miles, Allan
See Dellinger, Allan Miles

Miles, Buddy
See Miles, George

Miles, Butch
See Thornton, Charles J.

Miles, Charles J.
See Thornton, Charles J.

Miles, Dee
See Miles, Wilson Daniel

Miles, Dorien K[lein] 1915- [CA]
American author
* Miles, Sylva [joint pseudonym with
Sylva Mularchyk]

Miles, Elliot
See Ludvigsen, Karl [Eric]

Miles, Frederic James 1869-? [LAO]
British writer and editor
* Rangefinder

Miles, Garry
See Cason, James

Miles, George 1948- [IBW]
American musician
* Miles, Buddy

Miles, Gertrude Elizabeth 1860-?
[NAA]
American author
* Arnold, Faith Stewart

Miles, Henry Adolphus 19th c. [HPPN]
American clergyman
* H. A. M.

Miles, Henry, Jr.   [IP]
American author
* Hermes

Miles, James Warley 1819?-?   [HPPN]
American missionary, educator, librarian
* J. W. M.
* M.

Miles, John 20th c.   [OBW]
American baseball player
* Miles, Mule

Miles, John
See   Bickham, Jack M[iles]

Miles, Josephine [Josie] 1900?-   [BWW]
American singer
* Flowers, Evangelist Mary
* Harris, Pearl
* Jones, Augusta

Miles, Keith
See   Tralins, S[andor] Robert [Bob]

Miles, Lily Pearl ?-1957   [SC]
American actress
* Shelby, Charlotte

Miles, Lizzie
See   Landreaux, Elizabeth Mary

Miles, Long Gone
See   Miles, Luke

Miles, Lotta
See   Court, Florence

Miles, Luke 1925-   [DAM]
American singer
* Miles, Long Gone

Miles, Luther
See   Mander, Lionel

Miles, [Maxine Frances] Mary [Forbes-Robertson] 1900?-   [HPPN]
British aircraft designer
* Blossom

Miles, Miska
See   Martin, Patricia Miles

Miles, Mule
See   Miles, John

Miles, Otis 1949-   [RO2]
American singer
* Williams, Otis

Miles, Otis O. 1858-1921   [HPPN]
American actor
* Berry, George

Miles, Peter
See   Perreau-Saussine, Gerald

Miles, Pliny 1818-1865   [FFF, PA]
American journalist
* Communipaw

Miles, Richard
See   Perreau-Saussine, Gerald

Miles, Sarah Elizabeth Appleton 1807-?
[HPPN]
American poet
* A.

Miles, Sibella [Hatfield] 1800-?   [IP]
British poet
* Hatfield, S. E.

Miles, Susan 1887-   [WWL]
British author
* Roberts, Ursula

Miles, Sylva [joint pseudonym with Sylva Mularchyk]
See   Miles, Dorien K[lein]

Miles, Sylva [joint pseudonym with Dorien K(lein) Miles]
See   Mularchyk, Sylva

Miles, Vera
See   Ralston, Vera

Miles, Vic
See   Levy, Victor Miles, Jr.

Miles, Wilson Daniel 1909-1976   [BE]
American baseball player
* Miles, Dee

Milestone, Lewis
See   Milstein, Lewis

Mileta
See   Jennings, Clotilda

Miletus, Rex
See   Burgess, Michael Roy

Miley, Bubber
See   Miley, James Wesley

Miley, James Wesley 1903-1932   [DAM, EJ, PMJ]
American jazz musician
* Miley, Bubber

[The] Milford Bard
See   Lofland, John

Milford, Jake
See   Milford, John

Milford, John 20th c.   [SMG]
American hockey manager
* Milford, Jake

Milforde, Marie
See   Fisher, Mary

Milhailovitch, Boris 1891-1963   [FC]
Russian-born producer
* Morros, Boris

Milic, Jan ?-1374   [WBD]
Moravian-born prelate
* Milic of Kremsier

Milic of Kremsier
See   Milic, Jan

Milinda
See   Menander

Militant
See   Sandburg, Carl [August]

[The] Militant Roman Collar
See   Groppi, [Rev.] James E.

[A] Military Chaplain
See   Fraser, Joshua

[The] Military Legend
See   MacArthur, Douglas

[A] Military Officer, J. C.
See   Caldwell, [Sir] James

[The] Military Ventriloquist
See   Whitaker, Thomas

Militello, Pietro
See   Natali, Alfred Maxim

Miljus, John Kenneth 1895-   [BE]
American baseball player
* [The] Big Serb

Milk, Harvey 1935?-1979   [TI 9-26-83]
American local government official
* [The] Mayor of Castro Street

Milk of Magnesia Phillips
See   Phillips, Alfred Noroton, Jr.

[The] Milk Snatcher
See   Thatcher, Margaret Hilda [Roberts]

Milkman Jim Turner
See   Turner, James Riley

Milkomane, George Alexis
Milkomanovich 1903-   [CA, CC, LC, WW]
Russian-born British physician and author
* Bankoff, George Alexis
* Borodin, George
* Braddon, George
* Conway, Peter
* Redwood, Alec
* Sava, George

Milkowski, Zygmunt 1824-1915   [WBD]
Polish author
* Jez, Teodor Tomasz

Milks, Herbert 1902-   [CEI]
Canadian-born hockey player
* Milks, Hib

Milks, Hib
See   Milks, Herbert

[The] Milkwoman of Bristol
See   Yearsley, Ann

Milky the Clown
See   Fox, Karrell

Mill
See   Butler, William Mill

[The] Mill Boy of the Slashes
See   Clay, Henry

Mill, C. R.
See   Crnjanski, Milos

Mill, Garrett
See   Miller, Margaret

[The] Mill Hand
See   Patch, Sam[uel]

Mill, Ian St. John
See   Mills, Terry Kenneth

Mill, John Stuart 1806-1873   [HPPN, IP, NPS]
British philosopher and author
* A.
* [The] Logic Chopping Machine
* [The] Saint of Rationalism
* Wickliffe

Milla y Vidaurre, Jose 1822-1882 [BI]
Guatemalan historian
* Gil, Salome

Millaird, M. Albert [PA]
Author
* Grimm, Baron

Millais, Ruth
See Mulholland, Rosa

Millan Diaz, Antonio 1947-1976 [GS]
Spanish bullfighter
* Carnicerito de Ubeda [Little Butcher
  from Ubeda]

Milland, Jack
See Truscott-Jones, Reginald

Milland, Ray
See Truscott-Jones, Reginald

Milland, Spike
See Truscott-Jones, Reginald

Millar, James Primrose Malcolm 1893-
[IAW]
Scottish-born author
* White, G. A.

Millar, John 1735-1801 [IP]
Scottish jurist and author
* Crito

Millar, Kenneth 1915-1983 [CA, CC,
EMD]
American author
* Macdonald, John
* Macdonald, John Ross
* Macdonald, Ross

Millar, Mary
See Wetton, Mary

Millar, Minna Henrietta Joy 1914-
[AW]
British-born author
* Collier, Joy

Millard, Alice
See Bullivant, Cecil Henry

Millard, Christopher Sclater 1872-?
[LC, WWL]
British author
* Mason, Stuart

Millard, E. E. 19th c. [IP, PA]
American author
* E. E. M.
* E. M. E.

Millard, Edward R. ?-1963 [BEW]
American theatrical performer
* Millard, Rocky

Millard, Harry W.
See Williams, Harry Millard

Millard, John [IP]
British author and librarian
* Coxe, Henry, Esq.

Millard, Joseph 20th c. [SFP]
Author
* Westwood, N. J.

Millard, Rocky
See Millard, Edward R.

Millard, Ursula
See Coulter, Ursula

Millarde, June Elizabeth 1899-1936
[BEW]
American actress
* Caprice, June

Millaud, M. Albert [PA]
Author
* Himery, Paul

Millay, Edna St. Vincent 1892-1950
[LC]
American author
* Boyd, Nancy

Millbank
See Hope, Thomas

Millbank, Anne Isabella 1792-1860 [SN]
Friend of British poet, Lord Byron
* Donna Inez
* Millpond, Miss
* Raby, Aurora

Millbank, F. T.
See Holmes, Geoffrey Andrew

Millbank, [Capt.] H. R.
See Ellis, Edward S[ylvester]

Millbank, Mrs. George [FFF]
Entertainer
* Paine, Lizzie

Millburn, Cynthia
See Brooks, Anne Tedlock

Millen, F. F. [IP]
American journalist
* Ardboe
* Trefoil
* Verdad

Millender, Dharathula Hood 1920-
[HPPN]
American teacher, librarian, author
* Millender, Dolly

Millender, Dolly
See Millender, Dharathula Hood

Miller, Abraham Joseph, Jr. 20th c.
[RO2]
American musician
* Miller, Onion

Miller, Al 20th c.
Auto racer
* Clean, Mr.

Miller, Albert 1913- [FFA]
Canadian singer
* [The] Canadian Burl Ives
* Mills, Alan

Miller, Alex
See Ford, Aleck

Miller, Alexander R. G. 1875?-1940
[BEW]
American theatrical performer
* Karson, Kit

Miller, Alfred W. 1898?-1983 [SI 12-5-
83]
American publicist and writer
* Hackle, Sparse Grey

Miller, Alice Duer
See Miller, Mrs. Henry Wise

Miller, Alice Moore 1916-1960 [SC]
American actress
* Moore, Alice

Miller, Allen L., III 1948- [GF]
American golfer
* [The] Other Miller

Miller, Alligator Bait
See Miller, William Mosley

Miller, Ann
See Collier, Lucille Ann

Miller, [Lady] Anna Riggs 1740-1781
[HPPN]
Irish author
* [An] English Woman

Miller, B. [PA]
Author
* B. M.

Miller, Bazy
See Miller, Ruth Elizabeth
[McCormick]

Miller, Benj.
See Loomis, Noel M[iller]

Miller, Benny
See Kaplan, Louis

Miller, Big
See Miller, Clarence H.

Miller, Big Clice
See Miller, Jessee

Miller, Bill 1920-1961 [CC, EMD, WW]
American author
* Daemer, Will [joint pseudonym with
  Robert (Bob) Wade]
* Masterson, Whit [joint pseudonym
  with Robert (Bob) Wade]
* Miller, Wade [joint pseudonym with
  Robert (Bob) Wade]
* Wilmer, Dale [joint pseudonym with
  Robert (Bob) Wade]

Miller, Bill 20th c. [BLB]
American criminal
* [The] Killer

Miller, Bing
See Miller, Edmund John

Miller, Bing
See Miller, John E.

Miller, Bob 1895-1955 [CWG]
American singer and songwriter
* Burnett, Bob
* Ferguson, Bob
* Kackley, Bob
* Palmer, Bill

Miller, Bozo
See Miller, Edward Abraham

Miller, Bronco Charlie
See Miller, Charles

Miller, Bruce 20th c. [SI 9-1-82]
American football player
* Miller, Juice

Miller, Buck
See Miller, Clarence

Miller, Buck
See Miller, Eddie

Miller, Bullet
See Miller, Frank Lee

Miller, Buzz
See Miller, Vernal Philip

Miller, Calliope
See Miller, George Frederick

Miller, Calvin E. 1914- [CWG]
American country-western performer
* Miller, Curley

Miller, Carl Grover 1893- [NAA]
American educator and author
* Ballard, Cyrus

Miller, Carmen 1944- [BF]
British actress
* Miller, Mandy

Miller, Charles 1850-? [HPPN]
American cowboy, soldier, adventurer
* Bronco Carlos
* Miller, Bronco Charlie

Miller, Charles 20th c. [SMG]
American football player
* Miller, Ookie

Miller, Charles Bradley 1868-1945 [BE]
American baseball player
* Miller, Dusty

Miller, Charles C. 1831-? [ALY]
American author
* Benson, P., Sr.

Miller, Charles Henry 1842-1922
[WBD]
American etcher, painter, author
* De Muldor, Carl

Miller, Christine
See Van Walree, Mrs. E. C. W.

Miller, Cincinnatus Heine 1848-1913
[BEW, HPPN, LC, PA, UH]
American poet and playwright
* Miller, Joaquin
* [The] Oregon Byron
* [The] Poet of the Sierras

Miller, Clarence 1923- [BBH]
American softball player
* Miller, Buck

Miller, Clarence H. 1923- [EJ]
American jazz musician
* Miller, Big

Miller, Cleo
See Miller, Cleophus, Jr.

Miller, Cleophus, Jr. 1951-
American football player
* Miller, Cleo

Miller, Cotton
See Miller, Hugh Stanley [Hughie]

Miller, Crab Bait
See Miller, William Mosley

Miller, Curley
See Miller, Calvin E.

Miller, Curly
See Miller, George

Miller, Cyclone
See Miller, Joseph H.

Miller, Dais
See Miller, Lloyd Tevis

Miller, Davy 20th c. [BLB]
American boxer and referee
* Miller, Yiddles

Miller, Deacon
See Miller, James B.

Miller, Dempsey 20th c. [OBW]
American baseball player
* Miller, Dimp

Miller, Dimp
See Miller, Dempsey

Miller, Doc
See Miller, Roy Oscar

Miller, Doggie
See Miller, George Frederick

Miller, Donna 20th c.
American actress
* Mills, Donna

Miller, Doris R.
See Mosesson, Gloria R[ubin]

Miller, Dots
See Miller, John Barney

Miller, Dusty
See Miller, Charles Bradley

Miller, Dusty
See Miller, Geoffrey

Miller, Dusty
See Miller, Thomas

Miller, E. F.
See Pohle, Robert W[arren], Jr.

Miller, E. G.
See Miller, Edward George

Miller, Eddie 20th c. [OBW]
American baseball player
* Miller, Buck

Miller, Eddie
See Lisbona, Edward

Miller, Edgar E. [FB]
American football player
* Miller, Rip

Miller, Edmund John 1894-1966 [AS,
DGS, PB]
American baseball player
* Miller, Bing

Miller, Edward 20th c. [EF]
American football player
* Miller, Shorty

Miller, Edward Abraham 1909-
American trencherman
* Miller, Bozo

Miller, Edward George 1883-1948 [SC]
American actor
* Miller, E. G.

Miller, Edward Robert 1916- [BE]
American baseball player
* Miller, Eppie

Miller, Edwin
See Max, Edwin

Miller, Elizabeth Beecher [NAA]
American journalist
* Beecher, Elizabeth [Betty]

Miller, Elizabeth Erwin
See Lobingier, Elizabeth Miller

Miller, Elizabeth Maxfield 1910- [CA]
American author, educator, translator
* Maxfield, Elizabeth

Miller, Emily [Huntington] [IP]
American author
* Purdy

Miller, Eppie
See Miller, Edward Robert

Miller, Ernest 1894?-1971 [DAM, EJ,
PMJ]
American jazz musician
* Miller, Punch
* Punch, Kid

Miller, Eschal 1918- [FC]
American actress
* Grey, Nan

Miller, Eugene 20th c. [BBH]
American football player
* Miller, Shorty

Miller, Eugenia
See Mandelkorn, Eugenia Miller

Miller, Eugenie Marie Gaude ?-1865
[IP]
French author
* Valrey, Max

Miller, Evelyn
See Berger, Evelyn Miller

Miller, F. F. 1834-? [PA]
Author
* Ardboe

Miller, Fish Bait
See Miller, William Mosley

Miller, Flash
See Miller, Leroy

Miller, Florence Fenwick 1854-? [LAO]
British author and editor
* Filomena

Miller, Foghorn
See Miller, George Frederick

Miller, Francis Trevelyn 1877-? [ALY]
American author
* Meunier, Francois

Miller, Frank
See Loomis, Noel M[iller]

Miller, Frank Lee 1886-1974 [BE]
American baseball player
* Miller, Bullet

Miller, Fred[erick Holman] 1886-1953
[BE]
American baseball player
* Miller, Speedy

Miller, Frederick [Walter Gascoyne]
1904- [CA]
New Zealand journalist
* [The] Gascon

Miller, G. R.
See Judd, Frederick Charles

Miller, Gameboy
See Miller, Samuel

Miller, Gar Bait
See Miller, William Mosley

Miller, Gary Neil 1934?-1973 [BEW,
FC, HPPN, HT]
American actor and singer
* Dunn, Michael
* Loveless, [Dr.] Miguelito

Miller, Gene
See Miller, Truman

Miller, Geoffrey 1952- [DC]
British cricketer
* Miller, Dusty
* Miller, Mills

Miller, George [IP]
Scottish author
* [A] Country Bookseller

Miller, George ?-1952 [HPPN]
*American theatrical manager and press
agent*
* Miller, Lefty

Miller, George 1909- [IBW]
American dancer
* Miller, Curly

Miller, George
See Moran, George

Miller, George Amos 1868-? [HPPN]
American clergyman and author
* Peggy Ann

Miller, George Frederick 1864-1909
[AS, BE]
American baseball player
* Miller, Calliope
* Miller, Doggie
* Miller, Foghorn

Miller, George Louquet 1934- [CA]
American clergyman and author
* Martin, Greg

Miller, H. V.
See Miller, Harry Vye

Miller, Hack
See Miller, James Eldridge

Miller, Hack
See Miller, Lawrence

Miller, Harriet Mann 1831-1918
[HPPN, WBD]
American ornithologist and author
* Gwynfryn
* Miller, Olive Thorne

Miller, Harry Vye 1907- [ART]
New Zealand painter
* Miller, H. V.

Miller, Heinie
See Miller, Henry

Miller, Helen Hill 1899- [CA]
American author
* Hill, Helen

Miller, Henry 1891- [HPPN]
American author
* [The] Expatriate

Miller, Henry 20th c. [EF]
American football player
* Miller, Heinie

Miller, Henry, Jr. ?-1927 [HPPN]
American actor
* Miller, Jack

Miller, Homer Virgil Milton 1814-1896
[HPPN]
American orator
* [The] Demosthenes of the Mountains

Miller, Hooks
See Miller, William Paul [Bill]

Miller, Hope Ridings
See Ridings, Hope Dupre

Miller, Hub
See Miller, Pleas

Miller, Hugh 1802-1856 [DEP, IP]
Scottish geologist and author
* [A] Geologist
* [A] Journeyman Mason
* One of the Scotch People
* [The] Stonemason of Cromarty

Miller, Hugh Stanley [Hughie]
1887-1945 [BE]
American baseball player
* Miller, Cotton

Miller, Isabel
See Routsong, Alma

Miller, J. Irwin 1909?-
American industrialist
* [The] Medici of the Middle West

Miller, Jack 1895-1941 [SC]
American actor
* Miller, Shorty

Miller, Jack
See Miller, Henry, Jr.

Miller, James [Jim] ?-1937 [BE]
American baseball player
* Miller, Rabbit

Miller, James 1703-1744 [HPPN, IP]
British evangelist, author, playwright
* [An] Englishman
* [A] Gentleman of Wadham College
* Harlequin-Horace

Miller, James B. 1866-1909 [EWG]
American gunfighter
* Miller, Deacon
* Miller, Killer
* Miller, Killin' Jim

Miller, James Edward 1913-
American jazz musician
* Miller, Sing

Miller, James Eldridge 1911-1966 [BE]
American baseball player
* Miller, Hack

Miller, James Russell 1840-1912
[HPPN]
American clergyman, author, poet
* [The] Modern Bunyan

Miller, Jason
See Miller, John

Miller, Jessee 1904- [BA]
American physician
* Miller, Big Clice

Miller, Jim
See Moss, Eugene

Miller, Jimmy 20th c. [HDM]
British actor, singer, director
* McColl, Ewan

Miller, Joan Maxine 1922- [BEW, TR]
American actress and singer
* Copeland, Joan

Miller, Joaquin
See Miller, Cincinnatus Heine

Miller, Jocko
See Miller, Joseph John

Miller, Joe
See Mottley, John

Miller, Joe, II
See Ballantyne, James

Miller, Joe, Jr.
See Westcott, Thompson

Miller, John 1939?- [IPA]
American playwright
* Miller, Jason

Miller, John
See Samachson, Joseph

Miller, John Anthony 1915- [BE]
American baseball player
* Miller, Ox

Miller, John Barney 1886-1923 [AS,
BE]
American baseball player
* Miller, Dots

Miller, John Cale 19th c. [IP]
British clergyman and author
* [A] Birmingham Clergyman

Miller, John E. 1903-1964 [AS]
American football player
* Miller, Bing

Miller, Joseph [Joe] 1684-1738 [DEL,
FFF, RH]
British comic actor
* [The] Father of Jests

Miller, Joseph 20th c.   [ASC]
American musician
* Miller, Taps

Miller, Joseph H. 1859-1916   [BE]
American baseball player
* Miller, Cyclone

Miller, Joseph John 1908?-1984   [WP 5-21-84]
American boxer, golfer, boxing official
* Miller, Jocko

Miller, Juice
See   Miller, Bruce

Miller, Kathlyn 1896-1933   [THR]
Scottish-born actress and singer
* Hilliard, Kathlyn

Miller, Ken[neth Albert] 1915-   [BE]
American baseball player
* Miller, Whitey

Miller, Killer
See   Miller, James B.

Miller, Killin' Jim
See   Miller, James B.

Miller, Lanora 1932-   [CA]
American editor and author
* Welzenbach, Lanora F.

Miller, Laura Owen
See   Bamberger, Laura Owen Miller

Miller, Lawrence 1894-1971   [BE, PB]
American baseball player
* Miller, Hack

Miller, Lawrence
See   Alais, Ernest W.

Miller, Lefty
See   Miller, George

Miller, Lefty
See   Miller, Ralph Henry

Miller, Leo Alphonso 1897-   [BE]
American baseball player
* Miller, Red

Miller, Leonard 1864-1939   [LC, TC, UH]
British author
* Merrick, Leonard
* [The] Novelist's Novelist

Miller, Leroy 20th c.   [OBW]
American baseball player
* Miller, Flash

Miller, Lloyd Tevis 1875-?   [IBW]
American physician
* Miller, Dais

Miller, Louis 1898-1962   [SC]
Actor
* Mills, Guy

Miller, Lowell Otto 1889-1962   [BE]
American baseball player
* Miller, Moonie

Miller, Lydia Falconer 1805-1876   [DEL, FFF, HFN, IP]
British author
* L. F. F. M.
* Myrtle, Harriet

Miller, M. 1741-1781   [IP]
British author
* [An] Englishwoman

Miller, Mandy
See   Miller, Carmen

Miller, Marc
See   Baker, Marceil Genee [Kolstad]

Miller, Margaret 20th c.   [SFL]
Author
* Mill, Garrett

Miller, Margaret J.
See   Dale, Margaret J[essy] Miller

Miller, Marilyn
See   Reynolds, Mary Ellen

Miller, Marilyn McMeen
See   Brown, Marilyn McMeen Miller

Miller, Marsha
See   Baker, Marceil Genee [Kolstad]

Miller, Martha
See   Ivan, Martha Miller Pfaff

Miller, Martin
See   Muller, Rudolph

Miller, Marvin
See   Mueller, Marvin

Miller, Mary [Ayer] 19th c.   [IP]
American author
* Luola

Miller, Mary [Gillies] 19th c.   [IP]
British author
* Myrtle, Harriet

Miller, Mary
See   Northcott, [William] Cecil

Miller, Mary Beth 1942-   [CA, SAT]
American author and actress
* Mary Beth

Miller, Mary Britton 1883-1975   [ANT, CA, LC]
American author and poet
* Bolton, Isabel

Miller, Mary Ester 1876-?   [CAN]
Canadian author
* Keith, Marion

Miller, Maud
See   McCormick, Mrs. Loudon

Miller, Max
See   Sargent, Thomas Henry

Miller, May
See   Hues, Mrs. Frank

Miller, Merrill
See   Miller, Morris

Miller, Mills
See   Miller, Geoffrey

Miller, Minnie [Willis] 1845-?   [DNA]
American author
* Baines, Minnie Willis

Miller, Mitch[ell William] 1911- [HPPN]
American musician, impresario, television personality
* [The] Bearded One

Miller, Moonie
See   Miller, Lowell Otto

Miller, Morris 1890-1957   [SC]
American actor
* De Costa, Morris

Miller, Morris 1919-   [CA, OP]
American opera singer
* Merrill, Robert
* Miller, Merrill

Miller, Mrs. Henry   [FFF]
Entertainer
* Heron, Bijou

Miller, Mrs. Henry Wise 1874-1942 [HPPN]
American author
* Miller, Alice Duer

Miller, Mrs. John A. 19th c.   [DNA, IP, PA]
American author
* Latimer, Faith

Miller, Nicole Puleo 1944-   [CA]
American author
* Puleo, Nicole

Miller, Norman 20th c.   [IBW]
American actor
* Miller, Porto Rico

Miller, Olive Thorne
See   Miller, Harriet Mann

Miller, Onion
See   Miller, Abraham Joseph, Jr.

Miller, Ookie
See   Miller, Charles

Miller, Otis Louis 1901-1959
American baseball player
* Miller, Otto

Miller, Otto
See   Miller, Otis Louis

Miller, Ox
See   Miller, John Anthony

Miller, P[eter] Schuyler 1912-1974 [ESF, WGT]
American author and critic
* McDermott, Dennis [joint pseudonym with Aubrey McDermott and Walter Dennis]
* Nihil

Miller, Perry 1944-   [RO2]
American musician
* Young, Jesse Colin

Miller, Piano
See   Lisbona, Edward

Miller, Pleas 20th c. [OBW]
American baseball player
* Miller, Hub

Miller, Poi
See Miller, Robert

Miller, Porto Rico
See Miller, Norman

Miller, Punch
See Miller, Ernest

Miller, R. S. 1936- [CA]
American author
* Huston, Fran

Miller, Rabbit
See Miller, James [Jim]

Miller, Ralph Henry 1899-1967 [BE]
American baseball player
* Miller, Lefty

Miller, Red
See Miller, Leo Alphonso

Miller, Red
See Miller, Robert

Miller, Rice
See Ford, Aleck

Miller, Richard
See Pietschmann, Richard John, III

Miller, Rip
See Miller, Edgar E.

Miller, Robert 1890-1947 [HPPN]
Austrian swindler, forger, counterfeiter
* Dante, Monsieur
* Duval, Robert
* Lustig, [Count] Victor
* [The] Man Who Sold the Eiffel
Tower
* Miller, Victor
* [The] Sultan of the Skin Trade

Miller, Robert 1927- [SMG]
American football coach
* Miller, Red

Miller, Robert 20th c. [EF]
American football player
* Miller, Poi

Miller, Roland Arthur 1918- [BE]
American baseball player
* Miller, Ronnie

Miller, Ronnie
See Miller, Roland Arthur

Miller, Roscoe Clyde 1876-1913 [BE]
American baseball player
* Miller, Roxy
* Miller, Rubberlegs

Miller, Roxy
See Miller, Roscoe Clyde

Miller, Roy Oscar 1883-1938 [BE]
American baseball player
* Miller, Doc

Miller, Rubberlegs
See Miller, Roscoe Clyde

Miller, Rudel Charles 1900- [BE]
American baseball player
* Miller, Rudy

Miller, Rudy
See Miller, Rudel Charles

Miller, Ruth
See Jacobs, Ruth Harriet

Miller, Ruth Elizabeth [McCormick]
1921-
American newspaper publisher
* Colonel McCormick's Capital Invader
* [The] Colonel's Lady
* Miller, Bazy
* [The] Princess

Miller, Samuel 20th c. [MM, PHM]
American underworld figure
* Miller, Gameboy

Miller, Seymour 1908- [ASC]
American musician
* Miller, Sy

Miller, Sheila 1936- [CA]
American author and poet
* Grawoig, Sheila
* Jurnak, Sheila
* Raeschild, Sheila

Miller, Shorty
See Miller, Edward

Miller, Shorty
See Miller, Eugene

Miller, Shorty
See Miller, Jack

Miller, Shrimp Bait
See Miller, William Mosley

Miller, Sing
See Miller, James Edward

Miller, Speedy
See Miller, Fred[erick Holman]

Miller, Susan 1946- [FC]
American actress
* Saint James, Susan

Miller, Sy
See Miller, Seymour

Miller, Taps
See Miller, Joseph

Miller, Thomas ?-1955 [HPPN]
British ship captain
* Miller, Dusty

Miller, Thomas 1807?-1874 [DEL,
DNNS, SN]
British author and poet
* [The] Basket Maker

Miller, Thomasene 1942- [BA]
American administrator
* Miller, Tommi

Miller, Tobias Ham [PA]
Author
* Uncle Toby

Miller, Tommi
See Miller, Thomasene

Miller, Truman 1924?-1963 [BEW]
Stage manager and actor
* Miller, Gene

Miller, Val 1942- [IAW]
British author
* Manning, Val

Miller, Velna Lou 1935- [BEW]
American actress and singer
* Miller, Wynne

Miller, Vernal Philip 1928- [BEW]
American dancer, choreographer, actor
* Miller, Buzz

Miller, Victor [Brooke] 1940- [CA]
American author, screenwriter, playwright
* Brooke, Joshua
* McCoy, Arch

Miller, Victor
See Miller, Robert

Miller, Wade [joint pseudonym with
Robert (Bob) Wade]
See Miller, Bill

Miller, Wade [joint pseudonym with Bill
Miller]
See Wade, Robert [Bob]

Miller, Ward Taylor 1884-1958 [BE]
American baseball player
* Miller, Windy

Miller, Warne
See Rathborne, St. George Henry

Miller, Warner 1838-1918 [HPPN]
American manufacturer and politician
* Miller, Wood Pulp

Miller, Warren 1921-1966 [BI]
American author
* Vail, Amanda

Miller, Whitey
See Miller, Ken[neth Albert]

Miller, Wild Bill
See Miller, William Francis [Bill]

Miller, William 1781?-1849 [FFF, HN]
American religious leader
* [The] American Prophet
* [The] Poet of Low Hampton

Miller, William 1810-1872 [HPPN]
Scottish poet
* Laureate of the Nursery

Miller, William 1928-1977 [FC, SW,
WEF]
Irish-born American actor
* Boyd, Stephen

Miller, William Francis [Bill] 1910-
[BE]
American baseball player
* Miller, Wild Bill

Miller, William Mosley 1909?- [BI,
HPPN]
Former congressional doorkeeper
* [The] King of the Hill
* Miller, Alligator Bait
* Miller, Crab Bait
* Miller, Fish Bait

Miller, William Mosley (cont.)
* Miller, Gar Bait
* Miller, Shrimp Bait

Miller, William Paul [Bill] 1926-   [BE]
American baseball player
* Miller, Hooks

Miller, Willie
See Ford, Aleck

Miller, Windy
See Miller, Ward Taylor

Miller, Wood Pulp
See Miller, Warner

Miller, Wright W[atts] 1903-   [AW, CA]
British author and editor
* North, Mark

Miller, Wynne
See Miller, Velna Lou

Miller, Yiddles
See Miller, Davy

Miller, Zachary Taylor 1878-?   [HPPN]
American rancher
* Miller, [Colonel] Zack

Miller, [Colonel] Zack
See Miller, Zachary Taylor

Milles, [Vilhelm] Carl [Emil]
See Anderson, Vilhelm Carl Emil

Millet, Francis Davis 1846-1912
[HPPN]
American artist
* [The] Bulgarian

Millet [or Mile], Jean Francois
1642?-1679   [SN, WBD]
Flemish painter
* Francisque
* [A] Jupiter in Sabots

Millet, Jean Francois 1814-1875
[HPPN]
French painter
* Francisque
* [The] Man With the Hoe
* [The] Patriarch of Barbizon
* [The] Story Telling Painter

Millet, Kadish 1923-   [ASC]
American composer
* Millet, Kay

Millet, Kay
See Millet, Kadish

[The] Millet of America
See Higgins, Eugene

[The] Millet of Literature
See Hardy, Thomas

[The] Millet without the Angelus
See Hardy, Thomas

Millett, Nigel Stansbury 1904-   [LAO]
British author
* Oke, Richard

Milleville, Mary Ghita Lindell 1895-
[HPPN]
French underground leader
* Lindell, Mary

Millican, Arthenia 1920-   [BA]
American educator
* Millican, Jackie

Millican, Jackie
See Millican, Arthenia

Millicent
See Jordon, Mildred Arlene

Millidus
See Marston, John

Milligan, Alice L. 20th c.   [PI]
Irish poet
* Olkyrn, Iris

Milligan, Ernest 20th c.   [PI]
Irish poet
* Carew, Will

Milligan, Frances J. G.
See Watkins, Frances Jane Grierson

Milligan, Jocko
See Milligan, John

Milligan, John 1861-1923   [AS, BE]
American baseball player
* Milligan, Jocko

Milligan, Mary 1882-1966   [SC]
Irish actress
* Milligan, Min

Milligan, Maurice Morton 1884-?
[HPPN]
American attorney
* Missouri's Tom Dewey

Milligan, Min
See Milligan, Mary

Milligan, Spike
See Milligan, Terence Alan

Milligan, Terence Alan 1918-   [AW, CA, TR]
British actor, director, author
* Milligan, Spike

Millikan, Robert Andrews 1868-1953
[HPPN]
American physicist
* [The] Conqueror of the Electron
* Millikan, Tinker

Millikan, Tinker
See Millikan, Robert Andrews

Milliken, Bobo
See Milliken, Robert Fogle [Bob]

Milliken, Robert Fogle [Bob] 1926-
[BE]
American baseball player
* Milliken, Bobo

Milliken, William Grawn 1922-
American politician
* Boy Scout Bill
* [The] Lollipop Governor
* Milquetoast, Governor

Millin, John D. 20th c.   [HPPN]
American boxer and bookmaker
* Becker, John

Millinder, Lucius 1900-1966   [DAM, PMJ, WWJ]
American bandleader
* Millinder, Lucky

Millinder, Lucky
See Millinder, Lucius

Millington, Philip   [FFF]
Author
* Cento

[The] Million Dollar Invalid
See Mantle, Mickey Charles

[The] Million Dollar Mermaid
See Kellerman, Annette

[The] Millionaire
See Gerry, Peter Goelet

[The] Millionaire Boy Angel
See Cohen, Alexander

Millionaire Charlie Matranga
See Matranga, Charles

[The] Millionaire for God
See Studd, Charles Thomas

[The] Millionaire Gorilla
See Capone, Al[phonse]

[The] Millionaire Hobo
See How, James Eads

[The] Millionaire of Tennis
See Laver, Rod[ney George]

[The] Millionaire Sheriff
See Baker, Anderson Yancey

[The] Millionaire Tramp
See How, James Eads

Millman, Harry ?-1937   [HPPN]
American underworld figure
* [The] Lone Wolf of the Underworld

[El] Millonario [The Millionaire]
See Segura, Vicente

Millor
See Fernandes, Millor

Millpond, Miss
See Millbank, Anne Isabella

Mills, Abbott Paige 1889-   [BE]
American baseball player
* Mills, Jack

Mills, Alan
See Miller, Albert

Mills, [Rev.] Alfred Wilson 1832-?
[HPPN]
British clergyman
* A. W. M.

Mills, Algernon Victor 1905-   [WW]
Author
* Latimer, Rupert

Mills, Charles 1788-1826   [IP]
British historian and author
* Ducas, Theodore

Mills, Clarine Billingsley 1902?-
[HPPN]
Wife of American Congressman, Wilbur Daigh Mills
* Mills, Polly

Mills, Cotton Mather, Esq.
See Gaskell, Elizabeth Cleghorn

Mills, Donna
See Miller, Donna

Mills, Dorothy
See Howard, Dorothy Gray

Mills, Eleanor 1888-1922 [HPPN]
American murder victim
* Mills, Gypsy Queen

Mills, Enos Abijah 1870-1922 [HPPN, WBD]
American author
* [The] Columbus of the Rockies
* [The] Father of the Rocky Mountain National Park

Mills, Faith
See Payne, Odessa Strickland

Mills, Ferocious Fred
See Mills, Freddie

Mills, Florence Winfrey 1895-1927 [IBW]
American singer, actress, dancer
* Baby Florence

Mills, Frank
See Ransom, Frank

Mills, Freddie 1919-1965 [WBC]
British boxer
* Mills, Ferocious Fred

Mills, Frederick Allen 1869-1948 [ASC, BEW, DAM]
American composer
* Mills, Kerry

Mills, Guy
See Miller, Louis

Mills, Gypsy Queen
See Mills, Eleanor

Mills, Hayley 1946- [HPPN]
British actress
* [The] English Pixie
* [The] Merry Mime

Mills, Howard Robertson 1910- [BE]
American baseball player
* Mills, Lefty

Mills, Hugh [Travers] 20th c. [CC]
Author
* Travers, Hugh

Mills, Jack
See Mills, Abbott Paige

Mills, Janet Melanie Ailsa 1894- [CA]
British author
* Challoner, H. K.

Mills, John 19th c. [IP]
British sportsman and author
* [A] Man of Fashion

Mills, John
See Mills, Lewis Ernest Watts

Mills, Joseph T. 1845-1916 [HPPN]
American actor
* Hayden, Joseph

Mills, Kerry
See Mills, Frederick Allen

Mills, Lefty
See Mills, Howard Robertson

Mills, Lewis Ernest Watts 1908- [CA]
British actor, producer, director
* Mills, John

Mills, Martin
See Boyd, Martin

Mills, Osmington
See Brooks, Vivian Collin

Mills, P'lla
See Mills, Priscilla

Mills, Polly
See Mills, Clarine Billingsley

Mills, Priscilla 1918-1964 [IBW]
American painter and sculptor
* Mills, P'lla

Mills, Robert 1781-1855 [HPPN]
American architect and engineer
* [The] Architect of Public Buildings
* [The] Architect of the Washington Monument

Mills, Samuel John 1783-1818 [FFF]
American clergyman
* [The] Father of Foreign Mission Work

Mills, Terry Kenneth 1949- [IAW]
British author
* Mill, Ian St. John

Mills, Wee Willie
See Mills, William Grant [Willie]

Mills, Wilbur Daigh 1909- [HPPN]
American politician
* [The] Arkansas Hunkerer
* Texas, Mr.

Mills, William Grant [Willie] 1877-1914 [BE]
American baseball player
* Mills, Wee Willie

Mills, Yaroslava Surmach 1925- [ICB]
American illustrator
* Yaroslava

Millsap, Marjorie 1911- [F2]
Actress
* Lee, Dorothy

Millsaps, Daniel W., III 1919- [IAW]
American author
* Nuki
* Web, Dan

Millspaugh, Charles Frederick 1854-? [ALY]
American botanist and author
* Pesthe

Millstein, Rose Silverman 1903?-1975 [CA]
Russian-born American author, journalist, playwright
* Silverman, Rose

Milman, Harry Dubois
See Coryell, John Russell

Milman, Henry Hart 1791-1868 [NPS]
Clergyman
* [The] Poet Priest

Miln, H. Crichton ?-1957 [MBF]
British author
* Crichton, Jack
* Harper, Gillis

Milnar, Albert Joseph 1913- [BE]
American baseball player
* Milnar, Happy

Milnar, Happy
See Milnar, Albert Joseph

Milne, A. A.
See Milne, Alan Alexander

Milne, Alan Alexander 1882-1956 [LC, TC, WWL]
British author and playwright
* A. A. M.
* Milne, A. A.

Milne, Frances Margaret 1846-? [PI]
Irish-born poet
* Frances, Margaret

Milne, John Erskine 1931- [ART]
British sculptor
* J. E. M.

Milne, Pete
See Milne, William James

Milne, William James 1925- [BE]
American baseball player
* Milne, Pete

Milner, Bill
See Milner, Charles

Milner, Charles 20th c. [EF]
American football player
* Milner, Bill

Milner, D. E.
See Milner, Donald Ewart

Milner, Donald Ewart 1898- [ART]
British artist
* Milner, D. E.

Milner, Florence Cushman 20th c. [NAA]
American author and editor
* Cushman, Evelyn

Milner, George
See Hardinge, George Edward Charles

Milner, Hammer
See Milner, John David

Milner, Henry
See Wodson, Harry Milner

Milner, J. 1744-1797 [PA]
Author
* J. M.

Milner, John 1752-1826 [IP, WBD]
British prelate
* [The] English Athanasius
* J. M., D. D., F. S. A., Rev.

Milner, John David 1949- [BE]
American baseball player
* Milner, Hammer

Milner, Marion [Blackett] 1900- [AW, CA, WD]
British psychoanalyst and author
* Field, Joanna

Milner, Michael
See Cooper, Saul

Milner, Moses Embree 1829-1876 [BI, HPPN]
American frontiersman
* California Joe

Milner, Thomas Picton 1822-1891 [HPPN]
American journalist and soldier of fortune
* Picton, Thomas
* Preston, Paul

Milner Gibson, Mrs. 19th c. [SN]
* Newcome, Mrs. Hobson

Milnes, Richard Monckton [First Baron Houghton] 1809-1885 [DEL, HPPN]
British author and poet
* [A] Layman
* Milnes, Single Speech

Milnes, Single Speech
See Milnes, Richard Monckton [First Baron Houghton]

Milnes, Thomas Wray 1894- [WWL]
British author, poet, playwright
* Jig-Saw

Milnor, William 19th c. [IP]
American author
* [A] Member

Milo 6th c. BC [HN]
Greek athlete
* [The] Italian Samson

Milo
See Borra, Luigi

Milo
See Boyle, John

[La] Milo
See Montague, Pansy

Milo, George
See Vescia, George Milo

Milonas, Rolf
See Myller, Rolf

Miloradowitch, Michael 1770-1820 [DNNF, FFF, RH]
Russian army officer
* [The] Murat of Russia
* [The] Russian Murat

Milos, Milos
See Milosevic, Milos

Milosevic, Milos 1941-1966 [SC]
Yugoslav-born actor
* Milos, Milos

Milosevich, Michael [Mike] 1915-1966 [BE]
American baseball player
* Milosevich, Mollie

Milosevich, Mollie
See Milosevich, Michael [Mike]

Milosz, Czeslaw 1911- [CA]
Polish poet and author
* Syruc, J.

Milquetoast, Governor
See Milliken, William Grawn

Milsen, Oscar
See Mendelsohn, Oscar [Adolf]

Milsom, Charles Henry 1926- [WD]
British author and journalist
* Weston, William

Milstead, Cowboy
See Milstead, George Earl

Milstead, George Earl 1903- [BE]
American baseball player
* Milstead, Cowboy

Milstein, Lewis 1895-1980
Russian-born film director
* Milestone, Lewis

Miltenberg
See Lafontaine, August Heinrich Julius

Miltiades 6th c. BC [FFF, SN]
Athenian general
* [The] Tyrant of the Chersonese

Milto 5th c. BC [WBD]
Greek beauty
* Aspasia

Milton, Byron 1931-1973 [IBW]
American racer
* Milton, Doc

Milton, Doc
See Milton, Byron

Milton, Ernest 1905- [NOJ]
American jazz musician
* Milton, Kid

Milton, Georges
See Michaud, Georges

Milton, Gladys Alexandra 20th c. [WW]
Author
* Carlyle, Anthony

Milton, Hamilton Pirie Matt 1938- [SWI]
British swimmer
* Milton, Tony

Milton, Jack
See Kimbro, John M.

Milton, John 1608-1674 [DEA, FFF, HN, HPPN, NPS, PA, SN]
British poet
* [The] Black Mouthed Zoilus
* [The] Blind Poet

Milton, John (cont.)
* [The] Blind Tiresias of Modern Times
* [The] British Homer
* [The] Defender of the People
* [The] Divine
* [The] Divine Milton
* [The] English Mastiff
* [The] Great Gospel Gun
* [The] Homer of Britain
* J. M.
* [The] Lady
* [The] Lady of Christ College
* [The] Lady of Christ's
* [The] Pedagogue
* [The] Prince of Poets
* [The] Rival of Homer
* [The] Samson Agonistes
* Thyrsis
* [The] Trader in Faction

Milton, John R. 1924- [IAW]
American author
* Garrard, Christopher
* Lewis, Carson

Milton, Kid
See Milton, Ernest

Milton, Mark
See Pelton, Robert W[ayne]

Milton, Mark
See Shepherd, S. Rossiter

Milton, Marmaduke, Esq.
See Dunster, [Rev.] Charles

[The] Milton of Germany
See Klopstock, Friedrich Gottlieb

[The] Milton of Painting
See Fussli, Johann Heinrich

Milton, Oliver
See Hewitt, Cecil Rolph

Milton, Robert
See Davidor, Robert

Milton, Saul 20th c. [SFL]
Author
* Flinders, Karl

Milton, Tommy 20th c.
Auto racer
* [The] Great Milton

Milton, Tony
See Milton, Hamilton Pirie Matt

Milton, [Rev.] William 19th c. [HPPN]
British clergyman
* W. M.

Miltoun, Francis
See Mansfield, Milburg Francisco

Milverton, Charles A.
See Penzler, Otto

Milwaukee Phil Alderisio
See Alderisio, Felix Anthony

Milwaukee's Most Powerful Gambler
See Wicks, Thomas

Mimenza Castillo, Ricardo 1888- [NAA]
Mexican poet, writer, publisher
* Blas, Ruy

Mimi
See Dancourt, Marie Anne Carton

Mimi
See Perrin, Jeannine

[A] Mimicke
See Shakespeare, William

Mimieux, Yvette 1942- [HPPN]
French actress
* Hollywood's Little Princess

Mimile
See Buisson, Emile

Mimnermus 7th c. BC [DNNS]
Greek poet
* [The] Smyrnean Poet

Mina, Lino Amalia Espos Y 1809-1832
[BLB]
Spanish-born murderer and thief
* Espos, Carolino

Minacore, Calogero 1910-
American underworld figure
* Little Big Man
* [The] Little Man
* Marcello, Carlos

Minahan, Cotton
See Minahan, Edmund Joseph

Minahan, Edmund Joseph 1882-1958
[BE]
American baseball player
* Minahan, Cotton

Minarcin, Buster
See Minarcin, Rudy Anthony

Minarcin, Rudy Anthony 1930- [BE]
American baseball player
* Minarcin, Buster

Minasi, Dom
See Minasi, Dominic

Minasi, Dominic 1943- [EJ7]
American jazz musician
* Minasi, Dom

Mince, Johnny
See Muenzenberger, John Henry

Mincher, Don[ald Ray] 1938- [PB]
American baseball player
* Mincher, Mule

Mincher, Mule
See Mincher, Don[ald Ray]

Mincho 1352-1431 [WBD]
Japanese painter
* Cho Densu

Mincieli, Rose Laura 1912- [CA]
American author, educator, librarian
* Ross, Laura

Mincius, John 11th c. [WBD]
Pope
* Benedict X

Mind, Gottfried [or Godefroi] 1768-1814
[DNNS, FFF, RH]
Swiss painter
* [The] Bernese Friedli
* [The] Raphael of Cats

[The] Mind of the School
See Aristotle

Mindt, Heinz R. 1940- [IAW]
German author
* Paturi, Felix R.

Minehaha, Cornelius
See Wedekind, Benjamin Franklin

Mineo, Art
See Mineo, Attilio

Mineo, Attilio 1918- [ASC]
American musician
* Mineo, Art

Miner, Budd
See Miner, William

Miner, California Billy
See Miner, William

Miner, Charles 1800-1865 [IP, PA]
American author and journalist
* Harwood, John
* Poor Robert the Scribe

Miner, Enoch Newton ?-1923 [DNA]
American author
* Typist, Topsy

Miner, Jane Claypool 1933- [CA]
American author
* Claypool, Jane
* Ladd, Veronica

Miner, Lefty
See Miner, Ray[mond Theadore]

Miner, Matthew
See Wallmann, Jeffrey M[iner]

[The] Miner of Perranzabuloe
See Murrish, John

Miner, Old Bill
See Miner, William

Miner, Ray[mond Theadore] 1897-1963
[BE]
American baseball player
* Miner, Lefty

Miner, Sarah Luella 1861-1935 [HPPN]
American missionary and educator
* [The] Best Informed Foreigner in
  China

Miner, Tony
See Miner, Worthington

Miner, Virginia Scott 1901- [IA]
American author
* Hoosier Hank
* Hoosier Hannah
* Kay, Phoebe
* Kiplinger, David
* Thatcher, Amelia
* Wilcox, Hannah Simms

Miner, William 1847-1913 [BLB]
American stage and train robber
* Anderson, George
* Anderson, Sam
* Edwards, G. W.
* Miner, Budd
* Miner, California Billy

Miner, William (cont.)
* Miner, Old Bill
* Morgan, William

Miner, Worthington 1900?-1982 [FIR]
*American television producer, scriptwriter
director*
* Miner, Tony

Minerva
See Blatt, Josephine

Minerva
See Montagu, Mary Wortley

Minerve, Geezil
See Minerve, Harold

Minerve, Harold 1922- [EJ7]
American jazz musician
* Minerve, Geezil

Mines, John Flavel 1835-1891 [FFF]
American author
* Oldboy, Felix

Mines, Samuel 1909- [WD]
American author and editor
* Field, Peter

Minevitch, Borrah 1902?-1955 [HPPN]
*American harmonica player and
entertainer*
* [The] Harmonica Rascal

Ming Huang 685-762 [BI]
Chinese emperor
* T'ang Hsuan-tsung

Ming the Merciless
See Sigoloff, Sanford C.

Mingle, Belle 1858-1900 [BEW]
American actress
* Archer, Belle

Mingston, R. Gresham
See Stamp, Roger

Mingus, Charles [Charlie] 1923?-1979
American jazz musician
* Jazz's Angry Man

Minh, Big
See Minh, Duong Van

Minh, Duong Van 1916-
South Vietnamese military leader
* Minh, Big

Mini Tank Hughes
See Hughes, Leroy

[The] Miniature King of Swing
See Short, Robert Waltrip [Bobby]

[The] Miniature Mimic
See Kupper, Beatrice

[The] Miniature Petrarch
See Bembo, Pietro

[The] Miniature Sandow
See Matthes, Oscar

Minier, Nelson [joint pseudonym with
Adrien (Pearl) Stoutenburg]
See Baker, Laura Nelson

Minier, Nelson [joint pseudonym with Laura Nelson Baker]
See Stoutenburg, Adrien [Pearl]

Miniggio, Riccardo 20th c. [WF]
Italian actor
* Ric

Minimus, Lord
See Hudson, Jeffrey

[A] **Minister**
See Badger, Stephen

[A] **Minister**
See Bold, [Rev.] John

[A] **Minister**
See Cecil, [Rev.] Richard

[A] **Minister**
See Dickinson, [Rev.] Jonathan

[A] **Minister**
See Logie, [Rev] William

[The] **Minister**
See Peel, [Sir] Robert

[The] **Minister** [code name]
See Pryzchodzien, Zdzislaw

[A] **Minister**
See Stabback, [Rev.] Thomas

[A] **Minister**
See Stonhouse, [Sir] James

[A] **Minister**
See Webster, Samuel

[A] **Minister, Chaplain in the Army**
See Whittle, John

[A] **Minister in Boston**
See Mather, Cotton

[A] **Minister in the Country**
See Lewis, [Rev.] John

[A] **Minister in the Country**
See Welchman, Edward

[A] **Minister of a Chapel of Ease**
See Gray, Andrew

[The] **Minister of Enthusiasm**
See Charles, Mike

[The] **Minister of Fashion**
See Laurent, Marie-Jeanne

[A] **Minister of Known Learning, Piety, and Integrity**
See Hamilton, [Rev.] Alexander

[A] **Minister of London**
See Hickes, George

[A] **Minister of Neither Syndicate**
See Coddington, Henry

[A] **Minister of That Church**
See Gordon [or Gordone], [Rev.] James

[A] **Minister of the Church**
See Johnson, Samuel

[The] **Minister of the Church**
See Leonard, Henry Charles

[A] **Minister of the Church of England**
See Dodd, William

[A] **Minister of the Church of England**
See Howard, John

[A] **Minister of the Church of England**
See Waterland, [Rev.] Joseph

[A] **Minister of the Church of England**
See Webster, George Edis

[A] **Minister of the Church of Ireland**
See Perceval, Arthur Philip

[A] **Minister of the Church of Scotland**
See Ballantyne, John

[A] **Minister of the Church of Scotland**
See Currie, John

[A] **Minister of the Church of Scotland**
See Irvine, Alexander

[A] **Minister of the Church of Scotland**
See Moncrieff, Alexander

[A] **Minister of the Church of Scotland**
See Wilson, William

[A] **Minister of the Established Church**
See Duncan, Henry

[A] **Minister of the Gospel**
See Clap, Nathaniel

[A] **Minister of the Gospel**
See Snow, [Rev.] Herman

[A] **Minister of the Gospel**
See Wilson, Joseph

[A] **Minister of the Interior**
See Whiting, Sydney

[The] **Minister of Their Parish**
See Clubbe, [Rev.] William

[La] **Ministerie**
See Babinot, Albert

[A] **Ministering Friend of the People Called Quakers**
See Foe, Daniel

Minkovitz, Moshe 1936- [CA]
Israeli anthropologist and author
* Shokeid, Moshe

Minkus, Aloysius Ludwig 1827-1890 [HPPN]
Austrian violinist and composer
* Minkus, Leon

Minkus, Leon
See Minkus, Aloysius Ludwig

Minnaar-Vos, Anna
See Vos, Anna Beyera

[The] **Minneapolis Tomboy**
See Berg, Patricia J. [Patty]

Minner, Lefty
See Minner, Paul Edison

Minner, Paul Edison 1923- [BE]
American baseball player
* Minner, Lefty

Minnesinger to Millionaires
See Lee, Ivy Ledbetter

Minnesota Fats
See Wanderone, Rudolf Walter, Jr.

Minnesota, Miss
See Shopp, Beatrice Bella

Minnesota's Potato King
See Schroeder, Henry

Mino da Fiesole 1429-1484 [BI]
Italian sculptor
* Mino di Giovanni

Mino di Giovanni
See Mino da Fiesole

Minogue, Dennis 20th c.
American singer, songwriter, baseball player
* Cashman, Terry

Minor
See Balbus, Lucius Cornelius

Minor, Dan 20th c. [NP]
American jazz musician
* Big D

Minor, Dryden
See O'Donnell, Francis Hugh

Minor, Fred 1913- [NOJ]
American jazz musician
* Minor, H. E.

Minor, H. E.
See Minor, Fred

Minority of One
See Stanhope, Charles [Third Earl of Stanhope]

Minoso, Minnie
See Minoso, Saturnino Orestes Arrieta Armas

Minoso, Saturnino Orestes Arrieta Armas 1922- [BE, IBW]
Cuban-born baseball player
* [The] Cuban Comet
* Minoso, Minnie
* [The] Speed Merchant
* White Sox Katzenjammer Kid

Minot, Laurence 1300?-1352 [HN]
British poet
* [The] English Tyrtaeos

Minski, Nikolai Maksimovich
See Vilenkin, Nikolai Maksimovich

Minsky, Betty Jane [Toebe] 1932- [CA]
American author
* Toby, Liz

Minson, Roland 20th c. [MEB]
American basketball player
* [The] Cat

[The] **Minstrel Maiden of Mobile**
See Harriss, Julia Mildred

[The] **Minstrel Man**
See Gersenfeld, Benjamin

[The] **Minstrel of the Border**
See Scott, [Sir] Walter

Mintell, Frank Otto 1886-1951 [BX, RBE]
German-born boxer
* Mantell, Frank

Minter, Davide C. 1892- [WWL]
British author and editor
* Caroline

Minter, Iverson 1936- [BWW, EJ7]
American singer
* Bey, Iverson
* Cryin' Red
* Fuller, Playboy
* Fuller, Richard Lee
* Fuller, Rocky
* Guitar Red
* James, Elmore, Jr.
* Louisiana Red
* Minter, Red
* Rockin' Red
* Walkin' Slim

Minter, Mary Miles
See Shelby, Juliet

Minter, Red
See Minter, Iverson

Minto-Cowen, Frances
See Munthe, Frances

Minton, Paula
See Litwinsky, Paul

Minton, Sherman 1890- [HPPN]
American politician
* [The] King of the New Dealers
* Shay

Minton, Yvonne 1942?- [HPPN]
American singer
* [The] Strawberry Blonde

Mintun, Jake
See Mintun, John

Mintun, John 20th c. [EF]
American football player
* Mintun, Jake

Minturn, Edward
See Judson, Edward Zane Carroll

Minturn, Edward
See Urner, Nathan Dane

Mintwood
See Wager, Mary A. E.

Mintz, Barney
See Mintz, Bernard D.

Mintz, Bernard D. 20th c. [HPPN]
American football player
* Mintz, Barney

Mintz, David 1927- [FC, TR]
American actor
* Knight, David

Mintz, Joan 1920- [BEW]
American publisher and writer
* Marlowe, Joan

Mintz, Joyce Lois 1933- [CA]
American author and editor
* Madison, Joyce

Minus
See Engh, Bjorg Larsen

[A] Minute Philosopher
See Kingsley, Charles

Minuto [Minute]
See Vargas y Gonzalez, Enrique

[The] Minx of the Movies
See Compson, Eleanor Luicime

Minzesheimer, Blanche 1891-1963 [BEW]
American theatrical performer
* Blanche, Belle

Miomandre, Francis de
See Durand, Francois

Mione, Peter 20th c. [BLB]
American underworld figure
* Muggins, Petey

Miorcec de Kerdanet, Daniel Louis Mathurin 1793-? [IP]
French attorney, librarian, author
* Pennec, R. P. Cyrille

Mir
See Muhammad Taki

Mira
See Brunet, Jean Joseph

Mirabeau, Barrel
See Riqueti, [Andre] Boniface [Louis]

Mirabeau, Comte de
See Riqueti, Honore Gabriel Victor

Mirabeau, Marquis de
See Riqueti, Victor

[The] Mirabeau of Brazil
See Andrada e Silva, Antonio de

[The] Mirabeau of the Gironde
See Vergniaud, Pierre Victurnien

[The] Mirabeau of the Markets
See Danton, Georges Jacques

[The] Mirabeau of the Mob
See Danton, Georges Jacques

[The] Mirabeau of the Sans Culottes
See Danton, Georges Jacques

Mirabeau Tonneau
See Riqueti, [Andre] Boniface [Louis]

Mirabeau, Tub
See Riqueti, Honore Gabriel Victor

Mirabeau, Vicomte de
See Riqueti, [Andre] Boniface [Louis]

Mirabehn [Sister Mira]
See Slade, Madeleine

Mirabel
See Daniel, Rosa

Mirabel, Doctor
See Churchill, John [First Duke of Marlborough]

Mirabella, Gesualdo 1915- [OP]
Italian producer, singer, actor
* Vassallo, Aldo Mirabella

Mirabilia
See Maraviglia, Guiseppe Maria

Mirabilis, Doctor
See Bacon, Roger

[The] Miracle Child
See Gortner, Hugh Marjoe Ross

[The] Miracle Doctor
See Demara, Ferdinand Waldo, Jr.

[The] Miracle Man
See Brown, Jerald Ray

[The] Miracle Man
See Kissinger, Henry Alfred

[The] Miracle Man
See Stallings, George Tweedy

Miracle Man from Maine
See Muskie, Ed[mund Sixtus]

[The] Miracle Man of Holland
See Croiset, Gerard

[The] Miracle Man of Milk
See Borden, Gail

[The] Miracle Man of the Rockies
See Albeck, Stan

[The] Miracle Man of the Western Front
See Kazanjian, Varaztad H.

[The] Miracle Man of Virginia Beach
See Cayce, Edgar

[The] Miracle of Nature
See Christina

[The] Miracle of Our Age
See Sidney, [Sir] Philip

[The] Miracle of the Age
See Bacon, Roger

[The] Miracle of Time
See Elizabeth I

Miracle Worker
See Kissinger, Henry Alfred

[The] Miraculous Child
See D'Artois, Henri Charles Ferdinand Marie

Miraglia, Emilio 20th c. [WF]
Italian director
* Brady, Hal

Miramant, Yves
See Romanette, Irmine

Mirambo ?-1885 [FFF]
East African chieftain
* [The] Napoleon of Africa

Mirana, Paul 20th c. [SG]
Boxer
* Moran, Pal

Miranda
See Falconer, Miranda Hicks

Miranda, Carmen
See Da Cunha, Maria Do Carmo

Miranda, Guillermo Perez 1926- [BE]
Cuban-born baseball player
* Miranda, Willie

Miranda, Isa
See Sampietro, Ines Isabella

Miranda, Javier
See Bioy-Casares, Adolfo

Miranda, Maria
See Krenz-Senior, Ethel Rosabelle

Miranda, Roque 1799-1843 [GS]
Spanish bullfighter
* Rigores [Precise One]

Miranda, Willie
See Miranda, Guillermo Perez

Miranda da Silva Filho, Sebastio 1952-
[AES]
Brazilian soccer player
* Mirandinha

Mirande, Yves
See Le Querrec, A. Charles

Mirandinha
See Miranda da Silva Filho, Sebastio

[The] Mirandola of His Age
See Digby, [Sir] Kenelm

Mircea ?-1418 [WBD]
Prince of Walachia
* [The] Great

Mirecourt, Eugene de
See Jacquot, Charles Jean Baptiste

Mirepoix, Camille 1926- [CA]
British author and journalist
* Adastra

Mirglip, Knarf
See Pilgrim, Frank

Miriam, [Sister]
See Gallagher, Margaret Miriam

Miriam
See Heath, Maggie E.

Miriam
See Mary Francis of Jesus, [Sister]

Miriam
See Przesmycki, Zenon

Miriam of the Holy Spirit, [Sister]
See Powers, Jessica

Miriam Teresa, [Sister]
See Demjanovich, Teresa

Mirko
See Basaldella, Mirko

Mirliter
See Boue de Villiers, Amable Louis

Mirmillo
See Gibbons, William

Miroeus
See Lemire, Aubert

Miron
See Hazeltine, Miron J.

Miroslava
See Stern, Miroslava

[The] Mirror of all Martial Men
See Montacute [or Montagu], Thomas
de

[The] Mirror of Chivalry
See Rupert

[The] Mirror of Courtesy
See Sidney, [Sir] Philip

[The] Mirror of Her Age
See Bradstreet, Anne

[The] Mirror of Justice
See Victoria

Mirror, Tom
See Estcourt, Richard

[The] Mirror Upholder of His Age
See Shakespeare, William

Mirus, Ludmilla 1905- [IAW]
Austrian-born author
* Egger, Ellen
* Mirus-Kauba, Ludmilla

Mirus-Kauba, Ludmilla
See Mirus, Ludmilla

Mirza, Huseyn Ali 1817-1892 [HPPN]
Founder of the Bahai sect
* Baha Ullah [Spendor of God]

Mirza Muhammad Ali 1676-1756
[WBD]
Nawab of Bengal
* Ali Vardi Khan
* Allahvardi Khan

Mirza, Nusrat Ali 1882-? [WWL]
Welsh author
* Marc, Elizabeth

[The] Misanthrope
See Bremer, Arthur Herman

[The] Misanthrope of Athens
See Timon

Mischakoff, Mischa
See Fischberg, Mischa

Mischievous Andy
See Jackson, Andrew

[The] Miscreant
See Jenkins, John

Miser
See Foe, Daniel

Misericordia
See Foe, Daniel

Miserocchi, Anna 20th c. [WF]
Italian actress
* Wart, Helen

Mises, Dr.
See Fechner, Gustav Theodor

Mishima, Yukio
See Hiraoka, Kimitake

Mishra, Vidhata 1934- [IAW]
Indian author
* Shrividhata

Miske, Billy
See Miskel, William

Miskel, William 20th c. [SG]
Boxer
* Miske, Billy

Misleader of the Papacy
See Gaetano [or Caetani], Benedetto

Mislen, John 20th c. [HPPN]
American hobo
* [The] Hardrock Kid
* [The] King of the Hoboes

Miso Dolos
See Leslie, Charles

Misosarum, Gregory
See Swift, Jonathan

Misostratus
See Taylor, John

Miss America, Mr.
See Marks, Albert A.

Miss Bess
See Farmer, Bess

Miss Dorothy
See De Guiche, Dorothy

Miss Frances
See Horwich, Frances R[appaport]

Miss George
See Sidus, Georgina

Miss Juliet
See Delf, Juliet

Miss Kimiko [code name used by
Japanese during World War II]
See Roosevelt, Franklin Delano

Miss Lil
See Prado, Katie

Miss Lillian
See Carter, Lillian [Gordy]

Miss Lillian
See De Guiche, Lillian

Miss Lou
See Bennett, Louise Simone

Miss M
See McDonald, Willie Ruth

Miss Mary
See Larkins, Mary

Miss Mit
See Talmadge, Mattie

Miss Nancy
See Oldfield, Anna

Miss Nina
See Duff, Nina

Miss P.
See Plumptre, Anne

Miss Ruth
See Dennis, Ruth

Miss Tessie
See Daroux, Tessie Wall

Miss Tommie
See Clark, Tommie

Miss Vicky
See Khaury, Victoria Budinger

Miss X
See Goodrich-Freer, Adela M.

Miss Z
See Cusseaux, Zulema

[The] Missing Link
See Hatch, Sidney Stewart

[The] Missing Witness
See Schepps, Sam[uel]

[A] Missionary
See Breck, James Lloyd

[The] Missionary Bishop of America
See Doane, George Washington

[The] Missionary Bishop of Melanesia
See Patteson, John Coleridge

[A] Missionary from the Honourable Society for Propagating the Gospel
See Wetmore, [Rev.] James

Mississippi Big Joe
See Williams, Joe

Mississippi Fred McDowell
See McDowell, Frederick

Mississippi Joe Callicott
See Callicott, Joe

Mississippi John Jackson
See Jackson, John H.

Mississippi Matilda
See Witherspoon, Matilda

[The] Mississippi Mockingbird
See Harris, Wynonie

[The] Mississippi Mudcat
See Bush, Guy Terrell

Mississippi Mudder
See McCoy, Charles [Charlie]

Mississippi Mudder
See McCoy, Joe

[The] Mississippi River Sharper
See Devol, George

Missoni, Ottavio
Italian fashion designer
* Missoni, Tai

Missoni, Tai
See Missoni, Ottavio

[The] Missouri Kid
See Rudolph, William [Bill]

Missouri's Tom Dewey
See Milligan, Maurice Morton

Mr. A.
See Rothstein, Arnold

Mr. Abe
See Rosenberg, Abraham

Mr. B
See Balanchivadze, Gyorgi Melitonovitch

Mr. B
See Eckstein, William Clarence

Mr. Big in Crime
See Accardo, Antonio Leonardo

Mr. Big of Tin Pan Alley
See Gershvin, Jacob

Mr. Bo
See Collins, Louis Bo

Mr. Buddy
See Durham, Edward Lee

Mr. C
See Chambers, Wallace

Mr. Charlie
See Cannon, Charles A.

Mr. Cliff
See Roberts, Clifford

Mr. D.
See Derham, William

Mr. D.
See Manley, Dexter

Mr. Dooley's Friend
See Clemens, Samuel Langhorne

Mr. Eli
See Robinson, Eli

Mr. Fonda's Baby Jane
See Fonda, Jane

Mr. Frank
See Richardson, Frank

Mr. Frederick
See Mellinger, Frederick N.

Mr. Joe
See Wright, Joseph, Sr.

Mr. Joe
See Zerilli, Joseph

Mr. John
See Harberger, John Pico

Mr. Kenneth
See Marlowe, Kenneth

Mr. Mack
See Lewis, Mack

Mr. Max
See Rosenberg, Max

Mr. Nino
See Schiavon, Beniamino

Mr. Nixon's Professor
See Kissinger, Henry Alfred

Mr. P.
See Prysock, Arthur

Mr. P. [[code name used during World War II]]
See Churchill, Winston Spencer

Mr. Rick
See Randall, Richard

Mr. Sam
See Rayburn, Sam Taliaferro

Mr. Seward's Pet
See Hale, Charles

Mr. T
See Telling, Edward Riggs

Mr. T.
See Tero, Lawrence

Mr. T.
See Tureaud, Lawrence

Mr. Walter
See Baird, Walter J.

Mr. X
See Barber, Miller

Mr. X
See Hoch, Edward D[entinger]

Mr. X
See Kennan, George Frost

Mr. X
See Meyer, Russ

Mr. X
See Rescigno, Xavier Frederick

Mr. Z.
See Haiduc, Motu

Misterioso, L'Angelo
See Harrison, George

Mistinguett
See Bourgeois, Jeanne Marie

[The] Mistletoe Politician
See Van Buren, Martin

Mistral, Gabriela
See Godoy Alcayaga, Lucila

Mistral, George
See Mistral, Jorge

Mistral, Jorge 1923-1972 [SC]
Actor
* Mistral, George

[The] Mistress of Misdirection
See Christie, Agatha [Mary Clarissa]

[The] Mistress of Sophisticated Slapstick
See Munston, Constance Sylvia

[The] Mistress of the Closeup
See Griffith, Corinne

Mistress of the White House
See Madison, Dorothy Payne Todd

Mitcham, Gilroy
See Newton, William Simpson

Mitchel, Jackson
See Matcha, Jack

Mitchel, John Purroy 1879-1918
[HPPN]
American politician and investigator
* Young Torquemada

Mitchel, Ormsby McKnight 1810-1862
[DNNF, DNNS, HPPN, SN]
American army officer and astronomer
* [The] Director
* Old Stars

Mitchell, Adam
See Pyle, Hilary

Mitchell, Adrian 1932- [CA, IAW]
British author, poet, playwright
* Hewitt, Ben
* Jones, Volcano
* Mudgeon, Apeman
* Treacle, Uncle

Mitchell, Agnes W. 19th c. [IP]
American author
* A. W. M.

Mitchell, Arthur Adam 1934- [IBW]
American choreographer
* Poet in Motion

Mitchell, Augustus William 1913- [BA]
American physician
* Mitchell, Mitch

Mitchell, Billy 1917?-1978 [FIR]
Entertainer
* Postime, Mr.

Mitchell, Blue
See Mitchell, Richard Allen

Mitchell, Bunny
See Mitchell, Martha

Mitchell, Cameron
See Mitzell, Cameron M.

Mitchell, Carolyn
See Thomason, Barbara Ann

Mitchell, Charles 20th c.
American banker
* Mitchell, Sunshine Charlie

Mitchell, Charles J.
See O'Dea, Patrick J.

Mitchell, Charlie
See Gordon, Steven

Mitchell, Charlotte Grimes 1872-?
[NAA]
American author
* Twain, Minerva Mark

Mitchell, Clarence M., III 1940- [IBW]
American politician
* [The] Lone Wolf Politician

Mitchell, Clarence M., Jr. 1911- [IBW]
American attorney, congressional lobbyist, former boxer
* [The] 101st Senator
* [The] Shamrock Kid

Mitchell, Clyde [house pseudonym, Ziff-Davis]
See Ellison, Harlan [Jay]

Mitchell, Clyde [joint pseudonym with Robert Silverberg] [house pseudonym, Ziff-Davis]
See Garrett, [Gordon] Randall [Philip David]

Mitchell, Clyde [joint pseudonym with Randall Garrett] [house pseudonym, Ziff-Davis]
See Silverberg, Robert

Mitchell, Cooney
See Mitchell, Nelson

Mitchell, Dolly
See Melton, Mrs. William

Mitchell, Donald Grant 1822-1908
[DEL, FFF, HFN, HPPN, IP, PA]
American author
* [A] Bachelor
* Caius
* D. G. M.
* Marvel, Ik [of Ike]
* Marvel, J. K.
* [An] Opera Goer
* Timon, John

Mitchell, Doris 20th c. [NBB]
American musician
* Lightnin'

Mitchell, Elizabeth Harcourt [PA]
Author
* E. H. R.

Mitchell, Ewan
See Janner, Greville Ewan

Mitchell, Frederick Francis
See Yapp, Frederick Francis

Mitchell, G. [PA]
Author
* One from the Plow

Mitchell, Gene
See Hoadley, H. O[rlo]

Mitchell, George 1899- [MY]
American jazz musician
* Mitchell, Mitch

Mitchell, Ginger
See Mitchell, Rhea

Mitchell, Gladys [Maude Winifred]
1901- [CA, CC, EMD]
British author
* Hockaby, Stephen
* Torrie, Malcolm

Mitchell, Gordon B. 1932- [DAM, EJ]
American jazz musician
* Mitchell, Whitey

Mitchell, Guy
See Cernick, Al

Mitchell, Helen
See McRuer, Helen

Mitchell, Helen Porter 1861-1931
[BBD, IPA, LC]
Australian opera singer
* Melba, Nellie

Mitchell, Isaac 1859-1912 [HPPN]
American editor and author
* Nelson, Joseph

Mitchell, Isabel Mary 1893- [AW]
Australian author
* Plain, Josephine

Mitchell, Jack
See Sellers, Connie Leslie, Jr.

Mitchell, James 1926- [AW, CA]
British author
* Munro, James

Mitchell, James Leslie 1901-1935 [LC, TC, TC1]
Scottish author, archaeologist, historian
* Gibbon, Lewis Grassic

Mitchell, John ?-1772 [IP]
British-born American physician and author
* [An] Impartial Hand

Mitchell, John 1794-1870 [DNA, IP, PA]
American author and clergyman
* Chester, John
* Graduate of Yale of the Class of 1821

Mitchell, John 1882-1951 [CCL]
Canadian author
* Slater, Patrick

Mitchell, John 19th c. [IP]
British author
* [A] Practical Printer

Mitchell, John 1946- [RO2]
British musician
* Mitchell, Mitch

Mitchell, John
See Lamy, Douglas N.

Mitchell, John Hanlon 1897-1953
[NAA]
Canadian author
* Hanlon, John

Mitchell, John Kearsley 1798-1858
[FFF]
American physician and poet
* [A] Yankee

Mitchell, John Kearsley 20th c. [HPPN]
Lover of American murder victim Dorothy Keenan
* Marshall, Mr.

Mitchell, John Newton 1913- [HPPN]
American attorney and politician
* [The] Nation's Chief Lawyer
* [The] Phantom President of the United States
* [The] President's Worst Friend

Mitchell, Joni
See Anderson, Roberta Joan

Mitchell, K. L.
See Lamb, Elizabeth Searle

Mitchell, Keith Moore 1927- [DAM, EJ, PMJ]
American jazz musician
* Mitchell, Red

Mitchell, Kerry
See Wilkes-Hunter, Richard

Mitchell, Langdon [Elwin] 1862-?
[NAA]
American playwright
* Varley, John Philip

Mitchell, Lemonte Felton 1939- [BA]
American personnel director
* Mitchell, Mitch

Mitchell, Lottie Pearl ?-1974 [IBW]
American civil rights leader
* AKA, Miss
* Lady Pearl
* NAACP, Miss

Mitchell, Madman
See Valiant, Jerry

Mitchell, Maggie
See Mitchell, Margaret Julia

Mitchell, Maggie
See Paddock, Mrs.

Mitchell, Margaret
See Marsh, Margaret Munnerlyn
Mitchell

Mitchell, Margaret Julia 1837-1918
[HPPN]
American author
* Mitchell, Maggie

Mitchell, Maria 1818-? [HPPN]
American astronomer
* M. M.

Mitchell, Martha 1941-
*Administrative aide to American president
Jimmy Carter*
* Mitchell, Bunny

**Mitchell, Martha Elizabeth Beall
Jennings** 1918- [HPPN]
*Wife of American attorney general, John
Mitchell*
* American Mouth of the Year
* Kalmbach, Doris
* [The] Last of the Great Southern
  Belles
* Mitchell, Marty
* [The] Mouth That Roared
* Watergate's Warbler

Mitchell, Marty
See Mitchell, Martha Elizabeth Beall
Jennings

Mitchell, Mary 1892-
Australian author
* Plain, Josephine

Mitchell, Melvin 1953- [BA]
American football player
* Brown, Bob

[The] Mitchell Meteor
See Morenz, Howarth William

Mitchell, Mitch
See Mitchell, Augustus William

Mitchell, Mitch
See Mitchell, George

Mitchell, Mitch
See Mitchell, John

Mitchell, Mitch
See Mitchell, Lemonte Felton

Mitchell, Myron 1899- [BX, RBE]
American boxer
* Mitchell, Pinkey

Mitchell, Nelson 1802-1875 [BI]
American farmer
* Mitchell, Cooney

Mitchell, Oliver 1876-1945 [BEW]
American producer, director, author
* Morosco, Oliver

Mitchell, P. J.
See Mitchell, Parren James

Mitchell, Paige
See Ginnes, Judith S.

Mitchell, Parren James 1938- [IBW]
American politician
* Mitchell, P. J.

Mitchell, Pinkey
See Mitchell, Myron

Mitchell, Priscilla 1941- [FCW]
American singer
* Sadina

Mitchell, R. C. [FFF, PA]
British writer
* Creighton, Rob
* Vigilant

Mitchell, R. J.
See Mitchell, Robert James

Mitchell, Red
See Mitchell, Keith Moore

Mitchell, Red
See Mitchell, William Dickie

Mitchell, Rhea 1905-1957 [SC]
American actress
* Mitchell, Ginger

Mitchell, Richard Allen 1930-1979
[DAM, EJ]
American jazz musician
* Mitchell, Blue

Mitchell, Robert 19th c. [PA]
Author
* Bomeair, D. H.

Mitchell, Robert James 1930- [ART]
British sculptor
* Mitchell, R. J.

Mitchell, Roscoe 20th c. [IBW]
American actor and comedian
* Mitchell, Scoey

Mitchell, Ruth
See Kornfeld, Ruth

Mitchell, S. Valentine
See Gammell, Susanna Valentine
Mitchell

Mitchell, [Dr.] S[ilas] Weir 1829-1914
[HPPN]
American physician, author, poet
* Chester, John

Mitchell, Samuel Latham 1764-1831
[HPPN]
Scientist and politician
* [The] Nestor of American Science

Mitchell, Scoey
See Mitchell, Roscoe

Mitchell, Scott
See Godfrey, Lionel Robert Holcombe

Mitchell, Stanley
See Albertini, Adalberto

Mitchell, Stephen Mix 1743-1835
[HPPN]
American jurist and statesman
* [The] Stalking Library

Mitchell, Sunshine Charlie
See Mitchell, Charles

Mitchell, Thomas 1836-? [HPPN]
British politician
* St. Petersburg
* T. M.

Mitchell, Thomas Peter 19th c. [IP]
British author
* Elmlicht, Twinrock, Esq.

Mitchell, Ugo 1883- [BX]
Italian-born boxer
* Kelly, Hugo

Mitchell, Whitey
See Mitchell, Gordon B.

Mitchell, William 18th c. [DNNF, RH,
SN]
Scottish tin-plate worker and author
* [The] Great Tinclarian Doctor

Mitchell, William [Bill] 1853-1928 [BI,
BLB]
American murderer
* Russell, Baldy

Mitchell, William [Billy] 1879-1936
[HPPN]
American military leader
* [The] Flying General
* [The] Pioneer of Air Power

Mitchell, William 19th c. [IP]
Scottish author
* [A] Free Church Elder

Mitchell, William 1916-1977 [BDF, FC,
WEF]
British actor
* Finch, Peter
* Finchy

Mitchell, William Dickie 1930- [CEI]
Canadian-born hockey player
* Mitchell, Red

Mitchell, Young
See Herget, John L.

Mitchell, Yvonne
See Joseph, Yvonne

Mitchell-Cotts, [Sir] William Campbell
1903?-1964 [BEW]
British actor
* Cotts, Campbell

Mitchelson, Marvin 1929?-
American attorney
* [The] Paladin of Palimony
* [The] Paladin of Paramours
* [The] Pioneer of Palomony
* [The] Prince of Palimony
* [The] Sultan of Split

Mitchill, Samuel Latham 1764-1831 [IP]
American scientist and author
* [A] Gentleman Residing in the City

[The] Mite Manager
See Huggins, Miller James

Mitelberg, Louis 1919- [WEC]
French cartoonist
* Tim

Mitford, John ?-1831 [FFF]
British journalist and poet
* Burton, Alfred

Mitford, Nancy 1904-1973 [CA]
British author
* Rodd, Nancy Freeman-Mitford

Mithridates I 2nd c. BC [WBD]
King of Parthia
* Arsaces VI

Mithridates II 2nd c. BC [WBD]
King of Parthia
* [The] Great

Mithridates VI Eupator 1st c. BC
[WBD]
King of Parthia
* [The] Great

[El] Mito [The Myth]
See Rodriguez, Carlos

Mitra, Sarada Prasanna 1865-1915
[NAD]
Spiritual teacher
* Trigunatita, [Swami]

[The] Mitre Courtier
See Lamb, Charles

[The] Mitred Ass
See Potier, Augustin

Mitred Dulness
See Parker, Samuel

[The] Mitred Layman
See O'Beirne, Thomas Lewis

Mitru, Alexandru 1914- [IAW]
Rumanian author
* Piraianu, Alexandru

Mitry, Jean
See Goetgheluck Le Rouge Taillard
Des Acres De Presfontaines, Jean Rene

Mitscher, Marc Andrew 1887-
American naval officer
* Air Mica [code name used during
World War II]
* [The] Flying Admiral

Mitscher, Marc Andrew (cont.)
* Mitscher, Mich
* Mitscher, Pete

Mitscher, Mich
See Mitscher, Marc Andrew

Mitscher, Pete
See Mitscher, Marc Andrew

Mitskevich, A. P. 20th c. [SFP]
Author
* Dneprov, Anatoly

Mitsuyori, Kimura 1559-1635 [WBD]
Japanese painter
* Sanraku, Kano

Mittarilli, Nicolo Gracome 1707-1777
[PA]
Author
* Benedetto, Giovanni

Mittelholzer, Edgar 1909-1965 [CW]
Guyanese-born author, playwright, poet
* Woodsley, H. Austin

Mitterling, Ralph 1890-1956 [BE]
American baseball player
* Mitterling, Sarge

Mitterling, Sarge
See Mitterling, Ralph

**Mitterrand, Francois Maurice Adrien
Marie** 1916-
French president
* Morland

Mitton, G. E.
See Scott, Geraldine Edith

Mitzell, Cameron M. 1918- [BEW, ITA]
American actor
* Mitchell, Cameron

Mitzou
See Izquierdo, Mitzou

Mivart, St. George Jackson 1827-1900
[DEA]
British author
* Drew, D'Arcy

Mix, Katherine Lyon [CA]
American author
* Lyon, Katherine

Mix, Tom 1880-1940 [HPPN]
American actor
* America's Favorite Cowboy
* Mason, Tex
* [The] Ralston Straight Shooter
* [The] World's Champion Cowboy

Mix, Tom
See Santoro, Salvatore

Mix-Up, Professor
See Fox, Karrell

Mixter, Elisabeth W.
See Morss, Elizabeth W.

Miyazaki, Toshio 20th c. [EE]
Japanese intelligence agent
* Tanni

Miyori, Kim
See Utsunomiya, Cheryl

Mize, John Robert 1913- [BE, BN, PB]
American baseball player
* [The] Big Cat
* Mize, Skippy

Mize, Skippy
See Mize, John Robert

Mizell, Vinegar Bend
See Mizell, Wilmer David

Mizell, Wilmer David 1930- [BE, PB]
American baseball player
* Mizell, Vinegar Bend

Mizerak, Miz
See Mizerak, Steve

Mizerak, Steve 20th c.
American billiard player
* Mizerak, Miz

Mizmoon
See Soltysik, Patricia

Mizner, Bill
See Mizner, Wilson

Mizner, Elizabeth Howard 1907- [CA]
American author
* Howard, Elizabeth

Mizner, Wilson 1876-1933 [HPPN]
*American gambler, entrepreneur,
playwright, author*
* [The] Amazing Mizner
* [The] Greatest Man About Town Any
Town Ever Had
* Mizner, Bill

Mizpah
See Lea, Henry Charles

M'Keown, Darby
See Donnelly, James

Mlad-Miltijad
See Djuricic, Uladen St.

M'Laggan, Alexander 18th c. [IP]
Scottish clergyman and author
* [A] Gentleman in the North

M'Lauchlan, Thomas 19th c. [IP]
Scottish author
* [An] Eye Witness

Mlckovsky, Raymond James 1916-1969
[BE]
American baseball player
* Mack, Ray

M'Lelland, George 19th c. [IP]
Scottish author
* [A] Friend to the Peace of the
Church of Scotland

Mlle. Rosalie
See Levasseur, Marie Claude Josephe

Mmcoatman
See Coatman, Maureen Margaret

M'Neill, Archibald 19th c. [IP]
Scottish author
* [A] Member of the Society of
Antiquaries of Scotland

Mnemon
See Artaxerxes II

Mnemonicus
See Nares, Robert

Mnesarete 4th c. BC [HPPN]
Greek courtesan
* Phryne

Mo, Billy
See Joachim, Peter Mico

Moan, Emmett 20th c. [EF]
American football player
* Moan, Kelly

Moan, Kelly
See Moan, Emmett

Moanin' Matty Bell
See Bell, Madison A.

Moatlodi
See Chamberlain, Joseph

Moberley, A. 19th c. [IP]
British poet
* [A] Wanderer

Moberly, C. A. E.
See Moberly, Charlotte Anne Elizabeth

Moberly, Charlotte Anne Elizabeth
1846-1937 [HPPN]
British author
* Moberly, C. A. E.

[The] Mobile Magician
See Cousy, Robert J. [Bob]

Mobley, Walt
See Burgess, Michael Roy

[The] Mob's Financial Genius
See Suchowljansky, Maier

Mobutu, Joseph Desire 1930- [BI, IBW]
President of Zaire
* [Le] Guide
* Mobutu, Sese Seko

Mobutu, Sese Seko
See Mobutu, Joseph Desire

Mocatta, Dorothy Allen 1900- [WWL]
British author
* Mocatta, Frances

Mocatta, Frances
See Mocatta, Dorothy Allen

[The] Mock Preacher
See Whitefield, George

[The] Mocking Bird of Our Parnassian Ornithology
See Byron, George Gordon Noel

Mocky, Jean-Pierre
See Mokiejeswki, Jean

Moco [Joint signature with Jorgen Mogensen]
See Cornelius, Siegfried

Moco [Joint signature with Siegfried Cornelius]
See Mogensen, Jorgen

Moctezuma, Matos 20th c. [TI 8-16-82]
Mexican archaeologist
* Moctezuma III

Moctezuma III
See Moctezuma, Matos

Modak, Manorama Ramkrishna
See Grove, Marguerite

[Il] Modanino
See Mazzoni, Guido

Model T Slim
See Mickle, Elmon

Model, Walther 1891-1945 [BDW]
German army officer
* [The] Fuehrer's Fireman
* [The] Lion of Defence

Modell, Merriam 1908- [BI, WW]
American author
* Piper, Evelyn

Modena, Maria
See Kreis, Erna

Modenos, John Philip
See Modinos, Ioannis Philip

Moderator
See Chatterton, Thomas

Moderator?
See Francis, [Sir] Philip

Modern
See Foe, Daniel

[The] Modern Admirable Crichton
See Burton, [Sir] Richard Francis

[The] Modern Antigone
See Bourbon, Marie Therese Charlotte de

[A] Modern Antique
See Byron, Medora Gordon

[The] Modern Aristophanes
See Foote, Samuel

[The] Modern Athenian
See Dickson, Samuel Henry

[The] Modern Baillet
See Arouet, Francois Marie

[The] Modern Belisarius
See McClellan, George Brinton

[The] Modern Buddhist
See Tripakon, Chao Phya

[The] Modern Bunyan
See Miller, James Russell

[The] Modern Burns
See Grieve, Christopher Murray

[The] Modern Cagliostro
See Sykowski, Abram

[A] Modern Calvinist
See Wyld, Robert S.

[The] Modern Cervantes
See Pereda, Jose Maria de

[The] Modern Charlemagne
See Bonaparte, Napoleon

[The] Modern Classicist
See Mies, Ludwig

[The] Modern Congreve
See Sheridan, Richard Brinsley

[The] Modern Croesus
See Morrison, James

[The] Modern Day Warrior
See Von Erich, Kerry

[The] Modern Dickens
See De Morgan, William

[A] Modern English Journalist
See Murray, William [First Earl of Mansfield]

[The] Modern Galen
See Fernel, Jean

[The] Modern Generation's Rudy Vallee
See Monroe, Vaughn Wilton

[A] Modern Genius
See Pennie, John Fitzgerald

[The] Modern Gracchus
See Riqueti, Honore Gabriel Victor

[The] Modern Greek
See Mudie, Robert

[The] Modern Hercules
See Sandow, Eugene

[The] Modern Hippolyta
See Maria Theresa

[The] Modern Hogarth
See Cruikshank, George

[The] Modern Hogarth
See Seymour, Robert

[The] Modern Indagator Invictissimus [Most Invincible Investigator]
See Disraeli, Isaac

[The] Modern Jugurtha
See Abd-el-Kader

[The] Modern K. O. King
See Chaney, George

[The] Modern King of Swing
See Rogers, Milton M.

[The] Modern Knight Errant
See Hoover, J[ohn] Edgar

[The] Modern Madonna Painter
See Carriere, Eugene

Modern Mercury
See Roosevelt, James

[The] Modern Messalina
See Catherine II

[The] Modern Miracle Worker
See Bodie, Sam

[The] Modern Moses
See Tubman, Harriet Araminta Ross Davis

[The] Modern Mozart
See Korngold, Erich Wolfgang

[The] Modern Muckraker
See Anderson, Jack[son Northman]

[The] Modern Newton
See Laplace, Pierre Simon de

[The] Modern Nimrod
See Bonaparte, Napoleon

[The] Modern Pict
See Bruce, Thomas

[The] Modern Pilate
See Philip IV [or Philippe]

[The] Modern Pliny
See Gesner, Konrad von

[The] Modern Plutarch
See La Mothe Le Vayer, Francois de

Modern Pythagorean
See Macnish, Robert

[The] Modern Quintus Curtius
See Aubert, Rene

[The] Modern Rabelais
See Maginn, William

[The] Modern Roscius
See Betty, William Henry West

[The] Modern Sage
See K'ang Yu-wei

[The] Modern Sesostris
See Bonaparte, Napoleon

[The] Modern Sisyphus
See Webster, Daniel

[The] Modern Stagirite
See Warburton, William

[A] Modern Troubadour
See O'Carroll, Patrick

[The] Modern Wagner
See Humperdink, Engelbert

[The] Modern Warwick
See Whitney, William Collins

[The] Modern Zoilus
See Perrault, Charles

Modernis, Santho
See Henri, Thomas

[The] Modernist Maestro
See Levy, Julien

Moders [or Meders?], Mary 1643-1673
[LFW]
British swindler
* [The] German Princess

Moderwell, Hiram K. 1888- [WWL]
American author
* Motherwell, Hiram

Modest Bill Walton
See Walton, William Theodore [Bill]

[The] Modest Mr. Guzik
See Guzik, Jake

Modesto
See Ruiz, Henry

Modestus
See Draper, [Sir] William

Modini, Robert 1919- [FC]
American actor
* Stack, Robert

Modinos, Ioannis Philip 1930- [OP]
American opera singer
* Modenos, John Philip

Modish, [Lady] Betty
See Oldfield, Anna

Modjeska [or Modrzejewska], Helena
See Bencla, Jadwiza [Opido]

Modjeski, Ralph
See Modrzejewski, Ralph

Modoc
See Doyle, Jefferson E. P.

Modrzejewski, Ralph 1861-1940 [WBD]
Polish-born engineer
* Modjeski, Ralph

[A] Modus
See Swift, Jonathan

Modzelewski, Big Mo
See Modzelewski, Ed

Modzelewski, Ed 20th c. [BBH]
American football player
* Modzelewski, Big Mo

Modzelewski, Little Mo
See Modzelewski, Richard [Dick]

Modzelewski, Mo
See Modzelewski, Richard [Dick]

Modzelewski, Richard [Dick] 1931-
[FB, SMG]
American football player and coach
* Modzelewski, Little Mo
* Modzelewski, Mo

Modzelewski, Stan 20th c. [MEB]
American basketball player
* Modzelewski, Stutz

Modzelewski, Stutz
See Modzelewski, Stan

Moe, Angelo
See Moe, Chris

Moe, Chris 1949- [RO2]
American musician
* Moe, Angelo

Moebius
See Giraud, Jean

Moeckl, Christiane 1947- [OP]
German opera singer
* Zinkler, Christiane

Moelk, Heinrich von 12th c. [SN]
German satirist
* [The] Juvenal of Chivalry

Moeller, Joseph Douglas 1943- [SMG]
American baseball player
* Moeller, Skeeter

Moeller, Lucky
See Moeller, W. E.

Moeller, Ron[ald Ralph] 1938- [BE]
American baseball player
* [The] Kid

Moeller, Skeeter
See Moeller, Joseph Douglas

Moeller, Sweat
See Moeller, Thomas

Moeller, Thomas 20th c. [RO2]
British musician
* Moeller, Sweat

Moeller, W. E. 1912- [FCW]
American music executive
* Moeller, Lucky

Moellin, Jacob ben Moses 1365?-1427
[BI]
German clergyman and educator
* Maharil

Moendved [or Menved]
See Eric VI [or VIII]

Moer, Paul
See Moerschbacher, Paul E.

Moers, Ellen 1928-1979 [CA]
American educator, critic, author
* Mayer, Ellen Moers

Moerschbacher, Paul E. •1916- [EJ]
American jazz musician
* Moer, Paul

Moeser, Justus 1720-1794 [SN]
German author, historian, jurist
* [The] Franklin of Germany

Moethu
See Jones, Thomas

Moffa, Ettore 1885?-1954 [BI]
Italian-American journalist
* Stanco, Italo

Moffa, Paolo 20th c. [WF]
Italian director
* Byrd, John

Moffat, A. S. 19th c. [IP]
American author
* A. S. M.

Moffat, Margaret
See Bury, Margaret

Moffatt, J. 19th c. [IP]
British author
* O.

Moffatt, James
See Hughes, Robert J.

Moffett, Anthony J. 1945?- [CBS]
American politician
* Moffett, Toby

Moffett, Toby
See Moffett, Anthony J.

Moffett, William 18th c. [HPPN]
Irish poet
* J. K.

Moffett, William Adger 1869-?
American military leader
* [The] South Carolina Gamecock

Moffitt, De Loyce 1906- [ASC]
American composer, conductor, arranger
* Moffitt, Deke

Moffitt, Deke
See Moffitt, De Loyce

Moffitt, Jack 1901?- [BI]
American columnist
* Yank, Jonathan

Moffitt, Little Miss
See King, Billie Jean Moffitt

Mofussillite
See Lang, Thomas

Mogador
See Chabrillan, Celeste Venard
[Comtesse de Moreton]

Mogensen, Jorgen 1922- [WEC]
Danish cartoonist and sculptor
* Moco [Joint signature with Siegfried
  Cornelius]

Moggridge, Helen 20th c. [ART]
British artist
* H. M. M.

Moggridge, J. H. 19th c. [IP]
British author
* [A] Monmouthshire Magistrate

Mogridge, George 1802-1854 [DEL,
DNNF, FFF, IP]
British author
* Holding, Ephraim
* Jaunt, Jeremy
* My Uncle Newberry
* Old Humphrey
* Parley, Peter
* Uncle Adam

Mogridge, Stephen 1915- [AW]
British author and journalist
* Stevens, Jill

Moguy, Leonide
See Maguilevsky, Leonide

Mohair Jack
See Garner, John Nance

Mohammed [or Mahomet] 570-632
[DEP, FF, FFF]
*Religious teacher and founder of
Mohammedanism*
* [The] Apostle of the Sword
* [The] Camel Driver of Mecca
* [The] Father of Believers
* [The] Prophet
* Thaumaturgus

Mohammed 1029-1072 [WBD]
Sultan of the Seljuk Turks
* Alp Arslan [Courageous Lion]

Mohammed 20th c.
Saudi Arabian prince
* Abu Sharein [Father of the Double
  Evil]

Mohammed Ahmed 1843?-1885 [DNNS,
WBD]
Moslem agitator
* [The] False Prophet
* [The] Mahdi

Mohammed, Elijah
See Bogan, Gulam

Mohammed ibn-Abdullah ?-1920 [WBD]
Somali religious leader
* [The] Mad Mullah

Mohammed ibn-Ibrahim 1119-1229?
[WBD]
Persian poet
* Attar [Druggist]
* Farid ud-din Attar

Mohammed Nadir Khan 1880-1933
[WBD]
King of Afghanistan
* Nadir Shah

Mohammed of Ghor
See Muizz-ad-din

Mohammed II [or Mahomet] 1430-1481
[DEP, FFF]
Sultan of Turkey
* [The] Conqueror
* [The] Father of Good Works
* [The] Great

Mohammed X 1445?-1500? [WBD]
King of Granada
* [The] Brave

Mohammed XI
See Abu Abdallah [or Abdullah]

Mohan, P. Nath
See Shastri, Prithvinath

Mohan, Rajneesh Chandra 1932?-
Indian spiritual teacher
* Bhagwan Shree Rajneesh [Good Sir
  Rajneesh]

Moharaj, Soncu 1931- [IAW]
Indian author
* Jyotirmoy, Ghosh Dastider

Mohaupt, Rosa [Gottlieb] 1905?-1952
[BI]
Austrian musician
* Phil, Theo

Mohawk
See Rowe, Nicholas

Mohenesto
See Avery, Henry M.

Mohican
See Fisher, Joseph E.

Mohieddin, Khaled 20th c.
Egyptian politician
* [The] Red Major

Mohler, Ernest Follette 1874-1961 [BE]
American baseball player
* Mohler, Kid

Mohler, Johann Adam 1796-1838
[HPPN]
German historian and theologian
* [The] Catholic Schleiermacher

Mohler, Kid
See Mohler, Ernest Follette

Mohlmann, [Father] Michael 1920?-
[CW]
Curacaon author and poet
* Van Nuland, Wim

Mohns, Diesel
See Mohns, Douglas Allen

Mohns, Douglas Allen 1933- [FHE]
Canadian-born hockey player
* Mohns, Diesel

Mohoao
See Fairburn, Edwin

Mohr, Clare Eloise 1901-1959 [SC]
American actress
* Del Mar, Claire

Mohr, Frederick
See Leidhof, Charles

Mohr, Gordon 1916- [CA]
American army officer and writer
* Mohr, Jack

Mohr, Jack
See Mohr, Gordon

Moi-Meme
See Coveney, [Sister] Mary

Moilan, Connecticut Slim
See Moilan, Tim

Moilan, Tim 20th c. [HPPN]
American hobo
* Moilan, Connecticut Slim

Moile, N. T. 19th c. [HPPN]
British poet
* Bliss, Henry

Moilenen, Big Louie
See Moilenen, Louis

Moilenen, Louis 1885-1913 [HPPN]
Finnish-American giant
* Moilenen, Big Louie
* [The] Tallest Man in the World

Moiloa, James Jantjies 1916- [IAW]
South African author and poet
* Ntate, J. J.

Moina
See Dinnies, Anna Peyre

Moina
See Ryan, [Father] Abram Joseph

Moinaux, Georges-Victor Marcel
1860-1929 [CD, EWL, WBD]
French author, playwright, poet
* Courteline, Georges
* [The] Mark Twain of France

Moineau, Max
See Sparrow, Malcolm Weethie

Moir, David Macbeth 1798-1851 [DEL,
RH]
British author and poet
* Delta
* Wauch, Mansie

Moise, Isaac 1796-1880 [WBD]
French attorney and politician
* Cremieux, Adolphe

Mojica, Jose 1896-1974 [CA]
Mexican-born Peruvian monk, author, actor
* Jose De Guadaloupe, [Brother]

Mojo
See Buford, George

Mokanna, al-
See Hakim ben Allah

Mokanna the Veiled
See Hakim ben Allah

Mokiejeswki, Jean 1929- [FC, WEF]
French director and actor
* Mocky, Jean-Pierre

Moko
See Mead, Sidney Moko

Mola di Roma
See Mola, Pierfrancesco

Mola, Pierfrancesco 1612-1666 [WBD]
Italian painter
* Mola di Roma

Moldwarp, Nicholas, B. A.
See Manning, Anne

[The] Mole
See Ray, James Earl

Mole, Fenton LeRoy 1925- [BE]
American baseball player
* Mole, Muscles

Mole, Irving Milfred 1898-1961 [DAM, EJ, PMJ]
American jazz musician
* Mole, Miff

Mole, Mathieu 1584-1656 [DNNS]
French jurist and politician
* [The] Pym of France

Mole, Miff
See Mole, Irving Milfred

Mole, Muscles
See Mole, Fenton LeRoy

Mole, William
See Younger, William Anthony

Molenda, Bo
See Molenda, John

Molenda, John 20th c. [EF]
American football player
* Molenda, Bo

Moleri
See Demoliere, M. Hippolyte Jules

Molesworth, Keith F. 1906-1966 [AS]
American football player
* Molesworth, Rabbit

Molesworth, Mary Louisa Stewart 1839-1921 [LC]
Dutch-born author
* Graham, Ennis

Molesworth, Rabbit
See Molesworth, Keith F.

Moliere
See Poquelin, Jean Baptiste

Moliere, Armande Gresinde Claire Elisabeth Bejart 1643-? [SN]
Wife of French playwright, Moliere
* Celimene

Moliere, Ernest 1902?- [NOJ]
American jazz musician
* Moliere, Kid

Moliere, Frank 1914- [NOJ]
American jazz musician
* Moliere, Li'l Papa

Moliere, Kid
See Moliere, Ernest

Moliere, Li'l Papa
See Moliere, Frank

[The] Moliere of Italy
See Goldoni, Carlo

[The] Moliere of Music
See Gretry, Andre Ernest Modeste

[The] Moliere of Spain
See Moratin, Leandro Fernandez

Molin, Charles
See Mayne, William [James Carter]

Molina, Manuel ?-1927 [GS]
Spanish bullfighter
* Algabeno-Chico [Little One from Algaba]

Molina y Martinez, Rafael 1880-1910 [GS]
Spanish bullfighter
* Lagartijo [Lizard]
* Lagartijo Chico [Little Lizard]

Molina y Sanchez, Rafael 1841-1900 [GS]
Spanish bullfighter
* Lagartijo [Lizard]

Molinar, Demostines 1933- [IBW]
Panamanian-born scuba diver
* Jones, Davy
* Molinar, Mo

Molinar, Mo
See Molinar, Demostines

Molineaux the Moor
See Molineaux, Tom

Molineaux, the Morocco Prince
See Wharton, Jim

Molineaux, Tom 1784-1818 [HPPN]
American boxer
* Molineaux the Moor

Molinera, Antonia
See Carillo, Rosita Felix

Molinos, Miguel de 1640-1697? [SN]
Spanish clergyman
* [The] Quietist

Molinsky, Joan Sandra 1935?- [DF 12-15-82, HPPN, JF, NW 10-10-83]
American comedienne
* Rivers, Joan

Moll
See Foe, Daniel

Mollegen, Anne Rush
See Smith, Anne Mollegen

Mollet, Guy 1905-1975
French government official
* [The] Reluctant Robespierre
* [The] Tactful Teacher

Mollie Myrtle
See Leonard, Agnes

Mollinedo y Savaria, Antonio Gonzalez 1745?-1812 [HPPN]
Spanish army officer
* Savaria, Antonio Gonzalez de

Mollison, A. P.
See Pincus, Abraham

Mollison, James Allan 1905-1959 [HPPN]
British aviator
* [The] Playboy of the Air

Molloy, Joseph Fitzgerald 1859-1908 [PI]
Irish author
* Wilding, Ernest

Mollwitz, Frederick August 1890-1967 [BE]
German-born baseball player
* Mollwitz, Fritz
* Mollwitz, Zip

Mollwitz, Fritz
See Mollwitz, Frederick August

Mollwitz, Zip
See Mollwitz, Frederick August

Molly
See Driscoll, Marian

Molnar, Ferenc
See Neumann, Ferenc

Molody, Konon Trofimovich 1923?-1970 [EE]
Intelligence agent for Russia
* Lonsdale, Gordon Arnold

Molon
See Apollonius

Moloney, Patrick 19th c. [PI]
Irish physician and poet
* Australis

Molony, [Master] Molloy
See Thackeray, William Makepeace

Molotov, Mysterious
See Skryabin, Vyacheslav Mikhailovich

Molotov, Vyacheslav Mikhailovich
See Skryabin, Vyacheslav Mikhailovich

Moltke, Hellmuth Karl Bernhard von 1800-1891 [DNNS, FFF, NPS, SN]
Prussian army officer
* Hellmuth the Taciturn
* [Der] Schweigsame
* [The] Silent One
* [The] Taciturn

Moltzer, Jacob 1503-1558 [PA]
Author
* Micyllus

Molyneaux, John William Henry   [PA]
Author
* J. W. H. M.

Molyneux
See Molyneux, Edward

Molyneux, Edward 1891-1974   [WFA]
British fashion designer
* Molyneux

Molyneux the Moor
See Molyneux, Tom

Molyneux, Tom 1784-?   [HPPN]
American boxer
* Molyneux the Moor

Mombrizio, Bonino 1424-1484   [PA]
Author
* Momritius

Momi, Winifred Lei 1899-   [AM]
American singer and actress
* Shaw, Winnie

Momo
See Mercado, Jose Ramon

[El] Momo
See Soto, Gabriel

Momonia
See Kickham, Charles Joseph

Mompesson, [Sir] Giles 17th c.   [SN]
British manufacturer
* Overreach, [Sir] Giles

Momritius
See Mombrizio, Bonino

Moms Musings
See Mahaffy-Wilson, Mary Ruth

Momsie
See Snyder, Ruth

Mon
See Pountney, Monica Brailey

Mon Droit
See Selden, Richard Ely, Jr.

Mon Soldat [My Soldier]
See Henry IV [or Henri]

Mona
See O'Mahony, Timothy J.

Mona, Alli 20th c.   [IBW]
American magician
* Prince Alli

Mona Lisa
See Gherardini, Lisa di Anton Maria

[Il] Monaco
See Lorenzo

[Il] Monaco [The Monk]
See Morandi, Giorgio

Monaco, James 1885-1945   [AM]
American composer
* Ragtime Jimmy

Monaco, Richard 1940-   [CA]
American author, poet, editor
* Robhs, Dwight

Monadnock
See Nicholas, Dr.

Monaghan, James 1891-   [IAW]
American author
* Monaghan, Jay

Monaghan, Jay
See Monaghan, James

Monaghan, John Joseph 1920-   [BX, RBE]
Irish boxer
* Monaghan, Rinty

Monaghan, Rinty
See Monaghan, John Joseph

[El] Monaguillo [The Altar Boy]
See Torres Jimenez, Andres

Monahan, Bubs
See Monahan, Harold

Monahan, Deane
See Steele, James

Monahan, Edward Francis 1928-   [BE]
American baseball player
* Monahan, Rinty

Monahan, Harold 20th c.   [SR]
Bobsled racer
* Monahan, Bubs

Monahan, Hart
See Monahan, Hartland Patrick

Monahan, Hartland Patrick 1951-   [HR]
Canadian-born hockey player
* Monahan, Hart

Monahan, John
See Burnett, William Riley

Monahan, Rinty
See Monahan, Edward Francis

Monar, Motilall Rooplalln 1944?-   [CW]
Guyanese poet and editor
* Greene, Eustace

[The] Monarch
See Giscard d'Estaing, Valery

[The] Monarch of American Arts
See Hemingway, Ernest

Monarch of Christendom
See Borghese, Camillo

[The] Monarch of Crosbiters
See Greene, Robert

[The] Monarch of Hampshire
See Williams, Israel

[The] Monarch of Leg Shackles
See Weiss, Ehrich

Monarch of Letters
See Selden, John

[The] Monarch of Mastication
See Wrigley, William, Jr.

[The] Monarch of Misrule
See Smith, Jefferson Randolph

[The] Monarch of Mont Blanc
See Smith, Albert Richard

[The] Monarch of Superpower
See Insull, Samuel

[The] Monarch of the Monte Man
See Jones, William

[The] Monarch of the Musical Kingdom
See Handel, Georg Friedrich

[The] Monarch of the Prairies
See Carson, Christopher

[The] Monarch of Theologians
See Alexander of Hales

Monardo, Meco 1939-   [RO2]
American entertainer
* Meco

Monbouquette, Monbo
See Monbouquette, William Charles

Monbouquette, William Charles 1936-
[SMG]
American baseball player
* Monbouquette, Monbo

Monceau, Lucie 1871?-1948   [BEW]
French actress
* Moreno, Marguerite

Moncho y Gilabert, Antonio 20th c.
[SFP]
Author
* Gautisolo, Miguel

Monck, Mary C. F.
See Munster, Mary C. F.

Monck, Tristam K.
See Maitland, T. G. Dowling

Monckton, Rose C. 19th c.   [HFN]
Author
* M.

Moncorge, Jean-Alexis 1904-   [BDF, OCF, WEF]
French actor
* Gabin, Jean

Moncrief, Robert 20th c.   [RO1]
American singer
* Edwards, Bobby

Moncrieff, Alexander 1695-1761   [HPPN]
Scottish clergyman
* [A] Minister of the Church of Scotland

Moncrieff, Ernest
See Chi, Richard Hu See-Yee

Moncrieff, [Sir] Henry 1750-1827   [PA]
Author
* Welwood

Moncrieff, [Sir] James Wellwood
1776-1851   [RH]
Scottish attorney and jurist
* [The] Whole Duty of Man

Moncrieff, Robert Hope 20th c.   [MBF]
British author
* Hope, Ascott R.

Moncrieff, William Thomas 1794-1857
[HPPN]
British playwright and producer
* Shuffleton, Thomas

Moncure, Jane Belk 1926- [SAT]
American educator and author
* Wannamaker, Bruce

Monda, Richard 20th c. [RO2]
American singer and songwriter
* Daddy Dewdrop

Mondale, Fighting Fritz
See Mondale, Walter Frederick

Mondale, Fritz
See Mondale, Walter Frederick

Mondale, Joan 20th c. [NW 7-23-84]
Wife of American vice president, Walter Mondale
* Joan of Art
* Mondale, Phony Joanie

Mondale, Phony Joanie
See Mondale, Joan

Mondale, Walter Frederick 1928- [TI 9-17-84]
American vice president
* Mondale, Fighting Fritz
* Mondale, Fritz

Monday Boanerges
See Cook, Flavius Josephus

[The] Monday Club
See Churchill, John Wesley

Monday, Michael
See Ginder, Richard

Monday, Paul
See Gadd, Paul

Monday, Rick
See Monday, Robert James, Jr.

Monday, Robert James, Jr. 1945- [PB, SMG, WWB]
American baseball player
* Monday, Rick

Mondelle, Wendayne
See Ackerman, Wendayne

Mondello, Nuncio 1910?- [EJ, PMJ, WWJ]
American jazz musician
* Mondello, Toots

Mondello, Toots
See Mondello, Nuncio

Mondeno [The Clean One]
See Garcia Jimenez, Juan

Mondey, David [Charles] 1917- [CA]
British air force officer and author
* Charles, David

Mondor
See Girard, Philippe

Mondose, Alex
See Onsmonde, Alexandre

Mondrian, Piet[er Cornelis] 1872-1944
Dutch painter
* [The] Dancing Madonna
* [The] Father of Neo-Plasticism

Mondschein, Irving 1925- [EJS]
American track and field athlete
* Mondschein, Moon

Mondschein, Moon
See Mondschein, Irving

Mondy, Pierre
See Cuq, Pierre

Monedero [The Minter]
See Marcos, Jesus

Monet, Claude 1840-1926
French painter
* Apostle of Flux
* [The] Gardener of Giverny
* Prophet of Light

Monett, Lireve
See Worrell, Everil

Money Bags Qualters
See Qualters, Thomas Francis [Tom]

Money, Brooks
See Money, Donald Wayne

Money, Donald Wayne 1947- [BE]
American baseball player
* Money, Brooks

[The] Money Maestro
See Heidt, Horace Murray

Money Maker and Hoopla Artist
See Higgins, Andrew Jackson

Money-Coutts, Francis 1851-? [WWL]
British author
* Coutts, Francis

Monfa, Henri Marie Raymond de Toulouse-Lautrec 1864-1901 [HPPN]
French painter, lithographer, illustrator
* Toulouse-Lautrec

Mong, Yuk 1908-1933 [SC]
Actor
* Fook, Monte

Monge, Isidro Pedroza 1951- [SMG]
Mexican-born baseball player
* Monge, Sid

Monge, Sid
See Monge, Isidro Pedroza

Monger, [Ifor] David 1908- [AW, CA]
Welsh physician and playwright
* Manngian, Peter
* Richards, Peter

Mongkut 1804-1868 [HPPN]
King of Siam
* Rama IV

[The] Mongolian Bonaparte
See Timur [or Timour]

[The] Mongoose
See McEwen, Tom

Mongre, [Dr.] Paul
See Hausdorff, Felix

[The] Mongrel
See Arnold, Benedict

Monheimer, A. [PA]
Author
* Hackle, B.

Monica, Maestro
See Monica, Manuel [or Antonio?]

Monica, Manuel [or Antonio?] 1731?-?
[CW]
Dominican poet and singer
* Monica, Maestro
* Monica, Meso

Monica, Meso
See Monica, Manuel [or Antonio?]

Monig, Christopher
See Crossen, Ken[dell Foster]

Monique
See Benoit, Alice P.

Monitor
See Daley, George William

Monitor
See Lee, Arthur

Monitor
See Levine, Isaac Don

Monitor, Elias
See Worcester, Noah

Monjo, F. N.
See Monjo, Ferdinand Nicolas, III

Monjo, Ferdinand Nicolas, III 1924-
[TCC]
American author
* Monjo, F. N.

[The] Monk
See Alfonso IV [or Alphonso]

[The] Monk
See Casimir I

[The] Monk
See Eustace

[The] Monk
See Hughes, Richard

[The] Monk
See Lewis, Matthew Gregory

[The] Monk
See Ramiro II

Monk [or Monkey]
See Ruth, George Herman

Monk, Alan
See Kendall, Willmoore

Monk, Galdo
See Riseley, Jerry B[urr, Jr.]

Monk, George [Duke of Albemarle]
1608-1670 [DEP, DNNS, SN]
British army officer
* Abdae
* Honest George
* Old George
* [The] Thinking Silent General

Monk, James Henry 19th c. [HFN]
Author
* J. H. M.

Monk, Maria 1817?-1850 [HPPN]
Canadian author
* [The] Lying Nun

[The] Monk of Bury
See Lydgate, John

[The] Monk of Disentis
See Placidus [a Spescha], [Father]

[The] Monk of Eisleben
See Luther, Martin

[The] Monk of the Golden Islands
See Cybo of Genoa

[The] Monk of Westminster
See Richard of Cirencester

[The] Monk of Wittenberg
See Luther, Martin

Monk, Thelonious Sphere 1920-1982
[IBW]
American jazz musician
* [The] High Priest of Bebop

[The] Monkey
See Campistron, Jean Galbert de

Monkey
See Petit Mere, Frederic du

[The] Monkey King
See Trefflich, Henry

[The] Monkey King of Saigon
See Crum, William J.

Monkey Shine Maynard
See Maynard, Don[ald]

[The] Monkey Trial Defendant
See Scopes, John Thomas

Monkland, George
See Whittet, George Sorley

Monkman, Phyllis
See Harrison, Phyllis

Monks, P.
See O'Donnell, John Francis

Monks, Victoria 1884-1927 [BMH]
British singer
* John Bull's Girl
* Little Victoria

Monkshood, G. F.
See Clarke, William James

Monmouth
See Henry V

Monmouth, Duke of
See Scott, James

Monmouth, Elizabeth H. [PA]
Author
* Homespun, Sophia

[A] Monmouthshire Magistrate
See Moggridge, J. H.

Monnet, Jean 1888-1979
French political economist
* [The] Father of Europe
* [The] Father of the European
Community

Monnow, Peter
See Croudace, Glynn

Monod, Rene
See Koch, Kurt E[mil]

Monola, Adelaide
See Hughes, Adelaide Manola [Mould]

Monomachus [Who Fights in Single Combat]
See Constantine IX

Monomachus
See Vladimir II

Mononen, Larry
See Mononen, Lauri Ilmari

Mononen, Lauri Ilmari 1950- [SMG]
Finnish-born hockey player
* Mononen, Larry

Monongo
See Clytus, John

Monophthalmos [The One-Eyed]
See Antigonus I

Monophthalmus [The One-eyed]
See Acacius

Monopoli
See Insanguine, Giacomo [Antonio Francesco Paolo Michele]

Monos
See Mangan, James Clarence

Monro, Alexander 1697-1767 [PA]
Author
* Primus

Monro, Gavin
See Monro-Higgs, Gertrude

Monro, Matt
See Parsons, Terry

Monro-Higgs, Gertrude 1905- [AW, WD]
British author
* Monro, Gavin

Monroe, Alex
American football player
* Monroe, Mole

Monroe, Carole 1944- [CA]
American author
* Dufrechou, Carole

Monroe, Donald 1888- [SFL, WGT]
American author
* Keith, Donald [joint pseudonym with Keith Monroe]

Monroe, Douglas Richmond
See Cohen, Paul Arthur

Monroe, Earl 1944- [BB, SR]
American basketball player
* Magic, Mr.
* [The] Pearl

Monroe, Ed[ward Oliver] 1893-1969
[BE]
American baseball player
* Monroe, Peck

Monroe, Elizabeth Kortright 1768-1830
[HPPN]
Wife of American president, James Monore
* [The] Beautiful American [La Belle Americaine]

Monroe, Forest
See Wiechmann, Ferdinand Gerhard

Monroe, George H. [FFF]
American journalist
* Templeton

Monroe, James 1758-1831 [FAP]
American president
* [The] Era of Good Feeling President
* [The] Last of the Cocked Hats

Monroe, John Alexander 1874-1942
[RBE]
Canadian boxer
* Munroe, Jack

Monroe, Keith 1917- [CA, SFL, WGT]
American author
* Cochran, Rice E.
* Colombo, Dale
* Keith, Donald [joint pseudonym with Donald Monroe]

Monroe, Lyle
See Heinlein, Robert A[nson]

Monroe, Marilyn
See Mortensen, Norma Jean

Monroe, Mole
See Monroe, Alex

Monroe, Muscle Throat
See Monroe, Vaughn Wilton

[The] Monroe of Punk
See Harry, Deborah

Monroe, Peck
See Monroe, Ed[ward Oliver]

Monroe, Vaughn Wilton 1912-1973
[HPPN]
American jazz musician
* [The] Modern Generation's Rudy Vallee
* Monroe, Muscle Throat
* [The] Voice of R. C. A.

Monroe, Vince
See Vincent, Monroe

Monroe, William [Bill] 1911- [CWG, FCW]
American country-western performer
* [The] Father of Bluegrass Music

Monrose, Louis
See Barizan, Louis Martial

Monseigneur
See Louis

Monsell, Margaret E[mma Irwin] 1917-
[WGT]
American author
* Irwin, Margaret E.

Monserrat, Mrs. George [FFF]
Entertainer
* Ottolengui, Helen

Monsieur
See Orleans, Philippe II d'

Monsieur Charles
See Chop, Max

Monsieur Charly
See Pompidou, Georges Jean Raymond

[Le] Monsieur de l'Orchestre
See Mortier, Arnold

Monsieur de Paris
See Sanson, Charles Henri

Monsieur Fou-roux
See Van Gogh, Vincent

Monsieur Joe
See Cesari, Joseph

Monsieur le Coadjuteur
See Gondi, Jean Francois Paul de

Monsieur le Duc
See Bourbon, Henri Jules de

Monsieur le Duc
See Bourbon, Louis Henri de

Monsieur le Prince
See Bourbon, Louis II de [Prince de Conde]

Monsieur X
See Howard, Joseph

Monsieur X
See Moutis, Patrice Des

Monsieur X
See Parodi, Alexandre

[The] Monster
See Howard, Frank Oliver

[The] Monster
See Jeffries

[The] Monster
See O'Connor, Charles [Chuck]

[The] Monster
See Radatz, Richard Raymond [Dick]

[The] Monster
See Williams, Renwick

[The] Monster from Arizona
See Goldwater, Barry [Morris]

[The] Monster Man
See Eddy, Everett

[The] Monster Man
See Mundus, [Captain] Frank

[The] Monster of Dusseldorf
See Kuerten, Peter

[A] Monster of Languages
See Mezzofanti, Giuseppe

[The] Monster of Manheim
See Fasig, Jack

[The] Monster of Nature
See Vega Carpio, Lope Felix de

[The] Monster of Sixty Third Street
See Mudgett, Herman Webster

Monster of Turpitude
See Gifford, William

[The] Monster of Vienna
See Brunner, Alois

Monsterhead
See Burtt, Steve

[El] Monstruo [The Monster]
See Rodriguez Sanchez, Manuel

Montacute [or Montagu], Thomas de 1388-1428   [HN, RH]
Fourth Earl of Salisbury
* [The] Mirror of all Martial Men

Montagna, Luigi 1887-1950 [BI, CU, FC, SC]
Italian-American actor
* [The] Bull
* Montana, Bull
* Montana, Louis

Montagu, Ashley 1905- [CA, WP 9-12-84]
British-born anthropologist and author
* Academicas Mentor
* [The] Alistaire Cook of Anthropology

Montagu, Basil 1770-1851   [HPPN]
British barrister, editor, author
* [A] Chancery Barrister
* [A] Lover of Order

Montagu, Charles [First Earl of Halifax] 1661-1715 [HPPN, SN]
British statesman and patron of the arts
* Bays, the Noble Celsus
* [A] Maecenas

Montagu, Elizabeth Robinson 1720-1800 [HPPN]
British author
* Fidget
* [A] Lady of the Last Century

Montagu, Gladys Helen Rachel Goldsmid 1879-1965 [HPPN]
Irish table tennis player
* [The] Dowager Lady Swaythling

Montagu, John [Fourth Earl of Sandwich] 1718-1792 [DNNF, DNNS, RH]
British diplomat
* Twitcher, Jemmy

Montagu, Mary Wortley 1689-1762 [DEA, DEL, FFF, HPPN, NPS, SN, UH]
British author and poet
* [The] Admirable Lady Mary
* Artemisia
* [The] Female Maecenas
* L. M. W. M., Rt. Hon.
* Minerva
* Sappho

Montagu, Matthew 18th c. [HPPN]
British poet
* M. M.

Montagu, Robert
See Hampden, John

Montague, Alphonsus Joseph-Mary Augustus 1880-1948 [BEW]
British-born historian and editor
* Summers, Rey

Montague, Basil 1770-1851 [PA]
Author
* [The] Water Drinker

Montague, Boom
See Montague, Hugh [Viscount Trenchard]

Montague, Bruce Alexander 1939- [IAW]
British author and playwright
* Alexander, Bruce
* Bruce, Martin
* O'Toole, Kate
* Savage, Oscar

Montague, C. E.
See Montague, Charles Edward

Montague, Charles Edward 1867-1928 [LC, TC]
Irish journalist, author, critic
* Montague, C. E.

Montague, Clinton
See George, H. Maria

Montague, Eleonora Louisa 1811-? [PA]
Author
* [The] Landgrave
* Russell, Margaret

Montague, Eleonora Louisa
See Hervey, Eleonora Louisa

Montague, Harold
See Smith, Harold

Montague, Harry
See Mann, Henry J.

Montague, Henry James
See Mann, Henry J.

Montague, Hugh [Viscount Trenchard] 1872-?
British military leader
* Montague, Boom

Montague, Jeanne
See Yarde, Jeanne Betty Frances Treasure

Montague, John
See Moore, LaVerne M.

Montague, Lisa
See Shulman, Sandra [Dawn]

Montague, Pansy 20th c. [THR]
Australian-born entertainer
* [La] Milo

Montaigne, Michel Eyquem de 1533-1592 [NPS]
French philosopher and author
* [The] Father of Modern Miscellanies

[The] Montaigne of Geneva
See Bonnivard, Francois de

Montalban, Ricardo
See Merino, Ricardo Montalban

Montalban Merino, Ricardo 1920-
[BEW]
Mexican-born actor
* Montalban, Ricardo

Montalte, Louis de
See Pascal, Blaise

Montana
See Williams, Reginald Gordon

Montana, Bull
See Montagna, Luigi

Montana, Louis
See Montagna, Luigi

Montana, Montie
See Mickel, Owen Harlan

[The] Montana Outlaw Boss
See Plummer, Henry

Montana, Patsy
See Blevins, Rubye

Montana Red Tate
See Tate, Don

Montana Slim
See Carter, Wilf

Montana, Small
See Gan, Benjamin

[The] Montana Wonder
See Kiecal, Stanislaus

Montanari, Sergio 20th c. [WF]
Italian film editor
* Hillman, Sergius

Montana's Fighting Redhead
See Beckman, Martin

Montand, Yves
See Livi, Ivo [or Yvo]

Montanez, Guillermo Naranjo 1948-
[BE, SMG, WWB]
Puerto Rican-born baseball player
* Montanez, Willie

Montanez, Willie
See Montanez, Guillermo Naranjo

Montani, Virgil 1880?-1956 [BEW]
Actor and dancer
* Clifford, Jack

Montano
See Arias, Benito

Montano Arriola, Gustavo 1917-
[WECO]
American cartoonist
* Arriola, Gus

Montansier, Marguerite
See Brunet, Marguerite

Montanus
See McGee, Thomas D'Arcy

Montanus
See Van der Berghe, Robert

Montauban
See St. Aubyn, [Sir] John

Montauban, G. de
See Greenough, William Parker

Montayne, Harold B. 20th c. [SFP]
Author
* Eaton, George L.

Montbard, Georges
See Loyes, Charles Auguste

Montbars 1645-? [DNNF, DNNS, FFF]
French buccaneer
* [The] Exterminator

Montclair, Dennis
See Sladen, Norman St. Barbe

Montclair, J. W.
See Weidemeyer, John William

[The] Montclair Mailman
See Cestone, Michael

Montcorbier, Francois de 1431?-1484?
[HPPN, NPS]
French poet
* Loges, Francois des
* Mouton, Michael [or Michel]
* Villon, Francois

Montdory
See Desgilberts, Guillaume

Monte Joe Lowe
See Lowe, Joseph

Monte, Toti Dal
See Meneghel, Antonietta

Montefusco, John Joseph, Jr. 1950-
[SMG]
American baseball player
* [The] Count

Monteith, Owen
See Hook, Samuel Clarke

Montejo, Manny
See Montejo, Manuel

Montejo, Manuel 1936- [BE]
Cuban-born baseball player
* Montejo, Manny
* Montejo, Pete

Montejo, Pete
See Montejo, Manuel

Monteleone, Thomas F. 1946- [CA]
American author and psychotherapist
* Martin, Mario, Jr.

Montella, Sonny
See Montella, William

Montella, William 20th c.
American underworld figure
* Montella, Sonny

Montemayor, Felipe Angel 1930- [BE]
Mexican-born baseball player
* Montemayor, Monty

Montemayor, Monty
See Montemayor, Felipe Angel

Monterey, Carlotta
See Taasinge, Hazel Neilson

Montero, Antonio Maria 1818-? [GS]
Spanish bullfighter
* [El] Zurdo [Lefthanded One]

Montero, Roberto Bianchi 1907- [FDG]
Italian director
* White, M. Robert

Monterose, Frank Anthony, Jr. 1927-
[EJ]
American jazz musician
* Monterose, J. R.

Monterose, J. R.
See Monterose, Frank Anthony, Jr.

Montes, Antonio 1876-1907 [HPPN]
Spanish bullfighter
* [El] Sordo

Montes, Emeterio
See Corretjer, Juan Antonio

Montes, Fabian
See De Elzaburu, Manuel

Montes, Francisco 1805-1851 [GS]
Spanish bullfighter
* Montes, Paquiro

Montes, Ismael 1861-1933 [HPPN]
President of Bolivia
* [El] Gran Presidente

Montes, Paquiro
See Montes, Francisco

Montesino [or Montesinos], Antonio
[HPPN]
Spanish missionary
* [The] Apostle of Puerto Rico
* [The] Father of the Laws of Burgos

Montespan, Marquise de
See Rochechouart, Francoise Athenais

Montessori, Maria 1870-1952
Italian physician and educator
* [La] Dottoressa

Monteux, Papa
See Monteux, Pierre

Monteux, Pierre 1875-1964
French conductor
* Dictator of the Baton
* [The] Genial Genius
* Monteux, Papa

Montez, Editha Gilbert
See Jackson, Editha Salomon

Montez, Lola
See Gilbert, Marie Dolores Eliza Rosanna

Montez, Maria
See Gracia Vidal de Santos Silas, Maria Africa Antonia

Montezuma
See Gauguin, [Eugene Henri] Paul

Montezuma I 1390?-1469 [HPPN]
Emperor of Mexico
* Ilhuicamia [Heavenly Archer]

Montezuma II 1480?-1520 [HPPN]
Emperor of Mexico
* Uei Tlatoani [One Who Speaks]
* Xocoyotzin [Furious One]

Montfleury
See Jacob, Zacharie

Montford, Charles L.
See Legate, Charles

Montford, Simon de 1150?-1218 [HN]
French military leader
* [The] French Maccabaeus

Montfort, Auguste 1913- [CA]
French author
* Le Breton, Auguste

Montfort, Simon de [Earl of Leicester]
1200?-1265 [HN, WBD]
British statesman and soldier
* Simon the Righteous

Montgaillard, Comte de
See Roques, Maurice Jacques

Montgelas, Maximilian Joseph von
See De Garnerin, Maximilian Joseph

Montgomerie, Alexander 1588-1661
[WBD]
Sixth Earl of Eglinton
* Greysteel

Montgomerie, Robert
See Alloway, Robert Morellet

Montgomery, Bernard Law 1887-1976
[CA, HPPN]
British military leader
* [The] Hero of El Alamein
* Montgomery of Alamein
* Monty

Montgomery, Bob 1919- [IBW]
American boxer
* Montgomery, Bobcat

Montgomery, Bobcat
See Montgomery, Bob

Montgomery, Buddy
See Montgomery, Charles F.

Montgomery, Charles F. 1930- [DAM,
EJ]
American jazz musician
* Montgomery, Buddy

Montgomery, Charles Montague
See Lauder, [Sir] Thomas Dick

Montgomery, Charlotte Baker 1910-
[IAW]
American author
* Baker, Charlotte

Montgomery, Constance
See Cappel, Constance

Montgomery, Douglass 1908-1966
[HPPN]
American actor
* Douglas, Kent

Montgomery, E. J.
See Montgomery, Evangeline Juliet

Montgomery, Eurreal Wilford 1906?-
[EJ, WWJ]
American jazz musician
* Montgomery, Little Brother

Montgomery, Evangeline Juliet 20th c.
[BA]
American business executive and artist
* Montgomery, E. J.

Montgomery, Florence 19th c. [HPPN]
British author
* F. C.

Montgomery, Florence 20th c. [F2]
Actress
* Arliss, Florence

Montgomery, George
See Lenz, George Montgomery

Montgomery, George Edgar 1856-?
[HPPN]
American journalist
* Clague
* Vixen

Montgomery, Gerard
See Moultrie, John

Montgomery, Gillespie 1920- [IPA]
American politician
* Montgomery, Sonny

Montgomery, Girard
See Moultrie, George

Montgomery, Harry 1867-1911 [HPPN]
American actor
* Montgomery, Scamp

Montgomery, Henry, Jr. 1904-1981
[BEW, F2, FC]
American actor, producer, director
* Montgomery, Robert

Montgomery, James 1771-1854 [DEA,
DLE1, DNNS, NPS, PA, SN]
Scottish poet
* Alcaeus
* [The] Bard of Sheffield
* J. M.
* [A] Poet
* Positive, Paul
* Sheffield, Classic
* Silvertongue, Gabriel

Montgomery, John Leslie 1925-1968
[DAM]
American jazz musician
* Montgomery, Wes

Montgomery, John Wilson 1835?-1911
[PI]
Irish author
* Sweet Bard of Bailieborough

Montgomery, L. M.
See Macdonald, Lucy Maude
Montgomery

Montgomery, L. M.
See Montgomery, Lucy Maude

Montgomery, Leslie Alexander
1873-1961 [LC]
Irish author
* Doyle, Lynn

Montgomery, Little Brother
See Montgomery, Eurreal Wilford

Montgomery, Lucy Maude 1874-1942
[LC]
Canadian author
* Montgomery, L. M.

Montgomery, Mamie Elizabeth 1891-
[IAW]
American author
* Wakefield, Elizabeth

Montgomery, Marian
See Halloway, Marian M. Runnels

Montgomery, Max
See Davenport, Guy [Mattison], Jr.

Montgomery, Monk
See Montgomery, William Howard

Montgomery, Monty
See Montgomery, Robert Edward

Montgomery of Alamein
See Montgomery, Bernard Law

Montgomery, Peggy 1918- [F2]
American actress
* Baby Peggy

Montgomery, Raymond A., Jr. 1936-
[CA]
American author
* Mountain, Robert

Montgomery, Richard 1736-1775 [HN]
British army officer
* [The] Wolf of America

Montgomery, Richmond Ames 1870-1950
[BI, NAA]
American clergyman and author
* Kilbourn, Timothy

Montgomery, Robert 1807-1855 [NPS]
Poet
* Montgomery, Satan

Montgomery, Robert
See Montgomery, Henry, Jr.

Montgomery, Robert Bruce 1921-1978
[CC, EMD, SF]
British author and composer
* Crispin, Edmund

Montgomery, Robert Douglass 1908-1966
[SC]
American actor
* Douglas, Kent

Montgomery, Robert Edward 1944-
[SMG]
American baseball player
* Montgomery, Monty

Montgomery, Roselle Mercier 20th c.
[NAA]
American poet and writer
* Allen, Glen

Montgomery, Rutherford George 1894-
[NAA, TCC]
American author
* Avery, A. A.
* Avery, Al
* Elder, Art
* Marshall, E. P.
* Proctor, Everitt

Montgomery, S. John
See Cohen, Paul Arthur

Montgomery, Satan
See Montgomery, Robert

Montgomery, Scamp
See Montgomery, Harry

Montgomery, Sonny
See Montgomery, Gillespie

Montgomery, Thomasina 1946-1970
[IBW, RO2]
American singer
* Terrell, Tammi

Montgomery, Wes
See Montgomery, John Leslie

Montgomery, William Howard 1921-1982
[DAM, EJ]
American jazz musician
* Montgomery, Monk

Monti, Luigi 1830-? [PA, SN]
Italian-born American educator
* Sampleton, Samuel
* [The] Young Sicilian

Monticola
See Bransby, James Hews

Montifaud, Marc de
See Quivogne de Montifaud, Marie
Amelie

Montigny, Lemoine
See Lemoine, Adolphe

**Montini, Giovanni Battista Enrico
Antonio Maria** 1897-1978 [CBS]
Pope
* Paul VI
* [The] Pilgrim Pope

Montluc, Seigneur de
See De Lasseran-Massencome, Blaise

Montmenil
See Le Sage, Rene-Andre

Montmorency, Anne de 1493-1567
[DNNF, FFF, HN]
Constable of France
* [The] Conqueror
* [The] Fabius of France
* [The] French Fabius

**Montmorency-Bouteville, Francois Henri
de** [Duc de Luxembourg] 1628-1695
[DNNS, SN]
French marshal
* [Le] Tapissier de Notre-Dame
* [The] Upholsterer of Notre Dame

Montoliu, Tete
See Montoliu, Vincente

Montoliu, Vincente 1933- [EJ7]
Spanish jazz musician
* Montoliu, Tete

Montorsoli, [Fra] Giovanni Angelo
1507?-1563 [BI]
Italian sculptor
* Poggibonsi, Angelo di Michele
d'Angelo da

Montos, Little Nick
See Montos, Nick George

Montos, Nick George 1916- [HPPN]
American burglar and jail breaker
* [The] Escaper
* Montos, Little Nick

Montoya, Joseph M. 1915-1978
American politician
* [The] Barefoot Boy from Pena Blanca
* Montoya, Little Joe

Montoya, Little Joe
See Montoya, Joseph M.

[A] Montreal Lady, A. E. B.
See Brooks, Annie Elston

Montreal, Young
See Billingkoff, Morris

Montreal's Liberace
See Richer, Donald [Donny]

Montrose, David 1904- [BX, EJS, RBE]
Russian-born boxer
* Brown, Newsboy

Montrose, David
See Graham, Charles Ross

Montrose, Duchess of 19th c. [FFF]
Racehorse owner
* Manton, Mr.

Montrose, Eddie
See Horwitz, Abraham

Montrose, First Marquis of
See Graham, James

Montrose, Graham
See MacKinnon, Charles Roy

Montrose, James St. David
See Appleman, John Alan

Montrose, Kate
See Faust, Mrs. A. J.

Montrose, Muriel
See Andrews, Muriel

Montrose, Second Marquis of
See Graham, James

Montross, David
See Backus, Jean L[ouise]

Monty
See Montgomery, Bernard Law

Monvel
See Boutet, Jacques Marie

Monzant, Ramon Segundo 1933- [BE]
Venezuelan-born baseball player
* Monzant, Ray

Monzant, Ray
See Monzant, Ramon Segundo

Moodie, Edwin
See Williams, Edwin Alfred

Moodnick, Ronald 1924- [EMT, FC, TR]
British actor
* Moody, Ron

Moody, Big Train
See Moody, John Clifford

Moody, Billy
See Peirce, Thomas

Moody, Clyde 1915- [CWG]
American country-western performer
* [The] Hillbilly Waltz King
* [The] Woodchopper

Moody, D. L.
See Moody, Dwight Lyman

Moody, Dwight Lyman 1837-1899
[HPPN, LC]
American evangelist and author
* Moody, D. L.
* [The] Worker in Souls

Moody, Granville 1812-1887 [FFF]
American clergyman and army officer
* [The] Fighting Parson

Moody, Handkerchief
See Moody, Joseph

Moody, John Clifford 1917- [IBW]
American football player
* Moody, Big Train

Moody, Joseph 1700-1753 [HPPN]
*American clergyman and involuntary
murderer*
* Moody, Handkerchief

Moody, Juice
See Moody, Keith

Moody, Keith 1953- [SMG]
American football player
* Moody, Juice

Moody, Michael David 1946- [ART]
British artist
* M.

Moody, Orville 1933- [GF, HPPN]
American golfer
* Moody, Sarge
* [The] Sarge
* [The] Unknown Soldier

Moody, Querulous
See Urquhart, David Henry

Moody, Ron
See Moodnick, Ronald

Moody, Sarge
See Moody, Orville

Moody, William Vaughan 1869-1910
[HPPN]
American educator, author, playwright
* [The] Man in the Iron Mask

Moolic, George Henry 1867-1915 [BE]
American baseball player
* Moolic, Prunes

Moolic, Prunes
See Moolic, George Henry

Moolson, Melusa
See Solomon, Samuel

Moon, Eleanor 19th c. [HPPN]
British author
* E. M.

[The] Moon Faced Senator from Worcester
See Hoar, George Frisbie

Moon, George P. 20th c. [MBF]
British author
* Pembury, Montague

Moon, J. J.
See Eckert, Ned

Moon, Jack
See Elliott, John B.

Moon, Lefty
See Moon, Leo

Moon, Leo 1899-1970 [BE]
American baseball player
* Moon, Lefty

[The] Moon Maniac
See Cook, DeWitt Clinton

[The] Moon Maniac
See Fish, Hamilton

[The] Moon Missionary
See Irwin, James B.

[The] Moon Over the Mountain Girl
See Smith, Kathryn Elizabeth [Kate]

Moonbeam, Governor
See Brown, Edmund Gerald, Jr.[Jerry]

Moonblood, Q.
See Stallone, Sylvester [Enzio]

[The] Moondog
See Freed, Alan

Moondog
See Hardin, Louis Thomas

Moone, Kid
See Moone, Nick

Moone, Nick 20th c. [RBE]
Boxer
* Moone, Kid

Mooney, Bernard 1897- [BBH]
American wrestling coach
* Mooney, Spike

Mooney, Canice [Albert James]
1911-1963 [CA]
Irish clergyman, librarian, author
* O Maonaigh, Cainneach

Mooney, Harry
See Goodchild, Harry

Mooney, Old
See Scott, Robert Falcon

Mooney, Paul 20th c. [IBW]
American author
* [The] Black Tornado

Mooney, Sam
See Giancana, Salvatore

Mooney, Spike
See Mooney, Bernard

Mooney, Tex
See Schupbach, O. T.

Mooney, Thomas 1806-1888 [FFF]
Irish journalist
* Trans-Atlantic

Moonlight Ace Fussell
See Fussell, Fred[erick Morris]

Moonlight, Captain
See Scott, Andrew George

Moonshine Kate Carson
See Carson, Rosa Lee

[The] Moor
See Sforza, Lodovico [or Ludovico]

Moor, D. S.
See Orlov, Dimitry Stakhiyevich

Moor, Emily
See Deming, Richard

[The] Moor of Venice
See Haywood, Spencer

Moor, Robert 20th c. [EOP]
Founder of religious cult
* De Grimston, Robert Moor Sylvester

Moorcock, Michael John 1939-1978
[CA, ESF, WGT]
British author
* Barclay, Bill
* Barrington, Michael [joint pseudonym with Barrington J(ohn) Bayley]
* Bradbury, E[dward] P.
* Colvin, James
* Reid, Desmond [house pseudonym]

Moore, Adelaide
See Valentine, Mrs.

Moore, Alexander Herman 1899-
[BWW]
American singer
* Moore, Whistling Alex
* Papa Chittlins

Moore, Alice
See Miller, Alice Moore

Moore, Alton 1908- [WWJ]
American jazz musician
* Moore, Slim

Moore, Alvin Earl 1953- [BR]
American baseball player
* Moore, Junior

Moore, Amos
See Hubbard, George Barron

Moore, Anacreon
See Moore, Thomas

Moore, Ancient Archie
See Wright, Archibald Lee

Moore, Andrew
See Binder, Frederick Moore

Moore, Andrew C., Jr. 1902-1971 [FB]
American football coach
* Moore, Scrappy

Moore, Anne Pegg 1716-1813 [FF]
Claimed to have fasted for 20 months
* [The] Fasting Woman of Tutbury

Moore, Annie Aubertine [Woodward]
1841-1929 [DNA]
American author and musician
* Forestier, Auber

Moore, Anon
See Galloway, James M.

Moore, Archie
See Wright, Archibald Lee

Moore, Arnold Dwight 1913?- [BWW, IBW]
American singer
* Blues, Mr.
* Moore, Eldermo
* Moore, Gatemouth

Moore, Arthur 20th c. [SFL]
Author
* Moore, Harris [joint pseudonym with Alf(red) Harris]
* Oriel, Antrim

Moore, Austin
See Muir, [Charles] Augustus

Moore, Barbara
See Lee, Barbara [Moore]

Moore, Bartholomew Figures 1801-1878
[FFF]
American attorney
* [The] Father of the North Carolina Bar

Moore, Benjamin Theophilus 19th c.
[HPPN]
British mathematician
* Alciphron

Moore, Bernyce Atz 1910?-1962 [BEW]
American theatrical performer
* Maye, Bernyce

Moore, Bertha B. 1890- [BI, HPPN]
American author
* Cannon, Brenda
* McCurry, Betsy

Moore, Beryl
See Smith Woods, Dorothy Beryl

Moore, Big Chief
See Moore, Russell

Moore, Big Sol
See Moore, Wayne

Moore, Blue Goose
See Moore, Eugene, Sr.

Moore, Brew
See Moore, Milton Aubrey, Jr.

Moore, Brian 1921?- [TI 9-19-83]
Irish-born author
* Bryan, Michael
* Marrow, Bernard

Moore, Bucky
See Moore, William

Moore, Bud
See Moore, Edgar Augustine

Moore, Bud
See Moore, Walter

Moore, Buster
See Moore, Robert

Moore, C. L.
See Moore, Catherine Lucile

Moore, Carl 20th c. [HPPN]
American jazz musician
* Moore, Deacon

Moore, Catherine Lucile 1911- [HFF, SFL, WGT]
American author
* Hammond, Keith [joint pseudonym with Henry Kuttner]
* Hastings, Hudson [joint pseudonym with Henry Kuttner]
* Liddell, C. H. [joint pseudonym with Henry Kuttner]
* Moore, C. L.
* O'Donnell, Lawrence [joint pseudonym with Henry Kuttner]
* Padgett, Lewis [joint pseudonym with Henry Kuttner]

Moore, Charles
See Moore, Reginald Charles Arthur

Moore, Charles Alexander [Charlie] 1901-1967 [HPPN]
American educator, author, philosopher
* Moore, Doc

Moore, Chief
See Moore, Euel Walton

Moore, Chuck
Author
* Stone, Willie

Moore, Clara [Jessup] 1824-1899 [FFF]
American author
* Moreton, Clara

Moore, Clara
See Scott, Clara

Moore, Clayton 1915?- [HPPN]
American actor
* [The] Lone Ranger
* [The] Man in the Mask

Moore, Clayton
See Brandner, Gary

Moore, Clayton
See Granbeck, Marilyn

Moore, Clement Clarke 1779-1863 [DLE1, SAT]
American author, theologian, poet
* Columella

Moore, Colleen
See Morrison, Kathleen

Moore, Cory
See Sturgeon, Wina

Moore, Crossfire
See Moore, Earl Alonzo

Moore, Cy
See Moore, William Austin

Moore, Cy
See Moore, William Wilcy

Moore, Daniel McFarlan 1869-1936 [HPPN]
American electrical engineer and inventor
* [The] Father of the Moore Tube

Moore, Danny
See Moore, Fred Henderson

Moore, Deacon
See Moore, Carl

Moore, Debby
See Maultsby, Emmaline

Moore, Dennie
See Moore, Florence

Moore, Dick[ie]
See Moore, John Richard, Jr.

Moore, Dick
See Moore, Leon Alfred

Moore, Dinty
See Moore, James

Moore, Dinty
See Moore, William H., III

Moore, Dobie
See Moore, Walter

Moore, Doc
See Moore, Charles Alexander [Charlie]

Moore, Donald 1910?-1984 [SI 4-23-84]
American basketball coach
* Moore, Dudley

Moore, Dudley 1936?- [TI 2-21-83]
British actor
* Cuddly Dudley
* [The] Megamidget
* [The] Wee Wonder

Moore, Dudley
See Moore, Donald

Moore, E. W.
See Kelly, George R.

Moore, Earl Alonzo 1878-1961 [BE]
American baseball player
* Moore, Crossfire

Moore, Edgar Augustine 1918- [CWG]
American country-western performer
* Moore, Bud

Moore, Edward 1835-1916 [WBD]
British scholar
* [The] Oxford Dante

Moore, Edward
See Muir, Edwin

Moore, Eldermo
See Moore, Arnold Dwight

Moore, Elizabeth
See Atkins, Meg Elizabeth

Moore, Elsie
See O'Loughlin, Louise T.

Moore, Emily H. [FFF, PA]
Author
* Mignonette

Moore, Erica Maria 20th c. [SFL]
Author
* Akira

Moore, Euel Walton 1908- [BE]
American baseball player
* Moore, Chief

Moore, Eugene, Jr. 1909- [BE]
American baseball player
* Moore, Rowdy

Moore, Eugene, Sr. 1885-1938 [BE]
American baseball player
* Moore, Blue Goose

Moore, Eugenia
See Ouick, Florence

Moore, Ezekiel, Jr. 1943- [EF, FR]
American football player
* Moore, Zeke

Moore, F. L. [PA]
Author
* F. L. M.

Moore, Farmer
See Moore, Raymond Leroy

Moore, Fenworth [house pseudonym] [Stratemeyer Syndicate]
See Stratemeyer, Edward L.

Moore, Florence 1907- [BEW]
American actress
* Moore, Dennie

Moore, Frances Sarah
See Mack, Elsie Frances [Wilson]

Moore, Francis 1657-1715? [EOP, NPS]
British physician, astrologer, educator
* Moore, Old

Moore, Fred Henderson 1934- [BA]
American attorney
* Moore, Danny

Moore, G. E.
See Moore, George Edward

Moore, Garry
See Morfit, Thomas Garrison

Moore, Gatemouth
See Moore, Arnold Dwight

Moore, George 1852-1933 [HPPN]
Irish author
* [The] Man of Wax

Moore, George 20th c. [HPPN]
American actor and male beauty contest winner
* Nude America, Mr.

Moore, George Edward 1873-1958 [LC]
British author and philosopher
* Moore, G. E.

Moore, George Henry 1811-1870 [PI]
Irish poet
* G. H. M.
* M.

Moore, George W. 19th c. [HPPN]
British humorist
* Moore, Wide Awake

Moore, Hannah [Hudson] 1857-1927
[DNA]
American author and journalist
* Moore, N. Hudson

Moore, Harold 1915- [HPPN]
American petty thief
* [The] Chiseler

Moore, Harris [joint pseudonym with
Arthur Moore]
See Harris, Alf[red]

Moore, Harris [joint pseudonym with
Alf(red) Harris]
See Moore, Arthur

Moore, Harry 20th c. [OBW]
American baseball player
* Moore, Mike

Moore, Harry R. 1888-1958? [IBW, SC]
American entertainer and boxer
* Bosco
* Moore, Kingfish
* Moore, Tim
* Noble, Kid
* Young Klondyke

Moore, Henry 1889-1967 [HPPN]
American actor and dancer
* Gordon, Gilbert

Moore, Idora [McClellan] 1843-1929
[DNA]
American author
* Hamilton, Betsy

Moore, Ivy Lee 1953- [SMG]
American football player
* Moore, Moe

Moore, J. E. ?-1958 [BLB]
American underworld figure
* Maddox, Claude
* Moore, Screwy

Moore, J. S. 19th c. [FFF, PA]
American writer
* Parsee Merchant

Moore, James 1869?-1952 [BI]
American restaurateur
* Moore, Dinty

Moore, James 1924-1970 [BWW, NBB]
American singer
* Harmonica Slim
* Harpo, Slim

Moore, James 1928- [CA]
British author, editor, translator
* Balfour, John

Moore, James 20th c. [OBW]
American baseball player
* Moore, Red

Moore, Jane L. [PA]
Author
* Ione

Moore, Jo-Jo
See Moore, Joe Gregg

Moore, Joan 1882-1972 [HPPN]
British fashion designer
* Moore, Tiger

Moore, Joe Gregg 1908- [BE]
American baseball player
* [The] Gause Ghost
* Moore, Jo-Jo

Moore, John 1644-1714 [SN]
British prelate and book collector
* [The] Father of Black Letter
Collectors

Moore, John 1807-1856 [PI]
British poet
* Brandy, Jonas
* [The] Hermit in Oscott
* Pleon
* Romeo

Moore, John C. [FFF]
American writer
* Snooks, Peter

Moore, John Edward 20th c. [HPPN]
American underworld figure
* Maddox, Claude
* Moore, Screwey

Moore, John Richard, Jr. 1925- [CA]
American actor and author
* Moore, Dick[ie]

Moore, John Travers 1908- [CA]
American author and poet
* Tripp, John

Moore, John Trotwood 1858-1929
[HPPN]
American editor and author
* Trotwood

Moore, Joseph Solomon 19th c. [PA]
American author
* Adersey Curiosibhoy

Moore, Julia A. 1847-1920 [PA, WBD]
American poet
* [The] Sweet Singer of Michigan

Moore, Junior
See Moore, Alvin Earl

Moore, Justina 19th c. [NPS]
Author
* Pritchard, Martin J.

Moore, Kenneth
See La Due, Hubert

Moore, Kieron
See O'Hanrahan, Kieron

Moore, Kingfish
See Moore, Harry R.

Moore, Lander
See Fensch, Thomas

Moore, LaVerne M. 1906-1972 [EG,
GF]
American golfer
* Montague, John
* [The] Mysterious Montague
* [The] Rake and Shovel Golfer

Moore, Leon Alfred 1924- [BA]
American writer and artist
* Moore, Dick
* Moore, Spats

Moore, Leonard Edward [Lenny] 1933-
[BA]
American football player
* Moore, Sput
* Moore, Sputnick

Moore, Lloyd Albert 1912- [BE]
American baseball player
* Moore, Whitey

Moore, M. Louise 19th c. [SFL]
Author
* [An] Untrammeled Free-Thinker

Moore, Maggie
See Williamson, Mrs. J. C.

Moore, Marianne Craig 1887-1972
[HPPN]
American educator, librarian, poet
* [The] First Lady of Poetry

Moore, Marna
See Reynolds, [Marjorie] Moira
Davison

Moore, Mary Tyler 1937- [HPPN]
American actress
* America's Favorite Television Wife

Moore, Melba
See Moorman, Beatrice

Moore, Memphis Pal
See Moore, Thomas Wilson

Moore, Merrill 1903- [HPPN]
American physician and poet
* [The] Psychiatrist Poet

Moore, Michael
See Harris, Herbert

Moore, Mike
See Moore, Harry

Moore, Milton Aubrey, Jr. 1924-1973
[DAM, EJ, EJ7]
American jazz musician
* Moore, Brew

Moore, Mr. Mary Tyler
See Tinker, Grant

Moore, Moe
See Moore, Ivy Lee

Moore, Mollie E.
See Davis, Mary Evelyn [Moore]

Moore, Monette 1902-1962 [BWW]
American singer
* [The] Girl of Smiles
* Mayes, Ethel
* Potter, Nettie
* Smith, Susie
* White, Grace

Moore, Mrs. Bloomfield H. [PA]
Author
* Ward, Mrs. H. O.

Moore, Muriel Sarah 20th c. [LAO]
British author
* Glynn, Bill

Moore, N. Hudson
See Moore, Hannah [Hudson]

Moore, Nell
See Morfit, Eleanor Borum [Little]

Moore, Nicholas 1918- [CA]
British author and poet
* Kelly, Guy

Moore, Nicholas
See Nicolaeff, Ariadne

Moore, Numa Smith 1928- [EJ]
American jazz musician
* Moore, Pee Wee

Moore, Old
See Moore, Francis

Moore, Oliver
See Perry, Oliver Curtis

Moore, Pee Wee
See Moore, Numa Smith

Moore, Pete[r] 20th c. [HPPN]
Canadian midget
* [The] World's Smallest Man

Moore, Pete
See Moore, Warren

Moore, Raymond Leroy 1926- [BE]
American baseball player
* Moore, Farmer

Moore, Red
See Moore, James

Moore, Reg
See Moore, Reginald Charles Arthur

Moore, Regina
See Dunne, Mary Collins

Moore, Reginald Charles Arthur 1930-
[WD]
British author, journalist, poet
* Moore, Charles
* Moore, Reg

Moore, Richard E. M. 1938- [ART]
British medical artist
* R. E. M. M.
* R. M.

Moore, Robert 1898?-1966 [NOJ]
American jazz musician
* Moore, Buster

Moore, Robert
See Williams, Robert Moore

Moore, Robert E. [Bobby] 1949- [FB,
SMG]
American football player
* Rashad, Ahmad

Moore, Robert L[owell], Jr. 1925- [BI,
CA]
American author
* Moore, Robin

Moore, Robin
See Moore, Robert L[owell], Jr.

Moore, Roger
See O'More, Rory

Moore, Rosalie
See Brown, Rosalie [Gertrude] Moore

Moore, Rowdy
See Moore, Eugene, Jr.

Moore, Russell 1912?- [DAM, EJ, WWJ]
American jazz musician
* Moore, Big Chief

Moore, Sally
See Moore, Sara Jane

Moore, Sara Jane 1930?- [HPPN]
*American who attempted to assassinate
President Gerald Ford*
* Moore, Sally

Moore, Scrappy
See Moore, Andrew C., Jr.

Moore, Scrappy
See Moore, William Allen

Moore, Screwey
See Moore, John Edward

Moore, Slim
See Moore, Alton

Moore, Spats
See Moore, Leon Alfred

Moore, Sput
See Moore, Leonard Edward [Lenny]

Moore, Sputnick
See Moore, Leonard Edward [Lenny]

Moore, Square
See Moore, Squire

Moore, Squire 20th c. [OBW]
American baseball player
* Moore, Square

Moore, Ted 1900?- [BI]
American wrestler
* French Angel

Moore, Terry
See Koford, Helen

Moore, Thomas 1779-1852 [DEL, FFF,
HPPN, NPS, PA, PI, SN]
Irish poet
* [The] Bard of Erin
* Brown, Thomas, the Younger
* Cribb, Tom
* [The] Fudge Family
* [An] Irish Man
* Jove's Poet
* [The] Lansdowne Laureate
* Little, Master
* Little, Poor
* Little, Thomas

Moore, Thomas (cont.)
* Moore, Anacreon
* Moore, Trumpet
* One of the Fancy
* [The] Pander of Venus
* Rock, Captain
* Rustifucius, Trismegistus
* Sweet, Melodious Bard
* T. M.
* That Piperly Poet of Green Erin
* [The] Young Catullus of His Day

Moore, Thomas
See Girolami, Enzo

Moore, Thomas Wilson 1894-1953 [BX,
RBE]
American boxer
* Moore, Memphis Pal

Moore, Tiger
See Moore, Joan

Moore, Tim
See Moore, Harry R.

Moore, Tomiwitta 1930- [IBW]
American actress
* Moore, Tommie

Moore, Tommie
See Moore, Tomiwitta

Moore, Tony 20th c. [MBF]
British author
* Morris, Tony

Moore, Trumpet
See Moore, Thomas

Moore, Wallace
See Conway, Gerard F.

Moore, Walter ?-1932 [MK]
American baseball player
* Moore, Dobie

Moore, Walter 1926- [EAR]
American auto racer
* Moore, Bud

Moore, Walter
See Wysocki, Waldemar

Moore, Walter Homer 1844-1917
[HPPN]
American clergyman
* [The] Beloved Dean

Moore, Warren 1939- [IBW, RO1]
American singer, musician, songwriter
* Moore, Pete

Moore, Wayne 1945- [SMG]
American football player
* Moore, Big Sol

Moore, Wentworth
See Mallock, William Hurrell

Moore, Whistling Alex
See Moore, Alexander Herman

Moore, Whitey
See Moore, Lloyd Albert

Moore, Wide Awake
See Moore, George W.

Moore, Wilbur 1916-1965 [AS]
American football player
* [The] Little Indian

Moore, Wild Willie
See Moore, Willie

Moore, [Rev.] William 1782-1848
[HPPN]
British clergyman
* W. M., of Mevagissey

Moore, William 1905?-1983
American radio and television host
* Potter, Peter

Moore, William 20th c. [EF]
American football player
* Moore, Bucky

Moore, William
See Wysocki, Waldemar

Moore, William Allen 1892-1964 [BE]
American baseball player
* Moore, Scrappy

Moore, William Austin 1905- [BE]
American baseball player
* Moore, Cy

Moore, William H., III 1900- [BBH]
American lacrosse coach
* Moore, Dinty

Moore, William Henry 1848-1923
[HPPN]
American capitalist and railroad promoter
* [The] Sphinx of the Rock Island

Moore, William Wilcy 1897-1963 [BE,
PB]
American baseball player
* Moore, Cy

Moore, Willie 20th c. [BWW]
American musician
* Moore, Wild Willie

Moore, Willie
See Moretti, William

Moore, Willie C. 1913-1971 [BWW]
American singer
* Boll Weenie Bill
* Boll Weevil Bill

Moore, Winston Lee 1919-1966 [CWG]
American country-western performer
* Willet, Slim

Moore, Zeke
See Moore, Ezekiel, Jr.

Moore-Brabazon, J. T. C. 20th c.
[PPN]
British pioneer motorist and aviator
* Brab

Moore-Marriott, George Thomas
1885-1949 [F2, FC]
British actor
* Marriott, Moore

Mooreau, M. [PA]
Author
* Beaubien

Moorer, Boom Boom
See Moorer, Elkcanna

Moorer, Elkcanna 20th c. [RBE]
American boxer
* Moorer, Boom Boom

Moorhead, James Kennedy 1806-1884
[HPPN]
American politician
* Old Slackwater

Moorhead, Scipio 1730-1773 [HPPN]
African servant and author
* S. M.

Moorhouse, Herbert Joseph 1882-
[NAA, WW]
Canadian author
* Moorhouse, Hopkins

Moorhouse, Hilda Vansittart 20th c.
[CAP]
British author
* Vansittart, Jane

Moorhouse, Hopkins
See Moorhouse, Herbert Joseph

Moorien, M. [PA]
Author
* Mariel

[The] Moorland Bard
See Bakewell, T.

Moorman, Beatrice 1945- [IPA, SSS]
American singer and actress
* Moore, Melba

Moorman, Maurice 20th c. [EF]
American football player
* Moorman, Mo

Moorman, Mo
See Moorman, Maurice

Moorman, Watt 1814?-1840? [HPPN]
American outlaw and feud leader
* [The] Chief of the Regulators
* [The] Colonel
* [The] Colonel Commandant
* [The] Man With the Hunting Horn

Moorshead, Henry
See Pine, Leslie Gilbert

[The] Moose
See Boros, Julius Nicholas

Moose John
See Walker, John Mayon [Johnny]

Moosh
See Shelley, William

Mopp, Maximilian 1885-1954 [BI]
Austrian painter
* Oppenheimer, Maximilian

Moppert, Gabrielle 1880-? [FC]
French actress
* Dorziat, Gabrielle

[The] Moppet Character Actress
See Jones, Marcia Mae

Mor, Cahal
See O'Conor, Charles Patrick

Mor, Eoghan
See Daly, Eugene P.

Mor, McCarthaigh
See Varian, Ralph

Mora, Chato [Pug-Nose Mora]
See Mora y Garcia, Jose Antonio

Mora, Josie 1948- [IAW]
American author
* Nada, Alivia

Mora, Vera
See Sesan, Karolina Vera

Mora, Victor 20th c. [WECO]
Spanish cartoonist
* Alcazar, Victor

Mora y Garcia, Jose Antonio 1926-
[GS]
Spanish bullfighter
* Mora, Chato [Pug-Nose Mora]

Moraes, Frank Robert 1907- [HPPN]
British editor, correspondent, author
* Ariel

Morais, Antonio de
See De Morais Silva, Antonio

[A] Moral Byron
See Procter, Bryan Waller

[The] Moral Censor of China
See Confucius [or K'ung Fu-tzu]

[The] Moral Columbus
See Dow, Neal

[The] Moral Gower
See Gower, John

[The] Moral Philosopher
See Morgan, Thomas

[The] Moral Surface
See Peel, [Sir] Robert

Morales, Esy
See Morales, Ishmael

Morales, Ishmael 1917-1950 [SC]
Puerto Rican-born actor and bandleader
* Morales, Esy

Morales, Jerry
See Morales, Julio Ruben

Morales, Jorge 20th c. [RBE]
American boxer
* Dynamita, Kid

Morales, Julio Ruben 1949- [BE, SMG,
WWB]
Puerto Rican-born baseball player
* Morales, Jerry

Morales, Luis de 1509?-1586 [FFF, RH,
WBD]
Spanish painter
* [The] Divine

Morales y Mula, Jose 1883-1939 [GS]
Spanish bullfighter
* Ostioncito [Little Oyster]

[The] Moralist of the Main
See Clemens, Samuel Langhorne

Moralisto, Poet Lariat of Carthage
See Dill, J. M.

Moran [RH, SN]
King of Ireland
* [The] Just

Moran, Albert Thomas 1912- [BE]
American baseball player
* Moran, Hiker

Moran, Bugs
See Moran, Carl William, II

Moran, Bugs
See Moran, George

Moran, Butterfingers
See Moran, Thomas B.

Moran, Carl William, II 1950- [SMG]
American baseball player
* Moran, Bugs

Moran, Carlo [PA]
Author
* Bloodgood, Harry

Moran, Charles B. 1879-1949 [AS, FB]
*American baseball player and umpire,
football coach*
* Uncle Charlie

Moran, Charles McMoran Wilson
See Wilson, Charles McMoran

Moran, D. [PA]
Author
* Murray, Dominick

Moran, Deedle
See Moran, Roy Ellis

Moran, George 1893-1957 [BLB]
American underworld figure
* Miller, George
* Moran, Bugs

Moran, George
See Searcy, George

Moran, Gertrude Augusta 1923- [BI,
HPPN]
American tennis player
* Moran, Gorgeous Gussie
* Moran, Gussie

Moran, Gorgeous Gussie
See Moran, Gertrude Augusta

Moran, Gussie
See Moran, Gertrude Augusta

Moran, Hiker
See Moran, Albert Thomas

Moran, James Edward 1900- [BX, RBE]
American boxer
* Goodrich, Jimmy

Moran, Judy
See Sellers, Connie Leslie, Jr.

Moran, Lois
See Dowling, Lois Darlington

Moran, Lord
See Wilson, Charles McMoran

Moran, Mabel O'Connell 1899-1952
[BI, HPPN]
American author
* O'Moran, Mabel

Moran, Mae
See Beaman, Lottie Kimbrough

Moran, Mary 1856?-1949 [BI]
Nun
* Mary Teresa, [Mother]

Moran, Michael 1794?-1846 [DIL, PI]
Irish composer, singer, poet
* [The] Last Gleeman
* Zozimus

Moran, Mike
See Ard, William [Thomas]

Moran, Owen 1884-1949 [BX, RBE]
British boxer
* [The] Fearless

Moran, Paddy
See Moran, Patrick Joseph

Moran, Pal
See Mirana, Paul

Moran, Pat
See Mudgett, Helen

Moran, Patrick Joseph 1887-1966 [HK]
Canadian-born hockey player
* Moran, Paddy

Moran, Pauline Theresa 1885-1952
[BEW, F1, F2]
American actress
* Moran, Polly

Moran, Polly
See Moran, Pauline Theresa

Moran, Roy Ellis 1884-1966 [BE]
American baseball player
* Moran, Deedle

Moran, Thomas B. 1892-1971 [BLB,
HPPN]
American pickpocket
* [The] Dean of Pickpockets
* Moran, Butterfingers

Morandi, Giorgio 1891?-1964
Italian painter
* [Il] Monaco [The Monk]

Morando, Paolo 1486-1522 [WBD]
Veronese painter
* [Il] Cavazzola [or Cavazzuola]

Morant, Breaker
See Morant, Harry H.

Morant, Harry H. ?-1899 [DLE1]
Australian army officer and poet
* [The] Breaker
* Morant, Breaker

Morasawa, Chiyo 20th c. [EE]
Japanese intelligence agent
* Osawa, Lola

Morata, Jaido
See Vickers, John

Moratin, Leandro Fernandez 1760-1828
[DNNF, FFF, SN]
Spanish playwright and poet
* [The] Moliere of Spain
* [The] Spanish Moliere

Moratorium Bill Lemke
See Lemke, William

Moravia, Alberto
See Pincherle, Alberto

Moravia, Charles
See Darlouze, Rene

Morawa, Michael
See Menzel, Roderich

Moray, Dugald
See Cumming-Skinner, Dugald
Matheson

Moray, John S.
See Cazauran, Augustus R.

Moray, Tiburce
See Grousset, Paschal

Morbee, Wilfried Oscar 1940- [HPPN]
Belgian athlete
* Massis, John

Morck, Paal 1876-1931 [EWL]
Norwegian-American author
* Rolvaag, O[le] E[dvaart]

Morco, Happy Jack
See Morco, John

Morco, John ?-1873 [BLB, EWG]
American gunfighter
* Morco, Happy Jack

**Mordaunt, Charles [Third Earl of
Peterborough]** 1658-1735 [FFF, HPPN]
British army and naval officer, diplomat
* [The] Hero of Barcelona
* Smith, Matthew

Mordaunt, Eleanor [or Elinor]
See Mordaunt, Evelyn May [Clowes]

Mordaunt, Evelyn May [Clowes]
1877?-1942 [TC, TC1, WW]
British author
* Mordaunt, Eleanor [or Elinor]
* Riposte, A.

Mordaunt, Mrs. F. S. [FFF]
Entertainer
* Fleming, Marion

Mordechai, Ben
See Gerber, Israel J[oshua]

Mordichai
See Nathan, Isaac

Mordvinoff, Nicolas 1911-1973 [CA]
*Russian-born American author, artist,
illustrator*
* Nicolas

More, Alexandre 1616-1670 [PA, SN]
Author
* [The] Ethiop
* Morus

More [or Mor], [Sir] Anthony
1512?-1576   [HPPN]
Flemish painter
* Moro, Antonio

More, Anthony
See Clinton, Edwin M.

More, Atherton
See Child, Herbert

More, Caroline [joint pseudonym with
Margaret Pitcairn Strachan]
See Cone, Molly [Lamken]

More, Caroline [joint pseudonym with
Molly (Lamken) Cone]
See Strachan, Margaret Pitcairn

More, Euston
See Bloomer, Arnold Euston More

More, Hannah 1745-1833   [DEA, DLE1,
HPPN, NPS, PA]
British author, poet, playwright
* Chip, Will
* [A] Giantess of Genius
* Laureate of the Bluestockings
* Our Little David
* [The] Tenth Muse
* Z.

More, Henry 1614-1687   [HPPN, NPS,
SN]
British clergyman and philosopher
* [The] Cambridge Platonist
* [The] Chrysostum of Christ's College
* [An] Intellectual Epicure
* [The] Man Mouse
* Philalethes, Alazonomastix

More, John
See Bubb, George [Baron Melcombe]

More, Macullum
See Campbell, George John Douglas
[Eighth Duke of Argyle]

More, Margareta
See Manning, Anne

More, Phantom
See Smith, James Moore

More the Great
See Fitzgerald, Gerald

More, [Sir] Thomas 1478-1535
British statesman and author
* King's Conscience
* King's Good Servant
* [A] Man for all Seasons
* [The] Mercy-Killer
* Merry Saint
* Saint for the Small
* Saint for the Time
* Saint for this Season
* Saint in Time of Turmoil
* Worthy of England

More, William
See Mickle, William Julius

Moreas, Jean
See Papadiamantopoulos, Iannis

Moreau, David Merlin 1927-   [AW, WD]
British business executive and author
* Merlin, David

**Moreau de Bellaing, Edouard Jacques
Marie Joseph** 1880-1952   [BI]
French poet
* Dyssord, Jacques

Moreau, Hegesippe 1810-1838   [NPS]
French poet
* Myosotis

Morecambe, Eric
See Bartholomew, [John] Eric

Morecamp, Arthur
See Pilgrim, Thomas

Moreclarke, [Sir] Maudcope, of Hull
See Henley, John

Morecroft, Thomas ?-1741   [SN]
* Wimble, Will

Morehead, Albert H[odges] 1909-1966
[CAP]
American author and editor
* Hodges, Turner

Morehead, David Michael 1943-   [BE]
American baseball player
* Morehead, Moe

Morehead, Moe
See Morehead, David Michael

Morehead, Moe
See Morehead, Seth Marvin

Morehead, Seth Marvin 1934-   [BE]
American baseball player
* Morehead, Moe

Moreira, Ruben 20th c.   [WECO]
Cartoonist
* Rubimor

Morel [The Moor]
See Deschamps, Eustache

Morel, Dighton
See Warner, Kenneth [Lewis]

Morel, Francois Xavier 20th c.   [FDG]
Belgian director
* Rental, J. W.

Morel, Henri 19th c.   [HPPN]
French author
* Martin, Eusebe

Morel, Jules
See Auriol, Vincent

Morel-Retz, Louis-Pierre 1825-1899
[WEC]
French painter and cartoonist
* Stop

Moreland, Margaret Elizabeth
See Cooksley, Margaret Elizabeth

Morell, Andre
See Mesritz, Andre

Morell, [Sir] Charles
See Ridley, James

Morell, Thomas 1703-1784   [HPPN]
British scholar and librettist
* Morellus
* T. M.

Morelle, Jay
See Martin, James

Morelle, Maureen
See Fullam, Maureen Nina

Morellet, Andre 1727-1819   [HPPN, SN]
French satirist
* Bite 'em
* Franklin, Benjamin

Morelli, Carlo
See Zanelli, Carlos

Morelli, Giovanni 1816-1891   [WBD]
Italian art critic
* Lermoliev, Ivan

Morelli, Mme.   [FFF]
Entertainer
* Cornalba, Mlle.

Morello, Pete
See Morello, Piddu

Morello, Piddu ?-1930   [HPPN, MM,
PHM]
American underworld figure
* [The] Boss of Bosses
* [The] Clutching Hand
* Morello, Pete

Morellus
See Morell, Thomas

Morely, Ralph
See Hinton, Henry L.

Moren, Hicks
See Moren, Lewis Howard

Moren, Lewis Howard 1883-1966   [BE]
American baseball player
* Moren, Hicks

Moren, Sally M[oore] 1947-   [CA]
American author
* Morgan, Jane

Morena, Berta
See Meyer, Berta

Morency, Buster
See Morency, Robert

Morency, Robert 1932-1937   [SC]
Actor
* Morency, Buster

Morency, Suzanne Giroux 1772-?   [PA]
Author
* Quillet, Dame

[El] Morenillo [Little Swarthy One]
See Jimenez, Juan

**Morenito de Algeciras [Little Dark One
from Algeciras]**
See Olive Rodas, Diego

Morenito de Valencia
See Puchol, Aurelio

Morenito de Seville, Gino
See Gilmore, Eugene, Airman

Moreno, Anthony 20th c. [DI]
French swindler
* [El] Chorro [The Fountain]

Moreno, Antonio 1879-1942 [GS]
Spanish bullfighter
* Moreno de Alcala [Moreno from Alcala]

Moreno, Bento
See Teixeira De Queiroz, Francisco

Moreno, Francisco 20th c. [FIR]
Actor
* Moreno, Paco

Moreno, Marguerite
See Monceau, Lucie

Moreno, Mario 1911- [FC, HPPN, IPA, OCF]
Mexican entertainer
* Cantinflas
* Mexico's Charlie Chaplin

Moreno, Martin
See Swartz, Harry [Felix]

Moreno, Paco
See Moreno, Francisco

Moreno, Pajarito
See Moreno, Ricardo

Moreno, Ricardo 20th c. [WBC]
Mexican boxer
* Moreno, Pajarito

Moreno, Rita
See Alverio, Rosita Dolores

Moreno, Sky Ball
See Moreno, Thomas

Moreno, Thomas 1895-1938 [SC]
American actor and stunt performer
* Moreno, Sky Ball

Moreno, Tomas 20th c. [GS]
Spanish bullfighter
* [El] Tempranillo [The Little Early One]

Moreno, Virginia [Reyes] 1925- [DLE]
Filipino poet and playwright
* Pile

Moreno, Wenceslas 1899- [BMH]
Spanish ventriloquist
* Senor Wences

Moreno, Yen Ye'
See Moreno Quintero, Omar Renan

Moreno de Alcala [Moreno from Alcala]
See Moreno, Antonio

Moreno del Moral, Jose 1884-1941 [GS]
Spanish bullfighter
* Lagartijillo-Chico [Tiny Lizard]

Moreno Quintero, Omar Renan 1953- [BR]
Panamanian-born baseball player
* Moreno, Yen Ye'

Moreno y Fernandez, Antonio 1866-1929 [GS]
Spanish bullfighter
* Lagartijillo [Little Lizard]

Morentz, Ethel Irene 1925- [CA, IAW]
American author, poet, educator
* Fischer, Jakob
* Morentz, Pat

Morentz, Pat
See Morentz, Ethel Irene

Morenz, Howarth William 1902-1937 [CEI, FHE, SR]
Canadian-born hockey player
* [The] Babe Ruth of Hockey
* [The] Canadian Catapault
* [L']Homme-Eclair [The Top Man]
* [The] Marvel of Hockey
* [The] Mitchell Meteor
* Morenz, Howie
* Morenz, Le Grand
* [The] Stratford Streak

Morenz, Howie
See Morenz, Howarth William

Morenz, Le Grand
See Morenz, Howarth William

Moresby, Louis
See Beck, Eliza Louisa Moresby

Moreskonich, Charles 1919- [BE]
American baseball player
* Metro, Charles [Charlie]

Moret, Gallo
See Moret, Rogelio Torres

Moret, Neil
See Daniels, Charles N.

Moret, Rogelio Torres 1949- [BE, SMG]
Puerto Rican-born baseball player
* Moret, Gallo
* Moret, Roger

Moret, Roger
See Moret, Rogelio Torres

Moreton, Andrew, Merchant
See Foe, Daniel

Moreton, Clara
See Bloomfield-Moore, Clara Sophia [Jessup]

Moreton, Douglas Arthur 1928- [IAW, WD]
British author
* Douglas, Arthur
* Douglas, Joyce

Moreton, John
See Cohen, Morton N[orton]

Moreton, Lee
See Boucicault, Dionysius Lardner

Moretti, Eleanor
See Rogers, Eleanor

Moretti, William 1894?-1951 [BLB, HPPN, PHM]
American underworld figure
* Moore, Willie
* Moretti, Willing Willie

Moretti, Willing Willie
See Moretti, William

[Il] Moretto
See Bonvicino, Alessandro [or Alexander]

[Il] Moretto da Brescia
See Bonvicino, Alessandro [or Alexander]

Moreux, Theophile 1867-1954 [HPPN]
French meteorologist and astronomer
* Theophile, Abbe

Morey, Charles
See Fletcher, Helen Jill

Morfit, Eleanor Borum [Little] 1917?-1974 [BI]
American interior decorator
* Moore, Nell

Morfit, Thomas Garrison 1915- [IPA, ITA]
American entertainer
* Moore, Garry

Morford, Henry 1823-1881 [HPPN, PA]
American author
* [An] Editor
* [The] Governor

Morgan, Alfred P[owell] 1889-1972 [CA, SAT]
American author, editor, manufacturer
* Powell, A. M.

Morgan, Allen D. 20th c. [SFP]
Author
* Smith, Hogan

Morgan, Angela
See Paine, Lauran [Bosworth]

Morgan, Arlene
See Paine, Lauran [Bosworth]

Morgan, Bassett
See Morgan, Grace Jones

Morgan, Bruce
See Hueston, Billy

Morgan, Charles [Langbridge] 1894-1958 [LC]
British author
* Menander

Morgan, Chester Collins [Chet] 1910- [BE]
American baseball player
* Morgan, Chick

Morgan, Chesty
See Wilczhowski, Lillian

Morgan, Chick
See Morgan, Chester Collins [Chet]

Morgan, Claire
See Highsmith, [Mary] Patricia

Morgan, Claudia
See Wupperman, Claudeigh Louise

Morgan, Commodore
See Morgan, John Pierpont

Morgan, Cy
See Morgan, Harry Richard

Morgan, Daniel 1736-1802 [HPPN]
American army officer
* [The] Hero of Cowpens

Morgan, Daniel 1830-1865 [DI]
Australian bushranger
* Bill the Jockey
* Down the Hill Jack
* Mad Dan the Murrimbidgee Terror
* Morgan, Mad

Morgan, De Wolfe
See Williamson, Thames Ross

Morgan, Dennis
See Morner, Stanley

Morgan, Diana 1921- [HPPN]
British author
* Blaine, Sara
* Tremaine, Linda

Morgan, Edward W. 1888-1930 [HPPN]
American actor and singer
* Gibson, Ted

Morgan, Edwin Willis [Eddie] 1914-
[BE]
American baseball player
* Morgan, Pepper

Morgan, Emanuel
See Bynner, Witter

Morgan, Frank
See Paine, Lauran [Bosworth]

Morgan, Frank
See Wupperman, Francis Philip

Morgan, Fred Troy 1926- [CA]
American author
* Bleeker, Mordecia

Morgan, G. J.
See Rowland, Donald Sydney

Morgan, Garrett A. 1875-1963 [HPPN]
American inventor
* [The] Father of the Breathing Helmet
* [The] Father of the Traffic Light

Morgan, Gene
See Schwartzkopf, Eugene

Morgan, Grace Jones 1885- [WWL]
American author
* Morgan, Bassett

Morgan, Gwladys M.
See Lyle, Gwladys M. [Morgan]

Morgan, Gwyneth
See Beal, Gwyneth Morgan

Morgan, Harold Lansford 1934- [DAM]
American jazz musician
* Morgan, Lanny

Morgan, Harriet
See Mencken, Henry Louis [Harry]

Morgan, Harry
See Bratsburg, Harry

Morgan, Harry Richard 1878-1962 [AS,
BE]
American baseball player
* Morgan, Cy

Morgan, Helen 1900-1941 [HPPN]
American singer and actress
* [The] Girl on the Piano
* Little Elsie
* [The] Queen of the Torch Singers

Morgan, Henry
See Von Ost, Henry Lerner

Morgan, Henry James 1842-1913 [CCL]
Canadian author
* [A] British Canadian

Morgan, Hilda Campbell 20th c. [LAO]
Welsh-born author
* Vaughan, Hilda

Morgan, Howard 1936- [EJ7]
American jazz musician
* Morgan, Sonny

Morgan, Irene
See Morse, Irl

Morgan, J. P.
See Morgan, John Pierpont

Morgan, James 19th c. [HFN]
Author
* J. M.

Morgan, James Appleton 1845-1928
[HPPN]
American attorney and scholar
* Appleton

Morgan, James Edward 1883- [BE]
American baseball player
* Morgan, Red

Morgan, Jane
See Cooper, James Fenimore

Morgan, Jane
See Moren, Sally M[oore]

Morgan, Jaye P.
See Morgan, Mary

Morgan, Jinx
See Morgan, Judith A[dams]

Morgan, Joan 1905- [BF]
British actress, author, playwright
* North, Iris
* Wood, Joan Wentworth

Morgan, John
See Paine, Lauran [Bosworth]

Morgan, John Hunt 1826-1864 [HPPN]
American Confederate guerrilla leader
* [The] Raider

Morgan, John Pierpont 1837-1913
[HPPN]
American banker and financier
* Morgan, Commodore
* Morgan, J. P.

Morgan, Joseph 1671?-1745? [HPPN]
British author
* [A] Traveler in Basaruah

Morgan, Joseph Leonard [Joe] 1943-
[IBW]
American baseball player
* Little Giant

Morgan, Judith A[dams] 1939- [CA,
IAW]
American author
* Adams, Judith
* Kragen, Jinx
* Morgan, Jinx

Morgan, Justina
See Freeman, Jean Todd

Morgan, Lady
See Morgan, Sydney Owenson

Morgan, Lanny
See Morgan, Harold Lansford

Morgan, Lee
See Hallbing, Kjell Kare

Morgan, Lewis Henry 1818-1881 [FFF,
HPPN]
American anthropologist
* [The] Father of American
  Anthropology
* Skenandoah

Morgan, Mad
See Morgan, Daniel

Morgan, Maggie
See Cone, Mrs.

Morgan, Margo
See Rockwood, Margaret

Morgan, Maria 1828-1892 [HPPN]
American author
* Morgan, Marie
* Morgan, Middy [or Midy]

Morgan, Marie
See Morgan, Maria

Morgan, Marjorie
See Chibnall, Marjorie [McCallum]

Morgan, Mary 1932- [RO1]
American singer
* Morgan, Jaye P.

Morgan, Mary Ellen [O'Brien] 20th c.
[CCL]
Canadian poet
* Nana

Morgan, McKayla
See Basile, Gloria Vitanza

Morgan, Memo
See Avallone, Michael [Angelo], Jr.

Morgan, Michael [joint pseudonym with
Dean M. Dorn]
See Carle, C. E.

Morgan, Michael [joint pseudonym with
C. E. Carle]
See Dorn, Dean M.

Morgan, Michael
See Morgenstern, Dan M[ichael]

Morgan, Michaela
See Basile, Gloria Vitanza

Morgan, Michele
See Roussel, Simone

Morgan, Middy [or Midy]
See Morgan, Maria

Morgan, Murray Cromwell 1916- [ANT, WW]
American author
* Murray, Cromwell

Morgan, Nicholas
See Morgan, Thomas Bruce

Morgan, Pepper
See Morgan, Edwin Willis [Eddie]

Morgan, Phillip
See Phillips, Morgan

Morgan, Piero
See Piccioni, Piero

Morgan, Plowboy
See Morgan, Tom Stephen

Morgan, Ralph
See Wupperman, Raphael Kuhner

Morgan, Ralph Jerome
See Selz, Ralph Jerome Von Braun

Morgan, Red
See Morgan, James Edward

Morgan, Robert
See Turner, Robert [Harry]

Morgan, Scott
See Kuttner, Henry

Morgan, Sharon A[ntonia] 1951- [CA]
American author
* Fufuka, Karama

Morgan, Shirley
See Kiepper, Shirley Morgan

Morgan, Shubel
See Brown, John

Morgan, Sonny
See Morgan, Howard

Morgan, Squire
See Henry Frederick

Morgan, Sydney Owenson 1778?-1859
[HPPN, PI, SN]
Irish author and poet
* [The] Irish De Stael
* Morgan, Lady
* Owenson, Sydney
* S. O.
* [The] Wild Irish Girl

Morgan, Ted
See De Gramont, Sanche

Morgan, Thomas ?-1743 [HPPN, SN]
British author and clergyman
* [The] Moral Philosopher

Morgan, Thomas Bruce 1926-1972 [CA]
American author
* David, Nicholas
* Morgan, Nicholas

Morgan, Thomas Christopher 1914-
[AW, WW]
British author
* Muir, John

Morgan, Thomas P. [Tom] 1864-1929
American author
* Daft, Tennyson J.

Morgan, Tiny
See Selz, Ralph Jerome Von Braun

Morgan, Tod
See Pilkington, Bert

Morgan, Tom
See Morganelli, Tom

Morgan, Tom Stephen 1930- [ALR, BE]
American baseball player
* Morgan, Plowboy

Morgan, Valerie
See Paine, Lauran [Bosworth]

Morgan, Virginia
See Mundis, Hester

Morgan, Wesley
See Bennett, Isadora

Morgan, Wild Bill
See Morgan, William

Morgan, William 20th c. [OBW]
American baseball player
* Morgan, Wild Bill

Morgan, William
See Miner, William

Morgan, William Forbes 1879-1937
[HPPN]
American banker and politician
* [The] Czar of the Liquor Industry
* [The] Liquor Czar

Morgan, William Sacheus 20th c.
[ALY]
Welsh-born author
* Webley, Pelagian

Morgan-Grenville, Gerard [Wyndham]
1931- [CA]
British author
* Ross, George

Morgan-Jones, David Sylvanus 1900-
[ART]
British painter
* Voel, David

Morganelli, Tom 1909- [MY]
American jazz musician
* Morgan, Tom

Morganfield, McKinley 1915-1983
[BWW, EJ]
American singer
* Boss Man
* [The] Living Legend
* Waters, Muddy

Morganstern, Carl 1859-? [THR]
American-born entertainer
* Hertz, Carl
* [The] King of Cards

Morganweck, Frank 1875-1941 [BB, BBH]
American basketball promoter, financier, manager
* [The] Connie Mack of Pro Basketball
* Morganweck, Morgie
* Morganweck, Pop

Morganweck, Morgie
See Morganweck, Frank

Morganweck, Pop
See Morganweck, Frank

Morgenstern, Albert 1926- [BEW]
American actor
* Sterne, Morgan

Morgenstern, Dan M[ichael] 1929-
[IAW]
German-born author
* Morgan, Michael

Morgenstern, Henrik 1856-1940 [WBD]
Hungarian historian
* Marczali, Henrik

Morgenthau, Commentator
See Morgenthau, Henry J.

Morgenthau, Hans J. 1904- [JL]
German-born political scientist and author
* [The] Father of Power Politics

Morgenthau, Henry 1856-1946 [HPPN]
German-American diplomat
* [The] Great Ambassador

Morgenthau, Henry J. 1891-1967
[BDW]
American government official
* Henry the Morgue
* Morgenthau, Commentator

Morhange, Charles-Henri Valentin
1813-1888 [BBD]
French musician and composer
* Alkan, Charles-Henri Valentin

Morhardt, Meredith Goodwin 1937-
[BE]
American baseball player
* Morhardt, Moe

Morhardt, Moe
See Morhardt, Meredith Goodwin

Mori, Ogai
See Mori, Rintaro

Mori, Rintaro 1862-1922 [BI]
Japanese author, playwright, critic
* Mori, Ogai

Morial, Dutch
See Morial, Ernest Nathan

Morial, Ernest Nathan 1929- [IBW]
American politician
* Morial, Dutch

Moriale, [Fra]
See D'Albano, Montreal

Moriarty, Denis Ignatius
See Daunt, William Joseph O'Neill

Moriarty, Ellen [FFF, PI]
British poet
* Ellice, Lucy
* Evangeline

Moriarty, John Singleton
See Moriarty, W[illia]m Daniel

Moriarty, Joseph 1911?-1979
American underworld figure
* Moriarty, Newsboy

Moriarty, Newsboy
See Moriarty, Joseph

Moriarty, Patrick Eugene 1804-1875
[FFF]
American clergyman and writer
* Ermite
* Hierophilos

Moriarty, Tom 1878-? [THR]
Irish-born comedian
* Stuart, Tom

Moriarty, W[illia]m Daniel 1877-?
[NAA]
American economist and author
* Darragh, Darrach
* Moriarty, John Singleton

Morice, Anne
See Shaw, Felicity

Morice, Dave 1946- [CA]
American author, playwright, poet
* Alphabet, Dr.
* Holland, Joyce

Morich, Stanton
See Griffith-Jones, George Chetwynd

Morien, Sydney
See Archibald, Edith Jessie [Mortimer]

Morier, James Justinian 1780-1849
[DEL, PA]
British author and diplomat
* Hajji Baba of Ispahan
* Persic, Peregrine

Morimura, Tadasi
See Yoshikawa, Takeo

Morin, Claire
See Dore, Claire [Morin]

Morin, Etienne 1899-1966 [MWD]
French playwright
* Passeur, Steve

Morin, Leo-Pol 1892- [NAA]
Canadian writer and composer
* Callihou, James

Morine, Hoder
See Conroy, John Wesley [Jack]

Moriner, Ida 1876-1937 [THR]
American actress
* Conquest, Ida

Morison, Eileen 1915- [FC]
American actress
* Morison, Patricia

Morison, Frank
See Ross, Albert Henry

Morison, John Hopkins 19th c. [HPPN]
American clergyman
* J. H. M.

Morison, Patricia
See Morison, Eileen

Morita, Noriyuki 20th c. [TI 7-2-84]
American actor
* Morita, Pat

Morita, Pat
See Morita, Noriyuki

Moritz 1572-1632 [WBD]
Landgrave of Hesse-Cassel
* [Der] Gelehrte [The Scholar]

Morkovin, Bela V.
See Morkovin, Boris V[ladimir]

Morkovin, Boris V[ladimir] 1882-1968
[CAP]
Russian-born author
* Morkovin, Bela V.

Morland
See Mitterrand, Francois Maurice
Adrien Marie

Morland, Bart
See Burrage, Edwin Harcourt

Morland, Dick
See Hill, Reginald [Charles]

Morland, George 1763-1804 [DEP,
DNNS, RH]
British painter
* [The] English Teniers

Morland, Nigel 1905- [CA, EMD, IAW]
British author and editor
* Dane, Mary
* De Sola, John
* Donavan, John
* Forrest, Norman
* Garnett, Roger
* Kimberley, Hugh
* McCall, John Corey
* McCall, Vincent
* Shepherd, Neal

Morland, Peter Henry
See Faust, Frederick [Schiller]

Morlay, Gaby
See Fumoleau, Blanche

Morley, Arthur Spencer
See Bangs, John Kendrick

Morley, Brian
See Bradley, Marion Zimmer

Morley, Charles 1855-1916 [BEW]
British-born actor
* Cartwright, Charles

Morley, Countess of 19th c. [PA]
Author
* Spruggins, Richard Sucklethum

Morley, Helen
See Brant, Alice [Dayrell]

Morley, John 1942- [ART]
British painter
* J. M.

Morley, Karen
See Linton, Mabel

Morley, Leroy 1906- [BB]
American basketball coach
* Morley, Stix

Morley, Mathew
See Meyer, John M.

Morley, Mrs.
See Anne

Morley, Ralph
See Hinton, Howard

Morley, Stix
See Morley, Leroy

Morley, Susan
See Cross, John Keir

Morley, Wilfred Owen
See Lowndes, Robert Augustine Ward

Morma
See Dickens, Elizabeth

Mormon Bill Delaney
See Delaney, William E. [Billy]

[The] Mormon Bishop
See King, William Henry

[The] Mormon Kid
See Christianson, Willard Erastus

[The] Mormon Pope
See Young, Brigham

Mormonenko, Grigori 1903- [FC, WEF]
Russian director
* Alexandrov, Grigori

Morna
See Ladd, Catherine Stratton

Mornard, Jacques
See Vandendreschd, Jacques Mornard

Mornay, [Dr.] Joseph C.
See Demara, Ferdinand Waldo, Jr.

**Mornay, Philippe de [Seigneur du
Plessis-Marly]** 1549-1623 [DNNF, RH,
WBD]
Supporter of the French Protestants
* Duplessis Mornay
* [The] Huguenot Pope
* [Le] Pape des Huguenots
* [The] Pope of the Huguenots

Morne, Mary
See Strong, Maryland

Morner, Fitz
See Sikes, William Wirt

Morner, Stanley 1910?- [FC, HPPN,
ITA, PMJ]
American actor
* Morgan, Dennis
* Stanley, Richard

Morning Glory, Miss
See Noguchi, Yone

Morning, Richard
See Zeising, Adolf

[The] **Morning Star of Reformation**
See Waldo, Pierre

[The] **Morning Star of Song**
See Chaucer, Geoffrey

[The] **Morning Star of Stepney**
See Burroughs, Jeremiah

[The] **Morning Star of the Reformation**
See Hus, Jan

[The] **Morning Star of the Reformation**
See Wycliffe [or Wyclif], John

[The] **Morning Star of the Reformation in Germany**
See Lollard, Walter

Mornington, Edor
See Roberts, Cecil Edric Mornington

[Il] **Moro**
See Sforza, Lodovico [or Ludovico]

Moro, Antonio
See More [or Mor], [Sir] Anthony

[El] **Morocho del Abasto [The Brown-Haired Man from the Market]**
See Gardes, Charles Romuald

Morogh, Dominick [FFF]
Entertainer
* Murray, Dominick

Morojo
See Douglas, Myrtle R.

Moroni-Celsi, Guido 1885-1962 [WECO]
Italian cartoonist
* Sterny, F.

Morosco, Oliver
See Mitchell, Oliver

Morotius
See Morozzo, Carlo Giuseppe

Morozzo, Carlo Giuseppe 1645-1729 [PA]
Author
* Morotius

[The] **Morphine Murderer**
See Harris, Carlyle W.

[La] **Morphise**
See O'Murphy, Louise

Morphy, Paul Charles 1837-1884 [HPPN]
American chess player
* [The] Pride and Sorrow of Chess

Morpurgo, [Baron] Hubert Louis de 1896- [HPPN]
Austrian tennis player
* Morpurgo, [Baron] Umberto L. de
* [The] Tilden of His Country

Morpurgo, Nelly
See Morpurgo, Pieternella

Morpurgo, Pieternella 1940- [OP]
Dutch opera singer
* Morpurgo, Nelly

Morpurgo, [Baron] Umberto L. de
See Morpurgo, [Baron] Hubert Louis de

Morr, Skip
See Coolidge, Charles William

Morra, Egidio 1906- [ASC]
Italian-born musician
* Morra, Gene

Morra, Gene
See Morra, Egidio

Morrah, Dermot [Michael Macgregor] 1896-1974 [CAP]
British journalist and author
* Yorkist

Morrall, Earl 1934- [HPPN, SMG]
American football player
* Earl the Pearl
* Morrall, Old Bones

Morrall, Old Bones
See Morrall, Earl

Morrell, H. H.
See Mackenzie, H. H.

Morrell, John
See Olsen, Thomas Carl Morrell

Morrell, Wallace
See Garrish, Harold J.

Morren, Theophil
See Hofmannsthal, Hugo [Laurenz August Hofmann Edler] Von

Morres, Hervey Redmond 1746?-1797 [PI]
Irish poet
* Lord M.

Morrie
See Turner, Morris

Morrill, Golightly
See Morrill, Gulian Lansing

Morrill, Gulian Lansing 1857-1928 [DNA]
American author and clergyman
* Morrill, Golightly

Morrill, Honest John
See Morrill, John Francis

Morrill, John Francis 1855-1932 [BE]
American baseball player and manager
* Morrill, Honest John

Morrill, Richard
See Schreck, Everett M.

Morris
See Bevere, Maurice

Morris, Al
See Guimares, Albert

Morris, Alan B. 1910- [BBH]
Canadian football player and coach
* Morris, Teddy

Morris, Alvin 1912?- [FC, PMJ]
American singer and actor
* Martin, Tony

Morris, Anthony Paschal 1849-? [WW]
Author
* Newton, Nat?

Morris, Arthur J. 1882?- [HPPN]
American attorney and banker
* [The] Father of Pay As You Go Budgeting
* [The] Father of the Morris Plan

Morris, Barboura 1932-1975 [SC]
American actress
* O'Neil, Barbour

Morris, Bert De Wayne 1914-1959 [FC]
American actor
* Morris, Wayne

Morris, Billy
See Vick, William A.

Morris, Bugs
See Bennett, Joseph Harley

Morris, C. A.
See Morris, Charles Alfred

Morris, Cannonball
See Morris, Edward

Morris, Captain
See Morris, Charles

Morris, Carl B. 1887-1951 [HPPN, SG]
American boxer
* [The] Original White Hope
* [The] Sapulpa Giant

Morris, Carrie Finnell 1893?-1963 [BEW]
American theatrical performer
* Finnell, Carrie

Morris, Charles 1740?-1838? [DEL]
British songwriter
* Morris, Captain

Morris, Charles 1784-1856 [WBD]
American naval officer
* [The] Statesman of the American Navy

Morris, Charles 1919- [IBW]
American community organizer
* Charles 37X
* Kenyatta, Charles

Morris, Charles Alfred 1898- [ART]
British painter
* Morris, C. A.

Morris, Charles Smith 1833-1922 [WW]
Author
* Allen, Hugh
* Ballard, J. D.
* Blake, Redmond?
* Dare, Roland
* Frazier, S. M.
* Inman, R[obert] R[andolph?]
* Kaine, George S.
* Lytton, Edward
* Murry, William
* Pastnor, Paul
* Pierce, Jo
* Preston, Paul
* Southard, J. H.
* Tripp, C. E.
* Vincent, E. L.

Morris, Clara
See Morrison, Clara

Morris, Corbet
See Thompson, Louis McClanahan

Morris, Dinah
See Evans, Elizabeth

Morris, Edward 1859-1937 [AS, BE]
American baseball player
* Morris, Cannonball

Morris, Elizabeth Woodbridge 1870-?
[NAA]
American author
* Woodbridge, Elizabeth

Morris, Elwin Gordon 1921- [CEI]
Canadian-born hockey player
* Morris, Moe

Morris, Eph
See Morris, Evan

Morris, Esther Hobart McQuigg
1814-1902 [HPPN]
American woman suffrage advocate
* Wyoming's Outstanding Deceased
  Citizen

Morris, Eugene 1947- [FB, IPA, SMG]
American football player
* Morris, Mercury

Morris, Eugenia Laura [Tuttle] 1833-?
[DNA]
Author
* Keith, Alyn Yates

Morris, Evan 20th c. [CSH]
American rowboat racer
* Morris, Eph

Morris, G. A.
See MacLean, Katherine

Morris, General
See Morris, George Pope

Morris, George 1913-1975 [SC]
American actor
* McGiver, John

Morris, George Pope 1802-1864 [DLE1]
American journalist and poet
* Morris, General

Morris, Gwendolen Sutherland [SFL]
Author
* Sutherland, Morris

Morris, Harold 20th c. [OBW]
American baseball player
* Morris, Yellowhorse

Morris, Harry 1918- [IBW]
Liberian-born industrialist and politician
* [The] Rubber King

Morris, Harry
See Birkenhead, Harry

Morris, Hugh
See Herman, Lewis

Morris, Isabelle Patricola 1886-1965
[HPPN]
American musician and singer
* Patricola, [Miss] Isabelle

Morris, James Humphrey 1926- [CA]
British author
* Morris, Jan

Morris, James M. 19th c. [HFN, NPS]
American author
* Pepper, K. N.

Morris, Jan
See Morris, James Humphrey

Morris, Jane
See Ardmore, Jane Kesner

Morris, John 1907?- [BI]
American cartoonist
* Morris, Milt

Morris, John [joint pseudonym with
John Hearne]
See Cargill, Morris

Morris, John [joint pseudonym with
Morris Cargill]
See Hearne, John

Morris, John Chester Brooks 1901-1970
[HPPN]
American actor
* Boston Blackie

Morris, John Scott [Jack] 1956-
American baseball player
* [The] Count

Morris, Johnnie
See Erickson, John Morris

Morris, Joseph Christopher Columbus
1903- [EJ, WWJ]
American jazz musician
* Columbus, Chris

Morris, Joseph Harley
See Bennett, Joseph Harley

Morris, Julian
See West, Morris L[anglo]

Morris, Kate ?-1918 [THR]
British actress
* Serjeantson, Kate

Morris, Katherine
See Pike, Mrs. F. A. M.

Morris, Kenneth 1879-1937 [SFL]
Author
* Morus, Cenydd

Morris, Lana
See Matthews, Pamela

Morris, Leo 1939- [EJ7]
American jazz musician
* Muhammad, Idris

Morris, Leonard Carter 1915- [HPPN]
American jazz musician
* Morris, Skeets

Morris, [Sir] Lewis 1833-1907 [NPS,
WWL]
British poet
* [The] Bard of Penrhyn
* [A] New Writer

Morris, Mary Philipse 1730-1825
[HPPN]
*Friend of American president George
Washington*
* Morris, Polly

Morris, Mercury
See Morris, Eugene

Morris, Michael 1942- [CAR]
Canadian painter
* Dot, Marcel
* General Idea, Miss
* Idea, Marcel

Morris, Milt
See Morris, John

Morris, Moe
See Morris, Elwin Gordon

Morris, Mrs. Austin W. [FFF]
Entertainer
* Toucey, Kate

Morris, Myron
See Stearns, Myron Morris

Morris, Nobuko
See Albery, Nobuko

Morris, Old Tom
See Morris, Thomas, Sr.

Morris, Olive 1884- [THR]
British actress
* Terry, Olive

Morris, Patrick [IP]
Canadian politician and author
* [A] Member of the H. of A. of
  Newfoundland

Morris, Patrick
See Bouchard De Montmerency,
William Geoffrey

Morris, Patsy 1930?-
American opponent of capital punishment
* [The] Queen of Death Row

Morris, Peter
See Lockhart, John Gibson

Morris, Polly
See Morris, Mary Philipse

Morris, Ralph 18th c. [WGT]
Author
* Daniel, John

Morris, Richard 1708-1792 [IP]
British astrologer and author
* Spot, Dick, the Conjuror

Morris, Robert 1734-1806 [HPPN]
British-American financier
* Bobby the Cofferer
* Bobby the Treasurer
* [The] Financier of the American
  Revolution
* [The] Great Financier
* [The] Merchant Prince
* [The] Patriot Financier

Morris, Robert 1818-? [FFF]
Author
* [The] Poet Laureate of Freemasonry

Morris, Robert 1911- [ASC]
American composer
* Miketta, Bob

Morris, Robert
See Gibbons, James Sloan

Morris, Robert Tuttle 1857-1945 [BI]
American surgeon
* West, Mark

Morris, Ruby Turner 1908- [CA]
American economist and author
* Norris, Ruby Turner

Morris, Ruth
See Webb, Ruth Enid Borlase Morris

Morris, Samuel 1700-1770? [FFF]
American clergyman
* [The] Father of Presbyterianism in Virginia

Morris, Samuel V. 1835-? [FFF, IP]
American attorney and poet
* Hoosier

Morris, Sara
See Burke, John [Frederick]

Morris, Sarah Elisabeth Woodbridge 1870-? [HPPN]
American author
* Woodbridge, Elisabeth

Morris, Skeets
See Morris, Leonard Carter

Morris, Stephen
See Nussbaum, Morris

Morris, Steveland 1950- [IBW, IPA, SSS]
American singer and composer
* [The] Man
* Wonder, Little Stevie
* Wonder, Stevie

Morris, Teddy
See Morris, Alan B.

Morris the Crasher
See Lieberman, Morris

Morris, Thomas, Jr. 1850-1875 [BWG, EG, GF]
Scottish golfer
* Morris, Young Tom

Morris, Thomas, Sr. 1821-1908 [BWG, EG, GF]
Scottish golfer
* Morris, Old Tom

Morris, Tom 1821-1908 [HPPN]
Scottish golfer
* [The] Nestor of Golf

Morris, Tony
See Moore, Tony

Morris, Wayne
See Morris, Bert De Wayne

Morris, William 1834-1896
British poet and social reformer
* Topsy

Morris, William
See Fluhrer, John L.

Morris, Yellowhorse
See Morris, Harold

Morris, Young Tom
See Morris, Thomas, Jr.

Morris-Goodall, Vanne 1909- [CA]
British author
* Goodall, Vanne Morris

Morrison, Adrienne
See Morrison, Mabel

Morrison, Arthur 1863-? [WWL]
British author
* Hewitt, Martin

Morrison, C. T.
See Morrison, Charles Theodore

Morrison, Charles Theodore 1936- [LBA]
American author
* Morrison, C. T.

Morrison, Chinese
See Morrison, George Ernest

Morrison, Clara 1846-1925 [BEW, FFF]
Canadian-born actress and writer
* Morris, Clara

Morrison, Crutchy
See Morrison, John

Morrison, Curley
See Morrison, Fred

Morrison, Duke
See Morrison, Marion Michael

Morrison, Dwight 20th c. [SMG]
American basketball player
* Morrison, Red

Morrison, E. 19th c. [HPPN]
British author
* [The] Worthy Patriarch of Howard Division

Morrison, Eula Atwood 1911- [CA, WD]
American author
* Atwood, Drucy
* Delmonico, Andrea

Morrison, Firpo
See Morrison, Lake

Morrison, Fred [SMG]
American football player
* Morrison, Curley

Morrison, Fred 1923- [IBW]
American underwater demolition expert
* Morrison, Tiz

Morrison, G. F.
See Bernstein, Gerry

Morrison, George 1891-1973 [SC]
American actor
* Morrison, Pete

Morrison, George Ernest 1862-1920 [HPPN]
Australian journalist
* Morrison, Chinese

Morrison, Gert W. [house pseudonym] [Stratemeyer Syndicate]
See Stratemeyer, Edward L.

Morrison, Heady 19th c. [PA]
Author
* Juvinell, Uncle

Morrison, Horizontal Bill
See Morrison, William Ralls

Morrison, Irving
See Morse, Irl

Morrison, James 19th c. [SN]
British financier
* [The] Modern Croesus

Morrison, Jeanette Helen 1927- [BDF, FC, IPA]
American actress
* Leigh, Janet

Morrison, Jim 1943-1971 [PRS]
American singer
* [The] Lizard King

Morrison, John 17th c. [PA]
Author
* Struys, John

Morrison, John 1749-1798 [IP]
Scottish poet and clergyman
* Musoeus

Morrison, John 19th c. [HFN, IP]
British author and clergyman
* [A] Clergyman

Morrison, John 20th c. [CEI]
Hockey player
* Morrison, Crutchy

Morrison, John A. 1919- [EJ]
American jazz musician
* Morrison, Peck

Morrison, John Dewey 1895-1966 [BE, BTB]
American baseball player
* Morrison, Jughandle Johnny

Morrison, Jughandle Johnny
See Morrison, John Dewey

Morrison, Kathleen 1900- [F1, F2]
American actress
* Moore, Colleen

Morrison, Lake 20th c. [HPPN]
American football player
* Morrison, Firpo

Morrison, Mabel 20th c. [FAA]
American actress
* Morrison, Adrienne

Morrison, Margaret Mackie ?-1973 [CA]
Scottish-born author
* Cost, March
* Morrison, Peggy

Morrison, Marion Michael 1907-1979 [BDF, F2, FC]
American actor
* [The] Duke
* Morrison, Duke
* Wayne, John

Morrison, Marsh 1902- [CA]
American chiropractor and author
* Marsh, Analyticus

Morrison, Mary
See Washburne, Mary B.

Morrison, Mary Jane [Whitney]
1832-1904 [DNA]
American author
* Wallis, Jenny

Morrison, Michael A. 1934- [ITA]
American producer and film executive
* Wayne, Michael A.

Morrison, Mrs. Lewis   [FFF]
Entertainer
* Wood, Rose

Morrison, Paul Fix 1902- [FC]
American actor
* Fix, Paul

Morrison, Peck
See Morrison, John A.

Morrison, Peggy
See Morrison, Margaret Mackie

Morrison, Pete
See Morrison, George

Morrison, [Jesse] Ray 20th c. [HPPN]
American football coach
* [The] Master of the Aerial Circus

Morrison, Red
See Morrison, Dwight

Morrison, Richard
See Lowndes, Robert Augustine Ward

Morrison, Richard C. 1937- [HPPN]
American burglar
* [The] Babbling Burglar

Morrison, Richard James 1795-1874
[DNNF, IP, RH, WBD]
British astrologer
* Zadkiel
* Zadkiel Tao Sze
* Zadkiel the Seer

Morrison, Robert
See Lowndes, Robert Augustine Ward

Morrison, Roberta
See Webb, Jean Francis

Morrison, Ross Zane
See Marinoni, Rosa Zagnoni

Morrison, Thomas James 20th c. [AW]
Scottish author
* Muir, Alan

Morrison, Tiz
See Morrison, Fred

Morrison, Toni
See Wofford, Chloe Anthony

Morrison, Velma Ford 1909- [CA]
American publisher and author
* Ford, Hildegarde

Morrison, Victor
See Glut, Donald F[rank]

Morrison, William 1888-1960 [SC]
Irish-born actor
* Rainey, Norman

Morrison, William
See Samachson, Joseph

Morrison, William Ralls 1825-1909
[HPPN]
American politician
* Morrison, Horizontal Bill

Morriss, J. H.
See Ghnassia, Maurice [Jean-Henri]

Morrissey, Deacon
See Morrissey, Frank Frederick

Morrissey, Frank Frederick 20th c.
[BE]
American baseball player
* Morrissey, Deacon

Morrissey, James [Jim] 1917- [HPPN]
American labor leader
* [The] Maritime Maverick

Morrissey, Jo-Jo
See Morrissey, Joseph Anselm

Morrissey, John 1831-1880 [SG]
Irish-American gambler, boxer, politician
* Old Smoke

Morrissey, John Albert [Jack]
1877-1936 [BE]
American baseball player
* Morrissey, King

Morrissey, Joseph Anselm 1904-1950
[BE]
American baseball player
* Morrissey, Jo-Jo

Morrissey, Joseph Laurence 1905-
[ESF, SFL, WGT]
American author
* Richards, Henry
* Saxon, Richard

Morrissey, King
See Morrissey, John Albert [Jack]

Morros, Boris
See Milhailovitch, Boris

Morrough, E. R. 20th c. [SFL]
Author
* Abu Nadaar

Morrow, Annie McIntyre 1860?-1935
[HPPN]
American prostitute and pioneer
* [The] Heroine of Bald Mountain
* Morrow, Pegleg Annie

Morrow, Betty
See Bacon, Elizabeth

Morrow, Bruce
See Meyerowitz, Bruce

Morrow, Buddy
See Zudekoff, Muni

Morrow, Charlotte
See Kirwan, Molly [Morrow]

Morrow, Dave 19th c.
American frontiersman
* Prairie Dog Dave

Morrow, Doretta
See Marano, Doretta

Morrow, Felix 1906- [EOP]
American publisher, editor, author
* Wilson, John C.

Morrow, Gilbert
See Gibbs, George

Morrow, Harry C. 1866-1938 [DIL]
Irish playwright and actor
* MacNamara, Gerald

Morrow, Honore McCue 1880?-1940
[HPPN]
American author
* Morrow, Honore Willsie

Morrow, Honore Willsie
See Morrow, Honore McCue

Morrow, Larry
Irish author
* Bellman

Morrow, May
See Carpenter, Anna May

Morrow, Muni
See Zudekoff, Muni

Morrow, Pegleg Annie
See Morrow, Annie McIntyre

Morrow, W. C.
See Morrow, William Chambers

Morrow, William Chambers 1853-1923
[HFF]
American author
* Morrow, W. C.

Morrow, William G. 1916?- [HPPN]
Canadian jurist
* [The] Judge of the North

Morsain, Antoine
See Leneru, Marie

Morse, Anne Christensen 1915- [CA]
American author
* Head, Ann

Morse, Brick
See Morse, Clinton R.

Morse, Bud
See Morse, Newell Obediah

Morse, Carol
See Yeakley, Marjory Hall

Morse, Charles Wyman 1856-1933
[HPPN]
American business executive
* [The] Ice King

Morse, Clinton R. 20th c. [HPPN]
American sportswriter
* Morse, Brick

Morse, Dolly
See Morse, Theodora

Morse, Ella Mae 1925- [HPPN]
American jazz singer
* [The] Cow Cow Boogie Girl

Morse, Emerante 1928- [BA]
Haitian-born educator
* Morse, Emy

Morse, Emy
See Morse, Emerante

Morse, F. L. 19th c. [IP]
American author
* F. L. M.

Morse, Freeman H. 1807-? [IP]
American statesman and author
* [The] American Consul at London

Morse, H[enry] Clifton, IV 1924- [CA]
American author
* Clifton Fourth

Morse, Hap
See Morse, Peter R.

Morse, Irl 1894- [NAA]
American editor, poet, critic
* Baldwin, Douglas
* Morgan, Irene
* Morrison, Irving

Morse, J. J. 1848-1919 [EOP]
Claimed to possess psychic powers
* [The] Bishop of Spiritualism

Morse, Jason 1821-1861 [IP]
American clergyman and author
* [The] Pastor

Morse, Jedediah 1761-1826 [FFF, IP, WBD]
American clergyman and author
* [The] Father of American Geography
* [An] Inhabitant of New England

Morse, Katharine Duncan 1888- [WGT]
American author
* Doane, Jerry

Morse, Lucy G.
Author
* Gibbons, Lucy

Morse, Martha Wilson 1900- [AW]
American author
* Wilson, Martha

Morse, Newell Obediah 1904- [BE]
American baseball player
* Morse, Bud

Morse, Oliver 1922- [BA]
American educator
* Morse, Red

Morse, Peter R. 20th c. [BE]
American baseball player
* Morse, Hap

Morse, Red
See Morse, Oliver

Morse, Red
See Morse, W.

Morse, Richard
See Eastman, Fred

Morse, Samuel Finley Breese 1791-1872
[FFF, HPPN, IP]
American inventor
* [An] American
* [The] American Leonardo
* B.
* Brutus
* [The] Father of the Telegraph

Morse, Sidney Edwards 1794-1871 [IP]
American journalist
* [An] American

Morse, Theodora 1890-1953 [ASC, DAM]
American lyricist
* Esrom, D. A.
* Morse, Dolly
* Terriss, Dorothy

Morse, W. 20th c. [EF]
American football player
* Morse, Red

Morse, Wayne Lyman 1900-1974
[HPPN]
American attorney, educator, politician
* [The] Lone Wolf of the Senate
* [The] Wrecker

Morse, Withrow 1880-? [NAA]
American chemist and writer
* Rankin, John

Morsell, Mrs. Herndon   [FFF]
Entertainer
* Burton, Lizzie

Morss, Elizabeth W. 1918- [CA]
American artist
* Mixter, Elisabeth W.

Mort, Vivian
See Cromie, Alice Hamilton

[The] Mortal Mystery
See Baker, George

Mortara, Edgar 1852-1940 [HPPN]
Italian monk
* Pius

Mortensen, Lee
See Mortensen, Leland

Mortensen, Leland 20th c. [BBH]
American horseshoe pitcher
* Mortensen, Lee

Mortensen, Norma Jean 1926-1962
[BDF, FC, WEF]
American actress
* Baker, Norma Jean
* Bernhardt in a Bikini
* Cheesecake, Miss
* Little Orphan Annie in Hollywood
* M. M.
* Monroe, Marilyn

Mortensson, Ivar 1857-1934 [WBD]
Norwegian author, journalist, theologian
* Mortensson-Egnund, Ivar

Mortensson-Egnund, Ivar
See Mortensson, Ivar

Morthland, Charles 18th c. [HPPN]
Scottish author
* C. M.

[The] Mortician
See Gotshalk, Len

Mortier, Arnold ?-1885 [IP, PA]
French critic
* [Le] Monsieur de l'Orchestre

Mortier, Marie Antoinette 1882-?
[WBD]
French author
* Aurel

Mortimer
See Cade, John [Jack]

Mortimer
See Murphey, J. M.

Mortimer, Chapman
See Chapman-Mortimer, William
Charles

Mortimer, Charles
See Chapman-Mortimer, William
Charles

Mortimer, Geoffrey
See Gallichan, Walter M.

Mortimer, Gilbert
See Gibbs, Montgomery

Mortimer, Grace
See Stuart, M. B.

Mortimer, Henry
See Rennie, John O. D.

Mortimer, January
See Gallichan, Walter M.

Mortimer, John 18th c. [IP]
British author
* J. M., Esq., F.R.S.

Mortimer, John [Clifford] 1923- [BI, WD]
British playwright and author
* Lincoln, Geoffrey

Mortimer, John Hamilton 1741-1779
[DEP, DNNS, RH]
British painter
* [The] English Salvator Rosa

Mortimer, Lee
See Lieberman, Mortimer

Mortimer, Lottie
See Paff, Mrs. Charles

Mortimer, Mary H.
See Coury, Louise Andree

Mortimer, Mrs. N. E.   [IP, PA]
American author
* Rayland, Rose

Mortimer, Penelope [Ruth] 1918- [CA, WD]
British author and columnist
* Dimont, Penelope
* Temple, Ann

Mortimer, Peter
See Roberts, Dorothy James

Mortimer, Roger 1287?-1330 [NPS]
* [The] King of Folly

Mortimer, Thomas 1730-1810 [IP]
British author
* Philanthropos

Morton, A. Q. 1919- [AW]
Scottish clergyman and author
* Kew, Andrew

Morton, Air Mail
See Morton, William H.

Morton, Anthony
See Creasey, John

Morton, Benny
See Morton, Henry Sterling

Morton, Billy
See Morton, Jackson

Morton, Bubba
See Morton, Wycliffe Nathaniel

Morton, Burley
See Morton, George

Morton, Carl Wendle 1944- [SMG]
American baseball player
* Morton, Mo

Morton, Charles 1819-? [DNNS]
Music hall manager
* [The] Father of the Halls

Morton, Charles
See Mudge, Carl

Morton, Craig 1943-
American football player
* Morton, Curly

Morton, Curly
See Morton, Craig

Morton, Eleanor
See Stern, Elizabeth Gertrude [Levin]

Morton, Flutes
See Morton, Norvel E.

Morton, G. A. 20th c. [NPS]
American author
* Aitken, Robert

Morton, George 20th c. [RO2]
American record producer
* Morton, Shadow

Morton, George 20th c. [IBW]
American horse trainer
* Morton, Burley

Morton, Guy, Jr. 1930- [BE]
American baseball player
* Morton, Moose

Morton, Guy Mainwaring 1896-1968
[LAO, LC, WW]
British author and playwright
* Forrest, Mark
* Traill, Peter

Morton, Guy Mainwaring
See Dunstan, Guy Mainwaring

Morton, H. V.
See Morton, Henry Canova Vollam

Morton, Helen Marie 1936- [CAR]
American artist
* Morton, Ree

Morton, Henry 1836-1902 [HPPN]
American scientist and educator
* [The] Committee

Morton, Henry Canova Vollam 1892-
[LC, TC]
British author
* Morton, H. V.

Morton, Henry Sterling 1907- [DAM,
EJ, NP]
American jazz musician
* Bones, Mr.
* Morton, Benny

Morton, Hugh 1865-1916 [BEW]
*American-born playwright, librettist,
lyricist*
* McLellan, Charles Morton Stewart

Morton, J. B.
See Morton, John [Cameron Andrieu]
Bingham [Michael]

Morton, Jackson 1794-1874
American politician
* Morton, Billy

Morton, James 1870?-1967 [CCL]
Canadian author
* Jingle, Jay

Morton, Jelly Roll
See La Menthe, Ferdinand Joseph

Morton, John 1724?-1777 [FFF]
American financier
* [The] Rebel Banker

**Morton, John [Cameron Andrieu]
Bingham [Michael]** 1893-1979 [BI, CA,
LC]
British author and columnist
* Beachcomber [newspaper column
  pseudonym, 1924-]
* Morton, J. B.

Morton, Joseph
See Richman, Al

Morton, Julius Sterling 1832-1902
[HPPN]
American agriculturist and politician
* [The] Father of Arbor Day

Morton, Kitty
See Condon, Catherine

Morton, Leah
See Stern, Elizabeth Gertrude [Levin]

Morton, Lee Jack, Jr. 1928- [SAT]
American illustrator
* Jac, Lee

Morton, Maxine
See West, Katherine

Morton, Mo
See Morton, Carl Wendle

Morton, Monica
See McCulley, Johnston

Morton, Moose
See Morton, Guy, Jr.

Morton, Mort, Jr.
See Meskin, Morton

Morton, Nails
See Morton, Samuel J.

Morton, Norvel E. 1900?-1962 [WWJ]
American jazz musician
* Morton, Flutes

Morton, Oliver Hazard Perry Throck
1823-1877 [HPPN]
American politician
* Perry, Oliver
* Sitting Bull
* [The] War Governor

Morton, Patience
See Govan, [Mary] Christine Noble

Morton, Patricia
See Golding, Morton J[ay]

Morton, Ree
See Morton, Helen Marie

Morton, Rob
See Dowd, Nancy

Morton, Samuel J. ?-1923 [BLB]
American underworld figure
* Morton, Nails

Morton, Sarah Wentworth Apthorp
1752?-1846 [FFF, HPPN, WBD]
American poet
* [The] American Mrs. Montague
* [The] American Sappho
* Philenia [or Phililenia?]

Morton, Shadow
See Morton, George

Morton, Sparrow
See Morton, William H.

Morton, Stanley
See Freedgood, Morton

Morton, Thomas 1764-1838 [SN]
British playwright
* [A] Troubler of Israel

Morton, William
See Ferguson, William Blair Morton

Morton, William Ferdinand Joseph
See La Menthe, Ferdinand Joseph

Morton, William H. 19th c. [BE]
American baseball player
* Morton, Sparrow

Morton, William H. 1909- [FB]
American football player
* Morton, Air Mail

Morton, William Thomas Green
1819-1868 [HPPN]
American dentist
* [The] Father of Anesthesia
* [The] Father of Etherization

Morton, Wycliffe Nathaniel 1931- [BE]
American baseball player
* Morton, Bubba

Mortson, Gus
See Mortson, James Angus Gerald

Mortson, James Angus Gerald 1925-
[CEI, FHE]
Canadian-born hockey player
* Mortson, Gus

Morum, William 20th c. [AW]
British author and playwright
* Smith, Surrey [joint pseudonym with
William Dinner]

Morus
See More, Alexandre

Morus, Cenydd
See Morris, Kenneth

Morvan, Yves 1909- [IAW]
French journalist and author
* Marin, Jean

Moryn, Moose
See Moryn, Walter Joseph

Moryn, Walter Joseph 1926- [BE]
American baseball player
* Moryn, Moose

Mosa
See Gribaldi, Matteo

Mosbacher, Bus
See Mosbacher, Emil, Jr.

Mosbacher, Buster
See Mosbacher, Emil, Jr.

Mosbacher, Emil, Jr. 1922- [HPPN]
American sailboat racer
* Mosbacher, Bus
* Mosbacher, Buster

Mosby, John S. 1833-1916 [HPPN]
*American attorney and Confederate
ranger*
* [The] Gray Ghost

Mosby, Mary Webster [Pleasants]
1791-1844 [BDSA, DNA]
American author
* Webster, M. M.

Moscato, Brother
See Moscato, Phillip

Moscato, Phillip 20th c.
American underworld figure
* Moscato, Brother

**Moscherosch [or Mosenrosh], Johann
Michael** 1601-1669 [WBD]
German author
* [The] Dreamer
* Von Sittewald, Philander

Moschitta, John 1946?- [WP 2-23-84]
American actor
* Mighty Mouth

Moschus
See Lovel, Robert

Moscovitch, Maurice
See Masskoff, Maurice

Moscovitch, Nathaniel 1905?- [FC]
American actor
* Madison, Nat
* Madison, Noel

[The] Moscow Sappho
See Rostopchin, [Countess] Eudoxie

Moscowitz, Jennie
See Silverstein, Jennie

Moscow's Mercenary Master
See Castro Ruz, Fidel

Mose
See Depond, Moise

Moseilma 7th c. [RH]
Claimed to be a prophet
* [The] Liar

Moseka, Aminata
See Woolridge, Anna Marie

Mosel, George Ault, Jr. 1922- [BEW]
American playwright
* Mosel, Tad

Mosel, Tad
See Mosel, George Ault, Jr.

Moseley, Hallam Reynold 1948- [DC]
West Indian cricketer
* [The] Black Flash
* Moseley, Mojo
* Moses the Lawgiver

Moseley, Mojo
See Moseley, Hallam Reynold

Moseley, Robert 1922- [FC, IPA, ITA]
American actor
* Madison, Guy

Moselly, Emile 1870-1918 [WBD]
French author
* Chenin, Emile

Mosenrosh, Johann Michael 1601-1669
[HPPN]
German satirist
* [The] Dreamer
* Sittewald, Philander von

Moser, Hans
See Juliet, Jean

Moser, Joseph 1748-1819 [IP]
British author
* [A] Barber
* Twig, Timothy, Esq.

Moser, Mike
See Moser, William J.

Moser, William J. 1916-1953 [HPPN]
American producer
* Moser, Mike

Moses [HPPN]
Prophet and law giver
* [The] Prince of Egypt

Moses
See Fowler, Moses Field

Moses
See Tubman, Harriet Araminta Ross
Davis

Moses, Anna Mary Robertson
1860?-1961 [HPPN]
American artist
* [The] Grand Old Lady of American
Art
* Moses, Grandma

Moses ben Nahman Gerondi 1194-1270?
[BI]
Spanish Hebraist and physician
* Nahmanides

Moses, Bob
See Parris, Bob

Moses, Faraway
See Huff, Jacob K.

Moses, Felix 19th c.
American peddler
* Old Mose

Moses, Grandma
See Moses, Anna Mary Robertson

Moses, Hilda Theresa 20th c. [BEW]
American actress
* Simms, Hilda

[The] Moses of America
See Weis, Isaac Mayer

[The] Moses of Athens
See Aristocles

[The] Moses of Mesopotamia
See Jacobus

[The] Moses of Our Age
See Zinzendorf, [Count] Nikolaus
Ludwig von

[The] Moses of the Mormons
See Strang, James Jesse

Moses, Peepsight
See Moses, Wallace [Wally]

Moses, Phoebe Anne Oakley 1860-1926
[AS, NN]
American sharpshooter
* Little Sure Shot
* Mozee, Annie
* Oakley, Annie

Moses, Richard 20th c. [HPPN]
German business executive and financier
* Merton, Richard

Moses, Robert 1889-1981 [HPPN]
*American city planning commissioner and
builder*
* [The] Man Who Gets Things Done
* [The] Master Builder
* New York City's Master Builder

Moses, Ruben
See Wurmbrand, Richard

Moses the Lawgiver
See Moseley, Hallam Reynold

Moses the Son of Jehoshar
See Ebel, Henry

Moses to Her People
See Tubman, Harriet Araminta Ross
Davis

Moses, W. S. 19th c. [IP]
British author
* A. M., Oxon

Moses, Wallace [Wally] 1910- [BN]
American baseball player
* Moses, Peepsight

Mosesson, Gloria R[ubin] 20th c. [CA]
American editor
* French, Kathryn
* Miller, Doris R.

Moshe, David
See Winkelman, Donald M.

Mosher, Frederick C. 1913- [IAW]
American author
* Fritz

Mosher, L. E. 19th c. [FFF, IP]
American writer
* Wagoner, Hank

Mosher, T. B.
See Mosher, Thomas Bird

Mosher, [Christopher] Terry 1942- [CA]
Canadian author and cartoonist
* Aislin

Mosher, Thomas Bird 1852-1923 [LC]
Publisher
* Mosher, T. B.

Moshesh 1790?-1870 [HPPN]
King of Basutoland
* [The] Father of the Basotho

Moshinski, Albert 1925- [EMT]
American director
* Marre, Albert

Mosier, Marilyn 1929- [BEW]
American actress, dancer, comedienne
* Lynn, Mara

Mosina, Czecho
See Mosina, Tarcisio

Mosina, Tarcisio 1951- [AES]
Yugoslav soccer player
* Mosina, Czecho

Mosk
See Moskowitz, Gene

Moskiman, Doc
See Moskiman, William Bankhead

Moskiman, William Bankhead 1879-1953
[BE]
American baseball player
* Moskiman, Doc

Moskowitz, Belle Lindner 1877-1933
[HPPN]
*American social worker and political
leader*
* [The] Mother of the Travelers Aid

Moskowitz, Gene 1921?-1982 [CA]
French film critic
* Mosk

Moskowitz, Harry 1900-1971 [DAM]
American musician and conductor
* Ford, Harry

Moskowitz, Harry 1904- [EJS]
American basketball coach
* Moskowitz, Jammy

Moskowitz, Jammy
See Moskowitz, Harry

Moskowitz, Sam 1920- [CA, CC]
American author and editor
* Martin, Sam

Moskvitin, Jurij
See Hansen, Jurij

Mosley, Baptiste 1893-1965 [NOJ]
American jazz musician
* Mosley, Bat

Mosley, Bat
See Mosley, Baptiste

Mosley, Lawrence Leo 1909- [EJ, PMJ,
WWJ]
American jazz musician
* [The] Man with the Funny Horn
* Mosley, Snub

Mosley, [Sir] Oswald [Ernald]
1896-1980 [CAP, HPPN]
British legislator and author
* Britain's Hitler
* European

Mosley, Rocky
See Mosley, Roxell, Jr.

Mosley, Roxell, Jr. 1958- [BA]
American boxer
* Mosley, Rocky

Mosley, Snub
See Mosley, Lawrence Leo

Mosonyi, Mihaly
See Brandt, Michael

[The] Mosquito Nun
See Asman, [Sister] Monica

Moss, Buddy
See Moss, Eugene

Moss, Charles ?-1802 [HPPN]
British clergyman
* C. M.
* [The] Clearer

Moss, Crazy Horse
See Moss, Robert

Moss, Eugene 1906- [BWW]
American singer
* Miller, Jim
* Moss, Buddy

Moss, Howard Glenn 1918- [WP 4-8-85]
American baseball player
* [The] Howitzer

Moss, John 20th c.
American poker player
* Moss, Texas Johnny

Moss, Mary 1826-1873 [HPPN]
*British-American actress and theatrical
manager*
* Keene, Laura

Moss, Nancy
See Moss, Robert [Alfred]

Moss, Robert [Alfred] 1903- [CAP]
British author
* Moss, Nancy
* Moss, Roberta

Moss, Robert 20th c. [SMG]
American football player
* Moss, Crazy Horse

Moss, Roberta
See Moss, Robert [Alfred]

Moss, Rose 1937- [CA]
South African-born educator and author
* Johannes, R.

Moss, Stirling 1929- [HPPN]
British auto racer
* [The] British Auto Ace

Moss, Texas Johnny
See Moss, John

Mossbank [code name used during
World War II]
See Laval, Pierre

Mosse, T. 18th c. [PI]
Irish poet
* T. M.

Mosser, Ann J. 1912-
American author
* Allwood, Edith
* Brown, M. E.
* Hall, B. K.
* Ressom, J. Ann

Mossi, Donald Louis 1929- [BE]
American baseball player
* [The] Sphinx

Mossman, Burt[on] 1867-? [EWG]
American law officer
* Mossman, Cap

Mossman, Cap
See Mossman, Burt[on]

Mossman, Dow 1943- [CA]
American author
* O'Quill, Scarlett

Mossman, [Rev.] John Timberley
19th c. [HPPN]
British clergyman
* [A] Disciple of Bishop Butler

Mossop, Henry 1729-1773 [NPS]
Playwright
* [The] Distiller of Syllables

Mossop, Irene
See Swatridge, Irene Maude [Mossop]

[The] Most Admired Man in America
See Graham, William Franklin [Billy]

**[The] Most Beautiful Blonde in the
World**
See Field, Margaret Cynthia

[The] Most Beautiful Girl on Radio
See Eden, Ann

**[The] Most Beautiful Woman in the
World**
See Griffith, Corinne

[The] Most Beautiful Woman in the World
See Hruba, Vera

[The] Most Beautiful Woman in the World
See Mangano, Silvana

[The] Most Brutal Gunman in Chicago
See McErlane, Frank

[The] Most Christian Doctor
See Charlier, Jean

[The] Most Christian Doctor
See De Cusa, Nicholas

[The] Most Christian King
See Charles I

Most Christian King
See Louis XI

Most Christian King
See Pepin III

[The] Most Conspicuous Controversialist of His Age
See Chillingworth, William

[The] Most Dangerous Negro in America
See Randolph, Asa Philip

[The] Most Distinguished Milkman
See Dewey, Thomas Edmund

[The] Most Eminent and Renowned Navigator
See Magalhaes, Fernao De

[The] Most Eminent English Jurist
See Coke, [Sir] Edward

[The] Most Eminent of News Broadcasters
See Thomas, Lowell Jackson

[The] Most Enlightened Doctor
See Lully, Raymond

Most Erudite of the Romans
See Varro, Marcus Terentius

Most Faithful Majesty
See John V

[The] Most Famous Folk Singer of his Race
See White, Josh[ua Daniel]

[The] Most Famous Loser
See DePalma, Ralph

[The] Most Famous Woman of Two Centuries
See Koenigsmark, Aurora

[The] Most Faultless of Poets
See Pope, Alexander

[The] Most Happy Fellow
See Reagan, Ronald Wilson

[The] Most Hated Man In China
See Doihara, Kenji

[The] Most Impudent Man Living
See Warburton, William

[The] Most Influential Artist of the Twentieth Century
See Ruiz, Pablo Diego Jose Francisco de Paula Juan Nepomuceno Cipriano

[The] Most Intelligent of American Sopranos
See Smith, Phyllis

[The] Most Learned Fool in Christendom
See James I

Most Learned of the Romans
See Varro, Marcus Terentius

[The] Most Listened-To Man In America
See Richards, Harold M. S.

[The] Most Methodical Doctor
See Bassol, John

[The] Most Original Composer of 20th Century Music
See Ives, Charles Edward

[The] Most Outstanding Jurist
See Pound, Roscoe

[The] Most Powerful Man in the Soviet Union
See Brezhnev, Leonid Ilich

[The] Most Powerful Man in the World
See Deterding, Hendrik Wilhelm August

[The] Most Profound Doctor
See Aegidius [or Giles] of Colonna

[The] Most Prolific Writer
See Hamilton, Charles Harold St. John

[The] Most Publicized Witch of the Century
See Falk, Sybil

[The] Most Remarkable Man on Earth
See Bodie, Sam

[The] Most Resolute Doctor
See St. Pourcain, Guillaume Durand de

[The] Most Segregated Negro in America
See Meredith, James

[The] Most Thoroughgoing British Skeptic of the Eighteenth Century
See Hume, David

[The] Most Universal Genius
See Arbuthnot, John

[The] Most Unpatriotic Man Alive
See Fox, Charles James

[The] Most Useful Man in the Diplomatic Service
See White, Henry

[The] Most Widely Understood Poet in America
See Kenny, Nicholas Napoleon [Nick]

Mostel, Samuel Joel 1915-1977 [BEW, EMT, IPA]
American actor
* Mostel, Zero

Mostel, Zero
See Mostel, Samuel Joel

Mostil, Bananas
See Mostil, John Anthony

Mostil, John Anthony 1896-1970 [DGS, PB]
American baseball player
* Mostil, Bananas

Mostyn, Sydney
See Russell, William Clark

Mostyn-Owen, Gaia
See Servadio, Gaia [Cecilia Gemmalina]

Mota, Manny
See Mota, Manuel Rafael

Mota, Manuel Rafael 1938- [BE, PB, SMG]
Dominican-born baseball player
* Mota, Manny
* Mota, Mickey
* Mota, Pee Wee

Mota, Mickey
See Mota, Manuel Rafael

Mota, Pee Wee
See Mota, Manuel Rafael

Motassem, Al- [HN]
Caliph
* [The] Eight

Motaung, Boy-Boy
See Motaung, Kaiser

Motaung, Kaiser 1944- [AES]
South African soccer player
* Motaung, Boy-Boy

Moten, Benny
See Moten, Clarence Lemont

Moten, Clarence Lemont 1916- [EJ]
American jazz musician
* Moten, Benny

Moth
See Buckingham, Joseph Tinker

Moth
See Fleming, [Robert] Peter

Mothell, Carroll Ray 1897- [MK]
American baseball player
* Mothell, Dink

Mothell, Dink
See Mothell, Carroll Ray

[A] Mother
See Bird, Sarah

[A] Mother
See Mott, Abigail

[The] Mother
See Richard, Mira

Mother Ann
See Lee, Ann

Mother Elizabeth
See Hesselblad, Maria Elizabeth

Mother Goose
See Bowen, Ruth J. Baskerville

Mother Goose
See Fleet, Thomas

Mother Goose
See Foster, Elizabeth

Mother Goose
See Perrault, Charles

Mother Hubbard
See Spenser, Edmund

Mother Julia
See Billiart, Marie R. J.

Mother Maybelle
See Carter, Maybelle

Mother MD
See Cilento, Phyllis Dorothy

[The] Mother of a Thousand Daughters
See Agnew, Eliza

[The] Mother of All the Doughboys
See Rossler, Ernestine

[The] Mother of American Tennis
See Outerbridge, Mary Ewing

[The] Mother of American Women's Swimming
See Epstein, Charlotte

[The] Mother of Beale Street
See Glover, Lilian Mae

[The] Mother of Believers
See Ayesha [or Ayeshah]

[The] Mother of Country Music
See Carter, Maybelle

[The] Mother of Detective Stories
See Rohlfs, Anna Katharine [Green]

[The] Mother of Freedom
See Zenger, Anna Catherine Maulin

[The] Mother of God
See Mary

[The] Mother of Gospel Music
See Smith, Willie Mae Ford

[The] Mother of Her Country
See Maria Theresa

[The] Mother of Her Country
See Victoria

[The] Mother of Hull House
See Addams, Jane

[The] Mother of Level Measurements
See Farmer, Fannie Merritt

[The] Mother of Methodism in the United States
See Heck, Barbara Ruckle

[The] Mother of Mod
See Quant, Mary

[The] Mother of Quakerism
See Fell, Margaret

[The] Mother of Smith College
See Smith, Sophia

[The] Mother of Thanksgiving
See Hale, Sarah Josepha Buell

[The] Mother of the American Legion
See Rossler, Ernestine

[The] Mother of the Blues
See Rainey, Gertrude Malissa Nix [Pridgett]

[The] Mother of the Camps
See Victoria [or Victorina]

[The] Mother of the Civil Rights Movement
See Parks, Rose

[The] Mother of the Confederacy
See Law, Sallie Chapman Gordon

Mother of the Faithful
See Ayesha [or Ayeshah]

[The] Mother of the Girl Scouts
See Low, Juliette Gordon

[The] Mother of the Gracchi
See Cornelia

[The] Mother of the Green Revolution
See Day, Dorothy

[The] Mother of the Irish Drama
See Gregory, [Lady] Isabella Augusta Persse

[The] Mother of the Kindergarten
See Blow, Susan Elizabeth

Mother of the Motherless
See Bojaxhiu, Agnes Gonxha

[The] Mother of the Mountains
See Hance, Margaret

[The] Mother of the Movies
See Cogan, Fanny Hay

[The] Mother of the Nation
See Mandela, Winnie

[The] Mother of the People
See Margaret [or Marguerite] of France

[The] Mother of the Red Cross
See Barton, Clarissa Harlowe

[The] Mother of the Salvation Army
See Booth, Catherine Mumford

[The] Mother of the Strip Tease
See Dennis, Ruth

Mother of the Sun-Bonnet Babies
See Melcher, Bertha Corbett

[The] Mother of the Travelers Aid
See Moskowitz, Belle Lindner

[The] Mother of the Vegetable Compound
See Pinkham, Lydia E.

Mother of the W. A. V. E. S.
See Smith, Margaret Chase

[The] Mother of the World
See Bojaxhiu, Agnes Gonxha

Mother To The Poorest of The Poor
See Bojaxhiu, Agnes Gonxha

Motherwell, Hiram
See Moderwell, Hiram K.

Motherwell, William 1797-1835 [IP]
Scottish poet and journalist
* Brown, Isaac

[The] Motion Picture Czar
See Hays, Will H.

Motion Picture, Mr.
See De Mille, Cecil B[lount]

[The] Motivation Mentor
See Packard, Vance Oakley

Motley, Arthur Harrison 1900-1984 [BI]
American publisher
* Motley, Red

Motley, Marion 1921- [HPPN, IBW]
American football player
* Motley, Tank
* Otto Graham's Bodyguard

Motley, Mary
See De Reneville, Mary Margaret Motley Sheridan

Motley, Red
See Motley, Arthur Harrison

Motley, Tank
See Motley, Marion

Motmot, Snik P.
See Tompkins, Everett Thomas

Motoko, Yamanobe 20th c. [HPPN]
Japanese wedding consultant and columnist
* [The] Dear Abby of Japan

Motolinicafoutli
See Davila Garibi, Jose Ignacio

[The] Motor City Cobra
See Hearns, Thomas

[The] Motor City Madman
See Nugent, Ted

Motor Mouth
See Young, Andrew Jackson, Jr.

[The] Motorcycle Ace
See Mann, Richard [Dick]

[The] Motorized Cowboy
See Bryan, Jimmy

Mott, Abigail [IP]
American author
* [A] Mother

Mott, Albert Julius 19th c. [IP]
British author
* Barrowcliffe, A. J.

Mott, Bitsy
See Mott, Elisha Matthew

Mott, Buster
See Mott, Norman

Mott, Edward Spencer 1844-1910 [WW]
Author
* Gubbins, Nathaniel
* Spencer, Edward

Mott, Elisha Matthew 1918-   [BE]
American baseball player
* Mott, Bitsy

Mott, James Wheaton 1883-1945
[HPPN]
American politician
* Mott, Tonguepoint

Mott, Jordan L.   [IP]
American inventor and author
* [A] Member of the Executive
Committee

Mott, Lucretia Coffin 1793-1880
[HPPN]
American social reformer
* [The] Advance Agent of Emancipation
* Builder of the Quaker Road
* [The] Flower of Quakerism
* Gentle Warrior
* Girl of Old Nantucket
* [The] Invincible Warrior
* Lady of Seneca Falls
* [The] Sweet Spirited Advocate of
Justice, Love and Humanity

Mott, Michael 1930- [DLE]
British poet and author
* Alston, Charles

Mott, Norman 20th c. [EF]
American football player
* Mott, Buster

Mott, Tonguepoint
See Mott, James Wheaton

Mott, Vincent Valmon 1916- [CA]
American economist and author
* St. Andre, Lucien

Motte, Mellish Irving ?-1881 [HPPN]
American clergyman
* M. I. M.

Motte, Peter
See Harrison, Richard [Motte]

**Motte-Guyon, Jeanne Marie Bouvier De
La** 1648-1717 [HPPN]
French mystic
* Guyon, Madame

Motteux, Peter Anthony
See Motteux, Pierre Antoine

Motteux, Pierre Antoine 1660?-1718
[HPPN, SN]
British playwright, translator, editor
* Clayton, Thomas
* Motteux, Peter Anthony
* Our Sturdy Teuton

Mottley, John 1692-1750 [IP, PA]
British author
* [A] Gentleman
* Miller, Joe
* Seymour, Robert, of the Inner Temple

Mottola, Tony 1918- [PMJ]
American musician
* Big, Mr.

Motton, Curt
See Motton, Curtell Howard

Motton, Curtell Howard 1940-   [BE]
American baseball player
* Motton, Curt

Mottram, R. H.
See Mottram, Ralph Hale

Mottram, Ralph Hale 1883-1971 [DLE1,
LC, TC]
British author
* Marjoram, J.
* Mottram, R. H.

Motz, Josephine 1891-1964 [SC]
American actress
* Taylor, Josephine

Moubray, Bonington
See Lawrence, John

**Mouhadjou [or Mahdjou], [Said]
Moustapha**
See Denard, Robert [Bob]

Mouillot, Gertrude
See Davison, Gertrude

Mould, Mrs. Henry S.   [FFF]
Entertainer
* Manola, Marion

Moule, Henry 1801-? [PA]
British clergyman and author
* [A] Country Parson

Moule, Joseph   [IP]
Scottish clergyman and author
* [A] Member of the Congregation

Moule, Winifred Ruby 1920- [TR]
British actress and singer
* Lee, Vanessa

Moules, Peter 20th c. [RO2]
British singer
* [The] Count

Moulie, Charles 1890- [WBD]
French author
* Sandre, Thierry

Mouligneau, Michel 1935- [IAW]
Belgian author
* De Guy Latteur

Moulin, Jean 1899-1943
French resistance leader
* Max [code name used during World
War II]

Moulin, Louis du 1603?-1680? [FFF]
Historian and author
* Philalethes, Irenaeus

Moulinet, Madame
See Weber, Jeanne

Moulson, [Captain] W. H. Baliol
19th c. [HPPN]
British army officer and author
* [A] Guernsey Militia Officer

Moulton, Albert Theodore 1886-   [BE]
American baseball player
* Moulton, Ollie

Moulton, Carl
See Tubb, Edwin Charles

Moulton, Charles
See Marston, William Moulton

Moulton, Ellen Louise Chandler
1835-1908 [FFF, HPPN, PA]
American poet
* Ellen Louise
* L. C. M.
* Louise Ellen
* Pomfret, Ellen Louise

Moulton, Mabel
See Noyes, Mrs. A. C.

Moulton, Ollie
See Moulton, Albert Theodore

Moultrie, George 19th c. [PA]
Author
* Montgomery, Girard

Moultrie, Gerard 19th c. [IP]
British clergyman and hymn-writer
* D. P.
* Desiderius Pastor
* M.

Moultrie, John 1799-1874 [IP]
British poet
* Montgomery, Gerard

Moune
See Virel Jean-Louis, Cecile Moumoune
de

Mounet, Jean Sully 1841-1916 [BEW]
French-born actor
* Mounet-Sully, Jean

Mounet-Sully, Jean
See Mounet, Jean Sully

Mounsey, Thomas 19th c. [IP]
British author
* T. M.

Mount Atlas
See O'Shea, John

Mount, Bessie
See Mount, John

Mount Cashel, Earl of 1791?-1883
[FFF]
Irish aristocrat
* [The] Father of the House of Lords

Mount, Elisabeth
See Dougherty, Betty

Mount, John 20th c. [HPPN]
American brothel proprietor
* Mount, Bessie
* Perkins, Mrs. Carlos
* [The] Respected Madam of Oxnard

Mount, Thomas Ernest 1895- [HPPN]
American author
* King, Oliver

Mount Washington
See Washington, Russell

[The] Mountain
See Danton, Georges Jacques

[The] Mountain
See Robespierre, Maximilien

[The] Mountain Brutus
See Tell, William

Mountain Charley
See Guerin, Elsa Jane Forrest

[The] Mountain Evangelist
See Jones, Sam[uel Porter]

Mountain Fern
See Williamson, LaVerne

Mountain, George Jehoshaphat
1789-1863 [CCL, IP]
Canadian author and clergyman
* [The] Bishop of Montreal
* [A] Catholic Christian

Mountain, Jacob 1750-1825 [IP]
American prelate and author
* Jacob, Lord Bishop of Quebec

Mountain, Jacob Henry Brooke 19th c.
[HFN, IP]
British author and clergyman
* J. H. B. M.

[The] Mountain Man
See Walton, Bill

Mountain Man Roberts
See Roberts, Dale

Mountain, Marian
See Wisberg, Marian Aline

Mountain Music Melton
See Melton, Clifford George

Mountain, Robert
See Montgomery, Raymond A., Jr.

[The] Mountain Tiger of Nepaul
See Ranjit [or Runjeet], Singh

[The] Mountaineer
See Alston, Joseph

Mountaineer
See Wright, Charles

Mountbatten, Louis 1900-1979 [HPPN]
British naval officer
* [The] Last Great Englishman
* Uncle Dickie

Mountbatten, Richard
See Wallmann, Jeffrey M[iner]

Mountcastle, Clara H. 1837-? [CCL]
Canadian author
* Sima, Caris

Mountcastle, Fanny
See Thorp, Mrs. Charles R.

[A] Mountebank in Criticism
See Warburton, William

Mountenay, Barclay de [IP]
British author
* B. A.

Mountfield, David
See Grant, Neil

[The] Mountie of American Corporate Chiefs
See Bradshaw, Thornton

Mountjoy, Desmond
See Chapman-Huston, D. M.

Mountjoy, Earl 16th c. [FFF]
British aristocrat
* [The] Kitchen Maid in Ireland

Mountjoy, Medicine Bill
See Mountjoy, William R. [Billy]

Mountjoy, William R. [Billy] 1857-1894
[BE]
American baseball player
* Mountjoy, Medicine Bill

Moura, Joaq 20th c.
Brazilian eccentric
* [The] Kisser

Mouravieff, Nicholas 1793-1866 [FFF]
Russian army officer and governor of Lithuania
* [The] Hangman of Lithuania

Mouray
See Merlin, Jean Raymond

Mourdaunt, Mrs. Frank [FFF]
Entertainer
* Wallace, Laura

Mourer, Marie-Louise-Jeanne 1922-1967
[BDF, OCF, WEF]
French actress
* Arley, Catherine
* Arley, Maryse
* Carol, Martine
* Mourer, Maryse

Mourer, Maryse
See Mourer, Marie-Louise-Jeanne

Mourier, Marguerite
See Boulton, Marjorie

[The] Mourner
See Mangan, James Clarence

Mouron, Adolphe Jean Marie 1901-1968
[BI]
French illustrator
* Cassandre, A. M.

Mousa, Said 1929?- [TI 6-6-83]
Palestinian leader
* Abu Mousa [Father of Moses]

[The] Mouse
See McFadden, Ken

Mouse, Mickey
See Ely, William Harvey Johnson

[The] Mousetrap Builder
See Crosby, Harry Lillis

Mouskos, Mikhail 1913-1977
Archbishop and president of Cyprus
* [The] Dark Priest
* Mack the Knife
* Makarios III

Moussard, Jacqueline 1924- [CA]
French author
* Cervon, Jacqueline

Mousse, Alfred
See Housset, Arsene

Moustache, Madame
See Dumont, Emma [or Eleanora]

Moustakas, Alkiviadis 1923- [CA]
American journalist
* Manos, Charley

[The] Mouth
See Clarke, Norham Pfardt

[The] Mouth
See Cohen, Howard

Mouth
See Duyn, Willem

[The] Mouth
See Le Brock, Kelly

[The] Mouth
See Scroggs, [Sir] William

[The] Mouth of the South
See Turner, Robert Edward, III

[The] Mouth That Roared
See Mitchell, Martha Elizabeth Beall Jennings

Mouthpiece
See Porter, Maurice Malcolm

Mouthy
See Southey, Robert

Moutis, Patrice Des 1919?-1975 [BI]
French gambler
* Monsieur X

Mouton, Marine Bob
See Mouton, Robert L.

Mouton, Michael [or Michel]
See Montcorbier, Francois de

Mouton, Robert L. 1892- [HPPN]
American politician
* [The] Louisiana Ram
* Mouton, Marine Bob

Mouvet, Maurice 1886?-1927 [BEW]
French dancer
* Maurice

[The] Movable Brahmin
See Richardson, Elliot Lee

Move Up Joe
See Gerhardt, John Joseph

[The] Movie Moppet
See Fellows, Edith

Movshovitz, Israel 1870-1939 [WBD]
Russian-born scholar
* Davidson, Israel

Mowat, Magnus 19th c. [HPPN]
Scottish author
* Lochnagar

Mowat, Robert Case 1913- [IAW]
British author
* Mowat, Robin

Mowat, Robin
See Mowat, Robert Case

Mowbray, Henry
See Sweeney, Harry E.

Mowbray, J. P.
See Wheeler, Andrew Carpenter

Mowbray, John
See Hadath, John Edward Gunby

Mowbray, John
See Vahey, John George Haslette

Mowbray, Thomas 18th c. [IP]
Scottish clergyman and author
* T. M.

Mowbray, W. J. 20th c. [MBF]
British author
* Gascoigne, Eric

Mower, Mrs. Fred [FFF]
Entertainer
* Page, Lutie

Mowrey, Alvin Ernest 1884-? [BI]
American printer
* De Vil, Anold

Mowrey, Harry Harlan 1884-1947 [BE]
American baseball player
* Mowrey, Mike

Mowrey, Mike
See Mowrey, Harry Harlan

Mowshay, Ben
See Summerfield, Woolfe

Moxmox, Hermene 1856-1935 [BI]
American Indian warrior
* Yellow Wolf

Moxon, Edward 1801-1858 [IP]
British poet and publisher
* E. M.

Moy
See O'Donnell, John

Moya, Natalie
See Mullaly, Natalie

Moya, Pedro 20th c. [GS]
Spanish bullfighter
* [El] Nino de la Capea [The Boy of
  the Bull-Capings]

Moyano, Sebastian 1495?-1550? [WBD]
Spanish conquistador
* Belalcazar [or Benalcazar], Sebastian
  de

Moyle, John 18th c. [HPPN]
British physician
* [A] Member of the College of
  Physicians

Moyle, Walter 1672-1721 [HPPN]
British barrister
* W. M., Esq.

Moyler, Freeman William, Jr. 1931-
[BA]
American business executive
* Moyler, Pancho

Moyler, Pancho
See Moyler, Freeman William, Jr.

Moyne
See Toussaint-Desessarts, Nicholas

Moyne, Bryan Walter Guinness 1905-
[IAW]
British author and poet
* Guinness, Bryan

Moynihan, [Daniel] Patrick 1927-
American politician
* Fighting Irishman
* Man in the Polka-Dot Tie
* [The] Mask of Liberalism
* Moynihan the Maverick
* Our Man at the UN
* [The] Warrior Intellectual

Moynihan the Maverick
See Moynihan, [Daniel] Patrick

Moyridge, George [FFF]
Author
* Uncle Adam

Moyse, Alphonse 1898?-1973 [HPPN]
American bridge player and columnist
* Moyse, Sonny

Moyse, Charles Ebenezer 1852-1924
[CCL]
Canadian playwright
* Titmarsh, Belgrave

Moyse, Sonny
See Moyse, Alphonse

Mozans, H. J.
See Zahm, John Augustine

Mozart, Franz Xaver Wolfgang
1791-1844 [WBD]
Austrian composer, musician, conductor
* Mozart, Wolfgang Amadeus

Mozart, George
See Gillings, David

**Mozart, Johannes Chrysostom
Wolfgangus Theophilus** 1756-1791 [HN,
SN, WBD, WP 9-30-84]
Austrian composer
* [The] Father of Modern Music
* Mozart, Wolferl
* Mozart, Wolfgang Amadeus
* [The] Raphael of Music
* [The] Raphael of Opera

Mozart, Maria Anna 1751-1829 [WBD]
Austrian musician
* Mozart, Nannerl

Mozart, Nannerl
See Mozart, Maria Anna

[The] Mozart of the Nineteenth Century
See Mendelssohn, [Jakob Ludwig] Felix

Mozart, Wolferl
See Mozart, Johannes Chrysostom
Wolfgangus Theophilus

Mozart, Wolfgang Amadeus
See Mozart, Franz Xaver Wolfgang

Mozart, Wolfgang Amadeus
See Mozart, Johannes Chrysostom
Wolfgangus Theophilus

Mozee, Annie
See Moses, Phoebe Anne Oakley

**Mozier, Aloysius Eugene Francis
Patrick** 1902- [BI, HPPN]
American pioneer
* America's Ambassador of Good Will
* Gardenseed, Patty

Mozley, Anne 19th c. [HPPN]
British author
* His Sister

[El] Mozo
See Herrera, Francisco de

Mozzi, Marco Antonio 1678-1736 [PA]
Author
* Mutius

Mphahlele, Ezekiel 1919- [CA]
South African author
* Eseki, Bruno

M'Pherson, Samuel ?-1743 [SN]
Scottish commander
* [A] Second Xenophon

Mraz, George 1944- [EJ7]
Czech-born jazz musician
* Mraz, Jiri

Mraz, Jiri
See Mraz, George

Mrazek, Bertha 1890-1924 [BI]
Belgian mystic
* Marasco, Georges

M'Rory, [Rev] Rory
See Lees, James Cameron

Mrs. A.
See Klasen, Gertrud Alexandra Dagmar
Lawrence

Mrs. B.
See Boscawen, Frances Glanville

Mrs. G.
See Griffiths, Kitty Anna

[The] Mrs. Hemans of America
See Sigourney, Lydia Howard Huntley

Mrs. L.
See Longworth, Alice Lee Roosevelt

Mrs. T
See Thatcher, Margaret Hilda [Roberts]

Mrs. Thomas's Favourite Husband
See Thomas, Alf

Mrs. Winchell's Little Boy
See Winchell, Walter

M'Taggart, J. M.
See M'Taggart, John M'Taggart Ellis

M'Taggart, John M'Taggart Ellis
1866-1925 [LC]
British lecturer and author
* M'Taggart, J. M.

Mu Minin, Ameru al-
See Brown, Eugene

Mu, Yang
See Wang, Ching Hsien

Muazzim, Prince
See Bahadur Shah I

Mubarak, Hosni 1928?-
Egyptian president
* [The] Court Jester
* Empty Face
* Sadat's Sadat

Mucius, Caius   [DNNF]
Roman patrician
* Scaevola

[The] Muckraker Emeritus
See Seldes, George

[The] Muckraker With a Mission
See Anderson, Jack[son Northman]

Mud Dauber Joe
See McCoy, Joe

Mudd, Alice F.   [PA]
Author
* Peach Bloom

Mudd, Richard 20th c.
American basketball player
* Mudd, Suds

Mudd, Suds
See Mudd, Richard

Mude, O.
See Gorey, Edward [St. John]

Mudford, William 1782-1848   [IP]
British journalist, translator, author
* Attalus
* Swammerdam, Martin Gribaldus

Mudge, Carl 20th c.
American actor
* Morton, Charles

Mudge, Henry 1806-1874   [IP]
British author
* [A] Foe to Ignorance
* L. A. C.
* One of Themselves
* [A] Surgeon, M. R. C. S.

Mudge, [Rev.] William 19th c.   [HPPN]
British clergyman
* [A] Country Clergyman

Mudgeon, Apeman
See Mitchell, Adrian

Mudgett, Helen 1934-   [EJ]
American jazz musician
* Moran, Pat

Mudgett, Herman W.
See White, William A[nthony] P[arker]

Mudgett, Herman Webster 1864?-1896
[BLB, DI, HPPN]
American murderer, robber, arsonist
* America's Most Prolific Murderer
* [The] Criminal of the Nineteenth
  Century
* Dr. Harry

Mudgett, Herman Webster (cont.)
* Gordon, Harry
* Holmes, H. H.
* Holmes, Harry Howard
* Howard, H. M.
* [The] Landlord of Holmes' Castle
* [The] Monster of Sixty Third Street

Mudie, Charles Edward 1818-1890
[NPS]
Library founder and poet
* C. E. M.

Mudie, Leonard
See Cheetham, Leonard M.

Mudie, Robert 1777-1842   [IP, PA]
Scottish naturalist and author
* Langshank, Laurence, Gent.
* [The] Modern Greek

[El] Mudo
See Fernandez Navarrete, Juan

Muehfeldt, Freddie 20th c.   [BLB]
American gangster
* [The] Kid

Muehlbach, Luise [or Louise]
See Mundt, Clara M.

Muelier
See Higgins, Charles Eli

Mueller, Adam Heinrich 1779-1829
[WBD]
German political economist
* Mueller von Nitersdorf

Mueller, Clarence Franklin 1899-1975
[BE, BI]
American baseball player
* Mueller, Heinie

Mueller, Dominik
See Schmitz, P.

Mueller, Donald Frederick 1927-   [BE]
American baseball player
* Mandrake the Magician

Mueller, Dorothy 1901-   [CA]
British-born author
* Bowick, Dorothy Mueller

Mueller, Emmett Jerome 1912-   [BE]
American baseball player
* Mueller, Heinie

Mueller, Ernst 1890-   [JL]
Austrian author
* Lothar, Ernest

Mueller, Ernst 20th c.   [SFL]
Author
* West, Julian

Mueller, Erwin 1911-   [HPPN]
German-American physicist and inventor
* [The] Father of the Field Emission
  Microscope

Mueller, Franz 19th c.   [HPPN]
German tailor and murderer
* [The] First Train Murderer

Mueller, Frederick 1867-1925   [BMH]
German-born gymnast and strongman
* Sandow, Eugen[e]
* [The] Strongest Man in the World

Mueller, Friedrich 1749-1825   [WBD]
German poet, painter, engraver
* Mueller, Maler

Mueller, Friedrich Max 1823-?   [IP]
German scholar and author
* [An] Alien
* Philindus

Mueller, Fritz 1821-1897   [HPPN]
German zoologist
* [The] Prince of Observers

Mueller, Gerald F[rancis] 1927-   [CA]
American author
* Roberto, [Brother]

Mueller, Gerhardt
See Bickers, Richard Leslie Townshend

Mueller, Gestapo
See Mueller, Heinrich

Mueller, Gussie
See Mueller, Gustave

Mueller, Gustave 1890-1965   [NOJ]
American jazz musician
* Mueller, Gussie

Mueller, Hawk
See Mueller, William Lawrence [Bill]

Mueller, Heinie
See Mueller, Clarence Franklin

Mueller, Heinie
See Mueller, Emmett Jerome

Mueller, Heinrich 1896-   [BDW, HPPN]
German Nazi leader
* [The] Father of the Bullet Decree
* Mueller, Gestapo

Mueller, Hermann 1876-1931   [WBD]
German politician
* Mueller-Franken

Mueller, Herr
See Louis Philippe

Mueller, Iron Man
See Mueller, Ray Coleman

Mueller, Johann 1436-1476   [PA, WBD]
German mathematician and astronomer
* Regiomontanus

Mueller, Johann Gottwerth 1743-1828
[HPPN]
German author
* Mueller von Itzehoe

Mueller, Johann von 1752-1809   [SN]
Swiss historian
* [The] Thucydides of Germany

Mueller, Karl 1819-?   [HPPN, IP]
German author
* Elling, Franz von
* Mylius, Otfried

Mueller, Maler
See Mueller, Friedrich

Mueller, Marvin 1913-1985 [FC]
American actor, radio and television announcer
* Miller, Marvin
* Warren, Charlie

Mueller, Merrill 1916-1980
American journalist
* Mueller, Red

Mueller, Ray Coleman 1912- [BE]
American baseball player
* Mueller, Iron Man

Mueller, Red
See Mueller, Merrill

Mueller, Therese 1855-1930 [WBD]
German opera singer
* Malten, Therese

Mueller von Itzehoe
See Mueller, Johann Gottwerth

Mueller von Koenigswinter
See Mueller, Wolfgang

Mueller von Nitersdorf
See Mueller, Adam Heinrich

Mueller, Wilhelm 1794-1827 [HPPN]
German poet
* Jocundus, Frater

Mueller, William Lawrence [Bill] 1920- [BE]
American baseball player
* Mueller, Hawk

Mueller, Wolfgang 1816-1873 [WBD]
German poet and author
* Mueller von Koenigswinter

Mueller-Franken
See Mueller, Hermann

Mueller-Guttenbrunn, Adam 1852-1923 [WBD]
Austrian author, playwright, theatre director
* Ignotus

Mueller-Harlin, Wolfgang Johannes 1940- [IAW]
German author
* Thomas, Manuel

Mueller-Tannewitz, Anna 1899- [IAW]
German author
* Juergen, Anna

Muench, Charles 1891- [HPPN]
French conductor
* France's Greatest Conductor

Muench-Bellinghausen, Eligius Franz Josef 1806-1872 [IP]
German poet
* Halm, Friedrich

Muenchausen, Baron
See Pearl, Jack

[The] Muenchausen in Modern Dress
See Means, Gaston Bullock

[The] Muenchausen of the West
See Crockett, David [Davy]

Muenster, Sebastian 1489-1552 [DNNS, HN, RH]
German theologian, geographer, mathematician
* [The] German Strabo
* [The] Strabo of Germany

Muensterberg, Maximilian
See Nentwich, Max

Muenzenberger, John Henry 1912- [EJ, PMJ, WWJ]
American jazz musician
* Mince, Johnny

Muetzelburg, Adolf 19th c. [HPPN]
German author
* Severin, Justus
* Weber, Karl

Muff, Goliah
See Thackeray, William Makepeace

Muffett, Billy Arnold 1930- [BE]
American baseball player
* Muffett, Muff

Muffett, Muff
See Muffett, Billy Arnold

[The] Muffled Spokesman
See Yakir, Pyotr

Mug, [Sister] Mary Theodosia 1860-1943 [DNA]
American author
* Maery, Helen

Mugabi, John 20th c.
Ugandan boxer
* [The] Beast

Muggable Mary
See Glatzle, Mary

Muggeridge, Edward James 1830-1904 [WBD, WEF]
British photographer
* Muybridge, Eadweard

Muggeson, Margaret Elizabeth 1942- [AW, IAW, WD]
British author
* Dickinson, Margaret
* Jackson, Everatt

Muggins
See Clemens, Samuel Langhorne

Muggins, Petey
See Mione, Peter

Muggins, William
See Selby, Charles

[El] Muhajir
See Jackmon, Marvin X.

Muhammad, Elijah
See Poole, Elijah

Muhammad Ghori
See Muizz-ad-din

Muhammad, Idris
See Morris, Leo

Muhammad, Matthew Saad
See Franklin, Matthew

Muhammad Taki ?-1810 [BI]
Indian poet
* Mir

Muhammad, Wallace Deen 20th c. [NW 4-9-84]
American Black Muslim leader
* Muhammad, Warith Deen

Muhammad, Warith Deen
See Muhammad, Wallace Deen

Muhammed, Hamidi 1837?-1905 [HPPN]
African trader and slave merchant
* Tip
* Tipoo Tib

Muhidin, Ahmet 15th c.
Ottoman, navigator and cartographer
* Re'is, Piri [Muhyi 'l-Din]

Muhlenberg, Devil Pete
See Muhlenberg, John Peter Gabriel

Muhlenberg, John Peter Gabriel 1746-1807 [HPPN]
American army officer
* Muhlenberg, Devil Pete

Muhlenberg, William Augustus 1796-1877 [HPPN, IP]
American clergyman and author
* Catholicus
* One of the Memorialists

Muich, Ignatius Andrew 1903- [BE]
American baseball player
* Muich, Joe

Muich, Joe
See Muich, Ignatius Andrew

Muinntire, Fear na
See Rooney, William

Muir, Alan
See Morrison, Thomas James

Muir, [Charles] Augustus 1892- [CA, CC, WD]
Scottish-born author
* Moore, Austin

Muir, Barbara K[enrick Gowing] 1908- [CA]
British author
* Kaye, Barbara

Muir, Dexter
See Gribble, Leonard R[eginald]

Muir, Edwin 1887-1959 [TLC]
Scottish poet and author
* Moore, Edward

Muir, Florence Roma 1891-1930 [HPPN]
British author
* Wilson, Romer

Muir, Helen
See Lennehan, Helen Theresa Eucharia Flaherty

Muir, Jane
See Petrone, Jane Muir

Muir, Jean
See Fullerton, Jean Muir

Muir, [Rev.] John 1722-1799 [HPPN]
British clergyman
* J. M.

Muir, John 1810-? [IP, PA]
Scottish scholar and author
* J. M.
* [A] Layman

Muir, John 1838-1914 [HPPN]
Scottish-American naturalist and author
* [The] Father of the Yosemite
* Great Ice Chief
* J. M.
* John o' Mountains
* [The] Protector of the Wilds

Muir, John
See Morgan, Thomas Christopher

Muir, Kenneth [Arthur] 1907- [CA]
British educator and author
* Finney, Mark

Muir, Marie Agnes 1904- [AW, CA]
British author
* Blake, Monica
* Clynder, Monica
* Kaye, Barbara
* Scott, Jean

Muir, Mary 20th c. [WWL]
British writer
* Mike

Muir, Thomas S. 19th c. [IP]
Scottish author
* T. S. M.
* Unda

Muir, Wardrop Openshaw 1878-1927
[MBF]
British author
* Lang, Stewart

Muir, William 19th c. [IP]
Scottish author
* [An] Attorney

Muirhead, Sara Alyne [Guynes] 1885-?
[BI]
American pioneer
* Sagsam, Angela

Muirhead, Thorburn
See Thorburn-Muirhead, James

Muizz-ad-din ?-1206 [WBD]
Sultan of Ghazni
* Mohammed of Ghor
* Muhammad Ghori

[El] Mukattem
See Crosby, Howard

Muks, Roberts
See Avens, Roberts

Muktanada, Swami 1908- [EOP]
Indian mystic and author
* Baba
* Paramahansa

Mul
See Muldoon, William H.

Mularchyk, Sylva 20th c. [CA]
American author
* Miles, Sylva [joint pseudonym with Dorien K(lein) Miles]

Mularczyk, Roman 1921- [CD]
Polish author
* Bratny, Roman

Mulargia, Edoardo 20th c. [WF]
Italian director
* Muller, Edward G.

Mulas, Pedro 19th c. [GS]
Spanish bullfighter
* [El] Fraile [The Friar]

Mulcahy, A. E. 1913-
American singer
* Dover, Fostoria
* [The] Queen of the Torchers

Mulcahy, Hugh Noyes 1913- [BE]
American baseball player
* [The] Losing Pitcher

Mulcahy, Lucille Burnett 20th c. [CA, SAT]
American author
* Hale, Helen

Mulchinock, William Pembroke
1820-1864 [PI]
Irish poet
* Heremon
* M.
* W. P. M.

Muldaur, Maria
See D'Amato, Maria Grazia Rosa
Domenica

Mulder, Connie
See Mulder, Cornelius

Mulder, Cornelius 1925?-
South African politician
* Mulder, Connie

Mulder, Herman
See Mulder, Johannes Hermanus

Mulder, Johannes Hermanus 1894-
[IWM]
Dutch composer and educator
* Mulder, Herman

Muldoon, Dennis
See Goodwin, George B.

Muldoon, Major
See McCartney, William H.

Muldoon, Omar
See Matusow, Harvey Marshall

Muldoon, Piggy
See Muldoon, Robert David

Muldoon, Robert David 20th c.
New Zealand prime minister
* Muldoon, Piggy

Muldoon, William 1846-1933 [HPPN]
American boxer, commissioner, promoter
* [The] Czar of Boxing
* [The] Father of American Boxing
* [The] Iron Duke

Muldoon, William (cont.)
* [The] Old Roman
* [The] Solid Man

Muldoon, William F. ?-1909 [HPPN]
American actor, dancer, singer
* Carroll, Irish Billy
* Carroll, William F.

Muldoon, William H. [IP, PA]
American journalist
* [The] Man about Town
* Mul

Muldowney, Cha Cha
See Muldowney, Shirley

Muldowney, Crash
See Muldowney, Shirley

Muldowney, Shirley 1940?- [HPPN]
American auto racer
* Muldowney, Cha Cha
* Muldowney, Crash

Muldrow, Baby Face
See Muldrow, Gail

Muldrow, Gail 20th c. [RO2]
American singer
* Muldrow, Baby Face

Mulesko, Angelo
See Oglesby, Joseph

Mulet, Paul
See Rivers, Louis

Mulflur, Mary 1958- [HPPN]
American golfer
* [The] First Lady Lion

Mulford, Prentice 1834-1891 [HPPN]
American journalist and author
* Dogberry

Mulford, Ralph 20th c.
Auto racer
* [The] Parson

Mulgan, Catherine
See Gough, Catherine

Mulholland, Howard 20th c. [HPPN]
American radio announcer
* H. M.

Mulholland, Rosa 1850-? [PI]
Irish poet and author
* Millais, Ruth
* R. M.

Mulier, Pieter 1637-1701 [WBD]
Dutch painter
* Cavaliere Tempesta

Mulkeen, Anne
See Marcus, Anne M[ulkeen]

Mulkor, Pioter
See Hlojzy, Nagel

Mullaly, Charles J. 1877-1949 [CAT]
American author and editor
* Goodwin, Francis
* Winslow, Paul

Mullaly, Mrs. W. S. [FFF]
Entertainer
* Weber, Lisa

Mullaly, Natalie 1900- [THR]
Irish-born actress
* Moya, Natalie

Mullane, Anthony John 1859-1944 [BE, DGS]
Irish-born American baseball player
* [The] Apollo of the Box
* Mullane, Count Tony

Mullane, Count Tony
See Mullane, Anthony John

Mullane, Margaret 1890-1953 [HPPN]
American dancer and singer
* Edson, Margaret

Mullaney, Patrick Francis 1847?-1893
[BDSA, DNA, IP, PI]
American author and educator
* Azarias, [Brother]
* B. A. M.

Mulla's Bard
See Spenser, Edmund

Mulle, Maude
See Bell, Mrs. A. M.

Mulleavy, Greg[ory Thomas] 1905-1980
[BE]
American baseball player
* Mulleavy, Moe

Mulleavy, Moe
See Mulleavy, Greg[ory Thomas]

Mullen, Bud
See Mullen, Francis

Mullen, C. J. J.
See Mullen, Cyril J.

Mullen, Cyril J. 1908- [CA]
American author
* Mullen, C. J. J.

Mullen, Dore
See Mullen, Dorothy

Mullen, Dorothy 1933- [CA]
American author
* Mullen, Dore

Mullen, Ford Parker 1917- [BE]
American baseball player
* Mullen, Moon

Mullen, Francis 20th c.
American government official
* Mullen, Bud

Mullen, M. [PA]
Author
* North, Oliver

Mullen [or Mullins?], Michael
1833-1869 [PI]
Irish-born clergyman and poet
* Fodhla, Ollamh
* M. C.

Mullen, Moon
See Mullen, Ford Parker

Mullen, Moon
See Mullen, Thomas Patrick

Mullen, Stanley [B.] 1911-1973 [WGT]
American author
* Beecher, Lee
* Beecher, Stanley
* Drummond, John Peter

Mullen, Thomas Patrick 1951- [SMG]
American football player
* Mullen, Moon

Mullenger, Donna Belle 1921-1986
[BDF, FC, WEF]
American actress
* Adams, Donna
* Reed, Donna

Mullens, Edward 1916- [EJ, WWJ]
American jazz musician
* Mullens, Moon

Mullens, Moon
See Mullens, Edward

Muller, Billex
See Ellis, Edward S[ylvester]

Muller, Brick
See Muller, Harold

Muller, Catherine Elise 1861-1929
[EOP]
Claimed to possess psychic powers
* Smith, Helene

Muller, Charles G[eorge] 1897- [CA, IAW]
American author
* Geoffrey, Charles
* Gilliland, Charles

Muller, Charles Louis 1815-1892 [WBD]
French painter
* Muller de Paris

Muller de Paris
See Muller, Charles Louis

Muller, Don[ald] 20th c. [HPPN]
American football player
* Muller, Mush

Muller, Edward G.
See Mulargia, Edoardo

Muller, Harold 1901-1962 [AS, FB]
American football player
* Muller, Brick

Muller, John E. [house pseudonym]
See Fanthorpe, R[obert] Lionel

Muller, John E. [house pseudonym]
See Glynn, Anthony Arthur

Muller, Mush
See Muller, Don[ald]

Muller, Paul 1898- [IWM]
Swiss composer
* Muller-Zurich, Paul

Muller, Paul
See King, Albert

Muller, Rudolph 1899- [FC]
Czech-born actor
* Miller, Martin

Muller-Zurich, Paul
See Muller, Paul

Mullican, Aubrey Wilson 1909-1967
[CWG, DAM]
American country-western performer
* [The] King of the Hillbilly Piano Players
* Mullican, Moon

Mullican, Dorothy 1906-1981
American actress
* Lane, Lola

Mullican, Moon
See Mullican, Aubrey Wilson

Mullican, Priscilla 1917- [PMJ]
American actress
* Lane, Priscilla

Mullican, Rosemary 1916- [PMJ]
American actress
* Lane, Rosemary

Mullidor
See Shakespeare, William

Mulligan, Big Joe
See Mulligan, Joseph Ignatius [Joe]

Mulligan, Cockeye
See Albin, David

Mulligan, Gerald Joseph [Gerry] 1927-
[EJ7]
American jazz musician
* Mulligan, Jeru

Mulligan, Hugh A. 1925- [IAW]
American-born author
* H. A. M.

Mulligan, Irish Jimmy
See Mulligan, Jimmy

Mulligan, James 1874?-1962 [BEW]
American theatrical performer
* Valdare, Sunny Jim

Mulligan, Jeru
See Mulligan, Gerald Joseph [Gerry]

Mulligan, Jimmy 20th c. [WP 6-12-85]
Boxer
* Mulligan, Irish Jimmy

Mulligan, Joseph Ignatius [Joe] 1913-
[BE]
American baseball player
* Mulligan, Big Joe

Mulligan, Martin 20th c.
Australian tennis player
* Mulligano, Martino

Mulligan, Morty Macnamara
See Maginn, William

Mulligan of Killballymulligan
See Thackeray, William Makepeace

Mulligan, Paddy
See Mulligan, Patrick

Mulligan, Patrick 1945- [AES]
Irish soccer player
* Mulligan, Paddy

Mulligano, Martino
See Mulligan, Martin

Mulliken, Robert S. 1896- [HPPN]
American physicist
* [The] Father of the Molecularorbital
Theory

Mullin, George Joseph 1880-1944 [BE]
American baseball player
* Mullin, Wabash George

Mullin, Wabash George
See Mullin, George Joseph

Mullinahone, Eileen
See Heffernan, Michael J.

Mullinahone, K.
See Kickham, Charles Joseph

Mullins, Ann
See Dally, Ann Gwendolen Mullins

Mullins, Jeff 1942- [BB]
American basketball player
* Mullins, Pork Chop

Mullins, Lawrence A. 1908-1968 [BI,
HPPN]
American football coach
* Mullins, Moon

Mullins, Moon
See Mullins, Lawrence A.

Mullins, Pork Chop
See Mullins, Jeff

Mullins, Richard 1926- [HPPN]
American author
* Wells, Michael

Mullins, Rossana E. ?-1878 [PA]
Author
* R. E. L.
* R. E. M.

Mullion, Mordecai
See Maginn, William

Mullion, Mordecai
See Wilson, John

Mullner
See Collin, Jacques Albin Simon

Mulock, Miss
See Craik, Dinah Maria Mulock

Multatuli
See Dekker, Eduard Douwes

[The] Multi-Media Person
See Brown, Mary Richardson

Mulvany, Charles Pelham 1835-1885
[PI]
Irish-born poet
* C. P. M., Sch.

Mulvey, Ruth Watt
See Harmer, Ruth Mulvey

Mumbles
See Horton, Walter

Mumford, Angelina S. 1830-? [FFF, PA]
American poet
* Picciola

Mumford, Ethel Watts
See Grant, Ethel Watts Mumford

Mummius
See Maginn, William

Mummius, Lucius 2nd c. BC [WBD]
Roman general and politician
* Achaicus

[The] Mummy
See Merrill, Jan

Mummy Daddy
See Khan, Javed Miandad

**Mumtaz Mahall [The Ornament of the
Palace]**
See Banu, Arjumand

Mun
See Leaf, [Wilbur] Munro

Muna el Hussein [Desire of Hussein]
See Gardiner, Toni

Munby, A. N. L.
See Munby, Alan Noel Latimer

Munby, Alan Noel Latimer 1913-1974
[HFF, SFL]
British author
* Munby, A. N. L.

Munby, Arthur Joseph 1828-1910
[DLE1]
British poet
* Brown, Jones

Munce, Ruth Hill 1898- [CAP, SAT]
American author
* Hill, Ruth Livingston

Munch, Andreas 1811-1884 [SN]
Norwegian poet and playwright
* Norway's First Skald

Munchausen, Baron
See Gernsback, Hugo

Munchausen, Baron
See Raspe, Rudolph E[rich]

[The] Muncie Mortar
See Bonham, Ron

Mundanschaffter, Juan Carlos 1916-
[FC]
Argentinian actor
* Thompson, Carlos

Munday, Anthony 1553-1633 [DEA,
DLE1, NPS]
British poet and playwright
* A. M.
* Balladino, Antonio
* Honos Alit Artes
* L. P.
* Old Anthony Now-Now
* Piot, Lazarus

Munday, John William 20th c. [SFP]
Author
* Seeley, Charles S.

Mundis, Hester 1938- [PW 9-21-84]
American author
* Morgan, Virginia

Mundt, Clara M. 1814-1873 [DNNF,
FFF, WBD]
German author
* Muehlbach, Luise [or Louise]

Mundungus
See Sharp, Samuel

Mundus, [Captain] Frank 1926?-
American shark fisherman
* [The] Monster Man

Mundus, Jakob
See Vetsch, Jakob

Mundviller, Joseph-Louis 1886- [DFM]
French cinematographer
* Meyer, George

Mundy, Bingo
See Mundy, Ronald

Mundy, Max
See Schofield, Sylvia Anne

Mundy, Mrs.
See Ouick, Florence

Mundy, Ronald 20th c. [RO1]
American singer
* Mundy, Bingo

Mundy, Sue
See Clark, M. Jerome

Mundy, Talbot
See Gribbon, William Lancaster

Mundy, W. P.
See Mundy, William Percy

Mundy, William Percy 1936- [ART]
British painter
* Mundy, W. P.

Munefusa, Matsuo 1644-1694 [HPPN]
Japanese poet and mystic
* Basho
* Matsuobasho

Munger, Al
See Unger, Maurice Albert

Munger, George David 1918- [BE]
American baseball player
* Munger, Red

Munger, Gordon C. 1891-1947 [SC]
American actor
* Daly, Pat

Munger, Hortense Roberta
See Roberts, Hortense Roberta

Munger, Red
See Munger, George David

Mungo
See Dyson, Jeremiah

Mungo
See Kentigern

Mungo, Raymond 1946- [CA]
American author
* Lunar, Dennis

Munguia, Miguel 20th c. [GS]
Spanish bullfighter
* [El] Inspirado [The Inspired One]

Muni, Narad
See Anand, Mulk Raj

Muni, Paul
See Weisenfreund, Muni

Munich's Favorite Son
See Strauss, Richard

Muniz, Manny
See Muniz Rodriquez, Manuel

Muniz Rodriquez, Manuel 1947- [SMG]
Puerto Rican-born baseball player
* Muniz, Manny

Munk, Kaj
See Petersen, Kaj Harald Leininger

Munkacsi, Martin 1895?-1963 [WFA]
Rumanian-born photographer
* [The] High Priest of Fashion in
  Motion

Munkacszy, Mihaly von
See Lieb, Michael

Munkittrick, Howard 1865-1928 [BBD,
BEW, EMT]
American composer
* Talbot, Howard

Munn, Big
See Munn, Wayne

Munn, Biggie
See Munn, Clarence Lester

Munn, Clarence Lester 1908-1975 [BI]
American football coach
* Munn, Biggie

Munn, Frank 1895-1953 [HPPN]
American singer
* [The] Golden Voice of Radio

Munn, Hart
See Hardy, C. Colburn

Munn, Marguerite 1870-? [WWL]
British author
* Bryant, M.

Munn, Meryl Lucile 1916- [CA]
American author
* Maguire, Anne
* Nearing, Penny

Munn, Wayne 20th c. [HPPN]
American wrestler
* Munn, Big

Munnings, Hilda ?-1974 [TR]
Dancer
* Sokolova, Lydia

Munns, Big Ed
See Munns, Les[lie Ernest]

Munns, Les[lie Ernest] 1908- [BE]
American baseball player
* Munns, Big Ed
* Munns, Nemo

Munns, Nemo
See Munns, Les[lie Ernest]

Munoz, Felipe 1951- [SWI]
Mexican swimmer
* Tibio [Luke-Warm]

Munoz, Joe
See Munoz, Jose

Munoz, Jose 1817-1856 [GS]
Spanish bullfighter
* Pucheta [Big Bouquet]

Munoz, Jose 20th c. [OBW]
American baseball player
* Munoz, Joe

Munoz, Juan Antonio 1922- [FDG]
Spanish director
* Bardem, Juan Antonio

Munoz Marin, Luis 1898?-1980 [HPPN]
Puerto Rican governor
* [The] Father of Operation Bootstrap
* God's Pamphleteer

Munoz y Gonzalez, Fermin 1879-1942
[GS]
Spanish bullfighter
* Corchaito [Little Cork]

Munoz y Marin, Bernardo 1895-1969
[GS]
Spanish bullfighter
* Carnicerito [Little Butcher]

Munro, C[harles] K[irkpatrick]
See MacMullan, Charles Walden
Kirkpatrick

Munro, Christy
See Taves, Isabella

Munro, David
See Devine, David McDonald

Munro, Duncan H.
See Russell, Eric Frank

Munro, H. H.
See Munro, Hector Hugh

Munro, Hector Hugh 1870-1916 [HFF,
LC, TC]
British author
* Munro, H. H.
* Saki

Munro, [Macfarlane] Hugh 20th c.
[CA, IAW]
Scottish author
* Farlane, Jason
* Jason
* Wyvis, Ben

Munro, James
See Cave, Roderick [George James
Munro]

Munro, James
See Mitchell, James

Munro, John C. 1924-1953 [HPPN]
American radio announcer
* Munro, Red

Munro, Kathryn
See Tupper, Kathryn Munro

Munro, Mary
See Howe, Doris Kathleen

Munro, Neil 1864-1930 [WW]
Author
* Foulis, Hugh

Munro, Red
See Munro, John C.

Munro [or Monro], Robert ?-1633
[WBD]
Scottish army officer
* [The] Black Baron

Munro, Robert
See Hale-Monro, John Robert

Munro, Ronald Eadie
See Glen, Duncan Munro

Munro-Noble, Maisie 1883-1945 [BEW,
EMT]
British actress and singer
* Gay, Maisie

Munroe, Charles E. 1849-1938 [HPPN]
American chemical engineer
* [The] Father of the Bazooka

Munroe, Elizabeth L[ee] 1900- [CA]
American poet
* Grenelle, Lisa

Munroe, Jack
See Monroe, John Alexander

Munroe, R.
See Cheyne, [Sir] Joseph Lister Watson

Munsel, Patrice
See Munsil, Patrice Beverly

Munsell, Joel 1809-1880 [IP]
American author
* Prynne, Arthur

Munsey, Cecil [Richard, Jr.] 1935-
[CA]
American educator and author
* Richardson, C.

Munshi
See Soomro, Mohammad Ibrahim

Munshi, Shehnaaz
See Skagen, Kiki

Munsil, Patrice Beverly 1925- [MS]
American opera singer
* Munsel, Patrice

Munson, Clarence Hanford 1883- [BE]
American baseball player
* Munson, Red

Munson, Joseph Martin Napoleon [Joe]
See Carlson, Joseph Martin Napoleon

Munson, Ona
See Wolcott, Ona

Munson, Red
See Munson, Clarence Hanford

Munson, Squatty
See Munson, Thurman Lee

Munson, Thurman Lee 1947-1979 [PB]
American baseball player
* Munson, Squatty

[A] Munster Farmer
See O'Sullivan, Farrar

Munster, Mary C. F. 1835?-1892 [PI]
Irish poet
* Monck, Mary C. F.
* Tiny

Munster, Minnie
See Burleigh, Harriet E.

Munston, Constance Sylvia 1898- [FC, HPPN]
British actress
* Lillie, Beatrice [or Bea]
* [The] Mistress of Sophisticated Slapstick
* Peel, Lady

Munter, Jeremias
See Fornel, Bror Edvard

Munthe, Frances 1915?- [AW, CA, WD]
British author
* Cowen, Frances
* Hyde, Eleanor
* Minto-Cowen, Frances

Muntz, Earl William 1914?- [HPPN]
American business executive and manufacturer
* Muntz, Madman

Muntz, [Isabelle] Hope 1907- [IAW]
Canadian-born author
* Langland, William

Muntz, James
See Crowcroft, Peter

Muntz, Madman
See Muntz, Earl William

Mur
See Murschetz, Luis Marian

Mura, Corrine
See Wall, Corinna

Murad [or Amurath] I 1319-1389 [HPPN]
Sultan of Turkey
* Khudavendighiar

Murad Efendi
See Werner, Franz von

Muraguri, Nicholas 1934- [IAW]
Kenyan author
* Ruheni, Mwangi

Muraire, Jules 1883-1946 [FC, WEF]
French actor
* Raimu

Murakami, Masanori 20th c. [TI 4-4-83]
Japanese-born baseball player
* Murakami, Mashi

Murakami, Mashi
See Murakami, Masanori

Muralto, Onuphrio
See Walpole, Horatio [Fourth Earl of Orford]

Murat
See Agca, Mehmet Ali

Murat, Joachim 1767?-1815 [DNNS, HN, HPPN, SN]
King of Naples
* [Le] Beau Sabreur
* [The] Dandy King
* Franconi, King
* [The] Good Swordsman
* [The] Handsome Swordsman
* [Un] Roi de Theatre
* [The] Theatrical King

[The] Murat of America
See Wheat, Chatham Roberdeau

[The] Murat of Russia
See Miloradowitch, Michael

[The] Murat of the Magyar Army
See Kinisi, Paul

[The] Murat of the Union Army
See Logan, John Alexander

Murator, Antonita 1879-1942 [BI]
Spanish nun
* Maria de la Virgen Dolorosa, [Mother]

Muratori, Ludovico Antonio 1672-1750
Italian scholar
* [The] Father of Italian History

Murcer, Bobby Ray 1946- [PB]
American baseball player
* Murcer, Okie

Murcer, Okie
See Murcer, Bobby Ray

Murch, Simeon T. 1880-1939 [BE]
American baseball player
* Murch, Simmy

Murch, Simmy
See Murch, Simeon T.

Murchison, Thomas Malcolm 1896-1962 [BE]
American baseball player
* Murchison, Tim

Murchison, Tim
See Murchison, Thomas Malcolm

Murcia [From Murcia]
See Jimenez y Najar, Bartolome

Murden, Eliza 19th c. [IP]
American poet
* [A] Lady of Charleston, S. C.

[The] Murder Paymaster
See Schepps, Sam[uel]

[The] Murderer of Milan
See Rauff, Walter

[The] Murdering Policeman
See Becker, Charles

[The] Murdering Sexton
See Piper, Thomas W.

Murdoch, Doc
See Murdoch, Donald Walter

Murdoch, Donald Walter 1956- [SMG]
Canadian-born hockey player
* Murdoch, Doc
* Murdoch, Murder

Murdoch, Frank
See Hitchcock, Francis

Murdoch, Mud
See Murdoch, Robert John

Murdoch, Murder
See Murdoch, Donald Walter

Murdoch, Robert John 1946- [SMG]
Canadian-born hockey player
* Murdoch, Mud

Murdoch, [Sir] Walter Logie Forbes 1874-? [DLE1]
Australian scholar and author
* Elzevir

Murdock, Ann
See Coleman, Irene

Murdock, Laurette P. 1900- [CA]
American author
* Eustis, Laurette

Murdock, William
See Humberger, William

Muredach, Myles
See Kelley, Francis Clement

Murff, John Robert 1921- [BE]
American baseball player
* Murff, Red

Murff, Red
See Murff, John Robert

Murfree, Mary Noailles 1850-1922 [SFL, WGT]
American author
* Craddock, Charles Egbert
* Denbry, R. Emmet?

Murgatroyd, Matthew
See Jones, James Athearn

Muriel, John Saint Clair 1909- [WW]
British author
* Dewes, Simon
* Lindsay, John

Murielle, Constance
See Bennett, Mrs. Clement

Murieta, Joaquin
See Carillo, Joaquin

Murillo, Edith
See Martinetti, Mme. Ignacio

Murillo, Gerardo 1873-1964 [BI]
Mexican painter
* Atl, Dr.

Murio-Celli, Mme.
See D'Elpeux, Ravin

Muris, Johannes de 14th c. [WBD]
British musical theorist, astronomer, mathematician
* Normanus

Muris, Johannes [or Julianus] de 14th c. [WBD]
French musical theorist
* De Francia

Murman, George
See Heirens, William

Murnau, F[riedrich] W[ilhelm]
See Plumpe, Friedrich Wilhelm

Murph the Surf
See Murphy, Jack Ronald

Murphey, Anna 1797-1860 [PA]
Author
* [An] Ennuyee

Murphey, Big Tim
See Murphey, Timothy

Murphey, J. M. [PA]
Author
* Mortimer

Murphey, Timothy ?-1928 [BLB, MM, PHM]
American politician
* Murphey, Big Tim

Murphy, Arthur 1727-1805 [IP]
Irish journalist and playwright
* Ranger, Charles, Esq.

Murphy, Audie 1924-1971 [BDW, HPPN]
American army officer
* America's Most Decorated Soldier
* Hero from Texas
* Murphy, Baby
* Murphy, Medals

Murphy, Audie, Jr.
See Meltzer, R.

Murphy, Baby
See Murphy, Audie

Murphy, Beatrice M. 1908- [CA]
American editor and author
* Campbell, Beatrice Murphy

Murphy, Big Tim
See Murphy, Timothy

Murphy, Billy
See Murphy, Thomas W.

Murphy, Billy J. 1921- [FB]
American football coach
* Murphy, Spook

Murphy, Brian 1949?-
American behavior therapist
* Sunshine, Leo

Murphy, Bridey
See Tighe, Virginia

Murphy, Buck
See Whitcomb, Ian

Murphy, Buzz
See Murphy, Robert R.

Murphy, C. L. [joint pseudonym with Lawrence A(gustus) Murphy]
See Murphy, Charlotte A[lice]

Murphy, C. L. [joint pseudonym with Charlotte A(lice) Murphy]
See Murphy, Lawrence A[gustus]

Murphy, Calvin 1948- [IBW]
American basketball player
* [The] Tiny Giant

Murphy, Charles 1887-? [HPPN]
American murderer
* Dalton, Charles
* Lindsay, Charles
* Simpson, Charles

Murphy, Charles 1907- [BB]
American basketball player
* Murphy, Stretch

Murphy, Charles Francis 1858-1924 [HPPN]
American politician and Tammany Hall official
* Murphy, Silent Charley

Murphy, Charles W. 1871-1950 [BBH]
American bicycle racer
* Murphy, Mile a Minute

Murphy, Charlotte A[lice] 1924- [CA]
American author and poet
* Murphy, C. L. [joint pseudonym with Lawrence A(gustus) Murphy]

Murphy, Cicero 1936- [IBW]
American billiard player
* [The] Brooklyn Kid

Murphy, Con
See Murphy, Cornelius

Murphy, Con
See Murphy, Cornelius B.

Murphy, Connie
See Murphy, Cornelius David

Murphy, Cornelius 20th c. [TI 7-16-84]
American law enforcement officer
* Murphy, Con

Murphy, Cornelius B. 1863-1914 [BE]
American baseball player
* Murphy, Con
* Murphy, Razzle Dazzle

Murphy, Cornelius David 1870-1945 [BE]
American baseball player
* Murphy, Connie

Murphy, Denis
See O'Leary, Joseph

Murphy, Dennis Jasper
See Maturin, Charles Robert

Murphy, Dummy
See Murphy, Herbert C.

Murphy, E[mmett] Jefferson 1926- [CA, SAT]
American author
* Murphy, Pat

Murphy, Edgar Gardner 1869-1913 [HPPN]
American clergyman and author
* McKready, Kelvin

Murphy, Emily F. 1868-1933 [NAA]
Canadian author
* Canuck, Janey

Murphy, Fido
See Murphy, Raymond

Murphy, Fireman
See Murphy, John Joseph

Murphy, Fordham Johnny
See Murphy, John Joseph

Murphy, Francis 1836-1907 [HPPN]
Irish-American temperance advocate
* [The] Apostle of Temperance

Murphy, Francis 1888-1961 [HPPN]
American actor
* Murphy, Senator

Murphy, Francis Stack 1807-1860 [PI]
Irish author
* Cresswell, Frank

Murphy, Frank 1893-1949 [HPPN]
Attorney General of the U. S.and Supreme Court Associate Justice
* Frank the Just
* [The] New Deal's Tom Dewey

Murphy, Frank J. 20th c. [BE]
American baseball player
* Murphy, Tony

Murphy, Gentle Willie
See Murphy, William N. [Willie]

Murphy, George Mollett 19th c. [IP]
British author
* [An] Unknown

Murphy, Grandma
See Murphy, John Joseph

Murphy, Guffer
See Murphy, John T.

Murphy, Harlem Tommy
See Murphy, Tommy

Murphy, Hazel
See Thurston, Hazel [Patricia]

Murphy, Herbert C. 1890- [BE]
American baseball player
* Murphy, Dummy

Murphy, Honest Eddie
See Murphy, John Edward

Murphy, Ike
See Burns, Isaac

Murphy, Irish Bob
See Conarty, Edward Lee

Murphy, Isaac Burns
See Burns, Isaac

Murphy, Jack Ronald 1937- [BI]
American thief
* Murph the Surf

Murphy, James [Jimmy] ?-1924
American auto racer
* [The] Natural
* [The] Smiling Irishman

Murphy, James 1839-? [PI]
Irish author and poet
* J. M.
* M.
* St. Molaing

Murphy, James 19th c. [PI]
Irish poet
* O'Murchadha, Shemus

Murphy, James J. ?-1875 [PI]
Irish clergyman and poet
* Fionbarra

Murphy, John
See Grady, Ronan Calistus, Jr.

Murphy, John B. 1857-1916 [HPPN]
American surgeon and educator
* [The] Father of the Murphy Button
* [The] Surgical Genius of His
  Generation

Murphy, John Daly
See Conlon, John Daly

Murphy, John Edward 1891-1969 [BE]
American baseball player
* Murphy, Honest Eddie

Murphy, John Joseph 1908-1970 [BE, PB]
American baseball player
* Murphy, Fireman
* Murphy, Fordham Johnny
* Murphy, Grandma

Murphy, John P. 1879-1914 [BE]
American baseball player
* Murphy, Soldier Boy

Murphy, John R. 1933?- [HPPN]
American newspaper editor and kidnap victim
* Murphy, Reg

Murphy, John T. 1900?-1964 [BEW]
American theatrical performer
* Murphy, Guffer

Murphy, Joseph
See Cohen, Jacob

Murphy, Juliette 1902-1973 [HPPN]
American dancer
* Johnson, Julie

Murphy, Katharine Mary 1840?-1885 [PI]
Irish poet
* Brigid
* Townsbridge, Elizabeth

Murphy, Kid
See Frascella, Peter

Murphy, Lawrence A[gustus] 1924- [CA]
American author
* Lawrence, Steven C.
* Murphy, C. L. [joint pseudonym with Charlotte A(lice) Murphy]

Murphy, Leo Joseph 1889-1960 [BE]
American baseball player
* Murphy, Red

Murphy, Louis J.
See Hicks, Tyler Gregory

Murphy, Lyle 1908- [ASC, DAM, EJ]
American jazz musician
* Murphy, Spud

Murphy, Mabel Ansley 1870-? [HPPN]
American author
* Lee, Anne S.

Murphy, May
See Fogg, May

Murphy, Medals
See Murphy, Audie

Murphy, Melvin E. 1915- [DAM, EJ, PMJ]
American jazz musician
* Murphy, Turk

Murphy, Mike
See Hribar, Erneytsck

Murphy, Mile a Minute
See Murphy, Charles W.

Murphy, Mrs. H. 19th c. [PI]
American poet
* Stanley, Eveleen

Murphy, Nonie Carol 1926- [CA]
American author and actress
* Caroll, Nonie

Murphy, Pat
See Bodie, Jack

Murphy, Pat
See Murphy, E[mmett] Jefferson

Murphy, Peter 1864-1889 [PI]
Irish poet
* O'Murchadha, Peadar

Murphy, Raymond 1905?- [BI]
American football scout
* Murphy, Fido

Murphy, Razzle Dazzle
See Murphy, Cornelius B.

Murphy, Red
See Murphy, Leo Joseph

Murphy, Reg
See Murphy, John R.

Murphy, Robert [Bob]
See Dunnell, Duke Foster

Murphy, Robert D. 1894- [CND, HPPN]
American diplomat
* McGowan, Lieutenant Colonel [code name used during World War II]
* [The] Troubleshooter

Murphy, Robert R. 1895-1938 [BE]
American baseball player
* Murphy, Buzz

Murphy, Rose 20th c. [PMJ]
American singer
* [The] Chee Chee Girl

Murphy, Senator
See Murphy, Francis

Murphy, Silent Charley
See Murphy, Charles Francis

Murphy, Soldier Boy
See Murphy, John P.

Murphy, Spook
See Murphy, Billy J.

Murphy, Spud
See Murphy, Lyle

Murphy, Stretch
See Murphy, Charles

Murphy, Thomas James
See Furlong, Patrick M.

Murphy, Thomas W. 1863-1939 [BX, RBE, WBC]
New Zealand boxer
* Murphy, Billy
* Murphy, Torpedo Billy

Murphy, Timothy 20th c. [HPPN]
Irish-American labor union racketeer
* Murphy, Big Tim

Murphy, Tommy 1885-1958 [RBE]
American boxer
* Murphy, Harlem Tommy

Murphy, Tony
See Murphy, Frank J.

Murphy, Torpedo Billy
See Murphy, Thomas W.

Murphy, Turk
See Murphy, Melvin E.

Murphy, William
See Nevelson, William

Murphy, William Henry 1869-1906 [BE]
American baseball player
* Murphy, Yale

Murphy, William N. [Willie] 20th c. [BE]
American baseball player
* Murphy, Gentle Willie

Murphy, Yale
See Murphy, William Henry

Murranka, Mary 1944- [WD]
British author
* McGrath, Mary

Murray
See Saunders, Robert

Murray, A. C. 20th c. [MBF]
British author
* Feveril, Hubert
* Gray, Andrew

Murray, Adrian 20th c. [MBF]
British author
* Gordon, Richard

Murray, Adrian
See Curran, Mona [Elisa]

Murray, Alfalfa Bill
See Murray, William Henry

Murray, Aline
See Kilmer, Aline

Murray, Ambrose Joseph 1913- [BE]
American baseball player
* Murray, Amby

Murray, Amby
See Murray, Ambrose Joseph

Murray, Andrew Nicholas 1880-1929
[MBF]
British author
* Arnold, Malcolm
* Deane, Vesey
* Islay, Nicholas

Murray, Anne 1947- [RO2]
Canadian singer
* [The] Singing Sweetheart of Canada

Murray, Arthur
See Teichman, Arthur

Murray, Athol 1892- [CSH]
Canadian clergyman and college founder
* Murray, Pere

Murray, Bearcat
See Murray, Jim

Murray, Beatrice
See Posner, Richard

Murray, Big Jim
See Murray, James Francis [Jim]

Murray, Braham
See Goldstein, Braham

Murray, Brian
See Bell, Brian

Murray, Bromley 19th c. [HPPN]
American author
* Landseer

Murray, Bud
See Murray, Julian

Murray, C. Geoffrey 20th c. [MBF]
British author
* Gray, Geoffrey
* Kingsford, Guy
* Loxley, Raymond

Murray, Charles T. [PA]
Author
* Wright, Samuel

Murray, Cocklebur Bill
See Murray, William Henry

Murray, Cromwell
See Morgan, Murray Cromwell

Murray, D. L.
See Murray, David Leslie

Murray, David 1955- [IBW]
American jazz musician
* Murray, Sunny

Murray, David Christie 1847-1907
[NPS]
Writer
* Merlin

Murray, David Leslie 1888-1962 [LC]
British author
* Murray, D. L.

Murray, David Stark 1900- [IAW]
British pathologist and author
* Brown, Irwin

Murray, Deacon
See Murray, Raymond Lee

Murray, Dominick
See Moran, D.

Murray, Dominick
See Morogh, Dominick

Murray, Donald
See Bloom, Murray

Murray, Donald
See Vivarelli, Piero

Murray, E. C. Greenville ?-1882 [PA]
Author
* [The] Roving Englishman

Murray, Edgar Joyce 1878-? [MBF]
British author
* Drew, Sidney
* Rover, Max

Murray, Edna [BLB]
American criminal
* [The] Kissing Bandit

Murray, Edna
See Rowland, Donald Sydney

Murray, Eustace Clare Grenville
1828?-1881 [FFF, HPPN, PA]
British journalist and author
* [The] Father of the Scandal Sheet
* Hope, Mark
* Member for Paris
* Scampington, Duke of
* Trois Etoiles

Murray, Frances
See Booth, Rosemary Frances

Murray, George Gilbert Aime 1866-1957
[HPPN]
American classical scholar and author
* [The] Foremost Greek Scholar

Murray, George King 1898-1955 [BE]
American baseball player
* Murray, Smiler

Murray, Gilbert
See Wycherley, Richard Newman

Murray, Hamilton
See Malden, Henry

Murray, Hon. Mrs.
See Aust, Sarah

Murray, Irene
See Witherspoon, Irene Murray

Murray, J. Harold
See Roulon, Harry

Murray, Jack 20th c. [CEI]
Hockey player
* Murray, Muzz

Murray, James Arthur 1927- [DAM]
American jazz musician
* Murray, Sunny

Murray, James Francis [Jim] 1898-
[BE]
American baseball player
* Murray, Big Jim

Murray, Jan
See Janofsky, Murray

Murray, Jeanne 1923- [BEW, IPA, TR]
American actress
* Stapleton, Jean

Murray, Jeremiah J. 1865-1922 [BE]
American baseball player
* Murray, Miah

Murray, Jill
See Walker, Emily Kathleen

Murray, Jim 20th c. [SMG]
Hockey team trainer
* Murray, Bearcat

Murray, Jim
See Murray, Philip Jesse, Jr.

Murray, Joan 1904- [AW]
British author
* Wildeblood, Joan

Murray, John 1741-1815 [FFF, WBD]
British-born clergyman
* [The] Father of American
  Universalism
* [The] Father of Universalism in
  America

Murray, John 1778-1843 [DNNF, FFF,
NPS, SN]
British publisher
* [The] Anak of Publishers
* [The] Coxcomb Bookseller
* [The] Emperor of the West

Murray, John
See MacMurray, John

Murray, John
See Pfeferstein, John

Murray, John F[rancis] 1923-1977 [CA,
CAP]
American author and playwright
* Backgammon, Daisy
* Carryaway, Nick
* Combs, Robert

Murray, John Fisher 1811-1865 [PI]
Irish physician and poet
* J. F. M.
* Maire

Murray, John Joseph 1884-1958 [AS,
BE]
American baseball player
* Murray, Red

Murray, John Wilson 19th c. [HPPN]
British detective
* Old Never Let Go

Murray, Johnny
See Sloves, Herman

Murray, Judith Sargent Stevens
1751-1820 [HPPN]
American playwright, poet, essayist
* Constantia

Murray, Julian 1888-1952 [SC]
American actor and director
* Murray, Bud

Murray, Julien A. Dolezai 1896-1947
[HPPN]
American actress
* Dolezai, Julien A.

Murray, K. F.
See Carlisle, Fred

Murray, Ken
See Court, Don

Murray, Ken
See Turner, Robert [Harry]

Murray, Leo 20th c. [GW]
American rodeo performer
* Murray, Pickhandle

Murray, Leslie 20th c. [SFL]
Author
* Leo, Bessie

Murray, Lieut.
See Ballou, Maturin Murray

Murray, Lindley 1745-1826 [WBD]
Scottish-American grammarian
* [The] Father of English Grammar

Murray, Louise Spigler 1875-1956 [F1, F2]
Actress
* Carver, Louise

Murray, Mae
See Koenig, Marie Adrienne

Murray, Mary ?-1960 [BI]
American librarian and nun
* Marietta, [Sister]

Murray, Miah
See Murray, Jeremiah J.

Murray, Michael
See McLaren, Moray [David Shaw]

Murray, Mrs. J. J. [FFF]
Entertainer
* Melville, Virginia

Murray, Mrs. John [FFF]
Entertainer
* Hawthorne, Grace

Murray, Muzz
See Murray, Jack

Murray, Nicholas 1803-1861 [DEL, FFF, PA]
American clergyman and author
* Kirwan

Murray, Pere
See Murray, Athol

Murray, Peter
See James, Peter

Murray, Philip Jesse, Jr. 1925- [FFA]
American singer
* Murray, Jim

Murray, Pickhandle
See Murray, Leo

Murray, Raymond Lee 1917- [BE]
American baseball player
* Murray, Deacon

Murray, Red
See Murray, John Joseph

Murray, Robert
See Graydon, Robert Murray

Murray, Robert
See Twyman, Harold William

Murray, Rosalind
See Toynbee, Rosalind

Murray, Ruth Hilary 1933- [CA]
Irish-born educator and author
* Finnegan, Ruth H.

Murray, Sinclair
See Sullivan, Edward Alan

Murray, Smiler
See Murray, George King

Murray, Sunny
See Murray, David

Murray, Sunny
See Murray, James Arthur

Murray, T. C.
See Murray, Thomas C.

Murray the K
See Kaufman, Murray

Murray, Thomas C. 1873-1959 [LC]
Irish playwright
* Murray, T. C.

Murray, W. H.
See Cream, [Dr.] Thomas Neil

Murray, William [First Earl of Mansfield] 1705-1793 [HPPN, NPS, WBD]
British jurist
* [The] Father of Modern Toryism
* [The] Founder of English Commercial Law
* [A] Modern English Journalist

Murray, William [Billy] 1877-1954 [HPPN]
American singer and entertainer
* [The] Camden Budgerigar
* [The] Denver Nightingale

Murray, William
See Graydon, William Murray

Murray, William Henry 1869-1956 [BLB, HPPN]
American politician
* Murray, Alfalfa Bill
* Murray, Cocklebur Bill
* [The] Sage of Tishomingo

Murray, William Henry Harrison 1840-1904 [HPPN]
American clergyman, sportsman, author
* Adirondack

Murray, William Waldie 1891-1956 [CCL]
Canadian author
* [The] Orderly Sergeant

Murray-Ford, Alice May [Harte-Potts] 1879-?
Author
* Le Breton, Mrs. John

Murray-Ford, Thomas 1854-? [SFL]
British author and editor
* Le Breton, Thomas

Murrel, John A. 1794-1844? [BLB, HPPN]
American bandit
* [The] Great Rogue
* [The] Great Western Land Pirate

Murrell, Elsie Kathleen Seth-Smith 1883- [CAP]
British author
* Seth-Smith, Elsie K.

Murrell, Phil 1933- [BB]
American basketball player
* Murrell, Red

Murrell, Red
See Murrell, Phil

Murrells, Joseph 1904- [IAW]
British author and songwriter
* Temple, Edith

Murrish, John 1818-1861 [HPPN]
British miner
* [The] Miner of Perranzabuloe

Murrow, Edward Roscoe
See Murrow, Egbert Roscoe

Murrow, Egbert Roscoe 1908-1965 [HPPN, WBD]
American television journalist
* [The] Best Known and Most Influential Commentator on World War II
* Murrow, Edward Roscoe

Murry, Colin
See Middleton-Murry, Colin

Murry, Ted
See Mencher, Murray

Murry, William
See Morris, Charles Smith

Murschetz, Luis Marian 1936- [IAW]
Austrian-born author and cartoonist
* Mur

Murtha, Fred
See Gershvin, Jacob

Musaeus 5th c. [WBD]
Greek poet
* Grammaticus

Musaeus, Johann Karl August 1735-1787 [FFF]
German author
* Schellenburg

Musaeus Palatinus
See Braithwaite, Richard

Musafir
See Tagore, Amitendranath

[Il] Musannif
See Mackenzie, C. F.

Muscadel
See Downey, Richard

Muschamp, Lila 1896?-1950   [BEW]
Actress
* Maravan, Lila

Muschamp, Thomas
See Lloyd-Thomas, Catherine

Muscipula, Sen.
See Collier, John

[The] Muscle Man
See Berra, Lawrence Peter

Muscle Moll
See Zaharias, Mildred Didrikson

Muscle Throat Monroe
See Monroe, Vaughn Wilton

Muscles, Mr.
See Jackson, Reginald [Reggie]

[The] Muscovy General
See Dalyell [or Dalzell], Thomas

[The] Muscular Marvel from Idaho
See Killebrew, Harmon Clayton

[The] Muscular Strongman
See Sick, Max

[La] Muse de la Patrie [The Country's Muse]
See Gay, Delphine

Muse, Lewis Anderson 1908-   [BWW]
American singer
* Muse, Rabbit

[La] Muse Limonadiere
See Bourette, Charlotte

[The] Muse of Cumberland
See Blamire, Susanna

[The] Muse of Greece
See Xenophon

[The] Muse of Tragedy
See Siddons, Sarah

Muse, Patricia [Alice] 1923-   [CA]
American author
* Walters, Nell

Muse, Rabbit
See Muse, Lewis Anderson

[The] Muses' Darling
See Fletcher, John

[The] Muses' Judge and Friend
See Walsh, William

[The] Muses' Pride
See Sackville, Charles [Sixth Earl of Dorset]

Musgrave, Philip
See Abbott, Joseph

Musgrave-Wood, John 1915-   [WEC]
British cartoonist
* Emmwood

Musgrove, Nancye 1893-   [THR]
British actress
* Stewart, Nancye

Mushafir, Kartikeya Skylark
See Tikekar, Shripad Ramchandra

Mushrush, Obadiah 1875-1938
American underworld figure
* Mertz, George

Musial, Stan[ley Frank]
See Musial, Stanislaus

Musial, Stanislaus 1920-   [BAB, SR]
American baseball player
* [The] Man
* Musial, Stan[ley Frank]
* Stan the Man

Music, Dr.
See Riley, Doug[las Brian]

Music Maker, Mr.
See Welk, Lawrence LeRoy

Musica, Arthur 20th c.   [DI]
American swindler
* Vernard, George

Musica, Dandy Phil
See Musica, Philip Mariana Fausto

Musica, Philip Mariana Fausto 1877-1938   [BLB, HPPN]
Italian-born American swindler
* Costa, Frank
* Coster, F[rank] Donald
* Girard, P. Horace
* Johnston, William
* Musica, Dandy Phil
* Smith, W. W.

[The] Musical Copy Cat
See Heidt, Horace Murray

[The] Musical Giant
See Stravinsky, Igor Feadorovich

[The] Musical Small-Coal Man
See Britton, Thomas

[The] Musical Star of Radio
See Klein, Evelyn Kaye

[The] Musician
See Bull, Ole Barnemann

[The] Musicianly Boxer
See Calhoun, Herman

Musick, John Roy 1848-1901   [HPPN]
American journalist and author
* Broadaxe, Benjamin

Musidora
See Converse, Harriet [Maxwell]

Musidora
See Roques, Jeanne

Musidorus
See Greville, Robert Fulke

Musidorus
See Way, B.

Musikara
See Parikh, Rasiklal Chhotalal

Muskerry, Major
See Dowe, William

Musketeer
See Barker, Arthur James

Musketoeren
See Wirtanen, Atos Kasimir

Muskett, Netta 1893-   [HPPN]
British author
* Hill, Anne

Muskie, Ed[mund Sixtus] 1914-
American politician
* [The] Democrat's New Underdog
* Humphrey's Polish Yankee
* Miracle Man from Maine
* [The] Non Candidate

Muskrat Bill Shipke
See Shipke, William M. [Bill]

Muslih-ud-Din [or Moslehedin] 1184?-1291   [DNNS, SN, WBD]
Persian poet
* [The] Nightingale of a Thousand Songs
* [The] Oriental Catullus
* [The] Oriental Homer
* Saadi [or Sadi]

[The] Muslim Pliny
See Qazwini, al-

Muso
See Suparto, Muso

Musoeus
See Cary, Henry Francis

Musoeus
See Morrison, John

Musolino, Vincenzo 20th c.   [WF]
Italian director
* Davis, Glen Vincent

Muspratt, Rosalie Helen 1906-1976 [HFF, SFL, WGT]
British author
* John, Jasper

Musquito ?-1825   [DI]
Australian bushranger
* [The] Black Napoleon

Mussa, Hawaja
See Smilansky, Moshe

Musselman, Johnson J. 1890-1958   [SC]
American actor and magician
* Aska the Magician

Musser, Benjamin 1889-   [HPPN]
American poet
* [The] Poet Laureate of New Jersey

Musset, [Louis Charles] Alfred de 1810-1857   [DNNS, HN, HPPN, NPS, RH]
French poet
* Alcide, Baron de M.
* Dupuis, [Mademoiselle] Athenais
* [The] French Byron

Mussey, Virginia T. H.
See Ellison, Virginia Howell

Mussi, Mary 1907-   [AW, CA]
British author
* Edgar, Josephine
* Howard, Mary

Mussiere, Luciene
See Meurisse, Lucien

Musso, George F. 20th c.　[FB]
American football player
* Musso, Moose

Musso, John, Jr. 1950-　[SMG]
American football player
* [The] Italian Stallion

Musso, Moose
See Musso, George F.

Mussolini, Benito 1883-1945　[CBS, NN]
Italian dictator
* [The] Bullfrog of the Pontine Marshes
* [Il] Duce

Mussot
See Arnould, Jean-Francois

Mussulli, Boots
See Mussulli, Henry W.

Mussulli, Henry W. 1917-1967　[EJ, PMJ]
American jazz musician
* Mussulli, Boots

Mustache George Huber
See Huber, George

Mustache Mike Contino
See Contino, Michael

Mustafa ibn-Abdallah 1600?-1658
[WBD]
Turkish historian and bibliographer
* Hajji Khalfah [Assessor Who Has
   Made the Pilgrimage]
* Katib Chelebi [Noble Secretary]

Mustafa [or Mustapha], Kemal
1881-1938　[CBS, WBD]
Turkish military leader and statesman
* Kemal Atatuerk
* Kemal Pasha

Mustafavi, Ruhollah 1900?-
Iranian head of state
* Hindi
* [The] Imam
* Khomeini, [Ayatollah] Ruhollah

Mustapha 1755-1808　[HN]
Sultan of Turkey
* Bairaktar [Standard Bearer]

Mustapha
See Gardiner, William Nelson

Musto, Barry 1930-　[AW, WD]
British author
* Simon, Robert

Musus
See Daniel, Samuel

Mutcheruon, James Albertus, Jr. 1941-
[BA]
American physician
* Mutcheruon, Ziggy

Mutcheruon, Ziggy
See Mutcheruon, James Albertus, Jr.

[The] Mute
See Fernandez Navarrete, Juan

Muter, Mela
See Mutermilch, Mela

Mutermilch, Mela 1873-1967　[JL]
Polish-born artist
* Muter, Mela

Mutesa, Edward, II 1924-1969
President of Uganda
* King Freddie

Muth, Conrad 1471?-1526　[WBD]
German scholar
* Mutian
* Mutianus Rufus, Conradus

Muti, Ornella
See Rivelli, Francesca

Mutian
See Muth, Conrad

Mutianus Rufus, Conradus
See Muth, Conrad

Mutius
See Mozzi, Marco Antonio

Mutrie, James J. [Jim] 1851-1938　[BE]
American baseball manager
* Mutrie, Truthful Jim

Mutrie, Truthful Jim
See Mutrie, James J. [Jim]

Mutt
See Ens, Jewel Willoughby

Muttle
See Brescher, Max

[The] Mutton Eating King
See Charles II

[The] Mutual Girl
See Phillips, Norma

Mutwa, Baba
See Mutwa, Gado Vusa Mazulu

Mutwa, Gado Vusa Mazulu 1922-
[IBW]
*South African witch doctor, sculptor,
painter*
* Mutwa, Baba

Mutz
See Kuenstler, Morton

Muwakkil, Salim
See Cannady, Alonzo James

Muybridge, Eadweard
See Muggeridge, Edward James

Muza, Irene ?-1909　[HPPN]
American actress
* Pascaline, Mademoiselle

Muzakova, Johanna [Rottova] 1830-1899
[CD]
Czech author
* Svetla, Karolina

Muziano, Girolamo 1528?-1592　[WBD]
Italian painter
* Bressano [or Brescianino], Girolamo

Muzio [or Mutio]
See Nuzio, Girolamo

Muzio, Claudia
See Muzzio, Claudina

Muzorewa, Abel Tendekayi 1925-
Prime Minister of Zimbabwe Rhodesia
* Muzorewa, Muzzy

Muzorewa, Muzzy
See Muzorewa, Abel Tendekayi

Muzquiz, Carlos 1906-1960　[SC]
Mexican actor
* Muzquiz, Compadre

Muzquiz, Compadre
See Muzquiz, Carlos

Muzzio, Claudina 1889-1936　[BBD]
Italian opera singer
* Muzio, Claudia

Muzzio, Girolamo 1496-1576　[PA]
Author
* Nuzio

Muzzy, Bertha
Author
* Bowen, B. M.

Muzzy, L. R.　[PA]
Author
* Aunt Prudence

Mwalimu [Teacher]
See Nyerere, Julius Kambarage

Mwamba, Pal
See Roberts, John S[torm]

Mwandishi [Composer]
See Hancock, Herbert Jeffrey [Herbie]

Mwanga
See Stark, Claude Alan

Mwynvawr, Morgan 872-1001　[SN]
Welsh prince and warrior
* [The] Courteous

My Admirable Crichton
See De Quincey, Thomas

My Baritone
See Lucy, [Sir] Henry William

My Book, Doctor
See Abernethy, John

My Brother's Brother
See Chekhov, Anton [Pavlovich]

My Fancy
See Baker, Mae Rose

My Little Portuguese
See Browning, Elizabeth Barrett

My Moral Clytemnestra
See Byron, Anne Isabella Milbanke

My Octogenarian Friend
See Nichols, John

My Pen
See Dunn, Caleb

My Philosophical Poet
See Alexander, [Sir] William [First Earl of Stirling]

My Sunship
See Suppiluliumas

My Uncle Newberry
See Mogridge, George

Myassin, Leonid Fedorovich 1895-1979
[CA]
Russian-born dancer and choreographer
* Massine, Leonide

Myatt, Foghorn
See Myatt, George Edward

Myatt, George Edward 1914- [BE]
American baseball player
* Myatt, Foghorn
* Myatt, Mercury
* Myatt, Stud

Myatt, Mercury
See Myatt, George Edward

Myatt, Nellie 20th c. [AW]
British author
* Kirkham, Nellie

Myatt, Stud
See Myatt, George Edward

Myconius [or Mykonius], Friedrich
See Mekum, Friedrich

Myconius [or Mykonius], Oswald
See Geishuesler, Oswald

Mycroft
See Holmes, Geoffrey Andrew

Myddleton, Robert
See Hebblethwaite, Peter

Myer, Albert J. 1829-1880 [HPPN]
American army officer
* [The] Father of the Weather Bureau

Myer, Buddy
See Myer, Charles Solomon

Myer, Charles Solomon 1904-1974 [BI,
DGS, PB]
American baseball player
* Myer, Buddy

Myers, Albert 1863-1927 [BE]
American baseball player
* Myers, Cod

Myers, Allen O. [FFF]
American writer
* Pickaway

Myers, Bessie Allen ?-1964 [HPPN]
American dancer
* Allen, Bessie

Myers, Blind Sam
See Myers, Sam

Myers, Bumps
See Myers, Hubert Maxwell

Myers, C. F.
See Fairbanks, Carol

Myers, Carl 20th c. [GW]
American rodeo performer
* Myers, Curly

Myers, Carol Fairbanks
See Fairbanks, Carol

Myers, Chief
See Myers, Robert L.

Myers, Chip
See Myers, Phil[ip] Leon

Myers, Cod
See Myers, Albert

Myers, Curly
See Myers, Carl

Myers, F. W. H.
See Myers, Frederic William Henry

Myers, Frederic William Henry
1843-1901 [LC]
British author and poet
* Myers, F. W. H.

Myers, Hap
See Myers, Harold Robert

Myers, Hap
See Myers, Ralph Edward

Myers, Harold Robert 1947- [CEI]
Canadian-born hockey player
* Myers, Hap

Myers, Harriet Kathryn
See Whittington, Harry [Benjamin]

Myers, Henry Harrison 1889-1965 [AS,
BE, PB]
American baseball player
* Myers, Hy

Myers, Howard L. 20th c. [SFP]
Author
* Foray, Verge

Myers, Hubert Maxwell 1912-1968 [EJ,
WWJ]
American jazz musician
* Myers, Bumps

Myers, Hy
See Myers, Henry Harrison

Myers, James E. 20th c. [ASC]
American composer
* DeKnight, Jimmy

Myers, John
See Bechtel, Ralph

Myers, L. H.
See Myers, Leopold Hamilton

Myers, Laurence E. 1858-1899 [AS,
BBH]
American track and field athlete
* Myers, Lon

Myers, Leopold Hamilton 1881-1944
[LC]
British author
* Myers, L. H.

Myers, Linwood Lincoln 1914- [BE]
American baseball player
* Myers, Lynn

Myers, Lon
See Myers, Laurence E.

Myers, Louis 1929- [BWW]
American singer
* Meyers, Louie

Myers, Lynn
See Myers, Linwood Lincoln

Myers, Mary Breed [Hawley] 19th c.
[BI]
American balloonist
* Carlotta

Myers, Mary Cathcart 1906- [AW]
British author
* Cathcart, Mary

Myers, Michael 20th c. [IPA]
American politician
* Myers, Ozzie

Myers, Ozzie
See Myers, Michael

Myers, P. Hamilton 1812-? [PA]
Author
* [The] First of the Knickerbockers

Myers, Pete
See Myers, Pierre E.

Myers, Phil[ip] Leon 1945- [EF, FR]
American football player
* Myers, Chip

Myers, Pierre E. 1928-1968 [HPPN]
American actor and radio personality
* Myers, Pete

Myers, Pop
See Myers, Theodore E.

Myers, Ralph Edward 1888-1967 [BE]
American baseball player
* Myers, Hap

Myers, Ramona 1909?- [PMJ]
American singer
* Davies, Ramona
* Ramona

Myers, Richard
See Myers, Richardson

Myers, Richardson 1901- [BEW]
American composer and producer
* Myers, Richard

Myers, Robert L. 20th c. [HPPN]
American football coach
* Myers, Chief

Myers, Sam 20th c. [WP 8-9-85]
American musician
* Myers, Blind Sam

Myers, Serious
See Myers, Wilson Ernest

Myers, Stanley 1918- [JL]
American playwright and critic
* Richards, Stanley

Myers, Theodore E. 1874-1954 [AS]
*American auto racing promoter and
official*
* Myers, Pop

Myers, Wilson Ernest 1906- [WWJ]
American jazz musician
* Myers, Serious

Mykolaitis, Vincas 1893- [EWL]
Lithuanian poet, author, playwright
* Putinas

Myler, Beebe
See Myler, Levar

Myler, Levar 1923?- [BI]
American business executive
* Myler, Beebe

Myles
See Smith, Robert

Myles, Devera
See Zucker, Dolores Mae Bolton

Myles, Symon
See Follett, Kenneth Martin

Mylin, Edward Everett 1895-1975 [BI, FB]
American football player and coach
* Mylin, Hook [or Hooks]

Mylin, Hook [or Hooks]
See Mylin, Edward Everett

Myline, William 18th c. [HPPN]
Scottish clergyman
* One of the Suffering Clergy of the Church of Scotland

Mylius, Otfried
See Mueller, Karl

Myller, Rolf 1926- [SAT]
German-born American author
* Brown, David
* Milonas, Rolf

Mylo
See Boyle, John

Mynn, Alfred 1807-1861 [EC]
British cricketer
* [The] Lion of Kent

Myosotis
See Moreau, Hegesippe

Myra
See Fairbanks, Mrs. A. W.

Myra
See Foe, Daniel

Myra
See Newburgh, Countess of

Myrander
See Stevenson, James Alexander

Myrddin, Fardd
See Jones, John Daniel

Myre, Louis Philippe 1948- [FHE]
Canadian-born hockey player
* Myre, Phil

Myre, Phil
See Myre, Louis Philippe

Myrick, David Luke 1916-1971 [CME, ECM, FCW]
American country-western performer
* [The] Man with a Million Friends
* Tyler, T. Texas

Myrivilis, Stratis
See Stamatopoulos, Stratis

Myrna Loy's Celluloid Husband
See Powell, William Horatio

Myron
See Holmes, Abiel

Myron, Paul
See Linebarger, Paul Myron Wentworth

Myrrha
See Downing, Mary

Myrtel, Hera
See Jacques, Marie-Louise Victorine [Grones]

Myrtil, Odette
See Quignard, Odette

Myrtle, Charles 20th c. [EF]
American football player
* Myrtle, Chip

Myrtle, Chip
See Myrtle, Charles

Myrtle, Harriet
See Miller, Lydia Falconer

Myrtle, Harriet
See Miller, Mary [Gillies]

Myrtle, Lewis
See Hill, George Canning

Myrtle, Marmaduke
See Addison, Joseph

Myrtle, Marmaduke
See Dermody, Thomas

Myrtle, Marmaduke
See Steele, [Sir] Richard

Myrtle, May
See Holden, Maria

Myrtle, Minnie
See Bryan, Sarah M. L.

Myrtle, Minnie
See Dyer, Minnie Theresa

Myrtle, Minnie
See Johnson, Anna C.

Myrtle, Mollie
See Bacon, Julia

Myrtle, Molly
See Hill, Agnes [Leonard]

Myslivecek [or Mysliweczek], Josef 1737-1781 [WBD]
Czech composer
* [Il] Boemo
* Venatorini

Mystagogus
See Woolston, Thomas

Mysterious Bachelor
See Clark, Dana Boardman

[The] Mysterious Billionaire
See Hughes, Howard R.

Mysterious Billy Smith
See Smith, Amos

[The] Mysterious Cyclops of Israeli Politics
See Dayan, Moshe

Mysterious Dave Mather
See Mather [or Mathers], David

Mysterious Jimmy Wilmott
See Wilmott, James

[The] Mysterious Kid
See Lewis, Elmer

Mysterious Mike Malone
See Malone, Michael F.

[The] Mysterious Montague
See Moore, LaVerne M.

[The] Mysterious Rhinestone Cowboy
See Coe, David Allan

Mystery
See Westmoreland, Maria Elizabeth [Jourdan]

[The] Mystery Man of Europe
See Zacharias, Basileois

[The] Mystery Man of International Finance
See Gulbenkian, Calouste S.

[The] Mystery Man of Panama
See Herz, Cornelius

[The] Mystery Man of Quatsino Sound
See Quantrill, William Clarke

[The] Mystery Professor
See Cohen, Paul Arthur

Mystic in the Theatre
See Duse, Eleanora

[The] Mystic Materialist
See Lane, Franklin Knight

Mystifizinsky, Deutobold Symbolizetti Allegoriowitsch
See Vischer, Friedrich Theodor von

Myth, M. Y. T. H.
See Nicolovius, Ludwig

[The] Mythical Monster
See Dun, Thomas

Mzee [Grand Old Man]
See Ngengi, Kamau wa

N

N.
See Nares, Robert

N.
See Nicolas, [Sir] Nicholas Harris

N.
See Northrup, C. B.

N.
See Nott, Josiah Clark

N.
See Noyes, George Rapall

N. A.
See Ames, Nathaniel

N. A.
See Ansell, Norah

N. A.
See Appleton, Nathan

N. B.
See Foe, Daniel

N. B. S.
See Shurtleff, Nathaniel Bradstreet

N. C. M. S. C.
See Cotes, Humphrey

N. F.
See Field, Nathaniel

N. H.
See Herrick, N.

N. H. N.
See Nicolas, [Sir] Nicholas Harris

N. K.
See Kay, Nora

N. L. F.
See Frothingham, Nathaniel Langdon

N. M.?
See McDevitt, Neil

N. N.
See Kenyon, John

N. N.
See Pennell, Elizabeth

N. O.
See Bentley, Richard

N. O., Ancien Missionaire
See Cuoq, Jean Andre

N. of Arkansas
See Noland, Charles Fenton Mercer

N. P. D.
See Gould, Benjamin Apthorp

N. P. W.
See Willis, Nathaniel Parker

N. S.
See Anstis, John

N. S.
See Nichols, John

N. S. F.
See Folson, [Rev.] Nathaniel Smith

N. T.
See Transidder, Nicholas

N. T.
See Truebner, Nicolas

N. T. G.
See Granlund, Nils Thor

N. T. R.
See Rao, N. T. Rama

N. W.
See Whittemore, Nathan

[A] N. Y. Detective
See Doughty, Francis W.

N. Y. Times Man
See Alden, William L.

Na Gopaleen [or Na gCopaleen], Myles
See O'Nuallain, Brian

Naa Parthasarathy, Naarayana-Parthasarathy 1932- [IAW]
Indian author and poet
* Alagan, Koodal
* Dheeran
* Manivannan
* Pon Mudi

NAACP, Miss
See Mitchell, Lottie Pearl

Naas, N.
See McDevitt, Neil

Nab, O. J.
See Souchon, Harry V.

Naber, Charles R.
See Hall, Frank Richards

[The] Nabob
See Alexander, James

Nabob
See Barnwell, Richard

[The] Nabob of Sob
See Ray, Johnnie

Nabokov, Peter [Francis] 1940- [CA]
American author
* Towne, Peter

Nabokov, Vladimir Vladimirovich 1899-1977 [ANT, CA, CD]
Russian-born American author, poet, playwright
* [The] Black Swan of Lac Leman
* Siren, V[ladimir]

Nabonidus 6th c. BC [WBD]
King of Babylonia
* [The] Antiquarian King

* Nabors, Big Nabe
See Nabors, Jesse Lee, Sr.

Nabors, Jesse Lee, Sr. 1940- [BA]
American educator
* * Nabors, Big Nabe

Nacchiante, Giacome [PA]
Author
* Naclautus

Nachez, Tivadar
See Naschitz, Theodor

Nacht, Max 1881-1973 [BI]
American author and journalist
* Nomad, Max

Nacional [National]
See Anllo y Orrio, Ricardo

Nacional
See Martinez, Octavio

Nacional II [National, the Second]
See Anllo y Orrio, Juan

Nack, James M. 1809-1879 [HPPN]
American poet
* [The] Deaf and Dumb Poet

Naclautus
See Nacchiante, Giacome

Nada, Alivia
See Mora, Josie

Nada Yolanda
See Sharpe, Pauline

Nadar
See Tournachon, [Gaspard] Felix

Nadasdy, [Count] Ferencz 16th c.
[HPPN]
Hungarian army officer
* [The] Black Hero

Nadel, Aaron 20th c. [SFP]
Author
* Marcellinus, Animianus

Nadel, Warren 1930- [ASC]
American composer
* Starr, Randy

Nader, Owen
See Ackerman, Forrest J[ames]

Nader, Ralph 1934- [HPPN]
American attorney, author, reformer
* [The] Consumer Advocate
* [The] Genius of the Negative
　Approach
* [The] National Ombudsman
* Open Issue Ralph
* [The] People's Lawyer
* [The] Premier Public Relations Man
　of the Age

Nader, Seena
See Ackerman, Forrest J[ames]

Nader, William, S. X. Q.
See Douglas, William

Nadie, X.
See Laboulaye, Edouard

Nadir, A. A.?
See Romanoff, Alexander
Nicholayevitch

Nadir, Hadiyah Joan
See Little, Joan

Nadir, Moishe
See Reiss, Isaac

Nadir Shah 1688-1747 [FFF, HPPN,
WBD]
King of Persia
* [The] Conqueror
* [The] Last of the Great Asian
　Conquerors
* Tahmasp Kuli Khan [Slave of
　Tahmasp]
* [The] Wallace of Persia

Nadir Shah
See Mohammed Nadir Khan

Nadir, William
See Douglass, William

Nadja
See Wanger, Beatrice

Nadler, Susan
See Gantry, Susan Nadler

Naftali, Ch.
See Brandwein, Chaim N[aftali]

Nagai, Kafu
See Nagai, Sokichi

Nagai, Sokichi 1879-1959 [WOA]
Japanese author and critic
* Nagai, Kafu

Nagaul, Joe
See Ferriola, Joseph

Nagel, Anne
See Dolan, Ann

Nagel, Endre 1909- [CAR]
Swedish painter
* Nemes, Endre

Nagele, Anton 1876-? [LAO]
German author
* Clavell, Stauffer

Nageleisen, Louis Marcellus 1887-1965
[BE]
American baseball player
* Nagelsen, Lou[is Marcellus]

Nagelsen, Lou[is Marcellus]
See Nageleisen, Louis Marcellus

Nagelson, Russell Charles 1944- [BE]
American baseball player
* Nagelson, Rusty

Nagelson, Rusty
See Nagelson, Russell Charles

Nagenda, Musa
See Howard, Moses L[eon]

Naghten, Frederick 1822-1845 [PI]
Irish poet
* [A] Late Graduate of Oxford

Nagle, Arthur
See Sullivan, Edmund

Nagle, J. E. [PA]
Author
* Cousin Nourma

Nagle, Judge
See Nagle, Walter Harold

Nagle, Kel
See Nagle, Kelvin David George

Nagle, Kelvin David George 1920- [EG,
GF]
Australian golfer
* Nagle, Kel

Nagle, Lucky
See Nagle, Walter Harold

Nagle, Walter Harold 1880-1971 [BE]
American baseball player
* Nagle, Judge
* Nagle, Lucky

Nagle-Healy, James Anthony 1916-
[IAW]
Irish author, actor, producer
* Hay, Nigel
* Healy, James N.

Nagler, A. M.
See Nagler, Alois M.

Nagler, Alois M. 1907- [BEW]
*Austrian-born educator, theatrical
historian, drama critic*
* Nagler, A. M.

Nagol [joint pseudonym with Virgil
Glen Logan]
See Logan, Lillian Mee

Nagol [joint pseudonym with Lillian
Mee Logan]
See Logan, Virgil Glen

Nagurski, Bronislau 1908- [FB, HPPN,
OCS]
Canadian-born American football player
* [The] Big Ukrainian
* [The] Bronk
* [The] Indomitable Bronk
* Nagurski, Bronko

Nagurski, Bronko
See Nagurski, Bronislau

Nahmanides
See Moses ben Nahman Gerondi

Naidorf, Mendel 1914- [EJS]
Argentinian chess master
* Najdorf, Miguel

Naidu, [Rama] Murti 20th c. [BL]
Indian strong man
* [The] Indian Hercules

Naidu, Sarojini [Chattopadhyay]
1879-1949 [LC]
Indian political leader and poet
* [The] Nightingale of India

Naigeon, Jacques Andre 1738-1810
[HN, SN]
French author
* [The] Inquisitor of Atheists

[The] Nailer
See Stevens, William [Bill]

Nailor, John 12th c. [HN]
British outlaw
* Little John

Naipaul, V. S.
See Naipaul, Vidiadhar Surajprasad

Naipaul, Vidiadhar Surajprasad 1932-
[LC]
British author
* Naipaul, V. S.

Nair, Krishnapillai Krishnan 1918-
[IAW]
Indian author
* Chaitanya, Krishna

Nair, V. Madhavan 1915- [IAW]
Indian author
* Mali

Nairne, Carolina Oliphant 1766-1845
[HPPN]
Scottish poet
* [The] Flower of Strathearn

Nairne, Frank 20th c. [HPPN]
American football player
* Nairne, Pop

Nairne, Pop
See Nairne, Frank

Nairne, William Murray 1756-1830
[SN]
Husband of Scottish songwriter, Carolina Nairne
* Kind Robin

Naish, Carrol Patrick 1901- [BEW]
American actor
* Naish, J. Carrol

Naish, J. Carrol
See Naish, Carrol Patrick

Naismith, Helen 1929- [CA]
American writer
* Eppie

Naismith, Horace
See Helmer, William J[oseph]

Naismith, James 1861-1939 [BBH]
Canadian-born American inventor of basketball
* [The] Father of Basketball

Naismith, Laurence
See Johnson, Laurence Bernard

Najam
See Shastri, Prithvinath

Najdorf, Miguel
See Naidorf, Mendel

Nakae, Noriko 1940- [CA]
Japanese artist and illustrator
* Ueno, Noriko

Nakashima, George Katsutoshi 1905-
[CA]
American designer and author
* Sundarananda [One who Delights in Beauty]

Nakasone, Yasuhiro 1918?- [TI 12-6-82, WP 10-14-82]
Japanese prime minister
* Weathervane

Naksok
See Sung-Tai, Kim

Nakulan
See Doraiswajy, Trivandrum Krishna Iyer

Naldi, Nita
See Dooley, Anita Donna

Nale Roxlo, Conrado 1898- [BI]
Argentine poet and humorist
* Chamico

Naleway, Chick
See Naleway, Frank

Naleway, Frank 1901-1949 [BE]
American baseball player
* Naleway, Chick

Nall, Hiram Abiff 1950- [CA]
American author and editor
* Wadinasi, Sedeka

Nallaperumal, Ravanasamudram Subbiah 1931- [IAW]
Indian author
* Charan, Sakthi

Nalle
See Valtiala, Kaarle-Juhani Bertel

Nalod, Edward
See Nolan, Edward

Nam Suk
See Ahn, Soo-gil

Namary, Genevieve ?-1956 [SC]
Canadian-born actress
* Blinn, Genevieve

Namath, Broadway Joe
See Namath, Joseph William [Joe]

Namath, Joseph William [Joe] 1943-
[FB, HPPN]
American football player
* Gerber, Mr.
* Joe Willie
* Namath, Broadway Joe

Namby-Pamby
See Philips, Ambrose

[The] Nameless Bard
See Mathias, Thomas James

[A] Nameless Nobleman
See Austin, Jane Goodwin

Namier, Julia 1893- [CA]
Russian-born author
* De Beausobre, Julia Mikhailovna

Namier, [Sir] Lewis
See Bernstein-Namierowski, Lewis

Namovicz, Gene Inyart 1927- [CA]
American author and librarian
* Inyart, Gene

Nana
See Morgan, Mary Ellen [O'Brien]

Nana Sahib
See Dandhu Panth

Nanak 1469-1538 [HPPN, WBD]
Indian religious leader
* Guru [Teacher]
* Nanak, Great Guru

Nanak, Great Guru
See Nanak

Nance, Bo
See Nance, James S.

Nance, Bud
See Nance, James

Nance, Doc
See Cooper, William G.

Nance, Dub
See Nance, W. A.

Nance, Floor Show
See Nance, Willis

Nance, James 1921?-
American government official
* Nance, Bud

Nance, James S. 1942- [FB]
American football player
* Nance, Bo

Nance, Kid
See Cooper, William G.

Nance, Ray
See Nance, Willis

Nance, W. A. 1918?- [BI]
American clergyman
* Nance, Dub

Nance, William G.
See Cooper, William G.

Nance, Willis 1913-1976 [DAM, IBW, PMJ]
American jazz musician
* Nance, Floor Show
* Nance, Ray

Nanchoff, Crazy Horse
See Nanchoff, George

Nanchoff, George 1954-
American soccer player
* Nanchoff, Crazy Horse

Nancita
See Reagan, Anne Frances Davis

Nanda Kumar
See Nuncomar

Nandakumar, Prema 1939- [CA]
Indian author
* Aswin

Nankin, Eileen 20th c. [OP]
American opera singer
* Shelle, Eileen

NanKivell, Joice M.
See Loch, Joice NanKivell

Nannary, May
See Dailey, May Nannary

Nannerella
See Magnani, Anna

Nanni, Giovanni
See Annius of Viterbo

Nano, Hervio
See Leach, Harvey

Nanton, Joseph [Joe] 1904-1946?
[DAM, EJ, PMJ]
American jazz musician
* Nanton, Tricky Sam

Nanton, Tricky Sam
See Nanton, Joseph [Joe]

Nanye'hi
See Ward, Nancy

Naoroji, Dadabhai 1825-1917 [DEP]
Indian political reformer
* [The] Father of Indian Nationalism
* [The] Grand Old Man of India

Nap
See Bonaparte, Napoleon

Napier, Alan
See Napier-Clavering, Alan

Napier, Buddy
See Napier, Skelton LeRoy

Napier, Buffalo
See Napier, Walter

Napier, [Sir] Charles 1786-1860 [NPS]
British naval officer
* Black Charlie

Napier, Diana
See Ellis, Molly

Napier, Elma 1892- [BI]
British author
* Garner, Elizabeth

Napier, Eudie
See Napier, Euthumn

Napier, Euthumn 1915- [MK]
American baseball player
* Napier, Eudie

Napier, Geoffrey
See Glemser, Bernard

Napier, Geraldine
See Glemser, Bernard

Napier, John 1550-1617 [HPPN]
Scottish astronomer and mathematician
* [The] Father of Logarithms

Napier, Macvey 1776-1847 [NPS, SN]
Scottish editor
* [The] Bacon Fly
* Napier, Supplement
* Naso, Macveius

Napier, Marita
See Jacobs, Marita

Napier, Mark
See Laffin, John [Alfred Charles]

Napier, Mary
See Wright, [Mary] Patricia

Napier, Priscilla 1908- [CA]
British author
* Hunt, Penelope
* Stewart, Eve

Napier, Skelton LeRoy 1889-1968 [BE]
American baseball player
* Napier, Buddy

Napier, Supplement
See Napier, Macvey

Napier, Walter 20th c. [EF]
American football player
* Napier, Buffalo

Napier, William
See Seymour, William Napier

Napier-Clavering, Alan 1903- [FC]
British-born actor
* Napier, Alan

Napjus, Alice James 1913- [CA]
American author
* Napjus, James

Napjus, James
See Napjus, Alice James

Naples, Al
See Naples, Aloysius Francis

Naples, Aloysius Francis 1927- [BE]
American baseball player
* Naples, Al

Napoleon, Art
See Sudhalter, Richard M[errill]

Napoleon, George 1914-1964 [WWJ]
American jazz musician
* Napoleon, Teddy

Napoleon le Petit
See Bonaparte, Charles Louis Napoleon

[The] Napoleon of Africa
See Mirambo

[The] Napoleon of Crime
See Worth, Adam

[The] Napoleon of Drury Lane
See Elliston, Robert William

[The] Napoleon of Essayists
See Greeley, Horace

[The] Napoleon of Finance
See Balfour, Jabez Spencer

[The] Napoleon of Finance
See Ouyrard, Gabriel Julien

[The] Napoleon of Finance
See Ward, Ferdinand

[The] Napoleon of Gas
See Addicks, John Edward O'Sullivan

[The] Napoleon of Guerilla Warfare
See Wingate, Orde

[The] Napoleon of Liverpool Finance
See Ranger, Morris

[The] Napoleon of Luzon
See MacArthur, Douglas

[The] Napoleon of Mexico
See Iturbide, Agusto

[The] Napoleon of Opera
See Spontini, Gasparo

[The] Napoleon of Oratory
See Gladstone, William Ewart

[The] Napoleon of Oratory
See Pitt, William [Earl of Chatham]

[The] Napoleon of Peace
See Louis Philippe

[The] Napoleon of Princeton
See McKinley, William

[The] Napoleon of Promoters
See Rickard, George Lewis

[The] Napoleon of Protection
See McKinley, William

[The] Napoleon of Slavery
See Calhoun, John Caldwell

[The] Napoleon of Temperance
See Dow, Neal

[The] Napoleon of the California Bar
See Delmas, Delphin Michael

[The] Napoleon of the Drama
See Bunn, Alfred

[The] Napoleon of the Drama
See Elliston, Robert William

[The] Napoleon of the Drama
See Frohman, Charles

[The] Napoleon of the East
See Mehemet [or Mohammed] Ali

[The] Napoleon of the Great Exodus
See Hirsch, Maurice de [or Moritz Von]

[The] Napoleon of the Indian Race
See Hinmaton-Yalaktit

[The] Napoleon of the North
See Comstock, Peter

[The] Napoleon of the Pacific
See Kamehameha I

[The] Napoleon of the Prize Ring
See Sayers, Tom

[The] Napoleon of the South
See Bingaman, Adam L.

[The] Napoleon of the Stump
See Polk, James Knox

[The] Napoleon of the Turf
See Bentinck, [Lord] George

[The] Napoleon of the Turf
See Johnson, William Ransom

[The] Napoleon of the West
See Burr, Aaron

[The] Napoleon of the West
See Russell, William Hepburn

Napoleon, Phil
See Napoli, Filippo

Napoleon, Prince
See Bonaparte, Napoleon Joseph Charles Paul

Napoleon, Teddy
See Napoleon, George

Napoleon the Little
See Bonaparte, Charles Louis Napoleon

Napoleon I
See Bonaparte, Napoleon

Napoleon II
See Bonaparte, Francois Charles Joseph [Duc de Reichstadt]

Napoleon III
See Bonaparte, Charles Louis Napoleon

Napoleon XIV
See Samuels, Jerry

Napoles, Jose
See Martequilla, Angel

Napoles Fajardo, Juan Cristobal 1829-1862 [CW]
Cuban poet and playwright
* [El] Cucalambe

Napoli, Filippo 1901- [WWJ]
American jazz musician
* Napoleon, Phil

Napoli, Vincent 20th c. [SFP]
Author
* Vincent

Napolitan, Louis 1895-1950 [BI]
Italian-American hairdresser
* Louis, M.

Napolitano, Dominick 20th c.
American underworld figure
* Napolitano, Sonny Black

Napolitano, Sonny Black
See Napolitano, Dominick

Nappey, Donald 1936- [DI]
British murderer
* [The] Black Panther
* Neilsen, Donald

Narain, Jai Prakash
See Narayan, Jayaprakash

Naramore, Gay Humboldt 19th c.
[DNA]
American poet
* Humboldt, Gay

Naranjo, Cholly
See Naranjo, Lazaro Ramon Gonzalo

Naranjo, Lazaro Ramon Gonzalo 1934-
[BE]
Cuban-born baseball player
* Naranjo, Cholly

Narayan, Jayaprakash 1902-1979 [CA]
Indian political leader and author
* J. P.
* Loknayak [The Peoples Hero]
* Narain, Jai Prakash

Narayan, R. K.
See Narayan, Rasipuram Krishnaswami

Narayan, Rasipuram Krishnaswami
1907?- [WYA]
Indian author
* Narayan, R. K.

Narbeth, Horace [BI]
British photographer
* Roye

Narcejac, Thomas
See Ayraud, Pierre

Narcissa
See Oldfield, Anna

Narcissa
See Temple, Elizabeth Lee

Narcisse, Louis H. 1921- [IBW]
American clergyman
* King Louis

[The] Narcissus of France
See Lamartine, Alphonse Marie Louis
de Prat de

Narell, Irena 1923- [CA]
Polish-born American author
* Penzik, Irena

Nares, Edward 1762-1848 [HFN, PA]
Author
* Cecil, William
* It Matters Not Who
* Thinks-I-To-Myself, Who?

Nares, Owen
See Ramsay, Owen Nares

Nares, Robert 1753-1829 [HPPN]
British philologist and librarian
* A. N.
* Investigator
* Mnemonicus
* N.
* [An] Oxonian Graduate
* Pericranium
* R. N.
* Wicliffe
* Wolscianus

Narino, Henry 1889-1965 [THR]
French-born actor and singer
* De Bray, Henry

Narjani, A. E.
See Bonaparte, Marie

Narleski, Cap
See Narleski, William Edward [Bill]

Narleski, William Edward [Bill]
1899-1964 [BE]
American baseball player
* Narleski, Cap

Narmer
See Menes, [or Mena]

[The] Narragansett
See Maynard, Horace

Narsanmor
See Sanchez Morales, Narciso

Narssius
See Van Naerssen, Jan

Narum, Buster
See Narum, Leslie Ferdinand

Narum, Leslie Ferdinand 1940- [BE,
SMG]
American baseball player
* Narum, Buster

Narvestad, Joerund 1894- [NAA]
Norwegian-born author and educator
* Jorgenson, Theodore

Nasby, [Rev.] Petroleum Vesuvius
See Locke, David Ross

Naschitz, Theodor 1859-1930 [JL]
Hungarian musician
* Nachez, Tivadar

Nascimento, Francisco Manoel do
1734-1819 [WBD]
Portuguese poet
* Elysio, Filinto

Naseli, Alberto 16th c. [BI, HPPN]
Italian actor
* Ganassa, Zan

Nash, B. A.
See Banash, Joseph

Nash, Beau
See Nash, Richard

Nash, Brian 1963?- [TI 11-26-84]
British musician
* Nasher

Nash, Chandler
See Hunt, Katherine Chandler

Nash, Charles 1942- [BB]
American basketball player
* Nash, Cotton

Nash, Clarence 1905?-1985 [WP 6-9-84]
Voice of cartoon character, Donald Duck
* Nash, Ducky

Nash, Cotton
See Nash, Charles

Nash, [Rev.] Daniel 1763-1836 [HPPN]
American clergyman
* Grant, Parson

Nash, Daniel
See Loader, William Reginald

Nash, Ducky
See Nash, Clarence

Nash, Eno
See Stevens, Austin N[eil]

Nash, Frank ?-1933 [BLB, HPPN]
American bank robber
* Nash, George
* Nash, Jelly

Nash, G. Murray 20th c. [EOP]
Author
* Black, Paul

Nash, George
See Nash, Frank

Nash, James Edwin 1945- [PB]
American baseball player
* Nash, Jumbo

Nash, Jelly
See Nash, Frank

Nash, John 1830-1901 [BMH]
British comedian
* [The] Laughing Blacksmith
* Nash, Jolly John

Nash, Jolly John
See Nash, John

Nash, Jumbo
See Nash, James Edwin

Nash, Kittie Delorme 1863-1932
[HPPN]
American director and producer
* Delorme, Kittie

Nash, Lemoine 1898-1969 [BWW]
American singer
* [The] Banjo Boy
* Nash, Lemon

Nash, Lemon
See Nash, Lemoine

Nash, Linell
See Smith, Linell Nash

Nash, Mary
See Ryan, Mary

Nash, N. Richard
See Nusbaum, Nathaniel Richard

Nash, Newlyn [joint pseudonym with Muriel Howe]
See Howe, Doris Kathleen

Nash, Newlyn [joint pseudonym with Doris Kathleen Howe]
See Howe, Muriel

Nash, [Frederic] Ogden 1902-1971 [HPPN]
American writer
* [The] Undisputed Master of Light Verse

Nash, Padder
See Sewart, Alan

Nash, Richard 1674-1762 [FF, HN, SN]
British fashion leader
* [Le] Grand Nash
* [The] King of Bath
* Nash, Beau

Nash, Simon
See Chapman, Raymond

Nash [or Nashe?], Thomas 1567-1601
[DEA, HPPN, NPS, PA, SN, WBD]
British author and playwright
* [The] Ape of Greene
* Capricio, Signior
* Confuter, Captain
* [The] Divel's Oratour
* [The] English Aretine
* Fouleweather, Adam
* [The] Gentleman Ragamuffin
* Glossomachicall, Thomas
* [The] Only Unicorne of the Muses
* Our English Rabelais
* Pasquil
* Pennilesse, Pierce
* Percevall, Plaine
* Scarlet, Thomas
* [The] Second Leviathan of Prose
* This Free Lance of Our Literature
* [The] True English Aretine
* [The] Very Baggage of New Writers
* Young Euphues
* Young Juvenal

Nash, Walter 1882-1968 [HPPN]
New Zealand statesman
* [The] Architect of New Zealand's Welfare State

Nash, Willard G.   [PA]
Author
* Dusty

Nash, William 19th c. [PI]
Irish poet
* Endymion

Nasher
See Nash, Brian

[The] Nashville Narcissus
See Lucas, Charles Fred

Nasi, Joseph [Duke of Naxos]
See Miguez, Joao

Nasmyth, Alexander 1758-1840 [WBD]
Scottish painter
* [The] Father of Scottish Landscape Art

Nasmyth, Patrick [or Peter?] 1787-1831
[DEP, FFF, SN]
Scottish painter
* [The] English Hobbema
* [The] Hobbema of Scotland
* [The] Scotch Hobbema

Naso, Macveius
See Napier, Macvey

Nason, Arthur Huntington 1877-?
[NAA]
American author and editor
* Van Dyke, Anthony

Nason, Leonard Hastings 1895- [WW]
Author
* Steamer

[The] Nassau Nugget
See Kazmaier, Richard W., Jr.

Nasser ben Hareth 6th c. [NPS]
* [The] Aesop of Arabia

Nasser, Gamal Abdel 1918-1970 [HPPN]
Egyptian president
* [The] Boss
* Camel Driver
* [The] Conquered Hero
* Egypt's Ataturk
* Egypt's Two-Faced Sphinx
* Man of Destiny
* Pharaoh In Shirtsleeves
* [El] Rayis
* [The] Strong Man of Egypt

Nasser's Poodle
See Sadat, Anwar

Nast, Conde 1874-1942 [HPPN]
American publisher
* [The] First of the Beautiful People

Nast, Elsa Ruth
See Watson, Jane Werner

Nast, Thomas 1840-1902 [HPPN]
American political caricaturist and illustrator
* Our Best Recruiting Sergeant

Nastase, Ilie 1949- [SA]
Rumanian tennis player
* [The] Bucharest Buffoon
* Intruder from the East
* Nastase, Nasty
* Rumanian Rhubarb

Nastase, Nasty
See Nastase, Ilie

Nasworthy, Frank
American skateboard designer
* Cadillac, Captain

Nat King Cole
See Coles, Nathaniel Adams

Nata Ye Yeithe
See Jones, Paul

Natale, Anthony 20th c. [BBH]
American horseshoe pitcher
* Natale, Ginger

Natale, Ginger
See Natale, Anthony

Natali, Agnes
See Heron, Agnes

Natali, Alfred Maxim 1915- [CA]
Italian-born American author
* Militello, Pietro

Natali, Fanny
See Heron, Fanny

Natchez
See Broonzy, William Lee Conley

Nate the Great
See Thurmond, Nate

Nathal, Mrs.   [FFF]
Entertainer
* Lester, Louise

Nathan
See Mendelssohn, Moses

Nathan, Annie
See Meyer, Annie Nathan

Nathan, Daniel 1905-1982 [CA, CC, EMD]
American author
* Dannay, Frederic
* Queen, Ellery [joint pseudonym with Manfred Lepofsky]
* Queen, Ellery, Jr. [joint pseudonym with Manfred Lepofsky]
* Ross, Barnaby [joint pseudonym with Manfred Lepofsky]

Nathan, G. J.
See Nathan, George Jean

Nathan, George Jean 1882-1958 [CAA, HPPN, LC]
American author and critic
* [The] Dean of Theatrical Criticism
* Hatteras, Owen [joint pseudonym with Henry Louis Mencken]
* Nathan, G. J.
* [The] Thersites of American Dramatic Critics

[The] Nathan Hale of the South
See Davis, Sam

Nathan, Isaac ?-1492 [PA]
Author
* Mordichai

Nathan, Max 1916-1968 [SC]
American actor
* Newmark, Stewart

Nathan, Vivian
See Firko, Vivia

[The] Natick Cobbler
See Colbath, Jeremiah Jones

[The] Natick Cobbler
See Wilson, Henry

Natick Eddie Casey
See Casey, Edward L.

Natick Eddie Mahan
See Mahan, Edward W.

Natif et Habitant du Pays de Virginie
See Beverley, Robert

[The] Nation Builder
See Weizmann, Chaim

Nation, Carry Amelia Moore Gloyd
1846-1911 [HPPN]
American temperance advocate
* [The] Advocate of Hatchetation
* [The] Lady With the Hatchet
* [The] Little Hatchet

Nation, William 18th c. [HPPN]
British clergyman
* [A] Lover of Truth and Peace

[The] National Ombudsman
See Nader, Ralph

[The] Nation's Chief Lawyer
See Mitchell, John Newton

[The] Nation's Hostess
See Madison, Dorothy Payne Todd

**[The] Nation's Most Redoubtable
Criminal Lawyer**
See Stryker, Lloyd Paul

[The] Nation's Number 1 Football Fan
See Nixon, Richard Milhous

[The] Nation's Top Child Star
See O'Brien, Angela Maxine

[A] Native American
See Hildreth, Richard

[A] Native Georgian
See Longstreet, Augustus Baldwin

[A] Native of America
See Parke, John

[A] Native of Boston
See Jackson, Jonathan

[A] Native of Boston
See Mather, Cotton

[A] Native of Boston
See Wheildon, William Willder

[A] Native of Craven
See Carr, William

[A] Native of Denmark
See Anderson, Andreas

[A] Native of New Brunswick
See Fisher, Peter

[A] Native of New England
See Leonard, Daniel

[A] Native of the Forest
See Apes, William

[A] Native of the South
See Cooper, Myles

[A] Native of the Town
See Ogden, James

[A] Native of Virginia
See McLeod, Daniel

Natonek, Hans 1892- [LAO]
Czech-born editor and author
* Nek

Natsume, Kinnosuke 1867-1916 [EWL,
TLC]
Japanese author
* Gudabutsu
* Natsume, Soseki

Natsume, Soseki
See Natsume, Kinnosuke

Natti, Mary Lee 1919- [CA, SFL]
American author
* Kingman, Lee

Natty
See Birnbaum, Nathan

[The] Natural
See Murphy, James [Jimmy]

[The] Natural
See Sandberg, Ryne

[The] Natural Force
See Swope, Herbert Bayard

[A] Naturalist
See Adams, Andrew Leith

[A] Naturalist
See Adams, Arthur

[A] Naturalist
See Broderip, William John

[A] Naturalist
See Colenso, William

[A] Naturalist
See Collingwood, Cuthbert

[A] Naturalist
See Garner, Robert

[A] Naturalist
See Hildreth, Samuel Prescott

[A] Naturalist
See Houghton, [Rev.] William

[The] Naturalist
See Jones, John Matthew

[A] Naturalist
See Knapp, John Leonard

[A] Naturalist
See Krasinski, Valerian

[The] Naturalist
See Lord, John Keast

[A] Naturalist
See Ober, Frederick Albion

[A] Naturalist
See Sclater, Philip Lutley

[The] Naturalist
See Strato [or Straton]

Nature Boy
See Ahbez, Eden

Nature Boy from Brooklyn
See Ahbez, Eden

Nature Boy Kirby
See Kirby, Roger

Nature's Darling
See Waller, Edmund

Nature's Glory
See Elizabeth I

Nature's Sternest Painter
See Crabbe, George

Nau, Jacques Jean David 1634-1671
[FFF]
French buccaneer
* L'Olonnois, Francois
* [The] Scourge of the Spaniards

Nau, John Antoine
See Torquet, Andre

[The] Naugatuck Nugget
See O'Shea, Frank Joseph

Naughton, Mortimer J. 1889?-1958
[BEW]
American actor
* Norton, Jack

Naughton, Owen 20th c. [WWL]
Irish author and editor
* O Neachtain, Eoghan

Nauni, Remigo 1521-1581 [PA]
Author
* Remi de Florence

Nauta, Renicus Dowe 1869-? [HPPN]
Dutch educator and author
* Navita

Nauticus
See Clowes, [Sir] William Laird

Nauticus
See Seaman, [Sir] Owen

Nauticus
See Waltari, Mika [Toimi]

Nauticus, Penzance
See Rosewall, James

Nava, Franz
See Rimbault, Edward Francis

Nava, Sandy
See Nava, Vincent P.

Nava, Vincent P. 1850-1906 [BE]
American baseball player
* Nava, Sandy

Navajo Sam
See Dittenhoefer, Sam

[A] Naval Officer
See Collingridge, Augustus

[A] Naval Officer
See Fisher, William

[A] Naval Peer
See Plunkett, Edward [16th Baron
Dunsany]

Naval Person [code name used during
World War II]
See Churchill, Winston Spencer

Navarchus [joint pseudonym with James Woods]
See Vaux, Patrick

Navarchus [joint pseudonym with Patrick Vaux]
See Woods, James

[The] **Navarrais**
See Charles II

Navarre, Andre
See Wright, Alexander

[The] **Navarre of the American Revolution**
See Butler, Thomas

Navarro, Fats
See Navarro, Theodore

Navarro, Joaquin 1873-1936 [GS]
Spanish bullfighter
* Quinito

Navarro, Julio Ventura 1936- [BE, SMG]
Puerto Rican-born baseball player
* Navarro, Whiplash

Navarro, Osvaldo 1893-1954 [WEC]
Brazilian cartoonist
* Osvaldo

Navarro, Ruben 20th c. [AES]
Argentinian soccer player
* [The] Hatchet

Navarro, Theodore 1923-1950 [DAM, EJ, PMJ]
American jazz musician
* Navarro, Fats

Navarro, Whiplash
See Navarro, Julio Ventura

Navarro Baldeweg, Juan 1939- [BI]
Spanish architect
* Enebe, Hans

Navarrus
See Azpeleneta, Martimius ab

Navasky, Victor S. 1932- [CA]
American author and editor
* Hirsch, William Randolph [joint pseudonym with Marvin Kitman and R. Lingeman]

Navcom, Mr.
See Lear, William Powell

[The] **Navigator**
See Henry [or Don Henrique]

Navin, Frank
American baseball team owner
* [The] Mandarin

Navita
See Nauta, Renicus Dowe

Navratilova, Martina 1957?- [NW 9-6-82]
Czech-born tennis player
* [The] Great Wide Hope
* [The] Iron Maiden
* Tini Linguini

[The] **Navvy Poet**
See McGill, Patrick

Navy Bill Ingram
See Ingram, Jonas Howard

[The] **Navy Hercules**
See Hajnos, John

Navy's Destroyer
See Bellino, Joseph [Joe]

Nawaz, Malik Sarfraz 1948- [DC]
Pakistani-born cricketer
* Nawaz, Saf

Nawaz, Saf
See Nawaz, Malik Sarfraz

Nawe, Izabella
See Binek, Izabella

Nawrot, Harriet 1903-1975 [SC]
American actress and roller skater
* McGuirk, Harriet

Naya, Koki 1940-
Japanese sumo wrestler
* Taiho [Great Bird]

Nayar, S.
See Doraiswajy, Trivandrum Krishna Iyer

Naylor, Eliot
See Frankau, Pamela

Naylor, James 1617?-1660
British clergyman
* [The] Incarnation of Christ

Naylor, Jerry 1939- [ECM]
American country-western performer
* Garrard, Jackie

Naylor, John 1920- [CA]
British astrologer and author
* Orion

Naylor, Roleine Cecil 1892-1966 [BE]
American baseball player
* Naylor, Rollie

Naylor, Rollie
See Naylor, Roleine Cecil

Naylor, [Rev.] William 19th c.
British clergyman
* Castigator

Nayudu, Cottari Kanakayia 1895-1967 [EC]
Indian cricketer
* [The] Indian Bradman

Nazarena, [Sister]
See Grotta, Julia

Nazareth, Peter 1940- [CA]
Ugandan-born author
* Wako, Mdogo

Nazarian, Nikki
See Nichols, Cecilia Fawn

[The] **Nazarite**
See Parr, Samuel

[The] **Nazi Hunter**
See Friedman, Toviah

[The] **Nazim of Necromantic Nudity**
See Goldbogen [or Goldenborgen], Avrom Hirsch

Nazimova, Alla
See Mazimoff, Alla

Nazzaro
See Nazzaro, Erminio

Nazzaro, Erminio 1912- [BMH]
Italian-born impressionist
* Nazzaro

NCA, Mr.
See Callaghan, Dennis

Ndugu
See Chancler, Leon

Neafie
See Purple, Edwin R.

Neagle, Anna
See Robertson, Marjorie

Neagu, Paul 1938- [CAR]
British sculptor
* Belmood, Husny
* Honeysuckle, Philip
* Larsocchi, Eduard
* Paidola, Anton

Neal, Adeline Phyllis 1894- [WW]
Author
* Grey, A. F.

Neal, Alice Bradley
See Bradley, Emily

Neal, Ebberle 1930-
American basketball player
* Neal, Jim

Neal, Ed
See Neal, William

Neal, Gavin
See Tubb, Edwin Charles

Neal, Harry
See Bixby, Jerome Lewis

Neal, Hilary
See Norton, Olive Marion [Claydon]

Neal, James [FFF]
British author
* Nemesis

Neal, James T[homas] 1936- [CA]
American geologist and author
* James, Thomas N.

Neal, Jennie [FFF]
Entertainer
* Garrison, Maude

Neal, Jim
See Neal, Ebberle

Neal, John 1793-1876 [DEL, DLE1, DNNF, HPPN, PA]
American author
* Adams, Will
* Allen, Paul
* J. N.
* O'Cataract, Jehu
* O'Cataract, John

Neal, John (cont.)
* Somebody, M. D. C.
* X. Y. Z.

Neal, Offa
See Neal, Theophilus Fountain

Neal, Patricia 20th c. [HPPN]
American actress
* Flagg, Fannie

Neal, Patricia
See Neal, Patsy Louise

Neal, Patsy Louise 1926- [HPPN]
American actress
* Neal, Patricia

Neal, [Sir] Paul [PA]
Author
* Sidrophel

Neal, Theophilus Fountain 1876-1950
[BE]
American baseball player
* Neal, Offa

Neal, William 20th c. [EF]
American football player
* Neal, Ed

Neale, Alfred Earle 1891-1973 [BE, BI,
FB]
American football player and coach
* Neale, Greasy

Neale, Alice Clay 1828-1863 [PA]
Author
* Alice

Neale, C. Goodliffe 20th c. [BS]
British magazine publisher
* Goodliffe the Magician

Neale, Erskine 1805-? [PA]
Author
* [A] Coroner's Clerk
* [A] Country Curate
* [A] Gaol Chaplain

Neale, Flora
See McLeod, Georgie A.

Neale, Greasy
See Neale, Alfred Earle

Neale, J. E.
See Neale, [Sir] John Ernest

Neale, [Sir] John Ernest 1890- [LC]
British author and educator
* Neale, J. E.

Neale, John Mason 1818-1866 [HPPN]
British hymn writer
* J. M. N.

Neale, Nettie
See Heath, Maggie E.

Neander
See Dryden, John

Neander, Johann August Wilhelm
See Mendel, David

[The] Neapolitan
See Tischbein, Johann Heinrich
Wilhelm

Nearing, Elizabeth [Custer] 1898?-
[ANT, CC]
American author
* MacVeigh, Sue

Nearing, John Scott 1912-1976 [SAT]
American author
* Scott, John

Nearing, Penny
See Munn, Meryl Lucile

Neave, A. H.
See Headley-Neave, Alice

Neaves, Charles 1800-1876 [HPPN]
Scottish poet
* [An] Old Contributor to Maga

Nebel, John 1912-1978 [HPPN]
American radio personality
* Nebel, Long John

Nebel, Long John
See Nebel, John

[Der] Nebelmeister
See Rosemeyer, Bernd

[The] Nebraska Wildcat
See Hudkins, Ace

Nebrensky, Alex
See Cooper, Parley J[oseph]

Nebrija [or Lebrija], Elio Antonio de
See Martinez de Jarava, Elio Antonio

Nebylitsyn, Vladimir 1930?-1972
[HPPN]
Russian psychologist and author
* Dmitrievich

[A] Necessitarian
See Allen, John

Neckam [or Necham], Alexander
1157-1217 [WBD]
British scholar
* Nequam

Necker, Jacques [or James] 1732-1804
[HN, SN]
French statesman and financier
* [A] Machiavelli
* [The] Virtuous Genevese

Necker, Olivier 1440?-1484 [WBD]
Adviser to King Louis XI of France
* Olivier le Dain [or le Daim]
* Olivier le Diable

Neckham [or Necham], Alexander
1157-1215 [HPPN]
British scholar
* Nequam [Wicked]

Ned of the Hills
See Drea, E. V.

Ned the Chimney-Sweeper
See Victor Amadeus II

Nederveen Hendriks, Wietske 20th c.
[IAW]
Dutch author and poet
* Wytske

Nedlo the Gypsy Violinist
See Olden, Charles

Nee, Brett de Bary 1943- [CA]
American author
* De Bary, Brett

Needham, David 1951- [RBE]
British boxer
* [The] Artful Dodger

Needham, Deerfoot
See Needham, Thomas J.

Needham, Marchamont 1620-1678 [NPS,
SN]
British author
* Britannicus
* [The] Cobbett of His Day
* Commonwealth Didapper
* [The] Goliath of the Philistines
* [The] Son of Belial

Needham, Marchmont
See Quincy, Josiah

Needham, T. H.
See Johnson, Thomas Burgeland

Needham, Thomas J. 1879-1926 [BE]
Irish-born American baseball player
* Needham, Deerfoot

Neef, Elton T.
See Fanthorpe, R[obert] Lionel

Neek, Hugh
See Olden, Charles

Neels, Marc 1922- [WECO]
Flemish cartoonist
* Sleen, Marc

Neely, Bob 1953- [SMG]
Canadian-born hockey player
* Neely, Waldo

Neely, Waldo
See Neely, Bob

[The] Neem
See Nemo, Henry

Neeper, Carolyn 1937- [CA]
American author
* Neeper, Cary

Neeper, Cary
See Neeper, Carolyn

Neera
See Radius, Anna [Zuccari]

Neerskov, Hans Kristian 1932- [CA]
Danish author and clergyman
* Kristian, Hans

Neethling, J. S.
See Neethling, Jacobus Stephanus

Neethling, Jacobus Stephanus 20th c.
[IAW]
South African author
* Neethling, J. S.
* Neethling, Kobus

Neethling, Kobus
See Neethling, Jacobus Stephanus

Neeves, Thyrza 1884- [THR]
British actress
* Norman, Thyrza

Nef, Evelyn Stefansson 1913- [CA]
American geographer and author
* Stefansson, Evelyn

Nefe, Gaspard 1514-1580 [PA]
Author
* Noevius

Neff, Felix 1798-1829 [DNNF, FFF, HN]
Swiss missionary
* [The] Apostle of the Alps

Neff, Hildegarde
See Knef, Hildegard

[The] Negotiator of the Gadsden Purchase
See Gadsden, James

Negri, Pola
See Chalupec, Apolonia

Negri, Red
See Negri, Warren

Negri, Warren 20th c. [EF]
American football player
* Negri, Red

[El] Negro
See Chamorro Rapoccioli, Fernando

[El] Negro
See Nino, Pedro Alonso

[The] Negro June Allyson
See Wallace, Ruby Ann

[The] Negro Moses
See Tubman, Harriet Araminta Ross Davis

[The] Negro Sappho
See Wheatley, Phillis

Negron Munoz, Mercedes 1895-1973 [CW]
Cuban poet
* Lair, Clara

Negus
See Theodore II

Negus Negusti [King of Kings]
See Mariem, Sahala

Nehand, L. O.
See Condon, [Dr.] John Francis

Nehemiah, Renaldo
American track and field athlete
* Nehemiah, Skeets

Nehemiah, Skeets
See Nehemiah, Renaldo

Nehru, Jawaharlal 1889-1964
Indian Nationalist leader
* [The] Fighter for Independence

Neidhart Fuchs [Neidhart the Fox]
See Neidhart von Reuenthal

Neidhart von Reuenthal 13th c. [WBD]
Bavarian knight and poet
* Neidhart Fuchs [Neidhart the Fox]

Neighbors, Cecil F. 1880-1964 [BE]
American baseball player
* Neighbors, Cy

Neighbors, Cy
See Neighbors, Cecil F.

Neil, [Judge] Henry 1863-? [NAA]
American author
* Everett, Marshall

Neil, Rose
See Harwood, Isabella

[The] Neil Simon of Off-Off Broadway
See Eyen, Tom

Neilan, Marshall 20th c.
Film director
* Neilan, Mickey

Neilan, Mickey
See Neilan, Marshall

Neilhams, Terence 1940- [FC]
British actor and singer
* Faith, Adam

Neill, A. S.
See Neill, Alexander Sutherland

Neill, Alexander Sutherland 1883-1973
[LC]
British educator and author
* Neill, A. S.

Neill, Beau
See Neill, Thomas Hewson

Neill, Beverly Louise 1929- [FC, IPA, ITA]
American actress
* Blake, Amanda

Neill, Jay Wesley 1965?- [TI 12-31-84]
American suspected of robbery and murder
* [The] Geronimo Killer

Neill, Patrick 1776-1851 [SN]
Scottish naturalist
* [The] Lean Man

Neill, Roy William
See De Gostrie, Roland

Neill, Thomas Hewson 1826-1885 [FFF]
American soldier
* Neill, Beau

Neilly, Senor
See Neily, Harry

Neilsen, Donald
See Nappey, Donald

Neilson, Cora
See Carver, Mrs. J. H.

Neilson, Francis
See Butters, Francis

Neilson, Helen
See Harris, Helen Potts

Neilson, James Anthony 1940- [CEI, FHE, HK]
Canadian-born hockey player
* [The] Chief

Neilson, Lilian Adelaide
See Brown, Elizabeth Ann

Neilson, Marguerite
See Tompkins, Julia [Marguerite Hunter Manchee]

Neilson, Perlita
See Sowden, Margaret

Neilson, Vernon
See Clarke, Percy A.

Neilson-Terry, Dennis
See Terry, Dennis

Neilson-Terry, Hazel 1918-1974 [SC, THR]
British actress
* Terry, Hazel

Neilson-Terry, Phyllis
See Terry, Phyllis

Neily, Harry 1881-? [HPPN]
American sporting editor
* Neilly, Senor
* [The] Skillful Neily [El Neily Manoso]

Neipris, Janet
See Wille, Janet Neipris

Neish, Duncan
See Allan, F. Carney

Neiswanger, Marion 1879-? [THR]
American playwright
* Fairfax, Marion

Neitz, Alvin James ?-1952 [HPPN]
American producer
* James, Alan

Nek
See Natonek, Hans

Nekola, Bots
See Nekola, Francis Joseph

Nekola, Francis Joseph 1907- [BE]
American baseball player
* Nekola, Bots

Nelhams, Terry 1942?-
British singer, actor, entrepeneur
* Faith, Adam

Nelken, Carmen 1902-1966 [HPPN]
American actress
* Donato, Magda

Nell of Old Drury
See Symcott, Margaret

Nellie
See Marsh, E.

Nelly
See Foe, Daniel

Nelms, Henning   [WW]
Author
* Talbot, Hake

Nelson, Abbott Willie
See Nelson, Willie

Nelson, Albert 1923- [BWW]
American singer
* King, Albert

Nelson, Albert Francis
See Horazdovsky, Albert W.

Nelson, Alec
See Aveling, Edward Bibbins

Nelson, Andrew [Andy] 20th c. [BE]
American baseball player
* Nelson, Peaches

Nelson, Babe
See Nelson, Robert Sidney [Bob]

Nelson, Baby Face
See Gillis, Lester

Nelson, Barry
See Nielson, Robert

Nelson, Barry
See Thomas, Reginald George

Nelson, Battling
See Nelson, Oscar Matthew

Nelson, Benjamin Earl 1938- [PRS, RO1]
American singer and songwriter
* King, Ben E.

Nelson, Berky
See Nelson, H. Viscount, Jr.

Nelson, Big Eye
See Nelson, Louis Delisle

Nelson, Big George
See Gillis, Lester

Nelson, Bob 1944- [BWW]
American singer
* Nelson, Chicago Bob

Nelson, Bull
See Nelson, William

Nelson, Byron 1912- [BWG, EG]
American golfer
* Lord Byron
* [The] Mechanical Man

Nelson, Charles A. 19th c. [FFF]
American journalist
* Chelsea

Nelson, Chicago Bob
See Nelson, Bob

Nelson, Country Willie
See Nelson, Willie

Nelson, Dad
See Nelson, William

Nelson, Darrin 20th c. [SI 8-30-82]
American football player
* Disco Darrin

Nelson, Dave
See Nelson, Davidson C.

Nelson, Davidson C. 1905-1946 [WWJ]
American jazz musician
* Nelson, Dave

Nelson, Dixie Kay 1933- [ITA, SW]
American actress
* Nelson, Lori

Nelson, Doc
See Nelson, George

Nelson, Dolorez Alexandria 1929-
[HPPN]
American jazz musician
* Alexandria, Lorez

Nelson, Earl 20th c. [BWW]
American musician
* Nelson, Louisiana Earl

Nelson, Earle Leonard 1897-1928 [DI, HPPN]
American murderer
* [The] Dark Stranger
* [The] Gorilla Murderer
* Wilson, Roger

Nelson, Eddie 1894-1940 [SC]
American actor
* Nelson, Sunkist

Nelson, [George] Emmett 1905-1967
[BE]
American baseball player
* Nelson, Ramrod

Nelson, Emmett 20th c. [BWW]
American musician
* Rush, Bobby

Nelson, Eric Hilliard 1940-1986 [DAM, IPA, ITA]
American singer and actor
* Nelson, Ricky

Nelson, Ethel Florence 1913?- [AW, CA]
Canadian-born author
* Nelson, Nina

Nelson, Evelyn 1918?- [PMJ]
American singer
* Baker, Bonnie
* Baker, Wee Bonnie

Nelson, Frankie
See Valerio, Michael

Nelson, Gene
See Berg, Leander

Nelson, George 20th c. [NW 4-23-84, TI 5-21-84]
American astronaut
* Nelson, Pinky

Nelson, George 20th c. [BBH]
American collegiate athletic trainer
* Nelson, Doc

Nelson, George
See Gillis, Lester

Nelson, Gertrude
See Bobin, John William [Jack]

Nelson, Glenn Richard 1924- [BE]
American baseball player
* Nelson, Rocky

Nelson, H. Viscount, Jr. 1939- [BA]
American educator and author
* Nelson, Berky

Nelson, Harold 1880-1965 [SC]
American actor and singer
* Reed, Gus

Nelson, Harriet Hilliard
See Snyder, Peggy Lou

Nelson, Harrison 1925?- [BWW]
American singer
* Harris, Peppermint

Nelson, Henry 18th c. [PI]
Irish poet
* H. N.

Nelson, Horace 1916?- [MY]
American jazz musician
* Nelson, Steady

Nelson, Horatio 1758-1805 [DNNS, FFF, HN]
British naval officer
* [The] Duke of Thunder
* [The] Embodiment of Sea Power
* [The] Hero of a Hundred Fights
* [The] Hero of the Nile
* [The] Hero of Trafalger

Nelson, Ira 1913?-1978 [FIR]
American country-western performer
* Nelson, Pop

Nelson, Iromeio 1902-1974 [BWW]
American singer
* Nelson, Romeo

Nelson, Jack
See Nelson, Jackson W.

Nelson, Jack Alton 1927-1978 [SMG]
American football coach
* Nelson, Jocko

Nelson, Jackson W. 1849-1910 [AS, BE]
American baseball player
* Nelson, Jack

Nelson, Jane
See Wright, M. Jane

Nelson, Jimmie
See Gillis, Lester

Nelson, Jimmy 1928- [HPPN]
American entertainer
* [The] Television Ventrioloquist

Nelson, Jimmy
See Irvin, Monford Merrill

Nelson, Jocko
See Nelson, Jack Alton

Nelson, Joseph
See Mitchell, Isaac

Nelson, Knute 1843-1923 [HPPN]
American politician
* [The] Little Corporal
* [The] Little Giant of Alexandria
* [The] Little Norwegian

Nelson, [Hugh] Lawrence 1907- [WW]
Author
* Trent, Peter

Nelson, Line Drive
See Nelson, Lynn Bernard

Nelson, Lori
See Nelson, Dixie Kay

Nelson, Louis Delisle 1885-1949 [DAM, EJ, WWJ]
American jazz musician
* DeLisle, Louis
* Nelson, Big Eye

Nelson, Louisiana Earl
See Nelson, Earl

Nelson, Lyle 20th c.
American biathlete
* Nelson, Vile Lyle

Nelson, Lynn Bernard 1905-1955 [BE]
American baseball player
* Nelson, Line Drive

Nelson, Marguerite
See Floren, Lee

Nelson, Michael Harrington 1921- [CA]
British author, television scriptwriter, interviewer
* Stratton, Henry

Nelson, Nina
See Nelson, Ethel Florence

Nelson, Oscar Matthew Battling 1882-1954 [HPPN]
Danish-American boxer
* [The] Battler
* [The] Durable Dane
* Nelson, Battling

Nelson, Oswald George 1907-1975 [CA, DAM, IPA]
American actor, producer, director
* Nelson, Ozzie

Nelson, Ozzie
See Nelson, Oswald George

Nelson, Papoose
See Nelson, Walter

Nelson, Peaches
See Nelson, Andrew [Andy]

Nelson, Peter
See Solow, Martin

Nelson, Pinky
See Nelson, George

Nelson, Pop
See Nelson, Ira

Nelson, Prince Roger 1958- [NW 4-29-84, TI 8-6-84]
American musician, singer, songwriter
* His Royal Badness
* [The] Kid
* Prince
* Skipper
* Starr, Jamie

Nelson, R. F.
See Nelson, Radell Faraday

Nelson, Radell Faraday 1931- [CA, ESF]
American author
* Elson, R. N.
* Nelson, R. F.
* Nelson, Ray

Nelson, Ramrod
See Nelson, [George] Emmett

Nelson, Ray[mond Nelson]
See Kellogg, Raymond N.

Nelson, Ray
See Nelson, Radell Faraday

Nelson, Red
See Horazdovsky, Albert W.

Nelson, Ricky
See Nelson, Eric Hilliard

Nelson, Robert Sidney [Bob] 1936- [BE]
American baseball player
* Nelson, Babe
* Nelson, Tex

Nelson, Rocky
See Nelson, Glenn Richard

Nelson, Roger Eugene 1944- [BE, PB, SMG]
American baseball player
* Nelson, Spider

Nelson, Romeo
See Nelson, Iromeio

Nelson, Roy
See Nelson-Smith, Alan Roy Vere

Nelson, Ruth 1914- [CA]
American educator and author
* McHugh, Ruth Nelson

Nelson, Sandy
See Egnatzik, Joseph

Nelson, Spider
See Nelson, Roger Eugene

Nelson, Steady
See Nelson, Horace

Nelson, Steve
See Bobin, John William [Jack]

Nelson, Steve
See Mesaros, Stjepan

Nelson, Sunkist
See Nelson, Eddie

Nelson, T. 20th c. [MBF]
British author
* Brown, Duncan

Nelson, Tex
See Nelson, Robert Sidney [Bob]

Nelson, Theophila 18th c. [HPPN]
British author
* [A] Young Gentlewoman

Nelson, Victor
See Bobin, John William [Jack]

Nelson, Vile Lyle
See Nelson, Lyle

Nelson, Virginia
See Tallent, Virginia

Nelson, Walter 20th c. [RO2]
American musician
* Nelson, Papoose

Nelson, William 1824-1862 [HPPN]
American army officer
* Nelson, Bull
* Nelson, Dad

Nelson, Willie 1933- [FCW, HPPN]
American singer and songwriter
* [The] King of Country Music
* Nelson, Abbott Willie
* Nelson, Country Willie

Nelson-Smith, Alan Roy Vere 1905- [WWL]
British author
* Nelson, Roy

Nemes, Endre
See Nagel, Endre

Nemesis?
See Francis, [Sir] Philip

Nemesis
See Harris, [Sir] Charles Alexander

Nemesis
See Neal, James

Nemesis
See Robbins, Alfred Farthing

Nemesis
See Watre, Antony

[The] Nemesis of Gamblers
See Jerome, William Travers

[The] Nemesis of Kinky Hair
See Walker, Sarah Breedlove

[The] Nemesis of Maria Monk
See Stone, William Leete

Nemeth, Janos 20th c. [BBH]
Hungarian-born water polo player
* Nemeth, Jim

Nemeth, Jim
See Nemeth, Janos

Nemiro, Beverly Anderson 1925- [CA]
American author
* Anderson, Beverly M.

Nemo
See Adams, Henry Gardiner

Nemo
See Browne, Hablot Knight

Nemo
See Coffin, Roland Folger

Nemo
See Coleman, Patrick James

Nemo
See Fox, George Wilder

Nemo
See Gordon, Francis S.

Nemo
See Harvey, Moses

Nemo
See Pelly, Gerald Conn

Nemo, Henry 1914- [PMJ]
American composer
* [The] Neem

Nemo, Omen
See Rehm, Warren S.

Nenadovic, Matija 1777-1854 [WBD]
Serbian clergyman and patriot
* Prota Matija

Nengudi, Senga
See Irons, Sue

Nennius 8th c. [DEP]
Welsh historian
* [The] British Hector

Nentwich, Max 1868-? [LAO]
German author and playwright
* Muensterberg, Maximilian

[The] Neologist
See Sands, Robert Charles

Neos Philopator [New Philopator]
See Ptolemy VII

[The] Nephew of an East India Director
See Bosanquet, Augustus

[The] Nephew of My Uncle
See Sweeney, Peter Barr

Nephew of the Almighty
See Brothers, Richard

Nepomuk
See Kiellman-Goeranson, [Rev.] Julius
Axel

Neptune
See Taylor, Benjamin Ogle

Neptune, Father
See Cavill, Dick

Neptunus
See Bruce, Benjamin

Nepveu, Andre 1881-1959 [WBD]
French author
* Durtain, Luc

Nepveu [or Neveu], Pierre ?-1542?
[WBD]
French architect
* Trinqueau

Nequam [Wicked]
See Neckham [or Necham], Alexander

Neri Tanfucio
See Fucini, Renato

Nericault, Philippe 1680-1754 [WBD]
French playwright
* Destouches, Philippe

Nerina, Nadia
See Judd, Nadine

Nero
See Bonaparte, Charles Louis Napoleon

Nero [Claudius Caesar Drusus Germanicus]
See Domitius Ahenobarbus, Lucius

[A] Nero
See Leclerc du Tremblay, Francois

[The] Nero of Germany
See Wenceslaus [or Wenceslas]

[The] Nero of Our Times
See Nixon, Richard Milhous

[The] Nero of Persia
See Sefi [or Sophi]

[The] Nero of the North
See Christian II

Nero, Paul
See Polnarioff, Kurt

Nero, Peter
See Nierow, Bernard

Nero Caesar, Tiberius Claudius ?-37?
[DEP, FFF, SN]
Roman emperor
* [The] Imperial Machiavelli
* [The] Prince of Hypocrites
* Tiberius

Nerone, Giuseppe ?-1925? [BLB, PHM]
American underworld figure
* [The] Cavalier
* Nerone, Joseph
* Pavia, Joe
* Spano, Tony

Nerone, Joseph
See Nerone, Giuseppe

Nerra
See Fulk III

Nerses 310?-374 [WBD]
Patriarch of Armenia
* [The] Great

Nerses 1098-1173 [WBD]
Patriarch of Armenia
* [The] Gracious

Neruda, Pablo
See Reyes Basualto, [Ricardo Eliezer]
Neftali

Nerval, Gaston
See Diez de Medina, Raul

Nerval, Gerard de
See Labrunie, Gerard

Nervo, Jimmy
See Holloway, James

[The] Nervous Greek
See Skizas, Lou[is Peter]

Nervy Nick Nichols
See Nichols, Charles Augustus

Nerys
See Prys Williams, Nerys Mair Sioned

Nesbit, Edith 1858-1924 [FFF, LC, TC]
British author and poet
* Bland, Fabian [joint pseudonym with
Hubert Bland]
* Carisbrooke

Nesbit, Evelyn
See Thaw, Evelyn Nesbit

Nesbit, Troy
See Folsom, Franklin [Brewster]

Nesbitt, Harry
See Horowitz, Harry

Nesbitt, Miriam Anne
See Skancke, Miriam Anne

Neshamith, Sara
See Dushnitzky-Shner, Sara

Nesmith, Robert I. 1891-1972 [CA]
American author
* Clarke, [Captain] Jafah

Nesmy, Jean
See Surchamp, Henry

Ness, Richard Derby [PA]
Author
* W. D.

Nessmuk
See Sears, George W.

Nester, L. O.
See Condon, [Dr.] John Francis

Nestle, John Francis 1912- [CA, IAW]
British author
* Falcon

Nestor 1056?-1114? [DNNS, HN, RH]
Russian historian and monk
* [The] Father of Russian History

Nestor
See Steele, [Sir] Richard

Nestor
See Wren, [Sir] Christopher

[The] Nestor Girl
See Rhodes, Billie

[The] Nestor of America
See Franklin, Ben[jamin]

[The] Nestor of American Botany
See Darlington, William

[The] Nestor of American Science
See Mitchell, Samuel Latham

[The] Nestor of American Science
See Silliman, Benjamin

[The] Nestor of Canadian Politicians
See Baldwin, Robert

[The] Nestor of Congregationalism
See Bacon, Leonard

[The] Nestor of English Authors
See Rogers, Samuel

[The] Nestor of English Scholarship
See Kennedy, Benjamin Hall

[The] Nestor of Europe
See Leopold I

[The] Nestor of German Philosophy
See Platner, Ernst

[The] Nestor of German Poesy
See Tiedge, Christoph August

[The] Nestor of German Sculptors
See Dannecker, John Heinrich

[The] Nestor of Golf
See Morris, Tom

[The] Nestor of Modern Italian Authors
See Maffei, Andrea

[The] Nestor of the Chemical Revolution
See Black, James

[The] Nestor of the Confederacy
See Stephens, Alexander Hamilton

[The] Nestor of the German American Journalists
See Preetorius, Emil

[The] Nestor of the German Book Trade
See Frommann, Friedrich Johannes

[The] Nestor of the Hampden County Bar
See Bates, William Gelston

[The] Nestor of the House of Commons
See Ellice, Edward

[The] Nestor of the Methodist Conference in India
See Bowen, George

[The] Nestor of the Mississippi Bar
See Campbell, Josiah Adams Patterson

[The] Nestor of the Patriots
See Hawley, Joseph

[The] Nestor of the Press
See Dana, Charles Anderson

[The] Nestor of the Rocky Mountains
See Carson, Christopher

Netamuxwe
See Bock, William Sauts

Netcher, Roszika Dolly 1892-1970　[BI]
American dancer
* Dolly, Rosie

Neteru, Atum
See Neteru-Crockett, Ulysses-Atum

Neteru-Crockett, Ulysses-Atum 1938-
[BA]
American educator and author
* Neteru, Atum

Netherclift, Beryl Constance 1911-
[IAW]
British author
* Mascall, Margery D.

Nethercott, Henrietta 19th c.　[PI]
Irish poet
* Henrietta

Neto, Edvaldo 20th c.　[AES]
Brazilian soccer player
* Vava

Nettell, Richard [Geoffrey] 1907-　[CAP, WD]
British author
* Kenneggy, Richard

Netterville, Luke
See O'Grady, Standish James

Nettl, John Peter 1926-1968　[CAP]
German-born author
* Norwood, Paul

Nettle, H.
See Jackson, William

Nettles, Bonnie Lu 20th c.　[EOP]
American religious cult leader
* Dale
* Peep
* Pooh
* Poop
* Wink

Neubauer, William Arthur 1916-　[CA]
American author
* Arthur, William
* Bennett, Christine
* Bligh, Norman
* Carter, Ralph
* Garrison, Joan
* Hathaway, Jan
* Marsh, Rebecca
* Newcomb, Norma
* Semple, Gordon

Neuber, Karoline Weissenborn 1697-1760
[HPPN]
German actress
* [Die] Neuberin

Neuberger, Sigmund 1872-1911　[BMH]
German-born magician and illusionist
* [The] Great Lafayette

[Die] Neuberin
See Neuber, Karoline Weissenborn

Neuburg, Victor [Benjamin] 1883-1940
[EOP]
British poet and editor
* Alfricobas
* Benjie
* Broyle, M.
* Byrde, Richard
* Crayne, Christopher
* Edwardes, Lawrence
* French, Arthur
* Pentreath, Paul
* Pyne, Nicholas
* Stevens, Harold
* Tarn, Shirley
* Vickybird
* Vincam, Frater Omnia
* White, Rold

Neuer, John S. 1880-?　[BE]
American baseball player
* Neuer, Tacks

Neuer, Tacks
See Neuer, John S.

Neuffer, Irene LaBorde 1919-　[CA]
American author
* LaBorde, Rene

Neumaier, Horst R. 1939-　[OP]
German opera singer
* Laubenthal Horst R.

Neuman, Butch
See Neuman, Paul William

Neuman, Paul William ?-1964　[BBH]
American basketball player and coach
* Neuman, Butch

Neumann, Ferenc 1878-1952　[JL, MWD]
Hungarian playwright and director
* Companion in Exile
* Gay Old Man
* Hermit of the Plaza Hotel
* Journeyman Playwright
* Molnar, Ferenc

Neumann, Fred A.
See Hamilton, F. Anthony

Neumann, Karl Friedrich
See Bamberger, Karl Friedrich

Neumann, Vera 1910-　[WFA]
American designer
* Vera

Neustadt, Bert
See Neustadt, Bertha Cummings

Neustadt, Bertha Cummings 1921?-1984
[WP 5-9-84]
American educator
* Neustadt, Bert

Neustadtl, Hermine
See Stich, Hermine Neustadtl

Neutron Jack Welch
See Welch, John

Neutze, Hanns Lothar 1930-1967
[HPPN]
American actor
* Lothar, Hanns

Neuville, Auguste
See Dubourg, Felix

Neuwert
See Nowaczynski, Adolf

[The] Nevada Commoner
See Jones, John Percival

Nevada, Emma
See Wixom, Emma

Nevada Jack Rose
See Rose, Jack

Nevada's Premier Road Agent
See Sharp, Milton

Nevads's Master Pimp
See Conforte, Joseph

Nevanlinna, Sinikka Sisko 1917-　[IAW]
Finnish author and poet
* Kallio, Sinikka
* Kallio-Visapaa, Sinikka

Nevaro
See Willkomm, Otto

Neve, Philip 18th c.　[HPPN]
British barrister
* One of the Magistrates of the Public Office in Great Marlborough

Nevelson, William 1885-1931　[HPPN]
American actor
* Murphy, William

Never Fail Burns
See Burns, William John

Nevers, Big Dog
See Nevers, Ernest A. [Ernie]

Nevers, C. O.
See Converse, Charles Crozat

Nevers, Ernest A. [Ernie] 1902-
[HPPN]
American football player
* Nevers, Big Dog

Neves, Tancredo 1911?- [TI 1-28-85]
Brazilian president
* [The] Great Conciliator

Nevetz
See Cox, Stephen Bernard

Neville, Anna
See Fairburn, Eleanor

Neville, Anne
See Farleigh, Elsie

Neville, Arthur [RM]
Musician
* Neville, Red

Neville, B[arbara] Alison [Boodson]
1925- [CA, CC, WW]
British author
* Candy, Edward

Neville, C. J.
See Franklin, Cynthia

Neville, Cecily [or Cicely] 15th c.
[DNNS, FFF]
Wife of Richard, Duke of York
* [The] White Rose of Raby

Neville, Derek 1911- [IAW]
British author and poet
* Salt, Jonathan

Neville, Henry 1620-1694 [WGT]
British author
* Van Sloetten, Henry Cornelius

Neville, [Thomas] Henry
See Gartside, Thomas Henry

Neville, Kris [Ottman] 1925- [ESF,
WGT]
American author
* Starke, Henderson

Neville, Lee
See Richards, Lela Horn

Neville, Margaret
See Smith, Margaret

Neville, Margot [joint pseudonym with
Neville (Goyder) Joske]
See Goyder, Margot

Neville, Margot [joint pseudonym with
Margot Goyder]
See Joske, Neville [Goyder]

Neville, Mary
See Foster, Mary A.

Neville, Mary
See Woodrich, Mary Neville

Neville, Naomi
See Toussaint, Allen

Neville, Red
See Neville, Arthur

Neville, Richard 1428-1471 [DEP, DHA,
HN]
Earl of Warwick
* [The] Kingmaker
* [The] Last of the Barons

Neville, Robert [HN]
* [The] Peacock of the North

Nevin, Evelyn C.
See Ferguson, Evelyn

Nevins, Francis, Jr. 20th c.
American author and attorney
* Nevins, Mike

Nevins, Mike
See Nevins, Francis, Jr.

Nevins, William 1797-1835 [HPPN]
American clergyman
* M. S.

Nevinson, H. W.
See Nevinson, Henry Woodd

Nevinson, Henry Woodd 1856-1941
[LC]
British author
* Nevinson, H. W.

Nevison, William 1640?-1684 [CEC]
British highwayman
* Swift Nicks

[The] New Adam
See Jesus Christ

[The] New Alexandre Dumas
See Feval, Paul Henri

[The] New Aristarchus
See Sallo, Denis de

New China Hand
See Kissinger, Henry Alfred

[The] New Constantine
See Louis XIV

[The] New Convert
See Foe, Daniel

[The] New David
See Wheeler, Wayne Bidwell

[The] New Dealer
See Roosevelt, Franklin Delano

[The] New Deal's Tom Dewey
See Murphy, Frank

[The] New Dress-Improver
See Wilde, Oscar [Fingal O'Flahertie
Wills]

New, Edward
See Russell, Matthew

[The] New Empress of the Blues
See Brown, Olive

[The] New England Cicero
See Webster, Daniel

[A] New England Farmer
See Lowell, John

[A] New England Housekeeper
See Howard, Caroline K.

[A] New England Man
See Paulding, James Kirke

[A] New England Minister
See Tyler, Bennet

[A] New England Minister, A. B.
See Hale, Edward Everett

[The] New England Mystic
See Dickinson, Emily Elizabeth

[A] New England Pastor
See Emmons, Nathanael

New England's Mafia Boss
See Patriarca, Raymond L. S.

[The] New Haldeman
See Haig, Alexander Meigs, Jr.

[The] New Haman of the Jews
See Fettmilch, Vincenz

[The] New Hampshire Demosthenes
See Webster, Daniel

[The] New Heresiarch
See Toland, Junius Janus

[The] New Home Run Champion
See Maris, Roger

[The] New Jan Garber
See Young, Sterling

New, Lloyd H. 1916- [HPPN]
American fashion designer
* Kiva, Lloyd

[The] New Luther
See Du Plessis, Armand Jean

[The] New Moses
See Anastasius

[The] New Orleans Nightingale
See Parker, Lavernia Smith

[The] New Populist
See Bumpers, Dale

[The] New Rockefeller
See Koretz, Leo

[The] New Samson
See Delamarre, Victor

[The] New Sesostris
See Bonaparte, Napoleon

[The] New Sultan of Swat
See Aaron, Henry Louis [Hank]

[The] New Timon
See Bulwer-Lytton, Edward Robert

New Whig
See Foe, Daniel

[The] New World Superman
See Peron, Juan Domingo

[A] New Writer
See Morris, [Sir] Lewis

[A] New Writer
See Wood, Charles

New Year's Eve, Mr.
See Lombardo, Gaetano Alberto

New York City's Master Builder
See Moses, Robert

New York City's Official Greeter of Famous People
See Whalen, Grover Aloysius

[A] New York Detective
See Brampton, James

New York Fats
See Wanderone, Rudolf Walter, Jr.

[A] New York Presbyter
See Smith, [Rev.] John Cotton

[A] New Yorker
See Curry, Daniel

New York's Foremost Obstetrician
See Francis, John Wakefield

New York's Honest Gambler
See Harrison, John

New York's Number 1 Model
See Hunt, Marcia Virginia

[The] New Ziegfeld
See Goldbogen [or Goldenborgen], Avrom Hirsch

[The] Newark Adonis
See Weinert, Charley

Newberger, Gabriel F. 1867?-1939 [HPPN]
American poet
* [The] Poet of the Ozarks

Newberger, Siegmund 1873-1911 [HPPN]
American actor and vaudeville performer
* [The] Great Lafayette

Newbern, Frances 1913?- [PMJ]
American singer
* Langford, Frances

Newberry, Francis 18th c. [HPPN]
British author
* [A] Commissioner of Taxes
* F. N.

Newberry, Oliver 1789-1860 [FFF]
American shipbuilder
* [The] Admiral of the Lakes
* [The] Steamboat King

Newbery, John 1713-1767 [DLE1, HPPN, SAT]
British author and publisher
* Aesop, Abraham
* [The] Publisher Extraordinary
* Telescope, Tom
* [The] Whirler

Newbold, Anna Heckscher 1898- [NAA]
American author and poet
* Baden, Katia

Newbold, Stokes
See Adams, Richard N[ewbold]

Newborn, Alexander
See Sykowski, Abram

Newborn, Venezuela 20th c. [IBW]
American editor
* Newborn, Vinnie

Newborn, Vinnie
See Newborn, Venezuela

Newbound, Bernard Slade 1930- [CA]
Canadian-born playwright
* Slade, Bernard

Newburgh, Countess of [SN]
* Myra

Newbury, Herbert
See Herbert, S. A. F.

Newby, George Eric 1919- [DLE]
British author
* Parker, James

Newby, P. H.
See Newby, Percy Howard

Newby, Percy Howard 1918- [LC]
British author
* Newby, P. H.

Newchurch, Harold Everett 1937- [IBW]
American journalist
* Newchurch, Tack Towne

Newchurch, Tack Towne
See Newchurch, Harold Everett

Newcomb, Ada
See Hamlin, Mrs. Paul

Newcomb, Bitter Creek
See Newcomb, George

Newcomb, Duane G[raham] 1929- [CA]
American author
* Firestone, Tom

Newcomb, Ellsworth
See Kenny, Ellsworth Newcomb

Newcomb, George ?-1895 [BLB, EWG]
American gunfighter
* Newcomb, Bitter Creek
* Slaughter's Kid

Newcomb, Kerry 1946- [CA]
American author
* Carrol, Shana [joint pseudonym with Frank Schaefer]
* Gentry, Peter [joint pseudonym with Frank Schaefer]
* Savage, Christina [joint pseudonym with Frank Schaefer]

Newcomb, Norma
See Neubauer, William Arthur

Newcomb, Simon 1835-1909 [HPPN]
Canadian-American astronomer and educator
* Tarr, Simon

Newcomb, Theresa
See Jackson, Mrs. T. J.

Newcombe, Donald 1926- [BE, PB]
American baseball player
* Newcombe, Newk

Newcombe, John 20th c.
American tennis player
* Newcombe, Newk

Newcombe, Louis
See Stobbs, John Louis Newcombe

Newcombe, Newk
See Newcombe, Donald

Newcombe, Newk
See Newcombe, John

Newcome, Colin
See Young, Fred W.

Newcome, Mrs. Hobson
See Milner Gibson, Mrs.

Newcomen, Thomas 1663-1729 [HPPN]
British blacksmith and inventor
* [The] Father of the Atmospheric Steam Engine

Newell, Charles Martin 1821-? [HPPN, PA]
American author
* Barnacle, [Captain] B.
* Barnacle, [Captain] Robert

Newell, Crosby
See Bonsall, Crosby Barbara [Newell]

Newell, Hope Hockenberry 1896-1965 [CA]
American author
* Hockenberry, Hope

Newell, Ma
See Newell, Marshall

Newell, Marshall 1871-1897 [AS, FB]
American football player
* Newell, Ma

Newell, Mrs. Atkins [FFF]
* Palma, [Signora] Sara

Newell, Peter 1862-1924 [HPPN]
American author and illustrator
* Hershey, Sheaf

Newell, Pinky
See Newell, William E.

Newell, Robert 1807-1869 [HPPN]
American pioneer in Oregon
* Doctor [or Doc]

Newell, Robert Henry 1836-1901 [DEL, DNNF, FFF]
American author and journalist
* Kerr, Orpheus C.

Newell, Rosemary 1922- [CA]
American author
* Gibson, Rosemary

Newell, Roy
See Raymond, Harold Newell

Newell, S. 1824-? [PA]
Author
* North, W. Savage

Newell, William 1804-1881 [HPPN]
American clergyman
* [The] Pastor
* W. N.

Newell, William E. 1920- [BBH]
American collegiate athletic trainer
* Newell, Pinky

Newfield, Maurice 1893-1949 [BI]
British physician
* Fielding, Michael

Newhall, C. S. [PA]
Author
* Carl

Newhall, [Lieut. Colonel] Frederick C.
19th c. [HPPN]
American army officer
* [A] Staff Officer

Newhall, James Robinson 1809-1893
[DNA]
American author and historian
* Oldpath, Obadiah

Newhall, Laura Eugenia 1861-? [DNA]
American author
* Halstead, Ada L.

Newhouser, Harold [Hal] 1921- [ARL,
BE]
American baseball player
* Prince Hal

Newil, Charles
See Basset, Adrien Charles Alexandre

Newkirk, Foster
See Tucker, John F[rancis]

Newland, Mary
See Oldland, Lilian

Newlight, [Rev] Aristarchus
See Fitzgerald, William

Newlight, Aristarchus
See Whately, Richard

Newlin, Margaret Rudd 1925- [CA,
WD]
American poet and critic
* Rudd, Margaret

Newlin, Maurice Milton [Maury] 1914-
[BE]
American baseball player
* Newlin, Mickey

Newlin, Mickey
See Newlin, Maurice Milton [Maury]

Newlon, [Frank] Clarke 1905?-1982 [BI,
CA, SAT]
American author
* Clarke, Michael

Newman, A.
See Pim, Herbert Moore

Newman, Adrien Ann 1941- [CA]
American author
* Arpel, Adrien

Newman, Allan Scott 1950?-1978
American entertainer
* Scott, William

Newman, Andy 20th c. [CMA]
Musician
* Newman, Thunderclap

Newman, Anthony 1941- [HPPN]
American musician and composer
* [The] Hip Harpsichordist

Newman, Bernard [Charles] 1897-1968
[CC, LC, WW]
British author
* Betteridge, Don

Newman, Brains
See Newman, David

Newman, Buddie
See Newman, C. B.

Newman, C. B. 20th c. [TI 8-13-84]
American politician
* Newman, Buddie

Newman, Clinton E. 20th c. [HPPN]
*American business executive and
accountant*
* Newman, Ting

Newman, Dangerous Dan
See Newman, Kenneth Daniel

Newman, David 1933- [DAM, EJ, IBW]
American jazz musician
* Newman, Brains
* Newman, Fathead

Newman, Ernest
See Roberts, William

Newman, Esta Maria Dodd 1928-1966
[HPPN]
American playwright
* Dodd, E. Marlowe

Newman, Eugene William 1845-?
[BDSA]
American author and journalist
* Savoyard

Newman, Fathead
See Newman, David

Newman, Frank
See Abrams, Sam[uel]

Newman, Henry Hardin 1894?- [BI]
American journalist
* Newman, Zipp

Newman, James Roy 1907-1966 [BI,
HPPN]
*American attorney, mathematician,
economist, author*
* Einstein's Editor
* Stryfe, Paul

Newman, John 20th c. [CA, WGT]
British author
* Johns, Kenneth [joint pseudonym with
  (Henry) Kenneth Bulmer]

Newman, John Henry 1801-1890 [HN,
PA]
British theologian
* Catholicus
* J. H. N.
* [The] Recluse of Edgbaston

Newman, Kenneth Daniel 1952- [SMG]
Canadian-born hockey player
* Newman, Dangerous Dan

Newman, Kenneth E. 20th c. [MBF]
British author and editor
* Clifford, Martin [house pseudonym]
* Conquest, Owen [house pseudonym]
* Richards, Frank [house pseudonym]

Newman, Leonard Hugh 1909- [HPPN]
British author
* [The] Butterfly Farmer

Newman, M. W. [PA]
Author
* [The] Exile of Erin

Newman, Margaret
See Potter, Margaret [Newman]

Newman, Meta [Pennock] 1891- [NAA]
American author and editor
* Pennock, Meta

Newman, Mona Alice Jean 1910- [WD]
British author
* Fitzgerald, Barbara
* Stewart, Jean

[The] Newman of America
See Hewit, Nathaniel Augustus

Newman, Oliver ?-1931 [HPPN]
British murderer
* Tiggy

Newman, Richard Brinsley
See Gifford, Franklin Kent

Newman, Scott 1950-1978 [HPPN]
American actor
* Scott, William

Newman, Thunderclap
See Newman, Andy

Newman, Ting
See Newman, Clinton E.

Newman, Zipp
See Newman, Henry Hardin

Newmar, Julie
See Newmeyer, Julia Charlene

Newmar, Rima
See Wagman, Naomi

Newmark, Benjamin 20th c. [HPPN]
American politician and criminal
* Newmark, Jew Ben

Newmark, Jew Ben
See Newmark, Benjamin

Newmark, Stewart
See Nathan, Max

[The] Newmarket Oracle
See Ogden

Newmeyer, Julia Charlene 1930?-
[BEW, FC, SW]
American actress, singer, dancer
* Newmar, Julie

Newnham-Davis, Col. 1854-? [NPS]
Author
* [The] Dwarf of Blood

Newport, Andrew
See Foe, Daniel

Newquist, Roy 1925- [SFL]
Author
* Sterland, Carl

Newsom, Bobo
See Newsom, Norman Louis

Newsom, Buck
See Newsom, Norman Louis

Newsom, Norman Louis 1907-1962 [AS, BN, PB]
American baseball player
* Newsom, Bobo
* Newsom, Buck
* Ol' Showboat

Newsome, Arden J[eanne] 1932- [CA]
American author and columnist
* Sebastian, Jeanne

Newsome, Dick
See Newsome, Heber Hampton

Newsome, Heber Hampton 1909-1965
[BE]
American baseball player
* Newsome, Dick

Newsome, Lamar Ashby 1910- [BE]
American baseball player
* Newsome, Skeeter

Newsome, Skeeter
See Newsome, Lamar Ashby

Newsons, Albert 1891- [WWL]
British author
* Bands, Paul

Newsreel
See Wong Hai Sheng

Newte, Thomas
See Thomson, William

Newton, A. E.
See Newton, Alfred Edward

Newton, Alfred Edward 1863-1940 [LC]
American book collector and author
* Newton, A. E.

Newton, Ark
See Newton, William

Newton, Charles E.
See Perine, C. E.

Newton, Clark
See Harmon, Jim

Newton, David C.
See Chance, John Newton

Newton, Doc
See Newton, Eustace James

Newton, Dwight Bennett 1916- [CA]
American author
* Bennett, Dwight
* Hardin, Clement
* Logan, Ford
* Temple, Dan

Newton, Eustace James 1877-1931 [BE]
American baseball player
* Newton, Doc

Newton, Fig
See Newton, Francis

Newton, Fig
See Newton, Irving

Newton, Fig
See Newton, Lloyd

Newton, Fig
See Newton, Robert Lee

Newton, Frances
See Denison, Muriel [Goggin]

Newton, Francis 1909- [HPPN]
American baker
* Newton, Fig

Newton, Francis
See Hobsbawm, Eric J[ohn Ernest]

Newton, Henry Chance 1854-1931
[BEW, THR]
British-born critic and playwright
* Carados
* Gawain

Newton, Henry Jotham 1823-1895
[HPPN]
American inventor
* [The] Father of the Dry Plate Process
  in America

Newton, I. M.
See Newton, Irene Margaret

Newton, Irene Margaret 1915- [ART]
British artist
* Newton, I. M.

Newton, Irving 1898?-1980 [FIR]
Actor
* Newton, Fig

Newton, [Sir] Isaac 1642-1727 [DEP, DNNS, HN]
British mathematician and philosopher
* [The] Priest of Nature

Newton, Jean
See Stich, Hermine Neustadtl

Newton, Judy Kay 20th c.
American singer
* Newton, Juice

Newton, Juice
See Newton, Judy Kay

Newton, Lloyd 1943- [IBW]
American air force officer
* Newton, Fig

Newton, Macdonald
See Newton, William Simpson

Newton, Michael 1951- [CA]
American author
* Cannon, John
* Kozlow, Mark J.
* Robinson, Vince

Newton, Nat?
See Morris, Anthony Paschal

[The] Newton of Harmony
See Rameau, Jean Philippe

Newton, R.
See Cave, Edward

Newton, Richard 1676-1753 [HPPN]
British clergyman
* [A] Presbyter of the Church of
  England

Newton, Robert Lee 1949- [SMG]
American football player
* Newton, Fig

Newton, Stu
See Whitcomb, Ian

Newton, Wayne 1942?-
American singer
* [The] Midnight Idol

Newton, [Rev.] William 1684?-1744
[HPPN]
British clergyman
* [A] Curate of the Diocese of
  Canterbury

Newton, William 20th c. [EF]
American football player
* Newton, Ark

Newton, William Simpson 1923- [CA]
British author
* Mitcham, Gilroy
* Newton, Macdonald

Ney, Marie
See Fix, Marie

Ney, Michel [Duc d'Elchingen]
1769-1815 [DEP, DHA, FF, NN]
French army officer
* [The] Bravest of the Brave
* [Le] Lion Rouge
* [Le] Plus Brave des Braves
* [Le] Rougeaud

Ney of the Confederacy
See Cheatham, Benjamin Franklin

Ney, Patrick
See Bolitho, [Henry] Hector

Ney, Wolfgang
See Harranth, Wolf

Neyland, James [Elwyn] 1939- [CA]
American author and playwright
* Jameson, Judith
* Romero, Gerry

Neyland, [General] Robert Reese, Jr.
[Bob] 1892-1941 [HPPN]
American army officer and football coach
* Football's Greatest Coach
* [The] General
* [The] Gridiron Brigadier

Ngagoyeanes, Nicholas 1939- [CA]
Greek-born journalist
* Gage, Nicholas

Ngengi, Kamau wa 1891?-1978
Kenyan president
* Kamau, Johnstone
* Kenyatta, Jomo
* Mzee [Grand Old Man]

Ngugi, James T[hiong'o] 1938- [CA, CLC]
Kenyan-born author and playwright
* Thiong'o, Ngugi wa

Nguyen Ai Quoc [Nguyen the Patriot]
See Nguyen That Thanh

Nguyen That Thanh 1890-1969 [HPPN]
Vietnamese Communist leader
* [The] Communist Father of Vietnam
* [The] Father of Vietnam
* Ho Chi Minh [He Who Enlightens]
* Lucius [code name used during World War II]
* Nguyen Ai Quoc [Nguyen the Patriot]
* North Vietnam's Militant Uncle
* [The] Peanut
* Tong Van So
* Uncle Ho

Nguyen Tuong Tam 1905?-1963 [BI]
Vietnamese author
* Nhat Linh

Nguyen-Anh ?-1820 [WBD]
King of Annam, Indo-China
* Gialong

Nhat Linh
See Nguyen Tuong Tam

Ni Fhaircheallaigh, Una
See O'Farrelly, Agnes

Ni Loinsigh, Brid 1913-1968 [SC]
Irish actress
* Lynch, Brid

Niall ?-405 [HN]
King of Ireland
* [The] Great
* [The] Hero of the Nine Hostages

Niall, Ian
See McNeillie, John

Niarhos, Constantine Gregory 1920-
[BE]
American baseball player
* Niarhos, Gus

Niarhos, Gus
See Niarhos, Constantine Gregory

Niatum, Duane
See McGinnis, Duane

Niazi, A. A. K. 20th c.
Pakistani army officer
* Niazi, Tiger

Niazi, Immie
See Niazi, Imran Ahmad Khan

Niazi, Imran Ahmad Khan 1952- [DC]
Pakistani cricketer
* Niazi, Immie

Niazi, Tiger
See Niazi, A. A. K.

Nibbelink, Cynthia 1948- [MA]
American poet and author
* Williams, Maggie

Nibbi, Gino 1896- [HPPN]
Italian art dealer, critic, author
* Medaro

[The] Nibbler
See Hibbler, Albert George

Niblo, Fred
See Nobile, Frederico

Nibor, Kay
See Tucker, Robin

Niboyet, Pauline Fortunio [PA]
Author
* Fortunio, P. N.

Nibrah
See Hardin, L. S.

Nic Leodhas, Sorche
See Alger, Leclaire [Gowans]

Nic Shiubhlaigh, Maire ?-1958 [HPPN]
Irish actress
* Price, Maire

Nicander
See Williams, Morris

Nicander, Edwin
See Rau, Nicander Edwin

Nicator
See Demetrius II

Nicator
See Seleucus I

Niccolo
See Isouard, Nicolas

Niccolo of Ferrara 13th c. [SN]
Italian aristocrat
* Azo

Nice, Captain
See Donohue, Mark

Nice Gun, Mr.
See Levine, Lou

Nice, Mr.
See Griffin, Merv[yn Edward, Jr.]

Nice Nikita
See Khrushchev, Nikita Sergeyevich

Nice, Steven 20th c. [CMA]
British musician
* Harley, Steve

Nicephorus II 913?-969 [HPPN]
Ruler of Eastern Roman Empire
* Phocas

Nicephorus III ?-1081 [HPPN]
Ruler of Eastern Roman Empire
* Botaniates

Nicetas
See Ignatius

Nicetas Acominatus ?-1215? [HPPN]
Byzantine historian
* Nicetas Choniates

Nicetas Choniates
See Nicetas Acominatus

Nicety
See Foe, Daniel

Nichevo
See Dawes, Angela Kathleen

Nicholas 4th c. [DNNF, HPPN, RH, UH]
Saint
* [The] Boy Bishop
* Kriss Kringle [or Christ Kinkle]
* Santa Claus [or Klaus]

Nicholas 16th c. [HN]
Count of Zriny
* [The] Leonidas of Hungary

Nicholas, Big Nick
See Nicholas, George Walker

Nicholas, Dr. [PA]
Author
* Monadnock

Nicholas, Don
See De Collibus, Nicholas

Nicholas, George Walker 1922- [EJ]
American jazz musician
* Nicholas, Big Nick

Nicholas, Joseph [Joe] 1883-1957 [EJ]
American jazz musician
* Nicholas, Wooden Joe

Nicholas of Flue
See Loewenbrugger, Nikolaus

Nicholas, Philip Norborne 1773-1849
[FFF]
American writer
* Agricola

Nicholas, William [joint pseudonym with Nicholas Palen (Nick) Thimmesch]
See Johnson, William O.

Nicholas, William [joint pseudonym with William O. Johnson]
See Thimmesch, Nicholas Palen [Nick]

Nicholas, Wooden Joe
See Nicholas, Joseph [Joe]

Nicholas I 800?-867 [DNNS, FFF, SN]
Pope
* [The] Great

Nicholas I [Nikolai Pavlovich]
1796-1855 [DEP, DHA, HN, HPPN]
Czar of Russia
* [The] Gendarme of Europe
* [The] Iron Czar
* [The] Iron Emperor

Nicholas II 1868-1918 [HPPN]
Czar of Russia
* [The] Little Father

Nicholas II
See Gerard of Burgundy

Nicholas III
See Orsini, Giovanni Gaetano

Nicholas IV
See Masci, Girolamo

Nicholas V
See Parentucelli [or da Sarzana], Tommaso

Nicholas V
See Rainalducci, Pietro

Nicholls, Anthony
See Parsons, Anthony

Nicholls, Charles Wilbur de Lyon
1854-1923 [DNA]
American author and clergyman
* Chauncey, Shelton

Nicholls, [Sir] George 1781-1865
[HPPN]
British author and banker
* [An] Overseer

Nicholls, Joan 1908-1945 [THR]
British actress
* Marion, Joan

Nicholls, Mary Ann 1846?-1888 [BL]
Prostitute and murder victim
* Nicholls, Polly

Nicholls, Muriel 1920?-1975? [BWW]
American singer
* Booze, Beatrice
* Booze, Wee Bea
* [The] Queen Bea of Blues Singers
* [The] See See Rider Blues Girl

Nicholls, Polly
See Nicholls, Mary Ann

Nichols, Adelaide
See Baker, Adelaide Nichols

Nichols, Adelbert ?-1921 [HPPN]
American minstrel
* Nichols, Del

Nichols, Alvin 1947- [BWW]
American singer
* Jones, B. B.
* Nichols, Youngblood

Nichols, Arthur Francis
See Meikle, Arthur Francis

Nichols, Barbara
See Nickeraeur, Barbara

Nichols, Catherine 19th c. [HPPN]
American poet
* [An] Old Prairie Hen

Nichols, Cecilia Fawn 1906- [CAP]
American author and playwright
* Nazarian, Nikki

Nichols, Charles Augustus 1869-1953
[AS, BAB, PB]
American baseball player
* Nichols, Kid
* Nichols, Nervy Nick

Nichols, Dale [William] 1904- [CAP]
American-born artist, designer, illustrator
* De Polman, Willem

Nichols, Dave
See Frost, Helen

Nichols, Del
See Nichols, Adelbert

Nichols, Dolan Levon 1930- [BE]
American baseball player
* Nichols, Nick

Nichols, Ernest Loring 1905-1965 [ASC,
BBD, DAM]
American jazz musician
* Nichols, Red

Nichols, Fan
See Hanna, Frances [Nichols]

Nichols, Frederick C. 19th c. [BE]
American baseball player
* Nichols, Tricky

Nichols, George Herbert Fosdike 1883-
[LAO]
British author and journalist
* Quex

Nichols, Jimmy
See Nicholson, James David

Nichols, John 1745-1826 [HPPN, NPS]
British editor
* [The] Censor General of Literature
* J. N.
* My Octogenarian Friend
* N. S.
* [The] Prosper Marchand of English
Literature
* Sylvanus
* Urban, Sylvanus

Nichols, John Conover 1896-1945
[HPPN]
American politician
* Nichols, Oklahoma Jack

Nichols, John Gough 1806-1873 [HPPN]
British editor, journalist, biographer
* J. G. N.

Nichols, Kid
See Nichols, Charles Augustus

Nichols, Lee 20th c. [EF]
American football player
* Nichols, Mike

Nichols, Lulu
See Peckham, Luella Nichols

Nichols, Mary Sergeant Gove 1810-?
[FFF]
American author
* Orme, Mary

Nichols, Mike
See Nichols, Lee

Nichols, Mike
See Peschkowsky, Michael Igor

Nichols, Nervy Nick
See Nichols, Charles Augustus

Nichols, Nicholas
See Lathe, Herbert William

Nichols, Nick
See Nichols, Dolan Levon

Nichols, Oklahoma Jack
See Nichols, John Conover

Nichols, Paul
See Dallis, Nicholas Peter

Nichols, Peter
See Youd, Christopher Samuel

Nichols, Rebecca S. Reed 1819-1903
[FFF]
American author and poet
* Cleaveland, Kate
* Ellen

Nichols, Red
See Nichols, Ernest Loring

Nichols, Richard William 1930- [ART]
American-born painter
* R. W. N.

Nichols, Scott
See Scortia, Thomas N[icholas]

Nichols, T. Nickle
See Nichols, Thomas

Nichols, Thomas [IP]
British author
* Nichols, T. Nickle

Nichols, Thomas 19th c. [IP, PA]
Author
* Asmodeus

Nichols, Tricky
See Nichols, Frederick C.

Nichols, Youngblood
See Nichols, Alvin

Nicholson, Alexandra 1957?- [HPPN]
American gymnast
* [The] Tramp Champ

Nicholson, Christina
See Nicole, Christopher Robin

Nicholson, Dorothy
See Smith, Gladys Mary

Nicholson, Eliza Jane Poitevent
1849-1896 [FFF, PA]
American writer
* Eliza
* Rivers, Pearl

Nicholson, Francis 1753-1844 [WBD]
British painter
* [The] Father of Water Color Painting

Nicholson, Henry Joseph Boone [IP]
British clergyman and author
* H. J. B. N.

Nicholson, J. D.
See Nicholson, James David

Nicholson, James David 1917- [BWW]
American singer
* Nichols, Jimmy
* Nicholson, J. D.

Nicholson, James William Augustus
1821-1887 [FFF]
American naval officer
* War Horse

Nicholson, Jane
See Steen, Marguerite

Nicholson, John 1730-1796 [NPS]
British bookseller
* Maps

Nicholson, John 1790-1843 [SN]
British poet
* [The] Airedale Poet

Nicholson, John 1821-1857 [HPPN]
British military officer and colonial administrator
* Seyn, Nikkul

Nicholson, John
See Lambert, John

Nicholson, John
See Parcell, Norman H[owe]

Nicholson, Louise [FFF]
Entertainer
* Nikita, Mlle.

Nicholson, Mal
See Nicholson, Mallagy

Nicholson, Mallagy 1909- [IBW]
Canadian-born business executive
* Nicholson, Mal

Nicholson, Margaret
See Shelley, Percy Bysshe

Nicholson, Margaret Beda [Larminie]
1924- [AW, CA, WD]
British author
* Yorke, Margaret

Nicholson, Mrs. Paul [FFF]
Entertainer
* Thornton, Adelaide

Nicholson, Nick
See Nicholson, Robert

Nicholson, Parson
See Nicholson, Thomas C.

Nicholson, Robert 20th c. [ITA]
American producer
* Nicholson, Nick

Nicholson, Swish
See Nicholson, William Beck

Nicholson, Thomas C. 1862-1917 [BE]
American baseball player
* Nicholson, Parson

Nicholson, William 1782-1849 [DEL, IP]
Scottish poet
* [The] Galloway Poet

Nicholson, William 1816-1865 [WBD]
Australian statesman
* [The] Father of the Australian Ballot

Nicholson, William Beck 1914- [DGS]
American baseball player
* Nicholson, Swish

Nicholson, [Sir] William Newzam Prior
1872-1949 [DBA]
British painter
* Beggarstaff, W.

Nichopoulos, George C. 1928?-
American physician who treated Elvis Presley
* Nick, Dr.

Nick
See Whitley, Jonas E.

Nick, Dr.
See Nichopoulos, George C.

Nick, Inocencio da Costa 1897- [BI]
Brazilian engraver
* Mestre, Noza

Nick the Greek
See Dandalos, Nicholas Andrea

Nick the Kick
See Lowery, Nick

Nick the Quick
See Werkman, Nick

Nickalls, Gully
See Nickalls, Guy Oliver

Nickalls, Guy Oliver 1899- [BI]
British rower
* Nickalls, Gully

Nickelplate
See Stein, Jules W. Arndt

Nickeraeur, Barbara 1932-1976 [HCA]
American actress
* Nichols, Barbara

Nickerson, Camille Lucie 1888- [FFA, IBW]
American singer
* [The] Louisiana Lady

Nickerson, Hammie
See Davis, Hammie

Nickerson, Susan D. [IP]
Author
* [A] Lady of Boston

Nicklaus, Big Jack
See Nicklaus, Jack William

Nicklaus, Jack William 1940- [EG, HPPN]
American golfer
* [The] Golden Bear
* Nicklaus, Big Jack
* Ohio Fats

Nicklin, Philip Holbrook 1786-1842 [FFF]
American author
* Prolix, Peregrine

Nicklin, Samuel Strang 1876-1932 [BE]
American baseball player
* [The] Dixie Thrush
* Strang, Samuel Nicklin

Nickolls, Robert Boucher 1743-1814 [IP]
British clergyman and author
* Eusebius

Nicks, Samuel 17th c. [HPPN]
British highwayman
* Nicks, Swift

Nicks, Swift
See Nicks, Samuel

Nickson, Hilda 1912- [IAW]
British author
* Pressley, Hilda
* Preston, Hilary

Nico
See Jungman, Nico

Nicol, Abioseh
See Nicol, Davidson [Sylvester Hector Willoughby]

Nicol, Ann
See Turnbull, Ann [Christine]

Nicol, Davidson [Sylvester Hector Willoughby] 1924- [CA, WD]
Sierra Leonean author
* Nicol, Abioseh

Nicol, Eric [Patrick] 1919- [AW, CA]
Canadian author and playwright
* Jabez

Nicol, Martha [IP]
British author
* [A] Lady

Nicolaeff, Ariadne 1915- [WD]
British playwright and translator
* Moore, Nicholas

Nicolai
See Kasatkin, Ivan

Nicolai, Christopher Friedrich 1733-1811 [NPS, SN]
German author
* Erz-Philister
* Erz-Philosopher

Nicolaie, Louis Francois 1811-1879 [WBD]
French playwright
* Clairville, Louis Francois

Nicolas
See Mordvinoff, Nicolas

Nicolas, Claire
See White, Claire Nicolas

Nicolas, Ernest 1834-1898 [BBD]
French opera singer
* Nicolini

Nicolas, F. R. E.
See Freeling, Nicolas

Nicolas, Jean 1740-1823 [DNNS]
French politician
* [The] Tartuffe of the Revolution

Nicolas, [Sir] Nicholas Harris 1799-1848 [FFF, HPPN]
British author and historian
* Clionas
* N.
* N. H. N.

Nicolas, P. ?-1649 [PA]
Author
* Peltrel

Nicolas, Sarah [Davison] 19th c. [IP]
British author
* [A] Soldier's Daughter

Nicole, Christopher Robin 1930- [AW, CA, IAW]
British author
* Cade, Robin
* Grange, Peter
* Logan, Mark
* Nicholson, Christina
* York, Andrew

Nicole, Claudette
See Messmann, John

Nicolini
See Nicolas, Ernest

Nicolino
See Grimaldi, Nicolo

Nicoll, [Henry] Maurice [Dunlop]
1884-1953 [ESF, SFL, WGT]
British author
* Swayne, Martin

Nicoll, [Sir] William Robertson
1851-1923 [NPS, WBD]
Scottish clergyman and editor
* Clear, Claudius
* Man of Kent
* O. O.
* Wace, W. E.

Nicollet, Joseph Nicolas 1786-1843
[HPPN]
French mathematician and explorer
* Herschel, [Sir] John

Nicolovius
See Loven, [Rev.] Nils

Nicolovius, Ludwig 1837-? [DNA]
Author
* Myth, M. Y. T. H.

Nicolson, John Urban 1885- [WW]
Author
* [The] King of the Black Isles

Nicolson, Victoria Mary
See Sackville-West, Victoria Mary

Nicomedes II 2nd c. BC [FFF, SN,
WBD]
King of Bithynia
* Epiphanes
* [The] Illustrious

Nicosia, Francesco M[ichael] 1933-
[CA]
*Italian-born American author and
educator*
* Nicosia, Franco M.

Nicosia, Franco M.
See Nicosia, Francesco M[ichael]

Nicoson, Angus 20th c. [BBH]
American basketball player and coach
* Nicoson, Nick

Nicoson, Nick
See Nicoson, Angus

Nicote, Piere 1625-1695 [PA]
Author
* Mendrock, William

Niebergall, Charles Arthur [Charlie]
1899- [BE]
American baseball player
* Niebergall, Nig

Niebergall, Nig
See Niebergall, Charles Arthur
[Charlie]

Niehaus, Mrs. C. H.
Author
* Armstrong, Regina

Niekro, Knucksie
See Niekro, Philip Henry

Niekro, Philip Henry 1939- [SMG]
American baseball player
* Niekro, Knucksie

Nielsen, Alice
See Ivarius, Alice

Nielsen, Arthur Charles 1897-1980
[HPPN]
American business executive
* [The] Father of the Nielsen Rating

Nielsen, Asta 1882-1972 [SC]
Danish actress and producer
* [Die] Asta

Nielsen, Bent Rosenkilde 1904- [ART]
Danish author, journalist, art critic
* Don Benito

Nielsen, Helen Berniece 1918- [CA, CC,
EMD]
American author and scriptwriter
* Giles, Kris

Nielsen, Jean Sarver 1922- [CA]
American author
* Sarver, Hannah

Nielsen, Virginia
See McCall, Virginia Nielsen

Nielson, Ingrid
See Bancroft, Iris [Nelson]

Nielson, Oscar M. 1882-1954 [AS, BX,
RBE]
Danish-born boxer
* [The] Durable Dane
* Nelson, Battling

Nielson, Robert 1925- [BEW, SW, TR]
American actor
* Nelson, Barry

Nielssen, Eric
See Ludvigsen, Karl [Eric]

Nieman, Butch
See Nieman, Elmer LeRoy

Nieman, Elmer LeRoy 1918- [BE]
American baseball player
* Nieman, Butch

Nieman, Fred
See Czolgosz, Leon

Niembsch von Strehlenau, Nikolaus
1802-1850 [WBD]
Hungarian-born poet
* Lenau, Nikolaus

Niemes, Jack
See Niemes, Jacob Leland

Niemes, Jacob Leland 1919-1966 [BE]
American baseball player
* Niemes, Jack

Niemeyer, Mrs. [FFF]
Entertainer
* Chalfaut, May

Niemi, Finn
See Niemi, Laurie

Niemi, Laurie 1925-1968 [AS]
American football player
* Niemi, Finn

Nieminen, Anna-Maija 1928- [IAW]
Finnish author
* Raittila, Anne-Maija

**Niemoeller, Martin Friedrich Gustav
Emil** 1892-1984 [WP 3-8-84]
German naval officer, clergyman, pacifist
* [The] Scourge of Malta

Niemoller, Ara
See Llerena, Mario

Nienaber, Christoffel Johannes Michael
1918- [IAW]
South African author
* Nienaber, Stoffel

Nienaber, Petrus Johannes 1910- [IAW]
South African author
* De Villiers, Ryno B.
* Rousseau, J. J.
* Van Niekerk, I. R.

Nienaber, Stoffel
See Nienaber, Christoffel Johannes
Michael

Nienstedt, Stanley Grover 1926- [BEW]
American actor and singer
* Grover, Stanley

Niepce, Joseph Nicephore 19th c.
[BBH]
French inventor
* [The] Father of Photography

Nierow, Bernard 1934- [EPM]
American musician
* Nero, Peter

Niese, Charlotte 1854-? [WBD]
German author
* Buerger, Lucian

Nieto, Jose 20th c. [FIR]
Actor
* Nieto, Pepe

Nieto, Manuel 1869-1942 [GS]
Spanish bullfighter
* Gorete [Little Cap]

Nieto, Pepe
See Nieto, Jose

Nietschmann, Herman 19th c. [HPPN]
German author
* Stein, Armin

Nietzsche, Friedrich Wilhelm 1844-1900
[HPPN]
German philosopher
* [A] Jesus in the Temple
* [The] Little Minister

Nieuwenhuysen, Van
See Vaez, Jean N. Gustave

Nievens, Big Daddy
See Nievens, Roosevelt

Nievens, Roosevelt 20th c.
American football coach
* Nievens, Big Daddy

Nifio de la Eterna Sonrisa
See Torres y Reina, Emilio

Nifio de Tomares
See Torres y Reina, Emilio

Niflot, Isidor 1881?-1950 [BI]
American wrestler
* Niflot, Jack

Niflot, Jack
See Niflot, Isidor

Nifo, Augustine 1473-1538 [PA]
Author
* Niphas

Nig, Capt'n
See Swafford, Johnny C.

Nigel 12th c. [WBD]
British monk and author
* Wireker, Nigel

Niger
See Fox, Charles James

Niger, Emilius
See Roumer, Emile

Niger, Samuel
See Charney, Samuel

Nigger Jack Pershing
See Pershing, John Joseph

Nigger Nate Raymond
See Raymond, Nate

Nigh, Bonnie Lenora 1926- [ITA]
American actress
* Nigh, Jane

Nigh, Jane
See Nigh, Bonnie Lenora

Nighbor, Dutch
See Nighbor, Frank

Nighbor, Frank 1893-1966 [FHE]
Canadian-born hockey player
* Nighbor, Dutch

Night, Friday
See Hurley, Zevonal Faye

[The] Night Ghost of Saint Trond
See Schnauffer, Heinz-Wolfgang

Night Train Lane
See Lane, Richard

[The] Nightclub Queen
See Guinan, Mary Louise Cecelia

Nighthawk
See Terry, Bob

Nighthawk, Robert
See McCollum, Robert Lee

Nighthood's New Prince
See Carson, John William [Johnny]

Nightingale, Anne Redmon 1943- [CA]
Author
* Redmon, Anne

Nightingale, Florence 1820-1910 [FFF, NN]
British nurse, hospital reformer, philanthropist
* Filomena, Saint
* [The] Lady with the Lamp

Nightingale, Joseph 1775-1824 [IP]
British poet
* [A] Committee Man
* Elagnitin, J.

[The] Nightingale of a Thousand Songs
See Muslih-ud-Din [or Moslehedin]

[The] Nightingale of India
See Naidu, Sarojini [Chattopadhyay]

[The] Nightingale of the Andes
See Chavarri, Emperatriz

[The] Nightingale of the Twrch
See Edwards, John

[The] Nightingale of Twickenham
See Pope, Alexander

[The] Nightingale of Wittenberg
See Luther, Martin

[The] Nightingale of Wittenberg
See Sachs, Hans

[The] Nightmare of Europe
See Bonaparte, Napoleon

Nightrate, Emil
See Spielmann, Peter James

Nigro, Laura 1947- [RO2]
American singer
* Nyro, Laura

Nihil
See Miller, P[eter] Schuyler

Niininen, Margit
See Toernudd, Margit

Nijbroek, Paul Armand 1938- [CW]
Surinamese poet
* Marlee, Paul

Nijsni, K. M.
See Cox-George, Noah Arthur William

Nik
See Lee, Francis Nigel

Nikita, Mlle.
See Nicholson, Louise

Nikodim
See Rotov, Boris Georgi'evich

Nikolai
See Jaruszewicz, Nikolai

Nikolais, Alwin 1912- [CR]
American choreographer
* Nikolais, Nik

Nikolais, Nik
See Nikolais, Alwin

Nil
See Whitling, Henry John

Nil Admirari, Esq.
See Shelton, Frederick William

Niland, Big John
See Niland, John H.

Niland, Gorgo
See Niland, John H.

Niland, Honest Tom
See Niland, Thomas James [Tom]

Niland, John H. 1944- [FB]
American football player
* Niland, Big John
* Niland, Gorgo

Niland, Thomas James [Tom] 1870-1950 [BE]
American baseball player
* Niland, Honest Tom

Nile, Dorothea
See Avallone, Michael [Angelo], Jr.

Nilense, Baron de
See Collin, Jacques Albin Simon

Nilense, Le Frere Jacques
See Collin, Jacques Albin Simon

Niles, Al
See Niles, Alban Isaac

Niles, Alban Isaac 1933- [BA]
American attorney
* Niles, Al

Niles, Harry 1881-1953 [BI]
American baseball player
* Niles, Hep

Niles, Hep
See Niles, Harry

Niles, Johnny
See Nilsson, Harry Edward, III

Niles, Willys
See Hume, John Ferguson

[El] Nili
See Manzano y Pelayo, Jose

Nill, George Charles 1881-1962 [BE]
American baseball player
* Nill, Rabbit

Nill, Rabbit
See Nill, George Charles

Nilla
See Carter, Abby [Allin]

Niller, Mary Ager [FFF]
Author and poet
* Luola

Nillo
See Curtiss, Abby Allin

Nilson, Alice 1924- [EJ7]
Swedish singer
* Babs, Alice

Nilson, Amabel Rhoda 1908- [AW]
New Zealand-born home economist and author
* Nilson, Bee

Nilson, Bee
See Nilson, Amabel Rhoda

Nilsson
See Nilsson, Harry Edward, III

Nilsson, Birgit
See Svensson, Marta Birgit

Nilsson, Harry Edward, III 1941-
[LRR, RO2]
American singer
* Niles, Johnny
* Nilsson

Nilsson, Usha Saksena 1930- [BI, CA]
Indian-born author
* Priyamvada, Usha

Nimble, Jack B.
See Burgess, Michael Roy

Nimitz, Chester W. 1885-1966
American military leader
* Cottonhead
* Zero Zero [code name used during World War II]

Nimrod
See Apperley, Charles James

Nimrod
See Reynolds, John Hamilton

Nimrod Junior
See Collins, George Edwin

Nimzowitsch, Arnold [or Aron?]
1886-1935 [HPPN]
Latvian chess player
* [The] Father of Modern Chess
* [The] Stormy Petrel of the Chess World

Nina
See Campbell-Quine, Nina

Nina V.
See Vickers, Antoinette L.

Nincom
See Applewhite, Marshall Herff

Nind, William 1810-1856 [IP]
British poet and clergyman
* W. N.

[A] Nine to Five Pro
See Beard, Frank

Ninety Six
See Voiselle, William Symmes

Ninety-Take Wyler
See Wyler, William [Willie]

Ninian ?-432? [FFF]
Saint
* [The] Apostle of the Picts

[El] Nino de la Capea [The Boy of the Bull-Capings]
See Moya, Pedro

Nino de la Estrella [Child of the Star]
See Zafon, Silvino

Nino de la Palma
See Ordonez, Cayetano

Nino de La Palma [Boy from La Palma]
See Ordonez y Aguilera, Cayetano

Nino de la Rose [Boy of the Rose]
See Mier Jimenez, Ramon

Nino, Pedro Alonso 1468-1505? [WBD]
Spanish navigator
* [El] Negro

[El] Nino Sabio [The Wise Child]
See Camino Sanchez, Francisco

Ninon
See MacKnight, Ninon

Ninon de Lenclos
See L'Enclos, Anne

Ninrod, Lady
See Thackeray, William Makepeace

Nion
See Wallace, Ian

Nipclose, [Sir] Nicholas, Bart.
See Garrick, David

Niphas
See Nifo, Augustine

Nips, Nick
See Bennett, John Michael

Nirala
See Tripathi, Surya Kant

Nirt, Red
See Trinder, Tommy

Nisard, Theodore
See Normand, Theodule-Eleazar-Xavier

Nisbet, George 1836-1926 [HPPN]
French slave dealer
* Digna, Osman

Nisbet, Richard 18th c. [IP]
British author
* [A] West Indian

Nisei of the Biennium
See Uchida, Yosh[ihiro]

Nishi, Kay
See Nishi, Kazuhiko

Nishi, Kazuhiko 1956?- [TI 4-16-84]
Japanese business exeucitve
* Nishi, Kay

Nishi, Noriko 1943-
Japanese-born fashion designer
* Noriko

Nishri, Zvi
See Orlvov, Zvi

Nisidas
See Urena de Mendoza, Nicolas

Niska, Maralin Fae
See Dice, Maralin Fae

Nisot, Mavis Elizabeth [Hocking] 1893-
[WW]
British author
* Penmare, William

Nissen, Greta
See Rutz-Nissen, Grethe

Nistico, Sal
See Nistico, Salvatore

Nistico, Salvatore 1940- [EJ7]
American jazz musician
* Nistico, Sal

Nitcholas, Nick
See Nitcholas, Otho James

Nitcholas, Otho James 1908- [BE]
American baseball player
* Nitcholas, Nick

Nitgenockle
See Galt, William Hamilton

[The] Nitpicker
See Hendricks, Harlan William

Nitram, Notca W.
See Acton, Martin William

[The] Nitrate King
See North, John Thomas

Nitsch, Helen Alice [Matthews] ?-1889
[DNA]
American author
* Owen, Catherine

Nitsua, Benjamin
See Austin, Benjamin Fish

Nitti, Frank ?-1944? [BLB, PHM]
American underworld figure
* [The] Enforcer

Nitze, Paul 1907?- [TI 11-18-85]
American arms control adviser
* [The] Silver Fox

Niva, Rosa
See Noel, Victoire

Nivedita, [Sister]
See Noble, Margaret Elizabeth

Niven, Frank 20th c. [BBH]
American horseshoe pitching promoter
* Niven, Hands

Niven, Hands
See Niven, Frank

Niven, Marian
See Alston, Mary Niven

Niven, Vern
See Grier, Barbara G[ene Damon]

Nix, Willie 1922- [BWW]
American singer
* Memphis Blues Boy

Nixon, Agnes Eckhardt 1927- [CLC]
American producer and screenwriter
* Queen of the Soaps

Nixon, Clint
See Hecht, Clinton James

Nixon, Edward John [IP]
British clergyman and author
* [A] Member of the Univ. of Camb.

Nixon, Elmo
See Nixon, Elmore

Nixon, Elmore 1933-1975? [BWW]
American singer
* Nixon, Elmo

[The] Nixon Family's Closest Friend
See Rebozo, Charles Gregory

Nixon, Hammie
See Davis, Hammie

Nixon, K.
See Nixon, Kathleen Irene [Blundell]

Nixon, Kathleen Irene [Blundell] 20th c. [CA]
British author and artist
* Nixon, K.

Nixon, Marni
American singer
* [The] Ghostess with the Mostest

Nixon, Patricia [or Pat]
See Nixon, Thelma Catherine Patricia Ryan

Nixon, Plastic Pat
See Nixon, Thelma Catherine Patricia Ryan

Nixon, Richard Milhous 1913- [FAP, HPPN, NN]
American president
* [The] Bela Lugosi of American Politics
* [The] Czar
* [The] Embattled President
* Gloomy Gus
* [The] Godfather
* [The] Houdini of American Politics
* Ike's Kissinger
* [The] Iron Butt
* King Richard
* [The] Nation's Number 1 Football Fan
* [The] Nero of Our Times
* Richard the Chicken-Hearted
* St. Richard the Commie Killer
* Searchlight [Secret Service code name]
* [The] Tarnished President
* Tricky Dick [or Dickie]
* Truthful, President

Nixon, Thelma Catherine Patricia Ryan 1912- [HPPN, TI 4-16-84]
Wife of American president, Richard Nixon
* Nixon, Patricia [or Pat]
* Nixon, Plastic Pat
* Starlight [Secret Service code name]

Nixon, Wm. Penn
See Tourgee, Albion W[inegar]

Nixon's Alter Ego
See Haldeman, Harry Robbins

Nixon's Favorite Coach
See Allen, George

Nixon's Keen Scythe
See Brinegar, Claude Strout

Nixon's Nixon
See Anagnostopoulos, Spiro Theodore

Nixon's Secret Agent
See Kissinger, Henry Alfred

Nixon's Svengali
See Kissinger, Henry Alfred

Nixson, Maisie Mayer 1890- [WWL]
British author
* Lennox, Edward

Niza, Marcos de ?-1558 [WBD]
French-born missionary and explorer
* Marcos, [Fray]

Nizovoy, Pavel
See Tupikov, Pavel Georgievich

Nizzi, Guido 1900- [SFL]
Italian-born author
* Nizzi, Skipper

Nizzi, Skipper
See Nizzi, Guido

Njoroje, Mungai 1926- [HPPN]
Kenyan physician
* Kenya's One Man Medical Program

Nkrumah, Kwame 1909-1972 [IBW]
Prime minister of Ghana
* Osagyefo [Redeemer]

No bel-esprit
See Lowell, John

NO, Dr.
See Many, Seth E[dward]

No, Dr.
See Treurnicht, Andries

No Flint Grey
See Grey, Charles [First Earl Grey]

No Hit Nolan
See Ryan, [Lynn] Nolan

No Kid Glover
See Glover, Frederick Austin [Freddie]

No Matter by Whom
See Ralph, James

No Name
See Burleigh, Cecil

No Neck Williams
See Williams, Walter Allen

[The] No Nonsense Lady
See Thatcher, Margaret Hilda [Roberts]

No Problems Ed
See Meese, Edwin, III

No Rap
See Brown, Lee Patrick

No Splash Browning
See Browning, David

Noack, Armond A. 1930- [ECM]
American country-western performer
* Noack, Eddie
* Wood, Tommy

Noack, Eddie
See Noack, Armond A.

Noah, Father
See Welles, Gideon

Noah, Major
See Noah, Mordecai Manuel

Noah, Mordecai Manuel 1785-1851 [FFF, HPPN, IP]
American journalist and politician
* Howard
* Malack, Muly
* Noah, Major

Noah W.
See Worcester, Noah

Noailles, Duchesse de 18th c. [DNNS, FFF, RH]
French courtier
* Etiquette, Madame

Noakes, John
See Taylor, Tom

[The] Nobel Laureate
See Shockley, [Dr.] William Bradford

Nobel, Phil
See Fanthorpe, R[obert] Lionel

Nobile, Frederico 1874-1948 [BDF, FC]
American director
* Niblo, Fred

Nobilis Mathematicus
See Dee, John

Nobis, Booger Red
See Nobis, Thomas H., Jr.

Nobis, Thomas H., Jr. 1943-
American football player
* Nobis, Booger Red

[The] Noble
See Alfonso VIII [or Alphonso]

[The] Noble
See Charles III

[The] Noble
See Frederick William

[El] Noble
See Sancho IV

[The] Noble
See Suleiman I [or Soliman]

[The] Noble American Who Could Meet the European Philosophers ...
See Carnes, Peter

[A] Noble Author
See Byron, George Gordon Noel

[The] Noble Buzzard
See Burnet, Gilbert

Noble, Charles
See Pawley, Martin Edward

Noble, Clarke Randolph 20th c. [BBH]
American baseball coach and collegiate athletic director
* Noble, Dudy

Noble, Clyde V.
See Fisher, Clyde V.

[A] Noble Commander in America
See Campbell, John [Fourth Earl of Loudoun]

Noble, Dudy
See Noble, Clarke Randolph

[A] Noble Duke
See St. John, Henry

[The] Noble Earl
See Butler, James [Second Earl of Ormonde]

Noble, James 1907- [MY]
American jazz musician
* Noble, Jiggs

Noble, James
See Holloway, Ernest A.

Noble, Jiggs
See Noble, James

Noble, John [Appelbe] 1914- [CA]
British-born mariner and author
* Jan
* Lookout

Noble, John
See Griffin, Frank

Noble, John
See Hubble, Leslie Arthur Burt

Noble, Kid
See Moore, Harry R.

Noble, Kitty
See Killingsworth, Katherine

[A] Noble Lord
See Byron, George Gordon Noel

[A] Noble Lord
See Campbell, John [Fourth Earl of Loudoun]

[A] Noble Lord
See Cooper, Anthony Ashley [Third Earl of Shaftsbury]

[A] Noble Lord
See Sackville, [Lord] George [First Viscount Sackville]

[A] Noble Lord and Eminent Lawyer
See Gore, John [Baron Annaly]

Noble, Margaret Elizabeth 1867-1911 [BI]
Irish disciple of Swami Vivekananda
* Nivedita, [Sister]

[A] Noble Peer
See Harley, Robert [First Earl of Oxford]

Noble, Rafael Miguel 1922- [BE, OBW]
Cuban-born baseball player
* Noble, Ray

Noble, Ray
See Noble, Rafael Miguel

Noble, Samuel 1859-? [WWL]
Scottish author and poet
* Nomie

[The] Noble Soul
See Khosru I [or Chosroes]

[The] Noble Wit of Scotland
See Mackenzie, [Sir] George

[A] Nobleman
See Hervey, John [Baron Hervey of Ickworth]

[A] Nobleman
See Russell, William

[A] Nobleman Abroad
See Granville, George [Lord Viscount Lansdowne]

[A] Nobleman of the Other Kingdom
See Perceval, [Sir] John [First Earl of Egmont]

[A] Nobleman's Son
See Barrett, T. W.

Nobles, Milton
See Tamey, Milton

Noblesse Oblige
See Evans, Howard

[The] Noblest Roman of the National Baseball Field
See Comiskey, Charles Albert

[The] Noblest Roman of Them All
See McMillin, Benton

[The] Noblest Roman of Them All
See Thurman, Allan Granbery

Nobody [The Writer]
See Maurice, John Frederick Denison

Nobody
See Robinson, James

Nobody, A.
See Browne, Gordon Frederick

Nobody, Nathan
See Yellott, George

Nobody, Nemo
See Fennell, James

Noceni, Erle
See Sellers, Connie Leslie, Jr.

Nocentelli, Breeze
See Nocentelli, Leo

Nocentelli, Leo 20th c. [RM]
Musician
* Nocentelli, Breeze

Noch Vaster [Even Firmer]
See Steendam, Jacob

Nock, Albert Jay 1872?-1945 [BI, HPPN]
American historian
* Journeyman

Nocona Slim Burnett
See Burnett, John

Nod Noll
See Cromwell, Oliver

Nodder, Frederick 1893?-1937 [HPPN]
British murderer
* Hudson, Frederick
* Nodder, Uncle Fred

Nodder, Uncle Fred
See Nodder, Frederick

Nodset, Joan L.
See Lexau, Joan M.

Noe, Amedee de 1819-1879 [FFF, RH, WBD]
French caricaturist
* Cham

[The] Noel Coward of Russia
See Kataev, Valentin Petrovich

[The] Noel Coward of Ventriloquists
See Bergen, Edgar

Noel, Ella Marguerite 1943- [OP]
American opera singer
* Noel, Rita

Noel, Hilda Bloxton, Jr.
See Schroetter, Hilda Noel

Noel, John
See Bird, Dennis Leslie

Noel, L.
See Barker, Leonard Noel

Noel, Lucie
See Leon, Elizabeth Lucie

Noel, Lucien 20th c.
French actor
* Noel Noel

Noel, Marie
See Rouget, Marie Melanie

Noel Noel
See Noel, Lucien

Noel, Rita
See Noel, Ella Marguerite

Noel, Victoire 1815-1903 [BBD]
French opera singer
* Niva, Rosa
* Stoltz, [Mademoiselle] Heloise
* Stoltz, Rosine
* Ternaux, Mademoiselle

Noel-Baker, Philip John
See Baker, Philip John

Noel-Cooper, George W.
See Cooper, George William Noel

Noel Hume, Ivor 1927- [IAW]
British-born archaeologist and author
* Akerman, Richard

Noelita Marie, [Sister]
See Blakely, Delois

Noevius
See Nefe, Gaspard

Nofziger, Franklin Curran 1924-
American political consultant
* Nofziger, Lyn

Nofziger, Lyn
See Nofziger, Franklin Curran

Nogaret de la Valette, Jean Louis de 1554-1642 [SN]
French courtier and politician
* Epernon, Duc d'
* [Le] Valet du Cardinal

Nogaret, Francois Felix 1740-1830 [IP]
French author
* Aristenete

Noguchi, Thomas T. 1927?- [NW 3-28-83]
Japanese-born pathologist
* Coroner to the Stars

Noguchi, Yone 1875-1947 [BI]
Japanese poet
* Morning Glory, Miss

Noguera, Magdalena
See Conde Abellan, Carmen

Nogues i Cases, Xavier 1873-1941 [WEC]
Spanish cartoonist and illustrator
* Babel

Nohain, Franc
See Le Grand, Franc

Noham, Cam
See McMahon, Heber

Nohnn, Joel
See Lennon, John

Noir, Jean
See Cassou, Jean

Nojiri, Kiyohiko 1897-1973 [CA]
Japanese author and historian
* Osaragi, Jiro

Nokes, George Augustus 1867-? [WWL]
British author
* Sekon, George Augustus

Nokes, James 17th c. [DNNS, SN]
British actor
* [The] Liston of His Age
* Nokes, Nurse

Nokes, Nurse
See Nokes, James

Nokes, William 18th c. [IP]
British author
* [A] Catholick

Nolamo, Stanley
See Cohen, Stanley Irving

[The] Nolan
See Bruno, Giordano

Nolan, Brian
See O'Nuallain, Brian

Nolan, Buddy
See Nolan, Clarence H.

Nolan, Chuck
See Edson, John Thomas

Nolan, Clarence H. 1917- [HPPN]
American pianist and theater organist
* Nolan, Buddy

Nolan, [Violet] Cynthia 1914- [WD]
Australian author
* Reed, Cynthia

Nolan, Dixie
See Scruggs, Irene

Nolan, Edward 1857-1919 [HPPN]
American actor
* Nalod, Edward

Nolan, Edward Sylvester 1857-1913 [BE]
American baseball player
* [The] Only Nolan

Nolan, Frederic 1871-1926 [HPPN]
American vaudeville performer
* Nolan, Fritz

Nolan, Frederick 1784-1864 [IP, PA]
Irish clergyman and author
* [A] Reformer
* Search, Sarah
* Vigors, N. A., Jun.

Nolan, Fritz
See Nolan, Frederic

Nolan, George Brent 1904- [FC]
Irish-born actor
* Brent, George

Nolan, Jeannette Covert 1897-1974 [CA, SAT]
American author and critic
* Tucker, Caroline

Nolan, Kathleen
See Schrum, Jocelyn

Nolan, Louis Edward [IP]
British army officer and author
* Garrard, Kenner

Nolan, Mary
See Robertson, Mary Imogene

Nolan, Mrs. James [FFF]
Entertainer
* Ryan, Kate

Nolan, No Hit
See Ryan, [Lynn] Nolan

Nolan, Stephen 1820?-1890 [PI]
Irish poet and barrister
* Elrington, Stephen Nolan
* S. N.
* S. N. E., jun.

Nolan, William F[rancis] 1928- [CA, WGT]
American author
* Anmar, Frank
* Cahill, Mike?
* Edwards, F. E.
* Phillips, Michael

Noland, Charles Fenton Mercer 1812-1858 [IP, PA]
American author
* N. of Arkansas
* Whetstone, Pete

Noland, John T. 1896-1931 [BLB, CEC, MM]
American underworld figure
* [The] Clay Pigeon of the Underworld
* Diamond, John Thomas [Jack]
* Diamond, Legs
* Hart, John
* Higgins, John

Nolarci, Vigilio
See Carnoli, Luigi

Nolde, Emil
See Hansen, Emil

Nolkejumskoi
See William Augustus

Noll
See Cromwell, Oliver

Noll
See Goldsmith, Oliver

Noll, Bink
See Noll, Lou Barker

Noll, John Francis 1875-? [NAA]
American clergyman and author
* J. F. N.

Noll, Lou Barker 1927- [CA]
American poet and editor
* Noll, Bink

Noll, Martin David 1912- [CA]
American author and poet
* Buxbaum, Martin

Nolly, Emile
See Detanger, Emile

Nomad
See Custer, George Armstrong

Nomad
See Grafton-Smith, Adele

Nomad, Max
See Nacht, Max

Nomdet, Nylla
See Tedmon, Allyn Henry

Nomelleni, Leo 1924-
Italian-born American football player
* [The] Lion

Nomentanus
See Crescentius, Johannes [or John]

Nomie
See Noble, Samuel

Nomistake
See Partee, W. B.

Nompar de Caumont, Antonin 1633-1723 [RH]
French soldier
* [The] Dancing Chancellor
* Lauzun, Duc de

[The] Non Candidate
See Muskie, Ed[mund Sixtus]

[A] Non Combatant
See Bushby, Henry Jeffreys

[A] Non Commissioned Officer
See Driggs, George W.

[The] Non Hero in His Own Cause
See Hiss, Alger

[A] Non Intrusionist
See Dunbar, George

[A] Non Juror
See Spinckes, Nathaniel

[The] Non Organization Man
See Delorean, John Zachary

[The] Non Stop Activist
See Fonda, Jane

[The] Non Such
See Hutchinson, Ann

[The] Non Violent Singer
See Baez, Joan

[A] Nonagenarian
See Emery, Sarah Anna [Smith]

[A] Nonagenarian
See Graves, Richard

Noname [house pseudonym]
See Enton, Harry

Noname
See Senarens, Luis Philip

Nonda
See Papadopoulos, Epaminondes

Nonnemaker, Gus
See Nonnemaker, Gustavus

Nonnemaker, Gustavus 20th c.   [EF]
American football player
* Nonnemaker, Gus

Nonnenkamp, Leo William 1911-   [BE]
American baseball player
* Nonnenkamp, Red

Nonnenkamp, Red
See Nonnenkamp, Leo William

Nonni
See Svensson, Jon Stefan

Nonnius
See Nunez, Ludwig

Nonomura, I-yetsu 1576?-1643   [BI]
Japanese painter
* Sotatsu

[The] Nonpareil
See Kelly, John

[The] Nonpareil
See Randall, Jack

[Sir] Nonsence, Gregory
See Taylor, John

Nontoiling Sedentary Conspirator
See Hillman, Sidney

Noon, Brian 1919-   [CA]
British artist, graphologist, poet
* Kurdsen, Stephen

Noon, Ed
See Avallone, Michael [Angelo], Jr.

Noon Ghunna
See Khan, Javed Miandad

Noon, T. R.
See Norton, Olive Marion [Claydon]

Noon, Thomas 1921-1968   [FC]
American actor
* Noonan, Tommy

Noonan, Chotsie
See Noonan, Virginia Louise

Noonan, Robert 1868-1911   [LC]
British author
* Tressell, Robert

Noonan, Suzanne Dobson 1911-
American actress
* O'Day, Molly

Noonan, Tommy
See Noon, Thomas

Noonan, Virginia Louise 1910?-1968
[F2, FC, HPPN]
American actress
* Noonan, Chotsie
* O'Neil, Sally

Noone, Edwina
See Avallone, Michael [Angelo], Jr.

Noone, Peter Blair Denis Bernard 1947-
[EPM, PRS, RO2]
British singer
* Herman

Noordung, Hermann
See Potocnik, Captain

Nora [or Norma]
See Aiken, Elizabeth

Norah
See McDougall, Margaret [Dixon]

Norbert, [Father]
See Parisot, Pierre

Norbert, W.
See Wiener, Norbert

Norbury, Earl of 19th c.   [DNNF, FFF, SN]
Irish jurist
* [The] Hanging Judge

Norcross, Elizabeth
See Gladstone, Arthur M.

Norcross, John
See Conroy, John Wesley [Jack]

[Le] Nord
See Colbert, Jean Baptiste de

Nord, Amiral [code name used during World War II]
See Abrial, [Vice Admiral]

Nord, Pierre
See Brouillard, Andre Leon

Nordau, Max Simon
See Suedfeld, Max Simon

Norden, Charles
See Durrell, Lawrence [George]

Norden, Christine
See Thornton, Mary

Norden, Helen Brown
See Lawrenson, Helen

Nordenhjelm   [DEP]
* [The] Father of Swedish Eloquence

Nordhausen, Richard 1868?-?   [WBD]
German author
* Caliban

Nordheim, Sondre 1825-1897   [BBH]
Norwegian-born skiing pioneer
* [The] Father of Ski Jumping and Slalom
* [The] Father of Skiing

Nordhof, Daniel Georg 1639-1691   [PA]
Author
* Polyhistor

Nordhoff, Charles 1830-?   [IP]
American journalist
* [A] Boy
* Holmes, Charles
* [A] Sailor
* [A] Sailor Boy

Nordica, Lillian
See Norton, Lillian

Nordicus
See Snyder, Louis L.

Nordling, Johan 19th c.   [HPPN]
Swedish author
* Grip, Halvor

Nordstrom, Andrew Arthur 1931-   [BE]
American baseball player
* Carey, Andy

Norell, Norman
See Levinson, Norman

Norena, Eide
See Hansen, Kaja Andrea Karoline Eide

Norfolciensis
See Greene, Robert

[The] Norfolk Boy
See Porson, Richard

[The] Norfolk Gamester
See Walpole, [Sir] Robert [First Earl of Orford]

Norfolk, Kid
See Ward, William [Willie]

Noriac, Jules
See Cairon, Jules

Noricus
See Tockler, Conrad

Noriko
See Nishi, Noriko

Nork, F.
See Korn, Friedrich

Norkey, Bhotia Tensing
See Bhutia, Tensing

Norma Jean
See Beasler, Norma Jean

[The] Norma Shearer of Sweden
See Gustafsson, Greta Lovisa

[The] Normal Little Boy
See Lord, Michael

[The] Norman
See William I

Norman, Ames
See Ames, Norma

Norman, Barbara 1927- [CA, WD]
American author and translator
* Makanowitzky, Barbara

Norman, Bill
See Norman, Henry Willis Patrick

Norman, Coniel 20th c. [SMG]
American basketball player
* Norman, Popcorn

Norman, Don[ald] 20th c. [RO2]
American musician and songwriter
* Storball, Don

Norman, F. M. 1833-? [NPS]
Naval officer and author
* Tower, Martello

Norman, Fredie Hubert 1942- [SMG]
American baseball player
* Norman, Top Cat

Norman, George 1896?-1947 [HPPN]
American entertainer
* [The] Creole Fashion Plate
* Norman, Karyl

Norman, Geraldine [Lucia] 1940- [CA]
British author
* Keen, Geraldine

Norman, Greg 1955?- [TI 7-2-84]
Australian golfer
* [The] Great White Shark

Norman, Harold Christopher Francis
1879-? [WWL]
British author
* Hill, Warren

Norman, Henry Willis Patrick
1910-1962 [BE]
American baseball player and manager
* Norman, Bill

Norman, J. H.
See Norman, John Henry

Norman, James
See Schmidt, James Norman

Norman, Jett
See Walker, Clint

Norman, Joe
See Heard, J[oseph] Norman

Norman, John
See Lange, John Frederick, Jr.

Norman, John Henry 1896- [ART]
British painter
* Norman, J. H.

Norman, Josephine
See Arrich, Josephine

Norman, Karyl
See Norman, George

Norman, Kerry
See Le Pelley, Guernsey

Norman, Louis
See Carman, [William] Bliss

Norman, Louis
See Whittemore, Don

Norman, Mrs. George
See Blount, Melesina Mary [Mackenzie]

Norman, Norman V.
See Norman-Burt, Norman V.

Norman, Philip
See Philips, George Norman

Norman, Pierre
See Connor, Joseph Patrick

Norman, Popcorn
See Norman, Coniel

Norman, Richard
See Briefer, Richard [Dick]

Norman, Robert
See Gardner, Maurice

Norman, Shin
See Norman, William

Norman, Steve
See Pashko, Stanley

Norman, Thyrza
See Neeves, Thyrza

Norman, Top Cat
See Norman, Fredie Hubert

Norman, Victor
See Ransome, L. E.

Norman, W. S.
See Wilson, N[orman] Scarlyn

Norman, William 1935-1976 [IBW]
American entertainer
* Fat Alburt

Norman, William 20th c. [OBW]
American baseball player
* Norman, Shin

Norman-Burt, Norman V. 1864-1943
[THR]
British actor and theatrical manager
* Norman, Norman V.

Normand, Cisco
See Normand, Emile R.

Normand, Emile R. 1936- [EJ7]
Canadian jazz musician
* Normand, Cisco

Normand, Mabel 1894-1930 [HPPN]
American actress
* [The] Funniest Woman of the Silent
  Screen

Normand, Mabel
See Fortescue, Mabel

Normand, Theodule-Eleazar-Xavier
1812-1888 [BBD]
French scholar
* Nisard, Theodore

Normannus
See Tonnies, Ferdinand Julius

Norman's Puppy Dog
See Hasslehoon, Renaldo

Normanus
See Muris, Johannes de

Normyx [joint pseudonym with Norman
Douglas]
See Douglas, Elsa Fitzgibbon

Normyx [joint pseudonym with Elsa
Fitzgibbon Douglas]
See Douglas, Norman

Norna
See Brooks, Mary Elizabeth [Aiken]

**Norodom Sihanouk [Varman], Samdech
Preah** 1922- [CA]
Cambodian ruler and author
* Sihanouk, Norodom

Norr, Isroy M. 1887-1962 [HPPN]
American press agent
* Norr, Roy M.

Norr, Roy M.
See Norr, Isroy M.

Norris, Alexander M.
See Nosseck, Max

Norris, Arthur 1911- [BA]
American educator
* Norris, Mae

Norris, Benjamin Franklin, Jr.
1870-1902 [LC, TC]
American author
* Norris, Frank

Norris, Clarence 1913- [IBW]
Defendant in celebrated "Scottsboro" trial
* Norris, Willie

Norris, Dad
See Norris, John F.

Norris, Dead Eye
See Norris, William James

Norris, Edgar Poe
See Kinnaird, Clark

Norris, Frank
See Norris, Benjamin Franklin, Jr.

Norris, George William 1861-1944
[HPPN, WBD]
American politician
* [The] Dean of the Liberals
* [The] Father of Public Utility
  Regulation
* [The] Father of The Twentieth
  Amendment
* [The] Greek Purist

Norris, Harris
See Swindell, Minnie Harris

Norris, Henry 1665-1731 [IP, NPS, SN]
British actor
* H. N.
* Heigh-Ho
* Jubilee Dicky
* Scrub, Dicky

Norris, [Sir] John ?-1746 [DNNF, FFF, SN]
British naval officer
* Foul Weather Jack

Norris, John 1657-1711 [DNNS, HN, RH]
British philosopher and clergyman
* [The] English Plato

Norris, John F. 1846-1926 [HPPN]
American actor
* Norris, Dad

Norris, Kid
See Norris, Walter Oster

Norris, Mae
See Norris, Arthur

Norris, Randal [IP]
British barrister and author
* R. N.

Norris, Ruby Turner
See Morris, Ruby Turner

Norris, Walter Oster 1904-1958 [BBH]
American lacrosse player and coach
* [The] Kid
* Norris, Kid

Norris, William
See Block, William Norris

Norris, William James 1951- [BWW]
American singer
* Norris, Dead Eye

Norris, Willie
See Norris, Clarence

Norroy
See Browne, H. F.

[The] Norskie
See Amundsen, Roald

[A] North American
See Dickinson, John

North, Andre
See Norton, Alice Mary

North, Andrew
See Norton, Alice Mary

North, Anison
See Wilson, May

North, Barclay
See Hudson, William Cadwalader

North, Bob
See Young, Harold

North, C. C. 1865-1926 [HPPN]
American actor
* North, Sport

North, [Major] Charles Napier 19th c. [HPPN]
British army officer
* [An] English Major in India

North, Charles W.
See Bauer, Erwin A.

North, Christopher
See Maginn, William

North, Christopher
See Wilson, John

North, Colin
See Bingley, David Ernest

North, Colonel
See Bullivant, Cecil Henry

[The] North Country Angler
See Doubleday, Thomas

North, Darby
See Madden, Daniel Owen

North, Edward 1820-? [IP]
American scholar
* Dix Quaevidi

North, Elisha 1771-1843 [DNA, IP]
American author and physician
* Uncle Toby

North, Eric
See Cronin, Bernard [Charles]

North, F. H.
See Pratt, Jacob Loring

North, Frederic [Second Earl of Guilford] 1732-1792 [IP]
British statesman and author
* Northelia

North, [Captain] George
See Balfour, Robert Louis

North, Gil
See Horne, Geoffrey

North, Grace May
See North-Monfort, Grace May

North, Hattie
See Johnson, Edith North

North, Howard
See Dudley-Smith, Trevor

North, Ingoldsby
See Urner, Nathan Dane

North, Iris
See Morgan, Joan

North, Jack
See Pentelow, John Nix

North, James
See Swanson, Dan

North, John ?-1819 [IP]
British author and book collector
* Palermo

North, John ?-1835 [HPPN]
American gambling house proprietor
* [The] South's Most Crooked Gambler

North, John Ringling 1903- [HPPN]
American circus impresario and executive
* [The] Greatest Showman Since Barnum

North, John Thomas 1844-1896 [DNNS, FFF]
British industrialist
* [The] Nitrate King

North, Jonathan David
See Cohen, Paul Arthur

North, Kit
See Wilson, John

North, Laurence
See Symon, James David

North, Leigh
See Phelps, Elizabeth Steward [Natt]

North, Lionel
See Northcroft, George J. H.

North, Marilla
See Wilson, Marilla

North, Mark
See Miller, Wright W[atts]

North, Oliver
See Mullen, M.

North, Paul 1889?-1968 [THR]
British artist and designer
* Shelving, Paul

North, Pearson
See Pearson, T. E.

North, Robert
See Withers, Carl A.

North, Roger 1650-1733 [IP]
British barrister and author
* [A] Person of Honour

North, Sara
See Bonham, Barbara Thomas

North, Sara
See Hager, Jean

North, Sheree
See Bethel, Dawn

North, Sport
See North, C. C.

[The] North Star
See Bailey, Frederick Augustus Washington

North, Theophila
See Hollins, Dorothea

North, [Sir] Thomas 1535?-1601? [HPPN]
British translator and author
* [The] First Master of English Prose

North Vietnam's Militant Uncle
See Nguyen That Thanh

North, W. Savage
See Newell, S.

North, William 1869-? [WW]
Author
* Rodd, Ralph
* Vanner, John

[The] North Wind
See Colbert, Jean Baptiste de

North-Monfort, Grace May 20th c.
[NAA]
American author
* North, Grace May
* Norton, Carol

[The] Northamptonshire Peasant Poet
See Clare, John

[The] Northamptonshire Poet
See Clare, John

[The] Northamptonshire Poet
See Plummer, John

Northcote
See Boulting, Sydney

Northcote, [Sir] Stafford Henry 1818-?
[IP]
British statesman and author
* West End, [Sir] Warwick

Northcott, Baldy
See Northcott, Laurence

Northcott, [William] Cecil 1902- [CA]
British clergyman and author
* Miller, Mary
* Temple, Arthur

Northcott, Laurence 1907- [CEI]
Canadian-born hockey player
* Northcott, Baldy

Northcroft, Dorothea M. 20th c.
[WWL]
British author
* Ford, D. M.

Northcroft, E. Florence ?-1914 [WWL]
British author
* Cheerful, [Mrs.] Mary

Northcroft, George J. H. [WWL]
British author
* North, Lionel

Northe, Margaret Scott Copeland
20th c. [NAA]
American musician, poet, editor
* Copeland, Margaret Scott

Northelia
See North, Frederic [Second Earl of
Guilford]

Northen, Hub
See Northen, Hubbard Elwin

Northen, Hubbard Elwin 1885-1947
[BE]
American baseball player
* Northen, Hub

Northend, William Dummer 1823-? [IP]
American attorney and author
* W. D. N.

[The] Northern Addison
See Mackenzie, Henry

[The] Northern Dante
See Ossian

Northern Gael
See Devlin, Joseph

[The] Northern Harlot
See Elizabeth Petrovna

[The] Northern Herodotus
See Sturluson, Snorro

Northern, Leslie [house pseudonym]
See Long, Frank Belknap

[A] Northern Man
See Ingersoll, Joseph Reed

**[The] Northern Man with Southern
Principles**
See Van Buren, Martin

[The] Northern Phidias
See Thorvaldsen, Bertel [or Albert]

[A] Northern Presbyter
See Lord, Nathan

[The] Northern Semiramis
See Catherine II

[The] Northern Semiramis
See Margaret

[The] Northern Star
See Peter I [Petr Alekseevich]

[The] Northern Telemaque
See Alexander I [Aleksandr Pavlovich]

[The] Northern Thor
See Alexander I [Aleksandr Pavlovich]

[The] Northern Victor
See Gustavus II

Northerner
See Hughes, William Jesse

Northey, Carrie
See Roma, Caro

Northey, Ronald James 1920-1971 [BE]
American baseball player
* [The] Round Man

Northgrave, Anne
See Tibble, Anne

Northmore, Elizabeth Florence
1906-1974 [CAP]
British author
* Stucley, Elizabeth

Northmore, Thomas 18th c. [IP]
British author and poet
* Phileleutherus Devoniensis

Northrop, George Howard 1888-1945
[BN]
American baseball player
* Northrop, Jake
* Northrop, Jerky Jake

Northrop, Jake
See Northrop, George Howard

Northrop, Jerky Jake
See Northrop, George Howard

Northrop, John K. 1896-1981 [HPPN]
*American designer and manufacturing
executive*
* [The] World's Last Great Aviation
Pioneer

Northrup, [Capt.] B. A.
See Hubbard, Lafayette Ronald

Northrup, C. B. 19th c. [IP]
American poet and politician
* [A] Gentleman of South Carolina
* N.
* [The] Outcast

Northrup, Darrell
See Weeks, James

Northrup, Doc
See Northrup, M. A.

Northrup, Edwin Fitch 1866-1940 [ESF,
SFL, WGT]
American author
* Pseudoman, Akkad

Northrup, M. A. 20th c. [BBH]
American wrestler
* Northrup, Doc

Northshield, Robert 20th c. [ET]
Producer and television scriptwriter
* Northshield, Shad

Northshield, Shad
See Northshield, Robert

[The] Northumberland Piper
See Allen, James

[The] Northumbrian Gentleman
See Tegner, Henry [Stuart]

[The] Northwest Lumber King
See Benson, Simon

[The] Northwest Mystic
See Callahan, Kenneth

Norton, Alice Mary 1912- [CA, HPPN,
MJA, WYA]
American author
* North, Andre
* North, Andrew
* Norton, Andre
* Norton, Andrew
* Weston, Allen [joint pseudonym with
Grace Weston Hogarth]

Norton, Alice Whitson 1897- [NAA]
American writer
* Barry, Alice Montgomery
* Slater, Elizabeth Anne

Norton, Andre
See Norton, Alice Mary

Norton, Andrew
See Norton, Alice Mary

Norton, Andrews 1786-1853 [HPPN]
American scholar and educator
* One Lately a Member of the
Immediate Government of the College

Norton, Barry
See De Biraben, Alfredo

Norton, Bess
See Norton, Olive Marion [Claydon]

Norton, Bram
See Bramesco, Norton J.

Norton, Brocky Jack
See Norton, J. S.

Norton, Browning
See Norton, Frank R. B.

Norton, Carol
See North-Monfort, Grace May

Norton, Caroline Elizabeth Sarah
1808-1877 [FFF, HPPN, IP, PA]
British author
* Aunt Carry
* Hi Ski Hi
* [The] Honorable Mrs. Norton
* Libertas
* Sheridan, C. E.
* Stevenson, Pierce
* Tic-tic, [Count] Horloge de

Norton, Charles Eliot 1827-1908
[HPPN, IP]
American author, editor, translator
* [The] Apostle of Culture
* C. E. N.

Norton, Charles Ledyard 1837-1909
[HPPN]
American author
* Cogswell, E.
* D'Estrian, P.
* Sienna, B. T.

Norton, Chico
See Norton, Forrest

Norton, Clothes
See Norton, Ned

Norton, Daniel 20th c. [RO1]
American singer
* Norton, Sonny

Norton, Edith Eliza Ames 1864-1929
[DNA, NAA]
American writer
* Dunn, Eliza
* Kent, Karlene

Norton, Edward 19th c. [IP]
British author
* Honestus

Norton, Emperor
See Norton, Joshua A.

Norton, Fighting Mary
See Norton, Mary Teresa

Norton, Fletcher [First Baron Grantley]
1716-1789 [NPS]
British jurist
* Doublefee, [Sir] Bullface

Norton, Forrest 20th c. [SMG]
American football team staff member
* Norton, Chico

Norton, Frank R. B. 1909- [WYA]
Author
* Norton, Browning

Norton, Homer Hill 1895-1965 [HPPN]
American football coach
* [The] Showdown Man

Norton, J. J. 1849-? [BE]
American baseball player and manager
* Carey, Thomas John [Tom]

Norton, J. S. 19th c. [BLB]
American sheriff's deputy
* Norton, Brocky Jack

Norton, Jack
See Naughton, Mortimer J.

Norton, [Rev.] Jacob 1764-1858 [HPPN]
American clergyman
* [A] Aged Clergyman of Massachusetts
* [An] Orthodox Clergyman of
  Massachusetts
* [A] Serious Inquirer

Norton, James 1606-1663 [IP, PA]
British author
* [A] Layman

Norton, Joshua A. 1819-1880 [HPPN]
*British-born American businessman and
eccentric*
* Emperor of California and Protector
  of Mexico
* Norton, Emperor
* Norton I
* Protector of Mexico

Norton, Lillian 1857-1914 [BBD, BEW,
FFF]
American opera singer
* Nordica, Lillian

Norton, Mary Teresa 1875?-1959
[HPPN, WP 7-17-85]
American politician
* Norton, Fighting Mary
* Washington's First Mayoress

Norton, Mrs. Florice
See Brame, Charlotte Mary

Norton, Ned 1882-1961 [HPPN]
American actor
* Norton, Clothes

Norton, Olive Marion [Claydon] 1913-
[AW, CA]
British author
* Neal, Hilary
* Noon, T. R.
* Norton, Bess
* Norway, Kate

Norton, Philip 19th c. [SFL]
Author
* Smith, Artegall

Norton, Richard Henry Brinsley
1892-1954 [HPPN]
American actor
* Lord, Grantley

Norton, Sonny
See Norton, Daniel

Norton, Sybil
See Cournos, Helen Kestner
Satterthwaite

Norton, Thomas 1532-1584 [FFF]
British barrister and poet
* Archcarnifex

Norton, Victor
See Dalton, Gilbert

Norton I
See Norton, Joshua A.

Norval
See Noyes, E. Herbert

Norval
See Scrymgeour, James

Norvil, Manning
See Bulmer, [Henry] Kenneth

Norville, Kenneth 1908- [EJ, PMJ, WWJ]
American jazz musician
* Norvo, Red

Norville, Mildred Bailey 1906-1951
[HPPN]
American jazz musician
* Bailey, Mildred
* [The] Rocking Chair Lady

Norvo, Red
See Norville, Kenneth

Norvus, Nervous
See Drake, Jimmy

Norway, Kate
See Norton, Olive Marion [Claydon]

Norway, Nevil Shute 1899-1960 [LC,
TC, TCL]
British author
* Shute, Nevil

Norway's First Skald
See Munch, Andreas

Norweb, Janetta [Scott] ?-1817 [IP]
British author
* Janetta

[The] Norwegian Doll
See Henie, Sonja

[The] Norwegian Sphinx
See Bratteli, Trygve

[The] Norwich Quaker
See Gurney, John

[The] Norwich Weaver Boy
See Fox, William Johnson

Norwood, Abraham 19th c. [PA]
Author
* Abraham

Norwood, Ellie
See Brett, Anthony

Norwood, John
See Stark, [Delbert] Raymond

Norwood, One Leg
See Norwood, Sam

Norwood, Paul
See Nettl, John Peter

Norwood, Peg Leg
See Norwood, Sam

Norwood, Pig
See Norwood, Sam

Norwood, R. D.
See Norwood, Sam

Norwood, Sam 1900?-1967? [BWW]
American singer
* Norwood, One Leg
* Norwood, Peg Leg
* Norwood, Pig
* Norwood, R. D.

Norwood, Victor G[eorge] C[harles]
1920- [CA, WD]
British author, playwright, poet
* Banton, Coy
* Baxter, Shane V.
* Bowie, Jim
* Brand, Clay
* Cody, Walt
* Colter, Shayne
* Corteen, Wes
* Dangerfield, Clint
* Dark, Johnny
* Destry, Vince
* Fargo, Doone
* Fisher, Wade
* Gearing-Thomas, G.
* Hampton, Mark
* Janson, Hank [house pseudonym?]
* Karta, Nat
* McCord, Whip
* Rand, Brett
* Regan, Brad
* Russell, Shane
* Shane, Mark
* Shane, Rhondo
* Strange, Dillon
* Tressidy, Jim
* Tyrone, Paul
* Willard, Portman

Norwood, Wheelbarrow
See Norwood, Willie

Norwood, Willie 1947- [SMG]
American basketball player
* Norwood, Wheelbarrow

[The] Nose Slitter
See Coke, Arundel

Nosegay Nan
See Abington, Mrs.

Nosey
See Cromwell, Oliver

Nosey
See Wellesley, Arthur

Nosille, Nalrah
See Ellison, Harlan [Jay]

Noss, Doc
See Noss, M. E.

Noss, M. E. ?-1949 [HPPN]
American prospector
* Noss, Doc

Nosseck, Max 1902-1972 [SC]
Polish-born actor, director, producer
* Norris, Alexander M.

Nostalgia
See Bentley, James William Benedict

[La] Nostalgilder
See Duse, Eleanora

Nostradamus
See Michel de Notredame

Nostradamus, Merlin
See Cobbe, Frances Power

[The] Nostradamus of Portugal
See Bandarra, Goncalo Annes

Nostro, Nick 20th c. [WF]
Italian director
* Howard, Nick

Nosworthy, A. L.
See Nosworthy, Ann Louise

Nosworthy, Ann Louise 1929- [ART]
Scottish-born artist
* Nosworthy, A. L.

[The] Not So Favorite Son
See Reagan, Ronald Wilson

Not So Secret Swinger
See Kissinger, Henry Alfred

Notabilis, Doctor
See Peter de l'Isle

[Il] Notaro
See Jacopo [or Giacomo] da Lentini

Noteveas
See Sanchez, Pedro

Notger [or Notker] 830?-912 [RH, SN, WBD]
Swiss monk
* Balbulus
* [Le] Begue
* [The] Stammerer

Nothing Venture
See Finney, Humphrey S.

Nothus [Bastard]
See Ochus

Notional, Nehemiah
See Lovering, John

Notker 952?-1022 [WBD]
Swiss-German scholar
* Labeo [The Thick-Lipped]

Notlep, Robert
See Pelton, Robert W[ayne]

Notley, Frances Eliza Millett 19th c.
[IP, NPS]
British author
* Derrick, Frances

Noto, John J. 20th c. [HPPN]
American underworld figure
* Noto, Rabbit

Noto, Lore
See Noto, Lorenzo

Noto, Lorenzo 1923- [BEW]
American actor and producer
* Noto, Lore

Noto, Rabbit
See Noto, John J.

Noto, Tony
See Pappadio, Andimo

Nott, Barry
See Hurren, Bernard John

Nott, Charles C. 19th c. [IP]
American soldier and author
* [An] Officer in the Field

Nott, Henry Junius 1797-1837 [DNA, HPPN, IP]
American author and educator
* Hopkins, Jeremiah
* [A] Journeyman Printer
* Singularity, Thomas

Nott, John 1751-1826 [IP]
British poet, scholar, physician
* Vestris, Mons., Sen.

Nott, Josiah Clark 1804-1873 [HPPN]
American ethnologist, physician, author
* N.

Nott, Samuel 1754-1852 [HPPN]
American clergyman and educator
* [The] Patriarch of the New England Clergy

[The] Nottingham Captain
See Brandreth, Jeremiah

Nottingham, Don 1949- [SMG]
American football player
* [The] Human Bowling Ball

[The] Nottingham Poet
See Bailey, Philip James

Notyre, Jack
See England, Cecil Louis

Noureddin-Mahmud 1116-1174 [FFF, HN, RH]
Sultan of Syria and Egypt
* [The] Scourge of Christians

Nourse, Alan E[dward] 1928- [CA]
American author, columnist, medical expert
* Dr. X
* Edwards, Al

Nous-Terre, Jean
See Gratiant, Gilbert

Nous-Tous, Jean
See Gratiant, Gilbert

Nouveau, Arthur
See Whitcomb, Ian

Novachovitch, Lippe Benzion 1856-1932
[HPPN, WBD]
Lithuanian-born author, poet, playwright
* Ben-Nez
* Benedict, Leopold
* [The] Ghetto Poet
* Winchevsky, Morris

Novack, George [Edward] 1905- [CA]
American author and lecturer
* Warde, William F.

Novaes, Guiomar 1895-1979
Brazilian pianist
* [The] Paderewska of the Pampas

Novag, Novi 20th c. [RM]
Musician
* Novi

Novak, Bert
See Capone, Umberto

Novak, Joseph
See Kosinski, Jerzy [Nikodem]

Novak, Kim
See Novak, Marilyn Pauline

Novak, Marilyn Pauline 1933- [BDF, FC, HPPN, HT]
American actress
* Hollywood's Melancholy Blonde
* Novak, Kim

Novak, Robert 20th c. [HPPN]
American columnist
* [The] Prince of Darkness

Novak, Rose 1940- [CA]
American author
* Rose, Marcia [joint pseudonym with Marcia Kamien]

Novakovsky, Alexander 1915- [CA]
Russian-born economist and author
* Nove, Alec

Novalis
See Hardenberg, Friedrich von

Novanglus
See Adams, John

Novarro, Fernandez Antonio
See Sykowski, Abram

Novarro, Ramon
See Samaniegos, Ramon Gil

Novarro the Magnificent
See Sykowski, Abram

Novarro Fernandez, [Count] Alexander
See Sykowski, Abram

Nove, Alec
See Novakovsky, Alexander

Novel, Edward
See De Maune, Edward

[The] Novelist Detective
See Rolfe, Maro Orlando

[The] Novelist of the Cattle Kingdom
See Rhodes, Eugene Manlove

[The] Novelist of the Far West
See Guthrie, Alfred Bertram, Jr.

[The] Novelist of the New Testament
See Douglas, Lloyd Cassel

[The] Novelist of Three Worlds
See Hueffer, Ford Madox

[The] Novelist of Wessex
See Hardy, Thomas

[The] Novelist's Novelist
See Miller, Leonard

Novella, Rita 1920- [FC]
Mexican actress, singer, dancer
* Drake, Dona
* Rio, Rita

Novelli, Enrico 1876-1943 [WEC]
Italian cartoonist, author, illustrator
* Yambo

Novelli, Mario 20th c. [WF]
Italian actor
* Freeman, Anthony

Novello, Armando 1888-1938 [BMH, SC]
Swiss-born actor and circus performer
* Toto the Clown

Novello, Clara A. 1818-? [PA]
Author
* Gigliucci, Countess

Novello, Don 1943- [CA]
American author, actor, comedian
* Sarducci, [Father] Guido
* Toth, Lazlo

Novello, Ivor
See Davies, Ivor Novello

Novello, Mary 1809-? [PA]
Author
* Baun, Kit, Mariner

Novello-Davies, Clara
See Davies, Clara

[Le] Noven de mon Oncle
See Collin, Jacques Albin Simon

Novi
See Novag, Novi

Novial, Alice 1889-1957 [BI]
American medical missionary
* Marie Suzanne, [Sister]

Novice, George William 19th c. [IP]
Scottish author
* [An] Artist

Novicius, Aloysius
See Logan, John Daniel

Novikoff, Lou[is Alexander] 1915-1970 [BE, PB]
American baseball player
* [The] Mad Russian

Novikov, Olga 1840-1925 [IP, WBD]
Russian journalist
* O. K.
* [A] Russian Lady

Novomirsky
See Gordin, Morris

Novotney, Ralph Joseph 1924- [BE]
American baseball player
* Novotney, Rube

Novotney, Rube
See Novotney, Ralph Joseph

Nowaczynski, Adolf 1876-1944 [CD]
Polish playwright and pamphleteer
* Neuwert
* Przyjaciel

Nowak, Mariette 1941- [CA]
American author
* Ronsman, M. M.

Nowatzke, Thomas M. [Tom] 1942-
American football player
* [The] Struggler

Nowedonah 1903?-1975 [BI]
American Indian lecturer
* Hunter, Lois

Nowel, Samuel ?-1688 [SN]
American clergyman
* [The] Fighting Chaplain

Nowell, Alexander 1507?-1602 [NPS]
British clergyman
* Bottled Beer

Nowell, Elizabeth Cameron 20th c. [SAT]
American author
* Cameron, Elizabeth
* Clemons, Elizabeth

Nowell, Harriett P. [Hardy] 19th c. [HPPN, IP]
American author
* Mannering, May

Nowers, [Rev.] James Henry 19th c. [HPPN]
British clergyman
* [A] Late Railway Chaplain

Nowicki, Janet Lynn 1953- [HPPN]
American figure skater
* Lynn, Janet

Nowlan, George 20th c. [ECM]
American country-western performer
* Davis, Danny
* Yankee Irishman

Nowlan, Phil[ip Francis] 1888-1940 [WGT]
American author
* Phillips, Frank

Nox, Owen
See Cory, Charles Barney

Noy, William 1842-? [IP]
British author
* Pendrea, W.
* W. N.

Noyce, Elisha 19th c. [PA]
Author
* Uncle John

Noye, William 1577-1634 [HPPN]
British barrister
* [The] Great Gamaliel of the Law

Noyes, Arthur
American chemist
* Noyes, Stinker

Noyes, Charles Henry 1849-1898 [HPPN, IP, PA]
American attorney and poet
* Ambrose, [Brother]
* Quiet, Charles

Noyes, E. Herbert [IP, PA]
American author
* Norval
* Saxon

Noyes, Edwin 19th c. [DI]
American swindler
* Horton, Charles Johnson

Noyes, George Rapall 1798-1868
[HPPN]
American scholar
* G. R. N.
* N.

Noyes, James Oscar 1829-? [FFF, IP]
American author
* Our Own Correspondent

Noyes, Jane [McElhinney] 19th c. [IP]
American actress and writer
* Clare, Ada

Noyes, MacLeod
See Palton, Francis T.

Noyes, Mrs. A. C. [FFF]
Entertainer
* Moulton, Mabel

Noyes, Mrs. J. F.
See McElhinney, Jane

Noyes, Stinker
See Noyes, Arthur

Noyes, Winfield Charles 1889- [BE]
American baseball player
* Noyes, Wynn

Noyes, Wynn
See Noyes, Winfield Charles

Noyes-Kane, Dorothy 1906- [CAP]
American author and columnist
* Sproul, Dorothy Noyes

Noziere, Fernand
See Weyl, Fernand

[The] NRA Czar
See Johnson, Hugh Samuel

Ntate, J. J.
See Moiloa, James Jantjies

Ntsoelengoe, Ace
See Ntsoelengoe, Patrick

Ntsoelengoe, Patrick 1956- [AES]
South African soccer player
* Ntsoelengoe, Ace

Nuad [HN]
Irish chieftain
* Silver Hand

Nubbins Colt
See Barnes, Seaborn

Nubin, Rosetta 1915?-1973 [EJ, PMJ]
American singer
* Tharpe, [Sister] Rosetta

Nucera, Marisa Lonette 1959- [CA]
American poet
* Marisa

Nude America, Miss
See Butner, Susan

Nude America, Mr.
See Moore, George

Nude Universe, Miss
See Everts, Kellie

Nude Universe, Miss
See Haines, Suzanne

Nuetzel, Charles [Alexander] 1934-
[ESF, SFL, WGT]
American author
* Augustus, Albert, Jr.
* English, Charles
* Rivere, Alec

**Nuevo Ciclon de Mexico [New Cyclone
of Mexico]**
See Arruza, Manolo

Nuff, Noah
See Bellaw, Americus Wellington

Nugator
See Carter, St. Leger L.

Nugent, Basil 1894-1968 [THR]
British actor
* Sydney, Basil

Nugent, John Peer 1930- [CA]
American author and journalist
* Exall, Barry

Nugent, Michael ?-1845 [PI]
Irish poet, author, critic
* M. N-g-t

Nugent, Nancy 1938- [CA]
American writer and photographer
* Hawke, Nancy

Nugent, Ted 1948?-
American singer
* [The] Motor City Madman

Nu'i
See Kamehameha I

Nuitter, Charles Louis Etienne
See Truinet, Charles Louis Etienne

Nukes, Matti
See Nykanen, Matti Ensio

Nuki
See Millsaps, Daniel W., III

Numano, Allen Stanislaus Motoyuki
1908- [IAW]
Japanese-born author and translator
* Corenanda, A. L. A.

Number 48
See Booth, Albert James, Jr.

Number 1
See Douglas, Leon

Number 1 Adelphi Terriss
See Lewin, William Charles

Number 1 Bride
See Johnson, Lynda Bird

[The] Number 1 Innkeeper
See Hilton, Conrad Nicholson

[The] Number 1 Pinup Girl
See Grasle, Elizabeth

Number One Reference Reviewer
See Cheney, Frances Neel

**[The] Number 1 Slim Woman of the
Air**
See Luther, Irene

Number 30
See Gehlen, Reinhard

Number 12, Mrs.
See Starbuck, Alicia Jo

Number 24
See Sonsteby, Gunnar

[The] Number 2 Nazi
See Goering, Herman Wilhelm

Numidicus
See Metellus, Quintus Caecilius

Numkena, Anthony 20th c.
American actor
* Holliman, Earl

[The] Nun of Duelmen
See Emmerich [or Emmerick], Anna
Katharina

[The] Nun of Kenmare
See Cusack, Mary Frances

[The] Nun of Kent
See Barton, Elizabeth

Nun, Richard 18th c. [PI]
Irish poet
* R. N., Trinity College?

Nuncomar ?-1775 [WBD]
Indian government official
* Nanda Kumar

Nunes, Joseph Q. 19th c. [IP]
American attorney and author
* [A] Diplomat

Nunes de Caceres, Jose 1772-1846
[CW]
Dominican author and poet
* [El] Fabulista Principiante

Nunez, Alcide 1884-1934 [WWJ]
American jazz musician
* Nunez, Yellow

Nunez, Francisco 20th c. [GS]
Spanish bullfighter
* Curillo

Nunez, Juan 19th c. [GS]
Spanish bullfighter
* Sentimientos [Sentiments]

Nunez, Ludwig 1555-? [PA]
Author
* Nonnius

Nunez, William Loring 19th c. [FFF]
Author
* Spencer, Major

Nunez, Yellow
See Nunez, Alcide

Nunez de Arce, Gaspar 1834-1903
[DNNS]
Spanish poet
* [The] Spanish Tennyson

Nunez de Balboa, Vasco 1475-1519
[HPPN]
Spanish explorer
* [The] Finder of the Pacific

**Nunez de Guzman, Fernan [or
Fernando]** 1470?-1553 [DNNS, SN,
WBD]
Spanish scholar
* [El] Comendador Griego
* [The] Greek Commentator
* [El] Pinciano

Nunez Heysham, W. 19th c. [BI]
British author and sportsman
* Aesop

Nunio [SN]
* [The] Lusian Scipio

Nunley, Maggie Rennert
See Rennert, Maggie

Nunn, Carlos
See Sykowski, Abram

Nunn, William Curtis 1908- [CA, WD]
American historian, poet, author
* Curtis, Will
* Twist, Ananias

Nunn May, Allan 20th c. [EE]
*British physicist and intelligence agent for
Russia*
* Alek [code name]

Nunnemacher, Mrs. Jacob [FFF]
Entertainer
* Webster, Lizzie

Nunquam
See Blatchford, Robert

Nunzio, Nicholas S. 20th c. [WP 9-10-
85]
American jurist
* Nunzio, No Nonsense

Nunzio, No Nonsense
See Nunzio, Nicholas S.

Nuppenau, Tonny Landy 1937- [OP]
Danish opera singer
* Landy, Tonny

Nur el Hussein [Light of Hussein]
See Halaby, Elizabeth

Nur, Queen
See Halaby, Elizabeth

Nura
See Ulreich, Nura Woodson

Nuraini
See Sim, Katharine [Thomasset]

Nureyev, Rudolf
See Hametovich, Rudolf

Nurmi, Paavo 1897-1973 [NN, SR, TF]
Finnish track and field athlete
* [The] Flying Finn
* [The] Phantom Finn

Nurmin
See Voronskii, Aleksandr
Konstantinovich

Nurse, Malcolm 1903-1959 [IBW]
West Indian-born diplomat
* Padmore, George A.

[The] Nurse of Antiquity
See Camden, William

[The] Nursing Mother of Philosophy
See Boufflers, Mme. de

[Le] Nus
See Buisson, Jean Baptiste

Nusbaum, Nathaniel Richard 1913-
[BEW, TR]
American playwright, author, producer
* Nash, N. Richard

Nusic, Branislav 1864-1938 [CD]
Serbian playwright and author
* Akiba, Ben

Nuss, Ralph 20th c. [DI]
American murderer
* Russell, Donald

Nussbaum, Al[bert F.] 1934?- [CA]
American bank robber and author
* Avellano, Alberto
* Frederick, Lee
* Hiller, Doris
* Martin, Albert
* Oreshnik, A. F.

Nussbaum, Morris 1897-1964 [SC]
American actor and director
* Ankrum, Morris
* Morris, Stephen

Nussbaum, Mrs.
See Pious, Minerva

Nussbaum, Pansy
See Pious, Minerva

Nutbrown, Maurice 20th c. [MBF]
British author
* Denbigh, Maurice

Nutchuk
See Oliver, Simeon

Nuthead, Dinah 17th c. [HPPN]
American printer
* America's First Female Printer

[The] Nutmeg of Delight
See Hussein

Nutt, Charles 1929-1967 [CA, HFF, SF]
American author
* Beaumont, Charles
* Beaumont, E. J.
* Grantland, Keith
* Lovehill, C. B.
* McNutt, Charles
* Phillips, Michael
* Tenneshaw, S. M. [house pseudonym]

Nutt, Commodore
See McNutt, George Washington
Morrison

Nutt, Lily Clive 1888- [AW]
British author
* Arden, Clive

Nuttall, Jeff 1933- [CA]
British author and poet
* Church, Peter
* Homoras

Nuttall, P. Austin 19th c. [HPPN]
British scholar and lexicographer
* P. A. N.

Nuttall-Smith, Margaret Emily Noel
1919- [ART, FBJ]
British illustrator
* Fortnum, Peggy
* P. F.

Nutter, Buzz
See Nutter, Madison

Nutter, Dizzy
See Nutter, Everett Clarence

Nutter, Edna May Cox-Oliver
1883?-1942 [BEW, F2, OCF]
American actress
* Oliver, Edna May

Nutter, Everett Clarence 1892-1958
[BE]
American baseball player
* Nutter, Dizzy

Nutter, Madison 20th c. [EF]
American football player
* Nutter, Buzz

Nutter, William H. 1875-1941 [HPPN]
American author and journalist
* Witherspoon, Halliday

Nutting, Mary Olivia 1831-1910 [DNA,
PA]
American author
* Barrett, Mary

Nuverbis
See Spotswood, Dillon Jordan

Nuvolari, Tazio [HPPN]
Auto racer
* [The] Flying Mantuan
* [Il] Maestro

Nuyen, France
See Vannga, France

Nuzio
See Muzzio, Girolamo

Nuzio, Girolamo 1496-1576 [WBD]
Italian author and diplomat
* Muzio [or Mutio]

Nxeleafrika, Mnguni
See Jaffe, Hosea

Nyberg, Julia Christina 1785-1854
[HPPN, PA]
Swedish author
* Euphrosyne
* Sveeadstroem

Nyblom, Carl Rupert 1832-1907 [HPPN]
Swedish poet, critic, translator
* C. R. N.
* Carlino

Nyblom, Lennart 1915?- [BI]
Swedish columnist
* Red Top

Nydahl, Mally
See Nydahl, Malvin J.

Nydahl, Malvin J. 1906-   [FB]
American football player
* Nydahl, Mally

Nye
See Bevan, Aneurin

Nye, Bill
See Nye, Edgar Wilson

Nye, Columbus
See Lowell, James Russell

Nye, Edgar Wilson 1850-1896 [FFF,
WBD]
American author
* Nye, Bill

Nye, Gerald P. 1892-1971 [HPPN]
*American newspaper editor, politician,
political reformer*
* [The] Instigator of the Teapot Dome
  Investigation

Nye, Harold G.
See Harding, Lee

Nye, James Warren 1814-1876 [HPPN]
American politician
* Gray Eagle

**Nye, Miriam [Maurine Hawthorn]
Baker** 1918-   [CA]
American author and columnist
* Baker, Miriam Hawthorn

Nye, Nelson C[oral] 1907-   [CA]
American author
* Colt, Clem
* Denver, Drake C.
* Rockingham, Montague

Nyerere, Julius Kambarage 1922-
Tanzanian president
* [The] Father of African Socialism

Nyers, Amelia Kathryn 1907-   [IA]
American writer
* Raw, Kathryn

Nyet, Mr.
See Gromyko, Andrei Andreyevich

Nykanen, Matti Ensio 1963?-   [NW 3-13-
84, SI 12-5-83]
Finnish ski jumper
* Nukes, Matti

Nyky
See Bickerstaffe, Isaac

Nyman, Nyls Wallace 1954-   [BE]
American baseball player
* Nyman, Rex

Nyman, Rex
See Nyman, Nyls Wallace

Nyren, Dorothy
See Curley, Dorothy Nyren

Nyro, Laura
See Nigro, Laura

Nystrom, Knuckles
See Nystrom, Thore Robert

Nystrom, Thore Robert 1952-   [SMG]
Swedish-born hockey player
* Nystrom, Knuckles

Nyvall, David 1863-?   [NAA]
Swedish-born educator, author, poet
* A. N.

O

O.
See Atkinson, [Rev.] Henry

O.
See James, Lionel

O.
See Moffatt, J.

O.
See O'Hagan, John

O.
See O'Leary, Joseph

O.
See Osgood, Samuel

O. A.
See Andersson, Oskar Emil

O. A. B.
See Brownson, Orestes Augustus

O and W [Oldest and Wisest]
See Reagan, Ronald Wilson

O. B.
See Brown, Ollie Lee

O. B.
See Obradovich, James Robert

O. B. C.
See Cole, Owen Blayney

O. B. F.
See Frothingham, Octavius Brooks

O. B. J.
See Johnson, Oliver B.

[The] O. B. T. Czar
See Samuels, Howard

O Breanndain, Cathaoir
See Brennan, Charles

O Ceallaigh, Sean
See O'Kelly, John J.

O Ceallaigh, Tomas
See O'Kelly, Thomas

O Ceithearnaigh, Seamus
See Carney, James [Patrick]

O Conaire, Padraic
See Conroy, Patrick

O Concheanainn, Tomas
See Concannon, Thomas

O Danachair, Caoimhin
See Danaher, Kevin

O Donnchadha, Tadhg
See O'Donoghue, Tadhg

O Dubh, Cathal
See Duff, Charles [St. Lawrence]

O Dubhghaill, Seamus
See Doyle, James J.

O Duinnin, Padraig
See Dinneen, Patrick Stephen

O Farachain, Roibeard
See Farren, Robert

O Flannghaile, Tomas
See Flannery, Thomas

O. H.
See Henwood, [Rev.] Oliver

O. H. I. O.
See Frankenstein, George L.

O. H. K. B.
See Boyd, Oliver H. K.

O hAimhirgin, Osborn
See Bergin, Osborn J.

O hAodha, Tomas
See Hayes, Thomas

[The] O. Henry Girl
See Hinkle, Agnes

O. Jr.
See Omsby, Waterman L., Jr.

O. K.
See Kelly, Jonathan Falconbridge

O. K.
See King, Oliver

O. K.
See Kireeff, O.

O. K.
See Novikov, Olga

O. K., Mr.
See Koischwitz, Max Otto

O. L. F.
See Foster, Olive [Leonard]

O. L. S.
See Russell, George William

O Laoghaire, Peadar
See O'Leary, Peter

O Maille, Micheal
See O'Malley, Michael

O Maonaigh, Cainneach
See Mooney, Canice [Albert James]

O Neachtain, Eoghan
See Naughton, Owen

O. O.
See Nicoll, [Sir] William Robertson

O. P. F.
See Buchanan, James

O. P. Q.
See Merry, Robert

O. R.
See Rand, Olive

O. S.
See Seaman, [Sir] Owen

O Seaghdha, Padraig
See O'Shea, Patrick J.

O Siochain, P[adraig] A[ugustine]
See Sheehan, Patrick Augustine

O. W. H.
See Holmes, Oliver Wendell

O. W. W.
See Wight, Orlando Williams

[The] Oak
See Connor, Roger

Oak Cliff T-Bone
See Walker, Aaron Thibeaux

Oak, Purushottam Nagesh 1917- [IAW]
Indian author
* Amarnath
* Hansraj Bhatia
* Peno
* Uttam

Oaker, Jane
See Peper, Minnie Dorothy

Oakes, A. H.
See Bunner, Henry Cuyler

Oakes, Elizabeth [PA]
Author
* Halfenstein, Ernest

Oakes, Ennis Talmadge 1886-1948 [BE]
American baseball player
* Oakes, Rebel

Oakes, [Sir] Harry 1873?-1943 [HPPN]
British-American murder victim
* [The] Boy from the Backwoods of
  Maine
* [The] Lad from Maine

Oakes, James 1807-1878 [FFF, PA]
Author
* Acorn

Oakes, Rebel
See Oakes, Ennis Talmadge

Oakes, Vanya
See Oakes, Virginia Armstrong

Oakes, Virginia Armstrong 1909- [BI]
American author
* Oakes, Vanya

Oakey, Elegant
See Hall, Abraham Oakey

Oakie, Jack
See Offield, Lewis Delaney

[The] Oakland Redhead
See Budge, [John] Don[ald]

Oakland, Vivian
See Anderson, Vivian

Oakland, Will
See Hinrichs, Herman

Oakley, Annie
See Moses, Phoebe Anne Oakley

Oakley, Daisy
See Harding, Mrs. Roger

Oakley, Eric Gilbert 1916- [CA]
British author and publisher
* Capon, Peter
* Grapho
* Gregson, Paul

Oakley, Frederick [PA]
Author
* Short, Joshua

Oakley, Mrs. J. R. [FFF]
Entertainer
* Vaughn, Cora

Oakly
See Garrick, David

[The] Oakmont Orator
See Dykes, James Joseph [Jimmy]

Oaksey, [Lord] John Geoffrey Tristram
1929- [IAW]
British author
* Audax
* Marlborough

Oaksmith, Elizabeth
See Smith, Elizabeth Oakes

Oakum, John
See Phillips, Walter Polk

Oakwood, Oliver
See Potts, Stacy Gardner

Oana, Henry Kauhane 1908- [BE]
American baseball player
* Oana, Prince

Oana, Prince
See Oana, Henry Kauhane

Oastler, Richard 1789-1861 [DEP,
DNNS, HN]
British social reformer
* [The] Factory King

Oates, Alice
See Titus, Tracy

Oates, C. T.
See Oates, Christine Tate

Oates, Christine Tate 1913- [ART]
British painter
* Oates, C. T.

Oates, [Captain] E. G. ?-1912 [HPPN]
British explorer and army officer
* Hayseed, Farmer
* Oates, Titus

Oates, Felix
See Catlin, George L.

Oates, Joyce Carol 1938- [CN]
American author, playwright, poet
* Fernandes/Oates

Oates, Titus 1620-1705 [HPPN, SN]
British imposter
* Corah
* [The] Knight of the Post
* Libni
* [The] Light of the Town
* [An] Orthodox Beast
* [The] Savior of His Country
* [The] Scorn of the Court
* Telltroth, Titus
* Thou Shred of a Loom

Oates, Titus
See Bell, Martin

Oates, Titus
See Oates, [Captain] E. G.

Oatley, Evelyn 1907-1942 [HPPN]
British actress
* Ward, Nita

Oats, Sergeant
See Vawter, J. B.

Oawi, Dwight Muhammed
See Braxton, Dwight

O'B.?
See O'Brien, M. E.

O'B
See O'Bryant, Tilmon Bunche

Obadele, Imari Abubakaru, I
See Henry, Richard

Obadia, Hakki
See Obadia, Heskel H.

Obadia, Heskel H. 1924- [IWM]
Iraqi-born musician
* Obadia, Hakki

O'Bail, John
See Garganwahgah

O'Banion, Deany [or Deanie]
See O'Bannion, Charles Dion

O'Banion, Dion
See O'Bannion, Charles Dion

O'Bannion, Charles Dion 1892-1924
[BLB, HPPN]
American underworld figure
* Chicago's Arch Criminal
* Gangdom's Favorite Florist
* O'Banion, Deany [or Deanie]
* O'Banion, Dion

Obata, Toshimitsu 1953-
Japanese sumo wrestler
* Kitanoumi

Obata, Yojiro
See Uetake, Yojiro

Obed, Elisha 1952- [IBW]
Bahamian boxer
* [The] Bahamian Fighting Machine

Obee, Lois 1909-1976 [FC, TR]
British actress
* Dresdel, Sonia

O'Beirne, Brian
See Donn-Byrne, Brian Oswald

O'Beirne, Thomas Lewis 1748-1823 [PI]
Irish poet and clergyman
* [The] Mitred Layman

[The] Obelisk
See Thurman, Allan Granbery

O'Bell, John
See Garganwahgah

Obenchain, Eliza Caroline [Calvert]
1856-? [DNA]
American author
* Hall, Eliza Calvert

Ober, Frederick Albion 1849-1913
[HPPN]
American ornithologist and author
* [A] Naturalist

Ober, Sarah Endicott 1854-? [DNA]
American author
* Herrick, Huldah

Oberhansli, Trudi
See Schlapbach-Oberhansli, Trudi

Oberholtzer, Peter
See Brannon, William T.

Oberlander, Andrew J. 1905-1968 [AS,
FB]
American football player
* Oberlander, Swede

Oberlander, Doc
See Oberlander, Hartman Louis

Oberlander, Hartman Louis 1864-1922 [BE]
American baseball player
* Oberlander, Doc

Oberlander, Swede
See Oberlander, Andrew J.

Oberlin, Flossie
See Oberlin, Frank Rufus

Oberlin, Frank Rufus 1876-1952 [BE]
American baseball player
* Oberlin, Flossie

Oberndorff, [Count] Charles 1876-?
[LAO]
German-born author
* Von Oberndorff, Carl

Oberon
See Hathorne, Nathaniel

Oberon
See Robinson, Mary Darby

Oberon
See Snow, Joseph

Oberon, Merle
See Thompson, Estelle Merle O'Brien

O'Berta, Dingbat
See Oberta, John

Oberta, John 20th c. [BLB]
American gangster
* O'Berta, Dingbat

Oberth, Hermann 1894- [HPPN]
German-American scientist
* [The] Father of Space Travel
* [The] Pioneer of Modern Astronautics

Obertraut, Johann Michael 17th c.
[SN]
Danish army officer
* [Der] Deutsche Michael

Obici, Amedeo 1877-1947 [HPPN]
Italian-American peanut industry pioneer
* [The] Peanut King

O'Billovich, Jack 20th c.
American football player
* O'Billovich, Mad Dog

O'Billovich, Mad Dog
See O'Billovich, Jack

O'Birds, John
See Burroughs, John

Obiter Dictum
See Anderson, James

O'Blather, Count
See O'Nuallain, Brian

Oboe, Peter
See Jacobs, Walter Darnell

Obolenski, [Prince] Dimitri Romanoff
See Gerguson, Harry

Oboler, Arch 1907- [HPPN]
American playwright, director, radio executive
* [The] Dean of American Radio
  Writers

O'Boogie, [Dr.] Winston
See Lennon, John

Obotunde, Ijimere
See Beier, Ulli

Obradovic, Dimitrije 1742?-1811 [WBD]
Serbian author
* Dositheus

Obradovich, Buffy
See Obradovich, James Robert

Obradovich, James Robert 1953- [SMG]
American football player
* O. B.
* Obradovich, Buffy

O'Brady, Frederic Michel Maurice
See Abel, Frederic Michel Maurice

O'Brian, Frank
See Garfield, Brian [Francis] Wynne

O'Brian, Hugh
See Krampe, Hugh Charles

O'Brien, A.
See Cream, [Dr.] Thomas Neil

O'Brien, Angela Maxine 1937- [FC, HPPN, IPA, SW]
American actress
* [The] Nation's Top Child Star
* O'Brien, Margaret

O'Brien, Attie
See O'Brien, Francis Marcella

O'Brien, Buck
See O'Brien, Thomas Joseph

O'Brien, Buckshot
See O'Brien, Ralph

O'Brien, C. G.
See O'Brien, Charlotte Grace

O'Brien, Charlotte Grace ?-1909 [WWL]
Irish author
* O'Brien, C. G.

O'Brien, Chewing Gum
See O'Brien, John J.

O'Brien, Clifford Edward 20th c. [SFL, WGT]
Author
* O'Brien, Larry Clinton

O'Brien, Conor Cruise 1917- [BI, CA]
Irish author and diplomat
* Cruise O'Brien, Conor
* O'Donnell, Donat

O'Brien, Cyril C[ornelius] 1906- [CA]
Canadian author, educator, composer
* Wilson, Crane

O'Brien, Daniel Webster 1833-1875
[HPPN]
American minstrel and theatrical producer
* Bryant, Dan

O'Brien, Darby
See O'Brien, John F.

O'Brien, Dave 1912-1969 [HPPN]
American actor
* O'Brien, Tex

O'Brien, Dave
See Fronabarger, David Poole

O'Brien, David 20th c. [HPPN]
American football player
* O'Brien, Little David
* O'Brien, Slingshot

O'Brien, David 20th c. [SFL]
Author
* Cameron, Berl [house pseudonym,
  Curtis Warren]
* Le Page, Rand [house pseudonym,
  Curtis Warren]
* Luna, Kris [house pseudonym, Curtis
  Warren]
* Shaw, Brian [house pseudonym, Curtis
  Warren]

O'Brien, David
See Herd, David

O'Brien, David Wright ?-1944 [ESF,
WGT]
American author
* Blade, Alexander [house pseudonym,
  Ziff-Davis]
* Cabot, John York
* Dennis, Bruce
* Farnsworth, Duncan
* Garson, Clee [house pseudonym, Ziff-
  Davis]
* Vardon, Richard

O'Brien, Dean D. [joint pseudonym
with Otto O(scar) Binder]
See Binder, Earl Andrew

O'Brien, Dean D. [joint pseudonym
with Earl Andrew Binder]
See Binder, Otto O[scar]

O'Brien, Dee
See Bradley, Marion Zimmer

O'Brien, Desmond
See King, Richard Ashe

O'Brien, Donough [Baron of Ibrickan]
?-1624 [WBD]
Irish politician
* [The] Great Earl

O'Brien, Dynamite Johnny
See O'Brien, John

O'Brien, E. G.
See Clarke, Arthur C[harles]

O'Brien, Edmond 1915-1985 [WP 5-10-
85]
American actor
* O'Brien, Tiger

O'Brien, Edward Joseph Harrington
1890- [WWL]
American author
* Middleton, Arthur

O'Brien, Edward Stevenson
See Butt, Isaac

O'Brien, Ellard John 1930- [CEI]
Canadian-born hockey player
* O'Brien, Obie

O'Brien, Flann
See O'Nuallain, Brian

O'Brien, Francis Marcella 1840-1883
[PI]
Irish poet
* O'Brien, Attie

O'Brien, Frank Aloysius 1894- [BE]
American baseball player
* O'Brien, Mickey

O'Brien, George 1900- [HPPN]
American actor
* [The] He Man Star of the Twenties and Thirties
* [A] Man's Man and the Idol of Women

O'Brien, Gladys ?-1920 [SC]
American actress
* Field, Gladys

O'Brien, Hod
See O'Brien, Walter Howard

O'Brien, Howard Vincent 1888-1947
[WW]
Author
* Perrin, Clyde

O'Brien, Jack
See Hagen, Joseph F.

O'Brien, James 1805-1864 [HPPN]
Irish journalist
* Bronterre, James

O'Brien, James C. 20th c. [HPPN]
American attorney
* O'Brien, Rope

O'Brien, James Nagle 1848-1879 [PI]
Irish author
* Shamus

O'Brien, Jane 1918- [FC]
American actress
* Bryan, Jane

O'Brien, Jennie
See Devlin, Joseph

O'Brien, Joey
See Aiuppa, Joseph John [Joe]

O'Brien, John 1836-1887 [FFF, WBD]
American comedian
* Raymond, John T.

O'Brien, John 1851-1931 [HPPN]
Irish sea captain and adventurer
* Alaska's Sea Captain
* O'Brien, Dynamite Johnny

O'Brien, John F. 1867-1892 [BE]
American baseball player
* O'Brien, Darby

O'Brien, John J. 1870-1913 [BE]
Canadian-born baseball player
* O'Brien, Chewing Gum

O'Brien, John K.
See Byrne, John K.

O'Brien, John V. 1836-1889 [HPPN]
American circus entrepreneur
* O'Brien, Pogey

O'Brien, Larry Clinton
See O'Brien, Clifford Edward

O'Brien, Little David
See O'Brien, David

O'Brien, M. E. 1772-? [PI]
Irish poet
* O'B.?

O'Brien, Margaret
See O'Brien, Angela Maxine

O'Brien, Marian P[lowman] 1915- [CA]
American author
* Bryan, Mavis

O'Brien, Marianne
See Judd, Mary Ann

O'Brien, Marty
See Sinatra, Francis Albert [Frank]

O'Brien, Mary 18th c. [PI]
Irish author and poet
* [A] Lady

O'Brien, Mary 20th c. [LRR]
British-born singer
* Springfield, Dusty

O'Brien, Michael J. ?-1930 [HPPN]
American minstrel
* [The] Senator

O'Brien, Mickey
See O'Brien, Frank Aloysius

O'Brien, Mrs. Joseph
Author
* Vorse, Mary Heaton

O'Brien, Obie
See O'Brien, Ellard John

O'Brien, Obie
See O'Brien, Thomas Edward

O'Brien, Pat
See O'Brien, William Joseph, Jr.

O'Brien, Patria Gene 1916-1970 [FC]
American actress
* Ellis, Patricia

O'Brien, Peter 1842-1914 [DEP]
Irish jurist
* Peter the Packer

O'Brien, Philadelphia Jack
See Hagen, Joseph F.

O'Brien, Pogey
See O'Brien, John V.

O'Brien, Queenie
See Thompson, Estelle Merle O'Brien

O'Brien, Ralph 1928-
American basketball player
* O'Brien, Buckshot

O'Brien, Ricard Baptist 1809-1885 [PI]
Irish clergyman, writer, poet
* Baptist

O'Brien, Robert C.
See Conly, Robert Leslie

O'Brien, Rope
See O'Brien, James C.

O'Brien, Saliee
See Janas, Frankie-Lee

O'Brien, Shots
See Brennan, Charles

O'Brien, Slingshot
See O'Brien, David

O'Brien, Tex
See O'Brien, Dave

O'Brien, Thomas 1851-1906 [PI]
Irish poet
* Clontarf

O'Brien, Thomas 19th c. [HPPN]
American swindler
* [The] King of the Bunko Men

O'Brien, Thomas Edward 1918-1978
[BE]
American baseball player
* O'Brien, Obie

O'Brien, Thomas Joseph 1882-1959
[BE]
American baseball player
* O'Brien, Buck

O'Brien, Tiger
See O'Brien, Edmond

O'Brien, Tom
See Aiuppa, Joseph John [Joe]

O'Brien, Virginia 1921- [HPPN]
American singer and comedienne
* [The] Tall Gal With the Deadpan

O'Brien, Walter Howard 1936- [EJ]
American jazz musician
* O'Brien, Hod

O'Brien, Widow
See Sheridan, John F.

O'Brien, William 1740?-1815? [PI]
Irish comedian and author
* Lusus, Larry, Esq.

O'Brien, William Joseph, Jr. 1899-1983
[F2, IPA]
American actor
* O'Brien, Pat

O'Brien, William Shoney 1825?-1878
[HPPN]
American financier and mine operator
* [The] Jolly Millionaire

O'Brien, William Smith 1803-1864 [PI]
Irish poet
* W. O'B.

O'Bryan, Leonel [Campbell] ?-1938 [BI]
American newspaper publisher
* Pry, Polly

O'Bryan, Ronald C. 1944?-1984 [TI 2-6-84, WP 3-31-84]
American murderer
* [The] Candy Man

O'Bryant, Tilmon Bunche 1920- [BA]
American law official and administrator
* O'B

O'Bryen, W. J.
See Wheeler-O'Bryen, Wilfrid James

O'Brynt, Jon
See Barnum, W[illiam] Paul

[An] Obscure and Nameless Bard in the Braes of Angus
See Gordon, Joseph

[The] Obscure Mr. Volstead
See Volsted, Andrew J.

[The] Obscure Philosopher
See Heraclitos [or Heraclitus]

Observation
See Adams, Samuel

Observator
See Blodget, Samuel

Observator, Charles
See Sabin, Elijah Robinson

Observator on Wharton
See Ritson, Joseph

Observer
See Bruce, Benjamin

[An] Observer
See Corry, John

Observer
See Drake, John Pode

[An] Observer
See Emory, John

[An] Observer
See McNaughton, James

Observer
See Rapmund, Joseph

[An] Observer
See Rutlidge, [Sir] John James

Observer
See Taylor, Benjamin Ogle

[The] Obsessive Poisoner
See Young, Graham Frederick

Obukhova, Lidiia Alekseevna 20th c. [SFL]
Author
* Obukhova, Lydia

Obukhova, Lydia
See Obukhova, Lidiia Alekseevna

O'Byrne, Dermot
See Bax, [Sir] Arnold [Edward Trevor]

O'Callaghan, Brigid 1870-1955 [BEW, PMJ]
American entertainer
* Friganza, Trixie

O'Callaghan, John Cornelius 1805-1883 [PI]
Irish poet
* Carolan
* Gracchus
* J. O'C.

O'Callaghan, Thomas O'Donnell 1845-?
[PI]
Irish-born poet and journalist
* Libertas

O'Callanan, David
See Holland, Denis

Ocampo, Victoria 1891?-1979 [CA]
Argentinian author, editor, translator
* [The] Queen of Letters

Ocantos, Carlos Maria 1860-?
Argentine author
* [The] Balzac of Argentina

O'Carolan, Turloch 1670-1738 [DNNS, SN]
Irish poet and musician
* [The] Irish Anacreon
* [The] Last True Bard of Ireland
* [The] Orpheus of the Green Isle

O'Carroll, Louis Ely 1864-? [PI]
Irish poet
* Hopper, Claude

O'Carroll, Marie-Madeleine Bernadette 1906- [BEW, FC, WEF]
British actress
* Carroll, Madeleine

O'Carroll, Patrick 19th c. [PI]
Irish poet
* [A] Modern Troubadour

O'Carroll, Ryan
See Markun, Patricia Maloney

Ocasek, Ric
See Otcasek, Richard

O'Casey, Sean
See Casey, John

O'Cataract, Jehu
See Neal, John

O'Cataract, John
See Neal, John

O'Cathasaigh, Donal
See Casey, Daniel J[oseph]

O'Cathasaigh, Shaun
See Casey, John

Occam [or Ockham], William of 1276?-1347 [DNNS, FFF, HN, NPS, UH]
British philosopher
* Invincibilis, Doctor
* [The] Invincible Doctor
* Princeps Nominalium
* [The] Singular Doctor
* Singularis, Doctor
* Venerabilis, Doctor
* Venerabilis Inceptor
* [The] Venerable Initiator

Occasional
See Bruce, Sanders D.

Occasional
See Forney, John Weiss

Occidente, Maria dell'
See Brooks, Maria Gowen

O'Cean, John
See Lennon, John

Ocean, Julian
See De Mesne, Eugene [Frederick]

[The] Ocean Shepherd
See Raleigh, [Sir] Walter

Oceans, Lucky
See Gosfield, Reuben

Ocelot Margie Gardner
See Gardner, Margery Aimee

Ochai, Hidehiko 1939-
Japanese martial artist
* Ochai, Hidy

Ochai, Hidy
See Ochai, Hidehiko

Ochiltree, Eddie
See Gemmels [or Gemble], Andrew

Ochs, Adolph Simon 1858-1935 [HPPN]
American newspaper publisher
* [The] Builder of Chattanooga
* [The] Watchdog of Central Park

Ochus 5th c. BC [WBD]
King of Persia
* Darius II
* Nothus [Bastard]

Ochus 4th c. BC [WBD]
King of Persia
* Artaxerxes III

Ock, Harold David 1912- [BE]
American baseball player
* Ock, Whitey

Ock, Whitey
See Ock, Harold David

Ockenfuss, Lorenz 1779-1851 [HPPN]
German naturalist and philosopher
* Oken, Lorenz

Ockenheim, Johannes
See Okeghem [or Ockeghem], Jean van

Ockey, Footie
See Okypch, Walter Andrew

Ockey, Walter Andrew
See Okypch, Walter Andrew

Ockleman, Constance Frances Marie 1919-1973 [BDF, FC, WEF]
American actress
* Keane, Constance
* Lake, Veronica
* [The] Peekaboo Girl

Ockrent, Christine 1944?- [WP 4-8-85]
French newscaster
* Queen Christine

Ockside, Knight Russ
See Underhill, Edward Fitch

O'Clery, Michael
See O'Clery, Tadhg

O'Clery, Tadhg 1575-1643 [WBD]
Irish clergyman and scholar
* O'Clery, Michael

O'Connell, Charles J. 20th c. [BBH]
American handball organization officer
* [The] Father of One Wall Handball

O'Connell, Charlie 1935- [HPPN]
American roller derby skater
* [The] Roller Derby King

O'Connell, Daniel 1775-1847 [DEP, HN, NPS, RH]
Irish political agitator
* [The] Big Beggarman
* Big O
* [The] Great O
* [The] Irish Agitator
* [The] Liberator
* [The] Uncrowned Monarch

O'Connell, Daniel
See Weil, Joseph R.

O'Connell, Daniel J. 1874-? [HPPN]
Irish-American detective
* Hard Rock

O'Connell, Dermie
See O'Connell, Dermott

O'Connell, Dermott [SMG]
American basketball player
* O'Connell, Dermie

O'Connell, John ?-1860? [PI]
Irish poet
* Roche, Matthew

O'Connell, John 1811-1858 [PI]
Irish poet
* M. P.
* Y.

O'Connell, John A. [PI]
Irish author
* Aloysius

O'Connell, Mary 1814-1897 [BI]
American nurse
* Anthony, [Sister]

O'Connell, Maurice 1802?-1853 [PI]
Irish poet
* Fion
* Ith
* M. O'C.
* McFinn, Denis
* O'Doggerell, Patrick
* O'Taffrail, Patrick

O'Connell, Peg
See Ahern, Margaret McCrohan

O'Connell, Philip
See Martin, James

O'Connell, R. F.
See Van De Gohm, Richard

O'Connell's Head Pacificator
See Steel, Tom

O'Conner, Barrett Willoughby 20th c. [NAA]
American author
* Willoughby, Barrett

O'Conner, Elizabeth
See McNamara, Barbara Willard

O'Conner, Roger [PA]
Author
* Rock, Captain

O'Connor, Alma Mabel 1927- [FC, ITA]
American actress
* Gillis, Ann

O'Connor, Bucky
See O'Connor, Frank

O'Connor, Bucky
See O'Connor, Paul

O'Connor, Buddy
See O'Connor, Herbert William

O'Connor, Cathal ?-1010 [HN]
King of Connaught
* O'Connor of the Bloody Hand

O'Connor, Charles [Chuck] 20th c.
[HPPN]
American wrestler
* [The] Monster

O'Connor, Claxton J. 1907- [BBH]
American lacrosse player and coach
* O'Connor, Okie

O'Connor, Clint
See Paine, Lauran [Bosworth]

O'Connor, Frank 1913-1958 [BB]
American basketball coach
* O'Connor, Bucky

O'Connor, Frank
See O'Donovan, Michael

O'Connor, Herbert William 1916- [CEI, FHE, HK]
Canadian-born hockey player
* O'Connor, Buddy

O'Connor, James F. [Jim] 1893?-1963
[BEW]
American journalist
* Knight, Gene

O'Connor, James Matthew 1865-1950
[BE]
American baseball player
* Connor, James Matthew [Jim]

O'Connor, John H. 1856-1931 [HPPN]
American actor
* Connor, Harry

O'Connor, John Joseph 1867-1937 [BE]
American baseball player
* O'Connor, Peach Pie

O'Connor, Liam
See Liddy, James [Daniel Reeves]

O'Connor, [Sister] Mary Catharine
20th c. [CAP]
American author and educator
* Farrell, Catharine

O'Connor of the Bloody Hand
See O'Connor, Cathal

O'Connor, Okie
See O'Connor, Claxton J.

O'Connor, Paddy
See O'Connor, Patrick Francis

O'Connor, Patrick
See Wibberley, Leonard [Patrick O'Connor]

O'Connor, Patrick Francis 1879-1950
[BE]
American baseball player
* O'Connor, Paddy

O'Connor, Patrick Joseph 1895?-1950
[BI]
American educator
* Elwarn, [Brother] Joseph

O'Connor, Patrick Joseph 1924- [AW, WD]
Irish poet and editor
* Fiacc, Padraic

O'Connor, Paul 1845?-? [PI]
American poet
* [The] Covington Poet

O'Connor, Paul 20th c. [HPPN]
American football player
* O'Connor, Bucky

O'Connor, Peach Pie
See O'Connor, John Joseph

O'Connor, Philip
See Bancroft, Marie Constant

O'Connor, Regina Mary 1898- [BI]
American poet and educator
* Mary Edwardine, [Sister]

O'Connor, Richard 1915-1975 [BI, CA]
American author, actor, journalist
* Archer, Frank
* Burke, John
* Wayland, Patrick

O'Connor, Sandra Day 1930?- [HPPN]
American Supreme Court justice
* [The] Bitch Queen
* [A] Person for All Seasons

O'Connor, Stacy
See Rollins, William

O'Connor, T. P.
See O'Connor, Thomas Power

O'Connor, Terrible Tommy
See O'Connor, Thomas

O'Connor, Thomas 1886-? [BLB]
Irish-born American murderer and robber
* O'Connor, Terrible Tommy

O'Connor, Thomas Power 1848-1929
[CBS, LC, NPS, WBD]
Irish journalist and politician
* [The] Father of the House of Commons
* O'Connor, T. P.
* Tay Pay

O'Connor, Vincent Clarence Scott
20th c. [WWL]
British author
* Odysseus

O'Connor, William 1891?-1964 [BEW]
Theatrical performer
* Conlin, Ray, Sr.

Oconomowoc
See Henshall, James A.

O'Conor, Charles Patrick 1837?-? [PI]
Irish author
* Mor, Cahal
* Thierna, Cairn

Oconostota [or Occonostota] ?-1785
[HPPN]
American Indian chief
* Great Warrior

Octavia
See Ives, Mary Alice

Octavianus, Gaius Julius Caesar
See Octavius, Gaius

Octavio, Francesco 1447-1490 [PA]
Author
* Cliophile

Octavius 937?-964 [CAL]
Pope
* John XII

Octavius 12th c. [WBD]
Antipope
* Victor IV

Octavius
See Hales, William

Octavius, Gaius ?-14 [HN, RH, SN]
Roman emperor
* Augustus
* [The] Father of His Country
* Heaven Born Youth
* Octavianus, Gaius Julius Caesar

October, John
See Portway, Christopher [John]

October, Mr.
See Jackson, Reginald [Reggie]

[An] Octogenarian
See Gutch, John Mathew

[An] Octogenarian
See Halliburton, Brenton

[An] Octogenarian
See Lower, Richard

[An] Octogenarian
See Roche, James

[An] Octogenarian
See Turner, [Rev.] Baptist Noel

Octopus
See Drachman, Julian M[oses]

[The] Octopus
See Marion, Martin Whiteford

O'Cuilleanain, Eilis Dillon 1920- [TBJ]
Irish author
* Dillon, Eilis

O'Cuirc, Henry
See Quirke, Henry

O'Daly, Cormac
See Forbes, Dick

Odam, Norman [WP 2-22-85]
American singer and musician
* [The] Ledge
* [The] Legendary Stardust Cowboy

O'Daniel, Iron Mike
See O'Daniel, John Wilson

O'Daniel, Janet 20th c. [WD]
American author
* Janet, Lillian [joint pseudonym with
  Lillian Ressler]

O'Daniel, John Wilson 1894-1975 [BI]
American military leader
* O'Daniel, Iron Mike

O'Daniel, Pappy
See O'Daniel, Wilbert Lee

O'Daniel, Wilbert Lee 1890-1969
[CWG, DAM]
*American country-western performer and
politician*
* O'Daniel, Pappy

O'Dare, Kerry
See Starr, Richard Harry

O'Day, Anita
See Colton, Anita

O'Day, Caroline Goodwin 1875-1943
[HPPN]
American politician
* [The] White House Pet

O'Day, Cathy
See Crane, Barbara [Joyce]

O'Day, Dawn
See Paris, Dawn Evelyeen

O'Day, Molly
See Noonan, Suzanne Dobson

O'Day, Molly
See Williamson, LaVerne

O'Day, Mrs. William [FFF]
Entertainer
* Wells, Sadie

O'Day, Peggy
See Reis, Peggy

[The] Odcombian Legstretcher
See Coryat, Thomas

[The] Odd Boy
See Tillotson, John

[An] Odd Fellow
See Duncan, James

[The] Odd Fellow
See Mackenzie, Peter

[The] Odd Fellow
See Souter, Joseph

Odd, Orvar
See Sturzen-Becker, Oscar Patrik

Odd-Man In
See Lindsay, John Vliet

Oddo, Sandra [Schmidt] 1937- [CA]
American writer
* Schmidt, Sandra

Odds and Ends
See Quevedo, Walter C.

O'Dea, Anne Caldwell 1867-1936 [PMJ]
American lyricist and librettist
* Caldwell, Anne

O'Dea, Lefty
See O'Dea, Paul

O'Dea, Patrick J. 1872-1962 [FB]
Australian-born American football player
* Mitchell, Charles J.

O'Dea, Paul 1920- [BE]
American baseball player
* O'Dea, Lefty

Odell, Carol [CAP]
Author
* Odell, Gill [joint pseudonym with
  Traviss Gill]

O'Dell, Digger
See Brown, John H.

O'Dell, Digger
See O'Dell, William Oliver [Billy]

O'Dell, Digger
See Smith, Herbert O'Dell

Odell, Gill [joint pseudonym with Carol
Odell]
See Gill, Traviss

Odell, Gill [joint pseudonym with
Traviss Gill]
See Odell, Carol

Odell, Jonathan 1737-1818 [CCL,
HPPN]
*Canadian-American poet, satirist,
physician, missionary*
* Poet Laureate to the Congress
* Querno, Camillo

O'Dell, Kenny
See Gist, Kenneth, Jr.

O'Dell, Mac 1916- [CWG]
American country-western performer
* [The] Old Country Boy

Odell, Minna 1857?-1940 [DNA]
American poet
* Irving, Minna

Odell, Shorty
See Schwartz, Solomon

O'Dell, William Oliver [Billy] 1933-
[BE, BTB]
American baseball player
* O'Dell, Digger

Odem, J.
See Rubin, Jacob A.

Oden, Curly
See Oden, Olaf

Oden, James Burke [Jimmy] 1903-1977
[BWW]
American singer
* Big Bloke
* Oden, Old Man
* Poor Boy
* St. Louis Jimmy

Oden, Olaf 20th c. [EF]
American football player
* Oden, Curly

Oden, Old Man
See Oden, James Burke [Jimmy]

Odenwald, Lefty
See Odenwald, Theodore Joseph [Ted]

Odenwald, Theodore Joseph [Ted]
1902-1965 [BE]
American baseball player
* Odenwald, Lefty

Odescalchi, Benedetto 1611-1689 [WBD]
Pope
* Innocent XI

Odetta
See Holmes, Odetta

Odette
See Fortin, Marie Des Neiges

Odette, Mary
See Goimbault, Odette

Odhar, Coinneach [Kenneth Ore] 16th c.
[EOP]
Scottish wizard
* [The] Brahan Seer

O'Dhu, Fergus
See Trotter, [Canon] John Crawford

Odier, Daniel 1945?-
Swiss author
* Delacorta

Odin
See Burvik, Mabel Odin

Odinga, Oginga 20th c. [TI 8-16-82]
Kenyan Tribal leader
* Double O, Mr.

Odington, Walter
See Walter of Evesham

Odman, Jeremiah
See Atkinson, D. H.

O'do [or U'do] 1042?-1099 [WBD]
Pope
* Urban II

Ododonus
See Wolton, Edward

O'Doggerell, Patrick
See O'Connell, Maurice

O'Doherty, Brian 1934- [CA]
Irish-born American author and artist
* Ireland, Patrick

O'Doherty, Eileen
See Walker, Anna

Odoherty, [Sir] Morgan
See Maginn, William

O'Doire, Annraoi
See Beechhold, Henry F[rank]

Odom, Andrew 1936- [BWW]
American singer
* B. B. Jr.
* Big Voice
* Blues Boy
* Odom, King
* Odom, Little Andrew
* Odom, Moonhead
* Odom, Voice

Odom, Blue Moon
See Odom, Johnny Lee

Odom, David Everett [Dave] 1918-
[BE]
American baseball player
* Odom, Porky

Odom, George P. 20th c.
* Odom, Maje

Odom, Heinie
See Odom, Herman Boyd

Odom, Herbert 1933- [IBW]
American boxer
* Doc O

Odom, Herman Boyd 1900- [BE]
American baseball player
* Odom, Heinie

Odom, Johnny Lee 1945- [PB, SMG, WWB]
American baseball player
* Odom, Blue Moon

Odom, King
See Odom, Andrew

Odom, Leprechaun
See Odom, Steve Talmage

Odom, Little Andrew
See Odom, Andrew

Odom, Maje
See Odom, George P.

Odom, Moonhead
See Odom, Andrew

Odom, Porky
See Odom, David Everett [Dave]

Odom, Steve Talmage 1952- [SMG]
American football player
* Odom, Leprechaun

Odom, Voice
See Odom, Andrew

Odon, Gerard [HN]
Medieval scholar
* Scolasticus, Doctor

O'Donald, Donald
See Cooksley, S[idney] Bert

[The] O'Donnell
See Duffy, [Sir] Charles Gavan

O'Donnell, C. L. 19th c. [HPPN]
British author
* [A] Bengal Civilian

O'Donnell, Cathy
See Steely, Ann

O'Donnell, Dick [joint pseudonym with
Don(ald) (Arthur) Thompson]
See Lupoff, Richard Allen [Dick]

O'Donnell, Dick [joint pseudonym with
Richard Allen (Dick) Lupoff]
See Thompson, Don[ald Arthur]

O'Donnell, Donat
See O'Brien, Conor Cruise

O'Donnell, Edward ?-1923 [BLB]
American gangster
* O'Donnell, Spike

O'Donnell, Emmett 1906-1971 [WA]
American military leader
* O'Donnell, Rosy

O'Donnell, Francis Hugh 1848-? [PI]
Irish poet
* Llenodo
* Minor, Dryden

O'Donnell [or O'Donell?], Hugh
1571?-1602 [HN]
Irish chieftain
* Red Hugh

O'Donnell, John ?-1874 [PI]
Irish poet and clergyman
* Moy

O'Donnell, John Francis 1837-1874 [PI]
Irish author and poet
* C.
* Caviare
* French, Emily
* J. F. O'D.
* Monks, P.
* West, Monckton

O'Donnell, John Thomas, Jr. 1899-1940
[SC]
American actor
* Ward, Hap, Jr.

O'Donnell, John Thomas, Sr. 1868?-1944
[BEW, SC]
American actor and producer
* Ward, Hap

O'Donnell, K. M.
See Malzberg, Barry N[orman]

O'Donnell, Klondike
See O'Donnell, William

O'Donnell, Lawrence [joint pseudonym
with Catherine Lucile Moore]
See Kuttner, Henry

O'Donnell, Lawrence [joint pseudonym
with Henry Kuttner]
See Moore, Catherine Lucile

O'Donnell, Mary
See Dillon, Thomas

O'Donnell, Peter 20th c. [MBF]
British author
* Barnes, John

O'Donnell, Roderick
See Boyle, John

O'Donnell, Rosy
See O'Donnell, Emmett

O'Donnell, Spike
See O'Donnell, Edward

O'Donnell, William 20th c.　[BLB, PHM]
American underworld figure
* O'Donnell, Klondike

O'Donnevan, Finn
See Sheckley, Robert

O'Donoghue, John 1813-1893　[PI]
Irish poet and author
* S. T. C. D.

O'Donoghue, Tadhg 20th c.　[WWL]
Irish poet and editor
* O Donnchadha, Tadhg

O'Donovan, Gerald
See O'Donovan, Jeremiah

O'Donovan, Jeremiah 1871-1942　[DIL]
Irish author
* O'Donovan, Gerald

O'Donovan, John 1921-　[CA]
Irish author, playwright, broadcaster
* Marsh, Andrew

O'Donovan, Michael 1903-1966　[CBS, LC, TC1]
Irish author
* O'Connor, Frank

O'Donovan, Mrs.
See Rossa, Mrs. O'Donovan

O'Donovan, P. M., Esq.
See Peacock, Thomas Love

O'Donovan Rossa, Jeremiah 1831-?　[PI]
Irish poet
* Jer

O'Donovan Rossa, Mary Jane 1845-?
[PI]
Irish poet
* Cliodhna
* M. J. I.

O'Doul, Francis Joseph [Frank]
1897-1969　[AS, DGS, PB]
American baseball player
* [The] Man in the Green Suit
* O'Doul, Lefty

O'Doul, Lefty
See O'Doul, Francis Joseph [Frank]

O'Dowd, Cornelius
See Lever, Charles James

O'Dowd, Darby
See Luby, Kate

O'Dowd, George Alan 1961?-　[NW 1-23-84, NW 5-16-83, TI 11-28-83, WP 3-6-83]
British singer and songwriter
* Boy George
* Lush, Lieutenant

O'Dowd, John 1856-?　[PI]
Irish poet
* Adonis
* [A] Sligo Suspect

O'Dowd, Mike 1895-1957　[BX, RBE]
American boxer
* [The] St. Paul Cyclone

O'Dowd, Phelim
See Fox, Patrick J.

O'Dreams, John
See Wallace, Henry

O'Dryskull, Teddy
See Mahony, Francis Sylvester

Odum, Mary Hunt McCaleb　[BDSA]
American author and poet
* L'Eclair

O'Dunn, Denis
See Cleary, Thomas Stanislaus

Odwell, Fred[erick William] 1872-1948
[BE]
American baseball player
* Odwell, Fritz

Odwell, Fritz
See Odwell, Fred[erick William]

Odysseus
See Eliot, [Sir] Charles

Odysseus
See Johnson, Donald McI[ntosh]

Odysseus
See O'Connor, Vincent Clarence Scott

Oecolampadius, Johannes
See Heussgen [or Huessgen], Johannes

Oecolampadius, Johannes
See Hussgen, Johannes

Oedipus
See Bassianus

Oehlenschlaeger, Adam Gottlob
1779-1850　[SN, WBD]
Danish poet and playwright
* [The] King of the Scandinavian
　Singers
* [The] Poet King of Scandinavia

Oehmke, Thomas Harold 1947-　[CA]
American author
* Plain, Warren

Oelrichs, Blanche Marie Louise
1890-1950　[BEW]
American actress, author, poet
* Strange, Michael

Oertel, Charles Frank [Chuck] 1931-
[BE]
American baseball player
* Oertel, Ducky
* Oertel, Snuffy

Oertel, Ducky
See Oertel, Charles Frank [Chuck]

Oertel, Philipp Friedrich Wilhelm
1798-1867　[WBD]
German author
* Von Horn, W. O.

Oertel, Snuffy
See Oertel, Charles Frank [Chuck]

Oester, Ron 20th c.
American baseball player
* [The] Blender

Oesteren, Friedrich Werner Van 1874-?
[LAO]
German author and poet
* Oestern, Fr. W. V.

Oestergren, Carl Ludvig 1842-1881
[HPPN]
Swedish poet
* Fjalar

Oestern, Fr. W. V.
See Oesteren, Friedrich Werner Van

Oestman, Nan Inger 1923-　[IAW]
Swedish author
* Inger, Nan

Oettinger, Louella 1880?-1972　[F2, FC, OCF]
American columnist
* Parsons, Louella O.

O'Faolain, Julia 20th c.　[CA, CN]
Irish author and translator
* Martines, Julia

O'Faolain, Sean
See Whelan, John

O'Farrell, M. J. 1832-?　[PA]
Author
* Irish Priest

O'Farrell, Talbot
See Parrot, William

O'Farrell, William 1904-　[CC]
Author
* Grew, William

O'Farrelly, Agnes 20th c.　[WWL]
Irish author
* Ni Fhaircheallaigh, Una

O'Farrill, Arturo 1921-　[ASC, DAM, EJ]
Cuban-born composer
* O'Farrill, Chico

O'Farrill, Chico
See O'Farrill, Arturo

O'Feeney, Francis 1883-1953
American actor, screenwriter, director, producer
* Ford, Francis [Frank]

O'Feeney, Sean 1895-1973
American director, producer, screenwriter
* Ford, John
* Ford, Pappy

Ofek, Uriel
See Popik, Uriel

Ofer, Harold ?-1978　[FIR]
Actor
* Renard, Roy

[The] Off Wheeler
See Harlan, James Jefferson

Offard, Cecil　[PA]
Author
* Thornton, Harold

Offerman, George, Sr. 1880-1938　[SC]
American actor
* [The] Original Singing Nut

Offerre, M.
See Shamir, Moshe

[The] Office Builder
See Meyer, Lou[is]

Office, Rollie
See Office, Rowland Johnnie

Office, Row
See Office, Rowland Johnnie

Office, Rowland Johnnie 1952- [BE, SMG]
American baseball player
* Office, Rollie
* Office, Row

[An] Officer
See Anbury, Thomas

[An] Officer
See Austin, Harry

[An] Officer
See Blakeney, William

[An] Officer
See Conway, Henry Seymour

[An] Officer
See Cunningham, J.

[An] Officer
See Douglas, Archibald Alexander

[An] Officer
See Glenie, James

[An] Officer
See Porter, [Sir] Robert Ker

[An] Officer
See Sherer, [Colonel] Moyle

[An] Officer
See Thrush, Thomas

[An] Officer
See Thurlow, Edward [First Baron Thurlow]

[An] Officer
See Trant, [Captain] William

[An] Officer in Col. Baillie's Detachment
See Thomson, William

[An] Officer in His Majesty's Service
See Wallace, Robert Grenville

[An] Officer in the Army of Wolfe
See Jones, James Athearn

[An] Officer in the Field
See Kirkland, Charles Pinckney

[An] Officer in the Field
See Nott, Charles C.

[An] Officer in the Guards
See Ayscough, George Edward

[An] Officer in the Hon. E. I. Co's Bengal Native Infantry
See Butler, John

[An] Officer in the Mil. and Civ. Service of the Hon. E. I. Co.
See Sleeman, [Sir] William Henry

[The] Officer in the Tower
See Baillie-Stewart, Norman

[An] Officer of Distinction
See Churchill, John [First Duke of Marlborough]

[An] Officer of Rank in the Squadron
See Berry, [Sir] Edward

[An] Officer of State
See Hartig, F.

[An] Officer of the Army at Detroit
See Whiting, Henry

[An] Officer of the British Army
See Drewe, Edward

[An] Officer of the Line
See Gardner, John Lane

[An] Officer of the Ninth Regiment
See Thompson, Charles William

[An] Officer of the Rear-Guard
See Boykin, Edward M.

[An] Officer of the Regiment
See Califf, Joseph M.

[An] Officer of the Royal Engineers
See Webber, Charles Edmund

[An] Officer of the Royal Navy
See Goldsmith, [Lieut.] Hugh Colvill

[An] Officer of the Volunteer Corps
See Fraser, Archibald Campbell

[An] Officer of Zouaves
See Cler, Jean Joseph Gustave

[An] Officer on Half Pay
See Dawkins, William Gregory

[A] Officer under that General
See Bullard, Henry Adams

[An] Officer Who Served in the Expedition
See Gleig, George Robert

[An] Officer who Served There
See Ireland, William W.

[An] Officer's Wife
See Carrington, Margaret Jirvin

[The] Official Witch of Los Angeles
See Huebner, Louise

Offield, Lewis Delaney 1903-1978 [CED, F2, FC]
American actor
* Oakie, Jack

Offord, Lenore Glen 1905- [CA]
American author
* Durrant, Theo [joint pseudonym]

Offutt, A. J.
See Offutt, Andrew Jefferson

Offutt, Andrew Jefferson 1934- [CA, ESF, SFL]
American author
* Cleve, John
* Douglas, Jeff [joint pseudonym with Douglas Bruce Berry]

Offutt, Andrew Jefferson (cont.)
* Offutt, A. J.
* Williams, J. X. [house pseudonym, Greenleaf Classics]

O'Fihely, Maurice ?-1513 [PA]
Author
* De Portu

O'Finn, Thaddeus
See McGloin, Joseph Thaddeus

O'Flaherty, Bernard 1823-1876 [FFF, PA]
Entertainer
* Williams, Barney

O'Flaherty, Charles ?-1828 [PI]
Irish poet
* C. O. F.
* O'Reilly, Rory

O'Flaherty, Hugh 20th c. [WP 2-2-83]
Irish priest
* [The] Scarlet Pimpernel Priest

O'Flaherty, John Benedict 1918- [CEI]
Canadian-born hockey player
* O'Flaherty, Peanuts

O'Flaherty, Peanuts
See O'Flaherty, John Benedict

O'Flaherty, T. M. M.
See Cohen, Paul Arthur

O'Flanagan, Theophilus 1762?-1814 [PI]
Irish poet
* MacBrady, Thady

O'Flinn, Peter
See Fanthorpe, R[obert] Lionel

O'Flynn, Fergus
See Ryan, James

O'Flynn, Honoria 1909- [ASC]
Irish composer
* Mack, Noreen

O'Flynn, Jimmy
See Graydon, Robert Murray

O'Flynn, Peter
See Fanthorpe, R[obert] Lionel

O'Fogarty, Fogarty
See Gosnell, Samuel

O'Francis, Mary [PA]
Author
* Blount, Margaret

[The] Often Wrong, Never in Doubt Man
See Evans, Michael K.

Og
See Shadwell, Thomas

Og, Liam
See O'Neill, William

O'Gahagan, [Major] Goliah
See Thackeray, William Makepeace

O'Galop [At the Gallop]
See Rossillon, Marius

Ogan, George F. 1912- [CA, SAT]
American author
* Castle, Lee [joint pseudonym with Margaret E. (Nettles) Ogan]
* Keefer, Catherine [joint pseudonym with Margaret E. (Nettles) Ogan]
* Ogan, M. G. [joint pseudonym with Margaret E. (Nettles) Ogan]
* Stowe, Rosetta [joint pseudonym with Margaret E. (Nettles) Ogan]

Ogan, M. G. [joint pseudonym with Margaret E. (Nettles) Ogan]
See Ogan, George F.

Ogan, M. G. [joint pseudonym with George F. Ogan]
See Ogan, Margaret E. [Nettles]

Ogan, Margaret E. [Nettles] 1923-1979 [CA, SAT]
American author
* Castle, Lee [joint pseudonym with George F. Ogan]
* Keefer, Catherine [joint pseudonym with George F. Ogan]
* Ogan, M. G. [joint pseudonym with George F. Ogan]
* Stowe, Rosetta [joint pseudonym with George F. Ogan]

Ogarkov, Nikolai 1918?-
Russian military leader
* [The] Father of the Modern Soviet Army

O'Gatty, Jimmy
See Agati, James

O'Gatty, Packey
See Agati, Pasquale

Ogawa, Pelorhanke Ai
See Anthony, Florence

Ogden 18th c. [HN]
Gambler
* [The] Newmarket Oracle

Ogden, Anna Cora 1819-1870 [PA]
French-born author and actress
* Berkeley, Helen
* Isabel

Ogden, Bud
See Ogden, Carlos

Ogden, C. K.
See Ogden, Charles Kay

Ogden, Carlos 1946- [BB]
American basketball player
* Ogden, Bud

Ogden, Charles Kay 1889-1957 [LC]
British author, editor, inventor of Basic English
* Ogden, C. K.

Ogden, Christol
See English, Thomas Dunn

Ogden, Curly
See Ogden, Warren Harvey

Ogden, James 18th c. [HPPN]
British author
* [A] Native of the Town

Ogden, R. L.   [PA]
Author
* Podgers

Ogden, Richard D'Orsay
See Maxwell, Richard

Ogden, Robert 1746-1826 [HPPN]
American attorney
* [The] Honest Lawyer

Ogden, Ruth
See Ide, Francis Otis [Ogden]

Ogden, Uzal 1744?-1822 [HPPN]
American clergyman
* [A] Citizen of the United States

Ogden, Warren Harvey 1901-1964   [BE]
American baseball player
* Ogden, Curly

Ogdoades
See Langey, Guillaume du Bellay

Oge, Erin
See Wilson, Robert A.

Oge, Hector
See McMullan, William John

O'Ghurkin, [Dr.] Winston
See Lennon, John

Ogier, Le Prieur
See Balzac, Jean Louis Guez de

Ogilby, [Rev.] Frederick ?-1878 [HPPN]
American clergyman
* [A] Citizen of New York

Ogilvie, Clare M.
See Clifford, Clare

Ogilvy, Arthur James 20th c. [SFL]
Author
* A. J. O.

Ogilvy, Gavin
See Barrie, [Sir] James Matthew

Ogle, Anne   [PA]
Author
* Owen, Ashelford

Oglesby, Joseph 1931- [CA]
American author
* Kain, Malcolm
* Mulesko, Angelo
* Vale, Lewis
* Woodson, Jeff

Oglesby, Richard James 1824-1899 [FFF, HPPN]
American politician
* Farmer's Dick
* Uncle Dick

Oglou, Mehmet Suleiman ?-1572? [HPPN]
Turkish poet
* Fuzuli

Ognall, Leopold Horace 1908- [AW, CA, CC]
Canadian-born author
* Carmichael, Harry
* Howard, Hartley

Ognev [or Ognyov?], N[ikolai]
See Rosanov [or Rozanov?], Mikhail Grigorievich

[The] O'Gorman Mahon
See Mahon, Charles James Patrick

O'Gorman, Samuel F.
See Cusack, Michael J[oseph]

Ogorzov, Paul 1913?-1941 [HPPN]
German railway worker and murderer
* [The] S. Bahn Murderer

O'Gotham, Bob
See Greely, Robert H.

O'Grada, Sean
See O'Grady, John [Patrick]

O'Grady, Elizabeth Anne 20th c. [AW, CA]
Australian photojournalist and author
* Scollan, E. A.

O'Grady, Elsie May 1893-1963 [HPPN]
American actress
* Grady, Elsie May

O'Grady, Felix
See Hadath, John Edward Gunby

O'Grady, John [Patrick] 1907- [CA]
Australian author
* Culotta, Nino
* O'Grada, Sean

O'Grady, Mac
See McGleno, Phillip

O'Grady, Rohan
See Skinner, June Margaret O'Grady

O'Grady, Sean 1959?-
American boxer
* [The] Bubblegum Bomber
* [The] Green Machine

O'Grady, Standish Hayes 1830?-? [PI]
Irish poet and scholar
* Hayes, S.

O'Grady, Standish James 1846-1928 [SFL, WGT]
Irish author
* Clive, Arthur
* Netterville, Luke

O'Grady, Tony
See Clemens, Brian Horace

Ogre de la Goutte d'Or
See Weber, Jeanne

Ogrodowski, Ambrose Francis 1912-1956 [BE]
American baseball player
* Ogrodowski, Brusie

Ogrodowski, Brusie
See Ogrodowski, Ambrose Francis

Ogunseye, Obalumi
See Garrett, Irving

Ogus, Joyce 1932- [TR]
British actress and dancer
* Blair, Joyce

Ogus, Lionel 1931- [TR]
Canadian actor, dancer, choreographer
* Blair, Lionel

O'Gwynn, James 20th c. [ECM]
American country-western performer
* [The] Smiling Irishman

Oh Gran, Gilbert
See Masso, Justo

Oh Red Washington
See Washington, George

Oh Yeah Rogers
See Aiverum, Timothy Louis

O'Hagan, Archibald
See Hofmannsthal, Hugo [Laurenz
August Hofmann Edler] Von

O'Hagan, John 1822-1890 [PI]
Irish author and poet
* Amelia, Carolina Wilhelmina
* Cuillinn, Sliabh
* J. O'H.
* O.

O'Hair, Iva N. Smith 20th c. [NAA]
American poet
* O'Hair, Nolanne

O'Hair, Nolanne
See O'Hair, Iva N. Smith

O'Hall, [Mayor] Von
See Hall, Abraham Oakey

O'Halloran, Laurence
See Halloran, Laurence Hynes

Ohanian, Krekor 1925- [FC, HPPN,
IPA]
American actor
* Connors, Michael
* Connors, Touch

O'Hanlon, George
See Rice, George

O'Hanlon, George Samuel 1874-1946
[SC]
American actor
* [The] King of Burlesque
* Rice, Sam

O'Hanlon, Jacklyn
See Meek, Jacklyn O'Hanlon

O'Hanlon, John 1821-1905 [PA, PI]
Irish author and clergyman
* [An] Irish Missionary Priest
* Lageniensis

O'Hanlon, Mary I.
See Kelly, Mary I.

O'Hannegan, Larry
See Harris, Lee O.

O'Hanrahan, Kieron 1925- [FC]
Irish actor
* Moore, Kieron

O'Hara, Abigail 1860?-1954 [BI]
American educator
* Mary Liguori, [Sister]

O'Hara, Barnes
See Banim, Michael, Jr.

O'Hara, Dale
See Gillese, John Patrick

O'Hara, David
See Snell, Roy Judson

[The] O'Hara Family [joint pseudonym
with Michael Banim; also used alone]
See Banim, John

[The] O'Hara Family [joint pseudonym
with John Banim; also used alone]
See Banim, Michael, Jr.

O'Hara, George
See Harrison, George

O'Hara, H. Percy ?-1918 [HPPN]
American director
* Meldon, H. Percy

O'Hara, James Francis 1875-1954 [BE]
American baseball player
* O'Hara, Kid

O'Hara, John [Henry] 1905-1970 [CA,
HPPN]
American author
* Delaney, Franey
* [The] Voice of the Hangover
Generation

O'Hara, Joy
See Farquar, Agnes Stephens

O'Hara, Kane ?-1782 [PI]
Irish poet
* St. Patrick's Steeple

O'Hara, Kareen
See Careddu, Stefania

O'Hara, Kenneth
See Walton, Bryce

O'Hara, Kevin
See Cumberland, Marten

O'Hara, Kid
See O'Hara, James Francis

O'Hara, Mary
See Alsop, Mary O'Hara

O'Hara, Maureen
See Brown, Maureen Fitzsimons

O'Hara, Scott [house pseudonym]
See MacDonald, John D[ann]

Ohara, Yutaka 1908- [IAW]
Japanese author
* Houn

O'Hara-Smith, George
See Harrison, George

O'Hare, Artful Eddie
See O'Hare, Edward J.

O'Hare, Edward J. 20th c. [HPPN]
*American attorney and dog track
operator*
* O'Hare, Artful Eddie

O'Hare, Roger
See Donnelly, James

O'Harris, Pixie
See Pratt, Rhona Olive

O'Harro, Mike 20th c.
American nightclub owner
* [The] Singles King of Washington

O'Hearn, Donald Edwin 1928- [FHE]
Canadian-born hockey player
* O'Hearn, Nipper

O'Hearn, Nipper
See O'Hearn, Donald Edwin

O'Henry, Henry
See Dominguez Aragones, Edmundo

O'Herlihy, Eileen 1922- [BEW]
Scottish-born actress
* Herlie, Eileen

O'Herlihy, Patrick 19th c. [PI]
Irish poet
* P. O'H.

O'Higgins, [Don] Ambrosio
See Higgins, Ambrose

O'Higgins, Bernardo 1778-1842 [WBD]
Chilean soldier and statesman
* [The] Liberator of Chile

O'Higgins, Hyacinth Hazel 1922?-1970
[EMT, FC]
British actress and singer
* Hazell, Hy

Ohio Fats
See Nicklaus, Jack William

[The] Ohio Gong
See Allen, William

[The] Ohio Kid
See Lytle, Donald

[The] Ohio Roscius
See Lyon, Louis

[An] Ohio Volunteer
See Foster, James

Ohio's Ace Investigator
See Slater, Ora E.

Ohira, Masayoshi 1910-1980
Japanese prime minister
* [The] Bull
* Otochan [Daddy]

Ohiyesa
See Eastman, Charles A[lexander]

Ohl, Hans
See Kusenberg, Kurt

Ohl, Maude 20th c. [BDSA]
American author and poet
* Andrews, Annulet

Ohm, Peter 1923- [FC]
British actor
* Vaughan, Peter

Ohnet, Georges
See Henot, Georges

Ohnothimagen
See Harrison, George

Ohon
See Barba, Harry

Ohsawa, Georges
See Sakurazawa, Yukikazu

Ohser, Erich 1903-1944 [WECO]
German cartoonist
* Plauen, E. O.

Oil Can Boyd
See Boyd, Dennis

Oil Can Eddie
See Sadlowski, Edward

Oil Can Lisciotti
See Lisciotti, Larry

[The] Oil King
See Koretz, Leo

[The] Oil King of the Pacific
See Gray, Augustine

Oil's Gadfly
See Mattei, Enrico

Ojeda, Chucho
See Ojeda, Jesus

Ojeda, Jesus 1892-1943 [SC]
Mexican actor
* Ojeda, Chucho

O'K.
See O'Keeffe, M. J.

Oka
See Kuzmowycz, Olha

Okada, Hideki
See Glassco, John [Stinson]

Okamoto, Kozo 1948?- [HPPN]
Japanese terrorist
* [The] Voice of Orion

Oke, Richard
See Millett, Nigel Stansbury

O'Keefe, Adelaide 1776-1855? [PI]
Irish poet
* Adelaide

O'Keefe, Dennis
See Flanagan, Edward Vanes, Jr.

O'Keefe, John 1747-1833 [NPS]
Irish playwright
* [The] English Moliere

O'Keefe, Joseph 20th c. [BLB, DI]
American underworld figure
* O'Keefe, Specs
* Williams, Paul

O'Keefe, Lester 1896- [ASC]
*American composer and advertising
executive*
* Form, Tom

O'Keefe, Specs
See O'Keefe, Joseph

O'Keeffe, Cornelius
See Meagher, Thomas Francis

O'Keeffe, Georgia
See Stieglitz, Georgia O'Keeffe

O'Keeffe, M. J. 19th c. [PI]
Irish poet
* O'K.

Okeghem [or Ockeghem], Jean van
1430?-1495 [HPPN]
Dutch composer
* Ockenheim, Johannes

O'Kelly, Bard
See O'Kelly, Patrick

O'Kelly, Dennis 1720?-1787 [NPS]
Racehorse owner
* Eclipse, Count

O'Kelly, Don
See Kelly, Donald Patrick

O'Kelly, John J. 20th c. [WWL]
Irish author
* O Ceallaigh, Sean

O'Kelly, Patrick 1754-1835 [HPPN]
Irish poet
* O'Kelly, Bard

O'Kelly, Thomas 20th c. [WWL]
Irish poet and author
* O Ceallaigh, Tomas

Oken, Lorenz
See Ockenfuss, Lorenz

O'Key
See Radwanski, Pierre A[rthur]

[The] Okie From Muskogee
See Haggard, Merle

Oklahoma Bob Albright
See Albright, Bob

Oklahoma Jack Clark
See Clark, Jim

Oklahoma Jack Nichols
See Nichols, John Conover

Oklahoma Peddler
See Gilles, Albert S[imeon], Sr.

Oklahoma's Singing Cowboy
See Autry, [Orvon] Gene

Oklahoma's Yodeling Cowboy
See Autry, [Orvon] Gene

Okrie, Frank Anthony 1896-1959 [BE]
American baseball player
* Okrie, Lefty

Okrie, Lefty
See Okrie, Frank Anthony

Oksanen
See Ahlqvist, August Engelbrekt

Oksaselta, A.
See Ahlqvist, August Engelbrekt

Okyo 1733-1795 [WBD]
Japanese painter
* Maruyama Okyo

Okypch, Walter Andrew 1920- [BE]
American baseball player
* Ockey, Footie
* Ockey, Walter Andrew

O'L.
See O'Leary, Joseph

Ol' Arkansas
See Warneke, Lonnie

Ol' Blue Eyes
See Sinatra, Francis Albert [Frank]

Ol' Cement Hands
See Caster, Richard

Ol' Diz
See Dean, Jay Hanna

Ol' Hap
See Chandler, Albert Benjamin

Ol' Ironsides
See Tobin, James Anthony [Jim]

[The] Ol' Maestro
See Anzelevitz [or Anzelwitz],
Benjamin

Ol' Man River
See Wright, Archibald Lee

[The] Ol' Redhead
See Barber, Walter Lanier

Ol' Showboat
See Newsom, Norman Louis

Olaf 11th c. [DNNS]
King of Sweden
* [The] Lap King

Olaf 13th c. [HN]
Poet
* [The] White Poet

Olaf Haraldsson
See Olaf II [or Olaus]

Olaf Haraldsson
See Olaf III [or Olaus]

Olaf Kyrre [The Quiet]
See Olaf III [or Olaus]

Olaf Magnusson
See Olaf IV

Olaf, Pierre
See Trivier, Pierre-Olaf

Olaf Sitricson ?-981 [WBD]
Danish king of Northumbria and Dublin
* [The] Red

Olaf Tryggvesson
See Olaf I

Olaf I ?-1095 [WBD]
King of Denmark
* Hunger

Olaf I 969-1000 [WBD]
King of Norway
* Olaf Tryggvesson

Olaf II [or Olaus] 992-1030 [HN,
WBD]
King of Norway
* [The] Fat

Olaf II [or Olaus] (cont.)
* Olaf Haraldsson
* [The] Saint
* Saint Olaf
* Skotkoenung [The Tax-King]

Olaf III [or Olaus] ?-1093 [FFF, RH, WBD]
King of Norway
* Olaf Haraldsson
* Olaf Kyrre [The Quiet]
* [The] Pacific

Olaf IV 1100?-1115 [WBD]
King of Norway
* Olaf Magnusson

Olai, Georgius 1598-1672 [HN, WBD]
Swedish poet
* [The] Father of Modern Swedish Poetry
* Stiernhielm [or Stjernhjelm], Georg

Olajuwon, Akeem Abdul 1963?- [SI 11-28-83, TI 4-18-83, WP 4-27-84]
Nigerian-born basketball player
* Akeem the Dream
* [The] Dream
* Little Moses
* Olajuwon, Jellybear

Olajuwon, Jellybear
See Olajuwon, Akeem Abdul

Olander, Joan Lucille 1933- [FC, ITA, SW, WP 9-9-83]
American actress
* Olander, Zaba
* Van Doren, Mamie

Olander, Zaba
See Olander, Joan Lucille

O'Lanus, Corry
See Stanton, John

O'Laoghaire, Liam
See O'Leary, Liam

Olausson, Rune Erland 1933- [IAW]
Swedish author
* Alm, Monica

Olbracht, Ivan
See Zeman, Kamil

Olchewitz, M.
Author
* Verne, Jules

Olcott, Chancellor John 1858?-1932 [BEW, WBD]
American-born actor, singer, songwriter
* Olcott, Chauncey

Olcott, Chauncey
See Olcott, Chancellor John

Olcott, Henry S. 1832-? [HPPN]
American author
* [A] Pew Holder

Olcott, Sidney
See Alcott, John S.

Olczewska, Maria
See Berchtenbreiter, Marie

[The] Old
See Gorm

[The] Old
See Haakon IV Haakonsson

Old Abe
See Lincoln, Abraham

Old Ace of Spades
See Lee, Robert Edward

Old Aches and Pains
See Appling, Lucius Benjamin

Old Actor
See Shelly, Mortimer M.

[The] Old Admiral
See Columbus, Christopher

Old Agamemnon
See Carrington, Edward

[The] Old Alcalde
See Roberts, Oran Milo

Old Alex
See Alexander, William Anderson [Bill]

Old Allegheny
See Colston, Raleigh Edward

Old Alphabet
See Beauregard, Pierre Gustave Toutant

Old Andy
See Johnson, Andrew

[An] Old Angler and Bibliopole
See Thomas, Boosey

Old Anthony Now-Now
See Munday, Anthony

Old Antiquarian
See Simpson, Edward

[The] Old Arbitrator
See Klimm, William Joseph

Old Aristides
See Bicknell, Joshua

[An] Old Army Surgeon
See Dickson, Samuel Henry

[The] Old Ascraean
See Hesiod

Old Athlete
See Larrette, C. H.

[An] Old Author in a New Walk
See Best, John Richard

[An] Old Bachelor
See Carrington, E.

Old Bachelor
See Curtis, George William

[An] Old Bachelor
See Garrison, William Lloyd

Old Bachelor
See Wirt, William

Old Bags
See Scott, John

Old Bags
See Vansittart, Nicholas

Old Bald
See Preston, John Thomas Lewis

Old Bandanna
See Thurman, Allan Granbery

Old Beeswax
See Semmes, Raphael

Old Ben
See Jonson, Ben[jamin]

Old Ben Wade
See Wade, Benjamin Franklin

Old Bill
See Rock De Fabeck, Arthur Charles

Old Bill Leanord
See Leanord, William

Old Bill Miner
See Miner, William

Old Billy
See Sherman, William Tecumseh

Old Billy Gray
See Gray, William

Old Bird
See Clarke, Cecil

Old Blinky Howe
See Howe, Gordon [Gordie]

Old Blizzard
See Loring, William Wing

[The] Old Block
See Delano, Alonzo

Old Blood and Butts
See Whitney, Bartholomew Reynolds

Old Blood and Guts
See Patton, George Smith, Jr.

Old Blunderbuss
See Saxbe, William B.

[An] Old Bohemian
See Strauss, Gustave Louis Maurice

Old Bonafide
See Louis XIV

Old Bones Brown
See Brown, Joe

Old Bones Morrall
See Morrall, Earl

Old Boney
See Bonaparte, Napoleon

[An] Old Boomerang
See Houlding, John Richard

Old Borax
See Dvorak, Antonin

Old Bore
See Beauregard, Pierre Gustave Toutant

Old Bory
See Beauregard, Pierre Gustave Toutant

Old Bottle Foster
See Foster, Joseph

[An] Old Boy
See Bellasis, Edward

Old Boy
See Blanchard, Edward Litt Laman

Old Boy
See Hughes, Thomas

Old Boy Cox
See Cox, George Barnstable

[The] Old Boy in Specs
See Davis, Matthew Livingston

Old Brains
See Halleck, Henry Wager

Old Broadbrim
See Rathborne, St. George Henry

[An] Old Brother Officer
See Leake, [Colonel] William Martin

Old Brown of Ossawatomie
See Brown, John

Old Bruin
See Adams, John [or James?] Capen

Old Bruin
See Perry, Matthew Calbraith

Old Buck
See Buchanan, James

Old Bucko
See Tracy, Spencer

[The] Old Buddha
See Tzu Hsi [or Tze-hsi]

Old Buena Vista
See Taylor, Zach[ary]

[The] Old Buffer
See Gale, Frederick

Old Bullion
See Benton, Thomas Hart

Old Burchell
See Burritt, Elihu

Old Bushman
See Wheelwright, W.

[An] Old Business Man
See Draper, George

[The] Old Cab Horse
See Hindenburg, Paul von

Old Cabinet
See Gilder, Richard Watson

Old Cap Collier
See Iron, Nathaniel Colchester

Old Cap Collier
See Sawyer, Eugene Taylor

Old Captain Ezekiel
See Greeley, Ezekiel

Old Carroll the Bard
See Daly, Eugene P.

Old Cartman
See Lyon, Isaac S.

[An] Old Catholic
See Coxe, Arthur Cleveland

[An] Old Cavalry Officer
See Carmichael, Charles Montauban

Old Celt
See Bottrell, W.

Old Chalk
See Chadwick, Henry

Old Chapultepec
See Scott, Winfield

Old Chatty Cheerful
See Martin, William

Old Chatty Cheerful
See Martyn, William

Old Chickamauga
See Steedman, James B.

Old Chief
See Clay, Henry

Old, Chilly
See Old, Christopher Middleton

Old Chinook
See Wise, Henry Alexander

Old Chocolate
See Williams, Feab. S.

Old, Christopher Middleton 1948-   [DC]
British cricketer
* Old, Chilly

Old Chrysanthemum
See Bernal, John Desmond

[An] Old Citizen
See De Beck, William L.

[An] Old Clothes Philosopher
See Brade, William

Old Club
See Colston, Raleigh Edward

Old Clubby
See Colston, Raleigh Edward

Old Cockeye
See Butler, Benjamin Franklin

Old Coins
See Rowell, A. S.

[The] Old Colonel
See Arnheim, Gus

Old Colonel Draper
See Draper, T. Waln-Morgan

[An] Old Colonist
See Wright, George

Old Colony
See Zabriskie, F. N.

[The] Old Commoner
See Stevens, Thad[deus]

[An] Old Conservative
See Palfrey, John Gorham

[An] Old Contributor
See Cudlip, Annie Thomas

Old Contributor [joint pseudonym with Julius Warren Lewis]
See Lewis, Harriet Newell

Old Contributor [joint pseudonym with Harriet Newell Lewis]
See Lewis, Julius Warren

[An] Old Contributor to Maga
See Neaves, Charles

Old Coonskin Davis
See Davis, Curt[is Benton]

[An] Old Cormorant
See Burdett, Constance

[An] Old Cornish Boy
See Christophers, Samuel Woolcock

[An] Old Cornish Woman
See Kelynack, Mary

Old Corporal
See Coan, Leander S.

[The] Old Country Boy
See O'Dell, Mac

Old Creepy Karpis
See Karpowicz, Alvin

Old Crome
See Crome, John

[The] Old Curmudgeon
See Ickes, Harold LeClair

[The] Old Curmudgeon of Labor
See Meany, [William] George

Old Dad
See Crosby, Harry Lillis

Old Daddy Tubman
See Tubman, William Vacanarat Shadrach

Old Daph
See Davenant, [Sir] William

Old Day Twiggs
See Twiggs, David Emanuel

Old Denmark
See Febiger, Christian

[The] Old Dessauer
See Leopold I

[The] Old Detective
See Rolfe, Maro Orlando

[The] Old Dino
See Rusk, [David] Dean

[An] Old Diplomatic Servant
See Parish, Henry Headly

[An] Old Diplomatic Servant
See Urquhart, David

[An] Old Divine
See Henry, Matthew

[The] Old Doctor
See Kennicott, John

[The] Old Dog
See Bartlett, Frederick Orin

[The] Old Dog
See Cunnington, Charles Leslie

Old Dog Ritter
See Ritter, Louis Elmer

Old Double Dome
See Brisbane, Arthur

Old Douro
See Wellesley, Arthur

Old Dreadnought
See Boscawen, Edward

Old Dutch Cleanser
See Blankenburg, Rudolph

[The] Old Dutch Faker
See Meegeren, Hans van

Old Eagle Eye
See Beckley, Jacob Peter [Jake]

Old Ebony
See Blackwood, William

Old Eight to Seven
See Hayes, Rutherford Birchard

[The] Old English Epigrammatist
See Heywood, John

Old Fag
See Bell, Robert Stanley Warren

[An] Old Farmer
See Lowell, John

Old Father Ephraim
See Poget [or Pagit?], Ephraim

Old Figgers
See Grosvenor, Charles Henry

Old Flintlock
See Hanson, Roger Weightman

Old Folks Arntzen
See Arntzen, Orie Edgar

Old Folks Kinder
See Kinder, Ellis Raymond

Old Folks Pillette
See Pillette, Herman

[An] Old Follower
See Chads, [Sir] Henry Ducie

Old Forty Eight Hours
See Doubleday, Abner

Old Forward
See Bluecher, Gebhard Leberecht von

[The] Old Fox
See Griffith, Clark Calvin

[The] Old Fox
See Parker, Ellis Howard

[The] Old Fox
See Soult, Nicolas Jean de Dieu

[The] Old Fox
See Washington, George

[The] Old Fox of the Balkans
See Pasic, Nikola

Old Frank
See Cheatham, Benjamin Franklin

[An] Old Friend and Servant of the Church
See Jones, William

Old Fritz
See Frederick II

Old Fritz Zivic
See Zivic, Ferdinand Henry John

Old Fuss and Feathers
See Scott, Winfield

Old George
See Monk, George [Duke of Albemarle]

[An] Old Georgia Lawyer
See Andrews, Garnett

Old Gimlet Eye
See Butler, Smedley Darlington

Old Gimpy Evans
See Evans, Robley Dunglison

Old Glad-Eye
See Gladstone, William Ewart

Old Glorious
See William III

Old Glory
See Burdett, [Sir] Francis

Old Goldy
See Goldwater, Barry [Morris]

Old Granddad Kinder
See Kinder, Ellis Raymond

Old Granny
See Harrison, William Henry

Old Gravel Voice
See Harmon, Ernest Nason

Old Gravity
See Thurlow, Edward [First Baron Thurlow]

[The] Old Gray Fox
See Case, Everett

Old Grimes
See Greene, Albert Gorton

Old Groaner
See Crosby, Harry Lillis

[The] Old Groaner
See Reeve, Edward H. [Ted]

Old Grog
See Vernon, Edward

Old Grover
See Cleveland, [Stephen] Grover

Old Hair and Teeth
See Shaw, George Bernard

Old Hand
See Strauss, Lewis L[ichtenstein]

Old Harlo
See Abbott, Charles Edwards

[An] Old Harrovian
See Straight, [Sir] Douglas

Old Harry
See Henry VIII

Old Harve Bailey
See Bailey, Harvey

[An] Old Hereditary Burgess, and Proprietor in Both City and Country
See Foulis, [Sir] James

[The] Old Hermit of Journalism
See Scripps, Edward Wyllis

[The] Old Hero
See Jackson, Andrew

Old Hewson the Cobbler
See Hewson, John

Old Hickory
See Jackson, Andrew

[The] Old Home Remedy
See Barger, Eros Bolivar

Old Honesty
See Lamb, Charles

Old Horace
See Walpole, Horatio [First Baron Walpole of Wolterton]

Old Hoss Ardner
See Ardner, Joseph A. [Joe]

Old Hoss Radbourn
See Radbourn, Charles Gardner

Old Hoss Stephenson
See Stephenson, Jackson Riggs

Old Hoss Twineham
See Twineham, Arthur W.

Old Humbug
See Benton, Thomas Hart

Old Humphrey
See Mogridge, George

Old Hurrygraph
See Robinson, James A.

Old Hutch
See Hutchinson, Benjamin Peters

Old Indestructible Hein
See Hein, Mel

[The] Old Indian
See Wynn, Early

[An] Old Inhabitant
See Horsburgh, James

[An] Old Inhabitant of British America
See Halliburton, Brenton

Old Iron Head
See Johnson, Roy

Old Iron Pants
See Cronkite, Walter Leland, Jr.

Old Iron Pants
See Johnson, Hugh Samuel

Old Iron Pants
See Meyer, Leo Robert

Old Iron Pants
See Skryabin, Vyacheslav Mikhailovich

Old Ironsides
See Stewart, Charles

Old Jack
See Jackson, Thomas Jonathan

Old Jack
See Jervis, John

Old Jacob
See James II

Old Jacob
See Tonson, Jacob

Old Jeb
See Stuart, James Ewell Brown

[That] Old Jew of Eton
See Rous [or Rowse], Francis

Old Jim Burnett
See Burnett, James

Old Jim Cummins
See Cummins, James Robert

Old Jock
See Wilson, John

Old Joe Clark
See Clark, Manuel D., Jr.

Old, John M.
See Bava, Mario

Old John W.
See Heisman, John William

Old Jonathan
See Doudeney, D. A.

Old Joseph
See Tuekakas

Old Jube
See Early, Jubal Anderson

Old Jubilee
See Early, Jubal Anderson

Old Kentuck
See Clay, Henry

Old Kill Devil
See Freeman, Austin

Old Kinderhook
See Van Buren, Martin

Old Knick
See Du Bois, Edward

[An] Old Lady
See Cahill, Frank

[An] Old Lady
See Dawson, A.

[The] Old Lady
See King, Billie Jean Moffitt

[The] Old Lamplighter
See Blake, Hector

Old Leatherface
See Chennault, Claire Lee

[An] Old Leeds Cropper
See Atkinson, D. H.

[The] Old Lefthander
See Sanders, Joseph L. [Joe]

Old Lev Saltonstall
See Saltonstall, Leverett

[An] Old Line Democrat
See Wilkes, George

Old Line Whig
See Williams, James

[The] Old Lion
See Darrow, Clarence Seward

[The] Old Lion
See Pitt, William [Earl of Chatham]

[The] Old Lion
See Roosevelt, Theodore [Teddy]

Old Mac McDonnell
See McDonnell, James Smith

[An] Old Maid
See Phillips, Miss

[An] Old Man
See Aldam, W. H.

[The] Old Man
See Alexander, William Anderson [Bill]

[The] Old Man
See Broz, Josip

[An] Old Man
See Collier, John Payne

[The] Old Man
See DiBella, Thomas

[The] Old Man
See Fangio, Juan Manuel

[The] Old Man
See Fry, Bob

[The] Old Man
See Grace, William Gilbert

[The] Old Man
See Green, David

[An] Old Man
See Head, [Sir] Francis Bond

[An] Old Man
See Johnston, Richard Malcolm

[The] Old Man
See Kalbfus, Edward Clifford

[An] Old Man
See Quincy, Josiah

[An] Old Man
See Skelton, Philip

[The] Old Man
See Travis, Walter J.

[An] Old Man
See White, Joseph M.

Old Man Bender
See Bender, John

Old Man Clanton
See Clanton, N. H.

Old Man Cotrelle
See Cotrelle, Louis

Old Man Eloquent
See Adams, John Quincy

[The] Old Man Eloquent
See Coleridge, Samuel Taylor

Old Man Eloquent
See Custis, George Washington Parke

[The] Old Man Eloquent
See Gladstone, William Ewart

[The] Old Man Eloquent
See Isocrates

[The] Old Man Eloquent
See Socrates

[The] Old Man Eloquent
See Wilson, John

[The] Old Man Eloquent of the Senate
See Hoar, George Frisbie

Old Man James
See James, Robert

Old Man Mac
See McDonnell, James Smith

Old Man Nyet
See Skryabin, Vyacheslav Mikhailovich

Old Man Oden
See Oden, James Burke [Jimmy]

[The] Old Man of the Gridiron
See Kenneally, George V.

[The] Old Man of the Mountain
See Hasan ibn-al Sabbah

[The] Old Man of the Mountain
See Roberts, Floyd

Old Man of the Mountain
See Rogers, Nathaniel P.

[The] Old Man of the Mountain
See Timmis, Brian

[The] Old Man of the Pay TV Business
See Brutoco, Ronald

Old Man River
See Boros, Julius Nicholas

[The] Old Man River
See Skelton, Jimmy

Old Man Rose's Lead Mine
See George, Hezekiah

Old Man Sunshine
See Tebbs, George William

Old Man Thunder
See Honda, Soichiro

Old Man With a Cane
See Shillaber, Benjamin Penhallow

[The] Old Marshal
See Chang Tso-lin

[The] Old Master
See Gaines, Joseph

[The] Old Master
See Gibson, Robert

[The] Old Master
See Oldfield, Berna Eli

[The] Old Master
See Papaleo, William

[The] Old Master
See Spencer, Frank Harding

Old Master Leavitt
See Leavitt, Dudley

Old Mathematics
See Humphreys, Andrew Atkinson

[An] Old Member of Parliament
See Glover, Richard

[An] Old Member of Parliament
See Hill, [Sir] Richard

[An] Old Member of Parliament
See Lee, Arthur

[An] Old Member of the Society
See Colet, John Annesley

Old Merry
See Hodder, Edwin

Old Mob
See Sympson, Thomas

[An] Old Modern
See Pegge, Samuel

[The] Old Mongoose
See Wright, Archibald Lee

Old Moore
See Andrews, Henry

Old Moore
See Whitman, Edward W.

Old Morality
See Smith, William Henry

Old Mortality
See Paterson, Robert

[The] Old Mortality in His Line
See Upcott, William

[The] Old Mortality of Pictures
See Vertue, George

Old Mose
See Moses, Felix

Old Mose Grove
See Grove, Robert Moses

Old Mother Hancock
See Hancock, John

[An] Old Mountaineer
See Scribner, J. P.

Old Needle Nose
See Hope, Leslie Townes

Old Nels Rockefeller
See Rockefeller, Nelson Aldrich

Old Never Let Go
See Murray, John Wilson

[An] Old New Yorker
See Duer, William Alexander

Old Nick
See Forgues, Paul Emile Durand

Old Nick
See Machiavelli, Niccolo [or Nicholas]

Old 98
See Harmon, Thomas D.

Old Noll
See Aurevilly, Leon Louis Frederic Jules, Barbey d'

Old Noll
See Cromwell, Oliver

Old Noll's Fiddler
See L'Estrange, [Sir] Roger

[A] Old Observer
See Hill, Rowland

[An] Old Officer
See Skelton, Philip

Old One Wing
See Martin, James Green

Old Ossawatomie
See Brown, John

Old Pam
See Temple, Henry John

Old Pancake
See Comstock, Henry Tomkins Paige

Old Pap Safety
See Thomas, George Henry

Old Pard
See Ballou, Noble Winfield

[An] Old Paris Man
See Thackeray, William Makepeace

Old Parlez
See Colston, Raleigh Edward

[An] Old Pastor
See Mackee, [Rev.] Thomas John

Old Patch
See Price, Charles

[An] Old Pen
See Wrangham, Francis

[An] Old Peninsular
See Boys, Thomas

[The] Old Perfesser
See Kyser, James Kern

Old Pete
See Longstreet, James

Old Pete Alexander
See Alexander, Grover Cleveland

Old Peveril
See Scott, [Sir] Walter

Old Phil Thompson
See Thompson, Philip Burton, Sr.

Old Poison Stewart
See Stewart, Nelson

[The] Old Political War Lord
See Daley, Richard Joseph

Old Polly
See Colston, Raleigh Edward

Old Ponder
See Wordsworth, William

Old Pop
See Popplewell, Thomas

Old Possum
See Eliot, Thomas Stearns

[An] Old Prairie Hen
See Nichols, Catherine

[The] Old Pretender
See Stuart, James Francis Edward

[An] Old Printer
See Dorrington, William

Old Private
See Gerrish, T.

Old Prob
See Abbe, Cleveland

Old Probabilities
See Abbe, Cleveland

[The] Old Professor
See Stengel, Charles Dillon

[The] Old Public Functionary
See Buchanan, James

Old Push
See Leathers, Thomas Paul

Old Pushmataha
See Leathers, Thomas Paul

Old Put
See Putnam, Israel

Old Q
See Douglas, William

Old Ranger
See Reynolds, John

[The] Old Redhead
See Godfrey, Arthur Michael

Old Reliable
See Carlson, Jules

Old Reliable
See Henrich, Thomas David

Old Reliable
See Start, Joseph

Old Reliable
See Thomas, George Henry

[An] Old Reporter
See Watts, Walter Henry

[An] **Old Resident**
See Armstrong, William

[An] **Old Resident**
See Porter, Albert H.

[The] **Old Revolutionary**
See De Valera, Eamon

[The] **Old Right Hander**
See Coon, Carleton A.

Old Robin
See Devereux, Robert [Third Earl of Essex]

Old Rock
See Benning, Henry Lewis

Old Rock Bottom
See Skryabin, Vyacheslav Mikhailovich

[The] **Old Roman**
See Benton, Thomas Hart

[The] **Old Roman**
See Comiskey, Charles Albert

[The] **Old Roman**
See Muldoon, William

[The] **Old Roman**
See Thurman, Allan Granbery

Old Rosey
See Rosecrans, William Starke

Old Rough and Ready
See Taylor, Zach[ary]

Old Round About
See Cleveland, Benjamin

Old Rowley
See Charles II

Old Saddlebags
See McDonald, Joseph Ewing

[An] **Old Sailor**
See Ames, Nathaniel

Old Sailor
See Barker, Matthew Henry

[An] **Old Sailor**
See Carter, Isaac

Old Sailor
See Coffin, Roland Folger

[The] **Old Sailor**
See Kenny, Nicholas Napoleon [Nick]

[An] **Old Salt**
See Sibbald, Thomas

Old Sanitary
See Yeatman, James

Old Sarah
See Churchill, Sarah Jennings

Old Sarge Street
See Street, Charles Evard

Old Sarum
See Salisbury, Marchioness of

[The] **Old Satyr**
See De Marguetel de Saint-Denis, Charles

[The] **Old Scotsman**
See McLendon, Gordon

Old Scout
See Merrill, H. R.

[The] **Old Settler**
See Lyman, Albert Robison

Old 77
See Grange, Harold E.

[The] **Old Shah**
See Pahlavi, Mohammad Reza

[The] **Old Shekarry**
See Leveson, Henry Astbury

[The] **Old Shoe**
See Wilson, Thornton Arnold

Old Shoebox Annie
See Smith, Mary Eleanor

Old Shoes Shoemaker
See Shoemaker, William

Old Si
See Small, Samuel White

Old Silver Leg
See Stuyvesant, Petrus

Old Silver Nails
See Stuyvesant, Petrus

Old Sink and Swim
See Adams, John

Old Sir Henry
See Vane, [Sir] Henry

Old Ski Nose
See Hope, Leslie Townes

Old Slackwater
See Moorhead, James Kennedy

Old Sleuth
See Halsey, Harlan Page

Old Sleuth
See Harbaugh, Thomas Chalmers

Old Slow Trot
See Thomas, George Henry

Old Slyboots
See Scott, James

Old Smoke
See Morrissey, John

[An] **Old Smoker**
See Stock, John

[An] **Old Soldier**
See Armstrong, John

[An] **Old Soldier**
See Butler, [Sir] William Francis

[An] **Old Soldier**
See Perry, David

Old Soupbone Hubbell
See Hubbell, Carl Owen

Old South
See Austin, Benjamin

Old Spades Lee
See Lee, Robert Edward

Old Spex
See Smith, Francis Henney

Old Spoons
See Butler, Benjamin Franklin

Old Squab
See Dryden, John

Old Square Toes
See George V

Old Stager
See Adams, William Taylor

[An] **Old Stager**
See Aspinwall, James

[An] **Old Stager**
See Field, Maunsell Bradhurst

Old Stars
See Mitchel, Ormsby McKnight

Old Stay Maker
See Thomson, Alexander

Old Steady
See Steedman, James B.

Old Stone
See Stone, Henry

Old Stone Hammer
See Metcalfe, Thomas

Old Stoneface
See Gromyko, Andrei Andreyevich

Old Stonefingers Stuart
See Stuart, Richard Lee

Old Stonewall Collins
See Collins, George M.

Old Straight
See Stewart, Alexander Peter

Old Straws
See Field, Joseph M.

Old Stubblebeard Grimes
See Grimes, Burleigh Arland

[An] **Old Student**
See Barling, [Rev.] John

Old Subtlety
See Fiennes, William [First Viscount Saye and Sele]

[The] **Old Swamp Fox**
See Marion, Francis

[An] **Old Teacher**
See Emerson, George Barrell

[An] **Old Teacher**
See Hosmer, Margaret

Old Tecump
See Sherman, William Tecumseh

Old Tecumseh
See Sherman, William Tecumseh

Old Thad
See Stevens, Thad[deus]

Old Three Stars
See Grant, Hiram Ulysses

Old Tick
See Douglas, William

Old Tige
See Anderson, George Thomas

Old Tige
See Cabell, William Lewis

Old Timer
See Merrill, James Milford

Old Times
See Davis, James D.

Old Tip
See Harrison, William Henry

Old Tippecanoe
See Harrison, William Henry

[The] Old Titanic Earth Son
See Webster, Daniel

Old To-morrow
See Macdonald, [Sir] John Alexander

Old Tom Jackson
See Jackson, Thomas Jonathan

Old Tom Morris
See Morris, Thomas, Sr.

Old Tomato Face
See Hartnett, Charles Leo

[The] Old Tomcat of the Keys
See Zurke, Robert [Bob]

Old Tommy
See Devin, Thomas C.

Old Tony
See Cooper, Anthony Ashley [First Earl of Shaftesbury]

[An] Old Tradesman
See Bailey, Thomas

[An] Old Traveller
See Buckingham, James Silk

[The] Old Trouper
See Koerber, Leila Marie

Old True Blue
See Richardson, Abram [or Arthur?] Harding

Old Tu'key Neck
See Stilwell, Joseph Warren

[The] Old Turfman
See Colden, Cadwallader R.

Old Tush
See Davies, Charles

[The] Old Tycoon
See Price, Sterling G.

[The] Old Tycoon
See Woodruff, Robert W. [Bob]

Old 'Un
See Durivage, Francis Alexander

Old United States
See Grant, Hiram Ulysses

Old Usufruct
See Tilden, Samuel Jones

Old Veto
See Cleveland, [Stephen] Grover

Old Veto
See Humphreys, Benjamin Grubb

Old Veto
See Johnson, Andrew

Old Veto
See Tyler, John

Old Vicar
See Warter, John Wood

[The] Old Viking
See Furuseth, Andrew

Old Virginny
See Fennimore, James

Old, Walter Gorn
See Old, Walter Richard

Old, Walter Richard 1864-1929 [EOP]
British author
* Old, Walter Gorn
* Sepharial

[The] Old War Horse
See Cook, Philip

[The] Old War Horse of Reform
See Blankenburg, Rudolph

Old War-Horse
See Devin, Thomas C.

[The] Old Warrior
See Adenauer, Konrad

[The] Old Wheel Horse of Democracy
See Medary, Samuel

[The] Old Whig
See Addison, Joseph

Old Whiskers
See Wiles, Greenbury F.

Old White Hat
See Greeley, Horace

[The] Old Whoremaster
See Heitler, Michael

Old Wicked
See Godfrey, Hollen

Old Wiggie
See Davidson, James

Old Wigs
See Dunstan, [Sir] Jeffrey

[The] Old Wizard
See Carver, George Washington

Old Wolf Adenauer
See Adenauer, Konrad

[The] Old Woman in the Red Cap
See Pabor, Charles Henry

Old Wrinkle-Boots
See Willis, Browne

[The] Old Yorkshire Turfman
See Herbert, Henry William

Old Zach
See Buchanan, James

Old Zach
See Taylor, Zach[ary]

Old Zeb Weaver
See Weaver, Zebulon

Oldacre, Cedric, of Saxe Normanby
See Warter, John Wood

Oldboy, Felix
See Mines, John Flavel

Oldbuck, Obadiah
See Toepffer, Rodolphe

Oldbug, Jonathan
See Withington, Leonard

Oldcastle, Alice
See Meynell, Alice [Christiana Gertrude Thompson]

Oldcastle, Humphrey
See Amhurst, Nicholas

Oldcastle, Humphrey
See St. John, Henry

Oldcastle, [Sir] John 1360?-1417 [FFF, HN, HPPN, SN]
Leader of religious sect in England
* Cobham, Baron
* [The] Father of Political Dissenters
* [The] Good Lord Cobham

Oldcastle, John [or Jonathan]
See Meynell, Wilfrid

Oldeboerrigter, Melle Johannes 1908-1976 [CAR]
Dutch painter
* Melle

Olden, Charles 1909?- [BMH, FC]
British entertainer
* Nedlo the Gypsy Violinist
* Neek, Hugh
* Ray, Ted

Olden, Georg 1921- [IBW]
American graphic artist
* [The] Dean of TV Art Directors

Oldenburg, Claes 1929- [HPPN]
Swedish-American journalist and sculptor
* [The] Mentor of the Pop Art Movement

[The] Oldest Authoress
See Pollock, Alice

[The] Oldest Cop on the Beat
See Devlin, [Lieut.] John J.

[The] Oldest Inhabitant
See Cabell, Julia [Mayo]

Oldest Inspector
See Bently, J.

[The] Oldest Man in America
See Smith, Charlie

[The] Oldest Man in the Sea
See Counsilman, James

[The] Oldest Rookie
See Alsup, William [Bill]

[The] Oldest School Inspector
See Bentley, Joseph

[The] Oldest Soldier
See Hershey, [General] Lewis B.

Oldfeld, Peter [joint pseudonym with P. Jacobsson]
See Bartlett, Vernon

Oldfeld, Peter, [joint pseudonym with Vernon Bartlett]
See Jacobsson, P.

Oldfield, Anna 1683-1730 [HPPN, RH, SN]
British actress
* Miss Nancy
* Modish, [Lady] Betty
* Narcissa
* Oldfield, Nance

Oldfield, Barney
See Oldfield, Berna Eli

Oldfield, Berna Eli 1878-1946 [AS, FC, HPPN]
American auto racer
* America's Legendary Speed King
* [The] Old Master
* Oldfield, Barney

Oldfield, Claude Houghton 1889-1961 [LAO, LC, TC]
British author
* Houghton, Claude

Oldfield, Nance
See Oldfield, Anna

Oldham, Derek
See Oldham, John Stephens

Oldham, Esso
See Oldham, Stephen

Oldham, Hugh R.
See Whitford, Joan

Oldham, John 1653-1683 [DEL, FFF, NPS, PA]
British poet
* Astrophel
* [The] English Juvenal
* Grubendol
* [The] Juvenal of England
* [The] Marcellus of Our Tongue

Oldham, John Cyrus 1893-1961 [BE, BN]
American baseball player
* Oldham, Red
* Oldham, Rube

Oldham, John Stephens 1893-1968 [SC]
British actor and opera singer
* Oldham, Derek

Oldham of Greystones, Dr.
See Henry, Caleb Sprague

Oldham, Red
See Oldham, John Cyrus

Oldham, Rube
See Oldham, John Cyrus

Oldham, Stephen 1948- [DC]
British cricketer
* Oldham, Esso

Oldland, Lilian 1905- [F2]
Actress
* Newland, Mary

Oldmeadow, E. J.
See Oldmeadow, Ernest James

Oldmeadow, Ernest James 1867-1949 [LC]
British author
* Oldmeadow, E. J.

Oldmixon, Georgina Sidus 1763?-1836 [FAA]
British-born actress
* George, Miss

Oldmixon, John 1673-1742 [HPPN, NPS]
British historian and pamphleteer
* [The] Author of the First Part
* Wilson, Charles

Oldmixon, Mrs.
See Sidus, Georgina

Oldpath, Obadiah
See Newhall, James Robinson

Oldring, Reuben Henry 1884-1961 [BE]
American baseball player
* Oldring, Rube

Oldring, Rube
See Oldring, Reuben Henry

Oldroyd, Richard ?-1664 [NPS]
British conspirator
* [The] Devil of Dewsbury

Olds, Ransom Eli 1864-1950 [HPPN]
American automobile manufacturer
* [The] Father of Oldsmobile and Reo
* [The] Father of the Popular-Priced Car

Oldschool, Oliver
See Dennie, Joseph

Oldschool, Oliver
See Sargent, Nathan

Oldstyle, Jonathan, Gent.
See Irving, Washington

Oldstyle, Oliver
See Paulding, James Kirke

Oldway, Oliver
See Foe, Daniel

Oldys, Alexander [SN]
British poet
* [The] English Scarron
* [The] Little Poet

Oldys, Francis
See Chalmers, George

Oldys, William 1696-1761 [HPPN, NPS, PA]
British antiquary
* Cooper, E.
* G.
* Hayward, Thomas

Oldys, William (cont.)
* [A] Prodigy of Literary Curiosity
* W. O., Esq.

Ole Bootnose Abel
See Abel, Sid[ney Gerald]

Ole Earl
See Long, Earl Kemp

Ole Red Eyes
See Crocetti, Dino

Ole-Luk-Oie [Olaf Shut-Eye]
See Swinton, [Sir] Ernest Dunlop

Olea, Maria Florencia Varas 1938- [CA]
Chilean author and journalist
* Varas, Florencia

Olearius
See Von Oleuschtaeger, Johann Daniel

O'Leary, Arthur ?-1854? [PI]
Irish poet
* A. O'L.

O'Leary, Big Jim
See O'Leary, James

O'Leary, Chester F.
See Kuehnelt-Leddihn, Erik [Ritter Von]

O'Leary, Daniel 1856-1922 [BE]
American baseball player
* O'Leary, Hustling Dan

O'Leary, Ellen 1831-1889 [PI]
Irish poet
* Eily
* Lenel

O'Leary, Hustling Dan
See O'Leary, Daniel

O'Leary, James ?-1926 [BLB]
American underworld figure
* O'Leary, Big Jim

O'Leary, John
See Panzram, Carl

O'Leary, Joseph 19th c. [PI]
Irish poet and journalist
* Murphy, Denis
* O.
* O'L.
* [A] Reporter

O'Leary, Liam 1910- [WD]
Irish author
* O'Laoghaire, Liam

O'Leary, Pat
See Guerisse, Albert

O'Leary, Peter 20th c. [WWL]
Irish author
* O Laoghaire, Peadar

Oleastro, Hieronimo ?-1563 [PA]
Author
* De Azambuya

Olehewitz, L. M. 1828-1905
French author
* Verne, Jules

Olemy, P. T.
See Baker, George

Olenius, Elsa Victoria 1896- [IAW]
Swedish author
* Bergius, Elsa Britt

Oleson, John 1899- [FC]
Canadian-born actor
* Qualen, John

Olga
See Erteszek, Olga

Olga
See Phillips, Olga Somech

Olguin Rangel, Eduardo 1918- [GS]
Mexican bullfighter
* [El] Fantasma [The Ghost]

O'Liathain, Sesu
See Lyons, John Maguire

[The] Oliday King
See Butlin, [Sir] Billy

Olinger, Robert A. 1841?-1881 [EWG]
American gunfighter
* [The] Big Indian

Oliphant, Carolina [Baroness Nairne]
1766-1845 [DLE1, DNNS, SN]
Scottish poet
* B. B.
* Bogan of Bogan, Mrs.
* [The] Flower of Strathearn

Oliphant, Elmer Q. 1892?- [BB, FB]
American basketball and football player
* Oliphant, Ollie

Oliphant, Kington Blair 1862?-1952 [BI]
Scottish historian
* Maxtone-Grahame, Margaret Ethel

Oliphant, Lawrence ?-1792 [SN]
*Father of Scottish poet, Carolina
Oliphant Nairne*
* [The] Auld Laird

Oliphant, Mrs. 1828-1897 [NPS]
Author
* Dunsmuir, Amy

Oliphant, Ollie
See Oliphant, Elmer Q.

Oliphant, William 1906- [PMJ]
American bandleader
* Osborne, Will

Olitski, Jules
See Demikovosky, Jevel

Oliva, Antonio Pedro 1940- [BE, WWB]
Cuban-born baseball player
* Oliva, Tony

Oliva, Tony
See Oliva, Antonio Pedro

Olivares, Conde de
See De Guzman, Gaspar [Duque de
Sanlucar]

Olive, Ison Prentice 1840-1886 [BLB]
American gunfighter
* Olive, Print

Olive, Martin 1958- [DC]
British cricketer
* Olive, Palm

Olive, May
See Wheeler, Mrs. S. T.

Olive, Palm
See Olive, Martin

Olive, Print
See Olive, Ison Prentice

Olive-Branch, [Rev] Simon
See Roberts, William

Olive Rodas, Diego 1872-1950 [GS]
Spanish bullfighter
* Morenito de Algeciras [Little Dark
One from Algeciras]

Oliven, Fritz 1874-? [LAO]
German author
* Rideamus

Oliver
See Gibbs, Oliver

Oliver
See Swofford, William Oliver

Oliver
See Vallarino, Vincent

Oliver, Al[bert, Jr.] 1946- [BE, PB]
American baseball player
* Scoop, Mr.

Oliver, Amy Roberta [Ruck] 1878-1978
[AW, CA, LAO]
British author
* Ruck, Amy Roberta
* Ruck, Berta

Oliver, Burton
See Burt, Olive Woolley

Oliver, C. W.
See Oliver, Charles William

Oliver, Chad
See Oliver, Symes Chadwick

Oliver, Charles
See Selz, Ralph Jerome Von Braun

Oliver, Charles William 1911- [ART]
American-born painter
* Oliver, C. W.

Oliver, Clarence
See LaGrone, Oliver

Oliver, Dean 20th c. [GW]
American rodeo performer
* Oliver, Wope

Oliver, Death
See Oliver, Stephen

Oliver, Dick
See Barrett, Tracey Souter

Oliver, Dora Dana 1881-? [NAA]
American writer
* Shipman, Elydia Foss

Oliver, Dude
See Oliver, Philip Robert

Oliver, Edith
See Goldsmith, Edith

Oliver, Edna May
See Cox-Oliver, Edna May

Oliver, Edna May
See Nutter, Edna May Cox-Oliver

Oliver, Edward S. 1916?-1961 [AS, EG,
GF]
American golfer
* Oliver, Porky

Oliver, Eli L. 1899- [HPPN]
*Vice-president of Labor's Nonpartisan
League*
* Oliver, Kiss Of Death

Oliver, Eugene [FFF]
Entertainer
* Revillo, Eugene

Oliver, Frederick Spencer 1866-1899
[SFL]
Author
* Phylos the Thibetan

Oliver, Gail
See Scott, Marian [Gallagher]

Oliver, Gay
See Owen, Garnet

Oliver, George
See Onions, [George] Oliver

Oliver, Gertrude Kent 20th c. [MBF]
British author
* Carr, Kent

[The] Oliver Goldsmith of America
See Taylor, Benjamin Franklin

Oliver, Harold 1898- [FHE]
Canadian-born hockey player
* Oliver, Harry

Oliver, Harry
See Oliver, Harold

Oliver, Henry Kemble
See Oliver, Thomas Henry

Oliver, Hugh ?-1569 [PA]
Author
* Witweyke

Oliver, James 1823-1908 [HPPN]
*Scottish-American foundry owner and
inventor*
* [The] Father of the Hardfaced Plow

Oliver, Jane
See Rees, Helen Christina Easson
[Evans]

Oliver, John Rathbone 1872-1943 [TC1]
American author
* Roland, John

Oliver, Joseph 1885-1938 [BBD, DAM,
IBW]
American jazz musician
* Oliver, King
* Papa Joe

Oliver, Kine
See Alexander, Alger

Oliver, King
See Oliver, Joseph

Oliver, Kiss Of Death
See Oliver, Eli L.

Oliver, Mark
See Tyler-Whittle, Michael Sidney

Oliver, Melvin James 1910- [DAM, EJ, IBW]
American jazz musician
* [The] Charming Vocalist
* Oliver, Sy

Oliver, Mert
See Oliver, Merton A.

Oliver, Merton A. 1917- [EJ]
American jazz musician
* Oliver, Mert

Oliver, Nathan, Esq.
See Blakey, Robert

Oliver, Nathaniel 1940- [BE, SMG]
American baseball player
* Oliver, Pee Wee

Oliver, Olly
See Oliver, Philip Robert

Oliver, Owen
See Flynn, [Sir] J. Albert

Oliver, Paul A. 1830-1912 [HPPN]
American Civil War officer and inventor
* [The] American Father of Dynamite

Oliver, Pee Wee
See Oliver, Nathaniel

Oliver, Pen
See Thompson, [Sir] Henry

Oliver, Peter 1741-1822 [HPPN]
British-American jurist
* Caractacus

Oliver, Peter
See Oliver, William Pynchon

Oliver, Philip Robert 1956- [DC]
British cricketer
* Oliver, Dude
* Oliver, Olly

Oliver, Porky
See Oliver, Edward S.

Oliver, Rebel
See Oliver, Thomas Noble [Tom]

Oliver, Rochelle
See Olshever, Rochelle

Oliver, Sherling
See McGowan, Francis Oliver

Oliver, Simeon 1903-
American author and illustrator
* Nutchuk

Oliver, Stephen 18th c. [RBE]
British boxer
* Oliver, Death

Oliver, Stephen
See Chatto, William Andrew

Oliver, Susan
See Gercke, Charlotte

Oliver, Sy
See Oliver, Melvin James

Oliver, Symes Chadwick 1928- [SF]
American anthropologist and author
* Oliver, Chad

Oliver, Temple
See Smith, Jeanie Oliver [Davidson]

Oliver, Thelma 20th c. [IBW]
Yoga disciple
* Kaur, Krishna

Oliver, Thomas Henry 1800-1885 [WBD]
American educator, composer, industrialist
* Oliver, Henry Kemble

Oliver, Thomas Noble [Tom] 1903- [BE]
American baseball player
* Oliver, Rebel

Oliver, Tim
See Wilkins, [Robert] Tim[othy]

Oliver, Vic
See Samek, Viktor Oliver

Oliver, William Pynchon 1821-1855 [PA]
Author
* Oliver, Peter

Oliver, Wope
See Oliver, Dean

Olivera, Hector 20th c. [HPPN]
Argentine theater organist
* [The] Wizard of Ahs

Oliveras, Frank
See Pesce, Franco

Oliveria, Flash
See Oliveria, Miranda

Oliveria, Miranda 20th c. [AES]
Soccer player
* Oliveria, Flash

Olivero, Magda
See Olivero, Maria Maddalena

Olivero, Maria Maddalena 1916- [OP]
Italian opera singer
* Olivero, Magda

Oliveroff, Andre
See Grymes, Oliver Smith

Oliver's Fiddler
See L'Estrange, [Sir] Roger

Olivia
See Briggs, Emily Edson

Olivier, Jacques
See Guyonnet, Jacques

Olivier, [Sir] Laurence 1907- [HPPN]
British actor, director, producer
* [The] Present Champion of the English Theater

Olivier le Dain [or le Daim]
See Necker, Olivier

Olivier le Diable
See Necker, Olivier

Olivo, Chi Chi
See Olivo, Federico Emilio

Olivo, Federico Emilio 1928- [BE]
Dominican-born baseball player
* Olivo, Chi Chi

Olkyrn, Iris
See Milligan, Alice L.

Ollapod
See Clark, Willis Gaylord

Ollapod
See Edwards, Thomas A.

Ollie Papa
See Thomas, Charles

Ollif, S. L. E. [NPS]
Author
* Elphinstone, Leslie

Olliver, Tom
See Graydon, William Murray

Ollivier, Claude 20th c.
British intelligence chief
* Jade Amicol

Ollrichs, Dorothy Jardon 1883-1966 [HPPN]
American singer
* Jardon, Dorothy

Olmedo, Alex
See Olmedo y Rodriguez, Alejandro

Olmedo y Rodriguez, Alejandro 1936- [HPPN]
Peruvian tennis player
* Olmedo, Alex

Olmedo y Vazquez, Antonio 1874-1901 [GS]
Spanish bullfighter
* Valentin

Olmo, Chico
See Olmo, Luis Francisco Rodriguez

Olmo, Harold P. 1909?- [HPPN]
American educator and viticulturist
* Grape, Mr.

Olmo, Jibaro
See Olmo, Luis Francisco Rodriguez

Olmo, Luis Francisco Rodriguez 1919- [BE, BN]
Puerto Rican-born baseball player
* Olmo, Chico
* Olmo, Jibaro

Olmo, Pedro
See Kutschmann, Walter

Olmstead, Agnes [Reasor] [BI]
American home economist
* Logan, Martha

Olmsted, Charlotte
See Kursh, Charlotte Olmsted

Olmsted, George La Moille 19th c. [HPPN]
American journalist
* La Moille, [Dr.] Tom G.

Olney, Oliver
See Des Voignes, Jules Verne

Olney, Ross Robert 1929- [IAW]
American author
* Wilson, Pat

Olofsson, Nils Phillip 1906?-1974 [BI]
American wrestler
* [The] Swedish Angel

Ologboni, Tejumola F.
See Taylor, Rockie

O'London, John
See Lynd, Robert

O'London, John
See Whitten, Wilfred

O'Loughlin, Louise T. [FFF]
Entertainer
* Moore, Elsie

Olsen, Albert William 1921- [BE]
American baseball player
* Olsen, Ole

Olsen, Alfred Johannes, Jr. 1884-1956 [SF]
American writer
* Olsen, Bob

Olsen, Arthur 1894- [BE]
American baseball player
* Olsen, Ole

Olsen, Bob
See Olsen, Alfred Johannes, Jr.

Olsen, Bud
See Olsen, Enoch

Olsen, Cruster Aud 1889-1938 [SC]
American actor
* Cruster, Aud

Olsen, D. B.
See Hitchens, Dolores [Birk]

Olsen, Enoch 20th c. [SMG]
American basketball player
* Olsen, Bud

Olsen, Harold G. 1895-1953 [AS]
American basketball player and coach
* Olsen, Ole

Olsen, Ib Spang 1921- [CA, SAT]
Danish-born author and illustrator
* Detine, Padre [joint pseudonym with Erik E. Frederiksen]

Olsen, John Edward [Jack] 1925- [CA]
American author
* Rhoades, Jonathan

Olsen, John Siguard 1892-1963 [BEW, EMT, IPA]
American entertainer
* Olsen, Ole

Olsen, Merlin 20th c. [HPPN]
American football player and actor
* Olsen, Mule

Olsen, Mule
See Olsen, Merlin

Olsen, Ole
See Olsen, Albert William

Olsen, Ole
See Olsen, Arthur

Olsen, Ole
See Olsen, Harold G.

Olsen, Ole
See Olsen, John Siguard

Olsen, Theodore Victor 1932- [CA, WD]
American author
* Stark, Joshua
* Storm, Christopher
* Willoughby, Cass

Olsen, Thomas Carl Morrell 1912- [IAW]
Scottish-born author
* Morrell, John

Olsen, Tracy 1940- [ITA]
American actress
* Carter, Tracy

Olsheski, Gail 1952- [CA]
Canadian author
* Henley, Gail

Olshever, Rochelle 1937- [BEW]
American actress
* Oliver, Rochelle

Olson, Ann Margret 1941- [BDF, FC, HT]
Swedish-born American actress
* Ann Margret

Olson, Bobo
See Olson, Carl

Olson, Carl 1928- [BI, RBE, WA]
American boxer
* Olson, Bobo

Olson, Eugene E. 1936- [CA]
American author
* Steiger, Brad

Olson, Helene Dean 20th c. [IAW]
American writer
* Betty

Olson, Henry Russell 1913- [ASC]
American musician
* Russell, Henry

Olson, Ivan Massie 1885-1965 [AS, BE]
American baseball player
* Olson, Ivy

Olson, Ivy
See Olson, Ivan Massie

Olson, Karl Arthur 1930- [BE]
American baseball player
* Olson, Ole

Olson, Marv[in Clement] 1907- [BE]
American baseball player
* Olson, Sparky

Olson, Merle Theodore 1937- [CA]
American poet and author
* Olson, Toby

Olson, Mrs.
See Christine, Virginia

Olson, Ole
See Olson, Karl Arthur

Olson, Olof 1838-1916 [BI]
American painter
* Krans, Olof

Olson, Robert G. 1913- [ASC]
American composer and educator
* Roberts, Jon
* Rollins, Glenn

Olson, Sparky
See Olson, Marv[in Clement]

Olson, Toby
See Olson, Merle Theodore

Olson, Willis S. 1930- [BBH]
American skier
* Billy the Kid

Olsson, Anna 1866-? [NAA]
Swedish-born author
* Aina

Olt, Arisztid
See Blasko, Bela Lugosi

Olugebefola, Ademola?
See Thomas, Harold Alexander

Olvera, Ernesto Hill
See Olvera Gonzalez, Hermengildo

Olvera Gonzalez, Hermengildo 1937-1967 [SC]
Mexican actor and musician
* Olvera, Ernesto Hill

Olvero Lara, Francisco 1883- [GS]
Mexican bullfighter
* Berrinches [Bad-Tempered]

Olwyn, Lady
See Wilson, Monique

Olympia, Mr.
See Zane, Frank

[The] Olympian
See Pericles

Olympic
See Hugo, Victor Marie

Olys
See Korbut, Olga

Oma, Lee
See Czjewski, Frank

O'Mahoney, Jacques 1919- [FC, ITA, SW]
American actor
* Mahoney, Jock

O'Mahoney, Rich
See Crozetti, Ruth G. Warner [Lora]

O'Mahoney, Thaddeus [PA]
Author
* A. M.

O'Mahony, C. K. 1884- [WWL]
British author
* Ellis, Julian
* Kingston, Charles

O'Mahony, Patrick
See Mahony, Patrick

O'Mahony, Timothy J. 1839-? [PI]
Irish poet
* Mona

Omahundro, J. B.
See Ingraham, Prentiss

O'Malley, C.
See Lever, Charles James

O'Malley, Ellen
See Jones, Ellen

O'Malley, Frank 1916- [SFL, WGT]
Author
* O'Rourke, Frank

O'Malley, J. Patrick
See O'Malley, Patrick H., Jr.

O'Malley, Kevin
See Hossent, Harry

O'Malley, Mary Dolling [Sanders]
1889?-1974 [CA, LC, TC]
British author
* Bridge, Ann

O'Malley, Michael 20th c. [WWL]
Irish author and editor
* O Maille, Micheal

O'Malley, Patrick H., Jr. 1891-1966
[F1]
Actor
* O'Malley, J. Patrick

Oman, Carola [Mary Anima] 1897-1978
[CA, HPPN]
British author
* Lenanton, C.
* Lenanton, Carola Mary Anima Oman

O'Mant, Hedley Percival Angelo
1899-1955 [MBF]
British author
* Clifford, Martin [house pseudonym]
* Conquest, Owen [house pseudonym]
* Hawke, [Captain] Robert
* Owen, Hedley
* Richards, Frank [house pseudonym]
* Scott, Hamilton
* Scott, Hedley

Omar Khayyam 1025-1123 [DEP,
DNNF, HPPN]
Persian poet
* [The] Astronomer Poet
* [The] Great Tentmaker
* [The] King of Wisdom
* [The] Persian Horace
* [The] Tentmaker

Omar Pasha
See Latas, Michael

Omar, the Magnificent
See Kotkin, David

Omar I 581-644 [DNNF, FFF, SN]
Caliph of the Mussulman empire
* [The] Commander of the Faithful
* [The] Emperor of Believers

O'Mara, Jim
See Fluharty, Vernon Lee

O'Mara, Pat
See O'Mara, Timothy Joseph

O'Mara, Timothy Joseph 1901- [NAA]
British-born author
* O'Mara, Pat

Omari, Cuthbert Kashingo 1936- [IAW]
Tanzanian sociologist and author
* Manne, Macho
* Mbali, Ona

Omchery
See Pillai, Narayana Narayana

O'Meagher, Patrick J.
See Meagher, Patrick J.

O'Meara, Dermand ?-1620 [PA]
Author
* Dermitius

O'Meara, Kathleen [PA]
Author
* Ramsay, Grace

O'Meara, Martin J. 1929?- [SI 3-12-84]
American businessman and yachtsman
* O'Meara, Max

O'Meara, Max
See O'Meara, Martin J.

Omedy, Eugene
See Roper, Neil Campbell Ommanney

Omega
See Bradbury, Ray [Douglas]

Omega
See Platt, [Rev.] Robert

Omer [or Omar] Pasha
See Lattas, Michael

Omiccioli, Palmina 1925- [FC, WEF]
Italian actress
* Rossi-Drago, Eleonora

Omichund
See Amir Chand

Omikron
See Cladel, Leon

Ommanney, F. D.
See Ommanney, Francis Downes

Ommanney, Francis Downes 1903- [LC]
British zoologist and author
* Ommanney, F. D.

[The] Omniscious Doctor
See Agrippa, [Cornelius] Heinrich

Omnium, Jacob
See Higgins, Matthew James

Omnivagant
See Wyman, Rufus

Omohundro, John 1943- [SMG]
American football trainer
* Johnny O

Omohundro, John B. ?-1880
American Indian scout and author
* Texas Jack

Omond, Thomas Stewart 19th c.
[HPPN]
British poet
* White, Thomas, Jr.

O'Moore, Barry
See Yost, Herbert A.

O'Moran, Mabel
See Moran, Mabel O'Connell

O'More
See Kennedy, Thomas

O'More, Peggy
See Blocklinger, Peggy O'More

O'More, Rory 17th c. [WBD]
Irish chieftain
* Moore, Roger

Omowale, Marina
See Maxwell, Marina

Ompteda, [Baron] Georg von 1863-1931
[WBD]
German author, poet, playwright
* Egestorff, Georg

Omsby, Waterman L., Jr. 1834-? [PA]
Author
* O. Jr.

Omulevskii
See Fedorov, Innokentii Vasilevich

O'Mulrenin, Richard Joseph 1832?-1906
[PI]
Irish poet
* Concobar, Clann
* Erionnach

O'Murchadha, Peadar
See Murphy, Peter

O'Murchadha, Shemus
See Murphy, James

O'Murphy, Louise 18th c. [HPPN]
Irish model
* [La] Morphise

O'N.
See O'Neill, Michael

On, Pe [BI]
Burmese journalist
* Tet Toe

On the Go
See Steimer, Francis Alfred

On The Spot Spooner
See Spooner, Ed

Onadipe, Kola
See Onadipe, Nathaniel Kolawole

Onadipe, Nathaniel Kolawole 1922-
[CA, TCC]
Nigerian author
* Kolon, Nita
* Onadipe, Kola

O'Nair, Mairi
See Evans, Constance May

Onassis, Ari
See Onassis, Aristotle [Socrates]

Onassis, Aristotle [Socrates] 1900?-1975
[HPPN, NY 3-15-75]
Greek tycoon
* Onassis, Ari
* Onassis, Daddy O.

Onassis, Daddy O.
See Onassis, Aristotle [Socrates]

**Onassis, Jacqueline Lee [Bouvier]
[Kennedy]** 1929-
*Widow of Greek tycoon A. Onassis and
American president J. Kennedy*
* Jackie O
* Lace [Secret Service code name]

[The] Once and Future Prime Minister
See Soares, Mario

Ondra, Anny
See Ondrakova, Anny

Ondrakova, Anny 1903-   [FC, OCF]
Polish-born actress
* Ondra, Anny

[The] One and Only
See Dukinfield, William Claude

One Arm Daily
See Daily, Hugh Ignatius

[The] One Armed Devil
See Kearny, Philip

One Armed John
See Wrencher, John Thomas

One Armed Phil
See Kearny, Philip

[The] One Armed Scout
See Crisp, Henry

**One Behind the Throne Greater than
the Throne Itself**
See Stuart, John [Third Earl of Bute]

[The] One Book Author
See Marsh, Margaret Munnerlyn
Mitchell

One Called an High Churchman
See Leslie, Charles

One Eye Babe
See Philip, Joseph

One Eye Dotson
See Dotson, Clarence

[The] One Eyed
See Hermippus

[The] One Eyed
See Zisca, John

One Eyed Connelly
See Connelly, James Leo

[The] One Eyed General
See Liu Po-Ch'eng

One Formerly Possessed of the Place
See Lacy, Willoughby

One from the Plow
See Mitchell, G.

One Grand Schmidt
See Schmidt, Ernest J.

[The] 101st Senator
See Mitchell, Clarence M., Jr.

[The] One in a Duo
See Wallard, Elizabeth

One in Retirement
See Todd, Henry Cook

One Intimately Acquainted With Him
See Mather, Cotton

**One Lately a Member of the Immediate
Government of the College**
See Norton, Andrews

One Leg Norwood
See Norwood, Sam

One Leg Paget
See Paget, Henry William [First
Marquess of Anglesey]

[The] One Legged Governor
See Stuyvesant, Petrus

One Lung Smith
See Smith, George

[The] One Man Army of Bataan
See Wermuth, Arthur

[The] One Man Cyclone
See Chapin, Harry

One Man Patriot
See Fish, Hamilton, Jr.

[The] One Man Trio
See Bonner, Weldon H. Philip

[The] One Man Trust Company
See Wilson, Charles Moseman

[The] One Million Dollar Mouth
See Cronkite, Walter Leland, Jr.

One Misco Dolos
See Leslie, Charles

One Nail Heiny
See Heiny, Thomas

One of a Literary Family
See Le Breton, Anna Letitia [Aikin]

One of America's Keenest Thinkers
See Royce, Josiah

One of Dr. Wheelock's Pupils
See Frisbie, Levi

One of H. M.'s Justices of the Peace
See Owen, Robert

One of her Sons
See Abbott, Jacob

One of her Sons
See Legge, Alfred Owen

One of His Candid Neighbors
See Bellamy, Joseph

One of his Children
See White, Mrs. M. E. [Harding]

One of His Congregation
See Proctor, Edna Dean

One of His Constituents
See Copleston, Edward

One of his Constituents
See Drummond, Henry

One of his Countrymen
See Cushing, Caleb

One of His Majesty's Chaplains
See Perceval, Arthur Philip

One of His Majesty's Servants
See Perceval, Arthur Philip

One of His Sons
See Gill, [Rev.] Thomas Howard

One of Ireland's Ballad Poets
See Forrest, John Lawrence

One of its Members
See Ash, Edward

One of No Party
See Grant, James

One of Plutarch's Men
See Adams, Samuel

One of the Alderman
See Combe, Harvey Christopher

One of the Alumni
See Inglis, John

One of the Barclays
See Otis, Eliza Henderson Bordman

One of the Boys
See Fitzgerald, Percy Hetherington

One of the Bunglers
See Ord, Lewis Redman

One of the Cock and Hen Club
See Steevens, George

**One of the Committee of the American
Academy**
See Bigelow, Jacob

One of the Country Party
See Webster, James

One of the Crazies
See Ginsberg, Allen

**One of the "Eighteen Millions of
Bores"**
See Wright, Elizur

One of the 80,000 Incorrigible Jacobins
See Rashleigh, [Sir] John Colman

One of the Family
See Page, R. Channing M.

One of the Family
See Williams, Joseph Hartwell

One of the Family of the Bowleses
See Bowles, William Lisle

One of the Fancy
See Moore, Thomas

One of the Gamest Players in the Game
See Merkle, Fred[erick Charles]

One of the Hearers
See Mather, Cotton

One of the Last Century
See Rose, William Stewart

One of the Magistrates of the Public Office in Great Marlborough
See Neve, Philip

One of the Majority
See Gall, [Rev.] James

One of the Members of the College
See Coote, Charles

One of the Memorialists
See Muhlenberg, William Augustus

One of the Ministers in Boston
See Mather, Cotton

One of the Ministers in the North Part of Boston
See Mather, Cotton

One of the Ministers of Edinburgh
See Inglis, John

One of the Old School
See Hawkins, [Rev.] William Bentinck Lethem

One of the Old School
See Seymour, Robert

One of the Party
See Taylor, F.

One of the People
See Burges, Tristram

One of the People
See Dibdin, Thomas Frognall

One of the People
See Hopkinson, Francis

One of the People
See Waddington, Alfred Penderill

One of the People
See Wirt, William

One of the People Called Christians
See Horne, George

One of the People Called Christians
See Waring, Jeremiah

One of the Pilgrims
See Truesdell, A. C. W.

One of the Professors
See Clark, Thomas

One of the Raiders
See Atkinson, G. W.

One of the Readers
See Mather, Samuel

One of the Scotch People
See Miller, Hugh

One of the Suffering Clergy of the Church of Scotland
See Myline, William

One of the Suffering Clergy There
See Cant, [Rev.] Andrew

One of the Trustees
See Ruggles, Samuel Bulkley

One of the World's Fastest Humans
See Metcalfe, Ralph

One of Their Brethren
See Walker, [Rev.] John

One of Them
See Abbott, Jacob

One of Them
See Marsh, Leonard

One of Them
See White, Mrs W. H.

One of Themselves
See Aston, C. Penrhyn

One of themselves
See Ballantyne, Robert Michael

One of Themselves
See Mackarness, John Fielder

One of Themselves
See Mudge, Henry

One of Themselves
See Thackeray, William Makepeace

One Play McAfee
See McAfee, George A.

One Recently Returned from the Enemy's Country
See Pollard, Edward Alfred

[The] One Recognized Leader in Organic Chemistry
See Adams, [Dr.] Roger

One Round Tilden
See Tilden, William Tatem, II

One Speech Lee
See Lee, Joshua Bryan

One That Has Had Experience of Them
See Mather, Cotton

One That Has Perused the Summer Morning's Conversation
See Chauncy, Charles

One That Holds Communion With the Church
See Humfrey, John

One That Once Was a Scholar to Him
See Mather, Cotton

[The] 1980 Kansas Pork Queen
See Schwartz, Cheri

One, Two, Three, Four
See Foe, Daniel

One Unconcerned
See Daddo, William

[The] One Watt Big Shot
See Henie, Thomas

One Well Acquainted With Some of the Travellers
See Gostling, William

[The] One Wheel Champion
See Frisoli, Dennis

One Who, As a Son With a Father, Served With Him in the Gospel
See Mather, Cotton

One Who has a Tear for Others as Well as Himself
See Currie, E.

One Who Has Impersonated Them
See Martin, Helena Faucit

One Who has Never Quitted Him for Fifteen Years
See Doris, Charles

One who has seen the Elephant
See Scribner, B. F.

One Who Has Served
See Drayson, Alfred Wilks

One who has served under Sir Charles Napier?
See Bunbury, Henry Charles

One Who Has Served Under Sir Charles Napier
See Malleson, [Lieut. Colonel] George Bruce

One Who has Served Under the Marquis of Dalhousie
See Allen, Charles

One Who Has Some There
See Seymour, Almira

One Who Has Stood Behind the Counter
See Pae, David

One Who has Whistled at the Plow
See Somerville, Alexander

One Who Heartily Desires the Order, Peace, and Purity of the Churches
See Fitch, Thomas

One Who Is Also an Elder
See Mant, Richard

One Who is But an Attorney
See Butt, George

One Who is Really an Englishman
See Smith, C. W.

One Who Knew Him
See Deane, Charles

One Who Knows
See Foster, Arnold

One Who Knows
See Pickett, Charles Edward

One Who Knows
See Wahab, Charles James

One Who Knows It
See Shute, Hardwick

One Who Knows Them
See Wilson, Thomas L. V.

One Who Loves the Souls of the Lambs
See Marks, Richard

One Who Respects Them
See Bury, James

One Who Values Christianity For Its Own Sake, etc.
See Darby, John Nelson

One Who Was Born in the Colony of Massachusetts Bay
See Prescott, Benjamin

One who was thar
See Scribner, B. F.

One Who Wishes Well to Him in Common With Mankind
See Clarke, [Rev.] John

O'Neal, Blackie
See O'Neal, Charles

O'Neal, Charles 1904?-
American author
* O'Neal, Blackie

Oneal, Elizabeth 1934- [SAT]
American author
* Oneal, Zibby

O'Neal, Ernie [RBE]
American boxer
* O'Neal, Pope

O'Neal, Oran Herbert 1899- [BE]
American baseball player
* O'Neal, Skinny

O'Neal, Pope
See O'Neal, Ernie

O'Neal, Reggie
See O'Neal, Regina

O'Neal, Regina 20th c. [BA]
American author and educator
* O'Neal, Reggie

O'Neal, Ryan 1940?- [HPPN]
American actor
* [The] Sheik of Malibu

O'Neal, Skinny
See O'Neal, Oran Herbert

O'Neal, Zelma
See Schroeder, Zelma

Oneal, Zibby
See Oneal, Elizabeth

O'Neale, Margaret L. [Peggy] 1796-1879 [HPPN]
American author
* Eaton, Peggy

O'Neddy, Philothie
See Donday, Auguste Marie

Oneida
See Dugan, James

[The] O'Neil
See O'Neil, Hugh [Earl of Tyrone]

O'Neil, Barbour
See Morris, Barboura

O'Neil, Buck
See O'Neil, John Jordan

O'Neil, Cackles
See O'Neil, Katherine

O'Neil, Carolan
See FitzGerald, Shafto Justin Adair

O'Neil, Dennis 1939- [WECO]
American cartoonist and editor
* O'Shaugnessey, Sergius

O'Neil, Eric
See Barnum, W[illiam] Paul

O'Neil, Happy
See O'Neil, Peter H., Jr.

O'Neil, Hugh [Earl of Tyrone] 1540-1616 [HPPN]
Irish revolutionist
* [The] O'Neil

O'Neil, John Jordan 1911- [MK]
American baseball player
* O'Neil, Buck

O'Neil, Katherine 1914-1957 [HPPN]
American dancer
* O'Neil, Cackles

O'Neil, Kerry
See McIntyre, John T[homas]

O'Neil, Kitty 20th c. [HPPN]
American comedian
* [The] Laughing Lady

O'Neil, Nance
See Lamson, Gertrude

O'Neil, Nancy
See Smith, Nancy

O'Neil, Peter H., Jr. ?-1912 [HPPN]
American musician
* O'Neil, Happy

O'Neil, Sally
See Noonan, Virginia Louise

O'Neil, Simon
See Simonelli, Giovanni

O'Neil, Wolf
See Halsey, Harlan Page

O'Neill, Agnes 1884-1957 [BI]
American educator
* Aquinas, [Sister] Thomas

O'Neill, Archie
See Henaghan, Jim

O'Neill, Buck
See O'Neill, Frank J.

O'Neill, Buckey
See O'Neill, William Owen

O'Neill, C. M.
See Wilkes-Hunter, Richard

O'Neill, Cabby
See O'Neill, Leo C.

O'Neill, Catherine 1816-1888 [BI]
Nun
* Therese Emmanuel, [Mother]

O'Neill, Charles 1821-1893 [HPPN]
American politician
* [The] Father of the House

O'Neill, [Brother] Columba
See O'Neill, John

O'Neill, Con 1484?-1559? [WBD]
First Earl of Tyrone
* Bacach [The Lame]

O'Neill, Daniel [PA]
Author
* D. O. N.

O'Neill, Dodie
See O'Neill, Dolores

O'Neill, Dolores 1917- [PMJ]
American singer
* O'Neill, Dodie

O'Neill, Egan
See Linington, Elizabeth

O'Neill, [Robert] Emmett 1918- [BE]
American baseball player
* O'Neill, Pinky

O'Neill, Father
See Dellacroce, Aniello

O'Neill, Francis J. 20th c. [ALR]
American baseball team owner
* O'Neill, Steve

O'Neill, Frank J. 1875-1958 [AS, FB]
American football player and coach
* O'Neill, Buck

O'Neill, Hattie
See Russell, Mrs. R. F.

O'Neill, Henrietta Bruce
See Boate, Henrietta

O'Neill, James Beaton 1913- [CEI]
Canadian-born hockey player
* O'Neill, Peggy

O'Neill, James Edward 1858-1915 [AS, DGS, PB]
Canadian-born baseball player
* O'Neill, Tip

O'Neill, James Keith 1920- [BF]
British actor
* Edwards, Jimmy

O'Neill, John 1829-? [PI]
Irish poet
* J. O'N.?
* L.

O'Neill, John 1848-1923 [BI]
American cobbler
* O'Neill, [Brother] Columba

O'Neill, John Robert 1823-1860 [PI]
Irish playwright and musician
* Vamp, Hugo

O'Neill, Lally ?-1908 [HPPN]
American actor
* La Rose, Harry

O'Neill, Leo C. 20th c. [BBH]
American basketball coach
* O'Neill, Cabby

O'Neill, Maire
See Allgood, Maire

O'Neill, [Sister] Mary Agatha 1886-
[CAT]
Canadian-born author
* Gaule, Beatrice

O'Neill, Michael 19th c. [PI]
Irish poet
* O'N.

O'Neill, Michael Joyce 1877-1959 [BE]
Irish-born baseball player
* Joyce, Mike

O'Neill, Mickey
See Dion, Clarence J. H.

O'Neill, Moira
See Skrine, Agnes

O'Neill, Peaches
See O'Neill, Philip Bernard

O'Neill, Peggy
See Eaton, Margaret O'Neill

O'Neill, Peggy
See O'Neill, James Beaton

O'Neill, Philip Bernard 1879-1955 [BE]
American baseball player
* O'Neill, Peaches

O'Neill, Pinky
See O'Neill, [Robert] Emmett

O'Neill, Rose Cecil 1874-1944 [HPPN,
TC]
American illustrator, poet, author
* [The] Kewpie Doll Lady
* Latham, O'Neill

O'Neill, Scott
See Scott, Peg O'Neill

O'Neill, Shane
See O'Neill, William

O'Neill, Steve
See O'Neill, Francis J.

O'Neill, Thomas 1923- [CEI]
Canadian-born hockey player
* O'Neill, Windy

O'Neill, Thomas Philip 1912- [BI]
American politician
* O'Neill, Tip

O'Neill, Tip
See O'Neill, James Edward

O'Neill, Tip
See O'Neill, Thomas Philip

O'Neill, William 1877-? [PI]
Irish poet
* Slieve-Margy

O'Neill, William 1927- [CA]
British-born educator and author
* Og, Liam
* O'Neill, Shane
* O'Remus, Seamus

O'Neill, William Owen 1860-1898
American military officer
* O'Neill, Buckey

O'Neill, Windy
See O'Neill, Thomas

Oneiropolos
See Johnstone, Charles

O'nerva, L.
See Madetoja, Onerva

Onesimus
See Courtier, Peter L.

Onetti, Juan Carlos 1909- [CLC]
Uruguayan author
* [The] Lone Wolf of Uruguayan
Letters

Onfroy de Breville, Jacques 1858-1931
[WEC]
French cartoonist and illustrator
* Job

Onghill
See Creswell, John

O'Niall
See Hughes, Terence McMahon

Onion Head
See Pericles

Onions, C. T.
See Onions, Charles Talbut

Onions, Charles Talbut 1873-1965 [LC]
British editor
* Onions, C. T.

Onions, [George] Oliver 1873-1961 [CC,
LC, TC]
British author
* Oliver, George

Onis, Curly
See Onis, Manuel Dominguez

Onis, Manuel Dominguez 1908- [BE]
American baseball player
* Onis, Curly
* Onis, Ralph

Onis, Ralph
See Onis, Manuel Dominguez

Onkel Adam
See Wetterbergh, Carl Anton

Onkel Danny
See Turell, Dan

Onkel Franz
See Frisch, Frank Francis

Onkel Tom
See Hevesi, Ludwig

Onkelos 1st c. [WBD]
Author
* [The] Proselyte

Onlooker
See Grange, Cyril

Onlooker
See Parsons, Edward

Onlooker
See Russell, George William Erskine

[The] Only
See Richter, Jean Paul Friedrich

[The] Only Aretino
See Accolti, Bernardo

[The] Only Nolan
See Nolan, Edward Sylvester

[The] Only Unicorn of the Muses
See Nash [or Nashe?], Thomas

O'Nolan, Brian
See O'Nuallain, Brian

Onorato, Glauco 20th c. [WF]
Italian actor
* Stark, Richard

Onoto Watanna
See Babcock, Winnifred Eaton

Onslow
See Calhoun, John Caldwell

Onslow, George 1731-1792 [NPS]
Politician and army officer
* Cocking, George [Little]

Onsmonde, Alexandre 1894-1972 [SC]
Belgian actor and singer
* Mondose, Alex

[An] Ontario Judge
See Hagarty, [Sir] John Hawkins

O'Nuallain, Brian 1911-1966 [AW, CAP,
DIL]
Irish author
* Barnabas, Brother
* Doe, John James
* Knowall, George
* Na Gopaleen [or Na gCopaleen],
Myles
* Nolan, Brian
* O'Blather, Count
* O'Brien, Flann
* O'Nolan, Brian

Onward Christian Cagle
See Cagle, Christian K.

Onwhyn, Thomas ?-1886 [NPS, PA]
Draughtsman and engraver
* Palette, Peter
* Weller, Samuel

Onyx
See Ward, Elizabeth Stuart [Phelps]

Onze Jan
See Hofmeyr, Jan Hendrik

Oogam, LeRoi
See Smith, LeRoi Tex

Oom Paul
See Kruger, Stephanus Johannes Paulus

Oom Paul Derringer
See Derringer, Paul

Oom Paul Krueger
See Krueger, Arthur William

Oom the Omnipotent
See Bernard, Pierre A.

Oo'ma [Great Lady]
See Ray, Dixy Lee

[The] Oomph Girl
See Sheridan, Clara Lou

Oor Rab
See Burns, Robert

Oosterbaan, Benjamin Gaylord [Bennie]
1906- [HPPN]
American football coach
* Relaxation, Mr.

Oosterman, Gordon 1927- [CA]
American educator and author
* Eastman, G. Don

O'Pagus, Arry
See Sommer, H. B

O'Pake
See Mallison, William M.

O'Pake, Mr.
See Beckner, Samuel W. E.

Opatoshu, David
See Opatovsky, David

Opatoshu, Joseph
See Opatovsky, Joseph

Opatovsky, David 1918- [TR]
American actor
* Opatoshu, David

Opatovsky, Joseph 1886-1954 [EWL]
Polish-born author
* Opatoshu, Joseph

Opdycke, John Baker 1878-1956 [ALY]
American author
* Opdyke, Oliver

Opdyke, Oliver
See Opdycke, John Baker

Opel, John R. 1926?- [TI 1-3-83]
American business executive
* [The] Brain

Open Issue Ralph
See Nader, Ralph

Open Mouth
See Desa, Giuseppe

Openshaw, G. H. 20th c. [MBF]
British author
* Gale, John
* Shaw, Dick
* Shaw, Justin
* Sterne, Duncan

Openshaw, John
See Connor, Joseph Patrick

[An] Opera Goer
See Mitchell, Donald Grant

[An] Opera Manager
See Maretzek, Max

Opera's Bad Girl
See Kalogeropoulos, Maria Anna Sofia
Cecilia

[The] Operations Man
See Baker, Robert Gene [Bobby]

[An] Operative
See Duffy, [Sir] Charles Gavan

Operti, Albert 1852-1927 [HPPN]
*Italian-American painter, caricaturist,
scenic designer*
* Roccabigliera, Jasper Ludwig

Ophiel
See Peach, Edward C.

Ophuls, Marcel
See Oppenheimer, Marcel

Ophuls, Max
See Oppenheimer, Max

Opie, John 1761-1807 [DEP, FFF, SN]
British painter
* [The] Cornish Wonder

Opimius
See Fitzhugh, William Henry

O'Pindar, Scriblerus Murtough
See Carey, William Paulet

[The] Opinion Forecaster
See Roper, Elmo

Opitz, Martin 1597-1639 [HPPN, RH,
SN, WBD]
German author and poet
* [The] Beau Brummel of Language
* [The] Dryden of Germany
* [The] Father of German Poetry
* [The] Father of Modern German
Poetry
* Opitz von Boberfeld
* [The] Restorer of German Poetry

Opitz von Boberfeld
See Opitz, Martin

[The] Opium Eater
See De Quincey, Thomas

Opp, Francis
See Oppenheimer, Francis J.

Oppenheim, E[dward] Phillips 1866-1946
[CC, EMD, HPPN, WW]
British author
* Partridge, Anthony
* [The] Prince of Storytellers
* [The] World's Most Prolific and
Popular Writer of Thrillers

Oppenheim, Jill 1940- [FC, HT, SW]
American actress
* St. John, Jill

Oppenheim, Joel Lester 1930- [DLE]
American poet
* Aquarius

Oppenheimer, Erika
See Fromm, Erika

Oppenheimer, Francis J. 1881-? [NAA]
American author
* Opp, Francis

Oppenheimer, J[ulius] Robert 1904-1967
[HPPN]
American physicist
* [The] Equivocal Hero of Science
* [The] Father of the A-Bomb
* Oppy [or Oppie?]
* [The] Troubled Pied Piper of Los
Alamos

Oppenheimer, Joel Lester 1930- [HPPN]
American poet
* Aquarian
* Hammer, Jacob

Oppenheimer, Joseph 1698-1738
German clergyman
* Jud Suess

Oppenheimer, Marcel 1927- [OCF]
German-born director
* Ophuls, Marcel

Oppenheimer, Max 1902-1957 [BDF,
FC, FD]
German director
* Ophuls, Max

Oppenheimer, Maximilian
See Mopp, Maximilian

Opper, Adolf 1825-1903 [JL]
Bohemian-born journalist
* De Blowitz, Henri

Opper, F.
See Opper, Frederick Burr

Opper, Frederick Burr 1857-1937
[HPPN]
American cartoonist and illustrator
* Opper, F.

[The] Opponent of Conspicuous Waste
See Veblen, Thorstein Bunde

Oppy [or Oppie?]
See Oppenheimer, J[ulius] Robert

OPS
See Rabago, Andres

Optic, Oliver [joint pseudonym with
Edward L. Stratemeyer]
See Adams, William Taylor

Optic, Oliver [joint pseudonym with
William Taylor Adams]
See Stratemeyer, Edward L.

[A] Optimist
See Kaye, [Sir] John William

Optimus, Doctor
See De Bulhoes, Fernando

**Opzoomer, Adele Sophia Cornelia van
Antal** 1857-1925 [NPS]
Dutch author
* Wallis, A. S. C.

O'Quill, Maurice
See Denslow, Martin Van Buren

O'Quill, Scarlett
See Mossman, Dow

O'Quinn, John 20th c. [EF]
American football player
* O'Quinn, Red

O'Quinn, Red
See O'Quinn, John

O'Quinn, Vithaldas H.
See Santesson, Hans Stefan

Oracle
See Pearce, Ethel Katherine

[The] Oracle of Common Law
See Plowden, Edmund

[The] Oracle of Delft
See Grotius, Hugo

[The] Oracle of Denmark
See Bernstorff, Johann Hartwig Ernst von

[The] Oracle of France
See Bernard of Clairvaux

[The] Oracle of God
See De Grimston, Mary Ann

[The] Oracle of Good-Sense
See Malherbe, Francois de

[The] Oracle of Law
See Coke, [Sir] Edward

[The] Oracle of Nuneaton
See Simpson, Thomas

[The] Oracle of the Church
See Bernard of Clairvaux

[L']Oracolo delle Battaglie
See Falcone, Aniello

Orage, A. R.
See Orage, Alfred Richard

Orage, Alfred Richard 1873-1934   [LC]
British editor, lecturer, author
* Orage, A. R.

Oram, Blanche 1866-?   [NPS]
Author and journalist
* White, Roma

Oram, John
See Thomas, Jack

Oram, Mona K.
See Grenville, Mrs. Arthur

Oran
See Otis, F. N.

O'Randa, Jack
See Stone, Ena Margaret

Orange
See Dekker, Thomas

Orange, Clyde
See Orange, Walter

Orange Juice
See Simpson, Orenthal James

[The] Orange King
See Harris, James Armstrong

Orange Moll
See Meggs, Mary

[The] Orange Phantom
See Easton, Gerry

Orange, Walter 1947-   [RO2]
American musician
* Orange, Clyde

Oraquill
See Bornemann, Mary

[The] Orator
See O'Rourke, James Henry

Orator Bronze
See Henley, John

Orator Jim O'Rourke
See O'Rourke, James Henry

[The] Orator of Free-Dirt
See Julian, George Washington

[The] Orator of Nature
See Henry, Patrick

[The] Orator of Secession
See Yancey, William Lowndes

[The] Orator of the Human Race
See Du Val-de-Grace, Jean [or Johann] Baptiste

Orator of the Revolution
See Henry, Patrick

Orb, Clay
See Conrow, Herbert

Orbes, Marceline 1873-1927   [BEW]
Spanish-born clown
* Marceline

Orbis, Victor
See Powell-Smith, Vincent [Walter Francis]

Orbison, Keck [joint pseudonym with Olive Orbison]
See Keck, Maud

Orbison, Keck [joint pseudonym with Maud Keck]
See Orbison, Olive

Orbison, Olive 20th c.   [WW]
Author
* Orbison, Keck [joint pseudonym with Maud Keck]

Orbison, Roy 20th c.   [CMA]
American singer
* [The] Voice

Orbit
See Hovley, Stephen Eugene

Orcagna
See Di Cione, Andrea

Orchard, Eliza
See Connor, Mrs. E. A.

[The] Orchid
See Marcos, Imelda

Orchid from the Outback
See Sutherland, Joan

[The] Orchid Lady
See Griffith, Corinne

[The] Orchid Lady of the Screen
See Griffith, Corinne

[The] Orchid Man
See Carpentier, Georges

[The] Orchid of the Screen
See Griffith, Corinne

Orczy, Baroness
See Barstow, Emma Magdalena Rosalina Marie Josepha Barbara

Orczy, Emmuska
See Barstow, Emma Magdalena Rosalina Marie Josepha Barbara

Ord, Lewis Redman 1856-1942   [CCL]
Canadian author
* One of the Bunglers

Ord, Robert
See Ostlere, Edith

Ordenana, Antonio Rodriguez 1920-
[BE]
Cuban-born baseball player
* Ordenana, Tony

Ordenana, Tony
See Ordenana, Antonio Rodriguez

[The] Orderly Sergeant
See Murray, William Waldie

[An] Orderly Serjeant
See Waters, E. W.

Ordinatissimus, Doctor
See Bassol, John

Ordonez, Cayetano 1928-   [HPPN]
Spanish bullfighter
* Nino de la Palma

Ordonez, Valeriano 1924-   [IAW]
Spanish author and poet
* Is-Orval

Ordonez y Aguilera, Cayetano 1904-1961
[GS]
Spanish bullfighter
* Nino de La Palma [Boy from La Palma]

Ordunez, E. A. 20th c.   [GW]
Rodeo performer
* Ordunez, Yaqui

Ordunez, Yaqui
See Ordunez, E. A.

Ordway, Roger
See Pauker, John

Oreco
See Rodrigues Martins, Waldemar

O'Reed, Maggie Teresa 1916-   [HPPN]
American comedienne, actress, singer
* [The] Big Mouth
* Raye, Martha

O'Regan, Katherine
See Melville, Kathleen

O'Reggae, [Dr.] Winston
See Lennon, John

[The] Oregon Byron
See Miller, Cincinnatus Heine

O'Reid, John Charles, Esq.
See Conder, Josiah

O'Reilly, [Sister] Amadeus 1864-? [PI]
Irish-born poet
* Romaine, John
* Shandonian

O'Reilly, Edward James 1830-1880 [PI]
Irish-born poet and attorney
* Clio

O'Reilly, Jack 20th c.
American sportscaster
* O'Reilly, Legs

O'Reilly, John 1907?- [BI]
American journalist
* O'Reilly, Tex

O'Reilly, Legs
See O'Reilly, Jack

O'Reilly, Mary M. 1865-? [HPPN]
American Assistant Director of the Mint
* [The] Sweetheart of the Treasury

O'Reilly, [Private] Miles
See Halpine, Charles Graham

O'Reilly, Montagu
See Andrews, Wayne

O'Reilly, Navan
See Franks, Tom

O'Reilly, Patrick Thomas 1876-? [PI]
American poet
* Aenid

O'Reilly, Rory
See O'Flaherty, Charles

O'Reilly, Terry 1952?-
Canadian hockey player
* Taz

O'Reilly, Tex
See O'Reilly, John

O'Reilly, Thomas F. ?-1887 [PI]
Irish poet
* Artane

O'Reilly, Tiger
See O'Reilly, William Joseph

O'Reilly, William Joseph 1905- [OCS]
Australian cricketer
* O'Reilly, Tiger

O'Rell, Max
See Blouet, Paul

Orellana, Francisco de 1500?-1549 [HPPN]
Spanish soldier and explorer
* [The] Discoverer of the Amazon

O'Remus, Seamus
See O'Neill, William

Orenburgsky, Sergey Ivanovich
See Gusev, Sergey Ivanovich

Oreshnik, A. F.
See Nussbaum, Al[bert F.]

[An] Orestes of Exile
See Stael, Anne Louise Germaine de

Orfebre Tapatio
See Ortiz Puga, Jose

Orfeo Italiano
See Crescentini, Girolamo

Orfila, Matthieu Joseph Bonaventure 1787-1853 [HPPN]
French chemist
* [The] Father of Toxicology

Orga, Ates
See D'Arcy-Orga, Ates

Orga, Irfan 1909- [AW]
Turkish-born author
* Riza, Ali

Organ, John 1925- [CA]
British author and illustrator
* Ashley, Graham
* Farrell, Desmond

[The] Organizer of the New Breed
See Thomas, John Peter

[The] Organizer of Victory
See Carnot, Lazare-Nicolas-Marguerite

Orgel, Doris 1929- [CA, SAT]
Austrian-born author
* Adelberg, Doris

Orgen, Jacob 1894-1927 [BLB, HPPN, PHM]
American underworld figure
* [The] Last of the Oldtime Gangsters
* Orgen, Little Augie

Orgen, Little Augie
See Orgen, Jacob

Orgeni, Aglaja
See St. Jorgen, Goerger

Orgill, Douglas 1922- [CA]
British author
* Gilman, J. D. [joint pseudonym with Jack Fishman]

[The] Orginial Bathing Girl
See Steadman, Vera

O'Riain, Liam P.
See Ryan, William Patrick

Oriana
See Anne of Denmark

Oricellarius
See Ruccellai, Benardo

Oriel, Antrim
See Moore, Arthur

Orient
See Kidder, Frederic

[The] Oriental Catullus
See Muslih-ud-Din [or Moslehedin]

[The] Oriental Homer
See Mansur [or Hasan?], Abul Qasim

[The] Oriental Homer
See Muslih-ud-Din [or Moslehedin]

[The] Oriental Populist
See Tanaka, Kakuei

Origen 185-253 [DNNS, FFF, HN, NPS]
Greek theologian
* Adamantius
* [The] Father of Biblical Criticism
* [The] Man of Steel

[The] Original Astronaut
See Glenn, John Herschel

[The] Original Authentic Folk Singer
See Kincaid, Bradley

[The] Original Dinah
See Waters, Ethel

[The] Original Disco Man
See Brown, James

[The] Original Editor
See Wade, John

[The] Original Energy Superbear
See Dines, James

[The] Original Gay 90's Gal
See Thomas, Lillian

[The] Original Genius
See Cook, Will Marion

[The] Original Glamour Girl
See Goodman, Theodosia

[The] Original "It" Girl
See Bisbee, Aileen

[The] Original Nonpareil
See Randall, Jack

[The] Original Radio Girl
See De Leath, Vaughn

[The] Original Raffles
See Leslie, George Leonidas

[The] Original Robinson Crusoe
See Selkirk [or Selcraig], Alexander

[The] Original Singing Cowboy
See Sprague, Carl T.

[The] Original Singing Nut
See Offerman, George, Sr.

[The] Original Tramp Cyclist
See Clark, P. L.

[The] Original White Hope
See Morris, Carl B.

[The] Originator of the Ice Cream Soda
See Green, Robert M.

O'Riley, Warren
See Richardson, Gladwell

Orinda
See Philips, Katherine

Orinifo, Mrs. [FFF]
Entertainer
* Tournier, Millie

Orion
See Hammerton, [Sir] John Alexander

Orion
See Keegan, James

Orion
See Naylor, John

Orion
See Sikes, William Wirt

Orion
See Tullock, W. W.

O'Riordan, Conal O'Connell 1874-1948 [BEW, HPPN, LC, TC]
Irish-born playwright, author, actor
* Connell, F. Norreys

Orizzonte
See Bloemen, Jan Frans van

Orkan, Wladyslaw
See Smreczynski, Franciszek

Orkan, Wladyslaw
See Szmaciarz-Smreczynski, Franciszek

Orlando
See Hall, James

Orlando
See Holland, Edwin Clifford

Orlando
See Wodhull, Michael

Orlando, Ada ?-1908 [HPPN]
American actress
* Marlow, Mary

Orlando, Emanuels 1927- [CW]
Surinamese poet
* Cyrano

Orlando, Pietro
See Scarne, John

Orlando the Fair
See Feilding, Robert

Orlans, Harold
See Orlansky, Harold

Orlansky, Harold 1921- [HPPN]
American educator and author
* Orlans, Harold

Orleanian
See Wharton, Edward Clifton

Orleans, Anne Marie Louise d'
1627-1693 [FFF, RH, SN]
Duchess of Montpensier
* [La] Grande Mademoiselle
* Mademoiselle

Orleans, Gaston Jean Baptiste d'
1608-1660 [SN]
Son of Henry IV of France
* Clerante

Orleans, Henri Eugene Philippe Louis d'
1822-? [HN]
Son of King Louis Philippe of France
* [L']Homme du Lit de Fer

Orleans, Louis Philippe Albert d'
1838-1894 [FFF]
Pretender to crown of France and author
* Langel
* Paris, Comte de

Orleans, Louis Philippe Joseph d'
1747-1793 [DHA, DNNF, HN]
French political leader
* Egalite, Monsieur

Orleans, Louis Philippe Joseph d'
(cont.)
* Egalite, Philippe
* Gamelle

Orleans, Philippe II d' 1674-1723 [NPS, SN]
Brother of King Louis XIV of France
* [The] Boaster of Crimes
* [A] Godless Regent
* Monsieur

Orlev, Uri
See Orlowski, Jerzy Henryk

Orley, John 1899- [IPA]
American poet and critic
* Tate, Allen

Orliac, Mme. J. M. S. [PA]
Author
* Daurignac, J. M. S.

Orlier, Blaise
See Sylvestre, [Joseph Jean] Guy

Orlik, Ivan A. 1898-1953 [SC]
Russian-born actor and dancer
* Orlik, Vanya

Orlik, Vanya
See Orlik, Ivan A.

Orloff, Max
See Crowcroft, Peter

Orlov, Dimitry Stakhiyevich 1883-1946 [WEC]
Russian cartoonist
* Moor, D. S.

Orlowski, Jerzy Henryk 1931- [CA]
Polish-born author
* Orlev, Uri

Orlvov, Zvi 1878-? [EJS]
Russian-born Israeli educator
* Nishri, Zvi

Orman, Felix
See Abraham, Gus

Ormandy, Eugene
See Blau, Jeno

Orme, Benjamin
See Japp, Alexander Hay

Orme, Denise
See Smither, Jessie

Orme, Eve 1894- [AW]
Irish-born author
* Day, Irene

Orme, K. 20th c. [MBF]
British author
* Clifford, Martin [house pseudonym]

Orme, Mary
See Nichols, Mary Sergeant Gove

Orme, Michael
See Greeven, Alice Augusta

Orme, Rowan
See Rowan-Hamilton, Sydney Orme

Orme, Waymon 1940- [BA]
American business executive
* Orme, Wayne

Orme, Wayne
See Orme, Waymon

Ormiston, Margaret
See Curle, M. O.

Ormiston, Roberta
See Fletcher, Adele [Whitely]

Ormond, Frederic
See Dey, Frederic Van Rensselaer

Ormond, Pierce 1467?-1539 [HN]
Lord lieutenant of Ireland
* Red Peter

Ormonde, Duke of
See Butler, James

Ormsbee, David
See Longstreet, [Henry] Stephen [Weiner]

Ormsby, Clara
See Lewis, Alma

Ormsby, Emmett T. 1895?-1962 [BI]
American umpire
* Ormsby, Red

Ormsby, John S. 1869-? [PI]
Irish-born poet
* Stanley

Ormsby, Red
See Ormsby, Emmett T.

Ormsby, Waterman L., Jr. 1834-? [FFF, PA]
American writer
* Lil

[An] Ornament of Italy
See Bentivoglio, Guido

Orndorff, Paul 20th c.
American wrestler
* Wonderful, Mr.

Orne, Philip
See Lowell, Francis Cabot

Ornest, Ota
See Ornstein, Ota

Ornig, Graef
See Ackerman, Forrest J[ames]

Ornis
See Winchester, Clarence

Ornskog, Sonen I.
See Arwidsson, Adolf Iwar

Ornstein, But
See Ornstein, George

Ornstein, George 1917?-1978 [FIR]
Film executive
* Ornstein, But

Ornstein, Honora 1883?-1975 [BI]
American pioneer
* Diamond Tooth Lil

Ornstein, J. L.
See Ornstein, Jacob Leonard

Ornstein, Jacob Leonard 1915- [CA]
American linguist and author
* Ornstein, J. L.
* Ornstein-Galicia, J[acob] L[eonard]

Ornstein, Ota 1912- [JL]
Czech director
* Ornest, Ota

Ornstein, Richard W. 1880-1963 [FC, WEF]
German director
* Oswald, Richard

Ornstein-Galicia, J[acob] L[eonard]
See Ornstein, Jacob Leonard

O'Rolfe, M., the Irish Novelist
See Rolfe, Maro Orlando

Orosmades
See Gray, Thomas

O'Rourke, Blackie
See O'Rourke, Francis James

O'Rourke, Charles C. 1917- [FB]
Canadian-born football player
* O'Rourke, Chuckin' Charley

O'Rourke, Charlie
See O'Rourke, James Patrick

O'Rourke, Chuckin' Charley
See O'Rourke, Charles C.

O'Rourke, Edmund 1813-1879 [DEL, PI, RH]
Irish playwright and actor
* Falconer, Edmund

O'Rourke, Francis James 1891- [BE]
Canadian-born baseball player
* O'Rourke, Blackie

O'Rourke, Frank
See O'Malley, Frank

O'Rourke, James Henry 1852-1919 [BAB, BBH, PB]
American baseball player
* [The] Orator
* O'Rourke, Orator Jim
* Uncle Jeems

O'Rourke, James Patrick 1937- [BE]
American baseball player
* O'Rourke, Charlie

O'Rourke, James Stephen 1889-1955 [BE]
American baseball player
* O'Rourke, Queenie

O'Rourke, John 1861-1882 [EWG]
American gunfighter and gambler
* Johnny Behind-the-Deuce

O'Rourke, John 19th c. [PI]
Irish author
* Evergreen, Anthony

O'Rourke, Joseph Leo, Sr. 1881-1956 [BE]
American baseball player
* O'Rourke, Patsy

O'Rourke, Mary 1901-1964 [HPPN]
American singer
* Peterson, Master Joe

O'Rourke, Orator Jim
See O'Rourke, James Henry

O'Rourke, Patsy
See O'Rourke, Joseph Leo, Sr.

O'Rourke, Queenie
See O'Rourke, James Stephen

O'Rourke, Rory
See Whitty, Michael James

O'Rourke, Ruth Carol 1914- [BEW, FC]
American actress
* Hussey, Ruth

O'Rourke, Sarah ?-1915 [HPPN]
American vaudeville performer
* Madame Wanda

O'Rourke, Timothy Patrick 1864-1938 [BE]
American baseball player
* O'Rourke, Voiceless Tim

O'Rourke, Voiceless Tim
See O'Rourke, Timothy Patrick

Orovida
See Pissarro, Orovida Camille

Orowitz, Eugene Maurice 1936?- [FC, SW]
American actor
* Landon, Michael
* Lane, Michael

Orphan Annie
See D'Aquino, Iva Ikuko [Toguri]

[The] Orphan of the Temple
See Bourbon, Marie Therese Charlotte de

[The] Orphan of the Temple
See Charlotte, Marie Therese

Orpheus in the Gray Shades
See Levine, James

[The] Orpheus of Arabia
See Farabi, Abu Nasr Mohammed al-

[The] Orpheus of Highwaymen
See Gay, John

[The] Orpheus of His Age
See Ariosto, Lodovico

[The] Orpheus of Scotland
See James I

[The] Orpheus of the Eighteenth Century
See Handel, Georg Friedrich

[The] Orpheus of the Green Isle
See O'Carolan, Turloch

Orr, Andrew 1822-? [PI]
Irish poet
* [An] Aghadowey Man
* Comberbach

Orr, Isaac 1793-1844 [FFF, PA]
American clergyman and writer
* Hambden
* Timoleon

Orr, James Lawrence 1822-1873 [SN]
American politician and diplomat
* [That] Prince of Demagogues

Orr, Mary
See Denham, Mary Orr

Orrell, Forrest Gordon 1917- [BE]
American baseball player
* Orrell, Joe

Orrell, Joe
See Orrell, Forrest Gordon

Orrente, Pedro 1570?-1644 [WBD]
Spanish painter
* [The] Spanish Bassano

Orrico, Carmen 1935- [FC, SW]
American actor
* Saxon, John

Orris
See Ingelow, Jean

Orrmont, Arthur 1922- [CA]
American author
* Hunter, Anson

Orsatti, Ernesto Ralph 1903-1968 [BE]
American baseball player
* Orsatti, Ernie

Orsatti, Ernie
See Orsatti, Ernesto Ralph

Orsay, Alfred Guillaume Gabriel d' 1801-1852 [DEP]
French artist and fashion leader
* [The] Last of the Dandies

Orsborne, Dod
See Orsborne, George Black

Orsborne, George Black 1904?-1957 [BI]
Scottish adventurer
* Orsborne, Dod

Orsi, Count
See Orsi, John F.

Orsi, John F. 20th c. [HPPN]
American football player and coach
* Orsi, Count

Orsin, Floro
See Townsend, Alice

Orsini, Giovanni Gaetano 1216?-1280 [NPS, SN, WBD]
Pope
* [The] Accomplished
* [Il] Compirito
* Nicholas III
* Son of a She-Bear

Orsini, Giulio
See Gnoli, Domenico

Orsini, Pietro Francesco 1649-1730 [HN]
Pope
* Benedict XIII
* [The] Pacificator of Europe

Orsini, Virginie
See Baudoin, Virginie [Mortemart-Boisse]

Orsino, Horse
See Orsino, John Joseph

Orsino, John Joseph 1938- [BE]
American baseball player
* Orsino, Horse

Orszagh, Pavol 1849-1921 [CD]
Slovak poet
* Hviezdoslav

Ort, Ana
See Andrews, Arthur [Douglas, Jr.]

Ort, Ivan
See Dodge, Ossian E.

Orta, Pedro 20th c. [SMG]
Cuban-born baseball player
* [The] Babe Ruth of Cuba

Ortea, Francisco Carlos 1845-1899
[CW]
Dominican author
* Franck, Dr.

Ortea, Virginia Elena 1866-1903 [CW]
Dominican-born author and playwright
* Kennedy, Elena

Ortega, Anthony Robert [Tony] 1928-
[HPPN]
American jazz musician
* Batman

Ortega, Filomeno Coronado 1939- [BE]
American baseball player
* Ortega, Kemo
* Ortega, Phil

Ortega, Frank Garcia 1889?-1967 [BI]
American columnist
* Hermida, Jorge

Ortega, Gaspar
See Benitez, Gaspar

Ortega, Kemo
See Ortega, Filomeno Coronado

Ortega, Phil
See Ortega, Filomeno Coronado

Ortega, Santiago 1917- [GS]
Spanish bullfighter
* Mejorcito [Best Little One]

Ortega y Ramirez, Antonio 1857-1910
[GS]
Spanish bullfighter
* [El] Marinero [The Sailor]

Orth, Albert Lewis 1872-1948 [BE]
American baseball player
* [The] Curveless Wonder

Orth, Bennington
See Hoar, Roger Sherman

Orth, Johann
See Salvator, John Nepomuk

Orth, Richard 1931- [CA, WD]
American author
* Anderson, Clifford [joint pseudonym with Robert Anderson and Clifford Irving]
* Carver, John
* Cummings, Richard
* Gardner, Richard [or Dic]

Orth, Richard
See Gardner, Richard [Dic]

Orthodox
See Foe, Daniel

[An] Orthodox Beast
See Oates, Titus

[An] Orthodox Clergyman of Massachusetts
See Norton, [Rev.] Jacob

[An] Orthodox Minister of the Gospel
See Whiton, James Morris

Orthodox, Moses
See Boyle, John [Earl of Cork and Orrery]

Ortin, Chato
See Ortin, Leopoldo

Ortin, Leopoldo 1893-1953 [SC]
Mexican actor
* Ortin, Chato

Ortis, Jacopo
See Foscolo, Niccolo

Ortiz, Ana Alicia 1957?-
Mexican-born actress
* Alicia, Ana

Ortiz, Angel 20th c. [RBE]
American boxer
* Ortiz, Ruby

Ortiz, Baby
See Ortiz, Olivrio Nunez

Ortiz, Elisabeth Lambert 1928- [CA]
British author
* Lambert, Elisabeth

Ortiz, J. M. 20th c. [GS]
Spanish bullfighter
* Gallito de Zafra [Little Rooster from Zafra]

Ortiz, Olivrio Nunez 1919- [BE]
Cuban-born baseball player
* Ortiz, Baby

Ortiz, Ruby
See Ortiz, Angel

Ortiz de Dominguez, Josefa 1768?-1829
[HPPN]
Mexican heroine and rebel
* [La] Corregidora

Ortiz De Montellano
See Ortiz De Montellano, Bernardo

Ortiz De Montellano, Bernardo 1899-
[NAA]
Mexican author
* Ortiz De Montellano

Ortiz Puga, Jose 1902- [GS]
Mexican bullfighter
* Orfebre Tapatio

Ortman, E[lmore] Jan 1884- [CAP]
American educator and author
* Ortman, Elmer John

Ortman, Elmer John
See Ortman, E[lmore] Jan

Ortmanns, Pauline Ronacher 1912-
[WEF]
Austrian actress
* Romance, Viviane

Ortner-Zimmerman, Toni 1941- [CA]
American poet
* Zimmerman, Toni

Orton, Arthur 1834-1898 [DI, HPPN,
WBD]
British imposter
* Castro, Thomas
* [The] Tichborne Claimant
* Tichborne, [Sir] Roger Charles

Orton, Harlow S. 1817-1895 [HPPN]
American orator
* [The] Hossier Orator

Orton, James 1826-? [HFN, PA]
Author
* Alastor

Orton, Joe
See Orton, John Kingsley

Orton, John Kingsley 1933-1967 [LC]
British playwright
* Orton, Joe

Orton, Joseph
See Strang, Jesse

Orton, Thora Margaret 20th c. [AW]
British author
* Colson

Ortuno Duplaix, Emilio 1933- [GS]
Spanish bullfighter
* Jumillano

Ortyx
See Eaton, David H.

Orvis, Kenneth
See Lemieux, Kenneth

Orwell
See Smith, Walter Chalmers

Orwell, George
See Blair, Eric Arthur

Ory, Edward 1886-1973 [ASC, DAM,
EJ]
American jazz musician
* Ory, Kid

Ory, Kid
See Ory, Edward

Oryah, Yehudith
See Schochet, J. Immanuel

O'Ryan, Julia M. 1823-1887 [PI]
Irish poet
* J. M. R.?

Os Porci
See Sergius I

Osadchey, Edward P. 20th c. [PHM]
American underworld figure
* Spitz, Eddie

Osagiede, Sunday 20th c. [SI 11-28-83]
Nigerian basketball player and coach
* Basket, Sunny

Osagyefo [Redeemer]
See Nkrumah, Kwame

Osander
See Allen, Benjamin

Osaragi, Jiro
See Nojiri, Kiyohiko

Osawa, Lola
See Morasawa, Chiyo

Osborn, Barbara M.
See Henkel, Barbara Osborn

Osborn, Duke
See Osborn, Robert

Osborn, Fred
See Osborn, Wilfred P.

Osborn, George, Esq.
See Wynne, John Huddleston

Osborn, Laughton 1809-1878 [HFN, HPPN]
American poet and playwright
* Alethitheras
* [A] Poet
* White, Charles Erskine, D.D.

Osborn, Robert 20th c. [EF]
American football player
* Osborn, Duke

Osborn, Wilfred P. 1883-1954 [BE]
American baseball player
* Osborn, Fred

Osborne, Adrienne
See Eisbein, Adrienne

Osborne, Albert Roy 1924- [CRI]
American political organizer
* Hassan, Jeru-Ahmed

Osborne, Alma 20th c. [SC]
Actress
* Delmar, Ethel

Osborne, Bobo
See Osborne, Lawrence Sidney

Osborne, Bud
See Osborne, Lennie

Osborne, Charles Humfrey Caulfeild 1891- [CA]
British educator and author
* Humfrey, C.

Osborne, Clancy
See Osborne, Clarence

Osborne, Clarence 20th c. [EF]
American football player
* Osborne, Clancy

Osborne, D. H.
See Osborne, Denis Henry

Osborne, David
See Silverberg, Robert

Osborne, Denis Henry 1919- [ART]
British painter
* Osborne, D. H.

Osborne, Dorothy [Gladys] Yeo 1917- [AW, CA, HPPN, WD]
British author
* Armour, Gladys
* Arthur, Gladys

Osborne, Edward
See Manning, Anne

Osborne, Ernest Preston 1893-1969 [BE]
American baseball player
* Osborne, Tiny

Osborne, George
See Silverberg, Robert

Osborne, George O. 1845-1926 [HPPN]
American prison warden
* [The] Father of Prison Reform in the United States

Osborne, James Henry 1949- [SMG]
American football player
* Osborne, Jaws

Osborne, Jaws
See Osborne, James Henry

Osborne, Jefferson
See Schroeder, J. W.

Osborne, Jimmie 1923-1957 [CM]
American country-western performer
* [The] Kentucky Folk Singer

Osborne, John D. [FFF]
American journalist
* Gamma
* Leoni, Leone

Osborne, Lawrence Sidney 1935- [BE]
American baseball player
* Osborne, Bobo

Osborne, Lennie 1881?-1964 [BEW, F1, F2]
American actor
* Osborne, Bud
* Osborne, Miles

Osborne, Mark
See Bayfield, William John

Osborne, Mark
See Bobin, John William [Jack]

Osborne, Michael 20th c. [RO2]
British musician
* Osborne, Oz

Osborne, Miles
See Osborne, Lennie

Osborne, Ossie
See Osborne, Wayne Harold

Osborne, Oz
See Osborne, Michael

Osborne, Sydney Godolphin 1808-1889 [DEL, PA, RH]
British author and clergyman
* S. G. O.

Osborne, Tiny
See Osborne, Ernest Preston

Osborne, Wayne Harold 1912- [BE]
American baseball player
* Osborne, Ossie

Osborne, Will
See Oliphant, William

Osbourne, John 1948- [RO2]
British singer
* Osbourne, Ozzie

Osbourne, Ozzie
See Osbourne, John

Oscar
See Griffin, Gerald

Oscar
See Sullivan, Rollin

Oscar [or Oskar] I
See Bernadotte, Joseph Francois

Oscar Fredrik
See Oscar II

Oscar, Henry
See Wale, Henry

Oscar of the Waldorf
See Tschirky, Oscar

Oscar II 1829-1907 [HPPN]
King of Sweden and Norway
* Oscar Fredrik

Oscard, Fernanda 1921- [BEW]
American talent representative
* Oscard, Fifi

Oscard, Fifi
See Oscard, Fernanda

Osceola
See Blixen, Karen [Christentze Dinesen]

Oscotean
See Kent, [William] Charles [Mark]

Oscotian
See Lawlor, Denis Shine

Oscotiensis
See Lawlor, Denis Shine

Osenburg, Richard 20th c. [SFP]
Author
* Lauler, Michael

Osey, Herr N.
See Weiss, Ehrich

Osgood, Charles 20th c. [WP 12-17-84]
American news correspondent
* Forest, Chuck

Osgood, Charles
See Wood, Charles Osgood, III

Osgood, Frances Sargent Locke
1811-1850   [FFF, HPPN]
American poet
* F. S. O.
* Florence

Osgood, Irene
See   Harvey, Irene

Osgood, Kate Putman   [PA]
Author
* Putman, Kate

Osgood, Samuel 1812-1880   [HPPN]
American clergyman
* O.
* S. O.

Osgood, Win
See   Osgood, Winchester D.

Osgood, Winchester D. 1870-?   [FB]
American football player
* Osgood, Win

O'Shaugnessey, Sergius
See   O'Neil, Dennis

O'Shea, Blackjack
See   Rellaford, Jack

O'Shea, Frank Joseph 1920-   [BE]
American baseball player
* [The] Naugatuck Nugget
* Shea, Spec

O'Shea, Jack
See   Rellaford, Jack

O'Shea, John 19th c.   [PI]
Irish poet
* Mount Atlas

O'Shea, Katherine [Kitty] 1845-1921
[HPPN]
*Wife of Irish nationalist leader, Charles
Stewart Parnell*
* [The] Uncrowned Queen of England

O'Shea, Kittie
See   Scanlan, Kate

O'Shea, Patrick J. 20th c.   [WWL]
Irish author and playwright
* O Seaghdha, Padraig

O'Shea, Sean
See   Tralins, S[andor] Robert [Bob]

O'Shea, Tessie 1914-   [BMH]
Welsh-born comedienne
* Two Ton Tessie

O'Sheel, Shaemas
See   Shields, James

Osiander, Andreas
See   Hosemann, Andreas

O'Siochfhradha, P. 20th c.
Irish author, scholar, politician
* Seabhac, An

Oski
See   Conti, Oscar

Osman Nuri Pasha 1837?-1900   [WBD]
Turkish army officer
* Ghazi, al- [The Conqueror]

Osman Pasha
See   Ripperda, Jan Willem

Osman, Thomas Embly 1826-?   [PA]
American author
* Ayers, Alfred

Osman I [or Othman] 1259-1326
[HPPN, RH, SN, WBD]
Founder of the Turkish empire
* [The] Conqueror
* Ghazi, al-
* [The] Victorious

Osmond, Andrew Philip Kingsford 1938-
[CA, WWS]
British author
* Reid, Philip [joint pseudonym with
   Richard Ingrams]

Osmun, Thomas Embly 1834-1902
[FFF]
American author and critic
* Ayres, Alfred

Osnovyanenko
See   Kvitka, Grigori Petrovich

Osofer, Phil
See   Maine, Harry Carlton

Osorgin, Mikhail Andreyevich
See   Ilyin, Mikhail Andreyevich

Osorio, Jeronymo 1506-1580   [NPS]
Portuguese historian and author
* [The] Cicero of Portugal

Osorio, Manuel Luiz 1808-1879   [NPS]
Brazilian army officer
* [The] Fabulous

Osram
See   Austin, A. Everett, Jr.

Ossenbrink, Luther W. 1915-   [CWG,
ECM]
American country-western performer
* [The] Arkansas Woodchopper
* Arkie

Ossian 3rd c.   [FFF, NPS, RH, SN]
Gaelic bard and warrior
* [The] Celtic Homer
* [The] Gaelic Homer
* [The] Glory of Scotland
* [The] Homer of the Celts
* [The] Northern Dante
* [The] Poet of the Vague

Ossian
See   Macpherson, James

Ossian
See   McAleese, Daniel

Ossian-Nilsson, Karl Gustav 1875-?
[WBD]
Swedish poet and author
* Ossiannilsson, Karl Gustav

Ossiannilsson, Karl Gustav
See   Ossian-Nilsson, Karl Gustav

Ossinger, June Eileen 20th c.   [CCL]
Canadian author
* Spencer, June Lydiard

Ossit
See   Deslandes, [Baroness] Madeleine
Annette Edme Angelique

Ossman, Sylvester Louis 20th c.   [PMJ]
Musician
* Ossman, Vess

Ossman, Vess
See   Ossman, Sylvester Louis

Ossola
See   Foster, Clement le Neve

Ossoli, Marchioness
See   Fuller, Margaret Sarah

Ossorio, Carlos 20th c.   [GS]
Venezuelan bullfighter
* Rayito [Little Beam]

[The] Ostade of Literary History
See   Wood, Anthony

Osteen, Champ
See   Osteen, James Champlin

Osteen, Claude Wilson 1939-   [PB, SMG]
American baseball player
* Osteen, Gomer

Osteen, Gomer
See   Osteen, Claude Wilson

Osteen, James Champlin 1877-1962
[BE]
American baseball player
* Osteen, Champ

Osten, M.   [PA]
Author
* Eyler, Emile

Osterberg, James Jewell [Jim] 1947-
[CMA, DAM]
American musician
* Pop, Iggy
* Stooge, Iggy

Ostergaard, Geoffrey Nielsen 1926-
[CA]
British political scientist and author
* Gerard, Gaston

Ostergard, Red
See   Ostergard, Robert Lund

Ostergard, Robert Lund 1898-   [BE]
American baseball player
* Ostergard, Red

Osterman, Edward ?-1920   [BLB, DI,
HPPN]
American underworld figure
* Eastman, Edward
* Eastman, Monk
* Osterman, Monk

Osterman, Jack
See   Rosenthal, Jack

Osterman, Monk
See   Osterman, Edward

Osterman, Paula Marie 1908-   [F2, FC]
American actress
* Torres, Raquel

Ostermann, Uri 1923- [CA]
German-born Israeli author and editor
* Avnery, Uri

Ostermayr, Paul 1909- [FDG]
German director
* May, Paul

Ostermueller, Frederick Raymond
1907-1957 [AS, BE]
American baseball player
* Ostermueller, Fritz

Ostermueller, Fritz
See Ostermueller, Frederick Raymond

Ostertag, Barna
See Ostertag, Bernard

Ostertag, Bernard 1902- [BEW]
American artists representative and actor
* Ostertag, Barna

Osterwald, Bibi
See Osterwald, Margaret Virginia

Osterwald, Margaret Virginia 20th c.
[BEW]
American actress
* Osterwald, Bibi

Ostioncito [Little Oyster]
See Morales y Mula, Jose

Ostlere, Edith 20th c. [THR]
Playwright and actress
* Ord, Robert

Ostlere, Gordon 1921- [DLE]
British author
* Gordon, Richard

Ostlund, Island
See Ostlund, Petur David

Ostlund, Petur David 1943- [EJ7]
American-born jazz musician
* Ostlund, Island

Ostrander, Isabel [Egenton] 1883?-1924
[CC, HPPN, WW]
American author
* Chipperfield, Robert Fox
* Chipperfield, Robert Orr
* Fox, David
* Grant, Douglas

Ostrander, Mrs. Clarence [FFF]
Entertainer
* Wentworth, Mae

Ostransky, Big Leroy
See Ostransky, Leroy

Ostransky, Leroy 1918-
American composer and educator
* Ostransky, Big Leroy

Ostrong [or Ostrog], Mikhail
See Pedachenko, Alexander

Ostrowski, Joseph Paul 1916- [BE]
American baseball player
* Ostrowski, Professor

Ostrowski, Professor
See Ostrowski, Joseph Paul

Ostrowsky
See Holmquist, Anders

Ostrus, Merrill 1919- [ASC]
American composer
* Staton, Merrill

Osty, Lucien Pierre Jean 1920-
French author
* Larteguy, Jean

O'Suilleabhain, Sean 1903- [CA]
Irish archivist and author
* O'Sullivan, Sean

O'Sullivan, Daniel ?-1919 [HPPN]
American actor
* Sanford, Charles

O'Sullivan, Denis Barrington
See Beresford, William

O'Sullivan, Dennis 1818-1907 [HPPN]
American soldier
* [The] Penny Plug

**O'Sullivan, Dennis Patrick Terence
Joseph** 1906-1971 [EJ, PMJ, WWJ]
American jazz musician
* Sullivan, Joe

O'Sullivan, Eugene 1892-1971 [FC]
British entertainer
* Gerrard, Gene

O'Sullivan, Farrar [HFN]
Author
* [A] Munster Farmer

O'Sullivan, Gilbert
See O'Sullivan, Raymond Edward

O'Sullivan, Michael John 1794-1845
[PI]
Irish poet and playwright
* M. J. S.
* Paddy from Cork
* Sullivan, M. J.

O'Sullivan, Paul 1917- [BEW]
*American producer, theatre manager,
press representative*
* Vroom, Paul

O'Sullivan, Raymond Edward 1946-
[RO2]
Irish-born singer
* O'Sullivan, Gilbert

O'Sullivan, Sean
See O'Suilleabhain, Sean

O'Sullivan, Seumas
See Starkey, James Sullivan

O'Sullivan, Timothy 1840?-1882 [HPPN]
American photographer
* America's Forgotten Photographer

O'Sullivan, Timothy
See Sullivan, Timothy Daniel

Osusky, Stefan 1889-1973 [CA]
Czech diplomat and author
* Argus

Osvaldo
See Navarro, Osvaldo

Oswald, Camera Eye
See Oswald, Henry

Oswald, E.
See Schulze-Smidt, Bernhardine

Oswald, Henry 20th c. [HPPN]
American police detective
* Oswald, Camera Eye

Oswald, Lee Harvey 1939-1963 [BLB,
HPPN]
*American who assassinated President
John F. Kennedy*
* Lee, O. H.
* [The] Man Who Killed Kennedy
* [The] Psychopath
* Rabbit, Ozzie

Oswald, Marguerite Claverie 1915?-
[HPPN]
*Mother of American presidential assassin,
Lee Harvey Oswald*
* [The] Accused Mother

Oswald, Maude
See Hawley, Mrs. D. R.

Oswald, Richard
See Ornstein, Richard W.

Oswalda, Ossi
See Staglich, Oswalda

Oswalt, Sabine
See MacCormack, Sabine G[abriele]

O'Taffrail, Patrick
See O'Connell, Maurice

Otcasek, Richard 20th c. [CMA]
American musician
* Ocasek, Ric

Otero, Reggie
See Otero, Regino Joseph Gomez

Otero, Regino Joseph Gomez 1915-
[BE]
Cuban-born baseball player
* Otero, Reggie

Otey, James Harvey 1800-1863 [HPPN]
American clergyman
* [The] Good Bishop

[The] Other
See Harvey, Edmund George

[The] Other Eye of Florence
See Cavalcanti, Guido

[The] Other Gentleman of Lincoln's Inn
See Edwards, Thomas

[The] Other Helmut
See Kohl, Helmut

[The] Other Miller
See Miller, Allen L., III

[The] Other One
See Bonaparte, Napoleon

Othere
See Windsor-Garnett, John Raynham

Otho
See Holland, Denis

Otis, Bass 1784-1861 [HPPN]
American painter and lithographer
* [The] Father of American Lithography

Otis, Belle
See Woods, C. H.

Otis, Bill
See Otis, Paul Franklin

Otis, Cannonball
See Otis, Harry George

Otis, Elisha Graves 1811-1861 [HPPN]
American inventor
* [The] Father of the Safety Elevator

Otis, Eliza Henderson Bordman
1796-1873 [PA]
American author
* One of the Barclays

Otis, F. N. [FFF]
American writer
* Oran

Otis, George
See Mellen, Ida M[ay]

Otis, Harrison Gray 1765-1848 [HPPN]
American statesman and attorney
* [An] Aged and Retired Citizen of
  Boston
* Antiquary
* [The] Urbane Federalist

Otis, [General] Harrison Gray
1837-1917 [HPPN]
*American army officer and newspaper
publisher*
* [The] Generalissimo of the Open Shop
  Forces in Los Angeles

Otis, Harry George 1886- [BE]
American baseball player
* Otis, Cannonball

Otis, James
See Kaler, James Otis

Otis, Johnny, Jr. 1953- [EJ7]
American jazz musician
* Otis, Shuggie

Otis, Paul Franklin 1889- [BE]
American baseball player
* Otis, Bill

Otis, Shuggie
See Otis, Johnny, Jr.

Otley, Barbara Kathleen 1918- [ART]
British painter
* Fiennes-Foster

Otochan [Daddy]
See Ohira, Masayoshi

O'Toole, [Father]
See Synnott, Ed. Fitzgerald

O'Toole, Bryan, Esq., of Gray's Inn
See Maginn, William

O'Toole, Kate
See Montague, Bruce Alexander

O'Toole, Laurence ?-1180 [HN]
Archbishop of Dublin
* [The] Father of His Country

O'Toole, Peter
See O'Toole, Seamus

O'Toole, Phelim
See Commins, Andrew

O'Toole, Rex
See Tralins, S[andor] Robert [Bob]

O'Toole, Seamus 1933- [CR]
Irish-born actor
* O'Toole, Peter

O'Toole, Terence
See Otway, Caesar

Otreb, Rudolf
See Fludd, Robert

Otrepieff, Gregory ?-1606? [HN]
Russian monk
* [The] Pretender
* [The] Warbeck of the North

O'Trigger, [Sir] Lucius
See Horne, Richard Henry

Otsuka, George
See Otsuka, Keiji

Otsuka, Keiji 1938- [EJ7]
Japanese jazz musician
* Otsuka, George

Ott, Maggie Glenn
See Ott, Virginia

Ott, Mel[vin Thomas] 1909-1958 [BE,
BTB]
American baseball player and manager
* Master Melvin

Ott, Peter
See Von Hildebrand, Dietrich

Ott, Virginia 1917- [CA]
American author
* Ott, Maggie Glenn

Ottaviano, Thomas 1936- [BEW]
American producer and director
* Cimber, Matt

Ottenheimer, Florette Regina 1924-
[BEW]
American actress
* Hayes, Maggie

Otter
See Alfred, H. J.

Ottesen, Thea Tauber 1913- [CA]
Hungarian-born educator and author
* Bank-Jensen, Thea

Ottman, Abigail Kane 1885-1966
[HPPN]
American actress
* Kane, Gail

Otto [SN]
Earl of Ascania and Ballenstedt
* [The] Rich

Otto [or Otho] ?-1339 [SN]
Duke of Austria
* [The] Jovial

Otto 1116-1190 [SN]
Margrave of Meissen
* [The] Rich

Otto 1204-1252 [WBD]
Margrave of Brandenburg
* [The] Child

Otto, August J. 1943- [FB]
American football player
* Otto, Gus

Otto, Franz
See Spamer, Johann Gottlieb Christian
Franz Otto

Otto Graham's Bodyguard
See Motley, Marion

Otto, Gus
See Otto, August J.

Otto of Bamberg 1060?-1139 [HPPN,
WBD]
Saint
* [The] Apostle of Pomerania
* [The] Father of the Monks

Otto the Terrible
See Preminger, Otto

Otto, Young
See Susskind, Arthur

Otto I [or Otho] 912-973 [DNNS, FFF,
SN]
*King of Germany and Holy Roman
emperor*
* [The] Great
* [The] Lion

Otto II ?-1253 [WBD]
Duke of Bavaria
* [The] Illustrious

Otto II [or Otho] 955-983 [FFF, HN,
SN]
Holy Roman emperor
* [The] Bloody
* [The] Pale Death of the Saracens
* [The] Red
* Rufus

Otto III [or Otho] 980-1002 [DEP,
DNNS, SN]
Holy Roman emperor
* [The] Wonder of the World

Otto IV [or Otho] 1175?-1218 [FFF,
RH, SN]
Holy Roman emperor
* [The] Proud

Ottoboni, Pietro 1610-1691 [CAL]
Pope
* Alexander VIII

Ottokar II 1230?-1278 [WBD]
King of Bohemia
* [The] Great

Ottolengui, Helen
See Monserrat, Mrs. George

Otway, Caesar 1780-1842 [HPPN]
Irish author
* O'Toole, Terence

Otway, Thomas 1651-1685 [SN]
British playwright
* Tom the Second

O'Tyne, Nicholas
See Foster, Leroy A.

Oubo, Irac
See Lohier, Michel

[De] Oude Heer Smits [Old Mr. Smits]
See Lindo, Mark Prager

Oudeis
See Darby, Christopher Lovett

Ouden, Willeminjte den 1918-
Dutch swimmer
* Ouden, Willy den

Ouden, Willy den
See Ouden, Willeminjte den

Oudenarde, Dominie Nicholas Aegidius
See Paulding, James Kirke

Oudin, Mrs. Eugene   [FFF]
* Parker, Louise

Oudraadt, Jean 1540-1606   [PA]
Author
* Gerobulus

Ouellette, Adeland 1911-   [CEI]
Canadian-born hockey player
* Ouellette, Eddie

Ouellette, Eddie
See Ouellette, Adeland

Oufkir, Mohammed 1918-1972   [HPPN]
Moroccan army officer
* [The] Almost Perfect Regicide

Ouick, Florence 19th c.   [DI]
American bandit
* [The] Belle of the Daltons'
* Bryant, Mrs.
* King, Tom
* Moore, Eugenia
* Mundy, Mrs.

Ouida
See Rame, Marie Louise

Oulahan, Richard 1825?-1895   [PI]
Irish poet
* [A] Stranger

Ouno
See Ashworth, T. M.

Ounskowsky, Mischa 1905-1967   [F2, FC]
Russian-born actor
* Auer, Mischa

Our American Cruikshank
See Johnston, David Claypole

Our Andy
See Johnson, Andrew

Our Battle Laureate
See Brownell, Henry Howard

Our Best Recruiting Sergeant
See Nast, Thomas

Our Bitter Patriot
See Dreiser, Theodore

Our Bob
See Reynolds, Robert Rice

Our Bob Taylor
See Taylor, Robert Love

Our Bold Briton
See Blackmore, [Sir] Richard

Our Brave Defender
See Harrison, William Henry

Our Carter
See Harrison, Carter H.

Our Champion for Homer
See Boileau-Despreaux, Nicolas

Our Chet
See Arthur, Chester Alan

Our Domestic Raphael
See Stothard, Thomas

Our English Corot
See Peppercorn, Arthur Douglas

Our English Homer
See Chaucer, Geoffrey

Our English Homer
See Warner, William

Our English Marcellus
See Henry

Our English Rabelais
See Nash [or Nashe?], Thomas

Our English Rochefoucault
See Stanhope, Philip Dormer

Our English Virgil
See Cowley, Abraham

Our Female Phidias
See Damer, Anne Seymour

Our Fritz
See Frederick William

Our Goldfish
See Gross, Michael

Our Gracie
See Stansfield, Grace

Our Gracie of the North
See Stansfield, Grace

Our Grover
See Cleveland, [Stephen] Grover

Our Hebrew Friend
See Rose, Julian

Our Jimmy
See Rolph, James, Jr. [Jimmy]

Our Lady of Mercy
See Tallien, Jeanne Marie Ignace Theresa

Our Lady of O
See Mary

Our Letter'd Polypheme
See Johnson, Samuel

Our Literary Whale
See Johnson, Samuel

Our Little David
See More, Hannah

Our Malmesbury Philosopher
See Hobbes, Thomas

Our Man at the UN
See Moynihan, [Daniel] Patrick

Our Marie
See Wood, Matilda Alice Victoria

Our Mary
See Anderson, Mary Antoinette

Our Mary
See Ewen, Mary Cecilia

Our Mary Ann
See Lee, Mary Ann

Our Member for Paris
See Labouchere, Henry

Our Mercurie
See Massinger, Philip

Our Mock Ovid
See Coypeau, Charles [Sieur d'Assouci]

Our Nation's First Educator
See Mann, Horace

Our Northern Homer
See Scott, [Sir] Walter

Our only General
See Wolseley, Garnet Joseph [First Viscount Wolseley]

Our Own Correspondent
See Noyes, James Oscar

Our Own Evarts
See Evarts, William Maxwell

Our Patrick Henry
See Kolb, Reuben Francis

Our Pindar
See Cowley, Abraham

Our Randy
See Churchill, Randolph Henry Spencer

Our Rarest Poet
See Sidney, [Sir] Philip

Our Scottish Bodoni
See Ballantyne, John

Our Second Ciceronian
See Southwell, Robert

Our Setting Sun
See Charles II

Our Spanish Cato
See Pratt, [Sir] Charles [First Earl Camden]

Our Special Correspondent
See Atkinson, George Francklin

Our Sturdy Teuton
See Motteux, Pierre Antoine

Our Talatamtana
See Harvey, Gabriel

Our Talisman
See Lippard, George

Our Taptharthrath
See Harvey, Gabriel

Our Teddy
See Roosevelt, Theodore [Teddy]

Our Tender
See Hamlen, Georgia

Our Tityrus
See Chaucer, Geoffrey

Our Will
See Shakespeare, William

Our Young Ascantus
See Shadwell, Thomas

Ouroussow, Eugenie 1908-1975 [CA]
Russian-born American educator,
administrator, author
* Lehovich, Eugenie Ouroussow

Oursler, [Charles] Fulton 1893-1952
[CC, EMD, TC1]
American playwright, journalist, author
* Abbot, Anthony
* Armstrong, April
* Frikell, Samri

Oursler, Grace Perkins 1900- [NAA]
American author
* Macy, Dora
* Perkins, Grace

Oursler, Will[iam Charles] 1913- [CA]
American author
* Gallager, Gale
* Marine, Nick

Oury, Gerard
See Tannenbaum, Max-Gerard Houry

Oury, Grant
See Oury, Granville Henderson

Oury, Granville Henderson 1825-1891
American politician
* Oury, Grant

Ousamequin [or Wousamequin] ?-1661
[HPPN]
Chief of the Wampanoaga Indians
* Massasoit

Ouseley, Gideon Jasper Richard
1835-1906 [WGT]
Author
* Theosopho

Ouseley, [Sir] William Gore 1797-1866
[HPPN]
British diplomat
* [An] Englishman

Ousley, Curtis 1935-1971 [EJ7, RM,
RO1]
American musician
* Curtis, King

[The] Outcast
See Northrup, C. B.

[The] Outdoor Girl of the Films
See McSweeney, Virginia

Outen, Chick
See Outen, William Austin

Outen, William Austin 1905-1961 [BE]
American baseball player
* Outen, Chick

Outerbridge, Mary Ewing 20th c.
[BBH, SA]
American tennis player
* [The] Mother of American Tennis

Outi
See Honkanen, Hilja Loviisa Valkeapaa

Outis, U. Donough
See White, Richard Grant

Outland, John H. 1871-1947 [FB]
American football player
* [The] Father of Kansas Relays

[The] Outlaw
See Edward

[The] Outlaw
See Jennings, Waylon

[The] Outlaw Queen
See Starr, [Myra] Belle [Shirley]

Outrageous, Captain
See Turner, Robert Edward, III

Outram, [Sir] James 1803?-1861 [DEP,
DNNS, HN]
British army officer
* [The] Bayard of India
* [The] Bayard of the East
* [The] Bayard of the Indian Army

[The] Outside Man
See Hides, Jack Gordon

Outside, Mr.
See Caroline, James Calvin

Outside, Mr.
See Davis, Glenn W.

[The] Outspoken Prime Minister
See Thatcher, Margaret Hilda [Roberts]

[The] Outstanding American Furniture
Maker of the 18th Century
See Fife, Duncan

[The] Outstanding Librarian of This
Century
See Clapp, Verner Warren

Ouvard, Jacques
See Guichardan, Roger Jean-Baptiste

[L']Ouvreuse du Cirque
See Gauthier-Villars, Henri

Ouyrard, Gabriel Julien 1770-1846 [SN]
French banker and merchant
* [The] Napoleon of Finance

Ovary, Geza
See Paskandi, Geza

Oved, Mosheh
See Good, Morris Edward

Oveissi, Gholam Ali 1919?-1984
Iranian military leader
* [The] Butcher of Teheran

Over, Yoi
See Fox, Charles John Frederick

Overacker, Le Roy 1931- [FC]
American actor
* Baby Le Roy

Overall, Jeff
See Overall, Orval

Overall, Orval 1881-1947 [BN]
American baseball player
* Overall, Jeff

Overholser, Wayne D. 1906- [AW, CA]
American author
* Daniels, John S.
* Leighton, Lee
* Roberts, Wayne
* Stevens, Dan J.
* Wayne, Joseph

[The] Overland Man
See Sutherland, John Bain

Overlin, Ken 1910- [HPPN]
American boxer
* [The] Illinois Thunderbolt

Overmire, Frank 1919- [BE, BTB, SMG]
American baseball player and coach
* Overmire, Stub [or Stubby]

Overmire, Stub [or Stubby]
See Overmire, Frank

Overreach, [Sir] Giles
See Mompesson, [Sir] Giles

[An] Overseer
See Nicholls, [Sir] George

Overstake, Eva Alaine 1918-1952
[CWG]
American country-western performer
* Martin, Judy

Overstreet, Bonaro Wilkinson 1902-
[NAA]
American poet
* Wilkinson, Bonara

Overstreet, Tommy 1937- [ECM]
American country-western performer
* Dean, Tommy

Overtheway, Mrs.
See Ewing, Juliana [Horatia Gatty]

Overton, Max
See Wilcox, Don

Overton, Richard 17th c. [HPPN]
British pamphleteer and satirist
* Marpriest, Martin

Overy, Claire May
See Bass, Clara May

Ovesen, Ellis
See Smith, Shirley M[ae]

Ovid
See Ovidius Naso, Publius

[The] Ovid of France
See Bellay, Joachim du

[The] Ovid of the English Nation
See Drayton, Michael

Ovidius Naso, Publius ?-17? [DEP,
WBD]
Roman poet
* [The] Master of Love
* Ovid

Ovstedal, Barbara
Author
* Laker, Rosalind

Owain, Owain 1929- [IAW]
Welsh author
* Herco
* Humphreys, John

Owanda
See Robinson, Edgar Williams

Owanda
See Robinson, Emma

Owen
See Appleton, Jesse

Owen, Arnold Malcolm 1916?- [BE, BI, PB]
American baseball player
* Owen, Mickey

Owen, Ashelford
See Ogle, Anne

Owen, Big Steve
See Owen, Stephen Joseph [Steve]

Owen, Bill
See Rowbotham, William

Owen, Caroline Dale
See Snedeker, Caroline Dale

Owen, Catherine
See Bowen, Catherine

Owen, Catherine
See Nitsch, Helen Alice [Matthews]

Owen, Charles 18th c. [HPPN]
British dissenter
* [An] Anonymous Clergyman

Owen, Clifford
See Hamilton, Charles Harold St. John

Owen, [Harry] Collinson 1882-1956 [WGT, WW]
Author
* Addison, Hugh
* Collinson, Owen?

Owen, D. E. 20th c. [MBF]
British author
* English, Don

Owen, Dean
See McGaughy, Dudley Dean

Owen, Edmund
See Teller, Neville

Owen, Frank 1893-1968 [ESF, HFF, WGT]
American author
* Abner, Gerald
* Braithwaite, Raymond
* Hung Long Tom
* Kent, Richard
* Williams, Roswell

Owen, Frank 1907?-1979 [CA]
British author and broadcaster
* Cato [joint pseudonym with Peter D(unsmore) Howard and Michael Foote]

Owen, Frank Malcolm 1879-1942 [BE]
American baseball player
* Owen, Yip

Owen, Freck
See Owen, Marv[in James]

Owen, Garnet 20th c. [IAW]
American author
* Oliver, Gay

Owen, Hedley
See O'Mant, Hedley Percival Angelo

Owen, Hugh
See Faust, Frederick [Schiller]

Owen, J. A.
See Visger, Jean A. Owen

Owen, Jack 1929- [AW]
British author
* Dykes, Jack

Owen, John 1560?-1622? [HPPN]
British author
* [The] British Martial
* Little Owen the Epigrammaker

Owen, John 1765-1822 [IP]
British clergyman and author
* Christian, Theophilus, Esq.
* [A] Suburban Clergyman

Owen, John Pickard
See Butler, Samuel

Owen, Joseph B. [PA]
Author
* Alter

Owen, Maggie
See Wadelton, Maggie Jeanne

Owen, Marsha
See Busby, Mabel Janice

Owen, Marv[in James] 1906- [BN]
American baseball player
* Owen, Freck

Owen, Mary Jane
See Brockway, Jennie M.

Owen, Mickey
See Owen, Arnold Malcolm

Owen, Norman
See Walters, J.

Owen, Richard
See Roberts, Edna

Owen, Robert 1771-1858 [HFN, HPPN, IP, NPS]
Welsh-born reformer, editor, philanthropist
* Celatus
* [The] Father of British Socialism
* One of H. M.'s Justices of the Peace

Owen, Robert Dale 1801-1877 [IP]
Scottish-born reformer
* [A] Citizen of the West

Owen, Robert N. [Bob]
See Geis, Richard E[rwin]

Owen, Roderic
See Fenwick-Owen, Roderic Franklin Rawnsley

Owen, Seena
See Auen, Signe

Owen, Stephen Joseph [Steve] 1898- [HPPN]
American football coach
* Owen, Big Steve
* Owen, Stout Steve

Owen, Stout Steve
See Owen, Stephen Joseph [Steve]

Owen, Tom
See Watts, Peter Christopher

Owen, Tom, the Bee Hunter
See Thorpe, Thomas Bangs

Owen, Vincent
See Cook, Fred Gordon

Owen, William 19th c. [IP]
Welsh philologist
* Meirion

Owen, William
See Pughe, William Owen

Owen, William Charles 1854-? [WWL]
British author
* Senex

Owen, Yip
See Owen, Frank Malcolm

Owens, A.
See Hersey, Harold

Owens, Alvis Edgar, Jr. 1929- [CME, CWG, DAM]
American country-western performer
* Owens, Buck

Owens, Arthur Neal 1899- [HPPN]
American surgeon
* [The] Father of Plastic Surgery

Owens, Artie 1953- [SMG]
American football player
* Owens, Flea

Owens, Bear
See Owens, James Philip

Owens, Black Widow
See Owens, Milton

Owens, Brick
See Owens, Clarence B.

Owens, Brigman 1943-
American football player
* Owens, Twiggy

Owens, Buck
See Owens, Alvis Edgar, Jr.

Owens, Charles M.
See Brown, Charles M.

Owens, Charles Wayne 1954?- [BI, SMG]
American football player
* Owens, Tinker

Owens, Clarence B. 1885?-1949 [BI, HPPN]
American baseball umpire
* Owens, Brick

Owens, Cotton
See Owens, Everett

Owens, Doye H. 1892-1962 [ASC]
American musician
* Owens, Tex

Owens, Eddie
See Abram, Eddie

Owens, Everett 1924- [EAR]
American auto racer
* Owens, Cotton

Owens, Fannie
See Lyons, Sophie

Owens, Flea
See Owens, Artie

Owens, Furman Lee 1910- [BE]
American baseball player
* Owens, Jack

Owens, Ike
See Owens, Isaiah

Owens, Iris 20th c.
Author
* Daimler, Harriet

Owens, Isaiah 20th c. [EF]
American football player
* Owens, Ike

Owens, Jack 20th c. [HPPN]
American singer
* [The] Cruising Crooner

Owens, Jack
See Owens, Furman Lee

Owens, James Alvin, Jr. 1948- [BA]
American business executive
* Owens, Mouse

Owens, James Cleveland 1913-1980 [BBH, CA, TF]
American track and field athlete
* [The] Ebony Antelope
* [The] Ebony Express
* Owens, Jesse

Owens, James Philip 1934- [BE]
American baseball player
* Owens, Bear

Owens, Jesse
See Owens, James Cleveland

Owens, Michael J. 1859-1923 [HPPN]
American glass manufacturer
* [The] Father of the Glass Industry
* [The] Glass Giant

Owens, Milton 1954- [RBE]
American boxer
* Owens, Black Widow

Owens, Mouse
See Owens, James Alvin, Jr.

Owens, Paul 1924- [SMG]
American baseball team personnel director
* [The] Pope

Owens, R. C.
See Owens, Raleigh C.

Owens, Raleigh C. 1933- [FB]
American football player
* Owens, R. C.

Owens, Raymond ?-1942 [MK]
American baseball player
* Owens, Smoky

Owens, Red
See Owens, Thomas Llewellyn

Owens, Richard
See Chentres, Federico

Owens, Robert 1941- [IBW]
American clergyman
* Owens, [Father] Vladimir

Owens, Rochelle
See Bass, Rochelle

Owens, Ruby 1908-1963 [CM]
American country-western performer
* Radio's Original Texas Cowgirl
* Texas Ruby

Owens, Smoky
See Owens, Raymond

Owens, Steve E. 1947- [FB, HPPN]
American football player
* [The] Booming Sooner
* Ki He Gha [Leader]

Owens, Tex
See Owens, Doye H.

Owens, Thelma 1905- [CA]
American author
* Grafton, Ann

Owens, Thomas Llewellyn 1874-1952 [BE]
American baseball player
* Owens, Red

Owens, Tinker
See Owens, Charles Wayne

Owens, Twiggy
See Owens, Brigman

Owens, [Father] Vladimir
See Owens, Robert

Owenson, Robert
See MacOwen, Robert

Owenson, Sydney
See Morgan, Sydney Owenson

[The] Owl
See Banghart, Basil

[The] Owl?
See Bennett, Charles Henry

[The] Owl
See Caballero, Guadalupe

[The] Owl
See Garner, John Nance

[The] Owl
See Hooton, Burt Carlton

[The] Owl
See Polizzi, Alfred

[The] Owl
See Smith, F[rancis] Hopkinson

Owl, Eugene
See Pilgrim, Thomas

Owl, Sebastian
See Thompson, Hunter S[tockton]

Owlglass, Dr.
See Blaich, Hans Erich

[The] Owner
See Scott, Robert Falcon

Ownes, James E., Jr. 1937- [BA]
American business executive
* Big O

Owney the Killer
See Madden, Owen

Owski
See Dingell, John David

Owsley
See Stanley, Augustus Owsley, III

[The] Ox
See Kratochvilova, Jarmila

[The] Ox
See Zampieri, Domenico

Oxberry, William 1784-1824 [DNNS, FFF, SN]
British poet, printer, publisher, publican, player
* [The] Five P's

Oxenbury, Helen
See Burningham, Helen Oxenbury

Oxenbury, Thomas Bernard 1904- [ART]
British artist
* T. B. O.

Oxenford, John 1812-1877 [IP, PA]
British playwright
* [An] English Play-Goer

Oxenham, Elsie
See Dunkerley, Elsie Jeanette

Oxenham, Henry Nutcombe 1829-? [HPPN]
British clergyman
* [An] Ex Puseyite

Oxenham, John
See Dunkerley, William Arthur

Oxenstierna, Axel Gustafsson 1583-1654 [NPS, SN]
Swedish statesman
* Aquila, Aquilonius
* [The] Eagle of the North

[The] Oxford Dante
See Moore, Edward

[An] Oxford Divine
See Burdon, [Rev.] Richard

Oxford, George 20th c.   [CMA]
American disc jockey
* Oxford, Jumpin' George

Oxford, Jane
See Williams, Elma Mary

Oxford, Jumpin' George
See Oxford, George

[An] Oxford Tutor
See Fowler, William Warde

Oxley, Kate
See Whitehead, Kate

Oxley, William 1939-   [CA]
British poet
* Hardy, Jason

Oxoniae Poeta Laureatus
See Skelton, John

[An] Oxonian
See Buxton, Harry John Wilmot

[The] Oxonian
See Metcalfe, Frederick

[An] Oxonian Graduate
See Nares, Robert

Oxoniensis
See Brooke, Henry

Oxoniensis
See Trench, Francis

Oy-vik
See Holmvik, Oyvind

Oyama, Mas
See Yong-I-Choy

Oyama, Masutatsu
See Yong-I-Choy

Oyler, Andrew Paul [Andy] 1880-?   [BE]
American baseball player
* Oyler, Pepper

Oyler, Pepper
See Oyler, Andrew Paul [Andy]

Oyra, Jan
See Wojcieszko, Jan

Oyster Joe Martina
See Martina, Joseph John [Joe]

Oyved, Moysheh
See Good, Edward

Oz, Amos
See Klausner, Amos

Ozaki, Milton K. 20th c.   [CC, WW]
American author
* Saber, Robert O.

[The] Ozark Bear
See Tesreau, Charles Monroe

Ozark, Daniel Leonard 1923-   [BE, PB]
American baseball coach and manager
* Ozark Ike

Ozark Ike
See Kiner, Ralph McPherran

Ozark Ike
See Ozark, Daniel Leonard

Ozark Ike
See Zernial, Gus Edward

Ozbekhan, Anne Binkley Rand 20th c.
[SAT]
American author
* Binkley, Anne

Ozbekhan, Anne Binkley Rand 20th c.
[TBJ]
American author
* Rand, Anne

Ozdemir 16th c.   [HN]
* [The] Iron Ogli
* [The] Turkish Samson

Ozdenak, Yasin Erol 1948-   [AES]
Turkish soccer player
* Yasin, Erol

Ozgun, Faruk
See Agca, Mehmet Ali

Oziosi [The Lazybones]
See Merry, Robert

Ozmer, Doc
See Ozmer, Horace Robert

Ozmer, Horace Robert 1901-   [BE]
American baseball player
* Ozmer, Doc

Ozone, Barbara Lynn 1942-   [RO1]
American singer and songwriter
* Lynn, Barbara

Ozy
See Rosset, Benjamin Charles

P

Asterisk (*) indicates assumed name.

P.
See Marsh, George Perkins

P.
See McDonald, Daniel

P.
See Palfrey, Cazneau

P.
See Peabody, Andrew Preston

P.
See Peabody, Ephraim

P.
See Pegge, Samuel

P.
See Polwhele, Richard

P.
See Poole, William Frederick

P.
See Putnam, George

P. A.
See Ainslie, Peter

P. A.
See Bernard, Pierre A.

P. A. N.
See Nuttall, P. Austin

P. A. P. O. I. L. A.
See Locke, John

P. B.
See Benjamin, Park

P. B. D.
See Duncan, Philip Bury

P. B. K., Cambridge, 1867
See Holmes, Oliver Wendell

P. B. S.
See Shelley, Percy Bysshe

P. B. St. J.
See St. John, Percy Bollingbroke

P. C.
See Cullen, P. J.

P. C. A.
See Aubry, Philippe

P. C. E.
See Littledale, Richard

P. C. S. S.
See Smythe, Percy Clinton Sydney [Viscount of Strangford]

P. C. W.
See Webb, Philip Carteret

P. D.
See Debaufre, Peter

P. D.
See Haughton, Percy Duncan

P. D. Q.
See Perez de Cuellar y Guerra, Javier

P. E.
See Pegge, Samuel

P. E. T.
See Trudeau, Pierre Elliott

P. F.
See Freneau, Philip Morin

P. F.
See Nuttall-Smith, Margaret Emily Noel

P. G.
See Gardner, Peter

P. G.
See Giggle, Philip

P. G.
See Gyllenhammar, Pehr

P. G.
See Pegge, Samuel

P. G. A.
See Audran, Prosper Gabriel

P. G. S.
See Smyth, Patrick G.

P. H.
See Hempton, Paul Andrew Keates

P. H.
See Hogarth, Arthur Paul

P. H.
See Horry, Pinckney

P. H., M. D.
See Hiffernan, Paul

P. I. X.
See Hallam, Douglas

P. J.
See Johnson, Pamela P.

P. J. G.
See Garrard, Peter John

P. K.
See Anstis, [Rev.] Matthew

P. K.
See Kirk, Phyllis Odeal

P. K.
See Rosegger, Petri Kettenfeier

P. L.
See Larkin, Peter O'Neill

P. L. K. [Plucky Little King]
See Hussein

P. M.
See MacGillivray, James Pittendrigh

P. M.
See Margaret Rose

P. M.
See Massinger, Philip

P. M.
See Middleton, Patrick

P. M.
See Mieg, Peter

P. M. E.
See Ellis, Phillis Marion

P. McD.?
See McDonald, Peter

P. McG.
See McEntee, P.

P. O. L.
See Guiney, Louise Imogen

P. O'D.
See Donovan, Peter

P. O'H.
See O'Herlihy, Patrick

P. P.
See Daniel, George

P. P.
See Rumohr, Theodore Wilhelm Kjerstrup

P. P., A Parish Clerk
See Arbuthnot, John

P. P. B. K.
See Littledale, Richard

P. P. C.
See Carpenter, Philip Pearsall

P. P. C. R.
See Watts, Thomas

P. P. J.
See Pickard Jenkins, Percy

P. P., M. A., Rev.
See Graves, Richard

P. P. P.
See Maginn, William

P. R.
See Page Roberts, James

P. R.
See Robertson, Patrick

P. S.
See Pegge, Samuel

P. S.
See Schaff, Philip

P. T.
See Thursby, Peter

P. T.
See Tobin, Patricia L.

[The] P. T. Barnum of Sports
See Pyle, Charles C.

P. T. T.
See Maginn, William

P. V. B.
See Bradshaw, Percival Vanner

P. W.
See Drew, Pierce William

P. W.
See Strasser, Bernard Paul

P. W. W.
See Wilson, Philip Whitwell

[The] P. X. Millionaire
See Wooldridge, William O.

P-Orridge, Genesis
See Megson, Neil Andrew

P-Shaw
See Shaw, George Bernard

[The] Pa
See Stevens, Siaka

Pa Chin
See Li Fei-kan

Pa, Choon
See Kwak, Chong Won

Pa He Haska
See Cody, William Frederick

Paaltjens, Piet
See Haverschmidt, Francois

Paar, Jack 1918-   [HPPN]
American television personality
* [The] Boy from Bronxville
* [The] Peck's Bad Boy of Yesteryear T. V.

Pab
See Blooman, Percy A.

Pablo, Augustus
See Swaby, Horace

[The] Pablo Casals of Lard Carvers
See Eichenaur, Franz Victor

Pabon Pabon, Rosemberg 20th c.
Colombian guerrilla leader
* Uno, Comandante

Pabor, Charles Henry 1846-1913   [BE]
American baseball player and manager
* [The] Old Woman in the Red Cap

Pabst, G. W.
See Pabst, George Wilhelm

Pabst, G. W.
See Wilhelm, Georg

Pabst, George Wilhelm 1885-1967   [FC]
German director
* Pabst, G. W.

PAC Man
See Melcher, John

Pac Man
See Paklin, Igor

Pace, Peter
See Burnett, David [Benjamin Foley]

Pace, William   [IP]
British poet
* [A] Clergyman of the Church of England

Pacelli, Eugenio Maria Giovanni 1876-1958   [CBS, WBD]
Pope
* [The] Fighting Pope
* Pius XII
* [The] Pope of Peace

Pachal, Clay
See Pachal, Clayton

Pachal, Clayton 1956-   [HR]
Canadian-born hockey player
* Pachal, Clay

Pacheco, Assis
See De Assis Pacheco, Armando

Pacheco, Luis
See Fatio, Louis

Pachin Marin
See Gonzalez Marin, Francisco

Paching, Resta   [IP]
British innkeeper and author
* [A] Gentleman in London

Pachter, Henry M[aximilian]
See Paechter, Henry M[aximilian]

[The] Pacific
See Amadeus VIII

[The] Pacific
See Frederick III

[The] Pacific
See Olaf III [or Olaus]

[The] Pacific
See Pedro II

[The] Pacific Cyclone
See Smith, Holland McTyeire

[Le] Pacificateur de la Vendee
See Hoche, [Louis] Lazarus

Pacificator
See Alexander, Richard Dykes

[The] Pacificator of Europe
See Orsini, Pietro Francesco

Pacificator of the Occident
See Gonzalez, Manuel

Pacifico, Don
See Temple, Henry John

Pacifico, [Dr.] Solomon
See Thackeray, William Makepeace

Pacificus
See Caspary, Alfred

Pacificus
See Giddings, Joshua Reed

Pacificus
See Hamilton, Alexander

Pacioli [or Paccioli], Luca 1450?-1520?   [WBD]
Italian mathematician
* Di Borgo, Luca

Paciorek, Thomas Marian 1946-   [SMG]
American baseball player
* Paciorek, Wimpy

Paciorek, Wimpy
See Paciorek, Thomas Marian

Pacis, Vicente Albano 1900-   [NAA]
Filipino editor
* Pradas, Virginia

Packard, Clarissa
See Gilman, Caroline [Howard]

Packard, Elon E. 1923-1977   [HPPN]
American playwright
* Packard, Packy

Packard, Frederick Adolphus 1794-1867   [HPPN, IP]
American attorney and author
* [A] Citizen of Pennsylvania
* [A] Member of the Board of Directors of Girard College

Packard, Gilian E. 1938-   [ART]
British artist
* G. E. P.

Packard, Packy
See Packard, Elon E.

Packard, Vance Oakley 1914- [HPPN]
American journalist, lecturer, author
* [The] Motivation Mentor

Packer, Alfred 1847-1907 [BLB, HPPN]
American murderer and robber
* [The] Colorado Cannibal
* [The] Maneater
* Schwartze, John

Packer, Joy [Petersen] 1905- [CA]
South African author
* Packer, Lady

Packer, Lady
See Packer, Joy [Petersen]

Packer, Vin
See Meaker, Marijane

Packford, C. W. [NPS]
Author
* Alma Mater

Paco De Oro [Paco the Golden One]
See Diez, Francisco

Paco Frascuelo
See Sanchez, Francisco

Paco d'Arcos, J.
See Correa da Silva, Joaquim Belford

Pacorro
See Anton, Francisco

Pacorro
See Diaz y Perez, Francisco

Padden, Brains
See Padden, Richard J. [Dick]

Padden, Gunner
See Padden, William

Padden, Richard J. [Dick] 1870-1922
[BN]
American baseball player
* Padden, Brains

Padden, William 20th c. [BLB]
American underworld figure
* Padden, Gunner

Paddie Kak
See Kirtland, Ethel Schwartz

Paddock, Charles W. 1900-1943 [BBH]
American track and field athlete
* [The] World's Fastest Human

Paddock, Mrs. [FFF]
Entertainer
* Mitchell, Maggie

Paddu, Antonio 1944- [BX]
Italian boxer
* Paddu, Tonino

Paddu, Tonino
See Paddu, Antonio

Paddy
See McCloskey, Henry

Paddy
See McCluskey, Henry

Paddy from Cork
See O'Sullivan, Michael John

Paddy, Scot, the Piper
See McMullan, William John

Paddy the Cope
See Gallagher, Patrick

Paddywhiski
See Fox, Will H.

Padecopeo, Gabriel
See Vega Carpio, Lope Felix de

Paden, Clifton 1874-1956 [SC]
American actor, playwright, screenwriter
* Emerson, John

[The] Paderewska of the Pampas
See Novaes, Guiomar

Paderewski, Ignace Jan 1860-1941 [MS]
Polish pianist
* [The] Lion of Paris

Padeson, Mary
See Magraw, Beatrice Irene [May]

Padget, Calvin Jackson
See Ferroni, Giorgio

Padgett, Desmond
See Von Block, Bela

Padgett, Don Wilson 1911- [BE]
American baseball player
* Padgett, Red

Padgett, Ernest Kitchen [Ernie]
1899-1957 [BE, PB]
American baseball player
* Padgett, Red

**Padgett, Lewis [joint pseudonym with
Catherine Lucile Moore]**
See Kuttner, Henry

**Padgett, Lewis [joint pseudonym with
Henry Kuttner]**
See Moore, Catherine Lucile

Padgett, Red
See Padgett, Don Wilson

Padgett, Red
See Padgett, Ernest Kitchen [Ernie]

Padgett, Ron 1942- [CA]
American poet
* Dangerfield, Harlan
* Veitch, Tom

Padilla [Small Oven]
See Garcia De La Flor, Angel

Padilla, Eduardo
See Figueroa, Eduardo

Padilla, Ezequiel
See Penaloza, Ezequiel Padilla

Padilla, Jose Gualberto 1829-1886 [CW]
Puerto Rican poet
* [El] Caribe

Padilla de Sanz, Trina 1880?-? [CW]
Puerto Rican poet
* [La] Hija del Caribe

[The] Padishah of the Padishah
See Canning, [Sir] Stratford [First
Viscount Stratford de Redcliffe]

Padjan, Jack 1888-1960 [SC]
Actor
* Duane, Jack

Padmore, George A.
See Nurse, Malcolm

[Il] Padovanino
See Varotari, Alessandro

[Il] Padovano
See Annibale

Padraig, Padraic Giolla
See Fitzpatrick, Patrick Vincent

[El] Padre de las Rosas
See Schoener, [Rev.] George

[The] Padre of Hollywood
See Dodd, Neal

[El] Padrino
See Alvero Cruz, Jose Medrano

[Il] Padrino [The Godfather]
See Fanfani, Amintore

[Il] Padrone
See Sinatra, Francis Albert [Frank]

Padula, Vicente 1900-1967 [SC]
Argentinian-born actor
* Padula, Vincent

Padula, Vincent
See Padula, Vicente

Padva, Vladimir
Musician
* Padwa, Vee

Padwa, Vee
See Padva, Vladimir

Padwell, Peter, Esq., of Padington
See Bullock, Christopher

Pae, David [IP]
Scottish author
* Memoriter
* One Who Has Stood Behind the
  Counter

Paechter, Henry M[aximilian] 1907-
[CA]
German-born historian and author
* Pachter, Henry M[aximilian]
* Rabasseire, Henry

Paetel, Erich 1875-? [LAO]
German editor and author
* Her, Erich

Paez, Ramon [IP]
American artist and author
* R. P., de Venezuela

Paff, Mrs. Charles [FFF]
Entertainer
* Mortimer, Lottie

Pafko, Andrew 1921- [BE, BN]
American baseball player
* [The] Brow
* Pafko, Handy Andy
* Pafko, Pruschka

Pafko, Handy Andy
See Pafko, Andrew

Pafko, Pruschka
See Pafko, Andrew

[The] Pagan
See Vedder, Elihu

Pagan, Isobel 1741-1821 [HPPN]
Scottish poet
* Pagan, Mother

Pagan, Jose
See Rivera, Jose

Pagan, Kristian
See Sebelien, John Robert Francis

Pagan, Mother
See Pagan, Isobel

Pagan y Ferrer, Gloria Maria 1920-
[CA]
Puerto Rican poet
* Palma, Marigloria

Paganelli [or Pignatelli], Bernardo
?-1153 [WBD]
Pope
* Eugenius III

Paganini, Nicolo 1782-1840 [SN]
Italian musician
* [The] Devil

[The] Paganini of the Tuba
See Phillips, Harvey G.

Pagano, Bartolomeo 1878-1947 [WEF]
Italian actor
* Maciste

Page, Abraham
See Holt, John Saunders

Page, Alan 1946- [IBW]
American football player
* Page, War Whoop

Page, Anita
See Pomares, Anita

Page, Arthur W.
See Wellington, Arthur

Page, Big 'Un
See Page, Walter

Page, Catherine 20th c. [AW]
Irish-born author
* Armstrong, Cathleen

Page, Cedric Daniel 1945- [BA]
American educator
* Page, Rick

[Un] Page de la Cour Imperiale
See Hilaire, Emile Marc

Page, Don
See Paige, Jose

Page, Eileen
See Heal, Edith

Page, Eleanor
See Coerr, Eleanor [Beatrice]

Page, Elizabeth Lawson 20th c. [IBW]
American educator
* Page, Hot Lips

Page, Emma
See Tirbutt, Honoria

Page, Evelyn 1902- [CA, WD, WW]
American author
* Scarlett, Roger [joint pseudonym with
Dorothy Blair]

Page, Fireman
See Page, Joseph Francis [Joe]

Page, [Sir] Francis 1718-1741 [HN, RH]
British jurist
* [The] Hanging Judge

Page, G. S.
See Galbraith, Georgie Starbuck

Page, Gale
See Rutter, Sally

Page, Gerald W[ilburn] 1939- [CA,
HFF, WGT]
American author and editor
* Grindle, Carleton
* Jones, Harold
* Lee, Eric
* Pembrooke, Kenneth
* Tifton, Leo

Page, Grover, Jr. 1918- [CA]
American author and librarian
* McGinnis, K. K.

Page, H. A.
See Japp, Alexander Hay

Page, Harlan O. 1887-1965 [AS, BB]
American basketball player
* Page, Pat

Page, Henri
See Duckett, William

Page, Horse
See Page, Walter

Page, Hot Lips
See Page, Elizabeth Lawson

Page, Hot Lips
See Page, Oran Thaddeus

Page, Jake
See Page, James K[eena], Jr.

Page, James K[eena], Jr. 1936- [CA]
American author and editor
* Page, Jake

Page, John 1744-1808 [HPPN]
*American Revolutionary patriot and
politician*
* Partridge, John

Page, John 19th c. [IP]
British poet
* Folio, Felix

Page, John Arthur 1910- [FC, ITA]
American actor
* Paige, Robert [Bob]

Page, John Percy 1877-1973 [CSH]
Canadian basketball coach
* Page, Papa

Page, Jose 1905-1967 [HPPN]
American actor and director
* Alvarado, Don

Page, Joseph Francis [Joe] 1917- [BE,
PB]
American baseball player
* [The] Gay Reliever
* Page, Fireman

Page, Kenneth Calvin
See Hogben, Lancelot Thomas

Page, Kirby 1890-1957 [HPPN]
American clergyman and pacifist
* [The] Itinerant Evangelist for Peace

Page, La Wanda 1920- [IBW]
American entertainer
* [The] Bronze Goddess of Fire

Page, LeRoy Robert 1906-1982 [BAB]
American baseball player
* Paige, LeRoy Robert
* Paige, Satchel

Page, Lips
See Page, Oran Thaddeus

Page, Lorna
See Rowland, Donald Sydney

Page, Lucille
See Berdell, Lucille

Page, Lutie
See Mower, Mrs. Fred

Page, Marco
See Kurnitz, Harry

Page, Mary
See Heal, Edith

Page, Norvell W. 1904-1961 [EMD,
ESF, WGT]
American author
* Craig, Randolph
* Stockbridge, Grant

[The] Page of State to the Muses
See Spenser, Edmund

[A] Page on Father Page
See Fitzgerald, Gerald M.

Page, Oran Thaddeus 1908-1954 [BWW,
DAM, EJ]
American jazz musician
* Page, Hot Lips
* Page, Lips
* Papa Snow White

Page, Papa
See Page, John Percy

Page, Pat
See Page, Harlan O.

Page, Patricia Kathleen 1916- [CA,
WD]
British-born poet and artist
* Cape, Judith
* Irwin, P. K.

Page, Patti
See Fowler, Clara Ann

Page, Paul 20th c. [HPPN]
American radio announcer
* [The] Voice of the 500

Page, Paul
See Hicks, Campbell U.

Page, R. Channing M. 19th c. [IP]
American author
* One of the Family

Page, Richard ?-1841 [PA]
British author
* Hardcastle, Daniel

Page, Rick
See Page, Cedric Daniel

Page, Stanton
See Fuller, Henry Blake

Page, Thomas [joint pseudonym with Daniel T. Streib]
See Jones, Robert Page

Page, Thomas [joint pseudonym with Robert Page Jones]
See Streib, Dan[iel Thomas]

Page, Tilsa
See Stubbs, Tilsa

Page, Vicki
See Avey, Ruby

Page, Walter 20th c. [NP]
American jazz musician
* Page, Big 'Un
* Page, Horse

Page, Walter Hines 1855-1918 [WBD]
American journalist
* Worth, Nicholas

Page, War Whoop
See Page, Alan

Page Roberts, James 1925- [ART]
British painter and sculptor
* P. R.

Pagery, Francois
See Klein, Gerard

Pages, Pedro 1916- [CA]
Spanish-born educator and author
* Alba, Victor

Paget, Debra
See Griffin, Debralee

Paget, Francis Edward 1806-? [FFF, PA]
British clergyman and author
* Churne, William
* F. E. P.

Paget, George Charles Henry Victor 1922- [CA]
British author
* Anglesey, Marquess of

Paget, Henry William [First Marquess of Anglesey] 1768-1854 [NN]
British army officer
* Paget, One Leg

Paget, John
See Aiken, John [Kempton]

Paget, Margaret
See Medlicott, Margaret P[aget]

Paget, One Leg
See Paget, Henry William [First Marquess of Anglesey]

Paget, R. L.
See Knowles, Frederic Lawrence

Paget, Violet 1856-1935 [HDM, LC, TC]
British author
* Lee, Vernon

Paget-Lowe, H[enry]
See Lovecraft, Howard Phillips

Pagett, Nicola
See Scott, Nicola

Pagliacci From Brooklyn
See Ticker, Reuben

[The] Pagliacci of the Piano
See Reichman, Joseph

Pagliaroni, James Vincent 1937- [BE]
American baseball player
* Pagliaroni, Pag

Pagliaroni, Pag
See Pagliaroni, James Vincent

Pagnanelli, George
See Derounian, Avodis Arthur

Pagnani, Andreina
See Gentili, Andreina

Pahaska
See Cody, William Frederick

Pahlavi, Ashraf 1920?-
Sister of Iranian shah, Mohammed Reza Pahlavi
* [The] Black Panther

Pahlavi, Mohammad Reza 1920-1980 [HPPN]
Iranian ruler
* [The] Bloodsucker
* [The] Bloodsucker of the Century
* [The] King of Kings
* [The] Old Shah

Pahlow, Mannfried Otto Siegfried 1926- [IAW]
German chemist and writer
* Hagen, Martin S.

Pahz, [Anne] Cheryl Suzanne
See Goldfeder, [Anne] Cheryl Suzanne

Pahz, James Alon
See Goldfeder, [Kenneth] James

Pai Ta-shun
See Peterson, Frederick

Paicovich, Yigal 1918- [CA]
Israeli politican and author
* Allon, Yigal
* Jephthah [code name]

Paidagogos, Petros
See Brickman, William W.

Paidola, Anton
See Neagu, Paul

Paiement, Wilf
See Paiement, Wilfred

Paiement, Wilfred 1955- [FHE, SMG]
Canadian-born hockey player
* Paiement, Wilf

Paige, Elbridge Gerry 1816-1859 [PA]
American author
* Dow Jr.

Paige, Evelyn
See Gold, Evelyn Paige

Paige, George L. 1885- [BE]
American baseball player
* Paige, Pat

Paige, Janis
See Jaden, Donna Mae

Paige, Jose 1900?-1967 [F2, FC, SC]
American actor
* Alvarado, Don
* Page, Don

Paige, Leo
See Cochrane, William E.

Paige, LeRoy Robert
See Page, LeRoy Robert

Paige, Mabel
See Roberts, Mabel

Paige, Norman
See Seltzer, Norman Murray

Paige, Pat
See Paige, George L.

Paige, Patsy
See Brilhante, Patricia

Paige, Robert [Bob]
See Page, John Arthur

Paige, Satchel
See Page, LeRoy Robert

Paikert, Imre 1917- [OP]
Hungarian opera singer
* Palos, Imre

Paikowski, Franciszek Andzej 1916- [HPPN]
Polish-American tennis player
* Parker, Frank

Paillere, Madeleine Dominique 1916- [CW]
Haitian poet, author, art critic
* Fraeniel

Pain, Tommy
See Paine, Thomas

Paine, A. G. Amye 1864-? [NAA]
British-born writer
* A. G. A. P.
* Clarke, Gertrude

Paine, Allie
See Paine, Alva

Paine, Alva 1919- [BB]
American basketball player
* Paine, Allie

Paine, Citizen Tom
See Paine, Thomas

Paine, Flip
See Paine, Phillips Steere

Paine, Guthrie?
See Tremaine, F[rederick] Orlin

Paine, Hammond
See Hook, H. Clarke

Paine, Harriet Eliza 1845-1910 [HPPN]
American author
* Chester, Eliza

Paine, J. Lincoln
See Kramish, Arnold

Paine, Lauran [Bosworth] 1916- [CA, ESF, HPPN, SFL, SFP]
American author
* Ainsbury, Ray
* Ainsbury, Roy
* Ainsworth, Ray
* Ainsworth, Roy
* Allen, Clay
* Almonte, Rosa
* Andrews, A. A.
* Armour, John
* Bartlett, Kathleen
* Batchelor, Reg
* Beck, Harry
* Bedford, Kenneth
* Benton, Will
* Bosworth, Frank
* Bovee, Ruth
* Bradford, Will
* Bradley, Concho
* Brennan, Will
* Carrel, Mark
* Carter, Nevada
* Cassidy, Claude
* Clark, Badger
* Clarke, Richard
* Clarke, Robert
* Custer, Clint
* Dana, Amber
* Dana, Richard
* Davis, Audrey
* Drexler, J. F.
* Duchesne, Antoinette
* Durham, John
* Fisher, Margot
* Fleck, Betty
* Frost, Joni
* Glendenning, Donn
* Glenn, James
* Gordon, Angela
* Gorman, Beth
* Hart, Francis
* Hayden, Jay
* Holt, Helen
* Houston, Will
* Howard, Elizabeth
* Howard, Troy
* Hunt, John
* Ingersol, Jared
* Kelley, Ray
* Kelly, Ray
* Ketchum, Jack
* Kilgore, John
* Liggett, Hunter
* Lucas, J. K.
* Lyon, Buck
* Martin, Bruce
* Martin, Tom
* Morgan, Angela
* Morgan, Arlene
* Morgan, Frank
* Morgan, John
* Morgan, Valerie
* O'Connor, Clint

Paine, Lauran [Bosworth] (cont.)
* St. George, Arthur
* Sharp, Helen
* Slaughter, Jim
* Standish, Buck
* Stuart, Margaret
* Thompson, Buck
* Thompson, Russ
* Thorn, Barbara
* Undine, P. F.

Paine, Leslie Harold William 1921-
[IAW]
British author
* Paine, Nicky

Paine, Lizzie
See Millbank, Mrs. George

Paine, Nicky
See Paine, Leslie Harold William

Paine, Phillips Steere 1930- [BE]
American baseball player
* Paine, Flip

Paine, Robert Treat, Jr. 1773-1811 [IP]
American attorney, poet, journalist
* Menander

Paine, Thomas 1697?-1757 [IP]
American clergyman and author
* Philopatria

Paine, Thomas 1736-1809
British-born politician and author
* America's First Liberal
* Common Sense
* Duchatelet
* [An] Englishman
* Forester
* Humanus
* [A] Layman
* [The] Man of Reason
* Pain, Tommy
* Paine, Citizen Tom
* [The] Press Agent for Revolution
* [The] Prophet and Martyr of Democracy

Painsworth, W. Harassing
See Ainsworth, William Harrison

Painter, Daniel
See Burgess, Michael Roy

[The] Painter Laureate of Vermont
See Lucioni, Luigi

Painter, Mary C. 1841-? [PA]
Author
* Dawdle, Dolly

[The] Painter of Coolness
See Hobbema, Minderhout

Painter of Happiness
See Dufy, Raoul

[The] Painter of Jansenism
See Champagne, Philippe de

[The] Painter of Loneliness
See Hopper, Edward

[The] Painter of Nature
See Belleau, Remi

[The] Painter of Pageants
See Cagliari [or Caliari?], Paolo

[The] Painter of Presidents
See Stuart, Gilbert Charles

Painter of Protest
See Shahn, Ben[jamin]

[The] Painter of Sunlight
See Hitchcock, George

[The] Painter of the Graces
See Appiani, Andrea

[The] Painter of the Graces
See Boucher, Francois

[The] Painter of the National Parks
See Widforss, Gunnar Mauritz

[The] Painter of the Soil
See Wood, Grant

[The] Painter Patriot
See Gainsborough, Thomas

Painter Pug
See Hogarth, William

[The] Painter Without a Label
See Weeks, James

[The] Painting Moralist
See Hogarth, William

[The] Painting Nun
See Kent, Corita

Painton, Ivan Emory 1909- [IAW]
American poet and painter
* Zarello, Florian

Pair, Ronald R. 20th c.
American inventor and entrepreneur
* R. P.

Pairault, Pierre 1922- [CA]
French author
* Wul, Stefan

Paisley, Tom
See Passailaigue, Thomas E.

Paisnel, Edward 1925?- [HPPN]
British criminal
* [The] Jersey Monster

Paiva, Djanira 1914- [HPPN]
Brazilian artist
* Djanira

Pak, Chan-Ki
See Park, Chan-Ki

Pak, Chong-Hui
See Park, Chung Hee

Pakenham, F. J. [IP]
British author
* F. J. P.

Pakenham, Francis Aungier 1905-
[HPPN, NN]
British diplomat
* Longford, Frank Pakenham
* Porn, Lord

Pakington, [Sir] John ?-1560 [SN, WBD]
British barrister and courtier
* Her Temperance
* Pakington, Lusty

Pakington, [Sir] John Somerset
See Russell, John Somerset

Pakington, Lusty
See Pakington, [Sir] John

Paklin, Igor 1964?- [SI 3-5-84]
Russian track and field athlete
* Pac Man

Pal, Rudrendra Kumar 1902- [IAW]
Indian physician and writer
* Parulkumar

Palacio, Jorge [BI]
Argentine cartoonist
* Faruk

Palacio, Lino 1910?- [WECO]
Argentinian cartoonist
* Flax

Paladan, Josephin
See Peladan, Joseph

[The] Paladin of Palimony
See Mitchelson, Marvin

[The] Paladin of Paramours
See Mitchelson, Marvin

Palaeologus
See John V [or VI]

Palaeologus
See John VII

Palaeologus
See John VIII

Palaeologus
See Manuel II

Palaeologus
See Michael IX

Palaeologus
See Michael VIII

Palamon
See Churchyard, Thomas

Palance, Jack
See Palanuik, Walter

Palander af Vega
See Palander, Louis

Palander, Louis 1842-1902 [WBD]
Swedish naval officer and Arctic explorer
* Palander af Vega

Palanuik, Walter 1920?- [FC, SW, WEF]
American actor
* Palance, Jack

Palazzeschi, Aldo
See Giurlani, Aldo

Palden, Thondup Namgyal 1923-
[HPPN]
Maharnai of Sikkim
* [The] Queen of the Mountain

Paldi, Zelda 1873-1935 [BEW]
American actress and playwright
* Sears, Zelda

[The] Pale Death of the Saracens
See Otto II [or Otho]

Paleface, Hugh
See Palliser, [Sir] Hugh

Palermo
See Heisterkamp, Peter

Palermo
See North, John

Palermo, Alex
See Palermo, Alfonse Lawrence

Palermo, Alfonse Lawrence 1929-
[BEW]
American director, choreographer, actor
* Palermo, Alex

Palermo, Blinky
See Palermo, Frank

Palermo, Bucky
See Palermo, Charles

Palermo, Charles 1932?-
American underworld figure
* Allen, Charlie
* Buck, Charlie
* Palermo, Bucky

Palermo, Frank 20th c.
American boxing promoter, convicted of extortion
* Palermo, Blinky

Palestrant, Simon S. 1907- [AW, CAP]
American author
* Edwards, Stephen
* Stevens, S. P.
* Strand, Paul E.

Palestrina, Giovanni Pierluigida
1525?-1594 [DEP, HN, HPPN, SN]
Italian composer
* [The] Father of Music
* [The] Michael Angelo of the Lyre
* [The] Prince of Music
* [The] Savior of Church Music

Palethorpe-Todd, Richard 1919- [BF]
Irish-born actor
* Todd, Richard

Palette, Billy
See Robinson, William

Palette, Peter
See Onwhyn, Thomas

Palevsky, Max 1924- [HPPN]
American electronics executive
* [The] Green Max

Paley, Babe
See Paley, Barbara Cushing

Paley, Barbara Cushing 1915?-1978
American socialite
* Paley, Babe

Paley, William 1743-1805 [IP]
British author
* [A] Friend of Religious Liberty

Palfray, Warwick 1787-1838 [IP]
American journalist
* Another Layman

Palfrey, Cazneau 19th c. [HPPN]
American clergyman
* P.

Palfrey, John Gorham 1796-1881
[HPPN, IP]
American scholar, clergyman, historian, politician
* [An] Alumnus
* [A] Free Soiler from the Start
* J. G. P.
* [An] Old Conservative

Palfrey, Sarah Hammond 19th c. [IP]
American author and poet
* Foxton, E.

Palgrave, [Sir] Francis
See Cohen, Francis

Palgrave, Francis Turner 1824-1897
[DEL]
British author and editor
* Thurston, Henry T.

Palica, Ervin Martin
See Pavliecivich, Ervin Martin

Palickar, Stephen J. 1896- [NAA]
American author and journalist
* Carr, Stephen J.
* Stephens, S. J.

Palingenesius
See Mauzolli, Pietro Angelo

Palinurus
See Connolly, Cyril [Vernon]

[The] Palinurus of the Revolution
See Adams, Samuel

Palisier, John 1885?-? [NOJ]
American jazz musician
* Palisier, Pujol

Palisier, Pujol
See Palisier, John

Pall, Ellen Jane 1952- [CA]
American author
* Hill, Fiona

Pall, Etienne
See Platel, Felix

Palladino, Joseph Anthony 1910- [BEW, TR]
American actor
* Faye, Joey

Palladio, Andrea 1518-1580 [HPPN]
Italian architect
* [The] Architect of Reason

Pallant, Norman C. 20th c. [SFP]
Author
* Crouch, Charles Alban

Pallante, Aladdin Abdullah Achmed Anthony 1913-1970 [SC]
American actor and comic singer
* Aladdin

[The] Pallas of Sweden
See Key, Ellen Karoline Sofia

Pallavera, Franco
See Soldati, Mario

Palli, Pitsa
See Hartocollis, Peter

Pallidini, Jodi
See Robbin, [Jodi] Luna

Palliser, Francis
See Wilson, Mary

Palliser, [Sir] Hugh 1721-1796 [IP]
British naval officer and author
* Paleface, Hugh

Palm, Clarence 20th c. [OBW]
American baseball player
* Palm, Spoony

Palm, Gene
See Palmisano, Luigi

Palm, Mike
See Palm, Myron

Palm, Mike
See Palm, Richard Paul

Palm, Myron 20th c. [EF]
American football player
* Palm, Mike

Palm, Richard Paul 1925- [BE]
American baseball player
* Palm, Mike

Palm, Spoony
See Palm, Clarence

Palma Giovane
See Palma, Jacopo

Palma, Jacopo 1480?-1528 [WBD]
Venetian painter
* Palma Vecchio
* [Il] Vecchio [The Elder]

Palma, Jacopo 1544-1628 [WBD]
Venetian painter
* [Il] Giovane [The Younger]
* Palma Giovane

Palma, Marigloria
See Pagan y Ferrer, Gloria Maria

Palma, [Signora] Sara
See Newell, Mrs. Atkins

Palma Vecchio
See Palma, Jacopo

Palma y Romay, Ramon de 1812-1860
[CW]
Cuban poet, playwright, author
* [El] Bachiller Alfonso de Maldonado

Palmara, Mimmo 20th c. [WF]
Italian actor
* Palmer, Dick

Palme, Olof 1927- [HPPN]
Swedish prime minister
* [The] Rebel Without a Pause

Palmeno [Man from Palma Del Rio]
See Garcia, Julio

Palmeno [Man from Palma Del Rio]
See Garcia, Manuel

Palmer
See Powers, Francis Gary

Palmer, Anna Campbell 1854-1928
[HPPN]
American author
* Archibald, Mrs. George

Palmer, B. C.
See Schmidt, Laura M[arie]

Palmer, Baldy
See Palmer, Edwin Henry [Eddie]

Palmer, Bernard 1914- [CA]
American author
* Runyan, John

Palmer, Betsy
See Hrunek, Patricia Betsy

Palmer, Bill
See Miller, Bob

Palmer, Bud
See Palmer, John S.

Palmer, Charlotte 19th c. [HPPN]
British author and educator
* [A] Preceptress

Palmer, Claude 1893- [HPPN]
British actor
* Allister, Claude

Palmer, Cleveland
See Bradley, William Aspenwall

Palmer, Daniel David 1845-1913
[HPPN]
Founder of a chiropractic school
* Palmer, Fish

Palmer, Dick
See Palmara, Mimmo

Palmer, Ding
See Palmer, Winthrop H.

Palmer, Edward Vance 1885-1959
[DLE1]
Australian author
* Daly, Rann

Palmer, Edwin F. 19th c. [HPPN]
American soldier
* [A] Volunteer

Palmer, Edwin Henry [Eddie] 1893-
[BE]
American baseball player
* Palmer, Baldy

Palmer, Elsie Pavitt 1922- [CA]
American author
* Palmer, Peter

Palmer, Fanny
See Palmer, Frances Flora Bond

Palmer, Fish
See Palmer, Daniel David

Palmer, Frances Flora Bond 1812?-1876
[HPPN]
British-American artist and lithographer
* Palmer, Fanny

Palmer, Fred 1851-1927 [BEW]
British-born actor
* Grove, Fred

Palmer, Gentleman
See Palmer, John

Palmer, George 20th c. [CCL]
Canadian poet and author
* 2571

Palmer, Gregg
See Lee, Palmer

Palmer, Gretta
See Clark, Gretta Palmer

Palmer, Hackle
See Key, R. Blake

Palmer, Halleck
See Watson, Evelyn Mabel

Palmer, Helen Marion
See Geisel, Helen

Palmer, Henrietta Eliza Vaughan
1856-1911 [LC]
British author
* Winter, John Strange

Palmer, Henry 1892-1924 [HPPN]
American actor
* Williams, Frank

Palmer, James Shedden 1810-1867
[FFF]
American naval officer
* Palmer, Pie Crust

Palmer, Jane
See Gilman, Ann

Palmer, John 1728-1768 [HPPN]
British actor
* Palmer, Gentleman

Palmer, John 1729-1790 [IP]
British clergyman and author
* [A] Friend to Religious Liberty

Palmer, John 1807-1837 [EOP]
Astrologer and editor
* Raphael II

Palmer, John
See Turpin, Richard [Dick]

Palmer, John Leslie 1885-1944 [CC,
EMD, LC]
British author
* Beeding, Francis [joint pseudonym
with Hilary Aidan St. George
Saunders]
* Haddon, Christopher
* Pilgrim, David [joint pseudonym with
Hilary Aidan St. George Saunders]

Palmer, John S. 1923- [CR]
*American basketball player, sportscaster,
local government official*
* Palmer, Bud

Palmer, John Williamson 1825-1906
[BDSA, DNA, NPS]
American physician, poet, author
* Coventry, John

Palmer, Laura
See Schmidt, Laura M[arie]

Palmer, Lilli
See Peiser, Maria Lilli

Palmer, Lucienne 20th c.   [BEW, TR]
British playwright and translator
* Hill, Lucienne

Palmer, Lynde
See Peebles, Mary Louise

Palmer, M.   [PA]
Author
* Varick

Palmer, Madelyn 1910-   [IAW]
Australian-born author
* Peters, Geoffrey

Palmer, Minnie
See Marx, Minnie Palmer

Palmer, Minnie
See Rogers, Mrs. John R.

Palmer, Mrs. James F. [Reynolds]
19th c.   [IP]
British author
* [A] Lady
* Raphael

Palmer, Nathaniel B. 1799-1877   [HPPN]
American ship captain and explorer
* America's Best Known Sea Captain

Palmer, P. K. ?-1973?   [SFL]
Author
* Parnell, Keith

Palmer, Pamela Lynn 1951-   [CA]
American poet
* Leigh, Palmer

Palmer, Patricia 1895-1964   [SC]
American actress
* Gibson, Margaret

Palmer, Pedlar
See Palmer, Thomas

Palmer, Peter
See Palmer, Elsie Pavitt

Palmer, Pie Crust
See Palmer, James Shedden

Palmer, Pot-Pie
See Sanford, Edward

Palmer, Raymond A[rthur] 1910-1977
[ESF, SF, WGT]
American editor and writer
* Gade, Henry [house pseudonym]
* Irwin, G. H.
* Patton, Frank
* Pelkie, Joe Walter
* Quitman, Wallace
* Steber, A. R.
* Steele, Morris J. [house pseudonym,
  Ziff-Davis]
* Webster, Robert N.
* Winters, Rae?

**Palmer, Roundell [First Earl of
Selborne]** 1812-1895   [HPPN]
British jurist and hymn writer
* [The] Solicitor General

Palmer, Stuart [Hunter] 1905-1968   [CC,
WW]
American author
* Stewart [or Stuart], Jay

Palmer, Thomas 1876-1949   [BX, RBE]
British boxer
* Little Box o' Tricks
* Palmer, Pedlar

Palmer, Tobias
See Weathers, Winston

Palmer, Tom
See Leird, Henry J.

Palmer, Vera Jane 1932?-1967   [BDF,
FC, IPA]
American actress
* Mansfield, Jayne

Palmer, W. F. 19th c.   [IP]
American author
* W. F. P.

Palmer, William   [IP]
Author
* English Correspondent
* Warhawk

Palmer, William 1825-1856   [CEC]
British murderer
* [The] Rugeley Poisoner

Palmer, [Sir] William 19th c.   [IP]
British clergyman and author
* [A] Member of the Church at Oxford
* [A] Member of the Church of
  England
* [A] Member of the Church of God at
  Oxford
* Umbra Oxoniensis

Palmer, William Claud Michel
1891?-1970   [F2, FC]
British actor
* Allister, Claud

Palmer, William Henry 1830-1878   [PA]
Author
* Heller, Robert

Palmer, William Thomas 1877-?   [WWL]
British author
* Kent, Christopher
* W. T. P.

Palmer, Winthrop H. 1906-1970   [BBH]
American hockey player
* Palmer, Ding

Palmerston, Firebrand
See Temple, Henry John

Palmerston, Viscount
See Temple, Henry John

Palmezeaux
See Cubieres, Michael

Palmier, Remo
See Palmieri, Remo

Palmieri, Remo 1923-   [EJ]
American jazz musician
* Palmier, Remo

Palmisano, Luigi 20th c.   [SFL, SFP]
Author
* Palm, Gene

Palmyra's Queen
See Stanhope, Hester Lucy

Paloemon
See Maginn, William

Palomares Del Pino, Francisco 20th c.
[GS]
Spanish bullfighter
* [El] Marino [The Mariner]

Palomo Linares [Palomo from Linares]
See Palomo Martinez, Sebastian

Palomo Martinez, Sebastian 1947-   [GS]
Spanish bullfighter
* Palomo Linares [Palomo from Linares]

Palos, Imre
See Paikert, Imre

Palsgrave, Goodman
See Frederick V

Palsgrave, Goody
See Elizabeth

Palsson, Hermann 1921-   [IAW]
Icelandic-born author
* Cadwr

Paltenghi, Madeleine
See Anderson, Madeleine Paltenghi

Paltock, Robert 1697-1767   [PA, WGT]
British author
* Bingfield, William, Esq.
* R. P.
* R. S., a Passenger in the Hector
* Wilkins, Peter

Palton, Francis T.   [PA]
Author
* Noyes, MacLeod

[A] Paltry Dunghill
See Hill, [Sir] John

Paludan-Muller, Frederik 1809-1876
[HPPN]
Danish poet
* Fritz

Paludo
See Chacon, Augustin

Pam
See Temple, Henry John

Pambelecito
See Cervantes, Jose

Pamela
See FitzGerald, Lady

Pamfili, Giovanni Battista 1574-1655
[WBD]
Pope
* Innocent X

Pamjean, Louis
See Bedford-Jones, Henry [James
O'Brien]

[The] Pampas Bull
See Gonzalez, Jose Froilan

Pamphili
See Eusebius of Caesarea

Pamplin, W. 19th c. [IP]
British botanist and author
* W. P.

[El] Pamplones [Man from Pamplona]
See Legurregui, Jose

Pan
See Beresford, Leslie

Pan, Peter
See Bartier, Pierre

[El] Panadero [The Baker]
See Carmona y Luque, Jose

Panaetius
See De Ferrare, Baptiste

Panajot, H.
See Chitov, Panajot,

Panam, Pauline Adelaide Alexandre
19th c. [IP]
Author
* [A] Young Greek Lady

Panama Al Brown
See Brown, Alphonse Theo

Panard, Charles-Francois 1694-1765
[DEP, FFF, SN]
French poet and playwright
* [The] Father of Modern French Song
* [The] La Fontaine of the Vaudeville

[The] Panard of the 19th Century
See Gouffe, Armand

[The] Panavision Kid
See Bowering, George

Panbourne, Oliver
See Rockey, Howard

Pancho
See Cook, Enoch

Pancho
See Rosquellas, Adolfo

Panchon [Big Belly]
See Gonzalez, Francisco

Pancoast, Ace
See Pancoast, Asa

Pancoast, Asa 1905- [ASC]
American musician
* Pancoast, Ace

Panconcelli-Calzia, Giulio 1878-? [LAO]
Italian-born educator and author
* G. P. C.

Pancridge Earl
See Jones, Inigo

Pandel, Ted 1935- [HPPN]
American pianist and composer
* Praxiteles

[The] Pander of Venus
See Moore, Thomas

Pandian, Nallappaswamy [BI]
Indian singer
* Vilathikulam, Swami

Pandit, Vijaya Lakshmi 1900- [CA]
Indian author
* [The] Lamp of India

Pandora
See Macartney, Edith Hyde Robbins

Pandora
See Maccheta, Blanche Roosevelt
[Tucker]

Pandya, Harish C.
See Post, H. Christian

Paner, George Washington 1871-1950
[BE]
American baseball player
* Paynter, George Washington

Panfili, Mirella 20th c. [WF]
Italian actress
* Sullivan, Mary

Pangborn, Edgar 1909-1976 [SFL, WGT]
American author
* Harrison, Bruce

Pangloss
See Hendie, Paul

Panica, John 1893- [BX, RBE]
American boxer
* Wilson, Johnny

Panikkar, K[avalam] Madhava 1895-1963
[CAP]
Indian author
* Chanakya
* Putra, Kerala

Panlilio, Yay [BI]
*American journalist and underworld
figure*
* Colonel Yay

Panneton, Philippe 1895-1960 [WBD]
Canadian author
* Ringuet

Panofsky, Erwin 1892-1968 [HPPN]
German-American educator and art critic
* [The] King of Art Historians

Panomita
See Beccadelli, Antonio

Panonius, Janus
See Cisinge, Johann

Panova, Vera [Federovna] 1905-1973
[CA]
Russian author, playwright, journalist
* Veltman, Vera

Panowski, Eileen [Janet] Thompson
1920- [CA, WD]
American author
* Thompson, Eileen

Pan's Tutor
See Rabinowitz, Jerome

Pansey
See Reid, Esther

Panshin, Alexei 1940- [ESF]
American author
* Adams, Louis J. A. [joint pseudonym
with Joe Louis Hensley]

Pansy
See Alden, Isabella Macdonald

Pansy
See Donisthorpe, Ida Margaret Loder

Pant, Dandhu 1825?-1860 [HPPN]
Indian rebel
* Sahib, Nana

Pantagruel
See Henry II [or Henri]

Pantagruel, Gargantua
See Chetwood, William Rufus

Pantaleon, Jacques ?-1264 [WBD]
Pope
* Urban IV

Pantarch
See Andrews, Stephen Pearl

Pantenius, Theodor Hermann 1843-?
[IP]
German author
* Hermann, Theodor

Panther at the Plate
See Aaron, Henry Louis [Hank]

[The] Panther Girl
See Fitzpatrick, Margaret

Panting, Arnold Clement ?-1917 [MBF]
British author and editor
* Arnold, Clement

Panting, James Harwood 20th c. [MBF,
WWL]
British author
* Heathcote, Claud

Pantolabus, Ponce
See Huntingdon, John

Panurge
See Chauvin [or Caulvin?], Jean

Panurge
See Scott, [Sir] William [Lord Stowell]

Panurgus
See Henry VII

Panza, Sancho
See Hopkins, Harry Lloyd

Panzarella, Anthony John 1915- [BEW]
American producer and director
* Parella, Anthony

Panzer, Paul Wolfgang
See Panzerbeiter, Paul

Panzerbeiter, Paul 1872-1958
German-born actor
* Panzer, Paul Wolfgang

[El] Panzon [The Belly]
See Soto, Roberto

Panzram, Carl 1891-1930 [BLB]
American murderer
* Allen, Jack
* Baldwin, Jeff
* Copper John, II
* Davis, Jeff
* O'Leary, John
* Rhoades, Jefferson

Paolella, Alfred 1905- [PMJ, WWJ]
American composer and bandleader
* James, Freddy
* Powell, Teddy

Paoli, Antonio 1872-1946 [HPPN]
Puerto Rican opera singer
* [The] King of Tenors
* [The] Tenor of Kings

Paoli, Betty
See Glueck, Barbara Elisabeth

Paoli, Corsica
See Paoli, Pasquale de

Paoli, Pasquale de 1726-1807 [DNNF,
FFF, SN]
Corsican patriot
* Paoli, Corsica

Paolinelli, Rinaldo Angelo 1895- [BE]
American baseball player
* Pinelli, Babe
* Pinelli, Ralph Arthur

Paolo, [Fra]
See Sarpi, Pietro

Paolotti, John
See Wilson, Guthrie Edward

Paolotto, [Fra]
See Ghislandi, [Fra] Vittore

Pap
See Paprocki, Thomas

Pap
See Price, Sterling G.

Pap-Hatchet
See Lyly, John

[Il] Papa [The Pope]
See Greco, Michele

[Un] Papa
See Hetzel, Pierre Jules

Papa Bear Banks
See Banks, Earl

Papa Bear Halas
See Halas, George Stanley

Papa Charlie
See Davis, Charlie

Papa Charlie
See McCoy, Charles [Charlie]

Papa Charlie Jackson
See Jackson, Charlie

Papa Chittlins
See Moore, Alexander Herman

Papa Doc
See Duvalier, Francois

Papa G.
See Gilbert, Sam

Papa General
See Torrijos, Omar

Papa George
See Lightfoot, Alexander

Papa Henry Brown
See Brown, Henry

Papa Jac
See Assunto, Jacob

Papa Jack
See Laine, George Vitelle

Papa Joe
See Oliver, Joseph

Papa John
See Joseph, John

Papa John
See Phillips, John

Papa John Creach
See Creach, John

Papa Johnny Torrio
See Torrio, John [Johnny]

Papa la Violette
See Bonaparte, Napoleon

Papa Mutt Carey
See Carey, Thomas

Papa Snow White
See Page, Oran Thaddeus

Papa Tono
See Alix, Juan Antonio

Papadiamantopoulos, Iannis 1856-1910
[CD, EWL, HDM]
Greek-born poet, playwright, author
* Moreas, Jean

Papadimitriou, Theodoros 1931- [CAR]
Greek sculptor
* Theodoros

Papadopoulos, Epaminondes 1927?- [BI]
Greek painter
* Nonda

Papailler, Hubert 1916- [CW]
Haitian poet and author
* Maria Mour, Jean Hubert

Papaleo, Anthony 1928- [BEW, FC, IPA]
American actor
* Franciosa, Anthony [Tony]

Papaleo, William 1922- [BX, HPPN,
RBE]
American boxer
* [The] Old Master
* Pep, Willie
* Will o' the Wisp

Papandreou, Dimetrios 1891-1949 [BI]
Greek archbishop and regent
* Damaskinos

Papanicolaou, George 1883-1962
[HPPN]
Greek-American physician
* [The] Father of the Pap Smear Test

Paparella, Attilio 1874-1944 [BBD]
Italian conductor and composer
* Parelli, Attilio

Papareschi, Gregorio ?-1143 [WBD]
Pope
* Innocent II

Papaverius
See De Quincey, Thomas

Pape, D. L.
See Pape, Donna [Lugg]

[Le] Pape des Huguenots
See Mornay, Philippe de [Seigneur du
Plessis-Marly]

Pape, Donna [Lugg] 1930- [CA]
American author
* Pape, D. L.

[El] Papelero [The Paper Seller]
See Alvarado Luvianos, Victor

[The] Paper King
See Law, John

Paper Saving Pope
See Pope, Alexander

Paperito
See Jiminez, Marcos

[The] Paperknife
See Tullock, W. W.

[The] Papermaker's Papermaker
See Warren, James LeRoy [Lee]

[The] Paperwork Pedant
See Westphal, Siegfried

[The] Paphlagonian
See Michael IV

Papi, Boom Boom
See Papi, Donna

Papi, Donna 20th c. [HPPN]
American wrestler
* Papi, Boom Boom

Papillon
See Charriere, Henri

Papineau, Louis Joseph 1786-1871 [HN]
French-Canadian politician
* [The] Canadian O'Connell

Papini, Giovanni 1881-1956 [CAT]
Italian author
* Falco, Gian

Papinian
See Inglis, Charles

Papirius Cursor
See Whitefoord, Caleb

Papirius, Lucius 4th c. BC [WBD]
Roman general and politician
* Cursor

Papirofsky, Joseph 1921- [BEW, EMT,
HPPN, IPA]
American director and producer
* Papp, Joseph
* [The] Populist and Imperialist

Papish, Frank Richard 1917-1965 [BE]
American baseball player
* Papish, Pap

Papish, Pap
See Papish, Frank Richard

Papke, William Herman [Billy]
1886-1936 [BX, RBE]
American boxer
* [The] Illinois Thunderbolt
* [The] Thunderbolt

Papoulkas, Sotirios 1943- [OP]
Greek opera singer
* Papulkas, Soto

Papp, Joseph
See Papirofsky, Joseph

Pappa Yalla
See Washington, Isidoe

Pappadio, Andimo 1914-1976 [BI]
American racketeer
* Noto, Tony

Pappas, Angelos 1883- [SFL]
Author
* Pappazisis, Evangelos

Pappas, George Stephen 1930- [WD]
Australian author and educator
* Justificus

Pappas, Gimpy
See Pappas, Milt[on Steven]

Pappas, Milt[on Steven] 1939- [PB]
American baseball player
* [The] Golden Greek
* Pappas, Gimpy

Pappazisis, Evangelos
See Pappas, Angelos

Paprika
See Holmvik, Oyvind

Paprocki, Thomas 1901-1973 [WEC]
American cartoonist
* Pap

Papulkas, Soto
See Papoulkas, Sotirios

Papus
See Encausse, Gerard

Papworth, John Buonarotti ?-1847 [IP]
British architect and author
* J. P.

Paquirri
See Rivera Perez, Francisco

Parabellum
See Grautoff, Ferdinand [Heinrich]

Paracelsus
See Dahl, Ellen Dinesen

Paracelsus, Philippus Aureolus
See Von Hohenheim, Theophrastus
Bombastus

Paradise, Mary
See Eden, Dorothy Enid

Paragraph, Peter
See Adair, James Makittrick

Paragraph, Peter
See Faulkner, George

[The] Paraguayan Connection
See Ricord, Auguste

[The] Parakeet
See Fuentes, Rigoberto

Parallax
See Robotham, Samuel Birley

Parallelogram of Passion
See Evans, Marian

[A] Paralytic Quacksalver
See Harvey, Gabriel

Paramahansa
See Muktanada, Swami

[The] Paramount Wildcat
See Rainey, Gertrude Malissa Nix
[Pridgett]

Parans, Cato
See Heber, Richard

Parasara
See De Silva, David

[A] Parasite of Genius
See Walpole, Horatio [Fourth Earl of
Orford]

[The] Paratrooper Pet
See Kaumeyer, Dorothy

Parbury, Kathleen Ophir Theodora
1901- [ART]
British sculptor
* K. O. T. P.

Parcell, Norman H[owe] 20th c. [SFL,
WGT]
British author
* Fairleigh, Christopher
* Nicholson, John
* Percival, Norman

Pardee, C. W. 1885-1975 [FIR, SC]
American actor, rodeo performer, trainer
* Pardee, Doc

Pardee, Doc
See Pardee, C. W.

Pardee, Gabby
See Pardee, John P. [Jack]

Pardee, John P. [Jack] 1936-
American football player
* Pardee, Gabby

Pardon, George Frederick 1824-1884
[DEL, FFF, IP, NPS, PA]
British author and critic
* Crawley, [Captain] Rawdon
* G. F. P.
* Pastel
* Quiet, George
* Redgap
* Uncle George

Pare, Ambroise 1517-1590 [DEP, DNNS,
HN]
French surgeon
* [The] Father of French Surgery

Pareja, Juan de 1606?-1670 [WBD]
Spanish painter
* [El] Esclavo [The Slave]

Parejito [Little Smooth One]
See Lopez Parejo, Francisco

Parella, Anthony
See Panzarella, Anthony John

Parelli, Attilio
See Paparella, Attilio

[The] Parent of Canal Navigation
See Egerton, Francis

[The] Parent of English Verse
See Waller, Edmund

Parent-Desbarres, Pierre Francois 1798-?
[IP]
French author and bookseller
* Saint Sylvestre, P. D. de

Parenthenopeus Hereticus
See Gordon, William

Parentucelli [or da Sarzana], Tommaso
1397?-1455 [WBD]
Pope
* Nicholas V

Pares, Marion Stapylton 1914- [AW,
CA]
British author
* Campbell, Judith

Paret, Benny
See Paret, Bernardo

Paret, Bernardo 1937-1962 [RBE, WBC]
Cuban-born boxer
* Paret, Benny
* Paret, Kid

Paret, Kid
See Paret, Bernardo

Paretti, Tony 20th c. [BLB]
American underworld figure
* [The] Shoemaker

Parfait, Paul 1841-? [HPPN]
French journalist
* Scott, Richard

Parfect, Ca. 18th c. [IP]
British clergyman and author
* [A] Clergyman

Parfouru, Paul Desire 1843-1917 [BEW]
French producer and actor
* Porel, Paul

Pargeter, Edith Mary 1913- [AW, CA,
CC]
British author
* Peters, Ellis

Parham, Charles Valdez 1913- [DAM,
EJ, WWJ]
American jazz musician
* Parham, Truck

Parham, Hartzell Strathdene 1900-1943
[EJ, PMJ, WWJ]
American jazz musician
* Parham, Tiny

Parham, Robert Randall 1943- [CA]
American poet and writer
* Roberts, Rand

Parham, Tiny
See Parham, Hartzell Strathdene

Parham, Truck
See Parham, Charles Valdez

[A] Pariah
See Cornwallis, Caroline Frances

Pariani, Bill
See Pariani, Cino

Pariani, Cino 20th c. [BBH]
Soccer player
* Pariani, Bill

Paricciuoli, Walter 1917- [BBH]
American soccer player
* Peters, Wally

Paridel, Sir
See Fane, Mildmay

Parikh, Rasiklal Chhotalal 1897- [IAW]
Indian author
* Musikara

Parilli, Babe
See Parilli, Vito

Parilli, Vito 1930- [FB, SMG]
American football player
* Parilli, Babe

Parin, A. P. L.
See Faxon, Henry W.

Pario, James 20th c. [SG]
Boxer
* Bazzano, Tommy

Paris
See Hervey, John [Baron Hervey of Ickworth]

Paris, Comte de
See Orleans, Louis Philippe Albert d'

Paris, Dawn Evelyeen 1918- [F2, FC]
American actress
* O'Day, Dawn
* Shirley, Anne

Paris, Diacre
See Francois de Paris

Paris, Firmin
See Hudon, Maxime

Paris, Francois de 1690-1727 [WBD]
French theologian
* Paris, Diacre

Paris, John
See Ashton-Gwatkin, Frank Trelawny Arthur

Paris, John Ayrton 1785-1856 [IP, PA]
British physician and author
* [A] Physician

Paris, Manuel
See Conesa, Manuel R.

Parise, J. P.
See Parise, Jean Paul

Parise, Jean Paul 1941- [CEI, SMG]
Canadian-born hockey player
* Parise, J. P.
* Parise, Jeep

Parise, Jeep
See Parise, Jean Paul

Parish, Henry Headly 19th c. [IP]
British diplomat and author
* [An] Old Diplomatic Servant

Parish, Margaret Holt 1937- [HPPN]
American librarian and author
* Holt, Margaret

[A] Parish Priest
See Aitken, Robert

[A] Parish Priest
See Faber, Frederick William

[A] Parish Priest
See Scudamore, [Rev.] William Edward

Parish the Healer
See Parish, W. T.

Parish, Townsend
See Pietschmann, Richard John, III

Parish, W. T. 1873-1946 [EOP]
British spiritual healer
* Parish the Healer

[A] Parish Waywarden
See Liddell, Thomas

[A] Parishioner
See Devotion, [Rev.] Ebenezer

[A] Parishoner
See Willett, Richard

Parisi, Dandy Jack
See Parisi, Jack

Parisi, Jack 1900?-1983 [HPPN, TI 1-10-83]
American underworld figure
* [The] Dandy
* Parisi, Dandy Jack

[The] Parisian
See Charlton, Mary

Parisian Bob Caruthers
See Caruthers, Robert Lee

Parisot, Pierre 1697-1769 [FFF, SN]
French missionary
* Norbert, [Father]

Parisse, Louis Peter 1911-1956 [BE]
American baseball player
* Parisse, Tony

Parisse, Tony
See Parisse, Louis Peter

Park, Andrew 1808-1863 [IP]
Scottish poet
* Wilson, James

Park, Arthur 20th c. [HPPN]
American hobo
* [The] King of the Hobos
* Park, Slow Motion Shorty

[The] Park Avenue Hillbilly
See Shay, Dorothy

Park, Chan-Ki 1928- [IAW]
Korean author
* Pak, Chan-Ki

Park, Charles Carroll 1860-1931 [DNA]
American author
* Gray, Carl

Park, Chung Hee 1917-1979 [CA]
South Korean president
* Pak, Chong-Hui
* [The] Patriarch? [code name]
* Takagi, Masao

Park, D. U.
See Woods, Clee

Park, Elm
See Dunbar, Charles Stuart

Park, Fanny 1852-? [WWL]
British author
* Heslop, F.

Park, James Allan 1763-1838 [HFN, IP]
British author and barrister
* [A] Layman

Park, John 1775-1852 [IP]
American educator and journalist
* [A] Fellow Sufferer

Park, John James 1795-1833 [IP]
British barrister and author
* Eunomus

Park, Jordan [joint pseudonym with Frederik Pohl]
See Kornbluth, Cyril M.

Park, Jordan [joint pseudonym with Cyril M. Kornbluth]
See Pohl, Frederik

Park, Maeva
See Dobner, Maeva Park

Park, Slow Motion Shorty
See Park, Arthur

Park, Tongsun 20th c.
South Korean businessman
* [The] Asian Great Gatsby

Park, William Hallock 1863-1939 [HPPN]
American physician
* [The] Conqueror of Diphtheria

Parke, F. [PA]
British author
* [The] London Hermit

Parke, Harry
See Einstein, Harry

Parke, James 1782-1868 [IP]
British author
* J. P.

Parke, John 1754-1789 [HPPN, IP]
American poet and soldier
* [A] Native of America

Parker, Ace
See Parker, Clarence McKay

Parker, Adele
See Von Ohl, Adele

Parker, Admiral
See Parker, Richard

Parker, Anthony
See Tull, Anthony

Parker, Beatrice
See Huff, Tom Elmer

Parker, Bently
See Benjamin, Park

Parker, Bert
See Ellison, Harlan [Jay]

Parker, Big Jim
See Parker, Jim

Parker, Big Train
See Parker, Thomas [Tom]

Parker, Bill
See Parsons, William

Parker, Bird
See Parker, Charles Christopher, Jr.
[Charlie]

Parker, Bonnie 1911-1934 [BLB]
American murderer and robber
* Suicide Sal

Parker, Buddy
See Parker, Raymond Klein

Parker, Caroline
See Fenton, Mrs. Charles

Parker, Cecelia 1932?- [FC, HPPN, ITA, SW]
American actress
* Andy Hardy's Sister
* Parker, Suzy

Parker, Cecil
See Schwabe, Cecil

Parker, Charles Christopher, Jr.
[Charlie] 1920-1955 [BBD, EJ, PMJ]
American jazz musician
* Parker, Bird
* Parker, Yardbird

Parker, Clarence McKay 1913- [FB]
American football player
* Parker, Ace

Parker, Clarence Perkins 1893-1967
[BE]
American baseball player
* Parker, Pat

Parker, Cobra
See Parker, David Gene [Dave]

Parker, David Gene [Dave] 1951-
[IBW]
American baseball player
* Parker, Cobra

Parker, David L[ambert] 1935- [CA]
American author and filmmaker
* Parker, Dee

Parker, Dee
See Parker, David L[ambert]

Parker, Dixie
See Parker, Douglas Wooley

Parker, Doc
See Parker, Harley Park

Parker, Dom Anselm 1880-? [WWL]
British clergyman and writer
* Stanislaus, Edward

Parker, [Sister] Dominic
See Parker, Marion Dominica Hope

Parker, Dorothy
See Rothschild, Dorothy

Parker, Douglas Wooley 1895- [BE]
American baseball player
* Parker, Dixie

Parker, Edgar Rudolph Randolph
1872-1952 [HPPN]
Canadian dentist
* [The] Great Tooth Tycoon
* Parker, Painless

Parker, Edmund Kealoha 1931?-
American martial artist
* [The] Father of United States Karate

Parker, Elizabeth [Chandler] 1856-?
[FFF]
American author
* Chandler, Bessie

Parker, Ellis Howard 1872?-? [HPPN]
American police detective
* [The] Old Fox

Parker, Ely 1828-1897 [HPPN]
American soldier, tribal leader, engineer
* Donehogawa

Parker, Eric 1870-? [HPPN]
British author and journalist
* Cheviot of the Field

Parker, Fitzgerald Sale 1863-? [NAA]
American clergyman, author, editor
* Teche, L. A.

Parker, Francis James 1913- [PB]
American baseball player
* Francis, Charles
* Parker, Salty

Parker, Frank
See Ciccio, Frank

Parker, Frank
See Paikowski, Franciszek Andzej

Parker, Frederick 19th c. [HFN, IP]
British author
* Heinfetter, Herman

Parker, Gatling Gun
See Parker, John Henry

Parker, Gilbert
See Albrecht, Gilbert Parker

Parker, Harley Park 1874-1941 [BE]
American baseball player
* Parker, Doc

Parker, Helen F. [PA]
Author
* H. F. P.

Parker, Henry Taylor 1867-1934 [BEW]
American critic
* H. T. P.

Parker, Herman 1932-1971 [BWW, DAM]
American singer
* Parker, Junior
* Parker, Little Junior

Parker, Hershel 1935- [CA]
American educator and author
* Willis, Samuel

Parker, Horatio William 1863-1919
[HPPN]
American educator, choir leader, composer
* America's Most Celebrated 19th
Century Composer

Parker, Isaac 1838-1896 [BLB]
American jurist
* [The] Hanging Judge

Parker, Jack
See Ruwe, Horace A.

Parker, James
See Newby, George Eric

Parker, Jean
See Green, Mae

Parker, Jean
See Sharat Chandra, Gubbi Shankara
Chetty

Parker, Jean
See Zelinska, Luis Stephanie

Parker, Jim 1934- [IBW]
American football player
* Parker, Big Jim

Parker, Joel
See Parker, Joseph Lee

Parker, John 1875-? [WWL]
British author
* J. P.

Parker, John
See Wyatt, John

Parker, John Henry 1866-? [HPPN]
American army officer
* Parker, Gatling Gun

Parker, John William, Jr. 1918- [EJ, PMJ, WWJ]
American jazz musician
* Parker, Knocky

Parker, Joseph Lee 1952- [FR]
American football player
* Parker, Joel

Parker, Junior
See Parker, Herman

Parker, Knocky
See Parker, John William, Jr.

Parker, Lavernia Smith 1925?- [DF 4-
21-83]
American singer and musician
* [The] New Orleans Nightingale

Parker, Lefty
See Parker, Paul

Parker, Lew
See Jacobs, Austin Lewis

Parker, Linda 20th c. [ECM]
American country-western performer
* [The] Sunbonnet Girl

Parker, Little Junior
See Parker, Herman

Parker, Lou
See Parker, Lutrelle

Parker, Louise
See Oudin, Mrs. Eugene

Parker, Lutrelle 1924- [BA]
American government official
* Parker, Lou

Parker, M. E. Frances
See Bellerby, [Mary Eireen] Frances

Parker, Marion Dominica Hope 1914- [WD]
British poet, author, critic, translator
* Hope, Marion
* Mary Dominic, [Sister]
* Parker, [Sister] Dominic

Parker, Matthew 1504-1575
British clergyman
* Parker, Nosey

Parker, Maude
See Child, Mrs. Richard Washburn

Parker, Maurice Wesley 1939- [SMG]
American baseball player
* Parker, Tiger

Parker, Mrs. Benton [FFF]
Entertainer
* Buchanan, Virginia

Parker, Mrs. Harry D. [FFF]
Entertainer
* Blair, Lottie

Parker, Mrs. Richard E. [FFF]
Entertainer
* Dillon, Fannie

Parker, Murray 1896-1965 [SC]
American actor
* Uncle Murray

Parker, Nathaniel 1922- [IBW]
American actor
* [El] Shadow Negro

Parker, Nosey
See Parker, Matthew

Parker, Painless
See Parker, Edgar Rudolph Randolph

Parker, Pat
See Parker, Clarence Perkins

Parker, Paul 20th c. [BLB]
American bank robber
* Parker, Lefty

Parker, Paul
See Blunt, Paul

Parker, Paul William Giles 1956- [DC]
Rhodesian-born cricketer
* Parker, Polly
* Parker, Porky

Parker, Pinky
See Ciccio, Frank

Parker, Polly
See Parker, Paul William Giles

Parker, Porky
See Parker, Paul William Giles

Parker, Raymond Klein 1913-1982 [FB, HPPN, SMG]
American football coach
* Parker, Buddy
* [The] Top Football Coach in America

Parker, Richard ?-1797 [HN]
British seaman
* Parker, Admiral

Parker, Robert 20th c. [SMG]
American basketball player
* Parker, Sonny
* Sonny P.

Parker, Robert
See Boyd, Waldo T.

Parker, Robert LeRoy 1866-1937 [BLB, EWG, HPPN]
American bank and train robber
* Cassidy, Butch
* Cassidy, George
* Ingerfield
* Lowe, Jim
* Maxwell
* Phillips, William T.

Parker, Rosa Abbott [FFF, PA]
Author
* Abbott, Rosa

Parker, Salty
See Parker, Francis James

Parker, Samuel 1640-1688 [SN]
British author
* Bayes, Mr.
* Mitred Dulness

Parker, Samuel Dunn ?-1873 [HPPN]
American attorney
* [The] Attorney of the Commonwealth

Parker, Sarah 1824-? [PI]
Irish-born poet
* [The] Irish Girl

Parker, Seth
See Lord, Phillips Haynes

Parker, Sonny
See Parker, Robert

Parker, Suzy
See Parker, Cecelia

Parker, Theodore 1810-1860 [FFF, HPPN]
American clergyman and author
* Blodgett, Levi
* T. P.

Parker, Thomas [Tom] 20th c. [OBW]
American baseball player
* Parker, Big Train

Parker, Tiger
See Parker, Maurice Wesley

Parker, [Captain] Tom
See Van Kuijik, Andreas Cornelis

Parker, Tomcat
See Parker, Willie

Parker, Will S.
See Porter, William Sydney [Bill]

Parker, Willard 1800-1884 [HPPN]
American physician and educator
* [The] Conqueror of Appendicitis

Parker, Willard
See Van Eps, Worster

Parker, William Frederick 1860-1918 [CCL]
Canadian poet
* Spatha

Parker, Willie 20th c. [NBB]
American singer
* Parker, Tomcat

Parker, Yardbird
See Parker, Charles Christopher, Jr. [Charlie]

Parkes, David 19th c. [HPPN]
British author
* Shemaya, Ebn

Parkes, Frank Kobina 1932- [AW]
Ghanaian author
* Dompo, Kwesi

Parkes, James William 1896- [IAW]
British clergyman and author
* Hadham, John

Parkes, Lucas
See Harris, John [Wyndham Parkes Lucas] Beynon

Parkes, Terence 1927- [AW]
British cartoonist
* Larry

Parkes, William Theodore ?-1908? [PI]
Irish poet
* Bradey, Barney

Parkes, Wyndham
See Harris, John [Wyndham Parkes Lucas] Beynon

Parkhurst, Charles 1842-1933 [HPPN]
American clergyman and political reformer
* [The] Scourge of Tammany Hall

Parkinson, Cornelia M. 1925- [CA]
American author
* Taylor, Day [joint pseudonym with Sharon Salvato]

Parkinson, Donna Jones 1902-1965 [HPPN]
American actress
* Earl, Donna

Parkinson, Elizabeth 1882-1922 [DAM]
American singer
* Parkinson, Parkina

Parkinson, H. B.
See Parkinson, Henry Broughton

Parkinson, Henry Broughton 1884-1970
[BF]
British director
* Parkinson, H. B.

Parkinson, John 1567-1650 [HPPN]
British herbalist
* Botanicus Regius Primarius

Parkinson, Parkina
See Parkinson, Elizabeth

Parkinson, Roger 1939-1978 [CA]
British author
* Holden, Matthew

Parkinson-Fortescue, Chichester Samuel
See Fortescue, Chichester Samuel

Parkman, Chin
See Parkman, [Dr.] George

Parkman, Francis 1788-1852 [HPPN]
American clergyman
* F. P.

Parkman, Francis, Jr. 1823-1893
[HPPN]
American historian and author
* F. P., Jr.
* [The] Historian of the Wilderness

Parkman, [Dr.] George ?-1849 [HPPN]
American educator
* Parkman, Chin

Parkman, John 1813-1883 [HPPN]
American clergyman
* J. P.

Parks
See Price, Charles

Parks, Aunt Jane
See Parks, Jane

Parks, Bert
See Jacobson, Bert

Parks, Elizabeth Robins 1865?-1952
[HPPN]
American actress and author
* Raimond, C. E.
* Robins, Elizabeth

Parks, Georgina 20th c. [CCL]
Canadian author
* Gabrielle

Parks, Jane ?-1967 [HPPN]
American radio personality
* Parks, Aunt Jane

Parks, Larry
See Klausman, Samuel

Parks, Larry
See Lundigan, William

Parks, Louise 20th c. [IBW]
American dance troupe leader
* Mama Lu

Parks, Rose
American civil rights activist
* [The] Mother of the Civil Rights
  Movement

Parks, Slicker
See Parks, Vernon Henry

Parks, Vernon Henry 1895- [BE]
American baseball player
* Parks, Slicker

Parkyakarkus
See Einstein, Harry

Parkyakarkus, Nick
See Einstein, Harry

Parkyn, Walter A. 1862-? [WWL]
British author
* Homo

Parley, Peter
See Bennett, John

Parley, Peter
See Goodrich, Samuel Griswold

Parley, Peter
See Kettell, Samuel

Parley, Peter
See Martin, William

Parley, Peter
See Mogridge, George

Parley, Peter
See Tegg, William

[The] Parliamentarian
See Luce, Robert

[The] Parliamentary Pilot
See Robert, Henry M.

Parliamentary Procedure
See Cannon, Clarence

Parlin, John
See Graves, Charles Parlin

Parlin, John
See Graves, John Parlin

Parlo, Dita
See Kornstadt, Grethe Gerda

Parly, Ticho
See Christiansen, Ticho Parly Frederik

Parma, Clemens
See Menzel, Roderich

Parmagini, Antonio 20th c. [HPPN]
Italian-American racketeer
* Parmagini, Black Tony

Parmagini, Black Tony
See Parmagini, Antonio

[The] Parmegiano of Auctioneers
See Lochee, John

Parmelee, LeRoy Earl 1907- [BE]
American baseball player
* Parmelee, Tarzan

Parmelee, Tarzan
See Parmelee, LeRoy Earl

Parmeno
See Lopez Pinillos, Jose

Parmer, J. N.
See Parmer, Jess Norman

Parmer, Jess Norman 1925- [WYA]
American author
* Parmer, J. N.

[Il] Parmigianino [or Parmigiano]
See Mazzuoli [or Mazzola], Girolamo
Francesco Maria

Parnell, Babe
See Parnell, Frederick

Parnell, Charles Stewart 1846-1891
[DEP, DHA, DNNS]
Irish statesman
* [The] Uncrowned King of Ireland

Parnell, Dusty
See Parnell, Melvin Lloyd

Parnell, Fanny
See Parnell, Frances Isabel

Parnell, Frances Isabel 1854-1882 [DIL,
PI]
Irish poet
* Aleria
* Parnell, Fanny

Parnell, Francis
See Pragnell, Festus

Parnell, Frank [WGT]
Author
* Francis, Gregory [joint pseudonym
  with James (Murdoch) MacGregor]
* Richardson, Francis [joint pseudonym
  with L. E. Bartle]

Parnell, Frederick 20th c. [EF]
American football player
* Parnell, Babe

Parnell, Frederick Russell 1889-1973
[BMH]
British ventriloquist
* Carr, Russ

Parnell, [Sir] Henry Brooke 1776-1844
[HPPN]
British statesman
* [Un] Membre du Parlement
  d'Angleterre

Parnell, Keith
See Palmer, P. K.

Parnell, Marvelous Mel
See Parnell, Melvin Lloyd

Parnell, Melvin Lloyd 1922- [BE]
American baseball player
* Parnell, Dusty
* Parnell, Marvelous Mel

Parnell, Paul 1734?-1810 [SN]
British farmer
* Philpott, Toby

Parnell, Red
See Parnell, Roy

Parnell, Roy 20th c. [OBW]
American baseball player
* Parnell, Red

Parnell, Thomas Frederick 1862-1957
[BMH, HPPN]
British ventriloquist
* [The] Father of the Profession
* [The] Father of Variety
* Russell, Fred

Parnell, Val
See Parnell, Valentine Charles

Parnell, Valentine Charles 1894- [THR]
British theatrical manager
* Parnell, Val

Parnham, James Arthur 1894-1963 [BE]
American baseball player
* Parnham, Rube

Parnham, Rube
See Parnham, James Arthur

Parnis, Mollie
See Livingston, Mollie Parnis

Parodi, Alexandre 1901- [HPPN]
*French delegate to United Nations
Security Council*
* Monsieur X

**Paroisse-Pougin, Francois-Auguste
Arthur** 1834-1921 [BBD]
French author and music critic
* Pougin, Arthur

Parolini, Gianfranco 20th c. [FDG]
Italian director
* Kramer, Frank

Parr, George 1826-1891 [EC]
British cricketer
* [The] Lion of the North

Parr, Harriet 1837-? [DEL, FFF]
British author
* Lee, Holme

Parr, [Dr.] John Anthony
See Anthony, [Dr.] E.

Parr, Julian F. 20th c. [SFP]
Author
* Ragatzy, Anton

Parr, Lucy 1924- [CA, SAT]
American writer
* Carroll, Laura

Parr, Old
See Parr, Thomas

Parr, Olive Katharine 1874-1955 [BI]
British author
* Chase, Beatrice

Parr, Robert
See Gardner, Erle Stanley

Parr, Samuel 1747-1825 [DEL, DEP,
DNNF, NPS]
British scholar
* [The] Birmingham Doctor
* Johnson, Brummagem
* [The] Man With a Wig
* [The] Nazarite
* Phileleutherus Norfolciensis

Parr, Samuel (cont.)
* Philopatris Varvicensis
* [The] Whig Johnson

Parr, Thomas 1483?-1635 [DEP, DNNS,
RH]
British centenarian
* Parr, Old

Parra, Luis 20th c. [GS]
Spanish bullfighter
* [El] Jerezano [The Man from Jerez]

Parra Duenas, Augustin 1924- [GS]
Spanish bullfighter
* Parrita [Little Parra]

Parran
See Garlow, Clarence Joseph

Parrao [Spreading]
See Hernandez y Castro, Joaquin

Parrestiastes
See De Coetlogon, Charles Edward

Parreta
See Vazquez, Jose

Parrhasius 5th c. BC [DEP, DNNS,
FFF]
Greek painter
* [The] King of Painters
* [The] Prince of Painters

[The] Parricide
See Henry V [or Heinrich]

[The] Parricide
See John [or Johannes] of Swabia

Parris, Bob 1944- [NAD]
American civil rights organizer
* Moses, Bob

Parris, Buddy
See Parris, Wendall Alexander

Parris, John 1917- [HPPN]
British author
* Lascelles, Alison

Parris, Wendall Alexander 1911- [BA]
American educator
* Parris, Buddy

Parrish, C. H.
See Parrish, Charles Henry

Parrish, Charles Henry 1899- [BA]
American sociologist
* Parrish, C. H.

Parrish, Eugene
See Harding, Donald Edward

Parrish, Judy
See Donohue, Dorothy Howell

Parrish, [Emma] Kenyon 1849-? [NAA]
American writer
* Gamelyn
* McCurdy, Nancy

Parrish, Larry 1943-
American attorney
* Clean, Mr.
* [The] Memphis Heat

Parrish, Mary
See Cousins, Margaret

Parrish, Mary Frances
See Fisher, Mary Frances Kennedy

Parrish, Wendal
See Merrill, James Milford

Parrita [Little Parra]
See Parra Duenas, Augustin

Parrondo, Tomas 1857-1900 [GS]
Spanish bullfighter
* [El] Manchao [The Spotted One]

Parrot, William 1878-1952 [BMH]
British comedian and singer
* McIver, Jock
* O'Farrell, Talbot

Parrott, Charles 1893-1940 [JF]
American actor, comedian, director
* Chase, Charley

Parrott, George 1871-1900 [BLB, EWG,
HPPN]
American bandit
* Curry, Big Nose
* Curry, Flat Nose
* Curry, George L.
* Dilly, Tom

Parrott, James [Jimmie] 20th c. [JF]
American director
* Parrott, Paul

Parrott, Jiggs
See Parrott, Walter E.

Parrott, Michael Everett Arch 1954-
[SMG]
American baseball player
* [The] Birdman

Parrott, Paul
See Parrott, James [Jimmie]

Parrott, Tacky Tom
See Parrott, Thomas William [Tom]

Parrott, Thomas William [Tom]
1868-1932 [BE]
American baseball player
* Parrott, Tacky Tom

Parrott, Walter E. 1871-1898 [BE]
American baseball player
* Parrott, Jiggs

Parry, Albert 1901- [CA]
Russian-born American author
* Leclerc, Victor

Parry, David Harold 1868-1950 [MBF]
British author
* Blake, [Captain] Wilton
* Pike, Morton

Parry, [Sir] Edward Abbott 1863-1943
[HPPN]
British playwright
* Parry, Judge

Parry, Emma Louisa 19th c. [HPPN]
British author
* [An] American Student Girl

Parry, Hugh J[ones] 1916- [CA, WD, WW]
American author
* Cross, James

Parry, John ?-1782? [NPS]
* [The] Blind Harper

Parry, John 1776-1851 [BBD]
Welsh musician
* Bardd Alaw [Master of Song]

Parry, John
See Whelpton, [George] Eric

Parry, John Humphreys 1787-1825
[HFN]
Author
* Griffinhoof, Anthony

Parry, Judge
See Parry, [Sir] Edward Abbott

Parry, Michel Patrick 1947- [HFF, WGT]
British author
* Cassaba, Carlos
* Fury, Nick
* Lee, Steve
* Lovecraft, Linda
* Pendragon, Eric

Parry, Owen 20th c. [EF]
American football player
* Parry, Ox

Parry, Ox
See Parry, Owen

Parsee Merchant
See Moore, J. S.

Parsifal
See Curl, James Stevens

[The] Parson
See Mulford, Ralph

Parson B.
See Betty, [Rev.] Joseph

Parson Frank
See Jacox, Francis

Parson, Jiggs
See Parson, William Edwin

[The] Parson of the Islands
See Thomas, Joshua

Parson, William Edwin 1885-1967 [BE]
American baseball player
* Parson, Jiggs

Parsons, Anthony 1893-1963 [MBF]
British author
* Nicholls, Anthony

Parsons, B. 20th c. [MBF]
British author
* Hunt, Maurice
* Young, Warwick

Parsons, Baby
See Parsons, Harriet

Parsons, Benjamin ?-1851 [HPPN]
American author
* [A] Christian Layman

Parsons, Buzz
See Parsons, Les

Parsons, C. L. 20th c. [BBH]
American sports editor and basketball organization officer
* Parsons, Poss

Parsons, David 1915- [THR]
British actor
* Tree, David

Parsons, Dixie
See Parsons, Edward Dixon

Parsons, Edward 1900- [IAW]
British-born author
* Onlooker

Parsons, Edward Dixon 1916- [BE]
American baseball player
* Parsons, Dixie

Parsons, Elizabeth 1749-1807 [WBD]
British imposter
* [The] Cock Lane Ghost

Parsons, Elsie Worthington [Clews] 1875-1941 [DNA]
American author and anthropologist
* Main, John

[The] Parson's Emperor
See Charles IV [or Karl]

Parsons, Gale
See Parsons, Gamaliel Leroy, Jr.

Parsons, Gamaliel Leroy, Jr. 1921- [BA]
American physician
* Parsons, Gale

Parsons, Gram
See Connor, Cecil

Parsons, Harriet 20th c. [F1]
Actress
* Parsons, Baby

Parsons, Julia Warth 19th c. [HPPN]
American author
* Warth, Julian

Parsons, Les 1950- [AES]
Canadian soccer player
* Parsons, Buzz

Parsons, Long Tom
See Parsons, Thomas Anthony [Tom]

Parsons, Louella 1880?-1972 [HPPN]
American columnist
* [The] Dean of Gossip Columnists
* Lolly

Parsons, Louella O.
See Oettinger, Louella

Parsons, Patrick 1912- [FC]
British actor
* Holt, Patrick

Parsons, Poss
See Parsons, C. L.

Parsons, Reuben ?-1875 [BLB]
American gambler
* [The] Great American Faro Banker

Parsons [or Persons?], Robert 1546-1610 [FFF, PA, SN]
British missionary and author
* Crowbuck, Robert
* Doleman, Robert
* Howlett, John
* Philopater, Andreas
* [A] Proteus

Parsons, Smiling Bill
See Parsons, William [Billy]

Parsons, Terry 1931?-1985 [WP 2-11-85]
British singer
* Monro, Matt

Parsons, Theophilus 1750-1813 [HPPN, SN]
American jurist
* [The] Giant of the Law
* [A] Member of the Boston Society of the New Jerusalem

Parsons, Thomas Anthony [Tom] 1939- [BE]
American baseball player
* Parsons, Long Tom

Parsons, Thomas William 1819-1892 [SN]
American poet
* [The] Poet

Parsons, Tom
See MacPherson, Thomas George

Parsons, William [Billy] 1878-1919 [F1, SC]
American actor and producer
* Parsons, Smiling Bill

Parsons, William 1933- [HPPN]
American composer and singer
* Parker, Bill

Parsons, William B. 1859-1932 [HPPN]
American engineer
* [The] Father of the New York Subway

Parsons-Irwin, Maureen 1935- [ART]
British artist
* Mia

Parsonus Rusticus
See McDaniel, Samuel Walton

Partch, Virgil Franklin, II 1916-1984 [WEC]
American cartoonist
* VIP

Partee, W. B. [PA]
Author
* Nomistake

Partenheimer, Harold Philip 1891-1971 [BE]
American baseball player
* Partenheimer, Steve

Partenheimer, Party
See Partenheimer, Stanwood Wendell

Partenheimer, Stan
See Partenheimer, Stanwood Wendell

Partenheimer, Stanwood Wendell 1922-
[BE]
American baseball player
* Partenheimer, Party
* Partenheimer, Stan

Partenheimer, Steve
See Partenheimer, Harold Philip

Parthenia
See Mazzolari, Guiseppe Marione

[The] Parthenope of Naples
See Vida, Marco Girolamo

Partheusa
See Elizabeth I

Parthian
See Grimshaw, Roland William Wrigley

Particular, Pertinax
See Watkins, Tobias

Partington, Doris 1893-1953 [BEW]
British-born actress
* Lytton, Doris

Partington, F. H.
See Yoxall, Harry Waldo

Partington, Mrs.
See Avery, Samuel Putnam

Partington, Mrs.
See Smith, Sydney

Partington, Ruth
See Shillaber, Benjamin Penhallow

[The] Partisan of Independence
See Adams, John

[The] Partisan of the Unpopular
See Darrow, Clarence Seward

Parton, Sara Payson Willis 1811-1872
[DEL, HPPN, WBD]
American author
* F. F.
* Fern, Fanny

Partridge, Anthony
See Oppenheim, E[dward] Phillips

Partridge, [Sir] Bernard 1861-1945
[BEW, LC, WEC]
British actor, cartoonist, painter
* Gould, Bernard

Partridge, Edward Bellamy 1877-1960
[BI, SFL, WGT]
American author
* Bailey, Thomas

Partridge, Eric Honeywood 1894-1979
[IAW]
British literary critic and lexicographer
* Denison, Corrie
* Vigilans
* [The] Word King

Partridge, Fez
See Partridge, Martin David

Partridge, John
See Page, John

Partridge, Kathleen
See Wooderidge, Kathleen Mabel

Partridge, Martin David 1954- [DC]
British cricketer
* Partridge, Fez

Parulkumar
See Pal, Rudrendra Kumar

Parulski, George R[ichard], Jr. 1954-
[CA]
American author
* Brian, Alan B.
* Taylor, George

Parva Laus [Little Laud]
See Laud, William

Parviz
See Ghylichkhani, Parviz

Parviz
See Khosru II [or Chosroes]

Parvus
See Helphand, Alexander

Pary, C. C.
See Gilmore, Christopher Cook

Pas de Deux
See Ecevit, Bulent

[The] Pasadena Flash
See Freeman, [Dr.] David

Pascal, Andre
See Rothschild, [Baron] Henri De

Pascal, Blaise 1623-1662 [RH]
French philosopher
* Montalte, Louis de
* Thaumaturgus

Pascal, Gabor 1894-1954 [BEW]
Hungarian-born director
* Pascal, Gabriel

Pascal, Gabriel
See Pascal, Gabor

[The] Pascal of Germany
See Hardenberg, Friedrich von

Pascaline, Mademoiselle
See Muza, Irene

Pascarel
See Warner, B. Ellison

Paschal, Nancy
See Trotter, Grace V[iolet]

Paschal II
See Bieda, Ranieri Da

Paschal II
See Ranieri

Paschal III
See Guido of Crema

Pascin, Jules
See Pincas, Julius

Pascoe, Amy Bennet 20th c. [EG]
British golfer
* Pascoe, Polly

Pascoe, Polly
See Pascoe, Amy Bennet

Pascoe, [Rev.] William Gluyas 1838-?
[HPPN]
British clergyman
* [A] Wesleyan Minister

Pascual
See Garcia Sanchez, Jesus

Pascual, Camilo Alberto 1934- [BE]
Cuban-born baseball player
* [The] Little Potato

Pascual y Olmos, Jose 1870-1943 [GS]
Spanish bullfighter
* [El] Valenciano [The Valencian]

Pascudniak, Pascal
See Lupoff, Richard Allen [Dick]

Pasdeloup, Jean-Marie
See Durben, Wolfgang Johannes Maria

[Il] Pasellino
See Stefano, Francesoc di

Pasha, Khalil Sheriff [PA]
Author
* Fridolin, Major

Pasha, Mohammed
See Howe, William Wirt

Pashang, Adolph J. 1895?-1968 [HPPN]
American clergyman
* Hall, Marquette

Pashayan, Charles 20th c. [WP 2-25-85]
American politician
* Pashayan, Chip

Pashayan, Chip
See Pashayan, Charles

Pashenberry
See Pashnick, Larry

Pashko, Stanley 1913- [CA]
American author
* Norman, Steve
* Robbins, Tony

Pashkovsky, Theodore 1874-1950 [BI]
Russian prelate
* Theophilus

Pashnick, Larry 20th c.
American baseball player
* Pashenberry
* Quiz
* Quiznick

Pasic, Nikola 1845?-1926 [WBD]
Serbian and Yugoslav statesman
* [The] Old Fox of the Balkans

[La] Pasionaria
See Ibarruri, Dolores

Pasiphilus
See Busche, Hermann von dem

Paskandi, Geza 1933- [IAW]
Rumanian-born poet, playwright, translator
* Ovary, Geza

Paskert, Dode
See Paskert, George Henry

Paskert, George Henry 1881-1959 [AS, BE, PB]
American baseball player
* Paskert, Dode

Pasko, W. W.   [FFF]
American writer
* Seneca

Pasquale, Geraldine Ann 1947- [RO1]
American singer
* Stevens, Dodie

Pasqualina, [Sister]
See Lehnert, Josephine

Pasquier, Bach
See Pasquier, Charles Joseph

Pasquier, Charles Joseph 1881?-1953 [BEW, SC]
French actor
* Bach, Fernand
* Pasquier, Bach

Pasquil
See Nash [or Nashe?], Thomas

Pasquin
See Allen, Paul

Pasquin, Anthony [Tony]
See Williams, John

Pasquin, Paul
See Tytler, Alexander Fraser [Lord Woodhouselee]

Pasquino
See McLaughlin, James Fairfax

Pasquinus, Petrus, C. P. M.
See Comber, [Rev.] Thomas

Pass, Joe
See Passalaqua, Joseph Anthony

Passaglia, Carlo 1812-1887 [HPPN]
Italian politician and author
* Filalete, Ernesto

Passailaigue, Thomas E. 1932- [CA, SAT]
American writer, singer, composer
* Bethancourt, T. Ernesto
* Paisley, Tom

Passalaqua, Joseph Anthony 1929- [EJ7]
American jazz musician
* Pass, Joe

[Le] Passant
See Hervilly, Ernest d'

Passante, Dom
See Fearn, John Russell

Passarelli, Eduardo 1900- [WEF]
Italian director
* De Filippo, Eduardo

[Il] Passatore
See Bellino

Passeau, Claude William 1909- [BN]
American baseball player
* Passeau, Deacon

Passeau, Deacon
See Passeau, Claude William

Passel, Anne W[onders] 1918- [CA]
American poet and writer
* Wonders, Anne

Passeur, Steve
See Morin, Etienne

Passfield, Baron
See Webb, Sidney James

Passingham, Kenneth 20th c. [SFP]
Author
* Slack

[The] Passion Orator
See Andrews, John Urkhardt

[The] Passionate Pilgrim
See Van Gogh, Vincent

[The] Passionate Skeptic
See Russell, Bertrand Arthur William

Passkey [Secret Service code name]
See King, Leslie Lynch, Jr.

Passmore, Aileen Esther
See Griffiths, Aileen Esther

Passy, Colonel
See De Wavrin, Andre

Pastel
See Pardon, George Frederick

Pasternak, K. F.
See Kraszewski, Jozef Ignacy

Pasternak, Mike 1936- [BI, JL]
British disc jockey
* Rosko, Emperor
* Rosko, [Le] President

Pasteur, Louis 1822-1895 [HPPN]
French chemist and educator
* [The] Father of Bacteriology
* [The] Father of Vaccination
* [The] Founder of Preventive Medicine

Pastnor, Paul
See Morris, Charles Smith

Paston, George
See Symonds, Emily Morse

Paston, [Sir] William 1378-1444 [HPPN, WBD]
British historian and jurist
* [The] Good Judge

[The] Pastor
See Chase, [Rev.] Moses

[A] Pastor
See Clarke, [Rev.] Pitt

[A] Pastor
See Dallas, Alexander Robert Charles

[A] Pastor
See Day, [Rev.] Pliny Butts

[A] Pastor
See Dibdin, Thomas Frognall

[A] Pastor
See Fox, [Rev.] Thomas Bayley

[The] Pastor
See Furness, William Henry

[A] Pastor
See Goulburn, [Rev.] Edward Meyrick

[The] Pastor
See Hedge, Frederic Henry

Pastor
See Horton, Sanford Jackson

[A] Pastor
See Matthews, [Rev.] Isaac Constantine

[The] Pastor
See Morse, Jason

[The] Pastor
See Newell, William

[The] Pastor
See Quint, [Rev.] Alonzo Hall

[A] Pastor
See Sargent, [Rev.] John Turner

[A] Pastor
See Spencer, Ichabod Smith

[The] Pastor
See Spotswood, John Boswel

[A] Pastor
See Spring, Gardiner

[A] Pastor
See Stokes, John Whitley

[The] Pastor
See Winkley, [Rev.] Samuel Hobart

Pastor, Antonio [Tony] 1837-1908
American actor and theatre manager
* [The] Father of Vaudeville

[The] Pastor at Malden
See Emerson, [Rev.] Joseph

Pastor, Juan ?-1894 [GS]
Spanish bullfighter
* [El] Barbero [The Barber]

[The] Pastor of St. Paul's, Haggerstone
See Stone, William

[The] Pastor of the Poor
See Cox, James R.

[The] Pastor of the Westminister Congregational Society, Providence
See Woodbury, [Rev.] Augustus

Pastor, Tony
See Halsey, Harlan Page

Pastor, Tony
See Pestritto, Antonio

Pastor X
See Johnson, Merle Allison

Pastor y Duran, Vicente 1879-1966 [GS]
Spanish bullfighter
* [El] Chico de la Blusa [The Boy of the Blouse]

Pastora Gomez, Eden 1936?-
Nicaraguan guerrilla leader
* Zero, Commander

Pastoret [Shepherd]
See Ferrer y Rodriguez, Francisco

Pastorini, Dan
See Pastorini, Dante Anthony, Jr.

Pastorini, Dante Anthony, Jr. 1949-
[FR]
American football player
* Pastorini, Dan

Pastorini, Signor
See Walmesley, Charles

Pastorius, Francis Daniel 1651-1719
[SN]
First settler of Germantown, Pa.
* [The] Pennsylvania Pilgrim

[A] Pastor's Wife
See Cowdy, Cecilia

[A] Pastor's Wife
See Hubbell, Martha Stone

Pastrano, Wilfred Raleigh 1935- [BX, RBE]
American boxer
* Pastrano, Willie

Pastrano, Willie
See Pastrano, Wilfred Raleigh

Pastrone, Giovanni 1883-1959 [OCF]
Italian director and producer
* Fosco, Piero

Pastry, Mr.
See Hearne, Richard

Paszkiewicz, Mieczyslaw 1925- [IAW]
Polish-born author and poet
* Wizbor, Jakub Horczak

Pat
See Kenny, P. D.

Pat, Al
See Joseph, Alexander Callow

[The] Pat Boone of Country Music
See Anderson, Bill

Patanne, Maria
See LaPietra, Mary

Patatero [Potato Seller]
See Cosio Tesero, Alberto

Patch, Jim 20th c. [GW]
American rodeo performer
* Patch, Scrapiron

Patch, Sam[uel] ?-1829 [HPPN]
American high diver
* [The] Jersey Jumper
* [The] Jumping Hero
* [The] Mill Hand

Patch, Scrapiron
See Patch, Jim

Patch, Wally
See Vinicombe, Walter

Patchett, M. E.
See Patchett, Mary Osborne Elwyn

Patchett, Mary Osborne Elwyn 1897-
[SFL, TCC]
Australian author
* Bruce, David
* Patchett, M. E.

Patchin, Patch
See Patchin, Steven Earl

Patchin, Steven Earl 1950- [BR]
American baseball player
* Patchin, Patch

Patek, Freddie Joe 1944- [BE, PB]
American baseball player
* [The] Flea
* Patek, Midge
* Patek, Moochie

Patek, Midge
See Patek, Freddie Joe

Patek, Moochie
See Patek, Freddie Joe

Patel, Dip
See Patel, Dipak Narshi

Patel, Dipak Narshi 1958- [DC]
Kenyan-born cricketer
* Patel, Dip
* Patel, Dipstick

Patel, Dipstick
See Patel, Dipak Narshi

Patelin
See Leclerc du Tremblay, Francois

Pateman, Kim
See Levin, Kim

Patenaude, Edgar Arnold 1949- [HR, SMG]
Canadian-born hockey player
* Patenaude, Rusty

Patenaude, Rusty
See Patenaude, Edgar Arnold

Patenotre, Jules
See Des Noyers, Jules Patenotre

[The] Patentee
See Shaw, [Rev.] Oliver Abbott

Pater Bursae Londoniensis
See Houblon, James

Pater, Elias
See Friedman, Jacob Horace

Pater Patrum
See Gregory of Nyssa

Pater, [Philip] Roger
See Hudleston, Gilbert Roger

Paterfamilias
See Higgins, Matthew James

Paterfamilias
See Tupper, Martin Farquhar

Paterson, A. B.
See Paterson, Andrew Barton

Paterson, Andrew Barton 1864-1941
[LC, WWL]
Australian songwriter and author
* [The] Banjo
* Paterson, A. B.
* Paterson, Banjo

Paterson, Anne
See Einselen, Anne Frances

Paterson, Banjo
See Paterson, Andrew Barton

Paterson, Huntley
See Ludovici, Anthony M[ario]

Paterson, Jackie 1920-1966 [WBC]
Scottish boxer
* Paterson, Li'l Jackie
* [The] Swattin' Scot

Paterson, James [NPS]
Author
* James, Croak

Paterson, Judith
See Jones, Judith Paterson

Paterson, Li'l Jackie
See Paterson, Jackie

Paterson, Paul 19th c. [PA]
Author
* Playfair, Hugo

Paterson, Robert 1715-1801 [HPPN, SN]
Scottish stonecutter
* Old Mortality

Paterson, Samuel 1728-1802 [NPS]
Author
* Coriat Junior

Paterson, William 1658-1719 [HPPN]
Scottish banker
* [The] Father of the Bank of England
* Medway, Lewis

Paterson, William 1745-1806 [HPPN]
Irish-American statesman, attorney, jurist
* [The] Father of the New Jersey Plan

Paterson, William 19th c. [HPPN]
British army officer
* [An] Amateur

Paterson, William Romaine 1870-?
[LAO]
Scottish-born author
* Swift, Benjamin

Pathe, Charles 1863-1957 [HPPN]
French film pioneer
* [The] Father of the Newsreel

[The] Pathfinder
See Fremont, John Charles

[The] Pathfinder of San Juan
See Mears, Otto

[The] Pathfinder of the Field
See Dear, H. C.

[The] Pathfinder of the Seas
See Maury, Matthew Fontaine

Patience
See Foe, Daniel

[The] Patient
See Albert IV

Patin, Guy 1601?-1672 [SN]
French physician
* [The] Rabelaisian Doctor

Patino, Simon Iturri 1863?-1947 [DF 4.
24-83, HPPN]
Bolivian industrialist and diplomat
* [The] Bolivian Tin King
* [The] Tin Hermit
* [The] Tin King

Patman, Anti Chain Store
See Patman, Wright

Patman, Wright 1893- [HPPN]
American politician
* [The] Father of the Bonus
* Patman, Anti Chain Store

Patmore, Coventry K. Dighton 1823-?
[PA]
Author
* [The] Unknown Eros

Paton, Emilie [PA]
Author
* Rozier, Jacques

Paton, [Sir Joseph] Noel [PA]
Scottish author and painter
* Strivelyne, Elsie

Paton Walsh, Gillian Honoinne Mary
1937?- [AW, SAT, TCC]
British author
* Paton Walsh, Jill

Paton Walsh, Jill
See Paton Walsh, Gillian Honoinne
Mary

Patriarca, Raymond L. S. 1908-
[HPPN]
American underworld figure
* New England's Mafia Boss

[The] Patriarch? [code name]
See Park, Chung Hee

[The] Patriarch of Airships
See Eckener, Hugo

[The] Patriarch of Barbizon
See Millet, Jean Francois

[The] Patriarch of Columbia
See Taylor, Thomas

[The] Patriarch of Dorchester
See White, John

[The] Patriarch of English Learning
See Grocyn, William

[The] Patriarch of Ferney
See Arouet, Francois Marie

[The] Patriarch of Harmony
See Porpora, Nicholas

[The] Patriarch of New England
See Cotton, John

[The] Patriarch of Shifters
See Greene, Robert

[The] Patriarch of the Hills
See Crawford, Abel

[The] Patriarch of the Indians
See Mayhew, Thomas

[The] Patriarch of the Mountains
See Crawford, Abel

[The] Patriarch of the New England
Clergy
See Nott, Samuel

[The] Patriarch of the Spanish Theater
See Encina [or Enzina], Juan Del

[The] Patriarch of Three Rivers
See Fall, Albert Bacon

Patrice, Ann
See Galbraith, Georgie Starbuck

[A] Patrician
See Hudson, Edward

[The] Patrician of Rome
See Pepin III

Patrician of the Romans
See Pepin III

Patricius
See Adler, Philip

Patricius
See Coen, John

Patricius
See Geoghigan, R.

Patricius and Magister Militum
See Theodoric

Patrick 389?-461? [DNNF, DNNS, FFF,
HPPN]
Saint
* [The] Apostle of Ireland
* Succat

Patrick
See Byrne, John [Patrick]

Patrick, [Father]
See Cummins, John Thomas Benedict

Patrick, [Brother] Benilde
See Feeney, Gerard Martin

Patrick, Diana
See Wilson, Desemea

Patrick, Frederick Murray 1916- [CEI,
FHE]
Canadian-born hockey player
* Patrick, Muzz

Patrick, Gail
See Fitzpatrick, Margaret

Patrick, Gilbert 20th c. [BBH]
Jockey
* Gilpatrick

[The] Patrick Henry of New England
See Phillips, Wendell

[The] Patrick Henry of the Philippines
See Quezon y Molina, Manuel Luis

Patrick, Jimmy
See Vizzini, Sal[vatore]

Patrick, John
See Avallone, Michael [Angelo], Jr.

Patrick, John
See Christ, Ronald John

Patrick, John
See Goggan, John Patrick

Patrick, Johnstone G[illespie] 1918-
[CA]
Scottish-born clergyman and author
* Forward, Luke
* Star Man's Padre

Patrick, Keats
See Karig, Walter

Patrick, Leal
See Stone, Patti

Patrick, Lester 1883-1960 [FHE]
Canadian-born hockey player
* Hockey, Mr.
* [The] Silver Fox

Patrick, Lilian 1889?-1962 [BEW]
British theatrical performer
* Diamond, Lillian

Patrick, Lilian
See Keogh, Lilian Gilmore

Patrick, Marion 1940- [ART]
British painter
* M. P.

Patrick, Max
See McCormack, James

Patrick, Muzz
See Patrick, Frederick Murray

Patrick, Nigel
See Wemyss, Nigel

Patrick of the King's Chekar Maister
See Tytler, Patrick Fraser

Patrick, Q. [joint pseudonym with
Richard Wilson Webb]
See Aswell, Mary Louise

Patrick, Q. [joint pseudonym with
Richard Wilson Webb]
See Kelly, Martha Mott [Patsy]

Patrick, Q. [joint pseudonym with Mary
L. Aswell, Martha Kelly, and Hugh
Wheeler]
See Webb, Richard Wilson

Patrick, Q. [joint pseudonym with
Richard Wilson Webb]
See Wheeler, Hugh Callingham

Patrick, Ted 1930-
*American "deprogrammer" of religious
cultists*
* Black Lightning
* Black Satan

Patricola
See Toland, Junius Janus

Patricola, [Miss] Isabelle
See Morris, Isabelle Patricola

Patridge, S. W.   [PA]
Author
* S. W. P.

[A] Patriot
See Guy, L.

[The] Patriot
See Russell, W[illiam] Clark

[The] Patriot Artist
See Trumbull, John

[The] Patriot Financier
See Morris, Robert

[The] Patriot for Freedom
See Zenger, John Peter

[The] Patriot King
See George III

[The] Patriot King
See St. John, Henry

[The] Patriot of Humanity
See Grattan, Henry

[The] Patriot Printer of 1776
See Bradford, William

[The] Patriot Sculptor
See Mestrovic, Ivan

[A] Patriotic Englishman
See Russell, W. P.

Patris, Louis
See Patsouras, Louis

Patritio
See Godolphin, Sidney

[The] Patron
See Starr, George

[The] Patron and Poet of the Restoration
See Sackville, Charles [Sixth Earl of Dorset]

[The] Patron and Poet of the Restoration
See Sackville, Charles [Sixth Earl of Dorset]

[The] Patron of All Teachers
See Lasalle, Jean Baptiste de

[The] Patron of the Fine Arts
See Medici, Lorenzo de

[The] Patron Saint of American Orchards
See Chapman, John

[The] Patron Saint of Courtesans
See Du Plessis, Marie [Rose Alphonsine Plessis]

[The] Patron Saint of Queens
See Elizabeth

[The] Patron Saint of Smiths and Artists
See Eloi [or Eligius]

[The] Patron Saint of the Haight-Ashbury
See Harris, Leon Preston

[The] Patron Saint of Wuerzburg
See Kilian

[The] Patroon
See Van Rensselaer, Stephen

Patry, M. 20th c.   [WBD]
British author
* Williams, Patry [joint pseudonym with D. Williams]

Patsauq, Markoosie 1942-   [CA]
Canadian author
* Markoosie

Patsouras, Louis 1931-   [CA]
American historian and author
* Patris, Louis

Patston, Doris
See Sheehan, Doris

Patsy
See Sayers, Arthur Bond

Patsy, Carolina Petty
See Cobbold, Elizabeth Knipe Clarke

Patt, Babe
See Patt, Maurice

Patt, Frank 1928-   [BWW]
American singer
* Honeyboy

Patt, Maurice 20th c.   [EJS]
American football player
* Patt, Babe

Patte, Harold 20th c.
American politician
* Patte, Porque

Patte, Porque
See Patte, Harold

Pattee, David E. 20th c.   [SFP]
Author
* Davis, Pat

Patten, Case L. 1876-1935   [BE]
American baseball player
* Patten, Casey

Patten, Casey
See Patten, Case L.

Patten, Clinton A. 20th c.   [WGT]
Author
* Rock, James

Patten, Edward Roy 1939-   [BA]
American entertainer
* Cousin Eds

Patten, George Washington 1808-1882
[HPPN]
American poet and soldier
* [The] Poet Laureate of the Army

Patten, Gilbert [or Gil]
See Patten, William George

Patten, J. Alexander 19th c.   [WGT]
Author
* Cobb, Clayton W.

Patten, Lewis B[yford] 1915-1981   [CA]
American author
* Ford, Lewis B.

Patten, William George 1866-1945
[HPPN, TC, WGT, WW]
American author
* Bell, Emerson
* Bellwood, Herbert
* Dangerfield, Harry
* MacLaren, Gordon
* Patten, Gilbert [or Gil]
* Patten, Wyoming Bill
* St. Dare, Julian
* Standish, Burt L.
* Wilder, William West

Patten, Wyoming Bill
See Patten, William George

Patterson, Anna Eliza 1882?-?   [HPPN]
American chorus girl
* Becker, Mrs. Jacob
* [The] Floradora Sweetheart
* Martin, Anne E.
* Martin, Mrs. Leon Gaines
* Patterson, Nan
* Randolph, Nan E.

Patterson, Anne Virginia [Sharpe]
1841-1913   [BI]
American journalist
* Gaines, Garry

Patterson, Arthur E. 20th c.   [SMG]
American baseball executive
* Patterson, Red

Patterson, Arthur W. 1888-   [WWL]
British author
* Davidson, Wilder Bristol

Patterson, Charlotte [Buist] 1942-   [CA]
American author
* Buist, Charlotte

Patterson, Cissie
See Patterson, Eleanor Medill

Patterson, Claude, Jr. 1925-1972   [BBH]
American bowler
* Patterson, Pat

Patterson, Daryl Alan 1943-   [SMG]
American baseball player
* Patterson, Pat

Patterson, Eleanor Medill 1884-1948
[HPPN, WBD]
American journalist and author
* Gizycka, Eleanor M.
* Patterson, Cissie

Patterson, Elmer Calvin 1888-1975   [SC]
American actor
* Patterson, Hank

Patterson, Hal 20th c.   [CFH]
Canadian football player
* Prince Hal

Patterson, Hank
See Patterson, Elmer Calvin

Patterson, Harry 1929-   [AW, CA, WD]
British author
* Fallon, Martin
* Graham, James
* Higgins, Jack
* Marlowe, Hugh

Patterson, Jane
See Britton, Mattie Lula Cooper

Patterson, Jim
See Longley, William Preston

Patterson, Jimmy Dale 1935- [CWG, DAM]
American singer and songwriter
* Patterson, Pat

Patterson, John 1856-1936 [BMH]
Scottish-born animal trainer
* Duncan, Professor

Patterson, John J. 1843-1920 [HPPN]
American business executive
* [The] Chief
* [The] Father of Scientific Salesmanship
* [The] Father of the Thief Catcher

Patterson, John W. 20th c. [OBW]
American baseball player
* Patterson, Pat

Patterson, Joseph Medill 1879-1946 [HPPN]
American newspaper publisher
* [The] Father of the Tabloid

Patterson, Lila
See Rainey, Gertrude Malissa Nix [Pridgett]

Patterson, Margaret
See Grant, Maude Margaret

Patterson, Nan
See Patterson, Anna Eliza

Patterson, Olive
See Rowland, Donald Sydney

Patterson, Ottilie
See Barber, Anna-Ottilie Patterson

Patterson, Pat
See Patterson, Claude, Jr.

Patterson, Pat
See Patterson, Daryl Alan

Patterson, Pat
See Patterson, Jimmy Dale

Patterson, Pat
See Patterson, John W.

Patterson, Pat
See Patterson, William Jennings Bryan

Patterson, Paula
See Holland, Margaret T.

Patterson, Peter 1932- [BI, WD]
British playwright
* Terson, Peter

Patterson, Red
See Patterson, Arthur E.

Patterson, Roy Lewis 1876-1953 [BE]
American baseball player
* [The] Boy Wonder

Patterson, Sarah 20th c. [IBW]
American boxing manager
* Patterson, Tiny

Patterson, Sheila 20th c. [IBW]
American basketball player
* Patterson, Too Tall

Patterson, Tiny
See Patterson, Sarah

Patterson, Too Tall
See Patterson, Sheila

Patterson, Troy
See Corvino, Ettore

Patterson, Vance 20th c. [BWW]
American musician
* Piano Red

Patterson, Virginia [Sharpe] 1841-1913 [DNA]
American author and journalist
* Gaines, Garry

Patterson, William Jennings Bryan 1901- [BE]
American baseball player
* Patterson, Pat

Patteson, Coley
See Patteson, John Coleridge

Patteson, John Coleridge 1827-1871 [HPPN]
New Zealand clergyman
* [The] Missionary Bishop of Melanesia
* Patteson, Coley

Patti, Adela Juana Maria 1843-1919 [PA]
Spanish-born opera singer
* Patti, Adelina

Patti, Adelina
See Patti, Adela Juana Maria

Patti, Carlotta
See De Muenck, Carlotta Patti

Pattie, Joseph 1856-1931 [HPPN]
American actor
* Pond, Charles

Pattieson, Peter
See Scott, [Sir] Walter

Pattin, Duck
See Pattin, Martin William

Pattin, Martin William 1943- [SMG]
American baseball player
* Pattin, Duck

Pattinson, Nancy Evelyn 20th c. [AW]
British author
* Asquith, Nan

Pattison, Dorothy Wyndlow 1832-1878 [PA, WBD]
British philanthropist
* Sister Dora

Patton, Big John
See Patton, John

Patton, Billy Joe 1922- [HPPN]
American golfer
* Unpredictable, Mr.

Patton, Charles H. 1901?-1962 [BEW]
American actor
* Sheldon, Jerry

Patton, Charley 1887-1934 [BWW]
American singer
* [The] Masked Marvel
* Peters, Charley

Patton, Cliff
See Patton, John

Patton, Frank
See Palmer, Raymond A[rthur]

Patton, Frank [house pseudonym]
See Shaver, Richard S[harpe]

Patton, Fred 1911- [IAW]
American producer and scriptwriter
* Guinn, Pat

Patton, Gene 20th c.
American television personality
* Gene Gene the Dancing Machine

Patton, George Smith, Jr. 1885-1945 [CND]
American military leader
* Old Blood and Guts

Patton, James Blythe 19th c. [NPS]
Author
* White, Edmund

Patton, John 1936- [DAM]
American musician
* Patton, Big John

Patton, John 20th c. [EF]
American football player
* Patton, Cliff

Patton, John 20th c. [PHM]
American underworld figure
* [The] Boy Mayor

Patton, Marion
See Waldron, Marion Patton

Patton's Peer
See Abrams, Creighton Williams

Patty, Budge
See Patty, Edward John

Patty, Edward John 1924?- [BI]
American tennis player
* Patty, Budge

Paturi, Felix R.
See Mindt, Heinz R.

Patyn, Ann
See Carli, Audrey

Patyn, William 1395?-1486 [WBD]
British prelate
* Waynflete [or Wainfleet], William of

Paufichet, Jules 1883?-1951 [FC, OCF, WEF]
French actor
* Berry, Jules

Pauker, John 1920- [CA]
Hungarian-born author and poet
* Griffiths, Robert L., III
* Ordway, Roger
* Rowley, Thomas
* Somes, Jethro

Pauker, Ted
See Conquest, [George] Robert [Acworth]

Paul
See Delaroche, [Hippolyte] Paul

Paul, [Father]
See Dhorme, Edouard

Paul [code name used during World War II]
See Dourlein, Pieter

Paul
See Granger, [Rev.] Arturus

Paul
See Hildebrand, Ray

Paul [code name used during World War II]
See Kiffer, Raoul

Paul, [Father]
See Sarpi, Pietro

Paul, [Brother]
See Sarpi, Pietro

Paul
See Saul of Tarsus

Paul, [Brother]
See Scanlan, Peter E.

Paul
See Scott, [Sir] Walter

Paul, Adrian
See McGeoch, Andrew Jackson

Paul, Arthur Stuart 1943- [CEI]
Canadian-born hockey player
* Paul, Butch

Paul, Auren
See Uris, Auren

Paul, Betty
See Percheron, Betty

Paul, Billy
See Williams, Paul

Paul, Bonnie Ann 1941- [BEW]
American actress, singer, dancer
* Scott, Bonnie

Paul, Butch
See Paul, Arthur Stuart

Paul, Cedar
See Davenport, Gertrude Mary

Paul, Cedar
See Paul, Gertrude Mary Davenport

Paul, Charles Kegan 1828-1902 [DEA]
British author and clergyman
* C. K. P.

Paul, Daniel
See Kessel, Lipmann

Paul, Elizabeth
See Crow, Donna Fletcher

Paul, Elliot Harold 1891-1958 [CC, WW]
American author and journalist
* Rutledge, Brett

Paul, Emily
See Eicher, [Ethel] Elizabeth

Paul, Ernest
See Focke, Ernest Paul Walter

Paul, F. W.
See Fairman, Paul W.

Paul, Fritz 1893-1962 [DFM]
German film set designer
* Herlth, Robert

Paul, Genay
See Webster, Ester Luise

Paul, Gertrude Mary Davenport 20th c.
[HPPN]
British translator
* Paul, Cedar

Paul, Hugo
See Litwinsky, Paul

Paul, James
See Kocsis, James C.

Paul James Francis, [Father]
See Wattson, Lewis Thomas

Paul, John 1747-1792 [HPPN, SN, WBD]
American naval officer
* [The] Bayard of the Sea
* [The] Founder of the American Navy
* Gray
* Jones, John Paul
* [Le] Prince Burliabled

Paul, John
See Webb, Charles Henry

Paul Jones of the South
See Semmes, Raphael

Paul, Judith Edison 1939- [CA]
American author
* Edison, Judith

Paul, Les
See Polfus, Lester

Paul, Lyn
See Belcher, Lynda Susan

Paul, M. B.
See Paul, Morrison Bloomfield

Paul, Marco
See Abbot, Jacob

Paul, Maury Henry Biddle 1890-1942
[HPPN]
American journalist and society editor
* Knickerbocker, Cholly

Paul, Melvin 1962?-
American boxer
* [The] Tank

Paul, Morrison Bloomfield 20th c.
[ITA]
Canadian-born director and cameraman
* Paul, M. B.

Paul of Aegineta
See Paulus Aegineta

Paul of the Cross
See Danei, Paolo Francesco

Paul of Thebes 230?-343? [HPPN, WBD]
Saint
* [The] Founder of Monasticism
* [The] Hermit

Paul of Venice
See Sarpi, Pietro

[The] Paul Revere of Ecology
See Commoner, Barry

Paul, Richard
See Wurst, Richard Paul

Paul, Robert
See Abelson, Robert

Paul, Robert
See Roberts, John G[aither]

Paul, Sheri
See Resnick, Sylvia [Safran]

Paul, Shorty
See Paul, [Dr.] William D.

Paul, Stefanie [or Taffy?] 1942- [HT]
American actress
* Powers, Stefanie

Paul the Aged
See Whitehead, Paul

Paul the Deacon
See Paulus, Diaconus

Paul, William
See Eicher, [Ethel] Elizabeth

Paul, [Dr.] William D. 1900?-1977
[HPPN]
American physician and inventor
* Paul, Shorty

Paul I 1754-1801 [DF 7-26-83, HPPN]
Czar of Russia
* [The] Mad Czar

Paul II
See Barbo, Pietro

Paul III
See Farnese, Alessandro

Paul IV
See Caraffa, Giovanni Pietro

Paul V
See Borghese, Camillo

Paul VI
See Montini, Giovanni Battista Enrico Antonio Maria

Paula
See Jackson, Jill

Paulding, Frederick
See Dodge, Frederick

Paulding, James Kirke 1778-1860 [DEL, FFF, HPPN, NPS, PA, WGT]
American author and poet
* Bull-us, Hector
* [A] Doubtful Gentleman

Paulding, James Kirke (cont.)
* Fairlamb, Sampson
* Langstaff, Launcelot [joint pseudonym with Washington Irving and William Irving]
* [A] New England Man
* Oldstyle, Oliver
* Oudenarde, Dominie Nicholas Aegidius
* Scott, [Sir] Walter
* Tickler, Timothy

Paulet, Harry 1719-1794 [NPS]
Eleventh Marquis of Winchester
* Sternpost, Admiral

Paulet, John 1598-1675 [WBD]
Fifth Marquis of Winchester
* [The] Great Loyalist

Paulet, Mlle. 17th c. [HN]
Friend of King Henry IV of France
* [La] Lionne

Pauli, Wolfgang 1900-1958 [HPPN]
Austrian-American physicist
* [The] Discoverer of the Exclusion Principle

Paulin, Doc
See Paulin, Ernest

Paulin, Ernest 1902?- [NOJ]
American jazz musician
* Paulin, Doc

Paulinetti, Professor
See Thurber, Philip Henry

Paulinus
See Priestley, Joseph

Paull, Harry Major 1854-? [MBF]
British author
* Blake, Paul

Paull, M. A.
See Ripley, Mrs. John

Paull, Minnie E. [Kenney] 1859-1895 [DNA]
American author
* Clifford, Ella

Paulo the Magic Clown
See Klingler, Paul

Paulsen, Gil
See Paulsen, Guilford Paul Hans

Paulsen, Guilford Paul Hans 1902- [BE]
American baseball player
* Paulsen, Gil

Paulson, Jack
See Jackson, C[aary] Paul

Paulson, John W. 1889-1952 [HPPN]
American actor
* Reynolds, Jack

Paultz, Billy 20th c.
American basketball player
* [The] Whopper

Paulus Aegineta 7th c. [SN]
Greek physician
* [The] Father of Obstetric Surgery
* Paul of Aegineta

Paulus de Santa Maria
See Halevi, Solomon

Paulus, Diaconus 8th c. [HPPN]
Lombard historian and monk
* Paul the Deacon

Paulus, Jan
See Malloch, George Reston

Paulus, Lucius Aemilius 3rd c. BC [HPPN]
Roman army officer
* Macedonicus

Paulus Servita
See Sarpi, Pietro

Paulus Venetus
See Sarpi, Pietro

Pauly, Rosa
See Pollak, Rose

Paumier, Alfred
See Hodgson, Alfred

Paun, Maggie
See Voysey, Margaret

Pauper et Ignotus
See Thatcher, John Wells

[The] Pausanias of Britain
See Camden, William

Pautuxie
See Davies, Mary Carolyn

[Le] Pauvre Diable
See Freron, Elie-Catherine

Pauw, Cornelis van 1739-1799 [HPPN]
Dutch author
* M. de P.

Pavageau, Alcide 1888-1969 [EJ, WWJ]
American jazz musician
* Pavageau, Slow Drag

Pavageau, Slow Drag
See Pavageau, Alcide

Pavan, Marisa
See Pierangeli, Marisa

Pavarotti, Luciano 1935- [MS]
Italian-born opera singer
* King of the High C's

Pavelich, Blackie
See Pavelich, Martin Nicholas [Marty]

Pavelich, Martin Nicholas [Marty] 1927- [FHE]
Canadian-born hockey player
* Pavelich, Blackie

Paveskovich, John Michael 1919- [BE]
American baseball player and manager
* Pesky, Johnny
* Pesky, Needlenose

Pavey, Don 1922- [CA]
British artist and author
* Adair, Jack

Pavia, Joe
See Nerone, Giuseppe

Pavia y Alburquerque, Manuel 1828?-1895 [DHA]
Spanish army officer
* [The] Dictator of a Day

Pavius
See Pouw, Pietro

Pavlenko, Petr Andreevich 1899-1951 [SFL]
Author
* Pavlenko, Piotr

Pavlenko, Piotr
See Pavlenko, Petr Andreevich

Pavletich, Donald Stephen 1938- [SMG]
American baseball player
* Pavletich, Pav

Pavletich, Pav
See Pavletich, Donald Stephen

Pavliecivich, Ervin Martin 1928- [BE]
American baseball player
* Palica, Ervin Martin

Pavlik, Evelyn Marie 1954- [CA]
American author
* Sheridan, Adora [joint pseudonym with Jane Fay Hong]

Pavlovich, Paul 1940?- [BI]
French author
* Ajar, Emile

Pavsic, Vladimir 1913- [EWL]
Slovene poet and playwright
* Bor, Matej

Pawelek, Porky
See Pawelek, Theodore John [Ted]

Pawelek, Theodore John [Ted] 1919-1964 [BE]
American baseball player
* Pawelek, Porky

Paweski, Piotr 1536-1612
Polish theologian and author
* Skarga, Piotr

Pawkie, James, Esq.
See Galt, John

Pawle, Gerald 1913- [CA]
British columnist
* Atticus

Pawley, Eric
See Pawley, Frederick Arden

Pawley, Frederick Arden 1907- [BEW]
American educator and architect
* Pawley, Eric

Pawley, Martin Edward 1938- [WD]
British author
* Noble, Charles
* Spade, Rupert

Pawlikowska, Marja [Kossak] 1899-1945
[CD]
Polish poet and playwright
* Jasnorzewska, Marja
* [The] Polish Sappho
* [The] Queen of Polish Lyricists

Pawlowska, Yoi
See Maraini, Yoi

Pawnee Bill
See Lillie, [Major] Gordon W.

Pawnee Bill
See Little, Gordon W.

Pawnee Bill Hedges
See Hedges, William

Pax
See Cholmondeley, Mary

Pax
See McDermott, Hugh Farrar

Paxinou, Katina
See Constantopoulos, Katina

Paxinou, Katina
See Konstantopoulou, Katina

Paxton, Gary 20th c. [RO1]
American singer
* Flip

Paxton, Jack
See Lawton, Sherman P[axton]

Paxton, John 1923- [IAW]
British author and editor
* Cherrill, Jack

Paxton, [Dr.] John
See Lawton, Sherman P[axton]

Paxton, Joseph Rupert 1827-1867
[DNA]
American attorney and author
* Roset, Hipponax

Paxton, Lois
See Low, Lois Dorothea

Paxton, Mary Jean Wallace 1930-
American biologist and author
* Wallace, [Sister] M. Jean

Paxton, Philip
See Hammett, Samuel Adams

Paxton, Sydney
See Hood, Sydney Paxton

Payaba, Abraham 18th c. [HPPN]
British author
* Robert, James

Paycheck, Johnny
See Lytle, Donald

Paye, Robert
See Long, Gabrielle Margaret Vere
[Campbell]

Payelle, Raymond-Gerard 1898-1971
[CA]
French author, critic, playwright
* Heriat, Philippe

Payes, Rachel C[osgrove] 1922- [CA]
American author
* Arch, E. L.
* Cosgrove, Rachel

Payn, James 1830-1898 [HPPN, PA]
British author
* Found Dead
* Sauzade, John S.

Payne, A. G. 19th c. [HPPN]
American author
* Browne, Phillis

Payne, Alan
See Jakes, John W[illiam]

Payne, Alban S. 1822-? [FFF, PA]
Author
* Spicer, Nicholas

Payne, Alma Smith
See Ralston, Alma

Payne, Andrew H. 20th c. [OBW]
American baseball player
* Payne, Jap

Payne, B. J.
See Payne, Betty

Payne, Betty 1950- [IBW]
American air force officer
* Payne, B. J.

Payne, Bit
See Payne, Esther

Payne, Bondy
See Payne, Esther

Payne, Buckner H. [PA]
Author
* Ariel

Payne, Cecil McKenzie 1922- [EJ7]
American jazz musician
* Payne, Zodiac

Payne, Coal Oil
See Payne, Henry B.

Payne, Crutchley
See Evans, Frank Howel

Payne, David L. ?-1884 [HPPN]
American pioneer
* [The] Father of Oklahoma Boomers

Payne, Doc
See Payne, William

Payne, Donald Gordon 1924- [CA, WD]
British author
* Cameron, Ian
* Gordon, Donald
* Marshall, James Vance

Payne, Emmy
See West, Emily Govan [Emmy]

Payne, Esther 20th c. [BA]
American social worker
* Payne, Bit
* Payne, Bondy

Payne, F. M.
See Carey, Thomas Joseph

Payne, F. M.
See English, Thomas Dunn

Payne, Harold
See Kelly, George C.

Payne, Hazel Belle [Saulisberry] 1892-
[WW]
Author
* Gay, Greer

Payne, Henry B. 1810-1896 [FFF]
American politician
* Payne, Coal Oil

Payne, J. Bertrand 19th c. [HFN]
Author
* J. B. P.

Payne, Jap
See Payne, Andrew H.

Payne, Jimmy 20th c. [SI 9-1-82]
American football player
* [The] Inflicter

Payne, John 1940- [SW]
Australian actor
* Thompson, Jack

Payne, [Brother] John
See Demara, Ferdinand Waldo, Jr.

Payne, Lewis
See Powell, Lewis Thornton

Payne, Lou
See Payne, William

Payne, Odessa Strickland 1857-?
[BDSA]
American author
* Mills, Faith

Payne, Percival 1926-1979 [DAM, EJ,
IBW]
American jazz musician
* Payne, Sonny

Payne, [Pierre Stephen] Robert
1911-1983 [CA]
British-born author
* Cargoe, Richard
* Devon, John Anthony
* Horne, Howard
* Tikhonov, Valentin
* Young, Robert

Payne, Roger 1739-1797 [SN]
British bookbinder
* [The] Coryphaeus of Bookbinders

Payne, Ronald Charles 1922-1963 [BI,
CCL]
British author and publisher
* Castle, John [joint pseudonym with
John William Garrod]

Payne, Sonny
See Payne, Percival

Payne, William [OBW]
American baseball player
* Payne, Doc

Payne, William 1873-1953 [HPPN]
American actor
* Payne, Lou

Payne, Winona [Wilcox] 1865?-1949
[BI]
American journalist
* Maxwell, Mrs.

Payne, Zodiac
See Payne, Cecil McKenzie

Paynter, [Commander] Charles
1791-1873 [HPPN]
British naval officer
* Philalethes

Paynter, George Washington
See Paner, George Washington

[Le] Paysan du Danube
See Legendre, Louis

Payson, George 1824-1893 [DNA, PA]
American author and attorney
* Fogie, Francis
* Raven, Ralph
* Romaine, Robert Dexter

Payson, [Lieut.] Howard
See Goldfrap, John Henry

Payton, Sweetness
See Payton, Walter Jerry

Payton, Walter Jerry 1954- [SMG]
American football player
* Payton, Sweetness
* Payton, Wonderful Walter

Payton, Wonderful Walter
See Payton, Walter Jerry

Paz, A.
See Goldfeder, [Kenneth] James

Paz, Zan
See Goldfeder, [Anne] Cheryl Suzanne

Paz-Soldan y Unanue, Pedro [PA]
Author
* De Arona, Juan

Pazzetti, Pat
See Pazzetti, Vincent J.

Pazzetti, Vincent J. 1890-1972 [FB]
American football player
* Pazzetti, Pat

Pea Ridge Day
See Day, Clyde Henry

Pea Soup Dumont
See Dumont, George Henry

Peabody, Andrew Preston 1811-1893
[HPPN]
*American clergyman, educator, editor,
publisher*
* A. P. P.
* P.

Peabody, Chub
See Peabody, Endicott

Peabody, Eddy 1912-1970 [SC]
American actor and musician
* [The] Banjo King
* King of the Banjo

Peabody, Elizabeth Palmer 1804-1894
[HPPN]
American educator
* E. P. P.
* [The] Grandmother of Boston

Peabody, Endicott 1920- [FB]
American football player
* [The] Baby Faced Assassin
* Peabody, Chub

Peabody, Ephraim 1807-1856 [HPPN]
American clergyman
* E. P.
* P.

Peabody, George 1795-1869 [HPPN]
*American businessman, philanthropist,
patriot*
* [The] Unofficial Ambassador

Peabody, Josephine Preston
See Marks, Mrs. L. S.

Peabody, Mrs. Mark
See Victor, Metta Victoria Fuller

Peabody, William Bourne Oliver
1799-1847 [HPPN]
American clergyman
* W. B. O. P.

Peace and Justice
See Webster, Noah

[The] Peace Archbishop
See Hunthausen, Raymond

Peace Bertha Von Suttner
See Von Suttner, Bertha

Peace, Charles Frederick 1832-1879
[CEC, HPPN]
British burglar and murderer
* [The] Banner Cross Murderer
* [The] King of the Lags
* [The] Master Criminal
* Thompson, Mr.
* Ward, John

[The] Peace Crusader
See Wallace, Henry A[gard]

Peace, Frank
See Cook, William Everett

Peaceable, Abel
See Foe, Daniel

[The] Peaceful
See Alexander II

[The] Peaceful
See Casimir I

[The] Peaceful
See Edgar [or Eadgar]

[The] Peaceful
See Kang-wang

[The] Peaceful Prelate
See Massillon, Jean Baptiste

Peaceful Valley Denzer
See Denzer, Roger

[The] Peaceful Warrior
See King, Michael Luther, Jr.

[The] Peacemaker
See Channing, William Ellery

[The] Peacemaker
See Edward VII

[The] Peacemaker
See Irenaeus

[The] Peacemaker
See Isabel [or Elizabeth]

Peacemaker
See Kissinger, Henry Alfred

[The] Peach
See Depew, Chauncey Mitchell

Peach Bloom
See Mudd, Alice F.

Peach Blossom 1918?- [HPPN]
Japanese geisha girl
* [The] Tokyo Geisha

Peach, Edward C. 20th c. [EOP]
Author
* Ophiel

Peach Pie O'Connor
See O'Connor, John Joseph

Peache
See Hernandez, Jose P. H.

Peaches
See Barker [or Hurd?], Francine

Peaches
See Greene, Linda

Peaches
See Hynes, Frances Heenan

Peaches
See Levy [or Levee?], Marian

Peachie, John 17th c. [HPPN]
British physician
* [A] Physician in the Country

Peachum, Polly
See Fenton, Lavinia [Duchess of
Bolton]

Peacock, George 1791-1858 [HPPN]
British mathematician, educator, author
* [A] Member of the First Syndicate

Peacock, Kenneth 1927-1980
British drama critic and theater manager
* Tynan, Kenneth

Peacock, Marie 1893- [THR]
British actress and singer
* Blanche, Marie

[The] Peacock of the North
See Neville, Robert

[The] Peacock Senator
See Conkling, Roscoe

Peacock, Thomas Love 1785-1866
[DEA, DEL, PA]
British author and poet
* O'Donovan, P. M., Esq.
* Peppercorn, Peter

Peak, June
See Peak, Junius

Peak, Junius 1845-1934 [HPPN]
American law officer
* Peak, June

Peake, Frederick Gerard 1886-1970
[HPPN]
British army officer and statesman
* Peake Pasha

Peake Pasha
See Peake, Frederick Gerard

Peaker, E. J.
See Peaker, Edra Jeanne

Peaker, Edra Jeanne 20th c. [ITA]
American actress, singer, dancer
* Peaker, E. J.

Peale, Patrick
See Seckendorf, Gustav Anton von

[The] Peanut
See Carter, James Earl, Jr. [Jimmy] →

[The] Peanut
See Nguyen That Thanh

[The] Peanut Bard
See Canning, Josiah Dean, of Gill

[The] Peanut Farmer
See Carter, James Earl, Jr. [Jimmy]

[The] Peanut King
See Gwaltney, Pembroke Decatur

[The] Peanut King
See Obici, Amedeo

[The] Peanut Man
See Carver, George Washington

Peanut, Mr.
See Carver, George Washington

[The] Peanut President
See Carter, James Earl, Jr. [Jimmy]

[The] Pear
See Harvey, William King

Pearce, A. H.
See Quibell, Agatha Hunt

Pearce, A[nn] Philippa
See Christie, Ann Philippa Pearce

Pearce, Al 1898?-1961 [HPPN]
American radio performer
* Blurt, Elmer

Pearce, Brian Leonard 1915- [AW,
IAW]
British author
* Farnborough
* Hussey, Leonard
* Redman, Joseph

Pearce, Charles Louis St. John 20th c.
[MBF]
British author
* Fairbanks, Nat

Pearce, Ducky
See Pearce, William C.

Pearce, Ethel Katherine 1856-? [WWL]
British journalist
* Discipulus
* Oracle

Pearce, Gracie
See Pearce, Grayson S.

Pearce, Grayson S. ?-1894 [BE]
American baseball player
* Pearce, Gracie

Pearce, Guy
See Pilley, Charles

Pearce, Henry 1777-1809 [HN, NN,
RBE]
British boxer
* [The] Game Chicken

Pearce, Pard
See Pearce, Walter

Pearce, Raymond Maplesden 1894-
[AW]
British physician and author
* Maplesden, Ray

Pearce, Walter 20th c. [EF, SMG]
American football player
* Pearce, Pard

Pearce, William C. 1885-1933 [BE]
American baseball player
* Pearce, Ducky

Pearce, Zachary 1690-1774 [SN]
British clergyman and critic
* Avaro
* Longinus the Pope

Peard, F. M. [PA]
Author
* F. M. P.

Pearl
See Joplin, Janis

[The] Pearl
See Monroe, Earl

[The] Pearl
See Washington, Dwayne

Pearl, Christie
See Perkins, Ellen M.

Pearl, Cora
See Crouch, Emma Elizabeth

Pearl, Cousin Minnie
See Cannon, Sarah Ophelia Colley

Pearl, Eric
See Elman, Richard Martin

Pearl, Esther Elizabeth
See Ritz, David

Pearl, Eula
See Ferrand, Eula Pearl

Pearl, Irene
See Guyonvarch, Irene Cecilia

Pearl, Jack 1895?- [FIR, HPPN]
American comedian and actor
* Muenchausen, Baron

Pearl, Jack
See Pearl, Jacques Bain

Pearl, Jack
See Perelmuth, Jacob Pincus

Pearl, Jacques Bain 1923- [SFL, WYA]
American author
* Pearl, Jack

Pearl, Lee
See Pearl, Leo J.

Pearl, Leo J. 1907- [ASC]
American composer
* Pearl, Lee

Pearl, Minnie
See Cannon, Sarah Ophelia Colley

[The] Pearl of Brittany
See Eleanor

[The] Pearl of Ireland
See Bridget [or Brigette]

[The] Pearl of Normandy
See Emma

[The] Pearl of the East
See Zenobia

[The] Pearl of York
See Clitherow, Margaret Middleton

[The] Pearl of Zealand
See Coomans, Joanna

Pearl, Pinky
See Perelmuth, Jacob Pincus

Pearle, Mary 1849-? [PI]
Irish-born poet
* M. M. D.

Pearlie Mae
See Bailey, Pearl

Pearlman, Irving Ralph 1898- [EJS]
American football player
* Pearlman, Red

Pearlman, Maurice 1911- [CA]
Israeli author and political adviser
* Pearlman, Moshe

Pearlman, Moshe
See Pearlman, Maurice

Pearlman, Red
See Pearlman, Irving Ralph

Pearlson, Marion S. 1922-1956 [SC]
American actress
* Richman, Marian

Pearlstein, Howard J. 1942- [CA]
American poet and author
* Rush, Joshua

Pearsall, Elizabeth Sill 19th c. [HPPN]
British poet
* E. S. H.

Pearse, Padraic
See Pearse, Patrick Henry

Pearse, Patrick Henry 1879-1916
[HPPN, WWL]
Author and editor
* MacPiarais, Padraic
* Pearse, Padraic

Pearse, Peter Hector
See Cohen, Paul Arthur

Pearson, Alec George 20th c. [MBF]
British author
* Linley, Julian
* Scott, [Captain] Russell

Pearson, Andrew Russel 1897-1969
[HPPN, IPA]
American journalist
* [The] Leading Muckraker of His Time
* Pearson, Drew
* Pearson, Pugnacious
* [The] Tenacious Muckraker

Pearson, Bert
See Pearson, Madison

Pearson, Charles M. 1920-1944 [FB]
American football player
* Lincoln, Abe
* Pearson, Senator
* Pearson, Stubby

Pearson, Columbus Calvin, Jr. 1932-
[DAM, EJ]
American jazz musician
* Pearson, Duke

Pearson, Dave
See Barraclough, David Pearson

Pearson, David P. [Dave]
See Pierson, David P.

Pearson, Diane
See McClelland, Diane Margaret

Pearson, Drew
See Pearson, Andrew Russel

Pearson, Duke
See Pearson, Columbus Calvin, Jr.

Pearson, Edmund Lester 1880-1937
[HPPN]
American editor, bibliographer, librarian
* [The] Librarian

Pearson, Eliphalet 1752-1826 [HPPN]
American educator
* Elephant

Pearson, Emily [Clemens] 19th c.
[DNA, HPPN, PA]
American author
* Ervie
* Pocahontas

Pearson, Francis Gates 1855-1942
[BEW]
British actor
* Gerald, Frank

Pearson, George C. 19th c. [HPPN]
American author
* [A] Penitent Peri

Pearson, Hoot
See Pearson, Montgomery Marcellus

Pearson, Karl 1857-1936 [HPPN]
British scientist and editor
* K. P.

Pearson, Lester Bowles, Jr. 1897-
Canadian prime minister
* Pearson, Mike

Pearson, Lon
See Pearson, Milo Lorentz

Pearson, Madison 20th c. [EF]
American football player
* Pearson, Bert

Pearson, Martin [joint pseudonym with
Donald A(llen) Wollheim]
See Kornbluth, Cyril M.

Pearson, Martin [joint pseudonym with
Cyril M. Kornbluth]
See Wollheim, Donald A[llen]

Pearson, Mike
See Pearson, Lester Bowles, Jr.

Pearson, Milo Lorentz 1939- [CA]
American author and educator
* Pearson, Lon

Pearson, Monte
See Pearson, Montgomery Marcellus

Pearson, Montgomery Marcellus 1909-
[BE, BN]
American baseball player
* Pearson, Hoot
* Pearson, Monte

Pearson, Preston 1945- [SMG]
American football player
* [The] Cinderella Man

Pearson, Pug
See Pearson, Walter Clyde

Pearson, Pugnacious
See Pearson, Andrew Russel

Pearson, Richard 1765-1836 [HPPN]
British physician
* [A] Member of the College of
Physicians

Pearson, Senator
See Pearson, Charles M.

Pearson, Shepperd
See Hadath, John Edward Gunby

Pearson, Stubby
See Pearson, Charles M.

Pearson, T. E. 20th c. [MBF]
British author
* North, Pearson

Pearson, Walter Clyde 1929- [HPPN]
American poker player
* Pearson, Pug

Peart, Biscuits
See Peart, Clarence

Peart, Clarence 20th c. [CSH]
Canadian lacrosse promoter
* Peart, Biscuits

Peary, Harold [or Hal]
See De Faria, Harrold Jesse Pereira

Peary, Marie Ahnighito
See Kuhne, Marie [Ahnighito Peary]

[The] Peasant
See Brueghel [or Bruegel], Pieter

[The] Peasant
See Traina, Giuseppe

[The] Peasant Bard
See Burns, Robert

[The] Peasant Bard
See Canning, Josiah Dean, of Gill

[The] Peasant Bard
See Cummings, Josiah D.

[The] Peasant Bard
See Hill, George

[The] Peasant Boy Philosopher
See Ferguson, James

[The] Peasant of Cotignola
See Attendolo, Giacomuzo d'

[The] Peasant of the Danube
See Legendre, Louis

[The] Peasant Painter of Sweden
See Hoerberg, Peter

[The] Peasant Philosopher
See Deubler, Konrad

[The] Peasant Poet of Northamptonshire
See Clare, John

[The] Peasant Poet of Suffolk
See Bloomfield, Robert

[The] Peasant Poetess
See Hamilton, Janet

[The] Peasant Pope
See Sarto, Giuseppe Melchiorre

[The] Peasants' King
See Casimir III

Pease, Alfa
See Crouse, Mrs. Charles E.

Pease, [Lt.] John
See Hoar, Roger Sherman

Pease, Lillie
See Chrissie, Mrs. Edward

Peat, Louisa [Watson] 20th c. [CCL]
Canadian author
* Herself

Peay, Benjamin Franklin 1931- [RO1]
American singer
* Benton, Brook

Pebbly Jack Glasscock
See Glasscock, John Wesley

Peccadille
See Bandovin, E.

Peccadille
See Doubled, Victor

Peccavi
See Holden, Beatrice [Paget]

Pecci, Gioacchino Vincenzo 1810-1903
[CBS, WBD]
Pope
* Leo XIII

Pechey, Archibald Thomas 1876-1961
[HPPN, LAO, WW]
British author and playwright
* Cross, Mark
* Valentine

Peck, Abe
See Peckolick, Abe

Peck, Annie S. 1850-1935 [HPPN]
American mountain climber
* [The] Lady Mountaineer

Peck, Dutch
See Peck, Hubert

Peck, Eileen
See Cline, Eileen Peck

Peck, Ellen [or Catherine?] 19th c.
[DNA, PA]
Author
* Pine, Cuyler

Peck, Ellen
See Crosby, Nellie

Peck, George Washington 1817-1859
[HPPN, PA]
American author and journalist
* Bigly, Cantell A.
* G. W. P.

Peck, George Wilbur 1840-1916 [HPPN]
American politician, editor, author
* McGrant, Terence

Peck, Hubert 1898- [BB]
American basketball player
* Peck, Dutch

Peck, I. X.
See Mason, Thomas

Peck, Julie 1926- [FC, IPA, ITA]
American actress and singer
* London, Julie

Peck, Leonard
See Hardy, C. Colburn

Peck, Lillie ?-1878 [PA]
Author
* Elliot, Ruth

Peck, Wallace
See Walter, Charles T.

Peck, William Henry 1830-1892
[HPPN]
American educator and author
* Brown, Mahlon A.

Peck, Winifred Frances [Knox] 20th c.
[WW]
Author
* Knox, Winifred Frances

Peckham, Luella Nichols ?-1932
[HPPN]
American vauderville performer
* Nichols, Lulu

Peckham, Richard
See Holden, Raymond [Peckham]

Peckinpah, Sam[uel] 1925-1984 [HPPN,
WP 12-29-84]
American film director
* [The] Master of Violence

Peckolick, Abe 1945- [CA]
American writer
* Peck, Abe

**[The] Peck's Bad Boy of Yesteryear T.
V.**
See Paar, Jack

Peck's Bad Girl
See Javal, Camille

Pecora, Santo
See Pecoraro, Santo J.

Pecoraro, Santo J. 1902- [EJ, PMJ,
WWJ]
American jazz musician
* Pecora, Santo

Pecsok, Mary Bodell 1919- [CA]
American author
* Bodell, Mary

Pedachenko, Alexander 19th c. [BL]
*Russian-born physician and murder
suspect*
* Konovalov, Vassily
* Luiskovo, Andrey
* Ostrong [or Ostrog], Mikhail
* [The] Russian Doctor

[The] Pedagogue
See Milton, John

[The] Pedantic Professor
See Sherman, Alex

Peddar Zaskq
See Twitchell, Paul

Peddell, Maud Clement 20th c. [NAA]
American playwright
* Clement, Kay

Pedder, James 1775-1859 [IP, PA]
British-born author
* Frank
* J. P.

Peden, Rachel Mason 1901- [IA]
American columnist
* R. F. D., Mrs.

Peden, Torchy
See Peden, William John

Peden, William John 1906- [BBH, CSH]
Canadian bicycle racer
* Peden, Torchy

Pederek, Simon
See Thomas, Peter

Pederneiras, Raul Paranhos 1874-1953
[WEC]
Brazilian cartoonist, author, educator
* Raul

Pedersen, Christiern 1480-1554 [HPPN]
Danish author
* [The] Father of Danish Literature

Pedersen, Knut 1859-1952 [LC, TCL]
Norwegian author and playwright
* Hamsun, Knut

Pedersen, Sven 1917- [CA]
Danish author
* Hassel, Sven

Pedersoli, Carlo 20th c. [WF]
Italian actor
* Spencer, Bud

Pederson, Carl 1895-1958 [BEW, CED,
EMT]
Danish actor, dancer, singer
* Brisson, Carl

Pederson, Lily ?-1919 [SC]
American actress
* Gray, Beata
* Gray, Betty

Pederson, Pullman G. 1920- [EJ]
American jazz musician
* Pederson, Tommy

Pederson, Tommy
See Pederson, Pullman G.

[A] Pedestrian
See Aiton, John

Pedestrian
See Wilson, Robert

[The] Pedlar Poet
See McFarlan, James

Pedler, Anne I. Stafford 1901- [HPPN]
British author
* Stafford, Anne

Pedler, Christopher Magnus Howard
1927- [ESF, SFL]
British author and scientist
* Pedler, Kit

Pedler, Kit
See Pedler, Christopher Magnus
Howard

Pedres [Big Pedro]
See Martinez Gonzalez, Pedro

Pedrick, Gale
See Pedrick, Harvey

Pedrick, Harvey 1906-1970. [HPPN]
American playwright
* Pedrick, Gale

Pedrick, Jean 1922- [CA]
American poet and author
* Kefferstan, Jean

Pedrick, Robert, Jr. 20th c. [RO2]
American singer
* John, Robert

Pedro 1334-1369 [DNNS, RH, SN]
King of Castile and Leon
* [The] Cruel

Pedro I 1320-1367 [DNNS, FFF, WBD]
King of Portugal
* [The] Just
* [The] Justiciary
* [The] Severe

Pedro II 1648-1706 [WBD]
King of Portugal
* [The] Pacific

Pedro III [or Peter] 1239-1285 [DNNS, SN, WBD]
King of Aragon
* [The] Great

Pedro IV [or Peter] 1319-1387 [FFF, SN, WBD]
King of Aragon
* [The] Ceremonious

Pedroes, Charles P. 20th c. [BE]
American baseball player
* Pedroes, Chick

Pedroes, Chick
See Pedroes, Charles P.

Pedrosa, Amilde 1920- [WEC]
Brazilian cartoonist
* Appe

Pedrucho [Big Pedro]
See Basauri Paguaga, Pedro

Pedrucho [Big Pedro]
See Garcia, Francisco

Peebles, Hap
See Peebles, Harry

Peebles, Harry 1913- [CM]
American concert promoter
* Peebles, Hap

Peebles, Mary Louise 1835-1915 [DNA, FFF]
American author
* Palmer, Lynde

Peebles, McKinley 1897- [BWW]
American singer
* Sweet Papa Stovepipe

Peebles, Paul
See Maverick, Augustus

Peebles, William 1767-1823 [IP, PA]
Scottish clergyman and poet
* [A] Clergyman of the Church of Scotland

Peed, Patricia Kelly ?-1973 [HPPN]
American Librarian
* Kelly, Pat

Peed, William Bartlett 1915- [HPPN]
American author
* Peet, Bill

Peek, Coyle, Jr. 1950- [IBW]
American auto racer
* Black Helmet

[The] Peekaboo Girl
See Ockleman, Constance Frances Marie

Peekskill Pete Cregan
See Cregan, Pete[r James]

Peel, Frederick 1888- [WW]
Author
* Slingsby, Rufus [joint pseudonym with Charles Siddle]

Peel, Hazel Mary [Wallis] 1930- [AW, CA]
British author
* Hayman
* Peel, Wallis

Peel, [Captain] Jonathan 1799-1854 [PA]
Author
* Dinks

Peel, Lady
See Munston, Constance Sylvia

Peel, Norman Lemon
See Hirsch, Paul

Peel, Orange
See Peel, [Sir] Robert

Peel, Parsley
See Peel, [Sir] Robert

Peel, [Sir] Robert 1750-1830 [HPPN, SN]
British calico printer
* Peel, Parsley

Peel, [Sir] Robert 1788-1850 [FFF, IP, NPS, RH, SN]
British statesman
* Fitzborn
* Jenny
* Judas
* [The] Leonidas of the Day
* [The] Minister
* [The] Moral Surface
* Peel, Orange
* [The] Run Away Spartan
* [The] Spinning Spoon

Peel, Wallis
See Peel, Hazel Mary [Wallis]

Peele, Biscuits
See Peele, Clarence

Peele, Clarence 20th c. [BBH, CSH]
Canadian lacrosse player
* Peele, Biscuits

Peele, George 1558-1596 [DEA, SN]
British playwright and poet
* [The] Atlas of Poetrie
* G. P.
* Pyeboard, George

Peelon, Nancie 1910- [HPPN]
American educator and projectionist
* [The] Hubris Kid

Peep
See Nettles, Bonnie Lu

Peepers, Mr.
See Cox, Wallace Maynard [Wally]

Peeping Tom
See Kettell, Samuel

Peeping Tom
See Knapp, Henry Ryder

Peeradeal, Paul Puck
See Smith, [Sir] William Cusack, Bart.

Peeradeal, Peter Puck
See Smith, [Sir] William Cusack, Bart.

Peerce, Jan
See Perelmuth, Jacob Pincus

Peerless Annabelle
See Buchan, Annabelle W.

Peerless Hal Chase
See Chase, Harold Harris [Hal]

[The] Peerless Leader
See Bryan, William Jennings

[The] Peerless Leader
See Chance, Frank Leroy

Peers, Donald 1909?-1973 [FIR]
British singer
* [The] Cavalier of Song

Peers, Edgar Allison ?-1952 [BI]
British author and educator
* Truscot, Bruce

Peers, Frank 1874-? [THR]
British lyricist, composer, entertainer
* Leo, Frank

Peerson, Eliza O. [PA]
Author
* Aliqua

Peery, George A. 1906- [BE]
American baseball player
* Peery, Red

Peery, Red
See Peery, George A.

Peeslake, Gaffer
See Durrell, Lawrence [George]

Peet, Bill
See Peed, William Bartlett

Peete, Charles [Charlie] 1931-1956 [BE, IBW]
American baseball player
* Peete, Mule

Peete, Mule
See Peete, Charles [Charlie]

Peeters, Pete 1958?- [NW 1-17-83]
Canadian-born hockey player
* [The] Doctor

Peetie Wheatstraw's Brother
See Gordon, Jimmy

Peetie Wheatstraw's Buddy
See Ray, Harmon

Peg Leg Elliot
See Elliot, Frank

Peg Leg Howell
See Howell, Joshua Barnes

Peg Leg Lonergan
See Lonergan, Richard

Peg Leg Norwood
See Norwood, Sam

Peg Leg Sam
See Jackson, Arthur

Peg Pete
See Jackson, Arthur

Pegalle
See Rousseau, Jean-Jacques

Pegasus
See Benson, Nathaniel Anketell

Pegge, Samuel 1704-1796 [IP, SN]
British antiquary
* [An] Antiquary
* Echard, L.
* G.
* Gemsege, Paul
* L. E.
* [A] Late Very Learned and Reverend Divine
* [An] Old Modern
* P.
* P. E.
* P. G.
* P. S.
* [A] Ploughist
* Portius
* Row, T.
* S. P.
* Senex
* Vicarius Cantianus

Peggy Ann
See Miller, George Amos

Peggy la Pazza [Crazy Peggy]
See Guggenheim, Peggy

Pegleg Annie Morrow
See Morrow, Annie McIntyre

Pegler, Bud
See Pegler, [James] Westbrook

Pegler, Mabel Kelly 1900-1954 [HPPN]
American actress
* Kelly, Mabel

Pegler, Peg
See Pegler, [James] Westbrook

Pegler, [James] Westbrook 1894-1969 [HPPN]
American journalist and author
* [The] Angry Man of the Press
* [The] Human Saddle Sore
* [The] Master of the Epithet
* Pegler, Bud
* Pegler, Peg
* Pegler, Westy
* Pegler, Wrong Westbrook

Pegler, Westy
See Pegler, [James] Westbrook

Pegler, Wrong Westbrook
See Pegler, [James] Westbrook

Pegulu, Francois Fortune Louis 1901?- [HPPN]
French swindler
* De Robin, General

Peguy, Charles Pierre 1873-1914 [EWL, TLC]
French poet, journalist, philosopher
* Baudouin, Charles Pierre
* Baudouin, Marcel
* Deloire, Pierre

Pei, I. M.
See Pei, Ieoh Ming

Pei, Ieoh Ming 1917- [CR]
Chinese-born architect and city planner
* Pei, I. M.

Peichl, Gustav 1928- [WEC]
Austrian cartoonist and architect
* Ironimus

Peignot, Etienne Gabriel 1767-1849 [IP]
French author
* Rambler, Jacques

Peil, Charles Edward 1908?-1962 [BEW]
Actor
* Jones, Johnny

Peintre du Bonheur
See Dufy, Raoul

Peirce, Augustus 1802-1849 [IP]
American physician and author
* Poeta, Enginae Societatis

Peirce, Benjamin 1809-1881 [IP]
American mathematician and author
* Benjamin the Florentine
* Yamen, Ben

Peirce, Bradford Kinney 1819-? [IP]
American clergyman and author
* B. K. P.
* [The] Chaplain

Peirce, Charles Sanders 1839-1914 [HPPN]
American physicist, mathematician, philosopher
* [The] Father of Pragmatism

Peirce, George Howard 1842-? [HPPN]
American author
* Howard, G.

Peirce, I. [IP]
American author
* [A] Wanderer

Peirce, James 1673-1726 [IP]
British clergyman and author
* [A] Dissenter in the Country

Peirce, Thomas 1786-1850 [HPPN]
American poet
* [A] Citizen of Cincinnati
* Horace in Cincinnati
* Moody, Billy
* [The] Printer's Devil

Peiresc, Nicolas Claude Fabi de 1580-1637 [SN]
French scholar
* [The] Attorney General of the Republic of Letters

Peirson, Eliza O. 19th c. [IP]
American journalist
* Aliqua

Peiser, Maria Lilli 1914-1986 [BDF, TR, WEF]
German-born actress
* Palmer, Lilli

Peitz, Heinie
See Peitz, Henry Clement

Peitz, Henry Clement 1870-1943 [AS, BE]
American baseball player
* Peitz, Heinie

Peking's Vicar in the Balkans
See Hoxha, Enver

Pekin's Indispensable Man
See Chou En-Lai

Pekin's Man for All Seasons
See Chou En-Lai

Peladan, Joseph 1858-1918 [HPPN, WBD]
French author
* Paladan, Josephin
* Sar

Peladeau, Pierre 1925?-
Canadian publisher
* Pile o Dough

Pelaez, Cesareo 1932?-
Cuban-born magician
* Marco the Magi

Pelagius II ?-590 [DHA]
Pope
* Infallible

Pelau
See Auguste, Arsene

Pelayo, Luis 20th c. [HPPN]
Spanish taxi driver and bullfight heckler
* Ronquillo [Little Hoarse One]

Pele
See Arantes Do Nascimento, Edson

Peledo
See Chacon, Augustin

Peletier, Andrew Arthur 1884-1921 [BX, HPPN, RBE]
Canadian-born boxer
* Pelkey, Arthur

Pelham, Alfred Montgomery 1900- [IBW]
American accountant and college administrator
* Fix It, Mr.

Pelham, George 1766-1827 [NPS]
Bishop of Lincoln
* [The] Dandy Bishop

Pelham, George
See Pellew, George

Pelham, [Sir] Henry 1695-1754 [NPS]
British statesman
* [The] Bulwark of the State

Pelham, John 1838-1863 [HPPN, SN]
American army officer
* [The] Boy Major
* [The] Gallant

Pelham, M.
See Phillips, [Sir] Richard

[The] Pelican
See Leonard, Joe

Pelican
See Pellegrini, Carlo

Pelican, A.
See Gerard, James Watson

Pelide, Nicole 1902-1926 [HPPN]
American actor
* Marni, Nicole

Pelikan, Leopeldina Alize Elianore
1891-1931 [BEW]
German-born aerial performer
* Elitza
* Leitzel, Lillian

Pelin, Elin
See Ivanov, Dimiter

Pelissier, H. G.
See Pelissier, Harry Gabriel

Pelissier, Harry Gabriel 1874-1913
[BMH]
British entertainer
* Pelissier, H. G.

Pelissier De Bujac, Jacques Etienne
1904-1972 [FC]
American actor
* Cabot, Bruce

Pelkey, Arthur
See Peletier, Andrew Arthur

Pelkey, Eddie 1895?-1983 [WP 2-26-83]
American pool player
* Pelkey, Fast Eddie

Pelkey, Fast Eddie
See Pelkey, Eddie

Pelkie, Joe Walter
See Palmer, Raymond A[rthur]

Pelkington, John 1916-
American basketball player
* Pelkington, Stretch

Pelkington, Stretch
See Pelkington, John

Pelkonen, Elina
See Honkanen, Hilja Loviisa Valkeapaa

Pell, Ferris 19th c. [IP]
American attorney and author
* Publicola

Pell, Franklyn
See Pelligrin, Frank E.

Pell, Henry ?-1902? [HPPN]
American outlaw
* Pell, Long Henry
* Thompson, Henry

Pell, John W.
See Fish, Hamilton

Pell, Long Henry
See Pell, Henry

Pell, Robert
See Hagberg, David J[ames]

Pell, Robert Conger 1835?-1868 [DNA, IP]
American author
* Evelyn, Chetwood, Esq.

Pellan, Alfred
See Pelland, Alfred

Pelland, Alfred 1906- [CAR]
Canadian painter
* Pellan, Alfred

Pellegrin
See Fouque, Friedrich Heinrich Karl
de La Motte

Pellegrini, Carlo 1838-1889 [FFF, HN, RH, WEC]
British caricaturist
* Ape
* Jehu Junior
* Pelican
* Singe

Pellegrini, Pompeo
See Standen, Antony

Pellerano Castro, Arturo Bautista
1865-1916 [CW]
West Indian poet, author, playwright
* Byron

Pelletier, Alexis 1837-1910 [DNA]
Canadian author and clergyman
* Luigi
* St. Aime, Georges

Pelletier, Marcel 20th c. [SMG]
French-born hockey player and coach
* [The] Gypsy Goalie

Pelletier, Marie-Therese 1886?-1934
[BEW]
French-born actress
* Pierat, Marie-Therese

Pellew, George 1860?-1892 [EOP]
Attorney and author, who claimed to possess psychic powers
* Pelham, George

Pelley, Smelly
See Pelley, William Dudley

Pelley, William Dudley 1890-1965
[HPPN]
American author
* [The] Leader of Men
* Pelley, Smelly

Pellicanus, Konrad
See Kuerschner, Konrad

Pellicarius
See Marbode, M.

Pellicer, Pina
See Lopez Llergo, Josefina Pellicer

Pelligrin, Frank E. 20th c. [WW]
Author
* Pell, Franklyn

Pellisson-Fontanier, Paul 1624-1693
[HN, SN]
French author
* Convertisseur
* [The] King's Convertisseur

Pelly, Gerald Conn 1865-1900 [PI]
Irish poet
* Cieppe, G.
* Gerald
* Nemo
* Tormer, Cill

Peloncillo Jack Chamberlain
See Chamberlain, Samuel E.

Peloquin, Robert Dolan [Bob] 1928?-
[HPPN]
American detective
* [The] Jet Age Super Sleuth

Pelot, Pierre 1945- [ESF]
French author
* Suragne, Pierre

Pelovitz, Morton Herbert 1925- [EJ]
American jazz musician
* Herbert, Mort

Peltier, Florence
See Leonard, Florence Peltier

Pelto, Bert
See Pelto, Pertti J[uho]

Pelto, Pertti J[uho] 1927- [CA]
American author and anthropologist
* Pelto, Bert

Pelton, Beverly Jo 1939- [CA]
American author
* Jensen, Jo

Pelton, Robert W[ayne] 1937- [CA]
American author
* Arthur, Tiffany
* Martin, Kevin
* Martin, Robert W.
* Milton, Mark
* Notlep, Robert
* Sonero, Devi

Peltonen, Vihtori 1869-1913 [WBD]
Finnish playwright and poet
* Linnankoski, Johannes

Peltrel
See Nicolas, P.

Pelty, Barney 1880-1939 [EJS]
American baseball player
* [The] Yiddish Curver

[The] Pelvis
See Presley, Elvis Aron

Pelz, Edward 1800-1876 [IP]
German author
* Welp, Treumund

Pelzer, Leon ?-1922 [DI]
German-born Belgian murderer
* Preitel, Albert
* Vaughan, Henry

Pember, Arthur [IP]
American author
* A. P.

Pember-Devereux, Margaret R[ose Roy McAdam] 1877-? [WGT]
Author
* Devereux, Roy

Pemberton
See Adams, Charles Francis

Pemberton, Charles Reece 1790-1840
[IP]
British actor and poet
* [A] Sailor

Pemberton, Col. 19th c.   [IP, PA]
British officer and author
* Leo

Pemberton, Edgar   [IP]
British author
* Berton, P. M.

Pemberton, Edward Loines 19th c.
British philatelist
* [The] Father of Scientific Philately

Pemberton, Israel 1715-1779   [FFF]
American Quaker leader
* [The] King of the Quakers
* Wampum, King

Pemberton, Renfrew
See   Busby, F. M.

Pembroke, George
See   Prud'homme, George

Pembroke, Thomas
See   Hopkinson, Henry Thomas [Tom]

Pembrooke, Kenneth
See   Page, Gerald W[ilburn]

Pembury, Bill
See   Groom, Arthur William

Pembury, Grosvenor
See   Haydon, N. G.

Pembury, Montague
See   Moon, George P.

Pemjean, Lucian
See   Bedford-Jones, Henry [James O'Brien]

Pen, A., Esq.
See   Leech, John

Pen Amber, Joan 1945?-1982   [FIR]
Therapist and film technician
* PenAmber, Asha

Pen Dragon, Anser, Esq.
See   Ireland, William Henry

[The] Pen of the Revolution
See   Jefferson, Thomas

Pen, Steel
See   Penn, Colonel

Pena, Bubba
See   Pena, Robert

Pena, Robert 20th c.   [EF]
American football player
* Pena, Bubba

Pena Rego, Jesus 20th c.   [WECO]
Spanish cartoonist
* Suso

Penaloza, Ezequiel Padilla 1890-
[HPPN]
Mexican attorney and statesman
* Padilla, Ezequiel

PenAmber, Asha
See   Pen Amber, Joan

Penaranda, Enrique
See   Castillo, Enrique Penaranda

Penarth, Wyn
See   Plummer, Clare [Emsley]

[A] Pencil
See   Forrester, Alfred Henry

Pencil
See   Sowden, [Sir] William John

Penck, A. R.
See   Winkler, Ralf

Pencovic, Francis Heindswater 20th c.
[EOP]
Leader of American religious cult
* Krishna Venta

Pendarves, G. G.
See   Trenery, Gladys Gordon

Pendennis
See   Kelly, Denis

Pendennis, Arthur, Esquire
See   Thackeray, William Makepeace

Pendenys, Arthur
See   Humphreys, Arthur Lee

Pender, Doris
See   Lomas, Doris

Pender, Lex
See   Pendower, Jacques

Pender, Margaret T. 19th c.   [PI]
Irish poet and author
* Colleen
* M.
* M. T. P.
* Marguerite

Pendergast, Boss
See   Pendergast, Thomas J. [Tom]

Pendergast, Thomas J. [Tom] 1872-1945
[HPPN]
American political boss
* Pendergast, Boss

Pendergrass, Theodore [Teddy] 1951-
[IBW]
American singer, musician, composer
* Svengali
* Teddy Bear

Penders, Marilyn
See   Pendower, Jacques

Pendle, Nicholas
See   Birtill, George Arthur

Pendleton, Conrad Padraic
See   Kidd, Walter Evans

Pendleton, Don[ald Eugene] 1927-   [CA]
American author
* Britain, Dan
* Gregory, Stephan

Pendleton, Edward ?-1858   [HPPN]
American gambling house proprietor
* [The] Boss of the Bleeding Heart

Pendleton, George Hunt 1825-1889
[FFF, HPPN, SN]
American politician
* [The] Father of Civil Service Reform
* Gentleman George

Pendower, Jacques 1899-1976   [AW, CA, MBF]
British author
* Carstairs, Kathleen
* Curtis, Tom
* Dower, Penn
* Jacobs, T[homas] C[urtis] H[icks]
* Pender, Lex
* Penders, Marilyn
* Penn, Anne
* Stagg, James

Pendragon
See   McMartin, L. E.

Pendragon
See   Sampson, Henry

Pendragon, Eric
See   Parry, Michel Patrick

Pendray, G[eorge] Edwards 1901-
[NAA, WGT]
American author, journalist, editor
* Edwards, Gawain

Pendrea, W.
See   Noy, William

Penelope, [Viscountess] Ligonier 18th c.
[HPPN]
American author
* Emilia

Penfeather, Amabel
See   Cooper, James Fenimore

Penfeather, Amabel
See   Cooper, Susan Fenimore

Penfield, A.   [IP]
American financier and author
* A. P.

Penfield, Cornelia
See   Lathrop, Cornelia Sterrett
[Penfield]

Pengelly, William 1812-?   [IP]
British geologist and author
* [A] Geologist
* Y. M.

Penguin [code name]
See   Ahern, Thomas

[The] Penguin
See   Brothman, Abraham

[The] Penguin
See   Cey, Ronald Charles

[The] Penguin
See   Leonard, Joe

Penhafirme, Count of
See   Sartorius, [Sir] G. R.

Penholder
See   Eggleston, Edward

Peniakoff, Vladimir 1897-   [BDW]
Belgian-born British army officer
* Popski

Penick, Clifton Hewitt 1885-   [NAA]
American journalist
* McGuire, P.

Penick, Mary Frances 1931- [CME, CWG]
American country-western performer
* Davis, Skeeter

Penick, [Issac] Newt[on] 1859-1945 [HPPN]
American educator
* [The] Man to Whom Hall-Moody Owes Most

[A] Penitent Peri
See Pearson, George C.

[The] Penitent Thief
See Dismas [or Dismes]

Penkethman [or Pinkethman], William ?-1725 [HPPN]
British comedian
* [The] Idol of the Rabble
* Pinkey

Penklub
See Lange, Carl Gustav Albert

Penlake, Richard
See Salmon, Percy R.

Penman
See Hallock, Charles

[The] Penman of the Revolution
See Dickinson, John

Penmare, William
See Nisot, Mavis Elizabeth [Hocking]

Penn
See Jillette, Penn

Penn
See Perrine, William

Penn, Anne
See Pendower, Jacques

Penn, Arthur
See Bunner, Henry Cuyler

Penn, Arthur
See Matthews, James Brander

Penn, Christopher
See Lawlor, Pat[rick Anthony]

Penn, Colonel [FFF]
British army officer
* Pen, Steel

Penn, Mr.
See Colwell, Stephen

Penn, Rachel
See Willard, Caroline McCoy [White]

Penn, Ruth Bonn
See Rosenberg, Ethel [Clifford]

Penn, William 1644-1718 [HPPN, SN]
British Quaker leader and founder of Pennsylvania
* [The] Father of Pennsylvania
* That Jesuit

Penn, William 1776-1845? [IP, NPS]
British author
* Anglus, Phil
* [The] Rajah of Vaneplysia
* [An] Undergraduate

Penn, William
See Evarts, Jeremiah

Penn-Gaskell, Patricia 1916- [THR]
British actress
* Hilliard, Patricia

Pennage, E. M.
See Finkel, George [Irvine]

Pennanen, Lea Airi-Sirkka 1929- [IAW]
Finnish author
* Pikkumolliainen, Leena

Pennant, Thomas 1726-1798 [HPPN]
British traveler, naturalist, antiquary
* [A] Welch Freeholder

Pennec, R. P. Cyrille
See Miorcec de Kerdanet, Daniel Louis Mathurin

Penneck, Henry 1762-1834 [HPPN]
British physician
* Doseall, Dr.

Penneck, Henry 1800-1862 [IP]
British clergyman and author
* Bayle, Mr.

Pennecuik, Alexander 1652-1722 [IP]
Scottish poet and botanist
* A. P., M.D.

Pennell, Elizabeth 1855-1936 [HPPN]
American author
* [A] Greedy Woman
* N. N.

Pennell, Joseph [NPS]
Artist
* A[rtist] U[nknown]

Penner, Bumps
See Pinter, Josef

Penner, Eleanor May 1909-1946 [HPPN]
American actress
* Mae, Eleanor

Penner, Joe
See Pinter, Josef

Penner, Wanna Buy a Duck
See Pinter, Josef

Pennes, Jean 1894- [WEC]
French cartoonist
* Sennep, J.

Penney, Annette Culler 1916- [CA]
American author
* Culler, Annette Lorena

Penney, J. C.
See Penney, James Cash

Penney, James Cash 1876-1971 [HPPN]
American merchant
* Penney, J. C.

Penney, William, [Lord Kinloch] 1801-1872 [IP]
Scottish author
* [A] Layman

Penni, Giovanni Francesco 1488?-1528? [SN]
Italian painter
* [Il] Fattore [The Steward]

Pennibb
See Sibley, Inez K.

Pennick, Jack
See Pennick, Ronald

Pennick, Ronald 1895?-1964 [BEW]
American actor
* Pennick, Jack

Pennie, Frank 20th c.
American football player
* Pennie, Ox

Pennie, John Fitzgerald 1782-1848 [IP]
British author, actor, poet
* [A] Modern Genius
* Sylvaticus

Pennie, Ox
See Pennie, Frank

Pennier, Henry George 1904- [HPPN]
Canadian logger
* [The] Half Breed Logger

[The] Penniless
See Frederick I

[The] Penniless
See Maximilian I

[The] Penniless
See Walter

Pennilesse, Pierce
See Nash [or Nashe?], Thomas

Penniman, Major
See Denison, Charles Wheeler

Penniman, Major
See Dennison, Charles W.

Penniman, Richard Wayne 1932- [EJ, SSS, WP 11-12-84]
American singer
* [The] Bronze Liberace
* [The] Georgia Peach
* [The] King of Rock and Roll
* Little Richard
* [The] Queen of Rock and Roll

Pennington, Ann 1895?-1971 [AM, HPPN]
American actress and dancer
* [The] Dimpled Doll of Broadway
* Pennington, Penny
* [The] Shimmy Queen

Pennington, George Louis 1896- [BE]
American baseball player
* Pennington, Kewpie

Pennington, Kewpie
See Pennington, George Louis

Pennington, Mrs. S. 18th c. [IP]
British author
* S. P.

Pennington, Patience
See Pringle, Elizabeth Waties [Allston]

Pennington, Penny
See Galbraith, Georgie Starbuck

Pennington, Penny
See Pennington, Ann

Pennington, Richard 1904-   [CCL]
Canadian poet
* Peterley, David

Pennington, Stuart
See Galbraith, Georgie Starbuck

Pennington-Richards, C. M. 1911-   [BF]
British director
* Richards, Pennington

Pennochio, Tommy 20th c.   [CEC]
American underworld figure
* [The] Bull

Pennock, Herb[ert Jefferis] 1894-1948
[ALR, BAB, BE]
American baseball player
* [The] Knight of Kennett Square
* [The] Squire of Kennett Square

Pennock, Meta
See Newman, Meta [Pennock]

Pennot, [Rev.] Peter
See Round, William Marshall Fitz

Pennoyer, Clarence 1896?-1950   [BI]
American journalist
* Pennoyer, Pete

Pennoyer, Pete
See Pennoyer, Clarence

[The] Pennsylvania Farmer
See Dickinson, John

[A] Pennsylvania Farmer
See Powel, John Hare

[The] Pennsylvania Kid
See Wilson, Richard

[The] Pennsylvania Pilgrim
See Pastorius, Francis Daniel

[A] Pennsylvania Sailor
See Macpherson, John

[A] Pennsylvanian
See Kane, John Kintzing

Pennsylvania's Boss of Bosses
See Penrose, Boies

Penny, Johnny 20th c.   [RBE]
American boxer
* Pinney, Johnny

[The] Penny Plug
See O'Sullivan, Dennis

Penny, Prudence
See Goldberg, Hyman

Penny, Richard
See Lasser, David

Penny, William 19th c.   [PA]
Author
* Denarius

[The] Pennyless
See Frederic IV

Pennyman, John 17th c.   [IP]
British author
* Ang., Phil

Peno
See Oak, Purushottam Nagesh

Penrose, Boies 1860-1921   [HPPN]
American politician
* [The] Gutter Nietzschean
* Pennsylvania's Boss of Bosses
* Penrose, Boss

Penrose, Boss
See Penrose, Boies

Penrose, [Sir] Charles Vinicombe
1759-1830   [IP]
British naval officer and author
* [A] Flag Officer

Penrose, Elizabeth [Cartwright]
1790-1837   [DEL, FFF, RH]
British author
* Markham, Mrs.

Penrose, John 1778-1859   [IP, NPS]
British clergyman and author
* Senior
* [A] Trinitarian

Penrose, Llewellyn
See Eagles, John

Penrose, Margaret [house pseudonym]
[Stratemeyer Syndicate]
See Stratemeyer, Edward L.

Penrose, Spencer 1865-1939
American business executive
* [The] White Eagle

Penruddock, John ?-1655   [HPPN]
British rebel
* [The] Father of Penruddock's Rising
* [The] Father of the Wiltshire
  Rebellion

Penry, John 1559-1593   [PA]
British author
* Marprelate, Martin
* Priest, Martin

[El] Pensador Mexicano
See Fernandez de Lizardi, Jose Joaquin

Penseval, Guy
See Darley, George

[The] Pensioned Dauber
See Hogarth, William

[The] Pensioner
See Abercromby, James [First Baron
Dunfermline]

[The] Pentagon Spokesman
See Friedheim, Jerry W.

Pentecost, Hugh
See Philips, Judson Pentecost

Pentecost, Martin
See Hearn, John

[La] Pentecote Vivante
See Mezzofanti, Giuseppe

Pentelow, John Nix 1872-1931   [MBF]
British author and editor
* Clifford, Martin [house pseudonym]
* Huntingdon, Harry
* North, Jack
* Randolph, Richard
* Richards, Frank [house pseudonym]
* Ryle, Randolph
* West, John

Pentland, Mary
See Tilton, Mrs. E. L.

Pentreath, Doll 1686-1777   [RH]
* [The] Last who Spoke Cornish

Pentreath, Paul
See Neuburg, Victor [Benjamin]

Pentrill, Frank
See Rafferty, Mrs. William

Pentweazle, Ebenezer
See Smart, Christopher

Pentz, Jacob   [PA]
Author
* Gopher

Penzik, Irena
See Narell, Irena

Penzler, Otto 1942-   [CA]
German-born author
* Adler, Irene
* Ferrier, Lucy
* Gregory, Stephen
* Milverton, Charles A.

People, Granville Church 20th c.   [WW]
Author
* Church, Granville

[The] People's Advocate
See Dawes, Charles Gates

[The] People's Artist
See Douglas, Emory

People's Artist of the Republic
See Ivanov, Mikhail Mikhailovich

[The] People's Attorney
See Brandeis, Louis Dembitz

[The] People's Author
See Clemens, Samuel Langhorne

People's Capitalist
See Long, Russell Billiu

[The] People's Captain
See Garibaldi, Giuseppe

[The] People's Champion
See Clay, Cassius Marcellus, Jr.

[The] People's Cherce
See Walker, Frederick E.

[The] People's Choice
See Williams, Theodore Samuel [Ted]

[The] People's Democrat
See Hearst, William Randolph

[The] People's Friend
See Gordon, William

[The] People's Friend
See Marat, Jean Paul

[The] People's Friend
See Robespierre, Maximilien

Peoples, James E. [Jimmy] 1863-1920
[BN]
American baseball player
* Peoples, Kid

Peoples, Kid
See Peoples, James E. [Jimmy]

[The] People's King
See Lorraine, Henry I [or Henri] de

[The] People's Laureate
See Riley, James Whitcomb

[The] People's Lawyer
See Brandeis, Louis Dembitz

[The] People's Lawyer
See Nader, Ralph

[The] People's Poet
See Wilcox, Ella Wheeler

[The] People's Pope
See Wojtyla, Karol

[The] People's President
See Cleveland, [Stephen] Grover

[The] People's President
See Jackson, Andrew

[The] People's Prince
See Charles [Philip Arthur George]

[The] People's Will
See Pitt, William [Earl of Chatham]

[The] People's William
See Gladstone, William Ewart

[The] People's William
See Pitt, William [Earl of Chatham]

Peoples, Woodrow 1943-   [FB]
American football player
* Peoples, Woody

Peoples, Woody
See Peoples, Woodrow

Pep, Willie
See Papaleo, William

Pepe
See Mejias, Jose

Pepe Hillo [Little Joe]
See Leal y Casado, Cayetano

Pepe-Illo [Little Joey]
See Delgado y Guerra, Jose

Peper, Minnie Dorothy 1880-?   [THR]
American actress
* Oaker, Jane

Pepete [Big Joe]
See Gallego Mateo, Jose

Pepete [Big Joe]
See Rodriguez Davie, Jose

Pepete [Big Joe]
See Rodriguez y Rodriguez, Jose

Pepin ?-640?   [WBD]
Frankish ruler
* [The] Elder
* Pepin of Landern

Pepin of Herstal
See Pepin II

Pepin of Landern
See Pepin

Pepin II ?-714   [WBD]
Frankish ruler
* Pepin of Herstal

Pepin III 714?-768   [DNNS, HN, HPPN, SN]
King of the Franks
* [Le] Bref
* Most Christian King
* [The] Patrician of Rome
* Patrician of the Romans
* [The] Short

Pepino
See Carre, Freddy

Pepito the Spanish Clown
See Perez, Pepito

Pepitone, Joseph Anthony 1940-   [BE]
American baseball player
* Pepitone, Pepi

Pepitone, Pepi
See Pepitone, Joseph Anthony

Peploe, Denis Frederic Neil 1914-
[ART]
Scottish painter
* Denis P.

Peploski, Joseph Aloysius 1891-   [BE]
American baseball player
* Peploski, Pepper

Peploski, Pepper
See Peploski, Joseph Aloysius

Pepper, Bill
See Pepper, Curtis G.

Pepper Box Bartell
See Bartell, Richard William

Pepper, Choral 1918-   [CA]
American writer
* Lowe, Corke
* Rollins, Royce

Pepper, Curtis G. 1920-   [CA]
American author
* Pepper, Bill

Pepper, Frank S. 20th c.   [MBF]
British author
* Marshall, John
* Wilton, Hal

Pepper, Gary 1949-
British jazz musician
* Pepper, Woody

Pepper, George
See Martin, George

Pepper, Hugh McLaurin 1931-   [BE]
American baseball player
* Pepper, Laurin

Pepper, J. H. 19th c.   [HPPN]
British educator
* Professor

Pepper, Jack
See Culpepper, Edward

Pepper, Joan
See Wetherell-Pepper, Joan Alexander

Pepper, John
See Pogany, Joseph

Pepper, K. N.
See Morris, James M.

Pepper, Laurin
See Pepper, Hugh McLaurin

Pepper, Martin
See Krich, John

Pepper, Woody
See Pepper, Gary

Pepperbox, Peter
See Fessenden, Thomas Green

Peppercorn, Arthur Douglas 1847-1924
[DBA]
British painter
* Our English Corot

Peppercorn, H., M.D.
See Barham, Richard Harris

Peppercorn, Peter
See Peacock, Thomas Love

Peppergrass, Paul
See Boyce, John

Peppergrass, Paul
See McDougall, Margaret [Dixon]

Peppermint Cane
See Harris, Wynonie

Pepperpod, Pip
See Stoddard, Charles Warren

Peppin, Dad
See Peppin, George W.

Peppin, George W. 19th c.   [BLB]
American sheriff's deputy
* Peppin, Dad

Peppler, Alice Stolper
See Stolper, Alice

Pepys in Essex
See Tompkins, Herbert Winckworth

[The] Pepys of His Age
See De Bourdeille, Pierre

Pepys, Samuel 1633-1703   [DEA, DEP, DNNS, NPS, SN]
British author and politician
* [The] Father of Black Letter Lore
* [The] Prince of Gossips
* [The] Weather Glass of His Time
* [The] Weathercock of His Time

Pequot
See March, Charles W.

Per Aera
See Boothby, Frederick Lewis Maitland

Per Mare
See Boothby, Frederick Lewis Maitland

Peralta, Angela 1843?-1883 [FFF]
Mexican singer
* [The] Mexican Nightingale

Peralta, Goyo
See Peralta, Gregorio

Peralta, Gregorio 1935- [BX]
Argentinian boxer
* Peralta, Goyo

Peralta Seleron, Francisco 1900-1930
[GS]
Spanish bullfighter
* Facultades [Abilities]

[The] Perambulating Philosopher
See A Beckett, Gilbert Abbott

Perason, Arnett 20th c. [HPPN]
American football player
* Perason, Chink

Perason, Chink
See Perason, Arnett

Perceval, Arthur Philip 1800-1853 [IP]
British clergyman and author
* [A] Churchman
* [A] Minister of the Church of Ireland
* One of His Majesty's Chaplains
* One of His Majesty's Servants
* [A] Presbyter in the Diocese of
  Canterbury

Perceval, Charles George 1796-? [IP]
British clergyman and author
* [A] Country Clergyman
* [The] Rector of Calverton Bucks

**Perceval, [Sir] John [First Earl of
Egmont]** 1683?-1748 [HPPN, IP]
British political leader and author
* A.
* [A] Nobleman of the Other Kingdom

**Perceval, [Sir] John [Second Earl of
Egmont]** 1711-1770 [HPPN]
British politician
* [A] Gentleman in the Country

Perceval, Maxwell
See Perceval-Maxwell, Michael

Perceval, Spencer 1762-1812 [HPPN]
British statesman
* [A] Barrister

Perceval-Maxwell, Michael [WD]
Historian and author
* Perceval, Maxwell

Percevall, Plaine
See Nash [or Nashe?], Thomas

Perch, Philemon
See Johnston, Richard Malcolm

Percheron, Betty 1921- [THR]
British actress
* Paul, Betty

Percival
See Ralph, Julian E.

Percival
See Raphael, John N.

Percival, Arlene Walker 1919-1973
[HPPN]
American actress and casting director
* Walker, Arlene

Percival, Fanny
See Percy, Mrs. F. A.

Percival G.
See Irving, Peter

Percival, Hayward
See Hayward, Percy Roy

Percival, John 1779-1862 [FFF, WBD]
American naval officer
* Mad Jack
* Roaring Jack

Percival, Nelson
See Rymer, James Malcolm

Percival, Norman
See Parcell, Norman H[owe]

Percival, Thomas 1740-1804 [HPPN]
British physician
* [A] Gentleman of Manchester

Percival, Vincent
See Bonner, Carey

Percival, Walter C.
See Lingenfelter, Charles David

Percy, Charles Henry
See Smith, Dorothy Gladys

Percy, Edward
See Smith, Edward Percy

Percy, Eileen 1899- [HPPN]
Irish-American actress
* [The] Leading Lady of Silent Pictures

Percy, Florence
See Akers, Elizabeth [Chase]

Percy, Florence
See Allen, Elizabeth Akers

Percy, George
See Groves-Raines, George Percy

Percy, Henry 1364-1403 [DHA, DNNS,
SN]
British army officer
* Hotspur

Percy, Henry 1564-1632 [WBD]
Ninth Earl of Northumberland
* [The] Wizard Earl

Percy, [Sir] Hugh
See Smithson, Hugh

Percy, Marvin 1925- [ECM]
American singer and songwriter
* Rainwater, Marvin

Percy, Mrs. F. A. [PA]
Author
* Percival, Fanny

Percy, Reuben
See Byerley, Thomas

Percy, Sholto
See Byerley, Thomas

Percy, Sholto
See Robertson, Joseph Clinton

Percy, Thomas 1528-1572 [SN]
Seventh Earl of Northumberland
* Bladamour

Percy, Thomas 1729-1811 [HPPN, SN]
British author and poet
* Dromore, Thomas
* [The] Father of Poetical Taste
* Incog

Perdiguero Perez, Fernando 1929-
[IAW]
Spanish author
* Pin, Oscar

Perdita
See Robinson, Mary Darby

Perdomo y Heredia, Josefa Antonia
1834-1896 [CW]
Dominican poet
* Laura

Perdoni, Renso 1941- [FB]
Italian-born American football player
* Perdoni, Rock

Perdoni, Rock
See Perdoni, Renso

Perdue, Bolo
See Perdue, Willis

Perdue, Hubbard E. 1882-1968 [BE]
American baseball player
* [The] Gallatin Squash

Perdue, Willis 20th c. [HPPN]
American football player
* Perdue, Bolo

**Perdurabo, Frater [I Will Endure to the
End]**
See Crowley, Edward Alexander

[Le] Pere aux Rondeaux
See Davaux, Jean Baptiste

Pere de la Patrie
See Suger

[Le] Pere de la Patrie
See Vincent de Paul

[Le] Pere de la Pensee
See Catinat, Nicholas

Pere de l'Eloquence
See Jean [or Jehan] de Meung

[Le] Pere de l'Histoire de France
See Duchesne, Andre

[Le] Pere des Lettres
See Francis I or [Francois]

[Le] Pere du Peuple
See Louis XII

[Le] Pere Duchesne
See Hebert, Jacques Rene

[Le] Pere Enfantin
See Enfantin, Barthelemy Prosper

[Le] Pere Joyeux du Vaudeville
See Basselin, Olivier

Pere la Pudeur
See Berenger, Rene

Pereda, Jose Maria de 1833-1906
[HPPN]
Spanish author
* [The] Modern Cervantes

Peregoy, Calvin
See McClary, Thomas Calvert

Peregoy, George Weems
See Mencken, Henry Louis [Harry]

[La] Peregrina
See Avellaneda y Arteaga, Gertrudis
Gomez de

Peregrine, [Brother]
See Blewitt, John Octavius

Peregrine
See Deutscher, Isaac

Peregrinus
See Vincent of Lerins

Peregrinus, Petrus 13th c. [HPPN]
French scientist and soldier
* Peter de Mariacourt
* Peter the Pilgrim

Pereira, Harold Bertram 1890- [CA]
British author
* Askari, Hussaini Muhammad
* Yeates, Mabel

Pereira, Jacob Rodrigue 1715-1780
[WBD]
Spanish educator
* Pereire, Jacob Rodrigue

Pereira, Jonathan 1804-1853 [IP]
British physician and author
* J. P.

Pereira, Nunez Alvarez 1360-1431
[FFF, RH, SN]
Portuguese army officer and diplomat
* [The] Cid of Portugal
* [The] Portuguese Cid

Pereira, W. D.
See Pereira, Wilfred Dennis

Pereira, Wilfred Dennis 1921- [SFL]
British author
* Pereira, W. D.

Pereira de Souza, Washington Luiz
1869-1957 [WBD]
Brazilian statesman
* Luiz, Washington

Pereira Teixeira de Vasconcelos,
Joaquim 1879-1952 [BI]
Portuguese poet
* Teixeira de Pascoais

Pereire, Jacob Rodrigue
See Pereira, Jacob Rodrigue

Perelman, Cultured
See Shulman, Max

Perelman, Eliezer ?-1922 [TI 11-22-82]
Russian-born scholar
* Ben-Yehuda, Eliezer

Perelman, S. J.
See Perelman, Sidney Joseph

Perelman, Sidney Joseph 1904-1979
[BEW, IPA, LC]
American playwright and author
* Perelman, S. J.
* [El] Sid

Perelmuth, Jacob Pincus 1904-1984
[BBD, WP 12-17-84]
American opera singer
* Joyce, Randolph
* Pearl, Jack
* Pearl, Pinky
* Peerce, Jan
* Pierce, John
* Robinson, Paul

[The] Perennial Cecil
See De Mille, Cecil B[lount]

[The] Perennial Smart Alec of the
Movies
See Haines, William

Perera, Padma
See Hejmadi, Padma

Pereria Saromenho, Auguste ?-1878
[PA]
Author
* Abdallah

Peres, Shimon
See Persky, Shimon

Peresitch, [Colonel] 20th c. [CND]
Yugoslav military leader
* Hope, Mr. [code name used during
World War II]

Pereszlenyi, Martin 1918- [BEW]
Hungarian writer
* Esslin, Martin

Peretti, Felice 1521-1590 [HN, WBD]
Pope
* [The] Second Founder of Rome
* Sixtus V

Peretto
See Pomponazzi, Pietro

Peretz, Yitskhok Leybush 1852-1915
[MWD]
Polish author and poet
* [The] Colossus of Yiddish Literature
* [The] Father of Yiddish Literature

Perevozchikova, Maria Petrovna
1866-1954 [BEW]
Actress
* Lilina, Maria Petrovna

Perey, Lucien
See Herpin, Clara Adele Luce

Perez, Angel 1908- [BI]
American business executive
* Perez, Joe

Perez, Atanasio Rigal 1942- [PB, SMG,
WWB]
Cuban-born baseball player
* Perez, Doggie
* Perez, Tony

Perez, Cap
See Perez Rodriguez, Carlos Andres

Perez, Doggie
See Perez, Atanasio Rigal

Perez, Gino
See Perez, Isidro

Perez, Isidro 1959?-1983 [NW 10-17-83]
Mexican-born boxer
* Perez, Gino

Perez, Joe
See Perez, Angel

Perez, Jose Maria 20th c.
Spanish cartoonist
* Peridis

Perez, Juan
See Wellman, Manly Wade

Perez, Manuel ?-1884 [GS]
Spanish bullfighter
* [El] Relojero [The Watch-Maker]

Perez, Martin Roman 1947- [SMG]
American baseball player
* Perez, Taco

Perez, Pascual Gross 1957- [WP 8-16-84]
Dominican-born baseball player
* Perez, Perimeter

Perez, Pepito 1896-1975 [FIR, SC]
Spanish-born actor
* Pepito the Spanish Clown

Perez, Perimeter
See Perez, Pascual Gross

Perez, Taco
See Perez, Martin Roman

Perez, Tony
See Perez, Atanasio Rigal

Perez, Victor 1911-1942 [BX, RBE,
WBC]
Tunisian boxer
* Perez, Young
* [The] Tunis Terror

Perez, Young
See Perez, Victor

Perez Davila, Luis [BI]
Mexican dancer
* Luisillo

Perez de Cuellar y Guerra, Javier
1920?- [WP 5-9-82]
United Nations secretary general
* P. D. Q.

Perez de Guzman, Alphonso [or Alonso]
1258?-1320? [DNNF, FFF, WBD]
Spanish army officer
* [El] Bueno
* [The] Spanish Brutus

Perez de Leon, Hermina 1894-1953
[SC]
Mexican actress
* Derba, Mimi

Perez Rodriguez, Carlos Andres 1922?-
Venezuelan president
* Perez, Cap

Perez Vega, Reynaldo 20th c. [NW 4-2-84]
Nicaraguan army officer
* [El] Perro [The Dog]

Perez y Hoyos, Angel 1898- [GS]
Spanish bullfighter
* Angelillo de Triana [Little Angel of Triana]

[The] Perfect
See John II

[The] Perfect Ballplayer
See Sisler, George Harold

[The] Perfect Cure
See Stead, James Henry

[The] Perfect Fool
See Leopold, Isaiah Edwin

[The] Perfect Man
See Sandow, Eugene

[The] Perfect Master
See Ji, Maharaj

Perfect Pete
See Rozelle, Alvin Ray

Perfect, Peter
See Gregg, Peter

[The] Perfect Player
See Sisler, George Harold

[The] Perfect Prince
See John II

[The] Perfect Publisher
See Knopf, Alfred A.

[The] Perfect Stooge
See Bergen, Edgar

[The] Perfect Woman with the Form Divine
See Kellerman, Annette

Perforatus
See Borde, Andrew

[The] Perfume Burglar
See Wajcieckowski, Earl

Perfume Jack McKernan
See McKernan, John Leo

Pergamos
See Adams, Richard Newton

Pergarth, Peter
See Goddard, Norman Molyneux

Perhaps
See Horsley, Samuel

Peri, Jacopo 1561-1633 [BBD]
Italian composer
* [Il] Zazzerino

Pericas
See Lora Trejo, Francisco

Pericles 5th c. BC [DEP, NPS, SN]
Athenian statesman
* [The] G. O. M. of Athens
* [The] Olympian
* Onion Head
* Schinocephalus

Pericoli, Niccolo 1485-1550 [WBD]
Italian sculptor and architect
* [Il] Tribolo

Pericranium
See Nares, Robert

Peridis
See Perez, Jose Maria

Perier, Auguste Casimir 1811-1878 [WBD]
French politician
* Casimir Perier, Auguste

Perier, Francois
See Pilu, Francois

Periere, Inez
See Huntington, Mrs. Wright

Peries, Lester James 1921- [DFM]
Ceylonese director
* Ceylon's Satyajit Ray

Perigord, A. B.
See Raisson, Horace Napoleon

Peril, Milton R.
See Jones, Francis

[Le] Perin
See Daly, [John] Augustin

Perine, C. E. [PA]
Author
* Newton, Charles E.

Period, Pertinax and Co.
See Buckingham, Joseph Tinker

[The] Peripatetic Miss Rufsvold
See Rufsvold, Margaret Irene

Periquin
See Espinosa de los Monteros, Armando

Periwinkle, Paul
See St. John, Percy Bollingbroke

Periwinkle, Peter
See Fessenden, Thomas Green

Periwinkle, Tribulation
See Alcott, Louisa May

[A] Perjur'd Prince
See Louis XI

Perk, Abner
See Twombly, Alexander Stevenson

Perkerson, Medora [Field] 20th c. [WW]
Author
* Field, Medora

Perkins, Abigail
See Kaler, James Otis

Perkins, Admirable
See Perkins, [Commander] Albert

Perkins, [Commander] Albert 1908-
[HPPN]
British constable and bodyguard of Queen Elizabeth II
* Perkins, Admirable

Perkins, Alice 1872-? [THR]
American actress
* Lonnon, Alice

Perkins, Augustus Thorndike 19th c.
[HPPN]
American attorney and genealogist
* A. T. P.

Perkins, Buck
See Perkins, Clayton

Perkins, Charles Nelson 1936- [HPPN]
Australian civil rights activist and welfare director
* Australia's Martin Luther King

Perkins, Charles Sullivan [Charlie] 1905-
[BE]
American baseball player
* Perkins, Lefty

Perkins, Clayton 20th c. [FCW]
American musician
* Perkins, Buck

Perkins, Cy
See Perkins, Ralph Foster

Perkins, Don[ald A.] 20th c.
American football player
* Perkins, Perk

Perkins, Eli
See Landon, Melville De Lancey

Perkins, Eliza 19th c. [IP]
British author
* [A] Lady

Perkins, Ellen M. 19th c. [IP]
American author
* Pearl, Christie

Perkins, Erasmus
See Cannon, George

Perkins, Faith
See Bramer, Jennie [Perkins]

Perkins, Fearless Frances
See Perkins, Frances

Perkins, Frances 1882-1965 [HPPN]
American Secretary of Labor
* [The] Brahmin Reformer
* [The] Liberal Politician
* [The] Loquatious Linguist Whom Labor Loves
* Perkins, Fearless Frances

Perkins, Frederick Beecher 19th c. [IP, PA]
American author and librarian
* Budlong, Pharaoh

Perkins, George Douglas 1840-1914
[HPPN]
American politician
* Uncle George

Perkins, George Walbridge 1862-1920 [HPPN]
American politician
* [The] Dough Moose

Perkins, Grace
See Oursler, Grace Perkins

Perkins, Henry 19th c. [IP]
British accountant and author
* [An] Experienced Clerk

Perkins, Jacob 1766-1849 [HPPN]
American inventor
* America's Most Prolific Inventor

Perkins, James Handasyd 1810-1849 [HPPN]
American author
* J. H. P.

Perkins, Joe Willie 1913- [BWW]
American singer
* Perkins, Pinetop

Perkins, John 18th c. [HPPN]
American astronomer
* [An] Enquirer

Perkins, Justin 1805-1869 [WBD]
American missionary
* [The] Apostle of Persia

Perkins, Kenneth 1890- [WWL]
American author
* Phillips, King

Perkins, Lefty
See Perkins, Charles Sullivan [Charlie]

Perkins, Long Tom
See Perkins, Thomas Handasyd

Perkins, Mrs. Carlos
See Mount, John

Perkins, Newton Stephens 1925- [CA]
American sportswriter
* Perkins, Steve

Perkins, O. C. 20th c.
American singer
* Perkins, Perk

Perkins, Perk
See Perkins, Don[ald A.]

Perkins, Perk
See Perkins, O. C.

Perkins, Pinetop
See Perkins, Joe Willie

Perkins, Ralph Foster 1896-1963 [BE, PB]
American baseball player
* Perkins, Cy

Perkins, Richard
See Fellows, Dick

Perkins, Sam 20th c.
American basketball player
* [The] Plastic Man

Perkins, Steve
See Perkins, Newton Stephens

Perkins, Thomas Handasyd 1764-1854 [HPPN]
American merchant
* Perkins, Long Tom

Perkins, Violet Lilian 20th c. [SFL, WGT]
Author
* Leslie, Lilian [joint pseudonym with Arthur Leslie Hood]

Perkins, Virginia Chase 1902- [CAP, WD]
American author
* Chase, Virginia Lowell

Perle, George
See Perlman, George

Perley
See Poore, Benjamin Perley

Perley, Mrs. Frank [FFF]
Entertainer
* Glenn, Ida

Perlinger, Jeff 1953- [SMG]
American football player
* Perlinger, Pearl

Perlinger, Pearl
See Perlinger, Jeff

Perlman, George 1915- [CA]
American composer and author
* Perle, George

Perlman, Jess 1891- [CA]
American poet
* Gray, Philip

Perlmutter, Mawruss
See Welch, Lou

Perls, Frederick S[alomon] 1893?-1970 [CA, HPPN]
German-born author and psychotherapist
* Perls, Fritz

Perls, Fritz
See Perls, Frederick S[alomon]

Perne, Andrew 1596-1654 [NPS]
British clergyman
* [A] Doctor of Hypocrisie

Pernoll, Henry Hubbard 1888-1944 [BE]
American baseball player
* Pernoll, Hub

Pernoll, Hub
See Pernoll, Henry Hubbard

Peron, Eva Duarte 1919?-1952 [HPPN]
Wife of Argentinian president, Juan Peron
* Peron, Evita
* Saint Evita

Peron, Evita
See Peron, Eva Duarte

Peron, Isabel [or Isabelita]
See Peron, Maria Estela Martinez de

Peron, Juan Domingo 1895-1974 [HPPN]
President of Argentina
* [The] New World Superman
* [The] Strong Man of Argentina
* [El] Viejo [The Old One]

Peron, Maria Estela Martinez de 20th c. [HPPN, TI 1-23-84, TI 2-27-84, TI 9-19-83]
Argentine president
* [The] First Woman President of the Western Hemisphere
* Martinez, Isabel
* Martinez, Isabelita
* Peron, Isabel [or Isabelita]

Peronne
See Thompson, Ellen Perronet

Peropadre, Miguel 20th c. [GS]
Spanish bullfighter
* Cincovillas [Five Villas]

Perot, H. Ross 1930- [HPPN]
American business executive and philanthropist
* [The] Texas Computer Millionaire

Perotin 12th c. [BBD]
French composer
* Perotinus Magnus

Perotinus Magnus
See Perotin

Perowne, Barry
See Atkey, Philip

Peroy
See Ayxela y Torner, Pedro

[The] Perpetual Adolescent of American Poetry
See Pound, Ezra [Loomis]

[The] Perpetual Candidate
See Cleveland, [Stephen] Grover

Perpetual Motion
See Jackson, Henry

[The] Perpetual Secretary
See Thompson, Charlie

Perrault, Charles 1628-1703 [NPS, PA, SN]
French author
* Homer's Fastest Friend
* Immortal Pindar's Foe
* [The] Modern Zoilus
* Mother Goose

Perrault, Claude 1613-1688 [NPS]
French architect and scientist
* Lubin

Perrault, Giles
See Peyroles, Jacques

Perrault, Jumping Joe
See Perrault, Paul Joseph

Perrault, Paul Joseph 20th c. [BBH]
American skier
* Perrault, Jumping Joe

Perreard, Suzanne Louise Butler 1919-
[SAT]
British-born author
* Butler, Suzanne

Perreau, Ghislaine 1941- [FC, ITA, SW]
American actress
* Perreau, Gigi

Perreau, Gigi
See Perreau, Ghislaine

Perreau, Henri 20th c. [DI]
French murderer and robber
* Cotton, Mr.
* De Tourville, Henri

Perreau-Saussine, Gerald 1938- [CA, FC]
American actor, author, screenwriter
* Miles, Peter
* Miles, Richard

Perreault, Miche
See Perreault, Robert

Perreault, Robert 1931- [CEI]
Canadian-born hockey player
* Perreault, Miche

Perrenial President
See Tubman, William Vacanarat
Shadrach

Perrers [or Pierce?], Alice ?-1400
[DNNF, FFF, RH]
Mistress of King Edward III of England
* [The] Lady of the Sun

Perri, Leslie
See Wilson, Doris Marie Claire
Baumgardt Pohl

Perricas
See Toulet, Paul Jean

Perrier, Anna 19th c. [IP, PA]
Irish author
* [An] Irish Woman

Perrier, Jules
See Michiels, Alfred John Xavier

Perrier, Rose-Marie
See Casias, Rose-Marie Perrier

Perriman, Florence ?-1936 [EOP]
Author who claimed to possess psychic powers
* Faustina, Madame

Perrin, Claude Victor [Duc de Bellune]
1766-1841 [WBD]
French army officer
* Victor [or Victor-Perrin], Claude

Perrin, Clyde
See O'Brien, Howard Vincent

Perrin, Jack
See Rayart, Jack Perrin

Perrin, Jeannine 1926- [HPPN]
American jazz musician
* Mimi

Perrin, Lefty
See Perrin, William Joseph [Bill]

Perrin, William Joseph [Bill] 1911-1974
[BE]
American baseball player
* Perrin, Lefty

Perrine, John Grover 1885-1948 [BE]
American baseball player
* Perrine, Nig

Perrine, Nig
See Perrine, John Grover

Perrine, William 20th c. [HPPN]
American newspaper columnist
* Penn

Perrinot, Jeanne 1906- [THR]
French actress and singer
* Aubert, Jeanne

Perris, Samuel 19th c. [HPPN]
American criminal
* Perris, Worcester Sam

Perris, Worcester Sam
See Perris, Samuel

Perritt, Pol
See Perritt, William Dayton

Perritt, William Dayton 1892-1947 [AS, BE]
American baseball player
* Perritt, Pol

[El] Perro [The Dog]
See Perez Vega, Reynaldo

Perron, General
See Aullier, Pierre

Perrone, Count
See Perrone, Matteo

Perrone, Matteo 1883-1932 [HPPN]
American dancer and singer
* Perrone, Count

Perrone, Sam
See Perrone, Santo

Perrone, Santo ?-1966 [PHM]
American underworld figure
* Perrone, Sam

Perrot, Gervase
See Jones, Arthur Llewellyn

Perrugia, Vincenzo 20th c. [DI]
Italian robber
* Leonard

Perry, A. T. 1887- [WGT]
Ukrainian-born British author
* Ack-Lak, General

Perry, Albert 20th c. [GW]
American rodeo performer
* Perry, Coyote

Perry, Annette
See Perry, Antoinette

Perry, Antoinette 1888-1946 [SC]
American actress and director
* Perry, Annette

Perry, Aulcie 20th c. [IBW]
American-born basketball player
* Ben Avraham, Elisha

Perry, Barbara Fisher
See Fisher, Barbara

Perry, Bob
See Perry, Melvin Gray

Perry, Brighton
See Benchley, Robert [Charles]

Perry, Brighton
See Sherwood, Robert Emmet

Perry, Cicero R. 1822-1898 [HPPN]
American soldier
* Perry, Rufe

Perry, Clair Willard 1887- [NAA]
American author
* Perry, Clay

Perry, Clay
See Perry, Clair Willard

Perry, Clifford Albyn 1891-1937 [EMT]
British-born actor, producer, director
* Cliff, Laddie

Perry, Coyote
See Perry, Albert

Perry, David 19th c. [IP]
American soldier and author
* [An] Old Soldier

Perry, Dick 1922- [SFL]
Author
* Winfield, Dick

Perry, Edgar A.
See Poe, Edgar Allan

Perry, Elaine
See Frueauff, Elaine Storrs

Perry, Eleanor 1915?-1981 [CA]
American author and screenwriter
* Bayer, Oliver Weld

Perry, Ernest Thomas 1908- [ART]
Irish-born painter
* E. P.

Perry, Fletcher 1927- [BI, FB, IBW]
American football player
* Joe the Jet
* Perry, Joe
* Perry, Jolting Joe

Perry, Gaylord Jackson 1938- [HPPN]
American baseball player
* [The] Spitball Pitcher

Perry, Harry Dennies
See Ingraham, Prentiss

Perry, Henry G. [IP]
American journalist
* Regryph

Perry, Irene
See Brady, Irene

Perry, Irma
See Le Gallienne, Irma Hinton

Perry, James Black 1845-1936 [CCL]
Canadian author
* Weir, Logan

Perry, James Curtis
See Perry, Oliver Curtis

Perry, Joe
See Perry, Fletcher

Perry, Jolting Joe
See Perry, Fletcher

Perry, Joseph Franklin 1846-1909
[DNA]
American author and physician
* Ashmont
* Frank, Dr.

Perry, Junebug
See Perry, Vernon, Jr.

Perry, Lincoln Theodore 1892?-1985
[BI, F2, FC, HPPN]
American entertainer
* Stepin Fetchit
* [The] White Man's Negro

Perry, Margaret
See Frueauff, Margaret Hall

Perry, Martin Henry 1903- [AW]
British author
* Martyn, Henry

Perry, Matthew Calbraith 1794-1858
[HPPN]
American naval officer
* [The] Great Commodore
* Old Bruin

Perry, Melvin Gray 1934- [BE]
American baseball player
* Perry, Bob

Perry, Montanye 20th c. [NAA]
American author
* Lambert, Marion

Perry, Mrs. E. C. 19th c. [IP]
Author
* Hall, Elfin

Perry, Nancy Ling 1948?-1974 [HPPN]
American radical terrorist group member
* Fahiza

Perry, Ned
See Perryan, Noel

Perry, Neil James 1958- [DC]
British cricketer
* Perry, Ziggy

Perry, Oliver
See Morton, Oliver Hazard Perry
Throck

Perry, Oliver Curtis 1864-1930 [BLB]
American train robber
* Moore, Oliver
* Perry, James Curtis

Perry, Oliver Hazard 1785-1819
[HPPN]
American naval officer
* [The] Hero of Lake Erie
* [The] Tragic Commodore

Perry, Ritchie [John Allen] 1942- [CA]
British author
* Allen, John

Perry, Rufe
See Perry, Cicero R.

Perry, Rufus
See Gibson, Walter B[rown]

Perry, Ruth 1892-
Author
* Campion, Rose [joint pseudonym with
  Arthur LeRoy Kaser and Jean Lee
  Latham]

Perry, Socks
See Perry, William Henry [Hank]

Perry, Vernon, Jr. 1953- [SMG]
American football player
* Perry, Junebug

Perry, Vic[tor] 1920-1974 [SC]
British-born actor
* [The] World's Greatest Pickpocket

Perry, W. A. [IP]
American journalist
* Silalicum

Perry, William 1819-1881 [FFF, RBE]
British boxer
* [The] Tipton Slasher

Perry, William 20th c.
American football player
* [The] Refrigerator

Perry, [Captain] William B.
See Brown, William Perry

Perry, William Henry [Hank] 1886-1956
[BE]
American baseball player
* Perry, Socks

Perry, William Stevens 1832-? [IP]
American clergyman and author
* W. S. P.

Perry, Ziggy
See Perry, Neil James

Perryan, Noel 17th c. [SN]
Hostler
* Colon
* Perry, Ned

Perryman, Art
See Perryman, Stephen Peter

Perryman, Emmett Key 1888-1966 [BE]
American baseball player
* Perryman, Parson

Perryman, Lavonia Lauren 20th c. [BA]
American journalist
* Perryman, Vonia

Perryman, Parson
See Perryman, Emmett Key

Perryman, Rufus G. 1892-1973 [BWW,
EJ]
American jazz musician
* Detroit Red
* Speckled Red

Perryman, Stephen Peter 1955- [DC]
British cricketer
* Perryman, Art

Perryman, Vonia
See Perryman, Lavonia Lauren

Perryman, William Lee [Willie] 1911-
[BWW]
American singer
* Boogie 'n' Blues, Mr.
* Feelgood, Doctor
* Piano Red

[The] Persecutor
See Rawson, Edward

Perseus, Peter
See Thackeray, William Makepeace

Pershing, Black Jack
See Pershing, John Joseph

Pershing, John Joseph 1860-1948
[CND]
American military leader
* Pershing, Black Jack
* Pershing, Nigger Jack

Pershing, Marie
See Schultz, Pearle Henriksen

Pershing, Mike 1947- [HPPN]
American undercover police trooper
* Sims, Billy

Pershing, Nigger Jack
See Pershing, John Joseph

[The] Persian Alexander
See Sandjar

[The] Persian Anacreon
See Hafiz, Mohammed

[The] Persian Horace
See Omar Khayyam

[The] Persian King
See Cyrus

[The] Persian Sage
See Aphraates, Jacob

[The] Persian Sage
See Apraates, Jacob

Persiani, Andre Paul Stephane 1927-
[EJ]
French jazz musician
* Persiany, Andre Paul Stephane

Persiany, Andre Paul Stephane
See Persiani, Andre Paul Stephane

Persic, Peregrine
See Morier, James Justinian

Persico, Carmine 1933?- [PHM]
American underworld figure
* [The] Snake

Persico, Salvatore Giuseppe 1893- [BE]
American baseball player
* Smith, Joe
* Smith, Salvatore Giuseppe

Persimmons
See Bennett, M., Jr.

Persis
See Haime, Agnes Irvine Constance
[Adams]

Persius
See Flaccus, Aulus Persius

Persius Flaccus, Aulus 34-62 [FFF, RH, SN]
Roman satirist
* [The] Ligurian Sage

Perske, Betty Joan 1924- [BDF, BEW, BI, EMT]
American actress
* Bacall, Betty
* Bacall, Lauren
* [The] Looks

Persky, Mordecai 1931- [CA]
American editor
* Persky, Mort

Persky, Mort
See Persky, Mordecai

Persky, Shimon 1923- [CA]
Israeli politician and author
* Peres, Shimon

[A] Person about Town
See Webb, Cornelius

[A] Person Concer'n'd
See Colbatch, John

[A] Person Concerned in Trade
See Butterworth, James

[A] Person for All Seasons
See O'Connor, Sandra Day

[A] Person lately about Town
See Webbe, Cornelius

Person, Muscles
See Person, Norman

Person, Norman 20th c. [GW]
American rodeo performer
* Person, Muscles

[A] Person of Honor
See Leonard, Daniel

[A] Person of Honour
See Ancillon, Charles

[A] Person of Honour
See North, Roger

[A] Person of Honour
See Pulteney, William [Earl of Bath]

[A] Person of Honour
See Southland, T.

[A] Person of Honour
See Swift, Jonathan

[A] Person of Honour
See Villiers, George

[A] Person of Note Who Resided Many Years There
See Robinson, John

[A] Person of Quality
See Hervey, John [Baron Hervey of Ickworth]

[A] Person of Quality
See Howard, Edward [Eighth Earl of Suffolk]

[A] Person of Quality
See Pomfret, John

[A] Person of Quality
See Scott, Sarah

[A] Person of Quality
See Swift, Jonathan

[A] Person Who Had Some Share in His Education
See Sheridan, Thomas

[A] Person Who Lived There Ten Years
See Fermin, Philippe

[A] Person Who Renounced Deism
See Grey, Francis

[A] Person Without A Name
See Lewis, Alethea [Brereton]

Persona Grata
See Abuza, Sophie

Persona Grata
See Reed, [Sir] Carol

[The] Personality Girl
See Hanshaw, Annette

Personality, Princess
See Matthews, Jessie

Personne
See Fontaine, Felix Gregory de

Personne
See Lynch, Mrs. Henry

Personne
See Wilkins, E. G. P.

Persons, Truman Streckfus 1924-1984 [HPPN, WP 8-27-84]
American author
* Capote, Truman

[The] Perspicuous Doctor
See Burleigh, [or Burley?], Walter

Perspicuus, Doctor
See Bonet, Nicholas

Persson, Harry Arnold 1920- [EJ]
Swedish jazz musician
* Arnold, Harry

[The] Persuasive Euphemius
See Walpole, [Sir] Robert [First Earl of Orford]

[A] Pert, Prim Prater of the Northern Race
See Wedderburn, Alexander [First Baron Loughborough]

Pertinax
See Geraud, [Charles Joseph] Andre

Pertinax
See Gerault, Charles

Pertinax
See Haws, Duncan

Pertinax, Publius Helvius 126-193 [DEP, FFF]
Roman emperor
* [The] Tennis Ball of Fortune

Pertinez, Zoilo 20th c. [GS]
Spanish bullfighter
* Terremoto [Big Earthquake]

Pertzel, Mrs. [FFF]
Entertainer
* Prescott, Marie

Perugini, Mark [NPS]
Author
* March Pane

Perugini, Signor
See Chatterton, John

[Il] Perugino
See Bartoli, Pietro Santi

[Il] Perugino
See Vannucci, Pietro

Perus, Francoise 1936- [IAW]
French-born author
* Cueva, Francoise
* Perus-Cueva, Francoise

Perus-Cueva, Francoise
See Perus, Francoise

[A] Peruvian Princess
See Issembourg D'Happoncourt, Francoise D' [Dame de Graffigny]

Pery, Edmund Sexton 18th c. [IP]
Author
* [An] Armenian in Ireland

Pesano, Alfred Manuel 1928- [BE, IPA, SMG]
American baseball player and manager
* Martin, Alfred Manuel
* Martin, Billy

[Il] Pesarese
See Cantarini [or da Pesaro], Simone

Pesce, Franco 20th c. [WF]
Italian actor
* Oliveras, Frank

Peschkowsky, Michael Igor 1931- [BEW, FC, FD]
German-born American entertainer and director
* Nichols, Mike

[Il] Pesellino
See Di Stefano, Francesco

Peshkov [or Pyeshkoff], Alexei Maximovich 1868-1936 [OCF, TC, TCL]
Russian author and playwright
* Chlamyda, Jehudiil
* Gorky, Maxim

Peskay, Edward 1899?-1978 [FIR]
Film industry pioneer
* Peskay, Pop

Peskay, Pop
See Peskay, Edward

Pesky, Johnny
See Paveskovich, John Michael

Pesky, Needlenose
See Paveskovich, John Michael

Pessen, Beth 1943- [CA]
American author
* Shub, Beth

[The] Pessimist With Hope
See Darrow, Clarence Seward

Pessl, Gabriela Elsa 1906- [BBD]
Austrian-born musician
* Pessl, Yella

Pessl, Yella
See Pessl, Gabriela Elsa

Pessoa, Fernando [Antonio Nogueira]
1888-1935 [WOA]
Portuguese poet
* Caeiro, Alberto
* De Campos, Alvaro
* Reis, Ricardo

Pesta, Richard 1945?- [HPPN]
American self-appointed crime fighter
* Sticky, Captain

Pestalozzi
See Peters, Bernard

Pesthe
See Millspaugh, Charles Frederick

Pestleman Jack
See Keats, John

Pestritto, Antonio 1907-1969 [EJ, PMJ,
WWJ]
American jazz musician
* Pastor, Tony

Pestromi, Julia 1873?-1973 [HPPN]
Mexican Indian entertainer
* [The] Ape Woman

[The] Pet of the Fancy
See Curtis, Dick

[The] Pet of the Palace
See Stratton, Charles Sherwood

[The] Pet of the Year
See Lanza, Isabel

Petaja, Emil [Theodore] 1915- [ESF]
American author
* Pine, Theodore [joint pseudonym with
Henry L. Hasse]

Pete
See Longstreet, James

Pete
See Pierpont, Harry

Pete the Hermit
See Howard, Peter

Peter [HN]
Bishop of Argos
* Thaumaturgus

Peter ?-1012 [CAL]
Pope
* Bucca Porci [Pig's Snout]
* Sergius IV

Peter ?-1785 [HPPN]
German foundling
* [The] Wild Boy

Peter [or Pietro] 406-450 [FFF, HN]
Saint
* Chrysologus
* Golden Speech
* [The] Golden Tongued

Peter 19th c. [DNNS, RH]
Calabrian robber chief
* [The] Emperor of the Mountains

Peter
See Cockburn, [Rev.] William

Peter
See Foe, Daniel

Peter
See Lockhart, John Gibson

Peter
See Simon

Peter Claver 1580-1654 [WBD]
Saint
* [The] Apostle of the Negroes

Peter de l'Isle [HN]
Medieval scholar
* Notabilis, Doctor

Peter de Mariacourt
See Peregrinus, Petrus

Peter Lee, Sidney 20th c.
British forger
* [The] Magician

Peter o' the Painch
See Robinson, Patrick

Peter of Amiens 1050?-1115? [SN,
WBD]
French monk
* [The] Hermit

Peter [or Pierre] of Cluny 1092?-1156
[FFF, HN, WBD]
French-born monk
* Peter of Montboissier
* Venerabilis, Doctor
* [The] Venerable Doctor

Peter of Mantua
See Guarneri, Pietro Giovanni

Peter of Montboissier
See Peter [or Pierre] of Cluny

Peter of Pontefract
See Graves, Richard

**Peter of Tarentaise [Pietro di
Tarantasia]** 1245-1277 [CAL, HN]
Pope
* Famosissimus, Doctor
* Innocent V

Peter of Venice
See Guarneri, Pietro

[The] Peter Pan of Politics
See Brown, Edmund Gerald, Jr.[Jerry]

[The] Peter Pan of Pop
See Jackson, Michael Joseph

Peter, Parson
See Peters, Samuel Andrew

Peter, R. C.
See Peter, Robert Charles

Peter, Robert Charles 1888- [ART]
British painter and engraver
* Peter, R. C.

Peter the Great
See Pund, Henry R.

Peter the Great
See Rozelle, Alvin Ray

[The] Peter the Great of Egypt
See Mehemet [or Mohammed] Ali

Peter the Great Showman
See Ustinov, Peter Alexander

Peter the Headstrong
See Stuyvesant, Petrus

**Peter the Hermit of the Abolitionist
Movement**
See Lundy, Benjamin

Peter the Packer
See O'Brien, Peter

Peter the Paragon
See Sweeney, Peter Barr

Peter the Pilgrim
See Peregrinus, Petrus

Peter the Plowman
See Mercer, [Major] James

Peter, William 1788-1853 [IP]
British poet and politician
* [A] Layman

Peter I [Petr Alekseevich] 1672-1725
[DNNS, SN, WBD]
Czar of Russia
* [The] Great
* Mikhailov, Peter
* [The] Northern Star

Peter I 1844-1921 [HPPN]
King of Serbia
* Karageorgevich

Peter III 1728-1762 [HPPN]
Czar of Russia
* Feodorovich, Petr

Peterkiewicz, Jerzy
See Pietrkiewicz, Jerzy

Peterkin, Alexander 1781-1846 [IP, PA]
Scottish poet, barrister, antiquary
* Alumnus Edinensis
* Anti Harmonicus
* Civis

Peterkin, Daisy 1884-1952 [BEW]
American theatrical performer
* Dazie, Mademoiselle

Peterley, David
See Pennington, Richard

Peterman, Roberta 1930- [IPA, OP]
American opera singer
* Peters, Roberta

Peters, Alexander
See Hollander, Zander

Peters, Arthur Anderson 1913-1979
[CA]
American author
* Peters, Fritz

Peters, Barney
See Bauer, Erwin A.

Peters, Bernadette
See Lazzara, Bernadette

Peters, Bernard 1827-? [FFF, PA]
American editor
* Pestalozzi

Peters, Bill
See McGivern, William P[eter]

Peters, Brock
See Fisher, Brock

Peters, Bryan
See George, Peter [Bryan]

Peters, Caroline
See Betz, Eva Kelly

Peters, Charley
See Patton, Charley

Peters, Clarice
See Kwock, Laureen

Peters, Curtis Arnoux, Jr. 1904?-1968
[CA, HPPN, LC]
American cartoonist
* Arno, Curt
* Arno, Peter

Peters, Donald L. 1925- [CA]
American educator and author
* Peters, Leslie

Peters, Elizabeth 1926- [SW]
American actress
* Evans, Mary Ann
* Peters, Jean

Peters, Elizabeth
See Mertz, Barbara [Gross]

Peters, Ellis
See Pargeter, Edith Mary

Peters, Forest 20th c. [EF]
American football player
* Peters, Frosty

Peters, Fred
See Tuite, Frederick P.

Peters, Fritz
See Peters, Arthur Anderson

Peters, Frosty
See Peters, Forest

Peters, Gary Charles 1937- [PB]
American baseball player
* Peters, Pete

Peters, Geoffrey
See Palmer, Madelyn

Peters, Geoffrey
See Trippe, Peter

Peters, Herman Wolfe 1919- [HPPN]
American football player
* Peters, Laddie

Peters [or Peter?], Hugh 1599-1660
[DNNS, HN]
British clergyman
* Cromwell's Mad Chaplain
* [The] Pulpit Buffoon

Peters, Jane Alice 1908-1942 [BDF, F1,
FC, HPPN]
American actress
* Lombard, Carole
* [The] Queen of Screwball Comedies

Peters, Jean
See Peters, Elizabeth

Peters, Jeremy
See Smith, Thomas Lacey

Peters, John William 1893-1932 [BE]
American baseball player
* Peters, Shotgun

Peters, L. T. [joint pseudonym with Jo-
Ann Klainer]
See Klainer, Albert S.

Peters, L. T. [joint pseudonym with
Albert S. Klainer]
See Klainer, Jo-Ann

Peters, Laddie
See Peters, Herman Wolfe

Peters, Lane
See Lapidus, Elaine

Peters, Lawrence
See Davies, Leslie Purnell

Peters, Leslie
See Peters, Donald L.

Peters, Linda
See Catherall, Arthur

Peters, Ludovic
See Brent, Peter [Ludwig]

Peters, Marcia
See Gouled, Vivian G[loria]

Peters, Maureen 1935- [AW, CA, WD]
Welsh-born author
* Black, Veronica
* Darby, Catherine
* Rothman, Judith
* Whitby, Sharon

Peters, Oscar C. 1886- [BE]
American baseball player
* Peters, Rube

Peters, Pete
See Peters, Gary Charles

Peters, Phillis
See Wheatley, Phillis

Peters, Roberta
See Peterman, Roberta

Peters, Rube
See Peters, Oscar C.

Peters, Russell Dixon 1914- [BE]
American baseball player
* Peters, Rusty

Peters, Rusty
See Peters, Russell Dixon

Peters, S. H.
See Porter, William Sydney [Bill]

Peters, S. T.
See Brannon, William T.

Peters, Samuel Andrew 1735-1826 [IP]
American author
* [A] Gentleman of the Province
* Peter, Parson
* Viator, John, Esq.

Peters, Shotgun
See Peters, John William

Peters, Steven
See Geiser, Robert L[ee]

Peters, Susan
See Carnahan, Suzanne

Peters, W. A. 1841-? [IP, PA]
American journalist
* Bronson, Doctor
* Sloper, Joel

Peters, W. C.
See Peters, William Cumming

Peters, Wally
See Paricciuoli, Walter

Peters, William Cumming 1805-1866
[DAM]
*British-born musician, composer, music
publisher*
* Peters, W. C.

Petersen, Allan Ernest 1918- [BA]
American businessman
* Petersen, Pete

Petersen, Eugenie 1899- [EOP]
Russian-born educator and author
* Indra Devi

Petersen, Gwenn Boardman 1924- [CA]
British-born author
* Boardman, Gwenn R.

Petersen, Kaj Harald Leininger
1898-1944 [BEW]
Danish playwright and clergyman
* Munk, Kaj

Petersen, Pete
See Petersen, Allan Ernest

Petersen, Robert Storm 1882-1949
[WEC]
Danish cartoonist, painter, actor, author
* Storm P.

Petersen, Toni Phil 1932?-1985
Danish ballerina
* Lander, Toni

Petersham, Miska
See Petersham, Petrezselyem Mikaly

Petersham, Petrezselyem Mikaly
1888-1960 [CA]
*Hungarian-born American author and
illustrator*
* Petersham, Miska

Petersilea, Carlyle 1844-1903 [SFL, WGT]
Author
* Von Himmel, Ernst

Peterson, Anna
See Rundquist, Anna Olivia

Peterson, Beatrice Sofia Mathilda 1916- [FC]
American actress
* Brooke, Hillary

Peterson, Buddy
See Peterson, Carl Francis

Peterson, Cap
See Peterson, Charles Andrew

Peterson, Carl Francis 1925- [BE]
American baseball player
* Peterson, Buddy

Peterson, Cassandra 20th c.
American television personality
* Elvira

Peterson, Charles Andrew 1942- [BE]
American baseball player
* Peterson, Cap

Peterson, Charles Jacob 1819-1887 [DNA]
American author and publisher
* Randolph, J. Thornton

Peterson, Corinna 1923- [AW]
British author
* Cochrane, Corinna

Peterson, Crockey
See Peterson, Howard G.

Peterson, Firecracker
See Peterson, Herman

Peterson, Fred Ingels 1942- [BE, PB]
American baseball player
* Peterson, Fritz

Peterson, Frederick 1859-1938 [HPPN]
American neurologist and poet
* Pai Ta-shun

Peterson, Frederick Valdemar ?-1983 [WP 10-18-83]
American politician
* Peterson, Val

Peterson, Fritz
See Peterson, Fred Ingels

Peterson, Harding 1930- [SMG]
American baseball player and manager
* Peterson, Pete

Peterson, Herman ?-1975 [BBH]
American trapshooter
* Peterson, Firecracker

Peterson, Howard G. 1939?- [BI, HPPN]
American auto racer
* Peterson, Crockey

Peterson, James
See Zeiger, Henry A[nthony]

Peterson, Jeanne Whitehouse
See Whitehouse, Jeanne

Peterson, Jim
See Crawford, William [Elbert]

Peterson, John Victor 20th c. [WGT]
Author
* Valding, Victor [joint pseudonym with Allan Ingvald Benson]

Peterson, Judge Kenneth 1966- [IBW]
American musician
* Peterson, Lucky

Peterson, Lenka
See Isacson, Betty Ann

Peterson, Lucky
See Peterson, Judge Kenneth

Peterson, Margaret
See Fischer, Margaret Ann Peterson

Peterson, Marvin 1948- [IBW]
American jazz musician
* Hannibal

Peterson, Master Joe
See O'Rourke, Mary

Peterson, Maud Howard
See Hoopes, Mary Howard

Peterson, Pete
See Peterson, Harding

Peterson, Pete
See Peterson, Wilbur

Peterson, Ralph Howard 1915?-1976 [BI]
American journalist and television newscaster
* Howard, Ralph

Peterson, Robert E[ugene] 1928- [CA]
American author
* Saya, Peter

Peterson, Roger Tory 1908?-
American author and illustrator of bird guides
* King Penguin

Peterson, Val
See Peterson, Frederick Valdemar

Peterson, Wilbur 1915-1960 [SC]
American actor
* Peterson, Pete

Petie, Haris
See Petty, Roberta

Petiot, Henry John Felix Marcel 1897-1946? [DI, HPPN]
French murderer
* [The] Super Bluebeard
* Valery, Henry

Petiot, Henry Jules 1901-1965 [CAT, EWL]
French author
* Daniel Rops

Petipa, Marius 1819-1910 [HPPN]
Russian choreographer and ballet dancer
* [The] Father of the Classic Ballet

Petit, Adrien 1500-? [PA]
Author
* Coelicus

[Le] Petit Albert
See Albert [Count of Bollstadt]

Petit, Anne-Marie 1938- [FC]
French actress
* Petit, Pascale

[Le] Petit Bernard
See Bernard, Solomon

Petit, Buddy
See Crawford, Joseph

[Le] Petit Caporal
See Bonaparte, Napoleon

[The] Petit Chef
See Sukulov, Victor

[Le] Petit Fils de Voltaire
See About, Edmond Francois Valentin

Petit, Francois
See Landru, Henri Desire

[Le] Petit Homme Rouge
See Vizetelly, Ernest Alfred

Petit, Lizzie
See Cutler, P. C.

[Le] Petit Manteau Bleu
See Champion, Edme

Petit Mere, Frederic du 19th c. [IP]
French author
* Monkey

Petit, Pascale
See Petit, Anne-Marie

[Le] Petit Roi de Bourges
See Charles VII

Petite, Mademoiselle
See Bari-Dussot, Comtesse

[La] Petite Nellie
See Liddy, Eleanor Jane

Petkov, Khristo Botyov 1847-1876 [WBD]
Bulgarian patriot and poet
* Botyov, Khristo

Peto
See White, Stanley

Peto, James
See White, Stanley

Petofi, Sandor
See Petrovics, Sandor

Petosky, Fred Lee 1911- [BE]
American baseball player
* Petosky, Ted

Petosky, Ted
See Petosky, Fred Lee

Petracco, Francesco 1304-1374 [FFF, HPPN, NPS, WBD]
Italian poet
* [The] Father of Humanism
* Petrarch
* [The] Prince of Italian Poets
* [The] Prince of the Sonnet
* [The] Tuscan Imp of Fame

Petrarch
See Petracco, Francesco

[The] Petrarch of Catalonia
See March, Ausias

[The] Petrarch of England
See Sidney, [Sir] Philip

[The] Petrarch of France
See Ronsard, Pierre de

[The] Petrarch of Spain
See Vega, Garcilasso de la

Petre, Olinthus
See Maginn, William

Petri, Elio
See Petri, Eraclio

Petri, Eraclio 1929- [FDG]
Italian director
* Petri, Elio

Petri, Gerlacus
See Gerlac, Peterson

Petri, Olaus [or Olaf] 1493-1552
[HPPN]
Swedish reformer
* [The] Luther of Sweden

Petri, Sjurd Peeters 1527-1597 [PA]
Author
* Suffridus

Petrie, Mildred McClary 1912- [CA]
Canadian-born author
* Tymeson, Mildred McClary

Petrie, Rhona
See Buchanan, Marie

Petrie, Susan
See Seffernick, Susan M.

Petrilli, Dominick ?-1953 [PHM]
American underworld figure
* [The] Gap

Petrillo, James Caesar 1892-1984
[HPPN, WP 10-25-84]
American labor union leader
* Little Caesar

Petro Bey
See Mavromichalis, Petros

Petrocelli, Americo Peter 1943- [BE,
SMG]
American baseball player
* Petrocelli, Rico

Petrocelli, Orlando R[alph] 1930- [CA]
American publisher and author
* Dyer, Brian [joint pseudonym with
   Brian Rothery]

Petrocelli, Rico
See Petrocelli, Americo Peter

Petrolle, Billy 1905- [BX, RBE]
American boxer
* [The] Fargo Express

Petrone, Jane Muir 1929- [CA]
American author
* Muir, Jane

**[El] Petronio de los Toreros [The
Petronio of the Bullfighters]**
See Gaona y Jimenez, Rodolfo

Petronius
See Larsen, Erik

Petronius, Caius [or Gaius] 1st c. [FFF,
RH, SN]
Roman courtier
* Arbiter Elegantiae [or Elegantiarum]
* [A] Roman Beau Brummel

[The] Petronius of France
See Jolyot de Crebillon, Claude Prosper

Petronius, Pasquin
See Riley, Isaac

Petroselli, Luigi 1932?-
Italian politician
* Bananas, Joe

Petrosian, Tigran 1929?-1984 [NW 8-27-
84]
Russian chess player
* [The] Tiger

Petrosino, Joseph 1860-1909 [HPPN]
Italian-American detective
* Simoni, Guglielmo de

Petrosky, James 1927- [BE]
American baseball player
* Clark, James [Jim]

Petrov
See Vasilev, Zhelio

Petrov, Eugene [or Yevgeni]
See Katayev, Yevgeni Petrovich

Petrov, Stepan Gavrilovich 1868-1934
[BI]
Russian author
* Skitaletz

Petrova, Olga
See Harding, Muriel

Petrovics, Sandor 1823-1849 [WBD]
Hungarian poet
* Petofi, Sandor

Petrovitsch [or Petrovic], George
1766?-1817 [HN, WBD]
Serbian peasant leader
* Black George
* Czerny Djordje
* Karageorge [or Karadjordje]

Petrovna, Elizabeth 1709-1762
Empress of Russia
* [The] Infamous Harlot of the North

Petrovskaya, Kyra
See Wayne, Kyra Petrovskaya

Petrovsky, Boris
See Beauchamp, Kathleen Mansfield

Petrovsky, N.
See Poltoratzky, N[ikolai] P[etrovich]

Petrus a Gandavo
See Van Der Moere, Peeter

Petry, Daniel Joseph 1958- [SMG]
American baseball player
* Petry, Peaches

Petry, Peaches
See Petry, Daniel Joseph

Petschler, Erik 20th c.
Swedish director
* [The] Swedish Mack Sennett

Petterino, Arturo 1920?- [HPPN]
Italian-American head waiter
* Arturo
* [The] Dean of Maitre d's

Pettersson, H. Bertil N. 1932- [IAW]
Swedish author
* Malm, Margaretha

Pettes, George William 19th c. [IP, PA]
American poet
* G. W. P.

[The] Petticoat Pet
See Van Buren, Martin

Pettie [or Petty], Edna May 1875?-1948
[BEW, CED, EMT]
American actress and singer
* May, Edna

Pettie's Boy
See McCollum, Robert Lee

Pettigrew, Leola B. 1893- [BWW]
American singer
* Grant, Coot
* Grant, Leola B.
* Hunter, Patsy

Pettinger, Cowboy
See Pettinger, Eric

Pettinger, Eric 20th c. [CEI]
Canadian-born hockey player
* Pettinger, Cowboy

Pettingill, Amos
See Harris, William Bliss

Pettit, Lefty
See Pettit, Leon Arthur

Pettit, Lefty
See Pettit, [George William] Paul

Pettit, Leon Arthur 1902- [BE]
American baseball player
* Pettit, Lefty

Pettit, [George William] Paul 1931-
[BE]
American baseball player
* Pettit, Lefty

Pettitt, Mrs. [FFF]
Entertainer
* Buckingham, Fanny Louise

Pettus, William T. ?-1924 [MK]
American baseball player
* Pettus, Zack

Pettus, Zack
See Pettus, William T.

Petty, Jesse Lee 1894-1971 [BE]
American baseball player
* [The] Silver Fox

Petty, King
See Petty, Richard

Petty, Richard 1938?- [HPPN]
American auto racer
* [The] King
* [The] King of the Road
* King Richard
* Petty, King
* [The] Stock Car Racing King

Petty, Roberta 1915- [CA]
American artist and illustrator
* Petie, Haris

Petty, [Sir] William 1623-1687 [DNNS, HPPN, SN]
British statistician and political economist
* L.
* [The] Universal Genius

Petty, [Sir] William 1737-1805 [FFF, RH, SN]
British statesman
* Lansdowne, Marquis of
* Malagrida

Petzholdt, J. [PA]
Author
* Philalethes

Peu-a-Peu
See Leopold

Peverett, David 20th c. [RM, RO2]
British musician
* Lonesome Dave

[The] Peveril of the Peak
See Scott, [Sir] Walter

Pevsner, Naum Neemia 1890- [CAP]
Russian-born sculptor and author
* Gabo, Naum

[A] Pew Holder
See Olcott, Henry S.

Peyo
See Culliford, Pierre

Peyroles, Jacques 1931- [BI]
French journalist
* Perrault, Giles

Peyronney, Vicomtesse de 1841-? [FFF]
French author
* Etincelle
* Letoriere, Georges
* Trilby

Peyton, Benny
See Peyton, Benton E.

Peyton, Benton E. 1890?-1965 [WWJ]
American jazz musician
* Peyton, Benny

Peyton, Green
See Wertenbaker, G. Peyton

Peyton, John Lewis 1825?- [HPPN]
American author
* [A] State Agent

Peyton, K. M.
See Peyton, Kathleen Wendy [Herald]

Peyton, Kathleen Wendy [Herald] 1929-
[AW, CA, WD]
British author
* Herald, Kathleen
* Peyton, K. M.

Peyzaret, Richard 20th c. [WEC]
French cartoonist
* F'Murr

Pezet, [Dr.] F.
See Zauner, Franz Paul

Pezold, Larry
See Pezold, Lorenz Johannes

Pezold, Lorenz Johannes 1893-1957
[BE]
American baseball player
* Pezold, Larry

Pezza, Michele 1771?-1806 [WBD]
Italian gangleader
* Angelo, [Fra]
* Diavolo, [Fra]

Pezzolo, Francesco Stefano 1887-1961
[BE, PB]
American baseball player
* Bodie, Frank Stephan
* Bodie, Ping

Pezzullo, John 1911- [BE]
American baseball player
* Pezzullo, Pretzels

Pezzullo, Pretzels
See Pezzullo, John

Pfaal, Hans
See Poe, Edgar Allan

[Der] Pfaffen Kaiser
See Charles IV [or Karl]

Pfalzgraf, Dr.
See Marwedi, Friedrich Carl

Pfalzgraf, Florence Leighton 1902-
[WW]
Author
* Leighton, Florence

Pfeferstein, John 1906- [BEW]
American playwright, lyricist, composer
* Murray, John

Pfeffer, Big Jeff
See Pfeffer, Francis Xavier

Pfeffer, Dandelion
See Pfeffer, Nathaniel Frederick

Pfeffer, Edward Joseph 1888-1972 [BE]
American baseball player
* Pfeffer, Jeff

Pfeffer, Francis Xavier 1882-1954 [BE]
American baseball player
* Pfeffer, Big Jeff

Pfeffer, Jeff
See Pfeffer, Edward Joseph

Pfeffer, Nathaniel Frederick 1860-1932
[BE]
American baseball player
* Pfeffer, Dandelion

Pfeifenkopf, Jacob 1922?-1976 [BI]
American photo processor
* Fenko, Jack

Pfeifer, Allan Cameron 1896- [BEW]
American press representative
* Dalzell, Allan C.

Pfeiffer, C. Boyd 1937- [IAW]
American author
* Fletcher, Scott

Pfeiffer, Emil Charles 19th c. [HPPN]
American athlete
* [A] Port Oar

Pfeiffer, Ida Laura 1797-1858 [HPPN, PA]
German author
* [The] Queen of the Dead Hands
* Ryer

Pfeiffer, Jane Cahill 1933?-
American television executive
* Attila the Nun
* [The] Ayatullah
* Clean, Mrs.
* St. Jane

Pfeiffer, Johann Gregor 18th c. [WGT]
Author
* Auletes, Grazianus Agricola

Pfeiffer, Marcella
See Syracuse, Marcella Pfeiffer

Pfeiffer, Tillie
See Fuber, Mrs. Edward

Pfeil, Donald J. 20th c. [ESF, WGT]
American author
* Arrow, William [house pseudonym, Ballantine Books]

Pfeister, Jack
See Pfiestenberger, John Theodore Joseph [Jack]

Pfiestenberger, John Theodore Joseph [Jack] 1878-1953 [AS, BE]
American baseball player
* Jack the Giant Killer
* Pfeister, Jack

Pfirman, Charles H. 1891- [HPPN]
American baseball umpire
* Pfirman, Cy

Pfirman, Cy
See Pfirman, Charles H.

Pfizenmayer, Edna Warren Mason 1885-
[NAA]
American writer
* Mason, Edna Warren

Pflaum, Susanna Whitney
See Pflaum-Connor, Susanna [Whitney]

Pflaum-Connor, Susanna [Whitney]
1937- [CA]
American educator and author
* Pflaum, Susanna Whitney

Pfoutz, Shirley Eclov 1922- [CA]
American author
* Eclov, Shirley

Pfund, Lee
See Pfund, LeRoy Herbert

Pfund, LeRoy Herbert 1919- [BE]
American baseball player
* Pfund, Lee

Pfyl, Meinhard Charles 1884-1945 [BE]
American baseball player
* Pfyl, Monte

Pfyl, Monte
See Pfyl, Meinhard Charles

Phaedra
See Inghirami, Tommaso

Phaedra
See Long, Linda

Phaintin' Phil Scott
See Suffling, Philip

Phal, Louis 1897-1925 [BX]
Senegalese-born boxer
* Siki, Battling
* [The] Singular Senegalese

Phalaris?
See Francis, [Sir] Philip

Phalaris Junior
See Boyle, Charles [Fourth Earl of Orrery]

Phantastes
See Hazlitt, William

Phantasus
See Maximilian Joseph

[The] Phantom
See Javier, [Manuel] Julian Liranzo

[The] Phantom Billionaire
See Hughes, Howard R.

[The] Phantom Finn
See Nurmi, Paavo

[The] Phantom Major
See Stirling, David

[The] Phantom President of the United States
See Mitchell, John Newton

Pharaoh
See Louis XIV

Pharaoh In Shirtsleeves
See Nasser, Gamal Abdel

Pharboeus
See Verwey, Hans

Pharez, Bransby William 1870-1961 [HPPN]
British entertainer
* Williams, Bransby

Pharoah, Jaarone
See Jenkins, Gus

Pharr, Robert D[eane] 1916- [CA]
American author
* Washington, C.

Phazma
See Field, Matthew C.

Pheasant, [Dr.] Lundy
See Cooper, Robert Andrew

Phel
See Cannon, Sarah Ophelia Colley

Phelan, Arthur Thomas 1887-1964 [BE]
American baseball player
* Phelan, Dugan

Phelan, Dick
See Phelan, James D.

Phelan, Dugan
See Phelan, Arthur Thomas

Phelan, James D. 1854-1931 [BE]
American baseball player
* Phelan, Dick

Phelan, Jeremiah
See King, Charles Daly

Phelge, Nanker [joint pseudonym with Keith Richards]
See Jagger, Michael Philip

Phelge, Nanker [joint pseudonym with Michael Philip Jagger]
See Richards, Keith

Phelon, Mira M. 20th c. [SFL]
Author
* [The] Phelons [joint pseudonym with William P. Phelon]

Phelon, William P. 20th c. [SFL]
Author
* [The] Phelons [joint pseudonym with Mira M. Phelon]

[The] Phelons [joint pseudonym with William P. Phelon]
See Phelon, Mira M.

[The] Phelons [joint pseudonym with Mira M. Phelon]
See Phelon, William P.

Phelps, Arthur 1890?-1933? [BWW]
American singer
* Blind Arthur
* Blind Blake
* Gorgeous Weed
* James, Billy
* Martin, Blind George

Phelps, Babe
See Phelps, Ernest Gordon

Phelps, Blimp
See Phelps, Ernest Gordon

Phelps, Cornelius Carman 1840-1885 [BE]
American baseball player
* Phelps, Neal

Phelps, Digger
See Phelps, Richard

Phelps, Elizabeth [Stuart] 1815-1852 [DNA]
American author
* Trusta, H.

Phelps, Elizabeth Steward [Natt] ?-1920 [DNA]
American author
* North, Leigh

Phelps, Elizabeth Stuart
See Ward, Elizabeth Stuart [Phelps]

Phelps, Ernest Gordon 1908- [BE, DGS, PB]
American baseball player
* Phelps, Babe
* Phelps, Blimp

Phelps, Frederic
See McCulley, Johnston

Phelps, George H[amilton] 1854-? [WGT]
Author
* Tangent, Patrick Quinn

Phelps, L. L. [PA]
Author
* Alpha

Phelps, Neal
See Phelps, Cornelius Carman

Phelps, Richard 20th c. [BI]
American basketball coach
* Phelps, Digger

Phelps, S. B.
See Griswold, Frances Irene [Burge]

Phelps, W. D. [PA]
Author
* Webfoot

[The] Phenom
See Clyde, David

[The] Phenomenal Presiding Elder
See Wilson, John Alfred Baynum

Phil, Theo
See Mohaupt, Rosa [Gottlieb]

Phil-Arguros
See Foe, Daniel

Phil-Porney
See Mandeville, Bernard de

Philadelphia Jack O'Brien
See Hagen, Joseph F.

Philadelphia, Jacob
See Meyer, Jacob

[The] Philadelphia Lady
See Anderson, Marian

[The] Philadelphia Witch
See Favato, Carino

[A] Philadelphian
See Williams, W.

Philadelphia's Jean Valjean
See Burke, William

Philadelphia's Murdering Faith Healer
See Bolber, Morris

Philadelphia's Top Loan Shark
See Sindoni, Francesco Gaetano

Philadelphos [Brother-Lover]
See Ptolemy II

Philadelphus
See Attalus II

Philadelphus
See Bannister, Saxe

Philadelphus
See Curteis, [Rev.] Thomas

Philadelphus
See Mather, Increase

Philador
See Greene, Robert

Philagathos
See Stiles, Ezra

Philagathus ?-1013? [WBD]
Antipope
* John XVI

Philagathus
See Dexter, John Haven

Philalethes
See Abbott, Thomas Kingsmill

Philalethes
See Alting, Albertus Samuel Carpentier

Philalethes
See Amhurst, Nicholas

Philalethes
See Babcock, James Staunton

Philalethes
See Bentley, Richard

Philalethes
See Cameron, [Rev.] John

Philalethes
See Challoner, [Rev.] Richard

Philalethes
See Comrie, Alexander

Philalethes
See Curteis, [Rev.] Thomas

Philalethes
See Echard, Laurence

Philalethes
See Findlay, Robert

Philalethes
See Gough, John

Philalethes
See Hill, [Sir] Richard

Philalethes
See Horton, [Sir] Robert John Wilmot

Philalethes
See John [or Johann] Nepomuk Maria Joseph

Philalethes
See Jones, John

Philalethes
See Leslie, Charles

Philalethes
See Mather, Cotton

Philalethes [or Lover of Truth]
See Maule, Thomas

Philalethes
See Paynter, [Commander] Charles

Philalethes
See Petzholdt, J.

Philalethes
See Pomfret, John

Philalethes
See Portsmouth, Henry

Philalethes
See Spring, Samuel

Philalethes
See Stothert, William

Philalethes
See Turner, George

Philalethes
See Twining, Thomas

Philalethes
See Webb, F.

Philalethes
See Williams, Elisha

Philalethes, Alazonomastix
See More, Henry

Philalethes Cantabrigiensis
See Jackson, John

Philalethes Cantabrigiensis
See Jurin, James

Philalethes Cantabrigiensis
See Kaye, John

Philalethes Cantabrigiensis
See Turton, Thomas

Philalethes, Eugenius
See Vaughan, Thomas

Philalethes, Eugenius, Jr.
See Samber, Robert

Philalethes, Irenaeus
See Moulin, Louis du

Philalethes, M.A., Oxon
See Fellowes, Robert

Philalethes, Mencius
See Annet, Peter

Philalethes Rusticans
See Shepherd, Richard

Philalethes Rusticus
See Asplin, William

Philanar
See Taylor, John

Philander
See Cameron, [Rev.] John

Philander
See Sheehan, John

Philander
See Wright, James

Philanglia
See Scott, James

[A] Philanthropist
See Harris, Josiah

[The] Philanthropist
See Howard, John

Philanthropos
See Fellows, John

Philanthropos
See Forster, John

Philanthropos
See Ladd, William

Philanthropos
See Mortimer, Thomas

Philanthropos
See Rhees, [Rev.] Morgan John

Philanthropos
See Wakefield, Thomas

Philanthropos
See Wells, Seth Young

Philanthropos Londonensis
See Scott, Daniel J. U. D.

Philanthropos, Theophilus
See Hall, David

Philanthropos, Theophilus
See Poole, Robert

Philanthropus
See Locke, John

Philanthus
See Sharpe, John, Jr.

Philaret
See Drozdov, Vasili Mikhailovich

Philaret
See Romanov, Fedor Nikitich

Philarete
See Manwood, Thomas

Philaretes
See Cooper, John Gilbert

Philaretus
See Curll, Edmund

Philaretus
See Toplady, Augustus Montagu

Philargos, Petros 1339-1410 [HN, WBD]
Pope
* Alexander V
* Refulgidus, Doctor

Philbert, Dominique 1967?- [NW 4-18-83]
American artist
* ERO

Philbin, Silent Steve
See Philbin, Stephen H.

Philbin, Stephen H. 1888-1973 [FB]
American football player
* Philbin, Silent Steve

Philbrick, John Dudley 1818-1886 [HPPN]
American educator
* [The] Superintendent of Public Schools

Philbrick, Mary ?-1917 [HPPN]
American actress
* Uart, Marie

Philby, Harold 1912-
British intelligence agent for Russia
* Philby, Kim

Philby, Kim
See Philby, Harold

Philecclesia
See Davis, [Rev.] Charles Henry

Phileleuth Bangor, V. E. B.
See Foxcroft, Thomas

Phileleuthere de Leipzig
See Bentley, Richard

Phileleutheros
See Fell, John

Phileleutheros Orielensis
See Davidson, John

Phileleutherus Cantabrigiensis
See Herne, Thomas

Phileleutherus Devoniensis
See Northmore, Thomas

Phileleutherus Lipsiensis
See Bentley, Richard

Phileleutherus Norfolciensis
See Parr, Samuel

Phileleutherus Vigorniensis
See Cardale, Paul

Philemon
See Coventry, Henry

Philenia [or Phililenia?]
See Morton, Sarah Wentworth Apthorp

Philes, George P. 1828-? [PA]
Author
* Silentiarius, Paulus

Philhellene
See Aristobulus I

Philibert I 1464-1482 [WBD]
Duke of Savoy
* [The] Hunter

[An] Philibin
See Pollock, John H[ackett]

Philidor
See Danican, Francois Andre

Philindus
See Mueller, Friedrich Max

Philip ?-34 [WBD]
Son of Herod, King of Judea
* Herod Philip

Philip 1st c. [DNNS]
Early Christian deacon
* [The] Evangelist

Philip [Marcus Julius Philippus] 204-249
[WBD]
Roman emperor
* [The] Arabian

Philip [or Philippe] 1342-1404 [DNNS, SN, WBD]
First Duke of Burgundy
* [The] Bold
* [Le] Hardi

Philip [or Philippe] 1396-1467 [DNNS, SN, WBD]
Third Duke of Burgundy
* [Le] Bon
* [The] Good
* [The] Great Duke of the West

Philip 1504-1567 [DNNS]
Landgrave of Hesse
* [The] Magnanimous

Philip 1921-
British prince
* Keith, [code name]

Philip
See Metacomet

Philip, Gerard 1922-1959 [BDF, WEF]
French actor
* Philipe, Gerard

Philip, James 1858-1911 [BI]
American rancher and conservationist
* Philip, Scotty

Philip, John 1775-1851 [HPPN]
British missionary
* [The] Liberator of Africa

Philip, Joseph 1879-1960 [NOJ]
American jazz musician
* One Eye Babe

Philip, Lotte Brand
See Foerster, Lotte B[rand]

Philip, Scotty
See Philip, James

Philip the King
See Marston, Philip Bourke

Philip I [or Philippe] 1052-1108 [FFF, HN, SN]
King of France
* [The] Amorous

Philip I [or Philippe] 1478-1506 [DNNS, SN, WBD]
King of Spain
* [The] Handsome

Philip II [or Philippe] 1165-1223 [FFF, HN, SN]
King of France
* Augustus
* [The] Gift of God
* [The] Magnanimous

Philip II 1527-1598 [HN, SN]
King of Spain
* [The] Demon of the South
* Radirobanes

Philip III [or Philippe] 1245-1285
[DNNS, HN, SN]
King of France
* [The] Bold
* [The] False Coiner
* [Le] Hardi

Philip IV [or Philippe] 1268-1314
[DNNS, SN, WBD]
King of France
* [Le] Bel
* [The] Fair
* [A] Malignant Plant
* [The] Modern Pilate

Philip V [or Philippe] 1294?-1322
[DNNS, HN, WBD]
King of France
* [Le] Long
* [The] Tall

Philip V 1683-1746 [DNNF, DNNS, SN]
King of Spain
* Baboon, Philip
* [A] Bigot

Philip VI [or Philippe] 1293-1350 [HN, SN]
King of France
* [Le] Bien Fortune
* [The] Fortunate

Philipe, Gerard
See Philip, Gerard

Philipp, Adolph 1864-1936 [BEW]
German-born playwright, composer, actor
* Briquet, Jean

Philipp, Elliot Elias 1915- [CA, WD]
British physician and author
* Embey, Philip
* Havil, Anthony
* Medicus II
* Tempest, Victor

Philippe, Claudius Charles 1911?-1978
British-born caterer
* Philippe of the Waldorf

Philippe of the Waldorf
See Philippe, Claudius Charles

Philippi [or Philippson?] 1506-1556
[DNNS, SN, WBD]
German historian
* [The] Prophet of the Syrians
* [The] Protestant Livy
* Sleidan [or Sleidanus], John [or Johannes]

Philippi, Mark
See Bender, Arnold

Philippicus
See Bardanes

[The] Philippines' George Washington
See Quezon y Molina, Manuel Luis

Philips, Albert Edwin 1845-? [DNA]
American author
* Alberton, Edwin

Philips, Ambrose 1675?-1749 [NPS, SN, WBD]
British poet and playwright
* Macer
* Namby-Pamby

Philips, George Norman 1888?- [MBF]
British author
* Fremlin, Victor
* Norman, Philip
* Skene, Anthony [Juan]

Philips, John 1676-1709 [NPS]
Poet
* Pomona's Bard

Philips, Judson Pentecost 1903- [CC, EMD, WW]
American author
* Pentecost, Hugh

Philips, Katherine 1631-1664 [DEL, HPPN, NPS, SN, WBD]
British poet
* [An] English Sappho
* [The] Incomparable Orinda
* [The] Matchless Orinda
* Orinda
* [The] Sappho of England

Philips, Log Hall
See Philips, Mardin Wilson

Philips, Mardin Wilson 1806-1889 [HPPN]
American author, reformer, agriculturist
* Philips, Log Hall
* [The] Sage of Log Hall

Philips, Thomas
See Davies, Leslie Purnell

Philipse, Frederick 1626-1702 [HPPN]
Dutch-American millionaire
* [The] Dutch Millionaire

Philiscos 3rd c. BC [HN, SN]
Alexandrian poet
* Homer the Younger

Philisides
See Sidney, [Sir] Philip

[The] Philistine
See Spender, John Alfred

Philistor
See Pinkerton, John

Philkins, Ike
See Bowen, William Abraham

Phillatins
See Storer, David

Phillifent, John Thomas 1916-1976 [IAW, SF, SFL]
British author
* Colson, Dorothea
* Johnson, Alan
* Rackham, John

Phillimon, Harriet Eleanor [PA]
Author
* H. E. P.

Phillimore, Francis
See Meynell, Alice [Christiana Gertrude Thompson]

Phillip, Nobbie
See Phillip, Norbert

Phillip, Norbert 1948- [DC]
West Indian cricketer
* Phillip, Nobbie
* Phillip, Zidi

Phillip, Zidi
See Phillip, Norbert

Phillippe, Charles Louis 1872?-1952 [AS, DGS, PB]
American baseball player
* Phillippe, Deacon

Phillippe, Deacon
See Phillippe, Charles Louis

Phillipps, Ambrose Lisle, Esq.
See De Lisle, Ambrose Lisle March Phillipps

Phillips, Alan
See Stauderman, Albert P[hilip]

Phillips, Alan Meyrick Kerr 1916- [CA]
British author
* Phillips, Mickey

Phillips, Albert Abernathy 1904-1964 [BE]
American baseball player
* Phillips, Buz

Phillips, Alexander Forbes 1866-1917 [WWL]
British author and playwright
* Forbes, Athol

Phillips, Alfred Noroton, Jr. 1894- [HPPN]
American manufacturer and politician
* Phillips, Milk of Magnesia

Phillips, Anne G[arvey] 1929- [CA]
American educator and author
* Dye, Anne G.

Phillips, Ardith Lowell 20th c. [BBH]
American basketball coach
* Phillips, Pete

Phillips, Arthur Osborne 1894- [HPPN]
American impostor
* [The] Fake Doctor
* Phillips, Doc

Phillips, Aubrey Clyde 20th c. [SMG]
American football player and coach
* Phillips, Red

Phillips, Barton 20th c. [HPPN]
American bank robber
* Phillips, Whitey

Phillips, Barty
See Phillips, Elizabeth Margaret Ann

Phillips, Batt
See Phillips, W. J.

Phillips, Bill
See Phillips, Merlyn J.

Phillips, Bubba
See Phillips, John Melvin

Phillips, Bum
See Phillips, Oail

Phillips, Bunny
See Phillips, O. A.

Phillips, Buz
See Phillips, Albert Abernathy

Phillips, Clara 1899-? [LFW]
American murderer
* [The] Tiger Woman

Phillips, Clarence Lemuel 1908- [BE]
American baseball player
* Phillips, Red

Phillips, Dad
See Phillips, Festus

Phillips, Damon Roswell 1919- [BE]
American baseball player
* Phillips, Dee

Phillips, David Atlee 1922- [CA]
American intelligence officer, editor, author
* St. George, David [joint pseudonym with Georgi Markov]
* Spelvin, George

Phillips, David Graham 1867-1911 [DLE1]
American author and journalist
* Graham, John

Phillips, Dee
See Phillips, Damon Roswell

Phillips, Dennis John Andrew 1924- [AW, CA, CC]
British author
* Chambers, Peter
* Chester, Peter

Phillips, Doc
See Phillips, Arthur Osborne

Phillips, Elizabeth Margaret Ann 1933- [IAW]
British author
* Phillips, Barty

Phillips, Esther
See Jones, Esther Mae

Phillips, Festus 1872-1955 [SC]
American actor and makeup artist
* Phillips, Dad

Phillips, Flip
See Filipelli, Joseph Edward

Phillips, Flip
See Phillips, Joseph Edward

Phillips, [Rev.] Forbes ?-1917 [HPPN]
American playwright
* Forbes, Athol

Phillips, Frank
See Nowlan, Phil[ip Francis]

Phillips, Fuzz
See Phillips, Leo

Phillips, George Searle 1817-1889 [DEL, DNNF, FFF]
British-born author and journalist
* Searle, January

Phillips, George Spencer [PA]
Author
* Dix, J. R.

Phillips, Gerald William 1884- [WW]
Author
* Huntingdon, John

Phillips, Gordon 1890- [LAO]
British journalist
* Lucio

Phillips, H. C.
See Honey, Philip

Phillips, Harold Ross 1919-1972 [PB]
American baseball coach and manager
* Phillips, Lefty

Phillips, Harvey G. 1939- [HPPN]
American educator
* [The] Paganini of the Tuba
* Tuba, Mr.

Phillips, Horace 1853-? [BE]
American baseball manager
* Phillips, Hustling Horace

Phillips, Horace 20th c. [MBF]
British author and editor
* Duke, Derek
* Hope, Walter
* Stanton, Marjorie

Phillips, Howard S. 1894- [NAA]
British-born editor and writer
* Rivas, Guillermo

Phillips, Hugh 1886- [WWL]
British author
* Hughes, Philip

Phillips, Hustling Horace
See Phillips, Horace

Phillips, Irna ?-1974 [ET]
Scriptwriter
* [The] Queen of the Soaps

Phillips, Irv[ing W.] 1908- [SAT]
American cartoonist, illustrator, author
* Sabuso

Phillips, Ivan Keith 1943- [OP]
American scenic and lighting designer
* Phillips, Van

Phillips, J. B.
See Phillips, John Bertram

Phillips, [Doctor] J. P.
See Durand, J. P.

Phillips, Jack
See Sandburg, Carl [August]

Phillips, Jack Dorn 1921- [BE]
American baseball player
* Phillips, Stretch

Phillips, James [Jim] 1936- [FB, SMG]
American football player and coach
* Phillips, Red

Phillips, James Atlee 1915- [TCCM]
American author
* Atlee, Philip

Phillips, James R.
See Jennett, Richard P.

Phillips, James W. 1922- [CA]
American author
* Eblis, J. Philip
* McLaughlin, Bill

Phillips, Jerome C.
See Cleveland, Philip Jerome

Phillips, John 1832?-1883 [HPPN]
Portuguese-American frontiersman
* Phillips, Portugee

Phillips, John 1941- [DAM]
American singer
* Papa John

Phillips, John
See Marquand, John Phillips

Phillips, John Bertram 1906- [LC]
British author and prelate
* Phillips, J. B.

Phillips, John Henry, Sr. 1877-1948
[NOJ]
American jazz musician
* Fischer, Johnny

Phillips, John Melvin 1930- [BE, SMG]
American baseball player
* Phillips, Bubba

Phillips, Joseph Edward 1915- [HPPN]
American jazz musician
* Phillips, Flip

Phillips, Kate
See Goldney, Kate

Phillips, Kathleen 20th c. [CA, SAT]
Author
* Cole, Annette [joint pseudonym with
  Barbara A(nnette) Steiner]
* D'Andrea, Kate [joint pseudonym
  with Barbara A(nnette) Steiner]

Phillips, King
See Perkins, Kenneth

Phillips, Lefty
See Phillips, Harold Ross

Phillips, Leo 1916?-1977 [FIR]
American jazz musician
* Phillips, Fuzz

Phillips, Leon
See Gerson, Noel Bertram

Phillips, Lin 1947- [RO2]
American musician
* Phillips, Spike

Phillips, Mac
See Phillips, Maurice J[ack]

Phillips, Mandane
See Halley, Mandane Phillips

Phillips, Mark [joint pseudonym with
Laurence M(ark) Janifer]
See Garrett, [Gordon] Randall [Philip
David]

Phillips, Mark [joint pseudonym with
Randall Garrett]
See Harris, Larry M[ark]

Phillips, Maurice J[ack] 1914- [CA]
American author
* Phillips, Mac

Phillips, Merlyn J. 20th c. [CEI]
Canadian-born hockey player
* Phillips, Bill

Phillips, Michael
See Nolan, William F[rancis]

Phillips, Michael
See Nutt, Charles

Phillips, Michael Joseph 1937- [WD]
American poet, critic, writer
* Fairplay, Roger
* Swift, Farguar

Phillips, Michelle
See Gilliam, Holly

Phillips, Mickey
See Phillips, Alan Meyrick Kerr

Phillips, Milk of Magnesia
See Phillips, Alfred Noroton, Jr.

Phillips, Miss 19th c. [PA]
Author
* [An] Old Maid

Phillips, Morgan 16th c. [PA, SN]
Welsh author
* Morgan, Phillip
* [The] Sophister

Phillips, Mrs. Henry [FFF]
Entertainer
* Castleton, Kate

Phillips, Nibs
See Phillips, Thomas Neil

Phillips, Norma 1893-1931 [HPPN]
American actress
* [The] Mutual Girl

Phillips, O. A. 20th c. [BI]
American automobile dealer
* Phillips, Bunny

Phillips, O. A.
See Phillips, Oail

Phillips, Oail 1923?- [BI, SMG]
American football coach and manager
* Phillips, Bum
* Phillips, O. A.

Phillips, Olga Somech 1901- [AW]
British author
* Olga

Phillips, Osborne
See Barcynski, Leon Roger

Phillips, Pauline Esther [Friedman]
1918- [CA]
American columnist
* Dear Abby
* Phillips, Popo
* Van Buren, Abigail

Phillips, Pete
See Phillips, Ardith Lowell

Phillips, Peter [house pseudonym]
See Browne, Howard

Phillips, Phil
See Baptiste, John Phillip

Phillips, Philip 1834-1895 [WBD]
American singer and music publisher
* [The] Singing Pilgrim

Phillips, Pop
See Phillips, R. H.

Phillips, Popo
See Phillips, Pauline Esther [Friedman]

Phillips, Portugee
See Phillips, John

Phillips, R. H. 20th c. [CSH]
Canadian lacrosse promoter
* Phillips, Pop

Phillips, Red
See Phillips, Aubrey Clyde

Phillips, Red
See Phillips, Clarence Lemuel

Phillips, Red
See Phillips, James [Jim]

Phillips, [Sir] Richard 1767-1840 [DEL, FFF, HFN]
British journalist
* Adair, James
* Barrow, [Rev.] S.
* Blair, [Rev.] David
* Bossut, M. L'Abbe
* Clarke, [Rev.] C. C.
* Common Sense
* Goldsmith, [Rev.] J.
* Pelham, M.

Phillips, Richard
See Dick, Philip K[indred]

Phillips, Rog
See Graham, Roger Phillips

Phillips, Rosina
See Gingold, Hermione Ferdinanda

Phillips, Sid 1907-1973
British musician and composer
* King of the Clarinet

Phillips, Silver Bill
See Phillips, William Corcoran

Phillips, Spike
See Phillips, Lin

Phillips, Steve
See Whittington, Harry [Benjamin]

Phillips, Stretch
See Phillips, Jack Dorn

Phillips, Tay
See Phillips, William Taylor

Phillips, Thomas ?-1774 [HPPN]
British clergyman
* T. P. S. C. T.

Phillips, [Sir] Thomas 1792-1872 [HPPN]
British antiquary
* T. P.

Phillips, Thomas Neil 1880-1923 [BBH]
Canadian-born hockey player
* Phillips, Nibs

Phillips, Tom 1888-1941
British naval officer
* Thumb, Tom

Phillips, Tom
See Drotning, Phillip T[homas]

Phillips, Tully 1864-1943 [HPPN]
American actor
* Marshall, Tully

Phillips, Van
See Phillips, Ivan Keith

Phillips, Vel
See Phillips, Velvalea R.

Phillips, Velvalea R. 1924- [IBW]
American politician
* Phillips, Vel

Phillips, W.
See Dodge, Wendell Phillips

Phillips, W. J. 20th c. [CEI]
Canadian-born hockey player
* Phillips, Batt

Phillips, Walter Polk 1846-1920 [DNA, PA]
American journalist
* Oakum, John

Phillips, Walter Shelley 1867-1940 [HPPN]
American artist and author
* [El] Comancho
* Wi-chash-ta-Ish-nah-nah

Phillips, Ward
See Lovecraft, Howard Phillips

Phillips, Watts [PA]
Author
* Balfour, Fairfax

Phillips, Wendell 1811-1884 [HPPN, SN]
American abolitionist
* [The] Brahmin Radical
* [The] Patrick Henry of New England

Phillips, Whitey
See Phillips, Barton

Phillips, Whoa Bill
See Phillips, William Corcoran

Phillips, William 1864-1943 [HCA, SC]
American actor
* Marshall, Tully

Phillips, William Corcoran 1868-1941 [BE]
American baseball player
* Phillips, Silver Bill
* Phillips, Whoa Bill

Phillips, William T.
See Parker, Robert LeRoy

Phillips, William Taylor 1933- [BE]
American baseball player
* Phillips, Tay

Phillips-Birt, Douglas 1920-1977 [CA]
British author
* Argus
* Hextall, David
* Hogarth, Douglas

Phillipson, Christopher Paul 1952- [DC]
British cricketer
* Phillipson, Phillipo

Phillipson, Phillipo
See Phillipson, Christopher Paul

Phillpotts, [Mary] Adelaide [Eden] 1896- [LC, WD]
British author, poet, playwright
* Ross, Mary Adelaide Eden

Phillpotts, Eden 1862-1960 [CC, EMD, LC]
British author, poet, playwright
* Hext, Harrington

Philly Jilly Carlton
See Carlton, Stephen Norman

Philly Joe Jones
See Jones, Joseph Rudolph

Philmore, R.
See Howard, Herbert Edmund

Philo
See Ballou, Ellis

Philo
See Frend, William Hugh Clifford

Philo Britannia, Mrs.
See Foe, Daniel

Philo Criticus
See Hare, Francis

Philo Judaeus 1st c. [DEP, DNNF, DNNS, HPPN]
Hellenistic philosopher
* [The] Jewish Plato
* Philo of Alexandria

Philo Musa
See Currie, James

Philo Nauticus
See Halloran, Laurence Hynes

Philo of Alexandria
See Philo Judaeus

Philo Pacificus
See Wallcut, [Rev.] Robert Folger

Philo Royalist
See Foe, Daniel

Philo Ruggles
See Adams, John

Philo Scotus
See Ainslie, Philip Barrington

Philobiblicus Cantabrigiensis
See Chapman, John

Philobiblius
See Brockett, Linus Pierpont

Philobiblius
See Watson, Richard

Philobiblos
See Ireland, Alexander

Philobiblos
See Rodd, Thomas, Sr.

Philochelidon
See Forster, Thomas

Philochristus
See Abbott, Edwin Abbott

Philoclea
See Devereux, Penelope

Philocosmos
See Clark, Hamlet

Philocriticus Cantabrigiensis
See Jackson, John

Philodicaius
See Young, Thomas

Philoeunomos
See Sherman, Roger

Philogenes Panedonius
See Braithwaite, Richard

Philokalist
See Wierzbicki, Felix Paul

Philokalus
See Sporon, Benjamin G.

Philolaos
See Tloupas, Philolaos

Philolethus
See Lozano, [Don] Pedro

Philologer, A. B.
See Sterne, Laurence

Philologos [A Lover of Words]
See Bailey, Nathan

Philologus
See Spira, Francis

Philomath
See Franklin, Ben[jamin]

Philomath
See Walsh, Michael Paul

Philomath, T. N.
See Swift, Jonathan

Philomath: Oxoniensis
See Walker, Richard

Philomela
See Rowe, Elizabeth

Philomena
See Roe, Elizabeth Singer

Philomessus
See Locher, Jacob

Philometor
See Antiochus VIII

Philometor
See Attalus III

Philometor
See Demetrius III

Philometor [Mother-Lover]
See Ptolemy VI

Philomneste, Junior
See Brunet, Gustave

Philomon
See Marsden, John Howard

Philomythes
See Gonzalez, Gonzalo

Philonagnostes Criticus
See Herne, Thomas

Philonous
See Berenger, Richard

Philopacificus
See Worcester, Noah

Philoparthen, Esdras
See Wharton, [Sir] George

Philopater, Andreas
See Parsons [or Persons?], Robert

Philopator
See Antiochus IX

Philopator [Father-Lover]
See Ptolemy IV

Philopator
See Seleucus IV

Philopator Neos Dionysos
See Ptolemy XII [or X]

Philopator Philometor Caesar
See Ptolemy XV [XIV or XVI]

Philopatria
See Lee, Rachel Frances Antonina Dashwood

Philopatria
See Paine, Thomas

Philopatris Varvicensis
See Parr, Samuel

Philopatrius
See Dove, David James

Philopis
See Marsh, James

Philopoemen 3rd c. BC [DEP, DNNS, SN]
Greek army officer
* [The] Last of the Greeks

Philopoliteius
See Skene, [Sir] John

Philorthos
See Johnstone, George

Philorthos
See Poole, William Frederick

Philos Harmoniae
See McNemar, Richard

Philosinensis
See Medhurst, Walter Henry

[Le] Philosophe des Dames
See Caro, Elme Marie

[Le] Philosophe Inconnu
See Saint Martin, Louis Claude de

[The] Philosopher
See Alfonso X [or Alphonso]

[The] Philosopher
See Alfred [or Alured]

[The] Philosopher
See Annius Verus, Marcus

[The] Philosopher
See Bentham, Jeremy

[The] Philosopher
See Constantine

Philosopher
See Contarini, Marc Antoine

[The] Philosopher
See De Serment, Louise Anastasie

[The] Philosopher
See Edward [or Eadward]

[The] Philosopher
See Justin

[The] Philosopher
See Leo VI

[The] Philosopher
See Malchus

[The] Philosopher
See Seneca, Marcus Lucius Annaeus

[The] Philosopher
See Sorrell, Vic[tor Garland]

[The] Philosopher of Change
See Bergson, Henri

[The] Philosopher of Chelsea
See Carlyle, Thomas

[The] Philosopher of China
See Confucius [or K'ung Fu-tzu]

Philosopher of City Life
See Runyon, [Alfred] Damon

[The] Philosopher of Democracy
See Jefferson, Thomas

[The] Philosopher of Disenchantment
See Schopenhauer, Arthur

[The] Philosopher of Ferney
See Arouet, Francois Marie

Philosopher of Librarianship
See Ranganathan, Shiyali Ramamrita

[The] Philosopher of Madness
See Laing, Ronald David

[The] Philosopher of Malmesbury
See Hobbes, Thomas

[The] Philosopher of Persia
See Avicenna [or Abou-ibn-Sina]

[The] Philosopher of Samosata
See Lucian

[The] Philosopher of Sans Souci
See Frederick II

[The] Philosopher of Sunshine and Rain
See Griffith, Lawrence Rector

[The] Philosopher of the Absolute
See Hegel, Georg Wilhelm Friedrich

[The] Philosopher of the Arabs
See Kindi, al- [Abu Yusef al-Kindi]

[The] Philosopher of the Christians
See Aristocles

Philosopher of the Constitution
See Madison, James

[The] Philosopher of the Unknown
See Saint Martin, Louis Claude de

[The] Philosopher of Wimbledon
See Horne, John

[The] Philosopher Prince
See Frederick II

[The] Philosopher with the Golden Thigh
See Pythagoras

[The] Philosophic Bard
See Euripides

[The] Philosophical
See Strode, Ralph

Philosophus Anglorum
See Athelard of Bath

Philosophus Teutonicus
See Boehme, Jacob

Philostratus
See Foster, Thomas

Philotas
See Devereux, Robert [Third Earl of Essex]

Philotesis
See Roberts, Daniel

Philp, Kenward 19th c. [FFF]
American writer
* Flaneur

Philpot, Bud
See Philpot, Eli

Philpot, Eli 19th c. [HPPN]
American stagecoach driver
* Philpot, Bud

Philpot, J. H.
See Philpot, Joseph Henry

Philpot, Joseph Henry 1850-1939 [SFL, WGT, WWL]
British author
* Lafargue, Philip
* Philpot, J. H.

Philpot, J. P. 19th c. [HPPN]
American author
* Legalist

Philpott, Margaret 1903- [F2]
American actress
* Bellamy, Madge

Philpott, Toby
See Parnell, Paul

Philps, Arthur Carlton 1880-1942 [BMH, THR]
British entertainer
* Carlton
* [The] Great Carlton
* [The] Human Hairpin

Philroye, Humphrey
See Steele, [Sir] Richard

Philygeia
See Foe, Daniel

Phin
See Thayer, Ernest Lawrence

Phineas
See Hanifin, John M.

Phipps, Beatrix
See Kemp, Mrs. Maurice F.

Phipps, [Sir] Constantine 1656-1723 [SN]
Chancellor of Ireland
* [The] Impudent

Phipps, [Sir] Constantine Henry [First Marquis of Normanby] 1797-1863 [HPPN]
British statesman and author
* Irish Operator

Phipps, Joyce Irene 1910-1979 [EMT, FC]
British actress
* Grenfell, Joyce

Phipps, Margaret
See Tatham, Laura

Phipson, Joan
See Fitzhardinge, Joan Margaret

Phiseldeck
See Schmidt, Christoph

Phisterer, Frederick 1836-1909 [HPPN]
German-American politician
* [The] Father of the National Guard of New York

Phiz
See Browne, Hablot Knight

Phiz
See Walsh, Michael Paul

Phiz, Francis
See Smedley, Francis Edward [Frank]

Phlogobombos, Terentius
See Judah, Samuel Benjamin Helbert

Phocas
See Nicephorus II

Phocian
See Hamilton, Alexander

Phocion
See Curtis, George Ticknor

Phocion
See Hartley, Thomas

Phocion
See Smith, William Loughton

Phoebe
See Bentley, Joanna

Phoebus
See Gaston III

Phoenix
See Martin, [Sir] Henry

Phoenix Donald Weaver
See Weaver, William [Bill]

Phoenix, John
See Maylem, John

Phoenix, John, Gentleman
See Derby, George Horatio

[The] Phoenix of His Age
See Kindi, al- [Abu Yusef al-Kindi]

[The] Phoenix of Literature
See Grotius, Hugo

[The] Phoenix of Spain
See Vega Carpio, Lope Felix de

[The] Phoenix of the World
See Sidney, [Sir] Philip

[The] Phoenix of these Late Times
See Welby, Henry

[The] Phoenix of Wit
See Rabelais, Francois

[The] Phoney Faker
See Demara, Ferdinand Waldo, Jr.

[The] Phoney Ph. D.
See Hewitt, Marvin

Phonograph Jimmy McGraw
See McGraw, James

[The] Phonograph Singer
See Whitehouse, Fred

Phony Joanie Mondale
See Mondale, Joan

Photius Junior
See Sherlock, William

Phra
See Arnold, Edwin Lester

[The] Phrasemaker
See Wilson, [Thomas] Woodrow

[A] Phrenologist
See Tichborne, Thomas

Phryne
See Mnesarete

Phrynicus 2nd c. [WBD]
Greek grammarian
* Arabius

Phucher, Itothe
See Chittenden, Hiram Martin

Phusin, Kate
See Ruskin, John

Phyfe, Duncan
See Fife, Duncan

Phylos the Thibetan
See Oliver, Frederick Spencer

Phypps, Hyacinthe
See Gorey, Edward [St. John]

Physcon [Big-Belly]
See Ptolemy VIII [or VII]

[A] Physician
See Allen, John

[A] Physician
See Bullar, Joseph

[A] Physician
See Cook, N. F.

[A] Physician
See Couper, Robert

[A] Physician
See Dickson, Samuel Henry

[A] Physician
See Forster, Thomas

[A] Physician
See Hoskyns, John

[A] Physician
See Jackson, Rowland

[A] Physician
See Mackenzie, James

[A] Physician
See Paris, John Ayrton

[A] Physician in the Country
See Peachie, John

[A] Physician in the West Indies
See Grainger, James

[A] Physician in Town
See Cox, Daniel

[A] Physician of Charleston, South Carolina
See Dickson, Samuel Henry

[A] Physician of Philadelphia
See Horner, William Edmunds

[The] Physician to Corporate Bodies
See Lee, Ivy Ledbetter

[The] Physician's Physician
See Da Costa, Jacob Mendez

[Un] Physicien Voyageur
See Forster, Thomas

Physick, Edward Harold 1878-1972 [SFL, WGT]
British author
* Visiak, E. H.

Physick, Philip Syng 1768-1837 [FFF, WBD]
American surgeon
* [The] Father of American Surgery

Physics
See Crawford, Samuel W.

Physicus
See Archelaus of Athens

Physioc, Jessica Eskridge [Thomas] 1861?-1948 [BI, HPPN]
American actress
* Thomas, Virginia

Piaf, Edith
See Gassion, Edith Giovanna

Piani, Giuseppe Francesco 1880-? [BI]
Italian-American missionary
* Plainfield, Joseph Franklin

[A] Pianist
See Gottschalk, Louis Moreau

[The] Pianner Kid
See Lopez, Vincent

Piano, Celeste
See Lykiard, Alexis [Constantine]

Piano Legs Gore
See Gore, George F.

Piano Legs Hickman
See Hickman, Charles Taylor

[The] Piano Playing Baron
See Samek, Viktor Oliver

[The] Piano Prince of New Orleans
See Booker, James Carroll, III

Piano Red
See Harrison, Vernon

Piano Red
See Patterson, Vance

Piano Red
See Perryman, William Lee [Willie]

Piano Sam Vinson
See Vinson, Sam

Piano Slim
See Burton, Willard

Piatigorsky, Gregor 1903-1976 [CR, MS]
Russian musician
* Piatigorsky, Grischa
* [The] Russian Casals

Piatigorsky, Grischa
See Piatigorsky, Gregor

Piatt, Iron Man
See Piatt, Wiley Harold

Piatt, Louise Kirby 1812-1864 [FFF]
American author
* Smith, Bell

Piatt, Wiley Harold 1874-1946 [BE]
American baseball player
* Piatt, Iron Man

Piatti, Girolomo 1547-1591 [PA]
Author
* Platus

Piazza, Ben
See Piazza, Benito Daniel

Piazza, Benito Daniel 1934- [BEW]
American actor and writer
* Piazza, Ben

Pic
See Higgins, Charles S.

Pic, Ulysse [PA]
Author
* Lux, Adam

Pica, Peter
See Aldiss, Brian W[ilson]

Pica, Phineas
See Buckingham, Edwin

Picander
See Henrici, Christian Friedrich

Picard, Dorothy Young 1906- [CA]
American author
* Croman, Dorothy Young

Picariello, Fredrick Anthony 1940- [RO1]
American singer
* Cannon, Boom Boom
* Cannon, Freddy

Picaroon
See Ballantyne, John

Picart, Stephen [or Etienne] 1631-1721 [FFF, RH, SN]
French engraver
* [The] Roman

[The] Picasso of Children's Books
See Sendak, Maurice

[The] Picasso of Flowers
See Teshigahara, Sofu

Picasso of the Camera
See Weston, Edward

[The] Picasso of the Contemporary Drama
See Ionesco, Eugene

Picasso, Pablo [Ruiz]
See Ruiz, Pablo Diego Jose Francisco de Paula Juan Nepomuceno Cipriano

Piccadilly
See Gerard, Pierre S.

Piccadilly, Lord
See Douglas, William

[The] Piccadilly Patriot
See Burdett, [Sir] Francis

Piccinino, Jacopo ?-1465 [SN]
Italian army officer
* [The] Thunderbolt of War

Picciola
See Mumford, Angelina S.

Piccioni, Piero 20th c. [WF]
Italian composer
* Morgan, Piero

Piccolo, Fillippo ?-1769 [PA]
Author
* Lo

Piccolo, L. Brian 1943-1970 [FB]
American football player
* Piccolo, Pic

Piccolo Pete Elko
See Elko, Peter

Piccolo, Pic
See Piccolo, L. Brian

Pichegru, Charles 1761-1804 [SN]
French army officer
* [The] Savior of His Country

Pichon, Fats
See Pichon, Walter

Pichon, Thomas ?-1781 [PA]
Author
* Tyrrell, Thomas Signis

Pichon, Walter 1906-1967 [WWJ]
American jazz musician
* Pichon, Fats

Picinich, Val
See Picinich, Valentine John

Picinich, Valentine John 1896-1942
[BE]
American baseball player
* Picinich, Val

Pick, Lupu 1886-1931 [DFM]
German director and actor
* Lupu-Pick

Pick, Mr.
See Scoville, Joseph A.

Pick, Robert 1898-1978 [CA]
Austrian-born American author, editor, translator
* Richter, Valentin

Pickard, Dad
See Pickard, Obey

Pickard, Hannah Maynard [Thompson]
1812-1844 [CCL]
Canadian author
* [A] Lady

Pickard, Obey ?-1958 [DAM]
American musician
* Pickard, Dad

Pickard Jenkins, Percy 20th c. [ART]
Welsh designer and painter
* P. P. J.

Pickaway
See Myers, Allen O.

Pickel, Konrad 1459-1508 [HPPN, WBD]
German poet
* Celtis [or Celtes], Conradus
* [The] German Arch Humanist

Pickelherring
See Reynolds, Robert

Pickem, Peter
See Stearns, Harold Edmund

Picken, Andrew 1788-1833 [DLE1, NPS]
British author
* Keelivine, Christopher
* Picken, Dominie Legacy

Picken, Andrew
See Galt, John

Picken, Dominie Legacy
See Picken, Andrew

Picken, Henry
See Harkin, Hugh

Picken, Mary Brooks 1886- [NAA]
American author
* Joan, Mary
* Madison, Marilyn
* McCleary, Eleanor
* Wells, Jane Warren

Pickens, Andrew 1739-1817 [HPPN]
American army officer
* [The] Gamecock
* Skyagunsta
* [The] Wizard of Tomassee

Pickens, Buster
See Pickens, Edwin Goodwin

Pickens, Edwin Goodwin 1916-1964
[BWW]
American singer
* Pickens, Buster

Pickens, Slim
See Burns, Eddie

Pickens, Slim
See Lindley, Louis Bert, Jr.

Pickering, Dick
See Pickering, Urbane Henry

Pickering, Edward C. 1846-1919
[HPPN]
American astronomer
* [The] Father of the New Astronomy

Pickering, Ellen [PA]
Author
* Daniel, Mrs. Mackenzie

Pickering, Henry White 19th c. [HPPN]
American scholar and broker
* [A] Teacher

Pickering, Oliver Dan 1870-1952 [BE]
American baseball player
* Pickering, Ollie

Pickering, Ollie
See Pickering, Oliver Dan

Pickering, Percival
See Stirling, Anna Maria Diana
Wilhelmina [Pickering]

Pickering, Stephen 1947- [CA]
American author
* Ben Avraham, Chofetz Chaim

Pickering, Urbane Henry 1899-1970
[BE]
American baseball player
* Pickering, Dick

Pickering, William 1796-1854 [SN]
British publisher
* Discipulus Aldi

Picket
See Tomlinson, B. W.

Pickett, Bobby 1940- [RO1]
American singer and songwriter
* Pickett, Boris

Pickett, Boris
See Pickett, Bobby

Pickett, Charles Edward 19th c.
[HPPN]
American author
* One Who Knows

Pickett, Wilson 1941- [IBW]
American singer and songwriter
* [The] Wicked

Pickford, Gladys
See Smith, Gladys Mary

Pickford, Jack
See Smith, Jack

Pickford, Lottie
See Smith, Lottie

Pickford, Mary
See Smith, Gladys Mary

Pickle, Peregrine
See Akenside, Mark

Pickle, Peregrine
See Upton, George Putnam

Pickle, Prometheus
See Bush, William

Pickle the Spy
See Macdonell, Alastair Ruadh

Pickles, Frank K. 1893- [WWL]
Scottish writer
* Quiz

Pickles, M[abel] Elizabeth 1902- [CAP, WD]
British author
* Burgoyne, Elizabeth

Pickney, Thomas 1750-1828 [HPPN]
American attorney, soldier, politician
* Achates

Pickup, Clarence William 1897- [BE]
American baseball player
* Pickup, Ty

Pickup, Ty
See Pickup, Clarence William

Pickwick
See Dickens, Charles

Pickwoad, William 1912-1976 [TR]
British actor
* Mervyn, William

Pickworth, H. O. 1920- [EG]
Australian golfer
* Pickworth, Ossie

Pickworth, Ossie
See Pickworth, H. O.

Pico, John Baptist 1688-1740 [HN]
Italian educator
* [The] Dante of Philosophy

Picone, Babe
See Picone, Mario Peter

Picone, Mario Peter 1926- [BE]
American baseball player
* Picone, Babe

Picou, Alphonse
See Ghnassia, Maurice [Jean-Henri]

Picou, Alphonse Floristan 1879-1961
[IBW]
American jazz musician
* Picou, Peak

Picou, Peak
See Picou, Alphonse Floristan

Picquet, Francois 1708-1781 [FFF]
Missionary
* [The] Great Jesuit of the West

Picton, Bernard
See Knight, Bernard

Picton, Nina 20th c. [WGT]
Author
* Dearborn, Laura

Picton, Thomas 1822-1891 [DNA, FFF, PA]
American journalist
* [An] Ex Editor
* Gothamite
* Juvenile
* Preston, Paul
* [Le] Viola

Picton, Thomas
See Milner, Thomas Picton

Pictor Ignotus [Painter Unknown]
See Blake, William

[The] Pictorial Historian of Aboriginal America
See Catlin, George

[The] Pictorial Historian of the Civil War
See Brady, Mathew B.

Picture Maker's Picture Maker
See Capra, Frank

[The] Picturesque Explorer of the United States
See Lanman, Charles

Picus, John Quinn 1884-1946 [AS, BE]
American baseball player
* Quinn, John Picus [Jack]

Pidgeon, William Edwin 1909- [WEC]
Australian painter, illustrator, cartoonist
* Wep

Pie Crust Palmer
See Palmer, James Shedden

[The] Pie Lady
See Reveron, Saundra

Piechota, Al
See Piechota, Aloysius Edward

Piechota, Aloysius Edward 1914- [BE]
American baseball player
* Piechota, Al

Pieculewicz, Charles 20th c. [HPPN]
American football player
* Pieculewicz, Peck

Pieculewicz, Peck
See Pieculewicz, Charles

Pied Piper
See Williams, Dorian

[The] Pied Piper of Boston
See Ponzi, Carlo

[The] Pied Piper of Contentment
See Coue, Emile

[The] Pied Piper of Harlem
See Edinboro, Arlington

[The] Pied Piper of Love
See White, Barry

[The] Pied Piper of Rock 'n' Roll
See Freed, Alan

[The] Pied Piper of the A. E. F.
See Foster, Roland

Piegan Phil
See Sheridan, Philip Henry

Pieh, Cy
See Pieh, Edwin John

Pieh, Edwin John 1886-1945 [BE]
American baseball player
* Pieh, Cy

Piemontese, Alessio
See Ruscelli, Girolamo

Pieralisi, Virna 1937- [FC]
Italian actress
* Lisi, Virna

Pierangeli, Anna Maria 1932-1971 [FC, IPA]
Italian actress
* Angeli, Pier

Pierangeli, Marisa 1932- [FC, ITA, SW]
Italian actress
* Pavan, Marisa

Pierat, Marie-Therese
See Pelletier, Marie-Therese

Pierce, Abel Head 1834-1900 [BLB]
American cattle baron
* Pierce, Shanghai

Pierce, Billie
See Goodson, Wilhelmina Madison

Pierce, Carl Webster 1898- [NAA]
American playwright and actor
* Applebud, Adam

Pierce, Dede
See Pierce, Joseph De Lacrois

Pierce, Edith Gray 1893- [CA]
American author
* Gray, Marian

Pierce, Edward Lillie 19th c. [HPPN]
American attorney
* E. L. P.

Pierce, Emma
See Schulz, Mrs. Warren

Pierce, Franklin 1804-1869 [FAP, SN]
American president
* Handsome Frank
* Purse
* [The] Reluctant President
* Young Hickory

Pierce, George Foster 1811-1884 [BDSA]
American author, clergyman, educator
* [The] Demosthenes of Southern Methodism

Pierce, Jane Means Appleton 1806-1863
Wife of American president, Franklin Pierce
* [The] Shadow In the White House

Pierce, Jennings 1897- [HPPN]
American radio announcer
* J. P.

Pierce, Jo
See Manning, William Henry

Pierce, Jo
See Morris, Charles Smith

Pierce, John
See Perelmuth, Jacob Pincus

Pierce, John Leonard, Jr. 1921- [CA]
German-born author
* Bramlett, John

Pierce, John Robinson 1910- [CA, ESF]
American author
* Coupling, J. J.
* Roberts, John

Pierce, Joseph De Lacrois 1904-1973 [DAM, EJ7, IBW]
American jazz musician
* Pierce, Dede

Pierce, Katherine
See St. John, Wylly Folk

Pierce, Lefty
See Pierce, Ray[mond Lester]

Pierce, Lillian Elizabeth ?-1964 [HPPN]
American actress and singer
* McClure, Peggy

Pierce, Marvin 20th c. [HPPN]
American football player
* Pierce, Monk

Pierce, Marvin 20th c. [RO2]
American musician
* Pierce, Merve

Pierce, Mary Cunningham [Fitzgerald] 1908- [BI]
American author
* Cunningham, Mary

Pierce, Merve
See Pierce, Marvin

Pierce, Monk
See Pierce, Marvin

Pierce, Ray[mond Lester] 1897-1963 [BE]
American baseball player
* Pierce, Lefty

Pierce, Ronald 1938- [SW]
American actor
* Ely, Ron

Pierce, Samuel R. 20th c. [NW 9-13-82]
American government official
* Pierce, Silent Sam

Pierce, Shanghai
See Pierce, Abel Head

Pierce, Silent Sam
See Pierce, Samuel R.

Pierce, Thomas 1786-1850 [PA]
Author
* Horace in Cincinnati
* Idestone

Pierce, William 20th c. [TI 2-18-85]
American author and leader of white supremacist group
* Macdonald, Andrew

Piercy, Mrs.   [FFF]
Entertainer
* Dargon, Augusta

Piercy, Wild Bill
See Piercy, William Benton

Piercy, William Benton 1896-1951   [BE]
American baseball player
* Piercy, Wild Bill

Pieretti, Chick
See Pieretti, Marino Paul

Pieretti, Marino Paul 1920-   [BE]
Italian-born baseball player
* Pieretti, Chick

Pierian Dick
See Harvey, Richard

Pierleoni, Pietro ?-1138   [WBD]
Antipope
* Anacletus II
* [The] Jewish Pope

Piermarini
See Malacrida, Marchese

Piero di Cosimo 1462-1521   [WBD]
Florentine painter
* Piero di Lorenzo

Piero di Giovanni 1370?-1425   [BI, HPPN]
Italian painter
* Lorenzo, Don
* Lorenzo Monaco [Lorenzo the Monk]

Piero di Lorenzo
See Piero di Cosimo

Pierotti, Piero 1912-   [FDG]
Italian director
* Stanley, Peter E.

Pierozzi, Antonio 1389-1459   [WBD]
Saint
* Antoninus
* De Forciglioni, Antonio

Pierpont, Harry 1906-1934   [HPPN]
American bank robber and outlaw
* Pete

Pierre ?-1180   [HN]
Medieval scholar
* Mangeur [or Comeston]

Pierre, [Abbe]
See Groues, Henri Antoine

[The] Pierre Cardin of Korea
See Kim, Andre

Pierre et Paul
See Lourdoneix, Paul de

Pierre, Paul
See Calle, Paul

Pierre Benoit, Louis Marie 1936-   [CW]
Haitian poet and author
* Fardin, Dieudonne

Pierrepoint, Albert
See Andrews, Allen

Pierrepont
See Church, William Conant

Pierro, Wild Bill
See Pierro, William Leonard [Bill]

Pierro, William Leonard [Bill] 1926-
[BE]
American baseball player
* Pierro, Wild Bill

Pierrot
See Arnold, George

Pierrot, Marseilles
See Roggiero, Pierre

Piers, Ashdown [joint pseudonym with John James Pitcairn]
See Freeman, Richard

Piers, Ashdown [joint pseudonym with Richard Freeman]
See Pitcairn, John James

Pierson, David P. 1855-1922   [BE]
American baseball player
* Pearson, David P. [Dave]

Pierson, Dick
See Pierson, Edmund Dana

Pierson, Edmund Dana ?-1922   [BE]
American baseball player
* Pierson, Dick

Pierson, John H[erman] G[roesbeck] 1906-   [CA]
American author and economist
* Hand, John

Pierson, Walter
See McCulley, Johnston

Pierson, Wild Bill
See Pierson, William Morris [Bill]

Pierson, William Morris [Bill] 1899-1959   [BE]
American baseball player
* Pierson, Wild Bill

Pieseio
See Beardslee, L. A.

Piestre, Fernand Anne 1845-1924 [WBD]
French painter
* Cormon

Piet
See Retief, Pieter

Piet, Anthony Francis
See Pietruszka, Anthony Francis

Piet, Tony
See Pietruszka, Anthony Francis

Pieters, Eddie 1936?-   [CW]
Curacaon author and playwright
* Heyliger

Pieterszoon, Jan
See Sweelinck [or Swelinck], Jan Pieters

Pieterszoon, Nicolaes 1593?-1674?
[WBD]
Dutch anatomist
* Tulp, Claes Pieterszoon

Pietkowski, Masha 1925?-   [HPPN]
Polish survivor of Nazi concentration camp
* Fenelon, Fania

Pietrangeli, Nicki
See Pietrangeli, Nicola

Pietrangeli, Nicola 20th c.
Italian tennis player
* Pietrangeli, Nicki

Pietri, Dorando 20th c.   [TI 8-20-84]
Italian marathon runner
* Pietri, Wrong Way

Pietri, Wrong Way
See Pietri, Dorando

Pietrkiewicz, Jerzy 1916-   [ESF, SFL]
Polish author
* Peterkiewicz, Jerzy

Pietro Aquila 1350-1420   [HN]
Medieval scholar
* Scotus Minor
* Sufficens, Doctor

Pietrosante, Nicholas V. [Nick] 1937-
American football player
* [The] Plunger

Pietruszka, Anthony Francis 1906-   [BE, HPPN]
American baseball player
* Piet, Anthony Francis
* Piet, Tony
* Pietruszka, Whitey
* Tony the Silent

Pietruszka, Whitey
See Pietruszka, Anthony Francis

Pietschmann, Richard John, III 1940-
[CA]
American author and columnist
* Miller, Richard
* Parish, Townsend

Piette, Charles Joseph Ghislain 1885-1948   [BI]
Belgian clergyman and historian
* Maximin, [Father]

[Le] Pieux
See Frederick II

[Le] Pieux
See Louis I

[Le] Pieux [The Pious]
See Louis VII

[Le] Pieux
See Robert II

Piez, Charles William 1892-1930   [BE]
American baseball player
* Piez, Sandy

Piez, Sandy
See Piez, Charles William

Pifer, Whispering Bill
See Pifer, William

Pifer, William 20th c. [HPPN]
American motorcyclist
* Pifer, Whispering Bill

Piff, Charles 1930- [TR]
British actor
* Kay, Charles

Piffleheap
See Wilson, [James] Harold

Piffoel, Doctor
See Dudevant, Amandine Aurore Lucile
Dupin

Pig, Edward
See Gorey, Edward [St. John]

Pig Iron Kelley
See Kelley, William Darragh

[The] Pig Man
See Gustafson, Jim

Pig 'n' Whistle Red
See McTell, Willie Samuel

[The] Pig Woman
See Gibson, Jane

Pigalle, Jean Baptiste 1714-1785 [DEP,
DNNS, SN]
French sculptor
* [The] French Phidias

Pigault de l'Epiney 1753-1835 [WBD]
French author
* Pigault-Lebrun

Pigault-Lebrun
See Pigault de l'Epiney

[The] Piggly Wiggly Man
See Saunders, Clarence

Piggot, Mostyn T. [NPS]
Author
* Plum, Medium Tem

Piggott, C. M.
See Guido, [Cecily] Margaret

Piggy, Miss
See Schwartz, Cheri

Pigmeat Pete
See Wilson, Wesley

Pigmy Dick
See Harvey, Richard

Pignatari, Baby
See Pignatari, Francisco

Pignatari, Francisco 1917?-1977
Brazilian industrialist
* Pignatari, Baby

Pignatelli, Antonio 1615-1700 [WBD]
Pope
* Innocent XII

Pigot, John Edward 1822-1871 [PI]
Irish poet
* Fermoy
* Firinne
* Gall

Pigott, Anthony Charles Shackleton
1958- [DC]
British cricketer
* Pigott, Lester

Pigott, E. F. S. [FFF]
British writer
* Chat-Huant

Pigott, Lester
See Pigott, Anthony Charles Shackleton

Pigott, Mimi 1905?-1966 [THR]
British actress, singer, dancer
* Crawford, Mimi

Pigott, William 1870-1943 [LC]
British author
* Wales, Hubert

Pigozzi, Luciano 20th c. [WF]
Italian actor
* Collins, Alan

Pigtail Billy Riley
See Riley, William James [Billy]

Pihos, Big Dog
See Pihos, Peter L.

Pihos, Peter L. 1923- [FB]
American football player
* Pihos, Big Dog

Pijuan-Manotoc, Au-Au
See Pijuan-Manotoc, Aurora

Pijuan-Manotoc, Aurora 1950?- [TI 5-
28-84]
Philippine politician
* Pijuan-Manotoc, Au-Au

Pike, Albert 1809-1891 [HPPN]
American attorney, soldier, author
* Casca

Pike, Charles R.
See Bulmer, [Henry] Kenneth

Pike, Charles R.
See Harknett, Terry

Pike, Frances West [Atherton] 1819-?
[DNA]
American author
* Athern, Anna

Pike, James 1834-1867 [HPPN]
American law enforcement officer
* Pike of the Texas Rangers

Pike, Lip
See Pike, Lipman Emanuel

Pike, Lipman Emanuel 1845-1893 [AS,
BE, HPPN]
American baseball player
* Baseball's First Professional Player
* Pike, Lip

Pike, Mary Caroline [FFF, PA]
Author
* Hyde, Sidney

Pike, Mary Hayden Green 1827-1908
[FFF]
American author
* Langdon, Mary

Pike, Mary Hayden Green (cont.)
* May, Ida
* Story, Sydney A., Jr.

Pike, Morton
See Parry, David Harold

Pike, Mrs. [FFF]
Entertainer
* Sackett, Millie

Pike, Mrs. F. A. M. [PA]
Author
* Morris, Katherine

Pike, Noah W. 1838-? [PA]
Author
* Gordox

Pike of the Texas Rangers
See Pike, James

Pike, Robert L.
See Fish, Robert L.

Pike, William Ernest 20th c. [MBF]
British author and editor
* Conquest, Owen [house pseudonym]
* James, Ernest
* Richards, Frank [house pseudonym]

Pikestaff
See Baker, Thomas

Pikkumolliainen, Leena
See Pennanen, Lea Airi-Sirkka

Pilate, Pontius
See Walsh, Michael Paul

Pilbeam, Margery 1919- [BF]
British actress
* Pilbeam, Nova

Pilbeam, Nova
See Pilbeam, Margery

Pilcher, Rosamunde 1924- [AW, CA,
WD]
British author and playwright
* Fraser, Jane

Pile
See Moreno, Virginia [Reyes]

Pile, D. W. 20th c. [MBF]
British author
* Webber, Stawford

Pile o Dough
See Peladeau, Pierre

Pilgrim
See Brotherton, Edward

[The] Pilgrim
See Daniel

[A] Pilgrim
See Harsha, David Addison

[A] Pilgrim
See Wright, Frederick

Pilgrim, Anne
See Allan, Mabel Esther

[The] Pilgrim Bard
See Cummings, Scott

Pilgrim, David [joint pseudonym with Hilary Aidan St. George Saunders]
See Palmer, John Leslie

Pilgrim, David [joint pseudonym with John Leslie Palmer]
See Saunders, Hilary Aidan St. George

Pilgrim, Derral
See Zachary, Hugh

Pilgrim, Frank 1926- [CW]
Guyanese journalist, playwright, broadcaster
* Mirglip, Knarf

[The] Pilgrim from Hannibal
See Clemens, Samuel Langhorne

[The] Pilgrim Good Intent
See Worcester, Noah

[A] Pilgrim of Seventy
See Cox, John

Pilgrim, Paul
See Strodach, Paul Zeller

Pilgrim, Peter
See Bird, Robert Montgomery

[The] Pilgrim Pope
See Montini, Giovanni Battista Enrico Antonio Maria

Pilgrim, Thomas ?-1882 [DNA, HPPN]
American author
* Morecamp, Arthur
* Owl, Eugene

Pilgrim, William Lepper 1859-1918 [THR]
British actor
* Abingdon, W. L.

Pilgrimen
See Strussenfelt, Ulrika Sofia von

Pilio, Gerone
See Whitfield, John Humphreys

Pilk, Henry
See Campbell, Ken

Pilkington, Bert 1902-1953 [BX, RBE]
American boxer
* Morgan, Tod

Pilkington, Betty 20th c. [CA]
American journalist
* Alsterlund, Betty

Pilkington, Cynthia
See Horne, Cynthia Miriam

Pilkington, M. 18th c. [HPPN]
Irish author
* [The] Draper

Pillai, Narayana Narayana 1924- [IAW]
Indian author and playwright
* Omchery

[The] Pillar of Doctors
See William of Champeaux

[The] Pillar of the American Turf
See Belmont, August, Sr.

[The] Pillar of the Constitution
See Webster, Daniel

Pilleteri, Tony 1917- [BX, RBE]
American boxer
* [The] Garfield Gunner
* Larkin, Tippy

Pillette, Dee
See Pillette, Duane Xavier

Pillette, Duane Xavier 1922- [BE]
American baseball player
* Pillette, Dee

Pillette, Herman 1895-1960
American baseball player
* Pillette, Old Folks

Pillette, Old Folks
See Pillette, Herman

Pilley, Charles 1885- [LAO]
British barrister and journalist
* Pearce, Guy

Pillion, Cecil Randolph 1894-1962 [BE]
American baseball player
* Pillion, Squiz

Pillion, Squiz
See Pillion, Cecil Randolph

Pillow, Gideon Johnson 1806-1878 [SN]
American army officer
* [The] Liberator of Missouri

Pillsbury, Charles A. 1842-1899 [HPPN]
American flour miller
* [The] Father of New Process Milling

[The] Pillsbury Doughboy
See Hoyt, [Dewey] Lamarr

Pillsbury, John Sargent 1828-1901 [HPPN]
American milling executive and politician
* [The] Father of the University of Minnesota

Pilney, Andrew James 1913- [BE]
American baseball player
* Pilney, Anoy

Pilney, Anoy
See Pilney, Andrew James

Pilnyak, Boris
See Vogau, Boris Andreyevich

Pilon, Germain 1515?-1590 [FFF, RH, SN]
French sculptor
* [The] Father of French Sculpture

Pilot, James [FB]
American football player
* Pilot, Preacher

Pilot, Preacher
See Pilot, James

[The] Pilot Who Said No
See Heck, Michael

[The] Pilot who Weathered the Storm
See Pitt, William

Pilotin, Michael 20th c. [SFP]
Author
* Spriel, Stephen

[The] Pilot's General
See Quesada, Elwood R.

Pilou
See Bardot, Louis

Pilu, Francois 1919- [FC]
French actor
* Perier, Francois

Pim, Herbert Moore 1883- [WWL]
British author
* Newman, A.

Pimpernel
See Beaver, W. H.

Pin, Oscar
See Perdiguero Perez, Fernando

Pin-Tin
See Craveri, Sebastiano

Pinafore [Secret Service code name]
See Ford, Elizabeth Bloomer Warren [Betty]

Pinaud, Pierrette Ignace 1833-1908 [HPPN]
French actress
* Favart, Marie

Pincas, Julius 1885-1930 [WEC]
American artist
* Pascin, Jules

Pincay, Laffit 20th c.
Jockey
* [The] Pirate

Pinchback, Pinch
See Pinchback, Pinckney Benton Stewart

Pinchback, Pinckney Benton Stewart 19th c. [HPPN]
American gambler, carpetbagger, politician
* Pinchback, Pinch

Pincherle, Alberto 1907- [CLC]
Italian author, critic, playwright
* Moravia, Alberto

Pinchot, Gifford 1865-1946 [HPPN]
American politician and forestry expert
* [The] Father of American Forestry
* [The] Father of Conservation

[El] Pinciano
See Nunez de Guzman, Fernan [or Fernando]

Pinckert, Jeane 1918- [IPA]
American clairvoyant
* Dixon, Jeane

Pinckney, Barbara Biffinger Pfeiffer 1940?- [TI 3-3-86]
American author
* Pinckney, Callan

Pinckney, Blackguard Charlie
See Pinckney, Charles

Pinckney, Callan
See Pinckney, Barbara Biffinger Pfeiffer

Pinckney, Charles 1758?-1824 [BDSA, HPPN]
American statesman and author
* Pinckney, Blackguard Charlie
* Republican
* [A] South Carolina Federalist

Pincus, Abraham 1909?-1956 [BI]
American playwright
* Mollison, A. P.

Pincus, Barry Allen 1949?- [NY 12-1-85]
American composer and singer
* Manilow, Barry

Pincus, Gregory 1903- [HPPN]
American biologist
* [The] Father of the Birth Control Pill

Pincus, Jacob 1838-1918 [EJS]
American horse trainer and jockey
* Jacob the Silent

Pindar 5th c. BC [DNNS, FFF, HN, HPPN, NPS]
Greek poet
* [The] Dircaean Swan
* [The] Great Theban
* [The] Prince of Lyric Poets
* [The] Theban Bard
* [The] Theban Eagle
* [The] Theban Garden Swan
* [The] Theban Lyre

[The] Pindar, Horace, and Virgil of England
See Cowley, Abraham

[The] Pindar of England
See Cowley, Abraham

[The] Pindar of England
See Gray, Thomas

[The] Pindar of England
See Villiers, George

[The] Pindar of France
See Dorat, Jean

[The] Pindar of France
See Lebrun, Ponce Denis Ecouchard

[The] Pindar of France
See Ronsard, Pierre de

[The] Pindar of Italy
See Chiabrera, Gabriello

Pindar, Pat
See Battier, Henrietta

Pindar, Paul
See Akerman, John Yonge

Pindar, Peter?
See Lawler, C. F.

Pindar, Peter
See Wolcot, John

Pindar, Peter, Jr.
See Ellenwood, Henry S.

Pindaricus
See Slow, Jonathan

Pindemonte, Ippolito 1753-1828 [SN]
Italian poet
* [The] Italian Gray

Pinder, Callie
See Pinder, Cyril

Pinder, Cyril 1946- [IBW]
American football player
* Pinder, Callie

Pinder, J. M.
See Pinder, John Michael

Pinder, John Michael 1948- [ART]
British artist
* Pinder, J. M.

Pine, Arthur 1917- [ASC]
American public relations executive
* Richards, Jay

Pine, Cuyler
See Peck, Ellen [or Catherine?]

Pine, Leslie Gilbert 1907- [CA]
British author
* Moorshead, Henry

Pine, M. S.
See Finn, [Sister] Mary Paulina

Pine, Theodore [joint pseudonym with Emil (Theodore) Petaja]
See Hasse, Henry L.

Pine, Theodore [joint pseudonym with Henry L. Hasse]
See Petaja, Emil [Theodore]

Pine, William
See Harknett, Terry

Pineapple, Johnny
See Kaonohi, David

Pineau, Gabriel du 1573-1644 [DEP, FFF, SN]
French jurist
* [The] Cato of Anjou
* [The] Father of the People

Pinelli, Babe
See Paolinelli, Rinaldo Angelo

Pinelli, Ralph Arthur
See Paolinelli, Rinaldo Angelo

Pinelo
See De Leon, Antonio

Pinero, A. W.
See Pinero, [Sir] Arthur Wing

Pinero, [Sir] Arthur Wing 1855-1934 [LC]
British playwright
* Pinero, A. W.

Pinetop
See Sparks, Aaron

Pineux-Duval, Eugene Emmanuel 1808-1885 [WBD]
French painter
* Amaury-Duval, Eugene Emmanuel

[The] Pineville Painter
See Smith, William A.

Pinewood Tom
See White, Josh[ua Daniel]

[The] Piney Woods Thoreau
See Lovett, Eddie

Ping Pong
See Thompson, William Henry

[The] Ping Pong Diplomat
See Braithwaite, George

Pinheiro, Agbello 20th c. [SI 11-28-83]
Nigerian basketball coach
* Uncle P

Pinheiro, Paulo Henrique Barbara 1933- [IAW]
Brazilian author
* Barbara, Paulo Henrique

Piniella, Louis Victor 1943- [PB]
American baseball player
* Piniella, Piney

Piniella, Piney
See Piniella, Louis Victor

[The] Pink Lady
See Tout, Hazel Dawn

[The] Pink of the Press
See Willis, Nathaniel Parker

[The] Pink Powder Puff
See Guglielmi Di Valentina D'Antonguolla, Rodolpho Alfonso Raffaelo P.

Pink, Wal
See Pink, Walter Augustus

Pink, Walter Augustus 1862?-1922 [HPPN]
British playwright and actor
* Pink, Wal

Pink Whiskers
See Lewis, James Hamilton

Pinkerton, Allan 1819-1884 [HPPN]
Scottish-American detective
* Allen, [Major] E. J.
* America's Pioneer Detective
* [The] Eye

Pinkerton, Big Bill
See Pinkerton, William A.

Pinkerton, John 1758-1826 [DEA, DEL, HPPN]
Scottish author and historian
* Bennet, H., M.A.
* Heron, Robert
* Philistor
* Vindex

Pinkerton, W. Anson
See Steele, Henry

Pinkerton, William A. 1846-1923 [HPPN]
American detective
* Pinkerton, Big Bill

Pinkey
See Penkethman [or Pinkethman], William

Pinkham, Lydia E. 1819-1883 [HPPN]
American manufacturer
* [The] Mother of the Vegetable
  Compound

Pinkney, Miles
See Carre, Thomas

Pinkney, William 1764-1822 [HPPN]
American attorney, orator, statesman
* Caius
* Decius

Pinkston, Clarence 1900-1965 [BBH]
American swimming coach
* Pinkston, Pinky

Pinkston, Pinky
See Pinkston, Clarence

Pinkwater, Daniel Manus 1941- [IAW]
American author and illustrator
* Duck, Captain
* Lome, Mike
* Tress, Arthur

Pinky
See Humphrey, Hubert Horatio

Pinna y Ruiz, Donna Teresa
See Preston, William

Pinneberg, Rentier
See Hauser, Carl

Pinner, Joma
See Werner, Herma

[The] Pinner Miser
See Dancer, Daniel

Pinney, Johnny
See Penny, Johnny

Pinnix, Hannah Courtney [Baxter]
1851-1931 [DNA]
Author
* Kerr

Pinnock, [Rev.] William ?-1885 [HPPN]
British clergyman
* [A] Friend to Youth

Pino, E.
See Wittermans, Elizabeth [Pino]

Pintard, John 1759-1844 [HPPN]
American merchant and philanthropist
* [The] Father of Historical Societies in
  America

Pinter, Harold 1930- [CA]
British playwright and actor
* Baron, David

Pinter, Josef 1904-1941 [BEW, FC]
Hungarian-born American comedian
* Penner, Bumps
* Penner, Joe
* Penner, Wanna Buy a Duck

Pinto, Cecilia 20th c. [WEC]
Brazilian cartoonist
* Cica

Pinto, Jacqueline Harris 1927- [WD]
British author
* Blairman, Jacqueline

Pinto, Peter
See Bernstein, Eric [Lennard]

Pinto, Ziraldo Alves 1932- [WEC]
Brazilian cartoonist
* Ziraldo

Pinturicchio, Bernardo
See Betti [or Di Biagio?], Bernardino

Pinza, Ezio
See Pinza, Fortunato

Pinza, Fortunato 1892?-1957 [BBD, FC]
Italian-born American opera singer
* Pinza, Ezio

Pio. Padre [da Pietralcini]
See Forgione, Francesco

Pioche de la Vergne, Marie Madeleine
1634-1693 [SN]
French author
* [The] Fog
* La Fayette, Comtesse de

Pioggi, Louis 20th c. [BLB]
American underworld figure
* Louie the Lump

Piomingo
See Robinson, John

Pioneer
See Yates, Raymond Francis

[The] Pioneer Educator
See Hinsdale, Burke Aaron

[The] Pioneer of African Nationalism
See Johnson, James

[The] Pioneer of Air Power
See Mitchell, William [Billy]

[The] Pioneer of Colortype Printing
See Regensteiner, Theodore

[The] Pioneer of Financial Research
See Poor, Henry Varnum

[The] Pioneer of Modern Astronautics
See Oberth, Hermann

[The] Pioneer of Palomony
See Mitchelson, Marvin

[The] Pioneer of Renewal
See Ellard, Gerald

[The] Pioneer of Rolling Carts
See Sharp, James

[The] Pioneer of the Meat Industry
See Swift, Gustavus Franklin

Pioneer of the Modern Novel
See Evans, Marian

[The] Pioneer Plantsman
See Banister, John

[The] Pioneer Voice of America
See Brown, Charles Brockden

Piot, Lazarus
See Munday, Anthony

Piot, Lazarus
See Silvayn, Alexander

Piotrowska, Gabryela 1860-1921 [HPPN]
Polish actress and playwright
* Zapolska, Gabryela

[The] Pious
See Albert [or Albrecht]

[The] Pious
See Albert IV

[The] Pious
See Annius Verus, Marcus

[The] Pious
See Canute II

[The] Pious
See Edward VI

[The] Pious
See Eric IX

[The] Pious
See Ernest I [or Ernst]

[The] Pious
See Frederick III

[The] Pious
See Henry

[The] Pious
See Leopold III

[The] Pious
See Lothair I

[The] Pious
See Louis I

[The] Pious
See Robert II

[The] Pious
See Skippon, Philip

[The] Pious
See William I

Pious Jeems
See Gordon, James

[The] Pious Jimmy
See Carter, James Earl, Jr. [Jimmy]

Pious John
See Wanamaker, John

Pious, Minerva 1909- [HPPN, JF]
Russian-American actress and mimic
* Nussbaum, Mrs.
* Nussbaum, Pansy
* Rabinowitz, Gypsy Rose
* Rappaport, Blossom
* [The] Ruth Draper of Radio

[The] Pious Schoolmaster of Skippack
See Dock, Christopher

[Il] Piovano
See Arlotto Mainardi

Piozzi, Hester Lynch Salusbury
1741-1821 [HPPN, SN]
Welsh author
* Anna Matilda
* [An] Idle Gossip
* Matilda
* Thrale, Mrs.

Pipe Line Disney
See Disney, Wesley Ernest

Piper, A. G.
See Lewis, Julius Warren

Piper, [Sir] David Towry 1918- [AW]
British author
* Towry, Peter

Piper, Evelyn
See Modell, Merriam

Piper, Louis B. 20th c. [IBW]
American fashion designer
* Piper, Scotty

Piper, Peter
See Langbehn, Theo

Piper, Roger
See Fisher, John [Oswald Hamilton]

Piper, Scott 1954- [SMG]
American football player
* Clutch, Mr.

Piper, Scotty
See Piper, Louis B.

Piper, Thomas W. ?-1876 [HPPN]
American sexton and murderer
* [The] Murdering Sexton

Piper, Watty
See Bragg, Mabel Caroline

Piper, William Thomas, Sr. 1881-1970
[HPPN]
American aviation magnate
* [The] Henry Ford of Aviation

Pipes, Jeemes, of Pipesville
See Massett, Stephen C.

Pipgras, George 1899- [BN]
American baseball player
* [The] American Peasant
* [The] Danish Viking

Pipkin, Lefty
See Pipkin, Robert

Pipkin, Robert 20th c. [OBW]
American baseball player
* Pipkin, Lefty

Pipo
See Sofman, Gustave

Pippen, Cotton
See Pippen, Henry Harold

Pippen, Henry Harold 1910- [BE]
American baseball player
* Pippen, Cotton

Pipper, Pippia
See Whaling, Thornton

Pippi de Gianuzzi, Giulio 1492?-1546
[FFF, RH, WBD]
Italian painter
* [The] Roman
* Romano, Giulio

Pippin, Parley
See Bartlett, M. R.

Pipps, Mr.
See Leigh, Percival

Piquet, Francois 1708-1781 [DEP, DNNS]
Clergyman
* [The] Apostle of the Iroquois

Piquetort, Jean
See Routhier, [Sir] Adolphe Basile

Piraianu, Alexandru
See Mitru, Alexandru

[The] Pirate
See Pincay, Laffit

[The] Pirate King
See Khizr

[The] Pirate of the Gulf
See Lafitte, Jean

[The] Pirate Patriot
See Cheng Ch'eng-kung

[The] Pirate Preacher
See McIntire, Carl

[El] Pireo
See Cano Ruiz, Manuel

Pires, Joe
See Stout, Robert Joe

Pirie, Alexander K. 1942- [EG]
Scottish golfer
* Pirie, Sandy

Pirie, Sandy
See Pirie, Alexander K.

Pirie-Gordon, C. H. C.
See Pirie-Gordon, Charles Harry
Clinton

Pirie-Gordon, Charles Harry Clinton
1883-1969 [SFL, WGT]
British author
* Pirie-Gordon, C. H. C.
* Prospero and Caliban [joint
  pseudonym with Frederick William
  Serafino Austin Rolfe]

Piro, Frank 1920?- [BI]
American dancer
* Piro, Killer Joe

Piro, Killer Joe
See Piro, Frank

[Il] Pisanello
See Pisano, Antonio

Pisani, Carmen
See Frapolli, Madame

Pisano, Andrea 1270?-1348 [WBD]
Italian sculptor
* Da Pontedera, Andrea

Pisano, Antonio 1397?-1455? [WBD]
Veronese painter
* [Il] Pisanello
* Pisano, Vittore

Pisano, Leonardo
See Fibonacci, Leonardo

Pisano, Little Augie
See Carfano, Anthony

Pisano, Vittore
See Pisano, Antonio

Piscator
See Elliott, William

Piscator
See Lascelles, Robert

Piscator
See Lathy, Thomas P.

Piscator
See Walton, Izaak

Piscator, Paganus
See Fisher, Payne

Piscinarius
See Wier, Johannes

Pise, Charles Constantine 1802-1866
[HPPN]
American clergyman
* Her Brother In Law

[The] Pisistratos of Rome
See Caesar, [Gaius] Julius

Pismire, Osbert
See Hivnor, Robert

Pissarro, Camille 1830-1903 [HPPN]
French painter
* [The] Impressionist Printmaker
* [The] Unexplored Impressionist

Pissarro, Orovida Camille 1893-1968
[DBA]
British painter and etcher
* Orovida

[The] Pistol
See Rulewski, Jan

Pistol Pete
See Brennan, Peter J.

Pistol Pete
See Eaton, Frank

Pistol Pete Albright
See Albright, Thomas

Pistol Pete Maravich
See Maravich, Peter

Pistol Pete Reiser
See Reiser, Harold Patrick

Pistol Pete Wisniewski
See Wisniewski, Henry

Pistone, Joseph D. 20th c.
American FBI undercover agent
* Brasco, Don

Pistorius, Pieter 1920- [IAW]
South African author
* Hendriks, P. G.

Pitarra, Serafi
See Soler, Frederic

Pitati, Bonifazio di 1487-1553 [HPPN]
Italian painter
* Veneziano, Bonifazio
* Veronese, Bonifazio

Pitawall, Ernst
See Dedenroth, Eugen Hermann

Pitcairn, Frank
See Cockburn, [Francis] Claud

Pitcairn, John James 1860-1936 [CC, EMD, WGT]
British physician and author
* Ashdown, Clifford [joint pseudonym with Richard Freeman]
* Piers, Ashdown [joint pseudonym with Richard Freeman]

Pitcher
See Binstead, Arthur M.

Pitcher, Evelyn G[oodenough] 1915- [CA]
American author and educator
* Goodenough, Evelyn

Pitcher, Gladys 1890- [CAP]
American editor
* Adams, Betsy
* Wentworth, Barbara
* Weston, Ann

Pitcher, Molly
See McCauley, Mary Ludwig Hays

Pitcher, William John Charles 1859?-1925 [BEW]
Designer and artist
* Wilhelm, C.

Pitchford, Richard Valentine 1895-1973 [BI]
Welsh-born American magician
* Cardini

Pitchfork Ben Tillman
See Tillman, Benjamin Ryan

Pitchin' Paul Christman
See Christman, Paul C.

[The] Pitching Poet
See Kenna, Ed[ward Benninghaus]

Pith, Peter
See Smith, Sydney

Pithawalla, Maneck B. 1886- [WWL]
Indian poet
* Ruby

Pitkin, Sylvia Sherman 1895- [NAA]
American playwright
* Sherman, Sylvia

Pitko, Alex[ander] 1914- [BE]
American baseball player
* Pitko, Spunk

Pitko, Spunk
See Pitko, Alex[ander]

Pitlock, Lee Patrick Thomas 1947- [SMG]
American baseball player
* Pitlock, Skip

Pitlock, Skip
See Pitlock, Lee Patrick Thomas

Pitman, Margaret J. [PA]
Author
* Deane, Margery

[Il] Pitocchetto [The Beggar]
See Ceruti, Giacomo

Pitois, J. B. 1811-1877 [EOP]
Author
* Christian, Paul

Pitre, Cannonball
See Pitre, Didier

Pitre, Didier 1884-1934 [FHE, HK]
Canadian-born hockey player
* Pitre, Cannonball
* Pitre, Pit

Pitre, Pit
See Pitre, Didier

Pitt, Archie
See Selinger, Archie

Pitt, Diamond
See Pitt, Thomas

Pitt, Jeremy
See Wynne-Tyson, [Timothy] Jon [Lyden]

Pitt Lips Epps
See Epps, Eugene

Pitt, Mrs. H. M. [FFF]
Entertainer
* Addison, Fannie

Pitt, Thomas 1653-1726 [WBD]
British merchant and governor of Madras
* Pitt, Diamond

Pitt, Thomas [Lord Camelford] 1736?-1793 [HPPN]
British jurist
* [A] Cornishman

Pitt, Valerie
See Hall, Valerie

Pitt, William [Earl of Chatham] 1708-1778 [DEP, DNNS, HPPN, NPS, WBD]
British statesman
* [The] British Cicero
* [The] Distressed Statesman
* [The] Elder Pitt
* [The] Grand Old Man
* [The] Great Commoner
* Jowler
* [The] Loggerhead of London
* [The] Napoleon of Oratory
* [The] Old Lion
* [The] People's Will
* [The] People's William
* [The] Terrible Cornet of Horse
* [The] Young Marshal

Pitt, William 1759-1806 [FFF, HN, NPS, WBD]
British prime minister
* [An] Atlas
* Bottomless Pit
* [The] Heaven-Sent Minister
* [The] Pilot who Weathered the Storm
* [The] Younger Pitt

Pitt, William
See Wickliffe, Robert, Jr.

Pitt-Marson, Aileen 1912- [THR]
British actress
* Marson, Aileen

Pitt-Rivers, Augustus Henry
See Lane Fox, Augustus Henry

Pittard, Helene 1874-1953 [ESF, SFL, WGT]
French author
* Roger, Noelle

Pittenger, Clarke Alonzo 1899-1977 [BE]
American baseball player
* Pittenger, Pinky

Pittenger, Pinky
See Pittenger, Clarke Alonzo

Pittinger, Charles Reno 1871-1909 [AS, BE]
American baseball player
* Pittinger, Togie

Pittinger, Togie
See Pittinger, Charles Reno

Pittman, Jack [IBW]
American religious leader
* John the Prophet

Pittman, Key 1872-1940 [HPPN]
American miner and politician
* [The] Voice of Silver

Pittock, Joan [Hornby] 1930- [CA]
British author and educator
* Wesson, Joan

Pitts, Alabama
See Pitts, Edwin

Pitts, [Rev.] Alfred
See Watson, Johnny

Pitts, Charlie
See Wells, Samuel

Pitts, Donny
See Hathaway, Donny

Pitts, Edwin 20th c. [EF]
American football player
* Pitts, Alabama

Pitts, Eliza Susan 1898-1963 [BEW, HPPN]
American actress
* [The] Girl With the Ginger Snap Name
* Pitts, Zasu

Pitts, Frank 1943- [FB]
American football player
* Pitts, Riddler

Pitts, Herman Henry 1858-? [CCL]
Canadian author
* Brother Jonathan

Pitt's Loving Brother
See Grenville, Richard Temple [First Earl Temple]

Pitts, Riddler
See Pitts, Frank

Pitts, Zasu
See Pitts, Eliza Susan

Pittsburg Phil
See Smith, George

[The] Pittsburgh Candy King
See Clark, David Lytle

[The] Pittsburgh Hurricane
See Hunt, Robert [Bobby]

[The] Pittsburgh Kid
See Conn, William [Billy]

Pittsburgh Phil
See Smith, George Ellsworth

Pittsburgh Phil Strauss
See Strauss, Harry

[The] Pittsburgh Stealer
See Taveras, Franklin Fabian

[The] Pittsburgh Windmill
See Greb, Edward Henry

Pitusin
See Hurtado, Alfredo

Pius
See Metellus, Quintus Caecilius

Pius
See Mortara, Edgar

Pius II
See De Piccolomini, Enea Silvio

Pius III
See Todeschini-Piccolomini, Francesco

Pius IV
See Medici, Giovanni Angelo

Pius IX
See Mastai-Ferretti, Giovanni Maria

Pius V
See Ghislieri, Michele

Pius VI
See Braschi, Giovanni Angelo

Pius VII
See Chiaramonti, Luigi Barnaba

Pius VIII
See Castiglioni, Francesco Saverio

Pius X
See Sarto, Giuseppe Melchiorre

Pius XI
See Ratti, Ambrogio Damiano Achille

Pius XII
See Pacelli, Eugenio Maria Giovanni

Piute Pete
See Kaufman, Morris

Pixerecourt, Rene Charles Guilbert de
1773-1844 [DNNS, SN]
French playwright
* [The] Corneille of the Boulevards
* [The] Shakespeare of the Boulevards

[The] Pixie of Gasoline Alley
See Sachs, Edward Julius

Pixley, Frank M. [FFF]
American writer
* Podrida, Olla

Pizarro, Francisco 1475?-1541 [DNNS, FFF, RH]
Spanish explorer
* [The] Conqueror
* Conquistador

Pizer [or Kosminski?] 19th c. [BL]
Polish-born shoemaker and murder suspect
* Leather Apron

Pizzarelli, Bucky
See Pizzarelli, John

Pizzarelli, John 1926- [EJ7]
American jazz musician
* Pizzarelli, Bucky

Pizzarno, Madame [FFF]
Entertainer
* Giuri, Adele

Pizzat, Frank J[oseph] 1924- [CA]
American psychologist and author
* Venafro, Mark

Pizzo, John F. 1907-1952 [SC]
American actor and circus performer
* Little Bozo

Pizzo, Vito 1929- [EJ]
American jazz musician
* Price, Vito

Place, Benjamin
See Thring, Edward

Place, Francis 1771-1854 [HPPN]
British tailor and reformer
* [A] London Tailor

Place, Marian T[empleton] 1910- [CA, SAT]
American author
* White, Dale
* Whitinger, R. D.

Placere, Morris N.
See Gupta, Sushil Kumar

Placide, Alice
See Emmett, Mrs. Charles E.

Placide, Henry 1799-1870 [HPPN]
American actor
* [The] Stage's Most Convincing Actor

Placido
See Valdes, Gabriel de la Concepcion

Placidus [a Spescha], [Father] 1752-1833
Swiss monk and mountain climber
* [The] Monk of Disentis

Pladner, Emile 1906- [BX, RBE]
French boxer
* Pladner, Spider

Pladner, Spider
See Pladner, Emile

Plagiary, [Sir] Fretful
See Cumberland, Richard

Plaidy, Jean
See Hibbert, Eleanor Alice [Burford]

[The] Plain and Perspicuous Doctor
See Burleigh, [or Burley?], Walter

Plain Ben Jones
See Jones, Benjamin Allyn

[A] Plain Dealer
See Rushton, Thomas

[The] Plain Dealer
See Wycherly, William

[A] Plain Hand
See Hunt, Ezra Mundy

Plain, Henry
See Anderson, James

Plain, Josephine
See Mitchell, Isabel Mary

Plain, Timothy
See Blakie, G. W.

Plain, Timothy
See Threepland, Moncrieff

Plain, Warren
See Oehmke, Thomas Harold

Plainfield, Joseph Franklin
See Piani, Giuseppe Francesco

Planche, Matilda Anne
See Mackarness, Matilda Anne

Planchet, Roger Anthony 1923- [CWG]
Canadian country-western performer
* Rogers, Smiling Slim

Planck, Max Karl Ernst Ludwig
1858-1947 [HPPN]
German physicist
* [The] Father of the Quantum Theory

Plancus, Janus
See Bianchi, Giovanni

Plane, Anne
See Seymour, Marjorie F.

Planet
See Shakespeare, William

[The] Planet Prince
See Haggard, J. Harvey

Planinc, Milka 1924- [TI 1-30-84]
Yugoslavian prime minister
* [The] Margaret Thatcher of Yugoslavia

Plank, Edward Stewart 1875-1926 [BE, BTB]
American baseball player
* Plank, Gettysburg Eddie

Plank, Gettysburg Eddie
See Plank, Edward Stewart

[The] Plant Detective
See Douglas, David

[The] Plant Doctor
See Carver, George Washington

[The] Plant Explorer
See Hansen, Niels Ebbesen

Plant, Henry Bradley 1819-1899
[HPPN]
American railroad builder and industrialist
* [The] King of Florida

[The] Plant Magician
See Burbank, Luther

[The] Plant Wizard
See Burbank, Luther

Plantagenet
See Bromet, William

Plantagenet
See Geoffrey IV

Plantagenet, Edith 12th c. [DNNF, DNNS, SN]
Wife of David, Prince Royal of Scotland
* [The] Fair Maid of Anjou

Plantagenet, Edmund 1241?-1296
[DNNS, HN, WBD]
First Earl of Lancaster
* Crouchback

Plante, [Joseph] Jacques 1929- [CEI, FHE, HK]
Canadian-born hockey player
* Jake the Snake
* Plante, Omer

Plante, Omer
See Plante, [Joseph] Jacques

[A] Planter
See Long, Edward

Plantin, Christopher 1520?-1589 [SN]
Flemish typographer and printer
* [The] Cellini of Printing

Planty, Earl 20th c.
American educator and philatelist
* [The] Dean of First Day Cover Collectors

Planus et Perspicuus, Doctor
See Burleigh, [or Burley?], Walter

Plaskitt, Dorothy 1874?-1950 [THR]
British actress
* Hammond, Dorothy

Plastic Fantastic, Mr.
See Cavanaugh, Walter

[The] Plastic Historian
See Davidson, Jo

[The] Plastic Man
See Perkins, Sam

Plastic Pat Nixon
See Nixon, Thelma Catherine Patricia Ryan

Plastino, Al 20th c. [WECO]
Cartoonist
* Mik, Al

Platak, Joseph 1909?-1954 [AS]
American handball player
* [The] Blond Panther

Platel, Felix ?-1888 [PA]
French writer
* Ignotus
* Pall, Etienne

Platerito [Little Silversmith]
See Taravilla y Amoros, Gregorio

[El] Platero [The Silversmith]
See Garcia, Jose

Plath, Sylvia 1932-1963 [BI, CAP, LC]
American author and poet
* Lucas, Victoria

Platina
See Sacchi, Bartolommeo de'

[The] Platinum Bombshell
See Carpenter [or Carpentier?], Harlean

Platner, Ernst 1744-1818 [HN, SN]
German physician and philosopher
* [The] German Nestor of Philosophy
* [The] Nestor of German Philosophy

Plato [Broadshouldered]
See Aristocles

Plato
See Coventry, Henry

Plato
See De Quincey, Thomas

[The] Plato of Germany
See Jacobi, Friedrich Heinrich

[The] Plato of Germany
See Mendelssohn, Moses

[The] Plato of His Age
See Malebranche, Nicolas

[The] Plato of the Christian World
See Herder, Johann Gottfried von

[The] Plato of the Eighteenth Century
See Arouet, Francois Marie

[The] Plato of the Puritans
See Howe, John

Platon
See Levshin, Peter

[The] Platonic Puritan
See Howe, John

[The] Platonist
See Taylor, Thomas

Platonov, Andrei
See Klimentov, Andrei Platonovich

Plato's Master
See Socrates

Platoune
See Astell, Mary

Platov, Matvei Ivanovich, Count 1757-1818 [HPPN]
Russian soldier and nobleman
* Hetman of the Cossacks of the Don

Platt, Charles 1945- [ESF]
British author and editor
* St. James, Blakely [house pseudonym, Playboy Press]

Platt, Easy Boss
See Platt, Thomas Collier

Platt, Edward
See Greenberg, Edward

Platt, J. G.
See Platt, John Gerald

Platt, John Gerald 1892- [ART]
British painter, engraver, etcher
* Platt, J. G.

Platt, Kin 1911- [SFL]
Author
* York, Wesley Simon

Platt, Mizell George 1920- [BE]
American baseball player
* Platt, Whitey

Platt, Orville H. 1827-1905 [HPPN]
American statesman
* [The] Father of the Platt Amendment

Platt, [Rev.] Robert 1795-? [HPPN]
British clergyman
* Omega

Platt, Thomas Collier 1833-1910
[HPPN, NPS]
American politician
* Me Too
* Platt, Easy Boss

Platt, Whitey
See Platt, Mizell George

Platter, Felix 1536-1614 [HPPN]
French physician
* Beloved Son Felix

Platts, Beryl 1918- [CA]
British author and editor
* Seaton, Beryl

Platus
See Piatti, Girolomo

Plauen, E. O.
See Ohser, Erich

Plaut, Martin
See Marttin, Paul

Plautus
See Wilder, Alexander

Plawin, Paul 1938- [CA]
American author
* Godly, J. P.
* Steele, Dirk

[A] Play-Goer
See Ireland, Joseph N.

Playboy
See Reed, John [Silas]

[The] Playboy
See Reynolds, Robert Rice

Playboy Dick Cavill
See Cavill, Dick

[The] Playboy of New York
See Walker, James John [Jimmy]

[The] Playboy of the Air
See Mollison, James Allan

[The] Playboy of the Piano
See Rubinstein, Artur

[The] Playboy of the Western Wing
See Kissinger, Henry Alfred

Playboy of the Western World, Mr.
See Hefner, Hugh Marston

[The] Player
See Bach, Hans

Player, Eddie   [MBF]
British author
* Reid, Desmond [house pseudonym]

Player, Gary 1935-   [CR, HPPN]
South African golfer
* [The] Black Knight of the Fairways
* Golf's Black Knight

Player, Robert
See Jordan, Robert Furneaux

Player, [Sir] Thomas 17th c.   [SN]
* Rabsheka

[The] Player Who Is Never Caught
from Behind
See Bellino, Joseph [Joe]

Playfair, Hugo
See Paterson, Paul

Playfair, I.
See Wilde, Oscar [Fingal O'Flahertie
Wills]

Playfair, John 1748-1819 [HPPN]
Scottish mathematician and geologist
* [The] Proponent of the Huttonian
  Theory

Playfair, William 1759-1829 [HPPN]
Scottish author and inventor
* [Un] Anglais

[The] Playgirl of the Western World
See Johnson, Lucy

Pleasant, Cousin Joe
See Joseph, Pleasant

Pleasant Gardens Joe
See McDowell, Joseph

Pleasant Joe
See Joseph, Pleasant

Pleasant, Tommy Lee
See Smith, Pleasant

Pleasant Willy
See Shakespeare, William

Pleasants, Jack 1874-1923   [BMH]
British comedian
* [The] Bashful Limit

Pleasants, John Hampden 1797-1846
[HPPN]
American journalist and editor
* [The] Bayard of the Press

Pleasants, Mammy
See Pleasants, Mary Ellen Smith

Pleasants, Mary Ellen Smith 1812?-1904
[HPPN, IBW]
American abolitionist
* Pleasants, Mammy
* Smith, [Mrs.] Mary Ellen

Pleasure, King
See Beeks, Clarence

Pleban, Jerry J. 1957-   [HPPN]
American marine
* Pleban, Shorty

Pleban, Shorty
See Pleban, Jerry J.

[The] Plebeian Child of the Revolution
See Bonaparte, Napoleon

[The] Plebeian Count
See Riqueti, Honore Gabriel Victor

Pledge, Joe
See Polizio, Emetio

Pleigh, Phare
See Wiggin, James Henry

Pleil, Rudolf ?-1958 [HPPN]
German murderer
* [The] Best Death Maker

Plekhanov, Georgii Valentinovich
1856-1918 [HPPN]
Russian philosopher
* [The] Father of Russian Marxism

Plemiannikov, Roger Vadim 1928-
[BDF, FC, FDG]
French director
* Vadim, Roger

Plendello, Leo
See Saint, Andrew [John]

Plenipo, Rummer
See Prior, Matt[hew]

Plenthon, Gemistus
See Gemistus, Georgius

Plenthon, Georgius
See Gemistus, Georgius

Pleon
See Moore, John

Pleon, Alec 1911-   [BMH]
British comedian
* Funny Face

Plessis, Marie du
See Plessis, Rose Alphonsine

Plessis, Rose Alphonsine 1824-1847
[HPPN]
*Friend of French author, Alexandre
Dumas*
* Plessis, Marie du

Pletikosic, Ante 1939-   [AES]
Yugoslav soccer player
* Pletikosic, Tony

Pletikosic, Tony
See Pletikosic, Ante

Plews, Arthur Gordon Lane 1867-?
[THR]
British actor
* Poulton, A. G.

Pleydell, George
See Bancroft, George Pleydell

Pleydell, Paulus
See Crosbie, Andrew

Pleydell, Susan
See Senior, Isabel J[anet] C[ouper]
Syme

Plick et Plock
See Simenon, Georges [Joseph
Christian]

Plieksans, Janis 1865-1929 [EWL]
Latvian poet, playwright, translator
* Rainis, Janis

Plimmer, Charlotte 1916- [CA]
*American-born British author and
playwright*
* Denis, Charlotte [joint pseudonym
  with Denis Plimmer]

Plimmer, Denis 1914- [CA]
*Australian-born British author and
playwright*
* Denis, Charlotte [joint pseudonym
  with Charlotte Plimmer]

Plimsoll, Samuel 1824-1898 [DEP,
WBD]
*British politician, author, shipping
reformer*
* [The] Sailor's Friend

Plinius Secundus
See Rumsey, John

Plinth, Octavius   [IP]
American author
* [The] Rain Water Doctor

Pliny [Gaius Plinius Secundus] 23-79
[WBD]
Roman scholar
* [The] Elder

Pliny [Gaius Plinius Caecilius Secundus]
62-113 [WBD]
Roman politician
* [The] Younger

[The] Pliny of the East
See Ibn-Muhammed, Zakarija

Pliny the Youngest
See Wilson, Stanley Kidder

Plo
See Plowitz, Kurt

Plon-Plon
See Bonaparte, Napoleon Joseph
Charles Paul

Plotinus 205?-270 [RH]
Roman philosopher
* Thaumaturgus

[The] Plotter
See Ferguson, Robert

Ploug, Parmo Carl
See Rytter, Poul

Plough, Peter
See Barty, James S.

[A] Ploughist
See Pegge, Samuel

[A] Ploughman
See Burges, Tristram

Ploughman, John
See Spurgeon, Charles Haddon

Ploughman, Nina
See Sutcliffe, Pavella Dolores

[The] Ploughman of Madrid
See Isidore [or Isidro]

Ploughpenny
See Eric IV [or VI]

Ploughshare, Peter
See Beach, S. B.

Plover
See Wise, John S.

Plow 'em Under Wallace
See Wallace, Henry A[gard]

Plowden, Edmund 1518-1585 [NPS]
Jurist and author
* [The] Oracle of Common Law

Plowitz, Kurt 1912?-1969
American artist and stamp designer
* Plo

Plowman, Giles
See Sutcliffe, Joseph Robert

Plowright, William George Holroyd
1911-1977 [DI, EOP]
British swindler
* Roy, William
* Silver, Bill

Pluche, Jeames de la
See Thackeray, William Makepeace

Pluck, Christopher 20th c. [HPPN]
American barber and hairdresser
* [The] Father of the Haldeman Cut

Pluckrose, Henry [Arthur] 1931- [CA, SAT]
British educator and editor
* Cobbett, Richard

Pluff, Barbara Littlefield 1926- [CA]
American author
* Clayton, Barbara

Plug [code name]
See Presser, William

Plug, Percival, R. N.
See Hannay, James

Plugger Bill Martin
See Martin, William

Plum, J.
See Wodehouse, Pelham Grenville

Plum, Jennifer
See Kurland, Michael

Plum, Medium Tem
See Piggot, Mostyn T.

Plumb, Beatrice
See Hunzicker, Beatrice Plumb

Plumb, Hay
See Hay-Plumb, Edward

Plumb, J. H.
See Plumb, John Harold

Plumb, John Harold 1911- [LC]
British historian and author
* Plumb, J. H.

Plumb, Plumber
See Plumb, Ron

Plumb, Ron 1950- [SMG]
Canadian-born hockey player
* Plumb, Plumber

[The] Plumber
See DeCavalcante, Simone Rizzo

[The] Plume of War
See Sidney, [Sir] Philip

Plume, Sir
See Brown, [Sir] George

[The] Plumed Knight
See Blaine, James Gillespie

[The] Plumed Knight of the Confederacy
See Stuart, James Ewell Brown

Plumer, William 1759-1850 [FFF, HPPN, PA]
American statesman and author
* Cincinnatus
* Impartialis
* [A] Layman

Plumley, Ernest Frederick 1909- [AW, WD]
British playwright and actor
* Clevedon, John

Plumm, Norman D.
See Hornback, Bert G[erald]

Plummer, Ben
See Bingley, David Ernest

Plummer, Clare [Emsley] 1912- [AW, CA, HPPN, WD]
British author
* Emsley, Clare
* Penarth, Wyn

Plummer, Henry ?-1864 [HPPN]
American law officer
* [The] Montana Outlaw Boss

Plummer, John 1831-? [IP, PA]
British author and poet
* [The] Northamptonshire Poet

Plummer, Thomas Arthur 20th c. [WW]
Author
* Sarne, Michael

Plummy
See Dellbridge, John

Plumpe, Friedrich Wilhelm 1889-1931
[BDF, FC, FD]
German director
* Murnau, F[riedrich] W[ilhelm]

Plumptre, Annabella [IP]
British author
* [A] Lady

Plumptre, Anne [IP]
British author
* Miss P.

Plumptre, Edward Hayes 1821-1891
[HPPN]
British clergyman
* E. H. P.

Plumptre, John [IP]
British clergyman and author
* [A] Clergyman of the Church of England

Plunder
See McNally, Leonard

[The] Plunger
See Pietrosante, Nicholas V. [Nick]

Plunket, William Conyngham [First Baron Plunket] 1764-1854 [HPPN]
Irish barrister and jurist
* Sheelagh

Plunket, William Conyngham 1828-1897
[PI]
Irish poet and clergyman
* U. U. P.

Plunkett, Arthur Hume 19th c. [PI]
Irish poet
* A. H. P.

Plunkett, Edward [16th Baron Dunsany]
1808-1858 [HPPN]
Irish naval officer
* [A] Naval Peer

Plunkett, George Noble 1851-? [PI]
Irish poet
* Killeen

Plunkett, Henry Willoughby Grattan
1808-1889 [PI, RH]
Irish-born poet and playwright
* Frisbos
* Grattan, H. P.

Plunkett, J. M.
See Plunkett, Joseph Mary

Plunkett, James
See Kelly, James Plunkett

Plunkett, Joseph Mary 1887-1916 [LC]
Irish editor, poet, nationalist
* Plunkett, J. M.

Plunkett, Sarge
See Wier, A. M.

Plupy
See Shute, Henry Augustus

[Le] Plus Brave des Braves
See Ney, Michel [Duc d'Elchingen]

Plutarch 46?-120? [DNNS, FFF, SN]
Greek historian
* [The] Cheronean Sage

[The] Plutarch of France
See Le Vayer, Franocise De La Mothe

Plutonius
See Mehta, Rustam Jehangir

Plutus
See Bernhard, Georg

Plyades, [Rev. Mr.] Charles
See Churchill, Charles

Plymley, Peter
See Smith, Sydney

[The] Plymouth Sound
See White, James

Po Joe Williams
See Williams, Joe

[The] Po' Ol' Country Lawyer
See Ervin, Sam[uel James, Jr.]

Poage, Scott T[abor] 1931- [CA]
American engineer and author
* Scott, P. T.

Poague, William Robert 1899- [HPPN]
American educator and politician
* [The] Professor

Pocahontas
See Matoaka

Pocahontas
See Pearson, Emily [Clemens]

[The] Pocahontas of the West
See Ward, Nancy

Poccetti, Bernardino
See Barbatelli, Bernardino [or Bernardo]

Pocci, Franz Von 1803-1876 [WEC]
German cartoonist, illustrator, author
* [The] Hogarth of Bavaria

Poche
See Deschamps, Pierre Charles Ernest

Pochi Danari
See Maximilian I

[El] Pocho [The Rotten One]
See Alarcon, Alfonso

Pochonet, Dave
See Pochonet, Gerard

Pochonet, Gerard 1924- [EJ]
French jazz musician
* Pochonet, Dave

[The] Pocket Dictator
See Dollfuss, Engelbert

[The] Pocket Patton
See Harmon, Ernest Nason

[The] Pocket Rocket
See Richard, [Joseph] Henri

[The] Pocket Sims Reeves
See Powles, Matilda Alice

Pocock, Carmichael Charles 1920?-1979
British-born oil company executive
* Pocock, Mike

Pocock, Cyrene Sue 1896?-1964 [BEW]
American opera singer
* Van Gordon, Cyrena

Pocock, Mike
See Pocock, Carmichael Charles

Pocock, Nicholas Edward Julian 1951-
[DC]
Venezuelan-born cricketer
* Pocock, Pokers

Pocock, Patrick Ian 1946- [DC]
Welsh-born cricketer
* Pocock, Percy

Pocock, Percy
See Pocock, Patrick Ian

Pocock, Pokers
See Pocock, Nicholas Edward Julian

Pocoroba, Biff
See Pocoroba, Bill

Pocoroba, Bill 1953- [SMG]
American baseball player
* Pocoroba, Biff
* Pocoroba, Poco

Pocoroba, Poco
See Pocoroba, Bill

Podbielan, Bud
See Podbielan, Clarence Anthony

Podbielan, Clarence Anthony 1924-
[BE]
American baseball player
* Podbielan, Bud

Poderjay, Captain
See Poderjay, Ivan Ivanovich

Poderjay, Ivan Ivanovich 1899- [HPPN]
Slovenian confidence man
* [The] Bigamous Captain
* [The] Bolting Banker
* Poderjay, Captain

Podgajny, John Sigmund [Johnny] 1920-
[BE, PB]
American baseball player
* Podgajny, Specs

Podgajny, Specs
See Podgajny, John Sigmund [Johnny]

Podgers
See Ogden, R. L.

Podmarsh, Rollo
See Salter, Donald P. M.

Podmore, Periwinkle
See Bangs, John Kendrick

Podola, Guenther Fritz Erwin
1929?-1959 [HPPN]
German murderer
* Fisher, Mr.

Podoliak, Boris
See Kostiuk, Hryhory

Podoloff, Maurice [WP 8-16-81]
American hockey and basketball executive
* [The] Fiorello LaGuardia of Sports
* Podoloff, Poodles
* Podoloff, Pumpernickel

Podoloff, Poodles
See Podoloff, Maurice

Podoloff, Pumpernickel
See Podoloff, Maurice

Podrida, Olla
See Pixley, Frank M.

Poe, Edgar
See Levine, Philip

Poe, Edgar Allan 1809-1849 [EMD,
HPPN, NPS, PA, SN, WGT]
American author and poet
* [The] American Richard Savage
* [A] Bostonian
* E. A. P.
* Eddie
* [The] Father of Detection
* Israfel
* Marginalia
* Perry, Edgar A.
* Pfaal, Hans
* Pym, Arthur Gordon
* Quarles, Geoffrey
* Quickens, Quarles
* Reunet, Henri le
* [The] Wizard of Word Music

Poel, William
See Pole, William

Poe's Helen
See Whitman, Sarah Helen Power

[A] Poet
See Montgomery, James

[A] Poet
See Osborn, Laughton

[The] Poet
See Parsons, Thomas William

[The] Poet Adventurer
See Sandys, George

Poet and Saint
See Crashaw, Richard

[The] Poet at the Breakfast Table
See Holmes, Oliver Wendell

[The] Poet Bishop
See Taylor, Jeremy

[The] Poet Entertainer of the Ozarks
See Lucey, Thomas Elmore

[The] Poet From Nashville
See Hall, Tom T.

[The] Poet Genius of His People
See Dunbar, Paul Laurence

Poet in Motion
See Mitchell, Arthur Adam

Poet in Power
See Ecevit, Bulent

[The] Poet King
See James I

[The] Poet King of Scandinavia
See Oehlenschlaeger, Adam Gottlob

[The] Poet Laureate of California
See Coolbrith, Ida Donna

[The] Poet Laureate of California
See McGroarty, John Steven

[The] Poet Laureate of Democracy
See Riley, James Whitcomb

[The] Poet Laureate of Freemasonry
See Morris, Robert

[The] Poet Laureate of Georgia
See Stanton, Frank Lebby

[The] Poet Laureate of Harlem
See Hughes, [James] Langston

[The] Poet Laureate of His People
See Dunbar, Paul Laurence

[The] Poet Laureate of Modern Jazz
See Hendricks, John Carl

[The] Poet Laureate of New England
See Whittier, John Greenleaf

[The] Poet Laureate of New Jersey
See Musser, Benjamin

[The] Poet Laureate of Oxford
See Skelton, John

[The] Poet Laureate of Television
See Russell, Nipsey

[The] Poet Laureate of the Army
See Patten, George Washington

[The] Poet Laureate of the Bees
See Evans, John

[The] Poet Laureate of the Confederacy
See Timrod, Henry

[The] Poet Laureate of the Little Smokies
See Hickman, Herman M., Jr.

[The] Poet Laureate of the Railroad
See Fennell, Patrick

[The] Poet Laureate of the Revolution
See Esenin, Sergei Aleksandrovich

[The] Poet Laureate of the Sixth Circuit
See McCree, Wade H.

[The] Poet Laureate of the South
See Hayne, Paul Hamilton

Poet Laureate to the Congress
See Odell, Jonathan

[The] Poet Naturalist
See Thoreau, Henry David

[The] Poet 'o the Plains
See Eberhardt, John J.

[The] Poet of Armageddon
See Davidson, John

[The] Poet of Bran Meal and Pumpkins
See Graham, Sylvester

[The] Poet of Charleston
See Hayne, Paul Hamilton

[The] Poet of Childhood
See Eberhardt, John J.

[The] Poet of Childhood
See Field, Eugene

[The] Poet of Despair
See Thomson, James

[The] Poet of Duhallow
See Deady, John Christmas

[The] Poet of France
See Ronsard, Pierre de

[The] Poet of Greta Hall
See Southey, Robert

[The] Poet of Haslemere
See Tennyson, Alfred [First Baron Tennyson]

[The] Poet of His People
See Zunser, Eliakim

[The] Poet of Hygiene
See Dumas, Jean Baptiste Andre

[The] Poet of Ivy Wall
See Donoho, Thomas Seton

[The] Poet of Kings
See Ronsard, Pierre de

[The] Poet of Kirkintillock
See Watson, Walker

[The] Poet of Kissing
See Sidney, [Sir] Philip

[The] Poet of Languedoc
See Boe, Jacques

[The] Poet of Liberty
See Schiller, Johann Christoph Friedrich von

[The] Poet of Low Hampton
See Miller, William

[The] Poet of Methodism
See Wesley, Charles

[The] Poet of Nature
See Wordsworth, William

[The] Poet of Paris
See Fargue, Leon-Paul

[The] Poet of Poets
See Shelley, Percy Bysshe

[The] Poet of Princes
See Marot, Clement

[The] Poet of Reason
See Boileau-Despreaux, Nicolas

[The] Poet of St. Honore
See Beranger, Pierre Jean de

[The] Poet of the American Revolution
See Freneau, Philip Morin

[The] Poet of the Caucasus
See Lermontoff, Mikhail Yurievitch

[The] Poet of the Chase
See Somerville, William

Poet of the Chicago Slums
See Algren, Nelson

[The] Poet of the Common People
See Riley, James Whitcomb

[The] Poet of the Commonplace
See Longfellow, Henry Wadsworth

[The] Poet of the Confederacy
See Ryan, [Father] Abram Joseph

[The] Poet of the Damned
See Alighieri, Durante

Poet of the Depths
See Cousteau, Jacques-Yves

[The] Poet of the Excursion
See Wordsworth, William

[The] Poet of the Future
See Ronsard, Pierre de

[The] Poet of the Golden Gate
See Kirchoff, Theodore

Poet of the Hollow Tree
See Grimston, William

[The] Poet of the Inquisition
See Calderon de la Barca, Pedro

[The] Poet of the Moy
See Flanagan, Edward

[The] Poet of the Organ
See Crawford, Jesse

[The] Poet of the Ozarks
See Newberger, Gabriel F.

[The] Poet of the People
See Sandburg, Carl [August]

[The] Poet of the Piano
See Cavallaro, Carmen

[The] Poet of the Poor
See Crabbe, George

[The] Poet of the Revolution
See Mayakovsky, Vladimir Vladimirovich

[The] Poet of the Shenandoah Valley
See Lucas, Daniel Bedinger

[The] Poet of the Sierras
See Miller, Cincinnatus Heine

[The] Poet of the Slaves
See Castro Alves, Antonio de

[The] Poet of the Sword
See Skobeleff, Michael Dimitrievitch

[The] Poet of the Vague
See Ossian

[The] Poet of the Workshop
See Frazer, John de Jean

[The] Poet of Violence
See Chandler, Raymond

[The] Poet of Wicomisco
See Dennis, Amanda E.

[The] Poet of Wild Enchantment
See Coleridge, Samuel Taylor

[The] Poet Painter
See Rossetti, Dante Gabriel

[The] Poet Premier
See Ecevit, Bulent

[The] Poet Priest
See Milman, Henry Hart

[The] Poet Prince
See Frome, Anthony

[The] Poet Pug
See Pope, Alexander

[The] Poet Scout
See Crawford, J. W.

[The] Poet Sire of Italy
See Alighieri, Durante

[The] Poet Sportsman
See McLellan, Isaac

[The] Poet Squab
See Dryden, John

[The] Poet Wheelman
See Foster, S. Conant

[The] Poet With a Purpose
See Clem, Charles Douglas

Poet Wordy
See Wordsworth, William

Poeta, Enginae Societatis
See Peirce, Augustus

[Le] Poete des Rois
See Ronsard, Pierre de

[The] Poete Lacrymal
See Bouilly, Jean Nicolas

[The] Poetical Father of Waller
See Fairfax, Edward

[The] Poetical Milkmaid
See Yearsley, Ann

[A] Poetical Rochefoucault
See Davenant, [Sir] William

[A] Poetical Spagnoletto
See Grahame, James

[The] Poetry Lady
See Lawton, Ethel Chapin

[The] Poet's Parasite
See Warburton, William

[The] Poet's Poet
See Spenser, Edmund

[The] Poet's Publisher of America
See Fields, James Thomas

Poff, Alonzo M. 1870-1952   [SC]
American actor
* Poff, Lon

Poff, Lon
See Poff, Alonzo M.

Poffenberger, Boots
See Poffenberger, Cletus Elwood

Poffenberger, Cletus Elwood 1915-   [PB]
American baseball player
* Poffenberger, Boots

Pogany, Joseph   [BI]
American Communist leader
* Pepper, John

Poget [or Pagit?], Ephraim ?-1646   [SN]
Clergyman and author
* Old Father Ephraim

Poggel, Mary 1851-1907   [IA]
American author
* Ave
* Mary Salesia, [Sister]

Poggenburg, Edward Francis 1901?-1963
[BEW, HPPN]
American theatrical performer
* Archie the Manager
* Gardner, Ed

Poggi, Emil J. 1928-   [CA]
American educator and author
* Poggi, Jack

Poggi, Jack
See Poggi, Emil J.

Poggibonsi, Angelo di Michele d'Angelo da
See Montorsoli, [Fra] Giovanni Angelo

Pogo
See Gray, Patricia [Clark]

Pogodin, Nikolai Fyodorovich
See Stukalov, Nikolai Fyodorovich

Pogonatus
See Constantine IV

Pohl, Baruch 1838-1897   [BBD]
German impresario
* Pollini, Bernhard

Pohl, Frederik 1919-   [ESF, SF, WGT]
American author and editor
* Andrews, Elton V.
* Fleur, Paul
* Gottesman, S. D. [joint pseudonym with Cyril M. Kornbluth and Robert Lowndes]
* Gregor, Lee [joint pseudonym with Milton A. Rothman]
* Howard, Warren F.
* Judd, Cyril [joint pseudonym with Cyril M. Kornbluth]
* Lavond, Paul Dennis [joint pseudonym with J. Dockweiler, C. Kornbluth, R. Lowndes]
* Mariner, Scott [joint pseudonym with Cyril M. Kornbluth]
* Mason, Ernst
* McCann, Edson [joint pseudonym with Ramon Felipe San Juan Mario Alvarez Del Rey]
* McCreigh [or MacCreigh], James
* Park, Jordan [joint pseudonym with Cyril M. Kornbluth]
* Satterfield, Charles [joint pseudonym with Ramon Felipe San Juan Alvarez Del Rey]
* Wylie, Dirk [joint pseudonym with Joseph Harold Dockweiler and Cyril M. Kornbluth]

Pohle, Robert W[arren], Jr. 1949-   [CA]
American author
* Farnsworth, James
* Lee, Devon
* Miller, E. F.

Pohler, Joseph C. 1892-   [F2]
Actor
* Pollar, Gene

Pohlman, Max Edward 1911-   [IA]
American physician, playwright, author
* Benjamin, Claude
* Edwards, Max
* George, Marion E.

Pohorylles, Gerda 20th c.   [NY 9-22-85]
German photographer
* Taro, Gerda

Poignart, J.   [PA]
Author
* [L']Homme Qui-Let

Poile, Bud
See Poile, Norman Robert

Poile, Norman Robert 1924-   [CEI, FHE, HK]
Canadian-born hockey player
* Poile, Bud

Poincare, Raymond 1860-1934   [HPPN]
French statesman and writer
* [The] Hammer of the Germans

Poindexter, Albert 1902?-   [CWG, PMJ]
American country-western performer
* Dexter, Al

Poindexter, Buster
See Johansen, David

Poindexter, [Chester] Jennings 1910-
[BE]
American baseball player
* Poindexter, Jinx

Poindexter, Jinx
See Poindexter, [Chester] Jennings

Poindexter, Norwood 1926-   [DAM, EJ]
American jazz musician
* Poindexter, Pony

Poindexter, Pony
See Poindexter, Norwood

Poinsett, Joel Roberts 1779-1851
[HPPN, IP]
American statesman and author
* [A] Citizen of the United States
* [The] Secretary of War
* [A] South Carolinian

Poinsot, Antoine Edmond 1834-?   [IP]
French author
* Heilly, Georges d'

Pointed Arrow
See Jackson, Andrew

Pointer, Aaron Elton 1942-   [BE]
American baseball player
* Pointer, Hawk

Pointer, Bonnie
See Pointer, Patricia

Pointer, Hawk
See Pointer, Aaron Elton

Pointer, Patricia 1950- [EJ7]
American jazz musician
* Pointer, Bonnie

Pointkowski, Thomas Max 1926- [OP]
American opera singer
* Tipton, Thomas

Pointon, Robert
See Rooke, Daphne [Marie]

[La] Poire
See Louis Philippe

Poire, Emmanuel 1859-1909 [WEC]
French cartoonist
* D'Ache, Caran

Poiret, Paul 1879-1944 [HPPN]
French fashion designer
* [The] King of Fashion
* [The] Man Who Banned the Corset

Poirie, Jean-Aurele Pierre 1795-1855
[CW]
West Indian poet
* Saint Aurele, Poirie de

Poirier, Louis 1910- [EWL, TC1]
French author, playwright, poet
* Gracq, Julien

Poison, David
See Kotey, David

Poison Ivy Andrews
See Andrews, Ivy Paul

Poison Ivy Lee
See Lee, Ivy Ledbetter

Poison Joe Brennan
See Brennan, Joseph R.

[The] Poisoner
See Wainewright, Thomas Griffiths

[The] Poisoner
See Wu, Lady

Poisson, Raymond 1630?-1690 [HPPN]
French author and playwright
* Belleroche

Poitiers, Angele
See Fox, Hugh [Bernard, Jr.]

Poker Alice
See Tubbs, Alice Ivers

Poker Charley Farwell
See Farwell, Charles Benjamin

Poker Face
See Garner, John Nance

[A] Poker of Fun
See Lowell, Amy

Pol Pot
See Saloth Sar

POLA
See Watson, Pauline

Polachanin, Nicholas Joseph 1917- [BE]
American baseball player
* Polly, Nicholas Joseph [Nick]

Polacheck, Julian 1889-1927 [HPPN]
American dancer
* Alfred, Julian

Polaire, Mademoiselle
See Bouchard, Emilie Marie

Poland, Dorothy Elizabeth Hayward
1937- [AW, WD]
Welsh author
* Farely, Alison
* Hammond, Jane

Poland's Billy Mitchell
See Karpinski, Stanislaw

Polanski, Madame
See Goldberg, Nancy

Polatschek-Williams, Jolan
See Williams, Jolan

Polcher, Egon
See Anschel, Eugene

Polder, Markus
See Kruess, James

Poldowski
See Wieniawska, Irene Regine

[The] Pole
See Martin of Troppau

Pole, Michael de la 1330?-1389 [DNNF,
DNNS, HN]
First Earl of Suffolk
* [The] Beloved Merchant

Pole, Reginald 1500-1558 [HPPN]
British clergyman
* Cardinal of England

Pole, Thomas 1753-1829 [IP]
British clergyman and author
* [A] Friend to Education

Pole, William 1814-? [HFN]
British engineer and author
* Professor P.

Pole, William 1852-1934 [BEW, LC,
WBD]
British actor, director, producer
* Poel, William

Pole, William de la 1396-1450 [NPS]
Fourth Earl of Suffolk
* Jackanapes

Polemius
See Stanhope, James

Poles, E. 20th c. [OBW]
American baseball player
* Poles, Possum

Poles, Possum
See Poles, E.

Poles, Spot
See Poles, Spotswood

Poles, Spotswood 1887-1962 [MK]
American baseball player
* Poles, Spot

Polevoi, Boris
See Kampov, Boris Nikolayevich

Polexenes Digit Snift
See Hill, Benson Earle

Polfus, Lester 1916- [ECM, EJ]
American jazz musician
* Hot Rod Red
* Paul, Les
* Rhubarb Red

Polgar
See Kubelik, Jan

Polglase, Ann Eaton 1803-1865 [IP]
British author
* A. E. P.

Polhem, Christopher 1661-1751 [WBD]
Swedish engineer and inventor
* [The] Father of Swedish Mechanics

Polhill, Charles 18th c. [HPPN]
British author
* [A] Country Gentleman

Poli, Maurice 20th c. [WF]
Italian actor
* Greenwood, Monty

Poli, Umberto 1883-1957 [BI, EWL,
TCL]
Italian poet
* Saba, Umberto

Poliakoff, Vera 1911- [THR]
Russian-born actress
* Lindsay, Vera

Poliakoff, Vladimir 1881?-1956 [BI]
Russian-British publicist
* Augur

Poliakov, Samuel 1836-1888
Russian banker
* [The] Railroad King

Poliarchus
See Cotterell, [Sir] Charles

Poliarchus
See Henry IV [or Henri]

Policeman Paul
See Blyth, Harry

Policeman X
See Doherty, John

[The] Policy King
See Adams, Al[bert J.]

Polidor
See Guillaume, Ferdinando

Polidori, Louis Eustache ?-1830 [IP]
Italian physician and author
* Byron, Lord

Polienus Rhodiensis
See Barclay, John

Polin
See Marsales, Pierre Paul

Poling, Harold 20th c. [TI 3-26-84, TI 7-
18-83]
American business executive
* Poling, Red

Poling, Red
See Poling, Harold

Poliorcetes
See Demetrius I

Polis, Gregory Linn 1950- [SMG]
Canadian-born hockey player
* Polis, Indiana
* Polis, Pole-Eye

Polis, Indiana
See Polis, Gregory Linn

Polis, Pole-Eye
See Polis, Gregory Linn

[The] Polish Bayard
See Poniatowski, Jozef Anton

[The] Polish Byron
See Mickiewicz, Adam

[The] Polish Cato
See Reyten, Thaddeus

[The] Polish Franklin
See Czacki, Thaddeus [or Tadeusz]

[The] Polish Messiah
See Marcol, Czeslaw C.

[The] Polish Moliere
See Fredro, Alexander

[The] Polish Pindar
See Szymonowicz, Szymon

[The] Polish Prince
See Mazur, Richard F.

[The] Polish Prince
See Stemkowski, Peter David

[The] Polish Princess
See Young, Arlene

[The] Polish Puritan
See Gurowski, [Count] Adam

[The] Polish Pushkin
See Tuvim, Julian

[The] Polish Rifle
See Jaworski, Ron

[The] Polish Sappho
See Pawlikowska, Marja [Kossak]

[The] Polish Voltaire
See Krasicki, Ignatius

[The] Polite
See Grenville [or Granville], George
[Baron Lansdowne]

Polite and Learned Physician of Oxford
See Talbot, William

[The] Polite Lunatic
See Sullivan, James E.

Politella, Dario 1921- [CA, WD]
American author
* Granite, Tony
* Stewart, David

Polith, M. 19th c. [PA]
Author
* [A] Russian

Politian
See Ambrogini, Angelo

[The] Political Boss of all Russia
See Brezhnev, Leonid Ilich

[The] Political Debater
See Smith, Al[fred Emanuel]

[A] Political Economist
See Banfield, Thomas Charles

[The] Political Grimalkin
See Van Buren, Martin

[The] Political Legal Bandit
See Terry, [Judge] David Smith

[The] Political Minstrel
See Glazer, Joe

Political Parent
See Adams, Samuel

[The] Political Philosopher
See Smith, Thomas Vernon

[The] Political Savior of Virginia
See Walker, Gilbert Carlton

[A] Political Thor
See Farley, James Aloysius

[The] Political Trickster
See Segretti, Donald H.

[The] Politician
See Castiglia [or Seriglia?], Francesco

[The] Politician Achitophel
See Cooper, Anthony Ashley [First
Earl of Shaftesbury]

Politicus
See Kulski, Wladyslaw W[szebor]

Politicus
See MacRae, Archibald Oswald

Politzer, Heinrich 1910-1978 [CA]
Austrian-born author
* Politzer, Heinz

Politzer, Heinz
See Politzer, Heinrich

Poliuto
See Wilkie, Franc Bangs

Poliziano, Angelo
See Ambrogini, Angelo

Polizio, Emetio [BI]
American bookmaker
* Pledge, Joe

Polizzi, Alfred 1900- [BLB, MM, PHM]
Italian-born American underworld figure
* [The] Owl
* Polizzi, Big Al

Polizzi, Big Al
See Polizzi, Alfred

Polk, Bob
See Polk, James

Polk, James 1915- [BB]
American basketball coach
* Polk, Bob

Polk, James Knox 1795-1849 [FAP,
HPPN, SN]
American president
* [The] First Dark Horse
* [The] Napoleon of the Stump
* Young Hickory

Polk, Josiah F. 19th c. [IP]
American author
* Akroates

Polk, Leonidas 1806-1864 [HPPN]
American army officer and clergyman
* [The] Bishop of Louisiana
* [The] Fighting Bishop

Polk, Sahara Sarah
See Polk, Sarah Childress

Polk, Sarah Childress 1803-1891 [WP 1-
20-85]
*Wife of American president, James Knox
Polk*
* Polk, Sahara Sarah

Polka Dot Slim
See Vincent, Monroe

[The] Polka King
See Budry, Chester

Polkinghorne, Margaret 1939- [OP]
British opera singer
* Kingsley, Margaret

Pollack, Ben[jamin] 1904-1971 [HPPN]
American jazz musician
* [The] Father of Swing

Pollack, Michael John, Jr. 1939-
[BEW, FC]
American actor
* Pollard, Michael J.

Pollaiuolo, Simone 1454?-1508? [WBD]
Florentine architect
* [Il] Cronaca [The Chronicler]

Pollak, Felix 1909- [CA, HPPN]
Austrian-born poet
* Anselm, Felix
* [The] Master of Words and Guardian
  of Magazines

Pollak, Rose 1894- [JL]
Hungarian-born opera singer
* Pauly, Rosa

Polland, Madeleine A[ngela] 1918-
[TCC]
Irish-born author
* Adrian, Frances

Pollar, Gene
See Pohler, Joseph C.

Pollard, A. F.
See Pollard, Albert Frederick

Pollard, A. W.
See Pollard, Alfred William

Pollard, Albert Frederick 1869-1948
[LC]
British historian and author
* Pollard, A. F.

Pollard, Alfred William 1859-1944 [LC]
British author and editor
* Pollard, A. W.

Pollard, Benjamin 1780-1836 [HPPN]
American journalist and politician
* Brutus, Marcus

Pollard, Dock
See Pollard, Samuel

Pollard, Edward Alfred 1838-1872
[HPPN, IP]
American author and journalist
* [A] Distinguished Southern Journalist
* One Recently Returned from the
  Enemy's Country
* [The] Southern Spy
* [A] Southerner

Pollard, Frederick Douglass, Sr. 1894-
[FB, IBW]
American football player
* Pollard, Fritz

Pollard, Frederick, Jr. 20th c. [IBW]
*American football player, track and field
athlete*
* Pollard, Fritz

Pollard, Fritz
See Pollard, Frederick Douglass, Sr.

Pollard, Fritz
See Pollard, Frederick, Jr.

Pollard, Jim 1922- [BB]
American basketball player
* [The] Kangaroo Kid

Pollard, John X. [house pseudonym]
See Browne, Howard

Pollard, Michael J.
See Pollack, Michael John, Jr.

Pollard, Samuel 1938- [IBW]
American clergyman
* Pollard, Dock

Pollard, Snub
See Fraser, Harold

Pollente
See Charles IX

Polli, Crip
See Polli, Lou[is Americo]

Polli, Lou[is Americo] 1901- [BE]
American baseball player
* Polli, Crip

Pollini, Bernhard
See Pohl, Baruch

Pollini, Mme.
See Poole, Clara

Pollio
See Clifford, Thomas

Pollock, Alice 1868-1971 [HPPN]
British author
* [The] Oldest Authoress

Pollock, Anna
See Marble, Anna

Pollock, Courtnay 1877-? [WWL]
British author
* Maxwell, Edward

Pollock, Frederick 19th c. [HPPN]
British poet
* [An] Apprentice of Lincoln's Inn

Pollock, Guy
See Hamilton, Robert Douglas

Pollock, [Paul] Jackson 1912-1956
[HPPN]
American painter
* Jack the Dripper
* [The] Ultimate Abstraction

Pollock, John 18th c. [IP]
Scottish clergyman and author
* [A] Member of the Church of
  Scotland
* [A] Well Wisher of the Good-Old-
  Way

Pollock, John H[ackett] 1887- [WGT]
Author
* [An] Philibin

Pollock, Marshall 1901-1965 [HPPN]
American film editor
* Pollock, Mike

Pollock, Martin
See Gardner, Maurice

Pollock, Mary
See Blyton, Enid [Mary]

Pollock, Mike
See Pollock, Marshall

Polly, Nicholas Joseph [Nick]
See Polachanin, Nicholas Joseph

Polly the Weaver
See Johnson, Mary McDonough

Polnarioff, Kurt 1917-1958 [PMJ]
German-born American musician
* Nero, Paul

Polo, Articum
See Higinbotham, John D.

Polock Joe Saltis
See Saltis, Joseph

Polonius
See FitzGerald, Edward

Polonsky, Abraham 1910- [WW]
Author
* Hogarth, Emmett [joint pseudonym
  with Mitchell A. Wilson]

Polony, Raymond
See Machan, Tibor R[ichard]

Polovchak, Walter 1968?-
Russian-born defector
* [The] Littlest Defector

Polsby, Nelson W[oolf] 1934- [CA]
American political scientist and author
* Clun, Arthur

Poltoratzky, N[ikolai] P[etrovich] 1921-
[CA]
*Turkish-born American educator and
author*
* Petrovsky, N.

Poltroon, Milford
See Bascom, David

Poluflosboio, Lord
See Grosvenor, Richard [Lord
Belgrave]

Poluski, Byno 1908- [F2, FC]
British actress
* Ward, Polly

Polva, Anni
See Polviander, Anni Kyllikki

Polviander, Anni Kyllikki 1915- [IAW]
Finnish author
* Heino, Kyllikki
* Polva, Anni

Polwhele, Richard 1760-1838 [IP]
British clergyman and poet
* [A] Country Gentleman
* Eusebius Exoniensis
* P.
* R. P.
* [An] Undergraduate
* [A] Young Gentleman of Truro
  School

Polyaenus, Julius 2nd c. [SN]
Greek scholar
* [The] Macedonian

Polyanthus
See Wilson, John

Polybe
See Reinach, Joseph

Polycarp 72?-156? [HN]
Saint
* Doctor of Asia
* Doctor of the Holy Church of
  Smyrna

Polyglott, Pandemus, L. L. D.
See Maginn, William

Polygnotus 5th c. BC [FFF, RH, SN]
Greek painter
* [The] Father of Ecclesiastical History
* [The] Father of Historic Painting

Polyhistor
See Nordhof, Daniel Georg

Polyhistor
See Thordsen, Theodori

[The] Polyphemus of Literature
See Johnson, Samuel

Polyphile
See La Fontaine, Jean de

Polypus
See Barrett, Eaton Stannard

Polypus
See Wakefeld, Robert

Pomares, Anita 1910-
American actress
* Page, Anita

Pombal, Marques de
See Carvalho e Mello, Sebastiao Jose
de

Pomeran, David Sheldon 1931- [BEW]
American producer, director, playwright
* Sheldon, David

Pomerano, Castalio
See Braithwaite, Richard

Pomeranus
See Bugenhagen, Johann

Pomeranz, Joseph 1895-1955 [BEW]
Russian-born director
* Pomeroy, Jay

Pomeroy, Brick
See Pomeroy, Marcus Mills

Pomeroy, Eugene
See Donnelly, Thomas F.

Pomeroy, Florence Mary
See Powley, Florence Mary Pomeroy

Pomeroy, Hub[bard]
See Claassen, Harold

Pomeroy, Iola
See Howard, Mrs. L.

Pomeroy, Jay
See Pomeranz, Joseph

Pomeroy, Jesse 19th c.
American dime-novel enthusiast
* [The] Boston Boy Fiend

Pomeroy, Marcus Mills 1840-1896
[FFF, PA]
American journalist
* Pomeroy, Brick

Pomeroy, Pete
See Roth, Arthur J[oseph]

Pomeroy, Samuel Clarke 1816-1891
[HPPN]
American politician
* Pomeroy, Subsidy

Pomeroy, Subsidy
See Pomeroy, Samuel Clarke

Pometacom
See Metacomet

Pomfret, Baron
See Dame, Lawrence

Pomfret, Ellen Louise
See Moulton, Ellen Louise Chandler

Pomfret, Joan
See Townsend, Joan

Pomfret, John 1667?-1703 [HPPN, IP]
British poet
* [A] Person of Quality
* Philalethes

Pomfret, Peter
See Graves, Richard

Pommer, Dr.
See Bugenhagen, Johann

Pommerencke, Heinrich 20th c. [DI]
German murderer
* [The] Beast of the Black Forest

Pomona?
See Francis, [Sir] Philip

Pomona's Bard
See Philips, John

Pompeius Magnus, Sextus 1st c. BC
[WBD]
Roman soldier
* [The] Younger

Pompeo, John Anthony 1934- [EJ]
American jazz musician
* Rae, Johnny

Pompey [or Pompeius], Cneius
1st c. BC [DNNS, HN]
Roman general
* [The] Great
* Sampsiceranus, Alabarches, the
  Jerusalemite

Pompez, Alex
See Pompez, Allesandro

Pompez, Allesandro 20th c. [OBW]
American baseball player
* Pompez, Alex

Pompidou, Georges Jean Raymond
1911-1974 [HPPN]
President of France
* Monsieur Charly

Pompoan
See Cheng Sen

Pomponazzi, Pietro 1462-1525 [SN]
Italian philosopher
* Peretto

Pomponio, Leto
See Vilelleschi, Marchese Francesco

Pomponius, Lucius 1st c. BC [WBD]
Latin author
* Bononiensis [Of Bononia]

Pomponius, Titus 1st c. BC [HPPN]
Roman literary patron
* Atticus, Titus Pomponius

Pomposo
See Johnson, Samuel

Pomposus
See Butler, Dr.

Pomus, Doc
See Pomus, Jerome

Pomus, Jerome 1925- [PRS]
American songwriter
* Pomus, Doc

Pon Mudi
See Naa Parthasarathy, Naarayana-
Parthasarathy

Ponce de Leon, Rodrigo 1443-1492
[HN]
Spanish general
* [The] Marquis Duke of Cadiz

Ponchardier, Dominique
See Dominique, Antoine

Pond, Arlie
See Pond, Erasmus Arlington

Pond, Charles
See Pattie, Joseph

Pond, Ducky
See Pond, Raymond

Pond, Enoch 1791-1882 [HPPN]
American clergyman
* [A] Clergyman of Massachusetts

Pond, Erasmus Arlington 1872-1930
[BE]
American baseball player
* Pond, Arlie

Pond, Frederick Eugene 1856-1925
[DNA, FFF, PA]
American author
* Red Wing
* Wildwood, Will

Pond, George Edward 1837-1899 [FFF,
PA]
American editor and author
* Quilibet, Philip

Pond, L. W.
See Chute, Robert M.

Pond, Myron [PA]
Author
* [The] Commodore

Pond, Paul 1942?- [RO2, TR]
British actor and singer
* Jones, Paul

Pond, Raymond 1903-1982
American football coach
* Pond, Ducky

Pond, S. T. R. 20th c. [MBF]
British author
* Reay, Trevace

Pond, Wilf Pocklington 20th c. [NAA]
British-born editor
* Cottingham, Henry
* Cousans, S. W.
* Slight, John

Ponder, [Rev.] Peter
See Bell, William

Pondiac
See Pontiac

Poniatowski, Jozef Anton 1763-1814
[DNNF, FFF, IP]
Polish general
* [The] Bayard of Poland
* [The] Polish Bayard

Poningoe
See Dunn, Caleb

Poningoe
See Smith, Frances Shubael

Ponisi, Madame
See Hanson, Elizabeth

Pons, Alice Josephine 1904-   [BBD]
French-born opera singer
* Pons, Lily

Pons, Lily
See Pons, Alice Josephine

Ponselle, Carmela
See Ponzillo, Carmela

Ponselle, Rosa Melba
See Ponzillo, Rosa Melba

Ponsford, Ponny
See Ponsford, William Harold

Ponsford, William Harold 1900-   [EC]
Australian cricketer
* Ponsford, Ponny

Ponsin, Mlle.
See Prevost, Madame Henri

Ponsonby, Doris Almon 1907-   [CA, WD]
British author
* Rybot, Doris
* Tempest, Sarah

Ponsonby, Frederick George Brabazon
1815-?   [IP]
British barrister and playwright
* Roe, Richard

Ponsonby, [Sir] Henry Frederick
1825-1894?   [RH]
British statesman and author
* Sebastian

Ponsonby, Sarah 1755-1831   [HPPN]
Irish recluse
* Lady of the Vale
* Maid of Llangollen

Ponsonby, Spencer Cecil Brabazon
1824-?   [FFF, IP]
British author
* Bolton Row

Pont
See Laidler, Gavin Graham

Pont, Keith Rupert 1953-   [DC]
British cricketer
* Pont, Monty
* Pont, Plod

Pont, Monty
See Pont, Keith Rupert

Pont, Plod
See Pont, Keith Rupert

Pontacus
See Sacheverell, Henry

Pontano, Giovanni 1426-1503   [HPPN]
Italian humanist, poet, statesman
* Gioviano

Pontanus
See Dupont, Dennis

Ponte, Francesco da 1549-1592   [BI]
Italian painter
* Bassano, Francesco

Ponte, Jacopo [or Giacomo] da
1510-1592   [WBD]
Venetian painter
* Bassano, Jacopo [or Giacomo] da

Ponteach
See Pontiac

Pontecorvo, Gilberto 1919-   [BDF, FDG]
Italian director
* Pontecorvo, Gillo

Pontecorvo, Gillo
See Pontecorvo, Gilberto

Ponti, Diana da 16th c.   [HPPN]
Italian actress
* Lavinia

Pontiac 1720?-1769   [HPPN]
American Indian chief
* Pondiac
* Ponteach

Pontiac
See Boyle, John

Pontiac
See Knight, Oliver

Ponticus
See Aquila

[The] Pontiff of Bullfighting
See Gomez Ortega, Jose

[The] Pontiff of Calvinists
See Du Plessis, Armand Jean

Pontius, Brute
See Pontius, Miller

Pontius, Miller 20th c.
American football player
* Pontius, Brute

Pontormo, Jacopo da
See Carrucci, Jacopo

Pony Bob Haslam
See Haslam, Robert H.

Ponzi, Carlo 1878-1949   [BLB, DI, HPPN]
Italian-born swindler
* Bianchi, Charles
* [The] Great Ponzi
* [The] Pied Piper of Boston
* Ponzi, Charles
* Ponzi, Get Rich Quick
* [The] Slickest Swindler of Them All

Ponzi, Charles
See Ponzi, Carlo

Ponzi, Get Rich Quick
See Ponzi, Carlo

Ponzillo, Carmela 1892-   [BBD]
American opera singer
* Ponselle, Carmela

Ponzillo, Rosa Melba 1897-1981   [WBD]
American opera singer
* [The] Caruso in Petticoats
* Ponselle, Rosa Melba

Poodle
See Byng, Frederick

Pooh
See Nettles, Bonnie Lu

Pool, Harlin Welty 1908-1963   [BE]
American baseball player
* Pool, Samson

Pool, Maria L. 19th c.   [FFF, IP]
American writer
* Earnshaw, Catharine

Pool, Samson
See Pool, Harlin Welty

Poole, Buster
See Poole, James E.

Poole, Butcher Bill
See Poole, William

Poole, Clara   [FFF]
Entertainer
* Pollini, Mme.

Poole, [Captain] D. C. 19th c.   [HPPN]
American author
* [An] Indian Agent

Poole, Easy
See Poole, James Ralph [Jim]

Poole, Elijah 1897-1975   [HDM, IBW, IPA]
American Black Muslim leader
* Karriam, Elijah
* Messenger of Allah
* Muhammad, Elijah

Poole, Frederick King 1934-   [CA]
American writer and consultant
* Harris, Andrew

Poole, Gray Johnson 1906-   [CA]
American author and columnist
* Gray, Betsy

Poole, James E. 1915-   [FB]
American football player
* Poole, Buster

Poole, James Ralph [Jim] 1895-   [BE]
American baseball player
* Poole, Easy

Poole, Joseph   [RH]
British clergyman
* Fiddler Joss

Poole, Michael
See Poole, Reginald Heber

Poole, Peggy 1925-   [CA]
British poet and author
* Roche, Terry

Poole, Reginald Heber 1885-   [MBF, WW]
British author
* Heber, Austin
* Heber, Reginald
* Poole, Michael
* Thomas, Anthony
* Valentine, Henry

Poole, Richard 19th c.   [IP]
Scottish physician and author
* [An] Aged Layman

Poole, Robert 18th c. [HPPN]
British physician
* Philanthropos, Theophilus

Poole, Seth
See Riemer, George

Poole, Sophia [Lane] 19th c. [IP]
British author
* [The] Englishwoman
* His Sister

Poole, Thomas Wesley 1831?-1905
[CCL]
Canadian poet
* T. W. P.

Poole, Virginia Sherman 1919-1986
[BEW, FC, SW]
American actress
* Gilmore, Virginia

Poole, Vivian
See Jaffe, Gabriel Vivian

Poole, William ?-1855 [BLB, HPPN]
American murderer and gangleader
* Bill the Butcher
* Poole, Butcher Bill

Poole, William Frederick 1821-? [IP]
American librarian
* P.
* Philorthos

Pooler, James Anthony 1954- [SMG]
American football player
* Pooler, Pooh

Pooler, Pooh
See Pooler, James Anthony

Poolla, Tirupati Raju
See Raju, Poolla Tirupati

[The] Poolroom King
See Farrell, Frank

[The] Poolroom King
See Mahoney, James

Poop
See Nettles, Bonnie Lu

Poor, Agnes Blake 1842-1922 [DNA]
American author
* Prescott, Dorothy

Poor Bernard
See Bernard, Claude

Poor Bob
See Woodfork, Robert

Poor Boy
See Oden, James Burke [Jimmy]

Poor Charlie
See West, Charles [Charlie]

Poor Con
See Jackson, William

[The] Poor Devil
See Freron, Elie-Catherine

[The] Poor Fish Peddler
See Vanzetti, Bartolomeo

Poor, Henry Varnum 1812-1905
[HPPN]
American economist and publisher
* [The] Father of the Business Report
* [The] Pioneer of Financial Research

Poor Humphrey
See Hone, William

Poor Jim
See Rachell, James

Poor John Fitch
See Fitch, John

[The] Poor Little Rich Boy
See Hearst, William Randolph

Poor Little Rich Girl
See Hutton, Barbara

[The] Poor Little Rich Girl
See Vanderbilt, Gloria

[The] Poor Man's Celeste Holm
See Simpson, Elizabeth Sloan

[The] Poor Man's Counsellor
See Clark, Abraham

[the] Poor Man's Friend
See Couzens, James

[The] Poor Man's Friend
See Symcott, Margaret

[The] Poor Man's Priest
See Dolling, Robert William Radclyffe

[The] Poor Man's Shakespeare
See Griffith, David [Lewelyn] Wark

[The] Poor Man's Sterling Holloway
See Weaver, Winstead Sheffield
Glendening Dixon

Poor Poet-Ape
See Shakespeare, William

[The] Poor Potter
See Rogers, William

[The] Poor Priest
See Bernard, Claude

[The] Poor Priest
See Gorostiaga, [Father] Juan Atucha

Poor Richard
See Franklin, Ben[jamin]

Poor Robert the Scribe
See Miner, Charles

Poor Robin
See Herrick, Robert

Poor Robin
See Winstanley, William

[The] Poor Scholar
See Reid, [Thomas] Mayne

Poore, Benjamin Perley 1820-1887
[FFF, PA, WBD]
American journalist
* [The] Major
* Perley
* Raconteur

Poot, Huibert Cornelisz[oon] 1689-1733
[WBD]
Dutch poet
* [The] Dutch Hesiod

Pooter
See Hamilton, Alex

Pooton, James 1834-? [PA]
Author
* Unit, Matthew

Poots-Booby, Edna
See Larsen, Carl

Pop Boy Smith
See Smith, Clarence Ossie

Pop Gun Kelly
See Kelly, George R.

Pop, Iggy
See Osterberg, James Jewell [Jim]

[The] Popcorn King
See Redenbacher, Orville

Popcorn, Martha
See Falka, Martha

[The] Pope
See Barr, Alfred Hamilton, Jr.

[The] Pope
See Greco, Michele

[The] Pope
See Owens, Paul

[The] Pope
See Sinatra, Francis Albert [Frank]

Pope
See Strasberg, Lee

Pope, Albert A. 1843-1909 [HPPN]
American manufacturer
* [The] Founder of America's Bicycle
Industry

Pope, Alexander 1688-1744 [DEA,
DNNS, FFF, HPPN, IP, NPS, PPN, SN]
British poet
* [An] Ape
* Apoth
* [An] Apothecary
* [The] Bard of Twickenham
* Barnivelt, Esdras
* [The] Best Poet of England
* Distich, Dick
* [An] Eminent Hand
* [The] Empty Flask
* [The] English Horace
* [An] Eye Witness
* Gay, [Mr.] Joseph
* Gnatho
* Gunpowder Percy
* [A] Little Druid-Wight
* [A] Little Liar
* [The] Little Man of Twickenham
* [The] Little Nightingale
* Lord Peter
* [A] Lurking, Way-Laying Coward
* M.
* [The] Most Faultless of Poets
* [The] Nightingale of Twickenham
* [The] Poet Pug
* Pope, Paper Saving

Pope, Alexander (cont.)
* [The] Potentous Cub
* Sawney
* Scriblerus, Martinus
* Short, Bob
* [The] Sweet Swan of Thames
* That True Deacon of the Craft
* [The] Twickenham Bard
* Ultimus Romanorum
* [The] Wasp of Twickenham
* [A] Water Drinker

Pope, Augustus Russell 1819-1858 [HPPN]
American clergyman
* A. R. P.

Pope, Bucky
See Pope, Frank

Pope, Charles Henry 1841-1918 [DNA]
American author and clergyman
* Starcross, Roger

Pope, F. W. 20th c. [MBF]
British author
* Hulbert, Lloyd

Pope, Frank 20th c. [EF]
American football player
* Pope, Bucky

Pope, Henry 19th c. [PA]
American author and poet
* Gavilan, Peak

[The] Pope in Worsted Stockings
See Crabbe, George

Pope, Jane 1742-1818 [HPPN]
British actress
* Pope, Lively

Pope Joan
See John VIII

Pope, John 1822-1892 [FFF, SN]
American army officer
* Saddle-Bag John

Pope, Lively
See Pope, Jane

[The] Pope of Africa
See Carr, Burgess

[The] Pope of Catholic Action
See Sarto, Giuseppe Melchiorre

[The] Pope of Geneva
See Chauvin [or Caulvin?], Jean

[The] Pope of Peace
See Pacelli, Eugenio Maria Giovanni

[The] Pope of Philosophy
See Aristotle

[The] Pope of the Huguenots
See Du Plessis, Armand Jean

[The] Pope of the Huguenots
See Mornay, Philippe de [Seigneur du Plessis-Marly]

[The] Pope of the Reformation
See Chauvin [or Caulvin?], Jean

Pope, Paper Saving
See Pope, Alexander

Pope, Pat 1918- [THR]
British actress and singer
* Taylor, Pat

Pope Ray
See Burr, William Stacey

Pope-Hennessy, J. W.
See Pope-Hennessy, John Wyndham

Pope-Hennessy, John Wyndham 1913-
[LC]
British author
* Pope-Hennessy, J. W.

Popel, Stefan
See Bandera, Stefan

[The] Pope's Kaiser
See Charles IV [or Karl]

Popescu, Christine 1930- [CA, SAT]
British author
* Keir, Christine
* Pullein-Thompson, Christine

Popeye
See Simon, William

Popeye
See Zimmer, Don[ald William]

Popham, Vyvyan Wallis 1833-? [IP]
British clergyman and composer
* V. W. P.

Popiel, Paul
See Popiel, Poul Peter

Popiel, Poul Peter 1943- [HR]
Danish-born hockey player
* Popiel, Paul

Popik, Uriel 1926- [CA]
Israeli author, editor, translator
* Ofek, Uriel

[The] Popinjay
See Henry II [or Henri]

[The] Popish Duke
See James II

[The] Popish Midwife
See Cellier, Elizabeth

Poplicola
See Barre, Isaac

Poplicola
See Brown, Charles Brockden

Poplicola?
See Francis, [Sir] Philip

Poplicola, Valerius
See Adams, Samuel

Popov, Alexander Serafimovich 1863-?
[CD]
Russian author
* Serafimovich, Alexander

Popov, Dusko 1912?-1981 [HPPN, WP 4-2-83]
Yugoslav-born British intelligence agent
* Ivan
* [The] Real Life James Bond
* Tricycle

Popovic, Nenad D[ushan] 1909- [CAP]
Yugoslavian-born educator and author
* Spectator

Popovich, Paul 1940- [SMG]
American baseball player
* Popovich, Pop

Popovich, Pavel 20th c. [CND]
Russian cosmonaut
* Golden Eagle

Popovich, Pop
See Popovich, Paul

Popowski, Edward Joseph [Eddie] 1913-
[BE]
American baseball manager
* Popowski, Pop

Popowski, Pop
See Popowski, Edward Joseph [Eddie]

Popp, Augustin 1873-1943 [HPPN]
Austrian poet
* Waldeck, Heinrich Suso

Poppa [or Poppy] Hop
See Wilson, Harding

Popper, Frau [FFF]
Entertainer
* Menter, Sophie

Popper, Josef 1838-1921 [BI]
Austrian sociologist
* Lynkeus

Popplewell, Nigel Francis Mark 1957-
[DC]
British cricketer
* Popplewell, Poppers
* Popplewell, Pops

Popplewell, Poppers
See Popplewell, Nigel Francis Mark

Popplewell, Pops
See Popplewell, Nigel Francis Mark

Popplewell, Thomas ?-1790 [IP]
British singer and author
* Old Pop

Poppo ?-1048 [CAL]
Pope
* Damasus II

[The] Poppy Lady
See Michael, Miona

Pops, Mr.
See Fiedler, Arthur

Popski
See Peniakoff, Vladimir

Popularity Jack Doyle
See Doyle, [Sir] John

[The] Populist and Imperialist
See Papirofsky, Joseph

Populus
See Adams, Samuel

Poquelin, Jean Baptiste 1622-1673 [HN, SN, WBD]
French playwright
* Alceste

Poquelin, Jean Baptiste (cont.)
* [The] Anatomist of Humanity
* [The] Aristophanes of His Age
* [Le] Contemplateur
* [The] Father of French Comedy
* [The] French Aristophanes
* Gelaste
* [L']Hypochondre
* [The] King of Dramatists
* Moliere

Poquette, Pierre
See Poquette, Thomas Arthur

Poquette, Thomas Arthur 1951- [SMG]
American baseball player
* Poquette, Pierre

Por, Odon 1883- [WWL]
Author and journalist
* [Un] Gildista

Porat, Yosef
See Foerder, Heinz

Porcari, Constance Kwolek 1933- [CA]
American author
* Kwolek, Constance

Porcher, Mary F. Wickham
See Bond, Mary Fanning Wickham

Porcupine, Peter
See Cobbett, William

Pordage, Samuel 17th c. [SN]
* Mephibosheth

Pordenone, Giovanni Antonio da
See De Sacchi, Giovanni Antonio

Porel, Paul
See Parfouru, Paul Desire

Porges, Arthur 1915- [ESF, HFF, WGT]
American author
* Arthur, Peter
* Rogers, Pat

Pork Chop Hoffman
See Hoffman, John Edward

Pork Chop Lee
See Green, Lee

Pork Chop Mullins
See Mullins, Jeff

Pork Chop Smith
See Smith, Jerome

Porky Pig
See Vance, Cyrus Roberts

Porlock, Martin
See MacDonald, Philip

Porn, Lord
See Longford, Francis Aungier
Pakenham

Porphyro
See Bonaparte, Charles Louis Napoleon

Porphyrogenitus [Born in the Purple]
See Constantine VII

Porphyry
See Malchus

Porpora, Nicholas 1685?-1767? [HN]
Italian composer
* [The] Patriarch of Harmony

Porrata Doria de Rincon, Providencia
1910-1968 [CW]
Puerto Rican poet
* Rubens, Alma

Porrata Dorio de Aponte, Carmen 1911-
[CW]
Puerto Rican poet
* Demar, Carmen

Porsche, Ferdinand 1909- [CA]
German industrialist and author
* Porsche, Ferry

Porsche, Ferry
See Porsche, Ferdinand

**[The] Porson of Old English and French
Literature**
See Douce, Francis

Porson, Professor [joint pseudonym with
Robert Southey]
See Coleridge, Samuel Taylor

Porson, Professor [joint pseudonym with
Samuel Taylor Coleridge]
See Southey, Robert

Porson, Richard 1759-1808 [DNNS,
FFF, IP, NPS, SN]
British scholar and critic
* Cantabrigiensis
* [That] Coryphaeus of Learning
* Dawes, J. N.
* Devil Dick
* England, S.
* [The] Norfolk Boy
* Sundry Whereof

[A] Port Oar
See Pfeiffer, Emil Charles

Port, Wymar
See Judy, Will[iam Lewis]

Portaas, Herman Theodore 1886-1959
Norwegian poet
* Wildenwey, Herman Theodore

Portal, Ellis
See Powe, Bruce

Portal, [Rev.] George Raymond 19th c.
[HPPN]
British clergyman
* [A] London Clergyman

Portal, V. E. 1893- [WWL]
British author
* Bannisdale, V. E.

Porte
See Mathews, G. H.

Porte-Crayon
See Strother, David Hunter

[The] Porter
See DeLucia, Felice

Porter, Alan
See Clark, Ruth C[ampbell]

Porter, Albert H. 19th c. [HPPN]
American author
* [An] Old Resident

Porter, Alice
See Edwards, Margaret Marie

Porter, Allen 1895?-1944 [WWJ]
American jazz musician
* Porter, Yank

Porter, Alvin
See Rowland, Donald Sydney

Porter, Anna Marie 1780-1832 [HPPN]
British author
* [A] Young Lady

Porter, Anne Emerson 1816-? [IP]
American author
* Uncle Jerry

Porter, Callie Russell 1890-1980 [TI 12-
6-82]
American author
* M. T. F.
* Porter, Katherine Anne

Porter, Camanche Bill
See Porter, William

Porter, Cole 1893-1964 [HPPN]
American composer and lyricist
* [The] Elegant Hoosier Tunesmith

Porter, Countee Leroy 1903-1946
[HPPN, TLC]
American poet, author, playwright
* Cullen, Countee
* [The] Father of the Harlem
Renaissance

Porter, Curtis 1929- [EJ]
American jazz musician
* Hadi, Shafi

Porter, David 1780-1843 [HPPN, IP]
American naval officer and author
* [An] American Long Resident at
Constantinople
* [A] Fellow Citizen

Porter, David John 1948- [IAW]
British playwright
* Gladwyn, Edward

Porter, Dick
See Porter, Napoleon Bonaparte

Porter, Dorothy Louise Burnett 1905-
[IBW]
American author and librarian
* [The] Dean of Black Research
Bibliographers

Porter, Edwin S. 1870-1941 [HPPN]
American director and inventor
* [The] Father of the Western Movie

Porter, Eleanor [Hodgman] 1868-1920
[DNA]
American author
* Stuart, Eleanor

Porter, Elise 20th c. [THR]
American actress
* Bartlett, Elise

Porter, Freak Man
See Porter, George

Porter, Frederick 1871-? [MBF]
Scottish author and playwright
* Watson, Frederick

Porter, Geezer
See Porter, Howard

Porter, Gene Stratton
See Stratton, Geneva Grace

Porter, George 20th c. [RM]
Musician
* Porter, Freak Man

Porter, H. V.
See Porter, Henry V.

Porter, Harold Everett 1887-1936
[NAA, TC, WW]
American author
* Hall, Holworthy

Porter, Henry V. 1891-
American basketball executive
* Porter, H. V.

Porter, Howard 1948-
American basketball player
* Porter, Geezer

Porter, J. W. 1933- [BE]
American baseball player
* Porter, Jay

Porter, Jack Nusan
See Puchtik, Yakov Nusan

Porter, Jake
See Porter, Vernon

Porter, James 1753-1798 [PI]
Irish poet
* R.

Porter, Jane 1776-1850 [IP]
British author
* [An] Englishwoman
* J. P.

Porter, Jane 19th c. [CCL]
Canadian author
* [A] Lady

Porter, Jay
See Porter, J. W.

Porter, Katherine Anne
See Porter, Callie Russell

Porter, Kathryn
See Swinford, Betty [June Wells]

Porter, Lancelot 1882-? [CCL]
Canadian author
* Hewatson, Bob

Porter, Linn Boyd 1851-1916 [WGT]
American author
* Ross, Albert

Porter, Madeline 20th c.
American author
* Habersham, Elizabeth [joint pseudonym with Shannon Harper]
* James, Anna [joint pseudonym with Shannon Harper]

Porter, Mark
See Cox, James Anthony

Porter, Mark
See Leckie, Robert [Hugh]

Porter, Maurice Malcolm 1909- [AW]
British dentist and writer
* Mouthpiece

Porter, Mrs. Robert P. 19th c. [FFF, IP]
American writer
* Cress
* Detective's Daughter

Porter, Napoleon Bonaparte 1853-?
[DNA]
Author and railwayman
* Porter, Dick

Porter, Richard Twilley 1901-1974 [BE]
American baseball player
* Porter, Twitchy
* Porter, Wiggles

Porter, [Sir] Robert Ker 1780-1842 [IP]
British artist and author
* [An] Officer

Porter, Sheena
See Lane, Sheena Porter

Porter, Sugar
See Porter, Yvonne

Porter, T. B. 20th c. [GW]
American rodeo performer
* Porter, Teaberry

Porter, Teaberry
See Porter, T. B.

Porter, Twitchy
See Porter, Richard Twilley

Porter, Vernon 1910?- [WWJ]
American jazz musician
* Porter, Jake

Porter, Wiggles
See Porter, Richard Twilley

Porter, William
American frontiersman
* Porter, Camanche Bill

Porter, William Sydney [Bill] 1862-1910
[EMD, EWL, HPPN, WYA]
American author
* [The] American Maupassant
* Bliss, James L.
* Clark, Howard
* Dowd, T. B.
* Henry, O.
* Henry, Oliver
* Parker, Will S.
* Peters, S. H.

Porter, William Trotter 1809-1858
[FFF, PA]
American journalist
* York's Tall Son

Porter, Yank
See Porter, Allen

Porter, Yvonne 1942- [BA]
American community organizer
* Porter, Sugar

Porterfield, Bob
See Porterfield, Erwin Coolidge

Porterfield, Erwin Coolidge 1923-1980
[BE]
American baseball player
* Porterfield, Bob

Porteus, Fanny Wentworth Osborn
1849?-1934 [HPPN]
American actress
* Wentworth, Fanny

Portia
See Adams, Abigail Smith

Portius
See Pegge, Samuel

[The] Portly Master of the Involuntary Scream
See Hitchcock, Alfred Joseph

Portman, Arthur Fitzhardinge 1861-1940
[OCS]
British horse racing authority and editor
* Audax

Porto, Al[fred] 1926- [BE]
American baseball player
* Porto, Lefty

Porto, Lefty
See Porto, Al[fred]

Porto, Louis
See Rousseau, Camille

Portobello, Petronella
See Anderson, [Lady] Flavia

[The] Portrait in Sound
See Mester, Jorge

[The] Portrait Painter of Presidents
See Stuart, Gilbert Charles

[The] Portrayer of Brahmins
See Marquand, John Phillips

Portsmouth, Henry 1703-1780 [IP]
British author
* Catholicus
* Philalethes

[The] Portuguese Apollo
See De Camoens, Luiz

[The] Portuguese Cid
See Pereira, Nunez Alvarez

[The] Portuguese Fernandel
See Felipe, Alfredo

[The] Portuguese Horace
See Ferreira, Antonio

[The] Portuguese Joan of Arc
See Almeida, Brites de

[The] Portuguese Livy
See Barros, Joao de

[The] Portuguese Maecenas of Arts and Sciences
See Emanuel I [Manuel or Manoel]

[The] Portuguese Mars
See Alfonso [or Affonso] de Albuquerque

[The] Portuguese Moliere
See Silva, Antonio Jose da

[The] Portuguese Nostradamus
See Bandarra, Goncalo Annes

[The] Portuguese Nun
See Alcoforado, Marianna

[The] Portuguese Pindar
See Diniz da Cruz e Silva, Antonio

[The] Portuguese Plautus
See Vicente, Gil

[The] Portuguese Theocritus
See Sa de Miranda, Francisco da

[The] Portuguese Titian
See Sanchez Coello, Alonzo

Portway, Christopher [John] 1923-   [CA]
British author
* October, John

Posada, Leo
See Posada, Leopoldo Jesus

Posada, Leopoldo Jesus 1936-   [BE]
Cuban-born baseball player
* Posada, Leo
* Posada, Popy

Posada, Popy
See Posada, Leopoldo Jesus

Posateri, Mike 1900?-1977   [FIR]
Film set dresser and boxer
* Dundee, Mike

Posedel, Barnacle Bill
See Posedel, William John

Posedel, Chief
See Posedel, William John

Posedel, Porthole
See Posedel, William John

Posedel, Sailor Bill
See Posedel, William John

Posedel, William John 1906-   [PB]
American baseball player
* Posedel, Barnacle Bill
* Posedel, Chief
* Posedel, Porthole
* Posedel, Sailor Bill

Poser, Bob
See Poser, John Falk

Poser, John Falk 1910-   [BE]
American baseball player
* Poser, Bob

Posey, Alexander Lawrence 1873-1908 [HPPN]
American Indian editor and poet
* Harjo, Chinnubbie

Posey, C. W.
See Posey, Cumberland Willis, Sr.

Posey, Cum
See Posey, Cumberland Willis

Posey, Cumberland Willis 1890?-1946 [AS, MK]
American baseball player
* Posey, Cum

Posey, Cumberland Willis, Sr. 1858-? [IBW]
American businessman
* Posey, C. W.

Posey, Jo
See Hoffa, Josephine Poszywak

Posey, Sandy
See Sharp, Marthe

Positive, Paul
See Montgomery, James

Posner, Jacob D. 1883-   [WW]
Author
* Dean, Gregory

Posner, Richard 1944-   [CA, WD]
American author
* Craig, Jonathan
* Foster, Iris
* Murray, Beatrice
* Todd, Paul
* Wine, Dick

Posner, Victor 1919-   [HPPN]
American financial tycoon and stock manipulator
* [The] Corporate Raider
* [The] Favorite Ogre of Wall Street

Posorito [Little Match]
See Lopez Sibrian, Rodolfo Isidro

Possendorf, Hans
See Mahner-Mons, Hans

[The] Possum
See Jones, George

Possum, Peter
See Rowe, Richard

Possumtrot, Eli
See Ferguson, Robert B.

Post, A. H.
See Badger, Joseph E.

Post, Charles William 1854-1914 [HPPN]
American manufacturer
* [The] Post Toasties King
* [The] Postum King

Post, Dynamite
See Post, Seraphim

Post, Emily Price 1873-1960 [HPPN]
American author and columnist
* [The] Final Authority on Etiquette

Post, F. A.
See Post-Nikov, Feodor A.

Post, George B. 1837-1913   [HPPN]
American architect
* [The] Father of the Skyscraper

Post, H. Christian 1945-   [BA]
Tanzanian-born American business executive
* Pandya, Harish C.

Post, Henry 1948-   [CA]
American author
* Spot, Ryhen

Post, J. B.
See Post, Jerry Benjamin

Post, Jerry Benjamin 1937-   [SFL]
American author
* Post, J. B.

Post, Lydia [Minturn] 19th c.   [IP]
American author
* Barclay, Sydney

Post, Maveric
See Mapes, Victor

Post, Mortimer
See Blair, Walter

Post, Sarah L. 19th c.   [FFF, IP, PA]
American writer
* Graham, Rosa

Post, Seraphim 20th c.   [HPPN]
American football player
* Post, Dynamite

[The] Post Toasties King
See Post, Charles William

Post-Nikov, Feodor A. 1872-?   [NAA]
Russian-born editor and author
* Post, F. A.

Posta, Adrienne
See Poster, Adrienne

Poste, Denver
See Cox, Charles Roy

Postelnich, Joana
See Banu, Eugenia

Poster, Adrienne 1948-   [FC]
British actress
* Posta, Adrienne

[The] Posterior Osculator
See Bartlett, George

Posthaste?
See Shakespeare, William

Postime, Mr.
See Mitchell, Billy

Postl, Karl Anton 1793-1864 [DNA, HFN, HPPN, WBD]
Moravian-born author
* Hardman, Frederick
* Sealsfield, Charles
* Sidons, Charles

Postlethwayt, James 1688-1758 [IP]
British author
* J. P., Esq., F. R. S.

Postlethwayt, Malachy 1707?-1767 [IP]
British author
* [A] British Merchant

Postma, Magdalena Jacomina 1908-
[CA]
South African author
* Postma, Minnie

Postma, Minnie
See Postma, Magdalena Jacomina

[The] Postman Poet
See Capern, Edward

Poston, Charles Debrill 1825-1902
[HPPN]
American explorer and author
* [The] Father of Arizona

Poston, Doc
See Poston, Joseph E.

Poston, Joseph E. 1895?-1942 [WWJ]
American jazz musician
* Poston, Doc

[The] Postum King
See Post, Charles William

Pot, Philippe 1428-1494 [FF, FFF, HN, NPS, UH]
French prime minister
* [La] Bouche de Ciceron
* Cicero's Mouth

[The] Potamkin Girl
See Potamkin, Luba

Potamkin, Luba 1943?- [HPPN]
American model
* [The] Potamkin Girl

Potamkin, Victor A. 20th c. [HPPN]
American automobile dealer
* [The] Cadillac King of America

Potash, Abe
See Greenwald, Joe

Potato
See De Guiche, Lillian

[The] Potato King
See Ushijima, George

[The] Potato Mayor
See Shank, Samuel Lewis

Potato Quixote
See Alcott, Amos Bronson

[The] Potentous Cub
See Pope, Alexander

Pothecary, Raymond 20th c. [MBF]
British author
* Ford, Quinton

Pothouse Peggy
See Eaton, Margaret O'Neill

Potier, Augustin 17th c. [SN]
Bishop of Beauvais
* [The] Mitred Ass

Potiphar [joint pseudonym with J. F. Marrack]
See Hern, [George] Anthony

Potiphar [joint pseudonym with (George) Anthony Hern]
See Marrack, J. F.

Potiphar, Paul
See Curtis, George William

Potocki, Leon 19th c. [IP]
Polish author
* L. P.

Potocnik, Captain 20th c. [SFP]
Author
* Noordung, Hermann

Potoco [Large Pot]
See Villegas, Jose

Potokinova, Bohd. J.
See Botto, Jan

Potomac, Peter
See Hoopes, Roy

[The] Potsdam Pianist
See List, Eugene

Pott, Joseph Holden 1759-1847 [HPPN, IP]
British clergyman and author
* [A] Friend to the Principles of That Work
* Valentine

Pott, Lefty
See Pott, Nelson Adolph

Pott, Leon Vince Philip 1896-1913 [BMH]
British comedian
* Fragson, Harry

Pott, Nellie
See Pott, Nelson Adolph

Pott, Nelson Adolph 1899-1963 [BE]
American baseball player
* Pott, Lefty
* Pott, Nellie

Pottasch, Eleanor 20th c. [FIR]
American actress
* Barry, Eleanor

[The] Pottawatomie Giant
See Willard, Jess

Potten, Henry Thomas 1867-? [HPPN]
British clergyman and author
* Hibernia

Potter, Albert Knight 19th c. [IP]
American clergyman and author
* Six

Potter, Barnabas [or Barnaby?]
1578-1642 [SN]
British prelate
* [The] Puritanical Bishop

Potter, Bowie Knife
See Potter, John Fox

Potter, Faith
See Toperoff, Sam

Potter, George William, Jr. 1930- [AW, CA, CC]
American author
* Withers, E. L.

Potter, H. C.
See Potter, Henry C.

Potter, Henry C. 1904- [BEW]
American director and producer
* Potter, H. C.

Potter, Henry Glasford 19th c. [SAT]
British author
* Democritus

Potter, Hilda 1888- [THR]
British actress
* Bruce-Potter, Hilda

Potter, Horatio 1802?- [HPPN]
American clergyman
* [The] Bishop
* [The] Provisional Bishop

Potter, Jean
See Hoey, Jean Guran

Potter, John 1674?-1747 [HPPN]
British clergyman
* [The] Bishop of Oxford

Potter, John 1734-? [HPPN]
British physician and author
* [A] Late Deceased Satirist
* [A] Society of Gentleman

Potter, John Fox 1817-1899 [HPPN]
American politician
* Potter, Bowie Knife

Potter, Kathleen Jill 1932- [CA]
British author
* Kinder, Kathleen

Potter, Margaret [Newman] 1926- [AW, CA, SAT]
British author
* Betteridge, Anne
* Melville, Anne
* Newman, Margaret

Potter, Mary 1900- [ART]
British painter
* M. P.

Potter, Nettie
See Moore, Monette

Potter, Paul
See Congdon, Charles Taber

Potter, Paul Meredith
See Maclean, Walter A.

Potter, Peter
See Moore, William

Potter, Phillip A. 20th c.   [IBW]
American clergyman
* [The] Black Pope

Potter, Richard 1783-1835   [IBW]
American magician
* [The] Black Houdini
* [The] Man Salamander
* Professor of Legerdemain

Potter, Robert 20th c.   [ESF, SFL]
Australian author and clergyman
* Easterley, Robert and Wilbraham,
  John

Potter, Robert H. [Bob] 1902-   [BE]
American baseball player
* Potter, Squire

Potter, [Major] Roger Sherman
See Adams, Francis Colburn

Potter, Squire
See Potter, Robert H. [Bob]

Potthoff, Margot Maria 20th c.   [IAW]
German author
* Lundberg, Kai

Pottios, Mike
See Pottios, Myron J.

Pottios, Myron J. 1939-   [FB]
American football player
* Pottios, Mike

Pottle, F. A.
See Pottle, Frederick Albert

Pottle, Frederick Albert 1897-   [LC]
American educator and author
* Pottle, F. A.

Pottle, Gilbert Emery Bensley
1875?-1945   [BEW, F2, FC]
American actor and playwright
* Emery, Gilbert

Pottle, Juliet Wilbor Tompkins 1871-?
[NAA]
American author
* Tompkins, Juliet Wilbor

Potts, Arthur 20th c.   [WECO]
British cartoonist
* Spot

Potts, Harry 1869-1913   [HPPN]
British entertainer
* Fragson, Harry

Potts, James Henry 1848-?   [HPPN]
American clergyman
* [The] Deafman Eloquent

Potts, Philips, Esq.
See Maginn, William

Potts, Stacy Gardner 1799-1865   [DNA]
American author
* Oakwood, Oliver

Potts, Thomas Richard 1915-1944   [SC]
American actor
* Fiske, Richard

Potvin, Damase 1879-?   [NAA]
Canadian journalist and author
* Sainte Foy

Potvin, Jean Rene 1949-   [SMG]
Canadian-born hockey player
* Potvin, Potsy

Potvin, Potsy
See Potvin, Jean Rene

Poty 1580?-1648   [HPPN]
Brazilian Indian chief
* Camarao, Antonio Felippe

Potzin, Mike 20th c.   [HPPN]
American gambler and criminal
* Mike the Greek

Pou, Genevieve [Long] 1919-   [CC, WW]
Author
* Holden, Genevieve

Pouch, Captain
See Reynolds, John

Poueigh, Jean [Marie-Octave-Geraud]
1876-?   [BBD]
French composer and author
* Sere, Octave

Pougatcheff, Emilian 1726-1775   [HN]
Russian rebel leader
* [The] Pretender

[The] Poughkeepsie Seer
See Davis, Andrew Jackson

Pougin, Arthur
See Paroisse-Pougin, Francois-Auguste
Arthur

Pougny, Jean
See Puni, Ivan Albert

Poulton, A. G.
See Plews, Arthur Gordon Lane

Poulton, Harry 20th c.   [BBH]
Boxer
* Poulton, Kid

Poulton, Kid
See Poulton, Harry

Poulton, Ronald William 1889-1915
[OCS]
British rugby player
* Poulton Palmer, Ronald William

Poulton Palmer, Ronald William
See Poulton, Ronald William

Pouly
See Boudin y Martin, Pierre

Poum et Zette
See Simenon, Georges [Joseph
Christian]

Pound Cake McMullen
See McMullen, Kenneth Lee

Pound, Ezra [Loomis] 1885-1972   [CA,
CAA, HPPN]
American poet and critic
* Atheling, William
* Caged Panther
* E. P.
* [The] Expatriate American Poet
* Hemingway's Tutor
* Homesick Poet
* [The] Last Rower

Pound, Ezra [Loomis] (cont.)
* [The] Perpetual Adolescent of
  American Poetry
* Sightless Seer
* Venison, Alfred
* Voice of Silence

Pound, Reginald 20th c.   [WWL]
British writer
* Renthwaite, Robert

Pound, Roscoe 1870-1964   [HPPN]
American attorney, author, educator
* Grand Old Man of the Law
* Man With a Memory
* [The] Most Outstanding Jurist

Pound, Singleton
See Merland, Oliver

Pountney, Monica Brailey 20th c.
[ART]
British painter
* Mon

Poupard, Henri-Pierre 1901-   [BBD,
HDM]
French composer
* Sauguet, Henri

Pournelle, Jerry [Eugene] 1933-   [CA,
ESF, SFP]
American author
* Curtis, Wade

Poussin, Gaspar
See Dughet, Gaspar

Poussin, Nicolas 1594-1665   [HN, SN]
French painter
* [The] Intellectual Artist

[The] Poussin of England
See Cooper, Richard

[The] Poussin of France
See Dughet, Gaspar

Pouw, Pietro 1564-1611   [PA]
Author
* Pavius

Poveda y Armenteros, Francisco
1796-1879   [CW]
Cuban poet and playwright
* [El] Trovador Cubano

Povey, Charles 18th c.   [HPPN]
British author
* Ryley, [Sir] Heister

Pow, Johnny de
See Powers, John

Powder Face Eckert
See Eckert, Tom

Powder Horn Like
See Like, Jim

Powderly, Terence V. 1849-1924
[HPPN]
American labor union official
* [The] Knight of Labor

Powe, Bruce 1925-   [CA]
Canadian author
* Portal, Ellis

Powe, C. J.
See Powe, Cleophus Jaumah

Powe, Cleophus Jaumah 1910- [BA]
American business executive
* Powe, C. J.

Powel
See Price, Charles

Powel, John Hare 1786-1856 [HPPN]
American agriculturist
* [A] Pennsylvania Farmer

Powell, A. M.
See Morgan, Alfred P[owell]

Powell, Adam Clayton 1908-1972
[HPPN]
American politician and clergyman
* [The] King of Harlem

Powell, Adam Clayton, III 1946- [IBW]
American radio and television journalist
* Powell, Skipper

Powell, Albert 1900- [BF]
British actor
* Powell, Sandy

Powell, Altivia Edwards 1924- [IBW]
American singer and columnist
* [The] Left Bank Mother Confessor
* Powell, Buttercup

Powell, Arden 20th c. [EF]
American football player
* Powell, Tim

Powell, Big Judge
See Powell, John Stephen

Powell, Big Red
See Powell, Edward D.

Powell, Boche
See Powell, Edward D.

Powell, Boog
See Powell, John Wesley

Powell, Brian 1934- [CA]
Canadian educator and author
* Brian

Powell, Bud
See Powell, Earl

Powell, Buttercup
See Powell, Altivia Edwards

Powell, C. B.
See Powell, Clilan Bethany

Powell, Clilan Bethany 1894- [BA]
American physician
* Powell, C. B.

Powell, Clive 20th c. [LRR]
British jazz musician
* Fame, Georgie

Powell, Earl 1924-1966 [DAM, EJ, PMJ]
American jazz musician
* Powell, Bud

Powell, Edward D. 1912- [MK]
American baseball player
* Powell, Big Red
* Powell, Boche

Powell, Eleanor 1913- [HPPN]
American dancer and actress
* [The] World's Greatest Female Tap
Dancer

Powell, Eric Frederick William 1899-
[WD]
British author
* Rusholm, Peter

Powell, Everard Stephen, Sr. 1907-1976
[DAM, NP, PMJ]
American jazz musician
* Karweem, Musheed
* Powell, Rudy
* Powell, Tooty

Powell, [David] Frank 1845-1906
[HPPN]
American author and physician
* Fancy Frank
* [The] Mighty Medicine Man
* [The] Surgeon Scout
* White Beaver

Powell, Frank
See Ingraham, Prentiss

Powell, Geoffrey Stewart 1914- [CA]
British army officer and author
* Angus, Tom

Powell, Glennon 1947- [SMG]
American football team staff member
* Powell, Silky

Powell, Gordon 1922- [EJ, PMJ]
American jazz musician
* Powell, Specs

Powell, H. W. [PA]
Author
* M. E. M.

Powell, Jack
See Goodman, Jack

Powell, James Robert 1814-1883
[HPPN]
American pioneer
* [The] Duke of Birmingham

Powell, Jane
See Burce, Suzanne

Powell, Jimmy 20th c. [NP]
American jazz musician
* Powell, Neat

Powell, Jody
See Powell, Joseph Lester, Jr.

Powell, Joe 1952- [IBW]
American dancer
* Powell, Lovey Joe

Powell, John 1808?-1870 [HPPN]
American gambler
* [The] Honest Mississippi River
Gambler
* [The] Shining Knight of the Poker
Table

Powell, John 1876-1924 [HPPN]
American singer
* Leslie, James

Powell, John Stephen 1857-1921
[HPPN]
American jurist
* Powell, Big Judge

Powell, John Wesley 1941- [IPA, PB,
SMG]
American baseball player
* Powell, Boog

Powell, Joseph Lester, Jr. 1944?- [BI]
*Administrative aide to American president
Jimmy Carter*
* Powell, Jody

Powell, Lee
See Lee, Alfred E.

Powell, Lewis Thornton 1845-1865 [BI]
American conspirator
* Payne, Lewis

Powell, Lovey Joe
See Powell, Joe

Powell, Mary
See Manning, Anne

Powell, Melvin 20th c. [OBW]
American baseball player
* Powell, Put

Powell, Mousie
See Powell, Walter

Powell, Neat
See Powell, Jimmy

Powell, Neil
See Innes, Brian

Powell, Ollie 1890?-1928 [WWJ]
American jazz musician
* Powers, Ollie

Powell, Oscar Reginald 1884-? [CCL]
Canadian author
* Fairfax, Dick

Powell, Peewee
See Powell, William Ernest

Powell, Peter 1928-
American clergyman
* Powell, Stone Forehead

Powell, Philip Wayne 1913- [CA]
American historian and author
* Wayne, Philip

Powell, Piggie
See Powell, William Ernest

Powell, Pigmeat
See Powell, William Ernest

Powell, Put
See Powell, Melvin

Powell, Rabbit
See Powell, Raymond Reath

Powell, Ransom T. 19th c. [HPPN]
American military drummer
* Red Cap

Powell, Raymond Reath 1888-1962 [BE]
American baseball player
* Powell, Rabbit

Powell, Richard [Pitts] 1908- [CA]
American author
* Kirk, Jeremy

Powell, Richard Stillman
See Barbour, Ralph Henry

Powell, Ruben 20th c. [BBH]
American archer
* Flight Archer, Mr.

Powell, Rudy
See Powell, Everard Stephen, Sr.

Powell, Sandy
See Powell, Albert

Powell, Silky
See Powell, Glennon

Powell, Skipper
See Powell, Adam Clayton, III

Powell, Sonny
See Bester, Alfred

Powell, Specs
See Powell, Gordon

Powell, Stone Forehead
See Powell, Peter

Powell, Talmage 1920- [CA, WW]
American author
* McCready, Jack
* Talmage, Anne

Powell, Teddy
See Paolella, Alfred

Powell, Thomas 1809-1887 [HPPN]
American poet, playwright, journalist
* Diogenes
* Pungent, Pierce
* Trevor, Ernest

Powell, Tim
See Powell, Arden

Powell, Tiny
See Powell, Vance

Powell, Tooty
See Powell, Everard Stephen, Sr.

Powell, Vance 1928?- [BWW]
American singer
* Powell, Tiny

Powell, Walter 20th c. [BEW]
American orchestra leader
* Powell, Mousie

Powell, Wee Willie
See Powell, William Ernest

Powell, William ?-1803 [HN]
British eccentric
* [The] Highgate Prophet

Powell, William Ernest 1903- [MK]
American baseball player
* Powell, Peewee
* Powell, Piggie
* Powell, Pigmeat
* Powell, Wee Willie

Powell, William Horatio 1892- [HPPN]
American actor
* Myrna Loy's Celluloid Husband

Powell-Smith, Vincent [Walter Francis] 1939- [AW, CA, WD]
British author, reviewer, critic
* Elphinstone, Francis
* Justiciar
* Orbis, Victor
* Santa Maria

Power, Arthur
See Dudden, Arthur P[ower]

Power, Catherine
See DuBreuil, Elizabeth Lorinda

Power, Cecil
See Allen, [Charles] Grant [Blairfindie]

Power, David?
See Grady, Thomas

Power, Marguerite A. 19th c. [PA]
Author
* Honoria

Power, Mary 1881-1957 [CAT, CCL]
Canadian-born author
* Maura, [Sister]
* [A] Sister of Charity

Power, Michael
See Walker, David Esdaile

Power, Nelson
See Judd, Alfred

Power, Norman S[andiford] 1916- [CA]
British clergyman and author
* Kratos

Power, Paddy
See Power, [William Grattan] Tyrone, I

Power, Paul
See Vestergard, Luther

Power, Rex
See Langley, Roger

Power, Richard 1928-1970 [CAP]
Irish author
* De Paor, Risteard

Power, Samuel Browning [PA]
Author
* S. B. P.

Power, Susan C. Dunning 19th c. [FFF]
American author
* Dare, Shirley

Power, [William Grattan] Tyrone, I 1797-1841 [FAA]
Irish-born actor
* Power, Paddy

Power, William ?-1892 [HPPN]
American outlaw
* Evans, Joe
* Evans, Tim

Power-Ross, Robert W.
See Ross, Robert W.

Power-Waters, Brian 1922- [CA]
British-born American airline pilot and author
* Captain X

Powers, Anne
See Schwartz, Anne Powers

Powers, Barbara Hudson
See Dudley, Barbara Hudson

Powers, Bill
See Evans, Chris

Powers, C. F., Jr. 1923- [ITA]
American film executive
* Powers, Mike

Powers, Chester 20th c. [LRR]
American singer
* Valenti, Dino

Powers, Dick
See Sellers, Connie Leslie, Jr.

Powers, Ellis Foree 1906- [BE]
American baseball player
* Powers, Mike

Powers, Francis Gary 1929- [EE, HPPN]
American intelligence agent
* America's First Space Age Super Spy
* Palmer

Powers, George
See Infield, Glenn [Berton]

Powers, Grandmother
See Powers, Philip J.

Powers, Ike
See Powers, John Lloyd

Powers, J. F.
See Powers, James Farl

Powers, J. L.
See Glasby, John [Stephen]

Powers, James Farl 1917- [WYA]
American author
* Powers, J. F.

Powers, Jessica 20th c. [CAT]
American poet
* Miriam of the Holy Spirit, [Sister]

Powers, Jet
See Smith, James Marcus

Powers, John 20th c. [HPPN]
American politician
* Pow, Johnny de
* [The] Prince of Boodlers

Powers, John
See Holliday, John Henry

Powers, John A. 1923?-1980
American air force officer
* Powers, Shorty
* [The] Voice of Mission Control
* [The] Voice of the Astronauts

Powers, John J[ames] 1945- [CA]
American author
* Powers, John R.

Powers, John Lloyd 1906-1968 [BE]
American baseball player
* Powers, Ike

Powers, John R.
See Powers, John J[ames]

Powers, Johnny
See De Pow, Johnny

Powers, Julia
See Cox, Ida

Powers, Julius
See Cox, Ida

Powers, M. L.
See Tubb, Edwin Charles

Powers, Mala
See Powers, Mary Ellen

Powers, Margaret
See Heal, Edith

Powers, Mary Bullock 1878?-1948
[HPPN]
American recluse
* Cousin Mamie

Powers, Mary Ellen 1931- [FC, ITA, SW]
American actress
* Powers, Mala

Powers, Mike
See Powers, C. F., Jr.

Powers, Mike
See Powers, Ellis Foree

Powers, Mrs. William   [FFF]
Entertainer
* Booth, Rachel

Powers, Ollie
See Powell, Ollie

Powers, Philip J. 1853-1914 [BE]
American baseball player
* Powers, Grandmother

Powers, Richard
See Duryea, George

Powers, Richard M. 1921- [IBY]
American author, illustrator, painter
* Gorman, Terry

Powers, S. Rugeley   [PA]
Author
* S. R. P.

Powers, Shorty
See Powers, John A.

Powers, Stefanie
See Paul, Stefanie [or Taffy?]

Powerscourt, Sheila
See Wingfield, Sheila [Viscountess Powerscourt]

Powhatan
See Wa hun-sen-a-cawh [or Wahunsonacook]

Powis, Carl Edgar 1928- [BE]
American baseball player
* Powis, Jug

Powis, Jug
See Powis, Carl Edgar

Powis, William Herbert 1573?-1656
[HPPN]
British nobleman
* W. H., Mr.

Powles, Harry ?-1888 [BMH]
British comic singer
* Ball, Harry
* [The] Tramp Musician

Powles, Matilda Alice 1864-1952 [BMH, HPPN, THR]
British theatrical performer
* De Frece, Lady
* [The] Great Little Tilley
* [The] London Idol
* [The] Pocket Sims Reeves
* Tilley, Vesta

Powley, Faith Hinckley 1891- [NAA]
American author
* Jayne, Faith

Powley, Florence Mary Pomeroy 1892-
[CAP]
British poet
* Pomeroy, Florence Mary

Powley, Jean [Makins] 20th c. [WW]
Author
* Cardwell, Ann

Pownall, Henry 19th c. [HFN]
Author
* [An] Inhabitant

Pownall, Thomas 1722-1805 [HPPN]
British colonial administrator
* [An] Honourable Gentleman

Powys, [Rev.] Charles Richard 19th c.
[HPPN]
British clergyman
* [A] Gentleman of Oxford

Powys, J. C.
See Powys, John Cowper

Powys, John Cowper 1872-1963 [LC]
British author
* Powys, J. C.

Powys, Stephen
See De Lanty, Virginia

Powys, T. F.
See Powys, Theodore Francis

Powys, Theodore Francis 1875-1953
[LC, TC]
British author
* Powys, T. F.

Poy
See Fearon, Percy Arthur

Poynder, John 1779-1849 [PA]
Author
* [A] Layman

Poynter, James William 1885- [WWL]
British author
* Indicator

Poyntz, Launce
See Whittaker, Frederick

Poznanski, Alfred 1883?-1934 [BEW]
Polish-born playwright
* Savoir, Alfred

Pozo, Chano
See Pozo y Gonzales, Luciano

Pozo, Chino
See Pozo, Francisco

Pozo, Francisco 1915- [EJ]
Cuban-born jazz musician
* Pozo, Chino

Pozo y Gonzales, Luciano 1915-1948
[EJ]
Cuban-born jazz musician
* Pozo, Chano

Prabhupada, Bhaktivedanta 1896- [CA]
Indian spiritual teacher and author
* Bhaktivedanta, A. C.
* Bhaktivedanta Swami, A. C.

[A] Practical Chemist and Experienced Liquor Dealer
See Stephen, John

[A] Practical Farmer
See Armstrong, John

[A] Practical Gardener
See Fessenden, Thomas Green

[The] Practical Phrenologist
See Fowler, Orson Squire

[A] Practical Printer
See Mitchell, John

Practitioner of More Than Fifty Years' Experience in the Art of Angling
See Bartlett, John

Prada, Benny Kid
See Prada, Bernardo

Prada, Bernardo 1950- [RBE]
Colombian boxer
* Prada, Benny Kid

Pradas, Virginia
See Pacis, Vicente Albano

Praderito [Little Meadow]
See Diaz Del Busto, Severiano

Prado 19th c. [DI]
Murderer
* De Linska, [The] Count

Prado, Katie 1882-1957 [HPPN]
Austrian-American singer and bordello proprietress
* [The] Belle of New York
* Diamond-Tooth Lil
* Hildegard, Evelyn
* Miss Lil
* [The] Queen of the Bowery
* [The] Toast of the Barbary Coast
* [The] Voice of the St. Louis Fair

Prado, [Domase] Perez 1922- [EPM, IBW]
Cuban-born bandleader, arranger, composer
* [The] Mambo King
* [El] Rey del Mambo [The King of Mambo]

Praeceptor Germaniae
See Schwarzert, Philipp

Praeceptor Humilis
See West, Luther Shirley

Praed, Winthrop Mackworth 1802-1839 [DEL, FFF]
British poet
* Courtenay, Peregrine
* Joyeuse, Vyvian

Praestantissimus Mathematicus
See Brahe, Tycho

Praestantissimus Mathematicus
See Dee, John

Praetorius, Hieronymus
See Schulz [or Schulze], Hieronymus

Praetorius, Michael
See Schultheiss [or Schulz], Michael

Prager, Emanuel 20th c. [HPPN]
American jazz musician
* Prager, [Colonel] Manny

Prager, [Colonel] Manny
See Prager, Emanuel

[The] Pragmatic Humanist
See Young, Whitney Moore

Pragnell, Festus 1905- [ESF]
British author
* Parnell, Francis

Prairie Bird
See Willenan, M. W.

Prairie Dog Dave
See Morrow, Dave

Prairie Dog Finley
See Finley, Larry

[The] Prairie Star
See Bedra, Julie Marlene

[The] Prairie Tornado
See Roberts, Oral

Praize, Ann
See Blewett, Dorothy Emilie

Prajadhipok 1893-1941 [WBD]
King of Siam
* Rama VII

Prance, June E[lizebeth] 1929- [CA]
British-born author and illustrator
* Shaw, Elizabeth

Prateolus
See Duprean, Gabriel

Prather, Richard S[cott] 1921- [CA, CC, WW]
American author
* Knight, David
* Ring, Douglas

Pratt, Agnes Rothery 1888-1954 [BI, NAA]
American author
* Edwards, Agnes
* Rothery, Agnes Edwards

Pratt, Al[bert G.] 1847-1937 [BE]
American baseball manager
* Uncle Al

Pratt, Babe
See Pratt, Walter

Pratt, [Sir] Charles [First Earl Camden] 1714-1794 [SN]
British jurist and political leader
* Our Spanish Cato

Pratt, Charles 1830-1891 [HPPN]
American oil magnate and philanthropist
* [The] Father of Pratt Institute

Pratt, Charles E. ?-1885 [BBH]
American author and bicycling enthusiast
* Cycling's Elder Statesman

Pratt, Cornelia Atwood
See Comer, Cornelia Atwood

Pratt, D. E. H.
See Pratt, Derrick Edward Henry

Pratt, Daniel 1809-1887 [DNNF, DNNS, FFF]
American eccentric
* [The] Great American Traveller

Pratt, Del
See Pratt, Derrill Burnham

Pratt, Dennis 1897-1971 [EMT, FC, PMJ]
British-born actor and singer
* King, Dennis

Pratt, Derrick Edward Henry 1895- [ART]
British painter
* Pratt, D. E. H.

Pratt, Derrill Burnham 1888-1977 [BE]
American baseball player
* Pratt, Del

Pratt, E. J.
See Pratt, Edwin John

Pratt, Edwin John 1883-1964 [LC]
Canadian educator and poet
* Pratt, E. J.

Pratt, Eleanor Blake [Atkinson] 1899- [NAA, WW]
American author
* Atkinson, Eleanor Blake
* Blake, E. A.
* Blake, Eleanor

Pratt, Ella Ann [Farman] 1837-1907 [DNA]
American author
* Shepherd, Dorothea Alice

Pratt, F. Alcott 19th c. [FFF]
American author
* Demijohn

Pratt, [Murray] Fletcher 1897-1956 [ESF, SF, WGT]
American author
* Fletcher, George U.
* Lester, Irvin
* Ruby, B. F.

Pratt, Francis Ashbury 1827-1902 [HPPN]
American toolmaker and inventor
* [The] Father of Interchangeable Parts

Pratt, Francis Bruce [Frank] 1897- [BE]
American baseball player
* Pratt, Truckhorse

Pratt, Inga Stephens 20th c. [SFP]
Author
* Stephens, I. M.

Pratt, Jacob Loring 1835-1891 [DNA, PA]
American author and clergyman
* Campbell, Erving
* L. I.
* North, F. H.

Pratt, John 1931- [AW, CA]
British naval officer and author
* Winton, John

Pratt, L. Maria [PA]
Author
* Loring, Laurie

Pratt, Larry
See Pratt, Lester John

Pratt, Leonard E. 20th c. [MBF]
British author and editor
* Smith, Fenton

Pratt, Lester John 1887-1969 [BE]
American baseball player
* Pratt, Larry

Pratt, Rhona Olive 1903- [IAW]
Welsh-born author
* O'Harris, Pixie

Pratt, Samuel Jackson 1749-1814 [DEL, PA]
British author and poet
* Melmoth, Courtney

Pratt, Theodore 1901-1969 [ANT, BI, CC, TC1]
American author
* Brace, Timothy

Pratt, Truckhorse
See Pratt, Francis Bruce [Frank]

Pratt, Walter 1916- [CEI, FHE, HK]
Canadian-born hockey player
* Pratt, Babe

Pratt, William Henry 1887-1969 [BDF, BEW, F1]
British actor
* Karloff, Boris

Pratza, Nicholas 1904?-1973 [F2]
Rumanian-born actor
* Stuart, Nick

Pravda, Frantisek
See Hlinka, Vojtech

Praxiteles
See Pandel, Ted

Pray, Isaac Clark 1813-1869 [HPPN]
American journalist, playwright, actor
* Clerc, Pret of Le Pre aux Clercs
* [A] Journalist

[The] Praying Millionaire
See Johnson, Wallace

[The] Praying Puncher
See Cream, Arnold Raymond

Praz, Mario 1896-1982 [CA]
Italian author, editor, translator
* Alcibiade
* Di Guisa, Giano

Pre Adamite
See Hoar, George Frisbie

[The] Preacher
See Grande, Juan

[The] Preacher
See Short, Dewey

[The] Preacher of History
See Robinson, James Harvey

[The] Preacher President
See Garfield, James Abram

[The] Preaching Bishop
See Matthew, Tobias [or Tobie]

[The] Preaching Faro Dealer
See Skaggs, Elijah

[The] Preaching Weathercock
See Richardson, [Rev.] William

[The] Preaching Woman
See Sprague, Achsa W.

Prebble, John Edward Curtis 1915-
[CA]
British author
* Curtis, John

Prebble, Marjorie Mary Curtis 1912-
[CA]
British author
* Compton, Ann
* Conway, Denise
* Curtis, Marjorie

[The] Preceptor of Germany
See Schwarzert, Philipp

[A] Preceptress
See Palmer, Charlotte

Precocious Pencil
See Levine, Jack

[The] Precursor of Jimmy Hoffa
See Beck, David

[A] Predestinator
See Chauvin [or Caulvin?], Jean

[The] Predictor of Sociocracy
See Ward, Lester Frank

Preece, T. Evan [HN, RH]
Prophet of South Wales
* Shipton, Mother

Preedy, George
See Long, Gabrielle Margaret Vere
[Campbell]

Preetorius, Emil 1827-1905 [HPPN]
German-American journalist and publicist
* [The] Nestor of the German American
Journalists

Pregarty, John M. 1873-1931 [HPPN]
American actor and composer
* Lloyd, Evans

Preibisch, Mel[vin Adolphus] 1914-
[BE]
American baseball player
* Preibisch, Primo

Preibisch, Primo
See Preibisch, Mel[vin Adolphus]

Preitel, Albert
See Pelzer, Leon

Premchand, Munschi
See Srivastava, Dhanpat Rai

[The] Premier
See Disraeli, Benjamin

[Le] Premier Grenadier de France
See La Tour [or Latour] d'Auvergne,
Theophile Malo Corret de

**[Le] Premier Grenadier de la
Republique**
See La Tour [or Latour] d'Auvergne,
Theophile Malo Corret de

**[Le] Premier Maitre d'Hotel de la
Philosophie**
See Holbach, [Baron] Paul Henri
Dietrich d'

**[The] Premier Public Relations Man of
the Age**
See Nader, Ralph

Preminger, Otto 1906?-1986 [NW 5-5-86]
Austrian-born film director and producer
* Otto the Terrible

Premont, [Brother] Jeremy
See Willett, [Brother] Franciscus

Prenaier, Paul
See Sperry, Reginald

Prendergast 12th c. [HN]
Protector of MacGallapatrick of Ossory
* [The] Faithful Norman

Prendergast, Paul
See Jerrold, Douglas William

Prendergast, Paul
See Leigh, Percival

Prentice, Cecil 1903-1971 [BMH]
British entertainer
* Granada, Cecil

Prentice, Charles W. 1898- [THR]
Scottish-born composer
* Prentice, Jock

Prentice, Fry
See Prentice, Jo Ann

Prentice, Jo Ann 1933- [GF]
American golfer
* Prentice, Fry

Prentice, Jock
See Prentice, Charles W.

Prentice, [Rev.] Thomas 1702-1782
[HPPN]
American clergyman
* Simon the Farmer

[A] Prentise in the Divine Art of Poesy
See James I

Prentiss, Benjamin Mayberry 1819-1901
[HPPN]
American army officer
* [The] Hero of the Hornet's Nest

Prentiss, Charles 1774-1820 [HPPN]
American editor
* [A] Citizen of Massachusetts
* [A] Lover of the Truth
* Rover, Roderic

Prentiss, George Pepper
See Wilson, George Pepper

Prentiss, Karl
See Purdy, Ken William

Prentiss, Kitten
See Wilson, George Pepper

Prentiss, Mrs. 19th c. [PA]
Author
* Little Susy

Prentiss, Paula
See Ragusa, Paula

Prentiss, Seargent Smith 1808-1850
[HPPN]
American attorney and legislator
* [The] Whig Orator of the Old South

Presberg, Miriam Goldstein 1919- [CA,
WD]
American author
* Gilbert, Miriam

[A] Presbyter
See Addison, Berkeley

Presbyter
See Edwards, [Rev.] Edward

[A] Presbyter
See Hooper, [Rev.] Francis John
Bodfield

Presbyter
See Turner, Samuel Hulbeart

Presbyter Anglicanus
See Harris, Joseph Hemington

Presbyter Catholicus
See Harness, William

Presbyter, Ignotus
See Van Allen, William Harman

**[A] Presbyter in the Diocese of
Canterbury**
See Perceval, Arthur Philip

[A] Presbyter of the Church in Phila
See Lundy, John Patterson

[A] Presbyter of the Church of England
See Asplin, William

[A] Presbyter of the Church of England
See Austin, William

[A] Presbyter of the Church of England
See Bold, [Rev.] John

[A] Presbyter of the Church of England
See Boswell, [Rev.] John

[A] Presbyter of the Church of England
See Hall, Robert

[A] Presbyter of the Church of England
See Haywood, Thomas

[A] Presbyter of the Church of England
See Hunt, Brian

[A] Presbyter of the Church of England
See Jackson, John

[A] Presbyter of the Church of England
See Jones, William

[A] Presbyter of the Church of England
See Marshall, Nathaniel

[A] Presbyter of the Church of England
See Newton, Richard

[A] Presbyter of the Church of England
See Robertson, William

[A] Presbyter of the Church of England
See Sclater, William

[A] Presbyter of the Church of England
See Toplady, Augustus Montagu

[A] Presbyter of the Church of England
See Walker, Samuel

[A] Presbyter of the Church of England
See Whiston, Daniel

[A] Presbyter of the Diocese of London
See Berriman, William

[A] Presbyter of the Diocese of Maryland
See Jones, Norris M.

[A] Presbyter of the Diocese of Massachusetts
See Wainwright, Jonathan Mayhew

[A] Presbyter of the Diocese of Toronto
See Darling, William Stewart

[A] Presbyter of the Episcopal Church in Edinburgh
See Terrot, Charles Hughes

[A] Presbyter of the Suffering Church of Scotland
See Calder, [Rev.] Robert

[A] Presbyterian
See Blakie, Alexander

[The] Presbyterian Paul-Pry
See Edwards, Thomas

[The] Presbyterian Ulysses
See Campbell, Archibald

Prescot, Julian
See Budd, John

Prescott, Benjamin 1687-1777 [HPPN]
American clergyman
* One Who Was Born in the Colony of Massachusetts Bay

Prescott, Bobby
See Prescott, George Bertrand

Prescott, Caleb
See Bingley, David Ernest

Prescott, Dorothy
See Poor, Agnes Blake

Prescott, E. Livingston
See Jay, Edith K. Spicer

Prescott, George Bertrand 1931- [BE]
Panamanian-born baseball player
* Prescott, Bobby

Prescott, H. F. M.
See Prescott, Hilda Frances Margaret

Prescott, Hilda Frances Margaret 1896-1972 [LC]
British author
* Prescott, H. F. M.

Prescott, Marie
See Pertzel, Mrs.

Prescott, Paul J.
See Irons, Lettie Artley

Prescott, Thomas H.
See Blake, William O.

[The] Present Champion of the English Theater
See Olivier, [Sir] Laurence

[The] Present Pastor
See Burgess, Ebenezer

[The] Preserver
See Ptolemy I

[The] Preserver of His Country
See Lorraine, Francois de

[The] President
See Alderson, John

[The] President
See Chester, Harry

[The] President
See Cramp, John Mockett

President
See Sanden, Thomas

[The] President
See Sinclair, [Sir] John

[The] President
See Turner, Daniel

[The] President
See Wilder, Marshall Pinckney

[The] President
See Winthrop, Robert Charles

President Bob
See Spencer, Robert [Second Earl of Sunderland]

President De Facto
See Hayes, Rutherford Birchard

[Le] President Je Dis Ca
See Charton, Louis

[The] President Maker
See Clay, Henry

President, Mr.
See Shaw, [Warren] Wilbur

[The] President of Harvard University
See Quincy, Josiah

[The] President of Long Island
See Scott, John

[The] President of the College
See Raymond, John Howard

[The] President of the Derrieregarde
See Wilder, Alec

[The] President of the Royal College of Surgeons in England
See Green, John Henry

[The] President's Lawyer
See St. Clair, James

[The] President's Other Friend
See Abplanalp, Robert H.

[The] President's Preacher
See Graham, William Franklin [Billy]

[The] President's Rasputin
See Haldeman, Harry Robbins

[The] President's Worst Friend
See Mitchell, John Newton

Presko, Joseph Edward 1928- [BE]
American baseball player
* Presko, Little Joe

Presko, Little Joe
See Presko, Joseph Edward

Presland, John
See Bendit, Gladys Williams

Presle, Micheline
See Chassagne, Micheline

Presley, Bud
See Presley, George

Presley, Elvis Aron 1935-1977 [FCW, NN, RO1]
American singer
* Burrows, [Colonel] Jon [FBI code name]
* [The] Country Cat
* Elvis the Pelvis
* [The] Father of Rock 'n Roll
* [The] Heartbreak Kid
* [The] Hillbilly Cat
* Hillbilly on a Pedestal
* [The] King
* [The] King of Rock 'n Roll
* [The] Memphis Mesmerizer
* [The] Pelvis
* Swivel Hips

Presley, George 1922?- [BI]
American basketball coach
* Presley, Bud

[The] Press Agent for Revolution
See Paine, Thomas

Press, Red
See Press, Seymour

Press, Seymour 1924- [EJ]
American jazz musician
* Press, Red

Pressburger, Emeric 1902- [CA]
Hungarian-born author and screenwriter
* Imrie, Richard

Presser, Big Bill
See Presser, William

Presser, Charles 20th c. [SG]
Boxer
* Burke, Sailor

Presser, [Gerrit] Jacob 1899-1970
[CAP]
Dutch historian and author
* Drukker, J.
* Van Dam, J.
* Van Wageningen, J.

Presser, Janice 1946- [CA]
American author
* Greene, Janice Presser

Presser, William 20th c. [TI 5-2-83, WP
11-6-85]
American labor leader
* Plug [code name]
* Presser, Big Bill

Pressler, Franz 1927- [EJ]
Austrian jazz musician
* Fatty George

Pressley, Hilda
See Nickson, Hilda

Pressnell, Forest Charles 1906- [BE]
American baseball player
* Pressnell, Tot

Pressnell, Tot
See Pressnell, Forest Charles

Pressoir, Carlo
See Pressoir, Charles Fernand

Pressoir, Charles Fernand 1910-1973
[CW]
French-born poet and author
* Pressoir, Carlo

Prest, T. [PA]
Author
* Angelina

Prestel, Jim 20th c.
American football player
* Prestel, Primo

Prestel, Primo
See Prestel, Jim

Prester John
See Togrul Wang Khan

Presti, Tony
See Vander Linden, Anthony

Prestigiocomo, Pasquale 20th c. [BLB]
American underworld figure
* Presto, Pasquale

Prestnia, Frank 20th c. [RO2]
American musician
* Prestnia, Rocco

Prestnia, Rocco
See Prestnia, Frank

Presto
See Swift, Jonathan

Presto, Pasquale
See Prestigiocomo, Pasquale

Preston, Ann 1810?-1906 [BI]
Canadian servant
* Holy Ann

Preston, Arthur
See Hankins, Arthur Preston

Preston, Caroline F. [joint pseudonym
with Olive Augusta Cheney]
See Alger, Horatio, Jr.

Preston, Caroline F. [joint pseudonym
with Horatio Alger, Jr.]
See Cheney, Olive Augusta

Preston, Edward
See Guess, Edward Preston

Preston, Elliott W. 19th c. [HPPN]
British author
* Manfred

Preston, Frank 1860?-1939 [BEW]
*American producer and press
representative*
* Weadon, Percy

Preston, George
See Banks, Nancy Huston

Preston, George F.
See Warren, John Byrne Leicester
[Baron de Tabley]

Preston, Hilary
See Nickson, Hilda

Preston, Hugh
See Wilson, Derek Alan

Preston, J. 18th c. [HPPN]
British author
* [An] Elector

Preston, James 1913- [CAP]
Australian author
* James, Ronald

Preston, James
See Unett, John

Preston, John
See Buschlen, John Preston

Preston, John Thomas Lewis 19th c.
[HPPN]
American educator and army officer
* Old Bald

Preston, Mrs. M. J. [PA]
Author
* Junkin, Margaret

Preston, Newt
See Preston, Ray

Preston, Paul
See Cooper, Alfred Benjamin

Preston, Paul
See Milner, Thomas Picton

Preston, Paul
See Morris, Charles Smith

Preston, Paul
See Picton, Thomas

Preston, Ray 1954- [SMG]
American football player
* Preston, Newt

Preston, Richard
See Lindsay, Jack

Preston, Robert
See Meservey, Robert Preston

Preston, Roger [PA]
Author
* Widdrington, Roger

Preston, Terry
See Husky, Ferlin

Preston, Thomas Austin 1929?- [BI,
HPPN]
American gambler
* Amarillo Slim
* Arizona Slim

Preston, Walford
See Townley, Houghton

Preston, William 1753-1807 [PI]
Irish poet, playwright, attorney
* Pinna y Ruiz, Donna Teresa

Preston-Muddock, Joyce Emmerson
1843-1934 [EMD, WW]
British journalist and author
* Donovan, Dick

Prestopnik, Irving Henry 1912-1949
[NOJ, PMJ, WWJ]
American jazz musician
* Fazola, Faz
* Fazola, Irving Henry

[Il] Prete Genovese
See Strozzi [or Strozza], Bernardo

[Il] Prete Rosso
See Vivaldi, Antonio Lucio

[The] Pretender
See Cleveland, [Stephen] Grover

[The] Pretender
See Demetrius I

[The] Pretender
See Otrepieff, Gregory

[The] Pretender
See Pougatcheff, Emilian

Preti, Mattia 1613-1699 [WBD]
Italian painter
* [Il] Calabrese
* [Il] Cavaliere Calabrese

Pretorius, Hertha
See Kouts, Hertha Pretorius

[The] **Prettiest Carmen on Record**
See Swarthout, Gladys

[The] **Prettiest Three Million Dollar Corp. with Freckles in America**
See Kappelhoff, Doris von

[The] **Prettiest Union Spy**
See Fryer, Pauline Cushman

Pretty Boy
See Covay, Don

Pretty Boy Floyd
See Floyd, Charles Arthur

Pretty Fanny
See Kemble, Frances Anne [Fanny]

Pretty Peg
See Dank, Peg van

Pretty, Violet 1931?- [FC, SW]
British actress
* Heywood, Anne

Pretty Witty Nellie
See Symcott, Margaret

Pretzel, Karl
See Harris, Charles H.

Preuss, Phyllis 1939- [BWG, EG, GF]
American golfer
* Preuss, Tish

Preuss, Tish
See Preuss, Phyllis

Preville
See Dubus, Pierre-Louis

Previn, Andre
See Previn, George

Previn, George 1929- [JL]
American conductor
* Previn, Andre

[The] **Previous**
See William II [Friedrich Wilhelm Viktor Albert]

Prevost, Alain 1930?-1971 [CA]
French journalist and author
* D'Hugues, Varnac

Prevost, Antoine Francois 1697-1763 [HPPN]
French clergyman and author
* Prevost d'Exiles

Prevost d'Exiles
See Prevost, Antoine Francois

Prevost, Francis
See Battersby, Henry Francis Prevost

Prevost, Francis
See Prevost Battersby, H. F.

Prevost, Madame Henri [FFF]
Entertainer
* Ponsin, Mlle.

Prevost, Marcel
See Marcel, Eugene

Prevost, Marie
See Dunn, Marie Bickford

Prevost Battersby, H. F. 20th c. [WWL]
British author
* Prevost, Francis

[The] **Prewar Rocking Chair Sensation of Russia**
See Meyer, [Dr.] Alexander

Preyer, Polly
See Jamerson, Pauline [Thierry]

Prez Kenneth
See Kidd, Kenneth

Prezihov, Voranc
See Kuhar, Lovro

Priam
See Collins, C. J.

Price, Benton
See Wilson, Roger C.

Price, Beverley Joan 1931- [AW, WD]
New Zealand editor and author
* Randell, Beverley

Price, Charles 18th c. [BI, HN]
British banknote forger
* Bond
* Brank
* Old Patch
* Parks
* Powel
* Schutz
* Wigmore
* Wilmott

Price, Charles 20th c. [EF]
American football player
* Price, Cotton

Price, Clarence 1889-1968 [BB]
American basketball coach
* Price, Nibs

Price, Cotton
See Price, Charles

Price, Dennis
See Rose-Price, Dennistoun John Franklyn

Price, E. C. 19th c. [HPPN]
British author
* E. C. P.

Price, Edgar Hoffman 1898- [HFF, WGT]
American author
* Daly, Hamlin

Price, Edmund Enoch 1832?-1907 [HPPN]
American boxer
* Price, Ned
* [The] Tex Rickard of His Day

Price, Edwin Wathen 1847-1915 [BI]
British author, agriculturist, sportsman
* Ringwood

Price, Emerson Field 1902- [NAA]
American writer
* Hanley, Hugh

Price, Ernest Cutler 1891-1942 [BX, RBE]
American boxer
* Dillon, Jack
* Jack the Giant Killer

Price, Evadne
See Smith, Helen Zenna

Price, Frank J. 1860-? [ALY]
American author and editor
* Conway, Faulkner

Price, George [Henry] 1910-? [CAP]
Welsh-born clergyman, educator, author
* Price, Rhys

Price, Jack
See Price, Jacob A.

Price, Jacob A. 1907- [HPPN]
American racehorse breeder, owner, trainer
* Price, Jack

Price, Jennifer
See Hoover, Helen [Drusilla Blackburn]

Price, Jimmie
See White, John I[rwin]

Price, Joseph Charles 1854-1893? [IBW]
American clergyman and college administrator
* [The] Lion of the Lyceum

Price, Joseph Preston [Joe] 1897-1961 [BE]
American baseball player
* Price, Lumber

Price, Kate
See Duffy, Kate

Price, Kenny 1931- [ECM]
American country-western performer
* [The] Round Mound of Sound

Price, Leontyne
See Price, Mary Violet Leontine

Price, Lorain Manners 1910-1963 [HPPN]
American dancer
* Manners, Lorain

Price, Lucie Locke 1904- [CA, SAT, WD]
American artist and poet
* Locke, Lucie

Price, Lumber
See Price, Joseph Preston [Joe]

Price, Maire
See Nic Shiubhlaigh, Maire

Price, Mary Violet Leontine 1927- [IPA]
American opera singer
* Price, Leontyne

Price, Mrs. E. H. [FFF]
Entertainer
* Davenport, Fanny

Price, Nancy
See Maude, Lillian Nancy

Price, Ned
See Price, Edmund Enoch

Price, Nibs
See Price, Clarence

Price, Olive 1903- [CA, SAT]
American author and playwright
* Cherryholmes, Anne
* West, Barbara

Price, Pat 1955- [SMG]
Canadian-born hockey player
* Price, Pricey

Price, Pricey
See Price, Pat

Price, Ray Noble 1926- [CWG]
American country-western performer
* [The] Cherokee Cowboy

Price, Rhys
See Price, George [Henry]

Price, Robert 1900- [CA]
American educator, author, poet
* Drew, Morgan

Price, Sterling G. 1809-1869 [HPPN]
American army officer
* Dad
* [The] Old Tycoon
* Pap

Price, T. Rowe 20th c. [HPPN]
American financier, financial analyst, economist
* [The] Sage of Baltimore

Price, Virginia Williams 20th c. [NAA]
American writer
* Pride, Ginia

Price, Vito
See Pizzo, Vito

Price, Walter
See Wilson, Roger C.

Price, Walter Travis 1917- [BWW, NBB]
American singer
* Big Walter
* [The] Thunderbird from Coast to Coast

Price, William Raleigh 1875-? [NAA]
American educator and author
* Bonner, Raleigh

Price-Brown, John 1844-1938 [CCL]
Canadian author
* Bohn, Eric

Price-Mars, Jean 1876-1969 [CW]
Haitian author
* Mars, Jean Price

Priceman, James
See Kirkland, Winifred Margaretta

Prichard, Hesketh Vernon Hesketh
1876-1922 [WW]
British author
* Heron, H.

Prichard, K.
See Prichard, Kate O'Brien Hesketh

Prichard, Kate O'Brien Hesketh 20th c.
[EMD, WW]
Author
* Heron, E.
* Prichard, K.

Prichard, Katharine Susannah
See Throssell, Katharine Susannah Prichard

Priddy, Al
See Brown, Frederick Kenyon

[The] Pride and Sorrow of Chess
See Morphy, Paul Charles

Pride, Charley 1938- [FCW, RO2]
American country-western performer
* Pride, Country Charley

Pride, Country Charley
See Pride, Charley

Pride, Ginia
See Price, Virginia Williams

Pride, Hemphill P., II 1936- [BA]
American attorney
* Pride, Hempie

Pride, Hempie
See Pride, Hemphill P., II

[The] Pride of German Culture
See Goethe, Johann Wolfgang von

[The] Pride of Havana
See Luque, Adolfo

[The] Pride of Liberia
See Tubman, William Vacanarat Shadrach

[The] Pride of Pittsburgh
See Martin, Anne

[The] Pride of Pontypridd
See Thomas, Frederick Hall

[The] Pride of Pragmatists
See Haldeman, Harry Robbins

[The] Pride of the Ghetto
See Bernstein, Joseph [Joe]

Pride of the Met
See Ticker, Reuben

[The] Pride of the Phillipines
See Coleman, James L.

[The] Pride of the Rockies
See Devlan, Eugene

[The] Pride of the West Virginia Hills
See Martin, Nancy

[The] Pride of the Yankees
See Gehrig, [Henry] Lou[is]

Pride, Thomas ?-1658 [SN]
British parliamentary officer
* Pride, Yeasty
* [The] Purging Colonel

Pride, Yeasty
See Pride, Thomas

Pridgeon, Alan Paul 1954- [DC]
British cricketer
* Pridgeon, Pridge

Pridgeon, Pridge
See Pridgeon, Alan Paul

Pridvorov, Yefim 1883- [CD]
Russian poet
* Bedny, Demyan

[A] Priest
See Gilbey, Alfred

[The] Priest
See Konrad

[The] Priest
See Lamprecht

Priest Hater
See Eric II

Priest, John
See Kotschnig, John Walter

Priest, Martin
See Penry, John

[The] Priest of Nature
See Newton, [Sir] Isaac

[The] Priest of Nature
See Williams, David

[A] Priest of the Church of England
See Hooper, [Rev.] Richard

[A] Priest of the Congregation of the Holy Redeemer
See Cornell, J. H.

[A] Priest of the English Church
See Smith, Clement Ogle

[The] Priest of Volcanoes
See Hubbard, Bernard Rosecrans

Priestley, Clive Ryland 1892- [WW]
Author
* Ryland, Clive

Priestley, J. B.
See Priestley, John Boynton

Priestley, John Boynton 1894-1984
[BEW, CA, IPA, WP 8-16-84]
British playwright and author
* Goldsmith, Peter
* Jolly Jack
* Priestley, J. B.

Priestley, Joseph 1733-1804 [HPPN, SN]
British clergyman and chemist
* Clemens
* Liberius
* Paulinus
* Priestley, Proteus
* Turnabout, [Rev.] Secretary

Priestley, L. A. M.
See McCracken, Elizabeth A. M.

Priestley, Leslie Avoca 1908- [IWM]
British musician
* Carew, Leslie

Priestley, Proteus
See Priestley, Joseph

Priestley, Robert
See Wiggins, David

[A] Priestman
See Fitzpatrick, John

Prieto Barrera, Diego 1856-1918 [GS]
Spanish bullfighter
* Cuatro Dedos [Four Fingers]

Prieur de la Cote-d'Or
See Prieur-Duvernois, Claude Antoine

[Le] Prieur de Vendome
See Vendome, Philippe de

Prieur-Duvernois, Claude Antoine
1763-1827 [WBD]
French scholar and politician
* Prieur de la Cote-d'Or

[The] Prig
See Longueville, T.

Priggins, Peter
See Hewlett, Joseph T. J.

Prignani, Bartolommeo 1318-1389
[WBD]
Pope
* Urban VI

Priley, Margaret Hubbard 1909- [CA]
American author
* Hubbard, Margaret Ann

Prilukoff, Donat 20th c. [DI]
Russian murderer
* Zeiler, M.

Prim, Pop
See Prim, Raymond Lee

Prim, Raymond Lee 1906- [BE]
American baseball player
* Prim, Pop

Prima Donna Assoluta
See Sutherland, Joan

[A] Primcock
See Ralph, James

Prime, C. T.
See Prime, Cecil Thomas

Prime, Cecil Thomas 1909- [WYA]
Author
* Prime, C. T.

Prime, Edward Dorr Griffith 1814-1891
[FFF, HPPN, PA]
American clergyman and writer
* Eusebius
* His Son In Law

[The] Prime Irish Lad
See Randall, Jack

Prime, Lord
See Reynolds, Walter Doty

[The] Prime Minister
See Castiglia [or Seriglia?], Francesco

[The] Prime Minister of Mirth
See Wade, George Edward

Prime, Samuel Irenaeus 1812-1885
[FFF, HPPN, PA, WBD]
American clergyman and writer
* Irenaeus
* [A] Village Pastor

Prime, William Cowper 1825-1905 [PA]
Author
* W.

Primm, [Brother] Orrin
See Willett, [Brother] Franciscus

Primrose, [The Rev. Dr.] Charles
See Wilson, Benjamin

[The] Primrose Sphynx
See Disraeli, Benjamin

Primus
See Monro, Alexander

Primus Anglo Britannioe Episcopus
See Collier, Jeremy

Primus Baronetorum Angliae
See Bacon, [Sir] Nicholas

Prin, Marie 1908?-1953 [BL]
French artists' model
* Kiki of Montparnasse

[The] Prince
See Judah I [or Jehudah]

Prince
See Nelson, Prince Roger

Prince
See Salmon, Leon N.

Prince, Adelaide
See Rubenstein, Adelaide

Prince Albert
See Gore, Albert, Jr.

Prince Alli
See Mona, Alli

Prince, Arthur 1881-1948 [BMH]
British ventriloquist
* [The] Court Magician and
  Ventriloquist

Prince BS
See Andrew

[Le] Prince Burliabled
See Paul, John

Prince Charley
See Galloway, Charles Betts

[Le] Prince de la Critique
See Janin, Jules Gabriel

Prince, Dorris 1899-1927 [SC]
American actress
* Dare, Dorris

Prince Eddy
See Albert Victor

Prince, Edward Ernest 1858-? [NAA]
British-born writer
* Bessarion

Prince, F. T.
See Prince, Frank Templeton

Prince, Frank Templeton 1912- [MBL]
British poet
* Prince, F. T.

Prince Hal
See Chase, Harold Harris [Hal]

Prince Hal
See Henry V

Prince Hal
See Newhouser, Harold [Hal]

Prince Hal
See Patterson, Hal

Prince Hal
See Schumacher, Harold Henry

[The] Prince Imperial
See Bonaparte, Napoleon Eugene Louis
Jean Joseph

[The] Prince in Music
See Boethius, Anicius Manlius
Severinus

Prince, J. H.
See Prince, Jack Harvey

Prince, Jack Harvey 1908- [CA, SAT]
British-born author and illustrator
* Aquillo, Don
* Clinton, Jon
* Prince, J. H.
* Wardell, Dean

Prince, John 1751-1836 [HPPN]
American clergyman
* [A] Friend of the Christian Examiner
  and a Lover of Truth

Prince John
See Beauregard, Pierre Gustave Toutant

Prince John
See Hunt, John

Prince John
See Van Buren, John

Prince, John Critchley 19th c. [SN]
British poet
* [The] Bard of Hyde

Prince, John Tucker 19th c. [HPPN]
American author
* Syphax

Prince Kuroki
See Brezinski, Max Frederick

Prince Leonard
See Casley, Leonard

Prince, Nathan 1698-1748 [HPPN]
American scholar and clergyman
* [A] Fellow of Harvard College

[The] Prince of Accompanists
See Harty, [Sir] Hamilton

[The] Prince of Alchemy
See Rudolf II [or Rudolph]

[The] Prince of America
See Todd, John Payne

[The] Prince of American Letters
See Irving, Washington

[The] Prince of Ancient Comedy
See Aristophanes

[The] Prince of Artists
See Duerer, Albrecht [or Albert]

[The] **Prince of Beaux**
See Brummel, George Bryan

[The] **Prince of Beggars**
See Greene, Robert

[The] **Prince of Bible Commentators**
See Solomon bar Isaac

[The] **Prince of Bibliomaniacal Writers**
See Dibdin, Thomas Frognall

Prince of Biographers
See Boswell, James

[The] **Prince of Bohemian Artists**
See Mengs, Anton Rafael

[The] **Prince of Boodlers**
See Powers, John

[The] **Prince of Broadway**
See Cohan, George Michael

[The] **Prince of Buccaneers**
See Drake, [Sir] Francis

[The] **Prince of Car Thieves**
See Goldbaum, Michael

[The] **Prince of Caricaturists**
See Cruikshank, George

[The] **Prince of Castilian Poets**
See Garcilaso de la Vega

[The] **Prince of Centres**
See Wagstaff, Harold

[The] **Prince of Chitchat**
See Carson, John William [Johnny]

[The] **Prince of Cookery**
See Snowden, John

[The] **Prince of Coxcombs**
See Ligne, Charles Joseph

[The] **Prince of Critics**
See Aristarchus

[The] **Prince of Critics**
See Longinus, Dionysius Cassius

[The] **Prince of Dandies**
See Brummel, George Bryan

[The] **Prince of Dandies**
See Lewis, Matthew Gregory

[The] **Prince of Darkness**
See Barend, John

[The] **Prince of Darkness**
See Carson, John William [Johnny]

[The] **Prince of Darkness**
See Firbank, Louis

[The] **Prince of Darkness**
See Novak, Robert

[The] **Prince of Darkness**
See Van Rijn [or Ryn], Rembrandt Harmensz [or Harmenszoon]

[That] **Prince of Demagogues**
See Orr, James Lawrence

[The] **Prince of Destruction**
See Timur [or Timour]

[The] **Prince of Diplomatists**
See Talleyrand-Perigord, Charles Maurice de

[The] **Prince of Dribblers**
See Matthews, Stanley

[The] **Prince of Egypt**
See Moses

[The] **Prince of Erie**
See Fisk, James, Jr.

[The] **Prince of Flatworkers**
See Burke, William

[The] **Prince of Fools**
See Angoulevant

[The] **Prince of Forgers**
See Taylor, S. Allan

[The] **Prince of Gossips**
See Pepys, Samuel

[The] **Prince of Gourmets**
See Brillat-Savarin, Anthelme

[The] **Prince of Grammarians**
See Apollonius of Alexandria

[The] **Prince of Grammarians**
See Aristarchus

[The] **Prince of Hebrew Grammarians**
See Chajug, Jehuda

[The] **Prince of High Tobymen**
See Christie, Francis

[The] **Prince of Historians**
See Herrera, Antonio de

[The] **Prince of Homburg**
See Frederick II [Landgrave of Hesse-Homburg]

Prince of Humbugs
See Barnum, Phineas Taylor

[The] **Prince of Humorists**
See Clemens, Samuel Langhorne

[The] **Prince of Hypocrites**
See Nero Caesar, Tiberius Claudius

[The] **Prince of Interviewers**
See Senior, Nassau William

[The] **Prince of Italian Poets**
See Petracco, Francesco

[The] **Prince of Journalists**
See Greeley, Horace

[The] **Prince of Knickerbocker**
See Knickerbocker, Herman

[The] **Prince of Lawlessness**
See Quantrill, William Clarke

[The] **Prince of Letters**
See Saumaise, Claude

[The] **Prince of Liars**
See Mendez Pinto, Ferdinand

[The] **Prince of Light**
See Edison, Thomas Alva

[The] **Prince of Light**
See Jesus Christ

[The] **Prince of Literature**
See Han Yu

[The] **Prince of Losers**
See Cook, Frederick Albert

[The] **Prince of Lyric Poets**
See Duperier, Charles

[The] **Prince of Lyric Poets**
See Gongora y Argote, Luis de

[The] **Prince of Lyric Poets**
See Pindar

[The] **Prince of Lyrical Roman Poets**
See Horatius Flaccus, Quintus

[The] **Prince of Macaronies**
See Bussy, George [Fourth Earl of Jersey]

[The] **Prince of Mail Contractors**
See Reeside, James

[The] **Prince of Merchants**
See Stewart, Alexander Turner

[The] **Prince of Motown**
See Gaye, Marvin [Pentz]

[The] **Prince of Music**
See Palestrina, Giovanni Pierluigida

[The] **Prince of Neck-or-Nothing Novelists**
See Lever, Charles James

[The] **Prince of Negro Songwriters**
See Bland, James A.

[The] **Prince of New Comedy**
See Menander

[The] **Prince of Novelists**
See Fielding, Henry

[The] **Prince of Observers**
See Mueller, Fritz

[The] **Prince of Orators**
See Demosthenes

[The] **Prince of Painters**
See Apelles

[The] **Prince of Painters**
See Parrhasius

[The] **Prince of Palimony**
See Mitchelson, Marvin

[The] **Prince of Paragraphists**
See Greeley, Horace

[The] **Prince of Parliamentarians**
See Mell, Patrick Hues

[The] **Prince of Peace**
See Carnegie, Andrew

Prince of Peace
See Jesus Christ

[The] **Prince of Peace**
See King, Michael Luther, Jr.

[The] **Prince of Peace**
See Maximilian II

[The] **Prince of Pedagogues**
See Maginn, William

[The] **Prince of Philosophers**
See Aristocles

[The] **Prince of Physicians**
See Avicenna [or Abou-ibn-Sina]

[The] **Prince of Pistoleers**
See Hickok, James Butler

[The] **Prince of Players**
See Booth, Edwin Thomas

[The] **Prince of Players**
See Forrest, Edwin

[The] **Prince of Poets**
See Goethe, Johann Wolfgang von

[The] **Prince of Poets**
See Homer

[The] **Prince of Poets**
See Milton, John

[The] **Prince of Poets**
See Spenser, Edmund

[The] **Prince of Poets**
See Vergilius Maro, Publius

[The] **Prince of Poets in His Time**
See Spenser, Edmund

[The] **Prince of Politicians**
See Machiavelli, Niccolo [or Nicholas]

[The] **Prince of Portrait Engravers**
See Lignon, Etienne Frederic

[The] **Prince of Poyais**
See McGregor, Gregor

[The] **Prince of Priests**
See Henry V

[The] **Prince of Princes**
See George IV

[The] **Prince of Princes**
See Jesus Christ

[The] **Prince of Proconsuls**
See Lyautey, Louis Hubert Gonzalve

[The] **Prince of Publishers**
See Tonson, Jacob

[The] **Prince of Puke**
See Waters, John

[The] **Prince of Quacks**
See Balsamo, Giuseppe

[The] **Prince of Quarrellers**
See Caron, Pierre Augustin

[The] **Prince of Red-Nosed Comedians**
See Simmons, James

[The] **Prince of Restaurateurs**
See Rector, George

[The] **Prince of Roman Poets**
See Vergilius Maro, Publius

[The] **Prince of Sacred Bards**
See Homer

[The] **Prince of Satirists**
See Sachs, Hans

[The] **Prince of Sceptics**
See Hume, David

[The] **Prince of Schaghticoke**
See Knickerbocker, Herman

Prince of Scholastics
See Aquinas, Thomas [Thomas of Aquino]

[The] **Prince of Science**
See Tehuhe

[The] **Prince of Scoffers**
See Arouet, Francois Marie

[The] **Prince of Scum**
See Flynt, Larry

[The] **Prince of Showmen**
See Barnum, Phineas Taylor

[The] **Prince of Silesian Poets**
See Greif [Griphius or Gryphius], Andreas

[The] **Prince of Sophisticated Pornography**
See Hefner, Hugh Marston

[The] **Prince of Spanish Poetry**
See Vega, Garcilasso de la

[The] **Prince of Stinkers**
See Bartlett, George

[The] **Prince of Story-Tellers**
See Boccaccio, Giovanni

[The] **Prince of Storytellers**
See Oppenheim, E[dward] Phillips

[The] **Prince of the Air**
See Weiss, Ehrich

[The] **Prince of the American Theater**
See Cohan, George Michael

Prince of the Apostles
See Medici, Giovanni de

[The] **Prince of the Apostles**
See Simon

[The] **Prince of the Humanists**
See Gerhards, Gerhard [or Geert]

[The] **Prince of the New Pharisees**
See Gaetano [or Caetani], Benedetto

[The] **Prince of the Ode**
See Ronsard, Pierre de

Prince of the Oyster Pirates
See London, John Griffith [Jack]

[The] **Prince of the Peace**
See Godoy, Manuel de

[The] **Prince of the Piano-Forte**
See Gottschalk, Louis Moreau

[The] **Prince of the Rails**
See Lincoln, Robert Todd

[The] **Prince of the Sonnet**
See Bellay, Joachim du

[The] **Prince of the Sonnet**
See Petracco, Francesco

[The] **Prince of the Youth**
See Gonzalvo di Cordova, Hernandez

[The] **Prince of Thieves**
See Manolesco, George

Prince of Viana
See Charles IV

[The] **Prince of Wails**
See Carson, John William [Johnny]

[The] **Prince of Wails**
See Ray, John Alvin [Johnny]

[The] **Prince of Wails**
See William

[The] **Prince of Wales**
See Arthur, Chester Alan

[The] **Prince of Wicket-Keepers**
See Blackham, John McCarthy

[The] **Prince of Wit and Wisdom**
See Rogers, Will[iam Penn Adair]

[The] **Prince of Wits**
See Stanhope, Philip Dormer

Prince Ramiro
See Richard III

[The] **Prince Robber**
See Rupert

[The] **Prince Rupert of the Confederacy**
See Stuart, James Ewell Brown

[The] **Prince, the King, the Emperor of Quavers**
See Hawkins, [Sir] John

Prince, Thomas 1687-1758 [HPPN]
American clergyman and historian
* Her Father

Prince Tyrone
See English, Perry Tyrone, Jr.

Princefish
See Long, Russell Billiu

Princely Surrey
See Howard, Henry [Earl of Surrey]

Princeps Nominalium
See Occam [or Ockham], William of

Princeps Theologorum
See Aegidius [or Giles] of Colonna

[The] **Princess**
See Miller, Ruth Elizabeth [McCormick]

[The] **Princess**
See Winnemucca, Sarah

Princess Alice
See Longworth, Alice Lee Roosevelt

[The] **Princess of Ahlden**
See Sophia Dorothea

[The] **Princess of Black Poetry**
See Giovanni, Yolande Cornelia, Jr.

[The] Princess of Connemara
See Martin, Mary Letitia

[The] Princess of Situation Comedy
See Jacobs, Margaret

[The] Princess of the Blues
See Brown, Olive

Princess of the Press
See Barnett, Ida Baker Wells

[The] Princess of Wows
See Diana [Frances]

Princess Olive
See Serres, Olivia Wilmot

Princess, Patricia
See Richard, Ann B.

Princeton Charlie Reilly
See Reilly, Charles Thomas

[The] Principal Actor in the Watergate Coverup
See Dean, John, III

Principe de la Paz
See Godoy, Manuel de

Principe del Toreo [Prince of Bullfighting]
See Leal Kuri, Alfredo

Principiis Obsta
See Adams, Samuel

Pring-Mill, Robert D[uguid] F[orrest] 1924- [CA]
British educator and author
* Duguid, Robert

Pringle, Aileen
See Bisbee, Aileen

Pringle, Elizabeth Waties [Allston] 1845-1921 [DNA]
Author and historian
* Pennington, Patience

Pringle, John 1895?-1936 [BDF, BEW, F1, HPPN]
American actor
* Gilbert, John
* [The] Great Lover
* [The] Screen's Perfect Lover

Pringle, Laurence P. 1935- [CA, SAT]
American author, editor, photographer
* Edmund, Sean

Pringle, Thomas 1789-1834 [SN]
Scottish poet
* [The] Lamb

Pringle-Pattison, Andrew
See Seth, Andrew

Prinny
See George IV

Prins, Co
See Prins, Jacob

Prins, Jacob 1938- [AES]
Dutch soccer player
* Prins, Co

Printemps, Yvonne
See Wigniolle, Yvonne

[The] Printer's Devil
See Peirce, Thomas

Prior, Harry
See Knightley, D. G.

Prior, James
See Kirk, James Prior

Prior, Lulu
See De Nyse, Mrs. Edward

Prior, Matt[hew] 1664-1721 [HPPN, NPS, SN]
British poet and diplomat
* Plenipo, Rummer
* Rummer, Matt
* [The] Solomon of Bards
* [The] State Proteus

Prior, Samuel
See Galt, John

Priscian
See Hawtrey, Edward Craven

Priscianus
See Bentley, Richard

Priscilla
See Wakefield, Priscilla [Bell]

Prism, Brother
See Mathews, Charles

[The] Prison Playwright
See Brown, Rhozier Theopelius

[The] Prison Reformer
See Howard, John

[The] Prisoner of Chillon
See Bonnivard, Francois de

[The] Prisoner of Glatz
See Trenck, [Baron] Friedrich von der

[The] Prisoner of Ham
See Bonaparte, Charles Louis Napoleon

[The] Prisoner of Spandau
See Hess, Rudolf

[The] Prisoner of the Vatican
See Mastai-Ferretti, Giovanni Maria

[A] Prisoner of War
See Ely, Alfred

[A] Prisoner of War
See Erskine, C. M.

[The] Prisoner's Friend
See Beal, Abraham

[The] Prisoner's Friend
See Gilbert, Linda

Pritchard, Abisha 20th c. [EF]
American football player
* Pritchard, Bosh

Pritchard, Bosh
See Pritchard, Abisha

Pritchard, Buddy
See Pritchard, Harold William

Pritchard, Hannah 1711-1768 [HPPN]
British actress
* Vaughan, Miss

Pritchard, Harold William 1936- [BE]
American baseball player
* Pritchard, Buddy

Pritchard, John Laurence 1885- [WW]
Author
* Laurence, John

Pritchard, John Wallace 1912- [CA, ESF, SFL]
American author and psychologist
* Wallace, Ian

Pritchard, Marion 19th c. [HPPN]
British author
* A. M. Y.
* Amy

Pritchard, Martin J.
See Moore, Justina

Pritchard, Norman 1877-1929 [THR]
British actor
* Trevor, Norman

Pritchard, William Thomas 1909- [ESF, SFL, WGT]
British author
* Dexter, William

Pritchett, Florence
See Welles, Barbara

Pritchett, V. S.
See Pritchett, Victor Sawdon

Pritchett, Victor Sawdon 1900- [IPA, LC]
British author and critic
* Pritchett, V. S.

Pritkin, Ron 1920- [ASC]
American entertainer
* Terry, Ron

Private
See De Costa, Benjamin Franklin

[A] Private Detective
See Rathborne, St. George Henry

Private Eddie Fisher
See Fisher, Edwin Jack [Eddie]

[A] Private Gentleman
See Allan, Thomas

[A] Private Gentleman
See Wightman, O. G. R.

Private John
See Allen, John Mills

Private 19022
See Manning, Frederic

[A] Private of the 38th Artists' and Member of the Alpine Club
See Barrow, John

[A] Private Person
See Sharp, Granville

[A] Private Soldier
See Blessington, J. P.

[A] Private Soldier
See McElroy, John

Privateer
See Foster, Charles J.

Privett, Booger Red
See Privett, Sam

Privett, Sam 1858-1926 [GW]
American rodeo performer
* Privett, Booger Red

Privileged Lunatic
See Shaw, George Bernard

Priyamvada, Usha
See Nilsson, Usha Saksena

Pro Football, Mr.
See Halas, George Stanley

Pro Football's Most Controversial Coach
See Allen, George

Pro Golf's Beau Brummel
See Sanders, Doug[las]

Pro, [Father] Michael
See Pro Juarez, Miguel Augustin

Pro Juarez, Miguel Augustin 1893-1927
[HPPN]
Mexican clergyman and martyr
* God's Jester
* Pro, [Father] Michael

[A] Probationer of the Church of
Scotland
See Rae, William

Problematick, Jonathan
See Foe, Daniel

Probst, Colonel
See Probst, Otto

Probst, Nicholas David 1935- [BEW]
American actor
* Pryor, Nicholas

Probst, Otto 1889- [GF]
American collector of golf memorabilia
* Probst, Colonel

Probus
See Child, David Lee

Probus
See Drury, Joseph

Proby, P. J.
See Smith, James Marcus

Probyn, Elise
See McKibbon, J. E.

Probyn, John E.
See McKibbon, J. E.

Proceviat, Pro
See Proceviat, Richard Peter

Proceviat, Richard Peter 1946- [SMG]
Canadian-born hockey player
* Proceviat, Pro

Proclus 410-485 [RH]
Greek philosopher
* Thaumaturgus

Procop ?-1434 [WBD]
Hussite leader
* [The] Little

Procop [or Procopius], Andrew
1380?-1434 [DNNS, WBD]
Hussite leader
* [The] Great

Procope-Couteau, Michael 1684-1753
[PA]
Author
* Colteli

Procopio, Mariellen
See Grutz, Mariellen Procopio

[The] Procopius of France
See Siri, Victor

Procter, Adelaide Anne 1825-1864
[WBD]
British poet
* Berwick, Mary

Procter, Bryan Waller 1787-1874 [FFF,
HPPN, NPS, PA, SN]
British poet
* Cornwall, Baby
* Cornwall, Barry
* J. B.
* Jessamine, James
* [A] Moral Byron

Procter, Michael John 1946- [DC]
South African-born cricketer
* Procter, Prock

Procter, Prock
See Procter, Michael John

Proctor, Cub
See Proctor, James

Proctor, Edna Dean 1829-1923 [HPPN]
American poet and author
* One of His Congregation

Proctor, Everitt
See Montgomery, Rutherford George

Proctor, Ezekiel 1831-1907 [BI]
American Indian leader
* Proctor, Zeke

Proctor, Harley T. 1834-1907 [HPPN]
American soap industry pioneer
* [The] Father of Ivory Soap
* [The] Father of the Soap Industry

Proctor, Henry Hugh 1868-1933
[HPPN]
American clergyman
* [The] Father of Organized Alumni
Work at Fisk University

Proctor, James 20th c. [OBW]
American baseball player
* Proctor, Cub

Proctor, Mary 20th c. [HPPN, LAO]
Irish-born author
* [The] Lady of the Stars
* [The] Little Lady of the Stars

Proctor, Miller
See Huggins, Miller James

Proctor, Noah Richard 1900-1967 [BE]
American baseball player
* Proctor, Red

Proctor, Paul
See Samways, George Richmond

Proctor, Red
See Proctor, Noah Richard

Proctor, Richard A. 1837-1888 [FFF]
British author
* Five of Clubs

Proctor, Richard Wright 1816-1881
[HPPN]
British author
* Sylvan

Proctor, William 1872-1951 [HPPN]
American manufacturer and entomologist
* [The] Ivory Soap King

Proctor, Zeke
See Proctor, Ezekiel

Procureur de la Lanterne
See Desmoulins, [Lucie Simplice]
Camille [Benoit]

Prodgers, George 1892- [CEI, FHE]
Canadian-born hockey player
* Prodgers, Goldie

Prodgers, Goldie
See Prodgers, George

[The] Prodigal
See Albert VI

[The] Prodigious Spender
See Johnson, Lyndon Baines

[The] Prodigy at Thirteen
See Gampel, Lillit

[The] Prodigy of France
See Bude, Guillaume

[The] Prodigy of Learning
See Hahnemann, [Christian Friedrich]
Samuel

[A] Prodigy of Literary Curiosity
See Oldys, William

Prodpen, Pat
See Elliott, James

[The] Prof
See Blood, Ernest A.

[The] Prof
See Lindemann, Frederick Alexander

[The] Professional Troublemaker
See Hoffman, Abbott [Abbie]

[The] Professor
See Atkinson, Theodore Francis [Ted]

[The] Professor
See Cavill, Fred

[The] Professor
See Colonna, Gerard

[The] Professor
See Crandall, Milton

[A] Professor
See Gwilliam, John

Professor
See Leigh, Percival

Professor
See Pepper, J. H.

[The] Professor
See Poague, William Robert

[The] Professor
See Scarne, John

[The] Professor
See Scott, Benny

Professor
See Sityana, Alfred Mama Sikhefu

[The] Professor
See Smith, Oliver Prince

[The] Professor
See Verner, David

[The] Professor
See Whaling, Thornton

[The] Professor
See Wilson, [Thomas] Woodrow

[The] Professor
See Woodcock, Leonard

[The] Professor at the Breakfast Table
See Holmes, Oliver Wendell

[The] Professor of Botany
See Daubeny, Charles Giles Bridle

[The] Professor of Chess
See Sarratt, J. H.

[The] Professor of Dead and Living
Languages
See Holmes, Oliver Wendell

Professor of Legerdemain
See Potter, Richard

[A] Professor of Surgery
See Justamond, John Obadiah

Professor P.
See Pole, William

Professor X
See Boorstin, Daniel Joseph

Professor X
See Faulk, Odie B.

Proffitt, Josephine Moore 1914-1967
[ASC, BI]
American composer and author
* Dee, Sylvia

Profit and Loss
See Baker, James Loring

Profitabilis, Doctor
See Bonet, Nicholas

[The] Profound Doctor
See Bradwardine, Thomas

[The] Profound Doctor
See Middleton, Richard

Profumo, John 1915- [HPPN]
British politician
* [The] Head Waiter

Profundissimus, Doctor
See Aegidius [or Giles] of Colonna

Profundus, Doctor
See Bradwardine, Thomas

Profundus, Doctor
See Jacobus de Ascoli

Profundus, Doctor
See Middleton, Richard

Prog
See Scott, Thomas J.

Prognostes
See Fosco, Placide

[The] Prohibition Portia
See Willebrandt, Mabel Walker

[The] Projector
See Law, John

Prole, Lozania [joint pseudonym with
Charles Eade]
See Bloom, Ursula [Harvey]

Prole, Lozania [joint pseudonym with
Ursula (Harvey) Bloom]
See Eade, Charles

Prolix, Peregrine
See Nicklin, Philip Holbrook

[The] Prolocutor
See Stanhope, George

Prometheus
See Bush, William

Prometheus
See Steimer, Francis Alfred

[A] Prominent London Journalist
See Hill, Frank Harrison

Promitis, Mary 20th c. [HPPN]
American marathon dancer
* Hercules Mary

Promotion in the Church
See Angus, William

Pronzini, Bill 1943- [CA, TCCM]
American author
* Foxx, Jack
* Jeffrey, William
* Saxon, Alex

Proper, Adolph 1886?-1950 [BEW]
Austrian-born clown
* Robins, Adolph

[The] Proper Iconoclast
See Manet, Edouard

[The] Prophet
See Brothers, Richard

[The] Prophet
See Joachim

[The] Prophet
See Klimek, Tillie

[The] Prophet
See Lalawethika

[The] Prophet
See Mohammed [or Mahomet]

[The] Prophet
See Stephen of Cloyes

[The] Prophet Against Empire
See Blake, William

[The] Prophet and Martyr of
Democracy
See Paine, Thomas

[The] Prophet Daniel
See Foe, Daniel

[The] Prophet James
See Buck, James Smith

Prophet Joshua
See Creffeld, Edmund Franz

[The] Prophet of America
See Emerson, Ralph Waldo

Prophet of Light
See Monet, Claude

[The] Prophet of Romanticism
See Hardenberg, Friedrich von

[The] Prophet of San Francisco
See George, Henry

Prophet of the Midlands
See Lawrence, David Herbert

[The] Prophet of the Northwest
See Riel, Louis David

[The] Prophet of the Revolution
See Henry, Patrick

[The] Prophet of the Syrians
See Ephraem

[The] Prophet of the Syrians
See Philippi [or Philippson?]

[The] Prophet of the Syrians
See Syrus, Ephraem

[The] Prophetess
See Ayesha [or Ayeshah]

[The] Prophetess of Exeter
See Southcott, Joanna

Propolis Pete
See Wirth, Ed D.

[The] Proponent of Chance Results
See Feller, William

[The] Proponent of Isostasy
See Dutton, Clarence E.

[The] Proponent of the Huttonian
Theory
See Playfair, John

[A] Proprietor of India Stock
See Buckingham, James Silk

Proschko, Hermine Camille 19th c.
[HPPN]
German author
* Wittendorf, C.

[A] **Prose Ariosto**
See Bandello, Matteo [or Matthew]

[The] **Prose Burns of Ireland**
See Carleton, William

[The] **Prose Homer of Human Nature**
See Fielding, Henry

[The] **Prose Homer of the Great Ocean**
See Russell, William Clark

[The] **Proselyte**
See Onkelos

[The] **Prosk**
See Proski, Joe

Proski, Joe 1939- [SMG]
American basketball trainer
* [The] Prosk

Prosner, G. W.   [PA]
Author
* Z.

[The] **Prospector**
See Winkler, George E.

Prosper, John [joint pseudonym with
John C(hipman) Farrar]
See Buranelli, Prosper

Prosper, John [joint pseudonym with
Prosper Buranelli]
See Farrar, John C[hipman]

Prosper, Lincoln
See Cannon, Helen

[The] **Prosper Marchand of English
Literature**
See Nichols, John

Prosper of Aquitaine 5th c. [WBD]
Author
* Prosper Tiro

Prosper Tiro
See Prosper of Aquitaine

Prosperi, Francesco 20th c. [WF]
Director
* Shannon, Frank

Prosperity's Advance Agent
See McKinley, William

Prospero
See Douce, Francis

Prospero
See West, Tristram Frederick

Prospero and Caliban [joint pseudonym
with Frederick William Serafino Austin
Rolfe]
See Pirie-Gordon, Charles Harry
Clinton

Prospero and Caliban [joint pseudonym
with Charles Harry Clinton Pirie-
Gordon]
See Rolfe, Frederick William [Serafino
Austin Lewis Mary]

Proster, Adolph 1886-1950 [HPPN]
American actor
* Robins, A.

Prota Matija
See Nenadovic, Matija

[The] **Protagonist**
See Shakespeare, William

[A] **Protectionist**
See Elliot, John Lettsom

[The] **Protector**
See Cromwell, Oliver

[The] **Protector**
See Humphrey [Duke of Gloucester
and Earl of Pembroke]

[The] **Protector**
See Marshal, William

[The] **Protector**
See Richard III

[The] **Protector**
See Seymour, Edward

Protector and Defender of the Kingdom
See John of Lancaster

Protector of Mexico
See Norton, Joshua A.

[The] **Protector of Peru**
See San Martin, Jose de

Protector of the Indians
See Las Casas, Bartolome de

[The] **Protector of the Wilds**
See Muir, John

Protero, Dodi
See McIlraith, Dorothy Ann

Protesilaus
See Letellier, Francois Michel [Marquis
de Louvois]

[A] **Protestant**
See Billingsley, [Rev.] John

[A] **Protestant**
See McLean, Alexander

[A] **Protestant**
See Twort, Charles William

[A] **Protestant**
See Urquhart, David

[A] **Protestant**
See Wilson, David

[A] **Protestant Churchman**
See Ballard, J.

[A] **Protestant Clergyman**
See Wyatt-Edgell, [Rev.] Edgell

[A] **Protestant Dissenter**
See Bourn, Samuel

[A] **Protestant Dissenter**
See Christie, William

[A] **Protestant Dissenter**
See Gamble, John

[A] **Protestant Dissenter, a Friend to
Truth, Peace, and Liberty**
See Sladen, John

[The] **Protestant Duke**
See Scott, James

[A] **Protestant Episcopalian**
See Jay, William

[The] **Protestant Hero**
See Frederick II

[The] **Protestant Joiner**
See Colledge

[The] **Protestant Joiner**
See College, Stephen

[A] **Protestant Lady**
See Adams, Ann

[The] **Protestant Livy**
See Philippi [or Philippson?]

[The] **Protestant Martyr**
See Godfrey, [Sir] Edmundbury

[A] **Protestant Member of the
University of Oxford**
See Giles, John Allen

Protestant Neutrality
See Foe, Daniel

[A] **Protestant Nonconformist**
See Ash, Edward

[The] **Protestant Pope**
See Corsini, Lorenzo

[The] **Protestant Pope**
See Ganganelli, Giovanni Vincenzo
Antonio

[The] **Protestant Rector of Tixall,
Stafford**
See Webb, William

[A] **Protestant Watchman**
See Richardson, James

[The] **Protestant's Mouthpiece**
See Bayer, Johann

[A] **Protesting Catholic**
See Geddes, Alexander

Proteus
See Carvalho, S. S.

[The] **Proteus**
See Foote, Samuel

[A] **Proteus**
See Parsons [or Persons?], Robert

Proteus
See Steinmetz, Karl August Rudolf

[The] **Proteus of Man's Talents**
See Arouet, Francois Marie

[The] **Proteus of the Stage**
See Garrick, David

[The] **Proteus of These Their Talents**
See Arouet, Francois Marie

Prothero, Ron 20th c.
American scoutmaster and poet
* MacKrell, Claude

Protheroe, Cyril 20th c. [SFL]
Author
* Le Page, Rand [house pseudonym, Curtis Warren]

Protheroe, Ernest 20th c. [MBF]
British author
* Henley, P. A.

Prothro, Doc
See Prothro, James Thompson

Prothro, James Thompson 1893-1971 [BE, PB]
American baseball player
* Prothro, Doc

[The] Proto Martyr
See Stephen

[The] Proto Rebel
See Douglas, William

[The] Protomartyr of Britain
See Alban

[The] Protomartyr of the Scottish Reformation
See Hamilton, Patrick

Protovates Angliae
See Whittington [or Whitynton?], Robert

[The] Proud
See Albert I [or Albrecht]

[The] Proud
See Henry X

[The] Proud
See Otto IV [or Otho]

[The] Proud
See Tarquin II [or Tarquinius]

[The] Proud African
See Hall, Ian

[The] Proud Duke of Somerset
See Seymour, Charles [Sixth Duke of Somerset]

Proud, Miss
See Adams, Louisa Catherine Johnson

[The] Proudest Boast of the Caledonian Muse
See Scott, [Sir] Walter

[The] Proudest of the Proud
See Wedderburn, Alexander [First Baron Loughborough]

Proudfit, David L. [FFF, PA]
American author
* Arkwright, Peleg

Proudfit, Fairfax 1887- [BEW]
American educator, costume designer, writer
* Walkup, Fairfax Proudfit

Proudfoot, Walter
See Vahey, John George Haslette

Proudman, M. Eyre
See Lovely, Maureen Patey

Prough, Bill
See Prough, H. Clinton

Prough, H. Clinton 1888- [BE]
American baseball player
* Prough, Bill

Prout, Father
See Mahony, Francis Sylvester

Prout, G. Clifford
See Zuckerman, Buck Henry

Prout, Geoffrey 1894-? [MBF]
British author
* Spencer, Roland [joint pseudonym with Francis Alister Warwick]
* Valentine, Henry

Prouting, Frederick James [FFF]
British writer and editor
* Brown, Vandyke
* Verite sans Peur

Provence, Marcel
See Jouhandeau, Marcel Henri

Provenzano, Anthony 1917-
American underworld figure
* Provenzano, Tony Pro

Provenzano, Tony Pro
See Provenzano, Anthony

Providence [Secret Service code name]
See Eisenhower, David Dwight

[A] Provincial
See Godfrey, L. M.

Provine, Dutchy
See Provine, John William

Provine, John William 1866-1942 [HPPN]
American educator
* Provine, Dutchy

[The] Provisional Bishop
See Potter, Horatio

[The] Provisionals' Unknown Leader
See Twomey, Seamus

Prowler, Harley
See Masters, Edgar Lee

Prowse, R. O.
See Prowse, Richard Orton

Prowse, Richard Orton 1862-1949 [LC]
British author
* Prowse, R. O.

Proxmire, [Edward] William 1915- [CR]
American politician
* Billion Dollar Bill

[The] Proxy Fighter by Proxy
See Kirby, Allan Price

Prudden, Bonnie 1914?- [HPPN]
American physical culturist
* [The] Lady With Muscle

Prude, Agnes George 1905- [CA]
American choreographer, director, dancer, author
* De Mille, Agnes

Prudence Penny
See Malek, Leona [Alford]

Prudence Penny
See Young, Norma

Prudential
See Foe, Daniel

Prudentius, Aurelius Clemens 348-410? [DEP, SN]
Spanish poet
* [The] Virgil and Horace of the Christians

Prudhomme, Augie
See Prudhomme, John Olgus

Prudhomme, Don 20th c.
American auto racer
* [The] Snake

Prud'homme, George 1901-1972 [FIR, SC]
American actor and opera singer
* Pembroke, George

Prudhomme, John Olgus 1902- [BE]
American baseball player
* Prudhomme, Augie

Prudhomme, Rene Francois Armand 1839-1907 [CD]
French poet
* Sully-Prudhomme

Prudhon, Pierre-Paul
See Prudon, Pierre

Prudon, Pierre 1758-1823 [WBD]
French painter
* Prudhon, Pierre-Paul

Pruess, Earl Henry 1895- [BE]
American baseball player
* Pruess, Gibby

Pruess, Gibby
See Pruess, Earl Henry

Pruett, Gene 20th c. [GW]
American rodeo performer
* Pruett, Stiffy

Pruett, Hub
See Pruett, Hubert Shelby

Pruett, Hubert Shelby 1900- [BE, PB]
American baseball player
* Pruett, Hub
* Pruett, Shucks

Pruett, Shucks
See Pruett, Hubert Shelby

Pruett, Stiffy
See Pruett, Gene

Pruiett, Charles LeRoy 1883-1953 [BE]
American baseball player
* Pruiett, Tex

Pruiett, Tex
See Pruiett, Charles LeRoy

Pruitt, Alan
See Rose, Alvin Emanuel

Pruning Knife
See Allen, Henry Francis

Prus, Boleslaw
See Glowacki, Aleksander

Prusias I 3rd c. BC [WBD]
King of Bithynia
* [The] Lame

Prusias II 2nd c. BC [WBD]
King of Bithynia
* [The] Horseman

[The] Prussian Boot
See Bismarck, Otto Eduard Leopold von

[The] Prussian Leprechaun
See Leahy, Francis William [Frank]

[The] Prussian Pindar
See Willamow, Johann Gottlieb

Prussia's Uncrowned King
See Heydebrand Und Der Lasa, Ernst von

Prussing, M. Jean
See Burden, Jean

Prut, Constantin
See Ionescu, Constantin

Prutkov, Kozma
See Snodgrass, William DeWitt

Prutkov, Kozma [joint pseudonym with Vladimir Mikhailovich Zhemchuzhnikov]
See Zhemchuzhnikov, Aleksiei Mikhailovich

Prutkov, Kozma [joint pseudonym with Aleksiei Mikhailovich Zhemchuzhnikov]
See Zhemchuzhnikov, Vladimir Mikhailovich

Pry, Paul
See Byng, Frederick

Pry, Paul
See Hill, Thomas

Pry, Polly
See O'Bryan, Leonel [Campbell]

Pry, Solomon
See Fox, [Rev.] Thomas Bayley

Pryatel, Frank 1906?-1982 [FIR]
Radio personality
* Friend, Jimmy

Pryde, Anthony
See Weekes, Agnes Russell

Pryde, James Ferrier 1866-1941 [DBA]
British painter, lithographer, poster designer
* Beggarstaff, J.

Pryde, Peggy
See Woodley, Letitia Matilda

Pryer, Pauline
See Roby, Mary Linn

Prynne, Arthur
See Munsell, Joel

Prynne, Marginal
See Prynne, William

[The] Prynne of His Day
See Stubbs, Philip

Prynne, Voluminous
See Prynne, William

Prynne, William 1600-1669 [HPPN, NPS, RH, SN]
British pamphleteer
* [The] Brave Jersey Muse
* [The] Cato of the Age
* [The] Homer of the Isle
* Huntley, William
* Prynne, Marginal
* Prynne, Voluminous
* S. L.
* White, Matthew
* William the Conqueror

Prynne, William
See Butler, Samuel

Pryor, Aaron 20th c.
American boxer
* [The] Hawk

Pryor, Adel
See Wasserfall, Adel

Pryor, Bubba
See Pryor, James Edward

Pryor, Calvin Caffey 1928- [BA]
American attorney
* Pryor, Shag

Pryor, Jacqueline
See Williamson, Connie

Pryor, James Edward 1921- [BWW]
American singer
* Pryor, Bubba
* Pryor, Snooky

Pryor, Martha
See Waters, Ethel

Pryor, Nicholas
See Probst, Nicholas David

Pryor, Paul
See Taggard, E. T.

Pryor, Robert Stone
See Holland, Cecelia

Pryor, Roger 1901-1974 [HPPN]
American actor, musician, producer
* [The] Entertainment Jack of All Trades

Pryor, Shag
See Pryor, Calvin Caffey

Pryor, Snooky
See Pryor, James Edward

Prys Williams, Nerys Mair Sioned 1913- [DBA]
British painter and potter
* Nerys

Pryse, Hugh
See Pryse, John Hwfa

Pryse, John Hwfa 1910-1955 [BEW]
British-born actor
* Pryse, Hugh

Prysock, Arthur 1925- [IBW]
American singer
* Mr. P.

Pryzchodzien, Zdzislaw 20th c. [TI 10-31-83]
Polish intelligence agent
* [The] Minister [code name]

Przesmycki, Zenon 1861-1944 [WBD]
Polish editor and poet
* Miriam

Przybyszewski, Stanislaw 1868-1927 [MWD]
Polish editor, author, playwright
* [The] Founder of Polish Modernism

Przyjaciel
See Nowaczynski, Adolf

[The] Psalmsinger
See Adams, Samuel

Psenka, R. Jaromir 1875-? [NAA]
German-born author
* Dore, Gabriel

Pseudo Demetrius
See Demetrius I

[Der] Pseudo Doktor
See Bowers, Cholly

Pseudo Smerdis
See Gaumata

Pseudoman, Akkad
See Northrup, Edwin Fitch

Pseudoplutarch
See Charles I

Psifidis, Billy
See Psifidis, Vasillis

Psifidis, Vasillis 1944- [AES]
Greek soccer player
* Psifidis, Billy

Psigoloog
See Visser, Willem Johannes Conradie

[The] Psychiatrist Poet
See Moore, Merrill

[The] Psychic Engineer
See Jonsson, Olaf

[The] Psycho
See Barend, John

Psycho Ann
See Barrows, [Ruth] Marjorie

[The] Psychopath
See Oswald, Lee Harvey

Pteleon
See Grieve, Christopher Murray

Ptolemy 3rd c. BC [RH, WBD]
King of Macedonia
* Keraunos [or Ceraunus]
* [The] Thunderbolt

Ptolemy I 4th c. BC [FFF, HN, SN]
King of Egypt
* [The] Preserver
* Soter

Ptolemy II 3rd c. BC [HN]
King of Egypt
* Philadelphos [Brother-Lover]

Ptolemy III 3rd c. BC [HN, WBD]
King of Egypt
* Euergetes [Benefactor]

Ptolemy IV 3rd c. BC [HN, WBD]
King of Egypt
* Philopator [Father-Lover]

Ptolemy IX [or VIII] 1st c. BC [HN, WBD]
King of Egypt
* Lathyros
* Soter II

Ptolemy V 2nd c. BC [FFF, HN, SN]
King of Egypt
* Epiphanes
* [The] Illustrious

Ptolemy VI 2nd c. BC [WBD]
King of Egypt
* Philometor [Mother-Lover]

Ptolemy VII 2nd c. BC [WBD]
King of Egypt
* Neos Philopator [New Philopator]

Ptolemy VIII [or VII] 2nd c. BC [HN, WBD]
King of Egypt
* Euergetes II
* Physcon [Big-Belly]

Ptolemy X [IX or XI] 1st c. BC [WBD]
King of Egypt
* Alexander I

Ptolemy XI [X or XII] 1st c. BC [WBD]
King of Egypt
* Alexander II

Ptolemy XII [or X] 1st c. BC [HN, WBD]
King of Egypt
* Auletes [Flute Player]
* Philopator Neos Dionysos

Ptolemy XV [XIV or XVI] 1st c. BC [WBD]
Son of Cleopatra, Queen of Egypt
* Cesarion
* Philopator Philometor Caesar

P'u-yi, Henry
See Hsuan T'ung

Public Enemy Number 1
See Dillinger, John Herbert

Public Enemy Number 1
See Gillis, Lester

[The] Public Relations Genius
See Lee, Ivy Ledbetter

[The] Public Relations Pioneer
See Bruno, Henry Augustine

Public Utility, Mr.
See Sporn, Philip

Publicola
See Adams, John Quincy

Publicola
See Fox, William Johnson

Publicola
See Pell, Ferris

Publicola
See Smith, Sydney

Publicola
See Williams, D. E.

Publicola
See Williams, John

Publicus
See Fraleck, Edison Baldwin

Publicus Severus
See Dillon, [Sir] John Joseph

[A] Publisher
See Marston, Edward

[The] Publisher Extraordinary
See Newbery, John

[The] Publisher to the Victorians
See Fields, James Thomas

Publius
See Hamilton, Alexander

Publius
See Jay, John

Publius
See Madison, James

Publius
See Williams, Samuel B.

Publius Ovid
See Marston, John

Puccinelli, Count
See Puccinelli, George Lawrence

Puccinelli, George Lawrence 1906-1956 [BE]
American baseball player
* Puccinelli, Count

[La] Pucelle
See Joan of Arc [or Jeanne d'Arc]

Pucheta [Big Bouquet]
See Munoz, Jose

Puchol, Aurelio 1914-1953 [HPPN]
Spanish bullfighter
* Morenito de Valencia

Puchtik, Yakov Nusan 1944- [CA]
Russian-born American sociologist and author
* Porter, Jack Nusan

Puchungo
See Henriquez, Rafael Americo

Puck
See Ryan, William

[The] Puck of Commentators
See Steevens, George

[The] Puck of Literature
See Walpole, Horatio [Fourth Earl of Orford]

Puckett, Gary 1942- [RO2]
American singer
* Puckett, General

Puckett, General
See Puckett, Gary

Puckett, Lute
See Masters, Edgar Lee

Puddicombe, Anne Adaliza 1850?-1908 [NPS]
Author
* Raine, Allen

Puddler Jim Davis
See Davis, James John

[The] Pueblo Fireman
See Chiariglione, Andrew

Puechner, Ray 1935- [CA, WD]
American author
* Haddo, Oliver
* Tiger, Jack
* Victor, Charles B.

Puente, Ernest, Jr. 1925- [HPPN]
Puerto Rican-American jazz musician
* [The] Mambo Kid
* Puente, Tito

Puente, Ernest, Jr. 1925- [EJ]
American jazz musician
* Puente, Tito

Puente, Tito
See Puente, Ernest, Jr.

Puer, Formose
See Clodfelter, Noah J.

[The] Puerto Rican Pepper Pot
See San Juan, Olga

Pueterschein, Hermann
See Dwiggins, William Addison

Puetz, Ruth-Margret
See Doerkes, Ruth-Margret

Pufendorf, Samuel von 1632-1694 [WBD]
German jurist and historian
* Severinus de Monzambano

Puga, Ricardo [GS]
Spanish bullfighter
* [El] Cateto [The Yokel]

Puget, Pierre 1623-1694 [DNNF, DNNS, FFF, NPS]
French sculptor, painter, architect
* [The] French Michelangelo
* [The] Michael Angelo of France
* [The] Michael Angelo of Sculptors
* [Le] Michel Ange Francais

Pugh
See Pugh, Marshall Morrison

Pugh, Buzz
See Pugh, Jethro, Jr.

Pugh, Eliza Lofton [Phillips] 1841-?
[FFF, PA]
American writer
* Arria

Pugh, Gordon Scott 1909-1969 [BBH]
American lacrosse player and coach
* Pugh, Willie

Pugh, Jethro, Jr. 1944- [SMG]
American football player
* Pugh, Buzz

Pugh, Joe Bennie 1926-1960 [BWW]
American singer
* Forrest City Joe

Pugh, Marshall Morrison 20th c.
[HPPN]
Scottish author
* Pugh

Pugh, Roger 20th c. [MBF]
British author
* Rogers, Ben

Pugh, Willie
See Pugh, Gordon Scott

Pugh, Wynette 1942- [CME, HPPN, WP
9-30-83]
American country-western performer
* [The] First Lady of Country Music
* [The] Heartbreak Heroine of Country
  Music
* Queen Tammy
* Wynette, Tammy

Pughe, William Owen 1759-1835 [WBD]
Welsh antiquarian and lexicographer
* Owen, William

Puig y de la Puente, Francisco
1839-1917 [CW]
Cuban author
* Rosas, Julio

Pujo, Arsene Paulin 1861-1939 [HPPN]
American statesman
* [The] Forerunner of the Federal
  Reserve System

Pujol, Pierre Leon 1867-? [THR]
French playwright
* Flers, P. L.

Pul
See Tilgath-Pilneser

Pulaski, Casimir ?-1779 [DF 10-11-82]
American Revolutionary War hero
* [The] Father of the American Cavalry

Pulaski, Isme Beringer 1883?-1948
[BEW, BI]
American journalist, editor, critic
* Ibee
* Pulaski, Jack

Pulaski, Jack
See Pulaski, Isme Beringer

Pulaski, Leo ?-1937 [HPPN]
American actor
* Hoyt, Leo

Pulcher
See Claudius, Appius

Pulcher
See Claudius, Publius

Puleo, Nicole
See Miller, Nicole Puleo

Pulitzer, Herbert, Jr. 1930?- [TI 10-11-
82]
American publishing heir
* Pulitzer, Peter

Pulitzer, Margaret Leech
See Leech, Margaret

Pulitzer, Peter
See Pulitzer, Herbert, Jr.

Pullein-Thompson, Christine
See Popescu, Christine

Pullein-Thompson, Denis 1919- [LC]
British playwright
* Cannan, Denis

Pullein-Thompson, Diana
See Farr, Diana Pullein-Thompson

Pullein Thompson, Joanna Maxwell
1898-1961
British author
* Cannan, Joanna

Pullen, George Frederick [AW]
British translator
* Culpeper, Martin

Puller, Chesty
See Puller, Lewis B.

Puller, Lewis B. 20th c.
American military officer
* Puller, Chesty

Pulling, Albert Van Siclen 1891- [CA]
American author
* Pulling, Pierre

Pulling, Christopher Robert Druce 1893-
[CAP]
British author
* Druce, Christopher

Pulling, Pierre
See Pulling, Albert Van Siclen

Pullini, Adele Martinetti ?-1932 [HPPN]
American actress
* Martinetti, Adele

Pullman, George Mortimer 1831-1897
[HPPN]
American inventor and industrialist
* [The] Father of the Sleeping Car

Pully, B. S.
See Pully, Bernard Shaw

Pully, Bernard Shaw 1911?-1972 [JF]
American comedian
* Pully, B. S.

Pulos, William Leroy 1920- [IAW]
American psychologist and author
* Anderson, Alfred

[The] Pulpit Buffoon
See Peters [or Peter?], Hugh

[A] Pulpit Physician
See Sacheverell, Henry

Pulsford, Norman George 1902- [WW]
Author
* Trevor, A. C.

Pulsifer, D. 19th c. [PA]
Author
* Midgely, R. L.

Pulteney
See Amhurst, Nicholas

Pulteney, William [Earl of Bath]
1684-1764 [HPPN, IP, SN]
British political leader
* Cato, Marcus
* Curio
* D'Anvers, Caleb, of Gray's Inn
* [A] Member of the House of
  Commons
* [A] Person of Honour
* Squat, Squire
* That Weather Cock
* Trimmer, Will

Pulteney's Toad-Eater
See Vane, [Sir] Henry

Pultz, Adele 1874-1930 [THR]
American actress and singer
* Ritchie, Adele

Pulu
See Tiglath-Pileser III

Pulvertaft, Lalage Isobel 1925- [AW,
WD]
British author
* March, Hilary

[The] Pumper
See Longden, Johnny

Pumpernickel
See Weinstein, Sol

Pumpernickel Bill
See Troxell, William S.

Pumpkin, [Miss] Harriet
See Coutts, Harriet Mellon [Duchess of
St. Albans]

Pun Poan
See Cheng Sen

Punch
See Vassy, Gaston

Punch, Kid
See Miller, Ernest

Punch, Mr.
See Jerrold, Douglas William

Punchinello
See Blunt, Alexander

Punch's Commissioner
See Thackeray, William Makepeace

Puncuss, Pugagee
See McLlelan, George H. H.

Pund, Henry R. 1907- [FB]
American football player
* Peter the Great
* Pund, Peter

Pund, Peter
See Pund, Henry R.

Punderet
See Sanz Almenar

Punever, Peter
See Greenleaf, Lawrence N.

Pungent, Pierce
See Mahony, Francis Sylvester

Pungent, Pierce
See McLennan, J.

Pungent, Pierce
See Powell, Thomas

Puni, Ivan Albert 1892-1956 [CAR]
French painter
* Pougny, Jean

Punjabee
See Arnold, William Delafield

[A] Punk
See Cleopatra

Punnett, Ivar   [CC, WW]
Author
* Simons, Roger [joint pseudonym with
  Margaret Punnett]

Punnett, Margaret   [CC]
Author
* Simons, Roger [joint pseudonym with
  Ivar Punnett]

[El] Puno
See Gonzalez, Jaime

Punteret [Sharpshooter]
See Cecilio y Villanueva, Juan

[A] Pupil of the Late Dr. W. Hunter
See Trusler, John

Pupin, Michael Idvorsky 1858-1935
[HPPN]
*Hungarian-American physicist, author,
inventor*
* [The] Father of the Fluoroscope
* [The] Father of the X-ray Photograph

Pupper, Johann 1400?-1475 [WBD]
German monk and theologian
* Johannes von Goch

Puppet Master
See Kissinger, Henry Alfred

Puracal, John T[homas] 1931- [CA]
Australian economist and author
* Purcal, John T[homas]

Purcal, John T[homas]
See Puracal, John T[homas]

Purcell, Blondie
See Purcell, William Aloysius

Purcell, Estelle
See Fielders, Mrs. Frank M.

Purcell, Henry 1658-1695 [HPPN]
British musician and composer
* [The] Father of Anglican Church
  Music

Purcell, [Rev.] Henry 18th c. [HPPN]
American clergyman
* [A] Member of the Protestant
  Episcopal Association, in South
  Carolina

Purcell, J. S. 20th c. [MBF]
British author
* Stapleton, Maurice

Purcell, James A. 1906-1966 [BBH]
*American auto racing manager and
promoter*
* Purcell, Pat

Purcell, Pat
See Purcell, James A.

**Purcell, Victor William Williams
Saunders** 1896-1965 [CA, LC]
British author
* Buttle, Myra

Purcell, William Aloysius   [BE]
American baseball player and manager
* Purcell, Blondie

Purchase, Elspeth [Sandilands] 1940-
[CA]
*New Zealand-born British author and
playwright*
* Sandys, Elspeth

[A] Purchaser
See Donaldson, [Rev.] John William

Purdell, Reginald
See Grasdorf, Reginald

Purdie, Bernard 1939- [EJ7, LRR]
American jazz musician
* Purdie, Pretty

Purdie, Pretty
See Purdie, Bernard

Purdom, C. B.
See Purdom, Charles Benjamin

Purdom, Charles Benjamin 1883-1965
[BEW, LC]
British author and critic
* Purdom, C. B.

Purdy
See Miller, Emily [Huntington]

Purdy, Doc
See Purdy, George W.

Purdy, Everett Virgil 1904-1951 [BE]
American baseball player
* Purdy, Pid

Purdy, George W. 1859-1926 [HPPN]
American theatrical manager
* Purdy, Doc

Purdy, [Captain] Jim
See Gillelan, G[eorge] Howard

Purdy, Ken William 1913- [HPPN]
American author
* Prentiss, Karl

Purdy, Pid
See Purdy, Everett Virgil

[The] Pure
See Baffo

Pure, Simon
See Swinnerton, Frank Arthur

[The] Purging Colonel
See Pride, Thomas

[El] Puri
See Castellano Martinez, Agustin

[The] Purist of Language
See Malherbe, Francois de

[The] Puritan
See Abbot, George

[The] Puritan
See Boughton, George Henry

[The] Puritan
See Mies, Ludwig

[The] Puritan Captain
See Standish, Miles

[A] Puritan of the 19th Century
See Alden, Joseph Warren

[A] Puritan Pepys
See Sewall, Samuel

[The] Puritan Plato
See Howe, John

[The] Puritan Poet
See Whittier, John Greenleaf

[The] Puritanical Bishop
See Potter, Barnabas [or Barnaby?]

Purley, John
See Thomas, Reginald George

Purnell, Benjamin 1860?-1927 [HPPN]
American religious leader
* [The] King

Purnell, Idella 1901- [CA]
Mexican-born author
* Stone, Idella Purnell
* Stone, Ikey

Purnell, Jesse Rhoades 1879-1966 [BE]
American baseball player
* Purnell, Scrappy

Purnell, Keg
See Purnell, William

Purnell, Scrappy
See Purnell, Jesse Rhoades

Purnell, Thomas 19th c. [PA]
Author
* Q.

Purnell, William 1915-1965 [DAM, EJ,
WWJ]
American jazz musician
* Purnell, Keg

Purple, Edwin R. 1831-1879 [PA]
Author
* Neafie

[The] Purple Streak
See Boynton, Ben L.

Purpur, Clifford 1916- [CEI]
American-born hockey player
* Purpur, Fido

Purpur, Fido
See Purpur, Clifford

Pursch, Friedrich Traugott 1774-1820
[WBD]
German-born botanist and horticulturist
* Pursh, Frederick

Purse
See Pierce, Franklin

Pursh, Frederick
See Pursch, Friedrich Traugott

Purtell, William Patrick [Billy]
1886-1962 [BN]
American baseball player
* [The] Child Athlete

Purtill, Maurice 1916- [PMJ, WWJ]
American jazz musician
* Purtill, Moe

Purtill, Moe
See Purtill, Maurice

Purves, George
See Gray, Simon

Purwitsky, Marcus ?-1963 [EJS]
Russian-born South African horse trainer
* Purwitsky, Paddy

Purwitsky, Paddy
See Purwitsky, Marcus

Pusey, Edward Bouverie 1800-1882
[HPPN]
British clergyman and author
* [A] Bachelor of Divinity
* Champion of Orthodoxy
* E. B. P.

Push 'em Up Tony
See Lazzeri, Anthony Michael [Tony]

Pushcart Tony Cermack
See Cermack, Anton

Pushchin, Lev
See Gippius, Zinaida Nikolaievna

Pushful Joe
See Chamberlain, Joseph

Pushkin, Alexander Sergeivitch
1799-1837 [DNNF, FFF, IBW]
Russian poet
* Belkine, Ivan
* [The] Father of Russian Literature
* [The] Russian Byron

Pushy, Princess
See Von Reibnitz, Marie Christine

Putinas
See Mykolaitis, Vincas

Putman, Kate
See Osgood, Kate Putman

Putnam, Arthur Lee
See Alger, Horatio, Jr.

Putnam, Eleanor
See Bates, Harriet Leonora Vose

Putnam, George ?-1878 [HPPN]
American clergyman
* [A] Citizen of Boston
* P.

Putnam, George H[aven] 1844-1930
[WGT]
British-born American author
* G. H. P.

Putnam, George Palmer 1887-1950
[HPPN]
American publisher and author
* Bend, Palmer

Putnam, Henry ?-1827 [HPPN]
American attorney
* [A] Gentleman of South Carolina

Putnam, Isra
See La Spina, Greye Bragg

Putnam, Israel 1718-1790 [DNNF, FFF, HPPN, SN]
American army officer
* Old Put
* Putnam, Wolf

Putnam, J. Wesley
See Drago, Harry Sinclair

Putnam, John
See Beckwith, Burnham Putnam

Putnam, Kenneth
See Klass, Philip

Putnam, Lewis H. 19th c. [HPPN]
American author
* [A] Colored Man

Putnam, Mary Lowell 1810-1898 [DNA, PA]
American author
* Colvil, Edward

Putnam, Mary Traill Spence 1810-1898
[HPPN]
American author
* Colvil, Edward

Putnam, Mrs. S. W. [FFF]
Entertainer
* Amond, Nellie

Putnam, Rufus 1738-1824 [HPPN]
American pioneer settler
* [The] Father of Ohio

Putnam, S. W. [FFF]
Entertainer
* Sedgwick, Billy

Putnam, Sarah A. 1845-? [BDSA, FFF]
American author and poet
* Brock, Sallie A.
* Madison, Virginia

Putnam, Wolf
See Putnam, Israel

Putney, Gail J.
See Fullerton, Gail Putney

Putney, Henry M. 19th c. [FFF, PA]
American writer
* Snoggins

Puto
See Bate, Henry

Putra, Kerala
See Panikkar, K[avalam] Madhava

[Il] **Puttino** [The Boy]
See Leonardo, Giovanni

Puttock
See Aelfric

Puzzle "Nom"
See Tingley, Richard Hoadley

Puzzle, Peter
See Addison, Joseph

Puzzlem, Peter
See Herschel, Friedrich Wilhelm

Pyatt, Frederick Nelson 1953- [SMG]
Canadian-born hockey player
* Pyatt, Nelly

Pyatt, Nelly
See Pyatt, Frederick Nelson

Pycroft, Nita 1902- [THR]
British actress and singer
* Croft, Nita

Pyeboard, George
See Peele, George

Pygmalion
See Louis XIV

Pylades
See Gwinnett, Richard

Pyle, Cash and Carry
See Pyle, Charles C.

Pyle, Charles C. 1881-1939 [AS, FB, HPPN]
American football promoter
* [The] P. T. Barnum of Sports
* Pyle, Cash and Carry

Pyle, Firpo
See Pyle, Harlan Albert

Pyle, Harlan Albert 1905- [BE]
American baseball player
* Pyle, Firpo

Pyle, Harry Thomas 1861-1908 [BE]
American baseball player
* Pyle, Shadow

Pyle, Herbert Ewald 1910- [BE]
American baseball player
* Pyle, Lefty

Pyle, Hilary 1936- [CA]
Irish art critic and author
* Cullen, Peta
* Mitchell, Adam

Pyle, Lefty
See Pyle, Herbert Ewald

Pyle, Shadow
See Pyle, Harry Thomas

Pyles, Aitken
See McDavid, Raven I[oor], Jr.

Pylkowski, Henry 1911-1957   [AS, BX, RBE]
American boxer
* Risko, Babe
* Risko, Eddie

Pylodet, L.
See Leypoldt, Frederick

Pym, Arthur Gordon
See Poe, Edgar Allan

Pym, Beatrice Angela Carrington
20th c.   [THR]
British actress
* Cromwell, Cecil

Pym, John 1584-1643   [FFF, HN, SN]
British politician
* [The] English Aristides
* Pym, King

Pym, King
See Pym, John

[The] Pym of France
See Mole, Mathieu

Pym, T.
See Creed, Clara

Pynchon, Adeline Lobdell Atwater
20th c.   [NAA]
American writer
* Atwater, Caroline Lobdell

Pyne, John 17th c.   [SN]
Regicide
* [The] King of the West

Pyne, Nicholas
See Neuburg, Victor [Benjamin]

Pyne, William Henry 1770-1843   [BI, PA]
British author and painter
* Hardcastle, Ephraim

Pynnshurst
See Macleod, Xavier Donald

Pyricus 4th c. BC   [SN]
Painter
* [The] Ryparographer

Pyrocles
See Sidney, [Sir] Philip

Pyrrho
See McCabe, Ralph

Pythagoras 6th c.   [DEP, DNNS, RH]
Greek philosopher and mathematician
* Crotona's Sage
* [The] Long Haired Samian
* [The] Philosopher with the Golden Thigh
* [The] Sage of Crotona
* [The] Sage of Samos
* [The] Samian Sage

[A] Pythagorean
See Ludlow, Fitz-Hugh

[The] Pythagorean
See Tryon, Thomas

Python
See Dennis, John

Python
See Tyler, John

Python, Monty   [joint pseudonym]
See Gilliam, Terry [Vance]

Q

Asterisk (*) indicates assumed name.

Q.
See Barron, Alfred

Q
See Buckner, William Quinn

Q.
See Jerrold, Douglas William

Q
See Jones, Quincy Delight, Jr.

Q.
See Purnell, Thomas

Q.
See Quiller-Couch, [Sir] Arthur Thomas

Q.
See Rosenberg, Charles G.

Q.
See Yates, Edmund Hodgson

Q. B.
See Buckner, William Quinn

Q. F. Q.
See Quicksell, Q. F.

Q in the Corner
See Bayly, Thomas Haynes

Q. in the Corner
See Harris, John

Q. Q.
See Taylor, Jane

Q. X.?
See Young, Robert

Qadar, Basheer
See Alexander, Charles Khalil

Qazwini, al- 1203?-1283
Persian science writer
* [The] Medieval Pliny
* [The] Muslim Pliny

[A] Quack in Commentatorship
See Warburton, William

Quack Maurus
See Blackmore, [Sir] Richard

Quackenbush, Bill
See Quackenbush, Hubert George

Quackenbush, Hubert George 1922-
[CEI, FHE]
Canadian-born hockey player
* Quackenbush, Bill

Quad, Doctor
See Blackall, Christopher Rubey

Quad, M.
See Lewis, Charles Bertrand

[A] Quadragenarian
See Weaver, Robert

Quaesingus
See Cheng Sen

Quaid-i-azam [Great Leader]
See Jinnah, Mohammed Ali

Quake, Eartha
See Favory, Renne S.

[A] Quaker
See Forster, Josiah

Quaker Dolly Madison
See Madison, Dorothy Payne Todd

[The] Quaker Marytr
See Dyer, Mary

Quaker Meadows Joe
See McDowell, Joseph

[The] Quaker Poet
See Barton, Bernard

[The] Quaker Poet
See Scott, John

[The] Quaker Poet
See Whittier, John Greenleaf

[The] Quaker Poetess
See Lippincott, Martha Shepard

[The] Quaker Soldier
See Biddle, Clement

[The] Quaker Solon of Rochdale
See Bright, John

Qualen, John
See Oleson, John

Quallon
See Bradbury, Stephen Henry

Qualters, Marguerite 1895-1974 [SC]
American actress
* Qualters, Tot

Qualters, Money Bags
See Qualters, Thomas Francis [Tom]

Qualters, Thomas Francis [Tom] 1935-
[BE]
American baseball player
* Qualters, Money Bags

Qualters, Tot
See Qualters, Marguerite

Quang-yoo ?-265 [HN]
Chinese general
* [The] Mars of China

Quant, Mary 1934- [WFA]
British fashion designer
* [The] Mother of Mod

Quantrill, Charles [or Charley]
See Quantrill, William Clarke

Quantrill, William Clarke 1837-1865
[BLB, HPPN]
American murderer
* Hart, Charles
* [The] Mystery Man of Quatsino Sound
* [The] Prince of Lawlessness
* Quantrill, Charles [or Charley]

Quarantine
See Foe, Daniel

Quarles, Dizzy
See Quarles, Joseph James

Quarles, Francis 1592-1644 [NPS, SN]
Poet
* [The] Darling of Our Plebeian Judgments
* [The] Leveller in Poetry

Quarles, Geoffrey
See Poe, Edgar Allan

Quarles, Joseph James 1911- [BA]
American physician
* Quarles, Dizzy

[The] Quarreler
See Louis X

[The] Quarrelsome
See Henry II

Quarrier, Red
See Quarrier, Sidney

Quarrier, Sidney 20th c. [HPPN]
American football player
* Quarrier, Red

Quartararo, Gladys 20th c.
Actress
* Quartaro, Nena

Quartaro, Nena
See Quartararo, Gladys

Quarterback [code name used during World War II]
See Stilwell, Joseph Warren

Quarterback, Mr.
See Starr, Bryan Bartlett

Quarterback, Mr.
See Unitas, John[ny]

[The] Quarterback Who Never Made a Mistake
See Friedman, Benjamin [Benny]

Quarterly, Milton
See Coryell, John Russell

Quartermain, James
See Lynne, James Broom

Quatrelles
See L'Epine, Ernest Louis Victor Jules

Quay, Boss
See Quay, Matt[hew Stanley]

Quay, Donald 1920?-1976 [BI]
American sportswriter
* Quay, Luke

Quay, Luke
See Quay, Donald

Quay, Matt[hew Stanley] 1833-1904
[HPPN]
American politician and soldier
* Quay, Boss

Quayle, Mary Jane Ward 1905- [NAA]
American author
* Ward, Mary Jane

Quedens, Eunice 1912- [BEW, EMT, FC]
American actress
* Arden, Eve

[The] Queen
See Cubitt, Florence

[The] Queen
See Reagan, Anne Frances Davis

[The] Queen
See Spivey, Victoria Regina [Vicky]

[The] Queen
See Steinberg, Martha Jean Jones

Queen Alice
See Longworth, Alice Lee Roosevelt

Queen Anne's Great Captain
See Churchill, John [First Duke of Marlborough]

[The] Queen Bea of Blues Singers
See Nicholls, Muriel

Queen Bess
See Elizabeth I

Queen Bess Meyerson
See Meyerson, Bess

Queen, Billy Eddleman 1928- [BE]
American baseball player
* Queen, Doc

Queen Christine
See Ockrent, Christine

Queen Dick
See Cromwell, Richard

Queen, Doc
See Queen, Billy Eddleman

Queen Dolly Madison
See Madison, Dorothy Payne Todd

[The] Queen Dowager
See Madison, Dorothy Payne Todd

Queen Elizabeth's Favorite Sea Dog
See Drake, [Sir] Francis

Queen Elleezee
See Landreaux, Elizabeth Mary

Queen, Ellery [joint pseudonym with Daniel Nathan]
See Lepofsky, Manfred

Queen, Ellery [joint pseudonym with Manfred Lepofsky]
See Nathan, Daniel

Queen, Ellery
See Vance, John Holbrook [Jack]

Queen, Ellery, Jr.
See Holding, James [Clark Carlisle, Jr.]

Queen, Ellery, Jr. [joint pseudonym with Daniel Nathan]
See Lepofsky, Manfred

Queen, Ellery, Jr. [joint pseudonym with Manfred Lepofsky]
See Nathan, Daniel

Queen Helen
See Wills, Helen Newington

Queen Henry
See Henrietta Maria

Queen Marie of Hollywood
See Koerber, Leila Marie

Queen, Mrs. Frederick E. [FFF]
Entertainer
* Lascelles, Emma

[The] Queen of American Pop Music
See Egstrom, Norma Dolores

[The] Queen of Babylon
See Woffington, Margaret

[The] Queen of Beauty
See Somerset, Duchess of

[The] Queen of Blues
See Brown, Ada

[The] Queen of Bohemia
See McElhinney, Jane

Queen of Broadway
See Zimmerman, Ethel Agnes

[The] Queen of Camp
See Sontag, Susan

[The] Queen of Caprice
See Christina

[The] Queen of Carthage
See Leris, Claire Josephe

[The] Queen of Chicago Blues
See Taylor, Cora Walton

[The] Queen of Civil Rights
See Hurley, Ruby

[The] Queen of Coins
See Ford, Mary

[The] Queen of Confidence Women
See Crosby, Nellie

[The] Queen of Country Comedy
See Cannon, Sarah Ophelia Colley

[The] Queen of Country Music
See Deason, Muriel Ellen

[The] Queen of Country Music
See Lynn, Loretta

[The] Queen of Crime
See Christie, Agatha [Mary Clarissa]

[The] Queen of Crime
See Lyons, Sophie

[The] Queen of Death Row
See Morris, Patsy

[The] Queen of Diamonds
See Bonner, Antoinette

[The] Queen of Disco
See Gaines, La Donna Andrea

[The] Queen of Hearts
See Elizabeth

Queen of Hearts
See Keplinger, Mrs. E. M. Patterson

Queen of Hearts
See Madison, Dorothy Payne Todd

[The] Queen of Heaven
See Mary

[The] Queen of Heaven
See Voo-chee

[The] Queen of Horror
See Radcliffe, Anne Ward

[The] Queen of Jazz
See Abuza, Sophie

[The] Queen of Jazz
See Scruggs [or Winn?], Mary Elfrieda

[The] Queen of Kings
See Zauditu

[The] Queen of Letter-Writers
See Rabutin-Chantal, Marie de [Marquise de Sevigne]

[The] Queen of Letters
See Ocampo, Victoria

[The] Queen of Limbo
See Croney, Roz

[The] Queen of Nine Days
See Grey, [Lady] Jane

[The] Queen of Ohio
See Chadwick, Elizabeth [Bigley]

Queen of Palmyra
See Stanhope, Hester Lucy

[The] Queen of Paradox
See Mary, Queen of Scots

[The] Queen of Polish Lyricists
See Pawlikowska, Marja [Kossak]

[The] Queen of Protest
See Baez, Joan

[The] Queen of Queens
See Cleopatra

[The] Queen of Queens
See Stuart, Constance Cornell

[The] Queen of Republic Pictures
See Hruba, Vera

[The] Queen of Rock and Roll
See Penniman, Richard Wayne

[The] Queen of Rock 'n Rouge
See Furnier, Vincent Damon

[The] Queen of Romance
See Cartland, Barbara [Hamilton]

[The] Queen of Screwball Comedies
See Peters, Jane Alice

[The] Queen of Shepherds
See Elizabeth I

[The] Queen of Song
See Catalani, Angelica

[The] Queen of Soul
See Franklin, Aretha

[The] Queen of Soul
See Hightower, Donna

[The] Queen of Sporting Row
See Bulette, Julia C.

[The] Queen of Staccato
See Selika, Marie

[The] Queen of Swimming
See De Varona, Donna

[The] Queen of Tears
See Caroline Matilda

[The] Queen of Tears
See Mary Beatrice

[The] Queen of Technicolor
See Brown, Maureen Fitzsimons

Queen of Technicolor
See Gracia Vidal de Santos Silas, Maria Africa Antonia

[The] Queen of Tennis
See Washington, Ora

Queen of the Alligator Wrestlers
See Edstrom, Katherine

[The] Queen of the American Stage
See Duff, Mary Ann

[The] Queen of the American Stage
See Frost, Sarah Frances

[The] Queen of the Autoharp
See Carter, Maybelle

[The] Queen of the Badgers
See Lambert, May

[The] Queen of the Barbary Coast
See Daroux, Tessie Wall

[The] Queen of the Blues
See Dunn, Sara

[The] Queen of the Blues
See Edwards, Susie

[The] Queen of the Blues
See Jones, Ruth [Lee]

[The] Queen of the Blues
See Smith, Mamie

[The] Queen of the Blues
See Spivey, Victoria Regina [Vicky]

[The] Queen of the Blues
See Thomas, Blanche

[The] Queen of the Blues
See Waters, Ethel

[The] Queen of the Bowery
See Prado, Katie

[The] Queen of the British Box Office
See Stansfield, Grace

Queen of the B's
See Ankers, Evelyn

Queen of the B's
See Ball, Lucille

Queen of the B's
See Bitzer, Marjorie

[The] Queen of the Clinkers
See Hruba, Vera

[The] Queen of the Comstock
See Bowers, Eilley Orrum

[The] Queen of the Coon Shouters
See Campbell, Ada

[The] Queen of the Courts
See Riggs, Robert Larimore [Bobby]

Queen of the Cowgirls
See Smith, Frances Octavia

Queen of the Crystal Tank
See Webb, Ada

[The] Queen of the Dead Hands
See Pfeiffer, Ida Laura

[The] Queen of the Demi-Monde
See White, Lula [or Lulu]

[The] Queen of the Denver Red Lights
See Ready, Martha A. Thomson

Queen of the Desert
See Stanhope, Hester Lucy

[The] Queen of the Discotheques
See Gaynor, Gloria

[The] Queen of the East
See Zenobia

[the] Queen of the English Stage
See Brown, Elizabeth Ann

[The] Queen of the Folksingers
See Baez, Joan

[The] Queen of the Game Shows
See Mazeppa, Rose Marie

Queen of the Gospel Singers
See Jackson, Mahalia

Queen of the Gospel Song
See Jackson, Mahalia

[The] Queen of the Gypsies
See Adams, Rose

[The] Queen of the Hillbillies
See McCord, May Kennedy

[The] Queen of the Hoboes
See Denfield, Mick

Queen of the Hollywood Dress Extras
See Flowers, Bess

[The] Queen of the Ice
See Blanchard, Theresa Weld

[The] Queen of the Ice
See Henie, Sonja

[The] Queen of the Jukeboxes
See Jones, Ruth [Lee]

[The] Queen of the Kennels
See Wallis, Pauline

[The] Queen of the Lady Gamblers
See Dumont, Emma [or Eleanora]

[The] Queen of the Memphis Sound
See Thomas, Carla

[The] Queen of the Methodists
See Selina [Countess of Huntingdon]

[The] Queen of the Moaners
See Gibbons, Irene

[The] Queen of the Moaners
See Smith, Clara

[The] Queen of the Mountain
See Palden, Thondup Namgyal

[The] Queen of the Movies
See Smith, Gladys Mary

[The] Queen of the Night Clubs
See Alix, Liza Mae

[The] Queen of the Northern Seas
See Elizabeth I

[The] Queen of the Nudists
See Cubitt, Florence

[The] Queen of the Outlaws
See Starr, [Myra] Belle [Shirley]

[The] Queen of the Plaza
See Fuertes, Dolores Adios

[The] Queen of the Plaza
See Theodore, Adah Bertha

[The] Queen of the Prostitutes
See Cowan, Sarah

Queen of the Radio
See Guillot, Olga

Queen of the Red Lights
See Silks, Mattie

[The] Queen of the Ritz
See Auzello, Blanche Rubenstein

[The] Queen of the Rosewater
Administration
See Greenhow, Rose O'Neal

[The] Queen of the Row
See Younger, Pearl

[The] Queen of the Shoplifters
See Branch, Annie

[The] Queen of the Silent Serials
See White, Pearl

[The] Queen of the Skies
See Johnson, Amy

[The] Queen of the Sneak Thieves
See Branch, Annie

Queen of the Soaps
See Nixon, Agnes Eckhardt

[The] Queen of the Soaps
See Phillips, Irna

Queen of the Sob Sisters
See Seaman, Elizabeth [Cochrane]

Queen of the South
See Broil, Arlette B.

[The] Queen of the Speakeasies
See Guinan, Mary Louise Cecelia

[The] Queen of the Surf
See Williams, Esther

Queen of the Swashbucklers
See Fitzsimmons [or Fitzsimons?],
Maureen

[The] Queen of the Tenderloin
See Daroux, Tessie Wall

[The] Queen of the Torch Singers
See Morgan, Helen

[The] Queen of the Torchers
See Mulcahy, A. E.

[The] Queen of the Undress Circle
See Britton, Edith

[The] Queen of the Vampires
See Goodman, Theodosia

[The] Queen of the West
See Smith, Frances Octavia

[The] Queen of the Yodelers
See Bedra, Julie Marlene

[The] Queen of Thriller Writers
See Christie, Agatha [Mary Clarissa]

[The] Queen of Virgins
See Elizabeth I

Queen Poisoner
See Sherman, Lydia

Queen Rachel
See Canevaro, Barbara

Queen Sarah
See Churchill, Sarah Jennings

[The] Queen Square Hermit
See Bentham, Jeremy

Queen Tammy
See Pugh, Wynette

Queen Victoria's Favorite Composer
See Elgar, [Sir] Edward

Queen Willa
See Dickson, Willa

[The] Queen with the Heart of a King
See Elizabeth I

Queen Zarah
See Churchill, Sarah Jennings

Queen's Delight
See Raleigh, [Sir] Walter

[The] Queen's Earl of Desmond
See Fitzgerald, James

[The] Queen's Favorite Physician
See Arbuthnot, John

[The] Queen's Poisoner
See Rene, Master

Queerfellow, Quintin
See Clark, Charles

Queerquill
See Waggamon, Mary T.

[A] Quekett Clubman
See White, T. Chartres

Quencher, Mark
See Conolly, Charles M.

Queneau, Raymond 20th c.
French author
* Mara, Sally

Quennell, C. H.
See Quennell, Charles Henry Bourne

Quennell, Charles Henry Bourne
1872-1935 [LC]
Architect and author
* Quennell, C. H.

Quentin, Patrick [joint pseudonym with
Hugh Callingham Wheeler]
See Webb, Richard Wilson

Quentin, Patrick [joint pseudonym with
Richard Wilson Webb]
See Wheeler, Hugh Callingham

Quentin the Eagle
See Roosevelt, Quentin

Querard, Joseph-Maria 1797-1865 [PA]
Author
* D'Erquar, Mar. Jozon

Querculus
See Chesnan, Nicolas

Quercus
See Kingsley, O. A.

[El] Queretaro [The Man from
Queretaro]
See Sanroman, Ernesto

Querist
See Blennerhasset, Harman

Querno, Camillo 1470-1528 [NPS]
Italian poet
* [The] Antichrist of Wit

Querno, Camillo
See Odell, Jonathan

Query
See Brady, James T.

Query, Peter, Esq.
See Tupper, Martin Farquhar

Quesada, Elwood R. 1904-
American military officer
* [The] Pilot's General

Quesim
See Cheng Sen

Quesnay, Francois 1694-1774 [HPPN]
French physician and economist
* [The] European Confucius

Quesnay de Beaurepaire, Jules
1837-1923 [WBD]
French jurist and author
* De Glouvet, Jules

Quesne, Jacques Salbigoton 1778-1859
[HPPN]
French philosopher
* [The] Father of Psychism

Quesnel, Pierre 1699-1774 [WGT]
Author
* Rasiel de Selva, Hercule

Questal, Mae 20th c. [CED]
American entertainer
* [The] Betty Boop Girl

Question Mark
See Martinez, Rudy

Quetelet, Lambert Adolphe Jacques
1796-1874 [HPPN]
Belgian statistician and astronomer
* [The] Father of the Average Man
Theory

Quevedo
See Wright, R. W.

Quevedo, Raymond 1891?- [BI]
Trinidadian calypso singer
* Attila the Hun

Quevedo Redivivus
See Byron, George Gordon Noel

Quevedo, Walter C. [FFF, PA]
American writer
* Odds and Ends

Quex
See Nichols, George Herbert Fosdike

Queyroul, Henri 1857-1921 [BEW]
French-born playwright
* Keroul, Henri

Quezon y Molina, Manuel Luis
1878-1944 [HPPN]
Philippine president
* [The] Patrick Henry of the Philippines
* [The] Philippines' George Washington

Quibell, Agatha Hunt 1921- [AW, WD]
Canadian-born author
* Pearce, A. H.

Quichot, Dona
See Tomkiewicz, Mina

Quick, Amanda - see Krentz, Jayne

Quick, Annabelle 1922- [CA] CA #139
American translator
* MacMillan, Annabelle

Quick, Dorothy
See Meyer, Dorothy Quick

Quick Draw McGraw
See McGraw, Donnie

Quick Hands Torres
See Torres, Jose Luis

Quick, Ida
See Maurer, Mrs. George W.

Quick, John 1748-1831 [RH]
British comedian
* [The] Retired Diocletian of Islington

Quick, Lyman 1907- [EG, GF]
American golfer
* Quick, Smiley

Quick, Philip
See Strage, Mark

Quick, Smiley
See Quick, Lyman

Quick, Tom
See Wooldridge, George B.

Quickens, Quarles
See English, Thomas Dunn

Quickens, Quarles
See Poe, Edgar Allan

Quicksell, Howard 1901-1953 [WWJ]
American jazz musician
* Quicksell, Howdy

Quicksell, Howdy
See Quicksell, Howard

Quicksell, Q. F. 19th c. [HPPN]
American author
* Q. F. Q.

Quicksilver Bob Fulton
See Fulton, Robert

[The] Quicksilver King
See Bell, Thomas Frederick

Quid
See Fitzgerald, Robert Allan

Quid-Pro-Quo
See Smyth, Charles John

Quidam
See Meston, William

[Un] Quidam
See Turla, Leopoldo

Quidam
See Weintraub, Wiktor

Quiellens, Maurice 20th c. [RBE]
American boxer
* Quiellens, Tiger

Quiellens, Tiger
See Quiellens, Maurice

Quien Sabe?
See Bates, Harry Arthur

Quiet, Anthony
See Foe, Daniel

Quiet, Charles
See Noyes, Charles Henry

[The] Quiet Corruptor
See Remus, George

Quiet, George
See Pardon, George Frederick

Quiet Joe Knight
See Knight, Jonas William

[A] Quiet Looker-on.
See Foster, John

[The] Quiet Man
See Cooney, Gerry

[A] Quiet Man
See Fay, Theodore Sedgwick

[A] Quiet Man
See Thayer, Alexander Wheelock

Quiet Observer
See Wilson, Erasmus

[The] Quiet One
See Kray, Reginald [Reggie]

[The] Quiet Tiger
See Charles, Ezzard

[The] Quietist
See Molinos, Miguel de

Quietness
See Foe, Daniel

Quievreux, Jean-Francois 1926- [EJ7]
French jazz musician
* Gilson, Jef

Quigley, Aileen 1930- [IAW]
British author
* Fabian, Ruth
* Lindley, Erica

Quigley, Eileen Elliott
See Vivers, Eileen Elliott

Quigley, Ernest C. 1880-1968
Canadian-born basketball official
* Quigley, Quig

Quigley, Jane 1939- [TR]
American actress
* Alexander, Jane

Quigley, Joan 20th c. [CA]
American astrologer and author
* Star, Angel

Quigley, Margery 1886-
American author
* Clark, Margery [joint pseudonym with Mary E. Clark]

Quigley, Quig
See Quigley, Ernest C.

Quigley, Red
See Quigley, William

Quigley, Thomas James 1860-1913
[BEW]
American theatrical performer
* Seabrooke, Thomas Q.

Quigley, William 20th c. [EF]
American football player
* Quigley, Red

Quignard, Odette 1898- [BEW]
French actress
* Myrtil, Odette

Quijano, Rebecca 1952- [WP 12-26-84]
Witness in the assassination of Philippine leader, Benigno Aquino
* [The] Crying Lady

Quilibet, Philip
See Pond, George Edward

Quilici, Frank Ralph 1939- [BE]
American baseball player
* Quilici, Guido

Quilici, Guido
See Quilici, Frank Ralph

Quill
See Grange, Cyril

Quill, Barnaby
See Brandner, Gary

[The] Quill Man
See Johnson, William B.

Quill, Monica
See McInerny, Ralph

Quill, Timothy
See Warren, Arthur

Quillan, Edward [Eddie] 1907- [HPPN]
American actor and comedian
* [The] Googly Eyed Comedian

Quillem, Harry
See Kewen, Edward John Cage

Quiller, Andrew
See Bulmer, [Henry] Kenneth

Quiller-Couch, [Sir] Arthur Thomas
1863-1944 [CC, HPPN, LC, TC]
British author
* [The] Age of English Literature
* Q.

Quiller-Couch, Thomas 1826-? [HPPN]
British author
* Hook and Crook
* T. Q.

Quillet, Dame
See Morency, Suzanne Giroux

Quillinan, Dorothy Wordsworth
1804-1847 [HPPN]
British author
* Wordsworth, Dora

Quillinan, Edward 1791-1851 [NPS]
Poet
* [The] Heavy Horseman

Quilter, Eddie
See Woodman, Thomas

Quilty, Silver
See Quilty, Sylvester Patrick

Quilty, Sylvester Patrick 1891- [BBH, CSH]
Canadian football player
* Quilty, Silver

Quimber, Mario
See Alexander, Charles Khalil

Quimby, Phineas Parkhurst 1802-1866
[HPPN]
American mental healer
* [The] Forerunner of Christian Science
* [The] Forerunner of the New Thought
  Movement
* [The] Revealer of Spiritual Healing to
  This Age

Quin, Dan
See Lewis, Alfred Henry

Quin, James 1693-1766 [DNNS, NPS, RH]
Irish actor
* [The] Stage Leviathan
* [The] Whitfield of the Stage

Quin, Mike
See Ryan, Paul William

[La] Quina
See Hernandez Galicia, Joaquin

Quinault, Abraham Alexis 1693-1767
[HPPN]
French actor
* Dufresne

Quinault, Philippe 1635-1688 [HPPN]
French poet and playwright
* [The] Father of the Lyric Tragedy

Quince, Peter
See Day, George Harold

Quince, Peter
See Dexter, Timothy

Quince, Peter
See Story, Isaac

Quince, Peter Lum
See Ritchie, [Harry] Ward

Quincunx, [Ms.] Ramona J.
See Borgmann, Dmitri A[lfred]

Quincy, Edmund 1808-1877 [FFF, PA]
American writer
* Byles
* D. Y.

Quincy, Josiah 1744-1775 [FFF, IP, PA]
American author and patriot
* Calisthenes

Quincy, Josiah (cont.)
* Hyperion
* [An] Independent
* Mentor
* Needham, Marchmont
* [An] Old Man
* Sexby, Edward

Quincy, Josiah 1772-1864 [HPPN]
American attorney, statesman, educator
* [An] Alumnus
* [A] Citizen
* [A] Conservative Whig
* King Josiah the First
* [The] President of Harvard University

Quincy, Josiah 1802-1882 [HPPN]
American attorney and politician
* [The] Mayor
* [The] Reform Mayor of Boston

Quincy, Josiah 1859-1919 [HPPN]
American politician
* [The] Brahmin Democrat

Quincy, Josiah Phillips 1829-1910
[HPPN]
American attorney, author, poet
* J. P. Q.

Quincy, Samuel Miller 1833-? [IP, IP, PA]
American attorney and journalist
* [A] High Private
* [The] Man Who was a Private

Quinichette, Paul 1921- [PMJ]
American jazz musician
* Quinichette, Vice Pres

Quinichette, Vice Pres
See Quinichette, Paul

Quinito
See Navarro, Joaquin

Quinito
See Valverde y San Juan, Joaquin

Quinlan, Finners
See Quinlan, Thomas Aloysius

Quinlan, Red
See Quinlan, Sterling C.

Quinlan, Runty
See Quinlan, Walter

Quinlan, Skeet
See Quinlan, Voiney

Quinlan, Sterling C. 1916- [CA]
American author
* Quinlan, Red

Quinlan, Thomas Aloysius 1887-1966
[BE]
American baseball player
* Quinlan, Finners

Quinlan, Voiney 20th c. [EF]
American football player
* Quinlan, Skeet

Quinlan, Walter 20th c. [BLB, HPPN]
American gangster
* Quinlan, Runty
* [The] Runt

Quinn, [Sister] Bernetta
See Quinn, Roselyn Viola

Quinn, Edwin McIntosh 1906-1952?
[WWJ]
American jazz musician
* Quinn, Snoozer

Quinn, Elisabeth 1881-1962 [SAT]
American author and editor
* Adams, Dale
* Quinn, Vernon
* Vequin, Capini

Quinn, Ethel
See Russell, Lindsay Patricia

Quinn, James [Jim] 1890?- [HPPN]
American cowboy
* Chicago's Lone Cowhand

Quinn, James Aloysius ?-1924 [BLB]
American underworld figure
* Hot Stove Jimmy

Quinn, John Edward Pick 1884-1956
[BE]
American baseball player
* Quinn, Pit

Quinn, John Picus [Jack]
See Picus, John Quinn

Quinn, Kitty
See Wilkinson, Mrs. R. O.

Quinn, Maire Roden ?-1947 [BEW]
Irish-born actress
* Quinn, Mary

Quinn, Mary
See Quinn, Maire Roden

Quinn, Mary Bernetta
See Quinn, Roselyn Viola

Quinn, Paddy
See Quinn, Patrick

Quinn, Pat 20th c.
Hockey player and coach
* Crunch, Captain

Quinn, Patrick 19th c. [BE]
American baseball player
* Quinn, Paddy

Quinn, Pit
See Quinn, John Edward Pick

Quinn, Roselyn Viola 1915- [CA]
American author and educator
* Quinn, [Sister] Bernetta
* Quinn, Mary Bernetta

Quinn, Simon
See Smith, Martin William

Quinn, Snoozer
See Quinn, Edwin McIntosh

Quinn, Susan 1940- [CA]
American author
* Jacobs, Susan

Quinn, Vernon
See Quinn, Elisabeth

Quinn, Wellington Hunt 1918-1954 [BE]
American baseball player
* Quinn, Wimpy

Quinn, Wimpy
See Quinn, Wellington Hunt

Quino
See Lavado, Joaquin

Quinones, Adolfo 1955?- [NW 7-2-84]
American street dancer
* Shabba Doo

Quinones, Francisco Mariano 1830-1903
[CW]
Puerto Rican author
* Kadosh, A.

Quinpool, John
See Regan, John William

Quinquagenarius
See Faussett, Godfrey

Quinquampoix
See Foe, Daniel

Quint, [Rev.] Alonzo Hall 1828-?
[HPPN]
American clergyman
* [The] Pastor

Quint, Jeanne
See Benoliel, Jeanne Quint

Quint, Wilder Dwight 1863-1936 [DNA]
American journalist
* Dwight, Tilton

Quintana, Luis Joaquin 1951- [BE]
Puerto Rican-born baseball player
* Santos, Luis Joaquin

Quintana, Manuel Jose 1772-1857
[DEP, HN, SN]
Spanish poet and orator
* [The] Spanish Tyrtaeus
* [The] Tyrtaeus of Spain

Quintanilla, Chinito
See Quintanilla, Roberto

Quintanilla, Luis 1900- [NAA]
French-born author and poet
* Taniya, Kyn

**Quintanilla, Maria Aline Griffith y
Dexter, Condesa De**
See Griffith, Maria Aline

Quintanilla, Roberto 20th c. [RBE]
Mexican boxer
* Quintanilla, Chinito

Quintin, Rex
See Hardinge, Charles Wrexe

Quintinus Carbasius
See Beskow, [Baron] Bernhard Von

Quinton, John P[urcell] 1879-? [WGT]
British author
* MacBride, Melchoir

Quinton, Paul
See Wright, W. George

Quintus
See Crosby, Alpheus

Quintus Icilius
See Guichard [or Guischard], Karl
Gottlieb

Quinzano
See Conti, Giovanni-Francesca

Quir, Dr.
See Henley, John

Quirinius
See Acton, John Emerich Dalberg

Quirinus
See Dollinger, Johann Joseph Ignaz

Quirinus, Publius Sulpicius ?-21?
[HPPN]
Roman governor of Syria
* Cyrenius
* Cyrinus

Quirke, Henry 1847-? [PI]
Irish poet
* O'Cuirc, Henry

Quiroule, Pierre [Rolling Stone]
See Sayer, Walter William

Quisenberry, Dan
American baseball player
* [The] Quiz

Quisling, Vidkun 1887-1945 [HPPN]
Norwegian Fascist leader
* [The] Betrayer of Norway

Quisquilius
See Baker, George

Quist, Felicia
See Zametkin, Laura Kean

Quitman, Wallace
See Palmer, Raymond A[rthur]

Quittenton, Bertram 20th c. [MBF]
British author
* Quiz, Roland, Jr.

Quittenton, Richard Martin Howard
1833-1914 [MBF]
British author
* Quiz, Roland

Quivas, Manuel
See Quivers, Emanual

Quiver
See Dyson, Timothy J.

Quivers, Emanual 19th c. [IBW]
American pioneer
* Quivas, Manuel

Quivey, Grace 1873-1927 [BEW]
American singer
* Van Studdiford, Grace

Quivogne de Montifaud, Marie Amelie
1850-?
French author
* [The] Boccaccio of the Nineteenth
Century
* Montifaud, Marc de

Quixota, Arina Donna
See Foe, Daniel

[The] Quixote of the North
See Charles XII

[The] Quixotic Crusader
See Wallace, Henry A[gard]

Quiz
See Caswall, Edward

Quiz
See Dickens, Charles

Quiz
See Pashnick, Larry

Quiz
See Pickles, Frank K.

[The] Quiz
See Quisenberry, Dan

[The] Quiz Kid Extraordinary
See Coburn, Zerah

Quiz, Roland
See Quittenton, Richard Martin
Howard

Quiz, Roland, Jr.
See Quittenton, Bertram

Quiznick
See Pashnick, Larry

Quod, John
See Irving, John Treat

Quodlibets
See Hayman, Robert

Quoirez, Francoise 1935- [CA, FC, LC]
French author and playwright
* Sagan, Francoise

Quondam
See Stevens, Charles McClellan

[A] Quondam Oxonian and Carthusian
See Cabanel, Daniel

Quongti, Richard
See Macaulay, Thomas Babington [First
Baron Macaulay]

[The] Quotation Authority
See Bartlett, John

Quousque
See Atkins, Frederick Anthony

Quow
See McTurk, Michael

R

Asterisk (*) indicates assumed name.

R.
See Colfer, Rebecca B.

R.
See Porter, James

R
See Rees, [Morgan] Goronwy

R.
See Reilly, Thomas Devin

R.
See Richardson, James, Jr.

R.
See Ripley, Samuel

R.
See Robbins, Chandler

R.
See Rosselet, Andre

R [code name]
See Williams, Roy Lee

R. A.
See Allen, Richard

R. A.
See Allsop, Robert

R. A.
See Alsop, Richard

R. A. D.
See Daniell, Ralph Allen

R. A., Esq.
See Carte, [Rev.] Thomas

R. B.
See Baird, Robert

R. B.
See Barrett, Roderic

R. B.
See Beaver, Robert Atwood

R. B.
See Beverley, Robert

R. B.
See Blackwell, Robert

R. B.
See Bradford, Robert

R. B.?
See Burrowes, Robert

R. B.
See Crouch, Nathaniel

R. B. F.
See Fox, Robert Barclay

R. B. G.
See Ganly, Rosaleen Brigid

R. B. J.
See Jones, Robert Baker

R. B. S.
See Scott, Robert Bissett

R. C.
See Calder, [Rev.] Robert

R. C.
See Carter, Robert

R. C.
See Challoner, [Rev.] Richard

R. C.
See Chambers, Robert

R. C.
See Charruthers, Robert

R. C.
See Laurence, Richard

R. C. H.
See Hoare, [Sir] Richard Colt

R. D.
See De Courcy, Richard

R. D.
See Doyle, Richard

R. D. R.
See Maginn, William

R. D. W.
See Webb, Richard Davis

R. E.
See Ellis, Rufus

R. E., A Member of the Society
See Eddowes, [Rev.] Ralph

R. E. L.
See Mullins, Rossana E.

R. E. M.
See Mullins, Rossana E.

R. E. M. M.
See Moore, Richard E. M.

R. E. M. W.
See Whitaker, Rogers Ernest Malcolm

R. F.
See Fendt, Rene

R. F. A.
See Lee, Rachel Frances Antonina Dashwood

R. F., A. M.
See Farrington, [Rev.] Richard

R. F. D., Mrs.
See Peden, Rachel Mason

R. F. K.
See Kennedy, Robert Francis [Bobby]

R. F. P.
See Maginn, William

R. F. W.
See Wallcut, [Rev.] Robert Folger

R. G.
See Gough, Richard

R. G.
See Graham, Robert

R. G.
See Greene, Robert

R. G., a Clerk of the Court of Common Pleas
See Gardiner, R.

R. G., Junior
See Gough, Richard

R. G. W.
See White, Richard Grant

R. H.
See Hakluyt, Richard

R. H.
See Harvey, Richard

R. H.
See Hawker, Robert

R. H.
See Hobson, Robert

R. H. B.
See Bacon, Rufus Henry

R. H. B.
See Blades, R. H.

R. H. L.
See Humphrey, L. J.

R. H. L.
See Little, Richard Henry

R. H. S.
See Sandys, Richard Hill

R. H. S.
See Stoddard, Richard Henry

R. H. the E. of R.
See Wilmot, John

R. J.
See Jeffries, Richard

R. J. C.
See Reade, John

R. J. M.
Martin, Robert Jasper

R. K.
See Kent, Rockwell

R. K. M.
See Mackittrick, Richard Kendall

R. L.
See Davis, Thomas Osborne

R. L. B.
See Storer, Harriet G.

R. L. C.
See Carpenter, Russell Lant

R. L. S.
See Balfour, Robert Louis

R. M.
See Centlivre, Susanna Freeman

R. M.
See Moore, Richard E. M.

R. M.
See Mulholland, Rosa

R. M. B.
See Broadfield, Robina Margaret

R. M. C. E.
See Eagar, Richard Michael Cardwell

R. M. T. H.
See Bacon, Francis

R. N.
See Nares, Robert

R. N.
See Norris, Randal

R. N. C.
See Cust, Robert Needham

R. N. O.
See MacOwen, Robert

R. N., Trinity College?
See Nun, Richard

R. O. C.
See Cole, Rose Owen

R. P.
See Pair, Ronald R.

R. P.
See Paltock, Robert

R. P.
See Polwhele, Richard

R. P., de Venezuela
See Paez, Ramon

R. P. H. G.
See Howgrave-Graham, Robert P.

R. P. S.
See Stebbins, Rufus Phineas

R. R.
See Foe, Daniel

R. R.
See Hobbes, Thomas

R. R.
See Iyengar, K[odaganallur] R[amaswani] Srinivasa

R. R.
See Rantoul, Robert, Jr.

R. R.
See Reynolds, Ruth Evelyn Millicent

R. R. M.
See Madden, Richard Robert

R. R. R.
See Rusk, Robert Robertson

R. S.
See Foe, Daniel

R. S.
See Scott, John

R. S.
See Southwell, Robert

R. S.
See Starkey, Richard

R. S.
See Zinsser, Hans

R. S., a Passenger in the Hector
See Paltock, Robert

R. S. G. A.
See Anderson, Robert Stuart Guthrie

R. S. M.
See Mackenzie, Robert Shelton

R. T.
See Thomas, Ralph

R. T.
See Tyas, Robert

R. T. C.
See Cross, Roselle Theodore

R. T., Gent., of London
See Tofte, Robert

R. T. S.
See Maginn, William

R. V.
See Harvey, James

R. V., Cork
See Varian, Ralph

R. W.
See Ashton, Charles

R. W.
See Walker, Robert

R. W.
See Wheaton, Robert

R. W.
See Whitaker, Rogers Ernest Malcolm

R. W.
See White, Robert

R. W.
See Wright, Robert

R. W. B.
See Buchanan, Robert Williams

R. W. E.
See Emerson, Ralph Waldo

R. W. G.
See Gammon, Robert William

R. W., Jr.
See Wickliffe, Robert, Jr.

R. W. L.
See Lowrie, Randolph W.

R. W. N.
See Nichols, Richard William

R. W. S. W.
See Sackville-West, Reginald [Seventh Earl of De La Warr]

R. Y.
See Young, Robert

Raabe, Wilhelm 1831-1910 [WBD]
German poet and author
* Corvinus, Jakob

Ra'anan, Uri
See Frischwasser, Heinz Felix

Rab
See Abba Arika

Rab Roy Gaston
See Gaston, Robert

Rabagliati, Alberto
See Rabagliati-Vinata, Alberto

Rabagliati-Vinata, Alberto 1906-1974 [SC]
Italian actor and singer
* Rabagliati, Alberto

Rabago, Andres 1947- [WEC]
Spanish cartoonist
* OPS

Rabajos, Andy 20th c. [PMJ]
American singer
* Russell, Andy

Rabasseire, Henry
See Paechter, Henry M[aximilian]

Rabb, Theodore
See Rabinowicz, Theodore

Rabbi
See Judah I [or Jehudah]

Rabbi
See Strasberg, Lee

[The] Rabbi of Swat
See Solomon, Moses H.

Rabbie
See Towers, Maxwell

[The] Rabbit
See Huggins, Miller James

[The] Rabbit
See Stark, Ray

Rabbit, Ozzie
See Oswald, Lee Harvey

Rabbit, Peter
See Long, William Joseph

Rabbit That Stayed in the Hat
See Kissinger, Henry Alfred

[The] Rabbit's Foot Statesman
See Bryan, William Jennings

Rabbit's Foot Williams
See Coleman, Burl C.

Rabbitt, Eddie
See Thomas, Edward

Rabbotenus, Isaac
See Marnix, Philip Van [Baron Sainte Aldegonde]

Rabdau, Marianne
See Bakker-Rabdau, Marianne K[atherine]

Rabe, Ann C[rawford] Von 19th c. [WGT]
Author
* Von Degen

Rabe, Florence 1888-1954 [BEW, FC]
American actress
* Bates, Florence

Rabe, Folke
See Reinhold, Alvar Harald

Rabelais, Francois 1494?-1553 [FFF, NPS, RH, SN]
French satirist
* Alcofribas Nasier
* [Le] Cure de Meudon
* [The] Father of Ridicule
* [The] Idol of the Age
* [The] Lucian of France
* Mad Man
* [The] Phoenix of Wit
* [The] Ryparographer of Wits
* [The] Socrates of the French Renaissance

[The] Rabelais of England
See Sterne, Laurence

[The] Rabelais of England
See Swift, Jonathan

[The] Rabelais of Geneva
See Bonnivard, Francois de

[The] Rabelais of Germany
See Fischart, Johann

[The] Rabelais of Good Society
See Swift, Jonathan

[The] Rabelaisian Doctor
See Patin, Guy

Rabi, I. I.
See Rabi, Isidor Isaac

Rabi, Isidor Isaac 1898- [HPPN, IPA]
Austrian physicist
* [The] Father of the Resonance Method
* Rabi, I. I.

Rabia, Aliyah 1932- [EJ, IBW]
American singer
* Staton, Dakota
* Trucking Kid

Rabin, Fishy
See Rabinowitz, Philip

Rabin, Henry 1940- [HPPN]
American motorist and parking ticket delinquent
* [The] Top Scofflaw

Rabin, Philip
See Rabinowitz, Philip

Rabinowicz, Theodore 1937- [JL]
Czech-born historian and author
* Rabb, Theodore

Rabinowitsch, Lydia
See Kempner, Lydia Rabinowitsch

Rabinowitz, Gypsy Rose
See Pious, Minerva

Rabinowitz, Jerome 1918- [BEW, EMT, IPA]
American choreographer, dancer, director
* [The] Avante-Garde Diplomat
* Pan's Tutor
* Robbins, Jerome

Rabinowitz, Philip 20th c. [EJS]
American basketball player
* Rabin, Fishy
* Rabin, Philip

Rabinowitz, Solomon [or Sholem] J. 1859-1916 [HPPN, LC, TC, TLC]
Russian-born author and playwright
* Aleichem, Shalom
* [The] Jewish Mark Twain
* [The] Yiddish Mark Twain

Rabinowitz, William Edward 1915- [BEW]
American stage manager and director
* Ross, Bill

Rabito, Anthony 20th c.
American underworld figure
* Fish, Mr.

Raborg, Frederick A[shton], Jr. 1934- [CA]
American author and playwright
* Ashmore, Lewis
* Baldwin, Dick
* Bronson, Wolfe
* Kern, Canyon
* Mayfair, Bertha

Raboy, Emanuel 1914-1967 [WECO]
American cartoonist
* Raboy, Mac

Raboy, Mac
See Raboy, Emanuel

Rabsheka
See Player, [Sir] Thomas

Rabutin-Chantal, Marie de [Marquise de Sevigne] 1626-1696 [NPS]
French writer and fashion leader
* [The] Queen of Letter-Writers

Raby, Aurora
See Millbank, Anne Isabella

Raby, Derek Graham 1927- [CA]
British playwright
* Derrick, Graham

Racagni, Giovanni 1741-1822 [PA]
Author
* Maria, Giuseppe

Racan, Marquis de
See De Bueil, Honorat

[The] Race Driver Who Wouldn't Die
See Hurtubise, James [Jim]

[The] Racetrack King
See Dwyer, Philip

Rachel
See Ferguson, Rachel

Rachel, Mlle.
See Felix, Elizabeth Rachel [Elisa]

Rachell, James 1910- [BWW, NBB]
American singer
* Poor Jim
* Rachell, Yank

Rachell, Yank
See Rachell, James

Rachilde
See Vallette, Marguerite

Rachman, Stanley Jack 1934- [CA]
South African-born psychologist and author
* Durac, Jack

Racina, Thom 1946- [CA]
American author and playwright
* Anicar, Tom

Racine, Jean Baptiste 1639-1699 [DEP, DNNS, SN]
French poet
* Acante
* [L']Historien Trop Paye
* [L']Hypocrite Rimeur
* [The] Virgil of the French Drama

[The] Racine of Italy
See Trapassi, Pietro Antonio Domenico Bonaventura

[The] Racine of Music
See Sacchini, Antonio Maria Gaspare

Racine's Monkey
See Campistron, Jean Galbert de

[The] Racing Legend
See Von Horn, Eylard Theodore

Racing, Mr.
See Speers, James [Jim]

Rack, Edmund 1735-1787   [IP, NPS]
British author
* Eusebius
* [A] Friend to True Liberty

Racke, Henry 1883-1940   [SC]
American actor
* Gordon, C. Henry

Rackham, Arthur 1867-1939   [HPPN]
British illustrator
* [The] Gentle Humorist

Rackham, John ?-1720   [HPPN]
British pirate
* Calico Jack

Rackham, John
See Phillifent, John Thomas

Rackstraw, William Smyth 1823-1895
[BBD]
British music scholar
* Rockstro, William Smyth

Raconteur
See Poore, Benjamin Perley

Racot, Adolph   [PA]
Author
* Dancourt

Radak
See Kamchi, David

Radatz, Richard Raymond [Dick] 1937-
[BE, PB]
American baseball player
* [The] Monster

Radbourn, Charles Gardner 1853?-1897
[AS, BBH, PB]
American baseball player
* Radbourn, Old Hoss
* Radbourn, Rad

Radbourn, Dordy
See Radbourn, George B.

Radbourn, George B. 1856-1904   [BE]
American baseball player
* Radbourn, Dordy

Radbourn, Old Hoss
See Radbourn, Charles Gardner

Radbourn, Rad
See Radbourn, Charles Gardner

Radcliff, Raymond Allen 1902?-1962
[AS, DGS, PB]
American baseball player
* Radcliff, Rip

Radcliff, Rip
See Radcliff, Raymond Allen

Radcliffe, Alida G.   [IP]
Hymn writer
* A. G. R.

Radcliffe, Anne Ward 1764-1823   [NPS, SN]
British author
* [The] Queen of Horror
* [The] Salvator Rosa of British Novelists
* [The] Shakespeare of Romance Writers

Radcliffe, Double Duty
See Radcliffe, Theodore [Ted]

Radcliffe, [Henry] Garnett 1899-   [WW]
Author
* Travers, Stephen

Radcliffe, Henry
See Sims, Henry R.

Radcliffe, Jack
See Smith, Charles

Radcliffe, Janette
See Roberts, Janet Louise

Radcliffe, John 1650-1714   [NPS]
British physician
* Aesculapius

Radcliffe, Theodore [Ted] 1904-   [BI, MK]
American baseball player
* Radcliffe, Double Duty

Radcliffe, Virginia
See Hurst, Virginia Radcliffe

Radcliffe-Cooke, Charles Wallwyn
[NPS]
Author
* Gushington, Angelina

Rade, Paul Martin 1857-1940   [WBD]
German theologian
* Martin, Paul

Radebaugh, Roy 1910-1960   [BEW, FC]
American actor
* Cromwell, Richard

Radek, Karl Bernardovich
See Sobelsohn, Karl

Rademacher, Erich 20th c.   [BBH]
German swimmer and water polo player
* Rademacher, Ete

Rademacher, Ete
See Rademacher, Erich

Rader, David M. 1948-   [PB]
American baseball player
* Rader, Rooster

Rader, Douglas Lee 1944-   [BE, PB]
American baseball player
* Rader, Rojo
* Rader, Rooster
* [The] Red Rooster

Rader, Drew Leon 1901-   [BE]
American baseball player
* Rader, Lefty

Rader, Lefty
See Rader, Drew Leon

Rader, Lloyd E. 1907?-
American welfare department director
* [The] Sooner Huey Long

Rader, Rojo
See Rader, Douglas Lee

Rader, Rooster
See Rader, David M.

Rader, Rooster
See Rader, Douglas Lee

Raderman, Harry 20th c.   [HPPN]
American jazz musician
* [The] Man Who Made the Trombone Laugh

Radetzky Von Radetz, [Countess] Berta Leonarz De Harding 1902-   [AW]
German-born author
* Harding, Bertita

Radford, Richard F[rancis], Jr. 1939-
[CA]
American author
* Critchley, Lynne
* Lyndon, Amy

Radford, Ruby L[orraine] 1891-1971
[CA, SAT, WW]
American author
* Bailey, Matilda
* Ford, Marcia

Radha
See Smith, Mary

Radha, [Swami] Sivananda
See Hellman, Sylvia

Radiant [Secret Service code name]
See Reagan, Maureen

Radical
See Jones, Leslie Grove

[The] Radical Educationist
See Ironside, Isaac

[The] Radical Prophet of American Youth
See Zimmerman, Robert Allen

Radilovic, Julio 1928-   [WECO]
Yugoslav cartoonist
* Jules

Radimsky, Ladislaw 1898-1970   [CA]
Czech diplomat, editor, author
* Den, Petr

[The] Radio Priest
See Coughlin, [Father] Charles Edward

[The] Radio Rebel
See Smith, Al[fred Emanuel]

[The] Radio Stunt Man
See Whittington, Richard [Dick]

Radio's Cheerful Little Earful
See Little, John

Radio's Dream Girl
See Joy, Alice

Radio's First Announcer
See Cowan, Thomas H.

Radio's Greatest Commentator
See Kaltenborn, Hans von

Radio's Original Texas Cowgirl
See Owens, Ruby

Radio's Own Statue of Liberty
See Smith, Kathryn Elizabeth [Kate]

Radirobanes
See Philip II

Radisson, Pierre Esprit 1636?-1710
[HPPN]
French explorer and fur trader
* D'Esprit, Pierre
* [The] Father of the Hudson's Bay
  Company

Radius, Anna [Zuccari] 1846-1918   [BI]
Italian author
* Neera

Radla, Astrik 954?-1044?   [DNNF,
DNNS, FFF]
Saint
* Anastasius
* [The] Apostle of Hungary
* [The] Apostle of the Hungarians
* Astericus

Radley, Clive Thornton 1944-   [DC]
British cricketer
* Radley, Grizzly

Radley, Grizzly
See Radley, Clive Thornton

Radley, Harry John 1910-   [CEI]
Canadian-born hockey player
* Radley, Yip

Radley, Yip
See Radley, Harry John

Radmilovic, Paul
See Radmilovic, Paulo

Radmilovic, Paulo 1886-1968   [BBH,
SWI]
British swimmer
* Radmilovic, Paul
* Radmilovic, Raddy

Radmilovic, Raddy
See Radmilovic, Paulo

Rado, Agi
See Rado, Agnes

Rado, Agnes 1931-   [IWM]
Hungarian-born musician
* Rado, Agi

Rado, Alexander
See Radolfi, Sandor Alexander

Rado, James
See Radomski, James

Radocchia, Emilio Joseph 1932-   [ASC,
EJ]
American jazz musician
* Richards, Emil

Radolfi, Sandor Alexander 1900-1981
[EE, WWW]
Russian intelligence agent
* Albert [code name]
* Dora [code name]
* Kulichev, Ignati
* Rado, Alexander

Radomski, James 1939?-   [CA, CLC]
American lyricist, playwright, composer
* Rado, James

Radot, Valery 19th c.   [HPPN]
French author
* His Son In Law

Radwanski, Pierre A[rthur] 1903-   [CAP,
WD]
Canadian author and poet
* Al-Van-Gar
* Chochlik
* O'Key
* Radwanski-Szinagel, [Dr.] Pierre A.

Radwanski-Szinagel, [Dr.] Pierre A.
See Radwanski, Pierre A[rthur]

Radway, Ann
See Geis, Richard E[rwin]

Radyr, Tomos
See Stevenson, James Patrick

Radziwill, Catherine 1858-1941   [WBD]
Russian author
* Vassili, [Count] Paul

Radziwill, Nicholas 1515-1565   [WBD]
Prince of Nieswiez
* [The] Black

Radziwill, Olga
See Wettberg, Simolin

Radziwill, Stanislaus 20th c.   [BP]
Polish-born real estate investor
* Radziwill, Stash

Radziwill, Stash
See Radziwill, Stanislaus

Radzyminska, Jozefa 1921-   [IAW]
Polish author and poet
* Mieczyslawa

Rae, Charlotte
See Lubotsky, Charlotte Rae

Rae, Edna
See Gillooly, Edna Rae

Rae, Herbert
See Gibson, George Herbert Rae

Rae, Hugh C[rauford] 1935-   [AW, CA,
IAW]
Scottish author and playwright
* Crawford, Robert
* Houston, R. B.
* McGrath, Morgan
* Stern, Stuart
* Stirling, Jessica

Rae, Jack
See Sampley, Alton

Rae, Johnny
See Pompeo, John Anthony

Rae, Milford Andersen 1946-   [CA]
American author
* Rae, Rusty

Rae, Nan
See Clark, Nan

Rae, Rusty
See Rae, Milford Andersen

Rae, Scott
See Hammill, Cicely Mary

Rae, William   [IP]
Author
* [A] Probationer of the Church of
  Scotland

Raeburn, David
See Herring, Paul

Raeburn, Frances
See Kurstin, Frances Hedrick

Raeburn, [Sir] Henry 1756-1823   [WBD]
Scottish painter
* [The] Scottish Reynolds

Raeder, Cap
See Raeder, Robert

Raeder, Robert 1953-   [HR]
American hockey player
* Raeder, Cap

Raemsdonck
See De Ghesquiere, Joseph Jean

Raeschild, Sheila
See Miller, Sheila

Raether, Bud
See Raether, Harold Herman [Hal]

Raether, Harold Herman [Hal] 1932-
[BE]
American baseball player
* Raether, Bud

Raevsky, Iosif Moiseevich
See Gradus, Iosif Moiseevich

Rafael
See Valdivia, Rafael

Rafael, Beulah K. 1893?-1964   [BEW]
American theatrical performer
* Kennedy, Beulah

Rafael de Paula [Rafael from Paula]
See Soto Moreno, Rafael

Rafael, Juan Vicente
See Rivera Viera, [Padre] Juan

[The] Rafaelle of Auctioneers
See Leigh, George

Raffaelino del Garbo
See Capponi, Raffaello

Raffaelli, Giuliano 20th c.   [WF]
Italian actor
* Rafferty, Julian

Raffaellino
See Colle, Raffaello dal

Raffaello
See Santi [or Sanzio?], Raffaello

Raffalovich, George 1880-? [WWL]
British author
* Sands, Bedwin

Raffelock, David 1897- [CAP]
American author
* Locke, R. E.

Rafferty, Chips
See Goffage, John

Rafferty, Julian
See Raffaelli, Giuliano

Rafferty, Mrs. William 19th c. [PI]
Irish poet
* Pentrill, Frank

Rafferty, S. S.
See Hurley, John J[erome]

Raffety, Gordon Edward 1907- [NAA]
American author and poet
* Gray, John

Raffles Bill
See Aglassinger, Andreas

Raffles, Thomas 1788-1863 [IP]
British clergyman and author
* [A] Doctor of Divinity, But Not of
Oxford

Rafinesque, Constantine Samuel
1783-1840 [WBD]
Turkish-born naturalist
* Rafinesque-Schmaltz, Constantine
Samuel

Rafinesque-Schmaltz, Constantine Samuel
See Rafinesque, Constantine Samuel

Raft, George
See Ranft, George

Raftor, Catherine 1711-1785 [HPPN]
British actress
* Clive, Kitty

Rag, Captain
See Smith, Edmund Neale

Rag Emperor
See Everette, Samuel

[The] Rag Man
See Burrows, Hermann

Rag, Tag, and Bobtail
See Lees, James Cameron

Ragatzy, Anton
See Parr, Julian F.

[Il] Ragazzo
See Broschi, Carlo

Ragg, Alban E. 20th c. [CCL]
Canadian poet
* A. E. R.

Ragg, Thomas Murray 1897- [WW]
Author
* Thomas, Murray

Ragged Dick West
See West, Richard

Ragged, Hyder
See Biron, [Sir] Henry Chartres

[The] Ragged Lawyer
See Grover, Martin

Ragged Staff
See Coley, Rex

[The] Ragged Stranger
See Ryan, Edward Joseph

[The] Ragged Stranger Murderer
See Wanderer, Carl

[The] Ragin' Cajun
See Guidry, Ron[ald Ames]

Ragini Devi
See Sherman, Esther

Raglan, Baron
See Raglan, FitzRoy

Raglan, Baron
See Somerset, Fitzroy James Henry

Raglan, Clarence Eldon 1927- [CEI]
Canadian-born hockey player
* Raglan, Rags

Raglan, FitzRoy 1885-1964 [CA]
British author
* Raglan, Baron
* Somerset, FitzRoy Richard

Raglan, James
See Cornwall-Walker, Thomas James
Raglan

Raglan, Rags
See Raglan, Clarence Eldon

Ragland, John Morgan 1906-1946
[BEW, WA]
American theatrical performer
* Ragland, Rags

Ragland, Rags
See Ragland, John Morgan

Raglin, Alvin Redrick 1917-1955 [EJ,
WWJ]
American jazz musician
* Raglin, Junior

Raglin, Junior
See Raglin, Alvin Redrick

Ragonese, Don 1920- [ASC]
American composer, singer, musician
* Rodney, Don

Ragsdale, Bob 20th c. [GW]
American rodeo performer
* Ragsdale, Rags

Ragsdale, Lulah
See Ragsdale, Tallulah

Ragsdale, Rags
See Ragsdale, Bob

Ragsdale, Ray 1939- [ECM]
American singer and songwriter
* Stevens, Ray

Ragsdale, Tallulah 20th c. [NAA]
American author
* Ragsdale, Lulah

[The] Ragtime Girl
See Barlow, Maud

Ragtime Jimmy
See Monaco, James

Ragtime Jimmy Durante
See Durante, James Francis [Jimmy]

Ragtime Joe Howard
See Howard, Joseph

[The] Ragtime Kid
See Campbell, S. Brunson

[The] Ragtime King
See Greene, Gene

Ragtime Texas Thomas
See Thomas, Henry

Ragusa, Paula 1939- [BDF, FC, HT]
American actress
* Prentiss, Paula

Rahbeck, Knud Lyne 1760-1830 [SN]
Danish poet, author, critic
* [The] Maecenas of Danish Letters

Rahman, Abdul
See Wayman, Tony Russell

Rahman, [Sheikh] Mujibur 1911-
[HPPN]
Indian President of Bangla Desh
* [The] Father of Bangla Desh

Rahmer, Hans Sigismund 1924- [CA]
German-born clergyman and author
* Rayner, John Desmond

Rahner, Raymond M. 20th c. [CA]
*American actor, television performer,
author*
* Rayner, Ray

Rahsaan Roland Kirk
See Kirk, Ronald T.

Rahsepar
See Yar-Shater [or Yarshater], Ehsan
O[llah]

Rahv, Philip
See Greenberg, Ivan

Rai, Dewan Bahadur Dewan Jamiat
1861-? [HPPN]
Indian government official and author
* A. D. B.

**Raibolini, Francesco di Marco di
Giacomo** 1450?-1517? [BI, WBD]
Italian painter and goldsmith
* Francia, Franceso

Raiden
See Torikichi

[The] Raider
See Kilpatrick, [Hugh] Judson

[The] Raider
See Morgan, John Hunt

Raidler, Bill 20th c. [EWG]
American gunfighter
* Raidler, Little Bill

Raidler, Little Bill
See Raidler, Bill

[The] Rail Splitter
See Lincoln, Abraham

Railroad Bill
See Dorsey, Thomas A[ndrew] [Tommy]

[The] Railroad King
See Poliakov, Samuel

Railton, Patrick ?-1941?
British author
* Carleton, Patrick

[The] Railway King
See Corning, Erastus

[The] Railway King
See Gould, Jason

[The] Railway King
See Hudson, George

[The] Railway King
See Vanderbilt, William Henry

[The] Railway Reader
See Spedding, James

Raimann, Ferdinand 1790-1836 [WBD]
Austrian actor and playwright
* Raimund, Ferdinand

Raimar, Freimund
See Rueckert, Friedrich

Raimbourg, Andre 1917-1970 [FC, OCF, WEF]
French actor and singer
* Bourvil

Raimon, Louis Albert Alexandre 1922-
French hairstylist
* Alexandre

Raimond
See Hurlburt, William Henry

Raimond, C. E.
See Parks, Elizabeth Robins

Raimond, C. E.
See Robins, Elizabeth

Raimondi, Marcantonio 1475?-1534?
[WBD]
Italian engraver
* Marcantonio

Raimu
See Muraire, Jules

Raimund, Ferdinand
See Raimann, Ferdinand

Raimund, Golo
See Dannenberg, George

Rain, Jeramie
See Davis, Susan

[The] Rain Water Doctor
See Gardener, Sylvan

[The] Rain Water Doctor
See Plinth, Octavius

Rainalducci, Pietro ?-1333 [WBD]
Italian antipope
* Nicholas V

Rainbow [Secret Service code name]
See Reagan, Anne Frances Davis

Rainbow Bill Killefer
See Killefer, William Levier, Jr.

Raine, Allen
See Puddicombe, Anne Adaliza

Raine, Jack
See Raine, Thomas Foster

Raine, Nancy Greene 1943- [BBH]
Canadian skier
* Tiger of the Slopes

Raine, Richard
See Sawkins, Raymond H[arold]

Raine, Thomas Foster 1897- [BEW]
British actor
* Raine, Jack

Rainer, George
See Greenburger, Ingrid Elisabeth

Rainer, Jerome
See Goode, Gerald

Rainer, Julia
See Goode, Ruth

Rainer, Luise 1912-
Austrian actress
* [The] Viennese Teardrop

Raines, Ella
See Raubes, Ella Wallace

Raines, Tim 1961?-
American baseball player
* [The] Rock

Raines, Walter 1940- [BA]
American choreographer
* [The] Baron
* Sir Walter

Rainey, Bill G. 1926- [CA]
American author
* Rainey, Buck

Rainey, Buck
See Rainey, Bill G.

Rainey, Gertrude Malissa Nix [Pridgett]
1886-1939 [BWW, DAM, EJ]
American singer
* [The] Black Nightingale
* [The] Golden Necklace of the Blues
* Mama Can Can
* [The] Mother of the Blues
* [The] Paramount Wildcat
* Patterson, Lila
* Rainey, Ma
* Rainey, Madame
* Smith, Anne
* [The] Songbird of the South

Rainey, Ma
See Rainey, Gertrude Malissa Nix [Pridgett]

Rainey, Madame
See Rainey, Gertrude Malissa Nix [Pridgett]

Rainey, Memphis Ma
See Glover, Lilian Mae

Rainey, Norman
See Morrison, William

Rainey, Pa
See Rainey, William

Rainey, W. B.
See Blassingame, Wyatt Rainey

Rainey, William 20th c. [DAM, EJ, PMJ]
American entertainer
* Rainey, Pa

Rainger, Ralph
See Reichenthal, Ralph

Rainham, Thomas
See Barren, Charles

Rainis, Janis
See Plieksans, Janis

[The] Rainmaker
See Hatfield, Charles Mallory

Raintree, Lee
See Sellers, Connie Leslie, Jr.

Rainwater, Marvin
See Percy, Marvin

Rainy Day Smith
See Smith, John Thomas

Rais [or Retz], Gilles de 1404?-1440
[HPPN]
French soldier and mass murderer
* Bluebeard

Raisa, Rosa
See Burchstein, Rosa Raisa

Raisson, Horace Napoleon 1798-1854
[IP]
French author
* Perigord, A. B.

Raithby, John [IP]
British author
* [A] Member of Lincoln's Inn

Raittila, Anne-Maija
See Nieminen, Anna-Maija

Raj
See Kalra, Rajinder Mohan

Rajagopalacharia, Chakravarti 1879-1972
[WBD]
Indian politician
* C. R.
* [The] Tamil Mahatma

[The] Rajah
See Hornsby, Rogers

[The] Rajah
See Roy, Rammohun

[The] Rajah of Sarawak
See Brooke, [Sir] James

[The] Rajah of Vaneplysia
See Penn, William

Rajah, Raboid
See Boyd, Ray

Rajaram
See Iyengar, K[odaganallur]
R[amaswani] Srinivasa

Rajneesh, Acharya 1931-   [CA]
Indian mystic and author
* Rajneesh, Bhagwan Shree

Rajneesh, Bhagwan Shree
See Rajneesh, Acharya

Rajonsky, Milton M. 1924-   [IEJ]
American jazz musician
* Rogers, Shorty

Raju
See Ahmed, Raju

Raju, Poolla Tirupati 1904-   [CA]
Indian educator and author
* Poolla, Tirupati Raju

[The] Rake and Shovel Golfer
See Moore, LaVerne M.

[The] Rake of Piccadilly
See Douglas, William

Raker, Hugh
See Endfield, Cyril Raker

Raknes, Ola 1887-1975 [CAP]
Norwegian author
* Arnold, Carl

Rakosi, Carl 1903-   [CA]
German-born poet
* Rawley, Callman

Rakow, Edward Charles 1936-   [BE]
American baseball player
* Rakow, Rock

Rakow, Rock
See Rakow, Edward Charles

Rale, Nero
See Burgess, Michael Roy

Raleigh
See Lee, Arthur

Raleigh, Alan
See Brown, Elijah

Raleigh, Bones
See Raleigh, James Donald

Raleigh, Cecil
See Rowlands, Cecil

Raleigh, Elizabeth 1570-1647   [SN]
*Wife of British courtier, Sir Walter
Raleigh*
* [The] Lovely Bessie

Raleigh, James Donald 1926-   [CEI,
FHE]
Canadian-born hockey player
* Raleigh, Bones

Raleigh, Richard
See Kister, W. H.

Raleigh, Richard
See Lovecraft, Howard Phillips

Raleigh, W.
See St. John, Henry

Raleigh, [Sir] Walter 1552?-1618   [DEP,
DNNS, NPS, SN]
British courtier, explorer, statesman
* Elizabethan Skeptic
* [The] English Milo
* [The] Fox
* King's Snare
* [The] Knight of the Cloak
* Last Elizabethan
* Man of Two Worlds
* [The] Ocean Shepherd
* Queen's Delight
* [The] Renaissance Man
* [The] Shepherd of the Ocean
* That Great Lucifer
* Timias

Raleigh, Walter S. 18th c.   [PA]
Author
* W. S. R.

Raley, Rowena
See McCulley, Johnston

Ralp, Howard
See Bretherton, Ralph Harold

Ralph
See MacGregor, John

Ralph, James 1695?-1762   [HPPN, IP]
British journalist, playwright, poet
* [A] Gentleman of the Middle Temple
* [An] Impartial Inquirer
* Lilburne
* [A] Lover of Truth and Liberty
* No Matter by Whom
* [A] Primcock
* [A] Woman of Quality

Ralph, Jessie
See Chambers, Jessie Ralph

Ralph, Julian E. 1853-1903   [FFF, NPS]
American journalist
* German Barber
* Percival

Ralph, Mr. le Docteur
See Arouet, Francois Marie

[The] Ralph Nader of Microwaves
See Towne, Joseph

Ralph, Nathan
See Goldberg, Nathan Ralph

Ralph 124E41
See Ackerman, Forrest J[ames]

Ralph 124TL41
See Ackerman, Forrest J[ames]

Ralph Rover
See Ballantyne, Robert Michael

Ralston, Alma 20th c.   [CA]
American author
* Payne, Alma Smith

Ralston, Doc
See Ralston, Samuel Beryl

Ralston, Esther 1902-   [HPPN]
American actress
* [The] American Venus
* America's Youngest Juliet
* Baby Esther

Ralston, Gilbert A[lexander] 1912-   [CA]
American author
* Alexander, Gil

Ralston, Jan
See Dunlop, Agnes Mary Robertson

Ralston, Samuel Beryl 1885-   [BE]
American baseball player
* Ralston, Doc

[The] Ralston Straight Shooter
See Mix, Tom

Ralston, Thomas N.   [IP]
American clergyman and author
* Eureka

Ralston, Vera 1929?-   [BDF, FC, HT]
American actress
* Miles, Vera

Ralston, Vera Hruba
See Hruba, Vera

Ralston, William Chapman 1826-1875
[HPPN]
American banker and entrepreneur
* [The] First Gentleman of San
Francisco
* [The] Man Who Built San Francisco
* [The] Ruler of San Francisco

Ram Dass, [Baba] [Servant of God]
See Alpert, Richard

Ram, Immanuel
See Velikovsky, Immanuel

Ram John Holder
See Holder, John Wesley

Ram, Mr.
See Waterfield, Robert S.

Ram, Stopford James   [IP]
British clergyman and author
* Vernon, Ruth

Rama
See Gupta, Ram Chandra

Rama Rau, Santha
See Bowers, Santha Rama Rau

Rama I
See Chao P'ya Chakri

Rama III
See Chesda

Rama IV
See Mongkut

Rama IX
See Adulyadej, Bhumibol

Rama V
See Chulalongkorn

Rama VI
See Chao Fa Maha Vajiravudh

Rama VII
See Prajadhipok

Rama VIII
See Mahidol, Anata

Ramachakra, Yogi
See Atkinson, William Walker

Ramadhin, K. T. 1930- [EC]
West Indian cricketer
* Ramadhin, Sonny

Ramadhin, Sonny
See Ramadhin, K. T.

Ramage, Alan 1957- [DC]
British cricketer
* Ramage, Rod

Ramage, Jennifer 20th c. [WW]
Author
* Mason, Howard

Ramage, Rod
See Ramage, Alan

Ramakrishna, Sri
See Gadadhar

Ramal, Walter
See De La Mare, Walter [John]

Ramala, Pratap Roy
See Bhosale, Yeshwantrao P.

Ramamohana, Raya 1774-1833 [HPPN]
Indian reformer
* Rammohan, Roy

Ramanan
See Venkateswaran, Taruvai
Anantaramaseshan

Ramanujan, Molly 1932- [CA]
Indian-born author
* Daniels, Shouri
* Ramanujan, Shouri

Ramanujan, Shouri
See Ramanujan, Molly

Rambam
See Maimonides [or Moses ben
Maimon]

Rambam, Cyvia 1888-1982 [CA]
Polish-born ballet dancer and author
* Rambam, Myriam
* Ramberg [or Rambach], Myriam
* Rambert, Marie

Rambam, Myriam
See Rambam, Cyvia

Rambaud, Yveling
See Gilbert, Frederic

Rambaut, A. Beatrice 20th c. [WWL]
Irish author
* Romney, A. B.

Rambeau, Eddie
See Flurie, Edward Cletus

Rambeau, Marjorie 1889-1970 [FIR]
American actress
* [The] Bernhardt of the Klondike

Ramberg [or Rambach], Myriam
See Rambam, Cyvia

Rambert, Elmer Donald 1917- [BE]
American baseball player
* Rambert, Pep

Rambert, Marie
See Rambam, Cyvia

Rambert, Pep
See Rambert, Elmer Donald

Ramble, Robert
See Frost, John

[The] Rambler
See Barton, George

[A] Rambler
See Budworth, Joseph

[The] Rambler
See Deutzman, Lawrence F[rederick]

Rambler
See Fullerton, George Humphrey

Rambler
See Holden, Luther L.

[A] Rambler
See Simcox, George Augustus

Rambler
See Thatcher, John Wells

[A] Rambler Among the Tombs
See Shepherd, Samuel

[A] Rambler at Home
See Bird, Robert Montgomery

Rambler, Jacques
See Peignot, Etienne Gabriel

Ramblin' Bob
See McCollum, Robert Lee

Ramblin' Jack Elliott
See Adnopoz, Elliott Charles

Rambling King Floyd
See Floyd, Frank

Rambling Richard
See Egerton-Warburton, Rowland Eyles

Rambling Wreck
See Veeck, William Louis, Jr. [Bill]

[The] Rambling Yodeler
See Haley, William [Bill]

Rambo, Ms.
See Seegrist, Sylvia

Rambo, Pete
See Rambo, Warren Dawson

Rambo, Warren Dawson 1906- [BE]
American baseball player
* Rambo, Pete

**Ramboldini [or de Ramboldoni],
Vittorino** 1378-1446 [WBD]
Italian educator
* Vittorino da Feltre

Rambova, Natacha
See Shaunessy, Winifred

Rame, David
See Divine, Arthur Durham

Rame, Marie Louise 1839-1908 [SAT]
British author
* De La Ramee, [Marie] Louise
* Ouida

Rameau, Jean
See Labaigt, Laurent

Rameau, Jean Philippe 1683-1764?
[FFF, HN, SN]
French musician and composer
* [The] Newton of Harmony

Rameau, Leon
See Maurras, Charles-Marie-Photius

[La] Ramee
See Ramus, Pierre

Ramenghi, Bartolommeo 1484-1542
[WBD]
Italian painter
* [Il] Bagnacavallo

Ramey, Ben N. 1921-1977 [ESF]
American writer
* Hollis, H. H.

Raminagrobis
See Cretin, Guillaume

Ramirez, Alice Louise 20th c. [SFL]
Author
* Tiny Alice

Ramirez, Jose 1898- [GS]
Mexican bullfighter
* Gaonita [Little Gaona]

Ramirez, Orlando 1950- [BE]
Colombian-born baseball player
* Leal, Orlando

Ramirez, Ram
See Ramirez, Roger J.

Ramirez, Roger J. 1913- [ASC, WWJ]
Puerto Rican-born jazz musician
* Ramirez, Ram

Ramirez Alonso, Alfonso 1916- [GS]
Mexican bullfighter
* [El] Calesero [The Buggy Driver]

Ramirez-Sanchez, Ilyich 1947?-
Venezuelan-born terrorist
* Carlos
* [The] Jackal

Ramiro II ?-1147 [WBD]
King of Spain
* [The] Monk

Ramistella, John 1942- [PRS, RO2]
American singer and songwriter
* Rivers, Johnny

Ramler, Charles William 1725-1798
[SN]
German poet
* [The] German Horace

Rammelsberg, Kate [FFF]
Entertainer
* Rolla, Mlle.

Rammohan, Roy
See Ramamohana, Raya

Ramo, Simon 1913- [HPPN]
American electrical engineer
* [The] Father of the I. C. B. M.

Ramon
See Gomez de la Serna, Ramon

Ramon, Boris
See Hawkins, Peter

Ramon, Laon 1917-   [F2]
Actor
* Janney, Leon

Ramon, Paul
See McCartney, Paul

Ramona
See Myers, Ramona

Ramond
See Golodnotzky, Harry

Ramone, Dee Dee
See Colvin, Douglas

Ramone, Joey
See Hyman, Jeffrey

Ramone, Johnny
See Cummings, John

Ramone, Marky
See Bell, Mark

Ramone, Tommy
See Erdelyi, Tommy

Ramos, Armando 1948-   [BX, RBE]
American boxer
* Ramos, Mando

Ramos, Artur
See De Araujo Pereira, Artur Ramos

Ramos, Chucho
See Ramos, Jesus Manuel Garcia

Ramos, Jesus Manuel Garcia 1918-
[BE]
Venezuelan-born baseball player
* Ramos, Chucho

Ramos, Mando
See Ramos, Armando

Ramos, Pedro Guerra 1935-   [BE]
Cuban-born baseball player
* Ramos, Pete

Ramos, Pete
See Ramos, Pedro Guerra

Ramos, Sugar
See Ramos Zaqueira, Urtiminio

Ramos Lopez, Leopoldo 1913-   [GS]
Mexican bullfighter
* Ahijado del Matadero [God-Child of
  the Slaughter-House]

Ramos Zaqueira, Urtiminio 1941-   [BX,
RBE]
Cuban boxer
* Ramos, Sugar

Ramp, James 1898-   [NAA]
British-born author
* Ames, Woodforde

Rampa, Tuesday Lopsang
See Hoskins, Cyril Henry

Rampling, Anne
See Rice, Anne

Rampo, Edogawa
See Hirai, Taro

Ramsay, [Rev.] A. 18th c.   [HPPN]
British clergyman
* [A] Clergyman

Ramsay, Alexander 1754-1824   [FFF]
British-born anatomist
* [The] Caliban of Science

Ramsay, Allan 1686-1758   [DEL, FFF,
IP, SN]
Scottish poet
* Scot, Quod Ar.
* [The] Scottish Theocritus

Ramsay, Allan, Jr. 1713-1784   [HPPN,
IP]
Scottish painter and author
* Britannicus
* [A] Dilettante in Law and Politics
* Marcellus
* Steady
* Zero

Ramsay, Andrew John 1849?-1907
[DNA]
American poet
* Ramsay, J. R.

Ramsay, Andrew Michael 1686-1743
[FFF, RH, WBD]
Scottish author
* [The] Cavalier

Ramsay, Charlotte Lennox 1720-1804
[HPPN]
American poet and author
* [A] Young Lady

Ramsay, D.   [IP]
Author
* Hortensius

Ramsay, Fay
See Eastwood, Helen

Ramsay, Fox
See Ramsay, Maule

Ramsay, Fox Maule
See Maule, Fox

Ramsay, Grace
See O'Meara, Kathleen

Ramsay, J. R.
See Ramsay, Andrew John

Ramsay, [Rev.] James ?-1824   [HPPN]
Scottish clergyman
* [A] Friend of Truth and Peace

Ramsay, James 18th c.   [IP]
Scottish author
* [A] Gentleman

Ramsay, James 19th c.   [IP]
Scottish clergyman and author
* [A] Member of the Duddingston
  Curling Society

Ramsay, Joan
See Wilson, Louise Bruguiere Church

Ramsay, Maule 20th c.   [BBH]
Scottish-born sled dog racer
* Ramsay, Fox

Ramsay, Owen Nares 1888-1943   [F1,
F2, FC]
British actor
* Nares, Owen

Ramsay, Richard 1770?-1833?   [PI]
Irish poet
* Meek, Matthew

Ramsbottom, Dorothea Julia
See Thackeray, William Makepeace

Ramsbottom, Mrs.
See Hook, Theodore Edward

Ramsdell, James Willard 1918-1969
[BE]
American baseball player
* Willie the Knuck

Ramsden, E. H.
See Ramsden, Hartley

Ramsden, F. E.   [FFF]
American writer
* Kalula

Ramsden, Hartley 20th c.   [AW]
British author
* Ramsden, E. H.

Ramsden, Lewis
See Dowding, A. L.

Ramses III [or Rameses]   [DEP, WBD]
King of Egypt
* [The] Egyptian Solomon
* Rhampsinitus

Ramses V [or Rameses]   [HN]
King of Egypt
* Memnon

Ramsey, Alexander 1754-1824   [HPPN]
British-American physician
* [The] Caliban of Science

Ramsey, Alice Huyler 1887?-1983   [DF
9-14-83]
American motorist
* Woman Motorist of the Century

Ramsey, Buster
See Ramsey, Garrard

Ramsey, Chuck
See Ramsey, Lowell Wallace, Jr.

Ramsey, Eric
See Hagberg, David J[ames]

Ramsey, Garrard 20th c.   [EF]
American football player
* Ramsey, Buster

Ramsey, George?
See Dorsey, Thomas A[ndrew]
[Tommy]

Ramsey, John Montgomery
See Cohen, Paul Arthur

Ramsey, Joseph McCray 1890-   [NAA]
American editor
* J. M. R.

Ramsey, Lowell Wallace, Jr. 1952-
[FR]
American football player
* Ramsey, Chuck

Ramsey, Ronald 1938?- [BI]
American revolutionist
* Epstein, Joe Libre

Ramsey, Square Jaw
See Ramsey, William Thrace [Bill]

Ramsey, Thomas A. 1864-1906 [AS, BE, PB]
American baseball player
* Ramsey, Toad

Ramsey, Toad
See Ramsey, Thomas A.

Ramsey, William Thrace [Bill] 1921- [BE]
American baseball player
* Ramsey, Square Jaw

Ramskill, Valerie Patricia Roskams [AW, CAP, WD]
British author
* Brooke, Carol

Ramsome, [James] Stafford 1860-1931 [SFL]
Author
* Lewis, Caroline [joint pseudonym with (Edward) Harold Begbie and M. H. Temple]

Ramspeck, Robert 1890-1972 [HPPN]
American politician
* [The] Guardian of the Civil Service

Ramus, Pierre 1515-1572 [PA]
Author
* [La] Ramee

[La] Rana [The Frog]
See Verdugo, Rene Martin

Rana, J.
See Bhatia, Jamunadevi

Ranc, Arthur 1831-1908 [SN]
French politician
* Rock

Rance, Janet Mary 1928- [IAW]
British writer
* Graham, Janet

Rancher [code name]
See Williams, Roy Lee

[El] Ranchero [The Rancher]
See Aguilar Gonzalez, Jorge

Rand, Alissa 1905-1982
Russian-born American author
* Rand, Ayn

Rand, Anne
See Ozbekhan, Anne Binkley Rand

Rand, Ayn
See Rand, Alissa

Rand, Bill
See Engler, William George

Rand, Brett
See Norwood, Victor G[eorge] C[harles]

Rand, C. H. 19th c. [IP]
American? author
* Hazelton, Mabel

Rand, Ellen
See Fleming, Nellie

[The] Rand Goal Mine
See Geffin, Aaron

Rand, J. H.
See Holland, James R.

Rand, James S.
See Attenborough, Bernard George

Rand, John
See Reach, James

Rand, Lionel
See Van Clouser, Lionel

Rand, Olive 19th c. [IP]
American author and journalist
* O. R.

Rand, Sally 1904- [HPPN]
American fan dancer
* Fan-tastic Sally
* Her Sexellency

Rand, Sally
See Beck, Helen Gould

Rand, [Rev.] William 1700-1779 [HPPN]
American clergyman
* [A] Lover of Truth and Peace

Rand, William
See Roos, William

Randall, Addison Owen 1907-1945 [SC]
American actor
* Randall, Jack

Randall, Anne Frances
See Robinson, Mary Darby

Randall, Arkle
See Randall, Derek William

Randall, Bo
See Randall, W. D.

Randall, Bob
See Goldstein, Stanley B.

Randall, Clark 20th c.
Singer
* Tennille, Frank

Randall, Clay
See Adams, Clifton

Randall, Derek William 1951- [DC]
British cricketer
* Randall, Arkle

Randall, J. R. 19th c. [IP]
American poet
* J. R. R.

Randall, Jack 1794-1828 [NN, RBE]
British boxer
* [The] Nonpareil
* [The] Original Nonpareil
* [The] Prime Irish Lad

Randall, Jack
See Randall, Addison Owen

Randall, Janet [joint pseudonym with Robert W(illiam) Young]
See Young, Jan[et Randall]

Randall, Janet [joint pseudonym with Jan(et Randall) Young]
See Young, Robert W[illiam] [Bob]

Randall, Jean
See Hauck, Louise [Platt]

Randall, Joseph 1931-1970 [SC]
American stunt performer
* Starr, Randy

Randall, Mary
See Colver, Alice Mary [Ross]

Randall, Rae
See Salvason, Sigrum

Randall, Richard 20th c. [IBW]
American dog breeder, hair stylist, fashion designer
* Mr. Rick

Randall, Robert [joint pseudonym with Robert Silverberg]
See Garrett, [Gordon] Randall [Philip David]

Randall, Robert [joint pseudonym with Randall Garrett]
See Silverberg, Robert

Randall, Robert Lee 1948- [SMG]
American baseball player
* B. R.

Randall, Rona
See Shambrook, Rona

Randall, Steven
See Andrews, Clarence A[delbert]

Randall, W. D. 1909?- [BI]
American knife maker
* Randall, Bo

Randall, William
See Gwinn, William R.

Rande, Frank
See Scott, Charles

Randel, Adelaide
See Atwood, Mrs.

Randell, Benny 20th c. [BBH]
Boxer
* Randell, Red

Randell, Beverley
See Price, Beverley Joan

Randell, Red
See Randell, Benny

Randi, Don
See Schwartz, Don

Randi, James 1928- [EOP]
Canadian-born magician
* [The] Amazing Randi

Randle, Berdine Caronell 1929- [BA]
American educator
* Randle, Bert

Randle, Bert
See Randle, Berdine Caronell

Randle, Frank
See McEvoy, Arthur

Randle, Sonny
See Randle, Ulmo

Randle, Ulmo 1936- [FB]
American football player
* Randle, Sonny

Randles, Anthony V[ictor], Jr. 1942-
[CA]
American journalist
* Randles, Slim

Randles, E. 1760-1820 [IP]
British organist and author
* [The] Lyrist

Randles, Slim
See Randles, Anthony V[ictor], Jr.

Randolph, Arthur C.
See Greene, Alvin Carl

Randolph, Asa Philip 1889-1979 [CR,
HPPN, IBW]
American labor leader
* Black Labor, Mr.
* [The] Father of the Civil Rights
Movement
* [The] Grand Old Man of Black
Liberation
* [The] Most Dangerous Negro in
America
* St. Philip of the Pullman Porters
* Uncle Tom Number 2

Randolph, Big Jim
See Randolph, James Lyle

Randolph, Boots
See Randolph, Homer Louis, III

Randolph, Charles 19th c. [HPPN]
American author
* [An] American Citizen

Randolph, Dorothy
See Cohen, Dorothy

Randolph, Dorothy
See Mathewson, Dorothy Cohen

Randolph, Edmund Jennings 1753-1813
[HPPN]
American attorney and statesman
* [The] Attorney General

Randolph, Ellen
See Ross, Don

Randolph, Ellen
See Ross, William Edward Daniel

Randolph, Francis 1755-1831 [HPPN]
British clergyman
* Britannicus

Randolph, Geoffrey
See Ellis, Edward S[ylvester]

Randolph, Georgiana Ann 1908-1957
[CC, EMD, WGT]
American author and screenwriter
* Rice, Craig [joint pseudonym with
Salvatore A. Lombino]
* Sanders, Daphne
* Venning, Michael

Randolph, Gordon [joint pseudonym
with Sylvia Von Block]
See Von Block, Bela

Randolph, Gordon [joint pseudonym
with Bela Von Block]
See Von Block, Sylvia

Randolph, Homer Louis, III 20th c.
[CME]
American musician
* Randolph, Boots

Randolph, Irving 1909- [DAM, EJ, PMJ]
American jazz musician
* Randolph, Mouse

Randolph, [Lieutenant] J. H.
See Ellis, Edward S[ylvester]

Randolph, J. Thornton
See Peterson, Charles Jacob

Randolph, James Lyle 1930-1970 [IBW]
American disc jockey
* Randolph, Big Jim

Randolph, Jerry
See Brannon, William T.

Randolph, John 1773-1833 [FFF, HPPN,
SN]
American statesman
* Jack the Giant-Killer
* Little David
* Lord of Roanoke
* [The] Man with the Sling

Randolph, John
See Cohen, Emanuel Hirsch

Randolph, Josie Lee
See Beers, Mrs. J. Newton

Randolph, Lillian 20th c. [IBW]
American actress and conductor
* Madame Queen

Randolph, Marion
See Rodell, Marie F[reid]

Randolph, Mouse
See Randolph, Irving

Randolph, Nan E.
See Patterson, Anna Eliza

Randolph, Nancy
See McCarthy, Julia

Randolph, Nancy
See Robb, Inez [Callaway]

Randolph, Paschal Beverley 1825-?
[FFF, IP]
American author and editor
* Lee, Griffin
* [A] Rosicrucian

Randolph, Popsie
See Seezenais, William

Randolph, Randy
See Randolph, Zilner T.

Randolph, Richard
See Pentelow, John Nix

Randolph, Thomas, Jr. [Tom] 1943-
[IBW]
American track and field athlete
* Speed, Mr.

Randolph, Vance 1892- [CA]
American author, editor, folklorist
* Booker, Anton S.

Randolph, Zilner T. 1899- [MY]
American jazz musician
* Randolph, Randy

Random, Alan
See Kay, Ernest

Random, Alex
See Rowland, Donald Sydney

Rands, William Brighty 1823-1882
[DEL, DLE1, NPS, PA, SAT]
British author
* Browne, Matthew
* Fieldmouse, Timon
* Holbeach, Henry
* [The] Laureate of the Nursery
* Talker, T.

Randy Andy
See Andrew

Raney, Butch
See Raney, Gordon

Raney, Frank Robert Donald
See Raniszewski, Frank Robert Donald

Raney, Gordon ?-1953 [BBH]
American basketball player and coach
* Raney, Butch

Raney, Ribs
See Raniszewski, Frank Robert Donald

Raney, Sue
See Claussen, Raelene

Ranft, George 1895- [BDF, F2, FC]
American actor
* Raft, George

Ranganathan, Shiyali Ramamrita 1892-
[HPPN]
Indian librarian, educator, author
* Philosopher of Librarianship

Rangefinder
See Miles, Frederic James

Rangell, Johan Wilhelm 1894- [HPPN]
Finnish banker and political leader
* Rangell, Jukka

Rangell, Jukka
See Rangell, Johan Wilhelm

Rangely, E. R.
See Zachary, Hugh

Rangely, Olivia
See Zachary, Hugh

[The] Ranger
See Flack, Captain

Ranger Bill
See William, Joseph

Ranger, Charles, Esq.
See Murphy, Arthur

Ranger, Ken
See Creasey, John

Ranger, Morris [SN]
British speculator
* [The] Napoleon of Liverpool Finance

Ranger, Roger
See Freeman, James Midwinter

Ranieri 1050?-1118 [WBD]
Pope
* Paschal II

Raniszewski, Frank Robert Donald
1923- [BE]
American baseball player
* Raney, Frank Robert Donald
* Raney, Ribs

Ranjee
See Shahani, Ranjee

Ranji
See Ranjitsinhji, Kumar Shri

Ranjit [or Runjeet], Singh 1780-1839
[HN, WBD]
Maharaja
* [The] Lion of the Punjab
* [The] Mountain Tiger of Nepaul

Ranjitsinhji, Kumar Shri 1872-1933
[HPPN, NN]
Cricketer and Maharajah of Nawanagar
* [The] Black Prince of Cricketers
* Ranji

Rank, Otto
See Rosenfeld, Otto

Ranken, George 1838-1855 [IP]
British army officer and author
* [A] Soldier

Rankin, Arthur
See Davenport, Arthur Rankin

Rankin, Arthur McKee 1841-1914
[THR]
*Canadian-born actor and theatrical
manager*
* Henley, George

Rankin, Caroline 20th c.
Actress
* Rankin, Spike

Rankin, Fannie W. 19th c. [IP, PA]
Author
* F. W. R.

Rankin, Hugh Doak 20th c. [WGT]
American author
* Doak

Rankin, Jeannette 1880-1973 [HPPN]
American politician
* [The] First Woman in Congress

Rankin, John
See Morse, Withrow

Rankin, John Elliott 1882-? [HPPN]
American attorney and politician
* [The] Killer
* Rankin, T. V. A.

Rankin, Mrs. McKee [FFF]
Entertainer
* Blanchard, Kittie

Rankin, R. S. 1933- [BWW]
American singer
* Little T Bone
* Walker, T Bone, Jr.

Rankin, Ruth [DeLone] I[rvine] 1924-
[CA]
American author
* DeLone, Ruth

Rankin, Spike
See Rankin, Caroline

Rankin, Stella 1915- [ART]
British painter
* S. R.

Rankin, T. V. A.
See Rankin, John Elliott

Rankine, John
See Mason, Douglas R[ankine]

Rankine, William Birch 1858-1905
[HPPN]
American hydroelectrician
* [The] Father of Niagara Power

Ranking, B. Montgomerie 19th c. [IP]
British poet
* M. R.

Rann, John ?-1774 [DNNF, DNNS, RH]
British highwayman
* Sixteen-String Jack

Rannaill, Clan
See Grannell, Robert J.

Ranney, Agnes V. 1916- [BI, CA, SAT]
American author
* Reeves, Ruth Ellen

Ransenthaler, Peter 1929- [SW]
German actor
* Carsten, Peter

Ransford, Oliver Neil 1914- [AW]
British-born physician and author
* Wylcotes, John

Ransom, Frank 1870-1921 [BEW]
American actor
* Mills, Frank

Ransom, Jay Ellis 1914- [CA]
American author
* Adams, Henry T.

Ransom, John Crowe 1888- [CR]
American poet, critic, editor
* Ransom, Pappy

Ransom, Mike
See Ransom, Willard Blystone

Ransom, Olive
See Stephens, Kate

Ransom, Pappy
See Ransom, John Crowe

Ransom, Willard Blystone 1916- [BA]
American attorney
* Ransom, Mike

Ransome, Charles A.
See Rowe, John Gabriel

Ransome, L. E. 20th c. [MBF]
British author
* Clifford, Martin [house pseudonym]
* Hayes, Ivor
* Melbourne, Ivor
* Norman, Victor
* Richards, Frank [house pseudonym]
* Stirling, Tom

Ransome, Mrs. J. W. [FFF]
Entertainer
* Bordeaux, Ella

Ransome, Stephen
See Davis, Frederick Clyde

Ransome-Davies, Basil
See Colley, Iain

Rant, Tol E.
See Longyear, Barry Brookes

[The] Ranter
See Robins, John

Rantipole
See Bonaparte, Charles Louis Napoleon

Rantoul, Robert, Jr. 1805-1852 [HPPN]
American attorney and politician
* R. R.

Ranucci, Renato 1921- [BI, HPPN]
Italian comedian and songwriter
* Rascel, Renato

Ranulf of Chester
See Higden, Ranulf

Ranyard, Ellen Henrietta White
1810-1879 [DEL, FFF]
British author
* L. N. R.

Ranzini, Addis Durning 1909- [NAA]
American author and columnist
* Ames, Elinor

Rao, N. T. Rama 1923?-
Indian actor
* N. T. R.

Rao, Sridhar 1916- [EOP]
Leader of Indian religious sect
* Chidananda, Swami

**Raoul [code name used during World
War II]**
See Churchill, Peter

Raoul, Anthony
See Wilmot, Anthony

Raoul, M. ?-1274 [PA]
Author
* De Ferriers

**Rapagnetto-D'Annunzio, Gabriele
[original family surname?]**
See D'Annunzio, Gabriele

Rapallo, Mrs. S. F. Ludomilla [Schetky]
19th c. [IP]
British author
* His Daughter

Rapaport, Jerome L. 1928-   [CA]
American historian and author
* Clark, Jerome L.

Raper, Jack
See Raper, Julius Rowan

Raper, Julius Rowan 1938-   [CA]
American author
* Raper, Jack

Raphael
See Evans, Elizabeth Edson Gibson Du
Bois

Raphael
See Palmer, Mrs. James F. [Reynolds]

Raphael
See Santi [or Sanzio?], Raffaello

Raphael
See Smith, Robert Cross

Raphael, [Sister] Anna
See Fitzgerald, Anna A.

Raphael, Chaim 1908-   [CA, CC, WW]
British author
* Davey, Jocelyn
* Raphael, Rab

Raphael, Edwin
See Wakeley, Mr.

Raphael, Elaine
See Bolognese, Elaine Raphael
[Chionchio]

Raphael, Frederic [Michael] 1931-   [CA]
American-born author
* Caine, Mark [joint pseudonym with
Tom Maschler]

Raphael, Jay
See Josephs, Ray

Raphael, John N. 1868-1917   [BEW]
Playwright, critic, journalist
* Percival

Raphael, [Father] M.
See Goldgraber, Kenneth

[The] Raphael of Cats
See Mind, Gottfried [or Godefroi]

[The] Raphael of Domestic Art
See Wilkie, [Sir] David

[The] Raphael of England
See Reynolds, [Sir] Joshua

[The] Raphael of France
See Le Sueur [or Lesueur], Eustache

[The] Raphael of Holland
See Van Hemskerck, Martin

[The] Raphael of Holland
See Von Heemskerk [or Hemskerk],
Martin

[The] Raphael of Music
See Mozart, Johannes Chrysostom
Wolfgangus Theophilus

[The] Raphael of Opera
See Mozart, Johannes Chrysostom
Wolfgangus Theophilus

[The] Raphael of the Parc-aux-Cerfs
See Boucher, Francois

Raphael, Rab
See Raphael, Chaim

Raphael, Ralph B. 1856-1903   [BI]
American Zionist leader
* Raphael, Raphael Dov Ber

Raphael, Raphael Dov Ber
See Raphael, Ralph B.

Raphael, Sylvia 1938-   [LFW]
Israeli intelligence agent
* Roxbourgh, Patricia

Raphael II
See Palmer, John

Raphael III
See Medhurst, Mr.

Raphael IV
See Wakeley, Mr.

Raphael V
See Sparkes, Mr.

Raphael VI
See Cross, Robert C.

Raphaela, Cornelius [Nechi] 1914?-
[CW]
Curacaon author and poet
* Hernandez, Victor P.

Raphaelle
See Guertin, Raphaelle-Berthe

Rapid Robert Feller
See Feller, Robert William Andrew

Rapid, Young
See Brown, T. Allston

Rapidez, Kid
See Cruz, Alfredo

Rapier
See Watson, Alfred Edward Thomas

[The] Rapier of the North
See Chapdelaine, Ovila

Rapler, Rob
See Alexander, O. C.

Rapmund, Joseph 1862-?   [PI]
Irish poet
* Observer

Rapp, Butler 1898?-1931   [NOJ]
American jazz musician
* Rapp, Guye

Rapp, George
See Rapp, Johann Georg

Rapp, Goldie
See Rapp, Joseph Aloysius

Rapp, Goldie
See Rapp, Robert

Rapp, Guye
See Rapp, Butler

Rapp, Johann Georg 1757-1847   [HPPN]
German-born religious reformer
* Rapp, George

Rapp, Joseph Aloysius 1892-   [BE]
American baseball player
* Rapp, Goldie

Rapp, Louis 1909-1970   [PMJ]
American singer
* Wood, Barry

Rapp, Manny
See Rapp, Manuel

Rapp, Manuel 20th c.   [EF]
American football player
* Rapp, Manny

Rapp, Robert 20th c.   [EF]
American football player
* Rapp, Goldie

Rappaport, Barry 1909-1970   [HPPN]
American producer and singer
* Wood, Barry

Rappaport, Blossom
See Pious, Minerva

Rappaport, Frances 1908-   [HPPN]
American television personality
* Miss Frances

Rappaport, Semen Akimovich
See Rappaport, Solomon

Rappaport, Solomon 1863-1920   [BEW,
BI]
Yiddish author and playwright
* Ansky, S. A.
* Rappaport, Semen Akimovich

[The] Rapt Sage
See Aristocles

Rapuzzi, G. L. 20th c.   [SFP]
Author
* Gray, Woody
* Renna, G.

Raq
See Evens, Glyn Kinnaird

Raquenue, Izmael
See Zequiera y Arango, Manuel de

Rara
See Ravel, Maurice Joseph

Rare Ben
See Jonson, Ben[jamin]

Rare Sir Will
See Davenant, [Sir] William

Rarey, John Solomon 1827?-1866   [FFF]
American horse-tamer and author
* Scrutator

Rariden, Bedford Bill
See Rariden, William Angel

Rariden, William Angel 1888-1942   [BE]
American baseball player
* Rariden, Bedford Bill

Raro, Master
See Wieck, Friedrich

Rascel, Renato
See Ranucci, Renato

Rasch, C. M.
See Rasch, Catherine Margaret

Rasch, Catherine Margaret 1891- [ART]
British painter
* Rasch, C. M.

Raschi, Victor John Angelo 1919- [BE]
American baseball player
* [The] Springfield Rifle

Rascoe, Jesse Ed
See Bartholomew, Ed[ward Ellsworth]

Raset, Mickey
See Raset, Val

Raset, Val 1910-1977 [HPPN]
American choreographer
* Raset, Mickey

Rasey, Ruth M.
See Simpson, Ruth Mary Rasey

Rash, Dora Eileen Agnew [Wallace]
1897- [AW, CA]
British author
* Wallace, Doreen

Rashad, Ahmad
See Moore, Robert E. [Bobby]

Rasheed, [Rev.] Hakeem
See Jones, Clifford

Rashi
See Solomon bar Isaac

Rashid al-Din 1250?-1318 [WBD]
Arabic historian
* Tabib, al- [The Physician]

Rashleigh, [Sir] John Colman 1772-1847
[IP]
British politician and author
* One of the 80,000 Incorrigible
  Jacobins

Rasiel de Selva, Hercule
See Quesnel, Pierre

Raskin, Big Tubby
See Raskin, Morris

Raskin, Julius 1906- [EJS]
American basketball player
* Raskin, Little Tubby

Raskin, Little Tubby
See Raskin, Julius

Raskin, Morris 1906- [EJS]
American basketball coach
* Raskin, Big Tubby

Raskind, Richard 1935-
*American ophthalmologist and tennis pro
who underwent sex-change surgery*
* Richards, Renee

Rasley, John M. 1913- [ASC]
American composer
* Johnston, Randolph

Rasmussen, Deerfoot
See Rasmussen, Wayne

Rasmussen, Eric Ralph
See Rasmussen, Harold Ralph

Rasmussen, Harold Ralph 1952- [SMG]
American baseball player
* [The] Great Dane
* Rasmussen, Eric Ralph

Rasmussen, Juliana
See Galcai, Lalauga Malana Au Faoa
Taupou O. Tuffle Tuimanua

Rasmussen, Wayne 20th c.
American football player
* Rasmussen, Deerfoot

Rasofsky, Barnet David 1909-1967 [AS,
BX, EJS]
American boxer
* Ross, Barney

Raspe, Rudolph E[rich] 1737-1794
[WGT]
German author
* Munchausen, Baron
* Sarratt, H. J.

Rasputin, Grigori Efimovich 1871?-1916
[BL, HPPN]
Russian mystic
* [The] Holy Devil
* [The] Holy Satyr
* [The] Mad Monk

Rasputin, Maria
See Bern, Maria Rasputin Soloviev

[The] Rasputin of the Presidential Villa
See Lopez Rega, Jose

Rassoul, Mohammed
See Bogan, Gulam

Rastelli, Oreste 1900- [BMH]
Italian-born acrobat
* Voltige a la Richard

Rastelli, Philip 20th c.
American underworld figure
* Rastelli, Rusty

Rastelli, Rusty
See Rastelli, Philip

Rasulala, Thalmus
See Crowder, Jack

[The] Rat
See Herzog, Dorrel Norman Elvert

[The] Rat
See Linseman, Ken

[The] Rat
See Ratcliffe, [Sir] Richard

Rat
See Tourbillon, Robert Arthur

**[The] Rat Eyed Incarnation of
Attorneyism**
See Fouquier-Tinville, Antoine Quentin

Rata-Langa
See Galantara, Gabriele

Ratatoskr
See Blaich, Hans Erich

Ratazzi, Mme. 1830-? [PA]
Author
* D'Albans, Vicompte
* Stack, Baron

[The] Ratcliffe Highway Murderer
See Williams, John

Ratcliffe, James P.
See Mencken, Henry Louis [Harry]

Ratcliffe, Patricia 1940- [IAW]
British author
* King, Teri

Ratcliffe, Ratters
See Ratcliffe, Robert Malcolm

Ratcliffe, [Sir] Richard ?-1485 [SN]
* [The] Rat

Ratcliffe, Robert Malcolm 1951- [DC]
British cricketer
* Ratcliffe, Ratters

Ratcliffe, Samuel Kirkham 1868-?
[WWL]
American journalist
* Kirkman, Francis

Ratcliffe, Wilton Calvert 1903- [BEW]
American actor
* Graff, Wilton

Rath, E. J. [joint pseudonym with
Edith Rathbone (Jacobs) Brainerd]
See Brainerd, Chauncey Corey

Rath, E. J. [joint pseudonym with
Chauncey Corey Brainerd]
See Brainerd, Edith Rathbone [Jacobs]

Rathbone, Basil 1892-1967 [HPPN]
British actor
* [The] Man With the Finest Sneer in
  the Movies

Rathbone, Justus H. 1839-1889 [HPPN]
*American government clerk and fraternal
association activist*
* [The] Father of the Knights of
  Pythias

Rathbone, William 1819-? [IP, PA]
British merchant and author
* [The] Man of Business

Rathborne, St. George Henry 1854-1938
[DNA, NAA, WW]
American author
* Adams, Harrison
* Allen, Hugh
* Burton, Andy
* Carter, Herbert
* Clifton, Oliver Lee
* Dale, Dash
* Duncan, Duke
* Edwards, Ward
* Forbes, Aleck
* Howard, Jack
* Keene, Lieut.
* Langley, John Prentice
* Lawson, W. B.
* Leslie, Lawrence
* Manly, Marline
* Merrick, Mark
* Miller, Warne
* Old Broadbrim
* [A] Private Detective
* Robertson, Alex
* St. George, Harry
* Sharpe, Jack

Rathborne, St. George Henry (cont.)
* Stewart, Gordon
* Young Broadbrim

Rather, Bo
See Rather, David Elmer

Rather, David Elmer 1950- [SMG]
American football player
* Rather, Bo

Rathgeber, Ralph 1920- [BDF, BEW, FC]
American actor
* Meeker, Ralph

Rathjen, Carl H[enry] 1909- [IAW, SAT]
American author
* Russell, Charlotte
* Russell, Clinton

Ratigan, Eleanor Eldridge 1916- [CA]
American author
* Wharton, Virginia

[A] Rational Christian
See Leopold, Alexander

[The] Rationalist
See Baker, William

Ratisbonne, Louis Fortune Gustave 1827-1900 [WBD]
French author
* Trim

Ratner, Joann 1931- [BEW]
American actress
* Merlin, Joanna

Rato [Rat]
See Fittipaldi, Emerson

Ratoff, Gregory 1893- [HPPN]
Russian-American film director and actor
* Gregory the Great

Ratsch, Fred E. 1891-1933 [SC]
American actor
* Rooney, Pat

Rattazzi, [Princess] Marie Studolmine Bonaparte 1833-? [PI]
Irish-born poet, playwright, author
* Bernard, Camille
* D'Albeno, Vicomte
* De Kelmar, Louis
* Stock, Baron

Rattenberry, William A. 1857-1933 [SC]
American actor
* White, Bill

Rattenbury, John 19th c. [IP]
Author
* [A] Smuggler

Ratti, Ambrogio Damiano Achille 1857-1939 [CBS]
Pope
* Pius XI

Rattlebrain
See Halse, G.

Rattlehead, David
See Byrn, M. Lafayette

[The] Rattler
See Riley, Ken

Rattler, Morgan
See Banks, Percival Weldon

Rattler, Raby, Gent.
See Hall, Thomas

Rattlesnake Dick
See Barter, Richard

Rattlesnake Jack McGee
See McGee, John

Rattlesnake Jake Fallon
See Fallon, Charles

[The] Rattlesnake Murderer
See James, Robert

Rattlesnake Pete Lanihan
See Lanihan, Peter

Rattling Bill Longley
See Longley, William Preston

Rattray, Henrietta Barbara 20th c. [WWL]
British author
* Jehan, Noor

Rattray, Simon
See Dudley-Smith, Trevor

Rau, Bayone
See Rau, Douglas James

Rau, Douglas James 1948- [SMG]
American baseball player
* Rau, Bayone

Rau, Nicander Edwin 1877?-1951 [BEW]
American entertainer
* Nicander, Edwin

Raubenheimer, George Harding 1923- [AW, WD]
South African author and screenwriter
* Harding, George

Raubes, Ella Wallace 1921- [FC]
American actress
* Raines, Ella

Rauch, Billy
See Rauch, Russell

Rauch, Russell 1910- [PMJ]
American musician
* Rauch, Billy

Raucourt
See Saucerotte, Francoise-Marie Antoinette Josephe

Raudive-Maurina, Zenta 1897- [IAW]
Latvian-born author
* Maurina, Zenta

Raudman, Robert Joyce [Bob] 1942- [BE]
American baseball player
* Raudman, Shorty

Raudman, Shorty
See Raudman, Robert Joyce [Bob]

Rauff, Walter 1907?- [NW 8-29-83]
German Nazi leader
* [The] Murderer of Milan

Raul
See Pederneiras, Raul Paranhos

Rault, Walter
See Gorham, Maurice Anthony Coneys

Rauschenberg, Robert 1925- [HPPN]
American artist
* [The] Creator of Minimal Art

Rausse
See Franke, H. F.

Rautakallio, Pekka Olavi 1953- [SMG]
Finnish-born hockey player
* Rautakallio, Rocky

Rautakallio, Rocky
See Rautakallio, Pekka Olavi

Rautzhan, Clarence George 1952- [SMG]
American baseball player
* Rautzhan, Lance

Rautzhan, Lance
See Rautzhan, Clarence George

[The] Rav [The Rabbi]
See Soloveitehik, Joseph B.

Ravales, Robin 1935- [CW]
Surinamese poet and playwright
* Dobru, R.

Ravanel, Joseph 1869-1931
French mountain guide
* [Le] Rouge

Ravazza, Carl 1912?-1968 [HPPN, PMJ]
American singer and bandleader
* Ravell, Carl
* [The] Singing Maestro

[The] Rave
See Stallworth, Dave

Ravel, Maurice Joseph 1875-1937
French composer
* [The] Gallic Muse
* Master of Music
* Rara
* Riquet, Gomex le

Ravell, Carl
See Ravazza, Carl

[The] Raven
See Frey, A. R.

[The] Raven Knight
See Hunyadi, Janos [or Huniades, John]

Raven, Paul
See Gadd, Paul

Raven, Ralph
See Payson, George

Ravenel, Charles, Jr. 1938?-
American banker and politician
* Ravenel, Pug

Ravenel, John
See Upshur, Donald M.

Ravenel, Pug
See Ravenel, Charles, Jr.

Ravenglass, Hal
See Wood, Samuel Andrew

Ravenhall, Mrs.
See Keiser, Robert

Ravenscroft, Howard H. 1902-1969 [SC]
American actor
* Barcroft, Roy

Ravenswood
See Beebee, Charles Washington

Ravesteyn, Josse 1506-1571 [PA]
Author
* Tiletanus

Ravi, Bison
See Vian, Boris

Raviola, Antonio 20th c. [WECO]
Italian cartoonist
* Magnus

Ravlengherio, Francois 1539-1597 [PA]
Author
* Ruphelenguis

Raw, Kathryn
See Nyers, Amelia Kathryn

Raw Meat Bill
See Rodgers, Wilbur Kincaid

Rawford, W. C.
See Crawford, William [Elbert]

Rawhide [[code name]]
See Reagan, Ronald Wilson

Rawle, Francis ?-1727 [HPPN]
American author
* [A] Lover of His Country

Rawley, Callman
See Rakosi, Carl

Rawley, Charlotte 1894-1908 [SC]
American actress
* Mae, Jimsey

Rawlings, Harry
See Downing, George

Rawlings, J. R.
See McCulloch, J. H.

Rawlings, John W. 1892-1972 [PB]
American baseball player
* Rawlings, Red

Rawlings, Marjorie Kinnan
See Baskin, Marjorie Kinnan Rawlings

Rawlings, Martha 1942- [BA]
American educator
* Rawlings, Marti

Rawlings, Marti
See Rawlings, Martha

Rawlings, Red
See Rawlings, John W.

Rawlins, E[ustace]
See Barton, [Dr.] Eustace Robert

Rawlins, Judith [Judy]
See Riedel, Judith Ellen

Rawlins, Lester
See Rosenberg, Lester

Rawlinson, A. R.
See Rawlinson, Arthur Richard

Rawlinson, Arthur Richard 1894- [THR]
British playwright
* Rawlinson, A. R.

Rawlinson, Richard ?-1755 [IP]
British antiquary and author
* [An] Impartial Hand

Rawlinson, Thomas 1681-1725 [DEP, DNNS, SN]
British book collector
* Folio, Tom
* [The] Leviathan of Book-Collectors

Rawls, Katherine 1918- [BBH]
American swimmer and diver
* Rawls, Peggy

Rawls, Peggy
See Rawls, Katherine

Rawson, Albert Leighton 1829-1902 [DNA]
American author and artist
* Kadmus, G.

Rawson, Clayton 1906-1971 [AW, CA, CC]
American magician and author
* Merlini, [The] Great
* Towne, Stuart

Rawson, Edward 1615-1693 [HPPN]
British-American of Boston Colony
* [The] Persecutor

Rawson, George [IP]
British hymn writer
* [A] Leeds Layman

Rawson, Mrs. Harry 19th c. [IP]
British author
* [A] Lady

Rawston, George 19th c. [IP]
British author
* [An] Ex Dissenter

Ray
See Howard-Jones, Ray

Ray, Agnes
See Benjamin, Elizabeth Dundas [Bedell]

Ray, Aldo
See DaRe, Aldo

Ray, Allene
See Burch, Allene

Ray, Ambrose
See Ray, Tom

Ray, Andrew
See Aureli, Andrea

Ray, Anna Chapin 1865-1945 [BI]
American author
* Howard, Sidney

Ray, Baby
See Ray, Buford

Ray, Big Black
See Ray, Danny

Ray, Buddy
See Ray, Robert J.

Ray, Buford 1916- [FB, SMG]
American football player
* Ray, Baby

Ray, Cadillac
See Ray, Eddie

Ray, Carl 20th c. [HPPN]
American football player
* Ray, Mutt

Ray, Chesty Joie
See Ray, Joie

Ray, Danny 1934- [DAM]
American musician
* Ray, Big Black

Ray, De Witt Grinnell [PA]
Author
* Gray, Widett

Ray, Deborah
See Kogan Ray, Deborah

Ray, Dixy Lee 1914- [CR]
American politician and zoologist
* Oo'ma [Great Lady]

Ray, E. Henry
See Eisenhardt, Raymond Henry

Ray, Eddie 20th c.
American football player
* Ray, Cadillac

Ray, Elmer [BI]
American boxer
* Ray, Violent

Ray, Farmer
See Ray, Robert Henry

Ray, Felix
See Brubaker, Howard

Ray, Gabrielle
See Cook, Gabrielle

Ray, Harmon 1914- [BWW]
American singer
* Peetie Wheatstraw's Buddy
* Ray, Herman

Ray, Herman
See Ray, Harmon

Ray, Hugh L. 1884-1956 [AS, FB]
American football official
* Ray, Shorty

Ray, Ina
See Cowan, Odessa

Ray, Irene
See Beebe, Rachel Irene

Ray, Irene
See Sutton, Rachel Irene Beebe

Ray, Irv[ing Burton] 1864-1947　[BE]
American baseball player
* Ray, Stubby

Ray, Isaac 1807-1881　[HPPN]
American physician
* I. R.

Ray, Isom
See　Agee, Ray[mond Clinton]

Ray, James Earl 1928-　[BLB, HPPN]
American assassin of civil rights activist,
Martin Luther King, Jr.
* Bridgman, Paul
* [The] Camouflaged Killer
* Gault, Eric Starvo
* [The] Lovelorn Killer
* Lowmyer, Harvey
* [The] Mole
* Sneyd, Ramon George
* Willard, John

Ray, James Francis 1944-　[BE, PB]
American baseball player
* Ray, Sting

Ray, James Ralph 1893-1955　[BI]
American author and illustrator
* Ames, Jim

Ray, Jaybird
See　Ray, Otto

Ray, Jean
See　De Kremer, Jean Raymond

Ray, Jimmy
See　Genovese, James

Ray, John
See　Wray, John

Ray, John Alvin [Johnny] 1927-　[NN]
American singer
* [The] Prince of Wails

Ray, John Lamar 1944-　[IBW]
American attorney and politician
* Ray, St. Peter

Ray, Johnnie 1927-
American singer
* [The] Nabob of Sob

Ray, Johnny
See　Matthews, John

Ray, Joie 1884-　[BBH]
American track and field athlete
* Ray, Chesty Joie

Ray, Larry
See　Hayes, Larry Ray

Ray, Mutt
See　Ray, Carl

Ray, Nancy Louise 1918-　[CA]
Australian author
* Hunt, Nan

Ray, Nicholas
See　Kienzle, Raymond Nicholas

Ray, Otto ?-1976　[MK]
American baseball player
* Ray, Jaybird

Ray, R. J.
See　Brophy, Robert

Ray, Rena
See　Mary Rose, [Sister]

Ray, Rene
See　Creese, Irene

Ray, Robert Henry 1886-1963　[BE]
American baseball player
* Ray, Farmer

Ray, Robert J. 1919-　[ASC]
American composer
* Ray, Buddy

Ray, Russell
See　Strait, Raymond

Ray, St. Peter
See　Ray, John Lamar

Ray, Shorty
See　Ray, Hugh L.

Ray, Sting
See　Ray, James Francis

Ray, Stubby
See　Ray, Irv[ing Burton]

Ray, Ted
See　Olden, Charles

Ray, Terry 1915-　[FC, ITA, SW]
American actress
* Drew, Ellen

Ray, Thelma
See　Maud, Victoria

Ray, Tom 20th c.　[RO2]
American musician
* Ray, Ambrose

Ray, Violent
See　Ray, Elmer

Ray, Violet
See　Irvine, Edward James

Ray, Wesley
See　Gaulden, Ray

Ray, William Porter　[PA]
Author
* Tewksbury

Rayall, Mrs. A. ?-1854　[PA]
Author
* [A] Traveler

Rayart, Jack Perrin 1896-1968　[F1, F2]
Actor
* Perrin, Jack

Raybaud, Maxime　[IP, PA]
French author
* D'Alaux, Gustave

Rayburn, Sam Taliaferro 1882-1961
[HPPN]
American politician
* [The] Grand Old Man
* Mr. Sam

Raycraft, Stan
See　Shaver, Richard S[harpe]

Raye, Carol
See　Corkrey, Kathleen

Raye, Don
See　Wilhoite, Donald MacRae, Jr.

Raye, Martha
See　O'Reed, Maggie Teresa

Raye, Martha
See　Reed [or O'Reed?], Margaret
Theresa Yvonne

Rayer, Francis G. 20th c.　[SFP]
Author
* Longdon, George

Rayford, Big John
See　Rayford, John

Rayford, John 1943-　[RO2]
American musician
* Rayford, Big John

[El] Rayis
See　Nasser, Gamal Abdel

Rayito [Little Flash]
See　Del Pozo y Jimenez, Manuel

Rayito [Little Beam]
See　Ossorio, Carlos

Rayl, Jim 1941-　[BB]
American basketball player
* [The] Splendid Splinter

Rayland, Rose
See　Mortimer, Mrs. N. E.

Rayle, Geoffrey
See　McLean, Eric W.

[The] Rayleigh Bath Chair Murderer
See　Brown, Eric

Raymond, Arthur Lawrence 1882-1912
[BE, PB]
American baseball player
* Raymond, Bugs

Raymond, Augusta
See　Kidder, Mrs. Edward E.

Raymond, Bob
See　Infascelli, Roberto

Raymond, Bugs
See　Raymond, Arthur Lawrence

Raymond, Charles [joint pseudonym
with Raymond Koch]
See　Koch, Charlotte

Raymond, Charles [joint pseudonym
with Charlotte Koch]
See　Koch, Raymond

Raymond de Jesus, [Mother]
See　Dion, [Sister] Anita

Raymond de Saint-Gilles
See　Raymond IV

Raymond, E. V.
See　Gallun, Raymond Z[inke]

Raymond, Frenchy
See　Raymond, Joseph Claude Marc

Raymond, G. Alison
See Lanier, Alison Raymond

Raymond, Gene
See Guion, Raymond

Raymond, George Lansing 1839-1929
[DNA]
American author and educator
* Warren, Walter

Raymond, Grace
See Stillman, Annie Raymond

Raymond, Harold Newell 1884-1957
[ASC]
American composer
* Newell, Roy

Raymond, Harold R. 1925- [FB]
American football coach
* Raymond, Tubby

Raymond, Harry H.
See Truman, Harry H.

Raymond, Henry Augustus
See Scott, Sarah

Raymond, Henry Jarvis 1820-1869
[HPPN, SN]
American politician and journalist
* [The] Little Villain
* [A] Representative

Raymond, Henry S. [PA]
Author
* Bowline, Billy

Raymond, Hugh
See Michel, John B.

Raymond, Ida
See Tardy, Mary T.

Raymond, Jack
See Caines, John

Raymond, Jack
See Feder, George

Raymond, Joe
See Eintrach, Joseph R.

Raymond, Joe
See Rosinski, Joseph

Raymond, John Howard 1814-1878
[HPPN]
American educator
* [The] President of the College

Raymond, John T.
See O'Brien, John

Raymond, Joseph Claude Marc 1937-
[BE, PB]
Canadian-born baseball player
* Raymond, Frenchy

Raymond, Joseph H.
See Le Fontaine, Joseph [Raymond]

Raymond, Lee
See Hill, Mary Raymond

Raymond, Louise
See Daniels, Mrs.

Raymond, Lupe Victoria Jolie 20th c.
[BI]
Cuban singer
* La Lupe

Raymond, [Father] M.
See Flanagan, Joseph David Stanislaus

Raymond, Mary
See Keegan, Mary Heathcott

Raymond, Maurice 20th c. [HPPN]
American magician
* [The] Great Raymond
* [The] Master of Magic

Raymond, Mrs. Lewis   [FFF]
Entertainer
* May, Alice

Raymond, Nate 20th c. [DI]
American gambler
* Raymond, Nigger Nate

Raymond, Nigger Nate
See Raymond, Nate

Raymond, Paula
See Wright, Paula Ramona

Raymond, Rene 1906- [CC, EMD, WW]
British author
* Chase, James Hadley
* Docherty, James L.
* Grant, Ambrose
* Marshall, Raymond

Raymond, Robert
See Alter, Robert Edmond

Raymond, Rossiter Worthington
1840-1918 [DNA]
American author and engineer
* Gray, Robertson

Raymond the Great
See Saunders, Raymond

Raymond, Tubby
See Raymond, Harold R.

Raymond, Walter 1852-? [WWL]
British author
* Cobbleigh, Tom

Raymond, William Lee 1877-? [NAA]
American author
* X

Raymond IV ?-1105 [WBD]
Count of Toulouse
* Raymond de Saint-Gilles

Raynal, Abbe
See Raynal, Guillaume Thomas
Francois

Raynal, Guillaume Thomas Francois
1713-1796 [HPPN]
French author
* Raynal, Abbe

Raynal, Louis
See Hoffman, Josef

Rayne, Alan
See Tobin, James Edward

Rayner, Augustus Alfred 1894- [WW]
Author
* Hall, Whyte

Rayner, Chuck
See Rayner, Claude Earl

Rayner, Claire 1931- [AW, CA, WD]
British author and columnist
* Brandon, Sheila
* Chetwynd, Berry
* Lynton, Ann
* Martin, Ruth [house pseudonym]
* Saxe, Isobel

Rayner, Claude Earl 1920- [CEI, FHE,
HK]
Canadian-born hockey player
* Bonnie Prince Charlie
* Rayner, Chuck

Rayner, Guy
See Clarke, S. Dacre

Rayner, John Desmond
See Rahmer, Hans Sigismund

Rayner, Olive Pratt
See Allen, [Charles] Grant [Blairfindie]

Rayner, Ray
See Rahner, Raymond M.

Rayner, Richard
See McIlwain, David

Raynes, Frederica Rozelle Ridgway
1925- [IAW]
British author
* Castweazle, Eleanor

Raynor, George
See Rea, George James

Raynor, Hal
See Rubel, Henry Scott

Rayo
See Schmied, Rudolf

Rayola, Albert
See Capone, Umberto

Rayson, Paul
See Jennings, Leslie Nelson

Rayter, Joe
See McChesney, Mary F.

Razaf, Andy
See Razafinkeriefo, Andreamenentania
Paul

Razafinkeriefo, Andreamenentania Paul
1895-1973 [ASC, EJ, IBW]
American lyricist
* Crooning Andy
* Razaf, Andy

[El] Razi
See Ben-Fares, Almed

Razonador, Amable
See Henriquez y Alfau, Enrique

Razor Brain
See Tojo, Eiki

Rbg
See Ribbing, Sigurd

Rdd
See Ridderstad, Carl Fredrik

[II] Re
See Arantes Do Nascimento, Edson

[II] Re dei Cantatori
See Bernacchi, Antonio

Re Galantuomo
See Victor Emmanuel II

Re Lavrador [Farmer or Laborer King]
See Diniz

Rea, George James 1820-1864   [IP]
American minstrel
* Raynor, George

Rea, John Huntingdon 1909-1968   [FC]
American actor
* Ridgeley, John

Reach, James 20th c.   [WW]
Author
* Abbott, Bruce
* Bremer, Ward
* Manning, Hilda
* Rand, John
* Ressieb, George
* Sutton, Thomas
* West, Tom
* Williams, Pete
* Williams, Richard

Read, Brian [Ahier]
See Ahier, Brian

Read, Buck
See Read, Herbert

Read, E. A.
See Read, Edwin Alfred

Read, Edwin Alfred 1918-   [ART]
British stonemason and painter
* Read, E. A.

Read, George 1733-1798   [HPPN]
American senator
* [The] Champion of Equal
  Representation

Read, H. Y. 19th c.   [IP]
Canadian author
* [An] Actual Settler

Read, Herbert 1883-1970   [BB]
British-born American basketball player
* [The] Master Among Masters
* Read, Buck
* [The] Silver Fox

Read [or Reed?], James
See Malatesta, Guido

Read, Jan
See Read, John Hinton

Read, John Hinton 1917-   [AW, WD]
Australian-born author and playwright
* Read, Jan

Read, Melvin Dean 1922-   [CEI]
Canadian-born hockey player
* Read, Pee Wee

Read, Miss
See Saint, Dora Jessie [Shafe]

Read, O. 1886-   [WWL]
British journalist
* Reed, Hal

Read, Pee Wee
See Read, Melvin Dean

Read, William 1795?-1866   [PI]
Irish poet
* Eustace

Read, William 1820-?   [HPPN]
American physician
* [The] City Physician

Read-Tucker, L.
See Tucker, Loraine Read

Reade, Alfred Arthur 19th c.   [IP]
British author
* [A] Special Correspondent

Reade, Frances Lawson 20th c.   [CCL]
Canadian poet and author
* Langworthy, Yolande

Reade, Hamish
See Gray, Simon

Reade, John 1838-?   [IP]
Canadian clergyman, poet, journalist
* Home, J. F.
* J. R.
* R. J. C.

Reade, Lang
See Carter, David C[harles]

Reade, Regina
See Richardson, Randell

Reade, Rolf S.
See Rose, Alfred

Reade, William Winwood 1838-1875
[FFF]
British author
* Abati, Francesco

Reader, Paul
See Arce Robledo, Carlos De

[A] Reader Therein
See Cristadoro, Andrew

[The] Reading Baby Farmer
See Dyer, Amelia Elizabeth

[The] Reading Rifle
See Furillo, Carl Anthony

Ready, Martha A. Thomson 1846?-1929
[HPPN]
American brothel proprietress
* [The] Queen of the Denver Red
  Lights
* Silks, Mattie

Ready Money Spencer
See Spencer, Elihu

Reagan, Anne Frances Davis 1923-   [BP,
DF 3-7-83]
*Wife of American president, Ronald
Reagan*
* Nancita
* [The] Queen
* Rainbow [Secret Service code name]
* Reagan, Nancy

Reagan, Arthur 1882-?   [BE]
American baseball player
* Reagan, Rip

Reagan, Bobby
See Ruehle, George Robert

Reagan, Doctor
See Reagan, Ronald Wilson

Reagan, Dutch
See Reagan, Ronald Wilson

Reagan, Maureen 1941-   [WP 10-28-84]
*Daughter of American president, Ronald
Reagan*
* Radiant [Secret Service code name]

Reagan, Moon
See Reagan, [John] Neil

Reagan, Nancy
See Reagan, Anne Frances Davis

Reagan, [John] Neil 1909?-
*Brother of American president, Ronald
Reagan*
* Reagan, Moon

Reagan, Patricia 1953?-
*American actress and daughter of
President Ronald Reagan*
* Davis, Patti

Reagan, Rip
See Reagan, Arthur

Reagan, Ronald Prescott 1958-
*Son of American president, Ronald
Reagan*
* Reagan, Skip

Reagan, Ronald Wilson 1911-   [DF 3-7-
83, ET, FAP, HPPN, TI 3-3-86, TI 9-24-84,
TI 10-29-84, WP 9-16-85]
American president and former actor
* [The] Aging Right Wing Actor
* [The] Best Known Rancher in Santa
  Barbara, California
* Clean, Mr.
* [The] Defender
* [The] Doctor of Reality
* [The] Errol Flynn of the B's
* [The] Gipper
* [The] Great Communicator
* [The] Great Hero of American
  Conservatism
* [The] Great Persuader
* [The] Great Rondini
* [The] Most Happy Fellow
* [The] Not So Favorite Son
* O and W [Oldest and Wisest]
* Rawhide [[code name]]
* Reagan, Doctor
* Reagan, Dutch
* Reagan, Uncle
* Ronald the Right
* [The] Teflon President
* [The] Zippered Glipper

Reagan, Skip
See Reagan, Ronald Prescott

Reagan, Thomas [James] B[utler] 1916-
[AW, CA]
American author
* Thomas, Jim

Reagan, Uncle
See Reagan, Ronald Wilson

Reagan's Mr. Inside
See Darman, Richard G.

Reagan's Regan
See Regan, Donald Thomas

Real, Anthony
See Michel, F. Fernand

[The] Real Author of That Performance
See Witherspoon, John

[The] Real Jackal
See Tocnaye, Alain de Bougrenet de la

[The] Real Life James Bond
See Popov, Dusko

[The] Real Life Lolita
See Aadland, Beverly

[The] Real Life Raffles
See Mackay, George

[The] Real Mayor of Chicago
See Capone, Al[phonse]

[The] Real McCoy
See McCoy, Elijah J.

[The] Real McCoy
See McCoy, [Captain] William

[The] Real McCoy
See Selby, Norman

Ream, Vinnie
See Hoxie, Vinnie Ream

Reaney, James Crerar 1926- [AW]
Canadian author
* Spoonhill

[The] Reaper
See Glassner, Frank

Reardon, Beans
See Reardon, John Edward

Reardon, John Edward
American baseball official
* Reardon, Beans

Reason, Mr.
See Donaldson, James

Reason, Rex
See Roberts, Bart

[A] Reasoning Engine
See Clarke, Samuel

Reaves, John
See Reaves, Thomas Johnson

Reaves, Thomas Johnson 1950- [EF, FB]
American football player
* Reaves, John

Reavis, James Addison ?-1908 [BLB]
American swindler and forger
* De Arizonac, Baron
* De Los Colorados, Caballero
* [The] Red Baron of Arizona

Reavis, T. M. [FFF]
Advocated shifting U. S. capital to St. Louis, Mo.
* [The] Capital Mover

Reay, Evan
See Day, Alfred Ernest

Reay, Trevace
See Pond, S. T. R.

Rebak, H.
See Baker, Henry

Rebbeck, Elizabeth 19th c. [CCL]
Canadian author
* Catherina, Anna

[The] Rebbetzin [Rabbi's Wife]
See Jungreis, Esther

Rebecca
See Felix, Rachel

Rebecca
See Matoaka

[The] Rebel
See Bevan, Aneurin

[A] Rebel
See Eggleston, George Cary

Rebel
See Foe, Daniel

[The] Rebel Banker
See Morton, John

Rebel Duke of Ebbw Vale
See Bevan, Aneurin

[The] Rebel Girl
See Flynn, Elizabeth Gurley

[The] Rebel Governor
See Trumbull, Jonathan

[The] Rebel in a Wing Collar
See Coxey, Jacob Sechler

[The] Rebel of Salem
See Williams, Roger

[The] Rebel of Seventh Avenue
See Lolewski-Cassini, Oleg

[The] Rebel Poet
See Islam, Kazi Nazrul

[The] Rebel Spy
See Hardinge, Belle Boyd

[A] Rebel War Clerk
See Jones, John Beauchamp

[The] Rebel Without a Pause
See Palme, Olof

Rebelo, Marques
See Dias da Cruz, Eddy

Rebennack, Malcolm John 1940- [BI, NAD]
American singer
* Dr. John, the Night Tripper

[A] Rebenstein
See Bernstein, Aaron

Reberger, Crane
See Reberger, Frank Beall

Reberger, Frank Beall 1944- [BE]
American baseball player
* Reberger, Crane

Rebholz, Russ 20th c. [CFH]
American-born football player
* [The] Wisconsin Wrath

Reboul, Jean 1796-1864 [FFF, HPPN, PA, WBD]
French poet
* [The] Baker of Nimes
* [The] Baker Poet
* [Le] Boulanger de Nimes

Rebozo, Bebe
See Rebozo, Charles Gregory

Rebozo, Charles Gregory 1912- [BI, HPPN]
American real estate executive
* [The] Nixon Family's Closest Friend
* Rebozo, Bebe

Rebujina [Rumpus]
See Jimenez, Francisco

Recamier, Jeanne Francoise Julie Adelaide 1777-1849 [SN]
French society beauty
* [A] Second Helen

Recapper
See Abbott, Thomas C.

[A] Recent Missionary of the American Home Missionary Society...
See Cushman, [Rev.] Job

[Le] Rechin
See Fulk IV

Reckoner
See Strachan, John

[A] Recluse
See Clulow, William Benton

[The] Recluse of Edgbaston
See Newman, John Henry

[The] Recorder of the City of New York
See Horsmanden, Daniel

Recour, Charles
See Bott, Henry

[The] Recreator of Sherlock Holmes
See Gillette, William Hooker

Rectez, Ian
See Weisinger, Mort[imer]

[The] Rector
See Arundell, Francis Vyvyan Jago

[The] Rector
See Bedell, Gregory Thurston

[The] Rector
See Boggs, [Rev.] Edward B.

[The] Rector
See Coxe, Arthur Cleveland

[The] Rector
See Croswell, [Rev.] Harry

[The] Rector
See Egar, John H.

[The] Rector
See Gregory, Henry

[The] Rector
See Hoffman, [Rev.] Eugene Augustus

[The] Rector
See Lord, William Wilberforce

[The] Rector
See Sayers, [Rev.] Gilbert H.

[The] Rector
See Smith, [Rev.] John Cotton

[The] Rector
See Southard, [Rev.] Samuel Lewis

[The] Rector
See Tuttle, [Rev.] Isaac H.

[The] Rector
See Tyng, [Rev.] Dudley Atkins

[The] Rector and Bishop of the Diocese
See Doane, George Washington

Rector, Connie
See Rector, Cornelius

Rector, Cornelius 20th c. [OBW]
American baseball player
* Rector, Connie

Rector, George 1878-1947 [HPPN]
American restaurateur and author
* [The] Prince of Restaurateurs

[The] Rector of Calverton Bucks
See Perceval, Charles George

[The] Rector of Christ's Church, Watertown, Connecticut
See Reid, [Rev.] Horace Hall

[The] Rector of Fryerning
See Doyle, [Rev] Robert

[The] Rector of Lutterwoorth
See Wycliffe [or Wyclif], John

[The] Rector of St. Philip's Church
See Gadsden, Christopher Edwards

[The] Rector of the Church of the Advent
See Clark, [Rev.] Samuel Adams

Rector, Red
See Rector, William Eugene

Rector, William Eugene 1929- [CWG, DAM]
American country-western performer
* Rector, Red

[The] Red
See Amadeus VII

Red
See Brown, Angus

[The] Red
See Clare, Gilbert de

[The] Red
See Conrad

[The] Red
See Eric

[The] Red
See Fulk I

Red
See Lewis, [Harry] Sinclair

[The] Red
See Olaf Sitricson

[The] Red
See Otto II [or Otho]

[The] Red Admiral
See Beresford, Charles William De La Poer [First Baron Beresford]

[The] Red Barn Murderer
See Corder, William

[The] Red Baron
See Arledge, Roone

[The] Red Baron
See Berenson, Gordon Arthur

[The] Red Baron
See Berenson, Harold

[The] Red Baron
See Von Richthofen, Manfred

[The] Red Baron of Arizona
See Reavis, James Addison

[The] Red Baron of the S & L industry
See Knapp, Charles

Red Beard
See Frederick I [or Friedrich]

Red Beard
See Horush [Arouj, Horuc or Koruk]

Red Beard
See Khizr

Red Beard, Paul
See Kane, Paul

[The] Red Bishop
See Camara, Helder Pessoa

Red Buck Weightman
See Weightman, George

Red Butterfly
See Lauritsen, John [Phillip]

Red Cap
See Powell, Ransom T.

[A] Red Coat
See Sturrock, W.

[The] Red Colonel
See Guzman, Jacobo Arbenz

[The] Red Comyn
See Comyn, [Sir] John

[The] Red Countess
See Karolyi, Katalin Andrassy

Red Cross
See Grant, Charles

[The] Red Cross Knight
See George

[The] Red Dean
See Johnson, Hewlett

[The] Red Devil
See Jenatzy, Camille

Red Devil
See Wilborn, Nelson

Red Dog Dougherty
See Dougherty, Edward

[The] Red Douglas
See Douglas, Archibald

[The] Red Douglas
See Douglas, George

Red Eagle
See Weatherford, William

[The] Red Earl
See Burke [or Burgo?], Richard

Red Eye Hay
See Hay, James Alexander

Red Eye Jessie
See Bell, Jessie

[The] Red Feather Girl
See Bryant, Anita

[The] Red Fox
See Casimir I

[The] Red Fox
See Edgar [or Eadgar]

[The] Red Fox
See Hazelton, James

[The] Red Fox
See Jefferson, Thomas

[The] Red Fox
See Macliver, Colin

Red Fox Jackson
See Jackson, William Hicks

[The] Red Fox of Kinderhook
See Van Buren, Martin

[The] Red Fox of the Rio Grande Valley
See Creager, R. B.

Red Gallus Gene
See Talmadge, Eugene

[The] Red Hand
See Hughes, Terence McMahon

[The] Red Head
See Bow, Clara

[The] Red Head
See Godfrey, Arthur Michael

[The] Red Headed Kid from Wheeling
See Reuther, Walter Philip

[The] Red Headed Music Maker
See Hall, Wendell Woods

[The] Red Headed Rooster of the Rockies
See Belford, James Burns

[The] **Red Headed Tomboy**
See Berg, Patricia J. [Patty]

Red Herrings
See Seymour-Conway, Francis Charles

Red Hot Mama
See Abuza, Sophie

Red Hot Willie
See McTell, Willie Samuel

Red Hot Willie Glaze
See McTell, Willie Samuel

Red Hott Bergen
See Bergen, Stuart

Red Hugh
See O'Donnell [or O'Donell?], Hugh

Red Jack
See Almer, Jack

Red Jacket
See Sagoyewatha

Red Joe Lowe
See Lowe, Joseph

Red Ken Livingstone
See Livingstone, Ken[neth]

[The] **Red King**
See William II

[The] **Red Knight of Germany**
See Von Richthofen, Manfred

[The] **Red Light Bandit**
See Chessman, Caryl

[The] **Red Major**
See Mohieddin, Khaled

Red Mane
See Magnus

Red Mike Edson
See Edson, Merritt Austin

Red Mike Hylan
See Hylan, John F.

[The] **Red Monarch**
See Dzhugashvili, Iosif Vissarionovich

[The] **Red Napoleon**
See Zhukov, Georgi K.

Red Necktie Wearin
See Wearin, Otha Donner

Red Nelson
See Wilborn, Nelson

[The] **Red Pastor**
See Barth, Karl

Red Peter
See Ormond, Pierce

[The] **Red Petticoat General**
See Harrison, William Henry

Red Phil Davidson
See Davidson, Phil

Red Pope of Revolution
See DeLeon, Daniel

[The] **Red Priest**
See Vivaldi, Antonio Lucio

[The] **Red Prince**
See Frederick Charles

[The] **Red Prince**
See Salameh, Ali Hassan

Red Rat
See McDaniel, Ira C.

Red River Dave
See McEnery, David

[The] **Red Rooster**
See Rader, Douglas Lee

Red Rosa
See Luxemburg, Rosa

Red Rudi Dutschke
See Dutschke, Rudi

[The] **Red Shirt Hero**
See Garibaldi, Giuseppe

[The] **Red Spider**
See Staniak, Lucian

[The] **Red Spy Queen**
See Bentley, Elizabeth

[The] **Red Sultan**
See Abdul-Hamid II

Red Suspenders
See Talmadge, Herman Eugene

Red Ted Heslin
See Heslin, Ted

Red Ted Knight
See Knight, Ted

Red Top
See Nyblom, Lennart

Red Top Johnston
See Johnston, Wilfred Ivy

[The] **Red Tory**
See MacDonald, Flora

Red Wing
See Pond, Frederick Eugene

Red Wing, Princess
See St. Cyr, Lillian

[The] **Red Witch**
See Koch, Ilse

ReDaK
See Kimchi, David

Redax
See Vingedal, Sven Erik Axel

Redbarn, Thomas
See McEvoy, Bernard

Redbarn Wash
See Shaw, George Bernard

Redcam, Tom
See MacDermot, Thomas H.

Redd, Elvira 1930- [EJ7]
American jazz musician
* Redd, Vi

Redd, Vi
See Goldberg, Elvira Reod

Reddale, Frederic
See Reddall, Henry Frederick

Reddall, Henry Frederick 1856-1921
[DNA]
American journalist and musician
* Bantock, Miles
* Reddale, Frederic

Reddaway, W[illiam] Brian 1913- [CA]
British economist and author
* Academic Investor

Redder, George
See Drummond, Jack

Reddick
See Kidder, Joseph

Reddie, J. C.
See Campbell, James

Reddin, Kenneth Shiels 1895-1967
[DIL]
Irish author and playwright
* Sarr, Kenneth

Redding, Cannon Ball
See Redding, Richard

Redding, Otis 1941-1967 [PRS]
American singer and songwriter
* [The] King of Soul Singers

Redding, Richard 1891-1938? [MK]
American baseball player
* Redding, Cannon Ball

[The] **Redeemed Captive**
See Williams, John

Reden, Karl
See Converse, Charles Crozat

Redenbacher, Orville 1909- [HPPN]
American farmer and agriculturist
* [The] Popcorn King

Redfern, Buck
See Redfern, George Howard

Redfern, George Howard 1902-1964
[BE]
American baseball player
* Redfern, Buck

Redfern, Peter Irvine 1954- [SMG]
American baseball player
* Redfern, Red

Redfern, Red
See Redfern, Peter Irvine

Redfern, Ruth 1908- [F2]
Actress
* Hiatt, Ruth

Redfield, Clark
See McMorrow, Fred

Redfield, Jennifer
See Hoskins, Robert

Redfield, Malissa
See Elliott, Malissa Childs

Redfield, Martin
See Brown, Alice

Redgap
See Pardon, George Frederick

Redgate, John
See Kennedy, Adam

[The] Redhead
See Reuther, Walter Philip

[The] Redhead
See Ustinov, Dimitri

Redivivus, Joel Collier
See Veal, George

Redivivus, Quevedo, Jr.
See Wright, Robert William

Redlich, Marcellus Donald
See Von Redlich, Marcellus Donald A. R.

Redling, Nettie Radvanti 1900- [HPPN]
German author
* Seghers, Anna

Redman, Ben Ray 1896-1961 [AW, CC, WBD]
American author and journalist
* Lord, Jeremy

Redman, James W. 1915- [BA]
American union official
* Redman, Pep

Redman, Joseph
See Pearce, Brian Leonard

Redman, Pep
See Redman, James W.

Redmayne, Barbara
See Howe, Muriel

Redmayne, Mary Priestley 1902- [WWL]
British author
* Rodney, M.

Redmon, Ann 1925- [BA]
American educator and psychologist
* Ali, Fatima

Redmon, Anne
See Nightingale, Anne Redmon

Redmon, Jim 1947- [SMG]
American baseball player
* Redmon, Rat

Redmon, Rat
See Redmon, Jim

Redmond, Gus
See Redmond, Gustave

Redmond, Gustave 20th c. [EF]
American football player
* Redmond, Gus

Redmond, John McKittrick [Jack] 1910-1968 [BE]
American baseball player
* Redmond, Red

Redmond, Juanita
See Hipps, Juanita Redmond

Redmond, Red
See Redmond, John McKittrick [Jack]

Rednaxela
See Cropper, Margaret

Redo
See Hill, Anthony

Redondo y Dominguez, Jose 1818-1853 [GS]
Spanish bullfighter
* [El] Chiclanero [The Man from Chiclana]

Redpath, James 1833-1891 [FFF, PA]
Scottish-born journalist
* Berwick

Redruth, E.
See Edmonds, Richard, Jr.

Redstone, Sylvia
See Honnor, Sylvia Crofts

Redus, Frog
See Redus, Wilson R.

Redus, Wilson R. 1905- [MK]
American baseball player
* Redus, Frog

Redway, Ralph
See Hamilton, Charles Harold St. John

Redway, Ridley
See Hamilton, Charles Harold St. John

Redwin
See Day, Richard E.

Redwine, Skip
See Redwine, Wilbur

Redwine, Wilbur 1926- [ASC]
American musician
* Redwine, Skip

Redwing, Morris
See Merrill, James Milford

Redwood, Alec
See Milkomane, George Alexis Milkomanovich

Redwood, John
See Search, Preston Willis

Redwood, Ralph
See Holden, J. G. P.

Redwood, Rosaline
See Staples, Marjory Charlotte

Reece, Alphonso Son 1931- [DAM, EJ]
Jamaican-born jazz musician
* Reece, Dizzy

Reece, Alys [Tracy] 1912- [AW, WD]
British author
* Wingfield, Susan

Reece, Dizzy
See Reece, Alphonso Son

Reece, Reggie 20th c. [BBH]
Boxer
* Reece, Roughie

Reece, Roughie
See Reece, Reggie

Reed, A. C.
See Reed, Aaron Corthen

Reed, Aaron Corthen 20th c. [BWW]
American musician and singer
* Reed, A. C.

Reed, Alan
See Bergman, Teddy

Reed, Alexander Wyclif 1908- [CA]
New Zealand author
* Harlequin

Reed, Alison Touster 1952- [CA]
American poet
* Touster, Alison

Reed, Allan
See Eisfeld, Rainer

Reed, Allan?
See Rohr, Wolf Detlef

Reed, Andrew 1787-1862 [NPS]
Clergyman, philanthropist, hymn writer
* Douglas

Reed, B. Mitchel 20th c. [CMA]
American disc jockey
* B. M. R.
* [The] Boy on the Psychiatrist's Couch
* [The] Fastest Tongue in the West
* [The] Mad Monk in the Monastery

Reed, Bertie
See Reed, S. J.

Reed, Blair 20th c. [WW]
Author
* Ring, Adam

Reed, Bob 20th c.
American football player
* [The] Ski Cat

Reed, C. H. [PA]
Author
* Hazelton, Mabel

Reed, [Sir] Carol 1906-1976
British producer
* Persona Grata

Reed, Cynthia
See Nolan, [Violet] Cynthia

Reed, Czar
See Reed, Thomas Brackett

Reed, David V.
See Vern, David

Reed, Diz
See Reed, Howard Dean

Reed, Donald 1939- [IBW]
American army officer
* [The] Black Tiger

Reed, Donna
See Mullenger, Donna Belle

Reed, Edward Charles 1891- [WWL]
British author
* Brangwyn, Charles

Reed, Eliot [joint pseudonym with Charles Rodda]
See Ambler, Eric

Reed, Eliot [joint pseudonym with Eric Ambler]
See Rodda, Charles

Reed, Elizabeth Stewart 1914- [CA]
American author
* Stewart, Elizabeth Grey

Reed, Emeline [PA]
Author
* Roseau, Emie

Reed, Emmett X.
See King, Florence

Reed, Eunice 1928- [BA]
American educator
* Reed, Pat

Reed, Frank
See Ciorciolini, Marcello

Reed, Gus
See Nelson, Harold

Reed, Hal
See Read, O.

Reed, Howard Dean 1936- [BE]
American baseball player
* Reed, Diz

Reed, Isabella 1893?- [BEW, F2, FC]
British actress
* Elsom, Isobel

Reed, Ishmael 1938- [CN]
American author and poet
* Coleman, Emmett

Reed, Jean
See Hovick, June

Reed, Jerry
See Hubbard, Jerry Reed

Reed, John [Silas] 1887-1920 [HPPN, TLC]
American journalist, historian, poet, playwright
* [The] American Kipling
* Playboy

Reed, John S. 1939?- [TI 7-2-84]
American bank executive
* [The] Brat

Reed, Kit
See Reed, Lillian Craig

Reed, Lillian Craig 1932- [CA]
American journalist and author
* Reed, Kit

Reed, Lou
See Firbank, Louis

Reed, Lucy
See DeRidder, Lucille

Reed [or O'Reed?], Margaret Theresa Yvonne 1916- [BEW, EMT, IPA]
American actress, singer, comedienne
* Raye, Martha

Reed, Mary 1854-1943 [HPPN]
American missionary
* [The] Female Father Damien

Reed, Mary J. 1830-? [FFF]
American poet
* Roseau, Marie

Reed, Mrs. Samuel [FFF]
Entertainer
* Boeckel, Mary

Reed, Myrtle 1874-1911 [DNA, ICB]
American author and poet
* Green, Olive

Reed, Nathaniel 1862?-1950 [BI]
American reformed outlaw
* Texas Jack

Reed, Nora
See Hall, Vera

Reed, Pat
See Reed, Eunice

Reed, Peter [house pseudonym]
See MacDonald, John D[ann]

Reed, Peter Fishe 19th c. [HPPN]
American artist
* Reid, P. Fish

Reed, Peter Hugh 1892-1969
American author, reviewer, critic
* D'Esterre, Neville
* Girard, Paul

Reed, Robert
See Caille, Robert

Reed, Robert
See Rietz, John

Reed, Rosa
See Younger, Pearl

Reed, S. J. 1944?- [TI 5-23-83]
South African sailboat racer
* Reed, Bertie

Reed, Steve
See Le Gurdeur, Stephen

Reed, Thomas Brackett 1839-1902 [HPPN]
American politician
* Biddy
* Reed, Czar
* [The] Terrible Turk

Reed, Van [house pseudonym, Curtis Warren]
See Hughes, Den[n]is [Talbot]

Reed, Veronica
See Sherman, Theresa

Reed, Walter 1851-1902 [HPPN]
American army officer and physician
* [The] Doctor in Uniform

Reed-Smith, Ida 1868-? [NAA]
American author
* Warrington, Dan

Reeder, Cat
See Reeder, Tom

Reeder, Icicle
See Reeder, James Edward

Reeder, James Edward 1865-? [BE]
American baseball player
* Reeder, Icicle

Reeder, Nicholas [Nick]
See Herchenroeder, Nicholas

Reeder, Page, Sr. 1921?-1977 [FIR]
Radio producer and announcer
* Reeder, Scoop

Reeder, [Colonel] Red
See Reeder, Russell P., Jr.

Reeder, Russell P., Jr. 1902- [CA, SAT]
American army officer and author
* Reeder, [Colonel] Red

Reeder, Scoop
See Reeder, Page, Sr.

Reeder, Tom 1934- [CM]
American radio broadcaster
* Reeder, Cat

Reedman, Dinny
See Reedman, J. C.

Reedman, J. C. [EC]
Australian cricketer
* Reedman, Dinny

Reeds, F. Anton 20th c. [WGT]
Author
* Riker, Anthony

Reeman, Douglas [Edward] 1924- [AW, WD]
British author
* Kent, Alexander

Reems, Harry
See Streicher, Herbert

Reens, Mary
See Singleton, Betty

Rees, Dai
See Rees, David James

Rees, David
See Wignall, Trevor

Rees, David James 1913- [EG, GF]
Scottish golfer
* Rees, Dai

Rees, Dilwyn
See Daniel, Glyn [Edmund]

Rees, [Morgan] Goronwy 1909- [CA]
Welsh-born author, columnist, translator
* R

Rees, Grover, III 20th c. [TI 11-4-85]
American government official
* Rees, Rocky

Rees, Helen Christina Easson [Evans] 1903-1970 [CA]
British author
* Oliver, Jane

Rees, Ioan Bowen 1929- [CA]
Welsh author
* Rhys, Ioan

Rees, Joan 1927- [AW, WD]
British author
* Avery, June
* Bedford, Ann
* Strong, Susan

Rees, Melvin ?-1961 [DI]
American murderer
* [The] Sex Beast

Rees, Meriel
See Lambot, Isobel Mary

Rees, Rocky
See Rees, Grover, III

Rees, Stella
See Allen, Mrs. William W.

Reese, Della
See Early, Deloreese Patricia

Reese, Don 1951- [SMG]
American football player
* [The] Undertaker

Reese, Donk
See Reese, James Harrison

Reese, Harold Henry 1919- [BE, DGS, IPA]
American baseball player
* [The] Little Colonel
* Reese, Pee Wee

Reese, Harvey
See Roeder, Adolph

Reese, Heloise [Bowles] 1919-1977 [CA]
American columnist
* Heloise

Reese, James Harrison 1905- [SMG]
American baseball coach
* Reese, Donk

Reese, James Hymie
See Solomon, James Hymie

Reese, Jerry 20th c. [WP 2-11-85]
American wrestler
* Malumba, Voodoo

Reese, John [Henry] 20th c. [CA]
American author
* Carpenter, John Jo

Reese, Mason 1966?- [HPPN]
American actor
* [The] Borgasmord Kid
* [The] Seven Year Old Huckster

Reese, Pee Wee
See Reese, Harold Henry

Reeside, James 1789-1842 [HPPN]
Scottish-American businessman and mail contractor
* [The] Land Admiral
* [The] Prince of Mail Contractors

Reeve, Ada
See Isaacs, Adelaide Mary

Reeve, Arthur B[enjamin] 1880-1936 [HPPN]
American author
* [The] Creator of Craig Kennedy

Reeve, Clara 1729-1807 [SN, WGT]
British author
* C. R.
* Euphrasia

Reeve, Edward H. [Ted] 1902- [CSH]
Canadian journalist
* Fagan, Nutsy
* McGuffy, Moaner
* [The] Old Groaner
* Snippersnapper, Alice
* [The] Squire of Squawg Hollow

Reeve, Goodie 1898?-1978 [FIR]
Australian radio performer
* [The] First Lady of Sydney Radio

Reeve, Joel
See Cox, William R[obert]

Reeve, John ?-1540 [PA]
Author
* Melford

Reeve, Joseph 1937- [CA]
American author and journalist
* Albright, Joseph [Medill Patterson]

Reeve-Jones, Alan Edmond 1914- [AW, IAW]
Norwegian-born author, scriptwriter, lyricist
* Allen, Edmund
* Lunchbasket, Roger

Reeves, Amber
See Blanco White, Amber

Reeves, Clarence 20th c. [SG]
Boxer
* [The] Alabama Kid

Reeves, Daniel
See Liddy, James [Daniel Reeves]

Reeves, Daniel E. 1944- [FB]
American football player
* Reeves, Deacon Dan

Reeves, Deacon Dan
See Reeves, Daniel E.

Reeves, Del
See Reeves, [Franklin] Delano

Reeves, [Franklin] Delano 1933- [CWG, DAM, ECM]
American country-western performer
* [The] Dean Martin of Country Music
* Reeves, Del

Reeves, Fannie
See McDowell, Mrs. E. A.

Reeves, Gentleman Jim
See Reeves, James Travis [Jim]

Reeves, George
See Besselo, George

Reeves, Goebel 1899-1959 [ECM]
American country-western performer
* [The] Texas Drifter

Reeves, Gunner
See Reeves, Robert Edwin

Reeves, Helen Buckingham [Mathers] 1853-1920 [WGT, WW]
British author
* Lyall, David
* Mathers, Helen

Reeves, James
See Reeves, John Morris

Reeves, James Travis [Jim] 1923-1964 [BEW, ECM]
American singer and actor
* Bimbo Boy
* Reeves, Gentleman Jim

Reeves, John 1752-1829 [HPPN]
British barrister
* [A] Barrister
* [A] Lawyer

Reeves, John Morris 1909- [SFL, TCL]
British poet, author, critic
* Reeves, James

Reeves, Joyce
See Gard, Joyce

Reeves, Justin 20th c. [WGT]
Author
* Septama, Aladra

Reeves, Lawrence F. 1926- [CA]
American author
* Lyfick, Warren
* Seever, R.

Reeves, Marian Calhoun Legare 1854-? [DNA, FFF, PA]
American author
* Fadette

Reeves, Red
See Reeves, Reuben

Reeves, Reuben 1905- [WWJ]
American jazz musician
* Reeves, Red
* Reeves, River

Reeves, River
See Reeves, Reuben

Reeves, Robert Edwin 1904- [BE]
American baseball player
* Reeves, Gunner

Reeves, Ruth Ellen
See Ranney, Agnes V.

Reeves, Stephen [Steve] 1926- [HPPN]
American physical culturist and actor
* Ercole
* Shape
* Universe, Mr.
* World, Mr.

Refalo, [Hon.] John Philip
See Dunlop, James

[The] Referee
See Gordon, Archibald F.

[The] Reform Governor
See Cleveland, [Stephen] Grover

[The] Reform Mayor of Boston
See Quincy, Josiah

[The] Reform Pope
See Chauvin [or Caulvin?], Jean

[The] Reformed Gambler
See Green, Jonathan H.

[The] Reformed Michael Angelo
See Tibaldi, Pellegrino

[The] Reformed Minstrel
See Sutherland, Robert

[A] Reformed Stock Gambler
See Armstrong, William

[A] Reformer
See Nolan, Frederick

[The] Reformer of a Kingdom
See Knox, John

[The] Reformer of Astronomy
See Copernicus, Nicolaus

[The] Reformer of Empiricism
See Biran, Marie Francois Pierre
Gonthier de

[The] Refrigerator
See Bunker, Ellsworth

[The] Refrigerator
See Perry, William

Refugitta
See Harrison, Constance Cary

Refulgidus, Doctor
See Philargos, Petros

Regaldo, Hector 20th c.   [RO2]
Venezuelan musician
* Regaldo, Rudy

Regaldo, Rudy
See Regaldo, Hector

Regan, Brad
See Norwood, Victor G[eorge] C[harles]

Regan, Donald Thomas 1918-   [HPPN]
American government official
* [The] Barracuda
* Reagan's Regan
* [The] Treasury Boss
* [The] Treasury Chief

Regan, John William 1873-1945   [CCL]
Canadian author
* Quinpool, John

Regan, Kathleen Patricia 1920-1980
[BEW, TR]
American actress
* Medford, Kay

Regan, Phil[ip] 1908-   [HPPN]
American singer and actor
* [The] Singing Policeman

Regan, Phil[lip Raymond] 1937-   [BE,
PB]
American baseball player
* [The] Vulture

Regard, Paul
See Sheehan, Perley Poore

Regas, Panagiotis 1882-1974   [SC]
Greek-born actor
* Regas, Pedro

Regas, Pedro
See Regas, Panagiotis

Regaterin [The Little Bargainer]
See Boto y Recatero, Antonio

[El] Regatero [The Haggler]
See Lopez, Angel

Regazzoni, Clay
See Regazzoni, Gianclaudio Giuseppe

Regazzoni, Gianclaudio Giuseppe 1939-
[EAR]
Swiss auto racer
* Regazzoni, Clay

[The] Regenerator of Cookery
See Careme, Marie Antoine

Regenmeister
See Caracciola, Rudi

Regensteiner, Theodore 1868-1952
[HPPN]
German-American inventor and photo-
engraver
* [The] Pioneer of Colortype Printing

Reger, Erik
See Dannenberger, Hermann

Regester, Seeley
See Victor, Metta Victoria Fuller

[The] Reggae Master
See Marley, Robert Nesta [Bob]

[The] Reggae Musician
See Marley, Robert Nesta [Bob]

Reggie
See Connelly, Regina M.

Reggie No Dick
See Christie, John Reginald Halliday

Reggione, Michael ?-1932   [BLB]
American underworld figure
* Little Apples

Regibus, L. M.
See Foe, Daniel

Regillo
See De Sacchi, Giovanni Antonio

Reginald
See Burgess, Michael Roy

Reginald, R[obert]
See Burgess, Michael Roy

Reginaldus
See Regnauld, Valire

Regine
See Zylberberg, Regina

[El] Regio [The Gorgeous One]
See Lopez, Felix

Regio, Jose
See Dos Reis Pereira, Jose Maria

Regiomontanus
See Mueller, Johann

Regis
See Grise, Jeanne

Regis
See Whylock, R. M.

Regius
See Leroy, Louis

[The] Regius Professor of Divinity
See Hampden, Renn Dickson

[The] Regius Professor of Divinity
See Ince, William

Regnal, F.
See D'Erlanger, [Baron] Frederic A.

Regnauld, Valire 1543-1623   [PA]
Author
* Reginaldus

Regnault, Jeanne Julia 1854-1941
[WBD]
French actress
* Bartet, Jeanne Julia

Regnier
See Tousez, Francois Joseph Pierre

Regnier, Jeanne-Marie
See Khan, Noor Inayat

Regnier, Mathurin 1573-1613   [DNNS,
FFF, SN]
French poet
* [The] Father of French Satire

Regnier, Michel 1931-   [WECO]
Belgian cartoonist and editor
* Albert, Louis
* Greg

Rego, Anthony [Tony]
See DeRego, Anthony

Rego, Leonora 20th c.   [EOP]
Leader of religious cult
* Lalitananda, Swami

Regryph
See Perry, Henry G.

Rehan, Ada
See Crehan, Ada

Rehm, Warren S. 20th c.   [WGT]
Author
* Nemo, Omen

Rehn, Viktoria
See Kohn-Behrens, Charlotte

Rei, Kosumi
See Shibano, Takumi

Rei, Roumany
See Taylor, Tom

Reibel, Dutch
See Reibel, Earl

Reibel, Earl 1930-   [CEI]
Canadian-born hockey player
* Reibel, Dutch

Reiber, Frank Bernard 1909-   [BE]
American baseball player
* Reiber, Tubby

Reiber, Tubby
See Reiber, Frank Bernard

Reich, Edwin 1926-   [BEW]
American producer
* Rich, Eddie

Reich, Jacob 1875?-?   [HPPN]
American newspaper manager and police informer
* [The] King of the Newsboys
* Sullivan, Jack

Reich, Johannes Theodor 1906-   [HPPN]
Austrian director, producer, educator
* Reich, John

Reich, John
See Reich, Johannes Theodor

Reichardt, Frederic C. 1943-   [PB]
American baseball player
* Reichardt, Rick

Reichardt, Rick
See Reichardt, Frederic C.

Reichenau, Hermann Von 1013-1054
[HPPN]
German monk, poet, historian
* Contractus, Hermannus
* [The] Lame

Reichenbach, Berke
See Reichenbach, Harold

Reichenbach, Harold 20th c.   [SMG]
American baseball player
* Reichenbach, Berke

Reichenberg, Suzanne 1853-1924
[HPPN]
American actress
* De Bourgoing, Baroness

Reichenthal, Laura 1901-   [CN, LC, WD]
American author and poet
* Gottschalk, Laura Riding
* Jackson, Laura [Riding]
* Rich, Barbara [joint pseudonym with Robert Von Ranke Graves]
* Riding, Laura

Reichenthal, Ralph 1901-1942   [AM]
American composer
* Rainger, Ralph

Reichert, Herbert W[illiam] 1917-   [CA]
American educator, author, translator
* Schad, Wilhelm

Reichman, Arthur 1886-1944   [THR]
American playwright
* Richman, Arthur

Reichman, Harry 1895-1972   [BEW, EMT, PMJ]
American singer and actor
* Richman, Harry

Reichman, Joseph 1898-1970   [HPPN]
American pianist and orchestra leader
* [The] Pagliacci of the Piano

Reichner, Bix
See Reichner, S. Bickley

Reichner, S. Bickley 20th c.   [ASC]
American composer
* Reichner, Bix

Reichow, Corncob
See Reichow, Garet

Reichow, Garet 20th c.
American football player
* Reichow, Corncob
* Reichow, Gerry
* Reichow, Hayseed

Reichow, Gerry
See Reichow, Garet

Reichow, Hayseed
See Reichow, Garet

Reid, Breezy
See Reid, Floyd

Reid, Charles [Stuart] 1900-   [CA]
British author and journalist
* Davidson, John
* Martin, Francis
* Staurt, Charles

Reid, Charlotte T. 20th c.   [ET]
American politician and singer
* King, Annette

Reid, Christian
See Fisher, Frances C.

Reid, Christian
See Tiernan, Frances Christine [Fisher]

Reid, Desmond [house pseudonym]
See Bounds, S. J.

Reid, Desmond [house pseudonym]
See Browne, Noel

Reid, Desmond [house pseudonym]
See Burke, John [Frederick]

Reid, Desmond [house pseudonym]
See Chance, John Newton

Reid, Desmond [house pseudonym]
See Dolphin, Reginald Charles [Rex]

Reid, Desmond [house pseudonym]
See Douse, Anthony

Reid, Desmond [house pseudonym]
See Francis, Stephen D.

Reid, Desmond [house pseudonym]
See Garstin, A.

Reid, Desmond [house pseudonym]
See Hanson, V. J.

Reid, Desmond [house pseudonym]
See Lambe, F.

Reid, Desmond [house pseudonym]
See Martin, A. L.

Reid, Desmond [house pseudonym]
See McArdle, Brian

Reid, Desmond
See McNeilly, Wilfred Glassford

Reid, Desmond [house pseudonym]
See Moorcock, Michael John

Reid, Desmond [house pseudonym]
See Player, Eddie

Reid, Desmond [house pseudonym]
See Richards, Ross

Reid, Desmond [house pseudonym]
See Roberts, Lee

Reid, Desmond [house pseudonym]
See Robertson, Colin

Reid, Desmond [house pseudonym]
See Sowman, Gordon

Reid, Desmond [house pseudonym]
See Stagg, James

Reid, Desmond [house pseudonym]
See Story, Rosamond Mary

Reid, Desmond [house pseudonym]
See Teed, George Heber Hamilton

Reid, Edgeworth Blair 1920-   [BEW]
American actor
* Reid, Elliott

Reid, Ela 1907-1982   [CA]
British author and journalist
* Sen, Ela

Reid, Eleanor
See Smith, Constance Isabel

Reid, Elliott
See Reid, Edgeworth Blair

Reid, Esther 19th c.   [PA]
Author
* Pansey

Reid, Floyd 20th c.   [SMG]
American football player
* Reid, Breezy

Reid, Frances P[ugh] 1910-   [CA]
American author
* Allison, Marian

Reid, Hal
See Reid, James Hallock

Reid, Hartlaw
See Hardie, Robert

Reid, Helen Grace 20th c.   [NAA]
American author
* Carlisle, Helen Grace

Reid, Helen Rogers 1882-1970   [HPPN]
American newspaper owner and manager
* America's Lady Journalist

Reid, [Rev.] Horace Hall ?-1853
[HPPN]
American clergyman
* [The] Rector of Christ's Church, Watertown, Connecticut

Reid, Ike
See Cauldwell, Ike Reid

Reid, [Rev.] James 20th c.   [HPPN]
American clergyman
* [The] Chaplain of the Strip

Reid, James Hallock 1860?-1920   [BEW]
American playwright
* Reid, Hal

Reid, James Macarthur 1900-1970
[CAP]
Scottish author
* Walkinshaw, Colin

Reid, Jock
See Reid, John

Reid, John 18th c. [BBH]
Founder of American golf club
* [The] Father of American Golf
* Reid, Jock

Reid, John Cowie 1916-1972 [AW, CA]
New Zealand educator and author
* Caliban

Reid, Joseph 1954- [HPPN]
American poet and karate expert
* [The] Karate Poet

Reid, Max
See Reid, Maxwell

Reid, Maxwell 1903-1969 [SC]
American actor and musician
* Reid, Max

Reid, [Thomas] Mayne 1818-1883
[DLE1, HPPN, SAT, SFL]
American author and poet
* Beach, Charles
* Cannibal Jack
* [The] Poor Scholar

Reid, P. Fish
See Reed, Peter Fishe

Reid, Patricia Kimberly 1921?- [BEW,
FC, IPA]
American actress
* Stanley, Kim

Reid, Philip [joint pseudonym with
Andrew Philip Kingsford Osmond]
See Ingrams, Richard [Reid]

Reid, Philip [joint pseudonym with
Richard Ingrams]
See Osmond, Andrew Philip Kingsford

Reid, Robert 1773-1865 [HPPN]
Scottish antiquary and topographer
* Senex

Reid, Robert 1850-1922 [CCL]
Canadian poet
* Wanlock, Rob

Reid, Sandy
See Reid, William A.

Reid, Sarah Addington 1891- [NAA]
American author
* Addington, Sarah

Reid, T. W. [PA]
Author
* [The] Extinguished Exile

Reid, V. S.
See Reid, Victor Stafford

Reid, Victor Stafford 1913- [LC]
Jamaican author
* Reid, V. S.

Reid, Wallace Q.
See Goodchild, George

Reid, Whitelaw 1837-? [PA]
Author
* Agate

Reid, William A. 1857-? [BE]
Canadian-born baseball player
* Reid, Sandy

Reifsnyder, Reef
See Reifsnyder, Robert H.

Reifsnyder, Robert H. 1937- [FB]
American football player
* Reifsnyder, Reef

Reigle, Edmond 1924- [CEI]
Canadian-born hockey player
* Reigle, Rags

Reigle, Rags
See Reigle, Edmond

Reignolds, Kate
See Winslow, Mrs. Irving

Reile, Louis Anthony 1925- [IAW]
American author
* Curran, John

Reiling, Netty 1900- [TC]
German author
* Seghers, Anna

Reilley, Alexander Aloysius 1884-1968
[BE]
American baseball player
* Reilley, Duke
* Reilley, Midget

Reilley, Duke
See Reilley, Alexander Aloysius

Reilley, Midget
See Reilley, Alexander Aloysius

Reilly, Bernard James 1865-1930
[DNA]
Author and clergyman
* Yorke, Anthony

Reilly, Big Ed
See Reilly, Edward J.

Reilly, Brother
See Reilly, Edward J.

Reilly, Butt
See Reilly, Hugh

Reilly, Cab
See Reilly, T. D.

Reilly, Charles 1868-1938 [BE]
American baseball player
* Reilly, Josh

Reilly, Charles 20th c. [EF]
American football player
* Reilly, Mike

Reilly, Charles Thomas 1855-1937 [BE]
American baseball player
* Reilly, Princeton Charlie

Reilly, Death House
See Reilly, Edward J.

Reilly, Edward J. 20th c. [HPPN]
American attorney
* Reilly, Big Ed

Reilly, Edward J. (cont.)
* Reilly, Brother
* Reilly, Death House

Reilly, Edwin J. [PA]
Author
* Clio

Reilly, Frank D. ?-1919 [HPPN]
American actor
* Reilly, Happy

Reilly, Happy
See Reilly, Frank D.

Reilly, Helen [Abby Kieran] 1881?-1962
[CC, WW]
Author
* Abbey, Kieran

Reilly, Hugh 19th c. [RBE]
Boxer
* Reilly, Butt

Reilly, John Good 1858-1937 [BE, PB]
American baseball player
* Reilly, Long John

Reilly, Josh
See Reilly, Charles

Reilly, Long John
See Reilly, John Good

Reilly, Mary 1920- [BI]
American author
* McMullen, Mary

Reilly, Michael Francis 1910?-
American secret service agent
* Roosevelt's Shadow

Reilly, Mike
See Reilly, Charles

Reilly, Mrs. James [FFF]
Entertainer
* Templeton, May

Reilly, Philip C. 1878-1961 [BI]
American educator
* Columba, [Brother]

Reilly, Princeton Charlie
See Reilly, Charles Thomas

Reilly, Sidney
See Rosenblum, Sigmund G.

Reilly, Silver Bill
See Reilly, William

Reilly, T. D. 20th c.
American horseracing official
* Reilly, Cab

Reilly, Thomas Devin 1824-1854 [PI]
Irish poet
* R.
* T. R.

Reilly, William ?-1912 [HPPN]
American gambler
* Reilly, Silver Bill

Reilly, William K.
See Creasey, John

Reimann, Dutch
See Reimann, Harry

Reimann, Harry 20th c.   [BBH]
American basketball player
* Reimann, Dutch
* Reimann, Wally

Reimann, Wally
See Reimann, Harry

Reimar, Reinald
See Glasner, Adolf

Rein, Bo
See Rein, Robert

Rein, Orestes Pearle
See Rhyne, Orestes Pearle

Rein, Raphael Abramovitch 1880-?
[HPPN]
Russian historian
* Abramovitch, Raphael R.

Rein, Richard
See Smith, Richard Rein

Rein, Robert 1946?-
American football coach
* Rein, Bo

Reina, Gaetano ?-1930   [BLB]
American underworld figure
* Reina, Tom

Reina, Tom
See Reina, Gaetano

Reinach, Joseph 1856-1921   [BI, HPPN]
French politician and journalist
* Polybe

Reinbold, Adelheid 19th c.   [HPPN]
German author
* Berthold, Franz

[The] Reincarnated Troubadour
See Seeger, Pete[r R.]

Reindeer Bill Killefer
See Killefer, William Levier, Jr.

[La] Reine Blanche
See Mary, Queen of Scots

Reiner, Max
See Caldwell, [Janet] Taylor

Reiners, Dennis 20th c.   [GW]
American rodeo performer
* Reiners, Ringtail

Reiners, Ringtail
See Reiners, Dennis

Reinfeld, Fred 1910-1964   [CAP, SAT]
American author
* Young, Edward

Reinhardt, Django
See Reinhardt, Jean Baptiste

Reinhardt, Jean Baptiste 1910-1953   [EJ, PMJ]
Belgian-born jazz musician
* Reinhardt, Django

Reinhardt, Max
See Goldmann, Max

Reinhardt, S. Louis, Sr. 1899-   [EJS]
American football player
* Reinhardt, Spider

Reinhardt, Spider
See Reinhardt, S. Louis, Sr.

Reinhart, Charles Stanley 1844-1896
[SN]
American painter and illustrator
* Reinhart, Velveteen

Reinhart, Velveteen
See Reinhart, Charles Stanley

Reinhold, Alvar Harald 1935-   [IWM]
Swedish musician
* Rabe, Folke

Reinhold, C.
See Koestlin, Christian Reinhold

Reinhold, Ernest
See Britten, Emma Hardinge

Reinhoud
See D'Haese, Reinhoud

Reinicker, Walter [Wally]
See Smith, Walter

Reiniger, Robert Meredith 1902-   [BEW, EMT]
American composer, lyricist, librettist
* Willson, Meredith

Reinikka, Oliver Mathias 1901-   [CEI]
Canadian-born hockey player
* Reinikka, Rocco

Reinikka, Rocco
See Reinikka, Oliver Mathias

Reinmar der Alte
See Reinmar von Hagenau

Reinmar von Hagenau ?-1210?   [WBD]
Minnesinger and knight
* Reinmar der Alte

Reinser III
See Resnier, Andre Guillaume

Reinsmith, Richard
See Smith, Richard Rein

Reis, Fred 20th c.   [HPPN]
American criminal
* Dunbar, J. V.

Reis, Harrie Crane 1890-1939   [BE]
American baseball player
* Reis, Jack

Reis, Jack
See Reis, Harrie Crane

Reis, Peggy 1900-1964   [SC]
American actress and stunt performer
* O'Day, Peggy

Re'is, Piri [Muhyi 'l-Din]
See Muhidin, Ahmet

Reis, Ricardo
See Pessoa, Fernando [Antonio Nogueira]

Reiser, Chick
See Reiser, Joseph

Reiser, Harold Patrick 1919?-1981   [BE, BI, PB]
American baseball player
* Reiser, Pete
* Reiser, Pistol Pete

Reiser, Joseph 1914-
American basketball player
* Reiser, Chick

Reiser, Pete
See Reiser, Harold Patrick

Reiser, Pistol Pete
See Reiser, Harold Patrick

Reisigl, Bugs
See Reisigl, Jacob

Reisigl, Jacob 1887-1957   [BE]
American baseball player
* Reisigl, Bugs

Reisling, Doc
See Reisling, Frank Carl

Reisling, Frank Carl 1874-1955   [BE]
American baseball player
* Reisling, Doc

Reisor, Lawrence 20th c.   [HPPN]
American football player
* Reisor, Smack

Reisor, Smack
See Reisor, Lawrence

Reiss, Barbara Eve 1941-   [CA]
American poet
* Eve, Barbara

Reiss, Isaac 1885-1943   [BEW]
Austrian-born playwright
* Nadir, Moishe

Reit, Seymour 20th c.   [SAT]
American author, cartoonist, editor
* Reit, Sy

Reit, Sy
See Reit, Seymour

Reitci, Jack
See Reitci, John G[eorge]

Reitci, John G[eorge] 1922-1983   [CA, DF 4-26-83, WP 4-26-83]
American author
* Reitci, Jack
* Ritchie, Jack

Reitci, Rita Krohne 1930-   [CA]
American author
* Ritchie, Rita

Reiter, Virginia
See Reiterer, Virginia

Reiterer, Virginia 20th c.   [THR]
Italian actress
* Reiter, Virginia

Reith, Lord 1890-1971   [HPPN]
Scottish business executive
* [The] Father of the B. B. C.

Reitz, Heinie
See Reitz, Henry P.

Reitz, Henry P. 1867-1914 [BE]
American baseball player
* Reitz, Heinie

Reitz, Kenneth John 1951- [SMG]
American baseball player
* [The] Zamboni Machine

Reizenstein, Elmer Leopold 1892-1967
[EWL, LC, TC]
American playwright and author
* Rice, Elmer

Rejane, Gabrielle
See Reju, Gabrielle Charlotte

Rejaule y Toledo, Pedro Juan de 1578-?
[BI]
Spanish poet and playwright
* Turia, Ricardo de

Reju, Gabrielle Charlotte 1857-1920
[BEW, LC, THR]
French actress
* Rejane, Gabrielle

Rekai, Kati 1921- [CA]
Hungarian-born author
* Kati

Relampaguito [Little Lightning Flash]
See Gomez y Canete, Julio

Relaxation, Mr.
See Como, Pierino

Relaxation, Mr.
See Oosterbaan, Benjamin Gaylord
[Bennie]

[The] Relentless Borg
See Borg, Bjorn

Reles, Abraham [Abe] ?-1940 [BLB,
HPPN, MM, PHM]
*American underworld figure and police
informant*
* [The] Singing Canary
* Twist, Kid

Relgis, Eugene
See Siegler, Eugene

[A] Religious of CSMV
See Lawson, Ruth Penelope

[A] Religious Politician
See Adams, Samuel

[The] Religious Revolutionary
See Ikhnaton [or Akhenaten]

Reling, Jan
See Davis, Horace Bancroft

Relis, Harry
See Endore, [Samuel] Guy

Rellaford, Jack 1906-1967 [SC]
American actor
* O'Shea, Blackjack
* O'Shea, Jack

Rellihan, Gernie Floss Hunter 1888-
[IAW]
American poet
* Hunter, Gernie

[El] Relojero [The Watch-Maker]
See Perez, Manuel

Relonde, Maurice
See Jagendorf, M.

Relph, Harry 1868-1928 [BEW, BMH,
NN]
British comedian
* [The] Great Little Mackney
* Little Tich

[A] Reluctant Anachronism
See Winchell, Walter

[The] Reluctant President
See Pierce, Franklin

[The] Reluctant Robespierre
See Mollet, Guy

[The] Reluctant Signer
See Braxton, Carter

Rem Doxfud
See Hill, Anthony

Remacle, Stephane
See Javeau, Claude A.

Remar, Frits 1932- [IAW]
Danish author
* Dahl, John

Remark, Erich Paul 1898-1970 [EWL,
TCL]
German author
* Remarque, Erich Maria

[The] Remarkable Sir Richard
See Douglas, Richard

Remarque, Erich Maria
See Remark, Erich Paul

Remback, William
See Valigursky, Ed

Rembrandt
See Van Rijn [or Ryn], Rembrandt
Harmensz [or Harmenszoon]

[The] Rembrandt of Lard Carvers
See Eichenaur, Franz Victor

[The] Rembrandt of the Comic Strip
See Caniff, Milton Arthur

[The] Rembrandt of the Prairies
See Zuppke, Robert C.

[The] Rembrandt, of the West
See Remington, Frederic

**[The] Rembrandt or Raphael of the
Profession**
See Duval, Claude

Remenham, John
See Vlasto, John Alexander

Rementer, Butch
See Rementer, Willis J.

Rementer, Willis J. 20th c. [BE]
American baseball player
* Rementer, Butch

Remenyi, Ede
See Hoffmann, Ede

Remer, Helen 1877-1939 [THR]
American actress
* Ware, Helen

Remerond
See De Saulieu, Thierry

Remi [or Remigius] 439?-535? [HN,
HPPN, RH, WBD]
Saint
* [The] Apostle of the Franks
* Clovis
* [The] Great Apostle of the French
* [The] Second St. Paul

Remi de Florence
See Nauni, Remigo

Remi [or Remy], Georges 1907-1983
[CA, SAT]
Belgian author and illustrator
* Herge

Remi, Philippe de 1250?-1296 [SN]
French jurist
* Beaumanoir, Sire de
* [The] French Justinian

Remick, Ann 1935- [HPPN, IPA]
American actress
* America's Answer to Brigitte Bardot
* Remick, Lee

Remick, Lee
See Remick, Ann

Remington, Daisy
See Hines, Elizabeth Allison

Remington, Eliphalet 1793-1861 [HPPN]
American designer and manufacturer
* America's Master Gunsmith
* [The] Father of the Remington Pistol

Remington, Ella-Carrie 1914- [CA]
American author
* Alden, Carella

Remington, Frederic 1861-1909 [HPPN]
*American illustrtor, painter, sculptor, war
correspondent*
* [The] Rembrandt, of the West

Remington, Jemima
See Bevans, Florence Edith

Remington, Mark
See Bingley, David Ernest

Remiro, Joseph 1947- [HPPN]
American radical terrorist group member
* G. I. Joe

Remley, Frank 1902-1967 [SC]
American actor and musician
* Lewis, Elliott

Remmerswaal, Wilhelmus Abraham 1954-
Dutch-born baseball player
* Remmerswaal, Win

Remmerswaal, Win
See Remmerswaal, Wilhelmus Abraham

Remnant, Ernest 1910-1973 [BMH]
British comedian
* Wheeler, Jimmy

Remoh the Wizard
See Homer, Eugene M.

Rempe, Jim
American billiard player
* King James

Rempt, Jan Dirk 1907- [AW]
Dutch-born author
* De Jong Van Hage, T. P. Merkrid

Remsen, Ira 1846-1927 [HPPN]
American physician, chemist, educator
* [The] Discoverer of Saccharin

Remus, George 1873-? [MM]
German-born American underworld figure
* [The] Gentle Grafter
* King of the Bootleggers
* [The] Quiet Corruptor

Remy, Colonel
See Renault, Gilbert

Remy, Dominique 1886?- [NOJ]
American jazz musician
* Remy, T-Boy

Remy, L. B. 1869-1932 [HPPN]
American singer
* Uncle Lou

Remy, Pierre-Jean
See Angremy, Jean-Pierre

Remy, T-Boy
See Remy, Dominique

Remy, W. A.
See Mayer, Wilhelm

Rena
See Crossley, M. Louise Rodgers

Rena, Henry
See Rene, Henry

Rena, Kid
See Rene, Henry

Rena, Sally
See Rena, Sarah Mary

Rena, Sarah Mary 1941- [CA]
Scottish-born author
* Rena, Sally

Renad, Frederick
See Cooper, Frederick

[The] Renaissance Assassin
See Maglie, Salvatore Anthony

[The] Renaissance Man
See Raleigh, [Sir] Walter

Renaldo, Duncan
See Duncan, Renault Renaldo

Renan, Joseph Ernest 1823-1892 [SN]
French philologist and historian
* Leolin

[Le] Renard [The Fox]
See Louis XI

Renard, Celine [PA]
Author
* Maria, Jennie

Renard, Jules 1864-1910 [EWL]
French author
* Drauer

Renard, Rachelle
See Secor, Mrs. George J.

Renard, Roy
See Ofer, Harold

Renatus, Adamantius
See Woolston, Thomas

Renaud
See Crosneau, Maurice Arnold

Renaud, Mme. Rene [FFF]
Entertainer
* Hill, Rosa

Renault
See Laurent, Emmanuel

Renault, Gilbert 1905?-1984 [TI 8-13-84]
French intelligence official and author
* Remy, Colonel

Renault, Mary
See Chalians, Mary

Renault, Mary
See Challans, Mary

Renavent, George
See De Cheux, Georges

Renay, Diane
See Kushner, Renee Diane

Rencelaw, Brian
See Russell, Ray

Rency, Georges
See Stassart, Albert

Render, Bill
See Fletcher, Tex

Rendrag, Nitram
See Gardner, Martin

Rene, Googie
See Rene, Leon

Rene, Hans Evert
See Renerius, Hans-Evert

Rene, Henry 1900-1949 [DAM, EJ, WWJ]
American jazz musician
* Rena, Henry
* Rena, Kid

Rene, Jules
See De Cassamajor, Marquis

Rene, Leon 20th c. [RO1]
American musician
* Rene, Googie

Rene, Master 16th c. [HN]
Poisoned Jeanne d'Albret, mother of King Henri IV
* [The] Queen's Poisoner

Rene, Natalia 1908?-1977 [CA]
Russian dance historian, critic, author
* Roslavleva, Natalia

Rene, Roy
See Van Der Sluice, Harry

Rene the Red
See Levesque, Rene

Rene-Bazin, Marie 1883- [CAT]
French author
* Marie St. Justin, [Mother]

Rene I 1408?-1480 [DNNS, SN, WBD]
Titular King of Naples
* [Le] Bon Roi Rene
* [The] Good
* [The] Good King Rene
* [The] Last of the Troubadours

[The] Renegade
See Tyler, John

[The] Renegade Defender of the Maya
See Guerrero, Gonzalo

[The] Renegade Newspaper Heiress
See Hearst, Patricia Campbell [Patty]

Renerius, Hans-Evert 1941- [IAW]
Swedish author
* Rene, Hans Evert

Renfroe, Chico
See Renfroe, Othello Nelson

Renfroe, Gangster
See Renfroe, Othello Nelson

Renfroe, Martha Kay 1938- [CA]
American author
* Wren, M. K.

Renfroe, Othello Nelson 1923- [IBW, MK]
American baseball player
* Renfroe, Chico
* Renfroe, Gangster

Renger, Annemarie 1920?- [HPPN]
German politician
* Bundestag, Miss

Renggli, Josef
Swiss chef
* Renggli, Seppi

Renggli, Seppi
See Renggli, Josef

Renich, Helen T. 1916- [MA]
Chinese-born author
* Renich, Jill

Renich, Jill
See Renich, Helen T.

Renick, Cab
See Renick, Jesse

Renick, Jesse 1917- [BB]
American basketball player
* Renick, Cab

Renie
See Conley, Renie

Renier, Elizabeth
See Baker, Betty D[oreen Flook]

Renier, G. J.
See Renier, Gustaaf Johannes

Renier, Gustaaf Johannes 1892-1962 [LC]
Dutch-born historian and author
* Renier, G. J.

Reniff, Harold Eugene 1938- [BE]
American baseball player
* Reniff, Porky

Reniff, Porky
See Reniff, Harold Eugene

Renin, Paul
See Goyne, Richard

Renn, Casey
See Crim, Keith R[enn]

Renn, Ludwig
See Vieth Von Golssenau, Arnold
Friedrich

Renn, Thomas E[dward] 1939- [CA]
American author
* Strike, Jeremy

Renna, Big Bill
See Renna, William Beneditto

Renna, G.
See Rapuzzi, G. L.

Renna, William Beneditto 1924- [BE]
American baseball player
* Renna, Big Bill

Rennell, Thomas 1753-1840 [DEP,
DNNS, HN]
British clergyman
* [The] Demosthenes of the Pulpit

Renner, A. M.
See Gatterman, Eugen Ludwig

Renner, Karl 1870-1950 [WBD]
Austrian statesman and author
* Springer, Rudolf
* Synopticus

Rennert, Dutch
See Rennert, Laurence Henry, Jr.

Rennert, Laurence Henry, Jr. 1934-
[NLG]
American baseball official
* Rennert, Dutch

Rennert, Maggie 1922- [CA]
American author
* Nunley, Maggie Rennert

Rennie, Christopher
See Ambrose, Eric [Samuel]

Rennie, Eric Alexander 1909- [BEW]
British actor and director
* Rennie, Michael

Rennie, James Alan 1899-1969 [CAP]
Scottish author
* Cleland, Morton
* Denver, Boone
* MacFee, Maxwell

Rennie, John 1761-1821 [NPS]
Engineer and inventor
* Archimedes

Rennie, John O. D. 1875-1952 [SC]
Canadian actor
* Mortimer, Henry

Rennie, Michael
See Rennie, Eric Alexander

Renny
See Barber, Raymond

Reno, Clint
See Ballard, [Willis] Todhunter

Reno, Don 1926?-1984 [WP 10-17-84]
American musician and songwriter
* King of the Five String Banjo

Reno, Frank ?-1868 [BLB]
American outlaw
* Reno, Trick

Reno, Trick
See Reno, Frank

Reno, Wilk
See Reno, William

Reno, William ?-1868 [BLB]
American outlaw
* Reno, Wilk

Renoir, Pierre Auguste 1841-1919
French painter
* Master of the Human Form

Renou
See Rousseau, Jean-Jacques

Renouard, Antoine Augustin 1765-1853
[HPPN]
French bibliographer and bookseller
* [An] Amateur

Renould
See Arnould, Arthur

Rensa, Pug
See Rensa, Tony George

Rensa, Tony George 1901- [BE]
American baseball player
* Rensa, Pug

Renshaw, William Charles 1861-1904
[OCS]
British tennis player
* [The] Father of Modern Lawn Tennis

Rensie, Willis
See Eisner, Will[iam Erwin]

[The] Rent Shark
See Kaussen, Guenther

Rental, J. W.
See Morel, Francois Xavier

Renthwaite, Robert
See Pound, Reginald

Rentner, Ernest 20th c. [SMG]
American football player
* Rentner, Pug

Rentner, Pug
See Rentner, Ernest

Renton, Cam
See Armstrong, Richard

Renton, Julia
See Cole, Margaret Alice

Rentzel, Del
See Rentzel, Delos Wilson

Rentzel, Delos Wilson 1909- [HPPN]
American government official
* Rentzel, Del

Renzelman, Marilyn
See Ferguson, Marilyn

Renzi, Emma
See Scheepers, Emmerentia

Repo, Seppo 1947- [SMG]
Finnish-born hockey player
* [The] Fox

[A] Reporter
See O'Leary, Joseph

Repp, Ed[ward] Earl 1900- [SFL, WGT]
American author
* Buckner, Brad
* Cody, John
* Field, Peter

Reppeteau, Carey Harrison 1890-1957
[SC]
American actor
* Harrison, Carey

[A] Representative
See Raymond, Henry Jarvis

[A] Representative Peer
See Gardiner, Charles John [Earl of
Blessington]

[A] Republican
See Bliss, George

[Un] Republican
See Condorcet, Marie Jean Antoine
Nicholas De Caritat

Republican
See Pinckney, Charles

[A] Republican
See White, William Charles

[The] Republican Doctor
See Akenside, Mark

[The] Republican Martyr
See Marat, Jean Paul

Republican, Mr.
See Taft, Robert Alphonso [Bob]

[The] Republican on the Potomac
See Dewey, Thomas Edmund

[The] Republican Queen
See Sophie Charlotte

Repulski, Eldon John 1927- [BE]
American baseball player
* Repulski, Rip

Repulski, Rip
See Repulski, Eldon John

Rerre
See Gonzalez Buzon, Manuel

Resch, Chico
See Resch, Glenn Allan

Resch, Glenn Allan 1948- [BI, SMG]
Canadian-born hockey player
* Resch, Chico

Rescigno, Xavier Frederick 1913- [BE]
American baseball player
* Mr. X

Research
See Beilby, J. Wood

Reseda
See Robinson, Therese Albertine Louise
von Jakob

Resetar, Dorothy L. 1899?-1979
American actress
* Bergere, Dorothy

Reshevsky, Samuel 1911- [HPPN]
Polish-American chess master
* [The] Unofficial Chess Champion of
the Non-Communist World

[A] **Resident**
See Adamson, William Agar

[A] **Resident**
See Chittenden, Newton H.

[A] **Resident**
See Massary, Isabel

[A] **Resident Beyond the Frontier**
See Snelling, William Joseph

[The] **Resident Bootblack**
See Tempone, Joseph

[A] **Resident Clergyman**
See Hildesley, Mark

[A] **Resident M. A.**
See Weatherly, Frederick Edward

[A] **Resident of Paris**
See Lardner, Dionysius

[A] **Resident of St. John**
See Hooper, John

[A] **Resident of San Domingo**
See Fabens, Joseph Warren

Resilient Uncle
See Tubman, William Vacanarat
Shadrach

Reskind, John
See Wallmann, Jeffrey M[iner]

Resnick, Lee
See Resnick, Leon

Resnick, Leon 1923- [ASC]
American musician
* Resnick, Lee

Resnick, Sylvia [Safran] 1927- [CA]
American author and columnist
* Paul, Sheri

Resnier, Andre Guillaume 1729-1811
[WGT]
Author
* Reinser III

[The] **Resolute**
See Florio, John

[The] **Resolute Doctor**
See Baconthorp [Bacon or Bacondorp],
John

Resolutissimus, Dr.
See Dorandus de Sancto Porciano,
Gulielmus

Resolutissimus, Doctor
See Durand de St. Pourcain, Guillaume

[The] **Respectable Hottentot**
See Johnson, Samuel

[The] **Respected Madam of Oxnard**
See Mount, John

Ressel, Franco 20th c. [WF]
Italian actor
* Ressel, Frank

Ressel, Frank
See Ressel, Franco

Ressich, John [Sellar Matheson] 1877-?
[WW]
Author
* Baxter, Gregory [joint pseudonym
with Eric De Banzie]

Ressieb, George
See Reach, James

Ressler, Alice 1918- [CA]
American author
* Wayne, Alice

Ressler, Lillian 20th c. [WD]
Author
* Janet, Lillian [joint pseudonym with
Janet O'Daniel]

Ressom, J. Ann
See Mosser, Ann J.

Resta, Dario ?-1924
British-born auto racer
* [The] Conquering Invader
* [The] Foreign Invader

Restalrig
See Symons, J. B.

Restani, Big Bird
See Restani, Kevin

Restani, Kevin 1951- [SMG]
American basketball player
* Restani, Big Bird

Restaurador del Parnaso
See Melendez Valdes, Juan

Restelli, Dingo
See Restelli, Dino Paul

Restelli, Dino Paul 1924- [BE]
American baseball player
* Restelli, Dingo

Restif de La Bretonne
See Restif, Nicolas Edme

Restif, Nicolas Edme 1734-1806 [DNNS,
WBD]
French author
* [The] French Defoe
* Restif de La Bretonne
* [The] Rousseau of the Gutter
* [The] Voltaire of Chambermaids

Restitutor Orbis
See Aurelian [Claudius Lucius Valerius
Domitius Aurelianus]

Restless Daniel
See Foe, Daniel

Restless, Jimmy
See Hull, James

Restless, Tim
See Tyers, Thomas

[The] **Restless Troubadour**
See Belafonte, Harold George, Jr.
[Harry]

Reston, James 1910-
American journalist
* Reston, Scotty

Reston, Scotty
See Reston, James

[A] **Restoration Clergyman**
See Hudson, Charles

[The] **Restoration Rogue**
See Dangerfield, Thomas

[The] **Restorer of Cities**
See Sancho I

[The] **Restorer of Egyptian Freemasonry**
See Balsamo, Giuseppe

[The] **Restorer of French Liberty**
See Louis XVI

[The] **Restorer of German Poetry**
See Opitz, Martin

[The] **Restorer of Learning**
See Medici, Lorenzo de

[The] **Restorer of Leon**
See Alfonso V

[The] **Restorer of Letters**
See Heigius, Alexander

[The] **Restorer of Parnassus**
See Melendez Valdes, Juan

[The] **Restorer of Poland**
See Casimir I

[The] **Restorer of Science in Germany**
See Sturm, Johann Christoph

[The] **Restorer of the Protestantism of
France**
See Court, Antoine

[The] **Restorer of the Roman Empire**
See Aurelian [Claudius Lucius Valerius
Domitius Aurelianus]

[The] **Restorer of the Rosicrucian
Philosophy**
See Balsamo, Giuseppe

Reszke, Jean de
See Mieczislaw, Jan

Retcliffe, [Sir] John
See Goedsche, Hermann Ottomar
Friedrich

Rethberg, Elisabeth
See Sattler, Lisbeth

Retief, Pieter ?-1838 [HPPN]
South African Boer leader
* Piet

[A] Retired Barrister
See Ambler, Charles

[A] Retired Captain, R.N.
See Gardner, George H.

[The] Retired Diocletian of Islington
See Quick, John

[A] Retired Guardian
See Bradley, William

[A] Retired Officer
See Spens, J.

[A] Retired Practicioner
See Allen, John

Retla, Robert
See Alter, Robert Edmond

Retlaw
See Waldie, Walter S.

Retlaw, S. P.
See Steinhaeuser, Walter Philip

Retner, Beth A.
See Brown, Beth

Retnuh X
See Hunter, William F.

Retnyw, Werdna
See Winter, Andrew

Retort, Jack
See Hunt, Isaac

Retratos, Pintor de
See Lopez y Portana, Vicente

Rettig, Adolph John 1894-   [BE]
American baseball player
* Rettig, Otto

Rettig, Otto
See Rettig, Adolph John

Rettig, Thomas Noel [Tommy] 1941-
[HPPN]
American actor
* Lassie's Master

Retz, Cardinal de
See Gondi, Jean Francois Paul de

Retz, Catiline
See Gondi, Jean Francois Paul de

Retzlaff, Palmer 1931-   [FB]
American football player
* Retzlaff, Pete

Retzlaff, Pete
See Retzlaff, Palmer

Reuben
See Hawker, Robert Stephen

Reuben, George 1880-1945   [SC]
Russian-born actor
* McKay, George W.

Reubens, Paul
See Rubenfeld, Paul

Reuchlin, Johann 1455-1522   [HPPN]
German humanist
* Capnio [or Kapnio]

Reulbach, Big Ed
See Reulbach, Edward Marvin

Reulbach, Edward Marvin 1882-1961
[BE, PB]
American baseball player
* Lawson, Edward
* Reulbach, Big Ed

Reunet, Henri le
See Poe, Edgar Allan

Reurslag, Guurtje Johanna Hendrika
1886-   [LAO]
Dutch educator and author
* Riemens-Reurslag, J.

Reuss, Theodor ?-1924   [EOP]
German occultist
* Merlin, [Brother]
* Theodore, Charles

**Reuter, Heinrich Ludwig Christian
Friedrich** 1810-1874
German author
* Fritz

Reuter, Paul Julius von
See Josaphat, Israel Beer

Reuther, Walter Philip 1907-1970
[HPPN]
American labor leader
* Labor's Rugged Individualist
* [The] Red Headed Kid from Wheeling
* [The] Redhead

Rev. B
See Eisner, Betty Grover

Reval, Jacques
See Laver, James

**[The] Revealer of Spiritual Healing to
This Age**
See Quimby, Phineas Parkhurst

Reveille, Thomas
See Tirana, Rifat

Revel, Bernard 1885-1940   [HPPN]
Russian-American educator
* [The] Builder of American Jewish
  Orthodoxy
* [The] Father of Yeshiva College

Revel, Harry
See Floyd, Gilbert

Revel, Jean-Francois
See Ricard, Jean-Francois

[Le] Revele
See Artaud, Antonin

Revelle, Arthur Hamilton
See Engstroem, Arthur Hamilton

Revenell, Nicholas
See White, Frank James

Revere, M. P.
See Williamson, Alice Muriel
[Livingston]

Revere, Paul
See Abarbanell, Jacob Ralph

Revere, Paul
See Chandler, Douglas

Revere, Paul
See De Revoire, Paul

[The] Reverend
See Brezina, Greg

Reverend Billy
See Robinson, William

**[A] Reverend Divine of the Church of
England**
See McSparran, James

Reverend Ike
See Eikerenkoetter, Frederick J.

Reverend Levi
See Dryden, John

[The] Reverend Mr. Bob
See Herrington, Robert

Reverie, Reginald
See Mellen, Grenville

Revermort, J. A.
See Cramb, John Adam

Reveron, Saundra 1942-   [IBW]
American caterer
* [The] Pie Lady

Reverse, Sir
See Buller, [Sir] Redvers Henry

[The] Reversible Chancellor
See Bismarck, Otto Eduard Leopold
von

[La] Reverte
See Rodriguez, Augustin

Revertito [Little Reverte]
See Garcia Reverte, Manuel

Revier, Dorothy
See Velegra, Doris

[The] Reviewer
See Allibone, Samuel Austin

Revillo, Eugene
See Oliver, Eugene

Revilo
See Christianson, Oliver

Revilo
See Marshall, Oliver P.

Revilo, E. B.
See Byrne, Oliver

[The] Revlon Cosmetics King
See Revson, Charles Haskell

**[El] Revolucionario del Toreo [The
Revolutionary Bullfighter]**
See Belmonte y Garcia, Juan

[A] Revolutionary Soldier
See Collins, James

[A] Revolutionary Soldier
See Martin, James Sullivan

Revons, E. C.
See Converse, Charles Crozat

Revorg, Trebla
See Grover, Albert

Revson, Champagne Peter
See Revson, Peter Jeffrey

Revson, Charles Haskell 1906?-1975
[HPPN, NW 12-5-83]
American business executive
* [El] Exigente [The Demanding One]
* [The] Revlon Cosmetics King

Revson, Peter Jeffrey 1939-1974 [EAR, HPPN]
American auto racer
* [The] Glamour Boy of the Race Drivers
* Revson, Champagne Peter

Rewdgo, Deary
See Gorey, Edward [St. John]

Rexford, John
See Bailey, Prentiss

Rexroth, Kenneth 1905-1982
American painter, poet, philosopher
* [The] Last of the Great Bohemians

Rey, Alvino
See McBurney, Alvin

Rey, Anita
See Lorrnel, Marlise

[El] Rey del Mambo [The King of Mambo]
See Prado, [Domase] Perez

[El] Rey del Temple
See Solorzano Davalos, Jesus

Rey, Fernando
See Arambillet, Fernando

Rey, Frederico
See Koning, Fred Wittop

Rey, Hans Augusto
See Reyersbach, Hans Augusto

Rey, Louis-Etienne-Ernest 1823-1909
[BBD, HPPN]
French composer
* Reyer, Ernest
* Reyer, Louis-Etienne-Ernest

Rey, Pepe
See Cornyn, John Hubert

Rey, Roberto
See Colas Iglesias, Roberto

Rey, Russell [house pseudonym, Curtis Warren]
See Hughes, Den[n]is [Talbot]

Rey Tigre [King Tiger]
See Tijerina, Reies

Rey-Stolle, Alejandro 1910- [IAW]
Spanish author
* Xavier, Adro

Reyam
See Mayer, Charles Leopold

Reybaud, Marie Roch Louis 1799-1879
[HPPN, PA]
French author
* Clisson, Paul
* Dwrocher, Leon

Reyburn, Wallace [Macdonald] 1913-
[IAW]
New Zealand-born author
* Scott, William

Reyer, Ernest
See Rey, Louis-Etienne-Ernest

Reyer, Louis-Etienne-Ernest
See Rey, Louis-Etienne-Ernest

Reyersbach, Hans Augusto 1898-1977
[CA]
German-born illustrator and author
* Rey, Hans Augusto
* Uncle Gus

Reyes, Chucho
See Reyes Ferreira, Jesus

Reyes, Dr. [code name]
See Rogers, William Pierce

Reyes, Eva
See Ardura, Adaljina

Reyes, Fernando De Los 1930- [GS]
Mexican bullfighter
* Callao [Pebble]

Reyes, Miguel Angel
See Dilone, Miguel Angel

Reyes, Nap
See Reyes, Napoleon Aguilera

Reyes, Napoleon Aguilera 1919- [BE]
Cuban-born baseball player
* Reyes, Nap

Reyes Basualto, [Ricardo Eliezer] Neftali 1904-1973 [CLC, EWL, TCL]
Chilean poet
* [The] Latin Walt Whitman
* Neruda, Pablo

Reyes Ferreira, Jesus 1884-? [BI]
Mexican painter
* Reyes, Chucho

Reyhaud, [Madam] C.
See Arnaud, Henrietta

Reymond, Louis
See Daudet, Ernest

Reymont, Ladislas
See Reymont, Wladyslaw Stanislaw

Reymont, Wladyslaw Stanislaw 1867-1925 [TLC]
Author
* Reymont, Ladislas

Reyna, Ruth 1904- [IAW]
American author
* Abbott, Evelyn
* Abbott, Orrina
* Ana, Ray

Reynard
See Fox, Myron

Reynard
See Foxcroft, Francis [Frank]

Reynaud, Jacques
See Cisternes de Coutiras, Gabrielle Anne de

Reynold, Thomas, Physition
See Rhodion [or Roeslin], Eucharius

Reynolds, Adrian
See Long, Amelia Reynolds

Reynolds, Albert Pierce [Allie] 1915-
[BE, DGS, PB]
American baseball player
* Reynolds, Chief
* Superchief

Reynolds, Ann
See Bly, Carol

Reynolds, Bart
See Emblen, Donald Lewis

Reynolds, Buddy Lee
See Reynolds, Byron Leon

Reynolds, Burt
See Reynolds, Byron Leon

Reynolds, Byron Leon 1936- [HPPN]
American actor
* Buddy
* [The] Frog Prince
* Reynolds, Buddy Lee
* Reynolds, Burt
* Reynolds, Prince

Reynolds, Charles 1879?-1942 [BMH, THR]
British comedian
* Austin, Charles

Reynolds, Charles Alexander 1842-1876
[HPPN]
American hunter, guide, scout
* Reynolds, Lonesome Charley

Reynolds, Chief
See Reynolds, Albert Pierce [Allie]

Reynolds, Craig
See Enfield, Harold Hugh

Reynolds, Dallas McCord 1917- [CA, ESF, WGT]
American author
* Collins, Clark
* Mallory, Mark
* McCord, Guy
* Reynolds, Mack
* Ross, Dallas

Reynolds, Daniel Vance [Danny] 1919-
[BE]
American baseball player
* Reynolds, Squirrel

Reynolds, Debbie
See Reynolds, Mary Frances

Reynolds, Dickson
See Reynolds, Helen Mary Greenwood Campbell

Reynolds, [Rev.] E. Winchester 1827-?
[HPPN]
American clergyman
* [An] American Minister

Reynolds, Frank 1923-1983 [WP 7-21-83]
American reporter
* [The] Gray Ghost

Reynolds, G. W. M.
See Reynolds, George William
Macarthur

Reynolds, George William Macarthur
1814-1879 [HFF, PA]
British author
* Bos
* Master Timothy
* Reynolds, G. W. M.

Reynolds, Gertrude M. [Robins] 20th c.
[NPS]
Author
* Robins, G. M.

Reynolds, Hacksaw
See Reynolds, Jack

Reynolds, Helen Mary Greenwood Campbell 1884-1969 [CA, NAA]
Canadian author and illustrator
* Dickson, Helen
* Reynolds, Dickson

Reynolds, Helene
See Davenport, Helene

Reynolds, Herbert
See Rourke, Michael Elder

Reynolds, Horse
See Reynolds, Robert Odell

Reynolds, Ice
See Reynolds, Jerry

Reynolds, Jack 20th c.
American football player
* Reynolds, Hacksaw

Reynolds, Jack
See Jones, Jack

Reynolds, Jack
See Paulson, John W.

Reynolds, Jerry 20th c. [SI 11-28-83]
American basketball player
* Reynolds, Ice

Reynolds, John ?-1607 [HN]
Leader of a religious sect in Britain
* Pouch, Captain

Reynolds, John 1788-1865 [HPPN]
American scout and politician
* Old Ranger

Reynolds, John
See Whitlock, Ralph

Reynolds, John Cromwell 1810-1849
[HPPN]
American surgeon
* [The] Fighting Doctor

Reynolds, John Hamilton 1794-1842
[FFF, PI]
British poet
* Corcoran, Peter
* Herbert, Edward
* Nimrod

Reynolds, Joseph [FFF]
American railroad owner
* Diamond Joe

Reynolds, [Sir] Joshua 1723-1792
[DNNS, NPS, SN]
British painter
* [The] Bachelor Painter
* [The] Raphael of England

Reynolds, L. Major
See Leipiar, Louise

Reynolds, Liggett
See Simon, Robert Alfred

Reynolds, Lonesome Charley
See Reynolds, Charles Alexander

Reynolds, Lou
See Sebille, Louis

Reynolds, Mack
See Reynolds, Dallas McCord

Reynolds, Madge
See Whitlock, Ralph

Reynolds, Margaret Gertrude 19th c.
[PI]
Irish poet
* Sepperle

Reynolds, Marjorie
See Goodspeed, Marjorie

Reynolds, Marthe Lucy 1915- [HPPN]
American prostitute
* [The] Blonde Bum
* [The] Hoosier Hustler
* [The] Houri
* Reynolds, Roundheels

Reynolds, Mary Ellen 1898-1936 [BEW,
EMT, PMJ]
American actress, dancer, singer
* Miller, Marilyn

Reynolds, Mary Frances 1932- [BDF,
CR, EMT, FC]
American actress, singer, dancer
* [The] Iron Butterfly
* Reynolds, Debbie

Reynolds, [Marjorie] Moira Davison
1915- [CA]
American author
* Moore, Marna

Reynolds, Mollie
See Willis, Mollie R.

Reynolds, Mrs. James [FFF]
Entertainer
* Rivers, Olive

Reynolds, Myra Rolfe 20th c. [NAA]
American writer
* Alden, Betty [house pseudonym?]

Reynolds, N. O. 19th c. [HPPN]
American soldier
* Reynolds, Nage

Reynolds, Nage
See Reynolds, N. O.

Reynolds, Peter
See Horrocks, Peter

Reynolds, Peter
See Long, Amelia Reynolds

Reynolds, Prince
See Reynolds, Byron Leon

Reynolds, R. J.
See Reynolds, Robert James

Reynolds, Richard S. 1881-1955 [HPPN]
American aluminum manufacturer
* [The] Father of Metal Foil

Reynolds, Robert 17th c. [HPPN]
British comedian
* Pickelherring

Reynolds, Robert James 1959-
American baseball player
* Reynolds, R. J.

Reynolds, Robert Odell 20th c. [BBH]
American football player
* Reynolds, Horse

Reynolds, Robert Rice 1884-? [HPPN]
American politician
* Our Bob
* [The] Playboy

Reynolds, Ron
See Bradbury, Ray [Douglas]

Reynolds, Roundheels
See Reynolds, Marthe Lucy

Reynolds, Ruth Evelyn Millicent 1915-
[ART]
British painter and sculptor
* R. R.

Reynolds, Squirrel
See Reynolds, Daniel Vance [Danny]

Reynolds, Vivian
See Snyder, Mrs.

Reynolds, Walter Doty 1860-? [SFL,
WGT]
Author
* Prime, Lord

Reynolds, Walter H.
See Smith, Walter H.

Reynolds-Stephens, [Sir] William
See Stephens, William

Reys, Maria Everdina 1924- [EJ]
Dutch singer
* Reys, Rita

Reys, Rita
See Reys, Maria Everdina

Reysh, Tamen
See East, Henry Mortimer

Reyten, Thaddeus 18th c. [HN]
Resisted the partition of Poland
* [The] Polish Cato

Reywas, Mot
See Spivey, Thomas Sawyer

Rhadamanthus
See Butters, Francis

Rhaeticus [or Rheticus]
See Von Lauchen, Georg Joachim

Rhampsinitus
See Ramses III [or Rameses]

Rhangabe
See Michael I

[The] Rhapsody in Blue
See Frank, Clint

Rhapsody, Miss
See Wells, Viola Gertrude

Rhawn, Robert John [Bobby] 1919-
[BE]
American baseball player
* Rhawn, Rocky

Rhawn, Rocky
See Rhawn, Robert John [Bobby]

Rhea, Don 20th c.   [CM]
American radio broadcaster
* Uncle Don

Rhea, Nicholas
See Walker, Peter Norman

Rheal
See Cesena, Sebastian Gayet

Rheal, Sebastien
See Gayet, Sebastien

Rheam, Cy
See Rheam, Kenneth Johnston

Rheam, Kenneth Johnston 1893-1947
[BE]
American baseball player
* Rheam, Cy

Rhee, Jhoon 1932-
Korean-born martial artist
* [The] Father of American Tae Kwon Do

Rhees, [Rev.] Morgan John 1760-1804
[HPPN]
British-American clergyman
* Philanthropos

Rheinhardt, Rudolph H.
See Hempel, George

Rhem, Charles Flint 1903-   [BE, BN, PB]
American baseball player
* Rhem, Shad
* Rhem, Zorie

Rhem, Shad
See Rhem, Charles Flint

Rhem, Zorie
See Rhem, Charles Flint

Rhenanus, Beatus
See Birt, Theodor

Rhene Baton
See Baton, Rene

[The] Rhetorician
See Seneca, Marcus Lucius Annaeus

Rhett, Robert Barnwell
See Smith, Robert Barnwell

Rhiannon
See Mackworth, Cecily

Rhinde, William 18th c.   [HPPN]
British poet
* [An] Anti Hudibraston

Rhine, Alice Hyneman   [PA]
Author
* A. H. R.
* Alice

Rhine, Joseph A. 1895-   [HPPN]
American pioneer in research of extrasensory perception
* [The] E. S. P. Advocate

Rhines, Bunker
See Rhines, William P. [Billy]

Rhines, William P. [Billy] 1869-1922
[PB]
American baseball player
* Rhines, Bunker

[The] Rhinestone Rubinstein
See Liberace, Wladziu Valentino

Rhinewine, Abraham 1887-   [NAA]
Polish-born journalist and author
* Ero

Rhiney, Bambi
See Rhiney, Delores Francine

Rhiney, Delores Francine 20th c.   [IBW]
American fashion model
* Rhiney, Bambi

Rhinotmetus [With the Nose Cut Off]
See Justinian II

Rho, Stella
See Vitelleschi, Stella

Rhoades, Cornelia Harsen 1863-1940
[DNA]
American author
* Rhoades, Nina

Rhoades, Dusty
See Rhoades, Robert Barton

Rhoades, Geoffrey H. 1898-   [ART]
British painter
* G. H. R.

Rhoades, Jefferson
See Panzram, Carl

Rhoades, Jonathan
See Olsen, John Edward [Jack]

Rhoades, Judith G[rubman] 1935-   [CA]
American author
* Dilling, Judith

Rhoades, Nina
See Rhoades, Cornelia Harsen

Rhoades, Robert Barton 1879-1967   [BE, PB]
American baseball player
* Rhoades, Dusty

Rhodan, Forry
See Ackerman, Forrest J[ames]

Rhode, Austen
See Francis, Basil [Hoskins]

Rhode, John
See Street, Cecil John Charles

Rhode, Winslow
See Roe, F[rederic] Gordon

Rhodes
See Andronicus of Rhodes

Rhodes, Alfred ?-1948   [SC]
American actor
* Rhodes, Dusty

Rhodes, Billie 1894-   [CU]
American actress
* [The] Nestor Girl

Rhodes, Billy 1895-1967   [SC]
American actor
* Little, Billy

Rhodes, Cecil John 1853-1902   [HPPN, NPS]
British administrator and financier in South Africa
* [The] African Empire Builder
* [A] Colossus
* [The] Colossus of Africa
* [The] King of Diamonds

Rhodes, Donald Wayne 1954-   [SMG]
American football player
* Rhodes, Skid

Rhodes, Dusty
See Rhodes, Alfred

Rhodes, Dusty
See Rhodes, James Lamar

Rhodes, Dusty
See Rhodes, John Gordon

Rhodes, Dusty
See Rhodes, William Clarence [Bill]

Rhodes, Dusty
See Runnels, Virgil

Rhodes, Erik
See Sharpe, Ernest Rhoades

Rhodes, Ethmer Cletus 1913-1966
[CWG]
American country-western performer
* Rhodes, Slim

Rhodes, Eugene Manlove 1869-1934
[HPPN]
American author
* [The] Hired Man on Horseback
* [The] Novelist of the Cattle Kingdom

Rhodes, Fella
See Rhodes, William

Rhodes, Hari
See Rhodes, Harry

Rhodes, Harry 1932-   [BA]
American actor
* Rhodes, Hari

Rhodes, Helen   [NPS]
Composer and singer
* D'Hardelot, Guy

Rhodes, Izora 20th c.   [IBW]
American singer
* Two Tons of Fun

Rhodes, James Lamar 1927-   [BE, BI, PB]
American baseball player
* Rhodes, Dusty

Rhodes, John Gordon 1907-1960 [BE]
American baseball player
* Rhodes, Dusty

Rhodes, Laura
See Robinson, Lisa

Rhodes, Oakmead
See Burke, Thomas

Rhodes, Orville J. 1930- [ECM, RM]
American musician
* Rhodes, Red

Rhodes, Red
See Rhodes, Orville J.

Rhodes, Ruth 1896-1975 [SC]
American actress
* Lee, Ruth

Rhodes, Skid
See Rhodes, Donald Wayne

Rhodes, Slim
See Rhodes, Ethmer Cletus

Rhodes, William 20th c.
American football player
* Rhodes, Fella

Rhodes, William Clarence [Bill] 19th c.
[BE]
American baseball player
* Rhodes, Dusty

Rhodes, William Henry 1822-1876
[ESF, SFP]
American writer
* Caxton

Rhodes, Zandra Lindsey 1940- [WFA]
British fashion and textile designer
* [The] Girl with Green Hair

[The] Rhodian Master
See Ennius, Quintus

Rhodiginenus, Lingi Richiere 1450-1525
[PA]
Author
* Cielius

Rhodion [or Roeslin], Eucharius
1540-1598 [FFF]
British author
* Reynold, Thomas, Physition

Rhodopis
See Doricha

Rhody
See Burnside, Ambrose Everett

Rhody, Louis
See Rothkopf, Louis

[The] Rhomboid Rhetorician
See Goldbogen [or Goldenborgen],
Avrom Hirsch

Rhondda, [Viscountess] Margaret Haig
1884- [WWL]
British author
* Mackworth

Rhone, Cherokee 20th c.
American basketball player
* Rhone, Chief

Rhone, Chief
See Rhone, Cherokee

Rhone, Earnest 1953- [SMG]
American football player
* Rhone, Ironman

Rhone, Ironman
See Rhone, Earnest

[The] Rhone of Christian Eloquence
See Bossuet, Jacques Benigne

[The] Rhone of Christian Eloquence
See Hilary

[The] Rhone of Latin Eloquence
See Hilary

R'hoone, Lord
See Balzac, Honore de

Rhoscomyl, Owen
See Vaughan, Owen

Rhubarb, Colonel
See Worthington, Robert Lee [Bob]

Rhubarb Red
See Polfus, Lester

Rhuddlau, John
See Blanden, Charles Granger

Rhue, Morton
See Strassar, Todd

Rhum
See Sprogiani, Henrico

[The] Rhumba King
See Cugat, Xavier

Rhydderch, Ieuan
See Jones, Evan David

[A] Rhymer
See Bell, Thomas

[A] Rhymer
See Gatty, Alfred

[The] Rhyming Barber
See Di Giovanni, Domenico

Rhyndacenus
See Lascaris, Andreas Johannes [or
Janus]

Rhyne, Orestes Pearle 1885- [NAA]
American author and educator
* Rein, Orestes Pearle

Rhys, Horton [PA]
Author
* Imported Sparrow

Rhys, Ioan
See Rees, Ioan Bowen

Rhys, Megan
See Williams, Jeanne

Rhys-Jones, Dilys 1946- [TR]
British actress
* Watling, Dilys

[The] Rhythm and Blues King
See Frost, Frank Otis

Rhythm, Miss
See Brown, Ruth

Rhythm, Mr.
See Williams, Andre

Ribbans, Frederick Bolingbroke 19th c.
[HFN]
Author
* [A] Layman

Ribbentrop, Joachim 1893-1946
Nazi government official
* Von Ribbensnob
* Von Ribbentrop, Joachim

Ribbing, Sigurd 1816-? [HPPN]
Swedish author
* Rbg

Ribbonson, Horatio
See Shaw, George Bernard

Ribeiro, Antonio
See Guarghias, Aloysius George

Ribeiro, Joao Batista
See Fernandes, Joao Batista Ribeiro De
Andrade

Ribera, Jose 1588-1652 [SN, WBD]
Spanish painter
* [The] Little Spaniard
* Spagnoletto

Ribera, Lucas
See Cabrera, Luis

Riberio, Julio Cesar
See Riberio Vaughn, Julio Cesar

Riberio Vaughn, Julio Cesar 1845-1890
Brazilian author, journalist, philologist
* Riberio, Julio Cesar

Ric
See Miniggio, Riccardo

Ricard, Jean-Francois 1924- [CA]
French philosopher, critic, author
* Revel, Jean-Francois

Ricardel, Molly
See Boehnel, Molly

Ricardo
See McHale, Richard

Ricardo, Benito Concepcion 1954- [FR]
Paraguayan-born American football player
* Ricardo, Benny

Ricardo, Benny
See Ricardo, Benito Concepcion

Ricardo, Don
See Ridgely, Richard

Ricasoli, Bettino [Baron of Brolio]
1809-1880 [SN]
Italian statesman
* [The] Baron

Ricault, Charles Joseph de 1823-1899
[HPPN, WBD]
French historian and author
* D'Ricault, Charles
* Hericault, Charles d'

Ricca, Mops
See DeLucia, Felice

Ricca, Paul
See DeLucia, Felice

Riccardo, John 1924-
American automobile executive
* [The] Flamethrower

Ricci, [Curbastro] Gregorio 1853-1925 [HPPN]
Italian mathematician
* [The] Father of the Ricci Calculus

Ricci, Marie Nielli 1883-1970 [WFA]
Italian-born fashion designer
* Ricci, Nina

Ricci, Nina
See Ricci, Marie Nielli

Ricciarelli, Daniele 1509-1566 [SN, WBD]
Italian painter
* [Il] Braccatone
* [The] Breeches Maker
* Volterra, Daniele da

[IL] Riccio [The Curly-Haired]
See Briosco, Andrea

Riccio, Andrea
See Briosco, Andrea

Riccio, Domenico 1494-1567 [WBD]
Italian painter
* [Il] Brusasorci

Riccoboni, Adrienne 1930- [FC]
British actress
* Corri, Adrienne

Riccoboni, Lelio
See Riccoboni, Lodovico

Riccoboni, Lodovico 1675?-1753 [WBD]
Italian-born actor and playwright
* Riccoboni, Lelio

Riccoboni, Luigi 1674-1753 [PA]
Author
* Lelio

Riccobono, Joseph S. 1893?-1975 [BI]
American underworld figure
* Bono, Joe

Rice, Albert
See Leventhal, Albert Rice

Rice, Allison [joint pseudonym with Jane Rice]
See Allison, Ruth

Rice, Allison [joint pseudonym with Ruth Allison]
See Rice, Jane

Rice, Anne 20th c. [PW 2-15-85]
Author
* Rampling, Anne

Rice, Billy
See Greffly, Frederick

Rice, Brian K. 1932- [IAW]
British author
* Vigilans

Rice, Clive Edward Butler 1949- [DC]
South African-born cricketer
* Rice, Ricie

Rice, Craig [joint pseudonym with Georgiana Ann Randolph]
See Lombino, Salvatore A.

Rice, Craig [joint pseudonym with Salvatore A. Lombino]
See Randolph, Georgiana Ann

Rice, Daddy
See Rice, Thomas Dartmouth

Rice, Dan
See McLaren, Daniel

Rice, Daniel 1822-1900 [HPPN]
American circus clown
* [The] King of American Clowns
* [The] Shakespeare Clown

Rice, Del
See Rice, Delbert W.

Rice, Delbert W. 1922- [BE]
American baseball player
* Rice, Del

Rice, Desmond Charles 1924- [CA]
British author
* Meiring, Desmond

Rice, Dicey
See Rice, John Michael

Rice, Dorothy Mary 1913- [CA]
Irish-born author
* Borne, Dorothy
* Vicary, Dorothy

Rice, Edgar Charles 1892-1974 [BAB, DGS, PB]
American baseball player
* Man o' War
* Rice, Sam

Rice, Elinor
See Hays, Elinor Rice

Rice, Elmer
See Reizenstein, Elmer Leopold

Rice, George 1917- [FC]
American actor
* O'Hanlon, George

Rice, George Graham
See Herzig, Jacob Simon

Rice, Granny
See Rice, H. Grantland

Rice, H. Grantland 1880-1954 [FB]
American sportswriter
* Rice, Granny
* Wilson, James

Rice, Harold 20th c. [BS]
American educator and owner of silk magic business
* [The] Silk King

Rice, Harold Housten 1924- [BE]
American baseball player
* Rice, Hoot

Rice, Harvey 1800-1891 [HPPN]
American politician
* [The] Father of the Public School System in Ohio

Rice, Hoot
See Rice, Harold Housten

Rice, Howard 1897-1954 [SC]
American actor
* Carney, Don
* Uncle Don

Rice, Isaac Leopold 1850-1915 [HPPN, PA]
German-born American attorney, author, chess player
* Ecir
* [The] Father of the Rice Gambit

Rice, James 19th c. [SAT]
British author
* Legrand, Martin

Rice, Jane 20th c. [WGT]
Author
* Austin, Mary
* Rice, Allison [joint pseudonym with Ruth Allison]

Rice, Jim Crow
See Rice, Thomas Dartmouth

Rice, Joan Odette 1919- [AW]
British writer and broadcaster
* Hallam, Jay

Rice, John Michael 1949- [DC]
British cricketer
* Rice, Dicey

Rice, Mrs. Cale Young
Author
* Hegan, Alice Caldwell

[The] Rice Paddy Ranger
See Curless, Richard [Dick]

Rice, Ricie
See Rice, Clive Edward Butler

Rice, Rosella [FFF]
Writer
* Brooks, Chatty

Rice, Sam
See O'Hanlon, George Samuel

Rice, Sam
See Rice, Edgar Charles

Rice, Thomas Dartmouth 1808-1860 [DAM, DNNF, SN, WBD]
American songwriter and minstrel-show pioneer
* [The] Father of American Minstrelsy
* Rice, Daddy
* Rice, Jim Crow

Rice-Davies, Mandy
See Rice-Davies, Marylin

Rice-Davies, Marylin 1947?-
Involved in British political scandel
* Rice-Davies, Mandy

[The] Rich
See Canute II

Rich
See Fairfield, Richard Ivan

[The] Rich
See Fugger, Jakob, II

[The] Rich
See George

[The] Rich
See Louis IX

[The] Rich
See Otto

[The] Rich
See Otto

Rich, Barbara [joint pseudonym with Laura Reichenthal]
See Graves, Susan B[ernard]

Rich, Barbara [joint pseudonym with Robert Von Ranke Graves]
See Reichenthal, Laura

Rich, Bernard 1917-   [IEJ, PMJ, WWJ]
American jazz musician
* Baby Traps
* Rich, Buddy
* Traps the Drum Wonder

Rich, Buddy
See Rich, Bernard

Rich, C. B.
See Lewis, Leo Rich

Rich, Charley 20th c.   [HPPN]
American country-western performer
* [The] Silver Fox

Rich, Christopher ?-1714   [SN]
* Divito

Rich, D. Coleman
See Richardson, Darrell C.

Rich, Eddie
See Reich, Edwin

Rich, Edith J. R. 1878-1956   [BEW]
American editor and author
* Isaacs, Edith J. R.

Rich, Edmund
See Edmund

Rich, Gerry
See Brandon, Johnny

Rich, Henry K.
See Goddard, Norman Molyneux

Rich, Irene
See Luther, Irene

Rich, Jean
See Rinkoff, Barbara

Rich, John 1692-1761   [DNNF, DNNS, HPPN, SN]
British actor
* [The] Father of English Pantomime
* [The] Father of Harlequins
* Lun

[The] Rich Man's Norman Rockwell
See Wyeth, Andrew

Rich, Robert
See Trumbo, Dalton

Rich, Robert Felming 1883-?   [HPPN]
American politician
* Rich, Woolly Bob

Rich, Woodrow Earl 1917-   [BE]
American baseball player
* Rich, Woody

Rich, Woody
See Rich, Woodrow Earl

Rich, Woolly Bob
See Rich, Robert Felming

Richard
See Audin, J. M. V.

Richard, A. 1809-?   [PA]
Author
* Du Cental

Richard, Ann B. 1876-1949   [HPPN]
American costume designer and dancer
* Princess, Patricia

Richard, Anthony Tom
See Foe, Daniel

Richard, Bee-Bee
See Richard, Lee Edward

Richard, Bill
See Van Horn, Dale R.

Richard, Cliff
See Webb, Harold

Richard D.
See Dent, Richard

Richard, Francois   [WGT]
French author
* Richard-Bessiere, F. [joint pseudonym with Richard Bessiere]

Richard, George
See Stubbs, Harry C[lement]

Richard, [Joseph] Henri 1936-   [FHE]
Canadian hockey player
* [The] Pocket Rocket

Richard, J. R.
See Richard, James Rodney

Richard, Jacques 1952-   [SMG]
Canadian-born hockey player
* Costeau

Richard, James Robert
See Bowen, Robert Sydney

Richard, James Rodney 1950-   [BE, NLG]
American baseball player
* Richard, J. R.

Richard, Jean-Marius 1905-   [FC]
French screenwriter and director
* Carlo-Rim

Richard, Kent?
See Crossen, Ken[dell Foster]

Richard, Lee
See Le Pelley, Guernsey

Richard, Lee David 1926-   [BEW]
American actor
* Richardson, Lee

Richard, Lee Edward 1948-   [SMG]
American baseball player
* Richard, Bee-Bee

Richard, Marthe 1890?-1982
French politician and former intelligence agent
* Alouette [Skylark]

Richard, [Joseph Henri] Maurice 1921-   [CEI, FHE, SR]
Canadian hockey player
* [The] Babe Ruth of Hockey
* Richard, Rocket
* [The] Rocket

Richard, Mira 1878?-1973   [BI]
French religious leader
* [The] Mother

Richard Nixon With a Whistle
See Allen, George

Richard of Cirencester ?-1402   [DNNF, FFF, HN]
British historian
* [The] Monk of Westminster

Richard of Ely
See Fitzneale, Richard

Richard, Rocket
See Richard, [Joseph Henri] Maurice

Richard the Chicken-Hearted
See Nixon, Richard Milhous

Richard the Ruffian
See Afflis, Richard

Richard Yea and Nay
See Richard I

Richard, Zina
See Merante, Mrs. Louis

Richard-Bessiere, F. [joint pseudonym with Francois Richard]
See Bessiere, Richard

Richard-Bessiere, F. [joint pseudonym with Richard Bessiere]
See Richard, Francois

Richard I ?-996   [DNNS, WBD]
Duke of Normandy
* [The] Fearless

Richard I 1157-1199   [DHA, HN, HPPN, NPS, SN]
King of England
* [The] British Lion
* Coeur de Lion
* [The] Dickon of the Broom
* [The] Lion Hearted
* Richard Yea and Nay

Richard II ?-1026?   [DNNS, FFF, SN]
Duke of Normandy
* [The] Good

Richard II 1367?-1400   [HN, SN]
King of England
* Bordeaux
* [The] Coxcomb

Richard II (cont.)
* * [Le] Jeune Damoisel Richart
* * [The] Skinless Prince of Wales

Richard III 1452-1485 [FFF, SN, SN, WBD]
King of England
* * [The] Boar
* * Crouchback [or Crookback]
* * [The] Hog
* * Prince Ramiro
* * [The] Protector

Richards, Al
See Shubin, Seymour

Richards, Alfred [Luther] 1939- [CA]
American psychologist and author
* * Richards, Fred

Richards, Allen
See Rosenthal, Richard A.

Richards, Ann
See Kenton, Margaret Ann Borden

Richards, Anna M[atlock], Jr. 19th c. [SFL]
Author
* * A. M. R.

Richards, Beah
See Richardson, Beulah

Richards, Cannonball
See Richards, Frank

Richards, Charles 1912- [DAM, EJ, WWJ]
American jazz musician
* * Richards, Red

Richards, Charles
See Marvin, John T.

Richards, Clay
See Crossen, Ken[dell Foster]

Richards, Clifton James 1958- [DC]
British cricketer
* * Richards, Jack

Richards, Cornelia Holroyd [Bradley] 1822-1892 [DNA, FFF]
American author
* * Manners, Mrs.

Richards, Curley Top
See Richards, Ruby

Richards, Curtis
See Curtis, Richard [Alan]

Richards, David
See Bickers, Richard Leslie Townshend

Richards, Dick 20th c. [SFL]
Author
* * Wells, Barry

Richards, Dickinson W. 1895-1973 [HPPN]
American physician
* * [The] Father of Cardiac Catheterization

Richards, Duane
See Hurley, Vic

Richards, E. B.
See Bayley, Edwin Richard

Richards, Ellen Swallow
See Swallow, Elleen

Richards, Elvin 20th c. [EF]
American football player
* * Richards, Kink

Richards, Emil
See Radocchia, Emilio Joseph

Richards, Ezek
See Savage, John

Richards, Frances 1903- [ART]
British artist
* * F. R.

Richards, Francis [joint pseudonym with Richard (Orson) Lockridge]
See Lockridge, Frances Louise [Davis]

Richards, Francis [joint pseudonym with Frances Louise (Davis) Lockridge]
See Lockridge, Richard [Orson]

Richards, Frank 20th c.
American carnival performer
* * Richards, Cannonball

Richards, Frank [house pseudonym]
See Austin, Stanley E.

Richards, Frank [house pseudonym]
See Barnard, Richard Innes

Richards, Frank [house pseudonym]
See Barrie, S.

Richards, Frank [house pseudonym]
See Brooks, Edwy Searles

Richards, Frank [house pseudonym]
See Catchpole, William Leslie

Richards, Frank [house pseudonym]
See Cook, Fred Gordon

Richards, Frank [house pseudonym]
See Davis, A. W.

Richards, Frank [house pseudonym]
See Down, C. Maurice

Richards, Frank [house pseudonym]
See Duffy, Michael Francis

Richards, Frank [house pseudonym]
See Gibbons, William

Richards, Frank
See Hamilton, Charles Harold St. John

Richards, Frank [house pseudonym]
See Herman, Julius

Richards, Frank [house pseudonym]
See Hinton, Herbert Allan

Richards, Frank [house pseudonym]
See Hook, H. Clarke

Richards, Frank [house pseudonym]
See Hope, William Edward Stanton

Richards, Frank [house pseudonym]
See Kemp, Alec M.

Richards, Frank [house pseudonym]
See Kirkham, Reginald S.

Richards, Frank [house pseudonym]
See Newman, Kenneth E.

Richards, Frank [house pseudonym]
See O'Mant, Hedley Percival Angelo

Richards, Frank [house pseudonym]
See Pentelow, John Nix

Richards, Frank [house pseudonym]
See Pike, William Ernest

Richards, Frank [house pseudonym]
See Ransome, L. E.

Richards, Frank [house pseudonym]
See Samways, George Richmond

Richards, Frank [house pseudonym]
See Shepherd, S. Rossiter

Richards, Frank [house pseudonym]
See Twyman, Harold William

Richards, Frank [house pseudonym]
See Wood-Smith, Noel

Richards, Fred
See Richards, Alfred [Luther]

Richards, Fred Charles 1927- [BE]
American baseball player
* * Richards, Fuzzy

Richards, Fuzzy
See Richards, Fred Charles

Richards, George
See McManus, George

Richards, George Henry 1819-? [HPPN]
British naval officer
* * G. H. R.

Richards, Harold M. S. 1895?-1985
American evangelist
* * [The] Most Listened-To Man In America

Richards, Harvey D.
See Sainsbury, Noel Everingham

Richards, Henry
See Morrissey, Joseph Laurence

Richards, Henry
See Stoddard, Richard Henry

Richards, Hilda
See Hamilton, Charles Harold St. John

Richards, Hilda
See Wheway, John W.

Richards, I. A.
See Richards, Ivor Armstrong

Richards, Ivor Armstrong 1893-1979 [LC, TC]
British critic
* * [The] Guru of Cambridge
* * Richards, I. A.

Richards, J. R.
See Richards, James Rodney

Richards, Jack
See Richards, Clifton James

Richards, James Rodney 1950- [IBW]
American baseball player
* Richards, J. R.

Richards, Jay
See Pine, Arthur

Richards, Jeff
See Taylor, Richard Mansfield

Richards, Johnny
See Cascales, John

Richards, Kay
See Baker, Susan [Catherine]

Richards, Keith 1943- [CA]
British musician and songwriter
* Phelge, Nanker [joint pseudonym with Michael Philip Jagger]

Richards, Kenny
See Broderick, Richard L[awrence]

Richards, Kink
See Richards, Elvin

Richards, Lela Horn 1870-? [NAA]
American author
* Neville, Lee

Richards, Leslie
See Green, Richard

Richards, Lillian
See Richardson, Mrs. Leander

Richards, Linda Ann Judson 1841-1930 [HPPN]
American nurse
* America's First Trained Nurse

Richards, Mark
See Frischwasser, Heinz Felix

Richards, Mrs. George [FFF]
Entertainer
* Goodwin, Maude

Richards, Parke
See Fewell, Laura R.

Richards, Paul
See Buddee, Paul Edgar

Richards, Pennington
See Pennington-Richards, C. M.

Richards, Peter
See Monger, [Ifor] David

Richards, Phyllis
See Auty, Phyllis

Richards, Red
See Richards, Charles

Richards, Renee
See Raskind, Richard

Richards, Robert [Bob] 1926- [TF]
American track and field athlete
* [The] Vaulting Vicar

Richards, Ronald Charles William 1923- [AW, CA, WD]
British author and playwright
* Saddler, Allen
* Saddler, K. Allen

Richards, Ross 20th c. [MBF]
British author
* Mead, Matt
* Reid, Desmond [house pseudonym]

Richards, Ruby 20th c. [IBW]
American entertainer
* Richards, Curley Top

Richards, Sara Lippincott 1875-? [NAA]
American author
* Lippincott, Sara
* Stein, J. J.

Richards, Stanley
See Myers, Stanley

Richards, Stephen
See Stevens, Mark

Richards, Theodore W. 1868-1928 [HPPN]
American chemist and educator
* [The] Father of Isotopes

Richards, Thomas
See Bergman, Richard Thomas

Richards, Thomas Addison 1829-1900 [HPPN]
American landscape painter
* [The] Doughty of the South

Richards, William Upton [PA]
Author
* W. U. R.

Richardson, Abram [or Arthur?] Harding 1855-1931 [BE, DGS, PB]
American baseball player
* Old True Blue
* Richardson, Hardy

Richardson, Anne
See Roiphe, Anne Richardson

Richardson, Anthony 1899- [AW]
British author
* Currie, Thomas Stewart

Richardson, Antonio 1928- [BF]
British director
* Richardson, Tony

Richardson, Arleta
See Wright, Arleta

Richardson, Beth
See Gutcheon, Beth R[ichardson]

Richardson, Beulah 20th c. [IBW]
American actress, author, director
* Richards, Beah

Richardson, Bill
See Richardson, Hubert Leon

Richardson, C.
See Munsey, Cecil [Richard, Jr.]

Richardson, C. C.
See Richardson, Clarence Clifford

Richardson, Cha Cha
See Richardson, Michele

Richardson, Charles 1853-1927 [BI]
British author and sportsman
* Shotley

Richardson, Charles 19th c. [HPPN]
British evangelist
* [The] Lincolnshire Thrasher

Richardson, Claibe
See Richardson, Claiborne F.

Richardson, Claiborne F. 1929- [ASC]
American composer
* Richardson, Claibe

Richardson, Clarence Clifford 1918- [BWW]
American singer
* Richardson, C. C.
* Richardson, Peg

Richardson, Darrell C. 20th c. [SFP]
Author
* Rich, D. Coleman

Richardson, Earl H. 19th c. [HPPN]
American inventor
* [The] Father of the Electric Iron

Richardson, Edmund 1818-1886 [HPPN]
American cotton grower and dealer
* [The] Cotton King
* [The] World's Largest Cotton Planter

Richardson, Elliot Lee 1921?- [HPPN, WP 6-17-84]
American government official
* Clean, Mr.
* [The] Movable Brahmin
* Richardson, Muggsy

Richardson, Emory Aaron ?-1965 [IA]
American poet
* Big Rich

Richardson, Ethel Florence [Lindesay] 1870-1946 [CA]
Australian author
* Richardson, Henrietta
* Richardson, Henry Handel

Richardson, Flavia
See Thomson, Christine Campbell

Richardson, Francis [joint pseudonym with Frank Parnell]
See Bartle, L. E.

Richardson, Francis [joint pseudonym with L. E. Bartle]
See Parnell, Frank

Richardson, Frank 1950- [BA]
American artist
* Mr. Frank

Richardson, Gabriel 1759-1820 [SN]
Friend of Scottish poet, Robert Burns
* Brewer Gabriel

Richardson, Garnet 1933- [CSH]
Canadian curler
* Richardson, Sam

Richardson, George Tilton ?-1938 [DNA]
American journalist
* Tilton, Dwight

Richardson, Gladwell 20th c. [MBF]
British author
* Blacksnake, George
* Clarkson, Orman

Richardson, Gladwell (cont.)
* Grant, Maxwell [house pseudonym]
* Haines, John
* Jones, Calico
* Kent, Pete
* Kildare, Maurice
* O'Riley, Warren
* Warner, Frank
* Winslowe, John

Richardson, Grace Lee
See Dickson, Naida

Richardson, H. B. 20th c.   [SMG]
American baseball manager
* Richardson, Spec

Richardson, Hardy
See Richardson, Abram [or Arthur?]
Harding

Richardson, Harold Edward 1929-
[IAW]
American author
* Cumberland, Cass

Richardson, Henrietta
See Richardson, Ethel Florence
[Lindesay]

Richardson, Henry Handel
See Richardson, Ethel Florence
[Lindesay]

Richardson, Henry Handel
See Robertson, Ethel Florence
[Lindesay Richardson]

Richardson, Henry V-M 1923-   [CA]
American author
* Richardson, Vokes

Richardson, Hubert Leon 20th c.
American politician
* Richardson, Bill

Richardson, Isabella 1782-1878   [PA]
Author
* Shiels, Tibbie

Richardson, Israel Bush 1815-1862
[FFF]
American army officer
* Fighting Dick

Richardson, J. P.
See Richardson, Jiles Perry

Richardson, Jabez
See Day, Benjamin Henry

Richardson, James 1760-1850   [HPPN,
PA]
British author and clergyman
* Clericus Septentrionalis
* [A] Protestant Watchman
* Stevin, Adam

Richardson, James, Jr. 1817-1863
[HPPN]
American clergyman
* J. R.
* R.

Richardson, Jape
See Richardson, Jiles Perry

Richardson, Jiles Perry 1935-1959
[RO1]
American singer and songwriter
* [The] Big Bopper
* Richardson, J. P.
* Richardson, Jape

Richardson, John 1796-1852   [CCL]
Canadian poet
* [An] English Officer

Richardson, Julian 1916-   [IBW]
American printer and bookstore owner
* Richardson, Rich

Richardson, Leander   [FFF]
American writer
* Town Listener

Richardson, Lee
See Richard, Lee David

Richardson, Michele 1970?-   [SI 4-9-84]
Nicaraguan-born swimmer
* Richardson, Cha Cha

Richardson, Midge Turk 1930-   [CA]
American author
* Turk, Midge

Richardson, Mrs. Leander   [FFF]
Entertainer
* Andrews, Carrie
* Gilman, Ada
* Richards, Lillian

Richardson, Muggsy
See Richardson, Elliot Lee

Richardson, Nancy
See Lewis, LeAnn

[The] Richardson of Athens
See Thespis

Richardson, Peg
See Richardson, Clarence Clifford

Richardson, Rafe
See Richardson, Ralph

Richardson, Ralph 1902-1983   [CR]
British actor
* Richardson, Rafe

Richardson, Randell 1921-   [ASC]
American singer
* Reade, Regina
* Rogers, Rosalind

Richardson, Rich
See Richardson, Julian

Richardson, Robert
See Lewis, James W.

Richardson, Robert S[hirley] 1902-   [CA,
SAT]
American author
* Latham, Philip

Richardson, Sam
See Richardson, Garnet

Richardson, Samuel 1689-1761   [DEP,
DNNS, RH]
British author
* [The] English Marivaux

Richardson, Samuel (cont.)
* [The] Founder of the English
Domestic Novel
* [The] Shakespeare of Prose Fiction

Richardson, Sandy
See Richardson, Thomas F.

Richardson, Spec
See Richardson, H. B.

Richardson, Thomas F. 1907?-1980
American robber
* Richardson, Sandy

Richardson, Tony
See Richardson, Antonio

Richardson, Vokes
See Richardson, Henry V-M

Richardson, [Rev.] William 18th c.
[HPPN]
British clergyman
* [The] Preaching Weathercock

Richardson, William 18th c.   [DNNS]
Writer
* [The] Father of War Correspondents

Richardson's Killer
See Cora, Charles

Richardus Criticus Cantabrigiensis
See Bentley, Richard

Richbourg, John 20th c.   [CMA]
American disc jockey
* John R

Richelieu
See Robinson, William Erigena

Richelieu, Cardinal de
See Du Plessis, Armand Jean

Richelieu, Duc de
See De Vignerot du Plessis, Louis
Francois Armand

Richelieu, Peter
See Robinson, P. W.

Richelson, Geraldine 1922-   [CA, SAT]
American author
* Leander, Ed

Richenbacher, Edward 1890-1973
American aviator and businessman
* Ace of Aces
* Rickenbacker, Edward Vernon [Eddie]

Richer, Donald [Donny] 20th c.   [WFA]
Canadian fashion designer
* Montreal's Liberace

[The] Richest Man in America
See Astor, John Jacob

[The] Richest Man in Canada
See Bronfman, Samuel

[The] Richest Man in San Francisco
See Sharon, William [Bill]

[The] Richest Man in the World
See Bronfman, Edgar

[The] Richest Man in the World
See Getty, Jean Paul, Sr.

Richev, Robert Keith 1898- [HPPN]
American actor, playwright, producer, director
* Keith, Robert

Richey, David 1939- [CA]
American author
* Davey, John
* Johnson, Richard

Richey, Robert Keith 1898- [BEW]
American actor, playwright, director
* Keith, Robert

Richfield, Mai
See Ryan, Mrs. Thomas

[The] Richfield Reporter
See Hayes, Samuel Stewart

Richie
See Starkey, Richard

Richman, Abraham Samuel 1921- [EJ, PMJ]
American jazz musician
* Richman, Boomie

Richman, Ace
See Richman, Milton Harry

Richman, Al 1913- [CA]
British-born author
* Morton, Joseph
* Richmond, Al

Richman, Arthur
See Reichman, Arthur

Richman, Boomie
See Richman, Abraham Samuel

Richman, Harry
See Reichman, Harry

Richman, Marian
See Pearlson, Marion S.

Richman, Mark
See Richman, Marvin Jack

Richman, Marvin Jack 1927- [BEW]
American actor
* Richman, Mark

Richman, Milton Harry 1916- [CWG]
American country-western performer
* Richman, Ace

Richmond
See Sheppard, Jacob R.

Richmond, Al
See Richman, Al

Richmond, Bernice
See Robinson, Bernice [Nelke]

Richmond, Bill 1763-1829 [IBW]
American-born boxer
* [The] Black Terror

Richmond, Bud
See Richmond, Ray[mond S.]

Richmond, Charles D. 1935- [EJ]
American jazz musician
* Richmond, Dannie

Richmond, Dannie
See Richmond, Charles D.

Richmond, E. J.
See Richmond, Euphemia Johnson [Guernsey]

Richmond, Euphemia Johnson [Guernsey] 1825-? [DNA, HPPN]
American author
* Johnson, Effie
* Richmond, E. J.

Richmond, George
See Brister, Richard

Richmond, George
See Samways, George Richmond

Richmond, Grace
See Marsh, John

Richmond, H. B.
See Bungay, E. Newton

Richmond, Harry
See Boyle, Henry

Richmond, Hattie L.
See Canfield, Mrs. Eugene

Richmond, John Peter
See Carradine, Richmond Reed

Richmond, Kane
See Bowditch, Frederick W.

Richmond, Legh 19th c. [HFN]
Author and clergyman
* [A] Clergyman of the Church of England

Richmond, Mary
See Lindsay, Kathleen

Richmond, Ray[mond S.] 1896- [BE]
American baseball player
* Richmond, Bud

Richmond, Rod
See Glut, Donald F[rank]

Richmond, William
See Fell, William Richmond

Richmondiensis
See Duffield, Matthew Dawson

Richstein, Larry 20th c. [RM]
Musician
* Tabin, Rube

Richter, Emil Henry 1888-1934 [BE]
German-born baseball player
* Richter, Reggie

Richter, Ernst H. 1901-1959 [WGT]
German author
* Brown, William
* Terridge, Ernest

Richter, Eugen 1838-1906 [SFL]
Author
* Richter, Eugene

Richter, Eugene
See Richter, Eugen

Richter, Franz 1911?- [BI]
German Nazi leader
* Roessler, Fritz

Richter, Hugh 20th c. [EF]
American football player
* Richter, Pat

Richter, J. H.
See Richter-Altschaffer, John Hans

Richter, Jean Paul Friedrich 1763-1825 [DEP, RH, SN]
German author
* [Der] Einzige
* Jean Paul
* [The] Only
* [The] Unique

Richter, John ?-1974
American dancer and choreographer
* Cole, Jack
* [The] Father of Jazz Dance

Richter, Pat
See Richter, Hugh

Richter, Reggie
See Richter, Emil Henry

Richter, Valentin
See Pick, Robert

Richter, Vernon
See Hutchcroft, Vera

Richter-Altschaffer, John Hans 1901- [WD]
American economist and author
* Richter, J. H.

Richton, Addy
Radio scriptwriter
* Marston, Adelaide [joint pseudonym with Lynn Stone]

Ricimer ?-472 [HN]
Roman general
* [The] Roman King-Maker

Rickard, Cole
See Barrett, Geoffrey John

Rickard, Dink
See Rickard, George Lewis

Rickard, George Lewis 1870?-1929 [AS, BX, HPPN, OCS]
American boxing promoter
* [The] King of Sports Promoters
* [The] Magnificent Rube
* [The] Man with the Midas Touch
* [The] Master of Ballyhoo
* [The] Napoleon of Promoters
* Rickard, Dink
* Rickard, Tex

Rickard, Tex
See Rickard, George Lewis

Rickenbacker, Edward Vernon [Eddie]
See Richenbacher, Edward

Ricker, Elswyth Thane 20th c. [THR]
Playwright and author
* Thane, Elswyth

Rickert, Corinne Holt
See Sawyer, Corinne Holt

Rickert, Diamond Joe
See Rickert, Joseph Francis [Joe]

Rickert, Joseph Francis [Joe] 1876-1943
[BE]
American baseball player
* Rickert, Diamond Joe

Rickert, Marvin August 1921- [BE]
American baseball player
* Rickert, Twitch

Rickert, Shirley Jean 20th c. [FIR]
American entertainer
* Gilda

Rickert, Twitch
See Rickert, Marvin August

Rickerts, Helen 1923- [FC]
American actress
* Carter, Helena

Rickett, Frances 1921- [CA]
American author
* Kerrigan, Kate Lowe
* Winslow, Martha

Ricketts, Fred 1881-1945 [BI]
British composer and bandmaster
* Alford, Kenneth John

Rickey, [Wesley] Branch 1881-1965
[BE, HPPN, PB]
American baseball player, manager, executive
* [The] Brain
* [The] Mahatma

Rickles, Don 1926- [HPPN]
American comedian
* [The] Master of Insult Comedy
* [The] Merchant of Venom

Rickman, Thomas 1761-1834 [NPS]
Bookseller and author
* Clio

Rickover, Hyman 1900-1986 [JL]
American military leader
* [The] Father of the Atomic Submarine

Ricks, James 20th c. [MEB]
American basketball player
* Ricks, Pappy

Ricks, Jonathan
See Flanagan, Edward Vanes, Jr.

Ricks, Pappy
See Ricks, James

Rickword, [John] Edgell 1898-1982
[CA]
British author, editor, translator
* Mavin, John [joint pseudonym with Douglas Mavin Garman]

Rico, Alfredo Cruz 1944- [BE]
American baseball player
* Rico, Fred

Rico, Don
See Rico, Donato

Rico, Donato 1913?-1985
American comic book artist
* Rico, Don

Rico, Fred
See Rico, Alfredo Cruz

Ricord, Andre
See Ricord, Auguste

Ricord, Auguste 1911?- [HPPN]
French smuggler and racketeer
* [El] Commandante
* [The] Heroin Kingpin
* [The] Paraguayan Connection
* Ricord, Andre

Ricord, J. B. [FFF]
Author
* Madiana

Ricord, Philippe 1800-1889 [FFF]
American-born physician
* [The] Great American Doctor

Ricordi, Giulio 1840-1912 [WBD]
Italian composer
* Burgmein

Rictus, Jehan
See De Saint Amand, Gabriel Randon

Rictus, Jehan
See Saint Amand, Gabriel Randon de

Ridarelli, Robert Lewis 1942- [EPM, RO1]
American singer
* Rydell, Bobby

Riddel, James 18th c. [HPPN]
Scottish poet
* [A] Young Gentleman

Riddell, Charlotte Eliza Lawson [Cowan]
1832-1906 [HFF, HPPN, WGT, WW]
Irish author
* Hawthorne, Rainey
* Riddell, Mrs. J. H.
* Trafford, F. G.
* Trafford, F. G.

Riddell, John
See Ford, Corey

Riddell, Mrs. J. H.
See Riddell, Charlotte Eliza Lawson
[Cowan]

Riddell, Robert ?-1724 [SN]
Friend of Scottish poet, Robert Burns
* Glenriddell

Riddell, William Renwick 1852-?
[WWL]
Canadian author
* Williams, Rendall

Ridderstad, Carl Fredrik 1807-? [HPPN]
Swedish author and journalist
* Rdd

Riddery, Mac-an-t'sen
See Fitz Gibbon, Maurice

Riddick, Crow
See Riddick, Walter H.

Riddick, Margaret 20th c. [THR]
British actress
* Bennett, Faith

Riddick, Walter H. 20th c. [IBW]
American housing development planner
* Riddick, Crow

Riddle, B. N.
See Riddle, Bedford Neal

Riddle, Bedford Neal 1899- [BA]
American physician
* Riddle, B. N.

Riddle, Betsy [Freifrau Von Hutten]
1874-? [HPPN]
American author
* Von Hutten, Bettina

Riddle, Charles 20th c. [SMG]
American baseball scout
* Riddle, Chase

Riddle, Chase
See Riddle, Charles

Riddle, Hugh Joseph 1912- [ART, DBA]
British painter
* Riddle, Huseph

Riddle, Huseph
See Riddle, Hugh Joseph

Riddle, Jit
See Riddle, Marshall Lewis

Riddle, John Ludy 1905- [BE]
American baseball player
* Riddle, Mutt

Riddle, Marshall Lewis 1918- [MK]
American baseball player
* Riddle, Jit

Riddle, Mutt
See Riddle, John Ludy

Riddle, Richard
See Ainley, Richard

Riddle, Thomas Wilkinson 1886-?
[HPPN]
British clergyman and author
* T. W. R.

Riddolls, Brenda Harks 20th c. [AW]
British author
* English, Brenda H.

Rideamus
See Oliven, Fritz

Rideaux, Charles De Balzac 1900-
[WW]
Author
* Chancellor, John

Rideing, William Henry 1853-? [HPPN]
British-American journalist
* Wainwright, Alexander

Rider, Brett
See Gooden, Arthur Henry

Rider, Jane
See Lyons, Luella B.

Riderhood, Pleasant
See Slaughter, Mrs. M.

Ridge, John Rollin 1827-1867 [HPPN]
American Indian editor and poet
* Yellow Bird [Chess-quat-a-law-ny]

Ridgeley, John
See Rea, John Huntingdon

Ridgely, Richard 1910- [ASC]
American musician
* Ricardo, Don

Ridges, R.
See Smith, Bridges W.

Ridgeway
See Taylor, John Francis

Ridgeway, Algernon
See Wood, Anna Cogswell

Ridgeway, Philip
See Bower, Philip

Ridgley, Bebe
See Ridgley, William

Ridgley, William 1882-1961 [NOJ]
American jazz musician
* Ridgley, Bebe

Ridgway, Jason
See Lesser, Milton

[The] Riding Fool
See Hanneford, Edwin

Riding, Laura
See Reichenthal, Laura

Riding Master
See Grose, Francis

Ridings, Hope Dupre 1906- [NAA]
American writer
* Miller, Hope Ridings
* Vincent, Ann

Ridl, Buzz
See Ridl, Charles

Ridl, Charles 1920- [BB]
American basketball coach
* Ridl, Buzz

Ridley, James 1736-1765 [DEL, HFN, RH]
British author
* Horam, the Son of Asmar
* Morell, [Sir] Charles
* Van Scelter, Helter

Ridley, M. R.
See Ridley, Maurice Roy

Ridley, Maurice Roy 1890-1969 [LC]
British author and educator
* Ridley, M. R.

Ridley, Nat, Jr. [house pseudonym]
[Stratemeyer Syndicate]
See Stratemeyer, Edward L.

Ridlon, Marcia
See Balterman, Marcia Ridlon

Ridste, Frances Lillian Mary 1919-1948
[BEW, FC]
American actress
* Landis, Carole

Rie, May
See Crean, Mary Walsingham

Riebe, Hank
See Riebe, Harvey Donald

Riebe, Harvey Donald 1921- [BE]
American baseball player
* Riebe, Hank

Riedel, Judith Ellen 1936-1974 [SC]
American actress
* Rawlins, Judith [Judy]

Riedman, Sarah R[egal] 1902- [SAT]
Rumanian-born American author
* Gustafson, Sarah R.

Riefe, Alan 1925- [CA]
American author
* Hardin, J. D.
* Logan, Jake [house pseudonym,
  Playboy Press]
* Riefe, Barbara

Riefe, Barbara
See Riefe, Alan

Riefenstahl, Helene Bertha Amalie 1902-
[FDG]
German director
* Riefenstahl, Leni

Riefenstahl, Leni
See Riefenstahl, Helene Bertha Amalie

Riegel, Robert Henry 1914- [EG, GF]
American golfer
* Riegel, Skee

Riegel, Skee
See Riegel, Robert Henry

Riegels, Roy 20th c. [SR]
American football player
* Riegels, Wrong Way

Riegels, Wrong Way
See Riegels, Roy

Rieger, August 20th c. [WF]
German director
* Aurive, Jean Charles

Riel, Louis David 1844-1885 [FFF]
Canadian insurgent
* [The] Prophet of the Northwest

Riemens-Reurslag, J.
See Reurslag, Guurtje Johanna
Hendrika

Riemer, George 1920-1973 [CAP]
American author
* Poole, Seth
* Schirmerhorn, Clint

Rienzi, Cola di
See Gabrini, Niccolo

Riepenhausen, Christian 1789-1860
[WBD]
German painter, designer, etcher
* Riepenhausen, Johannes

Riepenhausen, Franz
See Riepenhausen, Friedrich

Riepenhausen, Friedrich 1786-1831
[WBD]
German painter, designer, etcher
* Riepenhausen, Franz

Riepenhausen, Johannes
See Riepenhausen, Christian

Ries, Lulu 20th c. [BEW]
American singer and actress
* Bates, Lulu

Riese, Felicia 1918- [FC]
British actress
* Roc, Patricia

Rieser, Henry [house pseudonym]
See MacDonald, John D[ann]

Rietz, John 1932-
American actor
* Reed, Robert

Rieux, A. de
See Carrat de Vaux, Alexandre

Riffe, Ernest
See Bergman, [Ernst] Ingmar

Rifkin, Shepard 1918- [CA, WD]
American author
* Logan, Jake [house pseudonym,
  Playboy Press]
* Michaels, Dale

Rifkin, Stanley Mark 1946?-
*American computer expert, accused of
fraud*
* Hansen, Mike

Rifle
See Butler, George H.

[The] Rifle
See Etcheverry, Sam

[The] Rifle
See Strickland, Roger

Rifle Jim Middleton
See Middleton, James Blaine [Jim]

Rift, Valerie
See Bartlett, Marie [Swan]

Riga, Nadine
See Evans, Nadine

**Rigau y Ros, Hyacinthe Francois
Honorat Mathias Pierre Martyr Andre**
1659-1743 [DEP, DNNS, WBD]
French painter
* [The] French Van Dyck
* Rigaud, Hyacinthe
* [The] Van Dyck of France

Rigaud, Hyacinthe
See Rigau y Ros, Hyacinthe Francois
Honorat Mathias Pierre Martyr Andre

Rigby
See Arrowsmith, Edmund

Rigby, Arthur
See Turner, William

Rigby, Edward
See Coke, Edward

Rigby, Richard 1722-1788 [NPS]
British politician
* Bloomsbury Dick

Rigdum Funnidos
See Ballantyne, John

Rigg, Diana 1938?-   [HPPN]
British actress
* Dame Diana

Rigg, Henry Kilburn 1911-1980   [CA]
American editor and author
* Kilburn, Henry

Riggins, John 20th c.
American football player
* [The] Diesel

Riggs, Betty
See Riggs, Mary Elizabeth

Riggs, Dorothy
See Riggs, Mary Elizabeth

Riggs, Elias 1810-1901   [HPPN]
American missionary
* E. R.

Riggs, Lee Aubrey 20th c.
American auctioneer
* Riggs, Speed

Riggs, Mary Elizabeth 1899-1975   [F1, FC, SC]
American actress
* Brent, Evelyn
* Riggs, Betty
* Riggs, Dorothy

Riggs, Mrs. George C.
Author
* Wiggin, Kate Douglas

Riggs, Robert Larimore [Bobby] 1918-
[DF 3-26-86, HPPN]
American tennis player
* [The] Chicken Plucker
* [The] Queen of the Courts
* [The] White Mohammed Ali

Riggs, Speed
See Riggs, Lee Aubrey

Righi, Massimo 20th c.   [WF]
Italian actor
* Dean, Max

Right Angled, Tri Angled Thurman
See Thurman, Allan Granbery

Right Cross
See Armstrong, Paul

[The] Right Hand Mind
See Robinson, Frances M.

Right Honourable Mendicant
See Fox, Charles James

[The] Right Reverend New Dealer
See Ryan, [Monsignor] John A.

Rigmarole, Crayon
See Sims, Alexander Dromgoole

Rignall, Lionel 1850?-1919   [BEW]
British-born actor and producer
* Rignold, Lionel

Rigney, Emory Elmo 1897-1972   [BE]
American baseball player
* Rigney, Topper

Rigney, Specs
See Rigney, William Joseph

Rigney, Topper
See Rigney, Emory Elmo

Rigney, William Joseph 1919-   [BE]
American baseball manager
* [The] Cricket
* Rigney, Specs

Rignold, Lionel
See Rignall, Lionel

Rignold, Marie
See D'Altra, Marie

Rignold, Willard ?-1913   [HPPN]
American singer
* Rivers, Walter

Rigolo
See Thieblin, Napoleon [or Nicolas?]
Leon

Rigoni, Orlando [Joseph] 1897?-   [CA, WD]
American author
* Ames, Leslie
* Bell, Carolyn
* Wesley, James

Rigores [Precise One]
See Miranda, Roque

Rigsby, Howard 1909-   [CA, WW]
American author
* Howard, Mark
* Howard, Vechel

Riis
See Bohr, Russell LeRoi

Riis, Jacob August 1849-1914   [HPPN]
Danish-American journalist and author
* [The] Friend of the Friendless

Rijsbergen, Wilhelmus 1952-   [AES]
Dutch soccer player
* Rijsbergen, Wim

Rijsbergen, Wim
See Rijsbergen, Wilhelmus

Riker, Anthony
See Reeds, F. Anton

Riker, Richard 1773-1822   [HPPN]
American society man
* [The] American Chesterfield

Rikhoff, James C. 1931-   [CA]
American author
* Cornwall, Jim
* Fargo, Joe
* Kincaid, Alan

Rikki
See Ducornet, Erica

Riley, Butch
See Riley, Thomas

Riley, Butt 1848?-?   [HPPN]
American criminal
* [The] King of the Hoodlums
* Riley, Butt

Riley, Butt
See Riley, Butt

Riley, Doug[las Brian] 1945-   [EJ7]
Canadian jazz musician
* Music, Dr.

Riley, Frank
See Ryhlick, Frank

Riley, Isaac 17th c.   [HPPN]
American publisher
* Petronius, Pasquin

Riley, Jack 1895-1933   [SC]
American actor
* Riley, Slim

Riley, James 1851?-1913   [BI]
American outlaw
* Middleton, Doc

Riley, James Whitcomb 1849-1916
[FFF, HPPN, SAT, WBD]
American author and poet
* [The] Burns of America
* [The] Children's Poet
* [The] Hoosier Poet
* [The] Hoosier Poet
* Johnson, Benjamin F., of Boone
* [The] People's Laureate
* [The] Poet Laureate of Democracy
* [The] Poet of the Common People

Riley, Ken 1947-   [SMG]
American football player
* [The] Rattler

Riley, Mary 1899-1927   [HPPN]
American singer
* [The] Girl From Kentucky

[The] Riley of the South
See Stanton, Frank Lebby

Riley, Pigtail Billy
See Riley, William James [Billy]

Riley, Slim
See Riley, Jack

Riley, Tex
See Creasey, John

Riley, Thomas 20th c.   [EF]
American football player
* Riley, Butch

Riley, William James [Billy] 1857-1887
[BE]
American baseball player
* Riley, Pigtail Billy

Riley, Willie 1866-?   [HPPN]
British author
* Leigh, W. Rye

Rill, Eli
See Schectman, Elias Maxwell

[The] Rillington Place Murderer
See Christie, John Reginald Halliday

Rimbault, Edward Francis 1816-   [PA]
Author
* Nava, Franz

Rimel, Duane [Weldon] 1915-   [CA]
American author
* Biggs, Peter
* Leggett, Eric

Rimel, Duane [Weldon] (cont.)
* Lemir, Andre
* Weldon, Rex

Rimington, R. S.
See Hardy, Robin

Rimmer, W. J.
See Rowland, Donald Sydney

Rinaldini, Angiolo
See Battisti, Eugenio

Rinaldo
See Edwards, James

Rindfleisch, Daniel 17th c.   [DSB]
Editor
* Bucretius, Danieles

Rindl, Robert 1892?-1961   [BI]
German-American journalist
* Ypsilon

Ring, Adam
See Reed, Blair

Ring, Douglas
See Prather, Richard S[cott]

Ring, Elizabeth 1912-   [CA]
British author
* Scott, Nerissa

[The] Ring Gorilla
See Bloom, Phil

Ring, Montague
See Aldridge, Amanda Ira

Ringbolt, Capt.
See Codman, John

Ringdahl, Mark
See Longyear, Barry Brookes

Ringelnatz, Joachim
See Boetticher, Hans

Ringer, Ada   [FFF]
Entertainer
* Knowles, Marie

Ringgold, Gene 1918-   [CA]
American author
* Lawrence, Kenneth G.
* Matteo, P. B., Jr.

Ringgold, Johnny 19th c.   [BLB]
American gunfighter
* Ringo, Johnny

Ringi, Kjell Arne Soerensen 1939-   [CA, SAT]
Swedish author and illustrator
* S-Ringi, Kjell

Ringlets
See Custer, George Armstrong

Ringletub, Jeremiah
See Styles, John

Ringling, Alfred J.
See Rungeling, Alfred J.

Ringling, Charles
See Rungeling, Charles

Ringling, John
See Rungeling, John

Ringmann, Christoph 1940-   [MS]
German musician
* Eschenbach, Christoph

[The] Ringmaster
See Mencken, Henry Louis [Harry]

Ringmaster of Fun City
See Lindsay, John Vliet

Ringo, Johnny
See Keevill, Henry J[ohn]

Ringo, Johnny
See Ringgold, Johnny

Ringold, Clay
See Hogan, [Robert] Ray

Ringoold, Fred
See Cerchio, Fernando

Ringuet
See Panneton, Philippe

Ringwood
See Price, Edwin Wathen

Ringwood, Ralph
See Hynes, Alfred D.

Rinho
See Shiki, Kazuhisa

Rink, Doris 1910-1925   [SC]
American actress
* Wynn, Doris

Rinker, Mildred 1907-1951   [BEW, CED]
American singer
* Bailey, Mildred
* [The] Rocking Chair Lady

Rinko, Irene 1896-1975   [HPPN]
American donor of home-baked cakes
* [The] Cake Lady

Rinkoff, Barbara 1923-   [HPPN]
American author and social worker
* Rich, Jean

Rinnan, Henry Oliver 20th c.   [EE]
Norwegian traitor
* Wist, Olav

Rinpoche [Precious Master]
See Tarthang Tulku

Rinzler, Carol Eisen 1941-   [CA]
American author
* Eisen, Carol G.

Rio, Frank 20th c.   [BLB, PHM]
American underworld figure
* Cline, Frank
* Gline, Frank
* Kline, Frank
* Rio, Slippery

Rio, Ramon Mercades del
See Vandendreschd, Jacques Mornard

Rio, Rita
See Novella, Rita

Rio, Slippery
See Rio, Frank

Riopelle, Howard Joseph 1922-   [CEI]
Canadian-born hockey player
* Riopelle, Rip

Riopelle, Rip
See Riopelle, Howard Joseph

Riordan, Bags
See Riordan, Mike

Riordan, Dan
See Cook, William Everett

Riordan, Irene 1903-1973   [FC]
American comedienne
* Ryan, Irene

Riordan, Mike 1945-   [SMG]
American basketball player
* Riordan, Bags

Rios, Aurelio
See Lopez, Aurelio Alejandro

Rios, Tere
See Versace, Marie Teresa Rios

Rios Montt, Ayatollah
See Rios Montt, Jose Efrain

Rios Montt, Jose Efrain 1927?-
Guatemalan president
* Rios Montt, Ayatollah

Riot, Pat
See Lewis, Thomas H.

Rip
See Connally, George Walter

Rip
See Hill, Rowland

Ripa, Alberto da ?-1551   [BBD]
Italian musician
* Mantovano, Alberto

Riperton, Minnie 1948-1980   [RO2]
American singer
* Davis, Andrea

Ripley, Allen Stevens 1952-   [SMG]
American baseball player
* Ripley, Rip

Ripley, Elmer 1891-   [BB]
American basketball player and coach
* Ripley, Rip

Ripley, George 1802-1880   [HPPN, IP]
American scholar and journalist
* [An] Alumnus of That School
* [The] Father of Brook Farm
* G. R.
* Its Pastor

Ripley, Jack
See Wainwright, John

Ripley, Julia C.
See Dorr, Julia Caroline Ripley

Ripley, Mrs. John   [NPS]
Author
* Paull, M. A.

Ripley, Ozark
See Thompson, John Baptiste De Macklot

Ripley, Rip
See Ripley, Allen Stevens

Ripley, Rip
See Ripley, Elmer

Ripley, Samuel ?-1847 [HPPN]
American clergyman
* R.

Ripman, Penelope ?-1973 [TR]
Actress, director, stage manager
* Jenner, Caryl

Ripman, Walter
See Rippmann, Walter

Ripon, John Scott
See Byerley, John Scott

Riposte, A.
See Mordaunt, Evelyn May [Clowes]

Rippay, Benjamin Wesley 1850-? [BE, DGS]
American baseball player
* Jones, Charles Wesley

Rippelmeyer, Raymond 1933- [SMG]
American baseball coach
* Rippelmeyer, Rip

Rippelmeyer, Rip
See Rippelmeyer, Raymond

[The] Ripper
See Roberts, Jack

Ripperda, Jan Willem 1680-1737 [WBD]
Dutch-born adventurer
* Osman Pasha

Ripperger, Henrietta
See Hawley, Henrietta Ripperger

Rippingale, Maureen 1935-1974 [SC]
British actress and dancer
* Lesley, Carole

Rippmann, Walter 1869-1947 [WBD]
British educator
* Ripman, Walter

Rippon, Angela 20th c.
British reporter
* [The] Barbara Walters of Britain

Rips, Ervine M[ilton] 1921- [CA]
American author
* Farnum, K. T.
* Lornquest, Olaf

Riq
See Atwater, Frederick Mund

Riquet, Gomex le
See Ravel, Maurice Joseph

Riqueti, [Andre] Boniface [Louis] 1754-1792 [DNNF, DNNS, FFF]
French soldier and politician
* Mirabeau, Barrel
* Mirabeau Tonneau
* Mirabeau, Vicomte de

Riqueti, Honore Gabriel Victor 1749-1791 [DHA, HN, SN]
French orator and revolutionary leader
* [The] Demosthenes of France
* [The] Hurricane

Riqueti, Honore Gabriel Victor (cont.)
* Mirabeau, Comte de
* Mirabeau, Tub
* [The] Modern Gracchus
* [The] Plebeian Count
* [The] Shakespeare of Eloquence
* [The] Tub

Riqueti, Victor 1715-1789 [DEP, DHA, SN]
French soldier and economist
* [L']Ami des Hommes
* [The] Friend of Man
* Mirabeau, Marquis de

Riqueti de Mirabeau, Sibylle Gabrielle Marie Antoinette 1850-1932 [FFF, WBD]
French author
* Gyp
* Martel de Janville, Comtesse de

Ris, Clement de 1750-1827 [SN]
* [Le] Comte de Gondreville

Risberg, Charles August 1894-1975 [BE, BI, PB]
American baseball player
* Risberg, Swede

Risberg, Swede
See Risberg, Charles August

Riscoe, Arthur
See Boorman, Arthur

Risdon, Elizabeth
See Evans, Elizabeth

Riseley, Jerry B[urr, Jr.] 1920- [CA]
American columnist and author
* Monk, Galdo

Rishton, William
See Wright, W. George

Rising, Perry Sumner 20th c. [BE]
American baseball player
* Rising, Pop

Rising, Pop
See Rising, Perry Sumner

Riskit, Jack
See Evans, John

Risko, Babe
See Pylkowski, Henry

Risko, Eddie
See Pylkowski, Henry

Risko, Johnny 1902-1953 [BX, HPPN]
American boxer
* [The] Cleveland Rubber Man
* Cleveland's Tireless Heavyweight
* [The] Rubber Man
* [The] Spoiler

Risner, James Robinson 1924?-
American air force pilot
* Risner, Robbie

Risner, Robbie
See Risner, James Robinson

[The] Risorgimento Revolutionary
See Mario, Jessie Meriton White

Ristare, Bo
See Linden, Erik Hugo Emanuel

Ristaud
See Cottin, Sophie

Ristori, Adelaide
See Capranica del Grillo, Marchioness

Rita
See Humphreys Booth, Eliza Margaret J. [Gollan]

Ritchard, Cyril
See Trimnell-Ritchard, Cyril

Ritcher, Rene 1910- [TR]
British actress
* Collier, Patience

Ritchey, Claude Cassius 1873-1951 [BE]
American baseball player
* Little All Right

Ritchie, Adele
See Pultz, Adele

Ritchie, Alvin 1890- [BBH, CFH]
Canadian football team builder
* [The] Silver Fox

Ritchie, Anna Cora [Ogden Mowatt] 1819-1870 [DLE1, DNA, IP]
American actress and author
* [An] Actress
* Berkley, [Mrs.] Helen
* Browning, Henry C.
* Isabel
* [A] Lady

Ritchie, Balfour 20th c. [MBF]
British author
* Baldwin, Basil

Ritchie, Barbara 20th c.
Author
* Arden, Barbie [joint pseudonym with Adrien (Pearl) Stoutenburg]

Ritchie, Bill
See Edgar, Frank Terrell Rhoades

Ritchie, David ?-1811 [SN]
Scottish pauper
* [The] Black Dwarf

Ritchie, David 1926-1952 [BX]
Australian boxer
* Sands, Dave

Ritchie, Douglas 1905-1967 [BDW, BI]
British radio broadcaster
* Britton, Colonel

Ritchie, Edwin 1931- [CA, WD]
American columnist and author
* Lewis, Voltaire

Ritchie, Jack
See Reitci, John G[eorge]

Ritchie, James Ewing 19th c. [IP]
American journalist
* Crayon, Christopher

Ritchie, John Simon 1957?-1979
British musician
* Vicious, Sid

Ritchie, [Sir] Lewis
See Da Costa Ricci, Lewis Anselmo

Ritchie, [Mary] Lily Munsell 1867-?
[NAA]
American author
* Briarly, Mary

Ritchie, Nellie Claire
See Stephens, Mrs. Thomas C.

Ritchie, Rita
See Reitci, Rita Krohne

Ritchie, Ruth 1900- [CA]
American author
* Juline, Ruth Bishop

Ritchie, Thomas 1778-1854 [SN]
American journalist
* [The] Father of Democracy in
  Virginia

Ritchie, [Harry] Ward 1905- [CA]
American author and poet
* Quince, Peter Lum

Ritchie, Willie
See Steffen, Gerhardt A.

Ritchie-Calder, Peter Ritchie
See Calder, Peter Ritchie

Ritiman, Louis Arthur 1880-1952 [BI]
French educator
* Athanase Emile, [Brother]

Ritson, Claire 1907- [DBA]
British painter
* Claire

Ritson, Isaac 1761-1789 [HPPN]
Scottish author
* [A] Young Shepherd

Ritson, Joseph 1752-1803 [DEL, HPPN,
IP, SN, SN]
British antiquary and critic
* Anti Scot
* [The] Antiquary of Poetry
* J. R.
* Justice
* [The] Learned Cabbage-Eater
* Observator on Wharton
* Sycorax
* [The] Word Catcher

Ritsos, Giannes
See Ritsos, Yannis

Ritsos, Yannis 1909- [CA]
Greek poet
* Ritsos, Giannes

Rittenhouse, David 1732-1792? [HN,
HPPN]
American astronomer
* [The] American Newton
* [The] Father of the Orrery

Ritter, Bud
See Ritter, Julius

Ritter, Dr.
See Schiller, Johann Christoph
Friedrich von

Ritter, Felix
See Kruess, James

Ritter, Hank
See Ritter, William Herbert

Ritter, Julius 20th c. [BBH]
American basketball player and coach
* Ritter, Bud

Ritter, Louis Elmer 1875-1952 [BE]
American baseball player
* Ritter, Old Dog

Ritter, Maurice Woodward 1906?-1974
[DAM, FC, PMJ]
American country-western performer
* Ritter, Tex

Ritter, Old Dog
See Ritter, Louis Elmer

Ritter, Sylvester 20th c.
American wrestler
* J. Y. D.
* [The] Junkyard Dog

Ritter, Tex
See Ritter, Maurice Woodward

Ritter, Theodore
See Bennet, Theodore

Ritter, William Herbert 1893-1964 [BE]
American baseball player
* Ritter, Hank

Rittman, Gertrud 20th c. [BEW]
German-born composer and arranger
* Rittman, Trude

Rittman, Trude
See Rittman, Gertrud

[The] Ritual Burial Murderess
See Conroy, Teresa Miriam

Ritvala, M.
See Waltari, Mika [Toimi]

Ritz, Al
See Joachim, Al

Ritz, David 1943- [CA]
American author
* Pearl, Esther Elizabeth

Ritz, Harry
See Joachim, Harry

Ritz, Jimmy
See Joachim, Jimmy

Ritz, Sally
See Henderson, Rosa [Rose]

Rius
See Del Rio, Eduardo

Rivail, Hippolyte Leon Denizard
1803-1869 [IP]
French author
* Kardec, Allan

[The] Rival of Homer
See Milton, John

[The] Rival of Sappho
See Lewis, Estelle Anna Blanche
Robinson

[A] Rival to the God of Harmonie
See Jonson, Ben[jamin]

Rivarol [or Rivaroli], Antoine 1753-1801
[HPPN]
French author
* Chevalier de Parcieux
* Comte de Rivarol

Rivas, Guillermo
See Phillips, Howard S.

Rivaz, Alice
See Golay, Alice

Rive, Jean Joseph 1730-1791 [SN]
French bibliographer
* [An] Ajax Flagellifer
* [The] Bull Dog of la Valliere
* [The] French Ritson

Rivella
See Manley, Mary de la Riviere

Rivelli, Francesca 1956?-
Italian actress
* [The] Italian Sex Bomb
* Muti, Ornella

Rivels, Charles 20th c. [BMH]
British acrobatic clown
* [The] Chaplin of the Trapeze

[The] River of Paradise
See Bernard of Clairvaux

Rivera, Bombo
See Rivera Torres, Jesus, Jr.

Rivera, Chita
See Figueroa Del Rivero, Dolores
Conchita

Rivera, Jim
See Rivera, Manuel Joseph

Rivera, Jose 20th c. [RBE]
American boxer
* Pagan, Jose

Rivera, Jungle Jim
See Rivera, Manuel Joseph

Rivera, Manuel Joseph 1922- [BE, PB]
American baseball player
* Rivera, Jim
* Rivera, Jungle Jim

Rivera, Scarlet
See Shea, Donna

Rivera Perez, Francisco 1948- [GS]
Spanish bullfighter
* Paquirri

Rivera Torres, Jesus, Jr. 1952- [SMG]
Puerto Rican-born baseball player
* Rivera, Bombo

Rivera Viera, [Padre] Juan 1885-1953
[CW]
Puerto Rican poet
* Rafael, Juan Vicente

Rivere, Alec
See Nuetzel, Charles [Alexander]

Rivers, Alfred J. 1925- [BA]
American business executive
* Rivers, Rip

Rivers, Elfrida
See Bradley, Marion Zimmer

Rivers, Georgia
See Clark, Marjorie

Rivers, Guy
See Simms, W[illiam] Gilmore

Rivers, Joan
See Molinsky, Joan Sandra

Rivers, Joe
See Ybarra, Jose

Rivers, John Milton 1948- [WWB]
American baseball player
* Mick the Quick
* Rivers, Mickey

Rivers, Johnny
See Ramistella, John

Rivers, [Rev.] Joseph
See Brookes, [Rev.] Joshua

Rivers, Larry
See Grossberg, Yitzroch Loiza

Rivers, Laurence
See Stebbins, Rowland

Rivers, Lord [RH]
Gambler
* [The] Wellington of Gamblers

Rivers, Louis 1922- [IBW]
American author
* Mulet, Paul

Rivers, Mickey
See Rivers, John Milton

Rivers, Olive
See Reynolds, Mrs. James

Rivers, Pearl
See Nicholson, Eliza Jane Poitevent

Rivers, Rip
See Rivers, Alfred J.

Rivers, Tex
See Lewins, C. A.

Rivers, Walter
See Rignold, Willard

Riverside, John
See Brooks, Noah

Riverside, John
See Heinlein, Robert A[nson]

Riverside Visitor
See Wright, Thomas

Riverton, Stein
See Elvestad, Sven

Riverton, Stein
See Elvstad, Sven

Rives, Amelie
See Troubetzkoy, Princess

Rives, Leigh
See Seward, William W[ard], Jr.

Rivett, Edith Caroline 1894-1958 [CC, EMD, LC]
British author
* Carnac, Carol
* Lorac, E. C. R.

Rivetta, Pietro Silvio [Conte di Solonghello] 1886-1952 [BI]
Italian author
* Toddi

Rivetus, Andreas, Junior
See Marvell, Andrew

Riviera, Jake
See Jakeman, Andrew

Riviere, Arthur Bernard 1899-1965 [BE]
American baseball player
* Riviere, Tink

Riviere, Curly
See Riviere, Fred

Riviere, Fred 1875-1935 [SC]
American actor
* Riviere, Curly

Riviere, Tink
See Riviere, Arthur Bernard

Rivington, Charles 19th c. [IP, PA]
British author
* Scrutator

Rivington, James 1724?-1802
American printer and bookseller
* J. R.

Rivington, James
See Hopkinson, Francis

Rivington, William 19th c. [IP, PA]
British author
* [A] Lay Member of the Committee
* [A] Layman

Rivinus, August Quirinus
See Bachmann, August Quirinus

Rivkin, Bobby 20th c.
American musician
* Bobby Z.

Rivoli, Mario 1943- [SAT]
American illustrator
* Koutoukas, H. M.
* Marasmus, Seymour

Rix, Donna
See Rowland, Donald Sydney

Rixey, Epp
See Rixey, Eppa P.

Rixey, Eppa Jeptha
See Rixey, Eppa P.

Rixey, Eppa P. 1891-1963 [BE, DGS, PB]
American baseball player
* Rixey, Epp
* Rixey, Eppa Jeptha
* Rixey, Jeptha

Rixey, Jeptha
See Rixey, Eppa P.

Rixon, Annie
See Studdert, Annie Louisa

Riza, Ali
See Orga, Irfan

Rizzi, Bruno 20th c. [NY 9-10-85]
Italian author
* Bruno R.

Rizzi, Bruno
See Gelli, Licio

Rizzi, Tony
See Rizzi, Trefoni

Rizzi, Trefoni 1923- [DAM, EJ]
American jazz musician
* Rizzi, Tony

Rizzo, Anthony 1937- [ASC]
American musician
* Rizzo, Bob

Rizzo, Bob
See Rizzo, Anthony

Rizzo, Frank Lazarro 1921- [HPPN, NW 1-24-83]
American politician
* [The] Big Bambino
* [The] Cisco Kid
* [The] Supercop
* Supercop
* [The] Toughest Cop in America

Rizzoti, Antonio
See Dragna, Jack

Rizzotti, Madame [FFF]
Entertainer
* Giuri, Marie

Rizzuto, Flea
See Rizzuto, Phil[lip Francis]

Rizzuto, Phil[lip Francis] 1918- [BE, BN, HPPN, PB]
American baseball player
* Rizzuto, Flea
* Rizzuto, Scooter
* [The] Scooter

Rizzuto, Scooter
See Rizzuto, Phil[lip Francis]

Ro Tae-yong
See Rutt, Richard

Roach, Charles H. 1860-1936 [HPPN]
American executive
* Roach, Dad

Roach, Dad
See Roach, Charles H.

Roach, Double Trouble
See Roach, Eugene

Roach, Eugene 20th c. [TI 2-25-85]
American checkers player
* Roach, Double Trouble

Roach, John
See Roche, John

Roach, Jonathan
See Endfield, Cyril Raker

Roach, Max
See Roach, Maxwell

Roach, Maxwell 1925- [EJ7]
American jazz musician
* Roach, Max

Roach, Portia
See Takakjian, Portia

Roach, Robert W. A. 1933- [WGT]
British author
* Jorgensson, A. K.

Roach, Roxy
See Roach, Wilbur C.

Roach, Skel
See Weichbrodt, Rudolph C.

Roach, Wilbur C. 1884-1947 [BE]
American baseball player
* Roach, Roxy

Road Runner
See Garr, Ralph Allen

[The] Road Runner
See Loftin, John

Road Runner Ferguson
See Ferguson, Rufus

Road Runner Williams
See Williams, Travis

[The] Roadbuilder
See MacKendrick, William Gordon

Roadrunner
See Cournoyer, Yvan Serge

Roane, Peter
See Campbell, C[larence] Samuel

Roane, Spencer 1762-1802 [BDSA]
American author and jurist
* Sidney, Algernon

Roaring Bill Hassamaer
See Hassamaer, William Louis [Bill]

Roaring Bob of the Garden
See Bensley, Robert

[The] Roaring Girl
See Frith, Mary

Roaring Jack
See Percival, John

Roaring Jake Griffith
See Griffith, Jacob Wark

Roark, Garland 1904- [CA]
American author
* Garland, George

Rob Donn
See Mackay, Robert

Rob Roy
See Macgregor, John

Rob Roy
See Macgregor, Robert

Robard, Jackson
See Wallmann, Jeffrey M[iner]

Robards, Sherman M[arshall] 1939-
[CA]
American journalist and author
* Robards, Terry

Robards, Terry
See Robards, Sherman M[arshall]

Robarge, John F. 1922- [CWG]
American country-western performer
* Roe, Tex

Robat [cult name]
See Buckland, Raymond

Robb, Alvis 20th c. [EF]
American football player
* Robb, Joe

Robb, Helen 1866-1937 [BEW]
American actress
* Lowell, Helen

Robb, Inez [Callaway] 1901?-1979 [CA]
American author and columnist
* Randolph, Nancy

Robb, Joe
See Robb, Alvis

Robb, John
See Robson, Norman

Robb, John S. 19th c. [FFF, IP]
American author and editor
* Solitaire
* [A] Tyke

[The] Robber
See Edward IV

[The] Robber Baron
See Gray, Harry

Robbie
See Robinson, Brooks [Calbert, Jr.]

Robbie of the Codes
See Robinson, Frances M.

Robbin, [Jodi] Luna 1936- [CA]
American author and illustrator
* Pallidini, Jodi

Robbins, Alfred Farthing 1856-? [FFF,
IP]
British author
* Clifton, Tom
* Dunheved
* Nemesis

Robbins, Austin 1944- [BB]
American basketball player
* Robbins, Red

Robbins, C. A
See Robbins, Clarence Aaron

Robbins, Chandler 1810-1882 [HPPN]
American clergyman
* Her Pastor
* R.

Robbins, Clarence Aaron 1888-1949
[WGT, WW]
American author
* Robbins, C. A
* Robbins, Tod

Robbins, Harold
See Kane, Francis

Robbins, Henry
See Slavitt, David Rytman

Robbins, Jerome
See Rabinowitz, Jerome

Robbins, June 20th c. [CA]
American poet
* Julie
* Julie of Colorado Springs

Robbins, Marty
See Robinson, Martin D.

Robbins, May Smith ?-1932 [HPPN]
American actress
* Smith, May

Robbins, Raleigh
See Hamilton, Charles Harold St. John

Robbins, Red
See Robbins, Austin

Robbins, Rollin
See Sherwood, Roland H.

Robbins, Ruth
See Schein, Ruth Robbins

Robbins, Tod
See Robbins, Clarence Aaron

Robbins, Tony
See Pashko, Stanley

Robby the Robber
See Robinson, Brooks [Calbert, Jr.]

Robe, Thomas 18th c. [HPPN]
British author
* Britannicus

Robeck, Geraldine Cecilia 1928- [CWG]
American country-western performer
* Lynn, Gerrie

Robello, Thomas Vardasco [Tommy]
1913- [BE]
American baseball player
* Robello, Tony

Robello, Tony
See Robello, Thomas Vardasco
[Tommy]

Roberds, Fred A. 1941- [ASC]
American composer, singer, actor
* Roberds, Smokey

Roberds, Smokey
See Roberds, Fred A.

Roberge, Joseph Albert Armand 1917-
[BE]
American baseball player
* Roberge, Skippy

Roberge, Skippy
See Roberge, Joseph Albert Armand

Roberson, Bo
See Roberson, Irvin

Roberson, Irvin 20th c. [EF]
American football player
* Roberson, Bo

Roberson, Marie
See Hamm, Marie Roberson

Roberson, Orlando 1910?- [WWJ]
American jazz musician
* Robeson, Orlando

Roberson, Rocky
See Roberson, Rudolph

Roberson, Rudolph 20th c. [IBW]
American athlete
* Roberson, Rocky

Robert ?-866 [WBD]
Count of Anjou
* [The] Strong

Robert, Chip
See Robert, Lawrence Wood, Jr.

Robert De Molesme 1028?-1111 [HPPN]
French clergyman and founder of the Cistercian Order
* Robert of Champagne
* Robert of Citeaux

Robert, Felix
See Cazenave, [or Cacenabe], Pierre

Robert Fleury
See Fleury, Joseph Nicolas Robert

Robert, Friedrich
See Ehlers, Friedrich Robert

[The] Robert Frost of the Paintbrush
See Wyeth, Andrew

Robert, Georges Achille Marie-Joseph 1875-? [HPPN]
French High Commissioner of Martinique and Guadeloupe
* Robert le Nazi

Robert, Henry M. 1837-1923 [HPPN]
American army officer and author
* [The] Parliamentary Pilot

Robert, James
See Payaba, Abraham

Robert, Karl
See Hartmann, Eduard von

Robert, Karl
See Meusnier, Georges

Robert, Lawrence Wood, Jr. 1887- [HPPN]
American construction engineer and politician
* Robert, Chip

Robert le Nazi
See Robert, Georges Achille Marie-Joseph

Robert, Lord Bishop of Sarum
See Drummond, Robert Hay

Robert of Anjou 1275-1343 [DNNS, HN]
King of Naples
* [The] Solomon of His Age
* [The] Wise

Robert of Champagne
See Robert De Molesme

Robert of Citeaux
See Robert De Molesme

Robert of Geneva 1342?-1394 [WBD]
Antipope
* Clement VII

Robert of Lincoln
See Grossetete, Robert

Robert the Devil
See Damiens, Robert Francois

Robert the Red
See Macgregor, Robert

Robert the Rhymer
See Williams, Alan Moray

Robert-Houdin, Jean Eugene 1805-1871 [HPPN]
French magician
* [The] Father of Modern Magic
* [The] Magic Man

Robert I ?-1035 [DNNF, DNNS, RH]
Duke of Normandy
* [The] Devil
* [Le] Diable
* [The] Magnificent

Robert I 1013?-1093 [HPPN]
Count of Flanders
* [The] Frisian

Robert I 1015-1085 [SN]
First Duke of Calabria
* [The] Cunning
* Guiscard
* [The] Terror of the Faithless

Robert I 1274-1329 [HN, WBD]
King of Scotland
* [The] Bruce
* Hob [or Hobbe], King
* [The] Joshua of Scotland
* [The] Summer King

Robert II [SN]
Count of Sicily
* [The] Terror of the Faithless

Robert II 971?-1031 [DNNS, FFF, RH]
King of France
* [Le] Pieux
* [The] Pious

Robert II 1054?-1134 [DNNF, HPPN, WBD]
Duke of Normandy
* Curt-Hose [Short-Shanks]
* Curtmantle

Robert II 1316-1390 [DNNS, NPS]
King of Scotland
* Blear Eye
* [The] Steward

Robert III
See Stewart, John

Roberta of Venice
See Di Camerino, Giuliana

Robertaille, Anthony F. 1879-1947 [BE]
American baseball player
* Robertaille, Chick

Robertaille, Chick
See Robertaille, Anthony F.

Roberthin, Robert 1600-1648 [IP]
British author
* Berintho

Robertjeot
See Sanderson, John

Roberto
See Greene, Robert

Roberto, [Brother]
See Mueller, Gerald F[rancis]

Roberts
See Harpe, Wiley

Roberts, Abraham
See Graubard, Abraham

Roberts, Andrew L. ?-1878 [BLB, DI, EWG]
American gunfighter
* Roberts, Buckshot

Roberts, Anthony
See Watney, John B[asil]

Roberts, Archie
See Roberts, Arthur J.

Roberts, Arthur Guy 1903- [WWL]
British author
* Clifford, Guy

Roberts, Arthur J. 20th c. [FB]
American football player
* Roberts, Archie

Roberts, Arthur O. 1923- [CA, SFL]
American author
* Cameron, Berl [joint pseudonym with John (Stephen) Glasby] [house pseudonym, Curtis Warren]
* Le Page, Rand [joint pseudonym with John (Stephen) Glasby] [house pseudonym, Curtis Warren]
* Lorraine, Paul [joint pseudonym with John (Stephen) Glasby] [house pseudonym, Curtis Warren]
* Mego, Al

Roberts, Bart 1928- [FC]
American actor
* Reason, Rex

Roberts, [Captain] Bartholomew 1682-1722 [HPPN, PW 1-6-86]
Welsh pirate
* Black Bart

Roberts, [Carl Eric] Bechhofer 1894-1949 [LC, WW, WWL]
British author
* Bechhofer, C. E.
* Ephesian

Roberts, Ben
See Eisenberg, Ben

Roberts, Big Jim
See Roberts, James Newson [Jim]

Roberts, Block Buster
See Roberts, Lenerte

Roberts, Bo
See Roberts, S. H.

Roberts, Brigham Henry 1857-1933 [HPPN]
Morman church leader
* [The] Defender of the Faith

Roberts, Buckshot
See Roberts, Andrew L.

Roberts, C. D. G.
See Roberts, [Sir] Charles George
Douglas

Roberts, Captain
See Hobart, Augustus C.

Roberts, Captain
See Hobart-Hampden, Augustus Charles

Roberts, Caroline Alice 19th c. [IP]
British poet
* C. A. R.

Roberts, Cecil Edric Mornington 1892-
[TC, WWL]
British author and playwright
* Beresford, Russell
* Mornington, Edor
* Seer

Roberts, Charles Emory 1918- [BE]
American baseball player
* Roberts, Red

Roberts, [Sir] Charles George Douglas
1860-1943 [LC, TLC]
Canadian author and poet
* [The] Father of Canadian Literature
* Roberts, C. D. G.

Roberts, Charles Luckeyeth 1887?-1968
[ASC, DAM, WWJ]
American jazz musician
* Roberts, Luckey

Roberts, Chip
See Roberts, L. R.

Roberts, Choo Choo
See Roberts, Eugene

Roberts, Clarence Ashley 1888-1963
[BE]
American baseball player
* Roberts, Skipper

Roberts, Clifford 1893?-1977
American golfer
* Mr. Cliff

Roberts, Cyril D. 1939- [IBW]
American insurance agent
* Roberts, Sonny

Roberts, Dale 1942- [BE]
American baseball player
* Roberts, Mountain Man

Roberts, Dan
See Ross, William Edward Daniel

Roberts, Daniel ?-1811 [IP]
British author
* Philotesis

Roberts, David
See Cox, John Roberts [Jack]

Roberts, Dell
See Fendell, Bob

Roberts, Don
See Ross, Don

Roberts, Dorothy James 1903- [CAP]
American author
* Mortimer, Peter

Roberts, Edith
See Roberts, Elizabeth [Kneipple]

Roberts, Edna 1912- [IAW]
British writer
* Finlay, Michael
* Hilton, Josephine
* Owen, Richard

Roberts, Edward 1904- [BF]
British director and screenwriter
* Dryhurst, Edward

Roberts, Edwin F. [PA]
Author
* Happy John

Roberts, Elizabeth [Kneipple] 20th c.
[CA]
Author
* Roberts, Edith

Roberts, Eric 1914- [AW, CA]
British author and playwright
* Robin

Roberts, Eugene 20th c. [EF]
American football player
* Roberts, Choo Choo

Roberts, Fireball
See Roberts, [Edward] Glenn, [Jr.]

Roberts, Florence Smythe 1878-1925
[HPPN]
American actress
* Smythe, Florence

Roberts, Floyd 20th c.
Auto racer
* [The] Old Man of the Mountain

Roberts, Frederick Sleigh 1832-1914
[HPPN, NN]
British military leader
* Bobs
* Bobs Bahadur
* Roberts of Kandahar, Pretoria and
  Waterford

Roberts, Gene 20th c.
American editor
* [The] Frog

Roberts, [Sir] George 1859-1950 [BI]
British hospital administrator
* Audax

Roberts, George
See Walters, Robert

Roberts, George Edward Theodore
1877-1953 [WW]
Author
* Goodridge Roberts, Theodore

Roberts, Glen
See Freeman, Leonard

Roberts, [Edward] Glenn, [Jr.]
1927?-1964 [AS, EAR, OCS]
American auto racer
* Roberts, Fireball

Roberts, Grant
See Wallmann, Jeffrey M[iner]

Roberts, Helen
See Hunter, Alberta

Roberts, Holt
See Draper, Ben

Roberts, Hortense Roberta 20th c. [CA]
American author
* Munger, Hortense Roberta

Roberts, Irene M. 1925?- [AW, CA,
WD]
British author
* Carr, Roberta
* Harle, Elizabeth
* Roberts, Ivor
* Rowland, Iris
* Shaw, Irene

Roberts, Ivor
See Roberts, Irene M.

Roberts, J. P. [PA]
Author
* Happy, John

Roberts, Jack 20th c. [HPPN]
American football player
* Jack the Ripper
* [The] Ripper

Roberts, James Hall
See Duncan, Robert Lipscomb

Roberts, James M. 1900-1945 [FB]
American football player
* Roberts, Red

Roberts, James Newson [Jim] 1895-
[BE]
American baseball player
* Roberts, Big Jim

Roberts, James William 1918- [CWG]
American singer
* Carson, James

Roberts, Jane 1929-1984 [CA]
American author
* Butts, Jane Roberts

Roberts, Janet Louise 1925- [CA]
American author
* Bronte, Louisa
* Danton, Rebecca
* Radcliffe, Janette

Roberts, Jason
See Bock, Fred

Roberts, Jim
See Bates, Barbara S[nedeker]

Roberts, Jim
See Caudle, James Robert

Roberts, Jimmy
See Edmeades, Robert Thomas

Roberts, Joan
See Seagrist, Josephine

Roberts, Joe
See Saltzman, Joseph [Joe]

Roberts, John 18th c. [IP, PA]
British author
* Anti Scriblerus Histrionicus
* [A] Stroling Player

Roberts, John 20th c. [HPPN]
American missionary
* White Robe

Roberts, John
See Bingley, David Ernest

Roberts, John
See Pierce, John Robinson

Roberts, John
See Swinerton, Thomas

Roberts, John G[aither] 1913- [CA]
American author
* Paul, Robert

Roberts, John Peter 1925- [IAW]
Welsh-born author
* Welsh, Robert

Roberts, John S[torm] 1936- [CA]
British author
* Anthony, John
* Lloyd, Jane
* Mwamba, Pal
* Storm, Anthony

Roberts, Johnny
See Robilotto, John

Roberts, Jon
See Olson, Robert G.

Roberts, Julian
See Bardens, Dennis [Conrad]

Roberts, K.
See Lake, Kenneth R[obert]

Roberts, Keith [John Kingston] 1935-
[CA, WGT]
British author
* Bevan, Alistair
* Kingston, John
* Stringer, David

Roberts, Ken
See Lake, Kenneth R[obert]

Roberts, Kenneth [Lewis] 1885- [CAA]
American author
* Kilgallen, Milton

Roberts, Kenneth
See Dent, Lester

Roberts, L. R. 20th c. [HPPN]
American football player
* Roberts, Chip

Roberts, Lawrence
See Fish, Robert L.

Roberts, Lee 20th c. [MBF]
British author
* Reid, Desmond [house pseudonym]

Roberts, Lee
See Martin, Robert [Lee]

Roberts, Lenerte 20th c. [IBW]
American realtor
* Roberts, Block Buster

Roberts, Lester A.   [IP]
American author
* [An] Artist

Roberts, Lionel
See Fanthorpe, R[obert] Lionel

Roberts, Lisa
See Turner, Robert [Harry]

Roberts, Lucille
See Gaillard, Lucile Roberts

Roberts, Luckey
See Roberts, Charles Luckeyeth

Roberts, Lynn 1922-
American actress
* Hart, Mary

Roberts, Mabel 1880?-1954 [BEW]
American actress
* Paige, Mabel

Roberts, MacLennan
See Terrall, Robert

Roberts, Maggie 19th c. [DNA, IP, PA]
American author
* Strebor, Eiggam

Roberts, Mark 20th c. [CA]
Author
* Derrick, Lionel [joint pseudonym with
  Chet Cunningham]

Roberts, Martin
See Wells, [Frank Charles] Robert

Roberts, Marty
See Schopp, Martin Robert

Roberts, Mary 1789-1864 [IP]
British author
* De Gleva, Mary

Roberts, Maurice 1905- [HPPN]
American hockey player
* Roberts, Moe

Roberts, McLean
See Machlin, Milton Robert

Roberts, Meade
See Mednick, Stanley Robert

Roberts, Moe
See Roberts, Maurice

Roberts, Moe
See Roberts, Morris

Roberts, Morris 1907- [CEI]
American hockey player
* Roberts, Moe

Roberts, Mountain Man
See Roberts, Dale

Roberts, Murray
See Graydon, Robert Murray

Roberts, Nancy
See Finley, Annette

**Roberts of Kandahar, Pretoria and
Waterford**
See Roberts, Frederick Sleigh

Roberts, Oral 1918?- [TI 2-17-86]
American evangelist
* [The] Prairie Tornado

Roberts, Oran Milo 1815-1898 [HPPN]
American soldier, statesman, jurist
* [The] Old Alcalde

Roberts, Philip Ilott 1872-1938 [DNA]
Author and clergyman
* Mann, A. Chester

Roberts, Ralph
See Barent, Ralph

Roberts, Rand
See Parham, Robert Randall

Roberts, [Sir] Randal H. 19th c.
[HPPN]
British author
* Light Cast

Roberts, Red
See Roberts, Charles Emory

Roberts, Red
See Roberts, James M.

Roberts, Rinalda
See Cudlipp, Edythe

Roberts, Robert Evan 1926- [BE]
American baseball player
* Roberts, Robin

Roberts, Robert Richford 1778-1843
[HPPN]
American missionary
* [The] Grandfather of the Missionaries

Roberts, Robin
See Roberts, Robert Evan

Roberts, Rose
See Calvert, Mrs. Louis

Roberts, S.   [IP]
British author
* [A] Llanbrynmair Farmer

Roberts, S. C.
See Roberts, [Sir] Sydney Castle

Roberts, S. H. 20th c.
American business executive
* Roberts, Bo

Roberts, Sally
See Dunn, Sara

Roberts, Sally
See Jones, Sally Roberts

Roberts, Samuel 1889?- [HPPN]
American gambler and procurer
* Roberts, Yellow

Roberts, Skipper
See Roberts, Clarence Ashley

Roberts, Snitcher
See Johnson, James

Roberts, Sonia Leslie 1934- [IAW]
British author
* Leslie, Robert
* Trevor, Charlotte

Roberts, Sonny
See Roberts, Cyril D.

Roberts, Suzanne 1931-　[CA]
American author
* Marath, Laurie
* Marath, Sparrow

Roberts, [Sir] Sydney Castle 1887-1966
[LC]
British educator and author
* Roberts, S. C.

Roberts, Terence
See Sanderson, Ivan T[erence]

Roberts, Theodore 1861-1928　[HPPN]
American actor
* Dad
* [The] Grand Old Man of the Screen

Roberts, Thom[as Sacra] 1940-　[CA]
American author
* Lawrence, Thomas

Roberts, Tom
See Thomas, R[obert] Murray

Roberts, Tom
See Thomas, Robert Murray

Roberts, Tommy 20th c.　[WFA]
British fashion designer
* Freedom, Mr.

Roberts, Ursula
See Miles, Susan

Roberts, Virginia
See Dean, Nell Marr

Roberts, Walt 20th c.　[IBW]
American football player
* [The] Flea

Roberts, Wayne
See Overholser, Wayne D.

Roberts, Will 20th c.　[BLB]
American train robber
* Dixon

Roberts, Will 20th c.　[ART]
Welsh painter
* Will R.

Roberts, William 1767-1849　[IP, PA]
British barrister and author
* Olive-Branch, [Rev] Simon

Roberts, William 1868-1959　[LC, TC]
British author and music critic
* Newman, Ernest

Roberts, William Hedley 1864-?　[THR]
British weightlifter
* Atlas

Roberts, Yellow
See Roberts, Samuel

Roberts-Jones, Phillipe John A. G.
1924-　[IAW]
Belgian author
* Jones, Phillipe

Robertshaw, [James] Denis 1911-　[AW,
CA]
British author
* Gaunt, Michael

Robertson, A. J.
See Robertson, Alfred

Robertson, Agnes
See Boucicault, Agnes Kelly Robertson

Robertson, Alex
See Rathborne, St. George Henry

Robertson, Alexander　[IP]
Scottish author
* Alister, R.

Robertson, Alexander Campbell 1887-
[BI]
American musician
* Robertson, Eck

Robertson, Alfred 1891-1948　[BB]
American basketball coach
* Robertson, A. J.

Robertson, Alfred 20th c.
American jockey
* Robertson, Robby

Robertson, Alice Alberthe 1871-?　[SFL,
WGT]
American author
* David, K.
* St. Luz, Berthe

Robertson, Amy
See Cooper, Robert Andrew

Robertson, Ben F. 1854-1884　[EWG]
American gunfighter and bank robber
* Burton, Ben F.
* Wheeler, Ben

Robertson, Bob
See Leone, Sergio

Robertson, Butch
See Robertson, Isaiah

Robertson, C. Alvin 1891-1943　[WWJ]
American jazz musician
* Robertson, Zue

Robertson, Colin 1906-　[MBF]
British author and playwright
* Reid, Desmond [house pseudonym]

Robertson, Constance [Pierrepont Noyes]
1897-　[ANT, CA, WD]
American author
* Scott, Dana

Robertson, Creole Pete
See Robertson, Peter

Robertson, Curtis 1865?-1900　[BI]
American murderer
* Charles, Robert

Robertson, Doc
See Robertson, Elbert K.

Robertson, E. Arnot
See Robertson, Eileen Arbuthnot

Robertson, E[ileen] Arnot
See Turner, Eileen Arbuthnot
Robertson

Robertson, Eck
See Robertson, Alexander Campbell

Robertson, Eileen Arbuthnot 1903-1961
[LC, TC]
British author
* Robertson, E. Arnot

Robertson, Elbert K. 20th c.　[IBW]
American inventor
* Robertson, Doc

Robertson, Ellis [joint pseudonym with
Robert Silverberg]
See Ellison, Harlan [Jay]

Robertson, Ellis [joint pseudonym with
Harlan (Jay) Ellison]
See Silverberg, Robert

Robertson, Elspeth
See Ellison, Joan Audrey [Anderson]

Robertson, Eric S. 19th c.　[HPPN]
British author
* [The] Editor

**Robertson, Ethel Florence [Lindesay
Richardson]** 1870-1946　[EWL, TC, TCL]
Australian author
* Richardson, Henry Handel

Robertson, Forbes
See Forbes-Robertson, [Sir] Johnston

Robertson, Frank C[hester] 1890-　[CA,
NAA]
American author
* Crane, Robert
* Field, Frank Chester
* Hill, King

Robertson, George Hepburn 1885?-1955
[HPPN]
*American auto racer, soldier, business
executive*
* [The] First Great Racer

Robertson, H. 19th c.　[IP]
Author
* [A] Scotch Episcopalian

Robertson, Helen
See Edmiston, Helen Jean Mary

Robertson, Henry 1890?-　[NOJ]
American jazz musician
* Robertson, Sleepy

Robertson, Henry D. 19th c.　[IP]
Author
* [A] Gentleman in the Service of the
East India Company

Robertson, Ian
See Forbes-Robertson, Ian

Robertson, Ignatius Loyola
See Knapp, Samuel Lorenzo

Robertson, Isaiah 1949-　[IBW]
American football player
* Robertson, Butch

Robertson, J.
See Frazer, John de Jean

Robertson, J. G.
See Robertson, John George

Robertson, J. M.
See Robertson, John Mackinnon

Robertson, Jaime 1944-   [RO2]
Canadian-born musician
* Robertson, Robbie

Robertson, James 1742-1814   [HPPN]
American pioneer
* [The] Father of Middle Tennessee

Robertson, James 1859-1936   [SC]
American actor
* Robertson, Scotty

Robertson, James B. 1909?-1966   [ASC, CWG]
American country-western performer
* Robertson, Texas Jim

Robertson, James Logie 1846-?   [WWL]
Scottish author and poet
* Haliburton, Hugh

Robertson, John 19th c.   [IP]
Scottish clergyman and author
* Topping, Godfrey

Robertson, John 19th c.   [CCL]
Canadian poet
* Scotus

Robertson, John
See Seeley, John Robert

Robertson, John George 1867-1933   [LC]
British author and educator
* Robertson, J. G.

Robertson, John Henry 1889-1965   [BE]
American baseball player
* Robinson, John Henry
* Robinson, Rube

Robertson, John Henry 1909-1965   [LC]
British author and journalist
* Connell, John

Robertson, John Mackinnon 1856-1933 [LC]
Scottish-born journalist and author
* Robertson, J. M.

Robertson, John Wilson 20th c.   [CCL]
Canadian poet
* Wilson, John

Robertson, John Wylie 1889-1966   [FC]
British actor
* Watson, Wylie

Robertson, [Rev.] Joseph 1726-1802 [HPPN]
British clergyman
* Eusebius
* Vicar of Lilliput

Robertson, Joseph 1811-1866   [IP]
Scottish antiquary
* Brown, James

Robertson, Joseph Clinton 1788-1852 [FFF]
British editor
* Percy, Sholto

Robertson, Keith [Carlton] 1914-   [CA, SAT, WW]
American author
* Keith, Carlton

Robertson, Lawson 1883-1951   [TF]
Scottish-born track and field athlete and coach
* Robertson, Robbie

Robertson, Margaret 1849-1935   [BEW]
British actress
* Kendal, [Dame] Madge

Robertson, Margery Ellen 1906-   [WD]
British author
* Thorp, Ellen
* Thorp, Morwenna

Robertson, Marion Gordon 1930?-   [BI]
American television performer and executive
* Robertson, Pat

Robertson, Marjorie 1904-1986   [BDF, BEW, FC, HPPN]
British actress
* Neagle, Anna

Robertson, Mary Imogene 1905?-1948 [BEW, F2, FIR]
American actress
* [The] Hard Luck Girl
* Nolan, Mary
* Wilson, Bubbles
* Wilson, Imogene

Robertson, Mrs. Donald   [FFF]
Entertainer
* Lewis, Catherine

Robertson, Oscar Palmer 1938-   [BB, HPPN]
American basketball player
* [The] Big O
* Robertson, Oz

Robertson, Oz
See Robertson, Oscar Palmer

Robertson, Pat
See Robertson, Marion Gordon

Robertson, Patrick 1794-1855   [IP]
Scottish poet and jurist
* P. R.

Robertson, Peter 1907-   [IBW]
American baseball player
* Robertson, Creole Pete

Robertson, R. R.
See Robertson, Richard Ross

Robertson, Rebecca
See Knief, Rebecca

Robertson, Richard Ross 1914-   [ART]
Scottish sculptor
* Robertson, R. R.

Robertson, Robbie
See Robertson, Jaime

Robertson, Robbie
See Robertson, Lawson

Robertson, Robby
See Robertson, Alfred

Robertson, S. M.
See Robertson, Sheila Macleod

Robertson, Sarah Franklin [Davis] 1845-1889   [DNA]
American author
* Carter, Ruth

Robertson, Scotty
See Robertson, James

Robertson, Seonaid Mairi 1912-   [ART]
Scottish-born artist
* S. M. R.

Robertson, Sheila Macleod 1927-   [ART]
British painter and sculptor
* Robertson, S. M.

Robertson, Sherrard Alexander 1919-1970   [BE]
Canadian-born baseball player
* Robertson, Sherry

Robertson, Sherry
See Robertson, Sherrard Alexander

Robertson, Sleepy
See Robertson, Henry

Robertson, Texas Jim
See Robertson, James B.

Robertson, Thomas Anthony 1897- [HPPN]
American agriculturist, business executive, author
* Tomasito, Don

Robertson, Thomas Beattie 1879-1936 [CCL]
Canadian author
* T. B. R.

Robertson, William 1721-1793   [IP]
Scottish clergyman
* [The] Historian of Rochdale
* [A] Presbyter of the Church of England

Robertson, Zue
See Robertson, C. Alvin

Robertson-Glasgow, R. C.
See Robertson-Glasgow, Raymond Charles

Robertson-Glasgow, Raymond Charles 1901-1965   [LC]
British author and cricket correspondent
* Robertson-Glasgow, R. C.

Robertsson, Sigurdur 1909-   [IAW]
Icelandic author and playwright
* Alfur Utangaros

Robeson, Eslanda Cardoza Goode 1896-1965   [IBW]
American pathologist, chemist, author
* Robeson, Essie

Robeson, Essie
See Robeson, Eslanda Cardoza Goode

Robeson, Kenneth [house pseudonym, Street & Smith]
See Bogart, William G.

Robeson, Kenneth [house pseudonym, Street & Smith]
See Daniels, Norman [A.]

Robeson, Kenneth [house pseudonym, Street & Smith]
See Dent, Lester

Robeson, Kenneth [house pseudonym, Street & Smith]
See Donovan, Laurence

Robeson, Kenneth [house pseudonym, Street & Smith]
See Ernst, Paul Frederick

Robeson, Kenneth [house pseudonym, Street & Smith]
See Goulart, Ron[ald Joseph]

Robeson, Kenneth [house pseudonym, Street & Smith]
See Hathaway, Alan

Robeson, Kenneth [house pseudonym, Street & Smith]
See Johnson, W. Ryerson

Robeson, Kenneth [house pseudonym, Street & Smith]
See Tepperman, Emile

Robeson of Rutgers
See Robeson, Paul

Robeson, Orlando
See Roberson, Orlando

Robeson, Paul 1898-1976 [HPPN]
American singer and actor
* Robeson of Rutgers

Robeson, Reed
See Robeson, Reeve

Robeson, Reeve 20th c. [IBW]
American businessman
* Robeson, Reed

Robespierre, Maximilien 1759?-1794 [HN, RH, SN]
French revolutionary leader
* [The] Cromwell of France
* [The] Incorruptible
* [The] King of Terror
* [The] Living Sophism
* [The] Mountain
* [The] People's Friend
* Robespierre, Seagreen
* [The] Seagreen Incorruptible

Robespierre, Seagreen
See Robespierre, Maximilien

Robey, [Sir] George
See Wade, George Edward

Robey, Ken
See Robitschek, Kurt

Robhs, Dwight
See Monaco, Richard

Robic, Ivo
See Robish, Eevo

Robidoux, Florent 1960-
Canadian-born hockey player
* Robidoux, Robey

Robidoux, Robey
See Robidoux, Florent

Robie, Anne A.
See Rolfe, Maro Orlando

Robilotto, John ?-1958 [BLB, PHM]
American underworld figure
* Roberts, Johnny

Robin
See Denard, Robert [Bob]

Robin
See Lyttle, Wesley Guard

Robin
See Roberts, Eric

[The] Robin Good-Fellow of the Stage
See Suett, Richard

[The] Robin Hood of Hunsrueck
See Bueckler, Johannes

[The] Robin Hood of Missouri
See James, Jesse Woodson

[The] Robin Hood of the Cookson Hills
See Floyd, Charles Arthur

[The] Robin Hood of the Forest
See Allen, Ethan

[The] Robin Hood of the Himalayas
See Singh, Kunwar Indrajit

[The] Robin Hood of The Little Blue
See James, Jesse Woodson

[The] Robin Hood of the Lowlands
See Macgregor, Robert

Robin Hood of the Sierras
See Carillo, Joaquin

Robin, Madeleine Marie 1918-1960
French opera singer
* Robin, Mado

Robin, Mado
See Robin, Madeleine Marie

Robin of Redesdale
See Hilyard, Robert

Robin, the Boy Wonder
See Gervis, Bert John, Jr.

Robin the Trickster
See Harley, Robert [First Earl of Oxford]

Robinet, Lee
See Browne, F. G.

Robinett, Stephen [Allen] 1941- [CA, WGT]
American author
* Hallus, Tak

Robins, A.
See Proster, Adolph

Robins, Adolph
See Proper, Adolph

Robins, Benjamin 1707-1751 [HPPN]
British engineer and ballistics expert
* [The] Father of Modern Gunnery

Robins, Denise [Naomi] 1897- [CA, WD]
British author and playwright
* French, Ashley
* Gray, Harriet
* Kane, Julia
* Wright, Francesca

Robins, Dorothy B.
See Robins-Mowry, Dorothy B[ernice]

Robins, Edward H.
See Haas, Edward

Robins, Elizabeth 1862-1952 [LC, TC, WW]
American actress and author
* Raimond, C. E.

Robins, Elizabeth
See Parks, Elizabeth Robins

Robins, Fenton
See Gammon, D. J.

Robins, G. M.
See Reynolds, Gertrude M. [Robins]

Robins, George [IP]
British author
* [An] Auctioneer

Robins, James ?-1836 [IP]
British publisher and bookseller
* Scott, Robert

Robins, John 17th c. [HPPN]
British farmer and religious fanatic
* [The] Ranter

Robins, Rollo
See Ellis, Edward S[ylvester]

Robins, Seelin
See Ellis, Edward S[ylvester]

Robins-Mowry, Dorothy B[ernice] 1921- [CA]
American author
* Robins, Dorothy B.

Robinson, Agnes Mary F.
See Duclaux, Agnes Mary Frances [Robinson]

Robinson, Alfred 1806-1895 [IP]
American author
* [An] American

Robinson, Alfred 1936?-
American political organizer
* Robinson, Skip

Robinson, Annie Douglas 1842-? [FFF]
American poet
* Douglas, Marian

Robinson, Arthur 1888-1935? [FDG]
American-born director
* Robison, Arthur

Robinson, Banjo
See Robinson, Ikey L.

Robinson, Bat
See Robinson, James

Robinson, Beezer
See Robinson, Bob

Robinson, Bernard Whitfield 1918-1972
[IBW]
American physician, naval officer, hospital administrator
* Robinson, Robby

Robinson, Bernice [Nelke] 1899-   [BI]
American author
* Richmond, Bernice

Robinson, Big Ike
See Robinson, Isaiah

Robinson, Big Jim
See Robinson, Nathan

Robinson, Bill 20th c.   [OBW]
American baseball player
* Robinson, Bojangles

Robinson, Bill
See Robinson, Luther

Robinson, Billy
See Robinson, Wilbert

Robinson, Black Rusie
See Robinson, James

Robinson, Blondie
See Robinson, Graydon

Robinson, Bob 20th c.   [GW]
American rodeo performer
* Robinson, Beezer

Robinson, Bojangles
See Robinson, Bill

Robinson, Brooks [Calbert, Jr.] 1937-
[HPPN, SMG]
American baseball player
* Impossible, Mr.
* Robbie
* Robby the Robber
* Robinson, Hoover
* [The] Vacuum Cleaner

Robinson, Budd
See Robinson, David

Robinson, Chaille Howard [Payne]
20th c.   [CA]
American author
* Kirby, Jean [house pseudonym, Whitman Publishing]
* Robinson, Kathleen

Robinson, Clara I. N. 19th c.   [IP]
British author
* Glubbins, Mrs.

Robinson, Cleophus 1932-   [IBW]
American clergyman and songwriter
* [The] King of Gospel Music

Robinson, Clyde ?-1915   [BE]
American baseball player
* Robinson, Rabbit

Robinson, Cornelius 1902-   [IBW]
American tour guide
* Robinson, Robby

Robinson, Cynthia 1946-   [SSS]
Musician
* Robinson, Ecco

Robinson, David 1915-   [CA]
American author, playwright, screenwriter
* Robinson, Budd

Robinson, Derek 1932-   [WD]
British author
* Robson, Dirk

Robinson, Doctor
See Hannegan, Dennis

Robinson, Dora 20th c.   [THR]
British theatrical business manager
* Fellowes-Robinson, Dora

Robinson, E. P.   [IP]
British author
* Jasper

Robinson, Ecco
See Robinson, Cynthia

Robinson, Ed 1882?-   [NOJ]
American jazz musician
* Robinson, Rabbit

Robinson, Eddie 1919-   [IBW]
American football player and coach
* Football, Mr.

Robinson, Edgar Williams 1794-1863
[PA]
Author
* Owanda

Robinson, Edward G.
See Goldenberg, Emanuel

Robinson, Edward N. 1873-1945   [FB]
American football coach
* Robinson, Robbie
* [The] Walter Camp of Brown Football

Robinson, Edwin Arlington 1869-1935
[HPPN]
American poet
* [A] Traditional Poet

Robinson, Edwin Meade 1878-?   [NAA]
American author and poet
* Robinson, Ted

Robinson, Eli 20th c.   [NP]
American jazz musician
* Mr. Eli

Robinson, Emma 1794-1863   [IP]
British author
* Owanda

Robinson, Esther 19th c.   [IP]
American journalist
* Warren, Esther

Robinson, Ezekial R. 20th c.   [IBW]
American magician
* Ezekiel the Great

Robinson, F. K 19th c.   [IP]
British philologist and author
* [An] Inhabitant

Robinson, F. Mabel 19th c.   [HPPN]
British author
* Griggs, W. Stephenson

Robinson, Fannie Clay 20th c.   [IBW]
Wife and business manager of American entertainer, Bill "Bojangles" Robinson
* Little Bo

Robinson, Fat
See Robinson, Freddy

Robinson, Fayette Lodawick 1818-1884
[HPPN]
American circus impresario
* Robinson, Yankee

Robinson, Frances
See Ladd, Marion Frances

Robinson, Frances M. 1906-   [HPPN]
Secretary to American army officer, Hugh S. Johnson
* [The] Right Hand Mind
* Robbie of the Codes

Robinson, Francis [Arthur] 1910-1980
[CA]
American opera executive and author
* Metropolitan Opera, Mr.

Robinson, Frank Isaac 1938-   [IBW]
American musician
* Robinson, Sugar Chile

Robinson, Frank M[alcolm] 1926-   [CA]
American author
* Benji, Thomas
* Courtney, Robert
* Walsh, James

Robinson, Frankie Walters 1859-1953
[HPPN]
American actress
* Bailey, Frankie

Robinson, Freddy 20th c.   [RBE]
American boxer
* Robinson, Fat

Robinson, Frederick 19th c.   [HPPN]
British army officer and author
* [A] Subaltern of Artillery

Robinson, Frederick John [Viscount Goderich and Earl of Ripon] 1782-1859
[DNNF, DNNS, SN]
British statesman
* Goderich, Goosey
* Robinson, Prosperity

Robinson, Geoffrey 1921-   [TR]
British actor
* Chater, Geoffrey

Robinson, George 20th c.   [OBW]
American baseball player
* Robinson, Sis

Robinson, George Geoffrey 1874-1944
[HPPN, LC]
British editor
* Dawson, George Geoffrey

Robinson, Good Rockin'
See Robinson, Louis Charles

Robinson, Graydon 1928-   [BBH, CSH]
Canadian bowler
* Robinson, Blondie

Robinson, Henrietta 1816-1905 [LFW]
American murderer
* [The] Veiled Murderess

Robinson, Herbert Spencer 20th c.
[CA]
American author
* Hespro, Herbert

Robinson, Herk
See Robinson, Spencer T.

Robinson, Hoover
See Robinson, Brooks [Calbert, Jr.]

Robinson, Ikey L. 1904- [WWJ]
American jazz musician
* Robinson, Banjo

Robinson, Inez Buck 1890-1957 [HPPN]
American actress
* Buck, Inez

Robinson, Isaiah 1892-1962 [NOJ]
American jazz musician
* Robinson, Big Ike

Robinson, Jack
See Michie, Archibald

Robinson, Jack
See Robinson, Robert

Robinson, Jack, Jr.
See Blair, David

Robinson, James 1713-1795 [IP]
British poet and actor
* Nobody

Robinson, James 1903-1957 [BWW]
American singer
* Bat the Humming-Bird
* Robinson, Bat

Robinson, James 1905-1970 [HPPN]
American actor
* Lang, Jimmy

Robinson, James 20th c. [OBW]
American baseball player
* Robinson, Black Rusie

Robinson, James A. 19th c. [PA]
Author
* Old Hurrygraph

Robinson, James D., III 1935-
American business executive
* Jimmy Three Sticks

Robinson, James Harvey 1863-1936
[HPPN]
American historian and educator
* [The] Preacher of History

Robinson, Jan M. 1933- [BI, SAT]
American author
* Flood, Flash

Robinson, Jill 1936- [CA]
American author
* Schary, Jill
* Zimmer, Jill Schary

Robinson, Jim
See Robinson, Nathan

Robinson, Jimmy Lee 1931- [BWW]
American singer
* Aliomar, Latif
* Lee, Jimmy
* Lee, Lonesome

Robinson, Joan [Mary] G[ale Thomas]
1910- [CA, SAT]
British author and illustrator
* Thomas, Joan Gale

Robinson, John ?-1927 [HPPN]
British murderer
* [The] Trunk Murderer

Robinson, John 1650-1723 [HPPN]
British clergyman
* [A] Person of Note Who Resided
  Many Years There

Robinson, John 1782-1833 [IP]
American author
* Piomingo

Robinson, John 18th c. [HPPN]
British physician and author
* J. R., M. D.

Robinson, John C. 1907- [IBW]
Ethiopian air force officer
* [The] Brown Condor

Robinson, John Henry
See Robertson, John Henry

Robinson, John Philo
See Crippen, [Dr.] Hawley Harvey

Robinson, John Philo, Jr.
See LeNeve, Ethel

Robinson, John Roosevelt [Jackie]
1919-1972 [HPPN]
American baseball player
* America's First Negro Big Leaguer

Robinson, Joseph T. 1872-1936 [HPPN]
American attorney and statesman
* [The] Co-author of the Robinson-
  Patman Act

Robinson, Josie
See Hayward, Mrs. Louis

Robinson, Kathleen
See Robinson, Chaille Howard [Payne]

Robinson, Kitty
See Kidd, Willie Mae

Robinson, L. C.
See Robinson, Louis Charles

Robinson, Lelia J. 19th c. [IP]
American author
* Clare, Ida

Robinson, Leonard [Len] 1951- [SMG]
American basketball player
* Robinson, Truck

Robinson, Lewis George 1886- [CC,
WW]
Author
* Braha, George
* Limnelius, George

Robinson, Lisa 1936- [CA]
American author
* Rhodes, Laura

Robinson, Louie, Jr. 1926- [CA]
American author and journalist
* Wyatt, James

Robinson, Louis Charles 1915-1976
[BWW]
American singer
* Robinson, Good Rockin'
* Robinson, L. C.

Robinson, Luther 1878-1949 [EMT,
HPPN, IPA, PMJ]
American actor and dancer
* Bojangles
* [The] King of Tap Dancers
* Robinson, Bill

Robinson, Mack
See Robinson, Matthew

Robinson, Madeleine
See Svoboda, Madeleine

Robinson, [Sister] Marian Dolores 1916-
[CA]
American psychologist and author
* Marian Dolores, [Sister]

Robinson, Martin D. 1925-1982 [ECM,
RO1]
American singer
* Robbins, Marty
* Teardrop, Mr.

Robinson, Mary 19th c. [DNNS, FFF,
NPS, RH]
*Wife of John Hatfield, who was executed
for forgery*
* [The] Beauty of Buttermere
* Mary of Buttermere

Robinson, Mary Darby 1758-1800
[DHA, FFF, HPPN, IP, SN, WGT]
British actress, author, poet
* Anna Maria
* Darby, Mary
* [The] English Sappho
* [The] Fair Perdita
* [A] Friend to Humanity
* Laura Maria
* Oberon
* Perdita
* Randall, Anne Frances
* Robinson, Perdita

Robinson, Matthew 20th c. [IBW]
American track and field athlete
* Robinson, Mack

Robinson, Mike 20th c. [IBW]
American basketball player
* Tiny Darkhorse

Robinson, Mogul
See Robinson, Remus G.

Robinson, Mrs. Forrest [FFF]
Entertainer
* Blair, Eugenia

Robinson, Mrs. George [FFF]
Entertainer
* Baldwin, Florence

Robinson, Nathan 1892-1976 [IBW, PMJ, WWJ]
American jazz musician
* Robinson, Big Jim
* Robinson, Jim

Robinson, Nugent 19th c. [FFF, IP]
American writer
* Clover, Sam
* Rugby, Nym

Robinson, P. W. 1893- [CA]
British-born author
* Richelieu, Peter

Robinson, Patricia Colbert 1923- [CA]
American author and playwright
* Duval, Margaret
* Macomber, Daria

Robinson, Patrick 1794-1855 [SN]
* Diminutive Peter
* Peter o' the Painch

Robinson, Paul 1944- [SMG]
American football player
* [The] Cactus Comet
* Robinson, Robby

Robinson, Paul
See Perelmuth, Jacob Pincus

Robinson, Perdita
See Robinson, Mary Darby

Robinson, Peter 1915- [HPPN]
American entertainer
* [The] Living Skeleton
* [The] World's Thinnest Man

Robinson, Peter 20th c. [WP 10-15-84]
British singer
* Marilyn

Robinson, Prosperity
See Robinson, Frederick John [Viscount Goderich and Earl of Ripon]

Robinson, Rabbit
See Robinson, Clyde

Robinson, Rabbit
See Robinson, Ed

Robinson, Ralph
See George III

Robinson, Ray
See Smith, Walker, Jr.

Robinson, Ray Charles 1930?- [BBD, BWW, LRR]
American musician
* Charles, Ray
* [The] Genius
* [The] Senior Diplomat of Soul

Robinson, Remus G. 20th c. [IBW]
American physician and school administrator
* Robinson, Mogul

Robinson, Richard Blundell 1905- [WW]
Author
* Leaderman, George

Robinson, Robbie
See Robinson, Edward N.

Robinson, Robbo
See Robinson, Robert Timothy

Robinson, Robby
See Robinson, Bernard Whitfield

Robinson, Robby
See Robinson, Cornelius

Robinson, Robby
See Robinson, Paul

Robinson, Robert 1927- [BB]
American basketball player
* Robinson, Jack

Robinson, Robert Murray 1949- [SMG]
American baseball player
* Robinson, Smokey

Robinson, Robert Timothy 1958- [DC]
British cricketer
* Robinson, Robbo

Robinson, Roland Edward 1912- [IAW]
Irish-born author and poet
* [The] Bastard from the Bush

Robinson, Rube
See Robertson, John Henry

Robinson, Samuel 19th c. [IP]
British scholar and author
* S. R.

Robinson, Shari
See McGuire, Leslie Sarah

Robinson, Sis
See Robinson, George

Robinson, Skindown
See Robinson, Walter

Robinson, Skip
See Robinson, Alfred

Robinson, Smith 1909- [IBW]
American editor
* Robinson, Smitty

Robinson, Smitty
See Robinson, Smith

Robinson, Smokey
See Robinson, Robert Murray

Robinson, Smokey
See Robinson, William

Robinson, Solon 1803-1880 [FFF, HPPN, IP, PA]
American author
* [The] King of the Squatters
* [A] Layman
* White, Blythe, Jr.

Robinson, Spencer T. 1941- [SMG]
American baseball executive
* Robinson, Herk

Robinson, Spider 1948- [CA]
American author
* Wyatt, B. D.

Robinson, Sugar Chile
See Robinson, Frank Isaac

Robinson, Sugar Ray
See Smith, Walker, Jr.

Robinson, Sylvia Vanderpool 1936- [RO2]
American singer and songwriter
* Sylvia

Robinson, T. H.
See Robinson, Theodore Henry

Robinson, Ted
See Robinson, Edwin Meade

Robinson, Theodore Henry 1881-1964 [LC]
British educator and author
* Robinson, T. H.

Robinson, Therese Albertine Louise von Jakob 1797-1870 [DEL, DNNF, HPPN, IP, RH]
German-born philologist and author
* Berthold, Ernst
* Reseda
* Talvi [or Talvj]

Robinson, [Sir] Thomas 18th c. [SN]
* Long Sir Thomas

Robinson, Thomas Romney 1792-1882 [HPPN]
British astronomer and inventor
* [The] Father of the Anemometer

Robinson, Truck
See Robinson, Leonard [Len]

Robinson, Vince
See Newton, Michael

Robinson, Walter 20th c. [OBW]
American baseball player
* Robinson, Skindown

Robinson, Wilbert 1863?-1934 [BAB, DGS, PB]
American baseball player and manager
* Fish, Billy
* Robinson, Billy
* Uncle Robbie [or Robby]

Robinson, William ?-1963 [BEW]
British theatrical performer
* Palette, Billy

Robinson, William 18th c. [SN]
British clergyman
* Reverend Billy

Robinson, William 1940- [PRS, RO2]
American singer and songwriter
* Robinson, Smokey

Robinson, William Ellsworth 1861-1918 [BMH]
American-born magician
* Ben Ali, Achmed
* Foo, Chung Ling
* Khan, Abdul
* Sahib, Nana
* Soo, Chung Ling
* Soo, Hop Ling

Robinson, William Erigena 1814-1892 [PA]
American author and journalist
* Richelieu

Robinson, William H. 1859-1894 [BE]
American baseball player
* Robinson, Yank

Robinson, William L. 19th c. [IP]
American author
* [A] Member of the Howard Association of New Orleans
* [A] Samaritan

Robinson, William Stevens 1818-1876 [FFF, IP, PA]
American author and journalist
* Bailey, Junior
* Boythorn
* Gilbert
* Kremlin
* Middlesex
* Warrington

Robinson, Yank
See Robinson, William H.

Robinson, Yankee
See Robinson, Fayette Lodawick

Robion, Jean
See Lanier, [Dr.] Clement

Robish, Eevo 1931- [RO1]
Yugoslav singer
* Robic, Ivo

Robison, Arthur
See Robinson, Arthur

Robison, Carson J. 1890-1957 [CWG]
American country-western performer
* [The] Granddaddy of the Hillbillies

Robison, David Victor 1911?-1978 [FIR]
Screenwriter
* David, Paul

Robison, John 1739-1805 [IP]
Scottish philosopher and author
* Cornelius

Robison, Mary 1865-1942 [BEW, F1, OCF]
Australian-born actress
* Robson, May

Robison, Nancy L[ouise] 1934- [SAT]
American author
* Johnson, Natalie

Robison, Ruth 20th c. [BEW]
American actress and producer
* Bailey, Ruth

Robison, Willard 1894-1968
American bandleader and singer
* [The] Evangelist of Rhythm

Robitschek, Kurt 1890-1950 [HPPN]
American producer
* Robey, Ken

Robjohn, William James 1843-1920 [BBD]
British-born musician
* Florio, Caryl

Robles Soler, Antonio 1897- [SFL, WGT]
Spanish author
* Antoniorrobles

Robley, Rob
See Robley, Wendell

Robley, Wendell 1916- [CA]
American author
* Robley, Rob

Robotham, Samuel Birley [FFF]
Astronomer and writer
* Parallax

Robson, Dirk
See Robinson, Derek

Robson, Frederick
See Brownbill, Thomas Robson

Robson, H. M.
See Robson, Hugh Mather

Robson, Henry 19th c. [IP]
British poet
* H. R.

Robson, Hugh Mather 1929- [ART]
British artist
* Robson, H. M.

Robson, May
See Robison, Mary

Robson, Norman 20th c. [SFL]
Author
* Robb, John

[The] Robson of the Halls
See Liston, Victor

Robson, Stuart
See Stuart, Henry Robson

Robson, William James 19th c. [IP]
British poet
* W. J. R.

[The] Robust
See Boufflers, Louis de

Robusti, Domenico 1560-1635 [BI]
Italian painter
* Tintoretto, Domenico
* [The] Younger

Robusti, Jacopo 1518-1594 [DNNS, HPPN, SN, WBD]
Italian painter
* [Il] Furioso
* [The] Thunderbolt of Painting
* Tintoret
* Tintoretto

Robusti, Marietta 1560-1590 [HPPN]
Venetian painter
* [La] Tintoretta

Roby, John 1793-1850 [IP]
British banker and author
* [An] Admirer of Walter Scott
* [An] Amateur of Fashion
* Byro

Roby, Mary Linn [CA]
American author
* Bradstreet, Vallerie
* D'Arcy, Pamela
* Grey, Georgina
* Pryer, Pauline
* Wilson, Mary

Robyn, Wee Willie
See Robyn, William

Robyn, William
Singer
* Robyn, Wee Willie

Roc Noir
See McDonald, Peter

Roc, Patricia
See Riese, Felicia

Rocca, Antonino 1923- [HPPN]
Italian wrestler
* Antonino the Great
* [The] Wrestler Who Never Loses

Roccabigliera, Jasper Ludwig
See Operti, Albert

Rocco, Gaetano 1914-1952 [SC]
American actor
* Tano, Guy

Roch, Dalby
See Webb, Ethel

Rocha, Adolfo 1907- [BI, HPPN]
Portuguese poet
* Torga, Miguel

Rocha, Ephraim 1923- [BB]
American basketball player
* Rocha, Red

Rocha, Red
See Rocha, Ephraim

Rochard, Henri
See Charlier, Roger H[enri]

Rochdale, Thomas
See Hinde, Alfred

[The] Rochdale Thunderbolt
See Bamford, Joseph

Roche, A. K. [joint pseudonym with Boche Kaplan]
See Abisch, Roslyn Kroop [Roz]

Roche, A. K. [joint pseudonym with Roslyn Kroop Abisch]
See Kaplan, Boche

Roche, Arthur Somers 1883-1935 [WW]
American author
* MacHaye, Eric

Roche, Eric
See Rochester, George Ernest

Roche, Frances Maria 1817?-? [PI]
Irish poet
* De Rupe

Roche, Hester
See Rochester, George Ernest

Roche, James 1770-1853 [DEL, PA, SN]
British author
* J. R.
* [An] Octogenarian
* [The] Roscoe of Cork

Roche, John 1813-1887 [FFF, WBD]
Irish-born American shipbuilder
* [The] Father of American Shipbuilding

Roche, John (cont.)
* [The] Father of Iron Shipbuilding in America
* Roach, John

Roche, John
See Le Roi, David [De Roche]

Roche, John Joseph [Jack] 1890- [BE]
American baseball player
* Roche, Red

Roche, Margaret Eleanor 1917- [HPPN]
American radio and television commentator
* McNellis, Maggi

Roche, Matthew
See O'Connell, John

Roche, Red
See Roche, John Joseph [Jack]

Roche, Terry
See Poole, Peggy

Rochechouart, Francoise Athenais 1641-1707 [SN]
Maid of honor to Queen Marie Therese
* Calypso
* Montespan, Marquise de
* Vashti

Rochefort, Bennett Harold
See Gilbert, Bennett Harold Rochefort

Rochefort, Harold
See Fenelon, Timothy Brendan

Rochefort, Julian 20th c. [MBF]
British author
* Stevens, Christopher

Rochefoucauld-Liancourt, Francois Alexandre Frederic, Duc de la 1747-1827 [IP]
French author
* [A] European

Rochelle
See Flacon, Joseph Henry

Rocher, Suzy [BI]
French entertainer
* Solidor, Suzy

Rochester
See Anderson, Edmund Lincoln [Eddie]

Rochester, Earl of
See Wilmot, John

[A] Rochester Fellow
See Scudder, Samuel Hubbard

Rochester, George Ernest 1905?- [MBF, SFL]
British author
* Beresford, John
* Chatham, Frank
* Frazer, Allison
* Furze, Barton
* Gaunt, Jeffrey
* Hale, Martin
* Kent, Elizabeth
* Roche, Eric
* Roche, Hester
* Smith, Hamilton
* West, Mary

[The] Rochester Israelite
See Sherenbeck, Mr.

Rochester, Mark
See Kent, [William] Charles [Mark]

Rochette, Raoul
See Rochetto, Raoul Desire

Rochetto, Raoul Desire 1790-1854 [PA]
Author
* Rochette, Raoul

Rochfort, Alfred
See Calhoun, Alfred R.

Rochon, Francois Jean 1953- [SMG]
Canadian-born hockey player
* Rochon, Frank

Rochon, Frank
See Rochon, Francois Jean

[The] Rock
See Averill, [Howard] Earl

[The] Rock
See Barbella, Rocco

[The] Rock
See Colavito, Rocco Domenico

[The] Rock
See Raines, Tim

Rock
See Ranc, Arthur

Rock
See Rockne, Knute Kenneth

[The] Rock
See Zeidel, Lawrence [Larry]

Rock, Blossom
See Blake, Marie

Rock, Blossom
See MacDonald, Edith

Rock, C. V.
See Rocken, Kurt Walter

Rock, Captain
See Moore, Thomas

Rock, Captain
See O'Conner, Roger

Rock, Captain, in London
See Whitty, J. M.

Rock, Charles
See De Fabeck, Arthur Charles Rock

Rock, Charles
See Rock De Fabeck, Arthur Charles

Rock, David John 1957- [DC]
British cricketer
* Rock, Jungle
* Rock, Rocky

Rock, Dr.
See Schmitt, Harrison Hagan

Rock, Dr.
See White, Charles

Rock, James
See Patten, Clinton A.

Rock, Jungle
See Rock, David John

Rock, Lester Henry
See Schwarzrock, Lester Henry

Rock, Magdalen
See Beck, Ellen

[The] Rock of Chickamauga
See Thomas, George Henry

[The] Rock of Notre Dame
See Rockne, Knute Kenneth

[The] Rock of the Marne
See McAlexander, Ulysses Grant

Rock, Pebbles
See Rock, Walter

Rock, R. W.
See Thompson, John C.

Rock, Richard
See Mainprize, Don[ald Charles]

Rock, Rocky
See Rock, David John

Rock, Walter 20th c.
American football player
* Rock, Pebbles
* Rock, Zeke

Rock, Zeke
See Rock, Walter

Rock De Fabeck, Arthur Charles 1866-1919 [BEW, HPPN]
Indian-born actor
* Old Bill
* Rock, Charles

Rockafeller, Harry J. 20th c. [BBH]
American collegiate athletic director
* Rockafeller, Rocky

Rockafeller, Rocky
See Rockafeller, Harry J.

Rockefeller, Bobo
See Rockefeller, Jeannette Edris

Rockefeller, David 1916?-
American banking executive
* D. R.

Rockefeller, Happy
See Rockefeller, Margaretta Large [Fitler Murphy]

Rockefeller, Jay
See Rockefeller, John D., IV

Rockefeller, Jeannette Edris 1917- [HPPN]
American wife of Winthrop Rockefeller
* Rockefeller, Bobo

Rockefeller, John D., IV 1937?-
American politician
* Rockefeller, Jay

Rockefeller, John Davison 1839-1937 [HPPN]
American industrialist and philanthropist
* John D.
* [The] Standard Oil King

Rockefeller, John Davison, III 1906-1978
American industrialist and philanthropist
* J. D. R. 3

Rockefeller, Margaretta Large [Fitler Murphy] 1926- [BI]
Wife of American vice president, Nelson Rockefeller
* Rockefeller, Happy

Rockefeller, Nelson Aldrich 1908-1979 [BI, HPPN]
American vice president
* Clean, Mr.
* [The] Dean of American Governors
* Rockefeller, Old Nels
* Rockefeller, Rocky
* [The] Spendthrift of Albany

Rockefeller, Old Nels
See Rockefeller, Nelson Aldrich

Rockefeller, Rocky
See Rockefeller, Nelson Aldrich

Rockefeller, William 1841-1922 [HPPN]
American business tycoon
* [The] Leader of the Oil Gang

Rocken, Kurt Walter 1906- [WGT]
German author
* Rock, C. V.
* Walter, Henry

[The] Rocket
See Larose, Claude

[The] Rocket
See Laver, Rod[ney George]

[The] Rocket
See Richard, [Joseph Henri] Maurice

Rocket, Captain
See Machado, Paulo Sergio Mastrotti

Rockey, Howard 1886-1934 [WW]
American author
* Bryce, Ronald
* Panbourne, Oliver

Rockfeller, Roger
See Deodato, Ruggero

[The] Rockford Sheik
See Mandella, Samuel R.

[The] Rockhampton Rocket
See Laver, Rod[ney George]

Rockin' Red
See Minter, Iverson

Rockin' Reggie Vincent
See Vincent, Reggie

Rockin' Robin
See Yount, Robin R.

Rockin' Sydney
See Semien, Sidney

[The] Rocking Chair Lady
See Norville, Mildred Bailey

Rockingham, [Sir] Charles
See Rohan-Chabot, Philippe Ferdinand Auguste de [Count de Jarnac]

Rockingham, Montague
See Nye, Nelson C[oral]

Rocklin, Ross Louis 1913- [CA]
American author
* Cente, H. F.
* Rocklynne, Ross
* Smith, Carlton

Rocklynne, Ross
See Rocklin, Ross Louis

Rockman, Maishe
See Rockman, Milton J.

Rockman, Milton J. [WP 11-6-85]
American underworld figure
* Rockman, Maishe

Rockne, Knute Kenneth 1888-1931 [HPPN]
American football coach
* [The] Great Man
* Rock
* [The] Rock of Notre Dame

Rocks
See Stone, Frederick Mather

Rockstro, William Smyth
See Rackstraw, William Smyth

Rockwell, Doc
See Rockwell, George L.

Rockwell, George E. 1926?- [HPPN]
American banker
* Banking's Technocrat

Rockwell, George L. 1889-1978 [HPPN]
American actor
* Rockwell, Doc

Rockwell, James Otis 1807-1831 [HPPN]
American poet
* J. O. R.

Rockwell, Kiffin Ayres
See Hayes, Kiffin Ayres

Rockwell, Mary L. Punderson 1897-1985 [WP 7-22-85]
Wife of American artist, Norman Rockwell
* Rockwell, Molly

Rockwell, Matt
See Rowland, Donald Sydney

Rockwell, Molly
See Rockwell, Mary L. Punderson

Rockwell, Norman Percival 1894-1980 [CR, HPPN]
American painter
* America's Most Beloved Artist
* [The] Lawrence Welk of American Painting

Rockwood
See Dykes, Thomas

Rockwood, Harry
See Young, Ernest A.

Rockwood, Margaret 1897-1962 [SC]
American actress and singer
* Morgan, Margo

Rockwood, Roy [house pseudonym] [Stratemeyer Syndicate]
See McFarlane, Leslie

Rockwood, Roy [house pseudonym] [Stratemeyer Syndicate]
See Stratemeyer, Edward L.

Rocky, Rockabye
See Barbella, Rocco

Roda Roda, Alexander Friedrich Ladislaus
See Rosenfeld, Alexander Friedrich Ladislaus

Rodale, J. I.
See Rodale, Jerome Irving

Rodale, Jerome Irving 1899-1971 [HPPN]
American natural foods advocate and magazine publisher
* Rodale, J. I.

Rodberg, Lillian 1936- [CA]
American author and columnist
* Boehme, Lillian R.

Rodd, Harriet Rashleigh 1779-1855 [HPPN]
British author
* H. R.

Rodd, Kylie Tennant 1912- [CA]
Australian author
* Tennant, Kylie

Rodd, Nancy Freeman-Mitford
See Mitford, Nancy

Rodd, Ralph
See North, William

Rodd, Thomas, Sr. 1763-1822 [IP]
British bookseller and author
* [The] Father of the Late Thomas Rodd
* Philobiblos
* [A] Young Gentleman

Rodd, William Henry 1816-? [IP]
British author
* [A] Local Preacher

Rodda, Charles 1891- [AW, CA, WW]
Australian-born author
* Holt, Gavin
* Low, Gardner
* Reed, Eliot [joint pseudonym with Eric Ambler]

Rodda, Joseph Tonkin 1834-? [IP]
British author
* Goldsworthy, Ralph

Rodda, Peter [Gordon] 1937- [CA]
South African-born playwright and poet
* Tudhope, Richard

Roddey, Philip Dale 1820-1897 [HPPN]
American merchant and army officer
* [The] Swamp Fox of the Tennessee Valley

Roddick, Ellen 1936- [CA]
American author and columnist
* Meade, Ellen

Roddy, John Gerald 1850?-? [PI]
Irish poet
* Clan-na-Rory
* Jo

Roddy the Rover
See De Blacam, Hugh [Aodh]

Roddy, William [PI]
Irish poet
* Derry Boy
* W.

Rode, [Jacques] Pierre [Joseph]
1774-1830 [SN]
French musician
* [The] Correggio of the Violin

Rodefer, Stephen 1940- [CA]
American poet and translator
* Calais, Jean

Rodeheaver, Homer Allan 1880-1956
[HPPN]
*American evangelist, hymn writer,
publisher*
* Rodey

Rodell, Marie F[reid] 1912-1975 [CA,
CC, WW]
American author, literary agent, editor
* Randolph, Marion

Rodenberg, Julius
See Levy, Julius

Roderick ?-711 [DEP, DNNS, SN]
King of the Visigoths
* [The] Last of the Goths

Rodes, Alfred 1905- [BMH]
Argentinian-born entertainer
* [L']enfant Paganini

Rodey
See Rodeheaver, Homer Allan

Rodgers, Andy
See Rodgers, Kenneth Andre Ian

Rodgers, Bill
See Rodgers, Wilbur Kincaid

Rodgers, Buck
See Rodgers, Francis G.

Rodgers, Buck
See Rodgers, Robert L. [Bob]

Rodgers, Francis G. 20th c.
American business executive
* Rodgers, Buck

Rodgers, Frank
See Infield, Glenn [Berton]

Rodgers, Franklin C. 1931- [FB]
American football coach
* Rodgers, Pepper

Rodgers, Ira E. 1895-1963 [AS, FB]
American football player
* Rodgers, Rat

Rodgers, James Charles [Jimmie]
1897-1933 [CWG]
American country-western performer
* America's Blue Yodeler
* [The] Father of Commercial Hillbilly
Music
* [The] Father of Country Music
* [The] Singing Brakeman

Rodgers, Joann Ellison 1941- [CA]
American journalist
* Scott, Eve

Rodgers, [Sir] John [Charles] 1906-
[IAW]
British politician and author
* Scrambled Ego

Rodgers, Kenneth Andre Ian 1934- [BE]
American baseball player
* Rodgers, Andy

Rodgers, Pepper
See Rodgers, Franklin C.

Rodgers, Rat
See Rodgers, Ira E.

Rodgers, Richard 1902- [HPPN]
American composer
* [The] Developer of the Plot Song

Rodgers, Robert L. [Bob] 1938- [PB]
American baseball player
* Rodgers, Buck

Rodgers, W. R.
See Rodgers, William Robert

Rodgers, Wilbur Kincaid 1887-1978
[BE]
American baseball player
* Raw Meat Bill
* Rodgers, Bill

Rodgers, William Robert 1909-1969
[LC]
Irish poet
* Rodgers, W. R.

Rodinson, Maxime 1915- [CA]
French author
* Ronsin, Jean

Rodman, Ella
See Church, Ella Rodman

Rodman, Emerson
See Ellis, Edward S[ylvester]

Rodman, Eric
See Silverberg, Robert

Rodman, Howard 20th c. [WF]
American screenwriter
* Simoun, Henri

Rodman, Maia
See Wojciechowska, Maia [Teresa]

Rodney, Bob
See Rodrigo, Robert

Rodney, Don
See Ragonese, Don

Rodney, M.
See Redmayne, Mary Priestley

Rodney, Marian C. Legare [Reeves]
19th c. [IP]
American author
* Fadette

Rodney, Red
See Chudnick, Robert

Rodomant
See Beethoven, Ludwig Van

[The] Rodomontade
See Clarke, Norham Pfardt

Rodrigo, Robert 1928- [CA]
British sportswriter and author
* Rodney, Bob

Rodrigues, Vilmar Silva 1931- [WEC]
Brazilian cartoonist
* Vilmar

Rodrigues Ferreira, Alexander 1756-1815
[FFF]
Brazilian traveller
* [The] Brazilian Humboldt

Rodrigues Martins, Waldemar 1937-
[AES]
Brazilian soccer player
* Oreco

Rodriguez, Angel
See Schmid, Charles Howard, Jr.

Rodriguez, Angel
See Schmid, Charles Howard, Jr.

Rodriguez, Antonio Hector 1920- [BE]
Cuban-born baseball player
* Rodriguez, Hec

Rodriguez, Augustin 1880?-? [HPPN]
Spanish bullfighter
* [La] Reverte
* Salome, Maria

Rodriguez, Aurelio Ituarte 1947- [BE]
Mexican-born baseball player
* Rodriguez, Leo

Rodriguez, Bobby
See Rodriguez, Roberto Munoz

Rodriguez, Braulio 20th c. [WECO]
Spanish cartoonist
* Bayo

Rodriguez, Brito
See Rodriguez, Sebastian

Rodriguez, Carlos [GS]
Venezuelan bullfighter
* [El] Mito [The Myth]

Rodriguez, Chi Chi
See Rodriguez, Juan A.

Rodriguez, Eliseo C. 1946- [SMG]
Puerto Rican-born baseball player
* Rodriguez, Ellie

Rodriguez, Ellie
See Rodriguez, Eliseo C.

Rodriguez, Fernando Pedro 1928- [BE]
Cuban-born baseball player
* Rodriguez, Freddy

Rodriguez, Freddy
See Rodriguez, Fernando Pedro

Rodriguez, Gonzalo 20th c.   [NW 2-25-85]
Colombian soccer team owner
* [El] Mejicano [The Mexican]

Rodriguez, Guillermo 1914-1951   [GS]
Peruvian bullfighter
* [El] Sargento [The Sergeant]

Rodriguez, Hec
See Rodriguez, Antonio Hector

Rodriguez, Jesus Rafael
See Hernaiz, Jesus Rafael

Rodriguez, Joaquin 1729-1800   [GS]
Spanish bullfighter
* Costillares [Big Ribs]

Rodriguez, Johnny
See Rodriguez, Juan Raul Davis

Rodriguez, Juan A. 1935-   [BI, BWG, GF, HPPN]
Puerto Rican golfer
* [The] Clown Prince of Golf
* Rodriguez, Chi Chi

Rodriguez, Juan Raul Davis 1952-
[ECM]
American country-western performer
* Rodriguez, Johnny

Rodriguez, Judith Green 1936-
Australian poet
* Green, Judith

Rodriguez, Leo
See Rodriguez, Aurelio Ituarte

Rodriguez, Nicholas Goodwin 1904?-
[WWJ]
Cuban-born jazz musician
* Rodriguez, Rod

Rodriguez, Roberto Munoz 1943-   [BE]
Venezuelan-born baseball player
* Rodriguez, Bobby

Rodriguez, Rod
See Rodriguez, Nicholas Goodwin

Rodriguez, Sebastian 1642-?   [IBW]
American musician
* Rodriguez, Brito

Rodriguez, Tito 1923-1973   [SC]
Actor, singer, bandleader
* [The] Frank Sinatra of Latin Music

Rodriguez Alvarez, Alejandro 1903-1965
[CA, EWL]
Spanish poet, playwright, screenwriter
* Casona, Alejandro

Rodriguez Davie, Jose 1867-1899   [GS]
Spanish bullfighter
* Pepete [Big Joe]

Rodriguez Sanchez, Guadalupe 1899-
[GS]
Mexican bullfighter
* Guero Guadalupe [Blonde Guadalupe]

Rodriguez Sanchez, Jose 1870-1922
[GS]
Spanish bullfighter
* Bebe Chico [Little Baby]

Rodriguez Sanchez, Manuel 1883-1923
[GS, SA]
Spanish bullfighter
* Manolete [Big Manuel]

Rodriguez Sanchez, Manuel 1917-1947
[GS, OCS]
Spanish bullfighter
* [The] Caliph of Cordoba
* Manolete [Big Manuel]
* [El] Monstruo [The Monster]

Rodriguez Ucares, Fray Jose 1725?-?
[CW]
Cuban poet and playwright
* [El] Capacho
* Capacho, Padre
* Ucres [or Ucares], Rodriguez

Rodriguez Valades, Jesus 1908-   [GS]
Mexican bullfighter
* Simonillo [Little Simon]

Rodriguez y Ortega, Joaquin 1903-
[GS, OCS]
Spanish bullfighter
* Cagancho

Rodriguez y Rodriguez, Jose 1824-1862
[GS]
Spanish bullfighter
* Pepete [Big Joe]

Rodt, Rudolf
See Eichrodt, Ludwig

Roducer, P.
See Harrison, George

Rodwell, James 19th c.   [IP, PA]
British author
* Uncle James

Rodziewiczowna, Marja 1863-1944   [CD]
Polish author
* Zmogas

Roe, A. V.
See Roe, Alliott Verdon

Roe, Alliott Verdon 1877?-?
American airplane manufacturer
* Roe, A. V.

Roe, [Frederick] Clay 1901-   [BE]
American baseball player
* Roe, Shad

Roe, E. P.
See Roe, Edward Payson

Roe, Edward Payson 1838-1888   [HPPN]
American author
* Roe, E. P.

Roe, Elizabeth Singer 18th c.   [HPPN]
British poet
* Philomena

Roe, Elwin Charles 1915-   [BE, PB]
American baseball player
* Roe, Preacher

Roe, F[rederic] Gordon 1894-   [CA, LAO, WD]
British author
* Criticus
* F. G. R.
* Rhode, Winslow
* Uncle Gordon

Roe, Harry Mason [house pseudonym]
[Stratemeyer Syndicate]
See Stratemeyer, Edward L.

Roe, Ivan 1917-   [AW, WD]
British author
* Savage, Richard

Roe, Leonard
See Douglas, John

Roe, M. S.
See Thomson, Daisy Hicks

Roe, Mary Abigail 1840?-?   [IP, PA]
American author
* Cornwall, C. M.

Roe, Owen
See Davis, Eugene

Roe, Preacher
See Roe, Elwin Charles

Roe, Richard
See Cowper, Francis Henry

Roe, Richard
See Ponsonby, Frederick George
Brabazon

Roe, Shad
See Roe, [Frederick] Clay

Roe, Tex
See Robarge, John F.

Roe, William J[ames] 1843-1915   [SFL, WGT]
American author
* Cervus, G. I.
* Genone, Hudor

Roebuck, John Arthur 1801-1879
[DNNS, NPS]
British politician
* I am Tear 'em
* Tear 'em

Roebuck, Peter Michael 1956-   [DC]
British cricketer
* Roebuck, Professor
* Roebuck, Roger

Roebuck, Professor
See Roebuck, Peter Michael

Roebuck, Roger
See Roebuck, Peter Michael

Roebuck, Theodore 20th c.   [HPPN]
American football player
* Roebuck, Tiny

Roebuck, Tiny
See Roebuck, Theodore

Roeder, Adolph 1857-?   [ALY]
American author and clergyman
* Reese, Harvey

Roeder, Pat
See Ellison, Harlan [Jay]

Roederer, [Comte] Pierre Louis
1754-1835 [HPPN]
French economist and politician
* [Un] Americain Residant a Vienne

Roehrich, William 1912- [TR]
American actor and author
* Roerick, William

Roelas [Ruelas], Juan de las 1560?-1625
[WBD]
Spanish painter
* [El] Clerigo

Roelvaag, O. E.
See Roelvaag, Ole Edvart

Roelvaag, Ole Edvart 1876-1931
[HPPN]
Norwegian-American educator and author
* Morck, Paal
* Roelvaag, O. E.

Roemer, Buddy
See Roemer, Charles, III

Roemer, Charles, III 1944?-
American businessman
* Roemer, Buddy

Roemers, Anna 1584-1651 [SN]
* [A] Dutch Sappho

Roerick, William
See Roehrich, William

Roese, John B. 1896-1959 [BI]
American educator
* Jerome, [Brother]

Roeser, Donald 20th c. [CMA]
Musician
* Dharma, Buck

Roessel-Waugh, C. C. [joint pseudonym
with Charles G. Waugh]
See Waugh, Carol-Lynn Roessel

Roessel-Waugh, C. C. [joint pseudonym
with Carol-Lynn Roessel Waugh]
See Waugh, Charles G.

Roesseler, Rudolf 1897-1958 [EE,
WWW]
*German publisher and intelligence agent
for Russia*
* Hermes
* Lucy [code name used during World
War II]

Roessler, Franz Anton 1746-1792 [BBD]
German composer
* Rosetti, Francesco Antonio

Roessler, Fritz
See Richter, Franz

Roest, Rust
See Elkan, Sophie

Roeter, Ada 1906- [HPPN]
American pianist and composer
* Rubin, Ada

Roeterdink, Hubert
See Roeterdink, Hubertus Johannus
Albertus

Roeterdink, Hubertus Johannus Albertus
1948- [IWM]
Dutch musician
* Roeterdink, Hubert

Roethke, Theodore 1908-1963 [MA]
American educator and poet
* Rothberg, Winterset

Roetter, Charles Frederick 1919- [CA]
German-born columnist and author
* Satiricus

Roffe
See Ericson, Rolf

Roffey, Maureen 1936- [SAT]
British author and illustrator
* Lodge, Maureen Roffey

Roffman, Sara
See Hershman, Morris

Rogan, Bullet Joe
See Rogan, Wilbur

Rogan, Wilbur 1893?-1967 [AS, MK]
American baseball player
* Rogan, Bullet Joe

Roge, Madame
See Bates, Charlotte Fiske

Roger
See Stephens, [Rev.] William

Roger
See Toutain, Jose

Roger Ferdinand
See Ferdinand, Roger

Roger, George Munroe [PA]
Author
* [The] Little Bugler

Roger, Mae Durham 20th c. [CA]
American author and librarian
* Durham, Mae

Roger, Noelle
See Pittard, Helene

Roger of Bruges
See Van der Weyde, Roger

Roger, Pierre 1291-1352 [WBD]
Pope
* Clement VI

Roger the Dodger
See Ward, Rodger

Roger, Victoriano 1898-1936 [HPPN]
Spanish bullfighter
* Valencia II

Roger I 1031-1101 [SN]
Count of Sicily and Calabria
* [The] Great Count
* [The] Terror of the Faithless

Rogers, Ben
See Pugh, Roger

Rogers, Buck
See Rogers, Everett

Rogers, Buck
See Rogers, Lee Otis

Rogers, Buck
See Rogers, Orlin Woodrow

Rogers, Buddy
See Rogers, Charles

Rogers, Charles 1904- [F2, FC, HPPN,
IPA]
American actor
* America's Boyfriend
* Rogers, Buddy

Rogers, Clara Kathleen 1844-1931 [BI,
NAA]
British-born singer, composer, author
* Doria, Clara

Rogers, D. J.
See Rogers, Dewayne Julius

Rogers, Dale Evans
See Smith, Frances Octavia

Rogers, Dewayne Julius 20th c. [IBW]
American singer
* Rogers, D. J.

Rogers, Don
See Degler, Claude

Rogers, Don
See Schieldge, Ernest

Rogers, Doris 1918?-1982 [FIR]
American entertainer
* Rogers, Red

Rogers, Doug
See Bradbury, Ray [Douglas]

Rogers, Duke?
See Williams, Egbert Austin

Rogers, Earl Andrus 1870-1922 [HPPN]
American attorney
* [The] Criminal's Best Friend

Rogers, Eleanor [FFF]
Entertainer
* Moretti, Eleanor

Rogers, Emmett
See McCloskey, John

Rogers, Emmett
See Sweet, Emmett Martine

Rogers, Everett 1891-1952 [NOJ]
American jazz musician
* Rogers, Buck

Rogers, Floyd
See Spence, William John Duncan

Rogers, Fred McFeely 1928- [CA]
*American television personality and
author*
* Rogers, Mister

Rogers, Fred O. 20th c.
American military officer
* Rogers, Tex

Rogers, Genevieve
See Aiken, Mrs. Frank E.

Rogers, Ginger
See McMath, Virginia Katherine

Rogers, Gus
See Solomon, Gus

Rogers, Hell Hound
See Rogers, Henry Huttleston

Rogers, Henry 1806-1877 [NPS, PA]
Author
* F. B.
* Greyson, R. E. H.
* Vindex

Rogers, Henry Bromfield 1802-1887
[HPPN]
American attorney
* [A] Conservative Whig

Rogers, Henry Huttleston 1840-1909
[HPPN]
American capitalist
* Rogers, Hell Hound

Rogers, James [Jimmy]
See Lane, James A.

Rogers, James Hotchkiss 1857-1940
[BI]
American musician and composer
* Campion, Edward

Rogers, John 1500-1555 [FFF, WBD]
British martyr
* [The] Deritend Martyr
* Matthew, Thomas

Rogers, John
See Rogers, Thomas Percy

Rogers, John
See Snow Cloud

Rogers, John Gray ?-1875 [HPPN]
American attorney
* J. G. R.

Rogers, John Jope 1816-1880 [HPPN]
British barrister
* J. J. R.

Rogers, John R. 1840?-1932 [HPPN]
American press representative
* Yours Merrily

Rogers, Joseph [Joe] 20th c. [HPPN]
American theatrical producer
* [The] Mayor of the Midway

Rogers, Keith
See Harris, Marion Rose [Young]

Rogers, Lee
See Wilson, Roger C.

Rogers, Lee Otis 1913- [BE]
American baseball player
* Rogers, Buck
* Rogers, Lefty

Rogers, Lefty
See Rogers, Lee Otis

Rogers, Lefty
See Rogers, Orlin Woodrow

Rogers, Levi 1887-1963 [BI]
Canadian rower and coxswain
* Rogers, Shotty

Rogers, Lorain [FFF]
Entertainer
* Thompson, Charlotte

Rogers, Loula K. [FFF]
Author
* Leola

Rogers, Mary Cecelia 1820-1841
[HPPN]
American murder victim
* Roget, Marie

Rogers, Mary Josephine 1882-1955 [BI]
American missionary
* Mary Joseph, [Mother]

Rogers, Max
See Solomon, Max

Rogers, Melva
See Graham, Roger Phillips

Rogers, Mick
See Glut, Donald F[rank]

Rogers, Milt
See Adelstein, Milton

Rogers, Milton M. 1924- [HPPN]
American jazz musician
* [The] Elder Statesman
* [The] Modern King of Swing
* Rogers, Shorty

Rogers, Mister
See Rogers, Fred McFeely

Rogers, Mrs. Charles S. [FFF]
Entertainer
* Vickers, Mattie

Rogers, Mrs. John R. [FFF]
Entertainer
* Palmer, Minnie

Rogers, Nat
See Rogers, William Richard

Rogers, Nathaniel P. 1794-1846 [FFF]
American journalist
* Old Man of the Mountain

Rogers, Oh Yeah
See Aiverum, Timothy Louis

Rogers, Orlin Woodrow 1912- [BE]
American baseball player
* Rogers, Buck
* Rogers, Lefty

Rogers, Packy
See Hazinski, Stanley Frank

Rogers, Pat
See Porges, Arthur

Rogers, Paul [Patrick] 1900- [CA]
American author and editor
* Hardwick, Homer

Rogers, Phillips
See Idell, Albert E.

Rogers, Red
See Rogers, Doris

Rogers, Robert
See Hamilton, Charles Harold St. John

Rogers, Rosalind
See Richardson, Randell

Rogers, Rosemary 1932- [CA, WD]
American author
* Mayson, Marina

Rogers, Roy
See Slye, Leonard

Rogers, Ruth 1890- [WW]
Author
* Alexander, Ruth

Rogers, Samuel 1763-1855 [DEP, FFF,
SN]
British poet
* [The] Banker Poet
* [The] Bard of Memory
* [The] Last English Maecenas
* [The] Maecenas of England
* [The] Nestor of English Authors

Rogers, Samuel Shepard 1943- [CA,
TR]
American playwright
* Shadow, Slim
* Shepard, Sam

Rogers, Sarah 1819-? [PA]
Author
* [A] Lady of New York

Rogers, Shorty
See Rajonsky, Milton M.

Rogers, Shorty
See Rogers, Milton M.

Rogers, Shotgun
See Rogers, Thomas Andrew

Rogers, Shotty
See Rogers, Levi

Rogers, Smiling Slim
See Planchet, Roger Anthony

Rogers, Stanley Frank
See Hazinski, Stanley Frank

Rogers, Steve
See Clarke, Percy A.

Rogers, Tex
See Rogers, Fred O.

Rogers, Thomas Andrew 1895-1936 [BE]
American baseball player
* Rogers, Shotgun

Rogers, Thomas Percy 1897- [IAW]
British author
* Rogers, John

Rogers, Timmie
See Aiverum, Timothy Louis

Rogers, Tom
See Edgar, Alfred

Rogers, W. G.
See Rogers, William Garland

Rogers, Wade
See Madlee, Dorothy [Haynes]

Rogers, Warren
See Brucker, Roger W[arren]

Rogers, Will[iam Penn Adair] 1879-1935
[HPPN]
American actor and comedian
* [The] Ambassador of Good Will
* [The] Cherokee Kid
* [The] Cowboy Philosopher
* [The] Man Who Can Say Anything
  and Make Everybody Like It
* [The] Prince of Wit and Wisdom
* [The] World's Number One
  Wisecracker

Rogers, William 18th c.
American potter
* [The] Poor Potter

Rogers, William
See Hawkins, Nehemiah

Rogers, William Garland 1896-1978
[WYA]
American author
* Rogers, W. G.

Rogers, William Pierce 1913-
American secretary of state
* Reyes, Dr. [code name]

Rogers, William Richard 1893- [MK]
American baseball player
* Rogers, Nat

Roget, John Lewis 19th c. [HPPN]
British author
* [A] Special Commissioner

Roget, Marie
See Rogers, Mary Cecelia

Roget, Peter Mark 1779-1869 [HPPN]
British physician, scholar, writer
* [The] Father of the Thesaurus

Roggiero, Pierre 1939- [HPPN]
French criminal
* Pierrot, Marseilles

Rognan, Roy ?-1943 [SC]
Actor and dancer
* Rognoni

Rognoni
See Rognan, Roy

Rogow, Lee 20th c. [SFP]
Author
* Ellis, Craig [house pseudonym]

Rogoz, Viorica-Georgina 1927- [IAW]
Rumanian author
* Huber

[A] Rogue of a Scot
See Erskine, John

Roguery, Doctor
See Smith, Thomas

Rohan, Louis Rene Edouard de
1734-1803 [SN]
French prelate
* [The] Hero of the Necklace

**Rohan-Chabot, Philippe Ferdinand
Auguste de** [Count de Jarnac] 19th c.
[HFN]
Author
* Rockingham, [Sir] Charles

Rohatyn, Felix 1929?-
American investment banker
* Felix the Fixer
* Fixit, Mr.

Rohe, Vera-Ellen Westmeyr 1926-1981
[FC, PMJ, SW]
American actress and dancer
* Vera Ellen

Rohen, Edward 1931- [CA, WD]
British poet and author
* Connors, Bruton

Rohl, Wolf Detlef
See Eisfeld, Rainer

Rohlfs, Anna Katharine [Green]
1846-1935 [HPPN, NAA, WW]
American author
* [The] Godmother of Detective Stories
* Green, Anna Katharine
* [The] Mother of Detective Stories

Rohling, Augustus W. 1861-1908
[HPPN]
American theatrical manager
* Hogan, Gus

Rohmer, Elizabeth Sax
See Ward, Rose Elizabeth Knox

Rohmer, Eric
See Scherer, Jean Marie Maurice

Rohmer, Sax
See Ward, Arthur Henry

Rohr, Wolf Detlef [WGT]
German author
* Caine, Geff?
* Coover, Wayne?
* Reed, Allan?

Rohrbach, Peter Thomas 1926- [WD]
American author
* Cody, James R.

Rohrlich, Ruby 20th c. [CA]
Canadian-born anthropologist and author
* Leavitt, Ruby R.
* Rohrlich-Leavitt, Ruby

Rohrlich-Leavitt, Ruby
See Rohrlich, Ruby

[Le] Roi
See Whitaker, Thomas

[Le] Roi Bourgeois
See Louis Philippe

[Le] Roi Citoyen
See Louis Philippe

[Un] Roi de Theatre
See Murat, Joachim

[Le] Roi des Barricades
See Louis Philippe

[Le] Roi des Braves
See Henry IV [or Henri]

[Le] Roi des Feuilletons
See Janin, Jules Gabriel

[Le] Roi des Halles
See Vendome, Francois de

[Le] Roi des Predicateurs
See Bourdaloue, Louis

[Le] Roi des Reptiles
See De la Ville, Bernard Germain
Etienne

[Le] Roi des Versailles
See Thiers, Louis Adolphe

[Le] Roi du Roi
See Du Plessis, Armand Jean

[Le] Roi Panade
See Louis XVIII

[Le] Roi Soleil
See Louis XIV

Roig, Anton Ambrose 1928- [BE]
American baseball player
* Roig, Tony

Roig, Tony
See Roig, Anton Ambrose

Roiphe, Anne Richardson 1935- [CA]
American author
* Richardson, Anne

Rojan
See Rojankovsky, Feodor Stepanovich

Rojankovsky, Feodor Stepanovich
1891-1970 [CA]
Russian-born author and illustrator
* Rojan

Rojas, Alejandro M. 1938- [PB]
Cuban-born baseball player
* Rojas, Minnie

Rojas, Cookie
See Rojas, Octavio Rivas

Rojas, Jose [GS]
Spanish bullfighter
* [El] Melenas [The Long-Haired One]

Rojas, Minnie
See Rojas, Alejandro M.

Rojas, Octavio Rivas 1939- [PB, SMG,
WWB]
Cuban-born baseball player
* Rojas, Cookie

Rojatt, Rick 1947-
Canadian stunt artist
* [The] Human Fly

Roker, A. B.
See Barton, Samuel

Roker, Granville William 1932- [EJ7]
American jazz musician
* Roker, Mickey

Roker, Mickey
See Roker, Granville William

Rola, Comte de
See Klossowski, Balthasar

Roland
See Zacherle, John

Roland, Arthur
See Kilbon, Roland

Roland, Gilbert
See Damaso De Alonso, Luis Antonio

Roland, John
See Oliver, John Rathbone

Roland, Marion
See Ross, Marion

Roland, Mary
See Lewis, Mary Christianna [Milne]

Roland, Nicholas
See Walmsley, Arnold Robert

[The] Roland of the Army
See Le Blond, Louis Vincent Joseph
[Comte de St. Hilaire]

Roland, Ruth 1893-1937 [CU]
American actress
* [The] Serial Queen

Roland de La Platiere, Jean Marie
1734-1793 [SN]
French revolutionary leader
* [The] Just

Roland de La Platiere, Jeanne Manon
1754-1793 [DEP, DNNS, FF]
French social leader
* [The] Circe of the Revolution

Roland-Manuel, Alexis
See Levy, Roland Alexis Manuel

Rolandow, G. W.
See Wutrich, Gottfried

Rolant, Rene
See Fanthorpe, R[obert] Lionel

Roldan, Enrique
See Garcia, Andres

Roles, Carl 20th c.
Horse trainer
* Roles, Slim

Roles, Slim
See Roles, Carl

Rolf, Frederick
See Friedrichs, Frederick

Rolfe, Father
See Rolfe, Frederick William [Serafino
Austin Lewis Mary]

**Rolfe, Frederick William [Serafino
Austin Lewis Mary]** 1860-1913 [LC,
SFL, TC]
British author
* Corvo, Baron
* Prospero and Caliban [joint
  pseudonym with Charles Harry
  Clinton Pirie-Gordon]
* Rolfe, Father

Rolfe, James 20th c. [BLB]
American politician
* Rolfe, Sunny Jim

Rolfe, Louise 20th c. [HPPN]
*Wife of American underworld figure,
Jack McGurn*
* [The] Blonde Alibi

Rolfe, Maro Orlando 1852-1925 [HPPN]
American author, journalist, historian
* [A] Civil War Captain
* [The] Detective Novelist
* Eflor, [Col.] Oram
* McHenry, [Col.] Oram R.
* [The] Novelist Detective
* [The] Old Detective
* O'Rolfe, M., the Irish Novelist
* Robie, Anne A.
* Rolfe, Sergeant?
* Rolker, A. W.?
* [The] Young Detective

Rolfe, Red
See Rolfe, Robert Abial

Rolfe, Robert Abial 1908-1969 [AS, BE,
PB]
American baseball player
* Rolfe, Red

Rolfe, Sergeant?
See Rolfe, Maro Orlando

Rolfe, Sunny Jim
See Rolfe, James

Rolker, A. W.?
See Rolfe, Maro Orlando

Rolla, Mlle.
See Rammelsberg, Kate

Rolle, Christian 1929- [CW]
West Indian poet
* Llero, Auguste

Rolle, Richard 1290?-1349 [SN, WBD]
British poet
* [The] Hermit of Hampole

Rolle, Tony 1960- [IBW]
American musician
* [The] Twentieth Century Mozart

[The] Roller Derby King
See O'Connell, Charlie

Rolleston, Thomas William Hazen
1857-? [PI]
Irish poet
* Kendal?

Rollicker, Harry
See Thackeray, William Makepeace

Rollin, Charles 1661-1741 [SN]
French educator
* [The] Bee of France
* Thucydides

Rollin, Frank A.
See Whipper, Frances E. Rollin

Rolling-Pin, Commodore
See Carter, John Hanson

Rollings, Red
See Rollings, William Russell

Rollings, William Russell 1904-1964
[BE]
American baseball player
* Rollings, Red

Rollington, Ralph
See Allingham, John W.

Rollins, Al
See Rollins, Elwin Ira

Rollins, Ellen Chapman [Hobbs]
1831-1881 [DNA, PA]
American author and historian
* Arr, E. H.

Rollins, Elwin Ira 1926- [CEI, FHE,
SMG]
Canadian-born hockey player
* Rollins, Al

Rollins, Glenn
See Olson, Robert G.

Rollins, Jack
See Rollins, Walter E.

Rollins, James Sidney 1812-1888
[HPPN]
American orator
* [The] Father of the University of
  Missouri
* [The] Silver Tongued Orator

Rollins, Kathleen 20th c. [EMD, WW]
Author
* Debrett, Hal [joint pseudonym with
  Davis Dresser]

Rollins, Montgomery 1867-1918 [DNA]
American author and banker
* Hay, Timothy

Rollins, Red
See Rollins, Richard John

Rollins, Richard John 1938- [BE]
American baseball player
* Rollins, Red

Rollins, Royce
See Pepper, Choral

Rollins, Sonny
See Rollins, Theodore Walter

Rollins, Theodore Walter 1929?- [DAM,
EJ, PMJ]
American jazz musician
* Rollins, Sonny

Rollins, Walter E. 1907-1973 [DAM]
American lyricist
* Rollins, Jack

Rollins, William 1897- [WW]
Author
* O'Connor, Stacy

Rollo [Rolf or Hrolf] 860?-931? [WBD]
Norse chieftain
* [The] Ganger [or Walker]

Rolls, Anthony
See Vulliamy, Colwyn Edward

Rolls, Charles Stewart 1877-1910
[HPPN]
British manufacturer and aviator
* [The] First English Victim

Rolls, M. M.   [PA]
Author
* His Mother

[The] Rolls Royce of Country Singers
See Jones, George

Rolo
See Greenhalgh, Fred

Rolph, C. H.
See Hewitt, Cecil Rolph

Rolph, James, Jr. [Jimmy] 1869-1934
[HPPN]
American shipowner, merchant, politician
* Our Jimmy
* Rolph, Sunny Jim

Rolph, Sunny Jim
See Rolph, James, Jr. [Jimmy]

Rolt, L. T. C.
See Rolt, Lionel Thomas Caswell

Rolt, Lionel Thomas Caswell 1910-1974
[HFF]
British author
* Rolt, L. T. C.

Rolvaag, O[le] E[dvaart]
See Morck, Paal

[The] Roly Poly Unionist
See Beck, David

Rolyat, Dan
See Taylor, Herbert

Rolyat, Jane
See McDougall, E. Jean [Taylor]

Roma, Caro 1866-1937 [HPPN]
American composer, author, singer
* Northey, Carrie

Roma, Clarice
See Hann, Roma

Roma, Lisa
See Trompeter, Lisa Roma

Romack, D. M.
See Hammack, Robert Dean Michael

[Le] Romain
See Dumont, Jean

[Le] Romain
See Hotteterre, Jacques

Romain, Rose
See Trebuchon, [Madame] Coutelier

Romain, Roy
See Romain, Royston

Romain, Royston 1918-   [SWI]
British swimmer
* Romain, Roy

Romaine, David
See Bohme, David M.

Romaine, John
See O'Reilly, [Sister] Amadeus

Romaine, Lawrence B. 1900-   [CAP]
American author
* [The] Weathercock

Romaine, Linton
See Lee, [Rev.] Albert

Romaine, Robert Dexter
See Payson, George

Romaine, [Rev.] William 1714-1795
[HPPN]
British clergyman
* [A] Late Commentator

Romains, Jules
See Farigoule, Louis

Roman, [Fra] ?-1571 [HPPN]
Italian monk and anthropologist
* [The] First Anthropologist

[The] Roman
See Dumont, Jean

[The] Roman
See Mignard, Pierre

[The] Roman
See Picart, Stephen [or Etienne]

[The] Roman
See Pippi de Gianuzzi, Giulio

[The] Roman
See Van Roomen, Adrian

[The] Roman Achilles
See Dentatus, Sicinius

[A] Roman Beau Brummel
See Petronius, Caius [or Gaius]

[A] Roman Catholic
See Ivers, Hardinge Furenzo

[A] Roman Catholic Clergyman
See Doyle, James Warren

[The] Roman Chaucer
See Ennius, Quintus

Roman, Daniel [David]
See Romanow, Daniel David

Roman, Eric
See Herzog, Eric

[The] Roman Hercules
See Commodus, Lucius Aelius

[The] Roman Hippocrates
See Celsus, Aulus Cornelius

Roman, Johan Helmich 1694-1758
[WBD]
Swedish musician and composer
* [The] Father of Swedish Music

Roman, Jose 1965?-   [NW 7-2-84]
American dancer
* Speedbreak, Mr.

[The] Roman King-Maker
See Ricimer

[The] Roman Roland
See Dentatus, Sicinius

[The] Roman Socrates
See Laelius, Gaius

[The] Roman Thucydides
See Sallust, Caius Crispus

Roman, William
See Wills, Garry

Romance, Franziska Magdalena
1830-1904 [HPPN]
Bohemian actress
* Janauschek, Fanny

Romance, Viviane
See Ortmanns, Pauline Ronacher

Romanette, Irmine 1895?-   [CW]
West Indian poet and author
* Miramant, Yves

Romani, Girolamo 1485-1566 [WBD]
Italian painter
* [Il] Romanino

[Il] Romanino
See Romani, Girolamo

Romanis, George Zackery
See Roumanis, George Zackery

Romanne-James, C.
See Romanne-James, Helena Constance

Romanne-James, Helena Constance
[LAO]
British author, editor, journalist
* Romanne-James, C.

Romano, Deane Louis 1927-   [HPPN]
American author
* Cairo, Jon

Romano, Deane Louis 1927-   [CA]
American author
* Cairo, Jon

Romano, Don
See Turner, Robert [Harry]

Romano, Emanuel
See Glicenstein, Emanuel

Romano, Giulio
See Gianuzzi, Giulio Pippi De'

Romano, Giulio
See Pippi de Gianuzzi, Giulio

Romano, Honey
See Romano, John Anthony

Romano, John Anthony 1934-   [BE]
American baseball player
* Romano, Honey

Romano, Paolo
See Alatri, Paolo

Romano, Sylvano 1882-1958 [HPPN]
American dancer
* Dale, Sylvano

Romanoff, [Prince] Alexander
See Sykowski, Abram

Romanoff, Alexander Nicholayevitch
1881-1945 [EMD, TC, WGT]
Russian-born British author
* Abdullah, Achmed
* Nadir, A. A.?

Romanoff, [Prince] Michael
See Gerguson, Harry

Romanoff, Mike
See Gerguson, Harry

Romanones, Countess of
See Griffith, Maria Aline

Romanov, Fedor Nikitich 1553?-1633
[WBD]
Patriarch of Moscow
* Philaret

Romanow, Daniel David 1921- [CA]
American author
* Roman, Daniel [David]

[The] Romantic Fiddler
See Trini, Anthony

[The] Romantic Revolutionary
See Mao Tse-tung

[The] Romantick Lady
See Burnett, Frances Eliza Hodgson

Romanus
See Lenihan, F. J.

Romanus, Agaedius 1247?-1316 [HPPN]
*Scholastic philosopher and general of the
Augustine order*
* Fundatissimus, Doctor

Romanus I ?-948 [HPPN]
Roman emperor
* Lecapenus

Romanus III 968?-1034 [HPPN]
Roman emperor
* Argyrus

Romanus IV ?-1071 [FFF, SN]
Byzantine emperor
* Diogenes

Romaunt, Christopher
See Bowman, J. M.

Romayne, Leicester
See Guimaraens, Manoel Pedro

Romberg, Sigmund 1887-1951 [HPPN]
Hungarian-American composer
* [The] American Successor to Johann
  Strauss

Romberger, Allen Isaiah 1927- [BE]
American baseball player
* Romberger, Dutch

Romberger, Dutch
See Romberger, Allen Isaiah

Rombro, Jacob 1858-1922 [DNA]
Russian-born author and labor leader
* Krantz, Philip

Rome, Alger [joint pseudonym with
Algirdas Jonas Budrys]
See Bixby, Jerome Lewis

Rome, Alger [joint pseudonym with
Jerome Lewis Bixby]
See Budrys, Algirdas Jonas

Rome, Anthony
See Albert, Marvin H.

Rome, Fred
See Toplis, Fred

Rome, Stewart
See Ryott, Septimus William

Romeike, Henry 1855-1903 [HPPN]
Russian-American businessman
* [The] Father of the News Clipping
  Service

Romeo
See Fellowes, George W.

Romeo
See Heffernan, Michael J.

Romeo
See Moore, John

Romeral
See Fernandez, Armando

Romero, Curro
See Romero Lopez, Francisco

Romero, Gary
See Catsos, Nicholas A.

Romero, Gerry
See Neyland, James [Elwyn]

Romero, Jose 1794-1858 [BI]
Chilean leader
* Zambo-Peluca

Romero Lopez, Francisco 1935- [GS]
Spanish bullfighter
* Romero, Curro

Romilly, [Sir] Samuel 1757-1818 [NPS]
British barrister and law reformer
* [The] Law's Expounder
* [The] State's Corrector

Rommel, Erwin 1891-1944 [CBS, CND]
German military leader
* Armored Knight
* [The] Desert Fox
* Gentleman of the Afrika Korps

Rommel, Marilyn Dayton 20th c.
[HPPN]
American journalist and author
* Rommel, Mimi

Rommel, Mimi
See Rommel, Marilyn Dayton

Romnes, Doc
See Romnes, Elwin N.

Romnes, Elwin N. 1909- [CEI, FHE,
HK]
American hockey player
* Romnes, Doc

Romney, A. B.
See Rambaut, A. Beatrice

Romney, Dick
See Romney, Ernest L.

Romney, Edana
See Rubenstein, Edana

Romney, Elwood 1911-1970 [BB]
American basketball player
* Romney, Woody

Romney, Ernest L. 1895-1969 [BB, FB]
American football and basketball coach
* Romney, Dick

Romney, George 1734-1802 [HPPN]
British painter
* [An] Eminent Painter

Romney, George 1907- [HPPN]
*American business executive and
politician*
* Romney, Lonesome George

Romney, Hugh 1936?- [HPPN]
American actor
* Gravy Wavy

Romney, Lonesome George
See Romney, George

Romney, Steve
See Bingley, David Ernest

Romney, Woody
See Romney, Elwood

Romo, Huevo
See Romo, Vicente Navarro

Romo, Vicente Navarro 1943- [BE,
SMG]
Mexican-born baseball player
* Romo, Huevo

Romoff, Woodrow Wilson 1918- [BEW]
American actor
* Romoff, Woody

Romoff, Woody
See Romoff, Woodrow Wilson

Romondt, Marcus
See Brandt, Johanna

Romp, Miss
See Bland, Dorothea

Romualdez, Benjamin 20th c.
*Filipino newspaper owner and provincial
governor*
* Romualdez, Kokoy

Romualdez, Kokoy
See Romualdez, Benjamin

Romulo, Carlos Pena 1899- [HPPN]
*Philippine army officer, educator,
journalist, statesman*
* [The] Defender of Freedom
* [The] Voice of Freedom

[The] Romulus of Brandenburg
See Henry I [or Heinrich]

Rona Rat
See Burstein, Rona

Rona, Victor 1936?-
Hungarian dancer
* [The] Hungarian Rhapsody

Ronald, David William 1937- [CA]
Scottish-born writer
* Williams, D.

Ronald, E. B.
See Barker, Ronald Ernest

Ronald, [Sir] Landon
See Russell, Landon R.

Ronald, Mary
See Arnold, Augusta [Foote]

Ronald the Right
See Reagan, Ronald Wilson

Ronalds, Danby
See Frankau, Ronald

Ronalds, Mary Teresa 1946- [IAW]
British author
* Sheridan, Teresa

Ronan, Erskine 20th c. [FHE]
Canadian hockey player
* Ronan, Skene

Ronan, Georgia
See Crampton, Georgia Ronan

Ronan, Skene
See Ronan, Erskine

Ronayne, Dominick 1770?-1835 [PI]
Irish poet and barrister
* Figaro in Dublin

Roncalli, Angelo Giuseppe 1881-1963
[CBS]
Pope
* John XXIII

[Le] Rondie
See Gaillard, Angier

Rondo, Father
See Davaux, Jean Baptiste

Ronet, E. ?-1972 [FIR]
French actress
* De Breteuil, Gilberte

Roney, Ruth Anne
See McMullin, Ruth R[oney]

Ronge [or Ronger], Florimond 1825-1892
[HPPN, WBD]
French composer
* [The] Father of Opera Bouffe
* Herve

Ronken, Harriet
See Lynton, Harriet Ronken

Ronn, Yuval 20th c. [SFL]
Author
* Ionel

Ronns, Edward
See Aarons, Edward S[idney]

[El] Ronquillo [The Raucous One]
See Lopez, Antonio

Ronquillo [Little Hoarse One]
See Pelayo, Luis

Ronsard, Pierre de 1524-1585 [DNNS,
NPS, RH, SN]
French poet
* [The] Apollo of the Fountain of
Muses
* [L']Apollon de la Source des Muses
[Apollo of the Fountain of Muses]
* [The] First Lyrist of France
* [The] French Chaucer
* [The] French Poet
* [The] Horace of France
* [The] King of Poets

Ronsard, Pierre de (cont.)
* [The] Petrarch of France
* [The] Pindar of France
* [The] Poet of France
* [The] Poet of Kings
* [The] Poet of the Future
* [Le] Poete des Rois
* [The] Prince of the Ode

Ronsin, Jean
See Rodinson, Maxime

Ronsman, M. M.
See Nowak, Mariette

Rood, Jack
See Van Horn, Dale R.

Rood, Ogden Nicholas 1831-1902
[HPPN]
American physicist and researcher
* [The] Father of American
Experimental Physics

Rooke, Daphne [Marie] 1914- [CA,
SAT]
South African-born author
* Pointon, Robert

Rooke, Harvard B.
See Herford, [Rev.] Brooke

Rooke, John 1781-1856 [HPPN]
British author
* Cumbriensis

Rooke, Valentine
See Brooke, Valentine

Rooks, George Brinton McClellan
See Ruckser, George Brinton McClellan

Rooney, Alderman
See Townley, Daniel O'Connell

Rooney, Arthur J. 1901- [BBH]
*American football team owner and
administrator*
* [The] Grand Old Man

Rooney, Barney
See Garvie, William

Rooney, Cobbs
See Rooney, Harry

Rooney, Harry 20th c. [EF]
American football player
* Rooney, Cobbs

Rooney, M. W. 19th c. [HFN]
Irish author and bookseller
* M. W. R.

Rooney, Mickey
See Yule, Joe, Jr.

Rooney, Pat
See Ratsch, Fred E.

Rooney, Pat, II 1880-1962 [HPPN]
American dancer and entertainer
* Vaudeville's Ageless Song and Dance
Man

Rooney, William 1873-1901 [PI]
Irish poet
* Ballinascorney
* Baltrasna

Rooney, William (cont.)
* Feltrim
* Fiachra, Hi
* Killester
* Knocksedan
* Laire, Criad
* Martin, Shel
* Muinntire, Fear na
* Ruadh, Sliabh
* Smoil, Glenn na

Roope, Cyril
See Roope, Graham Richard James

Roope, Graham Richard James 1946-
[DC]
British cricketer
* Roope, Cyril

Roos, Audrey [Kelley] 1912- [WW]
American author
* Kelley, Audrey
* Roos, Kelley [joint pseudonym with
William Roos]

Roos, Hans
See Meissner, Hans-Otto

Roos, Kelley [joint pseudonym with
William Roos]
See Roos, Audrey [Kelley]

Roos, Kelley [joint pseudonym with
Audrey (Kelley) Roos]
See Roos, William

Roos, Philipp Peter 1655?-1706 [HPPN]
German-born painter
* Mercurius
* Rosa di Tivoli

Roos, William 1911- [TCCM, WW]
American author
* Rand, William
* Roos, Kelley [joint pseudonym with
Audrey (Kelley) Roos]

Roosevelt, Babs
See Roosevelt, [Anna] Eleanor

Roosevelt, Blanche
See Maccheta, Blanche Roosevelt
[Tucker]

Roosevelt, Buddy
See Sanderson, Kent

Roosevelt, [Anna] Eleanor 1884-1962
[HPPN, NW 10-15-84]
*American lecturer, writer, and wife of
President Franklin Roosevelt*
* [The] Assistant President
* E. R.
* First Lady of the World
* Roosevelt, Babs
* Roosevelt, Granny
* [The] World's Most Admired Woman

Roosevelt, Franklin Delano 1882-1945
[CND, FAP, HPPN]
American president
* Admiral Q [code name used during
World War II]
* [The] Boss
* Cap'n
* Cargo [[code name used during World
War II]]

Roosevelt, Franklin Delano (cont.)
* Don Quixote [[code name used during World War II]]
* F. D. R.
* [The] Houdini in the White House
* King Franklin
* Miss Kimiko [code name used by Japanese during World War II]
* [The] New Dealer
* Sawbuck [[code name used during World War II]]
* [The] Sphinx
* [The] Squire of Hyde Park
* That Man in the White House

Roosevelt, Granny
See Roosevelt, [Anna] Eleanor

Roosevelt, Haroun al-
See Roosevelt, Theodore [Teddy]

Roosevelt, James 1907- [HPPN]
Eldest son of American president, Franklin Delano Roosevelt
* [The] Crown Prince of the New Deal
* Modern Mercury
* Son Jimmy

Roosevelt, Little Miss
See Longworth, Alice Lee Roosevelt

Roosevelt, Quentin 1897-1918 [HPPN]
American aviator and son of President Theodore Roosevelt
* Quentin the Eagle

Roosevelt, Robert Barnwell 1829-1906 [FFF, PA]
American author and politician
* Barnwell
* Zell, Ira

Roosevelt, Teedie
See Roosevelt, Theodore [Teddy]

Roosevelt, Theodore [Teddy] 1858-1919 [DNNS, FAP, HPPN]
American president
* [The] Bronco Buster
* [The] Bull Moose
* [The] Driving Force
* [The] Dynamo of Power
* Four Eyed Tenderfoot
* Four Eyes
* [The] Great White Chief
* [The] Happy Warrior
* [The] Hero of San Juan Hill
* [The] Man on Horseback
* [The] Man Who Would Be King
* [The] Meddler
* [The] Old Lion
* Our Teddy
* Roosevelt, Haroun al-
* Roosevelt, Teedie
* [The] Rough Rider
* [The] Sage of Princeton
* T. R.
* Teddy the First
* Telescope Teddy
* Terrible Teddy
* Theodore the Meddler
* Toothful Teddy
* [The] Trust Buster
* [The] Trust Busting President
* [The] Trust Slayer
* [The] Typical American

Roosevelt's Shadow
See Reilly, Michael Francis

Rooster
See Macropodio, Gino

Root Boy Slim
See Mackenzie, Foster, III

Root, Charles Henry 1899-1970 [BE, DGS, PB]
American baseball player
* Root, Chinski

Root, Chinski
See Root, Charles Henry

Root, Elihu 1845-1937 [HPPN]
American attorney and statesman
* [The] Internationalist

Root, Henry
See Donaldson, William

Root, Jack
See Ruthaly, Janos

Root of the Matter, Lord
See Hopkins, Harry Lloyd

Roote, Mike
See Fleischer, Leonore

Rootes, [Sir] William Edward 1894- [HPPN]
British manufacturer
* [The] Father of the Supercharger

[The] Rootin', Tootin', Ridin' Romeo of the Screen
See Lucid, Pate

[The] Rope
See Boyd, Robert Richard

[The] Rope Dancer
See De Grantmesnil, Yvo

Roper, Daniel Calhoun 1867-1943 [HPPN]
American attorney and politician
* [The] Chief Executioner

Roper, Elmo 1901-1971 [HPPN]
American public opinion surveyor and analyst
* [The] Opinion Forecaster

Roper, Laura Wood 1911- [CA, WD]
American author
* Wood, Laura N[ewbold]

Roper, Loring
See Colvin, Fred Herbert

Roper, Moses 19th c. [HPPN]
American slave
* [The] Chronic Runaway

Roper, Neil Campbell Ommanney 1941- [IAW]
Scottish-born poet and translator
* Omedy, Eugene

Roper, Ronnalie J. 1936- [CA]
American author
* Howard, Ronnalie Roper

Roper, Susan Bonthron 1948- [CA]
American author
* Brand, Susan

Roper, William L[eon] 1897- [CA]
American author
* Fry, David
* Sparkman, William

Ropes, Arthur Reed 1859-1933 [EMT]
British lyricist and librettist
* Ross, Adrian

Ropshin, V.
See Savinkov, Boris Viktorovich

Roquero Dominguez, Juan 1825-1885 [CW]
Cuban playwright
* Arrugado

Roques, Jeanne 1889-1957 [SC]
French actress and director
* Musidora

Roques, Maurice Jacques 1761-1841 [WBD]
French intelligence agent
* Montgaillard, Comte de

Rorvik, David M[ichael] 1946- [CA]
American author
* Davidson, Michael

Ros, Amanda McKittrick
See McKittrick, Anna Margaret

Rosa
See Jeffrey, Rosa Vertner

Rosa, Carl August Nicholas
See Rose, Carl August Nicholas

Rosa di Tivoli
See Roos, Philipp Peter

Rosa di Tivoli
See Ross, Philipp Peter

Rosa, Patti
See Buckingham, Jessie

Rosa, Salvator 1615-1673 [HN, WBD]
Italian painter and poet
* Salvatoriello
* [The] Shakespeare of Painting

Rosalind
See Daniel, Rosa

Rosalind
See Davis, Rosalind

Rosanov [or Rozanov?], Mikhail Grigorievich 1888-1938 [CD, LAO]
Russian author
* Ognev [or Ognyov?], N[ikolai]

Rosar, Buddy
See Rosar, Warren Vincent

Rosar, Warren Vincent 1914-1979 [BE, PB]
American baseball player
* Rosar, Buddy

Rosario, Angel Ramon 1945- [BE]
Puerto Rican-born baseball player
* Rosario, Jimmy

Rosario, Jimmy
See Rosario, Angel Ramon

Rosas, Julio
See Puig y de la Puente, Francisco

Rosavella
See Tucker, Blanch

Rosay, Francoise
See Bandy De Naleche, Francoise

Rosca, the Jester
See Marinoni, Rosa Zagnoni

Roscelin de Compiegne
See Roscellinus [or Rucelinus]

Roscellinus [or Rucelinus] 12th c.
[WBD]
Philosopher
* Roscelin de Compiegne

Roschildt, Alfred
See Sykowski, Abram

Roscius
See Garrick, David

Roscius Britannicus
See Betterton, Thomas

Roscius Britannicus
See Garrick, David

Roscius Britannicus
See Tarlton, Richard

[The] Roscius of England
See Betterton, Thomas

[The] Roscius of England
See Garrick, David

[The] Roscius of France
See Boyron, Michel [or Michael]

[The] Roscius of the Bowery
See Forrest, Edwin

Roscius, Quintus 1st c. BC [HPPN, SN]
Roman actor
* [The] Greatest of the Roman Comic
Actors
* [The] Jewel

Roscoe, Charles
See Rowland, Donald Sydney

Roscoe, Deane
See Yates, Frederic B.

Roscoe, John 1921- [WW]
Author
* Roscoe, Mike [joint pseudonym with
Michael Ruso]

Roscoe, Mike [joint pseudonym with
Michael Ruso]
See Roscoe, John

Roscoe, Mike [joint pseudonym with
John Roscoe]
See Ruso, Michael

[The] Roscoe of Cork
See Roche, James

Roscoe, William 1753-1831 [NPS]
Author and politician
* [The] Gillyflower of Liverpool

[The] Roscommon Giant
See Coffey, Jim

Rosdahl, Harrison 20th c. [EF]
American football player
* Rosdahl, Hatch

Rosdahl, Hatch
See Rosdahl, Harrison

Rose
See Kirwan, Rose

[The] Rose
See Margaret

[The] Rose
See Rosenman, Samuel Irving

[The] Rose
See Rozema, David Scott [Dave]

Rose, A. McGregor 1846-1898 [HPPN]
Scottish-Canadian journalist
* Gordon, A. M. R.

Rose, A. McGregor
See Gordon, Alexander McGregor Rose

Rose, A. N. Mount
See Japp, Alexander Hay

Rose, Alex
See Royz, Olesh

Rose, Alfred 20th c.
Author
* Reade, Rolf S.

Rose, Alvin Emanuel 20th c. [WW]
Author
* Pruitt, Alan

Rose, Anna Perrott
See Wright, Anna [Maria Louisa
Perrott] Rose

Rose, Arthur 1890-1968 [THR]
British actor
* Rose, Clarkson

Rose, Bald Jack
See Rosenzweig, Jacob

Rose, Billiard Ball Jack
See Rosenzweig, Jacob

Rose, Billy
See Rosenberg, William Samuel

Rose, Camille Davied 1893- [CAP]
American writer and editor
* Davied, Camille

Rose, Carl 1903-1971 [SAT]
American cartoonist and illustrator
* Cros, Earl

Rose, Carl August Nicholas 1843-1889
[WBD]
German operatic impresario
* Rosa, Carl August Nicholas

Rose, Chappie
See Rose, H. Chapman

Rose, Charles E. 1860-? [WWL]
British author
* Eddy, Charles

Rose, Clarkson
See Rose, Arthur

Rose, Della
See Bullion, Laura

Rose, [Lady] Dorothy Violet Frederica
1910- [AW]
British-born author and journalist
* Carrington, Dorothy

Rose, Edward Hampden ?-1810 [PI]
Irish poet
* [A] Foremast Man

Rose, Elizabeth Jane 1933- [BI]
British author
* Elizabeth

Rose, Florella
See Carlson, Vada F.

Rose, Francis [Frank]
See Fearn, John Russell

Rose, Fred 1897-1954 [ECM]
American songwriter and music publisher
* Dawson, Bart
* Jenkins, Floyd

Rose, Fred
See Rosenberg, Fred

Rose, Frederick W. 1849-? [WWL]
British author
* Martius

Rose, George 1817-1882 [DEL, FFF,
HPPN, RH]
British author
* Brown, Mrs.
* Sketchley, Arthur

Rose, H. Chapman 1907- [HPPN]
American attorney and politician
* Rose, Chappie

Rose, Hell Roarin'
See Rose, William Pinkney

Rose, Hilary
See MacKinnon, Charles Roy

Rose, Ian 1920- [WD]
Canadian physician and author
* Rose, Robert

Rose, Irving
See Browne, Ernest D.

Rose, J. H.
See Rose, John Holland

Rose, Jack 20th c. [BLB]
American underworld figure
* Billiard Ball Jack

Rose, Jack 20th c. [GW]
American rodeo performer
* Rose, Nevada Jack

Rose, Jennifer
See Weber, Nancy

Rose, John Holland 1855-1942 [LC]
British author and educator
* Rose, J. H.

Rose, Julian 1879-1935 [BMH]
American comedian
* Our Hebrew Friend

Rose, Kathleen Mary 1892?-1975 [FIR]
Entertainer
* Delores

Rose, Laurence F.
See Fearn, John Russell

Rose, Marcia [joint pseudonym with Rose Novak]
See Kamien, Marcia

Rose, Marcia [joint pseudonym with Marcia Kamien]
See Novak, Rose

Rose, Marie
See Brady, Alice

Rose Marie
See Carley, Rose Marie

Rose Marie
See Mazeppa, Rose Marie

Rose, Martha Emily [Parmelee] 1834-1923 [DNA]
American author
* Lee, Charles C.

Rose, Mary Kay 20th c. [HPPN]
American entertainer
* Lynn, Tracy

Rose, Mauri 1906- [HPPN]
American auto racer
* [The] Man With the Mustache
* [The] Top Wheel at the Brickyard

Rose, Morris
See Stacher, Joseph

Rose, [Iain] Murray 1939- [HPPN]
British swimmer
* [The] Undisputed Leader in Distance Freestyle Swimming

Rose, Nera
See Marion, Zelia

Rose, Nevada Jack
See Rose, Jack

[La] Rose Noire de Paris [The Black Rose of Paris]
See Landreaux, Elizabeth Mary

Rose [or Rosa] of Lima
See Flores, Isabel

[The] Rose of Tacloban
See Marcos, Imelda

Rose of the Cimarron
See Dunn, Rose

Rose of the Mountains
See Maphis, Rose Lee

[The] Rose of York
See Elizabeth

Rose, Pamela
See Koevoets, Pamela

Rose, Pete[r Edward] 1941- [BE, BI, PB]
American baseball player
* Hustle, Charlie

Rose, Philip
See Rosenberg, Philip

Rose, Phyllis
See Hoge, Phyllis

Rose, Polly
See Gottlieb, Polly Rose

Rose, Robert
See Rose, Ian

Rose, Upton
See Selz, Ralph Jerome Von Braun

Rose, Wendy 1948- [CA, SAT]
American author and illustrator
* Edwards, Bronwen Elizabeth
* Khanshendel, Chiron

Rose, William 1906- [HPPN]
American banker
* [The] Generous Lender

Rose, William Pinkney 19th c. [HPPN]
American army officer
* Rose, Hell Roarin'

Rose, William Stewart 1775-1843 [HPPN]
British scholar and translator
* One of the Last Century

Rose-Price, Dennistoun John Franklyn 1915-1973 [BEW, FC, OCF]
British actor
* Price, Dennis

Roseau, Emie
See Reed, Emeline

Roseau, Marie
See Reed, Mary J.

Rosebery, Lilian
See Routledge, Lilian

Roseboro, Gabby
See Roseboro, John H.

Roseboro, John H. 1933- [PB]
American baseball player
* Roseboro, Gabby

Rosebrough, Eli E. 19th c. [BE]
American baseball player
* Rosebrough, Zeke

Rosebrough, Zeke
See Rosebrough, Eli E.

Rosecrans, William Starke 1819-1898 [DNNS, SN]
American army officer
* Old Rosey
* Rosey

Rosedale, Ivan
See Ditmas, Francis Ivan Leslie

Rosedale, Valerie
See Harron, Don[ald]

Rosegger, P. K.
See Rosegger, Petri Kettenfeier

Rosegger, Peter
See Rosegger, Petri Kettenfeier

Rosegger, Petri Kettenfeier 1843-1918 [HPPN, WBD]
Austrian poet and author
* Kettenfeier, Petri
* Malser, Hans
* P. K.
* Rosegger, P. K.
* Rosegger, Peter

Roselinda
See White, Rose C. [King]

Roselle, Agnes 1870-1948 [BEW]
Canadian-born actress
* Knott, Roselle

Roselle, Amy
See Dacre, Mrs. Arthur

Roseller, David
See Timms, Edward Vivian

Roselli, John
See Sacco, Fillippo

Rosema, Rocky
See Rosema, Roger

Rosema, Roger 20th c. [EF]
American football player
* Rosema, Rocky

Roseman, Chief
See Roseman, James J.

Roseman, James J. 1856-? [BE, EJS]
American baseball player and manager
* Roseman, Chief

Rosemary
See Watson, Margaret

Rosemeyer, Bernd 1909-1938 [EAR]
German auto racer
* [Der] Nebelmeister

Rosemond, Manning Wyllard, Jr. 1918- [BA]
American dentist
* Rosemond, Max

Rosemond, Max
See Rosemond, Manning Wyllard, Jr.

Rosemonde
See Rostand, Louise Rose Etiennette

Rosen, Albert Leonard 1925- [BE, EJS, PB]
American baseball player
* Rosen, Flip

Rosen, Doc
See Stacher, Joseph

Rosen, Flip
See Rosen, Albert Leonard

Rosen, Frenchy
See Rosen, William

Rosen, Goodwin George 1912?- [BE, EJS]
Canadian-born baseball player
* Rosen, Goody

Rosen, Goody
See Rosen, Goodwin George

Rosen, Harry
See Siegel, Benjamin

Rosen, [Captain] James 1894?-
Actor
* [The] King of the Midgets

Rosen, Joseph
See Stacher, Joseph

Rosen, Julius
See Duffek, Nikolaus

Rosen, Lew
See Rosenthal, Lewis

Rosen, Martin Meyer
See Rosen, Moishe

Rosen, Max
See Rosenzweig, Maxie

Rosen, Michael 1946- [AW]
British author
* [The] Landgrave of Hesse

Rosen, Moishe 1932- [CA]
American clergyman and author
* Rosen, Martin Meyer

Rosen, Nig
See Siegel, Benjamin

Rosen, Nig
See Stromberg, Harry

Rosen, Stanley 20th c. [EJS]
American football player
* Rosen, Tex

Rosen, Tex
See Rosen, Stanley

Rosen, William 1882-1961 [EJS]
American horse trainer
* Rosen, Frenchy

Rosenbach, A. S.
See Rosenbach, Abraham Simon Wolf

Rosenbach, Abraham Simon Wolf
1876-1952 [LC]
American rare book dealer and author
* Rosenbach, A. S.

Rosenbaum, Borge 1909- [BBD, HPPN]
Danish-born pianist
* Borge, Victor
* [The] Unmelancholy Dane

Rosenbaum, Edward 20th c. [PHM]
American underworld figure
* Rosenbaum, Lucky Eddie

Rosenbaum, Hercel 1902-1937 [JL]
Polish author
* Drzewiecki, Henryk

Rosenbaum, Lucky Eddie
See Rosenbaum, Edward

Rosenberg, Aaron 20th c.
American football player
* Rosenberg, Rosy

Rosenberg, Abraham 1865-1944 [HPPN]
American co-founder of dried fruit packing concern
* Mr. Abe

Rosenberg, Alexander 20th c. [EJS]
American basketball player
* Rosenberg, Petey

Rosenberg, Ben 1885?-1983 [TI 1-24-83]
Russian-born painter
* Benn, Ben

Rosenberg, Charles G. 19th c. [PA]
Author
* Q.

Rosenberg, Charley Phil
See Green, Charles

Rosenberg, Elinor Blaisdell 1904-
[WGT]
American author
* Blaisdell, Anne
* Blaisdell, Elinor

Rosenberg, Ethel [Clifford] [CA, SAT]
American author
* Clifford, Eth
* Penn, Ruth Bonn

Rosenberg, Fred 20th c. [EE]
Polish-born intelligence agent for Russia
* Rose, Fred

Rosenberg, George 1864-1936 [ASC]
German-born composer
* Rosey, George

Rosenberg, Gill
See Koestler, Gisela Maria

Rosenberg, Harry 1903- [FC]
American singer
* [The] Street Singer
* Tracy, Arthur

Rosenberg, Ina 1937- [FC]
American actress
* Balin, Ina

Rosenberg, Jerold 1926-1955 [BEW, EMT]
American composer and lyricist
* Ross, Jerry

Rosenberg, John Paul [Jack] 1935-
[EOP, NAD]
American educator and developer of "est" therapy
* Erhard, Werner
* Frost, Jack

Rosenberg, Lefty Louis
See Rosenberg, Louis

Rosenberg, Leon Nikolaevich 1867-1924
[WBD]
Russian painter
* Bakst, Leon Nikolaevich

Rosenberg, Lester 1924- [TR]
American actor
* Rawlins, Lester

Rosenberg, Louis 20th c. [BLB]
American underworld figure
* Rosenberg, Lefty Louis

Rosenberg, Max 1867-1945 [HPPN]
American co-founder of dried fruit packing concern
* Mr. Max

Rosenberg, Michael 1943?- [BI]
American author
* Meeropol, Michael

Rosenberg, Nancy Sherman 1931- [CA, SAT]
American author
* Sherman, Nancy

Rosenberg, Petey
See Rosenberg, Alexander

Rosenberg, Philip 1921- [BEW, TR]
American producer
* Rose, Philip

Rosenberg, Robert 1948?- [BI, HPPN]
American educator
* Meeropol, Robert [or Robbie]

Rosenberg, Rosy
See Rosenberg, Aaron

Rosenberg, Seymour I. 1911- [HPPN]
American attorney and army officer
* Rosenberg, Si

Rosenberg, Si
See Rosenberg, Seymour I.

Rosenberg, William Samuel 1899-1966
[BEW, EMT, HPPN]
American producer and lyricist
* [The] Basement Barnum
* Rose, Billy

Rosenblatt, Fred 1914- [CA]
American author
* Dreyfus, Fred

Rosenblatt, Martin 1920- [FC]
Polish-American actor
* Martin, Ross

Rosenblatt, Richard Andrew 1925-
[BEW]
American stage manager, actor, director
* Grayson, Richard
* Martin, Richard A.

Rosenbloom, Max 1904-1956 [BX, EJS, RBE]
American boxer
* Rosenbloom, Slapsie Maxie

Rosenbloom, Slapsie Maxie
See Rosenbloom, Max

Rosenblum, Lawrence 1908- [CAP, WW]
American author
* Knight, Adam
* Lariar, Lawrence
* Lawrence, Michael
* Stark, Michael

Rosenblum, Sigmund G. 1874-? [JL]
Russian-born intelligence agent
* Reilly, Sidney

Rosenbusch, Harry
See Rosenbusch, Karl Heinrich Ferdinand

Rosenbusch, Karl Heinrich Ferdinand 1836-1914 [WBD]
German geologist
* Rosenbusch, Harry

Rosenfeld, Alexander Friedrich Ladislaus 1872-1945 [WBD]
Slavonian-born author and journalist
* Roda Roda, Alexander Friedrich Ladislaus

Rosenfeld, Beansie
See Bien, Samuel

Rosenfeld, Bobbie
See Rosenfeld, Fanny

Rosenfeld, Fanny 1903-1969 [BI, EJS]
Canadian track and field athlete
* Rosenfeld, Bobbie

Rosenfeld, Friedrich 1902- [IAW]
Austrian-born author
* Feld

Rosenfeld, Henry 1918?-
American writer
* Henry, Gig

Rosenfeld, Lev Borisovich 1883-1936 [JL, WBD]
Russian Communist leader
* Kamenev, Lev Borisovich

Rosenfeld, Louis Zara 1910- [NAA]
American author
* Zara, Louis

Rosenfeld, Lulla 1914- [CA]
American actress and author
* Adler, Lulla

Rosenfeld, Monroe H. 1861-1918 [DAM]
American composer
* Belasco, F.

Rosenfeld, Otto 1884-1939 [JL]
Austrian-born psychologist
* Rank, Otto

Rosenfeld, Sigmund
See Bien, Samuel

Rosenfelder, Charles H. 1947- [FB]
American football player
* Rosenfelder, Rosey

Rosenfelder, Rosey
See Rosenfelder, Charles H.

Rosenfield, Judith 1943- [CA]
American author
* Arcana, Judith

Rosenfield, Morris
See Alter, Moshe Jacob

Rosengren, Frank Duane 1926- [BEW]
American playwright
* Duane, Frank

Rosenheimer, Arthur 1916- [CA]
American author
* Knight, Arthur

[The] Rosenkavalier of Science
See Goethe, Johann Wolfgang von

Rosenkrantz, Linda 1934- [CA]
American author and columnist
* Damiano, Laila

Rosenkreutz, Christian 15th c. [HPPN]
Austrian secret society founder
* [The] Father of the Rosicrucians

Rosenman, Samuel Irving 1896- [HPPN]
American jurist and advisor to President Franklin Roosevelt
* [The] Rose
* Sammy the Rose

Rosenmeyer, Alan Otto 1921- [CA]
German-born American psychologist and author
* Ross, Alan O[tto]

Rosenow, August 20th c. [EF]
American football player
* Rosenow, Gus

Rosenow, Gus
See Rosenow, August

Rosenstein, Chicken Moe
See Rosenstein, Moses

Rosenstein, Moses 20th c. [HPPN]
American poultry dealer and racketeer
* Rosenstein, Chicken Moe

Rosenstock, Sami 1896-1963 [EWL, TCL]
Rumanian-born French poet and author
* Tzara, Tristan

Rosenthal, Alan 1936- [CA]
British-born author, producer, director
* Talkin, Gil

Rosenthal, Andrew 20th c. [CA]
Author
* Warren, Andrew [joint pseudonym with Warren (Stanley) Tute]

Rosenthal, Beansie
See Rosenthal, Herman

Rosenthal, Carolyn 20th c. [BEW]
American lyricist
* Leigh, Carolyn

Rosenthal, Elinor Marilyn 1932- [OP]
American opera singer
* Ross, Elinor

Rosenthal, Eugenie 1912- [BEW]
American lighting and scenic designer
* Rosenthal, Jean

Rosenthal, Frank 20th c. [TI 10-24-83]
American underworld figure
* Rosenthal, Lefty

Rosenthal, Hard Luck Herman
See Rosenthal, Herman

Rosenthal, Herman ?-1912 [BLB, HPPN]
American gambler
* Rosenthal, Beansie
* Rosenthal, Hard Luck Herman

Rosenthal, J. J. 1863?-1923 [HPPN]
American theatrical manager and talent representative
* Rosenthal, Jake

Rosenthal, Jack 1902?-1939 [BEW]
American comedian
* Osterman, Jack

Rosenthal, Jake
See Rosenthal, J. J.

Rosenthal, Jean
See Rosenthal, Eugenie

Rosenthal, Judi 1934- [CA]
American author
* K-Turkel, Judi
* Kesselman, Judi R.
* Kesselman-Turkel, Judi
* Turkel, Pauline

Rosenthal, Lefty
See Rosenthal, Frank

Rosenthal, Lewis 1856-1909 [DNA]
American journalist
* Rosen, Lew

Rosenthal, Linda 20th c.
American ballerina
* Merrill, Linda

Rosenthal, Lyova Haskell 1929- [BEW, FC, IPA]
American actress
* Grant, Lee

Rosenthal, M. L.
See Rosenthal, Macha Louis

Rosenthal, Macha Louis 1917- [WYA]
American author
* Rosenthal, M. L.

Rosenthal, Richard A. 1925- [CA, WW]
American author
* Richards, Allen

Rosenus, Alan [Harvey] 1940- [CA]
American author
* Middlebrook, David

Rosenzweig, Harry 20th c.
American politician
* [The] Diamond Man

Rosenzweig, Jacob 1875?-1947 [HPPN]
American gambler, clergyman, caterer
* Rose, Bald Jack
* Rose, Billiard Ball Jack

Rosenzweig, Maxie 20th c. [PAC]
American musician
* Rosen, Max

Roser, Bunny
See Roser, John Joseph

Roser, Emerson Corey 1918- [BE]
American baseball player
* Roser, Steve

Roser, John Joseph 1901- [BE]
American baseball player
* Roser, Bunny

Roser, Steve
See Roser, Emerson Corey

Rose's Lobbygow
See Schepps, Sam[uel]

Roset, Hipponax
See Paxton, Joseph Rupert

Rosetti, Francesco Antonio
See Roessler, Franz Anton

Rosevear, John 1936- [CA]
American author
* Circus, Jim

Rosewall, James 1797-1875 [HPPN]
British sailor
* Nauticus, Penzance

Rosewall, Kenneth Robert 1934-
Australian tennis player
* [The] Iron Man
* Rosewall, Muscles

Rosewall, Muscles
See Rosewall, Kenneth Robert

Rosewater, Frank 1856-? [SFL, WGT]
American author
* Mayoe, Franklin and Marian

Rosewell, [Rev.] Samuel 1679-1722
[HPPN]
British clergyman
* S. R.

Rosey
See Rosecrans, William Starke

Rosey, George
See Rosenberg, George

Roshanara
See Craddock, Olive

Rosi, Paolo 1928- [BX]
Italian-born boxer
* Rosi, Paulo

Rosi, Paulo
See Rosi, Paolo

Rosicrucian
See Frothingham, Washington

[A] Rosicrucian
See Randolph, Paschal Beverley

Rosicrucius
See Dibdin, Thomas Frognall

Rosie
See Swoyer, Anna Myrtle

Rosimond
See La Roze, Claude

Rosing, Bodil
See Hammerich, Bodil

Rosinski, Joseph 1929?-1982 [FIR]
Radio personality and actor
* Raymond, Joe

Rosio, Giovanni Vittorio 1577-1647
[PA]
Author
* Erythroeus, James Ficias

Rosius
See Koes, Friedrick

Roskam, Karel Lodewijk 1931- [IAW]
Dutch author
* Dutchman, Kalamu

Rosko, Emperor
See Pasternak, Mike

Rosko, [Le] President
See Pasternak, Mike

Roskolenko, Harry 1907-1980 [CA]
American author
* Ross, Colin

Roslavleva, Natalia
See Rene, Natalia

Roslyn, Guy
See Hatton, Joshua

Rosmer, Ernst
See Bernstein, Elsa

Rosmer, Milton
See Lunt, Arthur Milton

Rosmini-Serbati, Antonio 1797-1855
[DEP]
Italian philosopher
* [The] Italian Froebel

Rosmond, Babette 1921- [CA]
American author
* Arroway, Francis M.
* Campion, Rosamond

Rosner, Johnny 1895-1974 [EJS, RBE]
American boxer
* Rosner, Young

Rosner, Young
See Rosner, Johnny

Rosny, J. H. [joint pseudonym with
Seraphin Justin Francois Boex]
See Boex, Joseph-Henri Honore

Rosny, J. H. [joint pseudonym with
Joseph-Henri Honore Boex]
See Boex, Seraphin Justin Francois

Rosny aine, J. H.
See Boex, Joseph-Henri Honore

Rosny jeune, J. H.
See Boex, Seraphin Justin Francois

Rospigliosi, Giulio 1600-1669 [WBD]
Pope
* Clement IX

Rosquellas, Adolfo 1900- [HPPN]
*Argentine-American orchestra leader,
violinist, composer*
* Pancho

Ross, Adrian
See Ropes, Arthur Reed

Ross, Aircraftsman
See Lawrence, Thomas Edward

Ross, Alan O[tto]
See Rosenmeyer, Alan Otto

Ross, Albert
See Goldstein, Arthur D[avid]

Ross, Albert
See Porter, Linn Boyd

Ross, Albert Henry 1891- [SFL, WGT]
Author
* Morison, Frank

Ross, Alfred 1907?- [HPPN]
American musician
* America's Best Known Blood Donor

Ross, Allan
See Warwick, Alan Ross

Ross, Angus
See Giggal, Kenneth

Ross, Ann 1813-1895 [BI]
American nun
* Ross, [Mother] Xavier

Ross, Annie
See Short, Annabelle

Ross, Barnaby [joint pseudonym with
Daniel Nathan]
See Lepofsky, Manfred

Ross, Barnaby [joint pseudonym with
Manfred Lepofsky]
See Nathan, Daniel

Ross, Barney
See Rasofsky, Barnet David

Ross, Betsy Griscom 1752-1836 [HPPN]
American pioneer
* Claypool, Elizabeth
* Grimke, Elizabeth
* [The] Last of Philadelphia's Free
Quakers

Ross, Betty 1880-1947 [SC]
American actress
* Clarke, Betty Ross

Ross, Beverly Morgan 1914- [CWG,
DAM]
American country-western performer
* Ross, Buddy

Ross, Bill
See Rabinowitz, William Edward

Ross, Bitter Herb
See Ross, Herbert George

Ross, Buck
See Ross, Lee Ravon

Ross, Buddy
See Ross, Beverly Morgan

Ross, Buster
See Ross, Chester Franklin

Ross, Carlton
See Brooks, Edwy Searles

Ross, Catherine
See Beaty, Betty

Ross, Charles
See Lucania, Salvatore

Ross, Charles Henry 1836-1897 [FFF,
PA]
British author and artist
* Butt, Boswell, Esq.
* Sloper, Ally

Ross, Charles Isaiah 1925- [BWW, NBB]
American singer
* [The] Flying Eagle
* Ross, Doc [or Doctor]

Ross, Charles J.
See Kelly, Charles J.

Ross, Chester Franklin 1903-1982 [BE]
American baseball player
* Ross, Buster

Ross, Chuck 20th c.
American author
* Demos, Erik

Ross, Churchill
See Weigle, Ross

Ross, Clarissa
See Ross, William Edward Daniel

Ross, Colin
See Roskolenko, Harry

Ross, Croker Mountain
See Ross, [Sir] John

Ross, Curly
See Ross, Ernest Bertram [Ernie]

Ross, Dallas
See Reynolds, Dallas McCord

Ross, Dana
See Ross, William Edward Daniel

Ross, Diana
See Denney, Diana

Ross, Doc [or Doctor]
See Ross, Charles Isaiah

Ross, Dr.
See Campbell, Henry Colin

Ross, Don 20th c.
American author
* Dana, Rose
* Gilmer, Alice
* Randolph, Ellen
* Roberts, Don
* Ross, Marilyn
* Rossiter, Jane

Ross, Dunbar 1800?-1865 [DNA]
Irish-born author and politician
* Zeno

Ross, Edgar 1949- [RBE]
American boxer
* Ross, Mad Dog

Ross, Elinor
See Rosenthal, Elinor Marilyn

Ross, Elizabeth
See Kuebler-Ross, Elizabeth

Ross, Ellen [PA]
Author
* Brook, Nelsie

Ross, Ernest Bertram [Ernie] 1880-1950
[BE]
Canadian baseball player
* Ross, Curly

Ross, Eulalie Steinmetz 1910- [CA]
American author and librarian
* Steinmetz, Eulalie

Ross, Eva
See Henderson, Eva

Ross, Eva Florence
See Stevens, Mrs. Victor

Ross, Frank [Xavier], Jr. 1914- [CA]
American author
* Frank, R., Jr.

Ross, George
See Morgan-Grenville, Gerard
[Wyndham]

Ross, George
See Ross, Isaac

Ross, Gertrude Mary Astbury 1887-1957
[HPPN]
British theatrical performer
* Gitana, Gertie

Ross, Harold Wallace 1892-1951
[HPPN, LC]
American editor
* [The] Father of the "New Yorker"
* Ross, Roughhouse

Ross, Helaine
See Daniels, Dorothy

Ross, Helena
See Young, Patricia Helena

Ross, Herbert
See Tait, Herbert

Ross, Herbert George 1931-
American basketball player
* Ross, Bitter Herb

Ross, Howard
See Rossini, Renato

Ross, Ian
See Rossmann, John F[rancis]

Ross, Isaac 1907- [WD]
British playwright
* Ross, George

Ross, Ivan T.
See Rossner, Robert

Ross, J. H.
See Lawrence, Thomas Edward

Ross, J. L. W. 20th c. [CCL]
Canadian author
* Scugog

Ross, James [joint pseudonym with
Tony Halliwell]
See Darrington, Hugh

Ross, James [joint pseudonym with
Hugh Darrington]
See Halliwell, Tony

Ross, Jean
See Hewson, Irene Dale

Ross, Jerry
See Rosenberg, Jerold

Ross, [Sir] John 1777-1856 [HPPN]
Scottish explorer and naval officer
* Ross, Croker Mountain

Ross, John
See Coowescoowe [or Kooweskoowe]

Ross, Jonathan
See Rossiter, John

Ross, Joseph
See Wrzos, Joseph Henry

Ross, Katherine
See Walter, Dorothy Blake

Ross, Keith 1899-1960 [F2, FC]
American actor
* Keith, Ian

Ross, Lancelot Patrick 1906- [PMJ]
American singer
* Ross, Lanny

Ross, Lanny
See Ross, Lancelot Patrick

Ross, Laura
See Mincieli, Rose Laura

Ross, Laurence
See Hyland, Ann

Ross, Leah
See Webb, Mary Haydn

Ross, Lee
See Ross, Sam

Ross, Lee Ravon 1915- [BE]
American baseball player
* Ross, Buck

Ross, Leonard [Q.]
See Rosten, Leo C[alvin]

Ross, Lucas Tunia 20th c. [RO2]
American musician
* Ross, Tawl

Ross, Mad Dog
See Ross, Edgar

Ross, Marilyn
See Ross, Don

Ross, Marilyn
See Ross, William Edward Daniel

Ross, Marilyn Heimberg 1939- [CA]
American author
* Heimberg, Marilyn Markham

Ross, Marion 1898-1966 [SC]
American actress
* Roland, Marion

Ross, Martin
See Martin, Violet Florence

Ross, Mary Adelaide Eden
See Phillpotts, [Mary] Adelaide [Eden]

Ross, Mother
See Davies, Mrs. Christian

Ross, Mrs. W. S. [FFF]
Entertainer
* Wood, Lillian

Ross, Nancy
See DeRoin, Nancy

Ross, Nellie Tayloe 1876-1977 [HPPN]
American politician
* America's First Female Governor

Ross, Oriel
See Swinstead, Muriel

Ross, Patricia
See Baxter, Patricia E. W.

Ross, Patricia
See Wood, Patricia E. W.

Ross, Paul
See Crawford, William [Elbert]

Ross, Philipp Peter 1657-1705 [WBD]
German painter
* Rosa di Tivoli

Ross, Robert W. 1922- [CA]
American author and clergyman
* Power-Ross, Robert W.

Ross, Roughhouse
See Ross, Harold Wallace

Ross, Sam ?-1966 [HPPN]
American actor
* Ross, Lee

Ross, Shirley
See Gaunt, Bernice

Ross, Sutherland
See Callard, Thomas Henry

Ross, T. J.
See Ross, Theodore John

Ross, Tawl
See Ross, Lucas Tunia

Ross, Theodore John 1924- [SFL]
American author
* Ross, T. J.

Ross, Virginia
See Conolly, Mrs. Edward J.

Ross, W. E. D.
See Ross, William Edward Daniel

Ross, Ward
See Fearn, John Russell

Ross, William 18th c. [HPPN]
British author
* W. R.

Ross, William
See Gonzalez, Gonzalo

Ross, William Edward Daniel 1912-
[CA, SFL]
Canadian author
* Ames, Leslie
* Dana, Rose
* Dorset, Ruth
* Gilmer, Ann
* Randolph, Ellen
* Roberts, Dan
* Ross, Clarissa
* Ross, Dana
* Ross, Marilyn
* Ross, W. E. D.
* Rossiter, Jane
* Steel, Tex
* Williams, Rose

Ross, William Stewart 20th c. [WWL]
British author
* Saladin

Ross, William Wrightson Eustace
1894-1966 [CCL]
Canadian poet
* E. R.

Ross, [Mother] Xavier
See Ross, Ann

Ross, Z. H.
See Ross, Zola Helen

Ross, Zola Helen 1912- [CA, WW]
American author
* Arre, Helen
* Iles, Bert
* Ross, Z. H.

Ross-Church, Florence M. 19th c.
[FFF]
Author
* Marryatt, Florence

Ross-Craig, Stella 1906- [ART]
British artist
* S. R. C.

Ross-Macdonald, Malcolm J[ohn]
See Macdonald, Malcolm John Ross

Ross Williamson, Hugh 1901-1978 [CA]
British playwright
* Rossiter, Ian

Rossa, Mrs. O'Donovan [PA]
Author
* O'Donovan, Mrs.

Rosse, Ian
See Straker, John Foster

Rosse, Susanna
See Connolly, Vivian

Rossel, Roger
See Vandeputte, Roger

Rosselet, Andre 1915- [ART]
Swiss artist
* R.

Rossellino, Antonio
See Gamberelli, Antonio

Rossellino, Bernardo
See Gamberelli, Bernardo

Rossen, Punch
See Rossen, Ronnie

Rossen, Ronnie 20th c. [GW]
American rodeo performer
* Rossen, Punch

Rosser, Lee 20th c. [GW]
American rodeo performer
* Rosser, Rounder

Rosser, Rounder
See Rosser, Lee

Rosser, Thomas Lafayette 1836-1910
[HPPN]
American army officer
* [The] Savior of the Valley

Rosset, Barnet Lee, Jr. 1922- [BEW]
American editor
* Rosset, Barney

Rosset, Barney
See Rosset, Barnet Lee, Jr.

Rosset, Benjamin Charles 1910-1974
[CA]
Russian-born author
* Ozy

Rossetti, Christina Georgina 1830-1894
[FFF, SAT, WBD]
British poet
* Alleyn, Ellen

Rossetti, Dante Gabriel 1828-1882
[NPS, SN]
British painter and poet
* Hamlin
* [The] Poet Painter

Rossetti, Gabriele
See Citeriore, Vasto Abruzzo

Rossetti, Gino
See Rossetti, Louis A.

Rossetti, Louis A. 1930?- [BI]
American architect
* Rossetti, Gino

Rossetti, Minerva
See Rowland, Donald Sydney

Rossi, Aga
See Agarossi, Elena

Rossi, Francesco de' 1510-1563 [HPPN]
Italian painter
* Salviati, Cecco di

Rossi, Francis 20th c. [RO2]
British musician
* Rossi, Mike

Rossi, Francois
See Abiatt, Roland

Rossi, Giovanni Battista de' 1494-1540
[HPPN]
Italian painter
* [Il] Rosso
* [Il] Rosso Fiorentino

Rossi, Girolamo 1539-1607 [PA]
Author
* Rubens

Rossi, Jean Baptiste 1931- [PA, TCCM]
French author
* Japrisot, Sebastien

Rossi, Mike
See Rossi, Francis

Rossi, Salomone 1565?-1628? [WBD]
Italian-born composer
* [L']Ebreo

Rossi, Sanna Morrison Barlow 1917-
[CA]
American author
* Barlow, Sanna Morrison

Rossi, Tommy
See Cuiringione, Tommy

Rossi-Drago, Eleonora
See Omiccioli, Palmina

Rossignol, Felix Ludger 1839-1903
[BBD]
French composer
* Joncieres, Victorin de

Rossignol, Jean Antoine 1759-1802
[HN]
French army officer
* [The] Devil of Vendee

Rossillon, Marius 1880?-1946   [WEC]
French cartoonist
* O'Galop [At the Gallop]

Rossini, Gioachino Antonio 1792-1868
[DNNS, SN]
Italian composer
* [The] Swan of Pesaro

Rossini, Renato 20th c.   [WF]
Italian actor
* Ross, Howard

Rossiter, Anna M. S.   [PA]
Author
* Cushman, Lilla N.

Rossiter, Anthony 1926-   [ART]
British painter
* A. R.

Rossiter, Ian
See Ross Williamson, Hugh

Rossiter, Jane
See Ross, Don

Rossiter, Jane
See Ross, William Edward Daniel

Rossiter, John 1916-   [CA]
British author
* Ross, Jonathan

Rossiter, Oscar
See Skeels, Vernon H.

Rossiter, Will
See Williams, W. R.

Rossler, Ernestine 1861-1936 [HPPN]
Czech-born actress and opera singer
* [The] Grand Old Lady of Opera
* [The] Mother of All the Doughboys
* [The] Mother of the American Legion
* Schumann-Heink, Ernestine

Rossman, Evelyn
See Rothchild, Sylvia

Rossmann, John F[rancis] 1942-   [CA]
American author
* Ross, Ian

Rossner, Augusta
See Eddie, Augusta Rossner

Rossner, Robert 1932-   [CA]
American author and educator
* Ross, Ivan T.

[Il] Rosso
See Rossi, Giovanni Battista de'

[Il] Rosso Fiorentino
See De Rossi, Giovanni Battista

[Il] Rosso Fiorentino
See Rossi, Giovanni Battista de'

Rosso, Gustavo 1881-1950   [WEC]
Italian cartoonist and illustrator
* Gustavino [Little Gustave]

Rossoeus, Georgius Gulielmus
See Gifford, William

Rost, Hans Wilmsen L.
See Lauremberg, Johann

Rostand, Louise Rose Etiennette
1871-1953   [HPPN, WBD]
French poet
* Gerard, Rosemonde
* Rosemonde

Rostand, Robert
See Hopkins, Robert

Rosten, Leo C[alvin] 1908-   [AW, CA, LC]
American author and playwright
* Ross, Leonard [Q.]

Rostenkowski, Dan 1928?-   [NW 3-7-83]
American politician
* Rosty

Rostopchin, [Countess] Eudoxie
1811-1858   [HPPN]
Russian poet
* [The] Moscow Sappho

Rostrevor, George
See Hamilton, George Rostrevor

Rostron, P. R.
See Hulbert, Joan Margery

Rostron, Primrose
See Hulbert, Joan Margery

Rostropovich, Mstislav 1927?-
Russian musician
* Rostropovich, Slava

Rostropovich, Slava
See Rostropovich, Mstislav

Rosty
See Rostenkowski, Dan

Rotarius
See Kerekes, Tibor

Rotation Slim
See Hairston, George

Rotella, Domenico 1918-   [CAR]
Italian artist
* Rotella, Mimmo

Rotella, Mimmo
See Rotella, Domenico

Roth, Alexander
See Dunner, Joseph

Roth, Arthur J[oseph] 1925-   [CA]
American author
* Hoy, Nina
* Mara, Barney
* McGurk, Slater
* Pomeroy, Pete

Roth, Bobby
See Roth, Herman

Roth, Braggo
See Roth, Robert Frank

Roth, Christian 1945-   [IAW]
Swiss author and columnist
* Brdlbrmpft

Roth, Herman 20th c.   [OBW]
American baseball player
* Roth, Bobby

Roth, Holly 1916-1964   [CA, CC, EMD]
American author
* Ballard, K. G.
* Merrill, P. J.

Roth, Karen
See Sellers, Connie Leslie, Jr.

Roth, Lillian
See Rutstein, Lillian

Roth, Robert
See Sellers, Connie Leslie, Jr.

Roth, Robert Frank 1892-1936   [BE]
American baseball player
* Roth, Braggo

Roth, Sam 1903?-1951   [BI]
American ticket agent
* Broadway Sam

Roth, Samuel 1894-1974   [CA]
*Austrian-born American poet, editor,
publisher*
* Lockridge, Norman

Rothafel, Roxy
See Rothapfel, Samuel Lionel

Rothafel, S. L.
See Rothapfel, Samuel Lionel

Rothapfel, Samuel Lionel 1882-1936
[WA, WEF]
American theatre manager
* Rothafel, Roxy
* Rothafel, S. L.

Rothberg, Winterset
See Roethke, Theodore

Rothchild, Jeroboam 1885-1944   [JL]
French government official
* Mandel, Georges

Rothchild, Sylvia 1923-   [CA]
American author
* Rossman, Evelyn

Rothenfels, Emmy von
See Ingersleben, Emilie von

Rothenstein, Albert Daniel 1883-1953
[THR]
British artist and designer
* Rutherston, Albert Daniel

Rotherham, Thomas 1423-1500   [WBD]
British prelate
* Scott, Thomas

Rothermel, Bobby
See Rothermel, Edward Hill

Rothermel, Edward Hill 1870-?   [BE]
American baseball player
* Rothermel, Bobby

Rothery, Agnes Edwards
See Pratt, Agnes Rothery

Rothery, Brian 1934- [WD]
Irish author
* Dyer, Brian [joint pseudonym with
Orlando R(alph) Petrocelli]

Rothko, Mark
See Rothkowitz [or Rothkovich],
Marcus

Rothkopf, Louis 20th c. [PHM]
American underworld figure
* Rhody, Louis
* Zarumba, Louis

Rothkowitz [or Rothkovich], Marcus
1903-1970
Russian-born American artist
* Rothko, Mark

Rothmaler, Karl von
See Einem, Karl von

Rothman, Arnold 1925- [ITA]
American actor and writer
* Arnold, Danny

Rothman, Judith
See Peters, Maureen

Rothman, Milton A. 1919- [WGT]
American author
* Gregor, Lee [joint pseudonym with
Frederik Pohl]

Rothmuller, Aron Marko 1908- [CA]
*Yugoslav-born American opera singer and
educator*
* Kinor, Jehuda

Rothmund, Wilhelmino 1917- [BEW]
American actress
* Worth, Billie

Rothschild, Dorothy 1893-1967 [HPPN,
IPA]
American author
* Constant Reader
* Parker, Dorothy
* Rousseau, Helene

Rothschild, [Baron] Henri De 1872-1947
[HPPN]
French financier and playwright
* Pascal, Andre

Rothschild, J. Monroe 1891-1963 [SC]
American actor
* Childs, Monroe

Rothstein, Arnold 1882-1928 [BLB,
HPPN, MM]
American underworld figure
* A. A. R., Mr.
* A. R.
* [The] Big Bankroll
* Big, Mr.
* [The] Brain
* [The] Czar of the New York
Underworld
* [The] Dedicated Gambler
* [The] Man to See
* [The] Man Uptown
* [The] Master of Crime
* Mr. A.

Rothstein's Blonde Lure
See Keyes, Ruth

Rothweiler, Paul R[oger] 1931- [CA]
American author
* Curtis, Richard Hale
* Ruyerson, James Paul
* Scofield, Jonathan

Rothwell, Annie
See Christie, Annie Rothwell [Fowler]

Rothwell, Henry Talbot 1921- [AW]
British author
* Talbot, Henry

Rothwell, William H. 1880-1927 [BX,
RBE]
American boxer
* Corbett, Young

Roti, Bruno 20th c. [NW 2-13-84]
* [The] Bomber

Roti, Fred B. 20th c. [NW 2-13-84]
American politician
* Roti, Peanuts

Roti, Peanuts
See Roti, Fred B.

Rotov, Boris Georgi'evich 1929-1978
[BI]
Russian religious leader
* Nikodim

Rotrou, Jean de 1609-1650 [HN, SN]
French playwright
* [The] Father of the French Drama
* [The] Founder of the French Theatre

Rotsler, William 1926- [ESF, WGT]
American author and artist
* Arrow, William [house pseudonym,
Ballantine Books]
* Hall, John Ryder

Rotten, Johnny
See Lydon, John

[The] Rottenest American
See Fonda, Jane

Rotter, Elizabeth
Author
* Matthews, Laura

Rotton, [Rev.] John Edward Wharton
19th c. [HPPN]
British clergyman
* Chaplain

Roubillac, Louis Francois 1695-1762
[NPS]
French sculptor
* [The] Little Sculptor

Roudebush, Earl David 1891-? [BBH]
American basketball coach
* Roudebush, Roudie

Roudebush, Roudie
See Roudebush, Earl David

Rouel, Joseph Jules [PA]
Author
* J. J. R.

[Le] Rouge
See Ravanel, Joseph

[Le] Rougeaud
See Ney, Michel [Duc d'Elchingen]

Rouget, Marie Melanie 1883-? [BI]
French poet
* Noel, Marie

Rouget de Lisle, Claude Joseph
1760-1836 [HN, HPPN]
French army officer and composer
* [The] Father of the Marseillaise
* [The] Tyrtaeus of France

Rough and Ready
See Taylor, Zach[ary]

Rough Hewer
See Yates, Robert

Rough House Haynes
See Haynes, Leroy H.

[The] Rough Rider
See Roosevelt, Theodore [Teddy]

Roughsey, Dick 1921?- [ICB]
Australian illustrator
* Goobalathaldin [tribal name]

Rouher, Eugene 1813-1884 [FFF]
French prime minister
* Vice Emperor

Rouillon, Paul
See Malossis, Auguste Paul Poulet

Roulon, Harry 1891-1940 [SC]
American actor
* Murray, J. Harold

Roulston, Rolly
See Roulston, William Orville

Roulston, William Orville 1911- [CEI]
Canadian-born hockey player
* Roulston, Rolly

Roumanis, George Zackery 1929- [EJ]
American jazz musician
* Romanis, George Zackery

Roumer, Emile 1903- [CW]
Haitian poet
* Niger, Emilius

Roumi
See Aiwas, Dzati

Round House George Lehman
See Lehman, George

[The] Round Man
See Northey, Ronald James

[The] Round Mound of Rebound
See Barkley, Charles

[The] Round Mound of Sound
See Price, Kenny

[The] Round Mound of Sound
See Sawell, Larry

Round, William Marshall Fitz 1845-1906
[HPPN, PA]
American author and journalist
* Pennot, [Rev.] Peter
* Vevay, Paul

[The] Roundsman of the Lord
See Comstock, Anthony

Rounesville, Robert 1914-1974 [SC]
American actor and opera singer
* Field, Robert

Rountree, Ella Jackson 1936- [BA]
American educator
* Rountree, Ree

Rountree, Owen [joint pseudonym with
Steven M(ark) Krauzer]
See Kittredge, William

Rountree, Owen [joint pseudonym with
William Kittredge]
See Krauzer, Steven M[ark]

Rountree, Ree
See Rountree, Ella Jackson

Rourke, James
See Trimble, Louis P[reston]

Rourke, Louise Musgrave 20th c.
[WWL]
British author
* Dickerson-Watkins, L.

Rourke, Michael Elder ?-1933 [HPPN]
American lyricist and playwright
* Reynolds, Herbert

Rous [or Rowse], Francis 1579-1659
[SN]
British politician
* Another Proteus
* [That] Old Jew of Eton

Rous, Francis P. 1879-1970 [HPPN]
American medical researcher
* [The] Discoverer of the Cancer Virus
* [The] Father of the Blood Bank

Rous, Helen
See Shaw, Helen

Rous, Samuel Holland 1866-1947 [BI]
American singer
* Dudley, S. H.
* Kernell, Frank

Rouse, Raymond 1936- [AES]
Welsh soccer player
* Rouse, Vic

Rouse, Rebel
See Rouse, Stephen John

Rouse, Stephen John 1949- [DC]
Welsh-born cricketer
* Rouse, Rebel

Rouse, Vic
See Rouse, Raymond

Rousseau, Camille 1921- [CW]
West Indian poet
* Porto, Louis

Rousseau, Helene
See Rothschild, Dorothy

Rousseau, Henri 1844-1910 [WBD]
French painter
* [Le] Douanier

Rousseau, J. J.
See Nienaber, Petrus Johannes

Rousseau, Jean-Jacques 1712-1778
[DNNF, DNNS, HPPN, NPS, SN]
Swiss-French philosopher
* [The] Citizen of Geneva
* [The] Father of Sentiment
* J. J.
* Jean Jacques
* [The] Melancholy Jacques
* Pegalle
* Renou

Rousseau, Odette 1901-1974 [FIR, SC]
French actress and singer
* Florelle [or Florette?]

[The] Rousseau of China
See K'ang Yu-wei

[The] Rousseau of the Gutter
See Restif, Nicolas Edme

Rousseau, Victor
See Emanuel, Victor Rousseau

Roussel, Simone 1920- [BDF, FC, ITA]
French actress
* Morgan, Michele

Roussimoff, Andre 20th c.
French wrestler
* Andre the Giant

Roustabout
See Hoffmann, Phil

Routhier, [Sir] Adolphe Basile 1839-?
[ALY]
Canadian author
* Piquetort, Jean

Routledge, Lilian 20th c. [THR]
British actress
* Rosebery, Lilian

Routsong, Alma 1924- [CA]
American author
* Miller, Isabel

Rouverol, Jean
See Butler, Jean Rouverol

Roux, Paul Pierre 1861-1940 [CD,
EWL]
French poet and playwright
* [Le] Magnifique
* Saint Pol-Roux

Rouzier, Maximilien Louis Severin
1846-1927 [CW]
Haitian journalist and author
* Saint Mexant
* Semexant

Rover
See Gibson, Alfred

[The] Rover Center
See McEwan, John J.

Rover, Max
See Murray, Edgar Joyce

Rover, Roderic
See Prentiss, Charles

Rovin, Alex
See Russo, Albert

Rovin, Ben
See Clevenger, Ernest Allen, Jr.

[The] Roving Englishman
See Murray, E. C. Greenville

[A] Roving Printer
See Jones, John Beauchamp

Rovira
See Acha Sanz, Raul

Row, Saville
See Clark, Saville

Row, T.
See Pegge, Samuel

Rowan, David [Dave]
See Drohan, David

Rowan, Deirdre
See Williams, Jeanne

Rowan-Hamilton, Sydney Orme
1877-1949 [BI, LAO]
British author and playwright
* Orme, Rowan

Rowans, Virginia
See Tanner, Edward Everett, III

Rowbotham, Sheila 1943- [CA]
British author and political activist
* Turner, Sheila

Rowbotham, William 1914?- [BF, FC]
British comic actor
* Owen, Bill

Rowdy Bill Coughlin
See Coughlin, Bill

Rowdy Joe Lowe
See Lowe, Joseph

Rowdy Kate Rowe
See Rowe, Kathryn

Rowdy King of Comedy
See Dukinfield, William Claude

Rowdy Richard Bartell
See Bartell, Richard William

Rowe, Alice E.
See Rowe, John Gabriel

Rowe, Bolton
See Scott, Clement William

Rowe, Bolton
See Stephenson, Benjamin Charles

Rowe, Elizabeth 1674-1737 [DEL, PA]
British author
* Philomela

Rowe, Frank 20th c. [GW]
American rodeo performer
* Rowe, Little Beaver

Rowe, Harland Stimson 1896-1969 [BE]
American baseball player
* Rowe, Hypie

Rowe, Homie
See Rowe, Norman

Rowe, Hypie
See Rowe, Harland Stimson

Rowe, Imogene ?-1914 [HPPN]
American actress
* Van Dyke, Imogene

Rowe, John Gabriel 1873-? [MBF]
British author
* Austin, Mortimer
* Bright, James
* Dunstan, Gregory
* Ferris, Arthur
* Gabriel, John
* Lewis, Charles
* Ransome, Charles A.
* Rowe, Alice E.
* Walters, T. B.

Rowe, Kathryn 19th c. [BLB]
American madam
* Rowe, Rowdy Kate

Rowe, Little Beaver
See Rowe, Frank

Rowe, Lynwood Thomas 1910?-1961
[AS, BE, PB]
American baseball player
* Rowe, Schoolboy

Rowe, Margaret [Kevin] 1920- [CA]
Australian-born author
* Teresa Margaret, [Sister]

Rowe, Nicholas [FFF, PA]
American writer
* Mohawk

Rowe, Nicholas 1674-1718 [NPS]
British and poet playwright
* Bayes the Younger

Rowe, Norman 20th c. [GW]
American rodeo performer
* Rowe, Homie

Rowe, Richard 1828-1879 [DLE1]
British-born author
* Possum, Peter

Rowe, Rowdy Kate
See Rowe, Kathryn

Rowe, Samuel 1793-1853 [HPPN]
British clergyman
* [A] Member of the University of
Cambridge

Rowe, Saville
See Scott, Clement William

Rowe, Schoolboy
See Rowe, Lynwood Thomas

Rowe, Stephen
See Stares, John Edward Spencer

Rowe, Vivian C[laud] 1902-1978 [CA]
British author
* Hooton, Charles

Rowe, W. 20th c. [MBF]
British author
* Bingham, [Major] Arthur

Rowel, M.
See Thisted, V[aldemar] Adolph

Rowell, A. S. 19th c. [BDSA]
American author
* Old Coins

Rowell, Bama
See Rowell, Carvel William

Rowell, Carvel William 1916- [BE]
American baseball player
* Rowell, Bama

Rowen, Lady [Cult name]
See Buckland, Rosemary

Rowena
See Little, Sophia Louise Robbins

Rowing U. S. A., Mr.
See Goes, Clifford

Rowland, Betty Jane 20th c. [HPPN]
American entertainer
* [The] Ball of Fire

Rowland, Bo
See Rowland, John T.

Rowland, Clarence Henry 1879-1969
[AS, BTB, PB]
American baseball executive
* Rowland, Pants
* Svengali

Rowland, D. 1778-1859 [PA]
Author
* [A] Layman

Rowland, Donald Sydney 1928- [CA]
British author
* Adams, Annette
* Bassett, Jack
* Baxter, Hazel
* Benton, Karla
* Berry, Helen
* Brant, Lewis
* Bray, Alison
* Brayce, William
* Brockley, Fenton
* Bronson, Oliver
* Buchanan, Chuck
* Caley, Rod
* Carlton, Roger
* Cleve, Janita
* Court, Sharon
* Craig, Vera
* Craille, Wesley
* Dryden, John
* Fenton, Freda
* Field, Charles
* Garner, Graham
* Kroll, Burt
* Langley, Helen
* Lansing, Henry
* Lant, Harvey
* Lynn, Irene
* Madison, Hank
* Mason, Chuck
* McHugh, Stuart
* Morgan, G. J.
* Murray, Edna
* Page, Lorna
* Patterson, Olive
* Porter, Alvin
* Random, Alex
* Rimmer, W. J.
* Rix, Donna

Rowland, Donald Sydney (cont.)
* Rockwell, Matt
* Roscoe, Charles
* Rossetti, Minerva
* Scott, Norford
* Scott, Valerie
* Segundo, Bart
* Shaul, Frank
* Spurr, Clinton
* Starr, Roland
* Stevens, J. D.
* Suffling, Mark
* Talbot, Kay
* Travers, Will
* Vine, Sarah
* Vinson, Elaine
* Walters, Rick
* Webb, Neil

Rowland, E. G.
See Girolami, Enzo

Rowland, Grey
See Rowland-Brown, Lilian

Rowland, Iris
See Roberts, Irene M.

Rowland, John T. 1901?-1964 [BI]
American football player and coach
* Rowland, Bo

Rowland, Pants
See Rowland, Clarence Henry

Rowland, Roland 1918?-
British industrialist
* Rowland, Tiny

Rowland, Rozelle 20th c. [HPPN]
American entertainer
* [The] Baroness Empain
* [The] Golden Girl

Rowland, Tiny
See Rowland, Roland

Rowland, W.
See Winter, Holmes Edwin Cornelius

Rowland-Brown, Lilian 1863-? [LAO]
British author
* Rowland, Grey

**Rowland-Entwistle, [Arthur] Theodore
[Henry]** 1925- [CA, SAT]
British author
* Briquebec, John
* Ellis, Anyon
* Hall-Clarke, James
* Henry, T. E.
* Lawrence, J. T.

Rowlands, Cadwallader
See Hotten, John Camden

Rowlands, Cecil 1856-1914 [BEW]
Playwright
* Raleigh, Cecil

Rowlands, Effie Adelaide
See Albanesi, [Madame] Effie Maria
[Henderson]

Rowlands, John 1841-1904 [FFF, IPA]
Welsh explorer
* [The] Cortez of Africa
* Stanley, [Sir] Henry Morton

Rowlands, Peter
See Lovell, Mark

Rowles, Mary Elizabeth 20th c. [BEW]
American actress
* Rowles, Polly

Rowles, Polly
See Rowles, Mary Elizabeth

Rowley, Ames Dor[r]ance
See Lovecraft, Howard Phillips

Rowley, Charles, Jr. [PA]
Author
* Gilderoy, Roland

Rowley, Herbert 1883?-1964 [BEW]
Theatrical performer
* Bond, Bert

Rowley, Richard
See Williams, Richard Valentine

Rowley, Thomas
See Chatterton, Thomas

Rowley, Thomas
See Pauker, John

Rowse, A. L.
See Rowse, Alfred Leslie

Rowse, Alfred Leslie 1903- [LC]
British author and historian
* Rowse, A. L.

Rowson, Susanna Haswell 1762-1824
[HPPN]
Anglo-American author and actress
* America's First Best Selling Author

Rowswell, Albert K. 1884-1955 [HPPN]
American radio personality
* Rowswell, Rosey

Rowswell, Rosey
See Rowswell, Albert K.

Roxalana
See Davenport, Elizabeth

Roxanne
See Lennon, Florence

Roxbourgh, Patricia
See Raphael, Sylvia

[A] Roxbury Farmer
See Lowell, John

Roy
See Willis, Nathaniel Parker

Roy, Brandon
See Barclay, Florence Louisa
Charlesworth

Roy, Dan
See Lotinga, Ernest

Roy, Ewell Paul 1929- [CA]
*American agricultural economist and
author*
* Bonnette, Victor
* Lemoine, Ernest

Roy, Gordon
See Wallace, Helen

Roy, Hippolyte 1763-1829 [WFA]
French fashion designer
* Leroy

Roy, Jack
See Cohen, Jacob

Roy, John
See Durand, [Sir] H. Mortimer

Roy, Julien
See Macinnes, Tom

Roy, Jumbo
See Roy, Norm[an Brooks]

Roy, Lee
See Antonini, Leo

Roy, Liam
See Scarry, Patricia [Murphy] [Patsy]

Roy, Luxymon
See Homan, Samuel H.

Roy, Norm[an Brooks] 1928- [BE]
American baseball player
* Roy, Jumbo

Roy, Percy Gordon
See Wolfgang, Otto

Roy, Ralph
See Badger, Joseph E.

Roy, Ramala Pratap
See Bhosale, Yeshwantrao P.

Roy, Rammohun 1780-1833 [PA]
Author
* [The] Rajah

Roy, William
See Plowright, William George Holroyd

Royaards, Wilhelm 1867?-1929 [BEW]
Actor and director
* Royaards, William

Royaards, William
See Royaards, Wilhelm

[The] Royal Black Sheep
See Armstrong-Jones, Anthony Charles
Robert [Lord Snowdon]

[The] Royal Butcher
See Henry VIII

Royal, D.
See DuBreuil, Elizabeth Lorinda

[The] Royal Entertainer
See Sault, Wallace A. [Wally]

[A] Royal Field Leech
See Symonds, Francis Addington

[The] Royal Martyr
See Charles I

[The] Royal Martyr
See Edward [or Eadward]

[The] Royal Midas
See Dennis, John

Royal 'Prentice in the Art of Poesy
See James I

Royal, Ralph
See Abarbanell, Jacob Ralph

[The] Royal Saint
See Henry VI

Royal, Ted
See Dewar, Ted Royal

[The] Royal Violinist
See Southgate, Elsie

[The] Royal Wanderer
See Charles II

[The] Royalist Butcher
See De Lasseran-Massencome, Blaise

[Le] Royaliste Boucher
See Lasseran-Massencome [Seigneur de
Montluc]

Royall, Anne Newport 1769-1854
[HPPN]
American author
* Royall, Godless Anne

Royall, Godless Anne
See Royall, Anne Newport

Royalty's Favorite Entertainer
See Kaminsky [or Kominski?], David
Daniel

Royce, Ashley A.
See Hathorne, Nathaniel

Royce, Forrest 1911-1965 [SC]
American stunt performer
* Royce, Frosty

Royce, Frosty
See Royce, Forrest

Royce, Josiah 1855-1916 [HPPN]
American philosopher and educator
* One of America's Keenest Thinkers

Royce, Julian
See Gardner, Julian

Royce, Kenneth
See Gandley, Kenneth Royce

Royde, Frank
See Howroyd, Frank

Roye
See Narbeth, Horace

Royer
See Hastings, Louis Royer

Royer, Harry 1889-1951 [SC]
American actor
* Royer, Missouri

Royer, Missouri
See Royer, Harry

Royer, Robb 20th c. [RO2]
American musician and songwriter
* Wilson, Robb

Royster, Jeron Kennis 1952- [SMG]
American baseball player
* Bird, J.
* Royster, Jerry

Royster, Jerry
See Royster, Jeron Kennis

Royston, John Eric 1914- [BA]
American attorney
* [The] Judge

Royston, Roy
See Crowden, Roy

Royston, William Haylett 19th c.
[HFN]
Author
* W. H. R.

Royz, Olesh 1898-1976 [JL]
Polish-born American political figure
* Rose, Alex

Roze, Raymond
See Roze-Perkins, J. H. Raymond

Roze-Perkins, J. H. Raymond 1875-1920
[BBD]
British composer
* Roze, Raymond

Rozelle, Alvin Ray 1926- [CR, FB, IPA]
American football commissioner
* [The] Boy Commissioner
* Doughsmell, Pete
* Perfect Pete
* Peter the Great
* Rozelle, Pete
* St. Peter

Rozelle, Pete
See Rozelle, Alvin Ray

Rozelle, Richard 20th c. [RBE]
American boxer
* [The] Fly

Rozema, David Scott [Dave] 1956-
[SMG]
American baseball player
* [The] Rose
* Rozema, Rosie

Rozema, Rosie
See Rozema, David Scott [Dave]

Rozenberga, Elza 1865-1943 [CD]
Latvian poet and playwright
* Aspazija

Rozier, Jacques
See Paton, Emilie

Ruadh
See McAleese, Daniel

Ruadh, Sliabh
See Rooney, William

Ruano, Argimiro 1924- [CA]
Spanish-born author
* Ruano, Nazario

Ruano, Nazario
See Ruano, Argimiro

Rub
See Villiers, George

Rubashov, Schneor Zalman 1889-1974
[CA]
Israeli president, poet, historian
* Shazar, [Schneor] Zalman

Rubber Arm
See Connally, George Walter

[The] Rubber Duck
See Fries, William [Bill]

Rubber Face
See Skelton, [Richard] Red

[The] Rubber Hammer
See Skryabin, Vyacheslav Mikhailovich

[The] Rubber King
See Harter, Dow Watters

[The] Rubber King
See Morris, Harry

[The] Rubber Lion
See Blomberg, Werner von

[The] Rubber Man
See Risko, Johnny

Rubber Man McDole
See McDole, Roland Owen

Rubberlegs, Mr.
See Bolger, Ray[mond Wallace]

Rubbia, Carlo 1934?- [TI 10-29-84]
Italian physicist
* [The] Alitalia Scientist

Rubek, Sennoia
See Burke, John

Rubel, Edith
See Mapother, Edith Rubel

Rubel, Henry Scott 1898- [BI]
American clergyman and songwriter
* Raynor, Hal

Ruben, Lynsey 1951-
British composer and singer
* De Paul, Lynsey

Ruben, William S. 20th c. [SFL, WGT]
Author
* Shannon, Fred

Rubenfeld, Paul 1953?- [WP 8-2-85]
American comic actor
* Herman, Pee-wee
* Reubens, Paul

Rubens
See Rossi, Girolamo

Rubens, Alma
See Porrata Doria de Rincon,
Providencia

Rubens, Alma
See Smith, Alma

[The] Rubens of English Poetry
See Spenser, Edmund

[The] Rubens of France
See Delacroix, Ferdinand Victor Eugene

Rubens, Peter Paul 1577-1640 [HN,
RH]
Flemish painter
* [Le] Gentilhomme de la Peinture
* [The] Gentleman Painter

Rubenstein, Adelaide 1857?-1941 [BEW]
British actress
* Prince, Adelaide

Rubenstein, Edana 1919- [FC]
South African-born actress
* Romney, Edana

Rubenstein, Jacob 1911-1967 [HPPN,
JL]
*American nightclub owner who killed Lee
Harvey Oswald*
* [The] Assassin's Assassin
* Ruby, Jack

Rubenstein, Louis 1861-1931 [HPPN]
Canadian figure skater
* [The] Father of Figure Skating in
North America

Ruberto, John Edward 1946- [SMG]
American baseball coach
* Ruberto, Sonny

Ruberto, Sonny
See Ruberto, John Edward

Rubicon
See Lunn, Arnold [Henry Moore]

Rubimor
See Moreira, Ruben

Rubin, Ada
See Roeter, Ada

Rubin, Charles J. 1950- [CA]
American author
* Buzzle, Buck

Rubin, Cynthia Elyce 1944- [CA]
American author
* Alplaus, N. Y. [joint pseudonym with
Jerome Rubin]

Rubin, Gail 1942- [CA]
American author
* Bereny, Gail Rubin

Rubin, Harold 20th c. [HPPN]
*American adult bookstore and massage
parlor proprietor*
* Rubin, Weird Harold

Rubin, Harold
See Kane, Francis

Rubin, Jacob A. 1910-1972 [CA]
*Austrian-born American editor, journalist,
author*
* Odem, J.

Rubin, Jerome 20th c. [CA]
American author
* Alplaus, N. Y. [joint pseudonym with
Cynthia Elyce Rubin]

Rubin, Michael Stewart 1929- [BEW,
EMT, TR]
American playwright and librettist
* Stewart, Michael

Rubin, Weird Harold
See Rubin, Harold

Rubini, Diane 1890-1969 [SC]
American actress
* De Aubry, Diane

Rubino, Matthew 20th c.
American underworld figure
* Rubino, Mike

Rubino, Mike
See Rubino, Matthew

Rubinstein, Artur 1889- [HPPN]
Polish American pianist
* [The] Playboy of the Piano

Rubinstein, Chip
See Rubinstein, Matthew N.

Rubinstein, Hannah Golofski 1923-1974
[HPPN]
American fashion designer
* Klein, Anne

Rubinstein, Harry 1895-1974 [BEW,
EMT]
American composer and librettist
* Ruby, Harry

Rubinstein, Matthew N. 1921- [WFA]
American clothing manufacturer
* Rubinstein, Chip

Rubinstein, S[amuel] Leonard 1922-
[CA]
American author
* Weber, Rubin [joint pseudonym with
  Robert G. Weaver]

Rubinstein, Serge 1908-1955 [HPPN]
Russian swindler
* [The] Boy Wizard of International
  Finance
* [The] Boy Wonder of Wall Street

Rubio, Antonio 20th c. [GS]
Spanish bullfighter
* Macandro

[El] Rubio de Boston
See Tuck, Porter

**Rubio de Valencia [Redhead of
Valencia]**
See Villa y Mari, Francisco

Rubio, Julio
See Buyana, Mohamed

Rubios, Jose
See Maloney, Terry

Rubirosa, Porfirio ?-1965 [HPPN]
Dominican playboy and diplomat
* Rubirosa, Ruby

Rubirosa, Ruby
See Rubirosa, Porfirio

Rubruquis, Guillaume 1220?-1293
[HPPN]
French missionary and author
* William of Ruysbroeck [or Rubrouck]

Ruby
See Kavanagh, Rose

Ruby
See Pithawalla, Maneck B.

Ruby, B. F.
See Pratt, [Murray] Fletcher

Ruby, Harry
See Rubinstein, Harry

Ruby, Jack
See Rubenstein, Jacob

Ruby, Martin 1922- [CFH]
American-born football player
* Ruby, Rube

Ruby Nose
See Cromwell, Oliver

Ruby Robert Fitzsimmons
See Fitzsimmons, Robert Prometheus
[Bob]

Ruby, Rube
See Ruby, Martin

Ruby, Texas
See Fox, Ruby Owens

Ruby, Thelma
See Wigoder, Thelma

Ruccellai, Benardo 1449-1514 [PA]
Author
* Oricellarius

Ruchrath [or Ruchrad], Johannes
?-1481? [WBD]
German religious reformer
* John of Wesel

Ruck, Amy Roberta
See Oliver, Amy Roberta [Ruck]

Ruck, Berta
See Oliver, Amy Roberta [Ruck]

Ruckelshaus, Jill 1937?- [TI 7-11-83]
*Wife of EPA administrator, William
Ruckelshaus*
* [The] Gloria Steinem of the
  Republican Party

Rucker, Annabelle 1904-1967 [SC]
American actress
* Williams, Annabelle

Rucker, George Napoleon 1884-1970
[BE, PB]
American baseball player
* Rucker, Nap

Rucker, Henry 1921- [IBW]
American psychic
* [The] Ghost Breaker

Rucker, John Joel 1917- [BE]
American baseball player
* [The] Crabapple Comet

Rucker, Nap
See Rucker, George Napoleon

Ruckser, George Brinton McClellan
1863-1935 [BE]
American baseball player
* Rooks, George Brinton McClellan

Ruckstull, F[red] Wellington 1853-?
[NAA]
French-born writer and editor
* Arbeiter, Petronius

Rudd, Margaret
See Newlin, Margaret Rudd

Rudd, Mrs. 18th c. [DI]
British forger
* [The] Female Forger

Rudd, Steele
See Davis, Arthur Hoey

Rudd, W. L. 1845-? [HPPN]
British American soldier
* Colorado Chico
* Little Red

Rude, Ike 1894- [GW]
American rodeo performer
* Rude, Jitney

Rude, Jitney
See Rude, Ike

Rudel, Hans-Ulrich 1916-1982
German aviator
* [The] Eagle of the Eastern Front

Rudensky, Morris
See Friedman, Max Motel

Rudensky, Red
See Friedman, Max Motel

Rudensky, Rusty
See Friedman, Max Motel

[A] Ruder Burns
See Cunningham, Allan

Ruderman, Rudy
See Ruderman, Seymour George

Ruderman, Seymour George 1926-
[ASC]
American composer
* Ruderman, Rudy

Rudersdorff, Richard [FFF]
Entertainer
* Mansfield, Richard

Rudge, Letty 1862-1923 [THR]
British actress and dancer
* Lind, Letty

Rudhyar, Dane
See Chenneviere, Daniel

Rudie, Evelyn
See Bernauer, Evelyn Rudie

Ruding, Mrs. Walter [NPS]
Author
* Johnstone, Edith

Rudloff, Leo
See Von Rudloff, Alfred Felix

Rudnick, George ?-1940 [BLB, PHM]
American underworld figure
* Rudnick, Whitey

Rudnick, Whitey
See Rudnick, George

Rudolf
See Freund, Rudolf

Rudolf II [or Rudolph] 1552-1612
[DHA, FFF, SN]
Emperor of Germany
* [The] German Trimegistus
* [The] Hermes Trismegistus of
  Germany
* [The] Prince of Alchemy

Rudolph, Al[bert] 1894-1966 [AS, BX,
EJS]
American boxer
* McCoy, Al

Rudolph, Baldy
See Rudolph, Richard

Rudolph, Dutch
See Rudolph, John Herman

Rudolph, John Herman 1882-1967 [BE]
American baseball player
* Rudolph, Dutch

Rudolph, Lee [Norman] 1948- [CA]
American author and poet
* Cummings, Ann

Rudolph, Marvin 1938-1979 [BB]
American basketball official
* Hollywood, Mr.
* Rudolph, Mendy

Rudolph, Mendy
See Rudolph, Marvin

Rudolph, Richard 1887-1949 [BE, PB]
American baseball player
* Rudolph, Baldy

Rudolph, Skeeter
See Rudolph, Wilma Glodean Ward

Rudolph, William [Bill] ?-1905 [HPPN]
American bank robber
* Gorney, Charles
* [The] Missouri Kid

Rudolph, Wilma Glodean Ward 1940-
[BBH, IBW, SR]
American track and field athlete
* [The] Black Gazelle
* [The] Black Pearl
* [La] Gazelle
* [La] Gazelle Noire
* Rudolph, Skeeter
* Rudolph, Wondrous Wilma
* [The] World's Fastest Woman

Rudolph, Wondrous Wilma
See Rudolph, Wilma Glodean Ward

Rudomin, Esther
See Hautzig, Esther Rudomin

Rudstrom, Calvin 1895- [CA]
American author
* Rutstrum, Calvin

Rudy the Omelet Man
See Stanish, Rudolph

Rue, Jon Thoresen
See Tostenson, John

Rueckert, Friedrich 1788-1866 [WBD]
German poet
* Raimar, Freimund

Ruedi, Norma Paul
See Ainsworth, Norma

Ruef, Abraham [Abe] 1864-1936
[HPPN]
American political boss
* Ruef, Boss

Ruef, Boss
See Ruef, Abraham [Abe]

Ruegen, Hierclas 1873-1907 [HPPN]
French poet
* Guerin, Charles

Ruehle, George Robert 1932- [CWG]
American country-western performer
* Reagan, Bobby

Ruel, Herold Dominic 1896-1963 [AS, BE, PB]
American baseball player
* Ruel, Muddy

Ruel, Muddy
See Ruel, Herold Dominic

Rueleus, Mme. C. ?-1878 [PA]
Author
* Graviere, Caroline

Ruell, Patrick
See Hill, Reginald [Charles]

Ruellan, Andre 1922- [ESF]
French author
* Dupont, Kurt
* Louvigny, Andre
* Steiner, Kurt
* Vigan, Luc
* Wargar, Kurt

Ruether, Dutch
See Ruether, Walter Henry

Ruether, Walter Henry 1893-1970 [AS, BE, PB]
American baseball player
* Ruether, Dutch

Ruf, Frank 1909- [HCA]
American actor
* Faylen, Frank

Ruffacq, Walter 1901-1966 [HPPN]
American actor
* Ruffax, Walter

Ruffax, Walter
See Ruffacq, Walter

Ruffian, M.
See Hasek, Jaroslav [Matej Frantisek]

Ruffin, David 20th c. [IBW]
American singer, dancer, bandleader
* King David

Ruffin, Penelope 20th c. [IBW]
American tour guide
* Ruffin, Penny

Ruffin, Penny
See Ruffin, Penelope

Ruffin, Red
See Ruffin, Richard David

Ruffin, Richard David 1924- [BA]
American physician
* Ruffin, Red

Ruffing, Charles Herbert 1904-1986
[BE, DGS, PB]
American baseball player
* Ruffing, Red

Ruffing, Red
See Ruffing, Charles Herbert

[The] Ruffle
See Tegner, Henry [Stuart]

Ruffner, Budge
See Ruffner, Lester Ward

Ruffner, Lester Ward 1918- [CA]
American author
* Ruffner, Budge

Ruffner, William Henry 1824-1908
[HPPN]
American clergyman and educator
* [The] Horace Mann of the South

Ruffo, Titta
See Titta, Ruffo Cafiero

Rufsvold, Margaret Irene 1907- [HPPN]
American librarian, author, educator
* [The] Peripatetic Miss Rufsvold

Rufus
See Clare, Gilbert de

Rufus
See Otto II [or Otho]

Rufus
See Shakespeare, William

Rufus
See William II

Rufus the Red
See William II

Rugby, Nym
See Robinson, Nugent

[The] Rugeley Poisoner
See Palmer, William

Rugg, William Augustus 1789-1828
[HPPN]
British actor
* Conway, Handsome
* Conway, William Augustus

[The] Rugged Lion
See Ali

[The] Rugged Timon of the Elizabethan Drama
See Marston, John

Ruggiero, Benjamin 20th c.
American underworld figure
* Ruggiero, Lefty

Ruggiero, Lefty
See Ruggiero, Benjamin

Ruggles, Benjamin 1783-1857 [HPPN]
American politician
* [The] Wheel Horse of the Senate

Ruggles, John 1789-1874 [HPPN]
American politician
* [The] Father of the Patent Office

Ruggles, Samuel Bulkley 1800-? [HPPN]
American author
* One of the Trustees

Ruggles, Timothy 1711-1795 [HPPN]
American attorney, jurist, and politician
* [The] Brigadier

Ruhamah
See Scudamore, Lily

Ruhamah
See Skidmore, Harriet M.

Ruheni, Mwangi
See Muraguri, Nicholas

Ruhland, Stanley 20th c. [BEW]
American actor
* Gaige, Truman

Ruhlmann, Eugene Augustus 1861-1918
[BEW, BMH, CED]
American entertainer
* [The] Dandy Coloured Coon
* Stratton, Eugene

Ruhnke, Claude
See Ruhnke, Kent

Ruhnke, Kent 1952- [SMG]
Canadian-born hockey player
* Ruhnke, Claude

Ruiz, Antonio 1792-1860 [GS]
Spanish bullfighter
* [El] Sombrerero [The Hatter]

Ruiz, Chico
See Ruiz, Hiraldo Sablon

Ruiz, Henry 20th c.
Nicaraguan guerrilla leader
* Modesto

Ruiz, Hiraldo Sablon 1938-1972 [BE, PB]
Cuban-born baseball player
* Ruiz, Chico

Ruiz, Jose 20th c. [GS]
Spanish bullfighter
* [El] Calatraveno [The Man from Calatrava]

Ruiz, Juan 1283?-1351? [WBD]
Spanish poet
* [The] Archpriest of Hita

Ruiz, Manuel 20th c. [GS]
Spanish bullfighter
* Manili

Ruiz, Pablo Diego Jose Francisco de Paula Juan Nepomuceno Cipriano 1881-1973 [CA, HPPN]
Spanish-born painter and sculptor
* [The] Century's Greatest Artist
* [The] Founder of Cubism
* [The] Genius of Twentieth Century Art
* [The] Most Influential Artist of the Twentieth Century
* Picasso, Pablo [Ruiz]

Ruiz, Poppa
See Ruiz, Silvino

Ruiz, Silvino 20th c. [OBW]
American baseball player
* Ruiz, Poppa

Ruiz Camino, Carlos 1920-1966 [GS]
Mexican bullfighter
* Arruza, Carlos
* [El] Ciclon Mexicano [The Mexican Cyclone]

Ruiz De La Torre, Victor 1940- [GS]
Spanish bullfighter
* [El] Satelite [The Satellite]

Ruiz Soler, Antonio 1921- [HPPN]
Spanish dancer, choreographer, director
* Antonio

Ruiz y Vargas, Juan 1855-1910 [GS]
Spanish bullfighter
* Lagartija [The Rogue]

Rukeyser, Bud
See Rukeyser, M. S., Jr.

Rukeyser, M. S., Jr. 20th c. [ET]
Television executive
* Rukeyser, Bud

Rule, Ann 20th c. [NY 2-21-84]
American author
* Stack, Andy

Rule, William Harris 19th c. [PA]
Author
* W. H. R

Ruler, Alexander John 1936- [IAW]
British author
* Alexander, John

Ruler in Petticoats
See Elizabeth I

[The] Ruler of Florida
See Flagler, Henry Morrison

[The] Ruler of Kings
See Louis XIV

[The] Ruler of San Francisco
See Ralston, William Chapman

[The] Ruler of the Ausonian Lyre
See Ambrogini, Angelo

[The] Ruler of the Reading
See Gowen, Franklin Benjamin

Rulewski, Jan 20th c.
Polish labor leader
* [The] Pistol

Rulfs, Helen 1907?- [FC]
American actress
* Vinson, Helen

Rullianus
See Fabius Maximus, Quintus

Rulofsen, William Herman 19th c. [HPPN]
American author
* Herman, William

Ruman, Sig
See Rumann, Siegfried

Rumanian Rhubarb
See Nastase, Ilie

Rumann, Siegfried 1884?-1967 [F2, FC]
German actor
* Ruman, Sig

Rumball, Charles 19th c. [SFL, WGT]
Author
* Delorme, Charles

Rumbold-Gibbs, Henry St. John Clair 1909-1975 [AW, CA, CC]
British author
* Gibbs, Henry

Rumbold-Gibbs, Henry St. John Clair (cont.)
* Harvester, Simon
* Saxon, John

Rumford, Count
See Thompson, Benjamin [Count Rumford]

Rummer, Matt
See Prior, Matt[hew]

Rumohr, Theodore Wilhelm Kjerstrup 1807-? [HPPN]
Danish poet, playwright, author
* P. P.

Rumsey, Bert
See Rumsey, Burtis Harold

Rumsey, Burtis Harold 1892-1968 [SC]
American actor
* Rumsey, Bert

Rumsey, John 19th c. [CCL]
Canadian poet
* Plinius Secundus

Rumsey, Julian Sidney 1823-1886 [FFF]
American merchant
* [The] Father of Grain Inspection

Rumsey, Murray
See Rumshinsky, Murray

Rumsfeld, Donald 1932-
American politician
* Rumsfeld, Rummy

Rumsfeld, Rummy
See Rumsfeld, Donald

Rumshinsky, Murray 1907- [ASC]
American composer and conductor
* Rumsey, Murray

Rumyantsev, Mikhail 1902?-1983 [WP 4-4-83]
Russian circus clown
* Karandash [pencil]

[The] Run Away Spartan
See Peel, [Sir] Robert

Run Forever Kolb
See Kolb, Reuben Francis

Runciman, A., pinx
See Cummings, Albert Arratoon Runciman

Runciman, James Cochran Stevenson 1903- [LC]
British author and educator
* Runciman, [Sir] Steven

Runciman, John
See Aldiss, Brian W[ilson]

Runciman, [Sir] Steven
See Runciman, James Cochran Stevenson

Rundell, Mrs. 19th c. [RH]
Author
* [A] Lady

Rundle, Anne 20th c. [AW, CA, WD]
British author
* Lamont, Marianne

Rundle, Anne (cont.)
* Manners, Alexandra
* Marshall, Joanne
* Sanders, Jeanne

Rundquist, Anna Olivia 1871-1951 [MS]
Swedish-born opera singer
* Fremstad, Olive
* Peterson, Anna

Rundquist, Harry 20th c. [EF]
American football player
* Rundquist, Porky

Rundquist, Porky
See Rundquist, Harry

Runeskold-Baner, Johan Gustaf 1861-?
[NAA]
Swedish-born author
* Sagabard, Raven

Rungeling, Alfred J. 1853?-1916 [BEW]
American circus proprietor
* Ringling, Alfred J.

Rungeling, Charles 1864-1926 [BEW]
American circus proprietor
* Ringling, Charles

Rungeling, John 1866?-1936 [BEW,
HPPN]
American circus performer and proprietor
* [The] Circus King
* Ringling, John

Runkle, Bertha
See Bash, Mrs. Louis H.

Runkle, Janice 1953?-1981
American veterinarian
* Clark, M.

Runkle, Lucia Gilbert [PA]
Author
* Calhoun, Mrs.

Runnels, James Edward 1928- [BE, PB]
American baseball player
* Runnels, Pete

Runnels, Mrs. Frederick [FFF]
Entertainer
* Somerville, Amelia

Runnels, Pete
See Runnels, James Edward

Runnels, Virgil 20th c.
American wrestler
* Rhodes, Dusty

Running Bear
See George, Willie

Runnymede
See Disraeli, Benjamin

[The] Runt
See Quinlan, Walter

Runyan, John
See Palmer, Bernard

Runyan, Paul Scott 1908- [BWG, GF]
American golfer
* Little Poison

Runyon, Charles W. 1928- [CA]
American author
* West, Mark

Runyon, [Alfred] Damon 1880-1946
[HPPN]
American author and journalist
* Gentleman of Broadway
* Philosopher of City Life
* Runyon, Reporter
* [The] Sentimental Cynic

Runyon, Reporter
See Runyon, [Alfred] Damon

Rupert [Rupertus or Ruprecht] 650?-?
[WBD]
Saint
* [The] Apostle of the Bavarians

Rupert 1352-1410 [SN]
King of Germany
* [The] Straitened

Rupert 1619-1682 [DNNF, NPS, RH, SN]
*Duke of Bavaria and British royalist
general*
* [The] Brilliant
* [The] Mad Cavalier
* [The] Mirror of Chivalry
* [The] Prince Robber

[The] Rupert of Debate
See Stanley, Edward George Geoffrey
Smith

Rupert, Raphael Rudolph 1910- [CAP]
Hungarian-born writer
* Tatray, Istvan

Ruphelenguis
See Ravlengherio, Francois

Rupolo, Ernest ?-1964 [BLB, PHM]
American underworld figure
* [The] Hawk

Rupp, Adolph 1901- [BB, HPPN]
American basketball coach
* [The] Baron
* [The] Baron of Bluegrass
* [The] Man in the Brown Suit

Ruppert, Charles 1914- [FC, ITA, SW]
American actor
* Drake, Charles

Ruppert, Chester
See Graham, Roger Phillips

Ruppert, Four Straight Jake
See Ruppert, Jacob, Sr. [Jake]

Ruppert, Jacob, Sr. [Jake] 1867-1939
[HPPN]
*American soldier, politician, baseball club
owner*
* [The] Colonel
* Ruppert, Four Straight Jake

[A] Rupublican
See Russell, Jonathan

[Un] Rural
See De Cavagnac, G.

Rural
See Dunlap, M. L.

[A] Rural Dean
See Tatham, Arthur

[A] Rural Divine
See Bruce, Archibald

[The] Rural Postman of Bideford
See Capern, Edward

Ruric, Peter 20th c. [EMD]
Author
* Cain, Paul

Ruscelli, Girolamo ?-1566 [BI]
Italian scholar
* Piemontese, Alessio

Rusco, Bill
See Rusco, W. A.

Rusco, W. A. 1855-1931 [HPPN]
American producer and press agent
* Rusco, Bill

Rush, Andy
See Rush, Jess Howard

Rush, Benjamin 1745-1813 [HPPN]
American physician
* [The] Father of American Psychiatry

Rush, Bobby
See Nelson, Emmett

Rush, Jess Howard 1889- [BE]
American baseball player
* Rush, Andy

Rush, Joshua
See Pearlstein, Howard J.

Rush, Mary Jo
See Matthews, Mary Jo

Rush, Otis 1934- [BWW]
American singer
* Little Otis

Rush, William 1756-1833 [HPPN]
American sculptor
* [The] First Native Born American
Sculptor

Rushing, James Andrew [Jimmy]
1902-1972 [BWW, NP]
American singer
* Five By Five, Mr.
* Honey Bunny Boo
* Rushing, Little Jim

Rushing, Little Jim
See Rushing, James Andrew [Jimmy]

[The] Rushing Reporter
See Kisch, Egon Erwin

Rusholm, Peter
See Powell, Eric Frederick William

Rushton, Charles
See Shortt, Charles Rushton

Rushton, Thomas 18th c. [HPPN]
British poet
* [A] Plain Dealer

Rushton, Wattie
See Atwood, A. Watson

Rusie, Amos Wilson 1871-1942 [AS, BE, PB]
American baseball player
* [The] Hoosier Thunderbolt
* [The] Indiana Thunderbolt

Rusin, Jack
See Russin, Jack

Rusinol y Prats, Santiago 1861-1931 [BEW]
Spanish-born playwright and artist
* Rusinyol, Santiago

Rusinyol, Santiago
See Rusinol y Prats, Santiago

Rusk, [David] Dean 1909- [HPPN]
American politician
* [The] Old Dino

Rusk, Howard 1901- [CR]
American physician
* Live Again, Dr.

Rusk, Jeremiah McLain 1830-1893 [HPPN]
American secretary of Agriculture
* Uncle Jerry

Rusk, Robert Robertson 1879-? [HPPN]
Scottish lecturer and author
* R. R. R.

Ruskin, John 1819-1900 [DEA, DEL, PA]
British author and art critic
* [A] Graduate of Oxford
* J. R.
* Phusin, Kate

Ruslander, Mark 1933?- [HPPN]
American comedian
* [The] Capital's Comic
* Russell, Mark

Ruso, Michael 20th c. [WW]
Author
* Roscoe, Mike [joint pseudonym with John Roscoe]

Russ, Lavinia 1904- [CA]
American author and editor
* Faxon, Lavinia

Russ, Paula
See Ignatiev, Pauline

Russ, W. L. [FFF]
American writer
* Macswell

Russell
See Connell, Russell H.

Russell, Albert
See Bixby, Jerome Lewis

Russell, Alexander 1814-1876 [HPPN]
Scottish journalist and editor
* A. R.

Russell, Amanda
See Feldman, Ellen [Bette]

Russell, Andy
See Rabajos, Andy

Russell, Ann
See Dosch, Audrey Ann

Russell, Anna
See Russell-Brown, Anna Claudia

Russell, Arthur
See Goode, Arthur Russell

Russell, Baldy
See Mitchell, William [Bill]

Russell, Bertrand Arthur William 1872-1970 [HPPN]
British mathematician and philosopher
* [The] Passionate Skeptic

Russell, Big Jim
See Russell, James Wyman

Russell, Billy
See Brown, Adam George

Russell, Black
See Russell, John

Russell, Bob
See Russell, Sidney Keith

Russell, Bull Run
See Russell, [Sir] William Howard

Russell, Byron
See Russell, Patrick Joseph

Russell, C. 20th c. [MBF]
British author
* Clifford, Martin [house pseudonym]
* Wood, Geoffrey

Russell, Campy
See Russell, Michael

Russell, Charles Ellsworth 1906-1969 [ASC, DAM, EJ]
American jazz musician
* Russell, Pee Wee

Russell, Charles Marion 1865-1926 [HPPN]
American artist and sculptor
* [The] Cowboy Artist

Russell, Charlotte
See Rathjen, Carl H[enry]

Russell, Clarence Dixon 1890-1962 [BE]
American baseball player
* Russell, Lefty

Russell, Clinton
See Rathjen, Carl H[enry]

Russell, Curly
See Russell, Dillon

Russell, Dillon 1920- [EJ, PMJ]
American jazz musician
* Russell, Curly

Russell, Donald
See Nuss, Ralph

Russell, E. J. C.
See Russell, Edwin John Cumming

Russell, Edwin John Cumming 1939- [ART]
British sculptor
* Beauchamp, Mary Annette

Russell, Edwin John Cumming (cont.)
* Russell, E. J. C.
* Von Arnim, Mary Beauchamp

Russell, Elizabeth Mary 1866-1941 [WBD]
Australian-born author
* Elizabeth

Russell, Eric Frank 1905-1978 [ESF]
British author
* Craig, Webster
* Munro, Duncan H.

Russell, Erle?
See Wilding, Philip

Russell, Ernestine Jane Geraldine 1921- [AM]
American actress
* Russell, Jane

Russell, Ethel Harriman ?-1953 [HPPN]
American author
* Borden, Ethel

Russell, Ewell Albert 1889- [BE, PB]
American baseball player
* Russell, Reb

Russell, Fay
See Russell, Lafayette

Russell, Francis Chambers 1953- [FR]
American football player
* Chambers, Rusty

Russell, Frank 20th c. [OBW]
American baseball player
* Russell, Junior

Russell, Frank Alden 1908- [BI]
American poet, philosopher, radio personality
* Malone, Ted

Russell, Frank M. 1895-1972 [HPPN]
American television executive
* Russell, Scoop

Russell, Fred
See Parnell, Thomas Frederick

Russell, G[eorge] Oscar 1890- [HPPN]
American author
* Russell, Oscar George

Russell, G. W. E.
See Russell, George William Erskine

Russell, George William 1867-1935 [EWL, HPPN, TC, TLC]
Irish author, poet, playwright
* A. E.
* Aeon
* Gab
* O. L. S.
* Y. O.

Russell, George William Erskine 1853-1919 [LC, NPS]
British author and politician
* Onlooker
* Russell, G. W. E.

Russell, Glen David 1915-1973 [BE]
American baseball player
* Russell, Rip

Russell, Hanora Mary 1945- [HPPN]
Irish call girl and author
* Lefy, Nora
* Levy, Norma
* Russell, Norma

Russell, Hattie
See Labadie, Mrs. Francis

Russell, [Sir] Henry 19th c. [NPS]
Author
* Civis

Russell, Henry
See Levy, Henry

Russell, Henry
See Olson, Henry Russell

Russell, Honey
See Russell, John D.

Russell, Isaac Ed 1913- [EJ]
American jazz musician
* Russell, Snookum

Russell, J.
See Bixby, Jerome Lewis

Russell, James
See Craythorne, James

Russell, James
See Harknett, Terry

Russell, James Wyman 1912- [CWG]
American country-western performer
* Russell, Big Jim

Russell, Jane
See Russell, Ernestine Jane Geraldine

Russell, Jerry Sneak
See Russell, Samuel

Russell, John 1740-1817 [NPS]
Scottish clergyman
* Russell, Black

Russell, John 1795-1883 [NPS]
British clergyman
* [The] Sporting Parson

Russell, John 1885-1956 [WW]
Author
* Thrice, Luke

Russell, John
See Fearn, John Russell

Russell, John D. 1903-1973 [BB, BI, SMG]
American basketball player and coach
* Russell, Honey

Russell, [Lord] John Earl 1792-1878
[DEL, DNNF, NPS, SN]
British statesman and author
* Finality John
* [A] Gentleman who has Left his Lodgings
* [The] Lycurgus of the Lower House
* Skillett, Joseph

Russell, John Henry 1893-1972 [MK]
American baseball player
* Russell, Pistol

Russell, John J. 1886- [RBE]
American boxer
* Russell, Unk

Russell, John L. ?-1937 [SC]
American actor and director
* Lowell, John

Russell, John Somerset 1799-1880
[WBD]
British politician
* Pakington, [Sir] John Somerset

Russell, Jonathan 1771-1832 [IP]
American merchant, statesman, author
* [A] Rupublican

Russell, Joseph 1719-1804 [HPPN]
American merchant and shipowner
* [The] Duke

Russell, Junior
See Russell, Frank

Russell, Kathleen Barbara 1940- [ART]
Scottish-born painter
* K.

Russell, Ken 1927- [CR]
British film maker
* [The] British Orson Welles

Russell, Lafayette 20th c. [EF]
American football player
* Russell, Fay
* Russell, Reb

Russell, Landon R. 1873-1938 [BBD]
British conductor
* Ronald, [Sir] Landon

Russell, Lefty
See Russell, Clarence Dixon

Russell, Leon
See Wilson, Hank

Russell, Lillian
See Leonard, Helen Louise

Russell, Lindsay Patricia 20th c.
[WWL]
Author and poet
* Quinn, Ethel

Russell, Lloyd Opal 1913-1968 [BE]
American baseball player
* Russell, Tex

Russell, Lucy May
See Coryell, John Russell

Russell, Mabel
See Scott, Mabel

Russell, Margaret
See Montague, Eleonora Louisa

Russell, Mark
See Ruslander, Mark

Russell, Martin 1934- [CA]
British author
* Lester, Mark

Russell, Matthew 1834-? [PI]
Irish author, poet, clergyman
* Eulalie
* M. R.
* New, Edward
* W. L.

Russell, Michael 1952- [NBA, SMG]
American basketball player
* Russell, Campy

Russell, Morris Craw 1840-1913 [DNA]
American journalist
* Uncle Dudley

Russell, Mrs. R. F. [FFF]
Entertainer
* O'Neill, Hattie

Russell, Nipsey 20th c. [IBW]
American comedian
* Harlem's Son of Fun
* [The] Poet Laureate of Television

Russell, Norma
See Russell, Hanora Mary

Russell, Norma Hull Lewis 1902- [CA]
British author
* Hodgson, Norma

Russell, Oscar George
See Russell, G[eorge] Oscar

Russell, Owl
See Russell, William Henry

Russell, Patrick
See Sammis, John

Russell, Patrick Joseph 1884?-1963
[BEW]
Irish-born actor
* Russell, Byron

Russell, Pee Wee
See Russell, Charles Ellsworth

Russell, Pistol
See Russell, John Henry

Russell, R. 19th c. [HFN, IP]
British author
* [A] Middle Aged Citizen

Russell, Ray 20th c. [SFP]
Author
* Rencelaw, Brian
* Thorne, Roger

Russell, Raymond
See Balfour, William Raymond John
Evelyn

Russell, Raymond
See Fearing, Lilian Blanche

Russell, Reb
See Russell, Ewell Albert

Russell, Reb
See Russell, Lafayette

Russell, Rex
See Langdon, John [Franklin Coasten]

Russell, Richard [IP]
British physician and author
* Maevius

Russell, Richard 1723-1784 [HPPN]
British author
* [A] Friend to Female Beauty

Russell, Richard Brevard, Jr. 1897-1971
American politician
* [The] Great Parliamentarian

Russell, Rip
See Russell, Glen David

Russell, Ropes
See Russell, William Ellis [Bill]

Russell, Roy 1918- [CA]
British playwright and critic
* Gresham, Anthony

Russell, Rufus Rufty 1940?- [BI]
American cinematographer
* Russell, Rusty

Russell, Rusty
See Russell, Rufus Rufty

Russell, S. K.
See Russell, Sidney Keith

Russell, Samuel 1766-1845 [UH]
British actor
* Russell, Jerry Sneak

Russell, Sarah
See Laski, Marghanita

Russell, Sarah
See Wright, Mabel Osgood

Russell, Scoop
See Russell, Frank M.

Russell, Shane
See Norwood, Victor G[eorge] C[harles]

Russell, Sidney Keith 1914- [ASC, PMJ]
American lyricist
* Russell, Bob
* Russell, S. K.

Russell, Snookum
See Russell, Isaac Ed

Russell, Tex
See Russell, Lloyd Opal

Russell, Thomas [IP]
British author and clergyman
* A. S.

Russell, Thomas
See Laslett, Peter

Russell, Thomas O'Neill 1828-1908 [PI]
Irish author
* Tierney, Reginald

Russell, Unk
See Russell, John J.

Russell, W[illiam] Clark 1639-1683
[WBD]
British politician
* [The] Patriot

Russell, W. M. 19th c. [HFN, IP]
British author
* W. M. R.

Russell, W. P. 19th c. [HPPN]
British author and philologist
* [A] Patriotic Englishman

Russell, William [IP]
British author
* Warneford, Lieut.

Russell, William 1741-1793 [HPPN]
Scottish author
* [A] Nobleman

Russell, William 1798-? [HPPN]
Scottish-American educator
* W. R.

Russell, William 1860-? [IP, WW]
British author
* [A] Law Clerk
* [A] Custom-House Officer
* [A] Detective
* [A] Detective Police Officer
* [An] English Detective
* [A] French Detective
* Inspector F.
* Waters
* Waters, C.
* Waters, Thomas?

Russell, William Clark 1844-1911
[DLE1, HPPN, WWL]
British author
* Booth, Mrs. Letitia
* Mostyn, Sydney
* [The] Prose Homer of the Great
  Ocean
* [A] Seafarer

Russell, William Ellis [Bill] 1948- [PB,
SMG]
American baseball player
* Russell, Ropes
* Russell, Young Blood
* Super Rook

Russell, William Eustis 1857-1896
[HPPN]
American politician
* Billie the Kid
* [The] Boy Governor
* [The] Boy Mayor

Russell, William Felton [Bill] 1934-
[IBW]
*American basketball player, coach,
manager*
* Basketball, Mr.

Russell, William Henry 1802-1873
[HPPN]
American politician
* Russell, Owl

Russell, William Hepburn 1812-1872
[HPPN]
American business executive
* [The] Father of the Pony Express
* [The] Napoleon of the West

Russell, [Sir] William Howard
1820-1907 [SN]
British journalist
* Russell, Bull Run

Russell, Winifred Brent 20th c. [NAA]
American author
* Stait, Virginia

Russell, Young Blood
See Russell, William Ellis [Bill]

Russell-Brown, Anna Claudia 1911-
[BEW]
British actress, singer, lyricist
* Russell, Anna

Russhon, Charles 20th c.
American fighter pilot and photographer
* Russhon, Rush

Russhon, Rush
See Russhon, Charles

Russi, Luciano 1914- [IAW]
Italian author
* Ellerre

[A] Russian
See Polith, M.

Russian Bill Tattenbaum
See Tattenbaum, William

[The] Russian Brahms
See Medtner, Nikolai

[The] Russian Burns
See Koltzoff, Alexei Vasilievitch

[The] Russian Byron
See Pushkin, Alexander Sergeivitch

[The] Russian Casals
See Piatigorsky, Gregor

[The] Russian Connection
See Hammer, [Dr.] Armand

[The] Russian Doctor
See Pedachenko, Alexander

[A] Russian Lady
See Novikov, Olga

[The] Russian Lion
See Hackenschmidt, George

[The] Russian Lion
See Lesnevich, Gus

[The] Russian Livy
See Karamzin, Nicholas Michaelovitch

[The] Russian Messalina
See Catherine II

[The] Russian Murat
See Miloradowitch, Michael

[The] Russian Palestrina
See Bortniansky, Dmitri

[The] Russian Terrorist
See Zhelyabov, Andrei Ivanovich

[The] Russian Vampire
See Tarnowska, [Countess] Maria

[The] Russian Voltaire
See Somorokof [or Sumorokow],
Alexander Petrovitch

[The] Russian Walter Scott
See Zagoskin, Mikhail

Russia's Chess Teacher
See Schiffers, Emmanuel

Russia's New Chess Star
See Karpov, Anatoly

Russin, Babe
See Russin, Irving

Russin, Irving 1911- [ASC, EJ, PMJ]
American jazz musician
* Russin, Babe

Russin, Jack 20th c.
American jazz musician
* Rusin, Jack

Russo, Albert 1943- [IAW]
Belgian author and poet
* Rovin, Alex

Russo, Andy
See Russo, Anthony C.

Russo, Anthony C. 1903-1958 [EJ]
American jazz musician
* Russo, Andy

Russo, Giuseppe Luigi 1884-? [HPPN]
Italian educator and author
* Russo, Joseph Louis

Russo, Joseph Louis
See Russo, Giuseppe Luigi

Russo, Lefty
See Russo, Marius Ugo

Russo, Marius Ugo 1914- [BE]
American baseball player
* Russo, Lefty

Russo, Patricia Ellen 1945- [BEW]
American actress
* McCormack, Patty

Russo, Santo 1929- [EJ]
American jazz musician
* Russo, Sonny

Russo, Scarface Jock
See Russo, Victor

Russo, Sonny
See Russo, Santo

Russo, Victor 20th c. [DI]
American underworld figure
* Russo, Scarface Jock

[The] Russophobist
See Urquhart, David

Russworm
See Gluchen, Freidrich Wilhelm

[The] Rustic Bard
See Dinsmoor, Robert

Rusticus
See Bauer, Marius Alexandre Jacques

Rusticus
See Dell, John

Rusticus
See Hickling, George

Rusticus
See Jenkins, MacGregor

Rusticus
See Maurice, John Frederick Denison

Rusticus
See Wheatley, Richard

Rusticus
See Williams, [Rev.] St. George Armstrong

Rusticus, Gent.
See Furman, Garrit

Rustifucius, Trismegistus
See Moore, Thomas

Rustler, Robin
See Maclean, John

Rustyface
See Cunnington, Charles Leslie

Ruter, P. S. [IP]
American author
* [A] Virginia Physician

Rutgers, Lispenard
See Smith, Henry Erskine

Rutgers, Rudy
See Torborg, Jeffrey Allen

Rutgers van der Loeff, An[na] Basenau 1910- [SAT]
Dutch author and translator
* Bas, Rutger

Ruth
See Hill, Mrs. A. P. [Dawson]

Ruth, Babe
See Ruth, George Herman

[The] Ruth Draper of Radio
See Pious, Minerva

Ruth, George Herman 1895-1948 [AS, HPPN, OCS, SR]
American baseball player
* [The] Babe
* [The] Bambino
* [The] Idol of the American Boy
* [The] Mighty Bambino
* Monk [or Monkey]
* Ruth, Babe
* Ruth, Jidge
* Ruth, Two Head
* [The] Sultan of Swat

Ruth, Jidge
See Ruth, George Herman

Ruth, Two Head
See Ruth, George Herman

Ruthaly, Janos 1876-1963 [AS, BX, RBE]
Austrian-born boxer
* Root, Jack

Ruther, Bull
See Ruther, Wyatt

Ruther, Wyatt 1923- [EJ]
American jazz musician
* Ruther, Bull

Rutherford, Alison
See Cockburn, Alicia

Rutherford, Alvord 20th c. [AES]
American soccer player
* Rutherford, Skip

Rutherford, Austin 20th c. [GW]
American rodeo performer
* Rutherford, Buck

Rutherford, Buck
See Rutherford, Austin

Rutherford, Chas.
See Martin, Lawrence

Rutherford, Doc
See Rutherford, John William [Johnny]

Rutherford, Douglas
See McConnell, James Douglas Rutherford

Rutherford, Edward James 1927- [IAW]
British author
* Rutherford, Ward

Rutherford, Elman 1912?- [WWJ]
American jazz musician
* Rutherford, Rudy

Rutherford, John
See Baker, Evelyn Greenleaf

Rutherford, John William [Johnny] 1925- [BE]
Canadian-born baseball player
* Rutherford, Doc

Rutherford, Joseph Franklin 1869-1941 [WBD]
American religious leader
* Rutherford, Judge

Rutherford, Judge
See Rutherford, Joseph Franklin

Rutherford, Laurette 1914-1968 [SC]
American actress
* Arlen, Judith

Rutherford, Mark
See White, William Hale

Rutherford, Pat 20th c. [CA]
American author
* Hayford, Taria [joint pseudonym with June Haydon]

Rutherford, Rudy
See Rutherford, Elman

Rutherford, Skip
See Rutherford, Alvord

Rutherford, Ward
See Rutherford, Edward James

Rutherglen
See Macfarlane, Robert

Rutherston, Albert Daniel
See Rothenstein, Albert Daniel

Ruthin, Margaret
See Catherall, Arthur

Ruthven, Lord [HN]
Scottish aristocrat
* Greysteil

Ruthven, Richard David 1951- [SMG]
American baseball player
* Ruthven, Rufus

Ruthven, Rufus
See Ruthven, Richard David

Rutkowski
See Krasnodebski, Boleslaw

Rutland, Arthur
See Adcock, [Arthur] St. John

Rutland, Dodge
See Singleton, Betty

Rutledge, Brett
See Paul, Elliot Harold

Rutledge, [Dom] Denys
See Rutledge, Edward William

Rutledge, Edward William 1906- [CA, WD]
British clergyman and author
* Rutledge, [Dom] Denys

Rutledge, Marice [or Maryse]
See Hale, Marie Louise Gibson

Rutledge, Nancy 20th c. [BI, WW]
American author
* Bryson, Leigh

Rutlidge, [Sir] John James 18th c. [IP]
British author
* [An] Observer

Rutner, Mickey
See Rutner, Milton

Rutner, Milton 1920- [HPPN]
American baseball player
* Rutner, Mickey

Rutstein, Lillian 1910-1980 [FC]
American actress
* Roth, Lillian

Rutstrum, Calvin
See Rudstrom, Calvin

Rutt, M. E.
See Shah, Amina

Rutt, Richard 1925- [CA]
British-born clergyman and author
* Ro Tae-yong

Ruttan, Kate [McIntyre] 20th c. [CCL]
Canadian poet
* McIntyre

Rutter, Eileen Joyce 1945- [CA]
British author
* Chant, Joy

Rutter, Grace 1878?-1950 [BEW]
American actress
* Elliston, Grace

Rutter, John 1796-1851 [IP]
British barrister, printer, author
* [A] Constitutional Reformer

Rutter, Sally 1913?-1983 [FC, ITA]
American actress
* Page, Gale

Ruttkay, Arnold 1923- [IAW]
Hungarian-born author
* So, Bernat

Rutty, Herbert Waring 1857-1932 [THR]
British actor
* Waring, Herbert

Rutty, John 1698-1775 [IP]
Irish physician and author
* Catholicus, Johannes
* [An] Unworthy Member of that Community
* Utopiensis, Bernardus

Rutz-Nissen, Grethe 1906?- [F2, FC]
Norwegian actress
* Nissen, Greta

Ruwe, Horace A. 1893-1940 [HPPN]
American singer
* Parker, Jack

Ruxton, Buck
See Hakim, Bukhtyar Rustomji Ratanji

Ruxton, George Augustus Frederick 1821-1848 [HPPN]
British adventurer, soldier, frontiersman
* Ruxton, Young George

Ruxton, Young George
See Ruxton, George Augustus Frederick

Ruy-Blas, Eugene
See Lebeau, Eugene

Ruyerson, James Paul
See Rothweiler, Paul R[oger]

Ruysbroek, Jean de 1293-1381 [DNNF, FFF, HN, HPPN]
Flemish mystic
* [The] Admirable Doctor
* Blessed John
* [The] Divine Doctor
* Divinus, Doctor
* [The] Ecstatic Doctor
* Ecstaticus, Doctor

Ruyslinck, Ward
See De Belser, Reimond Karel Maria

Ruze
See Coiffier, Antoine

Ruzicka, Lavoslav 1887- [WBD]
Yugoslav-born chemist
* Ruzicka, Leopold

Ruzicka, Leopold
See Ruzicka, Lavoslav

Ruzkova, Jana 1943- [OP]
Czech opera singer
* Jonasova, Jana

[Il] Ruzzante
See Beolco, Angelo

Ryall, G. F. T.
See Ryall, George Francis Trafford

Ryall, George Francis Trafford 1887?-1979 [CA]
American columnist
* Audax Minor
* Ryall, G. F. T.

Ryall, William Bolitho 1890-1920 [LC, TC]
British author and journalist
* Bolitho, William

Ryan, [Father] Abram Joseph 1838-1886 [FFF, WBD]
American clergyman and poet
* Moina
* [The] Poet of the Confederacy
* [The] Tom Moore of the Confederacy

Ryan, Arthur 1852-? [PI]
Irish poet and clergyman
* A. R.

Ryan, Blondy
See Ryan, John Collins

Ryan, Buddy
See Ryan, James

Ryan, Bunny
See Ryan, Elizabeth

Ryan, Carroll
See Ryan, William Thomas

Ryan, Chew Tobacco
See Ryan, Frank

Ryan, Chico
See Ryan, Dave

Ryan, Connie
See Ryan, Cornelius Joseph

Ryan, Cornelius Joseph 1920- [BE, SMG]
American baseball player, coach, manager
* Ryan, Connie

Ryan, Cyclone
See Ryan, Daniel R.

Ryan, Dad
See Ryan, Edward

Ryan, Daniel R. 1866-1917 [BE]
Irish-born baseball player
* Ryan, Cyclone

Ryan, Dave 1948- [RO2]
American singer
* Ryan, Chico

Ryan, Edward ?-1883? [HPPN]
American gambler
* Ryan, Dad

Ryan, Edward Joseph ?-1920 [HPPN]
American murder victim
* [The] Ragged Stranger

Ryan, Elizabeth 1894-1979 [OET]
American tennis player
* Ryan, Bunny

Ryan, Frank 20th c. [PHM]
American underworld figure
* Ryan, Chew Tobacco

Ryan, Frederick 1876-1913   [DIL]
Irish journalist and editor
* Finian
* Irial

Ryan, Gerald   [FFF]
Entertainer
* Eyre, Gerald

Ryan, Get Rich Quick
See   Ryan, John

Ryan, Gulfport
See   Ryan, John Francis [Jack]

Ryan, Hermine Braunsteiner 1920?-
Austrian concentration camp guard during the Nazi era
* [The] Mare
* [The] Stomping Mare

Ryan, Irene
See   Riordan, Irene

Ryan, J.
See   Hanratty, James

Ryan, James 1855-?   [PI]
Irish-born poet
* Golma
* J. R.
* McGaura, Conner
* O'Flynn, Fergus

Ryan, James 1934-   [SMG]
American football coach
* Ryan, Buddy

Ryan, John 20th c.   [HPPN]
American betting commissioner and gambler
* Ryan, Get Rich Quick

Ryan, John 20th c.   [GW]
American rodeo performer
* Ryan, Paddy

Ryan, [Monsignor] John A. 1869-1945
[HPPN]
American clergyman, social reformer, author
* [The] Right Reverend New Dealer

Ryan, John Collins 1906-1959   [BE]
American baseball player
* Ryan, Blondy

Ryan, John D. 1897-   [BI, CAT]
American author
* Ernest, [Brother]

Ryan, John Fergus 1931-   [CA]
American author and playwright
* Thames, Jack

Ryan, John Francis [Jack] 1884-1949
[BE]
American baseball player
* Ryan, Gulfport

Ryan, John Joseph 1922?-   [FC, SW]
American actor
* Lord, Jack

Ryan, Joseph B. 1902-   [BBH]
Canadian football team manager
* Ryan, Rufus

Ryan, Kate
See   Nolan, Mrs. James

Ryan, Lew
See   Malone, Lew[is Aloysius]

Ryan, Lillie Eldridge 1851-1920   [HPPN]
American actress
* Eldridge, Lillie

Ryan, Little
See   Ryan, Melvin

Ryan, Marah Ellis
Author
* Martin, Ellis

Ryan, Margaret Mary 19th c.   [PI]
Irish poet
* Esmonde, Alice
* M. My. R.
* M. R.

Ryan, Mary 1885-1976   [HCA]
American actress
* Nash, Mary

Ryan, Melvin 1914-   [MY]
American singer
* Ryan, Little

Ryan, Merven J. 20th c.   [OBW]
American baseball player
* Ryan, Red

Ryan, Michael 1851-?   [PI]
Irish-born poet and clergyman
* Eithne
* M. J. R.

Ryan, Mrs. Thomas   [FFF]
Entertainer
* Conway, Mai
* Richfield, Mai

Ryan, [Lynn] Nolan 1947-   [BE, HPPN, PB]
American baseball player
* [The] Express
* Nolan, No Hit

Ryan, Norman 1895-1936   [BI]
Canadian gangster
* Ryan, Red

Ryan, P. J. 19th c.   [PI]
Irish poet and writer
* Barra, Gougane

Ryan, Paddy
See   Ryan, John

Ryan, Paul William 1906-1947   [WW]
Author
* Finnegan, Robert
* Quin, Mike

Ryan, Red
See   Ryan, Merven J.

Ryan, Red
See   Ryan, Norman

Ryan, Rosy
See   Ryan, Wilfred Patrick Dolan

Ryan, Rufus
See   Ryan, Joseph B.

Ryan, Sgt.
See   Coryell, John Russell

Ryan, Sheila
See   McLaughlin, Katherine Elizabeth

Ryan, Sweeney
See   Lett, William Pittman

Ryan, Thomas 1849-?   [PI]
Irish author
* Doodle
* [A] Drangan Boy
* T. R.

Ryan, Thomas J.   [BBH]
Bowler
* [The] Father of Fivepin Bowling

Ryan, Tim
See   Dent, Lester

Ryan, Tommy
See   Eboli, Thomas

Ryan, Tommy
See   Youngs, Joseph, Jr.

Ryan, W. S.
See   Smyth, William

Ryan, Wilfred Patrick Dolan 1898-
[BE]
American baseball player
* Ryan, Rosy

Ryan, William ?-1848   [HN]
Irish murderer
* Puck

Ryan, William 1851-1906   [BI]
American clergyman
* James, [Father]

Ryan, William Patrick 20th c.   [WWL]
Irish author
* O'Riain, Liam P.

Ryan, William Thomas 1839-?   [PI]
Canadian journalist and poet
* Ryan, Carroll
* [A] Wanderer

Ryba, Dominic Joseph 1903-1970   [BE, PB]
American baseball player
* Ryba, Mike

Ryba, Mike
See   Ryba, Dominic Joseph

Rybot, Doris
See   Ponsonby, Doris Almon

Ryckmans, Pierre 1935-   [CA]
Belgian art historian and author
* Leys, Simon

Rycon
See   Savery, Constance Winifred

Rydell, Bobby
See   Ridarelli, Robert Lewis

Rydell, Forbes [joint pseudonym with Helen B. Rydell]
See   Forbes, DeLoris [Florine] Stanton

Rydell, Forbes [joint pseudonym with
DeLoris (Florine) Stanton Forbes]
See Rydell, Helen B.

Rydell, Helen B.   [EMD, WW]
American author
* Rydell, Forbes [joint pseudonym with
DeLoris (Florine) Stanton Forbes]

Rydell, Wendell
See Rydell, Wendy

Rydell, Wendy 1927-1981 [CA, SAT,
WD]
American author
* Rydell, Wendell

Ryden, Ernest Edwin 1886- [NAA]
American clergyman and editor
* Augustson, Ernest

Ryder, Alfred
See Corn, Alfred Jacob

Ryder, [Sir] Don
See Ryder, [Sir] Sydney Thomas

Ryder, Elliot   [PA]
Author
* Ynetchi, Paul

Ryder, [Prof.] G. W.
See Grimm, Richard

Ryder, Jonathan
See Ludlum, Robert

Ryder, Michael Lawson 1927- [WD]
British writer
* Lawson, Michael

Ryder, Mitch
See Levise, William S., Jr. [Billy]

Ryder, Steven
See Edgar, Alfred

Ryder, [Sir] Sydney Thomas 1916- [BI]
British publisher and editor
* Ryder, [Sir] Don

Ryder, W. J. D.   [IP]
British author
* [A] Carthusian
* W. J. D. R.

Rydz, Edward 1886-1943 [BDW]
Polish statesman and army officer
* Smigly-Rydz, Edward

Rye, Anthony
See Youd, Christopher Samuel

Rye, Eugene Rudolph
See Mercantelli, Eugene Rudolph

Rye, Francis   [IP]
Canadian scholar
* F. R., of Barrie

Rye, Half-Pint
See Mercantelli, Eugene Rudolph

Rye, Michael
See Billsbury, Rye

Ryer
See Pfeiffer, Ida Laura

Ryer, Frederick R.   [PA]
Author
* Warwick

Ryerson, Adolphus Egerton 1803-1882
[HPPN]
Canadian clergyman and educator
* [The] Chief Superintendent of Schools

Ryerson, Lowell
See Van Atta, Winfred Lowell

Ryffe, Carlos Dee 1930?- [HPPN]
American author
* [The] Stooge

Ryhlick, Frank 20th c. [SFP]
Author
* Riley, Frank

Ryland, Clive
See Priestley, Clive Ryland

Ryland, John 1753-1825 [IP]
British clergyman and author
* J. R., Jun.

Ryland, John Collett 1723-1792   [IP]
British clergyman and author
* [A] Lover of Christ

Ryland, Lee
See Arlandson, Leone

Ryle, John 1817-? [HPPN]
British-American silk manufacturer
* [The] Father of the Silk Industry

Ryle, Randolph
See Pentelow, John Nix

Ryley, [Sir] Heister
See Povey, Charles

Rymer, James Malcolm 1814?-1884
[HPPN]
British author
* Bishop, Bertha Thorne
* Conroy, J. D.
* Errym, Malcolm J.
* Merry, Captain, U. S. N.
* Merry, Malcolm J.
* Percival, Nelson
* Urban, Septimus R.

Rymer, Thomas 1641-1713 [SN]
British literary critic
* Shakespeare's Critic

Rymnikski
See Suvorov [or Suwarof], Aleksandr
Vasilievich

Rynas, Stephen A. 20th c. [WGT]
Author
* Arr, Stephen

Rynders, Captain
See Rynders, Isaiah

Rynders, Isaiah 19th c. [HPPN]
American gambler and politician
* Rynders, Captain

Rynne, Patrick 1888?-1955 [BI]
American clergyman and educator
* Thomas, [Brother]

Ryott, Septimus William 1886?-1965
[F1, F2, FC]
British actor
* Rome, Stewart

[The] Ryparographer
See Pyricus

[The] Ryparographer of Wits
See Rabelais, Francois

Ryse, Sherwood
See Starey, Alfred B.

Ryskind, Morrie 1895- [CA]
*American playwright, screenwriter,
columnist*
* Wintergreen, John P.

Rytter, Poul 1813-1894 [WBD]
Danish poet and politician
* Ploug, Parmo Carl

Ryun, James Ronald [Jim] 1947-
[HPPN]
American track athlete
* [The] Kindergartner

Rywell, Martin 1905-1971 [CAP]
American author and editor
* Hemingway, Taylor
* Sears, Deane

Rzewuski, [Count] Henryk 1791-1866
[BI, HPPN]
Polish author
* Bejla, J.

Rzewuski, Stanislaw 17th c. [WBD]
Polish soldier
* [The] Grand Hetman of the Crown

S

S.
See Foe, Daniel

S.
See Scully, Vincent

S.
See Shepherd, Henry John

S.
See Skelton, John

S.
See Smith, Charles Card

S.
See Smith, Gerrit

S.
See Sparks, Jared

S.
See Tyler, William Clark

S.
See Webber, Samuel

S. A.
See Ayscough, Samuel

S. A. A.
See Allibone, Samuel Austin

S. A. F.
See Flint, Sara A.

S. A. H.
See Hurlbut, Stephen A.

S. A. L. E. M.
See Wyman, Mrs. John C.

S. A. M.
See Vestal, Herman Beeson

S. A. W.
See Walker, Samuel Abraham

S. B.
See Foe, Daniel

S. B.
See St. Barbe, Charles

S. B. G.
See Goslin, S. B.

S. B. P.
See Power, Samuel Browning

S. B. W.
See Wickins, Stephen B.

[The] S. Bahn Murderer
See Ogorzov, Paul

S. C.
See Carter, Samuel

S. C.
See Colliber, Samuel

S. C.
See Colvil, Samuel

S. C.
See Crampton, Sean

S. C. H.
See Hall, Samuel Carter

S. D.
See Ditcher, Selina

S. D.
See Downes, Samuel

S. D. A.
See Alexander, Samuel Davies

S. D. B.
See Bruce, Sanders D.

S. E. B.
See Brydges, Samuel Egerton

S. E. Y.
See McCarthy, Denis Florence

S. F.
See Furley, [Rev.] Samuel

S. F. C.
See Campion, John Thomas

S. F. D.
See Dunlap, Samuel Fales

S. F., Mrs.
See Egerton, Sara Fyge Field

S. F. S.
See Streeter, Sebastian Ferris

S. G.
See Gilman, Samuel

S. G.
See Gordon, Susan

S. G.
See Grascome, Samuel

S. G.
See Sandys, George

S. G. B.
See Bulfinch, Stephen Greenleaf

S. G. H.
See Howe, Samuel Gridley

S. G. O.
See Osborne, Sydney Godolphin

S. H.
See Cornish, James

S. H.
See Hall, Spencer

S. H.
See Tidmarsh, James

S. H. F.
See Fox, Sarah [Hustler]

S. J.
See Johnson, [Rev.] Samuel

S. J.
See Jones, Stephen

S. J.
See Tappan, Sarah [Jackson Davis]

S. J. H.
See Hale, Sarah Josepha Buell

S. J. J. F.
See Fox, S. J. J.

S. K.
See Kirby, K. Sarah N.

S. K. L.
See Lothrop, Samuel Kirkland

S. L.
See Longfellow, [Rev.] Samuel

S. L.
See Lounds, Stanley Samuel

S. L.
See Prynne, William

S. L. J.
See Jones, Sarah L.

S. M.
See Maer, Stephen

S. M.
See Martin, Selina

S. M.
See Melland, Sylvia

S. M.
See Moorhead, Scipio

S. M.
See Smedley, Menella Bute

S. M. A.
See Allen, Stephen Merrill

S. M. C.
See Anderson, Kathleen Agness Cicely

S. M. D.
See Davis, Sarah Matilda

S. M. R.
See Robertson, Seonaid Mairi

S. M. S.
See McCarthy, Mary Stanislaus

S. N.
See Elrington, Thomas

S. N.
See Nolan, Stephen

S. N. E., jun.
See Nolan, Stephen

S. O.
See Morgan, Sydney Owenson

S. O.
See Osgood, Samuel

[The] S. O. B. Who Can Use His Elbows
See Walker, Charles E.

S. P.
See Pegge, Samuel

S. P.
See Pennington, Mrs. S.

S. P. T.
See Tregelles, Samuel Prideaux

S. R.
See Rankin, Stella

S. R.
See Robinson, Samuel

S. R.
See Rosewell, [Rev.] Samuel

S. R. C.
See Ross-Craig, Stella

S. R. D.
See Drummond, Spencer Rodney

S. R. P.
See Powers, S. Rugeley

S. R. W.
See Wills, Samuel Richard

S. S.
See Clarkson, Anthony

S. S.
See Salisbury, Stephen

S. S. C.
See Conant, Silliman S.

S. S. D. D.
See Farr, Florence

S. S. E.
See Sperry, [Sally] Baxter

S. S. S.
See Simpson, S. S.

S. T.
See Knight, Charles

S. T.
See Timmins, Samuel

S. T.
See Walpole, Horatio [Fourth Earl of Orford]

S. T. A.
See Armstrong, Samuel Turell

S. T. C.
See Coleridge, Samuel Taylor

S. T. C. D.?
See Ingram, John Kells

S. T. C. D.
See O'Donoghue, John

S. T. P., Mr.
See Granatelli, Andrew [Andy]

S. U. S. and C. A. C.
See Bunbury, Henry William

S. W.
See Walker, Samuel

S. W.
See Ward, Sam[uel]

S. W.
See Watts, S.

S. W.
See Whiting, Sydney

S. W.
See Willard, Samuel

S. W., A. B.
See Walker, Samuel

S. W. B.
See Bush, Solon Wanton

S. W., Esq.
See Scott, [Sir] Walter

S. W. P.
See Patridge, S. W.

S-Ringi, Kjell
See Ringi, Kjell Arne Soerensen

Sa de Miranda, Francisco da 1495?-1558 [DNNS]
Portuguese poet
* [The] Portuguese Theocritus

Saadi [or Sadi]
See Muslih-ud-Din [or Moslehedin]

Saari, Uhro 20th c. [BBH]
American water polo coach
* Saari, Whitey

Saari, Whitey
See Saari, Uhro

Saba, Umberto
See Poli, Umberto

Sabalkanski [Crosser of the Balkans]
See Diebitsch, Hans Karl Friedrich, [Count]

Sabaroth, Ludwig de
See Sainte Lorette, Isnard de

Sabattis
See Gill, T. M.

[The] Sabbath Bard
See Grahame, James

[A] Sabbath School Teacher
See Wilson, Robert

Sabbatini, Andrea 1480?-1545 [WBD]
Italian painter
* Andrea da Salerno

Saben, Gertrude Chetwynd Shallcross 20th c. [WGT]
Author
* Saben, Gregory [joint pseudonym with Frederick Evelyn Burkitt]

Saben, Gregory [joint pseudonym with Gertrude Chetwynd Shallcross Saben]
See Burkitt, Frederick Evelyn

Saben, Gregory [joint pseudonym with Frederick Evelyn Burkitt]
See Saben, Gertrude Chetwynd Shallcross

Saber, Robert O.
See Ozaki, Milton K.

Saberhagen, Bret William 1964-
American baseball player
* Geisha

Sabeth, Adolph Joachim 1866-1952 [HPPN]
Bohemian-American politician
* [The] Dean of the House

Sabiad
See White, Stanhope

Sabich, Spider
See Sabich, Vladimir

Sabich, Vladimir 1943?-1976 [BI, HPPN]
American skier
* Sabich, Spider
* [The] Spider

Sabin, A. K.
See Sabin, Arthur Knowles

Sabin, Arthur Knowles 1879-1959 [LC]
British poet
* Sabin, A. K.

Sabin, Elijah Robinson 1776-1818 [IP]
American clergyman and author
* Observator, Charles

Sabin, Louis 1930- [SAT]
American author and editor
* Brandt, Keith

Sabin, Mark
See Fox, Norman Arnold

Sabine, Lorenzo 1803-1877 [IP]
American author
* Vindex

Sabine, Wallace C. W. 1868-1919
[HPPN]
American physicist and educator
* [The] Father of Architectural
  Acoustics

Sabine, William Henry Waldo 1903-
[WWL]
British author
* [The] White Friar

Sabini, John Anthony 1921- [AW, CA]
American author
* Anthony, John

Sabino
See Ballard, Edward

Sabinus
See Floridus, Francisco

Sabinus Vespasianus, Titus Flavius 40-81
[DNNS, RH, WBD]
Roman emperor
* [The] Darling of Mankind
* [The] Delight of Mankind
* Titus

[El] Sabio [The Learned]
See Alfonso X [or Alphonso]

[El] Sabio
See Ferdinand VI

[El] Sabio [The Wise]
See Sancho VI

[Le] Sablonnier [The Sand-Dealer]
See Frederick II

Sabo, Alex[ander]
See Szabo, Alexander

Sabo, Giz
See Szabo, Alexander

Sabourin, Anne Winifred 1910- [CA]
American author and nun
* Mary Justine, [Sister]
* Sabourin, Justine

Sabourin, Gary Bruce 1943- [HK]
Canadian-born hockey player
* Sabourin, Gaye

Sabourin, Gaye
See Sabourin, Gary Bruce

Sabourin, Justine
See Sabourin, Anne Winifred

Sabre, Dirk
See Laffin, John [Alfred Charles]

Sabre, Mark
See Thomas, William B. [Bill]

Sabretache
See Barrow, Albert Stewart

Sabu
See Dastagir, Sabu

Sabu, Frank
See Konadu, Samuel Asare

Sabuso
See Phillips, Irv[ing W.]

Sabut Jung [The Daring in War]
See Clive, Robert [Baron Clive of
Plassey]

Saca Bona
See Grimshaw, Ivan Gerould

Sacajawea [or Sacagawea] 1786?-1812?
[HPPN]
American Indian guide
* [The] Bird Woman

Sacastru, Martin
See Bioy-Casares, Adolfo

Saccas [Sack Bearer]
See Ammonius

Sacchi, Bartolommeo de' 1421-1481
[HPPN]
Italian humanist and historian
* Platina

Sacchini, Antonio Maria Gaspare
1735?-1786 [DEP, FFF, RH]
Italian composer
* [The] Racine of Music

Sacco, Fillippo 1905- [BLB]
Italian-born American underworld figure
* Roselli, John

Sacco, Lugee 1943- [RO1]
American singer and songwriter
* Christie, Lou

Sacco, Nicolo 1891-1927
Italian-born American political radical
* [The] Good Shoemaker

Sacerdote, Jenny 20th c. [WFA]
French fashion designer
* Madame Jenny

Sacharissa
See Sidney, Dorothy

Sacharuk, Lawrence William 1952-
[SMG]
Canadian-born hockey player
* Sacharuk, Satch

Sacharuk, Satch
See Sacharuk, Lawrence William

Sachem
See Hillhouse, William

Sachem, E. B.
See Creel, Stephen Melville

[The] Sachem of Tammany Hall
See Kelly, John

[The] Sachem of Tammany Hall
See Tweed, William Marcy

Sacher-Masoch, Aurora von 19th c.
[IP]
German author
* Dunajew, Wanda von

Sacheverell, Henry 1674?-1724 [HPPN,
IP, NPS, SN]
British clergyman
* Bungey, The Tow'ring High-Church
  Pope
* [The] High Church Trumpet
* Pontacus
* [A] Pulpit Physician
* Sacheverellio, Don, Knight of the
  Firebrand
* [The] Tongue Loosed Doctor
* [The] Zealous Doctor

Sacheverell, Lucy 17th c. [NPS]
Friend of British poet, Richard Lovelace
* Lucasta

Sacheverell, William 1638-1691 [HPPN]
British politician
* [The] First Whig

**Sacheverellio, Don, Knight of the
Firebrand**
See Sacheverell, Henry

Sachs, Albert Louis 1935- [CA]
South African author
* Sachs, Albie

Sachs, Albie
See Sachs, Albert Louis

Sachs, David
See Selznick, David

Sachs, Edward Julius 1927-1964 [EAR,
HPPN]
American auto racer
* [The] Clown Prince of Auto Racing
* [The] Pixie of Gasoline Alley
* Sachs, Fast Eddie

Sachs, Fast Eddie
See Sachs, Edward Julius

Sachs, Georgia
See Adams, Georgia Sachs

Sachs, Hans 1494-1576 [HN, RH, SN]
German poet
* [The] Cobbler Poet
* [The] Laureate of the Gentle Craft
* [The] Nightingale of Wittenberg
* [The] Prince of Satirists

Sachs, Nelly 1891- [HPPN]
German poet and playwright
* Leonie

**Sachsen, Amalie Frederike Auguste
Herzogin von** 1794-1870 [IP]
German playwright
* Heister, Amalie

Sack, Ethel 1895?-1957 [BEW]
American actress
* Cody, Ethel

Sack, Jack
See Sack, Jacob Bernard

Sack, Jacob Bernard 1902- [HPPN]
American football player
* Sack, Jack

Sack, O.
See Matz, Bertram Waldrom

[The] Sackamenna Kid
See Caen, Herb[ert]

Sackerman, Henry
See Kahm, Harold S.

Sackett, Grenville A.   [FFF]
American poet
* Alfred

Sackett, Grenville A. 19th c.   [HPPN]
American attorney
* [An] American

Sackett, Harry
See Dixon, Andrew

Sackett, Julia 1887-1975   [BEW, EMT, PMJ]
American actress and singer
* Sanderson, Julia

Sackett, Millie
See Pike, Mrs.

Sacks, Claire
See Sprague, Claire S[acks]

Sackville, Charles [Sixth Earl of Dorset] 1638-1706   [HPPN, NPS, SN]
British poet and statesman
* C. S.
* [The] Grace of Courts
* Harpalus
* [The] Muses' Pride
* [The] Patron and Poet of the Restoration

Sackville, Charles [Sixth Earl of Dorset] 1643-1706   [HPPN, SN]
British poet and statesman
* Harpalus
* [The] Patron and Poet of the Restoration

Sackville, Charles [Second Duke of Dorset] 1711-1769   [IP]
British author and poet
* C. S.

Sackville, Edward 17th c.   [SN]
British army officer
* Benaiah

Sackville, [Lord] George [First Viscount Sackville] 1716-1785   [HPPN]
British soldier
* Germain, George
* [A] Late Noble Commander
* [A] Noble Lord

Sackville, Thomas [Baron Buckhurst] 1536-1608   [SN]
British poet and diplomat
* Eugenius

Sackville-West, Reginald [Seventh Earl of De La Warr] 1817-?   [IP]
British author
* R. W. S. W.

Sackville-West, V.
See Sackville-West, Victoria Mary

Sackville-West, Victoria Mary 1892-1962 [CA, DBQ, LC, TC]
British author and poet
* Nicolson, Victoria Mary

Sackville-West, Victoria Mary (cont.)
* Sackville-West, V.
* Sackville-West, Vita

Sackville-West, Vita
See Sackville-West, Victoria Mary

Saco
See Meserve, Arthur Livermore

[Le] Sacre Monstre [The Sacred Monster]
See Buchinsky, Charles

Sacred Heart
See Alacoque, Margaret Mary

Sacrobosco, Johannes de
See Holywood, John

[The] Sad Sack
See Cantor, Philip

Sad Sack George Bartlett
See Bartlett, George

Sad Sam Jones
See Jones, Samuel Pond

Sad Sam Zoldak
See Zoldak, Samuel Walter

Sadat, Anwar 1918-1981
Egyptian president
* [The] Hero of the Crossing
* Nasser's Poodle

Sadat's Sadat
See Mubarak, Hosni

Sadaukai, Owusu
See Fuller, Howard

Saddle-Bag John
See Pope, John

Saddler, A. C. 1935-   [EG]
Golfer
* Saddler, Sandy

Saddler, Allen
See Richards, Ronald Charles William

Saddler, Dandy Sandy
See Saddler, Joseph

Saddler, Joseph 1926-   [BX, IBW, RBE]
American boxer
* Saddler, Dandy Sandy
* Saddler, Sandy

Saddler, K. Allen
See Richards, Ronald Charles William

Saddler, Sandy
See Saddler, A. C.

Saddler, Sandy
See Saddler, Joseph

Sadeur, Jacques
See De Foigny, Gabriel

Sadgrove, Sidney Henry 1920-   [AW, WD]
British playwright
* Torrance, Lee

Sadi, Fats
See Sadi, Lallemand

Sadi, Lallemand 1926-   [EJ]
Belgian jazz musician
* Sadi, Fats

Sadina
See Mitchell, Priscilla

Sadino, Elmano
See Bocage [or Boccage], Manuel Maria Barbosa du

Sadleir, Mary Anne 1820-1903   [PA, PI]
Irish poet
* Cootehill, M.
* Madden, M. A.

Sadleir, Michael
See Sadler, M. T. H.

Sadleir, William Digby ?-1858   [PI]
Irish poet and clergyman
* W. D. S.

Sadler, Clarice Laurence 20th c. [WWL]
British author
* Laurence, Clarice

Sadler, Haskell Robert 1935-   [BWW]
American singer
* Cool Papa

Sadler, Izetta Estelle 1875?-1934   [BEW]
American actress
* Mayhew, Stella

Sadler, J. 19th c.   [HPPN]
British author
* [A] Lock Keeper

Sadler, James Robert 1908-1967   [BMH]
British entertainer
* Desmonde, Jerry

Sadler, L. R. 19th c.   [IP, PA]
British author
* Larwood, Jacob

Sadler, M. T. H. 1888-   [WWL]
British author
* Sadleir, Michael

Sadler, Mark
See Lynds, Dennis

Sadler, T.
See Foe, Daniel

Sadlowski, Edward 1939-
American labor leader
* Oil Can Eddie

Sadowski, Robert Frank [Bob] 1937- [BE]
American baseball player
* Sadowski, Sid

Sadowski, Sid
See Sadowski, Robert Frank [Bob]

Sadyk Pasha
See Czajkowski, Michal

Saemund Sigfusson 1054?-1133 [RH, SN, WBD]
Icelandic clergyman and poet
* [The] Sage
* [The] Wise

Saerasmid
See Gardette, Charles Desmarais

Saetone [joint pseudonym]
See Camus, Albert

Saffah, al- [The Bloodshedder]
See Abbas, Abu-al-

Safford, Ann Eliza 1792-1856 [HPPN]
American author
* His Wife

Safford, Mary J. 19th c. [IP, PA]
American journalist
* M. S.

Safian, Jill
See Jacobs, Jill

Safka, Melanie 1947- [RO2]
American singer
* Melanie

Sagabard, Raven
See Runeskold-Baner, Johan Gustaf

[The] Sagacious Terrier
See Bruce, James

Sagadahoc
See Kidder, Frederic

Sagan, Francoise
See Quoirez, Francoise

Sagan, Leontine
See Schlesinger, Leontine

Sagaunash 1780?-1841 [BI]
American Indian chief
* Caldwell, Billy

[The] Sage
See Bernal, John Desmond

[The] Sage
See Buchanan, George

[Le] Sage
See Charles V

[Le] Sage
See John V [or Jean]

[Le] Sage
See Las Cases, Emmanuel Augustin Dieudonne de

[The] Sage
See Saemund Sigfusson

Sage, Agnes Carolyn 20th c. [ALY]
American author
* Sage, Agnes Carr

Sage, Agnes Carr
See Sage, Agnes Carolyn

[The] Sage and Serious Spenser
See Spenser, Edmund

Sage, Anna
See Cumpanas, Ana

Sage, Bernard Janin 1821-1902 [DNA]
American author and attorney
* Centz, P. C.

[Le] Sage de la Grande Armee
See Drouot, Antoine, [Comte]

Sage, Frances
See Satz, Frances

Sage, Juniper [joint pseudonym with Edith (Thacher) Hurd]
See Brown, Margaret Wise

Sage, Juniper [joint pseudonym with Margaret Wise Brown]
See Hurd, Edith [Thacher]

[The] Sage of Alexandria
See Euclid

[The] Sage of America
See Franklin, Ben[jamin]

[The] Sage of Anacostia
See Bailey, Frederick Augustus Washington

[The] Sage of Ashland
See Clay, Henry

[The] Sage of Ashland
See Lee, Henry

[The] Sage of Auburn
See Seward, William Henry

Sage of Ayot
See Shaw, George Bernard

[The] Sage of Baltimore
See Mencken, Henry Louis [Harry]

[The] Sage of Baltimore
See Price, T. Rowe

[The] Sage of Bolt Court
See Johnson, Samuel

[The] Sage of Chappaqua
See Greeley, Horace

[The] Sage of Chelsea
See Carlyle, Thomas

[The] Sage of Concord
See Alcott, Amos Bronson

[The] Sage of Concord
See Emerson, Ralph Waldo

[The] Sage of Crotona
See Pythagoras

[The] Sage of Emporia
See White, William Allen

[The] Sage of Gramercy Park
See Tilden, Samuel Jones

[The] Sage of Greystone
See Tilden, Samuel Jones

[The] Sage of Happy Valley
See Taylor, Alfred Alexander

[The] Sage of Hickory Hill
See Watson, Thomas Edward

[The] Sage of Kinderhook
See Van Buren, Martin

[The] Sage of Lindenwald
See Van Buren, Martin

[The] Sage of Log Hall
See Philips, Mardin Wilson

[The] Sage of McDuffie
See Watson, Thomas Edward

[The] Sage of Mississippi College
See Aven, Algernon Jasper

[The] Sage of Moberly
See Conroy, John Wesley [Jack]

[The] Sage of Monticello
See Jefferson, Thomas

[The] Sage of Montpelier
See Madison, James

[The] Sage of Mount Vernon
See Washington, George

[The] Sage of Nininger
See Donnelly, Ignatius [Loyola]

[The] Sage of Pittsfield
See Dawes, Henry Laurens

[The] Sage of Potato Hill
See Howe, Ed[gar Watson]

[The] Sage of Princeton
See Cleveland, [Stephen] Grover

[The] Sage of Princeton
See Roosevelt, Theodore [Teddy]

[The] Sage of Samos
See Pythagoras

[The] Sage of Sex
See Ellis, [Henry] Havelock

[The] Sage of Sinnissippi
See Lowden, Frank Orren

[The] Sage of Skinner Street
See Godwin, William

[The] Sage of Springfield
See Lincoln, Abraham

[The] Sage of Syracuse
See Archimedes

[The] Sage of the Hermitage
See Jackson, Andrew

[The] Sage of the Verduga Hills
See McGroarty, John Steven

[The] Sage of Tishomingo
See Murray, William Henry

[The] Sage of Uvalde
See Garner, John Nance

[The] Sage of Walden Pond
See Thoreau, Henry David

[The] Sage of Walpole
See Bird, Francis William

[The] Sage of Wheatland
See Buchanan, James

Sagendorph, Robb Hansell 1900-1970 [CA]
American author
* Weatherwise, Abe

Sager, Jane Olive 1914- [MY]
American jazz musician
* Sager, Si

Sager, Pony
See Sager, Samuel B.

Sager, Samuel B. 1847-? [BE]
American baseball player
* Sager, Pony

Sager, Si
See Sager, Jane Olive

[The] Sagest of Usurpers
See Cromwell, Oliver

Sagglehorne, Sadie
See Chaillie, Jean Humphrey

[The] Saginaw Kid
See Lavigne, George

Sagitta
See Mackay, John Henry

Sagittarius
See Katzin, Olga

Sagittarius
See Schutz, Heinrich

Sagoyewatha 1751?-1830 [FFF, WBD]
American Indian chieftain
* [The] Cowkiller
* Red Jacket

Sagsam, Angela
See Muirhead, Sara Alyne [Guynes]

Sah-nee-weh
See Hendricks, Namee

Sahafzadeh
See Efendi, Mohammed Esaad

Sahara Sarah Polk
See Polk, Sarah Childress

Sahib, Nana
See Pant, Dandhu

Sahib, Nana
See Robinson, William Ellsworth

Sahm, Douglas Saldana 1942- [RO2]
American singer and musician
* Sir Douglas

Saicho 767-822 [WBD]
Japanese religious leader
* Dengyo Daishi

Sa'id, Ali Ahmad 1930- [BI]
Lebanese poet
* Adonis

Said, Bob
See Said, Boris

Said, Boris 1932- [EAR]
American auto racer
* Said, Bob

Said, Laila
See Abou Saif, Laila

Saida
See LeMair, H[enriette] Willebeek

Saidie
See Williams, Sarah

Saidy, Fareed Milhem 1907-1982 [BEW, EMT]
American librettist
* Saidy, Fred

Saidy, Fred
See Saidy, Fareed Milhem

Saietta, Ignazio 20th c. [BLB, PHM]
American underworld figure
* Lupo, Joseph
* Lupo the Wolf

Sailer, Toni 1935?- [HPPN]
Austrian skier and actor
* [The] King of the Mountain
* Toni San the Terrific

Sailil
See Tullock, W. W.

Sailland, Maurice Edmond 1872-1956 [BI]
French gastronomist
* Curnonsky

[A] Sailor
See Falconer, William

[A] Sailor
See Fox, Franklin

[A] Sailor
See Larwood, Joshua

[A] Sailor
See Lindsay, William Schaw

[A] Sailor
See Nordhoff, Charles

[A] Sailor
See Pemberton, Charles Reece

Sailor Art Thomas
See Thomas, Arthur

Sailor Bill Posedel
See Posedel, William John

Sailor Billy Vincent
See Vincent, William J.

Sailor Bob Shawkey
See Shawkey, Bob

[A] Sailor Boy
See Nordhoff, Charles

Sailor Don Sauer
See Sauer, Don

Sailor Joe
See Simmons, Vivian

[The] Sailor Kid
See London, John Griffith [Jack]

[The] Sailor King
See William IV

Sailor, Leo 1895-1962
American actor
* Saylor, Sid

Sailor of the Unknown Seas
See Drake, [Sir] Francis

[The] Sailor Prince
See George V

Sailor Tom Sharkey
See Sharkey, Thomas Joseph

Sailor William
See William IV

[The] Sailor's Friend
See Plimsoll, Samuel

[The] Sailor's Friend
See Weston, Agnes

[The] Sailor's Lawyer
See Dana, Richard Henry, Jr.

Saimes, George 1941- [FB]
American football player
* Camus in Shoulder Pads
* [The] Existentialist Pass Defender

Sain, John Franklin [Johnny] 1917- [BE, BTB]
American baseball player
* [The] Man of a Thousand Curves

Sainpolis, John
See St. Polis, John

Sainsbury, Noel Everingham 1884-? [HPPN]
American author
* Richards, Harvey D.
* Wayne, Dorothy

[The] Saint
See Canute IV

[The] Saint
See Chin-tsou-jin

[The] Saint
See Edward VI

[The] Saint
See Eric IX

[The] Saint
See Ferdinand III

[The] Saint
See Henry II [or Heinrich]

[The] Saint
See Ladislas I

[The] Saint
See Olaf II [or Olaus]

[The] Saint
See St. Gaudens, Augustus

St. Agnes, [Sister]
See Finn, Emily

St. Aime, Georges
See Pelletier, Alexis

Saint Albin, J. S. C. de
See Collin, Jacques Albin Simon

Saint Amand
See Lacoste, Jean Amand

Saint Amand, Gabriel Randon de 1867-1933 [HPPN]
French poet
* Rictus, Jehan

Saint Amant, Marc Antoine Girard de
1594-1661 [HPPN]
French poet
* [The] Creator of Burlesque Poetry in
  France

[The] Saint Among Us
See Bojaxhiu, Agnes Gonxha

St. Anbeck, Roland
See Beck, Roland Stanley

St. Andre, Lucien
See Mott, Vincent Valmon

Saint, Andrew [John] 1946- [CA]
British writer
* Plendello, Leo

St. Angel, Marjorie 1920-1969 [SC]
American actress
* Holliday, Marjorie

Saint Archibald
See Bower, Archibald

Saint Aubain, Andreas Nicolai de
1798-1865 [WBD]
Danish author
* Bernhard, Karl

Saint Aubin, Horace de
See Balzac, Honore de

St. Aubyn, Alan
See Marshall, Frances

St. Aubyn, [Sir] John 1758-1839
British author
* Montauban

St. Aubyn, John Humphrey 1790-1857
[IP]
British clergyman and author
* Bouverie, Lionel

Saint Aude, Magloire
See Magloire, Clement, fils

Saint Aurele, Poirie de
See Poirie, Jean-Aurele Pierre

St. Barbe
See Sladen, Douglas

St. Barbe, Charles 1776-1849 [IP]
British antiquary and author
* C. S. B.
* S. B.

St. Basil
See Spence, [Sir] Basil Unwin

Saint Benjamin
See White, Richard Grant

Saint Bernard Croly
See Croly, George

St. Briavels, James
See Wood, James Playsted

St. Bruno, Albert Francis 1909- [CAP]
Australian-born author
* Bruno, Frank

Saint Cecilia
See Manigault, G.

St. Clair, Byrd Hooper 1905-1976 [CA]
American author
* Hooper, Byrd

St. Clair, Cecil
See Clark, Susie Champney

St. Clair, Clovis
See Skarda, Patricia Lyn

St. Clair, Elizabeth
See Cohen, Susan

St. Clair, Everett
See Mansell, Mrs. C. B.

St. Clair, Geek
See St. Clair, Robert B.

St. Clair, James 1921?- [HPPN]
American attorney
* Justice's Midwife
* [The] President's Lawyer
* [The] White House Lawyer

St. Clair, Katherine
See Huff, Tom Elmer

St. Clair, Leonard
See Cooper, Leonard

St. Clair, Mabel
See Hibbard, Carrie S.

St. Clair, Margaret 1911- [ESF, SF,
WGT]
American author
* Hazel, William?
* Hazzard, Wilton
* Seabright, Idris

St. Clair, Philip
See Howard, Munroe

St. Clair, Robert B. 1931- [FB]
American football player
* St. Clair, Geek

St. Clair, Rosalind 19th c. [IP]
British author
* [A] Lady

St. Clair, Victor
See Browne, George Waldo

St. Clair, William
See Ford, William

St. Claire, Ebba
See St. Claire, Edward Joseph

St. Claire, Edward Joseph 1921- [BE]
American baseball player
* St. Claire, Ebba

St. Claire, Yvonne
See Hall, Emma L.

Saint Cricq, Lorenzo de 19th c. [IP]
French author
* Marcoy, Paul

St. Cyr, Cyprian
See Bernstein, Eric [Lennard]

St. Cyr, Lili
See Van Schaak, Marie

St. Cyr, Lillian 1873-1974 [FI, SC]
American actress
* Red Wing, Princess

St. Dare, Julian
See Patten, William George

St. Denis le Cadet
See Allen, Paul

Saint Denis, Michel Jacques 1897-1971
[AW, CAP]
French-born producer, director, author
* Duchesne, Jacques

St. Denis, Ruth
See Dennis, Ruth

St. Denis, Teddie
See Denham, June Catherine Church

Saint Denis, Valia Maria [Suria] 20th c.
[AW]
Russian-born playwright
* Magito, Suria

Saint, Dora Jessie [Shafe] 1913- [AW,
CA, WD]
British author
* Read, Miss

St. E. A. of M. and S.
See Crowley, Edward Alexander

Saint Eden, Dennis
See Foster, Don[ald]

Saint Etienne
See De Villiers, Cosm

Saint Evita
See Peron, Eva Duarte

Saint Evremond, Seigneur de
See De Marguetel de Saint-Denis,
Charles

St. Felix, Marie
See Lynch, Harriet Louise

Saint for the Small
See More, [Sir] Thomas

Saint for the Time
See More, [Sir] Thomas

Saint for this Season
See More, [Sir] Thomas

[The] St. Francis of Methodism
See Asbury, Francis

[The] Saint Francis of Presbyterianism
See Makemie, Francis

St. Gaudens, Augustus 1848-1907
[HPPN]
Irish-American sculptor
* [The] Saint

St. George
See McGovern, George Stanley

St. George, Arthur
See Paine, Lauran [Bosworth]

St. George, David [joint pseudonym
with David Atlee Phillips]
See Markov, Georgi

St. George, David [joint pseudonym with Georgi Markov]
See Phillips, David Atlee

St. George, George
See Snow, Joseph

St. George, Harry
See Rathborne, St. George Henry

St. George, [Mother] Mary 20th c. [CCL]
Canadian author
* Douglas, Mary

Saint George, Mrs. A. 19th c. [IP]
British author
* [An] English Lady

St. George, Philip
See Avallone, Michael [Angelo], Jr.

Saint Gildas the Wise
See Gildas [or Gildus]

St. Guillaume de Gellone
See Guillaume d'Orange

St. Harriot, [Doktor] Tourneur
See Weil, Joseph R.

St. Helier, Ivy
See Aitchison, Ivy

St. Hereticus
See Brown, Robert McAfee

St. Hilaire, Marco de
See Hilaire, Emile Marc

Saint Hyacinthe, Cardonner 1684-1746 [PA]
Author
* De Themuseuil, Chevalier

Saint in Time of Turmoil
See More, [Sir] Thomas

St. Innocence, [Sister]
See Gerson, Vassily Vassilijevich

St. Jacques, Bertrand Hardouin 1600-1648 [HPPN]
French actor
* Guillot Gorju

St. Jacques, Raymond
See Johnson, James Arthur

St. Jacques, Sterling 1951?-
American fashion model and dancer
* St. Jacques, Swirling Sterling

St. Jacques, Swirling Sterling
See St. Jacques, Sterling

St. James
See Strang, James Jesse

St. James, Andrew
See Stern, James [Andrew]

St. James, Bernard
See Treister, Bernard W[illiam]

St. James, Blakely [house pseudonym, Playboy Press]
See Platt, Charles

St. James, Fred
See Sullivan, John Florence

St. James of Compostela
See James

Saint James, Susan
See Miller, Susan

St. Jane
See Pfeiffer, Jane Cahill

Saint Jerome
See Edmunds, George Franklin

St. Jimmy the Tempted
See Carter, James Earl, Jr. [Jimmy]

St. John, Al 1893-1963 [F1, FC, SC]
American actor
* Jones, Fuzzy Q.
* St. John, Fuzzy

St. John, Beatrice ?-1974 [HPPN]
American actress, director, producer
* St. John, Trissie

St. John, Beth
See John, Elizabeth Beaman

St. John, Betta
See Streidler, Betty

Saint John, Charles William George 1809-1856 [IP]
British author
* [A] Sportsman and Naturalist

St. John, Christopher Marie
See Marshall, Christabel

St. John, Claire
See Harrison, Claire

St. John, David
See Hunt, E[verette] Howard, Jr.

St. John, Dick
See Gosting, Richard

St. John, Elizabeth
See John, Elizabeth Beaman

St. John, Eugenia
See Berry, Martha Eugenia

St. John, Florence
See Marius, Madame

St. John, Fuzzy
See St. John, Al

St. John, Henry 1678-1751 [DEA, DEL, HPPN, IP, RH, SN]
British statesman and writer
* Bolingbroke, Proud
* Bolingbroke, Viscount
* Bull
* D'Anvers, Caleb, Esq.
* Gambol, Leud
* High Mettled Harry
* [A] Noble Duke
* Oldcastle, Humphrey
* [The] Patriot King
* Raleigh, W.
* St. John, Tumbler Harry
* [The] Salamander in My Eye
* Trott, John, Yeoman

St. John, Henry
See Cooper, Charles Henry St. John

St. John, Henry
See Creasey, John

St. John, J. Hector
See Crevecoeur, Michel Guillaume Jean de

St. John, James Augustus 1801-1875 [IP]
Scottish author
* [A] Layman

St. John, Jill
See Oppenheim, Jill

St. John, John
See Sale, Richard [Bernard]

St. John, Leonie [joint pseudonym with Nancy Harmon]
See Bayer, William

St. John, Leonie [joint pseudonym with William Bayer]
See Harmon, Nancy

St. John, Lily
See Johnson, Lilian Clara

St. John, Mabel
See Cooper, Charles Henry St. John

Saint John, Marguerite
See Wood, Mrs. G. M.

St. John, Mary ?-1830? [PI]
Irish poet
* Mary

St. John, Nellie
See Van Auken, Mrs. Henry

St. John, Nicole
See Johnston, Norma

St. John, Oliver 1598?-1673 [SN]
British jurist
* [The] Dark Lantern Man

St. John, Percy Bollingbroke 1821-1889 [HPPN, PA]
British author
* Boone, Henry L.
* Brougham, J. T.
* Cavendish, Harry
* Freeman, J. L.
* Hope, [Lady] Esther
* McKeen, Captain
* P. B. St. J.
* Periwinkle, Paul
* St. John, Warren

Saint John, Perse
See Leger, [Marie-Rene] Alexis Saint-Leger

St. John, Philip
See Alvarez Del Rey, Ramon Felipe San Juan Mario Silvio Enrico

St. John, Randolph
See Kleiner, Rheinhart

St. John, Sergius 18th c. [PA]
Author
* Grandfather

Saint John the Righteous
See Anderson, John Bayard

St. John, Theophilus, LL B.
See Clapham, Samuel

St. John, Trissie
See St. John, Beatrice

St. John, Tumbler Harry
See St. John, Henry

St. John, Warren
See St. John, Percy Bollingbroke

St. John, William Pope 1848-1897
[HPPN]
American banker
* [The] Apostle of Free Coinage for Silver

St. John, Wylly Folk 1908- [CA, SAT]
American author
* Fox, Eleanor
* Larson, Eve
* Pierce, Katherine
* Vincent, Mary Keith
* Williams, Michael

St. Jorgen, Goerger 1841-1926 [BBD]
Hungarian-born opera singer
* Orgeni, Aglaja

St. Joseph of Cupertino
See Desa, Giuseppe

St. Justin Marie, [Mother]
See Bazin, Marie Rene

St. Kames
See Townsend, S. Nugent

St. Kayne, Humphrey
See Crawfurd, Oswald John Frederick

St. L., Vic
See Hopkins, Squire D.

St. Laurence, A.
See Felkin, Alfred Laurence

St. Laurent, Ace
See St. Laurent, Andre

St. Laurent, Andre 1953- [SMG]
Canadian-born hockey player
* St. Laurent, Ace

Saint Laurent, Cecil
See Laurent-Cely, Jacques

Saint Laurent, Felix de
See Ambroise, Fernand

St. Laurent, Julie de 19th c. [NN]
Mistress of Edward, Duke of Kent
* Edward's French Lady

St. Laurent, Louis 1882-1973
Canadian prime minister
* Uncle Louis

Saint Laurent, Yves [Henri Donat Mathieu] 1936-
French fashion designer
* Y. S. L.

St. Leger, Elizabeth 18th c. [FFF, HN, RH]
Daughter of Arthur, Lord Doneraile
* [The] Female Freemason
* [The] Lady Freemason

Saint Leger, Fabien de
See Lebrun, Pauline Guyot

St. Leger, Francis Barry Boyle 1799-1829 [HPPN]
British barrister
* [The] Late Gilbert Earle, Esq.

St. Leon, Ernest ?-1891 [EWG]
American law officer
* Diamond Dick

Saint Leon, Francesca Cerrito 1821-? [HPPN]
Italian ballet dancer
* Cerrito, Fanny

St. Leon, [Count] Reginald de
See Du Bois, Edward

St. Lis [or Liz]
See Senlis, Simon

St. Louis
See Louis IX

[The] St. Louis born Flame of Paris
See Baker, Josephine Carson

St. Louis Jimmy
See Oden, James Burke [Jimmy]

St. Louis Mac
See Simmons, Mack

St. Lue, Comte de
See Bonaparte, Louis

St. Luz, Berthe
See Robertson, Alice Alberthe

Saint Marc Girardin, Francois Auguste
See Girardin, Marc

St. Mars, F.
See Atkins, Frank, Jr.

St. Mars, Gabrielle de 1779-1847 [NPS, PA]
French author
* Dash, Comtesse

St. Martin, Anna ?-1943 [HPPN]
American actress
* Lansing, Jessie

Saint Martin, Louis Claude de 1743-1803 [DNNS, FFF, HPPN, SN]
French philosopher
* [The] French Boehme
* [Le] Philosophe Inconnu
* [The] Philosopher of the Unknown
* [The] Unknown Philosopher

St. Maur, Harry [FFF]
American writer
* Almaviva

Saint Maure, Charles de 18th c. [HPPN]
French author
* [A] French Officer

St. Maure, Claude de 1610-1690 [SN]
Duke of Montausier
* Alceste?

Saint Meva
See Harris, Josiah

Saint Mexant
See Rouzier, Maximilien Louis Severin

St. Molaing
See Murphy, James

St. Mox, E. S.
See Ellis, Edward S[ylvester]

St. Myer, Ned
See Stratemeyer, Edward L.

[The] Saint of Rationalism
See Mill, John Stuart

[The] Saint of Selma
See Jemison, David Victor

[The] Saint of the Gutters
See Bojaxhiu, Agnes Gonxha

Saint Olaf
See Olaf II [or Olaus]

Saint Patrice
See Harden-Hickey, James

Saint Patrice
See Hickey, James Harden

St. Patrick's Steeple
See O'Hara, Kane

[The] St. Paul Cyclone
See O'Dowd, Mike

[The] St. Paul of Spiritualism
See Doyle, [Sir] Arthur Conan

[The] St. Paul Phantom
See Gibbons, Michael J. [Mike]

St. Paul, Sterner
See Meek, Sterner St. Paul

St. Peter
See Rozelle, Alvin Ray

St. Petersburg
See Mitchell, Thomas

St. Philip of the Pullman Porters
See Randolph, Asa Philip

Saint Pierre, Abbe de
See Castel, Charles Irenee

St. Pierre, Dorothy
See Curley, Dorothy Nyren

St. Pius
See Sarto, Giuseppe Melchiorre

Saint Pol-Roux
See Roux, Paul Pierre

St. Polis, John 1873-1946 [SC]
American actor
* Sainpolis, John

St. Pourcain, Guillaume Durand de ?-1333 [HPPN]
French clergyman
* [The] Most Resolute Doctor

St. Raymond, Anne
See Italiano, Anna Maria Luisa

Saint Real, Abbe de
See Vichard, Cesar

St. Reynard, Geoff
See Krepps, Robert W[ilson]

St. Richard the Commie Killer
See Nixon, Richard Milhous

St. Ritch, A. R.
See Stritch, Andrew F. Russell

Saint Robert
See Viard, Felix

St. Rosa
See Flores, Isabel

Saint Saphorin
See De Pesmes, Francois Louis

Saint Sevin, Joseph Barnabe 1727-1803
[BBD]
French musician and composer
* L'Abbe, Joseph Barnabe Saint-Sevin

Saint Simon
See De Roovroy, Claude Henri

Saint Subber, Arnold
See Subber, Arnold

Saint Sylvestre, P. D. de
See Parent-Desbarres, Pierre Francois

St. Tamara
See Kolba, Tamara

St. Ursula
See Blair, Mary E.

St. Vivant, M.
See Bixby, Jerome Lewis

St. Vladimir
See Vladimir I

St. Vrain, [Major] E. L.
See Manning, William Henry

Saint Without A Halo
See Simon

Sainte Beuve, C. A.
See Sainte Beuve, Charles Auguste

Sainte Beuve, Charles Auguste
1804-1869   [HPPN, IP, NPS]
French poet and critic
* Another Proteus
* B. S.
* Delorme, Joseph
* [The] Don Juan of Literature
* Sainte Beuve, C. A.

[The] Sainte Beuve of English Criticism
See Arnold, Matthew

Sainte Foy
See Potvin, Damase

Sainte John, Don
See Johnson, Wilbur

Sainte Lorette, Isnard de 19th c.   [IP]
French author
* Sabaroth, Ludwig de

Sainte Madeleine, [Sister]
See Longley, Lydia

Sainte Marie, Beverly 1942?-   [IPA]
Canadian-born singer
* Sainte Marie, Buffy

Sainte Marie, Buffy
See Sainte Marie, Beverly

Sainte-Gall, Auguste Amedee de
See Strich, Christian

Saintine
See Boniface, Joseph Xavier

[The] Saintlike S. O. B.
See Goff, John W.

Saionji, [Prince] Kimmochi 1849-1940
[HPPN]
Japanese statesman
* [The] Last Genro
* [The] Man Who Westernized Japan

Saisset-Schneider, Charlotte Elisabeth Germaine 1882-1942   [BDF, FC, FDG]
French director
* Dulac, Germaine

Saisson, Pierre [joint pseudonym with George Middleton]
See Bolton, St. George Guy Reginald

Saisson, Pierre [joint pseudonym with St. George Guy Reginald Bolton]
See Middleton, George

Saitch, Bruiser
See Saitch, Eyre

Saitch, Eyre 20th c.   [MEB]
American basketball player
* Saitch, Bruiser

Saito, Fred
See Saito, Hiroyuki

Saito, Hiroyuki 1917-   [CA]
Japanese author and journalist
* Saito, Fred

Saito, Michiko
See Fujiwara, Michiko

Sakall, Cuddles
See Szakall, Eugene Gero

Sakall, S. Z.
See Szakall, Eugene Gero

Sakata, Harold 1926?-1982   [FIR]
* Sakata, Oddjob

Sakata, Oddjob
See Sakata, Harold

Sakharov, Andrei Dmitrievich 1921-
[HPPN, WP 9-7-85]
Russian nuclear physicist
* [The] Father of the Soviet Hydrogen Bomb

Saki
See Munro, Hector Hugh

Saklatvala, Beram 1911-1976   [CA, WD]
British poet and author
* Marsh, Henry

Saks, Elmer Eliot
See Fawcett, F[rank] Dubrez

Saks, Gene
See Saks, Jean Michael

Saks, Jean Michael 1921-   [BEW]
American actor and director
* Saks, Gene

Sakurazawa, Yukikazu 1893-1966
[HDM, NAD]
Cultist and founder of macrobiotics
* Ohsawa, Georges

Sakyamuni [Sage of the Sakyas]
See Siddhartha

Sal, Dizzy
See Saldanha, Edward

Sala, George Augustus 1828-1895   [FFF, PA]
British author
* Cruiser, Benedict, M. M.
* G. A. S.

Salaam, Abdul
See McCallum, Leo

Salaam, Kalamu Ya
See Ferdinand, Val

Salaam, Liaqat Ali
See Clarke, Kenneth Spearman [Kenny]

[The] Salad Oil King
See De Angelis, Anthony

Saladin 1137?-1193
Sultan of Egypt
* [The] Great

Saladin
See Ross, William Stewart

Salahuddin, Daoud
See Belfield, David

Salamanca, D. F. Se
See Ingram, John H.

Salamanca, Don Felix de
See Ingram, John H.

Salamanca, Lucy
See Del Barco, Lucy Salamanca

[The] Salamander
See Cutts, John

[The] Salamander in My Eye
See St. John, Henry

[El] Salamanquino [The Man from Salamanca]
See Casas, Julian

Salamatullah
See Ullah, Salamat

Salameh, Ali Hassan 1943?-1979
Palestinian terrorist
* Abu Hassan
* [The] Red Prince

Salamone, Pat
See Livingston, Patrick

Salas, Lauro 1927-   [WBC]
Mexican boxer
* Salas, Little Lauro

Salas, Little Lauro
See Salas, Lauro

Salas, Paco
See Lago Severino, Francisco

Salas, Paco
See Severino, Francisco Lago

Salathiel
See Croly, George

Salavina
See Savane, Virgile

Salazar, Lazaro 1914-1957 [MK]
American baseball player
* [The] Blue Prince

Salchichon [The Sausage]
See Thomas

Saldanha, Edward 1934- [EJ]
Burmese-born jazz musician
* Sal, Dizzy

Saldivar, Vicente
See Garcia, Vicente Samuel Saldivar

Saldivar, Vicente
See Saldivar Garcia, Vincente Samuel

Saldivar Garcia, Vincente Samuel 1943-
[BX, RBE]
Mexican-born boxer
* Saldivar, Vicente

Sale, Aggie
See Sale, Forest

Sale, Charles Partlow 1885-1936 [BEW, CED, F2]
American comedian and author
* Sale, Chic

Sale, Chic
See Sale, Charles Partlow

Sale, Cornelius, Jr. 1917?-
American politician
* Byrd, Robert Carlyle

Sale, Forest 1911- [BB]
American basketball player
* Sale, Aggie

Sale, Richard [Bernard] 1911- [CA]
American author
* St. John, John

Saleeby, Caleb Williams 1878-? [LAO]
British physician and author
* Crusader
* Lens

Salerno, Anthony 1912?-
American gambler and loan shark
* Salerno, Fat Tony

Salerno, Fat Tony
See Salerno, Anthony

Salerno, Kid
See Durante, James Francis [Jimmy]

Sales, Soupy
See Hines, Milton

Saleski, Buffy
See Saleski, Kathleen

Saleski, Don 1949- [SMG]
Canadian-born hockey player
* [The] Bird

Saleski, Kathleen 1950-
American author
* Saleski, Buffy

[The] Salesman De Luxe
See Hammer, [Dr.] Armand

Saley, M. L. [FFF]
American writer
* Ditson, Dick

[The] Salian
See Conrad II

Salias de Turnemir, Elizaveta Vasil'evna [Sukhovo-Kobylina] 1815-1892 [BI]
Russian author
* Tur, Evgeniia

[The] Salic
See Conrad II

Salim, Ahmad Khatab
See Atkinson, A. K.

Salinas, Pedro
See Salinas Serrano, Pedro

Salinas Serrano, Pedro 1891- [HPPN]
Spanish literary critic
* Salinas, Pedro

Salinger, J. D.
See Salinger, Jerome David

Salinger, Jerome David 1919- [IPA, LC]
American author
* Salinger, J. D.

Salinger, Pierre Emil George 1925-
American journalist
* Lancer [code name]

Salisbury, Marchioness of 1749?-1835
[HN]
Grandmother of the prime minister
* Old Sarum

Salisbury, Marilla 1908?-
American track and field athlete
* Sunbonnet Sue

Salisbury, Stephen 1798-1884 [IP]
American attorney and author
* S. S.

Salisbury, W. [IP]
British clergyman and author
* [A] Country Parson

Salivarova, Zdena
See Skvorecka, Zdena Salivarova

Salkeld, Joseph 19th c. [IP]
American author
* [A] Candidate for Orders in the Church

Sallaska, Georgia Myrle 1933- [SFL]
American author
* Benedict, Myrle

Sallaway, Myrtle May 1893- [NAA]
American writer and poet
* Cousin Gene
* Sallaway, Peggy Gene

Sallaway, Peggy Gene
See Sallaway, Myrtle May

Sallee, Harry Franklin 1885-1950 [AS, BE, PB]
American baseball player
* Sallee, Slim

Sallee, Slim
See Sallee, Harry Franklin

Sallo, Denis de 1626-1669 [SN]
Founder of first literary journal
* [The] New Aristarchus

Sallust
See Crispus, Gaius Sallustius

Sallust, Caius Crispus 1st c. BC [NPS]
Roman historian
* [The] Roman Thucydides

[The] Sallust of France
See Vichard, Cesar

Sally Blind Frascone
See Frascone, Salvatore

Sally Bugs Briguglio
See Briguglio, Salvatore

Salma, Abu
See Karmi, Abdul Karim

Salmasius, Claudius
See Saumaise, Claude

Salmon, Annie Elizabeth [Martin] 1899-
[AW, CA, WD]
British author
* Ashley, Elizabeth
* Martin, Nancy

Salmon, Chico
See Salmon, Rutherford Eduardo

Salmon, Geraldine Gordon 1897- [WW]
Author
* Sarasin, J. G.

Salmon, Hamilton 1893-1962 [BB]
American basketball player
* Salmon, June

Salmon, June
See Salmon, Hamilton

Salmon, Leon N. 1845-? [IP, PA]
American author
* Ixion
* Prince

Salmon, Louis J. 1880-1965 [AS]
American football player
* Salmon, Red

Salmon, Mrs.
See Sawyer, Carrie M.

Salmon, Nathan Ucuzoglu
See Ucuzoglu, Nathan Salmon

Salmon, Percy R. 1872-? [WWL]
British author
* Penlake, Richard

Salmon, Red
See Salmon, Louis J.

Salmon, Rutherford Eduardo 1940-   [BE]
Panamanian-born baseball player
* Salmon, Chico

Salola, Eeero 1902-   [IAW]
Finnish author
* Diogenes
* Lauri
* Lauri, Pikku

Salome
See Converse, Harriet [Maxwell]

Salome, Maria
See Rodriguez, Augustin

Salomen, Edith 1849-?   [LFW]
American swindler
* Ava, [Madame] Vera P.
* Landsfeldt, Countess
* Sister Mary
* [The] Swami
* Theo the Swami

Salomon 13th c.   [HN]
* [The] Jew of Tewkesbury

Salomon, Janet Lynn [Nowicki] 1953-
[CA]
American figure skater and author
* Lynn, Janet

Salomons, Jean-Pierre 1909-   [FC]
French-born actor
* Aumont, Jean-Pierre

Salop, Lynne
See Hawes, Lynne Salop

Saloth Sar 1925?-
Cambodian premier
* Pol Pot

Saloth Sar 20th c.
Cambodian Communist leader
* Pol Pot

Salpeter, Mechel 1892-   [BEW, EMT]
American producer
* Gordon, Max

Salsbury, Mrs. Nate   [FFF]
Entertainer
* Samuels, Ray

Salsbury, Nate 1888-   [HPPN]
American author
* Ireland, Baron

Salt, Henry 1780-1827   [PA]
Author
* [A] Traveler

Salt, Jonathan
See Neville, Derek

[The] Salt King
See Corbett, John

[The] Salt of Art
See Buonarroti, Michelangelo [or
Michael Angelo]

Salt Rock Midkiff
See Midkiff, Ezra Millington

Salt, Sarah
See Hobson, Coralie [Von Werner]

Saltboy, Razor
See Louis, Ray Baldwin

Salten, Felix
See Salzmann, Siegmund

Salter, Cedric
See Knight, Francis Edgar [Frank]

Salter, Donald P. M. 1942-   [CA]
British author
* Podmarsh, Rollo

Salter, Edith A.   [FFF]
Author
* Howard, Assunta

Salter, Margaret Lennox
See Donaldson, Margaret

Salter, Mary D.
See Ainsworth, Mary D[insmore] Salter

Salter, Sy 1926-   [IBW]
American boxer
* Total Man

Salter, T. F. 19th c.   [PA]
Author
* T. F. S.

Saltikoff, W.   [PA]
Author
* Stchedrin, Nikolai

Saltis, Joseph 20th c.   [BLB, PHM]
American gangster
* Saltis, Polock Joe

Saltis, Polock Joe
See Saltis, Joseph

Saltonstall, Leverett 1893?-1979
American politician
* Saltonstall, Old Lev
* Saltonstall, Salty

Saltonstall, Old Lev
See Saltonstall, Leverett

Saltonstall, Salty
See Saltonstall, Leverett

Saltus, Edgar Evertson 1855-1921
[DNA]
American author
* Verelart, Myndart

Salty Dog Sam
See Collins, Samuel

Saltykov, Mikhail Evgrafovich 1826-1889
[WBD]
Russian author
* Shchedrin, N.

Saltzgaver, Jack
See Saltzgaver, Otto Hamlin

Saltzgaver, Otto Hamlin 1905-   [BE]
American baseball player
* Saltzgaver, Jack

Saltzman, Joseph [Joe] 1939-   [CA]
American author, producer, editor
* Laertes, Joseph
* Michaels, Joe
* Roberts, Joe

Saluste
See De Bueil, Honorat

Salustri, Carlo Alberto 1873-1950
[EWL]
Italian poet
* Trilussa

Salva, Pierre 1900?-1980
French gypsy leader
* King of the Gypsies of Europe

Salvadori, Joyce
See Lussu, Joyce [Salvadori]

Salvadori, Massimo
See Salvadori-Paleotti, Massimo

Salvadori, Max William
See Salvadori-Paleotti, Massimo

Salvadori-Paleotti, Massimo 1908-   [CA]
British-born educator and author
* Salvadori, Massimo
* Salvadori, Max William

Salvage, Jonas
See Walker, James

Salvason, Sigrum 1909-1934   [SC]
American actress
* Randall, Rae

Salvatierra, Juan Maria de 1648-1717
[HPPN]
Italian clergyman
* [The] Apostle of California

Salvato, Sharon 20th c.   [CA]
Author
* Taylor, Day [joint pseudonym with
Cornelia M. Parkinson]

Salvator
See Hervey, John Lewis

Salvator, John Nepomuk 1852-1891?
[HPPN]
*Archduke of Austria and Prince of
Tuscany*
* Orth, Johann

[The] Salvator Rosa of British Novelists
See Radcliffe, Anne Ward

[The] Salvator Rosa of the Sea
See Scott, Michael

Salvatoriello
See Rosa, Salvator

Salvetti, Amerigo
See Antelminelli, Alessandro

Salvi, Giovanni Battista 1605-1685
[WBD]
Italian painter
* [Il] Sassoferrato

Salvi, Paul
See DeLucia, Felice

Salviati, Cecco di
See De Rossi, Francesco

Salviati, Cecco di
See Rossi, Francesco de'

Salviati, Francesco
See De Rossi, Francesco

Salviati, Leonardo 1540-1589 [WBD]
Italian scholar
* Infarinato

Salvo, Gyp
See Salvo, Manuel

Salvo, Manuel 1913- [BE]
American baseball player
* Salvo, Gyp

Salzedo, Carlos
See Salzedo, Leon

Salzedo, Leon 1885-1961 [MS]
French musician
* Salzedo, Carlos

Salzer, Beeb
See Salzer, Clarence M., Jr.

Salzer, Clarence M., Jr. 1933- [OP]
American scenic and lighting designer
* Salzer, Beeb

Salzer, L. E.
See Wilson, Lionel

Salzman, Belle 1911-1971 [JF]
American comedian
* Barth, Belle

Salzmann, Siegmund 1869-1945 [SAT]
Hungarian-born author
* Finder, Martin
* Salten, Felix

Sam
See Grant, Hiram Ulysses

[The] Sam Adams of Philadelphia
See Thomson, Charles

Sam Bam Cunningham
See Cunningham, Sam[uel Lewis, Jr.]

Sam, Butch
See Sam, Robert

Sam, Long Haired
See Brown, Sam

Sam, Robert 20th c. [RO2]
American musician
* Sam, Butch

Sam the Maltser
See Adams, Samuel

Sam the Man
See Taylor, Samuel L.

Sam the Plumber
See DeCavalcante, Simone Rizzo

Sam the Sham
See Samudio, Domingo

Sam the Torch
See Scarlow, Samuel

Samachson, Joseph 1906- [CA, SAT, SF]
American author
* Miller, John
* Morrison, William
* Sterling, Brett [house pseudonym, Standard Magazines]

Samaniegos, Ramon Gil 1899-1968
[BDF, CED, F1]
Mexican-born actor
* Novarro, Ramon

Samarakis, Antonis 1919- [IAW]
Greek author
* Kyprianos, Iossif

[A] Samaritan
See Robinson, William L.

Samaroff, Olga
See Hickenlooper, Lucie Mary Olga
Agnes

Samarow, Gregor
See Meding, Oskar

Samatananda, Swami
See Anderson, Rod

Samber, Robert 18th c. [HPPN]
British author
* Philalethes, Eugenius, Jr.

Sambrot, William [Anthony] 1920-
[ESF, IAW]
American writer
* Ayes, Anthony
* Ayes, William

[The] Same Author
See Combe [or Coombe], William

[The] Same Compiler
See Massey, Lucy Fletcher

[The] Same Hand That Wrote the Packet of Letters to Dr. Waterland
See Staunton, William

[The] Same Old Coon
See Clay, Henry

[The] Same Old Mose
See Weinberger, Moses

[The] Same Young Mose
See Weinberger, Moses

Samek, Viktor Oliver 1898-1964 [BEW, BMH]
Austrian-born comedian and musician
* Brown, Harry
* [The] Continental Wizard
* Oliver, Vic
* [The] Piano Playing Baron

[The] Samian Poet
See Simonides

[The] Samian Sage
See Pythagoras

Samira [Beautiful Flower]
See Stahl, Eva

Sammartini [or San Martini], Giovanni Battista 1701-1775 [BBD]
Italian composer
* [Il] Milanese

Sammartini [or San Martini], Giuseppe 1693?-1770? [BBD]
Italian-born musician
* [Il] Londinese

Sammis, John 1942- [CA, SAT]
American author
* Russell, Patrick

Sammon, Winona 1909-1941
American actress
* Shannon, Peggy

Sammons, Fur
See Sammons, James

Sammons, Jack
See Sammons, James

Sammons, James 20th c. [HPPN, PHM]
American underworld figure
* Sammons, Fur
* Sammons, Jack

Sammons, William Taylor ?-1882
[HPPN]
British journalist
* Sly, Sam

[The] Sammy Glick of the Cold War
See Kissinger, Henry Alfred

Sammy the Publican
See Adams, Samuel

Sammy the Rose
See Rosenman, Samuel Irving

Samo, Mrs. [FFF]
Entertainer
* Seymour, Laura

Samoiloff, Louise Cripps
See Cripps, Louise Lilian

[The] Samosatian Philosopher
See Lucian

Samperi, Anthony 20th c. [SG]
Boxer
* [The] Gas House Tartar
* Young, Terry

Sampietro, Ines Isabella 1909- [BDF, FC, ITA]
Italian actress
* Miranda, Isa

Sample, Omer W. ?-1884 [HPPN]
American outlaw
* Lincoln, George
* Sample, Red

Sample, Red
See Sample, Omer W.

Sampleton, Samuel
See Monti, Luigi

Sampley, Alton 1899-1957 [SC]
American actor
* Rae, Jack

Sampliner, Louis H. 20th c. [WGT]
Author
* Blade, Alexander [house pseudonym, Ziff-Davis]

Sampsiceranus, Alabarches, the Jerusalemite
See Pompey [or Pompeius], Cneius

Sampson, Deborah 1760-1827 [BL, HPPN]
American soldier
* [The] Amorous Amazon
* [The] Blooming Boy
* Captain Molly
* Sampson, Ephraim
* Shirtliffe, Robert

Sampson, Edgar Melvin 1907- [WWJ]
American jazz musician
* [The] Lamb

Sampson, Emma Speed 1868-? [NAA]
American author
* Speed, Nell

Sampson, Ephraim
See Sampson, Deborah

Sampson, Henry 19th c. [PA]
Author
* Pendragon

Sampson, Linda Joy 1945- [RO1]
American singer
* Scott, Linda

Sampson, Ray 1898-1964 [SC]
American actor
* Mayo, Harry A.

Sampson, Richard Henry 1896-1973 [CC, EMD, LC]
British author
* Hull, Richard

Sampson, Sammy
See Broonzy, William Lee Conley

Sampson, Virginia Reid 1909-1955 [SC]
American actress
* Carver, Lynn

Sampson, William 1764-1830 [PI]
Irish poet and attorney
* Fortescue

Sams, Jessie Bennett 20th c. [IBW]
American author
* Sams, Veanie

Sams, Moose
See Sams, Ron

Sams, Ron 20th c. [SI 9-1-82]
American football player
* Sams, Moose

Sams, Veanie
See Sams, Jessie Bennett

Samsel, Helen Maring 1903- [NAA]
American poet
* Maring, Helen

Samson [FFF]
Biblical strongman
* [The] Hercules of the Jews
* [The] Jewish Hercules

Samson
See Clippinger, J. A.

Samson
See Von Elkenberg, Johann

[The] Samson Agonistes
See Milton, John

Samson, Deborah 1760-1827
American Revolutionary War soldier
* Shurtleff, Robert

Samson, George Alexander Gibb 1858-1918 [BEW, WBD]
British actor and stage manager
* Alexander, [Sir] George

Samson, George Whitefield 1819-? [HPPN]
American clergyman and educator
* [A] Teacher

[The] Samson of England
See Topham, Thomas

Samsonov, Samson
See Edelstein, Samson Iosifovich

Samudio, Domingo 1940?- [PRS, RM, RO1]
American singer
* Sam the Sham

[The] Samuel Adams of New Jersey
See Fisher, Hendrick

[The] Samuel Adams of North Carolina
See Harnett, Cornelius

Samuel, Athanasius Y.
See Samuel, Yeshue

Samuel, Valerie 1910- [THR]
British actress
* Tudor, Valerie

Samuel, Yeshue 1907- [HPPN]
Syrian clergyman and author
* Samuel, Athanasius Y.

Samuels, Alfred Sanford 1866-1913 [HPPN]
American singer
* Sanford, Fred

Samuels Bacon
See Samuels, Philip Francis

Samuels, Calvin 20th c. [RM]
Musician
* Samuels, Fuzzy

Samuels, E. A.
See Tiffany, E. A.

Samuels, Fuzzy
See Samuels, Calvin

Samuels, Howard 1919- [CR, HPPN]
American politician
* Howie the Horse
* [The] O. B. T. Czar

Samuels, Howie
See Hoffman, Abbott [Abbie]

Samuels, Ike
See Samuels, Samuel Earl

Samuels, Jerry 20th c. [RO1]
American singer and songwriter
* Napoleon XIV

Samuels, Joseph Jonas [Joe] 1905- [BE]
American baseball player
* Samuels, Skabotch

Samuels, Louis 1898-1961 [HPPN]
American actor
* Burton, Phil

Samuels, Miriam 1925- [FC]
British actress
* Karlin, Miriam

Samuels, Philip Francis 1881-? [WGT]
Author
* Samuels Bacon

Samuels, Ray
See Salsbury, Mrs. Nate

Samuels, Samuel Earl 1876-? [EJS]
American baseball player
* Samuels, Ike

Samuels, Skabotch
See Samuels, Joseph Jonas [Joe]

Samuels, Victor
See Banis, Victor J[erome]

Samuelson, Hedvig 1906-1931 [HPPN]
American murder victim
* Samuelson, Sammy

Samuelson, Julian 1878-1934 [BEW]
British playwright, producer, director
* Wylie, Julian

Samuelson, Morris Laurence 1880-? [THR]
British playwright and librettist
* Wylie, Lauri

Samuelson, Sammy
See Samuelson, Hedvig

Samways, George Richmond 1895- [MBF]
British author
* Clifford, Martin [house pseudonym]
* Conquest, Owen [house pseudonym]
* Linley, Mark
* Masters, Paul
* Proctor, Paul
* Richards, Frank [house pseudonym]
* Richmond, George

Samwell, Gertrude Constance 1860?-1946 [THR]
British actress
* Featherstonhaugh, Constance

Samwell-Smith, Paul 1943- [RO2]
British musician
* Samwell-Smith, Sam

Samwell-Smith, Sam
See Samwell-Smith, Paul

San Diego, Mr.
See Smith, C. Arnholt [Arnie]

San Francisco, Mr.
See Caen, Herb[ert]

San Francisco, Mr.
See Magnin, Cyril

San Juan, Olga 1927- [HPPN]
Puerto Rican-American dancer and actress
* [The] Puerto Rican Pepper Pot

San Martin, Jose de 1778-1850 [FFF, WBD]
South American patriot
* [The] Protector of Peru

San Souce
See McAfee, Nella Marshall

San Vicente y Navarro, Rufino 1880-1963 [GS]
Spanish bullfighter
* Chiquito de Begona [Little Fellow from Begona]

Sana
See Howard, Anna Holyoke [Cutts]

Sanborn, B. X.
See Ballinger, William Sanborn [Bill]

Sanborn, Duane 1914- [CA]
American author
* Bradley, Duane

Sanborn, Michael 20th c. [TI 3-28-83]
American drug dealer
* Barnswallow, Fred

Sanchez, Alice
See Stovall, Alice

Sanchez, Anna Maria 20th c. [WP 1-13-83]
Actress
* Del Rio, Vanessa

Sanchez, Antonio 20th c. [RBE]
American boxer
* Sanchez, Tony

Sanchez, Cocoa
See Sanchez, Ezequiel

Sanchez, Ezequiel 20th c. [RBE]
Puerto Rican boxer
* Sanchez, Cocoa

Sanchez, Francisco 1845-1924 [GS]
Spanish bullfighter
* Paco Frascuelo

Sanchez, Irma Hilga
See Eisemann-Schier, Ruth

Sanchez, Pablo 20th c. [GS]
Spanish bullfighter
* Barajitas [The Little Card Player]

Sanchez, Paul 1935- [TR]
American actor
* Sand, Paul

Sanchez, Pedro 19th c. [GS]
Spanish bullfighter
* Noteveas

Sanchez, Pedro
See Spalla, Ignazio

Sanchez, Salvador 1844-1898 [HPPN]
Spanish bullfighter
* Frascuelo

Sanchez, Sonia Knight 1934- [IBW]
American author, poet, playwright
* Mannan, Laila

Sanchez, Tony
See Sanchez, Antonio

Sanchez Caballero, Antonio 1831-1895 [GS]
Spanish bullfighter
* [El] Tato [The Stammerer]

Sanchez Coello, Alonzo 1515-1590 [DEP, FFF, SN]
Portuguese painter
* [The] Portuguese Titian
* [The] Titian of Portugal

Sanchez de Almodovar, Bachiller Toribo
See Del Monte y Aponte, Domingo

Sanchez De Leon, Leandro 1859-1914 [GS]
Spanish bullfighter
* Cacheta [Lever]

Sanchez Del Campo, Jose 1848-1925 [GS]
Spanish bullfighter
* Cara Ancha [Wide-Face]

Sanchez Morales, Narciso 1915- [IAW]
Spanish author
* Aletes
* Anteo
* Narsanmor

Sanchez Munoz, Gil 1380?-1446 [WBD]
Antipope
* Clement VIII

Sanchez Olivares, Luis 1927- [GS]
Colombian bullfighter
* Diamante Negro [Black Diamond]

Sanchez Rodriguez, Jose 1895-1957 [GS]
Spanish bullfighter
* Hipolito

Sancho
See Cunningham, John William

Sancho Garces
See Sancho I

Sancho Ramirez
See Sancho V

Sancho I ?-925 [HPPN]
King of Navarre
* Sancho Garces

Sancho I 1154-1212 [HN, WBD]
King of Portugal
* [The] City Builder
* [The] Father of His Country
* [The] Restorer of Cities

Sancho II ?-1072 [DNNS, WBD]
King of Castile
* [El] Fuerte
* [The] Strong

Sancho II 1208-1248 [WBD]
King of Portugal
* Capelo

Sancho III 970-1035 [DNNS, WBD]
King of Navarre
* [The] Great

Sancho IV ?-1076 [WBD]
King of Navarre
* [El] Noble

Sancho IV 1258-1295 [NPS, WBD]
King of Spain
* [El] Bravo
* [The] Great

Sancho V ?-1094 [HPPN]
King of Navarre
* Sancho Ramirez

Sancho VI ?-1194 [WBD]
King of Navarre
* [El] Sabio [The Wise]

Sancho VII ?-1234 [WBD]
King of Navarre
* [El] Fuerte [The Strong]

Sancho VIII ?-1234 [HPPN]
King of Navarre
* [El] Fuerte [The Strong]

Sancroft, William 1616-1693 [SN]
Archbishop of Canterbury
* Zadoc

Sancta Clara
See Davenport, Christopher

Sanction
See Johnston, [Sir] Reginald Fleming

Sanctuary, Brenda 1934- [WD]
British author and columnist
* Campbell, Bridget

Sand, George
See Dudevant, Amandine Aurore Lucile Dupin

Sand, Heinie
See Sand, John Henry

Sand, John Henry 1897-1958 [BE]
American baseball player
* Sand, Heinie

Sand, Jules
See Dudevant, Amandine Aurore Lucile Dupin

Sand, Jules
See Sandeau, [Leonard Sylvain] Jules

[The] Sand Lot Agitator
See Kearney, Denis

Sand, Marvin
See Sobell, Morton

Sand, Maurice
See Dudevant, Maurice

Sand, Paul
See Sanchez, Paul

Sand, Warren B.?
See Tremaine, F[rederick] Orlin

Sanda, Dominique
See Varaigne, Dominique

Sandars, Harry
See Stannard, William John

Sandaval, Jaime
See Marlowe, Dan J[ames]

Sanday, Edgar
See Faure, Edgar

Sandberg, Ryne 1960?-   [NW 9-10-84]
American baseball player
* [The] Natural

Sandblad-Haneson, Emelie Cecilia Sofia
1889-   [IAW]
Swedish author
* Torpare, Tord

Sandburg, Carl [August] 1878-1967
[CA, HPPN, SAT]
American poet and author
* Militant
* Phillips, Jack
* [The] Poet of the People
* Sandburg, Charles A.

Sandburg, Charles A.
See Sandburg, Carl [August]

Sandburg, Helga
See Crile, Helga Sandburg

Sandby, Paul 1725-1809   [HPPN, WBD]
British engraver and painter
* [The] Father of English Watercolor
* [The] Father of Watercolor Art

Sande, Earl H. 1898-1968   [HPPN]
American jockey
* [The] Great Jockey of the Golden
  Age of Sports
* Sande, Handy

Sande, Handy
See Sande, Earl H.

Sandeau, [Leonard Sylvain] Jules
1811-1883   [NPS]
Author
* Sand, Jules

Sandel, Cora
See Fabricius, Sara

Sandell, Lynn
See Wickdahl, Lillian

Sandelowsky, Manfred Neumann
See Hamilton, F. Anthony

Sanden, Thomas 18th c.   [PA]
Author
* [A] Layman
* President

Sander, Peter
See Szarvas, Peter

Sanderlin, Owenita [Harrah] 1916-   [CA]
American author
* Kenny, Kathryn

Sanders, Albert
See Davidson, David

Sanders, Alex 20th c.   [EOP]
Claimed to possess psychic powers
* King of the Witches

Sanders, Buck
See Frentzen, Jeffrey

Sanders, Butch
See Sanders, Roy Garvin

Sanders, Byrne Hope
See Sperry, Byrne Hope

Sanders, Charlie 1946-   [IBW]
American football player
* Deep, Charlie
* Sanders, Little Mackey

Sanders, Clarence 1952-   [SMG]
American football player
* Sanders, Mad Dog

Sanders, Colonel
See Sanders, Harland

Sanders, Daffy
See Sanders, Kenneth George

Sanders, Daniel Jackson 20th c.
[HPPN]
American clergyman, editor, educator
* Zeus

Sanders, Daphne
See Randolph, Georgiana Ann

Sanders, Daryl 20th c.
American football player
* Sanders, Skunk

Sanders, Deac
See Sanders, John Maurice

Sanders, Dinger
See Sanders, Homer J., II

Sanders, Dorothy Lucie 1917-   [CA]
Australian author
* Walker, Lucy

Sanders, Doug[las] 1933?-   [HPPN]
American golfer
* Pro Golf's Beau Brummel

Sanders, Ed 1939-   [CA]
American poet, editor, filmmaker
* Black, Hobart

Sanders, Edward S. 1914?-1936   [BEW]
American theatrical performer
* Abbott, Edward S.

Sanders, Farrell 1940-   [EJ7]
American jazz musician
* Sanders, Pharoah

Sanders, Harland 1890?-1980   [HPPN]
American business executive
* [The] Colonel
* [The] Fried Chicken King
* Sanders, Colonel

Sanders, Henry Russell 1905-1958   [AS,
SMG]
American football coach
* Sanders, Red

Sanders, Homer J., II 1967-   [HPPN]
American motorcycle racer
* Sanders, Dinger

Sanders, Jeanne
See Rundle, Anne

Sanders, Joe 1896-1965   [PMJ]
American bandleader
* [The] Old Lefthander

Sanders, John 20th c.   [SFL]
Author
* Comer, Ralph

Sanders, John Maurice 1950-   [SMG]
American football player
* Sanders, Deac

Sanders, Joseph L. [Joe] 1896-1965
[HPPN]
American jazz musician
* [The] Old Lefthander

Sanders, Josephine 1898-   [EMT]
American actress, dancer, singer
* Delroy, Irene

Sanders, Kenneth George 1941-   [BE]
American baseball player
* Sanders, Daffy

Sanders, Kent
See Wilkes-Hunter, Richard

Sanders, Leonard 1929-   [CA]
American author and journalist
* Thomas, Dan

Sanders, Little Mackey
See Sanders, Charlie

Sanders, Mad Dog
See Sanders, Clarence

Sanders, Mike 20th c.
American basketball player
* Sanders, Slew

Sanders, Noah
See Blount, Roy [Alton], Jr.

Sanders, Orban 20th c.   [EF]
American football player
* Sanders, Speed

Sanders, Pep
See Sanders, Roy Garvin

Sanders, Pharoah
See Sanders, Farrell

Sanders, Red
See Sanders, Henry Russell

Sanders, Roy Garvin 1892-1950   [BE]
American baseball player
* Sanders, Butch
* Sanders, Pep

Sanders, Roy L. 1894-   [BE]
American baseball player
* Sanders, Simon

Sanders, Satch
See Sanders, Thomas E.

Sanders, Scheree   [BI]
American singer
* Scheree

Sanders, Simon
See Sanders, Roy L.

Sanders, Skunk
See Sanders, Daryl

Sanders, Slew
See Sanders, Mike

Sanders, Speed
See Sanders, Orban

Sanders, Thomas 1904-1967 [FC]
British actor
* Conway, Tom

Sanders, Thomas E. 1938- [BI, IBW]
American basketball coach
* Sanders, Satch

Sanders, Vic
See Sanders, Wendell Rowan

Sanders, Wendell Rowan 1933- [BA]
American physician
* Sanders, Vic

Sanders, William 17th c. [DSB]
Scottish scientist and author
* Mathers, Patrick

Sanders, Winston P.
See Anderson, Poul [William]

Sanderson, Derek Michael 1946- [BI, HR]
Canadian hockey player
* Sanderson, Turk

Sanderson, [Ronald] Douglas 1922- [WW]
Author
* Brett, Martin
* Douglas, Malcolm

Sanderson, F. W.
See Sanderson, Frederick William

Sanderson, Frederick William 1857-1922 [LC]
British educator and author
* Sanderson, F. W.

Sanderson, H. P. 20th c. [SFP]
Author
* Carr, Joan

Sanderson, Happy
See Sanderson, Winfrey

Sanderson, Ivan T[erence] 1911-1973 [CA, SAT]
Scottish-born author
* Roberts, Terence

Sanderson, John 1783-1844 [PA]
Author
* Robertjeot

Sanderson, Julia
See Sackett, Julia

Sanderson, Kent 1898-1973 [F1, F2, SC]
American actor
* Roosevelt, Buddy

Sanderson, Lawrence H. 20th c.
American military aviator
* Sanderson, Sandy

Sanderson, Richard
See Burdon, [Rev.] Richard

Sanderson, Sabina W[arren] 1931- [CA]
American editor
* Fawcett, Marion

Sanderson, Sandy
See Sanderson, Lawrence H.

Sanderson, Turk
See Sanderson, Derek Michael

Sanderson, Wimp
See Sanderson, Winfrey

Sanderson, Winfrey 20th c.
American basketball coach
* Sanderson, Happy
* Sanderson, Wimp

Sandette
See Walsh, Marie A.

Sandford, Leila
See Hanshaw, Annette

Sandford, Marjorie 1910- [THR]
British actress and singer
* Dey, Marjorie

Sandford, Nell Mary 1936- [WD]
British author
* Dunn, Nell

Sandford, Samuel 17th c. [SN]
British actor
* [The] Spagnolet of the Theatre

Sandford, Stanley J. 1894-1961 [SC]
American actor
* Sandford, Tiny

Sandford, Tiny
See Sandford, Stanley J.

Sandiford, Marie 1876-1959 [BI]
American educator
* Mary Raymond, [Sister]

Sandison, Janet
See Cameron, Elizabeth Jane

Sandisson, Mr. de
See Bignon, Jean Paul

Sandjar 1117-1158 [DEP, FFF, SN]
Seljuke sultan
* [The] Alexander of Persia
* [The] Persian Alexander
* [The] Second Alexander

Sandlin, Joann S[chepers] De Lora 1935- [CA]
American author and sociologist
* De Lora, Joann S.

Sandman, Peter M[ark] 1945- [CA]
American author
* David, William

Sandor, Alfred
See Sandwina, Alfred Heymann

Sandor, Jean
See Simenon, Georges [Joseph Christian]

Sandoval Alarcon, Mario 20th c.
Guatemalan politician
* [The] Godfather

Sandow, Eugen[e]
See Mueller, Frederick

Sandow, Eugene 1867-1925 [HPPN]
German strong man
* Apollo
* [The] Great Sandow
* [The] Modern Hercules
* [The] Perfect Man
* [The] Strongest Man in the World

Sandown, Margaret
See Stone, Ena Margaret

Sandoz, Jules Ami 1857?-1928 [HPPN]
American pioneer
* Sandoz, Old Jules

Sandoz, Mari [Susette] 1901-1966 [BI, CA, SAT]
American author
* Macumber, Mari

Sandoz, Old Jules
See Sandoz, Jules Ami

Sandre, Thierry
See Moulie, Charles

Sandrocottus
See Chandra Gupta [Chandra Gupta Maurya]

Sands, Bedwin
See Raffalovich, George

Sands, Bobby 1954-1981 [HPPN]
Irish guerrilla leader
* [The] Hunger Striker

Sands, Dave
See Ritchie, David

Sands, Dave? [house pseudonym?]
See Walton, Bryce

Sands, Jimmy
See Santucci, Jimmy

Sands, John
See Hutchinson, William

Sands, Johnny
See Harp, John

Sands, Leo G[eorge] 1912- [CA]
American engineer and author
* Craig, Lee
* Helmi, Jack

Sands, Leonard
See Sellers, Connie Leslie, Jr.

Sands, Martin
See Burke, John [Frederick]

Sands, Piggy
See Sands, Sam

Sands, Robert Charles 1799-1832 [FFF, HPPN, PA]
American author and journalist
* Amphilogist
* Herbert, Francis, Esq.
* [The] Neologist

Sands, Sam 20th c. [OBW]
American baseball player
* Sands, Piggy

Sandwell, Bernard Keble 1876-1954 [BI]
Canadian journalist
* Van Gogh, Lucy

Sandwina, Alfred Heymann 1918- [BEW]
Hungarian-born actor
* Sandor, Alfred

Sandy, Max
See Saunders, Carl Maxon

Sandy, Stephen
See Sandys, Stephen

Sandys, Elspeth
See Purchase, Elspeth [Sandilands]

Sandys, George 1578-1644 [DEA, HPPN]
British author
* [The] Poet Adventurer
* S. G.

Sandys, George Windle
See Crawfurd, Oswald John Frederick

Sandys, K. [PA]
Author
* Syndas, Kate

Sandys, Oliver
See Evans, Marguerite Florence Helene Jervis

Sandys, Richard Hill 1801-? [HPPN]
British barrister
* R. H. S.

Sandys, Stephen 1935- [CA]
American author and poet
* Sandy, Stephen

Sane, Jacques Noel 1740-1832 [HN]
French naval engineer
* [Le] Vauban de la Marine

Sanford, Charles
See O'Sullivan, Daniel

Sanford, Edward 1809-? [PA]
Author
* Palmer, Pot-Pie

Sanford, Fred
See Samuels, Alfred Sanford

Sanford, George F. 1870-1938 [FB]
American football player and coach
* Sanford, Sandy

Sanford, John Elroy 1922- [CA, IBW, IPA]
American actor and comedian
* Chicago Red
* Foxx, Redd
* Sanford, Smiley

Sanford, Laura [PA]
Author
* Fanchon

Sanford, Major
See Edwards, Pierpont

Sanford, Sandy
See Sanford, George F.

Sanford, Smiley
See Sanford, John Elroy

Sanftleben, Adolar
See Hauser, Carl

Sang, Samantha
See Gray, Cheryl

Sangallo, Antonio Picconi da
See Cordiani, Antonio

Sangallo, Giuliano da
See Giamberti, Giuliano

Sangchilli, Baltazar
See Belenguer Hevoas, Baltazar

Sanger, Edward 1882-1956 [F2, FC]
British actor
* Herbert, Holmes

Sanger, George 1825-1911 [WBD]
British circus owner
* Lord George

Sanger, Herbert
See Hoffmann, Lothar

Sanger, John 1816-1889 [WBD]
British circus owner
* Lord John

Sangerson, Margaret Love
See Bedford-Jones, Henry [James O'Brien]

Sanghamita, [Sister]
See Canavarro, M. A. de S.

Sanglier des Ardennes
See La Marck, Guillaume [or William] de

Sangodare, Asjantenu
See Slory, Michael

Sangodeyi, Yommy 20th c. [SI 11-28-83]
Nigerian-born basketball player
* Basket, Yommy

Sangret, August ?-1943 [HPPN]
French-Canadian murderer
* [The] Wigwam Girl Murderer

Sangster, Ann
See Shennan, Victoria

Sangster, Jimmy 1927- [SFL]
Welsh-born author
* Sansom, John [joint pseudonym with Alfred Edgar]

Sangster, Margaret Elizabeth Munson 1838-1912 [HPPN]
American author, poet, editor
* M. E. M. S.

Sanguillen, Manny
See Sanguillen, Manuel DeJesus

Sanguillen, Manuel DeJesus 1944- [BE, SMG]
Panamanian-born baseball player
* Sanguillen, Manny

Sanicki, Butch
See Sanicki, Ed[ward Robert]

Sanicki, Ed[ward Robert] 1924- [BE]
American baseball player
* Sanicki, Butch

[A] Sanitarian
See Brown, Samuel Sneade

Sanjay, Rajendra
See Gupta, Rajendra Prasad

Sannazaro, Jacopo [or Giacomo] 1458-1530 [DEP, FFF, RH]
Italian poet
* Actius Sincerus
* [The] Christian Virgil

Sannella, Andy
See Sannella, Anthony

Sannella, Anthony 1900-1961? [WWJ]
American jazz musician
* Sannella, Andy

Sanraku, Kano
See Mitsuyori, Kimura

Sanroman, Ernesto 20th c. [GS]
Mexican bullfighter
* [El] Queretaro [The Man from Queretaro]

Sans Esprit, Monsieur
See Fielding, Henry

Sans Gene, Madame
See Lefebvre, Catherine Hubscher [Duchess of Dantzig]

Sans Malice
See Akakia, Martin

Sans Peur
See John [or Jean]

Sans Peur, Jean
See Babou, Hippolyte

Sans Terre
See John

Sansom, John [joint pseudonym with Jimmy Sangster]
See Edgar, Alfred

Sansom, John [joint pseudonym with Alfred Edgar]
See Sangster, Jimmy

Sanson, Charles Henri 18th c. [HPPN]
French executioner
* Monsieur de Paris

Sansovino, Andrea
See Contucci, Andrea

Sansovino, Jacopo
See Tatti, Jacopo

Santa Baby Hodge
See Hodge, Orville Enoch

Santa Bob
See Horek, Bob

Santa Claus
See Coleman, Leighton

Santa Claus [or Klaus]
See Nicholas

Santa Claus of the Manchester Poor
See Cheney, Sophie H.

Santa Maria
See Powell-Smith, Vincent [Walter Francis]

Santamaria, Mongo
See Santamaria, Ramon

Santamaria, Nick 1941- [RO1]
American singer
* Santo, Nick

Santamaria, Ramon 1922- [IBW]
Cuban-born jazz musician
* Santamaria, Mongo

Santana, Blas Silverio 1950- [SMG]
Dominican-born baseball player
* Santana, Chi Chi

Santana, Chi Chi
See Santana, Blas Silverio

Santander, Francisco de Paula
1792-1840 [HPPN]
Columbian army officer and politician
* [The] Founder of New Granada

Santayana, George
See Santayana y Borras, Jorge
Augustin Nicolas Ruiz de

**Santayana y Borras, Jorge Augustin
Nicolas Ruiz de** 1863-1952 [HPPN]
Spanish-American poet and philosopher
* Santayana, George

Santee, Collier
See Flexner, Stuart Berg

Santell, Alfred 1895- [WEF]
American director
* Sautell, Al

Santerre, Antoine Joseph 1752-1809
[SN]
French politician and army officer
* [The] Frothy General

Santerre, Ethelbert
See Einstein, Isidor

Santerre, Meme
See Gardez, Marie Catherine

Santesson, H. S.
See Santesson, Hans Stefan

Santesson, Hans Stefan ?-1975 [SF,
SFP]
American author and editor
* O'Quinn, Vithaldas H.
* Santesson, H. S.

Santi [or Sanzio?], Raffaello 1483-1520
[FFF, HPPN, RH, WBD]
Italian painter
* [The] Affable
* [The] Angel of the Sun
* [The] Divine
* Raffaello
* Raphael
* [The] Sociable Spirit

Santiago, Blackie
See Santiago, Lester

Santiago, Burnell 1915-1944 [NOJ]
American jazz musician
* [The] King of Boogie Woogie

Santiago, Captain
See Irurzun, Hugo

Santiago, Danny
See James, Daniel

Santiago, Isidro 1811-1851 [GS]
Spanish bullfighter
* Barragan [Coarse Wool Coat]

Santiago, Jose Guillermo 1928- [BE]
Puerto Rican-born baseball player
* Santiago, Pants

Santiago, Lester 1909-1965 [NOJ]
American jazz musician
* Santiago, Blackie

Santiago, Pants
See Santiago, Jose Guillermo

Santiago, Tomas [BI]
Philippine social worker
* Manila Boy

Santiel, Powerpack
See Santiel, Terral

Santiel, Terral 20th c. [RO2]
American musician
* Santiel, Powerpack

Santley, Joseph
See Mansfield, Joseph

Santly, Banjo
See Santly, Joseph H.

Santly, Joseph H. 1886-1962 [BEW]
*American theatrical performer and
songwriter*
* Santly, Banjo

[El] Santo
See Ferdinand III

Santo, John
See Hammer, Desideriu

Santo, Nick
See Santamaria, Nick

Santoni, Espartaco B. 20th c. [WF]
Italian actor
* Anthony, Robert

Santop, Louis
See Loftin, Louis Santop

Santoro, Salvatore 20th c. [WP 2-28-85]
American underworld figure
* Mix, Tom

Santos, Alfred?
See Tremaine, F[rederick] Orlin

Santos, Domingo
See Domingo, Pedro

Santos, Enrique 1859-1935 [GS]
Spanish bullfighter
* Tortero [Cake Maker]

Santos, Helen 1939- [AW]
British author
* Griffiths, Helen

Santos, Luis Joaquin
See Quintana, Luis Joaquin

Santos Pue, Gaston 1931- [GS]
Mexican bullfighter
* [El] Centauro Potosino [The Centaur
from San Luis Potosi]

[A] Sant'ring Bully
See James II

Santucci, Girolamo 20th c. [BLB, PHM]
American underworld figure
* Doyle, Bobby

Santucci, Jimmy 1922- [MY]
American jazz musician
* Sands, Jimmy

Sanville, Jean 1918- [CA]
American psychotherapist and author
* Livermore, Jean

Sanz Almenar 1853-1888 [GS]
Spanish bullfighter
* Punderet

[The] Sao Paolo Swallow
See Bueno, Maria Esther Andion

Saperstein, Abraham M. [Abe]
1901?-1966 [BB, EJS]
*American basketball coach and team
owner*
* [The] Barnum of Basketball
* Little Caesar

Sapiens
See Gildas [or Gildus]

Sapiens
See Laelius, Gaius

Sapiens, Doctor
See Wessel, Johann [or John]

Sapin, Ruth
See Hurwitz, Ruth [Sapinsky]

Sapira, Sylvia 1908-1981
American harpsichordist
* Marlowe, Sylvia

Sapon, Archie 20th c. [SG]
Boxer
* Bell, Archie

Sapor II 4th c. [HPPN]
King of Persia
* [The] Great

Sapper
See McNeile, Herman Cyril

Sapphira
See Barber, Mary

Sappho 7th c. BC [FFF, HN, WBD]
Greek poet
* [The] Tenth Muse

Sappho
See Montagu, Mary Wortley

Sappho
See Scuderi, Magdalen [or Madeleine]
de

[The] Sappho of Brabant
See Bijns [or Byns], Anna

[The] Sappho of Brabant
See Byns, Anna

[The] Sappho of England
See Philips, Katherine

[The] Sappho of Toulouse
See Isaure, Clemence

Sapte, W.
See Edwards, Robert Hamilton

[The] Sapulpa Giant
See Morris, Carl B.

Saqorewec, E.
See McElhanon, Kenneth Andrew

Sar
See Peladan, Joseph

Sara
See Blake, Sally Mirliss

Sara, [Col.] Delle
See Aiken, Albert W.

Sarac, Roger
See Caras, Roger A[ndrew]

Saraceni, Eugene 1902- [GME, OCS]
American golfer
* Knickers, Mr.
* Sarazen, Gene

Sarachek, Bernard 1913?- [BI, EJS]
American basketball player
* Sarachek, Red

Sarachek, Red
See Sarachek, Bernard

Sarah [Margaret] 1960-
Duchess of York
* Fergie

Sarah
See Felix, Sophie

[The] Sarah Bernhardt of the Cafe Concert
See Guilbert, Yvette

Sarandon, Susan
See Tomaling, Susan

Sarant, Alfred 20th c.
American espionage agent
* Dayton, Weldon Bruce

Sarasin, J. G.
See Salmon, Geraldine Gordon

Sarasqueta, Indalecio 1860-1928 [OCS]
Spanish pelota player
* Chiquito d'Eibar [Little Fellow from Eibar]

Saraswati, S. K.
See Saraswati, Sarasi Kumar

Saraswati, Sarasi Kumar 1908- [IAW]
Indian author
* Saraswati, S. K.

Sarazen, Dolores
See Hertzler, Edith DeVilliers

Sarazen, Gene
See Saraceni, Eugene

Sarban
See Wall, John William

Sarbievius
See Sarbiewski, Mathieu Cassimer

Sarbievius, Casimir
See Sarbiewski, Mathieu Cassimer

Sarbiewski, Mathieu Cassimer 1595-1640
[HPPN, PA]
Polish author
* Sarbievius
* Sarbievius, Casimir

Sarbrow, Cepre
See Barrows, P. S.

Sarcey, Francisque 1827-1899 [WBD]
French journalist and critic
* Binet, Satane

Sard Erasmus
See Blackburn, Douglas

Sardanapalus
See Ashurbanipal

[The] Sardanapalus of China
See Cheo-tsin

[The] Sardanapalus of Germany
See Wenceslaus [or Wenceslas]

Sardi, Ivan
See Szepes, Ivan

Sardina, Adolfo 1933?- [BI]
Cuban-born fashion designer
* Adolfo

Sardinias, Eligio 1910- [BX, RBE]
Cuban boxer
* Chocolate, Kid
* [The] Cuban Bon Bon

Sardon, F. J. [PA]
Author
* Carle

Sarducci, [Father] Guido
See Novello, Don

Sarfatti, Margherita 1886-1961 [WBD]
Italian author and critic
* Cidie
* [El] Sereno

[The] Sarge
See Matthews, Gary Nathaniel

[The] Sarge
See Moody, Orville

Sargent, Aaron A. 1827-1887 [FFF]
American politician and diplomat
* Sargent, Effigy

Sargent, Brian [Lawrence] 1927- [CA]
British music educator, author, composer
* Strange, N. Blair

Sargent, Charles Sprague 1841-1927
[HPPN]
American dendrologist
* C. S. S.

Sargent, Chic
See Sargent, Epes Winthrop

Sargent, Effigy
See Sargent, Aaron A.

Sargent, Ella S. [PA]
Author
* Elliott, Elinor

Sargent, Epes Winthrop 1872?-1938
[BEW]
Bahamian-born drama critic
* Chicot
* Sargent, Chic

Sargent, Gary 1954- [SMG]
American hockey player
* Sargent, Sarge

Sargent, Henry Jackson 1809-? [FFF, PA]
American poet
* Anonym, Walter
* Legatee, Residuary

Sargent, Horse Belly
See Sargent, Joseph Alexander [Joe]

Sargent, Joan
See Jenkins, Sara

Sargent, John Osborne 1811-1891
[HPPN]
American attorney and author
* Sherry, Charles
* Singleton, Captain

Sargent, [Rev.] John Turner ?-1877
[HPPN]
American clergyman
* Bronze Beethoven, A Looker On
* [A] Pastor

Sargent, Joseph
See Sargente, Giuseppe Daniel

Sargent, Joseph Alexander [Joe]
1893-1950 [BE]
American baseball player
* Sargent, Horse Belly

Sargent, Judith 1751-1820 [PA]
American author
* Constantia

Sargent, Lucius Manlius 1786-1867
[FFF, HPPN, PA]
American poet and journalist
* Amgis
* Sexton of the Old School
* Sigma

Sargent, Mrs. H. J. [FFF]
Entertainer
* Bailey, Hannah

Sargent, Nathan 1794-1875 [FFF, PA]
American author
* Oldschool, Oliver

Sargent, Richard
See Cox, Richard

Sargent, Sarge
See Sargent, Gary

Sargent, Thomas Henry 1895-1963
[BEW, FC]
British entertainer
* [The] Cheeky Chappie
* Miller, Max

Sargente, Giuseppe Daniel 1925- [FIR]
American director
* Sargent, Joseph

[El] Sargento [The Sergeant]
See Rodriguez, Guillermo

Sargeson, Frank
See Davey, Morris Frank

Sargon II [HPPN]
King of Babylon
* Sharrunkin [The Righteous King]

Sargon II 8th c. BC [HPPN]
King of Assyria
* Sharrukin [The Righteous King]

Sari
See Fleur, Anne

Sarin, Max Kenneth 1912-1967 [SC]
American actor
* MacSarin, Kenneth

Sarkar, Probhat Ranjan 1921- [EOP, NAD]
Indian educator and founder of religious sect
* Anandamurti, Shri

Sarkia, Kaarlo Teodor
See Sulin, Kaarlo Teodor

Sarkis
See Zabunyan, Serkis

Sarkisian, Cherilyn
See Sarkisian, Cheryl

Sarkisian, Cheryl 1946- [IPA, RO2, WP 12-27-83]
American singer
* Cher
* LaPierre, Cherilyn
* Mason, Bonnie Joe [or Bonny Jo]
* Sarkisian, Cherilyn

Sarle, Charles Spenser 20th c. [WWL]
British author and journalist
* Amory, Arthur R.

Sarlo
See King, Carroll E.

Sarma, Challa Radhakrishna 1929- [IAW]
Indian author
* Krishna

Sarment, Jean
See Bellemere, Jean

Sarmiento, Domingo Faustino 1811-1888
Argentine educator and statesman
* [The] Schoolmaster President

Sarmiento, Manny
See Sarmiento Aponte, Manuel Eduardo

Sarmiento Aponte, Manuel Eduardo 1956- [BR]
Venezuelan-born baseball player
* Sarmiento, Manny

Sarnat, Marshall
See Sarnatzky, Marshall

Sarnatzky, Marshall 1929- [CA]
American-born Israeli financial analyst and author
* Sarnat, Marshall

Sarne, Michael
See Plummer, Thomas Arthur

Sarnian
See Falla, Frank W.

Sarnoff, [General] David 1891-1971 [HPPN]
American army officer and radio and television executive
* [The] Controversial Pioneer
* [The] Genius of R. C. A.

Sarnoff, Jan
See Sarnoff, Janyc

Sarnoff, Janyc 1928- [HPPN]
American musician
* Sarnoff, Jan

Saroff, Morton 1924- [ITA]
American music executive
* Jay, Morty

[The] Sarong Girl
See Kaumeyer, Dorothy

Sarony, Leslie
See Frye, Leslie

Saroyan, William 1908-1981 [FFF, HPPN, SN, WBD]
American author and playwright
* Goryan, Sirak
* [The] Hero of Fresno's Armenian Community
* [The] Literary Pride of His Home Town

Sarpi, Paolo
See Sarpi, Pietro

Sarpi, Pietro 1552-1623 [FFF, NPS, SN, WBD]
Italian prelate
* Paolo, [Fra]
* Paul, [Father]
* Paul, [Brother]
* Paul of Venice
* Paulus Servita
* Paulus Venetus
* Sarpi, Paolo
* Servita

Sarr, Kenneth
See Reddin, Kenneth Shiels

Sarrapede, James 1904-1972 [PMJ, WWJ]
American jazz musician
* Lytell, Jimmy

Sarratt, H. J.
See Raspe, Rudolph E[rich]

Sarratt, J. H. 19th c. [HPPN]
British chess player, author, educator
* [The] Professor of Chess

Sarrazin, Jacques Michel Andre 1940- [ITA]
Canadian-born actor
* Sarrazin, Michael

Sarrazin, Michael
See Sarrazin, Jacques Michel Andre

Sarruf, Alexander 1908- [F2, FC]
Egyptian actor
* D'Arcy, Alex

Sarsfield
See McGee, Thomas D'Arcy

Sarsfield, C. P.
See Marshner, Connaught Coyne

Sarsi, Lotario
See Grassi, Orazio

Sarti, Giuseppe 1729-1802 [BBD]
Italian composer
* [Il] Domenichino

Sarti, Signor
See Knight, Ashton

Sarto, Andrea del
See D'Agnolo di Francesco, Andrea Domenico

Sarto, Ben
See Fawcett, F[rank] Dubrez

Sarto, Giuseppe Melchiorre 1835-1914 [CBS, DNNS, HPPN, WBD]
Pope
* [The] Peasant Pope
* Pius X
* [The] Pope of Catholic Action
* St. Pius

Sartorius
See Snyders, Johann

Sartorius, [Sir] G. R. 1790-? [PA]
Author
* Penhafirme, Count of

Sartre, Jean-Paul 1905-? [CR]
French philosopher and author
* [The] Father of Existentialism

Sarver, Hannah
See Nielsen, Jean Sarver

Sarvis, Andrew 20th c. [OBW]
American baseball player
* Sarvis, Smoky

Sarvis, Smoky
See Sarvis, Andrew

Sashun, Sigmund
See Sassoon, Siegfried [Lorraine]

Sashweight
See Manchester, William

Saslavsky, Luis 20th c. [WF]
Author
* Fourcade, Simon

Sass, Charles [FFF]
American writer
* Centaur

Sass, George Herbert 1845-1908 [FFF, PA]
American journalist and poet
* Grey, Barton

Sass, Job
See Foxcroft, George Augustus

Sassafras
See Welsh, Johnnie

Sassetta
See Di Giovanni, Stefano

[Il] **Sassoferrato**
See Salvi, Giovanni Battista

[Il] **Sassone**
See Hasse, Johann Adolf

Sassoon, Richa 1858-1927 [JL]
Indian-born publisher
* Beer, Rachel

Sassoon, Siegfried [Lorraine] 1886-1967
[CA, DLE1]
British poet and author
* Kain, Saul
* Lyre, Pinchbeck
* Sashun, Sigmund
* Tak Yussuf Hoff [Take Yourself Off]

Sassoon, [Sir] Victor 1881-1961
British financier
* Eve, Mr.
* Seymour, Val

Sasuly, Richard 1913- [CA]
American author and editor
* Furth, Alex

Satane, Paul
See Haill, Robert Godfrey

Satanella
See Burnham, Mary Hewins

Satchell, Clarence 20th c. [RO2]
American musician
* Satchell, Satch

Satchell, Satch
See Satchell, Clarence

Satchmo
See Armstrong, [Daniel] Louis

[El] **Satelite [The Satellite]**
See Ruiz De La Torre, Victor

Sather, Julia Coley Duncan 1940- [CA]
American author
* Duncan, Julia Coley

Sathima
See Benjamin, Bea

Satie, Erik
See Leslie-Satie, Alfred Erikit

Satin, Miss
See Mallarme, Stephane

Satiricus
See Roetter, Charles Frederick

Sato, Masahiko
See Satoh, Masahiko

Satoh, Masahiko 1941- [EJ7]
Japanese-born jazz musician
* Sato, Masahiko

Satprem
See Enginger, Bernard

Satre, Magnus 20th c. [BBH]
American skier
* [The] Iron Man

Satriano, Satch
See Satriano, Thomas Victor

Satriano, Thomas Victor 1940- [BE]
American baseball player
* Satriano, Satch

Satterfield, Charles [joint pseudonym
with Frederik Pohl]
See Alvarez Del Rey, Ramon Felipe
San Juan Mario Silvio Enrico

Satterfield, Charles [joint pseudonym
with Ramon Felipe San Juan Alvarez
Del Rey]
See Pohl, Frederik

Satterly, Weston
See Sunners, William

Satterthwaite, Franklin 1846-? [HPPN]
American author
* Larkfin

Satterwhite, Collen Gray 1920-1978
[ASC]
American musician
* Satterwhite, Tex

Satterwhite, Tex
See Satterwhite, Collen Gray

Sattin, Lonnie
See Staton, Alonzo Louis Lee

Sattler, Lisbeth 1894-1976 [BBD]
German opera singer
* Rethberg, Elisabeth

[The] **Saturday Fox**
See Meyer, Leo Robert

Saturday Night, Mr.
See Gleason, Herbert John

Saturn, Sergeant [house pseudonym]
See Friend, Oscar J[erome]

Saturn, Sergeant [house pseudonym]
See Merwin, [W.] Sam[uel], Jr.

Saturn, Sergeant [house pseudonym]
See Weisinger, Mort[imer]

[The] **Satyr**
See Charles II

Satz, Frances 1915-1963 [SC]
American actress
* Keating, Katherine
* Sage, Frances

**Saucerotte, Francoise-Marie Antoinette
Josephe** 1756-1815 [HPPN]
French actress
* Raucourt

Saucier, Hot Sauce
See Saucier, Kevin Andrew

Saucier, Kevin Andrew 1956-
American baseball player
* Saucier, Hot Sauce

Saud, Sulaimon
See Tyner, Alfred McCoy

Sauda
See Forsyth, William Langdon

Sauer, Don 20th c. [RBE]
Boxing promoter
* Sauer, Sailor Don

Sauer, Edward 1920- [BE]
American baseball player
* Sauer, Horn

Sauer, Horn
See Sauer, Edward

Sauer, Joseph 1901?-1982 [FC]
American actor
* Sawyer, Joseph

Sauer, Muriel Stafford 20th c. [CA]
American graphologist and author
* Stafford, Muriel

Sauer, Peter 1900?-1949 [BI, HPPN]
American wrestler
* Steele, Ray

Sauer, Sailor Don
See Sauer, Don

Sauget, Joseph Sylvestre 1871-1955 [BI,
NAA]
French-born naturalist and author
* Leon, [Brother]

Sauguet, Henri
See Poupard, Henri-Pierre

Saul
See Cromwell, Oliver

Saul
See Kovner, Saul

Saul, Beverly Jean 1928- [ITA, SW]
American actress
* Tyler, Beverly

Saul, Frank 1924-
American basketball player
* Saul, Pep

Saul of Tarsus ?-67? [DEP, FF, WBD]
Saint
* [The] Apostle of the Gentiles
* Paul

Saul, Oscar
See Halpern, Oscar Saul

Saul, Pep
See Saul, Frank

Sauls, Judi Lee 1947- [SW]
Actress
* Meredith, Lee

Sauls, Kirby 20th c. [EF]
American football player
* Sauls, Mac

Sauls, Mac
See Sauls, Kirby

Sault, R. O.
See Swan, Charles F.

Sault, Wallace A. [Wally] 1880-1959
[HPPN]
American actor
* [The] Royal Entertainer

Saumaise, Claude 1588-1658 [NPS, PA]
French scholar
* Alastor
* [The] Great Kill-Cow of Christendom
* [The] Great Pan

Saumaise, Claude (cont.)
* [The] Prince of Letters
* Salmasius, Claudius

Saunders, Allen 1899- [WECO]
American cartoonist
* Allen, Dale

Saunders, Ann Loreille 1930- [WD]
British author
* Cox-Johnson, Ann

Saunders, Caleb
See Heinlein, Robert A[nson]

Saunders, Carl Maxon 1890-1974 [CA]
American journalist
* Sandy, Max

Saunders, Carl McK.
See Ketchum, Philip

Saunders, Clarence 1881-1953 [HPPN]
American chain store operator
* [The] Keydoozler
* [The] Piggly Wiggly Man

Saunders, David [FFF]
Author
* [The] Shepherd of Salisbury Plain

Saunders, David
See Sontup, Dan[iel]

Saunders, Edward 1866-1910 [BMH]
British comedian, singer, songwriter
* Deane, Charles

Saunders, Frederick 1807-? [PA]
Author
* [An] Epicure

Saunders, Helen Holmes 1892-1950
[HPPN]
American actress
* Holmes, Helen

Saunders, Hilary Aidan St. George
1898-1951 [LC, TC, WW]
British author
* Beeding, Francis [joint pseudonym
  with John Leslie Palmer]
* Pilgrim, David [joint pseudonym with
  John Leslie Palmer]

Saunders, Ione
See Cole, Margaret Alice

Saunders, Jean 1932- [CA, WD]
British author
* Blake, Sally
* Innes, Jean
* Summers, Rowena

Saunders, Joe 1842-1884 [BMH]
British entertainer
* Leybourne, George

Saunders, John S. 1873?-1952 [BI]
American educator
* Arnold Edward, [Brother]

Saunders, Killer
See Saunders, Mark

Saunders, Lawrence [joint pseudonym
with Clarisy Musadore (Ogden) Davis]
See Davis, Burton

Saunders, Lawrence [joint pseudonym
with Burton Davis]
See Davis, Clarisy Musadore [Ogden]

Saunders, Margaret Bell 1894- [CCL]
Canadian author
* Bell, Margaret

Saunders, Mark 20th c. [BBH]
Boxer
* Saunders, Killer

Saunders, P.
See Cohen, Paul Arthur

Saunders, Raymond 1877-1948 [BI]
American magician
* Raymond the Great

Saunders, Red
See Saunders, Theodore

Saunders, Richard
See Franklin, Ben[jamin]

Saunders, Robert 1727-1783 [FFF]
British author
* Burlington
* Llewellyn
* Murray
* Spencer, Nat

Saunders, Rufus, The Sage of Rocky
Creek
See Lloyd, Francis Bartow

Saunders, Russell
See Wiley, Carl A.

Saunders, Russell Collier 1906- [BE]
American baseball player
* Saunders, Rusty

Saunders, Rusty
See Saunders, Russell Collier

Saunders, Theodore 1912-1981 [EJ,
WWJ]
American jazz musician
* Saunders, Red

Saunders, Theodore 20th c. [WW]
Author
* Scott, Denis [joint pseudonym with
  Mary Means]

Saunders, Wallace 20th c. [IBW]
American songwriter
* Saunders, Wash

Saunders, Wash
See Saunders, Wallace

Saunders, Wes
See Bounds, Sydney J[ames]

Saunter, Samuel
See Dennie, Joseph

Saura, Carlos
See Altares Saura, Carlos

Saurin, Jacques 1677-1730 [NPS]
French clergyman
* [The] Bossuet of the Protestant Pulpit

[The] Sausage Maker Murder
See Luetgert, Adolph Louis

Sauser-Hall, Frederic 1887-1961 [EWL,
LC, OCF]
French-born poet and author
* Cendrars, Blaise

Saussure, Rene de 20th c. [WBD]
Swiss-French philologist
* Antido

Sautel, Maureen Ann 1951- [CA]
American author
* McGinn, Maureen Ann

Sautell, Al
See Santell, Alfred

Sautereau, Barry 1932- [TR]
British actor
* Kent, Barry

Sauvage, Franck
See Horn, Maurice

Sauvage, Frere
See Wilde, William Charles Kingsley

Sauvage, Sieur du
See Brissot, Roland

Sauvageau, Juan 1917- [CA]
Canadian-born author
* Lavoix, Jean

Sauval, Henri 1620?-1669? [SN]
French historian
* [The] Stowe of France

Sauvolle, Le Moine 1617?-1701 [HPPN]
French Canadian politician
* [The] American Prodigy

Sauzade, John S.
See Payn, James

Sava, George
See Milkomane, George Alexis
Milkomanovich

Sava, Jimmy 1895-1960 [BEW]
American-born actor
* Savo, Jimmy

Savage, Adam
See Butters, Francis

Savage, Blake
See Goodwin, Harold Leland [Hal]

Savage, Catharine
See Brosman, Catharine Savage

Savage, Christina [joint pseudonym with
Frank Schaefer]
See Newcomb, Kerry

Savage, Christina [joint pseudonym with
Kerry Newcomb]
See Schaefer, Frank

Savage, D. S.
See Savage, Derek Stanley

Savage, David
See Hossent, Harry

Savage, David Earle, Jr. 1946- [EAR]
American auto racer
* Savage, Swede

Savage, Derek Stanley 1917- [MBL]
British critic
* Savage, D. S.

Savage, Ethel May Dell ?-1939 [HPPN]
British author
* Dell, Ethel M.

Savage, Fred
See Savage, Richard LeQuesne

Savage, George Martin 1849-1938
[HPPN]
American educator
* [The] Grand Old Man
* [The] Union's Grand Old Man

Savage, Gordon 1906- [CEI]
Canadian-born hockey player
* Savage, Tony

Savage, Houston
See DeBlasio, Gene

Savage, Ian
See Giggal, Kenneth

Savage Illogic
See Strauss, Lewis L[ichtenstein]

Savage, Joan
See Weisman, Joan

Savage, John 1828-1888 [FFF, PA]
Irish-born journalist, poet, playwright
* Richards, Ezek
* Touchstone

Savage, John
See Youngs, John

Savage, Laura
See Stephens, Francis George

Savage, Leslie
See Duff, Douglas Valder

Savage, Leslie H. 1922?-1958 [BI,
HPPN]
American author
* Stewart, Logan

Savage, M. J. 19th c. [PA]
Author
* [A] Lunar Wray

Savage, Marmion Wilmo 1805-1872 [PI]
Irish author and poet
* M. W. S.

Savage, Mary
See Dresser, Mary

[The] Savage Messiah
See Gaudier-Brzeska, Henri

Savage, Mildred [Spitz] 1919- [CA]
American author
* Barrie, Jane

Savage, Oscar
See Montague, Bruce Alexander

Savage, Richard [Fourth Earl Rivers]
1660?-1712 [HN]
British soldier
* Tyburn Dick

Savage, Richard
See Roe, Ivan

Savage, Richard LeQuesne 1955- [DC]
British cricketer
* Savage, Fred

Savage, Swede
See Savage, David Earle, Jr.

Savage Tom Thomas
See Thomas, Thomas W. [Tom]

Savage, Tony
See Savage, Gordon

Savalas, Aristotle 1925- [IPA, SW]
American actor
* Savalas, Telly

Savalas, George 1927-1985 [WP 10-3-85]
American actor
* Demosthenes

Savalas, Telly
See Savalas, Aristotle

Savane, Virgile 1865-1920? [CW]
West Indian author and poet
* Salavina

Savaria, Antonio Gonzalez de
See Mollinedo y Savaria, Antonio
Gonzalez

Savarin
See Courtine, Robert

Savelli, Cencio 13th c. [WBD]
Pope
* Honorius III

Savelli, Giacomo 1210?-1287 [WBD]
Pope
* Honorius IV

Saverine, Rabbit
See Saverine, Robert Paul

Saverine, Robert Paul 1941- [BE]
American baseball player
* Saverine, Rabbit

Savery, Constance Winifred 1897-
[IAW]
British author
* Cloberry, Elizabeth
* Rycon

Savi, E. W.
See Savi, Ethel Winifred Bryning

Savi, Ethel Winifred Bryning ?-1954
[LC]
British author
* Savi, E. W.

Savidge, Ralph Austin 1879-1959 [BE]
American baseball player
* [The] Human Whipcord

Savile
See Sotheran, Henry

Savile
See Sothern, Henry

**Savile, [Sir] George [Marquis of
Halifax]** 1633-1695 [DEA, SN]
British statesman
* Jotham
* T. W.
* [The] Trimmer
* W. C., Sir

Savile, [Sir] Henry 1549-1622 [SN]
British scholar
* [The] Lay Bishop

Savill, Roy 1921- [HPPN]
British author
* Stacey, Paul

Saville, Gus H.
See Truean, Augustus H.

Savin, Una
See Hepworth, Mrs. George H.

Savini-Brioni, Gaetano 20th c. [CR]
Italian fashion designer
* Brioni
* [The] Caesar of Style
* [The] Men's Dior

Savinio, Alberto
See Chirico, Andrea de

Savinkov, Boris Viktorovich 1879-1925
[BI, CD]
Russian terrorist and author
* Ropshin, V.

Savino, Guido di
See Andries, Guido

[The] Savior of Church Music
See Palestrina, Giovanni Pierluigida

[The] Savior of El Paso
See Haynes, Frederick

[The] Savior of Europe
See Kreuger, Ivar

[The] Savior of His Country
See Clay, Henry

[The] Savior of His Country
See Oates, Titus

[The] Savior of His Country
See Pichegru, Charles

[The] Savior of His Country
See Washington, George

[The] Savior of Paris
See Gallieni, Joseph Simon

[The] Savior of Protestantism
See Gustavus II

[The] Savior of Terre Haute
See Martin, Anne

[The] Savior of the Arts
See Sirovich, William Irving

[The] Savior of the Comstock Lode
See Sutro, Adolph Heinrich Joseph

[The] Savior of the Constitution
See Bloom, Sol

Savior of the DuPonts
See Du Pont, Alfred Irenee

[The] Savior of the Nation
See Cromwell, Oliver

Savior of the Texas League
See Hoskins, Dave

[The] Savior of the Valley
See Rosser, Thomas Lafayette

[The] Saviour of Rome
See Marius, Caius

[The] Saviour of Society
See Bonaparte, Charles Louis Napoleon

[The] Saviour of the Nations
See Wellesley, Arthur

[The] Saviour of the People
See FitzOsbert, William

[The] Saviour of the Punjab
See Lawrence, John Laird Mair [First Baron Lawrence]

Saviozzi, Adriana
See Mazza, Adriana

Savitch, Jessica 1948-1984 [NW 11-7-83, WP 10-25-83]
American journalist
* Honeybee

Savitch, Spider
See Savitch, Vladimir

Savitch, Vladimir 1945?-1976
American skier
* Savitch, Spider

Savitri Priya, [Swami]
See Lynott, Jessica

Savo, Jimmy
See Sava, Jimmy

Savoir, Alfred
See Poznanski, Alfred

Savoldi, Joseph A. 1909-1974 [FB]
Italian-born football player
* Savoldi, Jumpin' Joe

Savoldi, Jumpin' Joe
See Savoldi, Joseph A.

Savona, Leopoldo 20th c. [FDG]
Italian director
* Colman, L.

Savonarola, Girolamo Maria Francesco Matteo 1452-1498 [HPPN]
Italian clergyman and reformer
* [The] First Great Protestant
* [The] Meddlesome Friar

Savonarola, Jeremy
See Mahony, Francis Sylvester

Savory, C. H. 19th c. [HPPN]
British decorator
* [A] Decorator

Savory, Kenneth 1873?-1923 [BEW]
British-born comedian
* Douglas, Kenneth

Savory, [Sir] Reginald Arthur 1894- [AW]
British writer
* Ledsam

Savoy, Anne
See Brooks, Anne Sooy

Savoy, Ashton 20th c. [NBB]
American singer
* Conroy, Ashton

Savoy, Bert
See McKenzie, Everett

Savoy, Houston
See DeBlasio, Gene

Savoy, Mark
See Turner, Robert [Harry]

Savoyard
See Newman, Eugene William

Savransky, Moe
See Savransky, Morris

Savransky, Morris 1929- [BE]
American baseball player
* Savransky, Moe

Saw, Buck
See Aby, Joseph C.

Sawamura, Kunitaro
See Kato, Tomoichi

Saward, James Townsend 19th c. [HPPN]
British
* Jim the Penman

Sawatski, Carl Ernest 1927- [BE, PB]
American baseball player and manager
* Sawatski, Swats

Sawatski, Swats
See Sawatski, Carl Ernest

Sawbuck [[code name used during World War II]]
See Roosevelt, Franklin Delano

Sawdust Caesar Goering
See Goering, Herman Wilhelm

Sawell, Larry [IBW]
American disc jockey
* [The] Round Mound of Sound
* [The] Sugar Pie Guy
* [The] Tokyo Giant

Sawhill, John C. 1937- [HPPN]
American government official
* [The] Energy Deputy

Sawkins, Raymond H[arold] 1923- [CA]
British author
* Bernard, Jay
* Forbes, Colin
* Raine, Richard

Sawley, Petra
See Marsh, John

Sawney
See Pope, Alexander

Sawtelle, William Carter
See Graham, Roger Phillips

Sawtille, Mrs. E. W. 19th c. [PA]
Author
* Towne, Tracy

Sawtre, William ?-1401 [HN, HPPN]
British heretic
* [The] First English Martyr
* [The] First Victim in England

Sawyer
See Wirtanen, Atos Kasimir

Sawyer, Boss
See Sawyer, Philetus

Sawyer, Buddy
See Estep, Harold

Sawyer, Carl
See Schreuer, Carl

Sawyer, Carl Everett 1890-1957 [BE]
American baseball player
* Sawyer, Huck

Sawyer, Carrie M. 20th c. [EOP]
Claimed to possess psychic powers
* Salmon, Mrs.

Sawyer, [Dr.] Charles E. 20th c. [HPPN]
Physician to American president, Warren Harding
* Sawyer, Doc
* Sawyer, General

Sawyer, Corinne Holt 20th c. [CA]
American author
* Rickert, Corinne Holt

Sawyer, Country
See Sawyer, John

Sawyer, Doc
See Sawyer, [Dr.] Charles E.

Sawyer, Eugene Taylor 1846-1924 [EMD, WW]
American author
* Carter, Nicholas
* Collier, Old Cap

Sawyer, Frederick William 1810-? [FFF]
American legal writer
* Canty Carl
* Carl

Sawyer, General
See Sawyer, [Dr.] Charles E.

Sawyer, Helen Alton 20th c. [HPPN]
American artist
* Farnsworth, Helen

Sawyer, Huck
See Sawyer, Carl Everett

Sawyer, John 1953- [SMG]
American football player
* Sawyer, Country

Sawyer, John
See Foley, [Cedric] John

Sawyer, Joseph
See Sauer, Joseph

Sawyer, Mark
See Greenhood, [Clarence] David

Sawyer, Philetus 1816-1900   [HPPN]
American lumber magnate and politician
* Sawyer, Boss
* [The] Wisconsin Lumber King

Sawyer, Ray 1937-   [RO2]
American singer
* [The] Hook
* Hook, Dr.

Sawyer, Ruth
See Durand, Mrs. Albert C.

Sawyer, Walter Leon 1862-1915   [DNA]
American journalist and author
* Standish, Winn

Sawyers, Bo
See Sawyers, James

Sawyers, James 20th c.   [RO2]
American musician
* Sawyers, Bo

Sax, Adolphe
See Sax, Antoine Joseph

Sax, Antoine Joseph 1814-1894   [WBD]
Belgian musical instrument maker
* Sax, Adolphe

Sax, Christian 1714-1806   [PA]
Author
* Saxius

Saxbe, William B. 1916-   [HPPN]
American politician
* Old Blunderbuss

Saxe, Burton
See Sikes, William Wirt

Saxe, Isobel
See Rayner, Claire

Saxe, [Hermann] Maurice de 1696-1750
[SN, WBD]
French marshal
* [A] Homeric Ajax
* Marshal de Saxe
* [The] Turenne of Louis XV

Saxe, Templer
See Edeveain, Templer Edward

Saxifrage
See Thorne, Sheldon B.

Saxin, Pauline
See Saxon, Polly

Saxius
See Sax, Christian

Saxo, Grammaticus 1140?-1206   [HPPN]
Danish chronicler
* [The] Scholar

Saxo-Norman
See Yvelin, Albert [Baron de Beville]

[The] Saxon
See Emma

[The] Saxon
See Henry I [or Heinrich]

[The] Saxon
See Lothair II

Saxon
See Noyes, E. Herbert

Saxon, Alex
See Pronzini, Bill

Saxon, Arthur
See Hennig, Arthur

Saxon, Bill
See Wallmann, Jeffrey M[iner]

Saxon, Carl
See Day, A. Grove

[The] Saxon Duke
See John Frederick

[The] Saxon Giant
See Handel, Georg Friedrich

Saxon, Gladys Relyea 20th c.   [CA]
American author
* Borden, M.
* Seyton, Marion

Saxon, Harold
See Clint, Mabel Brown

[The] Saxon Hating Creole
See De Marigney, Bernard

Saxon, John
See Orrico, Carmen

Saxon, John
See Rumbold-Gibbs, Henry St. John
Clair

Saxon, John A.
See Bellem, Robert Leslie

Saxon, Lefty
See Saxon, Thomas

[The] Saxon Milton
See Caedmon

[The] Saxon Nymph
See Elstob, Elizabeth

Saxon, Peter [house pseudonym]
See Baker, William Arthur Howard

Saxon, Peter [house pseudonym]
See Martin, Thomas Hector

Saxon, Peter [house pseudonym]
See McNeilly, Wilfred Glassford

Saxon, Polly 1884-1949   [HPPN]
American actress
* Saxin, Pauline

Saxon, Richard
See Morrissey, Joseph Laurence

Saxon, Sky
See Marsh, Richard

Saxon, Thomas 20th c.   [OBW]
American baseball player
* Saxon, Lefty

Saxon, Van
See Granbeck, Marilyn

Saxon, Van
See Simpson, Evangeline M.

Saxon, Vin
See Haydock, Ron

Saxton, Judith
See Turner, Judy

Say
See Cheves, Langdon

[The] Say Hey Kid
See Mays, William Howard, Jr. [Willie]

Say, Hugh 16th c.   [BI]
British explorer
* Day, John

Say, Thomas 1787-1834   [HPPN]
*American conchologist entomologist,
zoologist*
* [The] Father of American Conchology
* [The] Father of American Descriptive
Entomology
* [The] Father of American Entomology
* [The] Father of American Zoology
* [The] Father of Descriptive
Entomology in America

Saya, Peter
See Peterson, Robert E[ugene]

Sayao, Bidu
See De Oliveira Sayao, Balduina

Saye, Joe
See Shulman, Joseph

Sayel, Saed ?-1982
*Military adviser to the Palestine
Liberation Organization*
* Abu Walid

Sayer, Gerard 1948-   [RO2]
British singer
* Sayer, Leo

Sayer, H. W.
See Sayer, Harold Wilfred

Sayer, Harold Wilfred 1913-   [ART]
British painter and etcher
* Sayer, H. W.

Sayer, Leo
See Sayer, Gerard

Sayer, Nancy Margetts 1913-   [WD]
British author
* Bradfield, Nancy

Sayer, Wal
See Sayer, Walter William

Sayer, Walter William 1892-   [MBF]
British author
* Quiroule, Pierre [Rolling Stone]
* Sayer, Wal

Sayers, Arthur Bond ?-1912   [HPPN]
American conductor
* Patsy

Sayers, Ben
See Sayers, Bernard

Sayers, Bernard 1857-1924   [EG]
Scottish golfer
* Sayers, Ben
* Sayers, Wee Ben

Sayers, Dorothy L[eigh] 1893-1957 [CC, WW]
Author
* Leigh, Johanna

Sayers, Edgar
See Edgar, Alfred

Sayers, Frances H. 19th c. [HPPN]
British poet
* Cecil, [Lady] Frances H.

Sayers, Gale Eugene 1943- [HPPN, IBW]
American football player
* Comet Gale
* [The] Galloping Gale
* [The] Kansas Cyclone
* Sayers, Magic

Sayers, [Rev.] Gilbert H. 19th c. [HPPN]
American clergyman
* [The] Rector

Sayers, James Denson 20th c. [MBF]
British author
* Bardwell, Denver

Sayers, Magic
See Sayers, Gale Eugene

Sayers, Tom 1826-1865 [BBH, PPN, RBE]
British boxer
* [The] Little Wonder
* [The] Napoleon of the Prize Ring

Sayers, Wee Ben
See Sayers, Bernard

Sayler, H. L.
See Sayler, Harry Lincoln

Sayler, Harry Lincoln 1863-1913 [WGT]
American author
* Lamar, Ashton
* Sayler, H. L.
* Stuart, Gordon
* Whitney, Elliott [joint pseudonym with Henry Bedford-Jones]

Sayles, Bartholomew
See Letory, John Bruno

Sayles, Edwin Booth 1892- [CAP]
American author
* Sayles, Ted

Sayles, Hezekiah, Jr. 1918-1974 [IBW]
American boxing manager
* Sayles, Kiah

Sayles, Kiah
See Sayles, Hezekiah, Jr.

Sayles, Ted
See Sayles, Edwin Booth

Saylor, Lefty
See Saylor, Phil[ip Andrew]

Saylor, Phil[ip Andrew] 1871-1937 [BE]
American baseball player
* Saylor, Lefty

Saylor, Sid
See Sailor, Leo

Sayre, Bud
See Sayre, Reginald

Sayre, Gordon
See Woolfolk, Josiah Pitts

Sayre, Reginald 1915?- [BI]
American model maker
* Sayre, Bud

Sbarbaro, Anthony 1897-1969 [ASC, EJ, WWJ]
American jazz musician
* Spargo, Tony

Sbernia
See Berni, Francesco

Scaasi, Arnold
See Isaacs, Arnold

Scabbitt, Governor
See Babbitt, Bruce

Scaccio, John
See Talamo, W.

Scaeva
See Stuart, Isaac William

Scaeva
See Stubbes, John

Scaevola
See Allen, John

Scaevola
See Mucius, Caius

Scafone, Jack, Jr. 1936- [RO1]
Canadian-born singer and songwriter
* Scott, Jack

Scaggs, Boz
See Scaggs, William Royce

Scaggs, William Royce 1944- [RO2]
American musician
* Scaggs, Boz

Scagnetti, Jack 1924- [CA]
American journalist
* Michael, James

Scaife, Arthur Hodgkin 19th c. [CCL]
Canadian author
* Bilir, Kim

Scala, Can Francesco della 1291-1329 [WBD]
Imperial vicar of Verona
* Scala, Cane Grande della

Scala, Cane Grande della
See Scala, Can Francesco della

Scala, Flaminio 17th c. [HPPN]
Italian playwright
* Flavio

Scala, Gia
See Scoglio, Giovanna

Scalchi, Sofia
See Lolli, Countess

[The] Scald
See Smellie, George

Scale, Elizabeth Barry 1889- [CU]
American actress
* Barriscale, Bessie

Scales, Prunella
See Illingworth, Prunella

Scalice, Frank ?-1957 [PHM]
American underworld figure
* Cheech, Don

Scaliger, Josephus Justus 1540-1609 [HN, RH]
Italian scholar
* [The] Father of Chronology

[The] Scaliger of the Age
See Warburton, William

Scalisi, Josefina 1932- [OP]
Argentinian opera singer
* Carini, Nina

[The] Scalp Buyer
See Hamilton, Henry

Scalpel
See Dixon, Edward Henry

Scalpel, Aesculapius
See Berdoe, Edward

Scalzi, Frank Joseph 1913- [BE]
American baseball player
* Scalzi, Skeeter

Scalzi, Skeeter
See Scalzi, Frank Joseph

Scammony, Frank
See Atterbury, Francis

Scampington, Duke of
See Murray, Eustace Clare Grenville

Scanderbeg
See Castriot [or Castriota?], George

Scanderbeg III
See Ahmed Bey Zogu

[The] Scandinavian Semiramis
See Margaret

Scandrett, Edward Milton 1941- [BA]
American sales manager
* Scandrett, Scan

Scandrett, Scan
See Scandrett, Edward Milton

Scanes, Mrs. A. E. *MB
Author
* Goodman, Maude

Scanlan, Doc
See Scanlan, William Dennis

Scanlan, Dreamy
See Scanlan, Frank Aloysius

Scanlan, Frank Aloysius 1890-1969 [BE]
American baseball player
* Scanlan, Dreamy

Scanlan, Kate [FFF]
Entertainer
* O'Shea, Kittie

Scanlan, Michael 1836-? [PI]
Irish-born poet
* Blake, Dionysius

Scanlan, Peter E. 1865?-1950 [BI]
American educator
* Paul, [Brother]

Scanlan, Walter 1892- [BI]
American singer
* Van Brunt, Walter John

Scanlan, William Dennis 1881-1949
[AS, BE]
American baseball player
* Scanlan, Doc

Scanlon, Barry
See Cole, Thomas F.

Scanlon, C. K. M.
See Eliot, G. F.

Scanlon, C. K. M. [house pseudonym]
See Gruber, Frank

Scanlon, Tom 20th c. [WP 2-10-85]
American newspaper editor and historian
* Dykes, Todd

Scannabecchi, Lamberto ?-1130 [WBD]
Pope
* Honorius II

Scannabue, Aristarco
See Baretti, Giuseppe Marc'Antonio

Scannell, Jan
See Scannell, Johannes Petrus

Scannell, Johannes Petrus 1916- [IAW]
South African author
* Scannell, Jan

Scantlan, Samuel William 1901- [IAW]
American clergyman and author
* Leumas, William S.

Scantlebury, Pat
See Scantlebury, Patricio Athelstan

Scantlebury, Patricio Athelstan 1925-
[BE, OBW]
Panamanian-born baseball player
* Scantlebury, Pat

Scantrel, Yves
See Suares, Andre

Scar Face Charlie Eliot
See Eliot, Charles William

Scarabaeus
See Badham, Charles David

Scaramuccio
See Lawrence, William John

Scarce, Guerrant McCurdy 1949-
[SMG]
American baseball player
* Scarce, Mac

Scarce, Mac
See Scarce, Guerrant McCurdy

Scarf, Maggi
See Scarf, Maggie

Scarf, Maggie 1932- [CA, SAT]
American author
* Scarf, Maggi

Scarface
See Capone, Al[phonse]

Scarface Al Brown
See Capone, Al[phonse]

Scarface Ed Brown
See Brown, Edward

Scarface Jock Russo
See Russo, Victor

Scarface, Tony
See Capone, Al[phonse]

Scarff, William
See Budrys, Algirdas Jonas

Scargill, Andy 20th c.
British labor leader
* King Arthur

Scarlatti, Alessandro 1659-1725 [NPS]
Italian composer
* [The] Founder of Modern Opera

**[The] Scarlet Pimpernel of the First
Amendment**
See Dershowitz, Alan

[The] Scarlet Pimpernel Priest
See O'Flaherty, Hugh

Scarlet, Rebecca
See Burt, Katharine Newlin

Scarlet, Thomas
See Nash [or Nashe?], Thomas

Scarlet, Will
See Meehan, Francis Joseph

Scarlett, Bill
See Swartz, William

**Scarlett, [Sir] James [First Baron
Abinger]** 1769-1844 [NPS, SN]
British jurist
* Briareus of the King's Bench
* Ex Officio Jemmy

Scarlett, Roger [joint pseudonym with
Evelyn Page]
See Blair, Dorothy

Scarlett, Roger [joint pseudonym with
Dorothy Blair]
See Page, Evelyn

Scarlow, Samuel 1888- [HPPN]
Russian-American arsonist
* Sam the Torch

Scarnato, Patrick Henry 1923-1982
American comedian
* Henry, Pat

Scarne, John 20th c. [HPPN]
American author
* Orlando, Pietro
* [The] Professor
* [The] Virtuous Card Shark

Scaronia
See D'Aubigne, Francoise

Scarpa, Salvatore 1918- [ASC]
American musician
* Donson, Don

Scarpelli
See Scarpelli, Furio

Scarpelli, Furio 20th c. [WF]
Screenwriter
* Scarpelli

Scarron, Paul 1610-1660 [HPPN, SN]
French poet, author, playwright
* [The] Creator of Burlesque Poetry in
France
* [The] Father of French Burlesque
* [The] Invalid Laureate

Scarrott, Michael
See Fisher, Arthur Stanley Theodore

Scarry, Patricia [Murphy] [Patsy] 1924-
[CA, SAT]
Canadian-born author
* Roy, Liam

Scarth, Silent
See Scarth, William

Scarth, William 20th c. [HPPN]
Canadian police officer
* Scarth, Silent

Scat Man Crothers
See Crothers, [Benjamin] Sherman
[Louis]

Schaaf, Eliane 1937- [OP]
French opera singer
* Manchet, Eliane

Schaaf, Marilyn Brooke Goffstein 1940-
[FBJ, ICB]
American author and illustrator
* Goffstein, M. B.

Schaber, Nicholas 1858-1936 [SC]
American actor
* Woods, Nick

Schabinger, Arthur A. 1889-1972
American basketball coach
* Schabinger, Schabie

Schabinger, Schabie
See Schabinger, Arthur A.

Schachner, Nat[han] 1895-1955 [ESF,
WGT]
American author
* Corbett, Chan
* Glamis, Walter

Schacht, Al[exander] 1892- [BE, HPPN,
SR]
American baseball player
* [The] Clown Prince of Baseball
* Goodman, Murray

Schacht, Henry 1887?-1964 [BEW]
American actor and educator
* Sharp, Henry

Schacht, Ray McKeown 1929- [CWG]
American country-western performer
* Stuart, Carl

Schachtel, Roger [Bernard] 1949- [CA]
American author
* Forrester, Marian

Schachterle, Nancy [Lange] 1925- [CA]
Canadian-born author
* Laing, Anne C.

Schad, Wilhelm
See Reichert, Herbert W[illiam]

Schadow, Gottfried 1764-1850 [WEC]
German sculptor, author, cartoonist
* Gillray, Paris

Schaefer, Frank 1936- [CA]
American author
* Carrol, Shana [joint pseudonym with Kerry Newcomb]
* Gentry, Peter [joint pseudonym with Kerry Newcomb]
* Savage, Christina [joint pseudonym with Kerry Newcomb]

Schaefer, Germany
See Schaefer, Herman A.

Schaefer, Herman A. 1878-1919 [AS, BE, PB]
American baseball player
* Schaefer, Germany

Schaefer, Herman, Jr. 20th c. [HPPN]
American billiards player
* Schaefer, Young Jake

Schaefer, Herman, Sr. 1855-1909 [HPPN]
American billiards champion
* [The] Wizard

Schaefer, Hildegard 1917- [IAW]
German author
* Gardener, Hilde

Schaefer, Jacob, Sr. 1855-1909 [AS]
American billiards player
* [The] Wizard

Schaefer, Robin
See Malzberg, Barry N[orman]

Schaefer, Vincent J. 1906- [HPPN]
American physicist and educator
* [The] Father of Artificial Rain

Schaefer, William Donald 20th c. [WP 9-14-84]
American politician
* Annoyed, Mayor

Schaefer, Young Jake
See Schaefer, Herman, Jr.

Schaeffer, Claude Frederic Armand 1898-1982 [CA]
French author, archaeologist, curator
* Schaeffer-Forrer, Claude F. A.

Schaeffer, E. Carroll 20th c. [BBH]
American swimmer
* Schaeffer, Midget

Schaeffer, Harry Edward 1924- [BE]
American baseball player
* Schaeffer, Lefty

Schaeffer, Lefty
See Schaeffer, Harry Edward

Schaeffer, Midget
See Schaeffer, E. Carroll

Schaeffer-Forrer, Claude F. A.
See Schaeffer, Claude Frederic Armand

Schafer, Gertrude 1880-1960 [SC]
American actress
* Bondhill, Gertrude

Schafer, Gus
See Stevens, Peter

Schafer, Harry C. 1846-1935 [BE]
American baseball player
* Schafer, Silk Stocking

Schafer, Kermit 1914-1979
American producer and publisher
* Blooper, Mr.

Schafer, Mabel 1910- [HPPN]
American cooking authority
* [The] Caramel Corn Queen
* Sister Mabel

Schafer, Pinny
See Schafer, William

Schafer, Silk Stocking
See Schafer, Harry C.

Schafer, William   [RBE]
Boxing agent
* Schafer, Pinny

Schaff, Philip 1819-? [HPPN]
Swiss-American theologian and educator
* P. S.

Schaffenberger, Kurt 1920- [WECO]
American cartoonist
* Wahl, Lou

Schakel, Pieter
See Balluseck, Daniel J. Von

Schakovskoy, [Princess] Zinaida 1908- [CA]
Russian-born author and poet
* Croise, Jacques

Schaldenbrand, Mary 1922- [CA]
American educator and author
* Mary Aloysius, [Sister]

Schalk, Cracker
See Schalk, Raymond William

Schalk, LeRoy John 1908- [BE]
American baseball player
* Schalk, Roy

Schalk, Raymond William 1892-1970 [AS, DGS, PB]
American baseball player
* Schalk, Cracker

Schalk, Roy
See Schalk, LeRoy John

Schaller, Biff
See Schaller, Walter

Schaller, Walter 1889-1939 [BE]
American baseball player
* Schaller, Biff

Schallick, August 1858-1937 [BE]
German-born baseball player
* Shallix, August
* Shallix, Gus

Schanfield, Lewis Maurice 1867-1941 [BEW, EMT, PMJ]
American actor, producer, director
* Fields, Lew

Schani
See Strauss, Johann, Jr.

Schanker, Elizabeth Holman 1906-1971 [HPPN]
American singer and actress
* Holman, Libby

Schardt, Big Bill
See Schardt, Wilburt

Schardt, Wilburt 1886-1964 [BE]
American baseball player
* Schardt, Big Bill

Scharein, Art[hur Otto] 1905-1969 [BE]
American baseball player
* Scharein, Scoop

Scharein, George Albert 1914- [BE]
American baseball player
* Scharein, Tom

Scharein, Scoop
See Scharein, Art[hur Otto]

Scharein, Tom
See Scharein, George Albert

Scharf, Boo-Boo
See Scharf, Herman

Scharf, Edward T. 1859-1937 [BE]
American baseball player
* Scharf, Nick

Scharf, Herman 1901-1963 [SC]
American actor and stunt performer
* Scharf, Boo-Boo

Scharf, Nick
See Scharf, Edward T.

Scharff, Lester 1895-1962 [SC]
American actor
* Sharpe, Lester

Scharlemann, Dorothy Hoyer 1912- [CA]
American author and playwright
* Sharon, Donna Haye

Schartenmeyer
See Vischer, Friedrich Theodor von

Schary, Dore
See Schary, Isidore

Schary, Isidore 1905?-1980
American screenwriter, playwright, producer
* [The] Boy Wonder of Hollywood
* Schary, Dore

Schary, Jill
See Robinson, Jill

Schattner, Martine 1911- [BEW, HPPN]
American publisher
* Schattner, Meyer

Schattner, Meyer
See Schattner, Martine

Schaub, Marilyn McNamara 1928- [CA]
American translator
* McNamara, [Sister] Marie Aquinas

Schauer, Alexander
See Dimitrihoff, Dimitri Ivanovich

Schauer, Rube
See Dimitrihoff, Dimitri Ivanovich

Schauffler, Henry Albert 1837-1905
[HPPN]
Clergyman and missionary
* [The] Apostle to the Slavs

Schauffler, Margaret Widdemer 20th c.
[WWL]
American author
* Widdemer, Margaret

Schaum, Rounsevelle W. 20th c. [CR]
American television executive and producer
* Schaum, Skip

Schaum, Skip
See Schaum, Rounsevelle W.

Schaumburg, Paul 1884- [WBD]
German author
* Burg, Paul

Schayes, Adolph 1928-
American basketball player
* Schayes, Dolph

Schayes, Dolph
See Schayes, Adolph

Schealtiel, Nochumm J.
See Schochet, J. Immanuel

Schechter, William 1934- [CA]
Austrian-born author
* Williams, Chester

Scheckter, Baby Bear
See Scheckter, Jody

Scheckter, Jody 1950?- [EAR]
South African auto racer
* [The] Fastest Rookie on the Road
* Scheckter, Baby Bear

Schectman, Elias Maxwell 1926- [BEW]
American actor, director, playwright
* Rill, Eli

Schectman, Oscar 20th c. [HPPN]
American basketball player
* Schectman, Ossie

Schectman, Ossie
See Schectman, Oscar

Schedel, Ferencz 1805-1875 [WBD]
Hungarian historian
* Toldy, Ferencz

Scheels, Rabode Hermann 1622-1662
[PA]
Author
* Schelius

Scheepers, Emmerentia 20th c. [OP]
South African opera singer
* Renzi, Emma

Scheer, Deborah A. 1955- [HPPN]
American entertainer
* Cousteau, Desiree

Scheer, Heinie
See Scheer, Henry William

Scheer, Henry William 1900- [EJS]
American baseball player
* Scheer, Heinie

Scheer, K. H.
See Scheer, Karl Herbert

Scheer, Karl Herbert 1928- [SF, WGT]
German author
* Scheer, K. H.
* Turbojew, Alexej

Scheer, Vincent Morris 1905- [BI, BX, EJS]
American boxer
* Callahan, Mushi [or Mushy]

Scheeren, Dutch
See Scheeren, Frederick

Scheeren, Frederick 1891- [BE]
American baseball player
* Scheeren, Dutch
* Scheeren, Fritz

Scheeren, Fritz
See Scheeren, Frederick

Scheff, Friederike
See Yager, Anna

Scheff, Fritzi
See Yager, Anna

Scheffer, Frederick
See King, William

Scheffler, Johannes 1624-1677 [WBD]
German poet and mystic
* Angelus Silesius

Schein, Ruth Robbins 1917- [TBJ]
American author
* Robbins, Ruth

Scheinblum, Milton 1927- [EJ]
American jazz musician
* Sheen, Mickey

Scheinman, Walter Witcover 1924-
[BEW]
American actor, director, educator
* Witcover, Walt

Schekeryk, Melanie Safka 1947?-
[HPPN]
American singer and songwriter
* Melanie

Scheler, Max Ferdinand 1874-1928
[HPPN]
German philosopher
* [The] Great Thinker

Schelius
See Scheels, Rabode Hermann

Schell, Bunny
See Schell, Rolfe F[inch]

Schell, Rolfe F[inch] 1916- [CA]
American author
* Schell, Bunny

Schelle, Gerard Anthony 1917- [BE]
American baseball player
* Schelle, Jim

Schelle, Jim
See Schelle, Gerard Anthony

Schelle, Werner
See Leszynski, Werner Jacques

Schellenburg
See Musaeus, Johann Karl August

Schellendorf, Hans Bronsart von
1830-1913 [HPPN]
German pianist and composer
* Bronsart, Hans von

Scheller, Aleksandr Konstantinovich
1838-1900 [BI]
Russian author
* Mikhailov, A.

Schelling, Ernest Henry 1876-1939
[HPPN]
American pianist, composer, conductor
* Schelling, Uncle Ernest

Schelling, Uncle Ernest
See Schelling, Ernest Henry

Schem, Lida Clara 1875-1923 [DNA]
American author
* Blake, Margaret

Schemanske, Buck
See Schemanske, Fred[erick George]

Schemanske, Fred[erick George]
1903-1960 [BE]
American baseball player
* Schemanske, Buck

Schembechler, Bo
See Schembechler, Glenn Edward

Schembechler, Glenn Edward 1929- [BI, FB]
American football coach
* Schembechler, Bo

[The] Schemer
See Drucci, Vincent

[The] Schemer, an Ally of the Meddler
See Trumbull, John

Schemm, Mildred Walker 1905- [CA]
American author
* Walker, Mildred

Schenck, Anita A[llen] 1909- [CA]
American author
* Allen, Anita

Schenck, Joseph M. 1882-1961 [HPPN]
American film producer
* Uncle Joe

Schenck, Leopold [FFF]
German editor
* Schreier, Captain

Schenck, Lillian Broderick 1895-1946
[HPPN]
American actress
* Broderick, Lillian

Schenck, William 1893-1924 [BX]
American boxer
* Brennan, Bill

Schenk, Frances Victoria 1908- [EMT]
American actress and singer
* Day, Frances

Schepens, Martin 1955- [DC]
British cricketer
* Schepens, Skep

Schepens, Skep
See Schepens, Martin

Scheper, Nancy
See Scheper-Hughes, Nancy

Scheper-Hughes, Nancy 1944- [CA]
American anthropologist and author
* Scheper, Nancy

Schepps, Sam[uel] 20th c. [HPPN]
American gambler
* [The] Beau Brummel of Vagrants
* [The] Missing Witness
* [The] Murder Paymaster
* Rose's Lobbygow

Schere, Monroe 1913- [CA]
American author
* Howard, Jessica
* Summerhill, J. K.
* Winter, Abigail

Scheree
See Sanders, Scheree

Scherer, Edmond 1815-1889 [FFF]
French journalist
* French Politician

Scherer, Jean Marie Maurice 1920-
[BDF, FC, FDG, HPPN]
French director
* Cordier, Gilbert
* [The] Grand Cartesian
* Rohmer, Eric

Scherer, Roy Harold, Jr. 1925-1985
[BDF, FC, IPA]
American actor
* [The] Baron of Beefcake
* Fitzgerald, Roy
* Hudson, Rock

Scherr, Marie 20th c. [SFL, WGT]
American author
* Cher, Marie

Schertzer [or Shertzer], Herman 1909-
[PMJ]
American jazz musician
* Schertzer, Hymie

Schertzer, Hymie
See Schertzer [or Shertzer], Herman

Schesler, Charles 1900-1953 [BE]
German-born baseball player
* Schesler, Dutch

Schesler, Dutch
See Schesler, Charles

Scheucher, Annemarie 1935- [OP]
Austrian costume designer and architect
* Skalicki, Amirei

Scheuerman, Margaret 20th c. [BEW]
American theatre executive
* Sherman, Margaret

Schiano, Anthony 20th c. [BI]
American detective
* Solo, Tony

Schiavon, Beniamino ?-1968 [BI]
American maitre d'hotel
* Mr. Nino

Schiavone, Andrea
See Medolla [or Meldolla], Andrea

Schick, George Baldwin Powell 1903-
[IAW]
American educator and author
* Baldwin, George

Schickel, Julia Whedon 1936- [CA]
American author
* Whedon, Julia

Schickele, Peter 1935- [CA]
American composer and author
* Bach, P. D. Q.

Schicklgrueber, Adolf
See Hitler, Adolf

Schieldge, Ernest 20th c. [BS]
American magician
* Rogers, Don

Schieri, Friedrich Franz 1922- [IWM]
German conductor and composer
* Schieri, Fritz

Schieri, Fritz
See Schieri, Friedrich Franz

Schiff, Else 1878?-1961 [BEW]
German actress and author
* Basserman, Else

Schiff, Sydney 1869?-1944 [LC, TC]
British author and translator
* Hudson, Stephen

Schiffers, Emmanuel 1850-1904 [HPPN]
Russian chess player
* Russia's Chess Teacher

Schiffmann, Meir 1918- [CA]
German-born American author
* Ben Horin, Meir

Schifrin, Boris 1932- [EJ7]
Argentinian-born jazz musician
* Schifrin, Lalo

Schifrin, Lalo
See Schifrin, Boris

Schildkraut, Joseph 1896- [FIR]
Austrian-born actor
* Schildkraut, Pepi

Schildkraut, Pepi
See Schildkraut, Joseph

Schillaci, Anthony
See Schillaci, Peter Paul

Schillaci, Peter Paul 1929- [CA]
American clergyman and author
* Schillaci, Anthony

Schiller, Craig 1951- [CA]
American author
* Schiller, Mayer

Schiller, Ella F. 1874-1961 [HPPN]
American actress
* Fontanbleau, Ella

Schiller, Henry Carl 19th c. [PA]
Author
* Grey, Anthony

Schiller, Johann Christoph Friedrich von
1759-1805 [HPPN, NPS, SN]
German poet and playwright
* [The] First Among German
  Dramatists
* [The] Poet of Liberty
* Ritter, Dr.
* Schmidt, Dr.
* [The] Shakespeare of Germany

Schiller, Mayer
See Schiller, Craig

Schiller, Rose Leiman
See Goldemberg, Rose Leiman

Schilling, August E. 1908-1957 [SC]
American actor
* Schilling, Gus

Schilling, Bertha 1869-1935 [BBD]
Swiss-born opera singer
* Breval, Lucienne

Schilling, George, Sr. 1886-1964 [NOJ]
American jazz musician
* Schilling, Happy

Schilling, Gus
See Schilling, August E.

Schilling, Happy
See Schilling, George, Sr.

Schillings, Elbert Isaiah 1900-1954 [BE]
American baseball player
* Schillings, Red

Schillings, Red
See Schillings, Elbert Isaiah

Schilperoort, Peter 1919- [EJ]
Dutch jazz musician
* Bronx, Pat

Schilsky, Austin 1897- [FC]
British actor
* Trevor, Austin

Schiltberger, Johannes 1380-? [BI]
German traveler
* Hans the Bavarian

Schimmelpenninck, Mary Anne Galton
1778-1856 [HPPN]
British author
* Launcelot, Dom Claude

Schindell, Cy
See Schindell, Seymore

Schindell, Seymore 1907-1948 [SC]
American actor
* Schindell, Cy

Schinderhannes
See Bueckler, Johannes

Schiner, Herbert Arthur 1918-1970 [JF, SC]
American actor
* Harmonica Herb
* Shriner, Herb

Schinocephalus
See Pericles

Schiott, Johannes 1914- [BEW]
American director
* Fearnley, John

Schiotz, Aksel 20th c.
Danish opera singer
* [The] Voice of Denmark

Schipa, Raffaele Attilio Amadeo 1889-1965 [MS]
Italian opera singer
* Schipa, Tito

Schipa, Tito
See Schipa, Raffaele Attilio Amadeo

Schire
See Gardner, E. D.

Schirick, Dutch
See Schirick, Harry Ernest

Schirick, Harry Ernest 1890-1968 [BE]
American baseball player
* Schirick, Dutch

Schirmer, Joe 1916?-1975 [FIR]
Musician
* King of the Banjo

Schirmerhorn, Clint
See Riemer, George

Schirock, Fred Alexander 1925- [CA]
Canadian-born hockey player, coach, author
* Shero, Fred [Alexander]

Schisgal, Oscar 1901- [CA, SAT, WW]
Belgian-born author and speechwriter
* Cole, Jackson
* Hardy, Stuart

Schittenhelm, Gisele Eve 1906?- [F2, FC, WEF]
German actress
* Helm, Brigette

Schjelderup, Gerik 20th c. [ART]
Irish artist and actor
* Gerik

Schlachter, Christopher 20th c. [HPPN]
American football player
* Schlachter, Red

Schlachter, Red
See Schlachter, Christopher

Schlachter, Susan
See Thaler, Susan

Schlamme, Martha
See Haftel, Martha

Schlapbach-Oberhansli, Trudi 1944- [CA]
Swiss author and illustrator
* Oberhansli, Trudi

Schlechter, Carl 1874-1918 [HPPN]
Austrian chess player
* [The] Drawing Master

Schlecker, Max 1930- [IWM]
Swiss publisher and editor
* Schleo

Schlee, Nicholaevna Sanina 1904- [WFA]
Russian-born fashion designer
* Valentina

Schleger, Hans 1898-1976 [BI, GA]
British graphic artist
* Zero

Schlei, Admiral
See Schlei, George Henry

Schlei, George Henry 1878-1958 [BE]
American baseball player
* Schlei, Admiral

Schleier, Gregory 1918-1974 [SC]
American actor
* Dixon, Paul
* [The] Mayor of Kneesville

Schlein, Miriam 1926- [CA, SAT, TCC]
American author
* Stanhope, Lavinia
* Weiss, Miriam

Schlemihl, Peter
See Thoma, Ludwig

Schlemihl, Peter
See Wood, George

Schleo
See Schlecker, Max

Schlesinger, Bruno Walter 1876-1962 [BBD, IPA]
German conductor
* Walter, Bruno

Schlesinger, Leontine 1889- [WEF]
Austrian-born director
* Sagan, Leontine

Schlesinger, Rudy
See Schlesinger, William Cordes

Schlesinger, William Cordes 1942- [BE]
American baseball player
* Schlesinger, Rudy

Schletz, Elke 1940- [FC]
German actress
* Sommer, Elke

Schley, Winfield Scott 1839-1911 [HPPN]
American naval officer
* [The] Mephistopheles of the Ocean

Schliebner, Dutch
See Schliebner, Frederick Paul

Schliebner, Frederick Paul 1894- [BE]
German-born baseball player
* Schliebner, Dutch

Schliemann, Heinrich 1822-1890 [HPPN]
German archaeologist
* [The] Digger of Lost Treasure
* [The] Man Who Resurrected Troy

Schlink, [Mother] Basilea
See Schlink, Klara

Schlink, Klara 1904- [CA]
German author and religious leader
* Basilea, [Mother]
* Schlink, [Mother] Basilea

Schlitzer, Biff
See Schlitzer, Victor Joseph

Schlitzer, Victor Joseph 1884-1948 [BE]
American baseball player
* Schlitzer, Biff

Schlock Rock's Godzilla
See Furnier, Vincent Damon

Schloesser, Hendrik 1943- [OP]
Dutch opera singer
* Van Ree, Jean

Schlosberg, H[ershel] J[oshua]
See May, Henry John

Schloss, Arthur David 1889-1966 [LC, TC]
British translator
* Waley, Arthur

Schloss, William 1914- [FC]
American director
* Castle, William

Schmalz, Herbert Gustave 1856-1935 [DBA]
British painter
* Angelico
* Carmichael, Herbert

Schmees, George Edward 1924- [BE]
American baseball player
* Schmees, Rocky

Schmees, Rocky
See Schmees, George Edward

Schmeisser, William C. [Bill] 1880-1941 [BBH]
American lacrosse coach
* Father Bill

Schmeling, Max[imilian Adolph Otto Siegfried] 1905- [BX, RBE]
German-born boxer
* [The] Black Uhlan

Schmeling, Max
See Klein-Luckow, Max

Schmid, Charles Howard, Jr. 1942- [HPPN]
American murderer
* Rodriguez, Angel

Schmid, Charles Howard, Jr. 1942- [BLB]
American murderer
* Rodriguez, Angel

Schmid, Eduard 1890-1966 [CD, EWL]
German author
* Edschmid, Kasimir

Schmid, Peter 16th c. [BI]
German printer and publisher
* Fabricius

Schmide, John Bernhardt Vander Kleine
20th c. [BEW]
American actor and stage manager
* Barney, Jay

Schmidt, Albert 1902- [WECO]
American cartoonist
* Smith, Al

Schmidt, Anton Franz 1893-1955 [WBD]
German playwright, author, critic
* Dietzenschmidt

Schmidt, Boss
See Schmidt, Charles

Schmidt, Butch
See Schmidt, Charles John

Schmidt, Butcher Boy
See Schmidt, Charles John

Schmidt, Charles 1880-1932 [BE]
American baseball player
* Schmidt, Boss
* Schmidt, Dutch

Schmidt, Charles John 1887-1952 [BE]
American baseball player
* Schmidt, Butch
* Schmidt, Butcher Boy

Schmidt, Christoph 1740-1801 [PA]
Author
* Phiseldeck

Schmidt, Claire Harman 1957- [CA]
British editor
* Harman, Claire

Schmidt, Crazy
See Schmidt, Frederick

Schmidt, Dr.
See Schiller, Johann Christoph
Friedrich von

Schmidt, Dorothea
See Wender, Dorothea

Schmidt, Dutch
See Schmidt, Charles

Schmidt, Eduard 1890-1966 [HPPN]
German author
* Edschmid, Kasimir

Schmidt, Ernest J. 1911-
American basketball player
* Schmidt, One Grand

Schmidt, Frank Elmer 1879-1952 [BE,
PB]
American baseball player
* Smith, Frank Elmer
* Smith, Nig

Schmidt, Frederick ?-1951 [BI]
German radio commentator
* Williams, Fred

Schmidt, Frederick 1866-1940 [BE]
American baseball player
* Schmidt, Crazy

Schmidt, Helmut 1918-
West German chancellor
* [The] Lip
* [Der] Macher [The Doer]

Schmidt, Helmut (cont.)
* Schmidt, Super
* Schmidt the Lip

Schmidt, Herman 20th c. [BE]
American baseball player
* Schmidt, Pete

Schmidt, Ilse ?-1963 [SC]
German actress and dancer
* Grace, Dinah

Schmidt, Jack 1909- [HPPN]
American thief
* Jack S.

Schmidt, James Norman 1912- [CA,
WW]
American author
* Norman, James

Schmidt, Kaspar 1806-1856 [WBD]
German philosopher
* Stirner, Max

Schmidt, Kate 1954-
American javelin thrower
* Kate the Great

Schmidt, Laura M[arie] 1952- [CA]
American poet and editor
* Palmer, B. C.
* Palmer, Laura

Schmidt, Maynard 1909- [HPPN]
American procurer and criminal
* [The] Short Pants Bully

Schmidt, One Grand
See Schmidt, Ernest J.

Schmidt, Otto Ernst 1862-1926 [WBD]
German author and playwright
* Ernst, Otto

Schmidt, Pete
See Schmidt, Herman

Schmidt, Sandra
See Oddo, Sandra [Schmidt]

Schmidt, Super
See Schmidt, Helmut

Schmidt the Lip
See Schmidt, Helmut

Schmidt, Wilhelm 1876-1952 [CD]
German playwright, author, poet
* Schmidtbonn, Wilhelm

Schmidt, Willy 1896- [WGT]
German author
* Gerhold, German

Schmidtbonn, Wilhelm
See Schmidt, Wilhelm

Schmidtke, Rudi
See Schmidtke, Ruediger

Schmidtke, Ruediger 1943- [BX]
German boxer
* Schmidtke, Rudi

Schmied, Rudolf 20th c. [BI]
Austrian mystic
* Rayo

Schmit, Jean-Pierre 1904- [IWM]
Luxembourgian musicologist
* Schmit, Jempy

Schmit, Jempy
See Schmit, Jean-Pierre

Schmitt, Harrison Hagan 1935- [BI,
HPPN]
American geologist and astronaut
* America, Captain
* [The] First Scientist in Space
* Rock, Dr.
* Schmitt, Jack

Schmitt, Jack
See Schmitt, Harrison Hagan

Schmitt, Paul 20th c.
German historian and intelligence officer
* Carell, Paul

Schmittberger, Max ?-1917 [HPPN]
American police officer
* [The] Famous Squealer

Schmitz, Bear Tracks
See Schmitz, John Albert

Schmitz, Ettore 1861-1928 [CD, EWL,
LC]
Italian author
* Svevo, Italo

Schmitz, Frances ?-1913 [HPPN]
American actress and singer
* Leslie, Frances

Schmitz, John Albert 1920- [BE, PB]
American baseball player
* Schmitz, Bear Tracks

Schmitz, P. 1871-? [HPPN]
Swiss author and editor
* Mueller, Dominik

Schmock, Helen H. 1909- [MA]
American author
* Bell, Steve
* Cloutier, Helen H.

Schmucke, Anne
See Strich, Christian

Schmuerz, Adolph
See Vian, Boris

Schnabel, Johann Gottfried 1690?-1750?
[WBD]
German author
* Gisander

Schnabel, Martha 1926- [HPPN]
American police officer
* Mama, Officer

Schnake
See Hauser, Carl

Schnaubelt, Franz Joseph 1914- [CA]
American author
* Joseph, Franz

Schnauffer, Heinz-Wolfgang 1922-1950
German military officer
* [The] Night Ghost of Saint Trond

Schneck, Stephen 1933- [CA]
American entertainer and author
* Bite, Ben
* Fite, Mack
* Kite, Larry
* Knight, James
* Lite, Jams
* Spit, Sam

Schneeweiss, Amalie 1839-1898 [WBD]
Opera singer
* Weiss, Amalie

Schneider, Abram Leopoldovich
1917-1984 [BEW]
Russian-born director
* Schneider, Alan

Schneider, Alan
See Schneider, Abram Leopoldovich

Schneider, Anna 20th c. [CA]
American author
* Sequoia, Anna

Schneider, Betty Vance Humphreys
1927- [AW, WD]
American labor economist and author
* Humphreys, B. V.

Schneider, Buzz
See Schneider, William

Schneider, Elmer Reuben 1919- [EJ]
American jazz musician
* Schneider, Moe

Schneider, Emanuel Sebastian 1853-1933
[BE]
American baseball player
* Snyder, Emanuel Sebastian
* Snyder, Redleg

Schneider, Ethel 1916-1964 [SC]
American actress
* Clark, Ethel

Schneider, Guenther 1890-1956 [BEW,
F1, FC]
American actor
* Arnold, Edward

Schneider, Hannes 1890-1955 [BBH,
HPPN]
Austrian-born skiing instructor
* [The] Developer of the Arlberg
Technique
* [The] Father of Modern Skiing

Schneider, Isidor 1896- [CAA]
Polish-born poet, author, editor
* I. S.

Schneider, Laurie
See Adams, Laurie

Schneider, Leonard Alfred 1925-1966
[CA, JL]
American comedian, actor, author
* Bruce, Lenny

Schneider, Louis 1805-1878 [WBD]
German actor and author
* Both, L. W.

Schneider, Moe
See Schneider, Elmer Reuben

Schneider, Romy
See Albach-Retty, Rosemarie

Schneider, William 1954- [HR]
American hockey player
* Schneider, Buzz

Schneider-Green, Ann 20th c. [OP]
British opera singer
* Green, Anna

Schneidman, Biff
See Schneidman, Herman

Schneidman, Herman 1913- [EJS]
American football player
* Schneidman, Biff

Schnellbacher, Claw
See Schnellbacher, Otto O.

Schnellbacher, Otto O. 1923- [FB]
American football player
* Schnellbacher, Claw

Schneyder, J. F.
See Taylor, [Frank Herbert] Griffin

Schnickelgruber
See Hirzel, Werner

Schnitter, Johannes
See Sneider, Johannes

Schnittkind, Henry Thomas 1888-
[NAA]
Lithuanian-born author
* Thomas, Henry

Schnitzer, Eduard 1840-1892 [WBD]
German traveler and explorer
* Emin Pasha, Mehmed

Schnitzler, Arthur 1862-1931 [CA]
Austrian author and playwright
* Anatol

[The] Schnoz
See Durante, James Francis [Jimmy]

Schnozzle
See Durante, James Francis [Jimmy]

Schnozzola
See Durante, James Francis [Jimmy]

Schochen, Muriel Betty 1920- [BEW]
American director, actress, educator
* Sharon, Muriel

Schochet, J. Immanuel 1935- [IAW]
Swiss-born clergyman and author
* Oryah, Yehudith
* Schealtiel, Nochumm J.

Schock, George
See Loose, Katharine Riegel

Schockeor, Urbain Jacques 1890-1928
[AS, BE]
American baseball player
* Shocker, Urban James

Schoeb, Erika 20th c. [SFL]
Author
* De Witt, Denise
* Levi, Aristotle
* Von Grau, Wernher

Schoeffel, Florence Blackburn [White]
1860-1900 [DNA]
American author
* Gilman, Wenona

Schoeffer, Peter 1425?-1503? [HPPN]
German printer
* [The] Father of Letter Founders
* [The] Father of Type Foundering

Schoen, Martin
See Schongauer, Martin

Schoenberg, Alfred 1868-1949 [BEW,
EMT, F2, HPPN]
German-born entertainer
* Shean, Al
* Shean, Mr.

Schoenberg, Arnold 1874-1951 [HPPN]
Austrian-born American composer
* Apostle of Atonality
* Copernicus of Music
* [The] Father of Twelve Tone Music
* Twelve-Tone Oddity

Schoendienst, Albert Fred 1923- [DGS,
PB, SMG]
American baseball player and manager
* Finn, Huckleberry
* Schoendienst, Red

Schoendienst, Red
See Schoendienst, Albert Fred

Schoenduv, A. L. 1858-? [PA]
Author
* A. L. S.

Schoene, Lotte
See Bodenstein, Charlotte

Schoenemann, Anna Elisabeth 1758-1817
[WBD]
*Friend of German poet, Johann
Wolfgang von Goethe*
* Schoenemann, Lili

Schoenemann, Lili
See Schoenemann, Anna Elisabeth

Schoenenberger, Gualtiero
See Schoenenberger, Walter Louis
Frederic

Schoenenberger, Walter Louis Frederic
1926- [IAW]
Swiss art historian and author
* Schoenenberger, Gualtiero

Schoener, [Rev.] George 20th c.
[HPPN]
American clergyman
* [El] Padre de las Rosas

Schoenfeld, William C. 1893- [ASC]
American composer and arranger
* Blake, Lowell
* Conrad, Hugh

Schoenfield, Eugene 1935- [NAD]
American physician
* Hippocrates, Dr.

Schoenhaus, Isadore 20th c. [HPPN]
American criminal and taxi driver
* Schoenhaus, Itch

Schoenhaus, Itch
See Schoenhaus, Isadore

Schoening, Alwina 1848-1925   [BBD]
American opera singer
* Valleria, Alwina

Schoepflin, Harl Vincent 1893-1968
[SF]
American author
* Vincent, Harl

Schofield, Ducky
See Schofield, John Richard

Schofield, John Richard 1935-   [BE]
American baseball player
* Schofield, Ducky

Schofield, Jonathan
See Streib, Dan[iel Thomas]

Schofield, Paul
See Tubb, Edwin Charles

Schofield, Sylvia Anne 1922-   [AW, CA, WD]
British author
* Matheson, Sylvia A.
* Mundy, Max

Scholander, Fredrik Wilhelm   [FFF]
Author
* Acharius

[The] Scholar
See Alfonso X [or Alphonso]

[The] Scholar
See Mejia Victores, Oscar Humberto

[The] Scholar
See Saxo, Grammaticus

[A] Scholar
See Wesley, Samuel

[The] Scholar Gypsy
See Wade, George Alfred

[The] Scholar Murderer
See Aram, Eugene

[The] Scholar of the Georgia Bar
See Hill, Walter Barnard

Scholar-like Shepherd
See Greene, Robert

Scholarios, Georgios 15th c.   [WBD]
Greek scholar and prelate
* Gennadius II

[The] Scholastic
See Epiphanius

[The] Scholastic Divine
See Anselm of Laon

[The] Scholastic Doctor
See Anselm of Laon

Scholasticus
See Evagrius

Scholasticus
See Leontius of Byzantium

Scholasticus
See Socrates

Scholasticus, Doctor
See Anselm of Laon

Scholefield, Edmund O.
See Butterworth, William Edmund, III

Scholefield, Lillia ?-1954   [BEW]
Playwright
* Field, Lila

[The] Scholiast
See Howe, Mark Antony De Wolfe

Scholl, Jerry
See Schutz, Joseph Willard

Scholtz, LeRoy 1928?-1986   [TI 1-6-86]
American entertainer
* Claus, Santa C.

Scholz, Winfried 20th c.   [SFP]
Author
* Sholes, W. W.

Scholze, Johann Sigismund 1705-1750
[BBD]
German composer
* Sperontes

Schomaker, Mary Zimmeth 1928-   [CA]
American author
* Zimmeth, Mary

Schomburg, Alex 1905-   [ESF]
American illustrator
* King of the Airbrush

Schonestein, David ?-1879   [PA]
Author
* Steune, Georges

Schonfield, Hugh J[oseph] 1901-   [CA, WD]
British historian and author
* Fielding, Hubert
* Hegesippus

Schongauer, Martin 1445?-1491   [WBD]
German engraver and painter
* Hipsch [or Huebsch] Martin
* Schoen, Martin

School Boy Baker
See Baker, Jimmy

School Master Camden
See Camden, William

[The] School Mistress
See Lloyd, Sarah

Schoolboy Cleve
See White, Cleve

Schoolcraft, Henry R. 1793-1864   [PA]
Author
* Colcroft, Henry Roeve

Schooler, Pop
See Schooler, Virgil E.

Schooler, Virgil E. 1904-1974   [HPPN]
American educator and coach
* Schooler, Pop

[The] Schoolgirl Songstress
See Kirkwood, Pat

[A] Schoolmaster
See Alcott, William Alexander

[A] Schoolmaster
See Bitzius, Albert

[The] Schoolmaster at Home
See Dugall, George

[The] Schoolmaster Comedian
See Hay, Will

Schoolmaster, John
See Doudna, Edgar G.

[The] Schoolmaster of Politics
See Wilson, [Thomas] Woodrow

[The] Schoolmaster of the Middle Ages
See Isidore of Seville

[The] Schoolmaster of the Republic
See Webster, Noah

[The] Schoolmaster President
See Sarmiento, Domingo Faustino

[The] Schoolmaster to America
See Webster, Noah

Schoolmiss Alfred
See Tennyson, Alfred [First Baron Tennyson]

[The] Schoolmistress to France
See Alcuin [or Albinus]

Schoonmaker, Ann 1928-   [CA]
American author
* Boyd, Ann S.

Schoonover, Gloria Jean 1928-   [FC, PMJ, SW]
American singer and actress
* Jean, Gloria

Schop, Le Baron
See Texier, Edward

Schopenhauer, Arthur 1788-1860   [SN]
German philosopher
* [The] Philosopher of Disenchantment

Schopenhauer, Felix Beglio 1925-1943
[HPPN]
Mexican-born bullfighter
* Guzman, Felix

Schopenhauer, Theophratus
See Krackowizer, E. W.

Schopfer, Jean 1868-1931   [TC]
Swiss-born author, playwright, historian
* Anet, Claude

Schopp, Martin Robert 1918-   [CWG]
American country-western performer
* Roberts, Marty

Schoppe, Howard Freeman 1902-1967
[HPPN]
American actor
* Freeman, Howard

Schorb, Edwin Marsh 1940-   [CA]
American author and poet
* Marsh, Edwin
* McGrath, Doyle

Schorr, Daniel 1916-   [HPPN]
American television newscaster
* [The] C. B. S. Bellwether
* C. B. S.'s All-Around Expert

Schosberg, Paul A. 1938- [CA]
American author
* Allyn, Paul

Schotte, John LeRoy 1912?- [EMT, PMJ]
American dancer and actor
* LeRoy, Hal

Schotte, Paulus
See Elbogen, Paul

Schrader, Alma 1918-1935 [HPPN]
American dancer
* Lee, Arlene

Schrader, August
See Simmel, August

Schrader, F. F. [FFF]
Journalist
* Keen, Royal

Schrage, Pops
See Schrage, Tom

Schrage, Tom 1947?-
American basketball player
* Schrage, Pops

Schragmueller, Elsbeth 20th c. [EE]
German intelligence agent
* [The] Beautiful Blonde of Antwerp
* [The] Blonde of Antwerp
* [The] Terrible Doctor Elsbeth
* Tiger Eyes

Schrall, Leo 20th c. [BBH]
American baseball coach
* Schrall, Scrapiron

Schrall, Scrapiron
See Schrall, Leo

Schramm, Tex
See Schramm, Texas E.

Schramm, Texas E. 20th c.
American football executive
* Schramm, Tex

Schreck, Everett M. 1897- [CAP]
American actor and author
* Morrill, Richard

Schreck, Max
See Abel, Alfred

Schreck, Ossee
See Schreckengost, Ossee Freeman

Schreckengost, Ossee Freeman
1875-1914 [BE]
American baseball player
* Schreck, Ossee

Schreiber, Barney
See Schreiber, David Henry

Schreiber, David Henry 1882-? [BE]
American baseball player
* Schreiber, Barney

Schreiber, Hermann O. L. 1920- [CA, WD]
Austrian historian and author
* Bassermann, Lujo
* Buehnau, Ludwig

Schreiber, Le Anne 1945?-
American sports editor
* Schreiber, Swivel Hips

Schreiber, Paul Frederick 1902- [BE]
American baseball player
* Schreiber, Von

Schreiber, Swivel Hips
See Schreiber, Le Anne

Schreiber, Von
See Schreiber, Paul Frederick

Schreier, Captain
See Schenck, Leopold

Schreiner, Olive [Emily Albertina]
1855-1920 [BI, LC]
South African author
* Iron, Ralph

Schreuer, Carl 1921- [BEW]
American producer and stage manager
* Sawyer, Carl

Schrieber, Helmut 1903?-1963 [BEW]
Magician
* Kalanag

Schrift, Shirley 1922- [BDF, BEW, FC]
American actress
* Winters, Shelley

Schrijver, Johannes van 16th c. [BI]
Belgian printer
* Grapheus, Johannes

Schrikker, Adriaan S. 20th c. [HPPN]
Luxembourg financial analyst
* [The] Chartist Pope

Schriner, David 1911- [CEI, FHE, HK]
Canadian-born hockey player
* Schriner, Sweeney

Schriner, Sweeney
See Schriner, David

Schriver, Pop
See Schriver, William F.

Schriver, William F. 1866-1932 [BE, PB]
American baseball player
* Schriver, Pop

Schroder, Helen 1904-1966 [CED, EMT, PMJ]
American actress and singer
* [The] Boop Boop A Doop Girl
* Kane, Helen

Schroeder, Frederick Rudolph 1921- [BBH, OET]
American tennis player
* Schroeder, Lucky
* Schroeder, Ted

Schroeder, Henry 1774-1853 [NPS]
British topographer and engraver
* Butterworth, William

Schroeder, Henry 1855-1928 [HPPN]
German-American agriculturist
* Minnesota's Potato King

Schroeder, Irene 1909-1931 [LFW]
American bandit and murderer
* Iron Irene

Schroeder, J. W. 1871-1932 [SC]
American actor
* Osborne, Jefferson

Schroeder, John Henry 1784-1883 [FFF]
German banker and financier
* [The] German Peabody

Schroeder, Lucky
See Schroeder, Frederick Rudolph

Schroeder, Pat 20th c.
American wrestler
* Kai, Lelani

Schroeder, Richard C. 20th c. [CA]
Columnist
* Alfred, Richard [joint pseudonym with Nathan Alfred Haverstock]

Schroeder, Rudolf 1885-?
American military aviator
* Schroeder, Shorty

Schroeder, Shorty
See Schroeder, Rudolf

Schroeder, Sophie [Buerger] 1781-1868 [NPS]
German actress
* [The] German Siddons

Schroeder, Ted
See Schroeder, Frederick Rudolph

Schroeder, Zelma 1907- [EMT]
American actress, singer, dancer
* O'Neal, Zelma

Schroedter, Adolf 1805-1875 [WEC]
German cartoonist and painter
* King of the Arabesque

Schroepfer, Arthur 1908-1962 [THR]
British actor and playwright
* Macrae, Arthur

Schroetter, Hilda Noel 1917- [CA]
American editor and writer
* Noel, Hilda Bloxton, Jr.

Schroll, Al[bert Bringhurst] 1933- [BE]
American baseball player
* Schroll, Bull

Schroll, Bull
See Schroll, Al[bert Bringhurst]

Schrum, Jocelyn 1933-
American actress
* Nolan, Kathleen

Schryver, Pieter 1661-1743 [PA]
Author
* Scriverius

Schubart, Fannie Kilbourne 20th c. [NAA]
American author
* Kilbourne, Fannie

Schubbert
See Strubberg, Friedrich Armand

Schubert, Emile H.
See Smith, Leonard B.

Schubiger, Anselm
See Schubiger, Josef Allis

Schubiger, Josef Allis 1815-1888   [BBD]
Swiss author
* Schubiger, Anselm

Schubin, Ossip
See Kirschner, Aloysia

Schuble, Heinie
See Schuble, Henry George

Schuble, Henry George 1906-   [BE]
American baseball player
* Schuble, Heinie

Schuchman, Joan 1934-   [CA]
American author
* Brenner, Isabel
* Jones, Miriam
* Jones, Zelda

Schuck, F. H. P.
See Schuck, Frederick Hugh Paul

Schuck, Frederick Hugh Paul 1916-
[SFL]
American author
* Schuck, F. H. P.

Schueler, Dorli-Maria 1940-   [OP]
German opera singer
* Chryst, Dorothea

Schuerholz, Fred Peter 1889-1975   [BE]
American baseball player
* Sherry, Fred Peter

Schuette, Conrad Herman Louis 1843-?
[ALY]
German-born clergyman and author
* T. O. F.

Schuetz, Dennis 20th c.   [CA]
Author
* Aldyne, Nathan [joint pseudonym
  with Michael McDowell]

Schuetz, Francoise-Jeanne 1861-1936
[BBD]
Russian opera singer
* Litvinne, Felia

Schuetze, Gladys Henrietta [Raphael]
1881-1946   [TC]
British author
* Leslie, Henrietta
* Mendl, Gladys

Schuh, Harry 20th c.
American football player
* Schuh, Horse

Schuh, Horse
See Schuh, Harry

Schulberg, B. P.
See Schulberg, Benjamin Percival

Schulberg, Benjamin Percival 1892-1957
[BEW]
American producer
* Schulberg, B. P.

Schulberg, Geraldine Brooks 1925-1977
[HPPN]
American actress
* Brooks, Geraldine

Schulefand, Richard 1929?-   [FC, ITA,
TR]
American actor
* Shawn, Dick
* Shawn, Richy

**Schulemberg, Erangard Melrose de
[Duchess of Kendal]** ?-1743   [DNNF,
DNNS, FFF]
Mistress of King George I of England
* [The] Maypole

Schulkers, Robert Franc 1890-1972   [BI]
American author and critic
* Hawkins, Sekatary

Schulman, L. M.
See Schulman, Lester Martin

Schulman, Lester Martin 1934-   [SFL]
American author and editor
* Schulman, L. M.

Schulmerich, Edward Wesley 1902-
[HPPN]
American football and baseball player
* Schulmerich, Ironhorse

Schulmerich, Ironhorse
See Schulmerich, Edward Wesley

Schult, Arthur William 1928-   [BE]
American baseball player
* Schult, Dutch

Schult, Dutch
See Schult, Arthur William

Schulte, Elaine L[ouise] 1934-   [CA]
American author
* Young, Elaine L.

Schulte, Frank 1882-1949   [AS, BE, PB]
American baseball player
* Schulte, Wildfire

Schulte, Fred William 1904-   [BE, PB]
American baseball player
* Schulte, Fritz

Schulte, Fritz
See Schulte, Fred William

Schulte, Ham
See Schultehenrich, Herman Joseph

Schulte, Herman Joseph
See Schultehenrich, Herman Joseph

Schulte, Leonard William [Len]
See Schultehenrich, Leonard William

Schulte, Wildfire
See Schulte, Frank

Schultehenrich, Herman Joseph 1912-
[BE]
American baseball player
* Schulte, Ham
* Schulte, Herman Joseph

Schultehenrich, Leonard William 1916-
[BE]
American baseball player
* Schulte, Leonard William [Len]

Schultheiss [or Schulz], Michael
1571-1621   [WBD]
German composer and author
* Praetorius, Michael

Schultz, Adolph George 1882?-1951   [BI]
American football player
* Schultz, Germany

Schultz, Barney
See Schultz, George Warren

Schultz, Bill
See Schultz, Robert Duffy [Bob]

Schultz, Buddy
See Schultz, Charles Budd

Schultz, Charles Budd 1950-   [SMG]
American baseball player
* Schultz, Buddy

Schultz, David [Dave] 1949-   [FHE,
SMG]
Canadian-born hockey player
* [The] Hammer

Schultz, David 20th c.
American wrestler
* Dr. D.

Schultz, Dode
See Schultz, Joseph Charles, Jr.

Schultz, Dutch
See Flegenheimer, Arthur

Schultz, Frederick Walter 1840-1917
[DNA]
American author
* Walter, Frederick

Schultz, George Warren 1926-   [BE, PB,
SMG]
American baseball player and coach
* Schultz, Barney

Schultz, Germany
See Schultz, Adolph George

Schultz, Germany
See Schultz, Joseph Charles, Sr.

Schultz, Harry
See Heinberg, Alexander

Schultz, Hart Merriam 1882-1970   [BI]
American Indian artist
* Lone Wolf

Schultz, Hoe
See Schultz, Joseph Charles, Jr.

Schultz, Howard Henry 1922-   [BE]
American baseball player
* Schultz, Steeple
* Schultz, Stretch

Schultz, James Willard 1859-1947
[YAB]
American author
* Anderson, W. B.
* Apikuni [Far-Off White Robe]

Schultz, Johann 1595-1645 [PA]
Author
* Scultetus

Schultz, Joseph Charles, Jr. 1918- [BE]
American baseball player and manager
* Schultz, Dode
* Schultz, Hoe

Schultz, Joseph Charles, Sr. 1893-1941
[BE]
American baseball player
* Schultz, Germany

Schultz, Louise 1921- [HPPN]
American actress
* [The] Serial Queen
* Stirling, Linda

Schultz, Pearle Henriksen 1918- [CA, SAT]
American author
* Pershing, Marie

Schultz, Robert Duffy [Bob] 1923- [BE]
American baseball player
* Schultz, Bill

Schultz, Steeple
See Schultz, Howard Henry

Schultz, Stretch
See Schultz, Howard Henry

Schultze, Carl Edward 1866-1939
[WECO]
American cartoonist
* Bunny

Schultze, Paul
See Langer, Alfons

Schulz, Adolph G. 1883-1951 [AS, FB]
American football player
* Schulz, Germany

Schulz, Albert C. 1889-1931 [BE]
American baseball player
* Schulz, Lefty

Schulz, Germany
See Schulz, Adolph G.

Schulz [or Schulze], Hieronymus
1560-1629 [BBD]
German composer
* Praetorius, Hieronymus

Schulz, Lefty
See Schulz, Albert C.

Schulz, Mrs. Warren [FFF]
Entertainer
* Pierce, Emma

Schulz Ewerth, Eckard 1924-1961 [SC]
Samoan-born actor and singer
* Tuala, Mario

Schulze, Alfred Otto Wolfgang
1913-1951 [CAR]
German painter
* Wols

Schulze-Boysen, Harro ?-1942 [BI]
German Communist spy
* Coro

Schulze-Smidt, Bernhardine 19th c.
[HPPN]
German author
* Oswald, E.

Schumacher, Harold Henry 1910- [BE, PB]
American baseball player
* Prince Hal

Schuman, Karen 20th c.
American editor
* Blossom

Schumann, Carl J. 1884-1946 [BE]
American baseball player
* Schumann, Hack

Schumann, Cecilia
See Schumann, Clara Josephine Wieck

Schumann, Chiara
See Schumann, Clara Josephine Wieck

Schumann, Clara Josephine Wieck
1819-1896 [SN]
*German pianist and wife of composer,
Robert Schumann*
* Cecilia
* Chiara
* Schumann, Cecilia
* Schumann, Chiara
* Schumann, Zilia
* Zilia

Schumann, Hack
See Schumann, Carl J.

Schumann, Maurice 1911- [IAW]
French author
* Sidobre, Andre

Schumann, Zilia
See Schumann, Clara Josephine Wieck

Schumann-Heink, Ernestine
See Rossler, Ernestine

Schupbach, O. T. 20th c. [EF]
American football player
* Mooney, Tex

Schura
See Kollontay, Alexandra

Schurgot, Helen 20th c. [BEW]
American actress and singer
* Scott, Helena

Schurman, Anna Maria von 1607-1678
[SN]
German scholar
* [The] Torch of Wisdom

Schuster, Arnold 1926?-1952 [HPPN]
*American police informer and murder
victim*
* [The] Good Citizen

Schuster, Broadway
See Schuster, William Charles

Schuster, Sabu
See Schuster, William Charles

Schuster, William Charles 1914- [BE, BN]
American baseball player
* Schuster, Broadway
* Schuster, Sabu

Schusterman, Ben 1906- [BEW]
American business executive
* Sommers, Ben

Schutte, Ethel 1896- [THR]
American actress and singer
* Shutta, Ethel

Schutz
See Price, Charles

Schutz, Emma
See Harrison, Louise

Schutz, Heinrich 1585-1672 [FFF]
German composer
* [The] Father of German Music
* Sagittarius

Schutz, Joseph Willard 1912- [ESF]
American author and diplomat
* Scholl, Jerry

Schutze, Gladys Henrietta 1881-?
[HPPN]
British author
* Leslie, Henrietta
* Mendl, Gladys

Schuyler, Keith C. 1919- [IAW]
American author
* Bradley, Brian K.

Schuyler, Philip John 1733-1804
[HPPN]
American army officer
* [The] Great Eye

Schuyler, Sonny 1913- [PMJ]
American singer
* Skylar, Sunny

Schwab, Charles M. [Charley] 1862-1939
[HPPN]
American industrialist
* [The] Steel Titan
* [The] Steel Tycoon
* [The] Tycoon You Love to Hate

Schwab, Dutch
See Schwab, Frank J.

Schwab, Frank J. 1895-1965 [AS, FB]
American football player
* Schwab, Dutch

Schwabacher, Henri Simon 1875-1937
[HPPN]
French author and playwright
* Duvernois, Henri

Schwabe, Cecil 1897- [FC]
British actor
* Parker, Cecil

Schwabe, Leo ?-1889 [FFF]
Philanthropist
* [The] Soldiers' Friend

Schwabe, William
See Cassidy, William L[awrence
Robert]

Schwalberg, Carol[yn Ernestine Stein]
1930- [CA]
American author
* Bolling, Hal
* Jenkins, Phyllis
* La Fontaine, Blanche
* Levy, Lorelei
* Shorter, Carl
* Stein, Charles
* Ullman, Barbara

Schwamb, Blackie
See Schwamb, Ralph Richard

Schwamb, Ralph Richard 1926- [BE]
American baseball player
* Schwamb, Blackie

Schwamm, George S. 1903-1966 [SC]
American stunt performer
* Schwamm, Tony

Schwamm, Tony
See Schwamm, George S.

Schwanbeck, Karl Adam 1845-1895
[HPPN]
American soldier and diplomat
* Adams, Charles

Schwandt, Wilbur 1914- [ASC]
American musician
* Swan, Don

Schwann, Duncan
See Swann, Duncan

Schwartz, Anne Powers 1913- [CA, SAT]
American author
* Powers, Anne

Schwartz, Bernard 1925- [BDF, FC, HT]
American actor
* Curtis, Tony

Schwartz, Betty 1927- [CA]
American author
* Black, Betty

Schwartz, Blab
See Schwartz, William Charles [Bill]

Schwartz, Charles Henry 1895-1925
[BLB]
American murderer and swindler
* Warren, Harold

Schwartz, Charles Henry
See Schwartzhof, Leon Henry

Schwartz, Cheri 20th c. [HPPN]
American promoter of pork sales
* [The] 1980 Kansas Pork Queen
* Piggy, Miss

Schwartz, Corporal Izzy
See Schwartz, Izzy

Schwartz, Don 1937- [EJ7]
American jazz musician
* Randi, Don

Schwartz, Frances 20th c. [CAP, WD]
Author
* Sylvin, Francis [joint pseudonym with Sylvia S(ybil) Seaman]

Schwartz, Izzy 1902- [HPPN]
American boxer
* Schwartz, Corporal Izzy

Schwartz, Jacob Lawrence 1912- [BEW]
American composer, lyricist, producer
* Lawrence, Jack

Schwartz, Jeremiah 1905- [HPPN]
American actor and comedian
* Devine, Andy

Schwartz, Jerome Lawrence 1915- [CA]
American playwright, director, producer
* Lawrence, Jerome

Schwartz, Jozua Marius Willem Van Der Poorten 1858-1915 [LC, TC, WW]
Dutch author
* Maartens, Maarten

Schwartz, Marchmont 1909- [EJS, FB]
American football player
* Schwartz, Marchy

Schwartz, Marchy
See Schwartz, Marchmont

Schwartz, Maurice 1890-1960 [HPPN]
Actor
* [The] Barrymore of the Yiddish Theatre
* [The] Leading Figure of the Yiddish Theater

Schwartz, Muriel A.
See Eliot, Thomas Stearns

Schwartz, Oscar 1889-1967 [CED, EMT]
American actor and singer
* Shaw, Oscar

Schwartz, Paula 1925- [CA]
American author and playwright
* Mansfield, Elizabeth
* Mansfield, Libby

Schwartz, Pop
See Schwartz, William August

Schwartz, Richard 1928- [EJ]
American jazz musician
* Sutton, Dick

Schwartz, Richard Henry 1888-1970
[HPPN]
American theatrical executive
* Henry, Dick

Schwartz, Solomon 1874?-1924 [SC]
American actor
* Odell, Shorty

Schwartz, William August 1864-1940
[BE]
American baseball player
* Schwartz, Pop

Schwartz, William Charles [Bill]
1884-1961 [BE]
American baseball player
* Schwartz, Blab

Schwartzdorf, Jacob 1909- [BEW]
American musical director, composer, conductor
* Blackton, Jay

Schwartze, John
See Packer, Alfred

Schwartzhof, Leon Henry 1887-1925
[HPPN]
Alsatian-American chemist and murderer
* [The] Doctor
* Schwartz, Charles Henry
* Stein, Mr.
* Warren, Harold

Schwartzkopf, Eugene 1892-1940 [SC]
American actor and bandleader
* Morgan, Gene

Schwartzmann, Leo Isaakovich
1868-1938 [CD]
Russian philosopher and critic
* Shestov, Leo

Schwarz, Agnes Sophie Becker 19th c.
[HPPN]
German author
* Becker, Sophie

Schwarz, Bertha 1855-1947 [BBD]
German opera singer
* Bianchi, Bianca

Schwarz, Jack
See Schwarz, Jacob

Schwarz, Jacob 1924- [CA]
Dutch author
* Schwarz, Jack

Schwarz, Vera Aleksandrovna
1895?-1966 [BI]
Russian literary critic
* Alexandrova, Vera

Schwarzenberg, Elisabeth
See Czernohorsky, Elisabeth

Schwarzendorf, Johann Paul Agidius
1741-1816 [HPPN, WBD]
French composer
* Martini il Tedesco
* Martini, Jean Paul Egide
* [Il] Tedesco [The German]

Schwarzeneggar, Arnold 1947-
Austrian bodybuilder
* [The] Austrian Oak

Schwarzert, Philipp 1497-1560 [DEP, HN, HPPN, WBD]
German religious reformer
* [The] German Proteus
* Melanchthon, Philip
* Melanthon
* Praeceptor Germaniae
* [The] Preceptor of Germany
* [The] Teacher of Germany

Schwarzkopf, Hans 1910- [BBD, OP]
American opera director and linguist
* White, John S.

Schwarzrock, Lester Henry 1912- [BE]
American baseball player
* Rock, Lester Henry

Schwegler, Paul 1911- [FB]
American football player
* Schwegler, Schweg

Schwegler, Schweg
See Schwegler, Paul

Schweickart, Russell L. 1935-
American astronaut
* Schweickart, Rusty

Schweickart, Rusty
See Schweickart, Russell L.

Schweidler, Abraham
See Meinhold, Johann Wilhelm

[Der] Schweigsame
See Moltke, Hellmuth Karl Bernhard
von

Schweiserthal, Helen 1888-1959 [HPPN]
American actress
* Kilduff, Helen

Schweitzer, Al[bert Casper] 1882-1969
[BE]
American baseball player
* Schweitzer, Cheese

Schweitzer, [Dr.] Albert 1875-1965
[HPPN]
French physician and scholar
* [The] Jungle Doctor
* [The] Man of Mercy

Schweitzer, Byrd Baylor
See Baylor, Byrd

Schweitzer, Cheese
See Schweitzer, Al[bert Casper]

Schweitzer, Johann-Friedrich 17th c.
[NAD]
Swiss scholar
* Helvetius

Schweizer, Marc 1931- [IAW]
French author
* Generoso, Marc-Antoine
* Geneve, Pierre
* Larista, Pepe
* Laurac, Serge

Schweizer, Richard Gene 1930- [BEW]
American actor, singer, dancer
* France, Richard

Schwend, Friedrich 1907?-
German Nazi police official
* Wendig, Dr.

Schwerin, Kurt Christoph von 1684-1757
[DEP, DNNF, DNNS]
Prussian army officer
* [The] Little Marlborough

Schwichtenberg, Wilbur 1912- [EJ, PMJ,
WWJ]
American jazz musician
* Bradley, Will

Schwitters, Cletus Lee 20th c.
Actor
* Keith, Byron

Sciacca, Anthony 1921- [EJ, PMJ]
American jazz musician
* Scott, Tony

[The] Scian Muse
See Simonides

Sciapiro, Michel 1891-1962 [ASC]
Russian-born musician
* Fielding, Michael

Scicolone, Sofia Villani 1934- [BDF,
BP, HPPN, SW, WEF]
Italian actress
* Lazarro, Sofia
* Loren, Sophia
* Stecchetto [The Stick]

Science Fiction, Mr.
See Ackerman, Forrest J[ames]

[The] Scientific Gadfly
See Babbage, Charles

[The] Scientific Statesman
See Burke, Edmund

[The] Scientist
See Goethe, Johann Wolfgang von

[The] Scintillating Sicilian
See Trippi, Charles L. [Charlie]

Scioppius, Gaspar 1576-1649 [NPS, PA,
SN]
German scholar
* [The] Attila of Authors
* [The] Grammatical Cynic
* Grammaticus, Caius

Scio's Blind Old Bard
See Homer

Scipio
See Tracy, Uriah

Scipio
See Watson, [John Hugh] Adam

Scipio
See Watson, John Hugh Adam

**Scipio Aemilianus Africanus
Numantinus, Publius Cornelius**
2nd c. BC [WBD]
Roman general
* [The] Younger

Scipio Africanus, Publius Cornelius
3rd c. BC [WBD]
Roman general
* [The] Elder

Scipio, Lucius Cornelius 3rd c. BC
[WBD]
Roman politician
* Barbatus

Scipion
See D'Arnal, Etienne

Scipione
See Bonichi, Gino

[The] Scissor King
See Mantooth, Lawrence

Scissor Sam Long
See Long, Samuel

[The] Scissors King
See Stecher, Joe

Sclanders, Doorn
See Fearn, John Russell

Sclater, Philip Lutley 1829-? [IP]
British naturalist and journalist
* [A] Naturalist

Sclater, Ruth Leigh 1895- [NAA]
American author
* Leigh, Ruth

Sclater, William ?-1626 [IP]
British clergyman and author
* [A] Presbyter of the Church of
England

[A] Sclavonian Nobleman in London
See Hill, [Sir] John

Scoffic, Lou[is] 1913- [BE]
American baseball player
* Scoffic, Weaser

Scoffic, Weaser
See Scoffic, Lou[is]

Scofield, David 1922- [HPPN]
British actor
* Scofield, Paul

Scofield, Jonathan
See Rothweiler, Paul R[oger]

Scofield, Jonathan
See Toombs, John

Scofield, Norma Margaret Cartwright
1924- [CA]
Canadian-born author and playwright
* Cartwright, N.

Scofield, [David] Paul 1922- [HPPN]
British actor
* [The] Introverted Englishman

Scofield, Paul
See Scofield, David

Scoggins, Jesse Leonard 1891-1923 [BE]
American baseball player
* Scoggins, Jim
* Scoggins, Lefty

Scoggins, Jim
See Scoggins, Jesse Leonard

Scoggins, Lefty
See Scoggins, Jesse Leonard

Scoglio, Giovanna 1934-1972 [FC]
Italian actress
* Scala, Gia

Scognamiglio, Vincenzio 1922?- [BEW,
TR]
Italian-born actor
* Gardenia, Vincent

Scolari, Paolo ?-1191 [WBD]
Pope
* Clement III

Scolasticus
See John II

Scolasticus, Doctor
See Alfred [or Alured]

Scolasticus, Doctor
See Buridan, Jean

Scolasticus, Doctor
See Castro Novo, Hugh de

Scolasticus, Doctor
See Odon, Gerard

Scollan, E. A.
See O'Grady, Elizabeth Anne

Scollin, James Arthur, Jr. 1951-
American disc jockey
* Scols

Scolnick, Sylvan 20th c. [BI]
American swindler and embezzler
* Big Cherry

Scols
See Scollin, James Arthur, Jr.

Scoop, Mr.
See Oliver, Al[bert, Jr.]

[The] Scooter
See Rizzuto, Phil[lip Francis]

Scopes, John Thomas 1900-1970
[HPPN]
American educator
* [The] Monkey Trial Defendant

Scopoli-Biasi, Isabella 1810-? [IP]
Italian author
* Mario S.

Scopulorum, Junipero
See Aschwanden, Peter

Scorchvillein
See Henry de Loundres

Scoresby, William 1760-1829 [IP]
British navigator and author
* [A] Voyager

[The] Scorn of the Court
See Oates, Titus

[The] Scorpion
See Lockhart, John Gibson

Scortia, Thomas N[icholas] 1926- [CA]
American author
* Kurz, Artur R.
* McDow, Gerald
* Nichols, Scott

Scortichini, Guido 20th c. [WF]
Italian actor
* Burke, Samson

[A] Scot
See Anderson, James

[The] Scot
See Thomson, Robert Brown [Bobby]

Scot, A. F.
See Japp, Alexander Hay

Scot, Alexander 1525?-1584? [DNNS, RH, SN]
Scottish poet
* [The] Anacreon of Ancient Scottish Poetry
* [The] Scottish Anacreon

Scot, Chesman
See Bulmer, [Henry] Kenneth

Scot, Quod Ar.
See Ramsay, Allan

Scot, Thomas 18th c. [HPPN]
British author
* Cotton, [Sir] Robert

[A] Scotch Banker
See Charles, George Drummond

[A] Scotch Episcopalian
See Robertson, H.

[The] Scotch Hobbema
See Nasmyth, Patrick [or Peter?]

[The] Scotch Justinian
See David I

[A] Scotch Minister's Daughter
See Whitehead, Mrs. S. R.

[A] Scotch Physician
See Adams, Francis

[A] Scotch Preacher
See Wood, [Rev.] James

[The] Scotch Sappho
See Cockburn, Catherine

Scotch What d'ye Call
See Baillie, Robert

[The] Scotch Wop
See Corrara, Joseph

Scotchburn, Vernon 1897-1957 [THR]
British actor and playwright
* Sylvaine, Vernon

[The] Scotian Petrarch
See Drummond, William

Scotland, James 1917- [CA]
Scottish author and playwright
* Emerson, Ronald
* Little, Kenneth

Scotland, Jay
See Jakes, John W[illiam]

Scotland's First World Champion
See Lynch, Benny

Scoto-Britannicus
See Anderson, James

[A] Scots Gentleman
See Carstairs, William

[The] Scotsman
See Sutherland, John Bain

Scott, Adam ?-1529 [DNNS, FFF, SN]
Scottish marauder
* [The] King of the Border
* [The] King of Thieves

Scott, Alastair
See Allen, Kenneth S[ydney]

Scott, Alma Olivia [ICB]
Author
* Travers, Georgia

Scott, Amanda
See Scott-Drennan, Lynne

Scott, Andrew
See Scotti, Andrea

Scott, Andrew George 1842-1876 [DI]
Irish-born Australian bushranger
* Moonlight, Captain

Scott, [Captain] Angus
See Colinski, A. J.

Scott, Anna [Kay] 1838-1923 [DNA]
Author
* Marston, Mildred

Scott, Anne 1651-1732 [SN]
Duchess of Monmouth
* Annabel

Scott, Anthony
See Dresser, Davis

Scott, Archer G.
See Larbalestier, Philip George

Scott, Arthur 1890-1949 [DAM, PMJ, WWJ]
American jazz musician
* Scott, Bud

Scott, Barbara Ann 1928- [HPPN]
Canadian figure staker
* Scott, Tinker

Scott, Benny 1945- [IBW]
American auto racer
* [The] Professor

Scott, Betty
See Scott, Blanche Stuart

Scott, Billy 1923- [BMH]
British entertainer
* Scott, Uke

Scott, Blanche Stuart 1886-1970
[HPPN]
American aviator
* America's First Female Aeroplane Soloist
* Scott, Betty
* [The] Tomboy of the Air

Scott, Bluff
See Scott, Lewis Nathanel

Scott, Bo
See Scott, Robert

Scott, Bonnie
See Paul, Bonnie Ann

Scott, Bud
See Scott, Arthur

Scott, Bullet
See Scott, Willie

Scott, C. P.
See Scott, Charles Prestwich

Scott, Casey
See Kubis, Pat

Scott, Charles 1839-1884 [HPPN]
American outlaw
* Rande, Frank
* Van Zandt, Charles

Scott, Charles Prestwich 1846-1932
[LC]
British newspaper editor and owner
* Scott, C. P.

Scott, Charlie 1947- [IBW]
American athlete
* Abdul-Aleem, Shaheed

Scott, Christopher John 1959- [DC]
British cricketer
* Scott, Rock

Scott, Churchill
See Jackson, Joseph [Francis Ambrose]

Scott, Clara ?-1909 [HPPN]
American vaudeville performer
* Moore, Clara

Scott, [Sir] Claude Edward 1804-1874
[IP]
British artist and author
* C. E. S., Sir

Scott, Clement William 1841-1904
[FFF, HPPN, PA]
British drama critic
* Almaviva
* Doe, John
* Rowe, Bolton
* Rowe, Saville

Scott, Clifford 1913- [IBW]
American racehorse trainer
* Scott, Scotty

Scott, Clyde 1924- [FB]
American football player
* Scott, Smackover

Scott, Cora Annett [Pipitone] 1931-
[CA, SAT]
American author
* Annett, Cora

Scott, Cyril Kay
See Wellman, Frederick Creighton

Scott, Dan [house pseudonym]
[Stratemeyer Syndicate]
See Barker, S[quire] Omar

Scott, Dan [house pseudonym]
[Stratemeyer Syndicate]
See Stratemeyer, Edward L.

Scott, Dana
See Robertson, Constance [Pierrepont Noyes]

Scott, Daniel ?-1806 [SN]
Brother of Scottish author, Sir Walter Scott
* Conacher

Scott, Daniel J. U. D. ?-1759 [HPPN]
British clergyman
* Philanthropos Londonensis

Scott, David Dundas 19th c. [IP]
Scottish author
* [A] Member of the Convention of Royal Burghs of Scotland

Scott, Deacon
See Scott, Lewis Everett

Scott, Denis [joint pseudonym with Theodore Saunders]
See Means, Mary

Scott, Denis [joint pseudonym with Mary Means]
See Saunders, Theodore

Scott, Dixon
See Scott, Walter

Scott, Elise Aylen 1904- [NAA]
Canadian writer
* Aylen, Elise

Scott, Ernest
See Groves, William E.

Scott, Ethel McCullough 20th c. [CA]
Author
* Clark, Garel [joint pseudonym with May Garelick]

Scott, Eve
See Rodgers, Joann Ellison

Scott, Evelyn 1893- [WW]
American author
* Souza, E[rnest]

Scott, Evelyn
See Dunn, Elsie

Scott, Farmer Bob
See Scott, Robert Walter

Scott, Floyd John 1898-1953 [BE]
American baseball player
* Scott, Pete

Scott, Frances V.
See Wing, Frances [Scott]

Scott Free Lincoln
See Lincoln, Warren

Scott, G. Forrester 20th c. [WWL]
Author
* Halsham, John

Scott, Genevia
See Sylvester, Hannah

Scott, George 19th c. [IP]
Scottish author
* [A] Friend of Truth

Scott, George C., Jr. 1944- [PB, SMG]
American baseball player
* [The] Boomer

Scott, Geraldine Edith 20th c. [LAO]
British author
* Mitton, G. E.

Scott, Gordon
See Werschkul, Gordon M.

Scott, Hamilton
See O'Mant, Hedley Percival Angelo

Scott, Hedley
See O'Mant, Hedley Percival Angelo

Scott, Hedley
See Young, Fred W.

Scott, Helen Myers 1876-? [WWL]
Scottish author
* Meldrum, Helen Myers

Scott, Helena
See Schurgot, Helen

Scott, Hugh Stowell 1862-1903 [LC]
British author
* Merriman, Henry Seton

Scott, Ivan
See Eppinoff, Ivan

Scott, J. W. Robertson
See Scott, John William Robertson

Scott, Jack
See Scafone, Jack, Jr.

Scott, Jack S.
See Escott, Jonathan

Scott, James 1649-1685 [DEP, DNNF, SN, WBD]
Claimant to British throne
* Absalom
* Azaria
* Crofts, James
* Fitzroy, James
* [The] Little Duke
* Monmouth, Duke of
* [The] Protestant Duke

Scott, James 1733-1814 [IP]
British clergyman and author
* Anti Sejanus
* Old Slyboots
* Philanglia

Scott, James 1888-1957 [BE, PB]
American baseball player
* Death Valley Jim

Scott, [Sir] James George 1851-1935
[BI]
British author and colonial administrator
* Yoe, Shway [or Schway?]

Scott, Jane
See McElfresh, [Elizabeth] Adeline

Scott, Jay 1924- [THR]
British theatrical designer
* Hutchinson Scott, Jay

Scott, Jean
See Muir, Marie Agnes

Scott, Jeffrey
See Usher, Shaun

Scott, Jeremy
See Dick, Kay

Scott, Jody 1923- [WW]
Author
* Scott, Thurston [joint pseudonym with George Thurston Leite]

Scott, John [FFF]
Horse trainer
* [The] Wizard of the North

Scott, John 1630?-1696 [HPPN]
British adventurer
* [The] President of Long Island

Scott, John 1730-1783 [IP, SN]
British author
* [The] Quaker Poet
* R. S.

Scott, John 1751-1838 [DEP, FFF, SN]
British jurist
* Eldon, Earl of

Scott, John (cont.)
* Old Bags
* [The] Stormy Petrel of Politics

Scott, John 1784-1821 [IP]
British journalist
* Benson, Edgeworth

Scott, John 1820-1907 [PA]
American author and soldier
* Barbarossa

Scott, John
See Nearing, John Scott

Scott, John F. 19th c. [IP]
American author
* Bones, Brudder

Scott, John Robert 19th c. [IP]
British author
* Falkland

Scott, John William Robertson 1866-1962 [LC]
British author and editor
* Scott, J. W. Robertson

Scott, Justin 20th c. [CA]
American author
* Blazer, J. S.

Scott, [George] Ken[neth] 1918- [HPPN]
Italian-American fashion designer and restaurateur
* Falconetto

Scott, Kerry
See Swanson, Harold Norling

Scott, L. N.
See Scott, Lewis Nathanel

Scott, Latayne Colvett 1952- [CA]
American author
* Colvett, Latayne

Scott, Lauren
See Frentzen, Jeffrey

Scott, Leader
See Baxter, Lucy E.

Scott, Lefty
See Scott, Marshall

Scott, Leslie
See Abullah, Zakariya

Scott, Lewis Everett 1892-1960 [AS, BE, PB]
American baseball player
* Scott, Deacon

Scott, Lewis Nathanel 1938- [BA]
American business executive
* Scott, Bluff
* Scott, L. N.

Scott, Linda
See Sampson, Linda Joy

Scott, Lizabeth
See Matzo, Emma

Scott, Lloyd
See Turner, George E[ugene]

Scott, Mabel 1872?-1908 [BEW]
Actress
* Russell, Mabel

Scott, Malcolm 1872-1929 [BMH]
British comedian
* [The] Woman who Knows

Scott, Marco
See Charlier, Roger H[enri]

Scott, Marian [Gallagher] 20th c. [WW]
Author
* Oliver, Gail
* Wolffe, Katherine

Scott, Marshall 1915-1964 [BE]
American baseball player
* Scott, Lefty

Scott, Martin
See Gehman, Richard Boyd

Scott, Mary [RH]
Daughter of Sir William Scott of Harden
* [The] Flower of Yarrow

Scott, Maxwell
See Staniforth, [Dr.] John William

Scott, Michael 1175?-1230? [HPPN]
Scottish scholar and astrologer
* [The] Wondrous Wizard

Scott, Michael 1789-1835 [IP, SN]
Scottish author
* Cringle, Tom
* [The] Salvator Rosa of the Sea

Scott, Mickey
See Scott, Ralph Robert

Scott, Mikado Milt
See Scott, Milt[on Parker]

Scott, Milt[on Parker] 1866-1938 [BE]
American baseball player
* Scott, Mikado Milt

Scott, Monica
See Baber, Monica Mary

Scott, Natalie Anderson
See Sokoloff, Natalie B.

Scott, Nerissa
See Ring, Elizabeth

Scott, Nicola 1945- [TR]
British actress
* Pagett, Nicola

Scott, Norford
See Rowland, Donald Sydney

Scott, O. R.
See Gottliebsen, Ralph Joseph

[The] Scott of Ireland
See Banim, John

[The] Scott of Painting
See Gilbert, [Sir] John

[The] Scott of the Sea
See Cooper, James Fenimore

Scott, P. T.
See Poage, Scott T[abor]

Scott, Peg O'Neill 20th c. [SFL, WGT]
American author
* O'Neill, Scott
* Werper, Barton [house pseudonym]

Scott, Pete
See Scott, Floyd John

Scott, Peter Dale 1929- [CA]
Canadian-born author
* Greene, Adam
* Sproston, John

Scott, Peter T. 20th c. [ESF, SFL, WGT]
American author
* Werper, Barton [house pseudonym]

Scott, Phaintin' Phil
See Suffling, Philip

Scott, Phil
See Suffling, Philip

Scott, Phillippa 1935- [BEW]
American actress
* Scott, Pippa

Scott, Pippa
See Scott, Phillippa

Scott, Portia Adele 1946- [BA]
American business executive
* Thomas, Pat A.

Scott, R. T. M.
See Maitland, Reginald T.

Scott, Ralph Robert 1947- [SMG, WWB]
German-born baseball player
* Scott, Mickey

Scott, Ralph Tuckett
See Maginn, William

Scott, Randolph
See Crane, Randolph

Scott, Raymond
See Warnow, Harry

Scott, Richard
See Parfait, Paul

Scott, Robert 20th c. [EF]
American football player
* Scott, Bo

Scott, Robert 20th c. [WGT]
British author
* Blue Wolf

Scott, Robert
See Robins, James

Scott, Robert Bissett 1774-1841 [IP]
British author
* R. B. S.

Scott, Robert Falcon 1868-1912 [HPPN]
British officer and explorer
* Mooney, Old
* [The] Owner

Scott, Robert Walter 1861-1929 [HPPN]
American politician and agriculturist
* Scott, Farmer Bob

Scott, Robin
See Wilson, Robin S[cott]

Scott, Rock
See Scott, Christopher John

Scott, Roland B. 1911- [IBW]
American physician
* [The] Father of Sickle Cell Anemia Research

Scott, Roney
See Gault, William Campbell

Scott, [Captain] Russell
See Pearson, Alec George

Scott, [Major] S. S.
See Harbaugh, Thomas Chalmers

Scott, Sarah ?-1795 [IP, PA]
British author
* [A] Gentleman on his Travels
* [A] Person of Quality
* Raymond, Henry Augustus

Scott, Scotty
See Scott, Clifford

Scott, Smackover
See Scott, Clyde

Scott, Stanley
See Fagerstrom, Stan

Scott, Steve
See Crawford, William [Elbert]

Scott, Stuart
See Aitken, William Russell

Scott, Thomas
See Rotherham, Thomas

Scott, Thomas Hamilton Maxwell 1833-1895? [PI]
Irish poet
* [A] Belfast Student

Scott, Thomas J. 19th c. [IP, PA]
American journalist
* Prog

Scott, Thomas Jefferson [Tom] 1912- [HPPN]
American composer and singer
* [The] American Troubadour

Scott, Thurston [joint pseudonym with Jody Scott]
See Leite, George Thurston

Scott, Thurston [joint pseudonym with George Thurston Leite]
See Scott, Jody

Scott, Tinker
See Scott, Barbara Ann

Scott, Titus
See Ingram, Thomas Theodore Scott

Scott, Tommy
See Woodward, Thomas Jones

Scott, Tony
See Sciacca, Anthony

Scott, Uke
See Scott, Billy

Scott, Valerie
See Rowland, Donald Sydney

Scott, Walter 1729-1799 [SN]
Father of Scottish author, Sir Walter Scott
* Fairford, Alexander

Scott, [Sir] Walter 1771-1832 [DEL, HPPN, RH, SN]
Scottish author and poet
* [The] Arioso of the North
* [A] Bard of Martial Lay
* [The] Black Hussar of Literature
* [The] Border Minstrel
* Borderer Between Two Ages
* [The] Caledonian Comet
* [The] Charmer of the World
* Cleishbotham, Jedediah
* Clutterbuck, [Captain] Cuthbert
* Croftangry, Chrystal
* Dryasdust, [The] Rev. Dr.
* [The] Duke of Darnick
* Duns Scotus
* Fairford, Alan
* [The] Father of the Historical Novel
* [The] Great Border Minstrel
* [The] Great Magician of the North
* [The] Great Minstrel
* [The] Great Unknown
* Grogg, Colonel
* [A] Homer of a Poet
* [The] Homer of Modern Days
* [The] Homer of the Novel
* [A] Layman
* [The] Magician
* [The] Magician of the North
* Malachi
* Malagrowther, Malachi
* [The] Mighty Minstrel
* [The] Minstrel of the Border
* Old Peveril
* Our Northern Homer
* Pattieson, Peter
* Paul
* [The] Peveril of the Peak
* [The] Proudest Boast of the Caledonian Muse
* S. W., Esq.
* [The] Shirra
* Sir Tristram
* Somnambulus
* [The] Superlative of My Comparative
* Templeton, Laurence
* [The] Visionary
* [The] Wizard of the North

Scott, Walter 1872-1954 [BI]
American adventurer
* Death Valley Scotty

Scott, Walter 1882-1915 [WWL]
Author
* Scott, Dixon

Scott, Walter
See Chestnutt, Edgar B.

Scott, [Sir] Walter
See Paulding, James Kirke

Scott, Walter
See Shearer, Lloyd

Scott, [Sir] Walter, Bart.
See Allen, John Carter

Scott, Warwick
See Dudley-Smith, Trevor

Scott, Wendell, Sr. 1922- [IBW]
American auto racer
* [The] Dean of Black Racing

Scott, Will[iam Matthew] 1894?-1964 [EMD]
British author and artist
* Watt, William

Scott, [Sir] William [Lord Stowell] 1745-1836 [HPPN, IP]
British jurist and author
* Chrysal
* Cinna
* Civis
* Panurge

Scott, William
See Newman, Allan Scott

Scott, William
See Reyburn, Wallace [Macdonald]

Scott, William B. [IP]
American author
* Diversity

Scott, William Bell 1811-? [EOP]
Scottish author and poet
* [The] Scottish Blake

Scott, William Henry
See Lawrence, John

Scott, William Lloyd 1915- [HPPN]
American politician
* [The] Dumbest Man in Congress

Scott, William R[alph] 1918- [CA]
American author and screenwriter
* Hill, Weldon

Scott, Willie ?-1958 [IBW]
American auto racer
* Scott, Bullet

Scott, Winfield 1786-1866 [DNNS, HPPN, NPS, SN]
American army officer
* [The] Hero of Chippewa
* Old Chapultepec
* Old Fuss and Feathers

Scott, Winifred Mary 20th c. [LAO]
British author
* Wynne, Pamela

Scott-Drennan, Lynne
Author
* Scott, Amanda

Scott-Fraser, Elizabeth
See Fraser, Elizabeth Bertha [Liz]

Scott-Heron, Gil 1949- [IBW]
American author, poet, musician
* Spiderman

Scott-James, R. A.
See Scott-James, Rolfe Arnold

Scott-James, Rolfe Arnold 1878-1959 [LC]
British author and editor
* Scott-James, R. A.

Scott-Moncrieff, C. K.
See Scott-Moncrieff, Charles Kenneth
Michael

**Scott-Moncrieff, Charles Kenneth
Michael** 1889-1930 [LC]
Scottish-born translator
* Scott-Moncrieff, C. K.

Scott-Taggart, Elizabeth Mary Josephine
1927- [ART]
British sculptor
* Est

Scott Thorn, Ronald
See Wilkinson, Ronald

Scotti, Andrea 20th c. [WF]
Italian actor
* Scott, Andrew

Scotti, Giulio Clemente 1602-1669
[WGT]
Author
* Europaeus, Lucius Cornelius

Scottie
See Wilson, Robert

[The] Scottish Anacreon
See Scot, Alexander

[The] Scottish Blake
See Scott, William Bell

[The] Scottish Boanerges
See Alexander, James

[The] Scottish Boanerges
See Haldane, Robert

[A] Scottish Farmer and Land Agent
See Loudon, John Claudius

[The] Scottish Giant
See Welsch, James

[The] Scottish Heliogabalus
See James I

[The] Scottish Hercules
See Bankier, William

[The] Scottish Hogarth
See Allan, David

[The] Scottish Homer
See Wilkie, William

[The] Scottish Hudibras
See Colvil, Samuel

[The] Scottish Marcellus
See Macdonald, [Sir] James

[The] Scottish Plato
See Stewart, Dugald

[The] Scottish Probationer
See Davidson, Thomas

[The] Scottish Reynolds
See Raeburn, [Sir] Henry

[The] Scottish Roscius
See Johnston, Henry Erskine

[The] Scottish Sidney
See Baillie, Robert

[The] Scottish Solomon
See James I

[The] Scottish Teniers
See Wilkie, [Sir] David

[The] Scottish Theocritus
See Ramsay, Allan

[The] Scottish Vandyke
See Jamesone, George

[The] Scottish Walpole
See Sharpe, Charles Kirkpatrick

[The] Scotts Irishman
See Bruce, William

Scotty
See Urquhart, C. H.

Scotty
See Wiseman, Scott

Scotus
See Robertson, John

Scotus, Johannes [or John] 815?-875?
[HN, RH, SN]
Medieval philosopher and theologian
* Erigena [The Irishman]
* [The] Last of the Platonists
* [The] Wise

Scotus Minor
See Pietro Aquila

Scourfield, J. H. 19th c. [HPPN]
British poet
* J. H. S.

[The] Scourge
See Tropea, Orassio [or Orazio]

[The] Scourge of Christians
See Noureddin-Mahmud

[The] Scourge of Europe
See Bonaparte, Napoleon

[The] Scourge of Fanaticism
See South, Robert

[The] Scourge of God
See Attila

[The] Scourge of God
See Charles VIII

[The] Scourge of God
See Genseric

[The] Scourge of God
See Timur [or Timour]

[The] Scourge of Grammar
See Jacob, Giles

[The] Scourge of Homer
See Zoilus [or Zoilos]

[The] Scourge of Infidels
See Khaled [or Khalid]

[The] Scourge of Malta
See Niemoeller, Martin Friedrich
Gustav Emil

[The] Scourge of Princes
See Aretino, Pietro

[The] Scourge of Scotland
See Edward I

Scourge of Spain
See Drake, [Sir] Francis

[The] Scourge of Tammany Hall
See Parkhurst, Charles

[The] Scourge of the Bootleggers
See Willebrandt, Mabel Walker

[The] Scourge of the District Police
See Blanton, Thomas Lindsay

Scourge of the Jews
See Hitler, Adolf

[The] Scourge of the Jews
See John of Capistrano

[The] Scourge of the Jews
See Torquemada, Tomas de

[The] Scourge of the Priests
See Farel, Guillaume

**[The] Scourge of the Propagators of the
Faith**
See Drelincourt, Charles

[The] Scourge of the Spaniards
See Nau, Jacques Jean David

[The] Scourge of the Spanish Main
See Teach, Edward

[The] Scourge of the Swastika
See Himmler, Heinrich

[The] Scourge of Wales
See Edward I

Scovel, Juy
See Fontana, Jean Pierre

Scovel, Mrs. [FFF]
Entertainer
* Fielding, May

Scovell, Edward [FFF]
* Scovello, Signor

Scovello, Signor
See Scovell, Edward

Scoville, Joseph A. 1815-1864 [DEL,
FFF, PA]
British author and journalist
* Barrett, Walter, Clerk
* Manhattan
* Pick, Mr.

Scrace, Richard
See Williamson, Lydia [Buckland]

Scrag, Gosling
See Lyttelton, George [First Baron
Lyttelton]

Scraggs, Milton Byron
See Williams, Richard Dalton

Scram, Arthur N.
See Guild, Leo

Scrambled Ego
See Rodgers, [Sir] John [Charles]

[The] Scrambler Amongst the Alps
See Whymper, Edward

Scramuzzo, Craig William 1950- [SMG]
American baseball player
* Scramuzzo, Moose

Scramuzzo, Moose
See Scramuzzo, Craig William

Scrannel, Orpheus
See Armstrong, Terence Ian Fytton

Scrap Iron Beecher
See Beecher, Ed[ward]

Scrap Iron Courtney
See Courtney, Clinton Dawson

Scrap Iron Kenna
See Kenna, Ed[ward Aloysious]

Scrap Iron Stinson
See Stinson, Gorrell R.

[The] Scrap Metal Sculptor
See Gibson, Jack

Scrappy Bill Joyce
See Joyce, William Michael

Scrappy, Mr.
See Carter, James Earl, Jr. [Jimmy]

[The] Scratch
See Becker, Charles

Scratchley, Harry
See Sherwood, John D.

Scratt, Ivan
See Scratuglia, Ivan

Scratuglia, Ivan 20th c. [WF]
Italian actor
* Scratt, Ivan

[The] Screamer
See Ankers, Evelyn

Screamin' Jay Hawkins
See Hawkins, Jalacy J.

Screamin' Scott Simon
See Simon, Scott

[The] Screen Queen
See Taylor, Elizabeth [Liz]

[The] Screen Tragedy Girl
See Baskette, Lena

Screeno
See Bailey, Howard Henry

[The] Screen's Bad Girl
See West, Mae

[The] Screen's Greatest Lover
See Guglielmi Di Valentina
D'Antonguolla, Rodolpho Alfonso
Raffaelo P.

[The] Screen's Perfect Lover
See Pringle, John

[The] Screwball Sculptor
See Irwin, Fenelon Arroyo Seco

Scribble
See Sowden, [Sir] William John

Scribble, Loquacious, Esq.
See Hamilton, [Dr.] Alexander

Scribble, Timothy
See Cowper, A.

Scribble, William
See Smyth, William

[The] Scribe
See Ezra [or Ezdras]

Scribe of the Dark Age
See Waugh, Evelyn

Scribe of the Indies
See Alvarez, Chanca Diego

[The] Scribe of the Revolution
See Jefferson, Thomas

Scribe, Simeon
See Black, Adam

Scriber, Peter
See Davis, Charles Augustus

Scriblerus, Martinus
See Pope, Alexander

Scriblerus, Martinus
See Swift, Jonathan

Scriblerus Maximus
See Dance, James

Scriblerus Oxoniensis
See Barham, Richard Harris

Scriblerus Redivivus
See Caswall, Edward

Scriblerus Secundus, H.
See Fielding, Henry

Scriblerus Tertius
See Cooke, Thomas

Scribner, B. F. 19th c. [IP]
American soldier and author
* One who has seen the Elephant
* One who was thar
* [A] Volunteer

Scribner, J. P. 19th c. [IP]
American author
* [An] Old Mountaineer

Scripps, E. W.
See Scripps, Edward Wyllis

Scripps, Edward Wyllis 1854-1926
[HPPN]
*American journalist and newspaper
publisher*
* [The] Father of Syndication
* [The] Old Hermit of Journalism
* Scripps, E. W.

[The] Script Doctor
See Towne, Robert

Scripturista
See Hart, [Rev.] William

Scrire. O. T. O. 4-7
See Gardner, Gerald Brosseau

Scrivener, Chuck
See Scrivener, Wayne Allison

[The] Scrivener of Crosbiters
See Greene, Robert

Scrivener, Wayne Allison 1947- [SMG,
WWB]
American baseball player
* Scrivener, Chuck

Scriverius
See Schryver, Pieter

Scroddles
See Mason, William

Scroggie, Marcus Graham 1901- [WD]
British engineer and writer
* Cathode Ray

Scroggs, [Sir] William 1623?-1683
[HPPN]
British jurist
* [The] Mouth

Scrope, George Julius Poulett
See Thomson, George Julius Poulett

Scrub, Dicky
See Norris, Henry

Scruggs, Baby
See Scruggs, Leazar

Scruggs, Faye 20th c. [RO1]
American singer
* Adams, Atomic
* Adams, Faye

Scruggs, Irene 1901- [BWW]
American singer
* Brown, Chocolate
* Little Sister
* Nolan, Dixie

Scruggs, Leazar 1921- [BWW]
American dancer
* Scruggs, Baby

Scruggs [or Winn?], Mary Elfrieda
1910-1981 [EJ, HPPN, PMJ]
American jazz musician
* Burleigh, [or Burley?] Mary Lou
* [The] Queen of Jazz
* Williams, Mary Lou
* Winn, Mary Lou

Scrum, R.
See Crumb, Robert

Scrutator
See Ensor, [Sir] Robert Charles

Scrutator
See Harlock, K. W.

Scrutator
See Horlock, Knightley William

Scrutator
See Jerram, Charles

Scrutator
See Labouchere, Henry

Scrutator
See Leech, Harper

Scrutator
See Loveday, John

Scrutator
See Macallan, Daniel

Scrutator
See MacColl, Malcolm

Scrutator
See McCall, John

Scrutator
See Measor, C. P.

Scrutator
See Rarey, John Solomon

Scrutator
See Rivington, Charles

Scrutton, Daphne 1922-   [FC]
British actress
* Anderson, Daphne

Scrymgeour, James 19th c.   [IP]
Scottish author
* Norval

Scrymgeour Wedderburn, Janet 1941-
[ART]
British sculptor and stained-glass window designer
* J. S. W.

Scudamore, Lily   [FFF]
American writer
* Ruhamah

Scudamore, [Rev.] William Edward
19th c.   [HPPN]
British clergyman
* [A] Parish Priest

Scudder, Horace Elisha 1838-1902
[HPPN, IP]
American editor and author
* Fellow, R.
* James, S. T.

Scudder, Kawliga
See Scudder, Pat

Scudder, Mildred Lee 1908-   [CA, TBJ]
American author
* Lee, Mildred

Scudder, Pat 20th c.   [GW]
American rodeo performer
* Scudder, Kawliga

Scudder, Samuel Hubbard 1837-1911
[HPPN]
American naturalist
* Lutterby, Francis
* [A] Rochester Fellow

Scudder, Vida D. 19th c.   [IP]
American? author
* Coit., Davida

Scuderi, Magdalen [or Madeleine] de
1607-1671   [DEP, DNNS, NPS, RH]
French poet
* [The] French Sappho
* Sappho
* [The] Tenth Muse

Scugog
See Ross, J. L. W.

[The] Scullor
See Taylor, John

Scully, Vincent 1810-1871   [PI]
Irish poet and politician
* S.
* Vis

Scully, William Charles 1855-1943
[DLE1]
South African poet and author
* Witwatersrand

[The] Sculptor of American History
See Kelly, James Edward

[The] Sculptor Poet
See Lucretius Carus, Titus

Sculptor, Satiricus, Esq.
See Ireland, William Henry

Scultetus
See Schultz, Johann

Scum
See Crumb, Robert

Scurlock, Doc
See Scurlock, Josiah G.

Scurlock, Josiah G. ?-1882?   [EWG]
American gunfighter
* Scurlock, Doc

Scythrop, Glowry
See Shelley, Percy Bysshe

Sczepkowski, Theodore Walter 1923-
[BE]
American baseball player
* Sepkowski, Theodore Walter [Ted]

Sdt, E.
See Skarstedt, Ernest Teofil

[The] Se Baptist
See Smith [or Smyth?], John

Se De Kay
See Kirke, Charles D.

Se-Gwoi-Don-Kwe 20th c.   [BI]
American Indian sculptor
* Wilson, Duffy

Sea
See Coffin, Roland Folger

[The] Sea Devil
See Von Luckner, [Count] Felix

Sea Dragon
See Drake, [Sir] Francis

[The] Sea Dreamer
See Korzeniowski, Teodor Jozef
Konrad Nalecz

[A] Sea Fielding
See Marryatt, Frederick

Sea Gull
See Chereshkova, Valentina
Vladimirovna

Sea Gull, Professor
See Gould, Joseph Ferdinand

[The] Sea King's Daughter
See Alexandra, Caroline Marie
Charlotte Louisa Julia

Sea Lion
See Bennett, Geoffrey [Martin]

Sea Lion Hall
See Clolo, Carlos

Sea Lion Hall
See Hall, Charles L.

Sea Lord
See Middleton, Anne

Sea Shell
See Clark, Jeremiah Simpson

Seab, Lenial
See Johnston, D. B. S.

Seabhac, An
See O'Siochfhradha, P.

Seaborn, [Captain] Adam
See Symmes, John Cleves

Seabright, Idris
See St. Clair, Margaret

Seabright, John
See Tubb, Edwin Charles

Seabrook, Ephraim Baynard 19th c.
[IP]
American author
* E. B. S.

Seabrook, Whitemarsh Benjamin
1795?-1855   [HPPN]
American author and politician
* [A] South Carolinian

Seabrooke, David
See Bedford-Jones, Henry [James
O'Brien]

Seabrooke, Edward   [FFF]
Entertainer
* Lee, Edward

Seabrooke, Thomas Q.
See Quigley, Thomas James

Seabury, Samuel 1729-1796   [DNA,
HPPN, IP]
American author and clergyman
* A. W.
* [A] Farmer
* Farmer, A. W.
* [A] Member of the Episcopal Church
* [A] Westchester Farmer

Seabury, Samuel 1801-1872   [HPPN]
American clergyman
* Farmer, A. W.

Seabury, Ynez 1909-1973   [FIR, SC]
American actress
* [The] Biograph Baby

Seacole, Mary ?-1881   [IBW]
Jamaican-born nurse
* [The] Yellow Doctress

Seadlund, John Henry 1910-1938   [BLB]
American murderer and kidnapper
* Anders, Peter

Seadoaghob, Nana 1936-   [WBC]
Thai boxer
* Kingpetch, Pone

[A] Seafarer
See Russell, William Clark

Seafield, Frank
See Grant, Alexander Henley

Seaford, Caroline
See Cook, Marjorie Grant

Seaforth
See Foster, George Cecil

Seaforth, A. Nelson
See Clarke, George Sydenham

Seagar, Joan
See Fearn, John Russell

Seager, Charles [FFF, IP]
British author
* Academicus

Seagrave, Barbara Ann Garvey
See Jackson, Barbara Ann Garvey
Seagrave

Seagraves, Gordon 1897-1965
American physician
* [The] Burma Surgeon

[The] Seagreen Incorruptible
See Robespierre, Maximilien

Seagrist, Josephine 1922- [BEW]
American actress and singer
* Roberts, Joan

Seagull, Barbara
See Herzstein, Barbara

Seale, John Barlow 18th c. [IP]
British scholar
* [A] Friend of the Author

Seale, Johnny Ray 1938- [BE]
American baseball player
* Durango Kid

Seales, Ray 1953?- [HPPN]
American boxer
* Seales, Sugar Ray

Seales, Sugar Ray
See Seales, Ray

Sealey, Leonard George William 1923-
[IAW]
British-born educator and author
* Britt, George

Seals, Danny 1950- [RO2]
American singer
* England Dan

Seals, Frank Junior 1942- [BWW, IBW]
American singer, songwriter, musician
* Seals, Son

Seals, Jim 20th c. [BWW]
American musician
* Seals, Son

Seals, Son
See Seals, Frank Junior

Seals, Son
See Seals, Jim

Sealsfield, Charles 1793-1864 [HPPN]
Moravian author
* Hardman, Frederick

Sealsfield, Charles
See Postl, Karl Anton

Sealy, Robert 1831-1862 [PI]
Irish-born poet
* Menippus

Seaman, Abel
See Chase, Frank Eugene

Seaman, Augustus [IP, PA]
American author
* Brick, Titus

Seaman, Elizabeth [Cochrane] 1867-1922
[BI]
American journalist
* Bly, Nellie
* Queen of the Sob Sisters

Seaman, [Sir] Owen 1861-? [WWL]
British author
* Nauticus
* O. S.

Seaman, Sylvia S[ybil] 1910- [CAP,
WD]
American author
* Sylvin, Francis [joint pseudonym with
Frances Schwartz]

Seamans, Apache Bill?
See Seamans, William

[A] Seaman's Friend
See Baker, Samuel

Seamans, William
American frontiersman
* Seamans, Apache Bill?

Seamark
See Small, Austin J.

Seames, C. O. 20th c. [IBW]
American tennis player
* Seames, Mother

Seames, Mother
See Seames, C. O.

Seamrog
See Hickey, Michael Patrick

Search, Edward
See Hazlitt, William

Search, Edward
See Tucker, Abraham

Search, John
See Ashhurst, William Henry

Search, John
See Binney, Thomas

Search, John
See Whately, Richard

Search Light
See Frank, Waldo David

Search, Preston Willis 1853-? [NAA]
American author and educator
* Redwood, John

Search, Sarah
See Nolan, Frederick

Search, Warner Christian
See Smith, Baron

Search, Warner Christian
See Smith, [Sir] William Cusack, Bart.

[The] Searcher
See Fludd, Robert

Searcher, Leland
See Hebbard, William Wallace

Searchlight
See Eardley-Wilmot, [Sir] Sydney
Marow

Searchlight [Secret Service code name]
See Nixon, Richard Milhous

Searcy, George ?-1949 [F2]
Actor
* Moran, George

Seare, Nicholas
See Whitaker, Rod

Searing, Laura C. Redden 1840-1923
[FFF]
American poet
* Glyndon, Howard

Searle, January
See Phillips, George Searle

Searle, Joyce Collins 1930- [HPPN]
American jazz musician
* Collins, Joyce

Searle, Kathryn Adrienne 1942- [CA,
SAT]
British author and illustrator
* Kathryn

Searle, Louise
See Hunter, Mrs. Henry

Searle, Mrs. Cyril [FFF]
Entertainer
* Eytinge, Rose

Searle, Ronald William Fordham 1920-
[DLE]
British artist, illustrator, author
* Shy, Timothy [joint pseudonym with
Dominic Bevan Wyndham Lewis]

Sears, Alfred Francis 19th c. [SFL]
Author
* Inca-Pablo-Ozollo

Sears, Deane
See Rywell, Martin

Sears, Edmund Hamilton 1810-1876
[HPPN]
American clergyman, author, hymn writer
* E. H. S.

Sears, Edward Isidore 1819-1876 [DNA,
PI]
Irish-born author and editor
* Chevalier, H. E.

Sears, Eleonora R. 1881-1968 [HPPN]
American athlete
* [The] Universal Female Athlete

Sears, George W. 1821-? [HPPN, IP]
American woodsman and author
* Nessmuk

Sears, Isaac 1730-1786 [SN]
American merchant
* Sears, King

Sears, John, Jr. 20th c. [TI 5-16-83]
American horse groomer
* Sears, Top Cat

Sears, Ken[neth Eugene] 1917- [BE]
American baseball player
* Sears, Ziggy

Sears, King
See Sears, Isaac

Sears, Mrs. Newton [PA]
Author
* Kismet

Sears, Richard Warren 1863-1914
[HPPN]
American retail merchant
* [The] Mail Order Magician

Sears, Top Cat
See Sears, John, Jr.

Sears, Zelda
See Paldi, Zelda

Sears, Ziggy
See Sears, Ken[neth Eugene]

Seastrom, Victor
See Sjoestroem, Victor

Seaton, Beryl
See Platts, Beryl

Seaton, George
See Stenius, George

Seaton, Mrs.
See Yates, Edmund Hodgson

Seattle Bill James
See James, William Lawrence

Seattle Frank
See DuBreuil, Elizabeth Lorinda

Seattle's Sensational Son
See Zioncheck, Marion A.

Seaver, George Thomas [Tom] 1944-
[NLG]
American baseball player
* [The] Franchise
* Terrific, Tom

Seaver, W. A. [PA]
Author
* Editors Drawer

Seawell, Molly Elliot 1860-1916 [FFF,
IP]
American author
* Foxhall
* Sydney

Seaworthy, [Captain] Gregory
See Gregory, James

Sebastian 1554-1578 [DNNS, SN]
King of Portugal
* [The] Madman

Sebastian
See Ponsonby, [Sir] Henry Frederick

Sebastian, Jeanne
See Newsome, Arden J[eanne]

Sebastian, John 1944- [RO2]
American singer
* Benson, John

Sebastian, Lee
See Silverberg, Robert

Sebastian, Margaret
See Gladstone, Arthur M.

Sebastiano del Piombo
See Luciani, Sebastiano

Sebelien, John Robert Francis 1858-?
[LAO]
Danish-born scientist and author
* Pagan, Kristian

Sebenthal, Roberta Elizabeth 1917-
[CA, WD]
American author and poet
* Kruger, Paul

Sebille, Louis ?-1950 [BI]
American aviator
* Reynolds, Lou

Sebley, Frances Rae 1921- [WD]
British author and critic
* Jeffs, Rae

Sebottendorf, Rudolf Freiherr von
See Glauer, Adam

Sebring, Jay
See Kummer, Thomas Jay

Sec
See Blow, Marya Mannes

Secchi, Luciano 1939- [WEC]
Italian cartoonist
* Bunker, Max

Seccombe, Joseph 1706-1760 [IP]
American clergyman and author
* Fluviatulis Piscator

SecDef
See Weinberger, Caspar

Seceder in Glasgow
See Smith, William

Sechrist, Doc
See Sechrist, Theodore O'Hara

Sechrist, Theodore O'Hara 1876-1950
[BE]
American baseball player
* Sechrist, Doc

Sechter, Simon 1788-1867 [BBD]
Austrian composer
* Heiter, Ernst

Seckendorf, Gustav Anton von
1775-1823 [FFF]
German author and playwright
* Peale, Patrick

Seckener, Mrs. James A. [FFF]
Entertainer
* Vogt, Marie

[The] Second Achilles
See Dentatus, Sicinius

[The] Second Adam
See Jesus Christ

[The] Second Alexander
See Sandjar

[The] Second Aristotle
See Achillini, Alessandro

[A] Second Aristotle
See Frederick II

[The] Second Augustine
See Aquinas, Thomas [Thomas of
Aquino]

[The] Second Brutus
See Medici, Francesco de

[A] Second Cato
See Hopital, Michel de l'

[The] Second Charlemagne
See Charles V

[A] Second Constantine
See James II

[The] Second Dauphin
See Louis de France

[The] Second Effulgence
See Gotescalc

[The] Second Founder of Rome
See Peretti, Felice

[A] Second Helen
See Recamier, Jeanne Francoise Julie
Adelaide

Second, Henry
See Harrison, Henry Sydnor

[The] Second Hogarth
See Bunbury, Henry William

[The] Second John
See Adams, John Quincy

[A] Second Johnson
See Coleridge, Samuel Taylor

[The] Second Leviathan of Prose
See Nash [or Nashe?], Thomas

[The] Second Man on the Moon
See Aldrin, Edwin E., Jr.

[A] Second Mars
See Della Rovere, Giuliano

[The] Second Moses
See Maimonides [or Moses ben
Maimon]

**[The] Second Mother of Everybody's
Children**
See Abbott, Grace

[The] Second Mrs. Simpson Sloan
See Simpson, Elizabeth Sloan

[A] Second Ovid
See Greene, Robert

[The] Second Parent of the Reformed Church
See John [or Johann]

[The] Second Parent of the Reformed Church
See John Frederick

[The] Second Pavlova
See Danilova, Alexandra

[The] Second Romulus
See Camillus, Marcus Furius

[The] Second Romulus of Brandenburg
See Albert I [or Albrecht]

[The] Second St. Augustine
See Hughes de St. Victor

[The] Second St. Paul
See Remi [or Remigius]

[A] Second Shakespeare
See Marlowe, Christopher

[The] Second Solomon
See Henry VII

[The] Second Solomon
See James I

Second Thoughts, Solomon
See Kennedy, John Pendleton

[The] Second Trajan
See Claudius II [Marcus Aurelius Claudius]

[The] Second Washington
See Clay, Henry

[The] Second Washington
See Juarez, Benito Pablo

[The] Second William Jennings Bryan
See Lee, Joshua Bryan

[A] Second Xenophon
See M'Pherson, Samuel

Secondsight, Solomon
See McHenry, James

Secor, Helena
See Tons, Helen

Secor, Mrs. George J.   [FFF]
Entertainer
* Renard, Rachelle

Secor, Rosa 1884-1922 [THR]
American actress
* Lynd, Rosa

Secrest, Meryle
See Beveridge, Meryle Secrest

[The] Secret President
See Wilson, Edith Bolling Galt

[The] Secret Sharer
See Dean, John, III

Secretary and General Agent
See Harris, N. Sayre

[The] Secretary of Nature
See Aristocles

[The] Secretary of Nature
See Aristotle

[The] Secretary of Nature
See Bacon, Francis [First Baron Verulam]

[The] Secretary of Nature
See Socrates

[The] Secretary of the Massachusetts Sabbath School Society
See Bullard, Asa

[The] Secretary of the New York Sabbath Committee
See Cook, Russell S.

[The] Secretary of the Society
See Stackhouse, [Rev.] Alfred Long

[The] Secretary of War
See Poinsett, Joel Roberts

Secrist, Kelliher [joint pseudonym with W. G. Secrist]
See Kelliher, Dan T.

Secrist, Kelliher [joint pseudonym with Dan T. Kelliher]
See Secrist, W. G.

Secrist, W. G. 20th c. [WW]
Author
* Secrist, Kelliher [joint pseudonym with Dan T. Kelliher]

Sectanus, Quintus
See Sergardi, Ludovico

[The] Sectional President
See Lincoln, Abraham

Secundus
See Lotich, Peter

Secundus, Asmodeus
See Sotheran, Charles

Secundus, Johannes
See Everaerts, Jan Nicolai

Secutor
See Slater, John Herbert

Sedan Chair
See McMinoway, Michael W.

Seddon, John P. 19th c. [IP]
British architect and author
* His Brother

Seddon, Richard John 1845-1906 [HPPN]
New Zealand prime minister
* King Dick

Sedges, John
See Buck, Pearl S[ydenstricker]

Sedgewick, Helen
See Brady, Helen

Sedgman, Frank 20th c. [OET]
Australian tennis player
* [The] Gentleman

Sedgwick, Anne Douglas
See Selincourt, Anne De

Sedgwick, Billy
See Putnam, S. W.

Sedgwick, Doomsday
See Sedgwick, William

Sedgwick, Duke
See Sedgwick, Henry Kenneth

Sedgwick, Henry Kenneth 1899-   [BE]
American baseball player
* Sedgwick, Duke

Sedgwick, James 1775-1851 [IP]
British barrister and journalist
* [A] Barrister

Sedgwick, John 1813-1864 [HPPN]
American army officer
* Uncle John

Sedgwick, Modwena
See Glover, Modwena

Sedgwick, Theodore, Jr. 1780-1839 [FFF]
American author and attorney
* [An] American

Sedgwick, Theodore, Sr. 1811-1859 [IP]
American author and attorney
* Veto

Sedgwick, William ?-1669? [SN]
British clergyman
* [The] Apostle of the Isle of Ely
* Sedgwick, Doomsday

[The] Seditious Jesuit
See Campion, Edmund

Sedley, Arthur Osborne Lionel ?-1897? [PI]
Irish author and poet
* Carolan, R.

Sedley, Catherine [Countess of Dorchester] ?-1692 [SN]
Mistress of King James II
* Dorinda

Sedley, [Sir] Charles 1639-1701 [HPPN, IP]
British playwright
* C. S., Sir
* Lisideius
* [The] Tibullus of His Age

Sedley, F.
See Fay, Theodore Sedgwick

Sedley, William [Bill] 19th c. [HPPN]
American boatman
* [The] King of the Flatboatmen

Sedley, William Henry 1806-1872 [HPPN]
British-American actor
* Sedley-Smith, William Henry

Sedley-Smith, William Henry
See Sedley, William Henry

Sedolin, Sture
See Hallstrom, Carl

Sedran, Barney
See Sedransky, Barney

Sedransky, Barney 1891-1969   [BB, EJS]
American basketball player
* Sedran, Barney

Sedric, Con-Con
See Sedric, Paul

Sedric, [Eu]gene 1907-1963   [EJ, PMJ, WWJ]
American jazz musician
* Sedric, Honey Bear

Sedric, Honey Bear
See Sedric, [Eu]gene

Sedric, Paul 20th c.   [EJ, WWJ]
American musician
* Sedric, Con-Con

Sedulius, Caius
See Casey, James

Seduro, Vladimir 1910-   [CA]
Russian-born author
* Hlybinny, Vladimir

Sedway, Moe
See Sedwitz, Morris

Sedwitz, Morris 20th c.   [BLB]
American underworld figure
* Sedway, Moe

Sedych, Andrei
See Zwibak, Jacques

See, Chad
See See, Charles Henry [Charlie]

See, Charles Henry [Charlie] 1896-1948
[BE]
American baseball player
* See, Chad

See, Henricus von
See Dilg, William

See, James W. 19th c.   [HPPN]
American author
* Chordal

See, Lisa 20th c.   [PW 8-19-83]
American author
* Highland, Monica

[The] See Me Tuesday Man
See Geen, Robert H.

[The] See See Rider Blues Girl
See Nicholls, Muriel

See, T. J.
See Carey, Thomas Joseph

Seebord, G. R.
See Soderberg, Percy Measday

Seeburg, Franz von
See Hacker, Franz

Seed and Plum Cakins
See Trusler, John

Seed, Cecile Eugenie 1930-   [WD]
South African author
* Seed, Jenny

Seed, Jenny
See Seed, Cecile Eugenie

Seed, Sheila Turner 1937?-1979   [CA]
American editor, writer, photographer
* Turner, Sheila R.

Seedo, Sonia
See Fuchs, Sonia Husid

Seeds, Robert Ira 1907-   [BE]
American baseball player
* Seeds, Suitcase Bob

Seeds, Suitcase Bob
See Seeds, Robert Ira

Seeger, Pete[r R.] 1919-   [FCW, HPPN]
American singer and songwriter
* America's Tuning Fork
* Bowers, Pete
* [The] Reincarnated Troubadour
* [The] Thomas Jefferson of Folk Music

Seegrist, Sylvia 1961?-   [WP 10-29-85]
Involved in shopping mall murder incident
* Rambo, Ms.

Seehaitch
See Hennessy, William Charles

[A] Seeker
See Greenwood, Francis William Pitt

[The] Seeker of Visions
See Lame Deer

Seelen, Arthur
See Seelenfreund, Arthur

Seelenfreund, Arthur 1923-   [BEW]
American actor and theatre bookseller
* Seelen, Arthur

Seeley, [Mr.] Blossom
See Gersenfeld, Benjamin

Seeley, Charles S.
See Munday, John William

Seeley, John Robert 1834-1895   [DEA, IP, PA]
British author
* Ecce Homo
* Robertson, John
* White, James

Seeley, Robert Benton 19th c.   [IP, PA]
British author
* [A] Layman

Seelin, Elpha 1913-1975   [HPPN]
American playwright
* Ellington, E. A.

Seelos, Annette
See Wallis, Blanche

Seelye, Sarah Emma
See Edmonds, Sarah Emma

[The] Seer
See Aven, Algernon Jasper

Seer
See Roberts, Cecil Edric Mornington

[The] Seer of Wellesley Hills
See Babson, Roger Ward

[The] Seeress of Prevorst
See Hauffe, Frederica

Seers, Eugene 1865-?   [NAA]
Canadian-born poet and author
* Dantin, Louis

Seestern
See Grautoff, Ferdinand [Heinrich]

Seever, R.
See Reeves, Lawrence F.

Seezenais, William 1920?-1978   [BI]
American photographer
* Randolph, Popsie

Seferiades, Georgios
See Seferiades, Giorgos Stylianou

Seferiades, Giorgos Stylianou 1900-1971
[CA, EWL, TCL]
Greek diplomat and poet
* Seferiades, Georgios
* Seferis, George

Seferis, George
See Seferiades, Giorgos Stylianou

Seff, Richard
See Siff, Richard Philip

Seffernick, Susan M. 1951-   [HPPN]
American entertainer
* Day, Windy
* Petrie, Susan

Sefi [or Sophi] ?-1642   [HN]
Sultan of Persia
* [The] Nero of Persia

Sefrit, Sallie Mulholland 1862-1941
[IA]
American writer and poet
* Waller, Virginia Harmon

Segal, Alfred 1883-?   [BI]
American columnist
* Cincinnatus

Segal, Marc 1887-1985   [HPPN, JL]
Russian painter
* Chagall, Marc
* [The] Midsummer Night's Dreamer

Segal, Robert 1957-   [BP]
American actor
* Benson, Robby

Segal, Samuel 20th c.   [EJS]
American wrestler
* Maccabee, Dan

Segale, Rose 1850-1941   [CAT]
Italian-born American author
* Blandina, [Sister]

Segall, Don 20th c.   [SFL]
Author
* August, Leo

Segall, Liliane 1939-   [CAR]
American artist
* Lijn, Liliane

Seghers, Anna
See Redling, Nettie Radvanti

Seghers, Anna
See Reiling, Netty

Seghi, Phillip Dominic 1918- [SMG]
Baseball manager
* Seghi, Swapper

Seghi, Swapper
See Seghi, Phillip Dominic

Segrave, Adolphus
See Hamerton, Philip Gilbert

Segre, Dan V[ittorio] 1922- [CA]
Italian-born Israeli author
* Bauduc, R.

[Il] Segretario
See Machiavelli, Niccolo [or Nicholas]

Segretti, Donald H. 1941- [HPPN]
American politician
* [The] Political Trickster

Seguier, Pierre [RH]
French prophet and clergyman
* [The] Danton of the Cevennes

Segundo, Bart
See Rowland, Donald Sydney

Segura, Francisco 1921- [BI]
Ecuadorian tennis player
* Segura, Pancho

Segura, Francisco
See Cano, Francisco Segura

Segura, Pancho
See Cano, Francisco Segura

Segura, Pancho
See Segura, Francisco

Segura, Vicente 1883- [GS]
Mexican bullfighter
* [El] Millonario [The Millionaire]

Segura y Campos, Antonio 1880-1930
[GS]
Spanish bullfighter
* Segurita [Little Segura]

Segurita [Little Segura]
See Segura y Campos, Antonio

Seguy, Pierre
See Stein-Schneider, Herbert

Seibel, Werner 1946- [IAW]
German author and poet
* Lebies, Rene

Seibold, Harry 1896-1965 [BE]
American baseball player
* Seibold, Socks

Seibold, Socks
See Seibold, Harry

Seid, Ruth 1913- [ANT, AW, CA]
American author and playwright
* Sinclair, Jo

Seide, Diane 1930- [CA]
American author
* Seidner, Diane

Seidenschmer, Jacob 1891?-1913
[HPPN]
American underworld figure
* Lewis, Whitey

Seidick, Kathryn A[melia] 1943- [CA]
American author
* Michaels, Kasey

Seidl, Lea
See Mayrseidl, Caroline

Seidlitz, Julius
See Jedteles, Itzig

Seidman, J. S.
See Seidman, Jacob Stewart

Seidman, Jacob Stewart 1901- [BEW]
American investor and accountant
* Seidman, J. S.

Seidner, Diane
See Seide, Diane

Seifert, Elizabeth
See Gasparotti, Elizabeth Seifert

Seiffert, Ernst 1892-1948 [BBD, EMT]
Austrian-born opera singer
* Tauber, Richard

Seiffert, Marjorie Allen 1885-? [HPPN]
American author
* Cypher, Angela

Seignobosc, Francoise 1897-1961 [CA,
MJA]
French author and illustrator
* Francoise

Seilhamer, George O. 19th c. [IP]
American journalist
* G. O. S.

Seinfel, Ruth
See Goode, Ruth

Seipel, Ignatz 1876-1932 [HPPN]
Austrian chancellor and diplomat
* [The] Christian Statesman

Seitz, Carolyn Jane 1928- [BEW]
American actress, singer, director
* Seitz, Dran

Seitz, Dran
See Seitz, Carolyn Jane

Seitz, Franz 20th c. [WF]
German screenwriter
* Laforet, Georg

Seitz, Peter
See Seitzick, Peter

Seitzick, Peter 1905-1983
American arbitrator
* Seitz, Peter

Seixas, Gershom 1746-1816 [HPPN]
American clergyman
* [The] Leading Spokesman for Jews

[The] Sejanus of England
See Villiers, George

Sejour, Victor
See Marcou-Ferrand, Juan Victor
Sejour

Sejour-Magloire, Francis L. 1940- [CW]
Haitian poet and author
* Magloire, Francis L.

Sekely, Steve
See Szekely, Istvan

Sekers, Miki
See Sekers, Nicholas

Sekers, Nicholas ?-1972 [WFA]
British fabric manufacturer
* Sekers, Miki

Sekon, George Augustus
See Nokes, George Augustus

Sekona, Fonomonu 20th c. [RBE]
Tongan boxer
* Sekona, Young

Sekona, Young
See Sekona, Fonomonu

Sekowski, Josef 1800-1858 [BI]
Polish author
* Brambeus, Baron

Seku, Yerba
See Hooi, Richard

Sekulovich, Mladen 1914- [BDF, HT,
SW]
American actor
* Malden, Karl

Selbach, Albert Karl 1872-1956 [AS,
BE, PB]
American baseball player
* Selbach, Kip

Selbach, Kip
See Selbach, Albert Karl

Selbig, Elise
See Ahlefeld, Charlotte Sophie Luise
Wilhelmine von

Selbini, Lalla ?-1942 [BMH]
Entertainer
* [The] Bathing Belle on the Bicycle

Selbit, P. T.
See Tibbles, Percy Thomas

Selborn, Clara
See Svendsen, Clara

Selby, Brit
See Selby, Robert Briton

Selby, Charles 1801-1863 [IP]
British comedian and playwright
* Muggins, William
* Tickletooth, Tabitha

Selby, Norman 1873-1940 [AS, BX,
HPPN, RBE]
American boxer
* [The] Corkscrew Kid
* McCoy, Charles
* McCoy, Kid
* [The] Real McCoy

Selby, Percival M.
See Short, Percival M.

Selby, Robert Briton 1945- [CEI, FHE]
Canadian-born hockey player
* Selby, Brit

Selcamm, George
See Machlis, Joseph

Selchow
See Lafontaine, August Heinrich Julius

Selden, Albert
See Seldon, Albert Wiggin

Selden, George
See Thompson, George Selden

Selden, John 1584-1654 [NPS, SN]
British jurist and statesman
* [The] Champion of Human Law
* [The] Learned Selden
* Monarch of Letters
* [A] Walking Library

Selden, Richard Ely, Jr. 1797-1868 [IP]
American farmer and bibliographer
* Mon Droit

Seldes, George 1890- [HPPN]
American journalist
* [The] Muckraker Emeritus

Seldes, Gilbert [Vivian] 1893-1970 [CA, WW]
American author
* Bluphocks, Lucien
* Cauliflower, Sebastian
* Johns, Foster
* Shaw, Vivian

Seldon, Albert Wiggin 1922- [BEW]
American composer, producer, lyricist
* Selden, Albert

Seldon-Truss, Leslie
See Truss, [Leslie] Seldon

Selenus, Gustavus
See Augustus

Seleucus I 4th c. BC [WBD]
King of the Seleucidae
* Nicator

Seleucus II 3rd c. BC [WBD]
King of the Seleucidae
* Callinicus

Seleucus III 3rd c. BC [WBD]
King of the Seleucidae
* Soter

Seleucus IV 2nd c. BC [WBD]
King of the Seleucidae
* Philopator

Seleucus VI 2nd c. BC [WBD]
King of the Seleucidae
* Epiphanes Nicator

[The] Self Appointed Supercop
See Bulit, Faik

[The] Self Made Novelist
See Ferber, Edna

Self-Made Curmudgeon
See Dukinfield, William Claude

[The] Self-Tormentor
See Hobbes, Thomas

Selfridge, Harry Godron 1864-1947 [HPPN]
British-American merchant
* Mile A Minute Harry

Selfridge, Thomas Oliver 1836-1924 [HPPN]
American naval officer and surveyor
* [The] Father of the Panama Canal

Selig, Allan H. 20th c. [SMG]
American baseball executive
* Selig, Bud

Selig, Bud
See Selig, Allan H.

Seligman, Jake 19th c.
American clothier
* Little Jake of Saginaw
* Seligman, Little Jake

Seligman, Little Jake
See Seligman, Jake

Seligman, Walter Herbert 1902- [OP]
German conductor
* Herbert, Walter

Selika, Marie 1852-1937 [IBW]
American singer
* [The] Queen of Staccato

Selim
See Knowles, James Sheridan

Selim
See Woodworth, Samuel

Selim the Persian
See Lyttelton, George [First Baron Lyttelton]

Selim II 1524?-1574 [DNNS]
Sultan of Turkey
* [The] Sot

Selimovic, Mehmed 1910-1982 [IAW]
Yugoslav author
* Mesa

Selina [Countess of Huntingdon] 1707-1791 [HPPN]
British religious leader
* [The] Queen of the Methodists

Selincourt, Anne De 1873-? [WWL]
British author
* Sedgwick, Anne Douglas

Selinger, Archie 1885-1940 [BEW]
Actor and director
* Pitt, Archie

Selkirk [or Selcraig], Alexander 1676-1721 [HPPN]
Scottish sailor and castaway
* [The] Original Robinson Crusoe

Selkirk, George Alexander 1908- [BE, BN, PB]
American baseball player
* Selkirk, Twink
* Selkirk, Twinkletoes

Selkirk, J. B.
See Brown, James

Selkirk, Jane [joint pseudonym with Mary Hamilton (Ilsley) Chapman]
See Chapman, John Stanton Higham

Selkirk, Jane [joint pseudonym with John Stanton Higham Chapman]
See Chapman, Mary Hamilton [Ilsley]

Selkirk, Twink
See Selkirk, George Alexander

Selkirk, Twinkletoes
See Selkirk, George Alexander

Sell, Elwood Lester 1897-1961 [BE]
American baseball player
* Sell, Epp

Sell, Epp
See Sell, Elwood Lester

Sell, Hildegarde Loretta 1906- [HPPN, IPA, PMJ]
American singer
* [The] First Lady of Supper Clubs
* Hildegarde
* [The] Incomparable Hildegarde

Sella, Ernestine E. 20th c. [CCL]
Canadian poet
* Ernestine

Sellar, Robert James Batchen 1893- [WWL]
British author
* Chalfont, Peter

Sellari, Girolamo de' 1501-1556 [WBD]
Italian painter
* Carpi, Girolamo da

Sellassie, Sahle
See Marian, Sahle Sellassie Berhane

Sellecca, Connie
See Sellecchia, Concetta

Sellecchia, Concetta 20th c.
American actress
* Sellecca, Connie

Sellen, Gustav
See Alvensleben, Karl Ludwig Friedrich Wilhelm Von

Sellers, Charles E. 1887-1934 [BEW, F2]
American entertainer
* Mack, Charles

Sellers, Con
See Sellers, Connie Leslie, Jr.

Sellers, Connie Leslie, Jr. 1922- [CA, SFL]
American author
* Adam, Don
* Adams, Rich
* Adonis, Michael
* Arana, Ric
* Bannion, Della
* Bates, Norman
* Bear, Joe
* Campbell, Fred
* Carre, Chuck
* Cellini, Cal
* Connaughton, Sam
* Conners, Selwyn
* Conniston, Sam
* Cotton, Jerri
* Crane, Robert
* Denning, Laurence

Sellers, Connie Leslie, Jr. (cont.)
* DeVries, Con
* Dilli, Rick
* Downs, Bill
* Elliot, C. S.
* Gentry, Arthur
* Hall, Marcia
* Hawk, Jack
* Herman, Louis
* Higgins, Martyn
* Hurst, Brian
* Jacobs, Steven
* Lang, Jim
* Lark, Jody
* Linsley, Ladd. E.
* Madden, Dick
* Menasco, John
* Mitchell, Jack
* Moran, Judy
* Noceni, Erle
* Powers, Dick
* Raintree, Lee
* Roth, Karen
* Roth, Robert
* Sands, Leonard
* Sellers, Con
* Sellers, Mary
* Selwyn, Chuck
* Shannon, Leonard
* Simbeaux, L. L.
* Stanton, Chuck
* Steele, Charles
* Trent, Lawrence
* Trent, Leo
* Tully, Tom
* Ward, Tom

Sellers, Isaiah 1802?-1864 [WBD]
American steamboat pilot and writer
* Twain, Mark

Sellers, Jingle Joints
See Sellers, Ron

Sellers, John 1924- [BWW, EJ]
American singer
* Brother John
* Frank, Johnny

Sellers, Mary
See Sellers, Connie Leslie, Jr.

Sellers, Naomi
See Flack, Naomi John White

Sellers, Oliver 1881-1952 [BE]
American baseball player
* Sellers, Rube

Sellers, Phil 1953-
American basketball player
* [The] Thrill

Sellers, Ron 1947- [FB]
American football player
* Sellers, Jingle Joints
* Sellers, Weasel

Sellers, Rube
See Sellers, Oliver

Sellers, Weasel
See Sellers, Ron

Sellings, Arthur
See Ley, Arthur Gordon

Sellon, Priscilla Lydia 1821-1876
[HPPN]
British religious leader
* [The] Superior of the Society

Sells, Ralph
See Selz, Ralph Jerome Von Braun

Selmair-Selwart, Antonio Franz Thaeus
1896- [BEW]
German actor
* Selwart, Tonio

Selman, Elsie Emily 1919- [IAW]
British author
* Taylor, Selman

Selman, John H. 1839-1896 [HPPN]
American pioneer
* Uncle John

Selmar
See Brinckman, Karl G.

Selmark, George
See Truss, [Leslie] Seldon

Selous, H. C. 19th c. [IP]
British author
* Spen, Kay

Selten, Morton
See Stubbs, Morton Richard

Seltzer, Bromo
See Seltzer, Leo A.

Seltzer, Joseph 1884-1981 [F2]
American actor
* Smith, Joe

Seltzer, Leo A. 20th c. [BBH]
American Roller Derby pioneer
* Seltzer, Bromo

Seltzer, Leon E[ugene] 1918- [CA]
American author
* Leigh, Eugene

Seltzer, Louis B[enson] 1897-1980 [CA]
American author, journalist, editor
* Cleveland, Mr.

Seltzer, Norman Murray 1935- [OP]
American opera singer
* Paige, Norman

Selvaggio, John R. 1937- [ASC]
American musician
* Carlo, Johnny

Selwart, Tonio
See Selmair-Selwart, Antonio Franz
Thaeus

Selway, Captain
See Heath, Neville George Clevely

Selwyn, Chuck
See Sellers, Connie Leslie, Jr.

Selywn, John H.
See Josephs, John

Selz, Jerome Braun von
See Selz, Ralph Jerome Von Braun

Selz, Ralph Jerome Von Braun 1909-
[BLB, HPPN]
American murderer
* Baronovich, Michael
* Fell, Slipton J.
* [The] Laughing Killer of the
  Woodside Glens
* Morgan, Ralph Jerome
* Morgan, Tiny
* Oliver, Charles
* Rose, Upton
* Sells, Ralph
* Selz, Jerome Braun von
* [The] Soldier of Fortune
* Wild, Faran

Selznick, David 1902-1965 [DBQ]
American producer
* Sachs, David

Sem
See Goursat, Georges

Sembach, Johannes
See Semfke, Johannes

Sembrich, Marcella
See Kochanska, Praxede Marcelline

Semenko, Dave 1957- [SMG]
Canadian-born hockey player
* Cement Head
* Semenko, Semenk

Semenko, Semenk
See Semenko, Dave

Semexant
See Rouzier, Maximilien Louis Severin

Semfke, Johannes 1881-1944 [HPPN]
German-American opera singer
* Sembach, Johannes

Semien, Ivory Lee
See Semien, Lee

Semien, Lee 1931- [BWW]
American singer
* King Ivory Lee
* Semien, Ivory Lee

Semien, Sidney 1938- [BWW, NBB]
American singer
* Count Rockin' Sydney
* Rockin' Sydney

Seminola
See Cox-George, Noah Arthur William

[The] Semiramis of the North
See Catherine II

[The] Semiramis of the North
See Christina

[The] Semiramis of the North
See Margaret

[The] Semitic Sacrifice
See Dreyfus, Alfred

Semkiw, Virlyana
See Bishop, Tetiana Kroitor

Semkiw, Virlyana
See Shevchuk, Tetiana

Semler, Johann Salomo 1725-1791
[DNNS, WBD]
German theologian
* [The] Father of German Rationalism

Semmes, Raphael 1809-1877 [DNNS, HPPN, SN]
American naval officer
* Old Beeswax
* Paul Jones of the South

[Il] Semolei
See Franco, Battista

Semon, Julia Melrose 1869-1932
[HPPN]
American dancer and singer
* Melrose, Julia

Semon, Ray
See Beane, Mrs. George A., Jr.

Sempell, Charlotte 1909- [CA]
German-born historian and author
* Klenbort, Charlotte

Sempill, Ernest 20th c. [MBF]
British author
* Coles, Detective Inspector
* Gale, Alan
* Michael, John
* Michael, Paul
* Storm, Michael
* Storm, Rupert

Semple, Dugald 1884-? [LAO]
Scottish author and naturalist
* Wheelhouse

Semple, Gordon
See Neubauer, William Arthur

Semple, Jesse B.
See Hughes, [James] Langston

Semproch, Baby
See Semproch, Roman Anthony

Semproch, Ray
See Semproch, Roman Anthony

Semproch, Roman Anthony 1931- [BE]
American baseball player
* Semproch, Baby
* Semproch, Ray

Sempronicus
See Foe, Daniel

Sempronius
See Wilbraham, Roger

Semyonov, Iron Pants
See Semyonov, Vladimir

Semyonov, Vladimir 20th c.
Russian diplomat
* Semyonov, Iron Pants

Sen, Ela
See Reid, Ela

Sena, Kesavachhandra 19th c. [HPPN]
Hindu author
* [An] Indian Theist

Senac, Felix 1815-1866 [HPPN]
American spy
* [The] Confederate Agent

Senarens, Lu
See Senarens, Luis Philip

Senarens, Luis Philip 1865-1939 [ESF, SF, WGT]
American author
* Clyde, Kit?
* Doughty, Frank?
* Earle, W. J.?
* Garne, Gaston?
* Howard, Capt.?
* [The] Jules Verne of America
* Noname
* Senarens, Lu
* Sparling, Ned?

Senate's Rising Star
See Long, Russell Billiu

[The] Senator
See Greco, Salvatore

[The] Senator
See McMillen, Thomas

[The] Senator
See O'Brien, Michael J.

[The] Senator from Boeing
See Jackson, Henry Martin

[The] Senator from Formosa
See Knowland, William Fife

[The] Senator from Pendergast
See Truman, Harry S.

[A] Senator of Thirty Years
See Benton, Thomas Hart

Senator Sam Ervin
See Ervin, Sam[uel James, Jr.]

Sencourt, Robert [Esmonde]
See George, Robert Esmonde Gordon

Sendak, Maurice 1928- [HPPN]
American book illustrator
* [The] Picasso of Children's Books

Sendall, E. [FFF, PA]
Author
* Caractacus

Sendelbach, J. W. [FFF]
Entertainer
* Shannon, Joseph W.

Sendrey, Alfred
See Szendrei, Aladar

Seneachie
See Maclean, Lachlan

Seneca
See Pasko, W. W.

Seneca
See Webster, Noah

Seneca, Marcus Lucius Annaeus
1st c. BC [HPPN]
Roman rhetorician
* [The] Philosopher
* [The] Rhetorician

[The] Seneca of the East
See Buzurg-Mihir

Senectissimus, Theobaldus, Esq.
See Lovecraft, Howard Phillips

Senectus
See Granger, Gideon

Senefelder, Aloys 1771-1834 [HPPN]
German inventor
* [The] Father of Lithography

Senerchia, Al 1907- [MY]
American jazz musician
* Senner, Al

Senerchia, Emanuel Robert 1931- [BE]
American baseball player
* Senerchia, Sonny

Senerchia, Sonny
See Senerchia, Emanuel Robert

Senesino, Francesco
See Bernardi, Francesco

Senet
See Anderson, James

Senex
See Bateman, Josiah

Senex
See Dix, John Adams

Senex
See Owen, William Charles

Senex
See Pegge, Samuel

Senex
See Reid, Robert

Senex
See Townshend, Horace

Senghor, Leopold Sedar 1906- [IBW]
President of Senegal
* [The] Father of the Constitution

Seninho
See Jardim, Arsenio

Senior
See Penrose, John

[The] Senior Curate of St Luke's, Berwick Street
See Whitehead, Henry

[The] Senior Diplomat of Soul
See Robinson, Ray Charles

Senior, Isabel J[anet] C[ouper] Syme 20th c. [CA]
Scottish-born author
* Pleydell, Susan

[The] Senior Minister of the West Church in Boston
See Lowell, Charles

Senior, Nassau William 1790-1864
[FFF, HPPN, PA]
British author and economist
* [A] Guardian
* [The] Prince of Interviewers
* Spinner, Red
* Uncle Hardy

[A] Senior Physician
See Burder, Thomas Harrison

[A] Senior Resident Member of the University of Oxford
See Golightly, Charles Portales

Senlis, Simon ?-1109 [HN]
Earl of Northampton and Huntingdon
* St. Lis [or Liz]

Sennachie
See Whyte, Donald

Sennep, J.
See Pennes, Jean

Senner, Al
See Senerchia, Al

Sennett, Mack
See Sinnott, Michael

Sennett, Ted
See Sinitsky, Ted

Sennott, George 19th c. [PI]
Irish-born author
* [A] Jacksonian Democrat

[The] Senor
See Lopez, Alfonso Raymond

Senor Wences
See Moreno, Wenceslas

Senorita LBJ
See Johnson, Lynda Bird

Sensenderfer, Count
See Sensenderfer, John Phillips Jenkins

Sensenderfer, John Phillips Jenkins 1847-1903 [BE]
American baseball player
* Sensenderfer, Count
* Sensenderfer, Sen-Sen

Sensenderfer, Sen-Sen
See Sensenderfer, John Phillips Jenkins

Sensitive, Samuel and Testy, Timothy
See Beresford, James

Sentelle, Leopold Theodore 1879-1923 [BE]
American baseball player
* Sentelle, Paul

Sentelle, Paul
See Sentelle, Leopold Theodore

Sentencing Sam Leibowitz
See Leibowitz, Samuel Simon

Senter, Florence H.
See Ellis, Florence Hawley

Sentimental Charley Utter
See Utter, Charles

[The] Sentimental Cynic
See Runyon, [Alfred] Damon

[The] Sentimental Gentleman of Swing
See Dorsey, Thomas A[ndrew] [Tommy]

[A] Sentimental Idler
See Leach, Harry Harwood

[A] Sentimental Philosopher
See Irving, Washington

Sentimientos [Sentiments]
See Nunez, Juan

Sentinel
See Bogart, William Henry

Sentry, John A.
See Budrys, Algirdas Jonas

Seoane, Manny
See Seoane, Manuel Modesto

Seoane, Manuel Modesto 1955- [SMG]
American baseball player
* Seoane, Manny

[The] Seoul Survivor
See Kim, Dae Jung

Sepharial
See Gorn-Old, Walter

Sepharial
See Old, Walter Richard

Sephi-Mirza
See Louis

Sepia
See Fryatt, Fanny

Sepia
See Holmvik, Oyvind

[The] Sepia Mae West
See Cox, Ida

[The] Sepia Mae West
See Fouche, Sam

[The] Sepia Slugger
See Barrow, Joseph Louis

Sepkowski, Theodore Walter [Ted]
See Sczepkowski, Theodore Walter

Sepperle
See Reynolds, Margaret Gertrude

Septama, Aladra
See Reeves, Justin

September, Anthony
See Mammarella, Anthony [Tony]

[A] Septuagenarian
See Cust, Emma Sophia [Edgecombe]

Sequel, Rodolfo 1954?- [TI 6-27-83]
Chilean labor leader
* [The] Chilean Lech Walesa

Sequoia, Anna
See Schneider, Anna

Sequoya [or Sequoyah] 1770?-1843 [WBD]
American Indian scholar
* Guess, George

Serafian, Michael
See Martin, Malachi

Serafimovich, Alexander
See Popov, Alexander Serafimovich

Serafin, Joseph Stanley 1895-1947 [BE]
American baseball player
* Cobb, Joseph Stanley [Joe]

Serafina Bacigalupi, Maria De La Concepcion Conchita 1861?-1940 [BEW]
Actress
* Conchita

Serafinowicz, Leszek 1899- [CD]
Polish poet and author
* Lechon, Jan

Seranus
See Harrison, Susie Frances [Riley]

[The] Seraphic Doctor
See Di Fidanza, Giovanni

[The] Seraphic Saint
See Bernardone, Giovanni Francesco

Seraphicus, Doctor
See Di Fidanza, Giovanni

Seraphina
See Feliciani, Lorenza

Seraphine de Senlis
See Louis, Seraphine

Serato, Massimo 20th c. [WF]
Italian actor
* Barracuda, John

Sere, Octave
See Poueigh, Jean [Marie-Octave-Geraud]

Serebriakoff, Victor 1912- [IAW]
British author
* Serry, Victor

Serebroff, Munia 1903- [BEW]
Russian-born actor, singer, director
* Seroff, Muni

[El] Sereno
See Sarfatti, Margherita

Seretean, Bud
See Seretean, M. B.

Seretean, M. B. [SMG]
American basketball manager
* Seretean, Bud

Sergardi, Ludovico 1660-1726 [PA]
Author
* Sectanus, Quintus

Sergeant B
See Butler, Robert

Sergeant, Emily Frances Adeline 1851-1904 [FFF]
British author and poet
* Adeline

Sergeyev, Lily 1918-
German intelligence agent
* Treasure [code name used during World War II]

Serghi, Cella
See Serghi Bogdan, Cella

Serghi Bogdan, Cella 1907- [IAW]
Rumanian author
* Serghi, Cella

Sergi, Arturo
See Kagan, Arthur

Sergiev, Ioann 1821-1908 [WBD]
Russian clergyman
* John of Kronshtadt [or Cronstadt]

Sergius I 635?-701 [NPS]
Pope
* Os Porci

Sergius II
See Hogsmouth, Peter

Sergius IV
See Peter

[The] Serial King
See Alyn, Kirk

[The] Serial Queen
See Roland, Ruth

[The] Serial Queen
See Schultz, Louise

Seriel, Jerome
See Vallee, Jacques

[A] Serious Engineer
See Temple, Anthony

[A] Serious Inquirer
See Norton, [Rev.] Jacob

Serjeant, Richard
See Van Essen, William

Serjeantson, Kate
See Morris, Kate

Serle, Ambrose 1742-1812 [HPPN]
British author
* [A] Christian Lately Departed

Serner, Martin G[unnar] 1886-1947
[WGT]
Swedish author
* Heller, Frank

Sernicoli, Davide
See Trent, Ann

Seroff, Muni
See Serebroff, Munia

Serov, Ivan A. 1908- [EE]
Russian secret police chief
* [The] Butcher
* Ivan the Terrible

[Le] Serpent
See Freron, Elie-Catherine

[The] Serpent of Old Nile
See Cleopatra

[The] Serpent of the Nile
See Cleopatra

Serpentinus
See Banck, Karl

Serpieres
See Guillevic, Eugene

Serra, Diana
See Cary, Peggy-Jean Montgomery

Serra, Junipero
See Serra, Miguel Jose

Serra, Miguel Jose 1713-1784 [WBD]
Spanish missionary in America
* Serra, Junipero

**Serranito [Little Fellow from the
Mountain]**
See Gonzalez y Delgado, Hilario

Serrano, Carlos 20th c. [GS]
Mexican bullfighter
* [El] Voluntario [The Ready One]

Serranus
See De Serres, Jean

Serranus
See Lambert, Francois

Serrell, Bonnie
See Serrell, William

Serrell, William 20th c. [OBW]
American baseball player
* Serrell, Bonnie

Serres, Olivia Wilmot 1772-1834
[HPPN]
British impostor
* Princess Olive

Serrifile, F. O. O.
See Holmes, William Kersley

Serry, Victor
See Serebriakoff, Victor

Sert, Misia
See Godebska, Marie Sophie Olga
Zenaide

Servacis
See Granier de Cassagnac, Paul de

Servadio, Gaia [Cecilia Gemmalina]
1928- [WD]
British author
* Mostyn-Owen, Gaia

Servant Jacob
See Chenault, Marcus Wayne

[The] Servant of India
See Joshi, Narayan M.

[The] Servant of Peace
See Hammarskjold, Dag Hjalmar Carl
Agne

**[The] Servant of the Lord O. W. L.
[Oh Wonderful Love]**
See Graham, James

[The] Servant of the People
See Eastman, Joseph Bartlett

[The] Servant of the Servants of God
See Gregory I

Servetus, Michael, M.D.
See Blair, Patrick

Service, Dr.
See Isendahl, Walther

Service, R. W.
See Service, Robert William

Service, Robert William 1876-1958 [LC,
UH]
British-born poet
* [The] Canadian Kipling
* [The] Kipling of Canada
* Service, R. W.

[The] Serving Knight
See McConnell, John Preston

Servita
See Sarpi, Pietro

Servius Tullius 6th c. BC [HN]
Legendary King of Rome
* [The] Commons' King

Servus Servorum Dei
See Gregory I

Serwischer, Kurt 1913-1979 [CA, TR]
Austrian actor
* Kasznar, Kurt S.

Sesan, Karolina Vera 1908- [IWM]
*Russian-born opera singer and
musicologist*
* Mora, Vera

Sesit, Mike
See Sesit, Myron F.

Sesit, Myron F. 20th c. [HPPN]
American football player
* Sesit, Mike

Sesostris
See Louis XIV

Sessi, Mathilde
See Erlanger, Baroness

Sessi, Walter Anthony 1918- [BE]
American baseball player
* Sessi, Watsie

Sessi, Watsie
See Sessi, Walter Anthony

Setanta ?-2? [HPPN]
Irish warrior
* [The] Achilles of the Gael
* Cuchulain
* Cullin, Cu

Setaro, Peter D. 1924- [ASC]
American composer
* Baxter, Larry

Sete, Bola
See De Andrada, Djalma

Seth, Andrew 1856-1931 [WBD]
Scottish philosopher
* Pringle-Pattison, Andrew

Seth, Ronald [Sydney] 1911- [CA]
British-born author
* Chartham, Robert

Seth, Will
See Bullock, William

Seth-Smith, Elsie K.
See Murrell, Elsie Kathleen Seth-Smith

Seth-Smith, Leslie James 1923- [AW]
British author
* Brabazon, James

Sethi, Denis
See Sethi, Narendra Kumar

Sethi, Narendra Kumar 1935- [IAW]
Indian-born author
* Sethi, Denis

Sethunsa, Khotso 1883- [IBW]
South African medical practitioner
* [The] Great One

Setis, Keal
See Stiles, Ezra

Seton, Alexander ?-1604? [HPPN]
Scottish alchemist
* [The] Cosmopolite

Seton, [Sir] Alexander [Sixth Earl of Eglinton] 1588-1661 [HPPN]
Scottish clergyman
* Greysteel
* Montgomerie, Alexander

Seton, Anya
See Chase, Anya Seton

Seton, Ernest Thompson
See Thompson, Ernest Evan Seton

Seton, Graham
See Hutchison, Graham Seton

Seton, William, Jr. 18th c. [HPPN]
Scottish author
* [A] Member of Parliament

Seton-Watson, Robert William 1879-1951
[BI, LAO]
British author
* Viator, Scotus

Setoun, Gabriel
See Hepburn, Thomas Nicoll

Setterburg, Gabriel 20th c. [SFP]
Author
* Crane, Eric

Settle, Edith
See Andrews, William Linton

Settle, Elkanah 1648-1724 [NPS, PA, SN]
British playwright and poet
* [The] City Laureate
* Codrus
* Doeg

Settle, Joe
See Settle, Josiah T.

Settle, Josiah T. 1850-? [IBW]
American attorney and government official
* Settle, Joe

Settlemire, Lefty
See Settlemire [Edgar] Merle

Settlemire [Edgar] Merle 1903- [BE]
American baseball player
* Settlemire, Lefty

[A] Settler, at Stratford
See Linton, John James Edmonstoune

Seume, Johann Gottfried 1763-1810
[SN]
German author and poet
* [Der] Spaziergaenger nach Syrakus

Seuphor, Michel
See Arp, Jean

Seure, Cecile Emilie 1874-1966 [SC]
French actress
* Sorel, Cecile

Seuss, Dr.
See Geisel, Theodor Seuss

Seven Beauties
See Frafuso, Pasqualino

[The] Seven Days' King
See Aniello, Tommaso

[The] Seven Foot Cowboy
See Harris, Homer William

Seven Mule Barnum
See Barnum, William Henry

[The] Seven Year Old Huckster
See Reese, Mason

Sevenoaks
See Edwards, Alfred S.

17F FrenchW
See Fleming, Ian [Lancaster]

[The] 17th Century Florence Nightingale
See Alkin, Elizabeth

Seventh Cat
See Fei, Tong

Seventy Four, Lord
See Lowther, [Sir] James

72 Cannon Chang
See Chang Chung-Ch'ang

Severance, Felix
See Laumer, March

[The] Severe
See Pedro I

Severin, Christian 1562-1647 [WBD]
Danish astronomer
* Longomontanus

Severin, Justus
See Muetzelburg, Adolf

Severino, Francisco Lago 1875-1974
[HPPN]
Spanish actor
* Salas, Paco

Severinsen, Carl 1927- [ASC, BI, DAM, HPPN]
American jazz musician
* Severinsen, Doc
* Severinsen, Little Doc
* [The] World's Greatest Trumpet Player

Severinsen, Doc
See Severinsen, Carl

Severinsen, Little Doc
See Severinsen, Carl

Severinus de Monzambano
See Pufendorf, Samuel von

Severn, David
See Unwin, David S[torr]

Severne, Christine
See Boulton, Anne

Severs, Jerome
See Wooley, John [Steven]

Severson, Fred 20th c. [BBH, CSH]
Canadian lacrosse player
* Severson, Whitey

Severson, Jeff 20th c.
American football player
* Severson, Peach

Severson, Peach
See Severson, Jeff

Severson, Whitey
See Severson, Fred

Severud, Lloyd 1918- [BBH]
American skier and coach
* Severud, Snoball

Severud, Snoball
See Severud, Lloyd

Severyanin, Igor
See Lotarev, Igor Vasilyevich

Sevier, Catherine Sherrill 1754?-1836
[HPPN]
American pioneer
* Bonny Kate

Sevilla, Melba
See Hoerner, Melba

Seville, David
See Bagdasarian, Ross

Sewall, Arthur 1835-1900 [HPPN]
American politician, shipbuilder, owner
* America's Last Sailing Ship Builder

Sewall, Bud
See Sewall, Grant

Sewall, [Rev.] Edmund Quincy ?-1866
[HPPN]
American clergyman
* E. Q. S.

Sewall, Grant ?-1978 [FIR]
Actor
* Sewall, Bud

Sewall, Henry Devereux 19th c.
[HPPN]
American author
* [An] Unitarian of New York

Sewall, Jonathan 1728-1796 [HPPN]
American attorney and author
* Coverley, [Sir] Roger de

Sewall, Joseph 1688-1769 [HPPN]
American clergyman
* [The] Weeping Prophet

Sewall, Samuel 1652-1730 [SN]
American jurist
* [A] Puritan Pepys

Sewall, Samuel Edmund 19th c. [HPPN]
American attorney
* Z.

Seward, Alexander T. [Alec] 1902-1972
[BWW]
American singer
* Blues Boy
* Blues King
* Georgia Slim
* Guitar Slim
* Seward, Slim

Seward, Anna 1747-1809 [DEL, HPPN]
British poet
* Benvolio
* Seward, Nancy
* [The] Swan of Lichfield

Seward, Calgary Red
See Seward, Roy

Seward, Edward William
See Sourhardt, Edward William

Seward, George F. 19th c. [HPPN]
American diplomat and author
* [The] Consul General in China

Seward, John
See Stephens, Francis George

Seward, Nancy
See Seward, Anna

Seward, Roy 20th c. [GW]
Rodeo performer
* Seward, Calgary Red

Seward, Slim
See Seward, Alexander T. [Alec]

Seward, W.
See Maginn, William

Seward, William Henry 1801-1872
[DEP, FFF]
American statesman
* [The] Sage of Auburn

Seward, William W[ard], Jr. 1913-
[CA]
American author
* Rives, Leigh

Sewart, Alan 1928- [CA]
British author
* Nash, Padder
* Well, Alan Stewart

Sewell, Arthur
See Whitson, John Harvey

Sewell, Brocard 1912- [CA]
British author and clergyman
* Jerome, Joseph

Sewell, Elizabeth Missing 1815-? [DEL]
British author
* [A] Lady

Sewell, Hetty Jane ?-1961 [HPPN]
American actress and author
* Dunaway, Hetty Jane

Sewell, James Luther 1901- [BE]
American baseball manager
* Sewell, Luke

Sewell, Luke
See Sewell, James Luther

Sewell, M.
See Sobell, Morton

Sewell, Rip
See Sewell, Truett Banks

Sewell, Truett Banks 1908- [BE, PB]
American baseball player
* Sewell, Rip

Sewgolum, Papwa
See Sewgolum, Susunker

Sewgolum, Susunker 1929?-1978 [EG]
South African golfer
* Sewgolum, Papwa

[The] Sex Beast
See Rees, Melvin

Sex Collector
See Kinsey, Alfred Charles

[A] Sexagenarian
See Beloe, William

[A] Sexagenarian
See Haight, Canniff

Sexby, Edward
See Quincy, Josiah

Sexten
See Augustine, Richard

Sexton, Annie
See Fitzachary, John Christopher

Sexton of the Old School
See Sargent, Lucius Manlius

Sexton, Virginia Staudt 1916- [CA]
American psychologist and author
* Staudt, Virginia

Sexy Rexy
See Clifton, Rex Allen

Sexy Rexy
See Harrison, Reginald Carey

Seybold, Ralph Orlando 1870-1921 [AS,
BE, PB]
American baseball player
* Seybold, Socks

Seybold, Socks
See Seybold, Ralph Orlando

Seydel, Mildred [Wooley] 20th c. [CA]
American publisher and author
* Seydell, Mildred

Seydell, Mildred
See Seydel, Mildred [Wooley]

Seyler, Athene
See Hannen, Athene

Seymour, A. J.
See Seymour, Arthur James

Seymour, Alan
See Wright, Sydney Fowler

Seymour, Alice [FFF]
Entertainer
* Hensel, Octavia

Seymour, Almira 19th c. [HPPN]
American poet and author
* One Who Has Some There

Seymour, Anne
See Eckert, Anne Seymour

Seymour, Arthur James 1914- [CW]
Guyanese author, poet, critic
* Seymour, A. J.

Seymour, Caroline [FFF]
Writer
* Spencer, Edward

Seymour, Charles [Sixth Duke of
Somerset] 1662-1748 [DNNS, HN,
HPPN, SN]
British statesman
* [The] Proud Duke of Somerset

Seymour, Cy
See Seymour, James Bentley

Seymour, Dorothy Jane Z[ander] 1928-
[CA]
American author
* Johnson, Eleanor

Seymour, Edward 1506?-1552 [HN, SN,
WBD]
First Duke of Somerset
* [The] Good Duke
* [The] Protector

Seymour, [Sir] Edward 1633-1708 [SN]
British politician
* Amiel

Seymour, Edward 1837-1877 [PA]
Author
* E. S.

Seymour, Edward
See Hiscocks, Richard

Seymour, Frederick H[enri] 1850-1913
[WGT]
American author
* Gilhooley, Lord

Seymour, George
See Erby, John J.

Seymour, Gordon
See Waldstein, Charles

Seymour, Henry
See Hartmann, Helmut Henry

Seymour, James
See Cunningham, James

Seymour, James Bentley 1872-1919
[AS, BE, DGS]
American baseball player
* Seymour, Cy

Seymour, Jane
See Fitzpatrick, Marjorie Seymour

Seymour, Jane
See Frankenberg, Joyce Penelope
Wilhimena

Seymour, John
See Turbayne, John

Seymour, Laura
See Samo, Mrs.

Seymour, Marjorie F. 20th c. [WWL]
British author
* Cynthia
* Plane, Anne

Seymour, Mary Alice [Ives] 19th c.
[DNA]
American author
* Hensel, Octavia

Seymour, Mary H. 1840-1881 [PA]
Author
* M. H. S.

Seymour, Miranda
See Sinclair, Miranda

Seymour, Mrs. William [FFF]
Entertainer
* Davenport, May

Seymour, Robert 1800?-1836 [HPPN]
British caricaturist and book illustrator
* [The] Modern Hogarth
* One of the Old School

Seymour, Robert, of the Inner Temple
See Mottley, John

Seymour, Stephen Andrew
See Cohen, Seymour

Seymour, Thomas 1896- [FC]
British director
* Forde, Walter

Seymour, Val
See Sassoon, [Sir] Victor

Seymour, Whitney North 1923- [HPPN]
American attorney
* [The] Guardian of the Government

Seymour, William Napier 1914- [CA]
British author
* Napier, William

Seymour-Conway, Francis Charles
1777-1842 [NPS]
Third Marquis of Hertford
* Red Herrings

Seymoure, Schnitz
See Liebstadter, Anschel B.

Seyn, Nikkul
See Nicholson, John

Seyssel, Claude de 1450-1520 [HN, RH]
French historian
* [The] Father of Modern French
  Literature

Seyton, Marion
See Saxon, Gladys Relyea

Sfondrati, Niccolo 1535-1591 [CAL]
Pope
* Gregory XIV

Sforza
See Attendolo, Giacomuzo d'

Sforza, James 1369-1424 [FFF, SN]
Italian army officer
* [The] Great

Sforza, Lodovico [or Ludovico]
1451-1510? [HN, NPS, SN]
Duke of Milan
* [The] Moor
* [IL] Moro

Sgarlato, Nico 1944- [IAW]
Italian author
* Castellano, Franco

Sgroi, Alfonso 20th c. [BLB]
American underworld figure
* [The] Butch

Shabazz, El-Hajj Malik el-
See Little, Malcolm

Shabba Doo
See Quinones, Adolfo

Shackelford, Lynn 1947- [SMG]
American sportscaster
* Shackelford, Shack

Shackelford, Shack
See Shackelford, Lynn

Shacket, Sheldon R[ubin] 1941- [CA]
American author
* Albran, Kehlog [joint pseudonym with
  Martin A. Cohen]

Shackleton, Abraham 1753-1818 [PI]
Irish poet and translator
* A. S.

Shackleton, C. C.
See Aldiss, Brian W[ilson]

Shackleton, Doris [Cavell] 1918- [CA]
Canadian author
* French, Doris

Shackleton, Elizabeth 18th c. [PI]
Irish poet
* E. S., Miss

Shackleton, [Sir] Ernest Henry
1874-1922 [HPPN]
British explorer
* [The] Incredible Voyager

Shackleton-Bailey, D[avid] R[oy]
See Bailey, D[avid] R[oy] Shackleton

Shad, Bob 20th c. [NBB]
American songwriter
* Ellen, Robert

Shade, Ellen [PA]
Author
* Ellwood, Ella

[The] Shade of Sir Robert Peel
See Gale, [Rev.] Henry

Shade, R. D. B. M. 1938- [EG]
Golfer
* Shade, Ronnie

Shade, Ronnie
See Shade, R. D. B. M.

Shade, Will 1898-1966 [BWW, EJ]
American jazz musician
* Brimmer, Son

Shadi, Dorothy Clotelle Clarke 1908-
[CA, WD]
American author, critic, translator
* Clarke, Dorothy Clotelle

[The] Shadow
See Ashe, Arthur

[The] Shadow
See Shed, Nevil

Shadow in the Sun
See Elizabeth I

[The] Shadow In the White House
See Pierce, Jane Means Appleton

Shadow, John
See Byrom, John

[El] Shadow Negro
See Parker, Nathaniel

[The] Shadow Shogun
See Tanaka, Kakuei

Shadow, Slim
See Rogers, Samuel Shepard

[The] Shadower
See Apollodorus

Shadrin, Nicholas
See Artamonov, Nikolai

Shadwell, Thomas 1640-1692 [DEA,
NPS, SN]
British author, playwright, poet
* MacFlecknoe
* Og
* Our Young Ascantus
* T. S.
* Thou Great Prophet of Tautology
* Tom the First
* [The] True Blue Protestant Poet

Shady Bill Leith
See Leith, William [Bill]

Shafer, Arthur Joseph 1889-1962 [BE]
American baseball player
* Shafer, Tillie

Shafer, Filomina
See Shafer, Mina

Shafer, Mina 1872-? [NAA]
American poet and writer
* Shafer, Filomina

Shafer, Phil 20th c.
Auto racer
* [The] Texas Terror

Shafer, Tillie
See Shafer, Arthur Joseph

Shaff, Monroe 20th c. [BEW]
American producer and stage manager
* Shaff, Monty

Shaff, Monty
See Shaff, Monroe

Shaffer, Anthony [Joshua] 1926- [CC,
EMD, WD]
British playwright and author
* Anthony, Peter [joint pseudonym with
  Peter (Levin) Shaffer]

Shaffer, George 1852-? [BE]
American baseball player
* Shaffer, Orator

Shaffer, Orator
See Shaffer, George

Shaffer, Peter [Levin] 1926- [CA, CC, EMD]
British playwright and author
* Anthony, Peter [joint pseudonym with Anthony (Joshua) Shaffer]

Shaftel, Albert S. 1912- [HPPN]
American army officer
* [The] Brooklyn Babbitt
* [The] Foist Lieutenant

Shaftesbury, Seventh Earl of
See Cooper, Anthony Ashley

Shaftsbury, Edmund
See Edgerly, Webster

Shaginyan, Marietta Sergeyevna 1888-1982 [CA]
Russian author and poet
* Dollar, Jimmy

Shah, Amina 1918- [CA]
Scottish-born author
* Rutt, M. E.

Shah Jehan
See Khorrum [or Khurram]

[The] Shah of Baabda
See Gemayel, Amin

Shahani, Ranjee 1904-1968 [CA]
Pakistani-born author
* Ranjee

Shahcolen, a Hindu Philosopher Residing in Philadelphia
See Knapp, Samuel Lorenzo

Shahn, Ben[jamin] 1898-1969 [HPPN]
Russian-born American painter and graphic artist
* [The] American Hogarth
* Ghetto Graduate
* Harper, Mr.
* Mellowed Militant
* Painter of Protest

Shahn, Bernarda Bryson
See Bryson, Bernarda

Shaiffer, Howard Charles 1918-1967 [SC]
American actor
* Shaiffer, Tiny

Shaiffer, Tiny
See Shaiffer, Howard Charles

Shainmark, Eliezer L. 1900-1976 [CA]
Polish-born American journalist
* Shainmark, Lou

Shainmark, Lou
See Shainmark, Eliezer L.

Shake-Scene
See Shakespeare, William

Shaker
See Adams, F. W.

Shaker
See Adams, Frederick W.

[The] Shakespeare Clown
See Rice, Daniel

Shakespeare de la Hollande
See Van den Vondel, Joost

Shakespeare in Petticoats
See Baillie, Joanna

[The] Shakespeare of Divines
See Taylor, Jeremy

[The] Shakespeare of Eloquence
See Riqueti, Honore Gabriel Victor

[The] Shakespeare of France
See Corneille, Pierre

[The] Shakespeare of Germany
See Grossmann, Gustavus Frederick William

[The] Shakespeare of Germany
See Kotzebue, August Friedrich Ferdinand von

[The] Shakespeare of Germany
See Schiller, Johann Christoph Friedrich von

[The] Shakespeare of Harmony
See Wagner, [Wilhelm] Richard

[The] Shakespeare of India
See Kalidasa

[The] Shakespeare of Japan
See Chikamatsu Monzaemon

[The] Shakespeare of Novelists
See Fielding, Henry

[The] Shakespeare of Painting
See Rosa, Salvator

[The] Shakespeare of Prose
See Austen, Jane

[The] Shakespeare of Prose Fiction
See Richardson, Samuel

[The] Shakespeare of Romance Writers
See Radcliffe, Anne Ward

[The] Shakespeare of Science Fiction
See Wells, Herbert George

[The] Shakespeare of Sweden
See Strindberg, [Johan] August

[The] Shakespeare of the Boulevards
See Pixerecourt, Rene Charles Guilbert de

Shakespeare, William 1564-1616 [DEP, FFF, HPPN, NPS, SN]
British playwright and poet
* Aetion
* [The] Bard of all Time
* [The] Bard of Avon
* [The] Divine
* Doron
* Drusus
* [The] English Terence
* Fancy's Child
* [The] Glory of the English Stage
* [The] Glory of the Human Intellect

Shakespeare, William (cont.)
* [The] God of Our Idolatry
* Great Heir of Fame
* [The] Homer of Dramatic Poets
* Honie-Tongued
* [The] Horace of Our Dramatic Poets
* [The] Immortal Bard
* [The] Incomparable
* Johannes fac Totum [Jack of All Trades]
* Laberius Crispinus, Rufus
* [The] Lord of the British Pandemonium
* Malevole
* [The] Matchless
* [A] Mimicke
* [The] Mirror Upholder of His Age
* Mullidor
* Our Will
* Planet
* Pleasant Willy
* Poor Poet-Ape
* Posthaste?
* [The] Protagonist
* Rufus
* Shake-Scene
* [The] Swan of Avon
* [The] Sweet Swan of Avon
* That Drunken Fool
* That Nimble Mercury
* [An] Upstart Crow
* W. H.
* [The] Young Apollo

Shakespeare, William V. 1912-1974 [FB]
American football player
* [The] Bard of Staten Island

[A] Shakespeare Without Genius
See Hardi, Alexandre

Shakespeare's Critic
See Rymer, Thomas

Shakespeare's Predecessor
See Greene, Robert

[The] Shakesperian Scholar
See White, Richard Grant

Shakey Jake
See Harris, James D. [Jimmie]

Shakur, Assata
See Chesimard, Joanne

Shakur, Zayd Malik
See Costan, James

Shaler, Bessie ?-1965 [HPPN]
American actress and singer
* Brice, Elizabeth

Shalhoub, Michel 1932- [BDF, FC, WEF]
Egyptian-born actor
* Sharif, Omar

Shallix, August
See Schallick, August

Shallix, Gus
See Schallick, August

Shallow, Robert
See Atkinson, Frank

Shalmaneser II [WBD]
King of Assyria
* Shulmanuasharid

Shalofsky, Henry 1926- [EJ]
British jazz musician
* Shaw, Hank

Shalom, Shin 1905- [BI]
Israeli poet and author
* Shapira, Shalom Yosef

Shalong, K.
See Earley, Karen

Sham Hero
See Harrison, William Henry

Sham, Sir
See Dawkins, Darryl

Shambles, Peter
See Stanhope, William [Second Earl of Harrington]

Shambrick, Otto H. 1864-1927 [BE]
American baseball player
* Shomberg, Otto H.

Shambrook, Rona 20th c. [AW]
British author and journalist
* Randall, Rona

Shamgar
See Shamir, Moshe

Shamir, Moshe 1921- [IAW]
Israeli author
* Keller, Asaph
* Offerre, M.
* Shamgar

Shamir, Yitzhak
See Yezernitzky [or Jazernicki], Yitzhak

Shamlu, Ahmad 1925- [CLC]
Iranian poet, critic, author
* Bamdad, A.
* Sobh, A.

Shamrock
See Downey, Joseph

Shamrock
See Walsh, John

Shamrock
See Williams, R. D.

Shamrock
See Williams, Richard Dalton

[The] Shamrock Kid
See Mitchell, Clarence M., Jr.

Shamus
See O'Brien, James Nagle

Shan, Yeh
See Wang, Ching Hsien

Shand, Captain
See Floyd, Gilbert

Shandley, Sallie
See Stivers, Mrs. J.

Shandoff, Zachari
See Zhandov, Zahari

Shandon
See Lonergan, Michael

Shandon, Captain
See Cheltnam, C. Smith

Shandonian
See O'Reilly, [Sister] Amadeus

Shands, H. G. 20th c. [BBH]
American basketball coach
* Shands, Pete

Shands, Pete
See Shands, H. G.

Shane, John
See Durst, Paul

Shane, Mae Worden 1871-1924 [HPPN]
American actress
* Worden, Mae

Shane, Mark
See Norwood, Victor G[eorge] C[harles]

Shane, Nevis
See Shearer, Sonia M.

Shane, Peggy
See Boyd, [Margaret] Woodward [Smith]

Shane, Rhondo
See Norwood, Victor G[eorge] C[harles]

Shane, Susannah
See Ashbrook, Harriette [Cora]

Shaner, Skinny
See Shaner, Walter Dedaker [Wally]

Shaner, Walter Dedaker [Wally] 1900- [BE]
American baseball player
* Shaner, Skinny

Shange, Ntozake
See Williams, Paulette

Shanghai Bill Hickok
See Hickok, James Butler

[The] Shanghai Chicken
See Devine, John

Shanghai Larry Sullivan
See Sullivan, Larry M.

Shank, Bud
See Shank, Clifford Everett, Jr.

Shank, Clifford Everett, Jr. 1926- [ASC, EJ, PMJ]
American jazz musician
* Shank, Bud

Shank, Cowboy Reuben
See Shank, Reuben

Shank, Reuben 20th c.
American boxer
* Shank, Cowboy Reuben

Shank, Samuel Lewis 1872-1927 [HPPN]
American politician
* [The] Auctioneer Mayor
* [The] Indianapolis Potato Mayor
* [The] Potato Mayor

Shanklin, Ronnie Eugene 1948- [SMG]
American football player
* Shanklin, Shank

Shanklin, Shank
See Shanklin, Ronnie Eugene

Shanks, Hank
See Shanks, Howard Samuel

Shanks, Howard Samuel 1890-1941 [AS, BE, PB]
American baseball player
* Shanks, Hank

Shanley, Doc
See Shanley, Henry Roat

Shanley, Henry Roat 1889-1934 [BE]
American baseball player
* Shanley, Doc

Shann, B. V. 20th c. [CAP]
Author
* Bevis, James [joint pseudonym with Marten Cumberland]

Shann, Renee 1907?-1979 [CA]
British author
* Gaye, Carol

Shannon, A. Donnelly
See Aitken, A. Donnelly

Shannon, Carl
See Hogue, Wilbur Owings

Shannon, Del
See Westover, Charles

Shannon, Dell
See Linington, Elizabeth

Shannon, Edward N. 1795?-1860 [PI]
Irish poet
* Volpi, Odoardo

Shannon, Elizabeth S. 1914-1959 [SC]
American actress
* Sundmark, Betty

Shannon, Ethel
See Jackson, Ethel Shannon

Shannon, Frank
See Prosperi, Francesco

Shannon, Frank
See Shine, Dennis Francis Joseph

Shannon, Frank E. 20th c. [BE]
American baseball player
* Shannon, Tod

Shannon, Fred
See Ruben, William S.

Shannon, Joseph W.
See Sendelbach, J. W.

Shannon, Leonard
See Sellers, Connie Leslie, Jr.

Shannon, Lori
See McClean, Don

Shannon, Lytle
See Shannon, Mary Jane

Shannon, M.
See Geddie, John

Shannon, Mary Jane ?-1964 [CCL]
Canadian author
* Shannon, Lytle

Shannon, Maurice Joseph 1895-1970 [BE]
American baseball player
* Shannon, Red

Shannon, Moonman
See Shannon, Thomas Michael [Mike]

Shannon, Peggy
See Sammon, Winona

Shannon, Red
See Shannon, Maurice Joseph

Shannon, Robert
See Wieder, Robert S[hannon]

Shannon, Spike
See Shannon, William Porter

Shannon, Terry
See Mercer, Jessie

Shannon, Thomas Michael [Mike] 1939- [BE, PB]
American baseball player
* Shannon, Moonman

Shannon, Tod
See Shannon, Frank E.

Shannon, William Porter 1878-1940 [BE]
American baseball player
* Shannon, Spike

Shantry, Brian Keith 1955- [DC]
British cricketer
* Shantry, Shants

Shantry, Shants
See Shantry, Brian Keith

Shantz, Billy
See Shantz, Wilmer Ebert

Shantz, Wilmer Ebert 1927- [BE]
American baseball player
* Shantz, Billy

Shanwa
See Haarer, Alec Ernest

Shapcott, Reuben
See White, William Hale

Shape
See Reeves, Stephen [Steve]

Shapira, Shalom Yosef
See Shalom, Shin

Shapiro, David 1934- [JF]
American comedian
* Frye, David

Shapiro, Dolph
See Sharp, Dolph

Shapiro, Gurrah
See Shapiro, Jacob

Shapiro, Jacob 20th c. [BLB, PHM]
American underworld figure
* Shapiro, Gurrah

Shapiro, Jane P.
See Zacek, Jane Shapiro

Shapiro, Max 1911?-1981
American editor, author, publisher
* Stuart, Monroe

Shapiro, Raphael
See Viscusi, Raphael

Shapiro, Sammy 1910-1975 [SC]
American actor, bandleader, musician
* Spear, Sammy

Shapiro, Samuel 1927- [CA]
American historian and author
* Falcon, Richard

Shapoff, S. R. 1918- [BI, EJS]
American horse trainer
* Shapoff, Skippy

Shapoff, Sherrill W. 1921-1960 [EJS]
American horse trainer
* Shapoff, Skeeter

Shapoff, Skeeter
See Shapoff, Sherrill W.

Shapoff, Skippy
See Shapoff, S. R.

Shappiro, Budd 20th c. [CAP]
American author
* Arthur, Budd

Shappiro, Herbert [Arthur] 1898?-1975 [BI, CAP]
American author, playwright, journalist
* Arthur, Burt
* Arthur, Herbert
* Herbert, Arthur

Shapur II [or Sapor] 309-379 [FFF, HN, WBD]
Persian king
* [The] Great
* [The] Shoulder Breaker
* Zoolactaf [or Dsulaktaf]

Sharat Chandra, Gubbi Shankara Chetty 1938- [CA]
Indian-born poet
* Parker, Jean

Shard, Diana
See Stearns, Peter N.

Share, James M. 1822-? [HPPN]
Irish poet
* Delaval, Barclay

[A] Shareholder
See Booth, Henry

Shareowner, Mr.
See Funston, George Keith

Sharett, Moshe
See Shertok, Moshe

Sharif, Omar
See Shalhoub, Michel

[The] Shark
See Cambronne, Luckner

Shark, Captain
See Fournier-Aubry, Fernand

Shark, Gill
See Gillese, John Patrick

[The] Shark of the Exchange
See Fordyce, Alexander

Sharkey, Jack
See Cervati, Giovanni

Sharkey, Jack
See Cukoschay [or Zukauskas], Joseph Paul

Sharkey, John Michael 1931- [CA]
American author and playwright
* Abbot, Rick
* Johnson, Mike

Sharkey, Little Jackie
See Cervati, Giovanni

Sharkey, Sailor Tom
See Sharkey, Thomas Joseph

Sharkey, Thomas Joseph 1873-1953 [BI, SC]
Irish-born boxer and actor
* Sharkey, Sailor Tom

Sharlach, Marie 1881-1938 [BEW]
Russian-born theatrical performer
* Dainton, Marie

Sharlie
See Hall, [Robert] Cliff[ord]

Sharman, Maisie
See Bolton, Maisie Sharman

Sharman, Miriam
See Bolton, Maisie Sharman

Sharon, Ariel 1928?-
Israeli army officer and government official
* [The] Bulldozer
* Sharon, Arik

Sharon, Arik
See Sharon, Ariel

Sharon, Donna Haye
See Scharlemann, Dorothy Hoyer

Sharon, Grandma
See Sharon, Mary Bruce

Sharon, Mary Bruce 1878?-1961 [HPPN]
American painter
* Sharon, Grandma

Sharon, Muriel
See Schochen, Muriel Betty

Sharon, Rose
See Grossman, Josephine Judith

Sharon, William [Bill] 1821-1885 [HPPN]
American politician and financier
* [The] King of the Comstock
* [The] Richest Man in San Francisco

Sharookman, Bozo
See Sharookman, Ed

Sharookman, Ed 20th c.
American football player
* Sharookman, Bozo

Sharp, Becky
See Bowen, Katherine Morrison Norwood [Kay]

Sharp, Blunt
See Sharp, George

Sharp, Conversation
See Sharp, Richard

Sharp, Dee Dee
See LaRue, Dione

Sharp, Dolph 1914- [CA]
American writer
* Shapiro, Dolph

Sharp, George 1950- [DC]
British cricketer
* Sharp, Blunt
* Sharp, Sharpie

Sharp, Giles
See Collins, Joseph

Sharp, Granville 1735-1813 [HPPN]
British philanthropist, reformer, abolitionist
* [A] Private Person

Sharp, Helen
See Paine, Lauran [Bosworth]

Sharp, [Sir] Henry 1869-? [WWL]
British author
* Ainsworth, Oliver

Sharp, Henry
See Schacht, Henry

Sharp, James 18th c. [HPPN]
British ironmaster and inventor
* [The] Pioneer of Rolling Carts

Sharp, James
See Kinghorn, Alexander Manson

Sharp, John 18th c. [HPPN]
British author
* J. S.

Sharp, Kevin 1959- [DC]
British cricketer
* Action Man
* Sharp, Razor

Sharp Knife
See Jackson, Andrew

Sharp, Luke
See Barr, Robert

Sharp, Margery
See Castle, Margery Sharp

Sharp, Marthe 20th c.
Singer
* Posey, Sandy

Sharp, Martin 1843-1910 [HPPN]
British historian
* Hume, Martin Andrew Sharp

Sharp, Milton 19th c. [HPPN]
American robber
* [The] Gentlemanly Bandit
* Nevada's Premier Road Agent

[The] Sharp One
See Bejart, Louis

Sharp, Razor
See Sharp, Kevin

Sharp, Richard 1760-1835 [DEL]
British author and poet
* Sharp, Conversation

Sharp, Robert [George] 20th c. [SFL]
Author
* Deegan, Jon J. [house pseudonym, Hamilton]

Sharp, Samuel 1700?-1778 [NPS]
Surgeon
* Mundungus

Sharp, Sharpie
See Sharp, George

Sharp, Sidney
See Mapes, Victor

Sharp, Thomas 1693-1758 [FFF]
British author
* Coventry Antiquary

Sharp, William 1855-1905 [HPPN, LC, WGT, WWL]
Scottish-born poet and author
* Brooks, W. H.
* Macleod, Fiona
* Siwaarmill, H. P.
* Tirebuck, W.

Sharpe, Alexander John 1814-1890 [BBD, HPPN]
British author
* A. J. E.
* Ellis, Alexander John

Sharpe, Bayard Heston 1881-1916 [BE]
American baseball player
* Sharpe, Bud

Sharpe, Bud
See Sharpe, Bayard Heston

Sharpe, C.
See Hough, Clara Sharpe

Sharpe, Charles Kirkpatrick 1781-1849 [PA, SN]
Scottish patron of the arts
* [An] Amateur
* [The] Scottish Walpole

Sharpe, D. Richard
See Shaver, Richard S[harpe]

Sharpe, Ernest Jack
See Sharpsteen, Ernest Jack

Sharpe, Ernest Rhoades 1906- [BEW]
American actor, singer, director
* Rhodes, Erik

Sharpe, Gregory 1713-1771 [HPPN]
British clergyman
* [A] Lover of Truth

Sharpe, Howard Lee 20th c. [BBH]
American basketball player and coach
* Sharpe, Sharpie

Sharpe, Jack
See Rathborne, St. George Henry

Sharpe, Jerome
See Decremps, Henri

Sharpe, John, Jr. 18th c. [HPPN]
British author
* Philanthus

Sharpe, Lancelot 1774-1851 [HPPN]
British clergyman
* L. S.

Sharpe, Lester
See Scharff, Lester

Sharpe, Lucretia
See Burgess, Michael Roy

Sharpe, Pauline 1925- [NAD]
Spiritual leader
* Nada Yolanda

Sharpe, Pepper
See Sharpe, Robert

Sharpe, Robert 20th c. [OBW]
American baseball player
* Sharpe, Pepper

Sharpe, Sharpie
See Sharpe, Howard Lee

Sharpe, Wilbur Chaplin 1864-1929 [HPPN]
American actor
* Wilbur, Caryl

Sharples, Robert 1913- [IWM]
British musician
* Earley, Robert

Sharpshooting Singer From Astoria
See Zimmerman, Ethel Agnes

Sharpsteen, Ernest Jack 1880-1976 [MA]
American poet and playwright
* Sharpe, Ernest Jack

Sharrock, Linda
See Chambers, Linda

Sharrock, Marian Edna Dormitzer 1897- [HPPN]
American author
* Dormie, M. A.

Sharrocks, Alfred Burgess 1919- [ART]
British artist
* A. B. S.

Sharrukin [The Righteous King]
See Sargon II

Sharrunkin [The Righteous King]
See Sargon II

Shashoua, Salim Samuel 1930- [IWM]
Iraqi-born attorney and broadcasting editor
* Shashoua, Shlomo

Shashoua, Shlomo
See Shashoua, Salim Samuel

Shastri, Prithvinath 1926- [IAW]
Indian author and playwright
* Manugupta
* Mohan, P. Nath
* Najam
* Vasistha, Mohan

Shati, Bent el-
See Abdel-Rahmen, Aisha

Shatt, Montague
See Strong, Latham C.

Shattuck, Ethel
See Greenman, Ethel

Shattuck, Lemuel 19th c. [HPPN]
American author, publisher, bookseller
* [The] Chairman of the Commissioners

Shattuck, Meredith M. 20th c. [BBH]
American roller skating organization officer
* Shattuck, Red

Shattuck, Red
See Shattuck, Meredith M.

Shattuck, Truly
See Etrulia, Claire

Shaughnessy, Clark D. 1892-1970 [BBH, HPPN]
American football coach
* [The] Father of the Modern T-Formation
* Shaughnessy, Soup

Shaughnessy, Francis Joseph [Frank] 1883-1969 [AS, CFH]
American baseball executive and football coach
* Shaughnessy, Shag

Shaughnessy, Joseph C. 1921?-1985 [WP 7-27-85]
American actor
* Shaughnessy, Mickey

Shaughnessy, Mickey
See Shaughnessy, Joseph C.

Shaughnessy, Shag
See Shaughnessy, Francis Joseph [Frank]

Shaughnessy, Soup
See Shaughnessy, Clark D.

Shaul, Frank
See Rowland, Donald Sydney

Shaunessy, Winifred 1897-1966 [SC]
American actress, dancer, screenwriter
* Hudnut, Winifred
* Rambova, Natacha

Shaute, Joseph Benjamin 1900-1970 [BE, PB]
American baseball player
* Shaute, Lefty

Shaute, Lefty
See Shaute, Joseph Benjamin

Shavelson, Lydia 1906- [THR]
British actress
* Sherwood, Lydia

Shaver, Buster
See Shaver, Floyd Herbert

Shaver, C. L.
See Shaver, Claude L.

Shaver, Claude L. 1905- [BEW]
American educator
* Shaver, C. L.

Shaver, Floyd Herbert 1905- [ASC]
American entertainer and musician
* Shaver, Buster

Shaver, Gaius 1910- [FB]
American football player
* Shaver, Gus

Shaver, Gus
See Shaver, Gaius

Shaver, Richard S[harpe] 1907-1975 [WGT]
American author
* Amherst, Wes
* Benson, Edwin
* Blade, Alexander [house pseudonym, Ziff-Davis]
* Dexter, Edwin?
* Dexter, Peter
* Dorot, Peter?
* Dorset, Richard
* Elclair, Mollie?
* English, Richard
* Irwin, G. H. [house pseudonym]
* Lohrman, Paul [house pseudonym, Ziff-Davis]
* Patton, Frank [house pseudonym]
* Raycraft, Stan
* Sharpe, D. Richard

[The] Shavetail
See Cantor, Philip

Shaw, Albert 20th c. [NBB]
American musician
* Shaw, Honey Boy

Shaw, Alfred 1842-1907 [EC]
British cricketer
* [The] Emperor of Bowlers

Shaw, Alfred 1874-1958
British-born baseball player
* Shaw, Shoddy

Shaw, Amelia M. 1863?-1934 [BEW]
Irish-born entertainer
* Summerville, Amelia

Shaw, Artie
See Arshawsky, Arthur Jacob

Shaw, Athenaeum
See Shaw, William Smith

Shaw, Barton
See Drummond, Patrick Hamilton

Shaw, Brian [house pseudonym, Curtis Warren]
See Fearn, John Russell

Shaw, Brian [house pseudonym, Curtis Warren]
See Griffiths, David Arthur

Shaw, Brian [house pseudonym, Curtis Warren]
See O'Brien, David

Shaw, Brian [house pseudonym, Curtis Warren]
See Tubb, Edwin Charles

Shaw, Buck
See Shaw, Lawrence T.

Shaw, Bundles
See Shaw, Everett

Shaw, Bynum G[illette] 1923- [WD]
American author and screenwriter
* Gillette, Bob

Shaw, Charles 1900- [WW]
Author
* Singer, Bant

Shaw, David
See Griffiths, David Arthur

Shaw, Dawn
See Shaw, Thelma

Shaw, Dick
See Openshaw, G. H.

Shaw, Dupee
See Shaw, Frederick Lander

Shaw, Elijah W. 1900- [WWJ]
American jazz musician
* Shaw, Lige

Shaw, Elizabeth
See Prance, June E[lizabeth]

Shaw, Elizabeth Jonia Leilokelani 1901-1921 [HPPN]
Hawaiian dancer
* Lokelani, [Princess] Lei

Shaw, Everett 20th c. [GW]
American rodeo performer
* Shaw, Bundles

Shaw, Felicity 1918- [CA, TCCM]
British author
* Morice, Anne

Shaw, Flora Louisa
See Lugard, Flora Louisa Shaw

Shaw, Frank H. 1878-? [MBF]
British author
* Cleveland, Frank
* Guthrie, Archibald
* Hammerton, Grenville
* Hubert, Frank

Shaw, Fred 1867-1918 [BMH]
British comic singer
* Sheridan, Mark

Shaw, Frederick Lander 1859-1938 [AS, BE, PB]
American baseball player
* Shaw, Dupee

Shaw, Fud
See Shaw, Robert

Shaw, George
See Bickham, Jack M[iles]

Shaw, George Bernard 1856-1950 [HPPN, LC, NPS, TC]
Irish playwright, author, critic
* Brother Bernardo
* Di Bassetto, Corno
* [The] Fighting Idealist
* Fitzthunder, Robespierre Marat
* G. B. S.
* [A] Genius Unquenched
* George B.
* Headmaster to the Universe

Shaw, George Bernard (cont.)
* [The] Irish Shakespeare
* [The] Jesting Apostle
* Larking, G. B.
* Man of the Century
* [The] Metaphysical Jester
* Methuselah
* Old Hair and Teeth
* P-Shaw
* Privileged Lunatic
* Redbarn Wash
* Ribbonson, Horatio
* Sage of Ayot
* Shaw, Typographical
* Victorian Stage Pulpiteer
* [The] Wag of Whitehall Court

Shaw, Glen Byam
See Shaw, Glencairn Alexander Byam

Shaw, Glencairn Alexander Byam 1904-
[BEW]
British actor and director
* Shaw, Glen Byam

Shaw, Grunting Jim
See Shaw, James Aloysius

Shaw, Hank
See Shalofsky, Henry

Shaw, Helen 1863?-1934 [BEW]
Irish-born actress
* Rous, Helen

Shaw, Henry Wheeler 1818?-1885
[DEL, DNNF, FFF]
American author
* Billings, Josh
* Uncle Esek

Shaw, Hollace
Singer
* Vivien

Shaw, Honey Boy
See Shaw, Albert

Shaw, Howard Elwin 1827-1924 [HPPN]
American politician
* [The] Silver Tongued Orator of
Lamoille

Shaw, Irene
See Roberts, Irene M.

Shaw, James Aloysius 1893-1962 [BE]
American baseball player
* Shaw, Grunting Jim

Shaw, Jane
See Evans, Jean Bell Shaw

Shaw, Janet
See Hanshaw, Annette

Shaw, Joan 1930- [EJ7]
American jazz musician
* Jones, Salena

Shaw, Joan
See DeCosta, Joan

Shaw, John 1778-1809 [HPPN]
American physician and poet
* Ithacus

Shaw, Justin
See Openshaw, G. H.

Shaw, Lawrence T. 1899-1977 [BI, FB]
American football coach
* Shaw, Buck
* [The] Silver Fox

Shaw, Lawrence Taylor [Larry] 1924-
[SFL, SFP]
American editor
* Destiny, Archibald
* Thor, Terry

Shaw, Lige
See Shaw, Elijah W.

Shaw, Marlena
See Burgess, Marlena

Shaw, Martin
See Martin, E. Le Breton

Shaw, Michael
See Wolfe, LeRoy E.

Shaw, Nate
See Cobb, Ned

Shaw nee aw kee [The Silver Man]
See Kinzie, John

Shaw, Oliver 1776-1849 [FFF]
American singer and songwriter
* [The] Blind Singer

Shaw, [Rev.] Oliver Abbott ?-1855
[HPPN]
American clergyman
* [The] Patentee

Shaw, Oscar
See Schwartz, Oscar

Shaw, Ralph Robert 1907- [HPPN]
American librarian, author, educator
* [The] Great Shaw
* Himself
* Uncle Ralph

Shaw, Robert 1908- [BWW]
American singer
* Shaw, Fud

Shaw, Sandie
See Goodrich, Sandra

Shaw, Sandra
See Balfe, Veronica

Shaw, Shoddy
See Shaw, Alfred

Shaw, Stanley Gordon 1884-1938?
[MBF]
British author
* Dare, Captain
* Gordon, S. S.
* Gordon, Stanley
* Heritage, John
* Strange, Harry
* Wallace, Gordon

Shaw, Susan
See Sloots, Patsy

Shaw, T. D. W.
See Shaw, Thelma

Shaw, [Private] T. E.
See Lawrence, Thomas Edward

Shaw, Thelma 1901- [CA]
American author and editor
* Shaw, Dawn
* Shaw, T. D. W.

Shaw, Thomas Edward
See Lawrence, Thomas Edward

Shaw, Typographical
See Shaw, George Bernard

Shaw, Victoria
See Elphick, Jeanette

Shaw, Vivian
See Seldes, Gilbert [Vivian]

Shaw, [Warren] Wilbur 1902-1954
[HPPN]
American auto racer
* President, Mr.

Shaw, William A. 1914?-1978 [HPPN]
American criminal
* Dillinger's Pal
* [The] Kid
* [The] Last of Dillinger's Boys

Shaw, William Harlan 1922- [CA]
American artist, author, educator
* Harlan

Shaw, William Smith 1778-1826 [HPPN]
American librarian
* Shaw, Athenaeum

Shaw, Winnie
See Momi, Winifred Lei

Shawe-Taylor, Desmond 20th c.
British music critic
* Galway, Peter

Shawkey, Bob 1890-
American baseball player
* Shawkey, Sailor Bob

Shawkey, Sailor Bob
See Shawkey, Bob

Shawlee, Joan
See Fulton, Joan

Shawmut
See Chamberlain, Nathan Henry

Shawn, Dick
See Schulefand, Richard

Shawn, Edwin Meyers 1891-1972 [CA,
HPPN]
American dancer and choreographer
* [The] Father of Modern Dance
* Shawn, Ted

Shawn, Frank S.
See Goulart, Ron[ald Joseph]

Shawn, Richy
See Schulefand, Richard

Shawn, Semas
See Gray, Whitley

Shawn, Ted
See Shawn, Edwin Meyers

[The] Shawnee Prophet
See Lalawethika

Shay
See Minton, Sherman

Shay, Arthur Joseph 1898-1951 [BE]
American baseball player
* Shay, Marty

Shay, Dorothy 1923-1978 [ECM]
American country-western performer
* [The] Park Avenue Hillbilly

Shay, Jerry
See Dzedzeji, Jerry

Shay, Marty
See Shay, Arthur Joseph

Shayback, Mr.
See Barrows, Samuel June

Shayback, Mrs.
See Barrows, Catherine Isabel

Shayne, Gordon
See Winter, Bevis

Shayne, Robert
See Dawe, Robert Shaen

Shazar, Rachel
See Katznelson-Shazar, Rachel

Shazar, [Schneor] Zalman
See Rubashov, Schneor Zalman

Shcharansky, Avital
See Stiglitz, Natalya

Shchedrin, N.
See Saltykov, Mikhail Evgrafovich

[The] She Majesty Generalissimo
See Henrietta Maria

[The] She Wolf
See Lincoln, Mary Todd

[The] She Wolf of France
See Isabella of France

[The] She Wolf of France
See Margaret [or Marguerite]

Shea, Donna 1950-
American musician
* Rivera, Scarlet

Shea, Francis 1912- [CEI]
American hockey player
* Shea, Pat

Shea, George Beverly 1909- [CWG]
Canadian-born singer
* America's Beloved Gospel Singer

Shea, John Edward 1874-1968 [BE]
American baseball player
* Shea, Nap

Shea, John Gerald 1906- [CA]
American author
* Fitzgerald, Jack

Shea, John Michael 1904-1956
American baseball player
* Shea, Joseph

Shea, Joseph
See Shea, John Michael

Shea, Nap
See Shea, John Edward

Shea, Pat
See Shea, Francis

Shea, Patrick Henry 1898- [BE]
American baseball player
* Shea, Red

Shea, Red
See Shea, Patrick Henry

Shea, Robert [Joseph] 1933- [CA]
American author
* Eulenspiegel, Alexander
* Glass, Sandra

Shea, Spec
See O'Shea, Frank Joseph

Shea, Timothy
See Knipe, Alden Arthur

Sheaffer, Louis
See Slung, Louis Sheaffer

Sheahan, D. B. 1843-? [PA]
Author
* Bun
* Critique

Sheahan, Henry Beston 1888- [TC]
American author and naturalist
* Beston, Henry

Shean, Al
See Schoenberg, Alfred

Shean, Mr.
See Schoenberg, Alfred

Sheard, Virginia [Stanton] ?-1943
[DNA]
Canadian author and poet
* Sheard, Virna

Sheard, Virna
See Sheard, Virginia [Stanton]

Shearer, Lloyd 20th c.
Magazine columnist
* Scott, Walter

Shearer, Moira
See King, Moira

Shearer, [Edith] Norma 1904-1983
Canadian-born actress
* American Beauty Rose
* First Lady of the Screen

Shearer, Sonia M. ?-1934 [DNA]
Author
* Shane, Nevis

Sheares, John 1766-1798 [PI]
Irish poet and barrister
* Dion
* J. S.

Shearing, Joseph
See Long, Gabrielle Margaret Vere [Campbell]

Shearouse, Florine W. 1898- [HPPN]
American lyricist
* Ashby, Florine

Shears, Billie
See Watson, O[scar] Michael

Shears, Billy
See Starkey, Richard

Shears, George Penfield 1890- [BN]
American baseball player
* Shears, Scissors

Shears, Scissors
See Shears, George Penfield

Sheats, Mary Boney 1918- [CA]
American author and religious educator
* Boney, Mary Lily

Shebbeare, John 1709-1788 [DEL]
British author
* Angeloni, Battista

Shebib, Donald 20th c. [WP 11-11-83]
Film director
* Everett, D. S.

Sheckard, Jimmy
See Sheckard, Samuel J. T.

Sheckard, Samuel J. T. 1878-1947 [AS]
American baseball player
* Sheckard, Jimmy

Sheckley, Robert 1928- [ESF, WGT]
American author
* Barbee, Phillips
* Lange, Ned
* O'Donnevan, Finn

Shed, Nevil 20th c.
American basketball player
* [The] Shadow

Shedley, Ethan I.
See Beizer, Boris

Sheehan, Biff
See Sheehan, Timothy James

Sheehan, Big Jim
See Sheehan, James Thomas [Jim]

Sheehan, D. B. 19th c. [PI]
Irish poet
* Bernards, Dene

Sheehan, Doris 1904?-1957 [HPPN]
British actress
* Patston, Doris

Sheehan, James Thomas [Jim] 1913-
[BE]
American baseball player
* Sheehan, Big Jim

Sheehan, John 1814?-1882 [FFF, PA, PI]
Irish poet and author
* Irish Whiskey Drinker
* J. G.?
* [The] Knight of Innishowen
* Philander

Sheehan, John J. 20th c. [BBH]
American boxer
* Sheehan, Tan

Sheehan, Michael Francis 1865-? [PI]
Irish poet
* [A] Child of Nature

Sheehan, Patrick Augustine 1905-
[CAP]
Irish barrister and author
* O Siochain, P[adraig] A[ugustine]

Sheehan, Perley Poore 1875-1943
[WGT]
American author
* Regard, Paul

Sheehan, Tan
See Sheehan, John J.

Sheehan, Timothy James 1868-1923
[BE]
American baseball player
* Sheehan, Biff

Sheehan, Valerie Harms 1940- [CA]
American author
* Harms, Valerie

Sheehy-Skeffington, Francis
See Skeffington, Francis

Sheelagh
See Plunket, William Conyngham [First Baron Plunket]

Sheelah
See Fletcher, A.

Sheeler, Mark
See Sheeler, Morris

Sheeler, Morris 1923- [ITA]
American actor
* Sheeler, Mark

Sheely, Bud
See Sheely, Hollis Kimball

Sheely, Earl Homer 1893-1952 [BE, PB]
American baseball player
* Sheely, Whitey

Sheely, Hollis Kimball 1920- [BE, PB]
American baseball player
* Sheely, Bud

Sheely, Whitey
See Sheely, Earl Homer

Sheen, Chris
See Shinfield, Christopher

Sheen, Fulton J[ohn]
See Sheen, Peter

Sheen, Martin
See Estevez, Ramon

Sheen, Mickey
See Scheinblum, Milton

Sheen, Peter 1895-1979 [CA]
American clergyman
* [The] Microphone of God
* Sheen, Fulton J[ohn]

Sheeny Mike Kurtz
See Kurtz, Michael

Sheeny Mike Vallinsky
See Vallinsky, Michael

[The] Sheepmaker
See Smith, Joseph

[The] Sheepmaker
See Smith, Joseph

Sheeran, Big Irish
See Sheeran, Frank

Sheeran, Frank 20th c.
American labor union official
* Sheeran, Big Irish

Sheet-Iron Jack
See Allen, John

Sheets, Frederick hill 1859-1928
[HPPN]
American clergyman
* [The] Happy Warrior

Sheffield, Classic
See Montgomery, James

Sheffield, Flora
See Sheffield-Cassan, Flora

Sheffield, George St. John 1842-1924
[HPPN]
American rowing coach
* [The] Grandfather of Yale Rowing

Sheffield, John [Duke of Buckingham and Earl of Mulgrave] 1648-1721 [SN]
British politician and poet
* All Pride, Lord

Sheffield, John [Johnny] 1931- [HPPN]
American actor
* Bomba
* Boy

Sheffield, Reginald
See Sheffield-Cassan, Reginald

Sheffield-Cassan, Flora 1902- [THR]
British-born actress
* Sheffield, Flora

Sheffield-Cassan, Reginald 1901-1957
[THR]
British-born actor
* Sheffield, Reginald

Shehu, Mehmet 1914?-1982
Albanian prime minister
* [The] Butcher

[The] Sheik
See Baldwin, Baldwin M.

[The] Sheik
See Harroun, Ray

[The] Sheik
See Kologlu, Nermin

Sheik al Jebal
See Hasan ibn-al Sabbah

Sheik, Kid
See Colar, George

Sheik Michael
See Taylor, Michael

[The] Sheik of Hollywood
See Wonderlich, Jerry

[The] Sheik of Malibu
See O'Neal, Ryan

Sheil, Lily 1908?- [HPPN]
British-American journalist and author
* Graham, Sheilah
* [The] Last of the Unholy Trio

Sheila E.
See Escovedo, Sheila

Sheinfeld, Leslie A. 1926- [CA]
Canadian-born educator and author
* Field, Leslie A.

Sheinwold, Patricia
See Fox-Sheinwold, Patricia

Shekerjian, Regina Tor 20th c. [SAT]
American author and illustrator
* Tor, Regina

Shekles, Gail 1918- [BEW, FC]
American actor
* Stevens, Craig

Shelasky, George Irving 1922- [BEW, TR]
American actor and singer
* Irving, George S.

Shelbourne, Cecily
See Goodwin, Suzanne

Shelby, Charlotte
See Miles, Lily Pearl

Shelby, Daniel
See Macher, Daniel J.

Shelby, James 1927- [BWW]
American singer
* Shelby, Son

Shelby, John 20th c.
American baseball player
* Shelby, T Bone

Shelby, Juliet 1902-1984 [F2]
American actress
* Minter, Mary Miles

Shelby, Son
See Shelby, James

Shelby, Susan
See Kinnicutt, Susan Sibley

Shelby, T Bone
See Shelby, John

Shelby's Man of Earth
See Anthony, John Alston

Sheldon, Alice Bradley 1915- [ESF, SFL, WGT]
American author and psychologist
* Bradley, Alice
* Sheldon, Raccoona
* Tiptree, James, Jr.

Sheldon, Ann [house pseudonym]
[Stratemeyer Syndicate]
See Stratemeyer, Edward L.

Sheldon, Billie
See Crumley, William H.

Sheldon, Bob Mitchell 1950- [SMG]
American baseball player
* Sheldon, Shellie

Sheldon, C. M.
See Sheldon, Charles Monroe

Sheldon, Charles Monroe 1857-1946
[LC]
American author and clergyman
* Sheldon, C. M.

Sheldon, David
See Pomeran, David Sheldon

Sheldon, Eleanor Bernert 1920-   [CA]
American sociologist and author
* Bernert, Eleanor H.

Sheldon, George E.
See Stahl, Le Roy

Sheldon, Georgie
See Downs, Sarah Elizabeth [Forbush]

Sheldon, Jerry
See Patton, Charles H.

Sheldon, John [house pseudonym]
See Bloch, Robert [Albert]

Sheldon, Lee
See Lee, Wayne Cyril

Sheldon, Muriel 1926-   [CA]
American author and illustrator
* Batherman, Muriel

Sheldon, Peter 1922-   [CA]
British author
* Gaddes, Peter

Sheldon, Raccoona
See Sheldon, Alice Bradley

Sheldon, Roy [house pseudonym,
Hamilton]
See Brunner, John [Kilian Houston]

Sheldon, Roy [house pseudonym,
Hamilton]
See Campbell, Herbert J.

Sheldon, Roy [house pseudonym,
Hamilton]
See Tubb, Edwin Charles

Sheldon, Scott
See Wallmann, Jeffrey M[iner]

Sheldon, Shellie
See Sheldon, Bob Mitchell

Sheldon, Walt[er J.] 1917-   [BI, CA]
American author
* Hardin, J. D.
* James, Walter S.
* Walker, Shel
* Walters, Shelly

Shell, Donnie 1952-   [BA]
American football player
* Shell, Neck

Shell, Neck
See Shell, Donnie

Shell, Virginia Law 1923-   [CA]
American author
* Law, Virginia W.

Shellabarger, Samuel 1888-1954   [ANT,
CC, WW]
American author
* Esteven, John
* Loring, Peter

Shelle, Eileen
See Nankin, Eileen

Shellenberger, Beechie
See Shellenberger, Dave

Shellenberger, Dave 20th c.   [GW]
American rodeo performer
* Shellenberger, Beechie

Shelley
See Yeo-Thomas, Forest Frederick
Edward

Shelley, A. Fishe
See Gerard, James Watson

Shelley, Frances
See Wees, Frances Shelley

Shelley, Lillian [joint pseudonym with
Shelly R(uth) Koppel]
See Koppel, Lillian

Shelley, Lillian [joint pseudonym with
Lillian Koppel]
See Koppel, Shelley R[uth]

Shelley, Mad
See Shelley, Percy Bysshe

Shelley, Percy Bysshe 1792-1822   [DEL,
DLE1, HN, HPPN, NPS, SN, WGT]
British poet
* Ariel
* [The] Atheist
* Fiske, Jonathan, P. B.
* FitzVictor, John
* [A] Gentleman of Oxford
* [A] Gentleman of the University of
Oxford
* [The] Hermit of Marlow
* Mallecho, Miching, Esq.
* Nicholson, Margaret
* P. B. S.
* [The] Poet of Poets
* Scythrop, Glowry
* Shelley, Mad
* [The] Snake

Shelley, Peter
See Dresser, Davis

Shelley, William ?-1931   [HPPN]
British murderer
* Moosh

Shellogg, Alec
See Shellogg, Frederick

Shellogg, Frederick 1916-1968   [AS]
American football player
* Shellogg, Alec

Shelly, Carol Lee 20th c.   [BS]
American magician
* Carroll, Shelley

Shelly, Mortimer M.   [PA]
Author
* Old Actor

Shelton, Andrew Kemper 1888-1954
[BE]
American baseball player
* Shelton, Skeeter

Shelton, Frederick William 1814-1881
[FFF]
American author and clergyman
* Nil Admirari, Esq.

Shelton, Gary 20th c.
American singer
* Shondell, Troy

Shelton, Julia Finley   [FFF]
Writer
* Lorrimer, Laura

Shelton, Lola
See Klaue, Lola Shelton

Shelton, Miles
See Wilcox, Don

Shelton, Skeeter
See Shelton, Andrew Kemper

Shelton, Suzanne
See Buckley, Suzanne Shelton

Shelton, Violet 1892-1970   [THR]
British actress
* Campbell, Violet

Shelving, Paul
See North, Paul

Shemaya, Ebn
See Parkes, David

Shemo, Stan
See Shemo, Stephen Michael

Shemo, Stephen Michael 1915-   [BE]
American baseball player
* Shemo, Stan

Shemus of Ullinagh
See McGrady, James

Shen Yen-ping 1896-   [EWL]
Chinese author
* Hsuan Chu
* Mao Tun [Contradiction]

Sheng Ke Gon 1969-   [HPPN]
Chinese mathematical wizard
* [The] Living Computer

Shennan, Victoria 1917-   [AW]
British writer
* Sangster, Ann

Shenshin, Afanasi Afanasievich
See Foeth, Afanasi Afanasievich

Shenstone, William 1714-1763   [NPS,
SN]
British poet
* Columella
* [The] Lord of Leasowes
* [The] Water Gruel Bard

Shep
See Sheppard, James

Shepard, Alan Bartlett, Jr. 1923-
[HPPN]
American astronaut
* [The] First American in Space
* Grand Old Man of Space

Shepard, Benjamin Henry Jesse Francis
1848-1927 [TC]
British-born American author and musician
* Grierson, Francis

Shepard, Hazel
See Smith, Helen Ainslie

Shepard, Leslie Albert
See Juhasz, Leslie Albert

Shepard, Mary
See Knox, [Mary] Eleanor Jessie

Shepard, Morgan Van Roorbach
1865-1947 [NAA, SFL]
American author and editor
* Martin, John

Shepard, Nathan [PA]
Author
* Key note

Shepard, Sam
See Rogers, Samuel Shepard

Shepard, William
See Walsh, William Shepard

Shephard, Bo
See Shephard, Norman

Shephard, Dorothea Alice
See Farman, Ella

Shephard, Michael
See Ludlum, Robert

Shephard, Norman 1897- [BB]
American basketball coach
* Shephard, Bo

Shepheard-Walwyn, Hugh Wallwyn
1874-? [WWL]
British author
* Venning, Normandy

Shepherd, Ann
See Kalish, Scheindel

Shepherd, Berisford 1917- [WWJ]
American jazz musician
* Shepherd, Shep

Shepherd, David Robert 1940- [DC]
British cricketer
* Shepherd, Shep

Shepherd, Donald [Lee] 1932- [CA]
American author, editor, literary agent
* Kevern, Barbara

Shepherd, Dorothea Alice
See Pratt, Ella Ann [Farman]

[The] Shepherd Earl of Cumberland
See Clifford, Henry de

Shepherd, Gordon
See Brook-Shepherd, Gordon

Shepherd, Henry John ?-1840 [HPPN]
British barrister
* S.

Shepherd, Joan
See Buchanan, Betty [Joan]

Shepherd, John
See Ballard, [Willis] Todhunter

Shepherd, John Neil 1943- [DC]
West Indian cricketer
* Shepherd, Shep
* Shepherd, Walter

[The] Shepherd Lord
See Clifford, Henry de

Shepherd, Neal
See Morland, Nigel

[The] Shepherd of Banbury
See Campbell, John

[The] Shepherd of Salisbury Plain
See Saunders, David

[The] Shepherd of the Ocean
See Raleigh, [Sir] Walter

Shepherd, Richard 1732-1809 [HPPN]
British clergyman
* Philalethes Rusticans

Shepherd, Robert Henry Wishart 1888-
[HPPN]
Scottish clergyman and author
* Wishart, Henry

Shepherd, S. Rossiter 20th c. [MBF]
British author and editor
* Milton, Mark
* Richards, Frank [house pseudonym]

Shepherd, Samuel 1799-1858 [HPPN]
British civil servant
* [A] Rambler Among the Tombs

Shepherd, Shep
See Shepherd, Berisford

Shepherd, Shep
See Shepherd, David Robert

Shepherd, Shep
See Shepherd, John Neil

[The] Shepherd to the Wordsmith
See Gold, Victor

Shepherd Tom
See Hazard, Thomas Robinson

Shepherd, Walter
See Shepherd, John Neil

Shepherd, William James 1933- [IAW]
Australian author
* James, Peregrine

Shepherd, William James Affleck
1867-1946 [WEC]
British cartoonist
* J. A. S.

[The] Shepherdess of Dauphiny
See Vincent, Isabeau

Shepley, Michael
See Shepley-Smith, Michael

Shepley, Ruth
See Smith, Beverly Chew

Shepley-Smith, Michael 1907-1961 [FC]
British actor
* Shepley, Michael

Sheppard, Charles 20th c. [GW]
American rodeo performer
* Sheppard, Snakehead

Sheppard, Eli
See Young, Martha

Sheppard, Elizabeth Sara 1830-1862
[DNNF, FFF, PA]
British author
* Berger, Elizabeth
* Kinkel, Madame

Sheppard, Gregory Wayne 1949- [SMG]
Canadian-born hockey player
* Sheppard, Shep

Sheppard, Jacob R. [PA]
Author
* Richmond

Sheppard, Jake O. 20th c. [CEI]
Canadian-born hockey player
* Sheppard, Johnny

Sheppard, James ?-1970 [RO1]
American singer and songwriter
* Shep

Sheppard, Johnny
See Sheppard, Jake O.

Sheppard, Lancelot C[apel] 1906- [CA]
British author and translator
* Capel, Roger

Sheppard, Lydia H. 19th c. [HPPN]
American author
* Llewellyn, E. L.

Sheppard, Morris 1875-1941 [HPPN]
American politician
* [The] Father of the Eighteenth
  Amendment

Sheppard, Shep
See Sheppard, Gregory Wayne

Sheppard, Snakehead
See Sheppard, Charles

Sheppard, T. G.
See Browder, Bill

Shepperd, John 1907- [FC]
American actor
* Strudwick, Shepperd

Sheps, Elias 1892-1963 [BI]
Journalist and poet
* Almi, A.

Sherashevski, Boris
See Brown, John J.

Sheraton, Neil
See Smith, Norman Edward Mace

Sherborne
See Disraeli, Isaac

[The] Sherborne Murderess
See Bryant, Charlotte

Sherdel, Wee Willie
See Sherdel, William Henry

Sherdel, William Henry 1896-1968 [AS, BE, PB]
American baseball player
* Sherdel, Wee Willie

Sherenbeck, Mr.
British actor
* [The] Rochester Israelite

Sherer, Albert 20th c.
American diplomat
* Sherer, Bud

Sherer, Bud
See Sherer, Albert

Sherer, [Colonel] Moyle 19th c. [HPPN]
British army officer
* [An] Officer

Sherid, Roy
See Sherid, Roydan Richard

Sherid, Roydan Richard 1908- [BE]
American baseball player
* Sherid, Roy

Sheridan [FFF]
* [The] Hero of Debt

Sheridan, Adora [joint pseudonym with Evelyn Marie Pavlik]
See Hong, Jane Fay

Sheridan, Adora [joint pseudonym with Jane Fay Hong]
See Pavlik, Evelyn Marie

Sheridan, Ann
See Sheridan, Clara Lou

Sheridan, C. E.
See Norton, Caroline Elizabeth Sarah

Sheridan, Clara Lou 1915-1967 [BDF, CU, FC]
American actress
* Hellar, Gloria
* [The] Oomph Girl
* Sheridan, Ann

Sheridan, Dinah
See Mec, Dinah

Sheridan, [Eu]gene [Anthony] 1896- [BE]
American baseball player
* Sheridan, Red

Sheridan, Helen Selina [Countess of Dufferin] 1807-1867 [RH, WBD]
British poet
* Gushington, Angelina
* Gushington, Impulsia

Sheridan, John 19th c. [PI]
Australian poet
* Eureka

Sheridan, John F. ?-1908 [HPPN]
American actor
* O'Brien, Widow

Sheridan, Lee [joint pseudonym with Michael Sheridan]
See Lee, Elsie

Sheridan, Lee [joint pseudonym with Elsie Lee]
See Sheridan, Michael

Sheridan, Lionel Astor 1927- [CA]
British barrister and author
* Shoy, Lee Ang

Sheridan, Mark
See Shaw, Fred

Sheridan, Mary
See Graham, Daphne

Sheridan, Michael 20th c. [CA]
American author
* Sheridan, Lee [joint pseudonym with Elsie Lee]

Sheridan, Mrs. W. H. [FFF]
Entertainer
* Davenport, Louise

Sheridan, Neill Rawlins 1921- [BE]
American baseball player
* Sheridan, Wild Horse

Sheridan, Philip Henry 1831-1888 [DNNS, FFF, SN]
American army officer
* Jack of Clubs
* Little Phil
* Piegan Phil

Sheridan, R. B. B.
See Vanbrugh, [Sir] John

Sheridan, Red
See Sheridan, [Eu]gene [Anthony]

Sheridan, Richard Brinsley 1751-1816 [DEA, PPN, RH, SN]
Irish playwright
* Asmodeo
* [The] Modern Congreve
* Sherry
* [A] Young Hercules

Sheridan, Teresa
See Ronalds, Mary Teresa

Sheridan, Thomas 1684-1738 [HPPN]
Irish author
* [A] Person Who Had Some Share in His Education

Sheridan, Thomas 1775-1817 [SN]
British poet
* Sparkle, Tom

Sheridan, Thomas
See Gillings, Walter

Sheridan, Wild Horse
See Sheridan, Neill Rawlins

[The] Sheriff
See Constable, Jimmy Lee

[The] Sheriff
See Young, Faron

Sheriff, Paul
See Shouvalov, Paul

Sheritier, M. 1809-? [PA]
Author
* Thomas, Paul

Sherling, Ed[ward Creech] 1897-1965 [BE]
American baseball player
* Sherling, Shine

Sherling, Shine
See Sherling, Ed[ward Creech]

Sherlock
See Southwick, Solomon

Sherlock, John Clinton 1904- [BE]
American baseball player
* Sherlock, Monk

Sherlock, Monk
See Sherlock, John Clinton

Sherlock, Thomas 1678-1761 [HPPN]
British clergyman
* [The] Country Parson
* [A] Gentleman

Sherlock, William 1641-1707 [PA]
Author
* Photius Junior

Sherman, Alex 1923- [FB, HPPN]
American football coach
* [The] Big Shrimp of Pro Football
* [The] Pedantic Professor
* Sherman, Allie

Sherman, Allan
See Copelon, Allan

Sherman, Allie
See Sherman, Alex

Sherman, Babe
See Sherman, Daniel L.

Sherman, Boogie-Woogie
See Sherman, Harry

Sherman, Charles 20th c. [BLB]
American underworld figure
* Sherman, Chink

Sherman, Charlotte A.
See Sherman, Jory [Tecumseh]

Sherman, Chink
See Sherman, Charles

Sherman, Daniel L. 1892- [BE]
American baseball player
* Sherman, Babe

Sherman, Eleanor Rae 1929- [CA]
American author and illustrator
* Fleuridas, Ellie Rae

Sherman, Elizabeth
See Friskey, Margaret Richards

Sherman, Esther 1894-1982
American-born dancer
* Ragini Devi

Sherman, Frank Dempster 1860-1916 [HPPN, SFL, WGT]
American author
* Carmen, Felix
* Two Wags [joint pseudonym with John Kendrick Bangs]

Sherman, Gail
See Dern, Peggy Gaddis

Sherman, Harry 1904?-1977 [FIR]
Entertainer
* Sherman, Boogie-Woogie

Sherman, James D. ?-1896 [EWG]
American gunfighter
* Talbot, Jim

Sherman, Joan
See Dern, Peggy Gaddis

Sherman, John 1613-1685 [HPPN]
British-American clergyman
* College Puritan

Sherman, John 1823-1900 [FFF, HPPN]
American statesman
* [The] Great Financier
* Honest John

Sherman, Jory [Tecumseh] 1932- [CA]
American author and columnist
* Anvic, Frank
* Martin, Cort
* Sherman, Charlotte A.
* Tarrant, Wilma

Sherman, Lydia 1830-1878 [LFW]
American murderer
* Queen Poisoner

Sherman, Margaret
See Scheuerman, Margaret

Sherman, Michael
See Lowndes, Robert Augustine Ward

Sherman, Nancy
See Rosenberg, Nancy Sherman

Sherman, Peter Michael
See Lowndes, Robert Augustine Ward

Sherman, Roger 1721-1793 [HPPN]
American legislator
* [The] Learned Shoemaker
* Philoeunomos

Sherman, Saul 20th c. [EF]
American football player
* Sherman, Solly

Sherman, Solly
See Sherman, Saul

Sherman, Sylvia
See Pitkin, Sylvia Sherman

Sherman, Theresa 1916- [IBY, ICB]
American illustrator
* Reed, Veronica

Sherman, Vermin
See Sherman, William Dade

Sherman, William Dade 1910- [HPPN]
American racketeer and petty thief
* Sherman, Vermin

Sherman, William Tecumseh 1820-1891
[DNNF, FFF, HPPN, SN]
American army officer
* [The] General Who Made Georgia
  Howl
* [The] Great Marcher
* Mad Tom

Sherman, William Tecumseh (cont.)
* Old Billy
* Old Tecump
* Old Tecumseh
* Uncle Billy
* [The] Vandal Chief

Shero, Fred [Alexander]
See Schirock, Fred Alexander

Sherock, Shorty
See Cherock, Clarence Francis

Sherren, Wilkinson 20th c. [WWL]
British author
* Fay, Nicholas

Sherriff, R. C.
See Sherriff, Robert Cedric

Sherriff, Robert Cedric 1896- [LC, TC]
British author and playwright
* Sherriff, R. C.

Sherrill, Dorothy 1901- [CA]
American author and illustrator
* Martin, April

Sherrington, Alf
See Burrage, Alfred Sherrington

Sherrod, Jane
See Singer, Jane Sherrod

Sherry
See Sheridan, Richard Brinsley

Sherry, Charles
See Sargent, John Osborne

Sherry, Fred Peter
See Schuerholz, Fred Peter

Sherry, Oliver
See Lobo, George Edmund

Shertok, Moshe 1894-1965 [WBD]
Israeli prime minister
* Sharett, Moshe

Sherwin, Jeannette
See Gorlitz, Jeannette

Sherwin, Sterling
See Hagen, John Milton

Sherwood, Alice
See Haslam, Mrs. Charles A.

[The] Sherwood Forester
See Hall, Spencer T.

Sherwood, John D. 1840-? [FFF]
American author
* Scratchley, Harry

Sherwood, Josephine 1884-1957 [FC]
American actress
* Hull, Josephine

Sherwood, Lydia
See Shavelson, Lydia

Sherwood, Margaret Pollock 1864-1955
[HPPN]
American author and educator
* Hastings, Elizabeth

Sherwood, Mary Elizabeth Wilson
[PA]
Author
* M. E. W. S.

Sherwood, Mary Martha 1775-1851
[SFL]
Author
* [A] Young Lady

Sherwood, Mary Neal [FFF]
Translator
* Sterling, John

Sherwood, Michael
See Weathers, Philip Joseph

Sherwood, Nelson
See Bulmer, [Henry] Kenneth

Sherwood, R. E.
See Sherwood, Robert Emmet

Sherwood, Robert Emmet 1896-1955
[LC, TLC]
American author and playwright
* Perry, Brighton
* Sherwood, R. E.

Sherwood, Roland H. 1902- [NAA]
American-born writer
* Robbins, Rollin

Shestov, Leo
See Schwartzmann, Leo Isaakovich

Sheva
See L'Estrange, [Sir] Roger

Shevchuk, Tetiana 1906- [CAP]
Canadian-born author
* Bishop, Tania Kroitor
* Semkiw, Virlyana

Shevchuk, Tetiana
See Bishop, Tetiana Kroitor

Shew, Bobby
See Joratz, Robert

Shewell, Mrs. L. R. [FFF]
Entertainer
* Skerrett, Rose

Shewring, Walter 1906- [CAT]
British author
* Francis, Hayward

Shibano, Takumi 20th c. [SFP]
Author
* Rei, Kosumi

Shibukawa, Gyo
See Yamasaki, Takeo

Shibusawa, [Viscount] Elichi 1840-1931
[HPPN]
Japanese banker
* [The] J. P. Morgan of Japan

Shiel, Lily 1908?- [CA, CR]
British-born columnist
* Graham, Sheilah

Shiel, M. P.
See Shiel, Matthew Phipps

Shiel, Matthew Phipps 1865-1947 [CC, EMD, LC]
British author
* Holmes, Gordon [joint pseudonym with Louis Tracy]
* Shiel, M. P.

[The] Shield of Rome
See Fabius Maximus Verrucosus, Quintus

[The] Shield of Rome
See Verrocosus, Quintus Fabius Maximus

[The] Shield of the Church
See Aubusson, Pierre d'

Shields, Ben[jamin Cowan] 1903-1982 [BE]
American baseball player
* Shields, Big Ben
* Shields, Lefty

Shields, Big Ben
See Shields, Ben[jamin Cowan]

Shields, Charlie 20th c. [OBW]
American baseball player
* Shields, Lefty

Shields, Cornelius 1895?-1981
American banker and yachtsman
* [The] Gray Fox of Long Island Sound

Shields, Ella
See Buscher, Ella

Shields, Francis LeRoy 1891-1961 [BE]
American baseball player
* Shields, Pete

Shields, George Oliver 1846-1925 [ALY, FFF]
American author
* Coquina

Shields, James 1886-? [HPPN]
American author
* O'Sheel, Shaemas

Shields, Lefty
See Shields, Ben[jamin Cowan]

Shields, Lefty
See Shields, Charlie

Shields, Mrs. Bernard G. [FFF]
Entertainer
* Bernard, Bessie

Shields, Pete
See Shields, Francis LeRoy

Shields, Sammy
See Young, Sammy

Shields, William Joseph 1888-1961 [BDF, FC, IPA]
Irish actor
* Fitzgerald, Barry

Shiels, Andrew 1793-1879 [CCL]
Canadian poet
* Albyn

Shiels, Doc
See Shiels, Tony

Shiels, Tibbie
See Richardson, Isabella

Shiels, Tony 20th c. [EOP]
Magician
* Shiels, Doc

Shiffert, Edith [Marcombe] 1916- [CA]
Canadian-born author and educator
* Marcombe, Edith Marion

Shifflett, Duck
See Shifflett, Garland Jessie

Shifflett, Garland Jessie 1935- [BE]
American baseball player
* Shifflett, Duck

Shifrin, Aleksandr Mikhailovich 1901-1951 [BI]
Russian-American publicist
* Werner, Max

Shiftesbury
See Cooper, Anthony Ashley [First Earl of Shaftesbury]

Shifty Dick Croker
See Croker, Richard

Shiga, Emperor
See Shiga, Naoya

Shiga, Naoya 1883-1971
Japanese author
* [The] Divine Novelist
* Shiga, Emperor

Shigeru, Tsuyuki
See Kirkup, James

Shih Chao-chi 1877-1958 [WBD]
Chinese diplomat
* Sze Sao-ke, Alfred

Shih Huang Ti 3rd c. BC [HPPN]
Chinese ruler
* Cheng, Prince
* Ching, Prince
* [The] First Emperor

Shih Mai-yu 1873-1954 [BI]
Chinese physician
* Stone, Mary

Shih-T'ao
See Tao-Chi

Shihab, Sahib
See Gregory, Edmund

Shiki, Kazuhisa 20th c.
Japanese sumo wrestler
* Genkaiho
* Rinho

Shillaber, Benjamin Penhallow 1814-1890 [FFF, HPPN]
American author
* Billaber, She P.
* Old Man With a Cane
* Partington, Ruth

Shillaber, Ruth West 1908-1955 [BEW]
American actress
* Weston, Ruth

Shillard-Smith, Christine Wetherill 1910-1986 [HPPN, NY 1-27-86]
American fashion designer
* Leser, Tina

Shilling, Cal
See Shilling, Carroll

Shilling, Carroll 1886?-1950 [BBH]
American jockey
* Shilling, Cal

Shiloh, Johnny
See Clem, John Lincoln

Shima, George
See Ushijima, George

Shimazaki, Haruki 1872-1943 [CA]
Japanese author and poet
* Shimazaki, Toson

Shimazaki, Toson
See Shimazaki, Haruki

Shimei
See Dryden, John

[The] Shimmy Queen
See Pennington, Ann

Shinault, Enoch Erskine 1892-1930 [BE]
American baseball player
* Shinault, Ginger

Shinault, Ginger
See Shinault, Enoch Erskine

Shinborn, Max 20th c. [LFW]
Swindler, bank robber, gambler
* [The] King of the Badgers
* Shindell, Baron

Shindell, Baron
See Shinborn, Max

Shine, Dennis Francis Joseph 1908- [SFL]
Author
* Shannon, Frank

Shiner, Dick 20th c.
American football player
* Shiner, Herbie

Shiner, Herbie
See Shiner, Dick

Shines, John Ned [Johnny] 1915- [BWW]
American singer
* Little Wolf
* Shoe Shine Johnny

Shinfield, Christopher 1908- [BMH]
British female impersonator
* Sheen, Chris

Shingle, Solomon?
See Bellaw, Americus Wellington

Shingle, Solon
See Dunn, Caleb

[The] Shining Knight of the Poker Table
See Powell, John

[The] Shining Light of the Yiddish Theater
See Kaminska, Ida

Shinkle, James D. 1897?-1973　[CA]
Author
* Shinkle, Tex

Shinkle, Tex
See Shinkle, James D.

Shinn, Earl 1837-1886　[PA]
Author
* Strahan, Edward

Shinso 1460?-1530?　[WBD]
Japanese painter
* Soami

Shinwell, Emmanuel 1884-　[NN]
British politician and labor leader
* Sinbad the Tailor

Ship Surgeon
See Burton, Leonard Lamming

Shipke, Muskrat Bill
See Shipke, William M. [Bill]

Shipke, William M. [Bill] 1882-1940
[BE]
American baseball player
* Shipke, Muskrat Bill

Shipley, David
See Holden, David [Shipley]

Shipley, Joseph Clark [Joe] 1935-　[BE]
American baseball player
* Shipley, Moses

Shipley, Joseph Twaddell 1893-　[WD]
American author
* Goliard, Roy

Shipley, Miriam Allen De Ford
1888-1975　[WGT]
American author
* De Ford, Miriam Allen

Shipley, Moses
See Shipley, Joseph Clark [Joe]

Shipman, Elydia Foss
See Oliver, Dora Dana

Shipman, Samuel 1883-1937　[HPPN]
American playwright
* Shipman, Shippie

Shipman, Shippie
See Shipman, Samuel

Shippen
See Adams, Samuel

Shippen, William ?-1742?　[HN, RH]
British politician
* [The] Incorruptible

Shippen, Zoe
See Varnum, Zoe Shippen

Shipton, Anna 19th c.　[PA]
Author
* A. S.

Shipton, Mother
See Preece, T. Evan

Shipton, Mother
See Shipton, Ursula Southiel

Shipton, Ursula Southiel 1488-1560?
[HPPN]
British witch
* Shipton, Mother

[The] Shipyard Bunyan
See Higgins, Andrew Jackson

Shirach, Baldur von 1907-　[BDW]
German Nazi leader
* Falk, Richard

Shiras, Wilmar H. 1908-　[WGT]
American author
* Howes, Jane

Shires, [Charles] Art[hur] 1907-1967
[BE, PB]
American baseball player
* Art[hur] the Great
* Whattaman

Shirey, Claire Lee 1898-1962　[BE]
American baseball player
* Shirey, Duke

Shirey, Duke
See Shirey, Claire Lee

Shirley
See Lever, Charles James

Shirley
See Skelton, [Sir] John

Shirley, Alvis Newman 1918-　[BE]
American baseball player
* Shirley, Tex

Shirley, Anne
See Paris, Dawn Evelyeen

Shirley, Ernest Raeford 1901-1955　[BE]
American baseball player
* Shirley, Mule

Shirley, Florence Henderson 1883-
[NAA]
American writer and editor
* Leigh, Magda

Shirley, James 1596-1666　[DEA, DEP,
DNNS, SN]
British playwright
* J. S.
* [The] Last Minstrel of the English
Stage

Shirley, Mule
See Shirley, Ernest Raeford

Shirley, Penn
See Clarke, Sarah J.

Shirley, R. O.
See Shirley, Ralph Oakley

Shirley, Ralph　[NPS]
Author
* Ireton, Rollo

Shirley, Ralph Oakley 1918-　[ART]
British potter and painter
* Shirley, R. O.

Shirley, Tex
See Shirley, Alvis Newman

Shiroyan, Haig Krikor 1891-　[IAW]
Armenian-born author and poet
* Anoushavan

[The] Shirra
See Scott, [Sir] Walter

Shirreffs, Gordon D[onald] 1914-　[CA,
SAT, WD]
American author
* Donalds, Gordon
* Flynn, Jackson
* Gordon, Stewart
* MacLean, Art

Shirtliffe, Robert
See Sampson, Deborah

Shiver, Chick
See Shiver, Ivey Merwin

Shiver, Ivey Merwin 1906-　[BE]
American baseball player
* Shiver, Chick

Sho-wa
See Hirohito

Shoals, Roger 20th c.
American football player
* Shoals, Turtle

Shoals, Turtle
See Shoals, Roger

Shocker, Urban James
See Schockeor, Urbain Jacques

Shockley, [Dr.] William Bradford 1910-
[HPPN]
British physicist
* [The] Nobel Laureate

Shoddy, Gretchen
See Hauser, Carl

[The] Shoe
See Shoemaker, William [Willie]

Shoe, Aminidab
See Bousell, John

Shoe, Lucy T.
See Meritt, Lucy Shoe

Shoe Shine Johnny
See Shines, John Ned [Johnny]

Shoecraft, Robert K. 1914-　[IBW]
Micronesian chief justice
* Shoecraft, Shoe

Shoecraft, Ruth Thane 1896-1976
[HPPN]
American actress
* McDevitt, Ruth

Shoecraft, Shoe
See Shoecraft, Robert K.

Shoeffel, Mrs. John　[FFF]
Entertainer
* Booth, Agnes

Shoeless Joe Jackson
See Jackson, Joseph Jefferson

[The] Shoemaker
See Paretti, Tony

Shoemaker, Old Shoes
See Shoemaker, William

Shoemaker, William [Willie] 1931-
American jockey
* [El] Maestro [The Teacher]
* [The] Shoe
* [The] Silent Shoe
* [El] Viejo [The Old One]
* [El] Zapatero [The Shoemaker]

Shoemaker, William 20th c.   [BLB]
American detective
* Shoemaker, Old Shoes

Shoeneck, Jumbo
See Shoeneck, Lewis N.

Shoeneck, Lewis N. 1862-?   [BE]
American baseball player
* Shoeneck, Jumbo

Shoenight, Aloise 1914-   [CA]
American poet
* Tracy, Aloise

Shoffner, Milburn James 1905-   [BE]
American baseball player
* Shoffner, Milt

Shoffner, Milt
See Shoffner, Milburn James

Shofner, Del
See Shofner, Delbert M.

Shofner, Delbert M. 1934-   [FB]
American football player
* Shofner, Del

Shofner, Frank Strickland 1920-   [BE]
American baseball player
* Shofner, Strick

Shofner, Grant Calvin 1932-   [CWG]
American country-western performer
* Smith, Cal

Shofner, Strick
See Shofner, Frank Strickland

Shogun of Dogs
See Tsunayoshi

Shogun of the Darkness
See Tanaka, Kakuei

Shokeid, Moshe
See Minkovitz, Moshe

Sholes, Christopher Latham 1819-1890
[HPPN, WP 3-9-85]
American inventor, printer, journalist
* [The] Father of the Typewriter

Sholes, W. W.
See Scholz, Winfried

Sholl, Anna McClure 20th c.   [WW]
Author
* Corson, Geoffrey

Sholto
See Mackenzie, Robert Shelton

Shomaker, Dianna 1934-   [CA]
American author and educator
* McDonald, Dianna

Shomberg, Otto H.
See Shambrick, Otto H.

Shomroni, Reuven
See Von Block, Bela

Shondell, Troy
See Shelton, Gary

Shone, Patric
See Hanley, James

Shonin, Shodo 8th c.   [HN]
Japanese religious leader
* [The] Buddhist St. Augustine

Shooshan, Chip
See Shooshan, Harry M., III

Shooshan, Harry M., III   [ET]
American government counsel
* Shooshan, Chip

[The] Shootin' Fool
See Drucci, Vincent

Shopp, Be Be
See Shopp, Beatrice Bella

Shopp, Beatrice Bella 1930-   [HPPN]
American beauty contest winner
* America of 1948, Miss
* Hopkins, Miss
* Minnesota, Miss
* Shopp, Be Be

Shor, Bernard 1904-1977   [BI]
American restaurateur
* Shor, Toots

Shor, Toots
See Shor, Bernard

Shore, Dinah
See Shore, Frances Rose

Shore, Edward William [Eddie] 1902-
[HPPN, SR]
Canadian-born hockey player
* [The] Babe Ruth of Hockey
* [The] Chief Assassin
* [The] Maniac
* [The] Wild Man

Shore, Edward William [Eddie] 1902-
[SR]
Canadian-born hockey player
* [The] Babe Ruth of Hockey

Shore, Frances Rose 1917-   [FC, IPA,
ITA]
American entertainer
* [The] Allied V-2
* Shore, Dinah

Shore, Hamby
See Shore, Sam Hamilton

Shore, Norman
See Smith, Norman Edward Mace

Shore, Philippa
See Holbeche, Philippa [Jack]

Shore, Sam Hamilton 1886-1918   [FHE]
Canadian-born hockey player
* Shore, Hamby

Shoreham, Lydia
See Chadwick, Elizabeth [Bigley]

Shores, Cyrus Wells 1844-1934   [EWG]
American gunfighter
* Shores, Doc

Shores, Doc
See Shores, Cyrus Wells

Shorsa, May
See Slater, May Wilson

[The] Short
See Pepin III

Short and Fat, Sampson
See Kettell, Samuel

Short, Annabelle 1930-   [EJ]
*British-born American singer and
songwriter*
* Ross, Annie

Short, Beth Campbell 1908-   [NAA]
American journalist
* Campbell, Beth

Short, Bob
See Barbauld, Anna Letitia

Short, Bob
See Longstreet, Augustus Baldwin

Short, Bob
See Pope, Alexander

Short, Charles Williams 19th c.   [PA]
Author
* C. W. S.

Short, Dewey 1898-   [HPPN]
American politician
* Jenny
* [The] Laughing Gas Man
* [The] Preacher

Short, Eleanor Talbot Kinkead 20th c.
[NAA]
American author
* Kinkead, Eleanor Talbot

Short, Elizabeth 1925?-1947   [BI, HPPN]
American murder victim
* [The] Black Dahlia

Short, J. D. 1902-1962   [BWW]
American singer
* Short, Jaydee
* Short, Jelly Jaw

Short, Jackson
See Hochstein, Peter

Short, Jaydee
See Short, J. D.

Short, Jelly Jaw
See Short, J. D.

Short, John Fulton 1932-   [HPPN]
American bullfighter and painter
* Fulton, John
* [The] Yanqui Matador

Short, Joshua
See Oakley, Frederick

Short, Luke
See Glidden, Frederick D[illey]

Short, Luke L. 1854-1893   [HPPN]
American gambler and law officer
* [The] Fighting Marshal

Short, Mary Asenath   [FFF, PA]
American poet
* True, Fanny

Short Pants
See Campagna, Louis

[The] Short Pants Bully
See Schmidt, Maynard

Short, Percival M. 1886-1955   [THR]
British theatrical manager
* Selby, Percival M.

Short, Robert Waltrip [Bobby] 1924-
[CR]
American singer
* [The] Midget King of Swing
* [The] Miniature King of Swing

Short, Roger, Jr.
See Eyen, Tom

Short, Thomas Vowler 1790-?   [HPPN]
British clergyman
* [A] Clergyman

Shortcut, Daisy
See Cohen, D. S.

Shorten, Charles Henry 1892-1965   [BE]
American baseball player
* Shorten, Chick

Shorten, Chick
See Shorten, Charles Henry

Shorter, Aylward 1932-   [CA]
British anthropologist and author
* Jensi, Muganwa Nsiku

Shorter, Carl
See Schwalberg, Carol[yn Ernestine Stein]

Shorter, Mrs. Clement
Author
* Siegerson, Dora

Shortfield, Luke
See Jones, John Beauchamp

Shorthouse, Rebecca
See Lea, Constance Nicholson

Shortstop, Mr.
See Marion, Martin Whiteford

Shortstuff, Mr.
See Macon, John Wesley

Shortt, Charles Rushton 1904-   [WW]
Author
* Rushton, Charles

Shorty George
See Johnson, James

Shoshone Mike
See Daggett, Mike

Shostakovich, Dmitri Dmitryevich
1906-1975   [HPPN]
Russian composer and pianist
* [The] Hero of Socialist Labor

[The] Shot
See Foley, Jack

[The] Shotgun Bandit
See Hogg, Irving

Shotgun Ben Thompson
See Thompson, Ben

Shotley
See Richardson, Charles

Shots, Kid
See Madison, Louis

Shotter, Ralph Champion 1907-   [FC, TR]
British actor
* Michael, Ralph

Shotton, Barney
See Shotton, Burton Edwin

Shotton, Burton Edwin 1884-1962   [BE, PB]
American baseball player and manager
* Shotton, Barney

[The] Shoulder Breaker
See Shapur II [or Sapor]

Shoulders, James Arthur [Jim] 1928-
[HPPN]
American rodeo performer
* [The] King of the Rodeo

Shoun, Clyde Mitchell 1912-1968   [AS, BE]
American baseball player
* Shoun, Hardrock

Shoun, Hardrock
See Shoun, Clyde Mitchell

Shouvalov, Paul 1903-1962   [FC]
Russian-born film art director
* Sheriff, Paul

Shoveller, Shove
See Shoveller, Stanley Howard

Shoveller, Stanley Howard 1882-1959
[OCS]
British field hockey player
* Shoveller, Shove

Shovlin, Brode
See Shovlin, John Joseph

Shovlin, John Joseph 1891-   [BE]
American baseball player
* Shovlin, Brode

Shovlin, Joseph Kenneth 1899?-1974
[FC, SC]
American actor
* Whalen, Michael

Show Business, Miss
See Abuza, Sophie

Showalter, Jackson Whipps 1860-1935?
[HPPN]
American chess player
* [The] Kentucky Lion

Showalter, Max 1917-   [FC, ITA, SW]
American actor and composer
* Adams, Casey

Showalter, Richard [Dick] 20th c.
[HPPN]
American jazz musician
* Walters, Dick

[The] Showdown Man
See Norton, Homer Hill

Shower, [Sir] Bartholomew ?-1701
[HPPN]
British barrister
* [A] Gentleman of the Inner Temple

Shower, Hudson 1919-   [BWW]
American singer
* Little Hudson

Showles, Mrs. William   [FFF]
Entertainer
* Marks, Sallie

Shoy, Lee Ang
See Sheridan, Lionel Astor

Shrake, Bud
See Shrake, Edwin

Shrake, Edwin 20th c.   [TI 1-16-84]
American author and sports columnist
* Shrake, Bud

Shrapnel, Henry 1761-1842   [HPPN]
British army officer and armament expert
* [The] Father of the Shrapnel Shell

Shreve, Lev
See Shreve, Leven Lawrence

Shreve, Leven Lawrence 1869-1942   [BE]
American baseball player
* Shreve, Lev

Shreve, Tiffany
See Everson, Carol

Shrewsbury, Ralph
See Jamieson, Leland Shattuck

[The] Shrimp
See Shrimpton, Jean

Shrimp Bait Miller
See Miller, William Mosley

Shrimpton, Jean 1943-
British fashion model
* [The] Shrimp

Shriner, Herb[ert] 1918-1970   [HPPN]
American television personality
* [The] Hoosier Hotshot

Shriner, Herb
See Schiner, Herbert Arthur

Shrinivasi, Asjantenu
See Lutchman, Martinus Haridat

Shriver, Harry C[lair] 1904-   [CA]
American author, editor, jurist
* Hornblower, Harry C.

Shriver, Harry Graydon 1896-   [BE]
American baseball player
* Shriver, Pop

Shriver, Pop
See Shriver, Harry Graydon

Shrividhata
See Mishra, Vidhata

[A] Shropshire Gentleman
See Foe, Daniel

Shroyer, Frederick 20th c. [SFP]
Author
* Freyer, Erick

Shtchirin, Jacob 1890- [BEW]
Russian-born actor, director, producer
* Ben-Ami, Jacob

Shteppa, Konstantin 1897?-1958 [BI]
Russian historian
* Godin, W.

Shu, Austin Chi-wei 1915- [CA]
Chinese-born compiler and translator
* Chi-wei
* Yang-jen

Shu Ch'ing-ch'un 1899-1966 [CA]
Chinese author and playwright
* Lao She
* Lau Shaw

Shu, Eddie
See Shulman, Edward

Shu-Jen, Chou 1881-1936 [CA]
Chinese author and educator
* Ch'o, Chou
* Hsun, Lu

Shub, Beth
See Pessen, Beth

Shuba, George Thomas 1924- [BE]
American baseball player
* Shuba, Shotgun

Shuba, Shotgun
See Shuba, George Thomas

Shubert, J. J.
See Szemanski, Jacob

Shubert, Lee
See Szemanski, Levi

Shubert, Sam S.
See Szemanski, Samuel

Shubin, Seymour 1921- [IAW]
American author
* Richards, Al

Shuckburgh, Charles 18th c. [IP]
British author
* [A] Gentleman of Gloucestershire

Shuff, Jean 1929?- [BEW, FC, TR]
British actress and singer
* Carson, Jeannie

Shuffle, Rube
See Heaton, Augustus Goodyear

Shufflebottom, Abel
See Southey, Robert

Shuffleton, Thomas
See Moncrieff, William Thomas

Shufflewick, Mrs.
See Jamieson, Rex

Shufflin' Phil Douglas
See Douglas, Philips Brooks

Shufflin' Sam
See Brown, Robert

Shugrue, Joe 1894-1961 [BX, RBE]
American boxer
* [The] Jersey Bobcat
* Shugrue, Young Joe

Shugrue, Young Joe
See Shugrue, Joe

Shula, Don[ald] 1930?- [HPPN]
American football coach
* Miami's Unmiraculous Miracle Worker

Shulberg, Alan
See Wilkes-Hunter, Richard

Shuler, James 20th c.
American boxer
* Black Gold

Shull, Margaret Anne Wyse 1940- [CA]
American author
* Shull, Peg
* Windsor, Annie

Shull, Peg
See Shull, Margaret Anne Wyse

Shulman, Edward 1918- [EJ, PMJ]
American jazz musician
* Shu, Eddie

Shulman, Joseph 1923- [EJ]
Scottish-born jazz musician
* Saye, Joe

Shulman, Max 1919- [HPPN]
American author and humorist
* Master of Undergraduate Humor
* Perelman, Cultured

Shulman, Sandra [Dawn] 1944- [CA]
British author
* Montague, Lisa

Shulmanuasharid
See Shalmaneser II

Shultz, George Pratt 1920- [HPPN]
American politician
* [The] Supercrat
* Washington's Scholar Athlete

Shultz, Gladys Denny 1895- [CA]
American author
* Gardner, Anne

Shultz, Toots
See Shultz, Wallace Luther

Shultz, Wallace Luther 1888-1959 [BE]
American baseball player
* Shultz, Toots

Shulvass, Moses A. 1909- [IAW]
Polish-born clergyman and author
* Meyerson, Tuvia

Shulz-Reichel, Fritz [BI]
German musician
* Crazy Otto

Shumsky, Zena Feldman 1926- [CA]
British-born author
* Collier, Jane
* Collier, Zena

Shumway, Lee
See Shumway, Leonard C.

Shumway, Leonard C. 1884-1959 [SC]
American actor
* Shumway, Lee

Shumway, Leslie Adelbert 20th c.
[HPPN]
American criminal
* Shumway, Lou

Shumway, Lou
See Shumway, Leslie Adelbert

[The] Shunt
See Hunt, James

Shupe, Bozo
See Shupe, James

Shupe, James 20th c. [HPPN]
American underworld figure
* Shupe, Bozo

Shura, Kashina 1937- [WFA]
Korean-born fashion designer
* Hardwick, Cathy

Shura, Mary Francis
See Craig, Mary Francis

Shurly, Ernest William 1888- [HPPN]
British author
* Hasler, Martin

Shurtleff, Bert
See Shurtleff, Bertrand

Shurtleff, Bertrand 20th c. [EF]
American football player
* Shurtleff, Bert

Shurtleff, Nathaniel Bradstreet ?-1874
[IP]
American antiquary
* N. B. S.

Shurtleff, Robert
See Samson, Deborah

Shushtary, John 1920- [CA]
British editor
* Canning, John

Shuster, Bud
See Shuster, E. G.

Shuster, E. G. 20th c. [IPA]
American politician
* Shuster, Bud

Shute, Denny
See Shute, Herman Densmore

Shute, Evan Vere 1905- [CCL]
Canadian author
* Jameson, Vere

Shute, Hardwick 19th c. [IP]
British clergyman and author
* One Who Knows It

Shute, Henry Augustus 1858-1943
[HPPN]
American humorist and author
* Plupy

Shute, Herman Densmore 1904-1974
[GF]
American golfer
* Shute, Denny

Shute, Nevil
See Norway, Nevil Shute

Shute, Walter 20th c. [MBF]
British author
* Edwards, Johnson
* Edwards, Walter
* Maxwell, Gordon
* Wentworth, Charles [house pseudonym]

Shutta, Ethel
See Schutte, Ethel

Shuttle Deus
See Kissinger, Henry Alfred

Shuttle Diplomat
See Kissinger, Henry Alfred

Shuttle, Job
See Weaver, Thomas

Shuttleworth, Kenneth 1944- [DC]
British cricketer
* Shuttleworth, Shut

Shuttleworth, Shut
See Shuttleworth, Kenneth

Shverubovich, Vasili Ivanovich 1875-1948
[BEW, BI]
Russian actor
* Kachalov, Vasili Ivanovich

Shy Di
See Diana [Frances]

Shy, Timothy [joint pseudonym with Ronald William Fordham Searle]
See Lewis, Dominic Bevan Wyndham

Shy, Timothy [joint pseudonym with Dominic Bevan Wyndham Lewis]
See Searle, Ronald William Fordham

Shy, Wally
See Cox, Wallace Maynard [Wally]

Shyer, Buddy
See Shyer, Melville

Shyer, Melville 1897-1968 [HPPN]
American director
* Shyer, Buddy

Siano, Fiore 20th c. [PHM]
American underworld figure
* Siano, Fury

Siano, Fury
See Siano, Fiore

Siano, Joe
See Valachi, Joseph Michael

Sib
See Ford, Aleck

Sibbald, Thomas 1810-1890 [CCL]
Canadian author
* [An] Old Salt

Sibbes, Richard 1577-1635 [SN]
British clergyman
* Humble and Heavenly-Minded

Sibbett, Monk
See Sibbett, Morgan

Sibbett, Morgan 1911- [HPPN]
American business executive and scholar
* Sibbett, Monk

Sibelius, Jean
See Sibelius, Johan Julius Christian

Sibelius, Johan Julius Christian
1865-1957 [BEW, IPA]
Finnish composer
* Sibelius, Jean

Sibelius, Johanna
See Freybe, Sibylle

Sibert, Willa 1873-1947 [EWL, HPPN]
American author, poet, critic
* Cather, Willa
* [The] Exponent of Integrity

Sibiriak
See Mamin, Dmitrii Narkisovich

Sibley, Ben 1876-? [THR]
Irish-born entertainer
* Albert, Ben

Sibley, Henry Hastings 1811-1891
[HPPN, IP]
American army officer and author
* [The] Father of Minnesota
* Hal a Dacotah
* Tall Pine
* Tall Trader
* [The] Walker in the Pines

Sibley, Inez K. 1908?- [CW]
Jamaican author
* Pennibb

Sibley, Susan
See Kinnicutt, Susan Sibley

Sibyl
See Martin, Sallie M. D.

[The] Sibyl of Europe
See Lieven, Dariya Khristoforovna

[La] Sibylle du Faubourg Saint-Germain
See Lenormand, Marie Anne Adelaide

Siccone ?-1003 [CAL]
Pope
* John XVII [or XVIII]

[The] Sicilian Anacreon
See Meli, Giovanni

[The] Sicilian Ox
See Aquinas, Thomas [Thomas of Aquino]

[The] Sicilian Theocritus
See Meli, Giovanni

Siciliano, Angelo 1893-1972 [HPPN, PE]
Italian-born body builder
* America's Most Perfectly Developed Man
* Atlas, Charles
* [The] World's Most Perfectly Developed Man

Siciliano, Mario 20th c. [WF]
Italian director
* Sirko, Marlon

Sick, Max 1882-1960?
Austrian strongman
* Maxick
* [The] Muscular Strongman

Sickert, Mrs. Cobden [NPS]
Author
* Amber, Miles

Sickles, Daniel Edgar 1825-1914
[HPPN]
American soldier and diplomat
* [The] Yankee King

[The] Sickly
See Henry III

Sickmann, Rocky
See Sickmann, Rodney

Sickmann, Rodney 1958-
American Marine who was held hostage in Iran
* Sickmann, Rocky

Sicto, C.
See Costi y Erro, Candido

[El] Sid
See Catlett, Sid L.

[El] Sid
See Perelman, Sidney Joseph

Siddhartha 6th c. BC [HPPN, WBD]
Indian philosopher and founder of Buddhism
* [The] Enlightened
* Gautama Buddha
* Sakyamuni [Sage of the Sakyas]

Siddle, Charles 1892- [WW]
Author
* Slingsby, Rufus [joint pseudonym with Frederick Peel]

Siddons, Belle ?-1881 [HPPN]
American gambler and spy
* Hallett, Mrs. Newton
* Verde, Lurline Monte
* Vestal, Madame

Siddons, James H.
See Stocqueler, Joachim Hayward

[The] Siddons of America
See Duff, Mary Ann

Siddons, Sarah 1755-1831 [HN]
British actress
* [The] Muse of Tragedy

Sidebottom, Arnold [Arnie] 1954- [DC]
British cricketer
* Thanold, Woofer

Siden, Captain
See Vairasse, Denis

Siderocrates
See Eisumenger, Samuel

Sidetes
See Antiochus VII

Sidetracked Home Executives [joint pseudonym with Pam Young]
See Jones, Peggy

Sidetracked Home Executives [joint pseudonym with Peggy Jones]
See Young, Pam

[The] Sidewalk Poet
See Crary, J. M.

Sidewalk Sam Guillemin
See Guillemin, Robert

[The] Sidewalk Statesman
See Smith, Al[fred Emanuel]

Sidey, James A. 19th c. [IP]
Author
* Crucelli, F.

Sidgwick, Cecily 20th c. [NPS]
Author
* Dean, Mrs. Andrew

Sidis, William James 1898- [NAA]
American author
* Folupa, Frank

Sidnal, Emma
See Freeman, Mrs. E. W.

Sidney
See Webster, Noah

Sidney [or Sydney?], Algernon 1622-1683 [NPS]
British statesman
* [The] British Cassius

Sidney, Algernon
See Adams, John Quincy

Sidney, Algernon
See Granger, Gideon

Sidney, Algernon
See Hale, Salma

Sidney, Algernon
See Roane, Spencer

Sidney, Algernon
See Waddington, Samuel Ferrand

Sidney, Dorothy 1617-1684 [WBD]
Countess of Sunderland
* Sacharissa

Sidney, E. W.
See Tucker, Nathaniel Beverley

Sidney, Edward William
See Tucker, Nathaniel Beverley

Sidney, Frank
See Warwick, Alan Ross

Sidney, Frank
See Warwick, Francis Alister

Sidney, Frank
See Warwick, Sidney

Sidney, George
See Bounds, S. J.

Sidney, George
See Greenfield, Sammy

Sidney, Jonathan
See Cooper, Emmanuel

Sidney, L. [IP]
British author
* Densyli

Sidney, Margaret
See Lothrop, Harriet Mulford Stone

Sidney, Mary 1561-1621 [NPS]
Sister of British poet, Sir Philip Sidney
* Urania

Sidney, Neilma
See Gantner, Neilma

Sidney, [Sir] Philip 1554-1586 [FFF, HN, NPS, SN]
British poet, statesman, soldier
* Astrophel
* [The] Blazing Starre of England's Glory
* [The] British Bayard
* Calidore
* [The] Chevalier Bayard of Our History
* [The] English Petrarch
* [The] Flower of Chivalry
* Illustrious Philip
* [The] Marcellus of the English Nation
* [The] Miracle of Our Age
* [The] Mirror of Courtesy
* Our Rarest Poet
* [The] Petrarch of England
* Philisides
* [The] Phoenix of the World
* [The] Plume of War
* [The] Poet of Kissing
* Pyrocles
* [The] Syren of this Latter Age
* [The] Warbler of Poetic Prose
* Zutpher Hero

Sidney, Samuel [IP]
British author
* Emigrant

Sidney, Scott
See Siggins, Scott

Sidney, Stuart?
See Avallone, Michael [Angelo], Jr.

Sidney, Sylvia
See Kosow, Sophia

Sidney-Fryer, Donald
See Fryer, Donald S[idney, Jr.]

Sidobre, Andre
See Schumann, Maurice

Sidonia, Ben
See Disraeli, Benjamin

Sidons, Charles
See Postl, Karl Anton

Sidrophel
See Lilly, William

Sidrophel
See Neal, [Sir] Paul

Sidrophel, Sir
See Walpole, [Sir] Robert [First Earl of Orford]

Sid's Stooge
See Knight, William

Sidus, Georgina ?-1835 [HPPN]
British actress and singer
* Miss George
* Oldmixon, Mrs.

Siebel, Frederick 1913- [ICB]
Austrian-born industrial designer and illustrator
* Siebel, Fritz

Siebel, Fritz
See Siebel, Frederick

Sieber, Sam Dixon 1931- [CA]
American author
* Kerr, Norman D.

Sieber's Boy
See Horn, Thomas [Tom]

Siebert, Albert Charles 1904-1939 [CEI, FHE, HK]
Canadian-born hockey player
* Siebert, Babe

Siebert, Babe
See Siebert, Albert Charles

Siebert, Eloise McElroy
See Hembling, Nina [Clark]

Siebert, Sonny
See Siebert, Wilfred Charles

Siebert, Wilfred Charles 1937- [BE, PB, SMG]
American baseball player
* Siebert, Sonny

Siedenschner, Jacob 20th c. [BLB]
American underworld figure
* Lewis, Whitey

Sieg, W. M.
See Wulff, Sigismund

Siege Gun Guilford
See Guilford, Jesse P.

Siegel, Abe J. 1914-1966 [BEW, SC]
American actor
* Stewart, David J.

Siegel, Benjamin 1884-1954 [BI]
American attorney and bridge expert
* Wentworth, W. W.

Siegel, Benjamin 1906-1947 [HPPN]
American underworld figure
* Rosen, Harry
* Rosen, Nig
* Siegel, Bugsy

Siegel, Benjamin 1914- [WD]
American author
* Benn, Matthew

Siegel, Bugsy
See Siegel, Benjamin

Siegel, Doris 20th c.   [CC, WW]
Author
* Wells, Susan

Siegel, Jack
See Siegel, Jacob

Siegel, Jacob 1913-   [CA]
American author
* Siegel, Jack

Siegel, Jerome 20th c.   [SFP]
Author
* Kenton, Bernard J.

Siegel, Mo
See Siegel, Morris J.

Siegel, Morris J. 1950-   [HPPN]
American entrepreneur
* [The] Celestial Seasonings Man
* Siegel, Mo

Siegen, Ludwig von 1609-?   [WBD]
German engraver
* Von Sechten

Siegerson, Dora
See Shorter, Mrs. Clement

Siegler, Eugene 1895-   [CA]
Rumanian-born author
* Relgis, Eugene

Siegmey
See Meyer, Siegbert

Siegvolk, Paul
See Mathews, Albert

Sieker, Lamartine P. 1848-1914   [HPPN]
American ranger and soldier
* Sieker, Lamb

Sieker, Lamb
See Sieker, Lamartine P.

Sielanski, Stanley ?-1955   [SC]
Polish-born actor
* Stanislaw, Stanley

Siemer, Cotton
See Siemer, Oscar Sylvester

Siemer, Oscar Sylvester 1901-1959   [BE]
American baseball player
* Siemer, Cotton

Sienkiewicz, Henryk [Adam Aleksander Pius] 1846-1916   [TLC]
Polish author and journalist
* Litwos

Sienna, B. T.
See Norton, Charles Ledyard

Sierbois, R. Q.
See Boissier, Jeane B. Prudence

Sierck, Detlef 1900-   [BDF, FC, FD]
Danish-born director
* Sirk, Douglas

Sierra, Vincente   [BI]
Uruguayan Communist spy
* Kent

Siet, Gloria 1930-   [OP]
American opera singer
* Lane, Gloria

Sieveking, Lance
See Sieveking, Lancelot De Giberne

Sieveking, Lancelot De Giberne 1896-1972   [LC]
British author and playwright
* Sieveking, Lance

Sievers, Roy Edward 1926-   [BE, DGS, PB]
American baseball player
* Sievers, Squirrel

Sievers, Squirrel
See Sievers, Roy Edward

Siew, William Leonard 1888-1977   [CA]
Lithuanian-born American journalist and author
* Laurence, William Leonard

Siface
See Grossi, Francesco Giovanni

Sifadda, Siful
See Wergeland, Henrik Arnold

Siff, Richard Philip 1927-   [BEW]
American talent representative
* Seff, Richard

Sifford, Charles [Charlie] 1923?- [HPPN]
American golfer
* [The] Jackie Robinson of Golf

Siffre, Michel 1940?-   [HPPN]
French speleologist
* [The] Time Juggler

Siffroi
See Bismarck, Otto Eduard Leopold von

Sig
See Webber, George Harris

Sigel, Franz 1824-1902   [FFF, SN]
German-born American army officer
* Dutchy

Sigel, Franz
See Kimberling, Hadley Siegel

Sigel, Mike 20th c.
American billiard player
* Hook, Captain

Siger de Brabant 13th c.
French theologian
* [The] Aristotle of the West

Sigerson, George 1839?-?   [PI]
Irish poet, scholar, scientist
* Erionnach
* Henry, Patrick
* [An] Ulsterman

Sigerson, Hester ?-1898   [PI]
Irish poet and author
* H.
* Uncle Remus

Sigfusdottir, Greta
See Sigfusdottir, Lara Margret

Sigfusdottir, Lara Margret 1910-   [IAW]
Icelandic author
* Sigfusdottir, Greta

Siggins, Scott 1872-1928   [SC]
Actor and director
* Sidney, Scott

Sighele, Mariantonietta 20th c.   [OP]
Italian opera singer
* Sighele, Mietta

Sighele, Mietta
See Sighele, Mariantonietta

Sightless Seer
See Pound, Ezra [Loomis]

Sigismund 1368-1437   [DNNF, RH, SN]
King of Germany
* [The] Balaam of Modern History
* [The] Light of the World
* Super Grammaticam

Sigismund 1427-1496   [SN]
Austrian monarch
* [The] Simple

Sigismund Zapolya [or Szapolyai]
See John II

Sigismund I 1467?-1548   [DNNS, FFF]
King of Poland
* [The] Great

Sigismund II 1520-1572   [FFF, RH, SN]
King of Poland
* Augustus

Siglin, Paddy
See Siglin, Wesley Peter

Siglin, Wesley Peter 1891-1956   [BE]
American baseball player
* Siglin, Paddy

Sigma
See Field, Julian Osgood

Sigma
See Sargent, Lucius Manlius

Sigma
See Sinclair, James

Sigma
See Straight, [Sir] Douglas

Signifyin' Mary Johnson
See Johnson, Mary

Signorelli, Luca d'Egidio di Ventura de 1441-1523   [WBD]
Italian painter
* Luca da Cortona

Signoret, Simone
See Kaminker, Simone

Sigoloff, Sanford C. 1931?-
American business executive
* Ming the Merciless

Sigourney, Lydia Howard Huntley 1791-1865   [HPPN, SN]
American author
* [The] American Hemans
* [The] Hemans of America
* L. H. S.
* [The] Mrs. Hemans of America

Sigourney, Lydia Howard Huntley
(cont.)
* Sigourney, Mrs.
* [The] Sweet Singer of Hartford

Sigourney, Mrs.
See Sigourney, Lydia Howard Huntley

Sigurd
See Hedenstierna, Alfred

Sigurd Mund [Mouth]
See Sigurd II

Sigurd I 1089?-1130   [WBD]
King of Norway
* [The] Crusader

Sigurd II 1134-1155   [WBD]
King of Norway
* Sigurd Mund [Mouth]

Sihanouk, Norodom
See Norodom Sihanouk [Varman],
Samdech Preah

Sikes, J. V. 20th c.   [HPPN]
American football player
* Sikes, Siki

Sikes, Olive [Logan] 1841-?   [IP]
American actress and author
* Chroniqueuse
* Logan, Olive

Sikes, Siki
See Sikes, J. V.

Sikes, Thomas 18th c.   [IP]
British clergyman and author
* [A] Country Clergyman

Sikes, William Wirt 1836-1883   [HPPN]
American author and journalist
* Brown, Boanerges
* Cobblestone, Sylvester, Jr.
* Cornwall, Ralph
* Dell, E. P.
* Dobb, James, Artist
* E. L. L.
* Gillespie, Ralph
* Harper, Charles Walker
* Howe, Seth
* [The] Idler
* Irving, Isaac V.
* James, Orlando
* Leonore
* Matsys, Quintin
* Morner, Fitz
* Orion
* Saxe, Burton
* Solemn One [The Wise]
* Starr
* Syles, Mrs.
* Wilhelm
* Wirt

Siki, Battling
See Phal, Louis

Sikorsky, Igor Ivan 1889-1972   [HPPN]
American engineer
* [The] Father of the Helicopter
* Uncle Igor

Silalicum
See Perry, W. A.

Silangan, Manuel
See Yabes, Leopoldo Y[abes]

Silas
See McCay, Winsor

Silas
See White, [Rev.] William

Silbajoris, Frank
See Silbajoris, Rimvydas

Silbajoris, Rimvydas 1926-   [CA]
Lithuanian-born educator and author
* Silbajoris, Frank

Silberbauer, Boom Boom
See Silberbauer, Charles

Silberbauer, Charles 1876-1953   [BI]
American police officer
* Silberbauer, Boom Boom

Silberberg, Leslie F[rances] Stone 1905-
[WGT]
American author
* Stone, Leslie F.

Silberman, Jerome 1934-   [BEW]
American actor
* Wilder, Gene

Silberschlag, Eisig 1903-   [IAW]
Austrian-born author
* Strong, Eric

Silberstein, Jay Jehiel 1936-   [CA]
Israeli-born author
* Zif, Jay Jehiel

Silbert, William M. 1921-   [ITA]
American entertainer
* Bradley, Bill

Silcott, Jane 1842-1895   [HPPN]
American Indian heroine
* Jane

[The] Silent
See William I

Silent Cal Benge
See Benge, Ray Adelphia

Silent Cal Coolidge
See Coolidge, [John] Calvin

Silent Charley Murphy
See Murphy, Charles Francis

Silent Frank Hinkey
See Hinkey, Frank A.

Silent Gates McGarragh
See McGarragh, Gates White

Silent Gene Hairston
See Hairston, Gene

Silent George Stone
See Stone, George Robert

Silent George Twombly
See Twombly, George Frederick

Silent Jake Volz
See Volz, Jacob Phillip [Jake]

Silent Jim Tatum
See Tatum, James Moore [Jim]

Silent Joe Martin
See Martin, Joseph Samuel [Joe]

Silent John Gillespie
See Gillespie, John Patrick

Silent John Hummel
See Hummel, John Edwin

Silent John Titus
See Titus, John Franklin

Silent John Whitehead
See Whitehead, John Henderson

[The] Silent Knight
See Gehringer, Charles Leonard

[The] Silent Laureate
See Bridges, Robert

[The] Silent Man
See Gehringer, Charles Leonard

[The] Silent Man
See Grant, Hiram Ulysses

Silent Mike Tiernan
See Tiernan, Michael Joseph

[The] Silent One
See Moltke, Hellmuth Karl Bernhard
von

[The] Silent Pole
See Kowalewskie, Stanislaus

Silent Sam Pierce
See Pierce, Samuel R.

Silent Sam, The Dancing Midget
See Davis, Sammy, Jr.

[The] Silent Scot
See Smith, Macdonald

[The] Silent Senator
See Sturgeon, Daniel

[The] Silent Shoe
See Shoemaker, William [Willie]

Silent Steve Philbin
See Philbin, Stephen H.

[The] Silent Swede
See Stenmark, Ingemar

[The] Silent Sycamore
See Byrd, Larry

Silent Tom Smith
See Smith, Tom

Silent Traveller
See Chiang Yee

Silent, William T.
See Jackson, John William, Jr.

Silentiarius, Paulus
See Philes, George P.

[The] Silentiary
See Anastasius I

Silicone Sally
See Smith, Sarah Anne

Silingsby, Maurice
See Urner, Nathan Dane

[The] Silk King
See Rice, Harold

[The] Silk Merchant
See Ibn-Ali-Hariri, Abu Mohammed Al Kasim

Silk Stocking Schafer
See Schafer, Harry C.

[The] Silken Lord
See Fitzgerald, Thomas

Silken Thomas
See Fitzgerald, Thomas

Silks, Mattie 1847-1929
American madam
* Queen of the Red Lights

Silks, Mattie
See Ready, Martha A. Thomson

Sill, Edward Rowland 1841-1887 [HPPN]
American poet and essayist
* Hedbrooke, Andrew

Sill, Richard 18th c. [IP]
British scholar
* Dirrill, Charles

Sillah, Mododou Baikoro 1935- [IAW]
Gambian writer
* Baikoro

Siller, Hilda [FFF]
American writer
* Hilda

Siller, Van
See Van Siller, Hilda

Silliman, Benjamin 1779-1864 [HPPN]
American scientist and author
* [The] Nestor of American Science

Silliman, George Joseph L. W. [PA]
Author
* Hannibal

[The] Sillographer
See Timon

Sills, Beverly
See Silverman, Belle Miriam

Sills, Gladys Wynne 1886-1964 [HPPN]
American actress
* Wynne, Gladys

Sills, Jennifer
See Lewis, Stephen

[The] Silly
See Charles VI

Silly Billy
See William Frederick

Silly Billy
See William IV

[The] Silly Duke
See Churchill, John [First Duke of Marlborough]

[The] Silly Kid
See Floyd, Frank

Silly Quirko
See Harvey, Gabriel

Silone, Ignazio
See Tranquilli, Secondo

Silsbee, [Rev.] William 19th c. [HPPN]
American clergyman
* W. S.

Siltanen, Risto 1958- [SMG]
Finnish-born hockey player
* [The] Incredible Hulk

Siluriensis
See Wilson, John

Siluriensis, Leolinus
See Jones, Arthur Llewellyn

[The] Silurist
See Vaughan, Henry

Silva, Antonio Jose da 1705-1739 [WBD]
Portuguese playwright
* [O] Judeu
* [The] Portuguese Moliere

Silva, Joseph
See Goulart, Ron[ald Joseph]

Silvani, Anita 20th c. [SFL, WGT]
Author
* A. F. S.

Silvanus
See Strasser, Bernard Paul

Silvanus, P. W.
See Strassar, Todd

Silvayn, Alexander 16th c. [FFF]
British author
* Piot, Lazarus

Silve, Claude
See Laforest-Divonne, Philomene De

Silver, Bill
See Plowright, William George Holroyd

Silver Bill Phillips
See Phillips, William Corcoran

Silver Billy Beldham
See Beldham, Billy

[The] Silver Captain
See Digby, [Sir] Henry

Silver Dick Bland
See Bland, Richard Parks

Silver Dollar Tabor
See Tabor, Horace Austin Warner

Silver Donald Cameron
See Cameron, Donald [Allan]

[The] Silver Fox
See Bierman, Bernard William [Bernie]

[The] Silver Fox
See Jehan, Jean

[The] Silver Fox
See Kidd, E. Culver

[The] Silver Fox
See Nitze, Paul

[The] Silver Fox
See Patrick, Lester

[The] Silver Fox
See Petty, Jesse Lee

[The] Silver Fox
See Read, Herbert

[The] Silver Fox
See Rich, Charley

[The] Silver Fox
See Ritchie, Alvin

[The] Silver Fox
See Shaw, Lawrence T.

[The] Silver Fox
See Snider, Edwin Donald

[The] Silver Fox
See Terry, William J.

[The] Silver Fox of the Northland
See Bierman, Bernard William [Bernie]

Silver, Fred
See Silverberg, Frederick

[The] Silver Haired Elderly Statesman of American Labor
See Meany, [William] George

Silver Hand
See Nuad

Silver Hands
See Ballardo, Ricardo

Silver Heels Marshall
See Marshall, John

Silver Kane
See Ledesma, Gonzales

Silver King of the Cowboys
See Gray, Gene

[The] Silver Masked Tenor
See White, Joseph M.

Silver, Monroe Burton 1933- [BEW]
American talent representative
* Silver, Monty

Silver, Monty
See Silver, Monroe Burton

Silver, Nicholas
See Faust, Frederick [Schiller]

Silver, Richard
See Bulmer, [Henry] Kenneth

Silver, Ruth
See Chew, Ruth

[The] Silver Sage
See Thomas, [John William] Elmer

[The] Silver Scot
See Armour, Thomas Dickson [Tommy]

Silver Snaffle III
See Cunningham, Margaret Isobel

Silver Spoon Butler
See Butler, Benjamin Franklin

[The] Silver Tongue
See Finch, Daniel [Second Earl of Nottingham]

[The] Silver Tongued
See Barry, Spranger

[The] Silver Tongued
See Bates, William

Silver Tongued
See Booth, Barton

[The] Silver Tongued
See Garrick, David

[The] Silver Tongued
See Hammond, Anthony

[The] Silver Tongued
See Smith, Henry

[The] Silver Tongued
See Sylvester, Joshua

[The] Silver Tongued and Golden Hearted
See Willard, Frances Elizabeth Caroline

Silver Tongued Josh Bryan
See Lee, Joshua Bryan

Silver Tongued Laurier
See Laurier, [Sir] Wilfrid

[The] Silver Tongued Orator
See Bell, Joshua Fry

[The] Silver Tongued Orator
See Bryan, William Jennings

[The] Silver Tongued Orator
See Dougherty, Daniel

[The] Silver Tongued Orator
See Kirkpatrick, John Milton

[The] Silver Tongued Orator
See Rollins, James Sidney

[The] Silver Tongued Orator of Lamoille
See Shaw, Howard Elwin

[The] Silver Tongued Orator of New Hampshire
See Gove, William Hazeltine

[The] Silver Tongued Orator of the South
See Baker, Alpheus

[The] Silver Tongued Orator of Wisconsin
See Fitch, Thomas

[The] Silver Tongued Sluggard of the Senate
See McCreery, Thomas C.

[The] Silver Tongued Spellbinder of the Pacific Coast
See Delmas, Delphin Michael

[The] Silver Trumpet of the House
See Deering, [Sir] Edward

Silver, W. A.   [PA]
Author
* Marsden, Frederick

Silver Whiskered Chapman
See Chapman, George

Silver Willy Hensel
See Hensel, [Rev. Dr.] Clarence

Silvera, Charles Anthony Ryan 1924-
[BE]
American baseball player
* Silvera, Swede

Silvera, Swede
See Silvera, Charles Anthony Ryan

Silverberg, Frederick 1936-   [ASC]
American composer and pianist
* Silver, Fred

Silverberg, Robert 1936-   [CA, ESF, WGT]
American author
* Aghill, Gordon [joint pseudonym with Randall Garrett]
* Arnette, Robert [house pseudonym, Ziff-Davis]
* Bethlen, T. D.
* Blade, Alexander [joint pseudonym with Randall Garrett] [house pseudonym, Ziff-Davis]
* Burke, Ralph [joint pseudonym with Randall Garrett]
* Chapman, Walker
* Clinton, Dirk
* Drummond, Walter
* Elliott, Don
* Greer, Richard [joint pseudonym with Randall Garrett] [house pseudonym, Ziff-Davis]
* Jarvis, E. K. [house pseudonym, Ziff-Davis]
* Jorgensen, Ivar [joint pseudonym with Randall Garrett] [house pseudonym, Ziff-Davis]
* Kastel, Warren [house pseudonym, Ziff-Davis]
* Knox, Calvin M.
* Malcolm, Dan
* Martin, Webber
* McKenzie, Ray?
* Merriman, Alex
* Mitchell, Clyde [joint pseudonym with Randall Garrett] [house pseudonym, Ziff-Davis]
* Osborne, David
* Osborne, George
* Randall, Robert [joint pseudonym with Randall Garrett]
* Robertson, Ellis [joint pseudonym with Harlan (Jay) Ellison]
* Rodman, Eric
* Sebastian, Lee
* Spencer, Leonard G. [joint pseudonym with Randall Garrett] [house pseudonym, Ziff-Davis]
* Tenneshaw, S. M. [joint pseudonym with Randall Garrett] [house pseudonym, Ziff-Davis]
* Thornton, Hall
* Vance, Gerald [joint pseudonym with Randall Garrett] [house pseudonym, Ziff-Davis]
* Watson, Richard F.

Silverblatt, Howard 1909-   [BEW, EMT, FC]
American actor, director, producer
* Da Silva, Howard

Silvercloud, A Detective Officer
See Brown, George Shaw

Silverheels, Jay
See Smith, Harold J.

Silverlake, Arthur 1905-   [F1, FC, HPPN, ITA]
American actor
* Bumstead, Dagwood
* Lake, Arthur

Silverlake, Florence 1905?-1980
American actress
* Lake, Florence

Silverman, Belle Miriam 1929-   [BBD, IPA, OP]
American opera singer
* Bubbles
* Sills, Beverly
* Silvery Bells

Silverman, Fred 1938?-
American television executive
* [The] Man with the Golden Gut

Silverman, George 20th c.   [EJS]
American basketball coach
* Silverman, Red

Silverman, Harriet ?-1975   [TR]
Columnist
* Silverman, Hattie

Silverman, Hattie
See Silverman, Harriet

Silverman, Jesse Ormand 1888-   [BE]
American baseball player
* Baker, Jesse Ormand

Silverman, Red
See Silverman, George

Silverman, Rose
See Millstein, Rose Silverman

Silverpen
See Meteyard, Eliza

Silvers, Phil
See Silversmith, Philip

Silversmith, Philip 1911?-1985   [BEW, IPA, SW]
American actor
* Silvers, Phil

Silverspoon, Dr.
See Witherspoon, John

Silverstein, Alvin 1933-   [CA, SAT]
American biologist, author, columnist
* Dr. A

Silverstein, Benjamin Irving 1919-
[BEW]
American union executive
* Irving, Ben

Silverstein, Bullet Joe
See Silverstein, Joseph L.

Silverstein, Jennie 1868?-1953 [BEW]
Rumanian-born actress
* Moscowitz, Jennie

Silverstein, Joseph L. 1898-1950 [EJS]
American football player
* Silverstein, Bullet Joe

Silverstein, Ralph S. 20th c. [EJS]
American wrestler
* Silverstein, Ruffy

Silverstein, Ruffy
See Silverstein, Ralph S.

Silverstein, Shel[by] 1932- [CA, SAT]
American author, illustrator, composer
* Uncle Shelby

Silverstone, Alan 1942?-
American business executive
* Uncle Al

Silverstone, Jonas T.
See Silverstone, Thomas

Silverstone, Thomas 1906- [BEW]
American attorney and producer
* Silverstone, Jonas T.

Silvertone, Mr.
See Martin, Freddy

Silvertongue, Gabriel
See Montgomery, James

Silvery Bells
See Silverman, Belle Miriam

Silvester, Frank
See Bingley, David Ernest

Silvestri, Hawk
See Silvestri, Kenneth Joseph

Silvestri, Kenneth Joseph 1916- [BE]
American baseball player
* Silvestri, Hawk

Silveti, Juan 1891-1956 [GS]
Mexican bullfighter
* [El] Tigre de Guanajuato [The Tiger
 from Guanajuato]

Silvette, Herbert 1907- [AW]
American author
* Dogbolt, Barnaby

Silvia
See Berkeley, Henrietta

Silvia, Charles 20th c. [BBH]
American swimmer and coach
* Silvia, Red

Silvia, Red
See Silvia, Charles

Silviana
See Wolff-Bekker, Elisabeth [Betje]

Silvius
See Balguy, John

Silvius [or Sylvius], Aeneas
See De Piccolomini, Enea Silvio

Sim, Georges
See Simenon, Georges [Joseph
Christian]

Sim, Katharine [Thomasset] 1913- [CA,
WW]
British author
* Nuraini

Sima, Caris
See Mountcastle, Clara H.

Simalo
See Loinger, Silvia Mary

Siman, E. E., Jr. 1921- [FCW]
*American music publisher, talent scout,
radio and recording executive*
* Siman, Si

Siman, Si
See Siman, E. E., Jr.

Simanskii, Sergei Vladimirovich 1877-?
[BI]
Patriarch of Russia
* Alexei

Simbeaux, L. L.
See Sellers, Connie Leslie, Jr.

Simcoe, Adolphus
See Thackeray, William Makepeace

Simcox, George Augustus [IP]
British playwright
* [A] Rambler

Simenon, Georges [Joseph Christian]
1903- [CA, EMD, HPPN, LC]
Belgian author
* Aramis
* Bobette
* Brulls, Christian
* Caraman, Georges
* D'Antibes, Germain
* Dersonnes, Jacques
* [La] Deshabilleuse
* D'Isly, Georges
* Dorsan, Luc
* Dorsange, Jean
* Du Perry, Jean
* Georges, Georges Martin
* Gut, Gom
* Kim
* Le Coq, Monsieur
* Plick et Plock
* Poum et Zette
* Sandor, Jean
* Sim, Georges
* Vialio, G.
* Vialis, Gaston

Simeon, Omer 1902- [MY]
American jazz musician
* Simeon, Simmie

Simeon, Simmie
See Simeon, Omer

Simmel, August 1815-1878 [IP]
German author
* Schrader, August

Simmonds, Michael Charles [Mike]
1934- [AW]
British author and journalist
* Essex, Frank

Simmons, Al
See Szymanski, Aloysius Harry

Simmons, Aloysius Harry
See Szymanski, Aloysius Harry

Simmons, Aloysius Harry
See Szymanski, Aloysius Harry

Simmons, Antennae Jimmy
See Simmons, Jimmy

Simmons, Blake
See Wallmann, Jeffrey M[iner]

Simmons, Bucketfoot Al
See Szymanski, Aloysius Harry

Simmons, Calvin 1950?-1982 [NW 9-6-82]
American conductor
* [The] Maestro Kid

Simmons, Catherine
See Duncan, Kathleen Mary

Simmons, Charles James [Jim] 1893-
[HPPN]
British Socialist leader
* [The] Soap Box Evangelist

Simmons, Cobra
See Simmons, Gary

Simmons, Connie
See Simmons, Cornelius

Simmons, Cornelius 1925-
American basketball player
* Simmons, Connie

Simmons, Daniel 1891-1966 [SC]
American actor
* Yowlachie, Chief

Simmons, David
See Gold, Alan R[obert]

Simmons, Dawn Langley
See Hall, Gordon Langley

Simmons, Edith ?-1917 [HPPN]
American vaudeville performer
* Creighton, Edith

Simmons, Edward
See Emerson, Edward

Simmons, Flat Jack
See Simmons, Jack

Simmons, Gary 1944- [SMG]
Canadian-born hockey player
* Simmons, Cobra

Simmons, [Rev.] George Frederick
1814-1855 [HPPN]
American clergyman
* G. F. S.
* [A] Member of the Same

Simmons, George W. 1815-1882 [IP]
American merchant and author
* [A] Friend to American Fnterprise

Simmons, George Washington 1885-1942
[BE]
American baseball player
* Simmons, Hack

Simmons, Hack
See Simmons, George Washington

Simmons, Hi
See Simmons, John

Simmons, Huey 1933-   [EJ7]
American jazz musician
* Simmons, Sonny

Simmons, Jack 1941-   [DC]
British cricketer
* Simmons, Flat Jack
* Simmons, Simmo

Simmons, James 1850-1923 [BMH, THR]
British actor and comic singer
* Fawn, James
* [The] Prince of Red-Nosed Comedians

Simmons, Jimmy 20th c.   [RM]
Musician
* Simmons, Antennae Jimmy

Simmons, John   [BBH]
American baseball coach
* Simmons, Hi

Simmons, Kim
See Duncan, Kathleen Mary

Simmons, Little Mack
See Simmons, Mack

Simmons, Lonnie
See Simmons, Samuel

Simmons, Mac
See Simmons, Mack

Simmons, Mack 1934-   [BWW]
American singer
* St. Louis Mac
* Simmons, Little Mack
* Simmons, Mac
* Sims, Mac

Simmons, Malcolm Early 1935-   [SMG]
American baseball player
* Simmons, Max

Simmons, Max
See Simmons, Malcolm Early

Simmons, Pat[rick Clement]
See Simoni, Patrick Clement

Simmons, Ruth
See Tighe, Virginia

Simmons, S. H.
See Simmons, Sylvia

Simmons, Samuel 1915?-   [WWJ]
American jazz musician
* Simmons, Lonnie

Simmons, Simba
See Simmons, Ted Lyle

Simmons, Simmo
See Simmons, Jack

Simmons, Sonny
See Simmons, Huey

Simmons, Stanley 1942?-   [HPPN]
American criminal
* [The] Fly

Simmons, Sylvia 20th c.   [CA]
American advertising executive and author
* Simmons, S. H.

Simmons, Ted Lyle 1949-   [SMG]
American baseball player
* Simmons, Simba

Simmons, Thomas ?-1808   [FFF]
British murderer
* [The] Man of Blood

Simmons, Vivian 1888-1965   [HPPN]
Canadian tattoo artist
* Sailor Joe

Simmons, William E. 1850-?   [PA]
Author
* W. E. S.

Simmons, William Hammatt 1812-1841
[IP]
American author
* Domal, C.
* Lockfast

Simmonseed, Johnny
See Hatfield, Bazil Muse

Simms, Billy
See Simms, W. H.

Simms, Ginny
See Sims, Virginia

Simms, Hilda
See Moses, Hilda Theresa

Simms, Larry 1934-   [HPPN]
American actor
* Dumpling, Baby

Simms, W[illiam] Gilmore 1806-1870
[FFF, HPPN, IP, PA]
American author
* [A] Collegian
* Cooper, Frank
* [The] Cooper of the South
* Isabel
* Rivers, Guy
* [The] Southern Cooper
* [A] Southron
* W. G. S.

Simms, W. H. 1856-?   [HPPN]
American gambler
* Simms, Billy

Simms, Yvonne 1928-   [AW]
British author and journalist
* Simon

Simnel, Lambert 1477?-1534   [HPPN]
British impostor
* Edward VI
* [The] False Earl of Warwick

Simon ?-67?   [DEP, DNNF, HPPN]
Saint
* Cephas
* Christ's Vicar On Earth
* Fisher of Men
* Fisherman Saint
* Kepha [Petros or Rock]
* Man of Fire
* Peter

Simon (cont.)
* [The] Prince of the Apostles
* Saint Without A Halo

Simon
See Allgood, Miles Clayton

Simon [joint pseudonym with Roger D'Este Burford]
See Blakeston, Oswell

Simon [joint pseudonym with Oswell Blakeston]
See Burford, Roger D'Este

Simon
See Cardenas, Simon

Simon
See Hooker, Henry Brown

Simon
See Simms, Yvonne

Simon, Abraham 1897-1957   [PMJ]
American bandleader
* Lyman, Abe

Simon, Billy
See Simon, Violet E.

Simon, Charlie May
See Fletcher, Charlie May Hogue

Simon, Cully
See Simon, John Cullen

Simon, Doc
See Simon, Neil

Simon, Edouard Etienne Antoine
1838-1913   [HPPN]
French journalist and politician
* Lockroy, Edourard Etienne Antoine

Simon, Emma [Couvely] 1848-?   [IP]
German author
* Vely, Emma

Simon, Francois 1895-1975   [BDF, F2, FC]
Swiss-born actor
* Simon, Michel

Simon, Gus 1881-1945   [SC]
German-born actor, songwriter, producer
* Edwards, Gus

Simon, Inge 1921-   [OP]
German-born opera singer
* Borkh, Inge

Simon, Joe 1947-   [IBW]
African singer and record producer
* Chokin' Kind

Simon, John
See Simon, Jovan Ivan

Simon, John Cullen 1918-   [CEI]
Canadian-born hockey player
* Simon, Cully

Simon, Joseph Philippe 1803-1891
[WBD]
French comedian and playwright
* Lockroy, Joseph Philippe

Simon, Jovan Ivan 1925- [BEW]
Yugoslav-born theatre critic
* Simon, John

Simon, Jules
See Suisse, Jules Francois Simon

Simon, Kaila 20th c.
Polish-born American author
* Simon, Kate

Simon, Kate
See Simon, Kaila

Simon, Kenneth
See Goldgraber, Kenneth

Simon, Lionel 1922- [CA]
American author and publisher
* Stuart, Lyle

Simon, Mae 20th c. [FIR]
American actress
* [The] Yiddish Sarah Bernhardt

Simon Magus 1st c. [HPPN]
Samarian sorcerer
* Simon the Magician
* [The] Supreme Power of God

Simon, Michel
See Simon, Francois

Simon, Mina Lewiton 1904-1970 [CAP, SAT]
American author and educator
* Lewiton, Mina

Simon, Neil 1927- [AN]
American playwright
* Simon, Doc

Simon of Sudbury
See Theobald [or Tybald], Simon

Simon, Paul Frederick 1941- [CLC, RO2]
American singer and songwriter
* Kane, Paul
* Landis, Jerry

Simon, Pazuza
See Simon, Stafford

Simon, Richard 1638-1712 [SN]
French theologian
* [The] Father of German Exegesis

Simon, Robert
See Musto, Barry

Simon, Robert Alfred 1897- [WW]
Author
* Reynolds, Liggett

Simon, S. J.
See Skidelsky, Simon Jasha

Simon, Scott 1948- [CMA]
Musician
* Simon, Screamin' Scott

Simon, Screamin' Scott
See Simon, Scott

Simon, Simone 1914- [HPPN]
French actress
* Europe's Sweetheart

Simon, Stafford 1908?-1960 [WWJ]
American jazz musician
* Simon, Pazuza

Simon, Sven
See Springer, Axel, Jr.

Simon the Farmer
See Prentice, [Rev.] Thomas

Simon the Magician
See Simon Magus

Simon the Righteous
See Montfort, Simon de [Earl of Leicester]

Simon the Skipper
See Hamilton, Thomas

Simon, Violet E. 20th c. [BBH]
American bowler
* Simon, Billy

Simon, William 1912- [HPPN]
American attorney, politician, government official
* [The] Energy Chief
* [The] Energy Czar
* [The] Federal Energy Chief
* Popeye

Simond, Louis 1767-1831 [IP]
Author
* [A] French Traveller

Simonds, Peter 1906- [CCL]
Canadian author
* Greaves, Richard

Simonds, William 1822-1859 [FFF]
American author
* Aimwell, Walter

Simone
See Benda, Pauline

Simone, Andre
See Katz, Otto

Simone, Nina
See Waymon, Eunice Kathleen

Simonelli, Giovanni 20th c. [WF]
Italian screenwriter
* O'Neil, Simon

Simonetta
See Cesario, Simonetta Colonna Di

Simonetta
See Di Cesaro, Simonetta

Simonetta
See Fabian, Alberta

Simonetta
See Vespucci, Simonetta Catteneo

Simoni, Guglielmo de
See Petrosino, Joseph

Simoni, Patrick Clement 1908-1968 [BE]
American baseball player
* Simmons, Pat[rick Clement]

Simonides 7th c. BC [DEP, SN]
Greek poet
* [The] Samian Poet

Simonides 6th c. BC [DNNS, RH, SN]
Greek poet
* [The] Cean Poet
* [The] Scian Muse

Simonillo [Little Simon]
See Rodriguez Valades, Jesus

Simonim, Wilhelmina Josephine [PA]
Author
* Haller, Gustave

Simons, Arthur D. 1919?-1979
American army officer
* [The] Bull

Simons, Bobby J. 1929?-1982
American singer and bandleader
* Simons, Tiny
* [The] Singing Canary

Simons, Butch
See Simons, Melbern Ellis

Simons, Claude, Jr. 1914-1975 [BI, FB]
American football player and coach
* Simons, Monk

Simons, Katherine Drayton Mayrant 1892- [CA]
American author and poet
* Mayrant, Drayton
* Maysi, Kadra

Simons, Lydia Lillybridge [IP]
British poet
* E. L.

Simons, Melbern Ellis 1900-1974 [BE]
American baseball player
* Simons, Butch

Simons, Monk
See Simons, Claude, Jr.

Simons, Roger [joint pseudonym with Margaret Punnett]
See Punnett, Ivar

Simons, Roger [joint pseudonym with Ivar Punnett]
See Punnett, Margaret

Simons, Sy
See Simons, Therlow Benjamin

Simons, Therlow Benjamin 1920- [BA]
American police official
* Simons, Sy

Simons, Tiny
See Simons, Bobby J.

Simonson, Mary Jane
See Wheeler, Mary Jane

Simos, Miriam 1951- [CA]
American author and playwright
* Starhawk

Simoun, Henri
See Rodman, Howard

Simpkin
See Webb, Arthur Patterson

Simpkin the Second, Poetic Recorder
See Broome, Ralph

Simpkins, Jonas
See Jewett, Benjamin E. G.

[The] Simple
See Charles III

[The] Simple
See Frederick III

[The] Simple
See Sigismund

[The] Simple Barefoot Wall Street Lawyer
See Willkie, Wendell Lewis

[The] Simple Lombard
See Di Castel, Guido

Simplicius
See Grant, [Sir] Charles

Simpson, Adele
See Smithline, Adele

Simpson [or Sampson?], Agnes 16th c. [DNNF]
Scottish woman executed for witchcraft
* [The] Wise Wife of Keith

Simpson, Archibald 18th c. [IP, PA]
Scottish author
* MacShinie, Gillespie

Simpson, Bertram Lennox 1877-? [WWL]
Author
* Weale, B. L. Putnam

Simpson, Bullet Joe
See Simpson, Harold Joseph

Simpson, Cass
See Simpson, Cassino

Simpson, Cassino 1902- [MY]
Italian-born jazz musician
* Simpson, Cass

Simpson, Charles 1874-1912 [HPPN]
American vaudeville performer
* Emmonds, Charles

Simpson, Charles
See Murphy, Charles

Simpson, Clarence 1915?- [BI]
American basketball coach
* Simpson, Snowy

Simpson, Duke
See Simpson, Thomas Leo

Simpson, Edith Eva 1902- [IAW]
American poet
* Felton, Eve

Simpson, Edward 1815-? [DI, DNNS, FFF, RH]
British manufacturer of counterfeit relics
* Flint Jack
* Fossil Willy
* Old Antiquarian

Simpson, Elizabeth Sloan 1917- [HPPN]
American model, fashion consultant, actress
* [The] First Lady of New York City
* [The] Poor Man's Celeste Holm
* [The] Second Mrs. Simpson Sloan

Simpson, Evan John 1901-1953 [BEW]
British-born actor, playwright, director
* John, Evan

Simpson, Evangeline M. 19th c. [FFF]
American author
* Saxon, Van

Simpson, Harold Joseph ?-1973 [BBH]
Canadian-born hockey player
* Simpson, Bullet Joe

Simpson, Harry Leon 1925- [BE]
American baseball player
* Simpson, Suitcase

Simpson, Hashknife
See Simpson, John Nicholas

Simpson, Helen [de Guerry]
See Browne, Helen de Guerry Simpson

Simpson, Jane [Cross] 1804-? [FFF]
British poet
* Gertrude

Simpson, Jane 1881-1935 [BEW]
American actress
* Wheatley, Jane

Simpson, Jerry 1842-1905 [HPPN]
American politician
* Simpson, Sockless
* Simpson, Sockless Jerry
* [The] Sockless Sage
* Sockless Socrates
* [The] Sockless Statesman

Simpson, John Hampson ?-1955 [WWL]
British author
* Hampson, John

Simpson, John Nicholas 19th c. [HPPN]
American cattle rancher
* Simpson, Hashknife

Simpson, Joseph 18th c. [HPPN]
British barrister
* [A] Barrister at Law

Simpson, Joseph 20th c. [CME]
American country-western performer
* Simpson, Red

Simpson, Judy 20th c. [CA]
American author
* Foxx, Rosalind [joint pseudonym with June Haydon]
* Logan, Sara [joint pseudonym with June Haydon]

Simpson, Louis 1923- [CW]
Jamaican-born poet
* Marontz, Louis Aston

Simpson, Maria
See Cahill, Frank

Simpson, Mike
See Simpson, Mitchell Louis

Simpson, Mitchell Louis 1916- [MY]
American jazz musician
* Simpson, Mike

Simpson, Myrtle L[illias] 1931- [CA]
British author
* Emslie, M. L.

Simpson, N. F.
See Simpson, Norman Frederick

Simpson, Norma 1926- [FC]
British actress
* Marsh, Carol

Simpson, Norman Frederick 1919- [BEW]
British playwright
* Simpson, N. F.

Simpson, O. J.
See Simpson, Orenthal James

Simpson, Orenthal James 1947- [FB, IPA, SMG]
American football player
* Juice
* Orange Juice
* Simpson, O. J.

Simpson, Ralph 1949-
American basketball player
* Simpson, Simp

Simpson, Red
See Simpson, Joseph

Simpson, Ruth Mary Rasey 1902- [CA]
American author and poet
* Rasey, Ruth M.

Simpson, Ryllis Barnes 1899?-1978 [FIR]
Dancer
* Hasoutra

Simpson, S. S. [IP]
American author
* S. S. S.

Simpson, [Rev.] Samuel 19th c. [HPPN]
British clergyman
* [A] Layman

Simpson, Shotgun
See Simpson, Tom

Simpson, Simp
See Simpson, Ralph

Simpson, Snowy
See Simpson, Clarence

Simpson, Sockless
See Simpson, Jerry

Simpson, Sockless Jerry
See Simpson, Jerry

Simpson, Stephen 1789-1854 [IP, PA]
American journalist
* Brutus

Simpson, Suitcase
See Simpson, Harry Leon

Simpson, Texas Bill
See Simpson, William Hood

Simpson, Thomas 1710-1761 [HPPN, IP]
British mathematician and author
* Hurlothrumbo
* [The] Oracle of Nuneaton

Simpson, Thomas Leo 1927- [BE]
American baseball player
* Simpson, Duke

Simpson, Tom 1952- [SMG]
Canadian-born hockey player
* Simpson, Shotgun

Simpson, W. Graham
See Coalfield, Jonathan

Simpson, Wallis Warfield 1896-1986
[HPPN]
*American wife of Edward VIII of
England*
* Simpson, Wally

Simpson, Wally
See Simpson, Wallis Warfield

Simpson, William 20th c. [ESF, SFL,
WGT]
American author
* Blot, Thomas

Simpson, William Hood 1888-1980
American military officer
* Simpson, Texas Bill

Sims, [Lieut.] A. K.
See Whitson, John Harvey

Sims, Alexander Dromgoole 1803-1848
[DNA]
American author
* Rigmarole, Crayon

Sims, Baby
See Sims, Stanley

Sims, Billy
See Pershing, Mike

Sims, Clarence 1891-1968 [BE]
American baseball player
* Sims, Pete

Sims, D. N.
See Sims, Denise Natalie

Sims, Denise Natalie 1940- [SFL]
British author
* Sims, D. N.

Sims, Duane B. 1941- [BE, PB, SMG]
American baseball player
* Sims, Duke

Sims, Duke
See Sims, Duane B.

Sims, Gameday
See Sims, Kenneth

Sims, George Robert 1847-1922 [FFF,
RH, WBD]
British journalist and playwright
* Dagonet

Sims, Henry R. 1893- [NAA]
American editor and politician
* Radcliffe, Henry

Sims, Howard 20th c. [WP 9-8-84]
American tap dancer
* Sims, Sandman

Sims, John Haley [Jack] 1925-1985
[DAM, EJ, PMJ]
American jazz musician
* Sims, Zoot

Sims, Kenneth 20th c. [SI 9-1-82]
American football player
* Sims, Gameday
* Sims, Moneybags

Sims, Mac
See Simmons, Mack

Sims, Moneybags
See Sims, Kenneth

Sims, Naomi 1947?- [HPPN]
American fashion model
* [The] Super Model

Sims, Pete
See Sims, Clarence

Sims, Peter 1938- [EJ]
American jazz musician
* La Roca, Pete

Sims, Phil[ip] 1933- [HPPN]
*American psychologist and consumer
advocate*
* [The] Black Ralph Nader

Sims, Sandman
See Sims, Howard

Sims, Stanley 20th c. [RBE]
Boxer
* Sims, Baby

Sims, Virginia 1916- [FC]
American singer
* Simms, Ginny

Sims, Zoot
See Sims, John Haley [Jack]

Sims-Errol, Leon 1881-1951 [THR]
Australian-born actor
* Errol, Leon

Simson, Archibald 19th c. [HFN]
Author
* Macshimi, Gillespie

Simson, Eric Andrew 1895- [WW]
Author
* Kirk, Laurence

Simson, Harold 1878-1944 [THR]
British composer
* Fraser-Simson, Harold

Simson, Lena Margaret 1869?-1957
[NAA]
British actress and author
* Ashwell, Lena

Sina, Sandy
See Messina, Santo

Sinatra, Dollie
See Sinatra, Natalie [Garaventi]

Sinatra, Francis Albert [Frank] 1915-
[HPPN, NN]
American singer and actor
* [The] Chairman of the Board
* [The] Dago
* Dr. Jekyll and Mr. Hyde
* Frankie Boy
* [The] General
* [The] Gov'nor
* King of the Ratpack
* [The] Leader

Sinatra, Francis Albert [Frank] (cont.)
* [The] Man
* O'Brien, Marty
* Ol' Blue Eyes
* [Il] Padrone
* [The] Pope
* [The] Swooner
* [The] Voice

Sinatra, Natalie [Garaventi] 1895?-1977
[BI]
*Mother of American singer and actor,
Frank Sinatra*
* Sinatra, Dollie

Sinbad
See Dingle, Aylward Edward

Sinbad the Tailor
See Shinwell, Emmanuel

Sinbaldi, Fosco
See Kacewgari, Romain

Sinbeth, Lesly
See Bennis, Wessel Johannes

[A] Sincere Friend of the People
See Lothian, Maurice

**[A] Sincere Lover of Our Protestant
Establishment**
See Bray, [Rev.] Thomas

**[A] Sincere Lover of the Church and
State**
See Webster, James

[A] Sincere Well Wisher to the Public
See Madan, Martin

Sincerity
See Foe, Daniel

Sincerus
See Adams, Samuel

Sinclair, Alasdair
See Clyne, Douglas George Wilson

Sinclair, Arthur
See McDonnell, Arthur

Sinclair, Bertha M[uzzy] 1874-1940
[WGT]
Author
* Bower, B. M.

Sinclair, Carrie Bell 1839-? [FFF, IP]
American poet
* Clara

Sinclair, Clarence
See Forshaw, Charles Frederick

Sinclair, Coll McLean 19th c. [CCL]
Canadian author
* Malcolm

Sinclair, Daisy
See Edwards, Margaret

Sinclair, Duncan
See Dunnett, Alastair MacTavish

Sinclair, Edith
See Favor, Mrs. Edward M.

Sinclair, Ellery
See Jemison, Louisa

Sinclair, Emil
See Hesse, Hermann

Sinclair, Gavin
See MacArthur, D[avid] Wilson

Sinclair, Grace
See Wallmann, Jeffrey M[iner]

Sinclair, Grant
See Drago, Harry Sinclair

Sinclair, Harry Ford 1876-1956 [HPPN]
American business executive
* Sinclair, Sinco

Sinclair, Heather
See Johnston, William

Sinclair, Ian
See Foley, [Cedric] John

Sinclair, James 19th c. [IP]
Scottish author
* Sigma

Sinclair, James
See Staples, Reginald Thomas

Sinclair, Jo
See Seid, Ruth

Sinclair, [Sir] John 1754-1835 [IP]
Scottish political reformer and author
* [The] President

Sinclair, Julian
See Sinclair, Mary Amelia St. Clair

Sinclair, Lottie
See Kennedy, Mrs. Frank

Sinclair, Mary
See Cook, Mary

Sinclair, Mary Amelia St. Clair
1865?-1946 [TLC]
British author and poet
* Sinclair, Julian
* Sinclair, May

Sinclair, May
See Sinclair, Mary Amelia St. Clair

Sinclair, Miranda 1948- [CA]
British author
* Seymour, Miranda

Sinclair, Mrs. E. V. [FFF]
Entertainer
* Clifford, Maude

Sinclair, Mrs. Harry [FFF]
Entertainer
* Vernon, Fanny

Sinclair, Rose
See Mendonca, Susan

Sinclair, Sinco
See Sinclair, Harry Ford

Sinclair, Upton [Beall] 1878-1968 [CA, SAT]
American author and politician
* Fitch, Clarke
* Garrison, Frederick
* Stirling, Arthur

Sinclair-Hill, Gerard Arthur 1896-1945 [BEW]
British director
* Hill, Sinclair

Sindall, B. R.
See Sindall, Bernard Ralph

Sindall, Bernard Ralph 1925- [ART]
British sculptor
* Sindall, B. R.

Sinderby, Donald
See Stephens, Donald Ryder

Sindici, [Maria] Magda Stuart 19th c. [NPS]
Author
* Vivaria, Kassandra

Sindona, Michele 1920- [HPPN, NW 9-13-82]
Italian financier and swindler
* Bonamico, Joseph
* God's Banker

Sindoni, Francesco Gaetano 1928-1980 [HPPN]
Italian-American underworld figure
* Philadelphia's Top Loan Shark
* Sindoni, Frank

Sindoni, Frank
See Sindoni, Francesco Gaetano

Sine
See Sinet, Maurice

Sined
See Kelly, Denis

Sinet, Maurice 1928- [WEC]
French cartoonist
* Sine

Sing Song, Jeffrey
See Foe, Daniel

Sing Wah
See Fortune, Robert

Sing-Sing
See Singer, William Robert

Singe
See Pellegrini, Carlo

[Le] Singe de Racine
See Campistron, Jean Galbert de

Singer, Adam
See Karp, David

Singer, Al 1907-1961 [EJS]
American boxer
* [The] Bronx Beauty

Singer, Alexander 1921-1967 [HPPN]
American producer and author
* Singer, Allie

Singer, Allie
See Singer, Alexander

Singer, Amanda
See Brooks, Janice Young

Singer, Bant
See Shaw, Charles

Singer, Bullet Bill
See Singer, William Robert

Singer, Burns
See Singer, James Hyman

Singer, Erno 1898?-1980 [BI]
Hungarian politician
* Gero, Erno

Singer, Guy
See Guisinger, Earl

Singer, I. J.
See Singer, Israel Joshua

Singer, Isaac Bashevis 1904- [CA, SAT]
Polish-born American author
* Bashevis, Isaac
* Warshofsky, Isaac

Singer, Isaac Merrit 1811-1875 [HPPN]
American inventor
* [The] Father of the Sewing Machine

Singer, Israel Joshua 1893-1944 [HPPN]
Polish-American author
* Singer, I. J.

Singer, James Hyman 1928-1964 [BI]
American poet and translator
* Singer, Burns

Singer, Jane Sherrod 1917- [CA, SAT]
American author
* Sherrod, Jane

Singer, Kurt D[eutsch]
See Deutsch, Kurt

[The] Singer of Catherine
See Derzhavin, Gavril

[The] Singer Throwing Machine
See Singer, William Robert

Singer, William Robert 1944- [BE, SMG]
American baseball player
* Billy No-No
* Sing-Sing
* Singer, Bullet Bill
* [The] Singer Throwing Machine

Singh, Kunwar Indrajit 1905?-1982 [WP 10-6-82]
Nepalese prime minister
* [The] Robin Hood of the Himalayas

Singh, Nain 19th c. [HPPN]
Indian spy
* A. K.

Singh, Raj
See Singh, Rajkumari

Singh, Rajkumari 1936?- [CW]
Guyanese poet and author
* Singh, Raj

Singh, Seth Shiv Dayal 1818-1878 [NAD]
Religious leader
* Swamiji Maharaj

Singh, Yoginder
See Agca, Mehmet Ali

Singin' Jack Smith
See Smith, Jack

Singin' Sam
See Frankel, Harry

[The] Singing and Dancing Juvenile
See Lane, Richard

[The] Singing Barber
See Fairburn, Werly

[The] Singing Bishop
See McCabe, Charles Cardwell

[The] Singing Brakeman
See Rodgers, James Charles [Jimmie]

[The] Singing Canary
See Reles, Abraham [Abe]

[The] Singing Canary
See Simons, Bobby J.

[The] Singing Capon
See Eddy, Nelson

[The] Singing Chaplain
See McCabe, Charles Cardwell

[The] Singing Christian
See White, Josh[ua Daniel]

[The] Singing Cowboy
See Autry, [Orvon] Gene

[The] Singing Duse
See Calvet, Rosa Emma

Singing Eagle
See Diego, Juan

[The] Singing Fisherman
See Horton, Johnny

[The] Singing Lady
See Wicker, Ireene Seaton

[The] Singing Maestro
See Ravazza, Carl

[The] Singing Millboy
See Hylton, John [Jack]

[The] Singing Nun
See Deckers, Jeannine

[The] Singing Pianist
See Erby, John J.

[The] Singing Pilgrim
See Phillips, Philip

[The] Singing Policeman
See Regan, Phil[ip]

[The] Singing Preacher
See White, Booker T. Washington

[The] Singing Ranger
See Snow, Clarence Eugene

Singing Sam
See Stevens, Sam

Singing Sam Chatmon
See Chatmon, Sam, Jr.

Singing Sandie
See Gordon, Alexander

[The] Singing Secretary
See McCabe, Charles Cardwell

[The] Singing Sheriff
See Young, Faron

[The] Singing Sibyl
See Victor, Metta Victoria Fuller

[The] Singing Star of the Movies
See Jones, Allan

[The] Singing Story Lady
See Wicker, Ireene Seaton

[The] Singing Sweetheart of Canada
See Murray, Anne

[The] Singing Troubador
See Lucanese, Dominic

[The] Singing Umpire
See Byron, William

Single, Celia
See Franklin, Ben[jamin]

Single Speech Hamilton
See Hamilton, William Gerard

Single Speech Hemphill
See Hemphill, Joseph

Single Speech Milnes
See Milnes, Richard Monckton [First Baron Houghton]

Single Tax Johnson
See Johnson, Tom Loftin

[The] Single Taxer
See George, Henry

[The] Singles King of Washington
See O'Harro, Mike

Singleton, Anne
See Benedict, Ruth

Singleton, Arthur, Esq.
See Knight, Henry Cogswell

Singleton, Arthur James 1898-1975
[DAM, EJ, PMJ]
American jazz musician
* Singleton, Zutty

Singleton, Benjamin 1809-1892 [IBW]
American pioneer
* Singleton, Pap

Singleton, Bert Elmer 1918- [BE]
American baseball player
* Singleton, Smoky

Singleton, Betty 1910- [CAP]
British author
* Reens, Mary
* Rutland, Dodge

Singleton, Big
See Singleton, Ron

Singleton, Captain
See Sargent, John Osborne

Singleton, E.
See Holden, Edward Singleton

Singleton, J. B.
See Singleton, James Benjamin, Sr.

Singleton, James Benjamin, Sr. 1902-
[BA]
American dentist
* Singleton, J. B.

Singleton, John Edward 1896-1937 [BE]
American baseball player
* Singleton, Sheriff

Singleton, Mary [Montgomerie Lamb]
19th c. [IP]
British poet
* Fane, Violet

Singleton, Mary
See Brooke, Frances [Moore]

Singleton, Pap
See Singleton, Benjamin

Singleton, Penny
See McNulty, Dorothy

Singleton, Ron 1952- [SMG]
American football player
* Singleton, Big

Singleton, Sheriff
See Singleton, John Edward

Singleton, Smoky
See Singleton, Bert Elmer

Singleton, William 19th c. [IP]
British author
* [A] Late Teacher
* [A] True Quaker

Singleton, Zutty
See Singleton, Arthur James

Singmaster, Elsie
See Lewars, Mrs. Harold

[The] Singular Doctor
See Occam [or Ockham], William of

[The] Singular Senegalese
See Phal, Louis

Singularis, Doctor
See Occam [or Ockham], William of

Singularity, Thomas
See Nott, Henry Junius

Sinhold Von Schutz, Philipp Balthasar
1657-1742 [WGT]
German author
* Creutzbergs, Amadei
* Ehrenkron, Irenico
* Von Faramond, Ludwig Ernst
* Von Wahrenberg, Constantino

Siniavskii, Andrei Donatovich 1925-
[BI]
Russian author
* Tertz, Abram

Sini'letta, Vic
See Smith, Victor A.

Sinister Sal Maglie
See Maglie, Salvatore Anthony

Sinitsky, Ted 1928- [CA]
American author
* Sennett, Ted

Sinjohn, John
See Galsworthy, John

Sinjun
See John, Elizabeth Beaman

Sinks, Rita Faye 1944- [CWG]
American country-western performer
* Faye, Rita

Sinkwich, Fireball Frankie
See Sinkwich, Frank

Sinkwich, Frank 1920- [FB]
American football player
* Sinkwich, Fireball Frankie

Sinn, Mrs. William E. [FFF]
Entertainer
* Tanner, Cora

Sinner Saved
See Huntington, William

[The] Sinner's Friend
See Mathew, Theobald

[The] Sinner's Friend
See Matthew, [Father] Theobald

Sinno, Big Sal
See Sinno, Salvatore

Sinno, Salvatore 20th c.
American underworld figure
* Sinno, Big Sal

Sinnott, Michael 1880-1960 [BEW, F1, FC, HPPN]
Canadian-born director and producer
* Goose, Father
* [The] King of Comedy
* Sennett, Mack

Sinoel
See Vies, Jen

Sinuss, Z.
See Skujins, Zigmunds

Siodmak, Curt
See Siodmak, Kurt

Siodmak, Kurt 1902- [FD, FDG]
German director
* Siodmak, Curt

Siodmak, Robert
See Siodmark, Robert

Siodmark, Robert 1900-1973 [SC]
American-born actor, producer, director
* Siodmak, Robert

Sion of Myrddin
See Williams, [Rev.] St. George Armstrong

Sioussat, Jean Pierre 1781-? [HPPN]
French White House official
* French John

Sipes, Leonard Raymond 1930- [CWG]
American country-western performer
* Collins, Tommy

Siple, Paul Allman 1908-1968 [HPPN]
American exporer, geologist, author
* [The] Boy Explorer

Sir, A.
See Sireborn, [Karl] Axel [Malte]

Sir Bob
See Walpole, [Sir] Robert [First Earl of Orford]

Sir Charles
See Thompson, Charles Phillip

Sir Chauncey
See Freeman, Ernie

Sir Douglas
See Sahm, Douglas Saldana

[The] Sir Joseph Banks of His Times
See Evelyn, John

[The] Sir Laurence Olivier of the White House
See Haig, Alexander Meigs, Jr.

Sir Len
See Slocombe, Philip Anthony

Sir Richard
See Cooley, Duff C.

Sir Rudi
See Bing, [Sir] Rudolf

Sir Timothy
See Keefe, Timothy John

Sir Toby
See Sutton, Scott

Sir Tristram
See Scott, [Sir] Walter

Sir Veto
See Johnson, Andrew

Sir Walter
See Davis, Walter

Sir Walter
See Raines, Walter

[Il] Siracusano
See Boi, Paolo

[The] Sire of Ossian
See Macpherson, James

[The] Sire of Steel
See Holley, Alexander Lyman

Sireborn, [Karl] Axel [Malte] 1915- [IAW]
Swedish author
* Sir, A.

[The] Siren of Sex
See West, Mae

[The] Siren of the Screen
See West, Mae

Siren, V[ladimir]
See Nabokov, Vladimir Vladimirovich

Siri, Victor 1615?-1685 [SN]
Italian monk and historian
* [The] Procopius of France

Sirica, John Joseph 1904- [HPPN]
American jurist
* Sirica, Maximum John
* [The] Watergate Judge

Sirica, Maximum John
See Sirica, John Joseph

Sirius
See Martyn, Edward

Sirk, Douglas
See Sierck, Detlef

Sirko, Marlon
See Siciliano, Mario

Sirois, Jigger
See Sirois, Leon Duray

Sirois, Leon Duray 1935- [EAR]
American auto racer
* Sirois, Jigger

Sirone
See Jones, Norris

Sirovich, William Irving 1882-1939 [HPPN]
American physician and politician
* [The] Savior of the Arts

Sirrom, Wes
See Weiss, Morris S[amuel]

Sirveaux, Jules 1882-1938 [OCF]
French actor
* Delphin

Siseman, E. J.
See Siseman, Ernest James

Siseman, Ernest James 1920- [ART]
British painter
* Siseman, E. J.

Sisines
See Archelaus

Sisk, John 1906- [HPPN]
American football player
* [The] Big Train

Sisko, Joseph Coffin 1920- [HPPN]
American army officer
* [The] Cisco Kid

Sisler, George Harold 1893-1973 [BE, DGS, HPPN, PB]
American baseball player
* [The] Perfect Ballplayer
* [The] Perfect Player
* Sisler, Gorgeous George

Sisler, Gorgeous George
See Sisler, George Harold

Sissle, Noble 20th c. [BWW]
American bandleader
* Brown, Willie

Sisson, C. J.
See Sisson, Charles Jasper

Sisson, Charles Jasper 1885-1966 [LC]
British editor, author, educator
* Sisson, C. J.

Sisson, Jack 18th c. [IBW]
American soldier
* Sisson, Prince
* Watson, Guy

Sisson, Prince
See Sisson, Jack

Sister Amy
See Archer-Gillian, Amy

Sister Dora
See Pattison, Dorothy Wyndlow

Sister Grace
See Kimmins, G. T.

Sister Louise
See Driver, Phyllis

Sister Mabel
See Schafer, Mabel

Sister Mary
See Meehan, Charles Patrick

Sister Mary
See Salomen, Edith

[A] Sister of Charity
See Power, Mary

[The] Sister of Shakespeare
See Baillie, Joanna

Sisti, Sebastian Daniel 1920-   [BE]
American baseball player
* Sisti, Sibby

Sisti, Sibby
See Sisti, Sebastian Daniel

Sisto Rosa
See Badalocchio, Sisto

Sistrunk, Manny
See Sistrunk, Manuel

Sistrunk, Manuel 1947-   [FR]
American football player
* Sistrunk, Manny

Sistrunk, Otis 1949-   [IBW]
American football player
* Sistrunk, Trunk

Sistrunk, Trunk
See Sistrunk, Otis

Sisyphus
See Barthelmes, [Albert] Wes[ley, Jr.]

[The] Sit Down Striker
See Hoffman, Clare E.

Sitaramiah, Venkataramiah 1899-   [IAW]
Indian author, poet, playwright
* Visee

Sitko, Emil M. 1923-1973   [FB, HPPN]
American football player
* Sitko, Red
* Sitko, Six Yards

Sitko, Red
See Sitko, Emil M.

Sitko, Six Yards
See Sitko, Emil M.

Sittewald, Philander von
See Mosenrosh, Johann Michael

Sitting Bull 1837?-1890   [HPPN]
American Indian chief
* [The] Champion of the Sioux

Sitting Bull
See Clarke, Robert D.

Sitting Bull
See Lawson, John Daniel

Sitting Bull
See Morton, Oliver Hazard Perry Throck

Sitting Bull
See Summerall, Charles Pelot

Sitting Bull
See Tatanka Yotanka

Sitwell, [Sir] Osbert 1892-   [HPPN]
British author, poet, satirist
* Miles

Sityana, Alfred Mama Sikhefu 1907-   [IAW]
South African author
* Professor

Sitzfleisch, Vladimir
See Spirer, Herbert F[rederick]

Siu Sin Far
See Eaton, Edith

Sivad
See Davis, Eugene

Sivananda, Swami
See Iyer, Kuppuswami

Sivasankara Pillai, Thakazhi 1912-   [IAW]
Indian author
* Thakazhi

Sivertsen, Cort 1622-1675   [HPPN, WBD]
Danish naval officer
* Adelaer, Cort Sivertsen

Sivoney, John L.
See Fontaine, Frank

Sivuca
See D'Oliviera, Severino

Siwaarmill, H. P.
See Sharp, William

Siward [Earl of Northumberland] ?-1055   [WBD]
Danish warrior
* [The] Strong

Six
See Potter, A. K.

Six
See Potter, Albert Knight

Six, [Father]
See Tranh-van-Luc

[The] Six Dollar A Game Quarterback
See Unitas, John[ny]

[A] Six Foot Suckling
See Fitzpatrick

Six, Jimmy
See Lewis, James Window

Six Shooter
See Spillane, Robert

Six Yards Sitko
See Sitko, Emil M.

Sixkiller, Alex 1951-   [FB]
American football player
* Sixkiller, Sonny

Sixkiller, Sonny
See Sixkiller, Alex

Sixteen-String Jack
See Rann, John

Sixtus IV
See Della Rovere, Francesco

Sixtus V
See Peretti, Felice

Sizemore, Barbara 1928?-   [HPPN]
American educator
* [The] Boat Rocker

Sizemore, Chris[tine] Costner 1927-   [CA]
American author
* Lancaster, Evelyn

Sizemore, Jimmy 1928-   [ECM]
American country-western performer
* Sizemore, Little Jimmy

Sizemore, Little Jimmy
See Sizemore, Jimmy

Sizemore, Pee Wee
See Sizemore, Ted Crawford

Sizemore, Runt
See Sizemore, Ted Crawford

Sizemore, Sizey
See Sizemore, Ted Crawford

Sizemore, Ted Crawford 1946-   [SMG]
American baseball player
* Sizemore, Pee Wee
* Sizemore, Runt
* Sizemore, Sizey

Sjoberg, Lars-Erik 1944-   [SMG]
Swedish-born hockey player
* Sjoberg, Shoe

Sjoberg, Shoe
See Sjoberg, Lars-Erik

Sjoeberg, Erik 1794-1828   [DNNF, FFF, RH]
Swedish poet
* Vitalis

Sjoeke, Eva 1926-   [FC]
Hungarian actress
* Bartok, Eva

Sjoestroem, Victor 1879-1960   [BEW, FC, FD]
Swedish actor and director
* Seastrom, Victor

Sjoholm, Peter 1948?-
Swedish singer and manager
* Holm, Peter

Skaerbaek
See Fuechsel, Franz

Skagen, Kiki 1943-   [CA]
American author
* Munshi, Shehnaaz

Skaggs, Brother
See Skaggs, Elijah

Skaggs, Elijah 1810-1870 [HPPN]
American gambler and confidence man
* Enterprising Elijah
* [The] Kentucky Card Sharp
* [The] Master Gambler
* [The] Preaching Faro Dealer
* Skaggs, Brother

Skald
See Cray, Edward

Skaldaspillir
See Eyvind Finnson

Skaldaspillir, Sigfridur
See Broxon, Mildred Downey

Skalicki, Amirei
See Scheucher, Annemarie

Skancke, Miriam Anne 1879-? [THR]
American actress
* Nesbitt, Miriam Anne

Skarbek, Krystyne 1915?-1952 [BI]
*Polish underground leader during World
War II*
* Armand, Jacqueline
* Granville, Christine

Skarda, Patricia Lyn 1946- [CA]
American author
* St. Clair, Clovis

Skarga, Piotr
See Paweski, Piotr

Skarstedt, Ernest Teofil 1854-? [NAA]
Swedish-born author
* Sdt, E.

[The] Skate
See Archibald, Nathaniel [Nate]

Skavronskaya, Marfa 1684?-1727
[HPPN]
Empress of Russia
* Alexievna, Catherine
* Catherine I

Skawonius, Ses
See Skawonius, Sven Erik

Skawonius, Sven Erik 20th c. [ART]
Swedish painter and theatre-set designer
* Skawonius, Ses

Skeat, W. W.
See Skeat, Walter William

Skeat, Walter William 1834-1912 [LC]
British philologist and author
* Skeat, W. W.

Skeels, Vernon H. 1918- [ESF]
American author and physician
* Rossiter, Oscar

Skeffington, Francis 1878-1916 [DIL]
Irish journalist
* Sheehy-Skeffington, Francis

Skeffington, [Sir] Lumley 1771-1850
[NPS]
British playwright
* Skipton, Skiff [or Skiffy]

Skeffington, [Sir] William ?-1535 [NPS]
Lord Deputy of Ireland
* [The] Gunner

Skeleton
See Gicheru, Samuel Mwangi

[The] Skeleton Specialist
See Williams Grant

Skelley, Joseph Harold 1891- [THR]
American actor
* Skelly, Hal

Skelly, Gentleman Jack
See Skelly, Jack

Skelly, Hal
See Skelley, Joseph Harold

Skelly, Jack 1870-1953 [BI]
American boxer
* Skelly, Gentleman Jack

Skelly, Madeleine 1904- [BEW]
American actress, producer, director
* Skelly, Madge

Skelly, Madge
See Skelly, Madeleine

Skelly, William Nugent ?-1852 [PI]
Irish poet
* W. N. S.

Skelton, Helter
See Skelton, [Richard] Red

Skelton, Herbert Sleath 1870-1921
[BEW, HPPN]
British actor and producer
* Sleath, Herbert

Skelton, Jimmy 1894?-1978 [FIR]
Musician
* [The] Old Man River

Skelton, John 1460?-1529 [DEL, HPPN,
PA, SN]
British poet
* Clout, Colin
* [A] Democratic Tory
* [The] Inventive Skelton
* Oxoniae Poeta Laureatus
* [The] Poet Laureate of Oxford
* S.
* [The] Vicar of Hell

Skelton, [Sir] John 1831-1897 [DEA]
Scottish author and editor
* Shirley

Skelton, Philip 1707-1787 [IP]
Irish clergyman and author
* [An] Old Man
* [An] Old Officer

Skelton, [Richard] Red 1913- [ASC, FC,
HPPN, IPA]
American comedian and actor
* America's Most Durable Clown
* Invincible Red
* Last of the Great American Clowns
* [The] Marcel Marceau of Television
* Rubber Face
* Skelton, Helter
* Television's Clown Prince

Skelton, Roger
See Horn, Peter [Rudolf Gisela]

Skenandoah
See Morgan, Lewis Henry

Skendo, Lumo
See Frasheri, Midhat

Skene, Anthony [Juan]
See Philips, George Norman

Skene, Felicia M. F. 19th c. [IP]
British poet
* F. M. F. S.

Skene, Harriet 18th c. [HPPN]
British author
* Baliol, Martha Bethune

Skene, James Henry 19th c. [IP]
British author
* [A] British Resident of Twenty Years
in the East

Skene, [Sir] John 1540-1617 [FFF]
Scottish advocate and writer
* Philopoliteius

**Skene-Melvin, [Lewis] David [St.
Columb]** 1936- [CA]
Canadian author
* Hill, Lew

Skerrett, Emma
See McClannin, Mrs. R. F.

Skerrett, Rose
See Shewell, Mrs. L. R.

Sketchley, Arthur
See Rose, George

Sketchley, Bud
See Sketchley, Harry Clement

Sketchley, Harry Clement 1919- [BE]
Canadian-born baseball player
* Sketchley, Bud

Skez
See Mackenzie, William Henry

[The] Ski Cat
See Reed, Bob

Ski, Mr.
See Clair, John, Jr.

Ski Nose
See Hope, Leslie Townes

Skiagraphos
See Apollodorus

Skian
See McMahon, Heber

Skibosh, Sky
See Skibosh, Thomas A.

Skibosh, Thomas A. 20th c. [SMG]
American baseball executive
* Skibosh, Sky

Skidelsky, Simon Jasha 20th c. [WW]
Author
* Simon, S. J.

Skidmore, Harriet M. 19th c. [FFF, IP, PA]
American writer
* Marie
* Ruhamah

Skidmore, Joseph, Sr. 18th c. [IP]
British author
* A. B.

Skikne, Larushka Mischa 1928-1973 [BDF, BEW, FC]
Lithuanian-born actor
* Harvey, Laurence

Skillett, Joseph
See Russell, [Lord] John Earl

[The] Skillful Neily [El Neily Manoso]
See Neily, Harry

Skillington, Nancy
See Talbot, Nancy Wilfreda Hewitt

Skillman, Ester Webster
See Webster, Ester Luise

Skillman, Isaac 1740-1799 [IP]
American clergyman and author
* [A] British Bostonian

Skimpole, Harold
See Hunt, [James Henry] Leigh

Skin and Bone
See Mahone, William

Skinflint, Obediah
See Harris, Joel Chandler

Skingle, Kenneth Thomas 1924- [EJ]
British jazz musician
* Graham, Kenny

[The] Skinless Prince of Wales
See Richard II

Skinner, Abby 19th c. [FFF]
American author
* Aunt Abby

Skinner, B. F.
See Skinner, Burrhus Frederic

Skinner, Burrhus Frederic 1904- [IPA]
American psychologist
* Skinner, B. F.

Skinner, Camp
See Skinner, Elisha Harrison

Skinner, Charles M. 1852-? [IP, PA]
American journalist
* Tramp

Skinner, Conrad Arthur 1889- [WW]
British author
* Maurice, Michael

Skinner, Dog
See Skinner, Robert R.

Skinner, Elisha Harrison 1897-1944 [BE]
American baseball player
* Skinner, Camp

Skinner, George 19th c. [HFN, IP, PA]
British author and clergyman
* Bernard, H. H.

Skinner, Hugh 20th c. [HPPN]
British ballet dancer
* Laing, Hugh

Skinner, I. G. M. 1890- [DBA]
British painter
* Jacquier

Skinner, Jennifer 1916-1962 [THR]
British actress
* Gray, Jennifer

Skinner, John 1744-1816 [IP, PA]
Scottish clergyman and author
* [A] Layman

Skinner, June Margaret O'Grady 1922- [AW, CA]
Canadian author
* O'Grady, Rohan

Skinner, Mose
See Brown, James E.

Skinner, Otis 1858-1942 [HPPN]
American actor
* [The] Dean of the American Stage
* [The] Dean of the American Theater

Skinner, Robert R. 1931- [PB]
American baseball player and manager
* Skinner, Dog

Skinner, Salmon 1818-1881 [IP, PA]
American journalist
* Amigo

Skip
See Batton, Clyde

Skipper
See Nelson, Prince Roger

Skipper, Betty
See Barr, Betty

Skippon, Philip 17th c. [SN]
British army officer
* [The] Pious

Skipton, Skiff [or Skiffy]
See Skeffington, [Sir] Lumley

Skipworth, Alison
See Groom, Alison

Skirt, Buckley
See Dress, Sue

Skitaletz
See Petrov, Stepan Gavrilovich

Skitt
See Taliaferro, Harden E.

Skittles
See Walters, Catherine

Skizas, Lou[is Peter] 1932- [BE]
American baseball player
* [The] Nervous Greek

Skladany, Joseph 20th c. [BBH]
American football player
* Skladany, Muggsy

Skladany, Muggsy
See Skladany, Joseph

Skobeleff, Michael Dimitrievitch 1843-1882 [SN]
Russian army officer
* [The] Poet of the Sword

Skoglund, Annika
See Banfield, Britt Annika

Skolimowski, Jerzy 1938- [CLC]
Polish director, screenwriter, editor
* Skolimowski, Yurek

Skolimowski, Yurek
See Skolimowski, Jerzy

Skoog, Myer 1926- [BB]
American basketball player
* Skoog, Whitey

Skoog, Whitey
See Skoog, Myer

Skookum Chuck
See Cumming, Robert Dalziel

Skopec, Buckshot
See Skopec, John S.

Skopec, John S. 1880-1912 [BE]
American baseball player
* Skopec, Buckshot

Skorpios, Antares
See Barlow, James William

Skotkoenung [The Tax-King]
See Olaf II [or Olaus]

Skowron, Moose
See Skowron, William Joseph, Jr.

Skowron, William Joseph, Jr. 1930- [BE, DGS, PB]
American baseball player
* Skowron, Moose

Skrine, Agnes 20th c. [WBD]
Irish poet
* O'Neill, Moira

Skrine, Mary Nesta 1905- [THR]
Irish playwright and author
* Farrell, M. J.

Skrine, Mary Nesta
See Keane, Mary Nesta [Skrine]

Skrine, Molly
See Keane, Mary Nesta [Skrine]

Skrote, Z.
See Skujins, Zigmunds

Skryabin, Vyacheslav Mikhailovich 1890-? [CND, IPA]
Russian diplomat
* Dunker [code name used during World War II]
* Kremlin's Kocktail Kid
* Kremlin's Old Reliable
* Molotov, Mysterious
* Molotov, Vyacheslav Mikhailovich
* Old Iron Pants
* Old Man Nyet
* Old Rock Bottom
* [The] Rubber Hammer
* Stone Ass

Skujins, Zigmunds 1926- [IAW]
Latvian author
* Sinuss, Z.
* Skrote, Z.
* Zigis

[The] **Skull**
See Canham, Charles Draper William

Skurdenis, Juliann V.
See Skurdenis-Smircich, Juliann
V[eronica]

Skurdenis-Smircich, Juliann V[eronica]
1942- [CA]
American author
* Skurdenis, Juliann V.

Skuse, Mrs.   [FFF]
Entertainer
* Whittingham, Mary

Skvorecka, Zdena Salivarova 1933-
[CA]
Czech-born singer, actress, publisher
* Salivarova, Zdena

Sky Ball Moreno
See Moreno, Thomas

Sky Hi Irvin
See Irvin, Leslie Leroy

Sky High Halsey
See Halsey, Schuyler

[The] **Sky Storming Yankee**
See Curtiss, Glenn Hammond

Skyagunsta
See Pickens, Andrew

Skylab's Mr. Fix-It
See Conrad, Charles

Skyland Scotty
See Wiseman, Scott

Skylar, Sunny
See Schuyler, Sonny

Skyrocket Jack Webster
See Webster, [Dr.] John White

Slack
See Passingham, Kenneth

Slack, Emilie ?-1932 [HPPN]
American actress
* Hayward, Emilie

Slack, Slacky
See Slack, Wilf[red Norris]

Slack, Wilf[red Norris] 1954- [DC]
West Indian cricketer
* Slack, Slacky

Slade, Adam
See Slade, Frank

Slade, Bernard
See Newbound, Bernard Slade

Slade, Brownie
See Slade, Eileen

Slade, Captain Jack
See Slade, Joseph Alfred

Slade, Daniel Denison 1823-1896 [DNA]
American author and physician
* Medicus

Slade, Eileen 1920- [MY]
American jazz musician
* Slade, Brownie

Slade, Frank 1875-? [DBA]
British painter
* Slade, Adam

Slade, Gordon 1904-1974 [BE]
American baseball player
* Slade, Oskie

Slade, Gurney
See Bartlett, Stephen

Slade, Jack
See Ballard, [Willis] Todhunter

Slade, Jack
See Slade, Joseph Alfred

Slade, Joseph Alfred 1824-1864 [BLB,
DI, EWG, HPPN]
American gunfighter
* Slade, Captain Jack
* Slade, Jack

Slade, Madeleine 1892?-1982 [DF 3-13-
83]
British-born disciple of Mahatma Gandhi
* Mirabehn [Sister Mira]

Slade, Maria Virginia Dale 19th c.
[HPPN]
American pioneer and vigilante
* Slade, Molly

Slade, Molly
See Slade, Maria Virginia Dale

Slade, Oskie
See Slade, Gordon

Sladek, John T[homas] 1937- [CA, ESF,
WGT]
American-born author
* Demijohn, Thom [joint pseudonym
with Thomas M. Disch]
* Knye, Cassandra [joint pseudonym
with Thomas M. Disch]

Sladen, Douglas 20th c. [WWL]
British author
* St. Barbe
* Wheelton, Brooke

Sladen, John 18th c. [HPPN]
British clergyman
* [A] Protestant Dissenter, a Friend to
Truth, Peace, and Liberty

Sladen, Norman St. Barbe ?-1969
[CAP]
British author and critic
* Bullingham, Rodney
* Montclair, Dennis

Slaettegard, Gunilla Lovisa
See Wallin, Gunilla Lovisa

Slagle, James Franklin 1873-1956 [BE,
PB]
American baseball player
* [The] Human Mosquito

Slagle, James Franklin (cont.)
* Slagle, Rabbit
* Slagle, Shorty

Slagle, Rabbit
See Slagle, James Franklin

Slagle, Shorty
See Slagle, James Franklin

Slaholt, Geswanouth 1899-1981 [SW]
Canadian-born actor
* George, [Chief] Dan

Slam, Sir
See Dawkins, Darryl

[The] **Slammer**
See Snead, Sam[uel Jackson]

Slammin Sam Snead
See Snead, Sam[uel Jackson]

Slaney, George Wilson 1884- [AW,
CAP, WW]
British author
* Woden, George
* Wouil, George

Slapsie Maxie Rosenbloom
See Rosenbloom, Max

[The] **Slasher**
See Atkinson, Theodore Francis [Ted]

Slate, John
See Fearn, John Russell

Slater, Duke
See Slater, Frederick E.

Slater, Eleanor 1903- [BI]
American educator
* Mary Eleanor, [Sister]

Slater, Elizabeth Anne
See Norton, Alice Whitson

Slater, Ernest ?-1942 [SFL, WGT, WWL]
British author
* Gwynne, Paul

Slater, Francis Carey 1876-1958 [LC]
South African author and poet
* Van Avond, Jan

Slater, Frederick E. 1898-1966 [AS]
American football player
* Slater, Duke

Slater, George 1845-? [IP, PA]
American journalist
* G. S.

Slater, John Herbert 20th c. [WWL]
British author
* Secutor

Slater, May Wilson 20th c. [PI]
Irish poet
* Shorsa, May

Slater, Nic
See Connolly, Charles M.

Slater, Ora E. 1870-1945 [HPPN]
American detective
* Ohio's Ace Investigator

Slater, Oscar
See Leschziner, Oscar

Slater, Patrick
See Mitchell, John

Slater, Samuel 1768-1835 [HPPN]
British-American manufacturer
* [The] Father of American
  Manufacture

Slater, Veronica
See Sullivan, Victoria

Slatinaru, Maria
See Buzurin, Maria

Slatoff, Stella B.
See Applebaum, Stella Balaban

Slattery, James 1948?-1974 [TR]
Actor
* Darling, Candy

Slaughter, Barney
See Slaughter, Byron Atkins

Slaughter, Byron Atkins 1884-1961 [BE]
American baseball player
* Slaughter, Barney

Slaughter, Country
See Slaughter, Enos Bradsher

Slaughter, Elizabeth Blythe 1893-1972
[F2, FC, SC]
American actress
* Blythe, Betty

Slaughter, Enos Bradsher 1916- [BE,
BI, PB]
American baseball player
* Slaughter, Country

Slaughter, Frank G[ill] 1908- [CA,
HPPN, LC, WD]
American author
* Terry, C. V.
* [The] Undisputed Master of Medical
  Fiction

Slaughter, Jean
See Doty, Jean Slaughter

Slaughter, Jim
See Paine, Lauran [Bosworth]

Slaughter, John Horton 1841-1922
[EWG, HPPN]
American gunfighter
* Don Juan
* Little Black John
* Slaughter, Texas John

Slaughter, John Horton 1841-1922
[HPPN]
American gunfighter
* Little Black John

[The] Slaughter Kid
See Lewis, Elmer

Slaughter, Marion T. 1883-1948 [CME,
CWG, PMJ]
American country-western performer
* Allen, Mack
* Ballard, Wolfe
* Calhoun, Jeff
* Carver, Al

Slaughter, Marion T. (cont.)
* Dale, Vernon
* Dalhart, Vernon
* Evans, Frank
* Harris, Harry
* King, Fred
* Little, Tobe
* [The] Lone Star Ranger
* Massey, Guy
* McAfee, B.
* McAfee, Carlos
* Vernon, Bill
* Watson, Tom
* White, Bob

Slaughter, Mickey
See Slaughter, Milton

Slaughter, Milton 20th c. [EF]
American football player
* Slaughter, Mickey

Slaughter, Mrs. M. [IP]
Author
* Riderhood, Pleasant

Slaughter, N. Carter 1885-1956 [BEW,
FC]
British actor and producer
* Slaughter, Tod

Slaughter, Texas John
See Slaughter, John Horton

Slaughter, Tod
See Slaughter, N. Carter

Slaughter's Kid
See Newcomb, George

Slavenska, Mia
See Corak, Mia

Slavic, Rosalind Welcher
See Welcher, Rosalind

Slavitt, David Rytman 1935- [AW, CA,
JL]
American author, poet, translator
* Robbins, Henry
* Sutton, Henry

Slavutych, Yar
See Zhuchenko, Yar

Slayback, Elbert 1901- [BE]
American baseball player
* Slayback, Scottie

Slayback, Scottie
See Slayback, Elbert

Slayback, Sly
See Slayback, William Grover

Slayback, William Grover 1948- [SMG]
American baseball player
* Slayback, Sly

**[The] Slayer of the Bulgarians
[Bulgaroctonus]**
See Basil II

Slayton, Deke
See Slayton, Donald Kent

Slayton, Donald Kent 1924- [BI, IPA]
American astronaut
* Slayton, Deke

Slayton, Foster Herbert 1902- [BE]
American baseball player
* Slayton, Steve

Slayton, Steve
See Slayton, Foster Herbert

Sleath, Herbert
See Skelton, Herbert Sleath

Sleech, John ?-1788 [IP]
British clergyman and author
* J. S., A. C.

Sleekhead
See A Beckett, Gilbert Abbott

Sleeman, [Sir] William Henry 1788-1856
[IP]
British officer and author
* [An] Indian Official
* [An] Officer in the Mil. and Civ.
  Service of the Hon. E. I. Co.

Sleen, Marc
See Neels, Marc

Sleep, Michael William 1955- [SMG]
Canadian-born hockey player
* Sleep, Sleeper
* Sleep, Zee

Sleep 'n Eat
See Best, Willie

Sleep, Sleeper
See Sleep, Michael William

Sleep, Zee
See Sleep, Michael William

Sleeper, Edward Peters 1900- [HPPN]
American Y. M. C. A. secretary
* Sleeper, Snoozer

Sleeper, John Sherburne 1794-1878
[DNA, PA]
American author
* Martingale, Hawser

Sleeper, Snoozer
See Sleeper, Edward Peters

Sleeper, Walter T. 19th c. [IP]
American author
* Uncle Walter

[The] Sleeping Clairvoyant
See Cayce, Edgar

[The] Sleeping Giant
See Cayce, Edgar

[The] Sleeping Preacher
See Baker, Rachel

[The] Sleeping Prophet
See Cayce, Edgar

Sleepy Bill Burns
See Burns, William Thomas

Sleepy Bill Johnson
See Johnson, William T.

Sleepy Jim Crowley
See Crowley, James H.

Sleepy John Estes
See Estes, John Adams

Sleepy Phil Knox
See Knox, Philander Chase

Sleidan [or Sleidanus], John [or Johannes]
See Philippi [or Philippson?]

Sleight, Elmer 20th c. [EF]
American football player
* Sleight, Red

Sleight, Red
See Sleight, Elmer

Slemp, Rita 1955-
American pilot
* Slemp, Roxi

Slemp, Roxi
See Slemp, Rita

Slender, Robert
See Freneau, Philip Morin

Slenker, Elmina [Drake] 1827-1909? [BDSA, DNA]
American author
* Aunt Elmina

Slesar, Henry 1927- [CA, ESF, WW]
American author
* Harson, Sley [joint pseudonym with Harlan (Jay) Ellison]
* Leslie, O. H.
* Street, Jay

Slice
See William Frederick

Slick, Colonel
See Tittle, Yelberton Abraham

Slick, Jersey
See Tichenor, Isaac

Slick, Jonathan
See Stephens, Ann Sophia Winterbotham

Slick, Sam
See Halliburton, Thomas Chandler

Slick, Sam, Jr.
See Avery, Samuel Putnam

Slick, Samuel
See Haliburton, Thomas Chandler

Slick Willie Sutton
See Sutton, William Francis [Willie]

[The] Slickest Swindler of Them All
See Ponzi, Carlo

Slidell, Alexander 1803-1848 [IP, PA, WBD]
American naval officer
* [The] American in England
* Mackenzie, Alexander Slidell
* [A] Young American

Slidell, Mrs. Edward 19th c. [IP]
British author
* Tytler, C. C. Fraser

Sliding Billy Hamilton
See Hamilton, William Robert

Slieve-Bloom
See Kelly, John Tarpey

Slieve-Margy
See O'Neill, William

Slievegallion
See Hepburn, David

Slievenamon
See Dollard, James Benjamin

Slievenamon
See Kickham, Charles Joseph

Slievenamon
See Meagher, John Francis

Slifka, Lewis 1920- [ASC]
American musician
* Spence, Lew

Slight, John
See Pond, Wilf Pocklington

[A] Sligo Suspect
See O'Dowd, John

Slim
See Gicheru, Samuel Mwangi

Slim
See Manchester, William

Slim Gray Gibson
See Gibson, Russell

Slim Jim
See Dukelan, George W.

Slim Jim Gavin
See Gavin, James Maurice

Slinfold
See Stuart, Mary F.

Slinger, Francisco 1933?- [CW]
Trinidadian singer and poet
* [The] Mighty Sparrow

Slingin' Sammy Baugh
See Baugh, Samuel A.

Slingsby, Jonathan Freke
See Waller, John Francis

Slingsby, Philip
See Willis, Nathaniel Parker

Slingsby, Rufus [joint pseudonym with Charles Siddle]
See Peel, Frederick

Slingsby, Rufus [joint pseudonym with Frederick Peel]
See Siddle, Charles

Slingshot Charley Taylor
See Taylor, Charley

Slipher, Vesto M. 1875-1969 [HPPN]
American astronomer
* [The] Father of the Red Shift Phenomenon

Slippers, Peggy
See Stevenson, Sara Yorke

Slippery Dick Connolly
See Connolly, Richard

Slippery Sam Tilden
See Tilden, Samuel Jones

Sliver, W. A. 19th c. [IP]
American playwright
* Marsden, Frederick

Sloan, Aloysius Martin 1927- [CEI, FHE, HK]
Canadian-born hockey player
* Sloan, Tod

Sloan, [Adam] Bruce 1914- [BE]
American baseball player
* Sloan, Fatso

Sloan, Fatso
See Sloan, [Adam] Bruce

Sloan, George [FFF]
Entertainer
* Knight, George S.

Sloan, Harry
See Yelding, Henry Edward

Sloan, J. Todhunter
See Sloan, James Forman

Sloan, James 19th c. [IP]
American author
* [An] American

Sloan, James Forman 1874-1933 [AS, BBH, BI, HPPN]
American jockey
* Sloan, J. Todhunter
* Sloan, Toad
* Sloan, Tod

Sloan, Larry 1923?- [HPPN]
American publisher
* [The] King of the Nonbooks

Sloan, Leni
See Sloan, Lenwood Ottis

Sloan, Lenwood Ottis 1948- [IBW]
American entertainer
* Sloan, Leni

Sloan, P. A.
See Sloan, Patrick Alan

Sloan, Patrick Alan 1908- [WD]
British economist and author
* Sloan, P. A.

Sloan, Paul H.
See Solataroff, [Dr.] H.

Sloan, Stephen
See Solomon, Stephen

Sloan, Toad
See Sloan, James Forman

Sloan, Tod
See Sloan, Aloysius Martin

Sloan, Tod
See Sloan, James Forman

Sloan, Tod
See Sloan, Yale Yeastman

Sloan, Yale Yeastman 1890-1956 [BE]
American baseball player
* Sloan, Tod

Sloane, Eric
See Hinrichs, Everard Jean

Sloane, Olive 1897?-1963   [THR]
British actress
* Baby Pearl

Sloane, Sara
See Bloom, Ursula [Harvey]

Sloat, Dwain Clifford 1918-   [BE]
American baseball player
* Sloat, Lefty

Sloat, Lefty
See Sloat, Dwain Clifford

Sloathful Bill Lattimore
See Lattimore, William Hershel [Bill]

Slocombe, Philip Anthony 1954-   [DC]
British cricketer
* Sir Len
* Slocombe, Slocs

Slocombe, Slocs
See Slocombe, Philip Anthony

Slocum, Frances 1773-1847   [HPPN]
Captive of American Indians
* Maconaquah
* [The] White Squaw

Slocum, Hi
See Clemens, Samuel Langhorne

Slocum, Mary S. F. 19th c.   [IP]
American author
* West, Willa

Slodtz, Rene Michael 1705-1764   [DEP, FFF, RH]
French sculptor
* [The] Michael Angelo of Sculptors

[The] Slogan Man
See Smythe, John Henry, Jr.

Sloggett, Nellie 1851-1923   [BI]
British author
* Cornwall, Nellie
* Tregarthen, Enys

Slokumb, Si
See Cheever, Henry P.

Sloluck, J. Milton
See Bierce, Ambrose [Gwinett]

Sloot, Marie 1853-?   [WWL]
Dutch author
* Melati Van Java

Sloots, Patsy 1929-   [FC]
British actress
* Shaw, Susan

Slop, Dr.
See Burton, John

Slop, Doctor
See Stoddart, [Sir] John

Sloper, Ally
See Ross, Charles Henry

Sloper, Joel
See Peters, W. A.

Sloper, Mace
See Leland, Charles Godfrey

Sloper, Margaret [Thayer] 1887?-1960 [BI]
American dance critic
* Lloyd, Margaret

Slory, Michael 1935-   [CW]
Surinamese poet
* Sangodare, Asjantenu

Slosberg, Mike
See Slosberg, Myron

Slosberg, Myron 1934-   [CA]
American author and advertising executive
* Slosberg, Mike

Slosson, Annie T. 19th c.   [IP]
American author
* [The] Youngest Member

Slote, Daniel 1830-1883   [IP]
American manufacturer and author
* Dan

Slotkin, Joseph ?-1929   [WGT]
British author
* Spie, Oliver?
* Tolz, Nick?

Slous, F. L. 19th c.   [IP]
British author
* [An] Awkward Man

[The] Slovak Liberalizer
See Dubcek, Alexander

Sloves, Herman 1899-1957   [RBE]
American boxer
* [The] Bronx Bone-Crusher
* Murray, Johnny

Slow Carus
See Tyson, Edward

Slow Drag Pavageau
See Pavageau, Alcide

Slow Joe Doyle
See Doyle, Judd Bruce

Slow, Jonathan 18th c.   [HPPN]
British clergyman and poet
* Pindaricus

Slow Kid Thompson
See Thompson, Ulysses

Slow Motion Shorty Park
See Park, Arthur

Slow Trot
See Thomas, George Henry

Slowitzky, Michael 1893-1962   [ASC]
American musician
* Edwards, Michael

Sluefoot Joe
See Gibson, Clifford

[The] Sluggard
See Louis V

Slumber, Baron
See Wodehouse, John

Slung, Louis Sheaffer 1912-   [CA]
American author and journalist
* Sheaffer, Louis

Slusser, George Edgar 1939-   [CA]
American author
* Anstey, Edgar

Sly, Albert 20th c.   [BLB]
American train robber
* Sly, Bertie

Sly, Bertie
See Sly, Albert

[The] Sly Fox
See Fox, Henry [First Baron Holland]

Sly, Jerry
See Stuart, John Todd

Sly, Sam
See Sammons, William Taylor

[The] Sly Sweeney
See Sweeney, Peter Barr

Slye, Leonard 1912-   [CWG, FC, HPPN, OCF]
American actor and singer
* [The] King of the Cowboys
* Rogers, Roy
* Weston, Dick
* [The] World's Top Boots and Saddle Star

Smada, Augusto
See Adams, William Augustus

Smadt, Jan 1895-   [BE]
American baseball player
* Smith, John W.

Smalacombe, John
See MacKay, Louis Alexander

Small, Austin J. ?-1929   [ESF, SFL, WW]
British author
* Seamark

[The] Small Beer Poet
See Fitzgerald, William Thomas

Small, Blind Freddie
See Small, Freddie

Small, Edna
See Ellis, Edna Small

Small, Ernest
See Lent, Blair

Small, Florence 20th c.   [DBA]
British painter
* Hardy, Florence Deric

Small, Freddie 1898?-   [NOJ]
American jazz musician
* Small, Blind Freddie

Small, George 19th c.   [DNA, FFF, PA]
American author and entertainer
* Bricktop

Small, John 18th c.   [IP]
Scottish author
* J. S., A Presbyter of the Episcopal Church of Scotland

Small Light Throop
See Throop, Enos Thompson

Small, Mary 20th c. [HPPN]
American personality
* Little Miss Bab-O

Small, Millie
See Smith, Millicent

[The] Small Paul Revere
See Ashbrook, John Milan

Small, Samuel White 1851-1931 [FFF]
American editor and clergyman
* Old Si

Small Shot Towers
See Towers, Joseph

Small, William
See Eversley, David Edward Charles

Smallage, George
See Smalridge, George

Smallens, Alexander
See Smolensk, Alexander

[The] Smallest Man in Baseball
See Davidson, Donald

Smalley, George W.   [PA]
Author
* G. W. S.

Smalls, Cliff
See Smalls, Clifton Arnold

Smalls, Clifton Arnold 1918-   [EJ7]
American jazz musician
* Smalls, Cliff

Smallwood, Jason
See Kisner, Jacob

Smalridge, George 1663-1719 [HPPN]
British prelate
* Smallage, George

Smaragdus
See Fitzpatrick, John

Smarrito
See Dati, Carlo Roberto

Smart, Anna Maria 18th c. [SN]
Wife of British poet, Christopher Smart
* [The] Lass with the Golden Locks

Smart, Christopher 1722-1771
British poet
* Midnight, [Mrs.] Mary
* Pentweazle, Ebenezer

Smart, Curly
See Smart, Wayne

Smart, J. Scott 1903-1960 [HPPN]
American actor
* [The] Fat Man

Smart, Wayne 1905?-1976 [BBH, BI]
American harness racing trainer and driver
* Smart, Curly

Smead, Mrs.   [PA]
Author
* Fay

Smead, Mrs.
See Cleaveland, Mrs. Willis M.

Smeaton, Fred
See Cook, Fred Gordon

Smeaton, Oliphant
See Smeaton, William Henry O.

Smeaton, William Henry O. 1856-1916
[WWL]
Scottish author and journalist
* Smeaton, Oliphant

Smedley, Edward 19th c. [HFN]
Editor, author, clergyman
* [A] Churchman

Smedley, Francis Edward [Frank]
1818-1864 [DEL, FFF, RH]
British author
* Fairleigh, Frank
* Phiz, Francis

Smedley, Menella Bute 19th c. [HFN,
PA]
Author
* M. S.
* S. M.

Smedley, Menella Bute 19th c. [PA]
Author
* M. S.

Smedsmo, Dale 1951- [SMG]
American hockey player
* Smedsmo, Smo

Smedsmo, Smo
See Smedsmo, Dale

Smee, Wentworth
See Burgin, George Brown

Smeed
See Taylor, [Joseph] Deems

Smeed, Frances
See Lasky, Jesse Louis, Jr.

Smeeton, George 19th c. [HFN]
Author
* Charfy, Guiniad

Smehoff, Aaron 20th c. [PHM]
American underworld figure
* Smiley, Allen

Smejkal, Frank John 1889-1950 [BE]
American baseball player
* Smykal, Frank John

Smek
See Magnus II

Smekalova, Hana 1918- [FC]
Franco-Czech actress
* Marly, Florence

Smelfungus
See Alexander, Patrick Proctor

Smelfungus
See Smollett, Tobias George

Smelfungus
See Sterne, Laurence

Smellie, George 1811-1896 [CCL]
Canadian poet
* [The] Scald

Smet, Eugenie Marie Joseph 1825-1871
[BI]
French nun
* Marie de la Providence, [Mother]

Smetana, Bedrich 1824-1884 [HPPN]
Czech musician
* [The] Father of the Czech Nationalist
  School of Composition

[The] Smiddy Muse
See Coyle, Matthew

Smidovich, Vikenti Vikentievich
1867-1943 [WBD]
Russian physician and author
* Veresaev, Vikenti

Smiff, O. P. Q. Philander
See Dowty, A. A.

Smiff, Sam
See Coutts, Tristram

Smigly-Rydz, Edward
See Rydz, Edward

Smik, Andrew J., Jr. 1914- [CWG]
American country-western performer
* Williams, Doc

Smik, Jessie Wanda 1919- [CWG]
American country-western performer
* Williams, Chickie

Smilansky, Moshe 1874-1953
Russian-born author
* Mussa, Hawaja

Smilansky, Yizhar
Israeli intelligence agent and author
* Yizhar, S.

Smile, R. Elton
See Smilie, Elton R.

Smiley, Allen
See Smehoff, Aaron

Smiley, Amelia 1869-1927 [HPPN]
American actress
* Bingham, Amelia

Smiley, Arthur Lee, Jr. 1925-1972
[DAM]
American country-western performer
* Smiley, Red

Smiley, Charles Wesley 1884- [ALY]
American author
* Cascadananda, Anagaraca

Smiley, Jim
See Spears, Raymond S[miley]

Smiley, Red
See Smiley, Arthur Lee, Jr.

Smilie, Elton R. 19th c. [SFL]
Author
* Smile, R. Elton

Smilin' Ed McConnell
See McConnell, Edward

Smiling Al Maul
See Maul, Albert Joseph

Smiling Albert Kesselring
See Kesselring, Albert

Smiling Bill Donovan
See Donovan, William Edward

Smiling Bill Parsons
See Parsons, William [Billy]

Smiling Billy Mason
See Mason, William C.

Smiling Bob Masterson
See Masterson, Robert

Smiling Bock Baker
See Baker, Charles

[The] Smiling Cobra
See Aubrey, James Thomas, Jr.

Smiling Frank Farnum
See Smith, William

[The] Smiling Irishman
See Murphy, James [Jimmy]

[The] Smiling Irishman
See O'Gwynn, James

Smiling Jack McGrath
See McGrath, John James

Smiling Jim Farley
See Farley, James Aloysius

Smiling Jimmy Sullivan
See Sullivan, James A.

Smiling Joe
See Joseph, Pleasant

Smiling Mickey Welch
See Welch, Michael F.

Smiling Slim Rogers
See Planchet, Roger Anthony

Smiling Stan Hack
See Hack, Stanley Camfield

Smirk, Mr.
See Turner, Francis

Smith
See Gow, [Captain] John

Smith
See Smith, Alice Maude

Smith
See Sultzer, Joseph

Smith, A. De Herries 1881-? [WWL]
Canadian author
* Finbar, Owen

Smith, A. J. M.
See Smith, Arthur James Marshall

Smith, Abbie Whitney 1919- [MA]
Canadian-born American author and poet
* Whitney, Abbie

Smith, Ach
See Smith, Anthony Charles

**Smith, Ada Beatrice Queen Victoria
Louisa Virginia Du Conge** 1895-1984
[IBW]
American entertainer
* Bricktop

Smith, Adam 1723-1790 [HPPN, SN]
Scottish economist
* Father Adam
* [The] Father of the Science of
 Political Economy

Smith, Adam
See Goodman, George J[erome]
W[aldo]

Smith, Adrian 1936- [BB]
American basketball player
* Smith, Odie

Smith, Al[fred Emanuel] 1873-1944
[HPPN]
American politician
* [The] Catholic Optimist
* [The] East Side Orator
* [The] Empire State Governor
* [The] Governor
* [The] Happy Warrior
* Hero of the Cities
* [The] Political Debater
* [The] Radio Rebel
* [The] Sidewalk Statesman
* [The] Unchosen

Smith, Al[phonse Eugene] 1928- [BE,
PB]
American baseball player
* Smith, Fuzzy

Smith, Al 1945- [FHE]
Canadian-born hockey player
* Smith, Smitty

Smith, Al
See Schmidt, Albert

Smith, Albert Richard 1816-1860
[DNNS, PA, RH]
British author and lecturer
* Biddle, Jasper
* [The] Monarch of Mont Blanc

Smith, Alexander 18th c. [HPPN]
British author
* Smith, Captain

Smith, Alexander
See Adams, John

Smith, Alexander Benjamin 1871-1919
[BE, EJS]
American baseball player
* Smith, Broadway Aleck

Smith, Alexis
See Smith, Gladys

Smith, Alf
See Smith, Alfred E.

Smith, Alfred Aloysius 1861?-1931 [LC,
TC, TC1]
British author and adventurer
* Horn, Alfred Aloysius
* Horn, Trader

Smith, Alfred E. 1873-1953 [FHE]
Canadian-born hockey player
* Smith, Alf

Smith, Alice Gustava 1899- [BI]
American poet and educator
* Maris Stella, [Sister]

Smith, Alice Maude 1867-? [NAA]
Canadian-born physician and playwright
* Broome, Sutton
* Smith
* Smith, Scoville

Smith, Allan E. 20th c. [CND]
Military leader
* [The] Duke of Wonsan

Smith, Allie Bagley 1889-1932 [HPPN]
American vaudeville performer
* Bagley, Allie

Smith, Alma 1897-1931 [F1, F2, FC]
American actress
* Rubens, Alma

Smith, Alvin K. 1926- [BWW]
American singer
* King, Al

Smith, Amos 1871-1937 [BBH, BX, RBE]
American boxer
* Smith, Billy
* Smith, Mysterious Billy

Smith, Andrew 1831?-1895 [HPPN]
Canadian-American manufacturer
* Mark
* Smith, Easy

Smith, Andrew 1836-1900 [WBD]
British-born engineer and inventor
* Hallidie, Andrew Smith

Smith, Andrew Latham ?-1926 [HPPN]
American football coach
* [The] Wonder Maker

Smith, Anne
See Rainey, Gertrude Malissa Nix
[Pridgett]

Smith, Anne Mollegen 1940- [CA]
American editor and writer
* Mollegen, Anne Rush

Smith, Annie [PA]
Author
* Herrin, Caller

Smith, Anthony Charles 1935- [IAW]
British author
* Smith, Ach

Smith, Art[hur] 1890-1926 [HPPN]
American aviator
* Indiana's Bird Boy

Smith, Artegall
See Norton, Philip

Smith, Arthur 18th c. [RBE]
Boxer
* [The] Gypsy

Smith, Arthur 1921- [DAM]
American bandleader and songwriter
* Smith, Guitar Boogie

Smith, Arthur 20th c. [ECM, FCW]
American country-western performer
* Smith, Fiddlin' Arthur

Smith, Arthur Douglas Howden
1887-1945 [BI]
American author
* Grant, Allen

Smith, Arthur F.   [FFF]
Entertainer
* Arthur, Joseph

Smith, Arthur James Marshall 1902-
[LC]
Canadian-born author and educator
* Smith, A. J. M.

Smith, Arthur L. 1942- [CA]
American educator and author
* Asante, Molefi K.

Smith [or Schmet], Augustine
See Gallitzin, Demetrius Augustine

Smith, B. F.
See Smith, Benjamin Franklin

Smith, Babycakes
See Smith, Jerry T.

Smith, Baldy
See Smith, William Farrar

Smith, Barbara Herrnstein 1932- [CA, WD]
American critic and editor
* Herrnstein, Barbara

Smith, Barbara Newman
See Darrow, Alice Vicki

Smith, Baron 19th c. [PA]
Author
* Search, Warner Christian

Smith, Barton 20th c. [EF]
American football player
* Smith, Barty

Smith, Barty
See Smith, Barton

Smith, Beetle
See Smith, Walter Bedell

Smith, Bell
See Piatt, Louise Kirby

Smith, Benjamin Franklin 20th c. [BA]
American educator
* Smith, B. F.

Smith, Bernard 1630-1708 [HPPN]
British organ builder
* Smith, Father

Smith, Bernard 20th c. [MBF]
British author and editor
* Campbell, Harry
* Heath, Bernard
* Martyn, Ivor
* Smith, Jack
* Williams, Fred J.

Smith, Bessie 1894-1937 [BWW]
American singer
* [The] Empress of the Blues

Smith, Beverly Chew 1892-1951 [HPPN]
American actress
* Shepley, Ruth

Smith, Big Clipper
See Smith, Maurice

Smith, Big Lee
See Smith, Lester

Smith, Billy 1903?-1963 [BEW]
Theatrical performer
* Smith, Little Billy

Smith, Billy
See Smith, Amos

Smith, Billy
See Thomas, Will Madison

Smith, Billy Ray 1935- [FB]
American football player
* Smith, Black Rabbit

Smith, Bingo
See Smith, Bobby

Smith, Black Rabbit
See Smith, Billy Ray

Smith, Blackjack
See Smith, Harry E.

Smith, Blue Smitty
See Smith, Claude

Smith, Boatswain
See Smith, G. C.

Smith, Bobby 1946- [NBA, SMG]
American basketball player
* Smith, Bingo

Smith, Bobus
See Smith, Robert

Smith, Bonecrusher
See Smith, James

Smith, Boo
See Smith, Bruce P.

Smith, Borax
See Smith, Francis Marion

Smith, Bridges W.   [PA]
Author
* Ridges, R.

Smith, Broadway Aleck
See Smith, Alexander Benjamin

Smith, Bruce P. 1920-1967 [FB]
American football player
* Smith, Boo

Smith, Bubba
See Smith, Charles Aaron

Smith, Bubba
See Smith, George

Smith, Buckhorse
See Smith, John

Smith, Bud
See Smith, Wallace

Smith, Buddy
See Smith, Ivan

Smith, Bull
See Smith, Louis

Smith, Bunty
See Smith, Frances

Smith, Buster
See Smith, Henry

Smith, Butch
See Smith, Wilton Leon

Smith, Byron Caldwell 1849-1877
[DNA]
American author and educator
* Maldclewith, Ronsby

Smith, C. Arnholt [Arnie] 1901-
[HPPN]
American business executive and fund raiser
* San Diego, Mr.

Smith, C. Busby
See Smith, John

Smith, C. L.
See Gascoigne, Mrs. C. L.

Smith, C. Manby 19th c. [PA]
Author
* Journeyman Printer

Smith, C. Pritchard
See Hoyt, Edwin P[almer], Jr.

Smith, C. U. 1901- [CA]
American author and poet
* Crowbate, Ophelia Mae

Smith, C. W. 19th c. [PA]
Author
* One Who is Really an Englishman

Smith, Caesar
See Dudley-Smith, Trevor

Smith, Cal
See Shofner, Grant Calvin

Smith, Campbell Sherston 1906- [THR]
British theatrical manager
* Williams, Campbell

Smith, Captain
See Smith, Alexander

Smith, Carl 1908?- [WWJ]
American jazz musician
* Smith, Tatti

Smith, Carlton
See Rocklin, Ross Louis

Smith, Carmichael
See Linebarger, Paul M[yron] A[nthony]

Smith, Carol Louise 1935- [EJ7]
American jazz musician
* Kaye, Carol

Smith, Caroline L. 19th c. [DNA, FFF, PA]
American author
* Aunt Carrie

Smith, Catfish
See Smith, Vernon

Smith, Catherine R. [Kay] 1925- [MA]
American writer
* Adams, Angela
* Andrews, Vickie

Smith, Cecil [Howard, III] 1917- [CA]
American columnist and playwright
* Howard, Cecil

Smith, Cedric 20th c.
American football player
* Smith, Pat

Smith, Charles ?-1932? [MK]
American baseball player
* Smith, Chino

Smith, Charles 1900-1967 [SC]
Scottish actor
* Radcliffe, Jack

Smith, Charles 1908- [THR]
British actor and singer
* Mayhew, Charles

Smith, Charles Aaron 1945- [FB, IPA, SMG]
American football player
* Smith, Bubba

Smith, Charles Card 1827-? [HPPN]
American author
* C. C. S.
* S.

Smith, Charles Edward 1950- [BA]
American football player
* Smith, Tank

Smith, Charles Henry 1826-1903 [FFF, PA, WBD]
American author
* Arp, Bill

Smith, Charles J. [FFF, PA]
Writer
* [The] Call Boy

Smith, Charles Marvin 1856-1927 [AS, BE]
Canadian-born baseball player
* Smith, Pop

Smith, Charles Mitchell 1855-? [NAA]
American writer
* Fowke, Gerard

Smith, Charles William 19th c. [HFN]
Author
* C. W. S.

Smith, Charlie 1842-? [HPPN]
American slave
* [The] Oldest Man in America

Smith, Charlie 20th c. [RBE]
Boxer
* Smith, Tombstone

Smith, Charlie
See Smith, Gideon

Smith, Charlotte 1749-1806 [FFF, HFN]
British author and poet
* Deene, Kenner

Smith, Cherry George 1956- [IBW]
American singer and songwriter
* Lynn, Cheryl

Smith, Chick
See Smith, John William

Smith, Chino
See Smith, Charles

Smith, Christopher Lyall 1958- [DC]
South African cricketer
* Smith, Kippy

Smith, Christopher Martin
See Forbes, Cabot L[owell]

Smith, Cladys 1908- [DAM, EJ, PMJ]
American jazz musician
* Smith, Jabbo

Smith, Clara 1894?-1935 [BWW]
American singer
* Green, Violet
* [The] Queen of the Moaners
* Smith, Jolly Clara
* [The] World's Champion Moaner

Smith, Clara Evelyn 1886- [THR]
British actress and singer
* Evelyn, Clara

Smith, Clarence 1904-1929 [DAM, EJ, PMJ]
American jazz musician
* Smith, Pinetop

Smith, Clarence Ossie 1892-1924 [BE]
American baseball player
* Smith, Pop Boy

Smith, Claude 1877-1921 [HPPN]
American vaudeville performer
* Kendall, Charles

Smith, Claude 20th c. [BWW]
American entertainer
* Smith, Blue Smitty

Smith, Claude M. 20th c. [BBH]
American collegiate athletic director
* Smith, Tad

Smith, Claudia Dell
Actress
* Dell, Claudia

Smith, Clay
See Smith, Claydes

Smith, Claydes [RO2]
American musician
* Smith, Clay

Smith, Clement Ogle 19th c. [PA]
Author
* [A] Priest of the English Church

Smith, Cleo
See Smith, Cleopherus

Smith, Cleo
See Smith, Cleveland

Smith, Cleopherus 1953- [SMG]
American baseball player
* Smith, Cleo

Smith, Cleveland 20th c. [OBW]
American baseball player
* Smith, Cleo

Smith, Clinton James 1913- [CEI, HK]
Canadian-born hockey player
* Smith, Snuffy

Smith, Clipper
See Smith, John

Smith, Clipper
See Smith, Maurice

Smith, Clyde
See Smith, George

Smith, Collie
See Smith, O'Neill Gordon

Smith, Columbia George
See Smith, George Allen

Smith, Constance [Connie] 1941- [FCW]
American country-western performer
* [The] Cinderella Girl of Country Music

Smith, Constance
See Smyth, Constance

Smith, Constance Isabel 1894- [WW]
Author
* Reid, Eleanor

Smith, Cordwainer
See Linebarger, Paul M[yron] A[nthony]

Smith, Cotton Ed
See Smith, Ellison DuRant

Smith, Cura
See Smith, Harold Raymond

Smith, Cyril
See Bruce-Smith, Cyril

Smith, D. H.
See Smith, David Henry

Smith, David [Larmer] 1899- [AW]
Scottish author
* Graham, Johnston

Smith, David [Jeddie] [Dave] 1942- [CA]
American author and poet
* Cornwell, Smith

Smith, David Henry 1947- [ART]
British artist
* Smith, D. H.

Smith, David MacLeod 1920- [CA]
Scottish author
* Dunbar, Edward
* Mariner, David

Smith, David Mark 1956- [DC]
British cricketer
* Smith, Smudger
* Smith, Smurf

Smith, Deaf
See Smith, Erastus

Smith, [Edgar] Dennis 20th c. [AW, WD]
Author
* Hathi

Smith, Doc
See Smith, Edward Elmer

Smith, Dodie
See Smith, Dorothy Gladys

Smith, Don[ald A.] 1946- [BB, SMG]
American basketball player
* Abdul-Aziz, Zaid
* [The] Kangaroo

Smith, Donald Alexander [First Baron Strathcona and Mount Royal] 1820-1914 [NPS]
Canadian administrator
* That Grand Old Man of Empire

Smith, Donald Robert 1890-1973 [FC]
American actor
* Armstrong, Robert

Smith, Donald Robin 1942- [OP]
Australian opera singer
* Donald, Robin

Smith, Doris 20th c. [IBW]
American fashion model
* Smith, Toukie

Smith, Dorothy
Actress
* Dwan, Dorothy

Smith, Dorothy [Stafford] 1905- [BI, CA, SAT]
British author
* Smith, Sarah Stafford

Smith, Dorothy Gladys 1896- [CA, LC, WD]
British author and playwright
* Anthony, C. L.
* Percy, Charles Henry
* Smith, Dodie

Smith, Dorothy June 20th c. [ITA]
American actress
* Vincent, June

Smith, Dorothy Loraine Blackburn [BEW]
American actress
* Blackburn, Dorothy

Smith, Dorothy Whitehill 1893- [HPPN]
American author
* Trent, Martha

Smith, Drifting
See Mickle, Elmon

Smith, Dutch
See Smith, Harold

Smith, E. E.
See Smith, Edward Elmer

Smith, E. J. 20th c. [EC]
British cricketer
* Smith, Tiger

Smith, Earl Sutton 1897- [BE, DGS, PB]
American baseball player
* Smith, Oil

Smith, Easy
See Smith, Andrew

Smith, Edith Lillian
See Webster, Edith Smith

Smith, Edmund Neale 1668-1710 [HN, SN]
British poet
* Rag, Captain
* Smith, Rag

Smith, Edward Elmer 1890-1965 [ESF, SF]
American author
* [The] Father of Space Opera
* Smith, Doc
* Smith, E. E.

Smith, Edward H. 1938- [CA]
American author
* Blair, Edward H.

Smith, Edward Percy 1891-1968 [BEW, LC]
British playwright
* Percy, Edward

Smith, Eleanor [FFF]
Writer
* Heatherbell

Smith, Eleanor 1875-1966 [SC]
American actress
* Lawson, Eleanor

Smith, Elephant
See Underhill, Cave

Smith, Elinor 20th c.
American aviator and author
* [The] Flying Flapper of Freeport

Smith, Elizabeth A. 19th c. [PA]
Author
* Chester, Elizabeth S.
* [A] Clergyman's Daughter
* Honey Bee

Smith, Elizabeth Bacheler 20th c. [BBH]
American bicycling organization founder
* Smith, Isabel

Smith, Elizabeth Oakes 1806-1893 [HPPN]
American author and poet
* Helfenstein, Ernest
* Oaksmith, Elizabeth

Smith, Elizabeth Thomasina [Meade] 1854-1914 [CC, EMD, WW]
British author
* Meade, L[illie] T[homas]

Smith, Ellison DuRant 1864-1944 [WBD]
American planter and politician
* Smith, Cotton Ed

Smith, Elmer Ellsworth 1868-1945 [DGS, PB]
American baseball player
* Smith, Mike

Smith, Elwood Hope 1904- [BE]
American baseball player
* Smith, Mike

Smith, Erastus 1787-1837 [HPPN]
American frontier scout
* Smith, Deaf

Smith, Ernest Brammah 1868?-1942 [EMD, LC, TC]
British author
* Bramah, Ernest

Smith, Essex
See Hope, [Frances] Essex [Theodora]

Smith, Eugene 1938- [BA]
American business executive
* Smith, Salt

Smith, Evelyn E. 1927- [SFL]
Author
* Lyons, Delphine C.

Smith, F[rancis] Hopkinson 1838-1915 [HPPN]
American author, painter, engineer
* [The] Owl

Smith, F. R. 1854-? [WWL]
British author
* Ackworth, John

Smith, Fannie N. 19th c. [DNA, PA]
American author
* Goldsmith, Christabel

Smith, Farmer
See Carten, Laura Paty

Smith, Farmer
See Smith, George Henry

Smith, Father
See Galitzin, Dimitri Augustine

Smith, Father
See Smith, Bernard

Smith, Fenton
See Pratt, Leonard E.

Smith, Fiddlin' Arthur
See Smith, Arthur

Smith, Fireball
See Smith, Theolic

Smith, Florence Margaret 1902-1971 [BI, CAP, LC]
British author and poet
* Smith, Stevie

Smith, Floyd 1917- [EJ]
American jazz musician
* Smith, Wonderful

Smith, Ford
See Friend, Oscar J[erome]

Smith, Fossil
See Smith, William

Smith, Frances 1912- [FC, SW]
American actress and singer
* Evans, Dale

Smith, Frances 1924- [EG]
British golfer
* Smith, Bunty

Smith, Frances C[hristine] 1904- [CA, SAT]
American author
* Smith, Jean

Smith, Frances Elizabeth 1832?-? [FFF]
American poet
* Fales, Fanny

Smith, Frances Octavia 1912- [CA, HPPN]
American actress, singer, lyricist, author
* Evans, Dale
* Queen of the Cowgirls
* [The] Queen of the West
* Rogers, Dale Evans

Smith, Frances Scott [Fitzgerald] 1921- [BI]
Daughter of American author F. Scott Fitzgerald
* Smith, Scottie Fitzgerald

Smith, Frances Shubael 1819-1887 [HPPN, PA]
American author
* [The] Chancellor
* Clootz, Caleb
* Crane, Ichabod, Jr.
* Daisey
* Devon, W. A.
* Maitland, James A.
* Poningoe
* Tenpin Boy
* Witch Hazel

Smith, Francis Henney 1812-1880 [HPPN]
American army officer
* Old Spex

Smith, Francis Marion 1846-1931 [HPPN]
American borax mine owner
* [The] Borax King
* Smith, Borax

Smith, Frank Elmer
See Schmidt, Frank Elmer

Smith, Frank Eugene 1865-1936 [BI]
American photographer
* Eugene, Frank

Smith, Frederick 20th c. [CA]
Musician
* Sonic, Fred

Smith, Frederick E[screet] 1922- [CA]
British author
* Farrell, David

Smith, Frederick Edwin [First Earl of Birkenhead] 1872-1930 [HPPN, PPN]
British statesman
* Ephesian
* F. E.

Smith, Frederick Escreet 1922- [HPPN]
British author
* Farrell, David

Smith, Frederick H. 1889- [BE]
American baseball player
* Smith, Klondike

Smith, Funny Papa
See Smith, John T.

Smith, Fuzzy
See Smith, Al[phonse Eugene]

Smith, G. C. 1782-1863 [HN]
Clergyman
* Smith, Boatswain

Smith, Gamaliel
See Bentham, Jeremy

Smith, Gentleman
See Smith, William

Smith, George [FFF]
"Plunger" on American racetrack
* Pittsburg Phil

Smith, George 18th c. [HPPN]
Irish author
* G. S.

Smith, George 1852-1930 [DNA]
Scottish-born author and jurist
* Smith, Clyde

Smith, George 19th c. [HPPN]
American gambler
* Smith, One Lung

Smith, George 1924- [BWW, NBB]
American singer
* Allen, George
* Big Walter
* Harmonica King
* Hip Cat
* Little Walter Jr.
* Smith, Harmonica
* Smith, Little George

Smith, George 1945- [IBW]
American football player
* Smith, Bubba

Smith, George Allen 1892-1965 [BE]
American baseball player
* Smith, Columbia George

Smith, George Ellsworth 1869?-? [HPPN]
American gambler
* [The] Ace of Gamblers
* Pittsburgh Phil
* Smith, Stag

Smith, George Gordon 1905?-1970 [HPPN]
British detective
* [The] Spy Catcher

Smith, George H[enry] 1922- [ESF, SFL, WGT]
American author
* Deer, M. J. [joint pseudonym with Mary J. Deer Smith]
* Hudson, Jan
* Jason, Jerry
* Smith, George Hudson
* Smith, Jan

Smith, George Henry 1871-1939 [BE]
American baseball player
* Smith, Heinie

Smith, George Henry 1873-1931 [HPPN]
American editor and author
* Smith, Farmer

Smith, George Hudson
See Smith, George H[enry]

Smith, George J. 1863-1927 [AS, BE]
American baseball player
* Smith, Germany

Smith, George Joseph 1872-1915 [HPPN]
British murderer
* [The] Amorous Antique Dealer
* [The] Brides in the Bath Murderer
* [The] Ladykiller
* Love, George Oliver
* Loyd, John
* Williams, Harry

Smith, George M. ?-1921 [HPPN]
American theatrical manager
* Smith, Pop

Smith, George O[liver] 1911- [ESF, WGT]
American author and engineer
* Long, Wesley

Smith, Gerald
See Smith, Gerland Oliver

Smith, Gerland Oliver 1896-1974 [SC]
British-born actor
* Smith, Gerald

Smith, Germany
See Smith, George J.

Smith, Gerrit 1797-1874 [HPPN]
American philanthropist
* S.
* X.

Smith, Gideon 20th c.
American football player
* Smith, Charlie

Smith, Gipsey
See Smith, Rodney

Smith, Gladys 1921- [TR, WEF]
Canadian-born actress
* Smith, Alexis

Smith, Gladys Mary 1893-1979 [CU, FC, HPPN, NN]
Canadian-born actress
* America's Sweetheart
* America's Sweetheart Emeritus
* Nicholson, Dorothy
* Pickford, Gladys
* Pickford, Mary
* [The] Queen of the Movies
* [The] World's Sweetheart

Smith, Goldwin 1823-1910 [HPPN, WWL]
British-born historian and author
* [The] Bystander
* [A] Layman

Smith, Grandfather
See Knight, Charles

Smith, Guitar Boogie
See Smith, Arthur

Smith, Gunboat
See Smyth, Edward J.

Smith, Gunboat
See Smythe, Edward J.

Smith, Guy
See Erby, John J.

Smith, H[arry] Allen 1907- [HPPN]
American journalist, humorist, author
* Vator, [Miss] Ella

Smith, H. W.
See Goldschmidt, [Dr.] Hans

Smith, Hal
See Smith, James Harrell

Smith, Hamilton
See Rochester, George Ernest

Smith, Hammond
See Smith, John Robert

Smith, Hap [or Happy]
See Smith, Henry Joseph

Smith, Harmonica
See Smith, George

Smith, Harold 1874-? [THR]
British author and entertainer
* Montague, Harold

Smith, Harold 1910- [WWJ]
American jazz musician
* Smith, Howard

Smith, Harold 20th c. [BBH]
American diver
* Smith, Dutch

Smith, Harold J. 1918-1980 [HPPN]
Canadian-Indian athlete and actor
* Silverheels, Jay
* Tonto

Smith, Harold J.
See Fields, Ross Eugene

Smith, Harold Raymond 1931- [BE]
American baseball player
* Smith, Cura

Smith, Harry Bache 1860-1936 [HPPN]
American librettist and lyricist
* America's Leading Librettist

Smith, Harry E. 1918- [FB]
American football player
* Smith, Blackjack

Smith, Heinie
See Smith, George Henry

Smith, Helen Ainslie 19th c. [HPPN]
American author
* Shepard, Hazel

Smith, Helen E. [FFF, PA]
American writer
* Gale, Ethel

Smith, Helen Zenna 20th c. [AW, WW]
British playwright, author, journalist
* Price, Evadne

Smith, Helene
See Muller, Catherine Elise

Smith, Henry 1550-1600 [FFF, NPS, RH]
British clergyman
* [The] Silver Tongued

Smith, Henry 1904- [EJ, PMJ, WWJ]
American jazz musician
* Smith, Buster

Smith, Henry Boynton 1815-1877 [HPPN]
American theologian
* [The] Hero of Reunion

Smith, Henry Erskine 1842?-1932 [DNA, NAA]
American author and playwright
* Rutgers, Lispenard

Smith, Henry Joseph 1883-1961 [BE]
American baseball player
* Smith, Hap [or Happy]

Smith, Henry Welles 1822-1881 [WBD]
American attorney
* Durant, Henry Fowle

Smith, Herbert Huntington 1851-? [ALY]
American author
* Huntington, H. S.

Smith, Herbert O'Dell 1915?-
American stunt performer
* O'Dell, Digger

Smith, Hezekiah Leroy Gordon 1909-1967 [ASC, DAM, EJ]
American jazz musician
* Smith, Stuff

Smith, Hildegarde Angell ?-1933 [DNA]
American author
* Angell, Hildegarde

Smith, Hogan
See Morgan, Allen D.

Smith, Holland McTyeire 1882-1967 [CND, HPPN]
American military leader
* [The] Father of Modern Amphibious Warfare
* [The] Pacific Cyclone
* Smith, Howlin' Mad

Smith, Honey Boy
See Woodbridge, Hudson

Smith, Hooley
See Smith, Reginald Joseph

Smith, Horace
See Smith, Horatio

Smith, Horatio 1779-1849 [WBD]
British poet
* Chatfield, Paul, M.D.
* Smith, Horace

Smith, Horton 1908-1963 [GF]
American golfer
* [The] Joplin Ghost

Smith, Howard
See Smith, Harold

Smith, Howard Van 1910- [CA]
American author
* Sommers, David

Smith, Howard Whitfield, Jr. 1914- [BEW]
American actor, stage manager, director
* Whitfield, Howard

Smith, Howlin'
See Smith, John T.

Smith, Howlin' Mad
See Smith, Holland McTyeire

Smith, Huey 1924- [RO1]
American musician
* Smith, Huey Piano

Smith, Huey Piano
See Smith, Huey

Smith, Hugh Fangar
See Fangareggi, Ugo

Smith, Hurricane
See Smith, Norman

Smith, Iain Crichton 1928- [DLE, WOA]
Scottish poet, author, playwright
* Mac A'Ghobhainn, Iain
* Mac A'Ghobhainn, Seamus

Smith, Ian 1919-
Rhodesian prime minister
* Good Old Smitty
* Iron Man Ian

Smith, Isabel
See Smith, Elizabeth Bacheler

Smith, Isadore Leighton Luce 1901-1985 [CA]
American author
* Leighton, Ann

Smith, Ivan 1919?-1981
American country-western performer
* Smith, Buddy

Smith, J.
See Collier, Jeremy

Smith, J. D. 20th c.
American football player
* [The] Wheatpicker

Smith, J. D.
See Smith, James David

Smith, [Prof.] J. Q.
See Burt, John P.

Smith, J. R. 20th c. [HPPN]
American football player
* Smith, Jackrabbit

Smith, J. T.
See Smith, John T.

Smith, Jabbo
See Smith, Cladys

Smith, Jack 1896-1933 [BEW, F1, IPA]
Canadian-born actor and producer
* Pickford, Jack

Smith, Jack 1898-1950 [BEW, SC]
American singer and actor
* Smith, Whispering Jack
* [The] Whispering Baritone

Smith, Jack 20th c. [GW]
American rodeo performer
* Smith, Singin' Jack

Smith, Jack
See Smith, Bernard

Smith, Jackrabbit
See Smith, J. R.

Smith, James 1887-1947 [BE]
American baseball player
* Bluejacket, James [Jim]

Smith, James 1935- [TR]
British actor
* Dale, Jim

Smith, James 1953- [WP 11-9-84]
American boxer
* Smith, Bonecrusher

Smith, James 20th c. [EF]
American football player
* Smith, Jetstream

Smith, James 20th c.
American political boss
* Smith, Sugar Jim

Smith, James 20th c. [RM, RO2]
American musician
* Smith, Smitty

Smith, James
See Mellilo, James

Smith, James A. 1876-? [BE]
American baseball player
* Smith, Stub

Smith, James Carlisle 1890-1966 [AS, BE, PB]
American baseball player
* Smith, Red

Smith, James David 1930- [BA]
American educator and artist
* Smith, J. D.

Smith, James Ellison 1910- [FC]
American actor
* Ellison, James

Smith, James Harrell 1923- [CWG]
American country-western performer
* Smith, Hal

Smith, James Henry ?-1907 [HPPN]
American millionaire
* Smith, Silent

Smith, James Hicks 1822-1882 [HPPN]
British barrister
* [An] Hereditary High Churchman

Smith, James Marcus 1938- [RO2]
American singer
* Powers, Jet
* Proby, P. J.

Smith, James Monroe 1888-1949 [HPPN]
American educator and embezzler
* Smith, Jingle Money

Smith, James Moore [SN]
* More, Phantom

Smith, James Oscar [Jimmy] 1926- [IBW]
American jazz musician
* Jazz Organ, Mr.

Smith, James Samuel 1875-? [THR]
British musician
* Mendel

Smith, Jan
See Smith, George H[enry]

Smith, Jane
See Cox, Ida

Smith, Jane Luella Dowd 1847-? [NAA]
American author
* Lell, Jennie
* Ulla

Smith, Jean
See Smith, Frances C[hristine]

Smith, Jeanette
See Walker, Jeanette S.

Smith, Jeanie Oliver [Davidson] 1836-1925 [DNA]
American author and poet
* Oliver, Temple

Smith, Jedediah Strong 1798-1831 [HPPN]
American explorer
* [The] Splendid Wayfarer

Smith, Jeff
See Jeffords, Jerome

Smith, Jefferson Randolph 1860-1898 [BLB, DI, HPPN]
American gambler and swindler
* [The] Great Thimble Rigger
* [The] King of the Frontier Con Men
* [The] Monarch of Misrule
* Smith, Soapy
* Wildest of the West

Smith, Jerome 1895- [NOJ]
American jazz musician
* Smith, Pork Chop

Smith, Jerome Van Crowninshield 1800-? [HPPN]
American author, physician, politician
* [A] Citizen of Massachusetts

Smith, Jerry Lee 20th c. [RO1]
American musician and songwriter
* Smith, Smoochee

Smith, Jerry T. 1943- [FB]
American football player
* Smith, Babycakes
* Smith, Shane

Smith, Jess[e] 1871-1923 [HPPN]
American political adviser
* Beau Jess of Washington Court House

Smith, Jetstream
See Smith, James

Smith, Jim [BI]
American football player
* Smith, Yazoo

Smith, Jimmy Dee
See Smith, Pleasant

Smith, Jingle Money
See Smith, James Monroe

Smith, Joe
See Liddell, James Andrew

Smith, Joe
See Persico, Salvatore Giuseppe

Smith, Joe
See Seltzer, Joseph

Smith [or Smyth?], John 1570?-1612 [SN, WBD]
British clergyman
* [The] Father of English General Baptists
* [The] Se Baptist

Smith, [Captain] John 1580-1631 [HPPN]
British adventurer and colonist
* [The] Father of Virginia
* Watson, Thomas

Smith, John 18th c. [NPS, SR]
British boxer
* Smith, Buckhorse

Smith, John 1880?-1918 [NOJ]
American jazz musician
* Smith, Sugar Johnny

Smith, John 1924- [AW, WD]
British author, poet, playwright
* Smith, C. Busby

Smith, John 20th c. [BBH]
American football player
* Smith, Clipper

Smith, John [joint pseudonym with Hoyt Hudson]
See Herrick, Marvin Theodore

Smith, John [joint pseudonym with Marvin Theodore Herrick]
See Hudson, Hoyt

Smith, John
See Lewis, John Delaware

Smith, John
See McKean, Henry Swasey

Smith, John
See Van Orden, Robert E.

Smith, [Rev.] John Cotton 1826-1862 [HPPN]
American clergyman
* [A] New York Presbyter
* [The] Rector

Smith, John, Esq.
See Smith, Seba

Smith, John Francis
See Gammon, John Francis

Smith, John Joseph [Jack]
See Coffey, John Joseph

Smith, John, Jr., of Arkansas
See Southworth, Sylvester S.

Smith, John Philip 1904?-1973 [HPPN]
American football coach and athletic director
* Smith, Little Clipper

Smith, John Robert 1933- [EJ7]
American jazz musician
* Hammond, Johnny
* Smith, Hammond

Smith, John Stores   [FFF]
Author
* Ackerlos, John

Smith, John T. 1890- [BWW]
American singer
* Howlin' Wolf
* Smith, Funny Papa
* Smith, Howlin'
* Smith, J. T.

Smith, John Thomas 1766-1833 [FFF, RH, SN]
British antiquary
* Smith, Rainy Day

Smith, John W.
See Smadt, Jan

Smith, John William 1892-1935 [BE]
American baseball player
* Smith, Chick

Smith, Johnston
See Crane, Stephen [Townley]

Smith, Jolly Clara
See Smith, Clara

Smith, Joseph   [SN]
British political organizer
* [The] Sheepmaker

Smith, Joseph [FFF]
American naval officer
* [The] Father of the Monitors

Smith, Joseph ?-1878 [SN]
British social reformer
* [The] Sheepmaker

Smith, Joseph 1805-1844 [HPPN]
American church founder
* [The] Father of the Mormons

Smith, Joseph [Joe] 1883?-? [HPPN]
American actor
* [The] Sunshine Boy

Smith, Joseph
See Sultzer, Joseph

Smith, Joseph Arthur 1848-1906 [BEW]
American playwright
* Arthur, Joseph

Smith, Joseph Edwards Adams 1822-1896 [PA]
American author
* Greylock, Godfrey

Smith, Julia Cleaver [joint pseudonym with Nichols Smith]
See Cleaver, Diane

Smith, Julia Cleaver [joint pseudonym with Diane Cleaver]
See Smith, Nichols

Smith, Katharine Grey [Hogg] 1876-1933 [DNA]
American author
* Grey, Katharine

Smith, Kathryn Elizabeth [Kate] 1909-1986 [HPPN]
American singer
* [The] Moon Over the Mountain Girl
* Radio's Own Statue of Liberty
* [The] Songbird of the South

Smith, Kay Nolte 1932- [CA]
American author and actress
* Gillian, Kay

Smith, Kenneth David 1956- [DC]
British cricketer
* Smith, Smithy

Smith, Kenny 20th c. [SI 11-28-83]
American basketball player
* [The] Jet

Smith, Kester 20th c. [RM]
Musician
* Smith, Smitty

Smith, King
See Louis Philippe

Smith, King Edward, III 1929- [CWG]
American country-western performer
* Smith, Smitty

Smith, Kippy
See Smith, Christopher Lyall

Smith, Klondike
See Smith, Frederick H.

Smith, L. D.   [FFF]
Author
* Dog Whip

Smith, L. H. 1916- [SFL, WGT]
Author
* Williams, Speedy

Smith, Lafayette
See Higdon, Hal

Smith, Larry 20th c. [RM]
Musician
* Smith, Legs Larry

Smith, Laura Newton Rundless 20th c. [IBW]
American singer
* Lee, Laura

Smith, Laura Rountree 1876-1924 [DNA]
American author
* June, Caroline Silver

Smith, Lawrence E. 1948- [FB]
American football player
* Smith, Tody

Smith, Lawrence Patrick 1894- [BE]
American baseball player
* Smith, Paddy

Smith, Lee
See Albion, Lee Smith

Smith, Legs Larry
See Smith, Larry

Smith, Lena [Kennedy] 1914- [CA]
British author
* Kennedy, Lena

Smith, Leonard B. 1915- [ASC]
American composer and conductor
* Bingley, Richard
* Hemingway, Chas.
* Schubert, Emile H.

Smith, LeRoi Tex 1934- [CA, HPPN]
American author
* Oogam, LeRoi
* Ugama, LeRoi
* Welch, Charles Scott

Smith, Lester 1898-1952 [NOJ]
American jazz musician
* Smith, Monk

Smith, Lester 1957- [HPPN]
American baseball player
* Smith, Big Lee
* Smith, Slim

Smith, Lew
See Floren, Lee

Smith, Lillian Boardman 1913?-1953 [HPPN]
American actress
* Boardman, Lillian

Smith, Linell Nash 1932- [CA, HPPN, SAT]
American author and illustrator
* Chenault, Nell
* Nash, Linell

Smith, Little Billy
See Smith, Billy

Smith, Little Billy
See Smith, William Russell

Smith, Little Clipper
See Smith, John Philip

Smith, Little George
See Smith, George

Smith, Lonnie 1933- [BA]
American writer and editor
* Kashif, Ghayth Nur

Smith, Lottie 1895-1936 [BEW, F1, F2]
Canadian-born actress
* Pickford, Lottie

Smith, Louis 20th c. [BE]
American baseball player
* Smith, Bull

Smith, Louis
See Barzini, Luigi Giorgio

Smith, Lyle 20th c. [GW]
American rodeo performer
* Smith, Rom

Smith, Mabel Louise 1924-1972 [BWW, EJ]
American singer
* Big Maybelle
* Webster, Mamie

Smith, Mac
See Smith, Macdonald

Smith, Macdonald 1880-1949 [GF]
Scottish-born golfer
* [The] Silent Scot
* Smith, Mac

Smith, Mamie 1883-1946 [BWW]
American singer
* [The] Queen of the Blues

Smith, Mandy
See Landreaux, Elizabeth Mary

Smith, Margaret [OP]
British opera singer
* Neville, Margaret

Smith, Margaret 1936?- [EG, GF]
American golfer
* Smith, Wiffi

Smith, Margaret
See Whittier, John Greenleaf

Smith, Margaret Chase 1898-
American politician
* Mother of the W. A. V. E. S.

Smith, Marguerite Alice Helene
1875-1957 [BEW, CED]
Belgian-born actress and opera singer
* Sylva, Marguerita

Smith, Marion C. [PA]
Author
* Couthony, Marion

Smith, Martin Cruz
See Smith, Martin William

Smith, Martin William 1942- [CA]
American author
* Carter, Nick
* Logan, Jake
* Quinn, Simon
* Smith, Martin Cruz

Smith, Marvin Harold 1900-1961 [BE]
American baseball player
* Smith, Red

Smith, Mary 1918- [AW, WD]
British author
* Drewery, Mary
* Radha

Smith, Mary Eleanor 1866-? [LFW]
American swindler and murderer
* Old Shoebox Annie

Smith, Mary Ellen 20th c. [CA, SAT]
American author
* Smith, Mike

Smith, [Mrs.] Mary Ellen
See Pleasants, Mary Ellen Smith

Smith, Mary Hopkins 20th c. [HPPN]
American missionary
* Smith, Sis

Smith, Mary J. Deer 20th c. [WGT]
American author
* Deer, M. J. [joint pseudonym with
  George H(enry) Smith]

Smith, Mary Pearsall 1864-1945
American-born author
* Logan, Mary

Smith, Mary Prudence [Wells]
1840-1930 [DNA]
American author
* Thorne, P.

Smith, Matthew
See Mordaunt, Charles [Third Earl of
Peterborough]

Smith, Matthew Hale 1810-1879 [FFF]
American author and clergyman
* Burleigh

Smith, Maurice 1899?-1984 [HPPN]
American football coach
* Smith, Big Clipper
* Smith, Clipper

Smith, May
See Robbins, May Smith

Smith, May Riley [PA]
Author
* M. L. R.

Smith, Michael 1939- [CA]
British psychologist and author
* Apter, Michael J[ohn]

Smith, Michael John 1942- [DC]
British cricketer
* Smith, Smudger

Smith, Midget
See Smith, William Joseph

Smith, Mike
See Smith, Elmer Ellsworth

Smith, Mike
See Smith, Elwood Hope

Smith, Mike
See Smith, Mary Ellen

Smith, Millicent 1946- [RO2]
Jamaican singer
* Small, Millie

Smith, Mr.
See Birch, Walter B.

Smith, Mr.
See Duleepsinhji, Kumar Shri

Smith, Mr.
See Lockwood, Ralph Ingersoll

Smith, Mr.
See Louis Philippe

Smith, Mona 1909- [FC]
Australian-born actress
* Barrie, Mona

Smith, Monk
See Smith, Lester

Smith, Moses 1932- [BWW]
American singer
* Smith, Whispering

Smith, Mrs.
See Yeardley, Martha Savory

Smith, Mrs. Adolphe Jerrold [FFF]
British writer
* Corisande

Smith, Mrs. Castle [PA]
Author
* Brenda

Smith, Mrs. F. B. [PA]
Author
* Fanfan

Smith, Mrs. John
See Arthur, Timothy Shay

Smith, Mrs. John A. [PA]
Author
* Aunt Esther

Smith, Mrs. M. B. 19th c. [DNA]
Author
* Wood, Hazel

Smith, Mrs. Spencer 19th c. [SN]
* Fair Florence

Smith, Mysterious Billy
See Smith, Amos

Smith, Nancy 1911- [THR]
Australian-born actress
* O'Neil, Nancy

Smith, Nathan Ryno 1797-1877 [BDSA]
American physician and author
* Viator

Smith, Neil 1949- [DC]
British cricketer
* Smith, Sam
* Smith, Smudger

Smith, Nichols 20th c. [NY 3-2-84]
American author and literary agent
* Smith, Julia Cleaver [joint pseudonym
  with Diane Cleaver]

Smith, Nig
See Schmidt, Frank Elmer

Smith, Noland 1943- [FB]
American football player
* [The] Super Gnat

Smith, Norma E[thel] 20th c. [NAA]
Canadian author and poet
* Bluenose

Smith, Norman 1923- [RO2]
British singer
* Smith, Hurricane

Smith, Norman Edward Mace 1914-
[WD]
British author
* Sheraton, Neil
* Shore, Norman

Smith, Norris 1881-1969 [IBW]
American-born actor and singer
* [The] Boy Baritone

Smith, O. C.
See Smith, Ocie Lee

Smith, Ocie Lee 1937- [DAM]
American singer
* Smith, O. C.

Smith, Odie
See Smith, Adrian

Smith, Oil
See Smith, Earl Sutton

Smith, Oliver Prince 1894?-1978
American military leader
* [The] Professor

Smith, One Lung
See Smith, George

Smith, O'Neill Gordon 1933-1959 [EC]
West Indian cricketer
* Smith, Collie

Smith, Ormond G. 1860-1933 [WGT]
American author
* Carter, Nick [joint pseudonym with John Russell Coryell] [house pseudonym]

Smith, Osborne Earl 1954- [BI, TI 1-31-83]
American baseball player
* Smith, Ozzie
* [The] Wizard of Oz

Smith, Otrie 1936- [BA]
American psychiatrist
* Hickerson, O. B.

Smith, Owen P. ?-1929 [BBH, HPPN]
American inventor of mechanical rabbit for dog racing
* [The] Father of Modern Greyhound Racing
* [The] Father of the Mechanical Rabbit

Smith, Ozzie
See Smith, Osborne Earl

Smith, Paddy
See Smith, Lawrence Patrick

Smith, Pat
See Smith, Cedric

Smith, Phenomenal
See Gammon, John Francis

Smith, Philosophy
See Smith, Thomas Vernon

Smith, Phyllis 1922?- [HPPN]
American singer
* Curtin, Phyllis
* [The] Most Intelligent of American Sopranos

Smith, Pinetop
See Smith, Clarence

Smith, Pinky
See Smith, Winthrop A.

Smith, Pleasant 1886-1969 [SC]
American actor and wrestler
* Pleasant, Tommy Lee
* Smith, Jimmy Dee

Smith, Pop
See Smith, Charles Marvin

Smith, Pop
See Smith, George M.

Smith, Pop Boy
See Smith, Clarence Ossie

Smith, Popgun
See Smith, William S.

Smith, Pops
See Smith, Russell T.

Smith, Pork Chop
See Smith, Jerome

Smith, R. C. 19th c. [HPPN]
British author
* Anglicus, Merlinus, Jr.
* Members of the Mercurie, etc.

Smith, Rabbi
See Smith, Thomas

Smith, Rag
See Smith, Edmund Neale

Smith, Rainy Day
See Smith, John Thomas

Smith, Raymond 1967?- [WP 10-29-85]
American football player
* [The] World

Smith, Raymond Harley 1945- [IAW]
American author
* Del Norte, Scott

Smith, Rebecca
See Lee, Rebecca Smith

Smith, Red
See Smith, James Carlisle

Smith, Red
See Smith, Marvin Harold

Smith, Red
See Smith, Richard Paul

Smith, Red
See Smith, Walter W[ellesley]

Smith, Red
See Smith, Willard Jehu

Smith, Reginald Joseph 1903?-1963 [CEI, FHE, HK]
Canadian-born hockey player
* Smith, Hooley

Smith, Richard Morris 1827-1896 [DNA]
American author
* Stanley, T. Lloyd

Smith, Richard Paul 1904- [BE]
American baseball player
* Smith, Red

Smith, Richard Rein 1930- [CA]
American author
* Bond, Ray
* Castle, Damon
* Collins, Cindy
* Crossan, Darryl
* Davis, Cliff
* Davis, Jim
* Green, Robert
* Lane, Sherry
* Rein, Richard
* Reinsmith, Richard
* Stradley, Mark
* Taylor, Ann
* Taylor, Brad
* Tower, Diana
* Walters, Chad

Smith, Riverboat
See Smith, Robert Walkup

Smith, Robert [DNNF]
* Smith, Bobus

Smith, Robert 1689-1768 [SN]
British mathematician and astronomer
* Black Smith of Trinity

Smith, Robert 1853-? [PI]
Irish poet
* Myles

Smith, Robert 1914- [AW]
British author and journalist
* Chattan, Robert

Smith, Robert 1938?- [BI]
American disk jockey
* Wolfman Jack

Smith, Robert A. 1870?-1943 [BBH]
American horse trainer
* Smith, Whistling Bob

Smith, Robert Barnwell 1800-1876 [BI, HPPN]
American politician
* [The] Father of Secession
* Rhett, Robert Barnwell

Smith, Robert Benjamin 1821-1894
American newspaper editor and politician
* Hilton, Robert Benjamin

Smith, Robert Charles 1938- [AW, CA]
British author
* Charles, Robert
* Leader, Charles

Smith, Robert Cross 1795-1832 [EOP]
British astrologer and author
* Raphael

Smith, Robert Dickie 1928- [IAW]
American clergyman and author
* Alexander, Justin

Smith, Robert Edward 1874-? [NAA]
American author and clergyman
* Brute, Q.

Smith, Robert Gray 1942- [WEC]
American cartoonist
* Graysmith, Robert

Smith, Robert Kimmel 1930- [CA, SAT]
American author
* Marks, Peter

Smith, Robert Walkup 1928- [BE]
American baseball player
* Smith, Riverboat

Smith, Robert Wilton 1881-1957 [BMH]
British comedian
* Wilton, Robb

Smith, Rodney 1860-1947 [HPPN]
British evangelist
* [The] Gipsy Boy
* Smith, Gipsey

Smith, Roger D. 1936- [FB]
American football player
* Smith, Zeke

Smith, Rom
See Smith, Lyle

Smith, Ron[ald] L[oran] 1936- [CA, WGT]
American author
* Loran, Martin [joint pseudonym with John Baxter]

Smith, Ronald Gregor 1913-1968 [CAP]
Scottish author
* Browne, Sam
* Maxwell, Ronald

Smith, Ross 1953- [SMG]
Canadian-born hockey player
* Smith, Smitty

Smith, Ross Alexander 1907-1937 [BEW]
American actor
* Alexander, Ross

Smith, Russell T. 1890-1966 [WWJ]
American jazz musician
* Smith, Pops

Smith, S. S.
See Williamson, Thames Ross

Smith, Sacheverell
See Darling, William Young

Smith, Salt
See Smith, Eugene

Smith, Salvatore Giuseppe
See Persico, Salvatore Giuseppe

Smith, Sam
See Smith, Neil

Smith, Samantha 20th c.
American student
* [The] Angel of Peace

Smith, Samuel 1857-? [BE]
American baseball player
* Smith, Skyrocket

Smith, Sarah 1832-1911 [LC]
British author
* Stretton, Hesba

Smith, Sarah Anne 1951- [HPPN]
American entertainer
* Silicone Sally

Smith, Sarah Pogson 19th c. [HPPN]
American author
* [A] Lady

Smith, Sarah Stafford
See Smith, Dorothy [Stafford]

Smith, Scottie Fitzgerald
See Smith, Frances Scott [Fitzgerald]

Smith, Scotty
See Lennox, George St. Leger Gordon

Smith, Scoville
See Smith, Alice Maude

Smith, Seba 1792-1868 [FFF, PA, WBD]
American author
* Downing, [Major] Jack
* Smith, John, Esq.

Smith, Shane
See Smith, Jerry T.

Smith, Shelley
See Bodington, Nancy [Hermione]

Smith, Sherrod Malone 1891-1949 [AS, BE]
American baseball player
* Smith, Sherry

Smith, Sherry
See Smith, Sherrod Malone

Smith, Shirley
See Curtis, E. J.

Smith, Shirley M[ae] 1923- [CA]
American author
* Ovesen, Ellis

Smith, Silent
See Smith, James Henry

Smith, Silent Tom
See Smith, Tom

Smith, Silver Willy
See Smith, William T.

Smith, Singin' Jack
See Smith, Jack

Smith, Sis
See Smith, Mary Hopkins

Smith, Skyrocket
See Smith, Samuel

Smith, Slim
See Smith, Lester

Smith, Smithy
See Smith, Kenneth David

Smith, Smitty
See Smith, Al

Smith, Smitty
See Smith, James

Smith, Smitty
See Smith, Kester

Smith, Smitty
See Smith, King Edward, III

Smith, Smitty
See Smith, Ross

Smith, Smitty
See Smith, William

Smith, Smitty
See Smith, William John

Smith, Smoochee
See Smith, Jerry Lee

Smith, Smudger
See Smith, David Mark

Smith, Smudger
See Smith, Michael John

Smith, Smudger
See Smith, Neil

Smith, Smurf
See Smith, David Mark

Smith, Snuffy
See Smith, Clinton James

Smith, Soapy
See Smith, Jefferson Randolph

Smith, Sookey
See Smith, William Sooy

Smith, Sophia 1796-1870 [HPPN]
American philanthropist
* [The] Mother of Smith College

Smith, Sosthenes
See Wells, Herbert George

Smith, Soule 19th c. [FFF]
American author
* Falcon

Smith, Stag
See Smith, George Ellsworth

Smith, Stevie
See Smith, Florence Margaret

Smith, Strata
See Smith, William

Smith, Stub
See Smith, James A.

Smith, Stuff
See Smith, Hezekiah Leroy Gordon

Smith, Sugar Jim
See Smith, James

Smith, Sugar Johnny
See Smith, John

Smith, Surrey [joint pseudonym with William Morum]
See Dinner, William

Smith, Surrey [joint pseudonym with William Dinner]
See Morum, William

Smith, Susie
See Moore, Monette

Smith, Sydney 1771-1845 [DEL, NPS, PA]
British author and clergyman
* Partington, Mrs.
* Pith, Peter
* Plymley, Peter
* Publicola

Smith, T. Carlyle
See Bangs, John Kendrick

Smith, T. D.
See Dudley-Smith, Trevor

Smith, Tab
See Smith, Talmadge

Smith, Tad
See Smith, Claude M.

Smith, Talmadge 1909-1971 [EJ, PMJ, WWJ]
American jazz musician
* Smith, Tab

Smith, Tangiers
See Smith, William

Smith, Tank
See Smith, Charles Edward

Smith, Tatti
See Smith, Carl

Smith, Tete
See Smith, William Ephraim

Smith, Theolic 20th c. [OBW]
American baseball player
* Smith, Fireball

Smith, [Sir] Thomas 1513-1577 [NPS]
Statesman and author
* [The] Glory of the Muses

Smith, Thomas 1558?-1625 [WBD]
British merchant
* Smythe, [Sir] Thomas

Smith, Thomas 1638-1710 [SN]
Philologist
* Roguery, Doctor
* Smith, Rabbi
* Smith, Tograi

Smith, Thomas J. 1830-1870 [EWG]
American law officer
* Bear River Tom

Smith, Thomas Lacey 1805-1875 [DNA]
Author and attorney
* Peters, Jeremy

Smith, Thomas Vernon 1890- [HPPN]
American politician
* [The] Political Philosopher
* Smith, Philosophy

Smith, Tiger
See Smith, E. J.

Smith, Tody
See Smith, Lawrence E.

Smith, Tograi
See Smith, Thomas

Smith, Tom 1878?-1957 [AS]
American horse trainer
* Smith, Silent Tom

Smith, Tombstone
See Smith, Charlie

Smith, Tony 1912- [HPPN]
American sculptor
* [The] Master of the Monumentalists

Smith, Tony 1927- [IBW]
American musician
* Tony the Terror

Smith, Toukie
See Smith, Doris

Smith, Trixie 1895-1943 [BWW]
American singer
* Ames, Tessie
* Lee, Bessie
* [The] Southern Nightingale

Smith, Verda T. 20th c.
American football player
* Smith, Vitamin T

Smith, Vernon 20th c.
American football player
* Smith, Catfish

Smith, Victor A. ?-1921 [SC]
American actor and circus performer
* Sini'letta, Vic

Smith, Vincent 1894-1952 [BI]
American monk
* Mary Simon, [Father]

Smith, Vitamin T
See Smith, Verda T.

Smith, W. B. [PA]
Author
* Etheridge, Kelsic

Smith, W. J.
See Smith, Walter James

Smith, W. W.
See Musica, Philip Mariana Fausto

Smith, Wade
See Snow, Charles Horace

Smith, Walker, Jr. 1920- [BX, IBW, WBC]
American boxer
* [The] Harlem Hotshot
* [The] Harlem Hurricane
* Robinson, Ray
* Robinson, Sugar Ray

Smith, Wallace 1929-1973 [BX, RBE]
American boxer
* Smith, Bud

Smith, Walter [BE]
American baseball player
* Reinicker, Walter [Wally]

Smith, Walter Bedell 1895- [BDW, HPPN]
American army officer
* [The] American Bulldog
* Bulldog
* [The] General Manager of the War
* Smith, Beetle

Smith, Walter Chalmers 1824-1908 [HPPN, NPS]
Scottish clergyman, hymn writer, poet
* Knott, Herman
* Orwell

Smith, Walter H. 1886-1930 [HPPN]
American actor and director
* Reynolds, Walter H.

Smith, Walter James 1917- [SFL]
British author
* Smith, W. J.

Smith, Walter O.
See Chattoram, Paul

Smith, Walter W[ellesley] 1905-1982 [BI, CA, IPA]
American sportswriter
* Smith, Red

Smith, Walter Whateley 1884-1947 [EOP]
British psychic researcher and author
* Carington, W[alter] Whateley

Smith, Ward
See Goldsmith, Howard

Smith, Webster
See Coleman, Clayton W[ebster]

Smith, Whispering
See Smith, Moses

Smith, Whispering Jack
See Smith, Jack

Smith, Whistling Bob
See Smith, Robert A.

Smith, Wib
See Smith, Wilbur Floyd

Smith, Wiffi
See Smith, Margaret

Smith, Wilbur Floyd 1886-1959 [BE]
American baseball player
* Smith, Wib

Smith, Willard Jehu 1892- [BE]
American baseball player
* Smith, Red

Smith, Willard L[aurence] 1927- [CA]
American author
* Laurence, Will

Smith, William 1655-1705 [HPPN]
British-American governor in Africa
* Smith, Tangiers

Smith, William 1727-1803 [HPPN]
Scottish clergyman, author, educator
* [A] Burgher
* Candidus
* Seceder in Glasgow

Smith, William 1730-1790 [DNNS, RH]
British actor
* Smith, Gentleman

Smith, William 1769-1839 [DNNS, FFF, HPPN, NPS, SN]
British geologist
* [The] Father of English Geology
* [The] Father of Geology
* Smith, Fossil
* Smith, Strata

Smith, William 1796?-1887 [FFF, SN]
American politician
* Extra Billy

Smith, William 1809-1907 [HPPN]
American pirate captor
* Uncle Billy

Smith, William 1831-1913 [HPPN]
Canadian-American manufacturer
* [The] Candy Boy
* Trade

Smith, William 1883-1961 [F2]
Actor
* Farnum, Franklyn
* Farnum, Smiling Frank

Smith, William 20th c. [RO2]
Canadian-born musician and songwriter
* Smith, Smitty

Smith, William
See Louis Philippe

Smith, William A. 1918?-
American artist
* [The] Pineville Painter

Smith, William Augustus 1874-1944 [BMH]
British comedian
* Bard, Wilkie

Smith, [Sir] William Cusack, Bart. 1776-1836 [PI]
Irish poet
* Peeradeal, Paul Puck
* Peeradeal, Peter Puck
* Search, Warner Christian

Smith, William Dale 1929- [CA]
American author
* Anthony, David

Smith, William Ephraim 1829-1890
American politician and military officer
* Smith, Tete

Smith, William Farrar 1824-1903 [FFF]
American army officer
* Smith, Baldy

Smith, William Henry 1825-1891 [DEP, DHA, DNNS]
British politician
* Old Morality

Smith, William Henry Joseph Berthol Bonaparte Bertholoff 1897-1973 [ASC, DAM, EJ]
American jazz musician
* [The] Lion
* Willie the Lion

Smith, William John 1950- [SMG]
Canadian-born hockey player
* Smith, Smitty

Smith, William Joseph 1899- [BX, RBE]
American boxer
* Smith, Midget

Smith, William Joseph Thomas 1920- [AW, IAW]
British author
* Ferrar, Gul

Smith, William Loughton 1745?-1812 [IP]
American statesman and author
* Phocion

Smith, William Russell 1815-1896 [HPPN]
American politician
* Smith, Little Billy

Smith, William S. 1816-1868 [HPPN]
American gunsmith, attorney, politician
* Smith, Popgun

Smith, William Sooy 1830-1916 [HPPN]
American army officer
* Smith, Sookey

Smith, William T. 20th c. [HPPN]
American politician
* Smith, Silver Willy

Smith, Willie 1939- [BE]
American baseball player
* Smith, Wonderful Willie

Smith, Willie Mae Ford 1906- [IBW]
American singer
* [The] Mother of Gospel Music

Smith, Wilton Leon 1945- [BA]
American physician
* Smith, Butch

Smith, Winthrop A. 1907- [BBH]
American lacrosse player and coach
* Smith, Pinky

Smith, Wonderful
See Smith, Floyd

Smith, Wonderful Willie
See Smith, Willie

Smith, Woodrow Wilson
See Kuttner, Henry

Smith, Yazoo
See Smith, Jim

Smith, Z. Z.
See Westheimer, David

Smith, Zeke
See Smith, Roger D.

Smith-Johannsen, Herman 1875-? [BBH]
Norwegian-born ski trail developer
* Smith-Johannsen, Jack Rabbit

Smith-Johannsen, Jack Rabbit
See Smith-Johannsen, Herman

Smith-Masters, Margaret 1869-? [LAO]
British author
* Le Fevre, Felicite

Smith-Thomas, Eleanor Mary Tydfil 1910- [THR]
Welsh-born actress and singer
* Fayre, Eleanor

Smith Woods, Dorothy Beryl 1904- [AW]
British author
* Moore, Beryl

Smithells, Anabel Doreen 20th c. [HPPN]
British author
* Boscawen, Linda

Smithells, Roger [William] 1905- [CAP]
British author
* Cash, Sebastian

Smither, Jessie 1884-1960 [BEW]
Actress
* Orme, Denise

Smithgall, Elizabeth
See Watts, Elizabeth [Bailey] Smithgall

Smithline, Adele 1903- [IPA]
American fashion designer
* Simpson, Adele

Smithson, Harriet Constance 1800-1854 [HPPN]
Irish actress
* Berlioz, Madame

Smithson, Hugh 1715-1786 [WBD]
First Duke of Northumberland
* Percy, [Sir] Hugh

Smithson, James
See Macie, James Lewis [or Louis]

Smithson, Noble 1841-? [ALY]
American author
* Freeman, Frank

Smithsonian, Dr.
See Henry, Joseph

Smithwick, Alfred Patrick 1927?-1973 [BBH]
Jockey
* Smithwick, Paddy

Smithwick, Paddy
See Smithwick, Alfred Patrick

Smits, Teo
See Smits, Theodore R[ichard]

Smits, Theodore R[ichard] 1905- [CA]
American author
* Smits, Teo

Smitts, Mr.
See Linds, Mark Prager

Smitz, Gaspar ?-1689 [SN]
Dutch painter
* Smitz, Magdalen

Smitz, Magdalen
See Smitz, Gaspar

Smoil, Glenn na
See Rooney, William

Smoke, Senor
See Lopez, Aurelio Alejandro

Smokehouse Charley
See Dorsey, Thomas A[ndrew] [Tommy]

Smokey Joe Finneran
See Finneran, Joseph Ignatius

Smokey Joe Martin
See Martin, William Joseph [Joe]

Smokey Joe Williams
See Williams, Joseph

Smokey Joe Wood
See Wood, Joseph

[The] Smokey Mountain Boy
See Acuff, Roy

Smokin' Joe
See Campbell, Joseph

Smokin' Joe Frazier
See Frazier, Joseph [Joe]

Smoky Babe
See Brown, Robert

[The] Smoky Eyed Beauty of the Silent Screen
See Logan, Jacqueline

Smolar, Boris 1897- [IAW]
Russian-born author and columnist
* Lewis, Ben

Smolens, Jay 1927- [BBD]
American music critic and editor
* Harrison, Jay

Smolensk, Alexander 1889-1972 [MS]
Russian-born conductor
* Smallens, Alexander

Smoll, Clyde Hetrick 1914- [BE]
American baseball player
* Smoll, Lefty

Smoll, Lefty
See Smoll, Clyde Hetrick

[The] Smollett of the Stage
See Farquhar, George

Smollett, Tobias George 1721-1771
[DNNF, FFF, IP, NPS, RH]
British author
* Alexander, Drawcansir
* Dustwich, Jonathan
* Smelfungus
* [The] Vagabond Scot

Smoot, Reed 1862-1941 [HPPN]
American politician and church leader
* [The] Harding Enthusiast

Smooth, Mr.
See Wallace, Jerry

Smothers, Abraham 20th c. [BWW, NBB]
American musician
* Smothers, Little Smokey

Smothers, Little Smokey
See Smothers, Abraham

Smothers, Otis 1929- [BWW]
American singer
* Smothers, Smokey

Smothers, Smokey
See Smothers, Otis

Smowrey, Henry Neitz 20th c. [BE]
American baseball player
* Smoyer, Henry Neitz

Smoyer, Henry Neitz
See Smowrey, Henry Neitz

Smreczynski, Franciszek 1876-1930
[HPPN]
Polish author, playwright, poet
* Orkan, Wladyslaw

[A] Smuggler
See Rattenbury, John

Smykal, Frank John
See Smejkal, Frank John

Smyres, Clancy
See Smyres, Clarence Melvin

Smyres, Clarence Melvin 1922- [BE]
American baseball player
* Smyres, Clancy

[The] Smyrnean Poet
See Mimnermus

Smyth, Alice M.
See Hadfield, Alice M[ary]

Smyth, Charles John 18th c. [IP]
British author
* Quid-Pro-Quo

Smyth, Constance 20th c. [ITA]
Irish-born actress
* Smith, Constance

Smyth, Edward J. 1887-1974 [BX, RBE]
American boxer
* Smith, Gunboat

Smyth, Frank 19th c. [FFF, IP]
American writer
* Werter, Max

Smyth, James Daniel 1893-1958 [BE]
American baseball player
* Smyth, Red

Smyth, John 1783-1854 [PI]
Irish-born poet
* Macgowan

Smyth, Patrick G. 1856?-? [PI]
Irish-born poet, author, journalist
* Green, Christopher
* P. G. S.

Smyth, Red
See Smyth, James Daniel

Smyth, William 1813-1878 [PI]
Irish author, actor, painter
* Ryan, W. S.
* Scribble, William

Smythe, C. Stafford 1921?-1971 [FHE]
Canadian hockey executive
* Smythe, Staff

Smythe, Conn
See Smythe, Constantine Falkland
Kerrys

Smythe, Constantine Falkland Kerrys
20th c. [FHE]
Canadian hockey executive
* [The] David Harum of Hockey
* Smythe, Conn

Smythe, Edward J. 1887-1974 [HPPN]
American boxer
* [The] Gunner
* Smith, Gunboat

Smythe, Florence
See Roberts, Florence Smythe

Smythe, George Sydney 19th c. [SN]
Author
* Averanche, Lionel

Smythe, James M. [IP]
American author
* [A] Southerner

Smythe, James P.
See McGarry, William Rutledge

Smythe, John Henry, Jr. 1883-?
[HPPN]
American slogan writer
* [The] Slogan Man
* Smythe, Slogan

Smythe, Maria Anne 1756-1837 [HPPN]
*Secret wife of George IV, King of
England*
* Fitzherbert, Mrs.

**Smythe, Percy Clinton Sydney [Viscount
of Strangford]** 1780-1855 [IP]
Irish author
* P. C. S. S.

Smythe, Samuel
See Dawes, Rufus

Smythe, Slogan
See Smythe, John Henry, Jr.

Smythe, Staff
See Smythe, C. Stafford

Smythe, [Sir] Thomas
See Smith, Thomas

Snaffle, Will, the Saddler
See Dunkin, Robert

Snaith, J. C.
See Snaith, John Collis

Snaith, John Collis 1876-1936 [LC, TC]
British author
* [The] Gloomy Scribe
* Snaith, J. C.

[The] Snake
See Persico, Carmine

[The] Snake
See Prudhomme, Don

[The] Snake
See Shelley, Percy Bysshe

[The] Snake Man
See Ditmars, Raymond Lee

Snake, William
See Araguy, Jean Raymond Eugene d'

Snap, Sylvanus
See Bergh, A. E.

Snapper Jack Garrison
See Garrison, Edward

[The] Snapping Turtle
See Glass, George Carter

[The] Snapping Turtle of the Ohio
See Fink, Mike

Snare, Richie
See Starkey, Richard

[The] Snark
See Wood, Starr

Snarley, Charley
See Clark, Charles

Snart, Charles 19th c. [HFN, IP]
British barrister and author
* [A] Gentleman Resident in the
  Neighborhood

Snavely, Carl Grey 1894?- [FB, HPPN]
American football coach
* Carolina's Snavely
* [The] Football Scholar
* King Carl

Snead, Austine ?-1888 [FFF]
American journalist
* Grundy, Miss

Snead, Fayette 19th c. [IP]
American journalist
* Fay

Snead, J. C.
See Snead, Jesse Carlyle

Snead, Jake
See Snead, Kenneth

Snead, Jesse Carlyle 1941- [GF]
American golfer
* Snead, J. C.

Snead, Kenneth 1923- [BA]
American physician
* Snead, Jake

Snead, Sam[uel Jackson] 1912- [BBH, BWG]
American golfer
* [The] Slammer
* Snead, Slammin Sam
* [The] West Virginia Hillbilly

Snead, Slammin Sam
See Snead, Sam[uel Jackson]

Sneaky Pete
See Kleinow, Pete

Sneddon, Robert William 1880-1944 [HPPN, NAA]
Scottish-American author
* Guillaume, Robert

Snedeker, Caroline Dale 1871-1956 [NAA, TCC]
American author
* Owen, Caroline Dale

Sneed, Eddie 20th c. [OBW]
American baseball player
* Sneed, Lefty

Sneed, Lefty
See Sneed, Eddie

Sneed, M. A. 19th c. [IP]
American journalist
* Grundy, Miss

Sneider, Johannes 1494?-1566 [WBD]
German religious reformer
* Agricola, Johannes
* Magister Islebius
* Schnitter, Johannes

Snekul, Heinrich Yale
See Lukens, Henry Clay

Snel, Billy
See Snell, William

Snell, Doc
See Snell, Walter Henry [Wally]

Snell, E. L. 20th c. [MBF]
British author
* Ellison, Ellis
* Ellsen, Ellis

Snell, Hannah 1723-1792 [DEP, RH]
British soldier
* [The] Female Marine
* Grey, James

Snell, Roy Judson 1878-? [NAA]
American author
* O'Hara, David

Snell van Royen
See Snellius, Willebrord

Snell, Walter Henry [Wally] 1889-1980 [BE]
American baseball player
* Snell, Doc

Snell, William 1938- [ASC]
American composer, author, illustrator
* Snel, Billy

Snellen, Happy Jack
See Snellen, John H.

Snellen, John H. 1859-1932 [HPPN]
Circus canvasman
* Snellen, Happy Jack

Snelling, Oswald Frederick 1916- [CA]
British author
* Frederick, Oswald

Snelling, William Joseph 1804-1848 [FFF, HPPN, IP, PA]
American journalist
* Bell, Solomon
* [A] Free Man
* [A] Resident Beyond the Frontier
* W. J. S.

Snellings, Rolland 20th c. [IBW]
American author
* Toure, Askia Muhammed

Snellius, Willebrord 1591-1626 [WBD]
Dutch mathematician
* Snell van Royen

Sneve, Virginia Driving Hawk 1933- [CA, SAT]
American author
* Driving Hawk, Virginia

Sneyd, Ramon George
See Ray, James Earl

Snider, Christopher ?-1770 [HN]
Killed by British soldiers
* [The] First Martyr of Liberty

Snider, Denton Jacques 1841-1925 [DNA]
American author, poet, educator
* Middling, Theophilus

Snider, Duke
See Snider, Edwin Donald

Snider, Edwin Donald 1926- [BE, HPPN, IPA, PB]
American baseball player
* [The] Duke
* [The] Duke of Brooklyn
* [The] Silver Fox
* Snider, Duke

Snider, Jacob ?-1866 [HPPN]
American inventor
* [The] Father of the Snider Rifle

Snider, John H. 20th c. [CCL]
Canadian poet and author
* Knight, Taylor C.

Sniff, Mr.
See Abisch, Roslyn Kroop [Roz]

Sniper
See Forty, Cecil Heber

Snipes, Rock
See Snipes, Wyatt Eure

Snipes, Roxy
See Snipes, Wyatt Eure

Snipes, Wyatt Eure 1896-1941 [BE]
American baseball player
* Snipes, Rock
* Snipes, Roxy

Snippersnapper, Alice
See Reeve, Edward H. [Ted]

Snod, E.
See Dodd, E. A.

Snoddy, Abbie [Llewellyn] [BI]
American columnist
* Llewellyn, Louise

Snodgrass, Fred Carlisle 1887-1974 [BE]
American baseball player
* Snodgrass, Snow

Snodgrass, Quintus Curtius
See Clemens, Samuel Langhorne

Snodgrass, Snow
See Snodgrass, Fred Carlisle

Snodgrass, Thomas Jefferson
See Clemens, Samuel Langhorne

Snodgrass, W. D.
See Snodgrass, William DeWitt

Snodgrass, William DeWitt 1926- [DLE, WD]
American poet, critic, translator
* Gardons, S. S.
* McConnell, Will
* Prutkov, Kozma
* Snodgrass, W. D.

Snoggins
See Putney, Henry M.

Snoilsky, Carl Johan Gustav 1841-? [NPS]
Swedish poet
* Trost, Sven

Snooks, Epaminondas T.
See Mason, C. P.

Snooks, Peter
See Moore, John C.

Snorter
See Connally, George Walter

Snouckaert, William 1510-1560 [PA]
Author
* Tenocarus

Snover, Bosco
See Snover, Colonel Lester

Snover, Colonel Lester 1895- [BE]
American baseball player
* Snover, Bosco

[The] Snow Baby
See Kuhne, Marie [Ahnighito Peary]

Snow, C. P.
See Snow, Charles Percy

Snow, Charles Horace 1877-? [WW]
Author
* Averill, H. C.
* Ballew, Charles
* Hardy, Russ
* Lee, Ranger
* Marshall, Gary
* Smith, Wade
* Wardle, Dan
* Wills, Chester

Snow, Charles Percy 1905-1980 [LC]
British author
* Snow, C. P.

Snow, Clarence Eugene 1914- [CME, DAM, ECM]
Canadian-born American country-western performer
* [The] Singing Ranger
* Snow, Hank
* [The] Yodeling Ranger

Snow Cloud 20th c. [BI]
American Indian chieftain
* Rogers, John

Snow, Donald Clifford 1917- [CA, SAT, WYA]
American author
* Fall, Thomas

Snow, Gilbert Wilson 1915?-1953 [BEW]
American actor
* Gill, Paul

Snow, Hank
See Snow, Clarence Eugene

Snow, Helen Foster 1907- [CA, WD]
American author and poet
* Wales, Nym

Snow, [Rev.] Herman 19th c. [HPPN]
American clergyman
* [A] Minister of the Gospel

Snow, Jackson
See Guerin, Elsa Jane Forrest

Snow, Jane
See Brandenburg, Margaret Johnston

Snow, Joseph 19th c. [PI]
Irish poet and journalist
* Oberon
* St. George, George

[The] Snow King
See Frederick V

[The] Snow King
See Gustavus II

Snow, Lida 1869?-1940 [BEW]
American actress
* McMillan, Lida

Snow, Lyndon
See Ansle, Dorothy Phoebe

Snow, Phoebe
See Gorsch, Marion Murray

Snow, Phoebe
See Laub, Phoebe

[The] Snow Queen
See Christina

[The] Snow Queen
See Elizabeth

Snow, Sandy
See Snow, William Alexander

Snow, Terry
See Woolsey, Maryhale

Snow, Theodore William ?-1862 [IP]
American clergyman and author
* La Touche, Geoffry

Snow, Valaida 20th c. [THR]
American actress and singer
* Valaida

Snow White [code name used during World War II]
See Soong, Mei-ling [or Mayling]

Snow, William 19th c. [IP]
British songwriter
* Wons, Mailliw

Snow, William Alexander 1946- [CEI]
Canadian-born hockey player
* Snow, Sandy

Snowden, Elmer Chester 1900-1973 [EJ, EJ7, IBW]
American jazz musician
* Snowden, Pops

Snowden, Fred 1937- [IBW]
American basketball coach
* [The] Fox

Snowden, James 1860-? [LAO]
British author and journalist
* Snowden, Keighley

Snowden, James Ross 1810-? [HPPN]
American author
* [The] Director of the Mint

Snowden, John 20th c. [IBW]
American editor and cooking school operator
* [The] Prince of Cookery

Snowden, Keighley
See Snowden, James

Snowden, Pops
See Snowden, Elmer Chester

[The] Snowshoe Expressman
See Johnson, Albert A.

[The] Snowshoe Itinerant
See Dyer, John Lewis

[The] Snowshoe Priest
See Baraga, Frederic

Snuff
See Stanhope, Charles

Snyder, Charles N. 1854-1924 [AS, BE]
American baseball player
* Snyder, Pop

Snyder, Christopher 1755?-1770 [HPPN]
American mob victim
* [The] First Martyr of the Revolution

Snyder, Clifford Gilpin 1917- [ECM, FCW]
American country-western performer
* Stone, Cliffie

Snyder, Colonel
See Snyder, Martin

Snyder, Cooney
See Snyder, Frank C.

Snyder, E. V.
See Snyder, Eugene Vincent

Snyder, Eloise C[olleen]
See Bartos, Eloise C[olleen]

Snyder, Emanuel Sebastian
See Schneider, Emanuel Sebastian

Snyder, Eugene Vincent 1943- [SFL]
American author
* Snyder, E. V.

Snyder, Fairmont
See Beebe, Ethel Fairmont

Snyder, Frank C. ?-1917 [BE]
Canadian baseball player
* Snyder, Cooney

Snyder, Frank Elton 1893-1962 [BE, PB]
American baseball player
* Snyder, Pancho

Snyder, Gene
See Snyder, M. G.

Snyder, Harry 1912- [HPPN]
American author
* Sterling, Hank

Snyder, James
See Synodinos, Dimitrios

Snyder, John 20th c.
American lobbyist
* Snyder, Magnum

Snyder, John
See Heyer, Adam

Snyder, Louis L. 1907- [CA]
American author and historian
* Nordicus

Snyder, M. G. 20th c. [IPA]
American politician
* Snyder, Gene

Snyder, Magnum
See Snyder, John

Snyder, Martin 20th c. [HPPN]
American racketeer
* [The] Gimp
* Snyder, Colonel
* Snyder, Moe

Snyder, Moe
See Snyder, Martin

Snyder, Mrs.   [FFF]
Entertainer
* Reynolds, Vivian

Snyder, Pancho
See Snyder, Frank Elton

Snyder, Peggy Lou 1912?-   [IPA, PMJ, SW]
American actress and singer
* Nelson, Harriet Hilliard

Snyder, Pop
See Snyder, Charles N.

Snyder, Redleg
See Schneider, Emanuel Sebastian

Snyder, Ruth ?-1928   [HPPN]
American murderer
* [The] Granite Woman
* Momsie

Snyder, Service
See Snyder, Victor

Snyder, Victor 1883-1926   [HPPN]
American actor
* Snyder, Service

Snyder, Wilbur 20th c.   [HPPN]
American wrestler
* [The] World's Most Scientific Wrestler

Snyders, Johann ?-1568   [PA]
Author
* Sartorius

So, Bernat
See Ruttkay, Arnold

Soa, Imamu Etheridge Knight
See Knight, Etheridge

Soame, [Sir] Henry F. R.
See Bunbury, [Sir] Henry Edward

Soami
See Shinso

[The] Soap Box Evangelist
See Simmons, Charles James [Jim]

[The] Soap King
See Hudson, Robert

Soaper, Senator
See Wade, Harry Vincent

Soapy Sam
See Wilberforce, Samuel

Soar, Albert 20th c.   [EF]
American football player
* Soar, Hank

Soar, Hank
See Soar, Albert

Soares, Chubby Cheeks
See Soares, Mario

Soares, Mario 20th c.
Portuguese premier
* [The] Once and Future Prime
  Minister
* Soares, Chubby Cheeks

Soares Correia, Artur Manuel 1950-
[AES]
Portuguese soccer player
* Artur

Sobchuk, Dennis 1954-
Hockey player
* [The] Greyhound

Sobchuk, Gene 1951-   [SMG]
Canadian-born hockey player
* Sobchuk, Geno

Sobchuk, Geno
See Sobchuk, Gene

Sobell, Morton 1917?-
American espionage agent
* Levitor, Morton
* Sand, Marvin
* Sewell, M.
* Solt, Morton
* Sowell, Morton

Sobelsohn, Karl 1885-?   [HPPN, JL]
Russian politician
* Radek, Karl Bernardovich
* Struthahn

Sober
See Johnson, Samuel

Sober One
See Johnson, Samuel

Sober, Pincus 1905-   [HPPN]
Polish-American track athlete
* Sober, Pinky

Sober, Pinky
See Sober, Pincus

Sobers, Garfield St. Auburn 1936-
[HPPN]
Barbados-born cricketer
* Sobers, Gary

Sobers, Gary
See Sobers, Garfield St. Auburn

Sobers, Wayne
See Sobers, Waynett A., Jr.

Sobers, Waynett A., Jr. 1937-   [BA]
American business executive
* Sobers, Wayne

Sobh, A.
See Shamlu, Ahmad

Sobhraj, Charles
See Sobhraj, Gurmukh

Sobhraj, Gurmukh 1944-?   [DI]
Vietnamese-born murderer and robber
* Gautier, Alain
* Sobhraj, Charles

Sobhuza II 1899?-1982
King of Swaziland
* [The] Bull
* [The] Father of His Country
* [The] Great Crocodile
* [The] Great Mountain
* [The] Inexplicable
* [The] Lion of Swaziland
* Son of the She Elephant

Sobieski, John
See John III

Sobkowiak, [Sister] Mary 1896?-   [NW
5-14-84]
American baseball enthusiast
* Baseball, [Sister] Mary

Soble, Jennie
See Cavin, Ruth [Brodie]

Sobotta, Kurt 1907-   [IAW]
German author
* Kurt, K. S.
* Straub, Otto

Soca Boca
See Grant, Robert

Soccer, Mr.
See Gonsalves, Bill

[The] Soccer Wizard
See Matthews, Stanley

Socci, Gianni
See Socci, Giovanni

Socci, Giovanni 1939-   [OP]
Italian opera singer
* Socci, Gianni

Socco the Bracer
See Gayles, Joseph

[The] Sociable Spirit
See Santi [or Sanzio?], Raffaello

**[The] Social Historian of the Cafe
Society**
See Beebe, Lucius

[The] Society Clown
See Grossmith, George, Jr.

Society Kid Hogan
See De Lorenzo, Salvatore

[A] Society of Gentleman
See Potter, John

[A] Society of Gentlemen
See Chambers, Ephraim

Socius Ejectus
See Baker, Thomas

Sock, A.
See Sulzberger, Arthur Ochs

Sockalexis, Chief
See Sockalexis, Louis Francis

Sockalexis, Louis Francis 1873-1913
[BE, PB]
American baseball player
* Sockalexis, Chief

Sockless Jerry Simpson
See Simpson, Jerry

[The] Sockless Sage
See Simpson, Jerry

Sockless Socrates
See Simpson, Jerry

[The] Sockless Statesman
See Simpson, Jerry

Socrates 5th c. BC [DEP, DNNS, FFF, NPS, SN]
Greek philosopher
* [The] Athenian Sage
* [The] Bearded Master
* [The] Midwife of Men's Thoughts
* [The] Old Man Eloquent
* Plato's Master
* [The] Secretary of Nature
* [The] Wisest Man of Greece

Socrates 5th c. [WBD]
Greek historian
* Scholasticus

[The] Socrates of His Age
See Gabrielli, Trifone

[The] Socrates of the French Renaissance
See Rabelais, Francois

[The] Socrates of the Jews
See Mendelssohn, Moses

[The] Socrates of the Musulmans
See Abou Hanifa

Soda Ash Johnny Horan
See Horan, John Michael

Soda Pop Jackson
See Jackson, Henry Martin

Soderberg, Percy Measday 1901-1969 [CAP]
British author
* Archer, S. E.
* Measday, George
* Seebord, G. R.
* Underhill, Peter

Soderland, M.
See Gandy, Mabel

[Il] Sodoma
See Bazzi, Giovanni Antonio de

[Il] Sodorna
See Bazzi, Giovanni Antonio de

Soederhjelm, Kai 1918- [IAW]
Finnish-born author
* Bergman, Jonas

Soerensen
See Vellejus, Andre Severin

Soeur Louise de la Misericorde
See Baume Le Blanc, Francoise Louise de la

Soeur Sourire [Sister Smile]
See Deckers, Jeannine

Sofi, Abou Moussah Djafar al-
See Geber

Sofia
See Zeiger, Sophia

Sofman, Gustave 1902-1970 [SC]
French actor and circus performer
* Pipo

[The] Soft Medusa
See Mary, Queen of Scots

Soft Soul, Ms.
See Marrs, Stella

Softly, Edgar
See Lovecraft, Howard Phillips

Softly, Edward
See Lovecraft, Howard Phillips

Sohailes
See Ahmed Ibn Hemdem Kiaya

Sohl, Gerald Allan [Jerry] 1913- [CA, ESF]
American author
* Butler, Nathan
* Sullivan, Sean Mei

Sohlke, Augustus 1865-1924 [BEW]
Director
* Sohlke, Gus

Sohlke, Gus
See Sohlke, Augustus

Sohr [or Sore], Martin 1486-1556 [WBD]
German musician and composer
* Agricola, Martin

[Il] Soiaro
See Gatti, Bernardino

Sojin
See Kamiyama, Sojin

[A] Sojourner
See Copleston, John Gay

Sokichi, Nagai 1879-1959
Japanese author
* Kafu, Nagai

Sokoloff, Melvin 1929- [EJ, PMJ]
American jazz musician
* Lewis, Mel

Sokoloff, Natalie B. 1906- [CAP]
Russian-born American author
* Scott, Natalie Anderson

Sokolov, Alexander V[sevolodovich] 1943- [CA]
Canadian-born author and educator
* Sokolov, Sasha

Sokolov, Nikolai 1903- [BI]
Russian painter
* Kukryniksky

Sokolov, Sasha
See Sokolov, Alexander V[sevolodovich]

Sokolova, Lydia
See Munnings, Hilda

Sokolova, Natasha
See Mahon, Natasha

Sol
See Soteldo, A. M.

Sola
See Anderson, Olive San Louie

Sola
See Tyler, Josephine

Solaita, Tolia 1947- [SMG, WWB]
Samoan-born baseball player
* Solaita, Tony

Solaita, Tony
See Solaita, Tolia

Solanito
See Solano, Ramon

Solano, Ramon 1933- [HPPN]
Spanish bullfighter
* Solanito

Solari, Andrea 1470-1527 [FFF, RH, SN]
Italian painter
* [Del] Gobbo
* [The] Humpback

Solari [or Solario], Christoforo 15th c. [WBD]
Italian sculptor and architect
* [Il] Gobbo [The Hunchback]

Solario, Antonio 1382-1455? [FFF, HN, SN]
Italian painter
* [The] Gypsy
* [Il] Zingaro

Solario, Isadore 20th c. [EJS]
American basketball coach
* Solario, Spin

Solario, Spin
See Solario, Isadore

Solaro, Antonio 1458?-1516? [HPPN]
Italian architect and sculptor
* Lombardo, Antonio

Solaro, Pietro 1435-1515 [HPPN]
Italian architect and sculptor
* Lombardo, Pietro

Solaro, Tullio 1455?-1532 [HPPN]
Italian architect and sculptor
* Lombardo, Tullio

Solataroff, [Dr.] H. ?-1921 [HPPN]
American playwright
* Sloan, Paul H.

Solbelli, Olga 1898-1976 [FIR]
Italian actress
* Sunbeauty, Olga

Solberg, David 1943-
American actor
* Soul, David

Solbert, Romaine G. 1925- [CA]
American author and illustrator
* Solbert, Ronni

Solbert, Ronni
See Solbert, Romaine G.

[El] Soldado
See Castro, Luis

[El] Soldado [The Soldier]
See Castro Sandoval, Luis

Soldano, Anthony 1927- [ASC]
American musician
* Dano, Tony

Soldati, Mario 1906- [CA]
Italian author, director, screenwriter
* Pallavera, Franco

[Il] Soldatino [The Little Soldier]
See Barazzutti, Corrado

[A] Soldier
See Diespecker, Richard E. Alan

[A] Soldier
See Goss, Warren Le

[A] Soldier
See Hill, A. F.

[A] Soldier
See Ranken, George

[A] Soldier
See Walker, Alexander

[A] Soldier
See Wilton, J. H.

[The] Soldier and the Sage
See Akiba Ben Joseph

Soldier Boy Curry
See Curry, George James

Soldier Boy Murphy
See Murphy, John P.

[The] Soldier of Fortune
See Selz, Ralph Jerome Von Braun

[The] Soldier of the Andes
See Espinosa, Juan

[The] Soldier Parson
See Caldwell, James

[A] Soldier's Daughter
See Nicolas, Sarah [Davison]

[The] Soldier's Friend
See Curtin, Andrew Gregg

[The] Soldiers' Friend
See Frederick Augustus

[The] Soldiers' Friend
See Schwabe, Leo

[The] Soldier's Friend
See Ward, Marcus Lawrence

[The] Soldier's Inspiration
See Grasle, Elizabeth

[The] Solemn Doctor
See Goethals, Henry

[The] Solemn Old Judge
See Hay, George Dewey

Solemn One [The Wise]
See Sikes, William Wirt

Solemnis, Doctor
See Goethals, Henry

Soler, Domingo
See Diaz Pavia, Domingo

Soler, Frederic   [IP]
Spanish author
* Pitarra, Serafi

Soler y Gisbert, Manuel 1913-1944
[GS]
Spanish bullfighter
* Vaquerito [Little Cowboy]

Soletanus, Matthoeus
See Tafuri, Malteo

[A] Solicitor
See Field, Edwin Wilkins

Solicitor
See Hodgkinson, Conway Loveridge

[The] Solicitor General
See Palmer, Roundell [First Earl of
Selborne]

[The] Solid Doctor
See Bradwardine, Thomas

[The] Solid Doctor
See Middleton, Richard

[The] Solid Man
See Muldoon, William

Solidity, Madame
See D'Aubigne, Francoise

Solidor, Suzy
See Rocher, Suzy

Solidus, Doctor
See Middleton, Richard

Soliman the Magnificent
See Jennens, Charles

Solitaire
See Fox, George Wilder

Solitaire
See Robb, John S.

[El] Solitario
See Estebanez Calderon, Serafin

[The] Solitary Monk
See Luther, Martin

[The] Solitary Singer
See Whitman, Walt[er]

Sollima, Sergio 1921-   [FDG]
Italian director
* Sterling, Simon

Solly, Samuel 1781-1847   [IP]
British author
* Ylloss

Solo, Jay
See Ellison, Harlan [Jay]

Solo, Tony
See Schiano, Anthony

Sologub, Fyodor
See Teternikov, Fyodor Kuzmich

Solomon   [UH]
King of Israel
* [The] Wise King

Solomon
See Cutner, Solomon

Solomon, Abba 1915-   [CA]
Israeli diplomat and author
* Eban, Abba
* Eban, Aubrey

Solomon bar Isaac 1040-1105
French clergyman and grammarian
* [The] Prince of Bible Commentators
* Rashi

Solomon, Charles 20th c.   [BLB, MM,
PHM]
American underworld figure
* Solomon, King

Solomon, Eddie, Jr. 1951-   [SMG]
American baseball player
* [The] King

Solomon, Fabulous Freddie
See Solomon, Freddie

Solomon, Freddie 1953-   [BA]
American football player
* Solomon, Fabulous Freddie

Solomon, Gus 1869-1908   [BEW, CED]
American actor
* Rogers, Gus

Solomon, Hans
See Solomon, Johann

Solomon, Herbert Jay 1930-   [EJ]
American jazz musician
* Mann, Herbie

Solomon, Hickory
See Solomon, Moses H.

Solomon, James B. 1921-1966   [SC]
American actor
* James, Ben

Solomon, James Hymie 1904-   [EJS]
American baseball player
* Reese, James Hymie

Solomon, Janis Little 1938-   [CA]
American writer
* Gellinek, Janis Little

Solomon, Johann 1933-   [EJ]
Austrian jazz musician
* Solomon, Hans

Solomon, King
See Solomon, Charles

Solomon, Max 1873-1932   [BEW, CED]
American actor
* Rogers, Max

Solomon, Moe
See Solomon, Moses H.

Solomon, Moses H. 1900-1966   [BE,
EJS]
American baseball player
* [The] Rabbi of Swat
* Solomon, Hickory
* Solomon, Moe

Solomon, Mrs. Fred   [FFF]
Entertainer
* Sutton, Mamie

[The] Solomon of Bards
See Prior, Matt[hew]

[The] Solomon of China
See Lee chee-men

[The] Solomon of England
See Henry VII

[The] Solomon of England
See James I

[The] Solomon of France
See Charles V

[The] Solomon of France
See Louis IX

[The] Solomon of Great Britain
See George III

[The] Solomon of His Age
See Robert of Anjou

Solomon, Samuel 1904-   [CA, WD]
British poet and translator
* Britindian
* Moolson, Melusa

Solomon, Saul 18th c.
South African merchant
* [The] Merchant King

Solomon, Saul 1816-1892
South African politician
* [The] Disraeli of South Africa

Solomon, Stephen 1936-   [CA]
American political scientist and author
* Sloan, Stephen

Solomons, Blanche
See Jackson, Editha Salomon

Solomons, Ikey, Jun.
See Thackeray, William Makepeace

[The] Solon of French Prose
See Balzac, Jean Louis Guez de

[The] Solon of French Prose
See Voiture, Vincent

[The] Solon of Parnassus
See Boileau-Despreaux, Nicolas

Solorzano Davalos, Jesus 1907-   [GS]
Mexican bullfighter
* [El] Rey del Temple

Soloveitehik, Joseph B. 1903?-   [TI 10-8-84]
American philosopher
* [The] Rav [The Rabbi]

Soloviev, Vladimir 1853-1900   [HPPN]
Russian philosopher
* [The] First Russian Philosopher

Solow, Martin 1920-   [CA]
American author
* Nelson, Peter

Solt, Morton
See Sobell, Morton

Soltan, Constance
See Dover, Constance

Solters, Julius Joseph
See Soltesz, Julius Joseph

Solters, Lemons
See Soltesz, Julius Joseph

Solters, Moose
See Soltesz, Julius Joseph

Soltesz, Julius Joseph 1906?-1975   [BE, HPPN, PB]
American baseball player
* Solters, Julius Joseph

Soltesz, Julius Joseph (cont.)
* Solters, Lemons
* Solters, Moose

Soltysik, Patricia 1950?-1974   [HPPN]
American radical terrorist group member
* [The] Female Brain of the S. L. A.
* Mizmoon

Solvay, Ernest 1838-1922   [HPPN]
Belgian manufacturing chemist
* [The] Carnegie of Belgium

Solwoska, Mara
See French, Marilyn

Solzhenitsyn, Aleksandr Isayevich 1918-   [HPPN]
Russian author
* [The] Boldest Man in the World
* [The] Exiled Soviet Author
* [The] Voice of Russian Conscience

Soma, Ito
See Doihara, Kenji

Soman, Shirley 1922-   [CA]
American author
* Camper, Shirley

Sombre, Samuel
See Gerard, James Watson

[El] Sombrerero [The Hatter]
See Ruiz, Antonio

Some French Angel
See De Salluste [or Salustius?], Guillaume

Somebody
See Byron, George Gordon Noel

Somebody, M. D. C.
See Neal, John

Somerby, Frederic Thomas 1814-1871   [DNA, PA]
American journalist
* Cymon

Somers
See Edwards, Harry Stillwell

Somers, Alexander 1861-?   [PI]
British author and solicitor
* Al So

Somers, Bart
See Fox, Gardner Francis

Somers, Carole
See Cosgrove, Judy

Somers, Jane
See Lessing, Doris

Somers, Jonathan Swift, III
See Farmer, Philip Jose

Somers, Paul
See Winterton, Paul

Somers, Rosalie
See Stephens, Harriet Marion

Somers, Suzanne
See Daniels, Dorothy

Somers, Suzanne
See Mahoney, Suzanne

Somerset, Duchess of   [HN]
* [The] Queen of Beauty

Somerset, Edward [Second Marquis of Worcester] 1601-1667   [SN]
British inventor
* Bezaliel

Somerset, Fitzroy James Henry 1788-1855   [HN]
British army officer
* [The] Invisible Commander
* Raglan, Baron

Somerset, FitzRoy Richard
See Raglan, FitzRoy

Somerset, Frances Thynne [Countess of Hertford] 1699-1754   [FFF]
British author
* Eusebia

Somerset, Henry Richard Charles 1849-1932   [HPPN]
British songwriter
* Lord Henry

Somerset, Isabella Caroline 1851-1921   [HPPN]
British philanthropist and prohibitionist
* Somerset, Lady Henry

Somerset, Lady Henry
See Somerset, Isabella Caroline

Somerset, Patrick
See Holme-Sumner, Patrick

Somerset, Wellington 19th c.   [IP]
British author and diplomat
* May Fly

Somerset, William 1090?-1143?   [HPPN]
British clergyman and historian
* William of Malmsbury

Somervell, D. C.
See Somervell, David Churchill

Somervell, David Churchill 1885-1965   [LC]
British historian and author
* Somervell, D. C.

Somerville
See Maugham, W[illiam] Somerset

Somerville, Alexander 1811-1885   [IP, PA]
Scottish politician and author
* One Who has Whistled at the Plow
* [The] Whistler
* [A] Workng Man

Somerville, Amelia
See Runnels, Mrs. Frederick

Somerville and Ross [joint pseudonym with Edith Anna Oenone Somerville]
See Martin, Violet Florence

Somerville and Ross [joint pseudonym with Violet Florence Martin]
See Somerville, Edith Anna Oenone

Somerville, Charles Ross 1903- [BI, GF]
Canadian golfer
* Somerville, Sandy

Somerville, Edith Anna Oenone
1858?-1949 [LC, TC]
Irish author
* Somerville and Ross [joint pseudonym
   with Violet Florence Martin]

Somerville, H. B.
See McComas, I. V.

Somerville, John 1765?- [HPPN]
Scottish baron and agriculturist
* [A] Friend To Order

Somerville, Rose M[aurer] 1908- [CA]
American sociologist and author
* Maurer, Rose

Somerville, Sandy
See Somerville, Charles Ross

Somerville, William 1675-1742 [SN]
British poet
* [The] Poet of the Chase

Somes, Jethro
See Pauker, John

[The] Sominex Kid
See Hayakawa, Samuel Ichiye

Sommer, Elke
See Schletz, Elke

Sommer, H. B 19th c. [IP]
American author
* O'Pagus, Arry

Sommer, Hans
See Zincke, Hans

Sommer, Richard Jerome 1934- [IAW]
American-born author and poet
* Henningsson, Rik

Sommers, Ben
See Schusterman, Ben

Sommers, David
See Smith, Howard Van

Sommers, Jane R.
See Jones, Cornelia

Sommers, Joseph Andrews 1866-1908
[BE]
American baseball player
* Sommers, Pete

Sommers, Kid
See Sommers, William

Sommers, Pete
See Sommers, Joseph Andrews

Sommers, William ?-1895 [BE]
Canadian baseball player
* Sommers, Kid

Sommerville, Andrew 19th c. [HPPN]
American soldier
* Sommerville, Faithful Andy
* Sommerville, Handy Andy

Sommerville, Andrew Henry [Andy]
See Summersgill, Henry Travers

Sommerville, Faithful Andy
See Sommerville, Andrew

Sommerville, Frankfort
See Story, A. M. Sommerville

Sommerville, Frankfort
See Story, Sommerville

Sommerville, Handy Andy
See Sommerville, Andrew

Somnambulus
See Scott, [Sir] Walter

[The] Somniferous Malloy
See Malloy, Michael [Mike]

**Somorokof [or Sumorokow], Alexander
Petrovitch** 1727?-1777 [DEP, DNNS,
RH]
Russian poet
* [The] Russian Voltaire

Somoza Debayle, Anastasio 1925-1980
Nicaraguan president
* [The] Last Marine
* Somoza Debayle, Tachito [or Tacho]

Somoza Debayle, Tachito [or Tacho]
See Somoza Debayle, Anastasio

Somoza Garcia, Anastasio 1896-1956
Nicaraguan president
* Somoza Garcia, Tacho

Somoza Garcia, Tacho
See Somoza Garcia, Anastasio

Somoza Portocarrero, Anastasio 1951?-
1980
*Son of Nicaraguan president, Anastasio
Somoza*
* Somoza Portocarrero, Tachito

Somoza Portocarrero, Tachito
See Somoza Portocarrero, Anastasio

Somtow, S. P.
See Sucharitkul, Somtow

Son Fewclothes
See Lewis, Robert

Son Jimmy
See Roosevelt, James

Son Joe
See Lawlars, Ernest

[The] Son of a Mandarin
See Haywood, Eliza [Fowler]

[The] Son of a Military Officer
See Bayley, Frederick W. N.

Son of a She-Bear
See Orsini, Giovanni Gaetano

[The] Son of Belial
See Needham, Marchamont

[A] Son of Candor
See Grenville, Richard Temple [First
Earl Temple]

Son of Harry
See Harrison, George

[The] Son of His Grandfather
See Harrison, Benjamin

[The] Son of Jupiter Ammon
See Alexander III

[A] Son of Liberty
See Adams, Samuel

[A] Son of Liberty
See Church, Benjamin

[A] Son of Martin Marprelate
See Walter, Thomas

Son of Sam
See Berkowitz, David R.

[The] Son of the Devil
See Ezzelino IV

[The] Son of the King
See Marko Kraljevic

[The] Son of the Last Man
See Charles II

[The] Son of the Man
See Bonaparte, Francois Charles Joseph
[Duc de Reichstadt]

[A] Son of the Marshes
See Visger, Jean A. Owen

[The] Son of the Saint
See Macaulay, Thomas Babington [First
Baron Macaulay]

Son of the She Elephant
See Sobhuza II

Son of the Soil
See Fletcher, Joseph Smith

Son of the Star
See Bar Cocheba, Simon

[A] Son of Thunder
See Irving, Edward

[The] Son of Toil
See Brown, Adam George

[A] Son of Truth and Decency
See Inglis, Charles

Son White Washington
See Washington, Edward

Soncinus
See Barbus, Paolo

Sonden, Anders Fredrik 19th c. [HPPN]
Swedish author
* A. F. S.

Sondergaard, Edith Holm 1900- [BEW,
FC, TR]
American actress
* Sondergaard, Gale

Sondergaard, Gale
See Sondergaard, Edith Holm

Sonero, Devi
See Pelton, Robert W[ayne]

[The] Song Symphonist
See Mahler, Gustav

[The] Songbird of the South
See Rainey, Gertrude Malissa Nix
[Pridgett]

[The] Songbird of the South
See Smith, Kathryn Elizabeth [Kate]

Songin, Butch
See Songin, Ed[ward]

Songin, Ed[ward] 1923?-1976 [BI, SMG]
American football player
* Songin, Butch

Sonia
See Hamburger, Ursula-Maria

Sonic, Fred
See Smith, Frederick

Sonica
See McAlpine, Robert W.

Sonnemann, Emmy
See Goering, Emmy

Sonnenberg, Dynamite Gus
See Sonnenberg, Gustave

Sonnenberg, Gustave 1898-1944 [FB]
American football player
* Sonnenberg, Dynamite Gus

Sonneveld, William
See Sonneveld, Wim

Sonneveld, Wim 1918-1974 [SC]
Dutch actor
* Sonneveld, William

Sonntag, Erik Nicholas 1925- [ART]
German-born sculptor and painter
* E. S.

Sonntag, Gertrud Walburga 1806-1854
[BBD]
German opera singer
* Sontag, Henriette

Sonntag, Uschi
See Wiegand, Ursula

Sonny
See Brown, Claude

Sonny Black Napolitano
See Napolitano, Dominick

Sonny Boy Williamson
See Ford, Aleck

Sonny Boy Williamson
See Williamson, John Lee

Sonny Ford Thomas
See Thomas, James

Sonny P.
See Parker, Robert

Sonny Red Kyner
See Kyner, Junior Sylvester

Sonny T
See Terrell, Saunders

Sono, Ephraim 1955- [SMG]
South African soccer player
* Sono, Jomo

Sono, Jomo
See Sono, Ephraim

Sonsteby, Gunnar 1918- [BDW]
Norwegian intelligence agent
* Broch
* Fjeld, Erling
* Kjaken
* Number 24

Sontag, George C.
See Contant, George

Sontag, Henriette
See Sonntag, Gertrud Walburga

Sontag, John
See Contant, John

Sontag, Susan 1933?- [PW 10-22-82]
American author and social critic
* [The] Dark Lady of American Letters
* [The] Queen of Camp

Sontup, Dan[iel] 1922- [CA]
American author
* Clarke, John
* Saunders, David

[Le] Sony'r Ra
See Blount, Herman

Soo, Chung Ling
See Robinson, William Ellsworth

Soo, Hop Ling
See Robinson, William Ellsworth

Soomro, Mohammad Ibrahim 1934-
[IAW]
Pakistani author
* Munshi

[The] Sooner Huey Long
See Rader, Lloyd E.

Soong, Mei-ling [or Mayling] 1899-
[CND]
Wife of Taiwanese president Chiang Kai-shek
* Chiang Kai-shek, Madame
* Snow White [code name used during World War II]

Soong, T. V.
See Soong [or Sung], Tse-Ven [or Tsu-wen]

Soong [or Sung], Tse-Ven [or Tsu-wen]
1891-1971 [BI, HPPN]
Chinese financier
* Soong, T. V.

Soper, Oro M. 1910?- [WWJ]
American jazz musician
* Soper, Tut

Soper, Tut
See Soper, Oro M.

Sophia Dorothea 1666-1726 [WBD]
Wife of King George I of England
* [The] Princess of Ahlden

Sophia, Mevrouw
See Macleod, Mevrouw Sophia

Sophie
See Gimbel, Sophie

Sophie Charlotte 1668-1705 [DEP,
DNNS, FFF]
Queen of Prussia
* [The] Republican Queen

Sophie of Saks Fifth Avenue
See Gimbel, Sophie

[The] Sophist
See Aelianus, Claudius

[The] Sophist
See Apollonius

[The] Sophister
See Phillips, Morgan

Sopho
See Home, Henry [Lord Kames]

Sophocardus
See Wishart [or Wiseheart?], George

Sophocles 5th c. BC [DNNS, FFF, NPS,
RH, UH]
Greek playwright
* [The] Athenian Bee
* [The] Attic Bee
* [The] Attic Homer
* [The] Bee of Athens
* [The] Bee of Attica

[The] Sophocles of the Dance
See Gioja, Gaetano

Sophonisba 3rd c. BC [HN]
Queen of Numidia
* [The] Catharine de Medici of Africa

Sophronion
See Dilke, [Sir] Charles

Sor, Fernando
See Sors, Fernando

Sorabji, Kaikhosru
See Sorabji, Leon Dudley

Sorabji, Leon Dudley 1892- [BBD]
British composer
* Sorabji, Kaikhosru

Sorbiere, Monsieur
See King, William

Sorcerer
See Kissinger, Henry Alfred

[El] Sordillo de Pereda
See Arco, Alonso del

[El] Sordo
See Montes, Antonio

[Il] Sordo del Barozzo
See Baglioni, Giovanni

Soreil, [Joseph] Arsene 1893- [IAW]
Belgian author
* Delaisne, Jean

Sorel, Agnes 1409?-1450 [DNNS, HN,
SN]
Mistress of King Charles VII of France
* [La] Dame de Beaute

Sorel, Byron
See Yatron, Michael

Sorel, Cecile
See Seure, Cecile Emilie

Sorel, Jean
See De Rochbrune, Jean

Sorel, Julia
See Drexler, Rosalyn

Sorel, W. J. 19th c. [IP, SAT]
British author
* Buskin, [Captain] Sock
* LeRos, Christian

Sorellina
See Mefford, Ditra Helena

Sorensen, Harald 1905- [BBH]
Norwegian-born skier, ski instructor, official, coach
* Sorensen, Pop

Sorensen, Pop
See Sorensen, Harald

Sorenson, Doc
See Sorenson, J. C.

Sorenson, Flemming 20th c. [WFA]
Danish-born fashion designer
* Flemming

Sorenson, J. C. 20th c. [GW]
American rodeo performer
* Sorenson, Doc

Sorey, Revie Cee, Jr. 1953- [SMG]
American football player
* Hollywood, Rock

Sorge, Anthony
See Valachi, Joseph Michael

Sorl, Ernest James [FFF]
Entertainer
* Sutton, Ernest

Sorokin, Pitirim A[lexandrovitch]
1889-1968 [CA]
Russian-born American sociologist and author
* Tchaadaieff

Soromenho, Augusto Pereira ?-1878 [IP]
Portuguese historian and author
* Abdallah

[The] Sorority Woman of the Year
See Stuart, Constance Cornell

Sorrell, Ace
See Sorrell, Vic[tor Garland]

Sorrell, Baby Doll
See Sorrell, Vic[tor Garland]

Sorrell, John A. 1904?-1984
Canadian hockey player
* [The] Frail Falcon

Sorrell, Lawyer
See Sorrell, Vic[tor Garland]

Sorrell, Vic[tor Garland] 1902- [HPPN]
American baseball player
* [The] Philosopher
* Sorrell, Ace
* Sorrell, Baby Doll
* Sorrell, Lawyer

Sorrells, Buckshot
See Sorrells, Marvin H.

Sorrells, Chick
See Sorrells, Raymond Edwin

Sorrells, Marvin H. 20th c. [GW]
American rodeo performer
* Sorrells, Buckshot

Sorrells, Raymond Edwin 1896- [BE]
American baseball player
* Sorrells, Chick
* Sorrells, Red

Sorrells, Red
See Sorrells, Raymond Edwin

[La] Sorrentina
See Frasca, Mary

Sors, Fernando 1778-1839 [BBD]
Spanish musician
* Sor, Fernando

Sortor, June Elizabeth 1939- [CA, SAT]
American author
* Sortor, Toni

Sortor, Toni
See Sortor, June Elizabeth

Sortun, Henrik 20th c. [EF]
American football player
* Sortun, Rick

Sortun, Rick
See Sortun, Henrik

Sorya, Francoise 1932- [BDF, FC, WEF]
French actress
* Aimee, Anouk
* Anouk

Soseki, Natsume
See Kinnosuke, Natsume

Soskin, V. H.
See Ellison, Virginia Howell

Sosthenes
See Coad, Frederick Roy

[A] Sot
See Massinger, Philip

[The] Sot
See Selim II

Sotatsu
See Nonomura, I-yetsu

Soteldo, A. M. [IP]
American journalist
* Sol

Soter [The Preserver]
See Antiochus I

Soter
See Attalus I

Soter [Preserver]
See Demetrius I

Soter
See Ptolemy I

Soter
See Seleucus III

Soter II
See Ptolemy IX [or VIII]

Sotheran, Charles 1847-? [IP, PA]
American author
* C. S.
* Colmolyn
* Secundus, Asmodeus
* Southernwood

Sotheran, Henry 1819-? [IP]
British author
* Savile

Sothern, Ann
See Lake, Harriette

Sothern, Edward Askew
See Stewart, Douglas

Sothern, Ella
See Willard, Mrs. Charles

Sothern, George Evelyn Augustus 1870-?
[THR]
British actor
* Sothern, Sam

Sothern, Georgia
See Anderson, Hazel

Sothern, Henry 1819-? [PA]
Author
* Savile

Sothern, Hugh 1882?-1947 [BEW, SC]
American actor
* Sutherland, Roy

Sothern, Janet Evelyn 20th c. [THR]
British actress
* Evelyn, Janet

Sothern, Jean
See Brannen, Jean

Sothern, Mrs. Lytton [FFF]
Entertainer
* Hewitt, Agnes

Sothern, Sam
See Sothern, George Evelyn Augustus

Sothoron, Allen Sutton 1893-1939 [BN]
American baseball player
* Sothoron, Fidge

Sothoron, Fidge
See Sothoron, Allen Sutton

Soto, Fernando 1920?-1980 [FIR]
Mexican actor
* Mantequilla

Soto, Gabriel [GS]
Mexican bullfighter
* [El] Momo

Soto, Juan ?-1871 [EWG]
American gunfighter
* [The] Human Wildcat

Soto, Roberto 1888-1960 [SC]
Mexican actor
* [El] Panzon [The Belly]

Soto Moreno, Rafael 1940- [GS]
Spanish bullfighter
* Rafael de Paula [Rafael from Paula]

Soubier, Cliff 20th c. [HPPN]
American radio performer
* Barnacle Bill the Sailor

Soubirous, Bernadette 1844-1879 [WBD]
Saint
* Bernadette of Lourdes

Soubise
See Blow, Katharine Cooke

Souchak, Burly Mike
See Souchak, Mike

Souchak, Mike 20th c.
American football player
* Souchak, Burly Mike

Souchock, Bud
See Souchock, Stephen

Souchock, Stephen 1919- [BE]
American baseball player
* Souchock, Bud

Souchon, Doc
See Souchon, Edmond, II

Souchon, Edmond, II 1897-1968 [EJ, EJ7]
American jazz musician
* Souchon, Doc

Souchon, Harry V. 1911?-1984 [WP 4-9-84]
American jazz authority and author
* Nab, O. J.

Soudley, Henry
See Wood, James Playsted

Souffrant, Jacques, ouvrier
See Ulbach, Louis

Soul Brother Number 1
See Brown, James

Soul, David
See Solberg, David

Soul, Jimmy
See McCleese, James

Soul, Lady
See Franklin, Aretha

[The] Soul Man
See Bland, Robert Calvin [Bobby]

[The] Soul of Empty Eminence
See Dodd, James William

[The] Soul of the Black Liberation Army
See Chesimard, Joanne

[The] Soul of the Fronde
See Longueville, Anne

Soulas, Josias de [Sieur de Primefosse] 1608?-1672 [WBD]
French actor
* Floridor

Soule, Minnie Meserve ?-1937 [EOP]
Claimed to possess psychic powers
* Chenoweth, Mrs.

Soule, Robert Homer 1900-1952 [HPPN]
American army officer
* Soule, Shorty

Soule, Shorty
See Soule, Robert Homer

Souli, Charles George
See Bedford-Jones, Henry [James O'Brien]

Soulouque
See Bonaparte, Charles Louis Napoleon

Soult, Marshall
See Knapp, Samuel Lorenzo

Soult, Nicolas Jean de Dieu 1769-1851 [DEP, DHA, FFF]
Marshal of France
* [The] Old Fox
* Vieux Renard

Soumarokov, Alexandre Petrovitch 1718-1777 [HPPN]
Russian poet
* [The] Russian Voltaire

Sound Money Glass
See Glass, George Carter

Soupbone
See Hines, Milton

Souphouse Charlie Bonaparte
See Bonaparte, Charles Joseph

[The] Sour Faced Clown
See Griebling, Otto

Sour Mash Daniels
See Daniels, [Harold] Jack

Souren, Y.
See Yohannessiantz, Souren

Sourhardt, Edward William 1867-1947 [AS, BE]
American baseball player
* Seward, Edward William

Sousa, John Philip 1854-1932 [WBD]
American bandleader and composer
* [The] March King

Sousa, [Frei] Luiz de
See Sousa Countinho, Manoel de

Sousa Countinho, Manoel de 1555-1632 [WBD]
Portuguese monk and author
* Sousa, [Frei] Luiz de

Soust de Borkenfeldt, Adolphe van 1824-1877 [IP]
Belgian poet and historian
* Jane, Paul

Souster, Raymond 1921- [CA, WD]
Canadian poet and author
* Holmes, John
* Holmes, Raymond

Soutar, Gwendoline Amy 1904- [AW]
British author
* Deane, Sonia

Souter, Joseph [IP]
Scottish playwright
* [The] Odd Fellow

[A] South Carolina Federalist
See Pinckney, Charles

[The] South Carolina Gamecock
See Moffett, William Adger

[The] South Carolina Gamecock
See Sumter, Thomas

[A] South Carolinian
See Hall, Robert Pleasants

[A] South Carolinian
See Middleton, Henry

[A] South Carolinian
See Poinsett, Joel Roberts

[A] South Carolinian
See Seabrook, Whitemarsh Benjamin

South, Clark
See Swain, Dwight V[reeland]

South, Edward Otha [Eddie] 1904-1962 [IBW]
American jazz musician
* Dark Angel of the Violin

South, Edwin
See Campbell, Bartley T.

South, Elma
See Cheesborough, Essie B.

South, Grace
See Clark, Gail

South, M. A.
See Atwood, Mary Ann

South, Robert 1634-1716 [SN]
British clergyman
* [The] Scourge of Fanaticism

South, Simeon
See Macgregor, J.

South, Theophilus
See Chitty, Edward

South Vietnam's Most Decorated Soldier
See Do Cao Tri

Southard, Helen Fairbairn 1906- [CA]
American psychologist and author
* Fairbairn, Helen

Southard, J. H.
See Morris, Charles Smith

Southard, [Rev.] Samuel Lewis 1819-1859 [HPPN]
American clergyman
* [The] Rector

Southcote, George
See Ashton, [Sir] George Grey

Southcott, Joanna 1750-1814 [HN, HPPN, SN]
British religious leader
* [The] Prophetess of Exeter
* [The] Spiritual Mother
* [The] Woman of Revelation XII

Southerland, Katherine Virden 20th c.
[WWL]
American author
* Virden, Katherine

Southerland, McCarthy 20th c.   [BA]
American clergyman
* McCarthy, Mac

Southerland, Myrtella
See Harkness, Edith Myrtella

[The] Southern
See Dowling, Bartholomew

[The] Southern Cooper
See Simms, W[illiam] Gilmore

[The] Southern Frontiersman
See Dale, Samuel

Southern Gael
See Locke, John

[The] Southern Gentleman
See Loden, James [Jimmie]

Southern, Jack
See Southworth, John Van Duyn

[A] Southern Matron
See Howard, Caroline K.

[The] Southern Nightingale
See Smith, Trixie

[A] Southern Physician
See Dickson, Samuel Henry

[A] Southern Planter
See Alston, Joseph

[A] Southern Pre-Emptor
See Winston, Thomas B.

Southern Sam Ervin
See Ervin, Sam[uel James, Jr.]

[The] Southern Scott
See Ariosto, Lodovico

[The] Southern Spy
See Pollard, Edward Alfred

Southern, Terry 1924?-   [CA, WD]
American author and screenwriter
* Kenton, Maxwell [joint pseudonym
  with Mason Hoffenberg]

[The] Southern Tycho
See Halley, Edmund

[A] Southerner
See Dake, Seymour R.

[A] Southerner
See Duke, Seymour R.

[A] Southerner
See Pollard, Edward Alfred

[A] Southerner
See Smythe, James M.

Southernwood
See Sotheran, Charles

Southey, Caroline Anne [Bowles]
1786?-1854   [HPPN, IP]
British poet
* A.

Southey, Caroline Anne [Bowles] (cont.)
* C.
* [The] Cowper of Our Modern
  Poetesses

Southey, Robert 1774-1843   [DEL, DEP,
DLE1, FFF, HPPN, IP, NPS, SN]
British author and poet
* [The] Ballad-Monger
* [The] Bard of the Bay
* Bion
* [The] Blackbird
* [The] Doctor
* [The] Epic Renegade
* Espriella, Manuel Alvarez
* [The] First Man of Letters in Europe
* Illustrious Conqueror of Common-
  Sense
* Inchiquin
* [A] Laureat
* Mouthy
* [The] Poet of Greta Hall
* Porson, Professor [joint pseudonym
  with Samuel Taylor Coleridge]
* Shufflebottom, Abel
* Turncoat

Southgate, Elsie 1890-1946   [BMH]
British musician
* [The] Royal Violinist

Southland, T. 17th c.   [HPPN]
British playwright
* [A] Person of Honour

**Southouse-Cheney, Reginald Evelyn
Peter** 1896-1951   [LC]
Irish author
* Cheney, Peter

[A] Southron
See Simms, W[illiam] Gilmore

[The] South's Avenging Angel
See Booth, John Wilkes

[The] South's Most Crooked Gambler
See North, John

Southside Johnny
See Lyon, Johnny

Southwell, Robert 1561-1595   [DEA, SN]
British poet
* Our Second Ciceronian
* R. S.

Southwick, Solomon 1773-1839   [DNA,
HPPN, IP]
American journalist
* Homespun, Henry
* Sherlock

Southwold, Stephen 1887-1964   [LC,
SFL, TC]
British author
* Bell, Neil
* Lambert, S. H.
* Martens, Paul
* Miles

Southwood, Marion 19th c.   [HPPN]
American author
* [A] Lady of New Orleans

Southworth, Billy 20th c.   [GSH]
American baseball player
* Billy the Kid

**Southworth, Emma Dorothy Eliza
[Nevitte]** 1818?-1899   [FFF]
American author
* E. D. E. N.

Southworth, John Van Duyn 1904-
[NAA]
American author and educator
* Southern, Jack

Southworth, Louis
See Grealey, Thomas Louis

Southworth, Sylvester S.   [IP, PA]
American author
* Smith, John, Jr., of Arkansas

Southworth, William H. [Billy] 1893-
[HPPN]
American baseball club manager
* Billy the Kid

Soutter, Fred
See Lake, Kenneth R[obert]

Souza, Carlos Estevao de 1921-   [WEC]
Brazilian cartoonist
* Estevao, Carlos

Souza, E[rnest]
See Scott, Evelyn

Souzay, Gerard
See Tisserand, Gerard Marcel

Sovine, Red
See Sovine, Woodrow Wilson

Sovine, Woodrow Wilson 1918-   [CME,
CWG, DAM]
American country-western performer
* Sovine, Red

Sowande, Fela 1905-   [IBW]
Nigerian-born composer
* [The] High Priest of Music

Sowden, Margaret 1933-   [TR]
British actress
* Neilson, Perlita

Sowden, Thomas 19th c.   [IP]
British author
* [A] Lancashire Lad

Sowden, [Sir] William John 1858-?
[HPPN, LAO]
Australian author
* Pencil
* Scribble

Sowder, Martin 1874-1931   [GW]
American rodeo performer
* Sowder, Thad

Sowder, Thad
See Sowder, Martin

Sowell, Morton
See Sobell, Morton

Sowells, Petey
See Sowells, Rich

Sowells, Rich 20th c. [SMG]
American football player
* Sowells, Petey

Sower, Christopher 1721-1784 [HPPN]
German-American pacifist and humanist
* [The] Bread Father [Der Brod Vater]

Sowerby, Arthur Lindsay McRae 1899-
[CAP]
British author and editor
* McRae, Lindsay

Sowerby, Githa
See Kendall, Katherine Githa

Sowman, Gordon 20th c. [MBF]
British author
* Reid, Desmond [house pseudonym]

[The] Soybean Chemist
See Julian, Percy Lavon

Soyinka, Akinwande Oluwole 1934-
[CLC, IBW, WOA]
Nigerian playwright, director, poet, author
* Soyinka, Wole

Soyinka, Wole
See Soyinka, Akinwande Oluwole

Sozzo
See Albina, Giuseppe

Spaatz, Carl 1891-1974 [WWW]
American air force officer
* Spaatz, Tooey

Spaatz, Tooey
See Spaatz, Carl

[The] Space Age Artist
See Forner, Raquel

Spacek, Mary Elizabeth 1950?- [BI]
American actress
* Spacek, Sissy

Spacek, Sissy
See Spacek, Mary Elizabeth

[The] Spaceman
See Lee, William Francis [Bill]

Spach, Louis Adolphe ?-1880 [IP, PA]
French historian
* Levater, Louis

Spade, Mark
See Balchin, Nigel [Marlin]

Spade, Rupert
See Pawley, Martin Edward

Spaeth, Helen Elizabeth 1924- [OP]
American opera singer
* Vanni, Helen Elizabeth

Spaeth, Sigmund Gottfried 1885-1965
[HPPN]
American musicologist, author, lecturer
* [The] Tune Detective

[Lo] Spagna
See Di Pietro, Giovanni

[The] Spagnolet of History
See Heylyn, Peter

[The] Spagnolet of the Theatre
See Cibber, Colley

[The] Spagnolet of the Theatre
See Sandford, Samuel

[Lo] Spagnoletto
See Garcia, Francisco Javier

Spagnoletto
See Ribera, Jose

Spagnolus, Baptista 1443-1516 [RH]
Italian poet
* [The] Mantuan

[Lo] Spagnuolo
See Crespi, Giuseppe Maria

[Lo] Spagnuolo dei Pesci
See Herrera, Francisco de

Spahn, Mary Attea 1929- [CA]
American author, poet, educator
* Attea, Mary

Spahn, Spahnie
See Spahn, Warren

Spahn, Warren 1922- [HPPN]
American baseball player
* Spahn, Spahnie

Spahnie Spahn
See Spahn, Warren

Spahr, Juerg 1925- [WEC]
Swiss cartoonist
* Juesp

Spaight, Richard Dobbs 1758-1802
[HPPN]
American statesman
* [The] Youngest of the Founding
Fathers

Spain, Hiram, Jr. 1936- [BA]
American attorney
* Spain, Sonny

Spain, John
See Adams, Cleve F[ranklin]

Spain, Sonny
See Spain, Hiram, Jr.

Spalatin, Georg
See Burckhardt, Georg

Spalding, Albert 1888-1953 [HPPN]
American violinist
* America's Own Violinist

Spalding, Charles Harry 1893-1950 [BE]
American baseball player
* Spalding, Dick

Spalding, Dick
See Spalding, Charles Harry

Spalding, Doctor
See Spalding, Gilbert R.

Spalding, Gilbert R. 1812-1880 [HPPN]
American circus entrepreneur
* Spalding, Doctor

Spalding, Henry D[aniel] 1915- [CA]
American author
* Sping, Dan

Spalding, John Lancaster 1840-1916
[DNA]
American author and clergyman
* Hamilton, Henry

Spalding, Keith
See Spalt, Karl Heinz G.

Spalding, Lucile
See Spalding, Ruth

Spalding, Ruth 20th c. [AW]
British author and playwright
* Jay, Marion
* Spalding, Lucile

Spalding, William 1809-1859 [IP]
Scottish author
* W. S.

Spalla, Ignazio 20th c. [WF]
Italian actor
* Sanchez, Pedro

Spalla, Joseph Salvatore 1923- [ITA]
American executive and producer
* Spalla, Rick

Spalla, Rick
See Spalla, Joseph Salvatore

Spalt, Karl Heinz G. 1913- [WD]
British author
* Spalding, Keith

[The] Spam Man
See Hormel, Jay Catherwood

**Spamer, Johann Gottlieb Christian
Franz Otto** 1820-? [HPPN]
German author, publisher, bookseller
* Otto, Franz

Span, Norman 20th c. [ASC]
West Indian composer and singer
* King Radio

Spang
See Spangler, Frank M.

Spang Gipe
See Huston, Henry Augustus

Spangenberg, Judith [Dunn] 1942- [CA,
SAT]
American author
* Dunn, Judy

Spangler, Frank M. 1881-1946 [WEC]
American cartoonist
* Spang

Spangler, Robert 20th c. [HPPN]
American stuntman
* Spangler, Spanky

Spangler, Spanky
See Spangler, Robert

[Der] Spangol
See Beethoven, Ludwig Van

Spangy
See Beethoven, Ludwig Van

[The] Spaniard
See Beethoven, Ludwig Van

[The] Spaniard
See Eugenie

[The] Spaniard
See Healy, Patrick Francis

Spanier, Francis Joseph 1906-1967
[DAM, WWJ]
American jazz musician
* Spanier, Muggsy

Spanier, Muggsy
See Spanier, Francis Joseph

Spanish
See Beethoven, Ludwig Van

Spanish
See Foe, Daniel

[The] Spanish Addison
See Feyjoo [or Feijoo] y Montenegro, Frey Benito

[The] Spanish Bassano
See Orrente, Pedro

[The] Spanish Bayard
See Garcia de Paredes, Diego

[The] Spanish Brutus
See Perez de Guzman, Alphonso [or Alonso]

[The] Spanish Byron
See Espronceda, Jose de

[The] Spanish Cellini
See Arfe y Villafane, Juan de

[The] Spanish Cicero
See Arguelles, Agustin

[The] Spanish Ennius
See Mena, Juan de

[The] Spanish Frank Sinatra
See Iglesias, Julio

[The] Spanish Grandee
See Duff, James

[The] Spanish Horace
See Argensola, Bartolome Leonardo de

[The] Spanish Horace
See Argensola, Lupercio Leonardo de

Spanish Jack
See Gonzales, Bli

[A] Spanish Jew from Alicant
See Edrehi, Israel

Spanish, Johnny
See Weyler, Joseph

[The] Spanish Livy
See Ginez de Sepulveda, Juan

[The] Spanish Michelangelo
See Cano, Alonso [or Alonzo]

[The] Spanish Moliere
See Moratin, Leandro Fernandez

[The] Spanish Mozart
See Arriaga, Juan Christosomo

[The] Spanish Petrarch
See Garcilaso de la Vega

[The] Spanish Petrarch
See Vega, Garcilasso de la

[The] Spanish Phoenix
See Vega Carpio, Lope Felix de

[The] Spanish Raphael
See Macip, Vicente Juan

Spanish Raymond Marquez
See Marquez, Raymond

[The] Spanish Shakespeare
See Calderon de la Barca, Pedro

[The] Spanish Sinatra
See Iglesias, Julio

[The] Spanish Tennyson
See Nunez de Arce, Gaspar

[The] Spanish Tyrtaeus
See Quintana, Manuel Jose

[The] Spanish Victor Hugo
See Zorilla, Jose

Spann, Charles Edward, III 1948-
[IBW]
American swimmer
* Spann, Little Eddie

Spann, Little Eddie
See Spann, Charles Edward, III

Spann, William Carter 1947- [HPPN]
Nephew of American president, James Earl Carter
* [The] Bad Peanut
* [The] Black Sheep

Spanner, Valerie
See Grayland, Valerie Merle [Spanner]

Spano, James
See Aiuppa, Joseph John [Joe]

Spano, Tony
See Nerone, Giuseppe

Spanpinato, Salvatore Willard 1942-
[RO2]
American singer
* Valentino, Sal

[La] Spara
See Spara, Hieronyma

Spara, Hieronyma ?-1659 [LFW]
Italian murderer
* [La] Spara

Sparando, Ace
See Sparando, Tony

Sparando, Tony 1906- [BBH]
American bowler
* Sparando, Ace

Spargo, Tony
See Sbarbaro, Anthony

Spark Plug Adams
See Adams, Earl John

Spark Plug, Miss
See Hobby, Olveta Culp

Sparkes, Joseph 19th c. [IP]
British author
* [A] Member

Sparkes, Mr. 1820-1875 [EOP]
Astrologer and editor
* Raphael V

Sparkia, Roy [Bernard] 1924- [CA]
American author
* Caine, Mitchell

Sparkle
See Theismann, Joseph

Sparkle, Sophie
See Hicks, Jennie E.

Sparkle, Tom
See Sheridan, Thomas

Sparkman, Edward A. 1883-1957 [BEW, FC]
Canadian-born actor
* Sparks, Ned

Sparkman, William
See Roper, William L[eon]

Sparks, Aaron 20th c. [BWW]
American musician
* Pinetop

Sparks, Don 20th c. [SMG]
American basketball team trainer
* Sparks, Sparky

Sparks, Godfrey
See Dickens, Charles

Sparks, Jared 1789-1866 [HPPN]
American historian
* S.

Sparks, Jesse Wadlington 1867-? [NAA]
American attorney and writer
* Jump, A.

Sparks, Mary [Crowninshield] 19th c.
[IP]
American author
* M. C. S.

Sparks, Merla Jean
See McCormick, Merla Jean

Sparks, Ned
See Sparkman, Edward A.

Sparks, Olive Ann Burns 20th c. [NY 8-31-84]
American author
* Burns, Olive Ann

Sparks, Sparky
See Sparks, Don

Sparks, Thomas Frank 1877-1937
American baseball player
* Sparks, Tully

Sparks, Timothy
See Dickens, Charles

Sparks, Tully
See Sparks, Thomas Frank

Sparling, Ned?
See Senarens, Luis Philip

Sparre, Nicolas ?-1761 [PA]
Author
* Hiersingius

Sparrow, Kid
See Gassion, Edith Giovanna

Sparrow, Malcolm Weethie 1862-1936
[CCL]
Canadian author
* Moineau, Max

Sparrow, Philip
See Steward, Samuel M.

Sparrow, Rory 20th c.
American basketball player
* [The] Buzzer Beater

Sparrowgrass, Mr.
See Cozzens, Frederick Swartwout

Sparshott, F. E.
See Sparshott, Francis Edward

Sparshott, Francis Edward 1926- [CA]
British-born Canadian author, poet,
philosopher
* Sparshott, F. E.

Spartacus
See Linton, William James

Spartacus, Deutero
See Fanthorpe, R[obert] Lionel

Spartacus, Tertius
See Burgess, Michael Roy

Spartanburg John McMakin
See McMakin, John Weaver

Spatha
See Parker, William Frederick

Spaulding, Buckskin Johnny
See Spaulding, John T.

Spaulding, Douglas
See Bradbury, Ray [Douglas]

Spaulding, Elbridge Gerry 1809-1897
[FFF, WBD]
American politician and banker
* [The] Father of Greenbacks

Spaulding, John T. ?-1926 [BI]
American hunter
* Spaulding, Buckskin Johnny

Spaulding, William 1809-? [PA]
Author
* W. S.

Spaulding, William Henry [Bill] 20th c.
[HPPN]
American football coach
* [The] Beloved Bruin

Spavento
See Hendie, Paul

Spavento, Don
See Cohn, Martin

Spavery
See Avery, Samuel Putnam

[Der] Spaziergaenger nach Syrakus
See Seume, Johann Gottfried

Speake, Robert Charles [Bob] 1930-
[BE]
American baseball player
* Speake, Spook

Speake, Spook
See Speake, Robert Charles [Bob]

Speaker, Spoke
See Speaker, Tristram E.

Speaker, Tris
See Speaker, Tristram E.

Speaker, Tristram E. 1888-1958 [AS,
DGS, PB]
American baseball player and manager
* [The] Gray Eagle
* Speaker, Spoke
* Speaker, Tris

Speakes, Catfish
See Speakes, Larry M

Speakes, Larry M 20th c. [DF 3-7-83]
American press secretary to American
president, Ronald Reagan
* Speakes, Catfish

Spear, Benjamin
See Henisch, Heinz K.

Spear, Sammy
See Shapiro, Sammy

Spear, W. [IP]
British author
* U. S. E.

Spearman, Clyde 20th c. [OBW]
American baseball player
* Spearman, Splo

Spearman, Elizabeth Fyfe 1901- [BI]
American author
* Spearman, Sheridan

Spearman, Henry 20th c. [OBW]
American baseball player
* Spearman, Splo

Spearman, Larna Kaye 1945- [BA]
American engineer
* Spearman, Lonnie

Spearman, Lonnie
See Spearman, Larna Kaye

Spearman, Sheridan
See Spearman, Elizabeth Fyfe

Spearman, Splo
See Spearman, Clyde

Spearman, Splo
See Spearman, Henry

Spears, Clarence W. 1894-1964 [AS,
FB]
American football player and coach
* Spears, Cupid
* Spears, Doc
* Spears, Fat

Spears, Cupid
See Spears, Clarence W.

Spears, Doc
See Spears, Clarence W.

Spears, Fat
See Spears, Clarence W.

Spears, Raymond S[miley] 1876-?
[NAA]
American author
* Smiley, Jim

Spec, Alonzo
See Thackeray, William Makepeace

Spec, Mr.
See Thackeray, William Makepeace

Speca, Robert [Bob] 20th c. [HPPN]
American domino player
* [The] Domino Wizard

[A] Special Commissioner
See Roget, John Lewis

[A] Special Correspondent
See Reade, Alfred Arthur

Special Duty Agent Three-Three
See Granville, Clive

Special K
See Kelser, Greg

Special K Jones
See Jones, Kendall Ray

[A] Special Reporter
See Allan, John

Speck, Dutch
See Speck, Norman

Speck, Norman 20th c. [EF]
American football player
* Speck, Dutch

Speck, Richard Benjamin
See Speck, Richard Franklin

Speck, Richard Franklin 1941- [BLB]
American murderer
* Brian, B.
* Lindbergh, Richard Franklin
* Speck, Richard Benjamin

Speckbacher, Joseph 1767-1820 [HPPN]
Austrian patriot
* [Der] Mann Vom Rinn

Speckled Red
See Perryman, Rufus G.

Spectacles, Timothy
See Foster, William C.

[The] Spectacular Rogue
See Means, Gaston Bullock

[The] Spectator
See Addison, Joseph

Spectator
See Bartlett, David W.

[A] Spectator
See Bartol, Cyrus Augustus

Spectator
See Bellew, Henry Walter

Spectator
See Popovic, Nenad D[ushan]

Spectator
See Walkley, Arthur Bingham

Spectator
See Wingate, W. H.

[A] Spectator of the Scenes
See Carroll, John

Spector, Isadore 20th c. [EJS]
American football player
* Spector, Spook

Spector, Phil 20th c. [CMA]
American record producer and songwriter
* [The] First Tycoon of Teen

Spector, Spook
See Spector, Isadore

[The] Speculator
See Durandus, Gulielmus

[The] Speculator King
See Livermore, Jesse Lauriston

Spedding, James 19th c. [HPPN]
Irish editor
* [The] Railway Reader

Speece, By
See Speece, Byron Franklin

Speece, Byron Franklin 1897- [BE]
American baseball player
* Speece, By

Speed
See Marvel, Carl Shipp

Speed Ball Cannon
See Cannon, Richard

Speed Demon
See Agati, Pasquale

Speed, F[rederick] Maurice 1912- [CA]
British author and film critic
* Deeps, Frederick
* Haffner, J. Lilliwhite

Speed, John 18th c. [IP]
British physician and author
* [An] Impartial Bystander
* Statutophilus

[The] Speed King of the Air
See Turner, [Colonel] Roscoe

[The] Speed Merchant
See Laviolette, Jean Baptiste

[The] Speed Merchant
See Minoso, Saturnino Orestes Arrieta Armas

Speed Merchant of the Pulps
See Burks, Arthur J.

Speed, Mr.
See Randolph, Thomas, Jr. [Tom]

Speed, Nell
See Sampson, Emma Speed

Speedbreak, Mr.
See Roman, Jose

Speer, Albert 1905-
German architect and Nazi leader
* [The] Architect of Nazism

Speer, Albert (cont.)
* [The] Feuhrer's Master Builder
* Mephistopheles

Speer, G. T.
See Speer, George Thomas

Speer, George Nathan 1886-1946 [BE]
American baseball player
* Speer, Kid

Speer, George Thomas 1891-1966 [DAM]
American singer
* Speer, G. T.

Speer, Jack 20th c. [SFP]
Author
* Bristol, John A.

Speer, Kid
See Speer, George Nathan

Speer, Lena Brock ?-1967 [DAM]
American singer
* Speer, Mom

Speer, Mom
See Speer, Lena Brock

Speers, James [Jim] 1882-1955 [CSH]
Canadian racehorse breeder
* Racing, Mr.

Speicher, Helen Ross [Smith] 1915-
[CA, SAT]
American author
* Abbott, Alice [joint pseudonym with Kathryn Kilby Borland]
* Land, Jane and Ross [joint pseudonym with Kathryn Kilby Borland]

Spektor, [Dr.] Adam
See Glut, Donald F[rank]

Spelling, Aaron 1926- [HPPN]
American television producer
* Big Four

Spellman, Leora 1891-1945 [SC]
American actress
* Spellmeyer, Leora

Spellmeyer, Leora
See Spellman, Leora

Spelman, Mary 1934- [CA]
American author
* Lockwood, Mary
* Towne, Mary

Spelvin, George
See Phillips, David Atlee

Spelvin, Georgina
See Graham, Chele

Spen, Kay
See Selous, H. C.

Spence, Alexander 20th c. [LRR]
Musician
* Spence, Skip

Spence, [Sir] Basil Unwin 1907-
[HPPN]
Scottish architect
* St. Basil

Spence, David 18th c. [HPPN]
Scottish author and banker
* [A] Member of the Society

Spence, Duncan
See Spence, William John Duncan

Spence, Elizabeth Isabella 1768-1832
[IP]
British author
* [A] Lady

Spence, George 1788-1851 [IP]
British barrister
* [A] Barrister of the Inner Temple

Spence, Harrison L. 1856-1908 [BE]
American baseball manager
* Spence, Harry

Spence, Harry
See Spence, Harrison L.

Spence, Hubert
See Longhurst, Percy William

Spence, J. A. D.
See Eliot, Thomas Stearns

Spence, James Mudie [IP, PA]
British author
* Leevitt, Don T. B.

Spence, John, Jr. ?-1851 [HPPN]
American physician and author
* [A] Young Physician

Spence, Joseph 1698-1768 [DEL, IP, SN]
British author
* Beaumont, [Sir] Harry
* Enceps, Pheso

Spence, Lew
See Slifka, Lewis

Spence, Skip
See Spence, Alexander

Spence, Thomas 1752-1814 [IP]
British educator and author
* Wishit, Mr.

Spence, William John Duncan 1923-
[WD]
British author
* Bowden, Jim
* Ford, Kirk
* Rogers, Floyd
* Spence, Duncan

Spencer
See Herz, Jerome Spencer [Jerry]

Spencer, Anne
See Bannister, Annie Bethel Scales

Spencer, Big Dee
See Spencer, Daryl Dean

Spencer, Brian 1949- [SMG]
Canadian-born hockey player
* Spencer, Spinner

Spencer, [Dr.] Bruce
See Abel, Alan [Irwin]

Spencer, Bud
See Pedersoli, Carlo

Spencer, Captain
See Tuite, Hugh

Spencer, Charles [Third Earl of Sunderland] 1674-1722 [HPPN]
British statesman and bibliophile
* Sundarius

Spencer, Charles [Charlie] 1955?-
[HPPN]
American basketball player
* Spencer, Magic Charlie

Spencer, Cornelia
See Yaukey, Grace S[ydenstricker]

Spencer, Daryl Dean 1929- [BE]
American baseball player
* Spencer, Big Dee

Spencer, [Rev.] E. 18th c. [HPPN]
British clergyman
* [A] Country Incumbent

Spencer, Edward
See Mott, Edward Spencer

Spencer, Edward
See Seymour, Caroline

Spencer, Edward
See Stares, John Edward Spencer

Spencer, Edward Russell 1884-1945
[BE]
American baseball player
* Spencer, Tubby

Spencer, Elihu 1721-1784 [FFF]
American clergyman
* Spencer, Ready Money

Spencer, Eliza 19th c. [IP]
American author
* Beverly, Elise

Spencer, Frank Harding 1890-1950
[HPPN]
American insurance executive
* [The] Old Master

Spencer, Fred
See Bretherton, Fred Spencer

Spencer, Gabriel ?-1598 [HPPN]
British actor
* Gabriel

Spencer, Geoffrey
See Wilson, Alexander [Douglas Chesney]

Spencer, George 1799-1864 [IP, PA, RH]
British clergyman and author
* Ignatius, [Father]

Spencer, Georgiana 18th c.
Duchess of Devonshire
* [The] Duchess of Dimples

Spencer, [Lord] H. 18th c. [IP]
British scholar
* Ironculus

Spencer, Harry 19th c.
Jockey
* [The] Iceman

Spencer, Henry ?-1406 [FFF, RH, SN]
Bishop of Norwich
* [The] Fighting Prelate

Spencer, Ichabod Smith 1798-1854 [IP]
American clergyman and author
* [A] Pastor

Spencer, Irvin James 1937- [CEI]
Canadian-born hockey player
* Spencer, Spinner

Spencer, Jake
See Kaplun, Jacob

Spencer, John 17th c. [HPPN]
British comedian
* Stockfisch, Hans

Spencer, John 1949- [DC]
British cricketer
* Spencer, Spud

Spencer, John
See Vickers, Roy

Spencer, John Charles [Lord Althorp]
1782-1845 [DNNS]
British politician
* Honest John [or Jack]

Spencer, June Lydiard
See Ossinger, June Eileen

Spencer, Leonard G. [joint pseudonym with Robert Silverberg] [house pseudonym, Ziff-Davis]
See Garrett, [Gordon] Randall [Philip David]

Spencer, Leonard G. [joint pseudonym with Randall Garrett] [house pseudonym, Ziff-Davis]
See Silverberg, Robert

Spencer, Lillian
See Clayburgh, Mrs. Edward

Spencer, Magic Charlie
See Spencer, Charles [Charlie]

Spencer, Maja
See Spencer, Mrs. William Loring [Nunez]

Spencer, Major
See Nunez, William Loring

Spencer, Major
See Spencer, William Loring

Spencer, Mr. [PA]
Author
* Allyn, Enylla

Spencer, Mrs. William Loring [Nunez]
19th c. [DNA]
Author
* Spencer, Maja

Spencer, Nat
See Saunders, Robert

Spencer, Norman D.
See Factor, John

Spencer, Oneill
See Spencer, William

Spencer, P. M.
See Spencer, Pamela Mary

Spencer, Pamela Mary 1924- [ART]
British artist
* Spencer, P. M.

Spencer, Parke
See Wright, Sewell Peaslee

Spencer, Ready Money
See Spencer, Elihu

Spencer, Robert [Second Earl of Sunderland] 1640-1702 [SN]
British politician
* President Bob

Spencer, Roland [joint pseudonym with Francis Alister Warwick]
See Prout, Geoffrey

Spencer, Roland [joint pseudonym with Geoffrey Prout]
See Warwick, Francis Alister

Spencer, Spinner
See Spencer, Brian

Spencer, Spinner
See Spencer, Irvin James

Spencer, Spud
See Spencer, John

Spencer, Tubby
See Spencer, Edward Russell

Spencer, Warren
See Lengel, William Charles

Spencer, William 1909-1944 [WWJ]
American jazz musician
* Spencer, Oneill

Spencer, William Loring 19th c.
[BDSA]
American author
* Spencer, Major

Spencer Meek, Margaret [Diston] 1925-
[CA]
Scottish-born author
* Meek, Margaret

Spender, J. A.
See Spender, John Alfred

Spender, John Alfred 1862-1942 [NPS]
British author
* Greville Minor
* [The] Philistine
* Spender, J. A.

Spendlove, G. H.
See Spendlove, Gerald Hugh

Spendlove, Gerald Hugh 1929- [ART]
British artist
* Spendlove, G. H.

[The] Spendthrift of Albany
See Rockefeller, Nelson Aldrich

Spener, Philipp Jakob 1635-1705
[HPPN]
German theologian
* [The] Father of Pietism

Spens, J. 19th c.   [IP]
Author
* [A] Retired Officer

Spenser, Edmund 1552-1599   [FFF, HPPN, NPS, RH, SN]
British poet
* Astrophel
* [The] Bard of Mulla's Silver Stream
* [The] Child of Fancy
* [The] Child of the Ausonian Muse
* Clout, Colin
* [The] Fairy Singer
* [The] Father of the Poets
* Immerito
* [The] King of Poets
* [The] Mighty Minstrel of Old Mole
* Mother Hubbard
* Mulla's Bard
* [The] Page of State to the Muses
* [The] Poet's Poet
* [The] Prince of Poets
* [The] Prince of Poets in His Time
* [The] Rubens of English Poetry
* [The] Sage and Serious Spenser

Spenser, Henry 1377-1399   [HPPN]
British clergyman
* [The] Fighting Prelate

Spenser, James
See Guest, Francis Narold

Spenser, [Sir] John 16th c.   [SN]
British politician
* Spenser, Rich

[The] Spenser of English Prose-Writers
See Taylor, Jeremy

[The] Spenser of His Age
See Fletcher, Phineas

Spenser, Rich
See Spenser, [Sir] John

Speranza
See Wilde, Jane Francesca Elgee

Speranza, Norma Jean 1935-   [RO1]
American singer
* Corey, Jill

Speraw, Birdie
See Speraw, Paul Bachman

Speraw, Paul Bachman 1893-1962   [BE]
American baseball player
* Speraw, Birdie
* Speraw, Polly

Speraw, Polly
See Speraw, Paul Bachman

Spero, Leopold 1887-   [WWL]
British author
* Hope, Cecil
* Managing Clerk

Spero, Robert 1862-1948   [BI]
American founder of Parents' Day
* Uncle Robert

Sperontes
See Scholze, Johann Sigismund

Sperry, [Sally] Baxter 1914-   [CA]
German-born American author
* S. S. E.

Sperry, Byrne Hope 1902-   [CA]
South African-born author and journalist
* Sanders, Byrne Hope

Sperry, Elmer A. 1860-1930   [HPPN]
American engineer, inventor, manufacturer
* [The] Father of the Gyroscope Compass

Sperry, J. E.
See Eisenstat, Jane Sperry

Sperry, Raymond, Jr. [house pseudonym] [Stratemeyer Syndicate]
See Stratemeyer, Edward L.

Sperry, Reginald   [FFF]
Prestidigitator
* Prenaier, Paul

Spes
See Campion, John Thomas

Spewack, Bella Cohen 1899-   [HPPN]
Hungarian-American playwright
* Cohen, Bella

Spewack, Samuel 1899-   [WW]
Author
* Abbott, A. A.

Speyrer, Charles W. 1949-   [FB]
American football player
* Speyrer, Cotton

Speyrer, Cotton
See Speyrer, Charles W.

[The] Sphinx
See Adenauer, Konrad

[The] Sphinx
See Baeza, Braulio

[The] Sphinx
See Brown, Lee Patrick

Sphinx
See Fox, Sarah [Hustler]

[The] Sphinx
See Gustafsson, Greta Lovisa

[The] Sphinx
See Leverson, Ada

[The] Sphinx
See Mossi, Donald Louis

[The] Sphinx
See Roosevelt, Franklin Delano

[The] Sphinx in Crepe
See Tarnowska, [Countess] Maria

[The] Sphinx of the Rock Island
See Moore, William Henry

Spicer, Anne Higginson 1871-?   [NAA]
American author and poet
* Anchusa

Spicer, Bart 1918-   [CC, WW]
Author
* Barbette, Jay

Spicer, Carmelita 1946-   [BA]
American business executive
* Spicer, Carmie

Spicer, Carmie
See Spicer, Carmelita

Spicer, Nicholas
See Payne, Alban S.

Spicer, Seth
See Gould, Benjamin F.

Spickler, Charles A[braham] 1880-? [WGT]
American author
* Brogan the Scribe

[The] Spider
See Guimard, [Marie] Madeleine

[The] Spider
See Sabich, Vladimir

Spider Bruce
See Mason, John

Spider Dan Goodwin
See Goodwin, Daniel

[The] Spider King
See Louis XI

Spider Man
See Goodwin, Daniel

[The] Spider of Tripoli
See Khadafi [or Qaddafi], [Colonel] Muammar el

Spider Sam
See McGhee, Walter Brown

[The] Spiderman
See Allen, Jimmy

Spiderman
See Scott-Heron, Gil

Spie, Oliver?
See Slotkin, Joseph

Spiegel, Clara Gatzert 1904-   [ANT]
American author
* Jaynes, Clare [joint pseudonym with Jane Rothschild Mayer]

Spiegel, Sam 1901?-1985   [NY 1-1-86]
Austrian-born producer
* Eagle, S. P.

Spiel, Hilde
See De Mendelssohn, Hilde Maria

Spielberg, Hanns von
See Zobeltitz, Hanns von

Spielman, Fred
See Spielman, Fritz

Spielman, Fritz 20th c.   [ASC]
Austrian-born composer
* Spielman, Fred

[Der] Spielmann
See Bach, Hans

Spielmann, M. H.
See Spielmann, Marion Harry Alexander

Spielmann, Marion Harry Alexander
1858-1948 [LAO, LC]
British author and critic
* M. H. S.
* Spielmann, M. H.

Spielmann, Peter James 1952- [CA]
American author
* Nightrate, Emil

Spielmann, Rudolf 1883-1942
Austrian chess player
* [The] Last Knight of the King's Gambit

Spike, Ethan
See Whittier, Matthew F.

Spiker, Ray
See Faust, Ray

Spikes
See Botts, Randolph

Spikes, Charley 20th c. [IBW]
American baseball player
* [The] Bogalusa Bomber

Spilhaus, Phyllis Margaret 20th c.
[IAW]
South African author
* Whiting Spilhaus, M.

Spillane, Bud
See Spillane, Robert

Spillane, Frank Morrison 1918- [CA,
CC, EMD]
American author
* Spillane, Mickey

Spillane, Mickey
See Spillane, Frank Morrison

Spillane, Robert 20th c. [TI 3-7-83]
American educator
* Six Shooter
* Spillane, Bud
* [The] Velvet Hammer

Spillius, Elizabeth Jane [Bott] 1924-
[AW]
Canadian-born anthropologist and author
* Bott, Elizabeth

Spillman, Barbara 1927- [FFA]
American singer
* Dane, Barbara

Spilotro, Anthony 20th c. [WP 3-6-83]
American underworld figure
* Spilotro, Tough Tony
* Tony the Ant

Spilotro, Tough Tony
See Spilotro, Anthony

Spilsbury, [Sir] Bernard Henry
1877-1947 [HPPN]
British pathologist
* [The] Ideal Scientific Witness

Spilsbury, Francis 18th c. [IP]
British author
* Yrubslips, F.

Spinckes, Nathaniel 1653?-1727 [IP]
British clergyman and author
* [A] Non Juror

Spinella, Barney 1893- [BBH]
Italian-born American bowler
* Spinella, Jumping Jack

Spinella, Jumping Jack
See Spinella, Barney

Spinelli, Evelita Juanita 1889-1941
[LFW]
American murderer
* [The] Duchess

Spinello Aretino
See Spinello, Luca

Spinello, Luca 1330?-1410 [WBD]
Florentine painter
* Spinello Aretino

Sping, Dan
See Spalding, Henry D[aniel]

Spinifex
See Martin, David

Spink, William 19th c. [IP]
British barrister and author
* [A] Member of the College of Justice

Spinks, Leon 1954?-
American boxer
* Spinks, Mess-Over

Spinks, Mess-Over
See Spinks, Leon

Spinner, Alice
See Fraser, Augusta Zelia

Spinner, Red
See Senior, Nassau William

Spinney, Chuck
See Spinney, Franklin

Spinney, Franklin 20th c. [TI 10-31-83]
American Defense Department analyst
* Spinney, Chuck

[The] Spinning Spoon
See Peel, [Sir] Robert

Spinossimus
See White, William, Jr.

Spinster
See Brooke, Frances [Moore]

Spinther
See Lentulus, Publius Cornelius

Spira, Francis ?-1548 [SN]
Italian attorney
* Philologus

[The] Spiral Ascensionist
See Ethardo

Spiral Groove
See Macdonald, Wilson

Spirer, Herbert F[rederick] 1925- [CA]
American author and educator
* Sitzfleisch, Vladimir

Spires, Arthur 1912- [BWW, NBB]
American singer
* Spires, Big Boy

Spires, Benjamin 1931- [BWW]
American musician
* Spires, Bud

Spires, Big Boy
See Spires, Arthur

Spires, Bud
See Spires, Benjamin

[The] Spirit
See Davis, Mickey

[The] Spirit of Hampden
See Fellowes, Robert

[The] Spirit of Nashville
See Collins, Lucretia

[The] Spirit of the Nation
See Meehan, Alexander S.

[The] Spirit of Tlatelolco
See Kissinger, Henry Alfred

[Lo] Spirito [The Ghost]
See Valente, Umberto

[The] Spiritual Coach
See Alpert, Richard

[The] Spiritual Father of Kant
See Hume, David

[The] Spiritual Mother
See Southcott, Joanna

Spiro, Edward 1908- [CA]
Austrian-born author
* Cookridge, E. H.

Spirt, Diana L[ouise] 1925- [CA]
American librarian and author
* Lembo, Diana L.

Spit, Sam
See Schneck, Stephen

[The] Spitball Pitcher
See Perry, Gaylord Jackson

Spitlera, Joseph P., Jr. 1938?- [NOJ]
American jazz musician
* Spitlera, Pee Wee

Spitlera, Pee Wee
See Spitlera, Joseph P., Jr.

Spitteler, Carl 1845-1924 [WBD]
Swiss author
* Tandem, Felix

Spittin' Bill Doak
See Doak, William Leopold

Spitz, Eddie
See Osadchey, Edward P.

Spitz, Mark Andrew 1950- [HPPN]
American swimmer
* [The] King of Amateur Swimming
* [The] King of Sports

Spitzer, Louis 1853-1894 [BBD]
Hungarian musician
* Hegyesi, Louis

Spivak, Charlie 1905?-1982
American musician and bandleader
* [The] Sweetest Trumpet in the World

Spivey, Addie 1910-1943 [BWW]
American singer
* May, Hannah
* Sweet Peas[e]

Spivey, Elton Island 1900-1971 [BWW]
American singer
* Spivey, Za Zu
* [The] Za Zu Girl

Spivey, Thomas Sawyer 1856-1938
[DNA]
American author and manufacturer
* Reywas, Mot

Spivey, Victoria Regina [Vicky]
1906-1976 [BWW]
American singer
* Lucas, Jane
* [The] Queen
* [The] Queen of the Blues

Spivey, Za Zu
See Spivey, Elton Island

Splane, Elza K.
See Temary, Elza

[The] Splendid Splinter
See Rayl, Jim

[The] Splendid Splinter
See Williams, Theodore Samuel [Ted]

[The] Splendid Wayfarer
See Smith, Jedediah Strong

Spo-Dee-O-Dee
See Theard, Sam

Spofforth, Frederick Robert 1853-1926
[EC, HPPN, OCS, WBD]
Australian cricketer
* [The] Demon
* [The] Demon Bowler

Spognardi, Andrea Ettore 1908- [BE]
American baseball player
* Spognardi, Andy

Spognardi, Andy
See Spognardi, Andrea Ettore

[The] Spoiled Darling of Spanish Romanticism
See Zorrilla y Moral, Jose

[The] Spoiler
See Howard, Kevin

[The] Spoiler
See Risko, Johnny

[The] Spoilt Child of Fortune
See Massena, Andre

[A] Spoilt Marmoset
See Foscolo, Niccolo

[The] Spokesman for the Beat Generation
See Ferlinghetti, Lawrence [Monsanto]

[The] Spokesman for the Lost Generation
See Hemingway, Ernest

Sponagle, Barry 20th c. [RBE]
Canadian boxer
* Sponagle, Kid

Sponagle, Kid
See Sponagle, Barry

Spondanus
See De Sponde, Jean

Spondee
See Tyler, William Clark

Sponge, Mr.
See Herbert, Henry William

Spontini, Gasparo 1774-1851 [HPPN]
Italian composer
* [The] Napoleon of Opera

Spoo-De-Odee
See Thread, Sam

[The] Spoon
See Witherspoon, James [Jimmy]

Spoon Stealer
See Butler, Benjamin Franklin

Spooner, Alden Jeremiah 1810-? [IP]
American journalist
* Testy, Tim

Spooner, Ed 20th c. [CSH]
Bicycle racing pioneer
* Spooner, On The Spot

Spooner, Edward 19th c. [IP]
British clergyman and author
* [A] Clergyman

Spooner, John D. 1937- [CA]
American author
* Brutus

Spooner, Lysander 1808-1887 [HPPN]
American attorney
* [The] Father of the Three Cent Stamp

Spooner, On The Spot
See Spooner, Ed

Spooner, William Archibald 1844-1930
[HPPN]
British clergyman and educator
* [The] Father of Spoonerisms

Spoonhill
See Reaney, James Crerar

Spoopendyke
See Huntly, Stanley

Sporkin, Stan[ley] 1932- [HPPN]
American attorney
* [The] Columbo of Wall Street

Sporn, Philip 1897?-1978
Austrian-born American industrialist
* Public Utility, Mr.

Sporon, Benjamin G. 18th c. [HPPN]
British author
* Philokalus

[The] Sporting Parson
See Russell, John

[The] Sports Impostor
See Bremen, Barry

[The] Sportsman
See Crosby, Harry Lillis

[A] Sportsman and Naturalist
See Saint John, Charles William George

[The] Sportsman Ventriloquist
See Clark, Johnson

Sporus
See Hervey, John [Baron Hervey of Ickworth]

Sposa, Demi James 1918?- [DF 11-29-82]
American television personality
* [The] Human Test Pattern
* James, Dennis

Spot
See Potts, Arthur

Spot, Dick, the Conjuror
See Morris, Richard

Spot, Ryhen
See Post, Henry

[The] Spotlight Kid
See Van Vliet, Don

Spotswood, Alexander 1676-1740
[HPPN, SN]
British colonial governor
* Cain, Tubal
* [The] Tubal Cain of America

Spotswood, Dillon Jordan 20th c.
[WGT]
Author
* Nuverbis

Spotswood, John
See Stanard, John Dandridge Spotswood

Spotswood, John Boswel 1808-? [IP]
American clergyman and author
* [The] Pastor

Spoturno, Francesco Giuseppe 1874-1934
[WBD]
Corsican-born French industrialist and newspaper owner
* Coty, Francois

Sprackling, Sprack
See Sprackling, William E.

Sprackling, William E. 1890- [FB]
American football player
* Sprackling, Sprack

Spradley, A. J. 1853-? [HPPN]
American detective and law officer
* Spradley, John

Spradley, John
See Spradley, A. J.

Sprafka, Galloping
See Sprafka, Joseph

Sprafka, Joseph 20th c. [HPPN]
American football player
* Sprafka, Galloping

Sprague, Achsa W. 1828?-1862 [HPPN]
American medium
* [The] Preaching Woman

Sprague, Bud
See Sprague, Mortimer E.

Sprague, Carl T. 1895- [ECM]
American country-western performer
* [The] Original Singing Cowboy

Sprague, Carter
See Merwin, [W.] Sam[uel], Jr.

Sprague, Charles 1791-1876 [HPPN, IP, PA]
American poet
* [The] Banker Poet
* C. S.

Sprague, Claire S[acks] 1926- [CA]
American educator and author
* Sacks, Claire

Sprague, Frank Julian 1857-1934 [WBD]
American engineer and inventor
* [The] Father of Electric Traction

Sprague, Mortimer E. 1904- [FB]
American football player
* Sprague, Bud

Sprague, Thomas A.
See Fish, Hamilton

Sprague, W. D. [joint pseudonym with Sylvia Von Block]
See Von Block, Bela

Sprague, W. D. [joint pseudonym with Bela Von Block]
See Von Block, Sylvia

Sprague, William Buell 1795-1876 [HPPN]
American clergyman
* [A] Clergyman of New England

Sprake, Leslie 20th c. [WWL]
British author
* Middle Wallop

Sprat
See George V

Sprat, James
See Hunt, [James Henry] Leigh

Spratt, Henry Lee 1888- [BE]
American baseball player
* Spratt, Jack

Spratt, Jack
See Cobb, Jack

Spratt, Jack
See Spratt, Henry Lee

Sprecher, Karl
See Bloch, David

Sprecher, Muggsy
See Sprecher, Robert J. [Bob]

Sprecher, Robert J. [Bob] 1921- [EJ]
American jazz musician
* Sprecher, Muggsy

Sprecher, William Gunther 1924- [ASC]
German-born musician
* Gunther, William

Spreckels, Anthony 1950?-1977 [FIR]
Producer
* Spreckels, Bunker

Spreckels, Bunker
See Spreckels, Anthony

Spreckels, Claus 1828-1908 [WBD]
German-born sugar manufacturer
* [The] Sugar King

Spreull, John 1657-1722 [SN]
Religious dissenter
* Bass John

Spriel, Stephen
See Pilotin, Michael

Sprigel, Olivier
See Avice, Claude

Sprigg, C[hristopher] St. John 1907-1937 [EMD, LC, TC]
British author and poet
* Caudwell, Christopher

Spring, Clifford 20th c. [BBH, CSH]
Canadian lacrosse player
* Spring, Doughy

Spring, Doughy
See Spring, Clifford

Spring, Elizabeth [Thompson] 19th c. [IP]
American author
* Her Daughter

Spring, Gardiner 1785-? [HPPN]
American clergyman
* [A] Pastor

Spring, Gerald M[ax] 1897- [CA]
German-born American educator and author
* Bodwell, Richard

Spring, Gordon 20th c. [BBH, CSH]
Canadian lacrosse promoter
* Spring, Grumpy

Spring, Grumpy
See Spring, Gordon

Spring, Miss
See Stuart, Constance Cornell

Spring, Philip
See Dobson, E. Philip

Spring, Samuel 1746-1819 [IP]
American clergyman and author
* Philalethes
* Theophilus

Spring, Thomas ?-1795? [PI]
Irish poet
* T. S.

Spring, Tom
See Winter, Thomas

Springall, Charles 1925- [FC]
British entertainer
* Drake, Charlie

[The] Springer
See Louis [or Ludwig]

Springer, Axel, Jr. 1942?-1980
German photojournalist
* Simon, Sven

Springer, Barbara 1871-1937 [SC]
Hungarian-born actress
* DeBozoky, Barbara

Springer, Marilyn Harris 1931- [CA]
American author
* Harris, Marilyn

Springer, Rudolf
See Renner, Karl

Springfield
See Kelly, Maurice Anthony

Springfield, David
See Lewis, Roy

Springfield, Dusty
See O'Brien, Mary

[The] Springfield Rifle
See Raschi, Victor John Angelo

Springmeyer, Charles E., Jr. 1912- [BEW]
American actor, stage manager, director
* Durand, Charles

Springs, Elliott White 1896-1959 [HPPN]
American author, military aviator, business executive
* Gish, Joe

Springsteen, Bruce 1949- [NW 12-20-82, TI 2-3-86, WP 9-13-84]
American singer
* [The] Blue Collar Troubador
* [The] Boss

Sprinkel, Beryl 20th c. [NW 4-23-83]
American government official
* Beryl the Peril

Sprinz, Joseph Conrad [Joe] 1902- [BE]
American baseball player
* Sprinz, Mule

Sprinz, Mule
See Sprinz, Joseph Conrad [Joe]

Sproat, Ebenezer ?-1805 [HPPN]
American army officer and jurist
* [The] Big Buckeye

Sprogiani, Henrico 1904?-1953 [BI]
French clown
* Rhum

Sproston, John
See Scott, Peter Dale

Sprott, Albert 20th c. [HPPN]
American football player
* Sprott, Pesky

Sprott, Pesky
See Sprott, Albert

Sproul, Dorothy Noyes
See Noyes-Kane, Dorothy

Sproul, William Cameron 1870-1928 [HPPN]
American manufacturer and politician
* [The] Father of Good Roads

Sproule, Ruth
See Lynch, Ruth Sproule

Sproule, Zibra
See Trask, George F.

Sproull, Lefty
See Sproull, Ralph

Sproull, Ralph 1893-   [BB]
American basketball player
* Sproull, Lefty

Sprout, Mr.
See Whiteing, Richard

Spruggins, Richard Sucklethum
See Morley, Countess of

Spun Yarn
See Loomis, Alfred Fullerton

Spunkey, Simon
See Fessenden, Thomas Green

Spurgeon, Charles Haddon 1834-1892
[DEL]
British author and clergyman
* Ploughman, John

Spurin-Calleia, Joseph 1897-1975   [BEW,
FC, HCA]
Maltese-born actor
* Calleia, Joseph

[The] Spurious Governor
See Livingston, William

Spurr, Clinton
See Rowland, Donald Sydney

Spurzheim, Johann Kaspar 1776-1832
[NPS, SN]
German physician
* Dousterswivel

Spy
See Ward, [Sir] Leslie

[The] Spy Catcher
See Smith, George Gordon

Spy in Washington
See Davis, Matthew Livingston

[The] Spy of the Cumberland
See Cushman, Pauline

Spykman, E. C.
See Spykman, Elizabeth Choate

Spykman, Elizabeth Choate 1896-1943
[TCC]
American author
* Spykman, E. C.

[The] Spymaster
See Hugel, Max

Spyropolous, Frieda 19th c.   [HPPN]
Syrian exotic dancer
* Little Egypt

Spyrou, Aristoklis Mathew 1886-?   [BI]
Greek patriarch
* Athenagoras I

[The] Squab Poet
See Dryden, John

Squanto 1585-1622   [HPPN]
*American Indian who befriended Pilgrim
settlers*
* Dark Pilgrim
* Tisquantum

Squarcialupi, Antonio 1416-1480   [BBD]
Italian musician
* Antonio degli Organi

Squarcialupo, Ignazio 16th c.   [SN]
Italian clergyman
* Griffarosto

[A] Square
See Abbott, Edwin Abbott

Square Jaw Ramsey
See Ramsey, William Thrace [Bill]

[The] Square Scourge of Washington
See Anderson, Jack[son Northman]

Squat, Squire
See Pulteney, William [Earl of Bath]

[A] Squatter
See Jones, John Beauchamp

Squatter Sovereignty
See Calhoun, John Caldwell

[The] Squaw Sachem of Pocasset
See Wetamoo

[The] Squealer
See Bioff, Willie

[La] Squelette des Graces
See Guimard, [Marie] Madeleine

Squibb, [Dr.] Edward Robinson
1819-1900   [HPPN]
*American pharmacist and drug
manufacturer*
* [The] Father of Modern Pharmacy
* [The] Father of the Pure Food and
Drug Act

Squibob
See Derby, George Horatio

Squier, Emma Lindsay
See Bransby, Emma Lindsay Squier

Squier, Ephraim George 1821-?   [DEL,
PA]
British author
* Bard, Samuel A.

Squier, Lucita
See Williams, Lucita Squier

[The] Squint-Eyed
See Barbieri, Giovanni [or Gian]
Francesco

Squinting Jack
See Wilkes, John

Squintum, Doctor
See Irving, Edward

Squintum, Doctor
See Whitefield, George

Squintum, Senior
See Whitfield, [Rev.] George

[The] Squire
See Adams, Derek John

[The] Squire
See Clark, Johnson

Squire
See Coleman, John Winston, Jr.

[The] Squire
See Howe, Lyman

Squire, J. C.
See Squire, John Collings

Squire, John Collings 1884-1958   [LC,
NAA]
British author and journalist
* Affable Hawk
* Eagle, Solomon
* Squire, J. C.

Squire, Miriam F.
See Leslie, Miriam Florence Folline

[The] Squire of Hyde Park
See Roosevelt, Franklin Delano

[The] Squire of Kennett Square
See Pennock, Herb[ert Jefferis]

[The] Squire of Sandringham
See Edward VII

[The] Squire of Squawg Hollow
See Reeve, Edward H. [Ted]

Squire, Ronald
See Squirl, Ronald

Squire Willy
See Buckley, William Frank, Jr. [Bill]

Squires, Eric
See Ball, Sylvia Patricia

Squires, Frederick 20th c.   [CAA]
American author
* Thumtack, Tom

Squires, Patricia
See Ball, Sylvia Patricia

Squires, Phil
See Barker, S[quire] Omar

Squires, Theodore 1907-1942   [BS]
American magician
* Anneman the Enigma
* Annemann, Theodore
* [The] Father of Modern Mental
Magic

Squirl, Ronald 1886-1958   [FC]
British actor
* Squire, Ronald

Squirrell, L. R.
See Squirrell, Leonard Russell

Squirrell, Leonard Russell 1893-   [ART]
British painter and etcher
* Squirrell, L. R.

Sreenivasapuram, Sesha Charlu 1921-
[IAW]
Indian author and poet
* Subhasree

Sri Aurobindo
See Ghose, Aurobindo

Sri-Rajputra
See Bera, Sudhir

Sriblerus, Martinus
See Arbuthnot, John

Srinivasan, S. 1900- [DFM]
Indian director and producer
* Vasan, S. S.

Srivastava, Dhanpat Rai 1881-1936 [BI]
Indian author
* Premchand, Munschi

Srzentich, Mirko 1934- [CCL]
Canadian poet
* Strong, Mike

Sse-ma-Thsian 1st c. [HN]
Chinese historian
* [The] Herodotus of China

Ssu-Ma, Ch'ien 2nd c. BC [HPPN]
Chinese historian
* [The] Grand Historian of China

Stabback, [Rev.] Thomas 1793-1850
[HPPN]
British clergyman
* [A] Minister

Stabile, Jack 20th c. [BLB]
American underworld figure
* Stabile, Stick 'em Up

Stabile, Stick 'em Up
See Stabile, Jack

Stabile, Stickum
See Stableford, Brian M[ichael]

Stabile, Theresa Maria 1919- [ASC,
PMJ]
American singer and composer
* Dawn, Dolly

Stabili, Francesco Degli 1257?-1327
[HPPN]
Italian poet and philosopher
* D'Ascoli, Cecco

Stableford, Brian M[ichael] 1948- [ESF,
HPPN]
British author and critic
* Craig, Brian [joint pseudonym with
Craig M. Mackintosh]
* Stabile, Stickum

Stabler, Jamie Latham ?-1882 [DNA,
PA]
American author
* Woodville, Jennie

Stabler, Ken 20th c.
American football player
* Stabler, Snake

Stabler, Snake
See Stabler, Ken

Staccato
See Kalisch, A.

Stacek, Albert John 1900- [BE]
American baseball player
* Stokes, Al[bert John]

Stacey, Paul
See Savill, Roy

Stacher, Doc
See Stacher, Joseph

Stacher, Joseph 1902- [BLB, MM]
Polish-born American underworld figure
* Goldman, Harry
* Harris, Doc
* Harris, J. P.
* Kent, George
* Rose, Morris
* Rosen, Doc
* Rosen, Joseph
* Stacher, Doc
* Stein, Joe J.
* Weiner, Doc

Stachys, Dimitris
See Constantelos, Demetrios J.

Stack, Andy
See Rule, Ann

Stack, Baron
See Ratazzi, Mme.

Stack, Frank H[untington] 1937- [CA]
American artist
* Sturgeon, Foolbert

Stack, Nicolete Meredith 1896- [CA]
American author
* Hill, Elleen
* Kenny, Kathryn [house pseudonym]
* Meredith, Nicolete

Stack, Philip 1900?-1948 [BI]
American poet
* Wahn, Don

Stack, Robert
See Modini, Robert

Stackhouse, [Rev.] Alfred Long
1811-1876 [HPPN]
British clergyman
* [The] Secretary of the Society

Stackhouse, Lefty
See Stackhouse, Wilburn Artist

Stackhouse, Mary Agnes 1878-1934
[CAT]
American author and poet
* Mary Angelita, [Sister]

Stackhouse, Ruby 20th c. [IBW]
American singer
* Andrews, Ruby

Stackhouse, Wilburn Artist 1911-1973
[GF]
American golfer
* Stackhouse, Lefty

Stacton, David [Derek] 1925-1968 [CA]
American author
* Boyd, Carse
* Clifton, Bud
* Dereksen, David

Stacy, Brian
See Browder, Bill

Stacy, Bruce
See Elliott, Bruce [Walter Gardner
Lively Stacy]

Stacy, Joel
See Dodge, Mary Elizabeth Mapes

Stacy, Terry
See Lea, Terrea

Stacy, Walter
See Elliott, Bruce [Walter Gardner
Lively Stacy]

Stadelman, S. L.
See Stadelman, Sara Lee

Stadelman, Sara Lee 1917- [CA]
American playwright and poet
* Harris, Sara Lee
* Stadelman, S. L.

Stael, Anne Louise Germaine de
1766-1817 [SN]
French author
* Corinne
* [An] Orestes of Exile

Staerback, Carl Georg 1828-? [HPPN]
Swedish author and historian
* Georg

[A] Staff Officer
See Newhall, [Lieut. Colonel] Frederick
C.

[A] Staff Officer
See Wilson, Thomas Fourness

[A] Staff Surgeon
See Henry, Walter

Stafford, Anne
See Pedler, Anne I. Stafford

Stafford, Caroline
See Watjen, Carolyn L. T.

Stafford, General
See Stafford, James Joseph

Stafford, Hanley
See Austin, John

Stafford, Harrison 20th c. [BBH]
American football player
* Stafford, Harry

Stafford, Harry
See Stafford, Harrison

Stafford, Harry Frank ?-1912 [HPPN]
American actor and author
* Stafford, Jim

Stafford, Heinie
See Stafford, Henry Alexander

Stafford, Henry Alexander 1891- [BE]
American baseball player
* Stafford, Heinie

Stafford, James Joseph 1868-1923 [BE]
American baseball player
* Stafford, General

Stafford, Jim
See Stafford, Harry Frank

Stafford, Jo 1920-
American singer
* Edwards, Darlene

Stafford, Linda 1943- [CA]
American author
* Crying Wind
* Lovequist, Gwendlelynn

Stafford, Muriel
See Sauer, Muriel Stafford

Stafford, Peter
See Tabori, Paul

Stafford, Tammy 1972- [HPPN]
American weight lifter
* [The] All American Girl
* Mighty Mite
* Supergirl

Stafford, William
See Tibbetts, William Nelson

Stafford-Northcote, Iris 1909- [THR]
Irish-born actress and singer
* Ashley, Iris

Staffordshire Knot
See Wrottesley, Arthur John Francis

[The] Stage Leviathan
See Quin, James

[The] Stage-Struck Hero
See Liston, Harry

[The] Stagecoach King
See Holladay, Benjamin

[The] Stage's Most Convincing Actor
See Placide, Henry

Stagg, Amos Alonzo 1862-1965 [BB, BBH]
American football and basketball coach
* Football's Old Man River
* [The] Grand Old Man of Football
* [The] Grand Old Man of the Midway
* Stagg, Lonnie
* [The] Unreconstructed Amateur

Stagg, J. R. 20th c. [MBF]
British author
* Barnet, John
* Harte, Oliver

Stagg, James 20th c. [MBF]
British author and journalist
* Johns, Gilbert
* Reid, Desmond [house pseudonym]

Stagg, James
See Pendower, Jacques

Stagg, John 19th c. [HPPN]
British poet
* [The] Blind Poet of Cumberland

Stagg, Lonnie
See Stagg, Amos Alonzo

Stagge, Jonathan [joint pseudonym with Hugh Callingham Wheeler]
See Webb, Richard Wilson

Stagge, Jonathan [joint pseudonym with Richard Wilson Webb]
See Wheeler, Hugh Callingham

[The] Stagirite
See Aristotle

Staglich, Oswalda 1899-1948 [SC]
German actress
* [The] German Mary Pickford
* Oswalda, Ossi

Stahan, Butch
See Stahan, Frank Ralph

Stahan, Frank Ralph 1915- [CEI]
Canadian-born hockey player
* Stahan, Butch

Stahl, Charles 1921- [HPPN]
Polish-American precious metal market expert
* [The] Gray Eminence
* [The] Metal Market Man

Stahl, Charles Sylvester 1873-1907 [AS, DGS, PB]
American baseball player
* Stahl, Chick

Stahl, Chick
See Stahl, Charles Sylvester

Stahl, Eva 1949-
Swedish nurse who served in Palestinian refugee camp, 1974-76
* Samira [Beautiful Flower]

Stahl, Fred Alan 1944- [CA]
American computer scientist and writer
* Feur, D. Cy

Stahl, Garland 1879-1922 [AS, BE, PB]
American baseball player and manager
* Stahl, Jake

Stahl, Heinrich
See Temme, Jodocus Donatus Hubertus

Stahl, Jake
See Stahl, Garland

Stahl, Jesse 20th c. [IBW]
American rodeo performer
* Stahl, Peerless

Stahl, Karl
See Goedeke, Karl

Stahl, Karl
See Goedke, Karl

Stahl, Le Roy 1908- [CAP]
American author
* Sheldon, George E.
* Wood, Kirk

Stahl, P. J.
See Hetzel, Pierre Jules

Stahl, Peerless
See Stahl, Jesse

Stahl, Pierre Jules
See Hetzel, Pierre Jules

Stahl-Nachbaur, Ernest
See Guggenheimer, Ernest

Stahr, Arthur
See Voight, Valeska

Stahr, Mme. Adolf W. T. [PA]
German author
* Lewald, Fanny

Staiger, Elizabeth Anne 1928- [BEW]
American actress and singer
* Staiger, Libi

Staiger, Libi
See Staiger, Elizabeth Anne

Stainback, George Tucker 1910- [BE, PB]
American baseball player
* Stainback, Tuck

Stainback, Macklin 1911- [CA]
American attorney and author
* Fleming, Macklin

Stainback, Tuck
See Stainback, George Tucker

Stainer, Leslie Howard 1893-1943 [BDF, BEW, WEF]
British actor, director, playwright
* Howard, Leslie

Staines, Trevor
See Brunner, John [Kilian Houston]

Stainforth, Frank [PA]
Author
* Forsith, Nat

Staing
See Vergoz, M.

Stainless Stephen
See Baynes, Arthur Clifford

Stainton, J. [NPS]
Journalist
* Looker-On

Stairs, Gordon
See Austin, Mary [Hunter]

Stait, Virginia
See Russell, Winifred Brent

Stakman, Elvin C. 1886?-1979
American plant pathologist
* Stakman, Stak

Stakman, Stak
See Stakman, Elvin C.

Stalberg, Carolina Vilhelmina 1803-1872 [HPPN]
Swedish author and poet
* Vilhelmina

Stalbrydge, Henry
See Bale, John

Stalcup, Sparky
See Stalcup, Wilbur

Stalcup, Wilbur 1910-1972 [BB]
American basketball coach
* Stalcup, Sparky

Staley, Gale
See Staley, George Gaylord

Staley, George Gaylord 1899- [BE]
American baseball player
* Staley, Gale

Staley, Harry
See Staley, Henry E.

Staley, Henry E. 1866-1910 [AS]
American baseball player
* Staley, Harry

Stalin, Joseph
See Dzhugashvili, Iosif Vissarionovich

[The] Stalking Library
See Mitchell, Stephen Mix

Stallard, Evan T. 1937- [PB]
American baseball player
* Stallard, Tracy

Stallard, Tracy
See Stallard, Evan T.

Stallcup, Red
See Stallcup, Thomas Virgil

Stallcup, Thomas Virgil 1922- [BE]
American baseball player
* Stallcup, Red

Staller, George Walborn 1916- [BE]
American baseball player
* Staller, Stopper

Staller, Stopper
See Staller, George Walborn

Stallings, Big Chief
See Stallings, George Tweedy

Stallings, George Tweedy 1867-1929
[BE, BTB]
American baseball player and manager
* [The] Miracle Man
* Stallings, Big Chief

Stallings, Margaret Elizabeth 1917-1955
[HPPN]
American actress
* Stallings, Meg

Stallings, Mary
See Evans, Mary Lorraine Stallings

Stallings, Meg
See Stallings, Margaret Elizabeth

Stallone, Sly
See Stallone, Sylvester [Enzio]

Stallone, Sylvester [Enzio] 1946- [BI,
CA]
American actor, director, screenwriter
* Moonblood, Q.
* Stallone, Sly

Stallworth, Bud
See Stallworth, Isaac

Stallworth, Dave 1941- [BB]
American basketball player
* [The] Rave

Stallworth, Isaac 1950- [BB]
American basketball player
* Stallworth, Bud

Stamatopoulos, Stratis 1892- [EWL]
Greek author
* Myrivilis, Stratis

Stambler, Helen
See Latner, Helen [Stambler]

Stamma of Aleppo
See Stamma, Philip

Stamma, Philip 18th c.
Syrian chess player
* Stamma of Aleppo

Stammel, Heinz-Josef 1926- [IAW]
German author
* Hagen, Christopher
* Lockhart, T. C.

[The] Stammerer
See Louis II

[The] Stammerer
See Michael II

[The] Stammerer
See Notger [or Notker]

Stamp, Roger 1913- [AW]
Scottish author
* Mingston, R. Gresham

Stampede
See Kelly, Jonathan Falconbridge

Stamper, Alex
See Kent, Arthur [William Charles]

Stamper, Pete
See Stamper, Wallace Logan

Stamper, Wallace Logan 1930- [CWG,
DAM]
American country-western performer
* Stamper, Pete

Stamps, Hulan 20th c. [OBW]
American baseball player
* Stamps, Lefty

Stamps, Lefty
See Stamps, Hulan

Stan the Man
See Musial, Stanislaus

Stan the Man
See Turner, Spurgeon, Jr.

Stanard, John Dandridge Spotswood
1905- [WWL]
American author and poet
* Spotswood, John

Stanco, Italo
See Moffa, Ettore

Standaert
See Bloemen, Pieter van

[The] Standard Bearer
See Maginn, William

[The] Standard Oil King
See Rockefeller, John Davison

Standen, Antony 16th c. [EE]
British intelligence agent
* Pellegrini, Pompeo

Stander, Andre Charles 1948?-1984 [TI
2-27-84]
South African bank robber
* Harris, Peter

Standfast, Silas
See Hillard, George Stillman

Standing, Dorothy 1909- [F2, FC,
HPPN]
British actress
* Hammond, Dorothy
* Hammond, Kay

Standing, John
See Leon, John

Standish, Buck
See Paine, Lauran [Bosworth]

Standish, Burt
See Cook, William Wallace

Standish, Burt L.
See Patten, William George

Standish, Burt L.
See Whitson, John Harvey

Standish, J. O.
See Horler, Sydney

Standish, John ?-1556 [SN]
Opposed translation of Bible into English
* Inkpot, Doctor

Standish, Miles 1584?-1656 [HPPN, SN]
American colonist
* [The] Hero of New England
* [The] Little Indian Fighter
* [The] Puritan Captain

Standish, Richard
See Goyne, Richard

Standish, Robert
See Gerahty, Digby George

Standish, Winn
See Sawyer, Walter Leon

Stanek, Al 1943- [BE]
American baseball player
* Stanek, Lefty

Stanek, Lefty
See Stanek, Al

Stanelli
See De Groot, Edward Stanley

Stanes, Muriel
See Stevens, Muriel Phyllis

Stanev, Emilian
See Stanev, Nikola [Stoyanov]

Stanev, Nikola [Stoyanov] 1907-1979
[CA]
Bulgarian author
* Stanev, Emilian

Stanfel, Rich 20th c. [SI 11-28-83]
American basketball player
* Stanfel, Standstill

Stanfel, Standstill
See Stanfel, Rich

Stanfield, Agnes
See McElhinney, Jane

Stanford, Jack 1900- [BMH]
British comic dancer
* [The] Dancing Fool

Stanford, John Keith 1892- [CA]
British author
* Issachar

Stanford, R. A. S. 1892-1971 [SC]
Actor
* Grahame, Bert

Stanford, Sally
See Busby, Mabel Janice

Stang, Judit 1921-1977 [CA]
Hungarian-born author and artist
* Varga, Judy

Stange Cop, Dr.
See Honey, Joel B.

Stangeland, Katharina Marie [Bech-Brondum] Michaelis 1872-1950 [EWL, TC]
Danish author
* Michaelis, Karin

Stanhope, Ada
See Bothner, Mrs. A.

Stanhope, Adeline
See Wheatcroft, Mrs. Nelson

Stanhope, Charles [Third Earl of Stanhope] 1753-1816 [NPS]
British politician and scientist
* Minority of One

Stanhope, Charles 1780-1851 [NPS]
Fourth Earl of Harrington
* Snuff

Stanhope, Douglas
See Duff, Douglas Valder

Stanhope, Eric
See Hamilton, Charles Harold St. John

Stanhope, George 1660-1728 [HPPN]
British clergyman
* [The] Prolocutor

Stanhope, Hester Lucy 1770-1839 [HN]
British eccentric
* Palmyra's Queen
* Queen of Palmyra
* Queen of the Desert

Stanhope, James 1673-1721 [HPPN]
British statesman and army officer
* Polemius

Stanhope, Lavinia
See Schlein, Miriam

Stanhope, Philip Dormer 1694-1773
[DEA, DEP, HPPN, NPS, SN, SN, WBD]
British statesman and author
* [A] Broad Bottom
* Broadbottom, Geffery
* Chester, [Sir] John
* Chesterfield, Fourth Earl of
* [An] English Gentleman
* FitzAdam, Adam
* [The] La Rochefoucauld of England
* [The] Maecenas and Petronius of His Age
* Our English Rochefoucault
* [The] Prince of Wits
* [A] Tea Table Scoundrel

Stanhope, William [Second Earl of Harrington] 1719-1779 [NPS]
British army officer and politician
* Shambles, Peter

Stanhouse, Don[ald Joseph] 1951-
American baseball player
* Stanhouse, Full Pack

Stanhouse, Full Pack
See Stanhouse, Don[ald Joseph]

Staniak, Lucian 1941?- [DI]
Polish murderer
* [The] Red Spider

Stanier, Maida Euphemia Kerr 1909-
[CA]
Scottish-born author, poet, playwright
* Culex

Staniforth, [Dr.] John William
1863-1927 [MBF]
British author
* Scott, Maxwell

Stanikowski, Stephan 1913-
Polish soccer player
* Stanis, Stephan

Stanis, Ber Nadette
See Stanislaus, Bernadette

Stanis, Stephan
See Stanikowski, Stephan

Stanish, Rudolph 1913- [HPPN]
American chef and banquet manager
* [The] Maestro of the Omelet
* Rudy the Omelet Man

Stanislaus, [Sister]
See Malone, Katie

Stanislaus, Bernadette 1953- [IBW]
American actress, fashion model, dancer
* Stanis, Ber Nadette

Stanislaus, Edward
See Parker, Dom Anselm

Stanislavsky, Konstantin Sergeivitch
See Alexeyev, Konstantin Sergeivitch

Stanislaw, Stanley
See Sielanski, Stanley

Stankiewicz, Michal
See Bystrzycki, Przemyslaw

Stankiewicz, Mike
See Stankiewicz, Myron

Stankiewicz, Myron 1935- [CEI]
Canadian-born hockey player
* Stankiewicz, Mike

Stanko, Steve 1918?- [BI]
American physical culturist
* Universe, Mr.

Stankunis, Lisa 20th c. [HPPN]
American wrestler
* [The] Butterfly

Stanky, Edward Raymond 1916- [BE, PB]
American baseball player and manager
* [The] Brat
* Stanky, Muggsy

Stanky, Muggsy
See Stanky, Edward Raymond

Stanlaws, Penrhyn
See Adamson, Penrhyn Stanley

Stanley
See Ormsby, John S.

Stanley, Alixe Russell
See Grant, Maude Margaret

Stanley, Alma Stuart
See De Garmo, Mrs. Charles

Stanley, Augustus Owsley, III 1935-
[HPPN, NAD]
American chemist
* Hippieland's Court Chemist
* [The] King of Acid
* [The] King of Psychopharmacology
* [The] L. S. D. King
* L. S. D., Mr.
* [The] L. S. D. Tycoon
* Owsley

Stanley, Barney
See Stanley, Russell

Stanley, Bennett
See Hough, Stanley Bennett

Stanley, Bigfoot
See Stanley, Robert William

Stanley, Buck
See Stanley, John Leonard

Stanley, Chuck
See Strong, Charles Stanley

Stanley, Dave
See Dachs, David

Stanley, Dean 1815-1881 [PA]
Author
* Anglicanus

Stanley, Diane 1943- [SAT]
American author and illustrator
* Zuromskis, Diane

Stanley, Digger
See Stanley, George

Stanley, Edward George Geoffrey Smith
1799-1869 [DEL, DNNF, FFF, HPPN]
British statesman and author
* Derby, 14th Earl of
* [The] Hotspur of Debate
* [The] Rupert of Debate
* Stanley, Scorpion

Stanley, Edward Henry Smith [15th Earl of Derby] 1826-1893 [HPPN]
British statesman
* [A] Living Statesman

Stanley, Eveleen
See Murphy, Mrs. H.

Stanley, Fay Grissom [Shulman] 1925-
[CA]
American author
* Fay, Stanley

Stanley, Ferdinando ?-1594 [SN]
Fifth Earl of Derby
* Amyntas?

Stanley, Francis
See Crocchiola, Francis Stanley

Stanley, Frank C. 1868-1910 [HPPN]
American singer
* Grinstead, William Stanley

Stanley, Frank C.
See Grinstead, William Stanley

Stanley, George 1883- [BX]
British boxer
* Stanley, Digger

Stanley, [Sir] Henry Morton
See Rowlands, John

Stanley, James 1607-1651 [WBD]
Seventh Earl of Derby
* [The] Martyr Earl

Stanley, John Leonard 1889-1940 [BE]
American baseball player
* Stanley, Buck

Stanley, John Wesley 1903- [MK]
American baseball player
* Stanley, Neck

Stanley, Kim
See Reid, Patricia Kimberly

Stanley, Marge
See Weinbaum, Stanley G[rauman]

Stanley, Marie
See West, Lillie

Stanley, Mickey
See Stanley, Mitchell Jack

Stanley, Milton O. 1940- [CM]
American radio program director
* Bailey, Bill

Stanley, Mitchell Jack 1942- [PB, SMG, WWB]
American baseball player
* Stanley, Mickey

Stanley, Neck
See Stanley, John Wesley

Stanley, Nick
See Stanley, Ralph

Stanley, Nora Kathleen Begbie Strange 1885?- [AW, CAP]
British author
* Strange, Nora K.

Stanley, Olin
See Honeywell, E. L.

Stanley, Paul
See Eisen, Stanley

Stanley, Peter E.
See Pierotti, Piero

Stanley, Phil
See Ind, Allison

Stanley, Phyllis
See Knapman, Phyllis

Stanley, Ralph 1914-1972 [SC]
American actor
* Stanley, Nick

Stanley, Reginald Fitz-Roy
See Cowtan, Robert

Stanley, Richard
See Morner, Stanley

Stanley, Robert
See Hamilton, Charles Harold St. John

Stanley, Robert William 1954-
American baseball player
* Stanley, Bigfoot

Stanley, Russell 1893-1971 [FHE, HK]
Canadian-born hockey player
* Stanley, Barney

Stanley, Scorpion
See Stanley, Edward George Geoffrey Smith

Stanley, T. Lloyd
See Smith, Richard Morris

Stanley, Warwick
See Hilton, John Buxton

Stanley, William 1647-1731 [HPPN]
British clergyman
* [A] Church of England Man
* Stentor

Stanley-Brown, Mary Garfield 1867-1947
Daughter of American president, James Garfield
* Stanley-Brown, Molly

Stanley-Brown, Molly
See Stanley-Brown, Mary Garfield

Stanli, Sue
See Meilach, Dona Z[weigoron]

Stannard, Henrietta Eliza Vaughan 1856-1911 [HPPN]
British author
* Whyte, Violet
* Winter, John Strange

Stannard, Lane
See Taurasi, James V., Sr.

Stannard, Russell 20th c. [MBF]
British author
* Mallinson, Russell

Stannard, William John ?-1880 [HPPN]
British author
* Sandars, Harry

Stannus, Austin
See Greaves, Clotilda

Stannus, Edris 1898- [THR]
Irish-born dancer
* De Valois, [Dame] Ninette

Stannus, [James] Gordon [Dawson] 1902- [CA]
British author
* Anthony, Gordon
* Jason

Stansberger, Richard 1950- [CA]
American poet and playwright
* Grant, Venzo

Stansbury, Alec
See Higgs, Alec Stansbury

Stansbury, Clayton Cresvell 1932- [BA]
American educator
* Stansbury, Czech

Stansbury, Czech
See Stansbury, Clayton Cresvell

Stansbury-Millett, Nigel ?-1946
Author
* Chandos, Dane [joint pseudonym with Peter Lilley]

Stansfeld, Anthony 20th c. [CC, WW]
Author
* Buckingham, Bruce [joint pseudonym with Peter Lilley]
* Chandos, Dane [joint pseudonym with Peter Lilley]

Stansfield, Grace 1898-1979 [CED, FC, HPPN]
British singer and comedienne
* Everybody's Gracie
* Fields, Gracie
* Our Gracie
* Our Gracie of the North
* [The] Queen of the British Box Office

Stansfield, Richard Habberton 1921- [CA]
British author
* Wainwright, David

Stansfield, Thomas 1908- [BMH]
British comedian
* Fields, Tommy
* London's Lancashire Comedian

Stanstead, John
See Groom, Arthur William

Stanton, Baby Bull
See Stanton, Leroy Bobby

Stanton, Borden?
See Wilding, Philip

Stanton, Buck
See Stanton, George Washington

Stanton, C. [PA]
Author
* C. S.

Stanton, Chuck
See Sellers, Connie Leslie, Jr.

Stanton, Coralie
See Hosken, Alice Cecil Seymour

Stanton, Dorothy
See Kaumeyer, Dorothy

Stanton, Edward
See Huntington, Edward Stanton

Stanton, Edwin McMasters 1814-1869 [HPPN]
American attorney and politician
* [The] Autocrat of Rebellion, Emancipation and Reconstruction

Stanton, Evan
See Hughes, [Rev.] Thomas Patrick

Stanton, Frank Lebby 1857-1927
[HPPN, WBD]
American journalist and poet
* [The] Poet Laureate of Georgia
* [The] Riley of the South

Stanton, George Washington 1906- [BE]
American baseball player
* Stanton, Buck

Stanton, John 1826-1871 [PA]
Author
* O'Lanus, Corry

Stanton, John
See Wallis, George C.

Stanton, Lee
See Stanton, Leroy Bobby

Stanton, Leroy Bobby 1946- [BE, PB]
American baseball player
* Stanton, Baby Bull
* Stanton, Lee

Stanton, Marjorie
See Phillips, Horace

Stanton, Paul
See Beaty, [Arthur] David

Stanton, Vance
See Avallone, Michael [Angelo], Jr.

Stanton, William
See Hope, William Edward Stanton

Stanwood, Brooks [joint pseudonym
with Susan Stanwood Kaminsky]
See Kaminsky, Howard

Stanwood, Brooks [joint pseudonym
with Howard Kaminsky]
See Kaminsky, Susan Stanwood

Stanwyck, Barbara
See Stevens, Ruby

Staples, Boo
See Staples, Cleotha

Staples, Bunnie
See Staples, Yvonne

Staples, Cleotha 1934- [IBW]
American singer
* Staples, Boo
* Staples, Roberta

Staples, Marjory Charlotte 20th c.
[AW]
New Zealand author
* Redwood, Rosaline

Staples, Pop
See Staples, Roebuck

Staples, Reginald Thomas 1911- [CA]
British author
* Bridges, Howard
* Sinclair, James
* Stevens, Robert Tyler

Staples, Roberta
See Staples, Cleotha

Staples, Roebuck   [IBW, RO2, SSS]
American singer
* Staples, Pop

Staples, Yvonne 1938- [IBW]
American singer
* Staples, Bunnie

Stapleton, D. [joint pseudonym with
Douglas Stapleton]
See Stapleton, Dorothy

Stapleton, D. [joint pseudonym with
Dorothy Stapleton]
See Stapleton, Douglas

Stapleton, Dorothy 20th c. [WW]
Author
* Stapleton, D. [joint pseudonym with
Douglas Stapleton]

Stapleton, Douglas 20th c. [WW]
Author
* Stapleton, D. [joint pseudonym with
Dorothy Stapleton]

Stapleton, Jean
See Murray, Jeanne

Stapleton, Kitty
See Bernard, Kitty

Stapleton, Maurice
See Purcell, J. S.

Stapleton, P. L. 1769-1829
French author
* Hus, Auguste

Stapleton, Pat[rick James] 1940- [FHE]
Canadian-born hockey player
* Stapleton, Whitey

Stapleton, Vivian S. 1921?- [BEW, EMT,
ITA]
American actress and singer
* Blaine, Vivian

Stapleton, Whitey
See Stapleton, Pat[rick James]

Stapleton, Zoe Margaret 20th c. [THR]
South African-born actress and dancer
* Gail, Zoe

Stapley, Richard
See Wyler, Richard

Stapulensis
See Lefevre d'Etaples, Jacques

**[The] Star and Luminary of Law and
Latern of Equity**
See Bartoli [or Bartolus]

Star, Angel
See Quigley, Joan

Star, Ely
See Jacob, Eugene

Star, Jean
See Lubanski, Jules Clement Ladislas

[The] Star Maker
See Edwards, Simon

[The] Star Maker
See Griffith, David [Lewelyn] Wark

Star Man's Padre
See Patrick, Johnstone G[illespie]

[The] Star of Africa
See Marseille, Hans Joachim

[The] Star of the East
See Aaron, Barney

[The] Star of the North
See Gustavus II

[The] Star of the Stuart Line
See James IV

Starbird, Kaye 1916- [CA, SAT]
American author
* Jennison, C. S.

Starbuck, Alicia Jo 1951-
American figure skater
* Number 12, Mrs.
* Starbuck, Jo Jo

Starbuck, Jo Jo
See Starbuck, Alicia Jo

Starbuck, Roger
See Comstock, Augustus

Starch Johnny
See Crowne, John

Starcross, Roger
See Pope, Charles Henry

[The] Stardust Kid
See Jones, David Robert Hayward

Stardust, Ziggy
See Jones, David Robert Hayward

Stares, John Edward Spencer 1947-
[IAW]
British author
* Rowe, Stephen
* Spencer, Edward

Starey, Alfred B.   [FFF]
Writer
* Ryse, Sherwood

Stargell, Papa
See Stargell, Wilver Dornell

Stargell, Pops
See Stargell, Wilver Dornell

Stargell, Willie
See Stargell, Wilver Dornell

Stargell, Wilver Dornell 1941- [BE,
HPPN, IPA, SMG]
American baseball player
* Gentle Ben
* Stargell, Papa
* Stargell, Pops
* Stargell, Willie

Starhawk
See Simos, Miriam

Staring, Adolph 1890- [HPPN]
Dutch art historian and author
* A. S.

Stark, Albert M. 1897- [EJS]
American basketball coach
* Stark, Dolly

Stark, Claude Alan 1935- [CA]
French-born American author
* Mwanga

Stark, Dolly
See Stark, Albert M.

Stark, Dolly
See Stark, Monroe Randolph

Stark, Elizabeth [Page] 1737-1814 [BI, HPPN]
American heroine
* Stark, Molly

Stark, Fortney H.
American politician
* Stark, Pete

Stark, James
See Goldston, Robert Conroy

Stark, John 1728-1822 [HPPN]
American army officer
* [The] Leonidas of America

Stark, John
See Godwin, John

Stark, Jonathan
See Marshall, H. P.

Stark, Joshua
See Olsen, Theodore Victor

Stark, Kathleen 1956?- [TI 8-27-84, WP 10-8-82]
American actress
* Cambridge, Mrs.
* Stark, Koo

Stark, Koo
See Stark, Kathleen

Stark, Lloyd Crow 1886-? [HPPN]
American politician
* Stark, Molly

Stark, Michael
See Rosenblum, Lawrence

Stark, Molly
See Stark, Elizabeth [Page]

Stark, Molly
See Stark, Lloyd Crow

Stark, Monroe Randolph 1885-1924 [BE]
American baseball player
* Stark, Dolly

Stark, Nancy [BI]
American author
* Steele, Addison

Stark, Pesach 1905- [JL]
Polish author
* Stryjkowski, Juljan

Stark, Pete
See Stark, Fortney H.

Stark, Phil
See Stork, Philipp

Stark, Ray 20th c.
American producer
* [The] Rabbit

Stark, [Delbert] Raymond 1919- [CA, WW]
American author and poet
* Norwood, John

Stark, Richard
See Onorato, Glauco

Stark, Richard
See Westlake, Donald E[dwin]

Starkad
See Holland, Syver Sigurdson

Starke, Henderson
See Neville, Kris [Ottman]

Starkey, Digbey Pilot 1806-1880 [PA, PI]
Irish poet and playwright
* Advena
* Menenius
* Theoria

Starkey, Geoffrey 15th c. [SN]
British author and clergyman
* [The] Grammarian

Starkey, James Sullivan 1879-1958 [EWL, LC, TC]
Irish poet
* O'Sullivan, Seumas

Starkey, Richard 1940- [BBD, IPA, OCF]
British musician and songwriter
* R. S.
* Richie
* Shears, Billy
* Snare, Richie
* Starr, Ringo

Starks, Kathryn 1922- [EJ, IPA]
American singer
* Starr, Kay

Starks, Lefty
See Starks, Otis

Starks, Otis 20th c. [OBW]
American baseball player
* Starks, Lefty

Starkweather, Charles 1940-1959 [DI]
American murderer
* Starkweather, Little Red

Starkweather, Little Red
See Starkweather, Charles

Starlight [Secret Service code name]
See Nixon, Thelma Catherine Patricia Ryan

Starling, John Crawford 1916- [BA]
American physician
* Starling, Ned

Starling, Marlon 20th c.
American boxer
* [The] Magic Man

Starling, Ned
See Starling, John Crawford

Starling, Thomas
See Hayton, Richard Neil

Starnagel, George Henry
See Steurnagel, George Henry

Starnes, Daniel [PA]
Author
* Mayfield, Frank

Starnes, Ebenezer ?-1870? [DNA]
American author
* Jones, [Dr.] Pleasant

Starobin, Mordecai 1902-1942 [HPPN]
American football player and coach
* Starobin, Mort

Starobin, Mort
See Starobin, Mordecai

Starowieyski, Franciszek 1930- [GA]
Polish graphic artist
* Byk, Jan

Starr
See Sikes, William Wirt

Starr, Angel
See Starr, Henry

Starr, Bart
See Starr, Bryan Bartlett

Starr, [Myra] Belle [Shirley] 1848-1889 [BLB, HPPN]
American outlaw
* [The] Bandit Queen
* [The] Female Jesse James
* [The] Outlaw Queen
* [The] Queen of the Outlaws

Starr, Blaze
See Fleming, Sissie

Starr, Bryan Bartlett 1934- [BI, FB, SMG]
American football player and coach
* Quarterback, Mr.
* Starr, Bart

Starr, Cecile 1921- [CA]
American filmmaker and editor
* Boyajian, Cecile

Starr, Chick
See Starr, William

Starr, Edwin
See Hatcher, Charles

Starr, Franklin 1915?-1972 [HPPN]
American radio announcer
* Starr, Lonny

Starr, Frederick 1858-1933 [HPPN]
American anthropologist and educator
* [The] Lone Star

Starr, George 20th c. [EE]
Intelligence agent
* [The] Patron

Starr, Handsome Johnny
See Starr, John

Starr, Henry 1873-1921 [CEC, EWG, HPPN]
American gunfighter
* [The] Bearcat
* [The] First Automobile Bandit
* Jackson, Frank
* [The] King of the Bank Robbers
* Starr, Angel

Starr, Henry
See Bingley, David Ernest

Starr, Iron Man
See Starr, Raymond Francis

Starr, Jamie
See Nelson, Prince Roger

Starr, John 20th c. [HPPN]
American wrestler
* Starr, Handsome Johnny

Starr, John
See Aycock, Roger Dee

Starr, John
See Counselman, Mary Elizabeth

Starr, John A.
See Gillese, John Patrick

Starr, Judy
See Gelfman, Judith S[chlein]

Starr, Julian
See Alger, Horatio, Jr.

Starr, Kay
See Starks, Kathryn

Starr, Laura B. [FFF]
American journalist
* Fanchon

Starr, Lonny
See Starr, Franklin

Starr, Mark
See Klein, Gerard

Starr, Mrs. George O. [FFF]
* Zarzel

Starr, Muriel
See MacIver, Muriel

Starr, Pearl
See Younger, Pearl

Starr, Randy
See Nadel, Warren

Starr, Randy
See Randall, Joseph

Starr, Raymond Francis 1906-1963 [BE]
American baseball player
* Starr, Iron Man

Starr, Richard Harry 1878-? [MBF, WW, WWL]
British author
* Essex, Captain
* Essex, Richard
* Godwin, Frank
* O'Dare, Kerry

Starr, Ringo
See Starkey, Richard

Starr, Roland
See Rowland, Donald Sydney

Starr, Tramp
See Wilson, William Carl

Starr, William 1911- [EJS]
American baseball player
* Starr, Chick

Starr-Hunt, Jack 1893?-1951 [BI]
American journalist
* Brackenridge, John

Starret, William
See McClintock, Marshall

Start, Clarissa
See Lippert, Clarissa Start

Start, Joseph 1842?-1927 [BE, PB]
American baseball player
* Old Reliable
* Start, Rocks

Start, Rocks
See Start, Joseph

Stasek, Antal
See Zeman, Antonin

Stasheff, Edward
See Korostasheffsky, Adolphe Borisovitch

Stashynsky, Bogdan 1931- [EE]
Russian intelligence agent
* Draeger, Siegfried

Stassart, Albert 1875-1951 [BI]
Belgian critic
* Rency, Georges

Stastny, Frank
See Stastny, Frantisek

Stastny, Frantisek 20th c.
Czech motorcyclist
* Stastny, Frank

Stasz, Clarice 20th c. [CA]
American sociologist and author
* Stoll, Clarice Stasz

[A] State Agent
See Peyton, John Lewis

[The] State Apothecary
See Beresford, John Claudius

[The] State Librarian
See Coggeshall, William Turner

[The] State Librarian of Connecticut
See Hoadley, Charles Jeremiah

[The] State Proteus
See Prior, Matt[hew]

[The] Staten Island Scot
See Thomson, Robert Brown [Bobby]

[The] State's Corrector
See Romilly, [Sir] Samuel

[A] "States"-man
See Childe, Edward Vernon

[The] Statesman Bishop
See Williams, John

[The] Statesman of the American Navy
See Morris, Charles

Statham, George
See Statham, John Brian

Statham, John Brian 1930- [EC]
British cricketer
* Statham, George

Statler, Ellsworth Milton 1863-1928 [HPPN]
American hotel proprietor
* America's Extraordinary Hotelman
* [The] Father of the Home Away From Home
* [The] Wheeling Bellboy

Staton, Alonzo Louis Lee [BEW]
American actor and singer
* Sattin, Lonnie

Staton, Dakota
See Rabia, Aliyah

Staton, Joseph [Joe] 1948- [BE]
American baseball player
* Staton, Slim

Staton, Merrill
See Ostrus, Merrill

Staton, Slim
See Staton, Joseph [Joe]

Statten, Vargo
See Fearn, John Russell

Statutophilus
See Speed, John

Statz, Arnold John 1897- [BE, BTB]
American baseball player
* Statz, Jigger

Statz, Jigger
See Statz, Arnold John

Staub, Daniel Joseph 1944- [PB, SMG, WWB]
American baseball player
* [Le] Grand Orange
* Staub, Rusty

Staub, Rusty
See Staub, Daniel Joseph

Stauderman, Albert P[hilip] 1910- [CA]
American author
* Phillips, Alan

Staudt, Virginia
See Sexton, Virginia Staudt

Stauffer, Don
See Berkebile, Fred D[onovan]

Staunton, Schuyler
See Baum, L[yman] Frank

Staunton, William 18th c. [HPPN]
British author
* [The] Same Hand That Wrote the Packet of Letters to Dr. Waterland

Staurt, Charles
See Reid, Charles [Stuart]

Stautner, Ernie 20th c.
American football player
* [The] Horse
* Stautner, Moose

Stautner, Moose
See Stautner, Ernie

Stavinsky, Serge Alexandre 1886-1934
[HPPN]
Russian-French swindler
* Stavisky, Sacha
* [The] Super Swindler

Stavisky, Sacha
See Stavinsky, Serge Alexandre

Stavropoulos
See Stavropoulos, George Peter

Stavropoulos, George Peter 20th c.
[WFA]
Greek-born fashion designer
* Stavropoulos

Stavros, Niko
See King, Florence

Stawell, Augustus
See Legge, Alfred Owen

[The] Stay Maker
See Thomson, Alexander

Stchedrin, Nikolai
See Saltikoff, W.

Stead, James Henry ?-1886 [HPPN]
British entertainer
* [The] Perfect Cure

Stead, Thistle Yolette 1902- [AW, WD]
Australian biologist and author
* Harris, Thistle Y.

Stead, W. T.
See Stead, William Thomas

Stead, William Thomas 1849-1912
[HPPN, LC]
British journalist
* [The] Crusader in Babylon
* Stead, W. T.

Steadman, [Capt] Dick
See Harbaugh, Thomas Chalmers

Steadman, Vera 1900- [HPPN]
American actress
* [The] Orginial Bathing Girl

Steady
See Ramsay, Allan, Jr.

Steady Eddie Lopat
See Lopatnyski, Edmund Walter

Steady Eddy Wolf
See Wolf, Eddy

Steady Freddie Lewis
See Lewis, Fred

Steady Pete Meegan
See Meegan, Pete[r J.]

Steady Roll Johnson
See Johnson, James

Steady Steve Vickers
See Vickers, Stephen James

Steagall, Red
See Steagall, Russell

Steagall, Russell [CME]
American country-western performer
* Steagall, Red

Stealingworth, Slim
See Wesselmann, Tom

[The] Steamboat King
See Newberry, Oliver

[The] Steamboat Sharper
See Devol, George

Steamer
See Nason, Leonard Hastings

Steamtrain Maury Graham
See Graham, Maurice

Stearns, Albert
See Stearns, Edgar Franklin

Stearns, Edgar Franklin 1879-? [ESF,
SFL, WGT]
American author
* Franklin, Edgar
* Stearns, Albert

Stearns, Frederick Kimball 1854-1928
[HPPN]
American traveler
* Detroit's Greatest Traveler

Stearns, Harold Edmund 1891-1943
[CA, HPPN]
American author and journalist
* America's Foremost Expatriate
* Doyle, Harold Edmund
* Lutetius
* Pickem, Peter

Stearns, J. N. [FFF]
American author
* Merry, Robert

Stearns, Myron Morris 1884- [NAA]
American author and editor
* Amid, John
* Morris, Myron

Stearns, Norman Thomas 1901- [MK]
American baseball player
* Stearns, Turkey

Stearns, Peter N. 1936- [IAW]
British-born author
* Shard, Diana

Stearns, Turkey
See Stearns, Norman Thomas

Stebbins, Dry Hole
See Stebbins, Grant Case

Stebbins, George Stanford 19th c.
[DNA, PA]
Author and physician
* Izax, Ikabod

Stebbins, Grant Case 1862-1925 [HPPN]
American oil prospector and driller
* Stebbins, Dry Hole

Stebbins, Mrs. S. B. [FFF]
American poet
* Bridges, Sallie

Stebbins, Robert
See Meyers, Sidney

Stebbins, Rowland 1882-1948 [BEW]
American producer
* Rivers, Laurence

Stebbins, Rufus Phineas 1810-1885
[HPPN]
American clergyman
* R. P. S.

Stebel, Sidney Leo 1924- [CA]
American author
* Bergson, Leo

Stebelski, Julian
See Stoberski, Zygmunt Julian

Steber, A. R. [house pseudonym, Ziff-
Davis]
See Graham, Roger Phillips

Steber, A. R.
See Palmer, Raymond A[rthur]

Stebnitski
See Leskov, Nikolai Semenovich

Stecchetti, Lorenzo
See Guerrini, Olindo

Stecchetto [The Stick]
See Scicolone, Sofia Villani

Stecher, Joe 20th c.
American wrestler
* [The] Scissors King

Steckling, Adri 20th c. [WFA]
American fashion designer
* Adri

Steding, Peggy 20th c. [SA]
American racquetball player
* Super Duper Tex

Stedman
See Kinney, Elizabeth C. [Dodge]

Stedman, Algernon Methuen Marshall
1856-1924 [WBD]
British publisher
* Methuen, [Sir] Algernon Methuen
  Marshall

Stedman, Charles
See Thomson, William

Stedman, Charles Ellery 1831-1905 [BI]
American physician and lithographer
* Chinks

Stedman, Edmund Clarence 1833-1908
[DEP, DNNS, FF]
American poet
* [The] Banker Poet

Stedman, Myrtle
See Lincoln, Myrtle

Steed, Mabel A. 1894- [WW]
Author
* Hughes, M. Alison

Steedman, James B. 1818-1883 [DNNS,
SN]
American army officer
* Old Chickamauga
* Old Steady

Steegmuller, Francis 1906- [CA, CC, TC1]
American author
* Keith, David
* Steel, Byron

Steel Arm Davis
See Davis, Walter

Steel Arm Johnny
See Taylor, John

Steel Arm Tyler
See Tyler, William

[The] Steel Butterfly
See Young, Gretchen Michaela

Steel, Byron
See Steegmuller, Francis

Steel, Howard
See Hayter, Cecil Goodenough

[The] Steel King
See Carnegie, Andrew

Steel, Kurt
See Steel, Rudolph Hornaday

[The] Steel Magnolia
See Carter, [Eleanor] Rosalynn Smith

[The] Steel Master
See Lewis, Essington

Steel, Robert
See Whitson, John Harvey

Steel, Rudolph Hornaday 1904-1946 [BI, WW]
American author
* Kagey, Rudolf
* Steel, Kurt

Steel, Tex
See Ross, William Edward Daniel

[The] Steel Titan
See Schwab, Charles M. [Charley]

Steel, Tom [HN]
* O'Connell's Head Pacificator

[The] Steel Tycoon
See Schwab, Charles M. [Charley]

Steel, Vernon
See Antonietti, Vernon

Steele, Addison
See Stark, Nancy

Steele, Addison
See Whitson, John Harvey

Steele, Addison, II
See Lupoff, Richard Allen [Dick]

Steele, Alice Garland
See Austin-Ball, Mrs. T.

Steele, Anne 1717-1778 [NPS]
Hymn writer
* Theodosia

Steele, Big Bill
See Steele, William Mitchell

Steele, Bob
See Bradbury, Robert

Steele, Captain
See Steele, [Sir] Richard

Steele, Charles
See Sellers, Connie Leslie, Jr.

Steele, Chester K.
See Stratemeyer, Edward L.

Steele, Curtis
See Tepperman, Emile

Steele, Dale
See Glut, Donald F[rank]

Steele, Daniel
See Chadwick, Charles

Steele, David Stanley 1941- [DC]
British cricketer
* Steele, Stainless

Steele, Dirk
See Plawin, Paul

Steele, Edward 1915- [MK]
American baseball player
* Steele, Stainless

Steele, Erskine
See Henderson, Archibald

Steele, Francesca Maria 1848-? [LAO]
British author
* Dale, Darley

Steele, Franklin 19th c. [HPPN]
American pioneer
* [The] First Citizen of St. Anthony

Steele, Fred I[rving] 1938- [CA]
American author
* Steele, Fritz

Steele, Fritz
See Steele, Fred I[rving]

Steele, Harwood Elmes Robert 1897- [CCL]
Canadian poet
* Steele, Howard

Steele, Henry 1931- [CA]
American economist and author
* Pinkerton, W. Anson

Steele, Howard [house pseudonym]
See Brooks, Leonard Harold

Steele, Howard [house pseudonym]
See Edgar, Alfred

Steele, Howard [house pseudonym]
See Marshall, Arthur C.

Steele, Howard
See Steele, Harwood Elmes Robert

Steele, Howard [house pseudonym]
See Symonds, Francis Addington

Steele, James 1890-1967 [HPPN]
American actor
* Kelly, Scotch

Steele, James 19th c. [HPPN]
American author
* Monahan, Deane

Steele, John Frederick 1946- [DC]
British cricketer
* Steele, Steeley

Steele, John Washington 1843?-1920 [FFF]
American industrialist
* Coal Oil Johnny

Steele, Larry 1916- [IBW]
American entertainer
* [The] Black Flo Ziegfeld

Steele, Louis 1911- [HPPN]
American composer and advertising executive
* Steele, Ted

Steele, Mary Q[uintard Govan] 1922- [CA, SAT, TBJ]
American author
* Gage, Wilson

Steele, Morris J. [house pseudonym, Ziff-Davis]
See Livingston, Berkeley

Steele, Morris J. [house pseudonym, Ziff-Davis]
See Palmer, Raymond A[rthur]

Steele, Pablo 1911- [HPPN]
Canadian clergyman and missionary
* [The] Agent for Change

Steele, Ray
See Sauer, Peter

Steele, [Sir] Richard 1672-1729 [DEA, DEL, DLE1, FFF, HPPN, PI, SN]
British author and playwright
* Bickerstaff, Isaac
* Edgar, [Sir] John
* [The] Father of English Periodical Literature
* [The] First of the British Periodical Essayists
* [A] Gentleman of the Army
* Hibernian Dick
* Hicks, Francis
* Impartial Hand
* Ironside, Nestor
* Jay
* Little Dicky
* [A] Member of the House of Commons
* Myrtle, Marmaduke
* Nestor
* Philroye, Humphrey
* Steele, Captain
* [A] Twopenny Author

Steele, Stainless
See Steele, David Stanley

Steele, Stainless
See Steele, Edward

Steele, Steeley
See Steele, John Frederick

Steele, Ted
See Steele, Louis

Steele, Tommy
See Hicks, Thomas

Steele, William [Bill]
See Gettinger, William A.

Steele, William Mitchell 1885-1949
[BE]
American baseball player
* Steele, Big Bill

Steelman, Farmer
See Steelman, Morris James

Steelman, Morris James 1875-1944 [BE]
American baseball player
* Steelman, Farmer

Steely, Ann 1923-1970 [FC]
American actress
* O'Donnell, Cathy

Steen, Frank
See Felstein, Ivor

Steen, Karl
See Daudet, Julie Rosalie Celeste

Steen, Malcolm Harold 1928- [CA]
American actor and author
* Steen, Mike

Steen, Marguerite 1894-1975 [CA]
British author and playwright
* Dryden, Lennox
* Nicholson, Jane

Steen, Mike
See Steen, Malcolm Harold

Steenberg, Rise 1913- [MS]
American opera singer
* Stevens, Rise

Steendam, Jacob 1616?-1672 [HPPN]
Dutch-American poet
* [The] First American Poet
* Noch Vaster [Even Firmer]

Steenie
See Villiers, George

Steeple Jack
See Aubin, Charles

Steer, Charlotte
See Hunter, Maud L[ily]

Steers, Les
See Steers, Lester

Steers, Lester 1917- [TF]
American track and field athlete
* Steers, Les

Steevens, G. W.
See Steevens, George Warrington

Steevens, George 1736-1800 [HPPN, PA, SN]
British Shakespearian commentator
* Alciphron
* Aldebaran
* Amner
* Annius Anglicanus
* Dowse, Ephraim
* H. B.
* One of the Cock and Hen Club
* [The] Puck of Commentators

Steevens, George Warrington 1869-1900 [LC]
British journalist
* Steevens, G. W.

Stefan, Karl 1884-? [HPPN]
American radio announcer and politician
* [The] Voice of the Radio

Stefani [or di Stefano], Ambrogio 15th c. [WBD]
Italian painter
* Borgognone, Ambrogio

Stefano, Francesoc di 1422?-1457 [HPPN]
Italian painter
* [Il] Pasellino

Stefansson, Evelyn
See Nef, Evelyn Stefansson

Stefansson, Klondike Stef
See Stefansson, Vilhjalmur

Stefansson, Magnus 1884-1942 [EWL]
Icelandic poet
* Arnarson, Oern

Stefansson, Vilhjalmur 1879-1962 [HPPN]
Icelandic-Canadian explorer
* Stefansson, Klondike Stef

Steffan, Alice Kennedy 1907- [CA]
American author
* Steffan, Jack

Steffan, Jack
See Steffan, Alice Kennedy

Steffan, Siobhan R.
See Goulart, Frances Sheridan

Steffanson, Con [house pseudonym]
See Cassiday, Bruce [Bingham]

Steffanson, Con [house pseudonym]
See Goulart, Ron[ald Joseph]

Steffen, Anthony
See De Teffe, Antonio

Steffen, Gerhardt A. 1891- [BX, RBE]
American boxer
* Ritchie, Willie

Steffens, Arthur 1873-? [MBF]
British author
* Cooper, Freemont
* Dee, Dare
* Glyn, Harrison
* Hale, Clement
* Hardy, Arthur S.
* Leigh, [Capt.] Arthur
* Walters, W. G.
* Wentworth, Charles [house pseudonym]

Steffens, [Joseph] Lincoln 1866-1936 [HPPN]
American journalist and reformer
* [The] King of the Muckrakers
* That Golden Rule Fellow

Stegeman, H. J.
See Stegeman, Herman J.

Stegeman, Herman J. 1891-1939 [FB]
American football coach
* Stegeman, H. J.

Stegeman, Sanford 20th c. [HPPN]
American football player
* Stegeman, Steg

Stegeman, Steg
See Stegeman, Sanford

Steger, Shelby 1906- [CA]
American author
* Loomis, Rae

Steichen, Edward 1880-1973 [HPPN]
American photographer
* [The] Master Photographer

Steid, Herman 19th c. [HPPN]
American criminal
* Marm's Poodle Dog

Steiger, Brad
See Olson, Eugene E.

Steimer, Francis Alfred 1854-? [FFF, PA]
Author
* On the Go
* Prometheus

Stein, Aaron Marc 1906- [CA, CC, EMD]
American author
* Bagby, George
* Stone, Hampton

Stein, Abe M. 1853-1920 [HPPN]
American actor
* Aiken, Sol

Stein, Armin
See Nietschmann, Herman

Stein, Bernard
See Kahlert, Karl F[riedrich]

Stein, Bird 1868-1944 [JL]
American educator
* Gans, Bird

Stein, Charles
See Schwalberg, Carol[yn Ernestine Stein]

Stein, Edith 1891-1942 [BI]
German philosopher
* Teresa Benedicta of the Cross, [Sister]

Stein, Frank N.
See Briefer, Richard [Dick]

Stein, George 1903-1967 [F1, F2, FC]
Polish-born actor
* Stone, George E.

Stein, Henrietta 1896-1971 [HPPN]
American shorthand expert
* Stein, Pinky

Stein, Henry Eugene 1945- [ESF, WGT]
American author
* Stine, Hank
* Whyte, Sibley

Stein, J. H. 20th c. [MBF]
British author
* Dixon, Don

Stein, J. J.
See Richards, Sara Lippincott

Stein, Jacob 20th c. [MM]
American underworld figure
* Drew, John

Stein, Jan
See Hegeler, Sten

Stein, Joe J.
See Stacher, Joseph

Stein, Johann Saville
See Stone, John Saville

Stein, Johnny
See Hountha, John Philip

Stein, Jules W. Arndt 1879?-? [HPPN, MM]
American underworld figure
* Adair, James Wilford
* Adair, John Wilson
* Arnold, J. W.
* Arnold, Jules
* Arnstein, Nicky
* Nickelplate

Stein, Julius Kerwin 1905- [BEW, EMT, ITA]
British-born composer and producer
* Styne, Jule

Stein, Justin Marion 1911- [BE]
American baseball player
* Stein, Ott

Stein, Lloyd 20th c. [BBH]
American athletic trainer
* Stein, Snapper

Stein, Mr.
See Schwartzhof, Leon Henry

Stein, Ott
See Stein, Justin Marion

Stein, Pinky
See Stein, Henrietta

Stein, Randy
See Stein, William Randolph

Stein, Robert Jack 1930-1980 [AM, EMT]
American actor, dancer, singer
* Van, Bobby

Stein, Snapper
See Stein, Lloyd

Stein, William Randolph 1953- [BR]
American baseball player
* Stein, Randy

Stein-Schneider, Herbert 20th c. [WP 3-6-83]
French-born clergyman
* Seguy, Pierre

Steinarr, Steinn
See Kristmundsson, Adalsteinn

Steinbeck, John [Ernst] 1902-1968 [CA, HPPN]
American author
* [The] Champion of the Downtrodden
* Glasscock, Amnesia

Steinberg, Aaron Zacharovich 1891-1975 [CA]
Russian-born British author and educator
* Avrelin, M.

Steinberg, Amy
See Douglas, Mrs. John

Steinberg, Edna 1905-1965 [SC]
Canadian-born actress
* Gregory, Edna

Steinberg, Elsy 1929- [FC]
American actress
* Stewart, Elaine

Steinberg, Hans Wilhelm 1899-1978 [MS]
German conductor
* Steinberg, William

Steinberg, Martha Jean Jones 20th c. [IBW]
American radio performer and community organizer
* Martha Jean, the Queen
* [The] Queen

Steinberg, Paul 1880-? [EJS]
American football player
* Steinberg, Twister

Steinberg, Saul 1940- [HPPN]
American business executive, entrepreneur, speculator
* Wall Street's Brash Outsider

Steinberg, Twister
See Steinberg, Paul

Steinberg, William
See Steinberg, Hans Wilhelm

Steinbrunner, Chris
See Steinbrunner, Peter Christian

Steinbrunner, Peter Christian 1933- [CA, SFL]
American author
* Christian, Peter
* Steinbrunner, Chris

Steindler, Robert A. 1920- [HPPN]
American editor and author
* Tremaine, Bob

Steiner, Abraham Albert 1921- [CA]
Czech-born American author
* Avni, Abraham Albert

Steiner, Barbara A[nnette] 1934- [CA, SAT]
American author
* Cole, Annette [joint pseudonym with Kathleen Phillips]
* D'Andrea, Kate [joint pseudonym with Kathleen Phillips]
* Daniel, Anne

Steiner, Gerolf 1908- [CA]
German educator and author
* Andereich, Justus
* Stuempke, Harald
* Wiederump, Trotzhard

Steiner, Jack 20th c. [WP 8-20-83]
American airline executive
* [The] Father of the 727

Steiner, James Harry 1917- [BE]
American baseball player
* Steiner, Red

Steiner, Kurt
See Ruellan, Andre

Steiner, Rebel
See Steiner, Roy

Steiner, Red
See Steiner, James Harry

Steiner, Roy 20th c. [EF]
American football player
* Steiner, Rebel

Steinfeldt, Battleaxe
See Steinfeldt, Harry M.

Steinfeldt, Harry M. 1876-1914 [BN]
American baseball player
* Steinfeldt, Battleaxe

Steinhaeuser, Walter Philip 1878-? [NAA]
American author and educator
* Retlaw, S. P.

Steinhauer, H. A. [PA]
Author
* Cozinski, Mary

Steinhausen, H.
See Gurster, Eugen

Steinitz, William 1837-1900 [HPPN]
Bohemian-American chess player
* [The] Chess Nut

Steinke, Jolly Bill
See Steinke, William

Steinke, William 1888-1958 [HPPN]
American radio personality
* Steinke, Jolly Bill

Steinmetz, Charles Proteus
See Steinmetz, Karl August Rudolf

Steinmetz, Christian 1882-1963 [BB]
American basketball player
* [The] Father of Wisconsin Basketball

Steinmetz, Eulalie
See Ross, Eulalie Steinmetz

Steinmetz, Karl August Rudolf 1865-1923 [HPPN, WBD]
American engineer
* [The] Electrical Wizard
* Proteus
* Steinmetz, Charles Proteus

Steinschneider, Heinrich 1869-1933 [EOP, NAD]
German psychic and astrologer
* [The] Devil's Prophet
* Hanussen, Erik Jan

Steinway, Henry Engelhard
See Steinweg, Heinrich Engelhard

Steinweg, Heinrich Engelhard 1797-1871 [WBD]
German-born piano manufacturer
* Steinway, Henry Engelhard

Steinwendner, Kurt 1920- [CAR]
Austrian artist
* Stenvert, Curt

Steinwert von Soest, Johannes 1448-1506
[BBD]
German composer
* Susato, Johannes

Stell, Mrs. Martin [FFF]
Entertainer
* Wheeler, Fanny

Stella
See Bagg, Stanley Clark

Stella
See Bowen-Graves, Mrs.

Stella
See Cox, Mary M.

Stella
See Devereux, Penelope

Stella
See Hanania, Stella

Stella
See Iron, Mrs. N. C.

Stella
See Johnson, Esther

Stella
See Lewis, Estelle Anna Blanche
Robinson

Stella C.
See Deacon, Leslie

Stella, Luciano 20th c. [WF]
Italian actor
* Kendall, Tony

Stelzle, Jacob Charles 1867-1919 [AS,
BE]
American baseball player
* Stenzel, Jacob Charles

Stembler, May
See Iasigi, Mrs. A. D.

Stemkowski, Peter David 1943- [SMG]
Canadian-born hockey player
* [The] Polish Prince
* Stemkowski, Stemmer

Stemkowski, Stemmer
See Stemkowski, Peter David

Stemp, Isay
See Stempnitzky, Isay

Stempasius
See Baron, Pierre

Stempnitzky, Isay 1922- [CA]
*Russian-born American business executive
and author*
* Stemp, Isay

Sten, Anna
See Sujakevitch, Anjuschka Stenski

Stender, Jan [BBH]
Dutch swimming coach
* [The] Hangman of Hilversum

Stendhal
See Beyle, Marie Henri

Stengel, Casey
See Stengel, Charles Dillon

Stengel, Charles Dillon 1889?-1975
[BAB, BE, OCS]
American baseball player and manager
* [The] Old Professor
* Stengel, Casey
* Stengel, Dutch

Stengel, Dutch
See Stengel, Charles Dillon

Stenius, George 1911-1979 [CA]
American, producer, director, screenwriter
* Seaton, George

Stenmark, Ingemar 20th c.
Swedish skier
* [The] Silent Swede

Stennett, Renaldo Antonio 1951- [BE,
SMG]
Panamanian-born baseball player
* Stennett, Rennie

Stennett, Rennie
See Stennett, Renaldo Antonio

Steno
See Vanzina, Stefano

Steno, Nicolas 1638-1687 [UH]
Danish geologist and anatomist
* [The] Father of Geology

Stensch, Gunther Siegmund 1924- [CA]
*German-born American biologist and
author*
* Stent, Gunther S[iegmund]

Stensland, Inger 1934?-1970 [BEW, FC]
Swedish-born actress
* Stevens, Inger

Stent, Gunther S[iegmund]
See Stensch, Gunther Siegmund

Stentor
See Stanley, William

Stentor, Ivy
See Keller, H. A.

Stenus
See Huxley, Herbert H[enry]

Stenvall, Alexis 1834-1872 [WBD]
Finnish playwright and author
* Kivi, Alexis

Stenvert, Curt
See Steinwendner, Kurt

Stenzel, Jacob Charles
See Stelzle, Jacob Charles

Step, Edward 1855-? [WWL]
British author
* Weston, James

[The] Stepfather of His Country
See Washington, George

[The] Stepfather of the Merit System
See Gillett, Frederick Huntington

Stephan, Agnes
See Kreuter-Trankel, Margot

Stephane, Roger
See Worms, Roger

Stephanowitch, Dantri
See De Riallo, J. Girard

Stephen ?-36?
Saint
* [The] Proto Martyr

Stephen
See Cox, Stephen Bernard

Stephen, Alexander R. 1954- [EG]
Scottish golfer
* Stephen, Sandy

Stephen, Buzz
See Stephen, Louis Roberts

Stephen Dushan
See Stephen Nemanya IX

Stephen, [Sir] George 1794-? [HFN, PA]
Author
* [An] Attorney
* Caveat Emptor

Stephen, [Sir] James Fitzjames
1829-1894 [DEL, PA]
British jurist and author
* [A] Barrister

Stephen, James Kenneth 1859-1892
[HPPN, WBD]
British poet
* J. K. S.

Stephen, John 19th c. [HPPN]
American businessman and author
* [A] Practical Chemist and Experienced
Liquor Dealer

Stephen, Joyce Alice 20th c. [AW]
New Zealand-born author
* Thomas, J. Bissell

Stephen, [Sir] Leslie 1832-1904 [BI,
DEA]
British author and philosopher
* [A] Don
* L. S.

Stephen, Louis Roberts 1944- [BE]
American baseball player
* Stephen, Buzz

Stephen, Mary
See Grimes, Katharine A.

Stephen Nemanya IX 1308?-1355
[WBD]
King of Serbia
* Stephen Dushan

Stephen of Cloyes 13th c. [HPPN]
French crusade leader
* [The] Prophet

Stephen of Moldavia 1433?-1504 [WBD]
Prince of Moldavia
* [The] Great

Stephen, Sandy
See Stephen, Alexander R.

Stephen I 979?-1038 [HN, WBD]
King of Hungary
* [The] Apostle of Hungary

Stephen II 1100-1131 [DNNS, FFF, HN]
King of Hungary
* [The] Lightning
* Thunder and Lightning
* [The] Thunderer

Stephen IX [or X]
See Frederick

Stephens, Alexander Hamilton 1812-1883
[HPPN, SN]
American politician
* [The] Dwarf Statesman
* [The] Little Pale Star from Georgia
* [The] Nestor of the Confederacy
* Stephens, Little Aleck

Stephens, Ann Sophia Winterbotham
1813-1886
American author, poet, editor
* Slick, Jonathan

Stephens, Arthur
See Agnew, Stephen Hamilton

Stephens, Buster
See Stephens, Vernon Decatur

Stephens, Casey
See Wagner, Sharon B.

Stephens, Catherine [Countess of Essex]
1794-1882 [HPPN]
British singer and actress
* Stephens, Kitty

Stephens, Charles
See Goldin, Stephen

Stephens, Charles Asbury 1844-1931
[DNA]
American author and scientist
* Stephens, Kit

Stephens, Clara 1870-1907 [BEW]
American actress
* Bloodgood, Clara

Stephens, Clifford 1953- [RBE]
American boxer
* Stephens, Randy

Stephens, David 18th c. [HPPN]
Irish author
* [A] Member of the Incorporated
  Society

Stephens, Donald Ryder 1898- [MBF,
SFL]
British author
* Sinderby, Donald

Stephens, Edna 1883- [THR]
American actress
* Goodrich, Edna

Stephens, Edward 17th c. [HPPN]
British author
* Christianus, Socrates

Stephens, Eve
See Ward Thomas, Evelyn Bridget
Patricia

Stephens, Frances
See Bentley, Margaret

Stephens, Francis George 19th c. [NPS]
Artist and author
* Savage, Laura
* Seward, John

Stephens, Francis H.
See Driscoll, Annette Sophia

Stephens, George 1800-1851 [HPPN, PI]
British playwright
* Dorset, St. George
* Dorset, St. John

Stephens, George 1922- [SMG]
American football team staff member
* Stephens, Tex

Stephens, Harold 20th c. [SMG]
American football player
* Stephens, Hayseed

Stephens, Harriet Marion 1823-1858
[FFF, PA]
Author
* H. M. S.
* Somers, Rosalie
* Ward, Marion

Stephens, Hayseed
See Stephens, Harold

Stephens, Henrietta Henkle 1909-1983
[CA]
American author and editor
* Buckmaster, Henrietta

Stephens, I. M.
See Pratt, Inga Stephens

Stephens, James 1882?-1950 [CA, DLE1]
Irish poet, playwright, author
* Esse, James

Stephens, James Anthony 1914- [BA]
American local government official
* Stephens, Palsy-Walsy

Stephens, James Walter 1883-1965 [BE]
American baseball player
* Stephens, Little Nemo

Stephens, Jeanne
See Hager, Jean

Stephens, John Lloyd 1805-1852
[HPPN]
American author
* [An] American

Stephens, Junior
See Stephens, Vernon Decatur

Stephens, Kate 1853-? [ALY]
American author
* Ransom, Olive

Stephens, Kenneth
See Agnew, Stephen Hamilton

Stephens, Kit
See Stephens, Charles Asbury

Stephens, Kitty
See Stephens, Catherine [Countess of
Essex]

Stephens, Lawrence Sterne 20th c.
[ESF, WGT]
American illustrator
* Lawrence
* Lawrence, Stephen

Stephens, Little Aleck
See Stephens, Alexander Hamilton

Stephens, Little Nemo
See Stephens, James Walter

Stephens, Louis 20th c. [EF]
American football player
* Stephens, Red

Stephens, Louise G. 1843-? [DNA]
American author
* Katharine

Stephens, Mike 1885?-1927? [NOJ]
American jazz musician
* [The] Father of Dixieland Drums
* Stephens, Ragbaby

Stephens, Mrs. Thomas C. [FFF]
Entertainer
* Ritchie, Nellie Claire

Stephens, Mrs. W. T. [FFF]
Entertainer
* Gray, Minnie Oscar

Stephens, Palsy-Walsy
See Stephens, James Anthony

Stephens, Peter
See Melekh, Igor Yakovlevich

Stephens, R. L.
See Hoch, Edward D[entinger]

Stephens, Ragbaby
See Stephens, Mike

Stephens, Randy
See Stephens, Clifford

Stephens, Red
See Stephens, Louis

Stephens, Reed
See Donaldson, Stephen R.

Stephens, Richard Waring 1912?- [BEW,
TR]
British actor
* Waring, Richard

Stephens, Rosemary 1924- [CA]
American author
* Carswell, Leslie

Stephens, S. J.
See Palickar, Stephen J.

Stephens, Tex
See Stephens, George

Stephens, Uriah Smith 1821-1882
[HPPN]
American labor leader
* [The] Father of the Knights of Labor

Stephens, Vernon Decatur 1920-1968
[AS, BE, HPPN, PB]
American baseball player
* Little Slug of the Boston Red Sox
* Stephens, Buster
* Stephens, Junior

Stephens, [Rev.] William 18th c.
[HPPN]
British clergyman
* Roger

Stephens, William 1862-1943 [WBD]
British sculptor
* Reynolds-Stephens, [Sir] William

Stephens, Woodford Cefis 20th c.
[BBH]
Horse trainer
* Stevens, Woody

Stephenson, Andrew M. 1946- [ESF]
British author and illustrator
* Ames

Stephenson, Benjamin Charles 19th c.
[FFF]
Playwright
* Rowe, Bolton

Stephenson, Calvin 20th c. [RO2]
American singer
* Stephenson, Dhaakk

Stephenson, Dhaakk
See Stephenson, Calvin

Stephenson, Dummy
See Stephenson, Reuben Crandol

Stephenson, George James ?-1888 [FFF]
British author and journalist
* Albion

Stephenson, Henry
See Garroway, Henry Stephenson

Stephenson, Honest John
See Stephenson, John

Stephenson, Jackson Riggs 1898- [BE,
BN, HPPN, PB]
American baseball player
* Stephenson, Old Hoss
* Stephenson, Warhorse
* Stevie

Stephenson, John 1809-1893 [HPPN]
Irish-American businessman
* Stephenson, Honest John

Stephenson, Old Hoss
See Stephenson, Jackson Riggs

Stephenson, Reuben Crandol 1869-1924
[BE]
American baseball player
* Stephenson, Dummy

Stephenson, Tarzan
See Stephenson, Walter McQueen

Stephenson, Valentine
See Hamlen, Georgia

Stephenson, Walter McQueen 1911-
[BE]
American baseball player
* Stephenson, Tarzan

Stephenson, Warhorse
See Stephenson, Jackson Riggs

Stephenson, [Sir] William Samuel 1896-
[BI]
British intelligence official
* Intrepid [code name]
* Little Bill

Stephson, Arthur Lee 1926- [NBB]
American musician
* Kansas City Red

Stepin Fetchit
See Perry, Lincoln Theodore

Stepka, Milan
See Benes, Jan

Stepniak
See Dragomanoff, Michael

Stepnyak [Son of the Steppe]
See Kravchinsky, Sergius Mikhailovich

Stepsure, Mephibosheth
See McCulloch, Thomas

Steptoe, Lydia
See Barnes, Djuna

Sterland, Carl
See Newquist, Roy

Sterling, Anthony
See Caesar, [Eu]gene [Lee]

Sterling, Babe ?-1921 [HPPN]
American vaudeville performer
* Marguerite, Babe

Sterling, Barry
See Lipton, Robert

Sterling, Brett [house pseudonym]
See Bradbury, Ray [Douglas]

Sterling, Brett [house pseudonym,
Standard Magazines]
See Hamilton, Edmond [Moore]

Sterling, Brett [house pseudonym,
Standard Magazines]
See Samachson, Joseph

Sterling, Edward 1773-1847 [DEL, NPS,
SN]
British journalist
* [The] Magus of the Times
* [The] Thunderer of the Times
* Vetus
* Whirlwind, Captain

Sterling, Ford
See Stitch, George Ford

Sterling, Hank
See Snyder, Harry

Sterling, Helen
See Hoke, Helen L.

Sterling, Jan [or Jane]
See Adriance, Jane Sterling

Sterling, Jean
See Taylor, Mary Virginia

Sterling, John 1806-1844 [FFF, HPPN]
British author and poet
* Archeus
* Elbett, Theodore

Sterling, John
See Sherwood, Mary Neal

Sterling, Richard
See Leggatt, Albert G.

Sterling, Robert
See Hart, William Sterling

Sterling, [Maria] Sandra
See Floren, Lee

Sterling, Simon
See Sollima, Sergio

Sterling, Stewart
See Winchell, Prentice

Sterling X
See Stuckey, Sterling

Sterling-Jones, M.
See Jones, Mary R.

[The] Stern
See Frederick

[The] Stern
See Harold III

Stern, Adolf
See Ernst, Adolf

Stern, Alfred 1899- [CA]
*Austrian-born American philosopher and
author*
* Alstern, Fred

Stern, Baroness [FFF]
French actress
* Croizette, Sophie

Stern, Bill 20th c. [FB]
Sportscaster
* Lateral Pass

Stern, Daniel
See De Flavigny, Marie Catherine
Sophie

Stern, David 1909- [ANT, WW]
American author
* Stirling, Peter

Stern, Detlef
See Strempel, Dora

Stern, Elizabeth
See Uhr, Elizabeth

Stern, Elizabeth Gertrude [Levin]
1889?-1954 [HPPN]
*Polish-born American author and social
worker*
* Morton, Eleanor
* Morton, Leah

Stern, Elsie Jean 1898-1953 [BI]
American composer
* Elsie Jean

Stern, G. B.
See Stern, Gladys Bertha [Bronwyn]

Stern, Georges 1882-1928 [EJS]
French jockey
* [The] King of the Derbies
* [The] King of the Jockeys

Stern, Gerd Jacob 1928- [CA]
German-born American sculptor and poet
* USCO

Stern, Gladys Bertha [Bronwyn] 1890-
[LC, TC]
British author
* Stern, G. B.

Stern, James [Andrew] 1904- [WD, WW]
British author and translator
* St. James, Andrew

Stern, Jay B. 1929- [CA]
American educator and author
* Kohavi, Y.

Stern, Joe 1894- [HPPN]
Austrian film director
* Von Sternberg, Joseph

Stern, Leonard 20th c. [HPPN]
American tennis player
* Stern, Shorty

Stern, Marie 1909- [CA]
American artist, author, illustrator
* Masha

Stern, Maximilian Enric 1926- [OP]
Israeli opera singer
* Ben-Schachar, Mordecai Enric

Stern, Miroslava 1930-1955 [SC]
Czech-born actress
* Miroslava

Stern, Paul Frederick
See Ernst, Paul Frederick

Stern, Philip Van Doren 1900- [CA, NAA, TC1]
American author
* Storme, Peter

Stern, Shorty
See Stern, Leonard

Stern, Stuart
See Rae, Hugh C[rauford]

Sternaman, Dutch
See Sternaman, Edward D.

Sternaman, Edward D. 1873-? [FB]
American football player
* Sternaman, Dutch

Sternberg, Alexander von
See Ungern-Sternberg, Alexander von

Sternberg, Jonas 1894-1969 [CA, WEF]
Austrian-born director
* Von Sternberg, Josef

Sterne, Carus
See Krause, Ernst Ludwig

Sterne, Duncan
See Openshaw, G. H.

Sterne, Emma Gelders 1894-1971 [CA, SAT]
American author
* Broun, Emily
* James, Josephine [joint pseudonym with Barbara Lindsay]

Sterne, Hedda
See Lindenberg, Hedda

Sterne, Karl
See Daudet, Julie Rosalie Celeste

Sterne, Laurence 1713-1768 [DEP, DNNF, FFF, HPPN, UH]
British author
* Bramin
* [The] English Rabelais
* [The] English Seneca
* Philologer, A. B.
* [The] Rabelais of England
* Smelfungus
* Yorick, Mr.

Sterne, Morgan
See Morgenstern, Albert

Sterne, Stuart
See Bloede, Gertrude

Sternpost, Admiral
See Paulet, Harry

Sterny, F.
See Moroni-Celsi, Guido

Sterrett, Charles Hurlbut 1889-1965 [BE]
American baseball player
* Sterrett, Dutch

Sterrett, Dutch
See Sterrett, Charles Hurlbut

Stesichorus 6th c. BC [FFF, SN]
Greek poet
* [The] Father of Choral Epode

Stet
See Welby, Thomas Earle

Stetson, Amos W. 19th c. [HPPN]
American banker
* A. W. S.

Stetson, Caleb 1793-1870 [HPPN]
American clergyman
* C. S.

Stetson, John Batterson 1830-1906 [HPPN]
American hat manufacturer
* [The] Father of the Ten Gallon Hat

Stetson, Mrs. John [FFF]
* Stokes, Katie

Stettinius, Edward Reilley, Jr. 1900-1949 [CND]
American secretary of state
* Collodion [code name used during World War II]

Steuart, Daniel 19th c. [PI]
Irish poet
* D. S.

Steuart, Richard D. 1878?-1951 [BI]
American journalist and historian
* Dulany, Carroll

Steuer, Max D. 1871-1940 [HPPN]
American attorney
* [The] Greatest Criminal Lawyer of His Time

Steune, Georges
See Schonestein, David

Steurnagel, George Henry 1873-1946 [BE]
American baseball player
* Starnagel, George Henry

Stevens, Alfred Peck 1839-1888 [BMH, WBD]
British entertainer
* [The] Great Vance
* Vance, Alfred Glenville

Stevens, Austin N[eil] 1930- [CA]
American author, editor, illustrator
* Austin, Stephen
* Nash, Eno

Stevens, Big Ed
See Stevens, Edward Lee

Stevens, Bill 1736-1781 [HPPN]
British boxer
* [The] Nailer

Stevens, Blaine
See Whittington, Harry [Benjamin]

Stevens, Casandra Mayo ?-1966 [ASC]
American composer and dancer
* Mayo, Cass

Stevens, Cat
See Georgiou, Stephen Demetre

Stevens, Cat
See Stevens, Charles A.

Stevens, Charles A. [PA]
Author
* Stevens, Cat

Stevens, Charles McClellan 1861-? [SFL]
Author
* Quondam

Stevens, Christopher
See Rochefort, Julian

Stevens, Christopher
See Tabori, Paul

Stevens, Clifford
See Weisse, Clifford Stevens

Stevens, Clysle 1927- [CA]
American poet
* Wade, John Stevens

Stevens, Con
See Stevens, Constantine Augustus Lucy

Stevens, Connie
See Ingolia, Concetta Ann

Stevens, Constance 1918- [BF]
British actress
* Gray, Sally

Stevens, Constantine Augustus Lucy 1900- [OCS]
Greyhound racing pioneer
* Stevens, Con

Stevens, Craig
See Shekles, Gail

Stevens, Dan J.
See Overholser, Wayne D.

Stevens, Dodie
See Pasquale, Geraldine Ann

Stevens, E. S.
See Drower, Ethel Stefana May

Stevens, Edward
See Cosgrove, Stephen E[dward]

Stevens, Edward Lee 1925- [BE]
American baseball player
* Stevens, Big Ed

Stevens, Elliot
See Stevens, Harold

Stevens, Fae Hewston
See Stevens, Frances Isted

Stevens, Frances Isted 1907- [AW, CAP]
Australian author
* Stevens, Fae Hewston

Stevens, Frances Moyer [Ross] 1895- [WW]
Author
* Hale, Christopher

Stevens, Francis
See Bennett, Gertrude Barrows

Stevens, Franklin 1933- [CA, SAT]
American author
* Franklin, Steve

Stevens, George 19th c. [PA]
Author
* Collins
* Whipple, Wade

Stevens, Harold 1909-1971 [HPPN]
American singer
* Stevens, Elliot

Stevens, Harold
See Neuburg, Victor [Benjamin]

Stevens, Harry
See Stevens, James Arthur [Jim]

Stevens, Henry 1819-1886 [HPPN]
American bibliophile
* G. M. B.
* Green Mountain Boy

Stevens, Hub
See Stevens, J. Hubert

Stevens, Inger
See Stensland, Inger

Stevens, J. D.
See Rowland, Donald Sydney

Stevens, J. Hubert 1890?-1950 [HPPN]
American bobsled racer
* Stevens, Hub

Stevens, Jake
See Stevens, Paul Eugene

Stevens, James Arthur [Jim] 1889-1966 [BE]
American baseball player
* Stevens, Harry

Stevens, Jane Greengold 1945- [CA]
American author
* Greengold, Jane

Stevens, Jennie 1878?-? [HPPN]
American outlaw
* Little Britches

Stevens, Jill
See Mogridge, Stephen

Stevens, Jimmy 20th c.
New Hebridean leader
* Stevens, Moly

Stevens, Joe 20th c. [WWJ]
American jazz musician
* Stevens, Ragababy

Stevens, John 1749-1838 [HPPN]
American inventor
* [The] Father of the Patent Law

Stevens, John 1919- [FC, SW]
American actor
* Brodie, Steve

Stevens, John 20th c. [SFL]
Author
* Hatfield, Frank

Stevens, John
See Tubb, Edwin Charles

Stevens, John H. 1820-1900 [HPPN]
Canadian pioneer
* [The] Father of Minneapolis

Stevens, K. T.
See Wood, Gloria

Stevens, Lee 1931- [BMH]
British female impersonator
* Avid, Alan
* [The] Bird with the Feathers

Stevens, Lynn
See Feeney, Franklin

Stevens, Mal
See Stevens, Marvin Allen

Stevens, Margaret Dean
See Aldrich, Bess Streeter

Stevens, Mark 1916?- [FC]
American actor
* Richards, Stephen

Stevens, Marvin Allen 1900?- [BI, FB]
American football player and coach
* Stevens, Mal

Stevens, Maurice
See Whitson, John Harvey

Stevens, Moly
See Stevens, Jimmy

Stevens, Mrs. Victor [FFF]
Entertainer
* Ross, Eva Florence

Stevens, Muriel Phyllis 1914- [ART]
British painter and illustrator
* Stanes, Muriel

Stevens, Onslow
See Stevenson, Onslow Ford

Stevens, Pam
See Gelberg, George

Stevens, Paul
See Gattoni, Paul Steven

Stevens, Paul Eugene 1900- [MK]
American baseball player
* Stevens, Jake

Stevens, Peter 20th c. [BLB]
American underworld figure
* Schafer, Gus

Stevens, Peter [joint pseudonym with Darlene (Stern) Geis]
See Geis, Bernard

Stevens, Peter [joint pseudonym with Bernard Geis]
See Geis, Darlene [Stern]

Stevens, Ragababy
See Stevens, Joe

Stevens, Ray
See Ragsdale, Ray

Stevens, Rise
See Steenberg, Rise

Stevens, Robert Tyler
See Staples, Reginald Thomas

Stevens, Ruby 1907- [BDF, BEW, F2]
American actress
* Stanwyck, Barbara

Stevens, S. P.
See Palestrant, Simon S.

Stevens, Sam 1939?-1984 [WP 8-18-84]
American singer and songwriter
* [The] Elvis Presley of the Gypsies
* [The] King of Gypsy Music
* Singing Sam

Stevens, Sarah
See Heenan, Mrs. John C.

Stevens, Siaka 1906?-
President of Sierra Leone
* [The] Pa

Stevens, Stella
See Eggleston, Estelle

Stevens, Thad[deus] 1773?-1868 [DNNS, FFF, HPPN, NPS, SN]
American politician
* [The] American Pitt
* [The] Arch Priest of Anti Masonry
* [The] Chief Old Woman
* Grand Old Man
* [The] Great American Commoner
* [The] Great Commoner
* [The] Old Commoner
* Old Thad

Stevens, Thomas ?-1835 [HPPN]
American farmer
* [The] Antebellum Georgian

Stevens, Walter 1877-1939 [BLB]
American underworld figure
* [The] Dean of Chicago Gunmen

Stevens, William [FFF]
Author
* Ain

Stevens, William [Bill] 1736-1781 [RBE]
British boxer
* [The] Nailer

Stevens, William [Carey] 1881-? [NAA]
American writer
* Twelve o'Clock

Stevens, William Christopher
See Allen, Stephen Valentine [Steve]

Stevens, Woody
See Stephens, Woodford Cefis

Stevens, Yvette Marie 1954- [IBW]
American singer
* Khan, Chaka

Stevenson
See Gaskell, Elizabeth Cleghorn

Stevenson, A[rthur] Lionel 1902-
[HPPN]
American educator and author
* Stevenson, Doc

Stevenson, Anne
See Elvin, Anne Katharine Stevenson

Stevenson, D. E.
See Stevenson, Dorothy Emily

Stevenson, Doc
See Stevenson, A[rthur] Lionel

Stevenson, Dorothy Emily 1892-1973
[SFL]
Scottish-born author
* Stevenson, D. E.

Stevenson, Florence 20th c. [CA]
American author and playwright
* Curzon, Lucia
* Faire, Zabrina

Stevenson, Graham Barry 1955- [DC]
British cricketer
* Stevenson, Moonbeam

Stevenson, J. P.
See Stevenson, James Patrick

Stevenson, James Alexander 1881-1937
[DBA]
British sculptor
* Myrander

Stevenson, James Patrick 1910- [CA,
WD]
Welsh-born clergyman and author
* Haldane-Stevenson, James Patrick
* Radyr, Tomos
* Stevenson, J. P.

Stevenson, John 1853-? [SFL, WGT]
American author
* Jackson, Stephen

Stevenson, John Hall
See Hall, John

Stevenson, John P.
See Grierson, Edward

Stevenson, Keith 1950- [DC]
British cricketer
* Stevenson, Stevo

Stevenson, Mary
See Kennedy, Mary Stevenson

Stevenson, Moonbeam
See Stevenson, Graham Barry

Stevenson, Mrs. Charles [FFF]
Entertainer
* Claxton, Kate

Stevenson, Onslow Ford 1902?- [BEW,
FC]
American actor and director
* Stevens, Onslow

Stevenson, Pierce
See Norton, Caroline Elizabeth Sarah

Stevenson, Robert Louis
See Balfour, Robert Louis

Stevenson, Sara Yorke 1847-? [ALY]
French-born author
* Slippers, Peggy

Stevenson, Steve
See Stevenson, Tommy

Stevenson, Steve
See Stevenson, Vincent M.

Stevenson, Stevo
See Stevenson, Keith

Stevenson, Tommy 1914?-1944 [WWJ]
American jazz musician
* Stevenson, Steve

Stevenson, Vincent M. 1884-1962 [AS,
FB]
American football player
* Stevenson, Steve

Stevenson, William 1925- [CA]
British author
* Chen Hwei

Stevenson, William Adell 1948- [IBW]
*American playwright and television
scriptwriter*
* Adell, Ilunga

Steventon, John
See Tarkington, John Stevenson

Steverino
See Allen, Stephen Valentine [Steve]

Stevie
See Stephenson, Jackson Riggs

Stevin, Adam
See Richardson, James

[The] Steward
See Robert II

[A] Steward
See Yates, Thomas

Steward, Alexander 1343?-1405? [HN,
WBD]
Earl of Buchan and Lord of Badenoch
* [The] Wolf of Badenoch

Steward, [Rev.] James
See Trumbull, Henry

Steward of Democracy
See Winant, John Gilbert

Steward, Sable 1876-? [THR]
British comedienne
* Fern, Sable

Steward, Samuel M. 20th c.
American author
* Sparrow, Philip

Stewart, A. C.
See Stewart, Agnes Charlotte

Stewart, Ace
See Stewart, Asa

Stewart, Agnes Charlotte 20th c. [TCC]
British author
* Stewart, A. C.

Stewart, Albert 1904-
Canadian-born hockey player
* Stewart, Babe

Stewart, Albert 20th c. [GW]
American rodeo performer
* Stewart, Whitey

Stewart, Alexander Charles 1867-1944
[CCL]
Canadian author
* A. C. S., Professor

Stewart, Alexander Peter 1821-1908
[HPPN]
American army officer and educator
* Old Straight

Stewart, Alexander Turner 1803-1876
[HPPN]
American merchant and philanthropist
* [The] Prince of Merchants

Stewart, Alfred Walter 1880-1947 [CC,
EMD, WW]
British author
* Connington, J[ohn] J[ervis]

Stewart, Andrew 1791-1872 [HPPN]
*American legislator and business
executive*
* Stewart, Tariff Andy

Stewart, Anita
See Converse, Anita Marie [Stewart]

Stewart, Anita
See Stewart, Anna May

Stewart, Anna May 1895-1961 [F1, F2,
FC]
American actress
* Stewart, Anita

Stewart, Asa 1869-1912 [BE]
American baseball player
* Stewart, Ace

Stewart, Babe
See Stewart, Albert

Stewart, Babs
See Stewart, Rosalind

Stewart, Black Jack
See Stewart, John Sherratt

Stewart, Blood
See Stewart, Clarence

Stewart, Bob 1950- [SMG]
Canadian-born hockey player
* Stewart, Stewie

Stewart, Bud
See Stewart, Edward Perry

Stewart, Bunky
See Stewart, Veston Goff

Stewart, Catherine
See Zeigle, Kate M.

Stewart, Charles [CEI, SMG]
Hockey player
* Stewart, Doc

Stewart, Charles 1778-1869 [HPPN]
American naval officer
* Old Ironsides

Stewart, Charles
See Zurhorst, Charles [Stewart, Jr.]

Stewart, Charles Eugene 1883-1934
[BE]
American baseball player
* Stewart, Tuffy

Stewart, Charlotte [NPS]
Author
* M'Aulay, Allan

Stewart, Clarence 1944- [BI]
American criminal
* Stewart, Blood

Stewart, Clinton [FFF]
American writer
* Walsingham

Stewart, David
See Politella, Dario

Stewart, David J.
See Siegel, Abe J.

Stewart, Doc
See Stewart, Charles

Stewart, Donald 1950- [IBW]
American circus performer
* Stewart, Keywash

Stewart, Dorothy Mary 1917-1965 [CA]
British author
* Elgin, Mary

Stewart, Douglas 1830-1880 [PA]
Author
* Dundreary, Lord
* Sothern, Edward Askew

Stewart, Dugald 1753-1828 [HN]
Scottish philosopher
* [The] Scottish Plato

Stewart, Edward Perry 1916- [BE]
American baseball player
* Stewart, Bud

Stewart, Elaine
See Steinberg, Elsy

Stewart, Eliza Daniel 1816-1908
[HPPN]
American temperance advocate and humanitarian
* Stewart, Mother

Stewart, Elizabeth Grey
See Reed, Elizabeth Stewart

Stewart, Elizabeth M. 19th c. [HPPN]
British author
* E. M. S.

Stewart, Eve
See Napier, Priscilla

Stewart, Evelyn
See Galli, Ida

Stewart, Frances
See Wilmot, James Reginald

Stewart, Fred 1946- [RO2]
American musician
* Stone, Fred

Stewart, Gabby
See Stewart, Glen Weldon

Stewart, Gene
See Hallowell, Russell F.

Stewart, Geraldine
See Barry, Mrs. Shiel

Stewart, Glen Weldon 1912- [BE]
American baseball player
* Stewart, Gabby

Stewart, Gordon
See Rathborne, St. George Henry

Stewart, Harold 20th c. [CA]
Australian poet
* Malley, Ern [joint pseudonym with James Phillip McAuley]

Stewart, Harris B[ates], Jr. 1922- [CA]
American oceanographer and author
* Benthic, Arch E.

Stewart, Hod
See Stewart, Horace

Stewart, Horace ?-1907
Canadian-born hockey player
* Stewart, Hod

Stewart, Humphrey John 1854-1932
[HPPN]
American composer and musician
* [The] Walter Damrosch of the Pacific Coast

Stewart, Isabella
See Chesne-Dauphine, Isabella

Stewart, J. C.
See Crossey, J. S.

Stewart, J. George 1891?-1970 [HPPN]
American engineer and architect
* [The] Architect of the Capital

Stewart, J. I. M.
See Stewart, John Innes Mackintosh

Stewart, Jackie 1939- [EAR]
Scottish auto racer
* [The] Flying Scot

Stewart, Jackie
See Stewart, John

Stewart, [Sir] James [IP]
Barrister and author
* [A] Lawyer

Stewart [or Stuart], James ?-1592 [SN, WBD]
Second Earl of Moray
* [The] Bonny Earl
* Young Waters

Stewart [or Stuart], James 1531?-1570
[DNNF, FFF, HN]
First Earl of Moray
* [The] Good Regent

Stewart, James L. 1913- [BDF, FC, WEF]
British actor
* Granger, Stewart

Stewart, James Maitland [Jimmy] 1908-
[HPPN]
American actor, aviator, army officer
* [The] Grand Old Man of the Aw Shucks School

Stewart [or Stuart], Jay
See Palmer, Stuart [Hunter]

Stewart, Jean
See Newman, Mona Alice Jean

Stewart, Jessie [IP]
Scottish poet
* J. S.

Stewart, John 1340?-1406 [WBD]
King of Scotland
* Robert III

Stewart, John 1749-1822 [DNNF, RH, SN]
British traveller
* Stewart, Walking

Stewart, John [William] 1920- [CA]
American author
* Cole, Jack

Stewart, John 1939- [HPPN]
Scottish auto racer and sports announcer
* [The] Flying Scot
* Stewart, Jackie

Stewart, John Allan 1838-? [FFF, PA]
American writer
* Taswert

Stewart, John Franklin 1894- [BE]
American baseball player
* Stewart, Stuffy

Stewart, John Innes Mackintosh 1906-
[CC, EMD, LC]
Scottish-born author
* Innes, Michael
* Stewart, J. I. M.

Stewart, John Sherratt 1917- [FHE, HK]
Canadian-born hockey player
* Stewart, Black Jack

Stewart, Judith Anne
See Maciel, Judi[th Anne]

Stewart, Kaye
See Howe, Doris Kathleen

Stewart, Kenneth Livingston 1894- [CC, WW]
Author
* Livingston, Kenneth

Stewart, Kerry
See Stewart, Linda

Stewart, Keywash
See Stewart, Donald

Stewart, Lefty
See Stewart, Walter Cleveland

Stewart, Leroy 1914- [DAM, EJ, PMJ]
American jazz musician
* Stewart, Slam

Stewart, Linda 20th c. [CA]
American author
* Stewart, Kerry
* Stewart, Sam

Stewart, Logan
See Savage, Leslie H.

Stewart, Logan
See Wilding, Philip

Stewart, Mack
See Stewart, William Macklin

Stewart, Margaret 1897- [BF, THR]
British actress
* Stuart, Madge

Stewart, Margaret
See Wilson, Margaret Campell

Stewart, Maria Stewart 19th c. [IP]
Scottish author
* [A] Chip of the Young Block

Stewart, Marie Kathryn 1882-1956
[BEW, F2, FC]
American actress
* Doro, Marie

Stewart, Martha
See Haworth, Martha

Stewart, Michael
See Rubin, Michael Stewart

Stewart, Mother
See Stewart, Eliza Daniel

Stewart, Mrs. Dugald 19th c. [NPS]
* Ivy

Stewart, Mrs. W. [IP]
British author
* E. S.

Stewart, Nancye
See Musgrove, Nancye

Stewart, Neb
See Stewart, Walter Nesbitt

Stewart, Neil 20th c. [WW]
Author
* Lombard, Nap [joint pseudonym with Pamela Hansford Johnson]

Stewart, Nels
See Stewart, Nelson

Stewart, Nelson 1902-1957 [FHE, HK]
Canadian-born hockey player
* Stewart, Nels
* Stewart, Old Poison

Stewart, Old Poison
See Stewart, Nelson

Stewart, Paul A. 1885- [IBW]
American scout program organizer
* Stewart, Pop

Stewart, Paula
See Zurndorfer, Dorothy Paula

Stewart, Pop
See Stewart, Paul A.

Stewart, Ralph Donald 1948- [SMG]
Canadian-born hockey player
* Stewart, Stewie

Stewart, Rattray
See Macbeath, Innis [Stewart]

Stewart, Rex
See Stewart, William

Stewart, Robert [Viscount Castlereagh]
1769-1822 [DNNS, FFF, NPS, SN]
British statesman
* Carotid Artery Cutting
* [The] Derrydown Triangle
* [An] Intellectual Eunuch

Stewart, Robert Armistead 1877-1950
[BI, HPPN]
American educator, author, poet
* Stuart, Gordon

Stewart, Rosalind 1922- [MY]
American singer
* Stewart, Babs

Stewart, Rose 1945- [RO2]
American musician
* Stone, Rose

Stewart, Sam
See Stewart, Linda

Stewart, Sandy
See Galitz, Sandra Ester

Stewart, Slam
See Stewart, Leroy

Stewart, Stephen 1869-? [THR]
British actor
* Ewart, Stephen T.

Stewart, Stewie
See Stewart, Bob

Stewart, Stewie
See Stewart, Ralph Donald

Stewart, Stuffy
See Stewart, John Franklin

Stewart, Sylvester 1944- [RO2]
American musician
* Stone, Sly

Stewart, Tariff Andy
See Stewart, Andrew

Stewart, Tuffy
See Stewart, Charles Eugene

Stewart, Veston Goff 1931- [BE]
American baseball player
* Stewart, Bunky

Stewart, Walking
See Stewart, John

Stewart, Walter Cleveland 1900- [BE, PB]
American baseball player
* Stewart, Lefty

Stewart, Walter Nesbitt 1918- [BE]
American baseball player
* Stewart, Neb

Stewart, Wendall
See Eklund, Gordon

Stewart, Whitey
See Stewart, Albert

Stewart, Will
See Williamson, John Stewart [Jack]

Stewart, William [IP]
Scottish author
* W. S., M.P.

Stewart, William 1907-1967 [IBW]
American jazz musician
* Stewart, Rex

Stewart, William Macklin 1913- [BE]
American baseball player
* Stewart, Mack

Stewart, William Morris 1827-1909
[HPPN]
American politician
* [The] Father of the 15th Amendment

Stewart-Cockerton, Josephine 1895-
[WWL]
British author
* Herne, Thomas

Stewer, Jan
See Coles, Albert

Sthalberg, George [IP]
Author
* [A] Gentleman Who Was a Swede

Stibbes, Agnes Jean 19th c. [FFF, IP]
American author
* Carra, Emma
* Fairfax, Ruth

Stice, J. U.
See Condon, [Dr.] John Francis

Stich, Hermine Neustadtl 1897- [NAA]
American journalist
* Neustadtl, Hermine
* Newton, Jean

[The] Stick
See Kovolick, Philip

Stick 'em Up Stabile
See Stabile, Jack

Stickland, Tiger Jim
See Strickland, James

Stickles, Montford 1938- [FB]
American football player
* Stickles, Monty

Stickles, Monty
See Stickles, Montford

Stickney, Caroline 19th c. [IP]
American author
* Landor, Charles

Stickney, Sarah
See Ellis, Mrs.

Sticky, Captain
See Pesta, Richard

Stiegel, Baron
See Stiegel, Henry William

Stiegel, Henry William 1729-1785
[HPPN]
German industrialist and manufacturer
* Stiegel, Baron
* Von Stiegel, Baron

Stiegele, Georg 1815-1868 [BBD]
German singer and composer
* Stigelli, Giorgio

Stieglitz, Georgia O'Keeffe 1887-
[HPPN]
American painter
* O'Keeffe, Georgia

Stiehm, Ewald O. 1885-1923 [FB]
American football coach
* Stiehm, Jumbo

Stiehm, Jumbo
See Stiehm, Ewald O.

Stier, John 1936?- [HPPN]
American jazz musician
* Edwards, Johnny

Stiernhielm [or Stjernhjelm], Georg
See Olai, Georgius

Stierwell, Jay
See Swicegood, Thomas L. P.

Stiff, Dorothy Aileen 1921- [AW]
British writer
* Kendal, June

Stigelli, Giorgio
See Stiegele, Georg

Stiger, Jim 20th c.
American football player
* Stiger, Smiley

Stiger, Smiley
See Stiger, Jim

Stiglitz, Natalya 20th c. [TI 2-17-86]
*Wife of Soviet dissident, Anatoli
Shcharansky*
* Shcharansky, Avital

Stiles, Bill
See Chadwell, William

Stiles, Ezra 1727-1795 [HPPN]
American clergyman and scholar
* Philagathos
* Setis, Keal

Stiles, Rolland Mays 1906- [HPPN]
American baseball player
* Lena

Stiles, William Larkin [Billy] ?-1908
[EWG]
American gunfighter
* Larkin, William

Stilicho, Flavius 359?-408 [RH]
Roman general and statesman
* [The] Last of the Romans

[The] Still
See Tacitus, Cornelius

Still, Andrew Taylor 1828-1917 [HPPN]
American physician
* [The] Father of Osteopathy

Still Bill Hill
See Hill, William C.

Still, William Grant 1895-1978 [IBW]
American composer and musician
* [The] Dean of Afro-American
  Composers

Stille, Karl
See Demme, Hermann Christoph
Gottfried

Stiller, Mauritz
See Stiller, Mosche [or Mowscha]

Stiller, Mosche [or Mowscha] 1883-1928
[FD]
Finnish director
* [The] Iron Duke
* Stiller, Mauritz

Stilling, Heinrich [or John Henry]
See Jung, Heinrich

Stillingfleet, Benjamin 1702-1771
[HPPN, IP]
British author
* [A] Farmer in Cheshire
* Krantzovius, Irenoeus

Stillman, Annie Raymond 1855-? [DNA]
American author
* Raymond, Grace

Stillman, Lou
See Ingber, Louis

Stillman, Samuel 1737-1807 [HPPN]
American clergyman
* Her Son

Stillman, W. O. 19th c. [IP]
American author
* W. O. S.

Stillman, William James 1828-1901
[HPPN]
American painter and journalist
* [The] American Pre Raphaelite

Stillwell, Frank
See Stillwell, T. C.

Stillwell, T. C. 1855-1882 [HPPN]
American outlaw
* Stillwell, Frank

Stillwell, William
See Krown, Kevin

[The] Stilt
See Chamberlain, Wilt[on Norman]

Stilton, W.
See Annet, Peter

Stilwell, Comanche Jack
See Stilwell, Simpson E.

Stilwell, Comanche John
See Stilwell, Simpson E.

Stilwell, Ethel
See Allan, Ethel Stilwell

Stilwell, Jack
See Stilwell, Simpson E.

Stilwell, Joseph Warren 1883-1946
[CND, HPPN, WA]
American military leader
* Inwall [code name used during World
  War II]
* Old Tu'key Neck
* Quarterback [code name used during
  World War II]
* Stilwell, Uncle Joe
* Stilwell, Vinegar Joe

Stilwell, Silas Moore 1800-1881 [FFF]
American politician
* Caucus, King

Stilwell, Simpson E. 1849-1903 [BI,
EWG, HPPN]
American attorney and army scout
* Stilwell, Comanche Jack
* Stilwell, Comanche John
* Stilwell, Jack
* Stilwell, Wildcat Jack

Stilwell, Uncle Joe
See Stilwell, Joseph Warren

Stilwell, Vinegar Joe
See Stilwell, Joseph Warren

Stilwell, Wildcat Jack
See Stilwell, Simpson E.

Stimmel, Archibald May [Archie]
1873-1958 [BE]
American baseball player
* Stimmel, Lumbago

Stimmel, Lumbago
See Stimmel, Archibald May [Archie]

Stimson, Frederic Jesup 1855-1943
[NAA]
American diplomat and author
* J. S. of Dale

Stimson, Henry Lewis 1867-1950
[HPPN]
*American Secretary of State and
Secretary of War*
* Stimy

Stimy
See Stimson, Henry Lewis

Stinchcomb, Gaylord R. 1896-1973 [BI,
FB]
American football player
* Stinchcomb, Pete

Stinchcomb, Pete
See Stinchcomb, Gaylord R.

Stinde, Julius 1841-? [IP]
Danish author
* Valmy, Alfred de

Stine, G[eorge] Harry 1928- [CA, SAT]
American author
* Correy, Lee

Stine, Hank
See Stein, Henry Eugene

Stine, Jovial Bob
See Stine, Robert Lawrence

Stine, Robert Lawrence 1943- [CA]
American author and editor
* Stine, Jovial Bob

Stine, Whitney Ward 1930- [CA]
American author
* McLeish, Garen
* Ward, Jonathon

Stiner, Alonzo L. 20th c. [HPPN]
American football coach
* Stiner, Lon

Stiner, Lon
See Stiner, Alonzo L.

Stinfalico, Eterio
See Marcello, Alessandro

Sting
See Sumner, Gordon Matthew

Stingo, John R.
See MacDonald, James Aloysius

Stinky
See Davis, Harry Albert

Stinson, Gorrell R. 1945- [SMG]
American baseball player
* Stinson, Scrap Iron

Stinson, Mrs. Frederick [FFF]
Entertainer
* Martinot, Sadie

Stinson, Scrap Iron
See Stinson, Gorrell R.

Stipetic, Werner H. 1942- [CA]
German screenwriter, producer, director
* Herzog, Werner

Stires, Garrett 1849-1933 [BE]
American baseball player
* Stires, Gat

Stires, Gat
See Stires, Garrett

Stirling, A. M. W.
See Stirling, Anna Maria Diana
Wilhelmina [Pickering]

**Stirling, Anna Maria Diana Wilhelmina
[Pickering]** 1865-1965 [CAP, LC]
British author
* Pickering, Percival
* Stirling, A. M. W.

Stirling, Arthur
See Sinclair, Upton [Beall]

Stirling, Bummer
See Stirling, Hugh

Stirling, David 1915- [BDW, WWW]
British military leader
* [The] Phantom Major

Stirling, Edward
See Lambert, Edward

Stirling, Fanny
See Hehl [or Kehl?], Mary Anne

Stirling, Gordon [SMG]
*American sportswriter and basketball
team president*
* Stirling, Scotty

Stirling, Hugh 1910- [CFH]
Canadian football player
* Stirling, Bummer

Stirling, James 1692-1770 [WBD]
Scottish mathematician
* [The] Venetian

Stirling, Jessica
See Coghlan, Margaret M.

Stirling, Jessica
See Rae, Hugh C[rauford]

Stirling, Linda
See Schultz, Louise

Stirling, Peter
See Stern, David

Stirling, Peter Lee 20th c. [RO2]
British singer
* Boone, Daniel

Stirling, Scotty
See Stirling, Gordon

Stirling, Tom
See Ransome, L. E.

Stirling, William 1818-? [HPPN]
Scottish nobleman
* Maxwell, [Sir] William Stirling
* [A] Traveller

Stirner, Max
See Schmidt, Kaspar

Stirnweiss, George Henry 1918?-1958
[AS, BE, PB]
American baseball player
* Stirnweiss, Snuffy

Stirnweiss, Snuffy
See Stirnweiss, George Henry

Stirrup
See Brent, Henry J.

Stitch, George Ford 1884?-1939 [BEW,
F1, F2]
American actor
* Sterling, Ford

Stitch, Wilhelmina
See Collie, Ruth

Stith, Edith Mae 1907- [BEW, IBW]
American singer, dancer, actress
* Barnes, Mae
* Brownskin Mama

Stith, Zoda 19th c. [IP]
American poet
* Elloie

Stitt, Edward 1924-1982 [DAM, EJ,
PMJ]
American jazz musician
* Stitt, Sonny

Stitt, J. M. 1930- [AW]
Scottish author
* Brunswick, James

Stitt, Sonny
See Stitt, Edward

Stivens, Dal
See Stivens, Dallas George

Stivens, Dallas George 1911- [SFL]
Author
* Stivens, Dal

Stivers, Jeremiah [FFF]
Entertainer
* Watson, Will

Stivers, Mark 20th c. [SFL]
Author
* Disrobeson, Kin I.

Stivers, Mrs. J. [FFF]
Entertainer
* Shandley, Sallie

Stivetts, Happy Jack
See Stivetts, John Elmer

Stivetts, John Elmer 1868-1930 [BE]
American baseball player
* Stivetts, Happy Jack

Sto
See Tofano, Sergio

Stobbs, John Louis Newcombe 1921-
[IAW]
British author
* Newcombe, Louis

Stoberski, Zygmunt Julian 1916- [IAW]
Polish author
* Boroniecki, Miroslaw
* Stebelski, Julian

Stobo, Edward John 1838-1918 [CCL]
Canadian author
* Aletheia

Stock, Baron
See Rattazzi, [Princess] Marie
Studolmine Bonaparte

[The] Stock Car Racing King
See Petty, Richard

Stock, Frederick
See Stock, Friedrich Wilhelm August

Stock, Friedrich Wilhelm August 1872-
1942
American conductor
* Stock, Frederick

Stock, John 19th c. [IP]
British author
* [An] Old Smoker

Stock, John Edmonds 1774-1835 [IP]
British author and physician
* [A] Layman

Stock, Joseph 1740-1813 [IP, PI]
Irish author and clergyman
* [An] Eye Witness

Stockard, Susan 1944- [SW]
American actress
* Channing, Stockard

Stockbridge, Frank Parker 1870-?
[NAA]
American author and journalist
* Johnson, Caleb

Stockbridge, Grant [house pseudonym]
See Gruber, Frank

Stockbridge, Grant [house pseudonym]
See Maitland, Reginald T.

Stockbridge, Grant
See Page, Norvell W.

Stockbridge, Grant [house pseudonym]
See Tepperman, Emile

Stockdale, Carl
See Stockdale, Carlton

Stockdale, Carlton 1874-1953 [SC]
American actor
* Stockdale, Carl

Stockdale, Percival 1736-1811 [FFF]
British author
* Agricola

Stocken, Frank 1867-1937 [THR]
British actor
* Lacy, Frank

Stocker, Helen 1887- [WWL]
British poet
* Cash, Helen

Stockfisch, Hans
See Spencer, John

Stockford, Lela E. 20th c. [CCL]
Canadian author
* Hamilton-Stockford, Joan

[The] Stocking-Foot Orator
See McKinley, William

Stockley, Cynthia
See Webb, Lilian Julian

Stockley, Mrs. Vesey [NPS]
Author
* Ford, Mrs. Gerard

Stockman, David A. 20th c. [DF 3-7-83]
American government official
* [The] Grim Reaper
* [The] Young Slasher

Stockton, Dick
See Stokvis, Dick

Stockton, F. R.
See Stockton, Francis Richard

Stockton, Francis Richard 1834-1902
[HPPN, LC]
American author
* Fort, Paul
* Stockton, F. R.

Stockton, Mrs. Frank R. 19th c. [FFF, IP]
American author
* Dunn, Deborah

Stockton, Richard 1764-1828 [HPPN]
American politician
* [The] Duke

Stockton, William T. 1812-1869 [BDSA]
American author and army officer
* Cor-de-Chasse

Stockwell, George A. 19th c. [IP, PA]
American author
* Archer

Stockwell, Mrs. L. R.   [FFF]
Entertainer
* Brandon, Ethel

[The] Stockyard Bluebeard
See Hoch, Johann

Stocqueler, Joachim Hayward   [IP]
British army officer and author
* Siddons, James H.

Stoddard, Betsy
See Zimmerman, Elizabeth S.

Stoddard, Charles [house pseudonym]
See Kuttner, Henry

Stoddard, Charles [house pseudonym]
See Strong, Charles Stanley

Stoddard, Charles Augustus 1833-?
[ALY]
American author
* Augustus

Stoddard, Charles Warren 1843-1909
[WBD]
American author and poet
* Pepperpod, Pip

Stoddard, [Major] Henry B.
See Ingraham, Prentiss

Stoddard, Richard Henry 1825-1903
[FFF, IP]
American poet and critic
* Lang, S.
* R. H. S.
* Richards, Henry

Stoddard, Sandol
See Warburg, Sandol Stoddard

Stoddard, William Osborne 1835-1925
[HPPN]
American inventor and author
* Forrest, [Col.] Chris

Stoddart, Jane T. 20th c. [WWL]
British author
* Lorner

Stoddart, [Sir] John 1773-1856 [DEL, PA]
British journalist
* J. S.
* Slop, Doctor

Stoddart, Thomas Tod   [IP]
Scottish author and poet
* [An] Angler

Stoeffler, Johann 1425-1531 [PA]
Author
* Stofflerinus

Stoepel, Helene 1862?-1937 [BEW]
American actress
* Heron, Bijou

Stoepfel, Mrs. Robert   [FFF]
Entertainer
* Heron, Matilda

Stofflerinus
See Stoeffler, Johann

Stoil, Michael Jon 1950- [CA]
German-born educator and author
* Augustine, Erich

Stojanov, Stojan
See Gancev, Stojan

Stokely, Wilma Dykeman 1920- [CA]
American author
* Dykeman, Wilma

Stoker, Abraham 1847-1912 [CC, EMD, LC]
British author
* Stoker, Bram

Stoker, Alan 1930- [CA, WD]
British author
* Evans, Alan

Stoker, Bram
See Stoker, Abraham

Stoker, H. G.
See Stoker, Hew Gordon Dacre

Stoker, Hew Gordon Dacre 1885-1966
[SC]
Irish-born actor and playwright
* Gordon, Hew
* Stoker, H. G.

Stoker, Willard
See Stoker, William Richard

Stoker, William Richard 1905- [TR]
British director
* Stoker, Willard

Stokes, Al[bert John]
See Stacek, Albert John

Stokes, Anthony 1736-1799 [HPPN]
British-American jurist
* [The] Chief Justice

Stokes, Big Mo
See Stokes, Maurice

Stokes, C. W. 19th c. [IP]
British author
* [A] London Merchant

Stokes, Cedric
See Beardmore, George

Stokes, Ella
See Doris, Mrs. John B.

Stokes, Francis William 1883- [WW]
Author
* Everton, Francis

Stokes, George 1789-1847 [IP]
British author
* Lay Member of the British and Foreign Bible Society

Stokes, Henry Sewell 1808-? [IP]
British poet
* H. S. S.

Stokes, J. Lemacks 19th c. [DNA]
Author and clergyman
* May, Reginald

Stokes, John Whitley [IP]
Irish clergyman and author
* [A] Pastor

Stokes, Katie
See Stetson, Mrs. John

Stokes, Manning Lee 20th c. [WGT, WW]
Author
* Ludwell, Bernice
* Manning, Lee

Stokes, Margaret MacNair 19th c. [IP]
Irish antiquary
* M. S.

Stokes, Maurice 1933-1970 [BB, IBW]
American basketball player
* Stokes, Big Mo
* Stokes, Mo

Stokes, Mo
See Stokes, Maurice

Stokes, Pee Wee
See Stokes, Tony

Stokes, Robert [Bob]
See Wilkening, Howard [Everett]

Stokes, Simpson
See Fawcett, F[rank] Dubrez

Stokes, Tony 20th c. [RBE]
American boxer
* Stokes, Pee Wee

Stokes, Whitley 1830-? [IP]
Irish barrister, historian, philologist
* W. S.

Stokes, William Brickly 1814-1897 [HPPN]
American soldier, attorney, politician
* [The] Eagle Orator

Stoki
See Stokowski, Leopold Anthony

Stokowski, Leopold
See Antoni, Boleslawowicz Stanislaw

Stokowski, Leopold Anthony 1882-1977 [PW 9-10-82]
British-born conductor
* Stoki

Stokvis, Dick 20th c. [SI 3-12-84]
American sportscaster
* Stockton, Dick

Stoll, Clarice Stasz
See Stasz, Clarice

Stoll, Dennis G[ray] 1912- [CA]
British author
* Craig, Denys

Stoll, [Sir] Oswald
See Gray, Oswald

Stolle, Ludwig Ferdinand 1806-1872 [HPPN]
German author
* Anders, Ludwig F.

Stollenwerck, Logan 20th c. [HPPN]
American football player
* Stollenwerck, Stolly

Stollenwerck, Stolly
See Stollenwerck, Logan

Stolper, Alice 1934- [IAW]
American author
* Peppler, Alice Stolper

Stolterfoth, Georg
See Bonus, Arthur

Stoltz, Adley 1946- [ITA]
American actress
* Dupont, Adley

Stoltz, [Mademoiselle] Heloise
See Noel, Victoire

Stoltz, Rosine
See Noel, Victoire

Stolz, Lois Meek 1891- [CAP]
American psychologist and author
* Meek, Lois Hayden

[The] Stomping Mare
See Ryan, Hermine Braunsteiner

Stona, Thomas ?-1792 [IP]
British clergyman and author
* [A] Dumpling-Eater

Stone, Alan [house pseudonym] [Stratemeyer Syndicate]
See Stratemeyer, Edward L.

Stone, Alan [house pseudonym] [Stratemeyer Syndicate]
See Svenson, Andrew E.

Stone, Arthur
See Gladstone, Arthur

Stone Ass
See Skryabin, Vyacheslav Mikhailovich

Stone, Barbara Haskins 1924?-1979 [CA]
British editor
* Haskins, Barbara

Stone, Ben W.
See Demara, Ferdinand Waldo, Jr.

Stone, Butch
See Stone, Henry

Stone, C. J. [IP]
British author
* Gibbon, Edwarda

Stone, Carol
See Stone, Fredeline Montgomery

Stone, Cecil Percival 19th c. [IP]
British army officer and author
* Enos

Stone, Cliffie
See Snyder, Clifford Gilpin

Stone, [Private] Dwight Elliot 1949?- [HPPN]
American soldier
* [The] Last Draftee in American History

Stone, Eddie
See Marblestone, Eddie

Stone, Elizabeth 19th c. [IP]
British author
* Menzies, Sutherland

Stone, Elna 20th c. [CA]
American author
* Daniel, Elna Worrell

Stone, Ena Margaret 1911- [IAW]
South African-born author
* O'Randa, Jack
* Sandown, Margaret

Stone, Ernest 20th c. [BMH]
British comedian
* Mack, Ernest

Stone, Eugenia 1879-1971 [CA, SAT]
American author
* Stone, Gene

Stone, Ezra
See Feinstone, Ezra Chaim

Stone Forehead Powell
See Powell, Peter

Stone, Fred
See Stewart, Fred

Stone, Fredeline Montgomery 1915- [BEW]
American actress and director
* Stone, Carol

Stone, Frederick Mather 1861-1932 [HPPN]
American attorney and politician
* Rocks

Stone, Gene
See Stone, Eugenia

Stone, George
See Stoneseifer, George

Stone, George E.
See Stein, George

Stone, George H. 1946- [PB]
American baseball player
* Stone, Stoney

Stone, George Robert 1876-1945 [EJS]
American baseball player
* Stone, Silent George

Stone, Grace Zaring 1896?- [ANT, CAP, CC]
American author
* Vance, Ethel

Stone, Hampton
See Stein, Aaron Marc

Stone, Henry ?-1653 [FFF, RH, SN]
British painter and sculptor
* Old Stone

Stone, Henry 1913- [PMJ]
American musician
* Stone, Butch

Stone, Henry Attie 1901-1956
American martial artist
* [The] Father of American Karate

Stone, Hoyt E[dward] 1935- [CA]
American author and clergyman
* Vernon, Eddie

Stone, I. F.
See Stone, Isador Feinstein

Stone, Idella Purnell
See Purnell, Idella

Stone, Ikey
See Purnell, Idella

Stone, Irving
See Tennenbaum, Irving

Stone, Isador Feinstein 1907- [CR, IPA]
American journalist and author
* Stone, I. F.
* Stone, Izzy

Stone, Izzy
See Stone, Isador Feinstein

Stone, J. L. 19th c. [IP]
American author
* [The] Hebrew Wood Chopper

Stone, Jeffery 20th c. [WP 2-17-85]
American baseball player
* Stone, Light Speed

Stone, Jesse 20th c.
Songwriter
* Calhoun, Charles

Stone, John Christopher 1923- [ART]
British artist
* J. C. S.

Stone, John Mack
See McCulley, Johnston

Stone, John Saville [FFF, IP, PA]
British author and musician
* Stein, Johann Saville

Stone, John Vernon 1918- [BE]
American baseball player
* Stone, Rocky

Stone, Jonathan Thomas 1905-1955 [AS, BE, PB]
American baseball player
* Stone, Rocky

Stone, Josephine Rector
See Dixon, Jeanne

Stone, Kate
See Holmes, Sarah Katherine Stone

Stone, Leslie F.
See Silberberg, Leslie F[rances] Stone

Stone, Light Speed
See Stone, Jeffery

Stone, Lucy 1818-1893 [HPPN]
American women's rights crusader
* Blackwell, Mrs. Henry
* [The] Voice of the Women's
  Movement

Stone, Lyle 1931- [IBW]
American athlete
* Stone, Toni

Stone, Lynn
Radio scriptwriter
* Marston, Adelaide [joint pseudonym
  with Addy Richton]

Stone, Marie
See Macdonald, Mrs. W. H.

Stone, Mary
See Shih Mai-yu

[The] Stone Mason of Tor House
See Jeffers, John Robinson

Stone, Mrs. S. C. 19th c. [IP]
American author
* Forester, Fleta

Stone, Oliver
See Bowdoin, William Goodrich

Stone, Patti 1926- [CA]
American author
* Patrick, Leal

Stone, Peter 20th c. [WF]
American screenwriter
* Werty, Quentin

Stone, Raymond [house pseudonym]
[Stratemeyer Syndicate]
See Stratemeyer, Edward L.

Stone, Richard
See Delaney, Jack J[ames]

Stone, Richard A. [house pseudonym]
[Stratemeyer Syndicate]
See Stratemeyer, Edward L.

Stone, Rocky
See Stone, John Vernon

Stone, Rocky
See Stone, Jonathan Thomas

Stone, Rose
See Stewart, Rose

Stone, Silent George
See Stone, George Robert

Stone, Simon
See Barrington, Howard

Stone, Sly
See Stewart, Sylvester

Stone, Stoney
See Stone, George H.

Stone, Stoney
See Stone, Wayne

Stone, Susan Berch 1944- [CA]
American author
* M
* Whitefield, Ann

Stone, Thomas H.
See Harknett, Terry

Stone, Tiger [or Tige]
See Stone, William Arthur

Stone, Toni
See Stone, Lyle

Stone, Wayne 20th c. [RO2]
Canadian-born musician
* Stone, Stoney

Stone, William 19th c. [IP]
British clergyman and author
* [The] Pastor of St. Paul's,
  Haggerstone

Stone, William Arthur 1901-1960 [BE]
American baseball player
* Stone, Tiger [or Tige]

Stone, William Joel 1848-1918 [WBD]
American politician
* Gum-Shoe Bill

Stone, William Leete 1792-1844 [HPPN]
American historian and journalist
* [The] Nemesis of Maria Monk

Stone, Willie
See Moore, Chuck

Stone, Zachary
See Follett, Kenneth Martin

Stonebraker, Homer 20th c. [BBH]
American basketball player
* Stonebraker, Stoney

Stonebraker, Stoney
See Stonebraker, Homer

Stonecastle, Henry
See Baker, Henry

Stoneclink
See Dale, Thomas F.

Stoneham, Charles Thurley 1895- [WW]
Author
* Thurley, Norgove

Stonehenge
See Walsh, John Henry

Stonehouse, Alpheus George Barnes
1862-1931 [HPPN]
Canadian circus entrepreneur
* Barnes, Al G.

Stonehouse, William Brocklehurst ?-1862
[IP]
British clergyman and author
* Fidelis

Stoneman, Ernest V. 1893-1968 [CWG, DAM]
American country-western performer
* Stoneman, Pop

Stoneman, Pop
See Stoneman, Ernest V.

Stoneman, Stoney
See Stoneman, William A.

Stoneman, William A. 1944- [PB]
American baseball player
* Stoneman, Stoney

[The] Stonemason of Cromarty
See Miller, Hugh

Stoner, Lil
See Stoner, Ulysses Simpson Grant

Stoner, Michael S. 1911-　[ASC]
American composer
* Stoner, Mickey

Stoner, Mickey
See Stoner, Michael S.

Stoner, Mother
See Stoner, Winifred Sackville

Stoner, Ulysses Simpson Grant
1899-1966　[BE]
American baseball player
* Stoner, Lil

Stoner, Winifred Sackville　[NAA]
Author and songwriter
* Stoner, Mother

Stoneseifer, George 1890-1928　[HPPN]
American singer
* Stone, George

Stonestreet, G. G. 19th c.　[IP]
British author
* Sussexiensis

[The] Stonewall of the West
See Cleburne, Patrick Ronayne

Stong, Clair L. 1902?-1975　[BI, CA]
American engineer, columnist, writer
* Stong, Red

Stong, Red
See Stong, Clair L.

Stonhouse, [Sir] James 1716-1795　[IP]
British clergyman and author
* [A] Minister

Stonier, George 20th c.
British author
* Fanfarlo
* Gurnard, Joseph

Stonor, Oliver 1903-　[CAP, HPPN]
British author, journalist, critic
* Bishop, E. Morchard
* Bishop, Evelyn Morchard
* Bishop, Morchard

[The] Stooge
See Ryffe, Carlos Dee

Stooge, Iggy
See Osterberg, James Jewell [Jim]

Stookey, Aaron W.
See Beatty, Jerome, Jr.

Stookey, Noel 1937-　[RO1]
American singer
* Stookey, Paul

Stookey, Paul
See Stookey, Noel

Stooping Jack Gorman
See Gorman, John F. [Jack]

Stoopnagle, [Colonel] Lemuel Q.
See Taylor, Frederick Chase

Stop
See Morel-Retz, Louis-Pierre

Stopelman, Francis
See Stoppelman, Frans

Stopes, Marie Carmichael 1880-1958
[HPPN, LAO]
Scottish author and scientist
* Carmichael, Marie
* Fay, Erica

Stopford, A. St. G. 19th c.　[PI]
Irish poet
* A. St. G. S.

Stopford Green, Mrs.
See Green, Alice Sophia Amelia
Stopford

Stoppard, Tom
See Straussler, Thomas

Stoppelman, Francis
See Stoppelman, Frans

Stoppelman, Frans 1921-　[CAP]
Dutch author
* Stopelman, Francis
* Stoppelman, Francis

Stoppelmoor, Cheryl 1951?-
American actress
* Ladd, Cheryl

[The] Stopper
See Calhoun, David

Storball, Don
See Norman, Don[ald]

Storer, David 19th c.　[IP]
American author
* Phillatins

Storer, Harriet G. 19th c.　[IP]
American author
* Doutney, Mrs. T. Narcisse
* R. L. B.

Storey, Edward Francis 1901-　[EG]
Golfer
* Storey, Eustace

Storey, Eustace
See Storey, Edward Francis

Storey, May Garcia 1868-1950　[HPPN]
American actress and costume designer
* Garcia, May

Storey, Red
See Storey, Roy Alvin

Storey, Roy Alvin 1918-　[CFH, HK]
*Canadian-born football and hockey
official*
* Storey, Red

Storey, Victoria Carolyn 1945-　[CA]
British author
* Martin, Vicky

[The] Stork
See Hendricks, Ted

[The] Stork
See Wilson, James

Stork Club, Mr.
See Billingsley, [John] Sherman

Stork, Mr.
See Michelman, Stanley

Stork, Philipp 1929-　[OP]
Canadian opera singer
* Stark, Phil

Storks
See Huxley, Thomas

Storm
See Townsend, Storm Diana

Storm, Anthony
See Roberts, John S[torm]

Storm, Brian [house pseudonym, Curtis
Warren]
See Holloway, Brian

Storm, Christopher
See Olsen, Theodore Victor

Storm, Duncan
See Floyd, Gilbert

Storm, Eric
See Tubb, Edwin Charles

Storm, Gale
See Cottle, Josephine

Storm, Hyemeyohsts 1935-　[CA]
American author
* Golden Silver

[The] Storm in Norman
See Van Lier, Norm[an, III]

Storm, Ivan
See Thomas, Reginald George

Storm, Jannick
See Jorgensen, J. S.

[The] Storm King
See Espy, James Pollard

Storm, Lesley
See Clark, Mabel Margaret [Cowie]

Storm, Mallory
See Fairman, Paul W.

Storm, Michael
See Sempill, Ernest

Storm P.
See Petersen, Robert Storm

Storm, Robert
See Trell, Max

Storm, Rupert
See Sempill, Ernest

Storm, Russell
See Williams, Robert Moore

Storm, Virginia
See Swatridge, Irene Maude [Mossop]

Storme, Peter
See Stern, Philip Van Doren

Storms, Andre 1911-
French author
* Castelot, Andre

Storms, Jacques 1914-
French playwright
* Castelot, Jacques

Stormy
See Lawrence, Stacy

Stormy Petrel
See Chandler, William Eaton

Stormy Petrel
See Kenny, Annie M.

**[The] Stormy Petrel of European
Politics**
See Mazzini, Giuseppe

[The] Stormy Petrel of Politics
See Brougham, Henry Peter

[The] Stormy Petrel of Politics
See Scott, John

[The] Stormy Petrel of the Art World
See Kent, Rockwell

[The] Stormy Petrel of the Chess World
See Nimzowitsch, Arnold [or Aron?]

[The] Stormy Voyager
See Wilkes, Charles

Storr, Catherine [Cole] 1913- [CA, SAT]
British author
* Adler, Irene
* Lourie, Helen

Storrs, George 1796-1879 [DNA, HPPN]
American author and clergyman
* Anthrops
* Homo Anthropos

Storti, Lin
See Storti, Lindo Ivan

Storti, Lindo Ivan 1906- [BE]
American baseball player
* Storti, Lin

Story, A. M. Sommerville 20th c.
[WGT, WWL]
Author
* Sommerville, Frankfort

Story, Adeline E. 19th c. [FFF, IP]
American writer
* Dixon, Helena

Story, E. M.
See Cassidy, James

Story, Isaac 1774-1803? [FFF, HPPN,
IP, PA, WBD]
American poet
* Headin, Beri
* Quince, Peter
* [The] Traveller

Story, Josephine
See Loring, Emilie [Baker]

[The] Story Lady
See Faulkner, Georgene

Story, Richard
See Gold, Horace Leonard

Story, Rosamond Mary 20th c. [MBF]
British author
* Jeskins, Richard
* Lee, Charles H.
* Lindsay, Josephine
* Reid, Desmond [house pseudonym]
* Tracy, Catherine
* Woods, Ross

Story, Sommerville 20th c. [HPPN]
German editor and journalist
* Sommerville, Frankfort

Story, Sydney A., Jr.
See Pike, Mary Hayden Green

[The] Story Telling Painter
See Millet, Jean Francois

Story, Thomas 1662?-1742 [IP]
British-born clergyman and author
* T. S.

Story, William Wetmore 1819-? [IP]
American poet and sculptor
* W. W. S.

[The] Storyteller
See Hall, Tom T.

[The] Stot
See Stuart, James

Stot, Joseph
See Whitworth, Robert

Stothard, Thomas 1755-1834 [SN]
British illustrator and painter
* [The] English Raphael
* Our Domestic Raphael

Stothert, James Augustine 19th c. [IP]
Scottish antiquary and poet
* [A] Member of the Gild

Stothert, William 19th c. [IP]
British clergyman and author
* Philalethes

Stotler, Bud
See Stotler, J. H.

Stotler, J. H. 20th c.
American horse trainer
* Stotler, Bud

Stott, Thomas 1755-1829 [PI, RH]
Irish poet
* Hafiz

Stoudenmire, Dallas 1843-1882 [HPPN]
American marshal and gunfighter
* [The] Lawman Turned Gunfighter

Stouder, O. C. 19th c. [IP]
American scholar
* Lancer

Stoughton, Blaine 20th c.
Hockey player
* Stoughton, Stash

Stoughton, Stash
See Stoughton, Blaine

Stout, Allyn McClelland 1904-1974 [BE,
HPPN]
American baseball player
* Stout, Fish Hook

Stout, Bert
See Stout, Herbert E.

Stout, Fish Hook
See Stout, Allyn McClelland

Stout Harry
See Henry VIII

Stout, Herbert E. 1905- [HPPN]
American composer and businessman
* Stout, Bert

Stout, Robert Joe 1936- [CA]
American author
* Pires, Joe

Stout Steve Owen
See Owen, Stephen Joseph [Steve]

Stoutenburg, Adrien [Pearl] 1916- [CA,
SAT, TBJ]
American author
* Arden, Barbie [joint pseudonym with
  Barbara Ritchie]
* Kendall, Lace
* Minier, Nelson [joint pseudonym with
  Laura Nelson Baker]

Stovall, Alice 1935- [HPPN]
American forger
* Mendez, Alice
* Sanchez, Alice

Stovall, Babe
See Stovall, Jewell

Stovall, Firebrand
See Stovall, George Thomas

Stovall, George Thomas 1878-1951 [BE,
PB]
American baseball player and manager
* Stovall, Firebrand

Stovall, Jesse Cranmer 1876-1955 [BE]
American baseball player
* Stovall, Scout

Stovall, Jewell 1907-1974 [BWW]
American singer
* Stovall, Babe

Stovall, Rawson 1973?- [TI 10-17-83]
American columnist
* Vid Kid

Stovall, Scout
See Stovall, Jesse Cranmer

Stovenour, June 1926- [FC, PMJ]
American actress
* Haver, June

Stover, Smokey
See Stover, Stewart

Stover, Stewart 20th c. [EF]
American football player
* Stover, Smokey

Stovey, Harry Duffield
See Stowe, Harry Duffield

Stovold, Andrew Willis 1953- [DC]
British cricketer
* Stovold, Squeak
* Stovold, Stov
* Stovold, Stovers

Stovold, Bubble
See Stovold, Martin Willis

Stovold, Martin Willis 1955-   [DC]
British cricketer
* Stovold, Bubble

Stovold, Squeak
See Stovold, Andrew Willis

Stovold, Stov
See Stovold, Andrew Willis

Stovold, Stovers
See Stovold, Andrew Willis

Stow, John 1525-1605   [DEP, FFF, IP, SN]
British historian
* [The] Herodotus of Old London
* [A] Lay Member of the Church of England
* Trudger and Trencher

Stowasser, Friedrich 1928-   [BI]
Austrian artist
* Hundertwasser, Fritz

Stowe, Harriet Beecher 1811-1896
[DEL, HPPN, IP]
American author
* [The] American Novelist
* Crowfield, Christopher
* [The] Crusader in Crinoline
* Henderson, Harry
* [The] Victorian Cinderella

Stowe, Harry Duffield 1856-1937   [BE, DGS]
American baseball player
* Stovey, Harry Duffield

[The] Stowe of France
See Sauval, Henri

Stowe, Rosetta [joint pseudonym with Margaret E. (Nettles) Ogan]
See Ogan, George F.

Stowe, Rosetta [joint pseudonym with George F. Ogan]
See Ogan, Margaret E. [Nettles]

Stowell, Hugh 1799-1865   [IP]
British clergyman and author
* [A] Clergyman

Stowell, William Scott 1745-1836   [IP, PA]
British author and jurist
* Civis

[The] Strabo of Britain
See Camden, William

[The] Strabo of Germany
See Muenster, Sebastian

Strabolgi, Bartolomeo
See Tucci, Niccolo

Strachan J[ohn] George 1910-
Canadian author
* George, Jay

Strachan, John 1778-1867   [IP, PA]
Scottish-born clergyman and author
* Reckoner

Strachan, Margaret Pitcairn 1908-   [CA, WD]
American author
* More, Caroline [joint pseudonym with Molly (Lamken) Cone]

Strachey, Barbara
See Halpern, Barbara Strachey

Straci, Joseph 20th c.   [PHM]
American underworld figure
* Stretch, Joe

Strader, John Gary 1932-   [HPPN]
American singer
* Gary, John

Strader, Norman 1902?-1956   [AS]
American football player
* Strader, Red

Strader, Red
See Strader, Norman

Stradley, Mark
See Smith, Richard Rein

Stradling, Matthew
See Mahoney, M. F.

Straesser, Joep
See Straesser, Joseph Willem Frederik

Straesser, Joseph Willem Frederik 1934-
[IWM]
Dutch composer
* Straesser, Joep

Strafford
See Johnson, Harriet Laight C.

Strage, Mark 1927-   [CA]
Manchurian-born American author
* Hazlitt, Joseph
* Quick, Philip

Strahan, Edward
See Shinn, Earl

Strahler, Michael Wayne 1947-   [SMG]
American baseball player
* Strahler, Spider
* [The] Thin Man

Strahler, Spider
See Strahler, Michael Wayne

Strahorn, Robert E.   [IP, PA]
American journalist
* Aleter, Esq.
* Alter Ego

Straight, [Sir] Douglas 1844-?   [IP, NPS, PA]
British author
* Daryl, Sidney
* [An] Old Harrovian
* Sigma

Straight Tongue
See Whipple, Henry Benjamin

Strain, R. W. M.
See Strain, Robert William Magill

Strain, Robert William Magill 1907-
[ART]
Irish-born painter
* Strain, R. W. M.

Straine, Doc
See Straine, James

Straine, James 20th c.   [BWW]
American entertainer
* Straine, Doc

Strait, Raymond 1924-   [CA]
American author
* Ray, Russell

[The] Straitened
See Rupert

Straiton, Edward Cornock 1917-   [CA]
Scottish veterinarian and author
* Vet, T. V.

Straker, John Foster 1904-   [CA]
British author
* Rosse, Ian

Strakosch, Avery
See Denham, Avery Strakosch

Stranahan, James Samuel Thomas
1808-1898   [HPPN]
American philanthropist
* [The] First Citizen of Brooklyn

Stranahan, Jason G. 20th c.
American lacrosse coach
* Stranahan, Stranny

Stranahan, Stranny
See Stranahan, Jason G.

Strand, Les
See Strandt, Leslie Roy

Strand, Mark
See Strand, Marthinius A.

Strand, Marthinius A. 1887-1965   [BBH]
Norwegian-born skiing organization founder and officer
* Strand, Mark

Strand, Paul E.
See Palestrant, Simon S.

Strandberg, Carl Vilhelm August
1818-1877   [WBD]
Swedish poet and journalist
* Talis Qualis

Strandt, Leslie Roy 1924-   [EJ]
American jazz musician
* Strand, Les

Strang, Herbert [joint pseudonym with Charles James L'Estrange]
See Ely, George Herbert

Strang, Herbert [joint pseudonym with George Herbert Ely]
See L'Estrange, Charles James

Strang, James Jesse 1813-1856   [HPPN]
American religious fanatic and author
* [The] Moses of the Mormons
* St. James

Strang, Jesse ?-1827   [BLB]
American murderer
* Orton, Joseph

Strang, John 1795-1863   [IP]
Scottish author
* [An] Invalid

Strang, Samuel Nicklin
See Nicklin, Samuel Strang

Strange, Alan Cochrane 1909- [BE]
American baseball player
* Strange, Inky

Strange, Dillon
See Norwood, Victor G[eorge] C[harles]

[The] Strange Friend
See Cox, Henry Hamilton

Strange, Harry
See Shaw, Stanley Gordon

Strange, Inky
See Strange, Alan Cochrane

Strange, [Sir] John 1696-1754 [IP]
British barrister and author
* [A] Barrister at Law

Strange, John Stephen
See Tillet, Dorothy [Stockbridge]

Strange, Joseph
See Crawfurd, Oswald John Frederick

Strange, Kemble
See McEnvoy, C. N.

[The] Strange Man of the Oglalas
See Tashunca-Uitco

Strange, Michael
See Oelrichs, Blanche Marie Louise

Strange, N. Blair
See Sargent, Brian [Lawrence]

Strange, Nora K.
See Stanley, Nora Kathleen Begbie
Strange

Strange, Philippa
See Coury, Louise Andree

Strangeglove, Dr.
See Stuart, Richard Lee

Strangelove, Dr.
See Brzezinski, Zbigniew

[The] Stranger
See Haggard, Merle

[A] Stranger
See Oulahan, Richard

[The] Stranger
See Walton, Bill

[The] Stranger in Parliament
See Whitty, Edward Michael

Stranger, Joyce
See Wilson, Joyce M[uriel Judson]

Stranger, Ralph
See Judson, Ralph

[The] Strangler
See Friedrich, Robert

Stranks, Charles James 1901- [AW]
British author
* Hillyer, Richard

Strap, Hugh
See Hughson [or Hewson], Hugh

Straparone, Joseph ?-1909 [HPPN]
Italian-American racketeer
* [The] King of Little Italy

Strapontin
See Burain, Paul

Strasberg, Lee 1901-1982 [JL]
Austrian-born actor and director
* [The] Father of Method Acting
* Pope
* Rabbi
* [The] Ultimate Shrink

Strassar, Todd 20th c.
American author
* Rhue, Morton
* Silvanus, P. W.

Strasser, Bernard Paul 1895- [CAP]
German-born author and clergyman
* P. W.
* Silvanus

Strataki, Anastasia 1938- [BBD]
Canadian opera singer
* Stratas, Teresa

Stratas, Teresa
See Strataki, Anastasia

Stratemeyer, Edward L. 1862-1930
[CAP, EMD, SAT]
American author
* Abbott, [Manager] Henry
* Adams, Harrison
* Alger, Horatio
* Appleton, Victor [house pseudonym] [Stratemeyer Syndicate]
* Appleton, Victor, II [house pseudonym] [Stratemeyer Syndicate]
* Barnum, Richard [house pseudonym] [Stratemeyer Syndicate]
* Bartlett, Philip A. [house pseudonym] [Stratemeyer Syndicate]
* Barton, May Hollis [house pseudonym] [Stratemeyer Syndicate]
* Beach, Charles Amory [house pseudonym] [Stratemeyer Syndicate]
* Bonehill, [Captain] Ralph
* Bowie, Jim
* Calkins, Franklin
* Carson, [Captain] James [house pseudonym] [Stratemeyer Syndicate]
* Chadwick, Lester [house pseudonym] [Stratemeyer Syndicate]
* Chapman, Allen [house pseudonym] [Stratemeyer Syndicate]
* Charles, Louis
* Cooper, James A.
* Cooper, John R. [house pseudonym] [Stratemeyer Syndicate]
* Daly, Jim
* Davenport, Spencer
* Dawson, Elmer A. [house pseudonym] [Stratemeyer Syndicate]
* Dixon, Franklin W. [house pseudonym] [Stratemeyer Syndicate]
* Duncan, Julia K. [house pseudonym] [Stratemeyer Syndicate]
* Edison, Theodore?
* Edwards, Julie
* Emerson, Alice B. [house pseudonym] [Stratemeyer Syndicate]

Stratemeyer, Edward L. (cont.)
* Ferris, James Cody [house pseudonym] [Stratemeyer Syndicate]
* Forbes, Graham B. [house pseudonym] [Stratemeyer Syndicate]
* Ford, Albert Lee
* Frank?
* Gordon, Frederick [house pseudonym] [Stratemeyer Syndicate]
* Hamilton, Ralph
* Hamilton, Robert W.
* Hardy, Alice Dale [house pseudonym] [Stratemeyer Syndicate]
* Harkaway, Hal
* Hawley, Mabel C. [house pseudonym] [Stratemeyer Syndicate]
* Henderley, Brooks [house pseudonym] [Stratemeyer Syndicate]
* Hicks, Harvey
* Hill, Grace Brooks [house pseudonym] [Stratemeyer Syndicate]
* Hope, Laura Lee [house pseudonym] [Stratemeyer Syndicate]
* Hunt, Francis [house pseudonym] [Stratemeyer Syndicate]
* Jack?
* Judd, Frances K. [house pseudonym] [Stratemeyer Syndicate]
* Keene, Carolyn [house pseudonym] [Stratemeyer Syndicate]
* Lawson, W. B.?
* Locke, Clinton W. [house pseudonym] [Stratemeyer Syndicate]
* Long, Helen Beecher [house pseudonym] [Stratemeyer Syndicate]
* Mackenzie, [Dr.] Willard
* Marlowe, Amy Bell [house pseudonym] [Stratemeyer Syndicate]
* Martin, Eugene [house pseudonym] [Stratemeyer Syndicate]
* Moore, Fenworth [house pseudonym] [Stratemeyer Syndicate]
* Morrison, Gert W. [house pseudonym] [Stratemeyer Syndicate]
* Optic, Oliver [joint pseudonym with William Taylor Adams]
* Penrose, Margaret [house pseudonym] [Stratemeyer Syndicate]
* Ridley, Nat, Jr. [house pseudonym] [Stratemeyer Syndicate]
* Rockwood, Roy [house pseudonym] [Stratemeyer Syndicate]
* Roe, Harry Mason [house pseudonym] [Stratemeyer Syndicate]
* St. Myer, Ned
* Scott, Dan [house pseudonym] [Stratemeyer Syndicate]
* Sheldon, Ann [house pseudonym] [Stratemeyer Syndicate]
* Sperry, Raymond, Jr. [house pseudonym] [Stratemeyer Syndicate]
* Steele, Chester K.
* Stone, Alan [house pseudonym] [Stratemeyer Syndicate]
* Stone, Raymond [house pseudonym] [Stratemeyer Syndicate]
* Stone, Richard A. [house pseudonym] [Stratemeyer Syndicate]
* Strayer, E. Ward
* Thorndyke, Helen Louise [house pseudonym] [Stratemeyer Syndicate]
* Warner, Frank A. [house pseudonym] [Stratemeyer Syndicate]

Stratemeyer, Edward L. (cont.)
* Webster, Frank V. [house pseudonym] [Stratemeyer Syndicate]
* West, Jerry [house pseudonym] [Stratemeyer Syndicate]
* Wheeler, Janet D. [house pseudonym] [Stratemeyer Syndicate]
* White, Ramy Allison [house pseudonym] [Stratemeyer Syndicate]
* Winfield, Allen?
* Winfield, Arthur M.
* Winfield, Edna
* Woods, Nat
* Young, Clarence [house pseudonym] [Stratemeyer Syndicate]

Stratford, Edmund
See Lechmere, Edmund

Stratford, Philip
See Bulmer, [Henry] Kenneth

[The] Stratford Streak
See Morenz, Howarth William

Strathesk, John
See Tod, John

Strato [or Straton] 3rd c. BC [HPPN]
Greek philosopher
* [The] Naturalist

Stratten, John
See Alldridge, John Stratten

Stratton, Charles Sherwood 1838-1883 [DNNS, FFF, HPPN, WBD]
American dwarf
* [The] Pet of the Palace
* Thumb, [General] Tom

Stratton, Chris
See Hubbard, Richard

Stratton, Eugene
See Ruhlmann, Eugene Augustus

Stratton, Gander
See Stratton, Monty Franklin Pierce

Stratton, Geneva Grace 1868-1924 [LC]
American author
* Porter, Gene Stratton
* Stratton-Porter, Gene
* [The] Woman Who Caught Bugs and Wrote Books

Stratton, Henry
See Nelson, Michael Harrington

Stratton, Monty Franklin Pierce 1912- [BE]
American baseball player
* Stratton, Gander

Stratton, Old Man
See Stratton, Winfield Scott

Stratton, Richard A. 1932-
American naval officer and Vietnam POW
* [The] Beak

Stratton, Thomas 18th c. [IP]
British compiler
* T. S.

Stratton, Thomas [joint pseudonym with Eugene DeWeese]
See Coulson, Robert [Stratton]

Stratton, Thomas [joint pseudonym with Robert (Stratton) Coulson]
See DeWeese, Eugene

Stratton, Winfield Scott 1848-1902 [HPPN]
American mine owner
* [The] Midas of the Rockies
* Stratton, Old Man

Stratton-Porter, Gene
See Stratton, Geneva Grace

Straub, Otto
See Sobotta, Kurt

Strauch, Katina [Parthemos] 1946- [CA]
American author and librarian
* Alexis, Katina

Straus
See Fields, J. M.

Straus, Dennis 20th c. [CA]
American author
* Ascher/Straus [joint pseudonym with Sheila Ascher]

Straus, Oscar
See Strauss, Oscar

Strauss, Dissenter
See Strauss, Lewis L[ichtenstein]

Strauss, Dutch
See Strauss, Joseph

Strauss, Frances 1904- [CAP]
American author
* Wiley, Bell

Strauss, Gustave Louis Maurice 1807?-1887 [HPPN]
Canadian author
* [An] Old Bohemian

Strauss, Harry ?-1941 [BLB, PHM]
American underworld figure
* Strauss, Pittsburgh Phil

Strauss in the Wind
See Strauss, Lewis L[ichtenstein]

Strauss, Johann 1867?-1939 [HPPN]
Austrian composer and conductor
* [The] Third

Strauss, Johann, Jr. 1825-1899
Austrian composer
* Emperor of the Waltz
* King of the Waltz
* Schani
* [The] Waltz King

Strauss, Johann, Sr. 1804-1849 [BBD]
Austrian composer and conductor
* Emperor of the Waltz
* [The] Father of the Waltz
* King of the Waltz
* [The] Waltz King

Strauss, Joseph 1844-1906 [EJS]
Hungarian-born American baseball player
* Strauss, Dutch

Strauss, Joseph B. 1870-1938 [HPPN]
American designer
* [The] Father of the Golden Gate Bridge

Strauss, Levi 1829-1902 [HPPN]
German-American designer and manufacturer
* [The] Father of the Levi

Strauss, Lewis L[ichtenstein] 1896-1974
American naval officer and government official
* Old Hand
* Savage Illogic
* Strauss, Dissenter
* Strauss in the Wind

Strauss, [Mary] Lucille Jackson 1908- [CAP]
American librarian and author
* Jackson, Lucille

Strauss, Oscar 1870-1954 [JL]
Austrian-born composer
* Straus, Oscar

Strauss, Pittsburgh Phil
See Strauss, Harry

Strauss, Richard 1864-1949
German conductor and composer
* [Ein] Heldenleben
* Master of the Orchestra
* Munich's Favorite Son

Strauss, Yawcob
See Adams, Charles Follen

Straussler, Thomas 1937- [CA, MWD, WOA]
British playwright
* Stoppard, Tom

Stravinsky, Igor Feadorovich 1882-1971 [HPPN]
Russian composer
* [The] Little Giant of Twentieth Century Music
* [The] Musical Giant

Stravinsky's Boswell
See Craft, Robert

Strawberry Bill Bernhard
See Bernhard, William Henry

[The] Strawberry Blonde
See Minton, Yvonne

Straws
See Field, Joseph M.

Straws, Jr.
See Field, Mary Katherine Keemle [Kate]

Strayer, E. Ward
See Stratemeyer, Edward L.

Strayer, Sara Barker ?-1986
American actress
* Wilson, Margery

Strayhorn, Swee'Pea
See Strayhorn, William [Billy]

Strayhorn, William [Billy] 1915-1967
[EJ, EJ7, IBW]
American jazz musician
* Strayhorn, Swee'Pea

Streaker, John A. 1859-? [BE]
American baseball player
* Stricker, Cub
* Stricker, John A.

Streamer, Col. D.
See Graham, Harry

Streamlet, [Rev.] Josiah
See Brookes, [Rev.] Joshua

Streatfield, [Rev.] Thomas 1777-1848
[HPPN]
British clergyman
* T. S.

Strebor, Eiggam
See Roberts, Maggie

Streefkerf, Hendrick
See Verkuyl, Gerrit

Streep, Mary Louise 1950?-
American actress
* Streep, Meryl

Streep, Meryl
See Streep, Mary Louise

Street, A. G.
See Street, Arthur George

Street, Alfred Billings 1811-1881
[HPPN]
American author and poet
* A. B. S. X.

Street, Arthur George 1892-1966 [CAP, LC]
British author
* Brian, James
* Street, A. G.

Street, Bobbie Lee 1944- [PAC, RO2]
American singer and songwriter
* Gentry, Bobbie

Street, C. J. C.
See Street, Cecil John Charles

Street, Cecil John Charles 1884-1964
[CC, EMD, HPPN, WGT]
British author
* Burton, Miles
* F. O. O.
* Rhode, John
* Street, C. J. C.
* X. X.

Street, Charles Evard 1882-1951 [AS, BE, PB]
American baseball player and manager
* Street, Gabby
* Street, Old Sarge

Street, G. S.
See Street, George Slythe

Street, Gabby
See Street, Charles Evard

Street, George Slythe 1867-1936 [LC]
British author
* Street, G. S.

Street, Jay
See Slesar, Henry

Street, Jonathan
See Tiner, John Hudson

Street, Lee
See Hampton, Kathleen

Street, Old Sarge
See Street, Charles Evard

Street, Robert
See Thomas, Gordon

[The] Street Rustler
See Woods, Oscar

[The] Street Singer
See Rosenberg, Harry

Streeter, Lefty
See Streeter, Samuel

Streeter, Samuel 1900- [MK]
American baseball player
* Streeter, Lefty

Streeter, Sebastian Ferris ?-1864
[HPPN]
American author
* S. F. S.

Streett, St. Clair 1887?-
American military aviator
* Streett, Wingbone

Streett, Wingbone
See Streett, St. Clair

Streib, Dan[iel Thomas] 1928- [CA, SFP]
American author
* Jones, J. Faragut
* Page, Thomas [joint pseudonym with Robert Page Jones]
* Schofield, Jonathan

Streicher, Herbert 20th c.
American actor
* Reems, Harry

Streidler, Betty 1930- [FC]
American actress
* St. John, Betta

Streisand, Barbara 1942- [AM]
American singer and actress
* Streisand, Barbra

Streisand, Barbra
See Streisand, Barbara

Strempel, Dora 19th c. [HPPN]
German author
* Stern, Detlef

Strenopoulos, Loukas Panteleemanos
1872-1951 [BI]
Greek archbishop
* Germanos

Strephon
See Bradbury, Edward

Stretch, Joe
See Straci, Joseph

Stretton, Charles
See Dyer, Charles [Raymond]

Stretton, Hesba
See Smith, Sarah

Stretton, Renshaw
See Dyer, Charles [Raymond]

Streuvels, Stijn
See Lateur, Frank

Stribling, Babe
See Stribling, Herbert G.

Stribling, Bill
See Stribling, Majure

Stribling, Herbert G. 1907?-1967 [BI]
American boxer
* Stribling, Babe

Stribling, Majure 20th c. [EF]
American football player
* Stribling, Bill

Stribling, T. S.
See Stribling, Thomas Sigismund

Stribling, Thomas Sigismund 1881-1965
[LC, TC]
American author
* Stribling, T. S.

Stribling, William Lawrence 1904-1933
[BX, RBE]
American boxer
* [The] Georgia Peach
* [The] King of the Canebrakes
* Stribling, Young

Stribling, Young
See Stribling, William Lawrence

Strich, Christian 1930- [CA]
Swiss editor
* Friedrich, Anton
* Jouvet, Jean
* Sainte-Gall, Auguste Amedee de
* Schmucke, Anne
* Sutter, Franz

Stricker, Cub
See Streaker, John A.

Stricker, John A.
See Streaker, John A.

Strickland, Bo
See Strickland, George Bevan

Strickland, D. A.
See Strickland, Donald Allen

Strickland, Donald Allen 1934- [CA]
American political scientist, educator, author
* Strickland, D. A.

Strickland, Enfield 1870?-1964 [BEW]
Theatrical performer
* Strickland, Rube

Strickland, George Bevan 1926- [BE]
American baseball player
* Strickland, Bo

Strickland, Howard 1952- [SMG]
American football player
* Strickland, Strick

Strickland, James 19th c.   [HPPN]
American cattle rancher
* Stickland, Tiger Jim

Strickland, Jane Margaret 19th c.
[HPPN]
British author
* Her Sister

Strickland, Joe
See Arnold, George W.

Strickland, Margot 1927-   [CA]
Spanish-born British author and actress
* Worth, Margaret

Strickland, Roger 1940-   [BB]
American basketball player
* [The] Rifle

Strickland, Rube
See Strickland, Enfield

Strickland, Strick
See Strickland, Howard

Stricklin, Al
See Stricklin, Alton Meeks

Stricklin, Alton Meeks 1908-   [BI]
American musician
* Stricklin, Al

[The] Strict
See Louis II

Stride, Elizabeth 1841?-1888   [BL]
Prostitute and murder victim
* Stride, Long Liz

Stride, Long Liz
See Stride, Elizabeth

Stride, Madeline 1909-   [THR]
British actress
* Gibson, Madeline

Strike but Hear
See Horne, John

Strike, Jeremy
See Renn, Thomas E[dward]

Strike, Mister
See Marichal, Juan Antonio Sanchez

Striker, Jake
See Striker, Wilbur Scott

Striker, Wilbur Scott 1933-   [BE]
American baseball player
* Striker, Jake

Strikha, Edvard
See Burevii, Kost'

Strincevich, Jumbo
See Strincevich, Nicholas Mihailovich

Strincevich, Nicholas Mihailovich 1915-
[BE]
American baseball player
* Strincevich, Jumbo

Strindberg, [Johan] August 1849-1912
[HPPN, UH, WBD]
Swedish playwright and author
* A. S.
* [The] Bedeviled Viking

Strindberg, [Johan] August (cont.)
* [The] Shakespeare of Sweden
* [The] Swedish Schopenhauer

Stringbean
See Akeman, David

Stringer, David
See Roberts, Keith [John Kingston]

Stringer, Moses 17th c.   [HPPN]
British author
* M. S.

Stripp, Jersey Joe
See Stripp, Joseph Valentine

Stripp, Joseph Valentine 1903-   [BE, PB]
American baseball player
* Stripp, Jersey Joe

[The] Stripper for Christ
See Everts, Kellie

Stritch, Andrew F. Russell 1869?-1905
[PI]
Irish poet
* Fionna, Flann
* St. Ritch, A. R.

Stritzl, Siegfried 1944-   [AES]
Yugoslav-born American soccer player
* Stritzl, Siggy

Stritzl, Siggy
See Stritzl, Siegfried

Strivelyne, Elsie
See Paton, [Sir Joseph] Noel

Strix
See Fleming, [Robert] Peter

Strix
See Howes, George W.

Strodach, Paul Zeller 1876-?   [NAA]
American clergyman and author
* Pilgrim, Paul

Strode, Ralph 14th c.   [DEL, SN]
British scholar and poet
* [The] Philosophical

Strode, Woodrow Wilson 1915-   [IBW]
American athlete and actor
* Strode, Woody

Strode, Woody
See Strode, Woodrow Wilson

[A] Stroling Player
See Roberts, John

[A] Stroller in Europe
See Wright, W. W.

[The] Strolling Player
See Guinness, [Sir] Alec

Strollo, Anthony C. 1899-1962   [BLB,
PHM]
American underworld figure
* Bender, Tony

Strom, Leslie Winter
See Winter, Leslie

Stromberg, Harry   [BLB, MM]
American underworld figure
* Rosen, Nig

Stromberg, Honey
See Stromberg, John

Stromberg, John 1853-1902   [BEW,
DAM]
American composer
* Stromberg, Honey

Stromme, Floyd Marvin 1916-   [BE]
American baseball player
* Stromme, Rock

Stromme, Rock
See Stromme, Floyd Marvin

[The] Strong
See Augustus II

[The] Strong
See Robert

[The] Strong
See Sancho II

[The] Strong
See Siward [Earl of Northumberland]

Strong, Anna Louise 1885-1970   [BI,
HPPN]
American journalist
* Anise

[The] Strong Arm
See Danton, Georges Jacques

Strong Bow
See Campbell, John Beautiste

[The] Strong Boy of Boston
See Sullivan, John L[awrence]

Strong, Charles [joint pseudonym with
Samuel Epstein]
See Epstein, Beryl [Williams]

Strong, Charles [joint pseudonym with
Beryl (Williams) Epstein]
See Epstein, Samuel

Strong, Charles Stanley 1906-1962
[CAT, NAA, SFL]
American author and editor
* Bartlett, Nancy
* Keats, Myron
* McClellan, William
* McKay, Kevin
* Stanley, Chuck
* Stoddard, Charles [house pseudonym]
* Sturdy, Carl

Strong, David
See McGuire, Leslie Sarah

Strong, Emilia Francis 1840-1904
British author
* Dilke, Lady

Strong, Eric
See Silberschlag, Eisig

Strong, [Rev.] George A. 1832-1912
[HPPN]
American author
* Henderson, Marc Antony

Strong, Harrington
See McCulley, Johnston

Strong, Hero
See Jones, Clara Augusta

Strong, J. J.
See Strong, Jeremy

Strong, James
See Hervey, Hedley

Strong, Jeremy 1949- [CA]
British author
* Strong, J. J.

Strong, John 1732-1798 [NPS]
* [The] Blind Mechanician

Strong, L. A. G.
See Strong, Leonard Alfred George

Strong, Latham C.   [PA]
Author
* Shatt, Montague

Strong, Lennox
See Grier, Barbara G[ene Damon]

Strong, Leonard Alfred George
1896-1958 [LC]
British author
* Strong, L. A. G.

[The] Strong Man
See Topham, Thomas

Strong Man McGillycuddy
See McGillycuddy, Valentine Trant
O'Connell

[The] Strong Man of Argentina
See Peron, Juan Domingo

[The] Strong Man of Egypt
See Nasser, Gamal Abdel

**[The] Strong Man of the Solomon
Islands**
See Kwaisulia

[The] Strong Man of Wall Street
See Whitney, Richard

Strong, Martin 18th c. [HPPN]
British scholar
* [A] Gentleman in the City

Strong, Maryland 1898-1935 [HPPN]
American actress
* Morne, Mary

Strong, Mike
See Srzentich, Mirko

Strong, Pat
See Hough, Richard [Alexander]

Strong, Shirley 20th c. [TI 7-30-84]
British track and field athlete
* Leotard Lady

Strong, Solange
See Hertz, Nellie Solange [Strong]

Strong, Spencer
See Ackerman, Forrest J[ames]

Strong, Susan
See Rees, Joan

[The] Strong Willed Mayor
See Daley, Richard Joseph

Strongblood, Casper
See Webster, David Endicott

Strongbow
See Clare, Gilbert de

Strongbow
See Clare, Richard de

Strongbow
See Fitzherbert, Richard

[The] Strongest Man in the World
See Cyr, Louis

[The] Strongest Man in the World
See Mueller, Frederick

[The] Strongest Man in the World
See Sandow, Eugene

[The] Strongest Man Who Ever Lived
See Cyr, Louis

Strongfellow, Professor
See Longfellow, Henry Wadsworth

Strongfort, Lionel
See Unger, Max

Strongheart, [Chief] Nipo
See Tahchenum, Neehahpouw

Strongin, Lynn 1939- [CA]
American author and poet
* Michaels, Lynn

Strongi'th'arm, Charles
See Armstrong, Charles Wicksteed

Stroock, Geraldine 1925-1977 [BEW,
FC, IPA]
American actress
* Brooks, Geraldine

Stroop, Helen E.
See Witty, Helen E. S[troop]

Strother, David Hunter 1817-1888
[DEL, DNNF, FFF]
American author and illustrator
* Porte-Crayon

Strother, Pat Wallace
See Wallace, Pat

Strothotte, Maurice Arnold 1865-1937
[BBD]
American musician
* Arnold, Maurice

Stroud, Albert
See Budrys, Algirdas Jonas

Stroud, Edwin Marvin 1939- [BE]
American baseball player
* [The] Creeper

Stroud, Ralph Vivian 1885- [BE]
American baseball player
* Stroud, Sailor

Stroud, Robert Franklin 1887-1963
[BLB]
American murderer
* [The] Birdman of Alcatraz

Stroud, Sailor
See Stroud, Ralph Vivian

Stroughter, Le Roy 1969- [IBW]
American trapeze performer
* Stroughter, Pee Wee

Stroughter, Pee Wee
See Stroughter, Le Roy

Strout, Richard L[ee] 1898- [CA]
American journalist
* T. R. B.

Strover, Dorothea 1900- [CA, WD]
British author and illustrator
* Tinne, Dorothea
* Tinne, E. D.

Strozzi [or Strozza], Bernardo
1581-1644 [WBD]
Italian painter and engraver
* [Il] Capuccino
* [Il] Prete Genovese

Strozzi, Filippo 1426-1491 [WBD]
Florentine banker
* [The] Elder

Strozzi, Giambattista 1488-1538 [WBD]
*Led attack against Medici family of
Florence*
* Filippo II

Strubberg, Friedrich Armand 1806-1889
[WBD]
German-born author
* Armand
* Schubbert

Struble, Virginia
See Burlingame, Virginia [Struble]

Struck, Dutch
See Struck, Raymond F.

Struck, Raymond F. 20th c. [BBH]
American basketball player and coach
* Struck, Dutch

Strudwick, Shepperd
See Shepperd, John

Struebe, Hermann 1879-? [CD, LAO]
German playwright, author, poet
* Burte, Hermann

Strug, Andrzej
See Galecki, Tadeusz

[The] Struggler
See Nowatzke, Thomas M. [Tom]

Strunck, Nicolas Adam 1640-1700 [SN]
German composer
* Archdiavolo

Strung, Norman 1941- [CA]
American author
* Barkee, Asouff
* Yaeger, Bart

Strunk, Jud
See Strunk, Justin Roderick, Jr.

Strunk, Justin Roderick, Jr. 1936- [BI,
RO2]
American singer and songwriter
* Strunk, Jud

Struss, Clarence Herbert 1909-
American baseball player
* Struss, Steamboat

Struss, Steamboat
See Struss, Clarence Herbert

Strussenfelt, Ulrika Sofia von 1801-1873
[HPPN]
Swedish author
* D. J. W. E.
* Pilgrimen

Struthahn
See Sobelsohn, Karl

Struther, Jan
See Maxtone Graham, Joyce
[Anstruther]

Struthers, Jeannie Gourley 1845-1928
[HPPN]
American actress
* Gourley, Jeannie

Strutt, Lord
See Charles II

Struttin' Jim Bottomley
See Bottomley, James Leroy

Struys, John
See Morrison, John

Strydonck, Victor van 1876-1953 [BDW]
Belgian army officer
* Strydonck de Burkel, Victor van

Strydonck de Burkel, Victor van
See Strydonck, Victor van

Stryfe, Paul
See Newman, James Roy

Stryjkowski, Juljan
See Stark, Pesach

Stryker, Dutch
See Stryker, Sterling Alpa

Stryker, Lloyd Paul 1885-1955 [HPPN]
American attorney and author
* [The] Knight With the Rueful
  Countenance
* [The] Nation's Most Redoubtable
  Criminal Lawyer

Stryker, Sterling Alpa 1895-1964 [BE]
American baseball player
* Stryker, Dutch

Strype, John 1643-1737 [HPPN]
British ecclesiastical historian and author
* Appendixmonger
* Dryasdust

Stuart, Alex
See Stuart, Vivian [Finlay]

Stuart, Alex R.
See Stuart, Richard Gordon

Stuart, Anthony
See Hale, Julian A[nthony] S[tuart]

Stuart, Athenian
See Stuart, James

Stuart, Beauty
See Stuart, James Ewell Brown

Stuart, Brian
See Worthington-Stuart, Brian Arthur

Stuart, Carl
See Schacht, Ray McKeown

Stuart, Charles
See MacKinnon, Charles Roy

Stuart, Charles Edward
See Allan, Charles Stuart Hay

**Stuart, Charles Edward Louis Philip
Casimir** 1720-1788 [DEP, DNNS, HPPN,
NPS, SN]
British prince
* Bonaventura, Father
* [The] Bonnie Chevalier
* Bonnie Prince Charlie
* Burke, Betty
* Charles Edward
* Count of Albany
* [The] Highland Laddie
* [The] King Over the Water
* [The] Young Adventurer
* [The] Young Chevalier
* [The] Young Pretender

Stuart, Charlotte 1863-? [THR]
British actress
* Granville, Charlotte

Stuart, Chauncey
See Stuart, William Alexander [Bill]

Stuart, Clay
See Whittington, Harry [Benjamin]

Stuart, Constance Cornell 1947?-
[HPPN]
*American White House press secretary
and staff director*
* [The] Queen of Queens
* [The] Sorority Woman of the Year
* Spring, Miss

Stuart, Cosmo
See Gordon-Lennox, Cosmo Charles

Stuart, D[orothy] M[argaret]
See Browne, Dorothy Margaret Stuart

Stuart, David
See Hoyt, Edwin P[almer], Jr.

Stuart, Don A.
See Campbell, John W[ood], Jr.

Stuart, Donald 20th c. [MBF]
British author and playwright
* Stuart, Ronald
* Verner, Gerald

Stuart, Eleanor
See Childs, Eleanor Stuart

Stuart, Eleanor
See Porter, Eleanor [Hodgman]

Stuart, English Jim
See Stuart, James

Stuart, Esme
See Claire, Amelie

Stuart, Fay
See Leonard, Nellie Mabel

Stuart [or Stewart], Frances Teresa
1647-1702 [WBD]
Mistress of King Charles II of England
* [La] Belle Stuart

Stuart, Frederick
See Tomlin, Eric Walter Frederick

Stuart, Giacomo Rossi 20th c. [WF]
Italian actor
* Stuart, Jack

Stuart, Gilbert 1746?-1786 [SN]
Scottish author and journalist
* Zoilus

Stuart, Gilbert Charles 1755-1828
[HPPN, SN]
American painter
* [The] American Stuart
* [The] Painter of Presidents
* [The] Portrait Painter of Presidents

Stuart, Gloria
See Finch, Gloria Stuart

Stuart, Gordon
See Bedford-Jones, Henry [James
O'Brien]

Stuart, Gordon
See Sayler, Harry Lincoln

Stuart, Gordon
See Stewart, Robert Armistead

Stuart, Harriet
See Lennox, Charlotte Ramsay

Stuart, Henry Benedict Maria Clemens
1725-1807 [DEP, DHA, SN]
King of England
* Henry IX
* [The] Last of the Stuarts
* York, Cardinal

Stuart, Henry Robson 1836-1903 [BEW]
American actor and producer
* Robson, Stuart

Stuart, Hod
See Stuart, Horace Hodgson

Stuart, Hod
See Stuart, William

Stuart, Horace Hodgson 1880-1907
[HK]
Canadian-born hockey player
* Stuart, Hod

Stuart, Ian
See MacLean, Alistair [Stuart]

Stuart, Ina 1907- [F2]
Actress
* La Roy, Rita

Stuart, Isaac William 1809-1861 [DNA]
American author and educator
* Scaeva

Stuart, Jack
See Stuart, Giacomo Rossi

Stuart, James ?-1851 [HPPN]
Australian outlaw
* Stuart, English Jim

Stuart, James 1533-1570 [HPPN]
Earl of Murray and Regent of Scotland
* [The] Good Regent

Stuart, James 1713-1788 [DNNF]
British painter and architect
* Stuart, Athenian

Stuart, James 1776-1849 [FFF]
Scottish traveller
* [The] Stot

Stuart, James Ewell Brown 1833-1864
[HPPN]
American army officer
* [The] Bible Class Man
* [The] Knight of the Golden Spurs
* Old Jeb
* [The] Plumed Knight of the
  Confederacy
* [The] Prince Rupert of the
  Confederacy
* Stuart, Beauty
* Stuart, Jeb

Stuart, James Francis Edward 1688-1766
[DEP, SN, WBD]
Son of King James II
* [The] Chevalier de St. George
* James Edward
* James III
* [The] King Over the Water
* [The] Old Pretender
* [The] Warming Pan Child
* [The] Warming Pan Hero

Stuart, Jane 1942- [CA]
American author and translator
* Juergensmeyer, Jane Stuart

Stuart, Jay Allison
See Tait, Dorothy

Stuart, Jean
See Leisenring, Margaret

Stuart. Jeanne
See Sweet, Jeanne

Stuart, Jeb
See Stuart, James Ewell Brown

Stuart, Jeff 1952- [RO2]
American musician
* Stuart, Wally

Stuart, John [Third Earl of Bute]
1713-1792 [HN, HPPN, NPS, SN]
British prime minister
* Another Machiavel
* Boot Jack
* One Behind the Throne Greater than
  the Throne Itself
* [The] Wire Master

Stuart, John
See Croall, John Alfred Louden

Stuart, John Davis [Johnny] 1901-1970
[BE]
American baseball player
* Stuart, Stud

Stuart, John Sobieski Stolberg
1795-1872 [HPPN]
*Son of British citizen who claimed to be
the son of Charles Edward Stuart*
* Count of Albany

Stuart, John Todd 1807-1885
American attorney
* Sly, Jerry

Stuart, Kenneth
See Wesander, Bjoern Kenneth

Stuart, Kirk
See Kincheloe, Charles

Stuart, Leslie
See Barrett, Thomas Augustine

Stuart, Leslie
See Marlowe, Kenneth

Stuart, Logan?
See Wilding, Philip

Stuart, Lyle 1922?- [HPPN]
American publisher
* [The] Bad Boy of Publishing

Stuart, Lyle
See Simon, Lionel

Stuart, M. B. [PA]
Author
* Mortimer, Grace

Stuart, Madge
See Stewart, Margaret

Stuart, Margaret
See Paine, Lauran [Bosworth]

Stuart, Marie
See Gaites, Steele

Stuart, Mary
See Mary, Queen of Scots

Stuart, Mary F. 20th c. [CCL]
Canadian poet
* Slinfold

Stuart, Maude
See Grubbs, Maude

Stuart, May 20th c. [THR]
British actress
* Leslie-Stuart, May

Stuart, Michael
See Thomas, Reginald George

Stuart, Monroe
See Shapiro, Max

Stuart, Morna 1905- [AW]
British author
* Campbell, C. J.

Stuart, Moses 1780-1852 [HPPN]
American scholar and theologian
* Civis
* [The] Father of Biblical Learning in
  America

Stuart, Mrs. Everard [FFF]
Entertainer
* Branscombe, Maud

Stuart, Nick
See Pratza, Nicholas

Stuart, Old Stonefingers
See Stuart, Richard Lee

Stuart, Otho
See Andreae, Otto Stuart

Stuart, Red
See Stuart, William

Stuart, Richard Gordon 1947- [ESF]
Scottish author
* Gordon, Stuart
* Stuart, Alex R.

Stuart, Richard Lee 1932- [BE, DGS,
HPPN, PB]
American baseball player
* [The] Boston Strangler
* [The] Iron Glove
* [The] Irrepressible Egoist
* Strangeglove, Dr.
* Stuart, Old Stonefingers
* Stuart, Stonefingers

Stuart, Robert 1785-1848 [HPPN]
Scottish-American Indian commissioner
* Friend of the Indian

Stuart, Ronald
See Stuart, Donald

Stuart, Sheila
See Baker, Mary Gladys Steel

Stuart, Sidney
See Avallone, Michael [Angelo], Jr.

Stuart, Stonefingers
See Stuart, Richard Lee

Stuart, Stud
See Stuart, John Davis [Johnny]

Stuart, Tom
See Moriarty, Tom

Stuart, V. A.
See Stuart, Vivian [Finlay]

Stuart, Vivian [Finlay] 1914- [CA, WD]
British author
* Allen, Barbara
* Finlay, Fiona
* Long, William Stuart
* Stuart, Alex
* Stuart, V. A.

Stuart, W. J.
See MacDonald, Philip

Stuart, Wally
See Stuart, Jeff

Stuart, Warren
See MacDonald, Philip

Stuart, William 20th c. [CBH, CEI,
CSH]
Canadian-born hockey player
* Stuart, Hod
* Stuart, Red

Stuart, William Alexander [Bill] 20th c.
[BE]
American baseball player
* Stuart, Chauncey

Stuart-Baker, Iris 1901- [THR]
British actress
* Baker, Iris

Stub
See Van Brocklin, Norm[an]

Stubbes, John 1541-1600 [DEL, PA]
British author
* Scaeva

Stubbing, Newton Haydn 1921- [CAR]
British painter
* Stubbing, Tony

Stubbing, Tony
See Stubbing, Newton Haydn

Stubbings, Hilda Uren
See U'Ren-Stubbings, Hilda

Stubborn Old Grover
See Cleveland, [Stephen] Grover

Stubbornness, General
See Chuikov, Vasily I.

Stubbs, Harry C[lement] 1922- [CA, ESF, SF]
American author
* Clement, Hal
* Richard, George

Stubbs, Morton Richard 1860-1939 [BEW, FC]
British actor
* Selten, Morton

Stubbs, Philip 15th c. [SN]
Puritan pamphleteer
* [The] Prynne of His Day

Stubbs, Tilsa 1926- [THR]
British actress
* Page, Tilsa

Stubby, Captain
See Fouts, Tom C.

Stuber, Abe
See Stuber, Emmett R.

Stuber, Emmett R. 1904- [FB]
American football coach
* Stuber, Abe

Stuber, Stanley I[rving] 1903- [CAP]
American author
* Erasmus, M. Nott

Stuckey, Sterling 1932- [IBW]
American author and historian
* Sterling X

Stucley, Elizabeth
See Northmore, Elizabeth Florence

Stucley, Lusty
See Stucley, [Sir] Thomas

Stucley, [Sir] Thomas 1525?-1578 [SN]
British adventurer
* Stucley, Lusty

Studd, Charles Thomas 1860-1931 [HPPN]
British cricket player and missionary
* [The] Millionaire for God

Studdert, Annie Louisa 1885- [AW]
Author
* Rixon, Annie

Studebaker, Don 20th c. [SFP]
Author
* Decles, Jon

[A] Student
See Brookes, S.

[A] Student
See Chittenden, Albert Jerome

[A] Student
See Forsyth, Ebenezer

Student
See Gosset, William Sealy

[A] Student at Law
See Knight, Frederick

[A] Student at Oxford
See Amhurst, Nicholas

[A] Student in Paris
See Gardner, Augustus Kingsley

Student in Physick and Astronomy
See Ames, Nathaniel

[The] Student Nurse of Danville
See Burchard, Samuel Dickinson

[A] Student of Harvard University
See Harris, Thaddeus Mason

[A] Student of Law
See Hunt, Frederick Knight

[A] Student of Occultism
See Hartmann, Franz

[A] Student of the Middle Temple
See Lucas, Henry

[A] Student of the Temple
See Bleuman, Jonathan

[A] Student of the Temple
See Leslie, Charles

Studer, Steven Paul 1953- [SMG]
American football player
* Studer, Stu

Studer, Stu
See Studer, Steven Paul

Studholme, Marie
See Lupton, Marie

Studley, Seymour L. 19th c. [BE]
American baseball player
* Studley, Warhorse

Studley, Warhorse
See Studley, Seymour L.

Studstill, Monkey
See Studstill, Pat[rick L.]

Studstill, Pat[rick L.] 1938-
American football player
* Studstill, Monkey

Stuempke, Harald
See Steiner, Gerolf

[The] Stuffed Prophet
See Cleveland, [Stephen] Grover

Stuffel, Paul Harrington 1927- [BE]
American baseball player
* Stuffel, Stu

Stuffel, Stu
See Stuffel, Paul Harrington

Stukalov, Nikolai Fyodorovich 1900-1962 [MWD]
Russian playwright
* Pogodin, Nikolai Fyodorovich

Stukeley, William 1687-1765 [HPPN, WBD]
British antiquary and author
* [The] Arch Druid
* Chyndonax

Stukus, Annis 20th c. [CFH]
Canadian football player and coach
* Stukus, Stuke

Stukus, Stuke
See Stukus, Annis

Stultifer, Morton
See Curtis, Richard [Alan]

[The] Stump Fingered
See Mark

[La] Stupenda [The Stupendous One]
See Sutherland, Joan

Stupid
See Brutus, Lucius Junius

[The] Stupid Boy
See Aquinas, Thomas [Thomas of Aquino]

Sturdivant, Snake
See Sturdivant, Thomas Virgil

Sturdivant, Thomas Virgil 1930- [BE, PB]
American baseball player
* Sturdivant, Snake

Sturdy, Carl
See Strong, Charles Stanley

Sturdy John
See Lilburne, John

Sturdy, William Allen 1840-? [DNA]
Author and educator
* Didwin, Isaac

Sture-Vasa, Mary
See Alsop, Mary O'Hara

Sturgeon, Daniel 1789-1878 [HPPN]
American politician
* [The] Silent Senator

Sturgeon, Foolbert
See Stack, Frank H[untington]

Sturgeon, Theodore Hamilton
See Waldo, Edward Hamilton

Sturgeon, Wina 20th c. [CA]
American author
* Moore, Cory

Sturges, Preston
See Biden, Edmond P.

Sturgill, Virgil Leon 1897- [NAA]
American writer and poet
* Edgewood, Henry

Sturgis, Colin [joint pseudonym with Mel(vin) Sturgis]
See Cole, Les[ter]

Sturgis, Colin [joint pseudonym with Les(ter) Cole]
See Sturgis, Mel[vin]

Sturgis, Frank A. 20th c. [HPPN]
Cuban-American defendant in Watergate trial
* Fiorini, Frank
* Hamilton, Edward

Sturgis, H. O.
See Sturgis, Howard Overing

Sturgis, Howard Overing 1855-1920 [LC]
British author
* Sturgis, H. O.

Sturgis, Mel[vin] 20th c. [WGT]
Author
* Sturgis, Colin [joint pseudonym with Les(ter) Cole]

Sturhahn, Cobbles
See Sturhahn, Herbert

Sturhahn, Herbert 20th c. [HPPN]
American football player
* Sturhahn, Cobbles

Sturluson, Snorro 1179-1241 [NPS]
Icelandic historian and poet
* [The] Northern Herodotus

Sturm, Johann Christoph 1507-1589 [DEP, FFF, SN]
German scholar
* [The] Cicero of Germany
* [The] German Cicero
* [The] Restorer of Science in Germany

Sturrock, Jeremy
See Healey, Benjamin James

Sturrock, W. 19th c. [CCL]
Canadian poet
* [A] Red Coat

Sturt, George 1863-1927 [BI, LC, TCL]
British author
* Bourne, George

Sturton, Hugh
See Johnson, Hugh Anthony Stephen

Sturtzel, Howard A[llison] 1894- [CA, SAT]
American author
* Annixter, Paul

Sturtzel, Jane Levington 1903- [CA, SAT]
American author
* Annixter, Jane
* Comfort, Jane Levington

Sturzen-Becker, Oscar Patrik 19th c. [HPPN]
Swedish author
* Odd, Orvar

Sturzwage, Leopold 1879-1968 [CAR]
French painter
* Survage, Leopold

Stutterin' Sam
See Copeland, Mary Dowell

Stutz, George 1893-1930 [BE]
American baseball player
* Stutz, Kid

Stutz, Kid
See Stutz, George

Stuyvesant, Alice [joint pseudonym with Charles Norris Williamson]
See Williamson, Alice Muriel [Livingston]

Stuyvesant, Alice [joint pseudonym with Alice Muriel (Livingston) Williamson]
See Williamson, Charles Norris

Stuyvesant, Peter
See Stuyvesant, Petrus

Stuyvesant, Petrus 1592?-1672 [HPPN, NPS, WBD]
Dutch administrator in America
* Hard Headed Pete
* Hardkopping Piet
* Headstrong Peter
* Old Silver Leg
* Old Silver Nails
* [The] One Legged Governor
* Peter the Headstrong
* Stuyvesant, Peter
* Wooden Leg

Stydahar, Joseph L. 1912- [FB]
American football player
* Stydahar, Jumbo Joe

Stydahar, Jumbo Joe
See Stydahar, Joseph L.

Styles, Frank Showell 1908- [CA, CC, SAT]
British author
* Carr, Glyn
* Howell, S.

Styles, John 1770-1860 [FFF]
British clergyman
* Ringletub, Jeremiah

Styles, Lena
See Styles, William Graves

Styles, William Graves 1897-1956 [BE]
American baseball player
* Styles, Lena

[A] Stylish Hard-Liner
See Begin, Menachem

Stylites, Simeon 390?-459 [HPPN]
Saint
* [The] Father of the Pillar Saints

Stylites, Simeon
See Caldwell, William A.

Stylla, Joanne
See Branden, Victoria [Fremlin]

Stymie
See Beard, Matthew

Styne, Jule
See Stein, Julius Kerwin

Stynes, Cornelius William 1868-1944 [BE]
American baseball player
* Stynes, Neil

Stynes, Neil
See Stynes, Cornelius William

Su Kuo-feng 20th c.
Chinese prime minister
* Hua Kuo-feng

Su Man-shu 1884-1918 [EWL]
Chinese poet and author
* Su Yuan-ying

Su Shih 1036-1101 [WBD]
Chinese poet and statesman
* Su Tung-po

Su Tung-po
See Su Shih

Su Yuan-ying
See Su Man-shu

Suardi, Bartolommeo 1460?-1536? [WBD]
Italian painter and architect
* [Il] Bramantino

Suares, Andre 1866-? [HPPN]
French poet, and critic
* Caedral
* [The] Knight Errant of Beauty
* Scantrel, Yves

Suarez, Carlos 1913- [GS]
Mexican bullfighter
* Tototoro [All Bull]

Suarez, Francisco [or Francois] 1548-1617 [DNNS, FFF]
Spanish theologian and philosopher
* [The] Last of the Schoolmen

Suarez Gomez, Roberto 1932?- [TI 2-25-85]
Bolivian cattleman and suspected drug dealer
* [The] King of Cocaine

Suarez Lynch, B. [joint pseudonym with Jorge Luis Borges]
See Bioy-Casares, Adolfo

Suarez Lynch, B. [joint pseudonym with Adolfo Bioy-Casares]
See Borges, Jorge Luis

Suavius, Leo
See Gohory, Jacques

[The] Sub Scribe to the Tribe of Adoniram
See Willis, John

[A] Sub-Utopian?
See Walker, Richard

[A] **Subaltern**
See Coke, Edward Thomas

[A] **Subaltern of Artillery**
See Robinson, Frederick

Subarra, Corrado Della ?-1154 [CAL]
Pope
* Anastasius IV

Subber, Arnold 1918- [BEW]
American producer
* Saint Subber, Arnold

Subhadra-Nandan
See Das, Prafulla Chandra

Subhasree
See Sreenivasapuram, Sesha Charlu

Sublett, Bubbles
See Sublett, John William

Sublett, John William 1902- [IBW]
American entertainer
* Sublett, Bubbles

[The] **Sublime Child**
See Hugo, Victor Marie

[The] **Sublime Dandy**
See Lewis, Meriwether

[The] **Sublime Fanatic**
See Dow, Neal

Sublimis et Illuminatus, Doctor
See Tauler, Johann

Subond, Valerie
See Grayland, Valerie Merle [Spanner]

Subotai [or Sabutai] 1172?-1245 [WBD]
Mongol general
* Bagatur [The Valiant]

[A] **Subscriber**
See Dickens, Charles

Subscription Jamie
See Mackintosh, [Sir] James

Subtilis, Doctor
See Duns Scotus, Johannes

Subtilissimus, Doctor
See Duns Scotus, Johannes

[The] **Subtle Doctor**
See Duns Scotus, Johannes

Subuh, Muhammad 1901- [EOP]
Indonesian mystic
* Bapak [Father]

[A] **Suburban Clergyman**
See Owen, John

[The] **Subway Shooter**
See Goetz, Bernhard Hugo

[The] **Subway Vigilante**
See Goetz, Bernhard Hugo

Succat
See Patrick

Success, Captain
See Arledge, Roone

[The] **Successor to Houdini**
See Baker, Steve

Sucharitkul, Somtow 20th c.
Thai author
* Somtow, S. P.

Sucher, Leonard 1906- [CR]
American columnist
* Lyons, Leonard

Suchowljansky, Maier 1902-1983 [BLB, HPPN]
Russian-born American underworld figure
* [The] Alfred Sloan of Organized Crime
* Lansky, Meyer
* Meyer the Bug
* [The] Mob's Financial Genius

Suck All Cream
See Clarke, Samuel

Suckert, Curzio 1898- [HPPN]
Italian author
* Malaparte, Curzio

Suckert, Kurt Erich 1898-1957 [CD, EWL]
Italian author, poet, playwright
* Malaparte, Curzio

Suckling, [Sir] John 1609-1642 [HPPN]
British poet, playwright, courtier
* [The] Father of Cribbage
* [The] Greatest Gallant of His Time

Suckling, John 1926- [TR]
British lighting designer and theatre consultant
* Wyckham, John

Suckling, Robert 1933- [TR]
British actor and director
* Chetwyn, Robert

Sudakis, Suds [or Sudsy]
See Sudakis, William Paul, Jr.

Sudakis, William Paul, Jr. 1946- [BE, SMG]
American baseball player
* Sudakis, Suds [or Sudsy]

Sudbury, Richard
See Gibson, Charles Hammond

Suddaby, [William] Donald 1900-1964 [ESF, LC, TCC]
British author
* Griff, Alan

Sudden Death Hill
See Hill, John Melvin

Sudden Sam McDowell
See McDowell, Samuel Edward Thomas

Suddith, Arnold Eugene 20th c. [BBH]
American basketball player
* Suddith, Sally

Suddith, Sally
See Suddith, Arnold Eugene

Suddlechop, Ursley
See Turner, Anne

Suddoth, J. Guy
See Erby, John J.

Suder, Pecky
See Suder, Pete[r]

Suder, Pete[r] 1916- [BE, PB]
American baseball player
* Suder, Pecky

Sudhalter, Richard M[errill] 1938- [CA]
American author and music critic
* Napoleon, Art

Sudhoff, John William 1874-1917 [BE]
American baseball player
* Sudhoff, Wee Willie

Sudhoff, Wee Willie
See Sudhoff, John William

Sudkamp, [Sister] Augustine
See Sudkamp, Cora May

Sudkamp, Cora May 1914- [IWM]
American music educator
* Sudkamp, [Sister] Augustine

Sudlow, Bessie
See Gunn, Mrs. Michael

Sudlow, Elizabeth Williams 1878-? [NAA]
Canadian-born journalist and author
* Waldus, Edythe

Sudorius
See Lesueur, Nicolas

Suds
See Lowe, William Herman

Sue, Eugene
See Sue, Marie Joseph

Sue, Marie Joseph 1804-1857 [NLC, WBD]
French author
* [The] French James Fenimore Cooper
* Sue, Eugene

Sue-Sand, Alexandre, fils
See Hamley, [Sir] Edward Bruce

Suedfeld, Max Simon 1849-1923 [WBD]
German physician and author
* Nordau, Max Simon

Suedfeld, Peter
See Field, Peter

Suess, Hans 1476?-1522 [HPPN, WBD]
German painter
* Kulmbach, Hans von

Suett, Richard 1755-1805 [NPS, SN]
Comedian
* Cherub Dicky
* [The] Robin Good-Fellow of the Stage

Sufana, Eugene 1928- [EJ]
American jazz musician
* Allen, Gene

[A] **Sufferer**
See Foe, Daniel

[A] **Sufferer**
See Wilson, Thomas

Sufficens, Doctor
See Pietro Aquila

Suffling, Mark
See Rowland, Donald Sydney

Suffling, Philip 1902- [RBE, SG]
British boxer
* Scott, Phaintin' Phil
* Scott, Phil

[A] Suffolk Clergyman
See Whitmore, John

Suffolk Coast
See Cooper, Ernest Read

[A] Suffolk Minister
See Harmer, [Rev.] Thomas

Suffridus
See Petri, Sjurd Peeters

Suga
See Yusuke, Suga

Sugar Bear Blanks
See Blanks, Larvell

Sugar Bear Clemons
See Clemons, Craig Lynn

Sugar Bear Crowder
See Crowder, Randy

Sugar Bear Hamilton
See Hamilton, Raymond Lee

Sugar Bear Young
See Young, Willie Lull

Sugar Beets
See Cummings, Fred

Sugar, Bert Randolph 1937- [CA]
American author
* Brooks, John
* Davis, Suzanne

Sugar Boy Dougherty
See Dougherty, Thomas James [Tom]

Sugar Boy Williams
See Williams, Joseph Leon [Joe]

Sugar Chile Robinson
See Robinson, Frank Isaac

[The] Sugar Daddy of Big Bankers
See Burns, Arthur Frank

Sugar Jim Henry
See Henry, Samuel James

Sugar Jim Smith
See Smith, James

Sugar Johnny Smith
See Smith, John

[The] Sugar King
See Havemeyer, Theodore A.

[The] Sugar King
See Spreckels, Claus

Sugar, Leo T. 1929- [FB]
American football player
* Sugar, Shug

Sugar Lip
See Hafiz, Mohammed

[The] Sugar Man
See Leonard, Ray Charles

[The] Sugar Pie Guy
See Sawell, Larry

Sugar Ray Leonard
See Leonard, Ray Charles

Sugar Ray Long
See Long, Russell

Sugar Ray Robinson
See Smith, Walker, Jr.

Sugar Ray Seales
See Seales, Ray

Sugar, Shug
See Sugar, Leo T.

[The] Sugar Tycoon of Jamaica
See Taylor, Simon

Sugarhouse Pete DiGiovanni
See DiGiovanni, Peter

Sugartail
See Harris, George Washington

Suger 1081?-1151 [WBD]
French statesman
* [The] Father of His Country
* Pere de la Patrie

Sugg, Buddy
See Sugg, P. A.

Sugg, P. A. 1908-1976 [HPPN]
American executive
* Sugg, Buddy

Suggs, Chick
See Suggs, Edward Murray

Suggs, Edward Murray 1901- [BX]
American boxer
* Suggs, Chick

Suggs, Simon
See Hooper, Johnson J.

Sugimoto, Tsunetaro 1879-1924 [SC]
Japanese-born actor
* Tomamoto, Thomas

Suhr, August Richard 1906- [BE]
American baseball player
* Suhr, Gus

Suhr, Gus
See Suhr, August Richard

Suicide Sal
See Parker, Bonnie

Suisse, Jules Francois Simon 1814-1896
[PA]
French author
* Simon, Jules

Suitcase Bob Seeds
See Seeds, Robert Ira

Suiter, Arlendo D. 1919- [ASC]
American composer
* Suiter, Don

Suiter, Don
See Suiter, Arlendo D.

Suitger ?-1047 [CAL]
Pope
* Clement II

Sujakevitch, Anjuschka Stenski 1908?-
[F2, FC]
Russian-born actress
* Sten, Anna

Sukeforth, Clyde LeRoy 1901- [BE]
American baseball player
* Sukeforth, Sukey

Sukeforth, Sukey
See Sukeforth, Clyde LeRoy

Sukenik, Yigael 1917- [CA]
*Israeli deputy prime minister,
archaeologist, author*
* Yadin, Yigael

Sukulov, Victor 20th c. [EE]
Latvian-born intelligence agent
* Kent, Edward
* [The] Petit Chef

Sularz, Bronislaw 1942- [AES]
Polish soccer player
* Sularz, Jerry

Sularz, Jerry
See Sularz, Bronislaw

Suleiman I [or Soliman] ?-1410? [FFF,
RH]
Sultan of Turkey
* [The] Noble

Suleiman II [or Soliman] 1493?-1566
[FFF, RH, WBD]
Sultan of Turkey
* Canuni
* [The] Conqueror
* [The] Law Giver
* [The] Lord of his Age
* [The] Magnificent

Sulin, Kaarlo Teodor 1902-1945 [EWL]
Finnish poet
* Sarkia, Kaarlo Teodor

Sulky
See Arcularius, Henry W.

Sulky
See Trimble, William Copeland

Sulla, Lucius Cornelius 2nd c. BC
[WBD]
Roman general and politician
* Felix

Sullivan
See McNamara, James B.

Sullivan, Alan 1868-1947 [BI, CCL]
Canadian author
* Murray, Sinclair

Sullivan, Barry
See Barry, Patrick

Sullivan, Big Mike
See Sullivan, Michael Joseph

Sullivan, Big Tim
See Sullivan, Timothy Daniel

Sullivan, Bonar 1924-1958   [FC]
American actor
* Colleano, Bonar, Jr.

Sullivan, Boston Tim
See Sullivan, Timothy P.

Sullivan, Brian
See Sullivan, Harry Joseph

Sullivan, Carl Mancel 1918-   [BE]
American baseball player
* Sullivan, Jack

Sullivan, Chub
See Sullivan, John Frank

Sullivan, Cynthia Jan 1937-   [GF]
American golfer
* Sullivan, Silky

Sullivan, Dan 20th c.   [BMH]
British strongman
* [The] Wonder of the Age

Sullivan, Daniel 1855-1910   [BEW]
American actor and playwright
* Sully, Daniel

Sullivan, Daniel C. 1857-1893   [BE]
American baseball player
* Sullivan, Link

Sullivan, Des
See Sullivan, Thomas Desmond

Sullivan, Eddie
See Collins, Edward Trowbridge, Sr.
[Eddie]

Sullivan, Edgar James 1890?-1957
[BEW]
British theatrical performer
* Colleano, Bonar, Sr.

Sullivan, Edmund 20th c.   [WWL]
British author
* Nagle, Arthur

Sullivan, Edward Alan 1868-1947   [CAN, WW]
Canadian author
* Murray, Sinclair

Sullivan, Edward Dean 1888-1938
[DNA]
American author and journalist
* Alum, Hardly

Sullivan, Edward Vincent 1902-   [CR, HPPN]
American television performer
* [The] Great Stone Face
* [The] Man in the Iron Mask
* [The] Unsmiling Irishman
* [The] Walking Mount Rushmore

Sullivan, Elizabeth 1902-   [F2, FC, OCF]
British-born American actress
* Lanchester, Elsa

Sullivan, Eric Harrison
See Hickey, Madelyn Eastlund

Sullivan, Frank 1910-1975   [SC, SW]
American actor
* Sully, Frank

Sullivan, Frank
See Dillinger, John Herbert

Sullivan, Frank Taylor 1929-   [CEI]
Canadian-born hockey player
* Sullivan, Sully

Sullivan, George James 1929-   [CEI, FHE, HK]
Canadian-born hockey player
* Sullivan, Red

Sullivan, George S. 1882-1927   [HPPN]
American vaudeville performer
* Tom the Midget

Sullivan, Harry Joseph 1919-1969   [SC]
American-born actor and opera singer
* Sullivan, Brian

Sullivan, Jack 1878-1947   [BX, RBE]
American boxer
* Sullivan, Twin

Sullivan, Jack
See Reich, Jacob

Sullivan, Jack
See Sullivan, Carl Mancel

Sullivan, James 1813-1856   [BI]
American boxer and promoter
* Sullivan, Yankee

Sullivan, James 19th c.
American dancer
* Sylvain, James

Sullivan, James [Jim] 1903-   [HPPN]
British rugby player
* Sully
* Young Sully

Sullivan, James A. 20th c.   [PHM]
American sheriff
* Sullivan, Smiling Jimmy

Sullivan, James E. 1864?-1931   [BEW]
Comedian
* [The] Polite Lunatic

Sullivan, James Frank 1853-1936   [ICB]
British illustrator
* Josef

Sullivan, Joe
See O'Sullivan, Dennis Patrick Terence
Joseph

Sullivan, John 1889?-1956   [BI]
Canadian boxer
* Sullivan, Spike

Sullivan, John Florence 1894-1956
[EMT, FC, HPPN, SC]
American entertainer
* Allen, Fred
* Huckle, Paul
* James, Freddie
* [The] King of the Quick Quip
* St. James, Fred
* Sullivan, Young

Sullivan, John Frank 1856-1881   [BE]
American baseball player
* Sullivan, Chub

Sullivan, John L[awrence] 1858-1918
[AS, BX, HPPN, RBE]
American boxer
* Big Casino
* [The] Boston Strong Boy
* [The] Great John L.
* John L.
* [The] Strong Boy of Boston

Sullivan, John Peter 1941-   [SMG]
American baseball player
* Sullivan, Sully

Sullivan, John Y. 1917-1967   [CWG, DAM]
American country-western performer
* Lonzo

Sullivan, Josephine 1880?-1962   [HPPN]
American theatrical performer
* Gassman, Josephine

Sullivan, Kid
See Tricamo, Stephen J.

Sullivan, Larry M. 20th c.   [HPPN]
American sports promoter and mining speculator
* Sullivan, Shanghai Larry

Sullivan, Lefty
See Sullivan, Paul Thomas

Sullivan, Link
See Sullivan, Daniel C.

Sullivan, Little Tim
See Sullivan, Timothy P.

Sullivan, Louis Henri 1856-1924
[HPPN]
American architect
* [The] Father of Modernism
* [The] Father of Modernism in
  Architecture

Sullivan, M. J.
See O'Sullivan, Michael John

Sullivan, Mark 1874-1952   [HPPN]
American journalist, columnist, commentator
* [The] Dean of Washington
  Correspondents
* [The] Friend of Presidents

Sullivan, Mary
See Panfili, Mirella

Sullivan, Maxine
See Williams, Marietta

Sullivan, Michael Joseph 1866-1906
[BE]
American baseball player
* Sullivan, Big Mike

Sullivan, Mike 1878-1937   [AS, BX, RBE]
American boxer
* Sullivan, Twin

Sullivan, Paul Thomas 1916-   [BE]
American baseball player
* Sullivan, Lefty

Sullivan, Peter 1951- [SMG]
Canadian-born hockey player
* Sullivan, Silky

Sullivan, Red
See Sullivan, George James

Sullivan, Robert Baldwin 1802-1853
[DNA, FFF]
Irish-born politician, jurist, author
* Cinna
* Legion

Sullivan, Rollin 1919- [CWG, DAM]
American country-western performer
* Oscar

Sullivan, Sean Mei
See Sohl, Gerald Allan [Jerry]

Sullivan, Shanghai Larry
See Sullivan, Larry M.

Sullivan, Sheila 1927- [CA]
British author and editor
* Bathurst, Sheila

Sullivan, Silky
See Sullivan, Cynthia Jan

Sullivan, Silky
See Sullivan, Peter

Sullivan, Sleeper
See Sullivan, Thomas Jefferson

Sullivan, Smiling Jimmy
See Sullivan, James A.

Sullivan, Spike
See Sullivan, John

Sullivan, Steve
See Tricamo, Stephen J.

Sullivan, Sully
See Sullivan, Frank Taylor

Sullivan, Sully
See Sullivan, John Peter

Sullivan, Thomas Desmond 1913- [GF]
American sportswriter
* Sullivan, Des

Sullivan, Thomas Jefferson ?-1899 [BE]
American baseball player
* Sullivan, Sleeper

Sullivan, Timothy Daniel 1827-? [PI]
Irish poet and politician
* O'Sullivan, Timothy
* T. D. S.

Sullivan, Timothy Daniel 1862-1913
[HPPN]
American politician
* [The] Big Feller
* [The] Last of the Big Time Grafters
* Sullivan, Big Tim

Sullivan, Timothy P. ?-1909 [HPPN]
American politician
* [The] Little Feller
* Sullivan, Boston Tim
* Sullivan, Little Tim

Sullivan, Twin
See Sullivan, Jack

Sullivan, Twin
See Sullivan, Mike

Sullivan, Vernon
See Vian, Boris

Sullivan, Victoria 1943- [CA]
American poet and playwright
* Slater, Veronica

Sullivan, William J., Sr. [Billy]
1875-1965 [HPPN]
American baseball player and manager
* [The] Father of the Catcher's Chest
Protector

Sullivan, Yankee
See Ambrose, James

Sullivan, Yankee
See Sullivan, James

Sullivan, Young
See Sullivan, John Florence

Sully
See Sullivan, James [Jim]

Sully, Daniel
See Sullivan, Daniel

Sully, Frank
See Sullivan, Frank

Sully, George 20th c.
Horse trainer
* Sully, Slim

Sully, George
See Busch, George

Sully, Jean Baptiste 1665-1701 [NPS]
French musician
* [Le] Buffon Odieux

Sully, Slim
See Sully, George

Sully-Prudhomme
See Prudhomme, Rene Francois
Armand

[The] Sulphur King
See Frasch, Herman

Sultan El Osman, Chareh
See Bullock-Webster, Llewelyn

[The] Sultan of Magic
See Wishner, Sam

[The] Sultan of Split
See Mitchelson, Marvin

[The] Sultan of Swap
See McKeon, Jack

[The] Sultan of Swat
See Ruth, George Herman

[The] Sultan of the Skin Trade
See Miller, Robert

Sultzer, Joseph 1884-1981 [JF]
American comedian
* Smith
* Smith, Joseph

Sulzberger, Arthur Hays 1891-1968
American newspaper publisher
* Aitchess, A.

Sulzberger, Arthur Ochs 1926?-
American newspaper publisher
* Sock, A.
* Sulzberger, Punch

Sulzberger, C. L.
See Sulzberger, Cyrus Leo, III

Sulzberger, Cyrus Leo, III 1912-
[WYA]
American author
* Sulzberger, C. L.

Sulzberger, Iphigene Ochs 1892?-
[HPPN]
American newspaper publisher
* [The] Grey Lady of the Times

Sulzberger, Punch
See Sulzberger, Arthur Ochs

Sumac, Yma
See Chavarri, Emperatriz

Summer, Brian
See DuBreuil, Elizabeth Lorinda

Summer, Donna
See Gaines, La Donna Andrea

[The] Summer King
See Amadeus

[The] Summer King
See Robert I

Summer, Marie
See Foucaux, Charlotte

Summerall, Charles Pelot 1867-1955
[HPPN]
American army officer
* Sitting Bull

Summerall, George 20th c. [FB]
American football player
* Summerall, Pat

Summerall, Pat
See Summerall, George

Summerdale
See Young, Alexander

Summerfield, Charles
See Arrington, Alfred W.

Summerfield, Charles
See Foster, Theodore

Summerfield, Joan 1921- [HPPN]
British dancer and actress
* Kent, Jean

Summerfield, Woolfe 1897- [WWL]
British author and barrister
* Mowshay, Ben

Summerforest, Ivy B.
See Kirkup, James

Summerhayes, Prudence
See Alan Turner, Violet Prudence

Summerhays, Reginald Sherriff 1881-?
[BI]
British horse breeder
* Gale, Martin

Summerhill, J. K.
See Schere, Monroe

Summerly, Felix
See Cole, [Sir] Henry

Summerly, Mrs. Felix
See Cole, Marian Fairman

Summers, A. Leonard 20th c. [WWL]
British author and journalist
* Cue

Summers, Blue Peter
See Summers, J. C.

Summers, Champ
See Summers, John J.

Summers, Colin
See Agnew, Stephen Hamilton

Summers, Colleen 1928- [ECM, RO1]
American singer
* Ford, Mary

Summers, Gordon
See Hornby, John [Wilkinson]

Summers, Hal
See Summers, Henry Forbes

Summers, Henry Forbes 1911- [CA]
British poet
* Summers, Hal

Summers, Hollis [Spurgeon, Jr.] 1916-
[CA, CN, WD]
American author and poet
* Hollis, Jim [joint pseudonym with
  Louis P(reston) Trimble]

Summers, J. C. 19th c. [HPPN]
American author
* Summers, Blue Peter

Summers, John A.
See Lawson, Horace Lowe

Summers, John J. 1948- [BR]
American baseball player
* Summers, Champ

Summers, Kickapoo
See Summers, Oron Edgar

Summers, Oron Edgar 1884-1953 [BE]
American baseball player
* Summers, Kickapoo

Summers, Rey
See Montague, Alphonsus Joseph-Mary
Augustus

Summers, Rowena
See Saunders, Jean

Summersales, Rowland 1912- [AW]
British author
* Gaines, Robert

Summersgill, Henry Travers 1876-1931
[BE]
American baseball player
* Sommerville, Andrew Henry [Andy]

Summerskill, Edith 1902?-1980?
British politician
* Dr. Edith

Summerville, Amelia
See Shaw, Amelia M.

Summerville, George J. 1892-1946
[BEW, F1, FC]
American actor
* Summerville, Slim

Summerville, Slim
See Summerville, George J.

Summey, James C. 1914-1976 [CWG,
ECM]
American country-western performer
* Cousin Jody

[The] Summoned
See Ferdinand IV

Sumner, Charles 1811-1874 [HPPN]
American politician
* [The] Bull of the Woods
* C. S.

Sumner, Charles
See Hall, Howard

Sumner, David [W. K.] 1937- [CA]
American author
* Kaiser, Bill

Sumner, Eldon
See Bruno, James Edward

Sumner, Gordon Matthew 1952?-
American singer, musician, composer
* Sting

Sumner, J. D.
See Sumner, John David

Sumner, John David 1924- [DAM]
American singer and songwriter
* Sumner, J. D.

Sumner, William Graham 1840-1910
[HPPN]
American educator, economist, sociologist
* [The] Forgotten Man
* Yale's Greatest Teacher

Sumter, Thomas 1734-1832 [HPPN, SN]
American army officer
* [The] Carolina Gamecock
* [The] Carolinian Gamecock
* [The] Gamecock
* [The] South Carolina Gamecock

[The] Sun God
See Louis XIV

Sun, Gus
See Klotz, Gustave Ferdinand

[The] Sun King
See Louis XIV

[The] Sun of Righteousness
See Jesus Christ

Sun Ra
See Blount, Herman

Sun Wen
See Sun Yat-sen

Sun Yat-sen 1866-1925 [HPPN, WBD]
Chinese statesman
* Chung Shan
* [The] Father of the Chinese Republic

Sun Yat-sen (cont.)
* [The] Father of the Revolution
* Sun Wen

Sunbeam
See McManus, Patrick

Sunbeam, Susie
See Mackarness, Matilda Anne

Sunbeauty, Olga
See Solbelli, Olga

[The] Sunbonnet Girl
See Parker, Linda

Sunbonnet Sue
See Salisbury, Marilla

[The] Sundance Kid
See Csonka, Lawrence R. [Larry]

[The] Sundance Kid
See Longbaugh, Harry

Sundaram
See Luhar, Tribhuvandas
Purushottandas

**Sundarananda [One who Delights in
Beauty]**
See Nakashima, George Katsutoshi

Sundarius
See Spencer, Charles [Third Earl of
Sunderland]

Sunday
See Talbot, Catherine

Sunday, Art[hur]
See Wacher, August

[The] Sunday Gentleman
See Foe, Daniel

Sunday, Johnny
See Meader, Vaughn

Sunday, Parson
See Sunday, William Ashley [Billy]

[A] Sunday Scholar
See Todd, W.

[A] Sunday School Superintendent
See Arnold, Alexander S.

Sunday, William Ashley [Billy]
1862-1935 [BE, HPPN, PB]
American evangelist and baseball player
* [The] Evangelist
* [The] Huckster of the Tabernacle
* Sunday, Parson

Sundback, Gideon 1880-1954 [HPPN]
*Swedish-American electrical engineer and
inventor*
* [The] Father of the Zipper

Sundmark, Betty
See Shannon, Elizabeth S.

Sundra, Smokey
See Sundra, Stephen Richard

Sundra, Stephen Richard 1910-1952
[BE]
American baseball player
* Sundra, Smokey

Sundry Whereof
See Porson, Richard

Sunesson, Lambert 1918- [IAW]
Swedish author
* Frykberg, August

Sung Chiao
See Chou, Eric

Sung, P. M.
See Chun, Jinsie K[yung] S[hien]

Sung-Tai, Kim 1907- [IWM]
Korean composer, educator, conductor
* Naksok

Sungei, Anak
See Brooke, Gilbert Edward

Sunkel, Lefty
See Sunkel, Thomas Jacob

Sunkel, Thomas Jacob 1912- [BE]
American baseball player
* Sunkel, Lefty

Sunna
See Larusdottir, Elinborg

Sunners, William 1903- [CAP]
American author
* Keith, Lee
* Satterly, Weston

Sunni-Ali, Fulani
See Boston, Cynthia Priscilla

[The] Sunny Gentleman
See Foe, Daniel

Sunny Jack Sutthoff
See Sutthoff, John Gerhard

Sunny Jim
See Watson, Johnny

Sunny Jim Bottomley
See Bottomley, James Leroy

Sunny Jim Callaghan
See Callaghan, Leonard James

Sunny Jim Coffroth
See Coffroth, James W. [Jimmy]

Sunny Jim Cosmano
See Cosmano, Vincenzo

Sunny Jim Dygert
See Dygert, James Henry

Sunny Jim Fitzsimmons
See Fitzsimmons, James Edward

Sunny Jim Hackett
See Hackett, James Joseph [Jim]

Sunny Jim Mallory
See Mallory, James Baugh [Jim]

Sunny Jim Rolfe
See Rolfe, James

Sunny Jim Rolph
See Rolph, James, Jr. [Jimmy]

Sunny Jim Valdare
See Mulligan, James

Sunny Jim Vandegrift
See Vandegrift, Alexander Archer

Sunny Jim Watson
See Watson, James Eli

Sunnyland Slim
See Luandrew, Albert

[The] Sunrise Poet
See Lanier, Sidney

Sunset Jimmy Burke
See Burke, James Timothy

Sunshine
See Abbott, Wenonah Stevens

Sunshine
See Hood, Dorothy Browning

Sunshine, Baby
See Flood, Pauline

[The] Sunshine Boy
See Dale, Charles

[The] Sunshine Boy
See Smith, Joseph [Joe]

Sunshine Charlie Mitchell
See Mitchell, Charles

Sunshine, Doc
See Warren, William A.

Sunshine, Leo
See Murphy, Brian

Sunshine, Marion
See Ijames, Mary Tunstall

Sunshine, Mr.
See Banks, Ernest [Ernie]

Sunshine, Silvia
See Brooks, Abbie M.

Suomalainen, Kari Yrjana 1920- [WEC]
Finnish cartoonist
* Kari

Suparto, Muso [BI]
Javanese Communist leader
* Muso

[The] Super Bluebeard
See Petiot, Henry John Felix Marcel

[The] Super Circus Girl
See Hartline, Mary

Super Duper Tex
See Steding, Peggy

Super Flanker Hayes
See Hayes, Robert Lee

Super Frog
See Du Hamel, Yvon

Super Gato Gonzalez
See Gonzalez, Rodolfo

[The] Super Gnat
See Smith, Noland

Super Grammaticam
See Sigismund

[The] Super Hippie
See Finkelstein, Peter Max

Super Joe
See Charboneau, Joe

Super K
See Kissinger, Henry Alfred

Super Kraut
See Kissinger, Henry Alfred

Super Mex
See Trevino, Lee

[The] Super Model
See Sims, Naomi

Super Rook
See Russell, William Ellis [Bill]

Super Santa
See Berman, Ed

[The] Super Soda Pop Peddler
See Kendall, Donald McIntosh

[The] Super Stinker
See Heiny, Thomas

Super Sub
See Kennedy, John Edward

[The] Super Swindler
See Stavinsky, Serge Alexandre

Super Tex
See Foyt, Anthony Joseph, Jr.

Superannuated Old Woman
See Harrison, William Henry

[The] Superb
See Hancock, Winfield Scott

Superbow
See Clements, Vassar

Superbrat
See McEnroe, John

Superbus
See Tarquin II [or Tarquinius]

Superchief
See Reynolds, Albert Pierce [Allie]

Supercop
See Rizzo, Frank Lazarro

[The] Supercrat
See Shultz, George Pratt

Supergirl
See Stafford, Tammy

Superhawk
See Begin, Menachem

Superhenry
See Kissinger, Henry Alfred

[The] Superintendant
See Fitzgerald, James Edward

[The] Superintendent
See Holyoke, Edward Augustus

[The] Superintendent of Public Schools
See Philbrick, John Dudley

[The] Superintendent of the Coast Survey
See Bache, Alexander Dallas

[The] Superior of the Society
See Sellon, Priscilla Lydia

[The] Superior Person
See Horsman, Edward

Superjew
See Epstein, Michael Peter

[The] Superlative of My Comparative
See Scott, [Sir] Walter

Supermac
See Macmillan, Harold

Superman
See Alyn, Kirk

Superman
See Bollerman, Howard

Superman
See Hartung, Clinton Clarence

[The] Superservant
See Valentino, Anthony

Superstar
See Kissinger, Henry Alfred

[The] Superstar of Pornoraphy
See Chambers, Marilyn

[The] Superstar of the Silents
See Swenson, Josephine May

Supervise [Secret Service code name]
See Truman, Harry S.

Suppiluliumas   [HPPN]
Hittite king
* [The] Charlemagne of the Near East
* Labarnas
* My Sunship

Supple, Gerald Henry 1823-1899   [PI]
Irish-born poet
* G. H. S.
* Torquil

Supporter of the Papal Omnipotence
See Borghese, Camillo

Supraner, Robyn 1930-   [CA, SAT]
American author
* Blake, Olive
* Frost, Erica
* Warren, Elizabeth

[The] Supreme Authority on English Usage
See Hall, Fitzedward

[The] Supreme Court's Emily Post
See Frankfurter, Felix

[The] Supreme Military Commander of the State
See Chu Teh

[The] Supreme Military Leader
See Castro, Cipriano

[The] Supreme Power of God
See Simon Magus

[El] Supremo
See Francia, Jose Gaspar Rodriguez

Sur, Atul Krishna 1904-   [IAW]
Indian author
* Chandravati
* Yama

Sura
See Lentulus, Publius Cornelius

Surabian, Zareh 20th c.   [EF]
American football player
* Surabian, Zeke

Surabian, Zeke
See Surabian, Zareh

Suragne, Pierre
See Pelot, Pierre

Suraiya, Jagdish Chatrabhuj 1946-
[IAW]
Indian author
* Suraiya, Jug

Suraiya, Jug
See Suraiya, Jagdish Chatrabhuj

Surchamp, Henry 1876-?   [CAT]
French author
* Nesmy, Jean

Sure Shot Dunlap
See Dunlap, Frederick C.

Surfaceman
See Anderson, Alexander

[A] Surgeon
See Abrahams, B.

[The] Surgeon General of Baseball
See Hyland, [Dr.] Robert F.

[A] Surgeon, M. R. C. S.
See Mudge, Henry

[The] Surgeon Scout
See Powell, [David] Frank

[The] Surgical Genius of His Generation
See Murphy, John B.

Surkont, Matthew Constantine 1922-
[BE]
American baseball player
* Surkont, Max

Surkont, Max
See Surkont, Matthew Constantine

Surly Sam
See Johnson, Samuel

Surmelian, Leon [Zaven] 1907-   [CAP]
Turkish-born author and educator
* Vandour, Cyril

Surrebutter, John, Esq.
See Anstey, John

[The] Surrey Pet
See Caffyn, William

Surrey, Richard
See Brooker, Bertram

[The] Surrey Vampire
See Haigh, John George

Surry, Colonel
See Cooke, John Esten

Surtees, Fanny 19th c.   [PA]
Author
* Cherith

Surtees, Robert Smith 1803-1864   [NPS]
Author
* Jorrocks, John

Survage, Leopold
See Sturzwage, Leopold

[The] Surveyor President
See Washington, George

Survilliers, Comte de
See Bonaparte, Joseph

[The] Survivor
See Fernyhough, Thomas

Susa, Charlotte
See Wagmuller, Charlotte

Susan
See Graham, [Maude Fitzgerald] Susan

Susato, Johannes
See Steinwert von Soest, Johannes

Susce, George Cyril Methodius 1908-
[BE]
American baseball player
* Susce, Good Kid

Susce, Good Kid
See Susce, George Cyril Methodius

Susie D.
See Drury, Susie

Suso
See Pena Rego, Jesus

Suso [or Seuse], Heinrich
See Berg, Heinrich

Suspensurus
See Lamb, Charles

[A] Sussex Clergyman
See Wise, [Rev.] Joseph

Sussex, Gordon
See Volk, Gordon

Sussex, Jasper
See Maginn, William

Sussexiensis
See Stonestreet, G. G.

Susskind, Arthur 1886-   [BX, EJS]
American boxer
* Otto, Young

Sussman, Cornelia Silver 1914-   [CA]
American author
* Jessey, Cornelia

Sutcliffe, Butch
See Sutcliffe, Charles Inigo

Sutcliffe, Charles Inigo 1915-   [BE]
American baseball player
* Sutcliffe, Butch

Sutcliffe, Edward Elmer 1863-1893 [BE]
American baseball player
* Sutcliffe, Sy

Sutcliffe, Joseph Robert 1911- [IAW]
British writer
* Plowman, Giles

Sutcliffe, Pavella Dolores 20th c.
[IAW]
British writer
* Ploughman, Nina

Sutcliffe, Peter 1946?-
British murderer
* [The] Yorkshire Ripper

Sutcliffe, Sy
See Sutcliffe, Edward Elmer

Suther, Flash
See Suther, John

Suther, John 20th c. [HPPN]
American football player
* Suther, Flash

Sutherland, Bill
See McCall, John

Sutherland, Conrad James 1901-? [BBH]
American lacrosse player and official
* Sutherland, Suds

Sutherland, Dizzy
See Sutherland, Howard Alvin

Sutherland, Duchess of 1869-? [NPS]
British author
* Fyffe, R. E.
* Gower, Erskine

Sutherland, [Dr.] Edwin H. 1883-1950
[HPPN]
American author, educator, criminologist
* [The] Dean of American
  Criminologists

Sutherland, Elizabeth
See Marshall, Elizabeth Margaret

Sutherland, Evelyn Greenleaf
See Baker, Evelyn Greenleaf

Sutherland, Gary Lynn 1944- [SMG]
American baseball player
* Sutherland, Suds

Sutherland, Harvey Scott 1894- [BE]
American baseball player
* Sutherland, Suds

Sutherland, Howard Alvin 1923- [BE]
American baseball player
* Sutherland, Dizzy

Sutherland, James T. 1870-1955 [BBH]
Canadian hockey pioneer
* [The] Father of Hockey

Sutherland, Joan 1929- [CR, HPPN]
Australian-born opera singer
* [The] Glorious Iceberg
* Orchid from the Outback
* Prima Donna Assoluta
* [La] Stupenda [The Stupendous One]

Sutherland, Jock
See Sutherland, John Bain

Sutherland, John Bain 1889-1948 [AS,
BI, FB, HPPN]
Scottish-born American football coach
* [The] Dour Scot
* [The] Overland Man
* [The] Scotsman
* Sutherland, Jock

Sutherland, Josie
See Mayo, Mrs. William H.

Sutherland, Lucy Christina 1864?-1935
[WFA]
British fashion designer
* Lucile

Sutherland, Morris
See Morris, Gwendolen Sutherland

Sutherland, Robert ?-1888 [FFF]
Entertainer and evangelist
* Hart, [Senator] Bob
* [The] Reformed Minstrel

Sutherland, Roy
See Sothern, Hugh

Sutherland, Suds
See Sutherland, Conrad James

Sutherland, Suds
See Sutherland, Gary Lynn

Sutherland, Suds
See Sutherland, Harvey Scott

Sutherland, Victoria ?-1913 [HPPN]
American actress
* Dennis, Victoria
* Howard, May

Sutherland, William
See Cooper, John Murray

Suthinee
See Ambhanwong, Suthilak

Suthpin, Barnacle Bill
See Suthpin, William Halstead

Suthpin, William Halstead 1887-
[HPPN]
American politician
* Suthpin, Barnacle Bill

Sutor, Harry G. 20th c. [BE]
American baseball player
* Sutor, Rube

Sutor, Rube
See Sutor, Harry G.

Sutro, Adolph Heinrich Joseph
1830-1898 [HPPN]
German-American engineer and politician
* [The] Father of the Sutro Tunnel
* [The] King of the Comstock
* [The] Savior of the Comstock Lode

Sutter, Captain
See Sutter, John Augustus

Sutter, Franz
See Strich, Christian

Sutter, John Augustus 1803-1880
[HPPN]
Swiss pioneer
* Sutter, Captain

Sutthoff, John Gerhard 1873-1942 [BE]
American baseball player
* Sutthoff, Sunny Jack

Sutthoff, Sunny Jack
See Sutthoff, John Gerhard

Suttles, Bubbles
See Suttles, George

Suttles, George 1901-1968 [MK]
American baseball player
* Suttles, Bubbles
* Suttles, Mule

Suttles, Mule
See Suttles, George

Suttles, Shirley [Smith] 1922- [CA]
American author
* Conger, Lesley

Sutton, Clarence R. 1931- [IBW]
American bobsled racer
* Sutton, Clay

Sutton, Clay
See Sutton, Clarence R.

Sutton, Cochise
See Sutton, Lloyd

Sutton, Dick
See Schwartz, Richard

Sutton, Donald Howard 1945- [SMG]
American baseball player
* Sutton, Elmer
* Sutton, Sut

Sutton, Eliza Warren 1865-1935 [SC]
American actress
* Warren, Eliza

Sutton, Elmer
See Sutton, Donald Howard

Sutton, Eric Graham Sutton 1892-
[WGT]
British author
* Marsden, Anthony

Sutton, Ernest
See Sorl, Ernest James

Sutton, Eugenia Geneva 1917- [SFL]
American author
* Sutton, Jean

Sutton, Henry
See Slavitt, David Rytman

Sutton, I. M.
See Coad, Frederick Roy

Sutton, Jean
See Sutton, Eugenia Geneva

Sutton, Jeff
See Sutton, Jefferson Howard

Sutton, Jefferson Howard 1913- [CA]
American author
* Sutton, Jeff

Sutton, John
See Tullett, Denis

Sutton, Kate 20th c. [HPPN]
American seafarer
* Sutton, Ma

Sutton, Lloyd 20th c. [BBH]
Boxer
* Sutton, Cochise

Sutton, Ma
See Sutton, Kate

Sutton, Mamie
See Solomon, Mrs. Fred

Sutton, Margaret Beebe
See Sutton, Rachel Irene Beebe

Sutton, Maurice Lewis 1927- [CA]
American author
* Sutton, Stack

Sutton, Penny
See Wood, Christopher [Hovelle]

Sutton, Pepe
See Sutton, Pierre Monte

Sutton, Pierre Monte 1947- [IBW]
*American broadcasting company executive
and publisher*
* Sutton, Pepe

Sutton, Rachel Irene Beebe 1903-
[HPPN]
American author
* Ray, Irene
* Sutton, Margaret Beebe

Sutton, Scott [PA]
Author
* Sir Toby

Sutton, Slick Willie
See Sutton, William Francis [Willie]

Sutton, Stack
See Sutton, Maurice Lewis

Sutton, Sut
See Sutton, Donald Howard

Sutton, Thomas
See Reach, James

Sutton, William 1877-1955 [SC]
American actor and magician
* [The] Great Fontonelle

Sutton, William Francis [Willie]
1901-1980 [BLB, CEC, DI, HPPN]
American bank robber
* [The] Actor
* [The] Babe Ruth of Bank Robbers
* Gordan, George
* Lynch, Edward
* Sutton, Slick Willie
* Willie the Actor

Sutton-Vane, V. H.
See Sutton-Vane, Vane Hunt

Sutton-Vane, Vane Hunt 1888-1963
[BEW, LC]
Playwright and actor
* Sutton-Vane, V. H.
* Vane, Sutton

**Suvorov [or Suwarof], Aleksandr
Vasilievich** 1729-1800 [HN, WBD]
Russian army officer
* [The] Invincible
* Italiski
* Rymnikski

Suydam, John Howard 1832-1909
[DNA]
American author and clergyman
* Knickerbocker, Jr.

Suzuki, Chiyoko 1930?- [HPPN]
Japanese-American actress and singer
* Suzuki, Pat

Suzuki, Guts
See Suzuki, Ishimatsu

Suzuki, Ishimatsu 1948- [RBE]
Japanese boxer
* Suzuki, Guts

Suzuki, Pat
See Suzuki, Chiyoko

Suzuki, Shuji 1927- [WEC]
Japanese cartoonist and illustrator
* Cho, Shinta

Suzuki, Zenko 1911?- [NW 10-25-82]
Japanese prime minister
* Fish, Mr.
* King Zenko the Ignorant

Suzy
See Mehle, Aileen

Svare, Harland 20th c.
Norwegian-American football coach
* [The] Swede

Svareff, [Count] Vladimir
See Crowley, Edward Alexander

Svarts, Helga 1890- [CD]
Swedish author and poet
* Martinson, Moa

Svedberg, Emanuel 1688-1772 [HN,
WBD]
Swedish scientist, philosopher, author
* [The] Apostle of the New Jerusalem
* Swedenborg, Emanuel

Svedberg, The
See Svedberg, Theodor

Svedberg, Theodor 1884-? [HPPN]
Swedish chemist
* Svedberg, The

Sveeadstroem
See Nyberg, Julia Christina

Sveinsson, Aslakur
See Indridason, Indridi

Sveinsson, Jon 1857-1944 [CAT]
Icelandic-born author
* Nonni

Svendsen, Caroline 1941?- [HPPN]
American boxer
* Svendsen, Sweet Caroline

Svendsen, Clara 20th c.
*Danish author and companion of Karen
Blixen*
* Selborn, Clara

Svendsen, Sweet Caroline
See Svendsen, Caroline

Svengali
See Pendergrass, Theodore [Teddy]

Svengali
See Rowland, Clarence Henry

[The] Svengali of Rock
See Good, Jack

[The] Svengali of Swat
See Lau, Charley

Svennberg, Olof Teodor 1852-? [THR]
Swedish actor
* Svennberg, Tore

Svennberg, Tore
See Svennberg, Olof Teodor

Svenson, Andrew E. 1910-1975 [CA,
SAT]
American author
* Dixon, Franklin W. [house
  pseudonym] [Stratemeyer Syndicate]
* Stone, Alan [house pseudonym]
  [Stratemeyer Syndicate]
* West, Jerry [house pseudonym]
  [Stratemeyer Syndicate]

Svensson, Jon Stefan 1857-1944 [BI]
Icelandic author
* Nonni

Svensson, Marta Birgit 1918- [OP]
Swedish opera singer
* Nilsson, Birgit

Svensson, Sven
See Bolay, Karl H.

Sverkers, Stig
See Foghammar, Stig Sverker

Sverre [or Swerro] 1152?-1202 [WBD]
King of Norway
* Sverre Sigurdsson

Sverre Sigurdsson
See Sverre [or Swerro]

Svetla, Karolina
See Muzakova, Johanna [Rottova]

Svevo, Italo
See Schmitz, Ettore

Svoboda, Madeleine 1916- [FC]
French actress
* Robinson, Madeleine

Swaby, Horace 20th c.
Jamaican musician
* Pablo, Augustus

Swacina, Harry Joseph 1881-1944 [BE]
American baseball player
* Swacina, Swats

Swacina, Swats
See Swacina, Harry Joseph

Swadling, Ann Pauline 1936- [OP]
British opera singer
* Howard, Ann

Swafford, Johnny C. 1920- [BA]
American author
* Lugman, Adbullah
* Nig, Capt'n

Swafford, Marthena [Funkhouser]
1845-1913 [BI]
American poet
* Bremer, Belle

Swagger, General
See Burgoyne, John

Swaim, Cy
See Swaim, John Hillary

Swaim, John Hillary 1874-1918 [BE]
American baseball player
* Swaim, Cy

Swain, Charles 1803-1874 [DEL]
British poet
* [The] Manchester Poet

Swain, Dwight V[reeland] 1915- [CA]
American author
* Carter, Nick
* South, Clark

Swain, E. G.
See Swain, Edmund Gill

Swain, Edmund Gill 1861-1938 [HFF]
British author
* Swain, E. G.

Swain, Frederick Dwight 1909- [HPPN]
American jazz musician
* Swain, Teeny

Swain, Garry
See Swain, Garth Frederick Arthur

Swain, Garth Frederick Arthur 1947-
[HR]
Canadian-born hockey player
* Swain, Garry

Swain, J. H., Jr.
See Hardin, John Wesley

Swain, Mack 1876-1935 [HPPN]
American actor
* Ambrose

Swain, Mark
See Clemens, Samuel Langhorne

Swain, Miriam
See Mason, Miriam Evangeline

Swain, Philip William 1889-1958 [BI,
HPPN]
American engineer and author
* Edwards, George

Swain, Teeny
See Swain, Frederick Dwight

Swales, Susan Matilda [Bradshaw]
1843-? [DNA]
American author
* Bell, Ernest

Swallow, Elleen 1842-1911 [HPPN]
American chemist and home economist
* Richards, Ellen Swallow

Swallow, Norman 1921- [AW, CA, WD]
British author
* Leather, George

Swallow, Silas Comfort 1839-1930
[HPPN]
American clergyman and politician
* [The] Fighting Parson

[The] Swami
See Jackson, Laura

[The] Swami
See Salomen, Edith

Swamiji Maharaj
See Singh, Seth Shiv Dayal

Swammerdam, Martin Gribaldus
See Mudford, William

Swamp Baby Wilson
See Wilson, Charles Woodrow [Charlie]

[The] Swamp Fox
See Marion, Francis

[The] Swamp Fox
See Vinson, Carl

Swamp Fox Campbell
See Campbell, Marion

[The] Swamp Fox of Mississippi
See Forrest, Nathan Bedford

**[The] Swamp Fox of the Tennessee
Valley**
See Roddey, Philip Dale

Swan, Annie S[hepherd] 1860-1943 [LC]
Scottish author
* Lyall, David

Swan, Charles F. [PA]
Author
* Sault, R. O.

Swan, Cormac 1916- [AW]
British physician and writer
* McCormac, Brian
* Tynan, Philip

Swan, Don
See Schwandt, Wilbur

Swan, [Colonel] James ?-1831? [HPPN]
American army officer
* [A] Late Member of the General
  Court

Swan, Marie
See Bartlett, Marie [Swan]

[The] Swan of Avon
See Shakespeare, William

[The] Swan of Cambray
See Fenelon, Francois de Salignac de la
Mothe

[The] Swan of Lichfield
See Seward, Anna

[The] Swan of Mantua
See Vergilius Maro, Publius

[The] Swan of Padua
See Algarotti, Francesco

[The] Swan of Pesaro
See Rossini, Gioachino Antonio

[The] Swan of the Meander
See Homer

[The] Swan of the Thames
See Taylor, John

Swan, [Sir] Simon, Bart.
See Fawcett, Joseph

Swander, Edward O. 1880-1944 [BE]
American baseball player
* Swander, Pinky

Swander, Pinky
See Swander, Edward O.

Swann, Donald [Ibrahim] 1923- [CA]
British songwriter and entertainer
* Tablet, Hilda

Swann, Ducky
See Swann, Henry

Swann, Duncan 1878-? [WWL]
British author
* Schwann, Duncan

Swann, Henry 1892- [BE]
American baseball player
* Swann, Ducky

Swann, Peggy
See Geis, Richard E[rwin]

Swanson, Arthur Leonard 1936- [BE]
American baseball player
* Swanson, Red

Swanson, Big Navy Claude
See Swanson, Claude Augustus

Swanson, Claude Augustus 1862-1939
[HPPN]
Secretary of the Navy
* Swanson, Big Navy Claude

Swanson, Dan 20th c. [WP 4-13-85]
American author
* North, James

Swanson, Gloria
See Swenson, Josephine May

Swanson, Harold Norling 1899- [HPPN]
American editor and author
* Scott, Kerry

Swanson, Logan
See Matheson, Richard [Burton]

Swanson, Red
See Swanson, Arthur Leonard

Swansson, Lars 1605-1669
Swedish poet
* Gyllenstierna, Erik
* Wivallius, Lars

Swanston, Baron
See Deeming, Frederick Bailey

Swanstrom, Nils
See Brannon, William T.

Swanswijk, L. G. 1924- [BI]
Dutch painter
* Lucebert

Swanwick, Anna 19th c. [PA]
Author
* A. S.

Swanwick, Catherine 19th c. [PA]
Author
* L.

Swanwick, John 18th c. [HPPN]
American author
* [A] Citizen of Philadelphia

Swarbrook, Frederick William 1950-
[DC]
British cricketer
* Swarbrook, Swarby

Swarbrook, Swarby
See Swarbrook, Frederick William

Swarsbrick, Robert 1740-1824 [HN]
* [The] Hermit of Lathom

Swarthout, Gladys 1904-1969 [HPPN]
American singer
* [The] Prettiest Carmen on Record

Swartz, Bud
See Swartz, Sherwin Merle

Swartz, Dan 1934- [BB]
American basketball player
* Swartz, Dogpatch

Swartz, Dazzy
See Swartz, Monroe

Swartz, Dogpatch
See Swartz, Dan

Swartz, Harry [Felix] 1911- [CA]
American author
* Moreno, Martin
* Valcoe, H. Felix

Swartz, Monroe 1897- [BE]
American baseball player
* Swartz, Dazzy
* Swartz, Monty

Swartz, Monty
See Swartz, Monroe

Swartz, Sherwin Merle 1929- [EJS]
American baseball player
* Swartz, Bud

Swartz, William ?-1978 [FIR]
Actor
* Scarlett, Bill

Swartze, Minna
See Adams, Minna

Swasey, Charles James 1847-1908 [BE]
American baseball player
* Sweasy, Charles James

Swasey, John B. 19th c. [DNA]
American author
* Ah-Chin-Le

Swatridge, Charles [John] 20th c. [CA, WW]
British author
* Charles, Theresa [joint pseudonym with Irene Maude (Mossop) Swatridge]
* Lance, Leslie

Swatridge, Irene Maude [Mossop]
[CA, WD, WW]
British author
* Chandos, Fay
* Charles, Theresa [joint pseudonym with Charles Swatridge]
* Mossop, Irene
* Storm, Virginia
* Tempest, Jan

[The] Swattin' Scot
See Paterson, Jackie

Swayne, Geoffrey
See Campion, Sidney Ronald

Swayne, Martin
See Nicoll, [Henry] Maurice [Dunlop]

Swayzee, Edwin 1903-1935 [WWJ]
American jazz musician
* Swayzee, King

Swayzee, King
See Swayzee, Edwin

Swearing Jack Waller
See Waller, John

Swears
See Wells, Ernest

Sweasy, Charles James
See Swasey, Charles James

[The] Sweater Girl
See Turner, Julia Jean Mildred Frances

Sweater, Mr.
See Como, Pierino

[The] Sweatshirt Kid
See Fischer, Robert James [Bobby]

Sweatt, George 1905- [IBW]
American baseball player
* Sweatt, Never

Sweatt, Never
See Sweatt, George

[The] Swede
See Gustavus I

[The] Swede
See Svare, Harland

Swedenborg, Emanuel
See Svedberg, Emanuel

Sweden's Glory
See Gustavus II

[The] Swedish Amazon
See Christina

[The] Swedish Angel
See Olofsson, Nils Phillip

[The] Swedish Dickens
See Bergman, Hjalmar [Fredrik Elgerus]

[The] Swedish Douglas Fairbanks
See Jahr, Adolf

[The] Swedish Express
See Hedberg, Anders

[The] Swedish Maccabaeus
See Gustavus II

[The] Swedish Mack Sennett
See Petschler, Erik

[The] Swedish Nightingale
See Lind, Johanna Maria

[The] Swedish Schopenhauer
See Strindberg, [Johan] August

Sweelinck [or Swelinck], Jan Pieters
1562-1621 [WBD]
Dutch musician and composer
* Pieterszoon, Jan

Sweeney, Barry
See Hand, Geoffrey Joseph Philip Macaulay

Sweeney, Brains
See Sweeney, Peter Barr

Sweeney, Charles 1922- [CA]
British author
* Sweeney, R. C. H.

Sweeney, Claire Cynthia 1928- [BEW]
American literary representative
* Degener, Claire S.

Sweeney, Daniel J. ?-1929 [HPPN]
American minstrel
* Sweeney, Jimmy

Sweeney, Harry E. 1882-1960 [SC]
Australian-born actor
* Mowbray, Henry

Sweeney, Jimmy
See Sweeney, Daniel J.

Sweeney, John J. 1860-? [BE]
American baseball player
* Sweeney, Rooney

Sweeney, Peter Barr 1825-1911 [HPPN]
American politician
* [The] Great Democratic Warwick
* [The] Nephew of My Uncle
* Peter the Paragon
* [The] Sly Sweeney
* Sweeney, Brains
* Sweeney, Spider
* Sweeney, Squire

Sweeney, R. C. H.
See Sweeney, Charles

Sweeney, Rooney
See Sweeney, John J.

Sweeney, Spider
See Sweeney, Peter Barr

Sweeney, Squire
See Sweeney, Peter Barr

Sweet, Adolphus Jean 1920- [BEW]
American actor and director
* Sweet, Dolph

Sweet Baby James
See Taylor, James

Sweet Bard of Bailieborough
See Montgomery, John Wilson

Sweet Bells Thompson
See Thompson, Mychal

Sweet, Blanche
See Wayne, Daphne

Sweet Caroline Svendsen
See Svendsen, Caroline

Sweet Charlie Brown
See Brown, Charlie

Sweet Daddy Grace
See Grace, Charles Manuel

Sweet, Dolph
See Sweet, Adolphus Jean

Sweet Due
See Duerod, Terry

Sweet Emma
See Barrett, Emma

Sweet Emma the Bell Gal
See Barrett, Emma

Sweet, Emmett Martine 1915-   [BEW]
American actor, producer, director
* Rogers, Emmett

Sweet E's
See Johnson, Evelyn

Sweet Eyes
See Chamanan, Kriangsak

Sweet, Jeanne 1908-   [THR]
British actress
* Stuart. Jeanne

[The] Sweet Little Fellow
See Van Buren, Martin

Sweet Lou Johnson
See Johnson, Louis Brown

Sweet Lou Whitaker
See Whitaker, Louis Rodman

Sweet Lovin Galloway
See Galloway, Charles

[The] Sweet Lyrist of Peter House
See Gray, Thomas

Sweet Mama Stringbean
See Waters, Ethel

Sweet, Melodious Bard
See Moore, Thomas

Sweet Nell
See Symcott, Margaret

Sweet Orange Barbour
See Barbour, Deleware

Sweet Papa Stovepipe
See Peebles, McKinley

Sweet Pea Jefferson
See Jefferson, Roy

Sweet Peas[e]
See Spivey, Addie

[The] Sweet Potato Man
See Carver, George Washington

[The] Sweet Singer of Hartford
See Sigourney, Lydia Howard Huntley

Sweet Singer of Israel
See David

[The] Sweet Singer of Michigan
See Moore, Julia A.

[The] Sweet Singer of the Temple
See Herbert, George

[The] Sweet Spirited Advocate of Justice, Love and Humanity
See Mott, Lucretia Coffin

[The] Sweet Swan of Avon
See Shakespeare, William

[The] Sweet Swan of Thames
See Pope, Alexander

Sweet Tongued
See Drayton, Michael

Sweet Vinny Bourne
See Bourne, Vincent

Sweet Warbler
See Lind, Johanna Maria

Sweet William
See Draper, William Henry

Sweet William
See William

[The] Sweetest Girl in Pictures
See Dantzler, Louise

[The] Sweetest Girl in the Movies
See Dantzler, Louise

[The] Sweetest Swinger in Minnie
See Carew, Rod[ney Cline]

[The] Sweetest Trumpet in the World
See Spivak, Charlie

[The] Sweetheart of Gospel
See Grant, Amy

[The] Sweetheart of the A. E. F.
See Bierbower [or Bierbauer], Elsie

[The] Sweetheart of the Foxholes
See Kaumeyer, Dorothy

[The] Sweetheart of the Soviet Sky
See Tereshkova, Valentina

[The] Sweetheart of the Treasury
See O'Reilly, Mary M.

Sweetland, Lester Leo 1901-1974   [BE]
American baseball player
* Sweetland, Sugar

Sweetland, Sugar
See Sweetland, Lester Leo

Sweetman, Elinor Mary 19th c.   [PI]
Irish poet
* E. S.

Sweetman, Grace 1865?-1962   [BEW]
American actress
* Filkins, Grace

Sweetman, Mary E. 1858?-1930   [THR]
Irish playwright and poet
* Francis, M. E.

Sweetser, Mary [Chisholm] 1894-   [CA]
American author
* Sweetser, Ted

Sweetser, Ted
See Sweetser, Mary [Chisholm]

[The] Sweetwater Express
See Windham, Barry

[The] Sweetwater Swatter
See Jenks, Verlin

Swellmore
See Thackeray, William Makepeace

Swemmer, B. Northling 1897-   [WWL]
South African author
* Africa, Ben

Swenke, August 20th c.
American horse trainer
* Swenke, Sarge

Swenke, Sarge
See Swenke, August

Swenson, Josephine May 1899?-1983
[BEW, FC, HPPN, IPA]
American actress
* [The] Superstar of the Silents
* Swanson, Gloria

Swenson, Peggy
See Geis, Richard E[rwin]

Swentor, Augie
See Swentor, August William

Swentor, August William 1899-   [BE]
American baseball player
* Swentor, Augie

Swetenham, Violet Hilda   [WD]
British author
* Drummond, V. H.

Swett, Charles A. 1868-?   [BE]
American baseball player
* Swett, Pop

Swett, Pop
See Swett, Charles A.

Swett, Portia 1887-   [BEW]
American educator
* Mansfield, Portia

Swett, William B. 19th c.   [HPPN]
American author
* [A] Deaf Mute

Sweven, Godfrey
See Brown, John Macmillan

Sweyn I [or Sueno] ?-1014   [HN, WBD]
King of Denmark
* Forkbeard

Sweyn II ?-1075   [WBD]
King of Denmark
* Estrithson

Swicegood, Thomas L. P. 1930- [CA]
American author
* Lowe, Charles K.
* Stierwell, Jay

Swift, Alexandra 1886-1936 [BEW]
British-born actress
* Carlisle, Alexandra

Swift, Anthony
See Farjeon, J[oseph] Jefferson

Swift, Augustus T.
See Lovecraft, Howard Phillips

Swift, Babe
See Swift, Leroy Russell

Swift, Benjamin
See McKimmey, James

Swift, Benjamin
See Paterson, William Romaine

Swift Bird
See Hare, William Hobart

Swift, Bryan
See Knott, William Cecil, Jr. [Bill]

Swift, Carolyn Ruth 1928- [CA]
American author
* Lenz, Carolyn Ruth Swift

Swift, David
See Kaufmann, John

Swift, Deane 1770?-? [PI]
Irish poet
* Marcus

Swift, Delia 19th c. [LFW]
American murderer and prostitute
* Fury, Bridget

Swift, Farguar
See Phillips, Michael Joseph

Swift, Gustavus Franklin 1839-1903 [HPPN]
American wholesaler
* [The] Pioneer of the Meat Industry

Swift, Jonathan 1667-1745 [DEA, DLE1, FFF, HN, HPPN, PA, SN]
British author
* Bickerstaff, Isaac, Esq.
* Cadenus
* [The] Copper Farthing Dean
* Dean, Mr.
* [The] Dean of St. Patrick's
* [A] Dissenter
* Draper, A.
* Drapier, M. B.
* Du Baudrier, Sieur
* [The] English Rabelais
* [The] Gloomy Dean
* Gulliver, Lemuel
* J. S. D. S. P.
* [The] Mad Parson
* Misosarum, Gregory
* [A] Modus
* [A] Person of Honour
* [A] Person of Quality
* Philomath, T. N.
* Presto
* [The] Rabelais of England
* [The] Rabelais of Good Society

Swift, Jonathan (cont.)
* Scriblerus, Martinus
* T. R. D. J. S. D. O. P. I. I.
* This Impious Buffoon
* Tripe, [Sir] Andrew
* Wagstaff, Simon

Swift, Jonathan
See Arbuthnot, John

Swift, Julian
See Applin, Arthur

Swift, Leroy Russell 1912- [BA]
American physician and business executive
* Swift, Babe

Swift, Lewis J.
See Gardner, Lewis J.

Swift, Merlin
See Leeming, Joseph

Swift Nicks
See Nevison, William

Swift, Patrick
See Mackenzie, William Lyon

Swift, Tom
See Kneafcy, Thomas

Swift Tony
See Vizzini, Sal[vatore]

Swift Walker Hubbard
See Hubbard, Gurdon Saltonstall

Swigart, Oad
See Swigart, Oadis Vaughn

Swigart, Oadis Vaughn 1915- [BE]
American baseball player
* Swigart, Oad

[The] Swimming Machine
See Wenden, Michael

[The] Swimming Nun
See Taylor, Stella

Swinburne, Algernon Charles 1837-1909 [DLE1, FFF, HPPN, PA, SN]
British poet
* Dennistown
* Maitland, Thomas
* Manners, Mrs. Horace
* Swinburne, Mad

Swinburne, [Sir] James [Ninth Baronet] 1858-1958 [HPPN]
British scientist and industrialist
* [The] Father of British Plastics

Swinburne, Mad
See Swinburne, Algernon Charles

Swinburne, Nora
See Johnson, Elinore

Swindell, Minnie Harris 1889- [IA]
American author
* Norris, Harris

[The] Swindler of the Century
See Koretz, Leo

[The] Swindler of the Century
See Means, Gaston Bullock

[The] Swindling Mayor
See Balfour, Jabez Spencer

Swinerton, Thomas ?-1554 [PA]
Author
* Roberts, John

Swinfen, [Rev.] John 18th c. [HPPN]
British dissenter
* [A] Clergyman in the City

Swinford, Betty [June Wells] 1927- [CA]
American author
* Haynes, Linda
* Porter, Kathryn
* Swinford, Bob
* Wells, June

Swinford, Bob
See Swinford, Betty [June Wells]

Swinford Boy
See Durkan, Patrick Francis

Swing Brother
See Burns, Eddie

Swing, Joseph May 1894- [HPPN]
American army officer
* Swing, Uncle Joe

Swing, Mr.
See Bondu, David [Dave]

Swing, Mrs.
See Bondu, Mayme

Swing, Uncle Joe
See Swing, Joseph May

[The] Swinger from Binger
See Bench, John Lee

Swings, Paul
See Swings, Polidore F. F.

Swings, Pol
See Swings, Polidore F. F.

Swings, Polidore F. F. 1906- [HPPN]
Belgian astrophysicist and educator
* Swings, Paul
* Swings, Pol

Swinnerton, Frank Arthur 1884-1982 [CA, HPPN]
British author, editor, critic
* Pure, Simon

Swinnock, George ?-1673 [HPPN]
British clergyman
* G. S.

Swinstead, Muriel 1907- [THR]
British actress
* Ross, Oriel

Swinton, E. D.
See Swinton, [Sir] Ernest Dunlop

Swinton, [Sir] Ernest Dunlop 1868-1951 [HPPN, LC, WGT]
British author
* Backsight-Forethought
* [The] Father of the Tank
* Ole-Luk-Oie [Olaf Shut-Eye]
* Swinton, E. D.

Swirbul, Jake
See Swirbul, Leon

Swirbul, Leon 20th c.
American aircraft company president
* Swirbul, Jake

Swirl, Anna
See Swirszczynska, Anna

Swirling Sterling St. Jacques
See St. Jacques, Sterling

Swirszczynska, Anna 20th c.
Polish poet and playwright
* Swirl, Anna

Swisher, Steven Eugene 1951- [SMG]
American baseball player
* Swisher, Swish

Swisher, Swish
See Swisher, Steven Eugene

[A] Swiss Gentleman
See Akenside, Mark

[The] Swiss Walter Scott
See Zoschokke

Swisshelm, Jane Grey   [FFF]
American writer
* Deans, Jennie

Swithin ?-862 [DEP]
Saint
* [The] Weeping Saint

Switzcky, Big Izzy
See Switzcky, Isadore

Switzcky, Isadore 20th c. [HPPN]
American poultry dealer and racketeer
* Switzcky, Big Izzy

Switzer, Alfalfa
See Switzer, Carl

Switzer, Benjamin 1880-1933 [SC]
Canadian-born actor and director
* Bertram, William

Switzer, Carl 1926-1959 [SC]
American actor
* Switzer, Alfalfa

Swivel Hips
See Presley, Elvis Aron

Swivel Hips Schreiber
See Schreiber, Le Anne

Swivett, R. G. O.
See Trippett, Frank

Swix, Mr.
See Wictorin, John

Swoboda, Rocky
See Swoboda, Ron[ald Alan]

Swoboda, Ron[ald Alan] 1944- [BE, PB]
American baseball player
* Swoboda, Rocky

Swofford, William Oliver 1945- [PRS, RO2]
American singer and songwriter
* Oliver

[The] Swooner
See Sinatra, Francis Albert [Frank]

Swope, Cornelius E. 19th c. [HPPN]
American author
* C. E. S.

Swope, Herbert Bayard 1882-1958
[HPPN]
American journalist
* [The] Natural Force

[The] Sword of Allah
See Khaled [or Khalid]

[The] Sword of God
See Khaled [or Khalid]

[The] Sword of Mars
See Attila

[The] Sword of Rome
See Marcellus, Marcus Claudius

[The] Sword of the Confederacy
See Jackson, Thomas Jonathan

[The] Sword of the Revolution
See Washington, George

Swoyer, Anna Myrtle 1921?- [BEW, EMT, HPPN, IPA]
American actress
* Rosie
* Walker, Nancy

Swoyer, Dewey Stewart 20th c. [BEW]
American entertainer
* Borto, Dewey

[The] Sybil of the Faubourg Saint Germain
See Le Normand, Marie

Sycophant, Lord
See Brooke, Henry [Lord Cobham]

Sycorax
See Ritson, Joseph

Sycowski, Abraham Albert   [BI]
Polish swindler
* Fernandez, [Count] Alexander Navarro
* Lados, Carlos

Sydell, Rose
See Emmett, Mrs. Charles E.

Sydenham, Thomas 1624-1689 [HN, SN, WBD]
British physician
* [The] British Hippocrates
* [The] English Hippocrates
* [The] Father of Modern Practice in Medicine

Sydenstricker, Absalom 1852-1931
[HPPN]
American missionary
* [The] Fighting Angel

Sydney
See Seawell, Molly Elliot

Sydney, Algernon
See Leigh, Benjamin Watkins

Sydney, Basil
See Nugent, Basil

Sydney, Carol
See Fraser, Shelagh

Sydney, Charles 1872?-1922 [BEW]
British-born actor
* Ainsworth, Sydney

Sydney, Cynthia
See Tralins, S[andor] Robert [Bob]

Sydney, Frank
See Warwick, Alan Ross

Sydney, Frank
See Warwick, Francis Alister

Sydney, Frank
See Warwick, Sidney

Sydney, Jon
See Brady, John Walter

[The] Sydney Smith of the Gallic Church
See Apollinaris Sidonius, Gaius Sollius

Sydney the Standard
See Acton, Cecil Russell

Sygrianus
See De Bologne, Michele

Sykes, Arthur Alkin 1861-? [HPPN, LAO]
British author
* Z. Y. Z.
* Zigzag
* ZYX

Sykes, Bobbi 1945- [IBW]
Australian political organizer
* Australia's Angela Davis

Sykes, Christopher [Hugh] 1907- [CA]
British author
* Waughburton, Richard [joint pseudonym with Robert Byron]

Sykes, Doc
See Sykes, Melvin

Sykes, George 1822-1880 [FFF]
American army officer
* Sykesey

Sykes, [Sir] Mark Masterman 1721-1823
[SN]
* Lorenzo

Sykes, Melvin 20th c. [OBW]
American baseball player
* Sykes, Doc

Sykes, Roosevelt 1906- [BWW]
American singer
* Bey, Roosevelt Sykes
* [The] Blues Man
* Bragg, Dobby
* [The] Honeydripper
* Johnson, Easy Papa
* Kelly, Willie

Sykesey
See Sykes, George

Sykowski, Abram 1892- [HPPN]
Polish-American swindler and confidence man
* Alex, [Count] Nevarre

Sykowski, Abram (cont.)
* Amedez, Maxim
* Dannot, Alexander
* Dannut, Charles Jadeaux
* [The] Dean of the Con Men
* Enrique, Della Valle
* Frimen, Max
* [The] Frog Man
* [The] Human Frog
* Kid Tiger
* Ladenis, Carlos
* Landeau, Max
* [The] Modern Cagliostro
* Newborn, Alexander
* Novarro, Fernandez Antonio
* Novarro the Magnificent
* Novarro Fernandez, [Count]
  Alexander
* Nunn, Carlos
* Romanoff, [Prince] Alexander
* Roschildt, Alfred

Syles, Mrs.
See Sikes, William Wirt

[The] Syllable Accenting American
See Weiss, Ehrich

Sylva, Carmen
See Elizabeth

Sylva, Ilena
See Thimblethorpe, Ilena

Sylva, Marguerita
See Smith, Marguerite Alice Helene

Sylvain, James
See Sullivan, James

Sylvain, Louise 1882-1970 [HPPN]
American actress
* Sylvie

Sylvaine, Vernon
See Scotchburn, Vernon

Sylvan
See Proctor, Richard Wright

[The] Sylvan Scribe
See Forbes, Seloftus D.

Sylvan, Urbanus
See Beeching, Henry Charles

Sylvander
See Burns, Robert

Sylvane, Andre
See Gerard, Paul Emile

Sylvanus
See Carleton, William

Sylvanus
See Nichols, John

Sylvaticus
See Pennie, John Fitzgerald

Sylvester, Arthur
See Tubbs, Arthur Lewis

Sylvester, Hannah 1900?-1973 [BWW]
American singer
* Harlem's Mae West
* Scott, Genevia

Sylvester, James Joseph
See Joseph, James

Sylvester, John
See Hawton, Hector

Sylvester, Joshua 1563-1618 [DEL,
DNNF, HPPN, RH, SN]
British poet and translator
* [The] Silver Tongued
* [A] True Nathaniel

Sylvester, Joshua
See Hotten, John Camden

Sylvester, Louise
See Mackey, Mrs. F. A.

Sylvester, Philip
See Worner, Philip Arthur Incledon

Sylvester II
See Gerbert

Sylvester III
See John

Sylvestre, [Joseph Jean] Guy 1918-
[CA]
Canadian librarian and author
* Bruneau, Jean
* Orlier, Blaise

Sylvestri, Armaud [PA]
Author
* Grimaud

Sylvestris
See Bernard de Chartres

Sylvia
See Douglas, Syble G.

Sylvia
See Henderson, Sylvia

Sylvia
See Robinson, Sylvia Vanderpool

Sylvia T
See Treadgold, Sylvia

Sylvianus
See Duke, [Rev.] William

Sylvie
See Sylvain, Louise

Sylvie
See Sylvie, Therese

Sylvie, Louise
See Mainquene, Louise

Sylvie, Therese 1883-1970 [OCF]
French actress
* Sylvie

Sylvin, Francis [joint pseudonym with
Sylvia S(ybil) Seaman]
See Schwartz, Frances

Sylvin, Francis [joint pseudonym with
Frances Schwartz]
See Seaman, Sylvia S[ybil]

Sylviolus
See Forestier, Antoine,

Sylvius
See Williamson, Hugh

Sylvius, C.
See Coscia, Silvio

Sylvius, Franciscus
See De la Boe, Franz

Sylvius, Jacobus
See Dubois, Jacques

Sym, Robert 1750-1844 [SN]
Scottish barrister
* Tickler, Timothy

[The] Symbolist Hero
See Fournier, Henri Alban

Symcott, Margaret 1642?-1691? [HN,
HPPN, NN, RH, WBD]
*British actress and mistress of King
Charles II*
* Gwyn [or Gwynne], Eleanor
* Gwyn [or Gwynne], Nell
* Nell of Old Drury
* [The] Poor Man's Friend
* Pretty Witty Nellie
* Sweet Nell

Syme, Robert 1795-? [FFF]
Scottish author
* Tickler, Timothy

Symington, Charlotte [PA]
Author
* Symington, Maggie

Symington, David 1904- [AW, CAP]
British author
* Halliday, James

Symington, Maggie
See Symington, Charlotte

Symington, Stuart 1901- [CR]
American politician
* [The] Big Bomber Boy

Symmes, John Cleves 1780-1829 [ESF,
SFL, WGT]
American author
* Seaborn, [Captain] Adam

Symmonds, John
See Gonzales, Bli

Symnes, Francis Edward 1851-1927
[HPPN]
Canadian clergyman
* Clark, Francis Edward

Symon, James David 1867-? [WWL]
British author
* North, Laurence

Symonds, Emily Morse ?-1936 [BEW,
LC]
British author and playwright
* Paston, George

Symonds, Francis Addington 1893-
[MBF, WWL]
British author and editor
* Danesford, Earle
* [A] Royal Field Leech
* Steele, Howard [house pseudonym]

Symonds, Margaret 1902- [THR]
British actress
* Davey, Nuna

Symons, A. J. A.
See Symons, Alphonse James Albert

Symons, Albert James Alroy
See Symons, Alphonse James Albert

Symons, Alphonse James Albert
1900-1941 [LC]
British author
* Symons, A. J. A.
* Symons, Albert James Alroy

Symons, [Dorothy] Geraldine 1909-
[CA, LC]
British author
* Groves, Georgina

Symons, J. B. 20th c. [WWL]
Scottish editor and poet
* Restalrig

Symons, Thomas William 1849-1920
[WBD]
American engineer
* [The] Father of the Barge Canal

[The] Symphony on Silver Skates
See Henie, Sonja

Symphony Sid
See Torin, Sidney

Sympson, Thomas ?-1691 [DI]
British highwayman
* Old Mob

Symus, the Pilgrim
See Cobb, Sylvanus, Jr.

Syncellus
See George

Syndas, Kate
See Sandys, K.

Synge, Don
See Edelstein, Hyman

Synge, J. M.
See Synge, John Millington

Synge, John Millington 1871-1909 [LC]
Irish author
* Synge, J. M.

Synnott, Ed. Fitzgerald 1873-? [WWL]
British author
* O'Toole, [Father]

Synodinos, Dimitrios 1919- [BI]
American columnist and former gambler
* Jimmy the Greek
* Snyder, James

Synopticus
See Renner, Karl

Syntax
See Ash, Edward Cecil

Syntax, Dr.
See Combe [or Coombe], William

Syntax, Doctor
See Gordon, Archibald F.

Syntax, Dr.
See Vizetelly, Francis Horace [Frank]

Syntax, John
See Dennett, Herbert Victor

Syphax
See Prince, John Tucker

Syphax, Burke 1910- [BA]
American physician
* Syphax, Mickey

Syphax, Mickey
See Syphax, Burke

Syr
See Allen, Samuel Adams

Syracuse, Marcella Pfeiffer 1930- [CA]
American author
* Pfeiffer, Marcella

[The] Syren of Antiquity
See Xenophon

[The] Syren of this Latter Age
See Sidney, [Sir] Philip

Syrokomla, Wladyslaw
See Kondratowicz, Ludwik Wladyslaw

Syruc, J.
See Milosz, Czeslaw

Syrus, Ephraem 308?-373? [HPPN]
Syrian theologian and poet
* [The] Prophet of the Syrians

Szabo, Alexander 1910- [BE]
American baseball player
* Sabo, Alex[ander]
* Sabo, Giz

Szabo, Istvan 1863-1924 [WBD]
Hungarian politician
* Szabo-Nagyatad

Szabo-Nagyatad
See Szabo, Istvan

Szacsvay-Feher, Tibor 1907- [IAW]
Hungarian author
* Feher, Tibor

Szadall, Szdke
See Szakall, Eugene Gero

Szajkowski, Zosa
See Frydman, Szajko

Szakall, Eugene Gero 1884-1955 [BEW,
FC, SC]
Hungarian-born actor
* Sakall, Cuddles
* Sakall, S. Z.
* Szadall, Szdke

Szalatna, Hubay von
See Huber, Eugen

Szaniawski, Jerzy 1886-1966 [MWD]
Polish playwright and author
* [The] Dean of Polish Dramatists

Szarvas, Peter 1933- [IWM]
Hungarian-born musician
* Sander, Peter

Szathmary, William 1924- [JF]
American comedian
* Dana, Bill
* Jimenez, Jose

Szatmary
See Szigligetti, Joseph

Sze Sao-ke, Alfred
See Shih Chao-chi

Szekely, Istvan 1889?-1979 [FC, FD]
Hungarian-born director
* Sekely, Steve

Szelenyi, Laszlo 1935- [IWM]
Hungarian-born musician
* Farago

Szemanski, Jacob 1878-1963 [EMT]
Lithuanian-born producer
* Shubert, J. J.

Szemanski, Levi 1873-1953 [EMT]
Lithuanian-born producer
* Shubert, Lee

Szemanski, Samuel 1876-1905 [EMT]
Lithuanian-born producer
* Shubert, Sam S.

Szendrei, Aladar 1884- [BBD]
Hungarian-born conductor and composer
* Sendrey, Alfred

Szenes, Andre 1895-1957 [BI]
*Hungarian-American author and
illustrator*
* Dugo, Andre

Szentes, Dorka
See Szentes, Dorotta

Szentes, Dorotta 17th c. [DI]
Hungarian murderer
* Szentes, Dorka

Szepes, Ivan 1930- [OP]
Italian opera singer
* Sardi, Ivan

Szigeti, Joseph 1892-1972 [MS]
Hungarian musician
* Szigeti, Joska

Szigeti, Joska
See Szigeti, Joseph

Szigligetti, Ede
See Szigligetti, Joseph

Szigligetti, Joseph 1814-1878 [HPPN,
PA]
Hungarian author
* Szatmary
* Szigligetti, Ede

Szmaciarz-Smreczynski, Franciszek
1876-1930 [CD]
Polish poet and author
* Orkan, Wladyslaw

Szydlow, Jarl
See Szydlowski, Mary Vigliante

Szydlowski, Mary Vigliante 1946- [CA]
American author
* Szydlow, Jarl
* Vigliante, Mary

Szymanski, Aloysius Harry 1902?-1956
[AS, BE, DGS, HPPN]
American baseball player
* [The] Duke of Milwaukee
* Simmons, Al
* Simmons, Aloysius Harry
* Simmons, Bucketfoot Al

Szymanski, Ignatius S.   [PA]
Author
* Harring, Harro

Szymonowicz, Szymon 1558-1629
[WBD]
Polish poet
* [The] Polish Pindar

Szymonowska, Marie 1790-?   [PA]
Author
* Woloweki

T

Asterisk (*) indicates assumed name.

T.
See Talbot, Catherine

T
See Tatlow, Tissington

T.
See Thorp, Joseph Peter

T.
See Tighe, Edward

T.
See Tormey, Michael

T.
See Tupper, Martin Farquhar

T.
See Tyler, Terry

T. A.
See Ashe, Thomas

T. B.
See Bates, Thomas

T. B.
See Belsham, Thomas

T. B.
See Benson, Arthur Christopher

T. B.
See Bowdler, Thomas

T. B.
See Bradbury, Thomas

T. B.
See Brightwell, Thomas

T. B.
See Buckridge, [Rev.] Theophilus

T. B.
See Bulfinch, Thomas

T. B.
See Burtt, Thomas

T. B.
See Foe, Daniel

T. B. A.
See Aldrich, Thomas Bailey

T. B. B.
See Baker, Thomas Bagnall

T. B. D.
See James, William Milbourne

T. B. F.
See Fox, [Rev.] Thomas Bayley

T. B., Gent.
See Barker, Thomas

T. B. O.
See Oxenbury, Thomas Bernard

T. B. R.
See Robertson, Thomas Beattie

T. C.
See Church, Thomas

T. C.
See Corbett, Thomas

T. C.
See Curteis, [Rev.] Thomas

T. C.
See Maginn, William

T. C. B.
See Bridges, Thomas Charles

T. C. C.
See Croker, Thomas Crofton

T. C. D.
See Dunphie, Charles James

T. C. G.
See Cary, Thomas Greaves

T. C. H.
See Hansard, Thomas Curson

T. C. I.
See Irwin, Thomas Caulfield

T. D.
See Dale, Thomas

T. D.
See Davis, Thomas Osborne

T. D.
See Dawson, Thomas

T. D.
See Dorsey, Thomas A[ndrew]
[Tommy]

T. D. M.
See McGee, Thomas D'Arcy

T. D. S.
See Sullivan, Timothy Daniel

T. D. W.
See Weld, Theodore Dwight

T. E.
See Edwards, Thomas

T. E.
See Ellwood, Thomas

T. E.
See Emes, Thomas

T. E.
See Foe, Daniel

T. F.
See Ashby, George

T. F.
See Falconer, [Rev.] Thomas

T. F.
See Faulkner, Robert Trevor

T. F.
See Fuller, Thomas

T. F. D.
See Dibdin, Thomas Frognall

T. F., One of the Bereaved Ones
See Foxcroft, Thomas

T. F. S.
See Salter, T. F.

T. G.
See Gib. T.

T. G.
See Gwin, Thomas

T. G. A.
See Appleton, Thomas Gold

T. G. C.
See Carroll, T. G.

T. H.
See Halpin, William

T. H.
See Hamilton, [Capt.] Thomas

T. H.
See Hardres, T.

T. H.
See Hewerdine, Thomas

T. H.
See Heywood, Thomas

T. H.
See Hill, Thomas

T. H.
See Hobbes, Thomas

T. H. C.
See Carter, Timothy H.

T. H. C.
See Corry, Thomas H.

T. H. E. A.
See Hallam, Arthur Henry

T. H. H.
See Harvey, Thomas Hingston

T. H. H.
See Howard, T. H.

T. H. L.
See Lowth, Thomas Henry

T. H., Pharmacop, Rustican
See Hickes, T.

T. H. W.
See White, Thomas

T. H. W.
See Wynne, Thomas H.

T. I.
See Irwin, Thomas Caulfield

T in Punch
See Thorp, Joseph Peter

T. J.
See James, Thornell Herbert

T. J.
See John, Thomas Edward

T. J. A.
See Arnold, Thomas James

T. J. M.
See Furlong, Patrick M.

T. K.
See Ken, Thomas

T. K.
See Kirkup, Thomas

T. K.
See Knight, T.

T. K.
See Kyd, Thomas

T. K. A.
See Arnold, Thomas Kerchever

T. L.
See Foe, Daniel

T. L.
See Laws, Tony

T. L. C.
See Cuyler, [Rev.] Theodore Ledyard

T. M.
See Martin, [Sir] Theodore

T. M.
See Maule, Thomas

T. M.
See May, Thomas

T. M.
See Meehan, Thomas

T. M.
See Middleton, Thomas

T. M.
See Mitchell, Thomas

T. M.
See Moore, Thomas

T. M.
See Morell, Thomas

T. M.
See Mosse, T.

T. M.
See Mounsey, Thomas

T. M.
See Mowbray, Thomas

T. M. B.
See Baker, T. M.

T. M. G.
See Gorman, Thomas Murray

T. N. T.
See Higgs, Dwight

T. N. T.
See Thomas, Cornelius Dickinson

T. O. F.
See Schuette, Conrad Herman Louis

T. P.
See Parker, Theodore

T. P.
See Phillips, [Sir] Thomas

T. P. S. C. T.
See Phillips, Thomas

T. Q.
See Quiller-Couch, Thomas

T. R.
See Reilly, Thomas Devin

T. R.
See Roosevelt, Theodore [Teddy]

T. R.
See Ryan, Thomas

T. R. B.
See Kinsley, Michael

T. R. B.
See Strout, Richard L[ee]

T. R. D. J. S. D. O. P. I. I.
See Swift, Jonathan

T. R. H.
See Higham, T. R.

T. S.
See Carlen, Rose Catharina

T. S.
See Krackowizer, E. W.

T. S.
See Shadwell, Thomas

T. S.
See Spring, Thomas

T. S.
See Story, Thomas

T. S.
See Stratton, Thomas

T. S.
See Streatfield, [Rev.] Thomas

T. S.
See Travers-Smith, Dorothea

T. S. G.
See Gueulette, Thomas Simon

T. S. H.
See Henderson, Thulia Susannah

T. S. K.
See King, Thomas Starr

T. S. M.
See Matthews, Thomas Soady

T. S. M.
See Muir, Thomas S.

T. T.
See Thackeray, William Makepeace

T. T.
See Tilton, Theodore

T. T.
See Tumulti, Thomas

T. V. F.
See Fosberry, Thomas Vincent

T. V.'s Annie Oakley
See Grayson, Betty Jeanne

T. W.
See Savile, [Sir] George [Marquis of Halifax]

T. W.
See Warland, Theodore

T. W.
See Watkins, Tobias

T. W.
See Webster, Thomas

T. W.
See Weed, Thurlow

T. W.
See Wilson, Thomas

T. W. B.
See Beaumont, Thomas Wentworth

T. W., Gent.
See Weaver, Thomas

T. W. H.
See Higginson, Thomas Wentworth Storrow

T. W. P.
See Poole, Thomas Wesley

T. W. R.
See Riddle, Thomas Wilkinson

T. Z.
See Adams, Samuel

Taabes, Kamil Amin
See Cohen, Elie

Taafe, Alice Frances 1896?- [F1, F2, FC]
American actress
* Terry, Alice

Taaffe, Michael
See Maguire, Robert Augustine Joseph

Taasinge, Hazel Neilson 1888-1970 [SC]
American actress
* Monterey, Carlotta

Tabaksblat, Alexander 1921- [OP]
Israeli conductor and composer
* Tarski, Alexander

Tabard, Geoffrey
See McNelly, Willis E[verett]

Tabard, Peter
See Blake, Leslie James

Tabarin
See Duval, Georges

Tabarin
See Girard, Antoine

[The] Tabasco Kid
See Elberfeld, Norman Arthur

Taber, Anthony Scott 1944- [CA]
American artist, cartoonist, author
* Anthony

Taber, Edward Timothy 1900- [BE]
American baseball player
* Taber, Lefty

Taber, Lefty
See Taber, Edward Timothy

Tabib, al- [The Physician]
See Rashid al-Din

Tabiensis
See Caynazzo, Jean

Tabin, Rube
See Richstein, Larry

Tablet, Hilda
See Swann, Donald [Ibrahim]

Tabor, E. 19th c. [NPS]
Author
* Cousin Alice

Tabor, Elizabeth McCourt Doe 1861-1935 [HPPN]
Wife of American industrialist, Horace Tabor
* Baby Doe

Tabor, Haw
See Tabor, Horace Austin Warner

Tabor, Horace Austin Warner 1830-1899 [HPPN]
American miner and industrialist
* Colorado's Bonanza King
* [The] Leadville Storekeeper Millionaire
* Tabor, Haw
* Tabor, Silver Dollar

Tabor, James Reubin 1916-1953 [BE, PB]
American baseball player
* Tabor, Rawhide
* Tabor, Rube

Tabor, Paul
See Tabori, Paul

Tabor, Rawhide
See Tabor, James Reubin

Tabor, Rube
See Tabor, James Reubin

Tabor, Silver Dollar
See Tabor, Horace Austin Warner

Tabori, Paul 1908-1974 [AW, CA, WD]
Hungarian-born British author, journalist, scriptwriter
* Hefner, Paul
* Stafford, Peter
* Stevens, Christopher
* Tabor, Paul

Tabourot, Jehan 1519?-1595? [BBD]
French author
* Arbeau, Thoinot

Tach
See Teach, Edward

[The] Taciturn
See Maximilian I

[The] Taciturn
See Moltke, Hellmuth Karl Bernhard von

Tacitus
See Darby, William

Tacitus
See Douglas, John

Tacitus
See Haines, Charles Glidden

Tacitus, Cornelius 54-117 [SN]
Roman orator, politician, historian
* [The] Still

[The] Tacitus of Sicily
See Falcandus, Hugo

Tack Towne Newchurch
See Newchurch, Harold Everett

Tackwell, Charles 20th c. [EF]
American football player
* Tackwell, Cookie

Tackwell, Cookie
See Tackwell, Charles

Tacky Tom Parrott
See Parrott, Thomas William [Tom]

[The] Tactful Teacher
See Mollet, Guy

[The] Tactician
See Aeneas

Tacuinus, Joannes
See Tridino, Johannes de Cereto de

Tad
See Dorgan, Thomas Aloysius

[Der] Tadler [The Fault-Finder]
See Gottsched, Johann Christoph

Tadrack, Moss
See Caryl, Warren

Tae-tsong I
See Lee chee-men

Taffrail
See Dorling, Henry Taprell

Taffy
See Llewellyn, D[avid] W[illiam] Alun

Taft, Big Bill
See Taft, William Howard

Taft, Helen Herron 1861-1943 [WP 1-20-85]
Wife of American president, William Howard Taft
* Taft, Nellie

Taft, Jim 1907?- [MY]
American jazz musician
* Taft, Slim

Taft, Nellie
See Taft, Helen Herron

Taft, Robert Alphonso [Bob] 1889-1953 [HPPN]
American politician
* Republican, Mr.

Taft, Slim
See Taft, Jim

Taft, William Howard 1857-1930 [HPPN]
American president and Supreme Court justice
* [The] Big Chief
* Taft, Big Bill

Tafuri, Malteo 1492-1585 [PA]
Author
* Soletanus, Matthoeus

Tag, Rag, and Bobtail, Messrs.
See Disraeli, Isaac

Taggard, E. T. 1839-? [PA]
Author
* Pryor, Paul

Taggart, Robert John 1890- [BE]
American baseball player
* Kelly, James Robert [Jim]

Taggart, William Stuart 1859-1925 [CCL]
Canadian author
* Bilton, Lance

Tagge, Jerry L. 1950- [FB]
American football player
* Tagge, Tags

Tagge, Tags
See Tagge, Jerry L.

Tagger, Theodor 1891-1958 [MGL]
Austrian playwright
* Bruckner, Ferdinand

Tagliapetra, Madame [HN]
* Carreno, Teresa

Tagliavini, Ferruccio 1914- [HPPN]
Italian opera singer
* [The] Graceful Tenor

Tagliere, Signor
See Tyler, George

Taglioni, Maria 1804-? [PA]
Author
* De Voisons, [Countess] Gilbert

Tagore, Amitendranath 1922- [CA]
Indian-born educator and author
* Musafir

Tagore, Rabindranath
See Thakura, Ravindranatha

Tah Gah Jute 1725?-1780 [WBD]
American Indian chieftain
* Logan, James [or John]

Tahan
See Griffin, Joseph K.

Tahchenum, Neehahpouw 1891-1966
[SC]
American actor
* Strongheart, [Chief] Nipo

Tahlaquah, David
See LeMond, Alan

Tahmasp Kuli Khan [Slave of Tahmasp]
See Nadir Shah

Taieb, Heliane 1929- [ESF]
French writer
* Verlanger, Julia

Taiho [Great Bird]
See Naya, Koki

Tail Gunner Joe
See McCarthy, Joseph Raymond

Taillandier, Rene Gaspard Ernest
1817-1879 [WBD]
French journalist and scholar
* Taillandier, Saint Rene

Taillandier, Saint Rene
See Taillandier, Rene Gaspard Ernest

Taillasson, Gaillard 1580-1647 [PA]
Author
* Mathalin

Taillevent, Michault
See Le Caron, Michault

[The] Tailor
See Campione, Marcello

Taine, Henri
See Taine, Hippolyte Adolphe

Taine, Hippolyte Adolphe 1828-1893
[HPPN]
French philosopher and critic
* Barnabe X
* Taine, Henri

Taine, John
See Bell, Eric Temple

Tainter, Charles Sumner 1854-1940
[HPPN]
American inventor
* [The] Father of the Dictating Machine

Taira, Koji
See Kiyomura, Koji

Taiso [Great Revival]
See Tsukioka, Yoshitoshi

Tait, Archibald Campbell 1811-? [IP,
PA]
Scottish clergyman and author
* [The] Bishop of London

Tait, Dorothy 1902?-1972 [CA]
American author and journalist
* Fairbairn, Ann
* Stuart, Jay Allison

Tait, Euphemia Margaret 20th c. [WW]
Author
* Ironside, John

Tait, George B. 20th c. [SFL, WGT]
Author
* Barclay, Alan

Tait, Herbert 1865-1934 [BEW]
Indian-born actor
* Ross, Herbert

Taitt, Doug[las John] 1902-1970 [BE]
American baseball player
* Taitt, Poco

Taitt, Poco
See Taitt, Doug[las John]

Taj Mahal
See Henry, Fredericks

Tajiri, Larry S.
See Tajiri, Taneyoshi

Tajiri, Taneyoshi 1914- [BEW]
American drama editor and critic
* Tajiri, Larry S.

Tak Yussuf Hoff [Take Yourself Off]
See Sassoon, Siegfried [Lorraine]

Takada, Kenzo 1940- [WFA]
Japanese-born fashion designer
* [The] Idea Man of French Ready-to-
Wear

Takagi, Masao
See Park, Chung Hee

Takahashi, Korekiyo
See Kawamura, Korekiyo

Takakjian, Portia 1930- [SAT]
American illustrator
* Johnston, Portia
* Roach, Portia
* Wiesner, Portia

Takamine, Jokichi 1854-1922 [HPPN]
Japanese-American chemical engineer
* [The] Father of Adrenalin

Takamiyama [Mountain of the Lofty
View]
See Kuhualua, Jesse

Take It Easy, Mr.
See Crosby, Harry Lillis

Takeda, James Tetsuzo 1900?- [BI]
Japanese clergyman and poet
* Tetsu

Taki
See Theodoracopulos, Peter

Takis
See Vassilakis, Panayotis

Tal, Joseph
See Gruenthal, Joseph

Tal-Coat, Pierre
See Jacob, Pierre

Talagrand, Jacques Louis
See Maulnier, Thierry

Talal bin Abdul Azziz al-Saud 1930?-
Saudi prince
* [The] Humanitarian Prince

Talamo, W. 20th c. [BLB]
American underworld figure
* Scaccio, John

Talazac
See Gambetta, Leon

Talbert, Coo Coo
See Talbert, Elmer

Talbert, Diron 20th c.
American football player
* Crunch, Captain

Talbert, Elmer 1900-1950 [NOJ]
American jazz musician
* Talbert, Coo Coo

Talbot, Bubby
See Talbot, Fred Lealand

Talbot, Carl
See Hipkins, Charles Hammond

Talbot, Carol Terry 1913- [CA]
American author
* Terry, Carol

Talbot, Catherine 18th c. [IP]
British author
* Sunday
* T.

Talbot, Charlene Joy 1928- [CA]
American author
* Lee, Lucy

Talbot, Charles 1660-1718 [NPS, SN]
Duke of Shrewsbury
* [The] Favorite of the Nation
* [The] King of Hearts

Talbot, Charles Remington 1849-1892
[DNA, HPPN, PA]
American author
* Brownjohn, John

Talbot, Charles Remington (cont.)
* John, John Brown
* Merriweather, Magnus

Talbot, Edmund Bernard
See Fitzalan-Howard, Edmund Bernard

Talbot, Elizabeth 1518-1608 [HN, SN, WBD]
Countess of Shrewsbury
* Bess of Hardwick
* [The] Lost Mistress

Talbot, Fred Lealand 1941- [BE]
American baseball player
* Talbot, Bubby

Talbot, George Foster 1819-? [IP]
American attorney and author
* [A] Layman

Talbot, Hake
See Nelms, Henning

Talbot, Hannah 19th c. [HPPN]
American author
* Danforth, Parke

Talbot, Henry
See Rothwell, Henry Talbot

Talbot, Howard
See Munkittrick, Howard

Talbot, Hugh
See Alington, Argentine Francis

Talbot, Jim
See Sherman, James D.

Talbot, John 1373-1453 [DEP, DNNS, RH]
First Earl of Shrewsbury
* [The] Achilles of England
* [The] English Achilles
* [The] Terror of France

Talbot, John William 1869-? [NAA]
American author and poet
* Anonymous

Talbot, Joseph Bovelle 1896-1973 [SC]
American actor and stunt performer
* Talbot, Slim

Talbot, Kay
See Rowland, Donald Sydney

Talbot, Lawrence
See Bryant, Edward [Winslow, Jr.]

Talbot, Lying Dick
See Talbot, Richard

Talbot, Lyle
See Henderson, Lisle

Talbot, Mary Anne 1778-1808 [HPPN]
British soldier
* [The] British Amazon

Talbot, Mary Lee Keister 20th c. [NAA]
American writer
* Dyer, Sabine

Talbot, Nancy Wilfreda Hewitt 1925- [ART]
British painter and stage designer
* Skillington, Nancy

Talbot, Richard 1630-1691 [DNNF, DNNS, HN]
Duke of Tyrconnel and Lord-Lieutenant of Ireland
* Talbot, Lying Dick

Talbot, Slim
See Talbot, Joseph Bovelle

Talbot, William 1659-1730 [HPPN]
British clergyman
* Polite and Learned Physician of Oxford

Talbot, William Henry Fox 1800-1877 [HPPN]
British photographer, philologist, archaeologist
* [The] Father of Photography

Talbot Kelly, C. E.
See Talbot Kelly, Chloe Elizabeth

Talbot Kelly, Chloe Elizabeth 1927- [ART]
British illustrator
* Talbot Kelly, C. E.

Talcott, John 1630-1688 [FFF]
Commanded troops in 1676 Indian War
* [The] Indian Fighter

Talcott, LeRoy Everett 1921- [BE]
American baseball player
* Talcott, Roy

Talcott, Mrs. Hersey Bradford [Goodwin] 19th c. [IP]
American author
* H. B. G.

Talcott, Roy
See Talcott, LeRoy Everett

Talender
See Bohse, August

Talent, Leo 1906- [ASC]
American musician
* Winters, Jack

[The] Talent of the Academy
See Aristotle

Talese, Gaetano 1932- [CA]
American author
* Talese, Gay

Talese, Gay
See Talese, Gaetano

Talfourd, Sarjeant
See Talfourd, [Sir] Thomas Noon

Talfourd, [Sir] Thomas Noon 1795-1854 [HPPN]
British playwright
* Talfourd, Sarjeant

Taliaferri, Buzz
See Taliaferro, Addison

Taliaferro, Addison 1936- [BA]
American hematologist
* Taliaferri, Buzz

Taliaferro, George 1927- [FB]
American football player
* Taliaferro, Scoop

Taliaferro, Hal 20th c.
American actor
* Wales, Wally

Taliaferro, Harden E. 1818?-1875 [DNA, IP]
American author
* Skitt

Taliaferro, Mike
See Taliaferro, Myron E.

Taliaferro, Myron E. 1941- [FB]
American football player
* Taliaferro, Mike

Taliaferro, Scoop
See Taliaferro, George

Talionis
See Foe, Daniel

Talis Qualis
See Strandberg, Carl Vilhelm August

[The] Talkative
See William II [Friedrich Wilhelm Viktor Albert]

Talkative Tom Blanton
See Blanton, Thomas Lindsay

Talker, T.
See Rands, William Brighty

[The] Talkies Only Rival
See Bodie, Sam

Talkin, Gil
See Rosenthal, Alan

[The] Talking Blues Boy
See Lunn, Robert

[The] Talking Blues Man
See Lunn, Robert

[The] Talking Man
See McGrady, James

[The] Tall
See Albert [or Albrecht]

[The] Tall
See Philip V [or Philippe]

[The] Tall Gal With the Deadpan
See O'Brien, Virginia

Tall Guy Bonventre
See Bonventre, Cesare

Tall Paul Hankins
See Hankins, Paul

Tall Pine
See Sibley, Henry Hastings

Tall, Stephen
See Crook, Compton N.

[The] Tall Sycamore of the Wabash
See Voorhees, Daniel Wolsey

[The] Tall Tactician
See McGillicuddy, Cornelius Alexander

[The] Tall Texan
See Gray, Claude

[The] Tall Texan
See Kilpatrick, Ben

Tall, Tom
See Guthrie, Tommie Lee

Tall Trader
See Sibley, Henry Hastings

Tallafierro, Gabriel
See Fox, Hugh [Bernard, Jr.]

Tallemant des Reaux, Gedeon 1619-1692
[SN]
French author
* [The] Calomniographe of His Age

Tallent, Virginia 1911-1968 [SC]
American actress
* Nelson, Virginia

Tallentyre, S. G.
See Hall, Evelyn Beatrice

[The] Tallest Man in the World
See Moilenen, Louis

Talleyrand-Perigord, Charles Maurice de
1754-1838 [DNNS, RH]
French statesman
* Bishop of Autun
* [The] Prince of Diplomatists

Tallien, Jeanne Marie Ignace Theresa
1774?-1831? [HN]
French lady of fashion and politician
* Our Lady of Mercy

Tallis [or Tallys], Thomas 1510?-1585
[DEP, DNNS, NN]
British composer and musician
* [The] Father of English Cathedral
  Music
* [The] Father of English Music

Tallu
See Bankhead, Tallulah

Tallulah's Papa
See Bankhead, William Brockman

Talma, Francois Joseph 1763-1826
[DNNS, HN]
French actor
* [The] French Roscius

Talma, Madame
See Vanhove, Charlotte

Talma, Mercedes
See Ford, Mary

[The] Talma of the Boulevards
See Lemaitre, Antoine Louis Prosper

Talmadge, Constance [Connie] 1900-1973
[HPPN]
American actress
* [The] Bette Davis of the Silent Era

Talmadge, Eugene 1884-1946
American politician
* [The] Boss
* Red Gallus Gene
* [The] Wild Man
* Wild Man From Sugar Creek

Talmadge, Herman Eugene 1913-
[HPPN]
American politician
* Gene's Boy
* Herman the Unhappy
* Red Suspenders
* Talmadge, Humman

Talmadge, Humman
See Talmadge, Herman Eugene

Talmadge, Mattie 1881?-1981
*Mother of American politician, Herman
Talmadge*
* Miss Mit

Talmadge, Richard
See Metzetti, Sylvester Ricardo

Talmage, Anne
See Powell, Talmage

Talmon, Thrace
See Hale, Edith

Talton, Marion Lee 1939-   [BE]
American baseball player
* Talton, Tim

Talton, Tim
See Talton, Marion Lee

Talun, Iron
See Talun, Wladyslaw

Talun, Wladyslaw 1918-
Polish wrestler
* Talun, Iron

Talvi [or Talvj]
See Robinson, Therese Albertine Louise
von Jakob

Tam
See Campbell, Thomas

Tam
See MacKellar, Thomas

Tam of the Cowgate
See Hamilton, [Sir] Thomas

Tama Jim Wilson
See Wilson, James

Tamai, Katsunori 1903-1960 [WBD]
Japanese soldier and author
* Hino, Ashihei

Tamara
See Drasin, Tamara Swann

[La] Tamara
See Karsavin, Tamara

Tamarin, Shirley Astor Glubok 1933-
[TBJ]
Author
* Glubok, Shirley

Tamate
See Chalmers, James

Tamayo y Baus, Manuel 1829-1898
[NLC]
Spanish playwright
* Estebanez, Joaquin

Tambs, Lewis Arthur
See Jones, Lewis Arthur

Tamer, James 1913-
American underworld figure
* Tamer, Occo

Tamer, Occo
See Tamer, James

[The] Tamer of Lightning
See Franklin, Ben[jamin]

Tamerlan a Lunettes
See Thiers, Louis Adolphe

Tamerlane [or Tamburlaine]
See Timur [or Timour]

Tames, Richard Lawrence 1946- [WD]
British economist, historian, author
* Lawrence, James

Tamey, Milton 1847-1924 [BEW]
American actor
* Nobles, Milton

[The] Tamil Mahatma
See Rajagopalacharia, Chakravarti

Tamiris, Helen
See Becker, Helen

Tamminen, Juhani 1950- [SMG]
Finnish-born hockey player
* Tamminen, Tommy

Tamminen, Tommy
See Tamminen, Juhani

Tammsaare, A. H.
See Hansen, Anton

Tammsaare, Anton
See Hansen, Anton

Tammuz, Benjamin
See Kammerstein, Benjamin

Tamo
See Bodhidharma

Tamor, Caspipini
See Duchi, Jacob

Tampa Red
See Woodbridge, Hudson

Tamulis, Vitautis Casimirus 1911-1974
[BE]
American baseball player
* Tamulis, Vito

Tamulis, Vito
See Tamulis, Vitautis Casimirus

Tan
See Bogoraz, Vladimir Germanovich

Tan Ku
See Bailey, George W.

[The] Tan Tarzan of Thump
See Barrow, Joseph Louis

Tan Yun
See Lin, Adet J[usu]

Tanaka, Aiko 1924- [HPPN]
*Japanese prostitute and brothel
proprietress*
* Crazy Mary

Tanaka, Kakuei 1918- [HPPN, TI 8-1-83, TI 10-24-83, TI 11-14-83]
Japanese prime minister
* [The] Chauvinist Prime Minister
* [The] Computerized Bulldozer
* Kaku San
* [The] Man Who Broke the Mold
* [The] Oriental Populist
* [The] Shadow Shogun
* Shogun of the Darkness

Tanaquil, Paul
See Le Clercq, Jacques George Clemenceau

Tanaquill
See Elizabeth I

Tandem, Felix
See Spitteler, Carl

Tandler, [Dr.] Leo
See Trebitsch, Isaac

Tandon, Horace B. A. Moquin [PA]
Author
* Fredol

Taney, Roger Brooke 1777-1864 [HPPN]
American Chief Justice of the Supreme Court
* Coody, King

T'ang Hsuan-tsung
See Ming Huang

Tangent, Patrick Quinn
See Phelps, George H[amilton]

Tangermann, Friedrich Wilhelm 1815-? [IP]
German author
* Granella, Victor

Tangle Eye
See Horton, Walter

Tanguay, Eva 1878-1947 [SC]
Canadian-born actress
* [The] I Don't Care Girl

Tania
See Bunke, Haydee Tamara

Tania
See Hearst, Patricia Campbell [Patty]

Tania B.
See Blixen, Karen [Christentze Dinesen]

Tanis
See Davies, Hilda A.

Taniya, Kyn
See Quintanilla, Luis

[The] Tank
See Paul, Melvin

Tankersley, Lawrence William 1901- [BE]
American baseball player
* Tankersley, Leo

Tankersley, Leo
See Tankersley, Lawrence William

Tankersley, Ruth McCormick 1921- [HPPN]
American editor, journalist, horsewoman
* Bazy

Tann, Jennifer 1939- [CA]
British author and screenwriter
* Booth, Geoffrey

Tannen, Julius 1881-1965 [JF]
Comedian
* [The] Human Chatterbox

Tannenbaum, Albert 20th c. [BLB]
American underworld figure
* Tannenbaum, Allie

Tannenbaum, Allie
See Tannenbaum, Albert

Tannenbaum, Max-Gerard Houry 1919- [FC, FDG]
French actor and director
* Oury, Gerard

[The] Tanner
See Wayne, Anthony

Tanner, Cora
See Sinn, Mrs. William E.

Tanner, Edward Everett, III 1921-1976 [BI, CA]
American author
* Dennis, Patrick
* Rowans, Virginia

Tanner, Elaine 1951- [BBH, CSH, SWI]
Canadian swimmer
* Mighty Mouse

Tanner, F. 18th c. [HPPN]
British author
* F. T.

Tanner, Gid
See Tanner, James Gideon

Tanner, Henry 19th c. [IP]
American author
* [An] Eye Witness

Tanner, James Gideon 1885-1960 [CWG, DAM, PMJ]
American country-western performer
* Tanner, Gid

Tanner, James T. 1858-? [NPS, THR]
British librettist
* [The] Father of Musical Comedy
* Leader, James

Tanner, John 1930-1963 [SC]
American actor
* Eager, Johnney

Tanner, John
See Edgar, John

Tanner, John
See Matcha, Jack

Tanner, John
See White Falcon

Tanner, Lightnin'
See Tanner, Paul

Tanner, Lina 1923- [IWM]
British musician
* Vincent, Lina

Tanner, Paul 1917- [MY]
American jazz musician
* Tanner, Lightnin'

[The] Tanner President
See Grant, Hiram Ulysses

Tanner, William Dean 1872-1922 [NY 3-21-86]
Irish-born director
* Taylor, William Desmond

Tanner-Rutherford, C.
See Winchester, Clarence

Tanni
See Miyazaki, Toshio

Tanny, Vic
See Iannidinardo, Victor

Tano, Guy
See Rocco, Gaetano

Tanswell, Albert Henry Silas Russell 1908- [BEW]
British-born actor and director
* Tanswell, Bertram

Tanswell, Bertram
See Tanswell, Albert Henry Silas Russell

Tante, Dilly
See Kunitz, Stanley [Jasspon]

Tantivy
See Judd, Harry

Tantrist
See Wesander, Bjoern Kenneth

Tanuma, Okitsugu 1719-1788 [HPPN]
Japanese statesman
* [The] Forerunner of Modern Japan

Tanzer, Arnold 1841-? [HPPN]
German-American author
* Detouche, Pierre

Tao-Chi 1630-1707 [BI]
Chinese painter
* Shih-T'ao

Tao-tse 6th c. BC [FFF, HN, SN]
Chinese philosopher
* [The] Epicurus of China

Tap, Casey
See Tapley, K. C.

Tap City Harris
See Harris, Arthur

Tapio, Pat Decker
See Kines, Pat Decker

[Le] Tapissier de Notre-Dame
See Montmorency-Bouteville, Francois Henri de [Duc de Luxembourg]

Tapley, K. C. 19th c. [CCL]
Canadian author
* Tap, Casey

Taplin, William 1730?-1807 [BI]
British author and sportsman
* Veteran Sportsman

Tappan, David 1753-1803 [IP]
American theologian and author
* Toletus

Tappan, Lewis 1788-1873 [IP]
American merchant and author
* [A] Gentleman in Boston

Tappan, Sarah [Jackson Davis] [IP]
American author
* S. J.

Tappe, El
See Tappe, Elvin Walter

Tappe, Elvin Walter 1927- [BE]
American baseball player and manager
* Tappe, El

Tapping, Sydney 1873-1941 [F1, F2, FC]
British actress
* Fairbrother, Sydney

Tapsky
See Cooper, Anthony Ashley [First Earl of Shaftesbury]

Tar, Gyula 1928- [OP]
Hungarian opera singer
* Tarnay, Gyula

Tara, John
See Michel, John B.

Taral, Fred 1867-1925 [BBH]
Jockey
* [The] Dutch Demon
* Little Casino

[Il] Tarantino
See Fago, Nicola

Tarasc, Gilbert
See Best, Tharratt Gilbert

Tarassoff [or Tarassov], Lev 1911- [BI, CA, EWL]
French author
* Troyat, Henri

Taravilla y Amoros, Gregorio 1882-1943 [GS]
Spanish bullfighter
* Platerito [Little Silversmith]

Tarbell, Ida Minerva 1875-1944 [HPPN]
American author and biographer
* [The] Dean of Woman Authors of America

Tarbert, Arlie
See Tarbert, Wilber Arlington

Tarbert, Wilber Arlington 1904-1946 [BE]
American baseball player
* Tarbert, Arlie

Tarbox, Increase Niles 1815-? [IP]
American clergyman and author
* Uncle George

Tarcisius 3rd c. [HPPN]
Saint
* [The] Boy Martyr of Rome

Tarde, Gabriel
See De Tarde, Gabriel

Tardieu, Andre Pierre Gabriel Amedee 1876-1945 [WBD]
French politician
* Villiers, George

Tardieu, Antoine Francois 1757-1822 [WBD]
French engraver
* [De L']Estrapade

Tardieu, Charles Jean 1765-1830 [WBD]
French painter
* Tardieu Cochin

Tardieu Cochin
See Tardieu, Charles Jean

Tardieu, Jules Romain 1805-1868 [IP, PA]
French author and poet
* Granella, Victor
* J. T., de Saint-Germain

Tardiveau, Rene Marie Auguste 1867-1926 [CD, TC]
French author
* Boylesve, Rene

Tardy George McClellan
See McClellan, George Brinton

Tardy, Mary T. 19th c. [DNA, IP]
American author and historian
* Raymond, Ida

Targ, William
See Torgownik, William

Tarheel Slim
See Bunn, Alden

Tariff Andy Stewart
See Stewart, Andrew

Tarita 1941?- [HPPN]
Tahitian actress
* [The] Cinderella of the South Seas

Tark the Shark
See Tarkanian, Jerry

Tarkanian, Jerry 1930-
American basketball coach
* Tark the Shark

Tarkenton, Cindy
See Tarkenton, Fran[cis] Asbury

Tarkenton, Fran[cis] Asbury 1940- [HPPN]
American football player
* Fran the Scram
* Tarkenton, Cindy

Tarkington, [Newton] Booth 1869-1946 [CAA, HPPN, TLC]
American author
* Corburton, John
* [The] Gentleman from Indianapolis
* Kilgalen, Milton
* Van Loot, Cornelius Obenchain
* Woodford, Cecil

Tarkington, John Stevenson 1832-1923 [DNA]
American author and attorney
* Steventon, John

Tarleton, Banastre 1754-1833
British military officer
* Tarleton, Bloody

Tarleton, Bloody
See Tarleton, Banastre

[Il] Tarlo
See Cecchi, Emilio

Tarlton, Richard ?-1588 [DEP, HPPN]
British comedian
* [The] English Roscius
* [The] Man of Happy Unhappy Answers
* Roscius Britannicus

Tarn, Pauline Mary 1877-1909 [BI]
French poet
* Vivien, Renee

Tarn, Shirley
See Neuburg, Victor [Benjamin]

Tarnacre, Robert
See Cartmell, Robert

Tarnawsky, Patricia W[arren] 1936- [CA]
American editor, author, poet
* Kilina, Patricia

Tarnay, Gyula
See Tar, Gyula

Tarne, Rosina
See Fearn, John Russell

[The] Tarnished President
See Nixon, Richard Milhous

Tarnower, Lydia 20th c. [BEW]
American editor
* Joel, Lydia

Tarnowska, [Countess] Maria 1878-1923 [LFW]
Russian murderer
* [The] Russian Vampire
* [The] Sphinx in Crepe

Taro, Gerda
See Pohorylles, Gerda

Tarpley, Brenda Mae 1944- [CME, ECM, RO1]
American singer
* Lee, Brenda
* Little Miss Dynamite

Tarquin II [or Tarquinius] 6th c. BC [FFF, RH, SN]
Legendary King of Rome
* [The] Proud
* Superbus

Tarr, Simon
See Newcomb, Simon

Tarrant, John
See Egleton, Clive [Frederick]

Tarrant, Wilma
See Sherman, Jory [Tecumseh]

Tarrok, Peer
See Zwerenz, Gerhard

Tarsis, Valerii Iakovievich 1900- [BI, WOA]
Russian author
* Veleriy, Ivan

Tarski, Alexander
See Tabaksblat, Alexander

Tarski, Alfred 1902- [JL]
Polish-born philosopher
* [The] Father of Logical Semantics

Tartaglia, Niccolo
See Fontana, Nicola

Tartarin
See Daudet, Alphonse

Tarthang Tulku 20th c. [EOP]
Leader of Tibetan religious sect
* Rinpoche [Precious Master]

Tartiere, Dorothy [Blackman] 1903- [BI]
American actress
* Tartiere, Drue

Tartiere, Drue
See Tartiere, Dorothy [Blackman]

Tarto, Joe
See Tortoriello, Joseph

Tartuffe, Kaiser
See William I [Wilhelm Friedrich Ludwig]

[The] Tartuffe of the Revolution
See Nicolas, Jean

Tarzan
See Heseltine, Michael

Tasco, Rai
See Tasco, Ridgeway

Tasco, Ridgeway 1917- [ITA]
American actor and announcer
* Tasco, Rai

Tashrak
See Zevin, Israel Joseph

Tashunca-Uitco 1849?-1877 [HPPN, WBD]
American Indian chief
* Crazy Horse
* [The] Strange Man of the Oglalas

Tasker, E. [IP]
American author
* E. T.

Tasma
See Couvreur, Jessie Catherine [Huybers]

[The] Tasmanian Devil
See Lee, Ron

Tassinari, Berte Danyell 1870-1917 [SC]
Italian-born actor
* Dansey, Herbert

Tasso, Torquato 1544-1595 [NPS, SN]
Italian poet
* [The] Bard of Chivalry
* [The] Father of Tuscan Poetry

Tassy, Tamas 1920- [IWM]
Hungarian-born composer, conductor, arranger
* Legrady, Thomas Theodore
* Thomas, Ted

Taswert
See Stewart, John Allan

Tatanka Yotanka 1837-1890 [HPPN]
American Indian Chieftain
* Sitting Bull

Tatch
See Teach, Edward

Tate, Allen
See Orley, John

Tate, B. H.
See Boyer, Bruce Hatton

Tate, Baby
See Tate, Charles Henry

Tate, Bennie
See Tate, Henry Bennett

Tate, Buddy
See Tate, George Holmes

Tate, Charles Henry 1916-1972 [BWW]
American singer
* Tate, Baby

Tate, Dimples
See Tate, Edward Christopher

Tate, Don 20th c. [GW]
American rodeo performer
* Tate, Montana Red

Tate, Edward
See Dransfield, Michael [John] Pender

Tate, Edward Christopher 1861-1932 [BE]
American baseball player
* Tate, Dimples
* Tate, Pop

Tate, Ellalice
See Hibbert, Eleanor Alice [Burford]

Tate, George Holmes 1914?- [EJ, NP, PMJ]
American jazz musician
* Tate, Buddy
* Tate, Moon

Tate, Hal
See Teitelman, Alex

Tate, Harry, Jr.
See Hutchison, Ronald

Tate, Henry [or Harry]
See Hutchison, Ronald Macdonald

Tate, Henry Bennett 1901-1973 [BE]
American baseball player
* Tate, Bennie

Tate, Lee Willie 1932- [BE]
American baseball player
* Tate, Skeeter

Tate, Margaret 1888?- [BBD, EMT]
British actress and singer
* Teyte, Maggie

Tate, Mary Anne
See Hale, Arlene

Tate, Montana Red
See Tate, Don

Tate, Moon
See Tate, George Holmes

Tate, Pop
See Tate, Edward Christopher

Tate, Richard
See Masters, Anthony

Tate, Robin
See Fanthorpe, R[obert] Lionel

Tate, Roosevelt 20th c. [OBW]
American baseball player
* Tate, Speed

Tate, Skeeter
See Tate, Lee Willie

Tate, Speed
See Tate, Roosevelt

Tate, Velma 1913- [CA]
American author
* Davenport, Francine
* Taylor, Valerie
* Young, Nacella

Tatham, Arthur 1809-1874 [IP]
British clergyman and author
* [A] Rural Dean

Tatham, Campbell
See Elting, Mary

Tatham, Laura 1919- [AW]
British author and journalist
* Martin, John
* Phipps, Margaret

Tati, Jacques
See Tatischeff, Jacques

Tatian 2nd c. [HPPN]
Assyrian clergyman
* [The] Apologist

Tatischeff, Jacques 1908-1982 [BDF, FC, IPA]
French director, writer, actor
* Tati, Jacques

Tatlow, Tissington 1876-? [LAO]
Irish-born clergyman, editor, writer
* T

[El] Tato [The Stammerer]
See Sanchez Caballero, Antonio

Tato de Mexico [Lisper from Mexico]
See Maldonado y Rodriguez, Edmundo

Tatray, Istvan
See Rupert, Raphael Rudolph

Tattenbaum, Russian Bill
See Tattenbaum, William

Tattenbaum, William ?-1881 [HPPN]
American outlaw
* Tattenbaum, Russian Bill

Tattersall, George 1817-1849 [IP]
British author
* Wildrake

Tattersall, John Cecil 1788-1812 [IP]
British clergyman and author
* Davus

Tattersall, Muriel Joyce 1931- [AW, CAP, WD]
British author
* Waud, Elizabeth

Tatti, Jacopo 1486-1570 [WBD]
Italian sculptor and architect
* Sansovino, Jacopo

Tattooed Knight
See Blaine, James Gillespie

[The] Tattooed Man
See Blaine, James Gillespie

Tatu, Elizabeth A. 1866-1944 [SC]
American actress
* Allyn, Lilly

Tatum, Earl 20th c. [NBA]
American basketball player
* [The] Black Jerry West

Tatum, Goose
See Tatum, Reece

Tatum, James Moore [Jim] 1913-[HPPN]
American football coach
* Tatum, Silent Jim

Tatum, Reece 1919?-1967 [AS, BB]
American basketball player
* [The] Clown Prince of Basketball
* Tatum, Goose

Tatum, Silent Jim
See Tatum, James Moore [Jim]

Taubenhaus, Eugene 1909- [BEW]
American actor, songwriter, business representative
* Doyle, Gene

Taubensee, Fred Joseph 1906-1955 [BE]
American baseball player
* Tauby, Fred Joseph

Tauber, Richard
See Seiffert, Ernst

Taubert, A.
See Hartmann, Agnes [Taubert] von

Taubes, Susan
See Feldmann, Susan Judith

Tauby, Fred Joseph
See Taubensee, Fred Joseph

Tauler, Johann 1300-1361 [DEP, HN, SN]
German mystic
* [The] Illuminated Doctor

Tauler, Johann (cont.)
* Illuminatus, Doctor
* Sublimis et Illuminatus, Doctor

Taunton, Eric
See Jones, Kenneth Westcott

Taunton, William Elias 18th c. [IP]
British scholar
* Touchstone, Timothy

Taurasi, James V., Sr. 20th c. [SFP]
Author
* Stannard, Lane
* Vincent, J. Harry

Taurog, Norman 1899-1981 [HPPN]
American actor and director
* Hollywood's Ace Man With Children
* Uncle Norman

Taurus
See Honey, Philip

Tausen, Hans 1494-1561 [DNNS, HN, RH]
Danish religious reformer
* [The] Danish Luther

Taussig, J. J. 20th c. [EJS]
American boxing manager and trainer
* Taussig, Moose

Taussig, Jacob 19th c. [HPPN]
American author
* [The] Emile Gaboriau of America

Taussig, Moose
See Taussig, J. J.

Tautphoeus, Jemima [Montgomery] [IP]
British author
* Cyrilla

Tavares, Antone 1950- [RO2]
American singer
* Tavares, Chubby

Tavares, Arthur 1949- [RO2]
American singer
* Tavares, Pooch

Tavares, Butch
See Tavares, Feliciano

Tavares, Chubby
See Tavares, Antone

Tavares, Feliciano 1953- [RO2]
American singer
* Tavares, Butch

Tavares, Loletha Elaine Falana 1945- [HPPN]
American singer, dancer, entertainer
* Falana, Lola

Tavares, Perry Lee 1954- [RO2]
American singer
* Tavares, Tiny

Tavares, Pooch
See Tavares, Arthur

Tavares, Tiny
See Tavares, Perry Lee

Taveau, A. L. [IP]
American poet
* Alton

Tavener, John Adam [Jackie] 1897-1969 [BN]
American baseball player
* Tavener, Rabbit

Tavener, Rabbit
See Tavener, John Adam [Jackie]

Taveral, John
See Howard, Robert Ervin

Taveras, Alex
See Taveras Betances, Alejandro A.

Taveras, Frank
See Taveras, Franklin Fabian

Taveras, Franklin Fabian 1950- [SMG]
Dominican-born baseball player
* [The] Pittsburgh Stealer
* Taveras, Frank

Taveras Betances, Alejandro A. 1955- [BR]
Dominican-born baseball player
* Taveras, Alex

Taverner
See Young, Alexander

Tavernier, Mrs. Albert [FFF]
Entertainer
* Van Cortlandt, Ida

Taves, Isabella 1915- [HPPN]
American author
* Munro, Christy

Tavis, Alec
See Dunnett, Alastair MacTavish

Taviss, Irene
See Thomson, Irene Taviss

Tavo, Gus [joint pseudonym with Martha Miller Pfaff Ivan]
See Ivan, Gustave E.

Tavo, Gus [joint pseudonym with Gustave E. Ivan]
See Ivan, Martha Miller Pfaff

Tawney, R. H.
See Tawney, Richard Henry

Tawney, Richard Henry 1880-1962 [LC]
British historian and author
* Tawney, R. H.

[The] Tawny
See Bonvicino, Alessandro [or Alexander]

[The] Tawny Yvette Guilbert
See Waters, Ethel

Taxil, Leo
See Jogand-Pages, Gabriel Antoine

Tay Pay
See O'Connor, Thomas Power

Tayama Katai
See Tayama Rokuya

Tayama Rokuya 1871-1930
Japanese author
* Tayama Katai

Tayler, Charles Benjamin 19th c. [IP]
British clergyman and author
* [A] Country Curate
* Temple, [Rev.] Allan

Tayler, E. D. [IP]
American author
* Jenkins, S. Joshua

Tayler, John James 1798-1869 [IP]
British clergyman and author
* J. J. T.

Tayler, Robert Walker 1812-1878
[HPPN]
American attorney and politician
* [The] Comptroller of the Treasury

Taylor, A. J. P.
See Taylor, Alan John Percivale

Taylor, Aaron [BWW]
American singer
* Taylor, Buddy

Taylor, Abraham 18th c. [HPPN]
British dissenter
* [A] Dissenting Country Gentleman

Taylor, Alan John Percivale 1906- [LC]
British historian and author
* Taylor, A. J. P.

Taylor, Albert Hoyt 1879-1961 [HPPN]
American physicist
* [The] Father of Radar

Taylor, Alec 1862-1943 [OCS]
British horse trainer
* [The] Wizard of Manton

Taylor, Alfred Alexander 1848-1931
[HPPN]
American politician
* [The] Knight of the Red Rose
* [The] Sage of Happy Valley
* Taylor, Uncle Alf

Taylor, [Capt.] Alfred B.
See Ingraham, Prentiss

Taylor, Allan 1897-1968 [BI]
American author
* Dwight, Allan

Taylor, Ann ?-1866 [IP]
British poet
* A.

Taylor, Ann
See Smith, Richard Rein

Taylor, Antonio Sanchez 1935- [BE,
SMG]
Cuban-born baseball player
* Taylor, Tony

Taylor, Arthur 1903- [BWW]
American singer
* Taylor, Montana

Taylor, Barbara G. 1942- [CA]
American editor and writer
* Desmarais, Barbara G.

Taylor, Bayard 1825-1878 [PA]
American author
* Echo Club

Taylor, Benjamin Franklin 1819-1887
[FFF, HPPN]
American author
* [The] Goldsmith of America
* [The] Oliver Goldsmith of America

Taylor, Benjamin Ogle [PA]
Author
* Neptune
* Observer
* Viator

Taylor, Bert Leston 1866-1921 [TC]
American columnist
* B. L. T.

Taylor, Bill
See Taylor, Joseph Cephus

Taylor, Blues
See Taylor, Johnny

Taylor, Bollicky
See Taylor, William Henry

Taylor, Bones
See Taylor, Hugh

Taylor, Brad
See Smith, Richard Rein

Taylor, Brenda Forbes 1909- [BEW]
British actress
* Forbes, Brenda

Taylor, Brewery Jack
See Taylor, John B.

Taylor, Bruce
See Yin, Leslie Charles Bowyer

Taylor, Bud
See Taylor, Charles B.

Taylor, Buddy
See Taylor, Aaron

Taylor, C. I.
See Taylor, Charles I.

Taylor, Candy Jim
See Taylor, James

Taylor, Cash
See Taylor, Joseph Cephus

Taylor, Charles A. 1864-1942 [HPPN]
American playwright
* [The] King of the Mellers

Taylor, Charles B. 1903-1962 [AS, BX,
RBE]
American boxer
* [The] Blond Terror of Terre Haute
* Taylor, Bud
* [The] Terre Haute Terror

Taylor, Charles Elmer 20th c.
American comedian
* Taylor, Rip

Taylor, Charles H. [Chuck] 1901-1969
[AS]
American basketball player and editor
* [The] Ambassador of Basketball

Taylor, Charles I. 1872-1922 [MK]
American baseball player
* Taylor, C. I.

Taylor, Charles R. S. 1915- [HPPN]
American musician and composer
* Taylor, Russ

Taylor, Charley 1894- [HPPN]
American hunting guide and slingsman
* Taylor, Slingshot Charley

Taylor, Chat
See Taylor, Robert William

Taylor, Chink
See Taylor, Leo Thomas

Taylor, Chip
See Voigt, James Wesley

Taylor, Christopher Lenard 1923- [BA]
American dentist
* Taylor, Horse

Taylor, Constance Lindsay 1907- [CA,
WW]
British author and playwright
* Cullingford, Guy

Taylor, Cora Walton 1935- [BWW, WP
6-11-85]
American singer
* [The] Queen of Chicago Blues
* Taylor, Koko

Taylor, Cyclone
See Taylor, Frederick Wellington

Taylor, D. M. 1915- [CM]
American radio broadcaster
* Taylor, Sammy

Taylor, [Rev.] Daniel 1684?-1748?
[HPPN]
American clergyman
* Jenkin, Griffin

Taylor, David Burt
See Cohen, Paul Arthur

Taylor, Day [joint pseudonym with
Sharon Salvato]
See Parkinson, Cornelia M.

Taylor, Day [joint pseudonym with
Cornelia M. Parkinson]
See Salvato, Sharon

Taylor, [Joseph] Deems 1885-1966
[HPPN]
American composer and music critic
* Smeed

Taylor, Deforrest Walker 1933- [BA]
American local government official
* Taylor, Don

Taylor, Demetria 1903-1977 [CA]
American author, educator, editor
* Merriman, Beth

Taylor, Doboy
See Taylor, Phillip

Taylor, Don
See Taylor, Deforrest Walker

Taylor, Dummy
See Taylor, Luther Haden

Taylor, Eddie 1923- [BWW]
American singer
* Taylor, Playboy

Taylor, Edgar 1793-1839 [IP]
British barrister and author
* Denton, H. B.

Taylor, Edward Lee 1897?-1955 [BI]
American aviator
* Taylor, Swanee

Taylor, Edward Samuel 19th c. [HPPN]
British clergyman
* [A] Graduate

Taylor, Elizabeth [Liz] 1932- [HPPN]
American actress
* [The] Screen Queen

Taylor, Elizabeth Jones 1854?-1885
[HPPN]
American rancher and lynching victim
* That Taylor Woman

Taylor, Elizabeth Tebbetts 20th c.
Author
* Tebbets-Taylor, Elizabeth

Taylor, Ellie
See Taylor, Ellis Clarence

Taylor, Ellis Clarence 1931- [BA]
American engineer
* Taylor, Ellie

Taylor, Erquiet 20th c. [EF]
American football player
* Taylor, Jake

Taylor, Estelle
See Boylan, Estelle

Taylor, Eva
See Gibbons, Irene

Taylor, F. 19th c. [HFN]
Author
* One of the Party

Taylor, Fatty
See Taylor, Roland

Taylor, Fiddling Bob
See Taylor, Robert Love

Taylor, Frederick 19th c. [IP]
British author
* Ballinasloe
* [A] Horse Dealer

Taylor, Frederick Chase 1897-1950 [BI,
SC]
American actor
* Stoopnagle, [Colonel] Lemuel Q.

Taylor, Frederick Wellington 1883?-1979
[BI, CEI, FHE, HK]
Canadian-born hockey player
* Taylor, Cyclone

Taylor, Frederick Winslow 1856-1915
[DEP, HPPN]
American engineer and efficiency expert
* [The] Father of Business Efficiency
* Taylor, Speedy

Taylor, Gay Stuart ?-1970 [BI]
British diarist
* Hurnscot, Loran

Taylor, George
See Hausrath, Adolf

Taylor, George
See Parulski, George R[ichard], Jr.

Taylor, George C. 1887- [BI]
American attorney
* Advocatus Diaboli

Taylor, [Rev.] George Henry 19th c.
[HPPN]
British clergyman
* [A] Village Curate

Taylor, George Watson 19th c. [IP]
British poet
* G. W. T.
* Watson, George

Taylor, [Frank Herbert] Griffin 1917-
[CA]
British-born author
* Schneyder, J. F.

Taylor, H. Baldwin
See Waugh, Hillary Baldwin

Taylor, Handsome Harry
See Taylor, Harry Warren

Taylor, Harry 1824-1901 [BI]
Anglo-Canadian hotel owner
* Taylor, Kamoose

Taylor, Harry
See Granick, Harry

Taylor, Harry Warren 1907-1969 [BE]
American baseball player
* Taylor, Handsome Harry

Taylor, Hartford Connecticut 1905-1963
[CWG]
American country-western performer
* Taylor, Harty

Taylor, Harty
See Taylor, Hartford Connecticut

Taylor, Hawk
See Taylor, Robert Dale

Taylor, Henry 1710?-1785 [IP]
British clergyman and author
* Ben Mordecai, Benjamin
* Indignatio

Taylor, Herbert 1872-1927 [BEW]
British actor
* Rolyat, Dan

Taylor, Horse
See Taylor, Christopher Lenard

Taylor, Hound Dog
See Taylor, Theodore

Taylor, Howard Langdon 1920-1974
[BI]
American author
* Taylor, Tim

Taylor, Hugh 20th c. [SMG]
American football coach
* Taylor, Bones

Taylor, Isaac 1787-1865 [IP]
British author
* I. T.

Taylor, J. G. 20th c. [BBH]
American sportswriter
* Taylor, Stink

Taylor, J. H.
See Taylor, John Henry

Taylor, J. R. 20th c. [SMG]
American football player
* Taylor, Tarz

Taylor, J. S.
See Taylor, James Spencer

Taylor, Jack 20th c. [CC]
Author
* Gray, Jonathan

Taylor, Jake
See Taylor, Erquiet

Taylor, James 1884-1948 [IBW, MK]
American baseball player
* Taylor, Candy Jim

Taylor, James 20th c. [HPPN]
American singer and songwriter
* Sweet Baby James

Taylor, James Spencer 1921- [ART]
British painter
* J. S. T.
* J. T.
* Taylor, J. S.

Taylor, James Wren 1898-1974 [BE, BI,
PB]
American baseball player and manager
* Taylor, Zack

Taylor, Jane 1783-1824 [IP, PA]
British author and poet
* Q. Q.

Taylor, Jelly
See Taylor, Olan

Taylor, Jeremy 1613-1667 [DEA, NPS,
PA, RH, SN]
British author and prelate
* Alexander, John
* [The] Beauty of Holiness
* [The] English Chrysostom
* J. T., D. D.
* [A] Layman
* [The] Poet Bishop
* [The] Shakespeare of Divines
* [The] Spenser of English Prose-Writers

Taylor, Jerome
See Krejci, Jerome

Taylor, Jesse
See Amidon, Bill [Vincent]

Taylor, Joe
See Taylor, William Michael

Taylor, Joe Carl 1921- [CWG]
American country-western performer
* [The] Cowboy Auctioneer

Taylor, John 1580-1654 [DEP, DNNF, FFF, IP, NPS]
British poet
* Ailo, Thorny
* Alexander, John, a Joyner
* Allde, Edward?
* Aqvaticvs, Mercvrivs
* [The] Chanticleere
* Eld, George?
* Mendsoale, My Heele
* Misostratus
* [Sir] Nonsence, Gregory
* Philanar
* [The] Scullor
* [The] Swan of the Thames
* Walker [?], Henry
* [The] Water Poet

Taylor, John 1753-1824 [DNA, IP]
American writer
* [A] Citizen of Virginia
* Curtius

Taylor, John 1767-1832 [IP]
British author
* Tonson, Monsieur

Taylor, John 1781-1864 [IP]
British publisher and author
* Verus

Taylor, [Chevalier] John 18th c. [HPPN]
British occultist
* Jones, Henry

Taylor, John 18th c. [SN]
Oculist
* Taylor, Liar

Taylor, John 19th c. [IP]
British author
* [A] Layman

Taylor, John [Alfred] 1931- [CA]
American poet and author
* Coppe, Abiezer
* Dupin, August Dupont
* Ward, Charles Dexter

Taylor, John 20th c. [OBW]
American baseball player
* Steel Arm Johnny

Taylor, John
See Magee, James

Taylor, John A. 19th c. [IP]
American attorney and author
* Fairchild, Paul

Taylor, John B. 1873-1900 [BE, PB]
American baseball player
* Taylor, Brewery Jack

Taylor, John Edward 1791-1844 [HPPN]
British journalist
* [The] Father of the Manchester Guardian

Taylor, John Francis 1849?-1902 [PI]
Irish poet and journalist
* Ridgeway

Taylor, John Henry 1871-1963 [GF]
British golfer
* Taylor, J. H.

Taylor, John M[axwell] 1930- [CA]
American diplomat and author
* Allen, Richard C.

Taylor, Johnny 20th c. [BWW]
American singer
* Taylor, Blues

Taylor, Johnny Lamar
See Young, Johnny

Taylor, Joseph Cephus 1926- [BE]
American baseball player
* Taylor, Bill
* Taylor, Cash

Taylor, Josephine
See Motz, Josephine

Taylor, Joyce Barbara 1921- [ART]
British artist
* J. B. T.

Taylor, Judson R.
See Halsey, Harlan Page

Taylor, Julia
See Worsley, Julia Taylor

Taylor, Just As Good
See Taylor, S. Allan

Taylor, Kamala [Purnaiya] 1924- [BI]
Indian author
* Markandaya, Kamala

Taylor, Kamoose
See Taylor, Harry

Taylor, Karen Malpede 1945- [CA]
American author and editor
* Malpede, Karen

Taylor, Kent
See Weiss, Louis

Taylor, Kingsize
See Taylor, Ted

Taylor, Koko
See Taylor, Cora Walton

Taylor, Laurette
See Cooney, Helen Laurette Magdalene

Taylor, Leo Thomas 1901- [BE]
American baseball player
* Taylor, Chink

Taylor, Les
See Taylor, Lionel

Taylor, Liar
See Taylor, John

Taylor, Linda 20th c. [HPPN]
American embezzler
* Chicago's Welfare Queen

Taylor, Lionel 1916- [ASC]
American musician
* Taylor, Les

Taylor, Little Johnny
See Young, Johnny

Taylor, Lois Dwight Cole
See Cole, Lois Dwight

Taylor, Luther Haden 1875?-1958 [AS, BE, PB]
American baseball player
* Taylor, Dummy

Taylor, Major
See Taylor, Marshall W.

Taylor, Malcolm 1943- [HPPN, SW]
British actor
* [The] Clockwork Top Banana
* McDowell, Malcolm

Taylor, Manton Robert 19th c. [IP]
Author
* [A] Clergyman

Taylor, Margaret
See Burroughs, Margaret Taylor

Taylor, Margaret
See Kenyon, [Margaret] Doris

Taylor, Margaret Stewart 20th c. [CA]
British author
* Collier, Margaret

Taylor, Marian Young 1909-1973 [CR]
American radio commentator
* Deane, Martha

Taylor, Marion Sayle 1889- [HPPN]
American radio lecturer and author
* [The] Voice of Experience

Taylor, Marshall W. 1878-1932 [BBH]
American bicycle racer
* Taylor, Major

Taylor, Mary A. 1844-1913 [HPPN]
American actress
* Markina, Mademoiselle
* Taylor, May

Taylor, Mary Ann 1912- [CA]
American author
* Bowe, Kate

Taylor, Mary Virginia 1912- [ASC]
American songwriter
* Sterling, Jean
* Wood, Sue

Taylor, May
See Taylor, Mary A.

Taylor, Michael 1937?- [HPPN]
British entertainer
* Sheik Michael

Taylor, Michael Angelo 18th c. [DNNS, HN, RH]
Barrister
* [The] Chicken

Taylor, Michael Norman Somerset 1942- [DC]
British cricketer
* Taylor, Tay

Taylor, Montana
See Taylor, Arthur

Taylor, Moose
See Taylor, William Michael

Taylor, Moses 1806-1882 [HPPN]
American banker and railroad operator
* [The] Financier of the Transatlantic Cable

Taylor, Mrs. Tom [PA]
Author
* Barker, Laura

Taylor, N. J. 1946- [BBH, CFH]
Canadian football team president
* Taylor, Piffles

Taylor, Newton
See Taylor, William Henry

Taylor, Norman
See Wood-Smith, Noel

Taylor of Norwich
See Borrow, George Henry

Taylor, Olan 20th c. [OBW]
American baseball player
* Taylor, Jelly

Taylor, Our Bob
See Taylor, Robert Love

Taylor, Pat
See Pope, Pat

Taylor, Pete
See Taylor, Vernon Charles

Taylor, Phillip ?-1871 [EWG]
American gunfighter
* Taylor, Doboy

Taylor, Phoebe [Atwood] 1909-1976
[CA, CC, EMD]
American author
* Tilton, Alice

Taylor, Piffles
See Taylor, N. J.

Taylor, Playboy
See Taylor, Eddie

Taylor, Ralph 1905-1951 [THR]
British actor
* Forbes, Ralph

Taylor, Red
See Taylor, Walter

Taylor, Richard 1919- [CA]
American educator and author
* Cronus, Diodorus

Taylor, Richard Mansfield 20th c.
[ITA, SW]
American actor
* Richards, Jeff

Taylor, Rip
See Taylor, Charles Elmer

Taylor, Robert 1923- [ECM]
American country-western performer
* Taylor, Tut

Taylor, Robert 1930- [SW]
Australian-born actor
* Taylor, Rod

Taylor, Robert
See Brough, Spangler Arlington

Taylor, Robert
See Brugh, Spangler Arlington

Taylor, Robert Dale 1939- [BE]
American baseball player
* Taylor, Hawk

Taylor, Robert Love 1850-1912 [HPPN]
American politician
* [The] Apostle of Sunshine
* [The] Knight of the White Rose
* Taylor, Fiddling Bob
* Taylor, Our Bob

Taylor, Robert William 1941- [DC]
British cricketer
* Taylor, Chat

Taylor, Rockie 1945- [BA]
American writer and editor
* Ologboni, Tejumola F.

Taylor, Rod
See Taylor, Robert

Taylor, Roland 1946- [NBA, SMG]
American basketball player
* Taylor, Fatty

Taylor, Roosevelt 1937- [FB]
American football player
* Taylor, Rosey

Taylor, Rosey
See Taylor, Roosevelt

Taylor, Russ
See Taylor, Charles R. S.

Taylor, S. Allan 1839-1913
Scottish-born forger
* [The] Prince of Forgers
* Taylor, Just As Good

Taylor, Sam
See Alex, Gus

Taylor, Sam
See Goodyear, Stephen Frederick

Taylor, Sammy
See Taylor, D. M.

Taylor, Samuel L. 1916- [EJ]
American jazz musician
* Sam the Man

Taylor, Selman
See Selman, Elsie Emily

Taylor, Seymour 1912- [ASC]
American musician
* Taylor, Sy

Taylor, Silas
See Domville, Silas

Taylor, Simon 1740-1813 [HPPN]
Jamaican sugar planter
* [The] Sugar Tycoon of Jamaica

Taylor, Slats
See Taylor, Virgil

Taylor, Slingshot Charley
See Taylor, Charley

Taylor, Speedy
See Taylor, Frederick Winslow

Taylor, Stella 1932?-
Former nun and expert swimmer
* [The] Swimming Nun

Taylor, Stink
See Taylor, J. G.

Taylor, Swanee
See Taylor, Edward Lee

Taylor, Sy
See Taylor, Seymour

Taylor, T.
See Foe, Daniel

Taylor, Tarz
See Taylor, J. R.

Taylor, Tay
See Taylor, Michael Norman Somerset

Taylor, Ted 20th c.
British singer
* Taylor, Kingsize

Taylor, Theodore 1916?-1975 [BI]
American musician
* Taylor, Hound Dog

Taylor, Theodore 1921- [CA]
American author and screenwriter
* Lang, T. T.

Taylor, Theodore
See Hotten, John Camden

Taylor, Thomas 1576-1633 [NPS]
British clergyman
* [A] Brazen Wall Against Popery
* [The] Illuminated Doctor
* Illuminatus, Doctor

Taylor, Thomas 1743-1833 [HPPN]
American army officer and pioneer
* [The] Patriarch of Columbia

Taylor, Thomas 1758-1835 [SN, WBD]
British scholar
* [The] Platonist

Taylor, Tim
See Taylor, Howard Langdon

Taylor, Tom 1817-1881 [IP]
British critic and playwright
* Mellot, Claude
* Noakes, John
* Rei, Roumany

Taylor, Tony
See Taylor, Antonio Sanchez

Taylor, Tucker Woodson 1854-1901 [BI]
American poet and educator
* Civis Americanus
* Hunter, William T.

Taylor, Tut
See Taylor, Robert

Taylor, Una Ashworth 19th c. [PI]
British-born poet and author
* A. H. R.

Taylor, Uncle Alf
See Taylor, Alfred Alexander

Taylor, Valerie
See Tate, Velma

Taylor, Vernon Charles 1927- [BE]
American baseball player
* Taylor, Pete

Taylor, Virgil ?-1978 [FIR]
Actor
* Taylor, Slats

Taylor, W. F. 19th c. [IP]
British author
* W. F. T.

Taylor, W. H. 19th c. [IP]
British author
* [A] Doctor of Physic

Taylor, W. T. 20th c. [MBF]
British author
* Bredon, John
* Gregory, Dave
* Whitehouse, Arch

Taylor, Walter 20th c. [IBW]
American track and field athlete
* Taylor, Red

Taylor, Walter G.
See Geibel, Adam

Taylor, Watson 19th c. [IP]
British author
* Cheakill, [Sir] Joseph, K. F., K. S.

Taylor, William Cooke 1800-1849
[HPPN]
Irish author
* Censor

Taylor, William Desmond
See Tanner, William Dean

Taylor, William Frederick 19th c.
[HFN]
Author
* W. F. T.

Taylor, William Henry 1855-1900 [BE]
American baseball player
* Taylor, Bollicky

Taylor, William Henry 1911- [DBA]
British painter, etcher, engraver
* Taylor, Newton

Taylor, William Michael 1929- [BE]
American baseball player
* Taylor, Joe
* Taylor, Moose

Taylor, Zach[ary] 1784-1850 [DNNF,
DNNS, SN]
American president and army officer
* [A] Brave Old Feller
* Old Buena Vista
* Old Rough and Ready
* Old Zach
* Rough and Ready

Taylor, Zack
See Taylor, James Wren

Taz
See O'Reilly, Terry

[The] Tazmanian Devil
See Hamel, Dean

Tchaadaieff
See Sorokin, Pitirim A[lexandrovitch]

Tchaikovsky, Telephones
See Konarsky, Matt

Tchernowitz, Chaim 1871-1949 [BI]
Russian-American scholar
* Tzair, Rav

Tchicaya, Gerald Felix 1931- [WOA]
Congolese poet
* U Tam'si

Tching
See Cheng Sen

Tching cong
See Cheng Sen

Te Rangi Hiroa 1880-1951 [HPPN]
New Zealand ethnologist
* Buck, [Sir] Peter Henry

Tea, Sir
See Lipton, Thomas

Tea Table
See Foe, Daniel

[A] Tea Table Scoundrel
See Stanhope, Philip Dormer

Teach, Edward ?-1718 [CEC, DI, HPPN,
WBD]
British pirate
* Blackbeard
* Blackbeard the Buccaneer
* [The] Scourge of the Spanish Main
* Tach
* Tatch
* Thatch

[A] Teacher
See Pickering, Henry White

[A] Teacher
See Samson, George Whitefield

[The] Teacher of Germany
See Schwarzert, Philipp

[The] Teacher of Millions
See Laubach, Frank Charles

[The] Teacher of the Catholic Church
See Dionysius

[The] Teacher President
See Garfield, James Abram

Teachout, Arthur John 1904- [BE]
American baseball player
* Teachout, Bud

Teachout, Bud
See Teachout, Arthur John

Teachwell, Mrs.
See Fenn, Eleanor

Teagarden, Big T
See Teagarden, Weldon Leo

Teagarden, Charlie 1913- [PMJ]
American jazz musician
* Teagarden, Little T

Teagarden, Clois Lee 1915- [EJ]
American jazz musician
* Teagarden, Cub

Teagarden, Cub
See Teagarden, Clois Lee

Teagarden, Jack
See Teagarden, Weldon Leo

Teagarden, Little T
See Teagarden, Charlie

Teagarden, Norma Louise
See Friedlander, Norma

Teagarden, Weldon Leo 1905-1964
[DAM, PMJ, WWJ]
American jazz musician
* Teagarden, Big T
* Teagarden, Jack

Teague, George Herbert 20th c. [WWL]
British author
* Galway, Herbert

Teague, John Jessop 1856-1929 [WW]
Author
* Gerard, Morice

Teague, Olin 1911?-1981
American politician and army officer
* Teague, Tiger

Teague, Tiger
See Teague, Olin

Teal, Allen Leslie 1933- [CEI, SMG]
Canadian-born hockey player
* Teal, Skip

Teal, G. Donn 1932- [WD]
American author
* Forsythe, Ronald

Teal, Skeeter
See Teal, Victor

Teal, Skip
See Teal, Allen Leslie

Teal, Victor 1949- [HR]
Canadian-born hockey player
* Teal, Skeeter

Team, Mr., of the Boston Braves
See Elliott, Robert Irving [Bob]

Tear 'em
See Roebuck, John Arthur

Teardrop, Mr.
See Robinson, Martin D.

Tearefowl, [Sir] Guzzledown
See Hogarth, William

Tearle, Conway
See Levy, Frederick

Tearle, Minnie [FFF]
Entertainer
* Conway, Minnie

Teasdale, Joseph 1936?-
American politician
* Teasdale, Walkin' Joe

Teasdale, Sara Filsinger
See Filsinger, Sara Teasdale

Teasdale, Walkin' Joe
See Teasdale, Joseph

Tebar Perez, Gregorio 1946-   [GS]
Spanish bullfighter
* [El] Inclusero [The Foundling]

Tebbets-Taylor, Elizabeth
See Taylor, Elizabeth Tebbetts

Tebbetts, Birdie
See Tebbetts, George Robert

Tebbetts, George Robert 1909?-   [BE,
IPA, PB]
American baseball player and manager
* Tebbetts, Birdie

Tebbs, George William 1873-?   [CCL]
Canadian poet and clergyman
* Old Man Sunshine

Tebeau, Charles Albert 20th c.   [BE]
American baseball player
* Tebeau, Pussy

Tebeau, George E. 1862-1923   [BE]
American baseball player
* Tebeau, White Wings

Tebeau, Oliver Wendell 1864-1918   [AS,
BE, PB]
American baseball player and manager
* Tebeau, Patsy

Tebeau, Patsy
See Tebeau, Oliver Wendell

Tebeau, Pussy
See Tebeau, Charles Albert

Tebeau, White Wings
See Tebeau, George E.

Tebell, Gus
See Tebell, Gustavus

Tebell, Gustavus 20th c.   [EF]
American football player
* Tebell, Gus

Teche, L. A.
See Parker, Fitzgerald Sale

Technicolor Tessie
See Ball, Lucille

**[The] Technological Father of the
Modern Steel Industry**
See Holley, Alexander Lyman

[The] Technological Merman
See Cousteau, Jacques-Yves

Tecosky, Morton 1914-   [BEW, FC, TR]
American director, producer, actor
* Da Costa, Morton

Tecumseh 1768?-1813   [HPPN]
American Indian chief
* [The] Last King of the Ohio

Ted the Terrific
See Williams, Theodore Samuel [Ted]

Teddy Bear
See Pendergrass, Theodore [Teddy]

Teddy Blue Abbott
See Abbott, E. C.

Teddy Boy Atkinson
See Atkinson, Theodore Francis [Ted]

Teddy the First
See Roosevelt, Theodore [Teddy]

Teddy the Jewboy
See Davis, Edward

[Il] Tedesco
See Elsheimer, Adam

[Il] Tedesco [The German]
See Schwarzendorf, Johann Paul
Agidius

Tedmon, Allyn Henry 1884-   [NAA]
American writer
* Allen, Ted
* Nomdet, Nylla

Tee-Van, Helen Damrosch 1893-1976
[SAT]
American artist, illustrator, writer
* Damrosch, Helen Therese

Teed, Cyrus Reed 1839-1908   [SFL,
WGT]
American author
* Chester, Lord
* Cyrus
* Koresh

Teed, George Heber Hamilton 1878-1939
[MBF]
Canadian-born author
* Brittany, Louis
* Hamilton, George
* Hamilton, Murray [joint pseudonym
  with Robert Murray Graydon]
* Reid, Desmond [house pseudonym]

[The] Teeger
See Dunlop, John Colin

[The] Teen-Age God-King
See Tutankhamen

[The] Teenyboppers' Super-puppy
See Cassidy, David

Teer, Barbara
Author
* Allister, Barbara

Teerius, Miss
See Horner, Mrs. Frederick

Teffi
See Buchinskaia, Nadezhda
Aleksandrovna [Lokhvitskaia]

Teffi, Nadezhda
See Lokhvitskaya, Nadezhda
Alexandrovna

Tefft, Lyman Beecher 1833-?   [ALY]
American author
* Vindex

[The] Teflon President
See Reagan, Ronald Wilson

Tegg, William 1816-1895   [NPS]
Author and publisher
* Parley, Peter

Tegner, Henry [Stuart] 1901-   [CA]
British author
* [The] Northumbrian Gentleman
* [The] Ruffle

Tehuhe ?-1200   [HN, RH, SN]
Chinese philosopher
* [The] Aristotle of China
* [The] Prince of Science

Tei Seiko
See Cheng Sen

[The] Teian Muse [or Poet]
See Anacreon

Teichelmann, Ebenezer 1859-1938
Mountain climber and photographer
* [The] Little Doctor

Teichman, Arthur 1895-   [JL]
American dancing instructor
* Murray, Arthur

Teichner, Hans H. 1908-1957   [BBH]
*American ski instructor and promoter of
skiing programs*
* Teichner, Peppi

Teichner, Peppi
See Teichner, Hans H.

Teilerian, Salomon 1896?-1960   [BI]
Armenian assassin
* Melikian, Saro

Teilhet, Darwin L[e Ora] 1904-1964
[ANT, ESF]
American author
* Fisher, Cyrus T.

Teitelman, Alex 1912-   [ASC]
American entertainer and composer
* Tate, Hal

Teitgen, Pierre Henri 1908-   [HPPN]
French political leader and educator
* Tristan

Teixeira De Pascoais, Joaquim
See Teixeira De Vasconcelos, Joaquim
Pereira

Teixeira De Queiroz, Francisco
1848-1919   [CD]
Portuguese author
* Moreno, Bento

**Teixeira De Vasconcelos, Joaquim
Pereira** 1877?-1952   [CD, EWL]
Portuguese poet and author
* Teixeira De Pascoais, Joaquim

Tejada, Raquel 1940?-   [FC, HT, IPA]
American actress
* Welch, Raquel

Tejn, Michael
See Klaehr, Mogens

Tekahionwake
See Johnson, Emily Pauline

Tekakwitha, Kateri 1656-1680   [WBD]
Saint
* [The] Lily of the Mohawks

Tekeli
See Hook, Theodore Edward

Tekulve, Kent
See Tekulve, Kenton Charles

Tekulve, Kenton Charles 1947- [SMG]
American baseball player
* Tekulve, Kent

Tela, Josephus
See Webb, Joseph

Telarius
See Webb, Foster

Telba
See Ablett, William

Telenga, Suzette 1915- [CA]
German-born author
* Yorke, Susan

[The] Telepathic Phenomenon
See Kraus, Josef

Telephone, Tom
See Cleary, Thomas Stanislaus

Telescope Teddy
See Roosevelt, Theodore [Teddy]

Telescope, Tom
See Newbery, John

Telescope, Tom, A. M.
See Goldsmith, Oliver

Teleshova, Elizabeth
See Eisenstein, [Madame] S. M.

Television, Mr.
See Berlinger, Milton

[The] Television Ventrioloquist
See Nelson, Jimmy

Television's Clown Prince
See Skelton, [Richard] Red

Television's International Man
See Frost, David

Television's Last Angry Man
See Klugman, Jack

Television's Tiny Terror
See Efron, Marshall

Telfair, Nancy
See DuBose, Louise Jones

Telfer, Dariel 1905- [CAP]
American author
* Forrest, Caleb

Telford, Thomas 1757-1834 [FFF]
Scottish poet
* Eskdale Tam

Telio, J.
See Joilet, Charles

Tell, Chef
See Erhardt, Friedemann Tell

Tell, Muni
See Griffin, Alice McClure

Tell, William 1282-1350 [HN, RH]
Legendary Swiss hero
* [The] Mountain Brutus

Tell, William
See Forrester, Arthur M.

Tellefsen, Carl 1854-1908 [BBH]
Norwegian-born skiing organization officer
* [The] Father of American Organized
  Skiing

Tellegen, Lou
See Van Dammeler, Isador Louis
Bernard

Teller, Edward 1908-
Hungarian-born American physicist
* [The] Father of the Hydrogen Bomb

Teller, Neville 1931- [IAW]
British author
* Owen, Edmund

Teller, Thomas
See Tuttle, George

Tellez, Gabriel 1570?-1648 [DNNF, RH,
WBD]
Spanish playwright
* Tirso de Molina

Tellier, Jacques
See Foy, Louis Andre

Telling, Edward Riggs 1919?- [TI 8-20-
84]
American business executive
* Mr. T

Telltale, George
See Holmes, Isaac Edward

Telltroth, Titus
See Oates, Titus

Telltruth, Paul
See Carey, George Seville

Telmann, Konrad
See Zitelmann, Konrad

Teluccini, Mario 16th c. [WGT]
Italian author
* [Il] Bernia

Telva, Marion
See Toucke, Marion

Temary, Elza 1905-1968 [SC]
American actress
* Splane, Elza K.

[Le] Temeraire
See Charles

Temme, Jodocus Donatus Hubertus
1798-1881 [WBD]
German jurist, criminologist, author
* Stahl, Heinrich

Temny
See Basil II [or Vasili]

[Un] Temoin Oculaire [An Eye-Witness]
See Bailly, Jean Sylvain

Temothie
See Escoffer, Tremim M.

[A] Temperate Drinker
See Gauntley, William

Temperate Fauvist
See Dufy, Raoul

Temperly, C. H. 18th c. [HPPN]
British poet
* C. H. T.

[The] Tempest
See Junot, Andoche

[A] Tempest Cleaving Swan
See Byron, George Gordon Noel

Tempest, Evelyn
See Cuming, Edward William Dirom

Tempest, J. Fletcher
See Fletcher, John Arthur

Tempest, Jan
See Swatridge, Irene Maude [Mossop]

Tempest, [Dame] Marie
See Etherington, Mary Susan

Tempest, Sarah
See Ponsonby, Doris Almon

Tempest, Stephen 18th c. [HPPN]
British author
* [A] Layman

Tempest, Theresa
See Kent, Louise Andrews

Tempest, Victor
See Philipp, Elliot Elias

[La] Tempete
See Junot, Andoche

Templaito [The Valiant One]
See Martinez, Julio

Templar
See Kent, [William] Charles [Mark]

Templar, John
See Garbutt, John L.

Templar, Maurice
See Groom, Arthur William

Temple, [Rev.] Allan
See Tayler, Charles Benjamin

Temple, Ann
See Mortimer, Penelope [Ruth]

Temple, Anthony 1723?-1795 [HPPN]
British clergyman
* [A] Serious Engineer

Temple, Arthur
See Northcott, [William] Cecil

Temple Bar
See Fox-Davies, Arthur Charles

Temple, Dan
See Newton, Dwight Bennett

Temple, Edith
See Murrells, Joseph

Temple, Elizabeth Lee ?-1736 [SN]
*Stepdaughter of British poet, Edward
Young*
* Narcissa

Temple, Geechie
See Temple, Johnny

Temple, Henry John 1784-1865 [DEP, DNNS, HN, HPPN]
British statesman
* Evergreen Pam
* Old Pam
* Pacifico, Don
* Palmerston, Firebrand
* Palmerston, Viscount
* Pam

Temple, Hope
See Davis, Hope

Temple, James
See Bell, Eric Temple

Temple, Johnny 1906-1968 [BWW]
American singer
* Temple, Geechie

Temple, Lafayette Parker 1911- [FFA]
American singer
* Temple, Pick

Temple, Launcelot
See Armstrong, John

Temple, Laura Sophia 1786-? [IP]
British poet
* L. S. T.

[The] Temple Leech
See Colman, George

Temple, M. H. 20th c. [SFL]
Author
* Lewis, Caroline [joint pseudonym with James S. Ransome and (Edward) Harold Begbie]

Temple, Mattie
See Clark, Mrs. Henry

Temple, Mr. Shirley
See Agar, John

Temple, Mrs. Edward P. [FFF]
Entertainer
* Winner, Polly

Temple, Neville
See Fane, Julian Charles Henry

Temple, Paul [joint pseudonym with James Douglas Rutherford McConnell]
See Durbridge, Francis

Temple, Paul [joint pseudonym with Francis Durbridge]
See McConnell, James Douglas Rutherford

Temple, Pick
See Temple, Lafayette Parker

Temple, Ralph
See Alexander, Robert William

Temple, Robin
See Wood, Samuel Andrew

Temple, Shirley
See Black, Shirley Temple

Temple, T. B.
See Banister, Thomas

Temple, Victoria
See Mason, Mrs. W. J.

Temple, [Sir] William 1628-1699 [DEA]
British poet
* W. T., Sir

Temple, [Rev.] William Johnstone 1746-1796 [HPPN]
British clergyman
* Biographicus

Temple-Ellis, N. A.
See Holdaway, Neville Aldridge

Templeton
See Monroe, George H.

Templeton, Dink
See Templeton, George

Templeton, Dink
See Templeton, Robert L.

Templeton, Faith
See Barber, Harriet Booner

Templeton, Fay
See West, Mrs. William

Templeton, Garry Lewis 1956- [SMG]
American baseball player
* Templeton, Jump Steady

Templeton, George ?-1980 [FIR]
Actor, director, producer
* Templeton, Dink

Templeton, Herminie
See Kavanagh, Herminie Templeton

Templeton, Horace
See Lever, Charles James

Templeton, Janet
See Hershman, Morris

Templeton, Jesse
See Goodchild, George

Templeton, Jump Steady
See Templeton, Garry Lewis

Templeton, Laurence
See Scott, [Sir] Walter

Templeton, May
See Reilly, Mrs. James

Templeton, Mrs. John [FFF]
Entertainer
* Vane, Alice

Templeton, Robert L. 1897?-1962 [AS, TF]
American track and field coach
* Templeton, Dink

Templeton, Ruth
See Bullivant, Margaret D.

Templeton, Timothy
See Adams, Charles Baker

Templeton, Tristram
See Davin, Nicholas Francis Flood

Templeton, W. P.
See Templeton, William Pettigrew

Templeton, William Pettigrew 1915- [BEW]
Scottish playwright
* Templeton, W. P.

Tempone, Joseph 1897- [HPPN]
American bootblack
* [The] Resident Bootblack

[The] Temporizing Statesman
See Whitelocke, Bulstrode

[El] Tempranillo [The Little Early One]
See Moreno, Tomas

Temujin [or Temuchin] 1162-1227 [HPPN, WBD]
Mongol chieftain
* Cambuscan
* Chinghiz Khan
* Genghis Khan
* Jenghiz Khan

Ten Cent Jimmy
See Buchanan, James

Ten Eyck, Edward H. 1879-1956 [AS]
American rower
* Ten Eyck, Ned

Ten Eyck, Ned
See Ten Eyck, Edward H.

10 4
See Correll, Victor Crosby

[A] Ten Pounder
See Mackenzie, Peter

[The] Ten Thousand Dollar Beauty
See Kelly, Michael Joseph

[The] Tenacious Muckraker
See Pearson, Andrew Russel

Tenant, Eleanor 20th c.
American tennis coach
* Tenant, Teach

Tenant, Teach
See Tenant, Eleanor

Tenax
See Lean, Garth Dickinson

Tenbrook, Harry
See Hansen, Henry Olaf

Tench, Charles Victor 1895- [NAA]
British-born writer
* C. V. T.
* Truscott, Charles

Tender Hawk
See Kissinger, Henry Alfred

Tendron, Marcel 1884-? [WBD]
French author
* Elder, Marc

Tenella
See Clarke, Mary Bayard Devereux

Tenenbaum, Joseph 1887- [NAA]
Polish-born physician and author
* Bendow, Josef

Tener, Martin J. 1935- [ASC]
American composer, author, educator
* Martins, Jay

Teneyck, Edward [PA]
Author
* Ed

Tenfjord, Johanne Marie [Glaever]
1918- [BI]
Norwegian author
* Holm, Hannebo

Teng Hsiao-ping [Little Peace]
See Kan Tse-kao

Tengberg, Violet 1920- [ART]
Swedish artist
* V. T.

Teniers, David 1582-1649 [WBD]
Flemish painter
* [The] Elder

Teniers, David 1610-1690 [WBD]
Flemish painter
* [The] Younger

[The] Teniers of Comedy
See Dancourt, Florent Carton

Tenn, William
See Klass, Philip

Tennant, Catherine
See Crozier, Kathleen Muriel [Eyles]

Tennant, Emma 1937- [ESF]
British author and editor
* Aydy, Catherine

Tennant, Kylie
See Rodd, Kylie Tennant

Tennant, Nora Jackson 1915- [CA]
British educator and author
* Jackson, Nora

Tennant, William 1784-1848 [IP]
Scottish poet and linguist
* Crookleg, W.

Tennenbaum, Irving 1903- [IPA, LC,
TC]
American author
* Stone, Irving

Tennent, Gilbert 1703-1764 [HPPN]
Irish-American clergyman
* [The] Central Figure of the Great
Awakening

Tennent, [Sir] James Emerson 1804-1869
[IP, PA]
Irish author
* Emerson, [Sir] James

Tenneshaw, S. M. [joint pseudonym
with Robert Silverberg] [house
pseudonym, Ziff-Davis]
See Garrett, [Gordon] Randall [Philip
David]

Tenneshaw, S. M. [house pseudonym,
Ziff-Davis]
See Geier, Chester S.

Tenneshaw, S. M. [house pseudonym,
Ziff-Davis]
See Hamilton, Edmond [Moore]

Tenneshaw, S. M. [house pseudonym,
Ziff-Davis]
See Lesser, Milton

Tenneshaw, S. M. [house pseudonym]
See Nutt, Charles

Tenneshaw, S. M. [joint pseudonym
with Randall Garrett] [house
pseudonym, Ziff-Davis]
See Silverberg, Robert

Tenness, George
See Delk, Robert Carlton

Tennessee
See Johnson, Andrew

Tennessee Ernie Ford
See Ford, Ernest Jennings

Tennessee Gabriel
See McGhee, Walter Brown

[The] Tennessee Plowboy
See Arnold, Richard Edward [Eddy]

[The] Tennessee Tailor
See Johnson, Andrew

[The] Tennessee Terror
See Hickman, Herman M., Jr.

Tennille
See Tennille, Toni

Tennille, Frank
See Randall, Clark

Tennille, Toni 1943-
American singer
* Tennille

Tennis Ball Head
See Hovley, Stephen Eugene

[The] Tennis Ball of Fortune
See Pertinax, Publius Helvius

Tennis, Mr.
See Jones, Perry

[The] Tennis Tycoon
See King, Billie Jean Moffitt

Tenno, Kwammu
See Kwammu

Tennov, Dorothy
See Tennow, Dorothy

Tennow, Dorothy 1928- [CA]
American psychologist and author
* Hoffman, D. T.
* Tennov, Dorothy

Tennyson, Alfred [First Baron
Tennyson] 1809-1892 [DEL, DEP, FFF,
NPS]
British poet
* Alcibiades
* [The] Bard of Arthurian Romance
* [The] English Virgil
* Merlin
* [The] Poet of Haslemere
* Schoolmiss Alfred
* Two Brothers [joint pseudonym with
Charles Tennyson]

Tennyson, Charles 1808-1879? [HPPN,
NPS]
British poet
* Turner, Charles Tennyson
* Two Brothers [joint pseudonym with
Alfred Tennyson]

Tennyson, Harold Alfred 1918- [MY]
American jazz musician
* Tennyson, Tenny

Tennyson, Joe ?-1926 [BMH]
British comedian
* Devine

Tennyson, Tenny
See Tennyson, Harold Alfred

Tenocarus
See Snouckaert, William

[The] Tenor
See Ticker, Reuben

[The] Tenor of Kings
See Paoli, Antonio

Tenor of the House
See Ticker, Reuben

Tenpin Boy
See Smith, Frances Shubael

[The] Tenpin Tattler
See Weinstein, Sam

Tenque, Gerard 1040?-1120? [HPPN]
Founder of religious military order
* Gerard the Blessed

Tensas, Madison
See Lewis, Henry Clay

Tenskwatawa
See Lalawethika

Tent, Ned
See Dennett, Herbert Victor

[The] Tenth Muse
See Bradstreet, Anne

[The] Tenth Muse
See Christina

[The] Tenth Muse
See De Gournay, Marie Lejars

[The] Tenth Muse
See De La Cruz, Juana Ines

[The] Tenth Muse
See Deshoulieres, Antoinette du Ligier
de la Garde

[The] Tenth Muse
See Gay, Delphine

[The] Tenth Muse
See Margaret [or Marquerite] of
Navarre

[The] Tenth Muse
See More, Hannah

[The] Tenth Muse
See Sappho

[The] Tenth Muse
See Scuderi, Magdalen [or Madeleine]
de

[The] **Tenth Muse**
See Vestris, Eliza Lucy

Tenth President of the World Republic
See Blair, Andrew

[The] **Tentmaker**
See Omar Khayyam

Teodomofilo
See Cardenas y Rodriguez, Nicolas

Teodorescu, Ion N. 1880-1967 [EWL, TCL]
Rumanian poet and author
* Arghezi, Tudor

Teofilus
See Loennquist, Carl Adolph

Tepper, M. B.
See Tepper, Matthew Bruce

Tepper, Matthew Bruce 1953- [SFL]
American composer and writer
* Tepper, M. B.

Tepperman, Emile 20th c. [SFL, SFP]
Author
* Robeson, Kenneth [house pseudonym, Street & Smith]
* Steele, Curtis
* Stockbridge, Grant [house pseudonym]

Ter Balkt, Herman Hendrik 1938- [IAW]
Dutch author
* Aos, Foel
* De Balker, Habakuk, II

Terada, Torahiko 1878-? [LAO]
Japanese physicist and writer
* Yosimura, Huyukiko

Teramond, Edmond Gautier de 1869-1957 [SFL]
Author
* Teramond, Guy de

Teramond, Guy de
See Teramond, Edmond Gautier de

Terek, A.
See Fors, Olga Dmitrievna

Terence
See Terentius Afer, Publius

[The] **Terence of England**
See Cumberland, Richard

Terentius Afer, Publius 2nd c. BC [BI]
Roman playwright
* Terence

Teresa, [Mother]
See Bojaxhiu, Agnes Gonxha

Teresa
See Viera Romera, Teresa de Jesus

Teresa Benedicta of the Cross, [Sister]
See Stein, Edith

Teresa, Big Vinnie
See Teresa, Vincent

Teresa Margaret, [Sister]
See Rowe, Margaret [Kevin]

Teresa of Avila 1515-1582 [HPPN]
Saint
* Theresa de Jesus

Teresa, Vincent 20th c.
American underworld figure
* Teresa, Big Vinnie

Tereshkova, Valentina 1937- [HPPN]
Russian cosmonaut
* [The] First Woman Cosmonaut
* [The] First Woman in Space
* [The] Sweetheart of the Soviet Sky

Terez
See Azevedo, Pedro d'

Terhune, Mary Virginia [Hawes] 1831-1922 [DNNF, FFF, WBD]
American author
* Harland, Marion

Terhune, Virginia Belle
See Van De Water, Virginia Belle Terhune

Terkel, Louis 1912- [HPPN]
American interviewer, actor, author
* Terkel, Studs

Terkel, Studs
See Terkel, Louis

Terlecki, Robert Joseph 1945- [SMG]
American baseball player
* Terlecki, Terk

Terlecki, Terk
See Terlecki, Robert Joseph

Termagant
See Foe, Daniel

[The] **Termagant of Spain**
See Farnese, Elizabeth

Termagant, [Madame] Roxana
See Thornton, Bonnell

Terme, Hilary
See Hay, Jacob

Termen, Leon 1896- [BBD]
Russian inventor
* Theremin, Leon

Ternaux, Mademoiselle
See Noel, Victoire

Terni, Fausta Cialente 1900- [CA]
Italian author
* Cialente, Fausta

Tero, Lawrence 20th c.
American actor and bodyguard
* Mr. T.

Terpander 7th c. BC [DEP, DNNS, FFF]
Greek musician and poet
* [The] Father of Greek Music

Terpigorev, Sergiei Nikolaevich 1841-1895 [BI]
Russian author
* Atava, Sergiei

Terr, Michael
See Terr, Mischa R.

Terr, Mischa R. 1899- [HPPN]
Russian composer and conductor
* Terr, Michael

Terrae Filius
See Garnham, Robert Edward

Terrae Filius
See Mangan, James Clarence

Terrail, Pierre du 1476-1524 [DNNF, DNNS, SN]
French hero
* Bayard, Seigneur de
* [Le] Chevalier Sans Peur et Sans Reproche
* [The] Flower of Chivalry
* [The] Good Knight Without Fear and Without Reproach

Terrall, Robert 1914- [CA]
American author
* Gonzales, John
* Halliday, Brett
* Kyle, Robert
* Roberts, MacLennan

Terranova, Ciro 1891-1938 [BLB, PHM]
Italian-born American underworld figure
* [The] Artichoke King

Terranova, Dino
See Vacirca, Corrado

[The] **Terre Haute Terror**
See Taylor, Charles B.

Terrell, St. John
See Eccles, George Clinton, Jr.

Terrell, Saunders 1911-1986 [BWW]
American singer
* Sonny T
* Terry, Sanders
* Terry, Sonny

Terrell, Tammi
See Montgomery, Thomasina

Terremoto [Big Earthquake]
See Pertinez, Zoilo

Terremoto de Malaga [Earthquake from Malaga]
See Martin Ramos, Baldomero

Terrence, Frederick J.
See Hayes, John F.

[The] **Terrible**
See Ivan IV Vasilievich

[The] **Terrible**
See Touhy, Rog[er]

[The] **Terrible Cornet of Horse**
See Pitt, William [Earl of Chatham]

[The] **Terrible Doctor Elsbeth**
See Schragmueller, Elsbeth

Terrible Fred Wittrock
See Wittrock, Frederick

[The] **Terrible Siren**
See Woodhull, Victoria Claflin

Terrible Ted Lindsay
See Lindsay, Robert Blake Theodore [Ted]

Terrible Ted Turner
See Turner, Robert Edward, III

Terrible Ted Williams
See Williams, Theodore Samuel [Ted]

Terrible Teddy
See Roosevelt, Theodore [Teddy]

Terrible Teddy Tetzlaff
See Tetzlaff, Teddy

Terrible Terry Allen
See Allen, Terry De La Mesa

Terrible Terry McGovern
See McGovern, John Terrence

Terrible Tim Witherspoon
See Witherspoon, Tim

Terrible Tommy Bolt
See Bolt, Tommy

Terrible Tommy O'Connor
See O'Connor, Thomas

Terrible Tommy Touhy
See Touhy, Tommy

[The] Terrible Turk
See Reed, Thomas Brackett

Terridge, Ernest
See Richter, Ernst H.

Terrific, Tom
See Seaver, George Thomas [Tom]

Terris, Norma
See Allison, Norma

Terris, Sid 1904- [EJS]
American boxer
* [The] Ghost of the Ghetto

Terriss, Dorothy
See Morse, Theodora

Terriss, Ellaline
See Lewin, Ellaline

Terriss, Number 1 Adelphi
See Lewin, William Charles

Terriss, William
See Lewin, Arthur

Terriss, William
See Lewin, William Charles

[The] Terror
See Cline, Donald Biff

[The] Terror
See Johnson, Daniel

[The] Terror
See Turner, C. T. B.

[The] Terror of France
See John

[The] Terror of France
See Talbot, John

[The] Terror of Pacific Street
See Kelly, Maggie

[The] Terror of the Faithless
See Robert I

[The] Terror of the Faithless
See Robert II

[The] Terror of the Faithless
See Roger I

[The] Terror of the Greeks
See Michieli [or Micheli], Dominico

[The] Terror of the Gulf
See Lafitte, Jean

[The] Terror of the House
See Hardin, Benjamin

[The] Terror of the Infield
See Dakoske, Edwin P.

[The] Terror of the Spanish Main
See Drake, [Sir] Francis

[The] Terror of the Tories
See Clinch, Joseph

[The] Terror of the World
See Attila

[The] Terror of Wall Street
See Engel [or Engels], George

[The] Terror to Road Agents
See May, D. B.

[The] Terrorist of the Rich
See Theodoracopulos, Peter

Terrot, Charles Hughes 1790-? [HPPN]
British prelate
* [A] Presbyter of the Episcopal Church in Edinburgh

Terry
See Duncan, Terence Edward

Terry
See Maloney, Francis [Joseph] T[erence]

Terry, Adonis
See Terry, William J.

Terry, Al
See Theriot, Allison Joseph

Terry, Alice
See Taafe, Alice Frances

Terry, Alice
See Terry, Ellen Alicia

Terry, Bob 1936- [BA]
American radio program director
* Nighthawk

Terry, Buddy
See Terry, Eldin

Terry, C. V.
See Slaughter, Frank G[ill]

Terry, Carol
See Talbot, Carol Terry

Terry, Clarence Agee 20th c. [IBW]
American football player
* Terry, Terrible

Terry, Dan
See Kostraba, Daniel

Terry, [Judge] David Smith 1823-1889 [HPPN]
American jurist, politician, duel fighter
* [The] California Desperado
* [The] Dueling Judge
* [The] Gentleman Killer
* [The] Political Legal Bandit

Terry, Dennis 1895-1932 [HPPN, THR]
British actor, theatrical manager, producer
* Dennis, Derrick
* Neilson-Terry, Dennis

Terry, Doc
See Adail, Terry

Terry, Don
See Locher, Donald

Terry, Edward Gordon 1872-1966 [LC]
British producer, director, stage designer
* Craig, Gordon

Terry, Eldin 1941- [IBW]
American jazz musician
* Terry, Buddy

Terry, Ellen Alicia 1847-1928 [HPPN]
British actress
* Terry, Alice

Terry, Florence 1854-1896 [HPPN]
British actress
* Floss

Terry, Hazel
See Neilson-Terry, Hazel

Terry, Henry Machu
See Imbert-Terry, [Sir] Henry Machu

Terry, Memphis Bill
See Terry, William Harold

Terry, Noel
See Wood-Smith, Noel

Terry, Olive
See Morris, Olive

Terry, Phyllis 1892- [THR]
British actress
* Neilson-Terry, Phyllis

Terry, Ron
See Pritkin, Ron

Terry, Rose
See Cooke, Rose Terry

Terry, Sanders
See Terrell, Saunders

Terry, Sarah Ballard 1819-1892 [HPPN]
British actress
* Yerrit, Miss

Terry, Saralee
See Kaye, Marvin [Nathan]

Terry, Sheila
See Clark, Kay

Terry, Sonny
See Terrell, Saunders

Terry, Terrible
See Terry, Clarence Agee

Terry the Blue-Eyed Irish Boy
See Casey, James

Terry Thomas
See Hoar-Stevens, Thomas Terry

Terry, Victoria Lawrence 1874?-1951
[HPPN]
British theatrical performer
* Victoria, Vesta

Terry, William
See Harknett, Terry

Terry, William Harold 1898- [BE]
American baseball player and manager
* Terry, Memphis Bill

Terry, William J. 1864-1915 [AS, NLG, PB]
American baseball player
* [The] Silver Fox
* Terry, Adonis

Terry, Zeb
See Terry, Zebulon Alexander

Terry, Zebulon Alexander 1891- [BE]
American baseball player
* Terry, Zeb

Terry-Lewis, Mabel
See Lewis, Mabel

Terson, Peter
See Patterson, Peter

Terstegge, Mabel Alice 1905- [CA]
American author and educator
* Georgiana, [Sister]

Tertz, Abram
See Siniavskii, Andrei Donatovich

Terwagne, Anne Joseph 1762-1817
[DNNS, WBD]
Heroine of the French Revolution
* [The] Amazon of Liberty
* [The] Amazon of the Revolution
* [La] Belle Liegeoise
* [The] Fury of the Gironde
* Theroigne de Mericourt

Terwilliger, Twig
See Terwilliger, Willard Wayne

Terwilliger, Willard Wayne 1925- [BE]
American baseball player
* Terwilliger, Twig

Terzian, Kathryn
See Cramer, Kathryn

Tesch, Al[bert John] 1891-1947 [BE]
American baseball player
* Tesch, Tiny

Tesch, Tiny
See Tesch, Al[bert John]

Teshigahara, Sofu 1901?-
Japanese flower arranger
* [The] Picasso of Flowers

Teshome, Alem 1952?- [IBW]
Ethiopian actress and producer
* Teshome, Ali

Teshome, Ali
See Teshome, Alem

Tesich, Steve
See Tesich, Stoyan

Tesich, Stoyan 1943?- [CA]
*Yugoslavian-born playwright and
screenwriter*
* Tesich, Steve

Tesla, Nikola 1856-1943 [HPPN]
*Croatian-American physicist, inventor,
electrician*
* [The] Eccentric Genius
* [The] Father of the Tesla Turbine
* [The] Genius Who Ushered in the
  Power Age
* [The] Man Who Invented the 20th
  Century

Tesone, William N. 1927- [ASC]
American composer and singer
* Duke, Billy

Tesreau, Charles Monroe 1889-1946
[AS, BN, PB]
American baseball player
* [The] Ozark Bear
* Tesreau, Jeff

Tesreau, Jeff
See Tesreau, Charles Monroe

Tessier, Ernest Maurice 1885-1973 [CC,
LC]
French author
* Dekobra, Maurice

Tessimond, A. S. J.
See Tessimond, Arthur Seymour John

Tessimond, Arthur Seymour John ?-1962
[LC]
British poet
* Tessimond, A. S. J.

Testa, Chicken Man
See Testa, Philip

Testa, Philip 20th c. [WP 2-28-85]
American underworld figure
* Testa, Chicken Man

Testerman, Don 1952- [SMG]
American football player
* Testerman, Hi Test

Testerman, Hi Test
See Testerman, Don

Testis
See Blondel, Maurice

Testis?
See Francis, [Sir] Philip

Testudo, Totty
See Wylde, Flora Frances

Testy, Tim
See Spooner, Alden Jeremiah

Teswod
See Dowsett, Joseph Morewood

Tet Toe
See On, Pe

Tete Bottee
See Comines [or Commines], Philippe
de

Teternikov, Fyodor Kuzmich 1863-1927
[CD, EWL]
Russian poet and author
* Sologub, Fyodor

Tetley, Mrs. William [FFF]
Entertainer
* Cushman, Josephine

Tetsu
See Takeda, James Tetsuzo

Tetsu
See Yamauchi, Tetsu

Tettelbach, Richard Morley [Dick] 1929-
[BE]
American baseball player
* Tettelbach, Tut

Tettelbach, Tut
See Tettelbach, Richard Morley [Dick]

Tettemer, John Moynihan 1876-1949
[BI]
American monk
* Ildefonso, [Father]

Tetzel, John [or Johann] 1465?-1519
[PA, SN]
German monk
* [A] Holy Autolycus
* Texelius

Tetzlaff, Teddy 20th c.
Auto racer
* Tetzlaff, Terrible Teddy

Tetzlaff, Terrible Teddy
See Tetzlaff, Teddy

Tetzner, Martha Helene 1872-? [LAO]
German author
* Von Einsiedel, R.

Tetzner, Ruth 1917- [IAW]
German author
* Hallard, Ruth

Teufelsdroeckh, Herr
See Carlyle, Thomas

Teuffel, Blanche Willis Howard 1847-
1898
American author
* Howard, Blanche W.

Teutha
See Jerdau, William

[The] Teutonic James Dean
See Buchholz, Robert Werner

[The] Teutonic Theosopher
See Boehme, Jacob

[The] Tewibble
See Clarke, Norham Pfardt

Tewksbury
See Ray, William Porter

Tex, Joe
See Arrington, Joseph, Jr.

[The] Tex Rickard of His Day
See Price, Edmund Enoch

Texas Bill Simpson
See Simpson, William Hood

Texas Billy Mays
See Mays, Billy Wayne

Texas Billy Thompson
See Thompson, William

Texas Binnie Barnes
See Barnes, Gertrude Maude

[The] Texas Computer Millionaire
See Perot, H. Ross

[The] Texas Doll Lady
See Weaver, Gustine Courson

Texas Dolly Brunson
See Brunson, Doyle

[The] Texas Drifter
See Reeves, Goebel

Texas Guitar Slim
See Winter, Johnny

[The] Texas Hanging Judge
See Bean, Roy

Texas Jack
See Broadwell, Richard L.

Texas Jack
See Omohundro, John B.

Texas Jack
See Reed, Nathaniel

Texas Jack Kraus
See Kraus, John William

Texas Jim Robertson
See Robertson, James B.

Texas John Slaughter
See Slaughter, John Horton

Texas Johnny Moss
See Moss, John

[The] Texas Kid
See Knuckles, Grafton

Texas, Miss
See Dennison, Jo-Carroll

Texas, Mr.
See Mills, Wilbur Daigh

[The] Texas Nightingale
See Barnes, Fae

[The] Texas Nightingale
See Wallace, Beulah Thomas

[The] Texas Peeping Tom
See Floyd, Charles Arthur

Texas Ranger
See Wallace, John

[The] Texas Rattlesnake
See Barrow, Clyde

Texas Red Adair
See Adair, Paul Neal

Texas Ruby
See Owens, Ruby

Texas Slim
See Hooker, John Lee

[The] Texas Terror
See Shafer, Phil

Texas Tessie
See Douglas, Lizzie

[The] Texas Titan
See Ling, James Joseph

Texas Tom Connally
See Connally, Thomas Terry [Tom]

Texas Tommy
See Dorsey, Thomas A[ndrew]
[Tommy]

[The] Texas Tornado
See DeBakey, Michael

[The] Texas Tornado
See Dennison, Jo-Carroll

[The] Texas Tornado
See Foyt, Anthony Joseph, Jr.

[The] Texas Tornado
See Zaharias, Mildred Didrikson

[The] Texas Troubadour
See Tubb, Ernest Dale

[The] Texas Wonder
See Hoffman, Frank J.

Texas's Last President
See Jones, Anson

Texelius
See Tetzel, John [or Johann]

Texier, Edward   [PA]
Author
* Kel-Kun
* Schop, Le Baron

Texier, John 20th c.   [HPPN]
French body builder
* France, Mr.

Textor, George Bernhardt 1888-1954
[BE]
American baseball player
* Textor, Tex

Textor, Tex
See Textor, George Bernhardt

Textu
See Duprey de la Ruffiniere, Pierre

Tey, Josephine
See Mackintosh, Elizabeth

Teyte, Maggie
See Tate, Margaret

Th. C.
See Child, Theodore

Thacker, Moe
See Thacker, Morris Benton

Thacker, Morris Benton 1934-   [BE]
American baseball player
* Thacker, Moe

Thacker, Page
See Burwell, Lettie M.

Thackeray, William Makepeace
1811-1863   [DEL, DLE1, HPPN, SAT,
WBD]
British author
* Benighted Irishman
* Brown, Mr.
* Byles, Growley
* Canterbury, Folkstone
* Clarence, Fitzroy
* Corks, John
* Espartero, Boldomero [or Baldomero]
* [The] F. C.
* [The] Fat Contributor
* Fitzboodle, George
* Fitzboodle, George Savage
* [A] Gentleman in Search of a Man-
Servant
* Gobemouche, M.
* Historical Painter
* [The] Honorable Wilhelmina Amelia
Skeggs
* Hugglestone, Leontius Androcles
* Jeames
* Jeames, Mr.
* [A] Lady of Fashion
* Melville, Lewis
* Merit, Modest
* Molony, [Master] Molloy
* Muff, Goliah
* Mulligan of Killballymulligan
* Ninrod, Lady
* O'Gahagan, [Major] Goliah
* [An] Old Paris Man
* One of Themselves
* Pacifico, [Dr.] Solomon
* Pendennis, Arthur, Esquire
* Perseus, Peter
* Pluche, Jeames de la
* Punch's Commissioner
* Ramsbottom, Dorothea Julia
* Rollicker, Harry
* Simcoe, Adolphus
* Solomons, Ikey, Jun.
* Spec, Alonzo
* Spec, Mr.
* Swellmore
* T. T.
* Tickletoby, Miss
* Titmarsh, M. A.
* Titmarsh, Michael Angelo
* Under Petty
* Wagstaff, Lancelot
* Wagstaff, Theophile
* Yellowplush, Charles, Esq.
* Yellowplush, Charles James

Thakazhi
See Sivasankara Pillai, Thakazhi

Thakura, Ravindranatha 1861-1941
[DLE1, EWL]
Indian poet, playwright, author
* [The] Bengal Shelley
* Tagore, Rabindranath

Thalberg, Irving Grant 1899-1936
[HPPN]
American producer
* [The] Boy Producer

Thalberg, Sigismund 1812-1871   [FFF]
Swiss-born musician and composer
* [The] Attila of the Piano

Thalberg, T. B.
See Corbett, Thalberg

Thaler, M. N.
See Kerner, Fred

Thaler, Susan 1939- [CA]
American author
* Schlachter, Susan

Thalestris
See Anne

Thames, C[hristopher] H.
See Lesser, Milton

Thames, Eve
See Thames, Uvena

Thames, Jack
See Ryan, John Fergus

Thames, [Sir] Timothy
See Khaury, Herbert Buckingham

Thames, Uvena 1944- [BA]
American educator
* Thames, Eve

Than, John A.
See Lynch, John A.

Thane, Elswyth
See Beebe, Elswyth Thane Ricker

Thane, Francois
See Hennesy, James Albert

Thanelian
See Coffin, Nathaniel W.

Thanet, Neil
See Fanthorpe, R[obert] Lionel

Thanet, Octave
See French, Alice

[The] Thanhouser Kid
See Eline, Marie

[The] Thanhouser Kidlet
See Badgley, Helen

Thanie, C. G.   [FFF]
American writer
* Clyde, Kate

Thanold, Woofer
See Sidebottom, Arnold [Arnie]

Tharaud, Lucien Rostaing, Jr. 1953-
[CA]
American poet
* Tharaud, Ross

Tharaud, Ross
See Tharaud, Lucien Rostaing, Jr.

Tharp, Corky
See Tharp, Tom

Tharp, Tom 20th c. [SMG]
American football player
* Tharp, Corky

Tharpe, [Sister] Rosetta
See Nubin, Rosetta

That Ad Glibber
See Allen, Stephen Valentine [Steve]

That Atheist Tamburian
See Marlowe, Christopher

That Bad Eartha
See Kitt, Eartha Mae

That Bright Luminary
See Darwin, Erasmus

That Candid Spoilsman
See Farley, James Aloysius

That Deep-Mouthed Boeotian
See Landor, Walter Savage

That Deep-Mouthed Theban
See Greathead, Bertie

That Drunken Fool
See Shakespeare, William

That Fox
See Antipas

That God of Clay
See Bonaparte, Napoleon

That Golden Rule Fellow
See Steffens, [Joseph] Lincoln

That Grand Old Man of Empire
See Smith, Donald Alexander [First
Baron Strathcona and Mount Royal]

That Great Lucifer
See Raleigh, [Sir] Walter

That High Towering Falcon
See Fitzgeoffrey, Charles

That Jesuit
See Penn, William

That Limping Old Bard
See Denham, [Sir] John

That Little Jap
See Inouye, Daniel Ken [Danny]

That Man in the White House
See Roosevelt, Franklin Delano

That Martial Macaroni
See Burgoyne, John

That Metromaniac Prince
See Frederick II

That Miserable Imp
See Mathias, Thomas James

That Modern Midas
See Lofft, Capel

That Nimble Mercury
See Shakespeare, William

That Nonpareil of Generals
See Mack von Leiberich, Karl

That Ohio Schoolteacher
See Alston, Walter Emmons

That Old Sentimentalist
See Held, John, Jr.

That Pellean Conqueror
See Alexander III

That Piperly Poet of Green Erin
See Moore, Thomas

That Rascal Freneau
See Freneau, Philip Morin

That Religious Machiavel
See Knox, John

**That Singular Splendor of the Italian
Race**
See Alighieri, Durante

That Taylor Woman
See Taylor, Elizabeth Jones

That True Deacon of the Craft
See Pope, Alexander

That Weather Cock
See Pulteney, William [Earl of Bath]

Thatch
See Teach, Edward

Thatcher, Amelia
See Miner, Virginia Scott

Thatcher, Eva
See Thatcher, Evelyn

Thatcher, Evelyn 1862-1942 [SC]
American actress
* [The] Irish Lady
* Thatcher, Eva

Thatcher, John Wells 1856-? [LAO]
British barrister and author
* Pauper et Ignotus
* Rambler

Thatcher, Julia
See Bensen, Donald R.

Thatcher, Margaret Hilda [Roberts]
1925- [HPPN, NN, SC, TI 6-20-83]
British prime minister
* Attila the Hen
* Britain's Iron Lady
* [The] Cold War Witch
* [The] Female Churchill
* [The] Grocer's Daughter
* [The] Iron Butterfly
* [The] Iron Lady
* [The] Iron Lady of British Politics
* [The] Iron Maiden
* [The] Milk Snatcher
* Mrs. T
* [The] No Nonsense Lady
* [The] Outspoken Prime Minister
* Thatcher, Mighty Maggie
* TINA [There is No Alternative]

Thatcher, Mighty Maggie
See Thatcher, Margaret Hilda [Roberts]

Thatcher, Moses 1842-1909 [HPPN]
American frontiersman
* Little Chief

Thatcher, Oxenbridge 1720-1765
[HPPN]
American author
* [A] British American

[The] Thaumaturge
See Dumond, Normand

Thaumaturgus
See Agatho

Thaumaturgus
See Alexander Leopold

Thaumaturgus
See Apollonius of Tyana

Thaumaturgus
See Bernardone, Giovanni Francesco

Thaumaturgus
See Gassner, Johann Joseph

Thaumaturgus
See Gregory of Neocaesarea

Thaumaturgus
See Isidore of Alexandria

Thaumaturgus
See Jamblichus

Thaumaturgus
See Mohammed [or Mahomet]

Thaumaturgus
See Pascal, Blaise

Thaumaturgus
See Peter

Thaumaturgus
See Plotinus

Thaumaturgus
See Proclus

Thaumaturgus
See Vincent de Paul

[The] Thaumaturgus of His Age
See De Bulhoes, Fernando

[The] Thaumaturgus of the Nineteenth Century
See Filumena

[The] Thaumaturgus of the West
See Bernard of Clairvaux

Thaw, Evelyn Nesbit 1885-1967 [HPPN, SC]
American actress
* [The] Girl in the Red Velvet Swing
* [The] Girl in the Swing
* Nesbit, Evelyn

Thaw, Harry Kendall 1871-1947 [HPPN]
American playboy and murderer
* [The] Mad Pittsburgh Playboy

Thayendanegea 1742-1807 [WBD]
American Indian chieftain
* Brant, Joseph

Thayer, Abbott H. 1849-1921 [HPPN]
American artist
* [The] Father of Thayer's Law

Thayer, Alexander Wheelock 1817-1897 [FFF]
American author and diplomat
* Diarist
* [A] Quiet Man

Thayer, Bob
See Holman, Joseph

Thayer, Charles [SMG]
Hockey team trainer
* Thayer, Skip

Thayer, Christopher Toppan ?-1880 [HPPN]
American clergyman
* C. T. T.

Thayer, Emma R[edington] Lee 1874-1973 [CAP, EMD, NAA]
American author and artist
* Thayer, Lee

Thayer, Ernest Lawrence 1863-1940
American author
* Phin

Thayer, Frederick C[lifton], Jr. 1924- [CA]
American author
* Walker, Jack

Thayer, Geraldine
See Daniels, Dorothy

Thayer, Jane
See Woolley, Catherine

Thayer, John 1758-1815 [HPPN]
American clergyman and missionary
* Turncoat, John

Thayer, Lee
See Thayer, Emma R[edington] Lee

Thayer, Mary Van Rensselear 1903-1983 [WP 12-14-83]
American columnist and author
* Flutterby, Madame
* Thayer, Molly

Thayer, Molly
See Thayer, Mary Van Rensselear

Thayer, Peter
See Ames, Rose Wyler

Thayer, Simeon 1737-1800 [HPPN]
American army officer
* [The] Hero of Fort Mifflin

Thayer, Skip
See Thayer, Charles

Thayer, Sylvanus 1785-1872 [HPPN, WBD]
American army officer and educator
* [The] Father of Military Education
* [The] Father of Technology in the United States
* [The] Father of the Military Academy
* [The] Father of the United States Military Academy
* [The] Father of West Point
* [The] Founder of West Point

Thayer, Tiffany Ellsworth 1902- [TC, WW]
American author
* Doe, John
* Ellsworth, Elmer, Jr.

Thayer, William Roscoe 1859-1923 [FFF]
American author
* Hermes, Paul

Thayson, Ernest 1878-1933 [HPPN]
Scottish-American actor
* Torrence, Ernest

Thearcher
See Hodgson, William Archer

Theard, Harry L., Jr. 1939- [OP]
American opera singer
* Theyard, Harry

Theard, Sam 20th c. [IBW]
American songwriter, dancer, comedian
* Spo-Dee-O-Dee

Theates
See Weintraub, Wiktor

[A] Theatrical Amateur
See Winston, James

[The] Theatrical King
See Murat, Joachim

[The] Theban Bard
See Pindar

[The] Theban Eagle
See Pindar

[The] Theban Garden Swan
See Pindar

[The] Theban Lyre
See Pindar

Thede, Marion Draughon 1903- [CAP]
American archivist and author
* Unger, Marion

Thee, Marek 1918- [CA]
Polish-born author
* Gdanski, Marek

Theimer, Joseph Michael 1923-1955 [EJ]
American jazz musician
* Timer, Joe

Theiner, George 1927- [CA]
Czech-born author
* George, Jonathan [joint pseudonym with John (Frederick) Burke]

Their Late Pastor
See Clark, [Rev.] Nelson

Their Latest Victim
See Habberton, John

Their Reverend Pastor
See Eells, [Rev.] Nathaniel

Their Vicar
See Edouart, [Rev.] Augustin Gaspard

Their Wellwisher
See Ide, Simeon

Theismann, Cheryl Brown 1948- [WP 1-28-85]
Wife of American football player, Joe Theismann
* Theismann, Shari

Theismann, Jawin' Joe
See Theismann, Joseph

Theismann, Joseph 1949-   [WP 1-28-85]
American football player
* Sparkle
* Theismann, Jawin' Joe

Theismann, Shari
See Theismann, Cheryl Brown

Thekla
See Mason, Caroline Atherton [Briggs]

Thelwall, Citizen
See Thelwall, John

Thelwall, John 1764-1834   [NPS, SN]
British author and political reformer
* Thelwall, Citizen
* Theophrastus, Sylvanus

Themaninthemoon
See Eagles, John

[The] Themistocles of Modern Greece
See Kanaris, Constantine

Thenon, Georges ?-1941   [BEW]
French author
* Thenon, Rip

Thenon, Rip
See Thenon, Georges

Theo Philo
See Foe, Daniel

Theo the Swami
See Salomen, Edith

Theobald
See Lovecraft, Howard Phillips

Theobald, Alfred Herbert
See Tubby, Alfred Herbert

Theobald, Lewis 1688-1744   [HPPN, NPS, SN]
British author, editor, playwright
* [The] King of Dunces
* Margites [The Booby]
* Tibbald, King
* Tibbald, Pedling

Theobald, Lewis, Jr.
See Lovecraft, Howard Phillips

Theobald, Ron[ald M.] 1943-   [PB]
American baseball player
* [The] Little General

Theobald [or Tybald], Simon ?-1381   [WBD]
British prelate
* Simon of Sudbury

Theobaldus
See Lovecraft, Howard Phillips

Theoc
See Child, Thomas Edward Theodore

Theocritus 3rd c. BC   [NPS]
Greek poet
* [The] Allan Ramsay of Sicily
* [The] Father of Pastoral Poetry

Theodamus
See Glass, Theodore

Theodoracopulos, Peter 1939?-   [PW 12-9-83, TI 8-20-84]
Society columnist
* Taki
* [The] Terrorist of the Rich

Theodorakis, Michalis 1925-   [CA]
Greek composer and musician
* Theodorakis, Mikis

Theodorakis, Mikis
See Theodorakis, Michalis

Theodore
See Kasa [or Kassa]

Theodore, Adah Bertha 1835?-1868   [FFF]
American actress
* Menken, Adah Isaacs
* [The] Queen of the Plaza

Theodore, Charles
See Reuss, Theodor

Theodore, King of Corsica
See Van Neuhoff, Baron

Theodore, Mademoiselle
See Crespe, Marie Madeleine

Theodore the Meddler
See Roosevelt, Theodore [Teddy]

Theodore I 1175-1222   [HPPN]
Emperor of Eastern Roman Empire
* Lascaris

Theodore II 1221-1258   [HPPN]
Emperor of Eastern Roman Empire
* Ducas
* Lascaris

Theodore II 1818-1868   [HPPN]
King of Abyssinia
* Negus

Theodoric 454-526   [DNNS, FFF, HPPN, WBD]
King of the Ostrogoths
* Dietrich von Bern [Theodoric of Verona]
* [The] Great
* Patricius and Magister Militum

Theodoros
See Papadimitriou, Theodoros

Theodorus
See Aristides [or Aristeides], Publius Aelius

Theodorus Philalethes
See Maule, Thomas

Theodosia
See Steele, Anne

Theodosius I 346-395   [DNNS, FFF, SN]
Roman emperor
* [The] Great

Theodosius II 401-450   [DNNS]
Byzantine emperor
* [The] Calligrapher

[The] Theologian
See Gregory of Nazianzus

[The] Theologian
See Isidore of Seville

[The] Theologian
See Treadwell, Daniel

Theologicus, Doctor
See Clemenges, Matthieu Nicholas de

Theologus
See Gregory of Nazianzus

Theone
See Artner, Marie Therese

Theophanes 758?-818   [WBD]
Saint
* [The] Confessor

Theophile
See Mandar, Michael Phillips

Theophile
See Viau, Theophile de

Theophile, Abbe
See Moreux, Theophile

Theophilus
See Duigenan, Patrick

Theophilus
See Pashkovsky, Theodore

Theophilus
See Spring, Samuel

Theophilus Secundus
See Wilberforce, Robert Isaac

Theophorus
See Ignatius

Theophrastos
See Tyrtamos

Theophrastus
See Creech, William

[The] Theophrastus of France
See La Bruyere, Jean de

Theophrastus, Sylvanus
See Thelwall, John

Theophylactus ?-1024   [CAL]
Pope
* Benedict VIII

Theophylactus 11th c.   [CAL]
Pope
* Benedict IX

Theoria
See Starkey, Digbey Pilot

Theos [The Divine]
See Antiochus II

Theos
See Antiochus VI

Theosopho
See Ouseley, Gideon Jasper Richard

Theotine
See Bayle, Marc Antoine

Theotokopoulos, Domenikos 1548?-1614?
[WBD]
Greek-born Spanish painter
* [El] Greco

Theremin, Leon
See Termen, Leon

Theresa de Jesus
See Teresa of Avila

Therese de Lisieux
See Martin, Therese

Therese Emmanuel, [Mother]
See O'Neill, Catherine

Therion, Master
See Crowley, Edward Alexander

Theriot, Allison Joseph 1922- [CWG]
American country-western performer
* Terry, Al

Theroigne de Mericourt
See Terwagne, Anne Joseph

Theron, Hilary
See Amos, Winsom

[The] Thersites of American Dramatic Critics
See Nathan, George Jean

Thesenga, Arnold Joseph 1914- [BE]
American baseball player
* Thesenga, Jug

Thesenga, Jug
See Thesenga, Arnold Joseph

Thespis 6th c. BC [FFF, RH, SN]
Greek poet
* [The] Father of Greek Tragedy
* [The] Father of the Greek Drama
* [The] Richardson of Athens

Theta
See Hughes, Terence McMahon

Theta
See Thorne, William

Theuerdank [Dear Thanks]
See Maximilian I

Thevenet, Claudine 1774-1837 [BI]
French nun
* Marie St. Ignatius, [Mother]

Thevenin, Denis
See Duhamel, Georges

Theyard, Harry
See Theard, Harry L., Jr.

T'Hezan, Arlette C. 1934- [OP]
French opera singer
* T'Hezan, Helia

T'Hezan, Helia
See T'Hezan, Arlette C.

Thiard, Pontus de 1521-1605 [DNNS, FFF, SN]
French poet
* [The] Anacreon of France
* [The] French Anacreon

Thibaud IV 922-978
Count of Blois
* [The] Impostor

Thibault, Jacques-Anatole-Francois 1844-1924 [EWL, IPA, LC]
French author, poet, critic
* France, Anatole

Thibault, Maralee G. 1924- [HPPN]
American broadcaster, journalist, author
* Davis, Maralee G.

Thibault, Pierre
See Felut, Maurice

Thibaut IV 1201-1253 [HN, SN]
Count of Champagne and King of Navarre
* [The] Father of French Poetry

Thibeaux, Acklin 1941- [IBW]
American sociologist
* Thibeaux, T-Bone

Thibeaux, T-Bone
See Thibeaux, Acklin

Thibodeaux, Keith 1950- [HPPN]
American actor
* Keith, Ricky

Thieblin, Napoleon [or Nicolas?] Leon ?-1888 [FFF, PA, RH]
British journalist and author
* Azamat Batuk
* Rigolo

[The] Thief
See Capuzzi, Nick

[The] Thief of Bad Gags
See Berlinger, Milton

Thiel, Max 1878?-1953 [BI]
American magician
* Maxino the Great

Thiele, Wilhelm 1890- [FD]
Austrian director
* Thiele, William

Thiele, William
See Thiele, Wilhelm

Thielemans, Jean 1922- [EJ, HPPN, PMJ]
Belgian-born jazz musician
* Thielemans, Jon
* Thielemans, Toots

Thielemans, Jon
See Thielemans, Jean

Thielemans, Toots
See Thielemans, Jean

Thielhelm, Emil 1950- [RO2]
American musician
* Thielhelm, Peppy

Thielhelm, Peppy
See Thielhelm, Emil

Thielman, Jack
See Thielman, John Peter

Thielman, John Peter 1879-1928 [BE]
American baseball player
* Thielman, Jack

[Der] Thier Wolff
See Wolff, Wilhelm

Thierna, Cairn
See O'Conor, Charles Patrick

Thiers, Louis Adolphe 1797-1877 [HN, HPPN]
French historian
* Attila le Petit
* Boum, General
* Cameleon
* Liberator of the Territory
* [Le] Roi des Versailles
* Tamerlan a Lunettes

Thiery, Herman 1912- [EWL]
Belgian poet, author, critic
* Daisne, Johan

Thies, Jake
See Thies, Vernon Arthur

Thies, Vernon Arthur 1926- [BE]
American baseball player
* Thies, Jake

Thijm, Karel J. L. Alberdingk 1864-? [HPPN]
Dutch author
* Van Deyssel, Lodewijk

Thimblethorpe, Ilena 1916- [THR]
British actress
* Sylva, Ilena

Thimblethorpe, June Sylvia 1926- [AW]
British author
* Thorpe, Sylvia

Thimmesch, Nicholas Palen [Nick] 1927- [CA, IAW]
American author
* Nicholas, William [joint pseudonym with William O. Johnson]

Thimonnier, Barthelemy 1793-1859 [HPPN]
French tailor and inventor
* [The] Father of the French Sewing Machine

[The] Thin Man
See Layden, Elmer

[The] Thin Man
See Strahler, Michael Wayne

Thin Man Watts
See Watts, Noble

[The] Thing
See Thomas, Lafayette Jerl

[The] Thinker
See Goethe, Johann Wolfgang von

Thinker, Theodore
See Woodworth, Francis Channing

[The] Thinking Man's Baritone
See Fischer, Albert Dietrich

[The] Thinking Man's Quarterback
See Griese, Robert Allen [Bob]

[The] Thinking Silent General
See Monk, George [Duke of Albemarle]

Thinks-I-To-Myself, Who?
See Nares, Edward

Thiong'o, Ngugi wa
See Ngugi, James T[hiong'o]

[The] Third
See Strauss, Johann

[The] Third Elias
See Luther, Martin

[The] Third Founder of Rome
See Marius, Caius

[The] Third Man of the Reformation
See Zwingli, Ulrich [or Huldreich]

[The] Third Romulus
See Marius, Caius

Third Round Diegel
See Diegel, Leo

Thirlmere, Rowland
See Walker, John

Thirlwell, George 1902-   [BEW]
British actor
* Turner, George

[The] Thirteen Inch Shell
See Bezdek, Hugo Frank

[The] Thirteenth Apostle
See John

31 Knot Burke
See Burke, Arleigh

This Bladder of Pride New-Blowne
See Harvey, Gabriel

This Execrable Erostratus
See Weston, Joseph

This Free Lance of Our Literature
See Nash [or Nashe?], Thomas

This Impious Buffoon
See Swift, Jonathan

This Mud Born Bubble
See Harvey, Gabriel

This Phoenix
See Hastings, Lord

This Phoenix Among Kings
See Frederick II

This Poetical Charlatan
See Wordsworth, William

This Political Parasite
See Wordsworth, William

This Ropemaker
See Harvey, Gabriel

This Trifler in Great Things
See Walpole, Horatio [Fourth Earl of Orford]

This Vain Braggadocio
See Harvey, Gabriel

Thisby [joint pseudonym with Dona M. Turner]
See Genovese, Vince

Thisby [joint pseudonym with Vince Genovese]
See Turner, Dona M.

Thisted, V[aldemar] Adolph 1815-1887 [SFL, WGT]
Author
* L. W. J. S.
* Rowel, M.

Thistle
See Middlemass, Hume

Thistle, Donald
See Brown, H. Clark

Thistle, Mel[ville William] 1914-   [CA]
Canadian author
* Bohr, Theophilus

Thistle, Timothy
See Ellsworth, O.

Thistleton, [The Hon.] Francis
See Fleet, William Henry

Thiusen, Ismar
See Macnie, John

Thody, Philip Malcolm Waller 1928- [IAW]
British author
* French, Don
* Graveyard, Aloysius

Thoelde, Johannes 17th c.   [HPPN]
German alchemist
* Valentinus, Basilius

Thoene, Peter
See Bihalji-Merin, Oto

Thoeny, John 1880-1948   [BE]
American baseball player
* Thoney, Bullet Jack
* Thoney, John

Thole, Carolus Adrianus Maria 1914- [ESF]
Dutch-born illustrator
* Thole, Karel

Thole, Karel
See Thole, Carolus Adrianus Maria

Thom, John Nichols 1796?-1838   [HPPN]
British eccentric
* Courtenay, [Sir] William

Thom, Robert
See Flatow, Robert

Thom, William 1799-1850   [DNNS, RH]
Scottish poet
* [The] Weaver Poet of Inverurie

Thoma, Frank 1896-   [BBH]
American bowler
* Thoma, Sykes

Thoma, Ludwig 1867-1921   [WBD]
German journalist and author
* Schlemihl, Peter

Thoma, Sykes
See Thoma, Frank

Thoman, Egbert S.
See Ellis, Edward S[ylvester]

Thomas 19th c.   [DHA]
Duke of Genoa
* Salchichon [The Sausage]

Thomas, [Brother]
See McGinty, Bonaventure Thomas

Thomas, [Brother]
See Rynne, Patrick

Thomas, Alf 20th c.   [BMH]
British comedian
* Mrs. Thomas's Favourite Husband

Thomas, Alfred 1870-?   [LAO]
Welsh clergyman and author
* Gwalia, Alfred

Thomas, Alfred 1911-1950 [HPPN]
American press agent
* Alfred, Tom

Thomas, Allison
See Fleischer, Leonore

Thomas, Alonzo 20th c.   [SMG]
American football player
* Thomas, Skip

Thomas, Alphonse 1899-   [BE, PB]
American baseball player
* Thomas, Tommy

Thomas, Alvin Clarence 1892?-   [HPPN]
American gambler
* [The] Derby Kid
* Thomas, Slim
* Thompson, Titanic

Thomas, Amos Leon, Jr. 1937-   [EJ7]
American jazz musician
* Thomas, Leone

Thomas, Andrea
See Hill, Margaret [Ohler]

Thomas, Ann 19th c.   [HFN]
Author
* Ann

Thomas, Annie
See Cudlip, Annie Thomas

Thomas, Anthony
See Poole, Reginald Heber

Thomas, Arthur 20th c.   [HPPN]
American wrestler
* Thomas, Sailor Art

Thomas, Augustus 1857-1934 [MWD]
American playwright
* [The] Dean of American Playwrights

Thomas, B.
See Johnson, Thomas Burgeland

Thomas, B. J.
See Thomas, Billy Joe

Thomas, Baby Face
See Thomas, Jesse

Thomas, Billy ?-1968   [HPPN]
American actor
* Buckwheat

Thomas, Billy Joe 1942- [PRS, RO2]
American singer
* Thomas, B. J.

Thomas, Blanche 1922-1977 [BWW]
American singer
* [The] Queen of the Blues

Thomas, Boosey [PA]
Author
* [An] Old Angler and Bibliopole

Thomas, Bud
See Thomas, John Tillman

Thomas, Bud
See Thomas, Luther Baxter

Thomas, Cairo
See Thomas, James

Thomas, Carl H.
See Doerffler, Alfred

Thomas, Carla 1942- [BWW, IBW, SSS]
American singer
* [The] Queen of the Memphis Sound

Thomas, Caroline
See Dorr, Julia Caroline Ripley

Thomas, Carolyn
See Duncan, Actea

Thomas, Charles 1900?- [NOJ]
American jazz musician
* Ollie Papa

Thomas, Charles 1918- [BB]
American basketball player
* Thomas, Red

Thomas, Charles 1925- [BWW]
American singer
* Davis, James [Jimmy]
* Maxwell Street Jimmy

Thomas, Chester David 1888-1953 [BE]
American baseball player
* Thomas, Pinch

Thomas, Clarence Franklin 1903-1952
[BE]
American baseball player
* Thomas, Lefty

Thomas, Claude Alfred 1890-1946 [BE]
American baseball player
* Thomas, Lefty

Thomas, Cornelius Dickinson 1920-1972
[CAP]
American author
* T. N. T.
* Thomas, Neal

Thomas, Cotton
See Jaxon, Frankie

Thomas, Craig 1942- [CA]
British author and educator
* Grant, David

Thomas, Curtis 20th c. [WW]
Author
* Kinney, Thomas

Thomas, Dan
See Sanders, Leonard

Thomas, Daniel B.
See Bluestein, Daniel Thomas

Thomas, Danny
See Jacobs, Amos

Thomas, David 1794-1882 [HPPN]
British-American iron master
* [The] Father of the American
   Anthracite Iron Industry

Thomas, David 1904- [MK]
American baseball player
* Thomas, Showboat

Thomas, David John 1959- [DC]
British cricketer
* Thomas, Teddy

Thomas, Dennis 20th c. [RO2]
American musician
* Dee Tee

Thomas, Derek
See Bogdanovich, Peter

Thomas, Doris
See Vancel, Doris

[The] Thomas Edison of Antiquity
See Archimedes

Thomas, [Philip] Edward 1878-1917
[LC]
British author
* Eastaway, Edward

Thomas, Edward 1941- [ECM]
American country-western performer
* Rabbitt, Eddie

Thomas, Elizabeth 1675-1730 [SN]
British author and poet
* Corinna

Thomas, Elizabeth 19th c. [WGT]
British author
* Bluemantle, [Mrs.] Bridget

Thomas, [John William] Elmer 1876-?
[HPPN]
American attorney and politician
* [The] Silver Sage

Thomas, Elton
See Ulman, Douglas Elton

Thomas, Ernest Lewis 1904- [DLE]
Welsh author
* Vaughn, Richard

Thomas, Eugene 1894- [WW]
Author
* Grey, Donald

Thomas, Fannie Crawford 1923- [IBW]
American singer and musician
* Thomas, Frantic Fay

Thomas, Fathead
See Thomas, George

Thomas, Fay Wesley 1904- [BE]
American baseball player
* Thomas, Scow

Thomas, Foots
See Thomas, Walter Purl

Thomas, Forrest 1881-? [BE]
American baseball player
* Thomas, Frosty

Thomas, Frank William 1898- [HPPN]
American football coach
* Thomas, Rat

Thomas, Frantic Fay
See Thomas, Fannie Crawford

Thomas, Frederick Hall 1886-1927 [BX,
RBE, WBC]
Welsh-born boxer
* [The] Pride of Pontypridd
* Welsh, Freddy
* [The] Welsh Wizard

Thomas, Frosty
See Thomas, Forrest

Thomas, G. K.
See Davies, Leslie Purnell

Thomas, Gary 20th c. [RBE]
American boxer
* Thomas, Tiger

Thomas, Gary Philip 1958- [DC]
British cricketer
* Thomas, Tight Lines

Thomas, George ?-1930 [WWJ]
American jazz musician
* Thomas, Fathead

Thomas, George Francis 19th c.
[HPPN]
American author
* Francis, George

Thomas, George Henry 1816-1870
[DNNS, FFF, HPPN, SN]
American army officer
* Old Pap Safety
* Old Reliable
* Old Slow Trot
* [The] Rock of Chickamauga
* Slow Trot
* Thomas, Lion Hearted
* Thomas, Pap
* Thomas, Uncle George
* Washington, George

Thomas, Gordon 1933- [CA, HPPN]
British author and editor
* Gordon, Tom
* James, Brian
* Street, Robert

Thomas, H. C.
See Keating, Lawrence A.

Thomas, Harlan C.
See Hale, William Harlan

Thomas, Harold Alexander 1941- [IBW]
American artist
* Olugebefola, Ademola?

Thomas, Heck
See Thomas, Henry Andrew

Thomas, Henry 1874-? [BWW]
American singer
* Thomas, Ragtime Texas

Thomas, Henry
See Johnson, Leslie

Thomas, Henry
See Schnittkind, Henry Thomas

Thomas, Henry
See Townsend, Henry

Thomas, Henry Andrew 1850-1912
[EWG]
American law officer
* Thomas, Heck

Thomas, Impeachment
See Thomas, John Parnell

Thomas, Isaiah 1750-1831 [HPPN, SN]
American printer
* [The] Baskerville of America
* [The] Didot of America

Thomas, Ivor
See Bulmer-Thomas, Ivor

Thomas, J. Bissell
See Stephen, Joyce Alice

Thomas, J. F.
See Fleming, Thomas J[ames]

Thomas, Jack 20th c. [SFL]
Author
* Oram, John

Thomas, James 1834-1882 [BI]
British author
* B. V.

Thomas, James 1926- [BWW]
American singer
* Thomas, Cairo
* Thomas, Son
* Thomas, Sonny Ford

Thomas, James, Jr. 1951- [EF, FR]
American football player
* J. T.

Thomas, James Leroy 1936- [BE]
American baseball player
* Thomas, Lee

Thomas, Jeannette Bell 1881-? [HPPN]
American folklorist
* [The] Traipsin' Woman

Thomas, Jeannette Grise 1935- [CA]
American author
* Grise, Jeannette

[The] Thomas Jefferson of Folk Music
See Seeger, Pete[r R.]

Thomas, Jesse 20th c. [BWW]
American musician
* Thomas, Baby Face

Thomas, Jim
See Reagan, Thomas [James] B[utler]

Thomas, Joan Gale
See Robinson, Joan [Mary] G[ale
Thomas]

Thomas, Joe 1902- [NOJ]
American jazz musician
* Brother Cornbread

Thomas, Joe
See Daly, Joseph

Thomas, John Daniel 1853-1930 [DNA]
Author and educator
* Crane, Ichabod

Thomas, John Parnell 1895- [HPPN]
American politician
* Thomas, Impeachment

Thomas, John Peter 1928- [CA, HPPN]
American author
* [The] Organizer of the New Breed
* Thomas, Piri

Thomas, John Richard 1881-1955
[HPPN]
American actor
* Thomas, Victor

Thomas, John Tillman 1929- [BE]
American baseball player
* Thomas, Bud

Thomas, [Rev.] John Wesley ?-1872
[HPPN]
British clergyman
* Anti Empiricus

Thomas, Josephine
See Henderson, Rosa [Rose]

Thomas, Joshua [FFF]
American clergyman
* [The] Parson of the Islands

Thomas, Julian 19th c. [HPPN]
British author
* [The] Vagabond

Thomas, K.
See Fearn, John Russell

Thomas, K. H.
See Kirk, Thomas Hobson

Thomas, Keith Marshall 1924- [BE]
American baseball player
* Thomas, Kite

Thomas, Kid
See Valentine, Thomas

Thomas, Kid
See Watts, Lou[is Thomas]

Thomas, Kite
See Thomas, Keith Marshall

Thomas, Lafayette Jerl 1928-1977
[BWW]
American singer
* [The] Thing

Thomas, Lawrence Buckley [PA]
Author
* L. B. T.

Thomas, Lee
See Floren, Lee

Thomas, Lee
See Thomas, James Leroy

Thomas, Lefty
See Thomas, Clarence Franklin

Thomas, Lefty
See Thomas, Claude Alfred

Thomas, Leo Raymond 1924- [BE]
American baseball player
* Thomas, Tommy

Thomas, Leone
See Thomas, Amos Leon, Jr.

Thomas, Lillian 1885-1969 [BWW, IBW]
American singer
* Baker, Fannie
* Brown, Lillian [or Lillyn]
* Elbrown
* Fernandez, Mildred
* [The] Indian Princess
* [The] Jazzbo Syncopator
* Jones, Maude
* [The] Kate Smith of Harlem
* [The] Original Gay 90's Gal
* [The] Youngest Interlocutor in the
World

Thomas, Lion Hearted
See Thomas, George Henry

Thomas, Louis 20th c. [EF]
American football player
* Thomas, Speedy

Thomas, Lowell Jackson 1892-1981
[BBH, HPPN]
American radio broadcaster, author, skier
* [The] Dean of World News
Broadcasters
* [The] Longest Running Newscaster in
History
* [The] Most Eminent of News
Broadcasters
* Thomas, Tommy
* [The] Voice of "Movietone News"

Thomas, Luther Baxter 1910- [BE]
American baseball player
* Thomas, Bud

Thomas, M. [PA]
Author
* Aptomas

Thomas, M. L.
See Jeier, Thomas

Thomas, Malcolm 1953- [FR]
American football player
* Thomas, Mike

Thomas, Manuel
See Mueller-Harlin, Wolfgang Johannes

Thomas, Marlo
See Jacobs, Margaret

Thomas, Martin
See Martin, Thomas Hector

Thomas, Mary Alice 20th c. [WWL]
Welsh author
* Eustace, Alice

Thomas, Maurice 1876-1961 [BDF,
BEW, FC]
French-born director
* Tourneur, Maurice

Thomas, Mervyn
See Curran, Mona [Elisa]

Thomas, Michael Tilson 1944- [CR]
American conductor
* [The] Lenny of the Seventies

Thomas, Michael Wolf 1945- [IAW]
German film editor
* Wolf, Dieter

Thomas, Mike
See Thomas, Malcolm

Thomas, Murray
See Ragg, Thomas Murray

Thomas, Neal
See Thomas, Cornelius Dickinson

Thomas, Norman Mattoon 1884-1968
[HPPN]
American politician, reformer, author
* America's Foremost Socialist

Thomas of Erceldoune
See Learmont, Thomas

Thomas of Woodstock 1355-1397 [SN]
Duke of Gloucester
* Cignus de Corde Benignus

Thomas, Olive
See Duffy, Olive

Thomas, Pap
See Thomas, George Henry

Thomas, Pat A.
See Scott, Portia Adele

Thomas, Paul
See Mann, Thomas

Thomas, Paul
See Sheritier, M.

Thomas, Peter 1928- [MA]
British-born author
* Pederek, Simon

Thomas, Philip Evan 1776-1861 [HPPN]
*American railroad promoter and
executive*
* [The] Father of the B. & O.

Thomas, Pinch
See Thomas, Chester David

Thomas, Piri
See Thomas, John Peter

Thomas, R[obert] Murray 1921- [CA]
American educator and author
* Roberts, Tom

Thomas, R. S.
See Thomas, Ronald Stuart

Thomas, Ragtime Texas
See Thomas, Henry

Thomas, Ralph 1840-? [DEL, FFF]
British bibliographer
* Hamst, Olphar

Thomas, Ralph 19th c. [HFN]
Author
* H. S.
* R. T.

Thomas, Ramblin'
See Thomas, Willard

Thomas, Rat
See Thomas, Frank William

Thomas, Red
See Thomas, Charles

Thomas, Red
See Thomas, Robert William

Thomas, Reginald George 1899-? [MBF]
British author
* Nelson, Barry
* Purley, John
* Storm, Ivan
* Stuart, Michael
* Wilson, Reg.

Thomas Rhymour of Ercildoune
See Learmont, Thomas

Thomas, Robert Murray 1921- [HPPN]
American educator and author
* Roberts, Tom

Thomas, Robert William 1898-1962
[BE]
American baseball player
* Thomas, Red

Thomas, Ronald Stuart 1913- [LC]
Welsh clergyman and poet
* Thomas, R. S.

Thomas, Ronald Wills 1910- [WW]
Author
* Bogar, Jeff
* Cadell, James
* Wills, Ronald

Thomas, Ross 1926- [AW, CA, EMD]
American author
* Bleeck, Oliver

Thomas, Rufus 1917?- [WP 8-14-85]
American singer
* [The] World's Oldest Teenager

Thomas, Sailor Art
See Thomas, Arthur

Thomas, Savage Tom
See Thomas, Thomas W. [Tom]

Thomas, Scow
See Thomas, Fay Wesley

Thomas, Sherilyn 1948- [CA]
American author
* Thomas, Sherry

Thomas, Sherry
See Thomas, Sherilyn

Thomas, Showboat
See Thomas, David

Thomas, Showboy
See Thomas, Worthia

Thomas, Skip
See Thomas, Alonzo

Thomas, Slim
See Thomas, Alvin Clarence

Thomas, Son
See Thomas, James

Thomas, Sonny Ford
See Thomas, James

Thomas, Speedy
See Thomas, Louis

Thomas, Stanley 1933- [CA]
British-born author
* Wyandotte, Steve

Thomas, T. F.
See Troy, Thomas F.

Thomas, Ted
See Tassy, Tamas

Thomas, Teddy
See Thomas, David John

Thomas the Bastard
See Fauconberg [or Falconberg],
Thomas

Thomas the Rhymer
See Learmont, Thomas

Thomas, Theodore 1835-1905 [HPPN]
German-American violinist and conductor
* [The] Founder of the Chicago
Symphony

Thomas, Theodore L. [Ted] 1920- [CA]
American author
* Lockard, Leonard

Thomas, Thomas W. [Tom] 1873-1942
[BE]
American baseball player
* Thomas, Savage Tom

Thomas, Tiger
See Thomas, Gary

Thomas, Tight Lines
See Thomas, Gary Philip

Thomas, Tommy
See Thomas, Alphonse

Thomas, Tommy
See Thomas, Leo Raymond

Thomas, Tommy
See Thomas, Lowell Jackson

Thomas, Uncle George
See Thomas, George Henry

Thomas, Vaughan 19th c. [HPPN]
British clergyman
* [A] Lover of Fine Arts

Thomas, Victor
See Thomas, John Richard

Thomas, Virginia
See Physioc, Jessica Eskridge [Thomas]

Thomas, Virginia Castleton
See Castleton, Virginia

Thomas, Wade Hamilton, Sr. 1922-
[BA]
American accountant
* [The] Lawyer

Thomas, Walter Purl 1907- [EJ, PMJ,
WWJ]
American jazz musician
* Thomas, Foots

Thomas, Will Madison 1905- [IBW]
American author
* Smith, Billy

Thomas, Willard 20th c. [BWW]
American musician
* Thomas, Ramblin'

Thomas, William 1832-1878 [BI]
Welsh clergyman and poet
* Islwyn

Thomas, William 1836?-? [HPPN]
American abolitionist
* Defensor

Thomas, William B. [Bill] 1934- [IAW]
American author
* Lowell, Alan
* Sabre, Mark
* Williams, Tom

Thomas, William M. 1878-1947 [BX, HPPN, RBE]
British boxer
* Broad, Kid

Thomas, Worthia 1907- [NOJ]
American jazz musician
* Thomas, Showboy

Thomasine
See Knight, Olivia

Thomasius, Christian 1655-1728 [SN]
German philosopher and jurist
* [The] Apostle of Enlightenment

Thomason, Alkali Ike
See Thomason, Ike

Thomason, Barbara Ann 1937-1966 [SC]
American actress
* Mitchell, Carolyn

Thomason, Ike [GW]
American rodeo performer
* Thomason, Alkali Ike

Thomason, John 20th c. [EF]
American football player
* Thomason, Stumpy

Thomason, Stumpy
See Thomason, John

Thomasson, H. L. 1903- [BI]
American dairy scientist
* Thomasson, Red

Thomasson, Red
See Thomasson, H. L.

Thomiris
See Mello, Francisco de

Thomond
See Hogan, Michael

Thompson, A. C.
See Meynell, Alice [Christiana Gertrude Thompson]

Thompson, Alexander Mattock 1861-1948 [LAO]
German-born playwright and journalist
* Dangle

Thompson, Alfred 1926- [EAR]
American auto racer
* Thompson, Speedy

Thompson, Alvin Clarence 1892-1974 [GF]
American gambler and golfer
* Thompson, Titanic

Thompson, Anthony A. 20th c. [ESF, SFL, WGT]
Author
* Alban, Anthony

Thompson, Ariadne 1910- [BI]
American author
* Van Matre, Paz

Thompson, Arthur Leonard Bell 1917-1975 [BI, CA]
British author
* Clifford, Francis

Thompson, Aundra 1953- [SMG]
American football player
* Thompson, Boomer

Thompson, Ayodele 1958- [TI 8-20-84]
British track and field athlete
* Thompson, Daley

Thompson, Ben 1843-? [HPPN]
American gambler and soldier
* Thompson, Shotgun Ben

Thompson, Bendigo
See Thompson, William

Thompson, Benjamin [Count Rumford] 1753-1814 [HPPN, NPS, PA, SN]
American-born physicist and adventurer
* [The] King of Fire
* [The] Knight of the White Eagle
* [The] Man of Stove
* Rumford, Count

Thompson, Beryl Antonia 1918-1970 [WEC]
British cartoonist
* Anton [joint pseudonym with Harold Thompson]

Thompson, Big Bill
See Thompson, William Hale

Thompson, Big Jim
See Thompson, James R.

Thompson, Big Sam
See Thompson, Samuel L.

Thompson, Billy 20th c. [SI 11-28-83]
American basketball player
* Thompson, World B.

Thompson, Boomer
See Thompson, Aundra

Thompson, Brute Force
See Thompson, George

Thompson, Buck
See Paine, Lauran [Bosworth]

Thompson, Carlos
See Mundanschaffter, Juan Carlos

Thompson, Cat
See Thompson, John A.

Thompson, Cecil 1905- [CEI, FHE, HK]
Canadian-born hockey player
* Thompson, Tiny

Thompson, Cecil Lewis 1904-1946 [AS, BX, RBE]
American boxer
* Thompson, Young Jack

Thompson, Charles 20th c. [SMG]
American baseball team scout
* Thompson, Tim

Thompson, Charles John Samuel 1862-1943 [SFL]
Author
* Thompson, Creswick J.

Thompson, Charles Lee 1857-? [BI]
American hunter
* Thompson, Wolfer

Thompson, Charles Phillip 1918- [EJ, WWJ]
American jazz musician
* Sir Charles

Thompson, Charles William 19th c. [HPPN]
British army officer
* [An] Officer of the Ninth Regiment

Thompson, Charlie 1729-1824 [HPPN]
Irish-American Secretary of the Continental Congress
* [The] Hand and Pen of the Congress
* [The] Perpetual Secretary

Thompson, Charlotte
See Rogers, Lorain

Thompson, China
See Lewis, Mary Christianna [Milne]

Thompson, Corner Memory
See Thompson, John

Thompson, Creswick J.
See Thompson, Charles John Samuel

Thompson, Cyclone
See Thompson, John

Thompson, Daley
See Thompson, Ayodele

Thompson, Daniel P. 19th c. [HFN]
American author
* [A] Member of the Vermont Bar

Thompson, David 1955- [IBW]
American basketball player
* Thompson, Hotshot

Thompson, Denman 1833-1911 [BEW]
American actor, playwright, producer
* Whitcomb, Joshua

Thompson, Derby Dick
See Thompson, Herbert John

Thompson, Derroll Lewis 1925- [FCW]
American country-western performer
* Adams, Derroll

Thompson, Don[ald Arthur] 1935- [CA]
American author and editor
* O'Donnell, Dick [joint pseudonym with Richard Allen (Dick) Lupoff]

Thompson, Don
See Thompson, Robert

Thompson, Donald Hoyt 1899?-1949
[BI]
American journalist
* Alden, Hoyt

Thompson, Dorothy
See Lewis, Mrs. Sinclair

Thompson, Edith 20th c. [WWL]
British author
* Tod, Evelyn

Thompson, Edward Anthony 1928-
[TCCM]
British author
* Lejeune, Anthony

Thompson, Eileen
See Panowski, Eileen [Janet] Thompson

Thompson, Eli 1924- [DAM, EJ, PMJ]
American jazz musician
* Thompson, Lucky

Thompson, Elizabeth V. ?-1921 [HPPN]
American actress
* Darling, Bessie

Thompson, Ellen Perronet 20th c.
[WWL]
British author
* Peronne

Thompson, Ernest Evan Seton 1860-1946
[LC, TC]
American author
* Seton, Ernest Thompson
* Thompson, Wolf

Thompson, Esau 1949- [IBW]
American disc jockey
* Thompson, Little Tiger

Thompson, Estelle Merle O'Brien
1911-1979 [BDF, IPA, WEF]
British actress
* Oberon, Merle
* O'Brien, Queenie

Thompson, Eugene Earl 1917- [BE]
American baseball player
* Thompson, Junior

Thompson, F. J. 19th c. [SN]
British army officer
* Thompson, Skikari

Thompson, Fat
See Thompson, James

Thompson, Francis Clegg
See Mencken, Henry Louis [Harry]

Thompson, Frank
American politician
* Thompson, Thompy

Thompson, Frank 20th c. [OBW]
American baseball player
* Thompson, Groundhog

Thompson, Franklin
See Edmonds, Sarah Emma

Thompson, Frederick B. 1836-1899
[HPPN]
American philanthropist
* Thompson, Uncle Fred

Thompson, George [PA]
Author
* Civis
* Greenhorn

Thompson, George 20th c. [MEB]
American basketball player
* Thompson, Brute Force

Thompson, George Selden 1929- [BI,
CA, SAT]
American author
* Selden, George

Thompson, Grace E. 20th c. [WWL]
British author
* Hope, Camilla

Thompson, Groundhog
See Thompson, Frank

Thompson, Harlan Howard 1894- [CAP,
SAT]
American author
* Holt, Stephen

Thompson, Harold 20th c. [WEC]
British cartoonist
* Anton [joint pseudonym with Beryl
  Antonia Thompson]
* Botterill, H.

Thompson, Harry
See Esmann, Harry

Thompson, [Sir] Henry 19th c. [FFF]
British author
* Oliver, Pen

Thompson, Henry
See Pell, Henry

Thompson, Herbert John 1881-? [BBH]
American horse trainer
* Thompson, Derby Dick

Thompson, Herman Lee 1923- [CWG]
American country-western performer
* Thompson, Tommy

Thompson, Hippolita ?-1933 [SC]
American actress
* Thompson, Polly

Thompson, Holy John
See Tostenson, John

Thompson, Hotshot
See Thompson, David

Thompson, Hugh 1943- [BWG]
American golfer
* Thompson, Rocky

Thompson, Hunter S[tockton] 1939-
[CA, IAW]
American author
* Duke, Raoul
* Owl, Sebastian

Thompson, J. J.
See Thompson, Jesse Jackson

Thompson, Jack
See Payne, John

Thompson, James 1884-1931 [HPPN]
American actor
* Thompson, Fat

Thompson, James Alfred 1893- [BE]
American baseball player
* Thompson, Shag

Thompson, James H.
See Freeman, Graydon La Verne

Thompson, James R. 1937- [TI 9-20-82]
American politician
* Clean, Mr.
* Thompson, Big Jim

Thompson, James W. 1935- [CA, MA]
American author, poet, dancer
* Altemese, Elethea
* Elethea, Abba

Thompson, James William ?-1881
[HPPN]
American clergyman
* J. W. T.

**Thompson, Jane Maude Evelyn De
Gourey Ireland** 1869-? [WWL]
British author
* Ireland, Maude

Thompson, Jay
See Thompson, Jennings Lewis, Jr.

Thompson, Jean M. 20th c. [NAA]
American author
* [The] Jack Frost Lady

Thompson, Jennings Lewis, Jr. 1927-
[ASC, BEW]
American composer, playwright, lyricist
* Thompson, Jay

Thompson, Jesse Jackson 1919- [IAW]
American author
* Thompson, J. J.

Thompson, Jimmy 1848-1931 [ECM]
American country-western performer
* Thompson, Uncle Jimmy

Thompson, Jocko
See Thompson, John Samuel

Thompson, John 1757-1843 [SN]
British auctioneer
* Thompson, Corner Memory
* Thompson, Memory

Thompson, John 1777-1799 [BDSA, PA]
American writer
* Casca
* Curtius
* Gracchus

Thompson, John 1876-1951 [AS, RBE]
American boxer
* Thompson, Cyclone

Thompson, John A. 1827-1876 [HPPN]
Norwegian-American mail carrier
* Thompson, Snowshoe

Thompson, John A. 1906- [BB]
American basketball player
* Thompson, Cat

Thompson, John Albert
See Tostenson, John

Thompson, John Baptiste De Macklot
1872-? [HPPN]
American author
* Ripley, Ozark

Thompson, John C. 19th c. [HPPN]
American soldier
* Rock, R. W.

Thompson, John Dall 1918-1971 [SC]
American actor
* Dall, John

Thompson, John Dudley 1898-1963 [BE]
American baseball player
* Thompson, Lee
* Thompson, Lefty

Thompson, John H. 1890- [NAA]
American author and editor
* Headen, John
* Johns, Thompson

Thompson, John Jenner 1918- [HPPN]
American actor
* Dall, John

Thompson, John P. ?-1895 [BE]
American baseball player
* Thompson, Tug

Thompson, John Samuel 1920- [BE]
American baseball player
* Thompson, Jocko

Thompson, John Taliaferro 1860-1940
[HPPN]
American army officer and inventor
* [The] Father of the Tommy Gun

Thompson, Joseph Parrish 1819-1879
[FFF, HPPN, PA]
American clergyman and author
* Berliner
* Egypt
* His Father

Thompson, Junior
See Thompson, Eugene Earl

Thompson, Lafayette Fresco 1902-1968
[BE, PB]
American baseball player
* Thompson, Tommy

Thompson, Lee
See Thompson, John Dudley

Thompson, Lefty
See Thompson, John Dudley

Thompson, Little Phil
See Thompson, Philip Burton, Jr.

Thompson, Little Tiger
See Thompson, Esau

Thompson, Long Sam
See Thompson, Samuel Tommy

Thompson, Louis McClanahan 1881-1951
[SC]
American actor
* Morris, Corbet

Thompson, Lucky
See Thompson, Eli

Thompson, Lurtis 20th c. [EF]
American football player
* Thompson, Tommy

Thompson, Lydia
See Henderson, Mrs. Alexander

Thompson, Madeline
See Greig, Maysie Coucher

Thompson, Marian Lee 1928- [EAR]
American auto racer
* Thompson, Mickey

Thompson, Marie M. 19th c. [PI]
Irish poet
* Ethne

Thompson, Mary Wolfe 1886- [CA]
American author
* Thompson, Wolfe

Thompson, Memory
See Thompson, John

Thompson, Mickey
See Thompson, Marian Lee

Thompson, Mr.
See Peace, Charles Frederick

Thompson, Moose
See Thompson, Wilbur

Thompson, Mrs. E. S. L. [PA]
Author
* Broderick, Mark

Thompson, Mrs. William [FFF]
American writer
* Clara Belle

Thompson, Mychal 1955?- [SI 8-23-82]
Bahamian-born basketball player
* Thompson, Sweet Bells

Thompson, Old Phil
See Thompson, Philip Burton, Sr.

Thompson, Percy Henry 1875?-1953
[BEW, BMH]
Theatrical performer
* Honri, Percy

Thompson, Peter [PA]
Author
* Dodger

Thompson, Philip Burton, Jr. 1845-1909
[HPPN]
American politician
* Thompson, Little Phil

Thompson, Philip Burton, Sr. 1821-?
[HPPN]
American attorney and politician
* Thompson, Old Phil

Thompson, Phillips [PA]
Author
* Briggs, Jimuel

Thompson, Phyllis Hoge
See Hoge, Phyllis

Thompson, Polly
See Thompson, Hippolita

Thompson, Polly
See Thomson, Mary Agnes

Thompson, Ralph 20th c. [EF]
American football player
* Thompson, Rocky

Thompson, Richard Wigginton 1809-1900
[FFF]
American politician
* [The] Ancient Mariner of the Wabash

Thompson, Robert 20th c. [EF]
American football player
* Thompson, Don

Thompson, Robert Hely 1854-? [PI]
Irish-born poet and playwright
* Blake, Robert

Thompson, Rocky
See Thompson, Hugh

Thompson, Rocky
See Thompson, Ralph

Thompson, Rupert Luckhart 1910-1971
[BE]
American baseball player
* Thompson, Tommy

Thompson, Russ
See Paine, Lauran [Bosworth]

Thompson, Samuel L. 1860-1922 [BE,
DGS, PB]
American baseball player
* Thompson, Big Sam

Thompson, Samuel Tommy 1908- [MK]
American baseball player
* Thompson, Long Sam

Thompson, Shag
See Thompson, James Alfred

Thompson, Shotgun Ben
See Thompson, Ben

Thompson, Skikari
See Thompson, F. J.

Thompson, Slow Kid
See Thompson, Ulysses

Thompson, Snowshoe
See Thompson, John A.

Thompson, Snowshoe
See Tostenson, John

Thompson, Speedy
See Thompson, Alfred

Thompson, Stephen
See Dell, Draycot Montagu

Thompson, Sue
See McKee, Eva Sue

Thompson, Sweet Bells
See Thompson, Mychal

Thompson, Sylvester 1937- [BWW]
American singer
* Johnson, Syl

Thompson, Texas Billy
See Thompson, William

Thompson, Thomas Phillips 1843-1933
[DNA]
British-born journalist
* Briggs, Jimuel

Thompson, Thompy
See Thompson, Frank

Thompson, Tim
See Thompson, Charles

Thompson, Tiny
See Thompson, Cecil

Thompson, Titanic
See Thompson, Alvin Clarence

Thompson, Tommy
See Thompson, Herman Lee

Thompson, Tommy
See Thompson, Lafayette Fresco

Thompson, Tommy
See Thompson, Lurtis

Thompson, Tommy
See Thompson, Rupert Luckhart

Thompson, Tug
See Thompson, John P.

Thompson, Ulysses 20th c. [BMH]
American entertainer
* Thompson, Slow Kid

Thompson, Uncle Fred
See Thompson, Frederick B.

Thompson, Uncle Jimmy
See Thompson, Jimmy

Thompson, Wallace Bixby, Jr. 1931-
[BA]
American dentist
* Dr. T.

Thompson, Wilbur 1921- [TF]
American track and field athlete
* Thompson, Moose

Thompson, William 1811-1880 [BI, RBE,
SG]
British boxer
* [The] Lion
* Thompson, Bendigo

Thompson, William 1845?-1888? [EWG]
British-born gunfighter
* Thompson, Texas Billy

Thompson, [Colonel] William 19th c.
[HPPN]
American army officer
* Governor Grover's Madcap Colonel

Thompson, William C. L.
See Edwards, William B[ennett]

Thompson, William Hale 1869?-1944
[BLB, PHM]
American politician with underworld ties
* Thompson, Big Bill

Thompson, William Henry 1881-1947
[BEW, F1, THR]
British actor
* Merson, Billy
* Ping Pong

Thompson, William R. [PA]
Author
* Mata

Thompson, William Tappan 1812-1882
[DLE1]
American author and journalist
* Jones, Major

Thompson, Wolf
See Thompson, Ernest Evan Seton

Thompson, Wolfe
See Thompson, Mary Wolfe

Thompson, Wolfer
See Thompson, Charles Lee

Thompson, World B.
See Thompson, Billy

Thompson, Young Jack
See Thompson, Cecil Lewis

Thoms, William John 1803-1885 [DLE1,
HFN, NPS]
British author
* Merton, Ambrose, Gent.

Thomson, A. A.
See Thomson, Arthur Alexander

Thomson, Ada 1929- [FC, TR]
British actress
* Merchant, Vivien

Thomson, Alexander 1744-1817 [SN]
* Old Stay Maker
* [The] Stay Maker

Thomson, Alexander 1817-1875 [NPS]
Scottish architect
* Thomson, Greek

Thomson, Arthur Alexander 1894-1968
[LC]
British author
* Thomson, A. A.

Thomson, Audrey
See Gwynn, Audrey Jean

Thomson, Beatrix
See Lindsay-Thomson, Beatrix

Thomson, Charles 1729-1824 [HPPN,
SN]
Irish-born American politician
* [The] Man of Truth
* [The] Sam Adams of Philadelphia
* Truth Teller

Thomson, Charles Wyville
See Charles, Wyville Thomas

Thomson, Christine Campbell 1897-
[HFF, MBF, SFP]
British author
* Alexander, Dair
* Campbell, Molly
* Hartley, Christine
* Richardson, Flavia

Thomson, Daisy Hicks 1918- [AW, WD]
Scottish author
* Roe, M. S.
* Thomson, Jonathan H.

Thomson, Derick Smith 1921- [CA,
WD]
Scottish poet and literary critic
* MacThomais, Ruaraidh

Thomson, Donald Walter 1906- [CCL]
Canadian author
* Dawson, Walter

Thomson, Dutch
See Thomson, Richard

Thomson, Edward
See Tubb, Edwin Charles

Thomson, Elihu 1853-1937 [HPPN]
British-American electrician and inventor
* [The] Beloved Scientist

Thomson, Floyd Harvey 1949- [SMG]
Canadian-born hockey player
* Thomson, White Pine

Thomson, George Julius Poulett
1797-1876 [WBD]
British geologist
* Scrope, George Julius Poulett

Thomson, George Malcolm 1899- [CA]
Scottish-born journalist and author
* MacDonald, Aeneas

Thomson, Greek
See Thomson, Alexander

Thomson, Irene Taviss 1941- [CA]
American sociologist and author
* Taviss, Irene

Thomson, J. A. K.
See Thomson, James Alexander Kerr

Thomson, James 1700-1748 [HPPN]
Scottish poet
* [A] Friend of the Author

Thomson, James 1834-1882 [NPS, WBD]
Scottish poet
* B. V.
* Bysshe Vanolis
* [The]Poet of Despair

Thomson, James Alexander Kerr
1879-1959 [LC]
Scottish-born scholar and author
* Thomson, J. A. K.

Thomson, James C[utting] 1909- [CA]
American musicologist and author
* Chase, Adam

Thomson, Joan
See Charnock, Joan Paget

Thomson, John 1778-1840 [DEP]
Scottish painter
* [The] Father of Scotch Landscape
  Painting

Thomson, [Rev.] John 18th c. [HPPN]
American clergyman
* [A] Member of the Said Synod

Thomson, John Cockburn 19th c.
[DNNF]
British author
* Wharton, Philip

Thomson, Jonathan H.
See Thomson, Daisy Hicks

Thomson, Katherine Byerley 1810-1862
[DEL, DNNF, FFF]
British author
* Grace, Eliza
* Wharton, Grace

Thomson, Louis
See Thomson, Louisa Emily

Thomson, Louisa Emily 1883- [DBA]
British painter, etcher, lithographer
* Thomson, Louis

Thomson, Mary Agnes 1885-1960
[HPPN]
American educator
* Thompson, Polly

Thomson, Meldrim 1912?-
American politician
* Half Mast Mel

Thomson, Mortimer Neal 1832?-1875
[WBD]
American author
* Doesticks, Q. K. Philander, P. B.

Thomson, Neil
See Johnson, Henry T.

Thomson, Ralph Methven 1875-? [NAA]
American poet and writer
* Methven, Ralph

Thomson, Richard ?-1613 [NPS]
Scholar and clergyman
* Thomson, Dutch

Thomson, Richard 1794-1865 [PA]
Author
* [An] Antiquary

Thomson, Robert Brown [Bobby] 1923-
[BE, PB]
Scottish-born baseball player
* [The] Flying Scot
* [The] Scot
* [The] Staten Island Scot

Thomson, Robert William 1822-1873
[HPPN]
British inventor
* [The] Father of the Pneumatic Tire

Thomson, Virgil 1896- [CR]
American composer, music critic, author
* [The] Virgil of American Musical
   History

Thomson, White Pine
See Thomson, Floyd Harvey

Thomson, William 1746-1817 [HPPN,
WGT]
British author
* [An] English Gentleman
* [The] Man in the Moon
* [The] Man of the People
* Newte, Thomas

Thomson, William (cont.)
* [An] Officer in Col. Baillie's
   Detachment
* Stedman, Charles

Thoney, Bullet Jack
See Thoeny, John

Thoney, John
See Thoeny, John

Thor
See Thurston, Robert Henry

Thor, Johannes
See Lang, Isaac

[The] Thor of the Ring
See Dempsey, William Harrison

Thor, Terry
See Shaw, Lawrence Taylor [Larry]

Thor, Tristan
See Lang, Isaac

Thorburn, Grant 1773?-1863 [FFF]
Scottish-born author
* Todd, Laurie

Thorburn, John
See Goldsmith, John Herman Thorburn

Thorburn-Muirhead, James 1899- [IAW]
Scottish-born author
* Muirhead, Thorburn

Thordsen, Theodori   [PA]
Author
* Polyhistor

Thore, T. E. J.
See Thore, Theophile Entienne Joseph

Thore, T. J. E.   [PA]
Author
* Baerger, W.

Thore, Theophile Entienne Joseph 1807-
1869
French author
* Buerger, W[illem]
* Thore, T. E. J.

Thoreau, Henry David 1817-1862
[HPPN, NPS]
American author
* [The] Concord Rebel
* [The] Hermit of Walden
* [The] Poet Naturalist
* [The] Sage of Walden Pond

Thorer, Konrad
See Greve, Felix Paul

Thorkelsson, Jon 1859-1924 [BI]
Icelandic historian and poet
* Fornolfur

Thorleif
See Veiby, John

Thormahlen, Hank
See Thormahlen, Herbert Ehler

Thormahlen, Herbert Ehler 1896-1955
[BE]
American baseball player
* Thormahlen, Hank
* Thormahlen, Lefty

Thormahlen, Lefty
See Thormahlen, Herbert Ehler

Thormanby
See Dixon, W. Willmott

Thormodsgard, Paul Gayton 1953-
[SMG]
American baseball player
* Thormodsgard, Thor

Thormodsgard, Thor
See Thormodsgard, Paul Gayton

Thorn, Barbara
See Paine, Lauran [Bosworth]

Thorn, Edgar
See MacDowell, Edward Alexander

Thorn, John 1947- [CA]
German-born American author
* Jones, Sanford W.

Thorn, Kate
See Jones, Clara Augusta

Thornberry, William A.
See Thornley, William A.

Thornborough, John 1551-1641 [NPS,
SN]
British clergyman
* Denarius Philosophorum

Thornborough, Laura
See Thornburgh, Laura

Thornburg, Elizabeth June 1921- [BEW,
OCF, SW]
American singer and actress
* [The] Blonde Bombshell
* Hutton, Betty

Thornburg, Marion 1919?- [FC, MY,
PMJ]
American singer and actress
* Hutton, Butch
* Hutton, Marion

Thornburgh, Laura 20th c. [NAA]
American author, film editor, director
* Thornborough, Laura

Thornbury, William A.
See Thornley, William A.

Thorndike, Helen Louise
See Adams, Harriet S[tratemeyer]

Thorndyke, Helen Louise [house
pseudonym] [Stratemeyer Syndicate]
See Stratemeyer, Edward L.

Thorndyke, Louise
See Boucicault, Agnes Kelly Robertson

Thorne, [Lt.] Alfred B.
See Aiken, Albert W.

Thorne, Alice
See Craythorne, Mrs. James

Thorne, B. K. Ted
See Thorne, B[liss] Kirby

Thorne, B[liss] Kirby 1916- [HPPN]
American journalist, author
* Thorne, B. K. Ted

Thorne, B[liss] Kirby (cont.)
* Thorne, Ted
* Vandal, Cameron

Thorne, Bradley D.
See Glut, Donald F[rank]

Thorne, Brinck
See Thorne, Samuel B.

Thorne, Dora
See Brame, Charlotte Mary

Thorne, Edouard
See Greve, Felix Paul

Thorne, Grace
See Coulter, Mrs. Frazer

Thorne, Guy
See Gull, Cyril Arthur Edward Ranger

Thorne, Harley?
See Brayman, James O.

Thorne, Hart
See Carhart, Arthur Hawthorne

Thorne, Ian
See Dikty, Julian May

Thorne, Jean Wright
See Dikty, Julian May

Thorne, John
See Thornton, John T.

Thorne, Kate
See Gray, Louisa M.

Thorne, Marion
See Thurston, Ida [Treadwell]

Thorne, Mrs. J. H.   [FFF]
Entertainer
* Meyer, Bonnie

Thorne, Nicola
See Ellerbeck, Rosemary [Anne L'Estrange]

Thorne, P.
See Smith, Mary Prudence [Wells]

Thorne, Ramsay
See Cameron, Lou

Thorne, Roger
See Russell, Ray

Thorne, Sabina 1927-   [CA]
American author
* Johnson, Sabina Thorne

Thorne, Samuel B. ?-1930   [FB]
American football player
* Thorne, Brinck

Thorne, Sarah
See Macknight, Sarah

Thorne, Sheldon B.   [IP]
American author
* Saxifrage

Thorne, Sterling
See Fuller, Dorothy Mason

Thorne, Ted
See Thorne, B[liss] Kirby

Thorne, Victor
See Jackson, Frederick

Thorne, Whyte
See Whiteing, Richard

Thorne, William 1558-1629   [FFF]
British scholar
* Theta

Thornet, Teresa A.
See Holloway, Anna

Thornhill, Claude E. 1893-1956   [AS, FB]
American football player and coach
* Thornhill, Tiny

Thornhill, Tiny
See Thornhill, Claude E.

Thornley, William A. 20th c.   [DBA]
British painter
* Thornberry, William A.
* Thornbury, William A.

Thornthwaite, J. A.   [IP]
British clergyman and author
* [A] Member of the Church of England

Thornton, Adelaide
See Nicholson, Mrs. Paul

Thornton, Andre 1949-   [BR]
American baseball player
* Thornton, Andy

Thornton, Andy
See Thornton, Andre

Thornton, Argonne Dense 1921-   [EJ]
American jazz musician
* Hakim, Sadik

Thornton, Big Mama
See Thornton, Willie Mae

Thornton, Bill 20th c.   [SMG]
American football coach
* Thornton, Thunder

Thornton, Bonnell 1724-1768   [IP]
British poet and journalist
* Birch, [Rev.] Bushby
* Critic and Censor General
* [A] Deputy
* Termagant, [Madame] Roxana
* Town, Mr.

Thornton, Buns
See Thornton, Charles Inglis

Thornton, Charles Bates 1913-   [CR]
American business executive
* Thornton, Tex

Thornton, Charles Inglis 1850-1929 [EC]
British cricketer
* Thornton, Buns

Thornton, Charles J. 1944-   [EJ7]
American jazz musician
* Miles, Butch
* Miles, Charles J.

Thornton, Cyril
See Hamilton, [Capt.] Thomas

Thornton, Edward
See Brooks, Edwy Searles

Thornton, Frank
See Ball, Frank

Thornton, Hall
See Silverberg, Robert

Thornton, Harold
See Offard, Cecil

Thornton, Jack
See Thornton, Lawrence

Thornton, John T. 1855-1911   [HPPN]
American vaudeville performer
* Thorne, John

Thornton, Lawrence 20th c.   [EF]
American football player
* Thornton, Jack

Thornton, Maimee
See Jeffrey-Smith, May Thornton

Thornton, Mary 1924-   [BF]
British actress and singer
* Norden, Christine

Thornton, Robert John 1758?-?   [HPPN]
British author
* [A] Lover of Social Order

Thornton, Tex
See Thornton, Charles Bates

Thornton, Thunder
See Thornton, Bill

Thornton, W. B.
See Burgess, Thornton Waldo

Thornton, William   [IP]
American author
* W. T.

Thornton, Willie Mae 1926-1984   [BWW, NBB, PRS]
American singer
* Thornton, Big Mama

Thorogood, Albert 1928?-   [BI]
British nonworker
* Thorogood, Idle Albert

Thorogood, Idle Albert
See Thorogood, Albert

Thorold, William James 1871-?   [CCL]
Canadian author
* Barron, Louie

Thorough
See Wentworth, [Sir] Thomas [First Earl of Stafford]

[The] Thorough Doctor
See Varro, William

Thorp, Edward 20th c.
Mathematician and gambler
* [The] Father of Card Counting

Thorp, Ellen
See Robertson, Margery Ellen

Thorp, Joseph Peter 1873-1962 [BI, HPPN, LAO, LC]
British journalist and critic
* Junius
* T.
* T in Punch

Thorp, Morwenna
See Robertson, Margery Ellen

Thorp, Mrs. Charles R. [FFF]
Entertainer
* Mountcastle, Fanny

Thorpe, Charles 19th c. [IP]
American author
* Champagne Charlie

Thorpe, Clarke Harrison
See Macdougall, Harrison Miller, Jr.

Thorpe, Dobbin
See Disch, Thomas M.

Thorpe, E. G.
See Thorpe, George

Thorpe, Elizabeth 20th c.
British intelligence agent
* Cynthia [code name used during World War II]

Thorpe, George 1916- [IAW]
British author
* Thorpe, E. G.

Thorpe, Henry 1841-? [IP, PA]
American author
* Walton

Thorpe, James Francis [Jim] 1888-1953 [HPPN]
American athlete
* Wa Tho Huck [Bright Path]

Thorpe, Kampa
See Bellamy, Elizabeth Whitfield

Thorpe, Richard
See Thorpe, Rollo Smolt

Thorpe, Rollo Smolt 1896- [FC, FD, WEF]
American director
* Thorpe, Richard

Thorpe, Sylvia
See Thimblethorpe, June Sylvia

Thorpe, Thomas Bangs 1815-1878 [IP, PA]
American journalist
* Logan
* Owen, Tom, the Bee Hunter
* Weiss, Lynde

Thorpe, Trebor
See Fanthorpe, R[obert] Lionel

Thorpe, Trevor
See Fanthorpe, R[obert] Lionel

Thorpe, William
See Vreeland, Frank

Thorson, Delos Russell 1906- [WW]
Author
* Christian, Kit [joint pseudonym with Sara Winfree Thorson]

Thorson, Sara Winfree 1906- [WW]
Author
* Christian, Kit [joint pseudonym with Delos Russell Thorson]

Thorstein, Eric
See Grossman, Josephine Judith

Thorton, [Mrs.] Bonnie
See Cox, Elizabeth

Thorvaldsen, Bertel [or Albert] 1770?-1844 [HN]
Danish sculptor
* [The] Northern Phidias

Thorwald, Juergen
See Bongartz, Heinz

Thou Great Prophet of Tautology
See Shadwell, Thomas

Thou Jackall
See Boswell, James

Thou Moral Washington of Africa
See Wilberforce, William

Thou Myron of the Age
See Garrard, George

Thou Shred of a Loom
See Oates, Titus

[The] Thoughtful Father
See Catinat, Nicholas

Thoyson, David 1864-1951 [SC]
Scottish-born actor
* Torrence, David

Thoyson, Ernest 1878-1933 [SC]
Scottish-born actor and singer
* Torrence, Ernest

[The] Thracian
See Leo I

[The] Thracian Dog
See Zoilus [or Zoilos]

Thrale, Mrs.
See Piozzi, Hester Lynch Salusbury

Thrasher, Buck
See Thrasher, Frank Edward

Thrasher, Frank Edward 1889-1938 [BE]
American baseball player
* Thrasher, Buck

Thrax [The Thracian]
See Maximinus, Gaius Julius Verus

Thread, Sam 1904?-1982 [FIR]
Songwriter and actor
* Spoo-De-Odee

[The] 3 Dog
See Davis, William Henry [Willie]

Three Finger Brown
See Brown, Mordecai Peter Centennial

Three Finger Brown
See Lucchese, Thomas Gaetano

Three Fingered Jack
See Dunlap, Jack

Three Fingered Jack
See Garcia, Manuel

Three Fingered Jack
See Hamilton, John

Three Fingered Jack
See White, William Jack

Three Fingered Jack McDowell
See McDowell, Jack

Three Fingers
See Fitzpatrick, Thomas

Three Fingers Coppola
See Coppola, Francesco Paolo

Three Minute Brumm
See Brumm, George Franklin

Three Star Hennessey
See Hennessey, George

Three to Nothing Jack
See Dalton, John P. [Jack]

Three Twelve
See Lucania, Salvatore

Threepland, Moncrieff ?-1838 [IP]
Scottish author
* Plain, Timothy

[A] Thrice Accursed Judas
See Beria, Lavrenti Pavlovich

Thrice, Luke
See Russell, John

Thrift, Vernon
See Hayward, Abraham

[The] Thrill
See Sellers, Phil

Thring, Edward 19th c. [IP, PA]
British clergyman, educator, author
* Place, Benjamin

[The] Thrissil
See James IV

Throckmorton, Job 1545-1601 [NPS]
Puritan pamphleteer
* Marprelate, Martin

Throckmorton, John Courtney 1753-1819 [SN]
* Benevolus

Throneberry, Marvelous Marv
See Throneberry, Marvin Eugene

Throneberry, Marvin Eugene 1933- [BE, PB]
American baseball player
* Throneberry, Marvelous Marv

Throop, Enos Thompson 1784-1874 [SN]
American politician
* Throop, Small Light

Throop, Small Light
See Throop, Enos Thompson

Thropp, Florence
See Bulkley, Mrs. Edward A.

Throssell, Katharine Susannah Prichard
1884- [LAO]
Australian author
* Prichard, Katharine Susannah

Thrower, Hammer
See Thrower, James

Thrower, James 20th c.
American football player
* Thrower, Hammer

Thrush, Thomas 19th c. [HPPN]
British naval officer
* [An] Officer
* Two Naval Officers

Thrysis
See Clough, Arthur Hugh

Thucydides
See Rollin, Charles

[The] Thucydides of Germany
See Mueller, Johann von

Thuitleru, Francois Jean 1653-1688
[PA]
Author
* Juvenon

Thumb, Thomas, Esq.
See Church, Benjamin

Thumb, Tom
See Alden, Darius Adner

Thumb, Tom
See Bonaparte, Charles Louis Napoleon

Thumb, Tom
See Phillips, Tom

Thumb, [General] Tom
See Stratton, Charles Sherwood

[The] Thumper
See Harris, Carrol Wayne

[The] Thumper
See Williams, Theodore Samuel [Ted]

Thumtack, Tom
See Squires, Frederick

Thuna, Lee
See Thuna, Leonora

Thuna, Leonora 1929- [CA]
American playwright
* Thuna, Lee

Thunder and Lightning
See Stephen II

Thunder and Lightning Williams
See Williams, David Rogerson

Thunder Bolt
See Foe, Daniel

[The] Thunder Maker
See Jones, Howard Harding

[The] Thunderbird from Coast to Coast
See Price, Walter Travis

[The] Thunderbolt
See Bajazet I [Bayazid or Bajasid]

[The] Thunderbolt
See Handel, Georg Friedrich

[The] Thunderbolt
See Papke, William Herman [Billy]

[The] Thunderbolt
See Ptolemy

Thunderbolt, Captain
See Ward, Fred

[The] Thunderbolt of France
See De Gontaut, Charles

[The] Thunderbolt of Italy
See Foix, Gaston de [Duc de Nemours]

[The] Thunderbolt of Painting
See Robusti, Jacopo

Thunderbolt of the Middle West
See May, Joseph

[The] Thunderbolt of War
See Piccinino, Jacopo

Thundercloud, Chief
See Daniels, Victor

Thundercloud, Chief
See Williams, Scott T.

Thundercloud, Katherine
See Witt, Shirley Hill

[The] Thunderer
See Gorovitz, Vladimir

[The] Thunderer
See Homer

[The] Thunderer
See Stephen II

[The] Thunderer of the Times
See Sterling, Edward

Thundering Jimmy Jenkins
See Jenkins, James

[The] Thundering Scot
See Knox, John

Thunders, Johnny
See Genzale, Johnny

Thundertentronckh, Arminius Von
See Arnold, Matthew

Thundy, Zacharias Pontian
See Thundyil, Zacharias Pontian

Thundyil, Zacharias Pontian 1936- [CA]
Indian-born author and clergyman
* Thundy, Zacharias Pontian

Thurber, Charles 19th c. [IP]
American author
* His Father

Thurber, Philip Henry 20th c.
American gymnast
* Paulinetti, Professor

Thurgood, Albert 1875?-1935 [OCS]
Australian soccer player
* Albert the Great

Thurland, Bilberry
See Hooten, Charles

Thurley, Norgove
See Stoneham, Charles Thurley

Thurlow, Edward [First Baron Thurlow]
1731?-1806 [HN, HPPN, SN]
British jurist and politician
* [An] Officer
* Old Gravity
* [The] Tiger

Thurman, Allan Granbery 1813-1895
[FFF, HPPN]
American politician
* [The] Gladstone of America
* [The] Noblest Roman of Them All
* [The] Obelisk
* Old Bandanna
* [The] Old Roman
* Thurman, Right Angled, Tri Angled

Thurman, Christa C[harlotte] Mayer
1934- [CA]
German-born author and museum curator
* Mayer, Christa Charlotte
* Mayer-Thurman, Christa C.

Thurman, Right Angled, Tri Angled
See Thurman, Allan Granbery

Thurman, Wallace 1902-1934 [CA, TLC]
American editor, author, playwright, poet
* Casey, Patrick
* Mandrake, Ethel Belle

Thurmond, Charlotte 1844-1934 [HPPN]
American pioneer and gambler
* Deno, Lottie

Thurmond, Nate 1941- [BB]
American basketball player
* Nate the Great

Thursby, Peter 1930- [ART]
British sculptor
* P. T.

Thursday's Child
See Kitt, Eartha Mae

[The] Thurso Baker
See Dick, Robert

Thurston, Arthur L. 20th c.
American aviation engineer
* Thurston, Mike

Thurston, Charles Mynn 1738-1812
[HPPN]
American clergyman, army officer, jurist
* [The] Warrior Parson

Thurston, David 1779-1865 [HPPN]
American author
* [A] Father

Thurston, Frederick C. 1933-   [FB]
American football player
* Thurston, Fuzzy

Thurston, Fuzzy
See Thurston, Frederick C.

Thurston, Harry
See Cowan, Marcus

Thurston, Hazel [Patricia] 1906-   [CA]
Irish-born author
* Murphy, Hazel

Thurston, Henry T.
See Palgrave, Francis Turner

Thurston, Hollis John 1899-1973   [BE, PB]
American baseball player
* Thurston, Sloppy

Thurston, Howard 1869-1936   [HPPN]
American magician and author
* Thurston the Great

Thurston, Howard
See Gibson, Walter B[rown]

Thurston, Ida [Treadwell] 1848-1918 [DNA]
American author
* Thorne, Marion

Thurston, Jane 20th c.   [BS]
American magician
* [The] Maid of Magic

Thurston, Laura M. Hawley 1812-1842 [FFF]
American poet and journalist
* Viola

Thurston, Mike
See Thurston, Arthur L.

Thurston, Oliver
See Flanders, Henry

Thurston, Robert Henry 1839-1903
American engineer and educator
* Thor

Thurston, Sloppy
See Thurston, Hollis John

Thurston the Great
See Thurston, Howard

Thury, [Mrs.] Ilona
See Konyechni, Ilona

Thynne, Francis
See Boteville, Francis

Thynne, Thomas ?-1682   [HN, RH, SN]
British aristocrat
* Issachar
* Tom of Ten Thousand

Thynne [or Boteville?], William ?-1546 [SN]
British scholar
* Aulicus

Thynne, William
See Boteville, William

Thyrsis
See Milton, John

Thyselius, Thorborg Elin Tryggvesdotter 1906-   [IAW]
Swedish author and poet
* Castenius, Sigrid

Thyson, A. C.
See Aitchison, George

Tiant, Lefty
See Tiant, Luis E.

Tiant, Luis E. 1906-1976   [MK]
American baseball player
* Tiant, Lefty

Tibaldi, Pellegrino 1527-1598   [SN, WBD]
Italian artist
* Da Bologna, Pellegrino
* [The] Reformed Michael Angelo

Tibbald, King
See Theobald, Lewis

Tibbald, Pedling
See Theobald, Lewis

Tibber, Robert
See Friedman, Eve Rosemary

Tibber, Rosemary
See Friedman, Eve Rosemary

Tibbetts, John C[arter] 1946-   [CA]
American author
* Ketch, Jack

Tibbetts, William
See Brannon, William T.

Tibbetts, William Nelson ?-1912   [HPPN]
American actor
* Stafford, William

Tibble, Anne 1912-1980   [CA]
British author
* Northgrave, Anne

Tibbles, Percy Thomas 1879-1938 [HPPN]
British magician
* Selbit, P. T.

Tibbs
See Dickens, Charles

Tibbs, Casey 20th c.   [GW]
American rodeo performer
* Midnight, Captain

Tibbs, Lillian Evans 1890-1967   [IBW]
American opera singer
* Evanti, [Madame] Lillian

Tiberiu, Farkas 1914-   [IWM]
Rumanian-born musician
* Levary, Tibor

Tiberius
See Nero Caesar, Tiberius Claudius

Tibet
See Gascard, Gilbert

Tibio [Luke-Warm]
See Munoz, Felipe

[The] Tibullus of France
See Desforges, Evariste Desire [Chevalier de Parny]

[The] Tibullus of His Age
See Sedley, [Sir] Charles

Tic-tic, [Count] Horloge de
See Norton, Caroline Elizabeth Sarah

Tich
See Amey, Ian

[The] Tichborne Claimant
See Orton, Arthur

Tichborne, [Sir] Roger Charles
See Orton, Arthur

Tichborne, Thomas   [IP]
British author
* [A] Phrenologist

Ticheburn, Cheviot
See Ainsworth, William Harrison

Tichenor, Isaac 1754-1838   [HPPN]
American politician
* Slick, Jersey

Tichenor, J. C.
See Kelly, George R.

Tick, Christy
See Furnari, Christopher

Tickell, Thomas 1686-1740   [IP]
British poet
* [A] Lady in England

Ticker, Reuben 1913-1975   [BBD, HPPN]
American opera singer
* Gambler at the Met
* [The] Golden Tenor
* [The] Met's Big Man
* [The] Met's Second Caruso
* Pagliacci From Brooklyn
* Pride of the Met
* [The] Tenor
* Tenor of the House
* Tucker, Richard
* [The] Unforgettable

Tickler, Timothy
See Paulding, James Kirke

Tickler, Timothy
See Syme, Robert

Tickletoby, Miss
See Thackeray, William Makepeace

Tickletooth, Tabitha
See Selby, Charles

Ticknor, George 1791-1871   [HPPN]
American scholar and author
* [Un] Citoyen Americain
* G. T.

Tico
See Harris, William

Tiddly
See Applewhite, Marshall Herff

Tiddy Doll
See Bonaparte, Napoleon

Tiddy Doll
See Grenville, George

Tiddy Doll
See Grenville, Richard Temple [First Earl Temple]

Tidman, Paul 19th c. [HPPN]
British compiler
* Evans, Mark

Tidmarsh, James [IP]
British author
* S. H.

Tidy, Theresa
See Graham, Elizabeth Susanna [Davenport]

Tieck, Johann Ludwig 1773-1853 [HFF, WGT]
German author
* Leberecht, Peter

Tiedge, Christoph August 1752-1841 [HN]
German poet
* [The] Nestor of German Poesy

Tielsch, Ilse 1929- [IAW]
Austrian author
* Tielsch-Felzmann, Ilse

Tielsch-Felzmann, Ilse
See Tielsch, Ilse

Tiempo, Cesar
See Zeitlin, Israel

T'ien-wang [Heavenly Prince]
See Hung Hsiu-ch'uan

Tieri, Frank 1904?-1981
American underworld figure
* Tieri, Funzi

Tieri, Funzi
See Tieri, Frank

Tiernan, Frances Christine [Fisher] 1846-1920 [BDSA, DNA]
American author
* Reid, Christian

Tiernan, Michael Joseph 1867-1918 [BE, DGS, PB]
American baseball player
* Tiernan, Silent Mike

Tiernan, Silent Mike
See Tiernan, Michael Joseph

Tierney, Cotton
See Tierney, James Arthur

Tierney, Gerald 1924- [FC, ITA, SW]
American actor
* Brady, Scott

Tierney, James Arthur 1894-1953 [BE]
American baseball player
* Tierney, Cotton

Tierney, John Lawrence 1892-1972 [CAP]
Australian author
* James, Brian

Tierney, Reginald
See Russell, Thomas O'Neill

Tietje, Leslie William 1911- [BE]
American baseball player
* Tietje, Toots

Tietje, Toots
See Tietje, Leslie William

Tifew, H. C.
See Fitch, William Edward

Tiffany, Charles 1812-1902 [HPPN]
American jewelry dealer
* America's Leading Jeweler

Tiffany, E. A. 1911- [CA]
American author
* Samuels, E. A.

Tiffany, Louis C. 1848-1933 [HPPN]
American artist
* [The] Father of Favrile Glass

Tiffin, Pamela
See Wonso, Pamela

Tifton, Leo
See Page, Gerald W[ilburn]

Tigar, Chad
See Levi, Peter

[The] Tiger
See Andretti, Mario

[The] Tiger
See Clemenceau, Georges

[The] Tiger
See Petrosian, Tigran

[The] Tiger
See Thurlow, Edward [First Baron Thurlow]

Tiger, Derry
See Ellison, Harlan [Jay]

Tiger, Dick
See Ihetu, Richard

[The] Tiger Earl
See Lindsay, Alexander

Tiger Eyes
See Schragmueller, Elsbeth

Tiger, Jack
See Puechner, Ray

Tiger Jack Fox
See Fox, John Linwood

Tiger Jim Stickland
See Strickland, James

Tiger, John
See Wager, Walter Herman

Tiger Lily
See Blake, Lillie Devereux

Tiger Man Cerdan
See Cerdan, Marcel

[The] Tiger of Alica
See Losada, Manuel

[The] Tiger of Central America
See Guardiola, Santos

[The] Tiger of Honduras
See Guardiola, Santos

[The] Tiger of Malaya
See Yamashita, Tomoyuki

[The] Tiger of Tacayuba [or Tacubaya?]
See Marquez, Leonardo

[The] Tiger of the Dim Trails
See Vasquez, Tiburico

[The] Tiger of the Philippines
See Yamashita, Tomoyuki

Tiger of the Slopes
See Raine, Nancy Greene

Tiger Tom
See Woodward, Thomas Jones

[The] Tiger Woman
See Judd, Ruth Marian McKinnell

[The] Tiger Woman
See Phillips, Clara

Tiggy
See Newman, Oliver

Tighe, Edward ?-1798? [PI]
Irish poet and politician
* T.

Tighe, Virginia 20th c. [EOP]
American believed to have been reincarnated
* Murphy, Bridey
* Simmons, Ruth

Tighe, William [IP]
Irish author
* [A] Father

Tight Lines Thomas
See Thomas, Gary Philip

Tiglath-Pileser III 8th c. BC [HPPN]
King of Assyria
* Pulu

Tigranes 1st c. BC [WBD]
King of Armenia
* [The] Great

[El] Tigre de Guanajuato [The Tiger from Guanajuato]
See Silveti, Juan

[The] Tigress
See Judd, Ruth Marian McKinnell

[The] Tigress
See Kalogeropoulos, Maria Anna Sofia Cecilia

[The] Tigress of Turin
See Lombardi, Lella

Tigrina
See Eide, Edith

Tihoti
See Calderon, George

Tijerina, Reies 20th c.
Mexican-American political organizer
* Rey Tigre [King Tiger]

Tikekar, Shripad Ramchandra 1901-
[AW]
Indian author
* Mushafir, Kartikeya Skylark

Tikhon
See Belyavin, Vasili Ivanovich

Tikhonov, Valentin
See Payne, [Pierre Stephen] Robert

Tiktiner
See Viterbo, Dina Tiktiner

Til, Sonny
See Tilghman, Earlington

Tilbury, John
See McGraw, James

Tilbury, Quenna
See Walker, Emily Kathleen

Tilbury, Tom
See Henley, Robert

Tilden, Big Bill
See Tilden, William Tatem, II

Tilden, Bryant P. 19th c. [HPPN]
American engineer
* Engineer

Tilden, Co Parcener
See Tilden, Samuel Jones

[The] Tilden of His Country
See Morpurgo, [Baron] Hubert Louis
de

Tilden, One Round
See Tilden, William Tatem, II

Tilden, Samuel Jones 1814-1886 [FFF,
HPPN, IP, SN]
American politician
* Crino
* [The] Graystone Sage
* Old Usufruct
* [The] Sage of Gramercy Park
* [The] Sage of Greystone
* Tilden, Co Parcener
* Tilden, Slippery Sam

Tilden, Slippery Sam
See Tilden, Samuel Jones

Tilden, William Tatem, II 1893-1953
[AS, HPPN, OET, SR]
American tennis player
* [The] Court Jouster
* King of the Nets
* Tilden, Big Bill
* Tilden, One Round

Tildsley, Peter 1898-1962 [BEW, FC]
British actor, author, theatre manager
* Haddon, Peter

Tilelli, Carmine Orlando 1930- [BX,
RBE]
American boxer
* Giardello, Joey

Tilesius, G.
See Gistl, Johannes N. Franz Xavier

Tileston, Mary Wilder [Foote] 19th c.
[IP, PA]
American author
* M. W. T.

Tiletanus
See Ravesteyn, Josse

Tilgath-Pilneser 8th c. BC [HPPN]
King of Syria
* Pul

Tilghman, Earlington 20th c. [RO1]
American singer
* Til, Sonny

Tilghman, Fast Draw
See Tilghman, William Matthew

Tilghman, William Matthew 1854-1924
[HPPN]
*American scout, buffalo hunter, law
officer*
* Tilghman, Fast Draw

Tilken, Felix 1860?-1921 [BEW, EMT,
PMJ]
Belgian-born composer
* Caryll, Ivan

Till, Bobo
See Till, Emmett Louis

Till, Emmett Louis 1941-1955 [IBW]
American lynching victim
* Till, Bobo

Till, Fred 1860-1927 [BEW]
British actor
* Lewis, Fred

Tillet, Auguste [IP]
French dentist and author
* Maury, J. C. F.

Tillet, Dorothy [Stockbridge] 1896-
[CC, WW]
Author
* Strange, John Stephen

Tillet, Maurice 20th c.
French wrestler
* [The] French Angel

Tilley, Vesta
See Powles, Matilda Alice

Tilling, Mabel 1880?-1957 [BEW]
British-born actress and playwright
* Constanduros, Mabel

Tillinghast, A. W.
See Tillinghast, Albert Warren

Tillinghast, Albert Warren 1875-1942
[GF]
*American golf course architect and golf
writer*
* Tillinghast, A. W.

Tillinghast, Joseph Leonard 1790-1840
[FFF]
American jurist and author
* Carroll
* Dion

Tillinghast, Oliver Louis 20th c. [BBH]
*American roller skating planner, builder,
flooring expert*
* Tillinghast, Tilli

Tillinghast, Tilli
See Tillinghast, Oliver Louis

Tillis, Fighting Cowboy
See Tillis, James

Tillis, James 1957?-
American boxer
* Tillis, Fighting Cowboy
* Tillis, Quick

Tillis, Quick
See Tillis, James

Tillman, Bad Dude
See Tillman, Russell

Tillman, Benjamin Ryan 1847-1918
[HPPN]
American politician
* [The] Agricultural Moses
* [The] Father of the Shell Manifesto
* Tillman, Pitchfork
* Tillman, Pitchfork Ben

Tillman, Nathaniel Patrick, Sr.
1898-1965 [IBW]
American educator
* Tillman, Tic

Tillman, Pitchfork
See Tillman, Benjamin Ryan

Tillman, Pitchfork Ben
See Tillman, Benjamin Ryan

Tillman, Russell 1946-
American football player
* Tillman, Bad Dude
* Tillman, Rusty

Tillman, Rusty
See Tillman, Russell

Tillman, Tic
See Tillman, Nathaniel Patrick, Sr.

Tilloch, Alexander 1759-1825 [FFF]
Scottish author and journalist
* Biblicus

Tillotson, Joe W. 20th c. [WGT]
Author
* Fuqua, Robert

Tillotson, John [IP]
British author
* [The] Odd Boy

Tillotson, Queena 1896-1951 [BBD]
American opera singer and author
* Mario, Queena

Tillray, Les
See Gardner, Erle Stanley

Tilly
See Kannan, Lakshmi

Tillyard, E. M. W.
See Tillyard, Eustace Mandeville
Wetenhall

Tillyard, Eustace Mandeville Wetenhall
1889-1962 [LC]
British author
* Tillyard, E. M. W.

Tilmon, James [Jim] 1934- [HPPN]
American aviator
* [The] Jet Age Renaissance Man

Tilt, Julia 19th c. [IP, PA]
British author
* Hamilton, May

Tiltman, Hugh Hessell 1897- [MBF]
British author
* Davenport, Tex
* Hessell, Henry

Tiltman, Ronald Frank 1901- [CAP]
British author and journalist
* Fraser, Ronald

Tilton, Alice
See Taylor, Phoebe [Atwood]

Tilton, Dwight
See Richardson, George Tilton

Tilton, James 1745-1822 [DNA, HPPN]
American author and surgeon
* Timoleon

Tilton, Liltin' Martha
See Tilton, Martha

Tilton, Martha 1915- [HPPN]
American singer and actress
* Tilton, Liltin' Martha

Tilton, Mrs. E. L. [FFF]
Entertainer
* Pentland, Mary

Tilton, Stephen Willis [IP, PA]
American poet and publisher
* Uncle Willis

Tilton, Theodore 1835-? [IP, PA]
American author and journalist
* Marmaduke, Sir
* T. T.

Tilton, Warren [IP]
American author
* Trifle

Tim
See Mitelberg, Louis

Tim Tom Conway
See Conway, Thomas Daniel

Timbs, John 1801-1875 [IP, PA]
British journalist, publisher, author
* Welby, Horace

Timbury, Jane 18th c. [IP]
British author
* Astell, [Hon.] Edward

Time Honored Lancaster
See John of Gaunt

[The] Time Juggler
See Siffre, Michel

Time, Mark
See Irwin, H. C.

[The] Time Traveler
See Wells, Herbert George

Timer, Joe
See Theimer, Joseph Michael

[The] Times Bee-Master
See Cumming, John

Timias
See Raleigh, [Sir] Walter

Timken, Henry 1831-1909 [HPPN]
German-American inventor and manufacturer
* [The] Father of the Tapered Roller Bearing

Timm, Cap
See Timm, L. C.

Timm, L. C. 20th c. [BBH]
American baseball coach
* Timm, Cap

Timmins, Samuel 19th c. [IP]
British author
* S. T.

Timmis, Brian 20th c. [CFH]
Football player
* [The] Old Man of the Mountain

Timms, Edward Vivian 1895- [WWL]
Australian author
* Dane, Zel
* Roseller, David

Timoleon
See Orr, Isaac

Timoleon
See Tilton, James

Timon 5th c. BC [HPPN]
Greek nobleman
* [The] Misanthrope of Athens

Timon 4th c. BC [HPPN]
Greek poet and philosopher
* [The] Sillographer

Timon
See Brydges, Grey

Timon
See Brydges, James [First Duke of Chandos]

Timon
See De la Haye, Louis Marie [Vicomte de Cormenin]

Timon, John
See Mitchell, Donald Grant

Timony, Arthur N.
See Vahey, John George Haslette

Timotheus 5th c. [NPS]
Bishop of Alexandria
* [The] Cat

Timothy
See Holmes, Sylvester

Timothy, a Country Boy
See Mellick, Henry George

Timrod, Henry 1829-1867 [HPPN, IP]
American poet and journalist
* Aglaus
* [The] Poet Laureate of the Confederacy

Timsol, Robert
See Bird, Frederic Mayer

Timur [or Timour] 1336-1405 [DEP, HN, RH]
Tartar conqueror
* [The] Destroying Prince
* [The] Firebrand of the Universe
* Ghengis Khan
* [The] Mongolian Bonaparte
* [The] Prince of Destruction
* [The] Scourge of God
* Tamerlane [or Tamburlaine]
* Timur Lenk [Timur the Lame]

Timur Lenk [Timur the Lame]
See Timur [or Timour]

[The] Tin Can Man of Pleasant Hill
See Goranson, Walter

[The] Tin Hermit
See Patino, Simon Iturri

[The] Tin King
See Patino, Simon Iturri

TINA [There is No Alternative]
See Thatcher, Margaret Hilda [Roberts]

Tincker, Mary Agnes [PA]
Author
* M. A. T.

Tincrowdor, Leo Queequeg
See Farmer, Philip Jose

Tindal, Henrietta Euphemia 19th c. [IP]
British author and poet
* Butler, Diana

Tindall, Frederick Cryer 1900- [IAW]
British author
* Mark, John

Tindall, William York 1903-1981 [CA]
American educator and author
* Yorick, A. P.

Tineman [or Tyneman] [One Who Loses]
See Douglas, Archibald

Tiner, John Hudson 1944- [CA]
American author
* Street, Jonathan

Ting Ling
See Chiang, Ping-chih

Tinglehoff, Henry Michael 1940- [FB]
American football player
* Tinglehoff, Mick

Tinglehoff, Mick
See Tinglehoff, Henry Michael

Tingley, Richard Hoadley 1856-? [NAA]
American author
* Lee, Ting
* Puzzle "Nom"

Tini Linguini
See Navratilova, Martina

[The] Tiniest Star in Films
See Flood, Pauline

Tinin
See Manuel, Jose

Tinker, C. B.
See Tinker, Chauncey Brewster

Tinker, Chauncey Brewster 1876-1963
[LC]
American author and educator
* Tinker, C. B.

Tinker, Gerald 1951- [SMG]
American football player
* Tinker, Tink

Tinker, Grant 1926- [HPPN]
American television executive
* Moore, Mr. Mary Tyler

[The] Tinker of Elstow
See Bunyan, John

Tinker, Tink
See Tinker, Gerald

Tinkham, George Holden 1870-?
[HPPN]
American politician
* [The] Big Game Hunter
* [The] Lion Hunter
* Wiskers

[The] Tinley Park Express
See Bettenhausen, Melvin E.

Tinman, Philippi Hamlin
See Wolcot, John

Tinne, Dorothea
See Strover, Dorothea

Tinne, E. D.
See Strover, Dorothea

Tinning, Bud
See Tinning, Lyle Forrest

Tinning, Lyle Forrest 1906-1961 [BE]
American baseball player
* Tinning, Bud

[El] Tino [The Tank]
See Blau Gisbert, Vicente

Tinquette, Miss
See Bourgeois, Jeanne Marie

Tinsley, Gaynell C. 1915- [FB]
American football player
* Tinsley, Gus

Tinsley, Gus
See Tinsley, Gaynell C.

Tinsley, Theodore 20th c. [SFP]
Author
* Grant, Maxwell [house pseudonym]

Tinto, Dick
See Goodrich, Frank Boott

Tinto, Dick
See Jones, Charles A.

Tinto, Gabriel
See Anthony, G. W.

Tintoret
See Robusti, Jacopo

[La] Tintoretta
See Robusti, Marietta

[La] Tintoretta
See Tintoretto, Marietta

Tintoretto
See Robusti, Jacopo

Tintoretto, Domenico
See Robusti, Domenico

Tintoretto, Marietta 1560-1590 [WBD]
Italian painter
* [La] Tintoretta

[The] Tintoretto of England
See Dobson, William

[The] Tintoretto of Switzerland
See Huber, Johann [or John] Rudolphe

Tiny
See Kelly, James

Tiny
See Munster, Mary C. F.

Tiny Alice
See Ramirez, Alice Louise

Tiny Darkhorse
See Robinson, Mike

[The] Tiny Giant
See Murphy, Calvin

Tiny Tim
See Khaury, Herbert Buckingham

Tiny Tim Woodruff
See Woodruff, Timothy Lester

Tiny Tina
See Hurd, Gloria

[El] Tio [The Uncle]
See Campora, Hector

Tio, Luis 1863?-1927 [NOJ]
Mexican-born jazz musician
* Tio, Papa

Tio, Papa
See Tio, Luis

[El] Tio Porsupuesto
See Bolivar, Simon

Tioga George Burns
See Burns, George Henry

Tip
See Marugg, Silvio A.

Tip
See Muhammed, Hamidi

Tipoo Tib [or Tip]
See Hamidi bin Muhammad

Tippecanoe
See Harrison, William Henry

[The] Tippecanoe Roarer
See Harrison, William Henry

Tipperariensis
See Hickie, Daniel B.

[A] Tipperary Man?
See Doheny, Michael

Tipple, Big Dan
See Tipple, Dan[iel Slaughter]

Tipple, Dan[iel Slaughter] 1890-1960
[BE]
American baseball player
* Tipple, Big Dan
* Tipple, Rusty

Tipple, Rusty
See Tipple, Dan[iel Slaughter]

Tippou-Saib 1749-1799 [PA]
Author
* Behadour

Tippy Toes Karras
See Karras, Alex[ander George]

Tiptoft, John 1427?-1470 [DNNS, HN, NPS, RH]
Earl of Worcester
* [The] Butcher of England
* [The] Cruel Judge

Tipton, Dukie
See Tipton, Eric Gordon

Tipton, Eric Gordon 1915- [BE, FB]
American football and baseball player
* [The] Blue Devil
* Eric the Red
* Tipton, Dukie

[The] Tipton Slasher
See Angone, Frank

[The] Tipton Slasher
See Perry, William

Tipton, Thomas
See Pointkowski, Thomas Max

Tiptree, James, Jr.
See Sheldon, Alice Bradley

Tipuca
See Wilson, T. P. Cameron

Tirabeque
See Lafuente [or La Fuente], Modesto

Tirado, Victor Manuel
See Tirado Lopez, Victor

Tirado Lopez, Victor 1940-
Mexican-born guerrilla leader in Nicaragua
* Tirado, Victor Manuel

Tirana, Rifat 1907?-1952 [BI]
Albanian-American economist
* Reveille, Thomas

Tiraqueau, Andre 1480-1588 [SN]
French jurist
* Bridlegoose, Judge

Tirbutt, Honoria 20th c. [TCCM]
British author
* Page, Emma

Tirebuck, W.
See Sharp, William

Tiria
See Bourke, James J.

Tiridates III 238?-314 [WBD]
King of Aremenia
* [The] Great

Tiroff, James [Jim] ?-1975 [SC]
Actor
* Harper, James

Tironi, Carla 1926- [IAW]
Italian author and photographer
* Cerati, Carla

Tirso de Molina
See Tellez, Gabriel

Tirzah, Mademoiselle
See Clewe, Belle Ragnar Parsons

Tisa, Benedict 20th c. [TI 11-1-82]
American FBI agent
* Benedict, James

Tisanthrope, Ter
See Gillespie, William Houyman

Tischbein, Johann Heinrich Wilhelm
1751-1829 [WBD]
German painter
* Goethe-Tischbein
* [The] Neapolitan

Tisdale, Wayman 20th c.
American basketball player
* Good Times Mr. T

Tisdom, James 20th c. [NBB]
American singer
* Tisdom, Smokestack

Tisdom, Smokestack
See Tisdom, James

Tish
See Bulwer-Lytton, Edward George
Earle Lytton

Tishbi, Elijah
See Levita, Elijah

Tisi [or Tisio], Benvenuto 1481?-1559
[WBD]
Italian painter
* Garofalo, Benvenuto da

Tisner
See Artis Gener, Aveli

Tisquantum
See Squanto

Tissant-Bernac, Mathieu
See Macbeath, Innis [Stewart]

Tisserand, Gerard Marcel 1920- [BBD,
OP]
French opera singer
* Souzay, Gerard

Tisserand, Jacques
See Barnes, Jim Weaver

Tissington, Anthony 18th c. [IP]
British author
* [A] Derbyshire Working Miner

Tissot, Jacques-Joseph 1836-1902
French artist
* Tissot, James

Tissot, James
See Tissot, Jacques-Joseph

Titan, Earl
See Fearn, John Russell

Titan of Babel
See Winchell, Walter

[The] Titan of Music
See Wagner, [Wilhelm] Richard

Titania
See Blixen, Karen [Christentze Dinesen]

Titcomb, Cannonball
See Titcomb, Ledell

Titcomb, Ledell 1865-1950 [BE]
American baseball player
* Titcomb, Cannonball

Titcomb, Timothy
See Holland, Josiah Gilbert

Tite Amedie Ardoin
See Ardoin, Amedie

Tite, Prince
See George II

Titi, Prince
See Frederick Louis

Titian
See Vecelli [or Vecellio], Tiziano

[The] Titian of France
See Blanchard, Jacques

[The] Titian of Portugal
See Sanchez Coello, Alonzo

Titmarsh, Belgrave
See Moyse, Charles Ebenezer

Titmarsh, M. A.
See Thackeray, William Makepeace

Titmarsh, Michael Angelo
See Thackeray, William Makepeace

Tito, Josip Broz
See Broz, Josip

[The] Tito of the Arab World
See Assad, Hafez

Titov, Nikolay Alexeyevitch 1800-1875
[BBD]
Russian composer
* [The] Grandfather of Russian Song

Titta, Ruffo Cafiero 1877-1953 [MS]
Italian opera singer
* [The] Lion of Pisa
* Ruffo, Titta

Titterington, Mrs. S. B. 19th c. [PA]
Author
* Graham, Grace

Titterton, W. R.
See Titterton, William Richard

Titterton, William Richard 1876-1963
[LC]
British author
* Titterton, W. R.

Titterwell, Timothy
See Kettell, Samuel

Tittle Tattle, [Sir] Fopling
See Foe, Daniel

Tittle, Y. A.
See Tittle, Yelberton Abraham

Tittle, Yelberton Abraham 1926- [FB,
IPA]
American football player
* Bald Eagle
* Slick, Colonel
* Tittle, Y. A.

Titus
See Dismas [or Dismes]

Titus
See Maginn, William

Titus
See Vespasianus, Titus Flavius Salinus

Titus Aurelius Fulvus Boionius Arrius
86-161 [WBD]
Roman emperor
* Antoninus Pius

Titus, Eve 1922- [CA, TBJ]
American author
* Lord, Nancy

Titus, John Franklin 1876-1943 [BE,
PB]
American baseball player
* Titus, Silent John

[The] Titus of Germany
See Joseph II

Titus, Silent John
See Titus, John Franklin

Titus, Tracy [FFF]
Entertainer
* Oates, Alice

Tityrus
See Chaucer, Geoffrey

Tivag
See Gavit, Daniel E.

Tivoli
See Bleakley, Horace William

Tivoli, Tony
See Vizzini, Sal[vatore]

[Il] Tizianello
See Vecelli, Tiziano

Tjader, Cal
See Tjader, Callen Radcliffe, Jr.

Tjader, Callen Radcliffe, Jr. 1925- [EJ,
PMJ]
American jazz musician
* Tjader, Cal

Tkaczuk, Edward Terrance 1920- [BE]
American baseball player
* Kazak, Edward Terrance

Tloupas, Philolaos 1924?- [BI]
Greek sculptor
* Philolaos

TNT
See Tubbs, Tony

Toal, Mike 1959- [SMG]
Canadian-born hockey player
* Toal, Toaler

Toal, Toaler
See Toal, Mike

[The] Toast of the Barbary Coast
See Prado, Katie

[The] Toastmaster General of the United States
See Jessel, George Albert [Georgie]

Toat
See Goldbogen [or Goldenborgen], Avrom Hirsch

Tobacco Bill Crosby
See Crosby, William R.

Tobacco Chewin' Johnny
See Lanning, John Young

[The] Tobacco Prince
See Lorillard, Pierre

Toberman, Charles 1880-1981 [HPPN]
American real estate developer
* Hollywood, Mr.

Tobey, David 1898- [EJS]
American basketball player and coach
* [The] Coach of Coaches
* Tobey, Pep

Tobey, Pep
See Tobey, David

Tobias, Katherine
See Gottfried, Theodore Mark

Tobias, Lenore 1912- [BEW]
American theatre party agent
* Tobin, Lenore

Tobik, David Vance 1953- [SMG]
American baseball player
* Tobik, Tobe

Tobik, Tobe
See Tobik, David Vance

Tobin, Abba Dabba
See Tobin, James Anthony [Jim]

Tobin, Daniel 19th c. [HPPN]
American gambler
* Tobin, Lucky Dan

Tobin, James Anthony [Jim] 1912-1969 [BE, BN, PB]
American baseball player
* Ol' Ironsides
* Tobin, Abba Dabba

Tobin, James Edward 1905-1968 [CAP]
American poet, editor, educator
* Rayne, Alan

Tobin, John H. 19th c. [IP, PA]
American journalist
* John of York

Tobin, John Martin [Johnny] 1906- [BE]
American baseball player
* Tobin, Tip

Tobin, Lenore
See Tobias, Lenore

Tobin, Lucky Dan
See Tobin, Daniel

Tobin, Marion Brooks 1916- [BE]
American baseball player
* Tobin, Pat

Tobin, Pat
See Tobin, Marion Brooks

Tobin, Patricia L. 1943- [BA]
American business executive
* P. T.

Tobin, Tip
See Tobin, John Martin [Johnny]

Tobler, Oscar 1897-1961 [EJS, RBE]
American boxer
* Jackson, Willie

Toby, Harriet
See Katzman, Harriet Joan

Toby, Liz
See Minsky, Betty Jane [Toebe]

Toby, M. P.
See Lucy, [Sir] Henry William

Toby, Simeon
See Trask, George F.

Toche, Raoul [PA]
Author
* Tovel, Raoul
* Triet, Robert
* Trinsome

Tockler, Conrad 1495-1530 [PA]
Author
* Noricus

Tocnaye, Alain de Bougrenet de la 1926- [HPPN]
French assassin
* [The] Real Jackal

Tod, Evelyn
See Thompson, Edith

Tod, George 19th c. [IP]
Scottish clergyman
* [A] Friend of the People

Tod, John 19th c. [IP]
Scottish author
* Strathesk, John

Tod, Osma Gallinger 1898-1982? [CAP]
American author
* Couch, Osma Palmer
* Gallinger, Osma Couch

Tod, Thomas 18th c. [HPPN]
Scottish author
* [The] True Briton

Todd, A. L.
See Todd, Alden

Todd, Alden 1918- [IAW]
American author
* Todd, A. L.

Todd, Ann
See Mayfield, Ann Todd

Todd, Anne Ophelia
See Dowden, Anne Ophelia [Todd]

Todd, Arthur 1914- [CED]
Canadian singer
* [The] Canadian Crosby
* Todd, Dick

Todd, Barbara Euphan 1890-1976 [TCC]
British author
* Bower, Barbara
* Euphan

Todd, Chapman C. 19th c. [HPPN]
American naval officer
* [The] Dewey of Manzanillo

Todd, Charles 1872-1955 [THR]
British actor and theatrical manager
* Windermere, Charles

Todd, Dick
See Todd, Arthur

Todd, Eric
See DuBreuil, Elizabeth Lorinda

Todd, H. E.
See Todd, Herbert Eatton

Todd, Henry Cook ?-1862 [CCL]
Canadian author
* One in Retirement
* [A] Traveller

Todd, Herbert 19th c. [IP]
British poet and clergyman
* Herbert, T.

Todd, Herbert Eatton 1908- [TCC]
British author
* Todd, H. E.

Todd, John M[urray] 1918- [CA]
British author
* Fox, John

Todd, John Payne 1792-? [HPPN]
Stepson of American president James Madison
* [The] Prince of America

Todd, [Rev.] Jonathan 1713-1791 [HPPN]
American clergyman
* [A] Member of the Consociation and Association

Todd, Laurie
See Thorburn, Grant

Todd, Margaret 1859-1918 [LC]
Scottish author
* Travers, Graham

Todd, Michael
See Goldbogen [or Goldenborgen], Avrom Hirsch

Todd, Nick
See Boone, Nick

Todd, Paul
See Posner, Richard

Todd, Paul Adrian 1953- [DC]
British cricketer
* Todd, Tubs

Todd, Richard
See Palethorpe-Todd, Richard

Todd, Ruthven 1914- [CC, WD]
American author and poet
* Campbell, R. T.

Todd, Sarah Manning
See Freeman, Jean Todd

Todd, Silas 18th c. [FFF]
Assistant of British evangelist, John Wesley
* [The] Good Samaritan of London

Todd, Thelma
See Lloyd, Alison

Todd, Tubs
See Todd, Paul Adrian

Todd, W. 19th c. [IP]
British author
* [A] Sunday Scholar

Toddi
See Rivetta, Pietro Silvio [Conte di Solonghello]

Todeschini-Piccolomini, Francesco 1439-1503 [CAL]
Pope
* Pius III

Todkill, Anas
See Cooke, John Esten

[The] Toe
See Groza, Louis

Toenes, Hal
See Toenes, William Harrel

Toenes, William Harrel 1917- [BE]
American baseball player
* Toenes, Hal

Toepfer, Wolfgang 1525?-1591? [BBD]
German author
* Figulus, Wolfgang

Toepffer, Rodolphe 1799-1846 [IP]
Swiss artist and author
* Oldbuck, Obadiah
* Vieux Bois, M.

Toernudd, Margit 1905- [IAW]
Finnish author
* Niininen, Margit

Tofano, Sergio 1886-1973 [WEC]
Italian cartoonist, filmmaker, actor
* Sto

Tofte, Arthur 1902- [IAW]
American author
* Andersson, Nic
* Babcock, Florence
* Boles, Nick

Tofte, Robert 16th c. [IP]
British author
* R. T., Gent., of London

Tofujin
See Kabashima, Katsuichi

Togae, Cedant Arma
See Adams, Samuel

Togliatti, Palmiro 1893-1964 [BI, HPPN]
Italian Communist leader
* Ercoli, Ercole
* [The] Italian Master of Maneuver

Togo, Hashimura
See Irwin, Wallace Admah

Togo, Mas
See Yong-I-Choy

Togrul Wang Khan 12th c. [HN]
Mongol chieftain
* Prester John

Toit, Jacob B. du 1877-? [HPPN]
South African poet
* Totius

Tojo, Eiki 1885-1948 [HPPN, WBD]
Japanese prime minister and army officer
* [The] Fiercest Hawk in Asia
* Razor Brain
* Tojo, Hideki

Tojo, Hideki
See Tojo, Eiki

Tokarski, E. F.
See Freund, Edward

Tokitsukaze
See Akiyoshi, Sadaji

Tokle, Torger 1920-1945 [BBH, HPPN]
Norwegian-born skier
* [The] Babe Ruth of Skiing
* [The] Flying Norseman

Tokohama, Charlie
See Grant, Charles

[The] Tokyo Geisha
See Peach Blossom

[The] Tokyo Giant
See Sawell, Larry

Tokyo Joe Eto
See Eto, Ken

Tokyo Rose?
See D'Aquino, Iva Ikuko [Toguri]

Tolan, Eddie 1908-1967 [BBH]
American track and field athlete
* [The] Midnight Express

Tolan, Michael
See Tuchow, Michael

Tolan, Robert [Bobby] 1945- [BA]
American baseball player
* B. T.
* Bobby T.

Toland, Gregg 1904-1948 [HPPN]
American cameraman
* [The] Creator of the Pan Focus

Toland, John
See Toland, Junius Janus

Toland, Junius Janus 1670-1722 [HPPN, IP, SN, WBD]
Irish author
* [Un] Anglois
* Britto-Batavius
* Eoganesius, Janus Junius
* Hierophilus
* [The] New Heresiarch
* Patricola
* Toland, John

Toland, Mary B. M. 19th c. [HPPN]
American author
* M. B. M. T.

Tolar, Cannonball
See Tolar, Charles G.

Tolar, Charles G. 1937- [FB]
American football player
* Tolar, Cannonball

Tolby, Arthur
See Infield, Glenn [Berton]

Tolchard, Roger William 1946- [DC]
British cricketer
* Tolchard, Tolly

Tolchard, Tolly
See Tolchard, Roger William

Tolderlund, Hother ?-1880 [IP]
Danish poet
* Lan, Viggo

Toldy, Ferencz
See Schedel, Ferencz

Tolentino, Arturo 1911?-
Philippine politician
* Tolentino, Turing

Tolentino, Turing
See Tolentino, Arturo

Toler, John [Earl of Norbury] ?-1831 [HN]
Irish jurist
* [The] Hanging Judge

[The] Tolerant Tiger
See Hiss, Alger

Toletus
See Tappan, David

Toliver, George
See Masselink, Ben

Tolkien, J. R. R.
See Tolkien, John Ronald Reuel

Tolkien, John Ronald Reuel 1892-1973 [HPPN, LC]
British author
* J. R. R. T.
* [The] Master of Middle Earth
* Tolkien, J. R. R.
* Tolleis

Toll, Frederick 18th c. [HPPN, IP]
British clergyman and author
* [A] Friend to the Established Church

Tolleis
See Tolkien, John Ronald Reuel

Tollemache, David 20th c. [WWL]
British author
* Lovell, Mark

Toller, Kate Caffrey
See Caffrey, Kate

Tollett, Charles Albert 20th c. [BA]
American physician
* C. A. T.

Tolliver, Steve 20th c. [ESF]
Author
* Davies, Fredric [joint pseudonym with Ron(ald C.) Ellik]

Tolmage, Gerald
See Gardner, Maurice

Tolman, Harriet [Smith] 19th c. [IP]
American author
* H. S. T.

Tolnai, Karoly
See De Tolnay, Charles Erich

Tolnai, Vagujhelyi Karoly
See De Tolnay, Charles Erich

Tolson, Chester Julius 1901- [BE]
American baseball player
* Tolson, Chick
* Tolson, Slug

Tolson, Chick
See Tolson, Chester Julius

Tolson, Dean 1951- [SMG]
American basketball player
* [The] Twig

Tolson, Dover
See Tolson, Marion

Tolson, Marion 1927- [IBW]
American racehorse trainer
* Tolson, Dover

Tolson, Slug
See Tolson, Chester Julius

Tolstoy, Leo
See Tolstoy, Lev Lvovich

Tolstoy, Leo
See Tolstoy, Lev Nikolayevich

Tolstoy, Lev Lvovich 1869-1945
Russian author
* Tolstoy, Leo

Tolstoy, Lev Nikolayevich 1828-1910
[LC]
Russian author
* Tolstoy, Leo

Tolz, Nick?
See Slotkin, Joseph

Tom
See Garfunkel, Art

Tom
See Vandover, Bud

Tom, Dick 1881-1923 [HPPN]
American actor
* Harry

[The] Tom Moore of France
See Amfrye, Guillaume

[The] Tom Moore of the Confederacy
See Ryan, [Father] Abram Joseph

Tom of Bedlam
See Milbourne, Luke

Tom of Ten Thousand
See Thynne, Thomas

[The] Tom Sawyer of Rock
See Deutschendorf, Henry John, Jr.

Tom the First
See Shadwell, Thomas

Tom the Midget
See Sullivan, George S.

Tom the Second
See Otway, Thomas

Tomacelli, Pietro ?-1404 [WBD]
Pope
* Boniface IX

Tomalin, Ruth 20th c. [WD]
British author and poet
* Leaver, Ruth

Tomaling, Susan 1946- [SW]
American actress
* Sarandon, Susan

Tomamoto, Thomas
See Sugimoto, Tsunetaro

Tomanek, Bones
See Tomanek, Richard Carl

Tomanek, Richard Carl 1931- [BE]
American baseball player
* Tomanek, Bones

Tomaras, William [Bill] 20th c. [BBH]
American wrestler and coach
* [The] Father of High School Wrestling

Tomasic, Niccolo 1802-1874 [WBD]
Italian author
* Tommaseo, Niccolo

Tomasito, Don
See Robertson, Thomas Anthony

Tomato Face Cullop
See Cullop, Henry

Tomato Face Lamabe
See Lamabe, John Alexander [Jack]

Tombo, Monsieur
See Armstrong, John

[The] Tomboy of the Air
See Scott, Blanche Stuart

[The] Tomboy With the Voice
See Kappelhoff, Doris von

[The] Tombs Angel
See Barberi, Maria

Tombs, Harry
See Walley, David Gordon

Tomes [A Bleeder or Carver]
See Vallot, Antoine

Tomfool
See Farjeon, Eleanor

Tomkiewicz, Mina 1917-1975 [CAP]
Polish-born journalist and author
* Meta
* Quichot, Dona

Tomkins, Isaac
See Brougham, Henry Peter

Tomkins, Jane Harrison 1841-1912
[DNA]
Author and poet
* Harrison, Jennie

Tomkins, Jasper
See Batey, Tom

Tomkins, Julia Marguerite Hunter Manchee 1909- [HPPN]
British author
* Neilson, Marguerite

Tomkins, S. Yewell 1909- [HPPN]
American actor
* Ewell, Tom

Tomkinson, Constance
See Weeks, Constance Tomkinson

Tomlin, Beadley 20th c. [EF]
American football player
* Tomlin, Tom

Tomlin, Eric Walter Frederick 1913-
[AW]
British author
* Stuart, Frederick

Tomlin, Felicity 1910- [TR]
British playwright
* Douglas, Felicity

Tomlin, Lily
See Tomlin, Mary Jean

Tomlin, Mary Jean 1939-
American comedienne and actress
* Tomlin, Lily

Tomlin, Pinky
See Tomlin, Truman

Tomlin, Tom
See Tomlin, Beadley

Tomlin, Truman 1908- [PMJ]
American composer, singer, bandleader
* Tomlin, Pinky

Tomline, F.
See Gilbert, [Sir] William Schwenck

Tomlins, Frederick Guest 1804-1867
[FFF]
British journalist
* Littlejohn

Tomlins, Keith Patrick 1957- [DC]
British cricketer
* Tomlins, Tommo

Tomlins, Thomas Edlyne 18th c. [IP]
British attorney and author
* [A] Barrister of the Inner Temple

Tomlins, Tommo
See Tomlins, Keith Patrick

Tomlinson, B. W. 19th c. [FFF, IP]
American author
* Picket

Tomlinson, Caroline [IP]
American author
* Aunt Carrie

Tomlinson, Frederick Charles 1867?-?
[CW]
Jamaican author
* Charles, Frederick

Tomlinson, H. M.
See Tomlinson, Henry Major

Tomlinson, Henry Major 1873-1958
[LC, TC]
British author
* Tomlinson, H. M.

Tomlinson, Ike
See Tomlinson, J. A.

Tomlinson, J. A. 20th c. [BBH]
American baseball coach
* Tomlinson, Ike

Tomlinson, Red
See Tomlinson, William G.

Tomlinson, William G. 20th c.
American military aviator
* Tomlinson, Red

Tomlison, Henry 1865-? [WWL]
British poet
* George, Henry Stephen

Tommaseo, Niccolo
See Tomasic, Niccolo

[The] Tommy Moore of France
See Beranger, Pierre Jean de

[The] Tommy Steele of Scotland
See Harvey, Alex

Tommy the Cork
See Corcoran, Thomas Gardiner

Tompion, Thomas 1639-1713 [SN, WBD]
British clockmaker
* [The] Father of Clock-Making
* [The] Father of English Watchmaking

Tompkins, Elizabeth Vreeland 1928?-
1985
American poet and radio personality
* Vreeland, Elizabeth

Tompkins, Everett Thomas 1931- [CA]
American author and columnist
* Motmot, Snik P.

Tompkins, Harry 20th c. [GW]
American rodeo performer
* Tompkins, Uppy

Tompkins, Herbert Winckworth 1867-?
[LAO]
British author and journalist
* Pepys in Essex

**Tompkins, Julia [Marguerite Hunter
Manchee]** 1909- [CA, WD]
British author
* Neilson, Marguerite

Tompkins, Juliet Wilbor
See Pottle, Juliet Wilbor Tompkins

Tompkins, Ron[ald Everett] 1944- [BE]
American baseball player
* Tompkins, Stretch

Tompkins, Stretch
See Tompkins, Ron[ald Everett]

Tompkins, Uppy
See Tompkins, Harry

Tompkins, Yewell 1909- [BEW, IPA,
ITA]
American actor
* Ewell, Tom

Toms, Tubby
See Toms, William L.

Toms, William L. 20th c. [BLB]
American journalist
* Toms, Tubby

Tomson, Graham R.
See Watson, Rosamund [Ball] Marriott

Tomson, Tommy
See Tomson, W. R.

Tomson, W. R. 20th c.
American advertising salesman
* Tomson, Tommy

Ton Duc Thang 1889?-1980
Vietnamese president
* Uncle Ton

Ton of Fun
See Barkley, Charles

Ton Ven
See Bordewijk, Ferdinand

Tonashi
See Harrington, Mark Raymond

Tonatiuh
See Alvarado, Pedro de

Tonawanda, Jackie 1948- [IBW]
American boxer
* [The] Female Ali

Toner, James
See Barry, Arthur

Tones, Joseph Meredith 19th c. [HPPN]
American author
* J. M. T.

Toney, Andrew 20th c. [NW 5-27-85]
American basketball player
* [The] Boston Strangler

Toney, Lemuel Gordon 1875-1941 [ASC,
BEW, CED]
American entertainer and songwriter
* Leonard, Eddie

Tong Van So
See Nguyen That Thanh

Tong, William 18th c. [HPPN]
British dissenter
* W. T.

Tongue, Cornelius 1800-1884 [IP, PA]
British author
* Cecil

[The] Tongue Loosed Doctor
See Sacheverell, Henry

Toni San the Terrific
See Sailer, Toni

Tonio K.
See Krikorian, Steve

Tonkin, Doc
See Tonkin, Harry Glenville

Tonkin, Harry Glenville 1881-1959 [BE]
American baseball player
* Tonkin, Doc

[Le] Tonkinois
See Ferry, Jules Francois Camille

Tonks, John 1927- [ART]
British sculptor
* J. T.

Tonna, Charlotte Elizabeth 1792-1846
[DEL, FFF, IP]
British author
* C. E.
* Charlotte-Elizabeth

Tonneman, Charles Richard 1881-1951
[BE]
American baseball player
* Tonneman, Tony

Tonneman, Tony
See Tonneman, Charles Richard

Tonnies, Ferdinand Julius 1855-? [LAO]
German educator and author
* Normannus

Tons, Helen [FFF]
Entertainer
* Secor, Helena

Tonsenius
See Townshend, Charles

Tonson, Jacob 1656?-1736 [HPPN, SN]
British publisher
* Old Jacob
* [The] Prince of Publishers

Tonson, Jacob
See Bennett, [Enoch] Arnold

Tonson, Monsieur
See Taylor, John

Tonti, Henri de 1650-1704 [HPPN, SN]
Explorer of the Mississippi Valley
* [The] Iron Hand
* Tonty of the Iron Hand

Tonto
See Smith, Harold J.

Tonty of the Iron Hand
See Tonti, Henri de

Tony
See Cholmondeley, Archer

Tony C.
See Conigliaro, Anthony Richard

Tony Ducks Corallo
See Corallo, Antonio

Tony Pro Provenzano
See Provenzano, Anthony

Tony the Ant
See Spilotro, Anthony

Tony the Aristocrat
See Genna, Antonio

Tony the Gentleman
See Genna, Antonio

Tony the Silent
See Pietruszka, Anthony Francis

Tony the Terror
See Smith, Tony

Too Mean Martin
See Martin, Harvey

Too Strong Boyd
See Boyd, Gregory Earl

Too Tall Jones
See Jones, Edward Lee

Too Tall Patterson
See Patterson, Sheila

Too Tight Henry
See Castle, Henry Lee

Too Tight Henry
See Townsend, Henry

Took, Belladonna
See Chapman, Vera

Took, Peregrine
See Took, Steve

Took, Steve 20th c. [CMA]
Musician
* Took, Peregrine

Tooke, Horne
See Horne, John

Tooke, Louise Mathews 1950- [CA]
American author
* Mathews, Louise

Tooke, William 1774-1820 [IP, PA]
British author and barrister
* M. M. M.

Tooker, Richard 1902- [WGT]
American author
* Lemke, Henry E.

Toole, Rex
See Tralins, S[andor] Robert [Bob]

Tooley, John 20th c. [IBW]
American playwright, producer, actor
* Ashby, John

Tooley, Nicholas
See Wilkinson, Nicholas

Tooley, Sarah Anne 20th c. [HPPN]
British author
* Leslie, Marion

Toom Tabard [Empty Jacket]
See Baliol [or Balliol], John

Toomay, Pat 20th c.
American football player
* Toomay, Ropes

Toomay, Ropes
See Toomay, Pat

Toombs, John 1927- [CA]
American author
* Kent, Fortune
* Scofield, Jonathan
* Wilde, Jocelyn
* Willoughby, Lee Davis

Toombs, Robert 1810-1885 [HPPN]
American politician
* [The] Georgia Fire Eater

Toonder, Martin
See Groom, Arthur William

Toorop, Annie Caroline 1891-1955 [CAR]
Dutch painter
* Toorop, Charley

Toorop, Charley
See Toorop, Annie Caroline

Tootell, Hugh ?-1745 [PA]
British author
* Dodd, Charles

Toothful Teddy
See Roosevelt, Theodore [Teddy]

Toothpick Ben Colvin
See Colvin, Ben[jamin]

Toothpick Sam Jones
See Jones, Samuel

[The] Tooz
See Matuszak, John

Top Balcony Belter
See Zimmerman, Ethel Agnes

Top Cat Jackson
See Jackson, Cubby

Top Cat Norman
See Norman, Fredie Hubert

Top Cat Sears
See Sears, John, Jr.

[The] Top Cop
See Webster, William Hedgcock

[The] Top Fashion Photographer
See Avedon, Richard

[The] Top Football Coach in America
See Parker, Raymond Klein

[The] Top Hatted Tragedian of Jazz
See Friedman, Theodore Leopold

[The] Top Scofflaw
See Rabin, Henry

[The] Top Wheel at the Brickyard
See Rose, Mauri

Toperoff, Sam 1933- [CA]
American author and poet
* Potter, Faith

Topham, Anthony 20th c. [RO2]
British musician
* Topham, Top

Topham, Thomas 1710-1753? [DNNS, FFF, RH]
British strongman
* [The] British Samson
* [The] English Milo
* [The] Samson of England
* [The] Strong Man

Topham, Top
See Topham, Anthony

Topi
See Vikstedt, Toivo Alarik

Toplady, Augustus Montagu 1740-1778 [FFF, IP]
British clergyman
* [An] Hanoverian
* Philaretus
* [A] Presbyter of the Church of England

Toplis, Fred 1874-? [THR]
British comedian
* Rome, Fred

Topol
See Topol, Chaim

Topol, Chaim 1935- [FC, SW]
Israeli actor
* Topol

Topolski, Feliks 1907- [ART]
Polish-born painter and draftsman
* F. T.

Toporcer, George 1899- [BE, PB]
American baseball player
* Toporcer, Specs

Toporcer, Specs
See Toporcer, George

Toppan, Jane
See Kelley, Nora

Topperwein, Elizabeth ?-1945 [AS]
American trapshooter
* Topperwein, Plinky

Topperwein, Plinky
See Topperwein, Elizabeth

Toppin, Rupe
See Toppin, Ruperto

Toppin, Ruperto 1941- [BE]
Panamanian-born baseball player
* Toppin, Rupe

Topping, Godfrey
See Robertson, John

Topping, Leo
See Leo, Bob

Topside, Papa
See Bond, George

Topsy
See Duncan, Rosetta

Topsy
See Morris, William

Tor, Regina
See Shekerjian, Regina Tor

Torakis, Louis 1928- [BEW]
American costume designer
* Travis, Michael

Torberg, Friedrich
See Kantor-Berg, Friedrich

Torbert, Carolyn 1938?- [BI]
American entertainer
* Barr, Candy

Torbett, Harvey Douglas Louis 1921-
[CA]
British author
* Dee, Henry
* Isis

Torbett, John Walter 1871-? [NAA]
American physician, poet, writer
* Uncle Peter

Torborg, Jeffrey Allen 1941- [SMG]
American baseball player
* Rutgers, Rudy

[The] Torch of Eloquence
See Masfar ben Bedreddin, Al-

[The] Torch of Pengwern
See Gwenwyn

[The] Torch of Wisdom
See Schurman, Anna Maria von

Torchy
See Hamilton, John Daniel Miller

Torday, Ursula 20th c. [CC, WD, WW]
British author
* Allardyce, Paula
* Blackstock, Charity
* Blackstock, Lee

Tordenskiol [Thunder Shield]
See Wessel, Peder

Torelli, Giuseppe 1721-1781 [IP]
Italian scholar and mathematician
* D'Arco, Ciu

Torello, James 1931-
American underworld figure
* Torello, Turk

Torello, Turk
See Torello, James

Torerito [Little Bullfighter]
See Bejarano y Carrasco, Rafael

Torga, Miguel
See Coelho Da Rocha, Adolfo

Torgeson, [Clifford] Earl 1924- [BE, PB]
American baseball player
* [The] Earl of Snohomish
* Torgeson, Torgie

Torgeson, Lavern 1929- [SMG]
American football coach
* Torgeson, Torgy

Torgeson, Torgie
See Torgeson, [Clifford] Earl

Torgeson, Torgy
See Torgeson, Lavern

Torgosi, Karlon
See Ackerman, Forrest J[ames]

Torgosi, Vespertina
See Ackerman, Forrest J[ames]

Torgownik, William 1907- [CA]
American publisher, author, poet
* Targ, William
* Yu, Charles

Torigi, Richard
See Tortorigi, Santo V.

Torikichi 19th c.
Japanese sumo wrestler
* Raiden

Torin, Sidney 1909- [BI]
American disk jockey
* Symphony Sid

Torkelson, Chester LeRoy 1894-1964
[BE]
American baseball player
* Torkelson, Red

Torkelson, Red
See Torkelson, Chester LeRoy

Torley, Luke
See Blish, James [Benjamin]

Torme, Mel[vin Howard] 1925-
American singer and songwriter
* Butterscotch, Mr.
* [The] Kid with the Gauze in His Jaws
* [The] Velvet Fog
* [The] Velvet Frog
* Wyatt, Wesley Butler

Torment, Mel
See Lennon, John

[The] Tormented Warrior
See Ludendorff, Erich Friedrich Wilhelm

Tormer, Cill
See Pelly, Gerald Conn

Tormey, Michael 1820-1893 [PI]
Irish poet
* Clericus
* T.

Torn, Elmore Rual, Jr. 1931- [BEW, FC, TR]
American actor and director
* Torn, Rip

Torn, Rip
See Torn, Elmore Rual, Jr.

[The] Tornado
See Wayne, Anthony

Tornado Jake Weimer
See Weimer, Jacob

Toro, Fermin 1807-1865 [FFF]
Venezuelan statesman and editor
* Kastos, Emiro

Torok, Lou 1927- [CA]
American author
* [The] Convict Writer

Torpare, Tord
See Sandblad-Haneson, Emelie Cecilia Sofia

Torphy, Red
See Torphy, Walter Anthony

Torphy, Walter Anthony 1891- [BE]
American baseball player
* Torphy, Red

Torquatus
See Jonson, Ben[jamin]

Torquemada
See Mathers, Edward Powys

Torquemada, Juan de [or John]
1388-1468 [HN]
Spanish monk and prelate
* Defender of the Faith

Torquemada, Tomas de 1420-1498
[HPPN]
Spanish clergyman and inquisitor general
* [The] Grand Inquisitor
* [The] Scourge of the Jews

Torquet, Andre 1873-1918 [WBD]
French poet and author
* Nau, John Antoine

Torquil
See Supple, Gerald Henry

Torquito [Little Torco]
See Vigiola Del Torco, Serafin

Torr, Iain
See MacKinnon, Charles Roy

Torr, Joan Rosita 1893?-1967 [LAO, LC]
British author
* Forbes, Rosita

Torrance, Baby Jack
See Torrance, Jack

Torrance, Jack 1912-1970 [TF]
American track and field athlete
* [The] Baby Elephant
* Torrance, Baby Jack

Torrance, Lee
See Sadgrove, Sidney Henry

[The] Torre of Poetry
See Gray, Thomas

Torre Lopez, Fernando 1927- [IAW]
Mexican-born author
* Grimaldo, Benjamin

Torrence, David
See Thoyson, David

Torrence, Ernest
See Thayson, Ernest

Torrens, [Lieut. Colonel] Henry D'Oyley
19th c.   [HPPN]
British army officer
* [A] Field Officer

Torrens, Robert 1780-1864   [IP]
Irish economist, naval officer politician
* [A] Member of the Political Economy
  Club

Torres, Alacran 20th c.   [BX, RBE]
Mexican boxer
* Torres, Efren

Torres, Don Gilberto Nunez 1915-   [BE]
Cuban-born baseball player
* Torres, Gil

Torres, Efren
See Torres, Alacran

Torres, Gil
See Torres, Don Gilberto Nunez

Torres, Jose Luis 1936-   [WBC]
Puerto Rican-born boxer
* Torres, Quick Hands

Torres, Kano
See Torres, Milton

Torres, Milton 1966?-   [NW 7-2-84]
American dancer
* Torres, Kano

Torres, Quick Hands
See Torres, Jose Luis

Torres, R. H.
See Hoffman, Burton Charles

Torres, Raquel
See Osterman, Paula Marie

Torres, Rosendo, Jr. 1948-   [SMG]
Puerto Rican-born baseball player
* Torres, Rusty

Torres, Rusty
See Torres, Rosendo, Jr.

Torres, Tereska [Szwarc] 20th c.   [CA,
WD]
French author
* Achard, George

Torres Jimenez, Andres 1945-   [GS]
Spanish bullfighter
* [El] Monaguillo [The Altar Boy]

Torres y Feria, Manuel de 1833-1892
[CW]
Cuban playwright
* De La Flor, Serafin

Torres y Reina, Emilio 1874-1947   [GS,
HPPN]
Spanish bullfighter
* Bombita [Little Bomb]
* Nifio de la Eterna Sonrisa
* Nifio de Tomares

Torres y Reina, Manuel 1884-1936   [GS]
Spanish bullfighter
* Bombita III [Little Bomb the Third]

Torres y Reina, Ricardo 1879-1936
[GS, OCS]
Spanish bullfighter
* Bombita [Little Bomb]

Torrey, Amos   [PA]
Author
* B. T.

Torrey, Elizabeth R. 19th c.   [HPPN]
American author
* Catius, Junior

Torrey, Henry Warren 19th c.   [HPPN]
American scholar
* H. W. T.

Torrey, Marjorie
See Chanslor, Marjorie Torrey [Hood]

Torrey, Therese Von Hohoff 1898?-1974
[CA]
American author and editor
* Hohoff, Tay

Torrey, Ware 1905-   [WW]
Author
* Crosby, Lee

Torri, Francesco 1891-   [BI]
Italian industrialist and painter
* Marinotti, Franco

Torriano, Hugh Arthur 1860-?   [WWL]
British author
* Marchmont, Frederick

Torrie, Malcolm
See Mitchell, Gladys [Maude Winifred]

Torrijos, Omar 20th c.   [NW 9-27-82]
Panamanian president
* Papa General

Torrio, John [Johnny] 1882-1957   [BLB,
HPPN, MM]
Italian-born American underworld figure
* [The] Father of Modern American
  Gangsterdom
* [The] Fox
* [The] Immune
* J. T.
* J. T.
* Langley, Frank
* McCarthy, J. T.
* Torrio, Little John
* Torrio, Papa Johnny
* Torrio, Terrible John

Torrio, Little John
See Torrio, John [Johnny]

Torrio, Papa Johnny
See Torrio, John [Johnny]

Torrio, Terrible John
See Torrio, John [Johnny]

Torro, Pel
See Fanthorpe, R[obert] Lionel

Torsi, Tristan
See Lang, Isaac

Torstensdotter, Elsa Viveca 1920-   [BDF,
WEF]
Swedish-born actress
* Lindfors, Viveca

Torsvan, Traven?
See Marut, Ret

Tortero [Cake Maker]
See Santos, Enrique

Tortoriello, Joseph 1902-   [EJ, PMJ,
WWJ]
American jazz musician
* Tarto, Joe

Tortorigi, Santo V. 1917-   [OP]
American opera singer
* Torigi, Richard

[The] Torture Murderess
See Baniszewski, Gertrude Wright

[A] Tory
See Adams, Samuel

[A] Tory
See Knatchbull-Hugessen, Edward
Hugessen [First Baron Bradbourne]

[A] Tory of the Old School
See Ward, Plumer

[The] Tory Terrier
See Churchill, John [First Duke of
Marlborough]

[The] Tory Traitor
See Honeyman, John

[The] Toscanini of the Pratfall
See Biden, Edmond P.

Tosh, Peter
See MacIntosh, Peter

Tosi, Carlo 1538-1584   [SN]
* Borromeo, Cardinal

Tosini, Michele
See Di Ridolfo, Michele

Toson, Shimazaki
See Haruki, Shimazaki

Tosswill, Leonard R. Major 1880-?
[WWL]
British author
* Kyrle

Tostenson, John 1827-1876   [BBH,
HPPN]
Norwegian-born skier
* Rue, Jon Thoresen
* Thompson, Holy John
* Thompson, John Albert
* Thompson, Snowshoe

Tot, Endre
See Toth, Endre

Totah, Knobby
See Totah, Nabil Marshall

Totah, Nabil Marshall 1930-   [EJ]
Jordanian-born jazz musician
* Totah, Knobby

[A] Total Abstainer
See Corder, Susanna

Total Man
See Salter, Sy

Toth, Andreas 1910?- [BDF, FD, WEF]
Hungarian-born director
* De Toth, Andre

Toth, Endre 1937- [CAR]
Hungarian artist
* Tot, Endre

Toth, Lazlo
See Novello, Don

Totham, Mary
See Breinburg, Petronella

Totila
See Baduila

Totius
See Toit, Jacob B. du

Toto
See De Curtis-Gagliardi, Antonio Furst

Toto
See Gerardin, Louis

Toto the Clown
See Novello, Armando

Tototoro [All Bull]
See Suarez, Carlos

Totten, Charles Adiel Lewis 1851-1908
[DNA, FFF]
American inventor and author
* Alcott, Ten

Totten, Satellite
See Totten, Willie

Totten, W. Fred 1905- [IAW]
American educator and author
* Worthington Ball, John

Totten, Willie 20th c. [WP 12-15-85]
American football player
* Totten, Satellite

Totts, Kid
See Blaise, Ed

Toucey, Kate
See Morris, Mrs. Austin W.

[The] Touch Doctor
See Greatrakes [or Greatorex],
Valentine

Touchatout
See Bienvenu, Leon

Touchdown Tony Adams
See Adams, Anthony L.

Touchdown Tony Baker
See Baker, Tony

[The] Touchdown Twin
See Bates, Mickey

[The] Touchdown Twin
See Caroline, James Calvin

Touch'em, Timothy
See Beck, Thomas

Touchstone
See Boote, Henry Ernest

Touchstone
See Burton, Claude Edward Cole-
Hamilton

Touchstone
See Durcie, John

Touchstone
See Savage, John

Touchstone, Timothy
See Aston, W.

Touchstone, Timothy
See Taunton, William Elias

Touchwood
See Garner, Katherine Minta

Toucke, Marion 1898?-1962 [BEW]
American opera singer
* Telva, Marion

[The] Tough Grandmother
See Vucanovich, Barbara

**[The] Tough Little Street Fighter from
Brooklyn**
See Hugel, Max

Tough Tony Anastasio
See Anastasio, Anthony

Tough Tony Capezio
See Capezio, Anthony

Tough Tony Foyt
See Foyt, Anthony Joseph, Jr.

Tough Tony Spilotro
See Spilotro, Anthony

[The] Tough Top Cop
See Webster, William Hedgcock

[The] Toughest Cop in America
See Rizzo, Frank Lazarro

Touhy, Black Roger
See Touhy, Rog[er]

Touhy, Rog[er] 1898-1959 [BLB, HPPN,
PHM]
American underworld figure
* [The] Terrible
* Touhy, Black Roger
* Touhy, Terrible

Touhy, Terrible
See Touhy, Rog[er]

Touhy, Terrible Tommy
See Touhy, Tommy

Touhy, Tommy 20th c. [BLB]
American underworld figure
* Touhy, Terrible Tommy

Toulet, Paul Jean 1867-1920 [HPPN]
French, poet, critic, author
* Perricas

Toulman, C.
See Crosland, Mrs. C.

Toulotte, E. L. J. 19th c. [IP]
French historian
* Gastine, Civique de

Toulouse Lautrec
See Curcio, Renato

Toulouse-Lautrec
See Monfa, Henri Marie Raymond de
Toulouse-Lautrec

Toumanova, Tamara
See Khacidovitch, Tamara

Toup, Jonathan 1713-1785 [IP]
British scholar and critic
* Toupius, Joannes

Toupius, Joannes
See Toup, Jonathan

Tourbillon, Ratsy
See Tourbillon, Robert Arthur

Tourbillon, Robert Arthur 1885-? [BLB,
DI, HPPN]
American swindler and robber
* Collins, Dapper Don
* Cromwall
* Hussey, Harry
* Rat
* Tourbillon, Ratsy

Toure, Askia Muhammed
See Snellings, Rolland

Toure, Kwame
See Carmichael, Stokeley

Toure, [Ahmed] Sekou 1922-1984 [TI 4-
9-84]
Guinean ruler
* [The] Big Elephant

Tourel, Jennie
See Davidson, Jennie

Tourgee, Albion W[inegar] 1838-1905
[SFL, WBD, WGT]
American author and politician
* Churton, Henry
* Henry, Edgar
* Nixon, Wm. Penn

Tournachon, [Gaspard] Felix 1820-1910
[BI, WEC]
French artist and balloonist
* Nadar

Tournebu, Adrien 1512-1565 [WBD]
French scholar
* Turnebe, Adrien

Tournefort, Joseph Pittou de 1656-1708
[DEP, HN]
French botanist
* [The] Father of Botany

Tourneur, Maurice
See Thomas, Maurice

Tournier, Luc
See Engels, Christiaan J. H.

Tournier, Millie
See Orinifo, Mrs.

Tournimparte, Alessandra
See Ginzburg, Natalia

Tousez, Francois Joseph Pierre
1807-1885 [HPPN]
French actor and educator
* Regnier

Toussain, Jacques 1547-? [SN]
French scholar
* [A] Living Library

Toussaint, Allen 20th c. [CMA]
American musician, songwriter, record producer
* Neville, Naomi
* Toussan

Toussaint, Gertrude
See Clark, Mrs. W. H.

Toussaint, Jackie
See Lourens-Koop, Adriana Luberta Klazina

Toussaint-Desessarts, Nicholas 1744-1810 [PA]
Author
* Moyne

Toussaint L'Ouverture, Pierre Dominique 1743-1803 [HPPN]
Haitian army officer
* [The] Black Napoleon
* [The] Liberator of Haiti

Toussan
See Toussaint, Allen

Tousseul, Jean
See Degee, Olivier

Touster, Alison
See Reed, Alison Touster

Tout, Hazel Dawn 1891?- [BEW, HPPN]
American actress
* Dawn, Hazel
* [The] Pink Lady

Toutain, Jose 20th c. [WECO]
Spanish cartoonist
* Roger

Touze, Pierre Francois 1799-1862 [BI]
French actor
* Bocage

Tovar, Cesar Leonardo 1940- [BE]
Venezuelan-born baseball player
* Tovar, Pepito

Tovar, Pepito
See Tovar, Cesar Leonardo

Tovel, Raoul
See Toche, Raoul

Tovell, Ruth Massey 1889-? [CAN]
Canadian author
* Massey, Ruth

Tovey, R. L.
See Tovey, Robert Lawton

Tovey, Robert Lawton 1924- [ART]
British painter
* Tovey, R. L.

Tower, Allen
See Coggeshall, John Allen

Tower, David Bates 1808-? [HPPN]
American educator
* [An] Eminent Practical Teacher

Tower, Diana
See Smith, Richard Rein

Tower, Don
See Bower, Donald E[dward]

[The] Tower Earl
See Fitzgerald, James

Tower, Joseph L.
See La Torre, Giuseppe

Tower, Martello
See Norman, F. M.

[The] Tower Murderer
See Whitman, Charles

Tower, Stella Mary [Hodgson] 1891- [WW]
Author
* Wolseley, Faith

Towers, Ivar [house pseudonym]
See Wilson, Richard

Towers, Ivars
See Kornbluth, Cyril M.

Towers, Joseph 1737-1799 [HPPN]
British dissenter
* Towers, Small Shot

Towers, Maxwell 1909- [CA]
Scottish-born author and poet
* Rabbie

Towers, Small Shot
See Towers, Joseph

Towers, Tricia
See Ivison, Elizabeth

Towery, Blackie
See Towery, Carlise

Towery, Carlise 1920-
American basketball player
* Towery, Blackie

Towgood, [Rev.] Micaiah 1700-1792 [HPPN]
British clergyman
* [A] Christian

Towle, Arthur 1887-1954 [FC]
British comedian and actor
* Lucan, Arthur

Towler, Daniel L. 1928- [FB]
American football player
* Towler, Deacon Dan

Towler, Deacon Dan
See Towler, Daniel L.

[The] Town Bull of Ely
See Cromwell, Oliver

[A] Town Councillor
See Duffy, [Sir] Charles Gavan

Town Crier
See Byrne, Charles A.

[The] Town Crier
See Woollcott, Alexander Humphreys

Town Listener
See Richardson, Leander

Town, Mr.
See Thornton, Bonnell

Towne, Ada 1868?-1931 [BEW]
American actress
* Fenton, Mabel

Towne, Artie
See Johnson, Henry

Towne, Babe
See Towne, Jay King

Towne, Jay King 1880-1938 [BE]
American baseball player
* Towne, Babe

Towne, Joseph 20th c. [HPPN]
American radar technician
* [The] Ralph Nader of Microwaves

Towne, Mary
See Spelman, Mary

Towne, Peggy
See Durante, Mary

Towne, Peter
See Nabokov, Peter [Francis]

Towne, Robert 20th c. [NW 3-26-84, NY 4-29-84, WP 3-29-84, WP 4-7-83]
American screenwriter and director
* [The] Script Doctor
* Vazak, P. H.

Towne, Stuart
See Rawson, Clayton

Towne, Tracy
See Sawtille, Mrs. E. W.

Townes, Charles H. 1915- [HPPN]
American physicist and educator
* [The] Father of the Laser
* [The] Father of the Maser

Townley, Arthur?
See Duganne, Augustine Joseph Hickey

Townley, Carol
See Townley-Parker, Caroline Townley

Townley, Daniel O'Connell 1824-1873 [FFF]
American author
* Rooney, Alderman

Townley, Houghton 20th c. [MBF]
British author
* Preston, Walford

Townley, Michael Vernon 20th c.
American suspected of involvement in Chilean assassination plot
* Williams

Townley, Thomas 18th c. [HPPN]
British author
* Grey, Oliver

Townley-Parker, Caroline Townley 1891- [WWL]
British author
* Townley, Carol

Towns, Forrest 1914- [BBH]
American track and field athlete
* Towns, Speck

Towns, Speck
See Towns, Forrest

Townsbridge, Elizabeth
See Murphy, Katharine Mary

Townsend, Alice   [PA]
Author
* Orsin, Floro

Townsend, Doris McFerran 1914-   [CA]
American author
* Clelland, Catherine
* McFerran, Ann
* McFerran, Doris

Townsend, Eric W.
See McLean, Eric W.

Townsend, [Dr.] Francis Everett
1867-1960   [HPPN]
American physician and humanist
* [The] Father of the Townsend Plan
* [The] Hammer of Thor

Townsend, George Alfred 1841-1914
[FFF, HPPN, PA]
American author and journalist
* Bouquet, Johnny
* Garth
* Gath
* Laertes

Townsend, George Henry 1835-1869
[PA]
British author
* [An] English Critic
* Green, John

Townsend, Happy
See Townsend, John

Townsend, Haworth Nottingham
1864-1927   [HPPN]
British-American insurance authority
* [The] King of the Marine Insurance
  Business

Townsend, Henry 1909-   [BWW]
American singer
* Thomas, Henry
* Too Tight Henry

Townsend, Ira Dance 1894-1965   [BE]
American baseball player
* Townsend, Pat

Townsend, James B[arclay] J[ermain]
1910-   [CA]
American author
* Livingston, Peter Van Rensselaer

Townsend, Joan 1913-   [IAW]
British author
* Pomfret, Joan

Townsend, John 1879-1963   [BE]
American baseball player
* Townsend, Happy

Townsend, John 1916-   [BB]
American basketball player
* [The] Houdini of the Hardwood

Townsend, John G., Jr. 1871-?   [HPPN]
American politician
* Townsend, Strawberry

Townsend, Lefty
See Townsend, Leo Alphonse

Townsend, Leo Alphonse 1891-   [BE]
American baseball player
* Townsend, Lefty

Townsend, Marion 1929-   [HPPN]
American singer
* Marlowe, Marion

Townsend, Mark
See Wallmann, Jeffrey M[iner]

Townsend, Mary Ashely [Van Voorhis]
1836?-1901   [FFF, HPPN, PA]
American poet
* Ashley, Mary
* Xariffa

Townsend, Pat
See Townsend, Ira Dance

Townsend, S. Nugent   [PA]
Author
* St. Kames

Townsend, Storm Diana 1937-   [ART]
British-born sculptor
* Storm

Townsend, Strawberry
See Townsend, John G., Jr.

Townsend, Virginia Frances 1836-1920
[FFF]
American author
* Cousin Virginia

Townsend, William Charles 1804-1850
[HPPN]
British barrister
* [A] Graduate of Oxford

Townshend, Champagne Charlie
See Townshend, Charles

Townshend, Charles 1674-1738   [HPPN,
PPN]
British statesman
* Tonsenius
* Townshend, Turnip

Townshend, Charles 1725-1767   [DNNS,
HPPN, WBD]
British politician
* Townshend, Champagne Charlie
* [The] Weathercock

Townshend, Charles
See Bronte, Charlotte

**Townshend, George [Fourth Viscount
and First Marquis Townshend]**
1724-1807   [HPPN]
British army officer
* Gesner, Sawney
* [An] Honorable Brigadier General
* MacAdam, Sawney
* Mackenzie, Sawney

Townshend, Horace 1750-1837   [PI]
Irish poet
* Senex

Townshend, Horace 1837-1904   [PI]
Irish poet and author
* Induna

Townshend, Richard
See Bickers, Richard Leslie Townshend

Townshend, Stephen 1860?-1914   [HPPN]
British actor and playwright
* Dennis, Will

Townshend, Turnip
See Townshend, Charles

Townson, Thomas 1715-1792   [HPPN]
British clergyman
* Mantuan

Towry, Peter
See Piper, [Sir] David Towry

Toxophilus
See Faddis, William L.

Toxopholite
See Lanigan, George Thomas

[The] Toy Bull Dog
See Courtney, Clinton Dawson

[The] Toy Bulldog
See Walker, Edward Patrick

[The] Toy Cannon
See Wynn, James Sherman [Jim]

[The] Toy Tiger
See Howatt, Garry Robert Charles

Toyen
See Cerminova, Marie

Toynbee, Arnold 1852-1883   [HPPN]
British historian and social reformer
* Father of Social Settlements

Toynbee, Lawrence 1922-   [ART]
British painter
* L. L. T.

Toynbee, Rosalind 1890-   [WWL]
British author
* Murray, Rosalind

Toyne, Clarice Joy 1906-   [HPPN]
British author
* Armido

Toyota
See Arima, Raido [or Yoriyuki]

Tozer, Basil John Joseph 20th c.
[WWL]
British author
* Villain, Regardant

Tozzo, Rocco 1895-1954   [AS, BX, RBE]
American boxer
* Kansas, Rocky

Traber
See Hoedel, Emil Heinrich Max

Trabert, Marion 1930-   [BBH]
American tennis player
* Trabert, Tony

Trabert, Tony
See Trabert, Marion

Trace, Al[bert J.]   [ASC]
American composer, conductor, singer
* Hart, Bob
* Watts, Clem

Tracewski, Richard Joseph 1935- [SMG]
American baseball player and coach
* Tracewski, Tracy
* Tracewski, Trixie

Tracewski, Tracy
See Tracewski, Richard Joseph

Tracewski, Trixie
See Tracewski, Richard Joseph

Tracey, Rah
See Tracey, Walter

Tracey, Thomas F.
See Flynn, Thomas W.

Tracey, Walter 20th c. [HPPN]
American football player
* Tracey, Rah

Trachsel, Myrtle Jamison 20th c.
[NAA]
American writer
* Jamison, Jane

Tracht, Doug 1951?- [WP 4-22-84]
American disc jockey
* [The] Greaseman

[The] Tractor King
See House, Eddie James, Jr.

Tracts, Hartley Wintney
See Gifford, F. O.

Tracy, Aloise
See Shoenight, Aloise

Tracy, Arthur
See Rosenberg, Harry

Tracy, Benjamin Franklin 1830-1915
[WBD]
American Secretary of the Navy
* [The] Father of the American Navy

Tracy, Catherine
See Story, Rosamond Mary

Tracy, Don[ald Fiske] 1905-? [CA]
American author
* Fuller, Roger

Tracy, Harry 20th c. [BLB]
American criminal
* [The] Mad Dog

Tracy, Hetty
See Williams, Mrs. Jesse

Tracy, Leland
See Tralins, S[andor] Robert [Bob]

Tracy, Louis 1863-1928 [CC, EMD,
WW]
British author and journalist
* Holmes, Gordon [joint pseudonym
with Matthew Phipps Shiel]

Tracy, Lucy Bradshaw 20th c. [NAA]
American writer
* Alden, Betty [house pseudonym?]

Tracy, Margaret [joint pseudonym with
Lawrence Klavan]
See Klavan, Drew

Tracy, Margaret [joint pseudonym with
Drew Klavan]
See Klavan, Lawrence

Tracy, Mrs. [FFF]
Entertainer
* Ethel, Agnes

Tracy, Powers
See Ward, Don[ald G.]

Tracy, Roger Sherman 1841-1926 [ESF,
SFL]
American author
* Hodge, T. Shirby

Tracy, Spencer 1900-1967 [HPPN]
American actor
* Old Bucko

Tracy, Uriah 1755-1807 [DNA]
American politician and author
* Scipio

Trade
See Smith, William

Trader, Ella King Newsom 19th c.
[HPPN]
American military nurse
* [The] Florence Nightingale of the
Southern Army

Trader Ike Williams
See Williams, Ike

[The] Trader in Faction
See Milton, John

Trader Jack McKeon
See McKeon, Jack

Trader Vic
See Bergeron, Victor Jules

[A] Tradesman
See Drinker, John

[A] Traditional Poet
See Robinson, Edwin Arlington

Tradleg, Nitram
See Geldart, Martin

Trafford, F. G.
See Riddell, Charlotte Eliza Lawson
[Cowan]

Trafford, F. G.
See Riddell, Charlotte Eliza Lawson
[Cowan]

Trafton, Adelina [FFF]
American author
* American Girl Abroad

Trafton, Edwin H. [PA]
Author
* Count, Noah

Trafton, George 1896-1971 [BBH]
American football player
* [The] Brute

Tragabuches [Tremendous Swallower]
See Ulloa, Jose

Tragaediographus
See Drayton, Michael

Tragett, Margaret Rivers 1885- [WWL]
British author
* Larminie, Margaret Rivers

Tragett, [Rev.] Thomas Heathcote
19th c. [HPPN]
British clergyman
* [A] Clergyman

[The] Tragic Commodore
See Perry, Oliver Hazard

Traglia, Luigi 1895?-1977
Italian cardinal
* [The] Living Archive

Tragus
See Bock, Hieronymus

Traherne, Michael
See Watkins-Pitchford, Denys James

Trahey, Jane 1923- [CA]
American author
* Erlanger, Baba

[The] Trail Blazer of Civilization
See Clum, John P.

Traill, Peter
See Dunstan, Guy Mainwaring

Traill, Peter
See Morton, Guy Mainwaring

Traill, Robert 1642-1716 [FFF, SN]
Scottish clergyman
* [The] Venomous Preacher

Trailrider
See Hyland, Ann

Train, Arthur 1875-? [WWL]
American author
* Lency, C.

Traina, Giuseppe 20th c. [BLB]
American underworld figure
* [The] Peasant

Traine, Gypsey
See Lovejoy, Mary Evelyn [Wood]

Trainor, Richard
See Tralins, S[andor] Robert [Bob]

Trainor, Thomas Weston 1922- [CEI]
Canadian-born hockey player
* Trainor, Wes

Trainor, Wes
See Trainor, Thomas Weston

[The] Traipsin' Woman
See Thomas, Jeannette Bell

[A] Traitor to Freedom
See Webster, Daniel

[The] Traitorous Hero
See Arnold, Benedict

Tralins, Robert S.
See Tralins, S[andor] Robert [Bob]

Tralins, S[andor] Robert [Bob] 1926-
[CA, WD]
American author
* Bixby, Ray Z.
* King, Norman A.

Tralins, S[andor] Robert [Bob] (cont.)
* Miles, Keith
* O'Shea, Sean
* O'Toole, Rex
* Sydney, Cynthia
* Toole, Rex
* Tracy, Leland
* Trainor, Richard
* Tralins, Robert S.
* Traube, Ruy
* Verdon, Dorothy

Tralow, Johannes 1882?-1968 [BI]
German author
* Low, Hanns

Tramback, Red
See Tramback, Stephen Joseph

Tramback, Stephen Joseph 1915- [BE]
American baseball player
* Tramback, Red

Tramel
See Martel, Felicien

Tramiel, Jack 1929?- [TI 1-3-83]
American business executive
* [The] Howard Hughes of
   computerdom

Tramin, A. G.
See Martin, Gloria Ann

Tramin, Ed
See Martin, Gloria Ann

Tramin, Lisa
See Martin, Gloria Ann

[The] Tramp
See Anderson, Arthur Henry

Tramp
See Skinner, Charles M.

[The] Tramp Champ
See Nicholson, Alexandra

[The] Tramp Musician
See Powles, Harry

[The] Tramp Poet
See Kemp, Harry Hibbard

Tramp, Tilbury
See Lever, Charles James

[El] Trampas [The] Trickster
See Garcia Hernandez, Hector

Tran Thi Phuong, [Madame] 20th c.
[HPPN]
Chinese massage parlor operator
* [The] Dragon Lady of Long Bihn

Tran-nam-Trung
See Tran-van-Tra

Tran-van-Tra 1913- [BI]
Vietnamese military leader
* Tran-nam-Trung

Tranh-van-Luc 1825-1899 [BI]
Annamese clergyman
* Six, [Father]

Trankel, Margot
See Kreuter-Trankel, Margot

Tranquilli, Secondo 1900- [CAP, EWL, IPA]
Italian author and playwright
* Silone, Ignazio

Tranquillity
See Foe, Daniel

Trans-Atlantic
See Mooney, Thomas

Transidder, Nicholas 1799-1875 [HPPN]
British author
* N. T.

[The] Translator
See Mathias, Thomas James

Translator General
See Holland, Philemon

[The] Translator of Michaelis
See Marsh, [Rev.] Herbert

[The] Translator of That Work
See Clifford, Robert

Transmarine
See Louis IV

Transue, Jacob
See Matheson, Joan

Trant, Erica
See Allen, Agnes [Banister]

Trant, Martin
See White, Trentwell Mason

Trant, [Captain] William 19th c.
[HPPN]
British army officer
* [An] Officer

Tranter, Nigel [Godwin] 1909- [CA, WWS]
Scottish author
* Tredgold, Nye

Trantina, Barbara 20th c. [BBH]
American swimmer
* Trantina, Bede

Trantina, Bede
See Trantina, Barbara

Trapassi, Pietro Antonio Domenico Bonaventura 1698-1782 [FFF, RH, WBD]
Italian poet and playwright
* Metastasio
* [The] Racine of Italy

Trapp, George 1949-
American basketball player
* Trapp, Heat

Trapp, Heat
See Trapp, George

Trappier, Arthur Benjamin 1910- [EJ, WWJ]
American jazz musician
* Trappier, Traps

Trappier, Traps
See Trappier, Arthur Benjamin

Traprock, Walter E.
See Chappell, George Shepard

Traps the Drum Wonder
See Rich, Bernard

Trash
See Tyler, William Clark

Trask, George F. 1797-1875 [FFF, PA]
Clergyman and author
* Sproule, Zibra
* Toby, Simeon

Trask, Helen
See Lowell, Joan

Trask, Jeremy
See Lacy, George Carleton

Trask, Kate 1853-1922 [DNA, FFF, WBD]
American author, poet, playwright
* Trask, Katrina

Trask, Katrina
See Trask, Kate

Trask, Merrill
See Colton, Mel

Traube, Ludwig
German physician
* [The] Father of Experimental
   Pathology

Traube, Ruy
See Tralins, S[andor] Robert [Bob]

Traudl
See Flaxman, Traudl

Traugott, Elizabeth Closs 1939- [CA]
American linguist and author
* Closs, Elizabeth

Trausti, Jon
See Magnusson, Guomundur

Travagliante, Lawrence J. 1950- [BI]
American disc jockey
* Kid Leo

Travascio, Nicholas Anthony 1925-1964
[EJ, PMJ]
American jazz musician
* Travis, Nick

[The] Travel Impresario
See Cook, Thomas

[A] Traveler
See Bavin, John

Traveler
See Clark, Mrs. H. K. U.

[A] Traveler
See Rayall, Mrs. A.

[A] Traveler
See Salt, Henry

[A] Traveler in Basaruah
See Morgan, Joseph

[The] Travelers' Guide
See Baedeker, Karl

[A] Traveling Bachelor
See Cooper, James Fenimore

[A] Traveling Showman
See Dilks, John M.

[The] Traveling Texan
See Walker, William Marvin [Billy]

[A] Traveller
See Bryant, William Cullen

[A] Traveller
See Campbell, John Francis

[The] Traveller
See Curtis, George William

Traveller
See Dowsett, Joseph Morewood

[A] Traveller
See Lee, Sarah [Willis Bowdich]

[A] Traveller
See Liddell, Thomas

[A] Traveller
See Stirling, William

[The] Traveller
See Story, Isaac

[A] Traveller
See Todd, Henry Cook

[A] Traveller in the East
See Malcolm, [Sir] John

[A] Traveller in the Tropics
See Ballou, Maturin Murray

[The] Travelling Netminder
See Conacher, Lionel Pretoria

[A] Travelling Physician
See Lefevre, [Sir] George William

Traven, B.?
See Marut, Ret

Traven, Beatrice
See Goldemberg, Rose Leiman

Traver, Robert
See Voelker, John Donaldson

Travers, Allan
See Travers, Aloysius Joseph

Travers, Aloysius Joseph 1892-1968
[BE]
American baseball player
* Travers, Allan

Travers, Bob
See Jones, Charley

Travers, Georgia
See Scott, Alma Olivia

Travers, Graham
See Todd, Margaret

Travers, Henry
See Heagerty, Travers John

Travers, Hugh
See Mills, Hugh [Travers]

Travers, Kenneth
See Hutchin, Kenneth Charles

Travers, Linden
See Lindon-Travers, Florence

Travers, P. L.
See Travers, Pamela Lyndon

Travers, Pamela Lyndon 1904?- [LC, TC]
British author and poet
* Travers, P. L.

Travers, Phebe [PA]
Author
* Aunt Florida

Travers, Richard C.
See Libb, Richard

Travers, Stephen
See Radcliffe, [Henry] Garnett

Travers, Virginia
See Coigney, Virginia

Travers, Will
See Rowland, Donald Sydney

Travers-Smith, Dorothea 20th c. [ART]
British painter
* T. S.

Traverse, Madlaine
See Businsky, Madlaine

Travies
See Travies De Villers, Charles-Joseph

Travies De Villers, Charles-Joseph
1804-1859 [WEC]
French cartoonist
* Travies

Travis, Gerry
See Trimble, Louis P[reston]

Travis, Jack
See Madden, [Jerry] David

Travis, [Dr.] John 20th c. [HPPN]
American physician
* [The] Father of Wellness

Travis, June
See Grabiner, June Dorothea

Travis, Lawrence
See Deutzman, Lawrence F[rederick]

Travis, Michael
See Torakis, Louis

Travis, Nick
See Travascio, Nicholas Anthony

Travis, Richard
See Justice, William

Travis, Walter J. 1862-1927 [BWG, EG, GF]
Australian-born golfer
* [The] Old Man

Traxler, Bingo Bob
See Traxler, Robert

Traxler, Robert 20th c.
American politician
* Traxler, Bingo Bob

Traylor, Bill 20th c. [IBW]
American painter
* Uncle Bill

Traynor, Alex
See Lagerwall, Edna

Traynor, Earl Richard ?-1944 [SC]
American actor
* Hogan, Earl
* Hogan, Hap

Traynor, Harold Joseph 1899-1972 [BE, DGS, PB]
American baseball player and manager
* Traynor, Pie

Traynor, Linda Borman 1950?-
American actress
* Lovelace, Linda

Traynor, Pie
See Traynor, Harold Joseph

Traz, Georges Albert Edouard De
1881-? [HPPN]
French author
* Fosca, Francois

Treacher, Arthur
See Veary, Arthur T.

Treacle, Uncle
See Mitchell, Adrian

Treadgold, Sylvia 1918- [ART]
British artist
* Sylvia T

Treadway, Red
See Treadway, Thadford Leon

Treadway, Thadford Leon 1920- [BE]
American baseball player
* Treadway, Red

Treadwell, Daniel 1791-1872 [SN]
American inventor
* [The] Theologian

Treadwell, John 1745-1823 [HPPN]
American politician
* [The] Father of the System of
Common School Education

Treasure [code name used during World
War II]
See Sergeyev, Lily

Treasure of Auchinleck
See Boswell, James

[A] Treasurer of a Corporation
See Cary, Thomas Greaves

[The] Treasury Boss
See Regan, Donald Thomas

[The] Treasury Chief
See Regan, Donald Thomas

Treat, Ida
See Bergeret, Ida Treat

Treat, Lawrence
See Goldstone, Lawrence Arthur

Trebelli, Zelia
See Gilbert, Zelia

Trebitsch, Isaac 1872?-1943 [EE]
Hungarian-born intelligence agent
* Chao kung, Abbot
* Lincoln, Isaac
* Tandler, [Dr.] Leo
* Trebitsch-Lincoln, Isaac

Trebitsch-Lincoln, Isaac
See Trebitsch, Isaac

Trebor
See Davis, Robert S.

Trebor
See Emmet, Robert

Trebor, Eidrah
See Hardie, Robert

Trebor, Snivig C.
See Givins, Robert Cartwright

Trebuchon, [Madame] Coutelier
1853-1929 [BI]
French author
* Romain, Rose

Trechmann, Emma 1909- [THR]
British actress
* Treckman, Emma

Trecker, Janice Law 1941- [CA]
American author
* Law, Janice

Treckman, Emma
See Trechmann, Emma

Treddles, Tumas
See Brymner, Douglas

Tredez, Alain 1926- [CA, TBJ]
French cartoonist, author, illustrator
* Trez, Alain

Tredez, Denise Laugier 1930- [CA, TBJ]
French author
* Trez, Denise

Tredgold, Nye
See Tranter, Nigel [Godwin]

[The] Tree
See West, Mary

Tree, David
See Parsons, David

Tree, Gregory
See Bardin, John Franklin

Tree, [Sir] Herbert Draper Beerbohm
See Beerbohm, Herbert

Tree, Lady
See Holt, Helen Maud

Trefflich, Henry 1908?-1978
American animal importer
* [The] Monkey King

Trefoil
See Millen, F. F.

Trefor, Eirlys
See Williams, Eirlys O[lwen]

Trefossa
See De Ziel, Henri Frans

Trefouret, Jeanne Alfredine 1859-1941
[BEW, WBD]
French actress
* Hading, Jane

Tregarthen, Enys
See Sloggett, Nellie

Tregelles, Samuel Prideaux 1813-1875
[HPPN]
British scholar
* S. P. T.

Tregellis, John
See Gowing, Sidney Floyd

Trehearne, Elizabeth [joint pseudonym
with Patricia Anne Maxwell]
See Albritton, Carol

Trehearne, Elizabeth [joint pseudonym
with Carol Albritton]
See Maxwell, Patricia Anne

Treibich, S. J.
See Treibich, Stephen John

Treibich, Stephen John 1936-1972 [SFL]
Author
* Treibich, S. J.

Treister, Bernard W[illiam] 1932- [CA]
American author
* St. James, Bernard

Trelawney, [Rev. Sir] Harry 1756-1834
[HPPN]
British clergyman
* Wildgoose, [Mr.] Geoffry

Trelawney, Hubert
See Tuite, Hugh

Trelawny, Anne
See Gibbons, Anne Trelawny

Trelawny, Edward ?-1630 [HN]
* [The] Honest Lawyer

Trelawny, Edward John 1792-1881
British adventurer
* [The] Younger Son

Treleaven, R. B.
See Treleaven, Richard Barrie

Treleaven, Richard Barrie 1920- [ART]
British artist
* Treleaven, R. B.

Trell, Max 20th c. [WECO]
American cartoonist
* Storm, Robert

Trelos, Tony
See Crechales, Anthony George

Tremaine, Bob
See Steindler, Robert A.

Tremaine, D. Lerium
See Bradbury, Ray [Douglas]

Tremaine, F[rederick] Orlin 1899-1956
[ESF, SFP, WGT]
American author and editor
* Beale, Anne?
* Frederick, Orlin
* Lane, Arthur
* Paine, Guthrie?
* Sand, Warren B.?
* Santos, Alfred?
* Van Lorne, Warner

Tremaine, Herbert
See Deuchar, Maude

Tremaine, Linda
See Morgan, Diana

Tremaine, Nelson 20th c. [WGT]
Author
* Van Lorne, Warner

Tremayne, Hartley
See Armour, R. Coutts

Tremayne, Jonathan
See Forrest-Webb, Robert

Tremayne, Peter
See Ellis, Peter Berresford

Tremblay, J. C.
See Tremblay, Jean Claude

Tremblay, Jean Claude 1939- [CEI,
FHE, HK]
Canadian-born hockey player
* Tremblay, J. C.

[The] Trembler
See Garcia

Trembly, Edward J. 1860-? [BE]
American baseball player
* Trumbull, Ed[ward J.]

Tremel, Mumbles
See Tremel, William Leonard [Bill]

Tremel, William Leonard [Bill] 1929-
[BE]
American baseball player
* Tremel, Mumbles

Tremendous, Sir
See Dennis, John

Tremenheere, [Rev.] William 1757-1838
[HPPN]
British clergyman
* [The] Vicar

Tremlett, Hurricane
See Tremlett, Timothy Maurice

Tremlett, Timothy Maurice 1956- [DC]
British cricketer
* Tremlett, Hurricane
* Tremlett, Tremers

Tremlett, Tremers
See Tremlett, Timothy Maurice

**Tremoille, [Vicomte] de Thouars [Prince
de Talmont]** 1460-1525 [WBD]
French army officer
* Chevalier sans Reproche

Trench, Francis 1805-1886 [NPS]
Clergyman and author
* Oxoniensis

Trenchard, Asa
See Watterson, Henry

Trenchard, John 1662?-1723 [FFF]
British author and journalist
* Cato
* Diogenes

Trenchard, Sarah
See Chanfrau, Mrs. H. T.

Trenck, [Baron] Friedrich von der 1726-1794 [HPPN]
Austrian military adventurer
* [The] Prisoner of Glatz

Trenery, Gladys Gordon 1885?-1938 [HFF, WGT]
British author
* Pendarves, G. G.

Trenpolpen, P. W.
See Courtney, William Prideaux

Trent, Al[phonso E.] 1905- [EJ]
American jazz musician
* Trent, Fonnie

Trent, Ann 20th c. [AW, IAW]
British author
* Blythe, Joyce
* Carlton, Ann
* Crosse, Elaine
* Desana, Dorothy
* Sernicoli, Davide

Trent, Clive?
See Emanuel, Victor Rousseau

Trent, Fonnie
See Trent, Al[phonso E.]

Trent, Gregory
See Williamson, Thames Ross

Trent, John
See Brown, LaVerne

Trent, Lawrence
See Sellers, Connie Leslie, Jr.

Trent, Leo
See Sellers, Connie Leslie, Jr.

Trent, Martha
See Smith, Dorothy Whitehill

Trent, Olaf
See Fanthorpe, R[obert] Lionel

Trent, Paul 1872-? [WWL]
British author
* Kaye, Wilmot

Trent, Peter
See Nelson, [Hugh] Lawrence

Trent, Philip
See Jones, Clifford

Trent, Roy
See Coe, Charles Francis

Trent, Timothy
See Malmberg, Carl

Trentworth, Fisher
See Ackerman, Forrest J[ames]

Trepagnier, Ernest 1885?-1968 [NOJ]
American jazz musician
* Trepagnier, Ninesse

Trepagnier, Ninesse
See Trepagnier, Ernest

Trepoff, Ivan
See Haubold, Herman Arthur

Trepper, Leopold 1904-1982 [EE, JL, WWW]
Polish-born intelligence agent
* [The] Big Chef
* Domb, Leiba
* Gilbert
* [The] Grand Chef

Tresham, Henry ?-1814 [HPPN]
Irish artist
* Britannicus

Tresilian, Liz
See Green, Elisabeth Sara

Tress, Arthur
See Pinkwater, Daniel Manus

Tressell, Robert
See Noonan, Robert

Tressidy, Jim
See Norwood, Victor G[eorge] C[harles]

Tressilian, Charles
See Atcheson, Richard

Trester, A. L.
See Trester, Arthur L.

Trester, Arthur L. 1878-1944
American basketball executive
* Trester, A. L.

Tretane
See Curgenoen, John Brendon

Treurnicht, Andries 1921?-
South African politician
* No, Dr.

Trevanian
See Whitaker, Rodney

Trevarthen, Hal P.
See Heydon, Joseph Kentigern

Trevelyan, G. M.
See Trevelyan, George Macaulay

Trevelyan, George Macaulay 1876-1962 [LC]
British historian and author
* Trevelyan, G. M.

Trevelyan, [Sir] George Otto 1838-1928 [DEA]
British author
* Broughton, H., B.C.S.

Trevelyan, Hilda
See Tucker, Hilda

Trevelyan, Katharine 1908- [CAP]
British author
* Goetsch-Trevelyan, Katharine

Trevelyan, Robert
See Forrest-Webb, Robert

Trevena, John
See Henham, Ernest George

Trevert, Edward
See Bubier, Edward Trevert

Treves, Kathleen
See Walker, Emily Kathleen

Trevethick, Richard 1771-1833 [DNNS]
British engineer
* [The] Father of the Locomotive

Trevi, Christina
See Benitez Trevino, Christina

Trevino, Bobby
See Trevino, Carlos Castro

Trevino, Carlos Castro 1945- [BE]
Mexican-born baseball player
* Trevino, Bobby

Trevino, Elizabeth B[orton] de 1904- [CA]
American author
* Borton, Elizabeth

Trevino, High Pressure Lee
See Trevino, Lee

Trevino, Lee 1939- [HPPN, SA]
American golfer
* [The] Merry Mexican
* Super Mex
* Trevino, High Pressure Lee

Trevision, Torquay
See Bedford-Jones, Henry [James O'Brien]

Trevitt, C. L., Literary Agent
See Johnson, William Geary

Trevor, A. C.
See Pulsford, Norman George

Trevor, Ann
See Trilnick, Annie

Trevor, Austin
See Schilsky, Austin

Trevor, Charlotte
See Roberts, Sonia Leslie

Trevor, Claire
See Wemlinger, Claire

Trevor, Edward
See Bulwer-Lytton, Edward Robert

Trevor, Edward
See Fane, Julian Charles Henry

Trevor, Elleston
See Dudley-Smith, Trevor

Trevor, Ernest
See Powell, Thomas

Trevor, Glen
See Hilton, James

Trevor, Joy
See Linskill, Doris Joy

Trevor, Norman
See Pritchard, Norman

Trevor, Ralph
See Wilmot, James Reginald

Trevor, Ross E.
See Crilly, Daniel

Trevor, Van
See Boulanger, Robert F.

Trevor, William
See Cox, William Trevor

Trevor-Roper, H. R.
See Trevor-Roper, Hugh Redwald

Trevor-Roper, Hugh Redwald 1914-
[LC]
British historian and writer
* Trevor-Roper, H. R.

Trew, Dighton
See Jones, J. G.

Trez, Alain
See Tredez, Alain

Trez, Denise
See Tredez, Denise Laugier

[The] Tri-State Terror
See Underhill, Wilbur

Trianero
See Jimenez, Juan

Triangle
See Bellew, Frank P. W.

[La] Trianita
See MacLean, Sallie

Triaquero, [Don] Gabriel
See Arouet, Francois Marie

Tribble, Ike
See Tribble, Israel

Tribble, Israel 1940- [BA]
American educator
* Tribble, Ike

[Il] Tribolo
See Pericoli, Niccolo

Triboniam
See Fraleck, Edison Baldwin

Triboulet
See Hotman, Francis

[The] Tribunal of the Terror
See Fouquier-Tinville, Antoine Quentin

Tribune
See Armstrong, Douglas Albert

Tribune of Liberty, Peace, and Justice
See Gabrini, Niccolo

[The] Tribune of the People
See Adams, Samuel

[The] Tribune of the People
See Babeuf, Francois Noel

[The] Tribune of the People
See Bright, John

[El] Tribuno Popular
See Deschamps, Eugenio

Tricamo, Stephen J. 1897- [BX, RBE]
American boxer
* Sullivan, Kid
* Sullivan, Steve

Trice, Borough
See Allen, Arthur Bruce

Trice, Marguerite Gwynne 1918- [FC, ITA]
American actress
* Gwynne, Anne

Trice, Rich[ard] 1917- [BWW]
American singer
* Fuller, Little Boy

Trice, Welly
See Trice, William Augusta [Willie]

Trice, William Augusta [Willie]
1910-1976 [BWW]
American singer
* Trice, Welly

Tricky Dick [or Dickie]
See Nixon, Richard Milhous

Tricky Dick Hyland
See Hyland, Richard

Tricky Dick McGuire
See McGuire, Richard

Tricky Sam Nanton
See Nanton, Joseph [Joe]

Tricotrin
See Henderson, N. J.

Tricycle
See Popov, Dusko

Tridino, Johannes de Cereto de 16th c.
[BI]
Italian painter
* Tacuinus, Joannes

Triebel, George W. 1855-1886 [BE]
American baseball player
* Creamer, George W.

Triem, Paul Ellsworth 1882- [WW]
Author
* Ellsworth, Paul

Triet, Robert
See Toche, Raoul

Trietsch, Hezzie
See Trietsch, Paul

Trietsch, Ken
See Trietsch, Ruby

Trietsch, Paul 1905?-1980
American musician
* Trietsch, Hezzie

Trietsch, Ruby 20th c. [JF]
American musician and composer
* Trietsch, Ken

Trifle
See Tilton, Warren

Trifle, Timothy
See Foe, Daniel

Trifolium
See McCarthy, Denis Florence

Trifonov, Georgy 1926- [BI]
Russian author and poet
* Dyomin, Mikhail

Trigg, [Colonel] Haiden C. 1834-1913
American dog breeder and author
* Full Cry

Trigg, Harry Davis 1927- [CA]
American author and television scriptwriter
* Clark, Parlin

Trigger Mike Coppola
See Coppola, Michael

[A] Triggite
See Liddell, Thomas

Trigunatita, [Swami]
See Mitra, Sarada Prasanna

Trihey, Harry
See Trihey, Henry Judah

Trihey, Henry Judah 1877-1942 [HK]
Canadian hockey player
* Trihey, Harry

Trilby
See Peyronney, Vicomtesse de

Trillo, Indio
See Trillo, Jesus Manuel

Trillo, Jesus Manuel 1950- [BE, SMG]
Venezuelan-born baseball player
* Marcano, Jesus Manuel
* Trillo, Indio
* Trillo, Manny

Trillo, Manny
See Trillo, Jesus Manuel

Trilnick, Annie ?-1970 [THR]
British actress
* Trevor, Ann

Trilussa
See Salustri, Carlo Alberto

Trim
See Baldwyn, Edward

Trim
See Ratisbonne, Louis Fortune Gustave

Trim, Corporal
See Bolger, Philip C[unningham]

Trim, Geoffrey Edward 1956- [DC]
British cricketer
* Trim, Trimy

Trim, Trimy
See Trim, Geoffrey Edward

Trimalcion
See Amoreux, Felix d' [Jules de Saint Felix]

Trimball, W. H.
See Mencken, Henry Louis [Harry]

Trimble, Jacquelyn W[hitney] 1927-
[CA]
American author
* Whitney, J. L. H.

Trimble, Louis P[reston] 1917- [CA, NAA, WW]
American author
* Brock, Stuart

Trimble, Louis P[reston] (cont.)
* Hollis, Jim [joint pseudonym with Hollis (Spurgeon) Summers]
* Rourke, James
* Travis, Gerry

Trimble, William Copeland 1851-? [PI]
Irish poet and journalist
* Sulky

Trimiar, Lady
See Trimiar [or Trimar?], Marion

Trimiar [or Trimar?], Marion 1953-
[IBW]
American boxer
* Trimiar, Lady
* Trimiar, Tyger

Trimiar, Tyger
See Trimiar [or Trimar?], Marion

Trimm, Thomas 1884-
German author, playwright, journalist
* Welk, Ehm

Trimm, Timothy
See Lespes, Napoleon

[The] Trimmer
See Savile, [Sir] George [Marquis of Halifax]

Trimmer, Eric James 1923- [AW, CA, WD]
British physician and author
* Jameson, Eric
* Lawson, [Dr.] Philip

Trimmer, Will
See Pulteney, William [Earl of Bath]

Trimnell-Ritchard, Cyril 1897-1977
[BEW]
Australian-born actor and director
* Ritchard, Cyril

Trinculo
See Wheeler, Andrew Carpenter

Trinder, Tommy 1909- [BMH]
British comedian
* Nirt, Red

Tring, A. Stephen
See Meynell, Laurence [Walter]

Trini, Anthony
Musician and singer
* [The] Romantic Fiddler

Trinidad, Corky
See Trinidad, Francisco D., Jr.

Trinidad, Francisco D., Jr. 1939- [CA]
Filipino-born cartoonist
* Trinidad, Corky

[A] Trinitarian
See Leavitt, Joshua

[A] Trinitarian
See Penrose, John

[A] Trinity Man
See Wright, Thomas

[A] Trinity Man
See Wright, Thomas

Trinkle, Sybil 1907-1947 [SC]
American actress
* Borden, Olive

Trinkolo, Boatswain
See Foe, Daniel

Trinqueau
See Nepveu [or Neveu], Pierre

Trinsome
See Toche, Raoul

Triolet, Elsa
See Blick, Elsa

Triot, P. A.
See Condon, [Dr.] John Francis

Trip, Tom
See Jones, Giles

Tripakon, Chao Phya 19th c. [HPPN]
Thai author
* [The] Modern Buddhist

Tripathi, Surya Kant 1899-1969? [BI]
Indian poet
* Nirala

Tripe
See Hamilton, Mrs.

Tripe, [Sir] Andrew
See Swift, Jonathan

Tripe, [Dr.] Andrew
See Wagstaffe, William

[The] Triple Threat Girl
See Gumm, Frances

Triple Threat Trippi
See Trippi, Charles L. [Charlie]

Triplet, William Samuel 1899- [SFL, WGT]
Author
* Bull, [Sergeant] Terry

Triplett, Ernie 20th c.
Auto racer
* [The] Blond Terror

Tripod
See Manchester, William

Tripp, C. E.
See Morris, Charles Smith

Tripp, [Rev.] Henry 19th c. [HPPN]
British clergyman
* [A] Clergyman

Tripp, John
See Moore, John Travers

Tripp, June Howard 1901- [EMT]
British actress, dancer, singer
* June

Tripp, Karen 1923- [AW, CA]
German-born author and poet
* Gershon, Karen

Tripp, Miles [Barton] 1923- [CA]
British author
* Brett, John Michael
* Brett, Michael

Tripp, Walter John 1874-? [WWL]
Author
* Carroder, C. H.

Trippa, Herr
See Agrippa, [Cornelius] Heinrich

Trippe, Peter [CC]
Author
* Peters, Geoffrey

Trippenmeker, Heinrich 1502-1560?
[HPPN, WBD]
German painter, engraver, goldsmith
* Albert of Westphalia
* Aldegrever, Heinrich

Trippett, Frank 1926- [CA]
American author and editor
* Swivett, R. G. O.

Trippetts, Mrs. Henry [FFF]
Entertainer
* Belden, Clara

Trippi, Charles L. [Charlie] 1922- [FB]
American football player
* [The] Scintillating Sicilian
* Trippi, Triple Threat

Trippi, Triple Threat
See Trippi, Charles L. [Charlie]

Trips, Captain
See Garcia, Jerry

Triscott, Edith Browning
See Allinson-James, Mrs.

Trismegistus [Thrice Greatest]
See Hermes

Trismegistus
See Whitney, Moses, Jr.

Trismegistus Secundus
See Bernard, [Sir] Thomas

Trissino, Giulio 16th c. [SN]
Son of Italian author, Giovanni Giorgio Trissino
* Agrilupo

Trissotin
See Cotin, Charles

Tristan
See Teitgen, Pierre Henri

Tritheim, Johannes 1462-1516 [HPPN]
German clergyman and bibliographer
* [The] Father of Bibliography

Tritheim, Johannes
See Heidendberg, Johannes

Triton, A. N.
See Barclay, Oliver R[ainsford]

[The] Triumphant Exciseman
See Walpole, [Sir] Robert [First Earl of Orford]

Trivier, Pierre-Olaf 1928- [BEW, TR]
French actor
* Olaf, Pierre

Trixie
See Lopez Ostoloza, Beatriz

Trobullfeld, Doctor
See Turberville, James

Trocchi, Alexander 1925- [CA]
Scottish author
* Lengel, Frances

Troels-Lund
See Lund, Troels Frederik

Trog
See Fawkes, Walter Ernest

Trogdon, William 20th c. [NW 2-7-83]
American author
* Least Heat Moon, William

Trognitz, Raymond William 1953?- [BI]
American hockey player
* Wild Willie

Trognon, A.
See Joinville, Francois Ferdinand
Philippe Louis Marie d'Orleans

Trois Etoiles [Three Stars]
See Mayer, Charles E. E.

Trois Etoiles
See Murray, Eustace Clare Grenville

[The] Trojan
See Evers, John Joseph

Trojanowicz, John M[ichael] 1936-
[CA]
American educator and author
* Troyanovich, John M[ichael]

Troll, Gustav
See Brestowski, Carl August

Trolley Line Butler
See Butler, John Stephen [Johnny]

Trollope, Frances 1780-1863 [DEA]
British author
* F. T.

Trollope, Susanna
See Maginn, William

Trollope, Theodosia 1810-1865 [DEA,
PA]
British author
* Garrow, Theodosia

Troloppe, Francis
See Feval, Paul Henri

Tromlitz, A. von
See Witzleben, Karl August Friedrich
von

Trommer, Lazarus 1888?-1957 [BI]
American engineer and author
* Aidline, Elbert

Trompeter, Lisa Roma 1892?-1965
[HPPN]
American singer
* Roma, Lisa

Tronche, Philippe 1929- [ESF]
French author and journalist
* Curval, Philippe

**Troncoso de la Concha, Manuel de
Jesus** 1878-1955 [CW]
Dominican author
* Buscon, Juan

Trone, Roland 20th c. [RO1]
American singer
* Don

[A] Trooper
See Adams, Francis Colburn

Tropea, Orassio [or Orazio] ?-1926?
[BLB, PHM]
American underworld figure
* [The] Scourge

Tropica
See Wolcott, Mary Adella

Trosky, Harold Arthur, Jr. [Hal]
See Troyavesky, Harold Arthur, Jr.

Trosky, Harold Arthur, Sr.
See Troyavesky, Harold Arthur, Sr.

Trosky, Hoot
See Troyavesky, Harold Arthur, Jr.

Trossi, Carlo Felice ?-1949 [EAR]
Italian auto racer
* Trossi, Didi

Trossi, Didi
See Trossi, Carlo Felice

Trost, Sven
See Snoilsky, Carl Johan Gustav

Trostl, Arturo 1952?- [BI]
American acrobat
* Arturo, Cookie

Trotere, Henry
See Trotter, Henry

Trotsky, Leon
See Bronstein, Lev Davidovich

Trott, John, Yeoman
See St. John, Henry

Trott-Plaid, John, Esq.
See Fielding, Henry

Trotter, C. H. 20th c.
Horse trainer
* Trotter, Tobe

Trotter, Canon John Crawford 1848-?
[HPPN]
Irish clergyman and author
* O'Dhu, Fergus

Trotter, Dale 20th c. [GW]
American rodeo performer
* Trotter, Trapper

Trotter, Grace V[iolet] 1900- [CA, SAT]
American author
* Paschal, Nancy

Trotter, Henry 1855-1912 [BBD]
British composer
* Trotere, Henry

Trotter, [Canon] John Crawford 1848-?
[LAO]
Irish clergyman and writer
* O'Dhu, Fergus

Trotter, Sallie
See Crawford, Sallie Wallace Brown

Trotter, Tobe
See Trotter, C. H.

Trotter, Trapper
See Trotter, Dale

Trottier, Bryan 1956- [SMG]
Canadian-born hockey player
* Trottier, Trots

Trottier, Trots
See Trottier, Bryan

Trotwood
See Moore, John Trotwood

Trotzendorf, Valentin
See Friedland, Valentin

[The] Troubador of the Violin
See Lande, Jules

[The] Troubadour
See Woods, Oscar

Troubetzkoy, Princess 1864?-1945
[BEW]
American author and playwright
* Rives, Amelie

**[The] Troubled Pied Piper of Los
Alamos**
See Oppenheimer, J[ulius] Robert

**[The] Troubled Troubadour of the
Forties**
See Haymes, Richard [Dick]

[A] Troubler of Israel
See Morton, Thomas

Troubles, Kid
See Bargordes, Benjamin

[The] Troubleshooter
See Murphy, Robert D.

Trousdale, William 1790-1872 [HPPN]
American soldier
* [The] War Horse of Sumner County

Trousse, Marguis de la ?-1648 [SN]
French aristocrat
* Alcidas

Trout, Dink
See Trout, Francis

Trout, Dizzy
See Trout, Paul Howard

Trout, Francis 1898-1950 [SC]
American actor and musician
* Trout, Dink

Trout, Kilgore
See Farmer, Philip Jose

Trout, Paul Howard 1915-1972 [BE, PB,
SMG]
American baseball player
* Trout, Dizzy

Trout, Rainbow
See Trout, Steve[n Russell]

Trout, Steve[n Russell] 1957-
American baseball player
* Trout, Rainbow

[El] Trovador Cubano
See Poveda y Armenteros, Francisco

Trovato, Ben
See Lover, Samuel

Trovatore
See Williams, William Francis

Trowbridge, John Townsend 1827-1916
[DEL, DNNF, FFF, HPPN]
American author
* [A] Contributor to the Atlantic
* Creyton, Paul

Trowell, Adjutant
See Dawes, Thomas

Troxell, William S. 1893?-1957   [BI]
American columnist
* Pumpernickel Bill

Troy, Bun
See Troy, Robert

Troy, Dasher
See Troy, John Joseph

Troy, Forrest 1933?-   [BI]
American journalist
* Troy, Frosty

Troy, Frosty
See Troy, Forrest

Troy, John Joseph 1856-1938   [BE]
American baseball player
* Troy, Dasher

Troy, Robert 1888-1918   [BE]
German-born baseball player
* Troy, Bun

Troy, Simon
See Warriner, Thurman

Troy, Thomas F. 1855-1937   [HPPN]
American minstrel
* Thomas, T. F.

Troyanovich, John M[ichael]
See Trojanowicz, John M[ichael]

Troyat, Henri
See Tarassoff [or Tarassov], Lev

Troyavesky, Harold Arthur, Jr. 1936-
[BE]
American baseball player
* Trosky, Harold Arthur, Jr. [Hal]
* Trosky, Hoot

Troyavesky, Harold Arthur, Sr. 1912-
[BE]
American baseball player
* Trosky, Harold Arthur, Sr.

Troyer, Byron L[eRoy] 1909-   [CA]
American author
* Hamilton, Dave

Truby, Bird Eye
See Truby, Harry Garvin

Truby, Harry Garvin 1870-1953   [BE]
American baseball player
* Truby, Bird Eye

Trucking Kid
See Rabia, Aliyah

Trucks, Butch
See Trucks, Claude Hudson

Trucks, Claude Hudson 20th c.   [RO2]
American musician
* Trucks, Butch

Trucks, Fire [or Fireball]
See Trucks, Virgil Oliver

Trucks, Virgil Oliver 1919-   [BE, PB]
American baseball player
* Trucks, Fire [or Fireball]

Trudeau, [Dr.] Edward Livingston
1848-1915   [HPPN]
American physician
* [The] Doctor Who Would Not Die

Trudeau, Garretson Beekman 1948-
[CA]
American cartoonist and author
* Trudeau, Garry B.

Trudeau, Garry B.
See Trudeau, Garretson Beekman

Trudeau, Pierre Elliott 1919-   [CR]
Canadian prime minister
* P. E. T.

Trudger and Trencher
See Stow, John

Trudix, Marty
See Truman, Ruth

[The] True Athenian
See Mehre, Harry J.

[The] True Blue Protestant Poet
See Shadwell, Thomas

[The] True Briton
See Tod, Thomas

[A] True Celt
See Davis, Thomas Osborne

[The] True Diana
See Elizabeth I

[The] True English Aretine
See Nash [or Nashe?], Thomas

True, Fanny
See Short, Mary Asenath

True Gun Hart
See Hart, William Woodrow [Bill]

True, Hiram L. 1845-1912   [DNA,
HPPN]
American author and physician
* Allen, Don

True, Hollis
See Chegwidden, T. C.

True, Kate
See Woods, Kate Tannant

[The] True Laureate of England
See Dibdin, Charles

True Love
See Foe, Daniel

[A] True Nathaniel
See Sylvester, Joshua

[A] True Patriot and Good Man
See Bowles, William Lisle

[The] True Prophet
See Longo, Bruce

[A] True Quaker
See Singleton, William

[A] True Son of the Church of England
See Asplin, William

True Thomas
See Learmont, Thomas

Truean, Augustus H. 1857-1908   [HPPN]
American actor and singer
* Saville, Gus H.

Trueblood, Newton A.   [BI]
American author
* Winter, Frank

Truebner, Nicolas 1817-?   [PA]
British author
* N. T.

Trueman, Fiery Fred
See Trueman, Fred

Trueman, Fred   [NN]
British cricketer
* Trueman, Fiery Fred

Truempy, Balz
See Truempy, Johann Balthasar

Truempy, Johann Balthasar 1946-
[IWM]
Swiss composer
* Truempy, Balz

Truesdell, A. C. W. 19th c.   [HPPN]
American author
* One of the Pilgrims

Truinet, Charles Louis Etienne
1828-1899   [BBD]
French author and librettist
* Nuitter, Charles Louis Etienne

Trujillo, Boom Boom
See Trujillo, Lorenzo

Trujillo, Chel
See Trujillo, Lorenzo L.

Trujillo, Lorenzo 20th c.   [RBE]
American boxer
* Trujillo, Boom Boom

Trujillo, Lorenzo L. 1906?-1962   [BEW]
Mexican actor
* Trujillo, Chel

Trujillo Molina, Rafael Leonidas
1891-1961   [HPPN]
Dominican army officer and politician
* [The] Dean of Dictators
* [The] Last Caesar

Trulock, Camilo Jose Cela 1916-
[HPPN]
Spanish author
* Cela, Camilo Joe

Truman, Bess
See Truman, Elizabeth Wallace

Truman, Elizabeth Wallace 1885-?
[HPPN]
Wife of American president, Harry S. Truman
* [The] Boss
* Truman, Bess

Truman, Harry H. 1866-1925 [BE]
American baseball player
* Raymond, Harry H.

Truman, Harry S. 1884-1972 [CND, FAP]
American president
* Give 'Em Hell Harry
* H. S. T.
* Haberdasher Harry
* High Tax Harry
* Hired Man of 150 Million People
* Kilting [code name used during World War II]
* [The] Man from Missouri
* [The] Man of Independence
* [The] Senator from Pendergast
* Supervise [Secret Service code name]

Truman, Marcus George 1890- [WW]
Author
* Beckett, Mark

Truman, Ruth 1931- [CA]
American author
* Trudix, Marty

Trumbauer, Frank[ie] 1900?-1956 [EJ, PMJ]
American jazz musician
* Trumbauer, Tram [or Trum]

Trumbauer, Tram [or Trum]
See Trumbauer, Frank[ie]

Trumble, Alfred [FFF]
American writer
* Babbler

Trumbo, Dalton 1905-1976 [CA, WD]
American screenwriter and author
* Jackson, Sam
* Rich, Robert

Trumbull
See Webster, Noah

Trumbull, Annie Eliot 1857-1949 [DNA]
American author, poet, playwright
* Eliot, Annie

Trumbull, Ed[ward J.]
See Trembly, Edward J.

Trumbull, Henry 19th c. [HPPN]
American author
* Steward, [Rev.] James

Trumbull, J. Hammond
See Trumbull, John

Trumbull, John 1750-1831 [HPPN]
American poet and jurist
* [The] Celebrated Author of "M'Fingal"
* [The] Meddler
* [The] Schemer, an Ally of the Meddler
* Trumbull, J. Hammond

Trumbull, John 1756-1843
American painter
* Colonial Limner
* Gentleman John
* [The] Patriot Artist

Trumbull, Jonathan 1710-1785 [HPPN, WBD]
American statesman
* Brother Jonathan
* [The] Rebel Governor

Trumbull, Matthew Mark 1826-1894 [HPPN]
British-American economist and author
* Trumbull, Wheelbarrow

Trumbull, Wheelbarrow
See Trumbull, Matthew Mark

Trumper, Hubert Bagster 1902- [CAP]
British author
* Bagster, Hubert

Trumpeter of Pitt
See Cobbett, William

Trumpeting Behemoth
See Hirt, Alois Maxwell

Trumps
See Dick, William Brisbane

Trumps
See McCollum, J. C.

Trundlett, Helen B.
See Eliot, Thomas Stearns

Trungpa, Chogyam
See Gyamtso, Choskyi

[The] Trunk Murderer
See Judd, Ruth Marian McKinnell

[The] Trunk Murderer
See Robinson, John

[The] Trunk Slayer
See Judd, Ruth Marian McKinnell

Truong Chinh [Long March]
See Dang Xuan Khu

Truscot, Bruce
See Peers, Edgar Allison

Truscott, Charles
See Tench, Charles Victor

Truscott-Jones, Reginald 1905?-1986 [BDF, F2, WEF]
Welsh-born actor and director
* Milland, Jack
* Milland, Ray
* Milland, Spike

Trusler, John 1735-1820 [HPPN]
British physician, clergyman, bookseller
* J. A.

Trusler, John (cont.)
* M. D. and F. R. S.
* [A] Pupil of the Late Dr. W. Hunter
* Seed and Plum Cakins

Trusler, Margaret
See Fisher, Margaret Trusler

Truss, [Leslie] Seldon 1892- [CA, CC]
British author
* Seldon-Truss, Leslie
* Selmark, George

[The] Trust Buster
See Roosevelt, Theodore [Teddy]

[The] Trust Busting President
See Roosevelt, Theodore [Teddy]

[The] Trust Slayer
See Roosevelt, Theodore [Teddy]

Trusta, H.
See Phelps, Elizabeth [Stuart]

[The] Trustee
See Foe, Daniel

[A] Trustee
See Whally, John

Trusty Anthony
See Aston, Anthony

[The] Truth
See Williams, Carl

Truth, Sojourner
See Van Wagener, Isabelle

Truth Teller
See Thomson, Charles

Truthful James
See Hennessy, William Charles

Truthful Jim Mutrie
See Mutrie, James J. [Jim]

Truthful, President
See Nixon, Richard Milhous

Truxtun, Thomas 1755-1822 [HPPN]
American ship captain
* America's Foremost Privateer Commander

Try-Davies, J.
See Hensley, Sophia Margaret [Almon]

Tryon, Thomas 1634-1703 [NPS]
Author and philosopher
* [The] Pythagorean

Tryon, William 1725-1788 [HPPN]
Irish trader
* [The] Great Wolf

Tsai Ch'un 1856-1875 [HPPN]
Chinese emperor
* T'ung Chi

Tsai T'ien [Glorious Succession]
See Kuang Hsu [or Kwang Hsu]

Ts'ao Yu
See Wan Chia-Pao

Tsatsos, Ioanna 1909- [CA]
Greek author and poet
* Tsatsos, Jeanne

Tsatsos, Jeanne
See Tsatsos, Ioanna

Tschegerleb
See Hafiz, Mohammed

Tschernek, Viktor 1913-   [IAW]
German author
* Bergauer, Johannes

Tschiffely, A. F.
See Tschiffely, Aime Felix

Tschiffely, Aime Felix 1895-1954   [LC]
Swiss-born author
* Tschiffely, A. F.

Tschirky, Oscar 1866-1950   [WBD]
Swiss-born hotel headwaiter
* Oscar of the Waldorf

Tschudi, Aegidius [or Gilg von]
1505-1572   [DNNS, WBD]
Swiss historian and theologian
* [The] Father of Swiss History

Tsedek, Moreh
See Carter, Ben

Tsederbaum, Iulii O. 1873-?   [JL]
Russian journalist and political theorist
* Martov, Julius

Tseng Chi-tse 1839-1890   [FFF, HPPN, WBD]
Chinese diplomat
* [The] Celestial Talleyrand
* Tseng, Marquis
* Tseng, Marshall

Tseng, Marquis
See Tseng Chi-tse

Tseng, Marshall
See Tseng Chi-tse

Tseng Yu-ho
See Ecke, Betty Tseng Yu-ho

Tseu, Yih Zan 1886-?   [HPPN]
Chinese educator and author
* Tyz, A. N.

Tshiamala, Kabasele ?-1983?   [CA]
Entertainer and songwriter
* Jeef, Kalle
* Kabasele, Joseph

Tsiang, T. F.
See Chiang T'ing Fu

Tsou Se-ling 20th c.   [DFM]
Chinese director
* Chu, Shih-ling

Tsu, Andrew Yu Yue 1887-   [HPPN]
Chinese clergyman and author
* Tsu, Y. Y.

Tsu, Y. Y.
See Tsu, Andrew Yu Yue

Tsubouchi, Shoyo
See Tsubouchi, Yuzo

Tsubouchi, Yuzo 1859-1935   [MWD]
Japanese director and playwright
* Tsubouchi, Shoyo

Tsukahara, Nobuo 1926-   [EJ7]
Japanese jazz musician
* Hara, Nobuo

Tsukinabe, Isao
See Vermeule, Cornelius Clarkson, III

Tsukioka, Yoshitoshi 1839-1892   [WECO]
Japanese artist
* Taiso [Great Revival]

Tsunayoshi 18th c.
Japanese shogun
* Shogun of Dogs

Tsung cheng Shih-lu
See Cheng Sen

Tsuruoka, Masami 1929-
Canadian martial artist
* [The] Father of Canadian Karate

Tsushima, Shuji 1909-1948   [BI, TCL]
Japanese author
* Dazai, Osamu

Tua Fault, Frank
See Bullock-Webster, Llewelyn

Tua, Teresina
See Felicita, Maria

Tuala, Mario
See Schulz Ewerth, Eckard

Tuan
See Campbell, John Beautiste

Tuann, Lucy H[siu-mei] C[hen] 1938-
[CA]
Taiwanese-born author
* Chen Jo-hsi

Tuathal, Cairn
See Davis, Eugene

[The] Tub
See Riqueti, Honore Gabriel Victor

Tuba, Mr.
See Phillips, Harvey G.

[The] Tubal Cain of America
See Spotswood, Alexander

Tubalcain
See Watson, Mary

Tubb, E. C.
See Tubb, Edwin Charles

Tubb, Edwin Charles 1919-   [CA, ESF, SF]
British author
* Adams, Chuck
* Armstrong, Anthony
* Bain, Ted
* Beecham, Alice
* Blake, Anthony
* Carey, Julian
* Carpenter, Morley
* Cary, Jud
* Clarkson, J. F.
* Dale, Norman
* Farrow, James S.
* Fenner, James R.
* Godfrey, R. H.
* Graham, Charles S.
* Gray, Charles

Tubb, Edwin Charles (cont.)
* Gridban, Volsted [house pseudonym, Scion Publications]
* Guthrie, Alan
* Holt, George
* Hunt, Gill [house pseudonym, Curtis Warren]
* Innes, Alan
* Jackson, E. F.
* Kent, Gordon
* Kern, Gregory [house pseudonym]
* Lamont, Duncan
* Lang, King [house pseudonym, Curtis Warren]
* Lantry, Mike
* Lawrence, P.
* Lawson, Chet
* Maclean, Arthur
* Maddox, Carl
* Martyn, Phillip
* Moulton, Carl
* Neal, Gavin
* Powers, M. L.
* Schofield, Paul
* Seabright, John
* Shaw, Brian [house pseudonym, Curtis Warren]
* Sheldon, Roy [house pseudonym, Hamilton]
* Stevens, John
* Storm, Eric
* Thomson, Edward
* Tubb, E. C.
* Wainwright, Ken
* Weight, Frank
* West, Douglas
* Wilding, Eric
* Winnard, Frank

Tubb, Ernest Dale 1914-1984   [ECM, FCW, TI 9-17-84, WP 9-7-84, WP 12-7-82]
American country-western performer
* [The] Gold Chain Troubador
* [The] Texas Troubadour

Tubbs, Alice Ivers 1851?-1930   [BI, HPPN]
American gambler
* Poker Alice

Tubbs, Arthur Lewis 1867-1946   [ALY, BI]
American playwright
* Sylvester, Arthur

Tubbs, Jerry 20th c.
American football player
* Tubbs, Tubby

Tubbs, Tony 20th c.
American boxer
* TNT

Tubbs, Tubby
See Tubbs, Jerry

Tubby, Alfred Herbert 1862-?   [LAO]
British physician and author
* Theobald, Alfred Herbert

Tubman, Harriet Araminta Ross Davis
1821-1913   [HPPN, IBW]
American abolitionist
* [The] Flame of Freedom
* [The] Modern Moses
* Moses

Tubman, Harriet Araminta Ross Davis
(cont.)
* Moses to Her People
* [The] Negro Moses

Tubman, Old Daddy
See Tubman, William Vacanarat
Shadrach

Tubman, William Vacanarat Shadrach
1895-1971 [HPPN]
Liberian president
* Perrenial President
* [The] Pride of Liberia
* Resilient Uncle
* Tubman, Old Daddy
* Uncle Shad

Tucci, Niccolo 1908- [CA]
*Swiss-born American author and
playwright*
* Strabolgi, Bartolomeo

Tuchow, Michael 20th c. [BEW]
American actor
* Tolan, Michael

Tuck, Dorothy
See McFarland, Dorothy Tuck

Tuck, Friar
See Tucker, Irwin St. John

Tuck, Porter 1932- [HPPN]
American bullfighter
* [El] Rubio de Boston

Tucker, Abraham 1705-1774 [DEL,
DNNF, FFF]
British author
* Comment, Cuthbert
* Search, Edward

Tucker, Agnes Kent Carruth 1910-
[AW]
American author
* Carruth, Agnes K.

Tucker, Ann
See Giudici, Ann Couper

Tucker, Blanch [PA]
Author
* Rosavella

Tucker, Bob
See Tucker, [Arthur] Wilson

Tucker, Caroline
See Nolan, Jeannette Covert

Tucker, Charlotte Maria 1821?-1893
[DNNF, RH, WBD]
British author
* A. L. O. E. [A Lady of England]

Tucker, Cissy 1874?-1941 [HPPN]
British actress
* Fitzgerald, Cissy

Tucker, Dan
See Tucker, Reasin

Tucker, Eleonora C. 1850-? [PI]
Canadian-born poet
* Deane, D. C.
* E. C. M.
* L. M.

Tucker, Foghorn
See Tucker, Thomas J.

Tucker, Gabe
See Tucker, Gaylord Bob

Tucker, Gaylord Bob 1915- [CWG,
DAM]
American country-western performer
* Tucker, Gabe

Tucker, George 1775-1861 [DLE1, DNA,
WGT]
American author and political economist
* Atterley, Joseph

Tucker, Georgina P. 1911- [CA]
American author
* Tucker, Gina

Tucker, Gina
See Tucker, Georgina P.

Tucker, Handsome Jack
See Tucker, John Randolph

Tucker, Herbert 1855-? [WWL]
South African author
* H. T.

Tucker, Hilda 1880-1959 [BEW]
Actress
* Trevelyan, Hilda

Tucker, Hubert Coutts ?-1921 [DBA]
British painter
* Coutts, Hubert

Tucker, Irwin St. John 1886-1982 [CA]
American clergyman, journalist, poet
* Tuck, Friar

Tucker, [Allan] James 1929- [AW, CA,
WD]
Welsh author and journalist
* Craig, David

Tucker, John F[rancis] 1871-? [ALY]
American author
* Newkirk, Foster

Tucker, John Randolph 1812-1883
[HPPN]
American naval officer
* Tucker, Handsome Jack

Tucker, Josiah [or Joseph?] 1711-1799
[HN]
British author, clergyman, economist
* Garlic, Parson

Tucker, LaCosta 20th c. [ECM]
American country-western performer
* LaCosta

Tucker, Lael
See Wertenbaker, Lael Tucker

Tucker, Link
See Bingley, David Ernest

Tucker, Loraine Read 1910- [ART]
British industrial designer
* Read-Tucker, L.

Tucker, Lorenzo 1907- [IBW]
American actor
* [The] Black Valentino

Tucker, Mary
See Clayton, Mrs. Albert

Tucker, Nathaniel Beverley 1784-1851
[FFF, PA]
American author
* Sidney, E. W.
* Sidney, Edward William

Tucker, Preston Thomas 1903-1956
[HPPN]
American auto manufacturing executive
* [The] Father of the Tucker Torpedo

Tucker, Reasin 19th c. [HPPN]
American pioneer
* Tucker, Dan

Tucker, Richard
See Ticker, Reuben

Tucker, Robin 1950- [CA]
American author and editor
* Nibor, Kay

Tucker, Saint George 1752-1827
[HPPN]
American attorney and educator
* [The] American Blackstone

Tucker, Samuel [IBW]
American magician
* [The] Great Sante

Tucker, Sophie
See Abuza, Sophie

Tucker, Tee
See Higgenbotham, Robert

Tucker, Thomas J. 1863-1935 [PB]
American baseball player
* Tucker, Foghorn

Tucker, Thurman Lowell 1917- [BE, PB]
American baseball player
* Joe E.

Tucker, Tommy
See Higgenbotham, Robert

Tucker, Tommy
See Higginbotham, Robert

Tucker, William George 1905-1964
[BWW, NBB]
American singer
* Barbee, John Henry

Tucker, [Arthur] Wilson 1914- [CA,
SFL, WGT]
American author
* Hoy Ping Pong
* Tucker, Bob
* Vaid, Sanford

Tucker-Fettner, Ann
See Giudici, Ann Couper

Tuckerman, Dusty
See Tuckerman, Earle

Tuckerman, Earle 20th c. [HPPN]
American singer
* Tuckerman, Dusty

Tuckerman, Joseph 1778-1840   [HPPN]
American clergyman
* [A] Gentleman in Boston
* J. T.

Tuckwell, Margaret 20th c.   [IAW]
British author
* Bacon, Margaret

Tudhope, Richard
See Rodda, Peter [Gordon]

Tudor, Antony 1909-   [HPPN]
British choreographer and ballet dancer
* [The] Man Without a Theory

Tudor, Frederic 1783-1864   [HPPN]
American merchant
* [The] Ice King

Tudor, Jasper [Earl of Pembroke and Duke of Bedford] ?-1495   [HPPN]
British soldier
* Jasper of Hatfield

Tudor, Mary
See Mary I

Tudor, Rowan
See Koster, Cornelius

Tudor, Tasha
See Burgess, Starling

Tudor, Valerie
See Samuel, Valerie

Tudoran, Radu
See Bogza, Nicolae

Tueart, Dennis 1949-   [AES]
British soccer player
* [The] Menace

Tuekakas 1790?-1871   [BI]
American Indian chief
* Old Joseph

Tuel, John E. 19th c.   [HPPN]
American author
* J. E. T.

[Der] Tuerken Louis
See Louis William I

Tuffley, Fred Eric Lewis 1855-1935   [BEW]
British-born actor
* Lewis, Eric

Tufin, Armand 1756-1793   [HPPN]
French army officer
* Armand, Charles

Tufts, Bowen Charleston 1911-1970   [FC]
American actor
* Tufts, Sonny

Tufts, Sonny
See Tufts, Bowen Charleston

Tufty, Barbara Jean 1923-   [IAW]
American author
* Jeans, Barbara

Tufverson, Agnes Colonia 1890-   [HPPN]
Norwegian-American attorney
* [The] Absent Corpus Delicti

Tugmutton, Timothy, Esq.
See Chorley, Charles

Tugwell, [Rev.] George 19th c.   [HPPN]
British author
* [A] Versemaker

Tugwell, Rexford Guy 1891-   [HPPN]
American Undersecretary of Agriculture
* American, Mr.
* [The] Barrymore of the Brain Trust

Tuite, Frederick P. 1885?-1963   [BEW]
American actor
* Peters, Fred

Tuite, Hugh 20th c.   [MBF]
British author
* Spencer, Captain
* Trelawney, Hubert

Tukesbury, Joe
See Wright, Joseph X.

Tulane, Anne
See Italiano, Anna Maria Luisa

Tulasne, Louis Rene 1815-1885   [WBD]
French botanist
* [The] Founder of Modern Mycology

Tuleja, Tad
See Tuleja, Thaddeus F[rancis]

Tuleja, Thaddeus F[rancis] 1944-   [CA]
American author
* Macao, Marshall
* Tuleja, Tad

Tull, Anthony 1912-   [THR]
British author and director
* Parker, Anthony

Tull, Jethro 1674-1741   [HPPN]
British author and agriculturist
* [The] Father of the Seed Drill

Tuller, Charles 1924?-   [HPPN]
American highjacker and government employee
* [The] Berserk Bureaucrat

Tullett, Denis 1928-   [WD]
British poet
* Sutton, John

Tullius Anglorum
See Lyly, John

Tulloch, [Sir] A. M.   [HN]
British writer
* Dalgetty, Dugald

Tullock, W. W. ?-1920   [WWL]
Author
* [The] Booktaster
* Bridge, Bonar
* Goosequill, Gregory
* Hill, Arthur
* Orion
* [The] Paperknife
* Sailil

Tully
See Cicero, Marcus Tullius

Tully, Ethel
See Dunlap, Ethel Margaret

Tully, J. M.
See Tully, Joyce Mary

Tully, Joyce Mary 20th c.   [ART]
British painter
* Tully, J. M.

Tully, Mrs. Richard Walton
Author
* Gates, Eleanor

Tully, Sam[uel] ?-1812   [HPPN]
American pirate and murderer
* Heathcoate, R.

Tully, Tom
See Sellers, Connie Leslie, Jr.

Tulp, Claes Pieterszoon
See Pieterszoon, Nicolaes

Tulsa Jack Blake
See Blake, John

Tulsa Red
See Fulson, Lowell

Tulsi Das 1532-1623   [HPPN]
Hindu poet and reformer
* [The] Greatest Poet of Medieval Hindustan

Tum-Tum
See Edward VII

Tumarin, Boris
See Tumarinson, Boris

Tumarinson, Boris 1910-   [BEW, TR]
Latvian-born actor, director, educator
* Tumarin, Boris

Tumble-Down Dick
See Cromwell, Richard

Tumbler Harry St. John
See St. John, Henry

[The] Tumbleweed Kid
See Curless, Richard [Dick]

[The] Tumbling Queen
See Matthews, JoAnn

Tuminaro, Angelo 20th c.   [PHM]
American underworld figure
* Tuminaro, Little Angie

Tuminaro, Little Angie
See Tuminaro, Angelo

Tummy
See Edward VII

Tumulti, Thomas ?-1872?   [PI]
Irish poet
* T. T.

[The] Tune Detective
See Spaeth, Sigmund Gottfried

Tuneful Harry
See Lawes, Henry

T'ung Chi
See Tsai Ch'un

Tung, Shamsuddin
See Tung, Tao Chang

Tung, Tao Chang 1923?- [BI]
Chinese journalist
* Tung, Shamsuddin

[The] Tunis Terror
See Perez, Victor

Tunnell, Emlen 1925-1975 [IBW]
American football player and coach
* [The] Gremlin

Tunnell, George N. 1903-1975 [PMJ, WWJ]
American singer
* Bon Bon

Tunnell, Mavis 1916- [THR]
British actress
* Clair, Mavis

Tunnell, Peggy Joye 20th c. [CWG]
American country-western performer
* Allen, Barbara

Tunney, Gene
See Tunney, James Joseph

Tunney, James Joseph 1897?-1978 [BI, BX, HPPN, RBE]
American boxer
* [The] Creamer
* [The] Fighting Marine
* Tunney, Gene

Tunnicliffe, Colin John 1951- [DC]
British cricketer
* Tunnicliffe, Tunners

Tunnicliffe, Howard Trevor 1950- [DC]
British cricketer
* Tunnicliffe, Pally

Tunnicliffe, Pally
See Tunnicliffe, Howard Trevor

Tunnicliffe, Tunners
See Tunnicliffe, Colin John

Tunstall, Alfred Moore 1863-1935 [HPPN]
American statesman
* [The] Dean of the Alabama Legislature
* [The] Gentleman from Hale
* Tunstall, Uncle Alf

Tunstall, Shana Barrett
See Tunstall, Velma [Barrett]

Tunstall, Uncle Alf
See Tunstall, Alfred Moore

Tunstall, Velma [Barrett] 1914- [CA, WD]
American poet
* Tunstall, Shana Barrett

Tuohy, Frank 1925- [HPPN]
British educator and author
* Tuohy, John Francis

Tuohy, John Francis
See Tuohy, Frank

Tupac Amaru
See Condorcanqui, Jose Gabriel

Tupikov, Pavel Georgievich 1882-? [HPPN]
Russian playwright and author
* Nizovoy, Pavel

Tupper, Kathryn Munro 20th c. [NAA]
Canadian poet
* Munro, Kathryn

Tupper, Martin Farquhar 1810-1889 [DEL, HPPN, PA]
British poet
* Paterfamilias
* Query, Peter, Esq.
* T.

Tupper, Mary
See Jones, Mary Tupper

Tur, Evgeniia
See Salias de Turnemir, Elizaveta Vasil'evna [Sukhovo-Kobylina]

Tur-Malka
See Greenberg, Uri Zvi

Turbayne, John 1914- [CA]
British author
* Seymour, John

Turberville, James ?-1570? [NPS]
Bishop of Exeter
* Trobullfeld, Doctor

Turbojew, Alexej
See Scheer, Karl Herbert

Turbulent, Tom
See Foe, Daniel

Turchin, Edward Lawrence [Eddie] 1917- [BE]
American baseball player
* Turchin, Smiley

Turchin, Smiley
See Turchin, Edward Lawrence [Eddie]

Turco, Lewis 1934- [MA]
American author
* Court, Wesli

Tureaud, Lawrence 1953?-
American actor
* Mr. T.

Turell, Dan 20th c. [IAW]
Danish poet
* Onkel Danny

[The] Turenne of Louis XV
See Saxe, [Hermann] Maurice de

Turgeon, Eugene Joseph 1897- [BE]
American baseball player
* Turgeon, Pete

Turgeon, Jean 1952- [WEC]
Canadian cartoonist
* Gite

Turgeon, [Madame] Leonida F. 1883- [NAA]
Canadian author
* Des Ormes, Renee

Turgeon, Pete
See Turgeon, Eugene Joseph

[El] Turia
See Barrios, Francisco

Turia, Ricardo de
See Rejaule y Toledo, Pedro Juan de

Turicchia, Signor
See Alunni, Corrado

[The] Turk
See Gonzaga, Ludovico di III

Turk, Chief
See Turk, Lucas Newton

Turk Gregory
See Hildebrand

Turk, Lucas Newton 1898- [BE]
American baseball player
* Turk, Chief

Turk, Midge
See Richardson, Midge Turk

Turkel, Pauline
See Kesselman, Judi R[osenthal]

Turkel, Pauline
See Rosenthal, Judi

Turkevich, Leonid 1877-1965 [BI]
American religious leader
* Leonty

Turkey Creek Johnson
See Johnson, Jack

Turkey Mike Donlin
See Donlin, Michael Joseph

Turkiewicz, Jim 1955- [SMG]
Canadian-born hockey player
* Turkiewicz, Turk

Turkiewicz, Turk
See Turkiewicz, Jim

[The] Turkish Samson
See Ozdemir

Turkson, Albertine Bowie 1950- [BA]
American attorney
* Turkson, Tina

Turkson, Tina
See Turkson, Albertine Bowie

Turkus, Burton 1902-1982 [NW 12-6-82]
American attorney
* Arsenic, Mr.

Turla, Leopoldo 1818-1877 [CW]
Cuban playwright and poet
* [Un] Quidam

Turleigh, Veronica
See Turley, Veronica

Turley, Bullet Bob
See Turley, Robert Lee

Turley, Robert Lee 1930- [BE, PB]
American baseball player
* Turley, Bullet Bob

Turley, Veronica 1903- [THR]
Irish-born actress
* Turleigh, Veronica

Turlough
See Hughes, Terence McMahon

Turlupin
See Legrand, Henri

Turmair [or Thurmayr], Johannes
1477-1534 [WBD]
Bavarian historian
* Aventinus, Johannes
* [The] Bavarian Herodotus

Turn Coat Meres
See Booth, Henry

Turn 'Em Loose Bruce
See Wright, Bruce McMarion

Turnabout, [Rev.] Secretary
See Priestley, Joseph

Turnbo, Kirk
See Turnbo, L. S.

Turnbo, L. S. 19th c. [HPPN]
American sheriff
* Turnbo, Kirk

Turnbull, Alex 20th c. [BBH]
Canadian lacrosse player
* Turnbull, Dad

Turnbull, Ann [Christine] 1943- [CA]
British author
* Nicol, Ann

Turnbull, Dad
See Turnbull, Alex

Turnbull, Dora Amy Elles Dillon
1878-1961 [CC, EMD, LC]
British author
* Delta
* Wentworth, Patricia

Turnbull, John Iglehart ?-1944 [BBH]
American lacrosse player
* [The] Babe Ruth of Lacrosse

Turnbull, Robert James 1775-1833
[WBD]
American author and attorney
* Brutus

Turnbull, William Barclay David Donald
1811-1863 [HFN, IP]
Scottish antiquary
* [A] Delver into Antiquity
* W. B. D. D. T.

Turncoat
See Southey, Robert

Turncoat, John
See Thayer, John

Turnebe, Adrien
See Tournebu, Adrien

Turner, Al 1929- [HPPN]
American arm wrestler
* [The] Godfather
* [The] King of the Hill
* Turner, Big Al

Turner, Alexander Freke
See Crawfurd, Oswald John Frederick

Turner, Alfred L. 1911- [HPPN]
American football player
* Turner, Warhorse

Turner, Anne ?-1615 [SN]
British murderer
* Dame Ursula
* Suddlechop, Ursley

Turner, B. K.
See Turner, Babe Kyro Lemon

Turner, Babe Kyro Lemon 1907-1972
[BWW]
American singer
* Black Ace
* Turner, B. K.
* Turner, Buck

Turner, Bake
See Turner, Robert

Turner, [Rev.] Baptist Noel 1739-1826
[HPPN]
British clergyman
* B. N. T.
* [An] Octogenarian

Turner, Big Al
See Turner, Al

Turner, Big Joe
See Turner, Joseph [Vernon]

Turner, Birdy
See Turner, David Roy

Turner, Blind Squire
See Darby, Theodore [Teddy]

Turner, Buck
See Turner, Babe Kyro Lemon

Turner, Bulldog
See Turner, Clyde

Turner, C. F.
See Turner, Fred

Turner, C. T. B. [NN]
Australian cricketer
* [The] Terror

Turner, Cactus Jack
See Turner, Jack

Turner, Carrie
See His, Mrs. Albert

Turner, Cecilia 1874-1924 [HPPN]
American actress and author
* Ellis, Cecilia

Turner, Charles Robert 1910- [BA]
American contractor
* Turner, Jack

Turner, Charles Tennyson
See Tennyson, Charles

Turner, Claramae
See Haas, Claramae

Turner, Clay
See Ballard, [Willis] Todhunter

Turner, Clyde 1919- [BI, HPPN, SMG,
WA]
American football player
* [The] Dog

Turner, Clyde (cont.)
* [The] Kid from Sweetwater
* Turner, Bulldog

Turner, Cora
See Mackamotzki, Kunigunde

Turner, Cotton
See Turner, Terrence Lamont

Turner, Curtis Morton 1924-1970 [BBH,
BI]
American auto racer
* Turner, Pops

Turner, Daddy
See Turner, Otis

Turner, Daniel 1710-1798 [HPPN, IP]
British author and clergyman
* [An] Impartial Hand
* [The] President

Turner, David Roy 1949- [DC]
British cricketer
* Turner, Birdy

Turner, Dona M. 1951- [CA]
American author
* Thisby [joint pseudonym with Vince
Genovese]

Turner, Dwight D. 20th c. [RO2]
American singer
* Turner, Spyder

Turner, E. C. 20th c. [OBW]
American baseball player
* Turner, Pop

Turner, Ed 20th c. [RBE]
American boxer
* Turner, Savage

Turner, Eileen Arbuthnot Robertson
1903- [WGT]
British author
* Robertson, E[ileen] Arnot

Turner, Ethel
See Curlewis, Ethel S. [Turner]

Turner, Florence 1885-1946 [SC]
American actress
* [The] Vitagraph Girl

Turner, Francis 1638?-1700 [SN]
British prelate
* Smirk, Mr.

Turner, Fred 1943- [CMA]
Musician
* Turner, C. F.

Turner, Frederick Jackson 1861-1932
[HPPN]
American historian
* America's Foremost Historian

Turner, George [IP]
British author
* Philalethes

Turner, George
See Thirlwell, George

Turner, George A. 1870-? [BE]
American baseball player
* Turner, Tuck

Turner, George E[ugene] 1925- [CA]
American author and illustrator
* Lowell, Tex
* Scott, Lloyd

Turner, Happy
See Turner, John C.

Turner, Harley 20th c. [SMG]
American football player
* Turner, Rocky

Turner, J. Fox 19th c. [IP]
British author
* Layne, Pyngle

Turner, Jack 20th c.
Auto racer
* Turner, Cactus Jack

Turner, Jack
See Turner, Charles Robert

Turner, James [IP]
British author
* Aristobulus

Turner, James Castle, Jr. 1917?- [WP
9-30-85]
American labor leader
* Labor, Mr.

Turner, James Riley 1904- [BE, PB]
American baseball player and coach
* Turner, Milkman Jim

Turner, Jerry
See Turner, John Webber

Turner, Joan 1922- [BMH]
Irish-born actress, singer, comedienne
* [The] Girl with a Thousand Voices
* [The] Whacky Warbler

Turner, John 20th c. [RM]
Musician
* Turner, Red

Turner, John C. 1896-1949 [ASC]
American musician
* Turner, Happy

Turner, John M. 19th c. [IP, PA]
American author
* Head, Archibald

Turner, John Victor 1900-1945 [CC,
MBF, WW]
British author
* Brady, Nicholas
* Hume, David

Turner, John Webber 1954- [SMG]
American baseball player
* Turner, Jerry

Turner, Joseph [Vernon] 1911-1985
[BWW, EJ, RO1, WP 12-1-85]
American singer
* Big Vernon
* [The] Boss of the Blues
* [The] King of the Shouters
* Turner, Big Joe
* [The] World's Greatest Blues Shouter

Turner, Joseph Mallord William
1775-1851 [NPS]
British painter
* [The] Blackbirdy

Turner, Josie
See Crawford, Phyllis

Turner, Judy 1936- [WD]
British author
* Saxton, Judith

Turner, Judy
See Turner, Julia Jean Mildred Frances

Turner, Julia Jean Mildred Frances
1920- [BDF, HPPN, SW, WEF]
American actress
* [The] Sweater Girl
* Turner, Judy
* Turner, Lana

Turner, L. F.
See Cohen, Paul Arthur

Turner, Lana
See Turner, Julia Jean Mildred Frances

Turner, Len
See Floren, Lee

Turner, Leopold McClintock 20th c.
[THR]
British journalist and theatre critic
* Godfrey-Turner, L.

Turner, Lida Larrimore 1897- [BI,
HPPN]
American author
* Larrimore, Lida

Turner, Lily 20th c. [BMH]
British singer
* Bush, Rose

Turner, Lloyd 1884- [BBH]
Canadian-born hockey player
* Hockey, Mr.

Turner, Mary
See Lambot, Isobel Mary

Turner, Milkman Jim
See Turner, James Riley

Turner, Morris 1924?- [BI, HPPN]
American cartoonist
* [The] Cartoonist With a Conscience
* Morrie

Turner, Orpha [PA]
Author
* Hammond, Orpha

Turner, Otis 1862-1918 [SC]
American actor and director
* Turner, Daddy

Turner, Peter Paul
See Jeffery, Grant

Turner, Philip [William] 1925- [FBJ,
IAW, TCC]
British author and playwright
* Chance, Stephen

Turner, Plum
See Turner, Richard

Turner, Pop
See Turner, E. C.

Turner, Pops
See Turner, Curtis Morton

Turner, Red
See Turner, John

Turner, Richard ?-1733 [SN]
Miser
* Turner, Plum

Turner, Robert [Harry] 1915- [CA]
American author
* Calhoun, Eric
* Klein, K. K.
* Lawson, Steve
* Lee, Parker
* Morgan, Robert
* Murray, Ken
* Roberts, Lisa
* Romano, Don
* Savoy, Mark

Turner, Robert 20th c. [SMG]
American football player
* Turner, Bake

Turner, Robert Edward, III 1939?- [TI
8-9-82]
*American business executive and yacht
racer*
* [The] Capsize Kid
* [The] Mouth of the South
* Outrageous, Captain
* Turner, Ted
* Turner, Terrible Ted
* Turner, Turnover Ted

Turner, Rocky
See Turner, Harley

Turner, [Colonel] Roscoe 1895-1970
[HPPN]
American aviator
* [The] Speed King of the Air

Turner, Samuel 1759-1801 [IP]
British diplomat and author
* [The] Ambassador

Turner, Samuel Hulbeart 1790-1861
[IP]
American clergyman and author
* Presbyter

Turner, Sandbag
See Turner, Sheadrick B.

Turner, Savage
See Turner, Ed

Turner, Sharon 1768-1847 [IP]
British historian and author
* [A] Layman

Turner, Sheadrick B. 1854-? [IBW]
American politician
* Turner, Sandbag

Turner, Sheila
See Rowbotham, Sheila

Turner, Sheila R.
See Seed, Sheila Turner

Turner, Spurgeon, Jr. 1924- [IBW]
American disc jockey
* Stan the Man

Turner, Spyder
See Turner, Dwight D.

Turner, Ted
See Turner, Robert Edward, III

Turner, Terrence Lamont 1881-1960
[BE]
American baseball player
* Turner, Cotton

Turner, Terrible Ted
See Turner, Robert Edward, III

Turner, Thomas Lovatt 1890-1962 [BE]
American baseball player
* Turner, Tink

Turner, Tina
See Bullock, Anna Mae

Turner, Tink
See Turner, Thomas Lovatt

Turner, Tuck
See Turner, George A.

Turner, Turnover Ted
See Turner, Robert Edward, III

Turner, W. J.
See Turner, Walter James Redfern

Turner, Walter 1866-1919 [HPPN]
British-American inventor
* America's Foremost Pneumatic
Engineer

Turner, Walter James Redfern
1889-1946 [LC, TC]
British author, poet, music critic
* Turner, W. J.

Turner, Warhorse
See Turner, Alfred L.

Turner, William 1520?-1568 [DEP]
British clergyman, physician, botanist
* [The] Father of English Botany

Turner, William 1870-1944 [BEW]
British comedian and playwright
* Rigby, Arthur

Turner, William Mason 1835-1877
American author, poet, physician
* Wylder, Lennox

Turnesa, William P. 1914- [BBH]
American golfer
* [The] Wedge

Turngren, Annette 1902-1980 [CA, WW]
American author
* Hopkins, A. T.

Turnhout, Gerard de
See Turnhout, Gheert Jacques

Turnhout, Gheert Jacques 1520?-1580
[BBD]
Dutch composer
* Turnhout, Gerard de

[The] Turnip-Hoer
See George I

Turnkey
See Lowe, [Sir] Hudson

Turnover Ted Turner
See Turner, Robert Edward, III

Turofsky, Riki
See Turofsky, Rita Nan

Turofsky, Rita Nan 1944- [OP]
Canadian opera singer
* Turofsky, Riki

Turpin, Ben
See Turpin, Bernard

Turpin, Ben
See Turpin, C. Murray

Turpin, Bernard 1869-1940 [FIR, HPPN, SC]
American actor
* [The] Crosseyed Comedian
* Turpin, Ben

Turpin, Big Dipper
See Turpin, Mel[vin]

Turpin, C. Murray 1878-? [HPPN]
American politician
* Turpin, Ben

Turpin, Dipper
See Turpin, Mel[vin]

Turpin, Mel[vin] 20th c. [SI 11-28-83, SI 12-5-83]
American basketball player
* Turpin, Big Dipper
* Turpin, Dipper

Turpin, Richard [Dick] 1705-1739 [DI, HN]
British robber
* [The] Flying Highwayman
* Palmer, John

Turpinszky, Bela 1933- [OP]
Hungarian opera singer
* Adolbert, Bela

Turquito
See Betruz, Miguel

Turrell, Big Jim
See Turrell, James Archie [Jim]

Turrell, Desmond 20th c. [HPPN]
British delinquent
* [The] King of the Teddy Boys

Turrell, James Archie [Jim] 1943-
[CAR]
American artist
* [The] Arch
* Turrell, Big Jim
* Turrell, Little Jimmie

Turrell, Little Jimmie
See Turrell, James Archie [Jim]

Turton, [Sir] Thomas 1764-1844 [IP]
British army officer and author
* [A] Country Gentleman

Turton, Thomas 1780-1864 [IP, PA]
British prelate and author
* Cantabrigiensis, Crito
* Clemens Anglicanus
* Philalethes Cantabrigiensis

Turton-Jones, Edith Constance [Bradshaw] 1904-1968 [CAP]
British author
* Gillespie, Susan

Turville, Henry
See Bullivant, Cecil Henry

[The] Tuscan Imp of Fame
See Petracco, Francesco

[The] Tuscan Poet
See Ariosto, Lodovico

[The] Tuscan Pony
See Fanfani, Amintore

Tuscarora John Barnwell
See Barnwell, John

Tusitala [Teller of Tales]
See Balfour, Robert Louis

[The] Tuskegee Cowboy
See Dawkins, Whit M.

Tusser, Thomas 1515?-1580 [RH, SN]
British poet
* [The] British Varro
* [The] Husbandman

Tustin, Elizabeth
See White, Celia

Tut, King
See Tut, Richard

Tut, Richard 20th c. [OBW]
American baseball player
* Tut, King

Tutankhamen [HPPN, NAD]
Egyptian pharaoh
* [The] Boy King
* Boy Pharaoh
* [The] Golden Monarch
* Golden Pharaoh
* King Tut
* Little Pharaoh
* [The] Teen-Age God-King

Tute, G. W.
See Tute, George William

Tute, George William 1933- [ART]
British artist
* Tute, G. W.

Tute, Warren [Stanley] 1914- [CA]
British author and playwright
* Warren, Andrew [joint pseudonym with Andrew Rosenthal]

Tuthall, William H. 1808-1880 [IP]
American attorney and author
* Anti Quary

Tuthill, Frank 1822-1865 [HPPN]
American journalist
* F. T.

[A] Tutor
See Jones, William

[A] Tutor and Fellow of a College in Oxford
See Bentham, Edward

Tutt, William Thayer 1902- [BBH]
American hockey organization officer
* [The] Father of the NCAA Hockey Tournament

Tuttiett, Mary Gleed ?-1923 [WWL]
British author and poet
* Gray, Maxwell

Tuttle, Charles Richard 1848-? [DNA]
Author and historian
* Clarke, Jean

Tuttle, E. C. 19th c. [FFF, IP]
British journalist
* Vernon, Judge

Tuttle, George 1804-1872 [DNA]
American author
* Teller, Thomas

Tuttle, Henry 20th c. [SG]
Boxer
* King Tut

Tuttle, [Rev.] Isaac H. 19th c. [HPPN]
American clergyman
* [The] Rector

Tuttle, Joseph Farrand [IP]
American clergyman and educator
* J. F. T.

Tutwiler, Julia Strudwick ?-1916
[HPPN]
American prison reformer
* [The] Angel of the Prisons

Tuvar, Lorenzo
See Armistead, Wilson

Tuvim, Judith 1921?-1965 [BDF, BEW,
EMT]
American actress and singer
* Holliday, Judy

Tuvim, Julian 1894-1953
Polish poet
* [The] Polish Pushkin

Tuyuchi
See Leito, Arturo

TV Slim
See Wills, Oscar

Twaddell, William ?-1840? [HPPN]
Scottish inventor
* [The] Father of Twaddell's
  Hydrometer

Twain, Mark
See Clemens, Samuel Langhorne

Twain, Mark
See Sellers, Isaiah

Twain, Minerva Mark
See Mitchell, Charlotte Grimes

Twain, Quarter
See Clemens, Samuel Langhorne

Tweed, Boss
See Tweed, William Marcy

Tweed, J. H.
See Knight, Vick R[alph], Jr.

Tweed, William Marcy 1823-1878 [CEC,
HPPN]
American politician
* [The] Sachem of Tammany Hall
* Tweed, Boss

Tweedale, J.
See Bickle, Judith Brundrett

Tweedsmuir, Baron
See Buchan, John

[The] Twelfth Man
See Gill, King

[The] 12 Million Dollar Man
See Amouzegar, Jamshid

Twelve o'Clock
See Stevens, William [Carey]

Twelve-Tone Oddity
See Schoenberg, Arnold

Twelveponies, Mary
See Cleveland, Mary

Twelvetrees, Helen
See Jurgen, Helen Marie

[The] Twentieth Century Borgia
See Archer-Gillian, Amy

[The] Twentieth Century Gabriel
See Hawkins, Erskine Ramsey

[The] Twentieth Century Minstrel
See Dyer-Bennet, Richard

Twentieth Century Moses
See Chaplin, Charles Spencer

[The] Twentieth Century Mozart
See Rolle, Tony

20/1631
See Upward, Allen

[The] Twickenham Bard
See Pope, Alexander

[The] Twig
See Tolson, Dean

Twig, Timothy, Esq.
See Moser, Joseph

Twigg, Lewis Harold 1937- [BA]
American physician
* Twigg, Tippy

Twigg, Tippy
See Twigg, Lewis Harold

Twiggs, David Emanuel 1790-1862
[HPPN]
American army officer
* Bengal Tiger
* [The] Horse
* Twiggs, Old Day

Twiggs, James 1933- [SFL]
Author
* Jameson, Twiggs

Twiggs, Old Day
See Twiggs, David Emanuel

Twiggy
See Hornby, Lesley

Twilight Ed Killian
See Killian, Edwin Henry

[The] Twin of Heavenlier Birth
See Beaumont, Francis

Twinberrow, William Henry 1877-?
[THR]
British actor
* Wolston, Henry

Twine, Chico
See Twine, Thomas, Sr.

Twine, Thomas, Sr. 1940- [BA]
American accountant
* Twine, Chico

Twineham, Arthur W. 1866-? [BE]
American baseball player
* Twineham, Old Hoss

Twineham, Old Hoss
See Twineham, Arthur W.

Twiney, Harrie
See Twiney, Harriette M. E.

Twiney, Harriette M. E. 1867-1953
[CW]
Jamaican poet
* Twiney, Harrie

Twining, Alexander Catlin 1801-1884
[HPPN]
American engineer
* [The] Engineer

Twining, Doc
See Twining, Howard Earle

Twining, Howard Earle 1894- [BE]
American baseball player
* Twining, Doc
* Twining, Twink

Twining, Louisa [IP]
British author
* L. T.

Twining, Thomas 1734-1804 [IP, SN]
British clergyman
* [The] Country Clergyman of the
  Eighteenth Century
* Philalethes

Twining, Twink
See Twining, Howard Earle

Twinkle Toes
See LeFlore, Ron[ald]

Twiss, Buddy
See Twiss, Clinton

Twiss, Clinton 1907-1952 [HPPN]
American announcer
* Twiss, Buddy

Twiss, Horace 1787-1849 [IP, NPS]
British barrister, author, politician
* Horatius

Twiss, Richard 1747-1821 [IP]
Author
* [An] Irish Traveller

Twiss, [Sir] Travers 1819-? [IP]
British barrister and author
* Corvinus

Twist, Ananias
See Nunn, William Curtis

Twist, Kid
See Reles, Abraham [Abe]

Twist, Kid
See Zwerbach, Max

[The] Twist King
See Evans, Ernest

Twist, Mr.
See Evans, Ernest

Twist-Wit, Christopher, Esq.
See Anstey, Christopher

[The] Twisting Vocalist
See Woodward, Thomas Jones

Twistleton-Wykeham-Fiennes, [Sir] Ranulph 1944- [WD]
British author
* Fiennes, Ranulph

Twistleton-Wykeham-Fiennes, Richard Nathaniel 1909- [WD]
British author and editor
* Fiennes, Richard

Twitchell, A. R.
See Brandon, Michael

Twitchell, Archie
See Brandon, Michael

Twitchell, Paul 20th c. [EOP]
American religious cult leader
* Peddar Zaskq

Twitchell, Twitch
See Twitchell, Wayne Lee

Twitchell, Wayne Lee 1948- [SMG]
American baseball player
* Twitchell, Twitch

Twitcher, Harry
See Brougham, Henry Peter

Twitcher, Jemmy
See Montagu, John [Fourth Earl of Sandwich]

Twitty, Conway
See Jenkins, Harold

Twm Shon Catti
See Jones, Thomas

Two Brothers [joint pseudonym with Julius Charles Hare]
See Hare, Augustus William

Two Brothers [joint pseudonym with Augustus William Hare]
See Hare, Julius Charles

Two Brothers [joint pseudonym with Charles Tennyson]
See Tennyson, Alfred [First Baron Tennyson]

Two Brothers [joint pseudonym with Alfred Tennyson]
See Tennyson, Charles

[The] Two Edged Knife
See Bilbo, Theodore Gilmore

Two Gun Alterie
See Alterie, Leland Verain

Two Gun Cohen
See Cohen, Morris A.

Two Gun Collins
See Collins, Harry Warren

Two Gun Crowley
See Crowley, Francis

[The] Two Gun Girl
See Guinan, Mary Louise Cecelia

Two Gun Guardino
See Guardino, Johnny

Two Gun Hart
See Capone, Vincenzo

Two Gun Pete
See Washington, Sylvester

202
See Christian, William

Two, Mr.
See Henry, Josiah F.

Two Naval Officers
See Thrush, Thomas

[The] Two Sisters [joint pseudonym with Sarah G. Walcott]
See Walcott, Eliza

[The] Two Sisters [joint pseudonym with Eliza Walcott]
See Walcott, Sarah G.

Two Sisters of the West [joint pseudonym with Catharine Ann (Ware) Warfield]
See Ware, Eleanor

Two Sisters of the West [joint pseudonym with Eleanor Ware]
See Warfield, Catharine Ann [Ware]

2571
See Palmer, George

[The] Two Time Loser
See Lowenstein, Allard Kenneth

Two Ton Baker
See Baker, Richard E.

Two Ton Tessie
See O'Shea, Tessie

Two Ton Tony Galento
See Galento, Tony

Two Tons of Fun
See Rhodes, Izora

Two Tons of Fun
See Wash, Martha

Two Wags [joint pseudonym with Frank Dempster Sherman]
See Bangs, John Kendrick

Two Wags [joint pseudonym with John Kendrick Bangs]
See Sherman, Frank Dempster

Two Way Corrigan
See Corrigan, Mark

Two Women of the West [joint pseudonym with Ella Marchant]
See Jones, Alice Ilgenfritz

Two Women of the West [joint pseudonym with Alice Ilgenfritz Jones]
See Marchant, Ella

Twogood, Forrest 1907-1972 [BB]
American basketball player and coach
* Twogood, Twogie

Twogood, Twogie
See Twogood, Forrest

Twombly, Alexander Stevenson 1832-?
[IP, PA]
American clergyman and author
* Perk, Abner

Twombly, Babe
See Twombly, Clarence Edward

Twombly, Clarence Edward 1896-1974
[BE]
American baseball player
* Twombly, Babe

Twombly, Cy
See Twombly, Edwin Parker

Twombly, Deacon
See Twombly, Henry B.

Twombly, Edwin Parker 1897?-1974
[BI]
American baseball player and coach
* Twombly, Cy

Twombly, George Frederick 1892- [BE]
American baseball player
* Twombly, Silent George

Twombly, Henry B. 1862-1955 [FB]
American football player
* Twombly, Deacon

Twombly, Silent George
See Twombly, George Frederick

Twomby, Louisa
See Meredith, Louisa

Twomey, Seamus 1920?- [HPPN]
Irish political leader
* [The] Provisionals' Unknown Leader

[A] Twopenny Author
See Steele, [Sir] Richard

Tworkov, Janice 1903- [BI]
American painter
* Biala

Twort, Charles William [IP]
British author
* [A] Protestant

Twyman, Gib
See Twyman, Gilbert Oscar, III

Twyman, Gilbert Oscar, III 1943- [CA]
American sportswriter
* Twyman, Gib

Twyman, Harold William 1898- [MBF]
British author
* Cartwright, A.
* Forge, John
* Murray, Robert
* Richards, Frank [house pseudonym]

Tyard, Pontus de 1521-1605 [DEP]
French poet
* [The] Anacreon of the French

Tyas, Robert 19th c. [IP]
British clergyman and author
* R. T.

Tyburn Dick
See Savage, Richard [Fourth Earl Rivers]

[A] Tycho Brahe
See Dyer, George

[The] Tycoon
See Lincoln, Abraham

[The] Tycoon You Love to Hate
See Schwab, Charles M. [Charley]

Tydeus
See Walpole, Horatio [Fourth Earl of Orford]

Tydus-Pooh-Pooh
See Bowring, [Sir] John

Tyers, Thomas 1726-1787 [IP]
British author
* Restless, Tim

[A] Tyke
See Robb, John S.

Tyler, A. E.
See Armstrong, [Annette] Elizabeth

Tyler, Alvin 20th c. [RM]
Musician
* Tyler, Red

Tyler, Audrey Patterson 20th c. [IBW]
American track and field athlete and coach
* Tyler, Mickey

Tyler, Bennet 1783-1858 [HPPN, IP]
American theologian and author
* [A] Consistent Churchman
* [A] New England Minister

Tyler, Beverly
See Saul, Beverly Jean

Tyler, Bonnie
See Hopkins, Gaynor

Tyler, Bubba
See Tyler, Lamar

Tyler, Daniel F. 19th c. [HPPN]
American author
* Uncle Ben

Tyler, David Gardiner 1846-1927
Son of American president, John Tyler
* Tyler, Gardie

Tyler, Gardie
See Tyler, David Gardiner

Tyler, George [FFF]
* Tagliere, Signor

Tyler, George Albert 1889-1953 [AS, BE, PB]
American baseball player
* Tyler, Lefty

Tyler, Harold McAfee 1896- [IBW]
American attorney
* Tyler, Tippy

Tyler, John [IP]
American author
* Python

Tyler, John 1790-1862 [FAP]
American president
* [The] Accidental President
* His Accidency
* Old Veto
* [The] Renegade
* Tyler, Too
* Young Hickory

Tyler, John Anthony [Johnnie] 1906-
[BE]
American baseball player
* Tyler, Ty Ty

Tyler, Josephine 19th c. [HPPN]
American author
* Sola

Tyler, Lamar 20th c. [SMG]
American football team trainer
* Tyler, Bubba

Tyler, Lefty
See Tyler, George Albert

Tyler, Lion [or Lyon] Gardiner 1853-1935
Son of American president, John Tyler
* Tyler, Lonie

Tyler, Lonie
See Tyler, Lion [or Lyon] Gardiner

Tyler, Mickey
See Tyler, Audrey Patterson

Tyler, Odette
See Kirkland, Elizabeth Lee

Tyler, Red
See Tyler, Alvin

Tyler, Robert [IP]
American author
* [A] Virginian

Tyler, Royall
See Tyler, William Clark

Tyler, Steel Arm
See Tyler, William

Tyler, T. Texas
See Myrick, David Luke

Tyler, Terry 1956-
American basketball player
* T.
* Tyler, Thunder

Tyler, Texas, Miss
See Dennison, Jo-Carroll

Tyler, Theodore
See Ziegler, Edward William

Tyler, Thunder
See Tyler, Terry

Tyler, Tippy
See Tyler, Harold McAfee

Tyler, Tom
See Burns, William

Tyler, Tom
See Marko [or Markoski?], Vincent

Tyler, Too
See Tyler, John

Tyler, Ty Ty
See Tyler, John Anthony [Johnnie]

Tyler, W. T.
See Hamrick, Samuel J.

Tyler, William 20th c. [OBW]
American baseball player
* Tyler, Steel Arm

Tyler, William Clark 1757-1826 [IP, NLC]
American jurist and author
* S.
* Spondee
* Trash
* Tyler, Royall
* Underhill, [Dr.] Updike

Tyler-Whittle, Michael Sidney 1927-
[CA]
British author
* Oliver, Mark
* Whittle, Tyler

Tyller, Jorge
See Avilez, Jose Daniel

Tymeson, Mildred McClary
See Petrie, Mildred McClary

Tynan, Katharine
See Hinkson, Katherine Tynan

Tynan, Kenneth
See Peacock, Kenneth

Tynan, Philip
See Swan, Cormac

Tyndale, William 1484?-1536 [DEA, HPPN]
British author and translator
* Hutchins, William
* W. T.

Tyner, Alfred McCoy 1938- [EJ7]
American jazz musician
* Saud, Sulaimon

Tyng, [Rev.] Dudley Atkins 1825-1858
[HPPN]
American clergyman
* [The] Rector

Tyng, Florence 19th c. [FFF, IP]
American author
* Florence

Typhoid Mary
See Mallon, Mary

[The] Typical American
See Roosevelt, Theodore [Teddy]

Typist, Topsy
See Miner, Enoch Newton

Tyran de Blanc
See Grimm, Friedrich Melchior von

[The] Tyrant
See Lincoln, Abraham

[The] Tyrant Basilides
See Ivan IV Vasilievich

[The] Tyrant of the Chersonese
See Miltiades

[The] Tyrant of the New England
See Andros, [Sir] Edmund

[The] Tyrant of Words and Syllables
See Malherbe, Francois de

Tyrconnel, Duchess of 17th c. [RH]
Wife of Richard Talbot, Lord-Lieutenant of Ireland
* [The] White Widow

Tyrone, Paul
See Norwood, Victor G[eorge] C[harles]

Tyrrell, Mary E. 1883-1944 [BEW]
American actress
* Grey, Jane

Tyrrell, Thomas Signis
See Pichon, Thomas

Tyrtaeus 7th c. BC [RH, SN]
Greek poet
* [The] Hobbler
* [The] Lame

[The] Tyrtaeus of France
See Rouget de Lisle, Claude Joseph

[The] Tyrtaeus of Germany
See Koerner, Karl Theodor [or Carl Theodore]

[The] Tyrtaeus of Spain
See Quintana, Manuel Jose

[The] Tyrtaeus of the British Navy
See Dibdin, Charles

Tyrtamos 4th c. BC [FFF, RH, SN]
Greek philosopher and scientist
* [The] Divine Speaker
* Theophrastos

Tyrwhitt, Gerald Hugh 1883-1950 [WBD]
British composer and painter
* Tyrwhitt-Wilson, Gerald Hugh

Tyrwhitt, Richard [IP]
British clergyman and author
* [A] Clergyman

Tyrwhitt-Wilson, Gerald Hugh
See Tyrwhitt, Gerald Hugh

Tyselling, Babe
See Tyselling, Richard

Tyselling, Richard 1910- [BB]
American basketball player and coach
* Tyselling, Babe

Tyshler, Alexandr Grigorievich 1898- [CAR]
Russian painter
* Dzhin-Dzhikh-Shivil

Tyson, A.
See Hersey, Harold

Tyson, Albert Thomas 1892-1953 [BE]
American baseball player
* Tyson, Ty

Tyson, Bertrand Oliver 1931- [BA]
American physician
* Tyson, Tram

Tyson, Cecil Washington 1914- [BE]
American baseball player
* Tyson, Turkey

Tyson, Coco
See Tyson, James

Tyson, Edward 1649-1708 [SN]
British physician
* Slow Carus

Tyson, Edwin Lloyd 20th c.
American radio and television broadcaster
* Tyson, Ty

Tyson, James 20th c. [RO1]
American singer
* Tyson, Coco

Tyson, John S. [IP]
American author
* [A] Citizen of Baltimore

Tyson, Teilo
See McFarlane, David

Tyson, Tram
See Tyson, Bertrand Oliver

Tyson, Turkey
See Tyson, Cecil Washington

Tyson, Ty
See Tyson, Albert Thomas

Tyson, Ty
See Tyson, Edwin Lloyd

Tyssen, Amhurst Daniel 1843-? [IP]
British barrister, antiquary, author
* A. D. T.

Tyssot de Patot, Simon 1655-1728? [SFL, WGT]
Author
* Bayle, Monsieur
* De Mesange, [Reverend] Pierre Cordelier Pierre
* Masse, James
* Massens, Jakob
* Massey, James

Tytla, Bill
See Tytla, Vladimir

Tytla, Vladimir 1904-1968 [WEC]
American animator
* Tytla, Bill

Tytler, Alexander Fraser [Lord Woodhouselee] 1747-1813 [IP]
Scottish scholar and author
* Pasquin, Paul

Tytler, Anne Fraser [IP, PA]
Scottish author
* A. F. T.

Tytler, Balloon
See Tytler, James

Tytler, C. C. Fraser
See Liddle, Christina Catherine Fraser Tytler

Tytler, C. C. Fraser
See Slidell, Mrs. Edward

Tytler, James 1747-1805 [FFF, HPPN, SN, WBD]
Scottish-born scholar
* Don Quixote, Jr.
* Tytler, Balloon

Tytler, Patrick Fraser 1791-1849 [HPPN]
Scottish historian and biographer
* Patrick of the King's Chekar Maister

Tytler, Sarah
See Keddie, Henrietta

Tytler, William 1711-1792 [HPPN]
Scottish historian and attorney
* Horatius
* Lucretius

Tyus, Ansa
See Tyus, Margaret

Tyus, Margaret 1947- [IBW]
American educator
* Tyus, Ansa

Tyz, A. N.
See Tseu, Yih Zan

Tzair, Rav
See Tchernowitz, Chaim

Tzara, Tristan
See Codrescu, Andrei

Tzara, Tristan
See Rosenstock, Sami

Tzavellas, Georges
See Tzavellas, Gheorghiou

Tzavellas, Gheorghiou 1916- [DFM]
Greek director
* Tzavellas, Georges

Tzimeas, John ?-1978 [FIR]
Actor
* Zimeas, John

Tzu Hsi [or Tze-hsi] 1835-1908 [HPPN, WBD]
Chinese empress dowager
* [The] Dragon Empress
* [The] Old Buddha
* Yehonala

U

[The] U Boat Killer
See Walker, Frederic

U. E.
See Edgcumbe, Ursula

[A] U. S. Detective
See Ellis, Edward S[ylvester]

U. S. E.
See Spear, W.

U Tam'si
See Tchicaya, Gerald Felix

U. U. P.
See Plunket, William Conyngham

Uale, Frank 1885-1927 [BLB, HPPN, PHM]
American underworld figure
* [The] Beau Brummell of the Brooklyn Underworld
* Yale, Frankie

Uart, Marie
See Philbrick, Mary

Ubertini, Francesco 1494?-1557 [WBD]
Italian painter
* [Il] Bachiacca

Ubique
See Gillmore, Parker

Ubique
See Guggisberg, [Sir] F. G.

Ubiquitous
See Brown, Tina

[The] Ubiquitous Financier of the Universe
See Mellon, Andrew William

Uccello, Paolo
See Di Dono, Paolo

Uccello, Paolo
See Dono, Paolo De

Uchida, Bomber
See Uchida, Shoji

Uchida, Shoji 20th c. [RBE]
Japanese boxer
* Uchida, Bomber

Uchida, Yosh[ihiro] 1920- [HPPN]
Nisei judoist and coach
* Nisei of the Biennium

Ucres [or Ucares], Rodriguez
See Rodriguez Ucares, Fray Jose

Ucuzoglu, Nathan Salmon 1951- [CA]
American author and philosopher
* Salmon, Nathan Ucuzoglu

Udall, Jan Beaney 1938- [CA, SAT]
American artist and author
* Beaney, Jan

Udall, John 1560?-1592 [NPS]
Puritan pamphleteer
* Marprelate, Martin

Udall, Lyn
See Keating, John Henry

Ueberroth, Harry 1909-1953 [BEW]
American actor
* Curtis, Alan

Uei Tlatoani [One Who Speaks]
See Montezuma II

Ueno, Noriko
See Nakae, Noriko

Uetake, Yojiro 20th c. [BBH]
Japanese wrestler and coach
* Obata, Yojiro

Ugama, LeRoi
See Smith, LeRoi Tex

Ugaro De Fox, Lucia
See Lockart, Lucia A[licia] Fox

[The] Ugliest Man in Canada
See Chapelski, Alex Samuel

[The] Ugliest Man in the World
See Webb, James

Ugolino [Count of Segni] 1147?-1241 [WBD]
Pope
* [The] Great
* Gregory IX

Ugolino da Pisa
See Gherardesca, Ugolino della [Conte di Donoratico]

Uhalt, Bernard Bartholomew 1910- [BE]
American baseball player
* Uhalt, Frenchy

Uhalt, Frenchy
See Uhalt, Bernard Bartholomew

Uhl, Friedrich Ludwig 1928- [OP]
Austrian opera singer
* Uhl, Fritz

Uhl, Fritz
See Uhl, Friedrich Ludwig

Uhl, Ruth
See Frank, Ruth Verd

[The] Uhlan King
See Alfonso XII

Uhland, Johann Ludwig 1787-1862 [SN]
German poet
* [The] Genre Poet of Germany

Uhle, George Ernest 1898- [BE, PB]
American baseball player
* [The] Bull

Uhle, Lefty
See Uhle, Robert Ellwood [Bob]

Uhle, Robert Ellwood [Bob] 1913- [BE]
American baseball player
* Uhle, Lefty

Uhr, Elizabeth 1929- [CA]
American author
* Stern, Elizabeth

Ukelele Ike
See Edwards, Cliff

Ukelele, Johnny
See Kaaihue, Johnny

Ukelele Kid
See Burse, Charlie

Ukrainka, Lesya
See Kvitka, Laryssa Petrovna

[The] Ukulele Ace
See Marvin, Johnny

[The] Ukulele Lady
See Breen, May Singhi

Ulacia, Gabino 1919- [IBW]
Cuban military leader
* Ulacia, Le Grande

Ulacia, Le Grande
See Ulacia, Gabino

Ulatowski, Clement Lambert 1886-1967
[BE]
American baseball player
* Clemens, Clem
* Clemens, Clement Lambert

Ulbach, Louis 1822-? [IP, PA]
French author and poet
* Ferragus
* Souffrant, Jacques, ouvrier

Ulbricht, Walter 1893-1973 [HPPN]
German Communist leader
* [The] Last Cold Warrior
* [The] Little Man With the Goatee

Ulfilas [or Uphilas] 311?-381? [HN, SN]
Bishop of the Goths
* [The] Apostle of the Goths

Ulisney, Michael Edward [Mike] 1917-
[BE]
American baseball player
* Ulisney, Slugs

Ulisney, Slugs
See Ulisney, Michael Edward [Mike]

Ulla
See Smith, Jane Luella Dowd

Ullah, Salamat 1913- [CA]
Indian educator and author
* Salamatullah

Ullithorne, Aida 20th c. [THR]
British actress
* Jenoure, Aida

Ullman, Allan 1909?-1982 [CA]
American author
* Alan, Sandy

Ullman, Barbara
See Schwalberg, Carol[yn Ernestine
Stein]

Ulloa, Jose 17th c. [GS]
Spanish bullfighter
* Tragabuches [Tremendous Swallower]

Ullrich, Carlos Santiago Castello 1922-
[BE]
Cuban-born baseball player
* Ullrich, Sandy

Ullrich, Sandy
See Ullrich, Carlos Santiago Castello

Ulman, Douglas Elton 1883-1939 [BEW,
HPPN, WEF]
American actor
* Aesop in Hollywood
* Fairbanks, Douglas, Sr.
* [The] Fourth Musketeer
* [The] King of Hollywood
* King of the Swashbucklers
* Thomas, Elton

Ulmar, Genevieve
See Cobb, Weldon J.

Ulmer, Blood
See Ulmer, James

Ulmer, James 1942-
American musician
* Ulmer, Blood
* Ulmer, Youngblood

Ulmer, Youngblood
See Ulmer, James

Ulreich, Nura Woodson 1899-1950
[IBY, ICB]
American author and illustrator
* Nura

Ulric, Lenore
See Ulrich, Lenore

Ulric Von Huetten
See Davis, Henry Winter

Ulrich, Charles, Jr.
See Galt, William Hamilton

Ulrich, Dutch
See Ulrich, Frank W.

Ulrich, Frank W. 1899-1929 [BE]
American baseball player
* Ulrich, Dutch

Ulrich, Lenore 1892-1970 [BEW, FC]
American actress
* Ulric, Lenore

[An] Ulsterman
See Sigerson, George

[The] Ultimate Abstraction
See Pollock, [Paul] Jackson

[The] Ultimate Free Lance
See Kissinger, Henry Alfred

[The] Ultimate Shrink
See Strasberg, Lee

Ultimus Anglorum
See Bedell, William

Ultimus Romanorum
See Congreve, William

Ultimus Romanorum
See Fox, Charles James

Ultimus Romanorum
See Gabrini, Niccolo

Ultimus Romanorum
See Hollis, Thomas

Ultimus Romanorum
See Johnson, Samuel

Ultimus Romanorum
See Pope, Alexander

Ultimus Romanorum
See Walpole, Horatio [Fourth Earl of
Orford]

Ultimus Scholasticorum, Doctor
See Biel [or Byll], Gabriel

Ultramontane
See John, Henry

Ulvaeus, Agnetha Faltskog 1950- [RO2]
Swedish singer
* Ulvaeus, Anna

Ulvaeus, Anna
See Ulvaeus, Agnetha Faltskog

Ulyanov, Vladimir Ilich 1870-1924
[HPPN, IPA, OCF]
Russian Communist leader
* [The] Father of the Russian
Revolution
* Lenin, Nicolai
* Lenin, Vladimir Ilyich

Ulyett, George 1851-1898 [EC]
British cricketer
* Ulyett, Happy Jack

Ulyett, Happy Jack
See Ulyett, George

[The] Ulysses
See Albert III [or Albrecht]

Ulysses
See Bliss, George Newman

Ulysses
See George III

Ulysses
See Graves, Samuel

Ulysses Cosmopolite
See Berkeley, George

Ulysses, Mohammed
See Gernsback, Hugo

[The] Ulysses of Bibliographers
See Mercier, Bartholomew

[The] Ulysses of the Highlands
See Cameron, [Sir] Evan

Umbach, Arnold J. 20th c. [BBH]
American wrestling coach
* Umbach, Swede

Umbach, Swede
See Umbach, Arnold J.

Umbehr, Otto 1902- [BI]
Austrian photojournalist
* Umbo

Umbellus, T.
See Eaton, David H.

Umber, George
See Findley, W.

Umbo
See Umbehr, Otto

Umbra Oxoniensis
See Palmer, [Sir] William

Umbrella Mike
See Boyle, Michael J.

[An] Umbrian Gozzoli
See Betti [or Di Biagio?], Bernardino

Umeko, Miss [code name used by
Japanese during World War II]
See Hull, Cordell

Umscheid, Christina Marie 1946- [MA]
German-born poet
* Christina Marie

Umstead, Roosevelt Thomas 1940- [BA]
American banker
* Unstead, Archie

Un
See   Second element of name

Un Flaneur
See Villiers, George William Frederick

Una
See Ford, Mary Anne McMullen

Una
See McMullen, Mary A.

Unada
See Gliewe, Unada [Grace]

Unamuno Y Jugo, Miguel de 1864-1936
[HPPN]
Spanish philosopher and author
* [The] Lone Heretic

[The] Uncaped Crusader
See Whitmore, George

[The] Unchosen
See Smith, Al[fred Emanuel]

Uncle Abe
See Lincoln, Abraham

Uncle Adam
See Mogridge, George

Uncle Al
See Pratt, Al[bert G.]

Uncle Al
See Silverstone, Alan

Uncle Alf Taylor
See Taylor, Alfred Alexander

Uncle Alf Tunstall
See Tunstall, Alfred Moore

Uncle Ben
See Crofton, Walter Cavendish

Uncle Ben
See Tyler, Daniel F.

Uncle Ben
See White, Rhoda E. [Waterman]

Uncle Bernie
See Meltzer, Bernard

Uncle Berry Williams
See Williams, Green Berry

Uncle Bill
See Alvord, William C.

Uncle Bill
See Traylor, Bill

Uncle Bill Wolsey
See Wolsey, William Franklyn

Uncle Billy
See Courtright, William

Uncle Billy
See Sherman, William Tecumseh

Uncle Billy
See Smith, William

Uncle Billy Workman
See Workman, William Henry

Uncle Charles
See Johnston, Charles Haven Ladd

Uncle Charles
See Mayer, Charles E. E.

Uncle Charlie
See Adams, Charles Francis

Uncle Charlie
See Moran, Charles B.

Uncle Cola
See Gentile, Nicola

Uncle Constantchin
See Anson, Adrian Constantine

Uncle Cyp
See Brasfield, L. L.

Uncle Dan
See Anderson, Frank

Uncle Dan
See Beard, Dan[iel Carter]

Uncle Dan
See Byron, Daniel E.

Uncle Dan
See Callaghan, Daniel I.

Uncle Dan
See Maskell, Dan

Uncle Dan'l
See Drew, Daniel

Uncle Dave Macon
See Macon, David Harrison

Uncle Dick
See Oglesby, Richard James

Uncle Dickie
See Mountbatten, Louis

Uncle Don
See Rhea, Don

Uncle Don
See Rice, Howard

Uncle Dud
See Leblanc, Dudley J.

Uncle Dudley
See Grover, Lucius Halen

Uncle Dudley
See Russell, Morris Craw

Uncle Ed
See Kempf, Edward J.

Uncle Ernest Schelling
See Schelling, Ernest Henry

Uncle Esek
See Shaw, Henry Wheeler

Uncle Ezra
See Barrett, Patrick J.

Uncle Ezra
See Kemp, Everett

Uncle Fred Nodder
See Nodder, Frederick

Uncle Fred Thompson
See Thompson, Frederick B.

Uncle Fudd
See McComb, Robert [Bob]

Uncle George
See Cohan, George Michael

Uncle George
See Pardon, George Frederick

Uncle George
See Perkins, George Douglas

Uncle George
See Tarbox, Increase Niles

Uncle George Thomas
See Thomas, George Henry

Uncle Gordon
See Roe, F[rederic] Gordon

Uncle Gus
See Reyersbach, Hans Augusto

Uncle Hardy
See Senior, Nassau William

Uncle Harry
See Habberton, John

Uncle Henry McDaniel
See McDaniel, Henry

Uncle Henry Warren
See Warren, Henry

Uncle Herbert
See Arthur, Timothy Shay

Uncle Ho
See Nguyen That Thanh

Uncle Igor
See Sikorsky, Igor Ivan

Uncle Jack
See Dey, John William

Uncle Jack
See Joel, Jack Bernato

Uncle Jake
See King, Oswin Kerryn

Uncle Jake
See McAlpine, Robert W.

Uncle James
See Rodwell, James

Uncle Jeems
See O'Rourke, James Henry

Uncle Jerry
See Porter, Anne Emerson

Uncle Jerry
See Rusk, Jeremiah McLain

Uncle Jesse
See Babb, Clement Edwin

Uncle Jimmie
See Doughty, James P.

Uncle Jimmy Thompson
See Thompson, Jimmy

Uncle Joe
See Barnes, Joseph [Joe]

Uncle Joe
See Cannon, Joseph Gurney

Uncle Joe
See Dzhugashvili, Iosif Vissarionovich

Uncle Joe
See Schenck, Joseph M.

Uncle Joe Stilwell
See Stilwell, Joseph Warren

Uncle Joe Swing
See Swing, Joseph May

Uncle John
See Aikin, John

Uncle John
See Chapman, Edwin O.

Uncle John
See McCormack, John W.

Uncle John
See Noyce, Elisha

Uncle John
See Sedgwick, John

Uncle John
See Selman, John H.

Uncle John Chisum
See Chisum, John Simpson

Uncle Johnny Williams
See Williams, Johnny

Uncle Jumbo
See Cleveland, [Stephen] Grover

Uncle Kwesi
See Lamptey, Jonathan Kwesi

Uncle Leopold
See Leopold I

Uncle Leroy
See Wood, Joseph

Uncle Lou
See Remy, L. B.

Uncle Louis
See St. Laurent, Louis

Uncle Mac
See McCulloch, Derek

Uncle Mark
See Hanna, Marcus Alonzo

Uncle Mark
See Lemon, Mark

Uncle Miltie
See Berlinger, Milton

Uncle Monty
See Hamilton-Wilkes, Edwin Montague

Uncle Mose
See Goldblatt, Mose

Uncle Murray
See Parker, Murray

Uncle Noah
See Brooks, Noah

Uncle Norman
See Taurog, Norman

Uncle P
See Pinheiro, Agbello

Uncle Paul
See Abbott, [Rev.] Edward

Uncle Paul
See Barham, Samuel, Jr.

Uncle Paul
See De Gournay, Paul F.

Uncle Paul
See Kruger, Stephanus Johannes Paulus

Uncle Peter
See Torbett, John Walter

Uncle Philip
See Hawks, Francis Lister

Uncle Ralph
See Shaw, Ralph Robert

Uncle Ray
See Coffman, Ramon Peyton

Uncle Remus
See Harris, Joel Chandler

Uncle Remus
See Kavanagh, Rose

Uncle Remus
See Sigerson, Hester

Uncle Robbie [or Robby]
See Robinson, Wilbert

Uncle Robert
See Lee, Robert Edward

Uncle Robert
See Spero, Robert

Uncle Sam
See Wilson, Samuel

Uncle Sam Grant
See Grant, Hiram Ulysses

Uncle Sam Ward
See Ward, Sam[uel]

Uncle Sam's Favorite Niece
See Kaumeyer, Dorothy

Uncle Shad
See Tubman, William Vacanarat Shadrach

Uncle Shelby
See Silverstein, Shel[by]

Uncle Skipper?
See Jordan, Charles [Charley]

Uncle Taffy
See Armstrong-Jones, Anthony Charles Robert [Lord Snowdon]

Uncle Tim
See Lower, Richard

Uncle Toby
See Cross, Wilbur Lucius

Uncle Toby
See Miller, Tobias Ham

Uncle Toby
See North, Elisha

Uncle Tom
See Bannon, Thomas Edward [Tom]

Uncle Tom
See Henson, Josiah

Uncle Tom Number 2
See Randolph, Asa Philip

Uncle Tom's Nephew
See Driver, Thomas

Uncle Ton
See Ton Duc Thang

Uncle Walter
See Cronkite, Walter Leland, Jr.

Uncle Walter
See Sleeper, Walter T.

Uncle Whit
See Chambers, [Jay David] Whittaker

Uncle Will
See Wells, William

Uncle Will, V. M.
See Crafts, Wilbur Fisk

Uncle Willis
See Tilton, Stephen Willis

Uncle Wip
See Cody, Wayne

Uncle Wip
See Willard, James A.

Uncle Yoolus
See Blegen, Julius P.

Uncles, Ewart Charles 1919- [ART]
British artist
* E. U.

Uncommercial Traveler
See Dickens, Charles

Unconditional Surrender Grant
See Grant, Hiram Ulysses

[The] Uncorruptible Commoner
See Marvell, Andrew

[The] Uncounseled
See Ethelred II

[The] Uncrownded King of Vaudeville
See Keith, Benjamin Franklin

[The] Uncrowned Champion
See Basilio, Italiano

Uncrowned King
See Blaine, James Gillespie

[The] Uncrowned King
See Edward VIII

[The] Uncrowned King
See Gordon, Charles George

[The] Uncrowned King of China
See Confucius [or K'ung Fu-tzu]

[The] Uncrowned King of Ireland
See Parnell, Charles Stewart

[The] Uncrowned King of Scotland
See Dundas, Henry

[The] Uncrowned Monarch
See O'Connell, Daniel

[The] Uncrowned Queen of American Womanhood
See Willard, Frances Elizabeth Caroline

[The] Uncrowned Queen of England
See O'Shea, Katherine [Kitty]

[The] Uncrowned Queen of the Blues
See Cox, Ida

Unda
See Muir, Thomas S.

Under Petty
See Thackeray, William Makepeace

Undercliffe, Errol
See Campbell, John Ramsey

Underdown, Emily 20th c. [NPS]
Author
* Chester, Norley

[An] Undergraduate
See Horne, George

[An] Undergraduate
See Penn, William

[An] Undergraduate
See Polwhele, Richard

[An] Undergraduate
See Whytehead, Thomas

Underhill, Cave 17th c. [IP]
British playwright
* Smith, Elephant

Underhill, Charles
See Hill, Reginald [Charles]

Underhill, Edward 16th c. [HN, SN]
Protestant supporter
* [The] Hot Gospeller

Underhill, Edward Bean [FFF]
American writer
* Fant, Eli

Underhill, Edward Fitch 1830-1898
American author
* Ockside, Knight Russ

Underhill, Peter
See Soderberg, Percy Measday

Underhill, [Dr.] Updike
See Tyler, William Clark

Underhill, Viola
See Wells, Viola Gertrude

Underhill, Wilbur 1897-1934 [BLB]
American bank robber
* [The] Tri-State Terror

[The] Undersea Explorer
See Cousteau, Jacques-Yves

[The] Undersigned
See Arnold, George

[The] Undertaker
See Reese, Don

[The] Undertaker
See Woodcock, Leonard

Underwood, Charlotte 1914- [BI]
American author
* Charles, Joan

Underwood, Deadly
See Underwood, Derek Leslie

Underwood, Derek Leslie 1945- [DC]
British cricketer
* Underwood, Deadly

Underwood, Grace 1911- [THR]
British actress
* Barry, Christine

Underwood, Keith Alfred 1934- [ART]
British artist
* K. A. U.

Underwood, Lewis Graham
See Wagner, C[harles] Peter

Underwood, Mavis Eileen 1916- [AW]
British author
* Kilpatrick, Sarah

Underwood, Michael
See Evelyn, [John] Michael

Underwood, Miles
See Glassco, John [Stinson]

Underwood, Mrs. S. K.
Author
* Kerr, Sophie

Underwood, T. R. ?-1835 [HPPN]
British artist and naturalist
* [A] Detenu

Undine, P. F.
See Paine, Lauran [Bosworth]

[The] Undisputed King of Basketball Comedy
See Lemon, Meadow George, III

Undisputed King of Handcuffs
See Weiss, Ehrich

[The] Undisputed Leader in Distance Freestyle Swimming
See Rose, [Iain] Murray

[The] Undisputed Master of Light Verse
See Nash, [Frederic] Ogden

[The] Undisputed Master of Medical Fiction
See Slaughter, Frank G[ill]

[The] Undisputed Queen of the Movies
See Grasle, Elizabeth

Unett, John 20th c. [HPPN]
British author
* Preston, James

[The] Unexplored Impressionist
See Pissarro, Camille

[The] Unfair Preacher
See Barrow, Isaac

[An] Unfermented Wine Communicant
See Coglan, John

[The] Unforgettable
See Ticker, Reuben

[The] Unforgettable Guerrilla
See Bunke, Haydee Tamara

[The] Unfortunate
See Apodaca, Juan Ruiz de

[The] Unfortunate
See Joseph II

Unger, Marion
See Thede, Marion Draughon

Unger, Maurice Albert 1917- [CA]
American educator and author
* Munger, Al

Unger, Max 1878-?
German-born strongman
* Strongfort, Lionel

Ungerer, Jean Thomas 1931- [CA, SAT, TBJ]
French-born author and illustrator
* Ungerer, Tomi

Ungerer, Tomi
See Ungerer, Jean Thomas

Ungern-Sternberg, Alexander von 1806-1868 [WBD]
Esthonian-born author
* Sternberg, Alexander von

[The] Ungodly
See Aetius of Antioch

[The] Unhappy Warrior
See Wallace, Henry A[gard]

Uni, Louis 1862-1928
French strongman
* Apollon

Uniacke, Evelyn Catherine 1884-
[WWL]
British author
* Clark, Catherine

Uniacke, Mary 19th c. [PI]
Irish poet
* M. U.

Unicus
See Bush, William

Unicus [Alone]
See Joergensen, Johannes

Uniformed Soldier
See Grant, Hiram Ulysses

[The] Unimperial President
See Madison, James

[The] **Unintentional Defaulter**
See Webster, Daniel

[The] **Uninvited Guest**
See Berman, Stanley

[An] **Union Army Officer**
See Wolford, Frank

Union Man Holke
See Holke, Walter Henry

Union Safeguard Grant
See Grant, Hiram Ulysses

[The] **Union's Grand Old Man**
See Savage, George Martin

[The] **Unique**
See Richter, Jean Paul Friedrich

Unit, Matthew
See Pooton, James

[An] **Unitarian**
See Beard, John Reilly

[A] **Unitarian**
See Gage, [Rev.] William Leonard

[An] **Unitarian**
See Ware, Henry, Jr.

[An] **Unitarian Minister**
See Aldred, Ebenezer

[An] **Unitarian of New York**
See Sewall, Henry Devereux

Unitas, John[ny] 1933-
American football player
* Johnny U
* Quarterback, Mr.
* [The] Six Dollar A Game Quarterback

United States Grant
See Grant, Hiram Ulysses

United We Stand Grant
See Grant, Hiram Ulysses

[The] **Universal Aristarchus**
See Hoskins, John

[The] **Universal Butt of all Mankind**
See Hill, [Sir] John

[The] **Universal Doctor**
See Alain de Lille [or Alan de l'Isle]

[The] **Universal Doctor**
See Aquinas, Thomas [Thomas of Aquino]

[The] **Universal Female Athlete**
See Sears, Eleonora R.

[The] **Universal Genius**
See Petty, [Sir] William

[The] **Universal Index and Living Cyclopaedia**
See Magliabecchi, Antonio [or Anthony]

[The] **Universal Penman**
See Bickham, George

[The] **Universal Philosopher**
See Harriot, Thomas

[A] **Universal Piece-Broker**
See Warburton, William

[The] **Universal Provider**
See Whiteley, William

[The] **Universal Spider**
See Louis XI

Universalis, Doctor
See Alain de Lille [or Alan de l'Isle]

Universalis, Doctor
See Albert [Count of Bollstadt]

Universalis, Doctor
See Aquinas, Thomas [Thomas of Aquino]

Universe, Mr.
See Reeves, Stephen [Steve]

Universe, Mr.
See Stanko, Steve

[An] **University Man**
See Carrington, George

[An] **University Pen**
See Howard, Luke

[A] **University Professor**
See Harvey, Alexander

[The] **University Rebel**
See Friend, William

Unk
See White, Cecil

[An] **Unknown**
See Murphy, George Mollett

[The] **Unknown Comic**
See Langston, Murray

[The] **Unknown Eros**
See Patmore, Coventry K. Dighton

[An] **Unknown Friend**
See Garden, George

[The] **Unknown Philosopher**
See Saint Martin, Louis Claude de

[The] **Unknown Soldier**
See Eckert, William Dole

[The] **Unknown Soldier**
See Moody, Orville

[The] **Unlikely Villain**
See Calley, [Lieut.] William Laws

[The] **Unloved One**
See Waugh, Auberon

[The] **Unmelancholy Dane**
See Rosenbaum, Borge

Uno
See Baker, George Melville

Uno, Comandante
See Pabon Pabon, Rosemberg

[The] **Unofficial Ambassador**
See Peabody, George

[The] **Unofficial Chess Champion of the Non-Communist World**
See Reshevsky, Samuel

[The] **Unofficial First Lady of Television**
See Emerson, Faye Margaret

Unofficial Observer
See Carter, John Franklin

Unpa
See Won-Sik, Lim

Unprecedented Strategist Grant
See Grant, Hiram Ulysses

Unpredictable, Mr.
See Patton, Billy Joe

Unquestionably Skilled Grant
See Grant, Hiram Ulysses

[The] **Unready**
See Ethelred II

[The] **Unreconstructed Amateur**
See Stagg, Amos Alonzo

[The] **Unreconstructed Expressionist**
See Benn, Gottfried

Unreconstructed Rebel
See Glass, George Carter

[The] **Unretired Psychologist**
See Martin, Lillie J.

Unruh, Big Daddy
See Unruh, Jesse Marvin

Unruh, Jesse Marvin 1923?-   [TI 4-21-86]
American politician
* Big Man on Campus
* Unruh, Big Daddy

Unseld, Westley 1947-   [IBW]
American basketball player
* [The] Jolly Green Giant

Unser Choe Hauser
See Hauser, Joseph John

Unser, Del
See Unser, Delbert Bernard

Unser, Delbert Bernard 1944-   [SMG]
American baseball player
* Unser, Del

Unser Fritz
See Frederick William

Unser, Robert [Bobby] 1934-   [HPPN]
American auto racer
* [The] Albuquerque Cowboy

[The] **Unsinkable Molly Brown**
See Brown, Margaret Tobin

[The] **Unsmiling Irishman**
See Sullivan, Edward Vincent

Unstead, Archie
See Umstead, Roosevelt Thomas

[The] **Untamed Heifer**
See Elizabeth I

[The] **Untaught Poetess**
See Leapor, Mary

Unterberg, David 1912?- [HPPN]
*American attorney and consumer's rights
advocate*
* [The] Condominium Gadfly
* Unterberg, Don Quixote

Unterberg, Don Quixote
See Unterberg, David

Unthank, Luisa-Teresa 1924- [AW, CA]
British-born writer
* Unthank, Tessa Brown

Unthank, Tessa Brown
See Unthank, Luisa-Teresa

Untouchable, Mr.
See Barnes, Leroy

[An] Untrammeled Free-Thinker
See Moore, M. Louise

Unwin, David S[torr] 1918- [AW, CA,
WD]
British author
* Severn, David

**[An] Unworthy Member of that
Community**
See Rutty, John

Upchurch, Boyd Bradfield 1919- [CA,
SF, WD]
American author
* Boyd, John

Upchurch, Jefferson Woodrow 1911-1971
[BE]
American baseball player
* Upchurch, Woody

Upchurch, Woody
See Upchurch, Jefferson Woodrow

Upcott, William 1779-1845 [SN]
British bibliographer
* [The] Old Mortality in His Line

Updike, John 1932- [CR]
American author
* [The] Andrew Wyeth of Literature

Updike, Wilkins 1786-1867 [IP]
American attorney and author
* [A] Landholder

Updyke, James
See Burnett, William Riley

Upham, Charles Wentworth 1802-1875
[HPPN]
American clergyman
* C. W. U.

Upham, Edward ?-1834 [IP]
British bookseller and author
* E. U.

Upham, Grace Le Baron [Locke]
1845-1916 [DNA]
American author
* Le Baron, Grace

Uphill Harold
See Wilson, [James] Harold

[The] Upholder of the Constitution
See Webster, Daniel

[An] Upholsterer
See Kay, A. J.

[The] Upholsterer of Notre Dame
See Montmorency-Bouteville, Francois
Henri de [Duc de Luxembourg]

Upp, George Henry 1883-1937 [BE]
American baseball player
* Upp, Jerry

Upp, Jerry
See Upp, George Henry

[An] Upper Graduate
See Geddes, Alexander

Upper, Joseph
See Harris, Joseph Upper

[An] Upper Servant
See Jones, John

[The] Upright
See Frederick IV

Upright, Dixie
See Upright, Roy T.

Upright, Roy T. 1926- [BE]
American baseball player
* Upright, Dixie

Upright Telltruth, Esq.
See Lamb, Charles

Upshaw, Mary Jane Stith [BDSA]
American poet
* Fielding, Fanny

Upshur, Abel Parker 1791-1844 [HPPN]
American jurist and statesman
* [A] Virginian

Upshur, Donald M. 1912-1950 [SC]
American actor and producer
* Ravenel, John

[The] Upside Down Comedian
See Lawrence, Joe

Upson, Dorothy Barbara 1904- [HPPN]
British author
* Fawcett, Barbara
* Furness, Elizabeth

Upson, Norma 1919- [CA]
American author
* Kimball, Nancy

[An] Upstart Crow
See Shakespeare, William

Upton, Francis Henry ?-1878 [HPPN]
American attorney
* [The] Advocate for the Captors

Upton, George Putnam 1834-1919
[WBD]
American journalist and music critic
* Pickle, Peregrine

Upton, John ?-1760 [IP]
British clergyman and author
* J. U.

Upton, Margaret 1894?-1957 [BEW]
American theatrical performer
* Joyce, Peggy Hopkins

Upton, Muscles
See Upton, Thomas Herbert [Tom]

Upton, Thomas Herbert [Tom] 1926-
[BE]
American baseball player
* Upton, Muscles

Upward, Allen 20th c. [WWL]
British author
* 20/1631

Upward, Edward Falaise 1903- [AW]
British author
* Chalmers, Allen

[El] Uqsor
See Borgmann, Dmitri A[lfred]

Urania
See Sidney, Mary

Urban, Louis John 1898- [BE]
American baseball player
* Urban, Luke

Urban, Luke
See Urban, Louis John

Urban, Septimus R.
See Rymer, James Malcolm

Urban, Septimus R.
See Urner, Nathan Dane

Urban, Sylvanus
See Bullen, A. H.

Urban, Sylvanus
See Nichols, John

Urban, Sylvanus, Gent.
See Cave, Edward

Urban II
See O'do [or U'do]

Urban III
See Crivelli, Uberto

Urban IV
See Pantaleon, Jacques

Urban V
See De Grimoard, Guillaume

Urban VI
See Prignani, Bartolommeo

Urban VII
See Castagna, Giovanni Battista

Urban VIII
See Barberini, Maffeo

Urbanczyk, Andrew Andrzej 1936-
[IAW]
Russian-born author
* A. U.

[The] Urbane Federalist
See Otis, Harrison Gray

Urbino, Levina [Buoncuore] 19th c.
[DNA, IP]
American author and educator
* Boncoeur, L.
* Cuore, L. B.
* Cuore, Lavinia Buon

Urbs Marmoris
See Campion, John Thomas

Urch, Elizabeth 1921- [WD]
British author
* Brogan, Elise

[The] Urchin
See Laud, William

Ure, George P. ?-1860 [CCL]
Canadian author
* [A] Member of the Press

Ure, Jean
See McCulloch, Sarah [or Sara?]

Urell, William Francis 20th c. [WW]
Author
* Francis, William

U'Ren, Hilda
See U'Ren-Stubbings, Hilda

Uren, Hilda
See U'Ren-Stubbings, Hilda

Uren, Malcolm John Leggoe 1900-
[AW]
Australian author
* Malcolm, John
* Matelot

U'Ren-Stubbings, Hilda 1914- [CA]
British-born writer and bibliographer
* Stubbings, Hilda Uren
* U'Ren, Hilda
* Uren, Hilda

Urena de Henriquez, Salome 1850-1897
[CW]
Dominican poet
* Herminia

Urena de Mendoza, Nicolas 1822-1875
[CW]
Dominican poet and folklorist
* Castulo
* Nisidas

Urfe, Honore d' 1567-1625 [HN, RH]
French author
* [The] Father of Pastoral Romance

Urgentissimus
See Foe, Daniel

Urich, Doc
See Urich, Richard

Urich, Richard 1929- [SMG]
American football coach
* Urich, Doc

Urick, Ed 20th c. [PMJ]
American singer and actor
* Ames, Ed

Urick, Gene 20th c. [PMJ]
American singer
* Ames, Gene

Urick, Joe 20th c. [PMJ]
American singer
* Ames, Joe

Urick, Vic 20th c. [PMJ]
American singer
* Ames, Vic

Urie, Mary Le Baron [Andrews]
1842-1894 [DNA]
Author
* Le Baron, Marie

Uriel
See Da Veiga Fontoura, Uriel

Uriel, Henry
See Faust, Frederick [Schiller]

Urim
See Atterbury, Francis

Uris, Auren 1913- [CA]
American author
* Paul, Auren

Urista, Alberto H. 1947- [CA]
Mexican-born author
* Alurista

Urmuz
See Codrescu, Andrei

Urn, Althea
See Ford, Consuelo Urisarri

Urner, Mabel Herbert
See Harper, Mabel Herbert

Urner, Nathan Dane 1839-1893 [DNA,
HPPN, PA, WGT]
American author and journalist
* Bainbridge, Bryant
* Brentford, Burke
* Campbell, Bartley
* Clancool, Clarence
* Courteney, Carl
* Gildersleeve, Professor
* Looker, O. N.
* Mentor
* Minturn, Edward
* North, Ingoldsby
* Silingsby, Maurice
* Urban, Septimus R.

Urquhart, C. H. 1855-? [FFF]
American writer
* Scotty

Urquhart, David 1805-1877 [HPPN, IP,
SN]
British diplomat
* [An] Old Diplomatic Servant
* [A] Protestant
* [The] Russophobist

Urquhart, David Henry 18th c. [IP]
British poet and clergyman
* Moody, Querulous

Urquhart, Guy
See McAlmon, Robert

Urquhart, Paul
See Black, Ladbroke Lionel Day

Urquhart, William Pollard 1815-? [IP]
Irish statesman and author
* [An] M. P.

Urrea, Lic. Blas
See Cabrera, Luis

Urrutia, Manuel 1900-1981 [HPPN]
Cuban president
* [The] Champion of Anti-Communism

Ursa Major
See Johnson, Samuel

Ursinus, Zacharias
See Beer [or Baer], Zacharias

Ursula, Sanna
See Honkanen, Hilja Loviisa Valkeapaa

Urtisius
See Wursteisen, Christian

Urwin, Ranald Keith 1942- [OP]
British opera singer
* Erwen, Keith

Urziceanu, Aura 1946- [EJ7]
Rumanian-born jazz musician
* Aura
* Lee, Aura

Us Two
See Warner, Richard

Uscatescu, George 1919- [IAW]
Rumanian-born author
* Aluta, Juan De

Uschner, Karl Richard Waldemar 1834-?
[IP]
German attorney and author
* Julian
* Klausner, Chr.

USCO
See Stern, Gerd Jacob

Useless, Ipecac, M.D.
See Houston, Eugene A.

[The] Useless Sole
See Grant, Hiram Ulysses

Usher, Charles 17th c. [IP]
British author
* C. U.

Usher, Frank Hugh 1909- [CA, WW]
British author
* Franklin, Charles
* Lester, Frank

Usher, Freeman L.
See Worcester, Noah

Usher, James 1720?-1772 [IP]
Irish author
* J. U.

Usher, Margo Scegge
See McHargue, Georgess

Usher, Shaun 1937- [CA]
British author
* Scott, Jeffrey

Ushewokunze, Herbert 20th c.
Zimbabwe Rhodesian government official
* Herbie the Herbalist

Ushijima, George 1863-1926 [HPPN]
Japanese-American agriculturist
* [The] Potato King
* Shima, George

Usikota
See Brinitzer, Carl

Usinulea
See Chauvin [or Caulvin?], Jean

Uspenskii, Petr Dem'yanovich 1878-1947 [LC]
Russian-born author
* Uspensky, P. D.

Uspensky, P. D.
See Uspenskii, Petr Dem'yanovich

Ussat, Dutch
See Ussat, William August

Ussat, William August 1904-1959 [BE]
American baseball player
* Ussat, Dutch

Usselmann, James 1876-1938 [WBD]
American actor
* Carew, James

Ustinov, Dimitri 1908?- [TI 11-22-82]
Russian politician
* [The] Redhead

Ustinov, Nicolai 1925- [MS]
Swedish opera singer
* Gedda, Nicolai

Ustinov, Peter Alexander 1921- [HPPN]
British actor and playwright
* [The] Lovable Egghead
* Peter the Great Showman

Uston, Kenneth 1934?-
American blackjack player
* [The] King of the Card Counters

Usuman Dan Fodio 1744-1817 [HPPN]
African religious leader
* Usuman, Shehu

Usuman, Shehu
See Usuman Dan Fodio

[The] Usurper
See Wang Mang

Utesov, Leonid 20th c. [HPPN]
Russian jazz band leader
* [The] King of Russian Jazz

Uticensis
See Cato, Marcus Porcius

Utilis, Doctor
See Lyra, Nicholas de

Utjesenovic, Juraj
See Martinuzzi, George

Utley, Fred Burton 1863-? [NAA]
Canadian writer
* Gordon, Ralph

Utley, Ralph
See Cairns, Huntington

Utley, Uldine 1912- [HPPN]
Clergyman
* [The] Joan of Arc of the Modern
  Religious World

Utopiensis, Bernardus
See Rutty, John

Utrerito [Little Fellow from Utrera]
See Garcia, Antonio

Utrillo, Lucie [Veau] 1878?-1965 [BI]
French painter
* Valore, Lucie

Utsunomiya, Cheryl 20th c.
Actress
* Miyori, Kim

Uttam
See Oak, Purushottam Nagesh

Utter, Charles 19th c. [HPPN]
Friend of American frontier scout, Wild Bill Hickok
* Utter, Colorado Charley
* Utter, Sentimental Charley

Utter, Colorado Charley
See Utter, Charles

Utter, Sentimental Charley
See Utter, Charles

Utterson, Edward Vernon 19th c. [IP]
British antiquary and editor
* E. V. U.

Uttley, Alice Jane [Taylor] 1884-1976
[CA, SAT]
British author
* Uttley, Alison

Uttley, Alison
See Uttley, Alice Jane [Taylor]

Uu, David
See Harris, David W.

Uvalde Jack
See Garner, John Nance

Uvedale, Christian
See Hill, [Sir] John

Uyeshiba, Morihei 1883-1969 [BBH]
Japanese martial artist
* [The] Father of Aikido

Uyesugi, Newton 1917- [HPPN]
Japanese-American optometrist
* [The] Father of the Contact Lens
* Wesley, Newton K.

Uzanne, Octave 19th c. [HPPN]
French editor and author
* [Un] Bibliophile

Uzcudun, Paolino 1899- [BX, HPPN]
Spanish boxer
* [The] Basque Sheepherder
* [The] Basque Woodchopper

Uzes, Duchesse d'
See De Rochechouart-Mortemart, Marie
Clementine

V

Asterisk (*) indicates assumed name.

V.
See Clive, Caroline [Meysey-Wigley]

V.
See Clive, Mrs. Archer

V.
See Valvano, Jim

V. B.
See Bourne, Vincent

V. B.
See Brooks, Vincent

V. B. K.
See Van Breda Kolff, Bill

V. B. K.
See Van Breda Kolff, Jan

V. C. C. W.
See Williams, Vivian Claud Craddock

V. F.
See Foot, Victorine Anne

V. N. G.
See Garrod, Violet Nellie

V. O. de B.
See Bishop, Vivien Oonah de Blois

V. T.
See Tengberg, Violet

V. W.
See Very, Washington

V. W. P.
See Popham, Vyvyan Wallis

Vaccarelli, Horn
See Vaccarelli, Joe J.

Vaccarelli, Joe J. 20th c. [RBE]
Boxing agent
* Vaccarelli, Horn

Vaccarelli, Paolo Antonini 20th c.
[BLB, PHM]
Italian-born American underworld figure
* Kelly, Paul

Vaccaro, Ernest B. 1905?-1979 [CA]
American journalist
* Vaccaro, Tony

Vaccaro, Tony
See Vaccaro, Ernest B.

Vacchi, Augustus Victor 1842-? [LAO]
French-born author
* La Bolina, Jack

Vace, Geoffrey
See Cave, Hugh B[arnett]

Vache, Ernest Lewis 1895-1953 [BE]
American baseball player
* Vache, Tex

Vache, Tex
See Vache, Ernest Lewis

Vachon, Rogatien Rosaire 1945- [FHE,
HK, SMG]
Canadian-born hockey player
* Vachon, Rogie

Vachon, Rogie
See Vachon, Rogatien Rosaire

Vacirca, Corrado 1904-1969 [SC]
Italian-born actor
* Terranova, Dino

[The] Vacuum Cleaner
See Robinson, Brooks [Calbert, Jr.]

Vacuus
See Davis, Thomas Osborne

Vacuus
See Mangan, James Clarence

Vaczek, Louis Charles 1913- [CA, WW]
Hungarian-born author
* Hardin, Peter

Vadianus, Joachim
See Von Watt, Joachim

Vadim, Roger
See Plemiannikov, Roger Vadim

Vadnais, Carol Marcel 1945- [SMG]
Canadian-born hockey player
* Vadnais, Vad

Vadnais, Vad
See Vadnais, Carol Marcel

Vaestberg, Anna Anderson 1832-?
[HPPN]
Swedish author and poet
* Anna A.

Vaeth, Martin
See Kummer, Frederic Arnold

Vaez, Jean N. Gustave 1812-? [PA]
Author
* Nieuwenhuysen, Van

Vaga, Perino del
See Buonaccorsi, Pietro

[The] Vagabond
See Badeau, Adam

Vagabond
See Blake, George

[The] Vagabond
See Thomas, Julian

[The] Vagabond Halfback
See McNally, John Victor

[The] Vagabond Lover
See Vallee, Hubert P[rior]

[The] Vagabond Scot
See Smollett, Tobias George

[The] Vagabond Violinist
See Compson, Eleanor Luicime

Vagg, Samuel 1826-1865 [HPPN]
American theatrical performer
* Collins, Sam

Vagramian, Aram 1921- [ASC]
American musician
* Vega, Al

Vagrant
See Duffus, Louis George

Vagrant
See Lehmann, Rudolf Chambers

[The] Vagrant Viking
See Freuchen, Peter

Vague, Vera
See Allen, Barbara Jo

Vahey, John George Haslette 1881-?
[WW, WWL]
British author
* Clandon, Henrietta
* Haslette, John
* Lang, Anthony
* Loder, Vernon
* Mowbray, John
* Proudfoot, Walter
* Timony, Arthur N.

Vahrer, M. [PA]
Author
* Frederick

Vaid, Sanford
See Tucker, [Arthur] Wilson

Vaidon, Lawdom
See Woolman, David S.

Vail, Amanda
See Miller, Warren

Vail, Dad
See Vail, Harry Emerson

Vail, Doc
See Vail, Robert Garfield [Bob]

Vail, Eric 1953- [SMG]
Canadian-born hockey player
* Vail, Train

Vail, Floyd 19th c. [FFF]
American writer
* Flambeau
* Valentine, Floyd

Vail, Harry Emerson 1859-1928 [BBH]
American rowing coach
* Vail, Dad

Vail, John Cooper [PA]
Author
* Allspice, Zekel

Vail, Kay Boyle 1903- [WGT]
Author
* Boyle, Kay

Vail, Melville 1906- [CEI]
Canadian-born hockey player
* Vail, Sparky

Vail, Philip
See Gerson, Noel Bertram

Vail, Robert Garfield [Bob] 1881-1953 [BE]
American baseball player
* Vail, Doc

Vail, Sparky
See Vail, Melville

Vail, Theodore Newton 1845-1920 [HPPN]
American business executive
* [The] Father of the A. T. & T.

Vail, Train
See Vail, Eric

Vails, Cheetah
See Vails, Nelson

Vails, Nelson 1960?- [TI 8-13-84]
American bicycle racer
* Vails, Cheetah

[The] Vain Tyrant
See Garrick, David

Vainall, Thomas
See Boyle, John [Earl of Cork and Orrery]

Vairasse, Denis 1630-1700 [WGT]
Author
* Siden, Captain

Vaka, Demetra
See Brown, Demetra Kenneth

Vala, Katri Wadenstroem
See Heikel, Karin Alice

Valachi, Joseph Michael 1904-1971 [BLB]
American underworld figure
* Cago, Joe
* Cargo, Joe
* Kato, Joe
* Siano, Joe
* Sorge, Anthony

Valaida
See Snow, Valaida

Valasco, David 1859-1931 [HPPN, JL, TLC]
American producer and playwright
* Belasco, David
* [The] Bishop of Broadway
* [The] Wizard of American Drama

Valbert, G.
See Cherbuliez, Victor

Valbonne, Jean
See Leprohon, Pierre

Valcoe, H. Felix
See Swartz, Harry [Felix]

Valda, [Mme.] Giulia
See Cameron, Julia

Valdare, Sunny Jim
See Mulligan, James

Valdarfer, Christofer
See Haslewood, Joseph

Valdarfer, Christopher
See Haslewood, Joseph

Valdeau, Vintie
See Wheeler, Mrs. James

Valdemoro
See Fernandez Perez, Angel

Valdes, Angel 1838-? [GS]
Peruvian bullfighter
* [El] Maestro [The Master]

Valdes, Gabriel de la Concepcion 1809-1844 [IBW, WBD]
Cuban poet
* Placido

Valdes, Jene
See Martinez, Eugenio R.

Valdes, Latigo
See Valdes, Rene Gutierrez

Valdes, Nelson P. 1945- [CA]
Cuban-born American educator and author
* Leyva, Ricardo

Valdes, Rene Gutierrez 1929- [BE]
Cuban-born baseball player
* Valdes, Latigo

Valdes, Rodrigo
See Valdez, Rodrigo

Valdes Machuca, Ignacio 1792-1851 [CW]
Cuban poet, playwright, journalist
* Desval

Valdespino, Hilario Borroto 1939- [BE]
Cuban-born baseball player
* Valdespino, Sandy

Valdespino, Sandy
See Valdespino, Hilario Borroto

Valdez, Carlos 1926- [EJ]
Cuban-born jazz musician
* Valdez, Potato

Valdez, Potato
See Valdez, Carlos

Valdez, Rodrigo 1946- [RBE]
Colombian boxer
* Valdes, Rodrigo

Valdez, Strico 20th c. [OBW]
American baseball player
* Valdez, Swat

Valdez, Swat
See Valdez, Strico

Valding, Victor [joint pseudonym with John Victor Peterson]
See Benson, Allan Ingvald

Valding, Victor [joint pseudonym with Allan Ingvald Benson]
See Peterson, John Victor

Valdivia, Rafael 1886?-1949 [BI]
Argentine caricaturist
* Rafael

Valdivia y Sisay, Aniceto 1859-1927 [CW]
Cuban playwright and poet
* Kostia, Conde

Vale
See Foe, Daniel

Vale, [Henry] Edmund [Theodoric] 1888-1969 [CAP]
Welsh author
* Bledlow, John

Vale et Fruere
See Baynes, John

Vale, Jerry
See Vitaliano, Genaro Louis

Vale, Keith
See Clegg, W. Paul

Vale, Lewis
See Oglesby, Joseph

Vale, Marguerite 20th c. [BEW]
Playwright
* Vale, Martin

Vale, Martin
See Vale, Marguerite

Valencak, Hannelore
See Mayer, Hannelore

Valencia
See Cuevas Roger, Victoriano

Valencia, Cookie
See Valencia, Jose

Valencia, Flaco [Skinny Valencia]
See Valencia Orozco, Ignacio

Valencia, Jose 20th c. [RBE]
American boxer
* Valencia, Cookie

Valencia II
See Roger, Victoriano

Valencia Orozco, Ignacio 1907- [GS]
Mexican bullfighter
* Valencia, Flaco [Skinny Valencia]

[El] Valenciano [The Valencian]
See Pascual y Olmos, Jose

Valens, Ritchie
See Valenzuela, Richard

Valente, Giorgio
See Vitalis, George

Valente, Umberto [MM]
American underworld figure
* [Lo] Spirito [The Ghost]

Valenti, Dino
See Powers, Chester

Valentin
See Olmedo y Vazquez, Antonio

Valentin, Karl
See Fey, Valentin Ludwig

Valentina
See Schlee, Nicholaevna Sanina

Valentine
See Congreve, William

Valentine
See Pechey, Archibald Thomas

Valentine
See Pott, Joseph Holden

Valentine, Alec
See Isaacs, Alan

Valentine, Benjamin Bennaton 1843-1926
[FFF, HPPN]
British-born journalist and playwright
* Fitznoodle, Francis
* Fitznoodle, Lord
* Iredale, John

Valentine, Bubba
See Valentine, Ellis Clarence

Valentine, Corky
See Valentine, Harold Lewis

Valentine, David
See Ludovici, Anthony M[ario]

Valentine, Douglas
See Williams, [George] Valentine

Valentine, Ellis Clarence 1954- [SMG]
American baseball player
* Valentine, Bubba

Valentine, Floyd
See Vail, Floyd

Valentine, Fred Lee 1935- [BE]
American baseball player
* Valentine, Squeaky

Valentine, Harold Lewis 1929- [BE]
American baseball player
* Valentine, Corky

Valentine, Helen 1909- [CAP]
American educator and author
* Valentine, [Sister] Mary Hester

Valentine, Henry
See Poole, Reginald Heber

Valentine, Henry
See Prout, Geoffrey

Valentine, James C[heyne] 1935- [CA]
American author
* Valentine, Tom

Valentine, Jane
See Meeker, Nellie J.

Valentine, Jimmy
See Hyatt, Henry

Valentine, Jimmy
See Lytell, Bert

Valentine, Jo
See Armstrong, Charlotte

Valentine, Joseph
See Valentino, Guiseppe

Valentine, [Sister] Mary Hester
See Valentine, Helen

Valentine, Mrs. [FFF, PA]
Entertainer
* Aunt Louisa
* Moore, Adelaide

Valentine 1014 [code name used during
World War II]
See Weiss, Louise

Valentine, Paul
See Daixel, William Wolf

Valentine, Raymond 1908- [WWJ]
American jazz musician
* Valentine, Syd

Valentine, Roger
See Duke, Donald Norman

Valentine, Squeaky
See Valentine, Fred Lee

Valentine, Syd
See Valentine, Raymond

Valentine, Thomas 1896-
American jazz musician
* Thomas, Kid

Valentine, Tom
See Valentine, James C[heyne]

Valentine, Val
See Gerich, Valentine

Valentino
See Garavani, Valentino

Valentino, Anthony 1943?- [HPPN]
American chauffeur
* [The] Superservant

Valentino, Guiseppe 1903-1948 [FC]
Italian-American cinematographer
* Valentine, Joseph

Valentino, Mark
See Busillo, Anthony

[The] Valentino of the 80's
See Iglesias, Julio

Valentino, Rudolph
See Guglielmi Di Valentina
D'Antonguolla, Rodolpho Alfonso
Raffaelo P.

Valentino, Sal
See Spanpinato, Salvatore Willard

Valentinov, Nikolai
See Vol'skii, Nikolai Vladislavovich

Valentinus, Basilius
See Thoelde, Johannes

Valentova, Ivona
See Gedzikova, Ivona

Valenzio, Rosalee 1911?-1964 [HPPN]
American theatrical performer
* Callahan, Billy

Valenzuela, Benjamin Beltran [Benny]
1933- [BE]
Mexican-born baseball player
* Valenzuela, Papelero

Valenzuela, Ismael 20th c.
Jockey
* Valenzuela, Milo

Valenzuela, Milo
See Valenzuela, Ismael

Valenzuela, Papelero
See Valenzuela, Benjamin Beltran
[Benny]

Valenzuela, Richard 1940?-1959 [LRR]
American musician
* Allens, Arvee
* Valens, Ritchie

Valera [y Acala-Galiano], Juan
1824-1905 [TLC]
Spanish author, poet, playwright
* Albornoz, Currita
* Filogyno, Eleutorio

Valeriano, Napoleon D[iestro]
1917?-1975 [CA]
*Filipino-born American army officer and
author*
* Valeriano Serrano, Napoleon Diestro

Valeriano Serrano, Napoleon Diestro
See Valeriano, Napoleon D[iestro]

Valerie
See Fould, Wilhelmine Josephine
Simonin

Valerie, Louis
See Barko, Louis

Valerio, Colonel
See Audisio, Walter

Valerio, Juan Francisco 1829?-1878
[CW]
Cuban author and playwright
* Valor y Fe, Narciso

Valerio, Michael 20th c. [SG]
Boxer
* Nelson, Frankie

Valerius
See Combe [or Coombe], William

Valerius?
See Francis, [Sir] Philip

Valerius, C.
See Mendes, Catulle

Valerius, Marcus 4th c. BC [SN]
Roman general
* Corvus [The Raven]

Valery, Henry
See Petiot, Henry John Felix Marcel

Valery, Joseph, Jr. 1934- [BWW]
American singer
* Blue, Joe
* Blue, Little Joe

Valestin, Edward Joseph 1908- [BE]
American baseball player
* Fallenstin, Ed[ward Joseph]
* Fallenstin, Jack

Valestra, John 20th c. [TI 11-1-82]
American government agent
* Vicenza, Mr.

[Le] Valet des Princes
See Froissart, Jean

[Le] Valet du Cardinal
See Nogaret de la Valette, Jean Louis
de

[The] Valet Poet
See Marot, Clement

[The] Valiant
See Alfonso VI [or Alphonso]

[The] Valiant
See John IV [or Jean]

Valiant, Gentleman Jerry
See Valiant, Jerry

Valiant, James [Jim] 20th c. [HPPN]
American wrestler
* [The] Irascible Easterner

Valiant, Jerry 20th c. [HPPN]
American wrestler
* Mitchell, Madman
* Valiant, Gentleman Jerry

Valiant, John 20th c. [HPPN]
American wrestler
* Valiant, Luscious John

[The] Valiant Lion
See Alep Arslan

Valiant, Luscious John
See Valiant, John

[The] Valiant Pilgrim
See Bunyan, John

Valigursky, Ed 20th c. [SFP]
Author
* Remback, William

Valiquette, Big Jack
See Valiquette, Jack

Valiquette, Jack 1956- [SMG]
Canadian hockey player
* Valiquette, Big Jack

Vallandigham, Clement L. 1820-1871
[HPPN]
American politician and peace advocate
* [The] First Copperhead

[The] Vallandingham of the South
See Foote, Henry Stuart

Vallarino, Vincent 1954?- [NW 1-10-83]
American art dealer and model
* Oliver

Valle-Inclan, Ramon Del
See Valle y Pena, Ramon Del

Valle y Pena, Ramon Del 1866-1936
[TCL]
Spanish author, playwright, poet
* Valle-Inclan, Ramon Del

Vallee, Hubert P[rior] 1901-1986 [AM,
BEW, CA, HPPN]
American actor and singer
* [The] Crooner
* [The] Vagabond Lover
* Vallee, Rudy

Vallee, Jacques 1939- [ESF]
French author
* Seriel, Jerome

Vallee, Rudy
See Vallee, Hubert P[rior]

Valleita, Leo
See Anselmi, Teodero

Vallejo Gonzalez, Carmen 1939- [OP]
Italian opera singer
* Gonzalez, Carmen Pagliaro

Valleria, Alwina
See Schoening, Alwina

Valles, Charles 20th c.
American jazz musician and disc jockey
* Maj
* Majharajah of Swirl
* Valles, China

Valles, China
See Valles, Charles

Vallesian, [Brother]
See Mallon, Henry J.

Vallette, Marguerite 1860?-1953 [WBD]
French author and critic
* Rachilde

Valli
See Van De Bovencamp, Valli

Valli, Alida
See Altenburger, Alida Maria

Valli, Frankie
See Castelluccio, Frank

Valli, Valli
See Knust, Valli

Valli, Virginia
See McSweeney, Virginia

Vallinsky, Michael 20th c. [HPPN]
American pickpocket
* Vallinsky, Sheeny Mike

Vallinsky, Sheeny Mike
See Vallinsky, Michael

Valliquietto, Margaret Rose 1911-
[EMT]
American actress, singer, dancer
* Knight, June

Vallot, Antoine 1594-1671 [SN]
French physician
* Tomes [A Bleeder or Carver]

Valmain, Frederic 1931- [AW]
French playwright and author
* Baulat, Paul
* Carter, James

Valmy, Alfred de
See Stinde, Julius

Valnay, Raoul
See Herve, Aime Marie Edouard

Valois, Georges
See Gressent, Alfred Georges

Valor y Fe, Narciso
See Valerio, Juan Francisco

Valore, Lucie
See Utrillo, Lucie [Veau]

Valpy, Francis H. 19th c. [HPPN]
British author
* Digamma

Valrey, Max
See Miller, Eugenie Marie Gaude

Valter, M. [PA]
Author
* Domino

Valtiala, Kaarle-Juhani Bertel 1938-
[IAW]
Finnish author
* Nalle

Valtin, Jan
See Krebs, Richard Julius Herman

Valur
See Fridriksson, Theodor

Valvano, Jim 1946?- [SI 12-5-83]
American basketball coach
* Coach V.
* Jimmy V.
* King Rat
* V.

Valverde y San Juan, Joaquin
1875-1918 [BBD]
Spanish-born composer
* Quinito

Valvrojenski, Bernard 1865-1959 [JL]
Lithuanian-born art historian and author
* B. B.
* Berenson, Bernard

Vambery, Armin
See Bamberger, Hermann

[The] Vamp
See Dietrich, Marie Magdalene

Vamp, Hugo
See O'Neill, John Robert

[The] Vamp Spy
See Zelle, Margarete Gertrude

[The] Vampire
See Lichtenberg, Byron

[The] Vampire Killer
See Haigh, John George

Vamvoras, Clyde 20th c.   [GW]
American rodeo performer
* Vamvoras, Vinegar Roan

Vamvoras, Vinegar Roan
See Vamvoras, Clyde

Van
See Bartlett, David W.

Van
See Vanbrugh, [Sir] John

Van
See   Second element of name for
further listings

Van Aeken [or Van Aken], Hieronymus
1450?-1516   [NPS, WBD]
Dutch painter
* Bosch, Hieronymus
* [The] Joyous

Van Allan, Richard
See Jones, Alan Philip

Van Allen, James 1914-   [HPPN]
American physicist
* [The] Discoverer of the Van Allen
  Belts

Van Allen, William Harman 1870-?
[WWL]
American author and clergyman
* Presbyter, Ignotus

Van Alstyne, Clayton Emery 1900-1960
[BE]
American baseball player
* Van Alstyne Spike

Van Alstyne Spike
See Van Alstyne, Clayton Emery

Van Anrooy, Francine 1924-   [CA]
Dutch author
* Van Anrooy, Frans

Van Anrooy, Frans
See Van Anrooy, Francine

Van Arden, J. Howard 1856-?   [PA]
Author
* Braddon, Paul

Van Arkel, Garret
See Buffett, Edward Payson

Van Arnam, Dave 20th c.   [SFP]
Author
* Archer, Ron [joint pseudonym with
  Theodore Edwin (Ted) White]

Van Arsdale, Wirt
See Davis, Martha [Wirt]

Van Artevelde, Jacob 1290-1345
[HPPN]
Flemish statesman and political leader
* [The] Brewer of Ghent

Van Atta, Russell 1906-   [BE]
American baseball player
* Van Atta, Sheriff

Van Atta, Sheriff
See Van Atta, Russell

Van Atta, Winfred Lowell 1910-   [CA,
WW]
American author
* Ryerson, Lowell

Van Augustine
See Abbott, John G.

Van Auken, Mrs. Henry   [FFF]
Entertainer
* St. John, Nellie

Van Avond, Jan
See Slater, Francis Carey

Van Bairle, Gaspard 1584-1648   [PA]
Author
* Barloeus

Van Bedacht, Rudy 1932-   [CW]
Surinamese poet, critic, journalist
* Verlooghen, Corly

Van Beever, Robert F. 20th c.   [SFL]
Author
* Gordon, Fritz [joint pseudonym with
  Fred(erick) G(ordon) Jarvis, Jr.]

Van Berg, Marion Harold ?-1971   [BBH]
American horse trainer
* Van, Mr.

Van Beverloo, Cornelis Guillaume 1922-
[CAR]
Dutch painter
* Corneille

Van, Billy
See Coppola, Vito

Van, Billy B.
See Vandegrift, Billy B.

Van, Bobby
See Stein, Robert Jack

Van Boxmeer, Boxy
See Van Boxmeer, John Martin

Van Boxmeer, John Martin 1952-
[SMG]
Canadian-born hockey player
* Van Boxmeer, Boxy

Van Breda Kolff, Bill 1922-   [BB, SMG]
American basketball player and coach
* V. B. K.
* Van Breda Kolff, Butch

Van Breda Kolff, Butch
See Van Breda Kolff, Bill

Van Breda Kolff, Jan 1951-   [SMG]
American basketball player
* V. B. K.

Van Breems, Beatrice Graham
1919?-1964   [HPPN]
American actress
* Graham, Virginia

Van Briggle, Margaret F[rances] Jessup
1917-   [CA]
American author
* Jessup, Frances

Van Brocklin, Norm[an] 1926-1983   [FB,
HPPN]
American football player and coach
* Dutch
* [The] Dutchman
* Stub

Van Brugge, Jan
See Joris, David

Van Brunt, Walter John
See Scanlan, Walter

Van Buren, Abigail
See Phillips, Pauline Esther [Friedman]

Van Buren, Deacon
See Van Buren, Edward Eugene

Van Buren, Edward Eugene 1870-1957
[BE]
American baseball player
* Van Buren, Deacon

Van Buren, John 1810-1866   [DNNS,
SN]
American attorney
* [The] Jove of Jolly Fellows
* [The] Jupiter Tonans of His Party
* Prince John

Van Buren, Martin 1782-1862   [DEP,
FAP, FFF, HPPN, NPS]
American president
* [The] American Talleyrand
* [The] Enchanter
* [The] Follower in the Footsteps
* [The] Fox
* [The] Fox of Kinderhook
* [The] Kinderhook Fox
* King Martin the First
* [The] Little Magician
* Little Matty
* Little Van
* [The] Machiavellian Belshazzar
* [The] Magician
* Matey
* [The] Mistletoe Politician
* [The] Northern Man with Southern
  Principles
* Old Kinderhook
* [The] Petticoat Pet
* [The] Political Grimalkin
* [The] Red Fox of Kinderhook
* [The] Sage of Kinderhook
* [The] Sage of Lindenwald
* [The] Sweet Little Fellow
* [The] Weasel
* Whiskey Van
* [The] Wizard of Kinderhook
* [The] Wizard of the Albany Regency
* Young Hickory

Van Buren, Raeburn
See Caplin, Alfred Gerald

Van Buren, Steve 20th c.
American football player
* Van Buren, Wham Bam

Van Buren, Wham Bam
See Van Buren, Steve

Van Calster, A. M. 20th c. [FDG]
Belgian director
* Calster, Og

Van Campen, Karl
See Campbell, John W[ood], Jr.

Van Clouser, Lionel 1909-1942 [SC]
American actor, songwriter, bandleader
* Rand, Lionel

Van Coevering, Jack
See Van Coevering, Jan Adrian

Van Coevering, Jan Adrian 1900-
[CAP]
Dutch-born author
* Van Coevering, Jack

Van Corstanje, Auspicius
See Van Corstanje, Charles

Van Corstanje, Charles 1913- [CA]
Dutch author
* Van Corstanje, Auspicius

Van Cortlandt, Ida
See Tavernier, Mrs. Albert

Van Cortlandt, Philip 1749-1831
[HPPN]
American soldier and politician
* [The] Great White Devil

Van Cott, J. M. 19th c. [HPPN]
American author
* J. M. V. C.

Van Dall, Harold?
See Budrys, Algirdas Jonas

Van Dam, J.
See Presser, [Gerrit] Jacob

Van Dam, Jose
See Van Damme, Joseph

Van Damme, Joseph 1940- [OP]
Belgian opera singer
* Van Dam, Jose

Van Dammeler, Isador Louis Bernard
1881-1934 [BEW, F2]
Dutch-born actor
* Tellegen, Lou

Van De Bovencamp, Valli 20th c. [IBY]
Rumanian-born illustrator and designer
* Valli

Van De Gohm, Richard 1919- [IAW]
British-born author
* Gohm, D. C.
* Gohm, Douglas
* O'Connell, R. F.

Van De Water, Virginia Belle Terhune
20th c. [NAA]
American author
* Terhune, Virginia Belle

Van Dekker, Albert 1904-1968
American actor
* Dekker, Albert

Van Den Bogaerde, Derek Niven 1920?-
[BDF, IPA, WEF]
British actor
* Bogarde, Dirk

Van den Bogaert, Martin ?-1694 [WBD]
Dutch sculptor
* Desjardins, Martin

Van Den Bosch, Anna Maria Tauscher
1855-1938 [BI]
Nun
* Mary Teresa of St. Joseph, [Mother]

Van Den Heuvel, Cornelisz A. 1931-
[CA]
American poet
* corneliszavandenheuvel

Van den Vondel, Joost 1587-1679 [NPS,
SN]
Dutch playwright and poet
* [The] Dutch Shakespeare
* Shakespeare de la Hollande

Van der Berghe, Robert ?-1580 [PA]
Author
* Montanus

Van der Faes, Pieter 1618-1680 [WBD]
Dutch painter
* Lely, [Sir] Peter

Van Der Hurk, Peter 1911- [NAD]
Dutch clairvoyant
* Hurkos, Peter

Van der Kun
See Lunaeus, Peter

Van Der Meer, Anton
See Van Der Meer, Antonius Wiebe

Van Der Meer, Antonius Wiebe 1908-
[IWM]
Dutch musician
* Van Der Meer, Anton

Van der Meer van Delft, Jan
See Vermeer, Jan

Van Der Meersch, Maxence
See Cardijn, Josef

Van der Mersch, Jean Andre 1734-1792
[DNNF]
Belgian patriot
* [The] Brave Fleming

Van Der Merwe, Derik
See Van Der Merwe, Frederik
Johannes

Van Der Merwe, Frederik Johannes
1924- [IWM]
South African musician
* Van Der Merwe, Derik

Van Der Moere, Peeter ?-1572 [BI]
Flemish educator
* Petrus a Gandavo

Van Der Niet, Hein 1901-1975 [HPPN]
Dutch actor
* Abbas, Ben

Van Der Niet, Hein (cont.)
* Dorn, Philip
* Dungen, Fritz van

Van Der Sluice, Harry 1891-1964
[HPPN]
American actor
* Rene, Roy

Van der Weyde, Roger 1455-1529 [FFF,
SN]
Flemish painter
* Roger of Bruges

Van Der Weyden, Roger 1400?-1464
[BI]
Flemish painter
* De La Pasture, Roger

Van Der Zee, Barbara Blanche 1932-
[IAW]
British author
* Griggs, Barbara

Van Deusen, Alonzo 19th c. [SFL]
Author
* [A] Capitalist

Van Deventer, Emma Murdock 20th c.
[EMD, WW]
American author
* Lynch, Lawrence L.

Van Devere, Trish
See Dressel, Patricia

Van Dewall, Johannes
See Kuehne, August

Van Deyssel, Lodewijk
See Thijm, Karel J. L. Alberdingk

Van Dine, Harvey 20th c. [HPPN]
Italian-American criminal
* [The] Little Songbird from Italy

Van Dine, S. S.
See Wright, Willard Huntington

Van Doesburg, Theo
See Kupper, Christiaan Emil Marie

Van Dongen, Cornelis Theodorus Marie
1877-1968 [CAR]
French painter
* Van Dongen, Kees

Van Dongen, Kees
See Van Dongen, Cornelis Theodorus
Marie

Van Doornik, Piet
See Fransen, Piet Frans

Van Doren, Dirck
See Dey, Frederic Van Rensselaer

Van Doren, Mamie
See Olander, Joan Lucille

Van Dorne, R.
See Wallmann, Jeffrey M[iner]

Van Dovski, Lee
See Lewandowski, Herbert

Van Duinkerken, Anton
See Asselbergs, W. J. M. A.

Van Dungen, Fritz 1905- [FC]
Dutch-born actor
* Dorn, Philip

Van Dusart, Eddie 1889-1929 [BX, RBE]
American boxer
* McGoorty, Eddie

[The] Van Dyck of France
See Rigau y Ros, Hyacinthe Francois Honorat Mathias Pierre Martyr Andre

Van Dyck, Philip 1680?-1752 [HPPN]
Dutch painter
* [The] Little Van Dyck

Van Dyke, Anthony
See Nason, Arthur Huntington

Van Dyke, Henry Jackson 1852-1933 [HPPN]
American clergyman, educator, author
* Vane, Henry

Van Dyke, Imogene
See Rowe, Imogene

Van Dyke, J.
See Edwards, Frederick Anthony

Van Dyke, W. S.
See Van Dyke, Woodbridge Strong, II

Van Dyke, Walter 1823-1905 [HPPN]
American politician
* [The] Father of the Union Party of California

Van Dyke, Woodbridge Strong, II 1887-1943 [SC]
American actor and director
* Van Dyke, W. S.

Van Dyne, Edith
See Baum, L[yman] Frank

Van Eijk, Kees 20th c. [WF]
Dutch actor
* Guilty, Joseph

Van Engelyom
See Lecomte, Jules

Van Eps, Worster 1912- [FC, ITA, SW]
American actor
* Parker, Willard

Van Erpe, Thomas 1584-1624 [WBD]
Dutch linguist
* Erpenius

Van Essen, William 1910- [AW, WD]
British physician and author
* Serjeant, Richard

Van Eyck, Jan [or John] 1385-1440 [DEP, FFF, RH]
Flemish painter
* [The] Father of Modern Oil Painting
* John of Bruges

Van Galder, Thomas 20th c. [EF]
American football player
* Van Galder, Tim

Van Galder, Tim
See Van Galder, Thomas

Van Geil, Mercury E. C. L.
See McGilvery, Laurence

Van Goeree, Irina
See Huygh-De Keuster, Maria-Frieda

Van Gogh, Lucy
See Sandwell, Bernard Keble

Van Gogh, Vincent 1853-1890 [HPPN]
Dutch painter, etcher, lithographer
* Monsieur Fou-roux
* [The] Passionate Pilgrim

Van Gordon, Cyrena
See Pocock, Cyrene Sue

Van Grasshoff, Carl Louis 1865-1919 [NAD]
Religious leader
* Heindel, Max

Van Haltren, George E. 1866-1945 [PB]
American baseball player
* Van Haltren, Rip

Van Haltren, Rip
See Van Haltren, George E.

Van Haren, Wouter
See Kolff, Roelof Coenraad

Van Hassen, Amy
See High-Smith, Domini

Van Heller, Marcus
See Zachary, Hugh

Van Hemskerck, Martin 1498-1574 [DEP, HN, RH]
Dutch painter
* [The] Raphael of Holland

Van Herp, Jacques 1923- [ESF]
Belgian critic, editor, author
* Jansen, Michel

Van Heusen, James [Jimmy]
See Babcock, Edward Chester

Van Hoddis, Jakob
See Davidsohn, Hans

Van Hoften, James 1945?- [NW 4-23-84, TI 4-23-84]
American astronaut
* Van Hoften, Ox

Van Hoften, Ox
See Van Hoften, James

Van Horn, Dale R. 1895- [NAA]
American author
* Covington, Chester
* Dale, V. R.
* Dalton, Howard
* Engell, Dee
* Lincoln, E. R.
* Richard, Bill
* Rood, Jack
* Vance, Gale
* Virginia, Daisy

Van Horn, Douglas 1944- [SMG]
American football player
* Van Horn, Reggie

Van Horn, Reggie
See Van Horn, Douglas

Van Horne, Harry Randall 1924- [ASC]
American composer and conductor
* Van Horne, Randy

Van Horne, Randy
See Van Horne, Harry Randall

Van Hulsteyn, Marda ?-1970 [THR]
South African-born actress
* Vanne, Marda

Van Iterson, S. R.
See Van Iterson, Siny Rose Van Der Breggen

Van Iterson, Siny Rose Van Der Breggen 20th c. [FBJ]
Dutch author
* Van Iterson, S. R.

Van Ith, Lily
See Friedli, Emilie Ida

Van Kampen, Oscar 1928?- [CW]
Surinamese author
* Banana, Azijn

Van Kriedt, David
See Kriedt, David N.

Van Kuijik, Andreas Cornelis 1909?-
Dutch-born business manager of Elvis Presley
* Parker, [Captain] Tom

Van Laerhoven, Robert Victor Flora 1953- [IAW]
Belgian author
* Ashmind, Kim

Van Lake, Turk
See Housepian, Vanig

Van Lake, Turk
See Hovsepian, Vanig

Van Lawick-Goodall, Jane 1934- [CA]
British ethologist and author
* Goodall, Jane

Van Lhin, Erik
See Alvarez Del Rey, Ramon Felipe San Juan Mario Silvio Enrico

Van Lier, Norm[an, III] 1947- [IBW]
American basketball player
* [The] Storm in Norman

Van Lierde, John 1907- [CAP]
Belgian-born author
* Van Lierde, Peter Canisius

Van Lierde, Peter Canisius
See Van Lierde, John

Van Loenen, Gabrielle
See Van Schaik-Willing, Jeanne Gabrielle

Van Loo, Carle
See Van Loo, Charles Andre

Van Loo, Charles Andre 1705-1765 [HPPN]
French painter
* Van Loo, Carle

Van Loot, Cornelius Obenchain
See Tarkington, [Newton] Booth

Van Lorne, Warner
See Tremaine, F[rederick] Orlin

Van Lorne, Warner
See Tremaine, Nelson

Van Maerlant, Jakob De Coster 13th c.
[HPPN]
Belgian poet
* [The] Father of Dutch Poetry
* [The] Father of Dutch Poets
* [The] Father of Flemish Poets

Van Matre, Paz
See Thompson, Ariadne

Van Mattimore, Richard 1899?-1976
[F2, FC]
American actor
* Arlen, Richard

Van Meegeren, Henricus Antonius
1889?-1947 [HPPN]
Dutch art forger
* Han

Van Meter, Homer ?-1934 [HPPN]
American outlaw
* Van Meter, Wayne

Van Meter, Wayne
See Van Meter, Homer

Van Mever, Piet
See Van Mever, Pieter Adriaan

Van Mever, Pieter Adriaan 1899-
[IWM]
Dutch musician
* Van Mever, Piet

Van, Mr.
See Van Berg, Marion Harold

Van Naerssen, Jan 1580-1637 [PA]
Author
* Narssius

Van Nally, Elsie
See Barrett, Rosa

Van Name, E. J. 20th c. [SFP]
Author
* Vanny, Jim

Van Neuhoff, Baron 1681-1756 [HPPN]
German adventurer
* Theodore, King of Corsica

Van Niekerk, I. R.
See Nienaber, Petrus Johannes

Van Noppen, Ina [Faye] W[oestemeyer]
1906- [CA]
American historian and author
* Woestemeyer, Ina Faye

Van Nuland, Wim
See Mohlmann, [Father] Michael

Van Offel, David 1919-1975 [SC]
British-born actor, director, playwright
* Daufel, Andre

Van Oort, Jan 1921- [CA]
Dutch author and illustrator
* Dulieu, Jean

Van Oostsanen, Jakob
See Cornelisz, Jakob

Van Oranje, Christina
See Maria Christina

Van Orden, Robert E. 1931- [FC, SW]
American actor
* Smith, John

Van Orden, William H. 19th c. [DNA]
American author
* James, Police Captain

Van P. Polanen 1936?- [CW]
Surinamese poet
* Dandilo, Kwame

Van Peteghem, Camille 1935- [OP]
Belgian opera singer
* Meghor, Camillo

Van Porter, Henry
See Correll, Charles J.

Van Ree, Jean
See Schloesser, Hendrik

Van Rensburg, Jaco
See Van Rensburg, Roelog Jacobus
Jansen

Van Rensburg, Roelf
See Van Rensburg, Roelog Jacobus
Jansen

Van Rensburg, Roelog Jacobus Jansen
1935- [IAW]
South African author
* Van Rensburg, Jaco
* Van Rensburg, Roelf

Van Rensselaer, Stephen 1764-1839
[HPPN, NPS]
American army officer and land owner
* [The] Patroon

Van Rensselar, Frederick 19th c.
[WGT]
Author
* Dey, Marmaduke

Van Rijn, Ignatius
See Ingram, Forrest L[eo]

Van Rijn [or Ryn], Rembrandt
Harmensz [or Harmenszoon] 1606-1669
[HPPN, WBD]
Dutch painter
* [The] Prince of Darkness
* Rembrandt

Van Robays, Bomber
See Van Robays, Maurice Rene

Van Robays, Maurice Rene 1914-1965
[BE]
American baseball player
* Van Robays, Bomber

Van Roemer, A. 1940?- [CW]
Surinamese poet
* Zamani

Van Roey, Leon 1921- [GA]
Danish cartoonist, illustrator, painter
* Leon
* Van Roy

Van Roomen, Adrian 1561-1615 [FFF,
RH]
Mathematician
* Adrianus Romanus
* [The] Roman

Van Rooy, Anton
See Van Rooy, Antonius Maria
Josephus

Van Rooy, Antonius Maria Josephus
1879-1932 [MS]
Dutch opera singer
* Van Rooy, Anton

Van Roy
See Van Roey, Leon

Van Ryssel, Paul
See Gachet, Paul Ferdinand

Van Saanen, Marie Louise
See Gibson, Marice Louise

Van Scelter, Helter
See Ridley, James

Van Schaak, Marie 1917- [HPPN]
American entertainer
* [The] Girl in the Bathtub
* St. Cyr, Lili

Van Schaik-Willing, Jeanne Gabrielle
1895- [IAW]
Dutch author
* Van Loenen, Gabrielle

Van Scheltinga, Theo
See Van Scheltinga, Tjeerd Daniel

Van Scheltinga, Tjeerd Daniel 1914-
Dutch chess player
* Van Scheltinga, Theo

Van See, John
See Vance, John Holbrook [Jack]

Van Shaick, John 1873-? [NAA]
American author and editor
* Johannes

Van Siller, Hilda 20th c. [WW]
Author
* Siller, Van

Van Slingerland, Nellie Bingham 1850-?
[DNA]
American author and playwright
* Bevans, Neile

Van Sloetten, Henry Cornelius
See Neville, Henry

Van Sluijters, Georges Joseph 1868-1943
[BI]
French artist
* De Feure, Georges

Van Someren, Liesje
See Lichtenberg, Elisabeth Jacoba

Van Stockum, Hilda 1908- [CA]
Dutch-born author, translator, illustrator
* Marlin, Hilda

Van Straubenzee, Clyde 1867-1934
[THR]
British theatrical manager
* Meynell, Clyde

Van Studdiford, Grace
See Quivey, Grace

Van Surdam, Dutch
See Van Surdam, Henderson

Van Surdam, Henderson 20th c. [FB]
American football coach
* Van Surdam, Dutch

Van Swearingen, Marmaduke 1754?-1810?
Chief of American Indian tribe
* Blue Jacket

Van Tassell, Cora
See Young, Mrs. Edwin

Van Tijn, Maartje
See Van Tijn, Mijntje Leentje

Van Tijn, Mijntje Leentje 1933- [IAW]
Dutch author
* Van Tijn, Maartje

Van Tricht, Elisabeth Emmy 1911-
[IAW]
Dutch author
* De Jong-Keesing, Elisabeth

Van Truesdale, Pheleg
See Adams, Francis Colburn

Van Tuyl, Rosealtha 1901- [SFL, WGT]
American author
* Van Tuyl, Zaara

Van Tuyl, Zaara
See Van Tuyl, Rosealtha

Van Twiller, Walter 1580?-1656? [SN]
Dutch colonial governor in America
* Walter the Doubter

Van Valey, Lyman 1853-1926 [HPPN]
American entertainer
* Christy, Dave

Van Valkenburg, Julia [FFF]
American writer
* Wayne, Gladys

Van Vechten, Abraham 1762-1823 [FFF, HPPN]
American attorney
* [The] Father of the Bar of the State
  of New York
* [The] Father of the New York Bar

Van Vechten, Carl 1880-? [CAA]
American author
* Atlas

Van Velthus, Jan
See Brunken, Ernest

Van Vleck, John 1899?-1980
American physicist
* [The] Father of Modern Magnetism

Van Vliet, Don 1941- [CMA, PRS, RM]
American singer and songwriter
* Beefheart, Captain
* [The] Spotlight Kid

Van Vogt, A. E.
See Van Vogt, Alfred Elton

Van Vogt, Alfred Elton 1912- [SF]
Canadian-born author
* Van Vogt, A. E.

Van Vogt, Edna Mayne Hull 1905-1975
[WGT]
American author
* Hull, E. Mayne

**Van Voorthuizen [or Voorthuyzen],
Louwrens** 1898-1968 [EOP]
Dutch religious leader
* Lou

Van Vormizeele, Eelco Voet 1942- [OP]
German opera singer
* Von Jordis, Eelco

Van Wagener, Isabelle 1797-1883 [IBW]
American abolitionist
* God's Fool
* [The] Libyan Sibyl
* Truth, Sojourner

Van Wageningen, J.
See Presser, [Gerrit] Jacob

Van Walree, Mrs. E. C. W. [PA]
Author
* Miller, Christine

Van Weddingen, Marthe 1924- [CA]
Belgian-born author
* Dumas, Claire

Van Winkle, Harold E. 1939- [ASC]
American composer
* Van Winkle, Rip

Van Winkle, Rip
See Van Winkle, Harold E.

Van Woeart, Alpheus
See Halloway, Vance

Van Wolzogen, Lodowijk 1642-1690
[PA]
Author
* Volzogenius

Van Wynkyn, Jan ?-1534? [WBD]
British printer
* Worde, Wynkyn de

Van Zandt, Charles
See Scott, Charles

Van Zandt, E. F.
See Cudlipp, Edythe

Van Zandt, Steve 20th c. [TI 10-7-85]
American composer and singer
* Little Steven

Van Zant, James E. 1898- [HPPN]
American politician
* [The] Father of the Bonus

Van Zeller, Claud 1905- [CA]
British clergyman and author
* Brother Choleric
* Van Zeller, Hubert
* Venning, Hugh

Van Zeller, Hubert
See Van Zeller, Claud

Van Zwienen, Ilse Charlotte Koehn
1929- [CA]
*German-born American author and
illustrator*
* Koehn, Ilse

Vanags, Martin 1947- [RO2]
German singer
* Kristian, Marty

Vanardy, Varick
See Dey, Frederic Van Rensselaer

VanBebber, Blackjack
See VanBebber, Jack Francis

VanBebber, Jack Francis 20th c. [BBH]
American wrestler
* VanBebber, Blackjack

Vanbrugh, [Dame] Irene
See Barnes, Irene

Vanbrugh, [Sir] John 1666-1726 [HPPN,
SN]
British playwright and architect
* Sheridan, R. B. B.
* Van

Vanbrugh, Prudence
See Bourchier, Prudence

Vanbrugh, Violet
See Barnes, Violet

Vance, Ag
See Vance, Walter Addington

Vance, Alfred Glenville
See Stevens, Alfred Peck

Vance, Arthur Charles 1893- [BI]
American baseball player
* Vance, Dazzy

Vance, Charles
See Goldblatt, Charles

Vance, Clara
See Denison, Mary Andrews

Vance, Clarence Arthur 1891-1961 [BE,
PB, SR]
American baseball player
* [The] Dazzler
* Vance, Dazzy

Vance, Clarice
See Black, Clara Ella

Vance, Cyrus Roberts 1917- [NW 9-27-82]
American attorney and diplomat
* Cyrus the Gray
* Porky Pig

Vance, Dazzy
See Vance, Arthur Charles

Vance, Dazzy
See Vance, Clarence Arthur

Vance, Dazzy
See Vance, Gene E.

Vance, Edgar
See Ambrose, Eric [Samuel]

Vance, Ethel
See Stone, Grace Zaring

Vance, Gale
See Van Horn, Dale R.

Vance, Gene E. 1947- [SMG]
American baseball player
* Vance, Dazzy
* Vance, Sandy

Vance, Gerald [joint pseudonym with
Robert Silverberg] [house pseudonym,
Ziff-Davis]
See Garrett, [Gordon] Randall [Philip
David]

Vance, Gerald [house pseudonym, Ziff-
Davis]
See Geier, Chester S.

Vance, Gerald [house pseudonym, Ziff-
Davis]
See Graham, Roger Phillips

Vance, Gerald [joint pseudonym with
Randall Garrett] [house pseudonym,
Ziff-Davis]
See Silverberg, Robert

Vance, Jack
See Kuttner, Henry

Vance, John Holbrook [Jack] 1916?-
[CA, EMD, TCCM, WGT]
American author
* Held, Peter
* Holbrook, John
* Queen, Ellery
* Van See, John
* Wade, Alan

Vance, Joseph Albert [Joe] 1905- [BE]
American baseball player
* Vance, Sandy

Vance, Nina
See Whittington, Nina Eloise

Vance, Sandy
See Vance, Gene E.

Vance, Sandy
See Vance, Joseph Albert [Joe]

Vance, Stan
See Vancini, Florestano

Vance the Great
See Stevens, Alfred Peck

Vance, Walter Addington 20th c. [BBH]
American basketball player
* Vance, Ag

Vancel, Doris 20th c. [WGT]
Author
* Thomas, Doris

Vancini, Florestano 1936- [FDG]
Italian director
* Vance, Stan

Vanda, Harry
See Wandan, Harry

Vandal, Cameron
See Thorne, B[liss] Kirby

[The] Vandal Chief
See Sherman, William Tecumseh

Vandalio
See Cetina, Gutierre de

Vandegrift, Alexander Archer 1887-1972
[HPPN]
American military officer
* [The] Guadalcanal General
* Vandegrift, Sunny Jim

Vandegrift, Billy B. 1870-? [THR]
American actor
* Van, Billy B.

Vandegrift, Margaret
See Janvier, Margaret Thomson

Vandegrift, Sunny Jim
See Vandegrift, Alexander Archer

Vandemann, Frederick H. 1873-1935
[BE]
American baseball player
* Abbott, Fred

Vandenberg, Harold Harris 1907- [BE]
American baseball player
* Vandenberg, Hy

Vandenberg, Hy
See Vandenberg, Harold Harris

Vandenberg, Philipp
See Hartel, Klaus Dieter

Vandenberg, Simon 1899- [BEW]
Belgian-born actor
* Abbott, Richard

Vandenburgh, Theodore H.   [PA]
Author
* Bunsby, Jack

Vandendreschd, Jacques Mornard 1904-
[BI, HPPN]
Belgian assassin
* Jacson, Frank
* Mornard, Jacques
* Rio, Ramon Mercades del

Vandeputte, Roger 1930- [OP]
Belgian conductor
* Rossel, Roger

Vander Linden, Anthony 1924- [BS]
American magician and bookseller
* [The] Continental Magician
* Presti, Tony

Vander Meer, John Samuel 1914- [BE,
HPPN]
American baseball player
* Double No-Hit
* [The] Double No-Hit Kid
* [The] Dutch Master

Vander Neck, J.
See Burgh, James

Vander Zee, James 1883- [IBW]
American photographer
* [The] Dean of Black Photographers

Vanderbilt, Commodore
See Vanderbilt, Cornelius

Vanderbilt, Cornelius 1794-1877 [WBD]
American industrialist
* Vanderbilt, Commodore

Vanderbilt, Cornelius, Jr. 1898- [NAA]
American author
* Lane, R.

Vanderbilt, Gloria 1924?- [HPPN]
American heiress
* [The] Poor Little Rich Girl
* Vanderbilt, Little Gloria

Vanderbilt, Little Gloria
See Vanderbilt, Gloria

Vanderbilt, William Henry 1821-1885
[SN]
American industrialist
* [The] Railway King

Vanderbundt, Skip
See Vanderbundt, William Gerard

Vanderbundt, William Gerard 1946-
[SMG]
American football player
* Vanderbundt, Skip

Vanderdecken
See Cooper, William

Vanderpoel, Aaron 1799-1871 [FFF]
American politician
* [The] Kinderhook Roarer

Vanderpool, Sylvia 1936- [RO1]
American singer
* Little Sylvia

**Vandersteen, Willibrord Jan Frans
Maria** 1913- [WECO]
Belgian cartoonist
* Vandersteen, Willy

Vandersteen, Willy
See Vandersteen, Willibrord Jan Frans
Maria

Vanderveen, Bareld Harmannus 1932-
[CA]
Dutch author and editor
* Vanderveen, Bart H.

Vanderveen, Bart H.
See Vanderveen, Bareld Harmannus

Vandivier, Fuzzy
See Vandivier, Robert

Vandivier, Robert 1903- [NBA]
American basketball player
* Vandivier, Fuzzy

Vandon, George
See Johnstone, George Harcourt [Third
Baron Derwent]

Vandour, Cyril
See Surmelian, Leon [Zaven]

Vandover, Bud 20th c. [HPPN]
American singer
* Tom

Vandover, Gordon 20th c. [HPPN]
American singer
* Harry

VanDusen, Conrad 1801?-1878 [CCL]
Canadian author
* Enemikeese

Vandyck in Little
See Cooper, Samuel

[The] Vandyck of England
See Dobson, William

[The] Vandyck of Sculpture
See Coysevox, Antoine

Vane, Alice
See Templeton, Mrs. John

Vane, Ann 1710-1736 [HPPN, SN]
Mistress of Frederick Lewis, son of King George II
* Frail, Lady
* [A] Lady of Quality
* Vanella

Vane, Bret
See Kent, Arthur [William Charles]

Vane, Derek
See Eaton-Back, Mrs. B.

Vane, [Sir] Henry 1589-1654 [HPPN, SN]
British statesman
* Old Sir Henry
* Pulteney's Toad-Eater

Vane, [Sir] Henry [Harry] 1612-1662 [HPPN, NPS]
British statesman
* Heron, Brother
* Young Sir Henry

Vane, Henry
See Van Dyke, Henry Jackson

Vane, Isabel
See Adams, Isabel Vane

Vane, Michael
See Humphries, Sydney Vernon

Vane, Roland
See McKeag, Ernest L[ionel]

Vane, Sutton
See Sutton-Vane, Vane Hunt

Vane, Volet
See Howell, Jane L.

Vanella
See Vane, Ann

Vanessa
See Vanhomrigh, Esther

Vaneuf, Andre
See Cohen, Sol B.

Vanglon, Henri 1875-1944 [CD]
French playwright
* Gheon, Henri

Vanguard
See Wood, Thomas Winter

Vanhomrigh, Esther 1690-1723 [NPS, UH]
Friend of British author, Jonathan Swift
* Vanessa

Vanhoutte, Marie-Leonie 20th c. [EE]
Intelligence agent
* Charlotte

Vanhove, Charlotte 1771-1860 [HPPN]
French actress
* Talma, Madame

Vanier, Bruce 1951- [HPPN]
American businessman
* Hood, Robin

[The] Vanilla Gorilla
See Lorenzen, Al

Vanini, Giulio Cesare
See Vanini, Lucilio

Vanini, Lucilio 1585-1619 [WBD]
Italian philosopher
* Vanini, Giulio Cesare

[The] Vanished Judge
See Crater, Joseph Force

Vanity
See Matthews, Denise

Vann, Joe
See Canzano, Joe

Vanne, Marda
See Van Hulsteyn, Marda

Vanner, John
See North, William

Vannga, France 1939- [SW]
French actress
* Nuyen, France

Vanni, Helen Elizabeth
See Spaeth, Helen Elizabeth

Vannucchi, Andrea Domenico D'Agnolo di Francesco di Luca 1486-1531 [HPPN]
Italian painter
* Del Sarto, Andrea
* [The] Faultless Painter

Vannucci, Pietro 1446-1523 [WBD]
Italian painter
* Della Pieve, Pier
* [Il] Perugino

Vanny, Jim
See Van Name, E. J.

Vanpeperstraete, Norbert 1912- [FDG]
Belgian director
* Benoit, Norbert

Vansart
See Vansittart, Charles

VanSickle, V. A.
See Carhart, Arthur Hawthorne

Vansittart, Charles *MB
British entertainer
* [The] Man With the Iron Grip
* Vansart

Vansittart, Jane
See Moorhouse, Hilda Vansittart

Vansittart, Nicholas 1766-1851 [HN]
British politician
* Old Bags

Van't Sant, Mien
See Van't Sant-Van Bommel, Aartje Wilhelmina

Van't Sant-Van Bommel, Aartje Wilhelmina 1901- [IAW]
Dutch author
* Van't Sant, Mien

Vanzetti, Bartolomeo 1888-1927
Italian-born American political radical
* [The] Poor Fish Peddler

Vanzi, Luigi 20th c. [WF]
Director
* Lewis, Vance

Vanzina, Stefano 1915- [FDG]
Italian director
* Steno

Vao Gogo, Emmanuel
See Fernandes, Millor

Vapnick, Richard Leon 1920-
British singer and music publisher
* James, Dick

Vaquerito [Little Cowboy]
See Soler y Gisbert, Manuel

Varaigne, Dominique 1948- [FC]
Actress
* Sanda, Dominique

Varas, Florencia
See Olea, Maria Florencia Varas

Varco, Joseph Vincent di 1911- [HPPN]
American underworld figure
* Little Caesar

Varconi, Victor
See Varkonyi, Mihaly

Varden, Evelyn
See Hall, Evelyn

Vardon, Richard
See O'Brien, David Wright

Vardon, Roger
See Delafosse, Frederick Montague

Vardre, Leslie
See Davies, Leslie Purnell

Vardys, V[ytautas] Stanley
See Zvirzdys, Vytautas

Vare y Garcia, Manuel 1894-1921 [GS]
Spanish bullfighter
* Varelito [Little Vare]

Varelito [Little Vare]
See Vare y Garcia, Manuel

Varelli, Alfredo 20th c. [WF]
Italian actor
* Farrell, Fred

Varelst, Simon [HN]
Painter
* [The] God of Flowers

Varenne, Alberic
See Laurent-Cely, Jacques

Varenov, Leonard 1911-1960 [MS]
American opera singer
* Warren, Leonard

Varesi, Gilda
See Conti, Gilda

Varga, Judy
See Stang, Judit

Vargas, Jose 20th c. [OBW]
American baseball player
* Vargas, Tetelo

Vargas, Teresa 1935- [OP]
Spanish opera singer
* Berganza, Teresa

Vargas, Tetelo
See Vargas, Jose

Vargas y Gonzalez, Enrique 1870-1930
[GS]
Spanish bullfighter
* Minuto [Minute]

Vari, Giuseppe 20th c. [WF]
Italian director
* Warren, Joseph

Varian, Elizabeth Willoughby 1830?-?
[PI]
Irish poet
* Finola

Varian, Ralph 1820?-1886 [PI]
Irish poet
* Duncathail
* Fionbarr
* Mor, McCarthaigh
* R. V., Cork

Varick
See Palmer, M.

Varick, Alfred 1881-1949 [F2, FC]
British actor
* Drayton, Alfred

Varick, James 1750?-1828 [HPPN]
American church leader
* [The] Father of the A. M. E. Zion
  Church

Varina
See Waring, Jane

Varina
See Waryng, Jane

Varipapa, Andy
See Varipapa, Antonio

Varipapa, Antonio 1891- [HPPN]
Italian-American bowler
* [The] Great Varipapa
* Varipapa, Andy

Varkonyi, Mihaly 1896- [FC]
Hungarian-born actor
* Varconi, Victor

Varley, John 1947- [CA]
American author
* Boehm, Herb

Varley, John Philip
See Mitchell, Langdon [Elwin]

Varma, Mahest Prasod 1918-
Indian leader of religious sect
* Yogi, Maharishi Mahesh

Varnadow, Peggy 1928- [FC]
American actress
* Dow, Peggy

Varnel, Marcel
See Le Bozec, Marcel

Varner, Buck
See Varner, Glen Gann

Varner, Glen Gann 1930- [BE]
American baseball player
* Varner, Buck

Varney, Dike
See Varney, Lawrence Delano

Varney, Gabriel
See Wainewright, Thomas Griffiths

Varney, Jim 1950?- [TI 1-20-86]
American actor
* Worrell, Ernest P.

Varney, Lawrence Delano 1880-1950
[BE]
American baseball player
* Varney, Dike

Varney, Pete
See Varney, Richard Fred

Varney, Richard Fred 1949- [SMG]
American baseball player
* Varney, Pete

Varnum, Joseph Bradley 1818-1874
[DNA]
American author and attorney
* Viator

Varnum, Zoe Shippen 1902- [IAW]
American author
* Shippen, Zoe

Varotari, Alessandro 1590-1650 [WBD]
Italian painter
* [Il] Padovanino

Varro, Marcus Terentius 1st c. BC
[DNNF, DNNS, FFF]
Roman scholar
* Most Erudite of the Romans
* Most Learned of the Romans

[The] Varro of Britain
See Camden, William

Varro, Publius Terentius 1st c. BC
[WBD]
Roman poet
* Atacinus

Varro, William 13th c. [DNNF, RH,
SN]
British scholastic philosopher
* Fundatus, Doctor
* [The] Thorough Doctor

Varus
See Clifford, Thomas

Vasan, S. S.
See Srinivasan, S.

Vasarely, Jean-Pierre 1934- [CAR]
French painter
* Yvaral

Vasaturo, Giuseppe 1900?-1964 [BEW,
FC]
Italian producer
* Amato, Giuseppe
* Amato, Peppino

Vasek, Vladimir 1867-1958 [CD, EWL]
Czech poet
* Bezruc, Petr

Vasey, George 19th c. [HFN]
Author and engraver
* [A] Beef Eater

Vashti
See Rochechouart, Francoise Athenais

Vasilev, Zhelio 20th c. [WP 10-14-84]
*Bulgarian implicated in plot to
assassinate Pope John Paul II*
* Petrov

Vasili, [Comte] Paul
See Adam, Juliette

Vasili, Paul
See Casal, Julian del

Vasiliu, Gheorghe 1881-1957 [EWL,
TCL]
Rumanian poet
* Bacovia, Gheorghe

Vasistha, Mohan
See Shastri, Prithvinath

Vasko, Elmer 1935- [CEI, FHE, HK]
Canadian-born hockey player
* Vasko, Moose

Vasko, Moose
See Vasko, Elmer

Vasquez, Tiburico ?-1875 [HPPN]
Mexican outlaw
* [The] Tiger of the Dim Trails

Vass, Fatty
See Vass, Frank

Vass, Frank ?-1917 [HPPN]
American actor
* Vass, Fatty

Vassa, Gustavus
See Equiano, Olaudah

Vassallo, Aldo Mirabella
See Mirabella, Gesualdo

Vassilakis, Panayotis 1925- [CAR]
Greek sculptor
* Takis

Vassili, [Count] Paul
See Radziwill, Catherine

Vassy, Gaston [PA]
Author
* Punch

Vasu, Nirmala-Kumara
See Bose, Nirmal Kumar

Vasudeva, Vishnudayal
See Bissoondoyal, Basdeo

Vatatzes
See John III

Vatel
See Deserres, Gaston

[Der] Vater des Deutschen Liedes [The Father of German Songs]
See Albert, Heinrich

Vathek
See Beckford, William

[The] Vatican Kissinger
See Benelli, Giovanni

[The] Vatican's Kissinger
See Casaroli, Agostino

Vatis, Tassi 20th c. [HPPN]
Greek-American millionaire and auto racing promoter
* [The] Greek

Vator, [Miss] Ella
See Smith, H[arry] Allen

[Le] Vauban de la Marine
See Sane, Jacques Noel

[The] Vauban of Sweden
See Dahlberg [or Dahlbergh], Erik Jonsson

Vaudeville's Ageless Song and Dance Man
See Rooney, Pat, II

Vaudeville's Dictator
See Keith, Benjamin Franklin

Vaudeville's Youngest Headliner
See West, Mae

Vaughan, Arkie
See Vaughan, Floyd E.

Vaughan, Arky
See Vaughan, Joseph Floyd

Vaughan, Auriel Rosemary Malet 1923-
[SFL, WGT]
Author
* Malet, Oriel

Vaughan, Carter A.
See Gerson, Noel Bertram

Vaughan, Dudley
See Johnson, Dudley Vaughan

Vaughan, Elizabeth
See Jones, Elizabeth Myfanwy

Vaughan, Floyd E. 1912- [HPPN]
American baseball player
* Vaughan, Arkie

Vaughan, Frankie
See Abelsohn, Frank

Vaughan, Glenn Edward 1944- [BE]
American baseball player
* Vaughan, Sparky

Vaughan, Henry 1622-1695 [DEL, DEP, DNNS]
Welsh poet
* [The] Silurist

Vaughan, Henry 1766-1844 [HPPN, IP]
British physician and poet
* H. H., Bart., Sir
* Halford, [Sir] Henry

Vaughan, Henry 1890- [BEW]
American actor and playwright
* Hull, Henry

Vaughan, Henry
See Pelzer, Leon

Vaughan, Hilda
See Morgan, Hilda Campbell

Vaughan, Jack 1949- [IBW]
American magician
* Goldfinger

Vaughan, John Walker 1925- [BEW]
American actor and director
* Vaughan, Stuart

Vaughan, Joseph Floyd 1912-1952 [AS, DGS, PB]
American baseball player
* Vaughan, Arky

Vaughan, Kate
See Candelin, Catherine

Vaughan, Lefty
See Vaughan, [Cecil] Porter

Vaughan, Leo
See Lendon, Kenneth Harry

Vaughan, Miss
See Pritchard, Hannah

Vaughan, Owen 20th c. [WGT]
Author
* Rhoscomyl, Owen

Vaughan, Pete
See Vaughan, Robert E.

Vaughan, Peter
See Ohm, Peter

Vaughan, [Cecil] Porter 1919- [BE]
American baseball player
* Vaughan, Lefty

Vaughan, Robert E. 20th c. [BBH]
American basketball coach
* Vaughan, Pete

Vaughan, Sarah [Lois] 1924- [EPM, PMJ]
American singer
* [The] Divine One
* [The] Divine Sarah
* Vaughan, Sassy

Vaughan, Sassy
See Vaughan, Sarah [Lois]

Vaughan, Sparky
See Vaughan, Glenn Edward

Vaughan, Stuart
See Vaughan, John Walker

Vaughan, Susie
See Candelin, Susan Mary Charlotte

Vaughan, Thomas 1622-1666 [DLE1, HPPN, NPS]
British poet and alchemist
* Anthroposophus
* Edwin
* Philalethes, Eugenius

Vaughan, Thomas 18th c. [NPS, SN]
Playwright
* Dangle
* [The] Dapper

Vaughan, Thomas 18th c. [PA]
Playwright
* Edwin

Vaughan, Yvonne 1949- [ECM, RO2]
American singer and songwriter
* Fargo, Donna

Vaughan Williams, Ralph
See Williams, Ralph

Vaughan Williams, Ursula 1911- [WD]
British author, poet, librettist
* Wood, Ursula

Vaughn, Ace
See Vaughn, Ralph Lincoln

Vaughn, Cora
See Oakley, Mrs. J. R.

Vaughn, Farmer
See Vaughn, Harry Francis

Vaughn, Frank
See James, Alexander Franklin

Vaughn, Fred[erick Thomas] 1918-1964 [BE]
American baseball player
* Vaughn, Muscles

Vaughn, Harry Francis 1864-1914 [BE, PB]
American baseball player
* Vaughn, Farmer

Vaughn, Hippo
See Vaughn, James Leslie

Vaughn, James Clayton, Jr. 1950?- [HPPN]
American murder suspect
* Bradley, William
* Cooper, James A.
* Franklin, Joseph Paul

Vaughn, James Leslie 1888-1966 [AS, DGS, PB]
American baseball player
* Vaughn, Hippo

Vaughn, Jap
See Vaughn, Tommy

Vaughn, Kate
See Kestin, Helen

Vaughn, Muscles
See Vaughn, Fred[erick Thomas]

Vaughn, Ralph Lincoln 1918- [BBH]
American basketball player
* Vaughn, Ace

Vaughn, Richard
See Thomas, Ernest Lewis

Vaughn, Theresa
See Mestayer, Mrs. W. A.

Vaughn, Tommy 20th c.
American football player
* Vaughn, Jap

Vaughn, Toni
See DuBreuil, Elizabeth Lorinda

Vaughn, Vivian 1902-1966 [SC]
American actress and singer
* Gould, Gypsy

Vaughn, William
See Von Brincken, Wilhelm

Vaulet, Clement 1876-? [WGT]
French author
* Vautel, Clement

[The] Vaulting Vicar
See Richards, Robert [Bob]

Vautel, Clement
See Vaulet, Clement

Vaux, C. Bowyer 19th c. [HPPN]
American author
* Dot

Vaux, Patrick 20th c. [WGT]
Author
* Navarchus [joint pseudonym with James Woods]

Vava
See Neto, Edvaldo

Vawter, J. B. 19th c. [HPPN]
American soldier and author
* Oats, Sergeant

Vawter, L. P. 1885- [NAA]
American artist and writer
* Capooch, Tony
* Doogin, Skinny
* Goode, Uncle Abner
* Leisure, Piddleton

Vayle, Valerie
See Brooks, Janice Young

[The] Vayn Pap-Hatchet
See Lyly, John

Vaysse, Charles 1910- [HPPN]
French author
* Fennell, Connie

Vaz, Gil
See Lenoir, Carlos

Vazak, P. H.
See Towne, Robert

Vazquez, Jose 19th c. [GS]
Spanish bullfighter
* Parreta

Veach, Peek-A-Boo
See Veach, William Walter

Veach, William Walter 1863-1937
American baseball player
* Veach, Peek-A-Boo

Veal, Coot
See Veal, Orville Inman

Veal, George 18th c. [HPPN]
British composer
* Collier, Joel
* Redivivus, Joel Collier

Veal, Mrs.
See Foe, Daniel

Veal, Orville Inman 1932- [BE]
American baseball player
* Veal, Coot

Veale, Thomas 1896?-1964 [BEW]
Theatrical performer
* Leslie, Tom

Veary, Arthur T. 1894-1975 [BEW, F2, FC]
British actor
* Treacher, Arthur

Veazie, Joseph [PA]
Author
* J. V. Z.

Veblen, Thorstein Bunde 1857-1929 [HPPN]
American social scientist and author
* [The] Opponent of Conspicuous Waste

Vecchi, Augustus Victor 1843-? [NPS]
Italian author
* Bolina, Jack la
* [The] Italian Marryat

[Il] Vecchio
See Amato, Giovanni Antonio d'

[Il] Vecchio [The Elder]
See Palma, Jacopo

Vecchio, Mary 20th c. [HPPN]
American prostitute
* [The] Hapless Hooker

Vecelli, Marco 1545-1616? [WBD]
Italian painter
* Marco di Tiziano

Vecelli [or Vecellio], Tiziano 1477-1576 [HPPN, WBD]
Italian painter
* [Da] Cadore
* [Il] Divino
* Titian

Vecelli, Tiziano 1579-? [WBD]
Italian painter
* [Il] Tizianello

Vedastus
See Webb, Foster

Vedder, Elihu 1836-1923 [HPPN]
American painter and illustrator
* [The] Pagan

Vedder, John K.
See Gruber, Frank

Vedette
See Boys, Thomas

Vedette
See Fitchett, William Henry

Vedette
See Hensman, Howard

Vedette
See Williams, [George] Valentine

Vee, Bobby
See Velline, Robert Thomas

Veeck, William Louis, Jr. [Bill] 1914- [HPPN]
American baseball team president
* [The] Bad Boy of Basebrawl
* [The] Happy Hustler
* Man With The Pink Hair
* [A] Midwestern Larry McPhail
* Rambling Wreck

[The] Veep
See Barkley, Alben William

Vega, Al
See Vagramian, Aram

Vega, David 20th c. [RO2]
American musician
* Vega, Dynamite

Vega, Dynamite
See Vega, David

Vega, Garcilasso de la 1503-1536 [HPPN]
Spanish poet
* [The] Petrarch of Spain
* [The] Prince of Spanish Poetry
* [The] Spanish Petrarch

Vega, [Señor] Juan de
See Cochrane, Charles

Vega, Lope de
See Vega Carpio, Lope Felix de

Vega, Luis 20th c. [TI 11-22-82]
American boxer
* [The] Bull

Vega, Memo
See Coruelio, Memo

Vega Carpio, Lope Felix de 1562-1635 [HN, HPPN, SN, WBD]
Spanish playwright and poet
* [The] Father of the Spanish Drama
* [El] Fenix de Espana
* [El] Licenciado Tome de Burguillos
* [The] Monster of Nature
* Padecopeo, Gabriel
* [The] Phoenix of Spain
* [The] Spanish Phoenix
* Vega, Lope de

Vega De Los Reyes, Rafael 1915- [HPPN]
Spanish bullfighter
* Gitanillo de Triana II

Vega De Los Reyes, Francisco 1903-1931 [GS]
Spanish bullfighter
* Gitanillo de Triana [Little Gypsy from Triana]

Vegetable, Dr.
See Ishizuka, Sagen

Vegg, Samuel 1827-1865 [BMH]
British comedian, singer, music hall manager
* Collins, Sam

Veheyne, Cherry
See Williamson, Ethel

Veiby, John 1860-? [BI]
American watchmaker
* Thorleif

Veidt, Conrad
See Weidt, Conrad

Veigelsberg, Hugo 1869-? [CD]
Hungarian critic, poet, publicist
* Ignotus

Veil, Bucky
See Veil, Frederick William

Veil, Frederick William 1881-1931 [BE]
American baseball player
* Veil, Bucky

[The] Veiled Murderess
See Robinson, Henrietta

[The] Veiled Prophet of Khorassan
See Hakim ben Allah

Veinshtein [or Weinstein], Garri Kimovich 1963- [NY 11-10-85, TI 11-18-85, WP 3-1-85]
Russian chess player
* [The] Boa Constrictor
* Kasparov, Garri Kimovich
* Kasparov, Gary

Veitch, Tom
See Padgett, Ron

Veits, Ulf
See Lindberg, Karl Sivert

Vejar, Chico
See Vejar, Francis

Vejar, Francis 20th c. [SG]
Boxer
* Vejar, Chico

Vel, Rob
See Velter, Robert

Velasco, Luis de 1500?-1564 [FFF]
Viceroy of Mexico
* [The] Father of New Spain

Velasquez, Loretta Janeta 1842-? [BDSA]
Cuban-born American heroine
* Buford, Harry T.

Velazco, Emil, Jr. 1924- [ITA]
American film executive
* Velazco, Robert E.

Velazco, Robert E.
See Velazco, Emil, Jr.

Velegra, Doris 1904- [F2]
Actress
* Revier, Dorothy

Veleriy, Ivan
See Tarsis, Valerii Iakovievich

Velez, Lupe
See Velez De Villalobos, Guadelupe

Velez, Otoniel 1950- [ALR]
Puerto Rican-born baseball player
* Velez, Otto

Velez, Otto
See Velez, Otoniel

Velez De Villalobos, Guadelupe 1909-1944 [CED, CU, IPA]
Mexican-born actress
* [The] Mexican Spitfire
* Velez, Lupe

Velikovsky, Immanuel 1895-1979 [AW, CA]
Russian-born author
* [The] Grand Old Man of the Fringe
* Ram, Immanuel

Velitchkova, Ljuba 1913- [BBD]
Bulgarian opera singer
* Welitsch, Ljuba

Vellejus, Andre Severin 1542-1616 [PA]
Author
* Soerensen

Velline, Robert Thomas 1943- [EPM, RO1]
American singer
* Vee, Bobby

Veloshkina, Irina 1925- [OP]
Russian opera singer
* Arkhipova, Irina

Velter, Robert 20th c. [WECO]
French cartoonist
* Vel, Rob

Veltman, Vera
See Panova, Vera [Federovna]

[The] Velvet Fog
See Torme, Mel[vin Howard]

[The] Velvet Frog
See Torme, Mel[vin Howard]

[The] Velvet Glove
See Ali, Zulfikar

[The] Velvet Glove
See Madison, Dorothy Payne Todd

[The] Velvet Hammer
See Spillane, Robert

[The] Velvet Steamroller
See Jacobs, Margaret

Vely, Emma
See Simon, Emma [Couvely]

Vemian, Alex Kirk 20th c. [WFA]
American jewelry designer
* Kirk, Alexis

Venable, Clark 1892- [SFL, WGT]
Author
* Clarke, Covington

Venable, Howard Phillip 1913- [BA]
American physician and author
* Drawoh, Phil

Venable, Lyn
See Venable, Marilyn

Venable, Marilyn 20th c. [SFP]
Author
* Venable, Lyn

Venables, Terry 20th c. [TCCM]
British author
* Yuill, P. B. [joint pseudonym with Gordon (Maclean) Williams]

Venafro, Mark
See Pizzat, Frank J[oseph]

Venance, Father
See Dongados, Jean Francois

Venard, [Brother]
See Gorman, Charles E.

Venator
See Elliott, William

Venatorini
See Myslivecek [or Mysliweczek], Josef

Vendome, Francois de 1616-1669 [DNNS, FFF, HN]
French officer and politician
* Beaufort, Duc de
* [The] King of the Markets
* [Le] Roi des Halles

Vendome, Philippe de 1655-1727 [WBD]
French army officer
* [Le] Prieur de Vendome

Vendrovskii, David Efimovich 1879-1971 [CA]
Russian author and translator
* Wendroff, Zalman
* Wendrowsky, Zalman

Vene-Cavanagh, Paul 1895- [THR]
British actor
* Cavanagh, Paul

Venerabilis, Doctor
See Bede [Baeda, or Beda]

Venerabilis, Doctor
See Hildebert

Venerabilis, Doctor
See Occam [or Ockham], William of

Venerabilis, Doctor
See Peter [or Pierre] of Cluny

Venerabilis Inceptor
See Occam [or Ockham], William of

[The] Venerable Bede
See Bede [Baeda, or Beda]

[The] Venerable Bede
See Eusebius of Caesarea

[The] Venerable Doctor
See Peter [or Pierre] of Cluny

[The] Venerable Doctor
See William of Champeaux

[The] Venerable Initiator
See Occam [or Ockham], William of

Veneralbilis, Doctor
See William of Champeaux

Venerandus, Doctor
See Gregory of Fonts

Veneris, James 1922-
American Korean War POW
* Wen

[The] Venetian
See Andrew III

[The] Venetian
See Stirling, James

[The] Venetian Addison
See Gozzi, Gaspare

Veneziano, Agostino
See De Musi, Agostino

Veneziano, Bonifazio
See Pitati, Bonifazio di

Venezis, Ilias
See Mellos, Ilias

[El] Venezolano [The Man from
Venezuela]
See Gonzalez, Pedro

Veni Vidi
See Croly, Jane Cunningham

Veniaminov, Ivan Evsieevich Popov
1797-1879 [BI]
Russian religious leader
* Innokentii

Venison, Alfred
See Pound, Ezra [Loomis]

Venkateswaran, Taruvai
Anantaramaseshan 1953- [IAW]
Indian poet
* Ramanan

Venn, Mary Eleanor 1908- [BI, HPPN]
American author
* Adrian, Mary

Venn, Topsy
See Cornell, Mrs. E. J.

Venner, Arthur
See Griswold, William McCrillis

Venner, J. G.
See Lewis, John Noel Claude

Vennew, Norman R.
See Wade, George Alfred

Venning, Corey 1924- [CA]
American author
* Hyde, Tracy Elliot

Venning, Hugh
See Van Zeller, Claud

Venning, John [HN]
* [The] Howard of Russia

Venning, Michael
See Randolph, Georgiana Ann

Venning, Normandy
See Shepheard-Walwyn, Hugh Wallwyn

Venn's Principal Fireman at Windsor
See Love, Christopher

Veno, Joseph Arthur 1891-1955 [BI]
American educator
* Adelphus Joseph, [Brother]

[The] Venomous Preacher
See Traill, Robert

Venora, Elena Sinaguglia 1932- [BEW]
American singer and actress
* Venora, Lee

Venora, Lee
See Venora, Elena Sinaguglia

Vento, Giuseppe Antonio
See Vizzini, Sal[vatore]

Vento, Joseph Angelo
See Vizzini, Sal[vatore]

Vento, Vincent M.
See Vizzini, Sal[vatore]

Ventura, Charlie
See Venturo, Charles

Ventura, Jeffrey
See Feinman, Jeffrey

Ventura, Lino
See Borrini, Angelo

Venturi, Denise Scott Brown
See Brown, Denise Scott

Venturi, Robert 1925?-
American architect
* [The] Guru of Chaos

Venturo, Betty Lou Baker 1928- [CA]
American author
* Baker, Betty

Venturo, Charles 1916- [EJ, PMJ, WWJ]
American jazz musician
* Ventura, Charlie

[The] Venus in Hollywood
See Bergman, Ingrid

Venus in Hollywood
See Dietrich, Marie Magdalene

Venuta, Benay
See Crooke, Venuta Rose

Venuti, Giuseppe 1904- [EJ]
American jazz musician
* Venuti, Joe

Venuti, Joe
See Venuti, Giuseppe

Vequin, Capini
See Quinn, Elisabeth

Vera
See Bottomley, Kate Madeline [Barry]

Vera
See Campbell, Lady Colin

Vera
See Dempster, C. L. H.

Vera
See Neumann, Vera

Vera, Billy
See McCord, William, Jr.

Vera, Carlos 1920- [HPPN]
Maxican bullfighter
* Canitas

Vera Ellen
See Rohe, Vera-Ellen Westmeyr

Verain, Leland
See Alterie, Leland Verain

Verax
See Alexander, Samuel

Verax
See Blakey, Robert

Verax
See Dunckley, Henry

Verax
See Forster, Thomas

Verax
See Godwin, William

Verax
See Warton, Thomas

Verban, Dutch
See Verban, Emil Matthew

Verban, Emil Matthew 1915- [BE, PB]
American baseball player
* [The] Antelope
* Verban, Dutch

Verbeck, Blanche Avicestill Harriman
1890- [NAA]
American author
* Harriman, Blanche Avicestill

Verble, Gene Kermit 1928- [BE]
American baseball player
* Verble, Satchel

Verble, Satchel
See Verble, Gene Kermit

Verborum, Architectus
See Bowyer, William

Vercors [code name used during World
War II]
See Bruller, Jean Marcel

Vercors
See Connolly, Cyril [Vernon]

Verd
See Verdier, Ed

Verdad
See Millen, F. F.

Verde, Lurline Monte
See Siddons, Belle

Verdel, Al[bert Alfred] 1921- [BE]
American baseball player
* Verdel, Stumpy

Verdel, Stumpy
See Verdel, Al[bert Alfred]

Verdello, Cordrac
See Harris, Richard

Verdery, Emily
See Battay, Emily Verdery

Verdi, Giuseppe 1813-1901 [SN]
Italian composer
* [The] Euripides of Italian Opera

Verdier, Ed 20th c. [WECO]
American cartoonist
* Verd

Verdon, Dorothy
See Tralins, S[andor] Robert [Bob]

Verdon, Gwen
See Verdon, Gwyneth Evelyn

Verdon, Gwyneth Evelyn 1926- [AM, BEW, EMT]
American actress, dancer, singer
* Verdon, Gwen
* [The] World's Fastest Tapper

Verdon, T. K.
See Verdon, Thomas Kirwan

Verdon, Thomas Kirwan 19th c. [PI]
Irish poet
* De Verdon, T. K.
* Verdon, T. K.

Verdu, Matilde
See Cela, Camilo Jose

Verdugo, Rene Martin 20th c. [TI 3-17-86]
Reputed Mexican drug smuggler
* [La] Rana [The Frog]

Verdy, Violette
See Guillerm, Nelly

Vere, Margaret
See Long, Gabrielle Margaret Vere [Campbell]

Verelart, Myndart
See Saltus, Edgar Evertson

Verelius, Olaus
See Werl, Olaf

Veren, Gilbert
See Keveren, A. G.

Verena, Sophie
See Alberti, Sophie [Moedinger]

Veresaev, Vikenti
See Smidovich, Vikenti Vikentievich

Verett, E.
See Evans, E. Everett

Verett, H. E. [joint pseudonym with Thelma D. Hamm Evans]
See Evans, E. Everett

Verett, H. E. [joint pseudonym with E. Everett Evans]
See Evans, Thelma D. Hamm

Verey, [Rev.] C.
See Crowley, Edward Alexander

Verga, Giovanni 1840-1922 [CA]
Italian author and playwright
* [The] Father of the Modern Realist Novel

Verghese, Thadikkal Paul 1922- [IAW]
Indian clergyman and author
* Gregorios, Paulos Mar

Vergil, Polydore 1475?-1555 [HPPN]
Italian-British historian and clergyman
* De Castello

Vergilius Maro, Publius 1st c. BC [DEP, FFF, NPS, SN]
Roman poet
* [The] Great Shepherd of the Mantuan Plains
* [The] Mantuan Bard
* [The] Mantuan Muse
* [The] Mantuan Swan
* [The] Prince of Poets
* [The] Prince of Roman Poets
* [The] Swan of Mantua
* Virgil [or Vergil]

Verginie, Jean Dimitre 1904-1970 [WFA]
French fashion designer
* Desses, Jean

Vergniaud, Pierre Victurnien 1753-1793 [HN]
French politician
* [The] Mirabeau of the Gironde

Vergoz, M. ?-1929 [HPPN]
American singer
* Staing

Verhagen, Jean 1924- [FC, ITA]
American actress
* Hagen, Jean

Verhoeff, Nico
See Verhoeff, Nicolaas Theodorus

Verhoeff, Nicolaas Theodorus 1904- [IWM]
Dutch musician
* Verhoeff, Nico

Verhuel
See Bonaparte, Charles Louis Napoleon

Veridicus
See Whitworth, Richard

Verin, Velko
See Inkiow, [Janakiev] Dimiter

Verion, Andre [BI]
Austrian art dealer and painter
* Verkauf, Willy

Verissimo, Jose
See Matos, Jose Verissimo Dias De

Verissimus
See Annius Verus, Marcus

Veritas
See Close, John

Veritas
See Hayward, Abraham

Veritas
See Walker, E. C.

Verite, Auguste
See Fournier, Jules

Verite sans Peur
See Prouting, Frederick James

Verkauf, Willy
See Verion, Andre

Verkhovynetz, M.
See Fedorovich, Nicholas

Verkuyl, Gerrit 1872-? [NAA]
Dutch-born clergyman and author
* Streefkerf, Hendrick

Verlaine, Paul [Marie] 1844-1896 [NLC]
French poet and author
* De Herlagnez, Pablo
* [The] Deplorable Verlaine

Verlanger, Julia
See Taieb, Heliane

Verle, Emy [FFF]
Entertainer
* Fursch-Madi, Mme.

Verlezza, Joseph 20th c. [TI 9-13-82]
American underworld figure
* Hooks, Joe

Verlooghen, Corly
See Van Bedacht, Rudy

Vermeer, Jan 1632-1675 [WBD]
Dutch painter
* Van der Meer van Delft, Jan

Vermeule, Cornelius Clarkson, III 1925- [CA]
Irish-born educator and author
* Tsukinabe, Isao

Vermigli, Pietro Martire 1500-1562 [HPPN]
Italian religious reformer
* Martyr, Peter

Vermilye, Kate 20th c. [ALY]
Irish-born author
* Jordan, Kate

Vermouth, Apollo C.
See McCartney, Paul

Vermretus
See Vernerey, Jean

Vern, David 1924- [ESF, SFL, WGT]
American author
* Blade, Alexander [house pseudonym, Ziff-Davis]
* Ellis, Craig [house pseudonym]
* Horn, Peter [house pseudonym, Ziff-Davis]
* Reed, David V.
* Woodruff, Clyde

Vernard, George
See Musica, Arthur

Verne, Adela
See Wurm, Adela

Verne, Alice
See Wurm, Alice

Verne, Hibbert
See Frazer-Hurst, Douglas

Verne, Jules 1828-1905 [HPPN]
French author
* [The] Father of Science Fiction

Verne, Jules
See Olchewitz, M.

Verne, Jules
See Olehewitz, L. M.

Verne, Karen
See Klinckerfuss, Ingabor Katrine

Verne, Mathilde
See Wurm, Mathilde

Verner, David 1894- [BS]
Canadian-born magician
* [The] Professor
* Vernon, Dai

Verner, Gerald
See Stuart, Donald

Vernerey, Jean [PA]
Author
* Vermretus

Vernet, Antoine Charles Horace
1758-1836 [WEC]
French caricaturist and painter
* Vernet, Carle

Vernet, Carle
See Vernet, Antoine Charles Horace

Vernet, Emile Jean Horace 1789-1863
[HPPN]
French painter
* Horace

Verneuil, Louis
See Collin Du Bocage, Louis Jacques
Marie

Verney, Sarah
See Holloway, Brenda W[ilmar]

Vernieres, Francois
See Baudovy, Michel-Aime

Vernon, Ada
See Dickinson, Susan E.

Vernon, Anne
See Vignaud, Edith Antoinette
Alexandrine

Vernon, Bill
See Slaughter, Marion T.

Vernon, Charles [or Charlie]
See Craven, Braxton

Vernon, Claire
See Breton-Smith, Clare

Vernon, Dai
See Verner, David

Vernon, Dorothy 1875-1970 [SC]
German-born actress
* Baird, Dorothy
* Burns, Dorothy

Vernon, Eddie
See Stone, Hoyt E[dward]

Vernon, Edward 1684-1757 [DEP, HN,
HPPN, SN]
British naval officer
* [A] Certain Eminent British Sailor
* Old Grog

Vernon, Edward 1757-1847 [WBD]
British prelate
* Harcourt, Edward

Vernon, Edward
See Coleman, Vernon

Vernon, Fanny
See Sinclair, Mrs. Harry

Vernon, Frank
See Vernon-Humphrey, Frank

Vernon, [Sir] George 16th c. [HN]
British jurist
* [The] King of the Peak

Vernon, George S[hirra] G[ibb] 1885-
[WGT]
Author
* George, Vernon

Vernon, Hardy
See Vernon, Marlborough

Vernon, Ida
See McGowan, Bridget

Vernon, James Barton 1918- [DGS, PB,
SMG]
American baseball player and coach
* Vernon, Mickey

Vernon, Judge
See Tuttle, E. C.

Vernon, Lee M.
See Von Block, Bela

Vernon, Marlborough 1859-1946 [HPPN]
American actor
* Vernon, Hardy

Vernon, Max
See Kellogg, Vernon Lyman

Vernon, Mickey
See Vernon, James Barton

Vernon, Olivia
See Bronte, Anne

Vernon, Peter
See Huddleston, Sisley

Vernon, Richard 1726-1800 [WBD]
British sportsman
* [The] Father of the Turf

Vernon, Rose
See Brant, Mrs. Luke

Vernon, Ruth
See Ram, Stopford James

Vernon, V.
See Hersey, Harold

Vernon-Humphrey, Frank 1875-1940
[THR]
British actor and producer
* Vernon, Frank

Vernor, D.
See Casewit, Curtis

Veron, Docteur
See Veron, Louis Desire

Veron, Louis Desire 1798-1867 [WBD]
French journalist
* Veron, Docteur

Veronese, Bonifazio
See Pitati, Bonifazio di

[The] Veronese of France
See Delacroix, Ferdinand Victor Eugene

Veronese, Paolo
See Cagliari [or Caliari?], Paolo

Verpilleux, A. E.
See Verpilleux, Emile Antoine

Verpilleux, Emile Antoine 1888-1964
[DBA]
British painter, engraver, illustrator
* Verpilleux, A. E.

VerPlanck, Billy
See VerPlanck, John Fenno

Verplanck, Gulian Crommalin 1786-1870
[PA]
Author
* Coody, Abimelech
* Herbert, Francis

VerPlanck, John Fenno 1930- [ASC, EJ]
American jazz musician
* VerPlanck, Billy

Verral, Charles Spain 1904- [CAP, SAT,
WD]
Canadian-born author
* Eaton, George L.

Verrall, A. W.
See Verrall, Arthur Woollgar

Verrall, Arthur Woollgar 1851-1912
[LC]
British educator and author
* Verrall, A. W.

Verrazano, Giovanni Da 1485?-1527
[HPPN]
Italian explorer
* [The] Explorer of the Atlantic Coast

Verret, Cajun
See Verret, Irving

Verret, Irving 1906?- [NOJ]
American jazz musician
* Verret, Cajun

Verrill, A[lpheus] Hyatt 1871-1954
[ESF, SFL, WGT]
American naturalist, explorer, author
* Ainsbury, Ray

Verrill, Virginia
See McLean, Virginia Katherine

Verrocchio [or Verocchio], Andrea del
See Di Michele Cione, Andrea

Verrocosus, Quintus Fabius Maximus
3rd c. BC [HPPN]
Roman army officer
* Cunctator [The Delayer]
* [The] Shield of Rome

Versace, Marie Teresa Rios 1917- [CA]
American author
* Rios, Tere

Versalles, Zoilo Casanova 1940- [BE,
HPPN, PB]
Cuban-born baseball player
* [The] Kid from Cuba
* Versalles, Zorro

Versalles, Zorro
See Versalles, Zoilo Casanova

Versatile, Val
See Enton, Harry

Verschaffelt, Pierre Antoine 1710-1793 [WBD]
Flemish sculptor
* Fiammingo, Pietro

Verschoyle, Winifred Mabel Letts 1882-? [HPPN]
British poet and author
* Letts, W. M.

[A] Versemaker
See Tugwell, [Rev.] George

Versois, Odile
See De Poliakoff-Baidaroff, Militza

Vert Gallant [Devoted Admirer]
See Henry IV [or Henri]

Vertot, Abbe de
See Aubert, Rene

Vertov, Dziga
See Kaufman, Denis Arkadievitch

Vertue, George 1684-1756 [SN]
British engraver and antiquary
* [The] Old Mortality of Pictures

Verus
See Brekell, [Rev.] John

Verus
See Brown, Robert

Verus
See Taylor, John

Verus
See Webb, Francis

Verus, Lucius Aurelius
See Commodus, Lucius Ceionius

Veruschka
See Lehndorff, Vera

Veruschka
See Von Lehndorff, Vera

Verval, Alain [joint pseudonym with Lawrence Montague Lande]
See Greenwood, Thomas

Verval, Alain [joint pseudonym with Thomas Greenwood]
See Lande, Lawrence Montague

Verwer, Hans
See Verwer, Johanna Elisabeth

Verwer, Johanna Elisabeth 1911- [AW]
Dutch critic, editor, author
* Johanson, Elisabeth
* Verwer, Hans

Verwey, Hans 1648-1692 [PA]
Author
* Pharboeus

Verwilghen, A[lbert-] Felix 1916- [CA]
British-born clergyman and author
* Yanagimura, Shimpu

[The] Very Baggage of New Writers
See Nash [or Nashe?], Thomas

Very, Jones 1813-1880 [HPPN]
American poet and author
* Emerson's Brave Saint
* J. V.

Very, Lydia Louisa Ann 19th c. [HPPN]
American poet
* L. L. A. V.

[A] Very Moderate Person, etc.
See Astell, Mary

Very, Washington 1815-1853 [HPPN]
American poet
* V. W.

Vesalius, Andreas 1514-1564 [HPPN]
Belgian anatomist
* [The] Father of Modern Anatomy

Vescia, George Milo 1909- [ITA]
American film set decorator
* Milo, George

Vesco, Robert Lee 1936- [HPPN]
American financier
* [The] Bootstrap Kid
* [The] Fugitive Financier

Veselitskaia, Lydiia Ivanovna 1857-? [BI]
Russian author
* Mikulich, V.

Vesenyi, Paul E. 1911- [CA]
Hungarian-born librarian and author
* Bod, Peter

Vesey, Denmark 1767?-1822 [HPPN]
American insurrectionist
* Vesey, Telemaque

Vesey, Paul
See Allen, Samuel [Washington]

Vesey, Telemaque
See Vesey, Denmark

Vespasian, Titus Flavius Sabinus 9-79 [HN, RH]
Roman emperor
* [The] Darling of Mankind
* Thaumaturgus

Vespasianus, Titus Flavius Salinus 40?-81 [HPPN]
Roman emperor
* Delight of Mankind
* Titus

Vespucci, Simonetta Catteneo 1459-1479? [HPPN]
Italian model
* Simonetta

Vesque von Puettlingen, Johann 1803-1883 [WBD]
Austrian composer
* Hoven, J.

Vessels, Billy W. 1931- [FB]
American football player
* Vessels, Curly

Vessels, Curly
See Vessels, Billy W.

Vestal, Herman Beeson 20th c. [SFP]
Author
* Beeson
* S. A. M.

Vestal, Madame
See Siddons, Belle

Vestal, Stanley 1887-1957 [TC, WW]
American author
* Campbell, Walter Stanley

Vestergard, Luther 1902-1968 [SC]
American actor
* Power, Paul

Vestey, [Lord] Samuel 1941?- [TI 9-26-83]
British aristocrat
* Vestey, Spam

Vestey, Spam
See Vestey, [Lord] Samuel

Vestris, Eliza Lucy 1797-1856 [NPS]
Actress
* [The] Tenth Muse

Vestris, Gaetano Apollino Balthazar 1729-1808 [DNNS, FFF, RH]
Italian dancer
* [The] God of Dancing
* [The] King of Dance

Vestris, Madame
See Bartolozzi, Lucia Elizabeth

Vestris, Madame
See Mathews, Lucia Elizabeth

Vestris, Mons., Sen.
See Nott, John

Vestvali, Felicita 1839-? [SN]
Opera singer
* [The] Magnificent Vestvali

Vet, T. V.
See Straiton, Edward Cornock

[A] Veteran
See Bunbury, Thomas

Veteran Observer
See Mansfield, Edward Deering

Veteran Sportsman
See Taplin, William

[A] Veteran Stager
See Grant, G.

[A] Veteran Traveller
See Wilson, William Rae

[The] Veteran's Friend
See Forbes, Charles R.

[The] Veterans' Nemesis
See Hoover, Herbert Clark

Veto
See Sedgwick, Theodore, Sr.

[The] Veto Governor
See Cleveland, [Stephen] Grover

[The] Veto Governor
See Winston, John Anthony

Veto, Madame
See [Josephe Jeanne] Marie Antoinette

[The] **Veto Mayor**
See Cleveland, [Stephen] Grover

Veto, Monsieur
See Louis XVI

[The] **Veto President**
See Cleveland, [Stephen] Grover

[The] **Veto President**
See Johnson, Andrew

Vetoyanis, Theodore 1908?-1984
American wrestler
* [The] Weeping Greek from Cripple
  Creek
* Zaharias, George

Vetri, Victoria 1944- [FC]
Australian actress
* Dorian, Angela

Vetsch, Jakob 20th c. [WGT]
Author
* Mundus, Jakob

**Vettergrund, Josephina Vilhelmina
Lundberg** 1830-? [HPPN]
Swedish author
* Lea

Vetus
See Sterling, Edward

Veuster, Joseph Damien de 1840-1889
[HPPN]
Belgian missionary
* Father Damien
* Kamiano, Father
* [The] Leper Priest

Vevay, Paul
See Round, William Marshall Fitz

Vexatus
See Blair-Fish, Wallace Wilfrid

Vexillum
See Banner, Hubert Stewart

Vey, Elinor
See Glover, Mrs. Eliot

Vezelay, Edith
See Davis, Edith Vezolles

Vezhinov, Pavel
See Gougov, Nikola Delchev

Vezina, Georges 1888?-1926 [BBH, SR]
Canadian-born hockey player
* [The] Chicoutimi Cucumber

Viadana, Lodovico
See Grossi, Lodovico

Vial, Gion
See Deplazes, Gion

Vialio, G.
See Simenon, Georges [Joseph
Christian]

Vialis, Gaston
See Simenon, Georges [Joseph
Christian]

Vian, Boris 1920-1959 [BI, TLC]
French author
* Ravi, Bison
* Schmuerz, Adolph
* Sullivan, Vernon
* Visi, Baron

Vian of the Cossack
See Vian, [Sir] Philip Louis

Vian, [Sir] Philip Louis 1894-1968
[HPPN]
British naval officer
* Vian of the Cossack

Viana, Nicholas 20th c. [BLB]
American underworld figure
* [The] Choir Boy

Vianney, Jean Baptiste Marie 1786-1859
[WBD]
Saint
* [The] Cure of Ars

Viard, Felix 1882-1967 [CW]
Haitian author
* Saint Robert

Viard, Henri Louis Luc 1921- [SFL,
WGT]
French author
* Ward, Henry

Viator
See Bright, Jonathan Huntington

Viator
See Forbes, Henry

Viator
See Hickey, Michael Patrick

Viator
See Smith, Nathan Ryno

Viator
See Taylor, Benjamin Ogle

Viator
See Varnum, Joseph Bradley

Viator, A.
See Aufrere, Anthony

Viator, John, Esq.
See Peters, Samuel Andrew

Viator, Scotus
See Seton-Watson, Robert William

Viator, Vacuus
See Hughes, Thomas

Viau, Lee
See Viau, Leon

Viau, Leon 1866-1947 [BE]
American baseball player
* Viau, Lee

Viau, Theophile de 1590-1626 [HPPN,
SN]
French poet
* [The] Coryphaeus of His Day
* [The] Creator of Burlesque Poetry in
  France
* Theophile

Viaud, [Dr.] Andre
See Auriol, Vincent

Viaud, Julien 1850?- [NW 1-2-84]
French author
* Loti, Pierre

Viaud, Louis Marie Julien 1850-1923
[CD, EWL, LC]
French author
* Loti, Pierre

Vic
See Forsythe, Clyde

Vic the Stick
See Correll, Victor Crosby

[The] **Vicar**
See Garrett, [Rev.] John

[A] **Vicar**
See Godson, [Rev.] John

[The] **Vicar**
See Haig, Alexander Meigs, Jr.

[The] **Vicar**
See Tremenheere, [Rev.] William

Vicar, Henry
See Felsen, Henry Gregor

Vicar of Bray
See Alleyn, Simon

[The] **Vicar of Cheshunt**
See Chapman, [Rev.] Richard

Vicar of Cudham
See Ayscough, Samuel

[The] **Vicar of Frome-Selwood**
See Bennett, William James

[The] **Vicar of Harewood**
See Hale, [Rev.] Richard

[The] **Vicar of Hell**
See Borde, Andrew

[The] **Vicar of Hell**
See Bryan, [Sir] Francis

[The] **Vicar of Hell**
See Cromwell, Thomas [Earl of Essex]

[The] **Vicar of Hell**
See Skelton, John

[The] **Vicar of Hell**
See Wolsey, Thomas

[The] **Vicar of Islington**
See Wilson, [Rev.] Daniel

Vicar of Lilliput
See Robertson, [Rev.] Joseph

[The] **Vicar of Penley**
See Foulger, [Rev.] Robert William

Vicar of Visuals
See Deaver, Michael

[The] **Vicar of Wakefield**
See Wilson, Benjamin

Vicarion, [Count] Palmiro
See Logue, Christopher

Vicarius Cantianus
See Pegge, Samuel

Vicars, Henry Edward 1888-1942 [CEC]
British criminal
* Flannelfoot
* Williams, Henry

Vicary, Dorothy
See Rice, Dorothy Mary

Vice Emperor
See Rouher, Eugene

Vice God
See Borghese, Camillo

Vice Pres Quinichette
See Quinichette, Paul

Vicente, Gil 1480?-1557? [HN, HPPN]
Portuguese playwright
* [The] Father of Portuguese Drama
* [The] Portuguese Plautus

Vicenza, Mr.
See Valestra, John

[The] Viceroy
See Churchill, Sarah Jennings

Vichard, Cesar 1639-1692 [FFF, HN, RH]
French historian
* Saint Real, Abbe de
* [The] Sallust of France

Vicious, Sid
See Ritchie, John Simon

Vick, Ernie
See Vick, Henry

Vick, Henry 20th c.
American football player
* Vick, Ernie

Vick, William A. ?-1919 [HPPN]
American vaudeville performer
* Morris, Billy

Vicker, Angus
See Felsen, Henry Gregor

Vickers
See Kaufman, Wallace

Vickers, Antoinette L. 1942- [CA]
American author and attorney
* Franchi, Eda
* Nina V.

Vickers, Harry Porter 1878-1958 [BE]
American baseball player
* Vickers, Rube

Vickers, John 19th c. [WGT]
Author
* Morata, Jaido

Vickers, Martha
See MacVicar, Martha

Vickers, Mattie
See Rogers, Mrs. Charles S.

Vickers, Roger Spencer
See Cohen, Paul Arthur

Vickers, Roy 1899-1965 [AW, EMD, WW]
British author
* Durham, David

Vickers, Roy (cont.)
* Kyle, Sefton
* Spencer, John

Vickers, Rube
See Vickers, Harry Porter

Vickers, Sarge
See Vickers, Stephen James

Vickers, Steady Steve
See Vickers, Stephen James

Vickers, Stephen James 1951- [SMG]
Canadian-born hockey player
* Vickers, Sarge
* Vickers, Steady Steve

Vicky
See Weisz, Victor

Vickybird
See Neuburg, Victor [Benjamin]

Vico, George Steve 1923- [BE]
American baseball player
* Vico, Sam

Vico, Sam
See Vico, George Steve

[A] Victim
See Benham, George Chittenden

[The] Victim of Instability
See Faithfull, Starr

Victoire [code name used during World War II]
See Carre, Mathilde [Belard]

Victor, Alexander F. 1879-1961 [HPPN]
American inventor
* [The] Master of His Master's Voice
* Victor, R. C. A.

Victor Amadeus II 1666-1732 [SN]
King of Sardinia
* [A] Genius
* Ned the Chimney-Sweeper

Victor, Charles B.
See Puechner, Ray

Victor [or Victor-Perrin], Claude
See Perrin, Claude Victor [Duc de Bellune]

Victor Emmanuel II 1820-1878 [DEP, HN, HPPN, SN]
King of Italy
* [The] Gallant King
* Guaff
* [The] Hero of Palestro
* [The] Honest King
* Honest Man King
* Re Galantuomo

Victor, Frances Fuller Barritt 1826-1902 [HPPN]
American author, editor, poet
* Barritt, Frances
* Dorothy D.
* Fane, Florence
* Fuller, Frances

[The] Victor Hugo of Painting
See Delacroix, Ferdinand Victor Eugene

Victor, Joan Berg 1937- [ICB]
American author and illustrator
* Berg, Joan

Victor, Josephine
See Guenczler, Josephine

Victor, Lucia
See Baker, Lucia Adelaide Victor

Victor, Metta Victoria Fuller 1831-1886 [FFF]
American author and poet
* Cushman, Corinne
* Edwards, Eleanor Lee
* Gray, Walter T.
* Kennedy, Rose
* Legrand, Louis, M.D.? [joint pseudonym with Orville J. Victor]
* Peabody, Mrs. Mark
* Regester, Seeley
* [The] Singing Sibyl

[The] Victor of a Hundred Battles
See Bonaparte, Napoleon

Victor, Orville J. 1827-1910
American author, historian, editor
* Legrand, Louis, M.D.? [joint pseudonym with Metta Victoria Fuller Victor]

Victor, R. C. A.
See Victor, Alexander F.

Victor, Sam
See Hershman, Morris

Victor, Verity
See Wright, E. M.

Victor II
See Gebhard

Victor III
See Dauferius

Victor IV
See Conti, Gregorio

Victor IV
See Octavius

Victoria [or Victorina] 3rd c. [DNNF, FFF]
Mother of Victorinus, one of the Thirty Tyrants of Rome
* [The] Mother of the Camps

Victoria 1819-1901 [DEP, DNNS, HN, NPS]
Queen of England
* Empress of India
* [The] Little Queen
* [The] Mirror of Justice
* [The] Mother of Her Country
* Wetter, Mrs.
* [The] Widow
* [The] Widow of Windsor

Victoria [Secret Service code name]
See Johnson, Claudia Alta [Taylor]

Victoria, Guadalupe
See Fernandez, Manuel Felix

Victoria, [Sister] M.
See Danforth, Ethel M.

Victoria, Tomas 16th c.   [FFF]
Spanish missionary to Guatemala
* [The] Elias of Guatemala

Victoria, Vesta
See Lawrence, Vesta

Victoria, Vesta
See Terry, Victoria Lawrence

[The] Victorian Cinderella
See Stowe, Harriet Beecher

Victorian Stage Pulpiteer
See Shaw, George Bernard

[The] Victorious
See Abu Jafar

[The] Victorious
See Charles VII

[The] Victorious
See Frederick I

[The] Victorious
See Joseph I

[The] Victorious
See Khosru II [or Chosroes]

[The] Victorious
See Ladislaus [or Lancelot]

[The] Victorious
See Osman I [or Othman]

[The] Victorious
See Waldemar II

Victory's Darling Child
See Massena, Andre

Vid Kid
See Stovall, Rawson

Vida, Marco Girolamo 1480?-1566
[DEP, DNNS, HPPN, SN]
Italian poet
* [The] Christian Virgil
* [The] Parthenope of Naples
* Vida, Marcus Hieronymous
* Virgilius Redivivus

Vida, Marcus Hieronymous
See Vida, Marco Girolamo

Vidacovich, Irving J. 1904-1966   [ASC,
SC, WWJ]
American jazz musician
* Cajun Pete
* Vidacovich, Pinky

Vidacovich, Pinky
See Vidacovich, Irving J.

Vidal, Eugene Luther, Jr. 1925-   [CA,
CC, EMD, HPPN]
American author
* Box, Edgar
* Hargrave, Leoni?
* [The] Masked Marvel of Modern
  Letters
* Vidal, Gore

Vidal, Gore
See Vidal, Eugene Luther, Jr.

Vidal, Jose Nicolas 1940-   [BE]
Dominican-born baseball player
* Vidal, Papito

Vidal, Papito
See Vidal, Jose Nicolas

Vidali, Vittorio
See Contreras, Carlos

Videla, Jorge Rafael 20th c.
Argentinian military leader
* [El] Hueso [The Bone]

Videlbias, Johannes
See Collin, Jacques Albin Simon

Video
See Couch, Jonathan

Video, Captain
See Wollman, Rodney

Vidette
See Doyle, Jefferson E. P.

Vidette
See Elliott, J. J.

Vidi
See Conant, William C.

Vidocq
See Hawkins, Charles Ashton

Vidocq, Eugene Francois 1775-1857
[HPPN]
French criminal and spy
* [The] Detective

Vidor, Florence
See Arto, Florence

Vieira da Cunha, Antonio Belisario
1896-1956 [WEC]
Brazilian cartoonist
* Belisario

[El] Viejo
See Herrera, Francisco de

[El] Viejo [The Old One]
See Peron, Juan Domingo

[El] Viejo [The Old One]
See Shoemaker, William [Willie]

Viela, Paul
See DeLucia, Felice

Viele, Egbert Ludovicus 1863-1937   [TC,
WBD]
American-born French poet
* Viele-Griffin, Francis

Viele-Griffin, Francis
See Viele, Egbert Ludovicus

Vien, Charles   [PA]
Author
* Hall, Robert

[The] Viennese Teardrop
See Rainer, Luise

Viera Romera, Teresa de Jesus   [BI]
Mexican dancer
* Teresa

Viereck, G. S.
See Viereck, George Sylvester

Viereck, George Sylvester 1884-1962
[HFF, NAA]
German author
* Corners, George F.
* Viereck, G. S.

Vies, Jen 1868-1949   [SC]
French actor
* Sinoel

Vieschouwer, Johann 1520-1562   [PA]
Author
* Carnarius

Viespi, Alexander 1931?-   [FC, HT, SW]
American actor
* Cord, Alex

Viete [or Vieta], Francois 1540-1603
[WBD]
French mathematician
* [The] Father of Algebra

Vieth Von Golssenau, Arnold Friedrich
1889-1979   [CD, HDM, TC]
German author
* Renn, Ludwig

[The] Vietnam Turncoat
See Garwood, Robert R.

Viett, George Frederic 1868-?   [NAA]
French-born poet and playwright
* Everett, Gifo G.
* Wegg De Norva, Silas

Vietta, Egon
See Fritz, Egon

Vieu, M.   [HN]
Author
* Halt, Robert

[Le] Vieux
See Aubert, Jacques

Vieux Bois, M.
See Toepffer, Rodolphe

[Un] vieux garcon
See Cynosuridis, Alphonse

Vieux, Marie 1917-1975   [CW]
Haitian author and playwright
* Colibri

Vieux Moustache
See Gordon, Clarence

Vieux Renard
See Soult, Nicolas Jean de Dieu

Vig
See McCarthy, Denis Florence

Vigan, Luc
See Ruellan, Andre

Vigara, Rafael Martin 1931-1958
[HPPN]
Spanish bullfighter
* [El] Zorro

Vigil, Lawrence
See Finnin, [Olive] Mary

Vigilans
See Le Grice, Charles Valentine

Vigilans
See Partridge, Eric Honeywood

Vigilans
See Rice, Brian K.

Vigilans sed Aequus
See Arnold, William Thomas

Vigilant
See Barker, Stanley

Vigilant
See Corlett, John

Vigilant
See Dixon, Sydenham

Vigilant
See Mitchell, R. C.

Vigilant
See Vosburg, F. W.

Vigilant Dove
See Kissinger, Henry Alfred

Vigiola Del Torco, Serafin 1889-1958
[GS]
Spanish bullfighter
* Torquito [Little Torco]

Vigliante, Mary
See Szydlowski, Mary Vigliante

Vigliotto, Giovanni
See Jipp, Fred

Vignaud, Edith Antoinette Alexandrine
1925- [FC, ITA, WEF]
French actress
* Vernon, Anne

Vigne d'Octon
See Vigne, Paul

Vigne, John 1885?- [NOJ]
American jazz musician
* Vigne, Ratty

Vigne, Paul 1859-1943 [WBD]
French author and politician
* Kerhouel, Gaetan
* Vigne d'Octon

Vigne, Ratty
See Vigne, John

Vignes, Jacques 1929?- [BI]
French cartoonist
* Elie

Vignola, Giacomo da
See Barocchio [or Barozzi], Giacomo

Vignoles, Etienne 1387-1442 [HN]
French general
* [La] Hire [The Growler]

Vignon, Claude
See Bouvier, Mme.

Vigo, Francis
See Vigo, Joseph Maria Francesco

Vigo, Jean
See Almereyda, Jean

Vigo, Joseph Maria Francesco
1747-1836 [WBD]
Italian-born fur trader and pioneer in America
* Vigo, Francis

[The] Vigo Voyeur
See Williams, Allen H.

Vigors, N. A., Jun.
See Nolan, Frederick

Viguers, Ruth Hill 1903-1971 [CA, CAP, SAT]
American editor and critic
* Hill, Ruth A.

Viking, Erl
See Martley, John

[The] Viking of Literature
See Bude, Guillaume

[The] Viking of Literature
See Gerhards, Gerhard [or Geert]

Viking, Ted
See Louwen, Jan

Viksnins, George J[uris] 1937- [CA]
Latvian-born American economist and author
* Kennecott, G. J.

Vikstedt, Toivo Alarik 1891-1930
[WEC]
Finnish cartoonist
* Topi

Vilathikulam, Swami
See Pandian, Nallappaswamy

Vildrac, Charles
See Messager, Charles

Vile Lyle Nelson
See Nelson, Lyle

Vilelleschi, Marchese Francesco [PA]
Author
* Pomponio, Leto

Vilenkin, Nikolai Maksimovich
1855-1937 [CD]
Russian poet and philosopher
* Minski, Nikolai Maksimovich

Viles, Walter 20th c. [MBF]
British author
* Beaumont, Brenchley

Vilhelmina
See Stalberg, Carolina Vilhelmina

Villa, Bobby
See Villa, Roberto

Villa, Francisco
See Arango, Doroteo

Villa, Joe
See Francavilla, Joe

Villa, Jose Garcia 1914- [CA]
Filipino-born poet, author, editor
* Doveglion

Villa, Mrs. Samuel B. [FFF]
Entertainer
* Wallace, Agnes

Villa, Pancho
See Arango, Doroteo

Villa, Pancho
See Guilledo, Francisco

Villa, Paul
See DeLucia, Felice

Villa, Roberto 20th c. [OBW]
American baseball player
* Villa, Bobby

Villa y Arilla, Nicanor 1869-1944 [GS]
Spanish bullfighter
* Villita [Little Villa]

Villa y Mari, Francisco 1884- [GS]
Spanish bullfighter
* Rubio de Valencia [Redhead of Valencia]

Villaard
See Beaumesnil, Henrietta Adelaide

[A] Village Apothecary
See Deacon, William Frederick

[The] Village Blacksmith
See Fitzsimmons, Robert Prometheus [Bob]

[A] Village Curate
See Glenn, William

[A] Village Curate
See Taylor, [Rev.] George Henry

[The] Village Idiot
See Hendricks, Harlan William

[A] Village Pastor
See Lawson, [Rev.] John

[A] Village Pastor
See Prime, Samuel Irenaeus

[The] Village Schoolmaster
See Dickinson, Charles M.

[The] Village Shoemaker
See Dickinson, Charles M.

[The] Village Utopian
See Bellamy, Edward

Villagran, Ce'sar
See Cabral, Ce'sar Augusto

Villain, Regardant
See Tozer, Basil John Joseph

Villain-Marais, Jean 1913- [BDF, WEF]
French actor
* Marais, Jean

Villanueva Parma, Luis 20th c. [SG]
Boxer
* Azteca, Kid

Villard, Frank
See Drouineau, Francois

Villard, Henry
See Hilgard, [Ferdinand] Heinrich [Gustav]

Villard, Jean 1896?-1982 [FIR]
Swiss singer and songwriter
* Gilles

Villars, Elizabeth
See Feldman, Ellen [Bette]

Ville, Bernard Germain Etienne de la
[Count Lacepede] 1756-1825 [HPPN]
French natural history researcher
* [The] King of Reptiles

Villegaignon, Chevalier de
See Durand, Nicholas

Villegas, Jose 1868-1927 [GS]
Spanish bullfighter
* Potoco [Large Pot]

Villehardouin, Geoffroi de 1150?-1212?
[DEP, FFF, HPPN, NPS, SN]
French historian
* [The] Father of French History
* [The] Father of French Prose
* [The] First of the French Historians
* [The] Xenophon of His Own History

Villemessant, Jean Hippolyte 1812-?
[PA]
Author
* Cartier

Villena, Enrique De 1384-1434 [HPPN]
Spanish author and scholar
* Aragon, Enrique de

Villeneuva, Arnaud de 1238-1314
[HPPN]
French chemist, astrologer, theologian
* [The] Father of Chemistry

Villeneuve 18th c. [WGT]
Author
* De Listonai, Mr.

Villette, Allis
See Ackerman, Forrest J[ames]

Villette, Pierre Marie Charles De
Bernard Du Grail de la 1804-1850
[HPPN]
French author
* Bernard, Charles de

Villiard, Paul 1910-1974 [CAP]
American author and photographer
* DeGros, J. H.

Villiers, Charles Pelham 1802-1898
[HPPN]
British statesman
* [The] Father of the House of
Commons

Villiers, George 1592-1628 [DNNF,
DNNS, HN]
First Duke of Buckingham
* [The] Sejanus of England
* Steenie

Villiers, George 1628-1687 [DEP, HPPN,
SN]
Second Duke of Buckingham
* [The] Alcibiades of His Time
* [A] Person of Honour
* [The] Pindar of England
* Rub
* Zimri

Villiers, George
See Tardieu, Andre Pierre Gabriel
Amedee

Villiers, George William Frederick
1800-1870 [IP]
Fourth Earl of Clarendon
* Un Flaneur

Villiers, Guy
See Goulding, Peter Geoffrey

Villinger, Hermine 19th c. [HPPN]
German author
* Willfried, H.

Villita [Little Villa]
See Villa y Arilla, Nicanor

Villon, Francois
See Montcorbier, Francois de

Villon, Jacques
See Duchamp, Gaston Emile

Villon, Pierre
See Gintzburger, Pierre

Vilmar
See Rodrigues, Vilmar Silva

Vinal, William Gould 1881-? [NAA]
American naturalist and author
* Cap'n Bill

Vinard, F. N.
See Vincent, Nathaniel Hawthorne

Vincam, Frater Omnia
See Neuburg, Victor [Benjamin]

Vincens, Mme. Charles 1840-1908
[WBD]
French author and critic
* Arvede Barine

Vincent 19th c. [HN]
Welsh religious leader
* [The] King of the Hills

Vincent
See Napoli, Vincent

Vincent, Ann
See Ridings, Hope Dupre

Vincent, Cecil
See Burton, Joan Eileen Veronica

Vincent, Charles 1851-1920 [SFL]
Author
* Mael, Peter [joint pseudonym with
Charles Causse]

Vincent, Clarence 1899-1960 [NOJ]
American jazz musician
* Vincent, Little Dud

Vincent de Paul 1581?-1660 [HPPN,
RH, SN]
Saint
* [The] Apostle of Organized Charity
* [The] Father of Your Country
* [Le] Pere de la Patrie
* Thaumaturgus

Vincent, E. L.
See Morris, Charles Smith

Vincent, E[lizabeth] Lee 1897- [CAP]
American psychologist and author
* Vincent, Leona

Vincent, Ellerton
See Logan, M. C.

Vincent, Elmore 20th c. [HPPN]
American comedian
* Fishface, [Senator] Frankenstein

Vincent, Frank
See Kirkham, Reginald S.

Vincent, Gene
See Craddock, Vincent Eugene

Vincent, Harl
See Schoepflin, Harl Vincent

Vincent, Heinrich Joseph
See Winzenhoerlein, Heinrich Joseph

Vincent, Irving B. 1909- [MK]
American baseball player
* Vincent, Lefty

Vincent, Isabeau [HN]
Prophetess
* [The] Shepherdess of Dauphiny

Vincent, J. Harry
See Taurasi, James V., Sr.

Vincent, Jack
See Grossman, Jack

Vincent, Jacques
See Dussaud, Angele

Vincent, John
See Alvarez Del Rey, Ramon Felipe
San Juan Mario Silvio Enrico

Vincent, John
See Farrow, R.

Vincent, John H. 1832-1920 [HPPN]
American clergyman and educator
* [The] Father of the American Sunday
School Movement
* [The] Father of the Chautauqua
Movement

Vincent, June
See Smith, Dorothy June

Vincent, Katharine
See Vincenti, Ella

Vincent, Lefty
See Vincent, Irving B.

Vincent, Leona
See Vincent, E[lizabeth] Lee

Vincent, Lina
See Tanner, Lina

Vincent, Little Dud
See Vincent, Clarence

Vincent, Mary Keith
See St. John, Wylly Folk

Vincent, Monroe 1919- [BWW]
American singer
* Calhoun, Mr.
* Monroe, Vince
* Polka Dot Slim

Vincent, Nathaniel Hawthorne 1889-
[ASC]
American composer and singer
* Kenbrovin, Jaan
* Vinard, F. N.

Vincent of Lerins ?-450? [WBD]
Saint
* Peregrinus

Vincent, Reggie 20th c. [RM]
Musician
* Vincent, Rockin' Reggie

Vincent, Rockin' Reggie
See Vincent, Reggie

Vincent, Sailor Billy
See Vincent, William J.

Vincent, Walter
See Vinson, Walter Jacobs

Vincent, William
See Holcroft, Thomas

Vincent, William J. 1896-1966 [SC]
American actor, stunt performer, boxer
* Vincent, Sailor Billy

Vincent, William R.
See Heitzmann, W[illia]m Ray

Vincent, Zacherie 1812-? [HPPN]
American Indian
* [The] Last of the Fullblooded Hurons

Vincenti, Ella 1919- [ITA]
American actress
* Vincent, Katharine

Vinciguerra, Francesca 1900- [TC]
American author
* Winwar, Frances

Vincson, Walter
See Vinson, Walter Jacobs

Vindex
See Adams, Samuel

Vindex
See Barker, Edmund Henry

Vindex
See Buet, Charles

Vindex
See Butler, John

Vindex?
See Francis, [Sir] Philip

Vindex
See Gibbons, William

Vindex
See Gordon, John M.

Vindex
See Loveday, John

Vindex
See Pinkerton, John

Vindex
See Rogers, Henry

Vindex
See Sabine, Lorenzo

Vindex
See Tefft, Lyman Beecher

Vindex
See Williams, [Rev.] St. George
Armstrong

[The] Vindicator
See De La Flechere, John William

Vindicator
See Harvey, William Woodis

Vindicator
See Hopkinson, Henry Thomas [Tom]

Vine, Sarah
See Rowland, Donald Sydney

Vine, William
See Youd, Christopher Samuel

Vinegar Bend Mizell
See Mizell, Wilmer David

Vinegar Bill Essick
See Essick, William Earl [Bill]

Vinegar, [Capt.] Hercules
See Fielding, Henry

Vinegar Joe Stilwell
See Stilwell, Joseph Warren

Vinegar Roan Vamvoras
See Vamvoras, Clyde

Vinegar, Tom
See Gregg, Andrew K.

Vinell, Sigrid Lidberg 1848-1885
[HPPN]
Swedish author
* Grane, Valfrid

Vinest, Shaw
See Longyear, Barry Brookes

Vingedal, Sven Erik Axel 1906- [IAW]
Swedish author and poet
* Redax

Vinicombe, Walter 1888-1971 [F2, FC]
British actor
* Patch, Wally

Viniello, Danny 1902-1958 [PMJ, WWJ]
American jazz musician
* Alvin, Danny

Vining, Elizabeth Gray 1902- [CA]
American author
* Gray, Elizabeth Janet

Vinkbooms
See Wainewright, Thomas Griffiths

Vinning, Pamelia S. [FFF]
Canadian writer
* Emilia
* Xenette

Vinokur, Grigory
See Weinrauch, Herschel

Vinson, Carl 1884?-1981
American politician
* Defense, Mr.
* [The] Swamp Fox

Vinson, Cleanhead
See Vinson, Eddie

Vinson, Eddie 1917- [EJ, PMJ, WWJ]
American jazz musician
* Cleanhead, Mr.
* Vinson, Cleanhead

Vinson, Elaine
See Rowland, Donald Sydney

Vinson, Ernest Augustus 1879-1951
[BE]
American baseball player
* Vinson, Rube

Vinson, Helen
See Rulfs, Helen

Vinson, Kathryn
See Williams, Kathryn Vinson

Vinson, Piano Sam
See Vinson, Sam

Vinson, Rex Thomas 1935- [ESF, SFL]
British author
* King, Vincent

Vinson, Rube
See Vinson, Ernest Augustus

Vinson, Sam 20th c. [BWW]
American musician
* Vinson, Piano Sam

Vinson, Walter Jacobs 1901-1975
[BWW]
American singer
* Jacobs, Walter
* Vincent, Walter
* Vincson, Walter

Vinton, V. V.
See Dale, Mrs. R. J.

Viola
See Downing, Frances Murdaugh
[Fanny]

[Le] Viola
See Picton, Thomas

Viola
See Thurston, Laura M. Hawley

Violet, M.
See Marryatt, Frederick

Violet, Ultra
See Collin-Dufresne, Isabelle

Violette
See Garrick, Marion Eva

Violetti
See Eva, Marion

[A] Violinist
See Blair, Willie

[A] Violinist
See Mackay, Eric

[Il] Violino
See Cortellini, Camillo

Violinsky, Solly
See Ginsberg, Sol

Viollis, Andree
See Ardenne de Tizac, Andree
Francoise Caroline d'

VIP
See Partch, Virgil Franklin, II

[The] Viper Girl
See Howard, Rosetta

Vipont, Charles
See Foulds, Elfrida Vipont

Vipont, Elfrida
See Foulds, Elfrida Vipont

Vipsania Agrippina
See Agrippina

Virchow, Hans Jakob Paul 1852-?
[HPPN]
German anatomist and author
* Hans

Virden, Katherine
See Southerland, Katherine Virden

Virdon, Quail
See Virdon, William C. [Bill]

Virdon, William C. [Bill] 1931-   [PB]
American baseball player
* Virdon, Quail

Virel Jean-Louis, Cecile Moumoune de
1918?-   [BI]
French singer
* Moune

Virey, Leopold
See Grousset, Paschal

Virga Dei
See Genseric

Virgil [or Vergil]
See Vergilius Maro, Publius

**[The] Virgil and Horace of the
Christians**
See Prudentius, Aurelius Clemens

Virgil, Laura
See Mainhall, Mrs. Henry

**[The] Virgil of American Musical
History**
See Thomson, Virgil

[The] Virgil of Dramatic Poets
See Jonson, Ben[jamin]

[The] Virgil of Prose
See Balfour, Robert Louis

[The] Virgil of the French
See Corneille, Pierre

[The] Virgil of the French Drama
See Racine, Jean Baptiste

Virgil, Osvaldo Jose 1933-   [BE, SMG]
*Dominican-born baseball player and
coach*
* Virgil, Ozzie

Virgil, Ozzie
See Virgil, Osvaldo Jose

**[Le] Virgile au Rabot [The Virgil of the
Plane]**
See Bellaut, Adam

Virgilius Redivivus
See Vida, Marco Girolamo

[The] Virgin Mary
See Mary

Virgin Modesty
See Wilmot, John

[The] Virgin Queen
See Elizabeth I

Virginia
See Davidson, Virginia E.

[The] Virginia Antiquary
See Bland, Richard

[The] Virginia Confederate
See Kelly, A. M.

Virginia, Daisy
See Van Horn, Dale R.

[The] Virginia Judge
See Kelly, Walter C.

[A] Virginia Physician
See Ruter, P. S.

[The] Virginia Rebel
See Bacon, Nathaniel

Virginia Revolutionist
See Madison, James

[A] Virginian
See Carruthers, William A.

[A] Virginian
See Tyler, Robert

[A] Virginian
See Upshur, Abel Parker

[A] Virginian Presbyter
See Bourne, George

Virginia's Tutelary Saint
See Matoaka

Virginius
See Brown, George M.

Virginius
See Connett, Eugene Virginius, III

Virlup, A. Kvazau
See Ackerman, Forrest J[ames]

Virtue, Lancaster
See Virtue, Vivian

Virtue, Vivian 1911-   [CW]
Jamaican poet and translator
* Virtue, Lancaster

[The] Virtuous Card Shark
See Scarne, John

[The] Virtuous Genevese
See Necker, Jacques [or James]

Virza, Edvarts
See Lieknis, Edvarts

Vis
See Scully, Vincent

Vischer, Friedrich Theodor von
1807-1887 [PA]
German author
* Mystifizinsky, Deutobold Symbolizetti
  Allegoriowitsch
* Schartenmeyer

Visconti, Galeazzo II 1320-1378 [SN]
Duke of Lombardy
* [The] Maecenas of His Time

Visconti, Luchino
See De Modrone, Luchino Visconti

Visconti, Matteo 1250-1323? [DNNS,
SN]
Lord of Milan
* [The] Great

Visconti, Teobaldo 1210-1276 [WBD]
Pope
* Gregory X

Viscusi, Raphael 20th c. [SI 4-16-84]
American restaurateur
* Shapiro, Raphael

Visee
See Sitaramiah, Venkataramiah

Visger, Jean A. Owen 20th c. [WWL]
British author
* Owen, J. A.
* [A] Son of the Marshes

Visi, Baron
See Vian, Boris

Visiak, E. H.
See Physick, Edward Harold

[The] Visionary
See Scott, [Sir] Walter

Viskardy, Nicholas 20th c. [WECO]
Cartoonist
* Cardy

Visser, A. J. J.
See Visser, Abraham Jacobus Johannes

Visser, Abraham Jacobus Johannes
1925- [IAW]
South African author
* Visser, A. J. J.

Visser, Willem Johannes Conradie 1920-
[IAW]
South African author
* Klinikus
* Psigoloog
* Visser, Willie

Visser, Willie
See Visser, Willem Johannes Conradie

Visto
See Jordan, W. S.

[The] Vitagraph Girl
See Turner, Florence

Vital, David
See Grossman, David

[The] Vital Spark
See Bismarck, Otto Eduard Leopold von

[The] Vital Spark
See Hill, Jenny

Vitaliano, Genaro Louis 1932- [RO1]
American singer
* Vale, Jerry

Vitalis
See Sjoeberg, Erik

Vitalis, George 1895- [BBD]
Greek composer and conductor
* Valente, Giorgio

[The] Vitamin Researcher
See McCollum, Elmer V.

Vitamin T Smith
See Smith, Verda T.

Vitamin Z
See Brzezinski, Zbigniew

Vitelleschi, Marchese [NPS]
Author
* Leto, Pomponio

Vitelleschi, Stella 1886- [THR]
British actress
* Rho, Stella

Vitellius, Aulus ?-69 [RH, SN]
Roman emperor
* [The] Flatterer
* [The] Glutton

Vitello, Erasmus
See Ciolek, Erazm

Viterbo, Dina Tiktiner 20th c. [WFA]
French fashion designer
* Tiktiner

Vitesse, Grande
See Walkerley, Rodney Lewis [De Burgh]

Vitet, Louis 1802-1873 [WBD]
French author and politician
* Vitet, Ludovic

Vitet, Ludovic
See Vitet, Louis

Vitezovic, Tomislav
See Kuehnelt-Leddihn, Erik [Ritter Von]

[El] Viti
See Martin Sanchez, Santiago

Vitols, Valdis
See Kikauka, Talis Talivaldis Tully

[The] Vitruvius of England
See Jones, Inigo

Vitt, Oscar Joseph 1890-1963 [AS]
American baseball player
* Vitt, Ossie

Vitt, Ossie
See Vitt, Oscar Joseph

Vitti, Monica
See Ceciarelli, Maria Luisa

Vitti, Ralph 1931?- [FC, SW]
American actor
* Dante, Michael

Vittorino da Feltre
See Ramboldini [or de Ramboldoni], Vittorino

Vittucci, Matteo [BI]
American dancer and dance teacher
* Matteo

Viva
See Hoffmann, Susan

Viva
See Williams, Eva

Vivaldi, Antonio Lucio 1678-1741 [HPPN]
Italian violinist, composer, clergyman
* [Il] Prete Rosso
* [The] Red Priest

Vivarelli, Piero [FDG]
Italian director
* Murray, Donald

Vivaria, Kassandra
See Sindici, [Maria] Magda Stuart

Vivarini, Bartolommeo
See Da Murano, Bartolommeo

Vivekananda, Swami
See Dutt, Narendra Nath

Vivers, Eileen Elliott 1905- [CA]
American home economist and author
* Quigley, Eileen Elliott

Vives, Juan Luis 1492-1540 [HPPN]
Spanish philosopher
* Vives, Ludovicus

Vives, Ludovicus
See Vives, Juan Luis

Vivian
See Lewes, George Henry

Vivian, C. T.
See Vivian, Cordy Tindell

Vivian, Cordy Tindell 1924- [BA]
American clergyman and author
* Vivian, C. T.

Vivian, Daisy
See Kenyon, Bruce

Vivian, Emily
See Kernell, Mrs. John

Vivian, Evelyn Charles H. 1882-1947 [ESF, HFF, WGT]
British author
* Cannell, Charles
* Mann, Jack

Vivian, Francis
See Ashley, [Arthur] Ernest

Vivian, Herbert 1865-? [WWL]
British author
* X.

Vivian, Lila
See Hicks, Edna

Vivian, The Coca Cola Girl
See Dragonette, Jessica

Viviano, Benedict T[homas]
See Viviano, Thomas Michael

Viviano, Thomas Michael 1940- [CA]
American author and clergyman
* Viviano, Benedict T[homas]

Vivien
See Shaw, Hollace

Vivien, Renee
See Tarn, Pauline Mary

Vivienne
See Entwistle, Florence Vivienne

Vivier, Colette
See Duval, Colette

Vixen
See Montgomery, George Edgar

Vizard, Stephen
See James, [David] Burnett [Stephen]

Vizardi, Ligio
See Diaz Ordonez, Virgilio

Vizetelly, Edmund [NPS]
Author
* Clare, Bertie

Vizetelly, Ernest Alfred 1853-1922 [WBD, WWL]
French author and journalist
* [Le] Petit Homme Rouge

Vizetelly, Francis Horace [Frank] 1864-? [ALY]
British-born author
* Syntax, Dr.

Vizzini, Sal[vatore] 20th c. [HPPN]
American undercover agent and police chief
* Cerra, [Major] Michael Anthony [or Mike]
* Kural, Ismet Musret
* Larkin, James Patrick
* Lombardi, Pasquale
* Patrick, Jimmy
* Swift Tony
* Tivoli, Tony
* Vento, Giuseppe Antonio
* Vento, Joseph Angelo
* Vento, Vincent M.
* Warner, Mike
* Warner, Theodore [or Ted]

Vlacic Ilir, Matija
See Flacius Illyricus, Matthias

Vlacich, Matthias 1520-1575 [HPPN]
German scholar
* Illyricus, Matthias Flacius

Vlad V 1430?-1476 [DI]
Hungarian ruler
* [The] Impaler

Vladeck, Charney
See Charney, Baruch

Vladimir I 956?-1015 [DNNS, HPPN, SN]
Grand Duke of Russia
* [The] Great
* St. Vladimir

Vladimir II 1053-1125 [WBD]
Russian ruler
* Monomachus

Vladimirov, Leonid
See Finkelstein, Leonid Vladimirovitch

Vlady
See Zabache, Wladimiro Bas

Vlady, Marina
See De Poliakoff-Baidaroff, Marina

Vlasek, June 1915- [FC]
American actress
* Lang, June

Vlasic, Bob
See Hirsch, Phil

Vlasto, John Alexander 1877-1958 [WW]
Author
* Alexander, John
* Remenham, John

Vocalis, Lambros Charles 1928- [BEW]
American stage manager, director, actor
* Forsythe, Charles

Voces Catholicae
See Dillon, Emile Joseph

Vodnoy, Matthew
See Vodnoy, Max

Vodnoy, Max 1892-1939 [SC]
Russian-born actor
* Vodnoy, Matthew

Voel, David
See Morgan-Jones, David Sylvanus

Voelker, John Donaldson 1903- [CA, CC, WD]
American author and jurist
* Traver, Robert

Voer, Jon Ur
See Jonsson, Jon

Vogau, Boris Andreyevich 1894-1938 [CD, EWL, TC]
Russian author
* Pilnyak, Boris

Vogel, Big Ed
See Vogel, Eddie

Vogel, Eddie 20th c. [PHM]
American underworld figure
* Vogel, Big Ed

Vogel, Harry Benjamin 1868-? [LAO]
New Zealand-born author
* Kinver, Richard

Vogel, [Dr.] Johannes
See Hofprediger, Johannes Martin Vogel

Vogel, Otto 20th c. [BBH]
American baseball coach
* Vogel, Otts

Vogel, Otts
See Vogel, Otto

Vogelland, Rico 1936?- [CW]
Surinamese poet, critic, editor
* Kross, Rudy

Vogelstein, Julie
See Braun-Vogelstein, Julie

Vogenitz, David George 1930- [AW, CA]
American author
* George, David

Vogler, Abt [or Abbe]
See Vogler, Georg Joseph

Vogler, Georg Joseph 1749-1814 [HPPN]
German organist, composer, author
* Vogler, Abt [or Abbe]

Vogt, Carl Henry 1895-1956 [BDF, BEW, F2]
American actor and director
* Calhern, Louis

Vogt, Marie
See Seckener, Mrs. James A.

Voiart, Anne E. Petitpain 1786-1866 [PA]
Author
* Elisa

[The] Voice
See Orbison, Roy

[The] Voice
See Sinatra, Francis Albert [Frank]

[A] Voice from Kentucky
See Coleman, William

[The] Voice Gorgeous
See Korjus, Miliza

[The] Voice of Denmark
See Schiotz, Aksel

[The] Voice of Doom
See Kaltenborn, Hans von

[The] Voice of Experience
See Taylor, Marion Sayle

[The] Voice of Flaming Youth
See Fitzgerald, F[rancis] Scott [Key]

[The] Voice of Freedom
See Henry, Patrick

[The] Voice of Freedom
See Romulo, Carlos Pena

[The] Voice of "Gangbusters"
See King, John Reed

[The] Voice of Leo
See Barker, Bradley

[The] Voice of Liberty
See Henry, Patrick

[The] Voice of Mission Control
See Powers, John A.

[The] Voice of "Movietone News"
See Thomas, Lowell Jackson

[The] Voice of New England
See Frost, Robert Lee

[The] Voice of Orion
See Okamoto, Kozo

[The] Voice of R. C. A.
See Monroe, Vaughn Wilton

[The] Voice of Russian Conscience
See Solzhenitsyn, Aleksandr Isayevich

[The] Voice of San Francisco
See Caen, Herb[ert]

Voice of Silence
See Pound, Ezra [Loomis]

[The] Voice of Silver
See Pittman, Key

[The] Voice of "Sky King"
See King, John Reed

[The] Voice of the Astronauts
See Powers, John A.

[The] Voice of the 500
See Page, Paul

[The] Voice of the Hangover Generation
See O'Hara, John [Henry]

[The] Voice of the Metropolitan
See Cross, Milton

[The] Voice of the Omaha Indians
See Bright Eyes

[The] Voice of the Radio
See Stefan, Karl

[The] Voice of the Revolution
See Henry, Patrick

[The] Voice of the St. Louis Fair
See Prado, Katie

[The] Voice of the Silent Majority
See Aurandt, Paul Harvey

[The] Voice of the South
See Blackmar, Armand Edward

[The] Voice of the Southland
See Lucas, Eugene

[The] Voice of the Uprooted
See Berkowitz, Itzhak Dov

[The] Voice of the Voiceless
See Anderson, Jack[son Northman]

[The] Voice of the Wehrmacht
See Ditmar, Karl

[The] Voice of the Women's Movement
See Stone, Lucy

[The] Voice of Wall Street
See Wachtel, Larry

[The] Voiceless Sinatra
See Johnson, Van

Voiceless Tim O'Rourke
See O'Rourke, Timothy Patrick

Voight, Valeska [PA]
Author
* Stahr, Arthur

Voigt, James Wesley 1940- [ECM]
American singer and songwriter
* Taylor, Chip

Voigt, Olen Edward 1899- [BE]
American baseball player
* Voigt, Ollie

Voigt, Ollie
See Voigt, Olen Edward

Voigt, William 1849?-1922 [DEP, DI]
Prussian shoemaker who masqueraded as an army officer
* [A] Captain of Koepenick

Voilemont, Comte de
See Esterhazy, Marie Charles Ferdinand Walsin

Voiselle, Big Bill
See Voiselle, William Symmes

Voiselle, William Symmes 1919- [BE, PB]
American baseball player
* Ninety Six
* Voiselle, Big Bill

[La] Voisin
See Deshayes, Catherine

Voiture, Vincent 1597-1648 [NPS, SN]
French courtier, poet, author
* [The] Great Letter-Writer
* [The] Solon of French Prose

Vojtech
See Adalbert [or Adelbert]

Vokes, Harry
See Langlin, Henry

Vokes, John Russell 1872-1924 [HPPN]
American vaudeville performer
* Vokes, Officer

Vokes, Officer
See Vokes, John Russell

Vokes, Rosina
See Clay, Mrs. Cecil

Volder, Willem de 1493-1568 [BI]
Dutch philosopher
* Gnapheus, Gulielmus

Volk, Gordon 1885- [WW, WWL]
British author
* Knotts, Raymond
* Sussex, Gordon

Volk, Hannah Marie
See Wormington, Hannah Marie

Volkmann, Richard von 1830-1889 [HPPN, WBD]
German surgeon, author, poet
* Leander, Richard
* Volkmann-Leander

Volkmann-Leander
See Volkmann, Richard von

Volkoff, Vladimir 1932- [CA]
French-born author, poet, playwright
* Barbare, Rholf
* Duloup, Victor

Volland, Louise Henriette 1716-1784 [BI, HPPN]
Friend of French philosopher, Denis Diderot
* Volland, Sophie

Volland, Sophie
See Volland, Louise Henriette

Vollmer, Louisa Smith 1898-1955 [HPPN]
American playwright
* Vollmer, Lula

Vollmer, Lula
See Vollmer, Louisa Smith

Volodarsky
See Goldstein, Moisei Markovich

Volonte, Claudio 20th c. [WF]
Italian actor
* Camaso, Claudio

Voloshin, Maximilian Aleksandrovich
See Kirienko-Voloshin, Maximilian Aleksandrovich

Volpe, Mops
See Volpe, Tony

Volpe, Robert R. 1943?- [HPPN]
American artist and police detective
* [The] Art Sleuth

Volpe, Tony 20th c. [BLB, PHM]
American underworld figure
* Volpe, Mops

Volpi, Odoardo
See Shannon, Edward N.

Volpone
See Godolphin, Sidney

Vol'skii, Nikolai Vladislavovich 1879-1964 [BI]
Russian author and journalist
* Valentinov, Nikolai
* Yurevsky, E.

Volsted, Andrew J. 1860-1947 [HPPN]
American attorney, legislator, prohibitionist
* [The] Father of the Volstead Act
* [The] Goat of the Wets
* [The] Obscure Mr. Volstead

Voltaggio, Vic
See Voltaggio, Vito Henry

Voltaggio, Vito Henry 1941- [ALR]
Baseball official
* Voltaggio, Vic

Voltaire
See Arouet, Francois Marie

[Le] Voltaire de Son Siecle
See Aretino, Pietro

[The] Voltaire of Chambermaids
See Restif, Nicolas Edme

[The] Voltaire of Germany
See Bauer, Bruno

[The] Voltaire of Germany
See Goethe, Johann Wolfgang von

[The] Voltaire of Germany
See Wieland, Christoph Martin

[The] Voltaire of Grecian Literature
See Lucian

[The] Voltaire of Poland
See Krasicki, Ignatius

[The] Voltaire of Science
See Boerhaave, Hermann

[The] Voltaire of the Sixteenth Century
See Gerhards, Gerhard [or Geert]

Volterra, Daniele da
See Ricciarelli, Daniele

[Il] Volterrano
See Franceschini, Baldassare

Voltige a la Richard
See Rastelli, Oreste

[El] Voluntario [The Ready One]
See Serrano, Carlos

[A] Volunteer
See Bruce, George

[A] Volunteer
See Douglas, John

Volunteer [Secret Service code name]
See Johnson, Lyndon Baines

[A] Volunteer
See Palmer, Edwin F.

[A] Volunteer
See Scribner, B. F.

Volusenus
See Wilson, Florence

Volz, Jacob Phillip [Jake] 1878-1962 [BE]
American baseball player
* Volz, Silent Jake

Volz, Silent Jake
See Volz, Jacob Phillip [Jake]

Volzogenius
See Van Wolzogen, Lodowijk

Von
See Second element of name for further listings

Von Adelheid, Auer
See Cosel, Charlotte von

Von Amyntor, Gerhard
See Gerhardt, Dagobert von

Von An Der Lan-Hochbrunn, Paul Eugen Josef 1863-1914 [BBD]
German conductor and composer
* Hartmann, Pater

Von Arnim, Liebet 20th c.
Daughter of Australian-born author, Elizabeth Mary Russell
* De Charms, Leslie

Von Arnim, Mary Beauchamp
See Russell, Edwin John Cumming

Von Aschendorf, Ignatz
See Korzeniowski, Teodor Jozef
Konrad Nalecz

Von Aulock, Andreas 20th c.
German military officer
* [The] Madman of St. Malo

Von Baudissin, Count   [NPS]
Author
* Von Schlicht, Baron

Von Benewyck, Jan 1594-1647   [PA]
Author
* Beverovicus

Von Bernbrunn, Karl Andreas 1789-1854
[HPPN]
American actor and impresario
* Carl, Karl

Von Berweck, Carl Gustav 1803-1871
[PA]
German author
* Von Guseck, Bornd

Von Betz, Matthew 1881-1938   [SC]
American actor
* Betz, Matthew

Von Block, Bela 1922-   [CA]
American author
* Black, Jonathan
* Chambertin, Ilya [joint pseudonym
  with Sylvia Von Block]
* Endfield, Mercedes
* Hennessey, Caroline [joint pseudonym
  with Sylvia Von Block]
* La Barr, Creighton
* Lucchesi, Aldo
* Meurice, Blanca
* Padgett, Desmond
* Randolph, Gordon [joint pseudonym
  with Sylvia Von Block]
* Shomroni, Reuven
* Sprague, W. D. [joint pseudonym
  with Sylvia Von Block]
* Vernon, Lee M.

Von Block, Sylvia 1931-   [CA]
American author
* Beaumont, Beverly
* Chambertin, Ilya [joint pseudonym
  with Bela Von Block]
* Clifford, Theodore
* Hennessey, Caroline [joint pseudonym
  with Bela Von Block]
* Randolph, Gordon [joint pseudonym
  with Bela Von Block]
* Sprague, W. D. [joint pseudonym
  with Bela Von Block]

Von Bluggen, Vander
See Knight, Charles

Von Bolanden, Konrad
See Bischoff, Joseph Edward Konrad

Von Bolvary, Geza
See Von Bolvary-Zahn, Geza Maria

Von Bolvary-Zahn, Geza Maria
1897-1961   [FDG]
Hungarian director
* Von Bolvary, Geza

Von Bonewell, Hendrick ?-1542   [PA]
Author
* Bonemelus

Von Boyle, Ackland
See Boyle, Acland

Von Brandenburg, Hugo   [SN]
German aristocrat
* [The] Great Baron

Von Braun, Wernher 1912-   [HPPN]
German-American physicist
* [The] Father of the V-2 Rocket

Von Brickel, Baron
See Becker, Charles

Von Brincken, Wilhelm 1891-1946   [SC]
German-born actor and director
* Beckwith, Roger
* Vaughn, William

Von Buttlar-Brandenfels, Johannes 1940-
[IAW]
German author
* Buttlar, Johannes

Von Castelhun, Friedl
See Marion, Frieda

Von Chelius, Oskar 1859-1923   [BBD]
German composer
* Berger, Siegfried

Von Chopnick, Professor
See Weil, Joseph R.

Von Cramm, Gottfried 1900-1976
German tennis player
* [The] Baron

Von Dalberg, Johann Kamera 1445-1503
[PA]
Author
* Dalburgius

Von Degen
See Rabe, Ann C[rawford] Von

Von Den Steinen, Robert
See Graf Wickenburg, Erik

Von Der Ahe, Chris
See Von Der Ahe, Christian Frederick
Wilhelm

**Von Der Ahe, Christian Frederick
Wilhelm** 1851-1913   [BE]
German-born baseball manager
* Von Der Ahe, Chris

Von Der Belin, Charles 1885-1936   [SC]
Belgian-born actor, producer, director
* Fallon, Charles

Von Der Butz, Philip 1883-1964   [F2]
Actor
* August, Edwin

Von der Clana, Heinrich
See Weiss, Albert Maria

Von der Linde, Philander
See Mencke [or Mencken], Johann
Burkhard

Von Der Ostsee, Johanne
See Falk, Johannes Daniel

**Von Dombrowski zu Papros und
Krusvic, Kathe** 1881-?   [ICB, SFL]
Austrian-born author and illustrator
* Dombrowski, Katrina
* K. O. S.

Von Drey, Howard
See Wandrei, Howard Elmer

Von Economo, C.
See Economo, Constantin

Von Einsiedel, R.
See Tetzner, Martha Helene

Von Elkenberg, Johann 18th c.
German strongman
* Samson

Von Erich, Kerry 20th c.   [NW 3-11-85]
American wrestler
* [The] Modern Day Warrior

Von Faramond, Ludwig Ernst
See Sinhold Von Schutz, Philipp
Balthasar

Von Fehmarn
See Lafrentz, Ferdinand William

Von Furstenberg, Betsy
See Von Furstenberg-Hedringen,
Elizabeth Caroline Maria Agatha
Felicitas

**Von Furstenberg-Hedringen, Elizabeth
Caroline Maria Agatha Felicitas** 1931?-
[BEW, CR, TR]
German-born actress
* Madcap Betsy
* Von Furstenberg, Betsy

Von Gerber, Francesca Mitzi Marlene
1930-   [FC, SW, WEF]
American actress
* Gaynor, Mitzi

Von Grau, Wernher
See Schoeb, Erika

Von Grimmelshausen, J. J. C.
See Von Grimmelshausen, Johann Hans
Jakob Christoffel

**Von Grimmelshausen, Johann Hans
Jakob Christoffel** 1622?-1676   [HPPN]
German author
* Von Grimmelshausen, J. J. C.

Von Grofe, Ferdinand Rudolph
1892-1972   [PMJ]
American composer and musician
* Grofe, Ferde

Von Gunther, Ilse [or Inge?] 1891-
[BBD]
Hungarian opera singer
* Ivoguen, Maria

Von Guseck, Bornd
See Von Berweck, Carl Gustav

Von Hassia, Henricus
See Langenstein, Heinrich

Von Heemskerk [or Hemskerk], Martin
1498-1574   [HPPN]
Dutch painter
* [The] Raphael of Holland

Von Heine, Baroness Gustav   [FFF]
Opera singer
* Klein, Regina

Von Hernreid, Paul George Julius 1908-
[BDF, WEF]
Austrian-born actor and director
* Henreid, Paul

Von Hildebrand, Dietrich 1889-1977
[CA]
German-born educator and author
* Ott, Peter

Von Himmel, Ernst
See Petersilea, Carlyle

Von Hohenberg, Luli 1909-   [FIR]
German-born actress
* Deste, Luli

Von Hohenheim, Theophrastus Bombastus 1493?-1541   [WBD]
Swiss-born physician
* Paracelsus, Philippus Aureolus

Von Holst, Gustavus Theodore 1874-1934   [BBD, WBD]
British composer and musician
* Holst, Gustav Theodore

Von Homberg, Otto
See Geise, [Dr.] Otto

Von Horn, Eylard Theodore ?-1948
[AS, HPPN]
American auto racer
* Horn, Ted
* [The] Racing Legend

Von Horn, W. O.
See Oertel, Philipp Friedrich Wilhelm

Von Huetten, Ulric
See Davis, Henry Winter

Von Hutten, Bettina
See Riddle, Betsy [Freifrau Von Hutten]

Von Ingerslaven, Emma   [PA]
Author
* Von Rotherfels, E.

Von Jordis, Eelco
See Van Vormizeele, Eelco Voet

Von Kaschnitz-Weinberg, Marie Luise 1901-1974   [CA]
German poet, author, playwright
* Kaschnitz, Marie Luise

Von Keller, Adalbert 1820-1882   [WBD]
Hungarian conductor and composer
* Keler, Bela

Von Klopp, Vahrah
See Malvern, Gladys

Von Kluge, Hans G. 1882-1944
German military leader
* Clever Hans

Von Koerber, Hans Nordewin 1886-
[CA]
German-born educator and author
* Euphemides, Aristes

Von Kolnitz, Alfred Holmes 1893-1948
[BE]
American baseball player
* Von Kolnitz, Fritz

Von Kolnitz, Fritz
See Von Kolnitz, Alfred Holmes

Von L., Detlev
See Liliencron, Friedrich [Axel Adolf]

Von Lang, Jochen
See Von Lang-Piechocki, Joachim

Von Lang-Piechocki, Joachim 1925-
[CA]
German author, editor, producer
* Von Lang, Jochen

Von Lauchen, Georg Joachim 1514-1576
[WBD]
German astronomer and mathematician
* Rhaeticus [or Rheticus]

Von Lehndorff, Vera 1943-
Actress and artist
* Veruschka

Von Lewinski, Fritz Erich 1887-   [WBD]
German army officer
* Mannstein, Fritz Erich von

Von Linden, E.
See May, Karl Friedrich

Von Losch, Emma ?-1898   [HPPN]
American prostitute
* Dutch Em

Von Losch, Marie Magdalene
See Dietrich, Marie Magdalene

Von Luckner, [Count] Felix 1881-1966
[HPPN]
German naval officer
* [The] Sea Devil

Von Muench-Bellinghausen, Eligius 1806-1871   [WBD]
German poet and playwright
* Halm, Friedrich

Von Neida, Stanley 1923-
American basketball player
* Von Neida, Whitey

Von Neida, Whitey
See Von Neida, Stanley

Von Nordenwald, Erich Oswald Hans Carl Stroheim 1885-1957   [BEW, F1, FC]
Austrian-born actor and director
* [The] Man You Love To Hate
* Von Stroheim, Erich

Von Oberndorff, Carl
See Oberndorff, [Count] Charles

Von Ohl, Adele 1885-1966   [SC]
American actress, stunt and rodeo performer
* Parker, Adele

Von Ohlen, Baron
See Von Ohlen, John

Von Ohlen, John 1941-   [EJ7]
American jazz musician
* Von Ohlen, Baron

Von Oleuschtaeger, Johann Daniel 1711-1778   [PA]
Author
* Olearius

Von Opel, Maria-Christina 1951?-
German heiress involved in drug smuggling operation
* Von Opel, Putzi

Von Opel, Putzi
See Von Opel, Maria-Christina

Von Ost, Henry Lerner 1915-   [CA]
American author, radio and television performer, comedian
* Morgan, Henry

Von Rachen, Kurt
See Hubbard, Lafayette Ronald

Von Redlich, Marcellus Donald A. R. 1893-   [NAA]
Austrian-born author and legal scholar
* Comes
* Diplomat
* Donaldus
* Redlich, Marcellus Donald

Von Regensburg, Berthold 1210-1272
[HPPN]
German clergyman
* [The] Chrysostom of the Middle Ages

Von Reibnitz, Marie Christine 1945-
[WP 4-17-85]
Czech-born princess
* Michael of Kent
* Pushy, Princess

Von Reinhold, Calvin
See Lutz, Calvin Jack Von Reinhold

Von Reinhold, Calvin
See Von Reinhold Lutz, Calvin Jack

Von Reinhold Lutz, Calvin Jack 1927-
[BEW]
Canadian dancer, choreographer, singer
* Von Reinhold, Calvin

Von Ribbensnob
See Ribbentrop, Joachim

Von Ribbentrop, Joachim
See Ribbentrop, Joachim

Von Richthofen, Manfred 1892-1918
[HPPN, NN]
German military aviator
* [The] Bloody Red Baron
* [The] Red Baron
* [The] Red Knight of Germany

Von Rotherfels, E.
See Von Ingerslaven, Emma

Von Rudloff, Alfred Felix 1902-   [CAT]
German-born American author and clergyman
* Rudloff, Leo

Von Scherler, Sasha
See Von Schoeler, Alexandra-Xenia Elizabeth Anne Marie Fiesola

Von Schlicht, Baron
See Von Baudissin, Count

Von Schmidt, Ferdinand   [PA]
Author
* Dranmor

Von Schoeler, Alexandra-Xenia Elizabeth Anne Marie Fiesola 1939-   [TR]
American actress
* Von Scherler, Sasha

Von Schwarzenfeld, Gertrude
See Cochrane De Alencar, Gertrude Emanuela Luise

Von Sechten
See Siegen, Ludwig von

Von Seyffertitz, Gustav 1863-1943   [SC]
Austrian-born actor and director
* Clonblough, G. Butler

Von Sittewald, Philander
See Moscherosch [or Mosenrosh], Johann Michael

Von Stackelberg-Treutlein, Freda Fanny Erica 1929-   [AW]
Estonian-born author
* Genter, Harry

Von Stade, Flicka
See Von Stade, Frederica

Von Stade, Frederica 1945?-
American opera singer
* Von Stade, Flicka

Von Sternberg, Josef
See Sternberg, Jonas

Von Sternberg, Joseph
See Stern, Joe

Von Stiegel, Baron
See Stiegel, Henry William

Von Storch, Anne B. 1910-   [CAP, SAT]
American author
* Malcolmson, Anne

Von Straschiripka, Johann
See Canon, Hans

Von Strehlenau, Nikolaus Niembsch 1802-1850   [HPPN]
Austrian poet
* Lenau, Nikolaus

Von Strensch, Gunther 1889-1963   [SC]
American actor, opera singer, director
* L'Estrange, Dick

Von Stroheim, Erich
See Von Nordenwald, Erich Oswald Hans Carl Stroheim

Von Suttner, Bertha 20th c.
Austrian baroness
* Von Suttner, Peace Bertha

Von Suttner, Peace Bertha
See Von Suttner, Bertha

Von Sydow, Carl Adolf 1929-   [BDF, IPA, OCF]
Swedish actor
* Von Sydow, Max

Von Sydow, Max
See Von Sydow, Carl Adolf

Von Teller, Ivan Dahl 20th c.   [BLB]
American swindler
* Anderson, Dutch
* Anderson, George

Von Tempski, Armine
See Ball, Armine

Von Theumer, Ernst 20th c.   [WF]
German director
* Welles, Mel

Von Thoma, Wilhelm Ritter 1892-1948
German military officer
* [The] Butcher of Guernica

Von Tilzer, Albert
See Gumm, Albert

Von Tilzer, Harry
See Gumm, Harry

Von Tromlitz, A.
See Von Witzleben, Karl Friedrich

Von Vohning
See Howard, Mrs. A. W. M.

Von Wahrenberg, Constantino
See Sinhold Von Schutz, Philipp Balthasar

Von Walhofen, Baroness   [FFF]
Entertainer
* Lucca, Pauline

Von Warthburgh, Alberto O. 1875-1914   [HPPN]
American director
* Warburg, Albert O.

Von Watt, Joachim 1484-1551   [WBD]
Swiss religious leader
* Vadianus, Joachim

Von Witzleben, Karl Friedrich 1773-1839   [PA]
Author
* Von Tromlitz, A.

Von Wohl, Ludwig 1903-1961   [EOP, SFL]
German-born astrologer and author
* De Wohl, Louis

Von Zaytz, Giovanni
See Zajc, Ivan

Von Zell, Harry 1906-   [HPPN]
American radio announcer and actor
* Giggles

Von Zesen, Philipp 1619-1689   [PA]
Author
* Coesius

Vonnegut, Bernard 1914-   [HPPN]
American physicist
* [The] Father of Artificial Rain

Vonnegut, Kurt, Jr. 1922-   [WGT]
American author
* Ferdinand

Voo-chee 7th c.   [FFF, HN, RH]
Widow of King Tae-tsong of China
* [The] Katherine de Medici of China
* [The] Queen of Heaven

Voorhees, Daniel Wolsey 1827-1897   [HPPN]
American politician
* [The] Tall Sycamore of the Wabash

Vorhees, Cy
See Vorhees, Henry Bert

Vorhees, Henry Bert 1874-1910   [BE]
American baseball player
* Vorhees, Cy

Vormius
See Worm, Olaus

Vorobeva, Maria 1892-   [BI]
French artist
* Marevna

Voronskii, Aleksandr Konstantinovich 1884-1937?   [BI]
Russian literary critic
* Nurmin

Vorse, Mary Heaton
See O'Brien, Mrs. Joseph

Vorster, Balthazar Johannes 1915-
South African prime minister
* Vorster, Jackboot John

Vorster, Jackboot John
See Vorster, Balthazar Johannes

Vorwarts, Marschall
See Bluecher, Gebhard Leberecht von

Vos, Anna Beyera 1919-   [IAW]
South African author
* Minnaar-Vos, Anna

Vos, Tonny
See Vos-Dahmen Von Buccholz, Tonny

Vos-Dahmen Von Buccholz, Tonny 1923-   [IAW]
Dutch author
* Vos, Tonny

Vosburg, F. W.   [FFF]
American writer
* Vigilant

Vosburgh, Alfred 1890-   [F1, F2]
Actor
* Whitman, Alfred

Vosburgh, Alfred
See Whitman, Gayne

Vose, Reuben 19th c.   [WGT]
Author
* Invisible Sam

Voskovec, George
See Voskovec, Jiri

Voskovec, Jiri 1905-   [BEW]
Czech-born actor, playwright, director
* Voskovec, George

Voss, Fatty
See Voss, Frank

Voss, Frank 1888-1917   [SC]
American actor
* Voss, Fatty

Voss, Tillie
See Voss, Walter

Voss, Walter 20th c. [SMG]
American football player
* Voss, Tillie

Voss, Werner 1897-1917
German fighter pilot
* [The] Flying Hussar
* [The] Hussar of Krefeld

Votre Solidite
See D'Aubigne, Francoise

Voudel, Jesse Vanden 1587-1679 [PA]
Author
* Justus

Vought, Chance M. 1890-1930 [HPPN]
American aircraft designer
* [The] Father of the Launching
  Catapult

Vovchok, Marc
See Marcovitch, M. A.

Vovchok, Marko
See Markovich, Mariia Aleksandrovna
[Velinskaia]

Vovsky, Salomon Mikhailovich
1890-1948 [BEW]
Russian actor and producer
* Mikhoels, Salomon

Vowinkel, John Henry 1884-1966 [BE]
American baseball player
* Vowinkel, Rip

Vowinkel, Rip
See Vowinkel, John Henry

Vox, Valentine
See Walsh, John Henry

[A] Voyager
See Benjamin, Park

[A] Voyager
See Hill, George

[A] Voyager
See Scoresby, William

[The] Voyager in Search of Europe
See Eliot, Thomas Stearns

Voyageur
See Allen, Cecil J[ohn]

[Un] Voyageur
See Dudevant, Amandine Aurore Lucile
Dupin

Voyant, Clair
See Ackerman, Forrest J[ames]

Voyle, Mary
See Manning, Rosemary Joy

Voynich, E. L.
See Voynich, Ethel Lilian Boole

Voynich, Ethel Lilian Boole 1864-1960
[LC]
British author
* Voynich, E. L.

Voysey, Margaret 1945- [CA]
British playwright and sociologist
* Paun, Maggie

Vradinnos, Zefiros
See Hatzidakis, Nicholas

Vrchlicky, Jaroslav
See Frida, Emil

Vrdolyak, Edward 1938?- [TI 4-23-83,
WP 3-26-84]
American politician
* Vrdolyak, Fast Eddie

Vrdolyak, Fast Eddie
See Vrdolyak, Edward

Vredenburg, Mona 1918- [THR]
British dancer and choreographer
* Inglesby, Mona

Vreeland, Elizabeth
See Tompkins, Elizabeth Vreeland

Vreeland, Frank 1891-1946 [BI, DNA]
American playwright
* Thorpe, William

Vriendt, Frans de 1520?-1570 [DNNS,
HN, WBD]
Flemish painter
* [The] Flemish Raphael
* Floris, Frans

Vrijman, Jan
See Hulsebos, Jan

Vronsky, Victoria 1909- [BBD]
Russian musician
* Vronsky, Vitya

Vronsky, Vitya
See Vronsky, Victoria

Vroom, Paul
See O'Sullivan, Paul

Vrugt, J. P. 1905-1960 [EWL]
Dutch author
* Blaman, Anna

Vucanovich, Barbara 1921?- [NW 9-6-82]
American politician
* [The] Tough Grandmother

Vucerovich, William 1918-1955 [AS,
EAR, HPPN]
American auto racer
* [The] Fresno Flash
* [The] Mad Russian
* Vukovich, Bill
* Vukovich, Vukie

Vugteveen, Verna Aardema 1911- [CA]
American author
* Aardema, Verna

Vujovic, Vladimir 1922- [FC]
French actor
* Auclair, Michel

Vukovich, Bill
See Vucerovich, William

Vukovich, Vukie
See Vucerovich, William

Vulliamy, Colwyn Edward 1886-1971
[CC, EMD, WW]
British author
* Rolls, Anthony

Vulpius, Melchior
See Fuchs, Melchior

Vulpius, Paul
See Fodor, Ladislaus

[The] Vulture
See Regan, Phil[lip Raymond]

Vuyk, Beb
See De Willigen, Elisabeth

Vynne, Eustace 1921?- [BI]
American yachtsman
* Vynne, Sunny

Vynne, Sunny
See Vynne, Eustace

Vyse, Bertie
See Beckett, Arthur

W

Asterisk (*) indicates assumed name.

W.
See Bowring, [Sir] John

W.
See Furlong, Thomas

W.
See Hebbe, Vendela Astrand

W.
See Prime, William Cowper

W.
See Roddy, William

W.
See Walker, James

W.
See Walker, Richard

W.
See Walker, Timothy

W.
See Walley, Samuel Hurd

W.
See Walsh, John Edward

W.
See Waters, John Charles

W.
See Webster, Thomas

W.
See Weld, Horatio Hastings

W.
See Whitman, Jason

W.
See Whitty, Michael James

W.
See Wigglesworth, Edward

W.
See Wrangham, Francis

W.
See Wray, Daniel

W. A.
See Allen, William

W. A. B.
See Butler, William Archer

W. A. C.
See Chatto, William Andrew

W. A. C.
See Copinger, Walter Arthur

W. A. D.
See Davis, William Augustus

W. A. D.
See Delamotte, William Alfred

W. A. D.
See Drummond, William Abernethy

W. A. D.
See Dwiggins, William Addison

W. A. W.
See Wallace, William A.

W. B.
See Ball, William

W. B.
See Barton, William

W. B.
See Bennett, William

W. B.
See Besant, [Sir] Walter

W. B.
See Blades, William

W. B.
See Blake, William

W. B.
See Boyne, William

W. B.
See Bromfield, William

W. B.
See Burge, William

W. B.
See Burton, Warren

W. B.
See Gay, John

W. B. A.
See Anthony, W. B.

W. B. B.
See Boyce, William Birmington

W. B. B.
See Buchanan, W. B.

W. B., D. D.
See Boyse, [Rev.] Joseph

W. B. D. D. T.
See Turnbull, William Barclay David Donald

W. B. F.
See Flower, [Rev.] William Balmbro

W. B. K.
See Kempling, William Bailey

W. B. L.
See Lapham, William Berry

W. B. L.
See Lord, W. B.

W. B. M.
See McCabe, William Bernard

W. B. O. P.
See Peabody, William Bourne Oliver

W. B. W.
See Whitmarsh, William Burt

W. C.
See Carleton, William

W. C.
See Chambers, [Sir] William

W. C.
See Cowley, William

W. C.
See Garrick, David

W. C. B.
See Bryant, William Cullen

W. C. B. W.
See Wyse, William Charles Bonaparte

W. C. C.
See Cotton, William Charles

W. C. C.
See Coward, William C.

W. C., Jun.
See Carleton, William, Jr.

W. C., M. D.
See Coward, William

W. C., Rev.
See Cole, William

W. C., Sir
See Savile, [Sir] George [Marquis of Halifax]

W. D.
See Darley, William

W. D.
See Day, W.

W. D.
See Drysdale, William

W. D.
See Duane, William

W. D.
See Dudeney, Wilfred

W. D.
See Dudgeon, William

W. D.
See Ness, Richard Derby

W. D. N.
See Northend, William Dummer

W. D. S.
See Sadleir, William Digby

W. D. W.
See Wilson, William Dexter

W. E.
See Emerson, William

W. E. A.
See Aytoun, William Edmonstoune

W. E. A. A.
See Axon, William Edward Armitage

W. E. F.
See Flaharty, W. E.

W. E. H.
See Heygate, William Edward

W. E. S.
See Simmons, William E.

W. E. W.
See Walker, W. E.

W. F.
See Falconer, William

W. F.
See Field, Edwin Wilkins

W. F.
See Field, William

W. F.
See Fiske, [Daniel] Willard

W. F. B.
See Bateman, William Fairbairn

W. F. P.
See Palmer, W. F.

W. F., Sir
See Fownes, [Sir] William

W. F. T.
See Taylor, W. F.

W. F. T.
See Taylor, William Frederick

W. G.
See Deacon, William Frederick

W. G.
See Gardner, William

W. G.
See Gauntley, William

W. G.
See Gell, [Sir] William

W. G.
See Grace, William Gilbert

W. G.
See Greene, William

W. G.
See Gregory, William

W. G. A.
See Allen, G. W.

W. G. B.
See Blaikie, William Garden

W. G. C.
See Clark, William George

W. G. D.
See Dix, William Giles

W. G. L.
See Mencken, Henry Louis [Harry]

W. G. S.
See Simms, W[illiam] Gilmore

W. H.
See Hennessy, William Charles

W. H.
See Herbert, William

W. H.
See Higgins, William

W. H.
See Hoare, William

W. H.
See Hornsell, William

W. H.
See Horsnell, William

W. H.
See Shakespeare, William

W. H. B.
See Bathurst, William Hiley

W. H. C.
See Channing, [Rev.] William Henry

W. H. D. A.
See Adams, William Henry Davenport

W. H. F.
See Furness, William Henry

W. H. H.
See Harvey, William Henry

W. H. H.
See Haseltine, W. H. H.

W. H. H.
See Herford, [Rev.] William Henry

W. H. J. W.
See Weale, William Henry James

W. H. L.
See Leeds, William Henry

W. H., Mr.
See Powis, William Herbert

W. H. R.
See Royston, William Haylett

W. H. R
See Rule, William Harris

W. H. W.
See Watts, Walter Henry

W. H. W.
See Whitmore, William Henry

W. H. W.
See Wyman, William Henry

W. I.
See Iago, William

W. J.
See Johnson, William

W. J. A. B.
See Bradford, William John Alden

W. J. B.
See Battersby, W. J.

W. J. B.
See Butler, William John

W. J. D.
See De La Mare, Walter [John]

W. J. D.
See Deane, William John

W. J. D. R.
See Ryder, W. J. D.

W. J. E. B.
See Bennett, William James

W. J. F.
See Fitzpatrick, William John

W. J. R.
See Robson, William James

W. J. S.
See Snelling, William Joseph

W. K.
See Kertland, William

W. K.
See Kingsford, William

W. K.
See Marston, John

W. L.
See Foe, Daniel

W. L.
See Lauder, William

W. L.
See Russell, Matthew

W. L. C.
See Collins, William Lucas

W. L. D.
See Dickinson, W. L.

W. L. K.
See Keese, William Linn

W. L. W.
See Webb, William Locock

W. M.
See Jones, Walter

W. M.
See Mackenzie, William

W. M.
See Milton, [Rev.] William

W. M., A Beneficed Priest
See Maskell, William

W. M., Esq.
See Moyle, Walter

W. M., of Mevagissey
See Moore, [Rev.] William

W. M. R.
See Russell, W. M.

W. N.
See Newell, William

W. N.
See Nind, William

W. N.
See Noy, William

W. N. S.
See Skelly, William Nugent

W. O., Esq.
See Oldys, William

W. O. S.
See Stillman, W. O.

W. O'B.
See O'Brien, William Smith

W. P.
See Dickens, Charles

W. P.
See Lunt, William Parsons

W. P.
See Pamplin, W.

W. P. C.
See Carey, William Paulet

W. P. C-y
See Carey, William Paulet

W. P. H.
See Hodgkinson, Wilfred Philip

W. P. L.
See Lunt, William Parsons

W. P. M.
See Mulchinock, William Pembroke

W. P. O.
See Walsh, William Pakenham

W. R.
See Hearst, William Randolph

W. R.
See Ross, William

W. R.
See Russell, William

W. R. G.
See Greg, William Rathburn

W. R. H.
See Hearst, William Randolph

W. S.
See Haring, G. W. H.

W. S.
See Silsbee, [Rev.] William

W. S.
See Spalding, William

W. S.
See Spaulding, William

W. S.
See Stokes, Whitley

W. S. J.
See Jordan, W. S.

W. S. L. S.
See Lach-Szyrma, Wladislaw Somerville

W. S. M.
See Mason, William Shaw

W. S., M.P.
See Stewart, William

W. S. P.
See Perry, William Stevens

W. S. R.
See Raleigh, Walter S.

W. T.
See Thornton, William

W. T.
See Tong, William

W. T.
See Tyndale, William

W. T. M.
See Meyler, Walter Thomas

W. T. P.
See Palmer, William Thomas

W. T., Sir
See Temple, [Sir] William

W. U. R.
See Richards, William Upton

W. W.
See Bloom, William

W. W.
See Whyte, William

W. W.
See Willis, William

W. W.
See Winstanley, William

W. W. C.
See Clapp, William Warland, Jr.

W. W. S.
See Story, William Wetmore

W. W. W.
See Waldron, William Watson

W. Y.
See Yates, William

Wa hun-sen-a-cawh [or Wahunsonacook]
1550?-1618 [WBD]
American Indian chieftain
* Powhatan

Wa Sha-Quon-Asin 1888-1938 [WBD]
Canadian-Indian author
* Grey Owl

Wa Sha-quon-asin
See Belaney, Archibald Stansfeld

Wa Tho Huck [Bright Path]
See Thorpe, James Francis [Jim]

Wabash George Mullin
See Mullin, George Joseph

Wabbes, Maria 20th c. [IBY]
Illustrator
* Florence

Wabun [East Wind]
See James, Marlise Ann

Wace, Robert 1120-1180 [PA]
Author
* Wistace, Grace

Wace, W. E.
See Nicoll, [Sir] William Robertson

Wachenheimer, Fred 1915- [JL]
*American television executive and
producer*
* Friendly, Fred W.

Wacher, August 1862-? [BE]
American baseball player
* Sunday, Art[hur]

Wachsmann, Franz 1906-1967 [FC, PMJ,
WEF]
German-born composer
* Waxman, Franz

Wachtel, Larry 20th c. [HPPN]
American financial analyst
* [The] Voice of Wall Street

Wachtel, Robert 20th c. [RM]
Musician
* Wachtel, Waddy

Wachtel, Waddy
See Wachtel, Robert

Wacky Joaquin Andujar
See Andujar, Joaquin

Waddel, Charles Carey 1868-1930 [WW]
Author
* Carey, Charles

Waddell, Evelyn Margaret 1918- [CA,
SAT, WD]
Canadian author
* Cook, Lyn

Waddell, George Edward 1876-1914
[AS, BE, PB]
American baseball player
* Waddell, Rube

Waddell, James 1739-1805 [FFF]
Irish-born American clergyman
* [The] Blind Preacher

Waddell, John 1854-1938 [HPPN]
Canadian-American civil engineer
* [The] Father of the Vertical Lift
 Bridge

Waddell, Reed 1859-1895 [HPPN]
American swindler and confidence man
* [The] Father of the Gold Brick
 Swindle

Waddell, Rube
See Waddell, George Edward

Waddell, Samuel J. 1879-1967 [LC]
Irish playwright
* Mayne, Rutherford

Waddell, William S.
See Andres, William Shackleford

Waddington, Alfred Penderill 1801-1872
[CCL]
Canadian author
* One of the People

Waddington, Miriam 1917- [CA]
Canadian author
* Merritt, E. B.

Waddington, Samuel Ferrand [IP]
British physician and author
* Sidney, Algernon

Waddles, Charleszetta Campbell 1912-
[HPPN, IBW]
American clergyman
* [The] Black Angel of the Poor
* Detroit's Black Angel
* Waddles, Mother

Waddles, Mother
See Waddles, Charleszetta Campbell

Wade, A. E.
See Wade, Arthur Edward

Wade, Abraham Lincoln 1880-1968 [BE]
American baseball player
* Wade, Ham

Wade, Alan
See Vance, John Holbrook [Jack]

Wade, Arthur Edward 1895- [ART]
Welsh painter
* Wade, A. E.

Wade, Benjamin Franklin 1800-1878
[HPPN]
American abolitionist and politician
* Wade, Bluff Ben
* Wade, Old Ben

Wade, Bill
See Barrett, Geoffrey John

Wade, Bluff Ben
See Wade, Benjamin Franklin

Wade, Doc
See Wade, Harold

Wade, Gale
See Wade, Galeard Lee

Wade, Galeard Lee 1929- [BE]
American baseball player
* Wade, Gale

Wade, George Alfred 1863-? [WWL]
British author
* [The] Scholar Gypsy
* Vennew, Norman R.

Wade, George Edward 1869-1954 [BEW,
EMT, F1]
British comic actor
* [The] Prime Minister of Mirth
* Robey, [Sir] George

Wade, Ham
See Wade, Abraham Lincoln

Wade, Harold 20th c. [RO2]
American musician
* Wade, Doc

Wade, Harry Vincent 1894- [BI]
American journalist
* Soaper, Senator

Wade, Henry
See Aubrey-Fletcher, [Sir] Henry
Lancelot

Wade, Herbert
See Wales, Hugh Gregory

Wade, Jacob Fields 1912- [BE]
American baseball player
* Wade, Whistlin' Jake

Wade, Jake
See Wade, Julius Jennings

Wade, Jennifer
See Wehen, Joy DeWeese

Wade, Joanna
See Berckman, Evelyn Domenica

Wade, John 19th c. [IP, PA]
British barrister and author
* J. W.
* [The] Original Editor

Wade, John Stevens
See Stevens, Clysle

Wade, Julius Jennings 20th c. [BBH]
American sportswriter and columnist
* Wade, Jake

Wade, Kit
See Carson, Xanthus

Wade, Malcolm 1914- [BB]
American basketball player
* Wade, Sparky

Wade, Old Ben
See Wade, Benjamin Franklin

Wade, Richard Frank 1899-1957 [BE]
American baseball player
* Wade, Rip

Wade, Rip
See Wade, Richard Frank

Wade, Robert [Bob] 1920- [CA, EMD,
WW]
American author
* Dalmer, Will [joint pseudonym with
 Bill Miller]
* Masterson, Whit [joint pseudonym
 with Bill Miller]
* Miller, Wade [joint pseudonym with
 Bill Miller]
* Wilmer, Dale [joint pseudonym with
 Bill Miller]

Wade, Robert [Bob]
See McIlwain, David

Wade, Rosalind Herschel 1909- [CAP,
WD]
British author and poet
* Carr, Catharine

Wade, Sparky
See Wade, Malcolm

Wade, Virginia 1946?- [HPPN]
British tennis player
* [The] Last of the Big Time Amateurs

Wade, Whistlin' Jake
See Wade, Jacob Fields

Wade, William C., Jr. 1945- [BA]
American physician
* Jamaludeen, Abdul Hamid

Wadekin, Karl-Eugen
See Waedekin, Karl-Eugen

Wadelton, Maggie Jeanne 1896- [BI,
HPPN, SFL]
Irish-American author
* Owen, Maggie
* Wadelton, Maggie-Owen

Wadelton, Maggie-Owen
See Wadelton, Maggie Jeanne

Wades in the Water 1871?-1947
[HPPN]
American Indian chief
* [The] Last of the Buffalo Hunters

Wadinasi, Sedeka
See Nall, Hiram Abiff

Wadkar, Hansa 1924-1971 [SC]
Indian actress
* Wadkar, Swan

Wadkar, Swan
See Wadkar, Hansa

Wadkins, Jerry Lanston 1951- [EG]
American golfer
* Wadkins, Lanny

Wadkins, Lanny
See Wadkins, Jerry Lanston

Wadler, Lucille 1906?- [NY 4-2-85]
American actress and producer
* Lortel, Lucille

Wadley, Wilfred John
See White, Frank James

Wadlow, M. Marie 20th c. [BBH]
American softball player
* Wadlow, Waddy

Wadlow, Robert Pershing 1918-1940
[HPPN]
American citizen, 9' tall
* [The] World's Tallest Man

Wadlow, Waddy
See Wadlow, M. Marie

Wadman, Elmer E. 19th c. [FFF, IP]
American writer
* Ellsworth

Waechter, Georg Philipp Ludwig Leonhard 1762-1837 [HPPN, NPS]
German soldier, educator, author
* Weber, Veit

Waedekin, Karl-Eugen 1921- [CA]
German educator and author
* Wadekin, Karl-Eugen

[The] Wag of Whitehall Court
See Shaw, George Bernard

Wagenhurst, Elwood Otto 1863-1946
[BE]
American baseball player
* Wagenhurst, Woodie

Wagenhurst, Woodie
See Wagenhurst, Elwood Otto

Wagenknecht, Edward [Charles] 1900-
[CA]
American author and editor
* Forrest, Julian

Wager, Mary A. E. 19th c. [FFF, IP, PA]
American author
* Mintwood

Wager, Michael
See Weisgal, Emanuel

Wager, Walter Herman 1924- [CA, IAW]
American author
* Herman, Walter
* Tiger, John

Waggamon, Mary T. [FFF]
American writer
* Fairie, Fanny
* Queerquill

[The] Waggish Welsh Judge
See Hardinge, George

Waggner, George
See Waggoner, George

Waggoner, George 1894- [FD]
American director
* Waggner, George

Waghorn, H. L.
See Horn, Holloway

Wagman, Naomi 1937- [CA]
Irsaeli-born writer
* Newmar, Rima

Wagmann, Adam 1905- [EWL]
Polish poet and author
* Wazyk, Adam

Wagmuller, Charlotte 20th c.
Actress
* Susa, Charlotte

Wagner, Albert 1869-1928 [BE]
American baseball player
* Wagner, Butts

Wagner, Aubrey 20th c.
American industrialist
* Wagner, Red

Wagner, Billy 1947- [HPPN]
American boxer
* Kelly, Billy
* Wagner, Kelly

Wagner, Broadway
See Wagner, Charles Thomas

Wagner, Bull
See Wagner, William George

Wagner, Butts
See Wagner, Albert

Wagner, C[harles] Peter 1930- [CA]
American author and editor
* Epafrodito
* Underwood, Lewis Graham

Wagner, Charles F. 1881-1943 [BE]
American baseball player
* Wagner, Heinie

Wagner, Charles Thomas 1912- [BE]
American baseball player
* Wagner, Broadway

Wagner, Cheekie [or Cheeks]
See Wagner, Leon Lamar

Wagner, Cosima 1837-1930
Wife of German composer, Richard Wagner
* [The] Delphic Oracle

Wagner, Daddy Wags
See Wagner, Leon Lamar

Wagner, Danny, Jr. 1968- [IBW]
American karate expert
* Wagner, Little Man

Wagner, Edward 1903?-1956 [BI, EJS]
American boxer
* Wagner, Kid

Wagner, Emmet ?-1977 [FIR]
Actor
* Wagner, Kid

Wagner, Ernest B. 20th c. [BBH]
American basketball coach
* Wagner, Griz

Wagner, Frank
See Wagner, Franklin A.

Wagner, Franklin A. 20th c. [BEW]
American choreographer, director, educator
* Wagner, Frank

Wagner, George Raymond 1915?-1963
[HPPN, SC, SR]
American wrestler
* Gorgeous George

Wagner, George Raymond (cont.)
* Gorgeous Georgeous
* [The] Human Orchid

Wagner, Griz
See Wagner, Ernest B.

Wagner, Gustav Franz 1912?-
German Nazi police official
* [The] Human Beast

Wagner, Hans 1872-? [LAO]
German author
* Wagner-Schoenkirch, Hans

Wagner, Hans
See Wagner, John Peter

Wagner, Heinie
See Wagner, Charles F.

Wagner, Honus
See Wagner, John Peter

Wagner, John Peter 1874-1955 [AS, BAB, BE]
American baseball player
* [The] Flying Dutchman
* Wagner, Hans
* Wagner, Honus

Wagner, Kelly
See Wagner, Billy

Wagner, Kid
See Wagner, Edward

Wagner, Kid
See Wagner, Emmet

Wagner, Leon Lamar 1934- [BE, DGS, PB]
American baseball player
* Wagner, Cheekie [or Cheeks]
* Wagner, Daddy Wags
* Wagner, Wag

Wagner, Little Man
See Wagner, Danny, Jr.

Wagner, Mark Duane 1954- [SMG]
American baseball player
* Wagner, Peanut

Wagner, Peanut
See Wagner, Mark Duane

Wagner, Red
See Wagner, Aubrey

Wagner, [Wilhelm] Richard 1813?-1883?
[HN, HPPN]
German composer
* [The] Michael Angelo of Opera
* [The] Shakespeare of Harmony
* [The] Titan of Music

Wagner, Robert F. 1877-1953 [HPPN]
German-American politician and legislator
* [The] Father of the Wagner Act

Wagner, Sharon B. 1936- [CA]
American author
* Stephens, Casey

Wagner, Wag
See Wagner, Leon Lamar

Wagner, William George 1887-1967
[BE]
American baseball player
* Wagner, Bull

Wagner-Schoenkirch, Hans
See Wagner, Hans

Wago, Bob Allotey 1943-   [RBE]
Ghanaian boxer
* Allotey, Bob

[The] Wagon Boy
See Corwin, Thomas

Wagon Tongue Adams
See Adams, Joseph Edward [Joe]

Wagon Tongue Keister
See Keister, William Hoffman

Wagoner, Hank
See Mosher, L. E.

Wagschal, Harry
See Goldfisch, Harry

Wagstaff, Harold 1891-1939   [OCS]
British rugby player
* [The] Prince of Centres

Wagstaff, Lancelot
See Thackeray, William Makepeace

Wagstaff, Simon
See Swift, Jonathan

Wagstaff, Theophile
See Thackeray, William Makepeace

Wagstaffe, Jeffrey
See Burroughs, Lewis

Wagstaffe, Launcelot
See Irving, Washington

Wagstaffe, Launcelot, Jr.
See Mackay, Charles

Wagstaffe, William 1685-1725   [IP]
British physician and author
* Crispin
* Tripe, [Dr.] Andrew

Wagstffe, John, Esq., of Wilbye Grange
See Mackay, Charles

Wah Kat Yu Ten [Beautiful Rainbow]
See Beauchamp, William Martin

Wahab, Charles James 19th c.   [IP]
British author
* One Who Knows

Wahl, Brick
See Wahl, Stephen Peters [Steve]

Wahl, Caedmon Thomas 1931-   [HPPN]
American clergyman and author
* Father Caedmon

Wahl, Lou
See Schaffenberger, Kurt

Wahl, Stephen Peters [Steve] 1919-
[HPPN]
American football coach
* Wahl, Brick

Wahl, Thomas [Peter] 1931-   [CA]
American clergyman and author
* Caedmon, [Father]

Wahl, Walter Dare
See Kalwara, Walter

Wahloo, Per 1926-1975   [CA]
Swedish author
* Wahloo, Peter

Wahloo, Peter
See Wahloo, Per

Wahls, Mike
See Wahls, Myron Hastings

Wahls, Myron Hastings 1931-   [BA]
American jurist
* Wahls, Mike

Wahn, Don
See Stack, Philip

[The] Wahoo Barber
See Crawford, Samuel Earl

Wahoo Sam Crawford
See Crawford, Samuel Earl

Waid, J. B. 1804-?   [CCL]
Canadian poet and author
* [The] Bard of Niagara

Wailer, Bunny
See Livingston, Neville

Wainer, Cord
See Dewey, Thomas B[lanchard]

Wainewright, Jeremiah 18th c.   [IP]
British physician and author
* [A] Member of the College of
  Physicians

Wainewright, Thomas Griffiths
1794-1852   [IP, NPS, SN, WBD]
British art critic and forger
* [The] Poisoner
* Varney, Gabriel
* Vinkbooms
* Weathercock, Janus

Wainscott, Cricket
See Blakely, Paul Lendrum

Wainwright, Alexander
See Rideing, William Henry

Wainwright, David
See Stansfield, Richard Habberton

Wainwright, Gordon Ray 1937-   [AW,
WD]
British educator and author
* Gordon, Ray

Wainwright, John 1921-   [TCCM]
British author
* Ripley, Jack

Wainwright, Jonathan Mayhew
1793-1854   [HPPN]
American clergyman
* [A] Presbyter of the Diocese of
  Massachusetts

Wainwright, Jonathan Mayhew
1883-1953   [HPPN]
American army officer
* Hero of Corregidor
* Wainwright, Skinny

Wainwright, Ken
See Tubb, Edwin Charles

Wainwright, Latham ?-1833   [IP]
British clergyman and author
* F. S. A.

Wainwright, Marie
See James, Mrs. Louis

Wainwright, Reader   [IP]
British barrister and author
* Another Barrister

Wainwright, Skinny
See Wainwright, Jonathan Mayhew

[Lieut] Wainwright Villiers, U. S. N.
See Cahill, Frank

Wainwright, Virginia 1891-   [HPPN]
American poet
* [The] Daisy Ashford of America

Wait
See Frankenstein, George L.

Wait [or Waite], Dash
See Wait, Frederick T.

Wait, Frederick T. 1853-1895   [EWG]
American gunfighter
* Wait [or Waite], Dash

Wait, Frona Eunice
See Colburn, Frona Eunice Wait

Wait, Simeon 17th c.   [SN]
Clergyman
* Magnano

Waite, A. E.
See Waite, Arthur Edward

Waite, Ada Lakeman 19th c.   [EOP]
*Wife of British scholar, Arthur Edward
Waite*
* Lucasta

Waite, Arthur Edward 1857-1942   [LC]
British poet and author
* Waite, A. E.

Waite, Bloody Bridles
See Waite, David Hanson

Waite, Charles ?-1951   [BI, SC]
Canadian actor and comedian
* Levance, Cal

Waite, David Hanson 1825-1901
[HPPN]
American politician
* Waite, Bloody Bridles

Waite, Deacon
See Waite, Frank E.

Waite, Frank E. 1906-   [CEI]
Canadian-born hockey player
* Waite, Deacon

Waite, Terry 1939?- [TI 12-2-85, WP 11-15-85]
Anglican lay worker
* [The] Anglican Henry Kissinger
* [The] Gentle Giant

Waite, Victor
See Makgill, [Sir] George

[The] Waiter
See DeLucia, Felice

Waitford, Hannah
See Hume, David

Wajcieckowski, Earl 1898-1926 [BLB, HPPN, MM, PHM]
American underworld figure
* [The] Father of the One-Way Ride
* Hymie the Polack
* [The] Perfume Burglar
* Weiss, Earl
* Weiss, Hymie
* Weiss, Little Hymie

Wajditsch Verbovac Von Doenhoff, [Baron] Gabriel 1888-1969 [BBD]
Hungarian-born American composer
* Wayditch, Gabriel

Wajsowna, Jadwiga
See Weiss, Pana

[The] Wake
See Hereward

Wake, Nancy 1916- [BDW]
Australian-born journalist and intelligence agent
* Andree, Madame
* Carlier, Lucienne

Wake, William 1657-1736? [IP]
British clergyman and author
* [A] Country Clergyman

Wakefeld, Robert ?-1537 [SN]
British scholar
* Polypus

Wakefield, Edward Gibbon 1796-1862 [IP]
British author
* [A] Member

Wakefield, Elizabeth
See Montgomery, Mamie Elizabeth

Wakefield, Homer 1865-1946 [BI]
American physician
* Locke, Prescott

Wakefield, Jean L.
See Laird, Jean E[louise]

Wakefield, John
See Darling, John

Wakefield, [Father] John
See Walsh, James Anthony

Wakefield, Priscilla [Bell] 1750-1832 [IP]
British author
* [A] Gentleman
* Priscilla

Wakefield, R. I.
See White, Gertrude M[ason]

Wakefield, Raymond ?-1919 [HPPN]
American vaudeville performer
* Eddy, Ray

Wakefield, Thomas 1752-1806 [IP]
British clergyman and author
* Philanthropos

Wakeford, William 1863-? [THR]
British theatrical manager
* Albert, William

Wakeley, Mr. ?-1853 [EOP]
Astrologer and author
* Raphael, Edwin
* Raphael IV

Wakeman, Annie
See Lathrop, Annie Wakeman

Wakenshaw, Janet Mackie 1951- [IAW]
Scottish journalist
* Fielding, Ann

Waking, Elizabeth
See Clagett, Sue Harry

Wako, Mdogo
See Nazareth, Peter

Wakoski, Diane 1937- [CA]
American poet
* Wakoski-Sherbell, Diane

Wakoski-Sherbell, Diane
See Wakoski, Diane

Waksman, Selman 1888-1973 [HPPN]
Russian-American biochemist
* [The] Discoverer of Streptomycin

Wakuman
See Wirgman, Charles

Walasiewicz, Stella 1911- [OCS]
Polish-born American sprinter
* Walsh, Stella

Walberg, George Elvin 1899-1978 [BE, PB]
American baseball player
* Walberg, Rube

Walberg, Rube
See Walberg, George Elvin

Walbrook, Anton
See Wohlbrueck, Adolf

Walch, Jakob
See Barbari, Jacopo de'

Walcott, Eliza [IP]
American poet
* [The] Two Sisters [joint pseudonym with Sarah G. Walcott]

Walcott, Eugene 20th c. [SG]
Boxer
* Meehan, Willie

Walcott, Jersey Joe
See Cream, Arnold Raymond

Walcott, Joe 1872-1935 [BX, RBE]
Barbadian-born boxer
* [The] Barbados Demon

Walcott, Josephine 19th c. [IP]
American author
* Havens, Cordelia

Walcott, Louis Eugene 1934- [IBW]
American musician, author, religious leader
* Farrakhan, Louis
* Louis X

Walcott, Mackenzie Edward Clarke 1822-? [IP]
British clergyman and poet
* M. E. C. W.

Walcott, Sarah G. [IP]
American poet
* [The] Two Sisters [joint pseudonym with Eliza Walcott]

Walczak, Ed[win Joseph] 1915- [BE]
American baseball player
* Walczak, Husky

Walczak, Husky
See Walczak, Ed[win Joseph]

Wald, Jerome Irving 1911- [HPPN]
American producer
* Wald, Jerry

Wald, Jerry
See Wald, Jerome Irving

Wald, Jerry
See Wald, Jervis

Wald, Jervis 1918?-1973 [PMJ]
American musician
* Wald, Jerry

Wald, Lillian D. 1867-1940
American humanitarian
* [The] Angel of Henry Street

Waldau, Max
See Hauenschild, Richard Georg Spiller von

Waldbauer, Albert Charles 1898- [BE]
American baseball player
* Waldbauer, Doc

Waldbauer, Doc
See Waldbauer, Albert Charles

Waldeck, Heinrich Suso
See Popp, Augustin

Waldemar [or Valdemar] 1281?-1319 [DNNS, WBD]
Margrave of Brandenburg
* [The] Great

Waldemar George
See Jarocinski, George

Waldemar I 1131-1182 [DNNS, SN, WBD]
King of Denmark
* [The] Great

Waldemar II 1170-1241 [WBD]
King of Denmark
* [The] Victorious

Waldemar IV 1320?-1375 [HPPN]
King of Denmark
* Atterdag

Walden, Ann Brevoort [Eddy]
1872?-1962 [BI]
American author
* Devoore, Ann

Walden, Walter 1870-? [NAA]
American author
* Irving, Miles

Walder, Herman 20th c. [IEJ]
American jazz musician
* Walder, Woody

Walder, Jimmy 20th c. [AES]
American soccer official
* [The] Dean of Referees

Walder, Woody
See Walder, Herman

Waldeyer, Wilhelm 1836-1921 [WBD]
German anatomist
* Waldeyer-Hartz, Wilhelm von

Waldeyer-Hartz, Wilhelm von
See Waldeyer, Wilhelm

Waldie, Charlotte Anne 1788-1859
[HFN, IP]
Scottish author
* [An] Englishwoman

Waldie, Walter S. 19th c. [IP]
American author
* Retlaw

Waldmueller, Robert
See Duboc, Edouard

Waldo, Cedric Dane
See Wolff, Cecil Drummond

Waldo, Dave
See Clarke, D[avid] Waldo

Waldo, E. Hunter
See Waldo, Edward Hamilton

Waldo, Edward Hamilton 1918-1985
[CA, ESF, HFF]
American author
* Ewing, Frederick R.
* Hunter, E. Waldo
* Sturgeon, Theodore Hamilton
* Waldo, E. Hunter
* Watson, Billy

Waldo, Hiram H. ?-1912 [HPPN]
American baseball promoter
* [The] Father of Baseball in the West

Waldo, James Curtis 1835-1901 [FFF]
American writer
* Linkinwater, Tim

Waldo, Leonard 1853-? [IP]
American astronomer and author
* L. W.

Waldo, Peter [IP]
British author
* [A] Layman

Waldo, Pierre 1120-1170 [HN]
Leader of religious sect
* [The] Morning Star of Reformation

Waldo, Ralph Emerson, III 1944- [CA]
American author, musician, composer
* Waldo, Terry

Waldo, Terry
See Waldo, Ralph Emerson, III

Waldorf, Lynn O. 1902- [FB]
American football coach
* Waldorf, Pappy

Waldorf, Pappy
See Waldorf, Lynn O.

Waldrip, Will
See Brock, Leonard Calvert

Waldron, Colin 1948- [SMG]
British soccer player
* Waldron, Waldo

Waldron, D'Lynn
See Waldron-Shah, Diane Lynn

Waldron, Francis Eugene 1905-1961
[BI]
American Communist leader
* Dennis, Eugene

Waldron, Francis Godolphin 18th c.
[IP]
British actor, editor, playwright
* F. G. W.

Waldron, George 1755-1840? [WBD]
Irish author
* Barrington, George

Waldron, Jack
See Baum, Jacob Kestem

Waldron, Kenny 20th c. [RBE]
American boxer
* Weldon, Kenny

Waldron, Marion Patton 20th c. [NAA]
American author
* Patton, Marion

Waldron, Waldo
See Waldron, Colin

Waldron, William Watson 19th c. [PI]
Irish poet
* W. W. W.

Waldron-Shah, Diane Lynn 1936- [CA]
American author
* Waldron, D'Lynn

Waldrop, Gid
See Waldrop, Gideon William
Winthrop, Jr.

Waldrop, Gideon William Winthrop, Jr.
1919- [ASC, BEW]
American composer, conductor, educator
* Waldrop, Gid

Waldseemueller, Martin 1470?-1518
[HPPN]
German cartographer
* Hylacomylus
* Ilacomilus

Waldstein, Charles 1856-1927 [WBD,
WWL]
American-born archaeologist
* Seymour, Gordon
* Walston, [Sir] Charles

Waldus, Edythe
See Sudlow, Elizabeth Williams

Wale, Henry 1891-1970 [FC]
British actor
* Oscar, Henry

Walenn, Cecil 1865?-1949 [THR]
British theatrical manager
* Barth, Cecil

Walentoski, Norman Edward 1917- [BE]
American baseball player
* Wallen, Norm[an Edward]

Wales, Geoffrey 1912- [ART]
British engraver
* G. W.

Wales, Henry Ware 1819-1856 [SN]
American scholar
* [A] Youth of Quiet Ways

Wales, Hubert
See Pigott, William

Wales, Hugh Gregory 1910- [CA]
American educator and author
* Wade, Herbert

Wales, Nym
See Snow, Helen Foster

Wales, Peleg
See Croffut, William A.

Wales, Wally
See Alderson, Floyd Taliaferro

Wales, Wally
See Taliaferro, Hal

Wales, Windy
See Knotts, Don

Walesa, Lech 1943?-
Polish labor leader
* Walesa, Leszek

Walesa, Leszek
See Walesa, Lech

Waley, Arthur
See Schloss, Arthur David

Walford, Bessy G. [IP, PA]
British author
* Walford, Flora

Walford, Christian
See Dilcock, Noreen

Walford, Cornelius ?-1885 [FFF, PA]
British author
* Junius

Walford, Flora
See Walford, Bessy G.

Walford, J. H. [FFF]
British writer
* Detached Badger

Walford, Thomas   [IP]
Author
* [An] Irish Gentleman

Walker, Aaron Thibeaux 1910-1975
[BWW, DAM, EJ]
American singer and songwriter
* [The] Daddy of the Blues
* Oak Cliff T-Bone
* Walker, T Bone

Walker, Albert Bluford 1926- [BE, PB, SMG]
American baseball player, manager, coach
* Walker, Rube

Walker, Alexander 19th c. [CCL]
Canadian poet
* [A] Soldier

Walker, Alvin 1954- [SMG]
American football player
* Walker, Skip

Walker, Anna 1891- [THR]
Irish actress
* O'Doherty, Eileen

Walker, Arlene
See Percival, Arlene Walker

Walker, Barbara K[erlin] 1921- [CA, SAT]
American author
* Kilreon, Beth

Walker, Beanie
See Walker, H. M.

Walker, Beau James
See Walker, James John [Jimmy]

Walker, Bee
See Walker, Bertha

Walker, Benjamin 19th c. [IP]
British author
* Albin, Rewk

Walker, Bertha 1908- [ASC]
American composer
* Walker, Bee

Walker, Bessie
See Henry, Bessie Walker

Walker, Big
See Walker, Edsell

Walker, Blind Willie
See Walker, Willie

Walker, Blue
See Walker, Tim

Walker, Bob 20th c. [GW]
American rodeo performer
* Walker, Cowboy

Walker, Bronc Man
See Walker, Enoch

Walker, C. 19th c. [IP]
British author
* Lottie

Walker, Charles 19th c. [IP]
British clergyman and author
* C. W.

Walker, Charles E. 20th c. [HPPN]
American lobbyist
* [The] S. O. B. Who Can Use His Elbows

Walker, Charles Herbert 1867-1947
[SC]
American actor
* Walker, Tex

Walker, Charles Thomas 1858-?   [HPPN]
American clergyman
* [The] Black Spurgeon of America

Walker, Chet 1940- [BB]
American basketball player
* [The] Jet

Walker, Chico
See Walker, Cleotha

Walker, Clarence 1951- [NBA, SMG]
American basketball player
* Walker, Foots

Walker, Clarence William 1889-1959
[AS, BE, PB]
American baseball player
* Walker, Tilly

Walker, Cleotha 1957-
American baseball player
* Walker, Chico

Walker, Clifton Reginald   [SFL]
Author
* Dixon, Richard

Walker, Clint 1927-
American actor
* Norman, Jett

Walker, Cowboy
See Walker, Bob

Walker, Curt
See Walker, William Curtis

Walker, Darrell 20th c.
American basketball player
* Walker, Sky

Walker, David Esdaile 1907-1968   [BI]
British journalist
* Esdaile, David
* Power, Michael

Walker, Dimples
See Wolke, Lillian

Walker, Dixie
See Walker, Ewart Gladstone

Walker, Dixie
See Walker, Frederick E.

Walker, Dixie
See Walker, James Roy

Walker, Dixie
See Walker, Richard

Walker, [Ewell] Doak, Jr. 1927- [FB, HPPN]
American football player
* [The] All American Mustang
* [The] Doaker
* [The] Little Man in Pro Football
* Walker, Doaker

Walker, Doaker
See Walker, [Ewell] Doak, Jr.

Walker, Douglas C. 1899?-1970 [AS, CFH, FB]
American football coach
* Walker, Peahead

Walker, E. C. 19th c. [IP]
American author
* Veritas

Walker, Edmund 1934?- [FC, TR]
British actor
* Kemp, Jeremy

Walker, Edsell 20th c. [OBW]
American baseball player
* Walker, Big

Walker, Edward Patrick 1901-1981
[BX, RBE]
American boxer
* [The] Toy Bulldog
* Walker, Mickey

Walker, Elocution
See Walker, John

Walker, Emily Kathleen 1913- [AW, WD]
British author
* Ash, Pauline
* Devon, Sarah
* Durham, Anne
* Ellis, Louise
* Lester, Jane
* Murray, Jill
* Tilbury, Quenna
* Treves, Kathleen
* Winchester, Kay

Walker, Emmeline Lisle   [FFF]
Author
* Lisle, Lester

Walker, Enoch 20th c. [GW]
American rodeo performer
* Walker, Bronc Man

Walker, Ewart Gladstone 1887-1965
[BE]
American baseball player
* Walker, Dixie

Walker, Filibuster
See Walker, William

Walker, Fleet
See Walker, Moses Fleetwood

Walker, Foots
See Walker, Clarence

Walker, Francis Amasa 1840-1897
[HPPN]
American economist and statistician
* [The] Father of the American Census

Walker, Frederic 1896- [HPPN]
British naval officer
* [The] U Boat Killer

Walker, Frederick E. 1910-1982 [BE, DGS, PB]
American baseball player
* [The] People's Cherce
* Walker, Dixie

Walker, Frederick Mitchell 1884-1958
American baseball player
* Walker, Mysterious

Walker, G. R. 19th c. [IP]
British author
* [An] Amateur

Walker, Gee
See Walker, Gerald Holmes

Walker, George 19th c. [IP]
British-born author
* Alpha

Walker, George 1915-1967 [MK]
American baseball player
* Walker, Schoolboy

Walker, George 20th c. [EF]
American football player
* Walker, Mickey

Walker, George Alfred 1807-1884 [FFF]
Welsh physician
* Walker, Graveyard

Walker, Gerald Holmes 1908-1981 [BE, PB]
American baseball player
* Walker, Gee

Walker, Gilbert Carlton 1833-1885 [HPPN]
American politician
* [The] Political Savior of Virginia

Walker, Glenn 20th c. [IBW]
American scientist
* Walker, Sonny

Walker, Graveyard
See Walker, George Alfred

Walker, H. M. 1884-1937 [HPPN]
American executive and playwright
* Walker, Beanie

Walker, Harry
See Waugh, Hillary Baldwin

Walker, Harry William 1918- [BE, PB, SMG]
American baseball player, manager, team owner
* [The] Hat

Walker, Harvey Willos 1906- [BE]
American baseball player
* Walker, Hub

Walker, Heather Eulalie 1908- [CED]
American actress
* Walker, Polly

Walker, Helen ?-1791 [SN]
Friend of Scottish author, Sir Walter Scott
* Deans, Jennie

Walker [?], Henry
See Taylor, John

Walker, Henry Augustus ?-1838 [HPPN]
American author
* H. A. W.

Walker, Herschel 1962?- [TI 12-13-82]
American football player
* [The] Franchise

Walker, Holly Beth
See Bond, Gladys Baker

Walker, Honey
See Walker, William

Walker, Hookey
See Walker, John

Walker, Hoss
See Walker, Jesse

Walker, Hub
See Walker, Harvey Willos

[The] Walker in the Pines
See Sibley, Henry Hastings

Walker, Ira
See Walker, Irma Ruth [Roden]

Walker, Irma Ruth [Roden] 1921- [CA]
American author
* Harris, Andrea
* Walker, Ira

Walker, J.
See Crawford, John Richard

Walker, J. Donald 1927- [NAD]
Spiritual teacher
* Kriyananda, [Swami]

Walker, Jack
See Thayer, Frederick C[lifton], Jr.

Walker, James [Jimmie]
American politician
* Beau James

Walker, James 1712-1793? [IP]
British clergyman and author
* Salvage, Jonas

Walker, James 1794-1874 [HPPN]
American clergyman, editor, college president
* [An] American
* J. W.
* W.

Walker, James 1912?-1949 [WWJ]
American jazz musician
* Walker, Jim Daddy

Walker, James Barr 1805-? [IP]
American clergyman and author
* [An] American Citizen

Walker, James John [Jimmy] 1881-1946 [HPPN]
American politician
* [The] Father of the New York State Boxing Bill
* [The] Playboy of New York
* Walker, Beau James
* [The] Wisecracker

Walker, James Roy 1893-1962 [BE]
American baseball player
* Walker, Dixie

Walker, Jeanette S. 1865-1952 [HPPN]
American singer
* Smith, Jeanette

Walker, Jerry Jeff
See Crosby, Ronald

Walker, Jesse 20th c. [OBW]
American baseball player
* Walker, Hoss

Walker, Jim Daddy
See Walker, James

Walker, John [DNNF, FFF]
British clerk
* Walker, Hookey

Walker, John 1732-1807 [DEL]
British lexicographer
* Walker, Elocution

Walker, [Rev.] John 1758-1823 [HPPN]
Irish clergyman
* One of Their Brethren

Walker, John 1781?-1859 [HPPN]
British druggist and inventor
* [The] Father of the Friction Match

Walker, John 1861-? [LAO]
British author
* Thirlmere, Rowland

Walker, John Mayon [Johnny] 1929- [BWW]
American singer
* Big Moose
* Moose John

Walker, Johnny Bull
See Bonica, John

Walker, Joseph
See McSpadden, Joseph Walker

Walker, Joseph Cooper 1762-1810 [IP]
Irish critic, author, historian
* [A] Member of the Arcadian Academy of Rome

Walker, Junior
See DeWalt, Autrey, Jr.

Walker, Katherine C. 19th c. [FFF, IP]
American author
* Kind, K. K.

Walker, Kenneth Francis 1924- [CA]
British-born physician and author
* Gifford-Jones, W.

Walker, Kenneth MacFarlane 1882-1966 [CA]
British physician and author
* MacFarlane, Kenneth

Walker, Kenny 20th c. [SI 12-5-83, SI 12-28-83]
American basketball player
* Walker, Sky

Walker, Lala
See Walker, Sally Butler

Walker, Lillian
See Wolke, Lillian

Walker, Lucy
See Sanders, Dorothy Lucie

Walker, Max
See Avallone, Michael [Angelo], Jr.

Walker, Mickey
See Walker, Edward Patrick

Walker, Mickey
See Walker, George

Walker, Mildred
See Schemm, Mildred Walker

Walker, Missy
See Walker, William

Walker, [Addison] Mort[imer] 1923-
[WECO]
American cartoonist
* Addison

Walker, Moses Fleetwood 1857-1924
[BE, IBW, OBW]
American baseball player
* Walker, Fleet

Walker, Mrs. D. M. F.   [FFF, IP, PA]
British author
* Mar, Helen

Walker, Mysterious
See Walker, Frederick Mitchell

Walker, Nancy
See Swoyer, Anna Myrtle

Walker, Obadiah 1616-1699 [HPPN]
British educator
* Ave-Maria, Obadiah

Walker, Patricius
See Allingham, William

Walker, Peahead
See Walker, Douglas C.

Walker, Peter Norman 1936-   [AW, CA]
British author
* Coram, Christopher
* Ferris, Tom
* Manton, Paul
* Rhea, Nicholas

Walker, Polly
See Walker, Heather Eulalie

Walker, Rachel
See Lenoir, Lucie

Walker, Richard 1791-1870 [WGT]
Author
* [A] Sub-Utopian?

Walker, Richard 19th c. [IP]
British botanist and author
* Philomath: Oxoniensis

Walker, Richard 19th c. [IP]
British author
* Basil
* W.

Walker, Richard 20th c. [TI 2-25-85]
American diplomat
* Walker, Dixie

Walker, Robert 18th c. [IP]
British author
* Bobbin, Tim, the Second

Walker, Robert 19th c. [IP]
British author
* R. W.

Walker, Robert 20th c. [HPPN]
American swindler
* Father Robert

Walker, Rose
See Dowsey, Rose Walker

Walker, Rowland 20th c.   [MBF, WWL]
British author
* Blair, Anthony
* Kenworthy, Hugh

Walker, Rube
See Walker, Albert Bluford

Walker, S. 19th c. [HPPN]
British author
* [The] Whistling Commercial

Walker, Sally Butler 1904-   [BA]
American business executive
* Walker, Lala

Walker, Samuel 18th c. [IP]
British clergyman and author
* [A] Presbyter of the Church of
  England
* S. W.
* S. W., A. B.

Walker, Samuel Abraham 19th c. [IP]
British clergyman and author
* S. A. W.

Walker, Sarah Breedlove 1867-1919
[HPPN]
American merchant and manufacturer
* [The] Nemesis of Kinky Hair

Walker, Schoolboy
See Walker, George

Walker, Shel
See Sheldon, Walt[er J.]

Walker, Sidney 1921-   [BX, IBW, RBE]
American boxer
* [The] Battlin' Shoeshine Boy
* Battling Beau Jack
* Beau Jack

Walker, Skip
See Walker, Alvin

Walker, Sky
See Walker, Darrell

Walker, Sky
See Walker, Kenny

Walker, Sonny
See Walker, Glenn

Walker, Stella Archer 20th c. [WD]
British author
* Archer-Batten, S.

Walker, Syd
See Kirkman, Sidney

Walker, T Bone
See Walker, Aaron Thibeaux

Walker, T Bone, Jr.
See Rankin, R. S.

Walker, T. Michael 1937- [CA]
American author
* White Elk, Michael

Walker, Tex
See Walker, Charles Herbert

Walker, Thomas 18th c. [HPPN]
American author
* Another Hand

Walker, Thomas 1850?-1934 [BEW,
HPPN]
British entertainer
* Walker, Whimsical

Walker, Tilly
See Walker, Clarence William

Walker, Tim 20th c. [RBE]
American boxer
* Walker, Blue

Walker, Timothy 1802-1856 [HPPN]
American attorney
* W.

Walker, W. E.   [IP]
British author
* W. E. W.

Walker, Whimsical
See Walker, Thomas

Walker, William 1824-1860 [HPPN]
American adventurer and filibuster
* [The] Green Eyed Man of Destiny
* [The] Grey Eyed Man of Destiny
* Walker, Filibuster
* Walker, Honey
* Walker, Missy

Walker, William 19th c. [NPS]
Australian author
* Cringle, Tom

Walker, William Curtis 1896-1955
[DGS]
American baseball player
* Walker, Curt

Walker, William Marvin [Billy] 1929-
[ECM, FCW]
American country-western performer
* [The] Masked Singer of Country
  Songs
* [The] Traveling Texan

Walker, William Sidney 1795-1846 [IP,
PA]
British author
* Haselfoot, Edward

Walker, William Sylvester 1846-?
[WWL]
Scottish author
* Coo-Ee

Walker, Willie 1896-1933 [BWW]
American singer
* Walker, Blind Willie

Walkerley, Rodney Lewis [De Burgh]
1905- [CAP]
British author
* Athos
* Vitesse, Grande

Walkin' Joe Teasdale
See Teasdale, Joseph

Walkin' Lawton Chiles
See Chiles, Lawton

Walkin' Slim
See Minter, Iverson

[The] Walking Gallows
See Hepenstall, Edward

[A] Walking Gentleman
See Grattan, Thomas Colley

[The] Walking Library
See Cameron, John

[A] Walking Library
See Hales, John

[The] Walking Library
See Longinus, Dionysius Cassius

[A] Walking Library
See Selden, John

[The] Walking Man
See Yost, Edward Frederick Joseph

[The] Walking Morgue
See Harper, Lucius Clinton

[The] Walking Mount Rushmore
See Sullivan, Edward Vincent

[The] Walking Museum
See Longinus, Dionysius Cassius

[The] Walking Parson
See Cooper, A. N.

[The] Walking Polyglot
See Agnesi, Maria Gaetana

[The] Walking Polyglot
See Mezzofanti, Giuseppe

Walkinshaw, Colin
See Reid, James Macarthur

Walkley, A. B.
See Walkley, Arthur Bingham

Walkley, Arthur Bingham 1855-1926
[LC, WWL]
British drama critic
* Spectator
* Walkley, A. B.

Walkup, Fairfax Proudfit
See Proudfit, Fairfax

Wall, Barbara 1911-   [CAT]
British author
* Lucas, Barbara

[The] Wall Climber
See Goodwin, Daniel

Wall, Corinna 1910-1965   [SC]
Actress and singer
* Mura, Corrine

Wall, G. 19th c.   [IP]
British botanist and author
* G. W.

Wall, Gummy
See Wall, Joseph Francis [Joe]

Wall, John William 1910-   [ESF, SFL, WGT]
British author
* Sarban

Wall, Joseph Francis [Joe] 1873-1936
[BE]
American baseball player
* Wall, Gummy

Wall, Max
See Lorimer, Maxwell George

Wall, Mrs. Henry   [FFF]
Entertainer
* Holt, Elise

Wall, Murray Wesley 1926-1971   [BE]
American baseball player
* Wall, Tex

Wall Street Bear in Europe
See Young, Samuel

Wall Street's Brash Outsider
See Steinberg, Saul

Wall Street's Favorite Bureaucrat
See Casey, William

Wall, Tessie
See Daroux, Tessie Wall

Wall, Tex
See Wall, Murray Wesley

Wallace, Agnes
See Villa, Mrs. Samuel B.

Wallace, Alexander Fielding 1918-   [CA, WD]
British author and translator
* Fielding, A. W.
* Fielding, Xan

Wallace, Babe
See Wallace, Emmitt

Wallace, Bad News
See Wallace, Edgar

Wallace, Beulah Thomas 1898-   [BWW]
American singer
* [The] Texas Nightingale
* Wallace, Sippie

Wallace, Bigfoot
See Wallace, William Alexander Anderson

Wallace, Bill
See Lally, William

Wallace, Billy 1880-1972   [HPPN]
American actor
* Wallace, Scratch

Wallace, Black
See Wallace, Charles

Wallace, Bobby
See Wallace, Roderick John

Wallace, Charles ?-1901   [HPPN]
American attorney and politician
* Wallace, Black

Wallace, Clarence Eugene 1890-1960
[BE]
American baseball player
* Wallace, Jack

Wallace, Cloris
See Leachman, Cloris W.

Wallace, Cookie
See Wallace, Roy Dean

Wallace, D. I. M.
See Wallace, Donald Ian Mackenzie

Wallace, David 1948-
American author
* Wallechinsky, David

Wallace, Dexter
See Masters, Edgar Lee

Wallace, Doc
See Wallace, Frederick Renshaw

Wallace, Donald Ian Mackenzie 1933-
[ART]
British artist
* Wallace, D. I. M.

Wallace, Doreen
See Rash, Dora Eileen Agnew [Wallace]

Wallace, Edgar 20th c.   [RBE]
American boxer
* Wallace, Bad News

Wallace, [Richard Horatio] Edgar
See Wallace, Walter

Wallace, [Lady] Eglantine 18th c.   [IP]
Scottish author
* E. W.

Wallace, Emmitt 20th c.   [IBW]
American entertainer and composer
* Wallace, Babe

Wallace, F. L.
See Wallace, Floyd L.

Wallace, Floyd L. 20th c.   [SF]
American author
* Wallace, F. L.

Wallace, Frederick Renshaw 1893-1964
[BE]
American baseball player
* Wallace, Doc

Wallace, George Corley 1919-   [CR, HPPN]
American politician
* [The] Fighting Little Judge
* [The] Headless Horseman
* Wallace, Lonesome George

Wallace, Gordon
See Shaw, Stanley Gordon

Wallace, Harry
See Atkinson, Harold Brown

Wallace, Harry Clinton 1882-1951   [BE]
American baseball player
* Wallace, Huck
* Wallace, Lefty

Wallace, Helen 20th c.   [WWL]
British author
* Roy, Gordon

Wallace, Henry 20th c.   [WWL]
Scottish author
* Chalom, John
* O'Dreams, John

Wallace, Henry A[gard] 1888-1965
[HPPN]
American vice president
* [The] Man With A Hoe
* [The] Peace Crusader
* [The] Quixotic Crusader
* [The] Unhappy Warrior
* Wallace in Wanderland
* Wallace, Plow 'em Under

Wallace, Henry Cantwell [Hank]
1866-1924 [HPPN]
American editor, publisher, politician
* [The] Farmer's Farmer

Wallace, Huck
See Wallace, Harry Clinton

Wallace, Ian 20th c. [NY 6-21-85]
Canadian clown
* Nion

Wallace, Ian
See Pritchard, John Wallace

Wallace in Wanderland
See Wallace, Henry A[gard]

Wallace, J. K. 1891-1950 [HPPN]
American union executive, musician, manufacturer
* Wallace, Spike

Wallace, Jack
See Wallace, Clarence Eugene

Wallace, James 18th c. [IP]
Scottish physician and author
* J. W., M. D.

Wallace, James Harold 1921- [BE]
American baseball player
* Wallace, Lefty

Wallace, Jean
See Wallasek, Jean

Wallace, Jennie
See Dobson, Mrs. Frank

Wallace, Jerry 1933- [ECM]
American singer and songwriter
* Smooth, Mr.

Wallace, John 20th c. [WW]
Author
* Aintree
* Grantham, Gerald
* Texas Ranger

Wallace, Laura
See Mourdaunt, Mrs. Frank

Wallace, Lefty
See Wallace, Harry Clinton

Wallace, Lefty
See Wallace, James Harold

Wallace, Lewis 1827-1905 [DNNS, FFF, SN]
American army officer, attorney, author
* Louisa

Wallace, Lonesome George
See Wallace, George Corley

Wallace, [Sister] M. Jean
See Paxton, Mary Jean Wallace

Wallace, May
See Maddox, May

Wallace, Mike
See Wallace, Myron

Wallace, Myron 1918- [IPA]
American television interviewer
* Wallace, Mike

Wallace, Nellie
See Liddy, Eleanor Jane

Wallace, Nigel
See Hamilton, Charles Harold St. John

[The] Wallace of Persia
See Nadir Shah

[The] Wallace of Switzerland
See Hofer, Andreas

[The] Wallace of Wales
See Glendower, Owen

Wallace, Pat 1929- [CA]
American author and poet
* Cloud, Patricia
* Latner, Pat Wallace
* Lord, Vivian
* Strother, Pat Wallace

Wallace, Paul
See Willens, Paul Norton

Wallace, Plow 'em Under
See Wallace, Henry A[gard]

Wallace, Rhody
See Wallace, Roderick John

Wallace, Richard
See Ind, Allison

Wallace, Robert
See Champion, D. L.

Wallace, Robert Grenville 19th c. [IP]
British soldier and author
* [An] Officer in His Majesty's Service

Wallace, Roderick John 1873-1960 [AS, BE, DGS]
American baseball player and manager
* Wallace, Bobby
* Wallace, Rhody

Wallace, Roger
See Charlier, Roger H[enri]

Wallace, Roy Dean 20th c. [RBE]
American boxer
* Wallace, Cookie

Wallace, Ruby Ann 1924- [BEW, CR, FC, IPA]
American actress
* Dee, Ruby
* [The] Negro June Allyson

Wallace, Scratch
See Wallace, Billy

Wallace, Sippie
See Wallace, Beulah Thomas

Wallace, Spike
See Wallace, J. K.

Wallace, Superfoot
See Wallace, William [Bill]

Wallace, Sylvan
See Ippoliti, Silvano

Wallace, Ted
See Kirkeby, Wallace Theodore

Wallace, Vince
See Gambino, Vincenzo

Wallace, Walter 1875-1932 [EMD, WGT]
British author
* Freeman, Richard [Dick]
* [The] King of Thrillers
* Wallace, [Richard Horatio] Edgar

Wallace, [Sir] William 1270?-1305
[DNNS, HN, RH]
Scottish patriot
* [The] Hammer and Scourge of England

Wallace, William [Bill] 20th c. [HPPN]
American karateist
* [The] King of Kicks
* Wallace, Superfoot

Wallace, William A.   [IP]
British author
* W. A. W.

Wallace, William Alexander Anderson
1817-1899 [HPPN]
American frontiersman
* Wallace, Bigfoot

Wallace-Clarke, George 1916- [WD]
British author
* Jaffa, George

Wallach, [Dr.] Louis C. 1886-1957 [BX, EJS, RBE]
American boxer
* Cross, Leach

Wallach, Meir 1867-1951 [JL]
Russian government official
* Litvinov, Maxim M.

Wallach, Meyer
See Finkelstein, Meyer

Wallack, James William 1795-1864
[FAA]
British-born actor
* [The] Elder Wallack

Wallack, John Johnstone 1820-1888
[FFF, WBD]
American-born actor and playwright
* Field, Allan
* Wallack, Lester

Wallack, Lester
See Wallack, John Johnstone

Wallard, Elizabeth 1910- [HPPN]
American educator and projectionist
* [The] One in a Duo

Wallard, Lee 1910-1963 [HPPN]
American auto racer
* [The] First Indy Four Hour Winner

Wallasek, Jean 1923- [FC]
American actress
* Wallace, Jean

Wallazz, Edmund A. 19th c. [HPPN]
American author
* E. A. W.

Wallcut, [Rev.] Robert Folger 1797-1884
[HPPN]
American clergyman
* Philo Pacificus
* R. F. W.

Wallechinsky, David
See Wallace, David

Wallek, Lee
See Johnson, Curt[is Lee]

Wallen, Norm[an Edward]
See Walentoski, Norman Edward

Wallenberg, Gustav 1904-1966 [SC]
Swedish-born actor and producer
* Wally, Gus

Wallenda, Karl 1905?- [HPPN]
German-American acrobat
* [The] Flying Wallenda

Waller, Brown
See Fraser, Waller Brown

Waller, Christopher Edward 1948- [DC]
British cricketer
* Waller, Wal

Waller, D. W.
See Wilmarth, Daniel

Waller, Edmund 1606-1687 [DEA, NPS,
SN]
British poet
* E. W.
* [The] Father of English Numbers
* [The] Inimitable
* [The] Master of the Feast
* Nature's Darling
* [The] Parent of English Verse

Waller, Fats
See Waller, Thomas Wright

Waller, John 1741-1802 [HPPN]
American clergyman
* [The] Devil's Adjutant
* Waller, Swearing Jack

Waller, John Francis 1810-1894 [DEL,
PA]
Irish author and poet
* Iota
* J. F. W.
* Slingsby, Jonathan Freke

Waller, John Francis 1883-1915 [BE]
American baseball player
* Waller, Red

Waller, Leslie 1923- [CA, WGT, WW]
American author
* Cody, C. S.
* Mann, Patrick

Waller, Lewis
See Lewis, William Waller

Waller, M. E.
See Waller, Mary Ella

Waller, Mary Ella 1855-1938 [LC]
American author
* Waller, M. E.

Waller, Max
See Warlomont, Maurice

Waller, P. H.
See Mahon, Patrick Herbert

Waller, Red
See Waller, John Francis

Waller, Sophia 17th c. [SN]
* Amoret?

Waller, Swearing Jack
See Waller, John

Waller, Thomas Wright 1904-1943
[ASC, BBD, HPPN, WWJ]
American jazz musician
* [The] Black Horowitz
* Waller, Fats

Waller, Virginia Harmon
See Sefrit, Sallie Mulholland

Waller, Wal
See Waller, Christopher Edward

Waller, [Sir] William 1597?-1668 [SN]
British army officer
* Arod
* William the Conqueror

Walley, David Gordon 1945- [IAW]
American author
* Tombs, Harry

Walley, Samuel Hurd 1805-1877 [IP]
American attorney, statesman, banker
* W.

Wallgren, Mon C.
See Wallgren, Monrad Charles

Wallgren, Monrad Charles 1891-
[HPPN]
American politician
* Wallgren, Mon C.

Wallin, Gunilla Lovisa 1938- [OP]
Swedish opera singer
* Slaettegard, Gunilla Lovisa

Wallin, Johan Olof 1779-1839 [HPPN]
Swedish poet, clergyman, hymn writer
* David's Harp of the North

Walling, Hubert 20th c. [HPPN]
American football player
* Walling, Wally

Walling, R. A. J.
See Walling, Robert Alfred John

Walling, Robert Alfred John 1869-1949
[LC]
British author
* Walling, R. A. J.

Walling, Wally
See Walling, Hubert

Wallington, George
See Figlia, Giorgio

Wallington, Lord
See Figlia, Giorgio

Wallis, A. S. C.
See Opzoomer, Adele Sophia Cornelia
van Antal

Wallis, B. and G. C.
See Wallis, George C.

Wallis, Blanche 1891-1918 [SC]
American actress
* Seelos, Annette

Wallis, Colonial
See Wallis, Frank Edwin

Wallis, Frank Edwin 1862-1929 [HPPN]
American architectural authority
* Wallis, Colonial

Wallis, George C. 20th c. [ESF, MBF,
SF]
British author
* Heath, Royston
* Stanton, John
* Wallis, B. and G. C.

Wallis, Geraldine McDonald 1925- [CA,
SAT]
American author and actress
* Campbell, Hope
* Hughes, Virginia
* McDonald, Cathy
* Wells, Helen

Wallis, Harold Joseph 1952- [SMG]
American baseball player
* Wallis, Tarzan

Wallis, Henry Marriage 20th c. [WWL]
British author
* Hilliers, Ashton

Wallis, Ik
See Laughton, Thomas R.

Wallis, Jenny
See Morrison, Mary Jane [Whitney]

Wallis, Mary Davis [Cook] [IP]
American author
* [A] Lady

Wallis, Pauline 1913?- [HPPN]
British dog racer
* [The] Queen of the Kennels

Wallis, Tarzan
See Wallis, Harold Joseph

Wallmann, Jeffrey M[iner] 1941- [CA]
American author
* Baxter, Phyllis
* Carter, Nick [house pseudonym]
* DaSilva, Leon
* Douglass, Amanda Hart
* Goering, Helga
* Graham, Carlotta
* Granby, Milton
* Heflin, Donald
* Jensen, Peter
* Miner, Matthew
* Mountbatten, Richard
* Reskind, John
* Robard, Jackson
* Roberts, Grant
* Saxon, Bill

Wallmann, Jeffrey M[iner] (cont.)
* Sheldon, Scott
* Simmons, Blake
* Sinclair, Grace
* Townsend, Mark
* Van Dorne, R.
* Wilson, Carole

Wallner, Christian Johannes 1948-
[IAW]
Austrian author
* Winkler, Johannes

Wallner, Franz
See Leidesdorf, Franz

Wallnutshire
See Foe, Daniel

Wallon, Jean ?-1882 [SN]
Author
* Colline

Wallop, Lucille Fletcher 1912- [CA]
American author
* Fletcher, Lucille

Wallopin Willie McCovey
See McCovey, Willie Lee

Wallraff, Guenter 20th c.
German journalist
* Esser, Hans

Walls, Ian Gascoigne 1922- [HPPN]
Scottish author
* Greenfingers, Mr.
* Lindsay, David

Walls, Peter 1926?-
Zimbabwe Rhodesian army officer
* Walls, Tommy

Walls, Tommy
See Walls, Peter

Wally, Gus
See Wallenberg, Gustav

Walmesley, Charles 1722-1797 [IP, PA]
British author and clergyman
* Pastorini, Signor

Walmoden
See Yarmouth, Countess of

Walmsley, Arnold Robert 1912- [CA]
British author
* Roland, Nicholas

Walmsley, Leo 1892- [WWL]
British author
* March Hare

Waln, Robert, Jr. 1797-1825 [IP]
American poet
* Atall, Peter
* [The] Hermit

Walneerg
See Knox, Thomas

Walpole, Horace
See Walpole, Horatio [Fourth Earl of Orford]

Walpole, Horatio [First Baron Walpole of Wolterton] 1678-1757 [SN]
British diplomat
* Old Horace

Walpole, Horatio [Fourth Earl of Orford] 1717-1797 [FFF, IP, NPS, SN, WBD, WGT]
British politician and author
* [The] Autocrat of Strawberry Hill
* [The] Frenchified Coxcomb
* H. W.
* Hill, Strawberry
* [The] Last of the Romans
* Lying Old Fox
* [A] Man
* Marshall, William
* Muralto, Onuphrio
* [A] Parasite of Genius
* [The] Puck of Literature
* S. T.
* This Trifler in Great Things
* Tydeus
* Ultimus Romanorum
* Walpole, Horace

Walpole, [Sir] Robert [First Earl of Orford] 1676-1745 [DNNF, HN, HPPN, NPS, SN]
British statesman
* Bluestring, Robin
* Brass, [Sir] Robert
* Courtely [or Courtley], [Sir] Robert
* Euphemius
* Flimnap
* [The] Grand Corrupter
* [The] Leviathan
* [The] Norfolk Gamester
* [The] Persuasive Euphemius
* Sidrophel, Sir
* Sir Bob
* [The] Triumphant Exciseman

Walraven
See Kaler, James Otis

Walraven, E. G.
See Jones, Emma Garrison

[The] Walrus
See Mackie, Albert D[avid]

Walsby, Charnock
See Heald, Leslie V.

Walser, Sam
See Howard, Robert Ervin

Walsh, Albert Edward 1887-1980 [FIR]
American director
* Walsh, Raoul

Walsh, Big Ed
See Walsh, Edward Augustine

Walsh, Big Moose
See Walsh, Edward Augustine

Walsh, Buck
See Walsh, Charles S.

Walsh, Charles 20th c. [SMG]
American football coach
* Walsh, Chile

Walsh, Charles S. 1901?-1950 [BBH, BI]
American rowing coach
* Walsh, Buck

Walsh, Chile
See Walsh, Charles

Walsh, Danny
See Walsh, Delano B.

Walsh, Dee
See Walsh, Thomas L.

Walsh, Delano B. 1945- [BA]
American engineer
* Walsh, Danny

Walsh, Edward Augustine 1881-1959
[BBH, BE, HPPN, PB]
American baseball player
* Walsh, Big Ed
* Walsh, Big Moose
* Walsh, Moose

Walsh, Flat
See Walsh, James

Walsh, Flora
See Hoyt, Mrs. Charles H.

Walsh, Frank
See March, Miles Standish

Walsh, Gillian Paton 1939- [HPPN]
British educator and author
* Walsh, Jill Paton

Walsh, J. M.
See Walsh, James Morgan

Walsh, James 1897- [CEI]
Canadian-born hockey player
* Walsh, Flat

Walsh, James
See Robinson, Frank M[alcolm]

Walsh, James Anthony 1867-1936
[CAT]
American author and clergyman
* Wakefield, [Father] John

Walsh, James Gerald 1919- [BE]
American baseball player
* Walsh, Junior

Walsh, James Morgan 1897-1952 [ESF, WGT, WW]
Australian-born author
* Hill, H. Haverstock
* Maddock, Stephen
* Walsh, J. M.

Walsh, Jill Paton
See Walsh, Gillian Paton

Walsh, Jimmy
See Walsh, Michael Timothy

Walsh, John 1835-1881 [PI]
Irish poet
* Boz
* [A] Cappoquin Girl
* J. J. W.
* J. W.
* Kilmartin
* Lismore
* Shamrock

Walsh, John Edward 1816-1869 [HPPN]
Irish barrister
* W.

Walsh, John Henry 1826-1888 [DEL, FFF, PA]
British author
* Stonehenge
* Vox, Valentine

Walsh, Johnny ?-1883 [BLB]
American gangleader
* Johnny the Mick

Walsh, Joseph Patrick [Joe] 1917- [BE]
American baseball player
* Walsh, Tweet

Walsh, Junior
See Walsh, James Gerald

Walsh, M. M. B. 20th c. [CA]
American author
* Walsh, Marnie

Walsh, Marie A. 19th c. [PA]
Author
* Sandette

Walsh, Marnie
See Walsh, M. M. B.

Walsh, Mary 1912- [HPPN]
American author
* Lavin, Mary

Walsh, Michael Paul 1866-1892 [PI]
Irish poet
* [A] Base Mechanic Wretch
* Buzz
* [A] Cashel Girl
* Gray, Louisa
* Philomath
* Phiz
* Pilate, Pontius

Walsh, Michael Timothy 1886-1947 [BE]
American baseball player
* Walsh, Jimmy
* Walsh, Runt

Walsh, Moose
See Walsh, Edward Augustine

Walsh, Mrs. John [FFF]
Entertainer
* Coleman, Kitty

Walsh, Raoul
See Walsh, Albert Edward

Walsh, Runt
See Walsh, Michael Timothy

Walsh, Stella
See Walasiewicz, Stella

Walsh, Thomas [Tom] ?-1910 [HPPN]
Irish-American carpenter and miner
* [The] Colorado Monte Cristo

Walsh, Thomas L. 1892- [BE]
American baseball player
* Walsh, Dee

Walsh, Tweet
See Walsh, Joseph Patrick [Joe]

Walsh, William 1663-1707 [SN]
British poet
* [The] Muses' Judge and Friend

Walsh, William Pakenham 1820-1902 [PI]
Irish clergyman, author, poet
* W. P. O.

Walsh, William Shepard 1854-1919 [HPPN]
American editor, critic, author
* Shepard, William

Walsh, William W. 1858-? [PA]
Author
* Fenwood, Harry
* Gellert

Walshe, Douglas 20th c. [MBF]
British author
* Carr, Adams

Walsingham
See McEwen, William Dalzell

Walsingham
See Stewart, Clinton

Walsingham, [Sir] Francis
See Arnall, William

Walster, Elaine Hatfield
See Hatfield, Elaine

Walston, [Sir] Charles
See Waldstein, Charles

Walston, Joseph
See Walston, Marie

Walston, Marie 1925- [CA]
American author
* Walston, Joseph

[The] Walt Disney of the Next Generation
See Finkelstein, Peter Max

[The] Walt Whitman of American Music
See Harris, Roy

Waltari, Mika [Toimi] 1908-1979 [CA]
Finnish author
* Nauticus
* Ritvala, M.

Walter 11th c. [HN, RH, SN]
Leader of the First Crusade
* [The] Penniless

Walter [code name used during World War II]
See Broz, Josip

Walter
See Henry VIII

Walter, Bruno
See Schlesinger, Bruno Walter

[The] Walter Camp of Brown Football
See Robinson, Edward N.

Walter, Chain Saw Maggie
See Walter, Maggie

Walter, Charles Russell 20th c. [BBH]
American basketball player
* Walter, Rut

Walter, Charles T. 19th c. [FFF]
American author
* Peck, Wallace

[The] Walter Damrosch of the Pacific Coast
See Stewart, Humphrey John

Walter, Dorothy Blake 1908- [CAP]
American author
* Blake, Katherine
* Blake, Kay
* Ross, Katherine

Walter, Frederick
See Schultz, Frederick Walter

Walter, Henry
See Rocken, Kurt Walter

Walter [or Walther], Johann
See Blanckenmueller, Johann

Walter, Lucy 1630?-1658 [HPPN]
Welsh mistress of Charles II of England
* Barlow, Mrs.
* Waters, Lucy

Walter, Maggie 1923?- [HPPN]
American anti-advertising advocate
* Walter, Chain Saw Maggie

Walter, Nancy
See Hagberg, Nancy

Walter of Evesham 14th c. [WBD]
British monk
* Odington, Walter

Walter of Swinbroke
See Baker, Geoffrey

Walter, Rut
See Walter, Charles Russell

[The] Walter Scott of Belgium
See Conscience, Hendrick

[The] Walter Scott of Hungary
See Josika, Miklos Nicholas

[The] Walter Scott of Italy
See Ariosto, Lodovico

[The] Walter Scott of the Middle Ages
See Froissart, Jean

Walter the Doubter
See Van Twiller, Walter

Walter, Thomas 1696-1728 [HPPN]
American clergyman
* [A] Son of Martin Marprelate

Walters, Alfred John 1892-1956 [BE]
American baseball player
* Walters, Roxy

Walters, Barbara 1931- [BP, HPPN]
American newscaster
* Elliott, Babs
* [The] First Lady of Talk

Walters, Big Stan
See Walters, Stan

Walters, Bucky
See Walters, William Henry

Walters, Catherine 19th c. [NN]
British courtesan
* Skittles

Walters, Chad
See Smith, Richard Rein

Walters, Dick
See Showalter, Richard [Dick]

Walters, Dick
See Walters, Vernon Anthony

Walters, Frankie 1859-1953 [SC]
American actress
* Bailey, Frankie
* [The] Girl with the Million Dollar
  Legs

Walters, [James] Fred 1912-1980 [BE]
American baseball player
* Walters, Whale

Walters, Gordon
See Locke, George [Walter]

Walters, Hugh
See Hughes, Walter Llewellyn

Walters, J. 20th c. [MBF]
British author
* Owen, Norman

Walters, John 1949- [DC]
British cricketer
* Walters, Welder

Walters, Kirby 20th c. [GW]
American rodeo performer
* Walters, Popcorn

Walters, Marvin M. 1882- [NAA]
American clergyman and writer
* Brinker, Martin

Walters, Maud 1910- [THR]
American actress and dancer
* Walters, Polly
* Walters, Teddy

Walters, Mule
See Walters, Stan

Walters, Nell
See Muse, Patricia [Alice]

Walters, Patricia Wheeler ?-1967
[HPPN]
American actress
* Wheeler, Patricia

Walters, Polly
See Walters, Maud

Walters, Popcorn
See Walters, Kirby

Walters, Rick
See Rowland, Donald Sydney

Walters, Robert [PA]
Author
* Roberts, George

Walters, Roxy
See Walters, Alfred John

Walters, Shelly
See Sheldon, Walt[er J.]

Walters, Stan 1948- [SMG]
American football player
* Walters, Big Stan
* Walters, Mule

Walters, T. B.
See Rowe, John Gabriel

Walters, Teddy
See Walters, Maud

Walters, Vernon Anthony 1917- [WP
12-16-85]
*American military officer and government
official*
* Walters, Dick

Walters, W. G.
See Steffens, Arthur

Walters, Warren
See Manning, William Henry

Walters, Welder
See Walters, John

Walters, Whale
See Walters, [James] Fred

Walters, William Henry 1909?- [BI,
DGS, PB]
American baseball player
* Walters, Bucky

Walthall, Henry B. 1878-1936 [HPPN]
American actor
* [The] Mansfield of the Screen
* Walthall, Wally

Walthall, Wally
See Walthall, Henry B.

Walther, David 1948- [HPPN]
American auto racer
* Walther, Salt

Walther, George 1946?-1974 [BI]
American boat racer
* Walther, Skipp

Walther, Salt
See Walther, David

Walther, Skipp
See Walther, George

Walthers, Jerrie
See Withers, Jane

Waltimore, Iain
See Waltman, William John

Waltman, William John 1905- [HPPN]
Dutch author
* Waltimore, Iain

Walton
See Thorpe, Henry

Walton, Bill 1952-
American basketball player
* [The] Mountain Man
* [The] Stranger

Walton, Bryce 1918- [ESF, WGT]
American author
* Franklin, Paul
* O'Hara, Kenneth
* Sands, Dave? [house pseudonym?]

Walton, Daniel James 1947- [BE]
American baseball player
* Walton, Mickey

Walton, Douglas
See Duder, J. Douglas

Walton, Evangeline
See Ensley, Wilma Evangeline

Walton, Francis
See Hodder, Alfred

Walton, Fred
See Heming, Frederick

Walton, Harry 20th c. [WGT]
Author
* Collier, Harry

Walton, Izaak 1593-1683 [DEL, FFF,
PA, SN]
British author
* Chalkhill, John
* [The] Compleat Angler
* [The] Father of Angling
* [The] First Professional English
  Biograhper
* [The] Gentle
* Piscator
* Walton, Meek

Walton, John 20th c. [DLE1]
Playwright
* Conway, Olive [joint pseudonym with
  Harold Brighouse]

Walton, Lloyd 1953- [SMG]
American basketball player
* Walton, Speedy

Walton, Luke
See Henderson, Bill

Walton, Mary Ellen
See Williams, Linda Sue

Walton, Meek
See Walton, Izaak

Walton, Mercy Dee 1915-1962 [BWW]
American singer
* Dee, Mercy

Walton, Michael Robert 1945- [HR]
Canadian-born hockey player
* Walton, Shakey

Walton, Mickey
See Walton, Daniel James

Walton, Modest Bill
See Walton, William Theodore [Bill]

Walton, Shakey
See Walton, Michael Robert

Walton, Speedy
See Walton, Lloyd

Walton, W. H. [PA]
Author
* Mansfield, Walworth

Walton, William Theodore [Bill] 1952-
[HPPN]
American basketball player
* Walton, Modest Bill

Walton, Zach
See   Zachary, Jonathan Thompson
Walton

Waltz, Jean Jacques 1873-1951 [BI, LAO]
French author
* Hansi

[The] Waltz King
See   King, Wayne Harold

[The] Waltz King
See   Strauss, Johann, Jr.

[The] Waltz King
See   Strauss, Johann, Sr.

Walworth, Alice
See   Graham, Alice Walworth

Walworth, Jeannette Ritchie 1837-1918 [HPPN, IP, PA]
American author
* Atom, Ann
* Haderman, Janet H.
* Haderman, Jeanette

Walz, Audrey 1907?-1983 [CC, WW]
American author
* Bonnamy, Francis

Wambsganss, William Adolph 1894- [BE]
American baseball player
* Wamby, William Adolph

Wamby, William Adolph
See   Wambsganss, William Adolph

Wampum, King
See   Pemberton, Israel

Wan Chia-Pao 1905- [MWD]
Chinese playwright
* Ts'ao Yu

Wan, [Mme.] Sul Te
See   Conley, Nellie

Wanamaker, John 1838-1922 [HPPN]
American retail merchant
* [The] Father of the Department Store
* [The] Father of the Grand Depot Store
* Pious John

Wanbaugh, Landis 1869-1911 [HPPN]
American actor
* McCord, Lewis

Wandan, Harry 1947- [RO2]
Dutch musician
* Vanda, Harry

[The] Wanderer
See   Barker, Matthew Henry

[The] Wanderer
See   Curtis, George William

Wanderer
See   D'Avigdor, Elim Henry

Wanderer
See   Dixon, William Scarth

[A] Wanderer
See   Flint, Susan C.

Wanderer
See   Gilbert, Jean

[The] Wanderer
See   Goethe, Johann Wolfgang von

[The] Wanderer
See   Lord, John Keast

[A] Wanderer
See   Moberley, A.

[A] Wanderer
See   Peirce, I.

[A] Wanderer
See   Ryan, William Thomas

[The] Wanderer
See   Watterston, George

Wanderer, Carl ?-1921 [HPPN]
American murderer
* [The] Butcher Boy
* [The] Hero Husband
* [The] Ragged Stranger Murderer

Wandering Eric Brook
See   Brook, Eric F.

[The] Wandering Jew
See   Aristeas

[The] Wandering Melodist
See   Incledon, Charles

[The] Wandering Minstrel
See   Wilson, Frederick

[A] Wandering Pilgrim
See   Dowling, Penelope

Wanderone, Rudolf Walter, Jr. 1913- [HPPN]
American pool player
* Minnesota Fats
* New York Fats

Wandrei, Howard Elmer 1909-1965 [WGT]
American author
* Coley, Robert
* Garron, Robert A.
* Graham, Howard
* Guernsey, H. W.
* Von Drey, Howard

[Der] Wandsbecker Bote
See   Claudius, Matthias

Waner, Lloyd James 1906-1982 [BE, DGS, HPPN, PB]
American baseball player
* Little Poison
* Warner, Muscles

Waner, Paul Glee 1903-1965 [BE, DGS, PB]
American baseball player
* Big Poison

Wang, C. T.
See   Wang Cheng-t'ing

Wang Chao-ming 1884-1944 [WBD]
Chinese politician
* Wang Ching-wei

Wang Cheng-t'ing 1882-1961 [WBD]
Chinese politician
* Wang, C. T.

Wang, Ching Hsien 1940- [CA]
Chinese-born educator and author
* Mu, Yang
* Shan, Yeh

Wang Ching-wei
See   Wang Chao-ming

Wang, Hui-Ming 1922- [CA]
Chinese-born wood engraver, calligrapher, translator
* H. M. W.

Wang Mang ?-23 [WBD]
Chinese emperor
* [The] Usurper

Wang Shou-jen 1472-1528? [WBD]
Chinese philosopher
* Wang Yang-ming

Wang Yang-ming
See   Wang Shou-jen

Wangara, Harun Kofi
See   Lawrence, Harold G.

Wangara, Malaika Ayo
See   Lawrence, Joyce Whitsett

Wangchuk, Anangavajra Khamsum
See   Govinda, Anagarika

Wanger, Beatrice 20th c. [NAA]
American-born writer
* Nadja

Wanger, Walter
See   Feuchtwanger, Walter

Wangner, Ellen D. 1874-? [NAA]
Canadian-born editor and author
* Jeffrey, Ellen

Wanlass, Chris
See   Wanlass, Cravens

Wanlass, Cravens 1926-
American inventor, engineer, computer scientist
* Wanlass, Chris

Wanlock, Rob
See   Reid, Robert

Wannamaker, Bruce
See   Moncure, Jane Belk

Wanner, Clarence Mellert 1884-1962 [BE]
American baseball player
* Wanner, Jack

Wanner, Jack
See   Wanner, Clarence Mellert

Wanninger, Paul Louis 1902- [BE]
American baseball player
* Wanninger, Pee Wee

Wanninger, Pee Wee
See   Wanninger, Paul Louis

Wanostrocht, Nicolas 1804-1876 [BI, NPS]
British author and cricketer
* Felix, Nicholas

Wanstall, Ken
See Green-Wanstall, Kenneth

Wantage, Baron
See Lindsay, Robert James

Wantland, Hal
See Wantland, Howell

Wantland, Howell 20th c. [EF]
American football player
* Wantland, Hal

Wanton, John 1672-1740 [HPPN]
American politician
* [The] Fighting Quaker

Wapens, Piet [Pete Weapons]
See Botha, Pieter

War Eagle
See Little Eagle

[The] War Governor
See Morton, Oliver Hazard Perry Throck

War Horse
See Nicholson, James William Augustus

[The] War Horse of Sumner County
See Trousdale, William

[The] War Horse of the Confederacy
See Longstreet, James

[The] War Poet
See Boker, George Henry

War Whoop Page
See Page, Alan

[The] War Women
See Hart, Nancy [Morgan]

[The] Warbeck of the North
See Otrepieff, Gregory

Warbeck, Perkin 1474-1499 [HN, HPPN, RH, SN]
Pretender to the crown of England
* [The] False Duke of York
* [The] Merchant of the Ruby
* [The] White Rose of England

Warbler, J. M.
See Cocagnac, Augustin Maurice-Jean

[The] Warbler of Poetic Prose
See Sidney, [Sir] Philip

[The] Warbling Banjoist
See Godfrey, Arthur Michael

Warborough, Martin Leach
See Allen, [Charles] Grant [Blairfindie]

Warbridge, C. W.
See Woods, Clee

Warburg, Albert O.
See Von Warthburgh, Alberto O.

Warburg, James Paul 1896-1969 [ASC, CAP]
American author
* Durfee, John
* Herrick, Wallace
* James, Paul

Warburg, Paul Moritz 1868-1952 [HPPN]
German-American banker
* [The] Father of the Federal Reserve System

Warburg, Sandol Stoddard 1927- [SAT]
American author
* Stoddard, Sandol

Warburton, Cotton
See Warburton, Irvine E.

Warburton, Irvine E. 1911-1982 [FB]
American football player and film editor
* Warburton, Cotton

Warburton, Joan 1920- [ART]
Scottish-born artist
* J. W.

Warburton, William 1698-1779 [HPPN, NPS, SN]
British prelate
* [An] Author
* [A] Blazing Star
* [A] Colossus of Literature
* [The] Great Preserver of Pope and Shakespeare
* [A] Hypercritic
* [The] Literary Bull-Dog
* [A] Literary Revolutionist
* [The] Modern Stagirite
* [The] Most Impudent Man Living
* [A] Mountebank in Criticism
* [The] Poet's Parasite
* [A] Quack in Commentatorship
* [The] Scaliger of the Age
* [A] Universal Piece-Broker

Ward, A. Sarsfield
See Ward, Arthur Henry

Ward, Artemus
See Browne, Charles Farrar

Ward, Arthur Henry 1883-1959 [ESF, HFF, SFL]
British author
* Furey, Michael
* Rohmer, Sax
* Ward, A. Sarsfield

Ward, Barbara
See Jackson, Barbara [Ward]

Ward, Bud
See Ward, Marvin Harvey

Ward, Burt
See Gervis, Bert John, Jr.

Ward, C. A. 19th c. [PI]
Irish poet
* Burghley, Feltham

Ward, Carrie
See Clarke-Ward, Carrie

Ward, Charles Dexter
See Taylor, John [Alfred]

Ward, Craig 1892-1979 [CA]
American astrologer and author
* MacCraig, Hugh

Ward, Diane
See Bunce, Corajane Diane

Ward, Don[ald G.] 1911- [CA]
American editor
* Tracy, Powers

Ward, E. D.
See Delaney, Edward Leo

Ward, E. D.
See Lucas, Edward Verrall

Ward, Edward 1660?-1731 [DEA]
British author and satirist
* E. W.

Ward, Elizabeth Campbell 1936- [CA]
American author
* Allen, E. C.

Ward, Elizabeth Honor [Shedden] 1926- [CA, WD]
British author
* Leslie, Ward S.

Ward, Elizabeth Rebecca 1881-? [BI, LC]
British author and poet
* Inchfawn, Fay

Ward, Elizabeth Stuart [Phelps] 1844-1911 [FFF, WGT]
American author
* Adams, Mary
* Onyx
* Phelps, Elizabeth Stuart

Ward, Eric
See Ebon, Martin

Ward, Fannie
See Buchanan, Fannie

Ward, Ferdinand 19th c. [FFF]
American speculator
* [The] Napoleon of Finance

Ward, Frank Gray 1867-1912 [BE]
American baseball player
* Ward, Piggy

Ward, Frank T. 1846-1921 [HPPN]
American entertainer
* Ward, Pop

Ward, Fred 1836-1870 [DI, HPPN]
Australian bushranger
* Thunderbolt, Captain

Ward, Frederick William Orde 1843-? [WWL]
British author
* Williams, F. Harald

Ward, Gabe
See Ward, Otto

Ward, Genevieve 1838-1922 [HPPN]
American actress and singer
* Guerrabelin, Genevieve

Ward, H. D. [PA]
Author
* Harvard Senior

Ward, H. O.
See Bloomfield-Moore, Clara Sophia
[Jessup]

Ward, Hap
See O'Donnell, John Thomas, Sr.

Ward, Hap, Jr.
See O'Donnell, John Thomas, Jr.

Ward, Harold 20th c. [SFL, SFP]
Author
* Zorro

Ward, Harry 20th c. [IBW]
American athlete
* Ward, Wu Fang

Ward, Harry
See De Michele, Angelo

Ward, Helene
See Kennedy, Helene Ward

Ward, Henry
See Viard, Henri Louis Luc

Ward, Henry Dana 1797-1884 [DNA]
American author and clergyman
* Harvard, Senior

Ward, Ideal
See Ward, William George

Ward, Ireland
See Widdemer, Irene

Ward, Jackie [RO1]
American singer
* Ward, Robin

Ward, James Harman 1806-1861
[HPPN]
American naval officer
* [The] Commissioner

Ward, James Warner 1807-1873 [FFF]
Writer
* Yorick

Ward, Janet
See Werner, Janet Anne

Ward, Janice
See Hartman, Rachel Frieda

Ward, Jay 20th c.
American television producer
* Britt, Ponsonby

Ward, Jem 1800-1884 [RBE]
British boxer
* [The] Black Diamond

Ward, Jennie
See Williams, Mrs. Odell

Ward, John
See Peace, Charles Frederick

Ward, John A. 20th c. [BE]
American baseball player
* Ward, Rube

Ward, John C. 20th c. [WWL]
Irish author and translator
* Mac An Bhaird, Seaghan

Ward, John Montgomery 1860-1925
[AS]
American baseball player
* Ward, Monte

Ward, Jonas
See Ard, William [Thomas]

Ward, Jonas
See Garfield, Brian [Francis] Wynne

Ward, Jonathon
See Stine, Whitney Ward

Ward, Joshua 1685-1761 [HN, NPS, SN]
British physician
* Ward, Spot

Ward, Kirwan
See Kirwan-Ward, Bernard Edward

Ward, [Sir] Leslie 1851-1922 [LC]
British illustrator
* Spy

Ward, Lester Frank 1841-1913 [HPPN]
American sociologist
* [The] Father of Telesis
* [The] Predictor of Sociocracy

Ward, Mabella Ann 19th c. [PA]
Author
* Dashaway, Kate

Ward, Maisie
See Ward, Mary Josephine

Ward, Marcus Lawrence 1812-1884
[HPPN]
American humanist
* [The] Soldier's Friend

Ward, Marian
See Williams, Mrs. Tony

Ward, Marion
See Stephens, Harriet Marion

Ward, Marion Inez Douglas 1885-
[LAO]
British author
* Fox, Marion

Ward, Martha Craft 1942- [CA]
American attorney and author
* Blue, Martha Ward

Ward, Marvin Harvey 1913-1968 [AS,
EG, GF]
American golfer
* Ward, Bud

Ward, Mary
See Holton, Mary Ward

Ward, Mary Jane
See Quayle, Mary Jane Ward

Ward, Mary Josephine 1889-1975 [CA]
British-born author and publisher
* Ward, Maisie

Ward, Melanie
See Curtis, Richard [Alan]

Ward, Melanie
See Lynch, Marilyn

Ward, Monte
See Ward, John Montgomery

Ward, Mrs. H. O.
See Moore, Mrs. Bloomfield H.

Ward, Nancy 1738-1822? [HPPN]
American Indian chief
* Nanye'hi
* [The] Pocahontas of the West

Ward, Nathaniel 1578?-1652 [FFF, PA,
WBD]
British-born clergyman and author
* De La Guard, Theodore

Ward, Nita
See Oatley, Evelyn

Ward, Ole
See Ward, Richard [Dick]

Ward, Otto 20th c. [JF]
American musician
* Ward, Gabe

Ward, Patrick J. 19th c. [PI]
Irish poet
* Doire

Ward, Peter
See Faust, Frederick [Schiller]

Ward, Philip 1938- [CA]
British author
* Greenfield, Darby

Ward, Piggy
See Ward, Frank Gray

Ward, Plumer 19th c. [HPPN]
British author
* [A] Tory of the Old School

Ward, Polly
See Poluski, Byno

Ward, Pop
See Ward, Frank T.

Ward, R. H.
See Ward, Richard Heron

Ward, R. Patrick
See Holzapfel, Rudolf Patrick [Rudi]

Ward, Richard [Dick] 1909-1966 [BE]
American baseball player
* Ward, Ole

Ward, Richard Heron 1910-1969 [LC]
British author and playwright
* Ward, R. H.

Ward, Robert
See Howard, Robert Ervin

Ward, Robert Spencer 1906- [BI]
American author and diplomat
* King, Evan

Ward, Robin
See Ward, Jackie

Ward, Rodger 1921- [HPPN]
American auto racer
* [The] Brakeless Wonder
* Roger the Dodger

Ward, Rose Elizabeth Knox 1886-
[SFL, WGT]
American author
* Knox, Lisbeth
* Rohmer, Elizabeth Sax

Ward, Rube
See Ward, John A.

Ward, Sam[uel] 1814-1884 [FFF, PA, SN]
American politician
* [The] King of the Lobby
* S. W.
* Ward, Uncle Sam

Ward, Sam
See Jacobs, George Herman

Ward, Seth 1928- [CME, HPPN]
American country-western performer
* [The] Dandy of Country Music
* Dean, Jimmy

Ward, Spot
See Ward, Joshua

Ward, Sylvia 1900- [THR]
British actress and singer
* Leslie, Sylvia

Ward, Thomas 1807-1873 [DNA, PA]
American poet
* Draw, Thom
* Flaccus

Ward, Tom
See Sellers, Connie Leslie, Jr.

Ward, Townsend [PA]
Author
* Logan

Ward, Uncle Sam
See Ward, Sam[uel]

Ward, Vera Hall
See Hall, Vera

Ward, Victoria
See Lefleur, Victoria

Ward, Warwick
See Mannon, W.

Ward, William [Willie] 1893- [BX, RBE]
Panamanian-born boxer
* Norfolk, Kid

Ward, William George 1812-1882 [DEP, WBD]
British theologian
* Ward, Ideal

Ward, Willie 1893- [HPPN]
American boxer
* Norfolk, Kid

Ward, Wu Fang
See Ward, Harry

Ward Thomas, Evelyn Bridget Patricia 1928- [AW, CA]
British author
* Anthony, Evelyn
* Evelyn, Anthony
* Stephens, Eve

Warde, Beatrice Lamberton 1900-1969
[SFL, WGT]
Author
* Beaujon, Paul

Warde, John 1912-1938 [HPPN]
American suicide victim
* [The] Man on the Ledge

Warde, Margaret
See Dunton, Edith Kellogg

Warde, William F.
See Novack, George [Edward]

Wardell, Dean
See Prince, Jack Harvey

Wardell, Edith 1869-1947 [BEW]
British actress
* Craig, Edith

Wardell, Etelka
See Heaton, Eva

Wardell, Henry Edward Gordon Godwin 1872-1966 [OCF]
British stage designer
* Craig, Edward Gordon

Wardell, Joseph 1909-
American comic actor
* Curly Joe
* DeRita, Joe

Warden, Colonel [code name used during World War II]
See Churchill, Winston Spencer

Warden, Florence
See James, Florence Alice [Price]

Warden, Francis
See Harrison, Mary Bennett

Warden, Gertrude
See Jones, Gertrude Warden

Warden, Jack 20th c.
American actor
* Costello, Johnny

Warden, Jack
See Lebzelter, Jack Warden

Warden, Jon[athan Edgar] 1946- [BE]
American baseball player
* Warden, Warbler

Warden, Warbler
See Warden, Jon[athan Edgar]

[The] Warden With a Conscience
See Baker, Juanita

Wardle, Dan
See Snow, Charles Horace

Wardle, Jane
See Hueffer, Oliver Madox

Wardrop, Bert
See Wardrop, Robert

Wardrop, David 20th c.
Author
* Kroge, Suds

Wardrop, Robert 1932- [SWI]
British swimmer
* Wardrop, Bert

Ware, Eleanor 1820-?
American author
* Two Sisters of the West [joint pseudonym with Catharine Ann (Ware) Warfield]

Ware, Eugene Fitch 1841-1911 [WBD]
American poet
* Ironquill

Ware, Helen
See Remer, Helen

Ware, Henry 1764-1845 [HPPN]
American clergyman
* H. W.

Ware, Henry, Jr. 1794-1843 [HPPN]
American clergyman, educator, author
* H. W., Jr.
* [An] Unitarian

Ware, John 1795-1864 [HPPN]
American physician
* J. W.

Ware, John
See Mabley, Edward [Howe]

Ware, Mary Harris [FFF]
Author
* Glenn, Gertrude

Ware, Monica
See Marsh, John

Ware, Wallace
See Karp, David

Wareham, John 20th c. [HPPN]
New Zealand-born founder of executive search organization
* [The] Corporate Headhunter

Wares, Buzzy
See Wares, Clyde Ellsworth

Wares, Clyde Ellsworth 1886-1964 [BE]
American baseball player
* Wares, Buzzy

Warfield, Catharine Ann [Ware] 1816-1877
American author
* Two Sisters of the West [joint pseudonym with Eleanor Ware]

Warfield, Patricia 1949- [BA]
American educator
* Warfield-Coppock, Nsenga

Warfield, Sandra
See Bornstein, Flora-Jean

Warfield-Coppock, Nsenga
See Warfield, Patricia

Wargar, Kurt
See Ruellan, Andre

Warhawk
See Calhoun, John Caldwell

Warhawk
See Clay, Henry

Warhawk
See Palmer, William

Warheit, I. A.
See Warheit, Israel Albert

Warheit, Israel Albert 1912-1973 [HPPN]
Canadian librarian and computer authority
* Warheit, I. A.

Warhol, Andy
See Warhola, Andrew

Warhol, Minnie
See Warhol, Ted

Warhol, Ted 20th c. [GW]
American rodeo performer
* Warhol, Minnie

Warhola, Andrew 1927- [BP, HPPN]
American painter and filmmaker
* Drella
* [The] Leader of the Pop Art Movement
* Warhol, Andy

Warhop, Chief
See Wauhop, John Milton

Warhop, Crab
See Wauhop, John Milton

Warhop, John Milton
See Wauhop, John Milton

Waring, Barbara
See Gibb, Barbara

Waring, C. H. 1819-1887 [HPPN]
British author
* C. H. W.

Waring, Fred 1900?-1984 [HPPN, TI 8-13-84]
American band and chorus leader
* America's Authentic Music Man
* [The] Man who taught America to sing

Waring, Herbert
See Rutty, Herbert Waring

Waring, Jane 19th c. [HPPN]
Irish friend of Jonathan Swift
* Varina

Waring, Jeremiah 1757-1829 [HPPN]
British Quaker
* One of the People Called Christians

Waring, Marcus H.
See Manning, William Henry

Waring, Richard
See Stephens, Richard Waring

Waring, William
See Harcourt, William

Warland, Allen
See Wollheim, Donald A[llen]

Warland, John
See Buchanan-Brown, John

Warland, John Henry ?-1872 [HPPN]
American author
* J. H. W.

Warland, Theodore ?-1864 [HPPN]
American clergyman
* T. W.

Warlick, Ernie 1933- [IBW]
American football player
* Warlick, Hands

Warlick, Hands
See Warlick, Ernie

[The] Warlike
See Charles XII

[The] Warlike
See Frederick I

[The] Warlike
See Henry II [or Henri]

Warlock, Peter
See Heseltine, Philip Arnold

Warlomont, Maurice 1860-1889 [HPPN]
Flemish author
* Waller, Max

[A] Warm Well Wisher to the Interests of General Christianity
See Cappe, [Rev.] Newcombe

Warmerdam, Cornelius 1915- [HPPN, TF]
American track and field athlete
* [The] Flying Dutchman
* Warmerdam, Dutch

Warmerdam, Dutch
See Warmerdam, Cornelius

[The] Warming Pan Child
See Stuart, James Francis Edward

[The] Warming Pan Hero
See Stuart, James Francis Edward

Warmley, Ernst
See Manson, James B.

Warmoth, Cy
See Warmoth, Wallace Walter

Warmoth, Wallace Walter 1893-1957 [BE]
American baseball player
* Warmoth, Cy

Warmth, Mr.
See Caldwell, Mike

Warneford, Lieut.
See Gunter, Archibald Clavering

Warneford, Lieut.
See Russell, William

Warneke, Country
See Warneke, Lonnie

Warneke, Dixie
See Warneke, Lonnie

Warneke, Lonnie 1909- [BE, HPPN]
American baseball player
* [The] Arkansas Humming Bird
* Ol' Arkansas

Warneke, Lonnie (cont.)
* Warneke, Country
* Warneke, Dixie

Warner, Albert
See Eichelbaum, Albert

Warner, Anna Bartlett 1827-1915 [DEL, DNNF, RH]
American author
* Lothrop, Amy

Warner, Augustine
See Byars, William Vincent

Warner, B. Ellison [FFF, PA]
American writer and clergyman
* Pascarel

Warner, B. F.
See Bowers, Warner Fremont

Warner, Charles
See Lickfold, Charles

Warner, Connie
See Warner, Cornell

Warner, Cornell 1948- [SMG]
American basketball player
* M
* Warner, Connie

Warner, Edgar 20th c. [NAD]
Psychic healer
* Karmu

Warner, Eliza A. 19th c. [HPPN]
American author
* A. H. K.

Warner, Esther S.
See Dendel, Esther [Sietmann Warner]

Warner, Fernandino 1703-1767? [HPPN]
British clergyman
* F. W.

Warner, Frances Lester
See Hersey, Frances Lester Warner

Warner, Frank
See Richardson, Gladwell

Warner, Frank A. [house pseudonym]
[Stratemeyer Syndicate]
See Stratemeyer, Edward L.

Warner, [George] Geoffrey John 1923- [CA, WD]
British author and artist
* Johns, Geoffrey

Warner, Glenn Scobey 1871-1954 [AS, FB, OCS]
American football coach
* Warner, Pop

Warner, Gloria
See Kelly, Gloria

Warner, Hannah
See Jewett, John Howard

Warner, Harry Morris
See Eichelbaum, Harry Morris

Warner, Helen Garnie 1846-? [DNA]
American author
* Harcourt, Helen

Warner, Henry Bryon
See Lickfold, Henry Bryon

Warner, Hoke Hayden 1894-1947 [BE]
American baseball player
* Warner, Hooks

Warner, Hooks
See Warner, Hoke Hayden

Warner, Indian
See Warner, Thomas

Warner, Jack
See Waters, John

Warner, Jack L.
See Eichelbaum, Jack L.

Warner, Jessie
See Clarance, Mrs. Edward

Warner, John 1736-1800 [HPPN]
British clergyman
* Anglus

Warner, Kenneth [Lewis] 1915- [CAP]
British author
* Morel, Dighton

Warner, L. T. [PA]
Author
* Leigh, Larry

Warner, Louis
See Weinberger, Louis

Warner, Matt
See Christianson, Willard Erastus

Warner, Matt
See Fichter, George S.

Warner, Mike
See Vizzini, Sal[vatore]

Warner, Muscles
See Waner, Lloyd James

Warner, [Sir] Pelham Francis 1873-1963
[OCS]
British cricketer
* Warner, Plum

Warner, Plum
See Warner, [Sir] Pelham Francis

Warner, Pop
See Warner, Glenn Scobey

Warner, Reginald Ernest 1905- [SFL]
Author
* Warner, Rex

Warner, Rex
See Warner, Reginald Ernest

Warner, Richard 1763-1857 [HPPN]
British clergyman and author
* Us Two

Warner, Samuel Louis
See Eichelbaum, Samuel Louis

Warner, Susan Bogert 1819-1885 [DEL, PA]
American author
* Wetherell, Elizabeth

Warner, Theodore [or Ted]
See Vizzini, Sal[vatore]

Warner, Thomas 1630?-1675 [WBD]
Governor of Dominica
* Warner, Indian

Warner, Virginia
See Brodine, Virginia Warner

Warner, Warren
See Warren, Samuel

Warner, William 1558?-1609 [SN]
British poet
* Our English Homer

Warner-Crozetti, R.
See Crozetti, Ruth G. Warner [Lora]

Warnes, Carlos 20th c. [WECO]
Cartoonist
* Bruto, Cesar

Warnock, Amelia Beers 1878-1956
[CCL]
Canadian poet
* Hale, Katherine

Warnow, Harry 1909?- [ASC, EJ, PMJ]
American bandleader
* Scott, Raymond

Warren, Accounts
See Warren, Lindsay Carter

Warren, Andrew [joint pseudonym with Warren (Stanley) Tute]
See Rosenthal, Andrew

Warren, Andrew [joint pseudonym with Andrew Rosenthal]
See Tute, Warren [Stanley]

Warren, Arthur [FFF]
American journalist
* Quill, Timothy

Warren, Baby Boy
See Warren, Robert Henry

Warren, Betty
See Hogan, Babette Hilda

Warren, Brett
See Breitberg, Louis

Warren, Butch
See Warren, Edward

Warren, Charlie
See Mueller, Marvin

Warren, Dave
See Wiersbe, Warren Wendell

Warren, David 1943- [CA]
American author
* Featherstone, D.

Warren, Earle 20th c. [NP]
American jazz musician
* Warren, Smiley

Warren, Edith [IBW]
American actress, singer, dancer
* Washington, Fredi

Warren, Edward ?-1878 [HPPN]
American physician
* E. W.

Warren, Edward 1939- [HPPN]
American jazz musician
* Warren, Butch

Warren, Eliza
See Sutton, Eliza Warren

Warren, Elizabeth
See Supraner, Robyn

Warren, Esther
See Robinson, Esther

Warren, Fiddlin' Kate
See Warren, Margie Ann

Warren, Francis Emroy 1844-1929
[WBD]
American politician
* [The] Father of Reclamation

Warren, Frederick Albert
See Bidwell, Austin

Warren, Frederick H. 1888- [WWL]
British author
* Warren, Henry

Warren, Harold
See Schwartz, Charles Henry

Warren, Harold
See Schwartzhof, Leon Henry

Warren, Harry
See Guaragna, Salvatore

Warren, Henry 1903- [ECM]
American country-western performer
* Warren, Uncle Henry

Warren, Henry
See Warren, Frederick H.

Warren, Hugh
See Manning, William Henry

Warren, Ina Russelle 1877?-1951 [BI]
American columnist
* Lincoln, Lucy

Warren, J. T.
See Manning, William Henry

Warren, James LeRoy [Lee] 1913-
[HPPN]
American machine tender
* [The] Papermaker's Papermaker

Warren, Jeff
See Jones, George Warren

Warren, John Byrne Leicester [Baron de Tabley] 1835-1895 [DEL, DLE1, PI]
British poet
* Lancaster, William
* Preston, George F.

Warren, John Russell 1886- [WW]
Author
* Coverack, Gilbert

Warren, Joseph 1741-1775 [HPPN]
American physician and army officer
* A True Patriot

Warren, Joseph
See Vari, Giuseppe

Warren, Josiah 1798-1874 [HPPN]
American inventor and reformer
* [The] Father of Anarchy
* [The] First American Anarchist

Warren, Lavinia
See Bump, Mercy Lavinia Warren

Warren, Leonard
See Varenov, Leonard

Warren, Lindsay Carter 1889- [HPPN]
American politician
* Warren, Accounts

Warren, Margie Ann 1922- [CWG, DAM]
American country-western performer
* Warren, Fiddlin' Kate

Warren, Mary
See Campion, Katherine

Warren, Mary Douglas
See Greig, Maysie Coucher

Warren, Mercy Otis 1728-1814 [HPPN]
American author, poet, playwright
* [The] First Lady of the Revolution
* Marcia

Warren, Ned
See Manning, William Henry

Warren, Patience
See Kelsey, Jeannette Garr [Washburn]

Warren, Peter Whitson 1941- [CA]
American author and artist
* Whitson

Warren, R.
See Ashton, Charles

Warren, Red
See Warren, Robert Penn

Warren, Robert Henry 1919-1977 [BWW]
American singer
* Warren, Baby Boy
* Williams, Johnny

Warren, Robert Penn 1905-
American author
* Warren, Red

Warren, Samuel 1807-1877 [WW]
British author
* Warner, Warren

Warren, Smiley
See Warren, Earle

Warren, Uncle Henry
See Warren, Henry

Warren, V. S.
See Manning, William Henry

Warren, Vernon
See Chapman, George Warren Vernon

Warren, Walter
See Raymond, George Lansing

Warren, William A. 1883-1938 [HPPN]
American radio personality
* Sunshine, Doc

Warrick, Marie Dionne 1940- [LRR]
American singer
* Warwick, Dionne

Warriner, Cornelia 20th c. [WW]
Author
* Crockett, James [joint pseudonym with James A. MacPhail]

Warriner, Thurman 20th c. [CC]
Author
* Troy, Simon

Warrington
See Robinson, William Stevens

Warrington, Dan
See Reed-Smith, Ida

Warrington, H. Jefferson
See Weil, Joseph R.

Warrington, Maris
See Billings, Edith S.

[The] Warrior
See Friend, Robert Bartmess

[The] Warrior
See Michael VI Stratioticus

[The] Warrior Drover
See Wayne, Anthony

[The] Warrior Intellectual
See Moynihan, [Daniel] Patrick

[The] Warrior Lady of Latham
See Charlotte

[The] Warrior of Freedom
See Garibaldi, Giuseppe

[The] Warrior of Today
See Jordan, Vernon Eulion, Jr.

[The] Warrior Parson
See Thurston, Charles Mynn

[The] Warrior Pope
See Della Rovere, Giuliano

[The] Warrior With a Heart
See Herbert, Anthony B.

Warrren, Charlie
See Donaldson, Dan

Warsh
See Warshaw, Jerry

Warshaw, Jerry 1929- [CA]
American illustrator
* Warsh

Warshofsky, Isaac
See Singer, Isaac Bashevis

Warstler, Harold Burton 1903-1964 [BE]
American baseball player
* Warstler, Rabbit

Warstler, Rabbit
See Warstler, Harold Burton

Wart, Helen
See Miserocchi, Anna

Wartenegg, Hanna
See Warzilek, Johanna

Warter, John Wood 1806-1878 [DEL, PA]
British author and clergyman
* Old Vicar
* Oldacre, Cedric, of Saxe Normanby

Warth, Julian
See Parsons, Julia Warth

Wartman, Frank Secord 1900?-1983 [WP 7-11-83]
American scientist and government official
* [The] Father of Titanium

Warton, Thomas 1728-1790 [HPPN, NPS, SN]
British poet and critic
* Honest Tom
* Menander
* Verax
* Whetham, John

Wartski, Maureen [Ann Crane] 1940- [CA]
Japanese-born American author
* Crane, M. A.

Warung, Price
See Astley, William

Warwick
See Ryer, Frederick R.

Warwick, A. H. 20th c. [CFH]
Canadian football player, coach, executive
* Warwick, Bert

Warwick, Alan Ross 20th c. [MBF]
British author
* Ross, Allan
* Sidney, Frank
* Sydney, Frank

Warwick, Anne
See Cranston, Ruth

Warwick, Bama
See Warwick, William Carl

Warwick, Bert
See Warwick, A. H.

Warwick, Bill
See Warwick, Firman Newton

Warwick, Charles
See McDonough, C. J.

Warwick, Dionne
See Warrick, Marie Dionne

Warwick, Dolores
See Frese, Dolores Warwick

Warwick, Eden
See Jabet, George S.

Warwick, Elsie
See Fullilove, Mrs. E. J.

Warwick, Firman Newton 1897- [BE]
American baseball player
* Warwick, Bill

Warwick, Francis Alister 20th c. [MBF]
British author
* Clifford, Martin [house pseudonym]
* Jardine, Warwick [house pseudonym]

Warwick, Francis Alister (cont.)
* Sidney, Frank
* Spencer, Roland [joint pseudonym with Geoffrey Prout]
* Sydney, Frank

Warwick, George
See Deeping, George Warwick

Warwick, Grant David 1921- [CEI, FHE, HK]
Canadian-born hockey player
* Warwick, Knobby

Warwick, Granville
See Griffith, David [Lewelyn] Wark

Warwick, Jarvis
See Garner, Hugh

Warwick, John
See Beattie, John McIntosh

Warwick, Jonathan Talbot
See Cohen, Paul Arthur

Warwick, Knobby
See Warwick, Grant David

Warwick, Pauline
See Davies, Betty Evelyn

Warwick, Robert
See Bien, Robert Taylor

Warwick, Sidney 1870-1953 [MBF]
British author
* Drayson, A. W.
* Sidney, Frank
* Sydney, Frank

Warwick, William Carl 1917- [EJ, WWJ]
American jazz musician
* Warwick, Bama

Waryman, Solomon
See Foe, Daniel

Waryng, Jane 17th c. [SN]
Friend of British satirist, Jonathan Swift
* Varina

Warzilek, Johanna 1939- [OP]
Austrian scenic and costume designer
* Wartenegg, Hanna

Wash A Kie 1798-1900 [HPPN]
American Indian warrior and statesman
* [The] Lone Pillar

Wash, Martha 20th c. [IBW]
American singer
* Two Tons of Fun

Wash, Mr.
See Washington, Sam

Wash, R.
See Cowlishaw, Ranson

[The] Washboard King
See King, Ernest

Washboard Sam
See Brown, Robert

Washboard Willie
See Hensley, William Paden

Washburn, Bryant
See Ludlow, Dwight

Washburne, Country
See Washburne, Joe

Washburne, Elihu Benjamin 1816-1867 [HPPN]
American politician
* [The] Watchdog of the Treasury

Washburne, Joe 1904-1974 [ASC, PMJ]
American musician
* Washburne, Country

Washburne, Mary B. [PA]
Author
* Morrison, Mary

Washer, Buck
See Washer, William

Washer, William 1882-1955 [BE]
American baseball player
* Washer, Buck

Washington, Alex
See Finkelstein, Mark

Washington, Berwell
See Cabell, James Branch

Washington, Buck
See Washington, Ford Lee

Washington, C.
See Pharr, Robert D[eane]

Washington, Clyde 20th c. [RBE]
American boxer
* Washington, Kid

Washington, D. C.
See Bender, D. C.

Washington, Diamond
See Washington, Leon

Washington, Didimus
See Washington, Richard

Washington, Dinah
See Jones, Ruth [Lee]

Washington, Dwayne 20th c. [SI 11-28-83, SI 12-5-83]
American basketball player
* [The] Pearl

Washington, Edward 1902-1964 [NOJ]
American jazz musician
* Washington, Son White

Washington, Edward Emmanuel
See Hill, David

Washington, Elsie 20th c.
Author and editor
* Welles, Rosalind

Washington, Ford Lee 1903-1955 [EJ, SC, WWJ]
American jazz musician and comedian
* Buck, Ford
* Washington, Buck

Washington, Fredi
See Warren, Edith

Washington, George 1732-1799 [BBH, DHA, FAP, SN, UH]
American president
* [The] American Cincinnatus
* [The] American Fabius
* [The] Atlas of America
* [The] Cincinnatus of the Americans
* [The] Cincinnatus of the West
* [The] Deliverer of America
* [The] Fabius of America
* [The] Farmer President
* [The] Father of His Country
* [The] Father of Pittsburgh
* [The] Flower of the Forest
* Harper
* Limey Stomper
* [The] Lovely Georgius
* [The] Old Fox
* [The] Sage of Mount Vernon
* [The] Savior of His Country
* [The] Stepfather of His Country
* [The] Surveyor President
* [The] Sword of the Revolution

Washington, George 20th c. [BWW]
American entertainer
* Washington, Oh Red

Washington, George
See Thomas, George Henry

Washington, George
See Washington, Sloane Vernon

Washington, Gladys J[oseph] 1931- [CA]
American author and educator
* Curry, Gladys J.

Washington, Grover, Jr. 1943- [IBW]
American jazz musician
* [The] Crossover King

Washington, Hap
See Washington, Harold Robert

Washington, Harold Robert 1935- [BA]
American attorney and educator
* Washington, Hap

Washington, Herbert 1941- [IBW]
American leader of military deserters organization
* Washington, Wash

Washington, Isabel 1871-1944 [THR]
American actress
* Irving, Isabel

Washington, Isidoe 1907?-1984 [BWW, WP 8-7-84]
American jazz musician
* Pappa Yalla
* Washington, Tuts

Washington, Jack
See Washington, Ronald

Washington, Joe 1953- [SMG]
American football player
* Washington, Joe Boy

Washington, Joe Boy
See Washington, Joe

Washington, Kid
See Washington, Clyde

Washington, Leon 1909- [WWJ]
American jazz musician
* Washington, Diamond

Washington, Leon H., Jr. 1907-1974
[IBW]
American publisher
* Washington, Wash

Washington, Mack
See Washington, William

Washington, [Catherine] Marguerite Beauchamp 1892-1972 [CAP]
American author
* Beaton, Anne
* Beauchamp, Pat
* Washington, Pat Beauchamp

[The] Washington of Africa
See Wilberforce, William

[The] Washington of Colombia
See Bolivar, Simon

[The] Washington of South America
See Bolivar, Simon

[The] Washington of the West
See Clark, George Rogers

[The] Washington of the West
See Harrison, William Henry

Washington, Oh Red
See Washington, George

Washington, Ora 1898-1971 [IBW]
American tennis player
* [The] Queen of Tennis

Washington, Pat Beauchamp
See Washington, [Catherine] Marguerite Beauchamp

Washington, Richard 20th c. [RM]
Musician
* Washington, Didimus

Washington, Rocky
See Washington, Roscoe

Washington, Ronald 1912-1964 [NP, WWJ]
American jazz musician
* Washington, Jack
* Washington, Weasel

Washington, Roscoe 20th c. [IBW]
American police officer
* Washington, Rocky

Washington, Russell 1946- [FB]
American football player
* Mount Washington

Washington, Sam 20th c.
American basketball player and manager
* Basketball, Mr.
* [The] Godfather of Basketball
* Wash, Mr.

Washington, Sloane Vernon 1907- [BE]
American baseball player
* Washington, George

Washington, Solomon 1836-1918
[HPPN]
American clergyman
* Gladden, Washington

Washington, Son White
See Washington, Edward

Washington, Sylvester 1906-1971 [IBW]
American police officer
* Two Gun Pete

Washington, Tuts
See Washington, Isidoe

Washington, Val
See Washington, Valores James

Washington, Valores James 1903- [IBW]
American politician and journalist
* Washington, Val

Washington, Wash
See Washington, Herbert

Washington, Wash
See Washington, Leon H., Jr.

Washington, Weasel
See Washington, Ronald

Washington, William 1908-1938 [WWJ]
American jazz musician
* Washington, Mack

[A] Washingtonian
See Lovett, John

Washington's Cinderella Woman
See McLean, Evalyn Walsh

Washington's Eminent Peanut Warehouser
See Carter, James Earl, Jr. [Jimmy]

Washington's First Mayoress
See Norton, Mary Teresa

Washington's Number One Farmer
See Bergland, Robert Selmer [Bob]

Washington's Other Monument
See Longworth, Alice Lee Roosevelt

Washington's Profumo
See Baker, Robert Gene [Bobby]

Washington's Resident Humorist
See Buchwald, Art[hur]

Washington's Scholar Athlete
See Shultz, George Pratt

[The] Washoe Seeress
See Bowers, Eilley Orrum

Wasmansdoff, Joyce 1928?-1972 [FIR]
American actress
* Lansing, Joi
* Loveland, Joy

Wasney, Henry 18th c. [HPPN]
British author
* F. A. S.
* [A] Wiltshire Clothier

Wason, Betty
See Hall, Elizabeth Wason

[The] Wasp of Twickenham
See Pope, Alexander

Wasself, Lucille 1887?-1921 [BBD]
American opera singer
* Marcel, Lucille

Wasserburg, Philipp 1827-1897 [PA, WGT]
Author
* Laicus, Phillipe

Wasserfall, Adel 1918- [CA]
Norwegian-born author
* Pryor, Adel

Wassersug, Joseph D. 1912- [CA]
American physician and writer
* Bradford [M.D.], Adam

Wast, Hugo
See Martinez Zuviria, Gustavo Adolfo

Wastle, William
See Lockhart, John Gibson

Wasylewski, Jan 1925- [CA]
American actor, author, playwright
* Merlin, Jan

Watanabe, Diagoro
See Kuhualua, Jesse

[The] Watch Dog of the Treasury
See Hagner, Peter

[The] Watch Dog of the Treasury
See Holman, William Steele

[The] Watchdog of Central Park
See Ochs, Adolph Simon

[The] Watchdog of the Treasury
See Blanton, Thomas Lindsay

[The] Watchdog of the Treasury
See Byrd, Harry Flood

[The] Watchdog of the Treasury
See Cannon, Joseph Gurney

[The] Watchdog of the Treasury
See Gallatin, [Abraham Alphonse] Albert

[The] Watchdog of the Treasury
See McCarl, John Raymond

[The] Watchdog of the Treasury
See Washburne, Elihu Benjamin

Watchman
See Draper, Warwick Herbert

[The] Water American
See Franklin, Ben[jamin]

[A] Water Drinker
See Lamb, Charles

[The] Water Drinker
See Montague, Basil

[A] Water Drinker
See Pope, Alexander

[The] Water Gruel Bard
See Shenstone, William

Water Gull
See Grenville, Richard Temple [First Earl Temple]

[The] Water Poet
See Taylor, John

[The] Water Rat
See Jones, Stephen [Phillip]

Water, Silas
See Loomis, Noel M[iller]

Waterfield, Buckets
See Waterfield, Robert S.

Waterfield, Rifle
See Waterfield, Robert S.

Waterfield, Robert S. 1920-   [FB, WP 3-26-83]
American football player
* Ram, Mr.
* Waterfield, Buckets
* Waterfield, Rifle

[The] Watergate Defendant
See Dean, John, III

[The] Watergate Guard
See Wills, Frank

[The] Watergate Judge
See Sirica, John Joseph

Watergate's Warbler
See Mitchell, Martha Elizabeth Beall Jennings

Waterhouse, Arthur
See Fearn, John Russell

Waterhouse, Benjamin 1754-1846 [HPPN]
American physician and educator
* [The] Father of Vaccination in America

Waterhouse, Keith [Spencer] 1929-   [CA]
British author, journalist, playwright
* Froy, Herald [joint pseudonym with Guy (Stephen) Deghy]
* Gibb, Lee [joint pseudonym with Guy (Stephen) Deghy]

Waterland, Daniel 1683-1740 [HPPN]
British clergyman
* [The] Doctor

Waterland, [Rev.] Joseph 17th c. [HPPN]
British clergyman
* [A] Minister of the Church of England

[The] Waterloo Hero
See Hill, Rowland [First Viscount Hill]

[The] Waterloo Hero
See Wellesley, Arthur

Waterman, Bic
See Joseph, Stephen M.

Waterman, Ida
See Francoeur, Ida Shaw

Waterman, [Rev.] Jotham ?-1836 [HPPN]
American clergyman
* A. B.
* Aquae Homo

Waterman, Lewis E. 1837-1901 [HPPN]
American inventor
* [The] Father of the Fountain Pen

Waterman, Nixon 1859-? [HPPN]
American author
* Martin, Peter

Waters
See Russell, William

Waters, Augustus   [PA]
Author
* Belshazzar

Waters, Blizzard
See Waters, Charlie

Waters, Bucky
See Waters, Raymond

Waters, C.
See Russell, William

Waters, Charlie 20th c.
American football player
* Waters, Blizzard

Waters, Chocolate
See Waters, Marianne

Waters, Chris
See Waters, Harold A[rthur]

Waters, Clara Erskine Clement 1834-1916 [HPPN]
American author
* Clement, Clara Erskine

Waters, Clarice C. 1874-1964 [HPPN]
American costume designer
* Madame Clarice

Waters, Clear
See Waters, Eddie

Waters, Daisy
See Waters, Doris

Waters, Doris 1904?-1978 [FIR]
British entertainer
* Waters, Daisy

Waters, E. W. 19th c. [HPPN]
American soldier and author
* [An] Orderly Serjeant

Waters, Eddie 20th c. [NBB]
American singer
* Waters, Clear

Waters, Ethel 1896-1977 [BWW, HPPN]
American singer and actress
* America's Foremost Ebony Comedienne
* Baby Star
* [The] Bronze Raquel Welch
* [The] Ebony Nora Bayes
* Jones, Mamie
* [The] Original Dinah
* Pryor, Martha
* [The] Queen of the Blues
* Sweet Mama Stringbean
* [The] Tawny Yvette Guilbert

Waters, Frank 20th c.
American football coach
* Waters, Muddy

Waters, Harold A[rthur] 1926-   [CA]
American educator and author
* Waters, Chris

Waters, John   [PA]
Author
* Flaccus

Waters, John 1894-   [BF, BI, FC]
British actor
* Warner, Jack

Waters, John 1946-   [HPPN]
American producer
* [The] Prince of Puke

Waters, John
See Carey, Henry

Waters, John
See Cary, Henry

Waters, John Charles 1830-1884 [PI]
Irish poet and physician
* W.

Waters, Lucy
See Walter, Lucy

Waters, Marianne 1949-   [CA]
American poet
* Waters, Chocolate

Waters, Monty
See Waters, Monville Charles

Waters, Monville Charles 1938-   [EJ7]
American jazz musician
* Waters, Monty

Waters, Muddy
See Morganfield, McKinley

Waters, Muddy
See Waters, Frank

Waters, Muddy, Jr.
See Buford, George

Waters, Raymond 1935-   [BB]
American basketball coach
* Waters, Bucky

Waters, Rosemary Elizabeth 1920- [AW]
British television producer and writer
* Horstmann, Rosemary

Waters, Thomas?
See Russell, William

Waterson, Light Horse Harry
See Watterson, Henry

Watford, Joel Albert 1906-   [AW]
British author
* Essex, Jon

Wathan, Duke
See Wathan, John David

Wathan, John David 1949-   [SMG]
American baseball player
* Wathan, Duke

Watjen, Carolyn L. T. 20th c. [CA]
American author
* Stafford, Caroline

Watkins, A. T. L.
See Watkins, Arthur Thomas Levi

Watkins, Alex 20th c. [WW]
Author
* Linklater, J. Lane

Watkins, Arthur Thomas Levi 1907-1965
[CA, LC]
Welsh-born playwright
* Watkins, A. T. L.
* Watkyn, Arthur

Watkins, Edward 1919?- [HPPN]
American bank robber
* Watkins, Fast Eddie

Watkins, Fast Eddie
See Watkins, Edward

Watkins, Frances Jane Grierson 1919-
[ART, DBA]
British artist
* Milligan, Frances J. G.
* Watkins, Peggy

Watkins, Gino
See Watkins, Henry George

Watkins, Henry George 1907-1932 [BI]
British explorer
* Watkins, Gino

Watkins, Joan C.
See Casale, Joan T[herese]

Watkins, Joe
See Watson, Mitchell

Watkins, Maurice 1956- [RBE]
American boxer
* Watkins, Termite

Watkins, Mel 1940- [CA]
American author
* Jackson, Franklin Jefferson

Watkins, Mrs. Charles A. [FFF]
Entertainer
* Gray, Ada

Watkins, Paula 1937- [BEW]
American actress and singer
* Wayne, Paula

Watkins, Peggy
See Watkins, Frances Jane Grierson

Watkins, Termite
See Watkins, Maurice

Watkins, Tobias 1780-1855 [DNA,
HPPN]
American author and physician
* Aegles
* Particular, Pertinax
* T. W.

Watkins-Pitchford, D. J.
See Watkins-Pitchford, Denys James

Watkins-Pitchford, Denys James 1905-
[CA, SAT, TCC]
British author and illustrator
* B B
* Traherne, Michael
* Watkins-Pitchford, D. J.

Watkinson, Frank 1925- [ART]
British sculptor, potter, painter
* Meretricious

Watkinson, Valerie
See Elliston, Valerie Mae [Watkinson]

Watkyn, Arthur
See Watkins, Arthur Thomas Levi

Watling, Dilys
See Rhys-Jones, Dilys

Watney, Bernard Martyn 1922- [AW]
British author
* Dolley, Marcus, J.

Watney, John B[asil] 1915- [CA]
British author
* Roberts, Anthony

Watre, Antony [PA]
Author
* Nemesis

Watrous, Harry Wilson 1857-1940
[HPPN]
American painter
* [The] American Meissonier

Watson, A. [PA]
Author
* De Younge, A.

Watson, A. J.
See Watson, Abram Joseph

Watson, Abram Joseph 1924- [EAR]
American auto racer
* Watson, A. J.

Watson, [John Hugh] Adam 1914- [CA]
British diplomat and author
* Scipio

Watson, Alan
See Watson, William Alexander Jardine

Watson, Alfred Edward Thomas
1849-1922 [BI, HPPN]
British journalist
* Rapier

Watson, Arthel 1923- [DAM]
American singer
* Watson, Doc

Watson, Billy
See Levie, Isaac

Watson, Billy
See Waldo, Edward Hamilton

Watson, Bobby
See Knucher, Robert Watson

Watson, Bootsie
See Watson, Douglas C.

Watson, [Sir] Brook 1735-1807 [FFF]
British soldier
* [The] Wooden Legged Commissary

Watson, Bryan Joseph 1942- [FHE,
SMG]
Canadian-born hockey player
* Watson, Bugsy

Watson, Bugsy
See Watson, Bryan Joseph

Watson, Bull
See Watson, Robert Jose

Watson, Charles 20th c.
American murderer
* Watson, Tex

Watson, Charles John 1885-1950 [BE]
American baseball player
* Watson, Doc

Watson, Claire
See McLamore, Claire

Watson, Deek
See Watson, Ivory

Watson, Doc
See Watson, Arthel

Watson, Doc
See Watson, Charles John

Watson, Douglas C. 20th c. [IBW]
American engineer
* Watson, Bootsie

Watson, Edmund Henry Lacon 1865-?
[LAO]
British author
* Lacon

Watson, Edwin 20th c.
*Administrative aide to Franklin Delano
Roosevelt*
* Watson, Pa

Watson, Elizabeth
See Boles-Watson, Elizabeth

Watson, Ella 1866-1888 [BLB, HPPN,
LFW]
American cattle thief
* Averill, Eva
* [The] Bandit Queen
* Maxwell, Cattle Kate
* Maxwell, Kate

Watson, Eve 1918- [THR]
British actress and singer
* Lister, Eve

Watson, Evelyn Mabel 1886- [NAA]
American author and poet
* Palmer, Halleck

Watson, Fly
See Watson, Thomas Sturges

Watson, Forbes ?-1871 [IP]
British botanist and author
* [A] Medical Man

Watson, Frank
See Ames, Francis H.

Watson, Frederick
See Porter, Frederick

Watson, Gayle Hudgens
See Hudgens, A[lice] Gayle

Watson, George
See Taylor, George Watson

Watson, George B. 19th c. [HPPN]
American author
* Lamp

Watson, George Bott Churchill [IP]
British physician and author
* Medicus

Watson, Guitar
See Watson, Johnny

Watson, Guy
See Sisson, Jack

Watson, Harold 1912?- [CW]
Jamaican poet and author
* Merson, H. A.

Watson, Harry E. 1898-1957 [HK]
Canadian-born hockey player
* Watson, Moose

Watson, Henrietta
See Boles-Watson, Henrietta

Watson, Henry Crocker Marriott
19th c. [WGT]
Author
* H. C. M. W.

Watson, Irving S.
See Mencken, Henry Louis [Harry]

Watson, Ivory 1909-1969 [SC]
American singer and actor
* Watson, Deek

Watson, J[ames] Wreford 1915- [CA, WD]
British poet, author, geographer
* Wreford, James

Watson, James [IP]
Scottish author
* [A] Member of the College of Justice

Watson, James ?-1820 [SN]
British author and editor
* [The] Doctor

Watson, James Eli 1864-1948 [HPPN]
American politician
* Watson, Sunny Jim
* [The] Wooden Shoe Statesman

Watson, James Lopez 1922- [IBW]
American politician and jurist
* Watson, Skiz

Watson, Jane Werner 1915- [CA, SAT, WW]
American author
* Bedford, A. N.
* Bedford, Annie North
* Hill, Monica
* Jasner, W. K.
* Nast, Elsa Ruth
* Werner, Elsa Jane
* Werner, Jane

Watson, Jean L. 19th c. [IP]
Scottish author
* J. L. W.

Watson, Jimmy
See Watson, Johnny

Watson, Joan
See Kaye, Violette

Watson, Joe 1943- [SMG]
Canadian-born hockey player
* Watson, Pumpkin
* Watson, Thundermouth

Watson, John [IP]
British author
* [A] Layman of the Church of England

Watson, John 1850-1907 [LC]
British-born author
* Maclaren, Ian

Watson, John H., MD
See Farmer, Philip Jose

Watson, John Hugh Adam 1914-
[HPPN]
British civil servant and author
* Scipio

Watson, John Reeves 1896-1949 [BE]
American baseball player
* Watson, Mule

Watson, Johnny 1867-1963 [BWW, NBB]
American singer
* Daddy Stovepipe
* Pitts, [Rev.] Alfred
* Sunny Jim
* Watson, Jimmy

Watson, Johnny 1935- [BWW, RO1]
American singer
* Watson, Guitar

Watson, Joseph K.
See Koff, Joseph

Watson, Julia 1943- [AW, CA, WD]
British author
* De Vere, Jane
* Fitzgerald, Julia
* Hamilton, Julia

Watson, L. J.
See Watson, Leslie Joseph

Watson, Le. De W.
See Wood, Richard Kennedy [Dick]

Watson, Lee
See Watson, Leland Hale

Watson, Leland Hale 1926- [BEW]
American theatrical lighting designer
* Watson, Lee

Watson, Leslie Joseph 1906- [ART]
British painter and landscape architect
* Watson, L. J.

Watson, Lillian Debra 1950- [BBH, SWI]
American swimmer
* Watson, Pokey

Watson, Mabel 1875?-1953 [BEW]
British actress
* Love, Mabel

Watson, Margaret [NPS]
Author
* Rosemary

Watson, Margaret
See Boles-Watson, Margaret

Watson, Mary 20th c. [WWL]
Scottish author
* Tubalcain

Watson, Milton 1894- [HPPN]
American baseball player
* Watson, Mule

Watson, Mitchell 1900-1969 [NOJ]
American jazz musician
* Watkins, Joe

Watson, Moose
See Watson, Harry E.

Watson, Mother
See Watson, Walter L.

Watson, Mrs. Robert A. 20th c. [NPS]
Author
* Cromarty, Deas

Watson, Mule
See Watson, John Reeves

Watson, Mule
See Watson, Milton

Watson, O[scar] Michael 1936- [CA]
American anthropologist and author
* Shears, Billie

Watson, Pa
See Watson, Edwin

Watson, Pauline 1925- [CA]
American author and columnist
* POLA

Watson, Pokey
See Watson, Lillian Debra

Watson, Pumpkin
See Watson, Joe

Watson, Reatha 1896?-1926 [BEW, F2, FC]
American actress
* La Marr, Barbara

Watson, Richard 1737-1816 [HPPN, IP]
British clergyman and author
* [A] Christian Whig
* [A] Consistent Protestant
* Philobiblius

Watson, Richard F.
See Silverberg, Robert

Watson, Robert Jose 1946- [BE, BI, PB]
American baseball player
* Watson, Bull

Watson, Robert R[utherford] 1917-
[CA]
American psychologist and author
* Holt, Robert R[utherford]

Watson, Rosamund [Ball] Marriott
1863-1911 [BI]
British poet
* Tomson, Graham R.

Watson, St. John
See Clarke, Percy A.

Watson, Skiz
See Watson, James Lopez

Watson, Solomon Lancelot Inglis 1901-
[THR]
British actor
* Lister, Lance

Watson, Sunny Jim
See Watson, James Eli

Watson, Tex
See Watson, Charles

Watson, Thomas
See Smith, [Captain] John

Watson, Thomas Edward 1856-1922
[HPPN]
American politician
* [The] Sage of Hickory Hill
* [The] Sage of McDuffie

Watson, Thomas Sturges 1949-
American golfer
* Watson, Fly

Watson, Thundermouth
See Watson, Joe

Watson, Tom
See Slaughter, Marion T.

Watson, Vernon 1886?-1949   [BEW, BI]
British actor
* King, Nosmo

Watson, Violet 1900-1972   [FC]
British actress
* Lyel, Viola

Watson, Virginia Cruse 20th c.   [NAA]
American editor and author
* West, Roger

Watson, Walker 1752-1854   [IP]
Scottish poet
* [The] Poet of Kirkintillock

Watson, Walter L. 1865-1898   [BE]
American baseball player
* Watson, Mother

Watson, Will
See Floren, Lee

Watson, Will
See Stivers, Jeremiah

Watson, William 1858-?   [NPS]
Poet
* Maitland, John Wilson

Watson, William Alexander Jardine
1933-   [CA]
Scottish educator and author
* Watson, Alan

Watson, William Lorimer 20th c.
[WWL]
British author
* Lorimer, Adam

Watson, William Robinson 1799-1864
[FFF]
American politician and writer
* Hamilton

Watson, Wylie
See Robertson, John Wylie

Watt, Elsie Gowans 1902-   [IAW]
Canadian writer
* Gowans, Elsa

Watt, Esme Violet 20th c.   [AW]
British author
* Jeans, Angela

Watt, Frank Marion 1902-1956   [BE]
American baseball player
* Watt, Kilo

Watt, Kilo
See Watt, Frank Marion

Watt, Mr. [code name used during
World War II]
See Wilson, [Sir] Henry Maitland

[The] Watt of America
See Evans, Oliver

Watt, William
See Scott, Will[iam Matthew]

Watt-Evans, Lawrence
See Evans, Lawrence Watt

Watters, Barbara H.
See Hunt, Barbara

Watters, H. E.
See Watters, Henry Eugene

Watters, Henry Eugene 1876-1938
[HPPN]
American educator
* Watters, H. E.

Watterson, Henry 1840?-1921   [FFF,
HPPN, PA, WBD]
American politician and journalist
* Henry of Navarre
* Marse Henry
* Trenchard, Asa
* Waterson, Light Horse Harry

Watterson, John William 1878-?   [WWL]
British author
* Cowley, Ramsay

Watterston, George 19th c.   [IP]
American author and librarian
* [A] Foreigner
* [The] Wanderer

Wattie
See Chisholm, Walter

Watts, Alan [Wilson] 1915-1973   [EOP]
*British-born American philosopher and
scholar*
* [The] Brain and the Buddha of
American Zen

Watts, Alaric Alexander 1799-1864
[HPPN]
British poet, editor, journalist
* [A] Magazine Editor

Watts, [Anna] Bernadette 1942-   [CA,
SAT]
British author and illustrator
* Bernadette

Watts, Bill 1939?-   [BI]
American wrestler
* Cowboy Bill

Watts, Charles H. 1902-1968   [SC]
American actor
* Watts, Cotton

Watts, Clem
See Trace, Al[bert J.]

Watts, Cotton
See Watts, Charles H.

Watts, Cueball
See Watts, Don[ald Earl]

Watts, Dodo
See Watts, Dorothy Margaret

Watts, Don[ald Earl] 1951-   [IBW, NBA,
SMG]
American basketball player
* Watts, Cueball
* Watts, Slick

Watts, Dorothy Margaret 1910-   [THR]
British actress
* Watts, Dodo

Watts, Elizabeth [Bailey] Smithgall
1941-   [CA]
American anthropologist and author
* Smithgall, Elizabeth

Watts, Ephraim
See Horne, Richard Henry

Watts, George Frederick 1817-1904
[HPPN]
British painter and sculptor
* George, F. W.

Watts, Herman 20th c.   [OBW]
American baseball player
* Watts, Lefty

Watts, Joan Alwyn 1921-   [ART]
British painter
* J. A. W.

Watts, John 1922-   [TR]
Canadian singer and actor
* Hanson, John

Watts, Lefty
See Watts, Herman

Watts, Lou[is Thomas] 1934-1970
[BWW]
American singer
* Lewis, Tommy
* Louis, Tommy
* Thomas, Kid

Watts, Mabel Pizzey 1906-   [CA, SAT]
British-born author
* Lynn, Patricia

Watts, Marilyn 1932-   [FC, SW]
American actress
* Corday, Mara

Watts, Noble 20th c.   [RO1]
American musician
* Watts, Thin Man

[The] Watts of Wales
See Williams, William

Watts, Overend
See Watts, Peter

Watts, Peter 1949- [CMA]
Musician
* Watts, Overend

Watts, Peter Christopher 1919- [CA]
British author
* Chisholm, Matt
* James, Cy
* Mackinlock, Duncan
* Owen, Tom

Watts, Phillips [IP]
British playwright and journalist
* Balfour, Felix

Watts, S. [IP]
British author
* S. W.

Watts, Slick
See Watts, Don[ald Earl]

Watts, Thin Man
See Watts, Noble

Watts, Thomas 1811-1869 [IP, PA]
British linguist and author
* P. P. C. R.

Watts, Walter Henry 19th c. [IP]
British journalist
* [An] Old Reporter
* W. H. W.

Watts, Walter Theodore 1832-1914 [LC]
British author
* Watts-Dunton, [Walter] Theodore

Watts-Dunton, [Walter] Theodore
See Watts, Walter Theodore

Wattson, Lewis Thomas 1864-1940 [BI]
American clergyman
* Paul James Francis, [Father]

Watzke, Alex 1880?-1918 [NOJ]
American jazz musician
* Watzke, King

Watzke, King
See Watzke, Alex

Wauch, Mansie
See Moir, David Macbeth

Wauchope, John [IP]
Scottish author
* J. W.

Waud, Elizabeth
See Tattersall, Muriel Joyce

Waugh, Auberon 1939?- [HPPN]
British author
* [The] Unloved One

Waugh, Carol-Lynn Roessel 1947- [CA]
American author
* Roessel-Waugh, C. C. [joint pseudonym with Charles G. Waugh]

Waugh, Charles G. 20th c. [CA]
American author
* Roessel-Waugh, C. C. [joint pseudonym with Carol-Lynn Roessel Waugh]

Waugh, Edwin 1817-1890 [PA, WBD]
British poet
* [The] Lancashire Burns
* [The] Lancashire Poet

Waugh, Evelyn 1903-1966
British author
* Scribe of the Dark Age

Waugh, Hillary Baldwin 1920- [CA, CC, EMD]
American author
* Grandower, Elissa
* Taylor, H. Baldwin
* Walker, Harry

Waugh, John 19th c. [IP]
American clergyman and author
* Chor-Episcopus

Waughburton, Richard [joint pseudonym with Christopher (Hugh) Sykes]
See Byron, Robert

Waughburton, Richard [joint pseudonym with Robert Byron]
See Sykes, Christopher [Hugh]

Wauhop, John Milton 1884-1960 [BE, PB]
American baseball player
* Warhop, Chief
* Warhop, Crab
* Warhop, John Milton

Wave
See Batchelder, Eugene

Waverley, Edward Bradwardine
See Croker, John Wilson

Waverly
See Wilson, A. J.

Wax, Emmanuel 1911-1983 [CA]
British literary agent, translator, author
* Wax, Jimmy

Wax, Jimmy
See Wax, Emmanuel

Wax, Rosalie [Amelia] H. 1911- [CA]
American anthropologist and author
* Hankey, Rosalie A.

Waxem of Wayback, Jedge
See Lampton, W. J.

Waxman, Albert 1875-1962 [BMH, THR]
Australian-born comedian
* [The] Australian Entertainer
* Whelan, Albert

Waxman, Franz
See Wachsmann, Franz

Way, Arthur S. 19th c. [IP]
British scholar and translator
* Avia

Way, B. 18th c. [IP]
British scholar
* Musidorus

Way, Charles 20th c. [EF]
American football player
* Way, Pie

Way, Elizabeth Fenwick 1920- [TCCM]
American author
* Fenwick, E. P.
* Fenwick, Elizabeth

Way, Fanny
See Way, Frances Elizabeth

Way, Frances Elizabeth 1871-? [DBA]
British painter
* Way, Fanny

Way, Isabel Stewart
See Bonnard, Isabel Stewart Way

Way, Lewis [IP]
British clergyman and author
* Basilicus

Way, Pie
See Way, Charles

Way, Robert E[dward] 1912- [CA]
South African-born author
* Black, David

Way, Wayne
See Humphries, Adelaide M.

Wayde, Bernard 20th c. [WW]
Author
* Collier, Old Cap

Wayditch, Gabriel
See Wajditsch Verbovac Von Doenhoff, [Baron] Gabriel

Waye, Ellen Jeanne 20th c. [AW]
Australian author
* Jose, Ellen J.

Wayfarer
See Cosens, Abner

Waylan, Mildred
See Harrell, Irene B[urk]

Wayland, Frederic Gregson 1906- [WWJ]
American jazz musician
* Wayland, Hank

Wayland, Hank
See Wayland, Frederic Gregson

Wayland, Heman Lincoln 1830-? [IP]
American clergyman and author
* Dobbs, [Rev.] Philetus

Wayland, Patrick
See O'Connor, Richard

Wayman, Dorothy [Godfrey] 1893-1975 [BI, CA, NAA]
American journalist, librarian, author
* Geoffrey, Theodate

Wayman, Tony Russell 1929- [CA]
British-born author
* Cardui, Van
* Cardui, Vanessa
* Rahman, Abdul

Waymon, Eunice Kathleen 1933- [EJ, IBW, SSS]
American singer
* [The] High Priestess of Soul
* Simone, Nina

Wayne, Alice
See Ressler, Alice

Wayne, Anderson
See Dresser, Davis

Wayne, Anthony 1745-1796 [DNNS, FFF, HPPN, SN]
American army officer
* Big Thunder
* [The] Black Snake
* [The] Chief Who Never Sleeps
* [The] Hero of Stony Point
* [The] Tanner
* [The] Tornado
* [The] Warrior Drover
* Wayne, Dandy
* Wayne, Drover
* Wayne, Mad Anthony
* [The] Wind

Wayne, Bobby
See Weintrop, Reuben

Wayne, Charles
See Liggett, Charles

Wayne, Charles J.
See Charles, James

Wayne, Charles Stokes 1858-? [NAA]
American author and playwright
* Hazeltine, Horace

Wayne, Chuck
See Jagelka, Charles

Wayne, Dandy
See Wayne, Anthony

Wayne, Daphne 1895?- [FC]
American actress
* [The] Biograph Blonde
* Sweet, Blanche

Wayne, David
See Balsiger, David W[ayne]

Wayne, David
See McMeekan, Wayne James

Wayne, Don 1949- [NW 10-7-85]
American actor
* D. J.
* Johnson, Don

Wayne, Donald
See Dodd, Wayne [Donald]

Wayne, Dorothy
See Sainsbury, Noel Everingham

Wayne, Drover
See Wayne, Anthony

Wayne, Duke
See Wayne, Robert

Wayne, Frances
See Bertocci, Chiarina Francesca

Wayne, Frances
See Wedge, Florence

Wayne, Gladys
See Van Valkenburg, Julia

Wayne, Helen
See Gill, Helen [Mabbott]

Wayne, John
See Morrison, Marion Michael

Wayne, Joseph
See Overholser, Wayne D.

Wayne, Kyra Petrovskaya 1918- [SAT]
Russian-born author
* Petrovskaya, Kyra

Wayne, Mad Anthony
See Wayne, Anthony

Wayne, Mary Penrose ?-1793 [HPPN]
Wife of American army officer, Anthony Wayne
* Wayne, Polly

Wayne, Michael A.
See Morrison, Michael A.

Wayne, Naunton
See Davies, Naunton

Wayne, Patricia
See Cutts, Patricia

Wayne, Paula
See Watkins, Paula

Wayne, Philip
See Powell, Philip Wayne

Wayne, Polly
See Wayne, Mary Penrose

Wayne, Richard
See Decker, Duane

Wayne, Robert 1904-1959 [HPPN]
American cinematographer and director
* Wayne, Duke

Waynflete [or Wainfleet], William of
See Patyn, William

Wayo, Charles Wesley
See Akakpo, Kofi

Ways, C. R.
See Blount, Roy [Alton], Jr.

Wazyk, Adam
See Wagmann, Adam

wbassett, Marnie
See Bassett, Flora Marjorie

Wead, Frank 1895-1947
American naval officer
* Wead, Spig

Wead, Spig
See Wead, Frank

Weadon, Percy
See Preston, Frank

Weafer, [Kenneth] Al[bert] 1914- [BE]
American baseball player
* Weafer, Hal

Weafer, Hal
See Weafer, [Kenneth] Al[bert]

Weale, Anne
See Blake, Andrea

Weale, B. L. Putnam
See Simpson, Bertram Lennox

Weale, William Henry James [IP]
British publisher and author
* W. H. J. W.

[The] Wealthiest Man of Antiquity
See Croesus

Weamys, Anna 17th c. [IP]
British poet
* A. W., Mrs.
* [A] Young Gentlewoman, Mrs. A. W.

Wearin, Otha Donner 1903- [HPPN]
American farmer and politician
* Wearin, Red Necktie

Wearin, Red Necktie
See Wearin, Otha Donner

Weary, Ogdred
See Gorey, Edward [St. John]

Weary Willie
See Kelly, Emmett

[The] Weasel
See Bessent, Fred Donald

[The] Weasel
See Cecil, William [First Baron Burleigh]

[The] Weasel
See Fratianno, James [Jimmy]

[The] Weasel
See Van Buren, Martin

[The] Weather Glass of His Time
See Pepys, Samuel

[The] Weathercock
See Aswad, al-

[The] Weathercock
See Romaine, Lawrence B.

[The] Weathercock
See Townshend, Charles

[The] Weathercock
See Windham, William

Weathercock, Janus
See Wainewright, Thomas Griffiths

[The] Weathercock of His Time
See Pepys, Samuel

Weatherford, William 1765?-1824 [BI, WBD]
American Indian chieftain
* Red Eagle

Weatherly, Frederick Edward 19th c. [IP]
British clergyman, poet, author
* [A] Resident M. A.

Weatherly, [Cyril] Roy 1915- [BE, PB]
American baseball player
* Weatherly, Stormy

Weatherly, Stormy
See Weatherly, [Cyril] Roy

Weatherly, William
See Wilkins, William

Weathers, Felicia Frances Theresa 1937-
[IBW]
American opera singer
* Weathers, Frankie

Weathers, Frankie
See Weathers, Felicia Frances Theresa

Weathers, Philip Joseph 1908- [IAW]
British director, playwright, author
* Sherwood, Michael

Weathers, Winston 1926- [CA]
American author
* Palmer, Tobias

Weathersby, Eliza
See Goodwin, Mrs. Nat C.

Weatherspoon, Nick 1950- [SMG]
American basketball player
* Weatherspoon, Spoon [or Spoonie]

Weatherspoon, Spoon [or Spoonie]
See Weatherspoon, Nick

Weatherstone, June Irene 1935- [CA]
Australian-born author
* Collins, June

Weathervane
See Nakasone, Yasuhiro

Weatherwise, Abe
See Sagendorph, Robb Hansell

[A] Weaver
See Bakewell, T.

Weaver, Ben J. 1900?-1949 [BI]
American horse owner and racer
* Weaver, Buck

Weaver, Bertrand 1908-1973 [CA]
Clergyman and writer
* Hunter, Paul

Weaver, Big Jim
See Weaver, James Dement

Weaver, Blind Curley
See Weaver, Curley James

Weaver, Buck
See Weaver, Ben J.

Weaver, Buck
See Weaver, Charles

Weaver, Buck
See Weaver, George Davis

Weaver, Buck
See Weaver, John O.

Weaver, Charles 1940- [EJ7]
American jazz musician
* Abdullah, Shakur

Weaver, Charles 20th c. [EF]
American football player
* Weaver, Buck

Weaver, Charley
See Arquette, Cliff[ord]

Weaver, Curley James 1906-1962
[BWW]
American singer
* Gordon, Slim
* Weaver, Blind Curley

Weaver, Doodles
See Weaver, Winstead Sheffield
Glendening Dixon

Weaver, Earl Sidney 1930- [WP 9-17-82]
American baseball manager
* [The] Certified Genius
* [The] Dream Weaver of 33rd Street
* [The] Earl of Baltimore

Weaver, Earle
See Willets, Walter E.

Weaver, Eddie 20th c.
American football player
* Weaver, Meat Cleaver

Weaver, Effie
See McVicker, Mrs. Horace

Weaver, Ella
See Whiteley, Mrs. John H.

Weaver, Elviry
See Weaver, June

Weaver, Farmer
See Weaver, William B.

Weaver, Fluss
See Weaver, James Brian [Jim]

Weaver, George Davis 1890-1956 [AS,
BE, HPPN, PB]
American baseball player
* Weaver, Buck
* [The] Whitest of the Black Sox

Weaver, Gertrude Renton 1884- [SFL,
WGT]
British author
* Colmore, G[eorge]
* Dunn, Gertrude

Weaver, Gustine Courson 1873-?
[HPPN, NAA]
American author
* Lady Gustine
* [The] Texas Doll Lady

Weaver, James 20th c. [EF]
American football player
* Weaver, Red

Weaver, James Brian [Jim] 1939- [BE]
American baseball player
* Weaver, Fluss

Weaver, James Dement 1903- [BE]
American baseball player
* Weaver, Big Jim

Weaver, John O. 1906-1978 [BI]
American radio and television newscaster
* Weaver, Buck

Weaver, June 1891?-1977 [FIR]
Entertainer
* Weaver, Elviry

Weaver, Katherine Grey Dunlap 1910-
[CA]
American author
* Weaver, Kitty

Weaver, Kitty
See Weaver, Katherine Grey Dunlap

Weaver, Lapland Willie
See Weaver, William [Bill]

Weaver, Mateman
See Greene, Alvin Carl

Weaver, Meat Cleaver
See Weaver, Eddie

Weaver, Monte
See Weaver, Montgomery Morton

Weaver, Montgomery Morton 1906-
[BE, PB]
American baseball player
* Weaver, Monte
* Weaver, Prof

Weaver, Old Zeb
See Weaver, Zebulon

Weaver, Orlie
See Weaver, Orville F.

Weaver, Orville F. 1888- [BE]
American baseball player
* Weaver, Orlie

Weaver, Pat
See Weaver, Sylvester, L., Jr.

Weaver, Paul Ford 1901- [BEW, TR]
American actor
* Ford, Paul

Weaver, Phoenix Donald
See Weaver, William [Bill]

[The] Weaver Poet of Inverurie
See Thom, William

Weaver, Prof
See Weaver, Montgomery Morton

Weaver, Red
See Weaver, James

Weaver, Robert [IP]
British clergyman and author
* [A] Quadragenarian

Weaver, Robert G. 20th c. [CA]
American author
* Weber, Rubin [joint pseudonym with
S(amuel) Leonard Rubinstein]

Weaver, Sigourney
See Weaver, Susan

Weaver, Susan 1950?- [WP 8-31-84]
American actress
* Weaver, Sigourney

Weaver, Sylvester, L., Jr. 20th c. [ET,
WP 8-31-84]
* [The] Father of the TV Talk Show
* Weaver, Pat

Weaver, Thomas [IP]
Author
* Shuttle, Job

Weaver, Thomas 1616-1663 [PI]
British poet
* T. W., Gent.

Weaver, Ward
See Mason, F[rancis] Van Wyck

Weaver, William [Bill] ?-1954 [BLB]
American robber
* Weaver, Lapland Willie
* Weaver, Phoenix Donald

Weaver, William B. 1865-1943 [BE]
American baseball player
* Weaver, Farmer

Weaver, Winstead Sheffield Glendening Dixon 1914- [HPPN, JF]
American actor and comedian
* [The] Poor Man's Sterling Holloway
* Weaver, Doodles

Weaver, Zebulon 1872-1948 [HPPN]
American attorney and politician
* Weaver, Old Zeb

Web, Dan
See Millsaps, Daniel W., III

Webb, A. C.
See Webb, Augustus Caesar

Webb, Ada [BMH]
Entertainer
* Queen of the Crystal Tank

Webb, Anthony 20th c. [SI 11-28-83]
American basketball player
* Webb, Spud

Webb, Anthony [joint pseudonym]
See Wilson, N[orman] Scarlyn

Webb, Arthur Patterson 1889- [WWL]
British author
* Simpkin

Webb, Augustus Caesar 1894- [SFL]
American author
* Webb, A. C.

Webb, Baby
See Webb, James

Webb, Bernard
See McCartney, Paul

Webb, Bill 1926- [BWW]
American singer
* Webb, Boogie Bill

Webb, Blanche A. [SFL]
Author
* Draper, Blanche A.

Webb, Bob 20th c.
Actor and former basketball player
* Webb, Spider

Webb, Boogie Bill
See Webb, Bill

Webb, Brenda Gail 1951-
American country-western performer
* Gayle, Crystal

Webb, Charles Henry 1834?-1905 [FFF, PA, WBD]
American poet and journalist
* Paul, John

Webb, Charles Hull 1843-? [FFF, IP]
American writer
* Caqueteur
* Cutting, Pierce
* Manley, Jack
* Marling, Matt

Webb, Chick
See Webb, William

Webb, Christopher
See Wibberley, Leonard [Patrick O'Connor]

Webb, Cleon Earl 1885-1958 [BE]
American baseball player
* Webb, Lefty

Webb, Clifton
See Hollenbeck, Webb Parmelee

Webb, Cornelius 19th c. [PA]
Author
* [A] Person about Town

Webb, Daniel 18th c. [HPPN]
British author
* [An] English Woolen Manufacturer

Webb, Dora
See Webb, Mahala Theodora

Webb, Dorothy Anna Maria 20th c. [WW]
Author
* March, Jermyn

Webb, Ellsworth 1931- [BX]
American boxer
* Webb, Spider

Webb, Ethel 1925- [IAW]
British-born author
* Roch, Dalby

Webb, Eve [Rudd] 1940?-
American artist
* Webb, Sasha

Webb, F. [IP]
British author
* Philalethes

Webb, Forrest
See Forrest-Webb, Robert

Webb, Foster 18th c. [IP]
British poet
* Telarius
* Vedastus

Webb, Francis 1735-1815 [IP]
British author
* Verus

Webb, Godfrey Edward Charles 1914- [AW]
British author
* England, Norman
* Godfrey, Charles

Webb, Hamilton Murrell 1889- [BI]
American boxing coach
* Webb, Spike

Webb, Harold 1940- [FC, LRR]
British singer
* Richard, Cliff

Webb, Jack Randolph 1920-1982 [HPPN, WW]
American actor, producer, director, author
* Farr, John
* Friday, [Sergeant] Joe
* Grady, Tex

Webb, James 20th c. [HPPN]
American entertainer
* [The] Ugliest Man in the World

Webb, James 20th c. [OBW]
American baseball player
* Webb, Baby

Webb, James Laverne 1909- [BE]
American baseball player
* Webb, Skeeter

Webb, James Watson 1802-1884 [HPPN, IP]
American politician and journalist
* [An] Amateur Traveller
* [The] Influential Editor

Webb, Jean Francis 1910- [CA, WD, WW]
American author
* Hamill, Ethel
* Morrison, Roberta

Webb, Jim
See Longley, William Preston

Webb, John Joshua 1847-1882 [EWG]
American gunfighter
* King, Samuel

Webb, Joseph 1735-1787 [IP, PA]
American author
* Tela, Josephus

Webb, Laura S. 19th c. [BDSA, IP]
American poet and educator
* Lee, Stannie

Webb, Lawrence Arthur 1906?- [WWJ]
American jazz musician
* Webb, Speed

Webb, Lefty
See Webb, Cleon Earl

Webb, Lilian Julian 1877-1936
Rhodesian author
* Stockley, Cynthia

Webb, Lionel
See Hershman, Morris

Webb, Lizbeth
See Wills-Webber, Lizbeth

Webb, Lucas
See Burgess, Michael Roy

Webb, Mahala Theodora 1887- [DBA]
British painter and sculptor
* Webb, Dora

Webb, Martha G.
See Wingate, Anne

Webb, Mary [WWL]
British author
* Meredith, Mary G.

Webb, Mary Haydn 1938- [CA]
American author
* Ross, Leah

Webb, Neil
See Rowland, Donald Sydney

Webb, Philip Carteret 1700-1770 [IP]
British antiquary and author
* [A] Gentleman of Lincoln's Inn
* [A] Member of the House of Commons
* P. C. W.

Webb, Red
See Webb, Samuel Henry

Webb, Richard Davis 19th c. [PI]
Irish poet
* R. D. W.

Webb, Richard Wilson [CC, EMD, WW]
British-born American author
* Patrick, Q. [joint pseudonym with Mary L. Aswell, Martha Kelly, and Hugh Wheeler]
* Quentin, Patrick [joint pseudonym with Hugh Callingham Wheeler]
* Stagge, Jonathan [joint pseudonym with Hugh Callingham Wheeler]

Webb, Robert Forrest
See Forrest-Webb, Robert

Webb, Ruth Enid Borlase Morris 1926- [AW, CA, WD]
Australian author
* Morris, Ruth

Webb, Samuel Henry 1924- [BE]
American baseball player
* Webb, Red

Webb, Sasha
See Webb, Eve [Rudd]

Webb, Sidney James 1859-1947
British economist
* Passfield, Baron

Webb, Skeeter
See Webb, James Laverne

Webb, Speed
See Webb, Lawrence Arthur

Webb, Spider
See Gohman, Fred Joseph

Webb, Spider
See Webb, Bob

Webb, Spider
See Webb, Ellsworth

Webb, Spider
See Webb, Travis

Webb, Spike
See Webb, Hamilton Murrell

Webb, Spud
See Webb, Anthony

Webb, Travis 20th c.
Auto racer
* Webb, Spider

Webb, W. T.
See Webb, William Thomas

Webb, William 19th c. [IP]
British clergyman and author
* [The] Protestant Rector of Tixall, Stafford

Webb, William 1902?-1939 [DAM, EJ, PMJ]
American jazz musician
* Webb, Chick

Webb, William H. 19th c. [IP, PA]
American author
* Magpie

Webb, William Locock 19th c. [IP]
British author
* W. L. W.

Webb, William Thomas 1918- [HFF]
British author
* Webb, W. T.

Webbe, Cornelius 19th c. [IP]
British author
* [A] Person lately about Town

Webbe, Gale D[udley] 1909- [CA]
American clergyman and author
* Cole, Stephen

Webber, Bert
See Webber, Ebbert T[rue]

Webber [or Weber], Bridgey
See Webber [or Weber], Louis

Webber, Charles Edmund 19th c. [IP]
British soldier and author
* C. E. W.
* [An] Officer of the Royal Engineers

Webber, Charles Wilkins 1819-1856 [HPPN, IP]
American naturalist, journalist, author
* Eimi, C. W.
* [A] Kentuckian
* Winterfield, Charles

Webber, Ebbert T[rue] 1921- [CA]
American author
* Webber, Bert

Webber, Edwin J. 1893-1968 [HPPN]
American composer and conductor
* Weber, Eddie

Webber, Frank
See Bushnell, William H.

Webber, Frederick 1889-1918 [HPPN]
American actor
* Weber, Rex

Webber, George Harris 1882- [NAA]
American educator and author
* Sig

Webber [or Weber], Louis 20th c. [HPPN]
American gambler
* Webber [or Weber], Bridgey
* Williams, Henry

Webber, Samuel 1797-1880 [IP]
American physician and author
* S.

Webber, Stawford
See Pile, D. W.

Webby
See Webster, Harold Tucker

Weber, Annemarie 1918- [IAW]
German author
* Henning, Katja

Weber, Brian 1947?- [NW 9-20-82]
American plaintiff in affirmative action trial
* [The] Blue Collar Bakke

Weber, Eddie
See Webber, Edwin J.

Weber, Hulda 1909- [IAW]
American author, poet, painter
* Katz, Hilda

Weber, Jeanne 1875-1910 [DI, LFW]
French murderer
* Bouchery, Madame
* Moulinet, Madame
* Ogre de la Goutte d'Or

Weber, Joe
See Weber, Morris

Weber, Karl
See Muetzelburg, Adolf

Weber, Lisa
See Mullaly, Mrs. W. S.

Weber, Morris 1867-1942 [PMJ]
American entertainer
* Weber, Joe

Weber, Nancy 1942- [CA]
American author
* Harmston, Olivia
* Rose, Jennifer
* West, Lindsay

Weber, Rex
See Webber, Frederick

Weber, Rubin [joint pseudonym with Robert G. Weaver]
See Rubinstein, S[amuel] Leonard

Weber, Rubin [joint pseudonym with S(amuel) Leonard Rubinstein]
See Weaver, Robert G.

Weber, Sarah Appleton 1930- [CA]
American educator and author
* Appleton, Sarah

Weber, Veit
See Waechter, Georg Philipp Ludwig Leonhard

Webfoot
See Phelps, W. D.

Webley, Pelagian
See Morgan, William Sacheus

Webster, Alice Jane Chandler 1876-1916 [LC, TC]
American author
* Webster, Jean

Webster, Black Dan
See Webster, Daniel

Webster, Bodus
See Webster, Cody

Webster, Chick
See Webster, John Robert

Webster, Cody 1970- [SI 9-6-82]
American little league baseball player
* Webster, Bodus

Webster, Daniel 1782-1852 [DNNS, HN, HPPN, SN]
American statesman
* All Eyes
* Black, Dan
* [The] Black Giant
* [The] Defender of the Constitution
* [The] Defender of the Union
* [The] Demosthenes of America
* [The] Eagle of the East
* [The] Expounder of the Constitution
* [The] God Like Daniel
* [The] Great Interpreter
* [The] Great Stone Face
* Icarus
* [The] Illustrious Defender
* Little Black Dan
* [The] Massachusetts Giant
* [The] Massachusetts Thunderer
* [The] Modern Sisyphus
* [The] New England Cicero
* [The] New Hampshire Demosthenes
* [The] Old Titanic Earth Son
* [The] Pillar of the Constitution
* [A] Traitor to Freedom
* [The] Unintentional Defaulter
* [The] Upholder of the Constitution
* Webster, Black Dan
* Webster, Immortal
* Webster, Indian Dan
* [The] Whig Gulliver

Webster, David Endicott 1929- [CA]
American author
* Strongblood, Casper

Webster, Edith Smith 20th c. [NAA]
American author
* Smith, Edith Lillian

Webster, Ester Luise 1898- [NAA]
American writer, editor, columnist
* Paul, Genay
* Skillman, Ester Webster

Webster, Ezekiel 1780-1829 [IP]
American attorney and author
* Cato

Webster, Frances 1876?-1951 [BI]
American circus performer
* Ethardo, Naomi

Webster, Frank V. [house pseudonym]
[Stratemeyer Syndicate]
See Stratemeyer, Edward L.

Webster, Gary
See Garrison, Webb B[lack]

Webster, George Edis 19th c. [HFN, IP]
British clergyman and author
* [A] Minister of the Church of England

Webster, Harold Tucker 1885-1952
[HPPN]
American cartoonist and satirist
* [The] Mark Twain of Cartoonists
* Webby

Webster, Immortal
See Webster, Daniel

Webster, Indian Dan
See Webster, Daniel

Webster, James 18th c. [IP]
Scottish clergyman and author
* One of the Country Party
* [A] Sincere Lover of the Church and State

Webster, Jean
See McKinney, Alice Jane Chandler Webster

Webster, Jean
See Webster, Alice Jane Chandler

Webster, Jennie Ellis Burdick 1882-?
[NAA]
American author and editor
* Burdick, Jennie Ellis

Webster, Jesse
See Cassill, Ronald Verlin

Webster, John Robert 1921- [CEI]
Canadian-born hockey player
* Webster, Chick

Webster, [Dr.] John White 1793-1850
[HPPN]
American chemist, educator, murderer
* J. W. W.
* Webster, Skyrocket Jack

Webster, Judge
See Webster, William Hedgcock

Webster, Julia Augusta 1837-1894
[DEA]
British author
* Home, Cecil

Webster, Lizzie
See Nunnemacher, Mrs. Jacob

Webster, Lucille 1886-1947 [F2]
American actress
* Gleason, Lucille

Webster, M. M.
See Mosby, Mary Webster [Pleasants]

Webster, Mamie
See Smith, Mabel Louise

Webster, Marvin 1952- [SMG]
American basketball player
* [The] Human Eraser

Webster, Mrs. John [FFF]
Entertainer
* McHenry, Nellie

Webster, Noah 1758-1843 [DNNS, FFF, HPPN, IP, SN]
American lexicographer and author
* Adam
* [An] American
* Aristides
* Aurelius

Webster, Noah (cont.)
* B.
* Candor
* Contented Freeman
* Curtius
* [A] Federalist
* Hampden
* Honorius
* Lover of Stability
* Marcellus
* Peace and Justice
* [The] Schoolmaster of the Republic
* [The] Schoolmaster to America
* Seneca
* Sidney
* Trumbull

Webster, Noah
See Knox, William [Bill]

Webster, Paul Frank 1909- [MY]
American jazz musician
* Webster, Webb

Webster, Pelatiah 1725-1795 [HPPN, IP]
American patriot and author
* [A] Citizen of Philadelphia
* [A] Citizen of the United States
* [A] Financier

Webster, Robert N.
See Palmer, Raymond A[rthur]

Webster, Samuel 1718-1796 [HPPN]
American clergyman
* [A] Minister

Webster, Skyrocket Jack
See Webster, [Dr.] John White

Webster, Speck
See Webster, William

Webster, Thomas 1780-1840 [IP]
British clergyman and author
* T. W.
* W.

Webster, Webb
See Webster, Paul Frank

Webster, William [OBW]
American baseball player
* Webster, Speck

Webster, William 1689-1758 [IP]
British clergyman and author
* [The] Draper
* [A] Draper of London
* [A] Friend to the Government
* Hooker, Richard, Esq., of the Inner Temple

Webster, William Hedgcock 1924?-
[HPPN]
American jurist
* [The] Top Cop
* [The] Tough Top Cop
* Webster, Judge

Wechsler, Moe
See Wechsler, Morris Louis

Wechsler, Morris Louis 1920- [EJ]
American jazz musician
* Wechsler, Moe

Weck, H-Bomb
See Weck, Henry

Weck, Henry 20th c. [CMA]
Musician
* Weck, H-Bomb

Weda [or Wegner], Richard
See Dallwitz-Wegner, Richard Von

Wedderburn, Alexander [First Baron Loughborough] 1733-1805 [HPPN, NPS, SN]
British jurist
* [The] Greatest Hypocrite in His Majesty's Dominions
* [A] Pert, Prim Prater of the Northern Race
* [The] Proudest of the Proud

Wedding, Alex
See Weiskopf, Grete

Wede
See Espy, Willard Richardson

Wedecee
See Caroe, William Douglas

Wedekind, Benjamin Franklin 1864-1918 [BEW, CA, LC, TLC]
German playwright, producer, actor
* Minehaha, Cornelius
* Wedekind, Frank

Wedekind, Frank
See Wedekind, Benjamin Franklin

Wedel, Gottschalk
See Zuccalmaglio-Waldbruehl, Wilhelm von

Wedell, Carl Heinrich 1712-1782 [DNNF, FFF, SN]
Prussian army officer
* Wedell, Leonidas

Wedell, Leonidas
See Wedell, Carl Heinrich

Wedemeyer, Albert C. 1897- [CND]
American military leader
* White, Mr. [code name used during World War II]

[The] Wedge
See Turnesa, William P.

Wedge, Florence 1919- [CA]
Canadian author
* Wayne, Frances

Wedgie
See Benn, Anthony Wedgwood

Wedgwood, [Dame] C. V.
See Wedgwood, Cicely Veronica

Wedgwood, Cicely Veronica 1910- [LC]
British author
* Wedgwood, [Dame] C. V.

Wedgwood, Edgar A. 1856-1920 [HPPN]
American sheriff
* [The] Kid Sheriff of Nebraska

Wedgwood, Josiah 1730-1795 [DNNS, HN, SN]
British potter
* [The] Father of English Pottery
* [The] Father of the Potteries

Wee Bea Booze
See Nicholls, Muriel

Wee Ben Sayers
See Sayers, Bernard

Wee Bobby Cruickshank
See Cruickshank, Bobby

Wee Bonnie Baker
See Nelson, Evelyn

Wee Charlie Barr
See Barr, Charles

Wee Georgie Wood
See Bramlett, George

[The] Wee Iceman
See Hogan, Benjamin William

Wee Jimmy
See Carter, James Earl, Jr. [Jimmy]

Wee Jimmy Clark
See Clark, James [Jimmy]

Wee Johnny
See Wilson, John

[The] Wee Scot
See Cruickshank, Bobby

[The] Wee Scot
See MacKay, Duncan McMillan

Wee Tommy Leach
See Leach, Thomas W.

Wee Willie Clark
See Clark, William Otis

Wee Willie Damman
See Damman, William Henry [Bill]

Wee Willie Keeler
See Keeler, William Henry

Wee Willie Ludolph
See Ludolph, William Francis [Willie]

Wee Willie Mains
See Mains, Willard Eben

Wee Willie Messino
See Messino, William

Wee Willie Mills
See Mills, William Grant [Willie]

Wee Willie Powell
See Powell, William Ernest

Wee Willie Robyn
See Robyn, William

Wee Willie Sherdel
See Sherdel, William Henry

Wee Willie Sudhoff
See Sudhoff, John William

Wee Willie Wilkin
See Wilkin, Wilbur

[The] Wee Wonder
See Moore, Dudley

Weed, Buddy
See Weed, Harold Eugene

Weed, Cy
See Weed, Randolph W.

Weed, Harold Eugene 1918- [EJ, PMJ]
American jazz musician
* Weed, Buddy

Weed, Leland T. 1901-1975 [SC]
American actor and singer
* Baker, Bob

Weed, Randolph W. 1883?-1964 [AS]
American rowboat racer
* Weed, Cy

Weed, Tad
See Weed, Thurlow

Weed, Thurlow 1797-1884 [PA]
American journalist and politician
* T. W.

Weed, Thurlow 20th c. [EF]
American football player
* Weed, Tad

Weed, Truman Andrew Wellington 1841-1927 [DNA]
American author and clergyman
* Wellington, Andrew

Weed, Walter H.
See Weil, Joseph R.

Weede, Robert
See Wiedefeld, Robert

Weeden, Charles Foster 1856-1928 [HPPN]
American clergyman
* Bishop of Congregational Churches

Weegee
See Fellig, Arthur

Weekes, Agnes Russell 1880-? [TC, WW]
British author
* Pryde, Anthony

Weekes, John Ernest 19th c. [IP]
British author
* J. E. W.

Weekley, Maurice Arden [WGT]
Author
* Arden, Rice

Weeks, Ada Mae 1900-1978 [THR]
American actress and dancer
* May, Ada

Weeks, Ans
See Weeks, Anson

Weeks, Anson 1898-1969 [HPPN]
American jazz musician
* Weeks, Ans

Weeks, Bill 20th c. [GW]
American rodeo performer
* Weeks, Crotcho

Weeks, Black Hoss
See Weeks, Guy

Weeks, Constance Tomkinson 1915-
[CA]
Canadian-born author
* Tomkinson, Constance

Weeks, Crotcho
See Weeks, Bill

Weeks, Guy 20th c. [GW]
American rodeo performer
* Weeks, Black Hoss

Weeks, Helen C. 19th c. [FFF, IP, PA]
American author
* Campbell, Helen
* Wheaton, Campbell

Weeks, James 1922- [HPPN]
American painter
* Northrup, Darrell
* [The] Painter Without a Label

Weeks, Marion
See Barron, Marion Weeks

Weeks, William Raymond 1783-1848
[DNA]
American author, clergyman, educator
* Bunyanus

Weems, J. Eddie, Jr.
See Weems, John Edward

Weems, John Edward 1924- [HPPN]
American journalist, educator, author
* Weems, J. Eddie, Jr.

Weems, Ted
See Weymes, Wilfred Theodore

**[The] Weeping Greek from Cripple
Creek**
See Vetoyanis, Theodore

[The] Weeping Philosopher
See Heraclitos [or Heraclitus]

[The] Weeping Prophet
See Sewall, Joseph

[The] Weeping Saint
See Swithin

Weeping Willie
See Winter, William

Weeping Willie Willoughby
See Willoughby, Claude William

Weeping Winifred
See Foe, Daniel

Weer, William
See Kaufman, Isadore

Weertz, Louis 1926- [EPM]
American musician
* Williams, Roger

Wees, Frances Shelley 1902- [CA]
Canadian author
* Shelley, Frances

Wef [Wild Eyed Fellow]
See Clifford, Christopher Craven

Wegg De Norva, Silas
See Viett, George Frederic

Wegier, Bayla 1927-1971 [FC]
Polish-French actress
* Darvi, Bella

Wehde, Biggs
See Wehde, Wilbur

Wehde, Wilbur 1906- [BE]
American baseball player
* Wehde, Biggs

Wehen, Joy DeWeese 20th c. [CA]
Malaysian-born author
* Wade, Jennifer

Wehl, Feodor
See Wehlen, Feodor zu

Wehlen, Feodor zu 1821-? [IP]
German author
* Wehl, Feodor

Wehmeyer, Lillian [Mabel] Biermann
1933- [CA]
American author and educator
* Biermann, Lillian

Wehr, Werner
See Gartmann, Heinz

Wei, Cho-ming 1888- [BI]
Chinese educator
* Wei, Francis

Wei, Francis
See Wei, Cho-ming

Wei, Rex Yue-Tien 1933- [AW, WD]
British author and poet
* Williams, Rex

Weichbrodt, Rudolph C. 1871-1958 [BE]
American baseball player
* Roach, Skel

Weidemeyer, John William 1819-1896
[DNA]
American author and publisher
* Montclair, J. W.

Weidenfeld, Jesse Marc 1919- [BEW]
American actor and comedian
* White, Jesse

Weidman, George E. 1861-1905 [AS,
BE]
American baseball player
* Weidman, Stump

Weidman, Stump
See Weidman, George E.

Weidt, Conrad 1892-1943 [WEF]
German-born actor
* Veidt, Conrad

Weigel, Ralph Richard 1921- [BE]
American baseball player
* Weigel, Wig

Weigel, Wig
See Weigel, Ralph Richard

Weight, Frank
See Tubb, Edwin Charles

Weightman, George ?-1895? [BLB,
EWG]
American bank and trainrobber
* Buck, Red
* Weightman, Red Buck

Weightman, Red Buck
See Weightman, George

Weightman, Wild Bill
See Weightman, William E.

Weightman, William E. 20th c. [EAR]
American auto racer
* Weightman, Wild Bill

Weigle, Marta
See Weigle, Mary Martha

Weigle, Mary Martha 1944- [CA]
American folklorist and author
* Weigle, Marta

Weigle, Ross 1901-1961
American actor
* Ross, Churchill

Weigum, Patricia Millicent 1929- [EJ]
American singer
* Yankee, Pat

Weihe, John Garibaldi 1862-1914 [BE]
American baseball player
* Weihe, Podgie

Weihe, Podgie
See Weihe, John Garibaldi

Weik, Legs
See Weik, Richard Henry

Weik, Richard Henry 1927- [BE]
American baseball player
* Weik, Legs

Weil, Josef 1828-1889 [WBD]
Bohemian-born poet and playwright
* Weilen, Josef von

Weil, Joseph R. 1875?-1976 [BI, HPPN]
American swindler
* Black, H. Huntington
* Chicago's Minister of Human Cupidity
* Dorrance, [Dr.] Richard T.
* Farnsworth, V. Timkin
* [The] Genius of Racing
* Lehigh, [Colonel] Rutherford B.
* Manningham, T. Raymond
* O'Connell, Daniel
* St. Harriot, [Doktor] Tourneur
* Von Chopnick, Professor
* Warrington, H. Jefferson
* Weed, Walter H.
* Weil, Yellow Kid
* Wilson, [Dr.] James R.

Weil, Roman L[ee] 1940- [CA]
American educator and author
* Worman, Eli

Weil, Yellow Kid
See Weil, Joseph R.

Weiland, Cooney
See Weiland, Ralph

Weiland, Lefty
See Weiland, Robert George

Weiland, Ralph 1904- [CEI, FHE, HK]
Canadian-born hockey player
* Weiland, Cooney

Weiland, Robert George 1905- [BE]
American baseball player
* Weiland, Lefty

Weilen, Josef von
See Weil, Josef

Weilenmann, Carl Woolworth 1889-1924
[AS, BE]
American baseball player
* Weilman, Carl Woolworth
* Weilman, Zeke

Weiler, Phyllis 1914- [FC]
American actress
* Brooks, Phyllis

Weill, Rene 1868-1952 [WBD]
French playwright
* Coolus, Romain

Weilman, Carl Woolworth
See Weilenmann, Carl Woolworth

Weilman, Zeke
See Weilenmann, Carl Woolworth

Weimer, Jacob 1873-1928 [AS, BE]
American baseball player
* Weimer, Tornado Jake

Weimer, Marguerite Josephine
1787-1867 [WBD]
French actress
* George, Mlle.

Weimer, Tornado Jake
See Weimer, Jacob

Weinbaum, Helen
See Kasson, Helen Weinbaum

Weinbaum, Stanley G[rauman]
1900?-1935 [ESF, WGT, WOA]
American author
* Jessel, John
* Stanley, Marge

Weinberg, Abe ?-1935 [PHM]
American underworld figure
* Weinberg, Bo

Weinberg, Bo
See Weinberg, Abe

Weinberg, Charles 1889-1955 [ASC]
American composer and conductor
* Wynn, Charles

Weinberg, Janet Hopson
See Hopson, Janet L[ouise]

Weinberg, Melvin 1925?-
*American swindler and government
witness in Abscam trials*
* [The] McDonald's of Con Men

Weinberg, Stephen Jacob 1891-1960
[BI, DI, HPPN]
American impostor
* [The] Amiable Swindler
* [The] Big Little Man from Brooklyn
* [The] Great Impostor
* [The] Impostor's Impostor
* Weyman, Stanley Clifford

Weinberger, Caspar 1917?- [NW 5-23-83,
NW 8-30-82, TI 12-20-82, WP 9-25-85]
American government official
* Cap the Cup
* Cap the Knife
* Cap the Ladle
* Cap the Shovel
* Cap the Suitcase
* [The] Defender
* SecDef

Weinberger, Harry 1924- [ART]
German-born artist
* H. W.

Weinberger, Louis 1881?-1949 [BI]
American attorney
* Warner, Louis

Weinberger, Moses 19th c. [HPPN]
*Hungarian-born American pioneer and
saloon keeper*
* [The] Same Old Mose
* [The] Same Young Mose

Weinberger, Moshe 1908- [CA]
Hungarian-born American author
* Carmilly, Moshe

Weinblatt, Mike
See Weinblatt, Myron

Weinblatt, Myron 20th c. [ET]
Television executive
* Weinblatt, Mike

Weiner, Doc
See Stacher, Joseph

Weiner, Edith 1943- [CA]
American journalist and editor
* Lederer, Edith Madelon

Weiner, Henri
See Longstreet, [Henry] Stephen
[Weiner]

Weiner, Margery Sarah 20th c. [AW]
British author
* Lake, Sarah

Weiner, Skip
See Weiner, Stewart

Weiner, Stewart 1945- [CA]
American author and editor
* Lebreo, Steward
* Lebreo, Stewart
* Weiner, Skip

Weiner, Yehudi 1929- [BBD]
American composer
* Wyner, Yehudi

Weinert, Charley 1895- [BX]
Hungarian-born boxer
* [The] Newark Adonis

Weinert, Lefty
See Weinert, Philip Walter

Weinert, Philip Walter 1901-1973 [BE]
American baseball player
* Weinert, Lefty

Weingarten, David 1902- [ASC]
American composer
* Gardner, Dave

Weingarten, Israel ?-1928 [HPPN]
American producer
* Weingarten, Izzy

Weingarten, Izzy
See Weingarten, Israel

Weingartner, Dutch
See Weingartner, Elmer William

Weingartner, Elmer William 1918- [BE]
American baseball player
* Weingartner, Dutch

Weinig, Jean Maria 1920- [CA]
American writer and poet
* Mary Anthony, [Mother]
* Weinig, [Sister] Mary Anthony

Weinig, [Sister] Mary Anthony
See Weinig, Jean Maria

Weinmann, Hans 1884-1960 [BI]
Czech industrialist
* Wyman, Hans

Weinrauch, Herschel 1905- [CAP]
Russian-born American author
* Vinokur, Grigory

Weinrich, Anna Katharina Hildegard
1933- [CA]
German-born anthropologist and author
* Mary Aquina, [Sister]

Weinstein, Aaron 1898-1967 [WGT]
American author
* Wyn, A. A.

Weinstein, Ellen R. 1939- [BEW]
American actress
* Weston, Ellen

Weinstein, Emanuel 1928-1975 [HPPN]
American cinematographer
* Wynne, Manny

Weinstein, Harry 1845-1933 [HPPN]
American eccentric and businessman
* Lee, Jacques L.

Weinstein, Leslie 20th c. [CMA]
American singer
* West, Leslie

Weinstein, Nathan Wallenstein
1903?-1940 [HPPN, LC, TC, TCL]
American author
* [The] Ironic Prophet
* West, Nathanael
* West, Pep

Weinstein, Sam 1914- [BBH]
American radio and television broadcaster
* [The] Tenpin Tattler

Weinstein, Sol 1928- [HPPN]
American journalist, scriptwriter, author
* Pumpernickel

Weinstock, Helen 1910- [CA]
American author
* Lewis, Francine
* Wells, Helen

Weinstock, Isadore 20th c. [EF]
American football player
* Weinstock, Izzy

Weinstock, Izzy
See Weinstock, Isadore

Weinstock, Jack 20th c.
American playwright and screenwriter
* Mareth, Glenville [joint pseudonym
  with William Gilbert Gomberg]

Weinstock, Lotus
See Weinstock, Marlene

Weinstock, Marlene 20th c. [NW 4-30-84]
American comedienne
* Weinstock, Lotus

Weinstock, Miklos Vary 1923?- [BI]
Hungarian singer
* Gafni, Miklos

Weintraub, Mickey
See Weintraub, Philip

Weintraub, Philip 1907- [BE, EJS]
American baseball player
* Weintraub, Mickey

Weintraub, Wiktor 1908- [IAW]
Polish-born author
* Quidam
* Theates

Weintrop, Reuben 1896-1968 [BMH]
British comedian and singer
* Fargo the Boy Wizard
* Flanagan, Bud
* Wayne, Bobby
* Winthrop, Robert

Weir, Ace
See Weir, Bob

Weir, Alice M.
See McLaughlin, Emma Maude

Weir, Bob 1947- [CMA]
Musician
* Weir, Ace

Weir, Henry Crichton 1857-? [PI]
Irish poet
* Crichton, Harry

Weir, Ike O'Neil 1867-1908 [BX, RBE]
Irish-born boxer
* [The] Belfast Spider

Weir, John
See Cross, Colin [John]

Weir, Leonard 1931- [BA]
American private investigator
* Al Hafeez, Humza

Weir, Logan
See Perry, James Black

Weir, Mordred
See Long, Amelia Reynolds

Weir, Rosemary 1905- [TCC]
South African-born author
* Bell, Catherine

Weir, Roy
See Weir, William Franklin [Bill]

Weir, Stan 1952- [SMG]
Canadian-born hockey player
* Weir, Stash

Weir, Stash
See Weir, Stan

Weir, William Franklin [Bill] 1911-
[BE]
American baseball player
* Weir, Roy

Weir, Woodrow [BBH]
American basketball player and coach
* Weir, Woody

Weir, Woody
See Weir, Woodrow

Weird Al Yankovic
See Yankovic, Al

Weird Beard Knight
See Knight, Russ

[The] Weird Guitar Player
See Bell, Ed[ward]

Weird Harold Rubin
See Rubin, Harold

Weirich, Bob 20th c.
Author
* Donnigan, Dregs

Weis, Arthur John 1903- [BE]
American baseball player
* Weis, Butch

Weis, Butch
See Weis, Arthur John

Weis, Isaac Mayer 1819-1900 [HPPN, WBD]
American clergyman
* [The] Moses of America
* Wise, Isaac Mayer

Weisberg, Roy B. 1893-1975 [SC]
Russian-born actor, director, screenwriter
* West, Billy

Weise, Clara Stock 19th c. [HPPN]
German author
* Cron, Clara

Weisenfreund, Muni 1895-1967 [F2, FC, HPPN, IPA]
Austrian-born actor
* [The] Man of Many Faces
* [The] Man Who Is Always Somebody
  Else
* Muni, Paul

Weiser, Bud
See Weiser, Harry Budson

Weiser, Harry Budson 1891-1961 [BE]
American baseball player
* Weiser, Bud

Weiser, Marjorie P[hillis] K[atz] 1934-
[CA]
American author
* Katz, Marjorie P.

Weisgal, Emanuel 1925- [BEW, TR]
American actor and director
* Wager, Michael

Weisgard, Leonard [Joseph] 1916- [CA, SAT]
American author and illustrator
* Green, Adam

Weisinger, Mort[imer] 1915- [SFP, WGT]
American author
* Garth, Will [house pseudonym]
* Geris, Tom Erwin
* Rectez, Ian
* Saturn, Sergeant [house pseudonym]

Weiskopf, Grete 20th c.
German author
* Wedding, Alex

Weisman, Alfred 1883-1972 [SC]
American actor
* White, Alfred H.

Weisman, Joan 1921- [MA]
American author
* Savage, Joan

Weiss, Albert Maria 1844-1925 [WBD]
German-born theologian and author
* Von der Clana, Heinrich

Weiss, Amalie
See Schneeweiss, Amalie

Weiss, Bernhard Siegfried 1697-1770
[HPPN]
German anatomist and educator
* Albinus

Weiss, Earl
See Wajcieckowski, Earl

Weiss, Edna
See Barth, Edna

Weiss, Ehrich 1874-1926 [BS, FC, HPPN, THR]
American magician
* Champion Jail Breaker
* [The] Handcuff King
* Houdini, Harry
* Houdini the Great
* [The] King of Cards
* [The] King of Esapologists
* [The] King of Handcuffs
* [The] Monarch of Leg Shackles
* Osey, Herr N.
* [The] Prince of the Air
* [The] Syllable Accenting American
* Undisputed King of Handcuffs

Weiss, Emanuel ?-1944 [PHM]
American underworld figure
* Weiss, Mendy

Weiss, Francesca 1885?-1975 [FIR]
Television performer
* Weiss, Mama

Weiss, George Martin 1894-1972 [BAB]
American baseball executive
* Weiss, Lonesome George

Weiss, Henry George 1898-1946 [NAA, SF]
Canadian-born writer
* Flagg, Francis

Weiss, Howard Peter 1927- [BEW]
American musician
* Howard, Peter

Weiss, Hymie
See Wajcieckowski, Earl

Weiss, Irving J. 1921- [CA]
American editor and writer
* Di Marco, Gino
* Forio, Robert

Weiss, John 1818-1879 [HPPN]
American clergyman
* J. W.

Weiss, Little Hymie
See Wajcieckowski, Earl

Weiss, Lonesome George
See Weiss, George Martin

Weiss, Louis 1907- [FC, ITA, SW]
American actor
* Taylor, Kent

Weiss, Louise 1893-1983 [HPPN]
French journalist
* Valentine 1014 [code name used
  during World War II]

Weiss, Lynde
See Thorpe, Thomas Bangs

Weiss, Mama
See Weiss, Francesca

Weiss, Mendy
See Weiss, Emanuel

Weiss, Miriam
See Schlein, Miriam

Weiss, Morris S[amuel] 1915- [CA]
American author and illustrator
* Higgins, Ink
* Sirrom, Wes

Weiss, Pana 20th c. [EJS]
Polish discus thrower
* Wajsowna, Jadwiga

Weiss, Paul 1901- [HPPN]
American philosopher and educator
* America's Foremost Speculative
  Philosopher

Weiss, Theo 1876-? [BMH, HPPN]
American magician
* Dash
* Hardeen
* Hardin
* [The] Legal Succesor of Houdini

Weisse, Clifford Stevens 1936- [BEW]
American talent representative
* Stevens, Clifford

Weissenberg, Alexis 1929- [MS]
Bulgarian-born musician
* Weissenberg, Sigi

Weissenberg, Sigi
See Weissenberg, Alexis

Weisshaus, Imre 1904-
Hungarian composer
* Arma, Paul

Weissman, Jack 1921- [CA]
American author
* Anderson, George

Weissman, Solly
See Weissman, William

Weissman, William 20th c. [BLB]
American underworld figure
* Weissman, Solly

Weissmuller, John[ny] 1904- [HPPN]
American swimmer and actor
* [The] Best of the Tarzans

Weisz, Herbert 1924- [TR]
Austrian-born director and actor
* Wise, Herbert

Weisz, Victor 1913-1966 [LC]
German-born cartoonist
* Vicky

Weitenkampf, Frank 1866-? [HPPN]
American librarian and author
* White, Frank Linstow

Weitz, George 1888?-1968 [EMT, PMJ]
American producer, director, writer
* White, George

Weitzel, Lawrence M. 1915- [HPPN]
American engineer
* [The] Mechanical Specialist

Weitzel, Sophy Winthrop 19th c. [IP,
PA]
American author
* Winthrop, Sophy

Weizman, Ezer 1925?- [WP 3-10-85]
Israeli government official
* Egypt, Mr.

Weizmann, Chaim 1874-1952 [HPPN]
President of Israel
* [The] Nation Builder

Wejp-Olsen, Werner 1938- [WEC]
Danish cartoonist
* WOW

Welber, Del
See Wilber, Delbert Quentin

Welburn, Vivienne
See Furlong, Vivienne Carole

Welby, Amelia Ball [Coppuck]
1819-1852 [DNA]
American poet
* Amelia

Welby, Henry 1554-1636? [NPS, SN]
British eccentric recluse
* [The] Hermit of Grub Street
* [The] Phoenix of these Late Times

Welby, Horace
See Timbs, John

Welby, John Robson ?-1964 [DI]
British murderer and robber
* Evans, Gwynne

Welby, Thomas Earle 1881-1933 [LC]
British author and journalist
* Stet

Welch, Alfred 1899-1952 [SC]
American actor
* Bond, Jack

Welch, Ann Courtenay Edmonds 1917-
[CA]
British author
* Douglas, Ann C.
* Edmonds, Ann C.

Welch, Bugger [or Booger]
See Welch, Frank Tiguer

Welch, Charles Scott
See Smith, LeRoi Tex

Welch, Dutch
See Welch, Herb[ert M.]

Welch, Ed
See Beck, H. O.

Welch, Edgar L[uderne] 1855-? [SFL,
WGT]
Author
* Gay, J. Drew
* Grip

Welch, Frank Tiguer 1897-1957 [BE,
BI]
American baseball player
* Welch, Bugger [or Booger]

[A] Welch Freeholder
See Jones, David

[A] Welch Freeholder
See Pennant, Thomas

Welch, General
See Welch, Rufus

Welch, Hawley 1907- [BBH, FH]
Canadian football player
* Welch, Huck

Welch, Herb[ert M.] 1900-1967 [BE]
American baseball player
* Welch, Dutch

Welch, Huck
See Welch, Hawley

Welch, Jean-Louise
See Kempton, Jean Welch

Welch, John 1935?- [TI 12-23-85]
American business executive
* Welch, Neutron Jack

Welch, Lou 20th c. [HPPN]
American radio comedian
* Perlmutter, Mawruss

Welch, Louise 1896-1980 [F1, F2]
American actress
* Carbasse, Louise
* Lovely, Louise

Welch, Marilyn 1933- [ASC]
American composer and entertainer
* Welch, Mitzie

Welch, Michael F. 1859-1941 [AS, DGS,
PB]
American baseball player
* Welch, Mickey
* Welch, Smiling Mickey

Welch, Mickey
See Welch, Michael F.

Welch, Mitzie
See Welch, Marilyn

Welch, Neutron Jack
See Welch, John

Welch, Pauline
See Bodenham, Hilda Morris

Welch, Raquel
See Tejada, Raquel

Welch, Ronald
See Felton, Ronald Oliver

Welch, Rowland
See Davies, Leslie Purnell

Welch, Rufus 1801-1856 [HPPN]
American circus entrepreneur
* Welch, General

Welch, Smiling Mickey
See Welch, Michael F.

Welch, Timothy L. 1935- [CA]
American author
* Cake, Patrick

Welcher, Rosalind 1922- [CA]
American author and illustrator
* Slavic, Rosalind Welcher

Welchman, Edward 1665?-1739 [IP]
British clergyman and author
* [A] Minister in the Country

Welcome, John
See Brennan, John N[eedham] H[uggard]

Weld, Horatio Hastings 1811-1888 [HPPN]
American clergyman and author
* Jones, Ezekiel
* W.

Weld, Matthew 19th c. [PI]
Irish poet
* Hartstonge, Matthew Weld

Weld, Susan Ker 1943- [BDF, FC, HT]
American actress
* Weld, Tuesday

Weld, Theodore Dwight 1803-? [IP]
American abolitionist reformer and author
* T. D. W.
* Wythe

Weld, Tuesday
See Weld, Susan Ker

Welday, Lyndon Earl 1879-1942 [BE]
American baseball player
* Welday, Mike

Welday, Mike
See Welday, Lyndon Earl

Weldon, [Sir] Anthony 1590-1655 [PA]
Author
* A. W., Sir

Weldon, Casey Bill
See Weldon, Will

Weldon, John 1875?-1963 [BEW, LC]
Irish actor, playwright, author
* MacNamara, Brinsley

Weldon, Kenny
See Waldron, Kenny

Weldon, Lillian
See Martin, Elizabeth

Weldon, Marvelous Mel
See Weldon, Melvin

Weldon, Melvin 20th c. [IBW]
American basketball player
* Weldon, Marvelous Mel

Weldon, Rex
See Rimel, Duane [Weldon]

Weldon, Robert 20th c. [WWL]
Irish poet
* Weldon, Roibeard

Weldon, Roibeard
See Weldon, Robert

Weldon, Will 1909- [BWW]
American singer
* [The] Hawaiian Guitar Wizard
* Kansas City Bill
* Levee Joe
* Weldon, Casey Bill

Welitsch, Ljuba
See Velitchkova, Ljuba

Welk, Ehm
See Trimm, Thomas

Welk, Lawrence LeRoy 1903- [HPPN]
American television personality and jazz musician
* [The] King of Musical Corn
* [The] Liberace of the Accordion
* Music Maker, Mr.

Welker, John Paul Pater 1946-
American entertainer
* Attle, John C.

Well, Alan Stewart
See Sewart, Alan

[The] Well Beloved
See Charles VI

[The] Well Beloved
See Louis XV

[The] Well Digger
See Matthews, Joseph W.

[The] Well Founded Doctor
See Aegidius [or Giles] of Colonna

[A] Well Known Author
See Lang, Andrew

[The] Well Known Gambler
See McDonald, Michael Cassius [Mike]

Well Languaged Daniel
See Daniel, Samuel

[The] Well of English Undefiled
See Chaucer, Geoffrey

[A] Well Wisher of the Good-Old-Way
See Pollock, John

[A] Well Wisher to His King and Country
See Whalley, George

[The] Well-Tempered Clavier
See Adenauer, Konrad

[A] Well-Wisher to the Good People of Great Britain
See Decker, [Sir] Matthew

[A] Well-Wisher to Trade
See Justice, Alexander

Welland, Colin
See Williams, Colin

Wellen, Edward [Paul] 1919- [CA, SFL]
American author
* Felder, Paul
* Gellert, Lew
* Killian, Larry

Wellens, Jan de 16th c. [BI]
Dutch painter
* Cock, Jan de

Weller
See Blanc, [Jean Joseph Charles] Louis

Weller, Bernard Williams 1870-? [LAO]
British author, critic, journalist
* B. W.

Weller, Calamity
See Weller, Luman Hamlin

Weller, Dorothy 20th c. [PW 3-30-84]
American author
* Bernard, Dorothy Ann
* Hale, Dorothea

Weller, George [Anthony] 1907- [CA]
American-born author and translator
* Wharf, Michael

Weller, Luman Hamlin 1833-1914 [FFF]
American politician
* Weller, Calamity

Weller, Samuel
See Onwhyn, Thomas

Welles, Albert 19th c. [HPPN]
American author
* [A] Descendant from One of the Early Puritanic Governors

Welles, Arthur 1893-1969 [HPPN]
American actor, dancer, singer
* Gray, Duncan

Welles, Barbara 1920?- [BI]
American radio commentator
* Pritchett, Florence

Welles, Gideon 1802-1878 [HPPN]
American politician, author, editor
* Noah, Father

Welles, Mel
See Von Theumer, Ernst

Welles, [George] Orson 1915-1985 [HPPN]
American actor, playwright, director, producer
* Jeeves, O. W.
* Your Obedient Servant

Welles, Rosalind
See Washington, Elsie

Wellesley, Arthur 1769-1852 [DEP, DNNS, NPS, SN]
British army officer and statesman
* [The] Achilles of England
* [The] Best of Cut-Throats
* [The] Captain of the Age
* [The] English Achilles
* Europe's Liberator
* [The] Great Duke
* [The] Hero of a Hundred Fights
* [The] Hero of the Peninsula
* [The] Iron Duke
* Nosey
* Old Douro
* [The] Saviour of the Nations
* [The] Waterloo Hero
* Wellington, Duke of

Wellesley, [Lord] Charles
See Bronte, Charlotte

Wellhouse, Frederick 1828-1911 [HPPN]
American horticulturist
* [The] Apple King

Welling, Sylvia
See Galloway, Sylvia

Wellington, Andrew
See Weed, Truman Andrew Wellington

Wellington, Arthur 1885-1968 [SC]
American actor
* Page, Arthur W.

[Le] Wellington des Joueurs
See Woodville, Anthony [Lord Rivers]

Wellington, Duke of
See Wellesley, Arthur

Wellington, John
See Farnill, Barrie

[The] Wellington of Gamblers
See Rivers, Lord

Wellman, Bert J. 20th c. [WGT]
Author
* [A] Law Abiding Revolutionist

Wellman, Frederick Creighton 1873-1960 [BI, CA]
American author and painter
* Scott, Cyril Kay

Wellman, Manly Wade 1903- [ESF, HFF, SFL]
American author
* Barclay, Gabriel [house pseudonym]
* Cotton, John
* Crow, Levi
* Ferney, Manuel
* Field, Gans T.
* Garth, Will [house pseudonym]
* Perez, Juan
* Wells, Hampton
* Wells, Wade

Wellman, Pearl 1910- [THR]
South African-born dancer
* Argyle, Pearl

Wells, Amos
See Blackmore, Amos

Wells, Anna Maria 1797-? [HPPN]
American poet
* A. M. W.

Wells, Barry
See Richards, Dick

Wells, Basil 1912- [ESF, WGT]
American writer
* Ellerman, Gene

Wells, Billy 1887-1967 [BX, RBE]
British boxer
* Wells, Bombardier Billy

Wells, Bombardier Billy
See Wells, Billy

Wells, Boomer
See Wells, Gregory DeWayne

Wells, Braxton
See Wollheim, Donald A[llen]

Wells, Carolyn 1870?-1942 [CC, EMD, WW]
American author
* Wright, Rowland

Wells, Charles 19th c. [HPPN]
British gambler and confidence man
* [The] Man Who Broke the Bank at Monte Carlo

Wells, Charles Jeremiah 1799?-1879 [DEL, WBD]
British poet and author
* Howard, H. L.

Wells, Conrad
See Fried, Abe

Wells, Dee
See Ayer, Alberta Constance [Chapman]

Wells, Devil
See Wells, Willie James

Wells, Dicky
See Wells, William

Wells, Ernest [NPS]
Journalist
* Swears

Wells, Gregory DeWayne 1954- [WP 10-2-84]
American baseball player
* Wells, Boomer

Wells, H. G.
See Wells, Herbert George

Wells, Hampton
See Wellman, Manly Wade

Wells, Helen [Weston] [BI]
American author
* Blake, Forest

Wells, Helen
See Wallis, Geraldine McDonald

Wells, Helen
See Weinstock, Helen

Wells, Herbert George 1866-1946 [CC, HPPN, LC, SF, TLC]
British author
* Bliss, Reginald
* [The] Critic of Progress
* Glockenhammer, Walter
* [The] Man Who Invented Tomorrow
* [The] Shakespeare of Science Fiction
* Smith, Sosthenes
* [The] Time Traveler
* Wells, H. G.

Wells, Hondo
See Whittington, Harry [Benjamin]

Wells, Hubert George
See Ackerman, Forrest J[ames]

Wells, J. Wellington
See De Camp, L[yon] Sprague

Wells, Jacqueline 1917- [SW]
American actress
* Bishop, Julie

Wells, Jane Warren
See Picken, Mary Brooks

Wells, Jessica
See Buckland, Raymond

Wells, John Jay [joint pseudonym with Juanita Ruth Wellons Coulson]
See Bradley, Marion Zimmer

Wells, John Jay [joint pseudonym with Marion Zimmer Bradley]
See Coulson, Juanita Ruth Wellons

Wells, Judge
See Wells, Lloyd C. A.

Wells, Julia Elizabeth 1935- [BDF, BEW, CA]
British actress, singer, author
* Andrews, Julie
* Edwards, Julie

Wells, June
See Swinford, Betty [June Wells]

Wells, Junior
See Blackmore, Amos

Wells, Kitty
See Deason, Muriel Ellen

Wells, Little Junior
See Blackmore, Amos

Wells, Lloyd C. A. 1924- [BA]
American photographer
* Wells, Judge

Wells, Mary 18th c. [NPS]
Actress
* Becky
* Cowslip

Wells, Mary P. [PA]
Author
* Thorne, P.

Wells, Michael
See Mullins, Richard

Wells, Michael John 1946- [EJ7]
British jazz musician
* Wells, Spike

Wells, Robert 1922- [ASC]
American composer and producer
* Levinson, Bob

Wells, [Frank Charles] Robert 1929-
[IAW]
British author
* Roberts, Martin

Wells, Robert
See Welsch, Roger L[ee]

Wells, Roy
See Downey, Raymond Joseph

Wells, Sadie
See O'Day, Mrs. William

Wells, Sam
See Chadwell, William

Wells, Samuel ?-1876 [EWG]
American gunfighter
* Pitts, Charlie

Wells, Seth Young 1767-1847 [HPPN]
American educator
* Philanthropos

Wells, Spike
See Wells, Michael John

Wells, Susan
See Siegel, Doris

Wells, Thornton
See Williams, T.

Wells, Tobias
See Forbes, DeLoris [Florine] Stanton

Wells, Viola Gertrude 1902- [BWW]
American singer
* Rhapsody, Miss
* Underhill, Viola

Wells, Wade
See Wellman, Manly Wade

Wells, William 1820-? [FFF, PA]
American author
* Uncle Will

Wells, William 1910- [ASC]
American jazz musician
* Wells, Dicky

Wells, William Charles 1757-1817 [PA]
Author
* Marius

Wells, Willie James 1908- [MK]
American baseball player
* Wells, Devil

Welp, Treumund
See Pelz, Edward

Welsch, James
Scottish strongman
* [The] Scottish Giant

Welsch, Roger L[ee] 1936- [CA]
American folklorist and author
* Wells, Robert

Welser, Albert
See Graw, William P.

Welsh, Charles 1850-1914 [DNA]
British-born author and editor
* McIvor, Ivor Ben

Welsh, Freddy
See Thomas, Frederick Hall

Welsh, H. 20th c. [CSH]
Canadian football promoter
* Welsh, Huck

Welsh, Huck
See Welsh, H.

Welsh, James J. 1866-? [BE]
American baseball player
* Welsh, Tub

Welsh, Johnnie 20th c. [HPPN]
American comedian
* Sassafras

[The] Welsh Parson
See Davis, James John

Welsh, Robert
See Roberts, John Peter

[The] Welsh Shakespeare
See Williams, Edward

Welsh, Susan
See Collins, Margaret [Brandon James]

Welsh, Tub
See Welsh, James J.

[The] Welsh Wizard
See Lloyd George, David

[The] Welsh Wizard
See Meredith, Billy

[The] Welsh Wizard
See Thomas, Frederick Hall

[The] Welsh Wonder
See Wilde, James [Jimmy]

Welskopf, Liselotte Elisabeth Charlotte
1901- [IAW]
German author
* Welskopf-Henrich, Liselotte

Welskopf-Henrich, Liselotte
See Welskopf, Liselotte Elisabeth
Charlotte

Welter, Blanca Rosa 1923?- [FC, IPA,
ITA]
Mexican-born actress
* Christian, Linda

Welty, S. F.
See Welty, Susan F.

Welty, Susan F. 1905- [CAP, SAT]
American author
* Welty, S. F.

Welwood
See Moncrieff, [Sir] Henry

Welzenbach, Lanora F.
See Miller, Lanora

Wemlinger, Claire 1909?- [FC, OCF]
American actress
* Trevor, Claire

**Wemyss, Francis [Ninth Earl of
Wemyss]** 1818-1914 [HPPN]
British political leader
* Cool of the Evening
* Elcho, Lord

Wemyss, Nigel 1913- [BF]
British actor and director
* Patrick, Nigel

Wen
See Veneris, James

Wen Ching
See Lim, Boon Keng

Wenceslas of Luxembourg 1337-1383
Duke of Brabant
* [The] Blue Duke

Wenceslaus 903?-935 [HPPN]
Saint
* Good King Wenceslaus

Wenceslaus [or Wenceslas] 1359?-1419
[DNNS, RH, SN]
King of Bohemia and Germany
* [The] Drunkard
* [The] Nero of Germany
* [The] Sardanapalus of Germany
* [The] Worthless

Wendelken-Wilson, Charles
See Wilson, Charles Edwin

Wendell, Bullet
See Wendell, Percy L.

Wendell, Percy L. 1889-1932 [FB]
American football player and coach
* Wendell, Bullet

Wendelstein
See Dobenek [or Dobneck], Johann

Wenden, Michael 1949- [SWI]
Australian swimmer
* [The] Swimming Machine

Wender, Dorothea 1934- [CA]
American educator and author
* Schmidt, Dorothea

Wendig, Dr.
See Schwend, Friedrich

Wendolin
See Durben, Wolfgang Johannes Maria

Wendorff, Arnold 1928?-1962 [BEW]
Theatrical performer
* Arnold, Eddie

Wendroff, Zalman
See Vendrovskii, David Efimovich

Wendrowsky, Zalman
See Vendrovskii, David Efimovich

Wendt, Fats
See Wendt, George

Wendt, George 1909?-1973 [FIR]
American jazz musician
* Wendt, Fats

Wene, Elmer H. 1892- [HPPN]
American politician and poultryman
* [The] Day Old Chick

Weng, Hsing Ching
See Weng, Wan-go

Weng, Wan-go 1918- [CA]
Chinese-born American author and filmmaker
* Weng, Hsing Ching

Wenger, Rose August 1892- [F1, F2, FC]
American actress
* Gibson, Helen

Wengrov, Charles
See Wengrovsky, Charles

Wengrovsky, Charles 1925- [CA]
American author
* Wengrov, Charles

Wenham, Jane ?-1730 [HPPN]
British witch
* [The] Last English Witch
* [The] Witch of Walkerne

Wenham, Jane
See Figgins, Jane

Wenkart, Henni
See Wenkart, Henny

Wenkart, Henny 1928- [CA]
Austrian-born publisher and author
* Wenkart, Henni

Wennerstrom, Genia Katherine 1930- [IBY, ICB]
American illustrator
* Genia

[The] Wensleydale Poet
See Barker, George William Michael Jones

Wensloff, Butch
See Wensloff, Charles William

Wensloff, Charles William 1915- [BE]
American baseball player
* Wensloff, Butch

Wentworth
See Canning, George

Wentworth, Barbara
See Pitcher, Gladys

Wentworth, Bessie
See Andrews, Elizabeth

Wentworth, Charles [house pseudonym]
See Bradley, Albert W.

Wentworth, Charles [house pseudonym]
See Clarke, Percy A.

Wentworth, Charles [house pseudonym]
See Shute, Walter

Wentworth, Charles [house pseudonym]
See Steffens, Arthur

Wentworth, Cy
See Wentworth, Marvin

Wentworth, Fanny
See Evans, Fanny Wentworth Osborn Porteus

Wentworth, Fanny
See Porteus, Fanny Wentworth Osborn

Wentworth, Herbert
See James, Herbert Wentworth

Wentworth, John 1815?-1888 [FFF, HPPN]
American politician
* [The] Chicago Giant
* Long John

Wentworth, John
See Child, Philip

Wentworth, Mae
See Ostrander, Mrs. Clarence

Wentworth, Martha
See Wentworth, Verna

Wentworth, Marvin 1905- [CEI]
Canadian-born hockey player
* Wentworth, Cy

Wentworth, Patricia
See Turnbull, Dora Amy Elles Dillon

Wentworth, Robert
See Hamilton, Edmond [Moore]

Wentworth, [Sir] Thomas [First Earl of Stafford] 1593-1641 [NPS, SN]
British statesman
* Black Tom Tyrant
* [The] Crown Martyr
* Thorough

Wentworth, Verna ?-1974 [SC]
American actress
* [The] Actress of One Hundred Voices
* Wentworth, Martha

Wentworth, W. W.
See Siegel, Benjamin

Wentworth, Walter
See Gilman, Bradley

Wentworth, William Charles 1793-1872 [WBD]
Australian politician
* [The] Australian Patriot

Wentz, Barney
See Wentz, Bryon

Wentz, Bryon 20th c. [EF]
American football player
* Wentz, Barney

Wenz, Fireball
See Wenz, Frederick Charles, Jr.

Wenz, Frederick Charles, Jr. 1941- [SMG]
American baseball player
* Wenz, Fireball

Wenzlaff, George 1946- [FC]
American actor
* Winslow, Foghorn
* Winslow, George

Wep
See Pidgeon, William Edwin

Werata, Tota
See Gadd, David Bernard Hallard

Werblin, David 1910?- [EJS]
American football team owner
* Werblin, Sonny

Werblin, Sonny
See Werblin, David

Werden, Percival Wheritt 1865-1934 [BE]
American baseball player
* Werden, Perry

Werden, Perry
See Werden, Percival Wheritt

Werdna, Retnyw
See Wynter, Andrew

Wergeland, Henrik Arnold 1808-1845 [SN, WBD]
Norwegian poet, playwright, patriot
* [The] Betrayer of the Fatherland
* [The] Holberg of Norway
* Sifadda, Siful

Werhas, John Charles [Johnny] 1938- [BE]
American baseball player
* Werhas, Peaches

Werhas, Peaches
See Werhas, John Charles [Johnny]

Werheim, John
See Fearn, John Russell

Werkman, Nick 1942- [BB]
American basketball player
* Nick the Quick

Werl, Olaf 1618-1682 [SN]
Swedish antiquary and historian
* [The] Coryphaeus of Northern Lore
* Verelius, Olaus

Werle
See Werle, Dan

Werle, Bugs
See Werle, William George

Werle, Dan 20th c. [ITA]
American costume designer
* Werle

Werle, William George 1920- [BE]
American baseball player
* Werle, Bugs

Wermuth, Arthur 20th c.
American military officer
* [The] One Man Army of Bataan

Werner
See Meany, Stephen Joseph

Werner, Buddy
See Werner, Wallace

Werner, Elsa Jane
See Watson, Jane Werner

Werner, Ernst
See Burstenbinder, Elisabeth

Werner, Franz von 1836-1881 [WBD]
Austrian-born poet and playwright
* Murad Efendi

Werner, Hans
See Blaze, Ange Henri

Werner, Herma 1926- [CA]
American author
* Cowen, Eve
* Pinner, Joma

Werner, Isaiah
See Douglass, Ellsworth

Werner, Jane
See Watson, Jane Werner

Werner, Janet Anne 20th c. [BEW]
American actress
* Ward, Janet

Werner, K.
See Casewit, Curtis

Werner, M. R.
See Werner, Morris Robert

Werner, Max
See Shifrin, Aleksandr Mikhailovich

Werner, Morris Robert 1897- [HPPN]
American author
* Werner, M. R.

Werner, Oscar Emil 1893-1953 [BI]
American journalist
* Werner, Wade

Werner, Oskar
See Bschliessmayer, Oskar Josef

Werner, Sacher S. 1898- [EJS]
Austrian horse trainer and harness racer
* Werner, Satch

Werner, Satch
See Werner, Sacher S.

Werner, Victor Emile 1894- [CA, WD]
American author
* Dallas, Vincent

Werner, Vivian 1921- [CA]
American author and journalist
* Jackson, Stephanie
* Lester, John

Werner, Wade
See Werner, Oscar Emil

Werner, Wallace 1935?-1964 [AS]
American skier
* Werner, Buddy

Werper, Barton [house pseudonym]
See Scott, Peg O'Neill

Werper, Barton [house pseudonym]
See Scott, Peter T.

Werschkul, Gordon M. 1927- [FC, ITA, SW]
American actor
* Scott, Gordon

Wert, Lynette L[emon] 1938- [CA]
American author
* LeMon, Lynn

Wertenbaker, G. Peyton 1907- [WGT]
American author
* Peyton, Green

Wertenbaker, Lael Tucker 1909- [CA]
American author
* Tucker, Lael

Werter, Max
See Smyth, Frank

Wertham, Fredric
See Wertheimer, Frederick Ignace

Wertheimer, Frederick Ignace 1895- [SFL]
German-born author
* Wertham, Fredric

Wertheimer, Leo 1862-1937 [WBD]
German philosopher
* Brunner, Constantin

Wertmueller, Lina
See Wertmueller Von Elgg, Arcangela

Wertmueller Von Elgg, Arcangela 1928- [CA, FDG]
Italian director and screenwriter
* Brown, George
* Wertmueller, Lina

Werty, Quentin
See Stone, Peter

Wertz, Del
See Wertz, Dwight Lewis

Wertz, Dwight Lewis 1891- [BE]
American baseball player
* Wertz, Del

Wertz, Henry Levi 1898- [BE]
American baseball player
* Wertz, Johnny

Wertz, Johnny
See Wertz, Henry Levi

Wesander, Bjoern Kenneth 1914- [CA]
British-born journalist and author
* Cox, P[atrick] Brian
* Stuart, Kenneth
* Tantrist

Weschcke, Carl L[ouis] 1930- [CA]
American author and publisher
* Gnosticus

Wescott, Frederick 1866-1941 [THR]
British comedian, author, theatrical manager
* Karno, Fred

Weslager, C. A.
See Weslager, Clinton Alfred

Weslager, Clinton Alfred 1909- [WYA]
American author
* Weslager, C. A.

Wesley, Art
See Grennell, Dean A.

Wesley, Charles 1707-1788 [FFF, HPPN]
British clergyman and hymn writer
* [The] Hymnist of the English Revival
* [The] Poet of Methodism

Wesley, Elizabeth
See McElfresh, [Elizabeth] Adeline

Wesley, James
See Rigoni, Orlando [Joseph]

Wesley, John 1703-1791 [HPPN]
British clergyman
* [The] Father of Methodism
* J. W.
* [A] Lover of Good English and Common Sense

Wesley, John 19th c. [HPPN]
American bank robber
* Hill, Harry

Wesley, Mary
See Eady, Mary Aline

Wesley, Newton K.
See Uyesugi, Newton

Wesley, Samuel 1662-1735 [NPS]
Clergyman and poet
* [A] Scholar

[A] Wesleyan Minister
See Pascoe, [Rev.] William Gluyas

Weslock, Nick
See Wisnock, Nick

Wessel, Horst 1907-1930 [HPPN]
German storm trooper
* [The] Father of Die Fahne Hoch

Wessel, Johann [or John] 1419-1489 [DNNF, DNNS, RH]
Dutch theologian and religious reformer
* Lux Mundi
* Magister Contradictionum
* [The] Master of Contradiction
* Sapiens, Doctor
* [The] Wise Doctor

Wessel, Peder 1691-1720 [HN, RH]
Norwegian naval officer
* [The] Danish Nelson
* Tordenskiol [Thunder Shield]

Wesselmann, Tom 20th c.
American artist
* Stealingworth, Slim

[The] Wessex Novelist
See Hardy, Thomas

Wessler, Bernard 1918- [BEW]
American actor
* West, Bernard

Wesso, Hans
See Wessolowski, Hans Waldemar

Wessolowski, Hans Waldemar 1882-? [SF]
German-born illustrator
* Wesso, Hans

Wesson, Joan
See Pittock, Joan [Hornby]

West, Adam
See Anderson, William

West, Adam
See Garrett, Sam

West, Al
See Hubbard, Al[len]

West, Angela 1933- [THR]
British actress
* Glynne, Angela

West, Annie
See Fields, Annie Adams

West, Anthony C. 1910-   [CN]
Irish author
* MacGrian, Michael

West, Avalon
See Chambers, Bertram Mordaunt

West, Barbara
See Price, Olive

West, Belf
See West, D. Belford

West, Benjamin 1750-1813   [NPS]
American astronomer and philosopher
* Bickerstaff, Isaac

West, Bernard
See Wessler, Bernard

West, Betty 1921-   [CA, SAT]
Author and illustrator
* Bowen, Betty Morgan

West, Big Jim
See West, Jim

West, Billy
See Weisberg, Roy B.

West, Buck
See West, Milton Douglas

West, Buster
See West, James

West, Buxton
See Champlin, Edwin Ross

West, C. P.
See Wodehouse, Pelham Grenville

West, Charles [Charlie] 1899-   [IBW]
American football player
* West, Prunes

West, Charles [Charlie] 1914-1976
[BWW]
American singer
* Poor Charlie

West, Charles Converse 1921-   [CA]
American author and theologian
* Barnabas

West, Chinese Tommy
See West, Thomas

West Country
See Dawson, Charles Kenneth

[A] **West Country Doctor**
See Cooper, Robert Andrew

West, Curly
See West, Granville

West, D. Belford 1896-   [FB]
American football player
* West, Belf

West, Dick
See West, Paul

West, Doc
See West, Harold

West, Dorothy Marie [Dottie] 1932-
[ECM]
American country-western performer
* [The] Country Sunshine

West, Douglas
See Tubb, Edwin Charles

West, Edgar
See Carr, Gordon

West, Elizabeth
See Wilson, Margaret

West, Emily Govan [Emmy] 1919-   [CA]
Author
* Payne, Emmy

West End, [Sir] Warwick
See Northcote, [Sir] Stafford Henry

West, George
See Crawford, George

West, Gertrude Ida 20th c.   [AW]
Belgian-born journalist and author
* West, Trudy

West, Gilbert Ashton 1883-?   [CCL]
Canadian poet
* Kap-o-Kaslo

West, Granville 1915?-1978   [FIR]
American country-western performer
* West, Curly

West, Harold 1915-1951   [EJ, WWJ]
American jazz musician
* West, Doc

West, Harold
See Wilson, Roger C.

West, Hi
See West, James

[A] **West India Merchant**
See Innes, William

[A] **West Indian**
See Nisbet, Richard

West, James 1884-1963   [BE]
American baseball player
* West, Hi

West, James 1902-1966   [SC]
American actor
* West, Buster

West, James
See Withers, Carl A.

West, Jerry 1938-   [SMG]
American basketball player and coach
* Clutch, Mr.

West, Jerry [house pseudonym]
[Stratemeyer Syndicate]
See Stratemeyer, Edward L.

West, Jerry [house pseudonym]
[Stratemeyer Syndicate]
See Svenson, Andrew E.

West, Jessamyn
See McPherson, Mrs. H. M.

West, Jim 20th c.   [RBE]
Australian boxer
* West, Big Jim

West, John
See Pentelow, John Nix

West, Joyce [Tarlton] 20th c.   [TCC]
New Zealand author
* Gilbert, Manu

West, Julian
See Mueller, Ernst

West, Katherine 1883-1936   [SC]
American actress
* Morton, Maxine
* Westner, Lillian

West, Keith
See Lane, Kenneth Westmacott

West, Kenyon
See Howland, Frances Louise

West, Kirkpatrick
See Harris, F[rank] Brayton

West, Lefty
See West, Weldon Edison

West, Leslie
See Weinstein, Leslie

West, Levon 1900-1968   [BI, HPPN]
American etcher and photographer
* Dmitri, Ivan

West, Lillie 1860-1939   [BEW, HPPN,
NAA]
American actress and drama critic
* Leslie, Amy
* Stanley, Marie

West, Lindsay
See Weber, Nancy

West, Luther Shirley 1899-   [IAW]
American author and poet
* Praeceptor Humilis

West, Mae 1893-1980   [HPPN]
American actress
* [The] Baby Vamp
* Diamond Lil
* Mast, Jane
* [The] Screen's Bad Girl
* [The] Siren of Sex
* [The] Siren of the Screen
* Vaudeville's Youngest Headliner

West, Mark
See Morris, Robert Tuttle

West, Mark
See Runyon, Charles W.

West, Marvin
See Goldfrap, John Henry

West, Mary 1964?-   [HPPN]
American basketball player
* [The] Tree

West, Mary
See Rochester, George Ernest

West, Michael
See Derleth, August [William]

West, Milton Douglas 1860-1929   [BE]
American baseball player
* West, Buck

West, Monckton
See O'Donnell, John Francis

West, Morris L[anglo] 1916-   [CA, WD]
Australian author and playwright
* East, Michael
* Morris, Julian

West, Mrs. William   [FFF]
Entertainer
* Templeton, Fay

West, Nancy Richard
See Westphal, Wilma Ross

West, Nathanael
See Weinstein, Nathan Wallenstein

West, Noel   [NPS]
Author
* Cox, M. B.

West, Paul 1890-1965   [HPPN]
American dancer and singer
* West, Dick

West, Pep
See Weinstein, Nathan Wallenstein

West, Prunes
See West, Charles [Charlie]

West, Ragged Dick
See West, Richard

West, Rebecca
See Fairfield, Cecily Isabel

West, Richard 1716-1742   [SN]
Friend of British poet, Thomas Gray
* Favonius

West, Richard 1871?-?   [BLB, HPPN]
American bank and trainrobber
* Little Dick
* West, Ragged Dick

West, Roger
See Watson, Virginia Cruse

West, Speedy
See West, Wesley Webb

West, Thomas 1577-1618   [WBD]
British colonial administrator in America
* De La Warr, Third Baron
* Delaware, Lord

West, Thomas 1859-1932   [SC]
American actor
* West, Chinese Tommy

West, Token
See Humphries, Adelaide M.

West, Tom
See Reach, James

West, Tristram Frederick 1911-   [IAW]
British scientist and writer
* Prospero

West, Trudy
See West, Gertrude Ida

West, Uta 1928-   [CA]
Polish-born American author
* Auden, Renee

West, Virgil Clifford 1931-   [IBW]
American dancer
* Beaver, Flash

[The] West Virginia Hillbilly
See Snead, Sam[uel Jackson]

West, Wallace 20th c.   [SFP]
Author
* Barlow, Roger

West, Ward
See Borland, Harold Glen [Hal]

West, Weldon Edison 1915-   [BE]
American baseball player
* West, Lefty

West, Wesley Webb 1924-   [CWG, DAM]
American country-western performer
* West, Speedy

West, Willa
See Slocum, Mary S. F.

West, William H.
See Flinn, William H.

West, William Henry 1824-1911
[HPPN]
American orator
* Blind Man Eloquent

West-Watson, Keith Campbell 20th c.
[WW]
Author
* Campbell, Keith

Westbrook, Chauncey Leon 1921-   [EJ]
American jazz musician
* Westbrook, Lord

Westbrook, Lord
See Westbrook, Chauncey Leon

Westbrook, Walter J. 20th c.   [BWW]
American singer
* Little Walter J.

[A] Westchester Farmer
See Seabury, Samuel

Westcombe, Charles
See Carr, Gordon

Westcott, Charles S.   [FFF, PA]
Author
* Homo

Westcott, Helen
See Hickman, Myrthas Helen

Westcott, John 1866-1941   [HPPN]
American producer
* Karno, Fred

Westcott, Kathleen
See Abrahamsen, Christine Elizabeth

Westcott, Netta
See Lupton, Netta

Westcott, Thompson   [PA]
Author
* Miller, Joe, Jr.

Westcott-Jones, K[enneth]
See Jones, Kenneth Westcott

Wester, Doris 1917-1960   [SC]
American actress
* Weston, Doris

Westerham, S. C.
See Alington, Cyril Argentine

Westermann, Professor
See Almquist, Karl Jonas Ludvig

Western, Barry
See Evans, Gwnfil Arthur

Western George
See Leslie, George Leonidas

[The] Western Hangman
See Jeffreys, George [First Baron Jeffreys of Wem]

Western, Hugh
See Hamill, Alfred Ernest

Western, Mark
See Crisp, Anthony Thomas [Tony]

Western Memorabilia
See Gowans, William

[The] Western Spy
See Dillon, John M[yles]

Westerzil, George J. 1891-1964   [BE]
American baseball player
* Westerzil, Tex

Westerzil, Tex
See Westerzil, George J.

Westfall, Eddie
See Westfall, Edwin Vernon

Westfall, Edwin Vernon 1940-   [FHE]
Canadian-born hockey player
* Westfall, Eddie

Westfield, Rick 20th c.   [RO2]
American musician
* Westfield, West

Westfield, West
See Westfield, Rick

Westford, Susanne
See Leonard, Susan

Westgate, John
See Bloomfield, Anthony John Westgate

Westgate, Lady
See Din, Salima

Westheimer, David 1917-   [CA]
American author
* Smith, Z. Z.

Westheimer, Ruth 1928?-   [TI 2-17-86]
American television personality
* Dr. Ruth

Westinghouse, George 1846-1914
[HPPN]
American inventor and industrialist
* [The] Father of the Air Brake
* [The] Inventive Wizard

Westlake, Donald E[dwin] 1933- [AW, CA, WGT]
American author
* Clark, Curt
* Coe, Tucker
* Culver, Timothy J.
* Cunningham, J. Morgan
* Stark, Richard

Westlake, Waldon Thomas 1920- [BE]
American baseball player
* Westlake, Wally

Westlake, Wally
See Westlake, Waldon Thomas

Westland, Lynn
See Joscelyn, Archie Lynn

Westley, George Hembert
See Hippisley, George

Westley, Helen
See Manney, Henrietta

Westley, John
See Conroy, John

Westmacott, Charles Malloy 1787-1868 [PA]
British author
* Blackmantle, Bernard

Westmacott, Mary
See Christie, Agatha [Mary Clarissa]

Westman, Habbakuk O.
See Ewbank, Thomas

Westman, Hab'k O.
See Ewbank, Thomas

Westminster, Duke of 19th c. [PPN]
British aristocrat
* Bend Or

Westmore, Buddy
See Westmore, George Hamilton

Westmore, George Hamilton 1916- [BEW]
American makeup consultant
* Westmore, Buddy

Westmoreland, Maria Elizabeth [Jourdan] 1815-? [FFF]
American author
* Mystery

Westmoreland, Reg[inald] [Conway] 1926- [CA, WD]
American author and journalist
* Conway, Ward

Westmoreland, William Childs 1914- [HPPN]
American army officer
* [The] Four Star Eagle Scout
* [The] Inevitable General
* Westy
* Wind Dummy Westy

Westner, Lillian
See West, Katherine

Weston, Agatha 1943- [IBW]
American singer and actress
* Weston, Kim

Weston, Agnes [NPS]
Founder of Royal Sailor's Rests
* [The] Sailor's Friend

Weston, Allen [joint pseudonym with Alice Mary Norton]
See Hogarth, Grace Weston

Weston, Allen [joint pseudonym with Grace Weston Hogarth]
See Norton, Alice Mary

Weston, Ann
See Pitcher, Gladys

Weston, Dick
See Slye, Leonard

Weston, Doris
See Wester, Doris

Weston, Edward 1886-1958
American photographer
* Picasso of the Camera

Weston, Ellen
See Hadani, Ami

Weston, Ellen
See Weinstein, Ellen R.

Weston, George W. 1863-1942 [HPPN]
American actor and director
* Weston, Kendal

Weston, Helen Gray
See Daniels, Dorothy

Weston, James
See Step, Edward

Weston, Joseph 18th c. [SN]
* This Execrable Erostratus

Weston, Kendal
See Weston, George W.

Weston, Kim
See Weston, Agatha

Weston, Mary
See Merritt, Onera Amelia

Weston, Paul
See Wetstein, Paul

Weston, Philip
See De Filippi, Amedeo

Weston, Robert P.
See Harris, Robert P.

Weston, Ruth
See Shillaber, Ruth West

Weston, W. Garfield 1898?-1978
Canadian business executive
* [The] Barnum of Bread

Weston, Warren
See Gale, Linn A. E.

Weston, William
See Milsom, Charles Henry

Westover, Charles 1939- [RO1]
American singer
* Shannon, Del

Westphal, Paul 1950- [SMG]
American basketball player
* Westphal, Westy

Westphal, Siegfried 1902?-1982 [WP 7-5-82]
German military officer
* [The] Paperwork Pedant

Westphal, Westy
See Westphal, Paul

Westphal, Wilma Ross 1907- [CA]
American author
* West, Nancy Richard

Westridge, Harold
See Avery, Harold

Westrup, Enrique Tomas 1879-? [NAA]
Mexican educator and author
* Wycliff

Westwater, [Sister] Agnes Martha 1929- [CA]
American-born author
* Earley, Martha

Westwick, Harry 1876-1957 [FHE, HK]
Canadian-born hockey player
* Westwick, Rat

Westwick, Rat
See Westwick, Harry

Westwood, Jennifer
See Chandler, Jennifer [Westwood]

Westwood, N. J.
See Millard, Joseph

Westwood, William John 1821-1846 [DI]
Australian bushranger
* Jackey Jackey

Westy
See Westmoreland, William Childs

Wet Wash Marshall
See Marshall, Preston

Wetamoo ?-1676 [HPPN]
American Indian
* [The] Squaw Sachem of Pocasset

Wetcheek, J. L.
See Feuchtwanger, Lion

Wetherby
See MacKillop, J.

Wethered, M. L.
See Wethered, Maud Llewellyn

Wethered, Maud Llewellyn 1898- [ART]
British sculptor, engraver, painter
* Wethered, M. L.

Wetherell, Dawson 19th c. [PI]
Irish poet
* C. C. V. G.

Wetherell, Elizabeth
See Warner, Susan Bogert

Wetherell, June 1909- [BI]
American author
* Frame, Patricia

Wetherell, Mrs. E. 1850-1891   [FFF]
American opera singer
* Abbott, Emma

Wetherell-Pepper, Joan Alexander 1920-
[CA]
British author
* Alexander, Joan
* Pepper, Joan

Wethern, George 20th c.   [HPPN]
American motorcyclist
* Baby Huey

Wetmore, [Rev.] James 18th c.   [HPPN]
American clergyman
* [A] Missionary from the Honourable
  Society for Propagating the Gospel

Wetmore, Joan
See   Deery, Joan

Wetstein, Paul 1912-   [PMJ]
American arranger and conductor
* Edwards, Jonathan
* Weston, Paul

Wettach, Adrien 1880-1959   [BEW, FC]
Swiss clown
* Grock

Wettberg, Simolin 1887?-1947   [BI]
Princess
* Radziwill, Olga

Wetter, Mrs.
See   Victoria

Wetterbergh, Carl Anton 1804-1889
[FFF, WBD]
Swedish author
* Onkel Adam

Wetton, Mary 1936-   [TR]
British actress and singer
* Millar, Mary

Wetty, Betty
See   Claymiller, Betty Day

Wetzel, Bonnie
See   Addleman, Bonnie Jean

Wetzel, Buzz
See   Wetzel, Charles Edward

Wetzel, Buzz
See   Wetzel, Franklin Burton

Wetzel, Charles Edward 1894-1941   [BE]
American baseball player
* Wetzel, Buzz

Wetzel, Franklin Burton 1893-1942
[BE]
American baseball player
* Wetzel, Buzz

Wetzel, George William 1868-1899   [BE]
American baseball player
* Wetzel, Shorty

Wetzel, Iron Man
See   Wetzel, J. C.

Wetzel, J. C. 20th c.   [HPPN]
American football player
* Wetzel, Iron Man

Wetzel, Shorty
See   Wetzel, George William

Weverka, Robert 1926-   [CA]
American author
* McMahon, Robert

Wexisnensis
See   Magnus, Jonas

Wexler, Irving 1888?-1952   [BLB, MM]
American underworld figure
* Gordon, Waxey

Wexler, Jerome [LeRoy] 1923-   [CA]
American author, illustrator, photographer
* Delmar, Roy

Wexler, Morris 20th c.   [MM]
American underworld figure
* Wexler, Mushy

Wexler, Mushy
See   Wexler, Morris

Weyand, Alexander M. 1892-   [FB]
American football player
* Weyand, Babe

Weyand, Babe
See   Weyand, Alexander M.

[The] Weyerhaeuser Baby
See   Weyerhaeuser, George

Weyerhaeuser, Frederick 1834-1914
[HPPN, WBD]
German-American businessman
* [The] Lumber King

Weyerhaeuser, George 1926-   [HPPN]
American kidnap victim
* [The] Weyerhaeuser Baby

Weygand, James Lamar 1919-   [IA]
American author
* [The] Indiana Kid
* James, Westbrook

Weyhing, August 1866-1955   [AS, PB]
American baseball player
* Weyhing, Cannonball
* Weyhing, Gus

Weyhing, Cannonball
See   Weyhing, August

Weyhing, Gus
See   Weyhing, August

Weyl, Fernand 1874?-1931   [BEW]
Playwright and critic
* Noziere, Fernand

Weyler, Butcher
See   Weyler y Nicolau, Valeriano

Weyler, Joseph ?-1919   [BLB]
American underworld figure
* Spanish, Johnny

Weyler y Nicolau, Valeriano 1830-1930
[HPPN]
Spanish army officer and governor
* Weyler, Butcher

Weyman, Stanley Clifford
See   Weinberg, Stephen Jacob

Weymes, Wilfred Theodore 1901-1963
[PMJ]
American bandleader
* Weems, Ted

Weymouth, Elizabeth Graham 1943-
American author
* Weymouth, Lally

Weymouth, Lally
See   Weymouth, Elizabeth Graham

Whack, Paddy
See   Fitzgibbon, John [Earl of Clare]

Whacker, John Bouche
See   Dabney, Virginius

[The] Whacky Warbler
See   Turner, Joan

[The] Whale
See   Hemmings, Edward Ernest [Eddie]

Whalen, Grover Aloysius 1886-1962
[HPPN]
American businessman and politician
* New York City's Official Greeter of
  Famous People

Whalen, Michael
See   Shovlin, Joseph Kenneth

Whaley, Barton Stewart 1928-   [CA]
American educator and author
* Barton, S. W.

Whaley, Buck
See   Whaley, Thomas

Whaley, Thomas 1766-1800   [BI]
Irish politician
* Whaley, Buck

Whaling, Thornton 1858-?   [ALY]
American clergyman and author
* Pipper, Pippia
* [The] Professor

Whalley, Dorothy 1911-   [CAP]
British author
* Cowlin, Dorothy

Whalley, George 18th c.   [HPPN]
British author
* [A] Well Wisher to His King and
  Country

Whally, John 18th c.   [HPPN]
British author
* [A] Trustee

Wharf, Michael
See   Weller, George [Anthony]

Wharmby, Margot 1910-   [AW, CA]
British author
* Winn, Alison [Osborn]

Wharton, Anthony
See   McAllister, Alister

Wharton, Baby Ray
See   Wharton, Ray

Wharton, Buck
See   Wharton, Charles M.

Wharton, Charles M. 1868-1949 [AS, FB]
American football player
* Wharton, Buck

Wharton, Edith
See Jones, Edith Newbald

Wharton, Edward Clifton 1827-1891
[DNA]
American author
* Orleanian

Wharton, Eliza
See Whitman, Elizabeth

Wharton, [Sir] George 1617-1681
[HPPN]
British soldier, poet, author
* Philoparthen, Esdras

Wharton, Grace
See Thomson, Katherine Byerley

Wharton, Henry 17th c. [PA]
Author
* Harmer, Anthony

Wharton, James
See Mencken, Henry Louis [Harry]

Wharton, Jim 1813-1856 [IBW]
American-born boxer
* Molineaux, the Morocco Prince

Wharton, Len
See Wharton, Thomas

Wharton, Philip
See Thomson, John Cockburn

Wharton, Ray 20th c. [GW]
American rodeo performer
* Wharton, Baby Ray

Wharton, Thomas 19th c. [HPPN]
American author
* Jones, Ethel

Wharton, Thomas 1927- [CEI]
Canadian-born hockey player
* Wharton, Len

Wharton, Virginia
See Ratigan, Eleanor Eldridge

Whately, Richard 1787-1863 [DEL, FFF, SN]
Irish author and clergyman
* [A] Country Pastor
* Konx Ompax
* Newlight, Aristarchus
* Search, John
* [The] White Bear

Whatley, David 20th c. [OBW]
American baseball player
* Whatley, Speed

Whatley, Fess
See Whatley, John Tuggle

Whatley, John Tuggle 1895- [IBW]
American bandleader
* Whatley, Fess

Whatley, Speed
See Whatley, David

What's the Use
See Chiles, Pearce Nuget

Whats-You-Call-Him, Clerk to the Same
See Anderson, Patrick

Whatshisname
See Massey, E. C.

Whattaman
See Shires, [Charles] Art[hur]

Whear, [Dr.] Rachael 1923- [AW]
British author
* Low, Rachael

Wheat, Buck
See Wheat, Zachariah Davis

Wheat, Chatham Roberdeau 1826-1862
[HPPN]
American army officer
* [The] Murat of America

Wheat, Mack
See Wheat, McKinley Davis

Wheat, Marvin 19th c. [HPPN]
American traveler
* Cincinnatus

Wheat, McKinley Davis 1893- [BE]
American baseball player
* Wheat, Mack

Wheat, Mr.
See Young, Milton R.

Wheat, Patte 1935- [CA, IAW]
American author
* Mahan, Pat
* Mahan, Patte Wheat

Wheat, Zachariah Davis 1888-1972 [BE, DGS]
American baseball player
* Wheat, Buck
* Wheat, Zack

Wheat, Zack
See Wheat, Zachariah Davis

Wheatbread, Paul 1946- [RO2]
American musician
* Wheatbread, Private
* Wheatbread, Wheaty

Wheatbread, Private
See Wheatbread, Paul

Wheatbread, Wheaty
See Wheatbread, Paul

Wheatcroft, Mrs. Nelson [FFF]
Entertainer
* Stanhope, Adeline

Wheatley, Agnes
See Cantor, Eli

Wheatley, H. B.
See Wheatley, Henry Benjamin

Wheatley, Henry Benjamin 1838-1917
[LC]
British author
* Wheatley, H. B.

Wheatley, Jane
See Simpson, Jane

Wheatley, Phillis 1753?-1784 [HPPN]
Afro-American poet
* [The] Negro Sappho
* Peters, Phillis

Wheatley, Richard 1831-? [FFF, HPPN]
British author and clergyman
* Copmanthorpe, Allan
* Gotham
* Justicia
* Rusticus

Wheatley, William [Bill] 1909- [BB, BBH]
American basketball player
* [The] Galloping Ghost

Wheaton, Campbell
See Campbell, Helen [Stuart]

Wheaton, Campbell
See Campbell, Henry Stuart

Wheaton, Campbell
See Weeks, Helen C.

Wheaton, Elwood Pierce 1914- [BE]
American baseball player
* Wheaton, Woody

[The] Wheaton Ice Man
See Grange, Harold E.

Wheaton, Robert 1826-1851 [HPPN]
American attorney
* R. W.

Wheaton, Woody
See Wheaton, Elwood Pierce

[The] Wheatpicker
See Smith, J. D.

Wheatstone, [Sir] Charles 1802-1875
[HPPN]
British physicist and inventor
* C. W.
* [The] Father of the Wheatstone Bridge

Wheatstraw, Little Peetie
See Hogg, Andrew

Wheatstraw, Peetie
See Bunch, William

Whedon, Julia
See Schickel, Julia Whedon

[The] Wheel Horse of the Senate
See Ruggles, Benjamin

Wheeler, Albert 1895- [BEW]
American actor
* Wheeler, Bert

Wheeler, Andrew Carpenter 1835?-1903
[DNA, FFF, HPPN, PA]
American journalist
* Crinkle, Nym
* J. P. M.
* Mowbray, J. P.
* Trinculo

Wheeler, Arthur L. 1872-1917 [AS, FB]
American football player
* Wheeler, Beef

Wheeler, Babe
See Wheeler, Harold

Wheeler, Beef
See Wheeler, Arthur L.

Wheeler, Ben
See Robertson, Ben F.

Wheeler, Benjamin Ide 1854-1927
[HPPN]
American educator
* Wheeler, Prexy

Wheeler, Bert
See Wheeler, Albert

Wheeler, Burton Kendall 1882-? [HPPN]
American politician
* [The] Great Liberal

Wheeler, C. C. [FFF, PA]
American writer
* Crispus

Wheeler, C. R.
See Wheeler, Carol Rosemary

Wheeler, Captain
See Ellis, Edward S[ylvester]

Wheeler, Carol Rosemary 1927- [ART]
British painter
* Wheeler, C. R.

Wheeler, Charles Stearns 1816-1843
[HPPN, PA]
American author
* C. S. W.
* Wheeler, Stern

Wheeler, Chris
See MacOwen, Arthur H.

Wheeler, David Hilton 1829-1902
[DNA]
American author, clergyman, educator
* Hilton, David

Wheeler, Don[ald Wesley] 1922- [BE]
American baseball player
* Wheeler, Scotty

Wheeler, Edward Lytton 1854?-1885?
[WW]
American author
* Lytton, Edward

Wheeler, Emily Frances 19th c. [FFF]
American author
* Winter, June

Wheeler, Fanny
See Stell, Mrs. Martin

Wheeler, Fighting Joe
See Wheeler, Joseph

Wheeler, Floyd Clark 1898-1968 [BE]
American baseball player
* Wheeler, Rip

Wheeler, George Dryden 1863-1939
[BMH]
British singer
* Dryden, Leo

Wheeler, George Harrison 1881-1918
[BE]
American baseball player
* Wheeler, Heavy

Wheeler, George L.
See Heroux, George L.

Wheeler, [Charles] Gidley 1938- [CA]
British author
* Gidley, Charles

Wheeler, Greyhound
See Wheeler, Wayne

Wheeler, Harold 20th c. [BBH]
American basketball coach
* Wheeler, Babe

Wheeler, Heavy
See Wheeler, George Harrison

Wheeler, [Dr.] Helen Rippier 1926-
[HPPN]
American educator, librarian, author
* [The] Dragon Lady

Wheeler, Hugh Callingham 1913- [CC,
EMD, WW]
Author
* Patrick, Q. [joint pseudonym with
  Richard Wilson Webb]
* Quentin, Patrick [joint pseudonym
  with Richard Wilson Webb]
* Stagge, Jonathan [joint pseudonym
  with Richard Wilson Webb]

Wheeler, James [Jim] 1873?-1974
[HPPN]
American animal dealer
* [The] Catman of the Yukon

Wheeler, Janet D. [house pseudonym]
[Stratemeyer Syndicate]
See Stratemeyer, Edward L.

Wheeler, Jimmy
See Remnant, Ernest

Wheeler, Joseph 1836-1906 [HPPN]
American politician and army officer
* [The] Little Hero
* Wheeler, Fighting Joe
* Wheeler, Little Joe

Wheeler, Joseph Trank 1868-? [ALY]
American author and editor
* Michael

Wheeler, Little Joe
See Wheeler, Joseph

Wheeler, Mary Jane 20th c. [CA]
American author
* Fowler, Mary Jane
* Simonson, Mary Jane

Wheeler, Mat
See Wittenwiler, Mathias

Wheeler, Mrs. James [FFF]
Entertainer
* Valdeau, Vintie

Wheeler, Mrs. S. T. [FFF]
Entertainer
* Olive, May

Wheeler, Off
See Harlin, J. J.

Wheeler, Patricia
See Walters, Patricia Wheeler

Wheeler, Prexy
See Wheeler, Benjamin Ide

Wheeler, Richard [Dick]
See Maynard, Richard Wheeler

Wheeler, Rip
See Wheeler, Floyd Clark

Wheeler, Scotty
See Wheeler, Don[ald Wesley]

Wheeler, Stern
See Wheeler, Charles Stearns

Wheeler, Teresa ?-1975 [SC]
Actress
* Cabaret Tess

Wheeler, Wayne 1950- [FB]
American football player
* Wheeler, Greyhound

Wheeler, Wayne Bidwell 1869-1927
[HPPN]
*American attorney, legislator,
prohibitionist*
* [The] Author of the Volstead Act
* [The] Hireling of the Anti-Saloon
  League
* [The] New David

Wheeler-O'Bryen, Wilfrid James 1898-
[THR]
British theatrical manager
* O'Bryen, W. J.

Wheelhouse
See Semple, Dugald

[The] Wheeling Bellboy
See Statler, Ellsworth Milton

Wheelock, Bobby
See Wheelock, Warren H.

Wheelock, Martha E. 1941- [CA]
American educator and author
* Alinder, Martha Wheelock

Wheelock, Warren H. 1864-1928 [BE]
American baseball player
* Wheelock, Bobby

Wheelton, Brooke
See Sladen, Douglas

Wheelwright, Esther 1696-1780 [BI]
Indian captive and nun
* Esther Marie Joseph, [Mother]

Wheelwright, W. [PA]
Author
* Old Bushman

Wheezer
See Hutchins, Bobby

Wheildon, William Willder 19th c.
[HPPN]
American journalist
* [The] Editor
* [A] Native of Boston

Whelan, Albert
See Waxman, Albert

Whelan, John
Author
* O'Faolain, Sean

Whelan, John 19th c. [DI]
Irish-born Australian bushranger
* Whelan, Rocky

Whelan, Rocky
See Whelan, John

Whellier, Alexander [RH]
Author
* Gifford, John, Esq.

Whelpley, James Davenport 1817-1872
[HPPN]
American journalist
* [A] Citizen of New York
* Horus
* J. D. W.

Whelpton, [George] Eric 1894-1981
[CA]
French-born author
* Lyte, Richard
* Parry, John

Whetham, John
See Warton, Thomas

Whetham, William Cecil Dampier
1867-1952 [TC1]
British historian and author
* Dampier, [Sir] William Cecil

Whetstone, Pete
See Noland, Charles Fenton Mercer

Wheway, John W. 20th c. [MBF]
British author
* Armitage, Vincent
* Richards, Hilda

Whewell, William 1795-1866 [HPPN]
*British philosopher, mathematician,
educator*
* [A] Member of Both Syndicates
* Whistle, Billy

Whicker, Kemp Caswell
See Wicker, Kemp Caswell

Whidborne, [Rev.] George Ferris 19th c.
[HPPN]
British clergyman
* [A] Clergyman of the Diocese of
Exeter

Whidby, Lulu 20th c. [BWW]
American entertainer
* White, Ella

[A] Whig
See Butler, John

[The] Whig
See Johnson, Samuel

[The] Whig Gulliver
See Webster, Daniel

[The] Whig Johnson
See Parr, Samuel

[A] Whig of '76
See Macomb, Robert

[A] Whig of the Old School
See Adams, Charles Francis

[A] Whig of the Revolution
See George III

[The] Whig Orator of the Old South
See Prentiss, Seargent Smith

Whigham, Haydn 1943- [HPPN]
American jazz musician
* Whigham, Jiggs

Whigham, Jiggs
See Whigham, Haydn

Whilk, Nat
See Lewis, Clive Staples

Whim Wham
See Curnow, [Thomas] Allen [Munro]

Whimsy, [Sir] Finical
See Worsley, [Sir] Richard

[The] Whip
See Blackwell, Ewell

Whipem, Benedick
See Harris, Richard

Whipper, Frances E. Rollin [IBW]
American author
* Rollin, Frank A.

Whipper, William 1805-1885 [HPPN]
American civil rights advocate
* [The] Father of the American Moral
Reform Society

[The] Whipping Post
See Livingston, William

Whipple, Clark D. ?-1963 [HPPN]
American conductor and musician
* Whipple, Doc

Whipple, Doc
See Whipple, Clark D.

Whipple, Edwin Percy 1819-1876
[HPPN]
American critic
* E. P. W.

Whipple, George Hoyt 1878-? [HPPN]
*American medical researcher and
educator*
* [The] Conqueror of Pernicious Anemia

Whipple, Henry Benjamin 1822-1901
[FFF]
American clergyman
* Straight Tongue

Whipple, Nelson S. 1882-1923 [SC]
American actor
* Dean, Nelson

Whipple, Squire 1804-1888 [FFF, HPPN]
American engineer
* [The] Father of American Bridge
Building
* [The] Father of Iron Bridges

Whipple, Wade
See Stevens, George

Whips, Andrea ?-1972 [SC]
American actress
* Feldman, Andrea

Whip's Lash
See Long, Russell Billiu

Whipster
See Bradley, Cuthbert

[The] Whirler
See Newbery, John

Whirlwind, Captain
See Sterling, Edward

Whisenton, Larry 1957- [SMG]
American baseball player
* Whisenton, Whizzer

Whisenton, Whizzer
See Whisenton, Larry

Whiskey Jim Greathouse
See Greathouse, James

Whiskey Van
See Van Buren, Martin

[The] Whispering Baritone
See Smith, Jack

Whispering Bill Anderson
See Anderson, Bill

Whispering Bill Barrett
See Barrett, William Joseph

Whispering Bill Pifer
See Pifer, William

Whispering Jack Smith
See Smith, Jack

Whispering Jimmie
See Ketcham, James

[The] Whispering Pianist
See Gillham, Art

Whispering Roy Hughes
See Hughes, Roy John

[The] Whispering Tenor
See Lucas, Eugene

Whistle, Billy
See Whewell, William

Whistlecraft, William and Robert
See Frere, John Hookham

[The] Whistler
See Engressia, Joe

[The] Whistler
See Somerville, Alexander

Whistler, George Washington 1800-1849
[HPPN]
American engineer
* Whistler, Pipes

Whistler, James Abbott McNeill
1834-1903 [HPPN]
American painter and etcher
* [The] Master of Limited Color

Whistler, Laurence 1912- [ART]
British engraver
* L. W.

Whistler, Lew[is]
See   Wissler, Lewis

Whistler, Pipes
See   Whistler, George Washington

Whistlin' Jake Wade
See   Wade, Jacob Fields

Whistling Alex Moore
See   Moore, Alexander Herman

Whistling Bob Smith
See   Smith, Robert A.

[The] Whistling Commercial
See   Walker, S.

[The] Whistling Coster
See   Mason, Fred

Whiston, Daniel 18th c.   [HPPN]
British clergyman
* [A] Presbyter of the Church of
  England

Whitaker, Charles Orbie 1893-1960
[SC]
Actor
* Whitaker, Slim

Whitaker, E. E. 20th c.   [ITA]
American theatre executive
* Whitaker, Whit

Whitaker, Joseph 1820-1895   [HPPN]
British publisher
* [The] Father of Whitaker's Almanac
* J. W.

Whitaker, Lily 1850-?   [DNA]
American poet
* Adidnac

Whitaker, Louis Rodman 1957-   [SMG]
American baseball player
* Whitaker, Sweet Lou

Whitaker, Pat
See   Whitaker, William H.

Whitaker, Pernell 20th c.   [SI 4-23-84]
American boxer
* Whitaker, Pete

Whitaker, Pete
See   Whitaker, Pernell

Whitaker, Popsie
See   Whitaker, Rogers Ernest Malcolm

Whitaker, Rod 1931-   [CA]
American author and educator
* Seare, Nicholas

Whitaker, Rodney 1925-   [NY 7-17-83]
Japanese-born American author
* Trevanian

Whitaker, Rogers Ernest Malcolm
1900-1981   [BI]
American editor and railroad buff
* Frimbo, E[rnest] M[alcolm]
* J. W. L.
* R. E. M. W.
* R. W.
* Whitaker, Popsie
* [The] World's Greatest Railroad Buff

Whitaker, Slim
See   Whitaker, Charles Orbie

Whitaker, Sweet Lou
See   Whitaker, Louis Rodman

Whitaker, Thomas 1883-1937   [BMH]
British ventriloquist
* Coram
* [The] Great Coram
* [The] Military Ventriloquist
* [Le] Roi

Whitaker, Whit
See   Whitaker, E. E.

Whitaker, William H. 1865-?   [BE]
American baseball player
* Whitaker, Pat

Whitbread, Jane
See   Levin, Jane Whitbread

Whitbread, Samuel 1758-1815   [SN]
British statesman
* [The] Brewer

Whitby, Sharon
See   Peters, Maureen

Whitcher, Frances Miriam Berry
1814-1852   [FFF, HPPN, PA]
American author
* Bedott, [Widow] Priscilla P.
* Whitcher, Frank
* [The] Widow Bedott

Whitcher, Frank
See   Whitcher, Frances Miriam Berry

Whitcomb, Ian 1941-   [CA]
British writer, singer, composer
* Bubb, Mel
* Murphy, Buck
* Newton, Stu
* Nouveau, Arthur

Whitcomb, Joshua
See   Thompson, Denman

Whitcomb, Kenneth G. 1926-   [ASC]
American composer, conductor, arranger
* Kenny, George

White
See   Anglus, Thomas

[The] White
See   Clitus

[The] White
See   Hugh [or Hugues]

White, Abe
See   White, Adel

White, Adam   [PA]
Author
* Arachnophilus

White, Adel 1906-   [BE]
American baseball player
* White, Abe

White, Alan 20th c.   [AW, CA, WD]
British author
* Fraser, James
* Whitney, Alec

White, Albert Eugene 1918-   [BE]
American baseball player
* White, Fuzz

White, Alexina B.   [FFF, PA]
American author
* Alba

White, Alfred H.
See   Weisman, Alfred

White, Alice
See   White, Alva

White, Allie
See   White, Thomas

White, Alva 1907-   [F2]
American actress
* White, Alice

White, Andy
See   White, Elwyn Brooks

White, Arthur 20th c.   [EF]
American football player
* White, Tarzan

White, Babe
See   White, Harold A.

White, Babington
See   Maxwell, Mary Elizabeth [Braddon]

White Backlash, Mr.
See   Maddox, Lester Garfield

White, Barry 1945-   [IBW]
American orchestra leader, singer,
composer
* [The] Pied Piper of Love

[The] White Bear
See   Whately, Richard

White, Beatrice 1901?-1963   [BEW]
American theatrical performer
* Curtis, Beatrice

White Beaver
See   Powell, [David] Frank

White, Belle
See   White, Isabella Mary

White, Benjamin Aspinwall ?-1866
[HPPN]
American physician
* B. A. W.

White, Bill
See   Gristy, Bill

White, Bill
See   Rattenberry, William A.

White, Blythe, Jr.
See   Robinson, Solon

White, Bob
See   Holland, Ray P.

White, Bob
See   Slaughter, Marion T.

White, Bob
See   White, Floyd Lester

White, Booker T. Washington 1906-1977
[BWW]
American singer
* [The] Singing Preacher
* White, Bucca [or Bukka]

White, Bucca [or Bukka]
See White, Booker T. Washington

White, Buck
See White, O'Neal

White, Byron Raymond 1917- [FB, OCS]
American football player and Supreme Court Justice
* White, Whizzer

White, C. H.
See Chaplin, Heman W.

White, Cecil 1900- [WEC]
Australian cartoonist
* Unk
* White, Unk

White, Cecil B.
See Christie, William H.

White, Celia 20th c. [AW]
British author
* Tustin, Elizabeth

White, Century
See White, John

White, Charles 1793-? [HPPN]
British soldier and author
* Corr, [Miss] Mary

White, Charles 1795-1861 [BI]
British author and sportsman
* Martingale

White, Charles 20th c. [TI 9-10-84]
British disc jockey and author
* Rock, Dr.

White, Charles
See White, James

White, Charles Albert [FFF, IP]
American composer
* Birch, Harry

White, Charles Erskine, D.D.
See Osborn, Laughton

White, Charles William 1906- [ANT]
American author
* White, Max

White, Charley
See Anchowitz, Charles

White, Charley
See Anschowitz, Charles

White, Charlotte [IP]
British poet
* C. W.

White, Cherokee
See White, Randolph Louis

White, Chief
See White, Randolph Louis

[The] White Chief of the Pawnees
See Lillie, [Major] Gordon W.

White, Claire Nicolas 1925- [CA]
Dutch-born American author and playwright
* Nicolas, Claire

White, Clara
See McCoy, Viola

White, Cleve 1928- [BWW]
American singer
* Schoolboy Cleve

White, Constance
See Howard, Charles J.

White, Constance M. 1903- [HPPN]
British author
* Howard, Constance

White, Dale
See Place, Marian T[empleton]

White, Deacon
See White, James Laurie

White, Deke
See White, George Frederick

[The] White Devil of Wallachia
See Castriot [or Castriota?], George

White, Doc
See White, Guy Harris

White, Duck
See White, James

White, Dwight 1949- [SMG]
American football player
* White, Mad Dog

White, E. B.
See White, Elwyn Brooks

[The] White Eagle
See McCoy, Tim

[The] White Eagle
See Penrose, Spencer

[The] White Earl
See Butler, James [Fourth Earl of Ormonde]

White, Edmund
See Patton, James Blythe

White, Edward Douglass 1845-1921
[HPPN]
American Supreme Court justice
* [The] Mentor of the Rule of Reason

White, Eliza A. 19th c. [IP, PA]
American author
* Alex

White Elk, Michael
See Walker, T. Michael

White, Ella
See Crippen, Catherine [Katie]

White, Ella
See Whidby, Lulu

White, Ellerton Oswald 1917-1971
[DAM, EJ, PMJ]
American jazz musician
* White, Sonny

White, Elwyn Brooks 1899-1985
[HPPN, IPA, LC, TC]
American author
* E. B. W.
* White, Andy
* White, E. B.
* White, En

White, En
See White, Elwyn Brooks

White, Eric 20th c. [BBH, CSH]
Canadian lacrosse player
* White, Rusty

[The] White Eyed Kaffir
See Chirgwin, George H.

[The] White Eyed Musical Moke
See Chirgwin, George H.

White Falcon 1780?-1847 [BI, HPPN]
American Indian chief
* Tanner, John

White, Father
See White, Harry Alexander

[The] White Flower
See Alighieri, Durante

White, Floyd Lester 1932- [CWG]
American country-western performer
* White, Bob

White Fox
See Hargrave, John

White, Frank James 1905-1960? [HPPN]
British confidence man and petty thief
* Colefax, Mortimer
* Gunnell, Vincent H.
* Hargreaves, Eustace Hamilton
* Hayward, Ian Spencer
* Revenell, Nicholas
* Wadley, Wilfred John

White, Frank Linstow
See Weitenkampf, Frank

[The] White Friar
See Sabine, William Henry Waldo

White, Fruit
See White, Morris

White, Fuzz
See White, Albert Eugene

White, G. A.
See Millar, James Primrose Malcolm

White, George
See Weitz, George

White, George Frederick 1872-1957
[BE]
American baseball player
* White, Deke

White, George M. 1805?-1900 [HPPN]
American gambler
* White, Major

White, George Savage 1784-? [HPPN]
British clergyman
* Amana

White, Georgia Atwood 1878?-1957 [BI]
American author
* Atwood, Dascomb

White, Gertrude M[ason] 1915- [CA]
American author
* Wakefield, R. I.

White, Gladys
See Henderson, Rosa [Rose]

White, Grace
See Moore, Monette

White, Guy Harris 1879-1969 [BE, DGS, PB]
American baseball player
* White, Doc

White, H. T.
See Engh, Rohn

White, Hannah 19th c. [HPPN]
American author
* [A] Lady

White, Harold A. 1894-1973 [FB]
American football player
* White, Babe

White, Harriet 19th c. [HFN, IP, PI]
Irish poet
* Harriet

White, Harry
See Whittington, Harry [Benjamin]

White, Harry Alexander 1898-1962 [EJ, WWJ]
American jazz musician
* White, Father

White, Henry ?-1836 [HPPN]
British clergyman
* H. W.

White, Henry 1850-1927 [HPPN]
American diplomat
* [The] Most Useful Man in the Diplomatic Service

White, Henry Kirke 1785-1806 [HPPN]
British poet
* [The] Boy Poet of Nottingham

White, Herbert [Martyn] Oliver 1885- [WW]
Author
* Martyn, Oliver

[The] White Hope Champion
See McCarty, Luther

[The] White House Hatchetman
See Colson, Charles W. [Chuck]

[The] White House Lawyer
See St. Clair, James

[The] White House Pet
See O'Day, Caroline Goodwin

[The] White House Reporter
See McClendon, Sarah

White House Tommy Corcoran
See Corcoran, Thomas Gardiner

White, Hubert
See Cobb, J. Storer

White, Hugh Lawson 1773-1840 [BDSA, HPPN]
American author, jurist, statesman
* [The] American Cato
* [The] Cato of America
* [The] Cato of the Senate

White, Hy
See White, Hyman

White, Hyman 1915- [WWJ]
American jazz musician
* White, Hy

White, Ida L. 19th c. [PI]
Irish poet
* Ida

White, Isabella Mary 1894-1972
British diver
* White, Belle

White, J. H.
See White, John Henry

White, Jack 20th c.
American director
* Black, Preston

White, James [IP]
British author
* [A] Gentleman, a Descendant of Dame Quickly

White, James [HN]
British politician
* [The] Plymouth Sound

White, James ?-1876 [HPPN]
American frontiersman and scout
* Chips, Buffalo
* White, Charles
* White, Jonathan

White, James 1804-1862 [IP]
Scottish clergyman and author
* [A] Country Curate
* J. W.

White, James 1840-1885 [NN]
Religious leader
* Jezreel, James Jershom

White, James 1953- [SMG]
American football player
* White, Duck

White, James
See Seeley, John Robert

White, James C. 1900- [HPPN]
American librarian
* [The] Buttinsky

White, James Dillon
See White, Stanley

White, James Laurie 1847-1939 [AS, BE, HPPN, PB]
American baseball player
* White, Deacon

White, Jesse
See Weidenfeld, Jesse Marc

White, Jewell Ryan 1943- [BA]
American labor leader
* J. W.
* White, Jule

White, Jo Jo
See White, Joseph

White, Jo-Jo
See White, Joyner Clifford

White, John ?-1760 [IP]
British clergyman and author
* [A] Gentleman

White, John 1574-1648 [DNNF, DNNS, SN]
British clergyman
* [The] Patriarch of Dorchester
* White, Patriarch

White, John 1590-1645 [DNNS, FFF, RH]
Welsh barrister and political writer
* White, Century

White, John 1846-? [IP]
British music printer, bookseller, author
* A. C. I. G. [A Cornishman in Gloucestershire]

White, John 1893- [BMH]
Scottish singer
* MacGregor, Sandy

White, John Duncan ?-1826 [BLB]
American murderer and pirate
* Marchant, Charles

White, John Henry 1909- [ART]
British sculptor
* White, J. H.

White, John I[rwin] 1902- [CA, CWG]
American country-western performer
* Johns, Whitey
* [The] Lone Star Ranger
* [The] Lonesome Cowboy
* Price, Jimmie

White, John S.
See Schwarzkopf, Hans

White, Johnny
See Bimstein, Morris

White, Jonathan
See White, James

White, Joseph 1946- [BB]
American basketball player
* White, Jo Jo

White, Joseph Blanco 1775-1841 [DEL, HPPN]
British author
* Blanco, Giuseppe
* [A] Clergyman of the Church of England
* [An] Irish Gentleman
* Leucadio Doblado, Don

White, Joseph M. 1790?-1839 [IP]
American politician, attorney, author
* [An] Old Man

White, Joseph M. 1891?-1959
American singer
* [The] Silver Masked Tenor

White, Josh[ua Daniel] 1915-1969 [BWW, HPPN]
American singer
* Barton, Tippy

White, Josh[ua Daniel] (cont.)
* [The] Most Famous Folk Singer of his Race
* Pinewood Tom
* [The] Singing Christian

White, Joyner Clifford 1909- [BE]
American baseball player
* White, Jo-Jo

White, Jude Gilliam 1947- [CA]
American author
* Deveraux, Jude

White, Jule
See White, Jewell Ryan

White, Katharine S. ?-1977
American author
* K. S. W.

White, Katherine Elizabeth 1916-1972 [FC]
American actress
* Wilson, Marie

White, Kevin Hagan 1929?-
American politician
* King Kevin
* Mayor De Luxe

[The] White King
See Charles I

White, [Oliver] Kirby 1884-1943 [BE]
American baseball player
* White, Redbuck

[The] White Knight
See Anagnostopoulos, Spiro Theodore

[The] White Knight
See Fitz Gibbon, Maurice

[The] White Knight
See Fitzgibbon, Edmund

[The] White Knight
See Hunyadi, Janos [or Huniades, John]

White, Lasses
See White, Lee Roy

White, Lee Roy 1888-1949 [SC]
American actor
* White, Lasses

White, Leonard
See Farjeon, J[oseph] Jefferson

White, Leonard Arthur 1919- [CEI]
Canadian-born hockey player
* White, Moe

White Lightning
See Donley, Doug

White Lightning Brown
See Brown, Charlie

White, Lula [or Lulu] 20th c. [HPPN]
West Indian brothel proprietress
* [The] Queen of the Demi-Monde

White, M. Robert
See Montero, Roberto Bianchi

White, Mad Dog
See White, Dwight

White, Major
See White, George M.

[The] White Man's Negro
See Perry, Lincoln Theodore

White, Manster
See White, Randy

White, Margaret Bourke 1906-1971 [HPPN]
American photographer
* [The] World's Foremost Photojournalist

White, Mary Helen ?-1923 [BEW]
Playwright
* Collingham, G. G.

White, Matthew
See Prynne, William

White, Matthew, Jr.
See Alden, William L.

White, Max
See White, Charles William

White, Melvin 1921- [IBW]
American actor and comedian
* White, Slappy

White, Meryon 20th c. [WWL]
British author
* White-Winton, Meryon

[The] White Milliner
See Jennings, Frances

White, Mr. [code name used during World War II]
See Wedemeyer, Albert C.

White, Moe
See White, Leonard Arthur

[The] White Mohammed Ali
See Riggs, Robert Larimore [Bobby]

White, Morris 1911- [WWJ]
American jazz musician
* White, Fruit

[The] White Mountain Giant
See Crawford, Ethan Allen

White, Mrs. Charles O. [FFF]
Entertainer
* Howard, Lillian

White, Mrs. Frank [FFF]
Entertainer
* Hall, Pauline

White, Mrs. Legrand [FFF]
Entertainer
* Maddern, Minnie

White, Mrs. M. E. [Harding] [IP]
American editor
* One of his Children

White, Mrs W. H. 19th c. [IP]
American author
* One of Them

White, Napoleon Bonaparte ?-1889 [HPPN]
American gambler
* White, Poley

White, O'Neal 1911- [GF]
American golfer
* White, Buck

White, Osmar Egmont Dorkin 1909- [CA]
Author and journalist
* Dentry, Robert

White, Patriarch
See White, John

White, Patricia Lorrainann 1928- [HPPN]
Canadian ballerina, educator, choreographer
* Wilde, Patricia

White, Patrick F. ?-1875 [PI]
Irish poet, writer, musician
* Black

White, Paul Hamilton Hume 1910- [CA]
Australian physician and author
* Jungle Doctor

White, Pearl 1889-1939 [HPPN]
American actress
* [The] Queen of the Silent Serials

[The] White Pele
See Zico, Arthur

White, Phyllis Dorothy [James] 20th c. [BI]
British author
* James, P. D.

White Pine Thomson
See Thomson, Floyd Harvey

[The] White Poet
See Olaf

White, Poley
See White, Napoleon Bonaparte

White, Princess 1881-1976 [BWW]
American singer
* [The] International Entertainer

White, Priscilla Maria Veronica 20th c. [LRR]
British singer
* Black, Cilla

[The] White Queen
See Mary, Queen of Scots

White, Quinten 1952- [EJ7]
American jazz musician
* White, Rocky

White Rabbit
See Yeo-Thomas, Forest Frederick Edward

White, Ramy Allison [house pseudonym] [Stratemeyer Syndicate]
See Stratemeyer, Edward L.

White, Randolph Louis 1897- [BA]
American publisher
* White, Cherokee
* White, Chief

White, Randy 20th c.
American football player
* White, Manster

[The] White Rat
See Herzog, Dorrel Norman Elvert

White, Ray
Boxer
* White, Windmill

White, Redbuck
See White, [Oliver] Kirby

White, Rhoda E. [Waterman]   [IP]
American author
* Uncle Ben

White, Richard Alan 1944-   [CA]
American author
* Cabral, Alberto

White, Richard Grant 1821-1885   [DEL, FFF, HPPN, IP, PA]
American author and critic
* [An] American Author
* [A] Learned Gorilla
* Outis, U. Donough
* R. G. W.
* Saint Benjamin
* [The] Shakesperian Scholar
* [A] Yankee

White Robe
See Roberts, John

White, Robert   [IP]
British poet
* R. W.

White, Rocky
See White, Quinten

White, Rold
See Neuburg, Victor [Benjamin]

White, Roma
See Oram, Blanche

[The] White Rose
See Elizabeth

White, Rose C. [King] 19th c.   [IP]
American poet
* Roselinda

[The] White Rose of England
See Warbeck, Perkin

[The] White Rose of Raby
See Neville, Cecily [or Cicely]

[The] White Rose of Scotland
See Gordon, [Lady] Catherine

[The] White Rose of York
See Courtney, Edward

White, Rusty
See White, Eric

[The] White Saint of India
See Bowen, George

White, Sally Joy
See White, Sarah Elizabeth

White, Sam
See White, Sanford B.

White, Sanford B. 1888-1964   [FB]
American football player
* White, Sam

White, Sarah Elizabeth 1845-1909   [DNA]
American author
* White, Sally Joy

[The] White Savage
See Girty, Simon

[The] White Savage
See Hunter, John Dunn

White, Sherm
See White, Sherman Eugene

White, Sherman Eugene 1948-   [FR]
American football player
* White, Sherm

White Shoes Johnson
See Johnson, William Arthur

White, Sidney 1864-1919   [BEW, FC]
American actor
* Drew, Sidney

White, Slappy
See White, Melvin

White, Solomon 1868-1955   [MK]
American baseball player
* King Solomon

White, Sonny
See White, Ellerton Oswald

White Sox Katzenjammer Kid
See Minoso, Saturnino Orestes Arrieta Armas

[The] White Squaw
See Slocum, Frances

[The] White Squaw of the Kanawha
See Bailey, Anne Hennis Trotter

White, Stanford 1853-1906   [HPPN]
American architect and murder victim
* America's Foremost Architect
* [The] Builder

White, Stanhope 1913-   [AW, CA, IAW]
British author
* Bana, Dan
* Sabiad

White, Stanley 1913-   [CA]
British author
* Krull, Felix
* Peto
* Peto, James
* White, James Dillon

White, T. Chartres 19th c.   [HPPN]
British author
* [A] Quekett Clubman

White, Tarzan
See White, Arthur

White, Terence Hanbury 1906-1964 [CA, SAT]
British author
* Aston, James

White, Tex
See White, Wilfred

White, Theodore Edwin [Ted] 1938- [CA, ESF, SFP]
American author
* Archer, Ron [joint pseudonym with Dave Van Arnam]
* Edwards, Norman [joint pseudonym with Terry (Gene) Carr]

White, Theodore Harold 1915-   [HPPN]
American journalist and author
* [The] Dean of American Reporters

White, [Mr.] Thom
See Elliott, Charles Wyllys

White, Thomas   [IP]
British author
* T. H. W.

White, Thomas 1582-1676   [FFF]
British philosopher and clergyman
* Candidus

White, Thomas 20th c.   [EF]
American football player
* White, Allie

White, Thomas, Jr.
See Omond, Thomas Stewart

White, Trentwell Mason 1901-   [WWL]
American author
* Trant, Martin

White, Unk
See White, Cecil

White, Walter 19th c.   [IP]
British author
* [A] Londoner

White, Whizzer
See White, Byron Raymond

White, Whizzer
See White, Wilford

White, Whoop-La
See White, William Henry

[The] White Widow
See Tyrconnel, Duchess of

White, Wilford 20th c.   [FB, SMG]
American football player
* White, Whizzer

White, Wilfred 20th c.   [CEI]
Hockey player
* White, Tex

White, Wilfrid 1903-   [BEW]
British actor
* Hyde-White, Wilfrid

White, [Rev.] William 1748-1836 [HPPN]
American clergyman
* Silas

White, William [Bill] 1934-   [IBW]
American sportscaster
* [The] Jackie Robinson of Broadcasting

White, William A[nthony] P[arker] 1911-1968   [CA, CC, EMD]
American author and critic
* Boucher, Anthony

White, William A[nthony] P[arker]
(cont.)
* Holmes, H. H.
* Mudgett, Herman W.

White, William Allen 1868-1944 [HPPN, WBD]
American author and journalist
* [The] Liberal Philosopher of the Middle West
* [The] Sage of Emporia

White, William Charles 1777-1818 [HPPN]
American actor, playwright, attorney, author
* [A] Republican

White, William Francis 1829-1891 [HPPN]
American pioneer
* Grey, William

White, William Hale 1831-1913 [LC, NPS, UH]
British author
* Rutherford, Mark
* Shapcott, Reuben

White, William Henry 1854-1911 [BE]
American baseball player
* White, Whoop-La

White, William Jack 20th c. [BLB, PHM]
American underworld figure
* Three Fingered Jack

White, William, Jr. 1934- [CA, WD]
American author, translator, poet
* Spinossimus

White, Windmill
See White, Ray

White Witch
See Foe, Daniel

[The] White Woman of the Genessee
See Jemison, Mary

White, Zebulon L. 19th c. [IP]
American author
* Z. L. W.

White, Zita
See Denholm, Therese Mary Zita White

White-Winton, Meryon
See White, Meryon

Whitebird, J[oanie]
See Green, Joan Elizabeth

[The] Whitechapel Whirlwind
See Bergman, Judah

[The] Whitechapel Windmill
See Bergman, Judah

Whitefeather, [Captain] Barabbas
See Jerrold, Douglas William

Whitefield, Ann
See Stone, Susan Berch

Whitefield, George 1714-1770 [FFF, IP, RH]
British religious leader
* [The] Mock Preacher
* Squintum, Doctor

Whitefoord, Caleb 1734-1810 [IP]
Scottish author
* Emendator
* Junia
* Papirius Cursor

Whiteford, Blackie
See Whiteford, John P.

Whiteford, John P. 1873-1962 [SC]
American actor
* Whiteford, Blackie

Whitefriar
See Hiscock, Eric

Whitehall, Harold 1905- [CAP]
British author, educator, playwright
* Fritz

Whitehead, Bud
See Whitehead, Rubin Angus

Whitehead, Burgess Urquhart 1910- [BE]
American baseball player
* Whitehead, Whitey

Whitehead, Commander
See Anderson, George Lee

Whitehead, Commander
See Whitehead, Walter Edward

Whitehead, Henry 19th c. [IP]
British clergyman and author
* [The] Senior Curate of St Luke's, Berwick Street

Whitehead, John Henderson 1909-1964 [BE]
American baseball player
* Whitehead, Silent John

Whitehead, John L., Jr. 1925- [IBW]
American air force officer and engineer
* Death, Mr.

Whitehead, Kate 1896- [WWL]
British author
* Oxley, Kate

Whitehead, Margaret della Rovere [ART]
British artist
* M. della R. W.

Whitehead, Mrs. C. B. 19th c. [IP, PA]
American author
* Jackson, Josephine

Whitehead, Mrs. S. R. [IP]
Author
* [A] Scotch Minister's Daughter

Whitehead, Paul 1709?-1774 [HPPN]
British poet
* Paul the Aged

Whitehead, Rubin Angus 20th c. [EF]
American football player
* Whitehead, Bud

Whitehead, Silent John
See Whitehead, John Henderson

Whitehead, Walter Edward 1908- [HPPN]
British business executive
* [The] Embodiment of Schweppervescence
* Whitehead, Commander

Whitehead, Whitey
See Whitehead, Burgess Urquhart

Whitehill, Walter Muir 1906?-1978
American historian and man of letters
* Boston, Mr.

Whitehorn, Arthur Lee
See Daney, Lee

Whitehorn, Katharine
See Lyall, Katharine Elizabeth

Whitehorn, Washington
See Bellaw, Americus Wellington

Whitehouse, Arch
See Taylor, W. T.

Whitehouse, Arch
See Whitehouse, Arthur George Joseph

Whitehouse, Arthur George Joseph 1895-1979 [CA, WW]
British-born author, cartoonist, journalist
* Whitehouse, Arch

Whitehouse, Charles Evis [Charlie] 1894-1960 [BE]
American baseball player
* Whitehouse, Lefty

Whitehouse, Flight
See Whitehouse, John

Whitehouse, Francis Cecil 1879-? [CCL]
Canadian poet
* Francisco, Ramon

Whitehouse, Fred 1895-1954
American vaudeville performer
* [The] Phonograph Singer

Whitehouse, Jeanne 1939- [CA]
American author
* Peterson, Jeanne Whitehouse

Whitehouse, John 1949- [DC]
British cricketer
* Whitehouse, Flight

Whitehouse, Lefty
See Whitehouse, Charles Evis [Charlie]

Whitehouse, W. F. 19th c. [IP, PA]
British author
* Agricola

Whiteing, Richard 1840-1928 [HPPN, IP, WWL]
British author
* Alb
* Sprout, Mr.
* Thorne, Whyte

Whitelaw, James 19th c. [HPPN]
British author
* Dove, Walter

Whiteley, John Peter 1955- [DC]
British cricketer
* Whiteley, Nimmo

Whiteley, Mrs. John H. [FFF]
Entertainer
* Weaver, Ella

Whiteley, Nimmo
See Whiteley, John Peter

Whiteley, William 1831-1907 [WBD]
British department store owner
* [The] Universal Provider

Whitelock, Louise [Clarkson] 1865-?
[WGT]
Author
* Clarkson, L.

Whitelocke, Bulstrode 1605-1675 [SN]
British politician
* [The] Temporizing Statesman

Whiteman, George Frederick Carl
1877-1958 [HPPN]
Australian actor, critic, theater manager
* Carroll, Sydney W.

Whiteman, Paul 1890-1967 [HPPN,
PMJ]
American jazz musician
* [The] Dean of American Popular
Music
* [The] King of Jazz
* Whiteman, Pops

Whiteman, Pops
See Whiteman, Paul

Whiteman, Sydney 1877-1958 [THR]
Australian-born critic, author, journalist
* Carroll, Sydney W.

[The] Whitest of the Black Sox
See Weaver, George Davis

Whitestock, Frank
See Brookfield, William Henry

Whitfield, [Rev.] George 1714-1740
[HPPN]
British clergyman
* Squintum, Senior

Whitfield, Howard
See Smith, Howard Whitfield, Jr.

Whitfield, John Humphreys 1906- [AW,
CA]
British educator and author
* Pilio, Gerone

Whitfield, Malvin Greston 1924- [IBW]
American track and field athlete
* Whitfield, Marvelous Mal

Whitfield, Marvelous Mal
See Whitfield, Malvin Greston

[The] Whitfield of Nova Scotia
See Alline, Henry

[The] Whitfield of the Stage
See Garrick, David

[The] Whitfield of the Stage
See Quin, James

Whitfield, Raoul 1898-1945 [CC, EMD]
American author
* Decolta, Ramon

Whitford, Annabelle
See Buchan, Annabelle W.

Whitford, Joan 1922?- [MBF]
British author
* Ford, Barry
* Oldham, Hugh R.

Whitford, Lawrence W. 20th c. [BBH]
American baseball coach
* Whitford, Mon

Whitford, Lee
See Coates, Walter John

Whitford, Mon
See Whitford, Lawrence W.

Whithorne, Emerson
See Whittern, Emerson

Whiting, Ed[ward C.]
See Zieber, Harry

Whiting, Henry 1790-1851 [IP]
American army officer and author
* [An] Officer of the Army at Detroit

Whiting, John 1655-1722 [HPPN]
British clergyman
* J. W.

Whiting, Little Billy
See Whiting, William Henry Chase

Whiting, Madcap Maggie
See Whiting, Margaret Eleanore

Whiting, Margaret Eleanore 1924-
[HPPN]
American singer and actress
* Whiting, Madcap Maggie

Whiting, Sadie Burt ?-1966 [HPPN]
American dancer
* Burt, Sadie

Whiting, Stanley
See Coffin, Lucius Powers

Whiting, Sydney 19th c. [IP, WGT]
British author
* [A] Minister of the Interior
* S. W.

Whiting, William Henry Chase
1824-1865 [HPPN]
American army officer
* Whiting, Little Billy

Whiting Spilhaus, M.
See Spilhaus, Phyllis Margaret

Whitinger, R. D.
See Place, Marian T[empleton]

Whitley, Crane
See Wilenchick, Clem

Whitley, George
See Chandler, Arthur Bertram

Whitley, Jonas E. 1849-? [IP, PA]
American author
* J. E. W.
* Nick

Whitling, Henry John 19th c. [IP]
British author
* Nil

Whitlock, Billy
See Essex, Frederick

Whitlock, Bob
See Whitlock, Von Varlynn

Whitlock, Buck
See Whitlock, Roy

Whitlock, John
See Codner, John

Whitlock, Ralph 1914- [CA, WD]
British author
* [The] Countryman
* Reynolds, John
* Reynolds, Madge

Whitlock, Roy 20th c. [SMG]
Canadian-born hockey player
* Whitlock, Buck

Whitlock, Von Varlynn 1931- [EJ]
American jazz musician
* Whitlock, Bob

Whitman, Alfred
See Vosburgh, Alfred

Whitman, Charles 1941-1966 [HPPN]
American murderer
* [The] Tower Murderer

Whitman, Edward W. 20th c. [EOP]
British astrologer
* Old Moore

Whitman, Elizabeth 1752-1788 [SN]
* [The] Coquette
* Wharton, Eliza

Whitman, [Walter] Frank[lin] 1924-
[BE]
American baseball player
* Whitman, Hooker

Whitman, Gayne 1890-1958 [SC]
American actor and screenwriter
* Vosburgh, Alfred

Whitman, Hooker
See Whitman, [Walter] Frank[lin]

Whitman, Jason 1799-1848 [HPPN]
American clergyman
* W.

Whitman, Jerry
See Winters, June

Whitman, John Lorin 1862-1926
[HPPN]
American prison guard and penologist
* [The] Beloved Jailer
* [The] Boy Guard

Whitman, Otis Dewey, Jr. 1924- [CME,
CWG, DAM]
American country-western performer
* Whitman, Slim

Whitman, Sarah Helen Power 1803-1878
[FFF, HPPN]
American poet
* Helen
* Poe's Helen

Whitman, Slim
See Whitman, Otis Dewey, Jr.

Whitman, Walt[er] 1819-1892 [DNNS,
FFF, HPPN, SN]
American poet
* [The] Good Gray Poet
* [The] Solitary Singer

Whitmarsh, William Burt 19th c. [IP]
British poet
* W. B. W.

Whitmire, Kathy 1947?- [TI 6-4-84]
American politician
* Whitmire, Tootsie

Whitmire, Tootsie
See Whitmire, Kathy

Whitmore, Cilla
See Gladstone, Arthur M.

Whitmore, George 1944?- [HPPN]
American accused assailant
* [The] Uncaped Crusader

Whitmore, H. 18th c. [WGT]
Author
* Gulliver, Lemuel, Junior

Whitmore, John 19th c. [IP]
British author
* [A] Suffolk Clergyman

Whitmore, William Henry 1836-? [IP]
American genealogist and politician
* W. H. W.

Whitnell, Barbara
See Hutton, Ann

Whitner, Edward Clarence 1916- [BE]
American baseball player
* Levy, Ed[ward Clarence]

Whitney, Abbie
See Smith, Abbie Whitney

Whitney, Adeline Dutton [Train] 1824-?
[IP]
American author
* A. D. T. W.

Whitney, Adeline Dutton [Train] 1824-?
[IP, PA]
American author
* Garney, Faith

Whitney, Alec
See White, Alan

Whitney, Arthur Carter 1906- [BE, PB]
American baseball player
* Whitney, Pinky

Whitney, Bartholomew Reynolds 1908-
[HPPN]
American army officer
* Old Blood and Butts

Whitney, Cap
See Whitney, Chauncey Belden

Whitney, Captain
See Whitney, James

Whitney, Chauncey Belden 1842-1873
[EWG]
American law officer
* Whitney, Cap

Whitney, Cornelius Vanderbilt 1899?-
American sportsman and industrialist
* Whitney, Sonny

Whitney, David
See Malick, Terrence

Whitney, Eli 1765-1825 [HPPN]
American inventor
* [The] Father of the Cotton Gin
* [The] Whittling Boy

Whitney, Elliott [joint pseudonym with
Harry Lincoln Saylor]
See Bedford-Jones, Henry [James
O'Brien]

Whitney, Elliott [joint pseudonym with
Henry Bedford-Jones]
See Sayler, Harry Lincoln

Whitney, Frank Thomas 1856-1943 [BE]
American baseball player
* Whitney, Jumbo

Whitney, Grasshopper Jim
See Whitney, James E.

Whitney, Hallam
See Whittington, Harry [Benjamin]

Whitney, Harry
See Kennedy, Patrick

Whitney, Henry Austin 19th c. [IP]
American author
* H. A. W.

Whitney, J. L. H.
See Trimble, Jacquelyn W[hitney]

Whitney, James ?-1693 [DI]
British highwayman
* [The] Jacobite Robber
* Whitney, Captain

Whitney, James E. 1856-1891 [AS,
DGS, PB]
American baseball player
* Whitney, Grasshopper Jim
* Whitney, Long Jim

Whitney, James S. 19th c. [HPPN]
American author
* [A] Member of the Board of
Education

Whitney, Jock
See Whitney, John Hay

Whitney, John Hay 1905?-1982
*American diplomat and newspaper
publisher*
* Whitney, Jock

Whitney, Julia 1919-1965 [HPPN]
American composer and singer
* Yulya

Whitney, Jumbo
See Whitney, Frank Thomas

Whitney, Long Jim
See Whitney, James E.

Whitney, Louisa [Goddard] 1819-1883
[IP]
American author
* L. W.

Whitney, Lucia
See Keller, Ethel May

Whitney, Lucia
See Kelley, Ethel [May]

Whitney, Moses, Jr. 1828-? [IP]
American author
* Trismegistus

Whitney, Moxam 1919- [ASC]
Canadian musician
* Whitney, Moxie

Whitney, Moxie
See Whitney, Moxam

Whitney, Peter
See Engle, Peter King

Whitney, Pinky
See Whitney, Arthur Carter

Whitney, Reid
See Armour, R. Coutts

Whitney, Richard 1889?- [HPPN]
American financier
* [The] Strong Man of Wall Street

Whitney, Sonny
See Whitney, Cornelius Vanderbilt

Whitney, Spencer
See Burks, Arthur J.

Whitney, Walter Langdon 1895-1958
[BI]
American author and press agent
* Lang, Don

Whitney, William Collins 1841-1904
[HPPN]
American politician
* [The] Modern Warwick

Whiton, James Morris 1833-? [IP]
American educator and author
* [An] Orthodox Minister of the Gospel

Whiton, James Nelson 1932- [CA]
American author and screenwriter
* Bolo, Solomon
* Boylan, Boyd

Whitshaw, Stella 1887- [THR]
Russian-born actress
* Arbenina, Stella

Whitson
See Warren, Peter Whitson

Whitson, John Harvey 1854-1936
[EMD, HPPN]
American author
* Carter, Nicholas?
* Garland, Luke
* Hazelton, Captain
* Hazelton, Colonel
* Merriwell, Frank
* Sewell, Arthur

Whitson, John Harvey (cont.)
* Sims, [Lieut.] A. K.
* Standish, Burt L.
* Steel, Robert
* Steele, Addison
* Stevens, Maurice
* Williams, Russell

Whitstable, George
See Lissenden, George B.

Whittaker, A. 17th c. [HN]
American clergyman
* [The] Apostle of Virginia

Whittaker, Charles
See Chambers, [Jay David] Whittaker

Whittaker, Doc
See Whittaker, Walt[er Elton]

Whittaker, Frederick 1838-1889 [WW]
British-born author
* Poyntz, Launce

Whittaker, Hudson
See Woodbridge, Hudson

Whittaker, Lucian   [SMG]
American basketball player
* Whittaker, Skippy

Whittaker, Norman 20th c. [BLB]
American swindler
* [The] Fox

Whittaker, Skippy
See Whittaker, Lucian

Whittaker, Walt[er Elton] 1894-1965
[BE]
American baseball player
* Whittaker, Doc

Whitted, George Bostic 1890-1942 [AS,
BE]
American baseball player
* Whitted, Possum

Whitted, Possum
See Whitted, George Bostic

Whittemore, Arthur 1916- [HPPN]
American pianist
* Whittemore, Buck

Whittemore, Buck
See Whittemore, Arthur

Whittemore, Don 20th c. [CA]
American author and film critic
* Norman, Louis

Whittemore, Nathan 18th c. [HPPN]
American almanac maker and publisher
* N. W.

Whitten, Wilfred ?-1942 [LC, WWL]
British author and editor
* O'London, John

Whittenton, Jesse [or Jess]
See Whittenton, Urshell

Whittenton, Urshell 1934- [EF, FB]
American football player
* Whittenton, Jesse [or Jess]

Whittern, Emerson 1884-1958 [DAM]
American composer
* Whithorne, Emerson

Whittet, George Sorley 20th c. [IAW]
Scottish-born author
* Jok
* Kerr, John O'Connell
* Monkland, George

Whittier, John Greenleaf 1807-1892
[DEL, HPPN, IP, PA]
American author and poet
* [The] Burns of America
* [The] Poet Laureate of New England
* [The] Puritan Poet
* [The] Quaker Poet
* Smith, Margaret
* [The] Wood Thrush of Essex

Whittier, Matthew F. 1812-1883 [FFF]
American author
* Spike, Ethan

Whittingham, Charlie 1913- [BBH]
American horse trainer
* [The] Bold Eagle

Whittingham, Mary
See Skuse, Mrs.

Whittington, C. L.
See Whittington, Columbus Lorenzo

Whittington, Columbus Lorenzo 1952-
[FR]
American football player
* Whittington, C. L.

Whittington, Harry [Benjamin] 1915-
[CA]
American author
* Carter, Ashley
* Harrison, Whit
* Holland, Kel
* Myers, Harriet Kathryn
* Phillips, Steve
* Stevens, Blaine
* Stuart, Clay
* Wells, Hondo
* White, Harry
* Whitney, Hallam

Whittington, Nina Eloise 20th c. [BEW]
American producer and director
* Vance, Nina

Whittington, Peter
See Mackay, James [Alexander]

Whittington, Richard [Dick] 1933?-
[HPPN]
American disc jockey
* [The] Radio Stunt Man

Whittington [or Whitynton?], Robert
15th c. [SN]
British grammarian and poet
* Protovates Angliae

Whittington-Egan, Richard 1924- [IAW]
British author
* Barrington, Nicholas
* Curzon, Charles
* Doughty, Nigel

Whittle, Emma
See Clark, Mrs. J. P.

Whittle, John 17th c. [HPPN]
British clergyman
* [A] Minister, Chaplain in the Army

Whittle, Tyler
See Tyler-Whittle, Michael Sidney

Whittlebot, Hernia
See Coward, [Sir] Noel [Pierce]

Whittlesey, Oscar C. 19th c. [IP, PA]
American author
* Bloomer, Ben

[The] Whittling Boy
See Whitney, Eli

Whittridge, Irwin Thomas 1908-1971
[SC]
American actor
* Goode, Jack

Whitty, Edward Michael 1827-1860 [IP]
British journalist
* [The] Stranger in Parliament

Whitty, J. B.
See Whitty, Michael James

Whitty, J. M. 19th c. [IP]
British journalist
* Rock, Captain, in London

Whitty, Michael James 1795-1827 [PI]
Irish poet and journalist
* M J. W.
* O'Rourke, Rory
* W.
* Whitty, J. B.

Whitwell, O'Brien 1870-1915 [BBD]
Irish composer
* Butler, O'Brien

Whitworth, Richard 18th c. [IP]
British politician and author
* Veridicus

Whitworth, Robert 18th c. [HPPN]
British author
* Stot, Joseph

[The] Whiz Kid
See Hutchins, Robert Maynard

Whiz, Walter
See Johnson, Curt[is Lee]

Whoa Bill Phillips
See Phillips, William Corcoran

[The] Whole Duty of Man
See Moncrieff, [Sir] James Wellwood

Whole Hog Hightower
See Hightower, Jim

[The] Whopper
See Paultz, Billy

Whyatt, Frances
See Boyd, Shylah

Whye, Felix
See Dixon, Arthur

Whylock, R. M. 20th c. [CCL]
Canadian poet
* Regis

Whymper, Edward 1840-1911 [HPPN]
British mountaineer and wood engraver
* [The] Conqueror of the Matterhorn
* [The] Scrambler Amongst the Alps

Whyms, Bo
See Whyms, Ronald

Whyms, Ronald 20th c. [RBE]
American boxer
* Whyms, Bo

Whysall, Dodger
See Whysall, W. W.

Whysall, W. W. [EC]
British cricketer
* Whysall, Dodger

Whyte, Donald 1926- [IAW]
Scottish author
* Sennachie

Whyte, Henry 1852?-1913 [WWL]
British author and folklorist
* Fioun

Whyte, Jerome
See Jerchower, Jerome Victor

Whyte, Rollin 20th c. [BBH]
American sailboat racer
* Whyte, Skip

Whyte, Sibley
See Stein, Henry Eugene

Whyte, Skip
See Whyte, Rollin

Whyte Tye
See Wingfield, Lewis

Whyte, Violet
See Stannard, Henrietta Eliza Vaughan

Whyte, William 18th c. [HPPN]
British poet
* W. W.

Whyte, William Pinkney 1824-1908
[HPPN]
American attorney and politician
* [The] Grand Old Man from Maryland
* Wi Chash Ta Ish Nan Nah

Whyte, [Viscount] Y. Melton
See Anderson, G. J. B.

Whytehead, Thomas 1815-1843 [IP]
British clergyman and hymn writer
* [An] Undergraduate

Whytforde, Richard 16th c. [SN]
* [The] Wretch of Sion

Whytock, Ora 1893-1955 [SC]
American actress
* Carew, Ora

Wi Chash Ta Ish Nan Nah
See Whyte, William Pinkney

Wi-chash-ta-Ish-nah-nah
See Phillips, Walter Shelley

Wibberley, Leonard [Patrick O'Connor]
1915- [CA, EMD, SAT]
Irish-born author
* Holton, Leonard

Wibberley, Leonard [Patrick O'Connor]
(cont.)
* O'Connor, Patrick
* Webb, Christopher

Wica, L.
See William

Wicher, Ernie
See Witcher, Ernie

Wick, Air
See Wick, Charles Z.

Wick, Carter
See Wilcox, Collin

Wick, Charles Z. 20th c.
American government official
* Wick, Air

Wick, Stuart Mary
See Freeman, Kathleen

Wickdahl, Lillian 20th c. [ASC]
American composer
* Sandell, Lynn

[The] Wicked
See Pickett, Wilson

[The] Wicked Lord Lyttelton
See Lyttelton, Thomas [Second Baron Lyttelton]

[The] Wicked Thief
See Gesmas [or Gestas]

[The] Wickedest Man in San Francisco
See Bierce, Ambrose [Gwinett]

[The] Wickedest Man in the World
See Crowley, Edward Alexander

Wickenden, William 19th c. [IP, PA]
British poet
* [The] Bard of the Forest

Wickenhauser, Mary 1916- [FC]
American actress
* Wickes, Mary

Wicker, Ireene Seaton 1905- [HPPN]
American singer
* [The] Singing Lady
* [The] Singing Story Lady

Wicker, Kemp Caswell 1906-1973 [BE]
American baseball player
* Whicker, Kemp Caswell

Wicker, Randolfe Hayden
See Hayden, C[harles] Gervin

Wicker, Thomas Grey 1926- [BI, CA, WD]
American author and journalist
* Connolly, Paul

Wickersham, Ned
See Wickersham, Ray

Wickersham, Ray 20th c. [BBH]
American softball player
* Wickersham, Ned

Wickes, Edward Zeus Franklin 19th c.
[DNA]
American author and physician
* Franklin, Edward Zeus

Wickes, Mary
See Wickenhauser, Mary

Wickham, Geoffrey Earle 1919- [ART]
British painter and sculptor
* G. E. W.

Wickham, Hilary Judith 1912- [ART]
British artist
* Hilary

Wickham, Jean 1903- [CA]
American author
* Gordon, Jean

Wickham, John 1923- [CW]
Barbadian author, critic, editor
* Wilsden, Clemensford

Wickham, M. F.
See Wickham, Mabel Frances

Wickham, Mabel Frances 1901- [ART]
British painter
* Wickham, M. F.

Wickham, Mary Fanning
See Bond, Mary Fanning Wickham

Wickham, Tony
See Wickham-Jones, Anthony

Wickham-Jones, Anthony 1922-1948
[BEW]
British actor
* Wickham, Tony

Wickins, Stephen B. 19th c. [IP]
British author
* S. B. W.

Wickliffe
See Mill, John Stuart

Wickliffe
See Winchester, Samuel Gover

Wickliffe, Charles Anderson 1788-1869
[HPPN]
American attorney and politician
* Wickliffe, Duke

Wickliffe, Duke
See Wickliffe, Charles Anderson

Wickliffe, John 1324?-1384 [HPPN]
British religious reformer
* Evangelicus, Doctor
* [The] Gospel Doctor
* [The] Morning Star of the Reformation

Wickliffe, Robert, Jr. ?-1850 [IP]
American author
* Pitt, William
* R. W., Jr.

Wickloe, Peter
See Duff, Douglas Valder

Wicks, Katharine Gibson 1893-1960
[IA]
American author
* Gibson, Katharine

Wicks, Thomas 19th c. [HPPN]
American gambler
* Milwaukee's Most Powerful Gambler

Wickstead, John 19th c. [IP]
British barrister and author
* [A] Fellow Townsman

Wicliffe
See Nares, Robert

Wictorin, John 1907-1969 [BBH]
*Swedish-born skiing organization supporter
and tournament official*
* Swix, Mr.

Widdemer, Irene 19th c. [IP]
American author
* Ward, Ireland

Widdemer, Mabel Cleland 1902-1964
[CA, SAT]
American author
* Cleland, Mabel
* Ludlum, Mabel Cleland

Widdemer, Margaret
See Schauffler, Margaret Widdemer

Widdrington, Roger
See Preston, Roger

[The] Wide Awake
See Louis VI

Wide Awake Moore
See Moore, George W.

[The] Wide Load from Leeds
See Barkley, Charles

Widenhofer, Robert 1943- [SMG]
American football coach
* Widenhofer, Woody

Widenhofer, Woody
See Widenhofer, Robert

Widerman, Robert 1926- [BEW]
French-born actor and singer
* Clary, Robert

Widforss, Gunnar Mauritz 1879-1934
[WBD]
Swedish-born painter
* [The] Painter of the National Parks

Widing, Juha Markku 1947-1985 [FHE,
HK, HR]
Finnish-born hockey player
* Widing, Whitey

Widing, Whitey
See Widing, Juha Markku

Widmark, Richard 1916?- [HPPN]
American actor
* [The] Young Man With a Sneer

Widmer, Mrs. Harry [FFF]
Entertainer
* Mayhew, Katie

Widner, Arthur L. 20th c. [WGT]
Author
* Lambert, Arthur

Widner, Wild Bill
See Widner, William Waterfield

Widner, William Waterfield 1867-1908
[BE]
American baseball player
* Widner, Wild Bill

[The] Widow
See Victoria

[The] Widow Bedott
See Whitcher, Frances Miriam Berry

[The] Widow Capet
See [Josephe Jeanne] Marie Antoinette

[The] Widow of Windsor
See Victoria

[The] Widow of Windy Nook
See Wilson, Mary

Wieand, Franklin Delano Roosevelt
1933- [BE]
American baseball player
* Wieand, Ted

Wieand, Ted
See Wieand, Franklin Delano Roosevelt

Wiechmann, Ferdinand Gerhard 1858-?
[ALY]
American chemist and author
* Monroe, Forest

Wieck, Friedrich 1785-1873 [SN]
* Raro, Master

Wiedefeld, Robert 1903-1972 [HPPN]
American actor and singer
* Weede, Robert

Wieder, Robert S[hannon] 1944- [CA]
American author
* Shannon, Robert

Wiederrecht, Martha Lucile 20th c.
[BEW]
American actress and singer
* Wright, Martha

Wiederump, Trotzhard
See Steiner, Gerolf

Wiegand, Ursula 1930- [IAW]
German author
* Sonntag, Uschi

Wiegel, Master Gabriel 1883-1929
[HPPN]
American actor
* Gabriel, Master

Wieland, Christoph Martin 1733-1813
[DNNF, DNNS, HN]
German poet and author
* [The] German Voltaire
* [Der] Meister
* [The] Voltaire of Germany

Wieman, Elton E. 1896-1971 [BBH, FB]
American football coach
* Wieman, Tad

Wieman, Tad
See Wieman, Elton E.

Wienecke, Gretchen Patricia 1932-
[BEW]
American singer, dancer, actress
* Wyler, Gretchen

Wiener, Francis de [or Franz] 1877-1937
[CD, WBD]
Belgian-born French playwright
* Croisset, Francis de

Wiener, Joan
See Bordow, Joan [Wiener]

Wiener, Norbert 1894-1964 [ESF, HPPN,
JL, WGT]
German-born mathematician and author
* [The] Father of Automation
* [The] Father of Cybernetics
* Norbert, W.

Wiener, Sam
See Dolgoff, Sam

Wiener, Thomas G[ustav] 1917- [CA]
Czech-born author
* Winner, Thomas G[ustav]

Wieniawska, Irene Regine 1880-1932
[BBD]
Belgian-born composer
* Poldowski

Wier, A. M. 19th c. [BDSA]
American writer
* Plunkett, Sarge

Wier, Johannes 1515-1588 [PA]
Author
* Piscinarius

Wier, Stuart Austin 1894- [NAA]
American author
* Austin, Stuart

Wiersbe, Warren Wendell 1929- [CA]
American clergyman and author
* Warren, Dave

Wiersma, Stanley M[arvin] 1930- [CA]
American author and poet
* Buning, Sietze

Wierzbicki, Felix Paul ?-1861 [IP]
Polish-born American author
* Philokalist

Wieselgren, Sigfrid 1843-? [HPPN]
Swedish author
* Horatio
* Wird, Sixten

Wiesengrund, Theodor 1903- [BBD]
German music theorist
* Adorno, Theodor
* Wiesengrund-Adorno, Theodor

Wiesengrund-Adorno, Theodor
See Wiesengrund, Theodor

Wiesner, Portia
See Takakjian, Portia

Wiesser, John Alexander ?-1935
[HPPN]
American actor
* Alexander, John

Wiest, Grace L.
See Deloughery, Grace L.

Wietelmann, Whitey
See Wietelmann, William Frederick

Wietelmann, William Frederick 1919-
[BE, SMG]
American baseball player and coach
* Wietelmann, Whitey

Wiezell, Richard John 1933- [HPPN]
American educator, editor, author
* Field, Andrew John

Wife of a Mormon Elder
See Ferris, Mrs. Benjamin G.

Wigan, Christopher
See Bingley, David Ernest

[The] Wigan Nightingale
See Booth, James

Wigg, T. I. G.
See McCutchan, Philip [Donald]

Wiggen, Henry J.
See Finkelstein, Mark

Wigger, Ralf Harolde 1899-1952? [FC]
American actor
* Harolde, Ralf

Wiggily, Uncle
See Goris, Albert

Wiggin, James Henry 1836-1900
[HPPN]
American clergyman and editor
* Pleigh, Phare

Wiggin, Kate Douglas
See Riggs, Mrs. George C.

Wiggins, Ava June 1934- [OP]
British opera singer
* June, Ava

Wiggins, David 1933- [AW]
British author and educator
* Priestley, Robert

Wiggins, Gerald Foster 1956- [EJ7]
American jazz musician
* Wiggins, J. J.

Wiggins, J. J.
See Wiggins, Gerald Foster

Wiggins, Thomas
See Bethune, Thomas Greene

Wigglesworth, Edward ?-1876 [HPPN]
American attorney
* E. W.
* W.

Wigglesworth, Margaret McKean 20th c.
[BBH]
American skier
* Wigglesworth, Marian

Wigglesworth, Marian
See Wigglesworth, Margaret McKean

Wigglesworth, Martin Francis 1926-
[AW]
British television and radio script writer
* Worth, Martin

Wiggs, Big Jim
See Wiggs, James Alvin [Jimmy]

Wiggs, James Alvin [Jimmy] 1876-1963
[BE]
Norwegian-born baseball player
* Wiggs, Big Jim

Wiggs, Johnny
See Hyman, John Wigginton

Wight, Emily [Carter] 1871-1939 [DNA]
American playwright
* Krag, Mary Miller

Wight, James Alfred 1916- [BI]
Scottish veterinarian and author
* Herriot, James

Wight, James Ambrose [FFF]
American clergyman and writer
* Ambrose

Wight, Lefty
See Wight, William Robert

Wight, Orlando Williams 1824-?
[HPPN]
American author
* O. W. W.

[A] Wight Skilled in Mathematics
See Williams, Dionysius

Wight, William Robert 1922- [BE]
American baseball player
* Wight, Lefty

Wightman, Frieda 1901?-1976 [HCA, THR]
Scottish-born actress
* Inescort, Frieda

Wightman, O. G. R. 18th c. [HPPN]
British author
* [A] Private Gentleman

Wighton, David 1863-? [THR]
British entertainer
* Devant, David

Wigmore
See Fabricius, Johan [Johannes]

Wigmore
See Price, Charles

Wignall, Anne 1912- [CA]
British author
* Acland, Alice
* Marreco, Anne

Wignall, Trevor 1883-1958 [MBF]
Welsh-born author
* Dene, Alan
* Rees, David

Wigniolle, Yvonne 1898- [BEW]
French actress and singer
* Printemps, Yvonne

Wigoder, Thelma 1925- [TR]
British actress
* Ruby, Thelma

Wigram, S. R. 19th c. [FFF]
American author
* Bee, Hookanit, Esq.

[The] Wigwam Girl Murderer
See Sangret, August

Wijnstroom, Christy
See Hoppen-Ram, Henderika
Wilhelmina Christina

Wikstrom, Maud 1946- [SW]
Swedish-born fashion model and actress
* Adams, Maud

Wilber, Babe
See Wilber, Delbert Quentin

Wilber, Bill
See McCoy, Joe

Wilber, Delbert Quentin 1919- [BE]
American baseball player
* Welber, Del
* Wilber, Babe

Wilberforce, Charles
See Maxwell, Robert

Wilberforce, Robert Isaac 1802-1857
[FFF]
British author and clergyman
* Theophilus Secundus

Wilberforce, Samuel 1805-1873 [DEP,
DNNS, SN]
Bishop of Oxford and Winchester
* Soapy Sam

Wilberforce, William 1759-1833 [DNNF,
NPS, RH, SN]
*British religious leader and antislavery
crusader*
* [The] Friend of Man
* [The] Man of Black Renown
* Thou Moral Washington of Africa
* [The] Washington of Africa

Wilbert, Christy
See Wilbert, William

Wilbert, William 1911?-1977 [BI]
American advertising executive
* Wilbert, Christy

Wilborn, Nelson 1907- [BWW]
American singer
* Dirty Red
* Red Devil
* Red Nelson

Wilbraham, Roger 1743-1829 [SN]
* Sempronius

Wilbur, Anna T. 1817-? [PA]
Author
* Leigh, Florence

Wilbur, Caryl
See Sharpe, Wilbur Chaplin

Wilbur, Gilligan
See Wilbur, John

Wilbur, Homer
See Lowell, James Russell

Wilbur, John 20th c.
American football player
* Wilbur, Gilligan

Wilby, Basil Leslie 1930- [AW, WD]
British author
* Knight, Gareth

Wilby, R. Hunt
See Eyster, William Reynolds

Wilc
See Wilczynski, Katerina

Wilcox, Collin 1924- [CA, HPPN]
American author
* Collins, Jeffrey
* Wick, Carter

Wilcox, David 1942- [FB]
American football player
* [The] Intimidator

Wilcox, Don 1908- [ESF, WGT]
American author
* Atomcracker, Buzz-Bolt
* Blade, Alexander [house pseudonym, Ziff-Davis]
* Eldon, Cleo
* Overton, Max
* Shelton, Miles

Wilcox, Ella Wheeler 1850-1919 [HPPN]
American poet and journalist
* [The] People's Poet

Wilcox, Hannah Simms
See Miner, Virginia Scott

Wilcox, Harry 20th c. [WW]
Author
* Derby, Mark

Wilcox, Howard 20th c. [BBH]
American auto racer
* Wilcox, Howdy

Wilcox, Howdy
See Wilcox, Howard

Wilcox, Jess
See Hershman, Morris

Wilcox, Jessica Arline 1925- [CA, HPPN]
American author, actress, model agency executive
* Conover, Jessica Arline Wilcox
* Jones, Candy

Wilcox, John 20th c. [CMA]
Musician
* Wilcox, Willie

Wilcox, L. A.
See Wilcox, Leslie Arthur

Wilcox, Leslie Arthur 1904- [ART]
British artist
* Wilcox, L. A.

Wilcox, Willie
See Wilcox, John

Wilcoxon, Harry 1905- [ITA]
British actor and producer
* Wilcoxon, Henry

Wilcoxon, Henry
See Wilcoxon, Harry

Wilczhowski, Lillian 20th c.
Polish-born entertainer
* Gabor, Chesty
* Morgan, Chesty
* [The] Zsa Zsa Gabor of Burlesque

Wilczynski, Katerina 1894- [ART, DBA]
British painter and etcher
* Wilc

Wild Bill Connelly
See Connelly, William Wirt [Bill]

Wild Bill Cummings
See Cummings, Bill

Wild Bill Davis
See Davis, William Strethen

Wild Bill Davison
See Davison, William

Wild Bill Donavan
See Donavan, William

Wild Bill Donovan
See Donovan, William Edward

Wild Bill Donovan
See Donovan, William Joseph

Wild Bill Douglas
See Douglas, William Orville

Wild Bill Elliott
See Elliott, Gordon

Wild Bill Ezinicki
See Ezinicki, William

Wild Bill Fitzsimmons
See Fitzsimmons, William

Wild Bill Hallahan
See Hallahan, William Anthony

Wild Bill Hancock
See Hancock, Bill

Wild Bill Hickok
See Hickok, James Butler

Wild Bill Hickok
See Hickok, William O.

Wild Bill Hunnefield
See Hunnefield, William Fenton

Wild Bill Hutchison
See Hutchison, William Forrest

Wild Bill Jennings
See Jennings, William P.

Wild Bill Kelly
See Kelly, William

Wild Bill Leard
See Leard, William Wallace [Bill]

Wild Bill Libby
See Libby, Willard Frank

Wild Bill Longley
See Longley, William Preston

Wild Bill Lovett
See Lovett, William L.

Wild Bill Luhrsen
See Luhrsen, William Ferdinand [Bill]

Wild Bill Mehlhorn
See Mehlhorn, William

Wild Bill Miller
See Miller, William Francis [Bill]

Wild Bill Morgan
See Morgan, William

Wild Bill Piercy
See Piercy, William Benton

Wild Bill Pierro
See Pierro, William Leonard [Bill]

Wild Bill Pierson
See Pierson, William Morris [Bill]

Wild Bill the Pony Express Rider
See Cody, William Frederick

Wild Bill Weightman
See Weightman, William E.

Wild Bill Widner
See Widner, William Waterfield

[The] Wild Boar of the Ardennes
See La Marck, Guillaume [or William] de

[The] Wild Boy
See Hauser, Kaspar

[The] Wild Boy
See Peter

Wild Bull McEver
See McEver, Eugene T.

[The] Wild Bull of the Pampas
See Firpo, Luis Angel

Wild Cat
See Coacoochee

Wild Charlie Wyatt
See Wyatt, Nathaniel Ellsworth

Wild Child Butler
See Butler, George

[The] Wild Colonial Boy
See Donahoe, Jack

[The] Wild Elk of the Wasatch
See Heusser, Edward Burleton

Wild, Faran
See Selz, Ralph Jerome Von Braun

Wild Goose Bill
See Condit, Samuel Wilbur

Wild, Henry 1684?-1734 [DEP, DNNF, DNNS]
British tailor who mastered seven foreign languages
* [The] Arabian Tailor
* [The] Learned Tailor

[The] Wild Hickory Nut
See Gibbons, Euell

Wild Horse Annie
See Johnston, Velma B.

Wild Horse Charlie Alexander
See Alexander, Charles W.

Wild Horse Crosby
See Crosby, Bob

[The] Wild Horse of the Osage
See Martin, John Leonard

Wild Horse Sheridan
See Sheridan, Neill Rawlins

[The] Wild Humorist of the Pacific Slope
See Clemens, Samuel Langhorne

[The] Wild Irish Girl
See Morgan, Sydney Owenson

Wild, Johann 1485-1554 [PA]
Author
* Ferus

Wild, Jonathan 1682?-1725 [HPPN]
British criminal
* [The] Great

[The] Wild Man
See Shore, Edward William [Eddie]

[The] Wild Man
See Talmadge, Eugene

Wild Man Fischer
See Fischer, Larry

[The] Wild Man from Hoboken
See Kennedy, Matthew Patrick

Wild Man From Sugar Creek
See Talmadge, Eugene

[The] Wild Man of American Literary Criticism
See Fiedler, Leslie A[aron]

[The] Wild Man of Brooklyn
See Barney, Rex

[The] Wild Man of Pop
See Hendrix, James Marshall [Jimi]

[The] Wild Methodist
See Abrams, Isaac

[The] Wild One
See Cottrell, Morganna Roberts

Wild, Reginald Leonard 1912- [AW]
British author
* Edwards, Leonard

Wild Rose
See Badger, Miss

[The] Wild Shaman of the Beat Generation
See Ginsberg, Allen

Wild Steed
See Long, Earl Kemp

Wild Willie
See Trognitz, Raymond William

Wild Willie Chaney
See Chaney, Willie

Wild Willie Moore
See Moore, Willie

Wildair, Harry
See Corbet, William John

Wildair, [Sir] Harry
See Farquhar, George

Wildbore, Charles ?-1802 [FFF, HPPN]
British clergyman, mathematician, writer
* Amicus
* Eumenes

Wildcat Jack Stilwell
See Stilwell, Simpson E.

Wilde, Cathrine
See Wilde, Cleo

Wilde, Cleo 1932- [HPPN]
American singer
* Wilde, Cathrine

Wilde, D. Gunther
See Hurwood, Bernhardt J[ackson]

Wilde, Hilary
See Breton-Smith, Clare

Wilde, James [Jimmy] 1892-1969 [BX, HPPN, OCS, RBE]
British boxer
* [The] Ghost with a Hammer in His Hand
* [The] Mighty Atom
* [The] Welsh Wonder

Wilde, Jane Francesca Elgee 1826?-1896 [CEC, PI]
Irish author and poet
* A.
* Ellis, John Fanshawe
* Speranza

Wilde, Jennifer
See Huff, Tom Elmer

Wilde, Jimmy
See Creasey, John

Wilde, Jocelyn
See Toombs, John

Wilde, Kathey
See King, Patricia

Wilde, Larry
See Wildman, Larry

Wilde, Oscar [Fingal O'Flahertie Wills] 1854-1900 [FFF, HPPN, LC, SAT]
Irish poet and playwright
* [The] Apostle of Aestheticism
* C. 3. 3.
* Melmoth, Sebastian
* [The] New Dress-Improver
* Playfair, I.

Wilde, Patricia
See White, Patricia Lorrainann

Wilde, Professor
See Elworthy, Albert Henry

Wilde, Richard Henry 1789-1847 [HPPN, PI]
Irish-born poet and politician
* De Lancy, FitzHugh
* Delaney, Fitzhugh

Wilde, Robert 17th c. [SN]
Author
* [The] Withers of the City

Wilde, Susie
See Adams, Mrs. Mark

Wilde, Vyvyan Beresford 1886-1967 [CA]
British author and translator
* Holland, Vyvyan [Beresford]

Wilde, William Charles Kingsley 1852-1899 [PI]
Irish poet and author
* Sauvage, Frere

Wildeblood, Joan
See Murray, Joan

Wildenwey, Herman Theodore
See Portaas, Herman Theodore

Wilder
See Fox, George Wilder

Wilder, Alec 1907- [HPPN]
American composer
* [The] President of the Derrieregarde

Wilder, Alexander 19th c. [FFF]
American journalist
* Merlin
* Plautus

Wilder, Billy
See Wilder, Samuel

Wilder, Cherry
See Grimm, Cherry Barbara

Wilder, Gene
See Silberman, Jerome

Wilder, Joan
See Lanigan, Catherine

Wilder, Katherine Loving Buell 1889- [WWL]
American author
* Buell, Wilder

Wilder, Marshall Pinckney 1798-1886 [HPPN]
American educator and author
* [The] President

Wilder, Rose
See Lane, Rose Wilder

Wilder, Samuel 1906- [FC, FD]
Austrian-born writer and director
* Wilder, Billy

Wilder, Stephen
See Lesser, Milton

Wilder, Thornton Niven 1897- [HPPN]
American author and playwright
* [The] Grand Old Novelist

Wilder, William West
See Patten, William George

[The] Wildest Indian
See Ishi

Wildest of the West
See Smith, Jefferson Randolph

Wildey, Thomas 1782-1868 [HPPN]
British-American cabinetmaker and organizer of fraternal order
* [The] Father of the I. O. O. F.

Wildfire
See Wyndham, [Sir] William

Wildfire, Madge
See Graham, Esther

Wildfire, Will
See Windham, William

[The] Wildflower of the Linden Field
See Clement, Lewis

Wildgoose, Geoffrey
See Graves, Richard

Wildgoose, [Mr.] Geoffry
See Trelawney, [Rev. Sir] Harry

Wilding, Anthony F. 20th c. [OET]
New Zealand-born tennis player
* Little Hercules

Wilding, Eric
See Tubb, Edwin Charles

Wilding, Ernest
See Molloy, Joseph Fitzgerald

Wilding, Philip 20th c. [ESF, SFL, WGT]
British author
* Fraser, Jefferson?
* Haynes, John Robert
* Marshall, Lloyd?
* Russell, Erle?
* Stanton, Borden?
* Stewart, Logan
* Stuart, Logan?

Wilding, Sten
See Liljenfors, Bennie Mads Carl

Wildman, Larry 1928- [JL]
American comedian and author
* Wilde, Larry

Wildon, R. G.
See Dowling, Richard

Wildrake
See Tattersall, George

Wilds, Honey
See Wilds, Lee Davis

Wilds, Lee Davis 1903?-1982
American country-western performer
* Wilds, Honey

Wildwood
See Winson, J. W.

Wildwood, Will
See Pond, Frederick Eugene

Wilenchick, Clem ?-1958 [SC]
Actor
* Whitley, Crane

Wiles, Domini
See High-Smith, Domini

Wiles, Greenbury F. 19th c. [HPPN]
American army officer
* Old Whiskers

Wiles, Joseph St. Clair 1914- [BA]
American pharmacologist
* Wiles, Sonny

Wiles, Sonny
See Wiles, Joseph St. Clair

Wiley, [Rev.] Allen 1797-1848 [HPPN]
American clergyman
* [A] Friend to Ministers

Wiley, Bell
See Strauss, Frances

Wiley, Carl A. 20th c. [WGT]
Author
* Saunders, Russell

Wiley, Charles A. 1925- [BI]
American bandmaster
* Wiley, Pete

Wiley, Coyote
See Wiley, Mark Eugene

Wiley, Doc
See Wiley, Washeba

Wiley, Flash
See Wiley, Fletcher Houston

Wiley, Fletcher Houston 1942- [BA]
American attorney
* Wiley, Flash

Wiley, John
See Graham, Roger Phillips

Wiley, Margaret L.
See Marshall, Margaret Lenore Wiley

Wiley, Mark Eugene 1948- [SMG]
American baseball player
* Wiley, Coyote

Wiley, Pete
See Wiley, Charles A.

Wiley, Stan
See Hill, John S[tanley]

Wiley, Washeba [OBW]
American baseball player
* Wiley, Doc

Wilford, Charles
See Dukes, Charles W.

Wilfred, Wilf
See Cude, Wilfred

Wilfrid, [Brother]
See Chatelain, Wilfrid

Wilhelm
See Benn, Mary

Wilhelm
See Brewer, William A.

Wilhelm
See Sikes, William Wirt

Wilhelm, C.
See Pitcher, William John Charles

Wilhelm, Charles Ernest 1929- [BE]
American baseball player
* Wilhelm, Spider

Wilhelm, Georg 1885-? [HPPN]
German film director
* Pabst, G. W.

Wilhelm, Irvin Key 1874-1936 [AS, BE, BN]
American baseball player
* Wilhelm, Kaiser
* Wilhelm, Little Eva

Wilhelm, James Hoyt 1923- [SMG]
American baseball player
* Wilhelm, Knuckles

Wilhelm, Kaiser
See Wilhelm, Irvin Key

Wilhelm, Kate
See Knight, Kate Wilhelm

Wilhelm, Knuckles
See Wilhelm, James Hoyt

Wilhelm, Little Eva
See Wilhelm, Irvin Key

Wilhelm, Spider
See Wilhelm, Charles Ernest

Wilhelmina
See Cooper, Wilhelmina [Behmenburg]

Wilhelmina Carolina 1683-1737 [HPPN]
Queen of Great Britain and Ireland
* Caroline of Ansbach

Wilhem, Guillaume-Louis
See Bocquillon, Guillaume-Louis

Wilhoite, Donald MacRae, Jr. 1909- [ASC, PMJ]
American songwriter
* Raye, Don

Wilkening, Howard [Everett] 1909- [CA]
American psychologist and author
* Stokes, Robert [Bob]

Wilkens, Leonard [Lenny] 1937- [HPPN]
American basketball player
* [The] Will o' the Wisp

Wilkens, Maybritt 1933?- [FC, SW]
Swedish actress
* Britt, May

Wilkerson, Claude 1955?- [TI 1-24-83]
American murderer
* Ches-ne-o-na-eh [The Man Who Kills the Wolves]

Wilkerson, Sergeant
See Demara, Ferdinand Waldo, Jr.

Wilkes, Ada
See McLeod, Mrs. J. F.

Wilkes, Charles 1798-1877 [HPPN]
American naval officer and explorer
* [The] Stormy Voyager

Wilkes, George 1817-1885 [HPPN]
American journalist, editor, publisher
* [An] Old Line Democrat

Wilkes, Jamaal 1953- [SMG]
American basketball player
* Wilkes, Silk

Wilkes, Jim 20th c.
American baseball player
* Wilkes, Junior

Wilkes, John 1727-1797 [HPPN, NPS]
British politician and author
* Borewell, Pego
* [Il] Bruto Iglese
* [The] Extraordinary Mr. Wilkes

Wilkes, John (cont.)
* [The] Idol of the Mob
* [A] Member of Parliament
* Squinting Jack

Wilkes, Junior
See Wilkes, Jim

Wilkes, Silk
See Wilkes, Jamaal

Wilkes, Thomas
See Derrick, Samuel

Wilkes, W. 20th c. [MBF]
British author
* Evelyn, A. W.

Wilkes-Hunter, Richard 1906- [AW, CA]
Australian author and journalist
* Ballard, Dean
* Brody, Marc
* Conrad, Tod
* Crane, Alex
* Douglas, Shane
* Dunn, James
* Gordon, Peter
* Mitchell, Kerry
* O'Neill, C. M.
* Sanders, Kent
* Shulberg, Alan

Wilkie, Aldon Jay 1914- [BE]
Canadian-born baseball player
* Wilkie, Lefty

Wilkie, [Sir] David 1785-1841 [DEP, RH, SN]
Scottish painter
* [The] Raphael of Domestic Art
* [The] Scottish Teniers

Wilkie, Franc Bangs 1832-1892 [DNA, FFF]
American author and journalist
* Poliuto

Wilkie, Lefty
See Wilkie, Aldon Jay

Wilkie, William 1721-1772 [DEL, FFF, RH]
Scottish poet
* [The] Homer of Scotland
* [The] Scottish Homer

Wilkin, Maria 19th c. [HPPN]
British author
* Maria

Wilkin, Wee Willie
See Wilkin, Wilbur

Wilkin, Wilbur ?-1973 [FB]
American football player
* Wilkin, Wee Willie

Wilkins, Alan Haydn 1953- [DC]
Welsh cricketer
* Wilkins, Wilki

Wilkins, Alonzo 1939-1972 [BBH, IBW]
American wheelchair basketball player
* Wilkins, Willie [or Willy]

Wilkins, Aminda Ann Badeau 20th c. [IBW]
American social worker
* Wilkins, Minnie

Wilkins, Dominique 1960?-
American basketball player
* Dunk, Dr.

Wilkins, E. G. P. [PA]
Author
* Personne

Wilkins, Harriet Annie 1829-1888 [FFF]
Canadian poet
* Harriet Annie

Wilkins, Henry George [BI]
British author
* Woodley, H. G.

Wilkins, Isaac 1741-1830 [PA]
Author
* Farmer, A. W.

Wilkins, Marilyn [Ruth] 1926- [CA]
American author
* Wilkins, Marne

Wilkins, Marne
See Wilkins, Marilyn [Ruth]

Wilkins, Mary E.
See Freeman, Mary Eleanor Wilkins

Wilkins, Mary Huiskamp Calhoun 1926- [TBJ]
American author
* Calhoun, Mary

Wilkins, Minnie
See Wilkins, Aminda Ann Badeau

Wilkins, Peter
See Paltock, Robert

Wilkins, Roy 1901-1981 [HPPN]
American civil rights advocate
* [The] Enormous Figure in the Movement
* [The] Last of the Giants

Wilkins, [Robert] Tim[othy] 1896- [BWW, NBB]
American singer
* Keghouse
* Oliver, Tim

Wilkins, Wilki
See Wilkins, Alan Haydn

Wilkins, William 1852-? [PI]
Irish poet and writer
* Weatherly, William

Wilkins, William A. [PA]
Author
* Greene, Hiram

Wilkins, Willie [or Willy]
See Wilkins, Alonzo

Wilkinson, Anna 1942- [TR]
British actress
* Carteret, Anna

Wilkinson, Bonara
See Overstreet, Bonaro Wilkinson

Wilkinson, Bud
See Wilkinson, Charles Burnham

Wilkinson, Buzz
See Wilkinson, Richard

Wilkinson, Charles Burnham 1916- [FB, HPPN, OCS]
American football coach
* [The] Golden Man of the Gridiron
* Wilkinson, Bud

Wilkinson, Cyril Theodore Anstruther 1884-1970 [OCS]
British field hockey player and cricketer
* Wilkinson, Wilkie

Wilkinson, Ellen 20th c. [PPN]
British politician
* Wilkinson, Red Ellen

Wilkinson, Fred 1894-1966 [THR]
British theatrical press representative
* Gratton, Fred

Wilkinson, Henry 1616-1690 [NPS]
British educator
* Dean Harry

Wilkinson, Henry, Jr. 1610-1675 [NPS, SN]
British politician
* Long Harry

Wilkinson, Iris Guiver 1906-1939 [LC, TCL]
New Zealand poet and author
* Hyde, Robin

Wilkinson, Jan 1931- [TR]
British actress
* Holden, Jan

Wilkinson, Jennie Gaudio 20th c. [IWM]
American musician
* Gaudio, Jennie

Wilkinson, John [Donald] 1929- [CA]
British clergyman and author
* Ironmaster, Maximus

Wilkinson, Lorna Hilda Kathleen 1909- [CAP]
British author
* Deane, Lorna

Wilkinson, Louis Umfreville 1881-1966 [LC]
British author
* Marlow, Louis

Wilkinson, Marguerite Ogden 1883-1928 [HPPN]
American poet
* Graves, Harley

Wilkinson, Mrs. Arthur P. [FFF]
Entertainer
* Dudley, Perle

Wilkinson, Mrs. R. O. [FFF]
Entertainer
* Quinn, Kitty

Wilkinson, Nicholas 1575?-1623 [HPPN]
British actor
* Tooley, Nicholas

Wilkinson, Percy Francis Hamilton
1912-   [AW, WD]
British author
* Wilkinson, Tim

Wilkinson, Red Ellen
See Wilkinson, Ellen

Wilkinson, Richard 1932-   [BB]
American basketball player
* Wilkinson, Buzz

Wilkinson, Ronald 1920-   [CA]
British physician and author
* Scott Thorn, Ronald

Wilkinson, Tate 1739-1803   [HPPN]
British actor, manager, author
* [The] Eighteenth Century Barnstormer

Wilkinson, Tim
See Wilkinson, Percy Francis Hamilton

Wilkinson, Wilkie
See Wilkinson, Cyril Theodore
Anstruther

Wilks, Brian 1933-   [CA]
British educator and playwright
* Hughes, Sam

Wilks, Cork
See Wilks, Theodore [Ted]

Wilks, Madge 1880-?   [THR]
British actress
* Fabian, Madge

Wilks, Theodore [Ted] 1915-   [BE, PB]
American baseball player
* Wilks, Cork

Will
See Lipkind, William

Will, Butch
See Will, Robert Lee

Will o' the Wisp
See Boswell, James

Will o' the Wisp
See Papaleo, William

[The] Will o' the Wisp
See Wilkens, Leonard [Lenny]

Will R.
See Roberts, Will

Will, Robert Lee 1931-   [BE]
American baseball player
* Will, Butch

Willadsen, Gene
See Lynn, Jane Thursten

Willamow, Johann Gottlieb 1736-1777
[SN]
Prussian poet
* [The] Prussian Pindar

Willard, Big Jess
See Willard, Jess

Willard, C. D.
See Diffin, Charles W[illard]

Willard, Caroline McCoy [White] 1853-?
[DNA, NPS]
American author
* Penn, Rachel

Willard, Charles
See Armstrong, John Byron

Willard, Cowboy Jess
See Willard, Jess

Willard, Frances Elizabeth Caroline
1839-1898   [HPPN]
*American educator, reformer, temperance
advocate*
* [The] Silver Tongued and Golden
  Hearted
* [The] Uncrowned Queen of American
  Womanhood

Willard, James A. 1889-1952   [HPPN]
American radio personality
* Uncle Wip

Willard, Jess 1881-1968   [BX, HPPN,
RBE, WBC]
American boxer
* [The] Kansas Giant
* [The] Pottawatomie Giant
* Willard, Big Jess
* Willard, Cowboy Jess

Willard, John
See Bolte, John Willard

Willard, John
See Clawson, John

Willard, John
See Ray, James Earl

Willard, Joseph 1798-1865   [HPPN]
American historian
* J. W.

Willard, Josiah Flynt 1869-1907   [EMD,
TC, WW]
American author
* Flynt, Josiah

Willard, Mrs. Charles   [FFF]
Entertainer
* Sothern, Ella

Willard, Portman
See Norwood, Victor G[eorge] C[harles]

Willard, Samuel 1775-1859   [HPPN]
American clergyman
* S. W.

Willart, C. A. 1879-1937   [HPPN]
American producer
* Willart, Doc

Willart, Doc
See Willart, C. A.

Willbanks, Alexander 20th c.   [HPPN]
American clergyman and evangelist
* [The] Black Billy Sunday

Willcox, J. K. Hamilton   [PA]
Author
* Fawcette, Wyliaume

Willcox, Orlando Bolivar 1823-1907
[FFF, PA]
American army officer and author
* March, Major
* March, Walter

Wille, Janet Neipris 1936-   [CA]
American playwright
* Neipris, Janet

Willebrands, Johannes 1910?-
Dutch cardinal
* [The] Flying Dutchman

Willebrandt, Mabel Walker 1889-1963
[HPPN, NW 9-5-83]
American attorney and politician
* [The] Prohibition Portia
* [The] Scourge of the Bootleggers

Willeford, Charles [Ray, III] 1919-
[CA, WD]
American author, poet, playwright
* Charles, Will

Willemer, Marianne von 1784-1860
[WBD]
*Friend of German poet, Johann
Wolfgang von Goethe*
* Zuleika

Willenan, M. W.   [PA]
Author
* Prairie Bird

Willens, Paul Norton 1938-   [BEW]
American actor, dancer, singer
* Wallace, Paul

Willer?
See Emshwiller, Ed[mund Alexander]

Willes, Irwin ?-1871   [FFF, RH]
British journalist
* Argus
* Argus the Exile

Willes, Jean
See Donahue, Jean

Willet, Mittens
See Aveling, Mrs. Henry

Willet, Slim
See Moore, Winston Lee

Willets, Walter E. 1924-   [CA]
American editor and author
* Weaver, Earle

Willett, Edward 1830-1889   [WW]
American author and editor
* Brent, Carl
* Henderson, J. Stanley

Willett, [Brother] Franciscus 1922-   [CA,
HPPN]
American author
* Bond, Ian
* Premont, [Brother] Jeremy
* Primm, [Brother] Orrin

Willett, Mrs.
See Coombe-Tennant, Winifred
Margaret Serocold

Willett, Richard 19th c.   [HPPN]
British author
* [A] Parishoner

Willetts, R. F.
See Willetts, Ronald Frederick

Willetts, Ronald Frederick 1915-
[WYA]
Author
* Willetts, R. F.

Willey, Abby
See Chamberlain, Mrs. R. B.

Willey, Bill
See Willey, David

Willey, Carl
See Willey, Carlton Francis

Willey, Carlton Francis 1931-   [BE]
American baseball player
* Willey, Carl

Willey, Chin
See Willey, Peter

Willey, David 20th c.   [BI]
American collector
* Willey, Bill

Willey, Norman 20th c.   [EF]
American football player
* Willey, Wildman

Willey, Peter 1949-   [DC]
British cricketer
* Willey, Chin
* Willey, Will

Willey, Robert
See Ley, Willy

Willey, Wildman
See Willey, Norman

Willey, Will
See Willey, Peter

Willfried, H.
See Villinger, Hermine

William ?-1406   [SN]
Duke of Austria
* [The] Delightful

William 11th c.   [NPS]
Count of Apulia
* Bras de Fer

William 1143-1214   [FFF, HN, RH]
King of Scotland
* [The] Lion

William 1196-1226   [DHA, DNNS]
Earl of Salisbury
* Longsword

William 1884-?   [HPPN]
Prince of Sweden
* Wica, L.

William 1982-
Son of Charles, Prince of Wales
* [The] Prince of Wails
* Sweet William

William
See Evarts, Jeremiah

William, Arnold
See Meadowcroft, Ernest [William]

William August Charles Frederick Adolf
1817-1905   [WBD]
Duke of Nassau
* Adolf of Nassau

William Augustus 1721-1765   [DEP,
DNNF, HPPN, NPS, SN]
Duke of Cumberland
* Billy the Butcher
* [The] Bloody Butcher
* [The] Bloody Duke of Cumberland
* [The] Butcher of Culloden
* Cumberland, Butcher
* Nolkejumskoi

William, David
See Williams, David

William Frederick 1776-1834   [DNNS,
HN, NPS]
Duke of Gloucester
* Silly Billy
* Slice

William, Joseph 1878-1939   [SC]
Actor
* Ranger Bill

William of Champeaux 1070?-1121
[DNNF, FFF, NPS]
French philosopher
* [The] Pillar of Doctors
* [The] Venerable Doctor
* Veneralbilis, Doctor

William of Malmsbury
See Somerset, William

William of Munster
See Kenealy, William

William of Orange
See William III

William of Ruysbroeck [or Rubrouck]
See Rubruquis, Guillaume

William of Wykeman [or Wickham]
1324-1404   [HPPN]
British prelate and statesman
* [The] Father of the English Public
  School System

William Powlett, Katherine 1911-
[ART]
British painter
* K. W. P.

William Rufus
See William II

[The] William Tell of the Tyrol
See Hofer, Andreas

William the Conqueror
See Kempe, William

William the Conqueror
See Prynne, William

William the Conqueror
See Waller, [Sir] William

William the Red
See Wright, William Simmons

William the Testy
See Kieft, William

William, Warren
See Krech, Warren William

William I ?-943   [DNNS, FFF, RH]
Duke of Normandy
* Longsword

William I 886-918   [WBD]
Duke of Aquitaine
* [The] Pious

William I 1027-1087   [DNNS, HN, RH]
King of England
* [The] Bastard
* [The] Conqueror
* [The] Norman

William I 1120-1166   [DNNS, HN, SN]
King of Sicily
* [The] Bad

William I 1533-1584   [DNNS, FFF, RH]
Prince of Orange
* [The] Father of the Dutch Republic
* [The] High Born Demosthenes
* [The] Silent

William I [Wilhelm Friedrich Ludwig]
1797-1888   [HN, RH, SN]
Emperor of Germany
* [The] Emperor of the German
  Kingdoms
* Kartaetschenprinz
* Tartuffe, Kaiser

William II 1056?-1100   [HN, HPPN, RH,
SN]
King of England
* [The] Red King
* Rufus
* Rufus the Red
* William Rufus

William II 1154-1189   [DNNS, HN, SN]
King of Sicily
* [The] Good

**William II [Friedrich Wilhelm Viktor
Albert]** 1859-1941   [DEP, HPPN]
Emperor of Germany
* [The] Bagman
* [The] Kaiser
* Kaiser Bill
* [The] Previous
* [The] Talkative
* [The] Young Man

William III 1650-1702   [DEP, DHA,
HPPN, PPN, SN]
King of England
* [The] Deliverer
* Dutch Billy
* Dutch William
* [The] Dutchman
* [The] Gallic Bully
* Old Glorious
* William of Orange

William IV 1532-1592   [WBD]
Landgrave of Hesse-Cassel
* [The] Wise

William IV 1765-1837   [DNNS, FFF,
HN, HPPN, NPS]
King of England
* [The] Flogster
* [The] Sailor King

William IV (cont.)
* Sailor William
* Silly Billy

William IV
See Friso, Charles Henry

William V 960?-1030 [WBD]
Duke of Aquitaine
* [The] Great

Williams
See Grover, William

Williams
See Townley, Michael Vernon

Williams, A. B. 1897?-1964 [BEW]
Theatrical performer
* Williams, Racehorse

Williams, A. C. 20th c. [IBW]
American disc jockey and glee club director
* Williams, Moohah

Williams, Ace
See Bamber, Wallace Eugene

Williams, Ace
See Williams, Robert Fulton

Williams, Al
See Williams, Almon Edward

Williams, Alan Moray 1915- [IAW]
British author and journalist
* Robert the Rhymer

Williams, Albert [Albie] 1917- [HPPN]
American reformed jewel thief and writer
* Cooper, Albert
* [The] Matinee Burglar
* [The] World's Foremost Jewel Thief

Williams, Albert O.
See Deeming, Frederick Bailey

Williams, Alex 19th c. [HPPN]
American politician
* Alexander the Great

Williams, Alexander ?-1917 [HPPN]
American police officer
* [The] Clubber

Williams, Allen H. 1906- [HPPN]
American entertainer
* [The] Vigo Voyeur

Williams, Alma Claire 1928- [OP]
American opera singer
* Barlow, Klara

Williams, Almon Edward 1914-1969
[BE]
American baseball player
* Williams, Al

Williams, Alva Mitchel 1882-1933 [BE]
American baseball player
* Williams, Rip

Williams, Andre 1936?- [BWW]
American singer
* Rhythm, Mr.
* Williams, Bacon Fat

Williams, Andrew 1906?- [PMJ]
American jazz musician
* Williams, Sandy

Williams, Andrew 20th c. [OBW]
American baseball player
* Williams, Stringbean

Williams, Andy
See Lavender, Glenn

Williams, Anna Bolles 1840-? [HPPN]
American author
* J. A. K.

Williams, Annabelle
See Rucker, Annabelle

Williams, Anson 1949?- [BI]
American actor
* Williams, Potsie

Williams, Anthony Sampson
See Cohen, Paul Arthur

Williams, August 1888-1964 [BE]
American baseball player
* Williams, Gloomy Gus

Williams, Augustine H. 1870-1890 [BE]
American baseball player
* Williams, Gus

Williams, Avril 1932- [TR]
British actress
* Elgar, Avril

Williams, Bacon Fat
See Williams, Andre

Williams, Barney
See Lebrowitz, Barney

Williams, Barney
See O'Flaherty, Bernard

Williams, Bay Boy
See Williams, Matthew

Williams, Bearcat
See Williams, John Overton

Williams, Bel
See Williams, Everett Belvin

Williams, Ben
See Williams, Robert Jerry

Williams, Benjamin 1831-1923 [WBD]
British painter
* Leader, Benjamin Williams

Williams, Berl 1919?-1978 [FIR]
Comedian
* Funny, Mr.

Williams, Bert
See Williams, Egbert Austin

Williams, Beryl
See Epstein, Beryl [Williams]

Williams, Bessie
See Henderson, Rosa [Rose]

Williams, Bessie
See McCoy, Viola

Williams, Big Boy
See Williams, Guinn

Williams, Big Cat
See Williams, Clarence

Williams, Big Cat
See Williams, Evan

Williams, Big Joe
See Williams, Joe

Williams, Bill
See Crawford, William [Elbert]

Williams, Bill
See Katt, William Henry

Williams, Billy
See Williams, Paul B.

Williams, Billy Dee
See December, William, Jr.

Williams, Billy Leo 1938- [HPPN]
American baseball player
* [The] Mechanical Man

Williams, Blazer
See Williams, Cecil

Williams, Blind Boy
See McGhee, Walter Brown

Williams, Blinky
See Williams, Sondra

Williams, Blue Jeans
See Williams, James Douglas

Williams, Booker
See Fleischer, Leonore

Williams, Boyd 20th c. [EF]
American football player
* Williams, Tex

Williams, Bransby 1870-1961 [BMH]
British entertainer
* [The] Actor Mimic
* [The] Hamlet of the Halls

Williams, Bransby
See Pharez, Bransby William

Williams, Brian 1904-1969 [BF]
British actor
* Williams, Hugh

Williams, Buddy
See Williams, George Henry

Williams, Bullet
See Williams, Jim

Williams, Burton 20th c. [EF]
American football player
* Williams, Cy

Williams, Buster
See Williams, Charles Anthony, Jr.

Williams, Butch
See Williams, Warren Milton

Williams, Buttons
See Williams, James Thomas

Williams, Cadillac
See Williams, Nelson

Williams, Campbell
See Smith, Campbell Sherston

Williams, Cap
See Williams, Marshall McDiarmid

Williams, Cara
See Kamiat, Bernice

Williams, Carbine
See Williams, David M.

Williams, Carl 20th c.
American boxer
* [The] Truth

Williams, Carol 1929- [WD]
American author
* Fenner, Carol

Williams, Cecil 1936?- [CW]
West Indian poet and playwright
* Williams, Blazer

Williams, Charles 1908?-1985 [NW 9-30-85]
American jazz musician
* Williams, Cootie

Williams, Charles
See Collier, James L[incoln]

Williams, Charles Anthony, Jr. 1942-
[EJ7]
American jazz musician
* Williams, Buster

Williams, Charles Hanbury 1709-1759
[FFF]
British author and diplomat
* Carl

Williams, Charles Henry 1896-1952
[MK]
American baseball player
* Williams, Lefty

Williams, Charles J. [PA]
Author
* Blue Jay

Williams, Charles Melvin 1908- [ASC, DAM, EJ]
American jazz musician
* Williams, Cootie

Williams, Charles Prosek 1947- [SMG]
American baseball player
* Williams, Knuck-Z

Williams, Charles Richard
See Malpass, Barbara Ann

Williams, Chester
See Schechter, William

Williams, Chickie
See Smik, Jessie Wanda

Williams, Chino 1934- [IBW]
American actor
* Williams, Fats

Williams, Claerwen 1938- [CA]
Australian-born author
* Lang, Maud

Williams, Clancy
See Williams, Clarence

Williams, Clarence 1942- [FB]
American football player
* Williams, Clancy

Williams, Clarence 1946- [SMG]
American football player
* Williams, Big Cat

Williams, Claude 1908- [EJ7, WP 1-1-85]
American jazz musician
* [The] Fiddler
* Williams, Fiddler

Williams, Claude Preston 1893-1959
[AS, BE, PB]
American baseball player
* Williams, Lefty

Williams, Clyde C. 1881-1974 [CAP, SAT]
American author
* Williams, Slim

Williams, Coe
See Harrison, C. William

Williams, Colin 1934- [CA]
British author and screenwriter
* Welland, Colin

Williams, Colonel Bill
See Williams, William [Bill]

Williams, Cootie
See Williams, Charles

Williams, Cootie
See Williams, Charles Melvin

Williams, Craig [OBW]
American baseball player
* Williams, Stringbean

Williams, Cris
See DeCristoforo, Romeo John

Williams, Cy
See Williams, Burton

Williams, Cy
See Williams, Fred

Williams, Cyclone
See Williams, Joseph

Williams, D. 20th c. [WBD]
British author
* Williams, Patry [joint pseudonym with M. Patry]

Williams, D.
See Ronald, David William

Williams, D. E. [PA]
Author
* Publicola

Williams, Dale
See Williams, Elisha Alphonso

Williams, Daniel Hale 1856-1931
[HPPN]
American surgeon
* [The] Father of the Heart Transplant

Williams, Danny
See McWilliam, Andrew

Williams, Dave 1954- [SMG]
Canadian hockey player
* Williams, Tiger

Williams, David 1738-1816 [NPS]
Clergyman
* [The] Priest of Nature

Williams, David 1926- [TR]
British actor and director
* William, David

Williams, David 1946- [EJ7]
West Indian jazz musician
* Williams, Happy

Williams, David Carter 1891-1962 [BE]
American baseball player
* Williams, Mutt

Williams, David M. 1901-1975
American inventor
* Williams, Carbine

Williams, David Rhys 20th c. [WGT]
Author
* Gan Index

Williams, David Rogerson 1776-1830
[HPPN]
American manufacturer, army officer, politician
* Williams, Thunder and Lightning

Williams, Dee
See Williams, Dewey Edgar

Williams, Denny
See Williams, Evon Daniel

Williams, Dewey Edgar 1916- [BE]
American baseball player
* Williams, Dee

Williams, Diamond
See Williams, James

Williams, Diamond George
See Williams, George Eddy

Williams, Dib
See Williams, Edwin Dibrell

Williams, Dino
See Williams Don[ald Reid]

Williams, Dionysius 1732?-1775 [HPPN]
British mathematician
* [A] Wight Skilled in Mathematics

Williams, Doc
See Smik, Andrew J., Jr.

Williams, Doc
See Williams, Henry L.

Williams Don[ald Reid] 1935- [BE]
American baseball player
* Williams, Dino

Williams, Don 20th c. [WP 9-30-83]
American country-western performer
* [The] Gentle Giant of Country Music

Williams, Dootsie
See Williams, Walter, Jr.

Williams, Dorian 1914- [IAW]
British author
* Pied Piper

Williams, Duke
See Williams, Walter Herman

Williams, E. C.
See Williams, Eric Cyril

Williams, E. N.
See Williams, Ernest Neville

Williams, Earl A. 1928- [IBW]
American businessman
* Williams, Skip

Williams, Earl Craig 1948- [SMG]
American baseball player
* Williams, Heavy

Williams, Ed
See Christian, William

Williams, Eddie
See Kilbridge, Patrick

Williams, Edith 1906- [THR]
American actress
* Barrett, Edith

Williams, Edward 1745-1826 [DEP,
DNNS, NPS, WBD]
Welsh poet
* [The] Cambrian Shakespeare
* Iolo Morgannwg
* [The] Welsh Shakespeare

Williams, Edward Francis 1903-1970
[CA]
British author and journalist
* Francis Williams, Lord

Williams, Edwin Alfred 1910- [AW, CC,
WW]
British author
* De Caire, Edwin
* Moodie, Edwin

Williams, Edwin Dibrell 1910- [BE]
American baseball player
* Williams, Dib

Williams, Egbert Austin 1874?-1922
[BEW, CED, IBW]
West Indian-born composer, actor, singer
* [The] Greatest Comedian on the
   American Stage
* [The] King of Laughter
* Rogers, Duke?
* Williams, Bert

Williams, Eirlys O[lwen] 20th c. [CAP]
Welsh author
* Trefor, Eirlys

Williams, Eleazar 1789?-1858 [HPPN]
Canadian Indian scout and missionary
* [The] Lost Dauphin
* Louis XVII

Williams, Elisha 1694-1755 [HPPN]
American clergyman
* [A] Lover of Truth and Liberty
* Philalethes

Williams, Elisha Alphonso 1855-1939
[BE]
American baseball player
* Williams, Dale

Williams, [Rev.] Elisha Scott 1757-1845
[HPPN]
American clergyman
* [A] Friend of Truth

Williams, Elizabeth
See Dohen, Dorothy

Williams, Elma Mary 1913- [HPPN]
British author
* Oxford, Jane

Williams, Emery H. 1931- [BWW]
American singer
* Detroit Jr.
* Williams, Little Junior

Williams, Ephie Augustus 1864-1940
[DNA]
American author and educator
* Angus

Williams, Eric Cyril 1918- [SFL]
British author
* Williams, E. C.

Williams, Ernest Neville 1917- [WYA]
Author
* Williams, E. N.

Williams, Esther 1923- [HPPN]
American model, actress, swimmer
* [The] Queen of the Surf

Williams, Ethlyne 1908- [F2]
Actress
* Claire, Ethlyne

Williams, Eva [FFF]
American writer
* Viva

Williams, Evan 1951- [HPPN]
American golfer
* Williams, Big Cat

Williams, Everett Belvin 1932- [BA]
American educator
* Williams, Bel

Williams, Evon Daniel 1899-1929 [BE]
American baseball player
* Williams, Denny

Williams, F. Harald
See Ward, Frederick William Orde

Williams, Fats
See Williams, Chino

Williams, Fats
See Williams, Frederick Richard

Williams, Feab. S. 20th c. [SG]
Boxer
* Godfrey, George
* Old Chocolate

Williams, Ferelith Eccles 1920- [SAT]
British author and illustrator
* Eccles

Williams, Fess
See Williams, Stanley R.

Williams, Fiddler
See Williams, Claude

Williams, Floyd 20th c. [NP]
American jazz musician
* Williams, Horsecollar

Williams, Fly
See Williams, James

Williams, Foster
See McCarthy, Foster J.

Williams, Fox
See Williams, George Dale

Williams, Franc
See Williams, Francis

Williams, Frances
See Jellinek, Frances

Williams, Frances B.
See Browin, Frances Williams

Williams, Francis 1910- [EJ7]
American jazz musician
* Williams, Franc

Williams, Frank
See Palmer, Henry

Williams, Fred 1888- [BE, DGS, PB]
American baseball player
* Williams, Cy

Williams, Fred 1913- [BE]
American baseball player
* Williams, Pap

Williams, Fred
See Schmidt, Frederick

Williams, Fred J.
See Smith, Bernard

Williams, Frederick 1865-1930 [BEW]
American actor
* Williams, Fritz

Williams, Frederick Benton
See Hamblen, Herbert Elliott

Williams, Frederick Richard 1956-
[SMG]
Canadian-born hockey player
* Williams, Fats

Williams, Frisky
See Williams, Ron

Williams, Fritz
See Williams, Frederick

Williams, Fritz
See Williams, Ron

Williams, Froggy
See Williams, James

Williams, G. Mennen 1911-
American politician
* Williams, Soapy

Williams, Gatenby
See Guggenheim, William

Williams, George Dale 1917- [EJ,
HPPN, PMJ]
American arranger and composer
* [The] Fox
* Williams, Fox

Williams, George Eddy 1940- [HPPN]
American robber
* [The] Chrome Revolver Bandit
* Williams, Diamond George

Williams, George Henry 1823?-1910
[FFF]
American politician
* Williams, Landaulet

Williams, George Henry 1891- [HPPN]
American locomotive engineer
* Williams, Buddy

Williams, George W. 19th c. [PA]
Author
* G. W. W.

Williams, Giggy
See Williams, Norwood

Williams, Gilbert M. 1917- [CA]
American author and director
* Wolfe, Michael

Williams, Gloomy Gus
See Williams, August

Williams, Gordon [Maclean] 1939-
[TCCM]
British author
* Yuill, P. B. [joint pseudonym with Terry Venables]

Williams, Gorgeous
See Williams, Nature

Williams, Graeme 20th c. [MBF]
British author
* Dent, Denis

Williams Grant 20th c. [HPPN]
American police officer
* [The] Skeleton Specialist

Williams, Grecian
See Williams, Hugh William

Williams, Green Berry 19th c.
American horse trainer
* Williams, Uncle Berry

Williams, Guinn 1900?-1962 [BEW, F1, FC]
American actor
* Williams, Big Boy

Williams, Gurney 1903?- [HPPN]
American cartoonist
* [The] Human Gagometer

Williams, Gus 20th c.
American basketball player
* [The] Wizard

Williams, Gus
See Leweck, Gustave Wilhelm

Williams, Gus
See Williams, Augustine H.

Williams, H. L. 19th c. [HPPN]
British author
* [An] Elector

Williams, Hank
See Williams, Hiram King

Williams, Happy
See Williams, David

Williams, Harold 1853-1926 [DNA, WGT]
American author and physician
* Afterem, George

Williams, Harrison 1920?-
American politician
* Williams, Pete

Williams, Harry
See Smith, George Joseph

Williams, Harry Millard 1928-1969
[SC]
American actor and producer
* Millard, Harry W.

Williams, Hawley
See Heyliger, William

Williams, Heavy
See Williams, Earl Craig

Williams, Henry
See Manville, William Henry

Williams, Henry
See Vicars, Henry Edward

Williams, Henry
See Webber [or Weber], Louis

Williams, Henry
See Williamson, Henry

Williams, Henry L. 1869-1931 [FB]
American football coach
* Williams, Doc

Williams, Herb
See Billerbeck, Herbert Schussler

Williams, Herbert 1914- [SFL]
Author
* H. W.

Williams, Hiram King 1923-1953 [ECM, HPPN, PAC, WP 12-7-82]
American country-western performer
* [The] Drifting Cowboy
* [The] Hillbilly Shakespeare
* [The] King of Country Music
* [The] King of Western Country Music
* Luke the Drifter
* Williams, Hank

Williams, Honolulu Johnny
See Williams, John Brodie [Johnny]

Williams, Horsecollar
See Williams, Floyd

Williams, Hot Rod
See Williams, John

Williams, Hugh
See Williams, Brian

Williams, Hugh Ernest Leo 1903-
[BEW]
British actor
* Williams, John

Williams, Hugh William 1773-1829
[NPS]
Painter
* Williams, Grecian

Williams, Idris Elgina 20th c. [ART]
British artist
* Aeron, Idris

Williams, Ike 1903- [HPPN]
American trader
* Williams, Trader Ike

Williams, Ike
See Williams, Isaiah

Williams, Inky
See Williams, Jay

Williams, Irene
See Gibbons, Irene

Williams, [Rev.] Isaac 1802-1865
Welsh clergyman and author
* B.

Williams, Isaiah 1912- [RBE]
American boxer
* Williams, Ike

Williams, Israel 1709-1788 [HPPN]
American politician and jurist
* [The] Monarch of Hampshire

Williams, J. R.
See Williams, James Robert

Williams, J. R.
See Williams, Jeanne

Williams, J. Walker
See Wodehouse, Pelham Grenville

Williams, J. X.
See Ludwig, Myles Eric

Williams, J. X. [house pseudonym, Greenleaf Classics]
See Offutt, Andrew Jefferson

Williams, Jac Lewis 1918- [IAW]
Welsh author
* Arthfab
* Isambard

Williams, James 1796-1869 [HPPN]
American editor and author
* Old Line Whig

Williams, James 1928- [FB]
American football player
* Williams, Froggy

Williams, James 1946-1973 [IBW]
American lacrosse player
* Williams, Poopie

Williams, James 20th c. [BI]
American basketball player
* Williams, Fly

Williams, James 20th c. [RO2]
American musician
* Williams, Diamond

Williams, James Douglas 1808-1880
[HPPN]
American politician
* Williams, Blue Jeans

Williams, James Edwards Lee [IBW]
American composer
* Lee, Bill

Williams, James Robert 1888-1957
[HPPN]
American cartoonist
* Williams, J. R.

Williams, James Thomas 1876-1965
[BE, PB]
American baseball player
* Williams, Buttons

Williams, Jane 1806-1885 [NPS]
Welsh historian and author
* Ysgafell

Williams, Jay 1914-1978 [SAT, WD]
American author
* Delving, Michael

Williams, Jay 20th c. [EF]
American football player
* Williams, Inky

Williams, Jay Jerome [WECO]
American cartoonist
* Alger, Edwin, Jr.

Williams, Jeanne 1930- [CA, SAT, WD]
American author
* Crecy, Jeanne
* Michaels, Kristin
* Rhys, Megan
* Rowan, Deirdre
* Williams, J. R.

Williams, Jim [OBW]
American baseball player
* Williams, Bullet

Williams, Jo Jo
See Williams, Joseph

Williams, Joan Mary Eileen 1916- [OP]
British programing advisor for opera company
* Ingpen, Joan

Williams, Joe 1903- [BWW, DAM, EJ]
American singer
* Hill, King Solomon
* Mississippi Big Joe
* Williams, Big Joe
* Williams, Po Joe

Williams, Joe
See Goreed, Joseph

Williams, Joel
See Jennings, John [Edward, Jr.]

Williams, John 1582-1650 [HPPN, SN]
British prelate and statesman
* [The] Chief of the Galenists
* [The] Statesman Bishop

Williams, John 1664-1729 [DNNF, DNNS, SN]
American clergyman
* [The] Redeemed Captive

Williams, John 1761-1818 [SN, WBD]
British-born author
* Pasquin, Anthony [Tony]

Williams, John 1773-1845 [PA]
Author
* Publicola

Williams, John 1789?-1811 [HPPN]
Irish murderer
* [The] Ratcliffe Highway Murderer

Williams, John 1796-1839 [HPPN]
British missionary
* [The] Apostle of Polynesia
* [The] Martyr of Erromango

Williams, John 1883-1951 [SC]
American actor
* Arthur, Johnny

Williams, John 1963?- [WP 6-13-85]
American basketball player
* Williams, Hot Rod

Williams, John
See Cook, William [Bill]

Williams, John
See Mackay, George

Williams, John
See Williams, Hugh Ernest Leo

Williams, John A[lfred] 1925- [CA]
American author, editor, scriptwriter
* Gregory, J. Dennis

Williams, John Babington 20th c. [WW]
Author
* Brampton, James?

Williams, John Brodie [Johnny]
1889-1963 [BE]
American baseball player
* Williams, Honolulu Johnny

Williams, John H. [PA]
Author
* Dadd, B.

Williams, John Joseph 1920- [BEW]
Canadian actor and playwright
* McLiam, John

Williams, John Overton 1905- [WWJ]
American jazz musician
* Williams, Bearcat

Williams, Johnny 1906- [BWW]
American singer
* Williams, Uncle Johnny

Williams, Johnny
See Hooker, John Lee

Williams, Johnny
See Warren, Robert Henry

Williams, Jolan [ART]
Austrian-born painter and graphic artist
* Polatschek-Williams, Jolan

Williams, Joseph 1876-? [MK]
American baseball player
* Williams, Cyclone
* Williams, Smokey Joe

Williams, Joseph 1920- [BWW]
American singer
* Williams, Jo Jo

Williams, Joseph Hartwell 19th c. [HPPN]
American author
* One of the Family

Williams, Joseph Leon [Joe] 1935- [BWW]
American singer
* Little Papa Joe
* Williams, Sugar Boy

Williams, Josephine 1864-1950 [SC]
American actress
* Winthrop, Joy

Williams, Jumpin' Joe
See Goreed, Joseph

Williams, June Deniece 1951- [IBW]
American singer and songwriter
* Williams, Niecy

Williams, Katherine
See Buck, Laura A.

Williams, Kathlyn 1884?-1960 [FIR]
American actress
* Kathlyn the Unafraid

Williams, Kathryn Vinson 1911- [WD]
American author
* Vinson, Kathryn

Williams, Kid
See Gutenko, John

Williams, King Fish
See Williams, Londell

Williams, Knuck-Z
See Williams, Charles Prosek

Williams, L. C. 1930-1960 [BWW]
American singer
* Lightnin' Jr.

Williams, Landaulet
See Williams, George Henry

Williams, Leaford Clemetson 1924- [BA]
Jamaican-born American government official
* Williams, Lee

Williams, Lee 1938- [BWW]
American singer
* Williams, Shot

Williams, Lee
See Williams, Leaford Clemetson

Williams, Lefty
See Williams, Charles Henry

Williams, Lefty
See Williams, Claude Preston

Williams, Leroy 20th c. [RBE]
American boxer
* Williams, Roy

Williams, Lester 1920- [NBB]
American singer
* Wintertime, Mr.

Williams, Lester 20th c. [SI 3-12-84]
American basketball player
* Williams, Shag

Williams, Lewis 1786-1842 [HPPN]
American politician
* [The] Father of the House

Williams, Linda Sue 1960- [HPPN]
American forger
* Blair, Hattie
* Walton, Mary Ellen

Williams, Little Junior
See Williams, Emery H.

Williams, Liza 1928- [CA]
American author
* Lehrman, Liza

Williams, Londell 1939- [BA]
American government official
* Williams, King Fish

Williams, Louis 1938- [OP]
American opera singer
* Hagen-William, Louis

Williams, Lucinda [IBW]
American track and field athlete
* Williams, Lucy

Williams, Lucita Squier 1899- [NAA]
American author
* Squier, Lucita

Williams, Lucy
See Williams, Lucinda

Williams, Lynn
See Hale, Arlene

Williams, M. B.
See Beresford-Williams, Mary E.

Williams, Maggie
See Nibbelink, Cynthia

Williams, Marietta 1911- [PMJ, WWJ]
American singer
* Sullivan, Maxine

Williams, Marsh
See Williams, Marshall McDiarmid

Williams, Marshall McDiarmid
1893-1935 [BE]
American baseball player
* Williams, Cap
* Williams, Marsh

Williams, Mary
See Barnes, Mrs. J. H.

Williams, Mary Lou
See Scruggs [or Winn?], Mary Elfrieda

Williams, Matthew 20th c. [IBW]
American artist
* Williams, Bay Boy

Williams, Meurig Mon 1925- [AW]
Welsh author
* Carrington, Michael

Williams, Michael
See St. John, Wylly Folk

Williams, Mike
See Ferrara, Romano

Williams, Milton 1936- [BA]
American educator
* El Kati, Mahmoud

Williams, Moohah
See Williams, A. C.

Williams, Morris [PA]
Author
* Nicander

Williams, Mrs. B. W. J. [FFF]
Writer
* Constance

Williams, Mrs. Jesse [FFF]
Entertainer
* Tracy, Hetty

Williams, Mrs. Odell [FFF]
Entertainer
* Ward, Jennie

Williams, Mrs. Tony [FFF]
Entertainer
* Ward, Marian

Williams, Mutt
See Williams, David Carter

Williams, Myrna 1905- [BDF, F2, FC]
American actress
* Loy, Myrna

Williams, Nathan Winslow 1860-1925
[DNA]
American author and attorney
* Dallas, Richard

Williams, Nature 20th c. [IBW]
American clown
* Williams, Gorgeous

Williams, Ned 1909- [CA]
South African-born author
* Harbin, Robert

Williams, Nelson 1917- [EJ]
American jazz musician
* Williams, Cadillac

Williams, Niecy
See Williams, June Deniece

Williams, No Neck
See Williams, Walter Allen

Williams, Nolan 1902?-1942? [NOJ]
American jazz musician
* Williams, Shine

Williams, Norman Neale, III 1943-
[SW]
American actor
* Kincaid, Aron

Williams, Norwood 1880?-? [NOJ]
American jazz musician
* Williams, Giggy

Williams, Orlando Cyprian 1883-1967
[LC]
British author and critic
* Williams, Orlo

Williams, Orlo
See Williams, Orlando Cyprian

Williams, Otis
See Miles, Otis

Williams, Pap
See Williams, Fred

Williams, Patrick J.
See Butterworth, William Edmund, III

Williams, Patry [joint pseudonym with
D. Williams]
See Patry, M.

Williams, Patry [joint pseudonym with
M. Patry]
See Williams, D.

Williams, Paul 1934- [RO2]
American singer
* Paul, Billy

Williams, Paul
See O'Keefe, Joseph

Williams, Paul B. 20th c. [BBH]
American baseball coach
* Williams, Billy

Williams, Paulette 1949-
American poet and playwright
* Shange, Ntozake

Williams, Pete
See Faulknor, Cliff[ord Vernon]

Williams, Pete
See Reach, James

Williams, Pete
See Williams, Harrison

Williams, Po Joe
See Williams, Joe

Williams, Poopie
See Williams, James

Williams, Pop
See Williams, Walter Merrill

Williams, Potsie
See Williams, Anson

Williams, Priscilla 1943- [IBW]
American trapeze artist
* Williams, Toni

Williams, Pug
See Williams, T. Ralph

Williams, R. D. [PA]
Author
* Shamrock

Williams, Rabbit's Foot
See Coleman, Burl C.

Williams, Racehorse
See Williams, A. B.

Williams, Ralph 1872-1958 [BBD]
British composer
* Vaughan Williams, Ralph

Williams, Rees Gephardt 1892- [BE]
American baseball player
* Williams, Steamboat

Williams, Reginald Gordon 1885-
[WWL]
British librarian and author
* Montana

Williams, Rendall
See Riddell, William Renwick

Williams, Renwick ?-1790 [DNNS, HN,
RH]
British criminal
* [The] Monster

Williams, Rex
See Wei, Rex Yue-Tien

Williams, Richard [house pseudonym]
See Baker, William Arthur Howard

Williams, Richard [house pseudonym]
See Chambers, Philip

Williams, Richard [house pseudonym]
See Dolphin, Reginald Charles [Rex]

Williams, Richard [house pseudonym]
See Francis, Stephen D.

Williams, Richard [house pseudonym]
See Franes, S. O.

Williams, Richard [house pseudonym]
See Hopkins, B.

Williams, Richard [house pseudonym]
See Marquis, M.

Williams, Richard
See Reach, James

Williams, Richard Dalton 1822-1862
[BDSA, PI]
Irish-born poet and editor
* D. N. S.
* [The] Haunted Man
* [The] Jealous Stoneybatter Man
* Scraggs, Milton Byron
* Shamrock

Williams, Richard Valentine 1877-1947
[DIL, SFL]
Irish poet and playwright
* Rowley, Richard

Williams, Rip
See Williams, Alva Mitchel

Williams, Road Runner
See Williams, Travis

Williams, Robert 1928- [IBW]
American actor
* Guillaume, Robert

Williams, Robert 1930?-1982 [FIR]
Radio and television singer and announcer
* Good Fellow, Johnny

Williams, Robert 20th c. [RBE]
American boxer
* Williams, Songbird

Williams, Robert 20th c.
American management consultant
* Williams, Rusty

Williams, Robert American 1886-1965
[HPPN]
American chemist
* [The] Isolator of Thiamin

Williams, Robert Fulton 1917- [BE]
American baseball player
* Williams, Ace

Williams, Robert Jerry 1954- [FR]
American football player
* Williams, Ben

Williams, Robert Moore 1907-1977
[CA, ESF, SF]
American author
* Browning, John S.
* Harmon, H. H.
* Jarvis, E. K. [house pseudonym, Ziff-Davis]
* Moore, Robert
* Storm, Russell

Williams, Roger 1604?-1683 [HPPN]
British founder of Rhode Island
* [The] Apostle of Toleration
* [The] Banished Preacher

Williams, Roger (cont.)
* [The] Indian's Friend
* [The] Rebel of Salem

Williams, Roger
See Weertz, Louis

Williams, Ron 1944- [BB, SMG]
American basketball player
* Williams, Frisky
* Williams, Fritz

Williams, Rose
See Ross, William Edward Daniel

Williams, Roswell
See Owen, Frank

Williams, Rowland 1818-1870 [HFN]
Author
* Camlan, Garonva

Williams, Rowland 1823-1905 [WBD]
Welsh poet
* Hwfa Mon

Williams, Roy
See Williams, Leroy

Williams, Roy Lee 20th c. [WP 11-6-85]
American labor union official
* R [code name]
* Rancher [code name]

Williams, Rubberlegs
See Williamson, Henry

Williams, Russell
See Whitson, John Harvey

Williams, Rusty
See Williams, Robert

Williams, S. L.
See Williams, Stephen Lionel

Williams, [Rev.] St. George Armstrong
19th c. [HPPN]
Welsh clergyman
* Clericus
* Rusticus
* Sion of Myrddin
* Vindex

Williams, Sampson N. 1921- [IBW]
American singer
* Williams, Viloski

Williams, Samuel B. 19th c. [HPPN]
American author
* Publius

Williams, Sandra [RO2]
American singer
* Blinky

Williams, Sandy
See Williams, Andrew

Williams, Sarah 1841-1868 [HPPN]
British poet
* Saidie

Williams, Scott T. 1898-1967 [SC]
American actor
* Thundercloud, Chief

Williams, Shag
See Williams, Lester

Williams, Sherley Anne 1944- [CA]
American author and poet
* Williams, Shirley

Williams, Shine
See Williams, Nolan

Williams, Shirley
See Williams, Sherley Anne

Williams, Shot
See Williams, Lee

Williams, Skip
See Williams, Earl A.

Williams, Slim
See Williams, Clyde C.

Williams, Smokey Joe
See Williams, Joseph

Williams, Soapy
See Williams, G. Mennen

Williams, Sol 1917-1985 [CME, CWG, DAM]
American country-western performer and actor
* Williams, Tex

Williams, Sondra 20th c. [IBW]
American singer
* Williams, Blinky

Williams, Songbird
See Williams, Robert

Williams, Sonnie
See Williams, W. Bill, Jr.

Williams, Speedy
See Smith, L. H.

Williams, Stanley R. 1894-1975 [BI, PMJ, WWJ]
American bandleader
* Williams, Fess

Williams, Steamboat
See Williams, Rees Gephardt

Williams, Stephen Lionel 20th c. [ART]
British artist
* Williams, S. L.

Williams, Stringbean
See Williams, Andrew

Williams, Stringbean
See Williams, Craig

Williams, Sugar Boy
See Williams, Joseph Leon [Joe]

Williams, Susan
See McCoy, Viola

Williams, T. [PA]
Author
* Wells, Thornton

Williams, T. Ralph 20th c. [BBH]
American wrestling coach
* Williams, Pug

Williams, T. Zachariah
See Johnson, Samuel

Williams, Tennessee
See Williams, Thomas Lanier

Williams, Terrible Ted
See Williams, Theodore Samuel [Ted]

Williams, Tex
See Williams, Boyd

Williams, Tex
See Williams, Sol

Williams, Theodore Samuel [Ted] 1918-
[BE, DGS, HPPN, PB]
American baseball player
* Ballgame, Teddy
* Baseball's Elder Statesman
* [The] Big Guy
* Champion of the Bat
* [The] Eternal Kid
* [The] .400 Hitter
* [The] Hit Kid
* Hit, Mr.
* [The] Kid
* King of the Home Run
* Luther, G. C.
* [The] People's Choice
* [The] Splendid Splinter
* Ted the Terrific
* [The] Thumper
* Williams, Terrible Ted
* [The] World's Richest Problem Child

Williams, Thomas 1779-1876 [FFF]
American clergyman and writer
* Egomet, Demens

Williams, Thomas [Andrew] 1931- [CA]
American educator, author, columnist
* Andreas, Thomas

Williams, Thomas Charles 1951- [SMG]
Canadian-born hockey player
* Williams, Vanderbilt

Williams, Thomas Lanier 1911-1983
[BEW, IPA, LC]
American playwright, author, poet
* Williams, Tennessee

Williams, Thunder and Lightning
See Williams, David Rogerson

Williams, Tiger
See Williams, Dave

Williams, Tina
See High-Smith, Domini

Williams, Tom
See Thomas, William B. [Bill]

Williams, Toni
See Williams, Priscilla

Williams, Trader Ike
See Williams, Ike

Williams, Travis 20th c.
American football player
* Williams, Road Runner

Williams, Tummus a
See Collier, John

Williams, Uncle Berry
See Williams, Green Berry

Williams, Uncle Johnny
See Williams, Johnny

Williams, [George] Valentine 1883-1946
[HPPN, WW]
British author
* Valentine, Douglas
* Vedette

Williams, Vanderbilt
See Williams, Thomas Charles

Williams, Viloski
See Williams, Sampson N.

Williams, Violet M.
See Boon, Violet Mary

Williams, Vivian Claud Craddock 1936-
[ART]
British author and illustrator
* V. C. C. W.

Williams, W. [PA]
Author
* [A] Philadelphian

Williams, W. Bill, Jr. 1939- [BA]
American sales manager
* Williams, Sonnie

Williams, W. F. [PA]
Author
* Blondell

Williams, W. R. 1867-1954 [ASC]
British-born American composer
* Rossiter, Will

Williams, Walter Allen 1943- [BE, PB]
American baseball player
* Williams, No Neck

Williams, Walter Herman 1906- [BA]
American business executive
* Williams, Duke

Williams, Walter, Jr. 20th c. [IBW]
American record company owner
* Williams, Dootsie

Williams, Walter Merrill 1874-1959
[BE]
American baseball player
* Williams, Pop

Williams, Warren Milton 1952- [HR,
SMG]
American hockey player
* Williams, Butch

Williams, Wash
See Williams, Washington J.

Williams, Washington J. 20th c. [BE]
American baseball player
* Williams, Wash

Williams, [Margaret] Wetherby [CA,
CC, WW]
Canadian-born British author
* Erskine, Margaret

Williams, William 1717-1791 [FFF, PA]
Welsh hymn writer and clergyman
* Caledfryn, Gwilym
* [The] Watts of Wales

Williams, William [Bill] 1898-1973
[BWW]
American singer
* Williams, Colonel Bill

Williams, William Francis 1836-? [FFF,
PA]
American writer
* Trovatore
* Wirt

Williams, William Holt [Billy]
1878-1915 [BMH]
Australian-born comic singer
* [The] Man in the Velvet Suit

Williams, Willie
See Ford, Aleck

Williams, Woodrow Wilson 1912- [BE]
American baseball player
* Williams, Woody

Williams, Woody
See Williams, Woodrow Wilson

Williamson, A. M.
See Williamson, Alice Muriel
[Livingston]

Williamson, Alice Muriel [Livingston]
1869-1933 [LC, WW]
American-born author
* De Crespigny, [Capt.] Charles [joint
pseudonym with Charles Norris
Williamson]
* De Savallo, Teresa [Marquesa
d'Alpens]
* Revere, M. P.
* Stuyvesant, Alice [joint pseudonym
with Charles Norris Williamson]
* Williamson, A. M.
* Williamson, [Mrs.] Harcourt

Williamson, B. L. 1927- [CM]
American recording executive
* Williamson, Slim

Williamson, C. N.
See Williamson, Charles Norris

Williamson, Charles Norris 1859-1920
[LC, WW]
British author
* De Crespigny, [Capt.] Charles [joint
pseudonym with Alice Muriel L.
Williamson]
* Stuyvesant, Alice [joint pseudonym
with Alice Muriel (Livingston)
Williamson]
* Williamson, C. N.

Williamson, Claude C[harles] H. 1891-?
[CAP]
British author
* Hope, Felix

Williamson, Connie 1930-1963 [SC]
American actress
* Pryor, Jacqueline

Williamson, Edward N. 1857-1894 [AS]
American baseball player
* Williamson, Ned

Williamson, Ellen Douglas 20th c. [CA]
American author
* Douglas, Ellen

Williamson, Ethel 20th c. [SFL, WGT]
Author
* Cardinal, Jane
* Veheyne, Cherry

Williamson, Fred R. 1938?- [BI, FB]
American football player and actor
* [The] Hammer
* Williamson, Hammer

Williamson, Geoffrey 1897- [CA]
British author
* Hastings, Alan

Williamson, H. S.
See Williamson, Harold Sandys

Williamson, Hammer
See Williamson, Fred R.

Williamson, [Mrs.] Harcourt
See Williamson, Alice Muriel
[Livingston]

Williamson, Harold Sandys 1892-
[ART]
British painter and designer
* Williamson, H. S.

Williamson, Henry 1907-1962 [BWW]
American singer
* Williams, Henry
* Williams, Rubberlegs

Williamson, Hugh 1735-1819 [HPPN]
American physician
* [A] Gentleman
* Sylvius

Williamson, Ivan B. 1911-1969 [AS, FB]
American football coach
* Williamson, Ivy

Williamson, Ivy
See Williamson, Ivan B.

Williamson, J. A.
See Williamson, James Alexander

Williamson, J. R.
See Williamson, John

Williamson, James
See Henderson, John William

Williamson, James Alexander 1886-1964
[LC]
British author and educator
* Williamson, J. A.

Williamson, John 20th c. [SMG]
American football player
* Williamson, J. R.

Williamson, John A.
See Henderson, John William

Williamson, John Lee 1914-1948 [DAM,
EJ, NBB]
American musician
* Williamson, Sonny Boy
* Williamson, Straw

Williamson, John Stewart [Jack] 1908-
[CA, WD]
American author and critic
* Stewart, Will

Williamson, LaVerne 1923- [ECM]
American country-western performer
* Lee, Dixie
* Mountain Fern
* O'Day, Molly

Williamson, Lydia [Buckland] 1860-1952
[CCL]
Canadian poet
* Scrace, Richard

Williamson, Mrs. J. C. [FFF]
Entertainer
* Moore, Maggie

Williamson, Ned
See Williamson, Edward N.

Williamson, Paul
See Butters, Paul Theophilus William

Williamson, Sarah E. Carmichael 19th c.
[HPPN]
American poet and author
* Carmichael, Sarah E.

Williamson, Slim
See Williamson, B. L.

Williamson, Sonny Boy
See Ford, Aleck

Williamson, Sonny Boy
See Williamson, John Lee

Williamson, Sonny Boy, Jr.
See Anderson, Clarence

Williamson, Straw
See Williamson, John Lee

Williamson, Thames Ross 1894- [TC,
WBD]
American author
* Dragpmet, Edward
* Fleming, Waldo
* Morgan, De Wolfe
* Smith, S. S.
* Trent, Gregory

Williamson, William Henry 1870-?
[LAO]
British author
* Bank, W. Dane
* Heath, W. Shaw

Williamson, Willie
See Ford, Aleck

Willibald, Graf
See Durben, Wolfgang Johannes Maria

Willibrord 658-739 [DNNS, FFF, SN]
Saint
* [The] Apostle of the Frisians
* Clement

Willie, Albert Frederic
See Lovecraft, Howard Phillips

Willie B
See Borum, William [Willie]

Willie C
See Cobbs, Willie

Willie C.
See Crawford, Willie Murphy

Willie, Frederick
See Lovecraft, Howard Phillips

Willie the Actor
See Sutton, William Francis [Willie]

Willie the Knuck
See Ramsdell, James Willard

Willie the Lion
See Smith, William Henry Joseph
Berthol Bonaparte Bertholoff

Willie the Wallop
See Mays, William Howard, Jr. [Willie]

Willing, Foy
See Willingham, Foy

Willing, Squaretoes
See Willing, Thomas

Willing, Thomas 18th c.
American merchant
* Willing, Squaretoes

Willing Willie Moretti
See Moretti, William

Willingham, Foy 1915- [ECM]
American country-western performer
* Willing, Foy

Willingham, Saundra 1942- [IBW]
American community organizer
* Melanie, [Sister]

Willington, James
See Goldsmith, Oliver

Willis, Aaron 1932- [BWW, NBB]
American singer
* Willis, Little Son

Willis, [George] Anthony Armstrong
1897-1976 [CA, CC, EMD]
Canadian-born author and playwright
* A. A.
* Armstrong, Anthony

Willis, Browne 1682-1760 [HPPN, SN]
British archeologist
* B. W., Esq., A Member of the
Society of Antiquaries
* Old Wrinkle-Boots

Willis, Charles
See Clarke, Arthur C[harles]

Willis, Charles William 1905-1962 [BE]
American baseball player
* Willis, Lefty

Willis, Chet
See Willis, Clarence

Willis, Chuck 1928-1958 [RO1]
American singer and songwriter
* King of the Stroll

Willis, Clarence 20th c. [RO2]
American musician
* Willis, Chet

Willis, Corinne Denneny 20th c. [CA]
American author
* Denning, Patricia

Willis, Goose
See Willis, Robert George Dylan

Willis, Guy
See Willis, James Ulysis

Willis, Hal, Student-at-Law
See Forrester, Charles Robert

Willis, Harold
See Willis, Robert George Dylan

Willis, Hope
See Mannix, Mary Walsh

Willis, J. H.
See Willis, John Henry

Willis, Jack
See Willis, Joshua F.

Willis, James Ulysis 1915- [CWG, DAM]
American country-western performer
* Willis, Guy

Willis, John 1616-1703 [SN]
* [The] glory and pride of the Presbyterian faction
* [The] Sub Scribe to the Tribe of Adoniram

Willis, John Henry 20th c. [ART]
British painter
* Willis, J. H.

Willis, John Howard 19th c. [CCL]
Canadian poet and author
* [A] Literary Lounger

Willis, Joshua F. 1920- [NOJ]
American jazz musician
* Willis, Jack

Willis, Julia A.
See Kempshall, Julia A.

Willis, Katherine ?-1724 [HPPN]
British author
* [A] Gentlewoman in the Country

Willis, Lefty
See Willis, Charles William

Willis, Lefty
See Willis, Les[ter Evans]

Willis, Les[ter Evans] 1908- [BE]
American baseball player
* Willis, Lefty
* Willis, Wimpy

Willis, Little Son
See Willis, Aaron

Willis, Little Son
See Willis, Malcolm

Willis, Lowell E.
See Davis, Horace Bancroft

Willis, Malcolm 20th c. [BWW]
American musician
* Willis, Little Son

Willis, Maud
See Lottman, Eileen

Willis, Mollie R. 1850-1928 [HPPN]
American actress
* Reynolds, Mollie

Willis, N[amby] P[amby]
See Willis, Nathaniel Parker

Willis, Nathaniel Parker 1806-1867
[FFF, HPPN, PA, SN]
American author and editor
* N. P. W.

Willis, Nathaniel Parker (cont.)
* [The] Pink of the Press
* Roy
* Slingsby, Philip
* Willis, N[amby] P[amby]
* Willis, Penciller

Willis, Penciller
See Willis, Nathaniel Parker

Willis, Robert George Dylan 1949-
[DC]
British cricketer
* Willis, Goose
* Willis, Harold
* Willis, Swordfish

Willis, Samuel
See Parker, Hershel

Willis, Swordfish
See Willis, Robert George Dylan

Willis, Ted 1918- [CA]
British author, playwright, screenwriter
* Dixon, George

Willis, Tex
See Howard, James

Willis, Walt 20th c. [SFP]
Author
* Bryan, Walter

Willis, William 1794-1870 [HPPN]
American historian
* W. W.

Willis, Wimpy
See Willis, Les[ter Evans]

Willis, Woodrick, Jr. 1941- [IBW]
American television newscaster
* Willis, Woody

Willis, Woody
See Willis, Woodrick, Jr.

Willkie, Wendell Lewis 1892-1944
[HPPN]
American attorney, politician, business executive
* [The] Barefoot Boy of Wall Street
* [The] Simple Barefoot Wall Street Lawyer

Willkomm, Otto 1887-1941 [SC]
American actor and acrobat
* Nevaro

Willman, Marianne 1940?-
American author
* Clark, Sabina

Willman, Tony 20th c.
Auto racer
* [The] Flying Dutchman

Willmore, Alfred 1899-1978 [DIL]
Irish playwright, actor, author
* MacLiammoir, Micheal

Willoughby, Barrett
See O'Conner, Barrett Willoughby

Willoughby, Cass
See Olsen, Theodore Victor

Willoughby, Claude William 1898- [BE]
American baseball player
* Willoughby, Weeping Willie

Willoughby, Elaine Macmann 1926-
[CA]
American author
* Macmann, Elaine

Willoughby, George
See Goldring, Douglas

Willoughby, [Sir] Henry Pollard 1796-?
[HPPN]
British baronet
* [An] English Landowner

Willoughby, Hugh
See Harvey, Nigel

Willoughby, Lee Davis
See Toombs, John

Willoughby, Weeping Willie
See Willoughby, Claude William

Willoughby-Higson, Philip John 1933-
[WD]
British historian and poet
* Higson, Philip John Willoughby

Wills, Bob 1906- [CWG]
American country-western performer
* [The] Daddy of Western Swing

Wills, Brember
See Le Couteur, Brember

Wills, Bump
See Wills, Elliot Taylor

Wills, Chester
See Snow, Charles Horace

Wills, Donna Sue
See Eisemann-Schier, Ruth

Wills, Elliot Taylor 1952- [SMG]
American baseball player
* Wills, Bump

Wills, Emily Grace 1861-1923 [HPPN]
American actress
* Barron, Grace

Wills, Frank 1948?- [HPPN]
American security guard
* [The] Watergate Guard

Wills, Garry 1935?-
American author
* Roman, William

Wills, Harry 1892-1958 [BX]
American boxer
* [The] Black Panther

Wills, Helen Newington 1907- [HPPN, OET]
American tennis player
* Little Miss Poker Face
* Queen Helen

Wills, James 1790-1868 [PI]
Irish poet and clergyman
* J. U. U.

Wills, Maurice Morning 1932- [HPPN, SMG]
American baseball player
* [The] Base Stealing King of the 1960's
* Wills, Maury
* Wills, Mouse [or Mousey]

Wills, Maury
See Wills, Maurice Morning

Wills, Mouse [or Mousey]
See Wills, Maurice Morning

Wills, Nat M.
See McGregor, Edward

Wills, Oscar 1916-1969 [BWW, NBB]
American singer
* TV Slim

Wills, Ronald
See Thomas, Ronald Wills

Wills, Samuel Richard ?-1905 [PI]
Irish poet
* S. R. W.

Wills, Thomas
See Ard, William [Thomas]

Wills-Webber, Lizbeth 1926- [THR]
British actress and singer
* Webb, Lizbeth

Willson, Frank Hoxie 1895-1964 [BE]
American baseball player
* Willson, Kid

Willson, Kid
See Willson, Frank Hoxie

Willson, Meredith
See Reiniger, Robert Meredith

Willson, Rini 1912-1966 [HPPN]
American actress and singer
* Zarova, Rini

Willson, Wingrove
See Light, Walter Herrod

Willy
See Colette, Sidonie Gabrielle

Willy
See Gauthier-Villars, Henri

Willy, Colette
See Colette, Sidonie Gabrielle

Willy o' the Hollins
See Gibson, William

Willy the Wisp
See Lindstrom, Willy

Wilma, Dana
See Faralla, Dorothy W.

Wilman, Buck
See Wilman, Joseph

Wilman, Joseph 1905-1969 [AS]
American bowler
* Wilman, Buck

Wilmarth, Daniel 1824?-1882 [HPPN]
American actor
* Waller, D. W.

Wilmer, Dale [joint pseudonym with Robert (Bob) Wade]
See Miller, Bill

Wilmer, Dale [joint pseudonym with Bill Miller]
See Wade, Robert [Bob]

Wilmore, Alfred 20th c. [OBW]
American baseball player
* Wilmore, Apple

Wilmore, Apple
See Wilmore, Alfred

Wilmot, Anthony 1933- [CA]
British author
* Raoul, Anthony

Wilmot, David 1814-1868 [HPPN]
American attorney and politician
* [The] Father of the Wilmot Proviso

Wilmot, Frank Leslie Thomson 1881-1942 [BI, DLE1, LAO]
Australian author
* Maurice, Furnley

Wilmot, James Reginald 1897- [WW]
Author
* Stewart, Frances
* Trevor, Ralph

Wilmot, John 1647-1680 [DNNF, FFF, HPPN, RH, SN]
British courtier and poet
* Bessus
* Dorimant
* R. H. the E. of R.
* Rochester, Earl of
* Virgin Modesty

Wilmot, John Eardley 1749-1815 [HPPN]
British barrister and author
* Junior

Wilmot, [Major] Walt
See Harbaugh, Thomas Chalmers

Wilmott
See Price, Charles

Wilmott, James 1814-1868 [HPPN]
American bank robber and safe cracker
* Wilmott, Mysterious Jimmy

Wilmott, Mysterious Jimmy
See Wilmott, James

Wilmshurst, Zavarr
See Bennett, William

Wilna, Elijah [or Elias] 1720-1797 [WBD]
Scholar
* Ben Solomon, Elijah [or Elias]
* Gaon Elijah of Wilna

Wilsden, Clemensford
See Wickham, John

Wilsey, Jay 1902- [F2]
Actor
* Buffalo Bill, Jr.

Wilshere, Vernon Sprague 1912- [BE]
American baseball player
* Wilshere, Whitey

Wilshere, Whitey
See Wilshere, Vernon Sprague

Wilshin, Sunday [or Sundae]
See Horne-Wishin, S.

Wilson, A. G. 20th c.
Horse trainer
* Wilson, Lex

Wilson, A. J. [FFF]
British cyclist and writer
* Waverly

Wilson, Ace
See Wilson, James [Jimmy]

Wilson, Al H. 1868-? [CED]
Actor
* Wilson, Metz

Wilson, Albert W. 1897-1949 [WWJ]
American jazz musician
* Wilson, Buster

Wilson, Albert William 1909- [AW]
British author
* Wilson, Yates

Wilson, Alexander [Douglas Chesney] 1893- [WW]
British author
* Spencer, Geoffrey

Wilson, Alexander Galbraith 1924- [BEW, EMT]
British composer, lyricist, librettist
* Wilson, Sandy

Wilson, Alice 20th c. [THR]
British actress
* De Winton, Alice

Wilson, Angus
See Johnstone-Wilson, Angus Frank

Wilson, Anthony [IP]
British author
* Bromley, Henry

Wilson, Art 1920- [IBW]
American baseball player
* Wilson, Octopus

Wilson, Arthur ?-1953 [IBW]
American actor and singer
* Wilson, Dooley

Wilson, Arthur Earl 1885-1960 [BE]
American baseball player
* Wilson, Dutch

Wilson, Augusta Jane Evans 1835-1909 [HPPN]
American author
* Evans, Augusta Jane

Wilson, Barbara 1932- [IAW]
British author
* Grayson, Laura

Wilson, Barbara
See Harris, Larry M[ark]

Wilson, Beau
See Wilson, Edward

Wilson, Belting Bert
See Wilson, Bertwin Hilliard

Wilson, Benjamin ?-1764 [SN]
Clergyman
* Primrose, [The Rev. Dr.] Charles
* [The] Vicar of Wakefield

Wilson, Bertwin Hilliard 1949- [SMG]
Canadian-born hockey player
* Wilson, Belting Bert

Wilson, Big Potatoes
See Wilson, Homer

Wilson, Billy
See Anderson, D. L.

Wilson, Black Jack
See Wilson, John Francis

Wilson, Bojum
See Wilson, Ernest Judson

Wilson, Bubbles
See Robertson, Mary Imogene

Wilson, Bud
See Wilson, Montgomery S.

Wilson, Bunny
See Wilson, Edmund

Wilson, Buster
See Wilson, Albert W.

Wilson, Butch
See Wilson, George

Wilson, Calvin T. 1928- [BA]
American jurist
* Wilson, Chico

Wilson, Camilla Jeanne 1945- [CA]
American author and journalist
* Wilson, Cammy

Wilson, Cammy
See Wilson, Camilla Jeanne

Wilson, Carol 1893-? [CEI, FHE]
Hockey player
* Wilson, Cully

Wilson, Carole
See Wallmann, Jeffrey M[iner]

Wilson, Caroline [Fry] 1787-1846 [IP]
British editor
* [The] Listener

Wilson, Cave
See Wilson, John

Wilson, Charles 1884-1966 [FC]
American actor
* Crehan, Joseph

Wilson, Charles
See Oldmixon, John

Wilson, Charles Edward 1886-1972
[HPPN]
American industrialist
* Wilson, Electric Charlie
* Wilson, Engine Charlie

Wilson, Charles Edwin 1938- [OP]
American conductor
* Wendelken-Wilson, Charles

Wilson, Charles Erwin 1890-1961
American automobile executive and government official
* Wilson, Engine Charlie

Wilson, Charles Kemmons 1912?-
[HPPN]
American hotel owner
* [The] Host With the Most

Wilson, Charles McMoran 1882-1977
[CA, CAP, HPPN]
British physician and author
* Moran, Charles McMoran Wilson
* Moran, Lord

Wilson, Charles Moseman 1858-1917
[HPPN]
American attorney
* [The] One Man Trust Company

Wilson, Charles Woodrow [Charlie]
1905- [BE]
American baseball player
* Wilson, Swamp Baby

Wilson, Charlotte
See Baker, Karle Wilson

Wilson, Chico
See Wilson, Calvin T.

Wilson, Chief
See Wilson, [John] Owen

Wilson, Chink
See Wilson, Howard William

Wilson, Christine
See Geach, Christine

Wilson, Christopher North 1785-1854
[HPPN]
Scottish journalist
* John

Wilson, Clarence Northon 1920- [BA]
American dentist
* Wilson, Red

Wilson, Claude 20th c. [GW]
American rodeo performer
* Wilson, Whip

Wilson, Clerow 1933- [IPA, SSS, SW]
American comedian
* Wilson, Flip

Wilson, Constance 20th c.
American actress
* Lewis, Connie

Wilson, Cora
See Conner, Mrs. J. W.

Wilson, Crane
See O'Brien, Cyril C[ornelius]

Wilson, Cully
See Wilson, Carol

Wilson, Daniel 1778-1858 [IP]
British clergyman and author
* [An] Absent Brother
* [The] Bishop
* D. W.
* Daniel, Bp. of Calcutta

Wilson, [Rev.] Daniel 1806-1886
[HPPN]
British clergyman
* [The] Vicar of Islington

Wilson, Daniel 1816-1892 [CCL, IP]
Scottish antiquary and poet
* D. W.
* Leina, Wil. D', Esq., of the Outer Temple

Wilson, Dave
See Floren, Lee

Wilson, David [IP]
British clergyman and author
* [A] Lover of Truth
* [A] Protestant

Wilson, David
See MacArthur, D[avid] Wilson

Wilson, Derek Alan 1935- [IAW]
British author
* Preston, Hugh

Wilson, Desemea 20th c. [WWL]
British author
* Patrick, Diana

Wilson, Diana
See Hunt, Diana

Wilson, Dick
See Wilson, Louis Sibbett

Wilson, Doc
See Wilson, Rudolph

Wilson, Don 20th c. [GW]
American rodeo performer
* Wilson, Spider

Wilson, Dooley
See Wilson, Arthur

Wilson, Doris Marie Claire Baumgardt Pohl 20th c. [WGT]
Author
* Perri, Leslie

Wilson, Dorothy Jean 1938- [CA]
American author
* Wilson, Jaye

Wilson, Duffy
See Se-Gwoi-Don-Kwe

Wilson, Duke
See Wilson, Robert Earl

Wilson, Dunc
See Wilson, Duncan Shepherd

Wilson, Duncan Shepherd 1948- [CEI]
Canadian-born hockey player
* Wilson, Dunc

Wilson, Dutch
See Wilson, Arthur Earl

Wilson, Dwayne E. S. 1937?-1978 [BI]
American singer
* Wilson, Fatman

Wilson, E. S. 20th c. [HPPN]
American football player
* Wilson, Puny

Wilson, Edith 1906- [BWW]
American singer and actress
* Aunt Jemima

Wilson, Edith Bolling Galt 1872-1961
[HPPN]
Wife of American president, Woodrow Wilson
* [The] First Lady of the Land
* [The] First Lady of the World
* [The] First Woman to Run the Government
* [The] Secret President

Wilson, Edmund 20th c.
American critic
* Wilson, Bunny

Wilson, Edward ?-1694 [NPS]
British aristocrat
* Wilson, Beau

Wilson, Edwin P. 1929?-
American intelligence agent
* [The] Ice Man
* McCormick, Philip

Wilson, Electric Charlie
See Wilson, Charles Edward

Wilson, Elizabeth
See Ivison, Elizabeth

Wilson, Engine Charlie
See Wilson, Charles Erwin

Wilson, Erasmus 1809-? [FFF, IP]
British surgeon and author
* Erasmus, W. J.
* Quiet Observer

Wilson, Ernest Judson 1899-1963 [MK]
American baseball player
* Wilson, Bojum
* Wilson, Jud

Wilson, Ethiop
See Wilson, William J.

Wilson, F. P.
See Wilson, Frank Percy

Wilson, F. T. 19th c. [IP]
British author
* Wright, Saul

Wilson, Fatman
See Wilson, Dwayne E. S.

Wilson, Flea
See Wilson, Peter Hugh L'Estrange

Wilson, Flip
See Wilson, Clerow

Wilson, Flip Flop
See Wilson, [James] Harold

Wilson, Florence 1500-1547 [PA]
Author
* Volusenus

Wilson, Florence 1894- [BBD]
Australian opera singer
* Austral, Florence

Wilson, Florence Roma Muir 1891-1930
[LC, TC]
British author
* Marichaud, Alphonse
* Wilson, Romer

Wilson, Francis 19th c. [IP]
British poet
* F. W.

Wilson, Francis Edward [Frank] 1902-
[BE]
American baseball player
* Wilson, Squash

Wilson, Frank Ealton 1869-1928 [BE]
American baseball player
* Wilson, Zeke

Wilson, Frank Percy 1889-1963 [LC]
British author and educator
* Wilson, F. P.

Wilson, Fred
See Girolami, Marino

Wilson, Frederick 19th c. [IP]
American author
* [The] Wandering Minstrel

Wilson, Frederick J. 19th c. [IP]
British journalist
* [A] Comprehensionist

Wilson, G. L. 19th c. [IP, PA]
American author
* Falkland, Frank

Wilson, Gary
See Wilson, James Garrett

Wilson, Gene ?-1962 [BEW]
Theatrical performer
* Lafferty, Wilson

Wilson, George ?-1951 [BF]
British director
* Wilson, Rex

Wilson, George 1818-1859 [IP]
Scottish physician and author
* Alumni of the University of Edinburgh

Wilson, George 20th c. [EF, HPPN]
American football player
* Wilson, Butch
* Wilson, Wildcat

Wilson, George
See Bland, George

Wilson, George
See Casharago, James [Jim]

Wilson, George
See McNally, Walter

Wilson, George Archibald 20th c. [BE]
American baseball player
* Wilson, Hickie

Wilson, George Frank 1889-1967 [BE]
American baseball player
* Wilson, Squanto

Wilson, George Peacock 1912-1973 [BE]
American baseball player
* Wilson, Icehouse

Wilson, George Pepper 1876-1902 [BE]
American baseball player
* Prentiss, George Pepper
* Prentiss, Kitten

Wilson, George Washington 1925-1974
[BE]
American baseball player
* Wilson, Ted [or Teddy]

Wilson, Giuseppe 1945- [AES]
British-born Italian soccer player
* Wilson, Pino

Wilson, Gomer Russell 1901-1946 [BE]
American baseball player
* Wilson, Tex

Wilson, Gordon Allan 1895-1970 [BBH, HK]
Canadian-born hockey player
* Wilson, Phat

Wilson, Gregory
See DeLamotte, Roy Carroll

Wilson, Guthrie Edward 1914- [WD]
New Zealand-born author
* Paolotti, John

Wilson, Gwendoline
See Ewens, Gwendoline Wilson

Wilson, H. W.
See Wilson, Halsey William

Wilson, Hack
See Wilson, Lewis Robert

Wilson, Hackenschmidt
See Wilson, Lewis Robert

Wilson, Halsey William 1868-1954
[HPPN]
American publisher
* Wilson, H. W.

Wilson, Hamilton K. 1922- [CWG, DAM]
American country-western performer
* Wilson, Smiley

Wilson, Hank 1941- [RO2]
American singer
* Russell, Leon

Wilson, Harding 1921-1975 [BWW]
American singer
* Poppa [or Poppy] Hop
* Wilson, Hop

Wilson, [James] Harold 1916-
British prime minister
* Britain's Question Mark
* Chairman Harold
* Childe Harold
* Elegant Anachronism
* Happy Harold
* Harold the Henpecked
* Labor's Gray Mystery
* Piffleheap
* Uphill Harold
* Wilson, Flip Flop

Wilson, Harry E. 1902- [BB, FB]
American basketball and football player
* Wilson, Light Horse Harry

Wilson, Harry Warden 1904-1966 [SC]
American actor
* Wilson, Ward

Wilson, Helen Helga 1902- [IAW]
Australian author
* Mayne, H. H.

Wilson, Henry 1812-1875 [HPPN]
American vice president
* [The] Cobbler
* [The] Natick Cobbler

Wilson, Henry
See Colbath, Jeremiah Jones

Wilson, [Sir] Henry Maitland 1881-1964 [CND]
British military leader
* Watt, Mr. [code name used during World War II]
* Wilson, Jumbo

Wilson, Henry Schutz 19th c. [HPPN]
British author
* Gray, Herbert

Wilson, Hickie
See Wilson, George Archibald

Wilson, Highball
See Wilson, Howard P.

Wilson, Homer 20th c. [BLB]
American bank robber
* Wilson, Big Potatoes

Wilson, Hop
See Wilson, Harding

Wilson, Howard P. 20th c. [BE]
American baseball player
* Wilson, Highball

Wilson, Howard William 20th c. [BE]
American baseball player
* Wilson, Chink

Wilson, Icehouse
See Wilson, George Peacock

Wilson, Ida Lewis 1841-? [HPPN]
American lighthouse keeper
* [The] Grace Darling of America

Wilson, Imogene
See Robertson, Mary Imogene

Wilson, Iris Higbie
See Engstrand, Iris [H.] Wilson

Wilson, J. Arbuthnot
See Allen, [Charles] Grant [Blairfindie]

Wilson, J. G.
See Wilson, John Gideon

Wilson, J. W.
See Kuhns, Marvin

Wilson, Jack
See Wovoka

Wilson, Jackie 1935?-1984 [DF 1-22-84, WP 1-23-84]
American singer
* Excitement, Mr.

Wilson, James [IP]
Scottish author
* Daft Jamie

Wilson, James 1795-1856 [IP, SN]
Scottish naturalist and author
* [An] Animal Painter
* Claudero, Son of Nimrod
* [The] Stork

Wilson, James 1835-1920 [HPPN]
Scottish-American Secretary of Agriculture
* Wilson, Tama Jim

Wilson, James [Jimmy] 1900-1947 [AS, BE, PB]
American baseball player and manager
* Wilson, Ace

Wilson, James 1933?-1977 [FIR]
Film executive
* Wilson, Skeet

Wilson, James
See Park, Andrew

Wilson, James
See Rice, H. Grantland

Wilson, James Edwin [IP, PA]
British author
* Lane, Chancery, Esq.
* Zinn, Sergeant

Wilson, James F. 20th c. [BBH]
American sports information director
* Wilson, Pepper

Wilson, James Falconer 1828-1895 [HPPN]
American politician
* Wilson, Jefferson Jim

Wilson, James Garrett 1877-1969 [BE]
American baseball player
* Wilson, Gary

Wilson, James Grant 1832-1914 [DNA, IP]
Scottish-born author, publisher, editor
* Grant, Allan [or Allen?]

Wilson, James Holbert 19th c. [HPPN]
British barrister
* [A] Member of the Inner Temple

Wilson, James Patriot 1769-1830 [HPPN]
American clergyman
* [A] Christian

Wilson, [Dr.] James R.
See Weil, Joseph R.

Wilson, Jasper
See Currie, James

Wilson, Jaye
See Wilson, Dorothy Jean

Wilson, Jefferson Jim
See Wilson, James Falconer

Wilson, Jerry
See Miali, Roberto

Wilson, Jessie Aitken [IP]
Scottish author
* His Sister

Wilson, Jim 1942?-
American wrestler
* [The] All American Boy

Wilson, John ?-1839 [NPS]
Apothecary
* Hornbook, Doctor

Wilson, John 1750-1821 [SN]
Scottish-born printer and author
* Wee Johnny

Wilson, John 1750-1826 [IP]
British poet
* J. W.
* J. W., Deceased, in Usum Amicorum

Wilson, John 1774-1855 [SN]
Scottish artist
* Old Jock

Wilson, John 1785-1854 [DEA, DEL, HN, IP, PA, SN, UH]
British author and poet
* [The] Admiral of the Lake
* Aquilius
* Austin, Arthur
* [The] Blackbird of Buchanan Lodge
* C. N.
* Crusty Christopher
* Eremus
* J. W.
* Kit
* Mathetes
* Mullion, Mordecai
* North, Christopher
* North, Kit
* [The] Old Man Eloquent
* Polyanthus
* Siluriensis

Wilson, John 19th c. [HPPN]
American pioneer
* Wilson, Cave

Wilson, John
See Robertson, John Wilson

Wilson, John Alfred Baynum 1848-? [HPPN]
American clergyman
* [The] Phenomenal Presiding Elder

Wilson, John B. 19th c. [HPPN]
American jurist
* Bautista, Juan

Wilson, John [Anthony] Burgess 1917- [AW, CA, CN]
British author, translator, critic
* Burgess, Anthony
* Kell, Joseph

Wilson, John C.
See Morrow, Felix

Wilson, John E. 20th c. [BBH]
American basketball player
* Wilson, Jumpin' Johnny

Wilson, John Francis 1912- [BE]
American baseball player
* Wilson, Black Jack
* Wilson, Strong Jack

Wilson, John Gideon 1876-1963 [LC]
Scottish-born bookseller
* Wilson, J. G.

Wilson, John Iliffe 1791-1861 [IP]
British author
* J. I. W.

Wilson, John Nicodemus 1890-1954
[BE]
American baseball player
* Wilson, Lefty

Wilson, John Park 1867-1932 [MBF]
British author
* Jackson, Julian

Wilson, Johnny
See Panica, John

Wilson, Joseph [IP]
American clergyman and author
* [A] Minister of the Gospel

Wilson, Joyce M[uriel Judson] 20th c.
[CA]
British author
* Stranger, Joyce

Wilson, Jud
See Wilson, Ernest Judson

Wilson, Juice
See Wilson, Robert Edward

Wilson, Julia
See Fox, Mrs. Charles F.

Wilson, Jumbo
See Wilson, [Sir] Henry Maitland

Wilson, Jumpin' Johnny
See Wilson, John E.

Wilson, June
See Badeni, June

Wilson, Jussem
See Wilson, Nelly

Wilson, Kate
See Lyons, Sophie

Wilson, Kenneth L. 1896?-1979 [BI,
HPPN]
*American sports executive and athletic
director*
* Wilson, Tug

Wilson, Kid
See Wilson, Wesley

Wilson, Kitty
See Wilson, Mary K.

Wilson, Lank
See Wilson, William Clarence

Wilson, Lee
See Lemmon, Laura Elizabeth

Wilson, Lefty
See Wilson, John Nicodemus

Wilson, Lefty
See Wilson, Ross Ingram

Wilson, Lefty
See Wilson, Roy Edward

Wilson, Lena 1898?-1939? [BWW]
American singer
* Coleman, Nelly

Wilson, Les[ter Wilbur] 1885-1967 [BE]
American baseball player
* Wilson, Tug

Wilson, Lewis Robert 1900-1948 [AS,
PB, SR]
American baseball player
* [The] Hacker
* Wilson, Hack
* Wilson, Hackenschmidt

Wilson, Lex
See Wilson, A. G.

Wilson, Light Horse Harry
See Wilson, Harry E.

Wilson, Lillian Brown 1886-1969
[HPPN]
American actress
* Brown, Lillian

Wilson, Lionel 1924- [CA]
American author, playwright, actor
* Blackton, Peter
* Ellis, Herbert
* Salzer, L. E.

Wilson, Lois 1895- [HPPN]
American actress
* [The] First Miss Alabama

Wilson, Louis Sibbett 1903-1965 [GF]
American golf course architect
* Wilson, Dick

Wilson, Louise Bruguiere Church 1902-
[NAA]
American writer and poet
* Ramsay, Joan

Wilson, Mabe
See Wilson, Maybelle

Wilson, Mamie 19th c. [IP, PA]
American author
* Clayton, May

Wilson, Margaret 1667-1685 [NPS]
* [The] Martyr of the Solway

Wilson, Margaret 1882-? [HPPN]
American author
* [An] Elderly Spinster
* West, Elizabeth

Wilson, Margaret Campell 1912- [IAW]
British author
* Stewart, Margaret

Wilson, Margery
See Strayer, Sara Barker

Wilson, Marie
See White, Katherine Elizabeth

Wilson, Marie B[eatrice] 1922- [CA]
American author
* Marie, Jeanne

Wilson, Marilla 1945- [IAW]
Australian author and poet
* North, Marilla

Wilson, Martha
See Morse, Martha Wilson

Wilson, Mary [IP]
Scottish author
* Palliser, Francis

Wilson, Mary ?-1963 [HPPN]
British murderer
* [The] Widow of Windy Nook

Wilson, Mary
See Lyons, Sophie

Wilson, Mary
See Roby, Mary Linn

Wilson, Mary Ann Ward 20th c.
[CWG]
American country-western performer
* Worth, Marion

Wilson, Mary K. 1927- [DAM]
American singer and songwriter
* Wilson, Kitty

Wilson, Matthias 1580-1656 [DEL, PA]
Author
* Knott, Edward

Wilson, May 20th c. [CCL]
Canadian author
* North, Anison

Wilson, May Lockwood 1908-1963
[HPPN]
American actress
* Kokin, Mabelle

Wilson, Maybelle 1870-1909 [HPPN]
American actress
* Wilson, Mabe

Wilson, Metz
See Wilson, Al H.

Wilson, Michael 20th c. [RM]
Musician
* Mick

Wilson, Mike
See Wilson, Samuel Marshall

Wilson, Miles 18th c. [SFL]
Author
* M. W.

Wilson, Mitchell A. 1913- [WW]
Author
* Hogarth, Emmett [joint pseudonym
  with Abraham Polonsky]

Wilson, Monique 20th c. [EOP]
Scottish occultist
* Olwyn, Lady

Wilson, Montgomery S. 1910?-1964
[BBH]
Ice skater
* Wilson, Bud

Wilson, Moose
See Wilson, Robert Earl

Wilson, Mrs. 1787-1846 [PA]
Author
* Fry, Caroline

Wilson, Mrs. A. J. 1836-? [PA]
Author
* Evans, Augusta

Wilson, Mrs. E. V. 19th c. [IP]
American author
* Farmer, May

Wilson, Mutt
See Wilson, William Clarence

Wilson, N[orman] Scarlyn 1901- [CA]
British author
* Norman, W. S.
* Webb, Anthony [joint pseudonym]

Wilson, Neil
See Wilson, Sammy O'Neil

Wilson, Nelly 1930- [CA]
Austrian-born author
* Wilson, Jussem

Wilson, Norris D. 1938- [CM]
American country-western performer,
songwriter, music publisher
* Wilson, Norro

Wilson, Norro
See Wilson, Norris D.

Wilson, Octopus
See Wilson, Art

Wilson, [John] Owen 1883-1954 [BE,
PB]
American baseball player
* Wilson, Chief

Wilson, Pat
See Olney, Ross Robert

Wilson, Penelope Coker
See Hall, Penelope C[oker]

Wilson, Pepper
See Wilson, James F.

Wilson, Peter C. 1913?-1984 [TI 6-18-84]
British auctioneer and business executive
* [The] Fastest Gavel in the West

Wilson, Peter Hugh L'Estrange 1958-
[DC]
British cricketer
* Wilson, Flea

Wilson, Phat
See Wilson, Gordon Allan

Wilson, Philip Whitwell 1875-? [WWL]
American author
* P. W. W.

Wilson, Pino
See Wilson, Giuseppe

Wilson, Plumpton [IP]
British clergyman and author
* [A] Country Clergyman

Wilson, Puny
See Wilson, E. S.

Wilson, R. A.
See Keiser, Robert

Wilson, R. A.
See Wilson, Robert Arthur

Wilson, Red
See Wilson, Clarence Northon

Wilson, Red
See Wilson, Robert James

Wilson, Reg.
See Thomas, Reginald George

Wilson, Rex
See Wilson, George

Wilson, Richard [IP]
British clergyman and author
* D. D., Cantab

Wilson, Richard 1713-1782 [HN, RH,
SN]
British painter
* [The] English Claude

Wilson, Richard 1920- [ESF, WGT]
American author and journalist
* Halibut, Edward
* Towers, Ivar [house pseudonym]

Wilson, Richard 20th c. [HPPN]
American hobo
* [The] King of the Hoboes
* [The] Pennsylvania Kid

Wilson, Richard Henry 1870-1948
[DNA]
American author and educator
* Fisguill, Richard

Wilson, Robb
See Royer, Robb

Wilson, Robert [IP]
British author
* Pedestrian

Wilson, Robert 1803-1882 [HPPN]
Scottish engineer and inventor
* [The] Father of the Screw Propeller

Wilson, Robert 1833-1912 [DNA]
Scottish-born author and clergyman
* Mapleton, Mark

Wilson, Robert 1889- [DBA]
Scottish-born painter
* Scottie
* Wilson, Scottie

Wilson, Robert 19th c. [HPPN]
British author
* [A] Sabbath School Teacher

Wilson, Robert A. 1820?-1875 [FFF, PI]
Irish journalist
* Allman, Jonathan
* Maglone, Barney
* Oge, Erin
* Young Ireland

Wilson, Robert Arthur 20th c. [ART]
British painter
* Wilson, R. A.

Wilson, Robert C. [Bob] 1916- [HPPN]
American politician
* Inside, Mr.

Wilson, Robert E. [Bobby] 20th c. [FB]
American football player
* [The] Mighty Midget of Corsicana

Wilson, Robert Earl 1935- [SMG]
American baseball player
* Wilson, Duke
* Wilson, Moose

Wilson, Robert Edward 1904-1964
[DAM, EJ, WWJ]
American jazz musician
* Wilson, Juice

Wilson, Robert James 1929- [BE]
American baseball player
* Wilson, Red

Wilson, Robert McNair 1882-? [CC,
WW, WWL]
British author
* Wynne, Anthony

Wilson, Roberta
American actress
* Kane, Diana

Wilson, Robin S[cott] 20th c. [WGT]
Author
* Scott, Robin

Wilson, Roger
See Nelson, Earle Leonard

Wilson, Roger C. 1912- [ASC]
American composer, conductor, arranger
* Ahrens, Thomas
* London, Stewart
* Price, Benton
* Price, Walter
* Rogers, Lee
* West, Harold

Wilson, Roger Harris Lebus 1920- [CA]
American author
* Harris, Roger

Wilson, Romer
See Muir, Florence Roma

Wilson, Romer
See Wilson, Florence Roma Muir

Wilson, Ross Ingram 1919- [CEI, SMG]
Canadian-born hockey player
* Wilson, Lefty

Wilson, Rossiere 1919-1959 [EJ, PMJ,
WWJ]
American jazz musician
* Wilson, Shadow

Wilson, Roy Edward 1896-1969 [BE]
American baseball player
* Wilson, Lefty

Wilson, Rudolph 20th c. [IBW]
American magician
* Wilson, Doc

Wilson, Sammy O'Neil 1935- [BE]
American baseball player
* Wilson, Neil

Wilson, Samuel 1766-1854 [WBD]
American meat packer
* Uncle Sam

Wilson, Samuel Marshall 1896- [BE]
American baseball player
* Wilson, Mike

Wilson, Sandra 1944- [CA]
British author
* Heath, Sandra

Wilson, Sandy
See Wilson, Alexander Galbraith

Wilson, Scottie
See Wilson, Robert

Wilson, Shadow
See Wilson, Rossiere

Wilson, Skeet
See Wilson, James

Wilson, Smiley
See Wilson, Hamilton K.

Wilson, Socks [or Sox]
See Wilson, Wesley

Wilson, Spider
See Wilson, Don

Wilson, Squanto
See Wilson, George Frank

Wilson, Squash
See Wilson, Francis Edward [Frank]

Wilson, Stanley Kidder 1879-? [WW]
Author
* Pliny the Youngest

Wilson, Steve
See Goldenberg, Emanuel

Wilson, Strong Jack
See Wilson, John Francis

Wilson, Swamp Baby
See Wilson, Charles Woodrow [Charlie]

Wilson, T. P. Cameron 1889-1918
[HPPN]
British poet and author
* Tipuca

Wilson, Tama Jim
See Wilson, James

Wilson, Ted [or Teddy]
See Wilson, George Washington

Wilson, Tex
See Wilson, Gomer Russell

Wilson, Thomas [IP]
British scholar
* [An] Amateur
* T. W.

Wilson, Thomas 1703-1784 [IP]
British clergyman and author
* [A] Sufferer

Wilson, Thomas Fourness [IP]
British army officer and author
* [A] Staff Officer

Wilson, Thomas L. V. 19th c. [IP]
American publisher
* One Who Knows Them

Wilson, Thornton Arnold 1921?-
American business executive
* [The] Old Shoe

Wilson, Tug
See Wilson, Kenneth L.

Wilson, Tug
See Wilson, Les[ter Wilbur]

Wilson, Virginia De Luce 1921- [BEW,
HPPN]
American actress, singer, dancer, painter
* De Luce, Virginia

Wilson, Ward
See Wilson, Harry Warden

Wilson, Warren 1909- [ITA]
American screenwriter, producer, actor
* Burke, Warren

Wilson, Wesley 1893-1958 [BWW,
DAM]
American singer
* Jenkins
* Pigmeat Pete
* Wilson, Kid
* Wilson, Socks [or Sox]

Wilson, Whip
See Wilson, Claude

Wilson, Whitney
See Lindberg, Arthur A.

Wilson, Wildcat
See Wilson, George

Wilson, William ?-1741 [IP]
Scottish clergyman and author
* [A] Minister of the Church of
Scotland

Wilson, William [Bill] ?-1871 [BLB,
EWG]
American law officer, gunfighter, gambler
* Bailey, William [Billy]

Wilson, William 1801-1860 [FFF, PA]
American journalist
* Alpin
* Grant, Allan

Wilson, William Abner 1864-1928
[HPPN]
American civic leader
* [The] Builder of the City of Houston

Wilson, William Carl 1885-1946 [IA]
American columnist
* Starr, Tramp

Wilson, William Clarence 1896-1962
[BN]
American baseball player
* Wilson, Lank
* Wilson, Mutt

Wilson, William Dexter 1816-? [HPPN]
American scholar
* W. D. W.

Wilson, William Griffith 1896-1971
[HPPN]
*American securities analyst and co-
founder of alcoholic support-group*
* Bill W.

Wilson, William J. 20th c. [IBW]
Journalist
* Wilson, Ethiop

Wilson, William Rae 1774-1849 [IP]
Scottish barrister and author
* [A] Veteran Traveller

Wilson, [Thomas] Woodrow 1856-1924
[FAP]
American president
* [The] Coiner of Weasel Words
* [The] Phrasemaker
* [The] Professor
* [The] Schoolmaster of Politics

Wilson, Yates
See Wilson, Albert William

Wilson, Zeke
See Wilson, Frank Ealton

Wilt the Stilt
See Chamberlain, Wilt[on Norman]

Wiltbye, John
See Blakely, Paul Lendrum

Wilton, Arthur 1944- [PRS, RM, RO2]
British musician
* Brown, Arthur
* [The] God of Hell Fire

Wilton, Hal
See Pepper, Frank S.

Wilton, J. H. 19th c. [IP]
British officer and author
* [A] Soldier

Wilton, Marie Effie 1839-1921 [HPPN]
British actress and theatrical manager
* Bancroft, Lady

Wilton, [Capt.] Mark
See Manning, William Henry

Wilton, Robb
See Smith, Robert Wilton

Wiltse, George LeRoy 1880-1959 [AS,
BE, PB]
American baseball player
* Wiltse, Hooks

Wiltse, Harold James [Hal] 1903- [BE]
American baseball player
* Wiltse, Whitey

Wiltse, Hooks
See Wiltse, George LeRoy

Wiltse, Lewis DeWitt 1871-1928 [BE]
American baseball player
* Wiltse, Snake

Wiltse, Snake
See Wiltse, Lewis DeWitt

Wiltse, Whitey
See Wiltse, Harold James [Hal]

[The] Wiltshire Antiquary
See Aubrey, John

[The] Wiltshire Bard
See Duck, Stephen

[A] Wiltshire Clothier
See Wasney, Henry

Wiltshire, George 1939- [IBW]
American auto racer
* [The] Lonesome Road Racer

[The] Wily
See Ferdinand V [or Ferdinand II of
Aragon]

Wimar, Carl
See Wimar, Karl Ferdinand

Wimar, Karl Ferdinand 1828-1862
[WBD]
German-born painter
* Wimar, Carl

Wimble, Will
See Morecroft, Thomas

Wimbrook, Francis
See Hernaman-Johnson, Francis

Wimhurst, Cecil Gordon [Eugene] 1905-
[AW, WW]
British author
* Brent, Nigel

Wimp, Kathryn Elizabeth 1920- [EJ]
American singer
* Davis, Kay

Winans, Katharine Brush 1903- [NAA]
American author
* Brush, Katharine

Winant, John Gilbert 1889-1947
American politician
* Steward of Democracy

Winar, Ernst
See Eichhorn, Wilhelm

Winch, Evelyn M.
See Winch, Marie Elizabeth Agnes

Winch, John
See Long, Gabrielle Margaret Vere
[Campbell]

Winch, Marie Elizabeth Agnes 20th c.
[WW]
Author
* Winch, Evelyn M.

Winchcomb, John 16th c. [DNNS, HN,
SN]
British clothier
* [The] Clothier of England
* Jack of Newbury

Winchell, Fred[erick Russell]
See Cook, Frederick Russell

Winchell, Prentice 1895- [CC, WW]
Author
* Collans, Dev
* De Bekker, Jay
* Dean, Spencer
* Sterling, Stewart

Winchell, Walter 1897-1972 [HPPN]
American journalist
* Aging Lion
* America's One Man Newspaper
* Busybody
* Great W. W.
* Mrs. Winchell's Little Boy
* [A] Reluctant Anachronism
* Titan of Babel

Winchester
See Henry III

Winchester, Arnold
See Curtis, Caroline Gardiner Cary

Winchester, Carroll
See Curtis, Caroline Gardiner Cary

Winchester, Clarence 1895- [IAW, MBF,
WWL]
British author
* Ornis
* Tanner-Rutherford, C.

Winchester, Hugh E.
See Wuensche, Edward Hugh

Winchester, Kay
See Walker, Emily Kathleen

Winchester, Mr.
See Wuensche, Edward Hugh

Winchester, Samuel Gover 1805-1841
[IP]
American clergyman and author
* Wickliffe

Winchevsky, Morris
See Novachovitch, Lippe Benzion

[The] Wind
See Wayne, Anthony

Wind Dummy Westy
See Westmoreland, William Childs

Windaybank, Stephen James 1956- [DC]
British cricketer
* Windaybank, Windy

Windaybank, Windy
See Windaybank, Stephen James

[The] Windemere Treasure
See Wordsworth, William

Winder, Mavis Areta 1907- [CA, WD]
New Zealand author
* Areta, Mavis
* Wynder, Mavis Areta

Windermere
See Hurd, Percy Angier

Windermere, Charles
See Todd, Charles

Windham, Barry 20th c.
American wrestler
* [The] Sweetwater Express

Windham, Basil
See Wodehouse, Pelham Grenville

Windham, William ?-1761 [IP]
British author
* [An] English Gentleman

Windham, William 1750-1810 [HPPN,
IP, NPS]
British statesman
* [An] Absented Member
* [The] Weathercock
* Wildfire, Will

Windisch, Gerard Roland
See Hill, Roy Leeuwenhoek Aloysius

Windle, Bill
See Windle, Willis Brewer

Windle, Mary Jane
See McLane, Mary Jane

Windle, Willis Brewer 1904- [BE]
American baseball player
* Windle, Bill

Windley, Peter Francis
See Cohen, Paul Arthur

**[The] Windmill with a Weathercock
Atop**
See Goodwin [or Goodwyn], John

Windsor
See Abbott, [Rev.] Edward

Windsor
See Henry VI

Windsor, Anne
See Dewey, Annette Barrett

Windsor, Annie
See Shull, Margaret Anne Wyse

Windsor, Barbara
See Deeks, Barbara

Windsor, Claire
See Cronk, Claire Viola

Windsor, Claire
See Hamerstrom, Frances

Windsor, Ernest Victor 1886- [WWL]
British writer
* Bartlemy

Windsor, Frank
See Birnage, Derek A. W.

Windsor, Marie
See Bertelson, Emily Marie

Windsor, Mary Catherine 1830-1914
[IBW]
American Civil War spy
* Aunt Kitty

Windsor, Rex
See Armstrong, Douglas Albert

Windsor-Garnett, John Raynham 1899-
[LAO, WWL]
Welsh-born author
* Othere

Windy Henry
See Comstock, Henry Tomkins Paige

Wine, Dick
See Posner, Richard

Wine Head Bender
See Bender, D. C.

Wine, Robert Paul [Bobby] 1938- [PB,
SMG]
American baseball player and coach
* Wine, Wino

Wine, Wino
See Wine, Robert Paul [Bobby]

Wine-Gar, Fran
See Wine-Gar, Frank

Wine-Gar, Frank 1901- [ASC]
American composer and educator
* Wine-Gar, Fran

Wineapple, Edward 1906- [EJS]
American baseball player
* Wineapple, Lefty

Wineapple, Lefty
See Wineapple, Edward

Wines, Enoch Cobb 1806-? [HPPN]
American educator and author
* [The] Commissioner

Wines, Frederick H. 1838-1912 [HPPN]
American clergyman and humanitarian
* [The] Father of the National
  Conference of Charities and
  Corrections

Winfield, Allen?
See Stratemeyer, Edward L.

Winfield, Arthur M.
See Stratemeyer, Edward L.

Winfield, Dick
See Perry, Dick

Winfield, Ed[ward] 1901?- [HPPN]
American auto racer
* [The] Father of Hot Rodding

Winfield, Edna
See Stratemeyer, Edward L.

Winfield, Leigh
See Youngberg, Norma Ione [Rhoads]

Winfindale, Judy 1914- [THR]
British actress
* Gunn, Judy

Winford, Cowboy
See Winford, James Head

Winford, James Head 1909- [BE]
American baseball player
* Winford, Cowboy

Winfrey, Mule
See Winfrey, Stan

Winfrey, Stan 20th c. [SMG]
American football player
* Winfrey, Mule

Winfrid [or Winfrith] 680-755 [DNNS, FF, FFF]
Saint
* [The] Apostle of Germany
* [The] Apostle of the Germans
* Boniface

Wing, Frances [Scott] 1907- [CAP]
American author
* Scott, Frances V.

Wing, James Egerton
See Bayfield, William John

Wing, Joseph Elwyn 1861-1915 [HPPN]
American farmer, lecturer, journalist
* Alfalfa Joe

Wingate, Anne 20th c.
American author
* Martin, Lee
* Webb, Martha G.

Wingate, Charles F. 1847-? [FFF, IP, PA]
American journalist
* Carlfried

Wingate, George Wood 1840-1928 [FFF]
American attorney and National Guard officer
* [The] Father of Rifle Practice

Wingate, Orde 1903-1944
British military officer
* [The] Napoleon of Guerilla Warfare

Wingate, W. H. 19th c. [IP]
British poet
* Spectator

[A] Winged Franklin
See Emerson, Ralph Waldo

Wingenbach, Charles Edward 1938- [HPPN]
American journalist, editor, author
* Liancourt, Raoul de

Wingfield, Frederick Davis 1899-1975 [BE]
American baseball player
* Wingfield, Ted

Wingfield, John 1792-1811 [IP, SN]
British officer and author
* Alonzo

Wingfield, Lewis   [FFF]
British journalist
* Whyte Tye

Wingfield, Sheila [Viscountess Powerscourt] 1906- [WD]
British author and poet
* Powerscourt, Sheila

Wingfield, Susan
See Reece, Alys [Tracy]

Wingfield, Ted
See Wingfield, Frederick Davis

Wingham, Charles Wing 1882-? [WWL]
British journalist
* Davids, Charles

Wingo, Absalom Holbrook 1898-1964 [BE]
American baseball player
* Wingo, Al
* Wingo, Red

Wingo, Al
See Wingo, Absalom Holbrook

Wingo, Ed[mund Armand]
See LaRiviere, Edmond

Wingo, Ivey Brown 1880-1941 [BE, PB]
American baseball player
* Wingo, Ivy

Wingo, Ivy
See Wingo, Ivey Brown

Wingo, Red
See Wingo, Absalom Holbrook

Wingrave, Anthony
See Wright, Sydney Fowler

Wingrove, Sybil Westmacott 1891- [F2]
Actress
* Grove, Sybil

Wingshot, Leo
See McKenna, Edward Lawrence

Winham, Lafayette Sylvester 1881-? [BE]
American baseball player
* Winham, Lave

Winham, Lave
See Winham, Lafayette Sylvester

Winiki, Ephriam
See Fearn, John Russell

Wininger, Bo
See Wininger, Francis G.

Wininger, Francis G. 1922-1967 [GF]
American golfer
* Wininger, Bo

Wink
See Nettles, Bonnie Lu

Wink, Josh
See Malloy, Marie Louise

Winkelbleich, Karl Georg 19th c. [HPPN]
German educator and radical
* Marlo, Karl

Winkelman, Donald M. 1934- [CA]
American author and poet
* Moshe, David

Winkey
See Egelshem, Wells

Winkler, Bull
See Winkler, Martin

Winkler, George E. 20th c. [CCL]
Canadian poet
* [The] Prospector

Winkler, Johannes
See Wallner, Christian Johannes

Winkler, Karl Gottfried Theodor 1775-1856 [IP]
German poet and composer
* Hell, Theodor

Winkler, Lillian ?-1932 [HPPN]
American singer
* Leonora, Lili

Winkler, Martin 1890?-1955? [NOJ]
American jazz musician
* Winkler, Bull

Winkler, Ralf 20th c.
German painter
* Penck, A. R.

Winkles, Bobby Brooks 1932- [PB]
American baseball manager
* Winkles, Winks

Winkles, Winks
See Winkles, Bobby Brooks

Winkley, [Rev.] Samuel Hobart 19th c.
[HPPN]
American clergyman
* [The] Pastor

Winkworth, Derek William 1924- [AW]
British writer
* 5029

Winlow, Alice Maud [Dudley] 1885-
[CCL]
Canadian poet
* A. M. W.

Winn, Alison [Osborn]
See Wharmby, Margot

Winn, Anona
See Winn-Wilkins, Anona

Winn, Breezy
See Winn, George Benjamin

Winn, George Benjamin 1897-1969 [BE]
American baseball player
* Winn, Breezy
* Winn, Lefty

Winn, Jane Frances
Author
* Fair, Frank

Winn, Lefty
See Winn, George Benjamin

Winn, Mary Lou
See Scruggs [or Winn?], Mary Elfrieda

Winn, William Edwin 20th c. [IBW]
American producer, educator, actor
* Alexandros, Alexis

Winn-Wilkins, Anona 20th c. [THR]
Australian-born actress and singer
* Winn, Anona

Winn-Winter, Jessie 20th c. [THR]
British actress
* Winter, Jessie

Winnard, Frank
See Tubb, Edwin Charles

Winne, Robert Bruce 1920- [FC, ITA,
SW]
American actor
* Hutton, Robert

Winnebrenner, Le Roy 1932- [HPPN]
American actor
* Baby Le Roy

Winnefred
See Gibson, Mary Frances

Winnemucca, Sarah 1844?-1891 [HPPN]
American Indian interpreter and educator
* [The] Princess

[The] Winner of the Indy 333 1/3
See Johncock, Gordon [Gordy]

Winner, Polly
See Temple, Mrs. Edward P.

Winner, Septimus 1827-1902 [BI, IP,
PA]
American composer
* Hawthorne, Alice

Winner, Thomas G[ustav]
See Wiener, Thomas G[ustav]

Winner, Viola Hopkins 1928- [CA]
American author
* Hopkins, Viola

Winney, Ken
See Marks, Winston K[itchener]

Winnfield Frog
See Long, Earl Kemp

Winnie
See Applewhite, Marshall Herff

Winnifrith, Joanna 1914- [FC]
British-born actress
* Lee, Anna

Winninger, Charles
See Winninger, Karl

Winninger, Karl 1884-1969 [BEW]
American actor
* Winninger, Charles

[The] Winningest Coach in the Nation
See Gaither, Alonzo Smith

Winogradsky, Barnet 1909- [BEW, EMT,
TR]
*Russian-born producer and theatre
manager*
* Delfont, Bernard

Winogradsky, Lew 1906- [JL]
*Russian-born British television and film
executive*
* Grade, [Sir] Lew

Winpisinger, William 1925?-
American labor leader
* Winpisinger, Wimpy

Winpisinger, Wimpy
See Winpisinger, William

Winscott, Edwin C. 1874-1947 [SC]
American actor
* Armand, Teddy V.

Winsett, John Thomas 1909- [BE]
American baseball player
* Winsett, Long Tom

Winsett, Long Tom
See Winsett, John Thomas

Winship, Elizabeth 1921- [CA]
American author and columnist
* Beth

Winslett, Hugh 20th c. [HPPN]
American football player
* Winslett, Wu

Winslett, Wu
See Winslett, Hugh

Winslow, Amos, Jr.
See Cobb, Sylvanus, Jr.

Winslow, Barry 20th c. [RO2]
American musician
* Winslow, Snoopy

Winslow, Dean Hendricks, Jr. 1934-1972
[CA]
American author, poet, journalist
* Winslow, Pete

Winslow, Donald
See Zoll, Donald Atwell

Winslow, Dorian
See Winston, Daoma

Winslow, Foghorn
See Wenzlaff, George

Winslow, Forbes Benignus 1810-1874
[IP]
British physician and author
* F. W.
* Medicus

Winslow, George
See Wenzlaff, George

Winslow, [Rev.] Hubbard 1800-1864
[HPPN]
American clergyman
* Evangelus Pacificus

Winslow, Martha
See Rickett, Frances

Winslow, Mrs. Irving [FFF]
Entertainer
* Reignolds, Kate

Winslow, Paul
See Mullaly, Charles J.

Winslow, Pete
See Winslow, Dean Hendricks, Jr.

Winslow, Rose Guggenheim 1881-?
[HPPN]
American poet and author
* Burr, Jane

Winslow, Snoopy
See Winslow, Barry

Winslow, Vernon 20th c. [CMA]
American disc jockey
* Daddy O, Doctor

Winslow, Walker [BI]
American author
* Maine, Harold

Winslowe, John
See Richardson, Gladwell

Winsome Winnie Judd
See Judd, Ruth Marian McKinnell

Winson, J. W. 20th c. [CCL]
Canadian author
* Wildwood

Winsor, Alfred 1881-? [BBH]
American hockey coach
* Winsor, Ralph

Winsor, Ralph
See Winsor, Alfred

Winstanley, William 1628?-1698 [WBD]
British author
* Poor Robin
* W. W.

Winsted, Huldah Lucile 20th c. [NAA]
Swedish-born poet and author
* Dakotan

Winston, Bobby
See Winston, Clarence

Winston, Bruce
See Bruce-Winston, Charles

Winston, Charles 1814-1864 [IP]
British artist and barrister
* [An] Amateur
* C. W.

Winston, Clarence 20th c. [OBW]
American baseball player
* Winston, Bobby

Winston, Daoma 1922- [SFL]
Author
* Winslow, Dorian

Winston, Harry 1896?-1978
American jewel merchant
* [The] King of Diamonds

Winston, James 18th c. [HPPN]
British author
* [A] Theatrical Amateur

Winston, John Anthony 1812-1871
[HPPN]
American politician
* [The] Veto Governor

Winston, Lena
See Chaffin, Lillie D.

Winston, Mike
See King, Florence

Winston, Moonie
See Winston, Roy C.

Winston, Robert Alexander 1907-1974
[CAP]
American author and aviator
* Fox, [Colonel] Victor J.

Winston, Roy C. 1940- [FB]
American football player
* Winston, Moonie

Winston, Sarah 1912- [CA, WD]
American author and poet
* Lorenz, Sarah E.

Winston, Thomas B. 19th c. [IP]
American author
* [A] Southern Pre-Emptor

Winteler de Weindeck, U. M. C.
[SFP]
Author
* Fighton, George Z.

Winter, Abigail
See Schere, Monroe

Winter, Andrew 1819-? [PA]
Author
* Retnyw, Werdna

Winter, Anna Maria 19th c. [PI]
Irish poet
* A. M. W.?
* A. W.?
* Anna Maria?

Winter, Bevis 1918- [CA, WW]
British author
* Bocca, Al
* Cagney, Peter
* Shayne, Gordon

Winter, Bud
See Winter, Lloyd

Winter, Calvin
See Copper, Frederic Taber

Winter, Elizabeth Campbell 1841-1922
[HPPN]
Scottish author
* Castelar, Isabella

Winter, Faith 1927- [ART]
British sculptor
* Ashe, Faith

Winter, Frank
See Trueblood, Newton A.

Winter, Fred 1922- [BB]
American basketball player
* Winter, Tex

Winter, George [IP]
British farmer and author
* Bramble, Benjamin

Winter, George Lovington 1878-1951
[AS, BE]
American baseball player
* Winter, Sassafrass

Winter, H. G. [joint pseudonym with
Desmond W. Hall]
See Bates, Harry Arthur

Winter, H. G. [joint pseudonym with
Harry Arthur Bates]
See Hall, Desmond Winter

Winter, Herbert
See Ellingford, Herbert Frederick

Winter, Holmes Edwin Cornelius
1851-1935 [DBA]
British painter
* Rowland, W.

Winter, Jessie
See Winn-Winter, Jessie

Winter, John Strange
See Palmer, Henrietta Eliza Vaughan

Winter, John Strange
See Stannard, Henrietta Eliza Vaughan

Winter, Johnny 1944- [BWW]
American singer
* Texas Guitar Slim

Winter, June
See Wheeler, Emily Frances

[The] Winter King
See Frederick V

Winter, Leslie 1940- [CA]
American author
* Strom, Leslie Winter

Winter, Lloyd 20th c. [BBH]
American track and field coach
* Winter, Bud

[The] Winter Queen
See Elizabeth

Winter, R. R.
See Winterbotham, Russell Robert

Winter, Sassafrass
See Winter, George Lovington

Winter, Tex
See Winter, Fred

Winter, Thomas 1795-1851 [RBE]
British boxer
* Spring, Tom

Winter, William 1836-1917 [FFF, HPPN,
PA]
American poet and critic
* Mercutio
* Weeping Willie

Winterbotham, Russell Robert 1904-1971
[CA, SAT]
American author
* Addy, Ted
* Bond, J. Harvey
* Hadley, Franklin
* Winter, R. R.

Winterfeld, Henry 1901- [TBJ]
German-born author
* Michael, Manfred

Winterfeld, Max 1879-1942 [BBD, BEW]
German composer
* Gilbert, Jean

Winterfield, Carl Georg August
1794-1852 [PA]
Author
* De Virigens

Winterfield, Charles
See Webber, Charles Wilkins

Wintergreen, John P.
See Ryskind, Morrie

Wintergreen, Warren
See Adamson, Joseph, III [Joe]

Wintermute, Slim
See Wintermute, Urgel

Wintermute, Urgel 1917- [BB]
American basketball player
* Wintermute, Slim

Winternitz, Roland 1904- [BEW]
Actor
* Winters, Roland

Winters, Bayla
See Winters, Bernice

Winters, Bernice 1921- [CA]
American poet and editor
* Winters, Bayla

Winters, Coddy
See Winters, Frank J.

Winters, Frank J. 1884-1944 [BBH]
American hockey player
* Winters, Coddy

Winters, Isadore L. 1887-? [HPPN]
American wrestler and coach
* Winters, Izzy

Winters, Izzy
See Winters, Isadore L.

Winters, Jack
See Talent, Leo

Winters, Janet Lewis 1899- [CAP]
American author and poet
* Lewis, Janet

Winters, Jesse 1899-1971 [MK]
American baseball player
* Winters, Nip

Winters, Jesse Franklin 1893- [BE]
American baseball player
* Winters, T-Bone

Winters, Jon
See Cross, Gilbert B.

Winters, June 1918- [ASC]
American composer and singer
* Whitman, Jerry

Winters, Linda 1918-1971 [SC]
American actress
* Comingore, Dorothy

Winters, Marjorie
See Henri, Florette

Winters, Nip
See Winters, Jesse

Winters, Rae?
See Palmer, Raymond A[rthur]

Winters, Roland
See Winternitz, Roland

Winters, Rosemary
See Breckler, Rosemary

Winters, Shelley
See Schrift, Shirley

Winters, T-Bone
See Winters, Jesse Franklin

Winters, Theodore 1823-1894
American horse breeder
* Black T

Wintertime, Mr.
See Williams, Lester

Winterton, Gayle
See Adams, William Taylor

Winterton, Paul 1908- [CA, CC, EMD]
British author and journalist
* Bax, Roger
* Garve, Andrew
* Somers, Paul

Winther, Richard 20th c. [EF]
American football player
* Winther, Wimpy

Winther, Wimpy
See Winther, Richard

Winthrop, Elizabeth
See Mahony, Elizabeth Winthrop

Winthrop, Fitz-John
See Winthrop, John

Winthrop, Gideon William 1919-
[HPPN]
American composer, conductor, educator
* Waldrop, Gid

Winthrop, John 1588-1649 [HPPN]
American colonial governor
* [The] American Nehemiah
* [The] Father of Massachusetts

Winthrop, John 1638-1707 [WBD]
American colonial governor
* Winthrop, Fitz-John

Winthrop, Joy
See Williams, Josephine

Winthrop, Laura 1825-? [FFF]
American author
* Hare, Emily

Winthrop, Robert
See Weintrop, Reuben

Winthrop, Robert Charles 1809-1894
[HPPN]
American politician
* [The] President

Winthrop, Robert Charles, Sr. 19th c.
[IP]
American statesman and author
* Blank Etcetera, Sen.

Winthrop, Sophy
See Weitzel, Sophy Winthrop

Wintle, Alfred Daniel 20th c. [SFL]
Author
* Cobb, Michael

Wintle, Anne 20th c. [CA]
British author
* Ellis, Olivia
* Francis, Anne

Wintle, Elizabeth Rhoda 1943- [SFL]
British author
* Lawrence, Louise

Wintle, Justin [Beecham] 1949- [CA]
British author
* Beecham, Justin

Wintle, Thomas 1737-1814 [HPPN]
British clergyman
* [A] Member of the University of Oxford

Winton, F. S.
See Harbaugh, Thomas Chalmers

Winton, Harry
See Harbaugh, Thomas Chalmers

Winton, John
See Pratt, John

Winton, [Capt] Walt
See Harbaugh, Thomas Chalmers

Wintringham, Clifton ?-1748 [IP]
British physician and author
* C. W., M. D.

Winwar, Frances
See Grebanier, Francesca Vinciguerra

Winwood, Brent
See Denny, John Thomas

Winwood, Estelle
See Goodwin, Estelle

Winwood, Mervyn 1943- [RO2]
British musician
* Winwood, Muff

Winwood, Muff
See Winwood, Mervyn

Winwood, Rett
See Corey, Francis Adelbert

Winzenhoerlein, Heinrich Joseph
1819-1901 [BBD]
German composer, singer, musical theorist
* Vincent, Heinrich Joseph

Wird, Sixten
See Wieselgren, Sigfrid

[The] Wire King of America
See Gates, John Warne

[The] Wire Master
See Stuart, John [Third Earl of Bute]

Wireker, Nigel
See Nigel

Wirgman, Charles 1833-1891 [WEC]
British journalist, artist, cartoonist
* Wakuman

Wirsen, Carl David 1842-? [HPPN]
Swedish poet and author
* C. D. W.

Wirt
See Sikes, William Wirt

Wirt
See Williams, William Francis

Wirt, Elizabeth Washington [Gamble]
1784-1857 [IP]
American author
* [A] Lady

Wirt, William 1772-1834 [HPPN, IP, PA]
American politician and author
* [The] British Spy
* Old Bachelor
* One of the People
* [A] Young Englishman
* [A] Young Gentleman of Rank

Wirt, Winola Wells 20th c. [CA]
American author
* Frazier, Sarah

Wirtanen, Atos Kasimir 1906- [IAW]
Finnish author
* Finn, Huck
* Musketoeren
* Sawyer

Wirth
See Haspinian, Jean

Wirth, Ed D. ?-1970 [BI]
American beekeeper and columnist
* Propolis Pete

Wirtz, Elwood Vernon 1897-1968 [BE]
American baseball player
* Wirtz, Kettle

Wirtz, Kettle
See Wirtz, Elwood Vernon

Wirz, [Captain] Henry 1822-1865 [HPPN]
Swiss-born American army officer
* Death on a Pale Horse

Wisbar, Frank
See Wysbar, Franz

Wisberg, Marian Aline 1923- [CA]
American author
* Mountain, Marian

[The] Wisconsin Lumber King
See Sawyer, Philetus

[The] Wisconsin Wrath
See Rebholz, Russ

Wisden, John 1826-1884 [EC]
British cricketer
* [The] Little Wonder

Wisdom
See Ehrlichman, John D.

Wisdom, Kenny
See Grogan, Emmett

Wisdom, Mother
See Lee, Ann

Wisdome, Thomas
See Dunbar, Charles Stuart

[The] Wise
See Aben-Ezra [or Esra]

[The] Wise
See Albert II

[The] Wise
See Albert IV

[The] Wise
See Alfonso X [or Alphonso]

[The] Wise
See Charles V

[The] Wise
See Che-Tsou

Wise
See Djang, Yuan Shan

[The] Wise
See Duns Scotus, Johannes

[The] Wise
See Frederick II

[The] Wise
See Frederick III

[The] Wise
See Gildas [or Gildus]

[The] Wise
See James I

[The] Wise
See John V [or Jean]

[The] Wise
See Laelius, Gaius

[The] Wise
See Las Cases, Emmanuel Augustin
Dieudonne de

[The] Wise
See Leo VI

[The] Wise
See Robert of Anjou

[The] Wise
See Saemund Sigfusson

[The] Wise
See Scotus, Johannes [or John]

[The] Wise
See William IV

Wise, Arthur 1923- [CA, CC]
British author
* McArthur, John

Wise, Buddy
See Wise, Robert Raymond

Wise, Casey
See Wise, Kendall Cole

Wise Charley McNary
See McNary, Charles Linza

Wise, Daniel 1813-1898 [DNA, FFF, PA]
American author and clergyman
* Cousin Clara
* Forrester, Francis, Esq.
* Lancewood, Lawrence

[The] Wise Doctor
See Wessel, Johann [or John]

[The] Wise Duchess
See Churchill, Sarah Jennings

Wise, Ernie
See Wiseman, Ernest

Wise, Harry
See Factor, John

Wise, Henry Alexander 1806-1876 [HPPN]
American army officer and politician
* [The] Harry Percy of the House
* Old Chinook

Wise, Henry Augustus 1819-1869 [DEL, HPPN]
American author
* [The] Chief of the Bureau of Ordnance
* Gringo, Harry

Wise, Herbert
See Weisz, Herbert

Wise, Isaac Mayer
See Weis, Isaac Mayer

Wise, James Waterman 1901- [NAA]
American author
* Analyticus

Wise, John 1652-1725 [HPPN]
American clergyman and author
* Amicus Patriae
* [The] First Great American Democrat

Wise, John S. [FFF, PA]
American writer
* Plover

Wise, Jonathan B.
See Colwell, Stephen

Wise, [Rev.] Joseph 18th c. [HPPN]
British poet
* [A] Sussex Clergyman

Wise, Kendall Cole 1932- [BE]
American baseball player
* Wise, Casey

[The] Wise King
See Solomon

Wise, Martha Hasel 1885-? [LFW]
American murderer
* [The] Borgia of America

Wise, Modoc
See Wise, Samuel W.

Wise, Nicholas Patrick Stephen 1802-1865 [HPPN]
British prelate
* Blougram, [Bishop]

Wise, Penny
See Caldwell, Evelyn

Wise, Ray 1906-1952 [JL]
American actor
* Mala

Wise, Robert A.
See Gebhart, Fred J.

Wise, Robert Raymond 1928-1955 [EJ]
American jazz musician
* Wise, Buddy

Wise, Samuel W. 1857-1910 [PB]
American baseball player
* Wise, Modoc

Wise, Vic
See Bloom, David Victor

[The] Wise Wife of Keith
See Simpson [or Sampson?], Agnes

[The] Wisecracker
See Walker, James John [Jimmy]

Wiseman, Ann [Sayre] 1926- [CA]
American author
* Denzer, Ann Wiseman

Wiseman, Ernest 1925- [FC]
British comedian
* Wise, Ernie

Wiseman, Mac
See Wiseman, Malcolm B.

Wiseman, Malcolm B. 1925- [ECM]
American country-western performer
* Wiseman, Mac

Wiseman, Myrtle Eleanor Cooper 1913-
[CWG]
American country-western performer
* Lulu Belle

Wiseman, Richard 1622?-1676 [HN]
British surgeon
* [The] Father of English Surgery

Wiseman, Scott 1909- [CWG, DAM,
HPPN]
American country-western performer
* Scotty
* Skyland Scotty

**[The] Wisest, Brightest, Meanest of
Mankind**
See Bacon, Francis [First Baron
Verulam]

[The] Wisest Fool in Christendom
See James I

[The] Wisest Man of Greece
See Socrates

[The] Wisest of the Bretons
See Gildas [or Gildus]

Wishart [or Wiseheart?], George
1513?-1546 [SN]
Scottish clergyman and martyr
* Sophocardus

Wishart, Henry
See Shepherd, Robert Henry Wishart

Wishit, Mr.
See Spence, Thomas

Wishner, Sam 20th c. [BS]
American magician
* [The] Sultan of Magic
* Zovello

Wiskers
See Tinkham, George Holden

Wisner, Edward 1860-1915 [HPPN]
American pioneer in land reclamation
* [The] Father of Reclamation

Wisniewski, Henry 20th c. [HPPN]
American football player
* Wisniewski, Pistol Pete

Wisniewski, Pistol Pete
See Wisniewski, Henry

Wisnock, Nick 1918- [CSH]
Canadian golfer
* Weslock, Nick

Wissler, Lewis 1868-1959 [BE]
American baseball player
* Whistler, Lew[is]

Wist, Olav
See Rinnan, Henry Oliver

Wistace, Grace
See Wace, Robert

Wistert, Albert A. 1920- [FB]
American football player
* Wistert, Ox

Wistert, Francis M. 1912- [FB]
American football player
* Wistert, Whitey

Wistert, Ox
See Wistert, Albert A.

Wistert, Whitey
See Wistert, Francis M.

[The] Witch
See Favato, Carino

[The] Witch Finder Generall
See Hopkins, Matthew

Witch Hazel
See Smith, Frances Shubael

Witch Hazel Bud
See Budd, William

[The] Witch of Eye
See Jourdemain, Marjory

[The] Witch of Walkerne
See Wenham, Jane

[The] Witch of Wall Street
See Green, Henrietta Howland
[Robinson]

Witcher, Ernie 20th c. [RBE]
American boxer
* Wicher, Ernie

Witchett, Joseph Leatherley 1792-1863
[FAA]
British-born American actor
* Cowell, Joe

[The] Witchfinder
See Hopkins, Matthew

Witcombe, Rick Trader 1943- [AW]
British screenwriter
* Marker, Clare

Witcover, Walt
See Scheinman, Walter Witcover

Witek, Mickey
See Witek, Nicholas Joseph

Witek, Nicholas Joseph 1915- [BE]
American baseball player
* Witek, Mickey

Witham, Marjorie Alexandra 1902-1970
[THR]
British actress
* Aubrey, Madge

Withem, Gary 1946- [RO2]
American musician
* Withem, Private

Withem, Private
See Withem, Gary

Wither, George 1588-1667 [NPS, SN]
Author
* Chronomastix
* [The] English Juvenal

Witherby, William 19th c. [HFN]
Author
* [A] Layman

Withers, Carl A. 1900-1970 [CA, SAT]
American author and editor
* North, Robert
* West, James

Withers, E. L.
See Potter, George William, Jr.

Withers, Georgette Lizette 1917- [OCF,
TR]
British actress
* Withers, Googie

Withers, Googie
See Withers, Georgette Lizette

Withers, Jane 1926- [AM, HPPN]
American actress
* Dixie's Dainty Dewdrop
* Josephine the Lady Plumber
* Walthers, Jerrie

Withers, [Rev.] John 18th c. [HPPN]
British clergyman
* [A] Citizen

[The] Withers of the City
See Wilde, Robert

Witherspoon, Halliday
See Nutter, William H.

Witherspoon, Irene Murray 1913- [CA]
American author
* Murray, Irene

Witherspoon, J. J.
See Wyman, Walter Forestus

Witherspoon, James [Jimmy] 1923-
[BWW, SSS]
American singer
* [The] Spoon

Witherspoon, John 1722-1794 [FFF,
HPPN]
Scottish clergyman
* [A] Citizen of the United States
* Druid
* [The] Real Author of That
Performance
* Silverspoon, Dr.

Witherspoon, Matilda 1914- [BWW]
American singer
* Mississippi Matilda

Witherspoon, Naomi Long
See Madgett, Naomi Long

Witherspoon, [Dr.] Orlando 19th c.
[HPPN]
American author
* Democritus, Junior

Witherspoon, Terrible Tim
See Witherspoon, Tim

Witherspoon, Tim 1959- [HPPN]
American boxer
* Witherspoon, Terrible Tim

Witherup, Anne Warrington
See Bangs, John Kendrick

Withington, Leonard 1789-? [FFF]
American author
* Oldbug, Jonathan

Withrow, Corky
See Withrow, Raymond Wallace

Withrow, Frank Blaine 1891-1966 [BE]
American baseball player
* Withrow, Kid

Withrow, Kid
See Withrow, Frank Blaine

Withrow, Raymond Wallace 1937- [BE]
American baseball player
* Withrow, Corky

Witkacy
See Witkiewicz, Stanislaw Ignacy

Witkiewicz, Stanislaw Ignacy 1885-1939
[MWD, WOA]
Polish author, playwright, philosopher
* Witkacy

Witkins, Alexander 1907-1961 [BEW, BMH]
South African-born theatrical performer
* Afrique

Witkowski, Daisy 1881-? [THR]
American-born comedienne
* Jerome, Daisy

Witkowski, Isador 1861-1927 [JL, LL]
German editor
* Harden, Maximilian

Witkowski, Sadie 1876-1950 [BEW]
American actress
* Jerome, Sadie

[The] Witling of Terror
See Barere de Vieuzac, Bertrand

Witt, George Adrian 1933- [BE]
American baseball player
* Witt, Red

Witt, Lawton Walter
See Wittkowski, Ladislaw Waldemar

Witt, Red
See Witt, George Adrian

Witt, Shirley Hill 1934- [CA]
American author
* Thundercloud, Katherine

Witt, Whitey
See Wittkowski, Ladislaw Waldemar

Witte, Glenna Finley 1925- [CA]
American author
* Finley, Glenna

[The] Wittenberg Monk
See Luther, Martin

Wittendorf, C.
See Proschko, Hermine Camille

Wittenwiler, Mathias 1842-1918 [HPPN]
American actor and entertainer
* Wheeler, Mat

Wittermans, Elizabeth [Pino] [CA]
Indonesian-born educator and author
* Pino, E.

Wittgenstein, Karl 19th c.
Austrian industrialist
* [The] Iron King

Wittgenstein, Ludwig 1889-1951 [HPPN]
German philosopher
* [The] Man With Qualities

Wittgenstein, Oberleutenant
See Khokhlov, Nicolai

Wittig, Hans
See Wittig, John Carl

Wittig, John Carl 1914- [BE]
American baseball player
* Wittig, Hans

Wittinghoff, Julienne 1764-1824 [HN]
Russian author and mystic
* [The] Grey Sister of Hearts

Wittkowski, Ladislaw Waldemar 1895-
[BE, PB]
American baseball player
* Witt, Lawton Walter
* Witt, Whitey

Wittlin, Tadeusz 1909- [CA, WD]
Polish-born American author, poet, historian
* Karniewski, Janusz
* Wittlin, Thaddeus [Andrew]

Wittlin, Thaddeus [Andrew]
See Wittlin, Tadeusz

Wittman, Steve
See Wittman, Sylvester J.

Wittman, Sylvester J. 1904- [OCS]
American aviator
* Wittman, Steve

Wittop, Freddy
See Koning, Fred Wittop

Wittrock, Frederick ?-1921 [DI]
American robber
* Wittrock, Terrible Fred

Wittrock, Terrible Fred
See Wittrock, Frederick

Witty, Helen E. S[troop] 1921- [CA]
American author, columnist, editor
* Stroop, Helen E.

Witwatersrand
See Scully, William Charles

Witwer, H. C.
See Witwer, Harry Charles

Witwer, Harry Charles 1890-1929
[HPPN]
American author
* Witwer, H. C.

Witweyke
See Oliver, Hugh

Witz
See Dingell, John David

Witzleben, Karl August Friedrich von
1773-1839 [WBD]
German author
* Tromlitz, A. von

Wivallius, Lars
See Swansson, Lars

Wixom, Emma 1859-1940 [BBD, FFF]
American opera singer
* Nevada, Emma

[The] Wizard
See Brooke, Alan F.

[The] Wizard
See Brookes, Norman Everard

Wizard
See Corlett, John

Wizard
See Cousy, Robert J. [Bob]

[The] Wizard
See Gibbons, Michael J. [Mike]

[The] Wizard
See Gregory, Andre

[The] Wizard
See Hoff, Bobby

[The] Wizard
See John III

[The] Wizard
See Schaefer, Herman, Sr.

[The] Wizard
See Schaefer, Jacob, Sr.

[The] Wizard
See Williams, Gus

[The] Wizard Dribbler
See Matthews, Stanley

[The] Wizard Earl
See Percy, Henry

Wizard, Mr.
See Herbert, Don[ald Jeffry]

[The] Wizard of Ahs
See Olivera, Hector

[The] Wizard of American Drama
See Valasco, David

[The] Wizard of Baseball
See McPhail, Leland Stanford

[The] Wizard of Berkeley
See Heinrich, Edward Oscar

[The] Wizard of Essex
See Dawson, Charles

[The] Wizard of Kinderhook
See Van Buren, Martin

[The] Wizard of Manton
See Taylor, Alec

[The] Wizard of Menlo Park
See Edison, Thomas Alva

[The] Wizard of Oz
See Smith, Osborne Earl

[The] Wizard of Spirit Lake
See Gilbert, Fred

[The] Wizard of the Albany Regency
See Van Buren, Martin

[The] Wizard of the Chorus Line
See Enos, William Berkeley

[The] Wizard of the Italian Renaissance
See Da Vinci, Leonardo

[The] Wizard of the North
See Scott, John

[The] Wizard of the North
See Scott, [Sir] Walter

Wizard of the Opera
See Menotti, Gian Carlo

[The] Wizard of the Saddle
See Forrest, Nathan Bedford

[The] Wizard of the Sea
See Kidd, [Captain] William

[The] Wizard of the Winged-T
See Hollis, Wilburn

[The] Wizard of the Wires
See Edison, Thomas Alva

[The] Wizard of Tomassee
See Pickens, Andrew

[The] Wizard of Utrecht
See Croiset, Gerard

[The] Wizard of Wacky Inventions
See Goldberg, Reuben Lucius

[The] Wizard of Westwood
See Wooden, John

[The] Wizard of Word Music
See Poe, Edgar Allan

Wizbor, Jakub Horczak
See Paszkiewicz, Mieczyslaw

Wjconnon
See Connon, William John

Wobbly Willie
See McKinley, William

Wockenfuss, Fuss
See Wockenfuss, Johnny Bilton

Wockenfuss, Johnny Bilton 1949-
[SMG]
American baseball player
* Wockenfuss, Fuss

Woddis, Hillel Chayim Keith 1914-
[IAW]
British author
* Woddis, Jack

Woddis, Jack
See Woddis, Hillel Chayim Keith

Wodehouse, John 1826-1902 [HN]
British statesman
* Kimberley, Earl of
* Slumber, Baron

Wodehouse, P. G.
See Wodehouse, Pelham Grenville

Wodehouse, Pelham Grenville 1881-1975
[ASC, BEW, CA]
British author, playwright, lyricist
* Brooke-Haven, P.
* Grenville, Pelham
* Plum, J.
* West, C. P.
* Williams, J. Walker

Wodehouse, Pelham Grenville (cont.)
* Windham, Basil
* Wodehouse, P. G.

Woden, George
See Slaney, George Wilson

Wodge, Dreary
See Gorey, Edward [St. John]

Wodhull, Michael 1740-1816 [HPPN]
British poet
* Orlando

Wodson, Harry Milner 1874-1952
[CCL]
Canadian author
* Milner, Henry

Woelflein, Heinrich 1470-1532 [PA]
Author
* Lupulus

Woestemeyer, Ina Faye
See Van Noppen, Ina [Faye]
W[oestemeyer]

Woffington, Margaret 1714?-1760
[HPPN]
Irish actress
* [The] Queen of Babylon
* Woffington, Peg

Woffington, Peg
See Woffington, Margaret

Wofford, Chloe Anthony 1931- [CA]
American author
* Morrison, Toni

Wohl, Burton 20th c. [SFL]
Author
* Hills, Baldwin

Wohl, James P[aul] 1937- [CA]
American author
* Coltrane, James

Wohlbrueck, Adolf 1900-1967 [BDF, F2, OCF]
Austrian-born actor
* Walbrook, Anton

Wohlford, James Eugene [Jim] 1951-
[BE]
American baseball player
* Wohlford, Wolfie

Wohlford, Wolfie
See Wohlford, James Eugene [Jim]

Wojciechowicz, Alexander 1915- [FB]
American football player
* Wojciechowicz, Wojie

Wojciechowicz, Wojie
See Wojciechowicz, Alexander

Wojciechowska, Maia [Teresa] 1927-
[CA, SAT]
Polish-born American author
* Larkin, Maia
* Rodman, Maia

Wojcieszko, Jan 1888- [THR]
Polish-born dancer
* Oyra, Jan

Wojnilower, Albert 20th c.
American economist
* Gloom, Dr.

Wojtek, Emerich Josef 1898- [FDG]
Austrian director
* Emo, E. W.

Wojtyla, Karol 1920- [CA]
Polish-born Pope and poet
* Gruda [A Clod of Earth]
* Jawien, Andrzej
* John Paul II
* [The] People's Pope

Wolcot, John 1738-1819 [DEL, HPPN, PA, WBD]
British author and poet
* Currycomb, Carnaby, Esq.
* Pindar, Peter
* Tinman, Philippi Hamlin

Wolcott, Mary Adella 1874?-? [CW]
Jamaican poet
* Tropica

Wolcott, Ona 1906?-1955 [F2, FC]
American actress
* Munson, Ona

Wolf, Aron 1817-1870 [BBD]
Dutch composer
* Berlijn, Anton

Wolf, Bear
See Wolf, Raymond

Wolf, Chicken
See Wolf, William Van Winkle

Wolf, Dieter
See Thomas, Michael Wolf

Wolf, Eddy 20th c.
American stilt walker
* Wolf, Steady Eddy

Wolf, Frederick
See Dempewolff, Richard F[rederic]

Wolf, George 1777-1840 [FFF]
American politician
* [The] Father of the Public School System of Pennsylvania

Wolf, Herr
See Hitler, Adolf

Wolf, Jay
See Wolf, Julius Rosenthal

Wolf, Julius Rosenthal 1929- [BEW]
American talent representative
* Wolf, Jay

[The] Wolf Lady
See Berg, Karlyn Atkinson

Wolf, Lefty
See Wolf, Walter Francis

Wolf, Markus 1923?-
East German intelligence agent
* Wolf, Mischa

Wolf, Miriam Bredow 1895- [CAP]
American medical secretary and author
* Bredow, Miriam

Wolf, Mischa
See Wolf, Markus

[The] Wolf of America
See Montgomery, Richard

[The] Wolf of Badenoch
See Steward, Alexander

[The] Wolf of France
See Louis XIV

[The] Wolf of Plinlimmon
See Gwenwyn

[The] Wolf of Wall Street
See Livermore, Jesse Lauriston

Wolf, Raymond 20th c. [HPPN]
American football player and coach
* Wolf, Bear

Wolf, Steady Eddy
See Wolf, Eddy

Wolf, Walter Francis 1900- [BE]
American baseball player
* Wolf, Lefty

Wolf, William Van Winkle 1862-1903
[BE, PB]
American baseball player
* Wolf, Chicken

Wolfe, Aaron
See Koontz, Dean R[ay]

Wolfe, Cedric
See Alais, Ernest W.

Wolfe, Charles 1791-1823 [PI]
Irish poet
* C. W.

Wolfe, Charles Keith 1943- [CA]
American author
* Henricks, Kaw

Wolfe, Eddie 20th c. [EJS]
American boxer
* Wolfe, Kid

Wolfe, George 1908- [EJS]
American basketball player
* Wolfe, Red

Wolfe, Harold 1931- [BB]
American basketball player
* Wolfe, Herc

Wolfe, Herc
See Wolfe, Harold

Wolfe, Kid
See Wolfe, Eddie

Wolfe, Laura [Guyol] 1884-1957 [BI]
American columnist
* Worth, Helen

Wolfe, LeRoy E. 1891?-1946 [BI]
American art critic
* Lewis, R. Edward
* Shaw, Michael

Wolfe, Lilian Lauferty 1887-1958 [IA]
American columnist
* Fairfax, Beatrice

Wolfe, Michael
See Williams, Gilbert M.

Wolfe, Polly
See Wolfe, Roy Chamberlain

Wolfe, Red
See Wolfe, George

Wolfe, Reginald
See Dibdin, Thomas Frognall

Wolfe, Roy Chamberlain 1888-1938
[BE]
American baseball player
* Wolfe, Polly

Wolfe, Sam
See Levy, Joseph [Joe]

Wolfe, Thomas Clayton 1900-1938
[HPPN]
American author
* [The] Hungry Gulliver

Wolfe, William [Willie] 1951?-1974
[HPPN]
American radical terrorist group leader
* Cujo

Wolfenden, George
See Beardmore, George

Wolff, Carl [or Karl?] 1860-1934 [CW]
Haitian author
* Carolus

Wolff, Cecil Drummond 20th c. [WGT]
Author
* Waldo, Cedric Dane

Wolff, David 20th c. [DFM]
Scriptwriter and director
* Maddow, Ben

Wolff, Frank
See Hermann, Frank

Wolff, Mary Evaline 1887-1964 [CAT,
TC]
American author and poet
* Madeleva, [Sister] M.
* Mary Madeleva, [Sister]

Wolff, Perry 20th c. [ET]
Television writer and producer
* Wolff, Skee

Wolff, Skee
See Wolff, Perry

Wolff, Victoria 1910- [IAW]
German-born author
* Martell, Claudia

Wolff, Wilhelm 1816-1887 [SN]
German sculptor
* [Der] Thier Wolff

Wolff, William Deakin 1902- [AW, WD]
British author and poet
* Martindale, Spencer

Wolff-Bekker, Elisabeth [Betje]
1738-1804 [BI, HPPN]
Dutch author, essayist, poet
* Silviana

Wolffe, Jabez 1877-1943 [EJS]
British distance swimmer, coach, and trainer
* Wolffe, Jappy

Wolffe, Jappy
See Wolffe, Jabez

Wolffe, Katherine
See Scott, Marian [Gallagher]

Wolffe, Yolande Mari 1940- [HPPN]
British jazz musician
* Bavan, Yolande

Wolfgang, Meldon John 1890-1947 [BE]
American baseball player
* Wolfgang, Mellie

Wolfgang, Mellie
See Wolfgang, Meldon John

Wolfgang, Otto 1898- [IAW]
Austrian-born author and poet
* Hill, Tom
* Roy, Percy Gordon

Wolfington, Iggie
See Wolfington, Ignatius

Wolfington, Ignatius 1920- [BEW]
American actor
* Wolfington, Iggie

Wolfman Jack
See Smith, Robert

Wolford, Frank 19th c. [HPPN]
American army officer and author
* [An] Union Army Officer

Wolfson, Victor 1910- [CA, WW]
American author and playwright
* Dodge, Langdon

Wolgast, Ad
See Wolgust, Adolphus

Wolgast, Midget
See Loscalzo, Joseph Robert

Wolgust, Adolphus 1888-1955 [BX, RBE,
WBC]
American boxer
* [The] Cadillac Wildcat
* [The] Dutchman
* [The] Michigan Wildcat
* Wolgast, Ad

Wolinski, David 20th c. [RO2]
American musician
* Wolinski, Hawk

Wolinski, Hawk
See Wolinski, David

Wolinsky, Dimples
See Wolinsky, Moey

Wolinsky, Moey ?-1943? [BLB, PHM]
American underworld figure
* Wolinsky, Dimples

Wolk, George 20th c. [SFL]
Author
* Graat, Heinrich

Wolke, Lillian 1888-1975 [CU, FIR, SC]
American actress
* Walker, Dimples
* Walker, Lillian

Wolkers-Ransome, J. E. M.
See Wolkers-Ransome, Joan Elizabeth
Margaret

**Wolkers-Ransome, Joan Elizabeth
Margaret** 1928- [ART]
British painter
* Wolkers-Ransome, J. E. M.

Wollersen, Florence 1893- [THR]
British actress
* Buckton, Florence

Wollheim, Donald A[llen] 1914- [CA,
ESF, WGT]
American author
* Cooke, Arthur [joint pseudonym with
 C. Kornbluth, R. Lowndes, J. Michel,
 E. Balter]
* Gordon, Millard Verne
* Grinnell, David
* Pearson, Martin [joint pseudonym
 with Cyril M. Kornbluth]
* Warland, Allen
* Wells, Braxton
* Woods, Lawrence [joint pseudonym
 with Robert Augustine Ward
 Lowndes, John Michel]

Wollman, [Dr.] Enrique?
See Mengele, [Dr.] Josef

Wollman, Rodney 1954?- [TI 6-6-83]
American video pirate
* Video, Captain

Wollstoncraft
See Godwin, Mary

Wolny, P.
See Janeczko, Paul B[ryan]

Woloweki
See Szymonowska, Marie

Wols
See Schulze, Alfred Otto Wolfgang

Wols, Frits
See Wong loi Sing, Eugene Wilfred

Wolscianus
See Nares, Robert

Wolseley, Faith
See Tower, Stella Mary [Hodgson]

**Wolseley, Garnet Joseph [First Viscount
Wolseley]** 1833-1913 [DNNS]
British army officer
* Our only General

[The] Wolsey of Hungary
See Martinuzzi, George

Wolsey, Thomas 1475?-1530 [NPS, SN]
British prelate and statesman
* [The] Boy Baccaleur
* [The] Butcher's Dog
* Hough No
* Mastiff Cur
* [The] Vicar of Hell

Wolsey, Uncle Bill
See Wolsey, William Franklyn

Wolsey, William Franklyn 1904-
[HPPN]
Canadian educator
* John I of Vancouver, Archbishop
* Wolsey, Uncle Bill

Wolstenholme, Stuart John 1947- [PRS]
British musician
* Wolstenholme, Woolly

Wolstenholme, Woolly
See Wolstenholme, Stuart John

Wolston, Henry
See Twinberrow, William Henry

Wolters, Reinder Albertus 1842-1917
[BE]
Dutch-born baseball player
* Wolters, Rynie

Wolters, Rynie
See Wolters, Reinder Albertus

Wolton, Edward 1492-1555 [PA]
Author
* Ododonus

Wolverton, Fighting Harry
See Wolverton, Harry

Wolverton, Harry 1873-1937
American baseball manager
* Wolverton, Fighting Harry

Womack, David A[lfred] 1933- [CA]
Canadian-born clergyman and author
* Buchan, David
* Yates, David O.

Womack, Dooley
See Womack, Horace Guy

Womack, Horace Guy 1939- [BE]
American baseball player
* Womack, Dooley

Womack, Ricky 20th c. [SI 4-23-84]
American boxer
* Womack, Wonderful

Womack, Sid[ney Kirk] 1896-1958 [BE]
American baseball player
* Womack, Tex

Womack, Tex
See Womack, Sid[ney Kirk]

Womack, Wonderful
See Womack, Ricky

[The] Woman Flogger
See Haynau, Julius Jakob von

[The] Woman in Black
See Gilbert, Marie Dolores Eliza
Rosanna

Woman in White
See Dix, Dorothea Lynde

Woman Motorist of the Century
See Ramsey, Alice Huyler

[The] Woman of Calvados
See Corday d'Armont, [Marie Anne]
Charlotte

[A] Woman of Quality
See Ralph, James

[The] Woman of Revelation XII
See Southcott, Joanna

[The] Woman of the Americas
See Gautier, Felisa De Rincon

[The] Woman Who Always Prays
See Duchesne, Rose Philippine

**[The] Woman Who Always Speaks Her
Mind**
See Cox-Oliver, Edna May

**[The] Woman Who Caught Bugs and
Wrote Books**
See Stratton, Geneva Grace

[The] Woman who Knows
See Scott, Malcolm

Woman Witch'd
See Foe, Daniel

Woman's Nemesis
See Wylie, Philip

Won-Sik, Lim 1919- [IWM]
Korean conductor and educator
* Unpa

Wonder, Alvin
See Lourie, Dick

Wonder Boy
See Kramer, Stanley E.

**[The] Wonder Boy of the Financial
District**
See Koretz, Leo

[The] Wonder Boy of the Speedways
See Fengler, Harlan

[The] Wonder Boy Preacher
See Burke, Solomon

[The] Wonder Child
See Hajos, Magdalena [or Marishka]

Wonder, Jak
See Ferguson, Peter K.

Wonder, Little Stevie
See Cauthen, Steve

Wonder, Little Stevie
See Morris, Steveland

[The] Wonder Maker
See Smith, Andrew Latham

[The] Wonder of the Age
See Sullivan, Dan

[The] Wonder of the World
See Albert IV

[The] Wonder of the World
See Frederick II

[The] Wonder of the World
See Gerbert

[The] Wonder of the World
See Otto III [or Otho]

Wonder, Stevie
See Morris, Steveland

Wonder, Wally
See Jones, Walter [Wally]

Wonder, William
See Kirwan, Thomas

Wonder Woman [code name]
See Barnes, Roberta

[The] Wonder Worker
See Gregory of Neocaesarea

[The] Wonderful
See Gongora y Argote, Luis de

[The] Wonderful Baritone
See De Melvin, Henri

[The] Wonderful Boy of Devizes
See Lawrence, [Sir] Thomas

[The] Wonderful Doctor
See Bacon, Roger

Wonderful, Mr.
See Davis, Sammy, Jr.

Wonderful, Mr.
See Orndorff, Paul

Wonderful, Mother
See Chanin, Myra

[A] Wonderful Quiz
See Lowell, James Russell

[The] Wonderful Soprano
See De Melvin, Henri

Wonderful Walter Payton
See Payton, Walter Jerry

Wonderful Willie Smith
See Smith, Willie

Wonderlich, Jerry 20th c.
Auto racer
* [The] Sheik of Hollywood

Wonders, Anne
See Passel, Anne W[onders]

[The] Wondrous Maid
See Joan of Arc [or Jeanne d'Arc]

Wondrous Wilma Rudolph
See Rudolph, Wilma Glodean Ward

[The] Wondrous Wizard
See Scott, Michael

Wong, Anna May
See Wong Liu Tsong

Wong, Elizabeth 1937- [AW]
Chinese writer
* Lien, Chi

Wong Hai Sheng 20th c.
Chinese cameraman
* Newsreel

Wong, Hin 1888- [LAO]
Journalist
* Huang Hsin Chao

Wong Liu Tsong 1907-1961 [BEW, F1, FC]
Chinese-American actress
* Wong, Anna May

Wong loi Sing, Eugene Wilfred 20th c. [CW]
Surinamese poet and author
* Wols, Frits

Wong, Pearl 20th c. [HPPN]
Chinese-American restaurateur
* [The] Dragon Lady of Broadway

Wong, Po Lan 1870-1972 [HPPN]
Chinese peddler
* Hong Kong Old Mary

Wong Tung Jim 1899- [FC, WEF]
Chinese-born cinematographer
* Howe, James Wong

Wons, Mailliw
See Snow, William

Wonso, Pamela 1942- [SW]
American actress
* Tiffin, Pamela

Woo, Chun Hoi 1936- [IAW]
Chinese author
* Four, Yer

Wood [code name used during World War II]
See Kolbe, Fritz

Wood, Alice 1873?-1949 [BEW, BMH]
Theatrical performer
* Lloyd, Alice

Wood, Anna Cogswell 20th c. [DNA]
American author
* Ridgeway, Algernon

Wood, Anthony 1632-1695 [SN]
British antiquary
* [The] Ostade of Literary History

Wood, Audrey Donella 1927- [BEW]
American choreographer, dancer, actress
* Wood, Deedee

Wood, Barbara Elaine 1923-1955 [HPPN]
American prostitute and murderer
* Graham, Barbara

Wood, Barry 1942- [DC]
British cricketer
* Wood, Sawdust

Wood, Barry
See Rapp, Louis

Wood, Barry
See Rappaport, Barry

Wood, Barry
See Wood, William B.

Wood, Batman
See Wood, Richard

Wood, Bo
See Wood, Charles

Wood, Bootie
See Wood, Mitchell, Jr.

Wood, Buddy
See Wood, Carl

Wood, Carl 1905-1948 [SC]
American actor
* Wood, Buddy

Wood, Carole
See Du Barry, Camille

Wood, Catherine
See Etchison, Birdie L[ee]

Wood, Charles 19th c. [HPPN]
British author
* [A] New Writer

Wood, Charles 20th c. [EF]
American football player
* Wood, Bo

Wood, Charles Asher 1909- [BE]
American baseball player
* Wood, Spades

Wood, Charles Dunning 1820-? [HPPN]
American author
* Dunning, Charles

Wood, Charles Osgood, III 1933- [CA]
American journalist and author
* Osgood, Charles

Wood, Charles Spencer 1900-1974 [BE]
American baseball player
* Wood, Doc

Wood, Charlotte Dunning 1858-? [HPPN]
American author
* Dunning, Charlotte

Wood, Christopher [Hovelle] 1935- [CA]
British author
* Dixon, Rosie
* Grape, Oliver
* Lea, Timothy
* Sutton, Penny

Wood, Clement 1888-1950 [NAA, WW]
American author and poet
* Dubois, Alan

Wood, Daisy 1877-1961 [BMH]
British entertainer
* Lancashire's Own Principal Boy

Wood, Dandy
See Wood, George A.

Wood, David Duffield 1838-1910 [DAM]
American organist and educator
* Wood, Duffle

Wood, Deedee
See Wood, Audrey Donella

Wood, Del
See Hazelwood, Adelaide

Wood, Dick
See Wood, Malcolm

Wood, Doc
See Wood, Charles Spencer

Wood, Doc
See Wood, John B.

Wood, Dorothy Adkins
See Adkins, Dorothy C.

Wood, Duffle
See Wood, David Duffield

Wood, Edgar A[llardyce] 1907- [CA, SAT, TCC]
Canadian author and illustrator
* Wood, Kerry

Wood, Ellen Price 1814-1887 [HPPN, NPS]
British author
* Ludlow, Johnny
* Wood, Mrs. Henry

Wood, Eric
See Campling, F. Knowles

Wood, Esther
See Brady, Esther Wood

Wood, Geoffrey
See Russell, C.

Wood, George 1799-1870 [PA]
Author
* Schlemihl, Peter

Wood, George A. 1858-1924 [AS, BE, PB]
American baseball player
* Wood, Dandy

Wood, Gloria 1919- [FC, ITA]
American actress
* Stevens, K. T.

Wood, Goggles
See Wood, Howard

Wood, Gordon D.
See DeMain, Gordon

Wood, Grant 1892-1942 [WBD]
American painter
* [The] Painter of the Soil

Wood, Hazel
See Smith, Mrs. M. B.

Wood, [Sir] Henry Joseph 1869-1944 [BBD, HPPN]
British conductor and composer
* Klenovsky, Paul

Wood, Horatio 19th c. [HPPN]
American clergyman
* H. W.

Wood, Howard 20th c.
American basketball player
* Wood, Goggles

Wood, [Rev.] James 19th c. [HPPN]
Scottish clergyman and author
* [A] Scotch Preacher

Wood, James Playsted 1905- [SAT]
American author
* St. Briavels, James
* Soudley, Henry

Wood, Jane
See Bokenham, Jane

Wood, Joan Wentworth
See Morgan, Joan

Wood, John ?-1870? [PI]
Irish poet
* De Waltram, Lanner

Wood, John B. ?-1883? [FFF, SN]
American printer and journalist
* [The] Great American Condenser
* Wood, Doc

Wood, John George 1827-1889 [RH]
British author and clergyman
* Forrest, George

Wood, John H., Jr. 1916?-1979
American jurist
* Wood, Maximum John

Wood, Joseph 1889-1985 [BE, PB]
American baseball player
* Wood, Smokey Joe

Wood, Joseph 20th c.
American musician
* Uncle Leroy

Wood, Julia Amanda [Sargent] 1825-1903 [DNA, PA]
American author
* Lee, Minnie Mary

Wood, Ken
See Cianfriglia, Giovanni

Wood, Kerry
See Wood, Edgar A[llardyce]

Wood, Kirk
See Stahl, Le Roy

Wood, Larry
See Wood, Marylaird

Wood, Laura N[ewbold]
See Roper, Laura Wood

Wood, Lillian
See Ross, Mrs. W. S.

Wood, Malcolm 20th c. [EF]
American football player
* Wood, Dick

Wood, Mary
See Bamfield, Veronica [Grissell]

Wood, Marylaird 20th c. [CA]
American writer
* Wood, Larry

Wood, Matilda Alice Victoria 1870-1922 [BEW, BMH, THR]
British theatrical performer
* [The] Bernhardt of the Music Halls
* Delmere, Bella
* Lloyd, Marie
* Our Marie

Wood, [Sir] Matthew 1768-1843 [HHF, HN, SN]
British jurist
* Absolute Wisdom

Wood, Maximum John
See Wood, John H., Jr.

Wood, Mitchell, Jr. 1919- [EJ]
American jazz musician
* Wood, Bootie

Wood, Mrs. G. M. [FFF]
Entertainer
* Saint John, Marguerite

Wood, Mrs. Henry
See Wood, Ellen Price

Wood, Natalie
See Gurdin, Natasha

Wood, Pat
See Baxter, Patricia E. W.

Wood, Patricia E. W. 20th c. [AW, WD]
British poet and playwright
* Ross, Patricia

Wood Pulp Miller
See Miller, Warner

Wood, Quality
See Wood, Violet

Wood, Richard [SMG]
American football player
* Wood, Batman

Wood, Richard Kennedy [Dick] 20th c. [NAA]
American writer
* Baker, Lon
* DuBois, Dick
* Watson, Le. De W.

Wood, Robert 20th c. [HPPN]
British murder trial defendant
* [The] Camden Town Murderer

Wood, Robert Paul 1931- [WD]
British film critic
* Wood, Robin

Wood, Robin
See Wood, Robert Paul

Wood, Roland A. [PA]
Author
* Beaulien

Wood, Rose
See Morrison, Mrs. Lewis

Wood, Rosie 1879-1944 [BMH, THR]
British entertainer
* Lloyd, Rosie

Wood, Roy Winton 1892- [BE]
American baseball player
* Wood, Woody

Wood, Samuel Andrew 1890- [MBF, WW]
British author and journalist
* Cross, Thomson
* Ravenglass, Hal
* Temple, Robin

Wood, Sara Bard Field 1882- [NAA]
American author and poet
* Field, Sara Bard

Wood, Sawdust
See Wood, Barry

Wood, Serry
See Freeman, Graydon La Verne

Wood, Smokey Joe
See Wood, Joseph

Wood, Spades
See Wood, Charles Asher

Wood, Starr 1870-1944 [DBA]
British caricaturist
* [The] Snark

Wood, Stuart 1957- [BP, RO1]
Scottish-born singer
* Wood, Woody

Wood, Sue
See Taylor, Mary Virginia

Wood, Thomas Winter 19th c. [NPS]
Author
* Vanguard

[The] Wood Thrush of Essex
See Whittier, John Greenleaf

Wood, Tommy
See Noack, Armond A.

Wood, Ursula
See Vaughan Williams, Ursula

Wood, Violet 1898- [AW]
British author
* Wood, Quality

Wood, W. S. [PA]
Author
* Merchant, Matthew

Wood, Wee Georgie
See Bramlett, George

Wood, Wilbur 1941- [SMG]
American baseball player
* Wood, Woody

Wood, William 1671-1730 [HPPN]
British ironmaster
* [The] Father of Wood's Metal

Wood, William B. 1910-1971 [FB]
American football player
* Wood, Barry

Wood, William Maxwell ?-1880 [HPPN]
American surgeon
* [The] Chief of the Bureau of
  Medicine and Surgery

Wood, William McDonald 1847-? [PA]
Author
* Jarvie, Nichol

Wood, Woody
See Wood, Roy Winton

Wood, Woody
See Wood, Stuart

Wood, Woody
See Wood, Wilbur

Wood De Vere, Clementine Duchene
1864-1954 [BBD]
French-born opera singer
* De Vere, Clementine Duchene

Wood-Seys, Roland Alexander 1854-1919
[DNA]
British-born author
* Cushing, Paul

Wood-Smith, Noel ?-1955? [MBF]
British author and editor
* Clifford, Martin [house pseudonym]
* Conquest, Owen [house pseudonym]
* Richards, Frank [house pseudonym]

Wood-Smith, Noel (cont.)
* Taylor, Norman
* Terry, Noel

Woodall, Al
See Woodall, Frank Alley

Woodall, Ellis O., Sr. 1927- [BA]
American educator
* Woodall, Woody

Woodall, Frank Alley 20th c. [EF]
American football player
* Woodall, Al

Woodall, Woody
See Woodall, Ellis O., Sr.

Woodard, J. H. [FFF]
American writer
* Jayhawker

Woodberry, Isaac Baker 1819-1858
[BBD]
American composer and music editor
* Woodbury, Isaac Baker

Woodbine, Jennie
See Blount, Annie R.

Woodbine Willie
See Kennedy, Geoffrey Anketell
Studdert

Woodbridge, Anne
See Fletcher, Frances

Woodbridge, Elisabeth
See Morris, Sarah Elisabeth
Woodbridge

Woodbridge, Hudson 1900?-1981 [BWW]
American singer
* Eager, Jimmy
* [The] Guitar Wizard
* Smith, Honey Boy
* Tampa Red
* Whittaker, Hudson

Woodbridge, Ruth
See Law, Ruth Helen

Woodbridge, Timothy 1784-1862 [FFF]
American clergyman
* [The] Blind Preacher

Woodbridge, Wylly 19th c. [HPPN]
American author
* [An] American Citizen

Woodbury, [Rev.] Augustus 1825-?
[HPPN]
American clergyman
* A. W.
* [The] Pastor of the Westminister
  Congregational Society, Providence

Woodbury, Isaac Baker
See Woodberry, Isaac Baker

[The] Woodchopper
See Moody, Clyde

Woodcock, John 1924- [ART]
British artist
* J. W.

Woodcock, Leonard 1911?-
American labor leader and diplomat
* [The] Professor
* [The] Undertaker

Woodcott, Keith
See Brunner, John [Kilian Houston]

Wooden Joe Nicholas
See Nicholas, Joseph [Joe]

Wooden, John 1910- [BB]
American basketball player and coach
* [The] India Rubber Man
* [The] Wizard of Westwood

Wooden Leg
See Stuyvesant, Petrus

[The] Wooden Legged Commissary
See Watson, [Sir] Brook

[The] Wooden Shoe Statesman
See Watson, James Eli

Woodensconce, Papernose, Esq.
See Brough, Robert Barnabas

Wooderidge, Kathleen Mabel 1914-
[HPPN]
British author
* Partridge, Kathleen

Woodfall, Memory
See Woodfall, William

Woodfall, William 1745-1803 [SN]
British journalist
* Woodfall, Memory

Woodfern, Winnie
See Gibson, Mary W. Stanley

Woodfield, Harry 20th c. [BBH]
American horseshoe pitcher
* Woodfield, Pop

Woodfield, Pop
See Woodfield, Harry

Woodford, Cecil
See Tarkington, [Newton] Booth

Woodford, [Irene] Cecile 1913- [AW,
IAW]
British author
* Barrie, Jane
* Douglas, Kim
* Lee, Veronica

Woodford, Jack
See Woolfolk, Josiah Pitts

Woodforde, James 19th c. [HPPN]
British author
* [A] Gentleman of Shropshire

Woodfork, Robert 1925- [BWW, NBB]
American singer
* Poor Bob

Woodfull, William Maldon 1897-1965
[EC]
Australian cricketer
* [The] Great Unbowlable

Woodham, Mrs. 1743-1803 [NPS]
Singer and actress
* Buck, Spencer

Woodham-Smith, Cecil Blanche
[Fitzgerald] 1896-1977 [CA, TC1]
British historian and author
* Gordon, Janet

Woodhead, A.
See Aldrich, Henry

Woodhead, Cynthia 20th c. [WP 7-31-84]
American swimmer
* Woodhead, Sippy

Woodhead, James 1851-1881 [BE]
British-born baseball player
* Woodhead, Red

Woodhead, Red
See Woodhead, James

Woodhead, Sippy
See Woodhead, Cynthia

Woodhouse, C. M.
See Woodhouse, Christopher Montague

Woodhouse, Christopher Montague 1917-
[MBL]
British author
* Woodhouse, C. M.

Woodhouse, Henry
See Casalegno, Mario Terenzio Enrico

Woodhouse, Martin 1932- [CA]
British author
* Charlton, John

Woodhull, Victoria Claflin 1838-1927
[HPPN]
American lecturer, author, editor
* [The] Terrible Siren

Woodin, H. L. 20th c. [SMG]
American football player
* Woodin, Whitey

Woodin, Whitey
See Woodin, H. L.

Woodland, Waif
See Blair, Caroline

Woodlawn, Holly
See Danhaki, Harold

Woodleigh, Dorma 1893- [THR]
British actress and dancer
* Leigh, Dorma

Woodley, David 20th c.
American football player
* Woodstrock

Woodley, H. G.
See Wilkins, Henry George

Woodley, Letitia Matilda 1869-? [THR]
British comedienne
* Pryde, Peggy

Woodley, Winifred
See Hedden, Worth Tuttle

Woodman, Cocoa
See Woodman, Dan[iel Courtenay]

Woodman, Dan[iel Courtenay] 1893-1962
[BE]
American baseball player
* Woodman, Cocoa

Woodman, Thomas 20th c. [MBF]
British author
* Quilter, Eddie

Woodpecker, Woody
See Brzezinski, Zbigniew

Woodrich, Mary Neville 1915- [CA,
SAT]
American author
* Neville, Mary

Woodroffe, Daniel
See Woods, Mrs. J. C.

Woodroffe, [Sir] John 1865-1936 [EOP]
British author and translator
* Avalon, Arthur

Woodrook, R. A.
See Cowlishaw, Ranson

Woodruff, Burt
See Woodruff, William H.

Woodruff, Clyde
See Vern, David

Woodruff, George 20th c. [BBH]
American football coach
* Woodruff, Kid

Woodruff, John 1915- [BBH]
American track and field athlete
* Woodruff, Long John

Woodruff, Josephine Constance 1909-
[F2, FC]
American actress
* Booth, Edwina

Woodruff, Julia Louisa Matilda [PA]
Author
* Jay, W. L. M.

Woodruff, Kid
See Woodruff, George

Woodruff, Long John
See Woodruff, John

Woodruff, Orville 1876-1937 [BE]
American baseball player
* Woodruff, Sam

Woodruff, Philip
See Mason, Philip

Woodruff, Robert W. [Bob] 1890?-
[HPPN]
American business executive
* [The] Boss
* Coke, Mr.
* [The] Old Tycoon

Woodruff, Robert W.
See Mencken, Henry Louis [Harry]

Woodruff, Sam
See Woodruff, Orville

Woodruff, Timothy Lester 1858-1913
American merchant and politician
* Woodruff, Tiny Tim

Woodruff, Tiny Tim
See Woodruff, Timothy Lester

Woodruff, William H. 1856-1934 [SC]
American actor
* Woodruff, Burt

Woodrum, Clifton Alexander 1887-
[HPPN]
American politician
* [The] Choirmaster of the House

Woods, A. H.
See Herman, Aladore

Woods, Al
See Dreeke, Frederick Ludwig

Woods, Al
See Woods, Alvis

Woods, Albert Herman [Al]
See Herman, Aladore

Woods, Alvis 1953- [ALR]
American baseball player
* Woods, Al

Woods, Big Boy
See Collins, Samuel

Woods, Buddy
See Woods, Oscar

Woods, C. H. [PA]
Author
* Otis, Belle

Woods, Charles Robert 1827-1885 [FFF]
American army officer
* Woods, Susan

Woods, Clee 1893- [CA]
American author
* Forest, Lee
* Park, D. U.
* Warbridge, C. W.

Woods, Constance
See McComb, Katherine Woods

Woods, Daddy
See Woods, Frank

Woods, Ethel 1878-? [BEW]
British actress
* Griffies, Ethel

Woods, Frank 20th c. [HPPN]
American film executive
* Woods, Daddy

Woods, Frederick 1932- [CA]
British author
* Ives, Lawrence

Woods, George Rowland 1915-1982
[BE]
American baseball player
* Woods, Pinky

Woods, Granville T. 1856-1910 [HPPN,
IBW]
American inventor
* [The] Dean of American Inventors
* [The] Father of the Synchronous
  Multiplex Railway Telegraph

Woods, James 19th c. [PI]
Irish poet
* Demos

Woods, James 20th c. [WGT]
Author
* Navarchus [joint pseudonym with Patrick Vaux]
* Yexley, Lionel

Woods, James Jerome [Jim] 1939- [BE]
American baseball player
* Woods, Woody

Woods, Jonah
See Woods, Olwen Spencer

Woods, Kate Tannant 19th c. [FFF]
American writer
* True, Kate

Woods, Lawrence [joint pseudonym with Donald A(llen) Wollheim]
See Lowndes, Robert Augustine Ward

Woods, Lawrence [joint pseudonym with Donald A(llen) Wollheim]
See Michel, John B.

Woods, Lawrence [joint pseudonym with Robert Augustine Ward Lowndes, John Michel]
See Wollheim, Donald A[llen]

Woods, Lawrence J. 20th c. [IBW]
American manufacturer
* [The] Chicago Carpet King

Woods, Leland
See Detzer, Karl

Woods, Mrs. J. C. 20th c. [NPS]
Author
* Woodroffe, Daniel

Woods, Nat
See Stratemeyer, Edward L.

Woods, Nick
See Schaber, Nicholas

Woods, Olando 1951- [RO2]
American musician
* Woods, Terrell

Woods, Olwen Spencer 1913- [AW]
British-born author
* Woods, Jonah

Woods, Oscar 1900-1956? [BWW]
American singer
* [The] Lone Wolf
* [The] Street Rustler
* [The] Troubadour
* Woods, Buddy

Woods, P. F.
See Bayley, Barrington J[ohn]

Woods, Percy 1909- [MY]
American singer
* Woods, Sonny

Woods, Pinky
See Woods, George Rowland

Woods, Rip
See Woods, Roosevelt, Jr.

Woods, Roosevelt, Jr. 1933- [BA]
American educator
* Woods, Rip

Woods, Ross
See Story, Rosamond Mary

Woods, Sara
See Bowen-Judd, Sara [Hutton]

Woods, Sonny
See Woods, Percy

Woods, Stockton
See Forrest, Richard S[tockton]

Woods, Stuart
See Lee, Stuart

Woods, Susan
See Woods, Charles Robert

Woods, Terrell
See Woods, Olando

Woods, William J. 1937-1968 [RO1]
American singer
* Little Willie John

Woods, Woody
See Woods, James Jerome [Jim]

Woodsley, H. Austin
See Mittelholzer, Edgar

Woodson
See James, Jesse Woodson

Woodson, B. J.
See James, Franklin

Woodson, Carter Godwin 1875-1950 [IBW]
American historian, author, editor
* [The] Father of Black History
* [The] Father of Modern Black History

Woodson, Jeff
See Oglesby, Joseph

Woodson, Kittie
See Mack, Mrs. Will H.

Woodson, Mary Blake 1886- [NAA]
American journalist
* Mayo, Mary

Woodson, Meg
See Baker, Elsie

Woodson, Mrs. W. L. [FFF]
Entertainer
* Fay, Lottie

Woodson, Richard Lee [Dick] 1945- [BE, PB]
American baseball player
* Woodson, Woody

Woodson, Woody
See Woodson, Richard Lee [Dick]

Woodstrock
See Woodley, David

Woodthorpe, Georgie
See Cooper, Mrs. Fred

Woodthorpe, Patricia Mariella 1928- [ART]
British painter and draftsman
* M. W.

Woodville, Anthony [Lord Rivers] 1442-1483 [SN]
* [Le] Wellington des Joueurs

Woodville, Jennie
See Stabler, Jamie Latham

Woodward, A. Aubertine 1841-? [PA]
American author
* Auber, Forrestier

Woodward, Calvin M. 1837-1914 [HPPN]
American author and educator
* [The] Father of Manual Training

Woodward, Edward [Emberlin] 20th c. [WW]
Author
* Grierson, Jane

Woodward, Grace Steele 1899- [CAP]
American author
* Doane, Marion S.

Woodward, Henry 1717-1777 [NPS]
Actor
* [The] Great Master in the Science of Grimace

Woodward, Henry Lovett [PA]
Author
* H. L. W.

Woodward, Ike
See Woodward, Isaiah Alfonso

Woodward, Isaiah Alfonso 1912- [BA]
American physician
* Woodward, Ike

Woodward, John 1665-1728 [SN]
Physician and antiquarian
* Fossile?

Woodward, John 1932?-
British naval officer
* Woodward, Sandy

Woodward, Joseph Janvier 1833-1884 [FFF]
American physician and author
* Janvier

Woodward, Lilian
See Marsh, John

Woodward, Patti 1880-1967 [BDF, F1, FC]
American actress
* Darwell, Jane

Woodward, Robert B. 1917- [HPPN]
American chemist
* [The] Father of Atabrine

Woodward, Sandy
See Woodward, John

Woodward, Tena Garrison 1883-1968 [IA]
American author
* Garrison, Anet

Woodward, Thomas Jones 1940- [IPA, RO2, SW]
Welsh-born singer
* Jones, Tom
* Scott, Tommy
* Tiger Tom
* [The] Twisting Vocalist

Woodward, William Frederick 1942- [BE, PB]
American baseball player
* Woodward, Woody

Woodward, Woody
See Woodward, William Frederick

Woodworth, Francis Channing 1812-1859 [DNA]
American author
* Thinker, Theodore

Woodworth, John 1768-1858 [HPPN]
American jurist
* [An] American Youth

Woodworth, Red
See Woodworth, Wade

Woodworth, Samuel 1784-1842 [DNA, SN]
American printer, journalist, author
* [The] American Goldsmith
* Selim

Woodworth, Wade 20th c. [HPPN]
American football player
* Woodworth, Red

Woody, Regina Jones 1894- [CA]
American dancer and author
* Devi, Nila

[The] Wool Carder President
See Fillmore, Millard

Wooldridge, George B. [PA]
Author
* Quick, Tom

Wooldridge, Lestocq Boileau 1851?-1920 [BEW]
Actor, theatre manager, playwright
* Lestocq, William

Wooldridge, William O. 1922?- [HPPN]
American soldier
* [The] Army's Topmost Sarge
* [The] Kickback King
* [The] P. X. Millionaire

Wooler, Thomas Jonathan 1786-1853 [PA]
Author
* Black Dwarf

Woolery, Clarence ?-1978 [FIR]
Singer
* Woolery, Pete

Woolery, Pete
See Woolery, Clarence

Wooley [or Woodley?], Charles [PA]
Author
* C. A. M. W.

Wooley, Edward Mott 1867-? [HPPN]
American author
* Bracefield, Richard

Wooley, John [Steven] 1949- [CA]
American author, editor, columnist
* Leslie, Robert B.
* Severs, Jerome

Wooley, Sheb
See Wooley, Shelby F.

Wooley, Shelby F. 1921- [ASC, CWG, DAM]
American singer, composer, actor
* Colder, Ben
* Wooley, Sheb

Woolf, George 1910-1946 [BBH, CSH]
Canadian-born jockey
* [The] Iceman

Woolf, [Adeline] Virginia 1882-1941 [DF 3-26-86]
British author
* [The] Goat

Woolf, Walter 1899- [THR]
American actor and singer
* King, Walter Woolf

Woolfolk, Josiah Pitts 1894-1971 [CA, NAA, WW]
American author
* Britt, Sappho Henderson
* Kennedy, Howard
* Sayre, Gordon
* Woodford, Jack

Woollcott, Alexander Humphreys 1887-1943 [BI, HPPN]
American author and journalist
* [The] Town Crier
* Woollcott, Louisa May

Woollcott, Louisa May
See Woollcott, Alexander Humphreys

Woolley, Catherine 1904- [AW, CA, MJA]
American author
* Thayer, Jane

Woolley, Edgar Montillion 1888-1963 [BEW, EMT, FC]
American actor and director
* Woolley, Monty

Woolley, Monty
See Woolley, Edgar Montillion

Woolly Bob Rich
See Rich, Robert Felming

Woolly Head
See Julian, George Washington

Woolman, David S. 1916- [CA]
American author and journalist
* Vaidon, Lawdom

Woolman, John 1720-1772 [HPPN]
American tailor, clergyman, abolitionist
* [The] Child of Light

Woolmer, Robert Andrew [Bob] 1948- [DC]
British cricketer
* Woolmer, Woolly

Woolmer, Woolly
See Woolmer, Robert Andrew [Bob]

Woolrich, Cornell
See Hopley-Woolrich, Cornell George

Woolrich, Daniel 20th c. [SFP]
Author
* Homes, Geoffrey

Woolridge, Anna Marie 1930- [IBW, SW]
American singer, actress, educator
* Lee, Gabby
* Lincoln, Abbey
* Moseka, Aminata
* Woolridge, Gabby

Woolridge, Gabby
See Woolridge, Anna Marie

Woolsey, Maryhale 1899- [ASC]
American author
* Hale, Eugenia
* Hale, Mary
* Snow, Terry

Woolsey, Roland Bert 1953- [FR]
American football player
* Woolsey, Rolly

Woolsey, Rolly
See Woolsey, Roland Bert

Woolsey, Sarah Chauncey 1835-1905 [FFF]
American author and poet
* Coolidge, Susan

Woolson, Constance Fenimore 1838-1894 [DNA, WBD]
American author
* March, Anne

Woolston, Thomas 1670-1733 [HPPN]
British deist
* Mystagogus
* Renatus, Adamantius

Woolwine, Laura [FFF]
Entertainer
* Bellini, Laura

Woolworth, Frank Winfield 1852-1919 [HPPN]
American merchant
* [The] Father of the Dime Store
* [The] Father of the Five and Ten

Woon
See Wotherspoon, Ralph

Wooten, Earl Hazwell 1924- [BE]
American baseball player
* Wooten, Junior

Wooten, Junior
See Wooten, Earl Hazwell

Wootten, Lawrence B. 1922- [EJ]
American jazz musician
* Wootten, Red

Wootten, Red
See Wootten, Lawrence B.

[The] Wop With the Mop
See Capone, Al[phonse]

Worblefister, Petunia
See Gribbin, Lenore S.

Worboys, Anne Eyre
See Worboys, Annette Isobel

Worboys, Annette Isobel 20th c. [AW, CA, WD]
New Zealand-born author
* Eyre, Annette
* Maxwell, Vicky
* Worboys, Anne Eyre

Worcester, Donald E[mmet]
See Makemson, Donald Emmet

Worcester, Leonard 1767-1846 [HPPN]
American clergyman
* Cephas

Worcester, Noah 1758-1837 [HPPN, PA]
American clergyman and author
* Monitor, Elias
* Noah W.
* Philopacificus
* [The] Pilgrim Good Intent
* Usher, Freeman L.

Worcester Sam Perris
See Perris, Samuel

[The] Worcester Speculator
See Fiske, Nathan

[The] Word Catcher
See Ritson, Joseph

[The] Word King
See Partridge, Eric Honeywood

Worde, Wynkyn de
See Van Wynkyn, Jan

Worden, Helen
See Cranmer, Helen Worden

Worden, Mae
See Shane, Mae Worden

Wordsdale, James ?-1767 [RH]
British painter and playwright
* Jemmy

Wordsworth, Christopher 1774-1846 [FFF]
British clergyman and scholar
* [The] Master of Trinity

Wordsworth, Dora
See Quillinan, Dorothy Wordsworth

Wordsworth, Favel Perry 1851-1888 [BE]
American baseball player
* Wordsworth, Red

Wordsworth, Red
See Wordsworth, Favel Perry

Wordsworth, William 1770-1850 [DEL, FFF, NPS, SN]
British poet
* [The] Bard of Rydal Mount
* [The] Blockhead
* [The] Clownish Sycophant
* [The] Converted Jacobin
* [The] Cumberland Poet
* [The] Farmer of a Lay
* [The] Great God Pan
* [The] Great Laker
* [The] Little Boatman
* [The] Lost Leader

Wordsworth, William (cont.)
* Old Ponder
* [The] Poet of Nature
* [The] Poet of the Excursion
* Poet Wordy
* This Poetical Charlatan
* This Political Parasite
* [The] Windemere Treasure

Worfel, W. G. 20th c. [SFL]
Author
* [The] Baron

[The] Worker in Souls
See Moody, Dwight Lyman

[A] Working Clergyman
See Mereweather, [Rev.] John Davies

[A] Working Man
See Carter, James

[A] Working Man
See Dixon, Thomas

Workman, Charles 20th c. [BLB, MM, PHM]
American underworld figure
* [The] Bug

Workman, Harry Hall 1899-1972 [BE]
American baseball player
* Workman, Hoge

Workman, Hoge
See Workman, Harry Hall

Workman, James 20th c. [SFL]
Author
* Dark, James

Workman, Raymond 1909?-1966 [AS]
American jockey
* Workman, Sonny

Workman, Sonny
See Workman, Raymond

Workman, Uncle Billy
See Workman, William Henry

Workman, William Henry 1839-1918 [HPPN]
American pioneer and civic leader
* Workman, Uncle Billy

[A] Workng Man
See Somerville, Alexander

Works, Judge
See Works, Ralph Talmadge

Works, Ralph Talmadge 1888-1941 [BE]
American baseball player
* Works, Judge

[The] World
See Smith, Raymond

World Citizen Number 1
See Davis, Garry

World Destroyer
See Hamilton, Edmond [Moore]

World, Mr.
See Reeves, Stephen [Steve]

[The] World Renowned Coon Shouter
See Abuza, Sophie

[The] World War Croesus
See McAdoo, William Gibbs

[The] World Wrecker
See Hamilton, Edmond [Moore]

[The] World's Champion Cowboy
See Mix, Tom

[The] World's Champion Moaner
See Smith, Clara

[The] World's Fair Mayor
See Harrison, Carter H.

World's Fairest, Miss
See Jergens, Adele Louisa

[The] World's Fastest Farmer
See Clark, James [Jimmy]

[The] World's Fastest Female Swimmer
See Fraser, Dawn

[The] World's Fastest Human
See Paddock, Charles W.

[The] World's Fastest Tapper
See Verdon, Gwyneth Evelyn

[The] World's Fastest Woman
See Rudolph, Wilma Glodean Ward

[The] World's First Black Combat Aviator
See Bullard, Eugene Jacques

[The] World's First Historian
See Cadmus of Miletus

[The] World's First Photographer
See Daguerre, Louis Jacques Nande

[The] World's Foremost Jewel Thief
See Williams, Albert [Albie]

[The] World's Foremost Photojournalist
See White, Margaret Bourke

[The] World's Funniest Woman
See Davis, Madonna Josephine

[The] World's Greatest Actor
See Blythe, John

[The] World's Greatest Alto Saxophone Player
See Dorsey, James [Jimmy]

[The] World's Greatest Blues Shouter
See Turner, Joseph [Vernon]

[The] World's Greatest Blues Singer
See Johnson, Alonzo

[The] World's Greatest Dribbler
See Haynes, Marques Oreole

[The] World's Greatest Eccentric Juggler
See Dukinfield, William Claude

[The] World's Greatest Female Tap Dancer
See Powell, Eleanor

[The] World's Greatest Gospel Singer
See Jackson, Mahalia

[The] World's Greatest Pickpocket
See Perry, Vic[tor]

[The] **World's Greatest Railroad Buff**
See Whitaker, Rogers Ernest Malcolm

[The] **World's Greatest Salesman**
See Girardi, Joe

[The] **World's Greatest Tenor**
See Caruso, Errico

[The] **World's Greatest Trumpet Player**
See Severinsen, Carl

[The] **World's Greatest Woman Athlete**
See Zaharias, Mildred Didrikson

[The] **World's Heaviest Man**
See Hughes, Robert Earl

[The] **World's Largest Cotton Planter**
See Richardson, Edmund

[The] **World's Last Great Aviation Pioneer**
See Northrop, John K.

[The] **World's Most Admired Woman**
See Roosevelt, [Anna] Eleanor

[The] **World's Most Dangerous Wrestler**
See Afflis, Richard

[The] **World's Most Famous Athlete**
See Arantes Do Nascimento, Edson

[The] **World's Most Perfectly Developed Man**
See Siciliano, Angelo

[The] **World's Most Prolific and Popular Writer of Thrillers**
See Oppenheim, E[dward] Phillips

[The] **World's Most Prolific Novelist**
See Cartland, Barbara [Hamilton]

[The] **World's Most Pulchritudinous Evangelist**
See McPherson, Aimee Semple

[The] **World's Most Scientific Wrestler**
See Snyder, Wilbur

[The] **World's Most Widely Syndicated Cartoonist**
See Lurie, Ranan R.

[The] **World's Number 1 Industrial Architect**
See Kahn, Albert

[The] **World's Number One Wisecracker**
See Rogers, Will[iam Penn Adair]

[The] **World's Oldest College Boy**
See Haines, William

[The] **World's Oldest Teenager**
See Thomas, Rufus

[The] **World's Richest Cop**
See Gilbert, Daniel A.

[The] **World's Richest Problem Child**
See Williams, Theodore Samuel [Ted]

[The] **World's Second Richest Man**
See Mellon, Andrew William

[The] **World's Smallest Man**
See Moore, Pete[r]

[The] **World's Strongest Man**
See Anderson, Paul

[The] **World's Strongest Teen-Ager**
See Gubner, Gary

[The] **World's Sweetheart**
See Smith, Gladys Mary

[The] **World's Tallest Economist**
See Galbraith, John Kenneth

[The] **World's Tallest Man**
See Hibe, Henry

[The] **World's Tallest Man**
See Wadlow, Robert Pershing

[The] **World's Tallest Woman**
See Allen, Sandy

[The] **World's Thinnest Man**
See Robinson, Peter

[The] **World's Top Boots and Saddle Star**
See Slye, Leonard

[The] **World's Wildest Tenor Man**
See Cobbs, Arnette

[The] **World's Wonder**
See Elizabeth I

[The] **World's Worst Guitarist**
See Bowman, Don

[The] **World's Youngest President**
See Duvalier, Jean-Claude

Worley, Frederick U. 19th c. [SFL, WGT]
Author
* Benefice

Worloou, Lambros 1915- [FC]
Greek-Egyptian singer
* Guetary, Georges

[The] **Worm**
See McCarter, Willie

Worm, Olaus 1588-1654 [PA]
Author
* Vormius

Worman, Eli
See Weil, Roman L[ee]

Wormington, Hannah Marie 1914- [CA]
American archaeologist and author
* Volk, Hannah Marie

Wormley, Cinda
See Kornblum, Cinda

Worms, Roger 1918?- [BI]
French journalist
* Stephane, Roger

Wormser, Richard [Edward] 1908-
[SFL, SFP]
Author
* Carter, Nick [house pseudonym]
* Friend, Ed

Worne, Duke
See Worne, Howard B.

Worne, Howard B. 1890-1933 [HPPN]
American director
* Worne, Duke

Worne, John
See Wylie, James

Worner, Philip Arthur Incledon 1910-
[AW]
British author
* Incledon, Philip
* Sylvester, Philip

Wornum, Miriam 1898- [AW]
American author
* Dennis, Eve

Wornum, Ralph Nicholson 1812-1877
[IP]
British artist and author
* [A] Layman

Worrell, Ernest P.
See Varney, Jim

Worrell, Everil 1893-1969 [HFF, WGT]
American author
* Monett, Lireve

Worrell, Jennie
See Hatfield, Mrs.

Worsley, Bruce
See Digby-Worsley, Bruce

Worsley, Gump
See Worsley, Lorne John

Worsley, Julia Taylor 1878-1976
[HPPN]
American actress
* Taylor, Julia

Worsley, Lorne John 1929- [CEI, FHE, HPPN, SR]
Canadian hockey player
* [The] Gumper
* [The] Lonely Hero of Hockey
* Worsley, Gump

Worsley, [Sir] Richard 1751-1805 [IP]
British antiquary
* Whimsy, [Sir] Finical

Worsnop, Wilfrid 1900-1966 [FC]
British actor
* Lawson, Wilfrid

[The] **Worst Actress of the Year**
See Grasle, Elizabeth

[The] **Worst Pope**
See Borgia, Rodrigo [or Rodriguez]

Worters, Roy 1900-1957 [FHE]
Canadian-born hockey player
* Worters, Shrimp

Worters, Shrimp
See Worters, Roy

Worth, Adam 1844-1902 [HPPN]
American criminal and thief
* Grau, Edouard
* [The] Napoleon of Crime

Worth, Amy
See Keller, David H[enry]

Worth, Billie
See Rothmund, Wilhelmino

Worth, Claude
See Holdsworth, Claude

Worth, Constance
See Howarth, Jocelyn

Worth, Dan
See Cruger, Paul

Worth, Gorham A. 1773-1856 [DNA]
American journalist and banker
* Jones, Ignatius

Worth, Helen
See Wolfe, Laura [Guyol]

Worth, Margaret
See Arvonen, Helen

Worth, Margaret
See Strickland, Margot

Worth, Marion
See Wilson, Mary Ann Ward

Worth, Martin
See Wigglesworth, Martin Francis

Worth, Nicholas
See Page, Walter Hines

Worth, Nigel
See Wright, Noel

Worth, Peter [house pseudonym, Ziff-Davis]
See Geier, Chester S.

Worth, Peter [house pseudonym, Ziff-Davis]
See Graham, Roger Phillips

Worth, Valerie
See Bahlke, Valerie Worth

Worthington, Allan Fulton 1929- [BE]
American baseball player
* Worthington, Red

Worthington, Mabel
See Blake, Mrs. O. W.

Worthington, Red
See Worthington, Allan Fulton

Worthington, Red
See Worthington, Robert Lee [Bob]

Worthington, Robert Lee [Bob] 1906-1963 [BN]
American baseball player
* Rhubarb, Colonel
* Worthington, Red

Worthington Ball, John
See Totten, W. Fred

Worthington-Smith, Hammett 1923-
[BA]
American educator
* H. W.

Worthington-Stuart, Brian Arthur
20th c. [WW]
Author
* Meredith, Peter
* Stuart, Brian

[The] Worthless
See Wenceslaus [or Wenceslas]

Worthy of England
See More, [Sir] Thomas

[The] Worthy Patriarch of Howard Division
See Morrison, E.

Wortis, Avi 1937- [CA, SAT]
American author
* Avi

Wortley, Charles Stuart [IP]
British army officer and author
* C. S. W., Captain the Honble.

Wortman, Buster
See Wortman, Frank

Wortman, Chuck
See Wortman, William Lewis

Wortman, Frank 1903-1970 [BLB]
American underworld figure
* Wortman, Buster

Wortman, Frank 20th c. [HPPN]
American film stage and scenery designer
* Wortman, Huck

Wortman, Huck
See Wortman, Frank

Wortman, William Lewis 1892- [BE]
American baseball player
* Wortman, Chuck

Worts, George Frank 1892- [WGT, WW]
American author
* Brent, Loring

Wosmek, Frances 1917- [CA]
American author and illustrator
* Brailsford, Frances

Wotherspoon, Ralph 1897- [WWL]
British author
* Woon

Wotton, William 1666-1726 [IP, NPS]
British scholar and clergyman
* [The] Boy Bachelor
* M. N.

Wotton, William, D.D.
See Astell, Mary

Woty, William 1731?-1791 [IP]
British poet
* Copywell, James

Wouil, George
See Slaney, George Wilson

[The] Would Be Truman Heir
See Carter, James Earl, Jr. [Jimmy]

[The] Would-be-Cromwell of America
See Adams, Samuel

[The] Wounded Hero
See Mantle, Mickey Charles

[The] Wounded Wonder
See Criqui, Eugene

Wovoka 1856?-1932 [WBD]
American Indian religious leader
* Wilson, Jack

WOW
See Wejp-Olsen, Werner

Wow the Wizard
See Fox, Karrell

Woxholt, Greta 1916- [FC]
Norwegian actress
* Gynt, Greta

Woy, Bucky
See Woy, William

Woy, William 1938- [BI]
American sports agent
* Woy, Bucky

Woyda
See Adamowicz, Adam

Woz
See Wozniak, Stephen

Wozniak, Stephen 1950?- [NW 5-30-83, NW 9-20-82]
American computer designer and business executive
* Woz

Wraith, W. J. 20th c. [CCL]
Canadian poet
* Alexander, Walter

Wrangel, Friedrich Heinrich Ernst von 1784-1877 [SN, WBD]
Prussian army officer
* Wrangel, Papa

Wrangel, Papa
See Wrangel, Friedrich Heinrich Ernst von

Wrangham, Francis 1769-1843 [IP]
British clergyman and author
* F. W
* Foote, Samuel, Jr.
* [An] Old Pen
* W.

[The] Wrangler
See Henry II

Wraxall, [Sir] Frederick Charles L. 1828-1865 [IP, PA]
British author
* Wraxall, Lascelles

Wraxall, Lascelles
See Wraxall, [Sir] Frederick Charles L.

Wray, Daniel 1701-1783 [HPPN]
British author
* W.

Wray, Fay 1907- [HPPN]
Canadian actress
* [The] Girl King Kong took a Shine to

Wray, James R. Ludlow 1894-1967 [AS, FB]
American football player and coach
* Wray, Lud

Wray, John 1628?-1705 [DNNS, HPPN, WBD]
British naturalist
* [The] Father of English Botany
* [The] Father of English Natural History
* Ray, John

Wray, John
See Malloy, John

Wray, Leopold
See Chatelain, Clara de Pontigny de

Wray, Lud
See Wray, James R. Ludlow

Wray, Mary   [IP]
British author
* [A] Lady

Wray, Reginald
See Home-Gall, William Benjamin

Wray, Roger
See Marriott, James William

Wray, W. Fitzwater 20th c. [WWL]
British author
* Kuklos

[The] Wrecker
See Hrechkosy, David John

[The] Wrecker
See Morse, Wayne Lyman

Wreford, James
See Watson, J[ames] Wreford

Wreford, John Reynell 19th c. [HPPN]
British hymn writer
* J. R. W.

Wren, [Sir] Christopher 1632-1723 [SN]
British architect
* Nestor

Wren, Ellaruth
See Elkins, Ella Ruth

Wren, Jenny
See Atkinson, Jane

Wren, Junior
See Wren, Lowe

Wren, Lowe 20th c. [EF]
American football player
* Wren, Junior

Wren, M. K.
See Renfroe, Martha Kay

Wren, P. C.
See Wren, Percival Christopher

Wren, Percival Christopher 1885-1941 [LC]
British author
* Wren, P. C.

Wrencher, Big John
See Wrencher, John Thomas

Wrencher, John Thomas 1923-1977 [BWW, NBB]
American singer
* One Armed John
* Wrencher, Big John

Wrenford, W. H. 19th c. [HPPN]
British author
* Master of the Usk Grammar School

[The] Wrestler Who Never Loses
See Rocca, Antonino

Wrestling's National Favorite
See Gagne, Verne

[The] Wretch of Sion
See Whytforde, Richard

Wrexe, Charles
See Hardinge, Charles Wrexe

Wrifford, Anson   [IP]
American author
* [An] Experienced Teacher

Wright, Ab
See Wright, Albert Owen

Wright, Albert 1912-1957 [AS, BX, RBE]
Mexican-born boxer
* Wright, Chalky

Wright, Albert Owen 1905-   [BE]
American baseball player
* Wright, Ab

Wright, Alexander ?-1940 [BMH]
Australian impressionist
* Navarre, Andre

Wright, Amos
See Magoun, Frederick Alexander

Wright, Anna [Maria Louisa Perrott] Rose 1890-1968 [CA]
American educator and author
* Rose, Anna Perrott

Wright, Archibald Lee 1916?- [BX, IBW, RBE, WP 9-20-85]
American boxer
* [The] Magnificent Mongoose
* Moore, Ancient Archie
* Moore, Archie
* Ol' Man River
* [The] Old Mongoose

Wright, Arleta 1923- [CA]
American author
* Richardson, Arleta

Wright, Armand Vincent 1896-1965 [SC]
American actor
* Wright, Curly

Wright, Arthur Justin 1889?-1954 [BI]
American painter
* Wright, Jud

Wright, Benjamin 1770-1842 [HPPN]
American engineer
* [The] Father of American Engineering

Wright, Bill
See Wright, Burnis

Wright, Bruce McMarion 1918-   [IBW]
American jurist and poet
* Turn 'Em Loose Bruce

Wright, Buckshot
See Wright, Forest Glenn

Wright, Buggy
See Wright, Clarence

Wright, Burnis 20th c. [OBW]
American baseball player
* Wright, Bill

Wright, Cat
See Wright, Rayfield

Wright, Ceylon
See Wright, Edward Yatman

Wright, Chalky
See Wright, Albert

Wright, Charles   [IP]
American author
* Mountaineer

Wright, Charles 1927- [EJ]
American jazz musician
* Wright, Specs

Wright, Charles Barstow 1822-1898 [HPPN]
American railroad president and financier
* [The] Father of Tacoma

Wright, Clarence 20th c. [OBW]
American baseball player
* Wright, Buggy

Wright, Clyde 1943- [PB]
American baseball player
* Wright, Skeeter

Wright, Curly
See Wright, Armand Vincent

Wright, Damon
See Ackerman, Forrest J[ames]

Wright, Dancer
See Wright, Elmo

Wright, Deacon
See Wright, William Simmons

Wright, Dick
See Wright, William James

Wright, Donna
See Martin, Kimberly Ann

Wright, E. M. 19th c. [IP]
American author
* Victor, Verity

Wright, Edward H. 20th c. [IBW]
American politician
* [The] Iron Master

Wright, Edward Yatman 20th c. [BE]
American baseball player
* Wright, Ceylon

Wright, Eleazar
See McNemar, Richard

Wright, Elinor Bruce 1921- [IAW]
British author
* Lyon, Elinor

Wright, Elizur 1804-1885 [HPPN, IP, WBD]
American actuary
* [A] Democrat of the Old School
* [The] Father of Legal-Reserve Life Insurance

Wright, Elizur (cont.)
* [A] Friend of the Road
* One of the "Eighteen Millions of Bores"

Wright, Elmo 1949- [FB]
American football player
* Wright, Dancer

Wright, Elsie
See Kaplan, Leigh Wright

Wright, Elsie N. 1907- [WW]
Author
* Grayson, [Capt.] J. J.

Wright, Enid Meadowcroft [LaMonte]
1898-1966 [CAP, SAT]
American author
* Meadowcroft, Enid LaMonte

Wright, Eugene Joseph [Gene] 1923-
[EJ7]
American jazz musician
* Wright, Senator

Wright, Farnsworth 1888-1940 [WGT]
American author
* Hard, Francis

Wright, Faye 1914- [CA]
American author
* Mata, Daya

Wright, Forest Glenn 1901- [BE, PB]
American baseball player
* Wright, Buckshot

Wright, Frances [Fanny] 1795-1852
[PA]
British-American author
* [An] Englishwoman

Wright, Frances J.
See Crothers, Jessie F[rances]

Wright, Francesca
See Robins, Denise [Naomi]

Wright, Frank Lloyd 1869-1959 [HPPN]
American architect and author
* America's Greatest Architect
* [The] Founder of the Taliesin Fellowship

Wright, Franklin
See Farmer, Henry

Wright, Frederick 1870-1941 [HPPN]
American actor
* Wright, Huntley

Wright, Frederick 19th c. [IP]
Irish-Canadian poet
* [A] Pilgrim

Wright, Frosty
See Wright, Paul W.

Wright, G. B.
See Wright, Gordon Butler

Wright, George [IP]
British author
* [An] Old Colonist

Wright, George 1877-1931 [THR]
British actor
* Bealby, George

Wright, Georgie
See Henley, Georgina

Wright, Gilbert Munger 1901- [SFL]
Author
* Lebar, John

Wright, Gordon Butler 1925- [ART]
British artist
* Wright, G. B.

Wright, Harry
See Wright, William Henry

Wright, Harry Wendell 1916-1954 [SC]
American actor and stunt performer
* Wright, Wen

Wright, Henry Press 19th c. [IP]
British clergyman and author
* [A] Crimean Chaplain

Wright, Hezekiah Hartley ?-1840 [IP]
American author
* [An] American

Wright, Huntley
See Wright, Frederick

Wright, J.
See Gifford, William

Wright, J. Hornsby 19th c. [IP]
British author
* [A] Charity Organizationist

Wright, Jack R.
See Finkelstein, Mark

Wright, James [IP]
British clergyman and author
* Philander

Wright, James A. 19th c. [HPPN]
American author
* [A] Layman

Wright, James Richard 1883- [NAA]
British-born writer
* Hart, J. E. T.

Wright, John [IP]
British author
* J. W.

Wright, John Geoffrey 1954- [DC]
New Zealand-born cricketer
* Wright, Wrighty

Wright, Joseph 1734-1797 [HN, WBD]
British painter
* Wright of Derby

Wright, Joseph, Jr. 1906- [CSH]
Canadian rowboat racer
* Wright, Young Joe

Wright, Joseph, Sr. 1864-1950 [CSH]
Canadian rowboat racer
* Mr. Joe

Wright, Joseph X. [FFF]
American writer
* Tukesbury, Joe

Wright, Jud
See Wright, Arthur Justin

Wright, Judith Grovner
See Bull, Lois

Wright, Julia McNair 1840-? [FFF]
American author
* Aunt Sophronia

Wright, Kenneth
See Alvarez Del Rey, Ramon Felipe
San Juan Mario Silvio Enrico

Wright, Lan
See Wright, Lionel Percy

Wright, Leroy 1918?-1959 [HPPN]
American rape trial defendant
* Wright, Roy

Wright, Lionel Percy 1923- [ESF, SFL, WGT]
British author
* Wright, Lan

Wright, Little Stevie
See Wright, Steve

Wright, Lucky
See Wright, William Simmons

Wright, Lucy Pauline [IP]
British poet
* L. P. W.

Wright, M. Jane 20th c. [OP]
American opera singer
* Nelson, Jane

Wright, Mabel Osgood 1859-1934
[ALY, WGT, WWL]
American author
* Barbara
* Russell, Sarah

Wright, Martha
See Wiederrecht, Martha Lucile

Wright, Mary [Booth] 1831-? [IP]
American author
* Carleton, Carrie

Wright, Mary Kathryn 1935- [EG, GF, GME]
American golfer
* Wright, Mickey

Wright, Mary M. 1894- [NAA]
American poet and author
* Lorraine, Lilith

Wright, Mary Pamela [Godwin] 1917-
[AW, CAP]
British author
* Bawn, Mary

Wright, Mickey
See Wright, Mary Kathryn

Wright, Nathan Edward 1943- [CWG, DAM]
American country-western performer
* Wright, Sonny

Wright, Nathan, Jr. 1923- [CA]
American educator and author
* Wright, Nathaniel, Jr.

Wright, Nathaniel, Jr.
See Wright, Nathan, Jr.

Wright, Noel 1890-1975 [SFL, WGT]
Author
* Worth, Nigel

Wright of Derby
See Wright, Joseph

Wright, Orlando 1921- [EJ]
American jazz musician
* Kaleem, Musa

Wright, [Mary] Patricia 1932- [CA]
British author
* Napier, Mary

Wright, Paul W. 20th c. [BBH]
American collegiate athletic director
* Wright, Frosty

Wright, Paula Ramona 1928?- [ITA]
American actress
* Raymond, Paula

Wright, Philip
See Hubble, Leslie Arthur Burt

Wright, R. R.
See Wright, Richard Robert, III

Wright, R. W. [PA]
Author
* Quevedo

Wright, Rasty
See Wright, Wayne Bromley

Wright, Rasty
See Wright, William S.

Wright, Rayfield 1945- [SMG]
American football player
* [The] Big Cat
* Wright, Cat

Wright, Richard 1764-1836 [IP]
British clergyman and author
* Beccaria Anglicus

Wright, Richard Robert, III 20th c.
[IBW]
American banker
* Wright, R. R.

Wright, Rita 1946- [IBW]
American singer, lyricist, songwriter
* Wright, Syreeta

Wright, Robert 18th c. [IP]
British author
* R. W.

Wright, Robert [joint pseudonym with
Robert Augustine Ward Lowndes]
See Ackerman, Forrest J[ames]

Wright, Robert [joint pseudonym with
Forrest J. Ackerman]
See Lowndes, Robert Augustine Ward

Wright, Robert B. 1915- [ASC]
American musician
* Bruce, Robert

Wright, Robert William 1816-1885
[DNA, IP]
American author and attorney
* Flaccus Horatius
* Redivivus, Quevedo, Jr.

Wright, Rowland
See Wells, Carolyn

Wright, Roy
See Wright, Leroy

Wright, Royston 1927- [CAR]
British artist
* Adzak, Roy

Wright, Ruth
See Kauffman, Ruth [Hammitt]

Wright, Samuel
See Murray, Charles T.

Wright, Sarah Anna [IP]
American author
* Aunt Sue

Wright, Saul
See Wilson, F. T.

Wright, Senator
See Wright, Eugene Joseph [Gene]

Wright, Sewell Peaslee 1897- [NAA]
American author
* Andrew, Thomas
* Cameron, Leigh
* Spencer, Parke

Wright, Silas 1795-1847 [HPPN]
American politician
* [The] Cato of the Senate

Wright, Skeeter
See Wright, Clyde

Wright, Sonny
See Wright, Nathan Edward

Wright, Specs
See Wright, Charles

Wright, Steve [RO2]
British singer
* Wright, Little Stevie

Wright, Sydney Fowler 1874-1965 [ESF,
LC, WGT]
British author and poet
* Fowler, Sydney
* Seymour, Alan
* Wingrave, Anthony

Wright, Syreeta
See Wright, Rita

Wright, Taffy
See Wright, Taft Shedron

Wright, Taft Shedron 1913- [BE, PB]
American baseball player
* Wright, Taffy

Wright, Ted
See Wright, Weldon

Wright, Tennessee
See Wright, Vester Richard

Wright, Thomas 1788-? [IP]
British author
* [The] Manchester Prison
  Philanthropist

Wright, Thomas 1810-1877 [IP]
British antiquary
* [An] Antiquary
* [A] Trinity Man

Wright, Thomas 1859-? [FFF, WWL]
British author
* Journeyman Engineer

Wright, Thomas (cont.)
* Riverside Visitor
* [A] Trinity Man

Wright, Vester Richard 1921?-1966 [AS]
American horse trainer
* Wright, Tennessee

Wright, W. George 20th c. [MBF]
British editor
* Bouchard, William
* Bryant, Bruce
* Grant, Howard
* Masterson, Val
* Quinton, Paul
* Rishton, William

Wright, W. W. 19th c. [IP]
American author
* [A] Stroller in Europe

Wright, Wayne Bromley 1895-1948 [BE]
American baseball player
* Wright, Rasty

Wright, Weaver
See Ackerman, Forrest J[ames]

Wright, Weldon 20th c. [EF]
American football player
* Wright, Ted

Wright, Wen
See Wright, Harry Wendell

Wright, Willard Huntington 1888-1939
[CC, EMD, LC]
American author, journalist, editor
* Van Dine, S. S.

Wright, William [IP]
Scottish clergyman and author
* [A] Lover of the Protestant Religion

Wright, William 1829-1898 [DNA]
American journalist
* De Quille, Dan

Wright, William Henry 1835-1895 [AS,
BAB, BBH, HPPN]
American baseball player and manager
* Baseball's First Pro
* [The] Father of Professional Baseball
* Wright, Harry

Wright, William James 1890-1952 [BE]
American baseball player
* Wright, Dick

Wright, William S. 1863-1922 [BE]
American baseball player
* Wright, Rasty

Wright, William Simmons 1880-1941
[BE]
American baseball player
* William the Red
* Wright, Deacon
* Wright, Lucky

Wright, Winifred 1910?-1950 [BEW]
Actress
* Melville, Winifred

Wright, Wrighty
See Wright, John Geoffrey

Wright, Young Joe
See Wright, Joseph, Jr.

Wright-Botchwey, Ro
See Wright-Botchwey, Roberta Yvonne

Wright-Botchwey, Roberta Yvonne 1946-
[BA]
American attorney and author
* Wright-Botchwey, Ro

Wright-Cooper, Richard 1893-1947
[THR]
British actor
* Cooper, Richard

Wrightsman, C. B.
See Wrightsman, Charles Bierer

Wrightsman, Charles Bierer 1895-   [CR]
American business executive
* Wrightsman, C. B.

Wrigley, George Watson 1873-1952
[BE]
American baseball player
* Wrigley, Zeke

Wrigley, William, Jr. 1861-1932
[HPPN]
American industrialist and manufacturer
* [The] Chewing Gum King
* [The] Chicle King
* [The] Monarch of Mastication

Wrigley, Zeke
See Wrigley, George Watson

[The] Writer of the Black National Anthem
See Johnson, J. Rosamond

Writewell, A. M.
See Close, John

Wroblewski, Jan
See Wroblewski, Ptaszyn

Wroblewski, Ptaszyn 1936-   [EJ]
Polish jazz musician
* Wroblewski, Jan

Wroe, Caleb ?-1728 [IP]
British clergyman and author
* [A] Country Minister

Wrong Old Orve
See Hodge, Orville Enoch

Wrong Way Corrigan
See Corrigan, Douglas George

Wrong Way Corrigan
See Corrigan, John

Wrong Way Marshall
See Marshall, Jim

Wrong Way Pietri
See Pietri, Dorando

Wrong Way Riegels
See Riegels, Roy

Wrong Westbrook Pegler
See Pegler, [James] Westbrook

Wronghead
See Jerrold, Douglas William

Wronker, Lili Cassel 1924-   [SAT]
German-born illustrator
* Cassel, Lili

Wronski, Jozef Maria
See Hoene, Jozef Maria

Wrottesley, Arthur John Francis 1908-
[CA]
British barrister and author
* Staffordshire Knot

Wroughton, Julia 1934-   [ART]
British painter
* J. W.

Wroughtwell, Faith
See Helphingstine, Mary J[ane]

Wroxham, Cecil
See Belfield, Harry Wedgwood

Wry-Mouthed
See Boleslav III

Wryde, Dogear
See Gorey, Edward [St. John]

Wrzaskala, Richard
See Wrzaskala, Ryszard Jozef

Wrzaskala, Ryszard Jozef 1932-   [IWM]
Polish-born musician
* Wrzaskala, Richard

Wrzos, Joseph Henry 1929-   [CA]
American author and editor
* Ross, Joseph

Wu, C. C.
See Wu Ch'ao-ch'u

Wu Ch'ao-ch'u 1886-1934 [WBD]
Chinese statesman
* Wu, C. C.

Wu, Lady ?-704 [HPPN]
Empress of China
* [The] Divine Empress
* [The] Poisoner

Wu, Nelson I[kon] 1919-   [CA]
Chinese-born educator and author
* Lu ch'iao

Wu Wen-Hsiu 1935-   [OP]
Taiwanese opera singer
* Wu, William

Wu, William
See Wu Wen-Hsiu

Wuelcker, Richard Paul 1845-1910
[WBD]
German theologian and author
* Wuelker, Richard Paul

Wuelker, Richard Paul
See Wuelcker, Richard Paul

Wuensche, Edward Hugh 1946?-
[HPPN]
American underworld figure and government witness
* Winchester, Hugh E.
* Winchester, Mr.

Wuestling, George 1903-1970
American baseball player
* Wuestling, Yatz

Wuestling, Yatz
See Wuestling, George

Wul, Stefan
See Pairault, Pierre

Wulff, Edgun Valdemar 1913-   [IBY, ICB]
American illustrator
* Edgun

Wulff, Sigismund   [IP]
German playwright
* Sieg, W. M.

Wunderkind
See Levine, James

[The] Wunderkind of Foggy Bottom
See Kissinger, Henry Alfred

[The] Wunderkind of Soviet Chess
See Karpov, Anatoly

Wunnakyawhtin U Ohn Ghine
See Maurice, David [John Kerr]

Wunsch, Josephine M. 1914-   [WD]
American author
* McLean, J. Sloan [joint pseudonym with Virginia M(ary) Gillette]

Wupperman, Claudeigh Louise 1912-
[BEW]
American actress
* Morgan, Claudia

Wupperman, Francis Philip 1890-1949
[F1, F2, FC]
American actor
* Morgan, Frank

Wupperman, Georgiana [Iversen] 20th c.
[BEW]
American actress
* Arnold, Grace

Wupperman, Raphael Kuhner 1882?-1956
[BEW, F2, SC]
American actor
* Morgan, Ralph

Wurm, Adela 1877-1952 [BBD]
British musician
* Verne, Adela

Wurm, Alice 1868-1958 [BBD]
British musician
* Verne, Alice

Wurm, Mathilde 1865-1936 [BBD]
British musician
* Verne, Mathilde

Wurman, Claude Olin 1927-1974   [SC]
American actor
* Justin, Morgan

Wurmbrand, Richard 1909-   [AW]
Rumanian-born clergyman and author
* Moses, Ruben

Wurmsaam, Vermelio
See Callenbach, Franz

Wurst, Richard Paul 19th c.   [IP]
American author
* Paul, Richard

Wursteisen, Christian 1544-1588 [PA]
Author
* Urtisius

Wurzbach, Constant 1818-1893 [WBD]
Austrian poet and author
* Constant, W.

Wutrich, Gottfried 1874-1914
Swiss-born American strongman
* Rolandow, G. W.

Wyandotte, Steve
See Thomas, Stanley

Wyant, Andrew R[obert] E[lmer]
1873-1964   [FB]
American football player
* Wyant, Polyphemus

Wyant, Polyphemus
See Wyant, Andrew R[obert] E[lmer]

Wyatt, B. D.
See Robinson, Spider

Wyatt, Ben
See Young, Fred W.

Wyatt, Gertrude 19th c. [IP]
British poet
* [A] Young Lady

Wyatt, James 18th c. [HPPN]
American author
* [A] Friend to Consistency

Wyatt, James
See Robinson, Louie, Jr.

Wyatt, Joe
See Wyatt, Loral John

Wyatt, John 1925- [CA]
British author
* Parker, John

Wyatt, John Whitlow 1907- [BE]
American baseball player
* Wyatt, Whit

Wyatt, Loral John 1901- [BE]
American baseball player
* Wyatt, Joe

Wyatt, Matthew Digby 1820-1877
[HPPN]
British architect
* [An] Architect

Wyatt, Nathaniel Ellsworth 1863-1895
[EWG, HPPN]
American gunfighter
* [The] Dashing Romeo of the
  Oklahoma Plains
* Wyatt, Wild Charlie
* Wyatt, Zip
* Yaeger, Dick

Wyatt, Pepper
See Wyatt, Ralph Arthur

Wyatt, Ralph Arthur 1920- [MK]
American baseball player
* Wyatt, Pepper

Wyatt, Wesley Butler
See Torme, Mel[vin Howard]

Wyatt, Whit
See Wyatt, John Whitlow

Wyatt, Wild Charlie
See Wyatt, Nathaniel Ellsworth

Wyatt, Wilma Winifred 1910?-1952
[CED, F2]
American actress
* Crosby, Dixie Lee
* Lee, Dixie

Wyatt, Zip
See Wyatt, Nathaniel Ellsworth

Wyatt-Edgell, [Rev.] Edgell 19th c.
[HPPN]
British clergyman
* [A] Protestant Clergyman

Wyatville, [Sir] Jeffry 1766-1840
[HPPN]
British architect
* [The] Architect to the King

Wybraniec, Peter F[rank] 1882- [WGT]
Author
* Leonhart, [Dr.] Raphael W.

Wyche, Joseph 18th c. [IP]
British author
* J. W., M. O. S. B.

Wyche, Lennon Douglas, Jr. 1946-
[BA]
American physician
* Wyche, Witchy

Wyche, Witchy
See Wyche, Lennon Douglas, Jr.

Wycherley, Bus
See Wycherley, Ralph

Wycherley, Ralph 1920- [CEI]
Canadian-born hockey player
* Wycherley, Bus

Wycherley, Richard Newman 20th c.
[LC]
Author
* Murray, Gilbert

Wycherly, Margaret
See De Wolfe, Margaret

Wycherly, Ronald 1941-1983
British singer
* Fury, Billy

Wycherly, William 1640?-1716 [SN]
British playwright
* [The] Plain Dealer

Wyckham, John
See Suckling, John

Wyckoff, Robert Fletcher 1923- [BEW,
TR]
*American theatrical designer and
producer*
* Fletcher, Robert

Wycliff
See Westrup, Enrique Tomas

Wycliffe, Bubba
See Wycliffe, Nathaniel Morton

Wycliffe [or Wyclif], John 1324-1384
[DEP, RH, SN]
British religious reformer
* [The] Evangelic Doctor
* Evangelicus, Doctor
* [The] Father of English Prose

Wycliffe [or Wyclif], John (cont.)
* [The] Gospel Doctor
* [The] Morning Star of the
  Reformation
* [The] Rector of Lutterwoorth

Wycliffe, John
See Bedford-Jones, Henry [James
O'Brien]

Wycliffe, Nathaniel Morton 1934-
[SMG]
American baseball player
* Wycliffe, Bubba

Wycoff, Leon 1903- [BEW, ITA, SW]
American actor
* Ames, Leon

Wyeth, Andrew 1917- [CR]
American painter
* [The] Rich Man's Norman Rockwell
* [The] Robert Frost of the Paintbrush

Wyeth, N. C.
See Wyeth, Newell Convers

Wyeth, Newell Convers 1882-1945
[WYA]
American author
* Wyeth, N. C.

[A] Wykehamist
See Ashley, John

[A] Wykehamist
See Gale, Frederick

Wykham, Helen
See Evans, Pamela

Wylcotes, John
See Ransford, Oliver Neil

Wyld, Robert S. 19th c. [HPPN]
Scottish author
* [A] Modern Calvinist

Wylde, Flora Frances 19th c. [IP]
Scottish? author
* Her Granddaughter
* Testudo, Totty

Wylde, Hazel
See Hotchkiss, Ella A.

Wylde, Katharine
See Colvill, Helen Hester

Wylder, Lennox
See Turner, William Mason

Wyler, Gretchen
See Wienecke, Gretchen Patricia

Wyler, Ninety-Take
See Wyler, William [Willie]

Wyler, Richard 1934- [FC]
American actor
* Stapley, Richard

Wyler, Rose
See Ames, Rose Wyler

Wyler, William [Willie] 1902-1981 [CR,
WP 8-5-85]
American director
* 40 Take Willie
* Wyler, Ninety-Take

Wylie, David 1811-1891 [CCL]
Canadian poet and author
* Y-le

Wylie, Dirk [joint pseudonym with C. Kornbluth, F. Kummer, F. Pohl]
See Dockweiler, Joseph Harold

Wylie, Dirk [joint pseudonym with Joseph Harold Dockweiler and Frederik Pohl]
See Kornbluth, Cyril M.

Wylie, Dirk [joint pseudonym with Joseph Harold Dockweiler]
See Kummer, Frederic Arnold

Wylie, Dirk [joint pseudonym with Joseph Harold Dockweiler and Cyril M. Kornbluth]
See Pohl, Frederik

Wylie, Francis E[rnest] 1905- [CA]
American author
* Wylie, Jeff

Wylie, I. A. R.
See Wylie, Ida Alexa Ross

Wylie, Ida Alexa Ross 1885- [LC, TC]
Australian-born author
* Wylie, I. A. R.

Wylie, James 1875-? [LAO]
British barrister and author
* Worne, John

Wylie, James Renwick 1861-1951 [BE]
American baseball player
* Wylie, Ren

Wylie, Jeff
See Wylie, Francis E[rnest]

Wylie, Julian
See Samuelson, Julian

Wylie, Laura [or Laurie]
See Matthews, Patricia [Brisco]

Wylie, Lauri
See Samuelson, Morris Laurence

Wylie, Philip 1902-1971 [HPPN]
American author
* Woman's Nemesis

Wylie, Ren
See Wylie, James Renwick

Wylie, Robert 18th c. [IP]
Scottish author
* [A] Gentleman in the City

Wylie, Wiggy
See Wylie, William Vance

Wylie, William Vance 1928- [CEI]
Canadian-born hockey player
* Wylie, Wiggy

Wyllie, George Ralston 1921- [ART]
Scottish sculptor
* G. R. W.

Wylwynne, Kythe
See Hyland, M. E. F.

Wyman, A. D. 20th c. [HPPN]
American football player
* Wyman, Pudge

Wyman, Edward G. 1900-1954 [HPPN]
American radio announcer
* Wyman, Jerry

Wyman, Hans
See Weinmann, Hans

Wyman, Jane
See Fulks, Sarah Jane

Wyman, Jerry
See Wyman, Edward G.

Wyman, Marc
See Howith, Harry

Wyman, Mrs. John C. [IP]
American author
* S. A. L. E. M.

Wyman, Pudge
See Wyman, A. D.

Wyman, Rufus ?-1842 [IP]
American physician and author
* Omnivagant

Wyman, Walter Forestus 1881-? [NAA]
American author
* Chapman, John
* Johnson, H. B.
* Maxwell, Herbert M.
* Witherspoon, J. J.

Wyman, William Henry 19th c. [IP]
American author
* W. H. W.

Wymark, Patrick
See Cheesman, Patrick

Wyn, A. A.
See Weinstein, Aaron

Wyn, Marjery
See Yeomans, Marjery

Wynd, Oswald [Morris] 1913- [AW, CA, WW]
Scottish author
* Black, Gavin

Wynder, Mavis Areta
See Winder, Mavis Areta

Wyndham, [Sir] Charles
See Culverwell, Charles

Wyndham, Esther
See Lutyens, Mary

Wyndham, Henry Penruddocke 1736-1819 [IP]
British author
* [A] Gentleman

Wyndham, J. [PA]
Author
* Merry, Doctor

Wyndham, John
See Harris, John [Wyndham Parkes Lucas] Beynon

Wyndham, Lee
See Hyndman, Jane Andrews [Lee]

Wyndham, Poppy
See Mackay, Elsie

Wyndham, Robert
See Hyndman, Robert Utley

Wyndham, [Sir] William 1687-1740 [SN]
British statesman
* Wildfire

Wynegar, Butch
See Wynegar, Harold Delano, Jr.

Wynegar, Harold Delano, Jr. 1956- [SMG, WWB]
American baseball player
* Wynegar, Butch

Wyner, Billie
See Cohen, Annie

Wyner, Yehudi
See Weiner, Yehudi

Wynette, Tammy
See Pugh, Wynette

Wynkoop, Matthew Bennett [IP]
American poet and printer
* [An] American

Wynman, Margaret
See Dixon, Ella Hepworth

Wynn, Alfred
See Brewer, Fredric [Aldwyn]

Wynn, Bert
See Gershvin, Jacob

Wynn, Cannon
See Wynn, James Sherman [Jim]

Wynn, Charles
See Weinberg, Charles

Wynn, Doris
See Rink, Doris

Wynn, Early 1920- [BI, DGS, HPPN, PB]
American baseball player
* [The] Old Indian
* Wynn, Gus

Wynn, Ed
See Leopold, Isaiah Edwin

Wynn, Frances Williams 1780?-1857 [IP]
British author
* [A] Lady of Quality

Wynn, Gus
See Wynn, Early

Wynn, James Sherman [Jim] 1942- [BE, PB, SMG]
American baseball player
* [The] Toy Cannon
* Wynn, Cannon

Wynn, May
See Hickey, Donna Lee

Wynn, Roberta Lee ?-1978 [FIR]
Acrobatic dancer
* [The] Dancing Doll of the South

Wynne, Anthony
See Wilson, Robert McNair

Wynne, Brian
See Garfield, Brian [Francis] Wynne

Wynne, Charles Whitworth
See Cayzer, Charles William

Wynne, Edward 1734-1784   [IP]
British barrister and author
* E. W.

Wynne, Emma [Moffett] 1844-?   [IP]
American author
* Lola

Wynne, Frank
See Garfield, Brian [Francis] Wynne

Wynne, George Robert 19th c.   [IP]
Irish? author
* G. R. W.

Wynne, Gladys
See Sills, Gladys Wynne

Wynne, John Huddleston 1743-1788
[IP]
*British printer, journalist, naval officer,
author*
* J. H. W.
* Osborn, George, Esq.

Wynne, Manny
See Weinstein, Emanuel

Wynne, May
See Knowles, Mabel Winifred

Wynne, May
See May, Winifred Jean

Wynne, Pamela
See Scott, Winifred Mary

Wynne, Thomas H. 19th c.   [IP]
British editor
* T. H. W.

Wynne-Tyson, Esme 1898-   [AW, CA]
British author, journalist, playwright
* Amanda
* De Morny, Peter
* Diotima

Wynne-Tyson, [Timothy] Jon [Lyden]
1924-   [CA]
British author
* Fourest, Michel
* Pitt, Jeremy

Wynter, Andrew   [IP, PA]
British author
* Werdna, Retnyw

Wynter, Dagmar 1930?-   [FC]
British actress
* Wynter, Dana

Wynter, Dana
See Wynter, Dagmar

Wynter, Sylvia 1932?-   [CW]
Cuban-born critic, playwright, author
* Carew, Wynter

Wynyard, Diana
See Cox, Dorothy Isobel

Wynyard, Talbot
See Hamilton, Charles Harold St. John

Wyoming Bill Patten
See Patten, William George

**Wyoming's Outstanding Deceased
Citizen**
See Morris, Esther Hobart McQuigg

Wyre, Alfred 20th c.   [BBH]
American athletic trainer
* Wyre, Duke

Wyre, Duke
See Wyre, Alfred

Wysbar, Franz 1899-1967   [FD, FDG,
WEF]
German director
* Wisbar, Frank

Wyse, Henry Washington 1918-   [BE,
PB]
American baseball player
* Wyse, Hooks

Wyse, Hooks
See Wyse, Henry Washington

Wyse, Thomas 1791-1862   [IP]
Irish statesman and diplomat
* Eldon, [Dr.] Abraham

Wyse, William Charles Bonaparte
19th c.   [IP]
British poet
* [A] Grand Nephew of Napoleon the
Great
* W. C. B. W.

Wyseman, Demetrius
See Dicke [or Duke?], Willis

Wyshner, Peter J. 1917-
American baseball player
* Gray, Pete

Wysocki, Colonel
See Kruszuk [or Kruszyk?], Florian

Wysocki, Waldemar 1915-1940   [HPPN]
American actor
* Moore, Walter
* Moore, William

Wysong, Biff
See Wysong, Harlin

Wysong, Harlin 1905-1951   [BE]
American baseball player
* Wysong, Biff

Wyspianski, Stanislaw 1869-1907
[MWD]
Polish poet and playwright
* [The] Creator of Modern Polish
Drama

Wyss, David
See Wyss, Johann Rudolf

Wyss, Johann Rudolf 1781-1830
[HPPN]
Swiss philosopher and librarian
* Wyss, David

Wyszynski, Stefan Cardinal 1901-1981
[HPPN]
Polish clergyman
* [The] Good and Zealous Pastor
* [A] Hero of the Church of Our
Times

Wythe
See Weld, Theodore Dwight

Wytske
See Nederveen Hendriks, Wietske

Wyvill, Fanny Susan 19th c.   [FFF]
American poet
* Brook, Fanshawe

Wyvis, Ben
See Munro, [Macfarlane] Hugh

Wyzewski, Theodore 1862-1917   [BBD]
Polish-born musicologist
* De Wyzewa, Theodore

X

X.
See Bowring, [Sir] John

X.
See Budgell, Eustace

X.
See Ellenwood, Henry S.

X
See Fawkes, Frank Attfield

X
See Fox-Davies, Arthur Charles

X.
See Jessopp, [Rev.] Augustus

X
See Kennan, George Frost

X
See Raymond, William Lee

X.
See Smith, Gerrit

X.
See Vivian, Herbert

X. H.
See Macpherson, Mrs. Brewster

X. L.
See Field, Julian Osgood

[The] X Rated Grandmother
See Avara, Mary

X 22
See Magriel, Paul

X. X.
See Street, Cecil John Charles

X. Y.
See Maclaurin, John

X. Y. Z.
See De Quincey, Thomas

X. Y. Z.
See Neal, John

X. Z.
See Gardiner, John Sylvester John

X. Z.
See Young, Robert

Xanrof, Leon
See Fourneau, Leon

Xanthopalus
See Callistus, Nicephorus

Xanthus, Xavier
See Laumer, March

Xariffa
See Townsend, Mary Ashely [Van Voorhis]

Xavier
See Boniface, Joseph Xavier

Xavier, [Father]
See Hurwood, Bernhardt J[ackson]

Xavier, [Mother]
See Mehegan, Catherine Josephine

Xavier, Adro
See Rey-Stolle, Alejandro

Xavier, Chico
See Xavier, Francisco Candido

Xavier, Francis [or Francisco] 1506-1552 [DNNS, FFF, HN]
Spanish missionary
* [The] Apostle of the Indies

Xavier, Francis
See Fish, Horace

Xavier, Francisco Candido 1910- [EOP]
Claimed to possess psychic powers
* Xavier, Chico

Xenette
See Vinning, Pamelia S.

Xeno
See Lake, Kenneth R[obert]

Xenomanes [A Lover of Travel]
See Bouchet, Jean

Xenophon 4th c. BC [DEP, RH, SN, UH]
Greek historian
* [The] Athenian Bee
* [The] Attic Muse
* [The] Bee of Athens
* [The] Muse of Greece
* [The] Syren of Antiquity

[The] Xenophon of His Own History
See Villehardouin, Geoffroi de

Xenophon XIII
See Maurras, Charles-Marie-Photius

Xerxes I 5th c. BC [WBD]
King of Persia
* [The] Great

Xiao Pingzi [The Little Bottle]
See Deng Xiaoping

XIE
See Edwards, Harry Stillwell

Xixx, [Ms.] Jezebel Q.
See Borgmann, Dmitri A[lfred]

Xocoyotzin [Furious One]
See Montezuma II

Xylander, Wilhelm
See Holtzmann, Wilhelm

Y

Y.
See Boyse, Samuel

Y.
See Frazer, John de Jean

Y.
See O'Connell, John

Y., Cork
See Buckley, Michael Bernard

Y. L. G.
See Ben Asher, Judah Loeb

Y. M.
See Pengelly, William

Y. N. L.
See Ball, Timothy Horton

Y. O.
See Russell, George William

Y. S. L.
See Saint Laurent, Yves [Henri Donat Mathieu]

[The] Y. W. C. A. Hostel Murderer
See Byrne, Patrick

Y. Y.
See Lynd, Robert

Y. Z.
See Johns, Tremenheere John

Y-le
See Wylie, David

Ya, P.
See Yakubovich, Peter Filipovich

Yabes, Leopoldo Y[abes] 1912- [CA]
Philippine author and editor
* Christian, A. B.
* Ibarra, Crisostomo
* Silangan, Manuel

Yablok, Indian
See Yablok, Julius

Yablok, Julius 20th c. [EJS]
American football player
* Yablok, Indian

Yablokoff, Herman
See Yablonik, Herman

Yablonik, Herman ?-1981
Polish-born actor, composer, playwright, director
* Yablokoff, Herman
* [The] Ziegfeld of the Jewish Stage

Yablonski, Jock
See Yablonski, Joseph A.

Yablonski, Joseph A. 1910-1969
American labor leader
* Yablonski, Jock

Yacco, Sada 20th c. [HPPN]
Japanese actress
* [The] Japanese Bernhardt

Yacconetti, Carlo 20th c. [SG]
Boxer
* Duane, Carl

Yack, Baby
See Yack, Norman

Yack, Norman 20th c. [BBH]
Boxer
* Yack, Baby

Yadin, Yigael
See Sukenik, Yigael

Yaeger, Bart
See Strung, Norman

Yaeger, Dick
See Wyatt, Nathaniel Ellsworth

Yaffe, Alan
See Yorinks, Arthur

Yaffe, Kadish 1897- [NAA]
Polish-born journalist
* Jaffe, Charles
* Kadish, I.

Yaffe, Morris 1921- [ITA]
American producer, director, actor
* Barr, Anthony

Yaffe, Richard 1903- [CA]
American journalist
* Chanan, Ben

Yager, Anna 1879-1954 [BBD, BEW]
Austrian-born opera singer
* Scheff, Friederike
* Scheff, Fritzi

Yaho
See Kitabatake, Miyo

Yahsin-che [Dumb Walking Man]
See Chiang Yee

Yakir, Pyotr 1923?- [HPPN]
Russian historian
* [The] Muffled Spokesman

Yakobson, Helen B[ates] 1913- [CA]
Russian-born American educator and author
* Bates, Helen L. Z.

Yakoub Beg 19th c. [DHA]
Led revolt against China in Kashgar
* Attalik Ghazi

Yakovlev, Aleksandr Ivanovich 1812-1870 [WBD]
Russian author
* Herzen [or Hertzen], Aleksandr Ivanovich
* Iskander

Yakovlev, Anatoli 20th c.
Russian espionage agent
* John

Yakub, Tasnim
See Memon, Fahmida

Yakubovich, Peter Filipovich 1860-1911
Author
* Ya, P.

Yakumo, Koizumi
See Hearn, [Patricios] Lafcadio [Tessima Carlos]

Yalag
See Ben Asher, Judah Loeb

Yale, Ad
See Yale, William M.

Yale, Frankie
See Uale, Frank

Yale, Linus 1821-1868 [HPPN]
American locksmith, inventor, manufacturer
* [The] Father of the Cylinder Lock

Yale, William M. 1870-1948 [BE]
American baseball player
* Yale, Ad

Yale's Greatest Teacher
See Sumner, William Graham

Yallup, Pat 1929- [ART]
South African-born painter and graphic designer
* Harvey, Pat

Yama
See Sur, Atul Krishna

Yamaguchi, Gogen 1909- [OCS]
Japanese karate expert
* [The] Cat

Yamamoto, Isoroku 1884-1943 [HPPN]
Japanese military leader
* [The] Foster Father of the Naval Air Corps
* [The] Man Who Menaced America

Yamamoto, Kansai 20th c.
Japanese fashion designer
* Kansai

Yamanaka, Sadao 1907-1938 [DFM]
Japanese director
* [The] Japanese Rene Clair

Yamani, [Sheikh] Ahmed Zaki 20th c.
[HPPN]
Saudi Arabian government official
* [The] Good Guy

Yamasaki, Takeo 1905- [IAW]
Japanese author
* Shibukawa, Gyo

Yamashita, Tomoyuki 1885-1946 [BDW, WWW]
Japanese army officer
* [The] Tiger of Malaya
* [The] Tiger of the Philippines

Yamashita, Tsutomu 1947- [BBD]
Japanese musician
* Yamash'ta, Stomu

Yamash'ta, Stomu
See Yamashita, Tsutomu

Yamauchi, Tetsu 20th c. [RM]
Musician
* Tetsu

Yambo
See Novelli, Enrico

Yamen, Ben
See Peirce, Benjamin

Yan
See Almeida Prado, Joao Fernando

Yanagimura, Shimpu
See Verwilghen, A[lbert-] Felix

Yancey, Arthur Henry 1891- [BI]
American contractor
* Yancey, Aytch

Yancey, Aytch
See Yancey, Arthur Henry

Yancey, Estella 1896- [BBW, WWJ]
American singer
* Yancey, Mama

Yancey, James Edward [Jimmy]
1898-1951 [BWW]
American singer
* Yancey, Papa

Yancey, Joseph J., Jr. [Joe] 1906-
[IBW]
American track and field coach
* [The] Coach of Champions

Yancey, Mama
See Yancey, Estella

Yancey, Papa
See Yancey, James Edward [Jimmy]

Yancey, William J. 1904-1971 [MK]
American baseball player
* Yancey, Yank

Yancey, William Lowndes 1814-1863
[HPPN]
American orator
* [The] Orator of Secession

Yancey, Yank
See Yancey, William J.

Yaney, Clyde A. 1910?-1978 [CWG]
American country-western performer
* Yaney, Skeets

Yaney, Skeets
See Yaney, Clyde A.

Yanez, Agustin 1904- [BI, HPPN]
Mexican author
* Delgadillo, Monico

Yang, C. K.
See Yang, Chuan-Kwang

Yang, Ch'u-yun
See Yeung Ku Wan

Yang, Chuan-Kwang 1935- [TF]
Formosan track and field athlete
* Yang, C. K.

Yang-jen
See Shu, Austin Chi-wei

Yanger, Benny
See Angone, Frank

Yank, Jonathan
See Moffitt, Jack

[A] Yankee
See Ingraham, Joseph Holt

[A] Yankee
See Mangan, James Clarence

[A] Yankee
See Mitchell, John Kearsley

[A] Yankee
See White, Richard Grant

[The] Yankee Arms Maker
See Colt, Samuel

[The] Yankee Clipper
See DeMaggio, Giuseppe Paolo, Jr.

[The] Yankee Clipper of the Accordion
See Contino, Richard [Dick]

[The] Yankee Doodle Dandy
See Cohan, George Michael

[The] Yankee Doodle Dandy
See Hancock, John

[The] Yankee Empire Builder
See Barrow, Edward Grant

[A] Yankee Farmer
See Lowell, John

Yankee Irishman
See Nowlan, George

Yankee Jonathan
See Hastings, Jonathan

[The] Yankee Killer
See Lary, Frank Strong

[The] Yankee King
See Sickles, Daniel Edgar

Yankee Ned
See Clark, George Edward

[The] Yankee Nonesuch
See Berra, Lawrence Peter

Yankee, Pat
See Weigum, Patricia Millicent

[The] Yankee Pedaler
See Hamilton, Pete[r]

[A] Yankee Prisoner
See Geer, John James

[The] Yankee Reformer
See Cheever, George Barrell

[The] Yankees' Old Pro
See Henrich, Thomas David

Yankovic, Al 20th c. [HPPN]
American entertainer
* Yankovic, Weird Al

Yankovic, Weird Al
See Yankovic, Al

Yanks, Byron 1928- [BBD]
American musician
* Janis, Byron

Yanne, Jean
See Gouye, Jean

Yannis, Michael
See Cacoyannis, Michael

Yannopoulos, Dino
See Yannopoulos, Konstantin

Yannopoulos, Konstantin 20th c. [OP]
Greek-born producer and stage-lighting designer
* Yannopoulos, Dino

Yanoff, Seymour L. 20th c.
American television executive
* Yanoff, Sy

Yanoff, Sy
See Yanoff, Seymour L.

Yanovsky, Basile S.
See Yanovsky, Vassily Semenovich

Yanovsky, V. S.
See Yanovsky, Vassily Semenovich

Yanovsky, Vassily Semenovich 1906-
[CA]
Russian-born American author
* Yanovsky, Basile S.
* Yanovsky, V. S.

[The] Yanqui Matador
See Short, John Fulton

Yap, Diosdado M. 1907- [IAW]
Filipino-born author
* Doc

Yapp, Frederick Francis 1878-1970 [BE]
American baseball player and manager
* Mitchell, Frederick Francis

Yar-Shater [or Yarshater], Ehsan O[llah]
1920- [CA, IAW]
Iranian-born educator and author
* Rahsepar

Yarborough, Cale
See Yarborough, William Caleb

Yarborough, James 20th c.
American football player
* Yarborough, Punjab

Yarborough, Punjab
See Yarborough, James

Yarborough, William Caleb 1939- [IPA]
American auto racer
* Yarborough, Cale

Yarbrough, Charles 1939- [BA]
American probation officer
* Yarbrough, Mickey

Yarbrough, James 20th c. [SI 11-7-83]
American football player
* Yarborough, Punjab
* Yarbrough, Squeaky

Yarbrough, Mickey
See Yarbrough, Charles

Yarbrough, Squeaky
See Yarbrough, James

Yarde, Jeanne Betty Frances Treasure
1925- [CA]
British author
* Hunter, Joan
* Montague, Jeanne

Yardley, Alice 1913- [IAW]
British educator and author
* Young, Angela

Yardley, Edward 18th c. [IP]
British clergyman and author
* E. Y.

Yardley, Herbert Osborne 1889-1958
American cryptographer
* [The] Father of American
  Cryptography

Yardley, John 19th c. [IP]
British author
* J. Y.

Yariv, Aharon 1921?- [HPPN]
Israeli intelligence officer
* [The] Master Spy

Yarmolinsky, Mrs. Avrahm 1895-
[HPPN]
American poet
* Deutsch, Babette

Yarmouth
See Bailey, Isaac H.

Yarmouth, Countess of 18th c. [SN]
Mistress of King George II
* Walmoden

Yarmy, Donald 1927-
American comic actor
* Adams, Don

Yarnall, Rusty
See Yarnall, Waldo Ward

Yarnall, Sophia
See Jacobs, Sophis Yarnall

Yarnall, Waldo Ward 1902- [BE]
American baseball player
* Yarnall, Rusty

Yaroslava
See Mills, Yaroslava Surmach

Yaroslavsky, Yemelyan
See Gubelman, Yemelyan

Yaroslaw, Bernard 1916- [IPA]
American radio interviewer
* Gray, Barry

Yarosz, Teddy
See Yarosz, Thaddeus

Yarosz, Thaddeus 1910-1974 [WBC]
American boxer
* Yarosz, Teddy

Yarrison, Byron Wardsworth 1896- [BE]
American baseball player
* Yarrison, Rube

Yarrison, Rube
See Yarrison, Byron Wardsworth

Yaryan, Clarence Everett 1893-1964
[BE]
American baseball player
* Yaryan, Yam

Yaryan, Yam
See Yaryan, Clarence Everett

Yashima, Taro
See Iwamatsu, Jun Atsushi

Yasin, Erol
See Ozdenak, Yasin Erol

Yasin, Khalid
See Young, Larry

Yastrzemski, Carl Michael 1939- [BE,
PB, SMG]
American baseball player
* Yaz

Yasui, Kenny 20th c.
American soldier
* York, Baby

Yates, A. G.
See Yates, Alan Geoffrey

Yates, Al[bert Arthur] 1945- [BE]
American baseball player
* Yates, Bunny

Yates, Alan Geoffrey 1923-1985 [CA]
British-born author
* Brown, Carter
* Yates, A. G.

Yates, Bill
See Yates, Floyd Buford

Yates, Bunny
See Yates, Al[bert Arthur]

Yates, David O.
See Womack, David A[lfred]

Yates, Dornford
See Mercer, Cecil William

Yates, Edmund Hodgson 1831-1894
[FFF, IP, PA]
British author and journalist
* Flaneur
* Lounger at the Clubs
* Q.
* Seaton, Mrs.

Yates, Elizabeth 1905- [CA]
American author
* McGreal, Elizabeth

Yates, Floyd Buford 1921- [WEC]
American cartoonist and editor
* Yates, Bill

Yates, Frederic B. 19th c. [IP, PA]
American author
* Roscoe, Deane

Yates, George Worthing 20th c. [WW]
Author
* Hunt, Peter [joint pseudonym with
  Charles Hunt Marshall]

Yates, Kenneth P., Ph. D.
See Hewitt, Marvin

Yates, M.
See Corkling, Mary Anne [Yates]

Yates, Mary E.
See Madigan, Mrs. H. P.

Yates, Mrs. Benjamin [FFF]
* Zoe, Mlle.

Yates, Raymond Francis 1895-1966 [BI,
HPPN, NAA, SAT]
American author
* Hall, Borden
* Pioneer

Yates, Robert [FFF]
American author
* Rough Hewer

Yates, Thomas 19th c. [IP]
British author
* [A] Steward

Yates, William 19th c. [IP]
Missionary, scholar, author
* W. Y.

Yatron, Michael 1921- [CA]
American author
* Sorel, Byron

Yaukey, Grace S[ydenstricker] 1899-
[ANT, CA, SAT]
American author
* Spencer, Cornelia

Yavits, Doc
See Yavits, Isadore

Yavits, Isadore 20th c. [EJS, HPPN]
American basketball player and coach
* Yavits, Doc
* Yavits, Izzy

Yavits, Izzy
See Yavits, Isadore

Yavorska, Lydia
See De Hubbenet, Lydia

Yaz
See Yastrzemski, Carl Michael

Ybarra, Jose 1892-1957 [BX, SG]
American boxer
* [The] Mexican Wildcat
* Rivers, Joe

Ybarra, T. R.
See Ybarra, Thomas Russell

Ybarra, Thomas Russell 1880-? [HPPN]
Venezuelan-American author
* Ybarra, T. R.

Yeabsley, Bert
See Yeabsley, Robert Watkins

Yeabsley, Robert Watkins 1893-1961
[BE]
American baseball player
* Yeabsley, Bert

Yeager, Buddy
See Yeager, John

Yeager, John 1918- [MY]
American jazz musician
* Yeager, Buddy

Yeager, Joseph F. 1875-1937 [BE]
American baseball player
* Yeager, Little Joe

Yeager, Little Joe
See Yeager, Joseph F.

Yeakley, Marjory Hall 1908- [CA]
American author
* Blair, Lucile
* Hall, Marjory
* Morse, Carol

Yeamans, Annie
See Griffiths, Annie

Yeamans, Eugenia Marguerite 1862-1906
[BEW]
Australian-born actress
* Yeamans, Jennie

Yeamans, Jennie
See Yeamans, Eugenia Marguerite

Yeardley, Martha Savory 1782-1851
[IP]
British author
* Smith, Mrs.

Yeargin, Grapefruit
See Yeargin, James Almond [Jim]

Yeargin, James Almond [Jim] 1902-1937
[BE]
American baseball player
* Yeargin, Grapefruit

Yearsley, Ann 1756-1806 [HN, PA]
British poet
* Lactilla
* [The] Milkwoman of Bristol
* [The] Poetical Milkmaid

Yeary, Lee Harvey 1939-
American actor
* Majors, Lee

Yeates, Mabel
See Pereira, Harold Bertram

Yeatman, James 1818-? [HPPN]
American sanitation advocate
* Old Sanitary

Yeatman, R. J.
See Yeatman, Robert Julian

Yeatman, Robert Julian 1898-1968 [LC]
British author
* Yeatman, R. J.

Yeaton, Charles Kendall 1911- [BEW]
American educator and director
* Yeaton, Kelly

Yeaton, Kelly
See Yeaton, Charles Kendall

Yeats, Jack
Artist
* Byrd, William

Yeats, W. B.
See Yeats, William Butler

Yeats, William Butler 1865-1939 [LC,
NPS]
Irish poet and playwright
* Ganconagh
* Yeats, W. B.

Yeats-Brown, F. C.
See Yeats-Brown, Francis Charles
Claypon

Yeats-Brown, Francis Charles Claypon
1886-1944 [LC]
British author
* Yeats-Brown, F. C.

Yechton, Barbara
See Krause, Lyda Farrington

Yeghiayan, Luisa Anais 1936- [OP]
French opera singer
* Bosabalian, Luisa Anais

Yeh, Wei-lien
See Yip, Wai-lim

Yehoash
See Bloomgarden, Solomon

Yehoash
See Blumgarten, Solomon

Yehonala
See Tzu Hsi [or Tze-hsi]

Yeiser, Sarah C. [Smith] [FFF]
American writer
* Aunt Charity
* Azelee

Yeldam, Walter S. 19th c. [PA]
British poet
* Cham, Aliph

Yelding, Henry Edward 1902-1971
[HPPN]
British stilt walker
* Sloan, Harry

Yellen, Jack
See Yellen, Selig

Yellen, Selig 1892- [BEW]
Polish-born lyricist and playwright
* Yellen, Jack

Yellott, Barbara Leslie 1915- [IAW]
American author and poet
* Jordan, Barbara Leslie

Yellott, George 1819-? [DNA]
American author
* Nobody, Nathan

Yellow Bird [Chess-quat-a-law-ny]
See Ridge, John Rollin

[The] Yellow Doctress
See Seacole, Mary

[The] Yellow Emperor
See Huang Ti

Yellow Hair
See Custer, George Armstrong

Yellow Kid Weil
See Weil, Joseph R.

Yellow Pages, Mr.
See Berry, Loren M.

Yellow Robe
See Frantz, Rosebud

Yellow Wolf
See Moxmox, Hermene

Yellowhorse, Chief
See Yellowhorse, Moses J.

Yellowhorse, Moses J. 1900-1964 [PB]
American baseball player
* Yellowhorse, Chief

Yellowplush, Charles, Esq.
See Thackeray, William Makepeace

Yellowplush, Charles James
See Thackeray, William Makepeace

Yemrof
See Formey, Jean Henri Samuel

Yen Hui-ch'ing 1877-1950 [HPPN,
WBD]
Chinese statesman
* Yen, W. W.

Yen, James Y. C.
See Yen Yang-ch'u

Yen Ping, Shen 1896?-1981 [CA]
Chinese clergyman, editor, author
* Dun, Mao

Yen, W. W.
See Yen Hui-ch'ing

Yen Yang-ch'u 1894- [WBD]
Chinese scholar
* Yen, James Y. C.

Yenda, Mit
See Adney, Timothy

Yendys, Sydney
See Dobell, Sydney Thompson

Yensid, Retlaw
See Disney, Walt[er Elias]

Yeo-Thomas, Forest Frederick Edward
1902-1964 [BDW, WWW]
British intelligence agent
* Shelley
* White Rabbit

Yeomans, Louisa
See King, Louisa Yeomans

Yeomans, Marjery 1909- [THR]
British actress and singer
* Wyn, Marjery

Yepremian, Garabed S. 1944- [FB]
Cyprian-born football player
* Yepremian, Garo

Yepremian, Garo
See Yepremian, Garabed S.

Yerby, Frank Garvin 1916- [IBW]
American author
* King of the Costume Novel

Yerex, Cuthbert
See Cuthbert, Estella Y.

Yerke, T. B.
See Yerke, Theodore Bruce

Yerke, Theodore Bruce 20th c. [WGT]
Author
* Fassbinder, Carlton J.
* Yerke, T. B.

Yerkes, Charles Carroll 1903-1950 [BE]
American baseball player
* Yerkes, Lefty

Yerkes, Charles Tyson 1837-1905
[HPPN]
American financier
* Chicago's Traction Boss

Yerkes, Lefty
See Yerkes, Charles Carroll

Yerrick, William John 1873-1936 [BE]
American baseball player
* Banks, William John [Bill]

Yerrit, Miss
See Terry, Sarah Ballard

Yerushalmi, Chaim
See Lipschitz, [Rabbi] Chaim U.

Yerushalmi, Gershon
See Harkavy, Zvi

Yerxa, Leroy 1915-1946 [ESF, SFP, WGT]
American writer
* Arno, Elroy
* Blade, Alexander [house pseudonym, Ziff-Davis]
* Casey, Richard [house pseudonym, Ziff-Davis]

Yesenin, Sergey
See Esenin, Sergei Aleksandrovich

Yeung Ku Wan 1861-1901 [BI]
Chinese revolutionist
* Yang, Ch'u-yun

Yewcic, Kibby
See Yewcic, Thomas J. [Tom]

Yewcic, Thomas J. [Tom] 1932- [BE]
American baseball player
* Yewcic, Kibby

Yewrownckie, Aunt
See Blinn, Mrs. Henry G.

Yexley, Lionel
See Woods, James

Yezernitzky [or Jazernicki], Yitzhak
1916?- [TI 9-12-83, TI 12-12-83]
Israeli prime minister
* Shamir, Yitzhak

[The] Yiddish Curver
See Pelty, Barney

[The] Yiddish Mark Twain
See Rabinowitz, Solomon [or Sholem] J.

[The] Yiddish Mark Twain
See Zevin, Israel Joseph

[The] Yiddish Sarah Bernhardt
See Simon, Mae

[Der] Yiddisher Vild-Kat
See Loeb, Albert Lorch

Yifter, Miruts 20th c.
Ethiopian track and field athlete
* Yifter the Shifter

Yifter the Shifter
See Yifter, Miruts

Yigal the Printer
See Hurvitz, Yigal

Yin, Leslie Charles Bowyer 1907- [CC, EMD, LC]
Chinese-born author
* Charteris, Leslie
* Taylor, Bruce

Yingling, Chink
See Yingling, Earl Hershey

Yingling, Earl Hershey 1888-1962 [BE]
American baseball player
* Yingling, Chink

Yingst, Henry Z. 1924- [CWG]
American country-western performer
* Zack, Jimmie

Yip, Wai-lim 1937- [CA]
Chinese-born educator, author, poet
* Yeh, Wei-lien

Yizhar, S.
See Smilansky, Yizhar

Ylla
See Koffler, Camilla

Ylloss
See Solly, Samuel

Ynetchi, Paul
See Ryder, Elliot

[The] Yodeling Cowgirl
See Blevins, Rubye

[The] Yodeling Ranger
See Snow, Clarence Eugene

Yodeling Slim Clark
See Clark, Raymond Le Roy

Yoder, Ernest Wolfe 1919- [HPPN]
American army officer
* Yoder, Yo Yo

Yoder, Yo Yo
See Yoder, Ernest Wolfe

Yoe, Shway [or Schway?]
See Scott, [Sir] James George

Yoelson, Asa 1886-1950 [BDF, BEW, EMT, HPPN]
American singer and actor
* [The] Immortal Jolson
* Jolson, Al
* Jolson, Jolie

Yoffe, Shlomo
See Yoffe, Solomon

Yoffe, Solomon 1909- [IWM]
Israeli composer
* Yoffe, Shlomo

Yogananda, Paramahansa
See Ghosh, Mukunda Lal

Yogi, Maharishi Mahesh
See Varma, Mahest Prasod

Yogiji, Harbhajan Singh Khalsa 1929-
[CA]
Indian-born religious leader and author
* Bhajan, Yogi

Yohannessiantz, Souren 1892?-1949 [BI]
Armenian-American philatelist
* Souren, Y.

Yohn, F. C.
See Yohn, Frederick Coffay

Yohn, Frederick Coffay 1875-1933
[HPPN]
American painter and illustrator
* Yohn, F. C.

Yokely, Laymon Samuel 1906- [MK]
American baseball player
* Yokely, Norman

Yokely, Norman
See Yokely, Laymon Samuel

Yoki
See King, Yolanda

Yokoi, Shoichi 1915?- [HPPN]
Japanese soldier and hermit
* [The] Hermit of Guam
* [The] Jungle Hermit

Yolanda
See Harris, Emily

Yolen, Will [Hyatt] 1908- [CA]
American author, journalist, playwright
* Lord, Phillips H.

Yong-I-Choy 1923-
Korean-born wrestler and martial artist
* Oyama, Mas
* Oyama, Masutatsu
* Togo, Mas

Yong-Tching 1677?-1735 [SN]
Emperor of China
* [The] Immortal

Yonge, Charlotte M. 1823-1901 [IP, NPS]
British historian and author
* Alma
* Aunt Charlotte

Yonge, Remington
See Doherty, Robert R.

Yoo, Grace S.
See Yoo, Young H[yun]

Yoo, Young H[yun] 1927- [CA]
Korean-born librarian and author
* Yoo, Grace S.

Yorick
See Ferrigni, Pietro Francesco Leopoldo Coccoluto

Yorick
See Hodgson, Ralph

Yorick
See Ivens, Michael William

Yorick
See Ward, James Warner

Yorick, A. P.
See Tindall, William York

Yorick, Mr.
See Sterne, Laurence

Yorinks, Arthur 1953- [CA, SAT]
American author and playwright
* Yaffe, Alan

York, Amanda
See Dial, Joan

York and Albany, Duke of
See Frederick Augustus

York, Andrew
See Nicole, Christopher Robin

York, Anton
See Zagat, Arthur Leo

York, Baby
See Yasui, Kenny

York, Cardinal
See Stuart, Henry Benedict Maria Clemens

York, James E. 1895- [BE]
American baseball player
* York, Lefty

York, Jeremy
See Creasey, John

York, Lefty
See York, James E.

York, Margaret Elizabeth 1927- [CA]
British author
* Abbey, Margaret
* Makepeace, Joanna

York, Richard Edward
See Cohen, Paul Arthur

York, Simon
See Heinlein, Robert A[nson]

York, Wesley Simon
See Platt, Kin

Yorke, Anthony
See Reilly, Bernard James

Yorke, Carol
See Bjorkman, Carol

Yorke, Carras
See Marshall, Arthur C.

Yorke, Curtis
See Lee, Susan Richmond

Yorke, Edith
See Byard, Edithe

Yorke, Henry Vincent 1905-1974 [EWL, LC, TC1]
British author
* Green, Henry

Yorke, Katherine
See Ellerbeck, Rosemary [Anne L'Estrange]

Yorke, Margaret
See Nicholson, Margaret Beda [Larminie]

Yorke, Oliver, Esq.
See Mahony, Francis Sylvester

Yorke, Onslow
See Dixon, William Hepworth

Yorke, Percy, Jr.
See Atkinson, Thomas, Jr.

Yorke, Philip [First Earl of Hardwicke] 1690-1764 [SN]
British jurist
* Gripus, Judge

Yorke, Roger
See Bingley, David Ernest

Yorke, Stephen
See Linskill, Mary

Yorke, Susan
See Ellinger, Suzette [Telenga]

Yorke, Suzy
See Burton, Joan Eileen Veronica

Yorkel, Hans
See Hall, Abraham Oakey

Yorkin, Alan 1926- [FC, FD, ITA]
American director
* Yorkin, Bud

Yorkin, Bud
See Yorkin, Alan

Yorkist
See Morrah, Dermot [Michael Macgregor]

York's Tall Son
See Porter, William Trotter

[A] Yorkshire Freeholder
See Bailey, Samuel

[The] Yorkshire Lad
See Foy, Tom

[The] Yorkshire Ripper
See Sutcliffe, Peter

[The] Yorkshire Witch
See Bateman, Mary Harker

Yoruba
See Guzman, Pablo

Yoseloff, Thomas 1913- [CA]
American author
* Young, Thomas

Yoshida Kaneyoshi 1283-1350
Japanese poet and author
* Yoshida Kenko

Yoshida Kenko
See Yoshida Kaneyoshi

Yoshikawa, Takeo 20th c. [EE]
Japanese intelligence agent
* Morimura, Tadasi

Yoshimuni 18th c.
Japanese shogun
* [The] Hawk Shogun

Yoshimura, Kimisaburo
See Yoshimura, Kozaburo

Yoshimura, Kozaburo 1911- [DFM]
Japanese director
* Yoshimura, Kimisaburo

Yoshinobu
See Hitotsubashi

Yoshkin, Nicolai 1907- [FC]
Russian actor
* Kosleck, Martin

Yosimura, Huyukiko
See Terada, Torahiko

Yost, Charles W. 1908?-1981
American diplomat
* [The] Gray Ghost

Yost, Edward Frederick Joseph 1926- [BE, SMG]
American baseball player and coach
* [The] Walking Man

Yost, Fielding H. 1871-1946 [AS, FB]
American football coach
* Yost, Hurry Up

Yost, Herbert A. 1880-1945
American actor
* O'Moore, Barry

Yost, Hurry Up
See Yost, Fielding H.

You, Dominique 1775-1830 [FFF]
Pirate
* Johnness

Youd, C. S.
See Youd, Christopher Samuel

Youd, Christopher Samuel 1922- [CA, DLE, SF]
British author
* Christopher, John
* Ford, Hilary
* Godfrey, William
* Graaf, Peter
* Nichols, Peter
* Rye, Anthony
* Vine, William
* Youd, C. S.

[The] Young
See Fulk V

[The] Young
See Louis II [or Ludwig]

[The] Young
See Louis VII

Young, A. S.
See Young, Andrew Sturgeon Nash

Young, Ado
See Young, M. Adrian

[The] Young Adventurer
See Stuart, Charles Edward Louis Philip Casimir

Young, Agatha
See Young, Agnes [Brooks]

Young, Agnes [Brooks] 1898-1974 [BI]
American author
* Young, Agatha

Young, Ahdele Carrine 1923- [CA]
American author
* Young, Carrie

Young, Al
See Young, John

Young, Alan
See Young, Angus

Young, Alexander 1800-1854 [HPPN]
American clergyman
* A. Y.

Young, Alexander 1836-1891 [DNA, HPPN]
American journalist and historian
* Summerdale
* Taverner

Young, Alexander
See Youngs, Basil Alexander

[A] Young American
See Slidell, Alexander

[The] Young American Roscius
See Cowell, Sam

[The] Young and Happy Husband
See Dowty, A. A.

Young, Andrew Jackson, Jr. 1932-
American diplomat
* Motor Mouth

Young, Andrew Sturgeon Nash 1924-
[LBA]
American author and editor
* Young, A. S.
* Young, Doc

Young, Angela
See Yardley, Alice

Young, Angus 1919- [FC, ITA, SW]
British-born actor
* Young, Alan

Young, Annie
See Dupuy, Eliza Ann

[The] Young Apollo
See Shakespeare, William

Young, Arlene 20th c. [HPPN]
American wrestler
* [The] Polish Princess

Young, Arthur 1741-1820 [HPPN]
British agriculturist
* [The] Father of Modern Agriculture

Young, Arthur Edward 1921- [BA]
American attorney
* Young, Pickles

Young, Austin 1885?-1954? [NOJ]
American jazz musician
* Young, Boots

Young, Babe
See Young, Norman Robert

Young Barney Aaron
See Aaron, Barney

Young, Billie 1936- [CA]
American author
* Ashe, Penelope [joint pseudonym with Robert W. Greene]

Young, Billy
See D'Arcy, Colin

Young Blood Russell
See Russell, William Ellis [Bill]

Young, Boots
See Young, Austin

Young, Brigham 1801-1877
American religious leader
* [The] Mormon Pope

Young Broadbrim
See Rathborne, St. George Henry

Young Broome Evans
See Evans, William

Young, Buddy
See Young, Claude H.

Young, Bull
See Young, John W.

Young, Caesar
See Young, Francis Thomas

Young, Candy
See Young, Canzetta

Young, Canzetta 1963- [IBW]
American track and field athlete
* Young, Candy

Young, Carrie
See Young, Ahdele Carrine

Young, Carter Travis
See Charbonneau, Louis [Henry]

Young, Catfish
See Young, Granville

Young, Catherine
See Klinckerfuss, Ingabor Katrine

[The] Young Catullus of His Day
See Moore, Thomas

Young, Charles A. 1865-1951 [AS]
American trapshooter
* Young, Sparrow

Young, Charles D.
See King, Alexander

Young, [Sir] Charles George 1795-1869
[HPPN]
British knight
* C. G. Y.

Young, Charlie 1951- [IBW]
American football player
* Young, Tree

Young, Chesley Virginia 1919- [CA]
American author
* Barnes, Chesley Virginia

[The] Young Chevalier
See Stuart, Charles Edward Louis Philip Casimir

Young, Chic
See Young, Murat Bernard

Young, Clarence [house pseudonym]
[Stratemeyer Syndicate]
See Stratemeyer, Edward L.

Young, Claude H. 1926-1983 [FB]
American football player
* Young, Buddy

Young Clay
See Frick, Henry Clay

[A] Young Clergyman
See Butler, Joseph

Young, Clifford M. 1902?-1950 [BI]
American advertising executive
* Young, Cy

Young, Cole 19th c. [HPPN]
American outlaw
* Estes, Cole

Young, Collier
See Bloch, Robert [Albert]

[A] **Young Cornish Gentleman**
See Foe, Daniel

[The] **Young Cub**
See Fox, Charles James

Young, Cy
See Young, Clifford M.

Young, Cy
See Young, Denton True

Young Cy
See Young, Irving Melrose

Young, Denton True 1867-1955 [AS, IPA, OCS]
American baseball player
* [The] Farmer
* Young, Cy

[The] **Young Detective**
See Rolfe, Maro Orlando

Young, Doc
See Young, Andrew Sturgeon Nash

Young, Donnie
See Lytle, Donald

Young, Dorothea Bennett 1924- [CA]
British author
* Bennett, Dorothea

Young, Duke
See Young, John Thomas

Young Dutch Sam
See Elias, Samuel

Young, E. H.
See Young, Emily Hilda

Young, Edward 1683-1765 [HPPN, NPS, SN]
British poet
* [The] Bard of Night
* Cynthio
* [The] Hoary Bard of Night

Young, Edward 20th c. [OBW]
American baseball player
* Young, Pep

Young, Edward
See Reinfeld, Fred

Young, Edward James 19th c. [HPPN]
American clergyman
* E. J. Y.

Young, Eileen 20th c. [ART]
British artist
* E. Y.

Young, Elaine L.
See Schulte, Elaine L[ouise]

Young, Elizabeth Jane 1910- [F2]
American actress
* Blane, Sally

Young, Elroy 1923- [BA]
American physician
* [The] Duke

Young, Emily Hilda 1880-1949 [HPPN, LC]
British author
* [The] Apostle of Quiet People
* Young, E. H.

[A] **Young Englishman**
See Wirt, William

Young, Eric Brett 20th c. [CC, WW]
Author
* Leacroft, Eric

Young, Ernest 1938?- [HPPN]
American hemophiliac
* [The] Man With 586 Blood Brothers

Young, Ernest A. 20th c. [WW]
American author
* Rockwood, Harry

Young, Etta
See Fritz, Etta Young

Young, Eugene Edward 1919- [EJ, NP, WWJ]
American jazz musician
* Young, Rabbit
* Young, Snookie

Young Euphues
See Nash [or Nashe?], Thomas

Young, Eve
See Chandler, Karen

Young, Everett
See Cosby, Yvonne Shepard

Young, Ewing ?-1841 [BI, HPPN]
American trapper and guide
* Joon, Joaquin

Young, Faron 1932- [ECM]
American country-western performer
* [The] Sheriff
* [The] Singing Sheriff

Young, Fay
See Young, Frank A.

Young, Francis Thomas ?-1904 [HPPN]
American distance runner, race-horse owner, bookmaker, murder victim
* Young, Caesar

Young, Frank A. 20th c. [IBW, OBW]
American sportswriter and baseball player
* [The] Dean of Black Sportswriters
* Young, Fay

Young, Frank W.
See Young, Fred W.

Young, Fred W. 20th c. [MBF]
British author
* Arnold, Frank
* Newcome, Colin
* Scott, Hedley
* Wyatt, Ben
* Young, Frank W.

Young, G. M.
See Young, George Malcolm

[A] **Young Gentleman**
See Church, Benjamin

[A] **Young Gentleman**
See Dawes, Thomas

[A] **Young Gentleman**
See Grady, Thomas

[A] **Young Gentleman**
See Riddel, James

[A] **Young Gentleman**
See Rodd, Thomas, Sr.

[A] **Young Gentleman of Oxford**
See Lechmere, Edmund

[A] **Young Gentleman of Rank**
See Wirt, William

[A] **Young Gentleman of Truro School**
See Polwhele, Richard

[A] **Young Gentleman of Winchester School**
See Lowth, Robert

[A] **Young Gentlewoman**
See Nelson, Theophila

[A] **Young Gentlewoman, Mrs. A. W.**
See Weamys, Anna

Young, George 1910-1972 [CSH]
Canadian swimmer
* [The] Catalina Kid

Young, George, Jr. 1933- [BA]
American radio announcer and producer
* Young, Toby

Young, George Malcolm 1882-1959 [LC]
British author
* Young, G. M.

Young George Ruxton
See Ruxton, George Augustus Frederick

Young, Gig
See Barr, Byron Ellsworth

Young, Gladys ?-1975 [NN]
Actress
* [The] First Lady of the Air

Young, Graham Frederick 1947- [HPPN]
British poisoner
* [The] Obsessive Poisoner

Young, Granville [WWJ]
American jazz musician
* Young, Catfish

[A] **Young Greek Lady**
See Panam, Pauline Adelaide Alexandre

Young, Gretchen Michaela 1913- [BDF, F1, FC, HPPN]
American actress
* [The] Iron Butterfly
* [The] Steel Butterfly
* Young, Loretta

Young, Ham
See Young, William Hamilton

Young, Harley E. 20th c. [SR]
American baseball player
* Cy the Third

Young, Harold 1881-1936 [SC]
American actor
* North, Bob

[A] Young Hercules
See Sheridan, Richard Brinsley

Young Hickory
See Hill, David Bennett

Young Hickory
See Pierce, Franklin

Young Hickory
See Polk, James Knox

Young Hickory
See Tyler, John

Young Hickory
See Van Buren, Martin

[The] Young Horace
See Jonson, Ben[jamin]

Young Hotspur
See Ingersoll, Ralph Isaacs

Young, Ida Melville ?-1920 [HPPN]
American actress
* Melville, Ida

Young Ireland
See Wilson, Robert A.

Young, Irving Melrose 1877-1935 [BE]
American baseball player
* Cy the Second
* Young Cy

Young, Isaac Heller 1809-1836 [BI]
American murderer
* Heller, Isaac

[The] Young Isis
See Cleopatra

Young Jack Hearne
See Hearne, John William

Young Jack Thompson
See Thompson, Cecil Lewis

Young Jake Schaefer
See Schaefer, Herman, Jr.

Young, James 1811-1883 [HPPN]
Scottish chemist
* [The] Father of the Paraffin Industry
* Young, Paraffin

Young, James Arthur 1927?- [HPPN]
American army officer
* [The] Man Who Would Not Die

Young, James Osborne 1912- [EJ, PMJ, WWJ]
American jazz musician
* Young, Trummy [or Trummie]

Young, Jan[et Randall] 1919- [CA, SAT, WD]
American author
* Randall, Janet [joint pseudonym with Robert W(illiam) Young]

Young, Jesse Colin
See Miller, Perry

Young, Jessica May Brewer 20th c. [NAA]
American poet
* Young, Jessica Morehead

Young, Jessica Morehead
See Young, Jessica May Brewer

Young, Joanne Mayhew 20th c. [NY 2-18-85]
American artist and gallery owner
* Mansion, Gracie

Young Joe Shugrue
See Shugrue, Joe

Young Joe Wright
See Wright, Joseph, Jr.

Young, John 1773-1837 [FFF, PA]
Canadian writer
* Agricola

Young, John 20th c. [EF]
American football player
* Young, Al

Young, John O. [Johnny] 1918-1974 [BWW]
American singer
* Young, Man

Young, John Russell 1840-1899 [FFF, HPPN]
American journalist
* Bizarre
* J. R. Y.

Young, John Thomas 1949- [SMG]
American baseball player
* Young, Duke

Young, John W. ?-1913 [SC]
American boxer and actor
* Young, Bull

Young, Johnny 1943- [BWW]
American singer
* Taylor, Johnny Lamar
* Taylor, Little Johnny

Young, Joseph ?-1888 [FFF]
American master of many trades and professions
* [The] Learned Weaver

Young, Joseph 1927- [BWW]
American singer
* Young, Mighty Joe

[The] Young Juvenal
See Lodge, Thomas

Young Juvenal
See Nash [or Nashe?], Thomas

Young Klondyke
See Moore, Harry R.

[A] Young Lady
See Bateman, Elizabeth Blower

[A] Young Lady
See Harvey, J.

[A] Young Lady
See Porter, Anna Marie

[A] Young Lady
See Ramsay, Charlotte Lennox

[A] Young Lady
See Sherwood, Mary Martha

[A] Young Lady
See Wyatt, Gertrude

Young, Larry 1940-1978 [EJ7, IBW]
American jazz musician
* Yasin, Khalid

Young, Lee
See Young, Leonidas Raymond

Young, Lemuel Floyd 1907-1962 [BE, HPPN]
American baseball player
* Young, Pep
* Young, Whitey

Young, Leonidas Raymond 1917- [EJ, PMJ, WWJ]
American jazz musician
* Young, Lee

Young, Lester Willis 1909-1959 [DAM, EJ, IBW]
American jazz musician
* [The] Father of Modern Jazz
* Young, Prez

[The] Young Lieutenant
See Harding, Elizabeth Ann

Young, Lloyd 20th c. [EF]
American football player
* Young, Sam

Young, Loretta
See Young, Gretchen Michaela

Young, M. Adrian 1946- [FB]
Irish-born football player
* Young, Ado

[The] Young Man
See Charles II

[A] Young Man
See Judd, [Rev.] Sylvester

[The] Young Man
See William II [Friedrich Wilhelm Viktor Albert]

Young, Man
See Young, John O. [Johnny]

[A] Young Man in Town
See Graves, Richard

[The] Young Man With a Sneer
See Widmark, Richard

[The] Young Marshal
See Chang Hsueh-liang

[The] Young Marshal
See Pitt, William [Earl of Chatham]

Young, Martha 20th c. [ALY]
American author
* Sheppard, Eli

Young, Mary Elizabeth ?-1953 [HPPN]
American actress
* MacDonald, Bettie

Young, Mary Elizabeth 1901?-1981
American columnist
* Haworth, Mary

Young, Mighty Joe
See Young, Joseph

Young, Milton R. 1898?-1983 [TI 6-13-83, WP 6-1-83]
American politician
* Wheat, Mr.

[The] **Young Mining Captain**
See Lean, Joseph F.

Young Mitchell
See Hegert, John L.

Young, Mrs. C. W. [NPS]
Author
* Doyle, Mina

Young, Mrs. Duncan [FFF]
Entertainer
* Braham, Leonora

Young, Mrs. Edwin [FFF]
Entertainer
* Van Tassell, Cora

Young, Murat Bernard 1901-1973 [CA]
American cartoonist
* Young, Chic

Young, Nacella
See Tate, Velma

[The] **Young Napoleon**
See McClellan, George Brinton

[A] **Young Native, R. A. D.**
See Daniell, Ralph Allen

Young, Nedrick
See Bessie, Alvah

Young, Noel 1922- [CA]
American author
* Elder, Leon

Young, Norma 1889-1974 [SC]
Actress
* Prudence Penny

Young, Norman Robert 1915- [BE]
American baseball player
* Young, Babe

Young, Pam 1943- [CA]
American author
* Sidetracked Home Executives [joint pseudonym with Peggy Jones]

Young, Paraffin
See Young, James

Young, Patricia Helena 1922- [IAW]
British author
* Ross, Helena

Young, Patsy
See Hanshaw, Annette

Young, Pep
See Young, Edward

Young, Pep
See Young, Lemuel Floyd

Young, Pep
See Young, Ralph

Young, Pep
See Young, William P.

Young, Percy M[arshall] 1912- [CA]
British author
* Marshall, Percy

Young Pete Mahovlich
See Mahovlich, Pete[r]

[A] **Young Physician**
See Spence, John, Jr.

Young, Pickles
See Young, Arthur Edward

[The] **Young Pretender**
See Stuart, Charles Edward Louis Philip Casimir

Young, Prez
See Young, Lester Willis

Young, R. [PA]
Author
* Guyon

Young, Rabbit
See Young, Eugene Edward

Young, Ralph 1890-1965
American baseball player
* Young, Pep

Young, Raymond A.
See Jones, Vernon

[The] **Young Renegade**
See Barish, Keith

Young, Ricardo
See Mature, Victor John

[The] **Young Richard Barthelmess**
See McCallister, Herbert Alonzo

Young, Robert 1800-? [PI]
Irish poet and author
* [The] Fermanagh True Blue

Young, Robert 18th c. [PI]
Irish poet
* Guhion
* Hugoni
* Q. X.?
* R. Y.
* X. Z.

Young, Robert
See Payne, [Pierre Stephen] Robert

Young, Robert W[illiam] [Bob] 1916-1969 [CA, SAT]
American author
* Randall, Janet [joint pseudonym with Jan(et Randall) Young]

[The] **Young Roscius**
See Betty, William Henry West

Young, Rose
See Harris, Marion Rose [Young]

Young, Sam
See Young, Lloyd

Young, Sammy 1874-? [THR]
Scottish comedian
* Shields, Sammy

Young, Samuel ?-1854 [PA]
Author
* Wall Street Bear in Europe

Young, Samuel 1821-1891 [HPPN]
American author
* [The] Literary Drayman

Young Sanford Houpe
See Houpe, Sanford

[A] **Young Scotsman**
See Boswell, James

[A] **Young Shepherd**
See Ritson, Isaac

[The] **Young Sicilian**
See Monti, Luigi

Young Sir Henry
See Vane, [Sir] Henry [Harry]

[The] **Young Slasher**
See Stockman, David A.

Young, Snookie
See Young, Eugene Edward

Young, Sparrow
See Young, Charles A.

[A] **Young Squire**
See Davis, Thomas Osborne

Young, Stephen
See Levy, Stephen

Young, Sterling ?-1974 [HPPN]
American jazz musician
* [The] New Jan Garber

Young, Stewart
See Burrage, Alfred McLelland

Young Subtlety
See Fiennes, Nathaniel

Young, Sugar Bear
See Young, Willie Lull

Young Sully
See Sullivan, James [Jim]

[The] **Young Swan**
See Chenier, Andre Marie de

Young Tarquin
See Charles II

Young, Terry
See Samperi, Anthony

Young, Thomas 1587-1655 [HPPN]
British clergyman and pamphleteer
* Junius, Thomas

Young, Thomas 1731?-1777 [HPPN]
American patriot and physician
* Philodicaius

Young, Thomas
See Yoseloff, Thomas

Young Thunderbolt
See Lea, Luke

Young, Toby
See Young, George, Jr.

Young Tom Morris
See Morris, Thomas, Jr.

Young Torquemada
See Mitchel, John Purroy

Young, Tree
See Young, Charlie

Young, Trummy [or Trummie]
See Young, James Osborne

[The] Young 'Un
See Burnham George P.

Young Veteran
See Hutton, Lawrence

Young, Waddy
See Young, Walter R.

Young, Walter R. 1916-1945 [AS, FB]
American football player
* Young, Waddy

Young, Warwick
See Parsons, B.

Young Waters
See Stewart [or Stuart], James

Young, Welton 20th c. [RO1]
American singer and songwriter
* Dean

Young, Whitey
See Young, Lemuel Floyd

Young, Whitney Moore 1921-1971
[HPPN]
American government official
* [The] Pragmatic Humanist

Young, Will
See Home-Gall, William Bolinbroke

Young, William ?-1757 [SN]
British author
* Adams, [Parson] Abraham

Young, William Hamilton 1836-1908
[HPPN]
American telegraph operator and executive
* Young, Ham

Young, William P. 20th c. [OBW]
American baseball player
* Young, Pep

Young Willie Dunn
See Dunn, Willie

Young, Willie Lull 1943- [SMG]
American football player
* Young, Sugar Bear

[The] Young Wolf
See Jenkins, Gus

[A] Young Woman
See Harrison, Susannah

Young Zoilus
See Dennis, John

[The] Young Zulu Kid
See Dimelfi, Giuseppe

Youngberg, Norma Ione [Rhoads] 1896-
[CA]
American author
* Winfield, Leigh

Youngblood, Arthur Clyde 1900-1968
[BE]
American baseball player
* Youngblood, Chief

Youngblood, Chief
See Youngblood, Arthur Clyde

[The] Younger
See Bingham, Peregrine

[The] Younger
See Cato, Marcus Porcius

[The] Younger
See Danton, Jean Pierre

[The] Younger
See James

[The] Younger
See Justin II

[The] Younger
See Mahaskah

[The] Younger
See Medici, Lorenzo de

[The] Younger
See Pliny [Gaius Plinius Caecilius Secundus]

[The] Younger
See Pompeius Magnus, Sextus

[The] Younger
See Robusti, Domenico

[The] Younger
See Scipio Aemilianus Africanus Numantinus, Publius Cornelius

[The] Younger
See Teniers, David

Younger, Baby Pearl
See Younger, Pearl

[A] Younger Brother
See Bailey, Samuel

Younger Brother
See Long, Earl Kemp

[The] Younger Brother of Oehlenschlaeger
See Grundtvig, Nikolai Frederik Saverni

Younger, Cole
See Younger, Thomas Coleman

Younger, Elizabeth 1913- [AW, CC]
British author
* Hely, Elizabeth

Younger, John Leo 1912?-1962 [BEW]
Australian theatrical performer
* Grant, Barney

Younger, Paul 1928- [FB, SMG]
American football player
* Younger, Tank

Younger, Pearl 1867-1925 [HPPN]
American prostitute and brothel proprietress
* [The] Canadian Lily
* [The] Queen of the Row

Younger, Pearl (cont.)
* Reed, Rosa
* Starr, Pearl
* Younger, Baby Pearl

[The] Younger Pitt
See Pitt, William

[The] Younger Son
See Trelawny, Edward John

Younger, Tank
See Younger, Paul

Younger, Thomas Coleman 1844-1916
[BI]
American outlaw
* Younger, Cole

Younger, William Anthony 1917-1962
[CC, WW]
Scottish poet and author
* Mole, William

[The] Youngest Interlocutor in the World
See Thomas, Lillian

[The] Youngest Member
See Slosson, Annie T.

[The] Youngest of the Founding Fathers
See Spaight, Richard Dobbs

[The] Youngest Signer
See Dayton, Jonathan

Youngs, Basil Alexander 1920- [OP]
British opera singer
* Young, Alexander

Youngs, John 1951?-
American actor
* Savage, John

Youngs, Joseph, Jr. 1870-1948 [AS, BX, RBE]
American boxer
* Ryan, Tommy

Youngs, Pep
See Youngs, Ross Middlebrook

Youngs, Ross Middlebrook 1897-1927
[BAB, CBS, DGS]
American baseball player
* Cobb, Ty, Jr.
* Youngs, Pep

Youngstrom, Adolph F. 1897-1968 [FB]
American football player
* Youngstrom, Swede

Youngstrom, Swede
See Youngstrom, Adolph F.

[A] Younker
See Cobb, Josiah

Yount, Ducky
See Yount, Herbert M.

Yount, Herbert M. 1889- [BE]
American baseball player
* Yount, Ducky

Yount, Robin R. 1955- [WP 3-5-83]
American baseball player
* Rockin' Robin

Yountis, Oliver ?-1892 [HPPN]
American outlaw
* Crescent Sam

Your Constant Reader
See Dickens, Charles

Your Gospel Singer
See MacHugh, Edward

Your Grace
See Hughes, Richard

Your Obedient Servant
See Welles, [George] Orson

Your Prime Saint
See Hutchinson, Thomas

Your Solidity
See D'Aubigne, Francoise

Yourcenar, Marguerite
See De Crayencour, Marguerite

Yours Merrily
See Rogers, John R.

Youssef-Ahmabadabi, Henry 1949-
[SMG]
Iranian-born football player
* Abadi, Henry

[The] Youth
See Almagro, Diego de

[A] Youth of Quiet Ways
See Wales, Henry Ware

[A] Youth of Thirteen
See Bryant, William Cullen

Yowa
See McMurray, Nancy A[rmistead]

Yowell, Carl Columbus 1902- [BE]
American baseball player
* Yowell, Sundown

Yowell, Sundown
See Yowell, Carl Columbus

Yowlachie, Chief
See Simmons, Daniel

Yoxall, Harry Waldo 1896- [CA, HPPN]
British publishing executive and author
* Partington, F. H.

[The] Ypsilanti Ripper
See Collins, John Norman

Ypsilon
See Rindl, Robert

Yram
See Forhan, Marcel Louis

Yrjo-Koskinen, Yrjo Sakari
See Forsman, Georg Zachris

Yrubslips, F.
See Spilsbury, Francis

Ysgafell
See Williams, Jane

Yu [Ta Yu] [HPPN]
Chinese emperor
* [The] Great Yu

Yu, Charles
See Torgownik, William

Yu Hung-chun 1898-1960 [BI]
Chinese premier
* Yui, O. K.

Yu, James T. C.
See Yu, Tsune-Chi

Yu Jih-chang 1882-1936 [WBD]
Chinese Christian leader
* Yui, David Z. T.

Yu, Tsune-Chi 1899- [HPPN]
Chinese diplomat and author
* Yu, James T. C.

Yuan, Mel
See De Bolt, James

Yui, David
See Yui, Ta-wei

Yui, David Z. T.
See Yu Jih-chang

Yui, O. K.
See Yu Hung-chun

Yui, Ta-wei [BI]
Chinese general
* Yui, David

Yuill, P. B. [joint pseudonym with Gordon (Maclean) Williams]
See Venables, Terry

Yuill, P. B. [joint pseudonym with Terry Venables]
See Williams, Gordon [Maclean]

Yuki
See Inoue, Yukitoshi

Yukon Bill
See Hayes, Catherine E. [Simpson]

Yukteswar Sri Babajhan, [Yogi]
See Douglas, John Lee

Yule, Joe, Jr. 1920- [ASC, BDF, FC, FIR]
American actor
* McGuire, Mickey
* [The] Mick
* Rooney, Mickey

Yulya
See Whitney, Julia

Yuma, Dan
See Dunham, Robert [Bob]

Yun, Mu
See Fee, Benjamin J.

Yunkel, Ramar
See Martin, Jose L[uis]

Yupanqui, Cusi 15th c. [HPPN]
Inca emperor
* [The] Greatest American of Pre-Columbian Days
* [The] Inca Pachacuti

Yupanqui, Manco Inca
See Manco Capac

Yurevsky, E.
See Vol'skii, Nikolai Vladislavovich

Yuriko
See Amemiya, Yuriko

Yurka, Blanche
See Jurka, Blanche

Yuro, Rosemarie 1941- [RO1]
American singer
* Yuro, Timi

Yuro, Timi
See Yuro, Rosemarie

Yusolfsky, John Gary 1937- [FC, HT]
American actor
* Lockwood, Gary

Yussel the Muscle
See Jacobs, Joe

Yusuke, Suga 1942- [WFA]
Chinese-born hairstylist
* Suga

Yvaral
See Vasarely, Jean-Pierre

Yvars, Sal
See Yvars, Salvador Anthony

Yvars, Salvador Anthony 1924- [BE]
American baseball player
* Yvars, Sal

Yvelin, Albert [Baron de Beville]
20th c. [NPS]
Author
* Saxo-Norman

Yver, Colette
See Huzard, Antoinette de Bergevin

Yves of Brittany 1253-1303 [WBD]
Saint
* [L']Avocat des Pauvres

Yvonne Aimee de Jesu, [Mother]
See Beauvais, Yvonne

Z

Asterisk (*) indicates assumed name.

Z.
See Adams, Samuel

Z
See Doherty, John

Z.
See Frazer, John de Jean

Z.
See Horne, George

Z
See Jefferys, William Hamilton

Z.
See More, Hannah

Z.
See Prosner, G. W.

Z.
See Sewall, Samuel Edmund

Z.
See Zetti, Italo

Z. L. W.
See White, Zebulon L.

[The] Z Man
See Zanders, Emanuel

Z. P.
See Mansfield, L. W.

Z. X.
See Gilland, James

Z. Y. Z.
See Sykes, Arthur Alkin

Z. Z.
See Zangwill, Louis

[The] Za Zu Girl
See Spivey, Elton Island

Zabache, Wladimiro Bas 1929- [EJ]
Spanish jazz musician
* Vlady

Zabad
See Cromwell, Oliver

Zabel, George W. 1891-1970 [AS]
American baseball player
* Zabel, Zip

Zabel, Steve G. 1948- [FB]
American football player
* Zabel, Zabe

Zabel, Zabe
See Zabel, Steve G.

Zabel, Zip
See Zabel, George W.

Zabelle, Flora
See Mangasarian, Flora

Zabotin, Colonel 20th c. [EE]
Russian intelligence agent
* Grant

Zabriskie, F. N. [PA]
Author
* Old Colony

Zabunyan, Serkis 1938- [CAR]
Turkish artist
* Sarkis

Zac, Pino
See Zaccaria, Pino

Zaccaria, Nicola Angelo
See Zachariou, Nicolas Angelos

Zaccaria, Pino 1930- [WEC]
Italian cartoonist and animator
* Zac, Pino

Zacchini, Edmondo 1894?-1981
Italian-born circus clown
* Zacchini, Papa

Zacchini, Papa
See Zacchini, Edmondo

Zacek, Jane Shapiro 1938- [CA]
American author and political scientist
* Shapiro, Jane P.

Zachak, Anna 1897-1973 [SC]
Hungarian-born actress
* Grey, Olga

Zachariadis, Nicolas 1900- [HPPN]
Greek Communist leader
* Koutvis

Zacharias, Basileois 1850-1936 [CBS, HPPN]
Turkish-born British financier and muntitions manufacturer
* [The] Mystery Man of Europe
* Zaharoff, Basil

Zacharias, Lee
See Zacharias, Lela Ann

Zacharias, Lela Ann 1944- [CA]
American author
* Zacharias, Lee

Zacharie de Lisieux, Pere 1582-1661
[WGT]
Author
* Firmiani, Petri
* Fontaines, Louis

Zachariou, Nicolas Angelos 1923- [OP]
Greek opera singer
* Zaccaria, Nicola Angelo

Zachary, Albert Myron 1917- [BE]
American baseball player
* Zachary, Chink

Zachary, Chink
See Zachary, Albert Myron

Zachary, Elizabeth
See Zachary, Hugh

Zachary, Hugh 1928- [CA, HPPN, SFL, WD]
American author
* Dexter, John.
* Gorman, Ginny
* Hughes, Zach
* Kane, Pablo
* Kanto, Peter
* Pilgrim, Derral
* Rangely, E. R.
* Rangely, Olivia
* Van Heller, Marcus
* Zachary, Elizabeth

Zachary, Jonathan Thompson Walton
1897-1969 [BE, DGS]
American baseball player
* Walton, Zach
* Zachary, Tom

Zachary Leo, [Brother]
See Meehan, Francis Joseph

Zachary, Rubin 1915- [HPPN]
American jazz musician
* Zachary, Zeke

Zachary, Tom
See Zachary, Jonathan Thompson
Walton

Zachary, Zeke
See Zachary, Rubin

Zacher, Elmer Henry 1883-1944 [BE]
American baseball player
* Zacher, Silver

Zacher, Silver
See Zacher, Elmer Henry

Zacherle, John 1918- [RO1]
American singer and television performer
* Roland

Zacherle, John C. 1919- [SFL, WGT]
American actor and author
* Zacherley

Zacherley
See Zacherle, John C.

Zachos, John Celivergos 1820-1898
[FFF]
American author, educator, clergyman
* Cadmus

Zack
See Keats, Gwendoline

Zack, Jimmie
See Yingst, Henry Z.

Zadig
See Hagarty, [Sir] John Hawkins

Zadkiel
See Lilly, William

Zadkiel
See Morrison, Richard James

Zadkiel Tao Sze
See Morrison, Richard James

Zadkiel the Seer
See Morrison, Richard James

Zadoc
See Sancroft, William

Zafon, Silvino 1908- [GS]
Spanish bullfighter
* Nino de la Estrella [Child of the Star]

Zag
See Zagorski, Jerzy

Zagat, Arthur Leo 1895-1948 [SFP,
WGT]
American author
* Alzee, Grendon?
* Conyers, Latham
* York, Anton

Zagorski, Jerzy 1907- [IAW]
Russian-born poet, author, playwright
* Magister, Juras
* Zag

Zagoskin, Mikhail 1789-1852 [NPS]
Russian author and playwright
* [The] Russian Walter Scott

Zaharias, Babe Didrikson
See Zaharias, Mildred Didrikson

Zaharias, George
See Vetoyanis, Theodore

Zaharias, Mildred Didrikson 1914-1956
[AS, GF, HPPN, MEB, TI 8-20-84]
*American golfer and track and field
athlete*
* Didrikson, Babe
* Muscle Moll
* [The] Texas Tornado
* [The] World's Greatest Woman
  Athlete
* Zaharias, Babe Didrikson

Zaharoff, Basil
See Zacharias, Basileois

Zahava, Irene 1951- [CA]
American author
* Levinson, Irene

Zahir ud-Din Muhammad 1483-1530
[WBD]
Emperor of India
* Baber [Babur or Babar]

Zahm, John Augustine 1851-1921
[DNA]
American author, clergyman, educator
* Mozans, H. J.

Zaidenberg, Arthur 1908?- [CA]
American author and artist
* Azaid

Zaidys, Pranas
See Gaida-Gaidamavicius, Pranas

Zain, C. C.
See Benjamin, Elbert

Zajc, Ivan 1831-1914 [BBD]
Croatian composer
* Von Zaytz, Giovanni

Zajdler, Zoe Girling 1907?- [HPPN]
Irish author and journalist
* Hare, Martin

Zale Gale
See Abbott, Wenonah Stevens

Zale, Tony
See Zaleski, Anthony Florian

Zalega
See Balucki, Michal

Zaleski, Anthony Florian 1913- [BX,
RBE]
American boxer
* [The] Man of Steel
* Zale, Tony

Zaleski, Henry 20th c. [HPPN]
American football player
* Zaleski, Zal

Zaleski, Zal
See Zaleski, Henry

Zalinski, Edmund Louis Gray 1849-1909
[HPPN]
American army officer and inventor
* [The] Father of the Pneumatic
  Dynamite Gun

Zamacois, Eduardo
See De Zamacois y Quintana, Eduardo

Zamani
See Van Roemer, A.

Zambo-Peluca
See Romero, Jose

Zambock, George
See Glasser, Allen

[The] Zamboni Machine
See Reitz, Kenneth John

Zamenhof, Lazarus Ludwig 1859-1917
[JL]
Polish oculist and philologist
* Esperanto, Dr.
* [The] Father of Esperanto

Zametkin, Laura Kean 1901?-1986
[HPPN, IPA, NY 3-2-86]
American author
* Field, Peter [joint pseudonym with
  Thayer Hobson]
* Hobson, Laura Z.
* Quist, Felicia

Zamora, Blackie
See Zamora, Porfiro

Zamora, Porfiro 1940- [RBE]
American boxer
* Zamora, Blackie

Zampieri, Domenico 1581-1641 [HN,
WBD]
Italian painter
* Domenichino
* [The] Ox

Zanardi-Landi, Elizabeth Marie
1904-1948 [FC]
Italian-born actress, playwright, author
* Landi, Elissa

Zanchin, Nino 20th c. [WF]
Italian director
* Andrews, Robert

Zanco, Manuel 1929- [NOJ]
American jazz musician
* Zanco, Moose

Zanco, Moose
See Zanco, Manuel

Zander, Jonas Gustaf Wilhelm
1835-1920 [HPPN]
Swedish physician
* [The] Father of Mechanotherapy

Zanderbergen, George
See Dikty, Julian May

Zanders, Emanuel 1951- [SMG]
American football player
* [The] Z Man

Zanders, Roosevelt Smith 1915- [IBW]
American chauffeur to celebrities
* [The] Czar

Zane, Frank 1942?-
American body builder
* Olympia, Mr.

Zanelli, Carlos 1897- [BBD]
Chilean-born opera singer
* Morelli, Carlo

Zangara, Joseph 1902-1933 [HPPN]
American assassin
* [The] Killer of Cermac

Zanguidi, Jacopo 1544-1574 [BI]
Spanish painter
* Bertoja, Jacopo

Zangwill, Israel 1864-1926 [DEA]
British author and playwright
* Bell, J. Freeman

Zangwill, Louis 1869-? [LAO]
British author
* Z. Z.

Zanni, Dom
See Zanni, Dominick Thomas

Zanni, Dominick Thomas 1932- [BE]
American baseball player
* Zanni, Dom

Zanuck, Darryl Francis 1902-1979
[DFM, HPPN]
American producer
* Canfield, Mark
* [The] Chief
* [The] Last of the Golden Age
  Producers

Zanville, Bernard 1913- [FC]
American actor
* Clark, Dane

[The] Zany of Debate
See Canning, George

[The] Zany of His Age
See Henley, John

[El] Zapatero [The Shoemaker]
See Shoemaker, William [Willie]

Zapolska, Gabrjela
See Korwin-Piotrowska, Gabrjela

Zapolska, Gabryela
See Piotrowska, Gabryela

Zapolya [Szapolyai]
See John I

Zara, Louis
See Rosenfeld, Louis Zara

Zarate, Fernando de
See Enriquez de Paz, Antonio

Zarchy, Harry 1912- [CA]
American educator and author
* Lewis, Roger

Zarchy, Rubin 1915- [EJ]
American jazz musician
* Zarchy, Zeke

Zarchy, Zeke
See Zarchy, Rubin

Zardis, Chester 1900- [WWJ]
American jazz musician
* Zardis, Little Bear

Zardis, Little Bear
See Zardis, Chester

Zarello, Florian
See Painton, Ivan Emory

Zarif, Margaret Min'imah 20th c. [MA]
American author and educator
* Boon-Jones, Margaret

Zarilla, Allen Lee 1919- [BE, PB]
American baseball player
* Zarilla, Zeke

Zarilla, Zeke
See Zarilla, Allen Lee

Zarnas, Augustus 20th c. [EF]
American football player
* Zarnas, Gus

Zarnas, Gus
See Zarnas, Augustus

Zarnecki, George 1915- [CA]
*Polish-born British art historian and
author*
* Zarnecki, Jerzy

Zarnecki, Jerzy
See Zarnecki, George

Zarova, Rini
See Willson, Rini

Zarovitch, [Princess] Vera
See Lane, Mary E. Bradley

Zarumba, Louis
See Rothkopf, Louis

Zarzel
See Starr, Mrs. George O.

Zass, Aleksandr [BL]
Russian strong man
* Zass, Samson

Zass, Samson
See Zass, Aleksandr

Zastrow, Erika
See Massey, Erika

Zaturenska, Maria
See Gregory, Mrs. Horace Marya

Zauchin, Norbert Henry 1929- [BE]
American baseball player
* Zauchin, Norm

Zauchin, Norm
See Zauchin, Norbert Henry

Zauditu 1876-1930 [HPPN]
Empress of Ethiopia
* [The] Queen of Kings

Zauner, Franz Paul 1876-? [LAO]
German writer
* Pezet, [Dr.] F.

Zavada, George 20th c.
American bank robber
* [The] King

Zavada, Joseph 1916?-1965 [HPPN]
American bank robber
* [The] King of the Bank Robbers

Zavavi, Aboul-Halcon 1168-1230 [PA]
Author
* Ibn-Maat

Zawadsky, Patience 1927- [CA]
American writer
* Hartman, Patience
* Lynne, Becky

Zawoluk, Robert 1930- [BB]
American basketball player
* Zawoluk, Zeke

Zawoluk, Zeke
See Zawoluk, Robert

Zayanskovsky, John Kremchek 1907-
[BEW]
American producer
* Kenley, John

Zazell, Miss
See Hefferman, Katherine

[Il] Zazzerino
See Peri, Jacopo

Zbyszko, Stanislaus
See Cyganiewicz, Stanislaus

Zdenek, Marilee 1934- [CA]
American author and actress
* Earle, Marilee

Zea, Francisco Antonio 1770-1822
[HPPN]
Colombian scientist and statesman
* [The] Franklin of Colombia

[The] Zealous Doctor
See Sacheverell, Henry

Zeani, Virginia
See Zehan, Virginia

Zeckendorf, William 1905- [HPPN]
American real estate broker
* [The] Big Operator

Zeckhausen, Henry Leopold 1903- [CA]
Austrian-born author
* Ellison, Henry Leopold

Zed
See Dienes, Zoltan Paul

Zedekiah
See Mattaniah

Zeene, Ben
See Davison, Leslie Loring

Zeffirelli, Franco
See Corsi, Gian Franco

Zeglio, Primo 1906- [FDG]
Italian director
* Creepy, Anthony
* Hopkins, Omar

Zehan, Virginia 1928- [OP]
Italian opera singer
* Zeani, Virginia

Zehetner, Francis C. 1902?-1960 [BI]
American clergyman and engineer
* Aubert of Jesus, [Brother]

Zehringer, Richard 1947- [RO2]
American singer and songwriter
* Derringer, Rick

Zeidel, Lawrence [Larry] 1928-   [FHE]
Canadian-born hockey player
* [The] Rock

Zeider, Bunions
See Zeider, Rollie Hubert

Zeider, Rollie Hubert 1883-1967 [BE, PB]
American baseball player
* Zeider, Bunions

Zeidler, Leatrice Joy 1899- [F2, FC]
American actress
* Joy, Leatrice

Zeiem, Lyle 1905-1967 [SC]
American actor
* Latell, Lyle

Zeiger, Henry A[nthony] 1930-   [CA]
American author
* Peterson, James

Zeiger, Sophia 1926- [IBY, ICB]
American illustrator
* Sofia

Zeigerman, Gerald 1939- [CA]
American author and columnist
* Gerald, Ziggy

Zeigfreid, Karl
See Fanthorpe, R[obert] Lionel

Zeigle, Kate M. 1850-? [PA]
Author
* Stewart, Catherine

Zeiler, M.
See Prilukoff, Donat

Zeising, Adolf 1810-1876 [HPPN]
German author
* Morning, Richard

Zeitlin, Dennis 1937?- [HPPN]
American pianist and psychiatrist
* Jazz, Dr.

Zeitlin, Israel 1906- [BI]
Argentine poet
* Tiempo, Cesar

Zekowski, Arlene 1922- [CA]
American author and poet
* Berne, Arlene
* Jans, Zephyr

Zelandus
See Bellamy, Jacobus

Zelaya, Roberto Ignacio 1945-   [CA]
Nicaraguan-born poet
* Aguila, Pancho

Zelazny, Roger [Joseph] 1937-   [ESF, WGT]
American author
* Denmark, Harrison

Zelden, Monk
See Zelden, Sam[uel]

Zelden, Sam[uel] 20th c. [HPPN]
American attorney
* Zelden, Monk

Zelenski, Tadeusz 1874-1942 [CD]
Polish critic, author, translator
* Boy

Zelia
See Byrne, Hannah

Zelide
See Charriere, Isabelle de

Zelig, Big Jack
See Alberts, William

Zelig, Jack
See Alberts, William

Zelinska, Luis Stephanie 1915- [HPPN]
American actress
* Parker, Jean

Zelinsky, Joseph F. 1901- [BBH]
Hungarian-born bowler
* Kissoff, Joseph F.

Zell, Ira
See Roosevelt, Robert Barnwell

Zell, Mrs.   [FFF]
Entertainer
* Mann, Rheta

Zelle, Margarete Gertrude 1876-1917
[BL, CBS, HPPN, LC]
Dutch-born intelligence agent for Germany
* Mata Hari
* [The] Vamp Spy

Zelmanowitz, Gerald Martin 20th c.
American underworld figure and government witness
* Maris, Paul

Zelver, Patricia [Farrell] 1923- [CA]
American author
* Farrell, Patricia

Zemach, Harve
See Fischtrom, Harvey

Zemach, Margot
See Fischtrom, Margot Zemach

Zeman, Antonin 1843-1931 [CD]
Czech author
* Stasek, Antal

Zeman, Bob
See Zeman, Edward

Zeman, Edward 20th c. [EF]
American football player
* Zeman, Bob

Zeman, Kamil 1882-1952 [CD, EWL]
Czech author
* Olbracht, Ivan

Zemaria
See Dos Santos, Zemaria

Zena, Harry
See Butler, George H.

Zenea, Juan Clemente 1832-1871   [CW]
Cuban poet, author, playwright
* [Un] Amigo de la Juventud
* Azucena, Adolfo de la
* Ego-Queque

Zenger, Anna Catherine Maulin
1704?-1751 [HPPN]
American newspaper editor and publisher
* [The] Mother of Freedom

Zenger, John Peter 1697-1746 [HPPN]
German-American newspaper editor and publisher
* [The] Apostle of a Free Press
* [The] Fighter for Freedom
* [The] Patriot for Freedom

Zeno [or Zenon] ?-491 [HPPN]
Byzantine emperor
* [The] Isaurian

Zeno
See Ross, Dunbar

Zenobia ?-273 [DEP, DNNF, HN]
Queen of Palmyra
* [The] Pearl of the East
* [The] Queen of the East

Zenobia, Alexandria
See Bronte, Anne

Zenogalache 1867?-1905 [HPPN]
American Indian horse thief and murderer
* [The] Apache Kid
* [The] Crazy One

Zenon [or Zeno], George Louis Francis
1900-1968 [WWJ]
American jazz musician
* Lewis, George

Zenos, G. M.
See Long, Harold B.

Zentner, Carola 1927- [CA]
German-born author and journalist
* Mason, Carola

Zeokinizul
See Louis XV

Zeppel, Nathan
See Zeppelovich, Nathan

Zeppelovich, Nathan 1915?- [HPPN]
Latvian-American inventor
* Zeppel, Nathan

Zequiera y Arango, Manuel de
1764-1846 [CW]
Cuban poet
* Armuna, Ezequiel
* Raquenue, Izmael

Zerby, Deborah [or Derby?] 1948- [HT, ITA, SW]
American actress
* Darby, Kim

Zere, Al
See Ablitzer, Alfred G.

Zerilli, Joseph 1898?-1977
American underworld figure
* Mr. Joe

Zernial, Gus Edward 1923- [BE, PB]
American baseball player
* Ozark Ike

Zernoudjy
See Eddya, Borhan

Zero
See Ramsay, Allan, Jr.

Zero
See Schleger, Hans

Zero, Commander
See Pastora Gomez, Eden

Zero, Kid
See Brimsek, Francis Charles [Frank]

Zero, Mr.
See Brimsek, Francis Charles [Frank]

Zero, Mr.
See Ledoux, Urbain

Zero Zero [code name used during World War II]
See Nimitz, Chester W.

Zeromski, Stefan 1864-1925   [CD, EWL]
Polish author and playwright
* Katerla, Jozef
* Zych, Maurycy

Zeta
See Cope, [Vincent] Zachary

Zeta
See Froude, James Anthony

Zeta
See Lovell, John

Zetford, Tully
See Bulmer, [Henry] Kenneth

Zethar
See Harvey, Francis

Zetti, Italo 1913-   [ART]
Italian artist
* Z.

Zettlein, George 1844-1905   [BE]
American baseball player
* [The] Charmer

Zeuner, Charles
See Zeuner, Heinrich Christoph

Zeuner, Heinrich Christoph 1795-1857
[BBD]
German-born American musician
* Zeuner, Charles

Zeus
See Sanders, Daniel Jackson

Zeuta, Hermann
See Holmes, Augusta Mary Jane

Zevaes, Alexandre
See Bourson, Gustave Alexandre

Zevi, Sabbatai 1626?-1676   [DI]
Turkish-born imposter
* Efferidi, Aziz Mehmed

Zevin, Israel Joseph 1872-1926   [WBD]
Russian-born journalist and author
* Tashrak
* [The] Yiddish Mark Twain

Zhabotinskii, Vladimir Evgen'evich
1880-1940   [BI, HPPN]
Russian Zionist leader
* Altalena

Zhandov, Zahari 1911-   [DFM]
Bulgarian director
* Shandoff, Zachari

Zhdanov, Andrei Aleksandrovich
1896-1948   [HPPN]
Russian army officer and government official
* [The] Architect of the Cominform

Zhelyabov, Andrei Ivanovich 1851-1882
[HPPN]
Russian revolutionary
* [The] Russian Terrorist

Zhemchuzhnikov, Aleksiei Mikhailovich
1821-1908   [BI, HPPN]
Russian poet
* Prutkov, Kozma [joint pseudonym with Vladimir Mikhailovich Zhemchuzhnikov]

Zhemchuzhnikov, Vladimir Mikhailovich
1830-1884   [BI, HPPN]
Russian poet
* Prutkov, Kozma [joint pseudonym with Aleksiei Mikhailovich Zhemchuzhnikov]

Zhivkov, Todor 1911-   [HPPN]
Bulgarian Communist leader
* Bulgaria's Loyal Pragmatist

Zhu Hongshen 1917?-
Chinese clergyman
* Chu, Vincent

Zhuchenko, Yar 1918-   [CA]
Russian-born author
* Slavutych, Yar

Zhukov, Georgi K. 1897-1974   [HPPN]
Russian military leader
* [The] Red Napoleon

Ziar, E. R.
See Ziar, Elizabeth Rosemary

Ziar, Elizabeth Rosemary 1919-   [ART]
British painter
* E. R. Z.
* Ziar, E. R.

Zibelman, Charles 1891-   [EJS]
American swimmer
* Zimmy, Charles

Zico, Arthur 1954?-
Brazilian soccer player
* [The] White Pele

Zieber, Harry 20th c.   [BE]
American baseball player
* Whiting, Ed[ward C.]

Ziegeld, Florenz 1867-1932   [HPPN, PMJ]
American producer
* [The] Lorenzo the Magnificent of the Stage
* Ziegfeld, Flo
* Ziegfeld, Ziggy

Ziegfeld, Flo
See Ziegeld, Florenz

[The] Ziegfeld of the Jewish Stage
See Yablonik, Herman

Ziegfeld, Ziggy
See Ziegeld, Florenz

Ziegler, Alan 1947-   [CA]
American author and poet
* Bona, Mercy

Ziegler, Anne
See Eastwood, Irene Frances

Ziegler, Buster
See Ziegler, John

Ziegler, Edward William 1932-   [ESF, SFL, WGT]
American author
* Tyler, Theodore

Ziegler, John 20th c.   [BBH]
American softball player
* Ziegler, Buster

Ziegler, Karen 1942-   [SW]
American actress
* Black, Karen

Ziegler, Ron[ald] 1939-   [HPPN]
American presidential press secretary
* Ziegler, Ziggy Ron

Ziegler, Shotgun
See Goetz, Fred

Ziegler, Ziggy Ron
See Ziegler, Ron[ald]

Zif, Jay Jehiel
See Silberstein, Jay Jehiel

Ziggy Ron Ziegler
See Ziegler, Ron[ald]

Zigis
See Skujins, Zigmunds

Zigzag
See Chapman, Eddie

Zigzag
See Sykes, Arthur Alkin

Zigzag, Mr., the Elder
See Archer, John Wykeham

Zilberg, Veniamin A. 1902-   [EWL]
Russian author
* Kaverin, Veniamin

Zilia
See Schumann, Clara Josephine Wieck

Zillah
See Macdonald, Zillah K[atherine]

Zilles, Antoine 1868-1932   [BEW]
Dutch-born actor
* Corrigan, Emmett

Zilveritch, Fanny 1909-   [FC]
Hungarian actress
* Gaal, Franceska

Zim
See Zimmerman, Eugene

Zim, Sonia Bleeker 1909-1971   [AW, CA]
Russian-born American author
* Bleeker, Sonia

Zimeas, John
See Tzimeas, John

Zimisces
See John I

Zimm, Louise Hasbrouck 1883- [NAA]
American author
* Hasbrouck, Louise Seymour

Zimmer, Charles Louis 1860-1949 [AS, BE, PB]
American baseball player
* Zimmer, Chief

Zimmer, Chief
See Zimmer, Charles Louis

Zimmer, Don[ald William] 1931- [PB, SMG]
American baseball player and manager
* Popeye
* Zimmer, Zim

Zimmer, Jessie 20th c. [HPPN]
American hosiery dealer
* Broadway's Queen of Stockings

Zimmer, Jill Schary
See Robinson, Jill

Zimmer, Zim
See Zimmer, Don[ald William]

Zimmerman, Arthur A. 1869-1936 [BBH]
American bicycle racer
* [The] Flying Yankee
* King of the Wheel
* Zimmerman, Zimmie

Zimmerman, Diana 1951- [HPPN]
American magician
* Diana the Enchantress

Zimmerman, Elizabeth S. 1884-1959 [SC]
American actress
* Stoddard, Betsy

Zimmerman, Ethel Agnes 1909-1984 [BEW, EMT, ITA, TI 2-27-84]
American singer and actress
* [The] Belter
* First Lady of the American Musical Theatre
* Leather-Lungs, Lady
* Madam Ambassador From and to Broadway
* [The] Merm
* Merman, Ethel
* Merman, Sureshot
* Queen of Broadway
* Sharpshooting Singer From Astoria
* Top Balcony Belter

Zimmerman, Eugene 1862-1935 [DNA]
Swiss-born author and cartoonist
* Zim

Zimmerman, Gerald Robert 1934- [SMG]
American baseball coach
* Zimmerman, Zim

Zimmerman, Heinie
See Zimmerman, Henry

Zimmerman, Henry 1887-1969 [BE]
American baseball player
* Zimmerman, Heinie

Zimmerman, Paul 20th c. [WP 10-19-84]
American sportswriter
* Dr. Z

Zimmerman, Robert Allen 1941- [CA, DAM, HPPN, LRR]
American singer and songwriter
* Dylan, Bob
* Grunt, Blindboy
* [The] Radical Prophet of American Youth

Zimmerman, Toni
See Ortner-Zimmerman, Toni

Zimmerman, Zim
See Zimmerman, Gerald Robert

Zimmerman, Zimmie
See Zimmerman, Arthur A.

Zimmermann, Werner 20th c. [SFL]
Author
* Douglas, Drake

Zimmerwal, Edmond
See Lozzi, Edmondo

Zimmeth, Mary
See Schomaker, Mary Zimmeth

Zimmy, Charles
See Zibelman, Charles

Zimri
See Villiers, George

Zinberg, Leonard 1911?-1968 [CC, EMD, TCCM]
American author
* April, Steve
* Lacy, Ed

Zincke, Hans 1837-1922 [BBD]
German composer
* Sommer, Hans

Ziner, Feenie
See Ziner, Florence

Ziner, Florence 1921- [CA]
American author
* Ziner, Feenie

Zingale, Carl 1895?-
American billiard player
* Kelly, Cue Ball

Zingara, Professor
See Leeming, Joseph

Zingaro
See Delany, William J.

[Il] Zingaro
See Solario, Antonio

Zink, John Smith 1929- [EAR]
American auto racer
* Zink, Junior

Zink, Junior
See Zink, John Smith

Zinken
See Hopp, Signe Marie

Zinkler, Christiane
See Moeckl, Christiane

Zinn, Sergeant
See Wilson, James Edwin

Zinoviev, Grigori Evseevich
See Apfelbaum, Hirsch

Zinsser, Hans 1878-1940 [BI, HPPN]
American bacteriologist
* R. S.

Zinzendorf, [Count] Nikolaus Ludwig von 1700-1760 [SN]
German-born religious leader
* [The] Moses of Our Age

Zioncheck, Marion A. 1900-1936 [HPPN]
Polish-American politician
* [The] Congressional Playboy
* Seattle's Sensational Son

Zipfel, Bud
See Zipfel, Marion Sylvester

Zipfel, Marion Sylvester 1938- [BE]
American baseball player
* Zipfel, Bud

Zipoli, Perlone
See Lippi, Lorenzo

Zipper Head
See Kramer, Gerald [Jerry]

[The] Zippered Glipper
See Reagan, Ronald Wilson

Zippo, Mr.
See Blaisdell, George G.

Ziraldo
See Pinto, Ziraldo Alves

Zisca, John 1360?-1424 [SN]
Bohemian army officer
* [The] One Eyed

Ziska
See Cummings, Amos Jay

Zitelmann, Konrad 1854-1897 [WBD]
German poet and author
* Telmann, Konrad

Zito, Salvatore 1933- [ASC]
American composer
* Zito, Torrie

Zito, Torrie
See Zito, Salvatore

Zivic, Charlie
See Affif, Charles

Zivic, Ferdinand Henry John 1913- [BI, HPPN]
American boxer
* Zivic, Fritzie
* Zivic, Old Fritz

Zivic, Fritzie
See Zivic, Ferdinand Henry John

Zivic, Old Fritz
See Zivic, Ferdinand Henry John

Zivyon
See Hoffman, Benzion

Ziyada, Marie 1891?-1941 [BI]
Egyptian author
* Copia, Isis

Ziz
See Furr, Toren

Zmaj
See Jovanovic, Jovan

Zmich, Ed[ward Albert] 1884-1950 [BE]
American baseball player
* Zmich, Ike

Zmich, Ike
See Zmich, Ed[ward Albert]

Zmogas
See Rodziewiczowna, Marja

Zobbau, M. [PA]
Author
* Castorim

Zobeltitz, Hanns von 1853-1918 [WBD]
German author
* Spielberg, Hanns von

Zocato [Left-Handed]
See Borrego Ruiz, Carlos

Zoe, Mlle.
See Yates, Mrs. Benjamin

Zoeller, Frank Urban 1952?-
American golfer
* Zoeller, Fuzzy

Zoeller, Fuzzy
See Zoeller, Frank Urban

Zoffani, John 1733-1810 [SN]
German-born painter
* [The] Dutch Hogarth

Zog I [or Zogu]
See Ahmed Bey Zogu

Zogbaum, Baird Leonard 1889?-1941
[HPPN]
American critic and poet
* Leonard, Baird

[The] Zoilos of Quinault
See Boileau-Despreaux, Nicolas

Zoilus [or Zoilos] 4th c. BC [DNNS,
HN, RH]
Greek grammarian
* Homeromastix
* Homer's Scourge
* [The] Scourge of Homer
* [The] Thracian Dog

Zoilus
See Dennis, John

Zoilus
See Lovecraft, Howard Phillips

Zoilus
See Stuart, Gilbert

Zoino, Vincent Edward 1928- [HPPN]
American actor
* Edwards, Vincent

Zolar
See King, Bruce

Zoldak, Sad Sam
See Zoldak, Samuel Walter

Zoldak, Samuel Walter 1918-1966 [BE]
American baseball player
* Zoldak, Sad Sam

Zolf, Larry 1934- [CA]
Canadian author and television journalist
* Jaded Observer

Zoll, Donald Atwell 1927- [CA]
American educator and author
* Winslow, Donald

Zoller, Israel 1881-1956 [BI]
Italian convert
* Zolli, Eugenio

Zolli, Eugenio
See Zoller, Israel

Zollinger, Gulielma 1856-1917 [DNA,
SAT]
American author
* Gladwin, William Zachary

Zollner, Henry 1893?- [HPPN]
American cotton rancher
* [The] Founder of Hobo Ranch

Zolotow, Charlotte [Shapiro] 1915- [BI,
TCC]
American author and editor
* Abbot, Sara
* Bookman, Charlotte

Zomerdijk, Hein
See Zomerdijk, Henricus Jacobus

Zomerdijk, Henricus Jacobus 1918-
[IWM]
Dutch musician
* Zomerdijk, Hein

Zomphier, Charles 1906-1973 [MK]
American baseball player
* Zomphier, Zomp

Zomphier, Zomp
See Zomphier, Charles

Zonik, Eleanor Dorothy 1918- [CA,
WD]
British playwright
* Glaser, Eleanor Dorothy

Zonis, Stuart Michael 1937- [BEW, FC]
American actor and singer
* Damon, Stuart

Zonnevylle, Michael J. F. 1854-1943
[HPPN]
American actor
* Kemble, Frank

Zook, Deborah
See Green, Deborah

Zoolactaf [or Dsulaktaf]
See Shapur II [or Sapor]

Zoophilus
See Blyth, Edward

Zorilla, Jose 1829-? [FFF]
Spanish poet
* [The] Spanish Victor Hugo

Zorina, Vera
See Hartwig, Eva Brigitta

Zorio, Vincent Edward 1928- [FC]
American actor
* Edwards, Vince

Zoroaster [or Zarathustra] [DEP, FFF,
SN]
Founder of the Magian religion
* [The] Bactrian Sage

Zorrilla y Moral, Jose 1817-1893
[HPPN]
Spanish playwright
* [The] Spoiled Darling of Spanish
  Romanticism

[El] Zorro
See Vigara, Rafael Martin

Zorro
See Ward, Harold

[El] Zorzal Crillo [The Native Thrush]
See Gardes, Charles Romuald

Zoschokke 1771-1848 [RH]
Swiss author
* [The] Swiss Walter Scott

Zouzou
See Ciarlet, Danielle

Zouzou
See Ciralet, Danielle

Zovello
See Wishner, Sam

Zoyara, Ella
See Kingsley, Omar

Zozimus
See Leyne, Maurice Richard

Zozimus
See Moran, Michael

[The] Zsa Zsa Gabor of Burlesque
See Wilczhowski, Lillian

Zsigmond, Vilmos 20th c. [WF]
Cinematographer
* Zsigmond, William

Zsigmond, William
See Zsigmond, Vilmos

Zsissly
See Albright, Malvin Marr

Zuber, Goober
See Zuber, William Henry

Zuber, William Henry 1913- [BE]
American baseball player
* Zuber, Goober

Zucca, Rita Louise 20th c.
*American-born propagandist during World
War II*
* Axis Sally

Zuccalmaglio-Waldbruehl, Wilhelm von
1805-1860 [SN]
* Wedel, Gottschalk

Zuccari, Anna Radius 1846-1918 [CD]
Italian author
* Neera

Zuck, Alexandra 1942- [FC, SW]
American actress
* Dee, Sandra

Zucker, Barney
See Zucker, William

Zucker, Dolores Mae Bolton 20th c.
[CA, HPPN]
American author and columnist
* Hill, Dee
* Hill, Devra Z.
* Myles, Devera

Zucker, William 1885?-1952 [BI]
American swimming coach
* Zucker, Barney

Zuckerman, Buck Henry 1930- [CA,
SW, WP 3-25-85]
American screenwriter and actor
* Henry, Buck
* Prout, G. Clifford

Zuckerman, Itzchak 20th c.
Polish resistance fighter
* Antek

Zuckerman, Norma Anna Bella
1931-1973 [SC]
American actress
* Crane, Norma

Zuckermann, Augusta 1890-1981 [BBD]
American musician
* Mana-Zucca

Zudekoff, Moe
See Zudekoff, Muni

Zudekoff, Muni 1919- [EJ, HPPN, PMJ,
WWJ]
American jazz musician
* Morrow, Buddy
* Morrow, Muni
* Zudekoff, Moe

Zuker, Barney
See Zuker, William

Zuker, Pop
See Zukor, Adolph

Zuker, William 20th c. [EJS]
American swimming coach
* Zuker, Barney

Zukerman, Pinchas 20th c.
Israeli musician
* Zukerman, Pinky

Zukerman, Pinky
See Zukerman, Pinchas

Zukor, Adolph 1873-? [HPPN]
American film producer
* [The] Henry Ford of the Movies
* Zuker, Pop

[The] Zula Kid
See Flammia, Michael

Zulano
See Harte, Jerome Alfred

Zulawski, Juliusz 1910- [IAW]
Polish author and poet
* J. Z.

Zulawski, Marek 1908- [ART, DBA]
Italian-born painter
* Marek

Zuleika
See Willemer, Marianne von

[The] Zulu Queen
See Chaka

Zumwalt, Elmo Russell, Jr. 1920-
American naval officer
* Zumwalt, Zoomie

Zumwalt, Oral 20th c. [GW]
American rodeo performer
* Zumwalt, Zumie

Zumwalt, Zoomie
See Zumwalt, Elmo Russell, Jr.

Zumwalt, Zumie
See Zumwalt, Oral

Zunic, Mad Matt
See Zunic, Matt

Zunic, Matt 1919-
American basketball player
* Zunic, Mad Matt

Zunich, Ralph 1910- [CEI]
American hockey player
* Zunich, Ricky

Zunich, Ricky
See Zunich, Ralph

Zuniga Villquiran, Jose 1950- [GS]
Colombian bullfighter
* Josellilo de Colombia [Little Joe from
Colombia]

Zunser, Eliakim 1836-1913 [HPPN]
Russian poet
* Badchen, Eliakim
* [The] Poet of His People

Zup
See Zuppke, Robert C.

Zupo, Frank Joseph 1939- [BE]
American baseball player
* Zupo, Noodles

Zupo, Noodles
See Zupo, Frank Joseph

Zuppke, Robert C. 1879-1957 [AS, BBH,
FB, HPPN]
German-born football player and coach
* [The] Little Dutchman
* [The] Rembrandt of the Prairies
* Zup
* Zuppke, Zupp

Zuppke, Zupp
See Zuppke, Robert C.

[El] Zurdo [Lefthanded One]
See Montero, Antonio Maria

Zurhorst, Charles [Stewart, Jr.] 1913-
[CA, SAT]
American author
* Stewart, Charles

Zurito [Little Wild Dove]
See De La Haba, Antonio

Zurito [Little Wild Dove]
See De La Haba Vargas, Gabriel

Zurito [Little Wild Dove]
See De La Habla, Manuel

Zurke, Robert [Bob] 1910-1944 [HPPN]
American jazz musician
* [The] Old Tomcat of the Keys

Zurndorfer, Dorothy Paula 1933-
[BEW]
American actress and singer
* Stewart, Paula

Zuromskis, Diane
See Stanley, Diane

Zuta, Jack ?-1928 [BLB]
American underworld figure
* Goodman, J. H.

Zutpher Hero
See Sidney, [Sir] Philip

Zvi, H.
See Harkavy, Zvi

Zvirzdys, Vytautas 1924- [CA]
*Lithuanian-born American political
scientist and author*
* Vardys, V[ytautas] Stanley

Zweibelsharf, David 1895- [BEW]
Russian-born actor
* Dank, David

Zweig, Stefan 1881-1942 [BI, HPPN]
Austrian author
* Branch, Stephen

Zweit, Adam
See Lovin, Roger Robert

Zwerbach, Max 1882-1908 [BLB]
American underworld figure
* Twist, Kid

Zwerenz, Gerhard 1925- [CA]
German author
* Tarrok, Peer

Zwibak, Jacques 1902- [CA]
Russian-born American author
* Sedych, Andrei

Zwilling, Dutch
See Zwilling, Edward Harrison

Zwilling, Edward Harrison 1888-1978
[BE, BI]
American baseball player
* Zwilling, Dutch

Zwillman, Abner 1899-1959 [BLB,
HPPN, MM, PHM]
American underworld figure
* [The] Man to See in New Jersey
* Zwillman, Longy

Zwillman, Longy
See Zwillman, Abner

Zwingli, Carl [PA]
Author
* Carlopago

Zwingli, Ulrich [or Huldreich]
1484-1531 [HPPN, SN]
Swiss religious reformer
* [The] Martin Luther of Switzerland
* [The] Third Man of the Reformation

Zworykin, Vladimir Kosma 1890?-1982
Russian-born scientist
* [The] Father of Television

Zych, Maurycy
See Zeromski, Stefan

Zylberberg, Regina 1929- [BI]
French singer, dancer, cabaret owner
* Regine

Zylis, Teresa Geralda 1935- [MS]
Polish opera singer
* Zylis-Gara, Teresa

Zylis-Gara, Teresa
See Zylis, Teresa Geralda

Zymirski, Michal
See Lyzwinski, Michal

Zyskind, Bruno 1901-1939 [JL]
Polish author
* Jasienski, Bruno

Zyx
See Hurtubise, Jacques

ZYX
See Sykes, Arthur Alkin

KEY TO SOURCE CODES

Detailed bibliographical information about the sources listed
below begins on page 1149.